Third Edition

Financial & Managerial Accounting for MBAs

PETER D. EASTON

ROBERT F. HALSEY

MARY LEA McANALLY

AL HARTGRAVES

WAYNE J. MORSE

Cambridge
BUSINESS PUBLISHERS

To my daughters, Joanne and Stacey
    —PDE

To my wife Ellie and children, Grace and Christian
    —RFH

To my husband Brittan and my children Loic, Cindy, Maclean, Quinn and Kay.
    —MLM

To my wife Aline.
    —AH

To my family and students.
    —WJM

Cambridge Business Publishers

FINANCIAL & MANAGERIAL ACCOUNTING FOR MBAs, Third Edition, by Peter D. Easton, Robert F. Halsey, Mary Lea McAnally, Al Hartgraves, and Wayne J. Morse.

Student Edition ISBN 978-1-61853-008-0

Bookstores & Faculty: to order this book, call **800-619-6473** or email **customerservice@cambridgepub.com.**

Students: to order this book, please visit the book's website and order directly online.

Printed in Canada.
10 9 8 7 6 5 4 3 2 1

PETER D. EASTON is an expert in accounting and valuation and holds the Notre Dame Alumni Chair in Accountancy in the Mendoza College of Business. Professor Easton's expertise is widely recognized by the academic research community and by the legal community. Professor Easton frequently serves as a consultant on accounting and valuation issues in federal and state courts.

Professor Easton holds undergraduate degrees from the University of Adelaide and the University of South Australia. He holds a graduate degree from the University of New England and a PhD in Business Administration (majoring in accounting and finance) from the University of California, Berkeley.

Professor Easton's research on corporate valuation has been published in the *Journal of Accounting and Economics, Journal of Accounting Research, The Accounting Review, Contemporary Accounting Research, Review of Accounting Studies,* and *Journal of Business Finance and Accounting.* Professor Easton has served as an associate editor for 11 leading accounting journals and he is currently an associate editor for the *Journal of Accounting Research, Journal of Business Finance and Accounting,* and *Journal of Accounting, Auditing, and Finance.* He is an editor of the *Review of Accounting Studies.*

Professor Easton has held appointments at the University of Chicago, the University of California at Berkeley, Ohio State University, Macquarie University, the Australian Graduate School of Management, the University of Melbourne, Tilburg University, National University of Singapore, Seoul National University, and Nyenrode University. He is the recipient of numerous awards for excellence in teaching and in research. Professor Easton regularly teaches accounting analysis and security valuation to MBAs. In addition, Professor Easton has taught managerial accounting at the graduate level.

ROBERT F. HALSEY is Professor of Accounting and Associate Dean of the Undergraduate School at Babson College. He received his MBA and PhD from the University of Wisconsin. Prior to obtaining his PhD he worked as the chief financial officer (CFO) of a privately held retailing and manufacturing company and as the vice president and manager of the commercial lending division of a large bank.

Professor Halsey teaches courses in financial and managerial accounting at both the graduate and undergraduate levels, including a popular course in financial statement analysis for second year MBA students. He has also taught numerous executive education courses for large multinational companies through Babson's school of Executive Education as well as for a number of stock brokerage firms in the Boston area. He is regarded as an innovative teacher and has been recognized for outstanding teaching at both the University of Wisconsin and Babson College.

Professor Halsey co-authors *Advanced Accounting* published by Cambridge Business Publishers. Professor Halsey's research interests are in the area of financial reporting, including firm valuation, financial statement analysis, and disclosure issues. He has publications in *Advances in Quantitative Analysis of Finance and Accounting, The Journal of the American Taxation Association, Issues in Accounting Education, The Portable MBA in Finance and Accounting,* the *CPA Journal, AICPA Professor/Practitioner Case Development Program,* and in other accounting and analysis journals.

Professor Halsey is an active member of the American Accounting Association and other accounting, analysis, and business organizations. He is widely recognized as an expert in the areas of financial reporting, financial analysis, and business valuation.

MARY LEA McANALLY is the Philip Ljundahl Professor of Accounting and Associate Dean for Graduate Programs at the Mays Business School. She obtained her Ph.D. from Stanford University and B. Comm. from the University of Alberta. She worked as a Chartered Accountant (in Canada) and is a Certified Internal Auditor. Prior to arriving at Texas A&M in 2002, Professor McAnally held positions at University of Texas at Austin, Canadian National Railways, and Dunwoody and Company.

Her research interests include accounting and disclosure in regulated environments, executive compensation, and accounting for risk. She has published articles in the leading academic journals including *Journal of Accounting and Economics, Journal of Accounting Research, The Accounting Review, Review of Accounting Studies,* and *Contemporary Accounting Research.* Professor McAnally received the Mays Business School Research Achievement Award in 2005. She is Associate Editor at *Accounting Horizons* and serves on the editorial board of *Contemporary Accounting Research* and is Guest Editor for the MBA-teaching volume of *Issues in Accounting Education* (2012). She is active in the American Accounting Association and its FARS section.

At Texas A&M, Professor McAnally teaches financial reporting, analysis, and valuation in the full-time and Executive MBA programs. Through the Mays Center for Executive Development, she works with corporate clients including Halliburton, AT&T, and Baker Hughes. She has also taught at University of Calgary, IMADEC (in Austria) and at the Indian School of Business, in Hyderabad. She has received numerous faculty-determined and student-initiated teaching awards at the MBA and executive levels. Those awards include the Beazley Award, the Trammell Foundation Award, the MBA Teaching Award (multiple times), the MBA Association Distinguished Faculty Award (three times), the Award for Outstanding and Memorable Faculty Member, and the Distinguished Achievement Award.

AL L. HARTGRAVES is Professor of Accounting at the Goizueta Business School at Emory University in Atlanta, Georgia. He is also a frequent Guest Professor at Johannes Kepler University in Linz, Austria and at the Helsinki School of Economics and Business Administration in Finland. His published scholarly and professional articles have appeared in The Accounting Review, Accounting Horizons, Management Accounting, Journal of Accountancy, Journal of Accounting and Public Policy and many other journals. Students at Goizueta Business School have selected him on six occasions to receive the Distinguished Educator Award. In 2002 he received Emory University's highest teaching award, The Scholar/Teacher Award, and in 2003 he was recognized as the Accounting Educator of the Year by the Georgia Society of CPAs. He has been recognized as an Outstanding Faculty Member in two editions of The Business Week Guide to the Best Business Schools. He is a Certified Public Accountant (inactive) and a Certified Management Accountant, having received the Certificate of Distinguished Performance on the CMA exam. He received his Ph.D. from Georgia State University.

WAYNE J. MORSE, a hiking and canoeing enthusiast, is Professor of Accounting at the Saunders College of Business at Rochester Institute of Technology. An author or co-author of more than fifty published papers, monographs, and textbooks, he was a founding member of the Management Accounting section of the American Accounting Association. His most notable writings are in the areas of learning curves, human resource accounting, and quality costs. He was a member of the IMA Committee on Research and an AICPA Board of Examiners subcommittee, and he has served on the editorial boards of Advances in Accounting, Trends in Accounting Education, Issues in Accounting Education, and Management Accounting Research. A Certified Public Accountant, he received his Ph.D. from Michigan State University. Prior to joining RIT, he was on the faculty of the University of Illinois, Duke University, the University of Tennessee, Clarkson University, and the University of Alabama-Huntsville.

Welcome to *Financial & Managerial Accounting for MBAs*. Our main goal in writing this book was to satisfy the needs of today's business manager by creating a contemporary, engaging, and user-oriented textbook. This book is the product of extensive market research including focus groups, market surveys, class tests, manuscript reviews, and interviews with faculty from across the country. We are grateful to the students and faculty who provided us with useful feedback during the preparation of this book.

TARGET AUDIENCE

Financial & Managerial Accounting for MBAs is intended for use in full-time, part-time, executive, and evening MBA programs that include a combined financial and managerial accounting course as part of the curriculum, and one in which managerial decision making and analysis are emphasized. This book easily accommodates mini-courses lasting several days as well as extended courses lasting a full semester.

INNOVATIVE APPROACH

Financial & Managerial Accounting for MBAs is managerially oriented and focuses on the most salient aspects of accounting. It teaches MBA students how to read, analyze, and interpret accounting data to make informed business decisions. This textbook makes accounting **engaging, relevant,** and **contemporary.** To that end, it consistently incorporates **real company data,** both in the body of each module and throughout assignment material.

FLEXIBLE STRUCTURE

The MBA curricula, instructor preferences, and course lengths vary across colleges. Accordingly and to the extent possible, the 24 modules that make up *Financial & Managerial Accounting for MBAs* were designed independently of one another. This modular presentation enables each college and instructor to "customize" the book to best fit the needs of their students. Our introduction and discussion of financial statements constitute Modules 1, 2, and 3. Module 4 presents the analysis of financial statements with an emphasis on profitability analysis. Modules 5 through 10 highlight major financial accounting topics including assets, liabilities, equity, and off-balance-sheet financing. Module 11 explains forecasting financial statements and Module 12 introduces simple valuation models. Module 13 introduces managerial accounting and is followed by a discussion of cost behavior and cost estimation in Module 14. Module 15 explains cost-volume-profit analysis while Module 16 focuses on using relevant costs to make business decisions. Job and process costing are covered in a single module, Module 17, followed by activity-based costing in Module 18 and the assignment of indirect costs in Module 19. The remaining modules, 20 through 24, highlight managerial accounting topics ranging from operational budgets and variance analysis to segment reporting, product pricing, and capital budgeting. At the end of the book, we include several useful resources. Appendix A contains Compound Interest tables. Appendix B details the process for preparing and analyzing the Statement of Cash Flow. Appendix C is an illustrative case that applies the techniques described in the financial accounting modules (1–12) to an actual company, Kimberly-Clark. Appendix D is a chart of accounts used in the book.

MANAGERIAL EMPHASIS

As MBA instructors, we recognize that the core MBA accounting course is not directed toward accounting majors. *Financial & Managerial Accounting for MBAs* embraces this reality. This book highlights **reporting, analysis, interpretation,** and **decision making.** In the financial accounting modules, we incorporate the following **financial statement effects template** when relevant to train MBA students in understanding the economic ramifications of transactions and their impact on all key financial statements. This analytical tool is a great resource for MBA students in learning accounting and applying it to their future courses and careers. Each transaction is identified in the "Transaction" column. Then, the dollar amounts (positive or negative) of the financial statement effects are recorded in the appropriate balance sheet or income statement columns. The template also reflects the statement of cash flow effects (via the cash column) and the statement of stockholders' equity effects (via the contributed capital and earned capital columns). The earned capital account is immediately updated to reflect any income or loss arising from each transaction (denoted by the arrow line from net income to earned capital). This template is instructive as it reveals the financial impacts of transactions, and it provides insights into the effects of accounting choices.

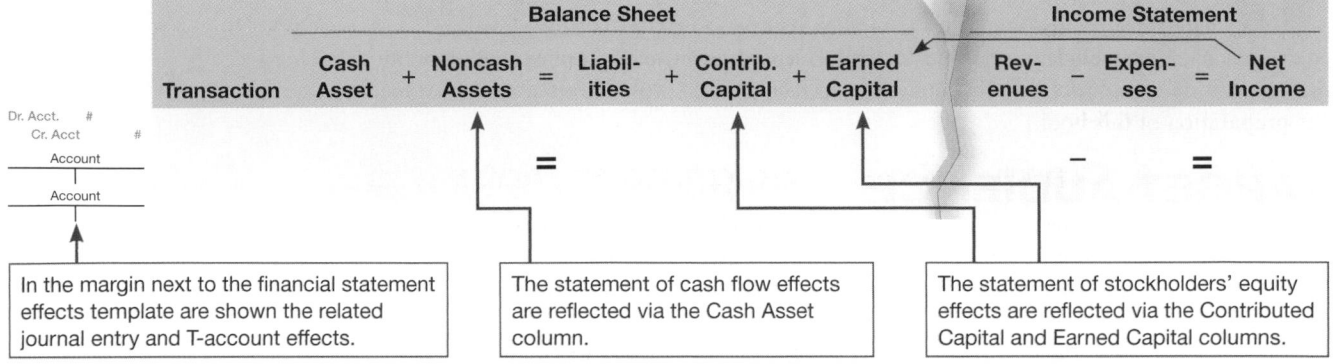

INNOVATIVE PEDAGOGY

Focus Companies for Each Module

In the financial accounting portion of the book, each module's content is explained through the accounting and reporting activities of real companies. To that end, each module incorporates a "focus company" for special emphasis and demonstration. The enhanced instructional value of focus companies comes from the way they engage MBA students in real analysis and interpretation. Focus companies were selected based on the industries that MBA students typically enter upon graduation. We apply a similar approach to the managerial accounting modules, but limited access to internal accounting information prevents us from illustrating all managerial accounting topics using real company data. We do, however, incorporate real world examples throughout each module. Each managerial accounting module is presented in context using real world scenarios from a variety of service, retail, and manufacturing companies. The following table lists focus companies by module.

MODULE 1 Berkshire Hathaway	**MODULE 10** Delta Airlines	**MODULE 19** Wells Fargo
MODULE 2 Apple	**MODULE 11** Procter & Gamble	**MODULE 20** Toyota
MODULE 3 Apple	**MODULE 12** Johnson & Johnson	**MODULE 21** Apple
MODULE 4 Target	**MODULE 13** Carbon Motors	**MODULE 22** Home Depot
MODULE 5 Pfizer	**MODULE 14** WalMart	**MODULE 23** IBM
MODULE 6 Cisco	**MODULE 15** Netflix	**MODULE 24** Viking Air
MODULE 7 Google	**MODULE 16** Nintendo	**APPENDIX B** Starbucks
MODULE 8 Verizon	**MODULE 17** Caterpillar	**APPENDIX C** Kimberly-Clark
MODULE 9 Aon	**MODULE 18** UPS	

Real Company Data Throughout

Market research and reviewer feedback tell us that one of instructors' greatest frustrations with other MBA textbooks is their lack of real company data. We have gone to great lengths to incorporate real company data throughout each module to reinforce important concepts and engage MBA students. We engage nonaccounting MBA students specializing in finance, marketing, management, real estate, operations, and so forth, with companies and scenarios that are relevant to them. For representative examples, **SEE PAGES 4-7, 5-5, 6-11.**

Decision Making Orientation

One primary goal of a MBA accounting course is to teach students the skills needed to apply their accounting knowledge to solving real business problems and making informed business decisions. With that goal in mind, Managerial Decision boxes in each module encourage students to apply the ma-terial presented to solving actual business scenarios. For representative examples, **SEE PAGES 5-16, 6-12, 8-23.**

Mid-Module and Module-End Reviews

Accounting can be challenging—especially for MBA students lacking business experience or previous exposure to business courses. To reinforce concepts presented in each module and to ensure student comprehension, we include mid-module and module-end reviews that require students to recall and apply the accounting techniques and concepts described in each module. For representative examples, **SEE PAGES 4-14, 5-19, 8-6.**

Excellent, Class-Tested Assignment Materials

Excellent assignment material is a must-have component of any successful textbook (and class). In keeping with the rest of the book, we used real company data extensively. We also ensured that assignments reflect our belief that MBA students should be trained in analyzing accounting information to make business decisions, as opposed to working on mechanical bookkeeping tasks. Assignments encourage students to analyze accounting information, interpret it, and apply the knowledge gained to a business decision. For representative examples, **SEE PAGES 4-36, 6-45, 9-41.**

THIRD EDITION CHANGES

Based on classroom use and reviewer feedback, a number of substantive changes have been made in this edition to further enhance the MBA students' experiences:

Financial Accounting Modules (1-12)

- **Updated Financial Data:** We have updated all Focus Company financial statements and disclosures to reflect each company's latest available filings. We have updated all assignments using real data to reflect each company's latest available filings and we have added many new assignments that also utilize real financial data and footnotes.
- **International Financial Reporting Standards (IFRS):** We have updated the IFRS Insight boxes and IFRS Alert boxes throughout the text to introduce students to the similarities and differences between U.S. GAAP and IFRS. We conclude each module with a summary of notable differences between IFRS and U.S. GAAP. We also added a new category of assignments, *IFRS Applications*, that require students to apply IFRS.
- **New Focus Companies:** We now utilize Target as the focus company of Module 4, AON Corporation as the focus company of Module 9, and Delta Airlines as the focus company in Module 10.
- **Treatment of cash.** We treat cash and cash equivalents as a nonoperating asset to reflect its increased use in a manner similar to short-term marketable securities. This change reflects changes in practice.
- **Accounting Quality.** We added a new section on accounting quality in Module 5. It describes measures of accounting quality and factors that mitigate accounting quality. We also provide a check list of items in financial statements that should be reviewed when analyzing financial statements.
- **Simplified treatment of income taxes:** We simplified the treatment of the income tax rate in Module 4; this carries through the ROE disaggregation analysis and in many other sections of the book.
- **Intercorporate Investments:** Consistent with recent changes in accounting standards, we have revised Module 7 to emphasize investors' control of securities and deemphasize the percentage of ownership as the determining factor in selecting the method used for financial reporting.
- **Equity Investments.** We expanded our coverage of equity investments with additional examples and explanation.
- **Credit Ratings:** We have expanded the section on Credit Ratings in Module 8 to add a discussion on trends in credit ratings. We have also updated the credit rating statistics to reflect the latest publication of Moody's Financial Metrics.

- **Noncontrolling Interest.** We added expanded discussion of noncontrolling interest, including accounting for noncontrolling interest, how its reported in the balance sheet and income statement, and the interpretation of related disclosures.
- **Revised Forecasting Module:** We have rewritten Module 11 on forecasting financial statements to help students understand the forecasting process; the revised module uses an actual analyst report on Procter & Gamble, together with the analysts' spreadsheets (from Morgan Stanley) to show how forecasting is performed in practice.
- **New Case Analysis.** New Appendix C illustrates a case analysis of the financial reporting, forecasting, and valuation of Kimberly-Clark Corporation.
- **New Regulations.** We highlight pending and proposed accounting standards and their likely effects, if passed. These include pending standards on financial statement presentation and leasing. This edition also reflects all accounting standards in effect since our last edition, including the new business combination and consolidation standard and goodwill impairment testing.

Managerial Accounting Modules (13-24)

- Over 25% of the assignment material is new.
- Most chapter-opening vignettes are new or revised. New feature companies include: Nintendo, Wells Fargo, IBM, and UPS.
- Most of the Business Insight Boxes are new or revised.
- Revised and shortened the section evaluating the illustration of job costing in Module 17. In addition, revised and shortened the section on Inventory Costs in Various Organizations.
- Revised the section on "Reasons for Budgeting" in Module 21 to include coverage of risk management.
- Added a new section on "Financial and Non-Financial Performance Measures" under Responsibility Accounting in Module 22.
- Added a new section on "Economic Value Added" in Module 23.

ONLINE INSTRUCTION AND HOMEWORK MANAGEMENT SYSTEM

 This supplement is ideal for distance/online/hybrid instruction, faculty responsible for large sections, and/or courses requiring independent learning. Available for an additional fee, this Web-based instruction and homework management system enables students to solve select assignments in each module and receive instant feedback. Assignments with a red check mark in the margin next to them are available in the online system. For more information, contact your sales representative.

SUPPLEMENT PACKAGE

For Instructors

Solutions Manual: Created by the authors, the *Solutions Manual* contains complete solutions to all the assignments in the text.

Test Bank: Written by the authors, the test bank includes multiple-choice items, matching questions, short essay questions, and problems.

Computerized Test Bank: This computerized version of the test bank enables you to add and edit questions; create up to 99 versions of each test; attach graphic files to questions; import and export ASCII files; and select questions based on type or learning objective. Provides password protection for saved tests and question databases and is able to run on a network.

PowerPoint: Created by the authors, the PowerPoint slides outline key elements of each module.

Website: All instructor materials are accessible via the book's Website (password protected) along with other useful links and information. www.cambridgepub.com

For Students

Student Solutions Manual: Created by the authors, the student solutions manual contains all solutions to the even-numbered assignment materials in the textbook. This is a **restricted** item that is only available to students after their instructor has authorized its purchase.

Website: Useful links are available to students free of charge on the book's website.

ACKNOWLEDGMENTS

This book benefited greatly from the valuable feedback of focus group attendees, reviewers, students, and colleagues. We are extremely grateful to them for their help in making this project a success.

Ashiq Ali, *University of Texas—Dallas*
Steve Baginski, *University of Georgia*
Dan Bens, *University of Arizona*
Denny Beresford, *University of Georgia*
Dennis Bline, *Bryant University*
John Briginshaw, *Pepperdine University*
Thomas Buchman, *University of Colorado—Boulder*
Mary Ellen Carter, *Boston College*
Judson Caskey, *UCLA*
Sandra Cereola, *James Madison University*
Sumantra Chakravarty, *CSU—Fullerton*
Betty Chavis, *CSU—Fullerton*
Agnes Cheng, *Louisiana State University*
Joseph Comprix, *Syracuse University*
Ellen Cook, *University of Louisiana*
Araya Debessay, *University of Delaware*
Roger Debreceny, *University of Hawaii*
Vicki Dickinson, *University of Mississippi*
Jeffrey Doyle, *University of Utah*
Joanne Duke, *San Francisco State University*
James Edwards, *University of South Carolina*
John Eichenseher, *University of Wisconsin*
Craig Emby, *Simon Fraser University*
Gerard Engeholm, *Pace University*
Kathryn Epps, *Kennesaw State University*
Mark Finn, *Northwestern University*
Tim Fogarty, *Case Western Reserve*
Richard Frankel, *Washington University*
Dan Givoly, *Pennsylvania State University*
Andy Garcia, *Bowling Green State University*
Julia Grant, *Case Western Reserve*
Karl Hackenbrack, *Vanderbilt University*
Michelle Hanlon, *MIT*
David Harvey, *University of Georgia*
Carla Hayn, *UCLA*
Frank Heflin, *Florida State University*
Elaine Henry, *University of Miami*
Judith Hora, *University of San Diego*
Herbert Hunt, *CSU—Long Beach*
Richard Hurley, *University of Connecticut*
Ross Jennings, *University of Texas*
Greg Jonas, *Case Western Reserve*

Greg Kane, *University of Delaware*
Zafar Khan, *Eastern Michigan University*
Saleha Khumawala, *University of Houston*
Marinilka Kimbro, *University of Washington—Tacoma*
Ron King, *Washington University*
Michael Kirschenheiter, *University of Illinois—Chicago*
Krishna Kumar, *George Washington University*
Lisa Kutcher, *University of Oregon*
Brian Leventhal, *University of Illinois—Chicago*
Pierre Liang, *Carnegie Mellon University*
Barbara Lougee, *University of San Diego*
Luann Lynch, *University of Virginia—Darden*
Michael Maier, *University of Alberta*
Ariel Markelevich, *Suffolk University*
Bruce McClain, *Cleveland State University*
Karen McDougal, *St. Joseph's University*
James McKinney, *University of Maryland*
Greg Miller, *University of Michigan*
Melanie Mogg, *University of Minnesota*
Steve Monahan, *INSEAD*
John Morris, *Kansas State University*
Dennis Murray, *University of Colorado—Denver*
Sandeep Nabar, *Oklahoma State University*
Ramesh Narasimhan, *Montclair State University*
Siva Nathan, *Georgia State University*
Doron Nissim, *Columbia University*
Shail Pandit, *University of Illinois—Chicago*
Susan Parker, *Santa Clara University*
William Pasewark, *Texas Tech*
Stephen Penman, *Columbia University*
Mark Penno, *University of Iowa*
Kathy Petroni, *Michigan State University*
Christine Petrovits, *New York University*
Kirk Philipich, *University of Michigan—Dearborn*
Morton Pincus, *UC—Irvine*
Kay Poston, *University of Indianapolis*
Grace Pownall, *Emory University*

Ram Ramanan, *University of Notre Dame*
David Randolph, *Xavier University*
Laura Rickett, *Kent State University*
Bruce Samuelson, *Pepperdine University*
Diane Satin, *CSU—East Bay*
Shahrokh Saudagaran, *University of Washington—Tacoma*
Andrew Schmidt, *Columbia University*
Stephen Sefcik, *University of Washington*
Galen Sevcik, *Georgia State University*
Lewis Shaw, *Suffolk University*
Kenneth Shaw, *University of Missouri*
Evan Shough, *UNC—Greensboro*
Paul Simko, *University of Virginia—Darden*
Kevin Smith, *University of Kansas*
Pam Smith, *Northern Illinois University*
Sri Sridharan, *Northwestern University*
Charles Stanley, *Baylor University*
Jens Stephan, *Eastern Michigan University*
Phillip Stocken, *Dartmouth College*
Sherre Strickland, *University of Massachusetts—Lowell*
Chandra Subramaniam, *University of Texas*
K.R. Subramanyam, *USC*
Gary Taylor, *University of Alabama*
Mark Taylor, *Case Western Reserve*
Suzanne Traylor, *SUNY—Albany*
Sam Tiras, *Louisiana State University*
Brett Trueman, *UCLA*
Jerry Van Os, *Westminster College*
Mark Vargus, *University of Texas—Dallas*
Robert Vigeland, *Texas Christian University*
Charles Wasley, *University of Rochester*
Greg Waymire, *Emory University*
Andrea Weickgenannt, *Xavier University*
Edward Werner, *Drexel University*
Jeffrey Williams, *University of Michigan*
David Wright, *University of Michigan*
Michelle Yetman, *UC—Davis*
Tzachi Zack, *Ohio State University*
Xiao-Jun Zhang, *UC—Berkeley*
Yuan Zhang, *Columbia University*
Yuping Zhao, *University of Houston*

Special thanks is extended to Vicki Dickinson for her contribution to this edition. In addition, we are extremely grateful to George Werthman, Jill Fischer, Jocelyn Mousel, Rich Kolasa, Debbie McQuade, Terry McQuade, and the entire team at Cambridge Business Publishers for their encouragement, enthusiasm, and guidance. Their market research, editorial development, and promotional efforts have made this book the best-selling financial & managerial accounting textbook in the MBA market.

Peter   Bob   Mary Lea   Al   Wayne

February 2012

BRIEF CONTENTS

About the Authors   iii

Preface   v

MODULE 1 Financial Accounting for MBAs   1-1

MODULE 2 Introducing Financial Statements and Transaction Analysis   2-1

MODULE 3 Accounting Adjustments and Constructing Financial Statements   3-1

MODULE 4 Analyzing and Interpreting Financial Statements   4-1

MODULE 5 Reporting and Analyzing Operating Income.   5-1

MODULE 6 Reporting and Analyzing Operating Assets   6-1

MODULE 7 Reporting and Analyzing Intercorporate Investments   7-1

MODULE 8 Reporting and Analyzing Nonowner Financing.   8-1

MODULE 9 Reporting and Analyzing Owner Financing.   9-1

MODULE 10 Reporting and Analyzing Off-Balance-Sheet Financing   10-1

MODULE 11 Forecasting Financial Statements   11-1

MODULE 12 Analyzing and Valuing Equity Securities   12-1

MODULE 13 Managerial Accounting for MBAs   13-1

MODULE 14 Cost Behavior, Activity Analysis, and Cost Estimation   14-1

MODULE 15 Cost-Volume-Profit Analysis and Planning.   15-1

MODULE 16 Relevant Costs and Benefits for Decision Making   16-1

MODULE 17 Product Costing: Job and Process Operations   17-1

MODULE 18 Activity-Based Costing, Customer Profitability, and Activity-Based Management   18-1

MODULE 19 Additional Topics in Product Costing   19-1

MODULE 20 Pricing and Other Product Management Decisions   20-1

MODULE 21 Operational Budgeting and Profit Planning.   21-1

MODULE 22 Standard Costs and Performance Reports   22-1

MODULE 23 Segment Reporting, Transfer Pricing, and Balanced Scorecard   23-1

MODULE 24 Capital Budgeting Decisions   24-1

APPENDIX A Compound Interest Tables. A-1

APPENDIX B Constructing the Statement of Cash Flows B-1

APPENDIX C Comprehensive Financial Accounting Case: Kimberly-Clark C-1

APPENDIX D Chart of Accounts with Acronyms D-1

Glossary. G-1

Index I-1

CONTENTS

MODULE 1
Financial Accounting for MBAs 1-1

Focus Company: Berkshire Hathaway 1-1
Reporting on Business Activities 1-4
Financial Statements: Demand and Supply 1-5
    Demand for Information 1-5
    Supply of Information 1-7
    International Accounting Standards and Convergence 1-8
Financial Statements 1-9
    Balance Sheet 1-10
    Income Statement 1-12
    Statement of Stockholders' Equity 1-14
    Statement of Cash Flows 1-15
    Financial Statement Linkages 1-15
    Information Beyond Financial Statements 1-16
    Choices in Financial Accounting 1-16
Mid-Module Review 1-18
Analysis of Financial Statements 1-18
    Return on Assets 1-18
    Components of Return on Assets 1-18
    Return on Equity 1-19
Financial Statements and Business Analysis 1-20
    Analyzing the Competitive Environment 1-20
    Analyzing the Broader Business Environment 1-22
Global Accounting 1-22
Module-End Review 1-23
Appendix 1A: Accessing SEC Filings 1-23
Appendix 1B: Accounting Principles and Governance 1-25
Assignments 1-31
Solutions to Review Problems 1-41

MODULE 2
Introducing Financial Statements and Transaction Analysis 2-1

Focus Company: Apple 2-1
Balance Sheet 2-3
    Balance Sheet and the Flow of Costs 2-3
    Assets 2-4
    Liabilities and Equity 2-6
Income Statement 2-11
    Recognition of Revenues and Expenses 2-12
    Reporting of Transitory Items 2-13
Statement of Stockholders' Equity 2-14
Statement of Cash Flows 2-15
    Statement Format and Data Sources 2-15
    Cash Flow Computations 2-17
Mid-Module Review 1 2-18
Articulation of Financial Statements 2-19
    Retained Earnings Reconciliation 2-19
    Financial Statement Linkages 2-20
Mid-Module Review 2 2-21
Transaction Analysis and Accounting 2-21
    Analyzing and Recording Transactions 2-22
    Adjusting Accounts 2-22
    Constructing Financial Statements 2-25
Global Accounting 2-29
Module-End Review 2-29
Appendix 2A: Additional Information Sources 2-30
Assignments 2-32
Solutions to Review Problems 2-45

MODULE 3
Accounting Adjustments and Constructing Financial Statements 3-1

Focus Company: Apple 3-1
Accounting for Transactions 3-4
    Financial Statement Effects Template 3-4
    Transaction Analysis 3-5
Mid-Module Review 1 3-8
Accounting Adjustments (Accruals) 3-8
    Prepaid Expenses (Assets) 3-9
    Unearned Revenues (Liabilities) 3-9
    Accrued Expenses (Liabilities) 3-10
    Accrued Revenues (Assets) 3-11
    Trial Balance Preparation and Use 3-12
Mid-Module Review 2 3-15
Financial Statement Preparation 3-15
    Income Statement 3-15
    Balance Sheet 3-16
    Statement of Stockholders' Equity 3-17
    Statement of Cash Flows 3-17
    Closing Process 3-20
Global Accounting 3-21
Module-End Review 3-21
Appendix 3A: Closing Process Using Journal Entries 3-22
Assignments 3-24
Solutions to Review Problems 3-35

MODULE 4
Analyzing and Interpreting Financial Statements 4-1

Focus Company: Target 4-1
Return on Equity (ROE) 4-4
Operating Return (RNOA) 4-5
    Operating Items in the Income Statement —NOPAT 4-5
Mid-Module Review 1 4-7
    Operating Items in the Balance Sheet —NOA 4-8
RNOA Disaggregation into Margin and Turnover 4-11
    Net Operating Profit Margin 4-11
    Net Operating Asset Turnover 4-12
    Trade-Off between Margin and Turnover 4-13
Mid-Module Review 2 4-14
    Further RNOA Disaggregation 4-15
Nonoperating Return 4-16
Financial Leverage Across Industries 4-17
    Limitations of Ratio Analysis 4-18
Global Accounting 4-19
Module-End Review 4-20
Appendix 4A: Nonoperating Return Component of ROE 4-21
Appendix 4B: Tools of Liquidity and Solvency Analysis 4-26
Appendix 4C: DuPont Disaggregation Analysis 4-30
Assignments 4-33
Solutions to Review Problems 4-54

MODULE 5
Reporting and Analyzing Operating Income 5-1

Focus Company: Pfizer 5-1
Operating Income Components 5-5
   Revenue and its Recognition 5-5
   Research and Development (R&D) Expenses 5-13
   Restructuring Expenses and Incentives 5-16
Mid-Module Review 1 5-19
   Income Tax Expenses and Allowances 5-19
Mid-Module Review 2 5-26
   Foreign Currency Translation Effects 5 26
Operating Components Below-The-Line 5-28
   Extraordinary Items 5-28
   Earnings Per Share 5-29
Accounting Quality 5-30
   Assessing and Remediating Accounting Quality 5-32
Global Accounting 5-33
Module-End Review 5-35
Appendix 5A: Expanded Explanation of Deferred Taxes 5-35
Assignments 5-37
Solutions to Review Problems 5-58

MODULE 6
Reporting and Analyzing Operating Assets 6-1

Focus Company: Cisco Systems 6-1
Accounts Receivable 6-3
   Allowance for Uncollectible Accounts 6-5
   Footnote and MD&A Disclosures 6-7
   Analysis Implications 6-8
Mid-Module Review 1 6-12
Inventory 6-13
   Capitalization of Inventory Cost 6-13
   Inventory Costing Methods 6-14
   Lower of Cost or Market 6-16
   Footnote Disclosures 6-17
   Financial Statement Effects of Inventory Costing 6-18
   Tools of Inventory Analysis 6-20
   LIFO Liquidations 6-25
Mid-Module Review 2 6-25
Property, Plant and Equipment (PPE) 6-26
   Capitalization of Asset Costs 6-26
   Depreciation 6-27
   Asset Sales and Impairments 6-30
   Footnote Disclosures 6-33
   Analysis Implications 6-33
Global Accounting 6-35
Module-End Review 6-36
Assignments 6-37
Solutions to Review Problems 6-52

MODULE 7
Reporting and Analyzing Intercorporate Investments 7-1

Focus Company: Google 7-1
Passive Investments 7-4
   Acquisition and Sale 7-5
   Fair Value versus Cost 7-5
   Investments Marked to Market 7-6
   Financial Statement Disclosures 7-7
   Investments Reported at Cost 7-9
Mid-Module Review 1 7-10
Investments with Significant Influence 7-11
   Accounting for Investments with Significant Influence 7-12
   Equity Method Accounting and ROE Effects 7-13

Mid-Module Review 2 7-16
Investments with Control 7-16
   Accounting for Investments with Control 7-16
Global Accounting 7-27
Module-End Review 7-28
Appendix 7A: Accounting for Derivatives 7-28
Assignments 7-32
Solutions to Review Problems 7-51

MODULE 8
Reporting and Analyzing Nonowner Financing 8-1

Focus Company: Verizon Communications 8-1
Current Liabilities 8-4
   Accounts Payable 8-4
   Accounts Payable Turnover (APT) 8-5
Mid-Module Review 1 8-6
   Accrued Liabilities 8-6
Mid-Module Review 2 8-10
   Current Nonoperating Liabilities 8-10
Mid-Module Review 3 8-11
Long-Term Nonoperating Liabilities 8-12
   Pricing of Debt 8-12
   Effective Cost of Debt 8-14
Reporting of Debt Financing 8-15
   Financial Statement Effects of Debt Issuance 8-15
   Effects of Discount and Premium Amortization 8-17
   Financial Statement Effects of Bond Repurchase 8-19
   Financial Statement Footnotes 8-20
Credit Ratings and the Cost of Debt 8-21
   What Are Credit Ratings? 8-22
   What Determines Credit Ratings? 8-23
   Any Trends with Credit Ratings? 8-24
   Trends in Financial Ratios Over Time 8-25
   Financial Ratios across Industries 8-25
Global Accounting 8-27
Module-End Review 8-28
Appendix 8A: Compound Interest 8-28
Appendix 8B: Economics of Gains and Losses on Bond Repurchases 8-32
Assignments 8-34
Solutions to Review Problems 8-46

MODULE 9
Reporting and Analyzing Owner Financing 9-1

Focus Company: Aon Corporation 9-1
Contributed Capital 9-4
   Classes of Stock 9-4
   Accounting for Stock Transactions 9-6
   Stock-Based Compensation 9-9
Mid-Module Review 1 9-15
Earned Capital 9-15
   Cash Dividends 9-16
Mid-Module Review 2 9-17
   Stock Dividends and Splits 9-17
Mid-Module Review 3 9-19
   Accumulated Other Comprehensive Income 9-19
Noncontrolling Interest 9-21
   Analysis and Interpretation of Noncontrolling Interest 9-23
   Summary of Stockholders' Equity 9-23
Equity Carve-Outs and Convertibles 9-24
   Sell-Offs 9-24
   Spin-Offs 9-25
   Split-Offs 9-26
   Analysis of Equity Carve-Outs 9-26
Mid-Module Review 4 9-27
   Convertible Securities 9-27

Global Accounting 9-29
Module-End Review 9-30
Assignments 9-30
Solutions to Review Problems 9-48

MODULE **10**
Reporting and Analyzing Off-Balance-Sheet Financing 10-1

Focus Company: Delta Air Lines 10-1

Leases 10-4
    Lessee Reporting of Leases 10-4
    Footnote Disclosure of Leases 10-6
    Capitalization of Operating Leases 10-7
Mid-Module Review 10-11
Pensions 10-12
    Reporting of Defined Benefit Pension Plans 10-12
    Balance Sheet Effects 10-12
    Income Statement Effects 10-14
    Footnote Disclosures—Components of Plan Assets and PBO 10-15
    Footnote Disclosures and Future Cash Flows 10-17
    Footnote Disclosures and Profit Implications 10-18
    Analysis Implications 10-19
    Other Post-Employment Benefits 10-20
Module-End Review 10-22
Appendix 10A: Amortization Component of Pension Expense 10-23
Appendix 10B: Special Purpose Entities (SPEs) 10-24
Appendix 10C: Lease Capitalization Using a Calculator and
                Present Value Tables 10-27
Assignments 10-29
Solutions to Review Problems 10-46

MODULE **11**
Forecasting Financial Statements 11-1

Focus Company: Procter & Gamble (P&G) 11-1

Forecasting Process 11-3
    Overview of Forecasting Process 11-3
    All-Important Revenues Forecast 11-5
    Identifying the Forecasting Steps 11-7
    Morgan Stanley Research Report 11-7
Step 1: Forecasting Revenues 11-8
    Factors Impacting Revenue Growth 11-8
    Forecasting Revenue Growth 11-12
Step 2: Forecasting Expenses 11-15
    Forecasting Operating Expenses 11-15
    Forecasting Nonoperating Expenses 11-16
    Forecasting Expenses for P&G 11-16
Step 3: Forecasting Assets, Liabilities and Equity 11-18
    Process of Forecasting Balance Sheet Items 11-19
    Forecasting Balance Sheet Items 11-21
Step 4: Adjust Forecasted Statements 11-26
    Adjust Forecasted Balance Sheet 11-27
Forecasting Statement of Cash Flows 11-28
Additional Forecasting Issues 11-30
    Multiyear Forecasting of Financial Statements 11-30
Mid-Module Review 11-33
Parsimonious Multiyear Forecasting 11-34
    Parsimonious Method for Forecasting 11-35
    Multiyear Forecasting with Parsimonious Method 11-35
Global Accounting 11-36
Module-End Review 11-36
Appendix 11A Morgan Stanley's Forecast Report on Procter &
                Gamble 11-36
Assignments 11-51
Solutions to Review Problems 11-71

MODULE **12**
Analyzing and Valuing Equity Securities 12-1

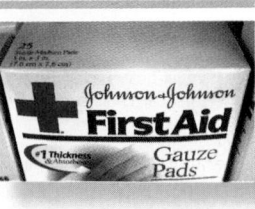

Focus Company: Johnson & Johnson 12-1

Equity Valuation Models 12-3
    Dividend Discount Model 12-3
    Discounted Cash Flow Model 12-3
    Residual Operating Income Model 12-4
Discounted Cash Flow (DCF) Model 12-4
    DCF Model Structure 12-4
    Steps in Applying the DCF Model 12-5
    Illustrating the DCF Model 12-5
Mid-Module Review 12-7
Residual Operating Income (ROPI) Model 12-8
    ROPI Model Structure 12-8
    Steps in Applying the ROPI Model 12-8
    Illustrating the ROPI Model 12-9
Managerial Insights from the ROPI Model 12-10
Assessment of Valuation Models 12-12
Global Accounting 12-13
Module-End Review 12-13
Appendix 12A: Johnson & Johnson Financial Statements 12-13
Appendix 12B: Oppenheimer Valuation of Procter & Gamble 12-15
Appendix 12C: Derivation of Free Cash Flow Formula 12-17
Assignments 12-18
Solutions to Review Problems 12-31

MODULE **13**
Managerial Accounting for MBAs 13-1

Focus Company: Carbon Motors Corporation 13-1

Uses of Accounting Information 13-3
    Financial Accounting 13-3
    Managerial Accounting 13-4
    Globalization of Accounting Standards 13-5
    Strategic Cost Management 13-5
Organizations: Missions, Goals, and Strategies 13-6
    Strategic Position Analysis 13-7
    Managerial Accounting and Goal Attainment 13-10
    Planning, Organizing, and Controlling 13-11
Mid-Module Review 13-12
    Competition and Its Key Dimensions 13-13
Cost Drivers 13-13
    Structural Cost Drivers 13-15
    Organizational Cost Drivers 13-15
    Activity Cost Drivers 13-16
Ethics in Managerial Accounting 13-17
    Codes of Ethics 13-18
    Corporate Governance 13-18
    Corporate Social Responsibility 13-19
Module-End Review 13-20
Assignments 13-20
Solutions to Review Problems 13-26

MODULE **14**
Cost Behavior, Activity Analysis, and Cost Estimation 14-1

Focus Company: Walmart 14-1

Cost Behavior Analysis 14-3
    Four Basic Cost Behavior Patterns 14-3
    Factors Affecting Cost Behavior Patterns 14-5
    Total Cost Function for an Organization or Segment 14-5
    Relevant Range 14-6
    Additional Cost Behavior Patterns 14-8
    Committed and Discretionary Fixed Costs 14-8

Mid-Module Review 14-10
Cost Estimation 14-10
    High-Low Cost Estimation 14-10
    Scatter Diagrams 14-12
    Least-Squares Regression 14-13
Additional Issues in Cost Estimation 14-15
    Changes in Technology and Prices 14-15
    Matching Activity and Costs 14-16
    Identifying Activity Cost Drivers 14-16
Alternative Cost Driver Classifications 14-16
    Manufacturing Cost Hierarchy 14-17
    Customer Cost Hierarchy 14-18
Module-End Review 14-20
Assignments 14-20
Solutions to Review Problems 14-31

MODULE 15
Cost-Volume-Profit Analysis and Planning 15-1

Focus Company: Netflix 15-1
Profitability Analysis 15-3
    Key Assumptions 15-3
    Profit Formula 15-4
Contribution and Functional Income Statements 15-6
    Functional Income Statement 15-6
    Analysis Using Contribution Margin Ratio 15-7
Break-Even Point and Profit Planning 15-8
    Determining Break-Even Point 15-8
    Profit Planning 15-8
    Cost-Volume-Profit Graph 15-10
    Profit-Volume Graph 15-10
    Impact of Income Taxes 15-12
Mid-Module Review 15-13
Multiple-Product Cost-Volume-Profit Analysis 15-13
    Sales Mix Analysis 15-14
Analysis of Operating Leverage 15-16
Module-End Review 15-18
Appendix 15A: Profitability Analysis with Unit and Nonunit Cost
              Drivers 15-19
Assignments 15-22
Solutions to Review Problems 15-35

MODULE 16
Relevant Costs and Benefits for Decision Making 16-1

Focus Company: Nintendo 16-1
Identifying Relevant Costs 16-3
    Relevance of Future Revenues 16-4
    Relevance of Outlay Costs 16-4
    Irrelevance of Sunk Costs 16-5
    Sunk Costs Can Cause Ethical Dilemmas 16-5
    Relevance of Disposal and Salvage Values 16-5
    Relevance of Opportunity Costs 16-6
Differential Analysis of Relevant Costs 16-6
Mid-Module Review 16-7
Applying Differential Analysis 16-8
    Multiple Changes in Profit Plans 16-8
    Special Orders 16-9
    Outsourcing Decisions (Make or Buy) 16-11
    Sell or Process Further 16-15
Use of Limited Resources 16-16
    Single Constraint 16-17
    Multiple Constraints 16-18
    Theory of Constraints 16-18
    Limitations of Decision Analysis Models 16-19
Module-End Review 16-20
Assignments 10-21
Solutions to Review Problems 16-34

MODULE 17
Product Costing: Job and Process Operations 17-1

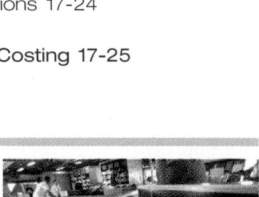

Focus Company: Caterpillar 17-1
Inventory Costs in Various
Organizations 17-3
Inventory Costs for Financial Reporting 17-4
    Product Costs and Period Costs 17-4
    Three Components of Product Costs 17-5
    A Closer Look at Manufacturing Overhead 17-7
The Production Environment 17-9
    Production Files and Records 17-10
Job Costing for Products and Services 17-10
    Job Costing Illustrated 17-11
    Statement of Cost of Goods Manufactured 17-15
    Overapplied and Underapplied Overhead 17-16
    Job Costing in Service Organizations 17-17
Mid-Module Review 17-19
Process Costing 17-20
    Cost of Production Report 17-20
    Weighted Average and First-In, First-Out Process Costing 17-23
    Process Costing in Service Organizations 17-24
Module-End Review 17-25
Appendix 17A: Absorption and Variable Costing 17-25
Assignments 17-30
Solutions to Review Problems 17-45

MODULE 18
Activity-Based Costing, Customer Profitability, and Activity-Based Management 18-1

Focus Company: UPS 18-1
Changing Cost Environment 18-3
Activity-based Costing 18-4
    ABC Product Costing Model 18-4
Traditional Product Costing and ABC Compared 18-6
    Applying Overhead with a Plantwide Rate 18-6
    Applying Overhead with Department Rates 18-7
    Applying Overhead with Activity-Based Costing 18-8
Mid-Module Review 18-11
    Limitations of ABC Illustration 18-12
    Comparing Traditional and Activity-Based Costing 18-12
ABC Implementation Issues 18-13
ABC and Customer Profitability Analysis 18-14
    Customer Profitability Profile 18-14
    ABC Customer Profitability Analysis Illustrated 18-14
Activity-Based Management 18-17
Module-End Review 18-18
Assignments 18-18
Solutions to Review Problems 18-35

MODULE 19
Additional Topics in Product Costing 19-1

Focus Company: Wells Fargo
Bank 19-1
Production and Service Department
Costs 19-3
Service Department Cost Allocation 19-4
    Direct Method 19-5
    Step Method 19-6
    Linear Algebra (Reciprocal) Method 19-8
    Dual Rates 19-8
Mid-Module Review 19-9
Lean Production and Just-in-Time Inventory Management 19-9
    Reducing Incoming Materials Inventory 19-10
    Reducing Work-in-Process Inventory 19-11

Reducing Finished Goods Inventory 19-12

Performance Evaluation and Recordkeeping with Lean Production and JIT 19-12

    Performance Evaluation 19-12

    Simplified Recordkeeping 19-14

Module-End Review 19-15

Assignments 19-15

Solutions to Review Problems 19-25

MODULE **20**
Pricing and Other Product Management Decisions 20-1

Focus Company: Toyota 20-1

Understanding the Value Chain 20-3

    Usefulness of a Value Chain Perspective 20-5

    Value-Added and Value Chain Perspectives 20-7

The Pricing Decision 20-7

    Economic Approaches to Pricing 20-7

    Cost-Based Approaches to Pricing 20-8

Mid-Module Review 20-11

Target Costing 20-11

    Target Costing Is Proactive for Cost Management 20-12

    Target Costing Encourages Design for Production 20-13

    Target Costing Reduces Time to Introduce Products 20-14

    Target Costing Requires Cost Information 20-14

    Target Costing Requires Coordination 20-14

    Target Costing is Key for Products with Short Life Cycles 20-15

    Target Costing Helps Manage Life Cycle Costs 20-15

Continuous Improvement Costing 20-16

Benchmarking 20-17

Module-End Review 20-18

Assignments 20-19

Solutions to Review Problems 20-26

MODULE **21**
Operational Budgeting and Profit Planning 21-1

Focus Company: Apple 21-1

Reasons for Budgeting 21-3

    Compel Planning 21-3

    Promote Communication and Coordination 21-3

    Provide a Guide to Action and Basis of Evaluation 21-4

    Aid in Risk Management 21-4

General Approaches to Budgeting 21-4

    Output/Input Approach 21-4

    Activity-Based Approach 21-5

    Incremental Approach 21-5

    Minimum Level Approach 21-6

Mid-Module Review 21-7

Master Budget 21-7

    Sales Budget 21-9

    Purchases Budget 21-10

    Selling Expense Budget 21-10

    General and Administrative Expense Budget 21-11

    Cash Budget 21-11

    Budgeted Financial Statements 21-13

    Finalizing the Budget 21-15

Budget Development in Manufacturing Organizations 21-15

    Production Budget 21-15

    Manufacturing Cost Budget 21-15

Budget Development and Manager Behavior 21-18

    Employee Participation 21-18

    Budgeting Periods 21-19

    Forecasts 21-19

    Ethics 21-20

    Open Book Management 21-20

Module-End Review 1 21-21

Module-End Review 2 21-22

Assignments 21-23

Solutions to Review Problems 21-37

MODULE **22**
Standard Costs and Performance Reports 22-1

Focus Company: Home Depot 22-1

Responsibility Accounting 22-3

    Performance Reporting and Organization Structures 22-4

    Types of Responsibility Centers 22-5

    Financial and Nonfinancial Performance Measures 22-6

Performance Reporting for Cost Centers 22-7

    Development of Flexible Budgets 22-7

    Flexible Budgets Emphasize Performance 22-8

Mid-Module Review 22-9

    Standard Costs and Performance Reports 22-9

Variance Analysis for Costs 22-10

    Establishing and Using Standards for Direct Materials 22-11

    Establishing and Using Standards for Direct Labor 22-13

    Establishing and Using Standards for Variable Overhead 22-15

    Fixed Overhead Variances 22-17

Performance Reports for Revenue Centers 22-17

    Inclusion of Controllable Costs 22-19

    Revenue Centers as Profit Centers 22-19

Module-End Review 22-21

Appendix 22A: Fixed Overhead Variances 22-21

Appendix 22B: Reconciling Budgeted and Actual Income 22-23

Assignments 22-24

Solutions to Review Problems 22-36

MODULE **23**
Segment Reporting, Transfer Pricing, and Balanced Scorecard 23-1

Focus Company: IBM 23-1

Strategic Business Segments and Segment Reporting 23-3

    Multilevel Segment Income Statements 23-4

    Interpreting Segment Reports 23-5

Mid-Module Review 23-7

Transfer Pricing 23-7

    Management Considerations 23-7

    Determining Transfer Prices 23-10

Investment Center Evaluation Measures 23-12

    Return on Investment 23-13

    Investment Center Income 23-15

    Investment Center Asset Base 23-15

    Other Valuation Issues 23-16

    Residual Income 23-16

    Economic Value Added 23-16

    Which Measure Is Best? 23-18

Balanced Scorecard 23-19

    Balanced Scorecard Framework 23-19

    Balanced Scorecard and Strategy 23-21

Module-End Review 23-22

Assignments 23-23

Solutions to Review Problems 23-38

MODULE **24**
Capital Budgeting Decisions 24-1

Focus Company: Viking Air 24-1

Long-Range Planning and Capital Budgeting 24-4

Capital Budgeting Models that Consider Time Value of Money 24-6

    Expected Cash Flows 24-6

    Manager Behavior and Expected Cash Flows 24-7

    Net Present Value 24-8

    Internal Rate of Return 24-9

Cost of Capital 24-10
Mid-Module Review 24-11
Capital Budgeting Models that do not Consider Time Value of
Money 24-11
    Payback Period 24-11
    Accounting Rate of Return 24-13
Evaluation of Capital Budgeting Models 24-14
Additional Aspects of Capital Budgeting 24-16
    Using Multiple Investment Criteria 24-16
    Evaluating Risk 24-16
    Differential Analysis of Project Cash Flows 24-17
    Predicting Differential Costs and Revenues for High-Tech
    Investments 24-17
Taxes in Capital Budgeting Decisions 24-20
    Depreciation Tax Shield 24-20
    Investment Tax Credit 24-21
Module-End Review 24-22
Appendix 24A: Time Value of Money 24-23
Appendix 24B: Table Approach to Determining Internal Rate of
                Return 24-28
Assignments 24-29
Solutions to Review Problems 24-41

APPENDIX **A**
Compound Interest Tables A-1

APPENDIX **B**
Constructing the Statement of Cash Flows B-1

Focus Company: Starbucks B-1
Framework for Statement of Cash
Flows B-3
    Operating Activities B-5
    Investing Activities B-5
    Financing Activities B-5
Cash Flow From Operating Activities B-6
    Steps to Compute Net Cash Flow from Operating Activities B-7
    Java House Case Illustration B-8
Cash Flows from Investing Activities B-11
    Java House Case Illustration B-11
Cash Flows from Financing Activities B-12
    Java House Case Illustration B-13
Summary of Net Cash Flow reporting B-13

    Supplemental Disclosures for Indirect Method B-14
    Java House Case Illustration B-14
Applications of Cash Flow Information B-15
    Usefulness of Classifications B-15
    Usefulness of the Statement of Cash Flows B-16
    Ratio Analyses of Cash Flows B-16
Appendix-End Review 1 B-18
Appendix B1: Direct Method Reporting for the Statement of Cash
            Flows B-19
Appendix-End Review 2 B-22
Assignments B-24
Solutions to Review Problems B-40

APPENDIX **C**
Comprehensive Financial Accounting Case C-1

Focus Company: Kimberly-
Clark C-1
Introduction C-3
Reviewing The Financial Statements C-4
    Income Statement Reporting and Analysis C-4
    Balance Sheet Reporting and Analysis C-12
    Off-Balance-Sheet Reporting and Analysis C-24
    Statement of Cash Flows Reporting and Analysis C-27
    Independent Audit Opinion C-28
Assessing Profitability and Creditworthiness C-29
    ROE Disaggregation C-30
    Disaggregation of RNOA—Margin and Turnover C-30
    Disaggregation of Margin and Turnover C-30
    Credit Analysis C-31
    Summarizing Profitability and Creditworthiness C-31
Forecasting Financial Statement Numbers C-32
Valuing Equity Securities C-35
    Multiyear Forecasting C-35
    Residual Operating Income Valuation C-37
    Sensitivity Analysis of Valuation Parameters C-38
    Assessment of the Valuation Estimate C-38
    Summary Observations C-38

APPENDIX **D**
Chart of Accounts with Acronyms D-1

Glossary G-1

Index I-1

Getty Images

BERKSHIRE HATHAWAY

Berkshire Hathaway owns numerous businesses that pursue diverse activities. The legendary Warren Buffett, the "Sage of Omaha," manages the company. Buffett's investment philosophy is to acquire and hold companies over the long run. His acquisition criteria, taken from Berkshire Hathaway's annual report, follow:

1. Large purchases (and large pretax earnings).

2. Demonstrated consistent earning power (future projections are of *no* interest to us, nor are 'turnaround' situations).

3. Businesses earning good returns on equity while employing little or no debt.

4. Management in place (we can't supply it).

5. Simple businesses (if there's lots of technology, we won't understand it).

6. An offering price (we don't want to waste our time or that of the seller by talking, even preliminarily, about a transaction when price is unknown).

At least three of Buffett's six criteria relate to financial performance. First, he seeks businesses with large and consistent earning power. Buffett is not only looking for consistent earnings, but earnings that are measured according to accounting policies that closely mirror the underlying economic performance of the business.

Second, Buffett focuses on "businesses earning good returns on equity," defined as income divided by average stockholders' equity: "Our preference would be to reach our goal by directly owning a diversified group of businesses that generate cash and consistently earn above-average returns" (Berkshire Hathaway annual report). For management to earn a good return on equity, it must focus on both income (financial performance) and equity (financial condition).

Third, Buffett values companies based on their ability to generate consistent earnings and cash. He focuses on *intrinsic value,* which he defines in each annual report as follows:

Intrinsic value is an all-important concept that offers the only logical approach to evaluating the relative attractiveness of

Financial Accounting for MBAs

LEARNING OBJECTIVES

LO1 Identify and discuss the users and suppliers of financial statement information. (p. 1-5)

LO2 Identify and explain the four financial statements, and define the accounting equation. (p. 1-9)

LO3 Explain and apply the basics of profitability analysis. (p. 1-18)

LO4 Describe business analysis within the context of a competitive environment. (p. 1-20)

LO5 Describe the accounting principles and regulations that frame financial statements. (p. 1-25)

investments and businesses. Intrinsic value can be defined simply: It is the discounted value of the cash that can be taken out of a business during its remaining life.

The discounted value Buffett describes is the present (today's) value of the cash flows the company expects to generate in the future. Cash is generated when companies are well managed and operate profitably and efficiently.

Warren Buffett provides some especially useful investment guidance in his Chairman's letter from a prior period's Berkshire Hathaway annual report:

> Three suggestions for investors: First, beware of companies displaying weak accounting. If a company still does not expense options, or if its pension assumptions are fanciful, watch out. When managements take the low road in aspects that are visible, it is likely they are following a similar path behind the scenes. There is seldom just one cockroach in the kitchen.
>
> Second, unintelligible footnotes usually indicate untrustworthy management. If you can't understand a footnote or

other managerial explanation, it's usually because the CEO doesn't want you to. Enron's descriptions of certain transactions still baffle me.

> Finally, be suspicious of companies that trumpet earnings projections and growth expectations. Businesses seldom operate in a tranquil, no-surprise environment, and earnings simply don't advance smoothly (except, of course, in the offering books of investment bankers).

This book will explain Buffett's references to stock option accounting and pension assumptions as well as a host of other accounting issues that affect interpretation and valuation of companies' financial performance. We will analyze and interpret the footnotes, which Buffett views as crucial to quality financial reporting and analysis. Our philosophy is simple: we must understand the intricacies and nuances of financial reporting to become critical readers and users of financial reports for company analysis and valuation.

Sources: Berkshire Hathaway *10-K Reports,* Berkshire Hathaway *Annual Reports; The Wall Street Journal,* January 2012.

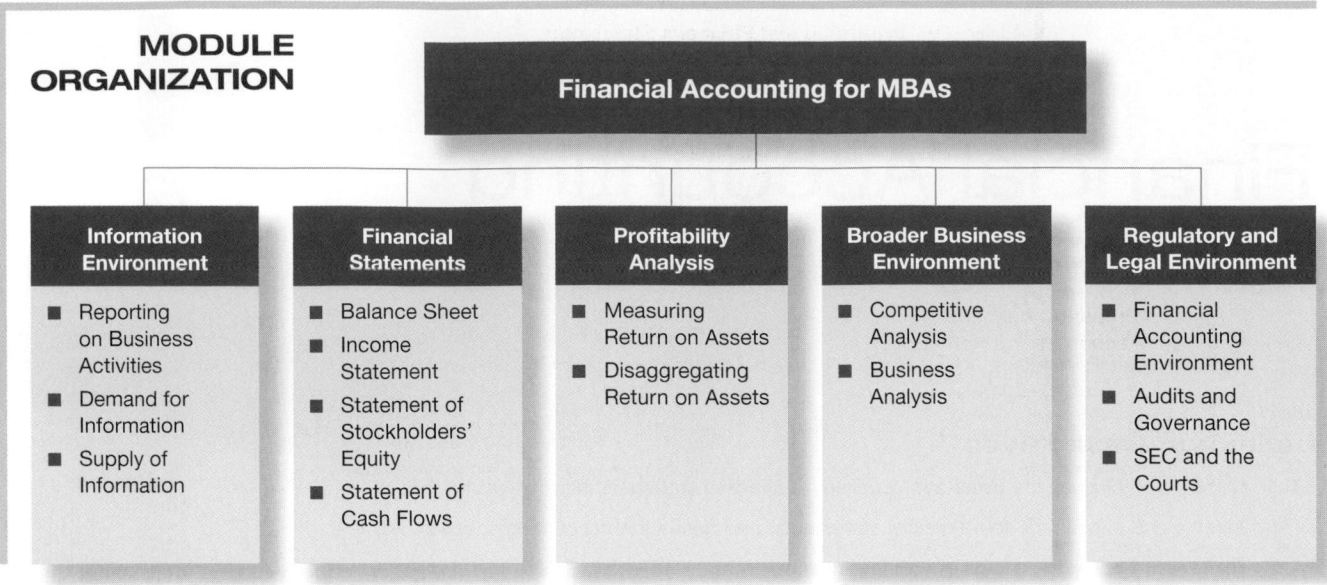

Financial accounting information serves many purposes. To understand this, imagine that we are a specific user of accounting information. For example, imagine we are a stock investor—how might we use accounting information to identify a stock to buy? Imagine we are a bond trader—how might we use accounting information to assess whether a company is able to repay its debt? Imagine we are a manager—how might we use accounting information to decide whether to acquire another company or divest a current division? Imagine we are an equity or credit analyst—how might we use accounting to assess and communicate an investment appraisal or credit report?

This book explains the concepts, preparation, and application of financial accounting information and, importantly, how decision makers use such information. Accounting information informs many decisions beyond the few listed above. In general, managers use financial accounting information to make operating, investing, and financing decisions. Investors and analysts use financial accounting information to help decide whether to buy or sell stock. Lenders and rating agencies use accounting information to help decide on a company's creditworthiness and lending terms. Regulators use accounting information to enact social and economic policies and to monitor compliance with laws. Legal institutions use accounting information to assess fines and reparations in litigation. Other decision makers rely on accounting information for purposes ranging from determining demands in labor union negotiations to levying damages for environmental abuses.

This module begins with an overview of the information environment that companies face, and it discusses the demand for and supply of financial information. We then review financial statements and explain what they convey about a company. Profitability is described next and is used as a focus of much of our application of accounting information. We conclude the module with an introduction to business analysis, which is an important part of drawing inferences from financial statements. We include (in the appendix) a discussion of the regulatory environment that defines current financial reporting for companies.

The remainder of the book can be broken into four parts–see figure at top of next page. Part 1 consists of Modules 1, 2 and 3 and offers an introduction of accounting fundamentals and the business environment. Part 2 consists of Module 4, which introduces analysis of financial statements. Although an aim of this book is to help us understand the application of financial statements, it is important that we understand their preparation. Thus, Part 3, which consists of Modules 5 through 10, describes the accounting for assets, liabilities, and equity; Appendix B covers accounting for cash flows. Part 4 consists of Modules 11 and 12, which explain the forecasting of accounting numbers and the valuation of common stock; Appendix C applies many of the analysis tools introduced in this book.

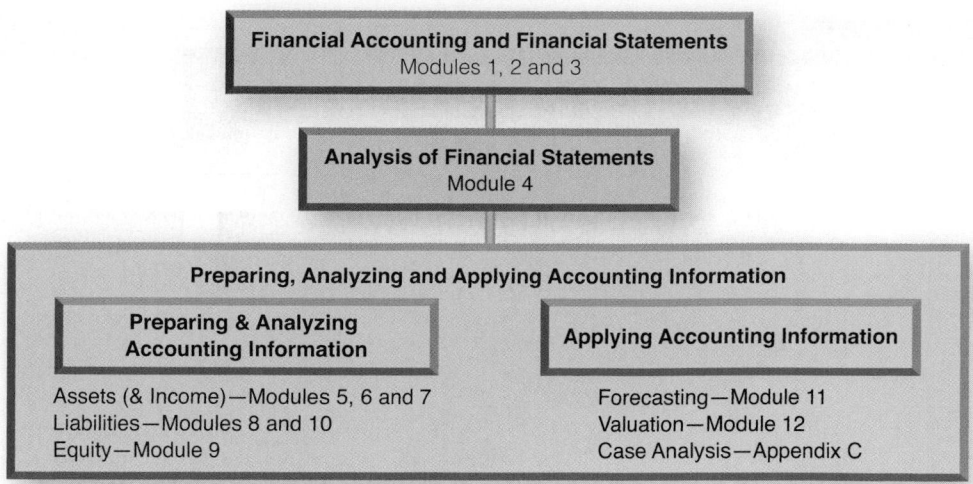

REPORTING ON BUSINESS ACTIVITIES

To effectively manage a company or infer whether it is well managed, we must understand the company's business activities. Financial statements help us understand these business activities. These statements report on a company's performance and financial condition, and reveal executive management's privileged information and insights.

Financial statements satisfy the needs of different users. The functioning of the accounting information system involves application of accounting standards to produce financial statements. Effectively using this information system involves making judgments, assumptions, and estimates based on data contained in the financial reports. The greatest value we derive from this information system as users of financial reports is the insight we gain into the business activities of the company under analysis.

To effectively analyze and use accounting information, we must consider the business context in which the information is created—see Exhibit 1.1. Without exception, all companies *plan* business activities, *finance* those activities, *invest* in those activities, and then engage in *operating* activities. Companies conduct all these activities while confronting *business forces*, including market constraints and competitive pressures. Financial statements provide crucial input for strategic planning. They also provide information about the relative success of those plans, which can be used to take corrective action or make new operating, investing, and financing decisions.

Exhibit 1.1 depicts the business activities for a typical company. The outer (green) ring is the planning process that reflects the overarching goals and objectives of the company within which strategic decisions are made. Those strategic decisions involve company financing, asset management, and daily operations. Apple, Inc., the focus company in Modules 2 and 3, provides the following description of its business strategy in its annual report:

Business Strategy   The Company is committed to bringing the best user experience to its customers through its innovative hardware, software, peripherals, services, and Internet offerings. The Company's business strategy leverages its unique ability to design and develop its own operating systems, hardware, application software, and services to provide its customers new products and solutions with superior ease-of-use, seamless integration, and innovative industrial design. The Company believes continual investment in research and development is critical to the development and enhancement of innovative products and technologies. In conjunction with its strategy, the Company continues to build and host a robust platform for the discovery and delivery of third-party digital content and applications through the iTunes Store... The Company is therefore uniquely positioned to offer superior and well-integrated digital lifestyle and productivity solutions.

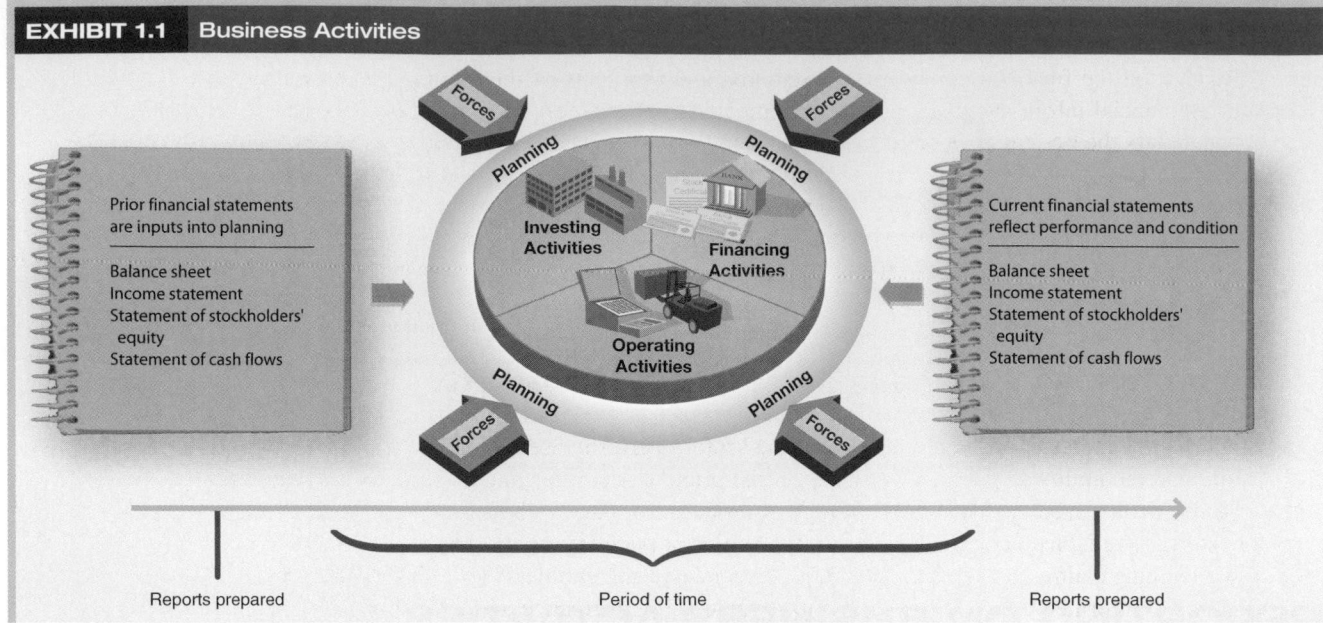

EXHIBIT 1.1   Business Activities

A company's *strategic* (or *business*) *plan* reflects how it plans to achieve its goals and objectives. A plan's success depends on an effective analysis of market demand and supply. Specifically, a company must assess demand for its products and services, and assess the supply of its inputs (both labor and capital). The plan must also include competitive analyses, opportunity assessments, and consideration of business threats.

Historical financial statements provide insight into the success of a company's strategic plan, and are an important input to the planning process. These statements highlight portions of the strategic plan that proved profitable and, thus, warrant additional capital investment. They also reveal areas that are less effective, and provide information to help managers develop remedial action.

Once strategic adjustments are planned and implemented, the resulting financial statements provide input into the planning process for the following year; and this process begins again. Understanding a company's strategic plan helps focus our analysis of financial statements by placing them in proper context.

FINANCIAL STATEMENTS: DEMAND AND SUPPLY

LO1 Identify and discuss the users and suppliers of financial statement information.

Demand for financial statements has existed for centuries as a means to facilitate efficient contracting and risk-sharing. Decision makers and other stakeholders demand information on a company's past and prospective returns and risks. Supply of financial statements is driven by companies' wish to lower their costs of financing and less obvious costs such as political, contracting, and labor. Managers decide how much financial information to supply by weighing the costs of disclosure against the benefits of disclosure. Regulatory agencies intervene in this process with various disclosure requirements that establish a minimum supply of information.

Demand for Information

The following broad classes of users demand financial accounting information:

- Managers and employees
- Investment analysts and information intermediaries
- Creditors and suppliers
- Shareholders and directors
- Customers and strategic partners
- Regulators and tax agencies
- Voters and their representatives

Managers and Employees

For their own well-being and future earnings potential, managers and employees demand accounting information on the financial condition, profitability, and prospects of their companies as well as comparative financial information on competing companies and business opportunities. This permits them to benchmark their company's performance and condition. Managers and employees also demand financial accounting information for use in compensation and bonus contracts that are tied to such numbers. The popularity of employee profit sharing and stock ownership plans has further increased demand for financial information. Other sources of demand include union contracts that link wage negotiations to accounting numbers and pension and benefit plans whose solvency depends on company performance.

Investment Analysts and Information Intermediaries

Investment analysts and other information intermediaries, such as financial press writers and business commentators, are interested in predicting companies' future performance. Expectations about future profitability and the ability to generate cash impact the price of securities and a company's ability to borrow money at favorable terms. Financial reports reflect information about past performance and current resources available to companies. These reports also provide information about claims on those resources, including claims by suppliers, creditors, lenders, and shareholders. This information allows analysts to make informed assessments about future financial performance and condition so they can provide stock recommendations or write commentaries.

Creditors and Suppliers

Banks and other lenders demand financial accounting information to help determine loan terms, loan amounts, interest rates, and required collateral. Loan agreements often include contractual requirements, called **covenants**, that restrict the borrower's behavior in some fashion. For example, loan covenants might require the loan recipient to maintain minimum levels of working capital, retained earnings, interest coverage, and so forth to safeguard lenders. Covenant violations can yield technical default, enabling the creditor to demand early payment or other compensation. Suppliers demand financial information to establish credit terms and to determine their long-term commitment to supply-chain relations. Both creditors and suppliers use financial information to monitor and adjust their contracts and commitments with a company.

Shareholders and Directors

Shareholders and directors demand financial accounting information to assess the profitability and risks of companies. Shareholders and others (such as investment analysts, brokers and potential investors) search for information useful in their investment decisions. **Fundamental analysis** uses financial information to estimate company value and to form buy-sell stock strategies. Both directors and shareholders use accounting information to evaluate managerial performance. Managers similarly use such information to request an increase in compensation and managerial power from directors. Outside directors are crucial to determining who runs the company, and these directors use accounting information to help make leadership decisions.

Customers and Strategic Partners

Customers (both current and potential) demand accounting information to assess a company's ability to provide products or services as agreed and to assess the company's staying power and reliability. Strategic partners wish to estimate the company's profitability to assess the fairness of returns on mutual transactions and strategic alliances.

Regulators and Tax Agencies

Regulators (such as the SEC, the Federal Trade Commission, and the Federal Reserve Bank) and tax agencies demand accounting information for antitrust assessments, public protection, price setting, import-export analyses, and setting tax policies. Timely and reliable information is crucial to effective regulatory policy, and accounting information is often central to social and economic policy. For example, governments often grant monopoly rights to electric and gas companies serving specific areas in exchange for regulation over prices charged to consumers. These prices are mainly determined from accounting measures.

Voters and Their Representatives

Voters and their representatives to national, state, and local governments demand accounting information for policy decisions. The decisions can involve economic, social, taxation, and other initiatives. Voters and their representatives also use accounting information to monitor government spending. We have all heard of the $1,000 hammer type stories that government watchdog groups uncover while sifting through accounting data. Contributors to nonprofit organizations also demand accounting information to assess the impact of their donations.

IFRS INSIGHT   **Development of International Standards**

The accounting standards explained in this book are consistent with generally accepted accounting principles (GAAP) primarily developed by the Financial Accounting Standards Board (FASB). A similar organization, the International Accounting Standards Board (IASB), develops a global set of International Financial Reporting Standards (IFRS) for preparation of financial statements. To increase comparability of financial statements and reduce reporting complexity, the Securities Exchange Commission (SEC), the FASB, and the IASB are committed to a process of convergence to one set of world accounting standards. As we progress through the book, we will provide IFRS Insight boxes like this to identify differences between GAAP and IFRS.

Supply of Information

In general, the quantity and quality of accounting information that companies supply are determined by managers' assessment of the benefits and costs of disclosure. Managers release information provided the benefits of disclosing that information outweigh the costs of doing so. Both *regulation* and *bargaining power* affect disclosure costs and benefits and thus play roles in determining the supply of accounting information. Most areas of the world regulate the minimum levels of accounting disclosures. In the U.S., publicly traded firms must file financial accounting information with the Securities Exchange Commission (SEC). The two main compulsory SEC filings are:

■ Form **10-K**: the audited annual report that includes the four financial statements, discussed below, with explanatory notes and the management's discussion and analysis (MD&A) of financial results.

■ Form **10-Q**: the unaudited quarterly report that includes summary versions of the four financial statements and limited additional disclosures.

Forms 10-K and 10-Q are available electronically from the SEC Website (see Appendix 1A). The minimum, regulated level of information is not the standard. Both the quantity and quality of information differ across companies and over time. We need only look at several annual reports to see considerable variance in the amount and type of accounting information supplied. For example, differences abound on disclosures for segment operations, product performance reports, and financing activities. Further, some stakeholders possess ample bargaining power to obtain accounting information for themselves. These typically include private lenders and major suppliers and customers.

Benefits of Disclosure

The benefits of supplying accounting information extend to a company's capital, labor, input, and output markets. Companies must compete in these markets. For example, capital markets provide debt and equity financing; the better a company's prospects, the lower is its cost of capital (as reflected in lower interest rates or higher stock prices). The same holds for a company's recruiting efforts in labor markets and its ability to establish superior supplier-customer relations in the input and output markets.

A company's performance in these markets depends on success with its business activities *and* the market's awareness of that success. Companies reap the benefits of disclosure with good news about their products, processes, management, and so forth. That is, there are real economic incentives for companies to disclose reliable (audited) accounting information enabling them to better compete in capital, labor, input, and output markets.

What inhibits companies from providing false or misleading good news? There are several constraints. An important constraint imposed by stakeholders is that of audit requirements and legal repercussions associated with inaccurate accounting information. Another relates to reputation effects from disclosures as subsequent events either support or refute earlier news.

Costs of Disclosure

The costs of supplying accounting information include its preparation and dissemination, competitive disadvantages, litigation potential, and political costs. Preparation and dissemination costs can be substantial, but companies have often already incurred those costs because managers need similar information for their own business decisions. The potential for information to yield competitive disadvantages is high. Companies are concerned that disclosures of their activities such as product or segment successes, strategic alliances or pursuits, technological or system innovations, and product or process quality improvements will harm their competitive advantages. Also, companies are frequently sued when disclosures create expectations that are not met. Highly visible companies often face political and public pressure, which creates "political costs." These companies often try to appear as if they do not generate excess profits. For example, government defense contractors, large software conglomerates, and oil companies are favorite targets of public scrutiny. Disclosure costs are higher for companies facing political costs.

The SEC adopted Regulation FD, or Reg FD for short, to curb the practice of selective disclosure by public companies (called *issuers* by the SEC) to certain shareholders and financial analysts. In the past, many companies disclosed important information in meetings and conference calls that excluded individual shareholders. The goal of this rule is to even the playing field for all investors. Reg FD reads as follows: "Whenever an issuer discloses any material nonpublic information regarding that issuer, the issuer shall make public disclosure of that information . . . simultaneously, in the case of an intentional disclosure; and . . . promptly, in the case of a non-intentional disclosure." Reg FD increased the cost of voluntary financial disclosure and led some companies to curtail the supply of financial information to all users.

International Accounting Standards and Convergence

The International Accounting Standards Board (IASB) oversees the development of accounting standards for a vast number of countries outside the U.S. More than 100 countries, including those in the European Union, require use of International Financial Reporting Standards (IFRS) developed by the IASB. For many years, IASB and the FASB operated as independent standard-setting bodies. In the early 2000s, pressure mounted for these two standard-setting organizations to collaborate and create one set of internationally acceptable standards. At a joint meeting in 2002, the FASB and the IASB each acknowledged their commitment to the development of high-quality, compatible accounting standards that could be used for both domestic and cross-border financial reporting. At that meeting, both the FASB and IASB pledged to use their best efforts to (a) make their existing financial reporting standards fully compatible as soon as practicable and (b) to coordinate their future work programs to ensure that once achieved, compatibility is maintained.

In May 2011, the SEC proposed a transition method to incorporate IFRS into the U.S. reporting system. The SEC delineated the perceived benefits and risks of the proposed method but did not lay out a definitive timeline for its implementation. Larger companies have begun to issue IFRS-compliant financial statements, and foreign private issuers on U.S. stock exchanges are currently permitted to file IFRS financial statements without reconciliation to U.S. GAAP as was previously required.

Are financial statements prepared under IFRS substantially different from those prepared under U.S. GAAP? At a broad level, the answer is no. Both are prepared using accrual accounting and utilize similar conceptual frameworks. Both require the same set of financial statements: a balance sheet, an income statement, a statement of cash flows, a statement of stockholders' equity, and a set of explanatory footnotes. That does not mean that no differences exist. However, the differences are typically technical in nature, and do not differ on broad principles discussed in this book. Indeed, recent accounting standards issued by the FASB and the IASB, such as the accounting for acquisitions of companies, were developed jointly and issued simultaneously to minimize differences as the two standard-setting bodies work toward harmonization of international standards.

At the end of each module, we summarize key differences between U.S. GAAP and IFRS. Also, there are a variety of sources that provide more detailed and technical analysis of similarities and differences between U.S. GAAP and IFRS. The FASB, the IASB, and each of the "Big 4" accounting firms also maintain Websites devoted to this issue. Search under IFRS and PwC, KPMG, EY and Deloitte. The two standard-setting bodies also provide useful information, see: FASB (**www.fasb.org/intl/**) and IASB (**www.iasb.org/Home.htm**).

BUSINESS INSIGHT   **Accounting Quality**

In the bear market that followed the bursting of the **dot.com** bubble in the early 2000s, and amid a series of corporate scandals such as Enron, Tyco, and WorldCom, Congress passed the **Sarbanes-Oxley Act,** often referred to as *SOX*. SOX sought to rectify perceived problems in accounting, including weak audit committees and deficient internal controls. Increased scrutiny of financial reporting and internal controls has had some success. A report by Glass, Lewis and Co., a corporate-governance research firm, shows that the number of financial restatements by publicly traded companies surged to a record 1,295 in 2005—which is one restatement for each 12 public companies, and more than triple the 2002 total, the year SOX passed. The Glass, Lewis and Co. report concluded that "when so many companies produce inaccurate financial statements, it seriously calls into question the quality of information that investors relied upon to make capital-allocation decisions" (**CFO.Com**). Bottom line: we must be critical readers of financial reports.

FINANCIAL STATEMENTS

LO2 Identify and explain the four financial statements, and define the accounting equation.

Companies use four financial statements to periodically report on business activities. These statements are the: balance sheet, income statement, statement of stockholders' equity, and statement of cash flows. Exhibit 1.2 shows how these statements are linked across time. A balance sheet reports on a company's financial position at a *point in time*. The income statement, statement of stockholders' equity, and the statement of cash flows report on performance over a *period of time*. The three statements in the middle of Exhibit 1.2 (period-of-time statements) link the balance sheet from the beginning to the end of a period.

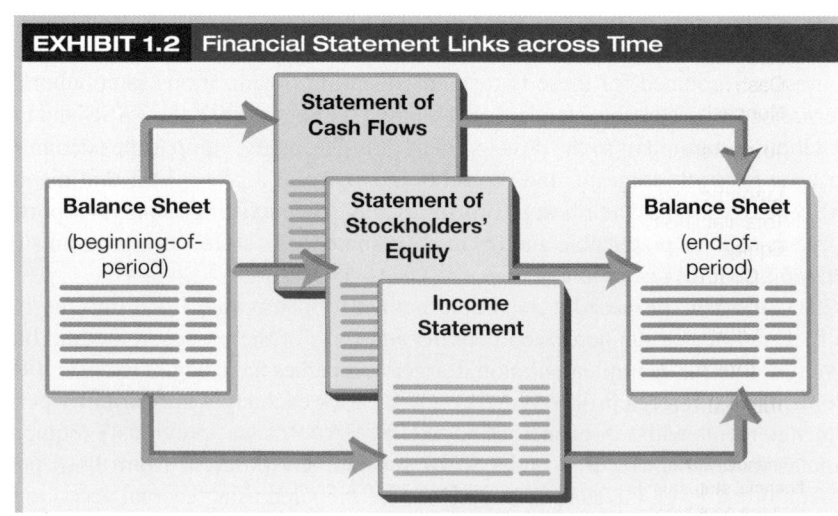

EXHIBIT 1.2   Financial Statement Links across Time

A one-year, or annual, reporting period is common and is called the *accounting,* or *fiscal, year.* Of course, firms prepare financial statements more frequently; semiannual, quarterly, and monthly financial statements are common. *Calendar-year* companies have reporting periods beginning on January 1 and ending on December 31. Berkshire Hathaway is a calendar-year company. Some companies choose a fiscal year ending on a date other than December 31, such as when sales and inventory are low. For example, Best Buy's fiscal year-end is always near February 1, after the busy holiday season.

Balance Sheet

A balance sheet reports a company's financial position at a point in time. The balance sheet reports the company's *resources* (*assets*), namely, what the company owns. The balance sheet also reports the *sources* of asset financing. There are two ways a company can finance its assets. It can raise money from shareholders; this is *owner financing.* It can also raise money from banks or other creditors and suppliers; this is *nonowner financing.* This means that both owners and nonowners hold claims on company assets. Owner claims on assets are referred to as *equity* and nonowner claims are referred to as *liabilities* (or debt). Since all financing must be invested in something, we obtain the following basic relation: *investing equals financing.* This equality is called the **accounting equation,** which follows:

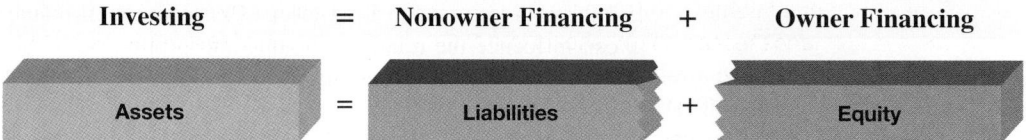

The accounting equation works for all companies at all points in time.

The balance sheet for Berkshire Hathaway is in Exhibit 1.3 (condensed). Refer to this balance sheet to verify the following amounts: assets = $372,229 million; liabilities = $209,295 million; and equity = $162,934 million. Assets equal liabilities plus equity, which reflects the accounting equation: investing equals financing.

Investing Activities

Balance sheets are organized like the accounting equation. Investing activities are represented by the company's assets. These assets are financed by a combination of nonowner financing (liabilities) and owner financing (equity).

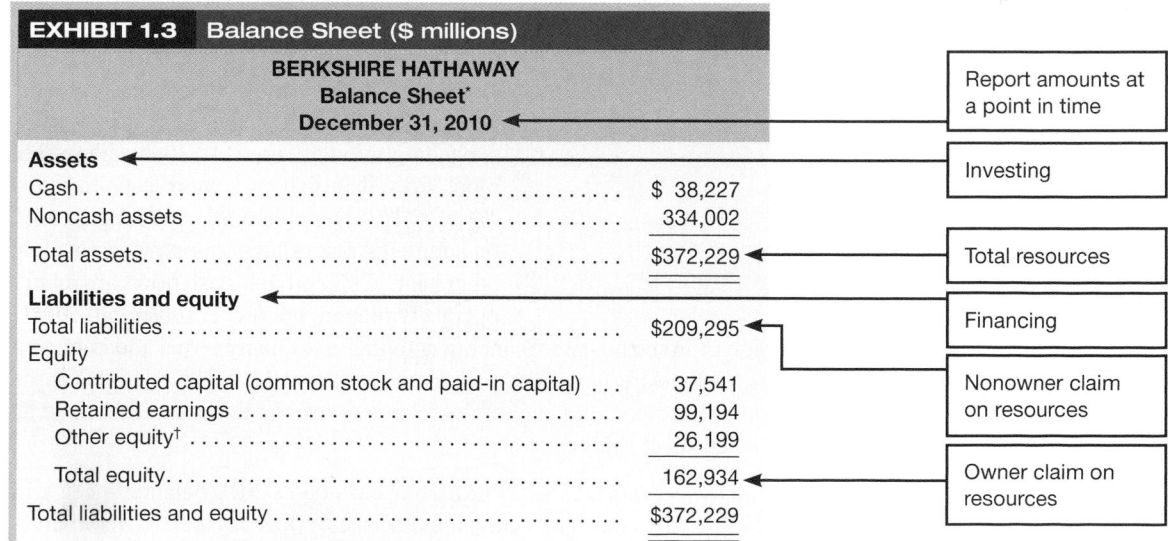

EXHIBIT 1.3	Balance Sheet ($ millions)	
BERKSHIRE HATHAWAY		
Balance Sheet*		
December 31, 2010		Report amounts at a point in time
Assets		Investing
Cash	$ 38,227	
Noncash assets	334,002	
Total assets	$372,229	Total resources
Liabilities and equity		
Total liabilities	$209,295	Financing
Equity		
Contributed capital (common stock and paid-in capital)	37,541	Nonowner claim on resources
Retained earnings	99,194	
Other equity†	26,199	
Total equity	162,934	Owner claim on resources
Total liabilities and equity	$372,229	

* Financial statement titles often begin with the word *consolidated.* This means that the financial statement includes a parent company and one or more subsidiaries, companies that the parent company owns and controls.

† For Berkshire Hathaway, other equity includes accumulated other comprehensive income and noncontrolling interests.

For simplicity, Berkshire Hathaway's balance sheet in Exhibit 1.3 categorizes assets into cash and noncash assets. Noncash assets consist of several asset categories (Module 2 explains the composition of noncash assets). These categories are listed in order of their nearness to cash. For example, companies own a category of assets called inventories. These are goods that the company intends to sell to its customers. Inventories are converted into cash when they are sold within a short period of time. Hence, they are classified as short-term assets. Companies also report a category of assets called property, plant and equipment. This category includes a company's office buildings or manufacturing facilities. Property, plant and equipment assets will be held for an extended period of time and are, therefore, generally classified as long-term assets.

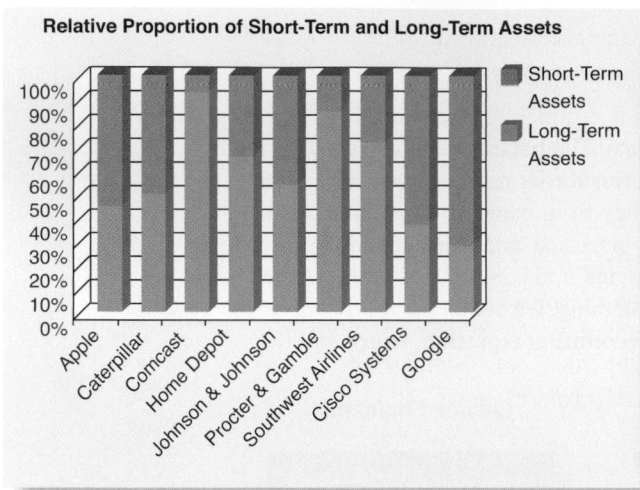

The relative proportion of short-term and long-term assets is largely determined by a company's business model. This is evident in the graph to the side that depicts the relative proportion of short- and long-term assets for several companies that we feature in this book. Companies such as Cisco and Google require little investment in long-term assets. On the other hand, Comcast and Procter & Gamble require a large investment in long-term assets. Although managers can influence the relative amounts and proportion of assets, their flexibility is somewhat limited by the nature of their industries.

Financing Activities

Assets must be paid for, and funding is provided by a combination of owner and nonowner financing. Owner (or equity) financing includes resources contributed to the company by its owners along with any profit retained by the company. Nonowner (creditor or debt) financing is borrowed money. We distinguish between these two financing sources for a reason: borrowed money entails a legal obligation to repay amounts owed, and failure to do so can result in severe consequences for the borrower. Equity financing entails no such legal obligation for repayment.

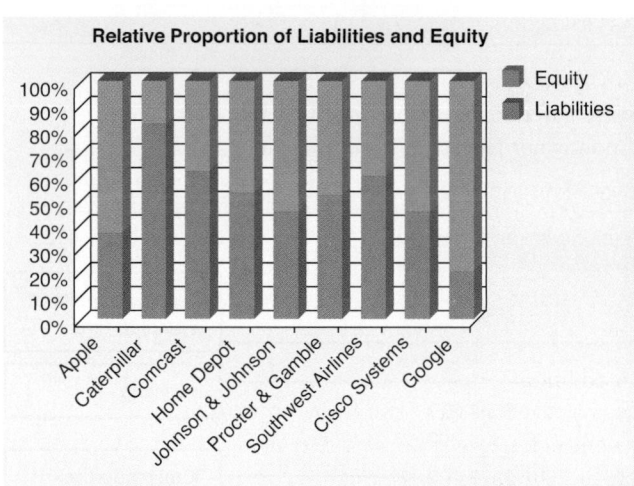

The relative proportion of nonowner (liabilities) and owner (equity) financing is largely determined by a company's business model. This is evident in the graph to the side, again citing many of the companies we feature as focus companies in this book. Google is a relatively new company that is expanding into new markets. Its business model is, therefore, more risky than that of a more established company operating in relatively stable markets. Google cannot afford to take on additional risk of higher nonowner financing levels. On the other hand, Caterpillar's cash flows are relatively stable. It can operate with more nonowner financing.

Our discussion of investing and financing activities uses many terms and concepts that we explain later in the book. Our desire here is to provide a sneak preview into the interplay among financial statements, manager behavior, and economics. Some questions that we might have at this early stage regarding the balance sheet follow:

■ Berkshire Hathaway reports $38,227 million of cash on its 2010 balance sheet, which is 10% of total assets. Many investment-type companies such as Berkshire Hathaway and high-tech companies such as Cisco Systems carry high levels of cash. Why is that? Is there a cost to holding too much cash? Is it costly to carry too little cash?

■ The relative proportion of short-term and long-term assets is largely dictated by companies' business models. Why is this the case? Why is the composition of assets on balance sheets for companies in the same industry similar? By what degree can a company's asset composition safely deviate from industry norms?

- What are the trade-offs in financing a company by owner versus nonowner financing? If nonowner financing is less costly, why don't we see companies financed entirely with borrowed money?

- How do shareholders influence the strategic direction of a company? How can long-term creditors influence strategic direction?

- Most assets and liabilities are reported on the balance sheet at their acquisition price, called *historical cost*. Would reporting assets and liabilities at fair values be more informative? What problems might fair-value reporting cause?

Review the Berkshire Hathaway balance sheet summarized in Exhibit 1.3 and think about these questions. We provide answers for each of these questions as we progress through the book.

IFRS INSIGHT Balance Sheet Presentation and IFRS

Balance sheets prepared under IFRS often classify accounts in reverse order of liquidity (lack of nearness to cash), which is the opposite of what U.S. companies do. For example, intangible assets are typically listed first and cash is listed last among assets. Also, equity is often listed before liabilities, where liabilities are again listed in order of decreasing liquidity. These choices reflect convention and *not* IFRS requirements.

Income Statement

An **income statement** reports on a company's performance over a period of time and lists amounts for revenues (also called sales) and expenses. Revenues less expenses yield the bottom-line net income amount. Berkshire Hathaway's income statement is in Exhibit 1.4. Refer to its income statement to verify the following: revenues = $136,185 million; expenses = $123,218 million; and net income = $12,967 million. Net income reflects the profit (also called earnings) to owners for that specific period.

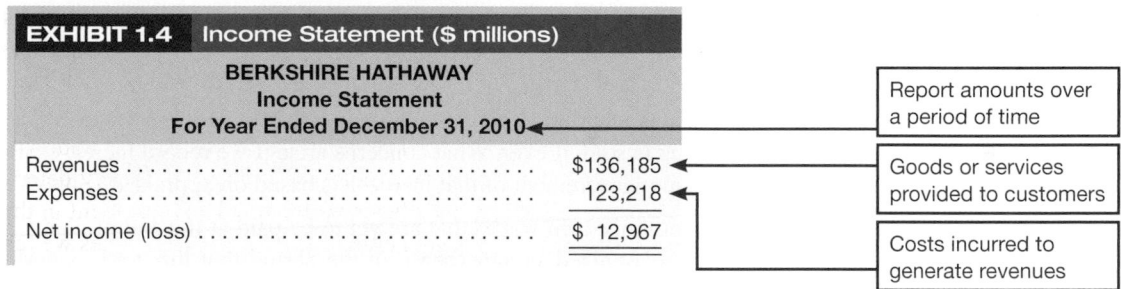

EXHIBIT 1.4 Income Statement ($ millions)

BERKSHIRE HATHAWAY Income Statement For Year Ended December 31, 2010		
Revenues	$136,185	
Expenses	123,218	
Net income (loss)	$ 12,967	

Report amounts over a period of time

Goods or services provided to customers

Costs incurred to generate revenues

Manufacturing and merchandising companies typically include an additional expense account, called cost of goods sold (or cost of sales), in the income statement following revenues. It is also common to report a subtotal called gross profit (or gross margin), which is revenues less cost of goods sold. The company's remaining expenses are then reported below gross profit. This income statement layout follows:

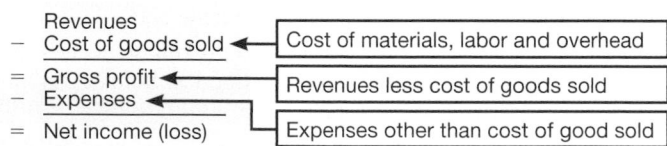

Revenues
− Cost of goods sold ← Cost of materials, labor and overhead
= Gross profit ← Revenues less cost of goods sold
− Expenses ←
= Net income (loss) ← Expenses other than cost of good sold

Operating Activities

Operating activities use company resources to produce, promote, and sell its products and services. These activities extend from input markets involving suppliers of materials and labor to a company's output markets involving customers of products and services. Input markets generate most *expenses*

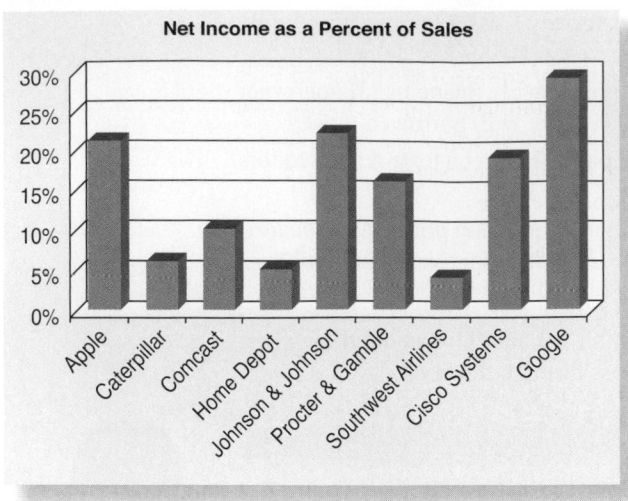

Net Income as a Percent of Sales

(or *costs*) such as inventory, salaries, materials, and logistics. Output markets generate *revenues* (or *sales*) to customers. Output markets also generate some expenses such as marketing and distributing products and services to customers. Net income arises when revenues exceed expenses. A loss occurs when expenses exceed revenues.

Differences exist in the relative profitability of companies across industries. Although effective management can increase the profitability of a company, business models play a large part in determining company profitability. These differences are illustrated in the graph (to the side) of net income as a percentage of sales for several companies.

Home Depot operates in a mature industry with little ability to differentiate its products from those of its competitors. Hence, its net income as a percentage of sales is low. **Southwest Airlines** faces a different kind of problem: having competitors that are desperate and trying to survive. Profitability will not return to the transportation industry until weaker competitors are no longer protected by bankruptcy courts. At the other end of the spectrum are **Apple**, **Cisco Systems** and **Google**. All three are dominant in their industries with products protected by patent laws. Their profitability levels are more akin to that of monopolists.

As a sneak preview, we might consider the following questions regarding the income statement:

■ Assume that a company sells a product to a customer who promises to pay in 30 days. Should the seller recognize the sale when it is made or when cash is collected?

■ When a company purchases a long-term asset such as a building, its cost is reported on the balance sheet as an asset. Should a company, instead, record the cost of that building as an expense when it is acquired? If not, how should a company report the cost of that asset over the course of its useful life?

■ Manufacturers and merchandisers report the cost of a product as an expense when the product sale is recorded. How might we measure the costs of a product that is sold by a merchandiser? By a manufacturer?

■ If an asset, such as a building, increases in value, that increase in value is not reported as income until the building is sold, if ever. What concerns arise if we record increases in asset values as part of income, when measurement of that increase is based on appraised values?

■ Employees commonly earn wages that are yet to be paid at the end of a particular period. Should their wages be recognized as an expense in the period that the work is performed, or when the wages are paid?

■ Companies are not allowed to report profit on transactions relating to their own stock. That is, they don't report income when stock is sold, nor do they report an expense when dividends are paid to shareholders. Why is this the case?

Review the Berkshire Hathaway income statement summarized in Exhibit 1.4 and think about these questions. We provide answers for each of these questions as we progress through the book.

BUSINESS INSIGHT   **Warren Buffett on Financial Reports**

"When Charlie and I read reports, we have no interest in pictures of personnel, plants or products. References to EBITDA [earnings before interest, taxes, depreciation and amortization] make us shudder—does management think the tooth fairy pays for capital expenditures? We're very suspicious of accounting methodology that is vague or unclear, since too often that means management wishes to hide something. And we don't want to read messages that a public relations department or consultant has turned out. Instead, we expect a company's CEO to explain in his or her own words what's happening." —Berkshire Hathaway annual report

Statement of Stockholders' Equity

The **statement of stockholders' equity** reports on changes in key types of equity over a period of time. For each type of equity, the statement reports the beginning balance, a summary of the activity in the account during the year, and the ending balance. Berkshire Hathaway's statement of stockholders' equity is in Exhibit 1.5. During the recent period, its equity changed due to share issuances and income reinvestment. Berkshire Hathaway classifies these changes into three categories:

- *Contributed capital*, the stockholders' net contributions to the company
- *Retained earnings*, net income over the life of the company minus all dividends ever paid
- *Other*, consists of amounts that we explain later in the book

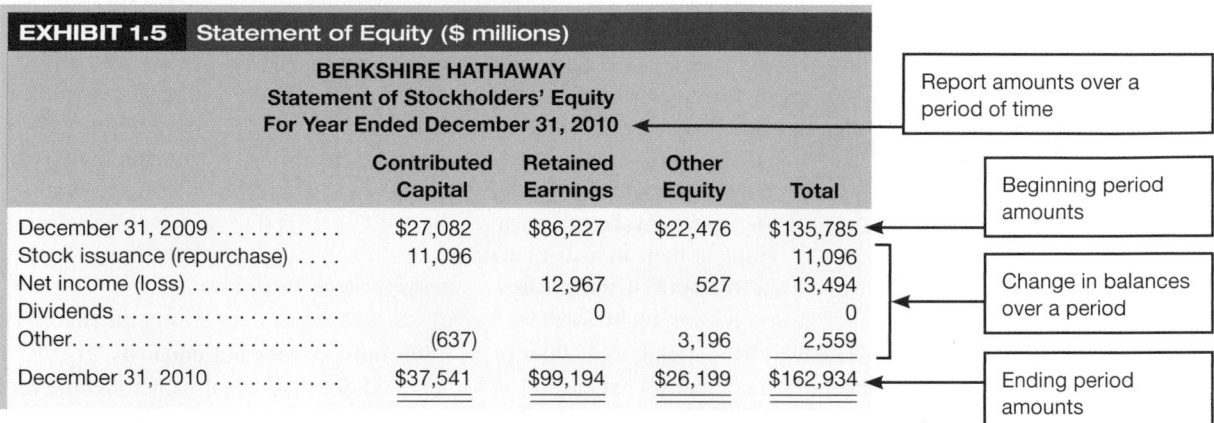

EXHIBIT 1.5	Statement of Equity ($ millions)			
BERKSHIRE HATHAWAY Statement of Stockholders' Equity For Year Ended December 31, 2010				
	Contributed Capital	Retained Earnings	Other Equity	Total
December 31, 2009	$27,082	$86,227	$22,476	$135,785
Stock issuance (repurchase)	11,096			11,096
Net income (loss)		12,967	527	13,494
Dividends		0		0
Other.	(637)		3,196	2,559
December 31, 2010	$37,541	$99,194	$26,199	$162,934

Report amounts over a period of time

Beginning period amounts

Change in balances over a period

Ending period amounts

Contributed capital represents the cash the company received from the sale of stock to stockholders (also called shareholders), less any funds expended for the repurchase of stock. Retained earnings (also called *earned capital* or *reinvested capital*) represent the cumulative total amount of income that the company has earned and that has been retained in the business and not distributed to shareholders in the form of dividends. The change in retained earnings links consecutive balance sheets via the income statement: Ending retained earnings = Beginning retained earnings + Net income − Dividends. For Berkshire Hathaway, its recent year's retained earnings increases from $86,227 million to $99,194 million. This increase of $12,967 million is explained by its net income of $12,967 million as Berkshire Hathaway paid no dividends in 2010.

RESEARCH INSIGHT **Are Earnings Important?**

A study asked top finance executives of publicly traded companies to *rank the three most important measures to report to outsiders.* The study reports that:

> "[More than 50% of] CFOs state that earnings are the most important financial metric to external constituents . . . this finding could reflect superior informational content in earnings over the other metrics. Alternatively, it could reflect myopic managerial concern about earnings. The emphasis on earnings is noteworthy because cash flows continue to be the measure emphasized in the academic finance literature."

The study also reports that CFOs view year-over-year change in earnings to be of critical importance to outsiders. Why is that? The study provides the following insights.

> "CFOs note that the first item in a press release is often a comparison of current quarter earnings with four quarters lagged quarterly earnings . . . CFOs also mention that while analysts' forecasts can be guided by management, last year's quarterly earnings number is a benchmark that is harder, if not impossible, to manage after the 10-Q has been filed with the SEC . . . Several executives mention that comparison to seasonally lagged earnings numbers provides a measure of earnings momentum and growth, and therefore is a useful gauge of corporate performance."

Thus, are earnings important? To the majority of finance chiefs surveyed, the answer is a resounding yes. (Source: Graham, et al., *Journal of Accounting and Economics,* 2005)

Statement of Cash Flows

The **statement of cash flows** reports the change (either an increase or a decrease) in a company's cash balance over a period of time. The statement reports on cash inflows and outflows from operating, investing, and financing activities over a period of time. Berkshire Hathaway's statement of cash flows is in Exhibit 1.6. Its cash balance increased by $7,669 million in the recent period: operating activities generated a $17,895 million cash inflow, investing activities reduced cash by $18,277 million, and financing activities yielded a cash inflow of $8,051 million.

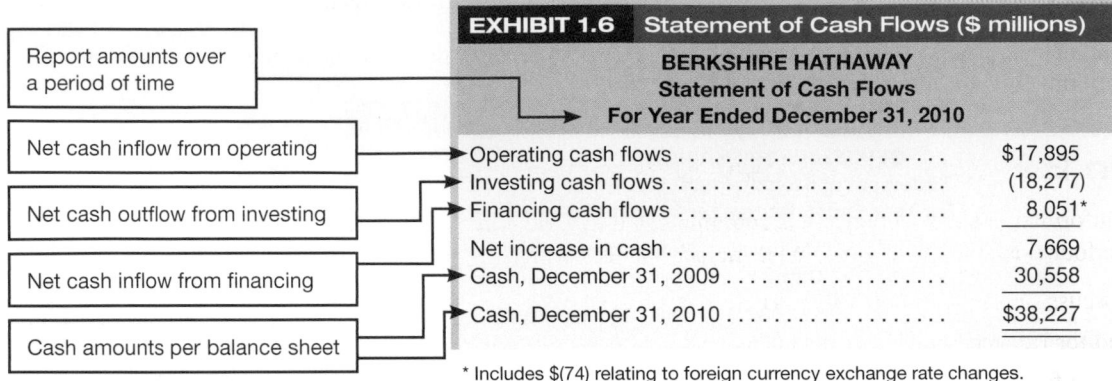

EXHIBIT 1.6   Statement of Cash Flows ($ millions)

BERKSHIRE HATHAWAY	
Statement of Cash Flows	
For Year Ended December 31, 2010	
Operating cash flows	$17,895
Investing cash flows	(18,277)
Financing cash flows	8,051*
Net increase in cash	7,669
Cash, December 31, 2009	30,558
Cash, December 31, 2010	$38,227

Report amounts over a period of time

Net cash inflow from operating

Net cash outflow from investing

Net cash inflow from financing

Cash amounts per balance sheet

* Includes $(74) relating to foreign currency exchange rate changes.

Berkshire Hathaway's operating cash flow of $17,895 million does not equal its $12,967 million net income. Generally, a company's net cash flow for a period does *not* equal its net income for the period. This is due to timing differences between when revenue and expense items are recognized on the income statement and when cash is received and paid. (We discuss this concept further in subsequent modules.)

Both cash flow and net income numbers are important for business decisions. Each is used in security valuation models, and both help users of accounting reports understand and assess a company's past, present, and future business activities. As a sneak preview, we might consider the following questions regarding the statement of cash flows:

■ What is the usefulness of the statement of cash flows? Do the balance sheet and income statement provide sufficient cash flow information?

■ What types of information are disclosed in the statement of cash flows and why are they important?

■ What kinds of activities are reported in each of the operating, investing and financing sections of the statement of cash flows? How is this information useful?

■ Is it important for a company to report net cash inflows (positive amounts) relating to operating activities over the longer term? What are the implications if operating cash flows are negative for an extended period of time?

■ Why is it important to know the composition of a company's investment activities? What kind of information might we look for? Are positive investing cash flows favorable?

■ Is it important to know the sources of a company's financing activities? What questions might that information help us answer?

■ How might the composition of operating, investing and financing cash flows change over a company's life cycle?

■ Is the bottom line increase in cash flow the key number? Why or why not?

Review the Berkshire Hathaway statement of cash flows summarized in Exhibit 1.6 and think about these questions. We provide answers for each of these questions as we progress through the book.

Financial Statement Linkages

The four financial statements are linked within and across periods—consider the following:

- The income statement and the balance sheet are linked via retained earnings. For Berkshire Hathaway, the $12,967 million increase in retained earnings (reported on the balance sheet) equals its net income (reported on the income statement) (see Exhibit 1.5). Berkshire Hathaway did not pay dividends in 2010.

- Retained earnings, contributed capital, and other equity balances appear both on the statement of stockholders' equity and the balance sheet.

- The statement of cash flows is linked to the income statement as net income is a component of operating cash flow. The statement of cash flows is also linked to the balance sheet as the change in the balance sheet cash account reflects the net cash inflows and outflows for the period.

Items that impact one financial statement ripple through the others. Linkages among the four financial statements are an important feature of the accounting system.

Information Beyond Financial Statements

Important financial information about a company is communicated to various decision makers through means other than the four financial statements. These include the following:

- Management Discussion and Analysis (MD&A)
- Independent Auditor Report
- Financial statement footnotes
- Regulatory filings, including proxy statements and other SEC filings

We describe and explain the usefulness of these additional information sources throughout the book.

Choices in Financial Accounting

Some people mistakenly assume that financial accounting is an exact discipline—that is, companies select the one proper accounting method to account for a transaction, and then follow the rules. The reality is that GAAP allows companies choices in preparing financial statements. The choice of methods often yields financial statements that are markedly different from one another in terms of reported income, assets, liabilities, and equity amounts.

People often are surprised that financial statements comprise numerous estimates. For example, companies must estimate the amounts that will eventually be collected from customers, the length of time that buildings and equipment will be productive, the value impairments of assets, the future costs of warranty claims, and the eventual payouts on pension plans. Following are examples of how some managers are alleged to have abused the latitude available in reporting financial results.

Company	Allegations
Adelphia Communications (ADELQ)	Founding Rigas family collected $3.1 billion in off-balance-sheet loans backed by Adelphia; it overstated results by inflating capital expenses and hiding debt.
Time Warner (TWX)	As the ad market faltered and AOL's purchase of Time Warner loomed, AOL inflated sales by booking revenue for barter deals and ads it sold for third parties. These questionable revenues boosted growth rates and sealed the deal. AOL also boosted sales via "round-trip" deals with advertisers and suppliers.
Bristol-Myers Squibb (BMY)	Inflated its 2001 revenue by $1.5 billion by "channel stuffing," or forcing wholesalers to accept more inventory than they could sell to get inventory off Bristol-Myers' books.
Enron	Created profits and hid debt totaling over $1 billion by improperly using off-the-books partnerships; manipulated the Texas power market; bribed foreign governments to win contracts abroad; manipulated California energy market.
Global Crossing (GLBC)	Engaged in network capacity "swaps" with other carriers to inflate revenue; shredded documents related to accounting practices.

continued

continued from prior page

Company	Allegations
Halliburton (HAL)	Improperly booked $100 million in annual construction cost overruns before customers agreed to pay for them.
Qwest Communications International (Q)	Inflated revenue using network capacity "swaps" and improper accounting for long-term deals.
Tyco (TYC)	Ex-CEO L. Dennis Kozlowski indicted for tax evasion; Kozlowski and former CFO Mark H. Swartz, convicted of taking unauthorized loans from the company.
WorldCom	Overstated cash flow by booking $11 billion in operating expenses as capital costs; loaned founder Bernard Ebbers $400 million off-the-books.
Xerox (XRX)	Falsified financial results for five years, overreported income by $1.5 billion.

Accounting standard setters walk a fine line regarding choice in accounting. On one hand, they are concerned that choice in preparing financial statements will lead to abuse by those seeking to gain by influencing decisions of financial statement users. On the other hand, standard setters are concerned that companies are too diverse for a "one size fits all" financial accounting system.

Enron exemplifies the problems that accompany rigid accounting standards. A set of accounting standards relating to special purpose entities (SPEs) provided preparers with guidelines under which those entities were or were not to be consolidated. Unfortunately, once the SPE guidelines were set, some people worked diligently to structure SPE transactions so as to narrowly avoid the consolidation requirements and achieve *off-balance-sheet* financing. This is just one example of how, with rigid standards, companies can adhere to the letter of the rule, but not its intent. In such situations, the financial statements are not fairly presented.

For most of its existence, the FASB has promulgated standards that were quite complicated and replete with guidelines. This invited abuse of the type embodied by the Enron scandal. In recent years, the pendulum has begun to swing away from such rigidity. Now, once financial statements are prepared, company management is required to step back from the details and make a judgment on whether the statements taken as a whole "fairly present" the financial condition of the company as is asserted in the company's audit report (see below).

Moreover, since the enactment of the **Sarbanes-Oxley Act,** the SEC requires the chief executive officer (CEO) of the company and its chief financial officer (CFO) to personally sign a statement attesting to the accuracy and completeness of the financial statements. This requirement is an important step in restoring confidence in the integrity of financial accounting. The statements signed by both the CEO and CFO contain the following declarations:

- Both the CEO and CFO have personally reviewed the annual report.
- There are no untrue statements of a material fact that would make the statements misleading.
- Financial statements fairly present in all material respects the financial condition of the company.
- All material facts are disclosed to the company's auditors and board of directors.
- No changes to its system of internal controls are made unless properly communicated.

The Sarbanes-Oxley Act (SOX) also imposed fines and potential jail time for executives. Presumably, the prospect of personal losses is designed to make these executives more vigilant in monitoring the financial accounting system. More recently, Congress passed *The Wall Street Reform and Consumer Protection Act* of 2010 (or the Dodd-Frank Act). Among the provisions of the act were rules that strengthened SOX by augmenting "claw-back" provisions for executives' ill-gotten gains.

MANAGERIAL DECISION **You Are the Product Manager**

There is often friction between investors' need for information and a company's desire to safeguard competitive advantages. Assume that you are a key-product manager at your company. Your department has test-marketed a potentially lucrative new product, which it plans to further finance. You are asked for advice on the extent of information to disclose about the new product in the MD&A section of the company's upcoming annual report. What advice do you provide and why? [Answer, p. 1-30]

MID-MODULE REVIEW

The following financial information is from Allstate Corporation, a competitor of Berkshire Hathaway's GEICO Insurance, for the year ended December 31, 2010 ($ millions).

Cash, ending year	$ 562
Cash flows from operations	3,689
Revenues	31,400
Stockholders' equity	19,044
Cash flows from financing	(6,071)
Total liabilities	111,830
Expenses	30,472
Noncash assets	130,312
Cash flows from investing	2,332
Net income	928
Cash, beginning year	612

Required

1. Prepare an income statement, balance sheet, and statement of cash flows for Allstate at December 31, 2010.
2. Compare the balance sheet and income statement of Allstate to those of Berkshire Hathaway in Exhibits 1.3 and 1.4. What differences do we observe?

The solution is on page 1-41.

ANALYSIS OF FINANCIAL STATEMENTS

This section previews the analysis framework of this book. This framework is used extensively by market professionals who analyze financial reports to evaluate company management and value the company's debt and equity securities. Analysis of financial performance is crucial in assessing prior strategic decisions and evaluating strategic alternatives.

LO3 Explain and apply the basics of profitability analysis.

Return on Assets

Suppose we learn that a company reports a profit of $10 million. Does the $10 million profit indicate that the company is performing well? Knowing that a company reports a profit is certainly positive as it indicates that customers value its goods or services and that its revenues exceed expenses. However, we cannot assess how well it is performing without considering the context. To explain, suppose we learn that this company has $500 million in assets. We now assess the $10 million profit as low because relative to the size of its asset investment, the company earned a paltry 2% return, computed as $10 million divided by $500 million. A 2% return on assets is what a much lower-risk investment in government-backed bonds might yield. The important point is that a company's profitability must be assessed with respect to the size of its investment. One common metric is the *return on assets* (ROA)—defined as net income for that period divided by the average assets for that period.

Components of Return on Assets

We can separate return on assets into two components: profitability and productivity. Profitability relates profit to sales. This ratio is called the *profit margin* (PM), and it reflects the net income (profit after tax) earned on each sales dollar. Management wants to earn as much profit as possible from sales.

Productivity relates sales to assets. This component, called *asset turnover* (AT), reflects sales generated by each dollar of assets. Management wants to maximize asset productivity, that is, to achieve the highest possible sales level for a given level of assets (or to achieve a given level of sales with the smallest level of assets).

Exhibit 1.7 depicts the disaggregation of return on assets into these two components. Profitability (PM) and productivity (AT) are multiplied to yield the return on assets (ROA). Average assets are commonly defined as (beginning-year assets + ending-year assets)/2.

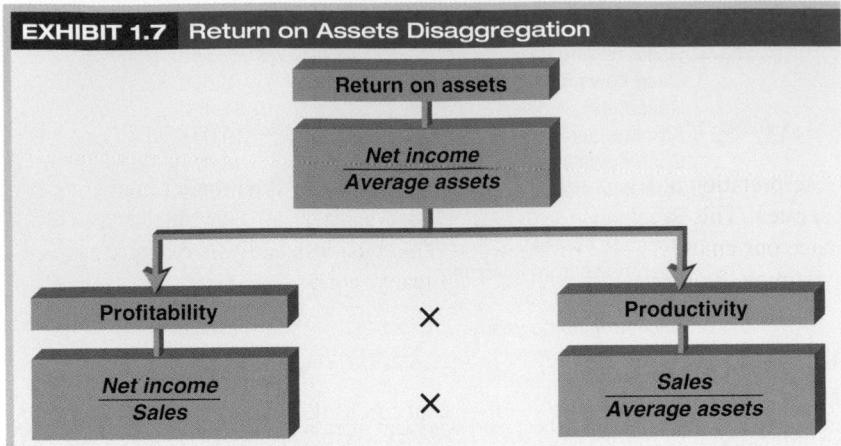

EXHIBIT 1.7   Return on Assets Disaggregation

There are an infinite number of combinations of profit margin and asset turnover that yield the same return on assets. To illustrate, Exhibit 1.8 graphs actual combinations of these two components for companies that we highlight in this book (each is identified by their ticker symbol). Retailers, like **Costco** (COST), **Best Buy** (BBY) and **TJX Companies** (TJX) are characterized by relatively low profit margins and a high turnover of their assets. The business models for other companies such as the pharmaceuticals [**Johnson & Johnson** (JNJ) and **Pfizer** (PFE)] require a larger investment in assets. These companies must earn a higher profit margin to yield an acceptable ROA. We might be surprised to see technology companies such as **Apple** in the group with high asset investments. Technology companies typically maintain a high level of cash and short-term investments on their balance sheets, which allows them to respond quickly to opportunities. The solid line represents those profitability and productivity combinations that yield a 10% return on assets.

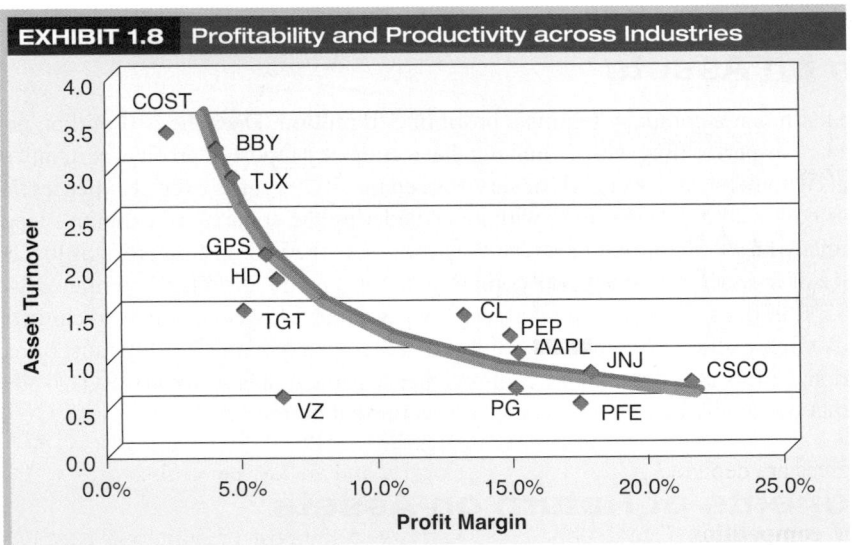

EXHIBIT 1.8   Profitability and Productivity across Industries

Return on Equity

Another important analysis measure is return on equity (ROE), which is defined as net income divided by average stockholders' equity, where average equity is commonly defined as (beginning-year equity + ending-year equity)/2. In this case, company earnings are compared to the level of stockholder (not total) investment. ROE reflects the return to stockholders, which is different from the return for the entire company (ROA).

MANAGERIAL DECISION | **You Are the Chief Financial Officer**

You are reviewing your company's financial performance for the first six months of the year and are unsatisfied with the results. How can you disaggregate return on assets to identify areas for improvement? [Answer, p. 1-31]

FINANCIAL STATEMENTS AND BUSINESS ANALYSIS

Analysis and interpretation of financial statements must consider the broader business context in which a company operates. This section describes how to systematically consider those broader business forces to enhance our analysis and interpretation. This business analysis can sharpen our insights and help us better estimate future performance and company value.

LO4 Describe business analysis within the context of a competitive environment.

Analyzing the Competitive Environment

Financial statements are influenced by five important forces that confront the company and determine its competitive intensity: (A) industry competition, (B) buyer power, (C) supplier power, (D) product substitutes, and (E) threat of entry (for further discussion, see Porter, *Competitive Strategy: Techniques for Analyzing Industries and Competitors*, 1980 and 1998).

EXHIBIT 1.9 | Competitive Forces within the Broader Business Environment

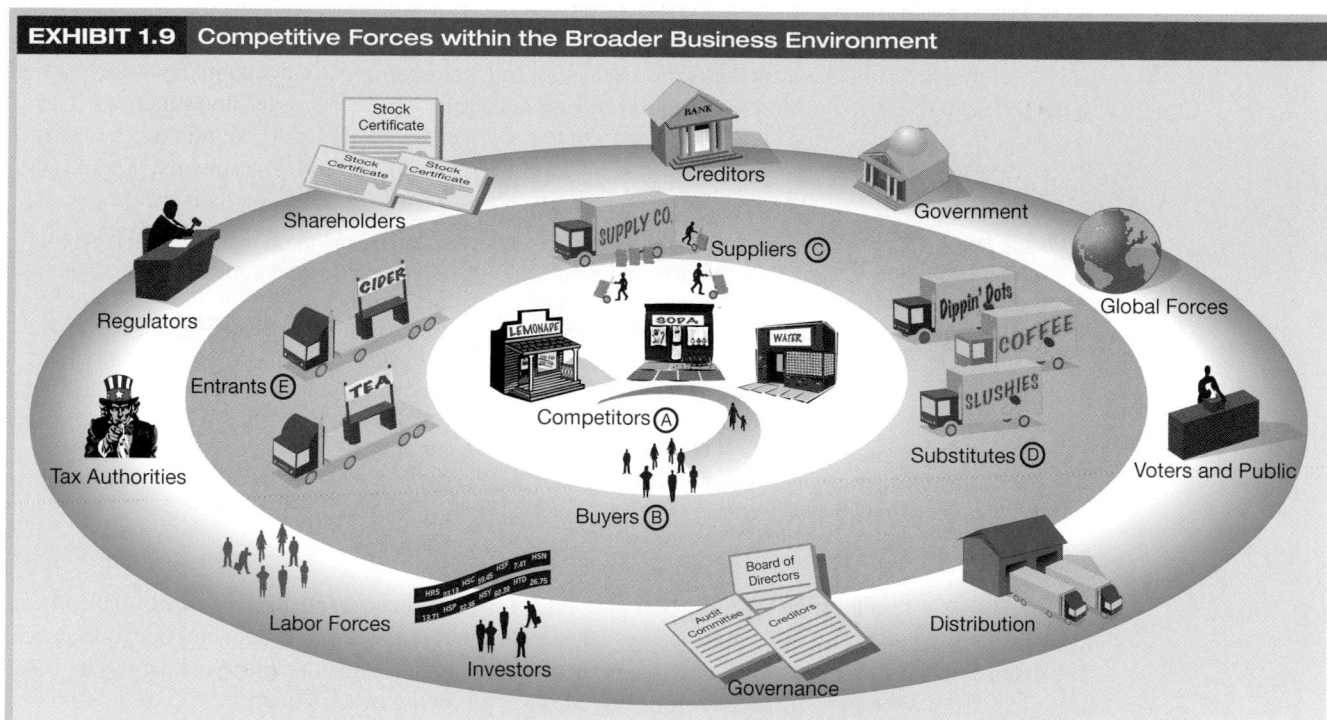

These five forces are depicted graphically in Exhibit 1.9 and are key determinants of profitability.

(A) **Industry competition** Competition and rivalry raise the cost of doing business as companies must hire and train competitive workers, advertise products, research and develop products, and engage in other related activities.

(B) **Bargaining power of buyers** Buyers with strong bargaining power can extract price concessions and demand a higher level of service and delayed payment terms; this force reduces both profits from sales and the operating cash flows to sellers.

(C) **Bargaining power of suppliers** Suppliers with strong bargaining power can demand higher prices and earlier payments, yielding adverse effects on profits and cash flows to buyers.

(D) **Threat of substitution** As the number of product substitutes increases, sellers have less power to raise prices and/or pass on costs to buyers; accordingly, threat of substitution places downward pressure on profits of sellers.

(E) **Threat of entry** New market entrants increase competition; to mitigate that threat, companies expend monies on activities such as new technologies, promotion, and human development to erect *barriers to entry* and to create *economies of scale*.

The broader business environment affects the level of profitability that a company can expect to achieve. Global economic forces and the quality and cost of labor affect the macroeconomy in which the company operates. Government regulation, borrowing agreements exacted by creditors, and internal governance procedures also affect the range of operating activities in which a company can engage. In addition, strategic plans are influenced by the oversight of equity markets, and investors are loathe to allow companies the freedom to manage for the longer term. Each of these external forces affects a company's strategic planning and expected level of profitability.

The relative strength of companies within their industries, and vis-à-vis suppliers and customers, is an important determinant of both their profitability and the structure of their balance sheets. As competition intensifies, profitability likely declines, and the amount of assets companies need to carry on their balance sheet likely increases in an effort to generate more profit. Such changes are revealed in the income statement and the balance sheet.

Applying Competitive Analysis

We apply the competitive analysis framework to help interpret the financial results of McLane Company. McLane is a subsidiary of Berkshire Hathaway and was acquired several years ago as explained in the following note to the Berkshire Hathaway annual report:

> On May 23, 2003, Berkshire acquired McLane Company, Inc., ("McLane") a distributor of grocery and food products to retailers, convenience stores and restaurants. Results of McLane's business operations are included in Berkshire's consolidated results beginning on that date. McLane's revenues in 2005 totaled $24.1 billion compared to $23.4 billion in 2004 and approximately $22.0 billion for the full year of 2003. Sales of grocery products increased about 5% in 2005 and were partially offset by lower sales to foodservice customers. McLane's business is marked by high sales volume and very low profit margins. Pretax earnings in 2005 of $217 million declined $11 million versus 2004. The gross margin percentage was relatively unchanged between years. However, the resulting increased gross profit was more than offset by higher payroll, fuel and insurance expenses. Approximately 33% of McLane's annual revenues currently derive from sales to Wal-Mart. Loss or curtailment of purchasing by Wal-Mart could have a material adverse impact on revenues and pre-tax earnings of McLane.

McLane is a wholesaler of food products; it purchases food products in finished and semifinished form from agricultural and food-related businesses and resells them to grocery and convenience food stores. The extensive distribution network required in this business entails considerable investment. Our business analysis of McLane's financial results includes the following observations:

■ **Industry competitors** McLane has many competitors with food products that are difficult to differentiate.

■ **Bargaining power of buyers** The note above reveals that 33% of McLane's sales are to Wal-Mart, which has considerable buying power that limits seller profits; also, the food industry is characterized by high turnover and low profit margins, which implies that cost control is key to success.

■ **Bargaining power of suppliers** McLane is large ($24 billion in annual sales), which implies its suppliers are unlikely to exert forces to increase its cost of sales.

■ **Threat of substitution** Grocery items are usually not well differentiated; this means the threat of substitution is high, which inhibits its ability to raise selling prices.

■ **Threat of entry** High investment costs, such as warehousing and logistics, are a barrier to entry in McLane's business; this means the threat of entry is relatively low.

Our analysis reveals that McLane is a high-volume, low-margin company. Its ability to control costs is crucial to its financial performance, including its ability to fully utilize its assets. Evaluation of McLane's financial statements should focus on that dimension.

Analyzing the Broader Business Environment

Quality analysis depends on an effective business analysis. Before we analyze a single accounting number, we must ask questions about a company's business environment such as the following:

■ *Life cycle* At what stage in its life is this company? Is it a start-up, experiencing growing pains? Is it strong and mature, reaping the benefits of competitive advantages? Is it nearing the end of its life, trying to milk what it can from stagnant product lines?

■ *Outputs* What products does it sell? Are its products new, established, or dated? Do its products have substitutes? How complicated are its products to produce?

■ *Buyers* Who are its buyers? Are buyers in good financial condition? Do buyers have substantial purchasing power? Can the seller dictate sales terms to buyers?

■ *Inputs* Who are its suppliers? Are there many supply sources? Does the company depend on a few supply sources with potential for high input costs?

■ *Competition* In what kind of markets does it operate? Are markets open? Is the market competitive? Does the company have competitive advantages? Can it protect itself from new entrants? At what cost? How must it compete to survive?

■ *Financing* Must it seek financing from public markets? Is it going public? Is it seeking to use its stock to acquire another company? Is it in danger of defaulting on debt covenants? Are there incentives to tell an overly optimistic story to attract lower-cost financing or to avoid default on debt?

■ *Labor* Who are its managers? What are their backgrounds? Can they be trusted? Are they competent? What is the state of employee relations? Is labor unionized?

■ *Governance* How effective is its corporate governance? Does it have a strong and independent board of directors? Does a strong audit committee of the board exist, and is it populated with outsiders? Does management have a large portion of its wealth tied to the company's stock?

■ *Risk* Is it subject to lawsuits from competitors or shareholders? Is it under investigation by regulators? Has it changed auditors? If so, why? Are its auditors independent? Does it face environmental and/or political risks?

We must assess the broader business context in which a company operates as we read and interpret its financial statements. A review of financial statements, which reflect business activities, cannot be undertaken in a vacuum. It is contextual and can only be effectively undertaken within the framework of a thorough understanding of the broader forces that impact company performance. We should view the above questions as a sneak preview of the types we will ask and answer throughout this book when we read and interpret financial statements.

GLOBAL ACCOUNTING

As we discussed earlier, the U.S. is among only a few economically developed countries (such as India, Singapore, and Russia) that do not use IFRS (a list is at **www.iasplus.com/country/useias.htm**). While laws and enforcement mechanisms vary across countries, the demand and supply of accounting information are governed by global economic forces. Thus, it is not surprising that IFRS and U.S. GAAP both prescribe the same set of financial statements. While account titles and note details differ, the underlying principles are the same. That is, U.S. GAAP and IFRS both capture, aggregate, summarize, and report economic activities on an accrual basis.

Given the global economy and liquid transnational capital markets, it is critical that we be conversant with both U.S. GAAP and IFRS. For this purpose, the final section of each module includes a summary of notable differences between these two systems of accounting for topics covered in that module. Also, each module has assignments that examine IFRS companies and their financial statements. By using a wide array of financial information, we will speak the language of accounting in at least two dialects.

MODULE-END REVIEW

Following are selected data from Progressive Corporation's 2010 10-K.

$ millions	2010
Sales............................	$14,963
Net income.......................	1,068
Average assets...................	20,600
Average stockholders' equity........	5,899

Required

a. Compute Progressive's return on assets. Disaggregate the ROA into its profitability and productivity components.

b. Compute Progressive's return on equity (ROE).

The solution is on page 1-42.

APPENDIX 1A: Accessing SEC Filings

All publicly traded companies are required to file various reports with the SEC, two of which are the 10-Q (quarterly financial statements) and the 10-K (annual financial statements). Following is a brief tutorial to access these electronic filings. The SEC's Website is **http://www.sec.gov**.

1. Following is the opening screen. Click on "Search for Company Filings" (highlighted below).

2. Click on company or fund name, ticker symbol, CIK (Central Index Key), file number, state, country, or SIC (Standard Industrial Classification).

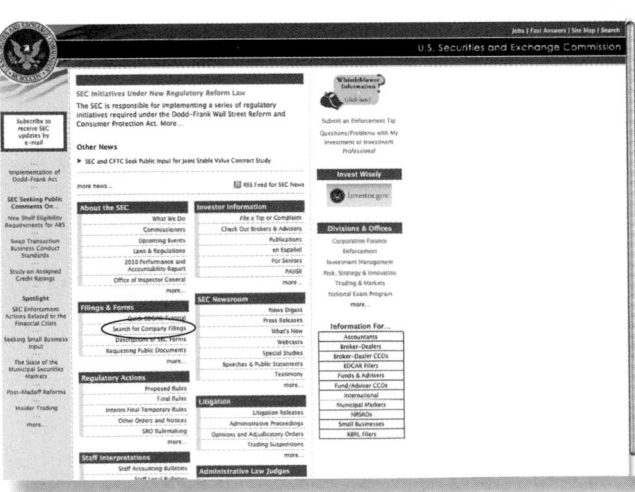

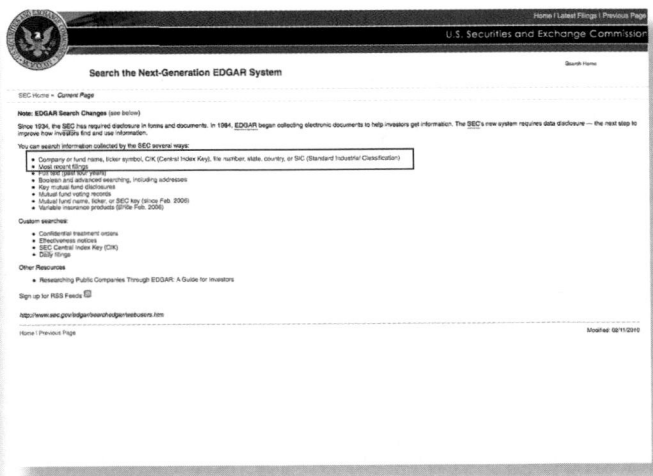

3. In **Company name**, type in the name of the company we are looking for. In this case, we are searching for Berkshire Hathaway. Then click enter.

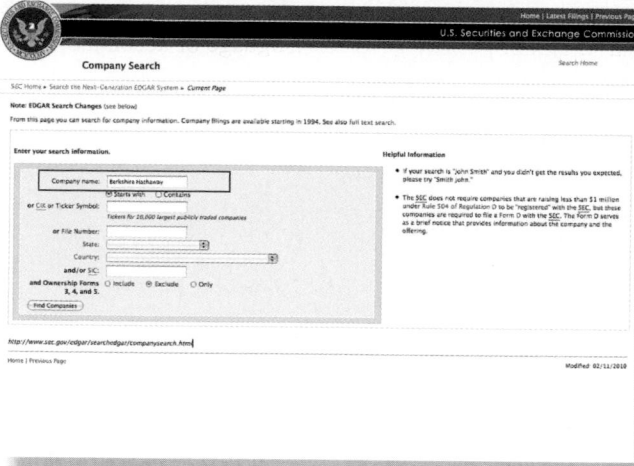

4. Several references to Berkshire appear. Click on the **CIK** (the SEC's numbering system) next to Berkshire Hathaway, Inc.

5. Enter the form number under "filing type" that we want to access. In this case we are looking for the 10-K.

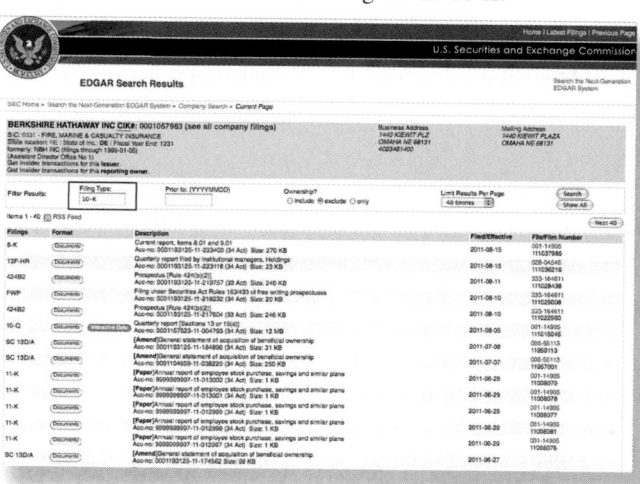

6. Click on the document link for the year that we want to access.

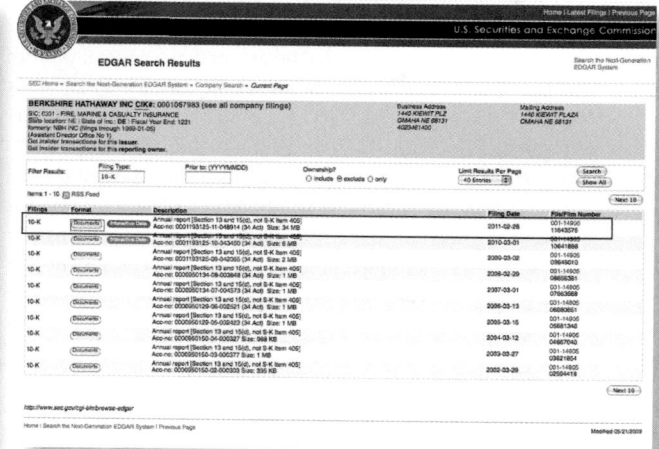

7. Exhibits relating to Berkshire Hathaway's 10-K filing appear; click on the 10-K document.

8. The Berkshire Hathaway 10-K will open up; the file is searchable.

9. Download an Excel file of the financial statement data by clicking on "Interactive Data."

10. Click on "View Excel Document" to view or download as a spreadsheet.

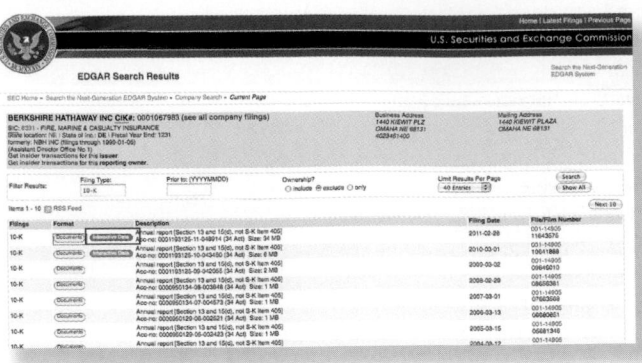

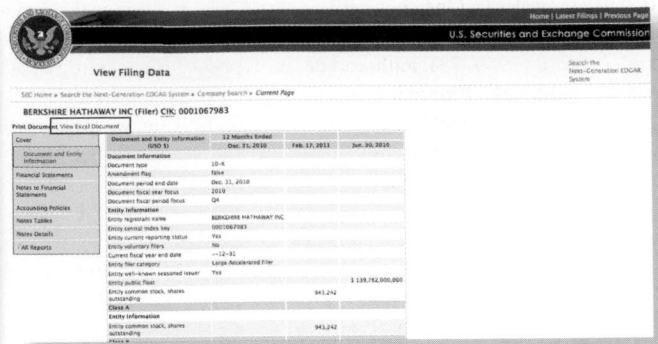

APPENDIX 1B: Accounting Principles and Governance

Financial Accounting Environment

LO5 Describe the accounting principles and regulations that frame financial statements.

Information in financial statements is crucial to valuing a company's debt and equity securities. Financial statement information can affect the price the market is willing to pay for the company's equity securities and interest rates attached to its debt securities.

The importance of financial statements means that their reliability is paramount. This includes the crucial role of ethics. To the extent that financial performance and condition are accurately communicated to business decision makers, debt and equity securities are more accurately priced. When securities are mis-priced, resources can be inefficiently allocated both within and across economies. Accurate, reliable financial statements are also important for the effective functioning of many other markets such as labor, input, and output markets.

To illustrate, recall the consequences of a breakdown in the integrity of the financial accounting system at **Enron**. Once it became clear that Enron had not faithfully and accurately reported its financial condition and performance, the market became unwilling to purchase Enron's securities. The value of its debt and equity securities dropped precipitously and the company was unable to obtain cash needed for operating activities. Within months of the disclosure of its financial accounting irregularities, Enron, with revenues of over $100 billion and total company value of over $60 billion, the fifth largest U.S. company, was bankrupt!

Further historical evidence of the importance of financial accounting is provided by the Great Depression of the 20th century. This depression was caused, in part, by the failure of companies to faithfully report their financial condition and performance.

Oversight of Financial Accounting

The stock market crash of 1929 and the ensuing Great Depression led Congress to pass the 1933 Securities Act. This act had two main objectives: (1) to require disclosure of financial and other information about securities being offered for public sale; and (2) to prohibit deceit, misrepresentations, and other fraud in the sale of securities. This act also required that companies register all securities proposed for public sale and disclose information about the securities being offered, including information about company financial condition and performance. This act became and remains a foundation for contemporary financial reporting.

Congress also passed the 1934 Securities Exchange Act, which created the **Securities and Exchange Commission** (SEC) and gave it broad powers to regulate the issuance and trading of securities. The act also provides that companies with more than $10 million in assets and whose securities are held by more than 500 owners must file annual and other periodic reports, including financial statements that are available for download from the SEC's database (**www.sec.gov**).

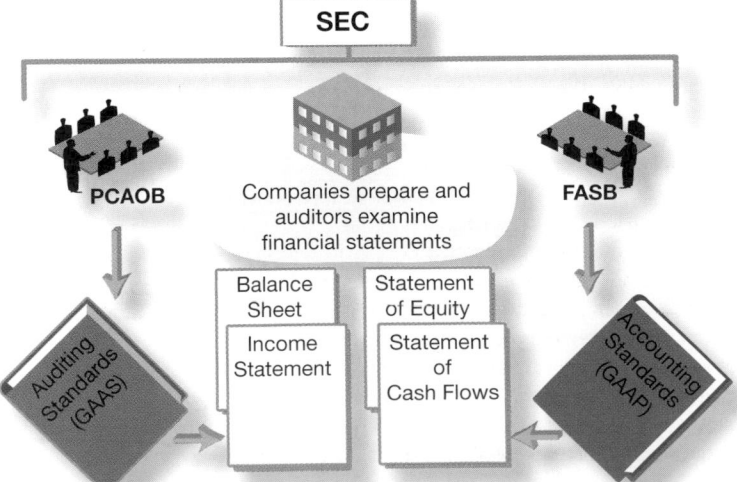

The SEC has ultimate authority over U.S. financial reporting, including setting accounting standards for preparing financial statements. Since 1939, however, the SEC has looked primarily to the private sector to set accounting standards. One such private sector organization is the American Institute of Certified Public Accountants (AICPA), whose two committees, the Committee on Accounting Procedure (1939–59) and the Accounting Principles Board (1959–73), authored the initial body of accounting standards.

Currently, the **Financial Accounting Standards Board (FASB)** sets U.S. financial accounting standards. The FASB is an independent body overseen by a foundation, whose members include public accounting firms, investment managers, academics, and corporate managers. The FASB has published over 150 accounting standards governing the preparation of financial reports. This is in addition to over 40 standards that were written by predecessor organizations to the FASB, numerous bulletins and interpretations, Emerging Issues Task Force (EITF) statements, AICPA statements of position (SOP), and direct SEC guidance, along with speeches made by high-ranking SEC personnel, all of which form the body of accounting standards governing financial statements. Collectively, these pronouncements, rules and guidance create what is called **Generally Accepted Accounting Principles (GAAP).**

The standard-setting process is arduous, often lasting up to a decade and involving extensive comment by the public, public officials, accountants, academics, investors, analysts, and corporate preparers of financial reports. The reason for this involved process is that amendments to existing standards or the creation of new standards affect the reported financial performance and condition of companies. Consequently, given the widespread impact of financial accounting, there are considerable economic consequences as a result of accounting changes. To influence the standard-setting process, special interest groups often lobby members of Congress to pressure the SEC and, ultimately, the FASB, on issues about which constituents feel strongly.

Audits and Corporate Governance

Even though key executives must personally attest to the completeness and accuracy of company financial statements, markets demand further assurances from outside parties to achieve the level of confidence necessary to warrant investment, credit, and other business decisions. To that end, companies engage external auditors to provide an opinion about financial statements. Further, companies implement a system of checks and balances that monitor managers' actions, which is called *corporate governance*.

Audit Report

Financial statements for each publicly traded company must be audited by an independent audit firm. There are a number of large auditing firms that are authorized by the SEC to provide auditing services for companies that issue securities to the public: PricewaterhouseCoopers, KPMG, Ernst & Young, Deloitte, RSM McGladrey, Grant Thornton, and BDO Seidman, to name a few. These firms provide opinions about financial statements for the large majority of publicly traded U.S. companies. A company's Board of Directors hires the auditors to review and express an opinion on its financial statements. The audit opinion expressed by Deloitte & Touche, LLP, on the financial statements of **Berkshire Hathaway** is reproduced in Exhibit 1.10.

The basic "clean" audit report is consistent across companies and includes these assertions:

- Financial statements are management's responsibility. Auditor responsibility is to express an *opinion* on those statements.

- Auditing involves a sampling of transactions, not investigation of each transaction.

- Audit opinion provides *reasonable assurance* that the statements are free of *material* misstatements, not a guarantee.

- Auditors review accounting policies used by management and the estimates used in preparing the statements.

- Financial statements *present fairly*, *in all material respects* a company's financial condition, in conformity with GAAP.

If the auditor cannot make all of these assertions, the auditor cannot issue a clean opinion. Instead, the auditor issues a "qualified" opinion and states the reasons a clean opinion cannot be issued. Financial report readers should scrutinize with care both the qualified audit opinion and the financial statements themselves.

The audit opinion is not based on a test of each transaction. Instead, auditors usually develop statistical samples to make inferences about the larger set of transactions. The audit report is not a guarantee that no misstatements exist. Auditors only provide reasonable assurance that the statements are free of material misstatements. Their use of the word "reasonable" is deliberate, as they do not want to be held to an absolute standard should problems be subsequently uncovered. The word *material* is used in the sense that an item must be of sufficient magnitude to change the perceptions or decisions of the financial statement user (such as a decision to purchase stock or extend credit).

The requirement of auditor independence is the cornerstone of effective auditing and is subject to debate because the company pays the auditor's fees. Regulators have questioned the perceived lack of independence of

EXHIBIT 1.10 Audit Report for Berkshire Hathaway

To the Board of Directors and Shareholders of Berkshire Hathaway Inc.

We have audited the accompanying consolidated balance sheets of Berkshire Hathaway Inc. and subsidiaries (the "Company") as of December 31, 2010 and 2009, and the related consolidated statements of earnings, cash flows and changes in shareholders' equity and comprehensive income for each of the three years in the period ended December 31, 2010. We also have audited the Company's internal control over financial reporting as of December 31, 2010, based on criteria established in Internal Control—Integrated Framework issued by the Committee of Sponsoring Organizations of the Treadway Commission. The Company's management is responsible for these financial statements, for maintaining effective internal control over financial reporting, and for its assessment of the effectiveness of internal control over financial reporting, included in the accompanying Management's Report on Internal Control over Financial Reporting. Our responsibility is to express an opinion on these financial statements and an opinion on the Company's internal control over financial reporting based on our audits.

We conducted our audits in accordance with the standards of the Public Company Accounting Oversight Board (United States). Those standards require that we plan and perform the audit to obtain reasonable assurance about whether the financial statements are free of material misstatement and whether effective internal control over financial reporting was maintained in all material respects. Our audits of the financial statements included examining, on a test basis, evidence supporting the amounts and disclosures in the financial statements, assessing the accounting principles used and significant estimates made by management, and evaluating the overall financial statement presentation. Our audit of internal control over financial reporting included obtaining an understanding of internal control over financial reporting, assessing the risk that a material weakness exists, and testing and evaluating the design and operating effectiveness of internal control based on the assessed risk. Our audits also included performing such other procedures as we considered necessary in the circumstances. We believe that our audits provide a reasonable basis for our opinions.

A company's internal control over financial reporting is a process designed by, or under the supervision of, the company's principal executive and principal financial officers, or persons performing similar functions, and effected by the company's board of directors, management, and other personnel to provide reasonable assurance regarding the reliability of financial reporting and the preparation of financial statements for external purposes in accordance with generally accepted accounting principles. A company's internal control over financial reporting includes those policies and procedures that (1) pertain to the maintenance of records that, in reasonable detail, accurately and fairly reflect the transactions and dispositions of the assets of the company; (2) provide reasonable assurance that transactions are recorded as necessary to permit preparation of financial statements in accordance with generally accepted accounting principles, and that receipts and expenditures of the company are being made only in accordance with authorizations of management and directors of the company; and (3) provide reasonable assurance regarding prevention or timely detection of unauthorized acquisition, use, or disposition of the company's assets that could have a material effect on the financial statements.

Because of the inherent limitations of internal control over financial reporting, including the possibility of collusion or improper management override of controls, material misstatements due to error or fraud may not be prevented or detected on a timely basis. Also, projections of any evaluation of the effectiveness of the internal control over financial reporting to future periods are subject to the risk that the controls may become inadequate because of changes in conditions, or that the degree of compliance with the policies or procedures may deteriorate.

In our opinion, the consolidated financial statements referred to above present fairly, in all material respects, the financial position of Berkshire Hathaway Inc. and subsidiaries as of December 31, 2010 and 2009, and the results of their operations and their cash flows for each of the three years in the period ended December 31, 2010, in conformity with accounting principles generally accepted in the United States of America. Also, in our opinion, the Company maintained, in all material respects, effective internal control over financial reporting as of December 31, 2010, based on the criteria established in Internal Control—Integrated Framework issued by the Committee of Sponsoring Organizations of the Treadway Commission.

DELOITTE & TOUCHE LLP

Omaha, Nebraska
February 25, 2011

auditing firms and the degree to which declining independence compromises the ability of auditing firms to challenge a client's dubious accounting.

The Sarbanes-Oxley Act contained several provisions designed to encourage auditor independence:

1. It established the **Public Company Accounting Oversight Board** (PCAOB) to oversee the development of audit standards and to monitor the effectiveness of auditors,
2. It prohibits auditors from offering certain types of consulting services, and requires audit partners to rotate clients every five years, and
3. It requires audit committees to consist of independent members.

Audit Committee

Law requires each publicly traded company to have a board of directors, where stockholders elect each director. This board represents the company owners and oversees management. The board also hires the company's executive management and regularly reviews company operations.

The board of directors usually establishes several subcommittees to focus on particular governance tasks such as compensation, strategic plans, and financial management. Governance committees are commonplace. One of these, the audit committee, oversees the financial accounting system. Exhibit 1.11 illustrates a typical organization of a company's governance structure.

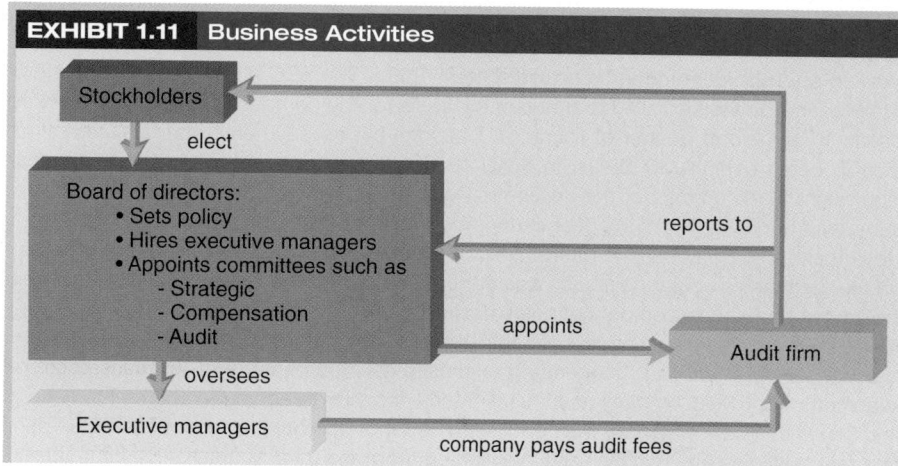

EXHIBIT 1.11   Business Activities

The audit committee must consist solely of outside directors, and cannot include the CEO. As part of its oversight of the financial accounting system, the audit committee focuses on **internal controls**, which are the policies and procedures used to protect assets, ensure reliable accounting, promote efficient operations, and urge adherence to company policies.

Regulatory and Legal Environment

The regulatory and legal environment provides further assurance that financial statements are complete and accurate.

SEC Enforcement Actions

Companies whose securities are issued to the public must file reports with the SEC (see **www.sec.gov**). One of these reports is the 10-K, which includes the annual financial statements (quarterly statements are filed on report 10-Q). The 10-K report provides more information than the company's glossy annual report, which is partly a marketing document (although the basic financial statements are identical). We prefer to use the 10-K because of its additional information.

The SEC critically reviews all of the financial reports that companies submit. If irregularities are found, the SEC has the authority to bring enforcement actions against companies that it feels are misrepresenting their financial condition (remember the phrase in the audit opinion that requires companies to "present fairly, in all material respects, the financial position of . . . "). One such action was brought against **Dell Inc.** and its executives in 2011. Following are excerpts from the SEC's complaint:

The Securities and Exchange Commission today charged Dell Inc. with failing to disclose material information to investors and using fraudulent accounting to make it falsely appear that the company was consistently meeting Wall Street earnings targets and reducing its operating expenses.

The SEC alleges that Dell did not disclose to investors large exclusivity payments the company received from Intel Corporation not to use central processing units (CPUs) manufactured by Intel's main rival. It was these payments rather than the company's management and operations that allowed Dell to meet its earnings targets. After Intel cut these payments, Dell again misled investors by not disclosing the true reason behind the company's decreased profitability...

The SEC's complaint, filed in federal district court in Washington, D.C., alleges that Dell Inc., Michael Dell, Rollins, and Schneider misrepresented the basis for the company's ability to consistently meet or exceed consensus analyst EPS estimates from fiscal year 2002 through fiscal year 2006. Without the Intel payments, Dell would have missed the EPS consensus in every quarter during this period...

The SEC's complaint further alleges that Dell's most senior former accounting personnel, including Schneider, Dunning, and Jackson engaged in improper accounting by maintaining a series of "cookie jar" reserves that it used to cover shortfalls in operating results from FY 2002 to FY 2005. Dell's fraudulent accounting made it appear that it was consistently meeting Wall Street earnings targets and reducing its operating expenses through the company's management and operations.

According to the SEC's complaint, Intel made exclusivity payments to Dell in order for Dell not to use CPUs manufactured by its rival—Advance Micro Devices, Inc. (AMD). These exclusivity payments grew from 10 percent of Dell's operating income in FY 2003 to 38 percent in FY 2006, and peaked at 76 percent in the first quarter of FY 2007. The SEC alleges that Dell Inc., Michael Dell, Rollins, and Schneider failed to disclose the basis for the company's sharp drop in its operating results in its second quarter of fiscal 2007 as Intel cut its payments after Dell announced its intention to begin using AMD CPUs. In dollar terms, the reduction in Intel exclusivity payments was equivalent to 75 percent of the decline in Dell's operating income. Michael Dell, Rollins, and Schneider had been warned in the past that Intel would cut its funding if Dell added AMD as a vendor. Nevertheless, in Dell's second quarter FY 2007 earnings call, they told investors that the sharp drop in the company's operating results was attributable to Dell pricing too aggressively in the face of slowing demand and to component costs declining less than expected.

The SEC's complaint further alleges that the reserve manipulations allowed Dell to materially misstate its earnings and its operating expenses as a percentage of revenue—an important financial metric that the Company itself highlighted—for over three years. The manipulations also enabled Dell to misstate materially the trend and amount of operating income of its EMEA segment, an important business unit that Dell also highlighted, from the third quarter of FY 2003 through the first quarter of FY 2005.

While not admitting to wrongdoing, Dell agreed to pay a penalty of $100 million to settle the SEC's charges. The SEC's oversight and powers of prosecution are an important check to help insure that companies' reports to investors "present fairly, in all material respects" their financial condition.

BUSINESS INSIGHT   Warren Buffett on Audit Committees

"Audit committees can't audit. Only a company's outside auditor can determine whether the earnings that a management purports to have made are suspect. Reforms that ignore this reality and that instead focus on the structure and charter of the audit committee will accomplish little. As we've discussed, far too many managers have fudged their company's numbers in recent years, using both accounting and operational techniques that are typically legal but that nevertheless materially mislead investors. Frequently, auditors knew about these deceptions. Too often, however, they remained silent. The key job of the audit committee is simply to get the auditors to divulge what they know. To do this job, the committee must make sure that the auditors worry more about misleading its members than about offending management. In recent years auditors have not felt that way. They have instead generally viewed the CEO, rather than the shareholders or directors, as their client. That has been a natural result of day-to-day working relationships and also of the auditors' understanding that, no matter what the board says, the CEO and CFO pay their fees and determine whether they are retained for both auditing and other work. The rules that have been recently instituted won't materially change this reality. What will break this cozy relationship is audit committees unequivocally putting auditors on the spot, making them understand they will become liable for major monetary penalties if they don't come forth with what they know or suspect."

—Warren Buffett, Berkshire Hathaway annual report

Courts

Courts provide remedies to individuals and companies that suffer damages as a result of material misstatements in financial statements. Typical court actions involve shareholders who sue the company and its auditors, alleging that the company disclosed, and the auditors attested to, false and misleading financial statements. Shareholder lawsuits are chronically in the news, although the number of such suits has declined in recent years. Stanford Law School's Securities Class Action Clearinghouse commented that "Two factors are likely responsible for the decline. First, lawsuits arising from the dramatic boom and bust of U.S. equities in the late 1990s and early 2000s are now largely behind us. Second, improved corporate governance in the wake of the Enron and WorldCom frauds likely reduced the actual incidence of fraud." Nevertheless, courts continue to wield considerable power. For example, the SEC and the New York District Attorney successfully brought suit against Adelphia Communications Corporation and its owners on behalf of the U.S. Government and numerous investors, creditors, employees and others affiliated with the company. The press release announcing the settlement read, in part:

Washington, D.C., April 25, 2005—The Securities and Exchange Commission today announced that it and the United States Attorney's Office for the Southern District of New York (USAO) reached an agreement to settle a civil enforcement action and resolve criminal charges against Adelphia Communications Corporation, its founder John J. Rigas, and his three sons, Timothy J. Rigas, Michael J. Rigas and James P. Rigas, in one of the most extensive financial frauds ever to take place at a public company.

In its complaint, the Commission charged that Adelphia, at the direction of the individual defendants: (1) fraudulently excluded billions of dollars in liabilities from its consolidated financial statements by hiding them on the books of off-balance sheet affiliates; (2) falsified operating statistics and inflated earnings to meet Wall Street estimates; and (3) concealed rampant self-dealing by the Rigas family, including the undisclosed use of corporate funds for purchases of Adelphia stock and luxury condominiums.

Mark K. Schonfeld, Director of the SEC's Northeast Regional Office, said, "This settlement agreement presents a strong, coordinated approach by the SEC and the U.S. Attorney's Office to resolving one of the most complicated and egregious financial frauds committed at a public company. The settlement provides an expedient and effective way to provide victims of Adelphia's fraud with a substantial recovery while at the same time enabling Adelphia to emerge from Chapter 11 bankruptcy."

The settlement terms of this action, and related criminal actions against the Rigas family, resulted in the following:

- Rigas family members forfeited in excess of $1.5 billion in assets derived from the fraud; the funds were used, in part, to establish a fund for the fraud victims.

- Rigas family members were barred from acting as officers or directors of a public company.

- John Rigas, the 80-year-old founder of Adelphia Communications, was sentenced to 15 years in prison; he applied for a Presidential pardon in January 2009 but was denied.

- Timothy Rigas, the ex-finance chief, was sentenced to 20 years and is currently serving time at a federal correctional complex in North Carolina.

GUIDANCE ANSWERS

MANAGERIAL DECISION   You Are the Product Manager

As a manager, you must balance two conflicting objectives—namely, mandatory disclosure requirements and your company's need to protect its competitive advantages. You must comply with all minimum required disclosure rules. The extent to which you offer additional disclosures depends on the sensitivity of the information; that is, how beneficial it is to your existing and potential competitors. Another consideration is how the information disclosed will impact your existing and potential investors. Disclosures such as this can be beneficial in that they inform investors and others about your company's successful investments. Still, there are many stakeholders impacted by your disclosure decision and each must be given due consideration.

MANAGERIAL DECISION   You Are the Chief Financial Officer

Financial performance is often measured by return on assets, which can be disaggregated into the profit margin (profit after tax/sales) and the asset turnover (sales/average assets). This disaggregation might lead you to review factors affecting profitability (gross margins and expense control) and to assess how effectively your company is utilizing its assets (the turnover rates). Finding ways to increase profitability for a given level of investment or to reduce the amount of invested capital while not adversely impacting profitability contributes to improved financial performance.

Superscript $^{A(B)}$ denotes assignments based on Appendix 1A (1B).

DISCUSSION QUESTIONS

Q1-1.   A firm's planning activities motivate and shape three types of business activities. List the three activities. Describe how financial statements can provide useful information for each activity. How can subsequent financial statements be used to evaluate the success of each of the activities?

Q1-2.   The accounting equation (Assets = Liabilities + Equity) is a fundamental business concept. Explain what this equation reveals about a company's sources and uses of funds and the claims on company resources.

Q1-3.   Companies prepare four primary financial statements. What are those financial statements and what information is typically conveyed in each?

Q1-4.   Does a balance sheet report on a period of time or at a point in time? Explain the information conveyed in the balance sheet.

Q1-5.   Does an income statement report on a period of time or at a point in time? Explain the information conveyed in the income statement.

Q1-6.   Does a statement of cash flows report on a period of time or at a point in time? Explain the information and activities conveyed in the statement of cash flows.

Q1-7.   Explain how a company's four primary financial statements are linked.

Q1-8.   Financial statements are used by several interested stakeholders. List three or more potential external users of financial statements. Explain how each constituent on your list might use financial statement information in their decision making process.

Q1-9.   What ethical issues might managers face in dealing with confidential information?

Procter & Gamble (PG)   **Q1-10.**^{A} Access the 2011 10-K for Procter & Gamble at the SEC's database of financial reports (**www.sec. gov**). Who is P&G's auditor? What specific language does the auditor use in expressing its opinion and what responsibilities does it assume?

Q1-11.^{B} Business decision makers external to the company increasingly demand more financial information from companies. Discuss the reasons why companies have traditionally opposed the efforts of regulatory agencies like the SEC to require more disclosure.

Q1-12.^{B} What are generally accepted accounting principles and what organizations presently establish them?

Enron   **Q1-13.**^{B} Corporate governance has received considerable attention since the collapse of Enron and other accounting-related scandals. What is meant by corporate governance? What are the primary means by which sound corporate governance is achieved?

Q1-14.^{B} What is the primary function of the auditor? In your own words, describe what an audit opinion says.

Q1-15.   Describe a decision that requires financial statement information, other than a stock investment decision. How is financial statement information useful in making this decision?

Q1-16.   Users of financial statement information are vitally concerned with the company's strategic direction. Despite their understanding of this need for information, companies are reluctant to supply it. Why? In particular, what costs are companies concerned about?

Q1-17.   One of Warren Buffett's acquisition criteria is to invest in businesses "earning good return on equity." The return on equity (ROE) formula uses both net income and stockholders' equity. Why is it important to relate net income to stockholders' equity? Why isn't it sufficient to merely concentrate on companies with the highest net income?

Q1-18. One of Warren Buffett's acquisition criteria is to invest in businesses "earning good return on equity, while employing little or no debt." Why is Buffett concerned about debt?

**Assignments with the ✅ in the margin are available in an online homework system.
See the Preface of the book for details.**

MINI EXERCISES

M1-19. Relating Financing and Investing Activities (LO2)

In a recent year, the total assets of Dell Inc. equal $38,599 million and its equity is $7,766 million. What is the amount of its liabilities? Does Dell receive more financing from its owners or nonowners? What percentage of financing is provided by Dell's owners?

Dell Inc. (DELL)

M1-20. Relating Financing and Investing Activities (LO2)

In a recent year, the total assets of Best Buy equal $17,849 million and its liabilities equal $10,557 million. What is the amount of Best Buy's equity? Does Best Buy receive more financing from its owners or nonowners? What percentage of financing is provided by its owners?

Best Buy (BBY)

M1-21. Applying the Accounting Equation and Computing Financing Proportions (LO2)

Use the accounting equation to compute the missing financial amounts (a), (b), and (c). Which of these companies is more owner-financed? Which of these companies is more nonowner-financed? Discuss why the proportion of owner financing might differ across these three businesses.

($ millions)	Assets	=	Liabilities	+	Equity
Hewlett-Packard..........................	$124,503	=	$83,722	+	$ (a)
General Mills..............................	$ 18,674	=	$ (b)	+	$ 6,612
Target.....................................	$ (c)	=	$28,218	+	$15,487

Hewlett-Packard (HPQ)

General Mills (GIS)

Target (TGT)

M1-22.[A] **Identifying Key Numbers from Financial Statements** (LO2)

Access the October 3, 2010, 10-K for Starbucks Corporation at the SEC's database for financial reports (**www.sec.gov**). What did Starbucks report for total assets, liabilities, and equity at October 3, 2010? Confirm that the accounting equation holds. What percent of Starbucks' assets is financed by nonowners?

Starbucks (SBUX)

M1-23.[A] **Verifying Linkages Between Financial Statements** (LO2)

Access the 2010 10-K for DuPont at the SEC's database of financial reports (**www.sec.gov**). Using its December 31, 2010, consolidated statement of stockholders' equity, prepare a table to reconcile the opening and ending balances of its retained (reinvested) earnings for 2010 by showing the activity in the account during the year.

E. I. DuPont de Nemours (DD)

M1-24. Identifying Financial Statement Line Items and Accounts (LO2)

Several line items and account titles are listed below. For each, indicate in which of the following financial statement(s) we would likely find the item or account: income statement (IS), balance sheet (BS), statement of stockholders' equity (SE), or statement of cash flows (SCF).

a. Cash asset	*d.* Contributed capital	*g.* Cash inflow for stock issued
b. Expenses	*e.* Cash outflow for capital expenditures	*h.* Cash outflow for dividends
c. Noncash assets	*f.* Retained earnings	*i.* Net income

M1-25. Identifying Ethical Issues and Accounting Choices (LO5)

Assume that you are a technology services provider and you must decide on whether to record revenue from the installation of computer software for one of your clients. Your contract calls for acceptance of the software by the client within six months of installation. According to the contract, you will be paid only when the client "accepts" the installation. Although you have not yet received your client's formal acceptance, you are confident that it is forthcoming. Failure to record these revenues will cause your company to miss Wall Street's earnings estimates. What stakeholders will be affected by your decision and how might they be affected?

M1-26.[B] **Understanding Internal Controls and Their Importance** (LO5)

The **Sarbanes-Oxley Act** legislation requires companies to report on the effectiveness of their internal controls. The SEC administers the Sarbanes-Oxley Act, and defines internal controls as follows:

"A process designed by, or under the supervision of, the registrant's principal executive and principal financial officers . . . to provide reasonable assurance regarding the reliability of financial reporting and the preparation of financial statements for external purposes in accordance with generally accepted accounting principles."

Why would Congress believe that internal controls are such an important area to monitor and report on?

EXERCISES

E1-27. Composition of Accounts on the Balance Sheet (LO2)

Target (TGT)

Answer the following questions about the Target balance sheet.

a. Accounts Receivable comprises a large proportion of its total assets. Why would a retailer such as Target report accounts receivable on its balance sheet?
b. Briefly describe the types of assets that Target is likely to include in its inventory.
c. What kinds of assets would Target likely include in its Property, Plant and Equipment?
d. Target reports about two-thirds of its total assets as long-term. Given Target's business model, why do we see it report a relatively high proportion of long-term assets?

 E1-28. Applying the Accounting Equation and Assessing Financial Statement Linkages (LO2)

Answer the following questions. (*Hint*: Apply the accounting equation.)

Intel (INTC)

a. Intel had assets equal to $63,186 million and liabilities equal to $13,756 million for a recent year-end. What was Intel's total equity at year-end? Why would we expect a company like Intel to report a relatively high proportion of equity vis-á-vis liabilities?

JetBlue (JBLU)

b. At the beginning of a recent year, JetBlue's assets were $6,549 million and its equity was $1,546 million. During the year, assets increased $44 million and liabilities decreased $(64) million. What was JetBlue's equity at the end of the year?
c. What balance sheet account provides the link between the balance sheet and the income statement? Briefly describe how this linkage works.

E1-29. Specifying Financial Information Users and Uses (LO1)

Financial statements have a wide audience of interested stakeholders. Identify two or more financial statement users that are external to the company. For each user on your list, specify two questions that could be addressed with financial statement information.

E1-30. Applying Financial Statement Relations to Compute Dividends (LO2)

Colgate-Palmolive (CL)

Colgate-Palmolive reports the following dollar balances in its retained earnings account.

($ millions)	2010	2009
Retained earnings	$14,329	$13,157

During 2010, Colgate-Palmolive reported net income of $2,203 million. What amount of dividends, if any, did Colgate-Palmolive pay to its shareholders in 2010? What percent of its net income did Colgate-Palmolive pay out as dividends in 2010?

E1-31. Computing and Interpreting Financial Statement Ratios (LO3)

Colgate-Palmolive (CL)

Following are selected ratios of Colgate-Palmolive for 2010 and 2009.

Return on Assets (ROA) Component	2010	2009
Profitability (Net income/Sales)	14%	15%
Productivity (Sales/Average net assets)................	1.4	1.5

a. Was the company profitable in 2010? What evidence do you have of this?
b. Is the change in productivity (asset turnover) a positive development? Explain.
c. Compute the company's return on assets (ROA) for 2010 (show computations).

E1-32. Computing Return on Assets and Applying the Accounting Equation (LO3)

Nordstrom, Inc. (JWN)

Nordstrom, Inc., reports net income of $613 million for its fiscal year ended January 2011. At the beginning of that fiscal year, Nordstrom had $6,579 million in total assets. By fiscal year-end 2011, total assets had grown to $7,462 million. What is Nordstrom's return on assets (ROA)?

E1-33.   Assessing the Role of Financial Statements in Society (LO1)

Financial statement information plays an important role in modern society and business.

  a. Identify two or more external stakeholders that are interested in a company's financial statements and what their particular interests are.

  b. What are *generally accepted accounting principles*? What organizations have primary responsibility for the formulation of GAAP?

  c. What role does financial statement information play in the allocation of society's financial resources?

  d. What are three aspects of the accounting environment that can create ethical pressure on management?

E1-34.   Computing Return on Equity (LO3)

Starbucks reports net income for 2010 of $945.6 million. Its stockholders' equity is $3,056.9 million and $3,682.3 million for 2009 and 2010, respectively.

Starbucks (SBUX)

  a. Compute its return on equity for 2010.

  b. Starbucks repurchased over $285 million of its common stock in 2010. How did this repurchase affect Starbucks' ROE?

  c. Why do you think a company like Starbucks repurchases its own stock?

PROBLEMS

P1-35.   Computing Return on Equity and Return on Assets (LO3)

The following table contains financial statement information for Wal-Mart Stores, Inc.

Wal-Mart Stores, Inc. (WMT)

($ millions)	Total Assets	Net Income	Sales	Equity
2011	$180,663	$16,389	$421,849	$68,542
2010	170,407	14,370	408,085	70,468
2009	163,429	13,381	404,254	65,285

Required

  a. Compute the return on equity (ROE) for 2010 and 2011. What trend, if any, is evident? How does Wal-Mart's ROE compare with the approximately 20% median ROE for companies in the Dow Jones Industrial average for 2011?

  b. Compute the return on assets (ROA) for 2010 and 2011. What trends, if any, are evident? How does Wal-Mart's ROA compare with the approximate 6.7% median ROA for companies in the Dow Jones Industrial average for 2011?

  c. What factors might allow a company like Wal-Mart to reap above-average returns?

P1-36.   Formulating Financial Statements from Raw Data (LO2)

Following is selected financial information from General Mills, Inc., for its fiscal year ended May 29, 2011 ($ millions).

General Mills, Inc. (GIS)

Revenue	$14,880.2
Cash from operating activities	1,526.8
Cash, beginning year	673.2
Stockholders' equity	6,612.2
Noncash assets	18,054.9
Cash from financing activities*	(865.3)
Cost of goods sold	8,926.7
Total expenses (other than cost of goods sold)	4,155.2
Cash, ending year	619.6
Total liabilities	12,062.3
Cash from investing activities	(715.1)

* Cash from financing activities includes the effects of foreign exchange rate fluctuations.

Required

a. Prepare the income statement, the balance sheet, and the statement of cash flows for General Mills for the fiscal year ended May 2011.

b. Do the negative amounts for cash from investing activities and cash from financing activities concern us? Explain.

c. Using the statements prepared for part *a*, compute the following ratios (for this part only, use the year-end balance instead of the average for assets and stockholders' equity):
   i. Profit margin
   ii. Asset turnover
   iii. Return on assets
   iv. Return on equity

P1-37.   **Formulating Financial Statements from Raw Data**   (LO2)

Abercrombie & Fitch
(ANF)

Following is selected financial information from **Abercrombie & Fitch** for its fiscal year ended January 29, 2011 ($ millions).

Noncash assets	$2,122
Total expenses (other than cost of goods sold)	2,062
Cash from investing activities.	(93)
Cash, ending year	826
Revenue	3,469
Total liabilities	1,057
Cash from operating activities	392
Cash from financing activities*	(143)
Cost of goods sold	1,257
Cash, beginning year	670
Stockholders' equity	1,891

* Cash from financing activities includes the effects of foreign exchange rate fluctuations.

Required

a. Prepare the income statement, the balance sheet, and the statement of cash flows for Abercrombie & Fitch for the fiscal year ended January 2011.

b. Do the negative amounts for cash from investing activities and cash from financing activities concern us? Explain.

c. Using the statements prepared for part *a*, compute the following ratios (for this part only, use the year-end balance instead of the average for assets and stockholders' equity):
   i. Profit margin
   ii. Asset turnover
   iii. Return on assets
   iv. Return on equity

P1-38.   **Formulating Financial Statements from Raw Data**   (LO2)

Cisco Systems, Inc.
(CSCO)

Following is selected financial information from **Cisco Systems, Inc.**, for the year ended July 31, 2010 ($ millions).

Cash, ending year	$ 4,581
Cash from operating activities	10,173
Sales.	40,040
Stockholders' equity	44,285
Cost of goods sold.	14,397
Cash from financing activities	621
Total liabilities	36,845
Total expenses (other than cost of goods sold)	17,876
Noncash assets	76,549
Cash used in investing activities	(11,931)
Net income.	7,767
Cash, beginning year	5,718

Required

a. Prepare the income statement, the balance sheet, and the statement of cash flows for Cisco Systems for the fiscal year ended July 31, 2010.

    b. Does the negative amount for cash from investing activities concern us? Explain.

    c. Using the statements prepared for part *a*, compute the following ratios (for this part only, use the year-end balance instead of the average for assets and stockholders' equity):

        i. Profit margin

        ii. Asset turnover

        iii. Return on assets

        iv. Return on equity

P1-39. **Formulating a Statement of Stockholders' Equity from Raw Data** (LO2)

Crocker Corporation began calendar-year 2011 with stockholders' equity of $100,000, consisting of contributed capital of $70,000 and retained earnings of $30,000. During 2011, it issued additional stock for total cash proceeds of $30,000. It also reported $50,000 of net income, and paid $25,000 as a cash dividend to shareholders.

Required

Prepare the 2011 statement of stockholders' equity for Crocker Corporation.

P1-40. **Formulating a Statement of Stockholders' Equity from Raw Data** (LO2)

Gap, Inc., reports the following selected information at January 30, 2010 ($ millions).

Contributed capital, Jan. 30, 2010......................	$2,990
Treasury stock, Jan. 30, 2010	(9,069)
Retained earnings, Jan. 30, 2010......................	10,815
Accumulated other comprehensive income, Jan. 30, 2010.....	155

Gap, Inc.
(GPS)

During fiscal year 2011, Gap reported the following:

1. Sale of stock .... $ 4
2. Purchase of stock 1,797
3. Net income 1,204
4. Cash dividends 252
5. Other comprehensive income..... 30

Required

Use this information to prepare the statement of stockholders' equity for Gap, Inc., for 2011.

P1-41. **Computing, Analyzing, and Interpreting Return on Equity and Return on Assets** (LO3)

Following are summary financial statement data for Kimberly-Clark for 2008 through 2010.

Kimberly-Clark (KMB)

KIMBERLY-CLARK CORPORATION (KMB)			
($ millions)	2010	2009	2008
Sales......................................	$19,746	$19,115	$19,415
Net income................................	1,843	1,884	1,690
Total assets...............................	19,864	19,209	18,089
Equity....................................	6,202	5,690	4,261

Required

a. Compute the return on assets and return on equity for 2009 and 2010 (use average assets and average equity), together with the components of ROA (profit margin and asset turnover). What trends do we observe? Which component appears to be driving the change in ROA over this time period?

b. KMB repurchased a large amount of its common shares in recent years at a cost of over $4.7 billion. How did this repurchase affect its return on equity?

P1-42. **Computing, Analyzing, and Interpreting Return on Equity and Return on Assets** (LO3)

Following are summary financial statement data for Nordstrom, Inc., for 2009 through 2011.

Nordstrom, Inc.
(JWN)

($ millions)	2011	2010	2009
Sales......................................	$9,700	$8,627	$8,573
Net income................................	613	441	401
Total assets...............................	7,462	6,579	5,661
Equity....................................	2,021	1,572	1,210

Required

Compute return on assets and return on equity for each year 2010 and 2011 (use average assets and average equity), together with the components of ROA (profit margin and asset turnover). What trends, if any, do we observe? Which component, if any, appears to be driving the change in ROA over this time period?

P1-43. Computing, Analyzing, and Interpreting Return on Equity (LO3)

Nokia (NOK)

Nokia manufactures, markets, and sells phones and other electronics. Total stockholders' equity for Nokia is €16,231 in 2010 and €14,749 in 2009. In 2010, Nokia reported net income of €1,850 on sales of €42,446.

Required

a. What is Nokia's return on equity for 2010?

b. What are total expenses for Nokia in 2010?

c. Nokia used cash to repurchase a large amount of its common stock during the period 2006 through 2008. What motivations might Nokia have for repurchasing its common stock?

P1-44. Comparing Abercrombie & Fitch and TJX Companies (LO3)

Abercrombie & Fitch (ANF)
TJX Companies (TJX)

Following are selected financial statement data from Abercrombie & Fitch (ANF—upscale clothing retailer) and TJX Companies (TJX—value-priced clothing retailer including TJ Maxx)—both dated the end of January 2011 or 2010.

($ millions)	Company	Total Assets	Net Income	Sales
2010	TJX Companies Inc.	$7,464		
2011	TJX Companies Inc.	7,972	$1,343	$21,942
2010	Abercombie & Fitch	2,822		
2011	Abercombie & Fitch	2,948	150	3,469

Required

a. Compute the return on assets for both companies for the year ended January 2011.

b. Disaggregate the ROAs for both companies into the profit margin and asset turnover.

c. What differences are observed? Evaluate these differences in light of the two companies' business models. Which company has better financial performance?

P1-45. Computing and Interpreting Return on Assets and Its Components (LO3)

McDonald's Corporation (MCD)

McDonald's Corporation (MCD) reported the following balance sheet and income statement data for 2008 through 2010.

($ millions)	Total Assets	Net Income	Sales
2008	$28,461.5		
2009	30,224.9	$4,551.0	$22,744.7
2010	31,975.2	4,946.3	24,074.6

Required

a. What is MCD's return on assets for 2009 and 2010? Disaggregate MCD's ROA into its net profit margin and its asset turnover.

b. What factor is mainly responsible for the change in MCD's ROA over this period?

P1-46. Disaggregating Return on Assets over Multiple Periods (LO3)

3M Company (MMM)

Following are selected financial statement data from 3M Company for 2007 through 2010.

($ millions)	Total Assets	Net Income	Sales
2007	24,694	4,096	24,462
2008	25,793	3,460	25,269
2009	27,250	3,193	23,123
2010	30,156	4,085	26,662

Required

a. Compute 3M Company's return on assets for 2008 through 2010. Disaggregate 3M's ROA into the profit margin and asset turnover for 2008 through 2010. What trends do we observe?

b. Which ROA component appears to be driving the trend observed in part a? Explain.

P1-47.[A]   **Reading and Interpreting Audit Opinions**   (LO5)

Apple Inc.'s 2010 financial statements include the following audit report from Ernst & Young LLP.

Apple Inc. (AAPL)

> **REPORT OF INDEPENDENT REGISTERED PUBLIC ACCOUNTING FIRM**
>
> The Board of Directors and Shareholders of Apple Inc.
>
> We have audited the accompanying consolidated balance sheets of Apple Inc. as of September 25, 2010 and September 26, 2009, and the related consolidated statements of operations, shareholders' equity and cash flows for the years then ended. These financial statements are the responsibility of the Company's management. Our responsibility is to express an opinion on these financial statements based on our audits.
>
> We conducted our audits in accordance with the standards of the Public Company Accounting Oversight Board (United States). Those standards require that we plan and perform the audit to obtain reasonable assurance about whether the financial statements are free of material misstatement. An audit includes examining, on a test basis, evidence supporting the amounts and disclosures in the financial statements. An audit also includes assessing the accounting principles used and significant estimates made by management, as well as evaluating the overall financial statement presentation. We believe that our audits provide a reasonable basis for our opinion.
>
> In our opinion, the financial statements referred to above present fairly, in all material respects, the consolidated financial position of Apple Inc. at September 25, 2010 and September 26, 2009, and the consolidated results of its operations and its cash flows for the years then ended, in conformity with U.S. generally accepted accounting principles.
>
> We also have audited, in accordance with the standards of the Public Company Accounting Oversight Board (United States), Apple Inc.'s internal control over financial reporting as of September 25, 2010, based on criteria established in Internal Control—Integrated Framework issued by the Committee of Sponsoring Organizations of the Treadway Commission and our report dated October 27, 2010 expressed an unqualified opinion thereon.
>
> /s/ Ernst & Young LLP
> San Jose, California
> October 27, 2010

Required

a. To whom is the report addressed? Why?

b. In your own words, briefly describe the audit process. What steps do auditors take to determine whether a company's financial statements are free from material misstatement?

c. What is the nature of Ernst & Young's opinion? What do you believe the word *fairly* means? Is Ernst & Young providing a guarantee to Apple's financial statement users?

d. What other opinion is Ernst & Young rendering? Why is this opinion important?

P1-48.   **Reading and Interpreting CEO Certifications**   (LO5)

Following is the CEO Certification required by the Sarbanes-Oxley Act and signed by Apple CEO Steve Jobs. Apple's Chief Financial Officer signed a similar form.

Apple Inc. (AAPL)

> **CERTIFICATIONS**
>
> I, Steven P. Jobs, certify that:
>
> 1.   I have reviewed this annual report on Form 10-K of Apple, Inc.;
>
> 2.   Based on my knowledge, this report does not contain any untrue statement of a material fact or omit to state a material fact necessary to make the statements made, in light of the circumstances under which such statements were made, not misleading with respect to the period covered by this report;
>
> 3.   Based on my knowledge, the financial statements, and other financial information included in this report, fairly present in all material respects the financial condition, results of operations and cash flows of the registrant as of, and for, the periods presented in this report;

continued

continued from prior page

4. The registrant's other certifying officer(s) and I are responsible for establishing and maintaining disclosure controls and procedures (as defined in Exchange Act Rules l3a-l5(e) and 15d-l5(e)) and internal control over financial reporting (as defined in Exchange Act Rules 13a-15(f) and 15d-15(f) for the registrant) and have:

(a) Designed such disclosure controls and procedures, or caused such disclosure controls and procedures to be designed under our supervision, to ensure that material information relating to the registrant, including its consolidated subsidiaries, is made known to us by others within those entities, particularly during the period in which this report is being prepared;

(b) Designed such internal control over financial reporting, or caused such internal control over financial reporting to be designed under our supervision, to provide reasonable assurance regarding the reliability of financial reporting and the preparation of financial statements for external purposes in accordance with generally accepted accounting principles;

(c) Evaluated the effectiveness of the registrant's disclosure controls and procedures and presented in this report our conclusions about the effectiveness of the disclosure controls and procedures, as of the end of the period covered by this report based on such evaluation; and

(d) Disclosed in this report any change in the registrant's internal control over financial reporting that occurred during the registrant's most recent fiscal quarter (the registrant's fourth fiscal quarter in the case of an annual report) that has materially affected, or is reasonably likely to materially affect, the registrant's internal control over financial reporting; and

5. The registrant's other certifying officer(s) and I have disclosed, based on our most recent evaluation of internal control over financial reporting, to the registrant's auditors and the audit committee of the registrant's board of directors (or persons performing the equivalent functions):

(a) All significant deficiencies and material weaknesses in the design or operation of internal control over financial reporting which are reasonably likely to adversely affect the registrant's ability to record, process, summarize, and report financial information; and

(b) Any fraud, whether or not material, that involves management or other employees who have a significant role in the registrant's internal control over financial reporting.

Date: October 27, 2010

By: /s/ STEVEN P. JOBS

Steven P. Jobs
Chief Executive Officer

Required

a. Summarize the assertions that Steve Jobs made in this certification.

b. Why did Congress feel it important that CEOs and CFOs sign such certifications?

c. What potential liability do you believe the CEO and CFO are assuming by signing such certifications?

P1-49.   Assessing Corporate Governance and Its Effects   (LO5)

General Electric (GE)

Review the corporate governance section of General Electric's Website (find and click on: "Our Company"; then, find and click on: "Governance").

Required

a. In your words, briefly describe GE's governance structure.

b. What is the main purpose of its governance structure?

IFRS APPLICATIONS

I1-50.   Applying the Accounting Equation and Computing Financing Proportions   (LO2)

The following table contains fiscal 2009 information for three companies that use IFRS. Apply the accounting equation to compute the missing financial amounts (a), (b), and (c). Which of these companies is more owner-financed? Which of these companies is more nonowner-financed? Discuss why the proportion of owner financing might differ across these three companies.

(Amounts in millions)	Assets	=	Liabilities	+	Equity	
OMV Group (France)	€ 21,415		€ 11,380		(a)	OMV Group
Ericsson (Sweden).	SEK 269,809		(b)		SEK 141,027	Ericsson
BAE Systems (UK).	(c)		£20,680		£4,727	BAE Systems

I1-51. **Computing Return on Equity and Return on Assets** (LO3)

The following table contains financial statement information for AstraZeneca, which is a global biopharmaceutical company focused on discovery, development, manufacturing and commercialization of medicines and is headquartered in London, UK.

AstraZeneca

($ millions)	Total Assets	Net Income	Sales	Equity
2007	$47,988	$5,969	$29,559	$14,915
2008	46,950	4,224	31,601	16,060
2009	54,920	7,490	32,804	20,821

Required

a. Compute the return on equity (ROE) for 2008 and 2009. What trend, if any, is evident? How does AstraZeneca's ROE compare with the approximately 17% median ROE for companies in the Dow Jones Industrial average for 2009?

b. Compute the return on assets (ROA) for 2008 and 2009. What trends, if any, are evident? How does AstraZeneca's ROA compare with the approximate 6.5% median ROA for companies in the Dow Jones Industrial average for 2009?

c. What factors might allow a company like AstraZeneca to reap above-average returns?

I1-52. **Computing and Interpreting Return on Assets and Its Components** (LO3)

Tesco PLC, which is one of the world's largest retailers and is headquartered in Cheshunt, U.K., reported the following balance sheet and income statement data for 2007 through 2009.

Tesco PLC

(£ millions)	Total Assets	Net Income	Sales
2007	£24,807	£1,899	£42,641
2008	30,164	2,130	47,298
2009	46,053	2,166	54,327

Required

a. What is Tesco's return on assets for 2008 and 2009?

b. Disaggregate Tesco's ROA metrics from part a into profit margin and asset turnover.

c. What factor is mainly responsible for the change in Tesco's ROA over this period?

MANAGEMENT APPLICATIONS

MA1-53. **Strategic Financing** (LO2)

You and your management team are working to develop the strategic direction of your company for the next three years. One issue you are discussing is how to finance the projected increases in operating assets. Your options are to rely more heavily on operating creditors, borrow the funds, or to sell additional stock in your company. Discuss the pros and cons of each source of financing.

MA1-54. **Statement Analysis** (LO3)

You are evaluating your company's recent operating performance and are trying to decide on the relative weights you should put on the income statement, the balance sheet, and the statement of cash flows. Discuss the information each of these statements provides and its role in evaluating operating performance.

MA1-55. **Analyst Relations** (LO2)

Your investor relations department reports to you that stockholders and financial analysts evaluate the quality of a company's financial reports based on their "transparency," namely the clarity and completeness of the company's financial disclosures. Discuss the trade-offs of providing more or less transparent financial reports.

MA1-56. **Ethics and Governance: Management Communications** (LO5)

The Business Insight box on page 1-13 quotes Warren Buffett on the use of accounting jargon. Many companies publicly describe their performance using terms such as "EBITDA" or "earnings purged of various expenses" because they believe these terms more effectively reflect their companies' performance than GAAP-defined terms such as net income. What ethical issues might arise from the use of such terms and what challenges does their use present for the governance of the company by shareholders and directors?

MA1-57.[B] **Ethics and Governance: Auditor Independence** (LO5)

The SEC has been concerned with the "independence" of external auditing firms. It is especially concerned about how large non-audit (such as consulting) fees might impact how aggressively auditing firms pursue accounting issues they uncover in their audits. Congress recently passed legislation that prohibits accounting firms from providing both consulting and auditing services to the same client. How might consulting fees affect auditor independence? What other conflicts of interest might exist for auditors? How do these conflicts impact the governance process?

SOLUTIONS TO REVIEW PROBLEMS

Mid-Module Review

Solution

1.

ALLSTATE CORPORATION
Income Statement
For Year Ended December 31, 2010

Revenues	$31,400
Expenses	30,472
Net income	$ 928

ALLSTATE CORPORATION
Balance Sheet
December 31, 2010

Cash	$ 562	Total liabilities	$111,830
Noncash assets	130,312	Stockholders' equity	19,044
Total assets	$130,874	Total liabilities and equity	$130,874

ALLSTATE CORPORATION
Statement of Cash Flows
For Year Ended December 31, 2010

Cash flows from operations	$3,689
Cash flows from investing	2,332
Cash flows from financing	(6,071)
Net increase (decrease) in cash	(50)
Cash, beginning year	612
Cash, ending year	$ 562

2. Berkshire Hathaway is a larger company; its total assets are $372,229 million compared to Allstate's assets of $130,874 million. The income statements of the two companies are markedly different. Berkshire Hathaway reports more than four times as much revenue ($136,185 million compared to $31,400 million). The difference in net income is also large; Berkshire Hathaway earned $12,967 million whereas Allstate reported net income of only $928 million.

Module-End Review

Solution

a. ROA = Net income/Average assets = $1,068/$20,600 = 5.2%. The profitability component is Net income/Sales = $1,068/$14,963 = 7.1%, and the productivity component is Sales/Average assets = $14,963/$20,600 = 0.73. Notice that 7.1% × 0.73 = 5.2%. Thus, the two components, when multiplied yield ROA.

b. ROE = Net income/Average stockholders' equity = $1,068/$5,899 = 18.1%.

Getty Images

APPLE

In 1985, the board of directors of Apple along with the new CEO John Sculley, dismissed Steve Jobs, Apple's co-founder. Fast forward 12 years—Apple is struggling to survive. After a series of crippling financial losses, the company's stock price is at an all-time low. In a complete about-face, the board asks Steve Jobs to return as interim CEO to begin a critical restructuring of the company's product line. True to form, Jobs shows up at his first meeting with Apple senior executives wearing shorts, sneakers, and a few days' beard growth. Sitting in a swivel chair and spinning slowly, Jobs begins quizzing the executives. "OK, tell me what's wrong with this place," asks Jobs. Mumbled replies and embarrassed looks ensue. Jobs cuts them short and jumps up: "It's the products! So what's wrong with the products?" Again, more weak answers and again Jobs cut them off. "The products SUCK!" he roars. "There's no sex in them anymore!"

Jobs was right—Apple was mired in a sea of problems, many stemming from a weak product line. The company's decision to design proprietary software that was often incompatible with Windows had relegated Apple to a niche player in the highly competitive, low-margin PC business. Years before, Microsoft had replicated the Mac operating system and licensed the software to PC manufacturers such as Dell. Apple's cumulative profit from 2001-2003 was an anemic $109 million and its prospects were dim.

That was then; this is now. Apple's iPod and iTunes sales quickly soared and comprised nearly 50% of Apple's revenues. However, today those products account for only 20% of its revenues. iPhone sales now top $25 billion annu-

ally, which is over one-third of total revenues. The effects of iPad sales will further reduce that percentage.

Apple's shares (ticker: AAPL) traded around $400 in 2011, a staggering 100 times the $4 they fetched fourteen years earlier when Jobs rejoined the team. Indeed, Apple's stock has more than doubled in price in the past two years, as the following price chart illustrates. The total stock market value of Apple stock (called the market capitalization or market cap) exceeded $373 billion in 2011.

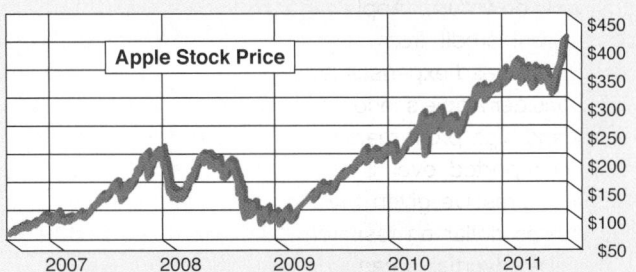

This module defines and explains the components of each financial statement: the balance sheet, the income statement, the statement of cash flows, and the statement of stockholders' equity. Let's begin with a sneak preview of Apple's financial statements.

Apple's balance sheet is very liquid as many of its assets can be readily converted to cash. Indeed, Apple holds over two-thirds of its assets in cash and marketable securities. Liquidity is important for companies like Apple that must react quickly to opportunities and changing market conditions. Like other technology companies, much of Apple's

Introducing Financial Statements and Transaction Analysis

LEARNING OBJECTIVES

LO1 Describe information conveyed by the financial statements. (p. 2-3)

LO2 Explain and illustrate linkages among the four financial statements. (p. 2-19)

LO3 Illustrate use of the financial statement effects template to summarize accounting transactions. (p. 2-21)

production is subcontracted. Consequently, Apple's property, plant and equipment make up only 6% of its assets.

On the financing side of its balance sheet, almost two-thirds of Apple's resources come from owner financing: from common stock sold to shareholders and from past profits that have been reinvested in the business. Technology companies such as Apple, which have uncertain product life-cycles and highly volatile cash flows, strive to avoid high debt levels that might cause financial problems in a business downturn. Apple's nonowner financing consists of low-cost credit from suppliers (accounts payable) and unpaid overhead expenses (accrued liabilities).

Consider Apple's income statement: driven by the popularity and high profit margins of iPods and iPhones, Apple recently reported over $18.3 billion of operating income. This is impressive given that Apple spends three cents of every sales dollar on research and development and runs expensive advertising campaigns.

Yet, companies cannot live by profits alone. It is cash that pays bills. Profits and cash flow reflect two different concepts, each providing a different perspective on company performance. Apple generated over $18.5 billion of cash flow from operating activities, and invested most of this cash flow in marketable securities. We review Apple's cash flows in this module.

Apple pays no dividends and its newly issued common stock relates primarily to executive stock options. These capital transactions are reported in the statement of stockholders' equity.

While it is important to understand what is reported in each of the four financial statements, it is also important to

know what is *not* reported. To illustrate, *Fortune* reported that "Jobs cut a deal with the Big Five record companies . . . to sell songs on iTunes, but they were afraid of Internet piracy. So Jobs promised to wrap their songs in Apple's *FairPlay*—the only copy-protection software that is iPod-compatible. Other digital music services such as Yahoo Music Unlimited and Napster reached similar deals with the big record labels. But Apple refused to license *FairPlay* to them. So those companies turned to Microsoft for copy protection. That means none of the songs sold by those services can be played on the wildly popular iPod. Instead, users of the services had to rely on inferior devices made by companies like Samsung and SanDisk that supported Microsoft's Windows Media format."

Apple's copy-protection software described above creates a barrier to competition that allows iPod to earn above-average profits. This represents a valuable resource to Apple, but it is not reported as an asset on Apple's balance sheet. Consider another example. Apple's software engineers write code and create software that will generate profits for Apple in the future. While this represents a valuable resource to Apple, it is not reported on the balance sheet because Apple expenses the software engineers' salaries when the code is written. Finally, Steve Jobs himself was a valuable unrecorded asset for Apple. We discuss these and other issues relating to asset recognition and measurement in this module.

Sources: Apple 2010 10-K; Apple 2010 Annual Report; *BusinessWeek*, 2006; *Fortune*, 2006 and 2012.

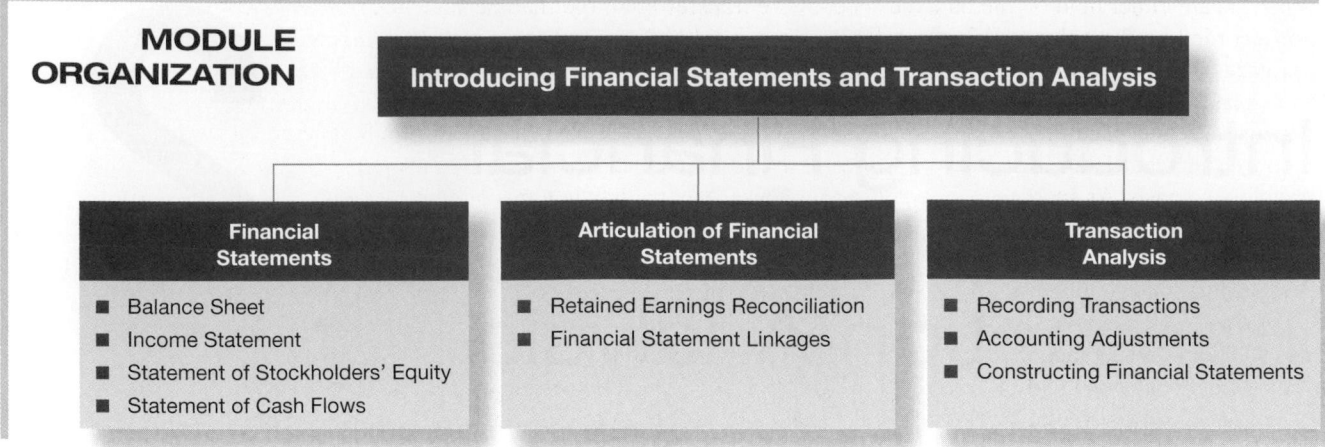

MODULE ORGANIZATION

Introducing Financial Statements and Transaction Analysis

Financial Statements	Articulation of Financial Statements	Transaction Analysis
■ Balance Sheet ■ Income Statement ■ Statement of Stockholders' Equity ■ Statement of Cash Flows	■ Retained Earnings Reconciliation ■ Financial Statement Linkages	■ Recording Transactions ■ Accounting Adjustments ■ Constructing Financial Statements

This module explains further the details of financial statements and how those statements articulate (relate to each other). Transaction analysis and accounting adjustments conclude the module.

BALANCE SHEET

LO1 Describe information conveyed by the financial statements.

The balance sheet is divided into three sections: assets, liabilities, and stockholders' equity. It provides information about the resources available to management and the claims against those resources by creditors and shareholders. The balance sheet reports the assets, liabilities and equity at a *point* in time. Balance sheet accounts are called "permanent accounts" in that they carry over from period to period; that is, the ending balance from one period becomes the beginning balance for the next.

Balance Sheet and the Flow of Costs

Companies incur costs to acquire resources that will be used in operations. Every cost creates either an immediate or a future economic benefit. Determining when the company will realize the benefit from a cost is paramount. When a cost creates an immediate benefit, such as gasoline used in delivery vehicles, the company records the cost in the income statement as an expense. When a cost creates a future economic benefit, such as inventory to be resold or equipment to be later used for manufacturing, the company records the cost on the balance sheet as an asset. Indeed, the definition of an asset is "a future economic benefit." An asset remains on the company's balance sheet until it is used up. When an asset is used up, the company realizes the economic benefit from the asset; that is, there is no future economic benefit left so there is no asset left. Then, the asset's cost is transferred from the balance sheet to the income statement where it is labeled an expense. This is why purchased assets are sometimes referred to as future expenses.

Companies expense certain costs, such as advertising, as they are incurred because even though the costs will likely bring future economic benefits, the related asset cannot be reliably measured. Exhibit 2.1 illustrates how costs flow from the balance sheet to the income statement.

EXHIBIT 2.1 Flow of Costs

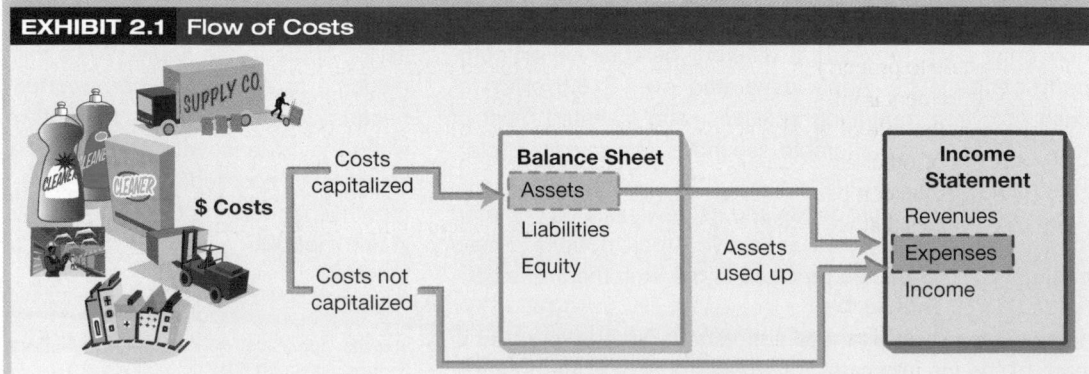

All costs are either held on the balance sheet or are transferred to the income statement. When costs are recorded on the balance sheet (referred to as *capitalized*), assets are reported and expenses are deferred to a later period. Once the company receives benefits from the assets, the related costs are transferred from the balance sheet to the income statement. At that point, assets are reduced and expenses are recorded in the current period. Tracking the flow of costs from the balance sheet to the income statement is an important part of accounting. GAAP allows companies some flexibility in transferring costs. As such, there is potential for abuse, especially when managers confront pressures to achieve income targets.

Corporate scandals involving **WorldCom** and **Enron** regrettably illustrate improper cost transfers designed to achieve higher profit levels. Neither company transferred costs from the balance sheet to the income statement as quickly as they should have. This had the effect of overstating assets on the balance sheet and net income on the income statement. In subsequent litigation, the SEC and the Justice Department contended that these companies intentionally overstated net income to boost stock prices. A number of senior executives from both Enron and WorldCom were sentenced to lengthy jail terms as a result of their criminal actions.

What does GAAP advise about the transfer of costs? Asset costs should transfer to the income statement when the asset no longer has any future economic benefit (which is when it no longer meets the definition of an asset). For example, when inventories are purchased or manufactured, their cost is recorded on the balance sheet as an asset called *inventories*. When inventories are sold, they no longer have an economic benefit to the company and their cost is transferred to the income statement in an expense called *cost of goods sold*. Cost of goods sold represents the cost of inventories sold during that period. This expense is recognized in the same period as the revenue generated from the sale. As another example, consider equipment costs. When a company acquires equipment, the cost of the equipment is recorded on the balance sheet in an asset called *equipment* (often included in the general category of property, plant, and equipment, or PPE). When equipment is used in operations, a portion of the acquisition cost is transferred to the income statement to match against the sales the equipment helped generate. To illustrate, if an asset costs $100,000, and 10% of it is used up this period in operating activities, then $10,000 of the asset's cost is transferred from the balance sheet to the income statement. This process is called *depreciation* and the expense related to this transfer of costs is called depreciation expense.

Assets

Companies acquire assets to yield a return for their shareholders. Assets are expected to produce economic benefits in the form of revenues, either directly, such as with inventory, or indirectly, such as with a manufacturing plant that produces inventories for sale. To create shareholder value, assets must yield income that is in excess of the cost of the funds used to acquire the assets.

The asset section of the **Apple** balance sheet is shown in Exhibit 2.2. Apple reports $75,183 million of total assets as of September 25, 2010, its year-end. Amounts reported on the balance sheet are at a *point in time*—that is, the close of business on the day of the report. An asset must possess two characteristics to be reported on the balance sheet:

1. It must be owned (or controlled) by the company.

2. It must confer expected future economic benefits that result from a past transaction or event.

The first requirement, owning or controlling an asset, implies that a company has legal title to the asset, such as the title to property, or has the unrestricted right to use the asset, such as a lease on the property. The second requirement implies that a company expects to realize a benefit from the asset. Benefits can be cash inflows from the sale of an asset or from sales of products produced by the asset. Benefits also can refer to the receipt of other assets such as an account receivable from a credit sale. Or, benefits can arise from future services the company will receive, such as prepaying for a year-long insurance policy. This requirement also implies that we cannot record an asset such as a brand name without a transaction to acquire it.

Current Assets

The balance sheet lists assets in order of decreasing **liquidity**, which refers to the ease of converting noncash assets into cash. The most liquid assets are called **current assets** and they are listed first. A

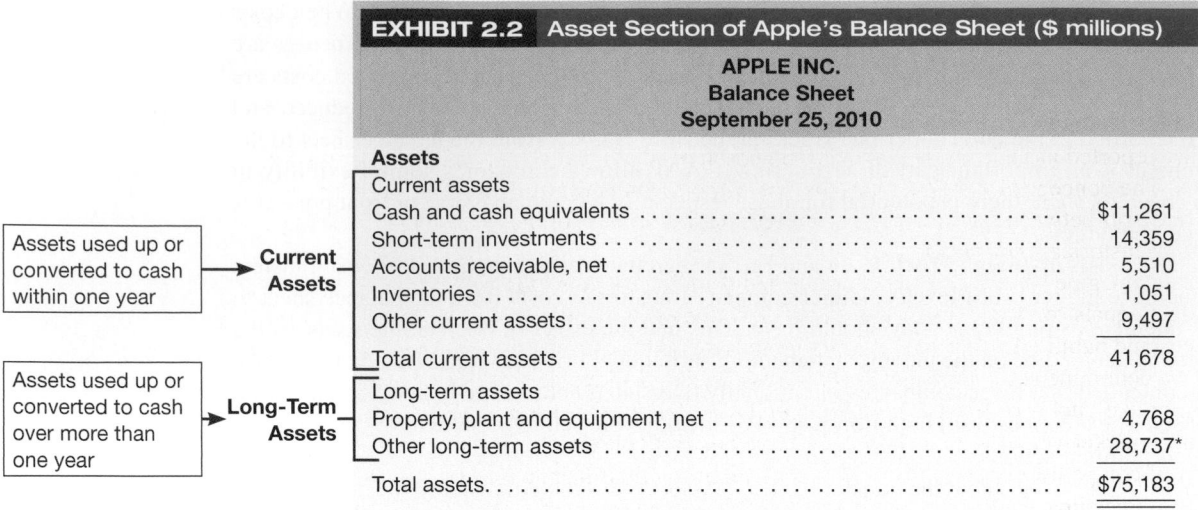

EXHIBIT 2.2   Asset Section of Apple's Balance Sheet ($ millions)

APPLE INC.
Balance Sheet
September 25, 2010

Assets	
Current assets	
Cash and cash equivalents	$11,261
Short-term investments	14,359
Accounts receivable, net	5,510
Inventories	1,051
Other current assets	9,497
Total current assets	41,678
Long-term assets	
Property, plant and equipment, net	4,768
Other long-term assets	28,737*
Total assets	$75,183

Assets used up or converted to cash within one year → **Current Assets**

Assets used up or converted to cash over more than one year → **Long-Term Assets**

*Includes $25,391 million of long-term marketable securities

company expects to convert its current assets into cash or use those assets in operations within the coming fiscal year.[1] Typical examples of current assets follow:

Cash—currency, bank deposits, and investments with an original maturity of 90 days or less (called *cash equivalents*);

Short-term investments—marketable securities and other investments that the company expects to dispose of in the short run;

Accounts receivable, net—amounts due to the company from customers arising from the sale of products and services on credit ("net" refers to the subtraction of uncollectible accounts);

Inventories—goods purchased or produced for sale to customers;

Prepaid expenses—costs paid in advance for rent, insurance, advertising and other services.

Apple reports current assets of $41,678 million in 2010, which is 55% of its total assets. The amount of current assets is an important measure of liquidity, which relates to a company's ability to make short-term payments. Companies require a degree of liquidity to operate effectively, as they must be able to respond to changing market conditions and take advantage of opportunities. However, current assets are expensive to hold (they must be stored, insured, monitored, financed, and so forth)—and they typically generate relatively low returns. As a result, companies seek to maintain only just enough current assets to cover liquidity needs, but not so much to unnecessarily reduce income.

Long-Term Assets

The second section of the balance sheet reports long-term (noncurrent) assets. Long-term assets include the following:

Property, plant and equipment (PPE), net—land, factory buildings, warehouses, office buildings, machinery, motor vehicles, office equipment and other items used in operating activities ("net" refers to subtraction of accumulated depreciation, the portion of the assets' cost that has been expensed);

Long-term investments—investments that the company does not intend to sell in the near future;

Intangible and other assets—assets without physical substance, including patents, trademarks, franchise rights, goodwill and other costs the company incurred that provide future benefits.

---

[1] Technically, current assets include those assets expected to be converted into cash within the upcoming fiscal year or the company's operating cycle (the cash-to-cash cycle), whichever is longer. Fortune Brands (manufacturer of Jim Beam Whiskey) provides an example of a current asset with a cash conversion cycle of longer than one year. Its inventory footnote reports: "In accordance with generally recognized trade practices, bulk whiskey inventories are classified as current assets, although the majority of such inventories, due to the duration of aging processes, ordinarily will not be sold within one year."

Long-term assets are not expected to be converted into cash for some time and are, therefore, listed after current assets.

Measuring Assets

Most assets are reported at their original acquisition costs, or **historical costs**, and not at their current market values. The concept of historical costs is not without controversy. The controversy arises because of the trade-off between the **relevance** of current market values for many business decisions and the **reliability** of historical cost measures.

To illustrate, imagine we are financial analysts and want to determine the value of a company. The company's value equals the value of its assets less the value of its liabilities. Current market values of company assets (and liabilities) are more informative and relevant to our analysis than are historical costs. But how can we determine market values? For some assets, like marketable securities, values are readily obtained from online quotes or from *The Wall Street Journal*. For other assets like property, plant, and equipment, their market values are far more subjective and difficult to estimate. It would be easier for us, as analysts, if companies reported credible market values on their balance sheet. However, allowing companies to report estimates of asset market values would introduce potential *bias* into financial reporting. Consequently, companies continue to report historical costs because the loss in reliability from using subjective market values on the balance sheet is considered to be greater than the loss in relevance from using historical costs.

It is important to realize that balance sheets only include items that can be reliably measured. If a company cannot assign a monetary amount to an asset with relative certainty, it does not recognize an asset on the balance sheet. This means that there are, typically, considerable "assets" that are not reflected on a balance sheet. For example, the well-known apple image is absent from Apple's balance sheet. This image is called an "unrecognized intangible asset." Both requirements for an asset are met: Apple owns the brand and it expects to realize future benefits from the logo. The problem is reliably measuring the expected future benefits to be derived from the image. Intangible assets such as the Coke bottle silhouette, the iPod brandname, and the Nike swoosh also are not on their respective balance sheets. Companies only report intangible assets on the balance sheet when the assets are purchased. Any internally created intangible assets are not reported on a balance sheet. A sizable amount of resources is, therefore, potentially omitted from companies' balance sheets.

Excluded intangible assets often relate to *knowledge-based* (intellectual) assets, such as a strong management team, a well-designed supply chain, or superior technology. Although these intangible assets confer a competitive advantage to the company, and yield above-normal income (and clear economic benefits to those companies), they cannot be reliably measured. This is one reason why companies in knowledge-based industries are so difficult to analyze and value.

Presumably, however, companies' market values reflect these excluded intangible assets. This can yield a large difference between the market value and the book (reported) value of a company's equity. This is illustrated in the following ratios of market value to book value (averages from 2011): Apple is 5.4 and Target is 2.3. These market-to-book values (ratios) are greater for companies with large knowledge-based assets that are not reported on the balance sheet, but are reflected in company market value (such as with Apple). Companies such as Target have fewer of these assets. Hence, their balance sheets usually reflect a greater portion of company value.

Liabilities and Equity

Liabilities and stockholders' equity represent the sources of capital the company uses to finance the acquisition of assets. In general, liabilities represent a company's future economic sacrifices. Liabilities are borrowed funds such as accounts payable and obligations to lenders. They can be interest-bearing or non-interest-bearing.

Equity represents capital that has been invested by the shareholders, either directly via the purchase of stock, or indirectly in the form of *retained earnings* that reflect earnings that are reinvested in the business and not paid out as dividends.

The liabilities and stockholders' equity sections of the Apple balance sheet are reproduced in Exhibit 2.3. Apple reports $27,392 million of total liabilities and $47,791 million of stockholders' equity as of its 2010 year-end.

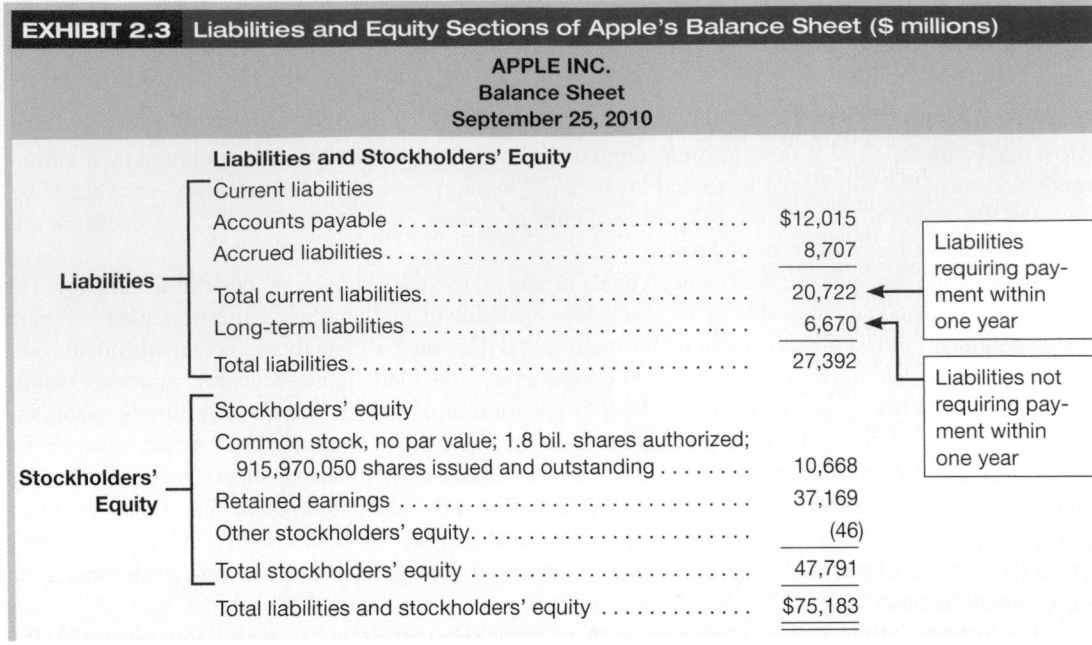

EXHIBIT 2.3 Liabilities and Equity Sections of Apple's Balance Sheet ($ millions)

APPLE INC.
Balance Sheet
September 25, 2010

Liabilities and Stockholders' Equity

Liabilities	Current liabilities	
	Accounts payable	$12,015
	Accrued liabilities	8,707
	Total current liabilities	20,722
	Long-term liabilities	6,670
	Total liabilities	27,392
Stockholders' Equity	Stockholders' equity	
	Common stock, no par value; 1.8 bil. shares authorized; 915,970,050 shares issued and outstanding	10,668
	Retained earnings	37,169
	Other stockholders' equity	(46)
	Total stockholders' equity	47,791
	Total liabilities and stockholders' equity	$75,183

Liabilities requiring payment within one year

Liabilities not requiring payment within one year

Why would Apple obtain capital from both borrowed funds and shareholders? Why not just one or the other? The answer lies in their relative costs and the contractual agreements that Apple has with each.

Creditors have the first claim on the assets of the company. As a result, their position is not as risky and, accordingly, their expected return on investment is less than that required by shareholders. Also, interest is tax deductible whereas dividends are not. This makes debt a less expensive source of capital than equity. So, then, why should a company not finance itself entirely with borrowed funds? The reason is that borrowed funds entail contractual obligations to repay the principal and interest on the debt. If a company cannot make these payments when they come due, creditors can force the company into bankruptcy and potentially put the company out of business. Shareholders, in contrast, cannot require repurchase of their stock, or even the payment of dividends. Thus, companies take on a level of debt that they can comfortably repay at reasonable interest costs. The remaining balance required to fund business activities is financed with more costly equity capital.

Current Liabilities

The balance sheet lists liabilities in order of maturity. Obligations that must be settled within one year are called **current liabilities**. Examples of common current liabilities follow:

Accounts payable—amounts owed to suppliers for goods and services purchased on credit.

Accrued liabilities—obligations for expenses that have been incurred but not yet paid; examples are accrued wages payable (wages earned by employees but not yet paid), accrued interest payable (interest that is owing but has not been paid), and accrued income taxes (taxes due).

Unearned revenues—obligations created when the company accepts payment in advance for goods or services it will deliver in the future; also called advances from customers, customer deposits, or deferred revenues.

Short-term notes payable—short-term debt payable to banks or other creditors.

Current maturities of long-term debt—principal portion of long-term debt that is due to be paid within one year.

Apple reports current liabilities of $20,722 million on its 2010 balance sheet.

Accounts payable arise when one company purchases goods or services from another company. Typically, sellers offer credit terms when selling to other companies, rather than expecting cash on delivery. The seller records an account receivable and the buyer records an account payable. Apple reports accounts payable of $12,015 million as of the balance sheet date. Accounts payable are relatively uncomplicated liabilities. A transaction occurs (inventory purchase), a bill is sent, and the amount owed is reported on the balance sheet as a liability.

Apple's accrued liabilities total $8,707 million. Accrued liabilities refer to incomplete transactions. For example, employees work and earn wages, but usually are not paid until later, such as several days after the period-end. Wages must be reported as expense in the period that employees earn them because those wages payable are obligations of the company and a liability (wages payable) must be set up on the balance sheet. This is an *accrual*. Other common accruals include the recording of liabilities such as rent and utilities payable, taxes payable, and interest payable on borrowings. All of these accruals involve recognition of expense in the income statement and a liability on the balance sheet.

Net working capital, or simply working capital, reflects the difference between current assets and current liabilities and is defined as follows:

$$\text{Net working capital} = \text{Current assets} - \text{Current liabilities}$$

We usually prefer to see more current assets than current liabilities to ensure that companies are liquid. That is, companies should have sufficient funds to pay their short-term debts as they mature. The net working capital required to conduct business depends on the company's **operating (or cash) cycle**, which is the time between paying cash for goods or employee services and receiving cash from customers—see Exhibit 2.4.

Companies, for example, use cash to purchase or manufacture inventories held for resale. Inventories are usually purchased on credit from suppliers (accounts payable). This financing is called **trade credit**. Inventories are sold, either for cash or on credit (accounts receivable). When receivables are ultimately collected, a portion of the cash received is used to repay accounts payable and the remainder goes to the cash account for the next operating cycle.

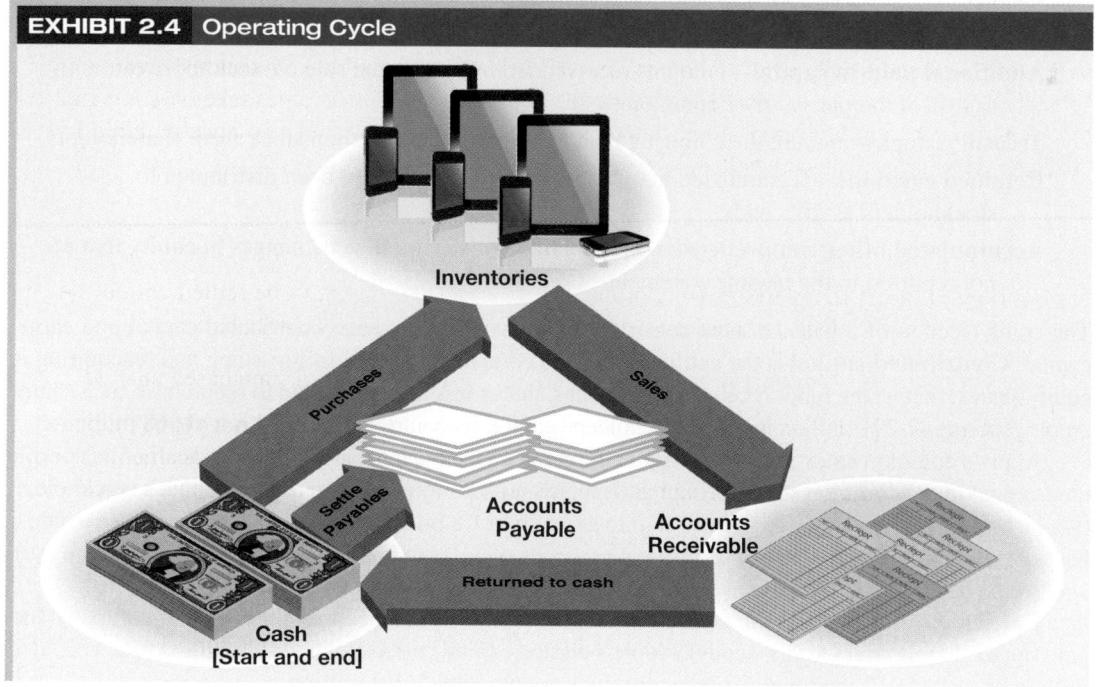

EXHIBIT 2.4 Operating Cycle

When cash is invested in inventory, the inventory can remain with the company for 30 to 90 days or more. Once inventory is sold, the resulting accounts receivable can remain with the company for another 30 to 90 days. Assets such as inventories and accounts receivable are costly to hold and, consequently, companies strive to reduce operating cycles with various initiatives that aim to:

- Decrease accounts receivable by better collection procedures
- Reduce inventory levels by improved production systems and management
- Increase trade credit to minimize the cash invested in inventories

Analysts often use the "cash conversion cycle" to evaluate company liquidity. The cash conversion cycle is the number of days the company has its cash tied up in receivables and inventories, less the number of days of trade credit provided by company suppliers.

Noncurrent Liabilities

Noncurrent liabilities are obligations due after one year. Examples of noncurrent liabilities follow:

Long-term debt—amounts borrowed from creditors that are scheduled to be repaid more than one year in the future; any portion of long-term debt that is due within one year is reclassified as a current liability called *current maturities of long-term debt*. Long-term debt includes bonds, mortgages, and other long-term loans.

Other long-term liabilities—various obligations, such as pension liabilities and long-term tax liabilities, that will be settled a year or more into the future.

Apple reports $6,670 million of noncurrent liabilities. As is typical of high-tech companies, Apple has no long-term debt. Instead, all of its noncurrent liabilities relate to deferred revenue and deferred taxes. Deferred (unearned) revenue arises when a company receives cash in advance of providing a good or service.

Stockholders' Equity

Stockholders' equity reflects financing provided from company owners. Equity is often referred to as *residual interest*. That is, stockholders have a claim on any assets in excess of what is needed to meet company obligations to creditors. The following are examples of items typically included in equity:

Common stock—par value received from the original sale of common stock to investors.

Preferred stock—value received from the original sale of preferred stock to investors; preferred stock has fewer ownership rights compared to common stock.

Additional paid-in capital—amounts received from the original sale of stock to investors in excess of the par value of common stock.

Treasury stock—amount the company paid to reacquire its common stock from shareholders.

Retained earnings—accumulated net income (profit) that has not been distributed to stockholders as dividends.

Accumulated other comprehensive income or loss—accumulated changes in equity that are not reported in the income statement.

Contributed Capital — (Common stock, Preferred stock, Additional paid-in capital, Treasury stock)

Earned Capital — (Retained earnings, Accumulated other comprehensive income or loss)

The equity section of a balance sheet consists of two basic components: contributed capital and earned capital. **Contributed capital** is the net funding that a company received from issuing and reacquiring its equity shares; that is, the funds received from issuing shares less any funds paid to repurchase such shares. Apple reports $47,791 million in total stockholders' equity. Its contributed capital is $10,668 million.

Apple's common stock is "no par" (see Exhibit 2.3). This means that Apple records all of its contributed capital in the common stock account and records no additional paid-in capital. Apple's stockholders (via its board of directors) have authorized it to issue up to 1.8 billion shares of common stock. To date, it has sold (issued) 915,970,050 shares for total proceeds of $10,668 million, or $11.65 per share, on average. Apple has repurchased no shares of stock to date.

Earned capital is the cumulative net income (loss) that has been retained by the company (not paid out to shareholders as dividends). Apple's earned capital (titled Retained Earnings) totals $37,169 million as of its 2010 year-end. Its other equity accounts total $(46) million.

Retained Earnings

There is an important relation for retained earnings that reconciles its beginning balance and its ending balance as follows:

	Beginning retained earnings
+	Net income (or − net loss)
−	Dividends
=	Ending retained earnings

This is a useful relation to remember. Apple's retained earnings increases (or decreases) each year by the amount of its reported net income (loss). If Apple paid dividends, it would decrease retained earnings, but Apple currently pays no dividends. (There are other items that can impact retained earnings that we discuss in later modules.) After we explain the income statement, we will revisit this relation and show how retained earnings link the balance sheet and income statement.

BUSINESS INSIGHT   **How Much Debt Is Reasonable?**

Apple reports total assets of $75,183 million, liabilities of $27,392 million, and stockholders' equity of $47,791 million. This reveals that it finances 36% of its assets with borrowed funds and 64% with shareholder investment. This is a lower percentage of nonowner financing than other companies such as Target and Procter & Gamble (P&G). Companies must monitor their financing sources and amounts. Too much borrowing is risky as borrowed amounts must be repaid with interest. The level of debt that a company can effectively manage depends on the stability and reliability of its operating cash flows. Companies such as P&G and Target can manage relatively high debt levels because their cash flows are relatively stable. Apple operates in an industry that changes rapidly. It cannot afford to take on too much borrowing risk.

($ millions)	Assets	Liabilities	Liabilities to Assets ratio	Equity	Equity to Assets ratio
Apple, Inc..............	$ 75,183	$27,392	36.4%	$47,791	63.6%
Cisco Systems, Inc..........	81,130	36,845	45.4%	44,285	54.6%
Gap, Inc..................	7,065	2,985	42.3%	4,080	57.7%
Procter & Gamble Co.........	128,172	66,733	52.1%	61,439	47.9%
Target Corporation...........	43,705	28,218	64.6%	15,487	35.4%

Book Value vs Market Value   Stockholders' equity is the "value" of the company determined by GAAP and is commonly referred to as the company's **book value**. This value is different from a company's **market value** (market capitalization or *market cap*), which is computed by multiplying the number of outstanding common shares by the per share market value. We can compute Apple's market cap by multiplying its outstanding shares at September 25, 2010, (915,970,050 shares) by its stock price on that date ($292.32), which equals $267.8 billion. This is considerably larger than its book value of equity on that date of $47,791 million. Book value and market value can differ for several reasons, mostly related to the recognition of transactions and events in financial statements such as the following:

■ GAAP generally reports assets and liabilities at historical costs, whereas the market attempts to estimate fair market values.

■ GAAP excludes resources that cannot be reliably measured (due to the absence of a past transaction or event) such as talented management, employee morale, recent innovations and successful marketing, whereas the market attempts to value these.

■ GAAP does not consider market differences in which companies operate, such as competitive conditions and expected changes, whereas the market attempts to factor in these differences in determining value.

■ GAAP does not usually report expected future performance, whereas the market attempts to predict and value future performance.

Presently for U.S. companies, book value is, on average, about two-thirds of market value. This means that the market has drawn on information in addition to that provided in the balance sheet and income statement in valuing equity shares. A major part of this information is in financial statement notes, but not all.

It is important to understand that, eventually, all factors determining company market value are reflected in financial statements and book value. Assets are eventually sold and liabilities are settled. Moreover, talented management, employee morale, technological innovations, and successful marketing are eventually recognized in reported profit. The difference between book value and market value is one of timing.

BUSINESS INSIGHT Apple's Market and Book Values

Apple's market value has historically exceeded its book value of equity (see graph below). Much of Apple's market value derives from intangible assets, such as brand equity, that are not fully reflected on its balance sheet, and from favorable expectations of future financial performance (particularly in recent years). Apple has incurred many costs, such as R&D, advertising, and promotion, that will probably yield future economic benefits. However, Apple expensed these costs (did not capitalize them as assets) because their future bene-fits were uncertain and therefore could not be reliably measured. Companies capitalize intangible assets only when those assets are purchased, and not when they are internally developed. Consequently, Apple's balance sheet and the balance sheets of many knowledge-based companies are, arguably, less informative about company value.

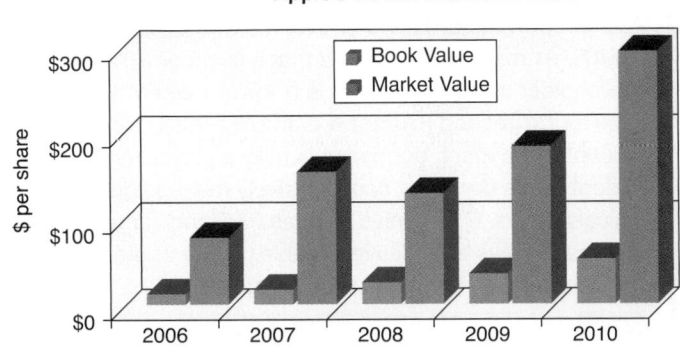

Apple's Market and Book Value

INCOME STATEMENT

The income statement reports revenues earned during a period, the expenses incurred to produce those revenues, and the resulting net income or loss. The general structure of the income statement follows:

	Revenues
−	Cost of goods sold
	Gross profit
−	Operating expenses
	Operating profit
−	Nonoperating expenses (+ Nonoperating revenues)
−	Tax expense
	Income from continuing operations
+/−	Nonrecurring items, net of tax
=	Net income

Apple's income statement from its 2010 10-K is shown in Exhibit 2.5. Apple reports net income of $14,013 million on sales of $65,225 million. This means that about $0.21 of each dollar of sales is brought down to the bottom line, computed as $14,013 million divided by $65,225 million. Apple's net income margin is higher than that of the average publicly-traded company, which reports about $0.06 in profit for each sales dollar. The remaining $0.79 of each sales dollar for Apple (computed as $1 minus $0.21) is consumed by costs incurred to generate sales. These costs include production costs (cost of sales), wages, advertising, research and development, equipment costs (such as depreciation), and taxes.

To analyze an income statement we must understand some terminology. **Revenues** (Sales) are increases in net assets (assets less liabilities) as a result of ordinary operating activities. **Expenses** are decreases in net assets used to generate revenues, including costs of sales, operating costs like wages and advertising (usually titled selling, general, and administrative expenses or SG&A), and nonoperating costs like interest on debt. The difference between revenues and expenses is **net income** when revenues exceed expenses, or **net loss** when expenses exceed revenues. The terms income, profit, and earnings are used interchangeably (as are revenues and sales).

EXHIBIT 2.5 Apple's Income Statement ($ millions)	
APPLE INC. **Income Statement** **For Year Ended September 25, 2010**	
Net sales.	$65,225
Cost of sales.	39,541
Gross margin	25,684
Operating expenses	
Research and development	1,782
Selling, general, and administrative	5,517
Total operating expenses	7,299
Operating profit	18,385
Other revenue and expense	
Interest and other income, net	155
Income before provision for income taxes.	18,540
Provision for income taxes.	4,527
Net income.	$14,013

Operating expenses are the usual and customary costs that a company incurs to support its operating activities. Those include cost of goods sold, selling expenses, depreciation expense, and research and development expense. Not all of these expenses require a cash outlay; for example, depreciation expense is a noncash expense, as are many liabilities such as wages payable, that recognize the expense in advance of cash payment. **Nonoperating expenses** relate to the company's financing and investing activities, and include interest expense, interest or dividend income, and gains and losses from the sale of securities. Business decision makers and analysts usually segregate operating and nonoperating activities as they offer different insights into company performance and condition.

> **Alert** The FASB has released a preliminary draft of a proposal to restructure financial statements to, among other things, better distinguish operating and nonoperating activities.

MANAGERIAL DECISION   You Are the Securities Analyst
You are analyzing the performance of a company that hired a new CEO during the current year. The current year's income statement includes an expense labeled "asset write-offs." Write-offs represent the accelerated transfer of costs from the balance sheet to the income statement. Are you concerned about the legitimacy of these expenses? Why or why not? [Answer, p. 2-32]

Recognition of Revenues and Expenses

An important consideration in preparing the income statement is *when* to recognize revenues and expenses. For many revenues and expenses, the decision is easy. When a customer purchases groceries, pays with a check, and walks out of the store with the groceries, we know that the sale is made and revenue should be recognized. Or, when companies receive and pay an electric bill with a check, they have clearly incurred an expense that should be recognized.

However, should Apple recognize revenue when it sells iPods to a retailer that does not have to pay Apple for 60 days? Should Apple recognize an expense for employees who work this week but will not be paid until the first of next month? The answer to both of these questions is yes.

Two fundamental principles guide recognition of revenues and expenses:

Revenue Recognition Principle—recognize revenues when *earned*.

Expense Recognition (Matching) Principle—recognize expenses when *incurred*.

These two principles are the foundation of **accrual accounting**, which is the accounting system used to prepare all GAAP-based financial statements. The general approach is this: first, recognize revenues in the time period they are earned; then, record all expenses *incurred* to generate those revenues during that same time period (this is called matching expenses to revenues). Net income is then correctly reported for that period.

Recognizing revenues when earned does not necessarily imply the receipt of cash. Revenue is e*arned* when the company has done everything that it is supposed to do. This means that a sale of goods on credit would qualify for recognition as long as the revenues are earned. Likewise, companies recognize an expense when it is *incurred*, even if no cash is paid. For example, companies recognize as expenses the wages earned by employees, even though they will not be paid until the next pay period. The company records an expense but pays no cash; instead, it records an accrued liability for the wages payable.

Accrual accounting requires estimates and assumptions. Examples include estimating how much revenue has been earned on a long-term contract, the amount of accounts receivable that will not be collected, the degree to which equipment has been "used up," the cleanup costs that a company must eventually pay for environmental liabilities, and numerous other estimates. All of these estimates and assumptions affect both reported net income and the balance sheet. Judgments affect all financial statements. This is an important by-product of accrual accounting. We discuss these estimates and assumptions, and their effects on financial statements, throughout the book.

MANAGERIAL DECISION   You Are the Operations Manager

You are the operations manager on a new consumer product that was launched this period with very successful sales. The Chief Financial Officer (CFO) asks you to prepare an estimate of warranty costs to charge against those sales. Why does the CFO desire a warranty cost estimate? What hurdles must you address in arriving at such an estimate? [Answer, p. 2-32]

Reporting of Transitory Items

To this point, we have only considered income from continuing operations and its components. A more complete income statement format is in Exhibit 2.6. The most noticeable difference involves two additional components of net income located at the bottom of the statement. These two components are specifically segregated from the "income from continuing operations" and are defined as follows:

1. **Discontinued operations** Gains or losses (and net income or loss) from business segments that are being sold or have been sold in the current period.

2. **Extraordinary items** Gains or losses from events that are both *unusual* and *infrequent* and are, therefore, excluded from income from continuing operations.

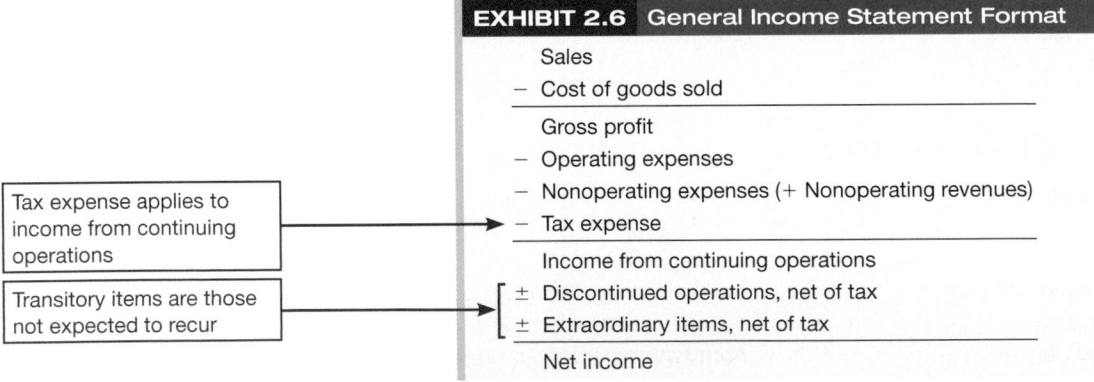

EXHIBIT 2.6   General Income Statement Format

Sales
− Cost of goods sold
Gross profit
− Operating expenses
− Nonoperating expenses (+ Nonoperating revenues)
− Tax expense
Income from continuing operations
± Discontinued operations, net of tax
± Extraordinary items, net of tax
Net income

Tax expense applies to income from continuing operations

Transitory items are those not expected to recur

These two components are segregated because they represent **transitory items**, which reflect transactions or events that are unlikely to recur. Many readers of financial statements are interested in *future* company performance. They analyze current-year financial statements to gain clues to better *predict* future performance. (Stock prices, for example, are based on a company's expected profits and cash flows.)

Transitory items, by definition, are unlikely to arise in future periods. Although transitory items can help us analyze past performance, they are largely irrelevant to predicting future performance. This means that investors and other users tend to focus on income from continuing operations because that is the level of profitability that is likely to **persist** (continue) into the future. Likewise, the financial press tends to focus on income from continuing operations when it discloses corporate earnings (often described as *earnings before one-time charges*).

IFRS INSIGHT	Balance Sheet and Income Statement under IFRS

U.S. GAAP and IFRS require a similar set of financial statements with similar formats. Both standards require current and long-term classifications for assets and liabilities, and both recognize revenues when earned and expenses when incurred. Although differences between U.S. GAAP and IFRS do exist at the "detailed level," there are at least three broader differences worth mention:

- GAAP makes no formal prescription for the balance sheet and the income statement; however, the SEC does prescribe the types of accounts and number of years that should be disclosed per Reg. S-X. This listing of required accounts is more detailed: Reg. S-X requires three years of comparative income statements whereas IFRS requires only two.

- GAAP requires the reporting of extraordinary items as a separate category of the income statement if they are unusual and infrequent; IFRS has no extraordinary item category.

- For items that are either unusual or infrequent, but not both, GAAP requires separate presentation in the income statement as a component of earnings from continuing operations; IFRS also requires disclosure of these items, but allows for such disclosure in footnotes to financial statements as an alternative to the income statement.

STATEMENT OF STOCKHOLDERS' EQUITY

The statement of stockholders' equity reconciles the beginning and ending balances of stockholders' equity accounts. The statement of stockholders' equity for **Apple** is shown in Exhibit 2.7.

EXHIBIT 2.7	Apple's Statement of Stockholders' Equity

APPLE INC.
Statement of Stockholders' Equity
For Year Ended September 25, 2010

($ millions)	Common Stock	Retained Earnings	Other Stockholders' Equity	Total Stockholders' Equity
Balance at September 26, 2009.	$ 8,210	$23,353	$77	$31,640
Common stock issued	2,458			2,458
Net income.		14,013		14,013
Dividends		0		0
Other.		(197)	(123)	(320)
Balance at September 25, 2010.	$10,668	$37,169	$(46)	$47,791

Apple's first equity component is common stock. The balance in common stock at the beginning of the year is $8,210 million. During 2010, Apple issued $2,458 million worth of common stock to employees who exercised stock options. At the end of 2010, the common stock account reports a balance of $10,668 million.

Apple's second stockholders' equity component is retained earnings. It totals $23,353 million at the start of fiscal 2010. During the year, it increased by $14,013 million from net income. Apple's retained earnings do not decrease for dividends because Apple pays no dividends; it also reports $(197) million of miscellaneous adjustments. The balance of retained earnings at year-end is $37,169 million.

In sum, total stockholders' equity begins the year at $31,640 million (including $77 million relating to miscellaneous accounts that increase total stockholders' equity) and ends fiscal 2010 with a balance of $47,791 million (including $(46) million relating to miscellaneous accounts that decrease total stockholders' equity) for a net increase of $16,151 million.

STATEMENT OF CASH FLOWS

The balance sheet and income statement are prepared using accrual accounting, in which revenues are recognized when earned and expenses when incurred. This means that companies can report income even though no cash is received. Cash shortages—due to unexpected cash outlays or when customers refuse to or cannot pay—can create economic hardships for companies and even cause their demise.

To assess cash flows, we must assess a company's cash management. Obligations to employees, creditors, and others are usually settled with cash. Illiquid companies (those lacking cash) are at risk of failure. Given the importance of cash management, companies must report a statement of cash flows in addition to the balance sheet, income statement, and statement of equity.

The income statement provides information about the economic viability of the company's products and services. It tells us whether the company can sell its products and services at prices that cover its costs and provide a reasonable return to lenders and stockholders. On the other hand, the statement of cash flows provides information about the company's ability to generate cash from those same transactions. It tells us from what sources the company has generated its cash (so we can evaluate whether those sources are persistent or transitory) and what it has done with the cash it generated.

Statement Format and Data Sources

The statement of cash flows is formatted to report cash inflows and cash outflows by the three primary business activities:

■ *Cash flows from operating activities* Cash flows from the company's transactions and events that relate to its operations.

■ *Cash flows from investing activities* Cash flows from acquisitions and divestitures of investments and long-term assets.

■ *Cash flows from financing activities* Cash flows from issuances of and payments toward borrowings and equity.

The combined cash flows from these three sections yield the net change in cash for the period. The three sections of the statement of cash flows relate to the income statement and to different parts of the balance sheet. These relations are highlighted in the table below:

Cash flow section	Information from income statement	Information from balance sheet	
Net cash flows from operating activities....	**Revenues** − **Expenses** = **Net income**	**Current operating assets** Long-term operating and all nonoperating assets	**Current operating liabilities** Long-term operating and all nonoperating liabilities Equity
Net cash flows from investing activities	Revenues − Expenses = Net income	Current operating assets **Long-term operating and all nonoperating assets**	Current operating liabilities Long-term operating and all nonoperating liabilities Equity
Net cash flows from financing activities	Revenues − Expenses = Net income	Current operating assets Long-term operating and all nonoperating assets	Current operating liabilities **Long-term operating and all nonoperating liabilities** **Equity**

Specifically, the three sections draw generally on the following information:

- **Net cash flows from operating activities** relate to the income statement and to the current asset and current liabilities sections of the balance sheet.
- **Net cash flows from investing activities** relate to the long-term assets section of the balance sheet.
- **Net cash flows from financing activities** relate to the long-term liabilities and stockholders' equity sections of the balance sheet.

These relations do not hold exactly, but they provide us a useful way to visualize the construction of the statement of cash flows.

In analyzing the statement of cash flows, we should not necessarily conclude that the company is better off if cash increases and worse off if cash decreases. It is not the change in cash that is most important, but the reasons behind the change. For example, what are the sources of cash inflows? Are these sources transitory? Are these sources mainly from operating activities? To what uses have cash inflows been put? Such questions and answers are key to properly using the statement of cash flows.

Exhibit 2.8 shows Apple's statement of cash flows. Apple reported $18,595 million in net cash inflows from operating activities in 2010. This is substantially greater than its net income of $14,013 million. The operating activities section of the statement of cash flows reconciles the difference between net income and operating cash flow. The difference is due to the add-back of depreciation, a noncash expense in the income statement, and other noncash expenses, together with year-over-year changes in operating assets and liabilities.

EXHIBIT 2.8 Apple's Statement of Cash Flows ($ millions)	
APPLE INC. **Statement of Cash Flows** **For Year Ended September 25, 2010**	
Operating activities	
Net income.	14,013
Adjustments to reconcile net income to cash generated by operating activities:	
Depreciation, amortization and accretion.	1,027
Stock-based compensation expense.	879
Deferred income tax expense.	1,440
Loss on disposition of property, plant and equipment.	24
Changes in operating assets and liabilities:	
Increase in accounts receivable.	(2,142)
Increase in inventories	(596)
Increase in vendor non-trade receivables.	(2,718)
Increase in other current assets.	(1,514)
Increase in other assets.	(120)
Increase in accounts payable.	6,307
Increase in deferred revenue	1,217
Increase in other liabilities.	778
Cash generated by operating activities.	18,595
Investing activities	
Purchases of marketable securities.	(57,793)
Proceeds from maturities of marketable securities	24,930
Proceeds from sales of marketable securities.	21,788
Purchases of other long-term investments.	(18)
Payments made in connection with business acquisitions, net of cash acquired.	(638)
Payments for acquisition of property, plant and equipment.	(2,005)
Payments for acquisition of intangible assets	(116)
Other.	(2)
Cash used in investing activities.	(13,854)
Financing activities	
Proceeds from issuance of common stock	912
Excess tax benefits from stock-based compensation.	751
Taxes paid related to net share settlement of equity awards.	(406)
Cash generated by financing activities.	1,257
Increase/(decrease) in cash and cash equivalents.	5,998
Cash and cash equivalents, beginning of the year	5,263
Cash and cash equivalents, end of the year	$11,261

Apple reports a net cash outflow of $13,854 million for investing activities, mainly for investments in marketable securities. Apple also generated $1,257 million from financing activities, mainly cash received when employees exercised their options to purchase common stock.

Overall, Apple's cash flow picture is strong. It is generating cash from operating activities and the sale of stock to employees, and is investing excess cash in marketable securities to ensure future liquidity.

Cash Flow Computations

It is sometimes difficult to understand why certain accounts are added to and subtracted from net income to yield net cash flows from operating activities. It often takes more than one pass through this section to grasp how this part of the cash flow statement is constructed.

A key to understanding these computations is to remember that under accrual accounting, revenues are recognized when earned and expenses when incurred. This recognition policy does not necessarily coincide with the receipt or payment of cash. The top line (net income) of the operating section of the statement of cash flows represents net (accrual) income under GAAP. The bottom line (net cash flows from operating activities) is the *cash profit* the company would have reported had it constructed its income statement on a cash basis rather than an accrual basis. Computing net cash flows from operating activities begins with GAAP profit and adjusts it to compute cash profit using the following general approach:

	Add (+) or Subtract (−) from Net Income
Net income............................	$ #
Add: depreciation expense	+
Adjust for changes in current assets	
Subtract increases in current assets	−
Add decreases in current assets	+
Adjust for changes in current liabilities	
Add increases in current liabilities	+
Subtract decreases in current liabilities ..	−
Cash from operating activities	$ #

Typically, net income is first adjusted for noncash expenses such as depreciation, and is then adjusted for changes during the year in current assets and current liabilities to yield cash flow from operating activities, or *cash profit*. The depreciation adjustment merely zeros out (undoes the effect of) depreciation expense, a noncash expense, which is deducted in computing net income. The following table provides brief explanations of adjustments for receivables, inventories, and payables and accruals, which are frequent sources of adjustments in this section:

	Change in account balance...	Means that...	Which requires this adjustment to net income to yield cash profit...
Receivables	Increase	Sales and net income increase, but cash is not yet received	Deduct increase in receivables from net income
	Decrease	More cash is received than is reported in sales and net income	Add decrease in receivables to net income
Inventories	Increase	Cash is paid for inventories that are not yet reflected in cost of goods sold	Deduct increase in inventories from net income
	Decrease	Cost of goods sold includes inventory costs that were paid for in a prior period	Add decrease in inventories to net income
Payables and accruals	Increase	More goods and services are acquired on credit, delaying cash payment	Add increase in payables and accruals to net income
	Decrease	More cash is paid than is reflected in cost of goods sold or operating expenses	Deduct decrease in payables and accruals from net income

BUSINESS INSIGHT	Insights into Apple's Statement of Cash Flows

The following provides insights into the computation of some amounts in the operating section of Apple's statement of cash flows in Exhibit 2.8 ($ millions).

Statement amount	Explanation of computation
Depreciation, amortization, and accretion $1,027	When buildings and equipment are acquired, their cost is recorded on the balance sheet as assets. Subsequently, as the assets are used up to generate revenues, a portion of their cost is transferred from the balance sheet to the income statement as an expense, called *depreciation*. Depreciation expense does not involve the payment of cash (that occurs when the asset is purchased). If we want to compute *cash profit*, we must add back depreciation expense to zero it out from income. The $1,027 in the second line of the statement of cash flows merely zeros out (undoes) the depreciation expense that was subtracted when Apple computed GAAP net income. Likewise, the next line (Stock-based compensation expense of $879) uses the same concept.
Increase in accounts receivable, $(2,142)	When a company sells goods *on credit*, it records revenue because it is earned, even though cash is not yet received. When Apple sold $2,142 of goods on credit, its revenues and net income increased by that amount, but no cash was received. Apple's cash profit is, thus, $2,142 less than net income. The $2,142 is subtracted from net income in computing net cash inflows from operations.
Increase in inventories, $(596)	When Apple purchases inventories, the purchase cost is reported on its balance sheet as a current asset. When inventories are sold, their cost is removed from the balance sheet and transferred to the income statement as an expense called cost of goods sold. If some inventories acquired are not yet sold, their cost is not yet reported in cost of goods sold and net income. The subtraction of $596 relates to the increase in inventories; it reflects the fact that cost of goods sold does not include all of the cash that was spent on inventories. That is, $596 cash was spent that is not yet reflected in cost of goods sold. Thus, the $596 is deducted from net income to compute *cash profit* for the period.
Increase in accounts payable, $6,307	Apple purchases much of its inventories on credit. The $6,307 increase in accounts payable reflects inventories that have been purchased, but have not yet been paid for in cash. The add-back of this $6,307 to net income reflects the fact that *cash profit* is $6,307 higher because $6,307 of accounts payable are not yet paid.

It is also helpful to use the following decision guide, involving changes in assets, liabilities, and equity, to understand increases and decreases in cash flows.

	Cash flow increases from	Cash flow decreases from
Assets.	Account decreases	Account increases
Liabilities and equity.	Account increases	Account decreases

The table above applies to all sections of the statement of cash flows. To determine if a change in each asset and liability account creates a cash inflow or outflow, examine the change and apply the decision rules from the table. For example, in the investing section, cash decreases when PPE assets increase. In the financing section, borrowing from a bank increases cash. Module 3 and Appendix B near the end of the book describe the preparation of the statement of cash flows in detail.

Sometimes the cash flow effect of an item reported in the statement of cash flows does not agree with the difference in the balance sheet accounts that we observe. This can be due to several factors. One common factor is when a company uses its own stock to acquire another entity. There is no cash effect from a stock acquisition and, hence, it is not reported in the statement of cash flows. Yet, the company does increase its assets and liabilities when it adds the acquired company's assets and liabilities to its balance sheet.

Knowledge of how companies record cash inflows and outflows helps us better understand the statement of cash flows. Determining how changes in asset and liability accounts affect cash provides an analytic tool *and* offers greater insight into managing a business. For instance, reducing the levels of receivables and inventories increases cash. Similarly, increasing the levels of accounts payable and accrued liabilities increases cash. Managing cash balances by managing other accounts is called *working capital management*, which is important for all companies.

MID-MODULE REVIEW 1

Following are account balances ($ millions) for Dell Inc. Using these data, prepare Dell's income statement and statement of cash flows for the fiscal year ended January 28, 2011. Prepare its balance sheet dated January 28, 2011.

Cash and cash equivalents, ending year	$13,913		Inventories	$ 1,301
Net cash provided by financing activities	474		Accounts payable	11,293
Long-term debt	5,146		Other stockholders' equity	(28,775)
Property, plant and equipment, net	1,953		Long-term investments	704
Other noncurrent assets	6,921		Other current assets	3,219
Accrued and other current liabilities	7,339		Retained earnings	24,744
Other noncurrent liabilities	6,204		Accounts receivable	10,136
Short-term investments	452		Selling, general and administrative expenses	7,302
Income tax expense	715		Research and development expenses	661
Net cash provided by operating activities	3,969		Cost of revenue	50,098
Paid-in capital	11,797		Net cash used in investing activities	(1,165)
Cash and cash equivalents, beginning year	10,635		Interest expense	83
Revenue	61,494			
Short-term debt	851			

The solution is on page 2-45.

ARTICULATION OF FINANCIAL STATEMENTS

LO2 Explain and illustrate linkages among the four financial statements.

The four financial statements are linked with each other and linked across time. This linkage is called **articulation**. This section demonstrates the articulation of financial statements using Apple.

Retained Earnings Reconciliation

The balance sheet and income statement are linked via retained earnings. Recall that retained earnings is updated each period as follows:

$$
\begin{array}{l}
\text{Beginning retained earnings} \\
\pm \ \text{Net income (loss)} \\
- \ \text{Dividends} \\
\hline
= \ \text{Ending retained earnings}
\end{array}
$$

Retained earnings reflect cumulative income that has not yet been distributed to shareholders. Exhibit 2.9 shows **Apple**'s retained earnings reconciliation for 2010.

EXHIBIT 2.9	Apple's Retained Earnings Reconciliation

APPLE INC.
Retained Earnings Reconciliation ($ millions)
For Year Ended September 25, 2010

Retained earnings, September 26, 2009		$23,353
Add:	Net income	14,013
Less:	Dividends	0
	Other adjustments	(197)
Retained earnings, September 25, 2010		$37,169

This reconciliation of retained earnings links the balance sheet and income statement.

In the absence of transactions with stockholders—such as stock issuances and repurchases, and dividend payments—the change in stockholders' equity equals income or loss for the period. The income statement, thus, measures the change in company value as measured by *GAAP*. This is not necessarily company value as measured by the *market*. Of course, all value-relevant items eventually find their way into the income statement. So, from a long-term perspective, the income statement does measure change in company value. This is why stock prices react to reported income and to analysts' expectations about future income.

Financial Statement Linkages

Articulation of the four financial statements is shown in Exhibit 2.10. Apple begins fiscal 2010 with assets of $47,501 million, consisting of cash for $5,263 million and noncash assets for $42,238 million. These investments are financed with $15,861 million from nonowners and $31,640 million from shareholders. The owner financing consists of contributed capital of $8,210 million, retained earnings of $23,353 million, and other stockholders' equity of $77 million.

Exhibit 2.10 shows balance sheets at the beginning and end of Apple's fiscal year on the left and right columns, respectively. The middle column reflects operating activities for 2010. The statement of cash flows explains how operating, investing, and financing activities increase the cash balance by $5,998 million from $5,263 million at the beginning of the year to $11,261 million at year-end. The ending balance in cash is reported in the year-end balance sheet on the right.

Apple's $14,013 million net income reported on the income statement is also carried over to the statement of shareholders' equity. The net income explains nearly all of the change in retained earnings reported in the statement of shareholders' equity because Apple paid no dividends in that year (other adjustments reduce retained earnings by $197 million).

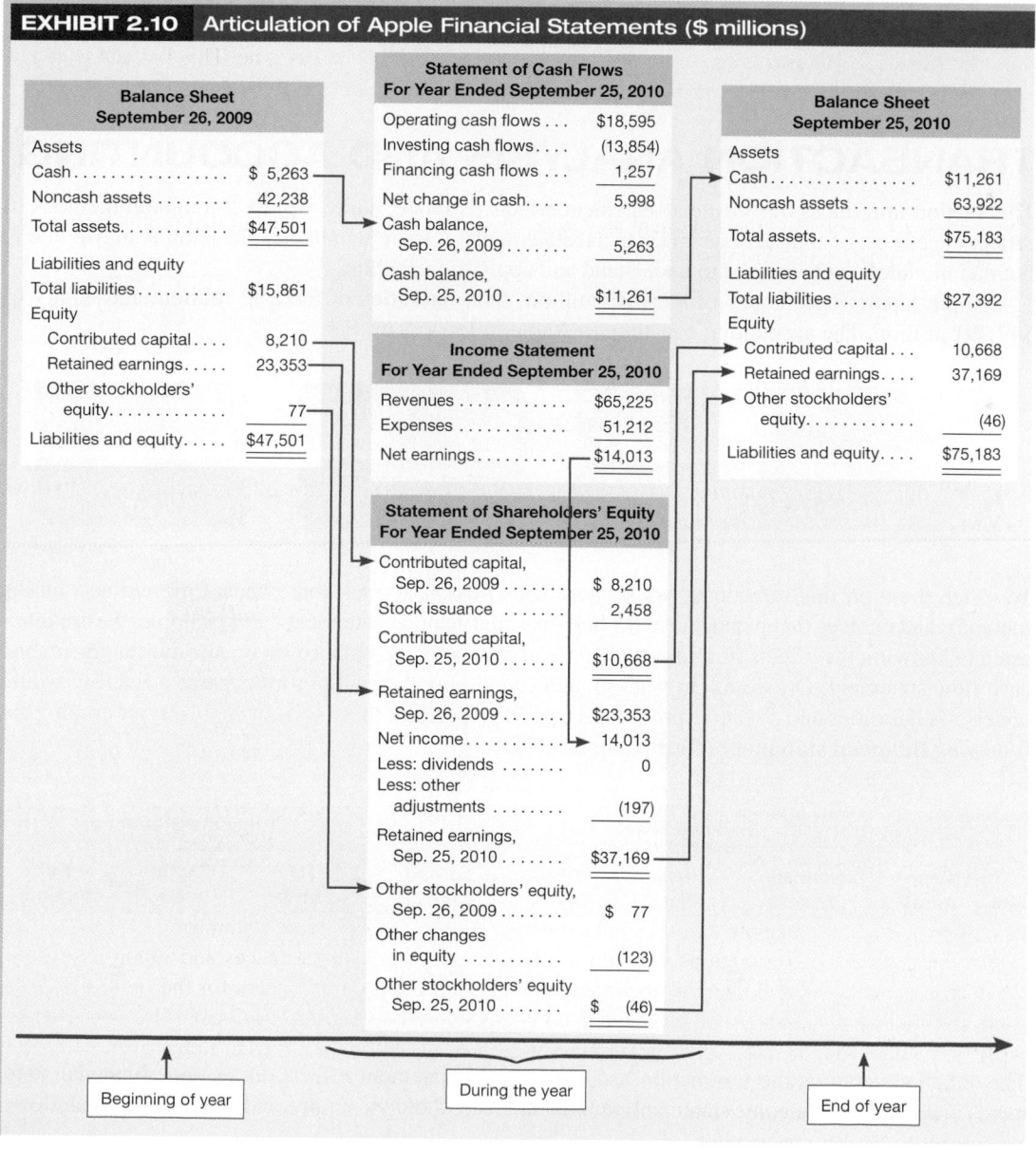

EXHIBIT 2.10   Articulation of Apple Financial Statements ($ millions)

Balance Sheet
September 26, 2009

Assets	
Cash	$ 5,263
Noncash assets	42,238
Total assets	$47,501
Liabilities and equity	
Total liabilities	$15,861
Equity	
Contributed capital	8,210
Retained earnings	23,353
Other stockholders' equity	77
Liabilities and equity	$47,501

Statement of Cash Flows
For Year Ended September 25, 2010

Operating cash flows	$18,595
Investing cash flows	(13,854)
Financing cash flows	1,257
Net change in cash	5,998
Cash balance, Sep. 26, 2009	5,263
Cash balance, Sep. 25, 2010	$11,261

Income Statement
For Year Ended September 25, 2010

Revenues	$65,225
Expenses	51,212
Net earnings	$14,013

Statement of Shareholders' Equity
For Year Ended September 25, 2010

Contributed capital, Sep. 26, 2009	$ 8,210
Stock issuance	2,458
Contributed capital, Sep. 25, 2010	$10,668
Retained earnings, Sep. 26, 2009	$23,353
Net income	14,013
Less: dividends	0
Less: other adjustments	(197)
Retained earnings, Sep. 25, 2010	$37,169
Other stockholders' equity, Sep. 26, 2009	$ 77
Other changes in equity	(123)
Other stockholders' equity Sep. 25, 2010	$ (46)

Balance Sheet
September 25, 2010

Assets	
Cash	$11,261
Noncash assets	63,922
Total assets	$75,183
Liabilities and equity	
Total liabilities	$27,392
Equity	
Contributed capital	10,668
Retained earnings	37,169
Other stockholders' equity	(46)
Liabilities and equity	$75,183

Beginning of year — During the year — End of year

MID-MODULE REVIEW 2

Refer to information in Mid-Module Review 1; assume that Dell reports the following balances for the prior year balance sheet and current year income statement. Prepare the articulation of Dell's financial statements from fiscal years 2010 to 2011 following the format of Exhibit 2.10.

Balance Sheet, January 29, 2010	
Assets	
Cash	$10,635
Noncash assets	23,017
Total assets	$33,652
Liabilities and Equity	
Total liabilities	$28,011
Equity	
Contributed capital	11,472
Retained earnings	22,110
Other stockholders' equity	(27,941)
Liabilities and equity	$33,652

Income Statement, For Year Ended January 28, 2011	
Revenues	$61,494
Expenses	58,859
Net earnings	$ 2,635

The solution is on page 2-46.

TRANSACTION ANALYSIS AND ACCOUNTING

LO3 Illustrate use of the financial statement effects template to summarize accounting transactions.

This section introduces our financial statement effects template, which we use throughout the book to reflect the effects of transactions on financial statements. A more detailed explanation is in Module 3, but that module is not required to understand and apply the template.

Apple reports total assets of $75,183 million, total liabilities of $27,392 million, and equity of $47,791 million. The accounting equation for Apple follows ($ million):

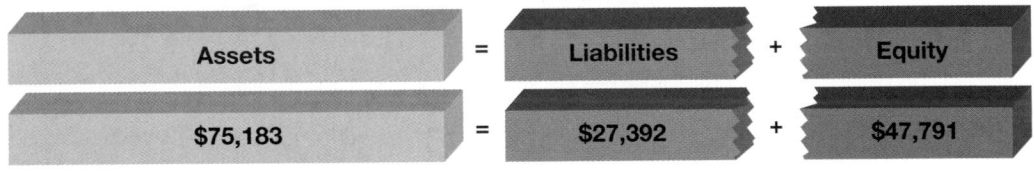

Assets	=	Liabilities	+	Equity
$75,183	=	$27,392	+	$47,791

We often draw on this relation to assess the effects of transactions and events, different accounting methods, and choices that managers make in preparing financial statements. For example, we are interested in knowing the effects of an asset acquisition or sale on the balance sheet, income statement, and cash flow statement. Or, we might want to understand how the failure to recognize a liability would understate liabilities and overstate profits and equity. To perform these sorts of analyses, we employ the following **financial statement effects template**:

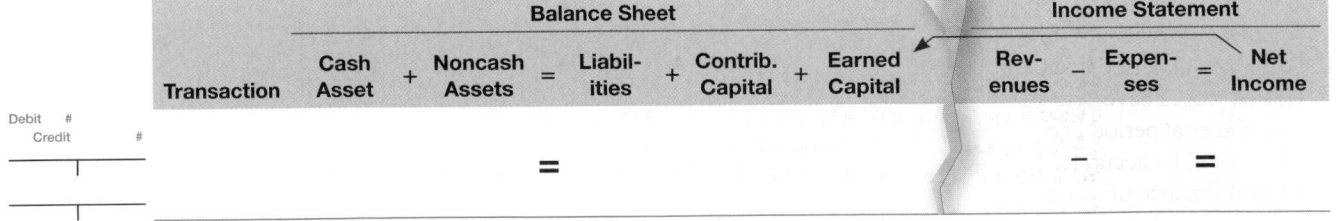

The template captures the transaction and its financial statement effects on the four financial statements: balance sheet, income statement, statement of stockholders' equity, and statement of cash flows.

For the balance sheet, we differentiate between cash and noncash assets so as to identify the cash effects of transactions. Likewise, equity is separated into the contributed and earned capital components. Finally, income statement effects are separated into revenues, expenses, and net income (the updating of retained earnings is denoted with an arrow line running from net income to earned capital). This template provides a convenient means to represent relatively complex financial accounting transactions and events in a simple, concise manner for both analysis and interpretation.

In addition to using the template to show the dollar effects of a transaction on the four financial statements, we also include each transaction's *journal entry* and *T-account* representation in the margin. We explain journal entries and T-accounts in Module 3; these are part of the bookkeeping aspects of accounting. The margin entries can be ignored without any loss of insight gained from the template. (Journal entries and T-accounts use acronyms for account titles; a list of acronyms is in Appendix C near the end of the book.)

The process leading up to preparing financial statements involves two steps: (1) recording transactions during the accounting period, and (2) adjusting accounting records to reflect events that have occurred but are not yet evidenced by an external transaction. We provide a brief introduction to these two steps, followed by a comprehensive example that includes preparation of financial statements (a more detailed illustration of this process is in Module 3).

Analyzing and Recording Transactions

All transactions affecting a company are recorded in its accounting records. For example, assume that a company paid $100 cash wages to employees. This is reflected in the following financial statement effects template.

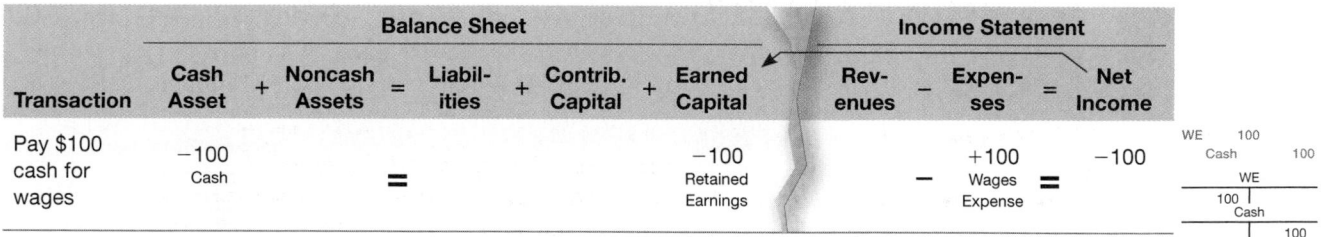

Cash assets are reduced by $100, and wages expense of $100 is reflected in the income statement, which reduces income and retained earnings by that amount. All transactions incurred by the company during the accounting period are recorded similarly. We show several further examples in our comprehensive illustration later in this section.

Adjusting Accounts

We must understand accounting adjustments (commonly called *accruals*) to fully analyze and interpret financial statements. In the transaction above, we record wages expense that has been earned by (and paid to) employees during the period. What if the employees were not paid for wages earned at period-end? Should the expense still be recorded? The answer is yes. All expenses incurred to generate, directly or indirectly, the revenues reported in the period must be recorded. This is the case even if those expenses are still unpaid at period-end. Failure to recognize wages expense would overstate net income for the period because wages have been earned and should be reported as expense in this period. Also, failure to record those wages at period-end would understate liabilities. Thus, neither the income statement nor the balance sheet would be accurate. Adjustments are, therefore, necessary to accurately portray financial condition and performance of a company.

There are four types of adjustments, which are illustrated in the following graphic. The two adjustments on the left relate to the receipt or payment of cash before revenue or expense is recognized. The two on the right relate to the receipt or payment of cash after revenue or expense is recognized.

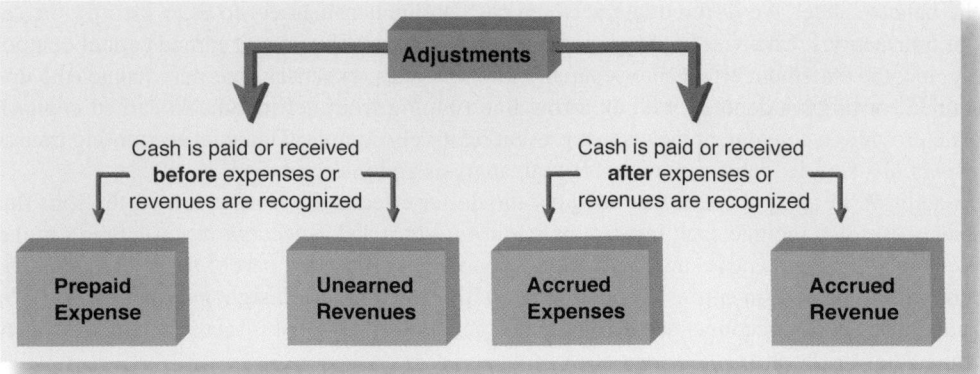

One of two types of accounts arise when cash is received or paid *before* recognition of revenue or expense.

> ***Prepaid expenses*** Prepaid expenses reflect advance cash payments that will ultimately become expenses; an example is the payment of radio advertising that will not be aired until sometime in the future.

> ***Unearned revenues*** Unearned revenues reflect cash received from customers before any services or goods are provided; an example is cash received from patrons for tickets to an upcoming concert.

To illustrate the adjustment required with prepaid expenses, assume that Apple pays $3,000 cash at the beginning of this year to rent office space, and that this allows Apple to use the space for the current year and two additional years. When paid, the prepaid rent is an asset for Apple (it now controls the space, which is expected to provide future benefits for its business). At the end of the first year, one-third of the Prepaid Rent asset is used up. Apple, therefore, removes that portion from its balance sheet and recognizes it as an expense in the income statement. The beginning-year payment and year-end expensing of the rental asset are recorded as follows:

	Balance Sheet							Income Statement		
Transaction	**Cash Asset**	+	**Noncash Assets**	=	**Liabilities**	+	**Contrib. Capital**	+	**Earned Capital**	**Revenues** − **Expenses** = **Net Income**

PPRNT 3,000
  Cash   3,000

PPRNT	
3,000	
Cash	
	3,000

a. Beginning-year $3,000 cash payment in advance of 3-year rent
−3,000 Cash   +3,000 Prepaid Rent   =   −   =

RNTE 1,000
  PPRNT 1,000

RNTE	
1,000	
PPRNT	
	1,000

b. Recognition of 1-year rent expense of $1,000
−1,000 Prepaid Rent   =   −1,000 Retained Earnings   −   +1,000 Rent Expense   =   −1,000

To illustrate unearned revenues, assume that Apple receives $5,000 cash in advance of providing services to a client. That amount is initially recorded as a liability for services owed the client. Later, when Apple provides the services, it can recognize that revenue since it is now earned. The receipt of cash and subsequent recognition of revenue are recorded as follows:

	Balance Sheet							Income Statement		
Transaction	**Cash Asset**	+	**Noncash Assets**	=	**Liabilities**	+	**Contrib. Capital**	+	**Earned Capital**	**Revenues** − **Expenses** = **Net Income**

Cash 5,000
  UR   5,000

Cash	
5,000	
UR	
	5,000

a. Receive $5,000 cash in advance for future services
+5,000 Cash   =   +5,000 Unearned Revenue   −   =

continued

	Balance Sheet						Income Statement		
Transaction	Cash Asset	+ Noncash Assets	= Liabilities	+ Contrib. Capital	+ Earned Capital		Revenues	− Expenses	= Net Income
b. Recognition of $5,000 services revenue earned			= −5,000 Unearned Revenue		+5,000 Retained Earnings		+5,000 Revenue −	=	+5,000

UR 5,000
REV 5,000
UR
5,000 |
REV
| 5,000

One of two types of accounts arise when cash is received or paid *after* recognition of revenue or expense.

>   ***Accrued expenses*** Accrued expenses are expenses incurred and recognized on the income statement, even though they are not yet paid in cash; an example is wages owed to employees who performed work but who have not yet been paid.

>   ***Accrued revenues*** Accrued revenues are revenues earned and recognized on the income statement, even though cash is not yet received; examples include accounts receivable and revenue earned under a long-term contract.

To illustrate accrued expenses, assume that $100 of wages earned by Apple employees this period is paid the following period. The period-end adjustment, and subsequent payment the following period, are both reflected in the following template.

	Balance Sheet						Income Statement		
Transaction	Cash Asset	+ Noncash Assets	= Liabilities	+ Contrib. Capital	+ Earned Capital		Revenues	− Expenses	= Net Income
Period 1: Accrue $100 wages expense and liability			= +100 Wages Payable		−100 Retained Earnings		−	+100 Wages Expense =	−100
Period 2: Pay $100 cash for wages	−100 Cash		= −100 Wages Payable				−	=	

WE 100
WP 100
WE
100 |
WP
| 100

WP 100
Cash 100
WP
100 |
Cash
| 100

Wages expense is recorded in period 1's income statement because it is incurred by the company and earned by employees in that period. Also, a liability is recorded in period 1 reflecting the company's obligation to make payment to employees. In period 2, the wages are paid, which means that both cash and the liability are reduced.

   To illustrate the accrual of revenues, assume that Apple is performing work under a long-term contract that allows it to bill the customer periodically as work is performed. At the end of the current period, it determines that it has earned $100,000 per contract. The accrual of this revenue and its subsequent collection are recorded as follows ($ 000s):

	Balance Sheet						Income Statement		
Transaction	Cash Asset	+ Noncash Assets	= Liabilities	+ Contrib. Capital	+ Earned Capital		Revenues	− Expenses	= Net Income
a. Accrual of $100 of earned revenue		+100 Accounts Receivable =			+100 Retained Earnings		+100 Revenue −	=	+100
b. Collection of account receivable	+100 Cash	−100 Accounts Receivable =					−	=	

AR 100
REV 100
AR
100 |
REV
| 100

Cash 100
AR 100
Cash
100 |
AR
| 100

Companies make these sort of adjustments to more accurately and completely report their financial performance and condition. Each of these adjustments is made by company managers and accountants based on the review of financial statements and information suggesting that adjustments are necessary to properly reflect financial condition and performance.

Constructing Financial Statements

We can prepare each of the four financial statements directly from our financial statement effects template. The balance sheet and income statement accounts, and their respective balances, can be read off the bottom row that totals the transactions and adjustments recorded during the period. The statement of cash flows and statement of stockholders' equity are represented by the cash column and the contributed and earned capital columns, respectively.

Illustration: Recording Transactions, Adjusting Accounts, and Preparing Statements

This section provides a comprehensive illustration that uses the financial statement effects template with a number of transactions related to Apple's 2010 financial statements shown earlier. These summary transactions are described in the far left column of the following template. Each column is summed to arrive at the balance sheet and income statement totals that tie to Apple's statements. Detailed explanations for each transaction are provided after the template. Then, we use the information in the template to construct Apple's financial statements.

		Balance Sheet					Income Statement		
Transaction	Cash Asset	+ Noncash Assets	= Liabil- ities	+ Contrib. Capital	+ Earned Capital		Rev- enues	– Expen- ses	= Net Income
Bal., Sept. 26, 2009	5,263	42,238	= 15,861	8,210	23,430		–		=
1. Sell com- mon stock for $2,458	+2,458 Cash		=	+2,458 Common Stock			–		=
2. Purchase $2,005 of PPE, financed by $2,005 of long-term debt		+2,005 PPE, net	= +2,005 Long-Term Debt				–		=
3. Purchase $40,137 of inventories on account		+40,137 Inventories	= +40,137 Accounts Payable				–		=
4. Sell inven- tories costing $39,541 for $65,225 on account		+65,225 Accounts Receivable	=		+65,225 Retained Earnings		+65,225 Sales	–	= +65,225
		−39,541 Inventory	=		−39,541 Retained Earnings			– +39,541 Cost of Goods Sold	= −39,541
5. Collect $63,083 of re- ceivables and pay $31,542 of accounts payable and other liabilities	+63,083 Cash	−63,083 Accounts Receivable	=				–		=
	−31,542 Cash		= −31,542 Accounts Payable				–		=

T-accounts (left margin):

```
Cash    2,458
   CS          2,458
        Cash
   2,458 |
        CS
        |  2,458

PPE     2,005
   LTD         2,005
        PPE
   2,005 |
        LTD
        |  2,005

INV    40,137
   AP         40,137
        INV
  40,137 |
        AP
        |  40,137

AR     65,225
   Sales      65,225
        AR
  65,225 |
        Sales
        |  65,225

COGS   39,541
   INV        39,541
        COGS
  39,541 |
        INV
        |  39,541

Cash   63,083
   AR         63,083
        Cash
  63,083 |
        AR
        |  63,083

AP     31,542
   Cash       31,542
        AP
  31,542 |
        Cash
        |  31,542
```

continued

	Balance Sheet						Income Statement		
Transaction	**Cash Asset**	**+ Noncash Assets**	**= Liabil- ities**	**+ Contrib. Capital**	**+ Earned Capital**		**Rev- enues**	**– Expen- ses**	**= Net Income**
6. Pay operating expenses and taxes (excluding depreciation) of $9,868	−9,868 Cash		=		−9,868 Retained Earnings			+9,868 – Operating Expenses	= −9,868
7. Accrue expenses of $931			+931 = Accrued Liabilities		−931 Retained Earnings			+931 – Operating Expenses	= −931
8. Purchase noncash assets for $18,288	−18,288 Cash	+18,288 Marketable Securities	=					–	=
9. Record depreciation of $1,027		−1,027 PPE, net	=		−1,027 Retained Earnings			+1,027 – Depreciation Expense	= −1,027
10. Record receipt of net investment income of $155	+155 Cash		=		+155 Retained Earnings			−155* – Investment Income	= +155
11. Record decrease in Other Assets and AOCI		−320 Other Assets	=		−320 Accumulated Other Comp. Income			–	=
Bal., Sept. 25, 2010	11,261	+ 63,922	= 27,392	+ 10,668	+ 37,123		65,225	– 51,212	= 14,013

*Apple reports investment income as an "addback" to other expenses.

Transaction Explanation Apple begins fiscal year 2010 with $47,501 million in total assets, consisting of $5,263 million of cash and $42,238 million of noncash assets. It also reports $15,861 million of liabilities and $31,640 million of stockholders' equity ($8,210 million of contributed capital and $23,430 million of earned capital, which includes other equity for this exhibit). During the year, eleven summary transactions occur that are described below.

1. **Owner Financing.** Companies raise funds from two sources: investing from shareholders and borrowing from creditors. Transaction 1 reflects issuance of common stock for $2,458 million. Cash is increased by that amount, as is contributed capital. Stock issuance (as well as its repurchase and any dividends paid to shareholders) does not impact income. Companies cannot record profit by trading in their own stock.

2. **Purchase PPE financed by debt.** Apple acquires $2,005 million of property, plant and equipment (PPE), and it finances this acquisition with a $2,005 million loan. Noncash assets increase by the $2,005 million of PPE, and liabilities increase by $2,005 million of long-term debt. PPE is initially reported on the balance sheet at the cost Apple paid to acquire it. When plant and equipment are used, a portion of the purchase cost is transferred from the balance sheet to the income statement as an expense called depreciation. Accounting for depreciation is shown in Transaction 9. The borrowing of money does not yield income, and repaying the principal amount borrowed is not an expense. Paying interest *on* liabilities, however, is an expense.

3. **Purchase inventories on credit.** Companies commonly acquire inventories from suppliers *on credit* (also called *on account*). The phrase "on credit" means that the purchase has not yet been paid for. A purchaser is typically allowed 30 days or more during which to make payment. When acquired in this manner, noncash assets (inventories) increase by the $40,137 million cost of the acquired inventory, and a liability (accounts payable) increases to reflect the amount owed to the supplier. Although inventories (iPods and iPhones, for example) normally carry a retail selling price that is higher than cost, this eventual profit is not recognized until inventories are sold.

4. **Sell inventories on credit.** Apple subsequently sells inventories that cost $39,541 million for a retail selling price of $65,225 million *on credit*. The phrase "on credit" means that Apple has not yet received cash for the selling price; cash receipt is expected in the future. The sale of inventories is recorded in two parts: the revenue part and the expense part. First, the sale is recorded by an increase in both revenues and noncash assets (accounts receivable). Revenues increase net income which, in turn, increases earned capital (via retained earnings). Second, the cost of inventories sold is removed from the balance sheet (Apple no longer owns those assets), and is transferred to the income statement as an expense, called *cost of goods sold*, which decreases both net income and earned capital by $39,541 (again, via retained earnings).

5. **Collect receivables and settle payables.** Apple receives $63,083 million cash from the collection of its accounts receivable, thus reducing noncash assets (accounts receivable) by that amount. Apple uses these proceeds to pay off $31,542 of its liabilities (accounts payable and other liabilities). Collecting accounts receivable does not yield revenue; instead, revenue is recognized when *earned* (see Transaction 4). Thus, recognizing revenue when earned does not necessarily yield an immediate cash increase.

6. **Pay cash for expenses.** Apple pays $9,868 million cash for expenses. This payment increases expenses, and reduces net income (and earned capital). Expenses are recognized when incurred, regardless of when they are paid. Expenses are both incurred and paid in this transaction. Transaction 7 is a case where expenses are recognized *before* being paid.

7. **Accrue expenses.** Accrued expenses relate to expenses that are incurred but not yet paid. For example, employees often work near the end of a period but are not paid until the next period. The company must record wages expense even though employees have not yet been paid in cash. The rationale is that expenses must be recorded in the period incurred to report the correct income for the period. In this transaction, Apple accrues $931 million of expenses, which reduces net income (and earned capital). Apple simultaneously records a $931 million increase in liabilities for its obligation to make future payment. This transaction is an accounting adjustment, or accrual.

8. **Purchase noncash assets.** Apple uses $18,288 million of its excess cash to purchase marketable securities as an investment. Thus, noncash assets increase. This is a common use of excess cash, especially for high-tech companies that desire added liquidity to take advantage of opportunities in a rapidly changing industry.

9. **Record depreciation.** Transaction 9 is another accounting adjustment. In this case, Apple recognizes that a portion of its plant and equipment is "used up" while generating revenues. Thus, it records a portion of the PPE cost as an expense during the period. In this case, $1,027 million of PPE cost is removed from the balance sheet and transferred to the income statement as depreciation expense. Net income (and earned capital) are reduced by $1,027 million.

10. **Record investment income.** Apple recognizes $155 of investment income in transaction 10. Profit increases by this same amount, resulting in an increase in retained earnings.

11. **Miscellaneous.** The final transaction is a miscellaneous adjustment to noncash assets and an earned capital account called accumulated other comprehensive income, which is distinct from retained earnings. We discuss this account in Module 9.

We can use the column totals from the financial statement effects template to prepare Apple's financial statements (in condensed form). We derive Apple's 2010 balance sheet and income statement from the template as follows ($ millions).

APPLE INC. Condensed Balance Sheet September 25, 2010	
Cash asset	$11,261
Noncash assets	63,922
Total assets.	$75,183
Liabilities.	$27,392
Contributed capital.	10,668
Earned capital	37,123
Total liabilities and equity	$75,183

APPLE INC. Condensed Income Statement For Year Ended September 25, 2010	
Revenues	$65,225
Expenses	51,212
Net income.	$14,013

We can summarize Apple's cash transactions from the cash column of the template. The cash column of the financial effects template reveals that cash increases by $5,998 million during the year from $5,263 million to $11,561 million; see the following statement. Items that contribute to this net increase are identified by the cash entries in that column (the subtotals for operating, investing, and financing sections are slightly different from actual results because of simplifying assumptions we make for our transactions example).

APPLE INC. Statement of Cash Flows ($ millions) For Year Ended September 25, 2010	
Operating cash flows (+ $31,541 − $9,868 + $155)................	$21,828
Investing cash flows...	(18,288)
Financing cash flows	2,458
Net change in cash...	5,998
Cash balance, Sep. 26, 2009.................................	5,263
Cash balance, Sep. 25, 2010.................................	$11,261

Apple's statement of stockholders' equity summarizes the transactions relating to its equity accounts. This statement follows and is organized into its contributed capital and earned capital categories of equity.

APPLE INC. Condensed Statement of Stockholders' Equity For Year Ended September 25, 2010			
($ millions)	Contributed Capital	Earned Capital	Total
Balance, September 26, 2009	$ 8,210	$23,430	$31,640
Issuance of common stock	2,458		2,458
Net income.............................		14,013	14,013
Miscellaneous..........................		(320)	(320)
Balance, September 25, 2010	$10,668	$37,123	$47,791

Apple's financial statements are abbreviated versions of those reproduced earlier in the module. We describe the preparation of financial statements and other accounting details at greater length in Module 3.

BUSINESS INSIGHT   **Controlling vs Noncontrolling Interest**

Financial statements are prepared on a *consolidated* basis. To consolidate a balance sheet, a company includes all the assets and liabilities of subsidiaries under its control. When a company controls a subsidiary, it directs all (100%) of the subsidiary's operations. But control does not mean 100% ownership; control can occur when a company owns the majority of a subsidiary's voting stock. For example, Verizon owns 55% of the voting stock of Verizon Wireless, a separate legal entity. This 55% gives Verizon voting control and Verizon is said to have a **controlling interest** in Verizon Wireless. The remaining 45% is owned by Vodafone, a UK telecom; Vodafone has a **noncontrolling interest** in Verizon Wireless. Now imagine if Verizon wanted to repaint the trucks in the Verizon Wireless fleet. Verizon would not paint only 55% of the trucks; it "controls" 100% of Verizon Wireless' trucks by virtue of its controlling interest, and it would paint all trucks. Consolidated financial statements reflect this notion of control. Verizon's balance sheet includes 100% of Verizon Wireless assets and liabilities. Because it owns only a 55% interest in Verizon Wireless assets and liabilities, Verizon reports the other 45% in equity as noncontrolling interest. The same logic applies to the income statement; that is, 100% of subsidiaries' revenues and expenses are included, and then the noncontrolling interest portion of net income is separated from net income at the bottom.

GLOBAL ACCOUNTING

Both GAAP and IFRS use accrual accounting to prepare financial statements. Although there are vastly more similarities than differences, we highlight below a few of the more notable differences for financial statements.

Balance Sheet The most visible difference is that the typical IFRS-based balance sheet is presented in reverse order of liquidity. The least liquid asset, usually goodwill, is listed first and the most liquid asset, cash, is last. The same inverse liquidity order applies to liabilities. There are also several detailed presentation and measurement differences that we explain in other modules. As one example, for GAAP-based balance sheets, bank overdrafts are often netted against cash balances. IFRS does not permit this netting on the balance sheet. However, the IFRS statement of cash flows *does* net the cash balance with any bank overdrafts and, thus, the cash balance on the statement of cash flows might not match the cash amount on the balance sheet.

Income Statement The most visible difference is that GAAP requires three years' data on the income statement whereas IFRS requires only two. Another difference is that GAAP income statements classify expenses by *function* and must separately report expenses applicable to revenues (cost of goods sold), whereas IFRS permits expense classification by *function* (cost of sales, selling and administrative, etc.) or by *type* (raw materials, labor, depreciation, etc.). This means, for example, that under IFRS, there is no requirement to report a cost of sales figure. Another difference is that no item can be classified as extraordinary under IFRS. Still another is that for items either unusual or infrequent, but not both, GAAP requires separate presentation in the income statement as a component of earnings from continuing operations. IFRS also requires disclosure of these items, but permits disclosure in notes to financial statements.

Statement of Cash Flows One of the more apparent differences between GAAP and IFRS is that a GAAP-based statement of cash flows classifies interest expense, interest revenue, and dividend revenue as operating cash flows, and dividends paid as financing cash flows. IFRS allows firms to choose from between the following two options:

1. Classify interest expense, dividends paid, interest revenue, and dividend revenue as operating cash flows, or

2. Classify interest expense and dividends paid as financing cash flows, and interest revenue and dividend revenue as investing cash flows.

MODULE-END REVIEW

At December 31, 2010, assume that the condensed balance sheet of Gateway shows the following.

Cash.....................	$ 80,000	Liabilities.................	$200,000
Noncash assets	270,000	Contributed capital.........	50,000
		Earned capital	100,000
Total assets..............	$350,000	Total liabilities and equity	$350,000

Assume the following summary transactions occur during 2011.

1. Purchase inventory of $80,000 on credit.
2. Pay employees $10,000 cash for wages earned this year.
3. Sell inventory costing $40,000 for $70,000 on credit.
4. Collect $15,000 cash from the accounts receivable in transaction 3.
5. Pay $35,000 cash toward the accounts payable in transaction 1.
6. Purchase advertising for $25,000 cash that will air next year.
7. Employees earn $5,000 in wages that will not be paid until next year.
8. Record $3,000 depreciation on its equipment.

Required

a. Record transactions 1 through 8 using the financial statement effects template.

b. Prepare the income statement and balance sheet for 2011.

c. Show linkage(s) between the income statement and the balance sheet.

The solution to the review problem is on page 2-46.

APPENDIX 2A: Additional Information Sources

The four financial statements are only a part of the information available to financial statement users. Additional information, from a variety of sources, provides useful insight into company operating activities and future prospects. This section highlights additional information sources.

Form 10-K

Companies with publicly traded securities must file a detailed annual report and discussion of their business activities in their Form 10-K with the SEC (quarterly reports are filed on Form 10-Q). Many of the disclosures in the 10-K are mandated by law and include the following general categories: Item 1, *Business;* Item 1A. *Risk Factors;* Item 2, *Properties;* Item 3, *Legal Proceedings;* Item 4, *Submission of Matters to a Vote of Security Holders;* Item 5, *Market for Registrant's Common Equity and Related Stockholder Matters;* Item 6, *Selected Financial Data;* Item 7, *Management's Discussion and Analysis of Financial Condition and Results of Operations;* Item 7A, *Quantitative and Qualitative Disclosures About Market Risk;* Item 8, *Financial Statements and Supplementary Data;* Item 9, *Changes in and Disagreements With Accountants on Accounting and Financial Disclosure;* Item 9A, *Controls and Procedures.*

Description of the Business (Item 1)

Companies must provide a general description of their business, including their principal products and services, the source and availability of required raw materials, all patents, trademarks, licenses, and important related agreements, seasonality of the business, any dependence upon a single customer, competitive conditions, including particular markets in which the company competes, the product offerings in those markets, and the status of its competitive environment. Companies must also provide a description of their overall strategy. Apple's partial disclosure follows:

> The Company is committed to bringing the best user experience to its customers through its innovative hardware, software, peripherals, services, and Internet offerings. The Company's business strategy leverages its unique ability to design and develop its own operating systems, hardware, application software, and services to provide its customers new products and solutions with superior ease-of-use, seamless integration, and innovative industrial design. The Company believes continual investment in research and development is critical to the development and enhancement of innovative products and technologies. In conjunction with its strategy, the Company continues to build and host a robust platform for the discovery and delivery of third-party digital content and applications through the iTunes Store. . . . Additionally, the Company's strategy includes expanding its distribution to effectively reach more customers and provide them with a high-quality sales and post-sales support experience. The Company is therefore uniquely positioned to offer superior and well-integrated digital lifestyle and productivity solutions.

Management's Discussion and Analysis of Financial Condition and Results of Operations (Item 7)

The management discussion and analysis (MD&A) section of the 10-K contains valuable insight into the company's results of operations. In addition to an executive overview of company status and its recent operating results, the MD&A section includes information relating to its critical accounting policies and estimates used in preparing its financial statements, a detailed discussion of its sales activity, year-over-year comparisons of operating activities, analysis of gross margin, operating expenses, taxes, and off-balance-sheet and contractual obligations, assessment of factors that affect future results and financial condition. Item 7A reports quantitative and qualitative disclosures about market risk. For example, Apple makes the following disclosure relating to its Mac operating system and its iPods, iPhones, iPads and other products.

The Company is currently the only maker of hardware using the Mac OS. The Mac OS has a minority market share in the personal computer market, which is dominated by makers of computers using competing operating systems, most notably Windows. The Company's financial condition and operating results substantially depend on its ability to continually develop improvements to the Mac platform to maintain perceived design and functional advantages. Use of unauthorized copies of the Mac OS on other companies' hardware products may result in decreased demand for the Company's hardware products, and materially adversely affect its financial condition and operating results.

Form 8-K

Another useful report that is required by the SEC and is publicly available is the Form 8-K. This form must be filed within four business days of any of the following events:

- Entry into or termination of a material definitive agreement (including petition for bankruptcy)
- Exit from a line of business or impairment of assets
- Change in the company's certified public accounting firm
- Change in control of the company
- Departure of the company's executive officers
- Changes in the company's articles of incorporation or bylaws

Outsiders typically use Form 8-K to monitor for material adverse changes in the company.

Analyst Reports

Sell-side analysts provide their clients with objective analyses of company operating activities. Frequently, these reports include a discussion of the competitive environment for each of the company's principal product lines, strengths and weaknesses of the company, and an investment recommendation, including financial analysis and a stock price target. For example, J.P. Morgan provides the following in its July 2011 report to clients on Apple:

J.P.Morgan

North America Equity Research
20 July 2011

Apple Inc.

This Party is Just Getting Started; Upside Parade Likely to Continue; Lifting Dec-12 PT to $525

Overweight

AAPL, AAPL US
Price: $376.85

▲ Price Target: $525.00
Previous: $450.00

With Overweight-rated Apple's stock, it is time for the value-like multiples to be rerated higher. We expect the stock to move higher in the near to mid term. Consistent with our preview, Apple reported a outstanding June quarter, and there appears no end to the upside parade. We believe the results likely restore the wow factor to the stock. In our view, the return of the wow factor, easing supply constraints, and pending new product cycles should jettison the fear that had been dogging valuation the last couple of months. We are raising our Dec-12 price target to $525, versus $450 previously.

- **A ridiculously big June quarter beat.** Apple reported major upside to Street consensus. Apple reported revenue/EPS of $28.6bn/$7.79, versus consensus of $25.0bn/$5.87. GM and OM were up more than 200 bps QoQ. As previewed, revenue upside from iPad and iPhone, combined with better component pricing and improved supply of iPads, drove a solid beat on the unit metrics. APAC growth of 247% was major upside driver, and we expect this trend to continue.

- **Whoa Nellie, those are big numbers.** June quarter unit shipments of 20.3M iPhones and 9.25M iPads beat our significantly above-consensus estimates of 19.6M and 8.7M. With iPhone, we think that carrier, geographic, enterprise, and dual mode GSM/CDMA expansion opportunities offer plenty of headroom for ongoing growth. As for the iPad, we expect the burst in units to ease investor concerns that competition or supply constraints would be a drag on growth. Mac results were in-line, but this performance should be put in perspective given the weak PC market (Mac units outgrow the broader PC market by a factor of five).

Price Performance

	YTD	1m	3m	12m
Abs	13.4%	16.7%	12.6%	52.2%

Credit Services

Several firms including Standard & Poor's (StandardAndPoors.com), Moody's Investors Service (Moodys.com), and Fitch Ratings (FitchRatings.com) provide credit analysis that assists potential lenders, investors, employees, and other users in evaluating a company's creditworthiness and future financial viability. Credit analysis is a specialized field of analysis, quite different from the equity analysis illustrated here. These firms issue credit ratings on publicly issued bonds as well as on firms' commercial paper.

Data Services

A number of companies supply financial statement data in easy-to-download spreadsheet formats. Thomson Reuters Corporation (**ThomsonReuters.com**) provides a wealth of information to its database subscribers, including the widely quoted *First Call* summary of analysts' earnings forecasts. Standard & Poor's provides financial data for all publicly traded companies in its *Compustat* database. This database reports a plethora of individual data items for all publicly traded companies or for any specified subset of companies. These data are useful for performing statistical analysis and making comparisons across companies or within industries. Finally, Capital IQ (www.CapitalIQ.com), a division of Standard & Poors, provides "as presented" financial data that conform to published financial statements as well as additional statistical data and analysis.

GUIDANCE ANSWERS

MANAGERIAL DECISION   You Are the Securities Analyst

Of special concern is the possibility that the new CEO is shifting costs to the current period in lieu of recording them in future periods. Evidence suggests that such behavior occurs when a new management team takes control. The reasoning is that the new management can blame poor current period performance on prior management and, at the same time, rid the balance sheet (and the new management team) of costs that would normally be expensed in future periods.

MANAGERIAL DECISION   You Are the Operations Manager

The CFO desires a warranty cost estimate that corresponds to the sales generated from the new product. To arrive at such an estimate, you must estimate the expected number and types of deficiencies in your product and the costs to repair each deficiency per the warranty provisions. This is often a difficult task for product engineers because it forces them to focus on product failures and associated costs.

Superscript [A] denotes assignments based on Appendix 2A.

DISCUSSION QUESTIONS

Q2-1. The balance sheet consists of assets, liabilities, and equity. Define each category and provide two examples of accounts reported within each category.

Q2-2. Explain how we account for a cost that creates an immediate benefit versus a cost that creates a future benefit.

Q2-3. GAAP is based on the concept of accrual accounting. Define and describe accrual accounting.

Q2-4. Analysts attempt to identify transitory items in an income statement. Define transitory items. What is the purpose of identifying transitory items?

Q2-5. What is the statement of stockholders' equity? What useful information does it contain?

Q2-6. What is the statement of cash flows? What useful information does it contain?

Q2-7. Define and explain the concept of financial statement articulation. What insight comes from understanding articulation?

Q2-8. Describe the flow of costs for the purchase of a machine. At what point do such costs become expenses? Why is it necessary to record the expenses related to the machine in the same period as the revenues it produces?

Q2-9. What are the two essential characteristics of an asset?

Q2-10. What does the concept of liquidity refer to? Explain.

Q2-11. What does the term *current* denote when referring to assets?

Q2-12. Assets are recorded at historical costs even though current market values might, arguably, be more relevant to financial statement readers. Describe the reasoning behind historical cost usage.

Q2-13. Identify three intangible assets that are likely to be *excluded* from the balance sheet because they cannot be reliably measured.

Q2-14. Identify three intangible assets that are recorded on the balance sheet.

Q2-15. What are accrued liabilities? Provide an example.

Q2-16. Define net working capital. Explain how increasing the amount of trade credit can reduce the net working capital for a company.

Q2-17. What is the difference between company *book value* and *market value*? Explain why these two amounts differ.

Q2-18. The financial statement effects template includes an arrow line running from net income to earned capital. What does this arrow line denote?

Assignments with the ✅ in the margin are available in an online homework system.
See the Preface of the book for details.

MINI EXERCISES

M2-19. Identifying and Classifying Financial Statement Items (LO1)
For each of the following items, indicate whether they would be reported in the balance sheet (B) or income statement (I).

a. Net income	*d.* Accumulated depreciation	*g.* Interest expense
b. Retained earnings	*e.* Wages expense	*h.* Interest payable
c. Depreciation expense	*f.* Wages payable	*i.* Sales

✅ **M2-20. Identifying and Classifying Financial Statement Items** (LO1)
For each of the following items, indicate whether they would be reported in the balance sheet (B) or income statement (I).

a. Machinery	*e.* Common stock	*i.* Taxes expense
b. Supplies expense	*f.* Factory buildings	*j.* Cost of goods sold
c. Inventories	*g.* Receivables	*k.* Long-term debt
d. Sales	*h.* Taxes payable	*l.* Treasury stock

M2-21. Computing and Comparing Income and Cash Flow Measures (LO1)
Penno Corporation recorded service revenues of $100,000 in 2012, of which $70,000 were on credit and $30,000 were for cash. Moreover, of the $70,000 credit sales for 2012, Penno collected $20,000 cash on those receivables before year-end 2012. The company also paid $25,000 cash for 2012 wages. Its employees also earned another $15,000 in wages for 2012, which were not yet paid at year-end 2012. (a) Compute the company's net income for 2012. (b) How much net cash inflow or outflow did the company generate in 2012? Explain why Penno's net income and net cash flow differ.

M2-22. Assigning Accounts to Sections of the Balance Sheet (LO1)
Identify each of the following accounts as a component of assets (A), liabilities (L), or equity (E).

a. Cash and cash equivalents	_____	*e.* Long-term debt	_____
b. Wages payable	_____	*f.* Retained earnings	_____
c. Common stock	_____	*g.* Additional paid-in capital	_____
d. Equipment	_____	*h.* Taxes payable	_____

✅ **M2-23. Determining Missing Information Using the Accounting Equation** (LO1)
Use your knowledge of accounting relations to complete the following table for Boatsman Company.

	2011	2012
Beginning retained earnings.....	$89,089	$?
Net income (loss)	?	48,192
Dividends	0	15,060
Ending retained earnings	69,634	?

M2-24. Reconciling Retained Earnings (LO1)

Johnson & Johnson (JNJ)

Following is financial information from Johnson & Johnson for the year ended January 2, 2011. Prepare the retained earnings reconciliation for Johnson & Johnson for the year ended January 2, 2011 ($ millions).

Retained earnings, Jan. 3, 2010......$70,306	Dividends......................	$5,804
Net earnings................... 13,334	Retained earnings, Jan. 2, 2011	?
Other retained earnings changes..... (63)		

M2-25. **Analyzing Transactions to Compute Net Income**   (LO1)

Wasley Corp., a start-up company, provided services that were acceptable to its customers and billed those customers for $350,000 in 2011. However, Wasley collected only $280,000 cash in 2011, and the remaining $70,000 was collected in 2012. Wasley employees earned $200,000 in 2011 wages that were not paid until the first week of 2012. How much net income does Wasley report for 2011? For 2012 (assuming no additional transactions)?

M2-26. **Analyzing Transactions Using the Financial Statement Effects Template**   (LO3)

Report the effects for each of the following transactions using the financial statement effects template.

a. Issue stock for $1,000 cash.
b. Purchase inventory for $500 cash.
c. Sell inventory in transaction b for $2,000 on credit.
d. Receive $2,000 cash toward transaction c receivable.

EXERCISES

E2-27. **Constructing Financial Statements from Account Data**   (LO1)

Barth Company reports the following year-end account balances at December 31, 2011. Prepare the 2011 income statement and the balance sheet as of December 31, 2011.

Accounts payable.	$ 16,000	Inventory	$ 36,000
Accounts receivable.	30,000	Land.	80,000
Bonds payable, long-term	200,000	Goodwill.	8,000
Buildings.	151,000	Retained earnings	60,000
Cash.	48,000	Sales revenue.	400,000
Common stock.	150,000	Supplies inventory	3,000
Cost of goods sold.	180,000	Supplies expense.	6,000
Equipment	70,000	Wages expense	40,000

E2-28. **Constructing Financial Statements from Transaction Data**   (LO1)

Baiman Corporation commences operations at the beginning of January. It provides its services on credit and bills its customers $30,000 for January sales. Its employees also earn January wages of $12,000 that are not paid until the first of February. Complete the following statements for the month-end of January.

Income Statement		Balance Sheet	
Sales.	$	Cash.	$
Wages expense	_____	Accounts receivable.	_____
Net income (loss)	$ _____	Total assets.	$ _____
		Wages payable.	$
		Retained earnings	_____
		Total liabilities and equity . . .	$ _____

E2-29. **Analyzing and Reporting Financial Statement Effects of Transactions**   (LO3)

M.E. Carter launched a professional services firm on March 1. The firm will prepare financial statements at each month-end. In March (its first month), Carter executed the following transactions. Prepare an income statement for Carter Company for the month of March.

a. Carter (owner) invested in the company, $100,000 cash and $20,000 in property and equipment. The company issued common stock to Carter.
b. The company paid $3,200 cash for rent of office furnishings and facilities for March.
c. The company performed services for clients and immediately received $4,000 cash earned.
d. The company performed services for clients and sent a bill for $14,000 with payment due within 60 days.
e. The company compensated an office employee with $4,800 cash as salary for March.
f. The company received $10,000 cash as partial payment on the amount owed from clients in transaction d.
g. The company paid $935 cash in dividends to Carter (owner).

E2-30.   Analyzing Transactions Using the Financial Statement Effects Template   (LO3)

Enter the effects of each of the transactions *a* through *g* from Exercise 2-29 using the financial statement effects template shown in the module.

Staples, Inc. (SPLS)

E2-31.   Identifying and Classifying Balance Sheet and Income Statement Accounts   (LO1)

Following are selected accounts for Staples, Inc.

a. Indicate whether each account appears on the balance sheet (B) or income statement (I).
b. Using the following data, compute total assets and total expenses.
c. Compute net profit margin (net income/sales) and total liabilities-to-equity ratio (total liabilities/ stockholders' equity).

($ millions)	Amount	Classification
Sales.	$24,545	
Accumulated depreciation	3,566	
Depreciation expense.	498	
Retained earnings	6,492	
Net income.	889	
Property, plant & equipment, net	2,148	
Selling, general & administrative expense	4,913	
Accounts receivable.	1,954	
Total liabilities.	6,960	
Stockholders' equity	6,951	

Target Corporation (TGT)

E2-32.   Identifying and Classifying Balance Sheet and Income Statement Accounts   (LO1)

Following are selected accounts for Target Corporation.

a. Indicate whether each account appears on the balance sheet (B) or income statement (I).
b. Using the following data, compute total assets and total expenses.
c. Compute net profit margin (net income/sales) and total liabilities-to-equity ratio (total liabilities/ stockholders' equity).

($ millions)	Amount	Classification
Total revenues	$67,390	
Accumulated depreciation	11,555	
Depreciation expense.	2,084	
Retained earnings	12,698	
Net income.	2,920	
Property, plant & equipment, net	25,493	
Selling, general & administrative expense	13,469	
Credit card receivables.	6,153	
Total liabilities.	28,218	
Stockholders' equity	15,487	

Abercrombie & Fitch (ANF)

TJX Companies (TJX)

E2-33.   Comparing Income Statements and Balance Sheets of Competitors   (LO1)

Following are selected income statement and balance sheet data from two retailers: Abercrombie & Fitch (clothing retailer in the high-end market) and TJX Companies (clothing retailer in the value-priced market).

Income Statement ($ millions)	ANF	TJX
Sales.	$3,469	$21,942
Cost of goods sold.	1,257	16,040
Gross profit.	2,212	5,902
Total expenses	2,062	4,559
Net income.	$ 150	$ 1,343

Balance Sheet ($ millions)	ANF	TJX
Current assets	$1,433	$5,100
Long-term assets	1,515	2,872
Total assets	$2,948	$7,972
Current liabilities	$ 559	$3,133
Long-term liabilities	498	1,739
Total liabilities	1,057	4,872
Stockholders' equity	1,891	3,100
Total liabilities and equity	$2,948	$7,972

a. Express each income statement amount as a percentage of sales. Comment on any differences observed between these two companies, especially as they relate to their respective business models.
b. Express each balance sheet amount as a percentage of total assets. Comment on any differences observed between these two companies, especially as they relate to their respective business models.
c. Which company has a higher proportion of stockholders' equity (and a lower proportion of debt)? What do the ratios tell us about relative riskiness of the two companies?

E2-34. Comparing Income Statements and Balance Sheets of Competitors (LO1)

Following are selected income statement and balance sheet data from two computer competitors: Apple and Dell. Apple (AAPL) Dell (DELL)

Income Statement ($ millions)	Apple	Dell
Sales	$65,225	$61,494
Cost of goods sold	39,541	50,098
Gross profit	25,684	11,396
Total expenses	11,671	8,761
Net income	$14,013	$ 2,635

Balance Sheet ($ millions)	Apple	Dell
Current assets	$41,678	$29,021
Long-term assets	33,505	9,578
Total assets	$75,183	$38,599
Current liabilities	$20,722	$19,483
Long-term liabilities	6,670	11,350
Total liabilities	27,392	30,833
Stockholders' equity	47,791	7,766
Total liabilities and equity	$75,183	$38,599

a. Express each income statement amount as a percentage of sales. Comment on any differences observed between the two companies, especially as they relate to their respective business models. (*Hint:* Apple's gross profit as a percentage of sales is considerably higher than Dell's. What aspect of Apple's business do we believe is driving its profitability?)
b. Express each balance sheet amount as a percentage of total assets. Comment on any differences observed between the two companies. Apple has chosen to structure itself with a higher proportion of equity (and a lower proportion of debt) than Dell. How does this capital structure decision affect our evaluation of the relative riskiness of these two companies?

E2-35. Comparing Income Statements and Balance Sheets of Competitors (LO1)

Following are selected income statement and balance sheet data for two communications companies: Comcast and Verizon. Comcast (CMCSA) Verizon (VZ)

Income Statement ($ millions)	Comcast	Verizon
Sales...................	$37,937	$106,565
Operating costs	29,957	91,920
Operating profit	7,980	14,645
Nonoperating expenses........	4,345	4,428
Net income.................	$ 3,635	$ 10,217

Balance Sheet ($ millions)	Comcast	Verizon
Current assets	$ 8,886	$ 22,348
Long-term assets	109,648	197,657
Total assets................	$118,534	$220,005
Current liabilities............	$ 8,234	$ 30,597
Long-term liabilities	65,723	102,496
Total liabilities	73,957	133,093
Stockholders' equity*.........	44,577	86,912
Total liabilities and equity	$118,534	$220,005

*Includes noncontrolling interest

a. Express each income statement amount as a percentage of sales. Comment on any differences observed between the two companies.
b. Express each balance sheet amount as a percentage of total assets. Comment on any differences observed between the two companies, especially as they relate to their respective business models.
c. Both Verizon and Comcast have chosen a capital structure with a higher proportion of liabilities than equity. How does this capital structure decision affect our evaluation of the riskiness of these two companies? Take into consideration the large level of capital expenditures that each must make to remain competitive.

E2-36. **Comparing Financial Information Across Industries** (LO1)

TJX Companies (TJX)
Apple Inc. (AAPL)

Use the data and computations required in parts a and b of exercises E2-33 and E2-34 to compare TJX Companies and Apple Inc.

a. Compare gross profit and net income as a percentage of sales for these two companies. How might differences in their respective business models explain the differences observed?
b. Compare sales versus total assets. What do observed differences indicate about the relative capital intensity of these two industries?
c. Which company has the higher percentage of total liabilities to stockholders' equity? What do these ratios imply about the relative riskiness of these two companies?
d. Compare the ratio of net income to stockholders' equity for these two companies. Which business model appears to yield higher returns on shareholder investment? Using answers to parts a through c above, identify the factors that appear to drive the ratio of net income to stockholders' equity.

E2-37. **Analyzing Transactions Using the Financial Statement Effects Template** (LO3)

Record the effect of each of the following transactions for Hora Company using the financial statement effects template.

a. Wages of $500 are earned by employees but not yet paid.
b. $2,000 of inventory is purchased on credit.
c. Inventory purchased in transaction b is sold for $3,000 on credit.
d. Collected $3,000 cash from transaction c.
e. Equipment is acquired for $5,000 cash.
f. Recorded $1,000 depreciation expense on equipment from transaction e.
g. Paid $10,000 cash toward a note payable that came due.
h. Paid $2,000 cash for interest on borrowings.

PROBLEMS

P2-38. **Constructing and Analyzing Balance Sheet Amounts from Incomplete Data** (LO1)

3M Company (MMM)

Selected balance sheet amounts for 3M Company, a manufacturer of consumer and business products, for three recent years follow.

$ millions	Current Assets	Long-Term Assets	Total Assets	Current Liabilities	Long-Term Liabilities	Total Liabilities	Stockholders' Equity*
2008	$ 9,598	$?	$25,793	$?	$9,550	$15,489	$10,304
2009	10,795	16,455	?	4,897	9,051	?	13,302
2010	?	17,941	30,156	6,089	8,050	14,139	?

* Includes noncontrolling interest

Required

a. Compute the missing balance sheet amounts for each of the three years shown.

b. What types of accounts would we expect to be included in current assets? In long-term assets?

P2-39. **Analyzing Transactions Using the Financial Statement Effects Template**   (LO3)

Sefcik Company began operations on the first of October. Following are the transactions for its first month of business.

1. S. Sefcik launched Sefcik Company and invested $50,000 into the business in exchange for common stock. The company also borrowed $100,000 from a local bank.
2. Sefcik Co. purchased equipment for $95,000 cash and purchased inventory of $40,000 on credit (the company still owes its suppliers for the inventory at month-end).
3. Sefcik Co. sold inventory costing $30,000 for $50,000 cash.
4. Sefcik Co. paid $10,000 cash for wages owed employees for October work.
5. Sefcik Co. paid interest on the bank loan of $1,000 cash.
6. Sefcik Co. recorded $500 of depreciation expense related to its equipment.
7. Sefcik Co. paid a dividend of $2,000 cash.

Required

a. Record the effects of each transaction using the financial statement effects template.

b. Prepare the income statement and balance sheet at the end of October.

P2-40. **Analyzing Transactions Using the Financial Statement Effects Template**   (LO3)

Following are selected transactions of Mogg Company. Record the effects of each using the financial statement effects template.

1. Shareholders contribute $10,000 cash to the business in exchange for common stock.
2. Employees earn $500 in wages that have not been paid at period-end.
3. Inventory of $3,000 is purchased on credit.
4. The inventory purchased in transaction 3 is sold for $4,500 on credit.
5. The company collected the $4,500 owed to it per transaction 4.
6. Equipment is purchased for $5,000 cash.
7. Depreciation of $1,000 is recorded on the equipment from transaction 6.
8. The Supplies account had a $3,800 balance at the beginning of this period; a physical count at period-end shows that $800 of supplies are still available. No supplies were purchased during this period.
9. The company paid $10,000 cash toward the principal on a note payable; also, $500 cash is paid to cover this note's interest expense for the period.
10. The company received $8,000 cash in advance for services to be delivered next period.

P2-41. **Comparing Operating Characteristics Across Industries**   (LO1)

Following are selected income statement and balance sheet data for companies in different industries.

$ millions	Sales	Cost of Goods Sold	Gross Profit	Net income	Assets	Liabilities	Stockholders' Equity	
Target Corp.	$67,390	$45,725	$21,665	$2,920	$43,705	$28,218	$15,487	Target (TGT)
Nike, Inc.	20,862	11,354	9,508	2,133	14,998	5,155	9,843	Nike (NKE)
Harley-Davidson. . . .	4,859	2,749	2,110	147	9,431	7,224	2,207	Harley-Davidson (HOG)
Cisco Systems	40,040	14,397	25,643	7,767	81,130	36,845	44,285	Cisco Systems (CSCO)

Required

a. Compute the following ratios for each company.
  1. Gross profit/Sales
  2. Net income/Sales
  3. Net income/Stockholders' equity
  4. Liabilities/Stockholders' equity

b. Comment on any differences among the companies' gross profit to sales ratios and net income as a percentage of sales. Do differences in the companies' business models explain the differences observed?

c. Which company reports the highest ratio of net income to equity? Suggest one or more reasons for this result.

d. Which company has financed itself with the highest percentage of liabilities to equity? Suggest one or more reasons why this company can take on such debt levels.

P2-42.   Comparing Cash Flows Across Retailers   (LO1)

Macy's (M)
Home Depot (HD)
Staples (SPLS)
Target (TGT)
Wal-Mart (WMT)

Following are selected accounts from the income statement and the statement of cash flows for several retailers.

| | | Net | Cash Flows from | | |
$ millions	Sales	Income	Operating	Investing	Financing
Macy's	$ 25,003	$ 847	$ 1,506	$ (465)	$ (1,263)
Home Depot, Inc.	67,997	3,338	4,585	(1,012)	(4,451)
Staples, Inc.	24,545	882	1,446	(472)	(938)
Target Corp.	67,390	2,920	5,271	(1,744)	(4,015)
Wal-Mart Stores	421,849	16,389	23,643	(12,193)	(12,028)

Required

a. Compute the ratio of net income to sales for each company. Rank the companies on the basis of this ratio. Do their respective business models give insight into these differences?

b. Compute net cash flows from operating activities as a percentage of sales. Rank the companies on the basis of this ratio. Does this ranking coincide with the ratio rankings from part *a*? Suggest one or more reasons for any differences you observe.

c. Compute net cash flows from investing activities as a percentage of sales. Rank the companies on the basis of this ratio. Does this ranking coincide with the ratio rankings from part *a*? Suggest one or more reasons for any differences you observe.

d. All of these companies report negative cash flows from financing activities. What does it mean for a company to have net cash *outflow* from financing?

P2-43.   Interpreting the Statement of Cash Flows   (LO1)

Wal-Mart (WMT)

Following is the statement of cash flows for Wal-Mart Stores, Inc.

WAL-MART STORES, INC. Statement of Cash Flows For Year Ended January 31, 2011 ($ millions)	
Cash flows from operating activities	
Net income	$ 16,993
Income from discontinued operations, net of tax.	(1,034)
Income from continuing operations	15,959
Adjustments to reconcile income from continuing operations to net cash provided by operating activities:	
Depreciation and amortizations	7,641
Deferred income taxes	651
Other operating activities	1,087
Changes in certain assets and liabilities, net of effects of acquisitions:	
Increase in accounts receivable	(733)
Increase in inventories.	(3,086)
Increase in accounts payable	2,557
Decrease in accrued liabilities.	(433)
Net cash provided by operating activities	23,643
Cash flows from investing activities	
Payments for property and equipment.	(12,699)
Proceeds from disposal of property and equipment	489
Investments and business acquisitions, net of cash acquired.	(202)
Other investing activities.	219
Net cash used in investing activities of continuing operations	(12,193)

continued

Cash flows from financing activities	
Net change in short-term borrowings	503
Proceeds from issuance of long-term debt	11,396
Payment of long-term debt	(4,080)
Dividends paid	(4,437)
Purchase of company stock	(14,776)
Payment of capital lease obligations	(363)
Other financing activities	(271)
Net cash used in financing activities	(12,028)
Effect of exchange rate changes on cash	66
Net (decrease) increase in cash	(512)
Cash at beginning of year	7,907
Cash at end of year	$ 7,395

Required

a. Why does Wal-Mart add back depreciation to compute net cash flows from operating activities?

b. Explain why the increase in receivables and inventories is reported as a cash outflow. Why do accounts payable provide a source of cash? Explain why the decrease in accrued liabilities is reported as a cash outflow.

c. Wal-Mart reports that it invested $12,699 million in property and equipment. Is this an appropriate type of expenditure for Wal-Mart to make? What relation should expenditures for PPE assets have with depreciation expense?

d. Wal-Mart indicates that it paid $14,776 million to repurchase its common stock in fiscal 2011 and, in addition, paid dividends of $4,437 million. Thus, Wal-Mart paid $19,213 million of cash to its shareholders during the year. How do we evaluate that use of cash relative to other possible uses for Wal-Mart's cash?

e. Provide an overall assessment of Wal-Mart's cash flows for 2011. In the analysis, consider the sources and uses of cash.

P2-44. **Interpreting the Statement of Cash Flows** (LO1)

Following is the statement of cash flows for Verizon.

Verizon (VZ)

VERIZON Statement of Cash Flows For Year Ended December 31, 2010 ($ millions)	
Cash Flows from Operating Activities	
Net income	$10,217
Adjustments to reconcile net income to net cash provided by operating activities:	
Depreciation and amortization expense	16,405
Employee retirement benefits	3,988
Deferred income taxes	3,233
Provision for uncollectible accounts	1,246
Equity in earnings of unconsolidated businesses, net of dividends received	2
Changes in current assets and liabilities, net of effects from acquisition or disposition of businesses:	
Accounts receivable	(859)
Inventories	299
Other assets	(313)
Accounts payable and accrued liabilities	1,075
Other, net	(1,930)
Net cash provided by operating activities	33,363
Cash Flows from Investing Activities	
Capital expenditures (including capitalized software)	(16,458)
Acquisitions of licenses, investments and businesses, net of cash acquired	(1,438)
Proceeds from dispositions	2,594
Net change in short-term investments	(3)
Other, net	251
Net cash used in investing activities	(15,054)

continued from prior page

Cash Flows from Financing Activities	
Repayments of long-term borrowings and capital lease obligations.	$ (8,136)
Increase (decrease) in short-term obligations, excluding current maturities	(1,097)
Dividends paid	(5,412)
Proceeds from access line spin-off	3,083
Other, net	(2,088)
Net cash used in financing activities	(13,650)
Increase (decrease) in cash and cash equivalents.	4,659
Cash and cash equivalents, beginning of year	2,009
Cash and cash equivalents, end of year	$ 6,668

Required

a. Why does Verizon add back depreciation to compute net cash flows from operating activities? What does the size of the depreciation add-back indicate about the relative capital intensity of this industry?

b. Verizon reports that it invested $16,458 million in property and equipment. These expenditures are necessitated by market pressures as the company faces stiff competition from other communications companies, such as Comcast. Where in the 10-K might we find additional information about these capital expenditures to ascertain whether Verizon is addressing the company's most pressing needs? What relation might we expect between the size of these capital expenditures and the amount of depreciation expense reported?

c. Verizon's statement of cash flows indicates that the company paid $8,136 million in debt payments. What problem does Verizon's high debt load pose for its ability to maintain the level of capital expenditures necessary to remain competitive in its industry?

d. During the year, Verizon paid dividends of $5,412 million but did not repay a sizeable portion of its debt. How do dividend payments differ from debt payments? Why would Verizon continue to pay dividends in light of cash demands for needed capital expenditures and debt repayments?

e. Provide an overall assessment of Verizon's cash flows for 2010. In the analysis, consider the sources and uses of cash.

P2-45.   Analyzing Transactions Using the Financial Statement Effects Template   (LO3)
On March 1, S. Penman (owner) launched AniFoods, Inc., an organic foods retailing company. Following are the transactions for its first month of business.

1. S. Penman (owner) contributed $100,000 cash to the company in return for common stock. Penman also lent the company $55,000. This $55,000 note is due one year hence.
2. The company purchased equipment in the amount of $50,000, paying $10,000 cash and signing a note payable to the equipment manufacturer for the remaining balance.
3. The company purchased inventory for $80,000 cash in March.
4. The company had March sales of $100,000 of which $60,000 was for cash and $40,000 on credit. Total cost of goods sold for its March sales was $70,000.
5. The company purchased future advertising time from a local radio station for $10,000 cash.
6. During March, $7,500 worth of radio spots purchased in transaction 5 are aired. The remaining spots will be aired in April.
7. Employee wages earned and paid during March total $15,000 cash.
8. Prior to disclosing the financial statements, the company recognized that employees had earned an additional $1,000 in wages that will be paid in the next period.
9. The company recorded $2,000 of depreciation for March relating to its equipment.

Required

a. Record the effect of each transaction using the financial statement effects template.

b. Prepare a March income statement and a balance sheet as of the end of March for AniFoods, Inc.

P2-46.   Analyzing Transactions Using the Financial Statement Effects Template   (LO3)
Hanlon Advertising Company began the current month with the following balance sheet.

Cash.	$ 80,000	Liabilities.	$ 70,000
Noncash assets	135,000	Contributed capital.	110,000
		Earned capital	35,000
Total assets.	$215,000	Total liabilities and equity	$215,000

Following are summary transactions that occurred during the current month.

1. The company purchased supplies for $5,000 cash; none were used this month.
2. Services of $2,500 were performed this month on credit.
3. Services were performed for $10,000 cash this month.
4. The company purchased advertising for $8,000 cash; the ads will run next month.
5. The company received $1,200 cash as partial payment on accounts receivable from transaction 2.
6. The company paid $3,400 cash toward the accounts payable balance reported at the beginning of the month.
7. Paid $3,100 cash toward this month's wages expenses.
8. The company declared and paid dividends of $500 cash.

Required

a. Record the effects of each transaction using the financial statement effects template.
b. Prepare the income statement for this month and the balance sheet as of month-end.

P2-47.   Reconciling and Computing Operating Cash Flows from Net Income   (LO1)

Petroni Company reports the following selected results for its current calendar year.

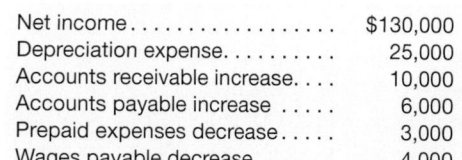

Net income..................	$130,000
Depreciation expense..........	25,000
Accounts receivable increase. . . .	10,000
Accounts payable increase	6,000
Prepaid expenses decrease.....	3,000
Wages payable decrease.......	4,000

Required

a. Prepare the operating section only of Petroni Company's statement of cash flows for the year.
b. Does the positive sign on depreciation expense indicate that the company is generating cash by recording depreciation? Explain.
c. Explain why the increase in accounts receivable is a use of cash in the statement of cash flows.
d. Explain why the decrease in prepaid expense is a source of cash in the statement of cash flows.

P2-48.   Analyzing Transactions Using the Financial Statement Effects Template   (LO3)

Werner Realty Company began the month with the following balance sheet.

Cash.......................	$ 30,000	Liabilities.....................	$ 90,000
Noncash assets	225,000	Contributed capital.............	45,000
		Earned capital `................	120,000
Total assets..................	$255,000	Total liabilities and equity........	$255,000

Following are summary transactions that occurred during the current month.

1. The company purchased $6,000 of supplies on credit.
2. The company received $8,000 cash from a new customer for services to be performed next month.
3. The company paid $6,000 cash to cover office rent for two months (the current month and the next).
4. The company billed clients for $25,000 of work performed.
5. The company paid employees $6,000 cash for work performed.
6. The company collected $25,000 cash from accounts receivable in transaction 4.
7. The company recorded $3,000 depreciation on its equipment.
8. At month-end, $2,000 of supplies purchased in transaction 1 are still available; no supplies were available when the month began.

Required

a. Record the effects of each transaction using the financial statement effects template.
b. Prepare the income statement for this month and the balance sheet as of month-end.

IFRS APPLICATIONS

I2-49.   Comparing Income Statements and Balance Sheets of Competitors   (LO1)

Following are selected income statement and balance sheet data from two European grocery chain companies: Tesco PLC (UK) and Ahold (The Netherlands).

Income Statements (for fiscal year ended)	Tesco February 26, 2011 (in £millions)	Ahold January 2, 2011 (in €millions)
Sales.	£60,931	€29,530
Cost of goods sold.	55,871	21,610
Gross profit.	5,060	7,920
Total expenses	2,405	7,067
Net income.	£ 2,655	€ 853

Balance Sheet (as of)	Tesco February 26, 2011 (in £millions)	Ahold January 2, 2011 (in €millions)
Current assets	£11,438	€ 5,194
Long-term assets	35,768	9,531
Total assets.	£47,206	€14,725
Current liabilities.	£17,731	€ 4,092
Long-term liabilities	12,852	4,723
Total liabilities.	30,583	8,815
Stockholders' equity	16,623	5,910
Total liabilities and equity	£47,206	€14,725

Required

a. Prepare a common-sized income statement. To do this, express each income statement amount as a percent of sales. Comment on any differences observed between the two companies. Ahold's gross profit percentage of sales is considerably higher than Tesco's. What might explain this difference?

b. Prepare a common-sized balance sheet. To do this, express each balance sheet amount as a percent of total assets. Comment on any differences observed between the two companies.

c. Ahold has chosen to structure itself with a higher proportion of equity (and a lower proportion of debt) than Tesco. How does this capital structure decision affect your assessment of the relative riskiness of these two companies?

I2-50.   **Interpreting the Statement of Cash Flows**   (LO1)

Following is the statement of cash flows for AstraZeneca, a multinational pharmaceutical conglomerate, headquartered in London, UK. The company uses IFRS for its financials and provides a conversion to U.S. $ as a convenience to investors.

ASTRAZENECA Consolidated Statement of Cash Flows For Year Ended December 31, 2009 ($ millions)	
Cash flows from operating activities	
Profit before tax	$10,807
Finance income and expense	736
Depreciation, amortization and impairment.	2,087
Increase in trade and other receivables.	(256)
Decrease in inventories	6
Increase in trade and other payables and provisions.	1,579
Other non-cash movements.	(200)
Cash generated from operations	14,759
Interest paid	(639)
Tax paid	(2,381)
Net cash inflow from operating activities.	11,739

continued

Cash flows from investing activities

Movement in short term investments and fixed deposits	$ (1,371)
Purchase of property, plant and equipment.	(962)
Disposal of property, plant and equipment	138
Purchase of intangible assets	(624)
Disposal of intangible assets	269
Purchase of non-current asset investments.	(31)
Disposal of non-current asset investments	3
Interest received.	113
Payments made by subsidiaries to non-controlling interests	(11)
Net cash outflow from investing activities	(2,476)
Net cash inflow/(outflow) before financing activities	9,263

Cash flows from financing activities

Proceeds from issue of share capital.	135
Repayment of loans	(650)
Dividends paid	(2,977)
Movement in short term borrowings	(137)
Net cash (outflow)/inflow from financing activities.	(3,629)
Net increase/(decrease) in cash and cash equivalents in the period	$ 5,634
Cash and cash equivalents at beginning of the period	4,123
Exchange rate effects.	71
Cash and cash equivalents at the end of the period.	$ 9,828

Required

a. Why does AstraZeneca add back depreciation to compute net cash flows from operating activities?

b. Explain why the increase in trade and other receivables is reported as a cash outflow and the decrease in inventories is reported as a cash inflow. Explain why trade and other payables and provisions are shown as a source of cash.

c. AstraZeneca reports that it invested $962 million in property and equipment. Is this an appropriate type of expenditure for AstraZeneca to make? What relation should expenditures for PPE assets have with depreciation expense?

d. AstraZeneca indicates that it paid dividends of $2,977 million. How do we evaluate that use of cash relative to other possible uses for AstraZeneca's cash?

e. Provide an overall assessment of AstraZeneca's cash flows for 2009. In the analysis, consider the sources and uses of cash.

MANAGEMENT APPLICATIONS

MA2-51. **Understanding the Company Operating Cycle and Management Strategy**   (LO1)

Consider the operating cycle as depicted in Exhibit 2.4, to answer the following questions.

a. Why might a company want to reduce its cash conversion cycle? (*Hint*: Consider the financial statement implications of reducing the cash conversion cycle.)

b. How might a company reduce its cash conversion cycle?

c. Examine and discuss the potential impacts on *customers* and *suppliers* of taking the actions identified in part *b*.

MA2-52. **Ethics and Governance: Understanding Revenue Recognition and Expense Recording**   (LO1)

Revenue should be recognized when it is earned and expense when incurred. Given some lack of specificity in these terms, companies have some latitude when applying GAAP to determine the timing and amount of revenues and expenses. A few companies use this latitude to manage reported earnings. Some have argued that it is not necessarily bad for companies to manage earnings in that, by doing so, management (1) can better provide investors and creditors with reported earnings that are closer to "core" earnings (that is, management purges earnings of components deemed irrelevant or distracting so that share prices better reflect company performance); and (2) can present the company in the best light, which benefits both shareholders and employees—a Machiavellian argument that "the end justifies the means."

a. Is it good that GAAP is written as broadly as it is? Explain. What are the pros and cons of defining accounting terms more strictly?

b. Assess (both pro and con) the Machiavellian argument above that defends managing earnings.

SOLUTIONS TO REVIEW PROBLEMS

Mid-Module Review 1

Solution

DELL INC.
Income Statement
For Fiscal Year Ended January 28, 2011

Revenue	$61,494
Cost of revenue	50,098
Gross margin	11,396
Operating expenses	
Selling, general, and administrative expenses	7,302
Research and development expenses	661
Total operating expenses	7,963
Operating income	3,433
Interest expense	83
Income before income taxes	3,350
Income tax expense	715
Net income	$ 2,635

DELL INC.
Statement of Cash Flows
For Fiscal Year Ended January 28, 2011

Net cash provided by operating activities	$ 3,969
Net cash used in investing activities	(1,165)
Net cash provided by financing activities	474
Net increase in cash and cash equivalents	3,278
Cash and cash equivalents, beginning of year	10,635
Cash and cash equivalents, ending of year	$13,913

DELL INC.
Balance Sheet
January 28, 2011

Assets		Liabilities and Equity	
Current assets		Current liabilities	
Cash and cash equivalents	$13,913	Short-term debt	$ 851
Short-term investments	452	Accounts payable	11,293
Accounts receivable	10,136	Accrued and other current liabilities	7,339
Inventories	1,301	Total current liabilities	19,483
Other current assets	3,219	Long-term debt	5,146
Total current assets	29,021	Other noncurrent liabilities	6,204
Property, plant, and equipment, net	1,953	Total liabilities	30,833
Long-term investments	704	Stockholders' equity	
Other noncurrent assets	6,921	Paid-in capital	11,797
		Retained earnings	24,744
		Other stockholders' equity	(28,775)
		Total stockholders' equity	7,766
Total assets	$38,599	Total liabilities and stockholders' equity	$38,599

Mid-Module Review 2

Solution

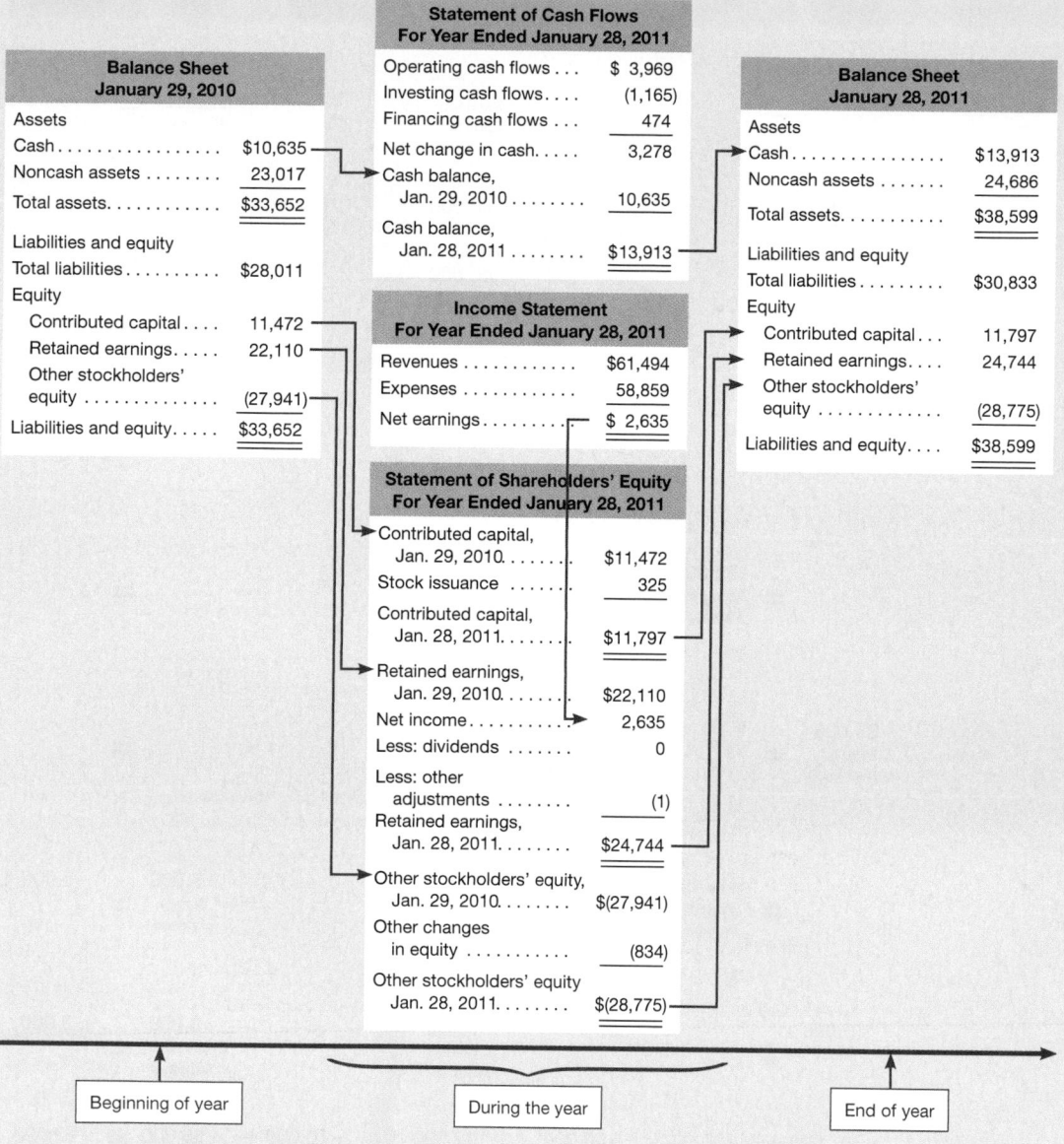

Module-End Review

Solution

a.

	Balance Sheet						Income Statement		
Transaction	Cash Asset	+ Noncash Assets	= Liabil- ities	+ Contrib. Capital	+ Earned Capital		Rev- enues	− Expen- ses	= Net Income
Beginning balance	+80,000	+270,000	= +200,000	+50,000	+100,000			−	=
1. Purchase inventory of $80,000 on credit		+80,000 Inventory	= +80,000 Accounts Payable					−	=

continued

	Balance Sheet						Income Statement		
Transaction	Cash Asset	+ Noncash Assets	= Liabil- ities	+ Contrib. Capital	+ Earned Capital		Rev- enues	− Expen- ses	= Net Income
2. Pay employees $10,000 cash for wages earned this year	−10,000 Cash		=		−10,000 Retained Earnings			+10,000 Wages Expense	−10,000
3. Sell inventory costing $40,000 for $70,000 on credit		+70,000 Accounts Receivable −40,000 Inventory	=		+70,000 Retained Earnings −40,000 Retained Earning		+70,000 Sales	− +40,000 Cost of Goods Sold	+70,000 −40,000
4. Collect $15,000 cash from the accounts receivable in transaction 3	+15,000 Cash	−15,000 Accounts Receivable	=				−	=	
5. Pay $35,000 cash toward the accounts payable in transaction 1	−35,000 Cash		= −35,000 Accounts Payable				−	=	
6. Purchase advertising for $25,000 cash that will air next year	−25,000 Cash	+25,000 Prepaid Advertising	=				−	=	
7. Employees earn $5,000 in wages that will not be paid until next year			= +5,000 Wages Payable		−5,000 Retained Earnings			− +5,000 Wages Expense	−5,000
8. Record $3,000 depreciation on its equipment		−3,000 PPE, net	=		−3,000 Retained Earnings			− +3,000 Depreciation Expense	−3,000
Ending balance	+25,000	+387,000	= +250,000	+50,000	+112,000		+70,000	− +58,000	= +12,000

b.

GATEWAY Income Statement For Year Ended December 31, 2011	
Revenues	$70,000
Expenses	58,000
Net income	$12,000

GATEWAY Balance Sheet December 31, 2011			
Cash.	$ 25,000	Liabilities.	$250,000
Noncash assets	387,000	Contributed capital.	50,000
		Earned capital (retained earnings)	112,000
Total assets.	$412,000	Total liabilities and equity	$412,000

c. The linkage between the income statement and the balance sheet is retained earnings. Each period, the retained earnings account is updated for net income less dividends paid. For this period, that updating follows.

GATEWAY Retained Earnings Reconciliation For Year Ended December 31, 2011	
Retained earnings, Dec. 31, 2010	$100,000
Add: Net income	12,000
Less: Dividends	(0)
Retained earnings, Dec. 31, 2011	$112,000

Getty Images

APPLE

Apple Computer launched the iPod in late 2001, arguably the most important product in the company's history. A basic hard-drive-based player, the iPod was not a new concept. Yet, Apple created a durable, slim, and sexy package, paired it with ear buds, and made the iPod a fashion statement as well as a great music player.

Marrying the hardware with the intuitive Apple-like software for navigation, the company had a winning combination. By the end of 2001, nearly 125,000 iPods had flown off the shelves. By 2010, Apple was selling over 50 million iPods per year and listeners had downloaded over 1 billion songs from iTunes—see graphic on opposite page.

Apple announced the introduction of the iPhone in 2007 and, later, the iPad in 2010. By the end of 2010, Apple was selling 40 million iPhones per year, and its sales exceeded $65 billion. Further, the income effect from selling iPads was just beginning and accounted for only 7.6% of Apple's revenues.

Since the introduction of the iPod, Apple's sales have increased by 1200% and its operating income, which was a $344 million operating loss in 2001, has grown to over $18 billion by 2011. In 2011, Apple's market capitalization was over $360 billion, 60% greater than Microsoft and second only to Exxon among U.S. companies.

To bring each iPod, iPhone and iPad to market, Apple must purchase component parts, manufacture them, hire sales personnel, pay advertisers, and distribute finished products. Each of these activities involves a transaction that Apple's accounting records must capture. The resulting financial statements tell the story of Apple's manufacturing and sales process in financial language.

This module explains how the accounting system captures business transactions, creates financial records, and aggregates the individual records to produce financial reports that we read and interpret in company 10-Ks. The resulting financial statements tell the story of Apple's business activities.

Sources: Apple 2010 10-K; *Fortune*, January 2007 and 2012.

Accounting Adjustments and Constructing Financial Statements

LEARNING OBJECTIVES

LO1 Analyze and record transactions using the financial statement effects template. (p. 3-4)

LO2 Prepare and explain accounting adjustments and their financial statement effects. (p. 3-8)

LO3 Explain and construct the trial balance. (p. 3-12)

LO4 Construct financial statements from the trial balance. (p. 3-15)

LO5 Describe the closing process. (p. 3-20)

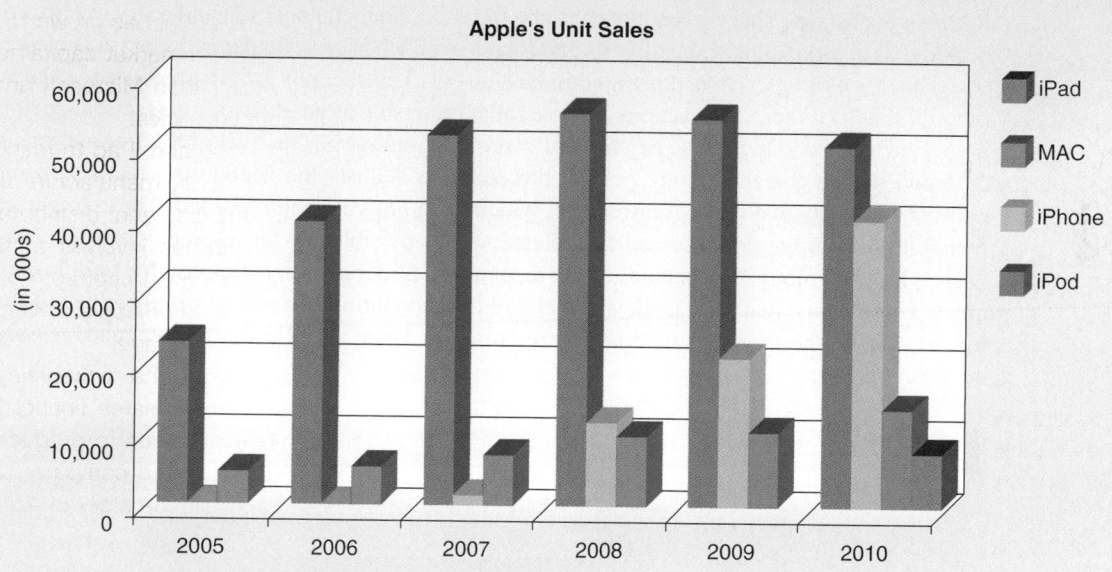

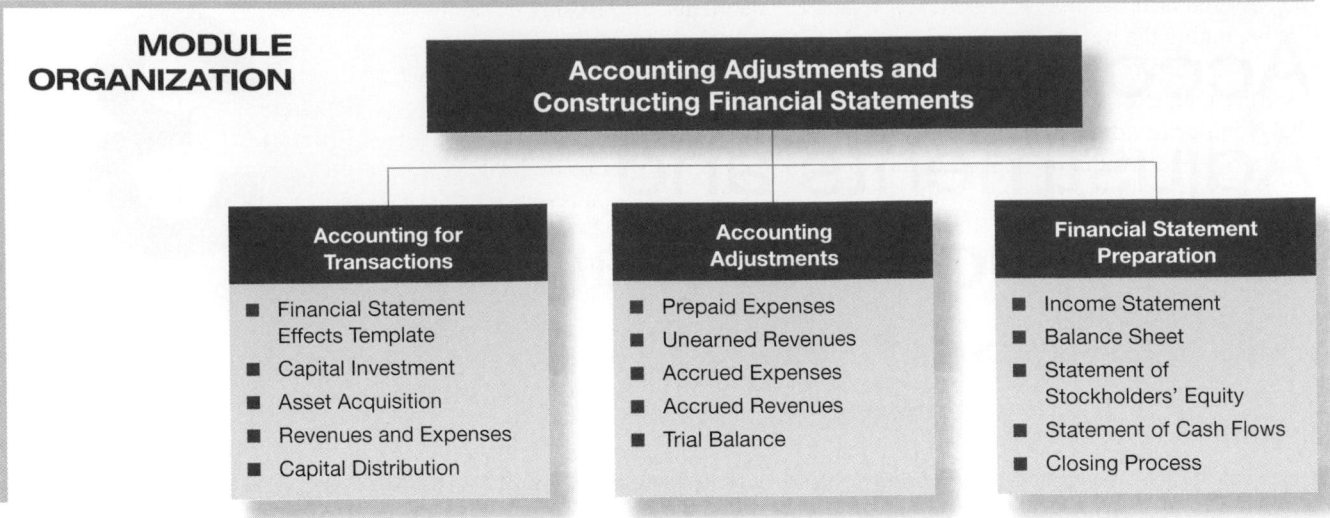

MODULE ORGANIZATION

Accounting Adjustments and Constructing Financial Statements

Accounting for Transactions	Accounting Adjustments	Financial Statement Preparation
■ Financial Statement Effects Template	■ Prepaid Expenses	■ Income Statement
■ Capital Investment	■ Unearned Revenues	■ Balance Sheet
■ Asset Acquisition	■ Accrued Expenses	■ Statement of Stockholders' Equity
■ Revenues and Expenses	■ Accrued Revenues	■ Statement of Cash Flows
■ Capital Distribution	■ Trial Balance	■ Closing Process

Financial statements report on the financial performance of a business using the language of accounting. To prepare these statements, companies translate day-to-day transactions into accounting records (called journals), and then record (post) them to individual accounts. At the end of an accounting period, each of these accounts is totaled, and the resulting balances are used to prepare financial statements. After the financial statements are prepared, the temporary (income statement) accounts are "zeroed out" so that the next period can begin anew—akin to clearing a scoreboard for the next game. Permanent (balance sheet) accounts continue to reflect financial position and carry over from period to period—akin to keeping track of wins and losses even when a particular scoreboard is cleared.

The *accounting cycle* is illustrated in Exhibit 3.1. Transactions are first recorded in the accounting records. Each of these transactions is, generally, the result of an external transaction, such as recording a sale to a customer or the payment of wages to employees. Once all of the transactions have been recorded during the accounting period, the company adjusts the accounting records to recognize a number of events that have occurred, but which have not yet been recorded. These might include the recognition of wage expense and the related wages payable for those employees who have earned wages, but have not yet been paid, or the recognition of depreciation expense for buildings and equipment. These adjustments are made at the end of the accounting period to properly adjust the accounting records before the financial statements are prepared. Once all adjustments are made, financial statements are prepared.

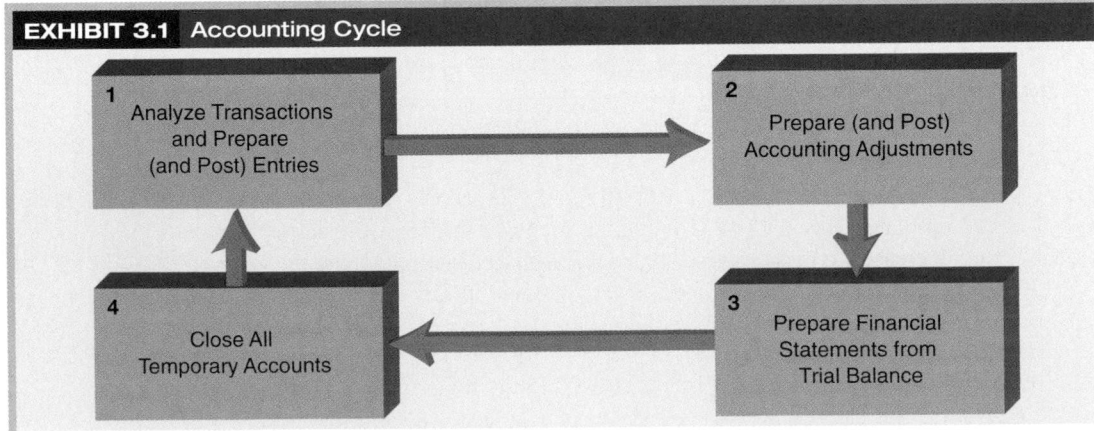

EXHIBIT 3.1 Accounting Cycle

1. Analyze Transactions and Prepare (and Post) Entries
2. Prepare (and Post) Accounting Adjustments
3. Prepare Financial Statements from Trial Balance
4. Close All Temporary Accounts

The purpose of Module 3 is to explain further details of the accounting cycle. Our illustration includes journalizing transactions, posting entries to accounts, adjusting those accounts, preparing unadjusted and adjusted trial balances, constructing financial statements, and closing out temporary accounts before beginning the next accounting period. We also show how to construct the statement of cash flows under both the direct and indirect methods. Some topics from Module 2 are repeated here for completeness (the template, accounting adjustments, and basic financial statement preparation, for example). This module provides a more detailed introduction to the accounting recordkeeping process. However, understanding topics in the other modules does not require knowledge of the details in this module.

Understanding the financial statement preparation process requires an understanding of the language used to record business transactions in accounting records. The recording and statement preparation processes are readily understood once we learn that language (of financial effects) and its mechanics (entries and posting). Even if we never journalize a transaction or prepare a financial statement, understanding the accounting process aids us in analyzing and interpreting accounting reports. Understanding the accounting language also facilitates our communication with business professionals within a company and with members of the business community outside of a company.

ACCOUNTING FOR TRANSACTIONS

This section explains how we account for and assess business transactions. We describe the financial statement effects template that we use throughout the book. We then illustrate its application to four main categories of business transactions.

LO1 Analyze and record transactions using the financial statement effects template.

Financial Statement Effects Template

Transaction analysis refers to the process of identifying, analyzing, and recording the financial statement effects of transactions. For this purpose, we use the following **financial statement effects template**.

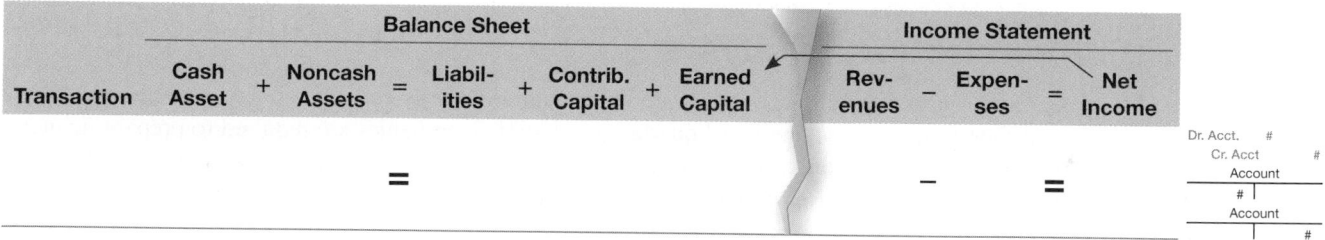

Each transaction is identified in the "Transaction" column. Then, the dollar amounts (positive or negative) of the financial statement effects are recorded in the appropriate balance sheet or income statement columns. The template also reflects the statement of cash flow effects (via the cash column) and the statement of stockholders' equity effects (via the contributed capital and earned capital columns). The retained earnings account, one of the accounts in earned capital, is immediately updated to reflect any income or loss arising from each transaction (denoted by the arrow line from net income to earned capital). This template is instructive as it reveals the financial impacts of transactions, and it provides insights into the effects of accounting choices.

T-Accounts and Journal Entries

The related journal entry and T-account effects are displayed in the margin next to the financial statement effects template. The **T-Accounts**, named for their likeness to a large 'T', are used to reflect increases and decreases to individual accounts. When a transaction occurs, it is recorded (*journalized*); once recorded, the specific accounts affected are updated in the accounting books (*general ledger*) of the company, and the affected accounts are increased or decreased. This process of continuously updating individual account balances is referred to as *posting* transactions to accounts. A T-account provides a simple illustration of the financial effects of each transaction.

Specifically, one side of the T-account is used for increases and the other for decreases. A convenient way to remember which side records increases is to recall the accounting equation: **Assets = Liabilities + Equity.** Assets are on the left side of the equation. So, the left side of an asset T-account records increases in the asset and the right side records decreases. Liabilities and equity are on the right side of the accounting equation. So, the right side of a liability and an equity T-account records increases and the left side records decreases. This relation is represented graphically as follows:

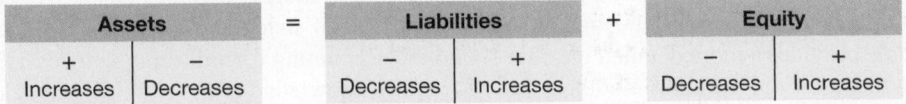

Journal entries also capture the effects of transactions. Journal entries reflect increases and decreases to accounts using the language of debits and credits. Debits and credits simply refer to the left or right side of a T-account, respectively. We can superimpose the descriptors of debit and credit on a T-account as follows.

Account Title	
Debit	Credit
(Left side)	(Right side)

The left side of the T-account is the "debit" side and the right side is the "credit" side. This holds for all T-accounts. Thus, to record an increase in an asset, we enter an amount on the left or debit side of the T-account—that is, we *debit the account*. Decreases in assets are recorded with an entry on the opposite (credit) side. To record an increase in a liability or equity account, we enter an amount on the right or credit side of the T-account—we *credit the account*. Decreases in liability or equity accounts are recorded on the left (debit) side.

In the margin of our financial statement effects template, we show the journal entry first, followed by the related T-accounts. In accounting jargon, this sequence relates to *journalizing* the entry and *posting* it to the affected accounts. The T-accounts represent the financial impact of each transaction on the respective asset, liability or equity accounts.

Transaction Analysis

This section uses **Apple Inc.** to illustrate the accounting for selected business transactions. The assumed time frame will be one fiscal quarter, as all public companies are required to prepare financial statements at least quarterly. We select transactions to illustrate four fundamental types of business activities: (1) financing the company, (2) asset acquisition, (3) revenue and expense recognition, and (4) dividend distribution. Next, we record accounting adjustments, prepare the financial statements, and close the books.

Capital Investment

Assume that Apple investors contribute $300 cash to the company in exchange for common stock. Apple's cash and common stock both increase. Recall that common stock is a component of contributed capital. The following financial statement effects template reflects this transaction. If cash financing was obtained from a bank instead of shareholders, the only change would be to increase liabilities by $300, not contributed capital.

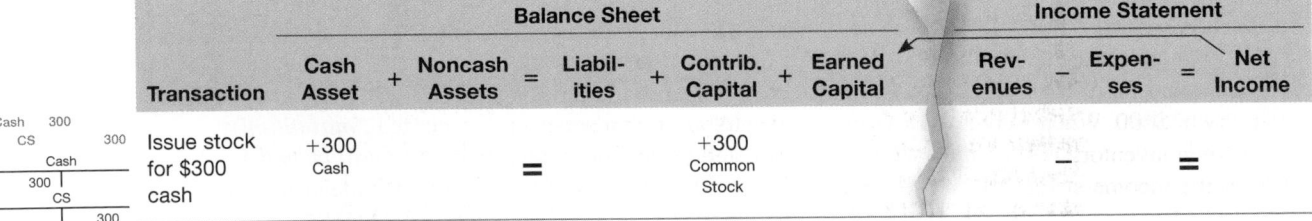

Journal Entry and T-Account

Although we will not repeatedly refer to journal entries and T-accounts, we will describe them for this first transaction. Specifically, the $300 debit equals the $300 credit in the journal entry: assets ($300 cash) = liabilities ($0) + equity ($300 common stock). This balance in transactions is the basis of *double-entry accounting*. For simplicity, we use acronyms (such as CS for common stock) in journal entries and T-accounts. (A listing of accounts and acronyms is located in Appendix C near the end of the book.) The journal entry for this transaction is

```
Cash.............................................  300
    CS (Common Stock) ..............................      300
```

Convention dictates that debits are listed first, followed by credits—the latter are indented.[1] The total debit(s) must always equal the total credit(s) for each transaction. The T-account representation for this transaction follows:

Cash		CS	
300			300

Cash is an asset; thus, a cash increase is recorded on the left or debit side of the T-account. Common stock is an equity account; thus, a common stock increase is recorded on the right or credit side.

Asset Acquisition

Assume that Apple purchases $2,000 worth of iPods from its supplier (we keep this illustration simple by ignoring Apple's manufacturing activities). When one company buys from another, it is normal to give a period of time in which to pay the obligation due, usually 30 to 60 days, or more. This purchase "on credit" (also called *on account*) means that Apple owes its supplier $2,000 for the purchase. Apple records the cost of the purchased iPods as an asset called inventories, which are goods held for resale. This acquisition of iPods on credit is recorded as follows.

	Balance Sheet								Income Statement					
Transaction	Cash Asset	+	Noncash Assets	=	Liabil- ities	+	Contrib. Capital	+	Earned Capital		Rev- enues	−	Expen- ses	=	Net Income
Purchase iPods for $2,000 on credit			+2,000 Inventory	=	+2,000 Accounts Payable							−		=	

```
INV    2,000
   AP       2,000

       INV
2,000 |
       AP
      | 2,000
```

Revenue and Expense Recognition

Assume that Apple sells iPods that cost $600 to a retailer for $700 on credit. The sale *on credit* means that the customer has not yet paid and Apple has a $700 account receivable. Can Apple record the $700 sale as revenue even though it has not collected any cash? The answer is yes. This decision reflects an important concept in accounting, called the **revenue recognition principle**. The revenue recognition principle prescribes that a company can recognize revenues provided that two conditions are met:

1. Revenues are *earned*, and
2. Revenues are *realized* or *realizable*.

Earned means that the company has done whatever it is required to do. In this case, it means that Apple has delivered the iPods to its retail customer. **Realized** or **realizable** means that the seller has either received cash or will receive cash at some point in the future. That is, Apple can recognize revenue if it expects to collect the $700 account receivable in the future.

Recording the $700 sale is only half the transaction. Apple must also record the decrease in iPod inventory of $600. When a company purchases inventory, it records the cost on the balance sheet as an asset. When inventory is sold, the "asset" is used up and its cost must be transferred from the balance sheet to the income statement as an expense. In particular, the expense associated with inventory is

---

[1] There can be more than one debit and one credit for a transaction. To illustrate, assume that Apple raises $300 cash, with $200 from investors and $100 borrowed from a bank. The resulting journal entry is:

```
Cash.............................................  300
    CS (common stock) ..............................      200
    NP (note payable)...............................      100
```

called cost of goods sold. Thus, the second part of Apple's revenue transaction is to remove the cost of the iPods from the balance sheet and recognize the cost of goods sold (an expense) in its income statement. This will record the cost of the inventory associated with this revenue.

Expenses are recorded as they are **incurred**. Once revenues are recognized (using the revenue recognition principle), we then record all related expenses incurred to generate those revenues *in the same period* that we recognize the revenue. This yields the proper measure of income for the period and is an application of accrual accounting.

The $700 sale of Apple iPods that cost $600 is recorded as follows.

		Balance Sheet						Income Statement		
Transaction	Cash Asset	+ Noncash Assets	= Liabil- ities	+ Contrib. Capital	+ Earned Capital		Rev- enues	– Expen- ses	= Net Income
Sell $700 of iPods on credit		+700 Accounts Receivable =			+700 Retained Earnings		+700 Sales	–	= +700
Record $600 cost of iPod sale		–600 Inventory =			–600 Retained Earnings			– +600 Cost of Goods Sold	= –600

(margin T-accounts)
```
AR        700
  Sales        700
      AR
700 |
    Sales
          |   700
COGS  600
  INV        600
    COGS
600 |
    INV
          |   600
```

The first part of this sales transaction records the $700 sale and the $700 increase in accounts receivable. Revenues are earned and therefore recognized even though no cash was received. The sale is reflected in the account receivable that will later be converted to cash. The increase in revenues increases income, which increases retained earnings.[2]

The second part of this sale transaction transfers the $600 in inventory on the balance sheet to the income statement as the cost of iPods sold. This entry increases expenses, and decreases both income and retained earnings. The transaction also reduces assets because Apple no longer owns the inventory; it is "used up."

Capital Distributions

Assume that Apple decides to pay $50 to its shareholders in the form of a cash dividend. Dividends are treated as a return of shareholders' investment. All transactions between the company and its shareholders are considered financing transactions. This includes payment of dividends, the issuance of stock, and any subsequent stock repurchase. Financing transactions affect only the balance sheet; they do not affect the income statement. Dividends are distributions of income. They represent the portion of income that the company chooses to distribute to shareholders—the portion that will no longer be retained. Thus, dividends reduce retained earnings. It is important to distinguish dividends from expenses—dividends are NOT an expense, they do not reduce net income. They are a distribution of net income; they reduce retained earnings. Apple's $50 dividend payment is reflected in the following template. (Companies typically record dividends in a separate dividends account and then later, in the closing process, this account is transferred to retained earnings. The template depicts dividends as a reduction of earned capital; more precisely, it is a reduction of retained earnings, which is part of earned capital. Alternatively, one could record dividends as an immediate reduction to retained earnings; the end result of both approaches is identical.)

		Balance Sheet						Income Statement		
Transaction	Cash Asset	+ Noncash Assets	= Liabil- ities	+ Contrib. Capital	+ Earned Capital		Rev- enues	– Expen- ses	= Net Income
Pay $50 cash for dividends	–50 Cash		=		–50 Dividends			–	=

(margin T-accounts)
```
DIV       50
  Cash         50
     DIV
50 |
    Cash
          |   50
```

---

[2] The retained earnings account is not automatically updated in most accounting software programs as our financial effects template illustrates. Instead, accountants transfer income to retained earnings using a journal entry as part of the closing process. We briefly explain the closing process near the end of this module and more fully in Appendix 3A.

MID-MODULE REVIEW 1

Assume that Symantec Corporation experienced the following six transactions relating to a capital investment, the purchase and sale of inventory, the collection of an account receivable, and the payment of an account payable.

1. Shareholders contribute $3,000 cash to Symantec in exchange for its common shares.
2. Symantec purchases $1,000 of inventory on credit.
3. Symantec sells $300 of inventory for $500 on credit.
4. Symantec collects $300 cash owed by customers.
5. Symantec pays $400 cash toward its accounts payable to suppliers.
6. Symantec pays $20 cash for dividends to its stockholders.

Required

Record each transaction in the financial statement effects template. Include journal entries for each account in the margin and post those entries to T-accounts.

The solution is on page 3-35.

ACCOUNTING ADJUSTMENTS (ACCRUALS)

Recognizing revenue when earned (even if not received in cash), and recording expenses when incurred (even if not paid in cash), are cornerstones of **accrual accounting**, which is required under GAAP.[3] Understanding accounting adjustments, commonly called *accruals*, is crucial to effectively analyzing and interpreting financial statements. In this module's Apple illustration, we recorded inventory as a purchase even though no cash was paid, and we recognized the sale as revenue even though no cash was received. Both of these transactions reflect accrual accounting. Some accounting adjustments affect the balance sheet alone (as with purchasing inventory on account). Other adjustments affect the balance sheet *and* the income statement (as with selling inventory on account). Accounting adjustments can affect asset, liability or equity accounts, and can either increase or decrease net income.

> **LO2** Prepare and explain accounting adjustments and their financial statement effects.

Companies make adjustments to more accurately report their financial performance and condition. For example, employees might not have been paid for wages earned at the end of an accounting period. Failure to recognize this labor cost would understate the company's total liabilities (because wages payable would be too low), and would overstate net income for the period (because wages expense would be too low). Thus, neither the balance sheet nor the income statement would be accurate.

Accounting adjustments yield a more accurate presentation of the economic results of a company for a period. Despite their generally beneficial effects, adjustments can be misused. Managers can use adjustments to bias reported income, rendering it higher or lower than it really is. Adjustments, if misused, can adversely affect business and investment decisions. Many recent accounting scandals have resulted from improper use of adjustments. Although outsiders cannot directly observe companies' specific accounting entries, their impact can be detected as changes in balance sheet and income statement accounts. Those changes provide signals for financial statement analysis. Consequently, understanding the accrual process will help us know what to look for as we analyze companies' financial reports. Exhibit 3.2 identifies four general types of accounting adjustments, which are briefly described below.

Prepaid expenses Prepaid expenses reflect advance cash payments that will ultimately become expenses. An example is the payment for radio advertising that will not be aired until sometime in the future.

Unearned revenues Unearned revenues reflect cash received from customers before any services or goods are provided. An example is cash received from patrons for tickets to an upcoming concert.

Accrued expenses Accrued expenses are expenses incurred and recognized on the income statement, even though they are not yet paid in cash. An example is wages owed to employees who performed work but who have not yet been paid.

---

[3] **Cash accounting** recognizes revenues when cash is received and expenses when cash is paid. This is not acceptable accounting under GAAP. However, small businesses that do not prepare financial reports for public investors and creditors sometimes use cash accounting.

Accrued revenues Accrued revenues are revenues earned and recognized on the income statement, even though cash is not yet received. Examples include sales on credit and revenue earned under a long-term contract.

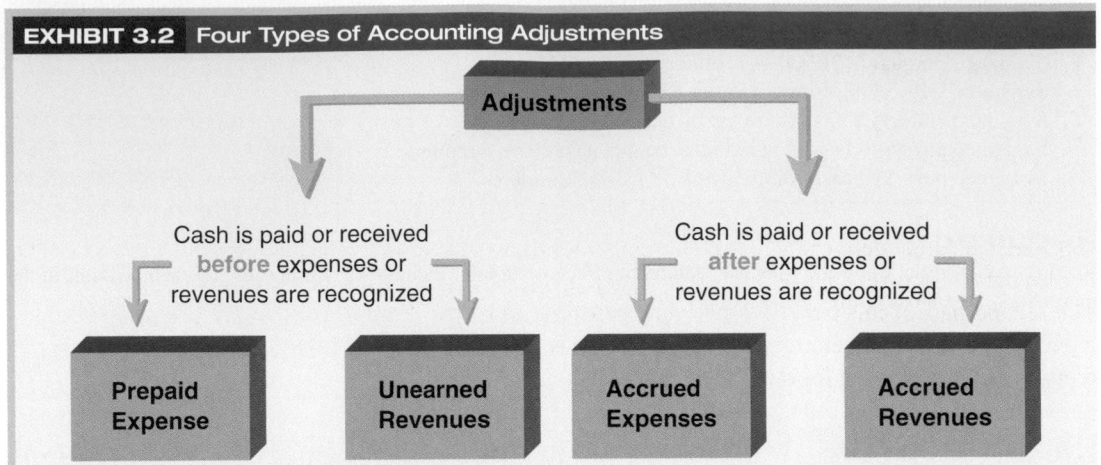

EXHIBIT 3.2 Four Types of Accounting Adjustments

The remainder of this section illustrates how Apple's financial statements would reflect each of these four types of adjustments.

Prepaid Expenses (Assets)

Assume that Apple pays $200 to purchase time on MTV for future iPod ads. Apple's cash account decreases by $200. Should the $200 advertising cost be recorded as an expense when Apple pays MTV, when MTV airs the ads, or at some other point? Under accrual accounting, Apple must record an expense when it is incurred. That means Apple should expense the cost of the ads when MTV airs them. When Apple pays for the advertisement, it records an asset; Apple "owns" TV time that will presumably provide future benefits when the ads air. In the interim, the cost of the ads is an asset on the balance sheet. Apple's financial statement effects template follows for this transaction. There is a decrease in cash and an increase in the advertising asset, titled prepaid advertising, when the ad time is paid for. At period-end, $50 of advertisements had aired. At that point, Apple must record an accounting adjustment to reduce the prepaid advertising account by $50 and transfer the cost to the income statement as advertising expense.

		Balance Sheet					Income Statement		
Transaction	Cash Asset	+ Noncash Assets	= Liabil- ities	+ Contrib. Capital	+ Earned Capital		Rev- enues	– Expen- ses	= Net Income
Pay $200 cash in advance for ad time	−200 Cash	+200 Prepaid Advertising =					–		=
Record $50 cost of ad air time		−50 Prepaid Advertising =			−50 Retained Earnings			+50 – Advertising = Expense	−50

Left margin T-accounts:
PPDA 200 / Cash 200
PPDA 200 | Cash 200
AE 50 / PPDA 50
AE 50 | PPDA 50

Unearned Revenues (Liabilities)

Assume that Apple receives $400 cash from a customer as advance payment on a multi-unit iPod sale to be delivered next month. Apple must record cash received on its balance sheet, but cannot recognize revenue from the order until earned, which is generally when iPods are delivered to the customer. Until then, Apple must recognize a liability called unearned or deferred revenue that represents Apple's obligation to fulfill the order at some future point. The financial statement effects template for this transaction follows.

	Balance Sheet						Income Statement		
Transaction	Cash Asset	+ Noncash Assets	= Liabil- ities	+ Contrib. Capital	+ Earned Capital		Rev- enues	− Expen- ses	= Net Income
Receive $400 cash in advance for iPod sale	+400 Cash		= +400 Unearned Revenue					−	=

Cash 400
UR 400
Cash
400 |
UR
| 400

Assume that Apple delivers the iPods a month later (but still within the fiscal quarter). Apple must recognize the $400 as revenue at delivery because it is now earned. Thus, net income increases by $400. The second part of this transaction is to record the cost of the iPods sold. Assuming the cost is $150, Apple reduces iPod inventory by $150 and records cost of goods sold by the same amount. These effects are reflected in the following template.

	Balance Sheet						Income Statement		
Transaction	Cash Asset	+ Noncash Assets	= Liabil- ities	+ Contrib. Capital	+ Earned Capital		Rev- enues	− Expen- ses	= Net Income
Deliver $400 of iPods paid in advance			= −400 Unearned Revenues		+400 Retained Earnings		+400 Sales	−	= +400
Record $150 cost of $400 iPod sale		−150 Inventory	=		−150 Retained Earnings			− +150 Cost of Goods Sold	= −150

UR 400
Sales 400
UR
400 |
Sales
| 400
COGS 150
INV 150
COGS
150 |
INV
| 150

Accrued Expenses (Liabilities)

Assume that Apple's sales staff earns $100 of sales commissions this period that will not be paid until next period. The sales staff earned the wages as they made the sales. However, because Apple pays its employees twice a month, the related cash payment will not occur until the next pay period. Should Apple record the wages earned by its employees as an expense even though payment has not yet been made? The answer is yes. The expense recognition principle requires Apple to recognize wages expense when it is *incurred*, even if not paid in cash. It must record wages expense incurred as a liability (wages payable). In the next period, when Apple pays the wages, it reduces both cash and wages payable. Net income is not affected by the cash payment; instead, net income decreased in the previous period when Apple accrued the wage expense.

	Balance Sheet						Income Statement		
Transaction	Cash Asset	+ Noncash Assets	= Liabil- ities	+ Contrib. Capital	+ Earned Capital		Rev- enues	− Expen- ses	= Net Income
Current pe- riod: Incur $100 of wages not yet paid			= +100 Wages Payable		−100 Retained Earnings			− +100 Wages Expense	= −100
Next period: Pay $100 cash for accrued wages	−100 Cash		= −100 Wages Payable					−	=

WE 100
WP 100
WE
100 |
WP
| 100
WP 100
Cash 100
WP
100 |
Cash
| 100

As another example of accrued expenses, assume that Apple rents office space and that it owes $25 in rent at period-end. Apple has incurred rent expense in the current period and that expense must be recorded this period. Failing to make this adjustment would mean that Apple's liabilities (rent payable) would be understated and its income would be overstated. The entry to record the accrual of rent expense for office space follows.

	Balance Sheet					Income Statement		
Transaction	Cash Asset	+ Noncash Assets	= Liabil- ities	+ Contrib. Capital	+ Earned Capital	Rev- enues	− Expen- ses	= Net Income
Incur $25 of rent not yet paid		=	+25 Rent Payable		−25 Retained Earnings		− +25 Rent Expense	= −25

RNTE 25
 RNTP   25
    RNTE
 25 |
    RNTP
       | 25

Accrued Revenues (Assets)

Assume that Apple delivers iPods to a customer in Boston who will pay next quarter. The sales price for those units is $500 and the cost is $400. Apple has completed its revenue earning process with this sale and must accrue revenue from the Boston customer even though Apple received no cash. Like all sales transactions, Apple must record two parts, the sales revenue and the cost of sales. The financial effects template for this two-part transaction follows.

	Balance Sheet					Income Statement		
Transaction	Cash Asset	+ Noncash Assets	= Liabil- ities	+ Contrib. Capital	+ Earned Capital	Rev- enues	− Expen- ses	= Net Income
Sell $500 of iPods on credit		+500 Accounts Receivable =			+500 Retained Earnings	+500 Sales	−	= +500
Record $400 cost of $500 iPod sale		−400 Inventory =			−400 Retained Earnings		− +400 Cost of Goods Sold	= −400

AR   500
 Sales   500
    AR
 500 |
    Sales
       | 500

COGS   400
 INV   400
    COGS
 400 |
    INV
       | 400

Summary of Accounting Adjustments

Adjustments are an important part of the accounting process and are crucial to accurate and informative financial accounting. It is through the accruals process that managers communicate information about future cash flows. For example, from accrual information, we know that Apple paid for a resource (inventories) that it has not yet sold. We know that suppliers have money owed to them (accounts payable) but Apple won't pay them until a future period. We know that revenues have been earned but cash is not yet received (accounts receivable). Those accruals tell us about Apple's past performance and, perhaps more importantly, about Apple's future cash flows. When used properly, accruals convey information about the past and the future that is useful in our evaluation of company financial performance and condition. Thus, we can use accrual information to more precisely value companies' equity and debt securities.

Not all managers are honest; some misuse accounting accruals to improperly recognize revenues and expenses. Abuses include accruing revenue before it is earned; and accruing expenses in the wrong period or in the wrong amount. These actions are fraudulent as they deliberately overstate or understate revenues and expenses and, thus, reported net income is incorrect. Safeguards against this type of managerial behavior include corporate governance systems (internal controls, accounting policies and procedures, routine scrutiny of accounting reports, and audit committees) and external checks and balances (independent auditors, regulatory bodies, and the court system). Collectively, these safeguards aim to protect interests of companies' internal and external stakeholders. When managers abuse accounting systems, tough and swift sanctions remind others that corporate malfeasance is unacceptable. Videos of police officers leading corporate executives to jail in handcuffs (the infamous "perp walk") send that message.

RESEARCH INSIGHT   **Accruals: Good or Bad?**

Researchers use accounting accruals to study the effects of earnings management on financial accounting. Earnings management is broadly defined as the use of accounting discretion to distort reported earnings. Managers have incentives to manage earnings in many situations. For example, managers have tendencies to accelerate revenue recognition to increase stock prices prior to equity offerings. In contrast, other research shows that managers decelerate revenue recognition to depress stock prices prior to a management buyout (where management repurchases common stock and takes the company "private"). Research also shows that managers use discretion when reporting special items to either meet or beat analysts' forecasts of earnings and/or to avoid reporting a loss. Not all earnings management occurs for opportunistic reasons. Research shows that managers use accruals to communicate private information about future profitability to outsiders. For example, management might signal future profitability through use of income-decreasing accruals to show investors that it can afford to apply conservative accounting. This "signaling" through accruals is found to precede stock splits and dividend increases. In sum, we must look at reported earnings in conjunction with other earnings quality signals (such as levels of disclosure, degree of corporate governance, and industry performance) to interpret information in accruals.

Trial Balance Preparation and Use

After Apple records all of its transactions, it must prepare financial statements so it can assess its financial performance and condition for the quarter. The following template shows a summary of Apple's transactions thus far.

LO3 Explain and construct the trial balance.

The first step in preparing financial statements is to prepare a **trial balance**, which is a listing of all accounts and their balances at a point in time. Its purpose is to prove the mathematical equality of debits and credits, provide a useful tool to uncover any accounting errors, and help prepare the financial statements. To prepare a trial balance we compile a listing of accounts and their balances, we determine whether that balance is a debit or credit, and then we check to ensure that the total of all debit balances equals the total of all credit balances. (If those totals do not agree, then an accounting error has occurred that must be identified and corrected.) The accounting adjustments at period-end, discussed earlier in this module, are set in dark green font.

Margin T-account entries (left column):

```
Cash    300
   CS       300
     Cash
   300 |
      CS
        | 300

INV    2,000
   AP      2,000
     INV
 2,000 |
      AP
        | 2,000

AR     700
   Sales    700
     AR
   700 |
     Sales
        | 700

COGS   600
   INV      600
     COGS
   600 |
      INV
        | 600

DIV     50
   Cash      50
     DIV
    50 |
     Cash
        | 50

PPDA   200
   Cash     200
     PPDA
   200 |
     Cash
        | 200

AE      50
   PPDA      50
     AE
    50 |
     PPDA
        | 50

Cash   400
   UR       400
     Cash
   400 |
      UR
        | 400

UR     400
   Sales    400
     UR
   400 |
     Sales
        | 400

COGS   150
   INV      150
     COGS
   150 |
      INV
        | 150

WE     100
   WP       100
     WE
   100 |
      WP
        | 100

RNTE    25
   RNTP      25
     RNTE
    25 |
     RNTP
        | 25

AR     500
   Sales    500
     AR
   500 |
     Sales
        | 500

COGS   400
   INV      400
     COGS
   400 |
      INV
        | 400
```

	Balance Sheet									Income Statement				
Transaction	Cash Asset	+	Noncash Assets	=	Liabilities	+	Contrib. Capital	+	Earned Capital	Revenues	−	Expenses	=	Net Income
Issue stock for $300 cash	+300 Cash			=			+300 Common Stock				−		=	
Purchase $2,000 of iPods on credit			+2,000 Inventory	=	+2,000 Accounts Payable						−		=	
Sell $700 of iPods on credit			+700 Accounts Receivable	=					+700 Retained Earnings	+700 Sales	−		=	+700
Record $600 cost of $700 iPod sale			−600 Inventory	=					−600 Retained Earnings		−	+600 Cost of Goods Sold	=	−600
Pay $50 cash for dividends	−50 Cash			=					−50 Dividends		−		=	
Pay $200 cash in advance for ad time	−200 Cash		+200 Prepaid Advertising	=							−		=	
Record $50 cost of ad air time			−50 Prepaid Advertising	=					−50 Retained Earnings		−	+50 Advertising Expense	=	−50
Receive $400 cash in advance for iPod sale	+400 Cash			=	+400 Unearned Revenue						−		=	
Deliver $400 of iPods paid in advance				=	−400 Unearned Revenue				+400 Retained Earnings	+400 Sales	−		=	+400
Record $150 cost of $400 iPod sale			−150 Inventory	=					−150 Retained Earnings		−	+150 Cost of Goods Sold	=	−150
Incur $100 of wages not yet paid				=	+100 Wages Payable				−100 Retained Earnings		−	+100 Wages Expense	=	−100
Incur $25 of rent not yet paid				=	+25 Rent Payable				−25 Retained Earnings		−	+25 Rent Expense	=	−25
Sell $500 of iPods on credit			+500 Accounts Receivable	=					+500 Retained Earnings	+500 Sales	−		=	+500
Record $400 cost of $500 iPod sale			−400 Inventory	=					−400 Retained Earnings		−	+400 Cost of Goods Sold	=	−400
Total	450	+	2,200	=	2,125	+	300	+	225	1,600	−	1,325	=	275

Entries for transactions involving accounting adjustments are set in dark green font.

The trial balance for Apple, which we assume to be as of December 31, 2012, follows.

APPLE Trial Balance December 31, 2012	Debit	Credit
Cash.	$ 450	
Accounts receivable.	1,200	
Inventory.	850	
Prepaid advertising.	150	
Accounts payable.		$2,000
Wages payable.		100
Rent payable		25
Unearned revenues		0
Common stock.		300
Dividends	50	
Sales.		1,600
Cost of goods sold.	1,150	
Wages expense	100	
Advertising expense.	50	
Rent expense	25	
Totals	$4,025	$4,025

The trial balance amounts consist of the ending balance for each of the accounts. For the Apple illustration, we total all transactions for each account listed in the template. To illustrate, cash has an ending balance of $450 ($300 − $50 − $200 + $400). Also, because cash is an asset (which is on the left-hand side of the balance sheet), it normally has a debit balance (which is on the left-hand side of the T-accounts). We can confirm the ending cash debit balance by totalling each of the cash T-account entries. Liabilities and equity accounts normally have credit balances (because they are on the right-hand side of the balance sheet), and we can confirm these ending credit balances by referring to individual account balances in the template. (See that Apple's trial balance includes all of the income statement accounts as well as the dividend account, but it does not include the retained earnings account from the financial statement effects template. This is because the template updates retained earnings immediately for each transaction. If we did include both the income statement accounts *and* retained earnings, we would double count all income statement transactions. Most companies' accounting systems do not update retained earnings immediately, which means the retained earnings balance [on the trial balance] is the beginning balance, which for our Apple example is zero.)

The trial balance shows total debits equal $4,025, which equals total credits. Accordingly, we know that all of the template transactions balance. We do not know, however, that all required journal entries have been properly included, or if Apple recorded entries that it should not have.

Precisely speaking, the trial balance above is an **adjusted trial balance**, prepared after all accounting adjustments have been recorded. In practice, we will also encounter an **unadjusted trial balance**, which is a trial balance prepared *before* the accounting adjustments are recorded. For the Apple example here, we show the following spreadsheet that contains the unadjusted and adjusted trial balances, along with middle columns containing the accounting adjustments. Remember that *financial statements are prepared from the adjusted trial balance*.

	APPLE Trial Balances December 31, 2012					
	Unadjusted		Adjustments		Adjusted	
	Debit	Credit	Debit	Credit	Debit	Credit
Cash....................................	$ 450				$ 450	
Accounts receivable......................	700		$ 500		1,200	
Inventory...............................	1,250			$ 400	850	
Prepaid advertising......................	200			50	150	
Accounts payable........................		$2,000				$2,000
Wages payable..........................		0		100		100
Rent payable		0		25		25
Unearned revenues		0				0
Common stock..........................		300				300
Dividends	50				50	
Sales..................................		1,100		500		1,600
Cost of goods sold......................	750		400		1,150	
Wages expense	0		100		100	
Advertising expense.....................	0		50		50	
Rent expense...........................	0		25		25	
Totals	$3,400	$3,400	$1,075	$1,075	$4,025	$4,025

MID-MODULE REVIEW 2

Refer to the transactions in Mid-Module Review 1. Assume that Symantec Corporation has the following two additional transactions (*a* and *b*) and four accounting adjustments (1 through 4).

a. Symantec pays $100 cash for current and future periods' rent of VoIP software.
b. Symantec receives $500 cash in advance from a client for consulting services.

1. As of period-end, Symantec had incurred rent expense of $30; $70 of the prepayment remains for future periods.
2. As of period-end, Symantec had earned $80 of the $500 paid in advance for consulting services.
3. Symantec employees earn $40 in wages that will not be paid until the next period.
4. Symantec provides $150 of services revenue but has not yet billed the client.

Required

Record each of the two accounting transactions and four adjustments using the financial statement effects template. Also record the journal entry for each in the margin and post each entry to T-accounts. Prepare a trial balance spreadsheet that contains columns for the unadjusted and adjusted trial balances and for the accounting adjustments. The unadjusted trial balance should reflect those transactions for Symantec from Mid-Module Review 1 and the two transactions *a* and *b* above.

The solution is on page 3-36.

FINANCIAL STATEMENT PREPARATION

LO4 Construct financial statements from the trial balance.

Financial statement preparation involves working with the accounts in the adjusted trial balance to properly report them in financial statements. There is an order to financial statement preparation. First, a company prepares its income statement using the income statement accounts. It then uses the net income number and dividend information to update the retained earnings account. Second, it prepares the balance sheet using the updated retained earnings account along with the remaining balance sheet accounts from the trial balance. Third, it prepares the statement of stockholders' equity. Fourth, it prepares the statement of cash flows using information from the cash account (and other sources).

Income Statement

Apple's income statement follows. Apple's trial balance reveals four income statement accounts. Those income statement accounts are called *temporary accounts* because they begin each accounting period with a zero balance. Apple's income statement also includes a line for gross profit because that subtotal is important to evaluate manufacturers' performance and profitability. Income for this quarterly period is $275 (we ignore taxes in this illustration).

APPLE Income Statement For Quarter Ended December 31, 2012	
Sales.	$1,600
Cost of goods sold.	1,150
Gross profit.	450
Wages expense	100
Advertising expense.	50
Rent expense	25
Net income.	$ 275

Retained Earnings Computation

Apple updates its retained earnings balance at period-end using income from the income statement and the dividend information from its trial balance. (For simplicity, we assume retained earnings is zero at the beginning of this period). This computation follows.

APPLE Retained Earnings Computation For Quarter Ended December 31, 2012	
Retained earnings, beginning of period	$ 0
Add: Net income (loss).	275
Deduct: Dividends.	50
Retained earnings, end of period.	$225

Balance Sheet

Once Apple computes the ending balance in retained earnings, it can prepare its balance sheet, which follows. Balance sheet accounts are called *permanent accounts* because their respective balances carry over from one period to the next. For example, the cash balance at the end of the current accounting period (ended December 31, 2012) is $450, which will be the balance at the beginning of the next accounting period (beginning January 1, 2013).

APPLE Balance Sheet December 31, 2012	
Assets	
Cash.	$ 450
Accounts receivable.	1,200
Inventory.	850
Prepaid advertising.	150
Total assets.	$2,650
Liabilities and Stockholders' Equity	
Liabilities	
Accounts payable.	$2,000
Wages payable.	100
Rent payable	25
Total liabilities	2,125
Stockholders' equity	
Common stock.	300
Retained earnings	225
Total stockholders' equity	525
Total liabilities and stockholders' equity.	$2,650

Statement of Stockholders' Equity

Apple uses the information pertaining to its contributed capital and earned capital categories to prepare the statement of stockholders' equity, as follows.

APPLE Statement of Stockholders' Equity For Quarter Ended December 31, 2012	Contributed Capital	Earned Capital	Total Stockholders' Equity
Beginning balance	$ 0	$ 0	$ 0
Stock issuance.	300		300
Net income (loss)		275	275
Dividends		(50)	(50)
Ending balance.	$300	$225	$525

Statement of Cash Flows

The statement of cash flows summarizes the cash-based transactions for the period and reports the sources and uses of cash. Each cash transaction represents an operating, investing, or financing activity.

Direct Method Presentation

To prepare the statement, Apple uses the Cash column of the financial statement effects template, see above. The following cash flow statement for Apple is based on the **direct method** for reporting operating cash flows. During the current period, Apple's cash increased by $450. Its increase in cash consists of a $200 net cash inflow from operating activities plus a $250 net cash inflow from financing activities. There were no investing activities during this period.

APPLE Statement of Cash Flows (Direct Method) For Quarter Ended December 31, 2012	
Operating activities	
Receipts from sales contracts	$400
Payments for advertising	(200)
Net cash flows from operating activities	200
Investing activities	
Net cash flows from investing activities.	0
Financing activities	
Issuance of common stock	300
Payment of cash dividends	(50)
Net cash flows from financing activities.	250
Net change in cash	450
Cash, beginning of period	0
Cash, end of period	$450

In practice, preparing a statement of cash flows is more complicated. Companies can have millions of transactions in the cash account and the task of classifying each transaction as operating, investing or financing would be costly and time-consuming. Instead, companies prepare the statement of cash flows using the current income statement and the balance sheets for the current and prior periods. The basic approach is to adjust net income to arrive at net cash flows from operating activities (the so-called *indirect method*) and then review changes in balance sheet accounts (by comparing the opening and ending balances) to arrive at net cash flows from investing and financing activities.

Indirect Method Presentation

There are two methods to display net cash flows from operating activities: the direct method and the indirect method. Both methods report the same net operating cash flow, the only difference is in presentation. Companies can choose which method to follow. Apple's simplified statement of cash flows above, is an example of the direct method. However, the **indirect method** is, by far, the most widely used method in practice today (over 98% of public companies use it). The indirect method computes operating cash flows *indirectly* by adjusting net income using the following format.

		Add (+) or Subtract (−) from Net Income
Adjustments for noncash revenues, expenses, gains and losses	Net income......................................	$ #
	Add: depreciation expense	+
	Adjust for changes in current operating assets	
	Subtract increases in current operating assets	−
	Add decreases in current operating assets	+
Adjustments for changes in noncash current operating assets and current operating liabilities	Adjust for changes in current operating liabilities	
	Add increases in current operating liabilities	+
	Subtract decreases in current operating liabilities	−
	Net cash flow from operating activities	$ #

Net income is first adjusted for noncash expenses such as depreciation and amortization, and is then adjusted for changes during the year in current operating assets and current operating liabilities to yield cash flow from operating activities, or *cash profit*. The depreciation adjustment merely zeros out (undoes the effect of) depreciation expense, a noncash expense, which is deducted in computing net income. The following table provides brief explanations of adjustments for receivables, inventories, and payables and accruals.

	Change in account balance . . .	Means that . . .	Which requires this adjustment to net income to yield cash profit . . .
Receivables	Increase	Sales and net income increase, but cash is not yet received	Deduct increase in receivables from net income
	Decrease	More cash is received than is reported in sales and net income	Add decrease in receivables to net income
Inventories	Increase	Cash is paid for inventories that are not yet reflected in cost of goods sold	Deduct increase in inventories from net income
	Decrease	Cost of goods sold includes inventory costs that were paid for in a prior period	Add decrease in inventories to net income
Payables and accruals	Increase	More goods and services are acquired on credit, delaying cash payment	Add increase in payables and accruals to net income
	Decrease	More cash is paid than that reflected in cost of goods sold or operating expenses	Deduct decrease in payables and accruals from net income

It is also helpful to use the following decision guide, involving changes in assets, liabilities, and equity, to understand increases and decreases in cash flows.

	Cash flow increases from	Cash flow decreases from
Assets......................	Account decreases	Account increases
Liabilities and equity...........	Account increases	Account decreases

Using this decision guide, we can determine the cash flow effects of the income statement and balance sheet information and categorize them into the following table for our Apple illustration.

Financial Element	Change	Source or Use	Cash Flow Effect	Classification on SCF
Current assets				
Accounts receivable	+ $1,200	Use	$(1,200)	Operating
Inventory.	+ 850	Use	(850)	Operating
Prepaid advertising.	+ 150	Use	(150)	Operating
Noncurrent assets				
PPE.	0		0	Investing
Accumulated depreciation . . .		Neither	0*	Operating
Current liabilities				
Accounts payable.	+ 2,000	Source	2,000	Operating
Wages payable.	+ 100	Source	100	Operating
Rent payable.	+ 25	Source	25	Operating
Long-term liabilities	0		0	Financing
Stockholders' equity				
Common stock.	+ 300	Source	300	Financing
Retained earnings				
Net income	+ 275	Source	275	Operating
Dividends	+ 50	Use	(50)	Financing
Total (net cash flow)			$ 450	

*Depreciation expense for the period, if present, is added to net income in computing cash flows from operating activities.

Increases in the three current operating assets reflect a use of cash, and are subtracted in the operating section of the statement of cash flows. Increases in noncurrent PPE assets also reflect a use of cash, which are classified as an investing activity. An increase in accumulated depreciation reflects the recording of depreciation expense in the income statement, which is a noncash expense that must be zeroed out (with an addition to net income) to yield cash profit. Increases in the three current operating liabilities reflect sources of cash, and are recorded as positive amounts in the statement of cash flows.

APPLE
Statement of Cash Flows (Indirect Method)
For Quarter Ended December 31, 2012

Operating activities	
Net income.	$ 275
Depreciation and other noncash expenses	0
Increase in accounts receivable	(1,200)
Increase in inventories	(850)
Increase in prepaid advertising.	(150)
Increase in accounts payable.	2,000
Increase in wages payable	100
Increase in rent payable	25
Net cash flows from operating activities	200
Investing activities	
Net cash flows from investing activities.	0
Financing activities	
Issuance of common stock	300
Payment of cash dividends	(50)
Net cash flows from financing activities.	250
Net change in cash.	450
Cash, beginning of period	0
Cash, end of period	$ 450

Issuance of common stock is a source of cash, and the payment of dividends to shareholders is a use of cash. Both of these are reflected in the financing section of the statement of cash flows. The financing section also reflects any increases or decreases in borrowings as sources or uses, respectively. The increase in retained earnings, resulting from net income, is a source of cash, but it is reported as an operating activity. (Components of the change in retained earnings, net income less dividends, are reflected in the statement of cash flows and, consequently, the change in retained earnings is already recognized.)

The sum of these elements yields a net increase in cash of $450. This is the same result we obtained earlier using the direct method. To reiterate, the indirect method represents a different presentation of the operating section only of the statement of cash flows. The investing and financing sections are identical under the direct and indirect approaches. Reporting these elements by operating, investing and financing activities yields the familiar form of the statement of cash flows previously shown.

Closing Process

The **closing process** refers to "zeroing out" the temporary accounts by transferring their ending balances to retained earnings. Recall, income statement accounts—revenues and expenses—and the dividend account are temporary accounts because their balances are zero at the end of each accounting period; balance sheet accounts carry over from period to period and are called permanent accounts. The closing process is typically carried out via a series of journal entries that successively zero out each revenue and expense account, and the dividend account, transferring those balances to retained earnings. The result is that all income statement accounts and the dividend account begin the next period with zero balances. The balance sheet accounts do not need to be similarly adjusted because their balances carry over from period to period. Recall the scoreboard analogy.

LO5 Describe the closing process.

Our financial statement effects template makes the closing process unnecessary because the template updates retained earnings with each revenue and expense entry. The arrow that runs from net income to retained earnings (part of earned capital) highlights the continual updating. To illustrate, recall the following entries that reflect Apple's initial sale of iPods on credit.

	Balance Sheet						Income Statement			
Transaction	**Cash Asset**	+ **Noncash Assets**	= **Liabil- ities**	+ **Contrib. Capital**	+ **Earned Capital**		**Rev- enues**	− **Expen- ses**	= **Net Income**	
Sell $700 of iPods on credit		+700 Accounts Receivable =			+700 Retained Earnings		+700 Sales	−	= +700	
Record $600 cost of $700 iPod sale		−600 Inventory =			−600 Retained Earnings			− +600 Cost of Goods Sold	= −600	

Sales of $700 increase net income by $700, which the template immediately transfers to retained earnings. Likewise, cost of goods sold reduces net income by $600, and this reduction is immediately carried to retained earnings. Consequently, the financial statement effects template always reports an updated retained earnings, making the closing process unnecessary.

It is important to distinguish our financial statement effects template from companies' accounting systems. The financial statement effects template and T-accounts are pedagogical tools that represent transactions' effects on the four financial statements. The template is highly stylized but its simplicity is instructive. In practice, managers use journal entries to record transactions and adjustments. The template captures these in summarized fashion. However, in practice, income statement transactions are not automatically transferred to retained earnings and retained earnings is not continuously updated. All companies perform the closing process—someone or some program must transfer the temporary account balances to retained earnings. Thus, it is important to understand the closing process and why companies "close" the books each period. We describe the mechanical details of the closing process in Appendix 3A.

The entire accounting process, from analysis of basic transactions to financial statement preparation to the closing process, is called the **accounting cycle**. As we discuss at the outset of this module and portray graphically in Exhibit 3.1, there are four basic processes in the accounting cycle.

First, companies analyze transactions and prepare (and post) entries. Second, companies prepare (and post) accounting adjustments. Third, financial statements are prepared from an adjusted trial balance. Fourth, companies perform the closing process. The analysis and posting of transactions is done regularly during each accounting period. However, the preparation of accounting adjustments and financial statements is only done at the end of an accounting period. At this point, we have explained and illustrated all aspects of the accounting cycle.

MANAGERIAL DECISION   **You Are the CFO**

Assume that you learn of the leakage of hazardous waste from your company's factory. It is estimated that cleanup could cost $10 million. Part 1: What effect will recording this cost have on your company's balance sheet and its income statement? Part 2: Accounting rules require you to record this cost if it is both probable and can be reliably estimated. Although the cleanup is relatively certain, the cost is a guess at this point. Consequently, you have some discretion whether to record it. Discuss the parties that are likely affected by your decision on whether or not to record the liability and related expense, and the ethical issues involved. [Answer 3-23]

GLOBAL ACCOUNTING

The way that accounting data are gathered and recorded does not differ across accounting standards. Thus, the accounting cycle in Exhibit 3.1 applies in countries using IFRS in the same manner as in the U.S. The difference is that companies create information systems that conform to the specific accounting rules in that country. For example, the rules for recording research and development (R&D) costs are different in the U.S. vis-à-vis Germany. Thus, the U.S. and the German company would each tailor their accounting systems to properly record R&D costs so that each company's financial statements comply with their respective countries' accounting standards. The accounting cycle of each company still involves transactions and adjustments and a closing process. The result is that identical R&D expenditures are classified differently and the resulting financial statements diverge.

    Large multinational companies often have subsidiaries in different countries. If a U.S. company has a foreign subsidiary, the foreign laws often require a domestic set of financial statements for tax, regulatory, banking, or other purposes. For example, Apple's 2011 10-K reports that it has two foreign subsidiaries, Apple Sales International and Apple Operations International, both incorporated in Ireland where IFRS is used. Both subsidiaries must prepare IFRS financial statements to file with the Irish Revenue Commission (the Irish equivalent of the IRS). During the closing process of the accounting cycle, Apple Inc. (the U.S. parent) must consolidate the two Irish subsidiaries, which means that all assets and liabilities of the two Irish subsidiaries are included on Apple Inc.'s balance sheet. Similarly, all of the revenues and expenses of the two Irish subsidiaries are included on Apple Inc.'s income statement. It would not be appropriate for a simple summing of accounts because of differences between IFRS and U.S. GAAP. Instead, Apple Inc. must convert IFRS financial statements to U.S. GAAP equivalent (as well as convert euros to U.S. dollars). To accomplish this, Apple Inc. might keep two sets of accounting records for subsidiaries, one set in GAAP and the other in IFRS. This is not as complicated as it might seem. Companies like Apple use sophisticated computer accounting systems and enterprise resource planning (ERP) systems that are capable of supporting multiple sets of accounting standards.

MODULE-END REVIEW

Refer to the transactions in Mid-Module Reviews 1 and 2. From those transactions, assume that Symantec Corporation prepares the following adjusted trial balance. Also assume its transactions are for the quarter ended December 31, 2012.

SYMANTEC Adjusted Trial Balance December 31, 2012		
	Debit	Credit
Cash.	$3,280	
Accounts receivable.	350	
Inventory.	700	
Prepaid rent	70	
Accounts payable.		$ 600
Wages payable.		40
Unearned revenues		420
Common stock.		3,000
Dividends	20	
Sales.		730
Cost of goods sold.	300	
Wages expense	40	
Rent expense	30	
Totals	$4,790	$4,790

Required

Prepare Symantec's income statement (including a separate retained earnings computation), statement of stockholders' equity, balance sheet, and statement of cash flows.

The solution is on page 3-37.

APPENDIX 3A: Closing Process Using Journal Entries

The idea of the closing process is to zero out all temporary accounts—all the income statement accounts and any dividend account. The balance in each temporary account is transferred to retained earnings leaving the temporary accounts with zero balances. That way, the temporary accounts are ready to capture transaction data for the next period. The closing process brings the retained earnings account up to date so that it accurately reflects the current period's income statement activity and dividends so that the balance sheet can be prepared. To illustrate, let's return to Apple's income statement.

Apple Income Statement For Quarter Ended December 31, 2012	
Sales.	$1,600
Cost of goods sold.	1,150
Gross profit.	450
Wages expense	100
Advertising expense.	50
Rent expense	25
Net income.	$ 275

The closing process transfers the ending balances for each of these income statement accounts, to retained earnings. The dividend account is a temporary account and therefore, it also must be closed to retained earnings. The journal entries, and the related T-accounts, follow for this three-step process.

1. Close all revenue accounts.

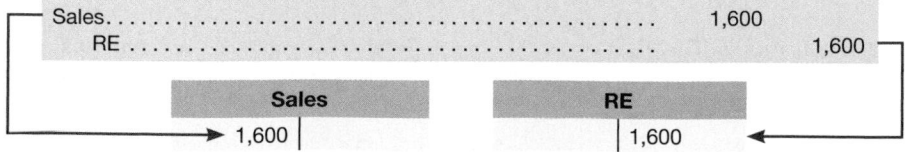

2. Close all expense accounts.

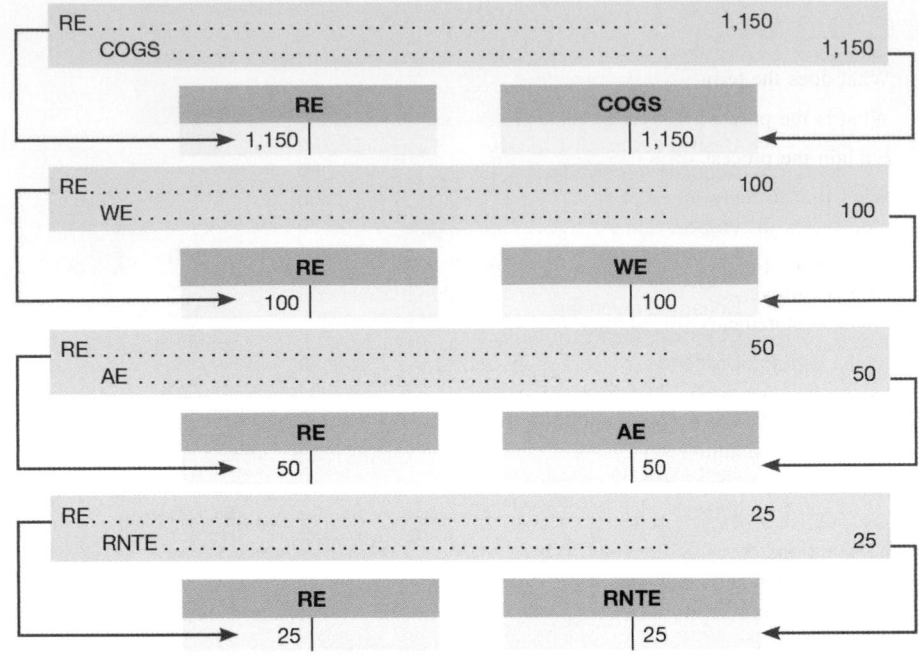

3. Close any dividend accounts.

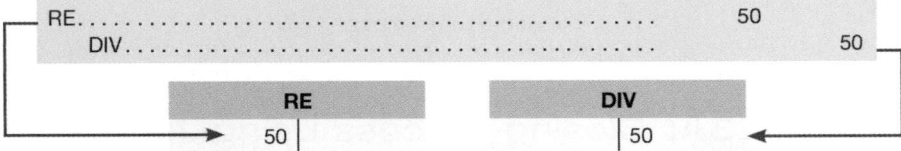

Apple must close one revenue account, four expense accounts, and a dividend account to retained earnings at the end of the period. The first closing entry transfers the $1,600 balance in the sales account to retained earnings. The closing entry debits sales for $1,600 (because the sales account has a $1,600 credit balance at period-end) and credits retained earnings. The second closing entry closes cost of goods sold ($1,150), wages expense ($100), advertising expense ($50), and rent expense ($25). The entry credits each of the expense accounts because their ending balances are debit balances. Third, the $50 dividend account balance is transferred to retained earnings. All the temporary accounts are now *closed*.

Retained earnings, which began the period with a zero balance, now reports a balance of $225, which equals net income for the period less the dividends paid to shareholders. This is the balance Apple reports in the stockholders' equity section of its balance sheet. Further, all of the income statement accounts (sales, cost of goods sold, wages expense, advertising expense, and rent expense) and the dividend account now show zero balances to begin the next period.

GUIDANCE ANSWERS

MANAGERIAL DECISION   You Are the CFO

Part 1: Liabilities will increase by $10 million for the estimated amount of the cleanup, and an expense in that amount will be recognized in the income statement, thus reducing both income and retained earnings (equity) by $10 million. Part 2: Stakeholders affected by recognition decisions of this type are often much broader than first realized. Management is directly involved in the decision. Recording this cost can affect the market value of the company, its relations with lenders and suppliers, its auditors, and many other stakeholders. Further, if recording this cost is the right accounting decision, failure to do so can foster unethical behavior throughout the company, thus affecting additional company employees.

Superscript ^A denotes assignments based on Appendix 3A.

DISCUSSION QUESTIONS

Q3-1. What does the term *fiscal year* mean?

Q3-2. What is the purpose of a general journal?

Q3-3. Explain the process of posting.

Q3-4. What four different types of adjustments are frequently necessary before financial statements are prepared at the end of an accounting period? Give at least one example of each type.

Q3-5. On January 1, Prepaid Insurance was debited for $1,872 related to the cost of a two-year premium, with coverage beginning immediately. How should this account be adjusted on January 31 before financial statements are prepared for the current month?

Q3-6. At the beginning of January, the first month of the accounting year, the Supplies account (asset) had a debit balance of $825. During January, purchases of $260 worth of supplies were debited to the account. At the end of January, $630 of supplies were still available. How should this account be adjusted? If no adjustment is made, describe the impact on (a) the income statement for January, and (b) the balance sheet prepared at January 31.

Q3-7. The publisher of *Accounting View*, a monthly magazine, received $9,720 cash on January 1 for new subscriptions covering the next 24 months, with service beginning immediately. (a) Use the financial statement effects template to record the receipt of the $9,720. (b) Use the template to show how the accounts should be adjusted at the end of January before financial statements are prepared for the current month.

Q3-8. Refer to Question Q3-7. Prepare journal entries for the receipt of cash and the delivery of the magazines.

Q3-9. Trombley Travel Agency pays an employee $475 in wages each Friday for the five-day work week ending on Friday. The last Friday of January falls on January 27. How should Trombley Travel Agency adjust wages expense on January 31, its fiscal year-end?

Q3-10. The Basu Company earns interest amounting to $360 per month on its investments. The company receives the interest revenue every six months, on December 31 and June 30. Monthly financial statements are prepared. Which accounts should Basu adjust on January 31?

Q3-11.^A What types of accounts are closed at the end of the accounting year? What are the three major steps in the closing process?

Assignments with the ✓ in the margin are available in an online homework system.
See the Preface of the book for details.

MINI EXERCISES

M3-12. **Assessing Financial Statement Effects of Transactions**   (LO1)
DeFond Services, a firm providing art services for advertisers, began business on June 1. The following accounts are needed to record the transactions for June: Cash; Accounts Receivable; Supplies; Office Equipment; Accounts Payable; Common Stock; Dividends; Service Fees Earned; Rent Expense; Utilities Expense; and Wages Expense. Record the following transactions for June using the financial statement effects template.

June 1   M. DeFond invested $12,000 cash to begin the business in exchange for common stock.
     2   Paid $950 cash for June rent.
     3   Purchased $6,400 of office equipment on credit.
     6   Purchased $3,800 of art materials and other supplies; the company paid $1,800 cash with the remainder due within 30 days.
   11   Billed clients $4,700 for services rendered.
   17   Collected $3,250 cash from clients on their accounts billed on June 11.
   19   Paid $3,000 cash toward the account for office equipment (see June 3).
   25   Paid $900 cash for dividends.
   30   Paid $350 cash for June utilities.
   30   Paid $2,500 cash for June wages.

M3-13. **Preparing Journal Entries and Posting** (LO1)

Refer to the information in M3-12. Prepare a journal entry for each transaction. Create a T-account for each account, and then post the journal entries to the T-accounts (use dates to reference each entry).

M3-14. **Assessing Financial Statement Effects of Transactions** (LO1)

Verrecchia Company, a cleaning services firm, began business on April 1. The company created the following accounts to record the transactions for April: Cash; Accounts Receivable; Supplies; Prepaid Van Lease; Equipment; Notes Payable; Accounts Payable; Common Stock; Dividends; Cleaning Fees Earned; Wages Expense; Advertising Expense; and Van Fuel Expense. Record the following transactions for April using the financial statement effects template.

April 1   R. Verrecchia invested $9,000 cash to begin the business in exchange for common stock.
2   Paid $2,850 cash for six months' lease on van for the business.
3   Borrowed $10,000 cash from bank and signed note payable agreeing to repay it in one year plus 10% interest.
4   Purchased $5,500 of cleaning equipment; the company paid $2,500 cash with the remainder due within 30 days.
5   Paid $4,300 cash for cleaning supplies.
7   Paid $350 cash for advertisements to run in the area newspaper during April.
21   Billed customers $3,500 for services performed.
23   Paid $3,000 cash toward the account for cleaning equipment (see April 4).
28   Collected $2,300 cash from customers on their accounts billed on April 21.
29   Paid $1,000 cash for dividends.
30   Paid $1,750 cash for April wages.
30   Paid $995 cash for gasoline used during April.

M3-15. **Preparing Journal Entries and Posting** (LO1)

Refer to the information in M3-14. Prepare a journal entry for each transaction. Create a T-account for each account, and then post the journal entries to the T-accounts (use dates to reference each entry).

M3-16. **Assessing Financial Statement Effects of Transactions and Adjustments** (LO1, 2)

Schrand Services offers janitorial services on both a contract basis and an hourly basis. On January 1, Schrand collected $20,100 cash in advance on a six-month contract for work to be performed evenly during the next six months.

a. Prepare the entry on January 1 to reflect the receipt of $20,100 cash for contract work; use the financial statement effects template.
b. Adjust the appropriate accounts on January 31 for the contract work done during January; use the financial statement effects template.
c. At January 31, a total of 30 hours of hourly rate janitor work was performed but unbilled. The billing rate is $19 per hour. Prepare the accounting adjustment needed on January 31, using the financial statement effects template. (The firm uses the account Fees Receivable to reflect revenue earned but not yet billed.)

M3-17. **Preparing Accounting Adjustments** (LO1, 2)

Refer to the information in M3-16. Prepare a journal entry for each of parts a, b, and c.

 M3-18. **Assessing Financial Statement Effects of Transactions and Adjustments** (LO2)

Selected accounts of Piotroski Properties, a real estate management firm, are shown below as of January 31, before any accounts have been adjusted.

	Debits	Credits
Prepaid Insurance	$6,660	
Supplies	1,930	
Office Equipment	5,952	
Unearned Rent Revenue		$ 5,250
Salaries Expense	3,100	
Rent Revenue		15,000

Piotroski Properties prepares monthly financial statements. Using the following information, adjust the accounts as necessary on January 31, using the financial statement effects template.

a. Prepaid insurance represents a three-year premium paid on January 1.
b. Supplies of $850 were still available on January 31.
c. Office equipment is expected to last eight years (or 96 months).

d. Earlier this month, on January 1, Piotroski collected $5,250 for six months' rent in advance from a tenant renting space for $875 per month.

e. Salaries of $490 have been earned by employees but not yet recorded as of January 31.

M3-19. Preparing Accounting Adjustments (LO2)

Refer to the information in M3-18. Prepare journal entries for each of parts *a* through *e*.

M3-20. Inferring Transactions from Financial Statements (LO1, 2)

Foot Locker, Inc., a retailer of athletic footwear and apparel, operates about 3,400 stores in the United States, Canada, Europe, Australia, and New Zealand. During its fiscal year ended in 2010, Foot Locker purchased merchandise inventory costing $3,555 ($ millions). Assume that Foot Locker makes all purchases on credit, and that its accounts payable is only used for inventory purchases. The following T-accounts reflect information contained in the company's fiscal 2009 and 2010 balance sheets ($ millions).

Foot Locker, Inc. (FL)

Inventories		Accounts Payable	
2009 Bal. 1,037		215	2009 Bal.
2010 Bal. 1,059		223	2010 Bal.

a. Use the financial statement effects template to record Foot Locker's 2010 purchases.

b. What amount did Foot Locker pay in cash to its suppliers during fiscal year 2010? Explain.

c. Use the financial statement effects template to record cost of goods sold for its fiscal year 2010.

M3-21. Preparing Journal Entries (LO1, 2)

Refer to the information in M3-20. Prepare journal entries for each of parts *a*, *b* and *c*.

M3-22. Preparing a Statement of Stockholders' Equity (LO4)

On December 31, 2011, the accounts of Leuz Architect Services showed credit balances in its Common Stock and Retained Earnings accounts of $30,000 and $18,000, respectively. The company's stock issuances for 2012 totaled $6,000, and it paid $9,700 in cash dividends. During 2012, the company had net income of $29,900. Prepare a 2012 statement of stockholders' equity for Leuz Architect Services.

M3-23.ᴬ Preparing Closing Journal Entries (LO5)

The adjusted trial balance at May 29, 2011, for General Mills includes the following selected accounts.

General Mills (GIS)

($ millions)	Debits	Credits
Net sales.		$14,880.2
Cost of goods sold.	$8,926.7	
Selling, general and administrative expense and other	3,087.8	
Interest expense, net	346.3	
Income tax expense.	721.1	
Retained earnings		8,122.4

Assume that the company has not yet closed any accounts to retained earnings. Prepare journal entries to close the temporary accounts above. Set up the needed T-accounts and post the closing entries. After these entries are posted, what is the balance of the Retained Earnings account?

M3-24. Inferring Transactions from Financial Statements (LO1, 2)

Lowe's is the second-largest home improvement retailer in the world with 1,749 stores. During its fiscal year ended in 2011, Lowe's purchased merchandise inventory at a cost of $31,735 ($ millions). Assume that all purchases were made on account and that accounts payable is only used for inventory purchases. The following T-accounts reflect information contained in the company's 2011 and 2010 balance sheets.

Lowe's Companies (LOW)

Merchandise Inventories		Accounts Payable	
2010 Bal. 8,249		4,287	2010 Bal.
2011 Bal. 8,321		4,351	2011 Bal.

a. Use the financial statement effects template to record Lowe's purchases during fiscal 2011.

b. What amount did Lowe's pay in cash to its suppliers during fiscal-year 2011? Explain.

c. Use the financial statement effects template to record cost of goods sold for its fiscal year ended in 2011.

M3-25.ᴬ Closing Journal Entries (LO5)

The adjusted trial balance as of December 31 for Hanlon Consulting contains the following selected accounts.

	Debits	Credits
Service Fees Earned		$80,300
Rent Expense	$20,800	
Salaries Expense	45,700	
Supplies Expense	5,600	
Depreciation Expense	10,200	
Retained Earnings		67,000

Prepare entries to close these accounts in journal entry form. Set up T-accounts for each account and record the adjusted trial balance amount in each account. Then, post the closing entries to the T-accounts. After these entries are posted, what is the balance of the Retained Earnings account?

EXERCISES

 E3-26. Assessing Financial Statement Effects of Adjustments (LO2)

For each of the following separate situations, prepare the necessary accounting adjustments using the financial statement effects template.

a. Unrecorded depreciation on equipment is $610.
b. The Supplies account has an unadjusted balance of $2,990. Supplies still available at the end of the period total $1,100.
c. On the date for preparing financial statements, an estimated utilities expense of $390 has been incurred, but no utility bill has yet been received or paid.
d. On the first day of the current period, rent for four periods was paid and recorded as a $2,800 debit to Prepaid Rent and a $2,800 credit to Cash.

Allstate Corp. (ALL)

e. Nine months ago, The Allstate Corporation sold a one-year policy to a customer and recorded the receipt of the premium by crediting Unearned Revenue for $624. No accounting adjustments have been prepared during the nine-month period. Allstate's annual financial statements are now being prepared.
f. At the end of the period, employee wages of $965 have been incurred but not paid or recorded.
g. At the end of the period, $300 of interest has been earned but not yet received or recorded.

E3-27. Preparing Accounting Adjustments (LO2)

Refer to the information in E3-26. Prepare journal entries for each accounting adjustment.

E3-28. Assessing Financial Statement Effects of Adjustments Across Two Periods (LO1, 2)

Engel Company closes its accounts on December 31 each year. The company works a five-day work week and pays its employees every two weeks. On December 31 Engel accrued $4,700 of salaries payable. On January 9 of the following year the company paid salaries of $12,000 cash to employees. Prepare entries using the financial statement effects template to (a) accrue the salaries payable on December 31; and (b) record the salary payment nine days later on January 9.

E3-29.ᴬ Preparing Accounting Adjustments (LO1, 2)

Refer to the information in E3-28. Prepare journal entries to accrue the salaries in December; close salaries expense for the year; and pay the salaries in January of the following year. Assume that there is no change in the pay rate during the year, and no change in the company's work force.

E3-30. Financial Analysis Using Adjusted Account Data (LO2)

Selected T-account balances for Bloomfield Company are shown below as of January 31, which reflect its accounting adjustments. The firm uses a calendar-year accounting period but prepares *monthly* accounting adjustments.

Supplies		Supplies Expense	
Jan. 31 Bal. 800		Jan. 31 Bal. 960	

Prepaid Insurance		Insurance Expense	
Jan. 31 Bal. 574		Jan. 31 Bal. 82	

Wages Payable		Wages Expense	
	Jan. 31 Bal. 500	Jan. 31 Bal. 3,200	

Truck		Accumulated Depreciation-Truck	
Jan. 31 Bal. 8,700			2,610 Bal. Jan. 31

a. If the amount in Supplies Expense represents the January 31 adjustment for the supplies used in January, and $620 worth of supplies were purchased during January, what was the January 1 beginning balance of Supplies?

b. The amount in the Insurance Expense account represents the adjustment made at January 31 for January insurance expense. If the original insurance premium was for one year, what was the amount of the premium and on what date did the insurance policy start?

c. If we assume that no beginning balance existed in either Wages Payable or Wages Expense on January 1, how much cash was paid as wages during January?

d. If the truck has a useful life of five years (or 60 months), what is the monthly amount of depreciation expense and how many months has Bloomfield owned the truck?

E3-31.   Assessing Financial Statement Effects of Adjustments   (LO2)

T. Lys began Thomas Refinishing Service on July 1. Selected accounts are shown below as of July 31, before any accounting adjustments have been made.

	Debits	Credits
Prepaid Rent	$5,700	
Prepaid Advertising	630	
Supplies	3,000	
Unearned Refinishing Fees		$ 600
Refinishing Fees Revenue		2,500

Using the following information, prepare the accounting adjustments necessary on July 31 using the financial statement effects template.

a. On July 1, the firm paid one year's rent of $5,700 in cash.

b. On July 1, $630 cash was paid to the local newspaper for an advertisement to run daily for the months of July, August, and September.

c. Supplies still available at July 31 total $1,100.

d. At July 31, refinishing services of $800 have been performed but not yet recorded or billed to customers. The firm uses the account Fees Receivable to reflect amounts due but not yet billed.

e. In early July, a customer paid $600 in advance for a refinishing project. At July 31, the project is one-half complete.

E3-32.   Preparing Accounting Adjustments and Posting   (LO2)

Refer to the information in E3-31. Prepare adjusting journal entries for each transaction. Set up T-accounts for each of the ledger accounts and post the journal entries to them.

E3-33.   Inferring Transactions from Financial Statements   (LO1)

The GAP is a global clothing retailer for men, women, children and babies. The following information   The Gap, Inc. (GPS)
is taken from the Gap's fiscal 2011 annual report.

Selected Balance Sheet Data	2011	2010
Inventories	$1,620	$1,477
Accounts Payable	1,049	1,027

a. The Gap purchased inventories totalling $8,918 million during 2011. Use the financial statement effects template to record cost of goods sold for The Gap's fiscal year ended 2011. (Assume that Accounts Payable is used only for recording purchases of inventories and all inventories are purchased on credit.)

b. What amount did the company pay to suppliers during the year? Record this with the financial statement effects template.

E3-34.   Inferring Transactions and Preparing Journal Entries   (LO1)

The GAP, Inc. (GPS)

Refer to the information in E3-33. Prepare journal entries for each transaction.

E3-35.ᴬ   Preparing Closing Journal Entries   (LO5)

The GAP, Inc. (GPS)

The adjusted trial balance of The GAP, Inc., dated January 29, 2011, contains the following selected accounts.

($ millions)	Debit	Credit
Net Sales		$14,664
Cost of Goods Sold	$8,775	
Operating Expenses.	3,921	
Interest Income, net		14
Income Tax Expense	778	
Retained Earnings (beginning of year) . . .		10,815

Prepare entries to close these accounts in journal entry form. Set up T-accounts for each of the ledger accounts and post the entries to them. After these entries are posted, what is the balance of the Retained Earnings account?

 E3-36.   Inferring Transactions from Financial Statements   (LO1, 2)

Costco Wholesale
Corporation (COST)

Costco Wholesale Corporation operates membership warehouses selling food, appliances, consumer electronics, apparel and other household goods at 582 locations across the U.S. as well as in Canada, the United Kingdom, Japan, Australia, South Korea, Taiwan, Mexico and Puerto Rico. As of its fiscal year-end 2010, Costco had approximately 60 million members. Selected fiscal-year information from the company's balance sheets follows.

Selected Balance Sheet Data ($ millions)	2010	2009
Merchandise inventories	$5,638	$5,405
Deferred membership income (liability)	869	824

a. During fiscal 2010, Costco collected $1,736 million cash for membership fees. Use the financial statement effects template to record the cash collected for membership fees.
b. Costco recorded merchandise costs (that is, cost of goods sold) of $67,995 in 2011. Record this transaction in the financial statements effects template.
c. Determine the value of merchandise that Costco purchased during fiscal-year 2011. Use the financial statement effects template to record these merchandise purchases. Assume all of Costco's purchases are on credit.

E3-37.   Inferring Transactions and Preparing Journal Entries   (LO1, 2)

Costco Wholesale
Corporation (COST)

Refer to the information in E3-36. Prepare journal entries for transactions in parts *a* through *c*.

 E3-38.ᴬ   Preparing Financial Statements and Closing Entries   (LO4, 5)

The adjusted trial balance for Beneish Corporation is as follows.

BENEISH CORPORATION Adjusted Trial Balance December 31	Debit	Credit
Cash.	$ 4,000	
Accounts receivable.	6,500	
Equipment	78,000	
Accumulated depreciation		$ 14,000
Notes payable		10,000
Common stock.		43,000
Retained earnings		20,600
Dividends	8,000	
Service fees earned		71,000
Rent expense	18,000	
Salaries expense	37,100	
Depreciation expense.	7,000	
Totals	$158,600	$158,600

a. Prepare Beneish Corporation's income statement and statement of stockholders' equity for year-end December 31, and its balance sheet as of December 31. The company paid cash dividends of $8,000 and there were no stock issuances or repurchases during the year.

b. Prepare journal entries to close Beneish's temporary accounts.

c. Set up T-accounts for each account and post the closing entries.

PROBLEMS

P3-39. **Assessing Financial Statement Effects of Transactions and Adjustments**   (LO2)

The following information relates to December 31 accounting adjustments for Koonce Kwik Print Company. The firm's fiscal year ends on December 31.

1. Weekly salaries for a five-day week total $1,800, payable on Fridays. December 31 of the current year is a Tuesday.
2. Koonce Kwik Print has $20,000 of notes payable outstanding at December 31. Interest of $200 has accrued on these notes by December 31, but will not be paid until the notes mature next year.
3. During December, Koonce Kwik Print provided $900 of printing services to clients who will be billed on January 2. The firm uses the account Fees Receivable to reflect amounts earned but not yet billed.
4. Starting December 1, all maintenance work on Koonce Kwik Print's equipment is handled by Richardson Repair Company under an agreement whereby Koonce Kwik Print pays a fixed monthly charge of $400. Koonce Kwik Print paid six months' service charge of $2,400 cash in advance on December 1, and increased its Prepaid Maintenance account by $2,400.
5. The firm paid $900 cash on December 15 for a series of radio commercials to run during December and January. One-third of the commercials have aired by December 31. The $900 payment was recorded in its Prepaid Advertising account.
6. Starting December 16, Koonce Kwik Print rented 400 square feet of storage space from a neighboring business. The monthly rent of $0.80 per square foot is due in advance on the first of each month. Nothing was paid in December, however, because the neighbor agreed to add the rent for one-half of December to the January 1 payment.
7. Koonce Kwik Print invested $5,000 cash in securities on December 1 and earned interest of $38 on these securities by December 31. No interest will be received until January.
8. Annual depreciation on the firm's equipment is $2,175. No depreciation has been recorded during the year.

Required

Prepare Koonce Kwik Print Company's accounting adjustments required at December 31 using the financial statement effects template.

P3-40. **Preparing Accounting Adjustments**   (LO2)

Refer to the information in P3-39. Prepare adjustments required at December 31 using journal entries.

P3-41. **Assessing Financial Statement Effects of Adjustments Across Two Periods**   (LO1, 2)

The following selected accounts appear in Sloan Company's unadjusted trial balance at December 31, the end of its fiscal year (all accounts have normal balances).

Prepaid Advertising	$ 1,200	Unearned Service Fees	$ 5,400
Wages Expense	43,800	Service Fees Earned.	87,000
Prepaid Insurance	3,420	Rental Income.	4,900

Required

a. Prepare Sloan Company's accounting adjustments at December 31, using the financial statement effects template and the following additional information.
   1. Prepaid advertising at December 31 is $800.
   2. Unpaid wages earned by employees in December are $1,300.
   3. Prepaid insurance at December 31 is $2,280.
   4. Unearned service fees at December 31 are $3,000.
   5. Rent revenue of $1,000 owed by a tenant is not recorded at December 31.

b. Prepare entries on January 4, of the following year, using the financial statement effects template to record
   1. Payment of $2,400 cash in wages.
   2. Cash receipt from the tenant of the $1,000 rent revenue.

P3-42.   Preparing Accounting Adjustments   (LO1, 2)

Refer to the information in P3-41. Prepare journal entries for parts *a* and *b*.

 P3-43.   Journalizing and Posting Transactions, and Preparing a Trial Balance and Adjustments   (LO1, 2, 3)

D. Roulstone opened Roulstone Roofing Service on April 1. Transactions for April follow.

Apr. 1   Roulstone contributed $11,500 cash to the business in exchange for common stock.
      2   Paid $6,100 cash for the purchase of a used truck.
      2   Purchased $3,100 of ladders and other equipment; the company paid $1,000 cash, with the balance due in 30 days.
      3   Paid $2,880 cash for two-year (or 24-month) premium toward liability insurance.
      5   Purchased $1,200 of supplies on credit.
      5   Received an advance of $1,800 cash from a customer for roof repairs to be done during April and May.
     12   Billed customers $5,500 for roofing services performed.
     18   Collected $4,900 cash from customers toward their accounts billed on April 12.
     29   Paid $675 cash for truck fuel used in April.
     30   Paid $100 cash for April newspaper advertising.
     30   Paid $2,500 cash for assistants' wages earned.
     30   Billed customers $4,000 for roofing services performed.

Required

a. Set up T-accounts for the following accounts: Cash; Accounts Receivable; Supplies; Prepaid Insurance; Trucks; Accumulated Depreciation–Trucks; Equipment; Accumulated Depreciation–Equipment; Accounts Payable; Unearned Roofing Fees; Common Stock; Roofing Fees Earned; Fuel Expense; Advertising Expense; Wages Expense; Insurance Expense; Supplies Expense; Depreciation Expense–Trucks; and Depreciation Expense–Equipment.

b. Record these transactions for April using journal entries.

c. Post these entries to their T-accounts (reference transactions in T-accounts by date).

d. Prepare an unadjusted trial balance at April 30.

e. Prepare entries to adjust the following accounts: Insurance Expense, Supplies Expense, Depreciation Expense—Trucks, Depreciation Expense—Equipment, and Roofing Fees Earned in journal entry form. Supplies still available on April 30 amount to $400. Depreciation for April was $125 on the truck and $35 on equipment. One-fourth of the roofing fee received on April 5, was earned by April 30.

f. Post adjusting entries to their T-accounts.

P3-44.   Assessing Financial Statement Effects of Transactions and Adjustments   (LO1, 2)

Refer to the information in P3-43.

Required

a. Use the financial statement effects template to record the transactions for April.

b. Use the financial statement effects template to record the adjustments at the end of April (described in part e of P3-43).

 P3-45.   Preparing an Unadjusted Trial Balance and Accounting Adjustments   (LO2, 3)

Pownall Photomake Company, a commercial photography studio, completed its first year of operations on December 31. General ledger account balances before year-end adjustments follow; no adjustments have been made to the accounts at any time during the year. Assume that all balances are normal.

Cash	$ 2,150	Accounts Payable	$ 1,910
Accounts Receivable	3,800	Unearned Photography Fees	2,600
Prepaid Rent	12,600	Common Stock	24,000
Prepaid Insurance	2,970	Photography Fees Earned	34,480
Supplies	4,250	Wages Expense	11,000
Equipment	22,800	Utilities Expense	3,420

An analysis of the firm's records discloses the following (business began on January 1).

1. Photography services of $925 have been rendered, but customers have not yet paid or been billed. The company uses the account Fees Receivable to reflect amounts due but not yet billed.

2. Equipment, purchased January 1, has an estimated life of 10 years.
3. Utilities expense for December is estimated to be $400, but the bill will not arrive or be paid until January of next year. (All prior months' utilities bills have been received and paid.)
4. The balance in Prepaid Rent represents the amount paid on January 1, for a 2-year lease on the studio it operates from.
5. In November, customers paid $2,600 cash in advance for photos to be taken for the holiday season. When received, these fees were credited to Unearned Photography Fees. By December 31, all of these fees are earned.
6. A 3-year insurance premium paid on January 1, was debited to Prepaid Insurance.
7. Supplies still available at December 31 are $1,520.
8. At December 31, wages expense of $375 has been incurred but not yet paid or recorded.

Required

a. Prepare Pownall Photomake's unadjusted trial balance at December 31.
b. Prepare its adjusting entries using the financial statement effects template.

P3-46. **Recording Adjustments with Journal Entries and T-Accounts**   (LO2, 3)
Refer to the information in P3-45.

Required

a. Prepare journal entries to record the accounting adjustments.
b. Set up T-accounts for each account and post the journal entries to them.

P3-47. **Preparing an Unadjusted Trial Balance and Accounting Adjustments**   (LO2, 3)
BensEx, a mailing service, has just completed its first year of operations on December 31. Its general ledger account balances before year-end adjustments follow; no adjusting entries have been made to the accounts at any time during the year. Assume that all balances are normal.

Cash	$ 2,300	Accounts Payable	$ 2,700
Accounts Receivable	5,120	Common Stock	9,530
Prepaid Advertising	1,680	Mailing Fees Earned	86,000
Supplies	6,270	Wages Expense	38,800
Equipment	42,240	Rent Expense	6,300
Notes Payable	7,500	Utilities Expense	3,020

An analysis of the firm's records reveals the following (business began on January 1).

1. The balance in Prepaid Advertising represents the amount paid for newspaper advertising for one year. The agreement, which calls for the same amount of space each month, covers the period from February 1 of this first year, to January 31 of the following year. BensEx did not advertise during its first month of operations.
2. Equipment, purchased January 1, has an estimated life of eight years.
3. Utilities expense does not include expense for December, estimated at $325. The bill will not arrive until January of the following year.
4. At year-end, employees have earned $1,200 in wages that will not be paid until January.
5. Supplies available at year-end amount to $1,520.
6. At year-end, unpaid interest of $450 has accrued on the notes payable.
7. The firm's lease calls for rent of $525 per month payable on the first of each month, plus an amount equal to 0.5% of annual mailing fees earned. The rental percentage is payable within 15 days after the end of the year.

Required

a. Prepare its unadjusted trial balance at December 31.
b. Prepare its adjusting entries using the financial statement effects template.

P3-48. **Recording Accounting Adjustments with Journal Entries and T-Accounts**   (LO2, 3)
Refer to information in P3-47.

Required

a. Prepare journal entries to record the accounting adjustments.
b. Set up T-accounts for each account and post the journal entries to them.

P3-49.[A] **Preparing Accounting Adjustments** (LO2, 4, 5)

Wysocki Wheels began operations on March 1 to provide automotive wheel alignment and balancing services. On March 31 the unadjusted trial balance follows.

WYSOCKI WHEELS Unadjusted Trial Balance March 31		
	Debit	Credit
Cash.............................	$ 1,900	
Accounts receivable.................	3,820	
Prepaid rent	4,770	
Supplies	3,700	
Equipment	36,180	
Accounts payable..................		$ 2,510
Unearned service revenue		1,000
Common stock.....................		38,400
Service revenue		12,360
Wages expense	3,900	
	$54,270	$54,270

The following information is also available.

1. The balance in Prepaid Rent was the amount paid on March 1 to cover the first six months' rent.
2. Supplies available on March 31 amounted to $1,720.
3. Equipment has an estimated life of nine years (or 108 months).
4. Unpaid and unrecorded wages at March 31 were $560.
5. Utility services used during March were estimated at $390; a bill is expected early in April.
6. The balance in Unearned Service Revenue was the amount received on March 1 from a car dealer to cover alignment and balancing services on cars sold by the dealer in March and April. Wysocki Wheels agreed to provide the services at a fixed fee of $500 each month.

Required

a. Prepare its accounting adjustments at March 31 in journal entry form.
b. Set up T-accounts and post the accounting adjustments to them.
c. Prepare its income statement for March and its balance sheet at March 31.
d. Prepare entries to close its temporary accounts in journal entry form. Post the closing entries to the T-accounts.

MANAGEMENT APPLICATIONS

MA3-50. **Preparing Accounting Adjustments and Financial Statements** (LO1, 2, 4)

Stocken Surf Shop began operations on July 1 with an initial investment of $50,000. During the first three months of operations, the following cash transactions were recorded in the firm's checking account.

Deposits

Initial investment by owner	$ 50,000
Collected from customers	81,000
Borrowings from bank	10,000
	$141,000

Checks drawn

Rent	$ 24,000
Fixtures and equipment.......	25,000
Merchandise inventory........	62,000
Salaries	6,000
Other expenses	13,000
	$130,000

Additional information:

1. Most sales were for cash, however, the store accepted a limited amount of credit sales; at September 30, customers owed the store $9,000.
2. Rent was paid on July 1 for six months.
3. Salaries of $3,000 per month were paid on the 1st of each month for salaries earned in the month prior.
4. Inventories were purchased for cash; at September 30, inventory of $21,000 was still available.
5. Fixtures and equipment were expected to last five years (or 60 months) with zero salvage value.
6. The bank charges 12% annual interest (1% per month) on the $10,000 bank loan. Stocken took the loan out July 1.

Required

a. Record all of Stocken's cash transactions and prepare any necessary adjusting entries at September 30. You may either use the financial statement effects template or journal entries combined with T-accounts.

b. Prepare the income statement for the three months ended September 30, and the balance sheet at September 30.

c. Analyze the statements from part b and assess the company's performance over its initial three months.

MA3-51. Analyzing Transactions, Impacts on Financial Ratios, and Loan Covenants (LO2)

Kadous Consulting, a firm started three years ago by K. Kadous, offers consulting services for material handling and plant layout. Its balance sheet at the close of the current year follows.

KADOUS CONSULTING Balance Sheet December 31			
Assets		**Liabilities**	
Cash..........................	$ 3,400	Notes payable	$30,000
Accounts receivable.............	22,875	Accounts payable...............	4,200
Supplies	13,200	Unearned consulting fees	11,300
Prepaid insurance...............	4,500	Wages payable..................	400
Equipment, gross...............	68,500	Total liabilities..................	45,900
Less: Accumulated		**Equity**	
depreciation	23,975	Common stock.................	8,000
Equipment, net.................	44,525	Retained earnings	34,600
Total assets....................	$88,500	Total liabilities and equity..........	$88,500

Earlier in the year Kadous obtained a bank loan of $30,000 cash for the firm. A provision of the loan is that the year-end debt-to-equity ratio (total liabilities to total equity) cannot exceed 1.0. Based on the above balance sheet, the ratio at December 31 of this year is 1.08. Kadous is concerned about being in violation of the loan agreement and requests assistance in reviewing the situation. Kadous believes that she might have overlooked some items at year-end. Discussions with Kadous reveal the following.

1. On January 1 of this year, the firm paid a $4,500 insurance premium for two years of coverage; the amount in Prepaid Insurance has not yet been adjusted.
2. Depreciation on equipment should be 10% of cost per year; the company inadvertently recorded 15% for this year.
3. Interest on the bank loan has been paid through the end of this year.
4. The firm concluded a major consulting engagement in December, doing a plant layout analysis for a new factory. The $6,000 fee has not been billed or recorded in the accounts.
5. On December 1 of this year, the firm received an $11,300 cash advance payment from Dichev Corp. for consulting services to be rendered over a two-month period. This payment was credited to the Unearned Consulting Fees account. One-half of this fee was earned but unrecorded by December 31 of this year.
6. Supplies costing $4,800 were available on December 31; the company has made no adjustment of its Supplies account.

Required

a. What is the correct debt-to-equity ratio at December 31?

b. Is the firm in violation of its loan agreement? Prepare computations to support the correct total liabilities and total equity figures at December 31.

MA3-52. **Ethics, Accounting Adjustments, and Auditors** (LO1, 2)

It is the end of the accounting year for Anne Beatty, controller of a medium-sized, publicly held corporation specializing in toxic waste cleanup. Within the corporation, only Beatty and the president know that the firm has been negotiating for several months to land a large contract for waste cleanup in Western Europe. The president has hired another firm with excellent contacts in Western Europe to help with negotiations. The outside firm will charge an hourly fee plus expenses, but has agreed not to submit a bill until the negotiations are in their final stages (expected to occur in another 3 to 4 months). Even if the contract falls through, the outside firm is entitled to receive payment for its services. Based upon her discussion with a member of the outside firm, Beatty knows that its charge for services provided to date will be $150,000. This is a material amount for the company.

Beatty knows that the president wants negotiations to remain as secret as possible so that competitors will not learn of the contract the company is pursuing in Europe. In fact, the president recently stated to her, "This is not the time to reveal our actions in Western Europe to other staff members, our auditors, or the readers of our financial statements; securing this contract is crucial to our future growth." No entry has been made in the accounting records for the cost of contract negotiations. Beatty now faces an uncomfortable situation. The company's outside auditor has just asked her if she knows of any year-end adjustments that have not yet been recorded.

Required

a. What are the ethical considerations that Beatty faces in answering the auditor's question?

b. How should Beatty respond to the auditor's question?

SOLUTIONS TO REVIEW PROBLEMS

Mid-Module Review 1

Solution

		Balance Sheet						Income Statement		
Transaction	Cash Asset	+ Noncash Assets	= Liabil-ities	+ Contrib. Capital	+ Earned Capital		Rev-enues	− Expen-ses	= Net Income
1. Issue stock for $3,000 cash	+3,000 Cash		=		+3,000 Common Stock			−	=
2. Purchase $1,000 of inventory on credit		+1,000 Inventory	= +1,000 Accounts Payable					−	=
3a. Sell inventory for $500 on credit		+500 Accounts Receivable	=		+500 Retained Earnings		+500 Sales	−	= +500
3b. Record $300 cost of inventory sold		−300 Inventory	=		−300 Retained Earnings			− +300 Cost of Goods Sold	= −300
4. Collect $300 cash owed by customers	+300 Cash	−300 Accounts Receivable	=					−	=
5. Pay $400 cash toward accounts payable	−400 Cash		= −400 Accounts Payable					−	=
6. Pay $20 cash for dividends	−20 Cash		=		−20 Dividends			−	=

Left margin T-accounts:

```
Cash    3,000
  CS          3,000
       Cash
3,000 |
  CS
      | 3,000
INV   1,000
  AP          1,000
       INV
1,000 |
  AP
      | 1,000
AR      500
  Sales       500
       AR
500 |
  Sales
      | 500
COGS    300
  INV         300
       COGS
300 |
  INV
      | 300
Cash    300
  AR          300
       Cash
300 |
  AR
      | 300
AP      400
  Cash        400
       AP
400 |
  Cash
      | 400
DIV     20
  Cash        20
       DIV
20 |
  Cash
      | 20
```

Mid-Module Review 2

Solution

Transaction	Balance Sheet						Income Statement				
	Cash Asset	+	Noncash Assets	=	Liabil- ities	+	Contrib. Capital	+	Earned Capital		
a. Pay $100 cash for current and future periods' rent	−100 Cash		+100 Prepaid Rent	=							
b. Receive $500 cash advance for future services	+500 Cash			=	+500 Unearned Revenues						
1. Record $30 of rental fees incurred			−30 Prepaid Rent	=					−30 Retained Earnings		
2. Record $80 of services earned				=	−80 Unearned Revenues				+80 Retained Earnings		
3. Incur $40 in wages to be paid next period				=	+40 Wages Payable				−40 Retained Earnings		
4. Provide $150 of services not yet billed to client			+150 Accounts Receivable	=					+150 Retained Earnings		

Income Statement columns:

Transaction	Revenues	−	Expenses	=	Net Income
a.		−		=	
b.		−		=	
1.		−	+30 Rent Expense	=	−30
2.	+80 Sales	−		=	+80
3.		−	+40 Wages Expense	=	−40
4.	+150 Sales	−		=	+150

T-accounts:

a. PPRNT 100 / Cash 100; PPRNT 100, Cash 100
b. Cash 500 / UR 500; Cash 500, UR 500
1. RE 30 / PPRNT 30; RE 30, PPRNT 30
2. UR 80 / Sales 80; UR 80, Sales 80
3. WE 40 / WP 40; WE 40, WP 40
4. AR 150 / Sales 150; AR 150, Sales 150

SYMANTEC Trial Balances

	Unadjusted Debit	Unadjusted Credit	Adjustments Debit	Adjustments Credit	Adjusted Debit	Adjusted Credit
Cash	$3,280				$3,280	
Accounts receivable	200		$150		350	
Inventory	700				700	
Prepaid rent	100			$ 30	70	
Accounts payable		$ 600				$ 600
Wages payable		0		40		40
Unearned revenues		500	80			420
Common stock		3,000				3,000
Dividends	20				20	
Sales		500		230*		730
Cost of goods sold	300				300	
Wages expense	0		40		40	
Rent expense	0		30		30	
Totals	$4,600	$4,600	$300	$300	$4,790	$4,790

*The $230 adjustment is a combination of the $150 and $80 adjustments.

Module-End Review

Solution

SYMANTEC
Income Statement
For Quarter Ended December 31, 2012

Sales.	$730
Cost of goods sold.	300
Gross profit.	430
Wage expense	40
Rent expense	30
Net income.	$360

SYMANTEC
Retained Earnings Computation
For Quarter Ended December 31, 2012

Retained earnings, beginning of period		$ 0
Add:	Net income (loss)	360
Deduct: Dividends		(20)
Retained earnings, end of period.		$340

SYMANTEC
Balance Sheet
December 31, 2012

Assets	
Cash.	$3,280
Accounts receivable.	350
Inventory.	700
Prepaid rent	70
Total assets.	$4,400
Liabilities and Stockholders' Equity	
Liabilities	
Accounts payable.	$ 600
Wages payable.	40
Unearned revenues	420
Total liabilities	1,060
Stockholders' equity	
Common stock.	3,000
Retained earnings	340
Total stockholders' equity	3,340
Total liabilities and stockholders' equity.	$4,400

SYMANTEC
Statement of Stockholders' Equity
For Quarter Ended December 31, 2012

	Contributed Capital	Earned Capital	Total Stockholders' Equity
Beginning balance	$ 0	$ 0	$ 0
Stock issuance.	3,000		3,000
Net income (loss)		360	360
Dividends		(20)	(20)
Ending balance.	**$3,000**	**$340**	**$3,340**

SYMANTEC
Statement of Cash Flows
For Quarter Ended December 31, 2012

Operating activities	
Net income	$ 360
Depreciation and other noncash expenses	0
Increase in accounts receivable	(350)
Increase in inventories	(700)
Increase in prepaid rent	(70)
Increase in accounts payable.	600
Increase in wages payable	40
Increase in unearned revenues.	420
Net cash flows from operating activities	300
Investing activities	
Net cash flows from investing activities.	0
Financing activities	
Issuance of common stock	3,000
Payment of cash dividends	(20)
Net cash flows from financing activities.	2,980
Net change in cash.	3,280
Cash, beginning of period	0
Cash, end of period	$3,280

Getty Images

TARGET

Target employs a number of financial measures to assess its overall performance and financial condition. These measures include ratios related to profitability and asset turnover as well as the return on invested capital. Analysts, too, use a variety of measures to capture different aspects of company performance to answer questions such as: Is it managed efficiently and profitably? Does it use assets effectively? Is performance achieved with a minimum of debt?

One fundamental measure is return on capital, which Warren Buffett, CEO of the investment firm Berkshire Hathaway, lists in his acquisition criteria cited in Module 1: "Our preference would be to reach our goal by directly owning a diversified group of businesses that generate cash and consistently earn above-average returns on capital." All return metrics follow the same basic formula—they divide some measure of profit by some measure of investment. A company's performance is commonly judged by its profitability. Although analysis of profit is important, it is only part of the story. A more meaningful analysis is to compare level of profitability with the amount of capital that has been invested in the business. The most common return measure is return on

equity (ROE), which focuses on shareholder investment as its measure of invested capital. By focusing on the *equity* investment, ROE measures return from the perspective of the common shareholder rather than the company overall. Target's ROE for 2011 was 18.94%, up from 15.26% two years prior.

This module focuses on analysis of return metrics. Beyond ROE, we put special emphasis on the return on net operating assets (RNOA), computed as net operating profit after tax (NOPAT) divided by average net operating assets (NOA). RNOA focuses on operating activities—operating profit relative to investment in net operating assets. It is important to distinguish operating activities from nonoperating activities because the capital markets value each component differently, placing much greater emphasis on operations. Target's RNOA has improved from 8.97% to 11.43% in the past three years.

RNOA consists of two components: profitability and asset productivity. Increasing either component increases RNOA. These components reflect on the first two questions we posed above: Is the company managed efficiently and profitably? Does it use assets effectively?

Analyzing and Interpreting Financial Statements

LEARNING OBJECTIVES

LO1 Compute return on equity (ROE) and disaggregate it into components of operating and nonoperating returns. (p. 4-4)

LO2 Disaggregate operating return (RNOA) into components of profitability and asset turnover. (p. 4-11)

LO3 Explain nonoperating return and compute it from return on equity and the operating return. (p. 4-16)

LO4 Compute and interpret measures of liquidity and solvency. (p. 4-26)

LO5 Describe and illustrate traditional DuPont disaggregation of ROE. (p. 4-30)

The profitability component of RNOA measures net operating profit after tax for each sales dollar (NOPAT/Sales), and is called the net operating profit margin (NOPM). Target's NOPM has increased from 4.25% to 5.04% in the past three years.

Asset productivity, the second component of RNOA, is reflected in net operating asset turnover (NOAT). NOAT is measured as sales divided by average net operating assets—it captures the notion of how many sales dollars are generated by each dollar of invested assets. Target has increased its NOAT from 2.11 to 2.27 in the past three years. Increasing the turnover for large asset bases is difficult, and NOAT measures tend to fluctuate in a narrow band. When companies are able to make a meaningful improvement in NOAT, however, it usually has a large impact on RNOA.

RNOA is an important metric in assessing the performance of company management. We can use the RNOA components, NOPM and NOAT, to assess how effectively and efficiently management uses the company's operating assets to produce a return.

The difference between ROE and RNOA is important for our analysis. Specifically, ROE consists of a return on operating activities (RNOA) *plus* a return on nonoperating activities, where the latter reflects how well the company uses borrowed funds. Companies can increase ROE by borrowing money and effectively using those borrowed funds. However, debt can increase the company's risk—where severe consequences can result if debt is not repaid when due. This is why Warren Buffett focuses on "businesses earning good returns on equity while employing little or no debt." For those companies that do employ debt, our analysis seeks to evaluate their ability to repay the amounts owed when due.

Over the years, analysts, creditors and others have developed hundreds of ratios to measure specific aspects of financial performance. Most of these seek answers to the root question: Can the company achieve a high return on its invested capital and, if so, is that return sustainable?

Sources: *Target 10-K, 2011; Berkshire Hathaway 10-K, 2010; The Wall Street Journal,* January 2011.

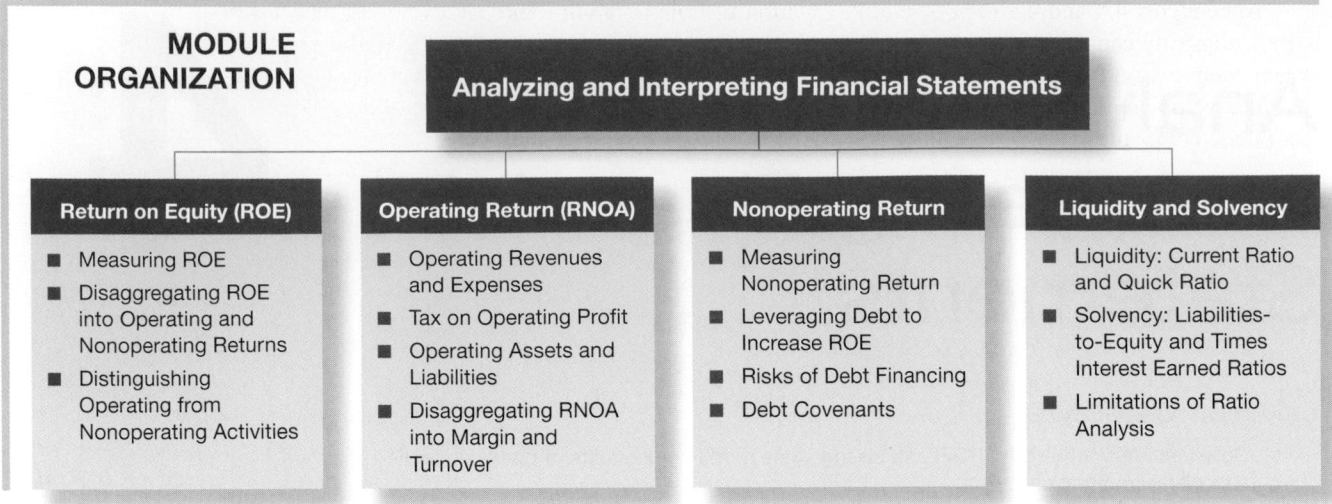

A key aspect of any analysis is identifying the business activities that drive company success. We pursue an answer to the question: Is the company earning an acceptable rate of return on its invested capital? We also want to know the extent to which the company's return on invested capital results from its operating versus its nonoperating activities. The distinction between returns from operating and nonoperating activities is important and plays a key role in our analysis.

Operating activities are the core activities of a company. They consist of those activities required to deliver a company's products or services to its customers. A company engages in operating activities when it conducts research and development, establishes supply chains, assembles administrative support, produces and markets its products, and follows up with after-sale customer services.

The asset side of a company's balance sheet reflects resources devoted to operating activities with accounts such as receivables, inventories, and property, plant and equipment (PPE). Operating activities are reflected in liabilities with accounts such as accounts payable, accrued expenses, and long-term operating liabilities such as pension and health care obligations. The income statement reflects operating activities through accounts such as revenues, costs of goods sold, and operating expenses such as selling, general, and administrative expenses that include wages, advertising, depreciation, occupancy, insurance, and research and development. Operating activities create the most long-lasting (persistent) effects on future profitability and cash flows of the company. Operations provide the primary value drivers for company stakeholders. It is for this reason that operating activities play such a prominent role in assessing profitability.

Nonoperating activities relate to the investing of cash in marketable securities and in other nonoperating investments. Nonoperating activities also relate to borrowings through accounts such as short- and long-term debt. These nonoperating assets and liabilities expand and contract to buffer fluctuations in operating asset and liability levels. When operating assets grow faster than operating liabilities, companies typically increase their nonoperating liabilities to fund the deficit. Later, these liabilities decline when operating assets decline. When companies have cash in excess of what is needed for operating activities, they often invest the cash temporarily in marketable securities or other investments to provide some return until those funds are needed for operations.

The income statement reflects nonoperating activities through accounts such as interest and dividend revenue, capital gains or losses relating to investments, and interest expense on borrowed funds. Nonoperating expenses, net of any nonoperating revenues, provide a nonoperating return for a company. Although nonoperating activities are important and must be managed well, they are not the main value drivers for company stakeholders.

We begin this module by explaining the return on equity (ROE). We then discuss in more detail how ROE consists of both an operating return (RNOA) and a nonoperating return. Next, we discuss the two RNOA components that measure profitability and asset turnover. We conclude this module with a discussion of nonoperating return, focusing on the notion that companies can increase ROE through judicious use of debt.

Appendixes 4A and 4B expand our explanation of nonoperating return by exploring how much debt a company can reasonably manage. For this purpose, we examine a number of liquidity and solvency metrics in Appendix 4B. As part of that analysis, we identify ratios that credit analysts typically use to develop credit ratings, which are key determinants of bond prices and the cost of debt financing for public companies.

RETURN ON EQUITY (ROE)

Return on equity (ROE) is the principal summary measure of company performance and is defined as follows:

$$ROE = \frac{\text{Net income}}{\text{Average stockholders' equity}}$$

ROE relates net income to the average investment by shareholders as measured by total stockholders' equity from the balance sheet.

LO1 Compute return on equity (ROE) and disaggregate it into components of operating and nonoperating returns.

BUSINESS INSIGHT	Which Net Income and Stockholders' Equity to Use?

Many companies have two sets of shareholders: those that own the common stock of the parent company (the company whose financial statements we review) and those that own shares in one or more of the parent company's subsidiaries (called "noncontrolling interest"). Current accounting standards require companies to identify the stockholders' equity relating to each group of shareholders and, likewise, the net income that is attributable to each. ROE is usually computed from the perspective of the parent's shareholders and, thus, the numerator is the net income that is attributable to the parent's shareholders and the denominator is the stockholders' equity of the parent's shareholders. We illustrate this difference for Walmart in our Mid-Module Review and discuss noncontrolling interests more fully in Module 7.

Warren Buffett highlights ROE as part of his acquisition criteria: "Businesses earning good returns on equity while employing little or no debt." The ROE formula can be rewritten in a way to better see the point Buffett is making (derivation of this ROE formula is in Appendix 4A):

ROE = Operating return + Nonoperating return

The equation above shows that ROE consists of two returns: (1) the return from the company's operating activities, linked to revenues and expenses from the company's products or services, and (2) the return from the company's use of debt, net of any return from nonoperating investments. Companies can use debt to increase their return on equity, but this increases risk because the failure to make required debt payments can yield many legal consequences, including bankruptcy. This is one reason why Warren Buffett focuses on companies whose return on equity is derived primarily from operating activities.

BUSINESS INSIGHT	Target's ROE and RNOA

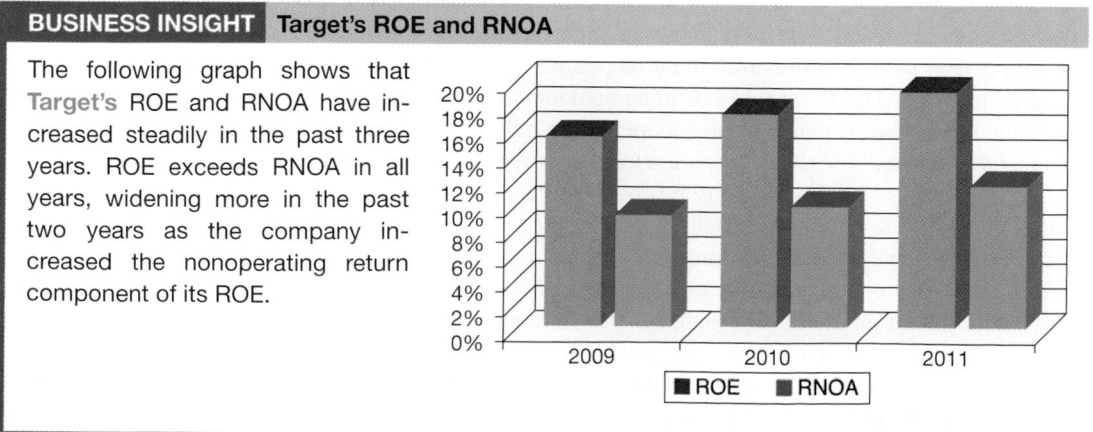

The following graph shows that Target's ROE and RNOA have increased steadily in the past three years. ROE exceeds RNOA in all years, widening more in the past two years as the company increased the nonoperating return component of its ROE.

OPERATING RETURN (RNOA)

Operating returns are reflected in the **return on net operating assets (RNOA)**, defined as follows:

$$\text{RNOA} = \frac{\text{Net operating profit after tax (NOPAT)}}{\text{Average net operating assets (NOA)}}$$

To implement this formula, we must first classify the income statement and balance sheet into operating and nonoperating components so that we can assess each separately. We first consider operating activities on the income statement and explain how to compute NOPAT. Second, we consider operating activities on the balance sheet and explain how to compute NOA.

Operating Items in the Income Statement —NOPAT

The income statement reports both operating and nonoperating activities. Exhibit 4.1 shows a typical income statement with the operating activities highlighted.

EXHIBIT 4.1 Operating and Nonoperating Items in the Income Statement
Typical Income Statement   **Operating Items Highlighted**
Revenues   **Cost of sales**

Gross profit
 Operating expenses
    Selling, general and administrative
    Asset impairment expense
    Gains and losses on asset disposal

Total operating expenses
Operating income   Interest expense   Interest and dividend revenue   Investment gains and losses
Total nonoperating expenses
Income from continuing operations before taxes   **Tax expense**
Income from continuing operations   Income (loss) from discontinued operations, net of tax (see Appendix 4A)
Consolidated net income   Less: consolidated net income attributable to noncontrolling interest (see Appendix 4A)
Consolidated net income attributable to parent shareholders

Operating activities are those that relate to bringing a company's products or services to market and any after-sales support. The income statement in Exhibit 4.1 reflects operating activities through revenues, costs of goods sold (COGS), and other expenses. Selling, general, and administrative expense (SG&A) includes wages, advertising, occupancy, insurance, research and development, depreciation, and many other operating expenses the company incurs in the ordinary course of business (some of these are often reported as separate line items in the income statement). Companies also dispose of operating assets, and can realize gains or losses from their disposal, or write them off partially or completely when they become impaired. These, too, are operating activities. Finally, the reported tax expense on the income statement reflects both operating and nonoperating activities. Later in this section we use Target's income statement to explain how to separately compute tax expense related to operating activities only.

Nonoperating activities relate to borrowed money that creates interest expense. Nonoperating activities also relate to investments such as marketable securities and other investments that yield interest or dividend revenue and capital gains or losses from any sales of nonoperating investments during the period. Often companies report income or loss from discontinued operations; which we consider as a nonoperating item on the income statement. ROE analysis is from the perspective of parent-company shareholders; thus, we also consider the portion of consolidated net income that is attributable to noncontrolling shareholders as a nonoperating item on the income statement.

Following is Target's 2011 income statement with the operating items highlighted. Target's operating items include sales, cost of sales, SG&A, and depreciation expense. Target's pretax operating income is $5,252 million. Its nonoperating activities relate to its borrowed money (interest expense) which yield pretax net nonoperating expense of $757 million.

TARGET Income Statement ($ millions) For Year Ended January 29, 2011	
Sales.	$65,786
Credit card revenues	1,604
Total revenues	67,390
Cost of sales.	45,725
Selling, general and administrative expenses	13,469
Credit card expenses	860
Depreciation and amortization	2,084
Earnings before interest expense and income taxes	5,252
Net interest expense	
Nonrecourse debt collateralized by credit card receivables.	83
Other interest expense	677
Interest income.	(3)
Net interest expense	757
Earnings before income taxes	4,495
Provision for income taxes.	1,575
Net earnings.	$ 2,920

Computing Tax on Operating Profit

Target's income statement reports net operating profit *before* tax (NOPBT) of $5,252 million. But, the numerator of the RNOA formula, defined previously, uses net operating profit *after tax* (NOPAT). Thus, we need to subtract taxes to determine NOPAT.

$$\textbf{NOPAT = NOPBT} - \textbf{Tax on operating profit}$$

The tax expense of $1,575 million that Target reports on its income statement pertains to both operating *and* nonoperating activities. To compute NOPAT, we need to compute the tax expense relating solely to operating profit as follows:

Tax on operating profit = Tax expense + (Pretax net nonoperating expense × Statutory tax rate)

Tax Shield

The amount in parentheses is called the *tax shield*, which are the taxes that Target saved by having tax-deductible nonoperating expenses (see Tax Shield box on the next page for details). By definition, the taxes saved (by the tax shield) do not relate to operating profits; thus, we must add back the tax shield to total tax expense to compute tax on operating profit. (For companies with nonoperating revenue greater than nonoperating expense, so-called *net nonoperating revenue*, the tax on operating profit is computed as: Tax expense − [Pretax net nonoperating revenue × Statutory tax rate]).

Applying this method, we see that Target had a tax shield of $280 million (computed as pretax net nonoperating expense of $757 million times its statutory tax rate of 37%) and tax on operating profit of $1,855 million (computed as $1,575 million + $280 million).[1] We subtract the tax on operating profit from the net operating profit before tax to obtain NOPAT. Thus, Target's net operating profit after tax is computed as follows ($ millions):

Net operating profit before tax (NOPBT)		$5,252
Less tax on operating profit		
Tax expense (from income statement)	$1,575	
Tax shield ($757 × 37%).	+280	(1,855)
Net operating profit after tax (NOPAT)		$3,397

[1] The statutory federal tax rate for corporations is 35% (per U.S. tax code). Also, most states and some local jurisdictions tax corporate income, and those state taxes are deductible for federal tax purposes. The *net* state tax rate is the statutory rate less the federal tax deduction. The tax rate on operating profit is the sum of the two. On average, the net state tax is about 2%; thus, we use 37% (35% + 2%) as the assumed tax rate on nonoperating expenses and revenues in our examples and assignments at the end of the module. The business insight boxes below explain that the tax rate on pretax profit will usually *not* be the assumed statutory rate (37%).

BUSINESS INSIGHT Tax Shield

Persons with home mortgages understand well the beneficial effects of the "interest tax shield." To see how the interest tax shield works, consider two individuals, each with income of $50,000 and each with only one expense: a home. Assume that one person pays $10,000 per year in rent; the other pays $10,000 in interest on a home mortgage. Rent is not deductible for tax purposes, whereas mortgage interest (but not principal) is deductible. Assume that each person pays taxes at 25%, the personal tax rate for this income level. Their tax payments follow.

	Renter	Home owner
Income before interest and taxes.	$50,000	$50,000
Less interest deduction	0	(10,000)
Taxable income	$50,000	$40,000
Taxes paid (25% rate).	$12,500	$10,000

The renter reports $50,000 in taxable income and pays $12,500 in taxes. The home owner deducts $10,000 in interest, which lowers taxable income to $40,000 and reduces taxes to $10,000. By deducting mortgage interest, the home owner's tax bill is $2,500 lower. The $2,500 is the *interest tax shield*, and we can compute it directly as the $10,000 interest deduction multiplied by the 25% tax rate.

BUSINESS INSIGHT Tax Rates for Computing NOPAT

In our examples and assignments, we assume the statutory tax rate is 37% as this is the approximate average combined federal and state tax rate for public companies. We can, as an alternative approach, compute a *company-specific* tax rate using the income tax footnote in the 10-K. For example, Target provides the following table in its 10-K for the year ended January 29, 2011:

Tax Rate Reconciliation	2011	2010	2009
Federal statutory rate.	35.0%	35.0%	35.0%
State income taxes, net of federal tax benefit	1.4	2.8	3.8
Other.	(1.3)	(2.1)	(1.4)
Effective tax rate.	35.1%	35.7%	37.4%

The federal statutory rate is 35.0%, and Target pays state taxes amounting to an additional 1.4% (it also reports reductions of 1.3% relating to "other" items). Thus, Target's effective tax rate (or average) for *all* of its income is the sum of all its taxes paid less benefits received, or 35.1%. However, the tax shield that we add back in computing NOPAT uses only *federal and state tax rates*. For Target, the company-specific tax rate that we can use to compute the tax shield is 36.4% (35.0% + 1.4%). It would be incorrect to use Target's 35.1% company-specific effective tax rate to compute NOPAT, as that rate includes both operating and nonoperating items. We discuss income tax more fully in Module 5.

MID-MODULE REVIEW 1

Following is the income statement of Walmart.

WALMART Income Statement ($ millions) For Fiscal Year Ended January 31, 2011	
Net sales.	$418,952
Membership and other income	2,897
Revenues, total.	421,849
Costs and expenses	
Cost of sales.	315,287
Operating, selling, general and administrative expenses.	81,020
Operating income.	25,542

continued

continued from prior page

Interest	
Debt	1,928
Capital leases	277
Interest income	(201)
Interest, net	2,004
Income from continuing operations before income taxes	23,538
Provision for income taxes	
Current	6,703
Deferred	876
Provision for income taxes, total	7,579
Income from continuing operations	15,959
Income (loss) from discontinued operations, net of tax	1,034
Consolidated net income	16,993
Less consolidated net income attributable to noncontrolling interest	(604)
Consolidated net income attributable to Walmart	$ 16,389

Required

Compute Walmart's net operating profit after tax (NOPAT). Assume a statutory rate of 37% applies to nonoperating expenses and revenues.

The solution is on page 4-54.

Operating Items in the Balance Sheet —NOA

RNOA relates NOPAT to the average net operating assets (NOA) of the company. We compute NOA as follows:

Net operating assets = Operating assets − Operating liabilities

To compute NOA we must partition the balance sheet into operating and nonoperating items. Exhibit 4.2 shows a typical balance sheet and highlights the operating items.

EXHIBIT 4.2 Operating and Nonoperating Items in the Balance Sheet	
Typical Balance Sheet **Operating Items Highlighted**	
Current assets	**Current liabilities**
Cash and cash equivalents	Short-term notes and interest payable
Short-term investments	Current maturities of long-term debt
Accounts receivable	**Accounts payable**
Inventories	**Accrued liabilities**
Prepaid expenses	**Unearned revenue**
Deferred income tax assets	**Deferred income tax liabilities**
Other current assets	Current liabilities of discontinued operations
Current assets of discontinued operations	
	Long-term liabilities
Long-term assets	Bonds and notes payable
Long-term investments in securities	Capitalized lease obligations
Property, plant and equipment, net	**Pension and other post-employment liabilities**
Capitalized lease assets	**Deferred income tax liabilities**
Natural resources	Long-term liabilities of discontinued operations
Equity method investments	
Goodwill and intangible assets	**Stockholders' equity**
Deferred income tax assets	All equity accounts
Other long-term assets	
Long-term assets of discontinued operations	Noncontrolling (minority) interest

Operating assets are those assets directly linked to operating activities, the company's ongoing (continuing) business operations. They typically include receivables, inventories, prepaid expenses, property, plant and equipment (PPE), and capitalized lease assets, and exclude short-term and long-term investments in marketable securities and any current and noncurrent assets that relate to discontinued operations. Equity investments in affiliated companies and goodwill are considered operating assets if they pertain to the ownership of stock in other firms linked to the company's operating activities (see Module 7). Deferred tax assets (and liabilities) are operating items because they relate to future tax deductions (or payments) arising from operating activities (see Module 5). We assume that "other" assets and liabilities, and "other" revenues and expenses, are operating unless information suggests otherwise. For example, details in footnotes might reveal that "other" includes nonoperating items. Or the company might explicitly indicate the "other" is nonoperating by reporting the item after a subtotal for income from operations. In these cases, we would consider the "other" as nonoperating.

Operating liabilities are liabilities that arise from operating revenues and expenses. For example, accounts payable and accrued expenses help fund inventories, wages, utilities, and other operating expenses; also, unearned revenue (an operating liability) relates to operating revenue. Similarly, pension and other post-employment obligations relate to long-term obligations for employee retirement and health care, which by definition are operating activities (see Module 10). Operating liabilities exclude bank loans, mortgages or other debt, which are nonoperating. Further, companies often use capitalized leases to finance long-term operating assets, and these capitalized lease liabilities are also nonoperating (see Module 10). Lastly, nonoperating liabilities include any current and noncurrent liabilities that relate to discontinued operations.

Nonoperating assets include cash and cash equivalents (see Business Insight box below) and investments in marketable securities, both short- and long-term. Nonoperating liabilities include interest bearing debt, both short- and long-term, and capitalized lease obligations. Finally, we consider all equity accounts nonoperating, including equity relating to noncontrolling interest.

BUSINESS INSIGHT   **Why is Cash a Nonoperating Asset?**

Most analysts consider cash as nonoperating because this account consists almost totally of "cash equivalents," which are short-term investments with a scheduled maturity of 90 days or less. Technically, the amount of cash needed to support routine business transactions is considered as operating and the remainder as a nonoperating short-term investment, similar to investments reported as marketable securities. If we know what portion of the cash balance supports operating activities, we would classify that as operating. Unfortunately, companies do not report that information and most analysts feel that it is probably a small portion. As a result, we, like others, treat the entire cash balance as nonoperating and recognize that we are probably understating net operating assets slightly.

The following is Target's balance sheets for 2011 and 2010. Its operating assets and operating liabilities are highlighted.

TARGET Balance Sheets		
(In millions)	Jan. 29, 2011	Jan. 30, 2010
Assets		
Cash and cash equivalents	$ 1,712	$ 2,200
Credit card receivables, net of allowance of $690 and $1,016	6,153	6,966
Inventory	7,596	7,179
Other current assets	1,752	2,079
Total current assets	17,213	18,424
Property and equipment		
Land	5,928	5,793
Buildings and improvements	23,081	22,152
Fixtures and equipment	4,939	4,743
Computer hardware and software	2,533	2,575
Construction-in-progress	567	502
Accumulated depreciation	(11,555)	(10,485)
Property and equipment, net	25,493	25,280
Other noncurrent assets	999	829
Total assets	$43,705	$44,533

continued

continued from prior page

Liabilities and shareholders' investment

Accounts payable.	$6,625	$6,511
Accrued and other current liabilities.	3,326	3,120
Unsecured debt and other borrowings	119	796
Nonrecourse debt collateralized by credit card receivables	—	900
Total current liabilities.	10,070	11,327
Unsecured debt and other borrowings	11,653	10,643
Nonrecourse debt collateralized by credit card receivables	3,954	4,475
Deferred income taxes.	934	835
Other noncurrent liabilities.	1,607	1,906
Total noncurrent liabilities.	18,148	17,859
Shareholders' investment		
Common stock.	59	62
Additional paid-in-capital.	3,311	2,919
Retained earnings.	12,698	12,947
Accumulated other comprehensive loss	(581)	(581)
Total shareholders' investment.	15,487	15,347
Total liabilities and shareholders' investment.	$43,705	$44,533

We assume that Target's "other" assets and liabilities are operating. We can sometimes make a finer distinction if footnotes to financial statements provide additional information. For now, assume that these "other" items reported in balance sheets pertain to operations.

Using Target's highlighted balance sheet above, we compute net operating assets for 2011 and 2010 as follows (recall that Net operating assets (NOA) = Total operating assets − Total operating liabilities).

Target ($ millions)	Jan. 29, 2011	Jan. 30, 2010
Operating assets		
Credit card receivables.	$ 6,153	$ 6,966
Inventory.	7,596	7,179
Other current assets.	1,752	2,079
Property and equipment, net	25,493	25,280
Other noncurrent assets.	999	829
Total operating assets	41,993	42,333
Operating liabilities		
Accounts payable.	6,625	6,511
Accrued and other current liabilities.	3,326	3,120
Deferred income taxes	934	835
Other noncurrent liabilities	1,607	1,906
Total operating liabilities.	12,492	12,372
Net operating assets (NOA).	$29,501	$29,961

To determine average NOA, we take a simple average of two consecutive years' numbers. Thus, return on net operating assets (RNOA) for Target for 2011 is computed as follows ($ millions).

$$RNOA = \frac{NOPAT}{Average\ NOA} = \frac{\$3,397}{(\$29,501 + \$29,961)/2} = 11.43\%$$

Target's 2011 RNOA is 11.43%. By comparison, Walmart's (its main competitor) RNOA is 15.63% (this computation is shown in Mid-Module Review 2), and the average for all publicly traded companies is about 8% for the past decade.

Recall that RNOA is related to ROE as follows: ROE = Operating return + Nonoperating return, where RNOA is the operating return. Thus, we can ask how do Target's RNOA and ROE compare? To answer this we need Target's 2011 ROE, which is computed as follows ($ millions).

$$\text{ROE} = \frac{\text{Net income}}{\text{Average stockholders' equity}} = \frac{\$2,920}{(\$15,487 + \$15,347)/2} = 18.94\%$$

In relative terms, Target's operating return (RNOA) is 60% (11.43%/18.94%) of its total ROE, which is slightly less than the average publicly traded company's percent of near 69%. Its nonoperating return of 7.5% (18.94% − 11.43%) makes up the remaining 40% of ROE.

Exhibit 4.3 provides a summary of key terms introduced to this point and their definitions.

EXHIBIT 4.3   Key Ratio and Acronym Definitions

Ratio	Definition
ROE: Return on equity	Net income/Average stockholders' equity
NOPAT: Net operating profit after tax	Operating revenues less operating expenses such as cost of sales, selling, general and administrative expense, and taxes; it excludes nonoperating revenues and expenses such as interest revenue, dividend revenue, interest expense, gains and losses on investments, discontinued operations, and income attributed to noncontrolling interest.
NOA: Net operating assets	Operating assets less operating liabilities; it excludes nonoperating items such as investments in marketable securities and interest-bearing debt.
RNOA: Return on net operating assets. . .	NOPAT/Average NOA
NNE: Net nonoperating expense	NOPAT − Net income; NNE consists of nonoperating expenses and revenues, net of tax, as well as any noncontrolling interest reported on the income statement.

RNOA DISAGGREGATION INTO MARGIN AND TURNOVER

LO2 Disaggregate operating return (RNOA) into components of profitability and asset turnover.

Disaggregating RNOA into its two components, profit margin and asset turnover, yields further insights into a company's performance. This disaggregation follows.

$$\text{RNOA} = \frac{\text{NOPAT}}{\text{Average NOA}} = \frac{\text{NOPAT}}{\text{Sales}} \times \frac{\text{Sales}}{\text{Average NOA}}$$

Net operating profit margin (NOPM)   Net operating asset turnover (NOAT)

Net Operating Profit Margin

Net operating profit margin (NOPM) reveals how much operating profit the company earns from each sales dollar. All things equal, a higher NOPM is preferable. NOPM is affected by the level of gross profit the company earns on its products (revenue minus cost of goods sold), which depends on product prices and manufacturing or purchase costs. NOPM is also affected by the level of operating expenses the company requires to support its products or services. This includes overhead costs such as wages, marketing, occupancy, and research and development. Finally, NOPM is affected by the level of competition (which affects product pricing) and the company's willingness and ability to control costs.

Target's net operating profit margin is computed as follows ($ millions).

$$\text{NOPM} = \frac{\text{NOPAT}}{\text{Revenues}} = \frac{\$3,397}{\$67,390} = 5.04\%$$

This result means that for each dollar of sales at Target, the company earns roughly 5.04¢ profit after all operating expenses and taxes. As a reference, the median NOPM for publicly traded companies during the past decade is about 6¢.

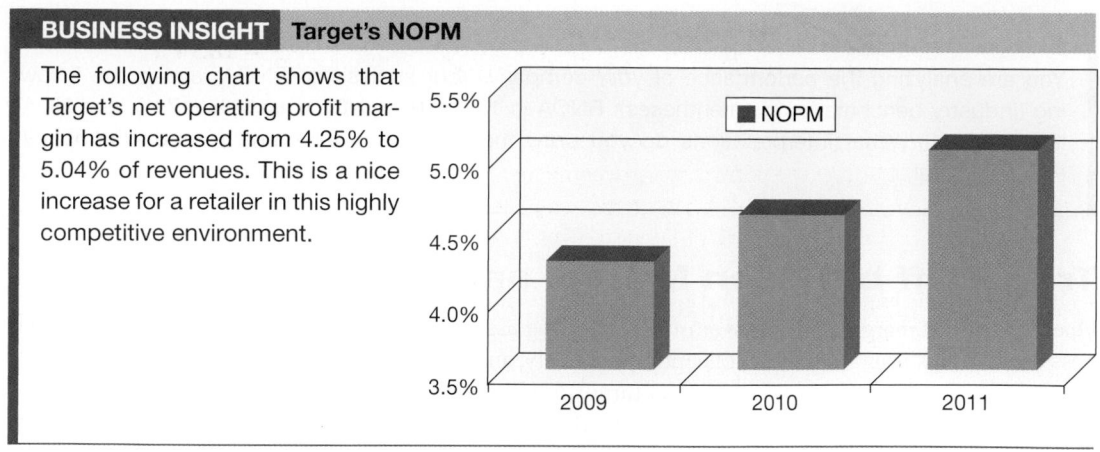

BUSINESS INSIGHT   Target's NOPM

The following chart shows that Target's net operating profit margin has increased from 4.25% to 5.04% of revenues. This is a nice increase for a retailer in this highly competitive environment.

Net Operating Asset Turnover

Net operating asset turnover (NOAT) measures the productivity of the company's net operating assets. This metric reveals the level of sales the company realizes from each dollar invested in net operating assets. All things equal, a higher NOAT is preferable. Target's net operating asset turnover ratio follows ($ millions).

$$\text{NOAT} = \frac{\text{Revenues}}{\text{Average NOA}} = \frac{\$67{,}390}{(\$29{,}501 + \$29{,}961)/2} = 2.27$$

This result means that for each dollar of net operating assets, Target realizes $2.27 in sales. As a reference, the median for publicly traded companies over the past decade is about $1.40.

NOAT can be increased by either increasing sales for a given level of investment in operating assets, or by reducing the amount of operating assets necessary to generate a dollar of sales, or both. Reducing operating working capital (current operating assets less current operating liabilities) is usually easier than reducing long-term net operating assets. For example, companies can implement strategies to collect their receivables faster, reduce their inventories, and delay payments to their suppliers. All of these actions reduce operating working capital and, thereby, increase NOAT. These strategies must be managed, however, so as not to negatively impact sales or supplier relations. Working capital management is an important part of managing the company effectively.

It is usually more difficult to reduce the level of long-term net operating assets. The level of PPE required by the company is determined more by the nature of the company's products or services than by management action. For example, telecommunications companies require more capital investment than do retail stores. Still, there are several actions that managers can take to reduce capital investment. Some companies pursue novel approaches, such as corporate alliances, outsourcing, and use of special purpose entities; we discuss some of these approaches in Module 10.

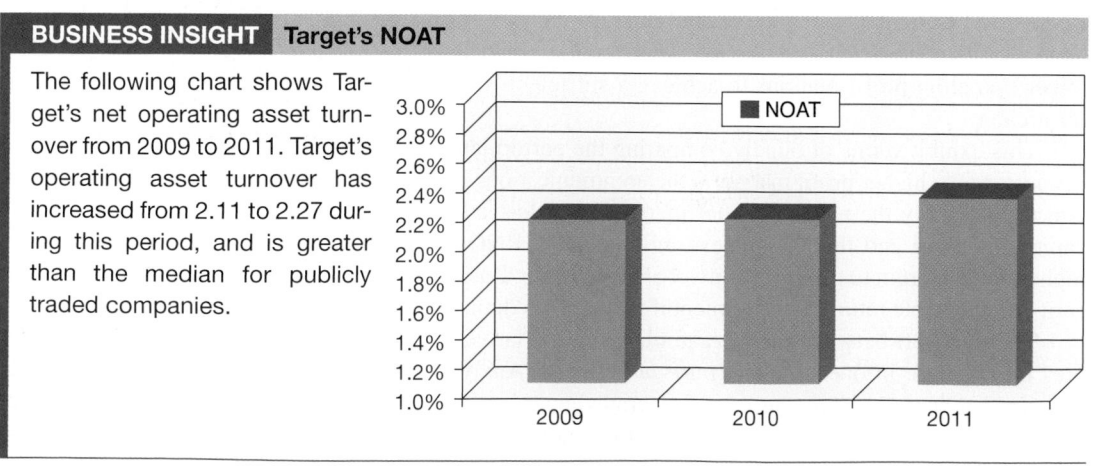

BUSINESS INSIGHT   Target's NOAT

The following chart shows Target's net operating asset turnover from 2009 to 2011. Target's operating asset turnover has increased from 2.11 to 2.27 during this period, and is greater than the median for publicly traded companies.

Trade-Off between Margin and Turnover

Operating profit margin and turnover of net operating assets are largely affected by a company's business model. This is an important concept. Specifically, an infinite number of combinations of net operating profit margin and net operating asset turnover will yield a given RNOA. This relation is depicted in Exhibit 4.4 (where the curved line reflects the median RNOA for all publicly traded companies during the most recent decade).

EXHIBIT 4.4   Profitability and Productivity across Industries

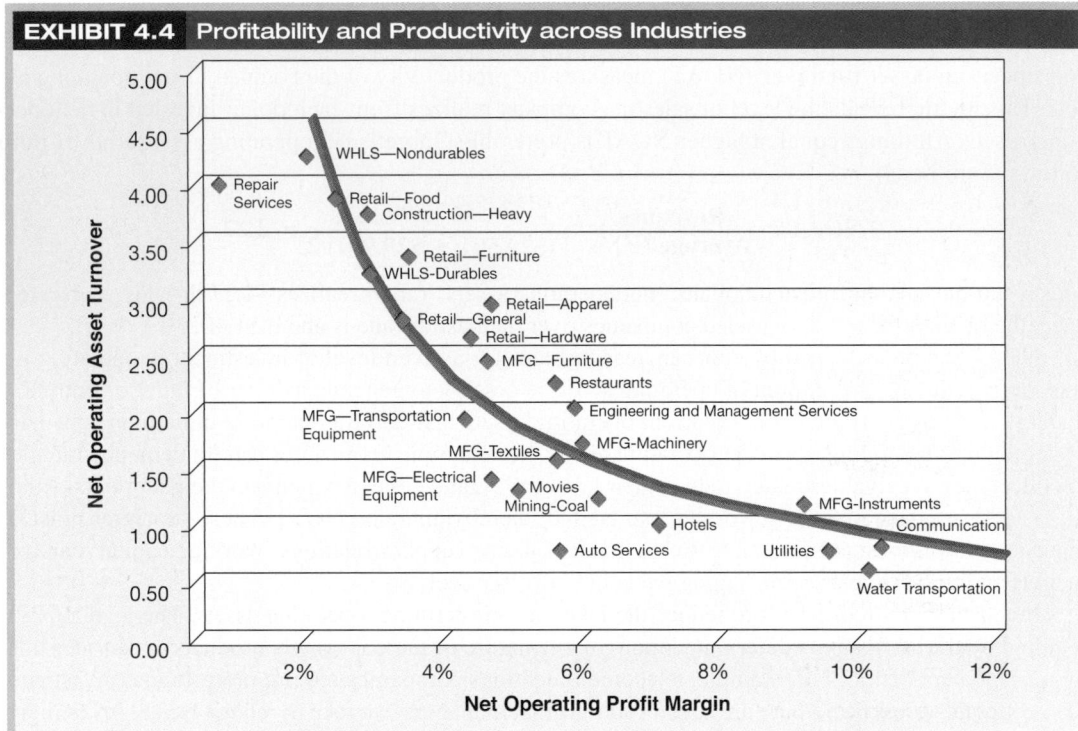

This exhibit reveals that some industries, such as communication and utilities, are capital intensive with relatively low net operating asset turnover. Accordingly, for such industries to achieve a required RNOA (to be competitive in the overall market), they must obtain a higher profit margin. On the other hand, companies such as wholesalers and retailers hold fewer assets and, therefore, can operate on lower operating profit margins to achieve a sufficient RNOA. This is because their asset turnover is far greater.

This exhibit warns of blindly comparing the performance of companies across different industries. For instance, a higher profit margin in the communications industry compared with the retailing industry is not necessarily the result of better management. Instead, the communications industry is extremely capital intensive and thus, to achieve an equivalent RNOA, communications companies must earn a higher profit margin to offset their lower asset turnover. Basic economics suggests that all industries must earn an acceptable return on investment if they are to continue to attract investors and survive.

The trade-off between margin and turnover is relatively straightforward when comparing companies that operate in one industry (*pure-play* firms). Analyzing conglomerates that operate in several industries is more challenging. Conglomerates' margins and turnover rates are a weighted average of the margins and turnover rates for the various industries in which they operate. For example, Caterpillar, Inc., is a blend of a manufacturing company and a financial institution (Caterpillar Financial

Services Corp.); thus, the margin and turnover benchmarks for Caterpillar on a consolidated basis are a weighted average of those two industries.

To summarize, ROE is the sum of the returns from operating (RNOA) and nonoperating activities. Further, RNOA is the product of NOPM and NOAT.

RESEARCH INSIGHT | **NOPM and NOAT Explain Stock Prices**

Research shows that stock returns are positively associated with earnings—when companies report higher than expected earnings, stock returns rise. Research also reports that the RNOA components (NOPM and NOAT) are more strongly associated with stock returns and future profitability than earnings (or return on assets) alone. This applies to the short-term market response to earnings announcements and long-term stock price changes. Thus, disaggregating earnings and the balance sheet into operating and nonoperating components is a useful analysis tool.

Source: Soliman, Mark T., *Use of DuPont Analysis by Market Participants* (October 2007), SSRN: ssrn.com/abstract=1101981.

MID-MODULE REVIEW 2

Following is the balance sheet of Walmart.

WALMART Balance Sheets		
(millions, except share data)	Jan. 31, 2011	Jan. 31, 2010
Cash and cash equivalents	$ 7,395	$ 7,907
Receivables, net	5,089	4,144
Inventories	36,318	32,713
Prepaid expenses and other	2,960	3,128
Current assets of discontinued operations	131	140
Total current assets	51,893	48,032
Property and equipment		
Land	24,386	22,591
Buildings and improvements	79,051	73,657
Fixtures and equipment	38,290	34,035
Transportation equipment	2,595	2,355
Construction in process	4,262	5,210
Property and equipment	148,584	137,848
Less accumulated depreciation	(43,486)	(38,304)
Property and equipment, net	105,098	99,544
Property under capital leases		
Property under capital leases	5,905	5,669
Less accumulated amortization	(3,125)	(2,906)
Property under capital leases, net	2,780	2,763
Goodwill	16,763	16,126
Other assets and deferred charges	4,129	3,942
Total assets	$180,663	$170,407
Short-term borrowings	$ 1,031	$ 523
Accounts payable	33,557	30,451
Accrued liabilities	18,701	18,734
Accrued income taxes	157	1,347
Long-term debt due within one year	4,655	4,050
Obligations under capital leases due within one year	336	346
Current liabilities of discontinued operations	47	92
Total current liabilities	58,484	55,543

continued

continued from prior page

Long-term debt	40,692	33,231
Long-term obligations under capital leases.	3,150	3,170
Deferred income taxes and other.	6,682	5,508
Redeemable noncontrolling interest.	408	307
Equity		
Preferred stock ($0.10 par value; 100 shares authorized, none issued)	—	—
Common stock ($0.10 par value; 11,000 shares authorized, 3,516 and 3,786		
issued and outstanding at January 31, 2011 and 2010, respectively)	352	378
Capital in excess of par value	3,577	3,803
Retained earnings	63,967	66,357
Accumulated other comprehensive income (loss)	646	(70)
Total Walmart shareholders' equity	68,542	70,468
Noncontrolling interest.	2,705	2,180
Total equity.	71,247	72,648
Total liabilities and equity	$180,663	$170,407

Required

1. Compute Walmart's net operating assets for 2011 and 2010.
2. Refer to Walmart's income statement and NOPAT from Mid-Module Review 1. Compute Walmart's return on net operating assets (RNOA) for 2011.
3. Compute Walmart's 2011 ROE. What percentage of Walmart's ROE comes from operations?
4. Disaggregate Walmart's 2011 RNOA into net operating profit margin (NOPM) and net operating asset turnover (NOAT).
5. Compare and contrast Walmart's ROE, RNOA, NOPM, and NOAT with those same measures computed in this module for Target. Interpret the results.

The solution is on page 4-55.

Further RNOA Disaggregation

While disaggregation of RNOA into net operating profit margin (NOPM) and net operating asset turnover (NOAT) yields valuable insight into factors driving company performance, analysts and creditors usually disaggregate those components even further. The purpose is to better identify the specific drivers of both profitability and turnover.

To disaggregate NOPM, we examine the gross profit on products sold and the individual expense accounts that affect operating profit as a percentage of sales (such as Gross profit/Sales and SG&A/Sales). These margin ratios aid comparisons across companies of differing sizes and across different time periods for the same company. We further discuss profit margin disaggregation in other modules that focus on operating results.

To disaggregate NOAT, we examine the individual balance sheet accounts that comprise NOA and compare them to the related income statement activity. Specifically, we compute accounts receivable turnover (ART), inventory turnover (INVT), property, plant and equipment turnover (PPET), as well as turnovers for liability accounts such as accounts payable (APT). Analysts and creditors often compute the net operating working capital turnover (NOWCT) to assess a company's working capital management compared to its competitors and recent trends. (Recall that operating working capital is calculated as current operating assets less current operating liabilities.) These turnover rates are further discussed in other modules that focus on operating assets and liabilities. Exhibit 4.5 provides a broad overview of ratios commonly used for component disaggregation and analysis.

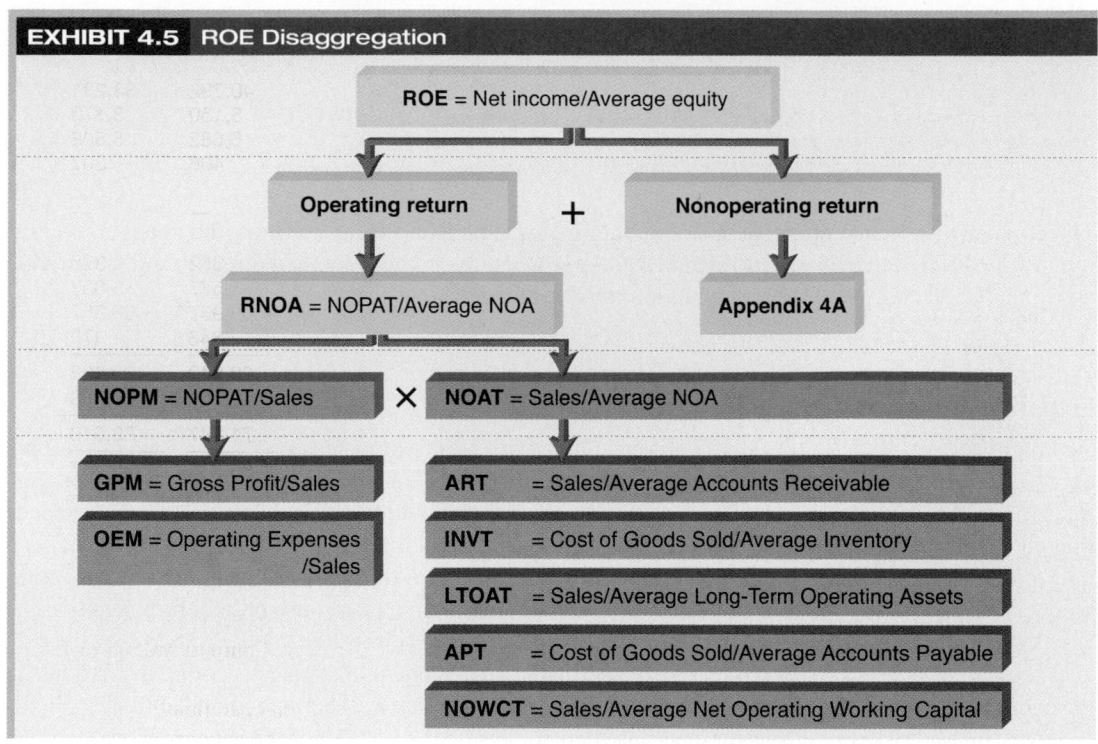

EXHIBIT 4.5 ROE Disaggregation

NONOPERATING RETURN

This section discusses a company's nonoperating return. In it's simplest form, the return on nonoperating activities measures the extent to which a company is using debt to increase its return on equity.

LO3 Explain nonoperating return and compute it from return on equity and the operating return.

Equity Only Financing

The following example provides the intuition for nonoperating return. Assume that a company has $1,000 in net operating assets for the current year in which it earns a 20% RNOA. It finances those assets entirely with equity investment (no debt). To simplify this example, we assume that taxes are 0%; later, we explain the impact of taxes. Its ROE is computed as follows:

$$
\begin{aligned}
\text{ROE} &= \text{Operating return} + \text{Nonoperating return} \\
&= \quad 20\% \quad + \quad 0\% \\
&= \quad 20\%
\end{aligned}
$$

Equity and Debt Financing

Next, assume that this company borrows $500 at 7% interest and uses those funds to acquire additional operating assets yielding the same 20% operating return as above. Its net operating assets for the year now total $1,500, and its profit is $265, computed as follows:

Profit from assets financed with equity ($1,000 × 20%)		$200
Profit from assets financed with debt ($500 × 20%)	$100	
Less interest expense from debt ($500 × 7%)	(35)	65
Net profit.		$265

We see that this company has increased its profit to $265 (up from $200) with the addition of debt, and its ROE is now 26.5% ($265/$1,000). The reason for the increased ROE is that the company borrowed $500 at 7% (and paid $35 of interest expense) and invested those funds in assets earning 20% (which generated $100 of profits). That difference of 13% ($65 profit, computed as [20% − 7%] × $500) accrues to shareholders. Stated differently, the company's ROE now consists of the following.

$$
\begin{aligned}
\textbf{ROE} &= \textbf{Operating return} + \textbf{Nonoperating return} \\
&= \qquad 20\% \qquad + \qquad 6.5\% \\
&= \qquad\qquad 26.5\%
\end{aligned}
$$

The company has made effective use of debt to increase its ROE. Here, we infer the nonoperating return as the difference between ROE and RNOA. This return can be computed directly, and we provide an expanded discussion of this computation in Appendix 4A.

Advantages and Disadvantages of Equity versus Debt Financing

We might further ask: If a higher ROE is desirable, why don't companies use the maximum possible debt? The answer is that creditors, such as banks and bondholders, charge successively higher interest rates for increasing levels of debt (see Module 8). At some point, the cost of the additional debt exceeds the return on the additional assets acquired from the debt financing. Thereafter, further debt financing does not make economic sense. The market, in essence, places a limit on the level of debt that a company can effectively acquire. In sum, shareholders benefit from increased use of debt provided that the assets financed with the debt earn a return that exceeds the cost of the debt.

Creditors usually require a company to execute a loan agreement that places varying restrictions on the company's operating activities. These restrictions, called *covenants*, help safeguard debtholders in the face of increased risk. Covenants exist because debtholders do not have a voice on the board of directors like stockholders do. These debt covenants impose a "cost" on the company beyond that of the interest rate, and these covenants are more stringent as a company increases its reliance on debt financing.

RESEARCH INSIGHT | **Ratio Behavior over Time**

How do RNOA and ROE behave over time? Following is a graph of these ratios (on average for a large set of firms) over the past decade. We see there is considerable variability in these ratios over time. The proportion of RNOA to ROE is greater for some periods of time than for others. Yet, in all periods for this large sample of firms, ROE exceeds RNOA. This is evidence of a positive effect, on average, for ROE from financial leverage.

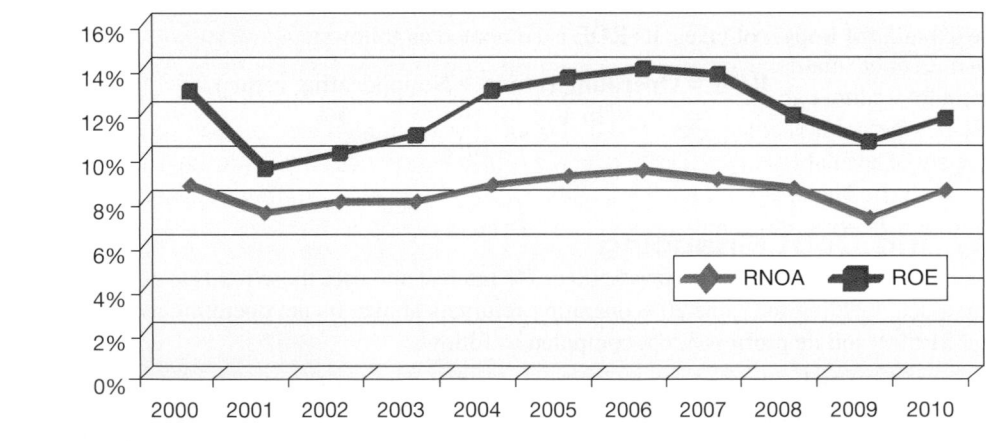

FINANCIAL LEVERAGE ACROSS INDUSTRIES

As we have seen, companies can effectively use debt to increase ROE with returns from nonoperating activities. The advantage of debt is that it typically is a less costly source of financing; currently the cost of debt is about 4% versus a cost of equity of about 12%, on average. Although it reduces financing costs, debt does carry default risk: the risk that the company will be unable to repay debt when it comes due. Creditors have several legal remedies when companies default, including forcing a company into bankruptcy and possibly liquidating its assets.

During the past decade, the median ratio of total liabilities to stockholders' equity, which measures the relative use of debt versus equity in a company's capital structure, is about 1.5 for publicly traded companies with sales over $500 million. This means that the average company is financed with about $1.50 of liabilities for each dollar of stockholders' equity. However, the relative use of debt varies considerably across industries as illustrated in Exhibit 4.6.

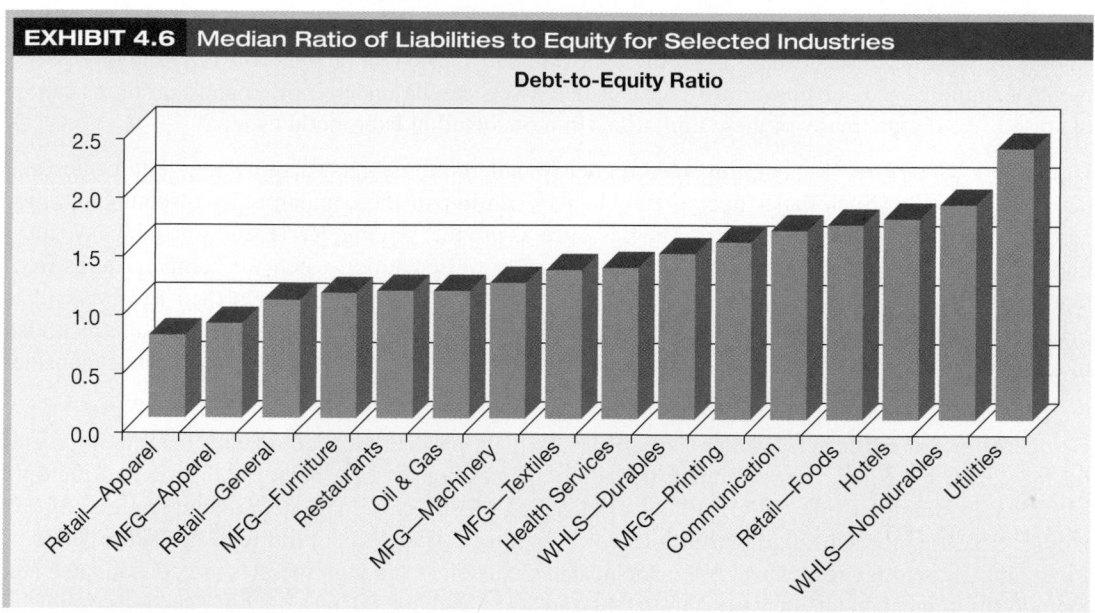

EXHIBIT 4.6 Median Ratio of Liabilities to Equity for Selected Industries

Companies in the utilities industry have a large proportion of debt. Because the utilities industry is regulated, profits and cash flows are relatively certain and stable and, as a result, utility companies can support a higher debt level. The hotel and nondurable wholesale industries also utilize a relatively high proportion of debt. However, these industries are not regulated, their market is more competitive and volatile and, consequently, their use of debt carries more risk. At the lower end of debt financing are retail and restaurant companies.

The core of our analysis relating to debt is the examination of a company's ability to generate cash to *service* its debt (that is, to make required debt payments of both interest and principal). Analysts, investors and creditors are primarily concerned about whether the company either has sufficient cash available or whether it is able to generate the required cash in the future to cover its debt obligations. The analysis of available cash and a company's ability to service its debt in the short run is called *liquidity analysis*. The analysis of the company's ability to generate sufficient cash in the long run is called *solvency analysis* (so named because a bankrupt company is said to be "insolvent").

Limitations of Ratio Analysis

The quality of financial statement analysis depends on the quality of financial information. We ought not blindly analyze numbers; doing so can lead to faulty conclusions and suboptimal decisions. Instead, we need to acknowledge that current accounting rules (GAAP) have limitations, and be fully aware of the company's environment, its competitive pressures, and any structural and strategic changes. This section discusses some of the factors that limit the usefulness of financial accounting information for ratio analysis.

GAAP Limitations Several limitations in GAAP can distort financial ratios. Limitations include:

1. **Measurability**. Financial statements reflect what can be reliably measured. This results in nonrecognition of certain assets, often internally developed assets, the very assets that are most likely to

confer a competitive advantage and create value. Examples are brand name, a superior management team, employee skills, and a reliable supply chain.

2. **Non-capitalized costs**. Related to the concept of measurability is the expensing of costs relating to "assets" that cannot be identified with enough precision to warrant capitalization. Examples are brand equity costs from advertising and other promotional activities, and research and development costs relating to future products.

3. **Historical costs**. Assets and liabilities are usually recorded at original acquisition or issuance costs. Subsequent increases in value are not recorded until realized, and declines in value are only recognized if deemed permanent.

Thus, GAAP balance sheets omit important and valuable assets. Our analysis of ROE and our assessment of liquidity and solvency, must consider that assets can be underreported and that ratios can be distorted. We discuss many of these limitations in more detail in later modules.

Company Changes Many companies regularly undertake mergers, acquire new companies and divest subsidiaries. Such major operational changes can impair the comparability of company ratios across time. Companies also change strategies, such as product pricing, R&D, and financing. We must understand the effects of such changes on ratios and exercise caution when we compare ratios from one period to the next. Companies also behave differently at different points in their life cycles. For instance, growth companies possess a different profile than do mature companies. Seasonal effects also markedly impact analysis of financial statements at different times of the year. Thus, we must consider life cycle and seasonality when we compare ratios across companies and over time.

Conglomerate Effects Few companies are pure-play; instead, most companies operate in several businesses or industries. Most publicly traded companies consist of a parent company and multiple subsidiaries, often pursuing different lines of business. Most heavy equipment manufacturers, for example, have finance subsidiaries (Ford Credit Corporation and Cat Financial are subsidiaries of Ford and Caterpillar respectively). Financial statements of such conglomerates are consolidated and include the financial statements of the parent and its subsidiaries. Consequently, such consolidated statements are challenging to analyze. Typically, analysts break the financials apart into their component businesses and separately analyze each component. Fortunately, companies must report financial information (albeit limited) for major business segments in their 10-Ks.

Fuzzy View Ratios reduce, to a single number, the myriad complexities of a company's operations. No scalar can accurately capture all qualitative aspects of a company. Ratios cannot meaningfully convey a company's marketing and management philosophies, its human resource activities, its financing activities, its strategic initiatives, and its product management. In our analysis we must learn to look through the numbers and ratios to better understand the operational factors that drive financial results. Successful analysis seeks to gain insight into what a company is really about and what the future portends. Our overriding purpose in analysis is to understand the past and present to better predict the future. Computing and examining ratios is one step in that process.

GLOBAL ACCOUNTING

An important aim of this module is to distinguish between operating and nonoperating items for the balance sheet and income statement. U.S. GAAP and IFRS generally account for items similarly, but there are certain disclosure differences worth noting.

The IFRS balance sheet is similar to its U.S. GAAP counterpart, with the visible exception for the frequent, but not mandatory, reverse ordering of assets and liabilities. However, one notable difference is that IFRS companies routinely report "financial assets" or "financial liabilities" on the balance sheet. We must assess these items. IFRS defines financial assets to include receivables (operating item), loans to affiliates or associates (can be operating or nonoperating depending on the nature of the transactions), securities held as investments (nonoperating), and derivatives (nonoperating). IFRS notes to financial statements, which tend to be more detailed than U.S. GAAP notes, usually detail what financial assets and liabilities consist of. This helps us accurately determine NOA and NNO.

The IFRS income statement usually reports fewer line items than U.S. GAAP income statements and, further, there is no definition of "operating activities" under IFRS. This means we must devote attention to classify operating versus nonoperating income components. Following is a table that shows common U.S. GAAP income statement items and their classification as operating (O) or nonoperating (N). This table also indicates which items are required for IFRS income statements.

Income Statement Line Items	Operating (O) or Nonoperating (N)	Required on IFRS Income Statement
Net sales	O	YES
Cost of sales	O	—
Selling, general and administrative (SG&A) expense	O	—
Provisions for doubtful accounts	O	—
Nonoperating income	N	—
Interest revenue and Interest expense	N	YES
Nonoperating expenses	N	—
Income before income taxes	O and N	—
Income tax expense	O and N	YES
Earnings on equity investments (associates and joint ventures)	O	YES
Income from continuing operations	O	—
Discontinued operations	N	YES
Income before extraordinary items	O and N	—
Extraordinary items, net of income tax	O or N	—
Net income	O and N	YES
Net income attributable to noncontrolling interest	N	YES
Net income attributable to controlling interest	O and N	YES
Earnings per share (Basic EPS and Diluted EPS)	O and N	YES

There is no requirement to report income from operations, yet many IFRS companies do so. However, items that are considered operating such as gains and losses on disposals of operating assets, or income from equity method investments, are often reported below the operating income line. We must examine IFRS income statements and their notes to make an independent assessment of what is operating. IFRS income statements usually report separately the other nonoperating revenues and expenses even though this is not required. We can better assess the nature of these items by reading the notes.

MODULE-END REVIEW

Refer to the income statement and balance sheet of **Walmart**, from Mid-Module Reviews 1 and 2 earlier in this module.

Required

1. Compute Walmart's nonoperating return for 2011.
2. Compute Target's nonoperating return for 2011 from the information reported in this module. Compare and contrast the nonoperating return for Walmart and Target. Interpret the results.
3. Compute Walmart's liabilities-to-equity ratio for 2011.
4. Compute Target's liabilities-to-equity ratio for 2011 from the balance sheet in this module. Compare and contrast the ratio to Walmart's liabilities-to-equity ratio. Interpret the results.

The solution is on page 4-55.

APPENDIX 4A: Nonoperating Return Component of ROE

LO3 Explain nonoperating return and compute it from return on equity and the operating return.

In this appendix, we consider the nonoperating return component of ROE in more detail. We also provide a derivation of that nonoperating return and discuss several special topics pertaining to it. We begin by considering three special cases of capital structure financing.

Nonoperating Return Framework

In the module, we infer the nonoperating return as the difference between ROE and RNOA. The nonoperating return can also be computed directly as FLEV × Spread, where FLEV is the degree of financial leverage and Spread is the difference between the assets' after-tax operating return (RNOA) and the after-tax cost of debt.

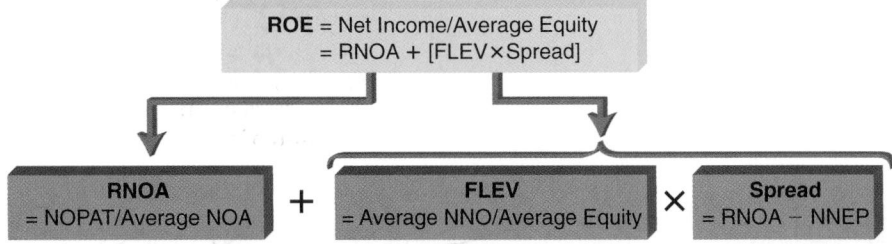

Exhibit 4A.1 provides definitions for each of the terms required in this computation.

EXHIBIT 4A.1 Nonoperating Return Definitions	
NNO: Net nonoperating obligations	Nonoperating liabilities (plus any noncontrolling interest reported on the balance sheet) less nonoperating assets
FLEV: Financial leverage	Average NNO/Average equity
NNE: Net nonoperating expense	NOPAT – Net income; NNE consists of nonoperating expenses and revenues, net of tax, as well as any noncontrolling interest reported on the income statement.
NNEP: Net nonoperating expense percent	NNE/Average NNO
Spread	RNOA – NNEP

Nonoperating Return—With Debt Financing, but Without Nonoperating Assets

To illustrate computation of the nonoperating return when the company has debt and equity financing (without nonoperating assets), let's refer to our example in this module of the company that increases its ROE through use of debt. (For this first illustration, view FLEV as the relative use of debt in the capital structure, and Spread as the difference between RNOA and the net nonoperating expense percent.) Again, assume that this company has $1,000 of equity, $500 of 7% debt, total assets of $1,500 that earn a 20% return, and a tax rate of 0%. The net income of this firm is $265, computed as follows:

Profit from assets financed with equity ($1,000 × 20%)		$200
Profit from assets financed with debt ($500 × 20%)	$100	
Less interest expense from debt ($500 × 7%)	(35)	65
Net profit		$265

This company's ROE is 26.5%, computed as $265/$1,000 (assuming income received at year-end for simplicity and average equity is $1,000). Its RNOA is 20%, FLEV is 0.50 (computed as $500 of average net nonoperating obligations divided by $1,000 average equity), and its Spread is 13% (computed as 20% less 7%). This company's ROE, shown with the nonoperating return being directly computed, is as follows:

$$ROE = RNOA + [\ FLEV\ \times\ Spread\ ]$$
$$= 20\%\ \ \ \ + [\ \ 0.50\ \ \ \times\ \ \ 13\%\ \ \ ]$$
$$= 26.5\%$$

We see that when a company's nonoperating activities relate solely to the borrowing of money (without nonoperating assets), FLEV collapses to the ratio of debt to equity, called the debt-to-equity ratio.

Nonoperating Return—Without Debt Financing, but With Nonoperating Assets

Some companies, such as many high-tech firms, have no debt, and maintain large portfolios of marketable securities. They hold these highly liquid assets so that they can respond quickly to new opportunities or react to competitive pressures. With high levels of nonoperating assets and no nonoperating liabilities, the net nonoperating obligations (NNO) has a negative sign (NNO = Nonoperating liabilities − Nonoperating assets). Likewise, FLEV is negative: Average NNO (−) / Average Equity (+). Further, net nonoperating expense (NNE = NOPAT − Net income) is negative because investment *income* is a negative nonoperating expense. However, the net nonoperating expense percent (NNEP) is positive because the negative NNE is divided by the negative NNO. *This causes ROE to be less than RNOA* (see computations below). We use the 2010 10-K of Intel to illustrate this curious result (Intel reports no noncontrolling interest).

Intel ($ millions, except percentages)	2010	2009	Average	Computation
NOA	$ 28,652	$ 29,232	$ 28,942	—
NNO	$(20,778)	$(12,472)	$(16,625)	—
Stockholders' equity	$ 49,430	$ 41,704	$ 45,567	—
Net income	$ 11,464	—	—	—
NOPAT	$ 11,250	—	—	—
NNE (NOPAT − Net income)	$ (214)	—	—	—
FLEV	(0.3648)	—	—	$(16,625)/$45,567
RNOA	38.87%	—	—	$11,250/$28,942
NNEP	1.29%	—	—	$(214)/$(16,625)
Spread	37.58%	—	—	38.87%-1.29%

Intel's NNO is negative because its investment in marketable securities exceeds its debt. Intel's ROE is 25.16%, and it consists of the following:

$$ROE = RNOA\ \ + [\ \ \ FLEV\ \ \ \times Spread\ \ \ ]$$
$$= 38.87\%\ \ + [\ \ -0.3648\ \times 37.58\%\ \ ]$$
$$= 38.87\%\ \ +\ \ \ \ \ \ \ \ \ \ [-13.71\%]$$
$$= 25.16\%$$

Intel's ROE is lower than its RNOA because of its large investment in marketable securities. That is, its excessive liquidity is penalizing its return on equity. The rationale for this seemingly incongruous result is this: Intel's ROE derives from operating and nonoperating assets. Intel's operating assets are providing an outstanding return (38.87%), much higher than the return on its marketable securities (1.29%). Holding liquid assets that are less productive means that Intel's shareholders are funding a sizeable level of liquidity, and sacrificing returns in the process. Why? Many companies in high-tech industries feel the need to maintain excessive liquidity to gain flexibility—the flexibility to take advantage of opportunities and to react quickly to competitor maneuvers. Intel's management, evidently, feels that the investment of costly equity capital in this manner will reap future rewards for its shareholders. Its 25.16% ROE provides some evidence that this strategy is not necessarily misguided.

Nonoperating Return—With Debt Financing and Nonoperating Assets

Most companies report both debt and investments on their balance sheets. If that debt markedly exceeds the investment balance, their ROE will look more like our first example (with debt only). Instead, if investments predominate, their ROE will look more like Intel's. It is important to remember that both the average NNO (and FLEV) and NNE can be either positive (debt) or negative (investments), and it is not always the case that ROE exceeds RNOA. We now compute nonoperating return for Target, a company with both debt and investments.

Nonoperating Return for Target

In Exhibit 4A.1, we define net nonoperating expense (NNE) as NOPAT − Net income. For Target, we can compute NNE as NOPAT of $3,397 million less net income of $2,920 million, which yields $477 million. More generally, NNE can include a number of nonoperating items such as interest expense, interest revenue, dividend income, investment gains and losses, income (loss) on discontinued operations and noncontrolling interest (if any); all net of tax. (Recall that the simple illustration at the beginning of this appendix *ignored taxes*, which meant NNE was equal to the $35 interest paid.)

To compute operating return (RNOA) we divided NOPAT from the income statement, by NOA from the balance sheet. Similarly, to compute the net nonoperating expense percent (NNEP), we divide NNE from the income statement by net nonoperating obligations from the balance sheet (NNO). Exhibit 4A.2 shows how a balance sheet can be reorganized into operating and nonoperating items.

EXHIBIT 4A.2   Simplified Balance Sheet

	Assets	**Liabilities**
Net operating assets (NOA) . . . . (assets – liabilities)	Current Operating Assets + Long-Term Operating Assets = Total Operating Assets	Current Operating Liabilities + Long-Term Operating Liabilities = Total Operating Liabilities
Net nonoperating obligations (NNO) . . . . (liabilities – assets)	Current Nonoperating Assets + Long-Term Nonoperating Assets = Total Nonoperating Assets	Current Nonoperating Liabilities + Long-Term Nonoperating Liabilities = Total Nonoperating Liabilities
		Equity Stockholders' Equity
Equity (NOA – NNO)	Total Assets	Total Liabilities and Equity

Net nonoperating obligations are total nonoperating liabilities less total nonoperating assets. The accounting equation stipulates that Assets = Liabilities + Equity, so we can adjust it to yield the following key identity:

Net operating assets (NOA) = Net nonoperating obligations (NNO) + Stockholders' equity

For Target, we compute NNO as follows:

Target ($ millions)	2011	2010
Nonoperating liabilities		
Unsecured debt and other borrowings	$ 119	$ 796
Nonrecourse debt collateralized by credit card receivables	—	900
L-T Unsecured debt and other borrowings	11,653	10,643
L-T Nonrecourse debt collateralized by credit card receivables	3,954	4,475
Total nonoperating liabilities.	15,726	16,814
Nonoperating assets		
Cash and cash equivalents	1,712	2,200
Short-term and long-term investments	0	0
Total nonoperating assets	1,712	2,200
Net nonoperating obligations (NNO)	$14,014	$14,614

Accordingly (drawing on NNE from the income statement and NNO from the balance sheet), we compute the net nonoperating expense percent (NNEP) as follows:

$$\text{Net nonoperating expense percent (NNEP)} = \frac{\text{Net nonoperating expense (NNE)}}{\text{Average net nonoperating obligations (NNO)}}$$

The net nonoperating expense percent (NNEP) measures the average cost of net nonoperating obligations. The denominator uses the average NNO similar to the return calculations (such as ROE and RNOA).

In the simple illustration from earlier in this appendix, that company's net nonoperating expense percent is 7%, computed as $35/$500, which is exactly equal to the interest rate on the loan. With real financial statements,

NNEP is more complicated because NNE often includes both interest on borrowed money and nonoperating income, and NNO is the net of operating liabilities less nonoperating assets. Thus NNEP often reflects an average return on nonoperating activities. For Target, its 2011 NNEP is 3.33%, computed as $477 million/[($14,014 million + $14,614 million)/2].

Target's 2011 RNOA is 11.43%, which means that net operating assets generate more return than the 3.33% cost of net nonoperating obligations. That is, Target earns a Spread of 8.10%, the difference between RNOA (11.43%) and NNEP (3.33%), on each asset financed with borrowed funds. By borrowing funds, Target creates leverage, which can be measured relative to stockholders' equity; that ratio is called financial leverage (FLEV). In sum, total nonoperating return is computed by the following formula:

$$\text{Nonoperating return} = \underbrace{\frac{\text{Average net nonoperating obligations (NNO)}}{\text{Average stockholders' equity}}}_{\text{FLEV}} \times \underbrace{(\text{RNOA} - \text{NNEP})}_{\text{Spread}}$$

Two points are immediately clear from this equation. First, ROE increases with the Spread between RNOA and NNEP. The more profitable the return on operating assets, the higher the return to shareholders. Second, the higher the debt relative to equity, the higher the ROE (assuming, of course, a positive Spread).

Target's 2011 Spread between RNOA and NNEP is 8.10%. It has average NNO of $14,314 million [($14,014 million + $14,614 million)/2] and average equity of $15,417 million [($15,487 million + $15,347 million)/2]. Thus, Target's ROE is as follows:

$$
\begin{array}{rcll}
\text{ROE} = & \text{Operating return} & + & \text{Nonoperating return} \\
= & 11.43\% & + & [\$14,314/\$15,417] \times [11.43\% - 3.33\%] \\
= & 11.43\% & + & [0.9285] \times [8.10\%] \\
= & & & 18.95\% \text{ (0.0001 rounding error)}
\end{array}
$$

Most companies report both debt and investments on their balance sheets. If that debt markedly exceeds the investment balance, their ROE will look more like our Target example (with net debt). Instead, if investments predominate, their ROE will look more like Intel's (with net investments). It is important to remember that both the average NNO (and FLEV) and NNE can be either positive (debt) or negative (investments), and it is not always the case that ROE exceeds RNOA.

Derivation of Nonoperating Return Formula

Following is the algebraic derivation of the nonoperating return formula, where NI is net income, SE is average stockholders' equity, and all other terms are as defined in Exhibits 4.3 and 4A.1.

$$
\begin{aligned}
\text{ROE} &= \frac{\text{NI}}{\text{SE}} \\[4pt]
&= \frac{\text{NOPAT} - \text{NNE}}{\text{SE}} \\[4pt]
&= \frac{\text{NOPAT}}{\text{SE}} - \frac{\text{NNE}}{\text{SE}} \\[4pt]
&= \left(\frac{\text{NOA}}{\text{SE}} \times \text{RNOA}\right) - \left(\frac{\text{NNO}}{\text{SE}} \times \text{NNEP}\right) \\[4pt]
&= \left(\frac{(\text{SE} + \text{NNO})}{\text{SE}} \times \text{RNOA}\right) - \left(\frac{\text{NNO}}{\text{SE}} \times \text{NNEP}\right) \\[4pt]
&= \left[\text{RNOA} \times \left(1 + \frac{\text{NNO}}{\text{SE}}\right)\right] - \left(\frac{\text{NNO}}{\text{SE}} \times \text{NNEP}\right) \\[4pt]
&= \text{RNOA} + \left(\frac{\text{NNO}}{\text{SE}} \times \text{RNOA}\right) - \left(\frac{\text{NNO}}{\text{SE}} \times \text{NNEP}\right) \\[4pt]
&= \text{RNOA} + \left(\frac{\text{NNO}}{\text{SE}}\right)(\text{RNOA} - \text{NNEP}) \\[4pt]
&= \text{RNOA} + (\text{FLEV} \times \text{Spread})
\end{aligned}
$$

Special Topics

The return on equity (ROE) computation becomes a bit more complicated in the presence of discontinued operations, preferred stock, and minority (or noncontrolling) equity interest. The first of these apportions ROE between operating and nonoperating returns, and the other two affect the dollar amount included in the denominator (average equity) of the ROE computation. Recall that ROE measures the return on investment for common shareholders. *The ROE numerator should include only the income available to pay common dividends and the ROE denominator should include common equity only, not the equity of preferred or minority shareholders.*

Discontinued Operations Discontinued operations are subsidiaries or business segments that the board of directors has formally decided to divest. Companies must report discontinued operations on a separate line, below income from continuing operations. The separate line item includes the net income or loss from discontinued operations along with any gains or losses on the disposal of discontinued net assets (see Module 5 for details). Although not required, many companies disclose the net assets of discontinued operations on the balance sheet to distinguish them from continuing net assets. If the net assets are not separated on the balance sheet, the footnotes provide details to facilitate a disaggregated analysis. These net assets of discontinued operations should be treated as nonoperating (they represent a nonoperating "investment" once they have been classified as discontinued) and their after-tax profit (loss) should be treated as nonoperating as well. Although the ROE computation is unaffected, the nonoperating portion of the ROE for the year will include the contribution of discontinued operations.

Preferred Stock The ROE formula takes the perspective of the common shareholder in that it relates the income available to pay common dividends to the average common shareholder. As such, preferred stock should not be included in average stockholders' equity in the denominator of the ROE formula. Similarly, any dividends paid on preferred stock should be subtracted from net income to yield the profit available to pay common dividends. (Dividends are not an expense in computing net income; thus, net income is available to both preferred and common shareholders. To determine net income available to common shareholders, we must subtract preferred dividends.) Thus, the presence of preferred stock requires two adjustments to the ROE formula.

1. Preferred dividends must be subtracted from net income in the numerator.
2. Preferred stock must be subtracted from stockholders' equity in the denominator.

This modified return on equity formula is more accurately labeled return on common equity (ROCE).

$$ROCE = \frac{\text{Net income} - \text{Preferred dividends}}{\text{Average stockholders' equity} - \text{Average preferred equity}}$$

Noncontrolling Interest When a company acquires controlling interest of the outstanding voting stock of another company, the parent company must consolidate the new subsidiary in its balance sheet and income statement (see Module 7). This means that the parent company must include 100% of the subsidiary's assets, liabilities, revenues and expenses. If the parent acquires less than 100% of the subsidiary's voting stock, the remaining claim of noncontrolling shareholders is reported on the balance sheet as a component of stockholders' equity called noncontrolling interest, and net income is separated into income attributable to company shareholders and that attributable to noncontrolling interests. *The ROE computation, then, should use the net income attributable to company shareholders divided by the average stockholders' equity where equity excludes noncontrolling interest.*

To illustrate the calculation of ROE, FLEV, and Spread in the presence of noncontrolling interest we consider the following selected balance sheet and income statement items from Walmart ($ millions).

	2011	2010	Average
Balance sheet items			
Net operating assets (NOA)	$114,040	$106,320	$110,180
Nonoperating liabilities.	$ 50,319	$ 41,719	$ 46,019
Less: Nonoperating assets.	(7,526)	(8,047)	(7,787)
Plus: Noncontrolling interest	2,705	2,180	2,443
NNO including noncontrolling interest	45,498	35,852	40,675
Equity (attributable to Walmart shareholders)	68,542	70,468	69,505
Total NNO and Equity.	$114,040	$106,320	$110,180
Income statement items			
Net operating profit after tax (NOPAT)	$ 17,222		
Net nonoperating expense (NNE).	(833)		
Net income attributable to Walmart shareholders	$ 16,389		

We then compute the following key ratios ($ millions):

RNOA	15.63%	($17,222/$110,180)
ROE	23.58%	($16,389/$69,505)
FLEV	0.585	($40,675/$69,505)
NNEP	2.05%	($833/$40,675)
Spread	13.58%	(15.63% − 2.05%)

We can also calculate NNE directly as follows ($ millions):

Interest, net before tax	$2,004
Less: Tax shield on interest, net at 37%	(741)
Interest, net after-tax	1,263
Less: Income from discontinued operations	(1,034)
Plus: Net income attributable to noncontrolling interest	604
Net nonoperating expense	$ 833

APPENDIX 4B: Tools of Liquidity and Solvency Analysis

Liquidity Analysis

Liquidity refers to cash availability: how much cash a company has, and how much it can raise on short notice. Two of the most common ratios used to assess the degree of liquidity are the current ratio and the quick ratio. Both of these ratios link required near-term payments to cash available in the near-term.

LO4 Compute and interpret measures of liquidity and solvency.

Current Ratio

Current assets are assets that a company expects to convert into cash within the next operating cycle, which is typically a year. *Current liabilities* are liabilities that come due within the next year. An excess of current assets over current liabilities (Current assets − Current liabilities), is known as *net working capital* or simply *working capital*.[2] Positive working capital implies that cash generated by "liquidating" current assets would be sufficient to pay current liabilities. The current ratio expresses working capital as a ratio and is computed as follows:

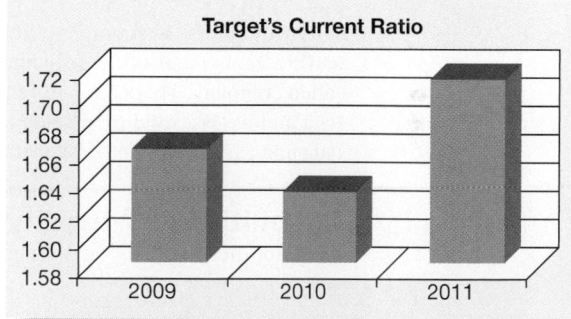

Target's Current Ratio

$$\text{Current ratio} = \frac{\text{Current assets}}{\text{Current liabilities}}$$

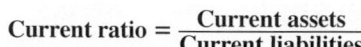

A current ratio greater than 1.0 implies positive working capital. Both working capital and the current ratio consider existing balance sheet data only and ignore cash inflows from future sales or other sources. The current ratio is more commonly used than working capital because ratios allow comparisons across companies of different size. Generally, companies prefer a higher current ratio; however, an excessively high current ratio indicates inefficient asset use. Furthermore, a current ratio less than 1.0 is not always bad for at least two reasons:

1. A cash-and-carry company (like a grocery store) can have potentially few current assets (and a low current ratio), but consistently large operating cash inflows ensure the company will be sufficiently liquid.

---

[2] Both operating assets and operating liabilities can be either current or long-term. "Current" means that the asset is expected to be used, or the liability paid, within the next operating cycle or one year, whichever is longer, which for most companies means a year. Using the current versus long-term nature of operating assets and liabilities we derive two types of net operating assets: net operating working capital (NOWC), and net long-term operating assets. Net operating working capital is defined as:

Net operating working capital (NOWC) = Current operating assets − Current operating liabilities

For Target, NOWC is $5,550 million for 2011 ($15,501 − $9,951).

2. A company can efficiently manage its working capital by minimizing receivables and inventories and maximizing payables. Walmart, for example, uses its buying power to exact extended credit terms from suppliers. Consequently, because it is essentially a cash-and-carry company, its current ratio is less than 1.0 and is sufficiently liquid.

The aim of current ratio analysis is to discern if a company is having, or is likely to have, difficulty meeting its short-term obligations. Target's current ratio for 2011 is 1.71 ($17,213 million/$10,070 million). Its current ratio has rebounded somewhat after three years of decline.

Quick Ratio

The quick ratio is a variant of the current ratio. It focuses on quick assets, which are assets likely to be converted to cash within a relatively short period of time. Specifically, quick assets include cash, marketable securities, and accounts receivable; they exclude inventories, prepaid assets, and other current assets. The quick ratio is defined as follows:

$$\text{Quick ratio} = \frac{\text{Cash + Marketable securities + Accounts receivables}}{\text{Current liabilities}}$$

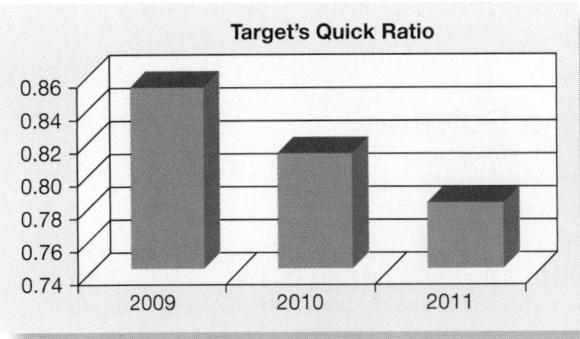

The quick ratio reflects on a company's ability to meet its current liabilities without liquidating inventories. It is a more stringent test of liquidity than the current ratio.

Target's 2011 quick ratio is 0.78 $\left(\frac{\$1,712 + \$6,153}{\$10,070}\right)$. Like the current ratio, Target's quick ratio has decreased steadily over the past three years, but the magnitude of this decline is minimal—see margin graph. It is not uncommon for a company's quick ratio to be less than 1.0. Although liquidity is not a major concern for Target, the decline in the quick ratio is something financial statement users would want to monitor.

Solvency Analysis

Solvency refers to a company's ability to meet its debt obligations, including both periodic interest payments and the repayment of the principal amount borrowed. Solvency is crucial because an insolvent company is a failed company. There are two general approaches to measuring solvency. The first approach uses balance sheet data and assesses the proportion of capital raised from creditors. The second approach uses income statement data and assesses the profit generated relative to debt payment obligations. We discuss each approach in turn.

Liabilities-to-Equity

The liabilities-to-equity ratio is a useful tool for the first type of solvency analysis. It is defined as follows:

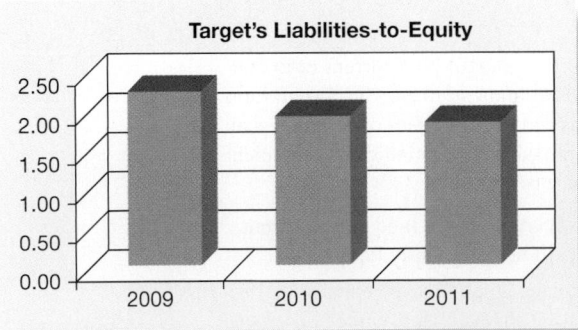

$$\text{Liabilities-to-equity ratio} = \frac{\text{Total liabilities}}{\text{Stockholders' equity}}$$

This ratio conveys how reliant a company is on creditor financing compared with equity financing. A higher ratio indicates less solvency, and more risk. Target's 2011 liabilities-to-equity ratio is 1.82 $\left(\frac{\$10,070 + \$18,148}{\$15,487}\right)$. This ratio has decreased over the past three years—see margin graph. Also, its ratio is slightly greater than 1.5, the median for publicly traded companies. (Because the numerator of this ratio includes the consolidated liabilities of the company, the denominator must use the company's total equity, which includes any noncontrolling interest reported on the balance sheet. Target does not report noncontrolling interest.)

A variant of this ratio considers a company's long-term debt divided by equity. This approach assumes that current liabilities are repaid from current assets (so-called self-liquidating). Thus, it assumes that creditors and stockholders need only focus on the relative proportion of long-term capital.

Times Interest Earned

The second type of solvency analysis compares profits to liabilities. This approach assesses how much operating profit is available to cover debt obligations. A common measure for this type of solvency analysis is the times interest earned ratio, defined as follows:

$$\text{Times interest earned} = \frac{\text{Earnings before interest and taxes}}{\text{Interest expense}}$$

The times interest earned ratio reflects the operating income available to pay interest expense. The underlying assumption is that only interest needs to be paid because the principal will be refinanced. This ratio is sometimes abbreviated as EBIT/I. The numerator is similar to net operating profits after tax (NOPAT), but it is *pretax* instead of after tax. We use earnings before net interest expense, that is, net of any other nonoperating income or expenses.

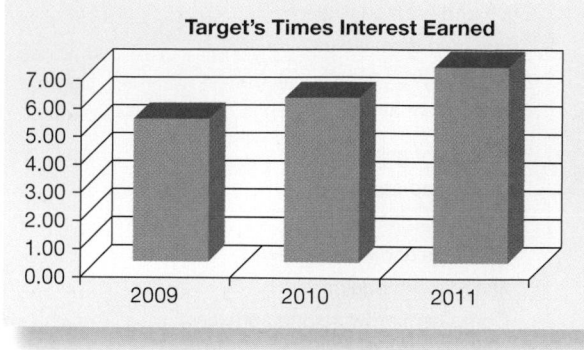

Management wants this ratio to be sufficiently high so that there is little risk of default. Target's 2011 times interest earned is a healthy 6.94, computed as $\frac{\$5,252}{\$757}$. This ratio has increased over the past three years—see margin graph. This result implies that Target could suffer a large decline in profitability and still be able to service its interest payments when due. Any solvency concerns we might have had relating to Target's lack of liquidity and relatively high debt load are mitigated by its earning power.

There are many variations of solvency and liquidity analysis and the ratios used. The basic idea is to construct measures that reflect a company's credit risk exposure. There is not one "best" financial leverage ratio. Instead, as financial statement users, we want to use measures that capture the risk we are most concerned with. It is also important to compute the ratios ourselves to ensure we know what is included and excluded from each ratio.

Vertical and Horizontal Analysis

Companies come in all sizes, which presents difficulties when making comparisons among firms or over time. There are several methods that attempt to overcome this obstacle.

Vertical analysis expresses financial statements in ratio form. Specifically, it is routine to express income statement items as a percent of net sales, and balance sheet items as a percent of total assets. Such *common-size financial statements* facilitate comparisons *across companies* of different sizes and comparisons of accounts within a set of financial statements.

Horizontal analysis is the scrutiny of financial data *across time*. Comparing data across two or more consecutive periods assists in analyzing trends in company performance and in predicting future performance.

Exhibits 4B.1 and 4B.2 present Target's common-size balance sheet and common-size income statement. We also present data for horizontal analysis by showing three years of common-size statements.

On the income side, Target's cost of goods sold has remained fairly constant over this three-year period. The improvement in Target's earnings before interest and taxes and net income has been the result of a reduction of credit card expenses. This, most likely, represents a reduction of credit losses on Target credit card receivables as the economy began to emerge from recession in 2011.

Target's total assets in dollars have decreased slightly since 2009. However, we are primarily interested in the composition of the balance sheet, or the proportion invested in each asset category. Specifically, liquidity has generally increased in the most recent year as cash and cash equivalents represent 3.9% of total assets in 2011, up from 2% in 2009. While receivables have decreased as a percent of total assets, inventories have increased, leaving total current assets relatively unchanged at 39% of total assets. Long-term assets have not changed markedly over these three years.

Target's short-term liabilities have remained constant over the three years with current liabilities representing 23% of total liabilities and equity. During this period, Target's long-term liabilities have decreased while its stockholders' equity has increased in relative terms. This is generally regarded as positive as it represents a corresponding reduction in debt. Overall, Target presents a relatively stable picture with reasonable percentages in all categories and a reduction in financial leverage.

EXHIBIT 4B.1   Common-Size Balance Sheets

TARGET
Common-Size Balance Sheets

	Amounts ($ millions)			Percentages*		
	2011	2010	2009	2011	2010	2009
Assets						
Cash and cash equivalents	$ 1,712	$ 2,200	$ 864	3.9%	4.9%	2.0%
Credit card receivables.	6,153	6,966	8,084	14.1	15.6	18.3
Inventory.	7,596	7,179	6,705	17.4	16.1	15.2
Other current assets.	1,752	2,079	1,835	4.0	4.7	4.2
Total current assets	17,213	18,424	17,488	39.4	41.4	39.6
Property and equipment						
Land	5,928	5,793	5,767	13.6	13.0	13.1
Buildings and improvements	23,081	22,152	20,430	52.8	49.7	46.3
Fixtures and equipment	4,939	4,743	4,270	11.3	10.7	9.7
Computer hardware and software	2,533	2,575	2,586	5.8	5.8	5.9
Construction-in-progress	567	502	1,763	1.3	1.1	4.0
Accumulated depreciation	(11,555)	(10,485)	(9,060)	(26.4)	(23.5)	(20.5)
Property and equipment, net	25,493	25,280	25,756	58.3	56.8	58.4
Other noncurrent assets.	999	829	862	2.3	1.9	2.0
Total assets.	$43,705	$44,533	$44,106	100.0%	100.0%	100.0%
Liabilities and shareholders' investment						
Accounts payable.	$ 6,625	$ 6,511	$ 6,337	15.2%	14.6%	14.4%
Accrued and other current liabilities.	3,326	3,120	2,913	7.6	7.0	6.6
Unsecured debt and other borrowings	119	796	1,262	0.3	1.8	2.9
Nonrecourse debt collateralized by credit card receivables	—	900	—	0.0	2.0	0.0
Total current liabilities	10,070	11,327	10,512	23.0	25.4	23.8
Unsecured debt and other borrowings	11,653	10,643	12,000	26.7	23.9	27.2
Nonrecourse debt collateralized by credit card receivables	3,954	4,475	5,490	9.0	10.0	12.4
Deferred income taxes.	934	835	455	2.1	1.9	1.0
Other noncurrent liabilities	1,607	1,906	1,937	3.7	4.3	4.4
Total noncurrent liabilities.	18,148	17,859	19,882	41.5	40.1	45.1
Shareholders' investment						
Common stock.	59	62	63	0.1	0.1	0.1
Additional paid-in-capital	3,311	2,919	2,762	7.6	6.6	6.3
Retained earnings.	12,698	12,947	11,443	29.1	29.1	25.9
Accumulated other comprehensive loss	(581)	(581)	(556)	(1.3)	(1.3)	(1.3)
Total shareholders' investment.	15,487	15,347	13,712	35.4	34.5	31.1
Total liabilities and shareholders' investment.	$43,705	$44,533	$44,106	100.0%	100.0%	100.0%

*Percentages are rounded to one decimal and, thus, might not exactly sum to totals and subtotals.

EXHIBIT 4B.2   Common-Size Income Statements

TARGET
Common-Size Income Statements

	Amounts ($ millions)			Percentages*		
	2011	2010	2009	2011	2010	2009
Sales.	$65,786	$63,435	$62,884	97.6%	97.1%	96.8%
Credit card revenues	1,604	1,922	2,064	2.4	2.9	3.2
Total revenues	67,390	65,357	64,948	100.0%	100.0%	100.0%
Cost of sales.	45,725	44,062	44,157	67.9	67.4	68.0
Selling, general and administrative expenses	13,469	13,078	12,954	20.0	20.0	19.9
Credit card expenses	860	1,521	1,609	1.3	2.3	2.5
Depreciation and amortization	2,084	2,023	1,826	3.1	3.1	2.8
Earnings before interest expense and income taxes	5,252	4,673	4,402	7.8	7.1	6.8
Net interest expense						
Nonrecourse debt collateralized by credit card						
receivables	83	97	167	0.1	0.1	0.3
Other interest expense	677	707	727	1.0	1.1	1.1
Interest income	(3)	(3)	(28)	(0.0)	(0.0)	(0.0)
Net interest expense	757	801	866	1.1	1.2	1.3
Earnings before income taxes	4,495	3,872	3,536	6.7	5.9	5.4
Provision for income taxes.	1,575	1,384	1,322	2.3	2.1	2.0
Net earnings	$ 2,920	$ 2,488	$ 2,214	4.3%	3.8%	3.4%

*Percentages are rounded to one decimal and, thus, might not exactly sum to totals and subtotals.

APPENDIX 4C: DuPont Disaggregation Analysis

Disaggregation of return on equity (ROE) into three components (profitability, turnover, and financial leverage) was initially introduced by the E.I. DuPont de Nemours and Company to aid its managers in performance evaluation. DuPont realized that management's focus on profit alone was insufficient because profit can be simply increased by additional investment in low-yielding, but safe, assets. Further, DuPont wanted managers to think like investors and to manage their portfolio of activities using investment principles that allocate scarce investment capital to competing projects in descending order of return on investment (the *capital budgeting approach*). The DuPont model incorporates this investment perspective into performance measurement by disaggregating ROE into the following three components:

LO5 Describe and illustrate traditional DuPont disaggregation of ROE.

1. Profitability
2. Turnover (asset utilization)
3. Financial leverage

Each of these measures is generally positive, in which case an increase in any one would increase ROE. A focus on these measures encourages managers to focus on *both* the balance sheet and the income statement. Such an analysis typically examines each of these components over time. Managers then seek to reverse adverse trends and to sustain positive trends.

Basic DuPont Model

The basic DuPont model disaggregates ROE as follows:

$$\text{ROE} = \frac{\text{Net income}}{\text{Average stockholders' equity}} = \frac{\text{Net income}}{\text{Sales}} \times \frac{\text{Sales}}{\text{Average total assets}} \times \frac{\text{Average total assets}}{\text{Average stockholders' equity}}$$

Profit Margin (PM)   Asset Turnover (AT)   Financial Leverage (FL)

These three components are described as follows:

- ■ **Profit margin** is the amount of profit that the company earns from each dollar of sales. A company can increase its profit margin by increasing its gross profit margin (Gross profit/Sales) and/or by reducing its expenses (other than cost of sales) as a percentage of sales.

- ■ **Asset turnover** is a productivity measure that reflects the volume of sales that a company generates from each dollar invested in assets. A company can increase its asset turnover by increasing sales volume with no increase in assets and/or by reducing asset investment without reducing sales.

- ■ **Financial leverage** measures the degree to which the company finances its assets with debt rather than equity. Increasing the percentage of debt relative to equity increases the financial leverage. Although financial leverage increases ROE (when performance is positive), debt must be used with care as it increases the company's relative riskiness (see our following discussion of financial leverage).

Return on Assets

The first two terms in the DuPont model, profit margin and asset turnover, relate to company operations and combine to yield return on assets (ROA) as follows:

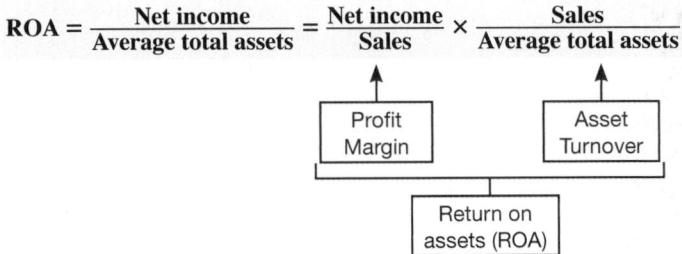

$$\text{ROA} = \frac{\text{Net income}}{\text{Average total assets}} = \frac{\text{Net income}}{\text{Sales}} \times \frac{\text{Sales}}{\text{Average total assets}}$$

Return on assets combines the first two terms in the ROE disaggregation, profit margin and turnover. It measures the return on investment for the company without regard to how it is financed (the relative proportion of debt and equity in its capital structure). Operating managers of a company typically grasp the income statement. They readily understand the pricing of products, the management of production costs, and the importance of controlling overhead costs. However, many managers do not appreciate the importance of managing the balance sheet. The ROA approach to performance measurement encourages managers to also focus on the returns that they achieve from the invested capital under their control. Those returns are maximized by a joint focus on both profitability and productivity.

Profitability

Profitability is measured by the profit margin (Net income/Sales). Analysis of profitability typically examines performance over time relative to benchmarks (such as competitors' or industry performance), which highlights trends and abnormalities. When abnormal performance is discovered, managers either correct suboptimal performance or protect superior performance. There are two general areas of profitability analysis: gross profit margin analysis and expense management.

Gross Profit Margin The gross profit margin (Gross profit/Sales) is crucial. It measures the gross profit (sales less cost of goods sold) for each sales dollar. Gross profit margin is affected by both the selling prices of products and their manufacturing cost. When markets are more competitive (or when products lose their competitive advantage), a company must reduce product prices to maintain market share and any increases in manufacturing costs cannot be directly passed on to customers; suggesting managers must focus on reducing costs. This might result in outsourcing of activities to lower labor costs and/or finding lower-cost raw materials. Such measures can yield a loss of product quality if not managed properly, which could further deteriorate the product's market position. Another strategy is to reduce product features not valued by the market. Focus groups of consumers can often identify these non-value-added product features that can be eliminated to save costs without affecting the product's value to consumers.

Expense Management Managers can focus on reducing manufacturing and/or administrative (*overhead*) expenses to increase profitability. *Manufacturing overhead* refers to all production expenses other than manufacturing labor and materials. These expenses include utilities, depreciation, and administrative costs related to manufacturing the product. *Administrative overhead* refers to all expenses not in cost of goods sold such as administrative salaries and benefits, marketing, legal, accounting, research and development. These overhead costs must be managed carefully as they can represent investments. Reductions in spending on advertising and research yield short-run, positive impacts on profitability, but can yield long-run deterioration in the company's market position. Likewise, requiring employees to work harder and longer can delay increases in wage-related costs, but the likely decline in employee morale can create long-run negative consequences.

Productivity

Productivity in the DuPont model refers to the volume of dollar sales resulting from each dollar invested in assets. When a decline in productivity is observed, managers have two avenues of attack:

1. Increase sales volume from the existing asset base, and/or
2. Decrease the investment in assets without reducing sales volume.

The first approach focuses on capacity utilization. Increasing throughput lowers per unit manufacturing costs as fixed costs are spread over a larger sales base. The second approach focuses on elimination of excess assets. That reduction increases cash and also reduces carrying costs associated with the eliminated assets.

Manager efforts to reduce assets often initially focus on working capital (current assets and liabilities). Receivables can be reduced by better credit-granting policies and better monitoring of outstanding receivables. Inventories can be reduced through just-in-time delivery of raw materials, elimination of bottlenecks in production to reduce work-in-process inventories, and producing to order rather than to estimated demand to reduce finished goods inventories. Companies can also delay payment of accounts payable to generate needed cash. Payables management is more art than science, and reductions must be managed with care so as not to threaten valuable supply channels.

Manager efforts to reduce long-term assets are more difficult. Recent years have witnessed an increase in use of corporate alliances, joint ventures, and activities that seek joint ownership of assets such as manufacturing, distribution, service facilities, and information technology (IT). Another strategy is to outsource production to reduce manufacturing assets. Outsourcing is effective provided the benefits from eliminating manufacturing assets more than offset the increased costs of purchasing goods from outsourced producers.

Financial Leverage

The third term in the DuPont model is financial leverage, the relative proportion of debt versus equity in the company's capital structure. Financial leverage in the DuPont model is measured by the ratio of average total assets to average stockholders' equity. An increase in this ratio implies an increase in the relative use of debt. This is evident from the accounting equation: assets = liabilities + equity. For example, assume that assets are financed equally with debt and equity. The accounting equation, expressed in percentage terms, follows: 100% = 50% + 50%, and the financial leverage of the company is 2.0 (100%/50%). If we increase the proportion of debt to 75% (decrease the proportion of equity to 25%), the financial leverage increases to 4.0 (100%/25%). The measure of financial leverage is important because debt is a contractual obligation (dividends are not), and a company's failure to make required debt payments can result in legal repercussions and even bankruptcy. As financial leverage increases, so do the required debt payments, along with the probability that the company is unable to meet its debt obligations in a business downturn.

ROA Adjustment in the Basic DuPont Model

The basic DuPont model is not entirely accurate, and adjusting the return on assets for the effect of interest addresses the inaccuracy.

Return on assets typically focuses on the operating side of the business (profit margin and asset turnover). Further, ROA is typically under the control of operating managers while the capital structure decision (the relative proportion of debt and equity) is not. Accordingly, an adjustment is often made to the numerator of ROA, and sometimes to the denominator. The numerator adjustment adds back the after-tax net interest expense (net of any other nonoperating revenues or expenses) and is computed as follows:

$$\text{ROA} = \frac{\text{Net income} + [\text{Interest expense } (1 - \text{Statutory tax rate})]}{\text{Average total assets}}$$

This adjusted numerator better reflects the company's operating profit as it measures return on assets exclusive of financing costs (independent of the capital structure decision). This adjusted ROA is typically reported by data collection services such as Compustat and Capital IQ, while the unadjusted is not. ("Statutory tax rate" in the ROA formula is the federal statutory tax rate *plus* the state tax rate net of any federal tax benefits; we use the 37% federal and state tax rates as explained in the NOPAT computation.)

The denominator adjustment is less common. That adjustment removes non-interest-bearing short-term liabilities (accounts payable and accrued liabilities) from total assets. The adjusted assets in the denominator are considered to better approximate the net assets that must be financed by long-term creditors and stockholders. In sum, adjustments to ROA move the numerator closer to net operating profit after-tax (NOPAT) and move the denominator closer to net operating assets (NOA). The resulting ROA ratio is then closer to the return on net operating assets (RNOA).

Illustration of DuPont Disaggregation

To illustrate DuPont disaggregation analysis, we use Target's income statement and balance sheet reported earlier in this module. Exhibit 4C.1 shows the computation for each component of the DuPont disaggregation analysis applied to Target.

EXHIBIT 4C.1   Computation of DuPont Disaggregation Analysis for Target

Ratio Component	Definition	Computation
Profit margin (PM).	$\dfrac{\text{Net income}}{\text{Sales}}$	$\dfrac{\$2,920}{\$67,390} = 4.33\%$
Asset turnover (AT).	$\dfrac{\text{Sales}}{\text{Average total assets}}$	$\dfrac{\$67,390}{(\$43,705 + \$44,533)/2} = 1.53$
Financial leverage (FL)	$\dfrac{\text{Average total assets}}{\text{Average total equity}}$	$\dfrac{(\$43,705 + \$44,533)/2}{(\$15,487 + \$15,347)/2} = 2.86$
Return on equity (ROE).	$\dfrac{\text{Net income}}{\text{Average total equity}}$	$\dfrac{\$2,920}{(\$15,487 + \$15,347)/2} = 18.94\%$
	or PM $\times$ AT $\times$ FL	or 4.33% $\times$ 1.53 $\times$ 2.86 = 18.94
Return on assets (Adjusted).	$\dfrac{\text{Net income} + \text{Interest expense} \times (1 - \text{Statutory Tax rate})}{\text{Average total assets}}$	$\dfrac{\{\$2,920 + [\$757 \times (1 - 37\%)]\}}{(\$43,705 + \$44,533)/2} = 7.70\%$

GUIDANCE ANSWERS

MANAGERIAL DECISION   You Are the CEO

Your company is performing substantially better than its competitors. Namely, your RNOA of 16% is markedly superior to competitors' RNOA of 10%. However, RNOA disaggregation shows that this is mainly attributed to your NOAT of 0.89 versus competitors' NOAT of 0.59. Your NOPM of 18% is essentially identical to competitors' NOPM of 17%. Accordingly, you will want to maintain your NOAT as further improvements are probably difficult to achieve. Importantly, you are likely to achieve the greatest benefit with efforts at improving your NOPM of 18%, which is only marginally better than the industry norm of 17%.

Superscript [A(B, C)] denotes assignments based on Appendix 4A (4B, 4C).

DISCUSSION QUESTIONS

Q4-1.   Explain in general terms the concept of return on investment. Why is this concept important in the analysis of financial performance?

Q4-2.[A]   (a) Explain how an increase in financial leverage can increase a company's ROE. (b) Given the potentially positive relation between financial leverage and ROE, why don't we see companies with 100% financial leverage (entirely nonowner financed)?

Q4-3.   Gross profit margin (Gross profit/Sales) is an important determinant of NOPAT. Identify two factors that can cause gross profit margin to decline. Is a reduction in the gross profit margin always bad news? Explain.

Q4-4. When might a reduction in operating expenses as a percentage of sales denote a short-term gain at the cost of long-term performance?

Q4-5. Describe the concept of asset turnover. What does the concept mean and why is it so important to understanding and interpreting financial performance?

Q4-6. Explain what it means when a company's ROE exceeds its RNOA.

Q4-7.ᴬ Discontinued operations are typically viewed as a nonoperating activity in the analysis of the balance sheet and the income statement. What is the rationale for this treatment?

Q4-8. Describe what is meant by the "tax shield."

Q4-9. What is meant by the term "net" in net operating assets (NOA).

Q4-10. Why is it important to disaggregate RNOA into operating profit margin (NOPM) and net operating assets turnover (NOAT)?

Q4-11. What insights do we gain from the graphical relation between profit margin and asset turnover?

Q4-12. Explain the concept of liquidity and why it is crucial to company survival.

Q4-13. Identify at least two factors that limit the usefulness of ratio analysis.

Q4-14.ᴬ Define (1) net nonoperating obligations and (2) the net nonoperating expense.

**Assignments with the ⊘ in the margin are available in an online homework system.
See the Preface of the book for details.**

MINI EXERCISES

M4-15. Identify and Compute Net Operating Assets (LO1)

Following is the balance sheet for Home Depot, Inc. Identify and compute fiscal year-end 2011 net operating assets.   Home Depot (HD)

(amounts in millions, except share and per share data)	January 30, 2011	January 31, 2010
Assets		
Current Assets		
Cash and cash equivalents	$ 545	$ 1,421
Receivables, net	1,085	964
Merchandise inventories	10,625	10,188
Other current assets	1,224	1,327
Total current assets	13,479	13,900
Property and equipment, at cost		
Land	8,497	8,451
Buildings	17,606	17,391
Furniture, fixtures and equipment	9,687	9,091
Leaseholder improvements	1,373	1,383
Construction in progress	654	525
Capital leases	568	504
	38,385	37,345
Less accumulated depreciation and amortization	13,325	11,795
Net property and equipment	25,060	25,550
Notes receivable	139	33
Goodwill	1,187	1,171
Other assets	260	223
Total assets	$40,125	$40,877

continued

continued from prior page

Liabilities and stockholders' equity		
Current liabilities		
Accounts payable	$ 4,717	$ 4,863
Accrued salaries and related expenses	1,290	1,263
Sales taxes payable	368	362
Deferred revenue	1,177	1,158
Income taxes payable	13	108
Current installments of long-term debt	1,042	1,020
Other accrued expenses	1,515	1,589
Total current liabilities	10,122	10,363
Long-term debt, excluding current installments	8,707	8,662
Other long-term liabilities	2,135	2,140
Deferred income taxes	272	319
Total liabilities	21,236	21,484
Stockholders' equity		
Common stock, par value $0.05; authorized: 10 billion shares; issued: 1.722 billion shares at January 30, 2011 and 1.716 billion shares at January 31, 2010; outstanding: 1.623 billion shares at January 30, 2011 and 1.698 billion shares at January 31, 2010	86	86
Paid-in capital	6,556	6,304
Retained earnings	14,995	13,226
Accumulated other comprehensive income	445	362
Treasury stock, at cost, 99 million shares at January 30, 2011 and 18 million shares at January 31, 2010	(3,193)	(585)
Total stockholders' equity	18,889	19,393
Total liabilities and stockholders' equity	$40,125	$40,877

M4-16.   Identify and Compute NOPAT   (LO1)

Home Depot (HD)

Following is the income statement for Home Depot, Inc. Compute NOPBT—net operating profit *before* tax. (*Hint:* Treat Home Depot's "other" income as nonoperating since the company classifies it as such in its income statement.) Compute NOPAT for 2011 using a combined Federal and State statutory tax rate of 37%.

(amounts in millions)	January 30, 2011
Net sales	$67,997
Cost of sales	44,693
Gross profit	23,304
Operating expenses:	
Selling, general and administrative	15,849
Depreciation and amortization	1,616
Total operating expenses	17,465
Operating income	5,839
Interest and other (income) expense:	
Interest and investment income	(15)
Interest expense	530
Other	51
Interest and other, net	566
Earnings before provision for income taxes	5,273
Provision for income taxes	1,935
Net earnings	$ 3,338

M4-17.   Compute RNOA, Net Operating Profit Margin, and NOA Turnover   (LO2)

Nordstrom, Inc.
(JWN)

Selected balance sheet and income statement information for Nordstrom, Inc., a department store retailer, follows.

Company ($ millions)	Ticker	2011 Revenues	2011 NOPAT	2011 Net Operating Assets	2010 Net Operating Assets
Nordstrom, Inc	JWN	$9,700	$693	$3,296	$3,390

a. Compute its 2011 return on net operating assets (RNOA).

b. Disaggregate RNOA into net operating profit margin (NOPM) and net operating asset turnover (NOAT). Confirm that RNOA = NOPM × NOAT.

M4-18.   Identify and Compute Net Operating Assets   (LO2)

Lowe's Companies, Inc. (LOW)

Following is the balance sheet for Lowe's Companies, Inc. Identify and compute its 2011 net operating assets (NOA).

LOWE'S COMPANIES, INC.		
($ millions, except par value)	January 28, 2011	January 29, 2010
Assets		
Current assets		
Cash and cash equivalents	$ 652	$ 632
Short-term investments	471	425
Merchandise inventory—net	8,321	8,249
Deferred income taxes—net.	193	208
Other current assets.	330	218
Total current assets	9,967	9,732
Property, less accumulated depreciation	22,089	22,499
Long-term investments	1,008	277
Other assets	635	497
Total assets.	$33,699	$33,005
Liabilities and Shareholders' Equity		
Current liabilities		
Current maturities of long-term debt	$ 36	$ 552
Accounts payable.	4,351	4,287
Accrued compensation and employee benefits.	667	577
Deferred revenue	707	683
Other current liabilities	1,358	1,256
Total current liabilities.	7,119	7,355
Long-term debt, excluding current maturities	6,537	4,528
Deferred income taxes—net.	467	598
Deferred revenue—extended protection plans	631	549
Other liabilities	833	906
Total liabilities	15,587	13,936
Shareholders' equity		
Preferred stock—$5 par value, none issued	—	—
Common stock—$.50 par value; Shares issued and outstanding:		
January 28, 2011, 1,354; January 29, 2010, 1,459	677	729
Capital in excess of par value	11	6
Retained earnings	17,371	18,307
Accumulated other comprehensive income.	53	27
Total shareholders' equity	18,112	19,069
Total liabilities and shareholders' equity.	$33,699	$33,005

M4-19.   Identify and Compute NOPAT   (LO2)

Lowe's Companies, Inc. (LOW)

Following is the income statement for Lowe's Companies, Inc. Compute its 2011 net operating profit after tax (NOPAT) assuming a 37% total statutory tax rate.

LOWE'S COMPANIES, INC.			
Fiscal years ended (In millions)	January 28, 2011	January 29, 2010	January 30, 2009
Net sales.	$48,815	$47,220	$48,230
Cost of sales.	31,663	30,757	31,729
Gross margin	17,152	16,463	16,501
Expenses			
Selling, general and administrative	12,006	11,737	11,176
Depreciation.	1,586	1,614	1,539
Interest—net.	332	287	280
Total expenses	13,924	13,638	12,995
Pre-tax earnings.	3,228	2,825	3,506
Income tax provision	1,218	1,042	1,311
Net earnings.	$ 2,010	$ 1,783	$ 2,195

M4-20.[C] **Compute and Interpret Disaggregation of Dupont Analysis Ratios**   (LO5)

Macy's, Inc. (M)

Selected balance sheet and income statement information for Macy's, Inc., a retailer, follows.

Company ($ millions)	Ticker	2011 Sales	2011 Net Income	2011 Assets	2010 Assets	2011 Stockholders' Equity	2010 Stockholders' Equity
Macy's	M	$25,003	$847	$20,631	$21,300	$5,530	$4,653

a. Compute Macy's 2011 return on equity (ROE).

b. Disaggregate ROE into profit margin, asset turnover, and financial leverage. Confirm that ROE = PM $\times$ AT $\times$ FL.

M4-21.   **Compute RNOA, Net Operating Profit Margin, and NOA Turnover for Competitors**   (LO2)

Abercrombie & Fitch (ANF)

TJX Companies (TJX)

Selected balance sheet and income statement information from Abercrombie & Fitch and TJX Companies, clothing retailers in the high-end and value-priced segments, respectively, follows.

Company ($ millions)	Ticker	2011 Sales	2011 NOPAT	2011 Net Operating Assets	2010 Net Operating Assets
Abercrombie & Fitch. . .	ANF	$ 3,469	$ 152	$1,032	$1,055
TJX Companies	TJX	21,942	1,364	2,072	1,937

a. Compute the 2011 return on net operating assets (RNOA) for both companies.

b. Disaggregate RNOA into net operating profit margin (NOPM) and net operating asset turnover (NOAT) for each company. Confirm that RNOA = NOPM $\times$ NOAT.

c. Discuss differences observed with respect to NOPM and NOAT and interpret these differences in light of each company's business model.

M4-22.[B] **Compute and Interpret Liquidity and Solvency Ratios**   (LO4)

Verizon (VZ)

Selected balance sheet and income statement information from Verizon follows.

($ millions)	2010	2009
Current assets	$ 22,348	$ 21,745
Current liabilities.	30,597	29,136
Total liabilities	133,093	142,764
Equity	86,912	84,143
Earnings before interest and taxes.	15,207	16,622
Interest expense.	2,523	3,102
Net cash flow from operating activities	33,363	31,390

a. Compute the current ratio for each year and discuss any trend in liquidity. What additional information about the numbers used to calculate this ratio might be useful in helping us assess liquidity?
Explain.

b. Compute times interest earned and the liabilities-to-equity for each year and discuss any noticeable
change. (The average liabilities-to-equity ratio for the telecommunications industry is 1.67.) Do you
have any concerns about Verizon's financial leverage and the company's ability to meet interest obligations? Explain.

c. Verizon's capital expenditures are expected to increase substantially as it seeks to respond to competitive pressures to upgrade the quality of its communication infrastructure. Assess Verizon's liquidity
and solvency in light of this strategic direction.

M4-23. **Compute Tax Rate on Operating Profit and NOPAT**   (LO2)

Selected income statement information for 2011 is presented below for Home Depot and Lowe's.

Home Depot (HD)

Lowe's Companies, Inc. (LOW)

Company ($ millions)	Ticker	Net Operating Profit Before Tax	Pretax Net Nonoperating Expense	Tax Expense	Statutory Tax Rate	Sales
Home Depot........	HD	$5,839	$566	$1,935	37%	$67,997
Lowe's	LOW	3,560	332	1,218	37%	48,815

a. Compute NOPAT for each company.

b. Compute NOPAT as a percent of sales for each company.

M4-24.[c] **Compute and Interpret Measures for DuPont Disaggregation Analysis**   (LO5)

Refer to the 2010 fiscal year financial data of 3M Company from P4-36 to answer the following requirements (perform these computations from the perspective of a 3M shareholder).

3M Company (MMM)

a. Compute the DuPont model component measures for profit margin, asset turnover, and financial
leverage.

b. Compute ROE. Confirm that ROE equals ROE computed using the component measures from part *a*
(ROE = PM × AT × FL).

c. Compute adjusted ROA (assume a tax rate of 37% and pretax net interest expense of $163).

EXERCISES

E4-25. **Compute and Interpret RNOA, Profit Margin, and Asset Turnover of Competitors**   (LO2)

Selected balance sheet and income statement information for drug store retailers CVS and Walgreen
follows.

CVS Caremark Corp (CVS)

Walgreen Co. (WAG)

Company ($ millions)	Ticker	2010 Sales	2010 NOPAT	2010 Net Operating Assets	2009 Net Operating Assets
CVS Caremark	CVS	$96,413	$3,777	$46,360	$45,889
Walgreen Co.........	WAG	67,420	2,145	14,921	14,140

a. Compute the 2010 return on net operating assets (RNOA) for each company.

b. Disaggregate RNOA into net operating profit margin (NOPM) and net operating asset turnover
(NOAT) for each company.

c. Discuss any differences in these ratios for each company.

E4-26. **Compute, Disaggregate, and Interpret RNOA of Competitors**   (LO2)

Selected balance sheet and income statement information for the clothing retailers, Abercrombie &
Fitch and The GAP, Inc., follows.

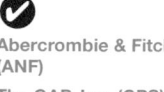

Abercrombie & Fitch (ANF)

The GAP, Inc. (GPS)

Company ($ millions)	Ticker	2011 Sales	2011 NOPAT	2011 Net Operating Assets	2010 Net Operating Assets
Abercrombie & Fitch...	ANF	$ 3,469	$ 152	$1,032	$1,055
The GAP............	GPS	14,664	1,195	2,419	2,318

a. Compute the 2011 return on net operating assets (RNOA) for each company.

b. Disaggregate RNOA into net operating profit margin (NOPM) and net operating asset turnover (NOAT) for each company.

c. Discuss any differences in these ratios for each company.

E4-27. Compute, Disaggregate, and Interpret RNOA of Competitors (LO2)

Nordstrom (JWN)
Limited Brands (LTD)

Selected balance sheet and income statement information for the clothing retailers Nordstrom and Limited Brands follows.

Company ($ millions)	Ticker	2011 Sales	2011 NOPAT	2011 Net Operating Assets	2010 Net Operating Assets
Nordstrom	JWN	$9,700	$693	$3,296	$3,390
Limited Brands	LTD	9,613	826	2,854	3,103

a. Compute the 2011 return on net operating assets (RNOA) for each company.

b. Disaggregate RNOA into net operating profit margin (NOPM) and net operating asset turnover (NOAT) for each company.

c. Discuss any differences in these ratios for each company. Identify the factor(s) that drives the differences in RNOA observed from your analyses in parts a and b.

E4-28. Compute, Disaggregate, and Interpret ROE and RNOA (LO1, 2)

Intel (INTC)

Selected fiscal year balance sheet and income statement information for the computer chip maker, Intel, follows ($ millions).

Company	Ticker	2010 Sales	2010 Net Income	2010 Net Operating Profit After Tax	2010 Net Operating Assets	2009 Net Operating Assets	2010 Stockholders' Equity	2009 Stockholders' Equity
Intel.	INTC	$43,623	$11,464	$11,250	$28,652	$29,232	$49,430	$41,704

a. Compute the 2010 return on equity (ROE) and the 2010 return on net operating assets (RNOA).

b. Disaggregate RNOA into net operating profit margin (NOPM) and net operating asset turnover (NOAT). What observations can we make about the company's NOPM and NOAT?

c. Compute the percentage of RNOA to ROE, and compute the company's nonoperating return for 2010.

E4-29. Compute, Disaggregate and Interpret ROE and RNOA (LO1, 2)

Macy's (M)

Selected balance sheet and income statement information from Macy's follows ($ millions).

Company	Ticker	2011 Sales	2011 Net Income	2011 Net Operating Profit After Tax	2011 Net Operating Assets	2010 Net Operating Assets	2011 Stockholders' Equity	2010 Stockholders' Equity
Macy's	M	$25,003	$847	$1,209	$11,491	$11,665	$5,530	$4,653

a. Compute the 2011 return on equity (ROE) and 2011 return on net operating assets (RNOA).

b. Disaggregate RNOA into net operating profit margin (NOPM) and net operating asset turnover (NOAT). What observations can we make about Macy's NOPM and NOAT?

c. Compute the percentage of RNOA to ROE, and compute Macy's nonoperating return for 2011.

E4-30. Compute, Disaggregate and Interpret ROE and RNOA (LO1, 2)

Cisco Systems (CSCO)

Selected balance sheet and income statement information from the software company, Cisco Systems, Inc., follows ($ millions).

Company	Ticker	2010 Sales	2010 Net Income	2010 Net Operating Profit After Tax	2010 Net Operating Assets	2009 Net Operating Assets	2010 Stockholders' Equity	2009 Stockholders' Equity
Cisco Systems	CSCO	$40,040	$7,767	$7,609	$19,708	$13,971	$44,267	$38,647

a. Compute the 2010 return on equity (ROE) and 2010 return on net operating assets (RNOA).

b. Disaggregate the RNOA from part a into net operating profit margin (NOPM) and net operating asset turnover (NOAT).

c. Compute the percentage of RNOA to ROE. Explain the relation we observe between ROE and RNOA, and Cisco's use of equity capital.

E4-31.[B] **Compute and Interpret Liquidity and Solvency Ratios** (LO4)

Selected balance sheet and income statement information from Comcast Corporation for 2010 and 2009 follows ($ millions).

Comcast Corporation (CMCSA)

	Total Current Assets	Total Current Liabilities	Pretax Income	Interest Expense	Total Liabilities*	Stockholders' Equity
2010	$8,886	$8,234	$6,104	$1,735	$74,100	$44,434
2009	3,223	7,249	5,106	2,044	69,922	42,811

*Includes redeemable noncontrolling interests

a. Compute the current ratio for each year and discuss any trend in liquidity. Do you believe the company is sufficiently liquid? Explain. What additional information about the accounting numbers comprising this ratio might be useful in helping you assess liquidity? Explain.

b. Compute times interest earned and the liabilities-to-equity ratio for each year and discuss any noticeable change.

c. What is your overall assessment of the company's liquidity and solvency from the analyses in parts a and b? Explain.

E4-32.[B] **Compute and Interpret Liquidity and Solvency Ratios** (LO4)

Selected balance sheet and income statement information from Verizon Communications, Inc., for 2010 and 2009 follows ($ millions).

Verizon Communications, Inc. (VZ)

	Total Current Assets	Total Current Liabilities	Pretax Income	Interest Expense	Total Liabilities	Stockholders' Equity
2010	$22,348	$30,597	$12,684	$2,469	$133,093	$86,912
2009	21,745	29,136	13,520	3,011	142,764	84,143

a. Compute the current ratio for each year and discuss any trend in liquidity. Do you believe the company is sufficiently liquid? Explain. What additional information about the accounting numbers comprising this ratio might be useful in helping you assess liquidity? Explain.

b. Compute times interest earned and the liabilities-to-equity ratio for each year and discuss any noticeable change.

c. What is your overall assessment of the company's liquidity and solvency from the analyses in parts a and b? Explain.

E4-33.[B] **Compute and Interpret Solvency Ratios for Business Segments** (LO2, 4)

Selected balance sheet and income statement information from General Electric Company and its two principal business segments (Industrial and Financial) for 2010 follows.

General Electric (GE)

($ millions)	Pretax Income	Interest Expense	Total Liabilities	Stockholders' Equity
Industrial segment	$15,166	$ 1,600	$ 95,729	$123,034
Financial segment	2,172	14,956	538,530	70,148
Other.........................	(3,130)[1]	(573)[2]	(7,241)[2]	(68,984)
General Electric Consolidated	$14,208	$15,983	$627,018	$124,198[3]

[1] Includes unallocated corporate operating activities.

[2] Includes intercompany loans and related interest expense; these are deducted (eliminated) in preparing consolidated financial statements.

[3] The consolidated equity equals the equity of the parent (industrial); this is explained in Module 7.

a. Compute times interest earned and the liabilities-to-equity ratio for 2010 for the two business segments (Industrial and Financial) and the company as a whole.

b. What is your overall assessment of the company's solvency? Explain. What differences do you observe between the two business segments? Do these differences correspond to your prior expectations given each company's business model?

c. Discuss the implications of the analysis of consolidated financial statements and the additional insight that can be gained from a more in-depth analysis of primary business segments.

E4-34.ᴬ **Direct Computation of Nonoperating Return**   (LO1, 3)

Walmart (WMT)

Refer to the income statement and balance sheet of Walmart, from Mid-Module Reviews 1 and 2.

a. Compute the FLEV and Spread for Walmart for 2011.

b. Use RNOA from Mid-Module Review 2, and the FLEV and Spread from part a, to compute ROE. Compare the ROE calculated in this exercise with the ROE from Mid-Module Review 2.

E4-35. **Compute NOPAT Using Tax Rates from Tax Footnote**   (LO1)

TJX Companies (TJX)

The income statement for TJX Companies, follows.

TJX COMPANIES Consolidated Statements of Income	
Fiscal Year Ended ($ thousands)	January 29, 2011
Net sales.	$21,942,193
Cost of sales, including buying and occupancy costs.	16,040,461
Selling, general and administrative expenses	3,710,053
Provision (credit) for computer intrusion related costs.	(11,550)
Interest expense, net	39,137
Income from continuing operations before provision for income taxes.	2,164,092
Provision for income taxes.	824,562
Income from continuing operations	1,339,530
Gain from discontinued operations, net of income taxes	3,611
Net income.	$ 1,343,141

TJX provides the following footnote disclosure relating to its effective tax rate:

	January 29, 2011
U.S. federal statutory income tax rate	35.0%
Effective state income tax rate.	4.1
Impact of foreign operations	(0.5)
All other	(0.5)
Worldwide effective income tax rate	38.1%

Compute TJX's NOPAT for 2011 using its income tax footnote disclosure.

PROBLEMS

P4-36. **Analysis and Interpretation of Profitability**   (LO1, 2)

3M Company (MMM)

Balance sheets and income statements for 3M Company follow.

Consolidated Statements of Income

Years ended December 31 (In millions)	2010	2009	2008
Net sales.	$26,662	$23,123	$25,269
Operating expenses			
Cost of sales.	13,831	12,109	13,379
Selling, general and administrative expenses	5,479	4,907	5,245
Research, development and related expenses	1,434	1,293	1,404
Loss from sale of businesses	—	—	23
Total operating expenses	20,744	18,309	20,051
Operating income.	5,918	4,814	5,218
Interest expense and income			
Interest expense	201	219	215
Interest income	(38)	(37)	(105)
Total interest expense.	163	182	110
Income before income taxes	5,755	4,632	5,108
Provision for income taxes.	1,592	1,388	1,588
Net income including noncontrolling interest.	4,163	3,244	3,520
Less: Net income attributable to noncontrolling interest	78	51	60
Net income attributable to 3M	$ 4,085	$ 3,193	$ 3,460

Consolidated Balance Sheets

At December 31 ($ millions, except per share amount)	2010	2009
Assets		
Current assets		
Cash and cash equivalents.	$ 3,377	$ 3,040
Marketable securities—current.	1,101	744
Accounts receivable—net of allowances of $98 and $109.	3,615	3,250
Inventories		
Finished goods	1,476	1,255
Work in process.	950	815
Raw materials and supplies	729	569
Total inventories	3,155	2,639
Other current assets.	967	1,122
Total current assets.	12,215	10,795
Marketable securities—noncurrent.	540	825
Investments	146	103
Property, plant and equipment.	20,253	19,440
Less: Accumulated depreciation	(12,974)	(12,440)
Property, plant and equipment—net.	7,279	7,000
Goodwill	6,820	5,832
Intangible assets—net	1,820	1,342
Prepaid pension benefits	74	78
Other assets.	1,262	1,275
Total assets.	$30,156	$27,250
Liabilities		
Current liabilities		
Short-term borrowings and current portion of long-term debt.	$ 1,269	$ 613
Accounts payable.	1,662	1,453
Accrued payroll.	778	680
Accrued income taxes	358	252
Other current liabilities	2,022	1,899
Total current liabilities	6,089	4,897

continued

continued from prior page

Long-term debt	**4,183**	5,097
Pension and postretirement benefits	**2,013**	2,227
Other liabilities	**1,854**	1,727
Total liabilities	**14,139**	13,948

Equity

3M Company shareholders' equity: Common stock, par value
$.01 per share; Shares outstanding—2010: 711,977,608;

Shares outstanding—2009: 710,599,119.......................	**9**	9
Additional paid-in capital	**3,468**	3,153
Retained earnings...	**25,995**	23,753
Treasury stock..	**(10,266)**	(10,397)
Accumulated other comprehensive income (loss)	**(3,543)**	(3,754)
Total 3M Company shareholders' equity......................	**15,663**	12,764
Noncontrolling interest.......................................	**354**	538
Total equity	**16,017**	13,302
Total liabilities and equity	**$30,156**	$27,250

Required

a. Compute net operating profit after tax (NOPAT) for 2010. Assume that the combined federal and state statutory tax rate is 37%.

b. Compute net operating assets (NOA) for 2010 and 2009. Treat noncurrent Investments as a nonoperating item.

c. Compute and disaggregate 3M's RNOA into net operating profit margin (NOPM) and net operating asset turnover (NOAT) for 2010. Demonstrate that RNOA = NOPM × NOAT.

d. Compute net nonoperating obligations (NNO) for 2010 and 2009. (*Hint:* Include noncontrolling interest from the balance sheet with NNO.) Confirm the relation: NOA = NNO + Stockholders' equity.

e. Compute return on equity (ROE) for 2010.

f. What is the nonoperating return component of ROE for 2010?

g. Comment on the difference between ROE and RNOA. What inference can we draw from this comparison?

P4-37.[B] **Analysis and Interpretation of Liquidity and Solvency**   (LO4)

3M Company (MMM)

Refer to the financial information of 3M Company in P4-36 to answer the following requirements.

Required

a. Compute the current ratio and quick ratio for 2010 and 2009. Comment on any observed trends.

b. Compute times interest earned and liabilities-to-equity ratios for 2010 and 2009. Comment on any noticeable changes.

c. Summarize your findings about the company's liquidity and solvency. Do you have any concerns about its ability to meet its debt obligations?

P4-38.[A] **Direct Computation of Nonoperating Return**   (LO1, 2, 3)

3M Company (MMM)

Refer to the financial information of 3M Company in P4-36 to answer the following requirements.

Required

a. Compute its financial leverage (FLEV) and Spread for 2010. Recall that NNE = NOPAT − Net income; remember to use stockholders' equity and net income for 3M's shareholders (excluding noncontrolling interests).

b. Assume that its return on equity (ROE) for 2010 is 28.74% and its return on net operating assets (RNOA) is 27.88%. Confirm computations to yield the relation: ROE = RNOA + (FLEV × Spread).

c. What do your computations of the nonoperating return imply about the company's use of borrowed funds?

 P4-39. **Analysis and Interpretation of Profitability**   (LO1, 2)

Best Buy Co., Inc.
(BBY)

Balance sheets and income statements for Best Buy Co., Inc., follow.

Consolidated Statements of Earnings

For Fiscal Years Ended ($ in millions)	February 26, 2011	February 27, 2010	February 28, 2009
Revenue	$50,272	$49,694	$45,015
Cost of goods sold	37,611	37,534	34,017
Restructuring charges—cost of goods sold	24	—	—
Gross profit	12,637	12,160	10,998
Selling, general and administrative expenses	10,325	9,873	8,984
Restructuring charges	198	52	78
Goodwill and tradename impairment	—	—	66
Operating income	2,114	2,235	1,870
Other income (expense)			
Investment income and other	51	54	35
Investment impairment	—	—	(111)
Interest expense	(87)	(94)	(94)
Earnings before income tax expense and equity in income of affiliates	2,078	2,195	1,700
Income tax expense	714	802	674
Equity in income of affiliates	2	1	7
Net earnings including noncontrolling interests	1,366	1,394	1,033
Net earnings attributable to noncontrolling interests	(89)	(77)	(30)
Net earnings attributable to Best Buy Co., Inc.	$ 1,277	$ 1,317	$ 1,003

Consolidated Balance Sheets

($ millions, except per share and share amounts)	February 26, 2011	February 27, 2010
Assets		
Current assets		
Cash and cash equivalents	$ 1,103	$ 1,826
Short-term investments	22	90
Receivables	2,348	2,020
Merchandise inventories	5,897	5,486
Other current assets	1,103	1,144
Total current assets	10,473	10,566
Property and equipment		
Land and buildings	766	757
Leasehold improvements	2,318	2,154
Fixtures and equipment	4,701	4,447
Property under capital lease	120	95
	7,905	7,453
Less accumulated depreciation	4,082	3,383
Net property and equipment	3,823	4,070
Goodwill	2,454	2,452
Tradenames, net	133	159
Customer relationships, net	203	279
Equity and other investments	328	324
Other noncurrent assets	435	452
Total assets	$17,849	$18,302

continued

continued from prior page

Liabilities and equity		
Current liabilities		
Accounts payable..	**$ 4,894**	$ 5,276
Unredeemed gift card liabilities	**474**	463
Accrued compensation and related expenses.........................	**570**	544
Accrued liabilities...	**1,471**	1,681
Accrued income taxes	**256**	316
Short-term debt	**557**	663
Current portion of long-term debt	**441**	35
Total current liabilities......................................	**8,663**	8,978
Long-term liabilities..	**1,183**	1,256
Long-term debt	**711**	1,104
Equity		
Best Buy Co., Inc. Shareholders' equity		
Preferred stock, $1.00 par value:		
Authorized—400,000 shares; issued and outstanding—none	**—**	—
Common stock, $0.10 par value:		
Authorized—1.0 billion shares; issued and outstanding—		
392,590,000 and 418,815,000 shares, respectively	**39**	42
Additional paid-in-capital	**18**	441
Retained earnings..	**6,372**	5,797
Accumulated other comprehensive income.........................	**173**	40
Total Best Buy Co., Inc. shareholders' equity.........................	**6,602**	6,320
Noncontrolling interests......................................	**690**	644
Total equity..	**7,292**	6,964
Total liabilities and equity.......................................	**$17,849**	$18,302

Required

a. Compute net operating profit after tax (NOPAT) for 2011. Assume that the combined federal and state statutory tax rate is 37%.

b. Compute net operating assets (NOA) for 2011 and 2010. (*Hint:* Treat the Equity and Other Investments and the Long-Term Liabilities as operating.)

c. Compute and disaggregate Best Buy's RNOA into net operating profit margin (NOPM) and net operating asset turnover (NOAT) for 2011; confirm that RNOA = NOPM × NOAT. The median NOPM and NOAT for companies in Best Buy's industry are 3.32% and 3.27%, respectively, yielding a median RNOA of slightly over 11%. Comment on NOPM and NOAT estimates for Best Buy in comparison to industry medians.

d. Compute net nonoperating obligations (NNO) for 2011 and 2010. Confirm the relation: NOA = NNO + Stockholders' equity.

e. Compute return on equity (ROE) for 2010.

f. Infer the nonoperating return component of ROE for 2010.

g. Comment on the difference between ROE and RNOA. What does this relation suggest about Best Buy's use of equity capital?

Best Buy (BBY)

P4-40.ᴮ Analysis and Interpretation of Liquidity and Solvency (LO4)

Refer to the financial information of Best Buy (BBY) in P4-39 to answer the following requirements.

Required

a. Compute Best Buy's current ratio and quick ratio for 2011 and 2010. Comment on any observed trends.

b. Compute Best Buy's times interest earned and its liabilities-to-equity ratios for 2011 and 2010. Comment on any noticeable change.

c. Summarize your findings about the company's liquidity and solvency. Do you have any concerns about Best Buy's ability to meet its debt obligations?

Best Buy (BBY)

P4-41.ᴬ Direct Computation of Nonoperating Return (LO1, 3)

Refer to the financial information of Best Buy (BBY) in P4-39 to answer the following requirements.

Required

a. Compute Best Buy's financial leverage (FLEV) and Spread for 2011; recall, NNE = NOPAT − Net income.

b. Assume that Best Buy's return on equity (ROE) for 2011 is 19.76% and its return on net operating assets (RNOA) is 18.86%. Confirm computations to yield the relation: ROE = RNOA + (FLEV × Spread).

c. What do your computations of the nonoperating return in parts a and b imply about the company's use of borrowed funds?

P4-42. **Analysis and Interpretation of Profitability**   (LO1, 2)

Balance sheets and income statements for Intel Corporation follow. Refer to these financial statements to answer the requirements.

Intel Corporation
(INTC)

INTEL CORPORATION Consolidated Statements of Income			
(in millions)	2010	2009	2008
Net revenue	$43,623	$35,127	$37,586
Cost of sales	15,132	15,566	16,742
Gross margin	28,491	19,561	20,844
Research and development	6,576	5,653	5,722
Marketing, general and administrative	6,309	7,931	5,452
Restructuring and asset impairment charges	—	231	710
Amortization of acquisition-related intangibles	18	35	6
Operating expenses	12,903	13,850	11,890
Operating income	15,588	5,711	8,954
Gains (losses) on equity method investments, net	117	(147)	(1,380)
Gains (losses) on other equity investments, net	231	(23)	(376)
Interest and other, net	109	163	488
Income before taxes	16,045	5,704	7,686
Provision for taxes	4,581	1,335	2,394
Net income	$11,464	$ 4,369	$ 5,292

INTEL CORPORATION Consolidated Balance Sheets		
(in millions, except par value)	2010	2009
Assets		
Current assets		
Cash and cash equivalents	$ 5,498	$ 3,987
Short-term investments	11,294	5,285
Trading assets	5,093	4,648
Accounts receivable, net of allowance for doubtful accounts of $28 ($19 in 2009)	2,867	2,273
Inventories	3,757	2,935
Deferred tax assets	1,488	1,216
Other current assets	1,614	813
Total current assets	31,611	21,157
Property, plant and equipment, net	17,899	17,225
Marketable equity securities	1,008	773
Other long-term investments	3,026	4,179
Goodwill	4,531	4,421
Other long-term assets	5,111	5,340
Total assets	$63,186	$53,095

continued

continued from prior page

Liabilities and stockholders' equity
Current liabilities

Short-term debt	$ 38	$ 172
Accounts payable	2,290	1,883
Accrued compensation and benefits	2,888	2,448
Accrued advertising	1,007	773
Deferred income on shipments to distributors	622	593
Other accrued liabilities	2,482	1,722
Total current liabilities	9,327	7,591
Long-term income taxes payable	190	193
Long-term debt	2,077	2,049
Long-term deferred tax liabilities	926	555
Other long-term liabilities	1,236	1,003

Stockholders' equity

Preferred stock, $0.001 par value, 50 shares authorized; none issued	—	—
Common stock, $0.001 par value, 10,000 shares authorized; 5,581 issued and 5,511 outstanding (5,523 issued and outstanding in 2009) and capital in excess of par value	16,178	14,993
Accumulated other comprehensive income (loss)	333	393
Retained earnings	32,919	26,318
Total stockholders' equity	49,430	41,704
Total liabilities and stockholders' equity	$63,186	$53,095

Required

a. Compute net operating profit after tax (NOPAT) for 2010. Assume that the combined federal and state statutory tax rate is 37%.

b. Compute net operating assets (NOA) for 2010 and 2009. (Hint: Assume that trading assets and long-term marketable equity securities are investments in marketable securities and are therefore, nonoperating assets; also, footnotes reveal that the other long-term investments are mainly loan receivables and are, therefore, operating.)

c. Compute RNOA and disaggregate it into net operating profit margin (NOPM) and net operating asset turnover (NOAT) for 2010. Comment on the drivers of RNOA.

d. Compute net nonoperating obligations (NNO) for 2010 and 2009. Confirm the relation: NOA = NNO + Stockholders' equity.

e. Compute return on equity (ROE) for 2010.

f. Infer the nonoperating return component of ROE for 2010.

g. Comment on the difference between ROE and RNOA. What does this relation suggest about Intel's use of equity capital?

 P4-43. **Analysis and Interpretation of Profitability** (LO1, 2)

Nordstrom, Inc.
(JWN)

Balance sheets and income statements for Nordstrom, Inc., follow. Refer to these financial statements to answer the requirements.

NORDSTROM, INC. Consolidated Statements of Earnings			
Fiscal Years Ended ($ millions)	2011	2010	2009
Net sales	$9,310	$8,258	$8,272
Credit card revenues	390	369	301
Total revenues	9,700	8,627	8,573
Cost of sales and related buying and occupancy costs	(5,897)	(5,328)	(5,417)
Selling, general and administrative expenses			
Retail	(2,412)	(2,109)	(2,103)
Credit	(273)	(356)	(274)
Earnings before interest and income taxes	1,118	834	779
Interest expense, net	(127)	(138)	(131)
Earnings before income taxes	991	696	648
Income tax expense	(378)	(255)	(247)
Net earnings	$ 613	$ 441	$ 401

NORDSTROM, INC. Consolidated Balance Sheets		
($ millions)	January 29, 2011	January 30, 2010
Assets		
Current assets		
Cash and cash equivalents	$1,506	$ 795
Accounts receivable, net	2,026	2,035
Merchandise inventories	977	898
Current deferred tax assets, net	236	238
Prepaid expenses and other	79	88
Total current assets	4,824	4,054
Land, buildings and equipment (net of accumulated depreciation of $3,520 and $3,316)	2,318	2,242
Goodwill	53	53
Other assets	267	230
Total assets	$7,462	$6,579
Liabilities and Shareholders' Equity		
Current liabilities		
Accounts payable	$ 846	$ 726
Accrued salaries, wages and related benefits	375	336
Other current liabilities	652	596
Current portion of long-term debt	6	356
Total current liabilities	1,879	2,014
Long-term debt, net	2,775	2,257
Deferred property incentives, net	495	469
Other liabilities	292	267
Shareholders' equity		
Common stock, no par value: 1,000 shares authorized; 218.0 and 217.7 shares issued and outstanding	1,168	1,066
Retained earnings	882	525
Accumulated other comprehensive loss	(29)	(19)
Total shareholders' equity	2,021	1,572
Total liabilities and shareholders' equity	$7,462	$6,579

Required

a. Compute net operating profit after tax (NOPAT) for 2011. Assume that the combined federal and state statutory tax rate is 37%.

b. Compute net operating assets (NOA) for 2011 and 2010.

c. Compute RNOA and disaggregate it into net operating profit margin (NOPM) and net operating asset turnover (NOAT) for 2011; confirm that RNOA = NOPM × NOAT. The median NOPM and NOAT for companies in Nordstrom's industry are 4.46% and 2.81%, respectively, yielding a median RNOA of slightly over 12%. Comment on NOPM and NOAT estimates for Nordstrom in comparison to industry medians.

d. Compute net nonoperating obligations (NNO) for 2011 and 2010. Confirm the relation: NOA = NNO + Stockholders' equity.

e. Compute return on equity (ROE) for 2011.

f. Infer the nonoperating return component of ROE for 2011.

g. Comment on the difference between ROE and RNOA. What does this relation suggest about Nordstrom's use of equity capital?

P4-44. **Analysis and Interpretation of Profitability** (LO1, 2)

Balance sheets and income statements for Kraft Foods, Inc., follow. Refer to these financial statements to answer the following requirements.

Kraft Foods, Inc. (KFT)

KRAFT FOODS, INC.
Income Statements

Years Ended December 31 (In millions)	2010	2009	2008
Net revenues	$49,207	$38,754	$40,492
Cost of sales	31,305	24,819	27,164
Gross profit	17,902	13,935	13,328
Selling, general and administrative expenses	12,001	8,784	8,613
Asset impairment and exit costs	18	(64)	1,024
Losses on divestitures, net	6	6	92
Amortization of intangibles	211	26	23
Operating income	5,666	5,183	3,576
Interest and other expense, net	2,024	1,237	1,240
Earnings from continuing operations before income taxes	3,642	3,946	2,336
Provision for income taxes	1,147	1,136	658
Earnings from continuing operations	2,495	2,810	1,678
Earnings and gain from discontinued operations, net of income taxes	1,644	218	1,215
Net earnings	4,139	3,028	2,893
Noncontrolling interest	25	7	9
Net earnings attributable to Kraft Foods	$ 4,114	$ 3,021	$ 2,884

KRAFT FOODS, INC.
Balance Sheets

December 31 (In millions, except per share amounts)	2010	2009
Assets		
Cash and cash equivalents	$ 2,481	$ 2,101
Receivables (net of allowances of $246 in 2010 and $121 in 2009)	6,539	5,197
Inventories, net	5,310	3,775
Deferred income taxes	898	730
Other current assets	993	651
Total current assets	16,221	12,454
Property, plant and equipment, net	13,792	10,693
Goodwill	37,856	28,764
Intangible assets, net	25,963	13,429
Prepaid pension assets	86	115
Other assets	1,371	1,259
Total assets	$95,289	$66,714
Liabilities		
Short-term borrowings	$ 750	$ 453
Current portion of long-term debt	1,115	513
Accounts payable	5,409	3,766
Accrued marketing	2,515	2,181
Accrued employment costs	1,292	1,175
Other current liabilities	4,579	3,403
Total current liabilities	15,660	11,491
Long-term debt	26,859	18,024
Deferred income taxes	7,984	4,508
Accrued pension costs	2,382	1,765
Accrued postretirement health care costs	3,046	2,816
Other liabilities	3,416	2,138
Total liabilities	59,347	40,742

continued

continued from prior page

Equity
Common Stock, no par value (1,996,537,778 shares issued in 2010 and
  1,735,000,000 shares issued in 2009) . . . .   —   —

	2010	2009
Additional paid-in capital	31,231	23,611
Retained earnings	16,619	14,636
Accumulated other comprehensive losses	(3,890)	(3,955)
Treasury stock, at cost	(8,126)	(8,416)
Total Kraft Foods shareholders' equity	35,834	25,876
Noncontrolling interest	108	96
Total equity	35,942	25,972
Total liabilities and equity	$95,289	$66,714

Required

  a. Compute net operating profit after tax (NOPAT) for 2010. Assume that the combined federal and state statutory tax rate is 37%.

  b. Compute net operating assets (NOA) for 2010 and 2009.

  c. Compute RNOA and disaggregate it into net operating profit margin (NOPM) and net operating asset turnover (NOAT) for 2011; confirm that RNOA = NOPM × NOAT. The median NOPM and NOAT for companies in KFT's industry are 6.22% and 1.66, respectively, yielding a median RNOA of 10.3%. Comment on NOPM and NOAT estimates for KFT in comparison to industry medians.

  d. Compute net nonoperating obligations (NNO) for 2010 and 2009. Confirm the relation: NOA = NNO + Stockholders' equity.

  e. Compute return on equity (ROE) for 2010.

  f. Infer the nonoperating return component of ROE for 2010.

  g. Comment on the difference between ROE and RNOA. What does this relation suggest about Kraft's use of debt?

P4-45.[B] **Analysis and Interpretation of Liquidity and Solvency**   (LO4)

Refer to the financial information of Kraft Foods, Inc., in P4-44 to answer the following requirements.   Kraft Foods, Inc.
(KFT)

Required

  a. Compute current ratio and quick ratio for 2010 and 2009. Comment on any observed trends.

  b. Compute times interest earned and its liabilities-to-equity ratios for 2010 and 2009. Comment on any noticeable change.

  c. Summarize your findings about the company's liquidity and solvency. Do you have any concerns about its ability to meet its debt obligations?

P4-46.[A] **Direct Computation of Nonoperating Return**   (LO1, 3)

Refer to the financial information of Kraft Foods, Inc., in P4-44 to answer the following requirements.   Kraft Foods, Inc.
(KFT)

Required

  a. Assume that 2010 net nonoperating expenses (NNE) are $(344) million and that 2010 RNOA is 7.18%. Compute financial leverage (FLEV) and Spread for 2010.

  b. Assume that 2010 return on equity (ROE) is 13.33%. Confirm computations to yield the relation: ROE = RNOA + (FLEV × Spread).

  c. What do your computations of the nonoperating return in parts a and b imply about the company's use of borrowed funds?

P4-47. **Analysis and Interpretation of Profit Margin, Asset Turnover, and RNOA for Several Companies**   (LO2)

Net operating profit margin (NOPM) and net operating asset turnover (NOAT) for several selected companies for the most recent year follow.

	NOPM	NOAT
Abbott Laboratories	13.83%	1.11
FedEx	3.60%	2.51
CVS Caremark	3.92%	2.09
Kraft	7.66%	0.94
Walgreen's	3.18%	4.64
Caterpillar	6.79%	1.18
Target	5.04%	2.27
Best Buy	2.76%	6.83

Abbott Laboratories (ABT)
FedEx (FDX)
CVS Caremark (CVS)
Kraft (KFT)
Walgreen's (WAG)
Caterpillar (CAT)
Target (TGT)
Best Buy (BBY)

Required

a. Graph NOPM and NOAT for each of these companies. Do you see a pattern that is similar to that shown in this module? Explain. (The graph in the module is based on medians for selected industries; the graph for this problem uses fewer companies than in the module and, thus, will not be as smooth.)

b. Consider the trade-off between profit margin and asset turnover. How can we evaluate companies on the profit margin and asset turnover trade-off? Explain.

 P4-48.^C **Compute and Analyze Measures for DuPont Disaggregation Analysis** (LO5)

Best Buy (BBY)

Refer to the fiscal 2011 financial data of Best Buy Co., Inc., in P4-39 to answer the following requirements.

Required

a. Apply the basic DuPont model and compute the component measures for profit margin, asset turnover, and financial leverage.

b. Compute ROE. Confirm that ROE equals ROE computed using the component measures from part *a* (ROE = PM × AT × FL).

c. Compute adjusted ROA (assume a tax rate of 37%).

P4-49.^C **Compute and Analyze Measures for DuPont Disaggregation Analysis** (LO5)

Kraft Foods (KFT)

Refer to the fiscal 2010 financial data of Kraft Foods in P4-44 to answer the following requirements.

Required

a. Apply the basic DuPont model and compute its component measures for profit margin, asset turnover, and financial leverage.

b. Compute ROE. Confirm that ROE equals ROE computed using the component measures from part *a* (ROE = PM × AT × FL).

c. Compute adjusted ROA (assume a tax rate of 37%). Compare the adjusted and unadjusted ROA ratios and explain why they differ.

 # IFRS APPLICATIONS

I4-50. **Compute, Disaggregate, and Interpret RNOA of Competitors** (LO2)

Shell Oil Company
Royal Dutch Shell
BP Limited

Shell Oil Company is the U.S.-based subsidiary of Royal Dutch Shell, a multinational oil company headquartered in The Hague, The Netherlands. BP Limited is a multinational oil company headquartered in London U.K. Selected balance sheet and income statement information and assumptions for both Shell and BP follow.

($ millions)	2009 Sales	2009 NOPAT	2009 Net Operating Assets	2008 Net Operating Assets
Shell Oil Company	$283,164	$11,793	$169,294	$148,070
BP Limited	243,173	16,800	138,275	125,834

a. Compute the 2009 return on net operating assets (RNOA) for each company.

b. Disaggregate RNOA into net operating profit margin (NOPM) and net operating asset turnover (NOAT) for each company.

c. Discuss any differences in these ratios for each company. What drives the differences in RNOA observed in parts *a* and *b*?

I4-51. **Compute, Disaggregate, and Interpret ROE and RNOA** (LO1, 2)

OMV Group

Headquartered in Vienna, OMV Group is Austria's largest oil-producing, refining and gas station operating company. Selected fiscal year balance sheet and income statement information and assumptions for OMV Group follows (€ thousands).

2009 Sales	2009 Net Income	2009 Net Operating Profit After Tax	2009 Net Operating Assets	2008 Net Operating Assets	2009 Stockholders' Equity	2008 Stockholders' Equity
€17,917,267	€716,931	€526,104	€13,002,350	€12,028,024	€10,034,785	€9,363,243

a. Compute the 2009 return on equity (ROE) and the 2009 return on net operating assets (RNOA).

b. Disaggregate RNOA into net operating profit margin (NOPM) and net operating asset turnover (NOAT).

c. Compute the percentage of RNOA to ROE, and compute OMV Group's nonoperating return for 2009.

I4-52.[B] **Compute and Interpret Liquidity and Solvency Ratios** (LO4)

Schneider Electric is a multinational energy company headquartered in Rueil-Malmaison, France. Se-lected balance sheet and income statement information and assumptions for 2008 and 2009 follows.

Schneider Electric

(€ millions)	Total Current Assets	Total Current Liabilities	Pretax Income	Interest Expense	Total Liabilities	Stockholders' Equity
2008..............	$8,778	$6,444	$2,266	$294	$13,756	$11,051
2009..............	9,731	6,162	1,208	323	13,761	11,888

a. Compute the current ratio for each year and discuss any trend in liquidity. Is the company sufficiently liquid? Explain. What additional information about the accounting numbers comprising this ratio might be useful in helping us assess liquidity? Explain.

b. Compute times interest earned and the liabilities-to-equity ratio for each year and discuss any notice-able change.

c. What is the overall assessment of the company's liquidity and solvency from the analyses in parts a and b? Explain.

I4-53. **Analysis and Interpretation of Profitability** (LO1, 2)

Wm Morrison Supermarkets plc is the fourth largest chain of supermarkets in the United Kingdom, headquartered in Bradford, England. Balance sheets and income statements for Morrison follow.

Wm Morrison Super-markets plc

WM MORRISON SUPERMARKETS plc
Consolidated statements of comprehensive income

52 weeks ended 31 January 2010 (£ millions)	2010	2009	2008
Turnover	£ 15,410	£ 14,528	£ 12,969
Cost of sales................................	(14,348)	(13,615)	(12,151)
Gross profit................................	1,062	913	818
Other operating income	65	37	30
Administrative expenses	(224)	(281)	(268)
Profits arising on fixed-asset transactions.........	4	2	32
Operating profit	907	671	612
Finance costs..............................	(60)	(60)	(60)
Finance income	11	44	60
Profit before taxation	858	655	612
Taxation	(260)	(195)	(58)
Profit for the period	£ 598	£ 460	£ 554

WM MORRISON SUPERMARKETS plc
Consolidated balance sheets

(£ millions)	2010	2009
Assets		
Non-current assets		
Property, plant and equipment.............................	£ 7,180	£ 6,587
Lease prepayments	257	250
Investment property[1]	229	242
Other financial assets[2]	—	81
	7,666	7,160
Current assets		
Stocks[3]...	577	494
Debtors[4]	201	245
Other financial assets....................................	71	—
Cash and cash equivalents	245	327
	1,094	1,066

continued

continued from prior page

Liabilities		
Current liabilities		
Creditors[5]	(1,845)	(1,915)
Other financial liabilities	(213)	(1)
Current tax liabilities	(94)	(108)
	(2,152)	(2,024)
Non-current liabilities		
Other financial liabilities	(1,027)	(1,049)
Deferred tax liabilities	(515)	(472)
Net pension liabilities	(17)	(49)
Provisions	(100)	(112)
	(1,659)	(1,682)
Net assets	£ 4,949	£ 4,520
Shareholders' equity		
Called-up share capital	£ 265	£ 263
Share premium	92	60
Capital redemption reserve	6	6
Merger reserve	2,578	2,578
Retained earnings and hedging reserve.	2,008	1,613
Total equity attributable to the owners of the Company	£ 4,949	£ 4,520

[1] Investment property is a nonoperating asset
[2] These are primarily marketable securities
[3] Stocks means inventories
[4] Debtors means accounts receivable
[5] Creditors means accounts payable

Required

a. Compute net operating profit after tax (NOPAT) for 2010 and 2009. Assume that marginal tax rates are 35.9% for 2010 and 36.0% for 2009.

b. Compute net operating assets (NOA) for 2010 and 2009.

c. Compute and disaggregate RNOA into net operating profit margin (NOPM) and net operating asset turnover (NOAT) for 2010 and 2009; assume that 2008 NOA is £4,666 million. Has the company's RNOA improved or worsened? Explain.

d. Compute net nonoperating obligations (NNO) for 2010 and 2009. Confirm the relation: NOA = NNO + Shareholders' equity.

e. Compute return on equity (ROE) for 2010 and 2009. (Shareholders' equity in 2008 is £4,378 million.)

f. What is the nonoperating return component of ROE for 2010 and 2009?

g. Comment on the difference between ROE and RNOA. What inference can we draw from this comparison?

I4-54.[B]   **Analysis and Interpretation of Liquidity and Solvency**   (LO4)

Wm Morrison Super-
markets plc

Wm Morrison Supermarkets plc is the fourth largest chain of supermarkets in the United Kingdom, headquartered in Bradford, England. Refer to the financial information for Morrisons in I4-53 to answer the following requirements.

Required

a. Compute the current ratio and quick ratio for 2010 and 2009. Comment on any observed trends.

b. Compute times interest earned and liabilities-to-equity ratios for 2010 and 2009. Comment on any noticeable changes.

c. Summarize the findings about the company's liquidity and solvency. Do we have any concerns about its ability to meet its debt obligations?

MANAGEMENT APPLICATIONS

MA4-55. Gross Profit and Strategic Management (LO2)

One way to increase overall profitability is to increase gross profit. This can be accomplished by raising prices and/or by reducing manufacturing costs.

Required

a. Will raising prices and/or reducing manufacturing costs unambiguously increase gross profit? Explain.

b. What strategy might you develop as a manager to (i) increase product prices, or (ii) reduce product manufacturing cost?

MA4-56. Asset Turnover and Strategic Management (LO2)

Increasing net operating asset turnover requires some combination of increasing sales and/or decreasing net operating assets. For the latter, many companies consider ways to reduce their investment in working capital (current assets less current liabilities). This can be accomplished by reducing the level of accounts receivable and inventories, or by increasing the level of accounts payable.

Required

a. Develop a list of suggested actions that you, as a manager, could undertake to achieve these three objectives.

b. Describe the marketing implications of reducing receivables and inventories, and the supplier implications of delaying payment. How can a company reduce working capital without negatively impacting its performance?

MA4-57. Ethics and Governance: Earnings Management (LO1)

Companies are aware that analysts focus on profitability in evaluating financial performance. Managers have historically utilized a number of methods to improve reported profitability that are cosmetic in nature and do not affect "real" operating performance. These methods are subsumed under the general heading of "earnings management." Justification for such actions typically includes the following arguments:

- Increasing stock price by managing earnings benefits shareholders; thus, no one is hurt by these actions.
- Earnings management is a temporary fix; such actions will be curtailed once "real" profitability improves, as managers expect.

Required

a. Identify the affected parties in any scheme to manage profits to prop up stock price.

b. Do the ends (of earnings management) justify the means? Explain.

c. To what extent are the objectives of managers different from those of shareholders?

d. What governance structure can you envision that might inhibit earnings management?

SOLUTIONS TO REVIEW PROBLEMS

Mid-Module Review 1

Solution

Walmart's NOPAT is computed as follows (in $ millions):

$$
\begin{aligned}
\text{NOPAT} &= \text{Operating profit before tax} - (\text{Tax expense} + [\text{Net interest expense} \times 37\%]) \\
&= \$25{,}542 - (\$7{,}579 + [\$2{,}004 \times 37\%]) \\
&= \$17{,}222
\end{aligned}
$$

Mid-Module Review 2

Solution ($ millions)

1.

	Jan. 31, 2011	Jan. 31, 2010
Operating assets		
Receivables, net	$ 5,089	$ 4,144
Inventories	36,318	32,713
Prepaid expenses and other	2,960	3,128
Property and equipment, net	105,098	99,544
Property under capital leases, net	2,780	2,763
Goodwill	16,763	16,126
Other assets and deferred charges	4,129	3,942
Total operating assets	173,137	162,360
Operating liabilities		
Accounts payable.	33,557	30,451
Accrued liabilities	18,701	18,734
Accrued income taxes	157	1,347
Deferred income taxes and other.	6,682	5,508
Total operating liabilities	59,097	56,040
Net operating assets (NOA).	$114,040	$106,320

2. $\text{RNOA} = \dfrac{\$17{,}222}{(\$114{,}040 + \$106{,}320)/2} = 15.63\%$

3. $\text{ROE} = \dfrac{\$16{,}389}{(\$68{,}542 + \$70{,}468)/2} = 23.58\%$

(Note: we use net income and stockholders' equity attributable to Walmart's shareholders.) Walmart's RNOA makes up 66% of its ROE, computed as 15.63%/23.58%.

4. $\text{NOPM} = \$17{,}222/\$421{,}849 = 4.08\%$

$\text{NOAT} = \dfrac{\$421{,}849}{(\$114{,}040 + \$106{,}320)/2} = 3.83$

5.

	ROE	RNOA	NOPM	NOAT
Target	18.94%	11.43%	5.04%	2.27
Walmart	23.58%	15.63%	4.08%	3.83

Walmart's higher ROE is driven by higher RNOA as the nonoperating return is similar (7.96% for WMT and 7.51% for TGT). Walmart's higher RNOA is the result of much higher NOAT, which more than offsets its lower NOPM.

Module-End Review

Solution ($ millions)

1. Walmart ROE = Operating return (RNOA) + Nonoperating return
   Using solutions from Mid-Module Review 2, and substituting, we get:
   23.58% = 15.62% + Nonoperating return
   7.96% = Nonoperating return
2. Target's ROE = Operating return (RNOA) + Nonoperating return
   18.94% = 11.43% + Nonoperating return
   7.51% = Nonoperating return
   Walmart's ROE is higher than Target's because of its higher RNOA. The nonoperating return is a function of both the relative amount of debt in their capital structures and the spread of the return on net operating assets

over the cost of that debt. Both companies are increasing their ROE by the use of financial leverage. Further analysis is warranted to investigate whether either company is taking on too much default risk by their use of debt.

3. Walmart's liabilities-to-equity ratio = Total liabilities/Total equity (We use total [consolidated] equity to be consistent with the consolidated liabilities in the numerator.)
   ($58,484 + $40,692 + $3,150 + $6,682)/$71,247 = 1.53

4. Target's liabilities-to-equity ratio = Total liabilities/Total equity
   ($10,070 + $18,148)/$15,487 = 1.82

While the liabilities-to-equity ratios for both companies are higher than for the average retail company (see: Exhibit 4.6), neither company's ratio is markedly out of line with medians for all publicly traded companies over the past decade. Further analysis is necessary to evaluate if that debt exposure is excessive. That additional analysis will examine the amount of projected debt payments (found in the long-term debt footnote) with projected net cash from operating activities.

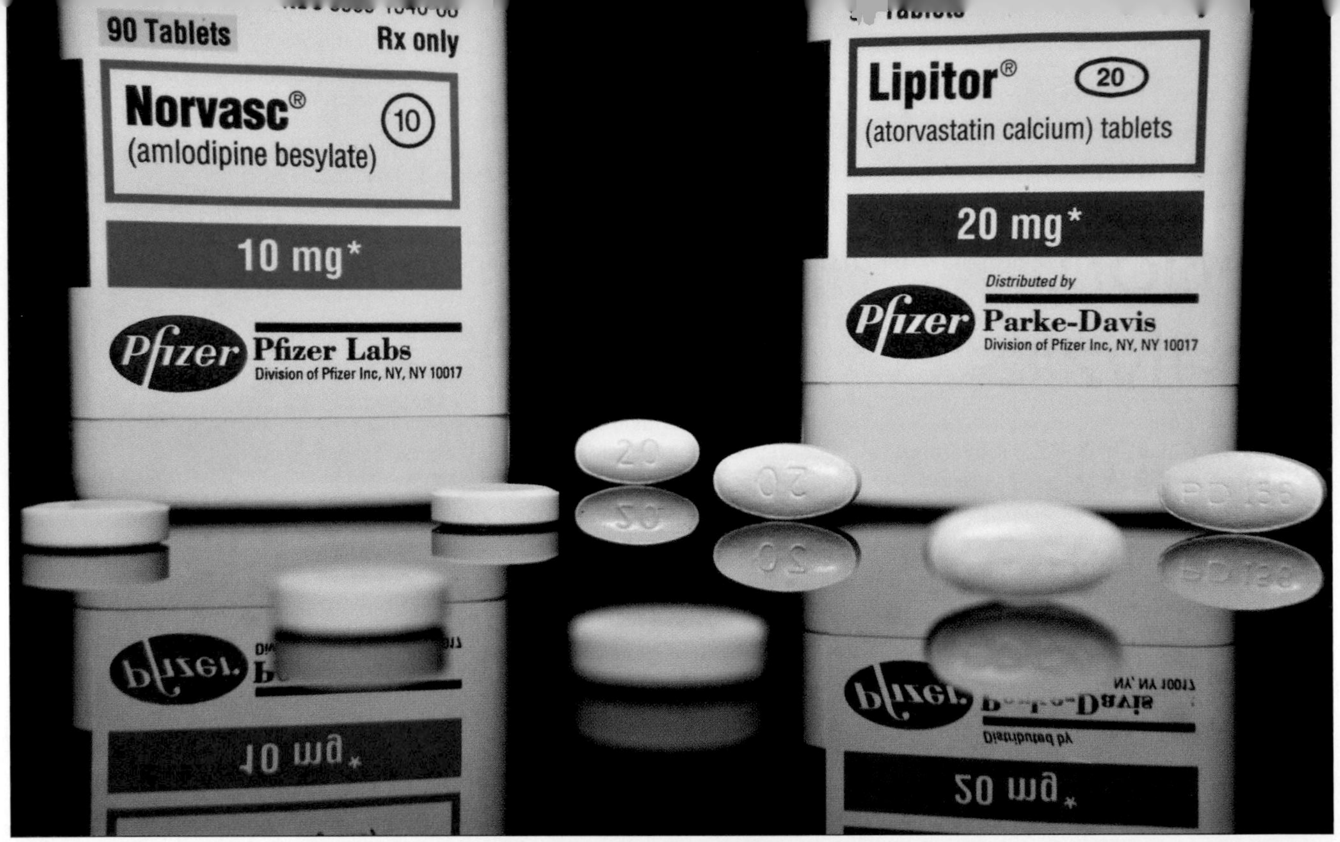

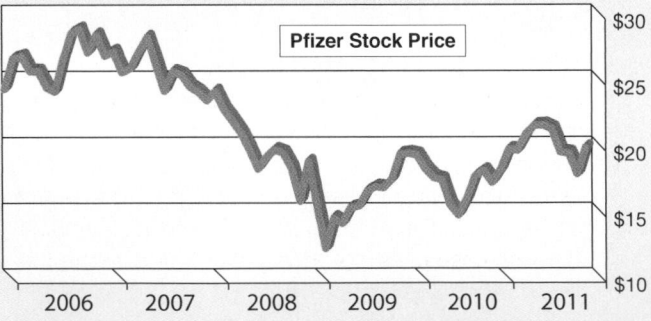

PFIZER

Pfizer's business is to discover, develop, manufacture and market leading prescription medicines. These endeavors define the company's operating activities and include research and development, manufacturing, advertising, sales, after-sale customer support, and all administrative functions necessary to support Pfizer's various activities.

Accounting for operating activities involves numerous estimates and choices, and GAAP often grants considerable latitude. To illustrate, consider the choice of when to recognize sales revenue. Should Pfizer recognize revenue when it receives a customer order? When it ships the drug order? Or, when the customer pays? GAAP requires that revenues be recognized when *earned*. It is up to the company to decide when that condition is met. This module identifies several revenue-recognition scenarios that are especially troublesome for companies, their auditors, regulators, and outside stakeholders.

Pfizer's key operating activity is its research and development (R&D). To protect its discoveries, Pfizer holds thousands of patents and applies for hundreds more each year. However, patents don't protect Pfizer indefinitely—patents expire or fail legal challenges and, then, Pfizer's drugs face competition from other drug manufacturers. In 2007, for example, Pfizer's sales of Zoloft and Norvasc declined by about $3.5 billion because patent protection expired on both drugs. Even the company's blockbuster drug, Lipitor,

with sales exceeding $10 billion in 2010 (16% of Pfizer's total revenues), is not a panacea for what ails Pfizer—the Lipitor patent expired in 2011.

Wall Street is not optimistic about Pfizer's ability to replace patents that will lapse over the next decade. While Pfizer's revenues have increased by over 40% in the past five years, its profits have decreased by about 57%, and Pfizer's stock price has fallen nearly 20% percent—see stock price chart below.

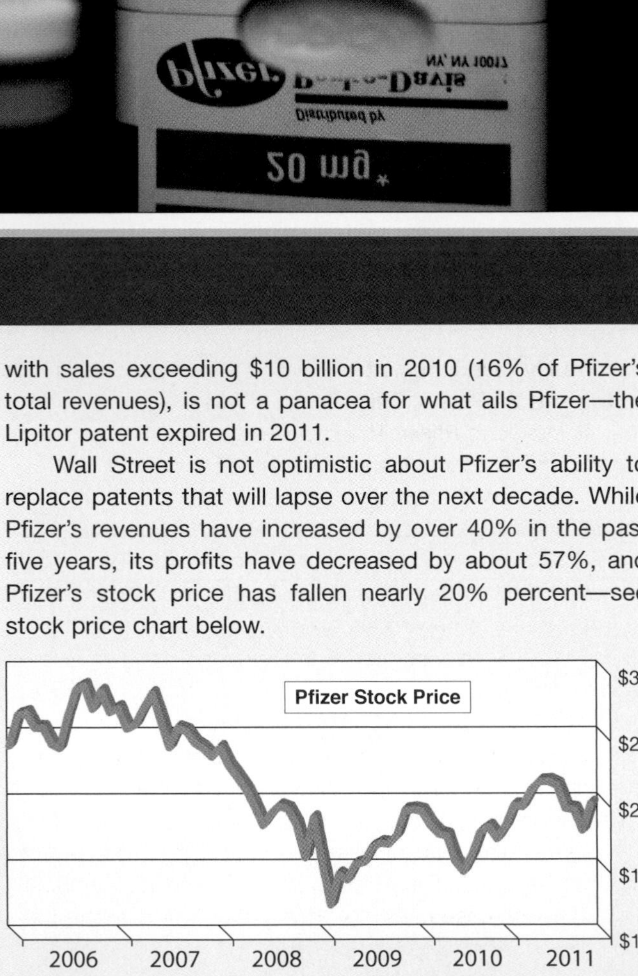

Although R&D activities generally yield future benefits and, thus, meet the criteria to be recorded as an asset, GAAP requires that companies expense most R&D costs. This creates balance sheets with significant "missing" assets. For example, the only asset that Pfizer has on its books specifically related to drugs that it has developed and

Reporting and Analyzing Operating Income

Module

5

LEARNING OBJECTIVES

LO1 Explain revenue recognition criteria and identify transactions of special concern. (p. 5-5)

LO2 Describe accounting for operating expenses, including research and development, and restructuring. (p. 5-13)

LO3 Explain and analyze accounting for income taxes. (p. 5-19)

LO4 Explain how foreign currency fluctuations affect the income statement. (p. 5-26)

LO5 Compute earnings per share and explain the effect of dilutive securities. (p. 5-29)

LO6 Explain accounting quality and identify areas for analysis. (p. 5-30)

is currently marketing is the legal cost of filing the patents with the U.S. Patent Office. Clearly this does not capture their full value to Pfizer. This module explains R&D accounting and the resulting financial statement implications.

Pfizer has restructured its business several times in an attempt to maintain operating profit. Restructurings typically involve two types of costs: severance costs relating to employee terminations and asset write-offs. GAAP grants leeway in how to account for restructuring activities. Should Pfizer expense the severance costs when the board of directors approves the layoffs? Or when the employees are actually paid? Or at some other point? This module discusses accounting for restructurings, including footnote disclosures that can help financial statement readers interpret restructuring activities.

A necessary part of operations is paying income taxes on profits earned. The IRS has its own rules for computing taxes owed. These rules, called the Internal Revenue Code, are different from GAAP. Thus, it is legal (and necessary) for companies to prepare two sets of financial reports, one for shareholders and one for tax authorities. In this module, we will see that tax expense reported on the income statement is not computed as a simple percentage of pretax income. The module also discusses the valuation allowance that is related to deferred tax assets, and explains how the allowance can markedly affect net income.

Earnings per share (EPS) is the most frequently quoted operating number in the financial press. It represents earnings that are available to pay dividends to common shareholders. Companies report two EPS numbers: basic and diluted. The latter represents the lower bound on EPS. It is important that we understand the difference between the two, and this module describes the two EPS computations.

Pfizer does business around the world, transacting in many currencies. Indeed, many of Pfizer's subsidiaries maintain their entire financial records in currencies other than the U.S. dollar. Consequently, to prepare its financial statements in $US, Pfizer must translate each transaction from foreign currencies into $US. This module describes the effects of foreign currency translation. When the dollar strengthens and weakens against other world currencies, a company's foreign revenues and expenses increase or decrease in $US value even if unit volumes remain unchanged. It is important to understand the mechanical relation between foreign exchange rates and income statement items if we are to properly analyze companies with global operations. This module considers these issues.

Sources: Pfizer 2010 10-K, Pfizer 2010 Annual Report; *Fortune*, January 2009; *BusinessWeek*, January 2009.

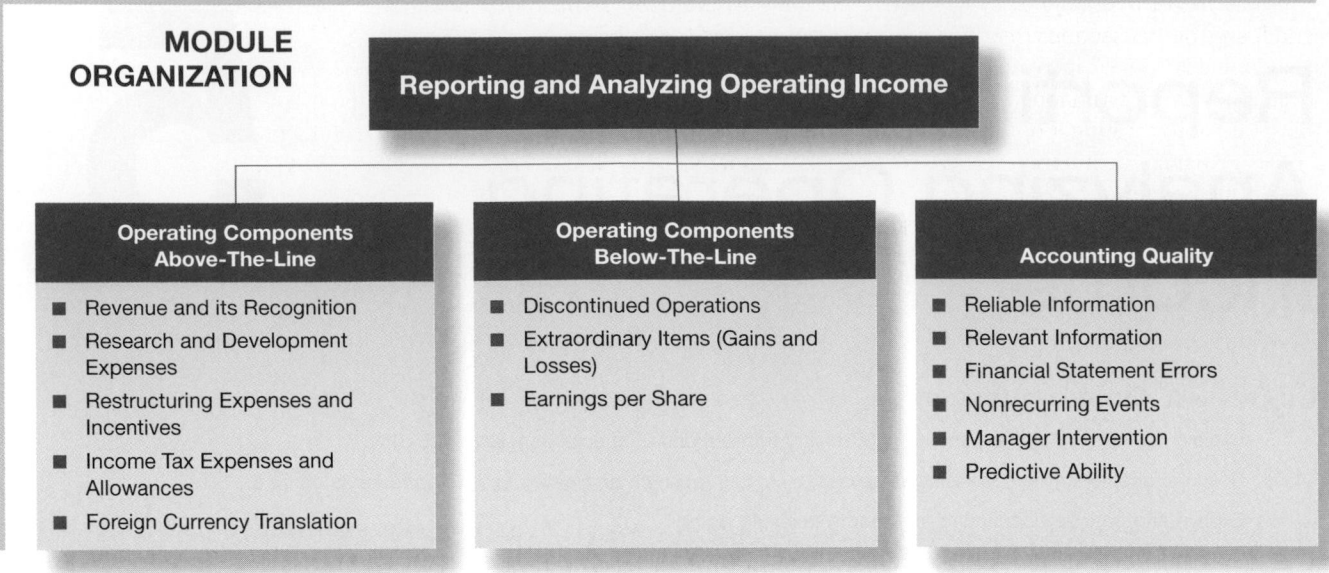

Operating activities refer to a company's primary transactions. These include the purchase of goods from suppliers, the conversion of goods into finished products, the promotion and distribution of goods, the sale of goods to customers, and post-sale customer support. For manufacturing companies, operating activities include the conversion of goods into finished products. The income statement reports on these operating activities such as sales, cost of goods sold, and selling, general, and administrative expenses. Because they are the lifeblood of any company, operating activities must be executed successfully for a company to consistently succeed.

Nonoperating activities relate to the borrowing of money and the ancillary investment activities of a company. They are not a company's primary activities.[1] These activities are typically reported in the income statement as interest revenues and expenses, dividend revenues, gains losses on sales of securities, and net income attributable to noncontrolling interest.

Proper identification of operating and nonoperating components is important for valuation of companies' equity (stock) and debt (notes and bonds). It is important, for example, to know whether company profitability results from operating activities, or whether poor operating performance is being masked by income from nonoperating activities. (We know that income from nonoperating activities usually depends on a favorable investment climate, which can be short-lived.)

Exhibit 5.1 classifies several common income components as operating or nonoperating.

EXHIBIT 5.1 Distinguishing Operating and Nonoperating Income Components	
Operating Activities	**Nonoperating Activities**
• Sales	• Interest revenues and expenses
• Cost of goods sold	• Dividend revenues
• Selling, general and administrative expenses	• Gains and losses on sales of investments
• Depreciation expense	• Investment write-downs
• Research and development expenses	• Gains and losses on debt retirement
• Restructuring expenses	• Gains and losses on discontinued operations
• Income tax expenses	• Allocation of profit to noncontrolling interest
• Extraordinary gains and losses	(previously titled "minority interest expense")
• Gains and losses on sales of operating assets	
• Foreign currency translation effects	
• Operating asset write-downs	
• Other income or expenses	

---

[1] Exceptions exist; for example, income derived from investments is operating income for financial-services firms such as banks and insurance companies. As another example, the income derived from financing subsidiaries of manufacturing companies, such as Ford Motor Credit and Caterpillar Financial, is part of operating income because these activities can be viewed as extensions of the sales process.

The list of operating activities above includes all the familiar operating items, as well as gains and losses on transactions relating to operating assets and the write-down of operating assets.[2] The list also includes "other" income statement items. We treat these as operating unless the income statement designates them as nonoperating or footnote information indicates that some or all of these "other" items are nonoperating. Footnotes are usually uninformative about "other" income statement items and "other" balance sheet items, and GAAP does not require specific disclosure of such items unless they are deemed *material*.[3]

We build our discussion of operating income around Pfizer's income statement (see Exhibit 5.2), which includes all of the typical operating accounts. We highlight the following topics in this module:

- Revenues
- Research and development expenses
- Restructuring expenses
- Income tax expenses

- Extraordinary gains and losses
- Earnings per share (EPS)
- Foreign currency translation effects

BUSINESS INSIGHT   **Ratios Across Industries**

Over time, industries evolve and reach equilibrium levels for operating activities. For example, some industries require a high level of selling, general and administrative (SG&A) expenses, perhaps due to high advertising demands or high occupancy costs. Other industries require intense research and development (R&D) expenditures to remain competitive. To a large extent, these cost structures dictate the prices that firms in the industry charge—each industry prices its product or service to yield a sufficient level of gross profit (sales less cost of sales) to cover the operating expenses and allow the industry to remain viable. Review the following table of selected operating margins for companies in various industries (NOPM is net operating profit margin as defined in Module 4).

	Gross profit/Sales	SG&A/Sales	R&D/Sales	NOPM
Cisco Systems, Inc. (CSCO)	64.0%	26.8%	13.2%	19.0%
Intel Corporation (INTC).	65.3%	14.5%	15.1%	25.8%
Pfizer Inc. (PFE)	76.0%	28.9%	13.9%	12.2%
Target Corp. (TGT)	32.1%	20.0%	0.0%	5.0%
Best Buy Co. Inc. (BBY)	25.1%	20.5%	0.0%	2.8%
Caterpillar Inc. (CAT)	28.7%	10.0%	4.5%	6.8%
Dell Inc. (DELL)	18.5%	11.9%	1.1%	4.4%
The Home Depot, Inc. (HD)	34.3%	23.3%	0.0%	5.4%
Nike, Inc. (NKE).	45.6%	32.1%	0.0%	10.0%
Cheesecake Factory Inc. (CAKE)	42.8%	5.8%	0.0%	5.6%

We see that Cisco, Intel and Pfizer report high gross profit margins. This does not necessarily suggest they are better managed than Dell. Instead, their industries require higher levels of gross profit to cover their high levels of SG&A and R&D. Dell, on the other hand, is in a highly price-competitive segment of the computer industry. To maintain its competitive advantage, Dell must control costs. Indeed, Dell reports among the lowest SG&A-to-sales ratio of the companies listed.

---

[2] To explain, a loss on the sale of equipment implies that the company did not depreciate the equipment quickly enough. Had the company recorded the "right" amount of depreciation over the years (that is, the amount of depreciation that perfectly matched the equipment's economic devaluation over time), the equipment's book value would have been exactly the same as its market value and no loss would have been recorded. Thus, we treat the loss on disposal in the same manner as depreciation expense—as operating. The same logic applies to write-downs of operating assets, which occur when the fair value of assets such as property and intangibles has declined below their book value.

[3] *Material* is an accounting term that means the item in question is important enough to make a difference to someone relying on the financial statements when making a business decision. Investors, for example, might find an item material if it is large enough to change their investment decision (whether to buy or sell the stock). This *materiality* judgment is in the eye of the beholder and this subjectivity makes materiality an elusive concept.

OPERATING INCOME COMPONENTS

Pfizer's 2010 income statement in Exhibit 5.2 highlights (in blue) the operating income components discussed in this module. We defer discussion of cost of goods sold (cost of sales) to Module 6, which focuses on inventories and other operating assets. Modules 2 and 4 discuss items typically included in selling, general and administrative (SG&A) expenses, and Module 7 addresses the accounts related to acquisitions of other companies (such as amortization of intangible assets, merger-related in-process research and development charges, noncontrolling interest, and discontinued operations).

EXHIBIT 5.2 Pfizer Income Statement	
(Millions, except per share data)	**2010**
Revenues.	$67,809
Costs and expenses	
Cost of sales.	16,279
Selling, informational and administative expenses.	19,614
Research and development expenses	9,413
Amortization of intangible assets	5,404
Acquisition-related in-process research and development charges	125
Restructuring charges and acquisition-related costs.	3,214
Other deductions—net	4,338
Income from continuing operations before provision for taxes on income	9,422
Provision for taxes on income.	1,124
Income from continuing operations	8,298
Discontinued operations—net of tax	(9)
Net income before allocation to noncontrolling interests.	8,289
Less: Net income attributable to noncontrolling interests	32
Net income attributable to Pfizer Inc..	$ 8,257
Earnings per common share—basic	
Income from continuing operations attributable to Pfizer Inc. common shareholders.	$ 1.03
Discontinued operations—net of tax	—
Net income attributable to Pfizer Inc. common shareholders	$ 1.03
Earnings per common share—diluted	
Income from continuing operations attributable to Pfizer Inc. common shareholders.	$ 1.02
Discontinued operations—net of tax	—
Net income attributable to Pfizer Inc. common shareholders	$ 1.02
Weighted-average shares—basic	8,036
Weighted-average shares—diluted	8,074

We begin by discussing revenue, including the revenue recognition criteria that companies must employ and improper revenue recognition that the SEC has recently challenged. Next, we discuss Pfizer's research and development expenses, restructuring charges, provision for taxes, effects of foreign currency fluctuations, extraordinary items, and earnings per share (EPS).

Revenue and its Recognition

LO1 Explain revenue recognition criteria and identify transactions of special concern.

Pfizer reports $67,809 million in revenue. This revenue represents the culmination of a process that includes the manufacture of the drugs, their promotion, the receipt of orders, delivery to the customer, billing for the sale amount, and collection of the amounts owed. At what point in this process should Pfizer recognize its revenue and the related profit? When the drugs are delivered to the customer? When payment is received? And, how should Pfizer treat sales discounts or rights of return?

IFRS INSIGHT   Income Statement Differences

IFRS allows companies to classify income statement items by nature (materials, labor, etc.) rather than by function (cost of goods sold, selling expenses, etc.). **Finmeccanica S.p.A.** is an Italian manufacturing conglomerate that operates in the defense, aerospace, transport and energy sectors. Its 2010 IFRS income statement classifies items by nature.

Finmeccanica SpA, Consolidated Income Statement (€ millions)	**2010**
Revenue	€18,695
Other operating income	627
Raw materials and consumables used	(6,316)
Purchase of services	(5,878)
Personnel costs	(4,772)
Amortisation, depreciation and impairment	(785)
Other operating expenses	(801)
Changes in inventories of work in progress, semi-finished and finished goods	(176)
Work performed by the Group and capitalized	638
	1,232
Finance income	850
Finance costs	(1,202)
Share of profit (loss) of equity accounted investments	(14)
Profit before taxes	866
Income taxes	(309)
Net profit	€ 557
Equity holders of the Company	€ 493
Minority interests	64
Net profit	€ 557

Because Finmeccanica classifies its income statement items by nature, there is no line item for cost of goods sold. Instead, the manufacturing and inventory costs recognized during the period are reported according to their nature (raw materials and consumables used, personnel costs, other operating expenses) along with the amount of the net change in inventories for the period. We see that other than raw materials and consumables used and the net change in inventories, all the operating costs combine product and period costs. For example, personnel costs include the salaries and wages for all staff from the manufacturing employees to the CEO.

GAAP specifies two **revenue recognition criteria** that must both be met for revenue to be recognized on the income statement. Revenue must be (1) **realized or realizable**, and (2) **earned**.[4] *Realized or realizable* means that the seller's net assets (assets less liabilities) increase. That is, the seller receives an asset, such as cash or accounts receivable, or satisfies a liability, such as deferred revenue, as a result of a transaction. The company does not have to wait to recognize revenue until after it collects the accounts receivable; the increase in the account receivable (asset) means that the revenue is realizable. *Earned* means that the seller has performed its duties under the terms of the sales agreement and that title to the product sold has passed to the buyer with no right of return or other contingencies.

---

[4] *SEC provides guidance for revenue recognition in Staff Accounting Bulletin (SAB) 101* (http://www.sec.gov/interps/account/sab101.htm) that states that revenue is realized, or realizable, and earned when *each* of the following criteria are met: (1) there is persuasive evidence that a sales agreement exists; (2) delivery has occurred or services have been rendered; (3) the seller's price to the buyer is fixed or determinable; and (4) collectibility is reasonably assured.

As long as Pfizer has delivered the drugs ordered by its customers, and its customers are obligated to make payment, Pfizer can recognize revenue. The following conditions would each argue *against* revenue recognition:

- *Rights of return exist,* other than due to routine product defects covered under product warranty.
- *Consignment sales,* where products are held on consignment until ultimately sold by the consignee.
- *Continuing involvement by seller in product resale,* such as where the seller has an obligation for future performance like product updates.
- *Contingency sales,* such as when product sales are contingent on product performance or further approvals by the customer.

Revenue is not recognized in these cases until the factors inhibiting revenue recognition are resolved.

Companies are required to report their revenue recognition policies in footnotes to their 10-K reports. Pfizer recognizes its revenues as follows:

> Revenue Recognition—We record revenue from product sales when the goods are shipped and title passes to the customer. At the time of sale, we also record estimates for a variety of sales deductions, such as sales rebates, discounts and incentives, and product returns.

Pfizer adopts the position that its revenues are *earned* when its products are shipped and the risks and rewards of the merchandise passes to its customers. At that point, Pfizer has done everything required and, thus, recognizes the sale in the income statement. Most companies recognize revenues using these same criteria. Pfizer does *not* recognize revenues for the gross selling price. Instead, Pfizer deducts that portion of gross sales that is likely to be refunded to customers through sales rebates, discounts and incentives (including volume purchases). Pfizer estimates the likely cost of those price reductions and deducts that amount from gross sales. Similarly, Pfizer does not recognize revenues for those products that it estimates will be returned, possibly because the drugs hit their expiration date before they are sold by Pfizer's customers. In sum, Pfizer recognizes revenues for products delivered to customers, and for only the sales price *net* of anticipated discounts and returns. This is why we often see "Revenues, net" on companies' income statements.

IFRS INSIGHT   **Revenue Recognition and IFRS**

Revenue is generally recognized under both U.S. GAAP and IFRS when the earning process is complete (when the seller has performed all obligations under the sales arrangement and no performance obligations remain) and benefits are realized or realizable. Further, there is extensive guidance under U.S. GAAP for specific industry transactions. That guidance is not present in IFRS. Moreover, public companies in the U.S. must follow additional guidance set by the SEC. Many believe that companies recognize revenue slightly earlier under IFRS than under GAAP.

Revenue Recognition and Risk Exposure

More than 70% of SEC accounting and auditing enforcement actions involve misstated revenues. The SEC's concern about aggressive (premature) revenue recognition prompted the issuance of a special *Staff Accounting Bulletin (SAB) 101* on the matter. The SEC provides the following examples of problem areas to assist companies in properly recognizing revenue:

- *Case 1: Channel stuffing.* Some sellers use their market power over customers to induce (or even require) them to purchase more goods than they actually need. This practice, called *channel stuffing*, increases period-end sales and net income. If no side agreements exist for product returns, the practice does not violate GAAP revenue recognition guidelines, but the SEC contends that revenues are misrepresented and that the practice is a violation of securities laws.

- *Case 2: Barter transactions.* Some barter transactions are concocted to create the illusion of revenue. Examples include the advertising swaps that dot-com companies have sometimes engaged in, and the excess capacity swaps of fiber optic communications businesses. The advertising swap relates to the simultaneous sale and purchase of advertising. The excess capacity swap relates to a company selling excess capacity to a competitor and, simultaneously, purchasing excess capacity from that competitor. Both types of swaps are exchanges of nearly identical services; they do not provide income or create an expense for either party. Further, these transactions do not represent a culmination of the normal earning process and, thus, the "earned" revenue recognition criterion is not met.

- *Case 3: Mischaracterizing transactions as arm's-length.* Transfers of inventories or other assets to related entities are typically not recognized as revenue until arm's-length sales occur. Sometimes, companies disguise non-arm's-length transactions as sales to unrelated entities. This practice is improper when the buyer is related to the seller, or the buyer is unable to pay for the merchandise other than from its resale. Revenue should not be recognized unless the sales process is complete, that is, goods have been transferred and an asset has been created (future payment from a solvent, independent party).

- *Case 4: Pending execution of sales agreements.* Sometimes companies boost current-period profits by recording revenue for goods delivered for which formal customer approval has yet to be received. The SEC's position is that if the company's practice is to obtain sales authorization, then revenue is *not* earned until such approval is obtained, even though product delivery is made and customer approval is anticipated.

- *Case 5: Gross versus net revenues.* Some companies use their distribution network to sell other companies' goods for a commission. There are increasing reports of companies that inflate revenues by reporting such transactions on a gross basis (separately reporting both sales and cost of goods sold) instead of reporting only the commission (typically a percentage of sales price). The incentives for such reporting are high for some dot.com companies and start-ups that believe the market prices of their stocks are based on revenue growth and not on profitability. Reporting revenues at gross rather than net could have enormous impact on the valuations of those companies. The SEC prescribes that such sales be reported on a net basis (see Business Insight on next page).

- *Case 6: Sales on consignment.* Some companies deliver goods to other companies with the understanding that these goods will be ultimately sold to third parties. At the time of delivery, title does not pass to the second company, and the second company has no obligation to make payment to the seller until the product is sold. This type of transaction is called a *consignment sale*. The SEC's position is that a sale has not occurred, and revenue is *not* to be recognized by the original company, until the product is sold to a third party. Further, the middleman (consignee) cannot report the gross sale, and can only report its commission revenue.

- *Case 7: Failure to take delivery.* Some customers may not take delivery of the product by period-end. In this case, revenue is *not* yet earned. The earning process is only complete once the product is delivered and accepted. An example is a layaway sale. Even though the product is ordered, and even partially paid for, revenue is not recognized until the product is delivered and final payment is made or agreed to be made.

- *Case 8: Nonrefundable fees.* Sellers sometimes receive fees that are nonrefundable to the customer. An example is a health club initiation fee or a cellular phone activation fee. Some sellers wish to record these cash receipts as revenue to boost current sales and income. However, even though cash is received and nonrefundable, revenue is not recognized until the product is delivered or the service performed. Until that time, the company reports the cash received as a liability (deferred revenue). Once the obligation is settled, the liability is removed and revenue is reported.

In sum, revenue is only recognized when it is earned and when it is realized or realizable. This demands that the seller has performed its obligations (no contingencies exist) and the buyer is an independent party with the financial capacity to pay the amounts owed.

| BUSINESS INSIGHT | Gross versus Net Revenues |

In 2011, Groupon, Inc., announced its intentions to offer stock to the public in an initial public offering (IPO). The company's original SEC registration statement disclosed that the company recorded revenue at the gross amount it received from selling Groupons (coupons). For example, when Groupon sold a restaurant gift certificate for $20, it would record the full amount of $20 even though a hefty portion (say $9 for example) is owed the restaurant owner. By recording revenues at "gross," Groupon did not comply with GAAP because it holds no inventory, does not determine the product or service price, and does not perform the service. The SEC intervened and Groupon restated revenues in an amended SEC filing in September 2011. Groupon now reports revenues at "net," which is the commission on sales, rather than the total value of online coupons. Returning to our restaurant example, Groupon's amended revenue would be $11, not $20. Footnote 2 of its latest SEC filing reports the following. Shortly after the amended filing, Groupon's Chief Operating Officer left the firm.

Revenues ($ 000s)	2008	2009	2010
As previously reported	$ 94	$30,471	$713,365
Restatement adjustment	(89)	(15,931)	(400,424)
As restated	$ 5	$14,540	$312,941

Percentage-of-Completion Revenue Recognition

Another revenue recognition challenge arises for companies with long-term sales contracts (spanning more than one period), such as construction companies, consultants, and defense contractors. For these companies, revenue is often recognized using the percentage-of-completion method, which recognizes revenue by determining the costs incurred under the contract relative to its total expected costs.

To illustrate, assume that Bayer Construction signs a $10 million contract to construct a building. Bayer estimates construction will take two years and will cost $7,500,000. This means the contract yields an expected gross profit of $2,500,000 over two years. The following table summarizes construction costs incurred each year and the revenue Bayer recognizes.

	Construction costs incurred	Percentage complete	Revenue recognized
Year 1	$4,500,000	$\frac{\$4,500,000}{\$7,500,000} = 60\%$	$10,000,000 × 60% = $6,000,000
Year 2	$3,000,000	$\frac{\$3,000,000}{\$7,500,000} = 40\%$	$10,000,000 × 40% = $4,000,000

This table reveals that Bayer would report $6 million in revenue and $1.5 million ($6 million − $4.5 million) in gross profit on the construction project in the first year; it would report $4 million in revenue and $1 million ($4 million − $3 million) in gross profit in the second year.

Next, assume that Bayer's client makes a $1 million deposit at the signing of the contract and that Bayer submits bills to the client based on the percentage of completion. The following table reflects the bills sent to, and the cash received from, the client.

	Revenue recognized	Client billed	Cash received
At signing	$ 0	$ 0	$1,000,000
Year 1	6,000,000	5,000,000	2,000,000
Year 2	4,000,000	4,000,000	7,000,000

At the signing of the contract, Bayer recognizes no revenue because construction has not begun and thus, Bayer has not earned any revenue. By the end of the second year, Bayer has recognized all of the contract revenue and the client has paid all monies owed per the accounts receivable. The following template captures Bayer Construction's transactions over this two-year period (M indicates millions).

Transaction	Balance Sheet						Income Statement		
	Cash Asset	+ Noncash Assets	= Liabil- ities	+ Contrib. Capital	+ Earned Capital		Rev- enues	− Expen- ses	= Net Income
Start of year 1: Record $1M deposit received at contract signing	+1M Cash		= +1M Unearned Revenue				−	=
Year 1: Record $4.5M construction costs	−4.5M Cash		=		−4.5M Retained Earnings		+4.5M Cost of Sales	−	= −4.5M
Year 1: Recognize $6M revenue on partly completed contract		+5M Accounts Receivable	= −1M Unearned Revenue		+6M Retained Earnings		+6M Revenue	−	= +6M
Year 1: Record $2M cash received from client	+2M Cash	−2M Accounts Receivable	=				−	=
Year 2: Record $3M construction costs	−3M Cash		=		−3M Retained Earnings		+3M Cost of Sales	−	= −3M
Year 2: Recognize $4M revenue for completed contract		+4M Accounts Receivable	=		+4M Retained Earnings		+4M Revenue	−	= +4M
Year 2: Record $7M cash received from client	+7M Cash	−7M Accounts Receivable	=				−	=

Revenue recognition policies for these types of contracts are disclosed in a manner typical to the following from the 2010 10-K report footnotes of **Raytheon Company**.

Revenue Recognition We account for our long-term contracts . . . using the percentage-of-completion accounting method. Under this method, revenue is recognized based on the extent of progress towards completion of the long-term contract . . . We generally use the cost-to-cost measure of progress for all of our long-term contracts . . . Under the cost-to-cost measure of progress, the extent of progress towards completion is measured based on the ratio of costs incurred-to-date to the total estimated costs at completion of the contract.

The percentage-of-completion method of revenue recognition requires an estimate of total costs. This estimate is made at the beginning of the contract and is typically the one used to initially bid the contract. However, estimates are inherently inaccurate. If the estimate changes during the construction period, the percentage-of-completion is computed as the total costs incurred to date divided by the *current* estimate of total anticipated costs (costs incurred to date plus total estimated costs to complete).

If total construction costs are underestimated, the percentage-of-completion is overestimated (the denominator is too low) and revenue and gross profit to date are overstated. The estimation process inherent in this method has the potential for inaccurate or, even, improper revenue recognition. In addition, estimates of remaining costs to complete projects are difficult for the auditors to verify. This uncertainty adds additional risk to financial statement analysis.

BUSINESS INSIGHT   **Disney's Revenue Recognition**

The **Walt Disney Company** uses a method similar to percentage-of-completion to determine the amount of production cost to match against film and television revenues. Following is an excerpt from its 10-K.

> Film and television costs include capitalizable production costs, production overhead, interest, development costs, and acquired production costs and are stated at the lower of cost, less accumulated amortization, or fair value. Film and television .... costs are expensed based on the ratio of the current period's revenues to estimated remaining total revenues (Ultimate Revenues). Ultimate Revenues include revenues that will be earned within ten years from the date of the initial theatrical release or ... the delivery of the first episode.

As Disney pays production costs, it records those costs on the balance sheet as inventory. Then, as film and television revenues are recognized, the company matches a portion of production costs (from inventory) against revenues in computing income. Each period, the costs recognized are equal to the proportion of total revenues recognized in the period to the total revenues expected over the life of the film or television show. Thus, estimates of both costs and income depend on the quality of Disney's revenue estimates, which are, likely, imprecise.

Recognition of Unearned Revenue

In some industries it is common to receive cash before recording revenue. Customers might pay in advance for special orders, make deposits for future services, or buy concert tickets, subscriptions, or gift cards. In those cases, companies must record unearned revenues, a liability, and only record revenue when those products and services are provided. Specifically, deposits or advance payments are not recorded as revenue until the company performs the services owed or delivers the goods. Until then, the company's balance sheet shows the advance payment as a liability (called unearned revenue or deferred revenue) because the company is obligated to deliver those products and services.

Unearned revenue is particularly common among technology companies that sell goods and services as packages. These sales are called "multi-element contracts," which are sales agreements that bundle goods and services that may or may not be delivered simultaneously. When delivery is delayed the company must record unearned revenue. Consider for example, the sale of an Apple iPad. The customer not only purchases the tablet hardware but the software integral to the iPad's function, additional software, and future software upgrades. How should Apple record revenue for such a multi-element contract? The short answer is that the total sales price is allocated among the elements of the contract and revenue is recognized (as it's earned) at different points in time for each element. Allocating the total sales price presents a challenge because elements often do not have stand-alone prices. GAAP allows companies to estimate selling prices for each element if sold separately and then allocate the total selling price ratably among the elements.

More specifically, assume that on September 26, 2010 (the first day of Apple's 2011 fiscal year), Apple sells 60 iPads to a customer and charges the total invoice amount of $36,000 to the customer's credit card (a cash transaction). Apple disclosed the following in its 10K:

> Beginning with initial sales of iPad in April 2010, the Company has also indicated it may from time-to-time provide future unspecified software upgrades and features free of charge to iPad customers. The Company's estimated selling price (ESP) for the embedded software upgrade right included with the sale of each iPad is $10. Amounts allocated to the embedded unspecified software upgrade rights are deferred and recognized on a straight-line basis over 24 months.

Apple records $36,000 cash and recognizes revenue on the hardware and software components of the sale. The estimated selling price of $600 for the future software upgrades (60 units at $10 per unit) is not earned at the point of sale. Instead, Apple records a liability (unearned revenue) for this amount. This means that revenue of $35,400 is immediately reported and $600 is reported over the ensuing 24 months. Apple prepares quarterly financial statements and will recognize $75 ($600 × 3/24) of the unearned revenue each quarter for two years. As revenue is earned, the unearned revenue account on the balance sheet is reduced and revenue is recorded in the income statement. The following template reflects the initial sales transaction and the subsequent first quarter accounting adjustment.

	Balance Sheet							Income Statement		
Transaction	Cash Asset	+	Noncash Assets	=	Liabil- ities	+	Contrib. Capital	+ Earned Capital	Rev- enues	− Expen- ses	= Net Income
Sep 26: Receive $36,000 cash advance for products	+36,000 Cash				+600 = Unearned Revenue			+35,400 Retained Earnings	+35,400 Revenue	−	= +35,400
Dec 26: Recognize three months' of unearned revenue					−75 = Unearned Revenue			+75 Retained Earnings	+75 Revenue	−	= +75

Cash   36,000
UR   600
Revenue 35,400

Cash
36,000 |
       | UR
       | 600
       | Rev
       | 35,400

UR   75
       | Rev   75
UR
75 |
   | Rev
   | 75

Apple's 2010 balance sheet reports the following liabilities (in millions):

Current liabilities
Accounts payable...	$12,015
Accrued expenses	5,723
Deferred revenue	2,984
Total current liabilities...	20,722
Deferred revenue– non-current	1,139
Other non-current liabilities	5,531
Total liabilities	$27,392

The company reports deferred revenue as both current and noncurrent liabilities. These relate to the revenue that will be earned in the coming year ($2,984 million) and in subsequent years ($1,139). These are substantial liabilities to Apple because many of its products are sold with guaranteed future services such as software upgrades and long-term service contracts. Each quarter, the unearned revenue account increases by the new sales and decreases as revenue is earned.

In June 2010, the FASB and IASB published a joint exposure draft (ED) on revenue recognition, *Revenue from Contracts with Customers*. These new revenue recognition rules are similar to the rules for multi-element contracts (described above). Companies must identify separate "performance obligations" within a contract and account for each individually. A performance obligation is an enforceable promise to transfer goods or services to the customer. The challenge for companies will be to identify the various performance obligations within a single contract. The core concept is whether or not a good or service is "distinct." It is distinct if the good or service 1) can be sold separately, 2) has a distinct function, and 3) has a distinct profit margin. A distinct good or service is accounted for as a separate performance obligation. If a good or service is not distinct, it is combined with other goods or services that form a distinct good or service. Companies recognize revenue as performance obligations are satisfied, that is, when the customer obtains control of the goods or services.

For construction projects the new rules will likely yield results similar to the percentage-of-completion accounting method described above. This is due to the fact that the various construction tasks are highly interrelated and are not routinely sold independently. The critical factor is whether 1) construction tasks are distinct and 2) control over the delivered goods and services is transferred to the customer continuously during the project (as opposed to at project completion). For example, if a company bills the customer throughout the project based either on measurable outputs such as milestones or on measurable inputs such as time and materials, then transfer of control is continuous and revenue will essentially be recognized on a percentage-of-completion basis. Nonetheless, many construction firms sent comment letters to the FASB / IASB, arguing that the new rules needlessly complicate revenue recognition and impose additional costs. The new rules could be required as soon as 2012, but the ultimate requirements and adoption dates will depend on additional due process by both boards.

Research and Development (R&D) Expenses

LO2 Describe accounting for operating expenses, including research and development, and restructuring.

R&D activities are a major expenditure for many companies, especially for those in technology and pharmaceutical industries. Pfizer's R&D costs, for example, make up 14% of revenues ($9,413 million/$67,809 million). These expenses include employment costs for R&D personnel, R&D materials and supplies, R&D related contract services, and R&D fixed-asset costs.

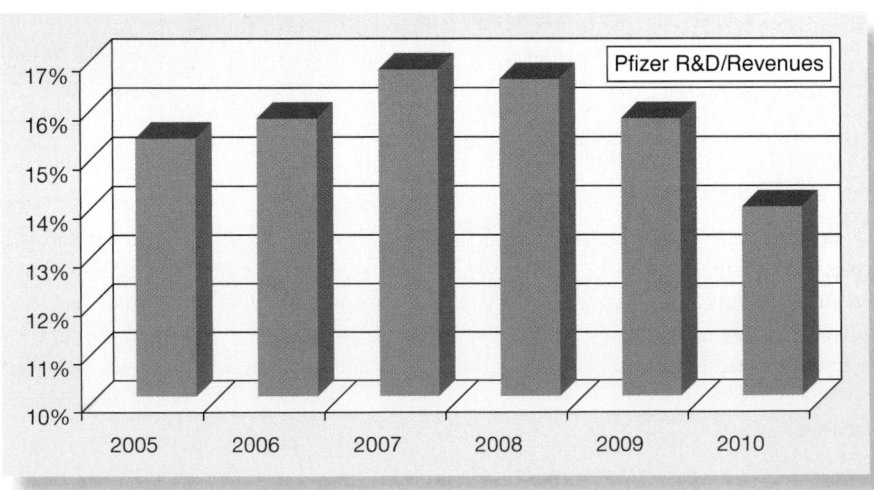

Accounting for R&D

Accounting for R&D is straightforward: R&D costs are expensed as incurred. The key issue is how to classify the expenses for financial reporting purposes. Salaries paid to researchers, and the depreciation and other expenses related to general-purpose research facilities, are accounted for in the usual manner (which is to expense salaries when paid and to capitalize and depreciate general-purpose research facilities). However, these expenses are totaled separately and are classified as R&D in the income statement rather than as SG&A. An exception to this general rule relates to the purchase of R&D assets that are only used for a specific project and then retired when that project is complete. These project-specific assets are expensed when purchased. Consequently, income is reduced in the year of acquisition (but higher in subsequent years) relative to what the company would have reported had the asset been capitalized and depreciated. (Project-specific assets are said to have no "alternate use." One alternate use could be reselling the asset. In that case, the asset is *not* considered project-specific and is accounted for like other long-term assets.)

Following is a footnote excerpt from **Pfizer**'s 2010 annual report related to its research and development expenditures:

> Research and development (R&D) costs are expensed as incurred. These expenses include the costs of our proprietary R&D efforts, as well as costs incurred in connection with certain licensing arrangements.

Pfizer capitalizes and depreciates general research facilities (those with alternate uses). All other R&D costs are expensed as incurred.

IFRS INSIGHT   Research and Development Expenses and IFRS

IFRS accounts for research costs and development costs separately. Research costs are always expensed. Development costs must be capitalized if all of the following conditions are affirmed:

- Technical feasibility of completing the intangible asset.
- Intention to complete the intangible asset.
- Ability to use or sell the intangible asset.
- Intangible asset will generate future economic benefits (the company must demonstrate the existence of a market or, if for internal use, the usefulness of the intangible asset).
- Availability of adequate resources to complete development.
- Ability to measure reliably the expenditure attributable to the intangible asset during its development.

U.S. GAAP allows for capitalization of costs related to the development of software for sale to third parties once the software achieves "commercial feasibility," but is silent on the capitalization of other intangible assets—thus, implicitly prescribing expensing of these assets.

Analysis of R&D

When R&D expenses are large, such as that for technology-based and pharmaceutical companies, a question arises as to how we should treat those expenses in our company analysis. If R&D outlays are expected to yield future benefits, companies would (conceptually) understate assets and income because GAAP requires expensing of R&D outlays. One approach is to capitalize and amortize the reported R&D expenses. To illustrate, assume that a company reports the following income statement:

Sales....................	$500
Expenses other than R&D . . .	350
R&D expenses	**100**
Net income (per GAAP)	$ 50

Next, assume that R&D expenses create economic benefits over the next five years. Accordingly, the method would treat the $100 R&D expenditures as an asset and amortize it over its useful life. Specifically, the adjusted balance sheet would reflect the $80 of unamortized R&D assets remaining, computed as $100 in R&D asset less $20 in R&D amortization (current-year equity is also $80 greater from the $80 of expenses postponed to future years). The adjusted income statement would reflect the $20 amortization of the $100 R&D asset as follows (computed as $100/5 years):

Sales....................	$500
Expenses other than R&D ...	350
R&D amortization	**20**
Net income..............	$130

This adjusted income makes the company look more profitable than GAAP would. (However, if the company is not experiencing abnormal growth and the $100 annual R&D expenditures continue as usual, then after the five-year initial amortization period the R&D amortization in the adjusted income statement will approximate the R&D expenses in the GAAP income statement.)

While this analysis might be conceptually appealing, it has problems. First, determining the proportion of R&D expenses that creates future economic benefits is extremely subjective. GAAP income statements do not distinguish between research and that of development and, instead, report them as one combined item. As users of financial reports, we have little basis to make such an allocation, let alone decide if outlays meet certain criteria. Second, there is considerable judgment in determining the period over which future economic benefits will occur. Some intangible assets such as patents are protected for specific lengths of time, but most other intangibles have no such defined period of potential benefit. Third, the manner in which future benefits will be realized is uncertain, so amortization of an R&D asset would be arbitrary. A straight-line method (as in our example above) would be easy, but would it reflect the asset's pattern of use?

For these reasons, we do not advise routinely creating pro forma net income and balance sheet numbers by capitalizing and amortizing R&D expenses. (An exception might be for growth companies that have yet to reach a steady level of R&D outlays, for companies with product breakthroughs, and for companies that require financial comparisons to IFRS-compliant reports.) Further, for companies that spend about the same amount each year on R&D, the income statement adjustment would be small. To see this, recall our example above: if the company spends $100 on R&D each year, then after five years, the amortization of previously capitalized amounts will be $100 (5 × $20) which is exactly the same as the R&D expense itself. However, the balance sheet adjustment can be more substantial as the R&D asset is "missing" entirely from the GAAP balance sheet (in the same way that benefits from the payment of wages or advertising are missing). Hence, when we compute ratios that involve income and assets (such as ROA or RNOA) or income and equity (such as ROE), the effects of expensing R&D are likely to overstate such ratios (from the absence of R&D assets in balance sheets).

A similar conclusion is reached in a recent study (Danielson and Press, "When Does R&D Expense Distort Profitability Estimates?" *Journal of Applied Finance*, 2005):

> . . . the accounting and finance literatures provide no guidance as to when potential distortion in accounting-based return measures makes an adjustment necessary. The expensing of R&D costs affects both the income statement and balance sheet, and therefore has an uncertain impact on a firm's accounting rate of return. It is possible for the income statement and balance sheet errors to cancel out—resulting in a small difference between adjusted and unadjusted accounting rates of return—even for a firm with high R&D costs. Thus, it is not obvious when complex and time-consuming adjustments for historical R&D costs are an essential step in a profitability analysis.

The study concludes that: "unadjusted ROA and adjusted (for R&D costs) ROA typically rank firm profitability in a similar order. Thus, unadjusted ROA is a reasonable proxy for firms' underlying economic profitability in many research applications, and complex adjustment procedures are often unnecessary."

Consequently, what analysis and/or adjustment for R&D expenses should we implement? Unfortunately, there is no simple computational adjustment. Instead, we begin our quantitative analysis by comparing common-sized R&D expenditures over time and across companies in the same industry (see Business Insight below). Differences in R&D outlays and marked departures from industry benchmarks call for further analysis. For our qualitative analysis, we look to the MD&A section of the 10-K, along with external sources of information, to gauge the effectiveness of the company's R&D efforts. Pharmaceutical companies typically disclose the drugs under development ("pipeline") as well as newly patented drugs. We can also evaluate new product introductions resulting from R&D expenditures. However, the disclosures for technology companies (and most other companies) are typically not as detailed. For those companies, we must seek information about new product introductions and other successes that management highlights in the MD&A.

BUSINESS INSIGHT   R&D at Pfizer and its Peers

Pfizer spent $9.4 billion in 2010 for R&D compared with its revenues of $67.8 billion, or about 13.9%. This reflects a high percent of revenues devoted to R&D for the pharmaceutical industry. Following is the R&D-expense-to-sales ratio for Pfizer and some of its competitors.

	2010	2009	2008
Pfizer	13.9%	15.7%	16.5%
Bristol-Meyers Squibb	18.3	19.4	19.8
Merck	23.9	21.3	20.1
Eli Lilly	21.2	19.8	18.9
Abbott Laboratories	10.6	8.9	9.1

Restructuring Expenses and Incentives

Restructuring expenses are substantial in many income statements. Because of their magnitude, GAAP requires enhanced disclosure, either as a separate line item in the income statement or as a footnote. Restructuring costs typically include three components:

1. Employee severance or relocation costs
2. Asset write-downs
3. Other restructuring costs

The first part, **employee severance or relocation costs**, represents accrued (estimated) costs to terminate or relocate employees as part of a restructuring program. To accrue those expenses, the company must:

- Estimate total costs of terminating or relocating selected employees; these costs might include severance pay (typically a number of weeks of pay based on the employee's tenure with the company), outplacement costs, and relocation or retraining costs for remaining employees.

- Report *total* estimated costs as an expense (and a liability) in the period the restructuring program is announced. Subsequent payments to employees reduce the restructuring accrual (the liability).

The second part of restructuring costs is **asset write-downs**, also called *write-offs* or *charge-offs*. Restructuring activities usually involve closure or relocation of manufacturing or administrative facilities. This can require the write-down of assets whose fair value is less than book value. For example, restructurings can necessitate the write-down of long-term assets (such as plant assets or goodwill) and of inventories. Recall that asset cost is first recorded on the balance sheet and is subsequently transferred from the balance sheet to the income statement as expense when the asset is used. The write-down of an asset accelerates this process for a portion, or all, of the asset cost. Write-downs have no cash flow effects unless the write-down has some potential tax consequences.

The third part of restructuring costs is typically labeled "Other" and includes costs of vacating duplicative facilities, fees to terminate contracts (such as lease agreements and service contracts), and other

BUSINESS INSIGHT Pfizer's Restructuring

Pfizer explains its restructuring efforts as follows in its 2010 10-K:

> We have incurred significant costs in connection with our cost-reduction initiatives (several programs initiated since 2005) and our acquisition of Wyeth on October 15, 2009. Since the acquisition of Wyeth, our cost-reduction initiatives that were announced on January 26, 2009 have been incorporated into a comprehensive plan to integrate Wyeth's operations, generate cost savings and capture synergies across the combined company. We are focusing our efforts on achieving an appropriate cost structure for the combined company. The components of restructuring charges associated with all of our cost-reduction initiatives and the acquisition of Wyeth follow:

(Millions of dollars)	Costs Incurred 2005-2010	Activity through December 31, 2010	Accrual as of December 31, 2010
Employee termination costs.	$ 8,846	$6,688	$2,158
Asset impairments	2,322	2,322	—
Other.	902	801	101
Total	$12,070	$9,811	$2,259

Financial statement effects of Pfizer's accounting for restructuring costs are illustrated in the following template ($ millions).

The template reflects five years' restructuring transactions. From 2005 to 2010, Pfizer estimated total restructuring costs of $12,070 million and discloses the three usual types of restructuring costs of employee termination, asset impairment, and other. Asset impairments ($2,322 million) do not involve cash. Pfizer shifts the asset cost from the balance sheet to the income statement (by increasing the assets' accumulated depreciation by $2,322 million). Employee termination and other costs will eventually be settled in cash and so Pfizer accrues $9,748 million on its balance sheet as a restructuring liability for those estimated costs (employee termination costs of $8,846 million plus other costs of $902 million). Over the five years, Pfizer pays $7,489 to settle the restructuring liability ($6,688 million + $801 million). GAAP requires disclosure of the initial liability, along with subsequent reductions or reversals of amounts not ultimately used. Pfizer includes the remaining $2,259 million in *Other current liabilities* ($1.6 billion) and *Other noncurrent liabilities* ($652 million) on its 2010 balance sheet.

exit costs (such as legal and asset-appraisal fees). Companies estimate and accrue these costs and reduce the restructuring liability as those costs are paid in cash.

The financial statement effects of restructuring charges can be large and frequent. We must remember that management determines the amount of restructuring costs and when to recognize them. As such, it is not uncommon for a company to time recognition of restructuring costs in a period when its income is already depressed. This behavior is referred to as a **big bath**.

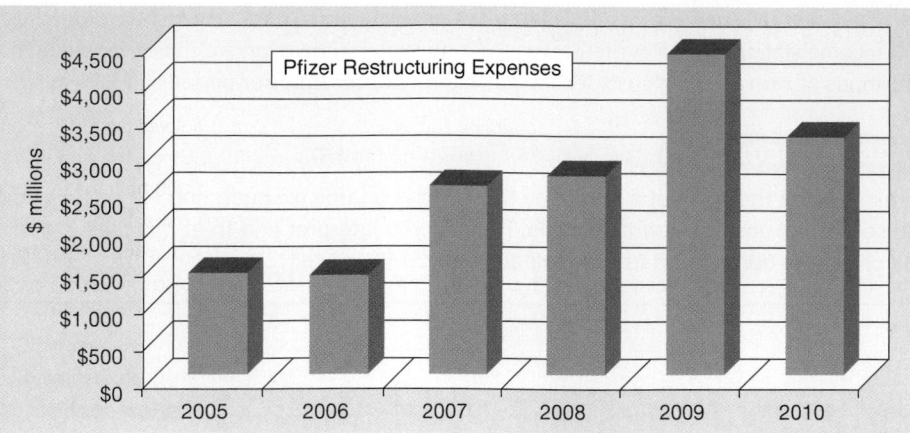

U.S. GAAP has relatively stringent rules relating to restructuring costs in an effort to mitigate abuses. For example, a company is required to have a formal restructuring plan that is approved by its board of directors before any restructuring charges are accrued. Also, a company must identify the relevant employees and notify them of its plan. In each subsequent year, the company must disclose in its footnotes the original amount of the liability (accrual), how much of that liability is settled in the current period (such as employee payments), how much of the original liability has been reversed because of original cost overestimation, any new accruals for unforeseen costs, and the current balance of the liability. This creates more transparent financial statements, which presumably deters earnings management.

RESEARCH INSIGHT   **Restructuring Costs and Managerial Incentives**

Research has investigated the circumstances and effects of restructuring costs. Some research finds that stock prices increase when a company announces a restructuring as if the market appreciates the company's candor. Research also finds that many companies that reduce income through restructuring costs later reverse a portion of those costs, resulting in a substantial income boost for the period of reversal. These reversals often occur when the company would have otherwise reported an earnings decline. Whether or not the market responds favorably to trimming the fat or simply disregards restructuring costs as transitory and, thus, as uninformative, managers have incentives to characterize such income-decreasing items as "one-time" on the income statement and routinely exclude such charges in non-GAAP, pro forma disclosures. These incentives often derive from contracts such as debt covenants and managerial bonus plans.

Restructuring costs are typically large and, as such, greatly affect reported profits. Our analysis must consider whether these costs are properly chargeable to the accounting period in which they are recognized. Following are some guidelines relating to the components of restructuring costs:

Employee Severance or Relocation Costs* and *Other Costs GAAP permits recognition of costs relating to employee separation or relocation that are *incremental* and that do not benefit future periods. Similarly, other accrued costs must be related to the restructuring and not to expenses that would otherwise have been incurred in the future. Thus, accrual of these costs is treated like other liability accruals. We must, however, be aware of over- or understated costs and their effect on current and future profitability. GAAP requires a reconciliation of this restructuring accrual in future years (see Business Insight on Pfizer's restructuring). A reconciliation reveals either overstatements or understatements: overstatements are followed by a reversal of the restructuring liability, and understatements are followed by further accruals. Should a company develop a reputation for recurring reversals or understatements, its management loses credibility.

Asset Write-downs Asset write-downs accelerate (or catch up) the depreciation process to reflect asset impairment. Impairment implies the loss of cash-generating capability and, likely, occurs over several years. Thus, prior periods' profits are arguably not as high as reported, and the current period's profit is not as low. This measurement error is difficult to estimate and, thus, many analysts do not adjust balance sheets and income statements for write-downs. At a minimum, however, we must recognize the qualitative implications of restructuring costs for the profitability of recent prior periods and the current period.

MANAGERIAL DECISION   **You Are the Financial Analyst**
You are analyzing the 10-K of a company that reports a large restructuring expense, involving employee severance and asset write-downs. How do you interpret and treat this cost in your analysis of the company's current and future profitability? [Answer, p. 5-37]

MID-MODULE REVIEW 1

Merck & Co., Inc., reports the following income statements for 2008 through 2010.

($ in millions)	2010	2009	2008
Sales.	$45,987	$27,428	$23,850
Costs, expenses and other			
Materials and production	18,396	9,019	5,583
Marketing and administrative	13,245	8,543	7,377
Research and development	10,991	5,845	4,805
Restructuring costs.	985	1,634	1,033
Equity income from affiliates.	(587)	(2,235)	(2,561)
Other (income) expense, net.	1,304	(10,668)	(2,318)
	44,334	12,138	13,919
Income before taxes.	1,653	15,290	9,931
Taxes on income	671	2,268	1,999
Net income.	$ 982	$13,022	$ 7,932

Required

1. Merck's revenue recognition policy, as outlined in footnotes to its 10-K, includes the following: "Revenues from sales of products are recognized when title and risk of loss passes to the customer." Evaluate Merck's revenue recognition policy.
2. Merck's research and development (R&D) efforts often require specialized equipment and facilities that cannot be used for any other purpose. How does Merck account for costs related to this specialized equipment and facilities? Would Merck account for these costs differently if they had alternate uses? Explain.
3. Merck reports restructuring expense each year. What are the general categories of restructuring expenses? How do accrual accounting and disclosure requirements prevent companies from intentionally overstating restructuring expenses in one year (referred to as taking a "big bath") and reversing the unused expenses in a future year?

The solution is on page 5-58.

Income Tax Expenses and Allowances

LO3 Explain and analyze accounting for income taxes.

Companies prepare financial statements for shareholders using GAAP. When these companies file their income tax returns, they prepare financial statements using the *Internal Revenue Code (IRC)*. These two different sets of accounting rules recognize revenues and expenses differently in many cases and, as a result, can yield markedly different levels of income. In general, companies desire to report lower income to taxing authorities than they do to their shareholders so that they can reduce their tax liability and increase after-tax cash flow. This practice is acceptable so long as the financial statements are prepared in conformity with GAAP and tax returns are filed in accordance with the IRC.

As an example, consider the depreciation of long-term assets. For shareholder reports, companies typically depreciate long-term assets using straight-line depreciation (meaning the same amount of depreciation expense is reported each year over the useful life of the asset). However, for reports sent to tax authorities, companies use an *accelerated* method of depreciation (meaning more depreciation is taken in the early years of the asset's life and less depreciation in later years). When a company depreciates assets at an accelerated rate for tax purposes, the depreciation deduction for tax purposes is higher and taxable income is lower in the early years of the assets' lives. As a result, tax payments are reduced and after-tax cash flow is increased. That excess cash can then be reinvested in the business to increase its returns to shareholders.

To illustrate, assume that Pfizer purchases an asset with a five-year life. It depreciates that asset using the straight-line method (equal expense per year) when reporting to shareholders and depreciates the asset at a faster rate (accelerated depreciation) for tax purposes. Annual (full year) depreciation expense under these two methods is depicted in Exhibit 5.3.

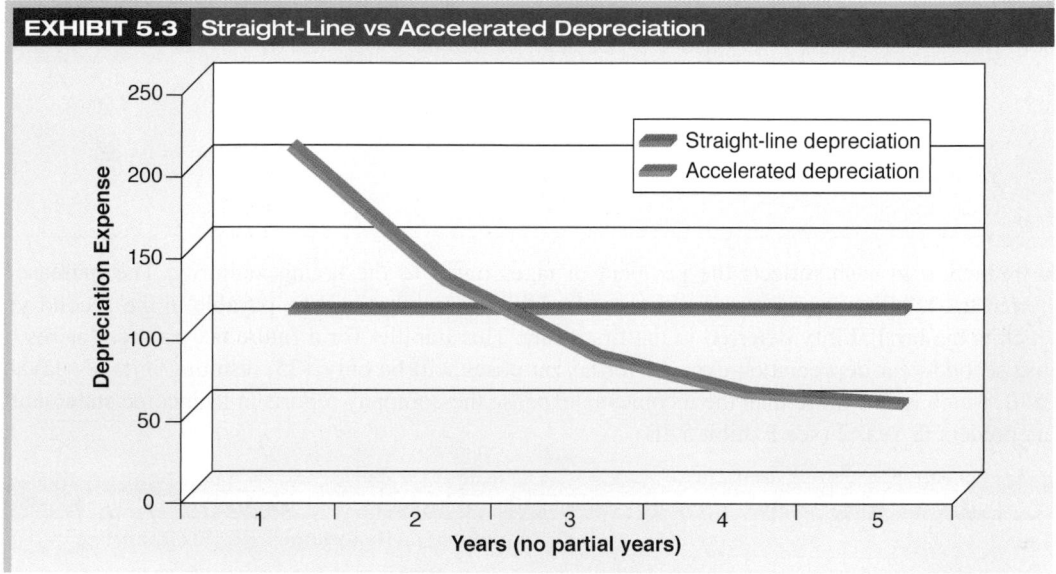

EXHIBIT 5.3 Straight-Line vs Accelerated Depreciation

During the first 2.5 years in this example, depreciation is higher in the company's tax returns than it is in its report to shareholders. In the last 2.5 years, this is reversed, with lower depreciation expense for tax purposes. Taxable income and tax payments are, therefore, higher during the last 2.5 years. The same total amount of depreciation is recognized under both methods over the five-year life of the asset. Only the timing of the recognition of the expense differs.[5]

We use this timing concept to illustrate the accounting for a **deferred tax liability**. Assume that a company purchases a depreciable asset with a cost of $100 and a two-year useful life. For financial reporting purposes (for GAAP-based reports for shareholders), it depreciates the asset using the straight-line method, which yields depreciation expense of $50 per year. For tax reporting (when filing income tax returns), it depreciates the asset on an accelerated basis, which yields depreciation deduction of $75 in the first year and $25 in the second year (the same total amount of depreciation is reported under the two depreciation methods; only the amount of depreciation reported per year differs). Assume that this company reports income before depreciation and taxes of $200 and that its tax rate is 40%. Its income statements, for both financial reporting and tax reporting, for the asset's first year are in Exhibit 5.4A.

---

[5] The Modified Accelerated Cost Recovery System (MACRS) is the current method of accelerated asset depreciation required by the United States income tax code. Under MACRS, all assets are divided into classes that dictate the number of years over which an asset's cost is "recovered" and the percentage of the asset cost that can be depreciated per year is fixed by regulation. For a five-year asset, such as in our example, the MACRS depreciation percentages per year are 20%, 32%, 19.2%, 11.52%, 11.52%, and 5.76%. MACRS assumes that assets are acquired in the middle of the year, hence a half-year depreciation in Year 1 and a half-year depreciation in Year 6. The point at which straight-line depreciation exceeds MACRS depreciation is after about 2.5 years as assumed in the example.

EXHIBIT 5.4A Year 1 Income Statements: Financial Reporting vs Tax Reporting		
Year 1	**Financial Reporting**	**Tax Reporting**
Income before depreciation	$200	$200
Depreciation.	50	75
Income before tax	150	125
Income tax (40%).	60 [expense]	50 [cash paid]
Net income.	$ 90	$ 75

This company records income tax expense and a related deferred tax liability for the first year as reflected in the following financial statement effects template:

Year 1	Balance Sheet						Income Statement		
Transaction	**Cash Asset**	+ **Noncash Assets**	= **Liabil- ities**	+ **Contrib. Capital**	+ **Earned Capital**		**Rev- enues**	− **Expen- ses**	= **Net Income**
Record tax expense: expense exceeds cash because of deferral of tax	−50 Cash		= +10 Deferred Tax Liability		−60 Retained Earnings			+60 Tax Expense	−60

TE   60
  DTL   10
  Cash   50
    TE
60 |
  DTL
        | 10
  Cash
        | 50

The reduction in cash reflects the payment of taxes owed to the taxing authority. The increase in deferred tax liability represents an estimate of additional tax that will be payable in the second year (which is the tax liability deferred in the first year). This liability for a future tax payment arises because second-year depreciation expense for tax purposes will be only $25, resulting in taxes payable of $70, which is $10 more than the income tax expense the company reports in its income statement to shareholders in Year 2 (see Exhibit 5.4B).

EXHIBIT 5.4B Year 2 Income Statements: Financial Reporting vs Tax Reporting		
Year 2	**Financial Reporting**	**Tax Reporting**
Income before depreciation	$200	$200
Depreciation.	50	25
Income before tax	150	175
Income tax (40%).	60 [expense]	70 [cash paid]
Net income.	$ 90	$105

At the end of Year 1, the company knows that this additional tax must be paid in Year 2 because the financial reporting and tax reporting depreciation schedules are set when the asset is placed in service. Given these known amounts, the company accrues the deferred tax liability in Year 1 in the same manner as it would accrue any estimated future liability, say for wages payable, by recognizing a liability and the related expense.

At the end of Year 2, the additional income tax is paid and the company's deferred tax liability is now satisfied. Financial statement effects related to the tax payment and expense in Year 2 are reflected in the following template:

Year 2	Balance Sheet						Income Statement		
Transaction	**Cash Asset**	+ **Noncash Assets**	= **Liabil- ities**	+ **Contrib. Capital**	+ **Earned Capital**		**Rev- enues**	− **Expen- ses**	= **Net Income**
Record tax expense: cash exceeds expense because deferred taxes are reversed	−70 Cash		= −10 Deferred Tax Liability		−60 Retained Earnings			+60 Tax Expense	−60

TE   60
DTL   10
  Cash   70
    TE
60 |
  DTL
10 |
  Cash
        | 70

The income tax expense for financial reporting purposes is $60 each year. However, the cash payment for taxes is $70 in Year 2; the $10 excess reduces the deferred tax liability accrued in Year 1.

This example demonstrates how accelerated depreciation for tax reporting and straight-line for financial reporting creates deferred tax liabilities. Other differences between tax reporting and financial reporting create other types of deferred tax accounts. **Deferred tax assets** arise when the tax payment is *greater* than the tax expense for financial reporting purposes (opposite of the illustration above).

Restructuring accruals are one source of deferred tax assets. In the year in which a company approves a reorganization plan, it will accrue a restructuring liability for estimated employee severance payments and other costs and it will write down assets to their market values (this reduces the net book value of those assets on the balance sheet). However, tax authorities do not recognize these accrual accounting transactions until they are realized. In particular, for tax purposes, restructuring costs are not deductible until paid in the future, and asset write-downs are not deductible until the loss is realized when the asset is sold. As a result, the restructuring accrual is not a liability for tax reporting until the company makes the payment, and the write-down of assets is not a deductible expense for tax purposes until the assets are sold. Both of these differences (the liability and the assets) give rise to a deferred tax asset. The deferred tax asset cost will be transferred to the income statement in the future as an expense when the company pays the restructuring costs and sells the impaired assets for a loss.

Another common deferred tax asset relates to **tax loss carryforwards**. Specifically, when a company reports a loss for tax purposes, it can carry back that loss for up to two years to recoup previous taxes paid. Any unused losses can be carried forward for up to twenty years to reduce future taxes. This creates a benefit (an "asset") for tax reporting for which there is no corresponding financial reporting asset. Thus, the company records a deferred tax asset but only if the company is "more likely than not" to be able to recoup past taxes. This depends on the company's assessment of whether it will have sufficient profits in the future.

Companies are required to establish a *deferred tax asset valuation allowance* for deferred tax assets when the future realization of their benefits is uncertain. The effect on financial statements of establishing such an allowance is to reduce reported assets, increase tax expense, and reduce equity (this is similar to accounting for the write-down of any asset). During 2010, Pfizer increased its valuation allowance from $353 million to $894 million. Increases in the valuation allowance reduce net income on a dollar-for-dollar basis. The increase in the valuation allowance during 2010, decreased net income by $541 million ($894 million − $353 million). These effects are reversed if the allowance is reversed in the future when, and if, realization of such tax benefits becomes more likely.

Disclosures Relating to Income Taxes

Pfizer's tax footnote to its income statement is shown in Exhibit 5.5. Pfizer's $1,124 million tax expense reported in its income statement (called the provision) consists of the following two components:

1. *Current tax expense.* Current tax expense is determined from the company's tax returns; it is the amount payable (in cash) to tax authorities (some of these taxes have been paid during the year as the company makes installments). Pfizer labels this "Current income taxes" and reports separate amounts for taxes to federal, state, local, and international tax authorities.

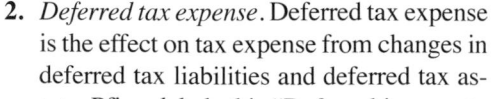

2. *Deferred tax expense.* Deferred tax expense is the effect on tax expense from changes in deferred tax liabilities and deferred tax assets. Pfizer labels this "Deferred income taxes" and reports separate amounts for deferrals related to U.S. and international tax rules.

In financial statement footnotes, companies must disclose the components of deferred tax liabilities and assets. Pfizer's deferred tax footnote to its balance sheet (shown in Exhibit 5.6) reports total deferred tax assets of $15,027 million and total deferred tax liabilities of $29,646 million. On the balance sheet companies report deferred tax assets and liabilities as either current or noncurrent based on

EXHIBIT 5.5	Income Tax Expense Footnote for Pfizer			
Year Ended December 31 (Millions of dollars)		**2010**	**2009**	**2008**
United States				
Current income taxes				
Federal		$(2,774)	$10,169	$ 707
State and local		(313)	71	154
Deferred income taxes				
Federal		2,033	(10,002)	106
State and local		(6)	(93)	(136)
Total U.S. tax (benefit) provision		(1,060)	145	831
International				
Current income taxes		2,258	1,539	2,115
Deferred income taxes		(74)	513	(1,301)
Total international tax provision		2,184	2,052	814
Total provision for taxes on income		$ 1,124	$ 2,197	$1,645

when the benefit (payment) is expected to be received (made). Companies are permitted to net some deferred tax assets and liabilities, and also to combine deferred taxes with other accounts on the balance sheet. Thus, for some companies, it is impossible to completely reconcile the tax footnote to the balance sheet. Many of Pfizer's deferred tax assets relate to accrued liabilities or asset write-downs arising from expenses included in financial reporting income, but not yet recognized for tax reporting (such as employee benefits and restructuring accruals). Pfizer has recorded a valuation allowance of $894 million. These various items all yield future reductions of the company's tax payments and are, therefore, classified as assets.

EXHIBIT 5.6	Deferred Taxes Footnote for Pfizer			
	2010 Deferred Tax		**2009 Deferred Tax**	
(Millions of dollars)	**Assets**	**(Liabilities)**	**Assets**	**(Liabilities)**
Prepaid/deferred items	$ 1,321	$ (112)	$ 1,330	$ (60)
Inventories	132	(59)	437	(859)
Intangibles	1,165	(17,104)	949	(19,802)
Property, plant and equipment	420	(2,146)	715	(2,014)
Employee benefits	4,479	(56)	4,786	(66)
Restructurings and other charges	1,359	(70)	884	(8)
Legal and product liability reserves	1,411	—	1,010	—
Net operating loss/credit carryforwards	4,575	—	4,658	—
Unremitted earnings	—	(9,524)	—	(7,057)
State and local tax adjustments	452	—	747	—
All other	607	(575)	744	(187)
Subtotal	15,921	(29,646)	16,260	(30,053)
Valuation allowance	(894)	—	(353)	—
Total deferred taxes	$15,027	$(29,646)	$15,907	$(30,053)
Net deferred tax liability		$(14,619)		$(14,146)

Pfizer's deferred tax liabilities relate to a varied assortment of items. As we illustrate above, Pfizer uses accelerated depreciation in its tax return, which results in a deferred tax liability of $2,146 million. The deferred tax asset relating to employee benefits arises from the accrual of pension expense for financial reporting, but has not yet been funded with cash contributions. The deferred tax liability relating to unremitted earnings results from investments that Pfizer has in affiliated companies. Pfizer reports income related to those investments, but the income is not taxable until the companies actually pay dividends to Pfizer. Thus, reported profit is greater than taxable income and a deferred tax liability is recognized (we discuss accounting for intercompany investments in Module 7). Pfizer will pay taxes on the subsidiaries' profits when the subsidiaries pay dividends in the future and then the deferred tax liability will be reduced. Finally, the deferred tax asset of net operating loss carryforwards relates to losses that Pfizer has reported for tax purposes that the company is carrying forward to reduce future tax liability as explained above.

Pfizer's 2010 income before tax is $9,422 million. Its tax expense of $1,124 million represents an effective tax rate of 11.9%. The *effective tax rate* is defined as tax expense divided by pretax income ($1,124 million/$9,422 million = 11.9%).[6] By comparison, the federal *statutory tax rate* for corporations (the rate prescribed in tax regulations) is 35%. Companies must provide a schedule that reconciles the effective tax rate (11.9% for Pfizer) with the Federal statutory rate of 35%. Following is the schedule that Pfizer reports in its 10-K.

Reconciliation of the U.S. statutory income tax rate to our effective tax rate for income from continuing operations follows:

Year Ended Dec. 31	2010	2009	2008
U.S. statutory income tax rate	35.0%	35.0%	35.0%
Earnings taxed at other than U.S. statutory rate	2.5	(9.3)	(20.2)
Resolution of certain tax positions	(26.4)	—	(3.1)
Sales of biopharmaceutical companies	—	(5.1)	(4.3)
U.S. healthcare legislation	2.8	—	—
U.S. research tax credit and manufacturing deduction	(2.3)	(1.3)	(1.2)
Legal settlements	0.4	(1.6)	9.0
Acquired IPR&D	0.5	0.2	2.1
Wyeth acquisition-related costs	0.5	2.4	—
All other—net	(1.1)	—	(0.3)
Effective tax rate for income from continuing operations	11.9%	20.3%	17.0%

In addition to federal taxes (paid to the IRS), companies also pay taxes to state, local, and foreign jurisdictions where they operate. These tax rates are typically lower than the statutory rate of 35%. In 2010, Pfizer's effective tax rate was reduced by 26.4% as a result of favorable rulings in litigation with taxing authorities. Also, several miscellaneous items increased Pfizer's effective tax rate by 3.3%, resulting in a net decrease of 23.1%.

In sum, Pfizer's effective tax rate for 2010 is 11.9%, which is 23.1 percentage points below the 35% statutory rate. In 2009, however, the effective tax rate was 20.3% and in 2008 it was 17%. Fluctuations, such as these, in the effective tax rate are not uncommon and highlight the difference between income reported under GAAP and that computed using multiple tax codes and tax incentives under which companies operate. Appendix 5A explains accounting for deferred taxes in more detail.

Analysis of Income Tax Disclosures

Analysis of deferred taxes can yield useful insights. Some revenue accruals (such as accounts receivable for longer-term contracts) increase deferred tax liabilities as GAAP income exceeds tax income (similar to the effect of using straight-line depreciation for financial reporting purposes and accelerated depreciation for tax returns).

An increase in deferred tax liabilities indicates that a company is reporting higher GAAP income relative to taxable income and can indicate the company is managing earnings upwards. The difference between reported corporate profits and taxable income increased substantially in the late 1990s, just prior to huge asset write-offs. *CFO Magazine* (November 2002) implied that such differences are important for analysis and should be monitored:

---

[6] This is the effective tax rate for *all* of Pfizer's income. In the previous module we compute the tax rate on operating profit by first deducting the taxes related to nonoperating income (or adding back the tax shield related to nonoperating expenses). The effective tax rate on total income, is a weighted average of the two rates (operating and nonoperating).

Fueling the sense that something [was] amiss [was] the growing gap between the two sets of numbers. In 1992, there was no significant difference between pretax book income and taxable net income . . . By 1996, according to IRS data, a $92.5 billion gap had appeared. By 1998 [prior to the market decline], the gap was $159 billion—a fourth of the total taxable income reported . . . If people had seen numbers showing very significant differences between book numbers for trading and tax numbers, they would have wondered if those [income] numbers were completely real.

Although an increase in deferred tax liabilities can legitimately result, for example, from an increase in depreciable assets and the use of accelerated depreciation for tax purposes, we must be aware of the possibility that such an increase arises from improper revenue recognition in that the company might not be reporting those revenues to tax authorities.

Adequacy of Deferred Tax Asset Valuation

Analysis of the deferred tax asset valuation account provides us with additional insight. This analysis involves (1) assessing the adequacy of the valuation allowance and (2) determining how and why the valuation account changed during the period and how that change affects net income.

When a company reports a deferred tax asset, the company implies that it will, more likely than not, receive a future tax benefit equal to the deferred tax asset. If the company is uncertain about the future tax benefit, it records an allowance to reduce the asset. How can we gauge the adequacy of a valuation allowance account? We might assess the reasons for the valuation account (typically reported in the tax footnote). We might examine other companies in the industry for similar allowances. We might also review the MD&A for any doubt on company prospects for future profitability.

We can quantify our analysis in at least three ways. First, we can examine the allowance as a percentage of the deferred tax assets. For **Pfizer**, this 2010 percentage is 5.62%; see below. We also want to gather data from other pharmaceutical companies and compare the sizes of their allowance accounts relative to their related deferred tax assets. The important point is that we must be comfortable with the size of the valuation account and remember that management has control over the adequacy and reporting of the allowance account (with audit assurances).

Pfizer ($ millions)	2010	2009
Deferred tax asset	$15,921	$16,260
Valuation allowance	$ 894	$ 353
Valuation allowance as a percent of total deferred tax asset	5.62%	2.17%

Second, we can examine changes in the allowance account. During a year, circumstances change and the company might be more or less assured of receiving the tax benefit. In that case, the company might decrease or increase its allowance account. The valuation allowance in 2010 is considerably larger than the previous year even though the deferred tax asset arising from net operating losses has decreased. This implies that during the year, Pfizer has revised downward the amount of net operating losses that the company expects to be able to use to reduce future taxes.

Third, we can quantify how a change in the valuation allowance affects net income and its effective tax rate (see Exhibit 5.7). To see this, recall that increases in the valuation allowance affect tax expense in the same direction, dollar for dollar. This in turn, affects net income (in the opposite direction) again, dollar for dollar. For Pfizer, its 2010 valuation allowance increased by $541 million ($353 million to $894 million), which increased tax expense and decreased net income by $541 million. This is not a large effect on income for Pfizer. However, changes in valuation allowances can have (and have had) marked effects on net income for numerous companies. One final note, reductions in the deferred tax asset valuation account can occur as a result of unused loss carryforwards; in that case, a company reduces the deferred tax asset and the related valuation allowance, which is similar in concept to the write-off of an account receivable discussed in Module 6. For our analysis, we must remember, however, that in the absence of expiring loss carryforwards, a company can increase current-period income by deliberately decreasing the valuation allowance. Knowing that such decreases can boost net income, companies might deliberately create too large a valuation allowance in one or more prior years and use it as a *cookie jar reserve* to boost income in future periods. We want to assess the details of the valuation account and changes therein from company footnotes and from the MD&A.

EXHIBIT 5.7	Effect of Deferred Tax Asset Valuation Account on Tax Expense	
Pfizer ($ millions)		**2010**
Change in valuation allowance.		$ 541
Impact of valuation allowance change on net income.		$ (541)
Income before tax		$9,422
Tax expense		$1,124
Effective tax rate (Tax expense/Income before tax)		11.9%
Tax expense before change in valuation account		$ 583
Effective tax rate before change in valuation account		6.2%

MID-MODULE REVIEW 2

Refer to the Merck & Co., Inc., 2010 income statement in Mid-Module Review 1. Merck provides the following additional information in footnotes to its 10-K.

Taxes on income consisted of:

Years Ended December 31 ($ in millions)	2010	2009	2008
Current provision			
Federal	$ 399	$ (55)	$1,054
Foreign	1,446	495	292
State	(82)	7	123
	1,763	447	1,469
Deferred provision			
Federal	764	2,095	419
Foreign	(1,777)	(437)	56
State	(79)	163	55
	(1,092)	1,821	530
	$ 671	$2,268	$1,999

Required

1. What is the total income tax expense that Merck reports in its 2010 income statement?
2. What amount of its total tax expense did (or will) Merck pay in cash (that is, what amount is currently payable)?
3. Explain how Merck calculates its income tax expense.

The solution is on page 5-59.

Foreign Currency Translation Effects

Many companies conduct international operations and transact business in currencies other than $US. It is common for companies to purchase assets in foreign currencies, borrow money in foreign currencies, and transact business with their customers in foreign currencies. Increasingly many companies have subsidiaries whose balance sheets and income statements are prepared in foreign currencies.

Financial statements prepared according to U.S. GAAP must be reported in $US. This means that the financial statements of any foreign subsidiaries must be translated into $US before consolidation with the U.S. parent company. This translation process can markedly alter both the balance sheet and income statement. We discuss income statement effects of foreign currency translation in this module; we discuss the effects on stockholders' equity in Module 9.

L04 Explain how foreign currency fluctuations affect the income statement.

Effects of Foreign Currency Transactions on Income

A change in the strength of the $US vis-à-vis foreign currencies has a direct effect on the $US equivalent for revenues, expenses, and income of the foreign subsidiary because revenues and expenses are translated at the average exchange rate for the period. Exhibit 5.8 shows those financial effects.

EXHIBIT 5.8	Income Statement Effects from Foreign Currency Movements		
	Revenues –	Expenses =	Net Income (or Loss)
$US Weakens.........	Increase	Increase	Increase
$US Strengthens	Decrease	Decrease	Decrease

Specifically, when the foreign currency strengthens (implying $US weakens), the subsidiary's revenues and expenses translate into more $US and, thus, reported income is higher than if the currencies had not fluctuated. On the other hand, when the $US strengthens, the subsidiary's revenues, expenses, and income decrease in $US terms. (The profit effect assumes that revenues exceed expenses; if expenses exceed revenues, a loss occurs, which increases if the $US weakens and decreases if the $US strengthens.)

Pfizer discusses how currency fluctuations affect its income statement in the following excerpt from footnotes to the company's 2010 10-K.

Revenues by Segment & Geographical Area ($ mil.)	Worldwide	US	International
Biopharmaceutical	$58,523	$25,962	$32,561
Diversified	8,966	2,981	5,985
Corporate and Other	320	103	217
	$67,809	$29,046	$38,763

Revenues increased . . . [partly due to] the favorable impact of foreign exchange, which increased revenues by approximately $1.1 billion, or 2%. Worldwide Biopharmaceutical revenues in 2010 were $58.5 billion, an increase of 29% compared to 2009, due to the weakening of the U.S. dollar relative to other currencies, primarily the Canadian dollar, Australian dollar, Japanese yen and Brazilian real, which favorably impacted Biopharmaceutical revenues by approximately $900 million, or 2%.

The $US weakened against many foreign currencies for several years preceding and including 2010. Thus, each unit of foreign currency purchased more $US. Therefore, revenues and expenses denominated in foreign currencies were translated to higher $US equivalents, yielding increased revenues and profits even when unit volumes remained unchanged. Pfizer also discloses that it attempts to dampen the effect that these fluctuations have on reported profit:

Foreign Exchange Risk   A significant portion of our revenues and earnings is exposed to changes in foreign exchange rates. We seek to manage our foreign exchange risk in part through operational means, including managing same-currency revenues in relation to same-currency costs and same-currency assets in relation to same-currency liabilities.

The phrase "operational means" indicates that the company structures its transactions in $US rather than a foreign currency or attempts to match same-currency revenues and expenses (or assets and liabilities) to minimize the effects of currency fluctuatinos. Foreign currency financial instruments are common and include forward and futures contracts, which lock in future currency values. We explain how these instruments (called derivatives) work in Appendix 7C. In sum, we must be cognizant of the effects of currency fluctuations on reported revenues, expenses, and profits for companies with substantial foreign-currency transactions.

OPERATING COMPONENTS BELOW-THE-LINE

Pfizer's income statement includes a subtotal labeled "income from continuing operations." Historically, this presentation highlighted the nonrecurring (*transitory*) portions of the income statement so that they could be eliminated to facilitate the projection of future profitability. The word "continuing" was meant to imply that income was purged of one-time items, as these were presented "below-the-line," that is, below income from continuing operations. Two categories of items are presented below-the-line:[7]

1. **Discontinued operations**   Net income (loss) from business segments that have been or will be sold, and any gains (losses) on net assets related to those segments sold in the current period.

2. **Extraordinary items**   Gains or losses from events that are both *unusual* and *infrequent*.

Discontinued operations are generally viewed as nonoperating, and we discuss their accounting treatment in Module 7. Explanation of the accounting for extraordinary items follows.

Extraordinary Items

Extraordinary items refer to events that are both unusual *and* infrequent. Their effects are reported following income from continuing operations. Management determines whether an event is unusual and infrequent (with auditor approval) for financial reporting purposes. Further, management often has incentives to classify unfavorable items as extraordinary because they will be reported separately, after income from continuing operations (*below-the-line*). These incentives derive from managers' beliefs that investors tend to focus more on items included in income from continuing operations and less on nonrecurring items that are not included in continuing operations.

GAAP provides the following guidance in determining whether or not an item is extraordinary:

■ *Unusual nature.* The underlying event or transaction must possess a high degree of abnormality and be clearly unrelated to, or only incidentally related to, the ordinary activities of the entity.

■ *Infrequency of occurrence.* The underlying event or transaction must be of a type that would not reasonably be expected to recur in the foreseeable future.

The following items are generally **not** reported as extraordinary items:

■ Gains and losses on retirement of debt[8]

■ Write-down or write-off of operating or nonoperating assets

■ Foreign currency gains and losses

■ Gains and losses from disposal of specific assets or business segment

■ Effects of a strike

■ Accrual adjustments related to long-term contracts

■ Costs of a takeover defense

Extraordinary items are reported separately (net of tax) and below income from continuing operations on the income statement.

---

[7] Prior accounting standards included a third category, **changes in accounting principles**. This category included voluntary and mandated changes in accounting policies utilized by a company, such as a change in the depreciation method. Under current GAAP, changes in accounting principles are no longer reported below-the-line. Instead, they are applied retrospectively (unless it is impractical to do so, in which case they are applied at the earliest practical date). No cumulative effect adjustment is made to income as was the case in prior standards. Instead, changes in depreciation methods are now accounted for as changes in estimates, which are applied prospectively.

[8] Until recently, gains and losses on debt retirement were treated as extraordinary items. To explain, understand that debt is accounted for at historical cost, just like the accounting for equipment. The *market price* of debt, however, is determined by fluctuations in interest rates. As a result, if a company retires (pays off) its debt before maturity, the cash paid to settle the debt often differs from the debt amount reported on the balance sheet, resulting in gains and losses on retirement. These gains and losses were formerly treated as extraordinary. Following passage of SFAS 145, these gains and losses are no longer automatically treated as extraordinary, but instead must be unusual and infrequent to be designated as extraordinary.

IFRS INSIGHT   Extraordinary Items and IFRS

IFRS does not permit the reporting of income and expense items as "extraordinary." The IASB justified its position in IAS1 as follows: "The Board decided that items treated as extraordinary result from the normal business risks faced by an entity and do not warrant presentation in a separate component of the income statement. The nature or function of a transaction or other event, rather than its frequency, should determine its presentation within the income statement. Items currently classified as 'extraordinary' are only a subset of the items of income and expense that may warrant disclosure to assist users in predicting an entity's future performance" (IAS1).

Earnings Per Share

LO5 Compute earnings per share and explain the effect of dilutive securities.

The income statement reports earnings per share (EPS) numbers. Most firms report two EPS numbers: basic and diluted. The difference between the two measures is shown in Exhibit 5.9.

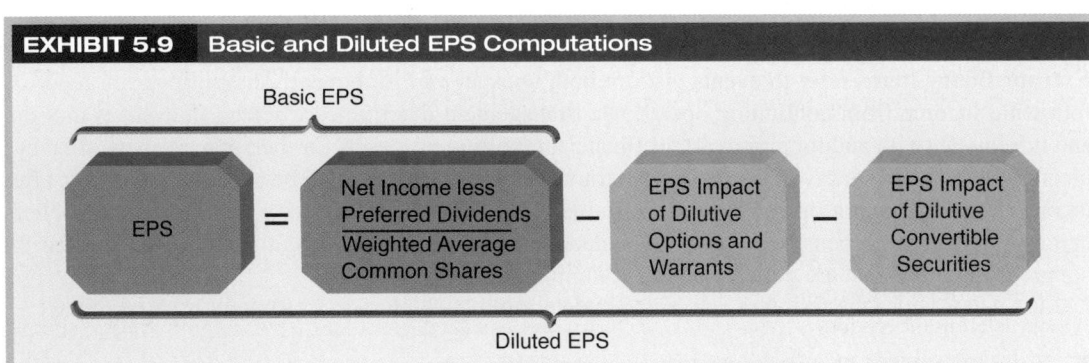

EXHIBIT 5.9   Basic and Diluted EPS Computations

Basic EPS is computed as: (Net income − Dividends on preferred stock)/Weighted average number of common shares outstanding during the year. Subtracting preferred stock dividends yields the income available for dividend payments to common shareholders. Computation of **diluted EPS** reflects the additional shares that would be issued if all stock options, warrants, and convertible securities had been converted into common shares at the beginning of the year or when issued, if issued during the year. Diluted EPS never exceeds basic EPS.

Pfizer reports Basic EPS of $1.03 in 2010 and Diluted EPS of $1.02. Given the near identical results for basic and diluted EPS, we know that Pfizer has few dilutive securities. **PDL Biopharma, Inc.**, however, reports a dilution of 26% in its EPS as evident from its following disclosure:

Fiscal year ended December 31 (in thousands, except per share)	2010	2009	2008
Basic net income per share	$ 0.73	$ 1.59	$ 0.58
Diluted net income per share	$ 0.54	$ 1.07	$ 0.47

PDL Biopharma reports the following dilutive effects on EPS:

(In thousands)	2010	2009	2008
Numerator			
Net income	$ 91,874	$189,660	$ 68,387
Add back interest expense for convertible notes, net of tax	5,087	7,079	10,450
Income used to compute net income per dilluted share	$ 96,961	$196,739	$ 78,837
Denominator			
Total weighted-average shares used to compute income per basic share	126,578	119,402	118,728
Effect of dilutive stock options	9	18	50
Restricted stock	103	42	10
Assumed conversion of convertible notes	52,111	64,938	49,081
Shares used to compute income per dilluted share from continuing operations and net income per dilluted share	178,801	184,400	167,869

Both the numerator and the denominator in the EPS calculation are affected by dilutive securities. If all the convertible notes had been exchanged for stock at the start of the year, the company would not have had to pay interest on these notes during the year. Therefore, the after-tax interest is added to net income in the numerator.

The denominator in the diluted earnings per share calculation presumes a worst case scenario that all employees holding options exercise their right to purchase common shares and all convertible notes are converted to common shares as of the beginning of the year. In that event, PDL Biopharma will issue an additional 52,223 thousand shares, thus increasing the denominator by that amount and reducing earnings per share from $0.73 to $0.54.[9]

Analysts and investors often use EPS figures to compare operating results for companies of different sizes under the assumption that the number of shares outstanding is proportional to the income level (that is, a company twice the size of another will report double the income and will have double the common shares outstanding, leaving EPS approximately equal for the two companies). This assumption is erroneous. Management controls the number of common shares outstanding and there is no relation between firm size and number of shares outstanding. Different companies also have different philosophies regarding share issuance and repurchase. For example, consider that most companies report annual EPS of less than $5, while Berkshire Hathaway reported EPS of $7,928 in 2010! This is because Berkshire Hathaway has so few common shares outstanding, not necessarily because it has stellar profits.

ACCOUNTING QUALITY

We conclude our coverage of operating income with a discussion of accounting quality. As we saw in earlier modules, there are at least two main uses of financial reports: evaluation and valuation. Financial statement readers use the reported numbers from financial statements along with information in the notes and Management Discussion and Analysis (MD&A), to evaluate company profitability, liquidity, solvency and other financial characteristics. Those users also evaluate its managers and board of directors with a view to assessing the results of past operating, investing and financing decisions. The evaluation of financial reports is also used to value the company, a process that includes forecasting operating, investing and financing results. In a later module we consider more fully the forecasting process. For now, it is important to understand that both uses of financial information (evaluation and valuation) demand high-quality accounting information.

LO6 Explain accounting quality and identify areas for analysis.

What is high-quality accounting information? Although there is not a single definition of high quality information, there are factors that enhance information quality.

Reliable High-quality accounting information is **reliable**. In particular, information is reliable when:

- Balance sheet numbers represent economic reality: all included assets will yield future economic benefits and there are no unrecorded assets; all liabilities are recorded and measured at economically appropriate amounts. Assets and liabilities are properly labeled and classified as current or noncurrent. Accounts have not been aggregated so as to obscure their true nature.

- Income statement numbers reflect economic earnings: revenues reflect all sales activity during the period and only those sales for that period; expenses are complete and properly measured. Items are properly labeled and any netting or aggregation of numbers does not obscure their true nature or amount.

- Reported cash flows accurately portray all of the cash that flowed in and out of the company during the period.

Relevant High-quality accounting information is **relevant**. In particular information is relevant when:

---

[9] The effects of dilutive securities are only included if they are, in fact, dilutive. Securities that are *antidilutive* would actually increase EPS, and are, thus, excluded from the computation. An example of an antidilutive security is employee stock options whose exercise price is greater than the stock's current market price. These *underwater* (or out-of-the-money) options are antidilutive and are, therefore, excluded from the EPS computation. PDL Biopharma provides the following explanation for this exclusion in its footnotes:

"We excluded 0.3 million, 2.5 million and 10.3 million of outstanding stock options from our diluted earnings per share calculations for the years ended December 31, 2010, 2009 and 2008, respectively, because the option exercise prices were greater than the average market prices of our common stock during these periods; therefore, their effect was anti-dilutive."

- Reported earnings and cash flow numbers can be used to forecast the amount and timing of future earnings and cash flows. This attribute is referred to as "relevance" and we return to it in our forecasting module.

- Footnotes provide additional quantitative and qualitative information that is accurate and complete. Sometimes a balance sheet or income statement number is not the best indicator of current value or is not predictive of future expectations. For example, LIFO inventory is reported on the balance sheet but the footnotes augment relevance by reporting the FIFO value of inventory.

There are several ways that accounting quality is diminished. (For a good discussion of this issue, see Dechow, P., and C. Schrand. "Earnings quality," The Research Foundation of CFA Institute. Charlottesville, VA 2004).

Unintentional Errors

We must understand that there are errors in financial statements. Two reports signed by external auditors (one concerning adequacy of the company's internal controls and one disclosing the audit opinion) provide some assurance that financial statements are free from material misstatement. However, those reports do not guarantee no errors; instead, they assert that any remaining errors are not large enough to affect the decisions of financial statement readers.

One-time Events

In the ordinary course of business, companies record one-time transactions that are not expected to recur. For example, a lawsuit is settled or commodity prices spike and the company earns a windfall profit. While these nonrecurring events are reliably measured and reported, by definition they cannot be used to predict future periods' events. Those specific line items are not relevant and our expectations about future earnings must not be swayed by such events. The challenge is in determining which items reported on the income statement are truly one-time events. Often companies highlight the existence of one-time items by reporting "pro forma" earnings in company financial statements and press releases. Pro forma income commonly begins with GAAP income from continuing operations (which excludes discontinued operations and extraordinary items), and then adjusts for other one-time items including restructuring charges, large gains and losses, and acquisition expenses (goodwill amortization and other acquisition costs). SEC Regulation G requires that companies reconcile such non-GAAP information to GAAP numbers so that financial statement readers can have a basis for comparison and can determine if the excluded items truly are one-time items. For example, in 2010 Merck & Co., Inc., reported the following "pro forma" (non-GAAP) information in its Form 10-K.

($ in millions)	2010
Pretax income as reported under GAAP	$ 1,653
Increase (decrease) for excluded items:	
Purchase accounting adjustments	9,007
Restructuring costs	1,986
Merger-related costs	396
Other items:	
Vioxx Liability reserve	950
Gain on AstraZeneca asset option exercise	(443)
Gain related to the MSP Partnership	—
Gain on Merial divestiture	—
Gain on distribution from AZLP	—
	13,549
Taxes on income as reported under GAAP	671
Estimated tax benefit (expense) on excluded items	1,798
Tax benefit from foreign entity tax rate changes	391
Tax charge related to U.S. health care reform legislation	(147)
Non-GAAP taxes on income	2,713
Non-GAAP net income	$10,836

This footnote indicates that Merck considers over $10 billion of net expenses, including the $2 billion restructuring costs, as one-time charges that, if included, portray an inaccurate picture of its performance during the period. Pfizer's non-GAAP income of $10,836 million is more than ten times larger than the reported GAAP income of $982.

RESEARCH INSIGHT **Pro Forma Earnings: Incidence and Outcomes**

In 2010, more than half the companies that comprise the Dow Jones Index reported non-GAAP numbers when reporting quarterly net income. *(See listing at: Larcker, D. and B. Tayan, "Pro Forma Earnings: What's Wrong with GAAP? August 20, 2010, http://ssrn.com/abstract=1678066.)* Despite the potential for abuse, investors often perceive certain non-GAAP earnings as more permanent than GAAP earnings because pro forma numbers allegedly provide better indication of future earnings power. For this reason, Wall Street analysts' earnings estimates typically use non-GAAP metrics, or "Street" earnings. Recent research reports two results that show how investors' use of pro forma earnings is changing. First, investors appear to pay more attention to pro forma earnings in the post-SOX period (after 2003), which suggests that SOX improved the credibility of non-GAAP disclosures. Second, investors discount earnings announcements in which managers make aggressive exclusions that are potentially misleading and, hence, stock values seem to reflect investors' ability to discern accounting quality. (Black, D., E. Black, T. Christensen, and W. Heninger "Has the Regulation of Pro Forma Reporting in the U.S. Changed Investors' Perceptions of Adjusted Earnings Disclosures?" November 23, 2010, http://ssrn.com/abstract=1818903)

Deliberate Manager Intervention

Ideally, all reported numbers are free from deliberate managerial intervention. This implies that the numbers are unbiased because managers have been impartial when choosing accounting policies and when exercising their discretion over reported numbers. However, history is rife with examples where this is not the case: managers can and do "manage" earnings and balance sheet numbers. Sometimes accounting quality is impugned because managers' intervention in the reporting process involves fraud. For example, in 2009, Ramalinga Raju, the CEO of Satyam (an Indian information-technology conglomerate), was arrested for reporting fictitious cash and profits of over $1 billion. However, more frequently, earnings management involves subtle, small increases in net income designed to achieve an outcome such as meeting analysts' forecasts or avoiding losses. While it is more often the case that "managed" earnings (and assets) are inflated, some managers underreport their true earnings (and assets). The highest quality accounting reports are free from biases in both directions; they are accurate because they are not over- or understated.

Reliable Numbers That Are Not Predictive

Companies can experience changes in economic events that impair the predictive ability of reliable numbers. For example, in June 2011, Marathon Oil announced that it was breaking the company into two new companies: Marathon Oil, which will engage in upstream oil and gas exploration and development activities, and Marathon Petroleum, which will run refineries and distribute products to retail and other customers. The company's 2010 financial statements, while reliable, were no longer relevant because the company's structure was so changed that users could not use its 2010 revenues and expenses to forecast 2011 net income. Expectations about future earnings were markedly altered.

Assessing and Remediating Accounting Quality

There is no tried and true formula for assessing accounting quality or for identifying earnings management. But, at a minimum, we can implement the following analysis and remediation techniques:

- Read both reports from the external auditor and take special note of any deviation from boilerplate language.
- Peruse the footnote on accounting policies (typically footnote 1) and compare the company's policies to its industry peers. Deviations from the norm can signal opportunism.

BUSINESS INSIGHT   Meeting or Beating Analysts' Forecasts

Missing analysts' earnings forecasts can cause stock prices to tumble. Therefore, managers aim to meet or beat the Street's expectation, sometimes resorting to earnings management involving accounting accruals, and other times using real actions (such as channel stuffing). These deliberate manager interventions reduce accounting quality. One way analysts and researchers detect potential earnings management is to identify unusual accruals and reversals (negative accruals) and quantify their effect on earnings. Of particular interest are unusual accruals that move EPS enough to meet or beat analysts' earnings forecasts; such accruals raise suspicion of managerial opportunism. Consider the case of Green Mountain Coffee; its consensus EPS forecast was $0.38 for the second quarter of fiscal 2011. When the company reported second-quarter earnings, they beat the consensus forecast by $0.10 per share, a 26% margin! The company's stock price shot up nearly 20% to $75.98. But a closer inspection of Green Mountain Coffee's financial statements reveals that the wide margin by which the company beat earnings forecast was not due to stellar performance but to an accounting anomaly. Its statement of cash flows reveals an unusual (negative) accrual of $22,259 thousand for sales returns for the second quarter of fiscal 2011. GAAP requires that firms report revenues net of anticipated sales returns. Companies use their historical experience with product returns to determine the sales returns expense (a debit on the income statement) with an offsetting entry to a sales-return allowance (a credit balance on the balance sheet). When customers return products, the company reduces the allowance for sales returns on the balance sheet. At the end of the quarter, the company estimates sales returns for the current quarters' sales, records the appropriate expense on the income statement, and updates the sales-return allowance. It is atypical for a company to have a negative expense for sales returns. A negative sales-return expense (a "reversal") increases revenues and earnings. This is what Green Mountain Coffee reported in 2Q 2011. On an after-tax basis, the reversal increased Green Mountain Coffee's net income by $14,468 thousand or about $0.10 per share (147,558,595 shares diluted outstanding at March 26, 2011). A skeptical analyst might conclude that it recorded a negative accrual to beat the Street's expectations. Such behavior hinders the quality of reported earnings.

- Examine changes in accounting policies. What would the company have reported absent the change? Did the new policy help it avoid reporting a loss or violating a debt covenant?

- Compare key ratios over time. Follow up on marked increases or decreases in ratios, read footnotes and the MD&A to see how management explains such changes. Follow up on ratios that do not change when a change is expected. For example, during the tech bubble, Worldcom, Inc., reported an expense-to-revenue ratio (ER ratio) of 42% quarter after quarter, despite the worsening of economic conditions. Later it was discovered that managers had deliberately underreported expenses to maintain the ER ratio. The lesson is that sometimes "no change" signals managerial intervention.

- Review ratios of competitors and consider macro economic conditions and how they have shifted over time. Are the ratios reasonable in light of current conditions? Are changes in the income statement aligning with changes on the balance sheet?

- Identify nonrecurring items and separately assess their impact on company performance and position. Take care when using pro forma numbers reported by the company.

- Recast financial statements as necessary to reflect an accounting policy(ies) that is more in line with competitors or one that better reflects economically relevant numbers. We illustrate recasting at several points in future modules. For example, we can convert LIFO inventory to FIFO and we can capitalize operating leases.

GLOBAL ACCOUNTING

We discussed the reporting of operating income, including revenue measurement and the timing of revenue recognition. However, companies reporting under IFRS are likely to recognize revenues earlier for the following three reasons:

BUSINESS INSIGHT	Pro Forma Income and Managerial Motives

The purported motive for reporting pro forma income is to eliminate transitory (one-time) items to enhance year-to-year comparability. Although this might be justified on the basis that pro forma income has greater predictive ability, important information is lost in the process. One role for accounting is to report how effective management has been in its stewardship of invested capital. Asset write-downs, liability accruals, and other charges that are eliminated in calculating pro forma income often reflect outcomes of poor management decisions. Our analysis must not blindly eliminate information contained in nonrecurring items by focusing solely on pro forma income. Critics of pro forma income also argue that the items excluded by managers from GAAP income are inconsistent across companies and time. They contend that a major motive for pro forma income is to mislead stakeholders. Legendary investor Warren Buffett puts pro forma in context: ***"When companies or investment professionals use terms such as 'EBITDA' and 'pro forma,' they want you to unthinkingly accept concepts that are dangerously flawed."*** (Berkshire Hathaway, Annual Report)

1. U.S. GAAP has specific guidance about what constitutes revenue, how revenue is measured, and the timing of its recognition. Also, U.S. GAAP has extensive, industry-specific revenue recognition guidelines. IFRS is not specific about the timing and measurement of revenue recognition and does not provide industry-specific guidance. With less detailed guidance, the general management preference for reporting income earlier will likely prevail.

2. A U.S. GAAP revenue-recognition criterion is that the sales price be fixed or determinable. This means that if a sale involves contingent consideration, no revenue is recognized until the contingency is resolved. IFRS considers the probability that economic benefits will flow to the seller and records such benefits as revenue if they can be reliably measured. This means contingent revenue is recognized earlier under IFRS.

3. For multiple-element contracts, both U.S. GAAP and IFRS allocate revenue based on relative fair values of the elements. However, IFRS requires fair-value estimates that are less restrictive.

For these reasons, our analysis of companies reporting under IFRS is likely to find more aggressive reporting and higher revenues (and net income). This front-loading of revenues is likely more pronounced for high revenue-growth companies and for industries with more multiple-element contracts.

We also discussed several expenses in this module, including research and development. There are differences between U.S. GAAP and IFRS for R&D. U.S. GAAP expenses all R&D costs whereas IFRS allows capitalization and subsequent amortization of certain development costs. For some companies and some industries this can create differences for both the balance sheet and income statement. For analysis purposes, we must review the R&D footnote of IFRS companies to determine the development costs capitalized for the period and the amount of amortization of previously capitalized costs. The difference between these two amounts represents the additional pretax expense that would be reported under U.S. GAAP. The IFRS intangible asset footnote reports the unamortized development costs, which represents the net asset that would not appear on a U.S. GAAP balance sheet (with the off-setting entries to deferred taxes and retained earnings).

The module also considered restructuring expenses. There are differences between IFRS and U.S. GAAP on restructuring, but most are minor. The following differences relate to timing:

■ Under IFRS, restructuring expense is recognized when there is a binding contract or a plan for the restructuring and if the affected employees expect the plan to be implemented. Under U.S. GAAP, restructuring expense can be recognized earlier because the trigger is managerial approval of a plan.

■ Under IFRS, compensation for employees who will be terminated is recognized when empl[...] are deemed redundant. Under U.S. GAAP, restructuring expense can be recognized later, [...] employees have been informed.

The following difference relates to the restructuring expense amount:

■ Consistent with other accruals under IFRS, a restructuring provision is reco[...] mate. This is usually the expected value or, in the case of a range of possi[...]

equally likely, the provision is recorded at the midpoint of the range. The U.S. GAAP estimate is at the most-likely outcome; and if there is a range of possible outcomes, the provision is recorded as the minimum amount of the range.

This means that the financial statement differences between IFRS and U.S. GAAP for restructurings cannot be predicted unequivocally. We must review the restructuring footnote; and remember that cumulative expense is the same under both reporting systems.

We also described tax expenses. There are three notable differences: two affect the income statement and one affects the balance sheet. With respect to the income statement:

1. Both U.S. GAAP and IFRS recognize deferred tax assets for timing differences and unused tax losses. However, under U.S. GAAP, a valuation allowance is set up if it is more likely than not (probability > 50%) that some portion of the deferred tax assets will not be utilized. Under IFRS, the deferred tax asset is only recognized to the extent that the future benefit is probable (probability > 50%). That is, there is no deferred tax asset if the company does not expect to earn enough taxable profit in the future to use the tax credit. This means there are no valuation allowances in IFRS (although sometimes a company reports the "unrecognized portion" of deferred tax assets). The net effect on income is identical but our review of an IFRS tax footnote will not involve assessing the adequacy of the allowance or the extent to which changes in the allowance affect net income.

2. Under IFRS, deferred tax assets on employee stock options are computed based on the options' intrinsic value at each reporting date. In contrast, GAAP uses historical value. This results in partial mark-to-market accounting for the IFRS deferred tax asset and introduces volatility in tax expense. We must review footnotes carefully to determine any potential income statement impact of IFRS revalued deferred tax assets.

With respect to the balance sheet, all deferred tax assets and liabilities are classified as long-term under IFRS. This will impact metrics and ratios that involve current assets and liabilities and could affect our comparative assessment of liquidity.

Finally, recall that separate reporting of extraordinary items is not permitted under IFRS. When comparing U.S. GAAP to IFRS, we include any extraordinary items with other expenses, according to their function.

MODULE-END REVIEW

Refer to the Merck & Co., Inc., 2010 income statement in the Mid-Module Review.

Required

1. Assume that during 2010 the $US weakened with respect to the currencies in which Merck conducts its business. How would that weakening affect Merck's income statement?
2. What is the difference between basic and diluted earnings per share?

The solution is on page 5-59.

APPENDIX 5A: Expanded Explanation of Deferred Taxes

The module provided an example of how different depreciation methods for tax and financial reporting create a deferred tax liability. That example showed that total depreciation over the life of the asset is the same under both tax and financial reporting, and that the only difference is the timing of the expense or tax deduction. Because depreciation differs each year, the amount at which the equipment is reported will differ as well for book and tax purposes (cost less accumulated depreciation is called *net book value* for financial reporting purposes and *tax basis* ~~for~~ tax purposes). These book vs tax differences are eliminated at the end of the asset's useful life.

~~To~~ understand this concept more completely, we modify the example from the module to include a third year. ~~that~~ the company purchases PPE assets at the start of Year 1 for $120. For financial reporting purposes, ~~uses~~ straight-line depreciation and records depreciation of $40 each year (with zero salvage). For tax purposes, assume that the company takes tax depreciation deductions of $60, $50, and $10. Exhibit 5A.1 reports the annual depreciation along with the asset's net book value and its tax basis, for each year-end.

EXHIBIT 5A.1	Book and Tax Depreciation and Carrying Value				
	Financial Reporting (Net Book Value)	Tax Reporting (Tax Basis)	Book vs Tax Difference	Deferred Tax Liability (Book vs Tax Difference × Tax Rate)	Deferred Tax Expense (Increase or Decrease in Deferred Tax Liability)
At purchase: PPE carrying value	$120	$120	$ 0	$ 0	
Year 1: Depreciation.	(40)	(60)			
End of Year 1: PPE carrying value . . .	80	60	$20	$ 8	$ 8
			($80 − $60)	($20 × 40%)	($8 − $0)
Year 2: Depreciation.	(40)	(50)			
End of Year 2: PPE carrying value . . .	40	10	$30	$12	$ 4
			($40 − $10)	($30 × 40%)	($12 − $8)
Year 3: Depreciation.	(40)	(10)			
End of Year 3: PPE carrying value . . .	0	0	$ 0	$ 0	$(12)
			($0 − $0)		($0 − $12)

The third column in Exhibit 5A.1 shows the "book-tax" difference, which is the difference between GAAP net book value and the tax basis at the end of each year. The fourth column shows the deferred tax liability at the end of each period, computed as the book-tax differences times the tax rate. We see from the fourth column that when the financial reporting net book value is greater than the tax basis, the company has a deferred tax liability on its balance sheet (as in Years 1 and 2). Companies' footnotes provide information about deferred taxes. For example, Pfizer's footnote reports a deferred tax liability (net) of $1,726 for its property, plant and equipment, which indicates that tax basis for PPE is less than GAAP net book value, on average, for Pfizer's PPE.

Accounting standards require a company to first compute the taxes it owes (per its tax return), then to compute any changes in deferred tax liabilities and assets, and finally to compute tax expense reported in the income statement (as a residual amount). Thus, tax expense is not computed as pretax income multiplied by the company's tax rate as we might initially expect. Instead, tax expense is computed as follows:

Tax Expense = Taxes Paid − Increase (or + Decrease) in Deferred Tax Assets + Increase (or − Decrease) in Deferred Liabilities

The far-right column in Exhibit 5A.1 shows the deferred tax expense per year, which is the amount added to, or subtracted from, taxes paid, to arrive at tax expense. If we assume this company had $100 of pre-depreciation income, its taxable income and tax expense (assuming a 40% rate) follows:

	Taxes Paid	Deferred Tax Expense	Total Tax Expense
Year 1	$16	$ 8	$24
	($100 − $60) × 40%		
Year 2	$20	$ 4	$24
	($100 − $50) × 40%		
Year 3	$36	$(12)	$24
	($100 − $10) × 40%		

In this example, the timing difference between the financial reporting and tax reporting derives from PPE and creates a deferred tax liability. Other differences between the two sets of books create other types of deferred tax accounts. Exhibit 5A.2 shows the relation between the financial reporting and tax reporting net book values, and the resulting deferred taxes (liability or asset) on the balance sheet.

EXHIBIT 5A.2	Sources of Deferred Tax Assets and Liabilities		
For Assets...			
Financial reporting net book value	> Tax reporting net book value	→	Deferred tax liability on balance sheet
Financial reporting net book value	< Tax reporting net book value	→	Deferred tax asset on balance sheet
For Liabilities...			
Financial reporting net book value	< Tax reporting net book value	→	Deferred tax liability on balance sheet
Financial reporting net book value	> Tax reporting net book value	→	Deferred tax asset on balance sheet

A common deferred tax asset relates to accrued restructuring costs (a liability for financial reporting purposes). Restructuring costs are not deductible for tax purposes until paid in the future and, thus, there is no accrual restructuring liability for tax reporting, which means it has a tax basis of $0. To explain how this timing difference affects tax expense, assume that a company accrues $300 of restructuring costs in Year 1 and settles the liability in Year 2 as follows:

	Financial Reporting (Net Book Value)	Tax Reporting (Tax Basis)	Book vs Tax Difference	Deferred Tax Asset (Book vs Tax Difference × Tax Rate)	Deferred Tax Expense (Decrease (or Increase) in Deferred Tax Asset)
Year 1: Accrue restructuring costs . . .	$(300)	$ 0			
End of Year 1: Liability book value . . .	$ 300	$ 0	$300	$120	$(120)
			($300 − $0)	($300 × 40%)	($120 − $0)
Year 2: Pay restructuring costs		$(300)			
End of Year 2: Liability book value . . .	$ 0	0	$ 0	$ 0	$120
			($0 − $0)	($0 × 40%)	($120 − $0)

Timing differences created by the restructuring liability yield a deferred tax asset in Year 1. Timing differences disappear in Year 2 when the company pays cash for restructuring costs. To see how tax expense is determined, assume that this company has $500 of pre-restructuring income; computations follow:

	Taxes Paid	Deferred Tax Expense	Total Tax Expense
Year 1	$200	$(120)	$ 80
	($500 − $0) × 40%		
Year 2	$ 80	$ 120	$200
	($500 − $300) × 40%		

Deferred tax accounts derive from timing differences between GAAP expenses and tax deductions. This creates differences between the net book value and the tax basis for many assets and liabilities. Pfizer's deferred tax footnote (see Exhibit 5.6) reports several deferred tax assets and liabilities that explain its book-tax difference and the tax basis. For example, in 2010, its deferred tax liability associated with PPE is $1,726 million ($2,146 million liability less $420 million asset). This reflects the cumulative tax savings to Pfizer from accelerated depreciation for its PPE. If we assume a tax rate of 35%, we can compute the book-tax difference for Pfizer's PPE as $4,931 million ($1,726 million/0.35). Its balance sheet reveals total PPE of $19,123, which implies that the tax basis for these assets is $14,192 million ($19,123 − $4,931).

GUIDANCE ANSWERS

MANAGERIAL DECISION   You Are the Financial Analyst

Typically, restructuring charges have three components: asset write-downs (such as inventories, property, plant, and goodwill), severance costs, and other restructuring-related expenses. Write-downs occur when the cash-flow-generating ability of an asset declines, thus reducing its current market value below its book value reported on the balance sheet. Arguably, this decline in cash-flow-generating ability did not occur solely in the current year and, most likely, has developed over several periods. It is not uncommon for companies to delay loss recognition, such as write-downs of assets. Thus, prior period income is, arguably, not as high as reported, and the current period loss is not as great as reported. Turning to severance and other costs, GAAP permits restructuring expense to include only those costs that are *incremental* and will *not* benefit future periods. The accrual of restructuring-related expenses can be viewed like other accruals; that is, it might be over- or understated. In future periods, the required reconciliation of the restructuring accrual will provide insight into the adequacy of the accrual in that earlier period.

DISCUSSION QUESTIONS

Q5-1.   What are the criteria that guide firms in recognition of revenue? What does each of the criteria mean? How are the criteria met for a company like Abercrombie & Fitch, a clothing retailer? How are the criteria met for a construction company that builds offices under long-term contracts with developers?

Q5-2.   Why are extraordinary items reported separately from continuing operations in the income statement?

Q5-3. What are the criteria for categorizing an event as an extraordinary item? Provide an example of an event that would properly be categorized as an extraordinary item and one that would not. How does this accounting treatment differ for IFRS?

Q5-4. What is the difference between basic earnings per share and diluted earnings per share? Are potentially dilutive securities always included in the EPS computation?

Q5-5. What effect, if any, does a weakening $US have on reported sales and net income for companies operating outside the United States?

Q5-6. Identify the three typical categories of restructuring costs and their effects on the balance sheet and the income statement. Explain the concept of a big bath and why restructuring costs are often identified with this event.

Q5-7. What is the current U.S. GAAP accounting treatment for research and development costs? How does this accounting treatment differ for IFRS? Why are R&D costs normally not capitalized under U.S. GAAP?

Q5-8. Under what circumstances will deferred taxes likely result in a cash outflow?

Q5-9. What is the concept of pro forma income and why has this income measure been criticized?

Q5-10. What is unearned revenue? Provide three examples of unearned revenue.

Assignments with the ✓ logo in the margin are available in an online homework system.
See the Preface of the book for details.

MINI EXERCISES

M5-11. **Computing Percentage-of-Completion Revenues**   (LO1)
Bartov Corporation agreed to build a warehouse for a client at an agreed contract price of $2,500,000. Expected (and actual) costs for the warehouse follow: 2012, $400,000; 2013, $1,000,000; and 2014, $500,000. The company completed the warehouse in 2014. Compute revenues, expenses, and income for each year 2012 through 2014 using the percentage-of-completion method. (Round percents to the nearest whole number.)

M5-12. **Applying the Financial Statement Effects Template.**   (LO1)
Refer to the information for Bartov Corporation in M5-11.

  a. Use the financial statement effects template to record contract revenues and expenses for each year 2012 through 2014 using the percentage-of-completion method.

  b. Prepare journal entries and T-accounts to record contract revenues and expenses for each year 2012 through 2014 using the percentage-of-completion method.

M5-13. **Assessing Revenue Recognition of Companies**   (LO1)
Identify and explain when each of the following companies should recognize revenue.

  a. The GAP: The GAP is a retailer of clothing items for all ages.

  b. Merck & Company: Merck engages in developing, manufacturing, and marketing pharmaceutical products. It sells its drugs to retailers like CVS and Walgreen.

  c. Deere & Company: Deere manufactures heavy equipment. It sells equipment to a network of independent distributors, who in turn sell the equipment to customers. Deere provides financing and insurance services both to distributors and customers.

  d. Bank of America: Bank of America is a banking institution. It lends money to individuals and corporations and invests excess funds in marketable securities.

  e. Johnson Controls: Johnson Controls manufactures products for the government under long-term contracts.

The GAP (GPS)

Merck & Company (MRK)

Deere & Company (DE)

Bank of America (BAC)

Johnson Controls (JCI)

M5-14. **Assessing Risk Exposure to Revenue Recognition**   (LO1)
BannerAD Corporation manages a Website that sells products on consignment from sellers. It pays these sellers a portion of the sales price, and charges a commission. Identify two potential revenue recognition problems relating to such sales.

M5-15. **Estimating Revenue Recognition with Right of Return**   (LO1)
The GAP offers an unconditional return policy. It normally expects 2% of sales at retail selling prices to be returned before the return period expires. Assuming that The GAP records total sales of $5 million for the current period, what amount of *net* sales should it record for this period?

The GAP (GPS)

M5-16. **Assessing Research and Development Expenses**   (LO2)
Abbott Laboratories reports the following (summary) income statement.

Abbott Laboratories (ABT)

Year Ended December 31 ($ millions)	2010
Net sales.	$35,167
Cost of products sold.	(14,665)
Research and development*	(4,038)
Selling, general and administrative	(10,376)
Pretax operating earnings	$ 6,088

* Includes acquired in process research and development.

a. Compute the percent of net sales that Abbott Laboratories spends on research and development (R&D). Compare this level of expenditure with the percentages for other companies that are discussed in the Business Insight box on page 5-4. How would you assess the appropriateness of its R&D expense level?

b. Describe how accounting for R&D expenditures affects Abbott Laboratories' balance sheet and income statement.

Bristol-Myers Squibb (BMY)

M5-17. Interpreting Foreign Currency Translation Disclosure   (LO4)

Bristol-Myers Squibb (BMY) reports the following table in its 10-K report relating to the change in sales from 2009 to 2010.

	Total Change	Analysis of % Change		
		Volume	Price	Foreign Exchange
U.S. net sales.	6%	3%	3%	—
Foreign net sales	(1)%	2%	(4)%	1%
Total net sales.	4%	2%	1%	1%

a. Did U.S. net sales increase or decrease during the year? By what percentage? How much of this change is attributable to volume versus price changes?

b. By what percentage did foreign net sales change during the year? How much of this change is attributable to volume versus price changes?

c. Why does the change in total net sales (4%) not equal the sum of the changes in U.S. (6%) and foreign net sales (−1%)?

M5-18. Analyzing Income Tax Disclosure   (LO3)

Dell Inc. (DELL)

Dell Inc. reports the following footnote disclosure to its 10-K report ($ millions).

The provision for income taxes consisted of the following:

Fiscal Year Ended	January 28, 2011
Federal	
Current	$597
Deferred	(95)
	502
State	
Current	66
Deferred	9
	75
Foreign	
Current	97
Deferred	41
	138
Total	$715

a. What amount of income tax expense does Dell report in its income statement for 2011?

b. How much of Dell's income tax expense is current (as opposed to deferred)?

c. Why do deferred tax assets and liabilities arise? How do they impact the tax expense that Dell reports in its 2011 income statement?

M5-19. Defining and Computing Earnings per Share (LO5)

Cleantech Solutions International reports the following information in footnotes to its 2010 Form 10-K.

Cleantech Solutions International (CLNT)

Net income available to common shareholders for basic and diluted net income per common share	$11,074,332
Weighted average common shares outstanding—basic	17,879,940
Effect of dilutive securities:	
Series A convertible preferred stock	4,980,272
Warrants	2,536,609
Weighted average common shares outstanding—diluted	25,396,821

a. Explain the concepts of basic and diluted earnings per share.
b. Compute basic and diluted EPS for 2010.
c. What is the effect of dilutive securities on EPS, in percentage terms?

M5-20. Assessing Revenue Recognition for Advance Payments (LO1)

Koonce Company operates a performing arts center. The company sells tickets for its upcoming season of six Broadway musicals and receives $420,000 cash. The performances occur monthly over the next six months.

a. When should Koonce record revenue for the Broadway musical series?
b. Use the financial statement effects template to show the $420,000 cash receipt and recognition of the first month's revenue.

M5-21. Reporting Unearned Revenue (LO1)

Target Corporation sells gift cards that can be used at any of the company's Target or Greatland stores. Target encodes information on the card's magnetic strip about the card's value, the date it expires (typically two years after issuance), and the store where it was purchased.

Target Corporation (TGT)

a. How will Target's balance sheet reflect the gift card? Will the balance sheet amount of these cards be classified as current or noncurrent?
b. When does Target record revenue from the gift card?

EXERCISES

E5-22. Assessing Revenue Recognition Timing (LO1)

Explain when each of the following businesses should recognize revenues:

a. A clothing retailer like The Limited.
b. A contractor like Boeing Company that performs work under long-term government contracts.
c. A grocery store like Supervalu.
d. A producer of television shows like MTV that syndicates its content to television stations.
e. A residential real estate developer that constructs only speculative houses and later sells these houses to buyers.
f. A banking institution like Bank of America that lends money for home mortgages.
g. A manufacturer like Harley-Davidson.
h. A publisher of magazines such as Time-Warner.

Limited (LTD)
Boeing Co. (BA)
Supervalu, Inc. (SVU)
MTV

Bank of America (BAC)
Harley-Davidson (HOG)
Time-Warner (TWX)

E5-23. Assessing Revenue Recognition Timing and Income Measurement (LO1)

Explain when each of the following businesses should recognize revenue and identify any income measurement issues that could arise.

a. RealMoney.Com, a division of TheStreet.Com, provides investment advice to customers for an up-front fee. It provides these customers with password-protected access to its Website where customers can download investment reports. RealMoney has an obligation to provide updates on its Website.
b. Oracle develops general ledger and other business application software that it sells to its customers. The customer pays an up-front fee for the right to use the software and a monthly fee for support services.
c. Intuit develops tax preparation software that it sells to its customers for a flat fee. No further payment is required and the software cannot be returned, only exchanged if defective.

TheStreet.Com (TSCM)

Oracle (ORCL)

Intuit (INTU)

d. A developer of computer games sells its software with a 10-day right of return period during which the software can be returned for a full refund. After the 10-day period has expired, the software cannot be returned.

E5-24. Constructing and Assessing Income Statements Using Percentage-of-Completion (LO1)

General Electric
Company (GE)

Assume that General Electric Company agreed in May 2011 to construct a nuclear generator for NSTAR, a utility company serving the Boston area. The contract price of $500 million is to be paid as follows: $200 million at the time of signing; $100 million on December 31, 2011; and $200 million at completion in May 2012. General Electric incurred the following costs in constructing the generator: $100 million in 2011, and $300 million in 2012.

a. Compute the amount of General Electric's revenue, expense, and income for both 2011 and 2012 under the percentage-of-completion revenue recognition method.

b. Discuss whether or not you believe the percentage-of-completion method provides a good measure of General Electric's performance under the contract.

 E5-25. Constructing and Assessing Income Statements Using Percentage-of-Completion (LO1)

On March 15, 2012, Frankel Construction contracted to build a shopping center at a contract price of $120 million. The schedule of expected (which equals actual) cash collections and contract costs follows:

Year	Cash Collections	Cost Incurred
2012	$ 30 million	$15 million
2013	50 million	40 million
2014	40 million	30 million
Total	$120 million	$85 million

a. Calculate the amount of revenue, expense, and net income for each of the three years 2012 through 2014 using the percentage-of-completion revenue recognition method. (Round percents to the nearest whole number.)

b. Discuss whether or not the percentage-of-completion method provides a good measure of this construction company's performance under the contract.

 E5-26. Interpreting the Income Tax Expense Footnote (LO3)

FedEx Corp (FDX)

The income tax footnote to the financial statements of FedEx Corporation follows.

The components of the provision for income taxes for the years ended May 31 were as follows:

($ millions)	2010	2009	2008
Current provision			
Domestic			
Federal	$ 36	$ (35)	$514
State and local	54	18	74
Foreign	207	214	242
	297	197	830
Deferred provision (benefit)			
Domestic			
Federal	408	327	31
State and local	15	48	(2)
Foreign	(10)	7	32
	413	382	61
Provision for income taxes.	$710	$579	$891

a. What is the amount of income tax expense reported in FedEx's 2010, 2009, and 2008 income statements?

b. What percentage of total tax expense is currently payable in each year?

c. One possible reason for the $408 million federal deferred tax expense in 2010 is that deferred tax liabilities increased during that year. Provide an example that gives rise to an increase in the deferred tax liability.

E5-27.   Identifying Operating Income Components   (LO2)

Following is the income statement information from Apollo Medical Devices. Identify the components that we would consider operating.

($ in thousands)	2010
Net sales.	$5,164,771
Cost of sales before special charges.	1,382,235
Special inventory obsolescence charge.	27,876
Total cost of sales.	1,410,111
Gross profit.	3,754,660
Selling, general and administrative expense	1,770,667
Research and development expense.	631,086
Merger and acquisition costs.	46,914
In-process research and development charges.	12,244
Litigation settlement.	16,500
Operating profit	1,277,249
Interest expense.	(67,372)
Interest income.	2,076
Gain on disposal of fixed assets	4,929
Impairment of marketable securities	(5,222)
Other income (expense), net	(2,857)
Earnings before income taxes	1,208,803
Income tax expense.	301,367
Net earnings.	$ 907,436

E5-28.   Identifying Operating Income Components   (LO2)

Following is the Deere & Company income statement for 2010.   Deere & Company (DE)

($ millions)	2010
Net Sales and Revenues	
Net sales.	$23,573.2
Finance and interest income	1,825.3
Other income	606.1
Total	26,004.6
Costs and Expenses	
Cost of sales.	17,398.8
Research and development expenses.	1,052.4
Selling, administrative and general expenses	2,968.7
Interest expense.	811.4
Other operating expenses	748.1
Total	22,979.4
Income of Consolidated Group before Income Taxes	3,025.2
Provision for income taxes.	1,161.6
Income of Consolidated Group	1,863.6
Equity in income of unconsolidated affiliates.	10.7
Net income.	1,874.3
Net income attributable to noncontrolling interests.	9.3
Net income attributable to Deere & Company.	$ 1,865.0

Notes:

- Income statement includes John Deere commercial and consumer tractor segment, a finance subsidiary that provides loan and lease financing relating to the sales of those tractors, and a health care segment that provides managed health care services for the company and certain outside customers.

- **Equity in income of unconsolidated affiliates** refers to income John Deere has earned on investments in affiliated (but unconsolidated) companies. These are generally investments made for strategic purposes.

a. Identify the components in its income statement that you would consider operating.

    b. Discuss your treatment of the company's finance and interest income that relates to financing of its John Deere lawn and garden, and commercial tractors.

E5-29. **Assessing the Income Tax Footnote**   (LO3)

Colgate-Palmolive (CL)

Colgate-Palmolive reports the following income tax footnote disclosure in its 10-K report.

Deferred Tax Balances at December 31 (In millions)	2010	2009
Deferred tax liabilities		
Intangible assets	$(463)	$(440)
Property, plant and equipment	(344)	(320)
Other	(116)	(157)
	(923)	(917)
Deferred tax assets		
Pension and other retiree benefits	471	389
Tax loss and tax credit carryforwards	130	153
Accrued liabilities	145	134
Stock-based compensation	108	103
Other	163	163
Valuation allowance	(1)	(2)
	1,016	940
Net deferred income taxes	$ 93	$ 23

    a. Colgate reports $344 million of deferred tax liabilities in 2010 relating to "Property." Explain how such liabilities arise.

    b. Describe how a deferred tax asset can arise from pension and other retiree benefits.

    c. Colgate reports $130 million in deferred tax assets for 2010 relating to tax loss and credit carryforwards. Describe how tax loss carryforwards arise and under what conditions the resulting deferred tax assets will be realized.

    d. Colgate has established a deferred tax asset valuation allowance of $1 million for 2010. What is the purpose of this allowance? How did the decrease in this allowance of $1 million from 2009 to 2010 affect net income?

    e. Colgate's income statement reports income tax expense of $1,117 million. Assume that cash paid for income tax is $1,123 million and that taxes payable increased by $64 million. Use the financial statement effects template to record tax expense for 2010. (*Hint*: Show the effects of changes in deferred taxes.)

E5-30. **Analyzing and Assessing Research and Development Expenses**   (LO2)

Advanced Micro Devices (AMD)
Intel Corp. (INTC)

Advanced Micro Devices (AMD) and Intel (INTC) are competitors in the computer processor industry. Following is a table ($ millions) of sales and R&D expenses for both companies.

AMD	R&D Expense	Sales	INTC	R&D Expense	Sales
2010	$1,405	$6,494	2010	$6,576	$43,623
2009	1,721	5,403	2009	5,653	35,127
2008	1,848	5,808	2008	5,722	37,586

    a. What percentage of sales are AMD and INTC spending on research and development?

    b. How are AMD and INTC's balance sheets and income statements affected by the accounting for R&D costs?

    c. How can one evaluate the effectiveness of R&D spending? Does the difference in R&D as a percentage of sales necessarily imply that one company is more heavily invested in R&D? Why might this not be the case?

E5-31. **Analyzing and Interpreting Foreign Currency Translation Effects**   (LO4)

Kellogg Co. (K)

Kellogg Co. reports the following table and discussion in its 2010 10-K.

The following tables provide an analysis of net sales and operating profit performance for 2010 versus 2009:

(Dollars in millions)	North America	Europe	Latin America	Asia Pacific	Corporate	Consolidated
2010 net sales	$8,402	$2,230	$923	$842	$—	$12,397
2009 net sales	$8,510	$2,361	$963	$741	$—	$12,575
% change—2010 vs. 2009:						
Volume (tonnage)	−2.5%	−2.4%	−3.4%	4.3%	—	−2.1%
Pricing/mix	0.6%	−0.3%	8.2%	−2.3%	—	0.8%
Subtotal—internal business	−1.9%	−2.7%	4.8%	2.0%	—	−1.3%
Foreign currency impact. . . .	0.6%	−2.8%	−8.9%	11.7%	—	−0.1%
Total change.	−1.3%	−5.5%	−4.1%	13.7%	—	−1.4%

(Dollars in millions)	North America	Europe	Latin America	Asia Pacific	Corporate	Consolidated
2010 operating profit	$1,554	$364	$153	$74	$(155)	$1,990
2009 operating profit	$1,569	$348	$179	$86	$(181)	$2,001
% change—2010 vs. 2009:						
Internal business.	−1.7%	8.2%	−2.4%	−29.5%	14.2%	−0.1%
Foreign currency impact. .	0.7%	−3.4%	−12.3%	15.2%	—	−0.5%
Total change.	−1.0%	4.8%	−14.7%	−14.3%	14.2%	−0.6%

Foreign exchange risk Our Company is exposed to fluctuations in foreign currency cash flows related to third-party purchases, intercompany transactions, and when applicable, nonfunctional currency denominated third-party debt. Our Company is also exposed to fluctuations in the value of foreign currency investments in subsidiaries and cash flows related to repatriation of these investments. Additionally, our Company is exposed to volatility in the translation of foreign currency earnings to U.S. Dollars. Primary exposures include the U.S. Dollar versus the British Pound, Euro, Australian Dollar, Canadian Dollar, and Mexican Peso, and in the case of inter-subsidiary transactions, the British Pound versus the Euro. We assess foreign currency risk based on transactional cash flows and translational volatility and enter into forward contracts, options, and currency swaps to reduce fluctuations in net long or short currency positions. Forward contracts and options are generally less than 18 months duration. Currency swap agreements are established in conjunction with the term of underlying debt issuances.

a. Before the effects of foreign currency rates, total consolidated sales decreased by 1.3% during 2010. What geographic segment accounted for this overall decline?

b. How did foreign currency exchange rates affect sales at each of the geographic segments? What can we infer about the strength of the U.S. dollar vis-à-vis the currencies in Kellogg's segments?

c. Operating profit declined modestly on a consolidated basis. Which geographic segments exhibited the lowest and which the highest change in profit during the year? Explain.

d. Describe how the accounting for foreign exchange translation affects reported sales and profits.

e. How does Kellogg Co. manage the risk related to its foreign exchange exposure? Describe the financial statement effects of this risk management activity.

E5-32. Interpreting Revenue Recognition for Gift Cards (LO1)

Footnotes to the 2010 annual report of Barnes & Noble disclose the following: Barnes & Noble (BKS)

The Barnes & Noble Member program entitles Members to receive the following benefits: 40% discount off the current hardcover Barnes & Noble store bestsellers, 20% discount off all adult hardcover books, 10% discount off Barnes & Noble sale price of other eligible items, unlimited free express shipping on orders made on Barnes & Noble.com, as well as periodic special promotions at Barnes & Noble stores and online at Barnes&Noble.com. The annual fee of $25.00 is non-refundable after the first 30 days. Revenue is recognized over the twelve-month period based upon historical spending patterns for Barnes & Noble Members.

a. Explain in layman terms how Barnes & Noble accounts for the cash received for its membership program. When does Barnes & Noble record revenue from this program?

b. How does Barnes & Noble's balance sheet reflect those membership fees?

c. Does the 40% discount affect Barnes & Noble's income statement when membership fees are received?

PROBLEMS

P5-33.   Analyzing and Interpreting Revenue Recognition Policies and Risks   {LO1}

Amazon.com (AMZN)

Amazon.com, Inc., provides the following explanation of its revenue recognition policies in its 10-K report.

> On January 1, 2010, we prospectively adopted ASU 2009-13, which amends Accounting Standards Codification ("ASC") Topic 605, Revenue Recognition. Under this new standard, we allocate revenue in arrangements with multiple deliverables using estimated selling prices (ESP) if we do not have vendor-specific objective evidence or third-party evidence of the selling prices of the deliverables. Estimated selling prices are management's best estimates of the prices that we would charge our customers if we were to sell the standalone elements separately.
>
> Sales of our Kindle e-reader are considered arrangements with multiple deliverables, consisting of the device, 3G wireless access and delivery for some models, and software upgrades. Under the prior accounting standard, we accounted for sales of the Kindle ratably over the average estimated life of the device. Accordingly, revenue and associated product cost of the device through December 31, 2009, were deferred at the time of sale and recognized on a straight-line basis over the two-year average estimated economic life.
>
> As of January 2010, we account for the sale of the Kindle as multiple deliverables. The revenue related to the device, which is the substantial portion of the total sale price, and related costs are recognized upon delivery. Revenue related to 3G wireless access and delivery and software upgrades is amortized over the average life of the device, which remains estimated at two years.
>
> Because we have adopted ASU 2009-13 prospectively, we are recognizing $508 million throughout 2010 and 2011 for revenue previously deferred under the prior accounting standard.

Required

a. What is a multiple-element contract? What product does Amazon sell that involves a multiple-element contract? Explain.

b. Explain how companies account for multiple-element contracts, in general.

c. Compare the accounting for the Kindle under the old and new accounting standards for revenue recognition. Amazon discloses that $508 million of previously deferred revenue will now be recognized earlier. Explain.

d. Assume that Amazon sells a Kindle with 3G capabilities for $180 and the company estimates a selling price (ESP) of $20 per unit for 3G access and future software upgrades. Compute the revenue that Amazon would recognize at the point of sale under the old and the new accounting standards.

e. Use the financial statement effects template to record the initial sale of a Kindle and the accounting adjustment required at the end of the first quarter for the new accounting standards.

P5-34.   Analyzing and Interpreting Income Tax Disclosures   {LO3}

Pfizer (PFE)

The 2010 income statement for **Pfizer** is reproduced in this module. Pfizer also reports the following footnote relating to its income taxes in its 2010 10-K report.

> **Deferred Taxes** Deferred taxes arise as a result of basis differentials between financial statement accounting and tax amounts. The tax effect of the major items recorded as deferred tax assets and liabilities, shown before jurisdictional netting, as of December 31 is as follows:

continued

(Millions of dollars)	2010 Deferred Tax Assets	(Liabilities)	2009 Deferred Tax Assets	(Liabilities)
Prepaid/deferred items.	$1,321	$ (112)	$1,330	$(60)
Inventories	132	(59)	437	(859)
Intangibles	1,165	(17,104)	949	(19,802)
Property, plant and equipment.	420	(2,146)	715	(2,014)
Employee benefits	4,479	(56)	4,786	(66)
Restructurings and other charges	1,359	(70)	884	(8)
Legal and product liability reserves	1,411	—	1,010	—
Net operating loss/credit carryforwards. . .	4,575	—	4,658	—
Unremitted earnings.	—	(9,524)	—	(7,057)
State and local tax adjustments.	452	—	747	—
All other	607	(575)	744	(187)
Subtotal	15,921	(29,646)	16,260	(30,053)
Valuation allowance	(894)	—	(353)	—
Total deferred taxes	$15,027	(29,646)	$15,907	(30,053)
Net deferred tax liability		$(14,619)		$(14,146)

Required

a. Describe the terms "deferred tax liabilities" and "deferred tax assets." Provide an example of how these accounts can arise.

b. Intangible assets (other than goodwill) acquired in the purchase of a company are depreciated (amortized) similar to buildings and equipment (see Module 7 for a discussion). Describe how the deferred tax liability of $17,104 million relating to intangibles arose.

c. Pfizer has many employee benefit plans, such as a long-term health plan and a pension plan. Some of these are generating deferred tax assets and others are generating deferred tax liabilities. Explain the timing of the recognition of expenses under these plans that would give rise to these different outcomes.

d. Pfizer reports a deferred tax liability labelled "unremitted earnings." This relates to an investment in an affiliated company for which Pfizer is recording income, but has not yet received dividends. Generally, investment income is taxed when received. Explain what information the deferred tax liability for unremitted earnings conveys.

e. Pfizer reports a deferred tax asset relating to net operating loss carryforwards. Explain what loss carryforwards are.

f. Pfizer reports a valuation allowance of $894 million in 2010. Explain why Pfizer has established this allowance and its effect on reported profit. Pfizer's valuation allowance was $353 million in 2009. Compute the change in its allowance during 2010 and explain how that change affected 2010 tax expense and net income.

P5-35. Analyzing and Interpreting Income Components and Disclosures (LO2)

The income statement for Xerox Corporation follows.

Xerox Corporation
(XRX)

Year ended December 31 (in millions)	2010	2009	2008
Revenue			
Equipment sales.	$ 3,857	$ 3,550	$ 4,679
Supplies, paper and other	3,377	3,096	3,646
Sales.	7,234	6,646	8,325
Service, outsourcing and rentals	13,739	7,820	8,485
Finance income	660	713	798
Total Revenues	21,633	15,179	17,608

continued

continued from prior page

Costs and Expenses			
Cost of sales.	4,741	4,395	5,519
Cost of service, outsourcing and rentals	9,195	4,488	4,929
Equipment financing interest	246	271	305
Research, development and engineering expenses	781	840	884
Selling, administrative and general expenses	4,594	4,149	4,534
Restructuring and asset impairment charges	483	(8)	429
Acquisition-related costs	77	72	—
Amortization of intangible assets	312	60	54
Other expenses, net	389	285	1,033
Total Costs and Expenses	20,818	14,552	17,687
Income (Loss) before Income Taxes, and Equity Income.	815	627	(79)
Income tax expense (benefit)	256	152	(231)
Equity in net income of unconsolidated affiliates.	78	41	113
Net income.	637	516	265
Less: Net income attributable to noncontrolling interests	31	31	35
Net income Attributable to Xerox	$ 606	$ 485	$ 230

Notes:

- The income statement includes sales of Xerox copiers and revenue earned by a finance subsidiary that provides loan and lease financing relating to the sales of those copiers.

- **Equity in net income of unconsolidated affiliates** refers to income Xerox has earned on investments in affiliated (but unconsolidated) companies.

Required

a. Xerox reports several sources of income. How should revenue be recognized for each of these business activities? Explain.

b. Compute the relative size of Sales revenue (total) and of revenue from Service, outsourcing and rentals. Hint: Scale each type of revenue by Total revenue. Which type of revenue grew more in 2010?

c. Xerox reports research, development and engineering expenses (R&D) each year. Compare R&D spending over the three years. Hint: Scale R&D by Total revenue each year. What might explain the change in 2010?

d. Xerox reports restructuring costs each year. (1) Describe the three typical categories of restructuring costs and the accounting for each. (2) How do you recommend treating these costs for analysis purposes? (3) Should regular recurring restructuring costs be treated differently than isolated occurrences of such costs for analysis purposes? (4) What does the $(8) expense in 2009 imply about one or more previous year's accruals?

e. Xerox reports $389 million in expenses in 2010 labeled as "Other expenses, net." How can a company use such an account to potentially obscure its actual financial performance?

P5-36.   Analyzing and Interpreting Income Tax Footnote   (LO3)

Ahold

Ahold, a grocery and retail company located in The Netherlands, reports the following footnote for income taxes in its 2010 annual report.

The following table specifies the current and deferred tax components of income taxes in the income statement:

For year ended (€ million)	2-Jan-11	3-Jan-10
Current income taxes		
Domestic taxes—the Netherlands	€169	€ 68
Foreign taxes		
United States	48	38
Europe—Other	4	11
Total current tax expense	221	117

continued

continued from prior page

Deferred income taxes		
Domestic taxes—the Netherlands	10	52
Foreign taxes		
United States	33	4
Europe—Other	7	(25)
Total deferred tax expense.	50	31
Total income tax expense.	€271	€148

The significant components of deferred income tax assets and liabilities are as follows, as of:

	2-Jan-11	3-Jan-10
Leases and financings	€222	€197
Pensions and other post-employment benefits	46	52
Provisions.	131	137
Derivatives and loans	7	6
Interest	35	36
Other.	52	27
Total gross temporary differences	493	455
Unrecognised temporary differences	(20)	(17)
Total recognised temporary differences.	473	438
Tax losses and credits	572	544
Unrecognised tax losses and credits.	(459)	(434)
Total recognised tax losses and credits.	113	110
Total deferred tax assets	586	548
Property, plant and equipment and intangible assets	(245)	(191)
Inventories	(103)	(92)
Other.	(5)	(9)
Total deferred tax liabilities.	(353)	(292)
Net deferred tax assets	€233	€256

Deferred income tax assets and liabilities are offset on the balance sheet when there is a legally enforceable right to offset current tax assets against current tax liabilities and when the deferred income taxes relate to income taxes levied by the same fiscal authority.

Required

a. What income tax expense does Ahold report in its 2010 income statement? How much of this expense is currently payable?

b. Ahold reports deferred tax liabilities relating to property, plant and equipment. Describe how these liabilities arise. How likely is it that these liabilities will be paid? Specifically, describe a scenario that will (i) defer these taxes indefinitely, and (ii) will result in these liabilities requiring payment within the near future.

c. Ahold reports a deferred tax asset relating to provisions. Footnotes to financial statements indicate that these provisions relate, in part, to self-insurance accruals. When a company self-insures, it does not purchase insurance from a third-party insurance company. Instead, it records an expense and related liability to reflect the probable payment of losses that can occur in the future. Explain why this accrual (provision) results in a deferred tax asset.

d. Ahold reports deferred tax assets relating to tax losses and credits. Explain how these arise and how they will result in a future benefit.

e. The company reports unrecognized temporary differences and unrecognized tax losses and credits. These are the IFRS equivalent of valuation allowances in U.S. GAAP. Why did the company set up these unrecognised portions of deferred tax assets? How did the increase in the combined unrecognized amounts from 2009 to 2010 affect net income? How can a company use these accounts to meet its income targets in a particular year?

P5-37.ᴬ **Analyzing and Interpreting Tax Footnote (Financial Statement Effects Template)** (LO3)

Under Armour, Inc., reports total tax expense of $40,442 (in thousands) on its income statement for year ended December 31, 2010, and paid cash of $38,773 (in thousands) for taxes. The tax footnote in the company's 10-K filing, reports the following deferred tax information.

Deferred tax assets and liabilities consisted of the following:

December 31 (In thousands)	2010	2009
Deferred tax assets		
State tax credits, net of federal tax impact	$ 1,750	$ —
Tax basis inventory adjustment	3,052	1,874
Inventory obsolescence reserves.	2,264	2,800
Allowance for doubtful accounts and other reserves.	8,996	7,042
Foreign net operating loss carryforward	10,917	9,476
Stock-based compensation.	8,790	5,450
Intangible asset	372	1,068
Deferred rent	2,975	1,728
Deferred compensation	1,449	1,105
Other.	2,709	3,151
Total deferred tax assets	43,274	33,694
Less: valuation allowance	(1,765)	—
Total net deferred tax assets	41,509	33,694
Deferred tax liabilities		
Prepaid expenses.	(1,865)	(1,133)
Property, plant and equipment.	(3,104)	(5,783)
Total deferred tax liabilities.	(4,969)	(6,916)
Total deferred tax assets, net.	$36,540	$26,778

Required

a. Under Armour's deferred tax assets increased during the most recent fiscal year. What explains the increase?

b. Did Under Armour's deferred tax liabilities increase or decrease during the most recent fiscal year? Explain how the change arose.

c. The company recorded a valuation allowance during 2010. This allowance relates to foreign net operating tax losses. Explain how tax losses give rise to deferred tax assets. Why does the company record a valuation account? What proportion of these losses, at December 31, 2010, does the company believe will likely expire unused?

d. Explain how the valuation allowance affected 2010 net income.

e. Use the financial statement effects template to record Under Armour's income tax expense for the fiscal year 2010 along with the changes in both deferred tax assets and liabilities. Assume that the amount needed to balance the tax transaction represents the amount payable to tax authorities.

P5-38. **Analyzing and Interpreting Restructuring Costs and Effects** (LO2)

Hewlett-Packard, Inc., reports the following footnote disclosure (excerpted) in its 2010 10-K relating to its restructuring programs.

Fiscal 2010 Acquisitions On July 1, 2010, HP completed the acquisition of Palm and initiated a plan to restructure the operations of Palm, including severance for Palm employees, contract cancellation costs and other items. The total expected cost of the plan is $46 million.

On April 12, 2010, HP completed the acquisition of 3Com. In connection with the acquisition, HP's management approved and initiated a plan to restructure the operation of 3Com, including

continued

severance costs and costs to vacate duplicative facilities. The total expected cost of the plan is $42 million. In fiscal 2010, HP recorded restructuring charges of approximately $18 million.

Fiscal 2010 ES Restructuring Plan On June 1, 2010, HP's management announced a plan to restructure its enterprise services business. The total expected cost of the plan that will be recorded as restructuring charges is approximately $1.0 billion, including severance costs to eliminate approximately 9,000 positions and infrastructure charges. For fiscal 2010, a restructuring charge of $650 million was recorded primarily related to severance costs. As of October 31, 2010, approximately 2,100 positions have been eliminated.

Fiscal 2009 Restructuring Plan In May 2009, HP's management approved and initiated a restructuring plan to structurally change and improve the effectiveness of several businesses. The total expected cost of the plan is $292 million in severance-related costs associated with the planned elimination of approximately 5,000 positions. As of October 31, 2010, approximately 4,200 positions had been eliminated.

Fiscal 2008 HP/EDS Restructuring Plan In connection with the acquisition of EDS on August 26, 2008, HP's management approved and initiated a restructuring plan to combine and align HP's services businesses, eliminate duplicative overhead functions and consolidate and vacate duplicative facilities. The restructuring plan is expected to be implemented over four years at a total expected cost of $3.4 billion.

The adjustments to the accrued restructuring expenses related to all of HP's restructuring plans described above for the twelve months ended October 31, 2010, were as follows:

In millions	Balance, October 31, 2009	Fiscal year 2010 charges (reversals)	Cash payments	Non-cash settlements & other adjustments	Balance, October 31, 2010
Fiscal 2010 acquisitions	$ —	$ 64	$ (20)	$ —	$ 44
Fiscal 2010 ES Plan:					
Severance	—	630	(55)	45	620
Infrastructure	—	20	(6)	(10)	4
Total 2010 ES Plan	—	650	(61)	35	624
Fiscal 2009 Plan	248	(5)	(177)	(9)	57
Fiscal 2008 HP/EDS Plan:					
Severance	747	236	(873)	(35)	75
Infrastructure	419	193	(185)	(19)	408
Total 2008 HP/EDS Plan	1,166	429	(1,058)	(54)	483
Total restructuring plans	$1,414	$1,138	$(1,316)	$(28)	$1,208

Required

a. Briefly describe the company's 2010 restructuring program. Provide two examples of common non-cash charges associated with corporate restructuring activities.

b. Using the financial statement effects template, show the effects on financial statements of the (1) 2010 restructuring charge of $1,138 million, and (2) 2010 cash payment of $1,316 million.

c. Assume that instead of accurately estimating the anticipated restructuring charge in 2010, the company overestimated them by $30 million. How would this overestimation affect financial statements in (1) 2010, and (2) 2011 when severance costs are paid in cash?

d. Consider the 2010 ES restructuring. The company reports that total charges will amount to $1 billion. What is the effect on the 2010 income statement from this restructuring? Why do investors care to know the total charge if it does not impact current-period earnings?

P5-39. Analyzing and Interpreting Income Tax Footnote (LO3)

Consider the following income tax footnote information for the E. I. du Pont de Nemours and Company. DuPont (DD)

Provision for Income Taxes

($ millions)	2010	2009	2008
Current tax expense (benefit)			
U.S. federal	$(109)	$23	$ 14
U.S. state and local	—	(9)	(3)
International	454	328	327
	345	342	338
Deferred tax expense (benefit)			
U.S. federal	245	57	210
U.S. state and local	3	1	—
International	66	15	(167)
	314	73	43
Provision for income taxes	$659	$415	$381

The significant components of deferred tax assets and liabilities are as follows:

($ millions)	2010 Asset	2010 Liability	2009 Asset	2009 Liability
Depreciation	$ —	$1,614	$ —	$1,515
Accrued employee benefits	3,731	81	3,899	98
Other accrued expenses	928	369	1,029	366
Inventories	273	154	197	148
Unrealized exchange gains	34	—	5	—
Tax loss/tax credit carryforwards/backs	2,680	—	3,023	—
Investment in subsidiaries and affiliates	41	279	45	275
Amortization of intangibles	53	636	80	558
Other	314	144	291	152
	8,054	$3,277	8,569	$3,112
Valuation allowance	(1,666)		(1,759)	
	$3,111		$3,698	

An analysis of the company's effective income tax rate (EITR) follows:

	2010	2009	2008
Statutory U.S. federal income tax rate	35.0%	35.0%	35.0%
Exchange gains/losses[1]	0.2	(2.6)	(0.2)
Domestic operations	(2.0)	(1.4)	(2.8)
Lower effective tax rates on international operations-net	(13.6)	(11.8)	(14.3)
Tax settlements	(1.8)	(0.2)	(1.8)
	17.8%	19.0%	15.9%

[1] Principally reflects the benefit of non-taxable exchange gains and losses resulting from remeasurement of foreign currency denominated monetary assets and liabilities.

Required

a. What is the total amount of income tax expense that DuPont reports in its 2010 income statement? What portion of this expense does DuPont expect to pay in 2011?

b. Explain how the deferred tax liability called "depreciation" arises. Under what circumstances will the company settle this liability? Under what circumstances might this liability be deferred indefinitely?

c. Explain how the deferred tax asset called "accrued employee benefits" arises. Why is it recognized as an asset?

d. Explain how the deferred tax asset called "tax loss/tax credit carryforwards/backs" arises. Under what circumstances will DuPont realize the benefits of this asset?

e. DuPont reports a 2010 valuation allowance of $1,666 million. How does this valuation allowance arise? How did the change in valuation allowance for 2010 affect net income? Valuation allowances typically relate to questions about the realizability of tax loss carryforwards. Under what circumstances might DuPont not realize the benefits of its tax loss carryforwards?

f. Dupont's footnote reports the effective income tax rates (EITR) for the three-year period. What explains the difference between the U.S. statutory rate and the company's EITR?

P5-40.   Assessing Revenue Recognition, R&D Expense, EPS, and Income Taxes (LO1, 2, 3, 5)
Following are the income statement and relevant footnotes from the 10-K of Intuit, Inc.   Intuit, Inc. (INTU)

INTUIT INC. CONSOLIDATED STATEMENTS OF OPERATIONS			
Twelve Months Ended July 31 (In millions, except per share amounts)	**2010**	**2009**	**2008**
Net revenue			
Product	$1,412	$1,376	$1,483
Service and other	2,043	1,733	1,510
Total net revenue	3,455	3,109	2,993
Costs and expenses			
Cost of revenue			
Cost of product revenue	144	156	154
Cost of service and other revenue	460	422	381
Amortization of acquired technology	49	59	55
Selling and marketing	976	907	841
Research and development	573	556	593
General and administrative	348	284	290
Amortization of other acquired intangible assets	42	42	35
Total costs and expenses	2,592	2,426	2,349
Operating income from continuing operations	863	683	644
Interest expense	(61)	(51)	(52)
Interest and other income	13	21	46
Gain on sale of outsourced payroll assets	—	—	52
Income from continuing operations before income taxes	815	653	690
Income tax provision	276	206	243
Net income from continuing operations	539	447	447
Net income (loss) from discontinued operations	35	—	30
Net income	$ 574	$ 447	$ 477
Basic net income per share from continuing operations	$ 1.71	$ 1.39	$ 1.36
Basic net income (loss) per share from discontinued operations	0.11	—	0.09
Basic net income per share	$ 1.82	$ 1.39	$ 1.45
Diluted net income per share from continuing operations	$ 1.66	$ 1.35	$ 1.32
Diluted net income (loss) per share from discontinued operations	0.11	—	0.09
Diluted net income per share	$ 1.77	$ 1.35	$ 1.41

The following table presents the composition of shares used in the computation of basic and diluted net income per share for the periods indicated.

Twelve Months Ended July 31 (In millions, except per share amounts)	**2010**	**2009**	**2008**
Denominator:			
Shares used in basic per share amounts:			
Weighted average common shares outstanding	316	322	329
Shares used in diluted per share amounts:			
Weighted average common shares outstanding	316	322	329
Dilutive common equivalent shares from stock options and restricted stock awards	9	8	10
Dilutive weighted average common shares outstanding	325	330	339

continued

continued from prior page

Revenue Recognition

We derive revenue from the sale of packaged software products, license fees, software subscriptions, product support, hosting services, payroll services, merchant services, professional services, transaction fees and multiple element arrangements that may include any combination of these items.

Product Revenue   We recognize revenue from the sale of our packaged software products and supplies when legal title transfers, which is generally when our customers download products from the Web, when we ship the products or, when products are delivered to retailers. We sell some products on consignment to certain retailers. We recognize revenue for these consignment transactions only when the end-user sale has occurred. For products that are sold on a subscription basis and include periodic updates, we recognize revenue ratably over the contractual time period.

Service Revenue   We recognize revenue from payroll processing and payroll tax filing services as the services are performed, provided we have no other remaining obligations to these customers.

Multiple Element Arrangements   We enter into certain revenue arrangements for which we are obligated to deliver multiple products and/or services (multiple elements). For these arrangements, which generally include software products, we allocate and defer revenue for the undelivered elements based on their vendor-specific objective evidence of fair value (VSOE). VSOE is the price charged when that element is sold separately. In situations where VSOE exists for all elements (delivered and undelivered), we allocate the total revenue to be earned under the arrangement among the various elements, based on their relative fair value.

Income Taxes

Differences between income taxes calculated using the federal statutory income tax rate of 35% and the provision for income taxes from continuing operations were as follows for the periods indicated:

Twelve Months Ended July 31 (In millions)	2010	2009	2008
Income from continuing operations before income taxes	$815	$653	$690
Statutory federal income tax	$285	$229	$242
State income tax, net of federal benefit	27	9	29
Federal research and experimentation credits	(8)	(20)	(7)
Domestic production activities deduction	(14)	(11)	(12)
Share-based compensation	4	4	—
Tax exempt interest	(2)	(5)	(12)
Effects of non-U.S. operations	(20)	—	—
Other, net	4	—	3
Total provision for income taxes from continuing operations	$276	$206	$243

Significant deferred tax assets and liabilities were as follows at the dates indicated:

July 31 (In millions)	2010	2009
Deferred tax assets		
Accruals and reserves not currently deductible	$ 30	$ 31
Deferred rent	10	12
Accrued and deferred compensation	18	1
Loss and tax credit carryforwards	63	46
Property and equipment	8	5
Share-based compensation	89	92
Other, net	4	11
Total deferred tax assets	222	198
Deferred tax liabilities		
Intangible assets	55	59
Other, net	1	5
Total deferred tax liabilities	56	64

continued

July 31 (In millions)	2010	2009
Total net deferred tax assets	166	134
Valuation allowance	(8)	(6)
Total net deferred tax assets, net of valuation allowance......	$158	$128

We have provided a valuation allowance related to the benefits of certain state and foreign net operating loss carryforwards that we believe are unlikely to be realized. The valuation allowance increased $2 million during the twelve months ended July 31, 2010, primarily due to state net operating loss carryforwards acquired in business combinations. These primarily California net operating loss carryforwards are unlikely to be realized as a result of the California legislation enacted in 2009 and effective for our fiscal 2012 which limits expected sources of future California taxable income for fiscal 2012 and beyond.

Required

a. Describe the differences in revenue recognition between product sales and after-sale services. How does the company recognize revenue for consignment sales? For products sold on a subscription basis? How is service revenue recognized?

b. Some of the company's sales involve multiple element arrangements. In general, what are these arrangements? How does the company account for such sales?

c. Intuit reports $573 million of Research and Development expense, up from $556 million in the prior year.

   i. What kind of research activities would we expect for a company like Intuit?

   ii. Given the kind of research activities described in part i, how does the accounting for Intuit's R&D costs differ from the way that those costs would have been accounted for had Intuit used IFRS for financial reporting?

d. Intuit's earnings per share (EPS) is $1.77 on a diluted basis, compared with its basic EPS of $1.82. What factor(s) accounts for this dilution?

e. Drawing on Intuit's income tax footnote, prepare a table in percentages showing computation of its effective tax rate for each of the three fiscal years. What tax-related items, if any, would we not expect to continue into fiscal year 2011?

f. Intuit reports deferred tax assets of $222 million.

   i. Describe how deferred tax assets relating to accruals arise.

   ii. Explain how deferred tax assets relating to loss carryforwards arise.

   iii. Intuit reports an increase of its deferred tax asset valuation allowance of $2 million in 2010. How does this affect Intuit's income?

P5-41. **Analyzing Unearned Revenue Disclosures** (LO1)

The following disclosures are from the August 29, 2010, annual report of Costco Wholesale Corporation.

Costco Wholesale (COST)

Revenue Recognition We generally recognize sales, net of estimated returns, at the time the member takes possession of merchandise or receives services. When we collect payment from customers prior to the transfer of ownership of merchandise or the performance of services, the amount received is generally recorded as deferred revenue on the consolidated balance sheets until the sale or service is completed. Membership fee revenue represents annual membership fees paid by our members. We account for membership fee revenue, net of estimated refunds, on a deferred basis, whereby revenue is recognized ratably over the one-year membership period.

Revenue ($ millions)	52 weeks ended August 29, 2010	52 weeks ended August 30, 2009	52 weeks ended August 31, 2008
Net sales..................	$76,255	$69,889	$70,977
Membership fees	1,691	1,533	1,506
Total revenue.............	$77,946	$71,422	$72,483

continued

continued from prior page

Current Liabilities ($ millions)	August 29, 2010	August 30, 2009
Short-term borrowings....................	$ 26	$ 16
Accounts payable........................	5,947	5,450
Accrued salaries and benefits	1,571	1,418
Accrued sales and other taxes.............	322	302
Deferred membership fees................	869	824
Current portion long-term debt	0	80
Other current liabilities...................	1,328	1,191
Total current liabilities..................	$10,063	$9,281

The components of the deferred tax assets and liabilities are as follows (in $ millions):

	August 29, 2010	August 30, 2009
Equity compensation	$112	$117
Deferred income/membership fees	118	94
Accrued liabilities and reserves	392	408
Other......................................	35	48
Total deferred tax assets	657	667
Property and equipment......................	414	403
Merchandise inventories	170	184
Total deferred tax liabilities..................	584	587
Net deferred tax assets	$ 73	$ 80

Required

a. Explain in layman terms how Costco accounts for the cash received for its membership fees.

b. Use the balance sheet information on Costco's Deferred Membership Fees liability account and its income statement revenues related to Membership Fees earned during 2010 to compute the cash that Costco received during 2010 for membership fees.

c. Use the financial statement effects template to show the effect of the cash Costco received during 2010 for membership fees and the recognition of membership fees revenue for 2010.

d. Costco reports a deferred tax asset related to deferred income/membership fees. Explain in layman terms how this asset arises. When will Costco receive the benefit associated with this asset?

IFRS APPLICATIONS

Dr. Reddy's Laboratories (RDY)

I5-42.   Assessing Research and Development Expenses   (LO2)

Dr. Reddy's Laboratories, an Indian pharmaceutical company whose stock is traded in the U.S., reports the following (summary) income statement (reported under IFRS).

Year Ended March 31 ($ millions)	2010
Revenues	$1,563
Cost of revenues	755
Selling, general and administrative	501
Research and development	84
Other (income) expense, net	179
Results from operations..................	$ 45*

*difference due to rounding

a. Compute the percent of revenues that Dr. Reddy's Laboratories spends on research and development (R&D). Compare this level of expenditure with the percentages for other companies that are discussed in the Business Insight box on page 5-4. How would you assess the appropriateness of its R&D expense level?

b. Describe how accounting for R&D expenditures affects Dr. Reddy's Laboratories' balance sheet and income statement. How would this accounting have been different if the company had reported under U.S. GAAP?

I5-43.   Assessing Research and Development Expenses   (LO2)

Finmeccanica S.p.A.

Headquartered in Rome, Italy, Finmeccanica S.p.A. is a multinational conglomerate operating in the defense and aerospace sectors. The company uses IFRS for its financial reports and disclosed the following in its 2010 annual report:

Development costs, net In € millions	December 31, 2010	December 31, 2009
Balance beginning of year	624	474
Development costs capitalised during the year	182	296
Amortisation	(68)	(84)
Impairment	(53)	(18)
Sales	(12)	(44)
Balance end of year	673	624

Required

a. Under IFRS, what six criteria did Finmeccanica have to meet in order to capitalize development costs?

b. The company reported total research and development R&D expenditures of €2,030 in 2010 and €1,982 in 2009. Assume that these amounts include the development costs capitalized during the year (above). What proportion of total R&D costs did the company capitalize in each year?

c. The development costs (intangible asset) is reduced by €53 in 2010 and €18 in 2009 for impairment. Explain how an intangible asset could become impaired. How did this impairment affect Finmeccanica's income statement in 2010? Is this an operating or a nonoperating item?

d. If Finmeccanica had always used U.S. GAAP to account for research and development costs, what would have been the difference in net income for 2010?

I5-44.   Assessing Research and Development Expenses   (LO2)

Finmeccanica S.p.A.

Headquartered in Rome, Italy, Finmeccanica S.p.A. is a multinational conglomerate operating in the defense and aerospace sectors. The company uses IFRS for its financial reports and disclosed the following in its 2010 annual report:

Research and development costs for Finmeccanica's Energy Sector for the year ended 31 December 2010 came to €38, up 6% over 2009 (€36). Research and development activities for the Energy Sector focused primarily on the following items in 2010:

- Gas turbines: AE94.3A turbine development projects to raise power, efficiency and operational flexibility, while complying with requirements on pollutants in exhaust gas, and projects to retrofit the AE94.2 turbine to increase the power and extend the life of the Class E turbine;
- Steam turbines: international projects investigating the behaviour of special materials (extremely high temperature steels and super alloys) with a view to developing the "ultrasupercritical" turbine (with a power rating in excess of 300 MW);
- Generators: development work on the new air-cooled 400-MVA model intended to complement the large, high-performance gas turbines.

Required

a. How are R&D costs accounted for under IFRS?

b. For each of the three energy sector R&D items described above, determine if the item meets the criteria for capitalization under IFRS.

I5-45.   Analyzing Unearned Revenue Transactions and Multiple-Element Arrangements   (LO1)

Research in Motion (RIMM)

Research in Motion reports the following financial statement data and footnote information.

Research in Motion Limited Consolidated Statements of Operations (USD $)			
	12 Months Ended		
In Millions, except per share data	Feb. 26, 2011	Feb. 27, 2010	Feb. 28, 2009
Revenue			
Hardware and other	$16,416	$12,536	$ 9,411
Service and software	3,491	2,417	1,654
Total revenue	19,907	14,953	11,065
Cost of sales			
Hardware and other	10,516	7,979	5,718
Service and software	566	390	250
Total cost of sales.	11,082	8,369	5,968
Gross margin	8,825	6,584	5,097
Operating expenses			
Research and development	1,351	965	685
Selling, marketing and administration . . .	2,400	1,907	1,495
Amortization	438	310	195
Litigation.	0	164	0
Total operating expenses	4,189	3,346	2,375
Income from operations	4,636	3,238	2,722
Investment income, net	8	28	79
Income before income taxes	4,644	3,266	2,801
Provision for income taxes.	1,233	809	908
Net income.	$ 3,411	$ 2,457	$ 1,893
Earnings per share			
Basic.	6.36	4.35	3.35
Diluted	6.34	4.31	3.30

Revenue Recognition

Multiple-element arrangements   The Company enters into revenue arrangements that may consist of multiple deliverables of its product and service offerings. The Company's typical multiple-element arrangements involve: (i) handheld devices with services and (ii) software with technical support services.

For the Company's arrangements involving multiple deliverables of handheld devices with services, the consideration from the arrangement is allocated to each respective element based on its relative selling price, using vendor-specific objective evidence of selling price (VSOE). In certain limited instances when the Company is unable to establish the selling price using VSOE, the Company attempts to establish selling price of each element based on acceptable third party evidence of selling price (TPE); however, the Company is generally unable to reliably determine the selling prices of similar competitor products and services on a stand-alone basis. In these instances, the Company uses best estimated selling price (BESP) in its allocation of arrangement consideration. The objective of BESP is to determine the price at which the Company would transact a sale if the product or service was sold on a stand-alone basis.

The Company regularly reviews VSOE, TPE and BESP, and maintains internal controls over the establishment and updates of these estimates. There were no material impacts to the amount of revenue recognized during the year, nor does the Company expect a material impact in the near term, from changes in VSOE, TPE or BESP.

Required

a. Research in Motion has sales contracts that consist of multiple deliverables bundled for one price. What are the two typical deliverables?

b. The footnotes report that, "Price protection is accrued as a reduction to revenue based on estimates of future price reductions, provided the price reduction can be reliably estimated and all other revenue recognition criteria have been met." Assume that the company believes that prices on the current Blackberry models will decrease by 10% in the coming year. Explain how the company would record this fact.

c. Explain in layman terms how Research in Motion records revenue from sales of bundled hardware and software.

d. Assume that a customer makes a volume purchase of 200 Blackberry Playbook tablets. The total discounted sales price is $480 per unit and the sale is on account. Because there is no reliable VSOE, RIM estimates a BESP of $476 for the hardware and services and of $84 for the software technical support. This second deliverable involves free future software upgrades for two years. Allocate the consideration received for the 200 units to each respective element in the arrangement, based on its relative selling price.

e. Use the financial statement effects template to record the original sale in part d., above, and the accounting adjustment at the end of the first fiscal year after the sale.

f. The income statement reports two types of revenue. Compare the relative magnitude of each revenue type. Hint: Scale each by total revenues.

g. The income statement reports cost of sales for both types of revenue. Which of the two has a higher gross margin? Explain why this might be the case.

MANAGEMENT APPLICATIONS

MA5-46. Managing Foreign Currency Risk   (LO4)

Fluctuations in foreign currency exchange rates can result in increased volatility of revenues, expenses, and profits. Companies generally attempt to reduce this volatility.

a. Identify two possible solutions to reduce the volatility effect of foreign exchange rate fluctuations.

b. What costs would arise if you implemented each of your solutions?

MA5-47. Ethics and Governance: Revenue Recognition   (LO1)

GAAP offers latitude in determining when revenue is earned. Assume that a company that normally required acceptance by its customers prior to recording revenue as earned, delivers a product to a customer near the end of the quarter. The company believes that customer acceptance is assured, but cannot obtain it prior to quarter-end. Recording the revenue would assure "making its numbers" for the quarter. Although formal acceptance is not obtained, the sales person records the sale, fully intending to obtain written acceptance as soon as possible.

a. What are the revenue recognition requirements in this case?

b. What are the ethical issues relating to this sale?

c. Assume you are on the board of directors of this company. What safeguards can you put in place to provide assurance that the company's revenue recognition policy is followed?

MA5-48. Ethics and Governance: Earnings Management   (LO2)

Assume that you are CEO of a company. Your company has reported a loss for the current year. Since it cannot carry back the entire loss to recoup taxes paid in prior years, it records a loss carryforward as a deferred tax asset. Your expectation is that future profitability will be sufficient to realize the tax benefits of the carryforward. Your chief financial officer approaches you with an idea to create a deferred tax valuation allowance that will reduce the deferred tax asset, increase tax expense for the year, and increase your reported loss. He reasons that the company's stock price will not be reduced markedly by the additional reported loss since a loss year has already been factored into the current price. Further, this deferred tax valuation allowance will create a reserve that can be used in future years to increase profit (via reversal of the allowance) if needed to meet analyst expectations.

a. What stakeholders are potentially affected by the CFO's proposal?

b. How do you respond to the proposal? Justify your response.

SOLUTIONS TO REVIEW PROBLEMS

Mid-Module Review 1

Solution

1. Revenues are only recognized when the earning process is complete. Merck delivers its product before the customer is obligated to make payment. Passage of title typically constitutes delivery. Merck's policy appears to be reasonable given its product and GAAP requirements.

2. All R&D related equipment and/or facilities that have no alternative use must be expensed under GAAP. Assets that have other uses are capitalized and depreciated like other plant assets. R&D costs are aggregated into one line item (research and development expense) on Merck's income statement. Other costs are reported under materials and production and/or marketing and administrative expenses.

3. Restructuring expenses generally fall into three categories: severance costs, asset write-offs, and other costs. Restructuring programs must be approved by the board of directors before they are recognized in financial statements. Further, companies are required to disclose the initial liability accrual together with the portion that was subsequently utilized or reversed, if any. Because the restructuring accrual is an estimate, overestimates and subsequent reversals are possible. Should the company develop a reputation for recurring reversals, it will lose credibility with analysts and other stakeholders.

Mid-Module Review 2

Solution
1. Total income tax expense is $671 million.
2. $1,763 million is currently payable or has already been paid during 2010.
3. Income tax expense is the sum of current taxes (that is, currently payable as determined from the company's tax returns) plus the change in deferred tax assets and liabilities. It is a calculated figure, not a percentage that is applied to pretax income. For 2010, reported tax expense was *reduced* by the deferred provision (a liability) of $1,092 million.

Module-End Review

Solution
1. Income statement accounts that are denominated in foreign currencies must be translated into $US before the financial statements are publicly disclosed. When the $US weakens, each foreign currency unit is worth more $US. Consequently, each account in Merck's income statement is larger because the dollar weakened. Because Merck reported *positive* earnings (a profit) for 2010, net income also would be larger.

2. Basic earnings per share is equal to net income (less preferred dividends) divided by the weighted average number of common shares outstanding during the period. Diluted EPS considers the effects of dilutive securities. In diluted EPS, the denominator increases by the additional shares that would have been issued assuming exercise of all options and conversion of all convertible securities. The numerator is also adjusted for any preferred dividends and/or interest that would not have been paid upon conversion.

Getty Images

Cisco Systems

Cisco Systems, Inc., manufactures and sells networking and communications products for transporting data, voice, and video within buildings, across town, and around the world. Cisco's products are everywhere; here are a few applications:

- Schoolchildren can view a virtual science experiment from a neighborhood center's Cisco-outfitted computer room.

- Airline passengers can check flight information and print boarding passes at convenient Cisco kiosks.

- Hospital nurses check medication levels at patients' bedsides using Cisco handheld devices and wireless networks.

- Auto designers in Japan, assembly technicians in the U.S., and component makers worldwide exchange manufacturing data over a Cisco network in real time.

- Police rely on citywide Cisco wireless networks to deliver fingerprint files, mug shots, and voicemail to mobile units.

- Customers call their banks' Cisco Internet Protocol (IP) based center, where account profiles appear to call agents.

- Companies shore up their databases with Cisco network security.

Cisco reported 2010 net income of $7.7 billion on $40 billion in sales, and a return on net operating assets (RNOA) of 45%. In 2001, Cisco reported a *loss* of $1 billion after recording $2.25 billion of restructuring costs, including costs related to the severance of 6,000 employees and the write-off of obsolete inventory and other assets.

Cisco's turnaround is remarkable. Sales have increased by over 60% in the past five years, and its return on net operating assets has remained at over 40% during this period, which reflects Cisco's effective asset (balance sheet) management. Recall that RNOA comprises both a profitability component and a productivity component (see Module 4). The productivity component (reflected in net operating asset turnover, NOAT) is measured as sales divided by average net operating assets. Effective management of operating assets is crucial to achieving a high RNOA. We focus on three important operating assets in this module: accounts receivable, inventories, and property, plant and equipment (PPE).

As part of their overall marketing efforts, companies extend credit to customers. At Cisco, for example, accounts receivable are an important asset because nearly all sales are on account. While favorable credit terms stimulate sales, the resulting accounts receivable are costly. First, accounts receivable are generally non-interest bearing and tie up a company's working capital in non-earning assets.

Reporting and Analyzing Operating Assets

LEARNING OBJECTIVES

LO1 Describe accounting for accounts receivable and the importance of the allowance for uncollectible accounts in determining profit. (p. 6-3)

LO2 Explain accounting for inventories and assess the effects on the balance sheet and income statement from different inventory costing methods. (p. 6-13)

LO3 Describe accounting for property, plant and equipment and explain the impacts on profit and cash flows from depreciation methods, disposals and impairments. (p. 6-26)

Second, receivables expose the company to collectibility risk—the risk that some customers won't pay. Third, companies incur the administrative costs associated with billing and collection. These costs must be weighed against the costs of other marketing tools, like advertising, sales incentives, and price discounts. Management of receivables is critical to financial success.

Inventories are significant assets at many companies, particularly for manufacturers such as Cisco, where inventories consist of raw materials (the basic product inputs), work in process (the cost of partially completed products), and finished goods (completed products awaiting sale). Inventories are also costly to maintain. The cost of buying and manufacturing the goods must be financed and inventories must be stored, moved, and insured. Consequently, companies prefer lower inventory levels whenever possible. However, companies must be careful to hold enough inventory. If they reduce inventory quantities too far, they risk inventory stock-outs, that is, not having enough inventory to meet demand. Management of inventories is also a critical activity.

Property, plant and equipment (PPE) is often the largest, and usually the most important, asset on the balance sheet. Companies need administrative offices, IT

and R&D facilities, regional sales and customer service offices, manufacturing and distribution facilities, vehicles, computers, and a host of other fixed assets. Fixed asset costs are substantial and are indirectly linked to sales and profits. Consequently, fixed-asset investments are often difficult to justify and, once acquired, fixed assets are often difficult to divest. Effective management of PPE assets usually requires management review of the entire value chain.

John Chambers, CEO of Cisco, recalls a conversation he once had with the legendary Jack Welch, former Chairman of GE. Following Cisco's announced restructuring program in 2001, Welch commented, "John, you'll never have a great company until you go through the really tough times. What builds a company is not just how you handle the successes, but it's the way you handle the real challenges." Cisco survived the tech bubble burst and is now reporting impressive financial results. To ensure future financial performance, however, Cisco must effectively manage both its income statement and its operating assets.

Sources: *BusinessWeek,* 2012, 2006 and 2003; Cisco Systems 10-K, 2011; Cisco Systems Annual Report, 2011; *Fortune,* April 2009.

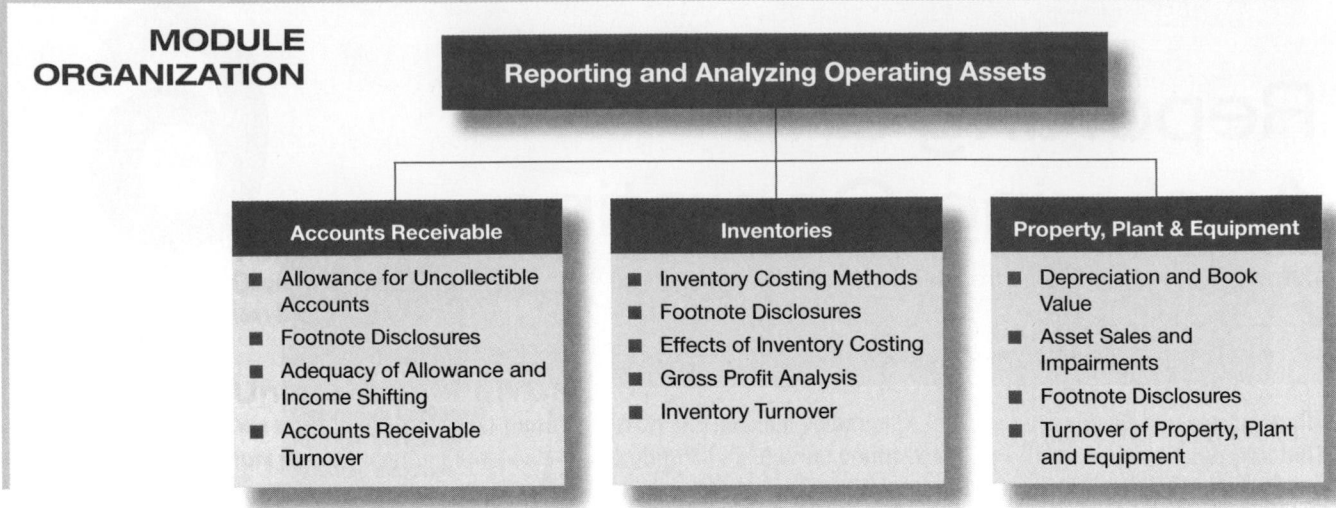

Managing net operating assets is crucial to creating shareholder value. To manage and assess net operating assets, we need to understand how they are measured and reported. This module describes the reporting and measuring of operating working capital, mainly receivables and inventories, and of long-term operating assets such as property, plant, and equipment. We do not discuss other long-term operating assets, such as equity investments in affiliated companies, investment in intangible assets, and nonoperating investments in marketable securities, as they are covered in other modules.

Receivables are usually a major part of operating working capital. They must be carefully managed as they represent a substantial asset for most companies and are an important marketing tool. GAAP requires companies to report receivables at the amount they expect to collect. This requires estimation of uncollectible accounts. The receivables reported on the balance sheet, and the expenses reported on the income statement, reflect management's estimate of uncollectible amounts. Accordingly, it is important that companies accurately assess uncollectible accounts and timely report them. It is also necessary that readers of financial reports understand management's accounting choices and their effects on reported balance sheets and income statements.

Inventory is another major component of operating working capital. Inventories usually constitute one of the three largest assets (along with receivables and long-term operating assets). Also, cost of goods sold, which flows from inventory, is the largest expense category for retailing and manufacturing companies. GAAP allows several methods for inventory accounting, and inventory-costing choices can markedly impact balance sheets and income statements, especially for companies experiencing relatively high inflation, coupled with slowly turning inventories.

Long-term plant assets are often the largest component of operating assets. Indeed, long-term operating assets are typically the largest asset for manufacturing companies, and their related depreciation expense is typically second only in amount to cost of goods sold in the income statement. GAAP allows different accounting methods for computing depreciation, which can significantly impact the income statement and the balance sheet. When companies dispose of fixed assets, a gain or loss may result. Understanding these gains and losses on asset sales is important as we assess performance. Further, asset write-downs (impairments) not only affect companies' current financial performance, but also future profitability. We must understand these effects when we forecast future income statements. This module considers all of these fixed asset accounting choices and consequences.

LO1 Describe accounting for accounts receivable and the importance of the allowance for uncollectible accounts in determining profit.

ACCOUNTS RECEIVABLE

Our focus on operating assets begins with accounts receivable. To help frame our discussion, we refer to the following graphic as we proceed through the module:

Income Statement	Balance Sheet	
Sales	Cash	Current liabilities
Cost of goods sold	Accounts receivable, net	Long-term liabilities
Selling, general & administrative	Inventory	
Income taxes	Property, plant, and equipment, net	Shareholders' equity
Net income	Investments	

The graphic highlights the balance sheet and income statement effects of accounts receivable. This section explains the accounting, reporting, and analysis of these highlighted items.

Retail companies transact mostly in cash. But other companies, including those that sell to other firms, usually do not expect cash upon delivery. Instead, they offer credit terms and have *credit sales* or *sales on account*.[1] An account receivable on the seller's balance sheet is always matched by a corresponding account payable on the buyer's balance sheet. Accounts receivable are reported on the seller's balance sheet at *net realizable value*, which is the net amount the seller expects to collect.

Sellers do not expect to collect all accounts receivable; they anticipate that some buyers will be unable to pay their accounts when they come due. For example, buyers can suffer business downturns that limit the cash available to meet liabilities. Then, buyers must decide which liabilities to pay. Typically, financially distressed companies decide to pay off liabilities to the IRS, to banks, and to bondholders because those creditors have enforcement powers and can quickly seize assets and disrupt operations, leading to bankruptcy and eventual liquidation. Buyers also try to cover their payroll, as they cannot exist without employees. Then, if there is cash remaining, buyers will pay suppliers to ensure continued flow of goods.

Accounts payable are *unsecured liabilities,* meaning that buyers have not pledged collateral to guarantee payment of amounts owed. As a result, when a company declares bankruptcy, accounts payable are comingled with other unsecured creditors (after the IRS and the secured creditors), and are typically not paid in full. Consequently, there is risk in the collectibility of accounts receivable. This *collectibility risk* is crucial to analysis of accounts receivable.

Cisco reports $4,929 million of accounts receivable in the current asset section of its fiscal year-end 2010 balance sheet.

$ millions	July 31, 2010
Cash and cash equivalents	$ 4,581
Investments	35,280
Accounts receivable, net of allowance for doubtful accounts of $235	4,929
Inventories	1,327
Deferred tax assets	2,126
Other current assets	3,178
Total current assets	$51,421

Cisco reports its receivables net of allowances for doubtful (uncollectible) accounts of $235 million. This means the total amount owed to Cisco is $5,164 million ($4,929 million + $235 million), but Cisco *estimates* that $235 million are uncollectible and reports on its balance sheet only the amount it expects to collect.

We might ask why buyers would sell to companies from whom they do not expect to collect. The answer is they would not have extended credit *if* they knew beforehand which companies would eventually not pay. For example, Cisco probably cannot identify precisely those companies that constitute the $235 million in uncollectible accounts. Yet, it knows from past experience that a certain portion of its

---

[1] An example of common credit terms are 2/10, net 30. These terms indicate that the seller offers the buyer an early-pay incentive, in this case a 2% discount off the cost if the buyer pays within 10 days of billing. If the buyer does not take advantage of the discount, it must pay 100% of the invoice cost within 30 days of billing. From the seller's standpoint, offering the discount is often warranted because it speeds up cash collections and then the seller can invest the cash to yield a return greater than the early-payment discount. The buyer often wishes to avail itself of attractive discounts even if it has to borrow money to do so. If the discount is not taken, however, the buyer should withhold payment as long as possible (at least for the full net period) so as to maximize its available cash. Meanwhile, the seller will exert whatever pressure it can to collect the amount due as quickly as possible. Thus, it is normal for there to be some tension between sellers and buyers.

receivables will prove uncollectible. GAAP requires companies to estimate the dollar amount of uncollectible accounts (even if managers cannot identify specific accounts that are uncollectible), and to report accounts receivable at the resulting *net realizable value* (total receivables less an allowance for uncollectible accounts).

Allowance for Uncollectible Accounts

Companies typically use an *aging analysis* to estimate the amount of uncollectible accounts. This requires an analysis of receivables as of the balance sheet date. Specifically, customer accounts are categorized by the number of days that the related invoices have been unpaid (outstanding). Based on prior experience, or on other available statistics, uncollectible percentages are applied to each category, with larger percentages applied to older accounts. The result of this analysis is a dollar amount for the allowance for uncollectible accounts (also called allowance for doubtful accounts) at the balance sheet date.

Aging Analysis

To illustrate, Exhibit 6.1 shows an aging analysis for a seller with $100,000 of gross accounts receivable at period-end. The current accounts are those that are still within their original credit period. As an example, if a seller's credit terms are 2/10, net 30, all invoices that have been outstanding for 30 days or fewer are current. Accounts listed as 1–60 days past due are those 1 to 60 days past their due date. This would include an account that is 45 days outstanding for a net 30-day invoice. This same logic applies to all categories.

EXHIBIT 6.1	Aging of Accounts Receivable		
Age of Accounts	**Receivable Balance**	**Estimated Percent Uncollectible**	**Estimated Uncollectible Accounts**
Current	$ 50,000	2%	$1,000
1-60 days past due	30,000	3	900
61-90 days past due	15,000	4	600
Over 90 days past due	5,000	8	400
Total	$100,000		$2,900

Exhibit 6.1 also reflects the seller's experience with uncollectible accounts, which manifests itself in the uncollectible percentages for each aged category. For example, on average, 3% of buyers' accounts that are 1–60 days past due prove uncollectible for this seller. Hence, the company estimates a potential loss of $900 for the $30,000 in receivables 1 to 60 days past due.

Reporting Receivables

The seller represented in Exhibit 6.1 reports its accounts receivable on the balance sheet as follows:

Accounts receivable, net of $2,900 in allowances $97,100

Assume that, as of the end of the *previous* accounting period, the company had estimated total uncollectible accounts of $2,200 based on an aging analysis of the receivables at that time. Also assume that the company did not write off any accounts receivable during the period. The *reconciliation* of its allowance account for the period follows:

Beginning allowance for uncollectible accounts . . . . $ 2,200
Add: Provision for uncollectible accounts (bad debts expense)   700
Less: Write-offs of accounts receivable   0
Ending allowance for uncollectible accounts . . . . $ 2,900

The aging analysis revealed that the allowance for uncollectible accounts is $700 too low and therefore, the company increased the allowance accordingly. This adjustment affects the financial statements as follows:

1. Accounts receivable are reduced by an additional $700 on the balance sheet (receivables are reported *net* of the allowance account).

2. A $700 expense, called bad debts expense, is reported in the income statement (usually part of SG&A expense). This reduces pretax profit by the same amount.[2]

The allowance for uncollectible accounts, a contra-asset account, increases with new provisions (additional bad debts expense) and decreases as accounts are written off. Individual accounts are written off when the seller identifies them as uncollectible. (A write-off reduces both accounts receivable and the allowance for uncollectible accounts as described below.) As with all permanent accounts on the balance sheet, the ending balance of the allowance account is the beginning balance for next period.

Writing Off Accounts

To illustrate the write-off of an account receivable, assume that subsequent to the period-end shown above, the seller receives notice that one of its customers, owing $500 at the time, has declared bankruptcy. The seller's attorneys believe that legal costs in attempting to collect this receivable would likely exceed the amount owed. So, the seller decides not to pursue collection and to write off this account. The write-off has the following effects:

1. Gross accounts receivable are reduced from $100,000 to $99,500.

2. Allowance for uncollectible accounts is reduced from $2,900 to $2,400.

After the write-off, the seller's balance sheet appears as follows:

Accounts receivable, net of $2,400 in allowances. $97,100

Exhibit 6.2 shows the effects of this write-off on the individual accounts.

EXHIBIT 6.2 Effects of an Accounts Receivable Write-Off			
Account	Before Write-Off	Effects of Write-Off	After Write-Off
Accounts receivable.	$100,000	$(500)	$99,500
Less: Allowance for uncollectible accounts.	2,900	(500)	2,400
Accounts receivable, net of allowance.	$ 97,100		$97,100

The balance of net accounts receivable is the same before and after the write-off. This is always the case. The write-off of an account is a non-event from an accounting point of view. That is, total assets do not change, liabilities stay the same, and equity is unaffected as there is no net income effect. The write-off affects individual asset accounts, but not total assets.

Let's next consider what happens when additional information arrives that alters management's expectations of uncollectible accounts. To illustrate, assume that sometime after the write-off above, the seller realizes that it has underestimated uncollectible accounts and that $3,000 (not $2,400) of the remaining $99,500 accounts receivable are uncollectible. The company must increase the allowance for uncollectible accounts by $600. The additional $600 provision has the following financial statement effects:

1. Allowance for uncollectible accounts increases by $600 to the revised estimated balance of $3,000; and accounts receivable (net of the allowance for uncollectible accounts) declines by $600 from $97,100 to $96,500 (or $99,500 − $3,000).

2. A $600 bad debts expense is added to the income statement, which reduces pretax income. Recall that in the prior period, the seller reported $700 of bad debts expense when the allowance account was increased from $2,200 to $2,900.

---

[2] Companies can also estimate uncollectible accounts using the *percentage of sales* method. The percentage of sales method computes bad debts expense directly, as a percentage of sales and the allowance for uncollectible accounts is estimated indirectly. In contrast, the aging method computes the allowance balance directly and the bad debts expense is the amount required to bring the allowance account up to (or down to) the amount determined by the aging analysis. To illustrate, if the company in Exhibit 6.1 reports sales of $100,000 and estimates the provision at 1% of sales, it would report a bad debts expense of $1,000 and an allowance balance of $3,200 instead of the $700 bad debts expense and the $2,900 allowance as determined using the aging analysis. The two methods nearly always report different values for the allowance, net accounts receivable, and bad debts expense.

Analyzing Receivable Transactions

To summarize, recording bad debts expense increases the allowance for uncollectible accounts, which affects both the *balance sheet* and *income statement*. Importantly, the financial statement effects occur when the allowance is estimated, and not when accounts are written off. In this way, bad debts expense is matched with sales on the income statement, and accounts receivable are reported net of uncollectible accounts on the balance sheet. Exhibit 6.3 illustrates each of the transactions discussed in this section using the financial statement effects template:

EXHIBIT 6.3   Financial Statement Effects of Key Accounts Receivable Transactions

		Balance Sheet				Income Statement		
Transaction	Cash Asset	+ Noncash Assets	= Liabil- ities	+ Contrib. Capital	+ Earned Capital	Rev- enues	− Expen- ses	= Net Income
a. Credit sales of $100,000		+100,000 Accounts Receivable =			+100,000 Retained Earnings	+100,000 Sales	−	= +100,000
b. Increase allowance for uncollectible accounts by $700		−700 Allowance for Uncollectible Accounts =			−700 Retained Earnings		+700 − Bad Debts Expense	= −700
c. Write off $500 in accounts receivable		−500 Accounts Receivable +500 = Allowance for Uncollectible Accounts					−	=
d. Increase allowance for uncollectible accounts by $600		−600 Allowance for Uncollectible Accounts =			−600 Retained Earnings		+600 − Bad Debts Expense	= −600

Left margin T-accounts:

AR 100,000 | Sales 100,000

AR
100,000 |
Sales
| 100,000

BDE 700 | AU 700

BDE
700 |
AU
| 700

AU 500 | AR 500

AU
500 |
AR
| 500

BDE 600 | AU 600

BDE
600 |
AU
| 600

Footnote and MD&A Disclosures

To illustrate the typical accounts receivable disclosure, consider Cisco's discussion of its allowance for uncollectible accounts (from its MD&A):

Allowances for Receivables and Sales Returns

The allowances for receivables were as follows (in millions, except percentages):

	July 31, 2010	July 25, 2009
Allowance for doubtful accounts	$235	$216
Percentage of gross accounts receivable	4.6%	6.4%
Allowance for lease receivables	$207	$213
Percentage of gross lease receivables	8.6%	10.7%
Allowance for loan receivables	$ 73	$ 88
Percentage of gross loan receivables	5.8%	10.2%

The allowances are based on our assessment of the collectibility of customer accounts. We regularly review the adequacy of these allowances by considering factors such as historical experience, credit quality, age of the receivable balances, and economic conditions that may affect a customer's

continued

ability to pay. In addition, we perform credit reviews and statistical portfolio analysis to assess the credit quality of our receivables. We also consider the concentration of receivables outstanding with a particular customer in assessing the adequacy of our allowances. Our allowance percentages declined in fiscal 2010 compared with fiscal 2009 due to improved portfolio management as we moved out of the challenging economic environment in fiscal 2009. Our allowance percentages for accounts receivable and lease receivables represent a return to approximately the levels we experienced prior to fiscal 2009, consistent with changes we have observed in the macroeconomic environment. If a major customer's creditworthiness deteriorates, or if actual defaults are higher than our historical experience, or if other circumstances arise, our estimates of the recoverability of amounts due to us could be overstated, and additional allowances could be required, which could have an adverse impact on our revenue.

Cisco's allowance for uncollectible accounts decreased as a percentage of gross receivables from the prior year, from 6.4% to 4.6%. As the economy emerged from recession in 2010, Cisco estimated that collectibility of its receivables would improve and then reduced its estimate of uncollectible accounts. This reduction increased income for that year. However, Cisco alludes to the level of estimation required and cautions the reader that additional allowances (provisions) could be required under certain circumstances, and that would adversely affect profit.

Cisco provides a footnote reconciliation of its allowance for uncollectible (doubtful) accounts for the past three years as shown in Exhibit 6.4.

EXHIBIT 6.4 Reconciliation of Cisco's Allowance for Uncollectible Accounts	
$ millions	**Allowance for Doubtful Accounts**
Year ended July 26, 2008	
Balance at beginning of fiscal year	$166
Provision	34
Write-offs and other	(23)
Balance at end of fiscal year	$177
Year ended July 25, 2009	
Balance at beginning of fiscal year	$177
Provision	54
Write-offs and other	(15)
Balance at end of fiscal year	$216
Year ended July 31, 2010	
Balance at beginning of fiscal year	$216
Provision	44
Write-offs and other	(25)
Balance at end of fiscal year	$235

Reconciling Cisco's allowance account provides insight into the level of the provision (expense) each year relative to the actual write-offs. Over the three-year period ended in 2010, Cisco wrote off $63 million of uncollectible accounts ($23 million + $15 million + $25 million) and increased its allowance by $132 million ($34 million + $54 million + $44 million), resulting in a net increase of $69 million ($235 million − $166 million). The allowance for uncollectible accounts as a percentage of gross accounts receivable was 4.6% in 2010, as the economy emerged from recession, about the same level that Cisco reported in 2008 as the economy entered recession.

Analysis Implications

This section considers analysis of accounts receivable and the allowance for uncollectible accounts.

Adequacy of Allowance Account

A company makes two representations when reporting accounts receivable (net) in the current asset section of its balance sheet:

1. It expects to collect the amount reported on the balance sheet (remember, accounts receivable are reported net of allowance for uncollectible accounts).
2. It expects to collect the amount within the next year (implied by the classification of accounts receivable as a current asset).

From an analysis viewpoint, we scrutinize the adequacy of a company's provision for its uncollectible accounts. If the provision is inadequate, the cash ultimately collected will be less than the net receivables reported on the balance sheet.

How can an outsider assess the adequacy of the allowance account? One answer is to compare the allowance account to gross accounts receivable for the company and for its competitors. For Cisco, the 2010 percentage is 4.6% (see above), a 28% decline from the level it reported in 2009. What does such a decline signify? Perhaps the overall economic environment has improved, rendering write-offs less likely. Perhaps the company has improved its credit underwriting or receivables collection efforts. The MD&A section of the 10-K report is likely to discuss such new initiatives. Or perhaps the company's customer mix has changed and it is now selling to more creditworthy customers (or, it eliminated a risky class of customers).

The important point is that we must be comfortable with the percentage of uncollectible accounts reported by the company. We must remember that management controls the size of the allowance account—albeit with audit assurances.

Income Shifting

We noted that the financial statement effects of uncollectible accounts transpire when the allowance is increased for new bad debts expense and not when the allowance is decreased for the write-off of uncollectible accounts. It is also important to note that management controls the amount and timing of the bad debts expense. Although external auditors assess the reasonableness of the allowance for uncollectible accounts, they do not possess management's inside knowledge and experience. This puts the auditors at an information disadvantage, particularly if any dispute arises.

Studies show that many companies use the allowance for uncollectible accounts to shift income from one year into another. For example, a company can increase current-period income by deliberately underestimating bad debts expense. However, in the future it will become apparent that the bad debts expense was too low when the company's write-offs exceed the balance in the allowance account. Then, the company will need to increase the allowance to make up for the earlier period's underestimate. As an example, consider a company that accurately estimates that it has $1,000 of uncollectible accounts at the end of 2011. Assume that the current balance in the allowance for uncollectible accounts is $200. But instead of recording bad debts expense of $800 as needed to have an adequate ($1,000) allowance, the company records only $100 of bad debts expense and reports an allowance of $300 at the end of 2011. Now if the company's original estimate was accurate, in 2012 it will write off accounts totaling $1,000. The write-offs ($1,000) are greater than the allowance balance ($300) and the company will need to increase the allowance by recording an additional $700 in 2012. The effect of this is that the company borrowed $700 of income from 2012 to report higher income in 2011. This is called "income shifting."

Why would a company want to shift income from a later period into the current period? Perhaps it is a lean year and the company is in danger of missing income targets. For example, internal targets influence manager bonuses and external targets set by the market influence stock prices. Or, perhaps the company is in danger of defaulting on loan agreements tied to income levels. The reality is that income pressures are great and these pressures can cause managers to bend (or even break) the rules.

Companies can just as easily shift income from the current period to one or more future periods by overestimating the current period bad debts expense and allowance for uncollectible accounts. Why would a company want to shift income to one or more future periods? Perhaps current times are good and the company wants to "bank" some of that income for future periods, sometimes called a *cookie jar reserve*. It can then draw on that reserve, if necessary, to boost income in one or more future lean years. Another reason for a company to shift income from the current period is that it does not wish to unduly inflate market expectations for future period income. Or perhaps the company is experiencing a very bad year and it feels that overestimating the provision will not drive income materially lower than it is. Thus, it decides to take a big bath (a large loss) and create a reserve that can be used in future periods. (Sears provides an interesting case as described in the Business Insight box.)

BUSINESS INSIGHT | **Sears' Cookie Jar**

A column several years ago in *The Wall Street Journal* reported on an equity analyst that asserted Sears' earnings growth was aided by a balance sheet maneuver of three years earlier that softened the impact of soaring levels of bad credit card debt. Namely, despite soaring credit losses, Sears had reported an earnings *increase*. How so? The analyst explained that Sears had markedly increased its allowance for uncollectible accounts in that earlier year (to a level twice that of similar companies) and had reported the related bad debts expense in that year when its earnings were high. The resulting reserve was much higher than needed. Then, when earnings were low, Sears charged its credit losses to the allowance for uncollectible accounts. However, since the balance of the allowance for uncollectible accounts was so large, no increase in that account was necessary and little or no bad debts expense was reported. Why is this a concern? The overstated reserve allowed Sears to prop up its earnings at a time when losses in its credit card unit were soaring. The analyst concluded that the increase in Sears' year-to-date earnings has depended entirely on its over-reserved allowance.

Use of the allowance for uncollectible accounts to shift income is a source of concern. This is especially so for banks where the allowance for loan losses is a large component of banks' balance sheets and loan loss expense is a major component of reported income. Our analysis must scrutinize the allowance for uncollectible accounts to identify any changes from past practices or industry norms and, then, to justify those changes before accepting them as valid.

Accounts Receivable Turnover and Average Collection Period

The net operating asset turnover (NOAT) is sales divided by average net operating assets. An important component of this measure is the **accounts receivable turnover (ART)**, which is defined as:[3]

Accounts Receivable Turnover = Sales/Average Accounts Receivable, gross

Accounts receivable turnover reveals how many times receivables have turned (been collected) during the period. More turns indicate that receivables are being collected more quickly.

A companion measure to accounts receivable turnover is the **average collection period (ACP)** for accounts receivable, also called *days sales outstanding*, which is defined as:

Average Collection Period = Accounts Receivable, gross/Average Daily Sales

where average daily sales equals sales divided by 365 days. The average collection period indicates how long, on average, the receivables are outstanding before being collected.[4]

To illustrate, Cisco's 2010 total net sales (products and services) are $40,040 million, gross accounts receivable are $5,164 million at year-end, and $3,393 million at the prior year-end (average is

---

[3] Technically, the numerator should be net credit sales because receivables arise from credit sales. Including cash sales in the numerator inflates the ratio. Typically, outsiders do not know the level of cash sales and, therefore, must use total sales to calculate the turnover ratio.

[4] The average collection period computation in this module uses *ending* accounts receivable. This focuses the analysis on the most current receivables. Cisco uses a variant of this approach, described in its MD&A section as follows: Accounts receivable/Average annualized 4Q sales (or AR/[(4Q Sales × 4)/365]). Arguably, Cisco's variant focuses even more on the most recent collection period because ending accounts receivable relate more closely to 4Q sales than to reported annual sales. Most analysts use the reported annual sales instead of the annualized 4Q sales because the former are easily accessed in financial statement databases. As an alternative, we could also examine average daily sales in *average* accounts receivable (Average accounts receivable/Average daily sales). The approach we use in the text addresses the average collection period of *current* (ending) accounts receivable, and the latter approach examines the average collection period of *average* accounts receivable. Finally, some analysts use "net" and not "gross" receivables. The concern with using net is that it introduces management's allowance policy as another variable in this analysis. The "correct" ratio depends on the issue we wish to investigate. It is important to choose the formula that best answers the question we are asking.

$4,278.5 million). Thus, its accounts receivable turnover is 9.36, computed as $40,040/$4,278.5, and its average collection period (days sales outstanding) is 47 days, computed as $5,164/($40,040/365 days).

The accounts receivable turnover and the average collection period yield valuable insights on at least two dimensions:

1. *Receivables quality* Changes in receivable turnover (and collection period) speak to accounts receivable quality. If turnover slows (collection period lengthens), the reason could be deterioration in collectibility. However, there are at least three alternative explanations:

    a. A seller can extend its credit terms. If the seller is attempting to enter new markets or take market share from competitors, it may extend credit terms to attract buyers.

    b. A seller can take on longer-paying customers. For example, facing increased competition, automobile and other manufacturing companies began leasing their products, thus reducing customers' cash outlays and stimulating sales. Moving away from cash sales and toward leasing reduced receivables turnover and increased the collection period.

    c. The seller can increase the allowance provision. Receivables turnover is sometimes computed using net receivables (after the allowance for uncollectible accounts). In this case, overestimating the provision reduces net receivables and increases the turnover ratio. Accordingly, the apparent improvement in turnover could be incorrectly attributed to improved operating performance rather than a decline in the quality of the receivables.

2. *Asset utilization* Asset turnover is an important financial performance measure used both by managers for internal performance goals, as well as by the market in evaluating companies. High-performing companies must be both effective (controlling margins and operating expenses) and efficient (getting the most out of their asset base). An increase in receivables ties up cash. As well, slower-turning receivables carry increased risk of loss. One of the first "low-hanging fruits" that companies pursue in efforts to improve overall asset utilization is efficiency in receivables collection.

The following chart shows the average collection period for accounts receivable of Cisco and four peer competitors that Cisco indentifies in its 10-K.

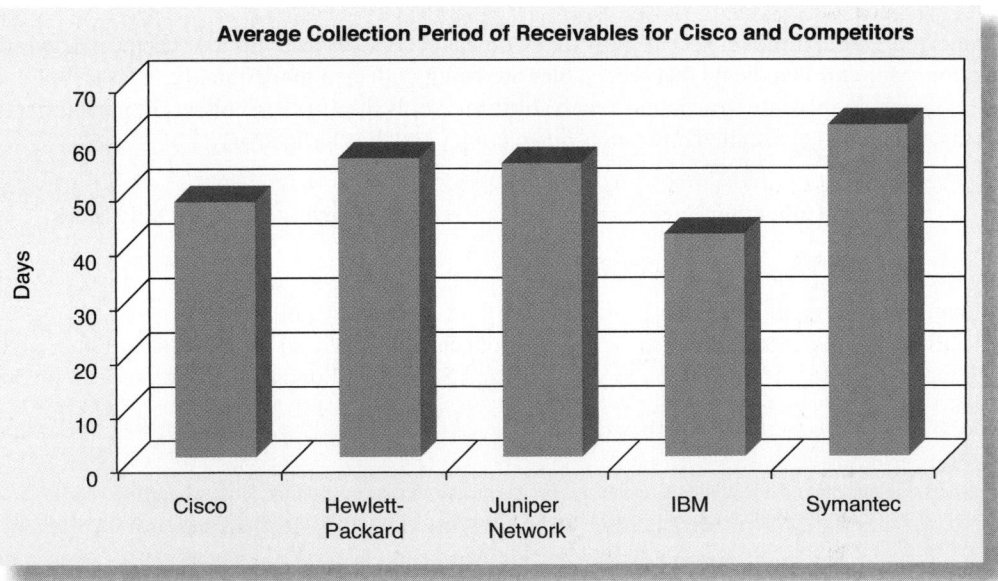

Cisco's average collection period of 47 days compares favorably with its primary competitors. Companies in this industry generally report average collection periods of 40–60 days.

To appreciate differences in average collection periods across industries, let's compare the average collection periods across a number of industries as follows:

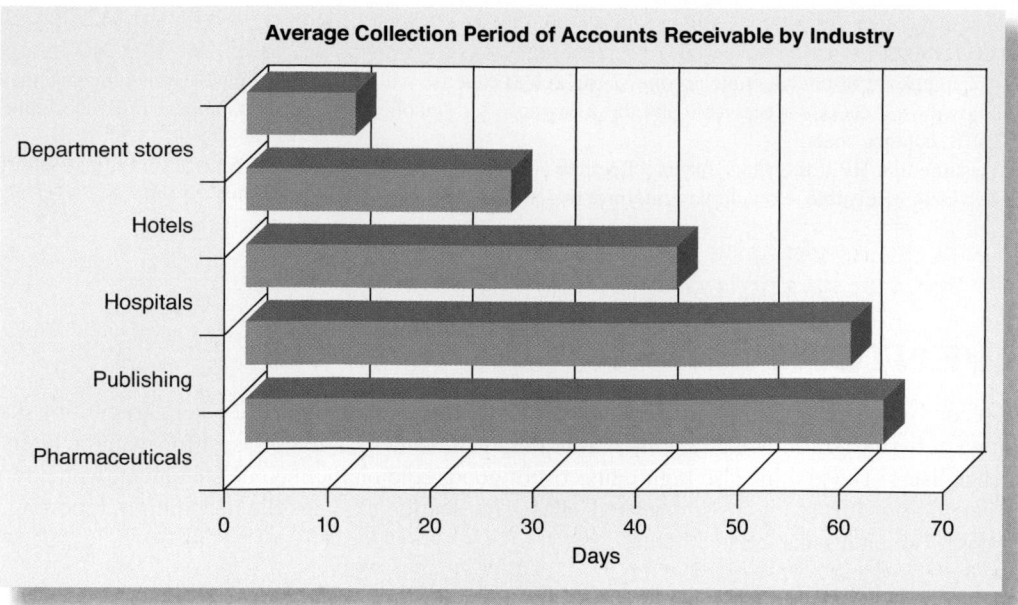

Department stores and hotels have the shortest collection periods. For those industries, receivables are minimal because sales are made mainly via cash, check or credit card. Most of the other industries in the table have collection periods ranging from 40 to 60 days. This corresponds with typical credit terms offered on commercial transactions. Pharmaceutical companies and hospitals have longer collection periods because they often require payment from third-party insurers and government agencies such as Medicare and the Veterans' Administration.

MANAGERIAL DECISION   You Are the Receivables Manager

You are analyzing your receivables turnover report for the period and you are concerned that the average collection period is lengthening. What specific actions can you take to reduce the average collection period? [Answer, p. 6-37]

MID-MODULE REVIEW 1

At December 31, 2012, assume that Hewlett-Packard had a balance of $770,000 in its Accounts Receivable account and a balance of $7,000 in its Allowance for Uncollectible Accounts. The company then analyzed and aged its accounts receivable as shown below. Assume that HP experienced past losses as follows: 1% of current balances, 5% of balances 1-60 days past due, 15% of balances 61–180 days past due, and 40% of balances over 180 days past due. The company bases its provision for credit losses on the aging analysis.

Current	$468,000
1–60 days past due	244,000
61–180 days past due	38,000
Over 180 days past due	20,000
Total accounts receivable	$770,000

continued

Required

1. What amount of uncollectible accounts (bad debts) expense will HP report in its 2012 income statement?
2. Show how Accounts Receivable and the Allowance for Uncollectible Accounts appear in its December 31, 2012, balance sheet.
3. Assume that HP's allowance for uncollectible accounts has maintained an historical average of 2% of gross accounts receivable. How do you interpret the current allowance percentage?

The solution is on page 6-52.

INVENTORY

LO2 Explain accounting for inventories and assess the effects on the balance sheet and income statement from different inventory costing methods.

The second major component of operating working capital is inventory. To help frame this discussion, we refer to the following graphic that highlights inventory, a major asset for manufacturers and merchandisers. The graphic also highlights cost of goods sold on the income statement, which reflects the matching of inventory costs to related sales. This section explains the accounting, reporting, and analysis of inventory and related items.

Income Statement	Balance Sheet	
Sales	Cash	Current liabilities
Cost of goods sold	Accounts receivable, net	Long-term liabilities
Selling, general & administrative	Inventory	
Income taxes	Property, plant, and equipment, net	Shareholders' equity
Net income	Investments	

Inventory is reported on the balance sheet at its purchase price or the cost to manufacture goods that are internally produced. Inventory costs vary over time with changes in market conditions. Consequently, the cost per unit of the goods available for sale varies from period to period—even if the quantity of goods available remains the same.

When inventory is purchased or produced, it is "capitalized." That is, it is carried on the balance sheet as an asset until it is sold, at which time its cost is transferred from the balance sheet to the income statement as an expense (cost of goods sold). The process by which costs are removed from the balance sheet is important. For example, if higher cost units are transferred from the balance sheet, then cost of goods sold is higher and gross profit (sales less cost of goods sold) is lower. Conversely, if lower cost units are transferred to cost of goods sold, gross profit is higher. The remainder of this section discusses the accounting for inventory including the mechanics, reporting, and analysis of inventory costing.

Capitalization of Inventory Cost

Capitalization means that a cost is recorded on the balance sheet and is not immediately expensed on the income statement. Once costs are capitalized, they remain on the balance sheet as assets until they are used up, at which time they are transferred from the balance sheet to the income statement as expense. If costs are capitalized rather than expensed, then assets, current income, and current equity are all higher.

For purchased inventories (such as merchandise), the amount of cost capitalized is the purchase price. For manufacturers, cost capitalization is more difficult, as **manufacturing costs** consist of three components: cost of direct materials used in the product, cost of direct labor to manufacture the product, and manufacturing overhead. Direct materials cost is relatively easy to compute. Design specifications list the components of each product, and their purchase costs are readily determined. The direct labor cost per unit of inventory is based on how long each unit takes to construct and the rates for each labor class working on that product. Overhead costs are also capitalized into inventory, and include the costs of plant asset depreciation, utilities, supervisory personnel, and other costs that contribute to manufacturing activities—that is, all costs of manufacturing other than direct materials and direct labor. (How these costs are assigned to individual units and across multiple products is a *managerial accounting* topic.)

When inventories are sold, their costs are transferred from the balance sheet to the income statement as cost of goods sold (COGS). COGS is then deducted from sales to yield **gross profit**:

$$\textbf{Gross Profit = Sales − Cost of Goods Sold}$$

The manner in which inventory costs are transferred from the balance sheet to the income statement affects both the level of inventories reported on the balance sheet and the amount of gross profit (and net income) reported on the income statement.

Inventory Costing Methods

Exhibit 6.5 shows the computation of cost of goods sold.

EXHIBIT 6.5	**Cost of Goods Sold Computation**
	Beginning inventory (prior period balance sheet)
+	Inventory purchased and/or produced
	Cost of goods available for sale
−	Ending inventory (current period balance sheet)
	Cost of goods sold (current period income statement)

The cost of inventory available at the beginning of a period is a carryover from the ending inventory balance of the prior period. Current period inventory purchases (or costs of newly manufactured inventories) are added to the beginning inventory balance, yielding the total cost of goods (inventory) available for sale. Then, the goods available are either sold, and end up in cost of goods sold for the period (reported on the income statement), or the goods available remain unsold and are still in inventory at the end of the period (reported on the balance sheet). Exhibit 6.6 shows this cost flow graphically.

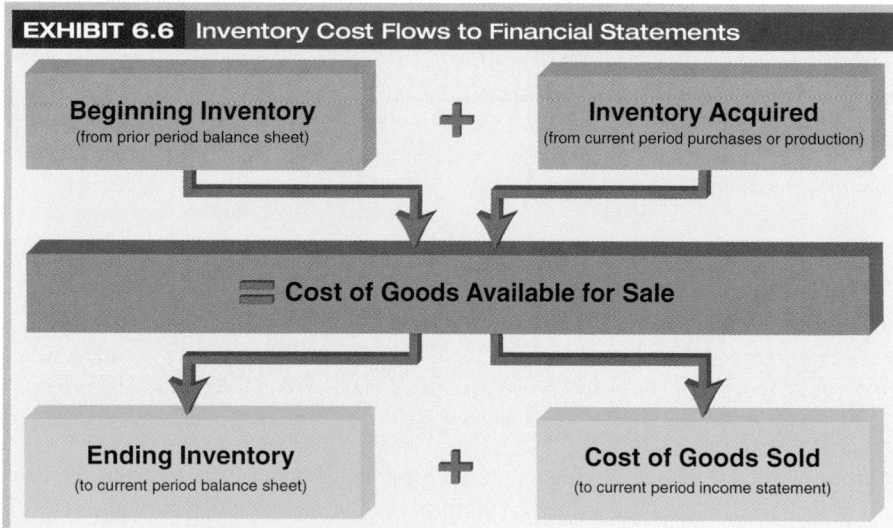

Understanding the flow of inventory costs is important. If all inventory purchased or manufactured during the period is sold, then COGS is equal to the cost of the goods purchased or manufactured. However, when inventory remains at the end of a period, companies must distinguish the cost of the inventories that were sold from the cost of the inventories that remain. GAAP allows for several options.

Exhibit 6.7 illustrates the partial inventory records of a company.

EXHIBIT 6.7 Summary Inventory Records			
Inventory on January 1, 2012.	500 units	@ $100 per unit	$ 50,000
Inventory purchased in 2012	200 units	@ $150 per unit	30,000
Total cost of goods available for sale in 2012	700 units		$ 80,000
Inventory sold in 2012	450 units	@ $250 per unit	$112,500

This company began the period with 500 units of inventory that were purchased or manufactured for $50,000 ($100 each). During the period the company purchased and/or manufactured an additional 200 units costing $30,000. The total cost of goods available for sale for this period equals $80,000.

The company sold 450 units during 2012 for $250 per unit for total sales of $112,500. Accordingly, the company must remove the cost of the 450 units sold from the inventory account on the balance sheet and match this cost against the revenues generated from the sale. An important question is which costs should management remove from the balance sheet and report as cost of goods sold in the income statement? Three inventory costing methods (FIFO, LIFO and average cost) are common and all are acceptable under GAAP.

First-In, First-Out (FIFO)

The FIFO inventory costing method transfers costs from inventory in the order that they were initially recorded. That is, FIFO assumes that the first costs recorded in inventory (first-in) are the first costs transferred from inventory (first-out). Applying FIFO to the data in Exhibit 6.7 means that the costs of the 450 units sold comes from *beginning* inventory, which consists of 500 units costing $100 each. The company's cost of goods sold and gross profit, using FIFO, is computed as follows:

Sales.	$112,500
COGS (450 @ $100 each).	45,000
Gross profit.	$ 67,500

The cost remaining in inventory and reported on the 2012 year-end balance sheet is $35,000 ($80,000 goods available for sale less $45,000 COGS). The following financial statement effects template captures the transaction.

		Balance Sheet				Income Statement		
Transaction	Cash Asset	+ Noncash Assets	= Liabil- ities	+ Contrib. Capital	+ Earned Capital	Rev- enues	– Expen- ses	= Net Income
Sold 450 units using FIFO costing (450 @ $100 each)		−45,000 Inventory =			−45,000 Retained Earnings		+45,000 Cost of Goods Sold	= −45,000

COGS 45,000
  INV   45,000

      COGS
45,000 |
        INV
          | 45,000

Last-In, First-Out (LIFO)

The LIFO inventory costing method transfers the most recent inventory costs from the balance sheet to COGS. That is, the LIFO method assumes that the most recent inventory purchases (last-in) are the first costs transferred from inventory (first-out). The company's cost of goods sold and gross profit, using LIFO, is computed as follows:

Sales.		$112,500
COGS: 200 @ $150 per unit	$30,000	
250 @ $100 per unit	25,000	55,000
Gross profit.		$ 57,500

The cost remaining in inventory and reported on the company's 2012 balance sheet is $25,000 (computed as $80,000 − $55,000). This is reflected in our financial statements effects template as follows.

	Balance Sheet						Income Statement		
Transaction	Cash Asset	+ Noncash Assets	= Liabil- ities	+ Contrib. Capital	+ Earned Capital		Rev- enues	− Expen- ses	= Net Income
Sold 450 units using LIFO costing (200 @ $150) + (250 @ $100)		−55,000 Inventory =			−55,000 Retained Earnings			+55,000 − Cost of Goods Sold	= −55,000

COGS 55,000
INV 55,000

COGS
55,000 |

INV
| 55,000

Average Cost (AC)

The average cost method computes the cost of goods sold as an average of the cost to purchase or manufacture all of the inventories that were available for sale during the period. To calculate the average cost of $114.286 per unit the company divides the total cost of goods available for sale by the number of units available for sale ($80,000/700 units). The company's sales, cost of sales, and gross profit follow.

Sales.......................................	$112,500
COGS (450 @ $114.286 per unit).................	51,429
Gross profit..................................	$ 61,071

The cost remaining in inventory and reported on the company's 2012 balance sheet is $28,571 ($80,000 − $51,429). This is reflected in our financial statements effects template as follows.

	Balance Sheet						Income Statement		
Transaction	Cash Asset	+ Noncash Assets	= Liabil- ities	+ Contrib. Capital	+ Earned Capital		Rev- enues	− Expen- ses	= Net Income
Sold 450 units using average cost method (450 @ $114.286)		−51,429 Inventory =			−51,429 Retained Earnings			+51,429 − Cost of Goods Sold	= −51,429

COGS 51,429
INV 51,429

COGS
51,429 |

INV
| 51,429

It is important to understand that the inventory costing method a company chooses is independent of the actual flow of inventory. The method choice determines COGS and ending inventory but not the actual physical inventory sold. For example, many grocery chains use LIFO inventory but certainly do not sell the freshest products first. (Companies do not frequently change inventory costing methods. Companies can adopt a new inventory costing method if doing so enhances the quality of the company's financial reports. Also, IRS regulations prohibit certain inventory costing method changes.)

Lower of Cost or Market

Companies must write down the carrying amount of inventories on the balance sheet *if* the reported cost (using FIFO, for example) exceeds market value (determined by current replacement cost). This process is called reporting inventories at the **lower of cost or market** and creates the following financial statement effects:

■ Inventory book value is written down to current market value (replacement cost), reducing inventory and total assets.

■ Inventory write-down is reflected as an expense (part of cost of goods sold) on the income statement, reducing current period gross profit, income, and equity.

To illustrate, assume that a company has inventory on its balance sheet at a cost of $27,000. Management learns that the inventory's replacement cost is $23,000 and writes inventories down to a balance of $23,000. The following financial statement effects template shows the adjustment.

	Balance Sheet							Income Statement		
Transaction	Cash Asset	+	Noncash Assets	=	Liabil- ities	+	Contrib. Capital	+	Earned Capital	
Write down inventory from $27,000 to $23,000.			−4,000 Inventory	=					−4,000 Retained Earnings	

Rev- enues	−	Expen- ses	=	Net Income
	−	+4,000 Cost of Goods Sold	=	−4,000

```
COGS   4,000
   INV      4,000
        COGS
 4,000 |
     INV
        | 4,000
```

The inventory write-down (a noncash expense) is reflected in cost of goods sold and reduces gross profit by $4,000. Inventory write-downs are included in cost of goods sold. They are *not* reported in selling, general, and administrative expenses, which is common for other asset write-downs. The most common occurrence of inventory write-downs is in connection with restructuring activities.

The write-down of inventories can potentially shift income from one period to another. If, for example, inventories were written down below current replacement cost, future gross profit would be increased via lower future cost of goods sold. GAAP anticipates this possibility by requiring that inventories not be written down below a floor that is equal to net realizable value less a normal markup. Although this still allows some discretion (and the ability to manage income), the auditors must assess net realizable value and markups.

> **IFRS INSIGHT**   Inventory Measurement under IFRS
>
> Like GAAP, IFRS measures inventories at the lower of cost or market. The cost of inventory generally is determined using the FIFO (first-in, first-out) or weighted average cost method; use of the LIFO (last-in, first-out) method is prohibited under IFRS.

Footnote Disclosures

Notes to financial statements describe the inventory accounting method a company uses. To illustrate, Cisco reports $1,327 million in inventory on its 2010 balance sheet as a current asset. Cisco includes a general footnote on inventory along with more specific disclosures in other footnotes. Following is an excerpt from Cisco's general footnote on inventories.

> **Inventories.** Inventories are stated at the lower of cost or market. Cost is computed using standard cost, which approximates actual cost, on a first-in, first-out basis. The Company provides inventory write-downs based on excess and obsolete inventories determined primarily by future demand forecasts. The write-down is measured as the difference between the cost of the inventory and market based upon assumptions about future demand and charged to the provision for inventory, which is a component of cost of sales. At the point of the loss recognition, a new, lower-cost basis for that inventory is established, and subsequent changes in facts and circumstances do not result in the restoration or increase in that newly established cost basis.

This footnote includes at least two items of interest for our analysis of inventory:

1. Cisco uses the FIFO method of inventory costing.
2. Inventories are reported at the lower of cost or market (LCM). For example, if the current value of Cisco's inventories is less than its reported cost, Cisco would set up an "allowance" for inventories, similar to the allowance for uncollectible accounts. The inventory allowance reduces the reported inventory amount to the current (lower) market value.

Cisco also includes a more detailed inventory footnote as follows:

Inventories ($ millions)	July 31, 2010	July 25, 2009
Raw materials	$ 217	$ 165
Work in process	50	33
Finished goods		
Distributor inventory and deferred cost of sales	$ 587	$ 382
Manufacturing finished goods	260	310
Total finished goods	847	692
Service-related spares	161	151
Demonstration systems	52	33
Total	$1,327	$1,074

This disclosure separately reports inventory costs by the following stages in the production cycle:

- *Raw materials and supplies* These are costs of direct materials and inputs into the production process including, for example, chemicals in raw state, plastic and steel for manufacturing, and incidental direct materials such as screws and lubricants.
- *Work in process* These are costs of partly finished products (also called work-in-progress).
- *Finished goods* These are the costs of products that are completed and awaiting sale.

Why do companies disclose such details about inventory? First, investment in inventory is typically large—markedly impacting both balance sheets and income statements. Second, risks of inventory losses are often high, due to technical obsolescence and consumer tastes. This is an important issue for a company such as Cisco that operates in a technology-sensitive industry. Indeed, Cisco reported a loss of over $2 billion in 2001 when the tech bubble burst, demand dried up, and the company had to write down unsalable inventories. Third, inventory details can provide insight into future performance—both good and bad. Fourth, high inventory levels result in substantial costs for the company, such as the following:

- Financing costs to hold inventories (when not purchased on credit or when held beyond credit period)
- Storage costs (such as warehousing and related facilities)
- Handling costs (including wages)
- Insurance costs

Consequently, companies seek to minimize inventory levels provided this does not exceed the cost of holding insufficient inventory, called stock-outs. Stock-outs result in lost sales and production delays if machines and employees must be reconfigured to fill order backlogs. Cisco's total inventories have remained at 2005 levels despite a $15.2 billion increase in sales.

Financial Statement Effects of Inventory Costing

This section describes the financial statement effects of different inventory costing methods.

Income Statement Effects
The three inventory costing methods yield differing levels of gross profit as Exhibit 6.8 shows.

EXHIBIT 6.8 Income Effects from Inventory Costing Methods			
	Sales	Cost of Goods Sold	Gross Profit
FIFO	$112,500	$45,000	$67,500
LIFO	112,500	55,000	57,500
Average cost	112,500	51,429	61,071

Recall that inventory costs rose during this period from $100 per unit to $150 per unit. The higher gross profit reported under FIFO arises because FIFO matches older, lower-cost inventory against current selling prices. To generalize: in an inflationary environment, FIFO yields higher gross profit than do LIFO or average cost methods.

In recent years, the gross profit impact from using the FIFO method has been minimal for companies due to lower rates of inflation and increased management focus on reducing inventory quantities through improved manufacturing processes and better inventory controls. The FIFO gross profit effect can still arise, however, with companies subject to high inflation and slow inventory turnover.

Balance Sheet Effects

In our illustration above, the ending inventory using LIFO is less than that reported using FIFO. In periods of rising costs, LIFO inventories are markedly lower than under FIFO. As a result, balance sheets using LIFO do not accurately represent the cost that a company would incur to replace its current investment in inventories.

Caterpillar (CAT), for example, reports 2010 inventories under LIFO costing $9,587 million. As disclosed in the footnotes to its 10-K (see below), if CAT valued these inventories using FIFO, the reported amount would be $2,575 million greater, a 27% increase. This suggests that CAT's balance sheet omits over $2,575 million in inventories.

Cash Flow Effects

Unlike for most other accounting method choices, inventory costing methods affect taxable income and, thus, taxes paid. When a company adopts LIFO in its tax filings, the IRS requires it to also use LIFO for financial reporting purposes (in its 10-K). This requirement is known as the *LIFO conformity rule*. In an inflationary economy, using FIFO results in higher taxable income and, consequently, higher taxes payable. Conversely, using LIFO reduces the tax liability.

Caterpillar, Inc., discloses the following inventory information in its 2010 10-K:

> Inventories are stated at the lower of cost or market. Cost is principally determined using the last-in, first-out (LIFO) method. The value of inventories on the LIFO basis represented about 70% of total inventories at December 31, 2010, 2009 and 2008.
>
> If the FIFO (first-in, first-out) method had been in use, inventories would have been $2,575 million, $3,022 million and $3,216 million higher than reported at December 31, 2010, 2009 and 2008, respectively.

CAT uses LIFO for most of its inventories.[5] The use of LIFO has reduced the carrying amount of 2010 inventories by $2,575 million. Had it used FIFO, its inventories would have been reported at $12,162 million ($9,587 million + $2,575 million) rather than the $9,587 million that is reported on its balance sheet as of 2010. This difference, referred to as the **LIFO reserve**, is the amount that must be added to LIFO inventories to adjust them to their FIFO value.

$$\text{FIFO Inventory} = \text{LIFO Inventory} + \text{LIFO Reserve}$$

This relation also impacts cost of goods sold (COGS) as follows:

$$\text{FIFO COGS} = \text{LIFO COGS} - \text{Increase in LIFO Reserve (or + Decrease)}$$

Use of LIFO reduced CAT's inventories by $2,575 million, resulting in a cumulative increase in cost of goods sold and a cumulative decrease in gross profit and pretax profit of that same amount.[6] Because CAT also uses LIFO for tax purposes, the decrease in pretax profits reduced CAT's cumulative

---

[5] Neither the IRS nor GAAP requires use of a single inventory costing method. That is, companies are allowed to, and frequently do, use different inventory costing methods for different types of inventory (such as spare parts versus finished goods).

[6] Recall: Cost of Goods Sold = Beginning Inventories + Purchases − Ending Inventories. Thus, as ending inventories decrease, cost of goods sold increases.

tax bill by about $901 million ($2,575 million × 35% assumed corporate tax rate). This had real cash flow consequences: CAT's cumulative operating cash flow was $901 million higher because CAT used LIFO instead of FIFO. The increased cash flow from tax savings is often cited as a compelling reason for management to adopt LIFO.

Because companies use different inventory costing methods, their financial statements are often not comparable. The problem is most serious when companies hold large amounts of inventory and when prices markedly rise or fall. To compare companies using different inventory costing methods, say LIFO and FIFO, we need to adjust the LIFO numbers to their FIFO equivalents or vice versa. For example, one way to compare CAT with another company that uses FIFO, is to add CAT's LIFO reserve to its LIFO inventory. As explained above, this $2,575 million increase in 2010 inventories would have increased its cumulative pretax profits by $2,575 million and taxes by $901 million. Thus, to adjust the 2010 balance sheet we increase inventories by $2,575 million, tax liabilities by $901 million (the extra taxes CAT would have had to pay under FIFO), and equity by the difference of $1,674 million (computed as $2,575 − $901).

To adjust CAT's 2010 income statement from LIFO to FIFO, we use the change in LIFO reserve. For CAT, the LIFO reserve decreased by $447 million during 2010, from $3,022 million in 2009 to $2,575 million in 2010. This means that had it been using FIFO, its COGS would have been $447 million higher, and 2010 gross profit and pretax income would have been $447 million lower. In 2010, CAT would have paid $156 million less in taxes had it used FIFO ($447 million × 35% assumed tax rate).

RESEARCH INSIGHT   **LIFO and Stock Prices**

The value-relevance of inventory disclosures depends at least partly on whether investors rely more on the income statement or the balance sheet to assess future cash flows. Under LIFO, cost of goods sold reflects current costs, whereas FIFO ending inventory reflects current costs. This implies that LIFO enhances the usefulness of the income statement to the detriment of the balance sheet. This trade-off partly motivates the required LIFO reserve disclosure (the adjustment necessary to restate LIFO ending inventory and cost of good sold to FIFO). Research suggests that LIFO-based income statements better reflect stock prices than do FIFO income statements that are restated using the LIFO reserve. Research also shows a negative relation between stock prices and LIFO reserve—meaning that higher magnitudes of LIFO reserve are associated with lower stock prices. This is consistent with the LIFO reserve being viewed as an inflation indicator (for either current or future inventory costs), which the market views as detrimental to company value.

Tools of Inventory Analysis

This section describes several useful tools for analysis of inventory and related accounts.

Gross Profit Analysis

The **gross profit margin (GPM)** is gross profit divided by sales. This important ratio is closely monitored by management and outsiders. Exhibit 6.9 shows the gross profit margin on Cisco's sales for the past three years.

EXHIBIT 6.9 Gross Profit Margin for Cisco			
Fiscal Year	**2010**	**2009**	**2008**
Product sales	$40,040	$36,117	$39,540
Product cost of goods sold	14,397	13,023	14,194
Gross profit.	$25,643	$23,094	$25,346
Gross profit margin.	64.0%	63.9%	64.1%

The gross profit margin is commonly used instead of the dollar amount of gross profit as the GPM allows for comparisons across companies and over time. A decline in GPM is usually cause for concern since it indicates that the company has less ability to pass on increased product cost to customers or that the company is not effectively managing product costs. Some possible reasons for a GPM decline follow:

- *Product line is stale*. Perhaps products are out of fashion and the company must resort to mark-downs to reduce overstocked inventories. Or, perhaps the product lines have lost their technological edge, yielding reduced demand.

- *New competitors enter the market*. Perhaps substitute products are now available from competitors, yielding increased pressure to reduce selling prices.

- *General decline in economic activity*. Perhaps an economic downturn reduces product demand.

- *Inventory is overstocked*. Perhaps the company overproduced goods and finds itself in an over-stock position. This can require reduced selling prices to move inventory.

- *Manufacturing costs have increased*. This could be due to poor planning, production glitches, or unfavorable supply chain reconfiguration.

- *Changes in product mix*. Perhaps the company is selling a higher proportion of low margin goods.

Cisco's gross profit margin on product sales increased by 0.1 percentage points (63.9% to 64.0%) over the past year. Following is Cisco's discussion of its gross profit taken from its 2010 10-K:

Gross Margin In fiscal 2010, our gross margin percentage increased by 0.1 percentage points compared with fiscal 2009, driven by a slightly higher product gross margin percentage coupled with an unchanged service gross margin percentage. The higher product gross margin percentage was primarily due to lower overall manufacturing costs, higher shipment volume, and favorable product mix. Partially offsetting the product gross margin increase were higher sales discounts and rebates, and lower product pricing. The service gross margin percentage remained unchanged from period to period with the increase in gross margin from technical support services being offset by a decline in gross margin for advanced services. Our product and service gross margins may be impacted by uncertain economic conditions as well as our movement into market adjacencies and could decline if any of the factors that impact our gross margins are adversely affected in future periods.

Cisco's gross profit margin increased in 2010 because of lower manufacturing costs, higher shipment volume, and favorable product mix. This increase was partially offset by increased sales discounts. There are a number of factors that can adversely affect gross profit margins: changes in product mix, introduction of new products at lower introductory prices to gain market share, increases in production costs, sales discounts, inventory obsolescence and warranty costs, and changes in production volume.

Competitive pressures mean that companies rarely have the opportunity to completely control gross profit with price increases. Improvements in gross profit on existing product lines typically arise from better management of supply chains, production processes, or distribution networks. Companies that succeed do so because of better performance on basic business processes. This is one of Cisco's primary objectives.

Inventory Turnover

Inventory turnover (INVT) reflects the management of inventory and is computed as follows:

$$\textbf{Inventory Turnover = Cost of Goods Sold/Average Inventory}$$

Cost of goods sold is in the numerator because inventory is reported at cost. Inventory turnover indicates how many times inventory turns (is sold) during a period. More turns indicate that inventory is being sold more quickly, which decreases the risk of obsolete inventory and increases liquidity.

Average inventory days outstanding (AIDO), also called *days inventory outstanding*, is a companion measure to inventory turnover and is computed as follows:

Average Inventory Days Outstanding = Inventory/Average Daily Cost of Goods Sold

where average daily cost of goods sold equals cost of goods sold divided by 365 days.[7]

For Cisco, cost of products sold, in 2010, is $11,620 million, inventory at year-end is $1,327 million, inventory at prior year-end was $1,074 million (average is $1,200.5 million). Thus, its inventory turnover is 9.7, computed as $11,620 million/$1,200.5 million, which implies that, in 2010, Cisco sold its average inventory 9.7 times. Its 2010 average inventory days outstanding is 42 days, computed as $1,327 million/($11,620 million/365 days), which implies that it takes Cisco 42 days to sell its year-end inventory.

Overall, analysis of inventory turnover and days outstanding is important for at least two reasons:

1. *Inventory quality.* Inventory turnover can be compared over time and across competitors. Higher turnover is viewed favorably, because it implies that products are salable, preferably without undue discounting (we would compare profit margins to assess discounting). Conversely, lower turnover implies that inventory is on the shelves for a longer period of time, perhaps from excessive purchases or production, missed fashion trends or technological advances, increased competition, and so forth. Our conclusions about higher or lower turnover must consider alternative explanations including the following:

   • Product mix can include more (or less) higher margin, slower turning inventories. This can occur from business acquisitions that consolidate different types of inventory.

   • A company can change its promotion policies. Increased, effective advertising is likely to increase inventory turnover. Advertising expense is in SG&A, not COGS. This means the additional advertising cost is in operating expenses, but the benefit is in gross profit and turnover. If the promotion campaign is successful, the positive effects in margin and turnover should more than offset the promotion cost in SG&A.

   • A company can realize improvements in manufacturing efficiency and lower investments in direct materials and work-in-process inventories. Such improvements reduce inventory and, consequently, increase inventory turnover. Although a good sign, it does not yield any information about the desirability of a company's product line.

2. *Asset utilization.* Companies strive to optimize their inventory investment. Carrying too much inventory is expensive, and too little inventory risks stock-outs and lost sales (current and future). Companies can make the following operational changes to reduce inventory.

   • Improved manufacturing processes can eliminate bottlenecks and the consequent buildup of work-in-process inventories.

   • Just-in-time (JIT) deliveries from suppliers, which provide raw materials to the production line when needed, can reduce the level of raw materials and associated holding costs.

   • Demand-pull production, in which raw materials are released into the production process when final goods are demanded by customers instead of producing for estimated demand, can reduce inventory levels. Dell Computer, for example, does not manufacture a computer until it receives the customer's order; thus, Dell produces for actual, rather than estimated, demand.

Reducing inventories reduces inventory carrying costs, thus improving profitability and increasing cash flows. The reduction in inventory is reflected as an operating cash inflow in the statement of cash flows.

---

[7] Similar to the average receivables collection period, this formula examines the average daily COGS in *ending* inventories to focus analysis on current inventories. One can also examine average daily COGS in *average* inventories (Average inventories/Average daily COGS). These two approaches address different issues: the first addresses the average days outstanding of *current ending* inventories, and the second examines the average days outstanding of *average* inventories. It is important that we first identify the issue under investigation and then choose the formula that best addresses that issue.

There is normal tension between the sales side of a company that argues for depth and breadth of inventory, and the finance side that monitors inventory carrying costs and seeks to maximize cash flow. Companies, therefore, seek to *optimize* inventory investment, not minimize it.

Following is a chart comparing Cisco's average inventory days outstanding with its peer companies.

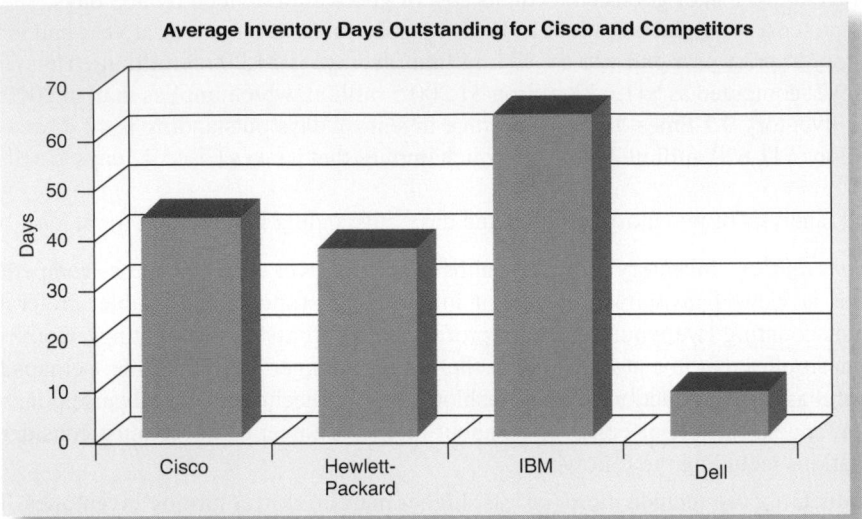

Cisco's average inventory days outstanding of 42 days compares favorably with its peers. Cisco's 2010 10-K provides the following comments regarding inventory management:

> We believe that in any rapidly shifting supply and demand environment such as the one we experienced in fiscal 2010, shifts in lead times, inventory levels, purchase commitments, and manufacturing outputs will occur. During fiscal 2010, we experienced longer than normal lead times on several of our products and we continue to see challenges at some of our component suppliers. This was attributable in part to increasing demand driven by the improvement in our overall markets. In addition, and similar to what is happening throughout the industry, the longer than normal lead times also stemmed from supplier constraints based upon their labor and other actions taken during the global economic downturn. While we may continue to experience longer than normal lead times, our lead times improved on the majority of our products in the second half of fiscal 2010, and at the end of fiscal 2010, product lead times to customers were within a normal range for the majority of our products. We have increased our efforts in procuring components in order to meet customer expectations, which have contributed to an increase in purchase commitments. If, however, lead times for key components lengthen further, our operating results for a particular future period could be adversely affected if we further increase our purchase commitments, which could lead to excess and obsolete inventory charges.

Dell's average inventory days outstanding of nine days is markedly lower than other companies shown in this graph. Dell has traditionally focused on excellence in this area, and views this as a competitive advantage. Dell's 2010 10-K reports the following:

> We utilize several suppliers to manufacture sub-assemblies for our products. Our efficient supply chain management allows us to enter into flexible and mutually beneficial purchase arrangements with our suppliers in order to minimize inventory risk. Consistent with industry practice, we acquire raw materials or other goods and services, including product components, by issuing to suppliers authorizations to purchase based on our projected demand and manufacturing needs. These

continued

purchase orders are typically fulfilled within 30 days and are entered into during the ordinary course of business in order to establish best pricing and continuity of supply for our production. The following table presents the components of our cash conversion cycle for the fourth quarter of each of the past three fiscal years. The slight increase in DSI from January 29, 2010, was primarily attributable to the optimization of our supply chain requiring an increase in strategic purchases of materials and finished goods inventory.

For Fiscal Quarter Ended	January 28, 2011	January 29, 2010	January 30, 2009
Days of sales outstanding	40	38	35
Days of supply in inventory	9	8	7
Days in accounts payable	(82)	(82)	(67)
Cash conversion cycle.	(33)	(36)	(25)

Dell describes its cash conversion cycle, which measures the days from initial investment of cash in inventories to collection of the receivable arising from credit sales and repayment of amounts due to inventory suppliers. Normally, this is a positive number. Companies continually strive to reduce the cash conversion cycle to reduce the amount of investment in net operating assets (NOA), thereby improving the return on net operating assets (RNOA) and increasing cash flow. For Dell, its cash conversion cycle is negative because the company takes longer to pay its suppliers than the time invested in inventories and receivables. This is mainly the result of Dell's manufacturing process that effectively reduces raw materials, work-in-process, and finished goods inventories. Bottom line: Dell's operating efficiency is generating excess cash that can be invested in operating assets to further increase profitability.

Returning to the average inventory days outstanding, it is instructive to compare this measure across selected industries.

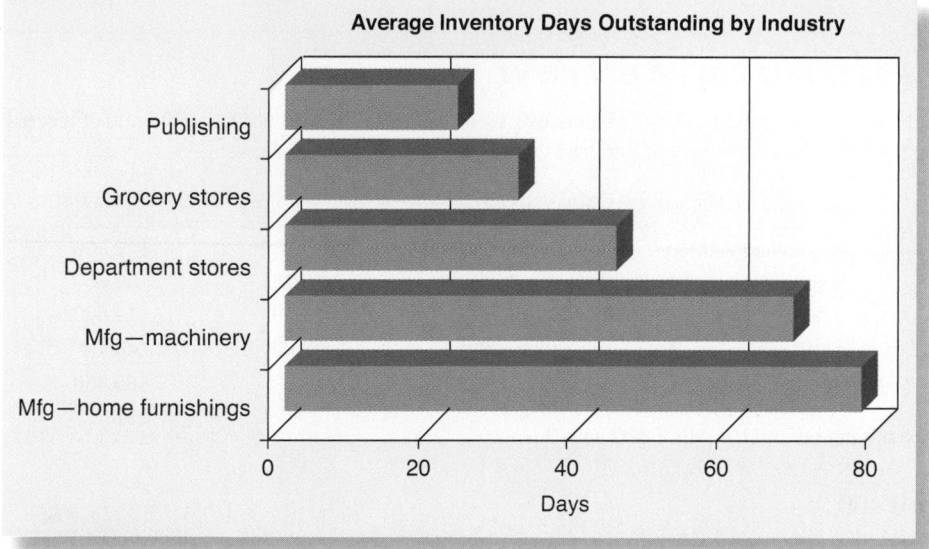

Publishing companies and grocery stores carry 20–30 days' inventory at any point in time. Inventories are low in the publishing industry because newspapers are printed and sold daily, and grocery stores do not carry large amounts of retail inventories. On the other hand, manufacturers must carry raw materials, work-in-process and finished goods inventories.

MANAGERIAL DECISION | **You Are the Plant Manager**

You are analyzing your inventory turnover report for the month and are concerned that the average inventory days outstanding is lengthening. What actions can you take to reduce average inventory days outstanding? [Answer, p. 6-37]

LIFO Liquidations

When companies acquire inventory at different costs, they are required to account for each cost level as a separate inventory pool or layer (for example, there are the $100 and $150 units in our Exhibit 6.7 illustration). When companies reduce inventory levels, older inventory costs flow to the income statement. These older LIFO costs are often markedly different from current replacement costs. Given the usual inflationary environment, sales of older pools often yield a boost to gross profit as older, lower costs are matched against current selling prices on the income statement.

The increase in gross profit resulting from a reduction of inventory quantities in the presence of rising costs is called **LIFO liquidation**. The effect of LIFO liquidation is evident in the following footnote from Newell Rubbermaid's 2010 10-K:

Inventory costs include direct materials, direct labor and manufacturing overhead, or when finished goods are sourced, the cost is the amount paid to the third party. Cost of certain domestic inventories (approximately 52.0% and 51.7% of gross inventory costs at December 31, 2010 and 2009, respectively) was determined by the LIFO method; for the balance, cost was determined using the FIFO method. As of December 31, 2010 and 2009, LIFO reserves were $30.1 million and $24.2 million, respectively. The net income recognized by the Company related to the liquidation of LIFO based inventories in 2010 and 2009 was $8.7 million and $16.9 million, respectively.

Newell Rubbermaid reports that reductions in inventory quantities in 2010 led to the sale (at current selling prices) of products that carried lower costs from prior years. As a result of these inventory reductions, COGS were lower, which increased income by $8.7 million.

MID-MODULE REVIEW 2

At the beginning of the current period, assume that Hewlett-Packard (HP) holds 1,000 units of a certain product with a unit cost of $18. A summary of purchases during the current period follows:

		Units	Unit Cost	Cost
Beginning Inventory		1,000	$18.00	$18,000
Purchases:	#1	1,800	18.25	32,850
	#2	800	18.50	14,800
	#3	1,200	19.00	22,800
Goods available for sale		4,800		$88,450

During the current period, HP sells 2,800 units.

Required
1. Assume that HP uses the first-in, first-out (FIFO) method for this product. Compute the product's cost of goods sold for the current period and the ending inventory balance.
2. Assume that HP uses the last-in, first-out (LIFO) method for this product. Compute the product's cost of goods sold for the current period and the ending inventory balance.
3. Assume that HP uses the average cost (AC) method for this product. Compute the product's cost of goods sold for the current period and the ending inventory balance.
4. As manager, which of these three inventory costing methods would you choose:
   a. To reflect what is probably the physical flow of goods? Explain.
   b. To minimize income taxes for the period? Explain.
5. Assume that HP utilizes the LIFO method and delays purchasing lot #3 until the next period. Compute cost of goods sold under this scenario and discuss how the LIFO liquidation affects profit.

The solution is on page 6-52.

PROPERTY, PLANT AND EQUIPMENT (PPE)

Many companies' largest operating asset is property, plant, and equipment. To frame our PPE discussion, the following graphic highlights long-term operating assets on the balance sheet, and selling, general and administrative expenses on the income statement. The latter includes depreciation and asset write-downs that match the assets' cost against sales derived from the assets. (Depreciation on manufacturing facilities is included in cost of goods sold.) This section explains the accounting, reporting, and analysis of PPE and related items.

LO3 Describe accounting for property, plant and equipment and explain the impacts on profit and cash flows from depreciation methods, disposals and impairments.

Income Statement
Sales
Cost of goods sold
Selling, general & administrative
Income taxes
Net income

Balance Sheet	
Cash	Current liabilities
Accounts receivable, net	Long-term liabilities
Inventory	
Property, plant, and equipment, net	Shareholders' equity
Investments	

Capitalization of Asset Costs

Companies capitalize costs as an asset on the balance sheet only if that asset possesses both of the following characteristics:

1. The asset is owned or controlled by the company and results from a past transaction.
2. The asset provides future expected benefits.

Owning the asset means the company has title to the asset as provided in a purchase contract. (Assets acquired under leases are also capitalized if certain conditions are met—see Module 10.) Future expected benefits usually refer to future cash inflows. Companies capitalize the full cost to acquire the

---

BUSINESS INSIGHT | **WorldCom and Improper Cost Capitalization**

WorldCom's CEO, Bernie Ebbers, and chief financial officer, Scott Sullivan, were convicted in 2005 of *cooking the books* so the company would not show a loss for 2001 and subsequent quarters. Specifically, WorldCom incurred large costs in anticipation of an increase in Internet-related business that did not materialize. Instead of expensing the costs as GAAP requires and reporting a loss in the WorldCom income statement, executives shifted the costs to the balance sheet. By capitalizing these costs (recording them on the balance sheet) as PPE, WorldCom was able to disguise these costs as assets, thereby inflating current profitability. Although the WorldCom case involved massive fraud, which is difficult for outsiders to detect, an astute analyst might have suspected something was amiss from analysis of WorldCom's long-term asset turnover (Sales/ Average long-term assets) as shown below. The obvious decline in turnover reveals that World-Com's assets constituted an ever-increasing percent of total sales during periods leading up to 2002. This finding does not, in itself, imply fraud. It does, however, raise serious questions that analysts should have posed to WorldCom executives in analyst meetings.

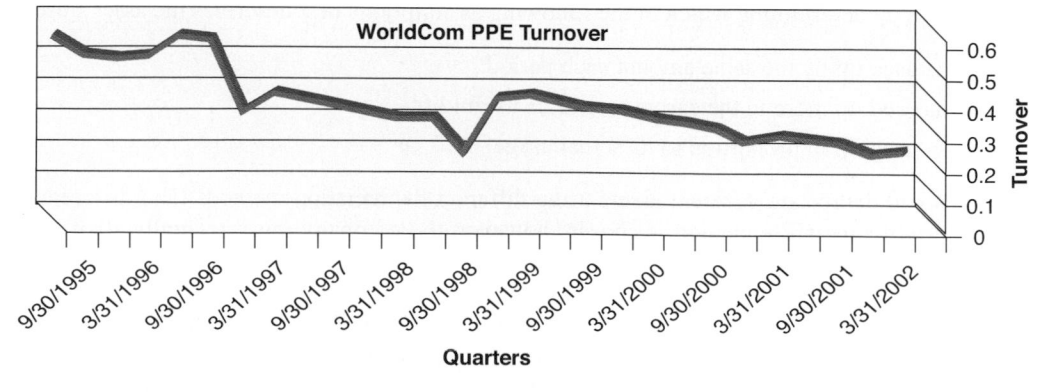

asset, including the purchase price, transportation, setup, and all other costs necessary to get the asset into service. This is called the asset's acquisition cost.

Companies can only capitalize asset costs that are *directly linked* to future cash inflows, and the costs capitalized as an asset can be no greater than the related expected future cash inflows. This means that if a company reports a $200 asset, we can reasonably expect that it will derive at least $200 in expected cash inflows from the use and ultimate disposal of the asset.

The *directly linked* condition for capitalization of asset cost is important. When a company acquires a machine, it capitalizes the cost because the company expects the machine's output to yield cash inflows from the sale of products associated with the machine and from the cash received when the company eventually disposes of the machine. On the other hand, when it comes to research and development (R&D) activities, it is more difficult to directly link expected cash inflows with the R&D expenditures because R&D activities are often unsuccessful. Further, companies cannot reliably estimate the future cash flows from successful R&D activities. Accordingly, GAAP requires that R&D expenditures be expensed when paid. Similar arguments are applied to advertising, promotion and wages to justify expensing of those costs. Each of these latter examples relates to items or activities that we generally think will create intangible assets. That is, we reasonably expect R&D efforts and advertising campaigns to produce results. If not, companies would not pursue them.

We also generally view employee activities as generating future benefits. Indeed, we often refer to the *human resources* (asset) of a company. However, the link between these items or activities and their outputs is not as direct as GAAP requires for capitalizing such costs. The nonrecognition of these assets is one reason why it is difficult to analyze and value knowledge-based companies and such companies are less suited to traditional ROE disaggregation analysis. Capitalization and non-capitalization of costs can markedly impact financial statements and our analysis inferences and assessment of a company as an investment prospect.

Depreciation

Once the cost of PPE is capitalized on the balance sheet as an asset, it must be systematically transferred from the balance sheet to the income statement as depreciation expense to match the asset's cost to the revenues it generates. The depreciation process requires the following estimates:

1. **Useful life**. Period of time over which the asset is expected to generate cash inflows or other measurable benefits
2. **Salvage value**. Expected disposal amount at the end of the asset's useful life
3. **Depreciation rate**. An estimate of how the asset will be used up over its useful life

Management must determine each of these factors when the asset is acquired. Depreciation commences immediately upon asset acquisition and use. Management also can revise estimates that determine depreciation during the asset's useful life.

The **depreciation base**, also called *nonrecoverable cost*, is the amount to be depreciated. The depreciation base is the acquisition cost less estimated salvage value. This means that at the end of the asset's useful life, only the salvage value remains on the balance sheet.

Depreciation method relates to the manner in which the asset is used up. Companies choose from three methods by determining which of the following assumptions best describes the asset's use:

1. Asset is used up by the same amount each period.
2. Asset is used up more in the early years of its useful life.
3. Asset is used up in proportion to its actual usage.

A company can depreciate different assets using different depreciation methods (and different useful lives). After a depreciation method is chosen, however, the company must generally stick with that method throughout the asset's useful life. This is not to say that companies cannot change depreciation methods, but changes must be justified as providing more useful financial reports.

The using up of an asset generally relates to physical or technological obsolescence. *Physical obsolescence* relates to an asset's diminished capacity to produce output. *Technological obsolescence* relates to an asset's diminished efficiency in producing output in a competitive manner.

All depreciation methods have the following general formula:

$$\text{Depreciation Expense} = \text{Depreciation Base} \times \text{Depreciation Rate}$$

Remembering this general formula helps us understand the depreciation process. Also, each depreciation method reports the same amount of depreciation expense *over the life of the asset*. The only difference is in the amount of depreciation expense reported *for a given period*. To illustrate, consider a machine with the following details: $100,000 cost, $10,000 salvage value, and a five-year useful life. We look at two of the most common methods of depreciation.

Straight-Line Method

Under the straight-line (SL) method, depreciation expense is recognized evenly over the estimated useful life of the asset as follows:

Depreciation Base	Depreciation Rate
Cost − Salvage value	1/Estimated useful life
= $100,000 − $10,000	= 1/5 years
= $90,000	= 20%

Depreciation expense per year for this asset is $18,000, computed as $90,000 × 20%. For the asset's first full year of usage, $18,000 of depreciation expense is reported in the income statement. (If an asset is purchased midyear, it is typically depreciated only for the portion of the year it is used. For example, had the asset in this illustration been purchased on May 31, the company would report $10,500 of depreciation in the first year, computed as 7/12 × $18,000, assuming the company has a December 31 year-end.) This depreciation is reflected in the company's financial statements as follows:

	Balance Sheet							Income Statement		
Transaction	Cash Asset	+	Noncash Assets	=	Liabil- ities	+	Contrib. Capital	+	Earned Capital	Rev- enues	−	Expen- ses	=	Net Income
Record $18,000 straight-line depreciation			−18,000 Accumulated Depreciation	=					−18,000 Retained Earnings			+18,000 Depreciation Expense	=	−18,000

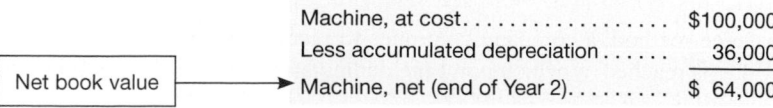

The accumulated depreciation (contra asset) account increases by $18,000, thus reducing net PPE by the same amount. Also, $18,000 of the asset cost is transferred from the balance sheet to the income statement as depreciation expense. At the end of the first year the asset is reported on the balance sheet as follows:

Machine, at cost.................	$100,000
Less accumulated depreciation......	18,000
Net book value ⟶ Machine, net (end of Year 1)........	$ 82,000

Accumulated depreciation is the sum of all depreciation expense that has been recorded to date. The asset **net book value (NBV)**, or *carrying value*, is cost less accumulated depreciation. Although the word value is used here, it does not refer to market value. Depreciation is a cost allocation concept (transfer of costs from the balance sheet to the income statement), not a valuation concept.

In the second year of usage, another $18,000 of depreciation expense is recorded in the income statement and the net book value of the asset on the balance sheet follows:

Machine, at cost.................	$100,000
Less accumulated depreciation......	36,000
Net book value ⟶ Machine, net (end of Year 2)........	$ 64,000

Accumulated depreciation of $36,000 now includes the sum of the first and second years' depreciation, and the net book value of the asset is now reduced to $64,000. After the fifth year, a total of $90,000 of accumulated depreciation will be recorded ($18,000 per year × 5 years), yielding a net book value for the machine of $10,000. The net book value at the end of the machine's useful life is exactly equal to the salvage value that management estimated when the asset was acquired.

Double-Declining-Balance Method

GAAP also allows *accelerated* methods of depreciation, the most common being the double-declining-balance method. This method records more depreciation in the early years of an asset's useful life (hence the term *accelerated*) and less depreciation in later years. At the end of the asset's useful life, the balance sheet will still report a net book value equal to the asset's salvage value. The difference between straight-line and accelerated depreciation methods is not in the total amount of depreciation, but in the rate at which costs are transferred from the balance sheet to the income statement.

For the double-declining-balance (DDB) method, the depreciation base is net book value, which declines over the life of the asset (this is why the method is called "declining balance"). The depreciation rate is twice the straight-line (SL) rate (which explains the word "double"). The depreciation base and rate for the asset in our illustrative example are computed as follows:

Depreciation Base	Depreciation Rate
Net Book Value = Cost − Accumulated Depreciation	2 × SL rate = 2 × 20% = 40%

The depreciation expense for the first year is $40,000, computed as $100,000 × 40%. This depreciation is reflected in the company's financial statements as follows:

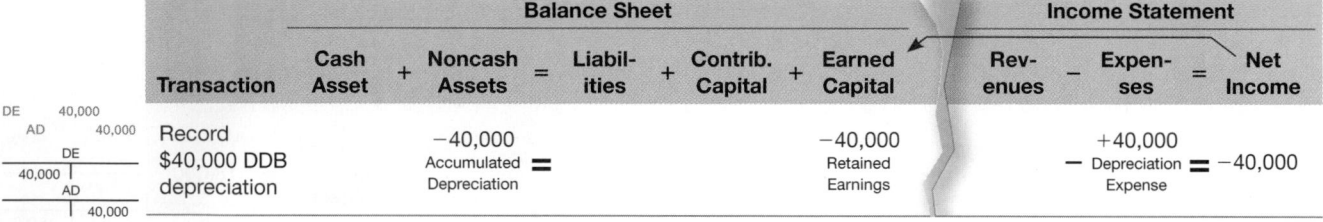

The accumulated depreciation (contra asset) account increases by $40,000 which reduces net PPE (compare this to the $18,000 depreciation under straight-line). This means that $40,000 of the asset cost is transferred from the balance sheet to the income statement as depreciation expense. At the end of the first year, the asset is reported on the balance sheet as follows:

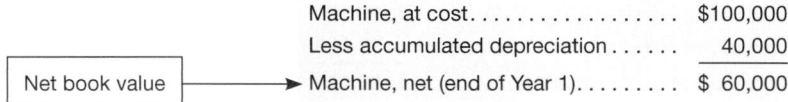

	Machine, at cost.................	$100,000
	Less accumulated depreciation......	40,000
Net book value	Machine, net (end of Year 1).........	$ 60,000

In the second year, the net book value of the asset is the new depreciable base, and the company records depreciation of $24,000 ($60,000 × 40%) in the income statement. At the end of the second year, the net book value of the asset on the balance sheet is:

	Machine, at cost.................	$100,000
	Less accumulated depreciation......	64,000
Net book value	Machine, net (end of Year 2).........	$ 36,000

Under the double-declining-balance method, a company continues to record depreciation expense in this manner until the salvage value is reached, at which point the depreciation process is discontinued.

This leaves a net book value equal to the salvage value, as with the straight-line method.[8] The DDB depreciation schedule for the life of this asset is in Exhibit 6.10.

EXHIBIT 6.10	Double-Declining-Balance Depreciation Schedule		
Year	Book Value at Beginning of Year	Depreciation Expense	Book Value at End of Year
1	$100,000	$40,000	$60,000
2	60,000	24,000	36,000
3	36,000	14,400	21,600
4	21,600	8,640	12,960
5	12,960	2,960*	10,000

*The formula value of $5,184 ($12,960 × 40%) is *not* reported because it would depreciate the asset below salvage value; only the $2,960 needed to reach salvage value is reported.

Exhibit 6.11 shows the depreciation expense and net book value for both the SL and DDB methods. During the first two years, the DDB method yields a higher depreciation expense compared to the SL method. Beginning in the third year, this pattern reverses and the SL method produces higher depreciation expense. Over the asset's life, the same $90,000 of asset cost is transferred to the income statement as depreciation expense, leaving a salvage value of $10,000 on the balance sheet under both methods.

EXHIBIT 6.11	Comparison of Straight-Line and Double-Declining-Balance Depreciation			
	Straight-Line		Double-Declining-Balance	
Year	Depreciation Expense	Book Value at End of Year	Depreciation Expense	Book Value at End of Year
1	$18,000	$82,000	$40,000	$60,000
2	18,000	64,000	24,000	36,000
3	18,000	46,000	14,400	21,600
4	18,000	28,000	8,640	12,960
5	18,000	10,000	2,960	10,000
	$90,000		$90,000	

All depreciation methods yield the same salvage value

Total depreciation expense over asset life is identical for all methods

Companies typically use the SL method for financial reporting purposes and an accelerated depreciation method for tax returns.[9] The reason is that in early years the SL depreciation yields higher income on shareholder reports, whereas accelerated depreciation yields lower taxable income. Even though this relation reverses in later years, companies prefer to have the tax savings sooner rather than later so that the cash savings can be invested to produce earnings. Further, the reversal may never occur—if depreciable assets are growing at a fast enough rate, the additional first year's depreciation on newly acquired assets more than offsets the lower depreciation expense on older assets, yielding a "permanent" reduction in taxable income and taxes paid.[10]

Asset Sales and Impairments

This section discusses gains and losses from asset sales, and the computation and disclosure of asset impairments.

---

[8] A variant of DDB allows for a change from DDB to SL at the point when SL depreciation exceeds that for DDB.

[9] The IRS mandates the use of MACRS (Modified Accelerated Cost Recovery System) for tax purposes. This method specifies the useful life for various classes of assets, assumes no salvage value, and generally uses the double-declining-balance method.

[10] A third, common depreciation method is **units-of-production**, which depreciates assets according to use. Specifically, the depreciation base is cost less salvage value, and the depreciation rate is the units produced and sold during the year compared with the total expected units to be produced and sold. For example, if a truck is driven 10,000 miles out of a total expected 100,000 miles, 10% of its nonrecoverable cost is reflected as depreciation expense. This method is common for extractive industries like timber and coal.

Gains and Losses on Asset Sales

The gain or loss on the sale (disposition) of a long-term asset is computed as follows.

$$\text{Gain or Loss on Asset Sale} = \text{Proceeds from Sale} - \text{Net Book Value of Asset Sold}$$

An asset's net book value is its acquisition cost less accumulated depreciation. When an asset is sold, its acquisition cost and related accumulated depreciation are both removed from the balance sheet and any gain or loss is reported in income from continuing operations.

Gains and losses on asset sales can be large, and analysts must be aware that these gains and losses are usually *transitory operating* income components. Financial statements do not typically report gains and losses from asset sales because, if the gain or loss is small (immaterial), companies include the item in selling, general and administrative expenses. Footnotes can sometimes be informative. To illustrate, **International Paper Company** provides the following footnote disclosure relating to the sale of its forestlands ($ millions):

> In the fourth quarter, the Company completed sales of 5.1 million acres of forestlands for $6.1 billion, including $1.4 billion in cash and $4.7 billion in installment notes, resulting in pre-tax gains totaling $4.4 billion.

International Paper sold forestlands, carried on its balance sheet at a net book value of $1.7 billion (computed as $6.1 billion sale less $4.4 billion gain), for $6.1 billion. The impacts on its financial statements follow:

Cash   1.4 Bil.
N.Rec.   4.7 Bil.
  PPE   1.7 Bil.
  Gain   4.4 Bil.

Cash
1.4 Bil. |
Notes Rec.
4.7 Bil. |
PPE
       | 1.7 Bil.
Gain
       | 4.4 Bil.

	Balance Sheet					Income Statement		
Transaction	Cash Asset	+ Noncash Assets	= Liabil- ities	+ Contrib. Capital	+ Earned Capital	Rev- enues	− Expen- ses	= Net Income
Sale of forestlands	+1.4 Bil. Cash	−1.7 Bil. Forestlands (PPE) +4.7 Bil. Notes Receivable =			+4.4 Bil. Retained Earnings	+4.4 Bil. Gain on Asset Sale	−	= +4.4 Bil.

Asset Impairments

Property, plant, and equipment (PPE) assets are reported at their net book values (original cost less accumulated depreciation). This is the case even if the market values of these assets increase subsequent to acquisition. As a result, there can be unrecognized gains hidden within the balance sheet.

On the other hand, if market values of PPE assets subsequently decrease—and the asset value is deemed to be permanently impaired—then companies must write off the impaired cost and recognize losses on those assets. **Impairment** of PPE assets is determined by comparing the asset's net book value to the sum of the asset's *expected* future (undiscounted) cash flows. If the sum of expected cash flow is greater than net book value, there is no impairment. However, if the sum of the expected cash flow is less than net book value, the asset is deemed impaired and it is written down to its current fair value (generally, the present value of those expected cash flows). Exhibit 6.12 depicts this impairment analysis.

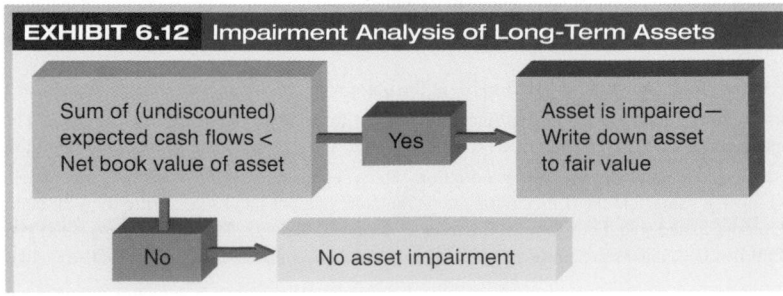

EXHIBIT 6.12   Impairment Analysis of Long-Term Assets

When a company takes an impairment charge, assets are reduced by the amount of the write-down and the loss is recognized in the income statement. To illustrate, a footnote to the 2011 10-K of **Starbucks Corporation** reports the following about asset impairments:

Asset Impairment When facts and circumstances indicate that the carrying values of long-lived assets may not be recoverable, we evaluate long-lived assets for impairment. We first compare the carrying value of the asset to the asset's estimated future cash flows (undiscounted). If the estimated future cash flows are less than the carrying value of the asset, we calculate an impairment loss based on the asset's estimated fair value. For store assets, the fair value of the assets is estimated using a discounted cash flow model based on future store revenues and operating costs, using internal projections . . . We recognized net impairment and disposition losses of $67.7 million, $224.4 million and $325.0 million in fiscal 2010, 2009 and 2008, respectively, primarily due to underperforming company-operated retail stores. The net losses in fiscal 2009 and 2008 include $129.2 million and $201.6 million, respectively, of asset impairments related primarily to the US and International store closures as part of Starbucks store portfolio rationalization which began in fiscal 2008.

Starbucks's pretax write-down of impaired assets affected its financial statements as follows:

	Balance Sheet							Income Statement			
Transaction	Cash Asset	+	Noncash Assets	=	Liabil-ities	+	Contrib. Capital	+	Earned Capital		Rev-enues	−	Expen-ses	=	Net Income
Write-down long-lived assets by $67.7 Mil.			−67.7 Mil. PPE	=					−67.7 Mil. Retained Earnings				+67.7 Mil. − Asset Impairment Expense	=	−67.7 Mil.

AIE   67.7 Mil.
PPE   67.7 Mil.

AIE
67.7 Mil.

PPE
67.7 Mil.

Starbucks wrote down the carrying value (net book value) of its long-lived assets by $67.7 million. This write-down accelerated the transfer of the asset's cost from the balance sheet to the income statement. Consequently, Starbucks recognized a pretax expense of $67.7 million in the current year rather than over time via the depreciation process.

It is important to note that management determines if and when to recognize asset impairments. Thus, there is room for management to opportunistically over- or underestimate asset impairments. Write-downs of long-term assets are often recognized in connection with a restructuring program.

Analysis of asset write-downs presents at least two potential challenges:

1. *Insufficient write-down.* Assets sometimes are impaired but an impairment charge is not recognized. This can arise if management is overly optimistic about future prospects or is reluctant to recognize the full impairment in income.

2. *Aggressive write-down.* This *big bath* scenario can arise if income is already very low in a given year. Management's view is that the market will not penalize the company's stock for an extra write-off when the year was already bad. Taking a larger impairment charge purges the balance sheet of costs that would otherwise hit future years' income.

GAAP does not condone either of these cases. Yet, because management must estimate future cash flows for the impairment test, it has some degree of control over the timing and amount of the asset write-off and can use that discretion to manage reported income.

IFRS INSIGHT   **PPE Valuation under IFRS**

Like GAAP, companies reporting under IFRS must periodically assess long-lived assets for possible impairment. Unlike the two-step GAAP approach, IFRS use a one-step approach: firms compare an asset's net book value to its current fair value (estimated as discounted expected future cash flows) to test for impairment and then reduce net book value to that fair value. Another IFRS difference is that PPE can be revalued upwards to fair value if fair value can be measured reliably.

Footnote Disclosures

Cisco reports the following PPE asset amounts in its balance sheet:

($ millions)	July 31, 2010	July 25, 2009
Property, plant and equipment, net	$3,941	$4,043

In addition to its balance sheet disclosure, Cisco provides two footnotes that more fully describe its PPE assets:

1. *Summary of Significant Accounting Policies.* This footnote describes Cisco's accounting for PPE assets in general terms:

Depreciation and Amortization Property and equipment are stated at cost, less accumulated depreciation and amortization. Depreciation and amortization are computed using the straight-line method over the following periods.

Buildings.	25 years
Building improvements.	10 years
Furniture and fixtures	5 years
Leasehold improvements	Shorter of remaining lease term or 5 years
Computer equipment and related software	30 to 36 months
Production, engineering, and other equipment	Up to 5 years
Operating lease assets	Based on lease term—generally up to 3 years

There are two items of interest in this disclosure: (a) Cisco, like most publicly traded companies, depreciates its PPE assets using the straight-line method (for tax purposes it uses an accelerated method). (b) Cisco provides general disclosures on the useful lives of its assets: 30 months to 25 years. We will discuss a method to more accurately estimate the useful lives in the next section.

2. *Supplemental balance sheet information.* This footnote provides a breakdown of Cisco's PPE assets by category as well as the balance in the accumulated depreciation account:

Property and equipment, net (millions)	July 31, 2010	July 25, 2009
Land, buildings, and building & leasehold improvements	$ 4,470	$ 4,618
Computer equipment and related software	1,405	1,823
Production, engineering, and other equipment	4,702	5,075
Operating lease assets.	255	227
Furniture and fixtures	476	465
	11,308	12,208
Less accumulated depreciation and amortization	(7,367)	(8,165)
Total	$ 3,941	$ 4,043

Analysis Implications

This section explains how to measure long-term asset utilization and asset age.

PPE Turnover

A crucial issue in analyzing PPE assets is determining their productivity (utilization). For example, what level of plant assets is necessary to generate a dollar of revenues? How capital intensive are the company and its competitors? To address these and similar questions, we use **PPE turnover**, defined as follows:

PPE Turnover (PPET) = Sales/Average PPE Assets, net

Cisco's 2010 PPE turnover is 10.0 ($40,040 million/[($3,941 million + $4,043 million)/2]). (We use net PPE in the computation above; arguments for using gross PPE are not as compelling as with receivables because managers have less latitude over accumulated depreciation vis-a-vis the allowance for uncollectibles.) This turnover places Cisco somewhat higher than most of its peers (see chart that follows).

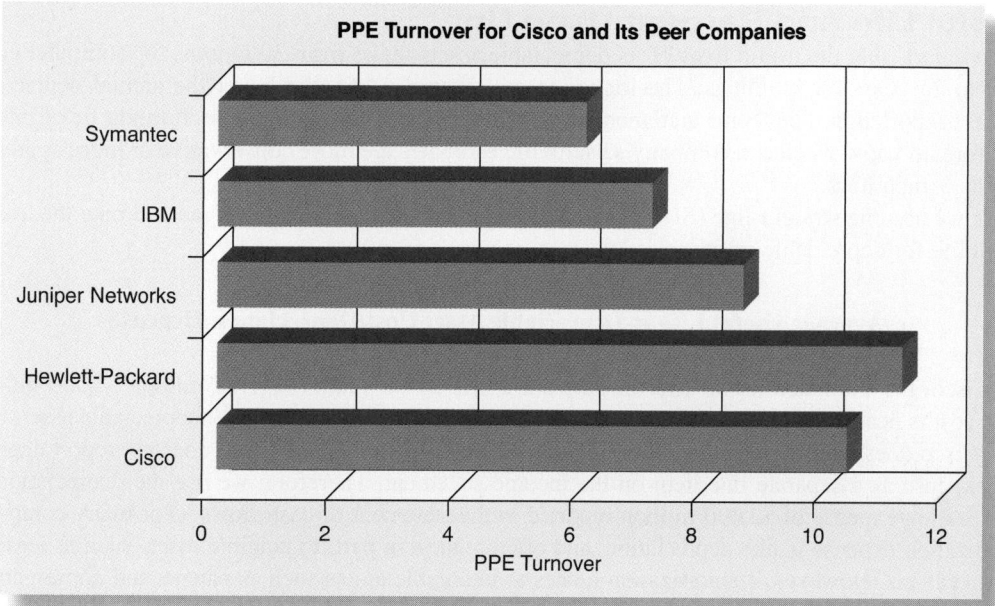

Higher PPE turnover is preferable to lower. A higher PPE turnover implies a lower capital investment for a given level of sales. Higher turnover, therefore, increases profitability because the company avoids asset carrying costs and because the freed-up assets can generate operating cash flow. (PPE turnover that is markedly higher than competitors may hint that the company leases equipment instead of owning it; see Module 10 for explanation.)

PPE turnover is lower for capital-intensive manufacturing companies than it is for companies in service or knowledge-based industries. To this point, consider the following chart of PPE turnover for selected industries.

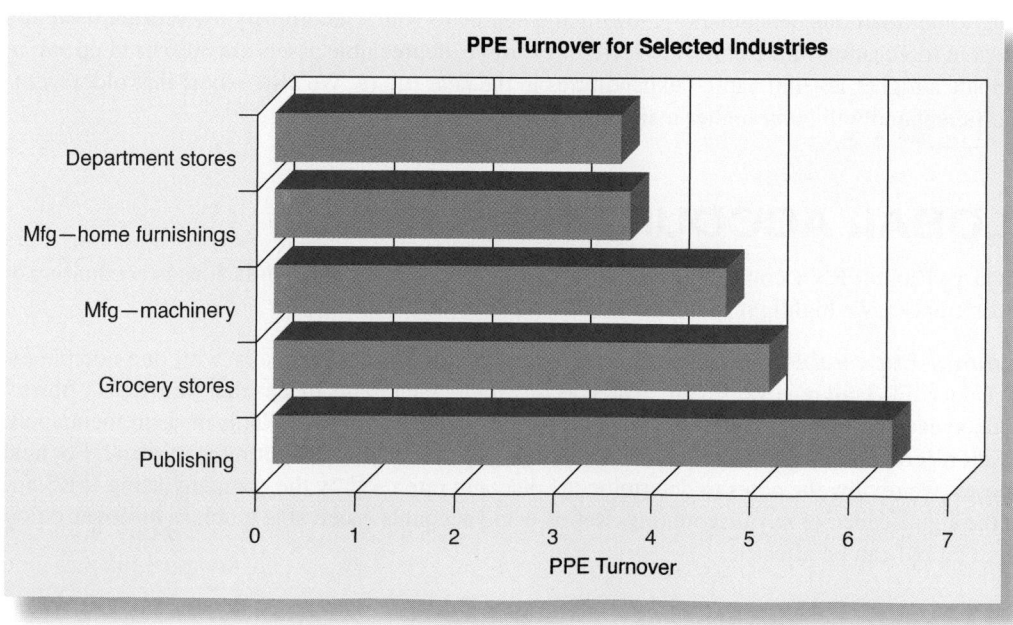

Publishers and grocery stores are not capital-intensive businesses. Their PPE turnover rates are, correspondingly, higher than for other industries.

MANAGERIAL DECISION   **You Are the Division Manager**

You are the manager for a main operating division of your company. You are concerned that a declining PPE turnover is adversely affecting your division's return on net operating assets. What specific actions can you take to increase PPE turnover? [Answer, p. 6-37]

Useful Life and Percent Used Up

Cisco reports that the useful lives of its depreciable assets range from 30 months for computer equipment to 25 years for buildings. The longer an asset's useful life, the lower the annual depreciation expense reported in the income statement and the higher the income each year. It might be of interest, therefore, to know whether a company's useful life estimates are more conservative or more aggressive than its competitors.

If we assume straight-line (SL) depreciation and zero salvage value, we can estimate the average useful life for depreciable assets as follows:

$$\text{Average Useful Life} = \text{Depreciable Asset Cost/Depreciation Expense}$$

For Cisco, the estimated useful life for its plant assets is 5.6 years ($11,308 million/$2,030 million). Land cost is nearly always excluded from gross PPE cost because land is a nondepreciable asset. However, Cisco does not provide a breakout of land cost in its footnotes and Cisco does not report depreciation expense as a separate line item on the income statement. Therefore, we use the depreciation and amortization expense of $2,030 million reported in the statement of cash flows. (For many companies, amortization expense is like depreciation, and often relates, in part, to tangible assets such as leasehold improvements. However, if amortization relates to intangible assets such as patents and copyrights, the amortization should be subtracted from total depreciation and amortization before estimating useful life.)

We can also estimate the proportion of a company's depreciable assets that have already been transferred to the income statement. This ratio reflects the percent of depreciable assets that are no longer productive—as follows:

$$\text{Percent Used Up} = \text{Accumulated Depreciation/Depreciable Asset Cost}$$

Cisco's assets are 65% used up, computed as $7,367 million/$11,308 million. If a company replaced all of its assets evenly each year, the percent used up ratio would be 50%. Cisco's depreciable assets are slightly older than this benchmark. Knowing the degree to which a company's assets are used up is of interest in forecasting future cash flows. If, for example, depreciable assets are 80% used up, we might anticipate a higher level of capital expenditures in the near future. We also expect that older assets are less efficient and will incur higher maintenance costs.

GLOBAL ACCOUNTING

Both GAAP and IFRS account similarly for operating assets. Although similarities in accounting dwarf any differences, we highlight some of the more notable differences.

Accounts Receivable Accounts receivable are accounted for identically with one notable exception. Under IFRS, all receivables are treated as *financial* assets. This means that future cash flows from accounts receivable must be discounted and reported at net present value. This measurement applies to both short-term and long-term receivables, assuming the effect of discounting is material. For analysis purposes, we review the notes to determine the discount rate used by the company using IFRS and assess the significance of any discounting. Ratios using accounts receivable (such as turnover ratios and current ratios) can be affected.

Inventory There are three notable differences in accounting for inventory:

1. IFRS does not permit use of the LIFO method; in this module, we discussed the needed adjustments when analyzing a company that uses LIFO.

2. Under U.S. GAAP, inventory is carried at lower of cost or market; under IFRS it is lower of cost or net realizable value. This means that GAAP inventory write-downs are larger than under IFRS because of the floor effect for market value, described earlier in the module. We analyze notes to determine if inventory write-downs are large. If so, GAAP cost of sales can be much higher, which can depress gross profit margins and operating income. This can impact ratios such as inventory turnover, but we cannot determine the direction, which depends on the relative size of the write-down and its impact on cost of sales versus total inventory. (When using LIFO, inventory write-downs are less frequent because the "cost" of LIFO inventory is the oldest costs, which are often low relative to current market replacement values.)

3. IFRS permits companies to reverse inventory write-downs; GAAP does not. This means that if markets recover and inventory previously "impaired" regains some or all of its value, it can be revalued upwards. IFRS notes disclose this revaluation, if material, which permits us to recompute inventory and cost of sales amounts that are comparable to GAAP.

Fixed Assets In accounting for fixed assets, four notable differences deserve mention:

1. GAAP requires the total cost of a fixed asset to be capitalized and depreciated over its useful life. Under IFRS, fixed assets are disaggregated into individual components and then each component is separately depreciated over its useful life. Thus, assets with components with vastly different useful lives, can yield depreciation expense using IFRS that is markedly different from that computed using GAAP. This means that income, and net book values of assets on the balance sheet, can differ for two otherwise identical companies using GAAP versus IFRS. Ratios using plant assets are also impacted. We must review notes regarding depreciation of asset components to make this assessment.

2. Property, plant and equipment can be carried at depreciated cost under U.S. GAAP and IFRS, but can be revalued at fair market value under IFRS. The latter will cause IFRS book values of PPE to be higher. Few companies have opted to revalue assets upwards but in some industries, such as real estate, the practice is common.

3. U.S. GAAP applies a two-step approach for determining impairments. Step 1: compare book value to *undiscounted* expected future cash flows; and Step 2: if book value is higher, measure impairment using *discounted* expected future cash flows. IFRS uses *discounted* expected future cash flows for both steps, which means IFRS uses one step. This results in more asset impairments under IFRS.

4. IFRS fair-value impairments for fixed assets can be reversed; that is, written back up after being written down. The notes to PPE articulate such reversals.

MODULE-END REVIEW

On January 2, assume that Hewlett-Packard purchases equipment that fabricates a key-product part. The equipment costs $95,000, and its estimated useful life is five years, after which it is expected to be sold for $10,000.

Required
1. Compute depreciation expense for each year of the equipment's useful life for each of the following depreciation methods:
   a. Straight-line
   b. Double-declining-balance
2. Show how HP reports the equipment on its balance sheet at the end of the third year assuming straight-line depreciation.
3. Assume that this is the only depreciable asset the company owns and that it uses straight-line depreciation. Estimate the useful life and the percent used up for this asset at the end of the third year.

4. Assume that HP estimates that, at the end of the third year, the equipment will generate $40,000 in cash flow over its remaining life and that it has a current fair value of $36,000. Is the equipment impaired? If so, what is the effect on HP's financial statements?

5. Instead of the facts in part 4, assume that, at the end of the third year, HP sells the equipment for $50,000 cash. What amount of gain or loss does HP report from this sale?

The solution is on page 6-53.

GUIDANCE ANSWERS

MANAGERIAL DECISION **You Are the Receivables Manager**

First, we must realize that extending credit is an important tool in the marketing of your products, often as important as advertising and promotion. Given that receivables are necessary, there are certain ways to speed their collection. (1) We can better screen the customers to whom we extend credit. (2) We can negotiate advance or progress payments from customers. (3) We can use bank letters of credit or other automatic drafting procedures that obviate billing. (4) We can make sure products are sent as ordered, to reduce disputes. (5) We can improve administration of past-due accounts to provide for more timely notices of delinquencies and better collection procedures.

MANAGERIAL DECISION **You Are the Plant Manager**

Companies need inventories to avoid lost sales opportunities; however, there are several ways to minimize inventory needs. (1) We can reduce product costs by improving product design to eliminate costly features that customers don't value. (2) We can use more cost-efficient suppliers; possibly producing in lower wage-rate parts of the world. (3) We can reduce raw material inventories with just-in-time delivery from suppliers. (4) We can eliminate production bottlenecks that increase work-in-process inventories. (5) We can manufacture for orders rather than for estimated demand to reduce finished goods inventories. (6) We can improve warehousing and distribution to reduce duplicate inventories. (7) We can monitor product sales and adjust product mix as demand changes to reduce finished goods inventories.

MANAGERIAL DECISION **You Are the Division Manager**

PPE is a difficult asset to reduce. Because companies need long-term operating assets, managers usually try to maximize throughput to reduce unit costs. Also, many companies form alliances to share administrative, production, logistics, customer service, IT, and other functions. These alliances take many forms (such as joint ventures) and are designed to spread ownership of assets among many users. The goal is to identify underutilized assets and to increase capacity utilization. Another solution might be to reconfigure the value chain from raw material to end user. Examples include the sharing of IT, or manufacturing facilities, outsourcing of production or administration such as customer service centers, and the use of special purpose entities for asset securitization (see Module 10).

DISCUSSION QUESTIONS

Q6-1. Explain how management can shift income from one period into another by its estimation of uncollectible accounts.

Q6-2. Why do relatively stable inventory costs across periods reduce the importance of management's choice of an inventory costing method?

Q6-3. Explain why using the FIFO inventory costing method will increase gross profit during periods of rising inventory costs.

Q6-4. If inventory costs are rising, which inventory costing method—first-in, first-out; last-in, first-out; or average cost—yields the (a) lowest ending inventory? (b) lowest net income? (c) largest ending inventory? (d) largest net income? (e) greatest cash flow, assuming the same method is used for tax purposes?

Q6-5. Even though it may not reflect their physical flow of goods, why might companies adopt last-in, first-out inventory costing in periods when costs are consistently rising?

Q6-6. In a recent annual report, Kaiser Aluminum Corporation made the following statement in reference to its inventories: "The Company recorded pretax charges of approximately $19.4 million because of a reduction in the carrying values of its inventories caused principally by prevailing lower prices for alumina, primary aluminum, and fabricated products." What basic accounting principle caused Kaiser Aluminum to record this $19.4 million pretax charge? Briefly describe the rationale for this principle.

Kaiser Aluminum
Corporation (KALU)

Q6-7. Why is depreciation expense necessary to properly match revenues and expenses?

Q6-8. How might a company revise its depreciation expense computation due to a change in an asset's estimated useful life or salvage value?

Q6-9. When is a PPE asset considered to be impaired? How is an impairment loss computed?

Q6-10. What is the benefit of accelerated depreciation for income tax purposes when the total depreciation taken over the asset's life is identical under any method of depreciation?

Q6-11. What factors determine the gain or loss on the sale of a PPE asset?

**Assignments with the ✔ in the margin are available in an online homework system.
See the Preface of the book for details.**

MINI EXERCISES

M6-12. Estimating Uncollectible Accounts and Reporting Accounts Receivable (LO1)
Mohan Company estimates its uncollectible accounts by aging its accounts receivable and applying percentages to various aged categories of accounts. Mohan computes a total of $2,100 in estimated uncollectible accounts as of its current year-end. Its Accounts Receivable has a balance of $98,000, and its Allowance for Uncollectible Accounts has an unused balance of $500 before any year-end adjustments.

a. What amount of bad debts expense will Mohan report in its income statement for the current year?
b. Determine the net amount of accounts receivable reported in current assets at year-end.

M6-13. Interpreting the Allowance Method for Accounts Receivable (LO1)
At a recent board of directors meeting of Ascot, Inc., one of the directors expressed concern over the allowance for uncollectible accounts appearing in the company's balance sheet. "I don't understand this account," he said. "Why don't we just show accounts receivable at the amount owed to us and get rid of that allowance?" Respond to the director's question; include in your response (a) an explanation of why the company has an allowance account, (b) what the balance sheet presentation of accounts receivable is intended to show, and (c) how accrual accounting (as opposed to the cash-basis accounting) affects the presentation of accounts receivable.

M6-14. Analyzing the Allowance for Uncollectible Accounts (LO1)
Following is the current asset section from the Kraft Foods, Inc., balance sheet.

Kraft Foods, Inc. (KFT)

$ millions	2010	2009
Cash and cash equivalents	$ 2,481	$ 2,101
Receivables (net of allowances of $246 in 2010 and $121 in 2009)	6,539	5,197
Inventories, net.	5,310	3,775
Deferred income taxes	898	730
Other current assets.	993	651
Total current assets	$16,221	$12,454

a. Compute the gross amount of accounts receivable for both 2010 and 2009. Compute the percentage of the allowance for uncollectible accounts relative to the gross amount of accounts receivable for each of those years.
b. Compute the relative size of net accounts receivable to total assets; the latter were $95,289 million and $66,714 million for 2010 and 2009, respectively. Interpret the quality of Kraft's receivables for 2010 compared to 2009. (As additional background, net earnings attributable to the company were $4,114 million and $3,021 million for 2010 and 2009, respectively.)

M6-15.   Evaluating Accounts Receivable Turnover for Competitors (LO1)

Procter & Gamble
(PG)

Colgate-Palmolive
(CL)

Procter & Gamble (PG) and Colgate-Palmolive (CL) report the following sales and accounts receivable balances ($ millions) for 2010 and 2009.

$ millions	Procter & Gamble		Colgate-Palmolive	
	Sales	Accounts Receivable	Sales	Accounts Receivable
2010.............	$78,938	$5,335	$15,564	$1,610
2009.............	76,694	5,836	15,327	1,626

a. Compute the accounts receivable turnover for both companies for 2010.
b. Identify and discuss a potential explanation for the difference between these competitors' accounts receivable turnover.

M6-16.   Computing Cost of Goods Sold and Ending Inventory under FIFO, LIFO, and Average Cost (LO2)

Assume that Gode Company reports the following initial balance and subsequent purchase of inventory.

Inventory balance at beginning of year	1,000 units @ $100 each	$100,000
Inventory purchased during the year	2,000 units @ $150 each	300,000
Cost of goods available for sale during the year	3,000 units	$400,000

Assume that 1,700 units are sold during the year. Compute the cost of goods sold for the year and the inventory on the year-end balance sheet under the following inventory costing methods:

a. FIFO
b. LIFO
c. Average Cost

M6-17.   Computing Cost of Goods Sold and Ending Inventory under FIFO, LIFO and Average Cost (LO2)

Bartov Corporation reports the following beginning inventory and inventory purchases.

Inventory balance at beginning of year	400 units @ $10 each	$ 4,000
Inventory purchased during the year	700 units @ $12 each	8,400
Cost of goods available for sale during the year	1,100 units	$12,400

Bartov sells 600 of its inventory units during the year. Compute the cost of goods sold for the year and the inventory on the year-end balance sheet under the following inventory costing methods:

a. FIFO
b. LIFO
c. Average Cost

M6-18.   Computing and Evaluating Inventory Turnover for Two Companies (LO2)

Abercrombie & Fitch
(ANF)

TJX Companies (TJX)

Abercrombie & Fitch (ANF) and TJX Companies (TJX) report the following information in their respective January 2011 10-K reports relating to their 2010 and 2009 fiscal years.

$ millions	Abercrombie & Fitch			TJX Companies		
	Sales	Cost of Goods Sold	Inventories	Sales	Cost of Goods Sold	Inventories
2010	$3,469	$1,257	$386	$21,942	$16,040	$2,765
2009	2,929	1,045	311	20,288	14,968	2,532

a. Compute the 2010 inventory turnover for each of these two retailers.
b. Discuss any difference you observe in inventory turnover between these two companies. Does the difference confirm your expectations given their respective business models? Explain. (Hint: ANF is a higher-end retailer and TJX sells more value-priced clothing.)
c. Describe ways that a retailer can improve its inventory turnover.

M6-19. Computing Depreciation under Straight-Line and Double-Declining-Balance (LO3)

A delivery van costing $18,000 is expected to have a $1,500 salvage value at the end of its useful life of five years. Assume that the truck was purchased on January 1. Compute the depreciation expense for the first two calendar years under the following depreciation methods:

a. Straight-line
b. Double-declining-balance

M6-20. Computing Depreciation under Straight-Line and Double-Declining-Balance for Partial Years (LO3)

A company with a calendar year-end, purchases a machine costing $145,800 on May 1, 2011. The machine is expected to be obsolete after three years (36 months) and, thereafter, no longer useful to the company. The estimated salvage value is $5,400. The company's depreciation policy is to record depreciation for the portion of the year that the asset is in service. Compute depreciation expense for both 2011 and 2012 under the following depreciation methods:

a. Straight-line
b. Double-declining-balance

M6-21. Computing and Comparing PPE Turnover for Two Companies (LO3)

Texas Instruments (TXN) and Intel Corporation (INTC) report the following information.

$ millions	Intel Corporation Sales	Plant, Property and Equipment, net	Texas Instruments Sales	Plant, Property and Equipment, net
2010	$43,623	$17,899	$13,966	$3,680
2009	35,127	17,225	10,427	3,158

a. Compute the 2010 PPE turnover for both companies. Comment on any difference observed.
b. Discuss ways in which high-tech manufacturing companies like these can increase their PPE turnover.

EXERCISES

E6-22. Estimating Uncollectible Accounts and Reporting Accounts Receivable (LO1)

LaFond Company analyzes its accounts receivable at December 31, and arrives at the aged categories below along with the percentages that are estimated as uncollectible.

Age Group	Accounts Receivable	Estimated Loss %
0–30 days past due	$ 90,000	1%
31–60 days past due	20,000	2
61–120 days past due	11,000	5
121–180 days past due	6,000	10
Over 180 days past due	4,000	25
Total accounts receivable	$131,000	

The unused balance of the allowance for uncollectible accounts is $520 on December 31, before any adjustments.

a. What amount of bad debts expense will LaFond report in its income statement for the year?
b. Use the financial statement effects template to record LaFond's bad debts expense for the year.
c. What is the balance of accounts receivable on its December 31 balance sheet?

E6-23. Analyzing and Reporting Receivable Transactions and Uncollectible Accounts (using percentage of sales method) (LO1)

At the beginning of the year, Penman Company had the following account balances.

Accounts Receivable	$122,000
Allowance for Uncollectible Accounts	7,900

During the year, Penman's credit sales were $1,173,000 and collections on accounts receivable were $1,150,000. The following additional transactions occurred during the year.

Feb. 17   Wrote off Nissim's account, $3,600.
May 28   Wrote off Weiss's account, $2,400.
Dec. 15   Wrote off Ohlson's account, $900.
Dec. 31   Recorded the bad debts expense assuming that Penman's policy is to record bad debts expense as 0.8% of credit sales. (*Hint*: The allowance account is increased by 0.8% of credit sales regardless of write-offs.)

Compute the ending balances in accounts receivable and the allowance for uncollectible accounts. Show how Penman's December 31 balance sheet reports the two accounts.

Hewlett-Packard
(HPQ)

E6-24.   Interpreting the Accounts Receivable Footnote (LO1)
Hewlett-Packard Company (HPQ) reports the following in its 2010 10-K report.

October 31 (In millions)	2010	2009
Accounts receivable.	$18,481	$16,537

HPQ footnotes to its 10-K provide the following additional information relating to its allowance for doubtful accounts.

For the fiscal years ended October 31 (In millions)	2010	2009	2008
Allowance for doubtful accounts—accounts receivable			
Balance, beginning of period	$629	$553	$226
Increase in allowance from acquisition.	7	—	245
Addition of bad debts provision	80	282	226
Deductions, net of recoveries.	(191)	(206)	(144)
Balance, end of period	$525	$629	$553

a. What is the gross amount of accounts receivables for HPQ in fiscal 2010 and 2009?
b. What is the percentage of the allowance for doubtful accounts to gross accounts receivable for 2010 and 2009?
c. What amount of bad debts expense did HPQ report each year 2008 through 2010 (ignore increase in allowance from acquisitions)? How does bad debts expense compare with the amounts of its accounts receivable actually written off? (Identify the amounts and explain.)
d. Explain the changes in the allowance for doubtful accounts from 2008 through 2010. Does it appear that HPQ increased or decreased its allowance for doubtful accounts in any particular year beyond what seems reasonable? As background, total assets were $124,503, $114,799 and $113,331 for 2010, 2009 and 2008, respectively, and net earnings attributable to the company were $8,761, $7,660 and $8,329 ($ millions).

E6-25.   Estimating Bad Debts Expense and Reporting Receivables (LO1)
At December 31, Sunil Company had a balance of $375,000 in its accounts receivable and an unused balance of $4,200 in its allowance for uncollectible accounts. The company then aged its accounts as follows:

Current	$304,000
1–60 days past due	44,000
61–180 days past due	18,000
Over 180 days past due	9,000
Total accounts receivable.	$375,000

The company has experienced losses as follows: 1% of current balances, 5% of balances 1–60 days past due, 15% of balances 61–180 days past due, and 40% of balances over 180 days past due. The company continues to base its allowance for uncollectible accounts on this aging analysis and percentages.

a. What amount of bad debts expense does Sunil report on its income statement for the year?
b. Show how Sunil's December 31 balance sheet will report the accounts receivable and the allowance for uncollectible accounts.

E6-26. **Estimating Uncollectible Accounts and Reporting Receivables over Multiple Periods**   (LO1)

Barth Company, which has been in business for three years, makes all of its sales on credit and does not offer cash discounts. Its credit sales, customer collections, and write-offs of uncollectible accounts for its first three years follow:

Year	Sales	Collections	Accounts Written Off
2009	$751,000	$733,000	$5,300
2010	876,000	864,000	5,800
2011	972,000	938,000	6,500

 a. Barth recognizes bad debts expense as 1% of sales. (Hint: This means the allowance account is increased by 1% of credit sales regardless of any write-offs and unused balances.) What does Barth's 2011 balance sheet report for accounts receivable and the allowance for uncollectible accounts? What total amount of bad debts expense appears on Barth's income statement for each of the three years?

 b. Comment on the appropriateness of the 1% rate used to provide for bad debts based on your analysis in part a.

E6-27. **Applying and Analyzing Inventory Costing Methods**   (LO2)

At the beginning of the current period, Chen carried 1,000 units of its product with a unit cost of $20. A summary of purchases during the current period follows:

	Units	Unit Cost	Cost
Beginning Inventory	1,000	$20	$20,000
Purchases: #1.	1,800	22	39,600
#2.	800	26	20,800
#3.	1,200	29	34,800

During the current period, Chen sold 2,800 units.

 a. Assume that Chen uses the first-in, first-out method. Compute both cost of goods sold for the current period and the ending inventory balance. Use the financial statement effects template to record cost of goods sold for the period.

 b. Assume that Chen uses the last-in, first-out method. Compute both cost of goods sold for the current period and the ending inventory balance.

 c. Assume that Chen uses the average cost method. Compute both cost of goods sold for the current period and the ending inventory balance.

 d. Which of these three inventory costing methods would you choose to:
1. Reflect what is probably the physical flow of goods? Explain.
2. Minimize income taxes for the period? Explain.
3. Report the largest amount of income for the period? Explain.

E6-28. **Analyzing an Inventory Footnote Disclosure**   (LO2)

General Electric Company reports the following footnote in its 10-K report.

General Electric
Company (GE)

December 31 (In millions)	2010	2009
Raw materials and work in process	$ 6,973	$ 7,581
Finished goods.	4,435	4,105
Unbilled shipments.	456	759
	11,864	12,445
Less revaluation to LIFO.	(404)	(529)
	$11,460	$11,916

The company reports its inventories using the LIFO inventory costing method.

 a. What is the balance in inventories reported on GE's 2010 balance sheet?

 b. What would GE's 2010 balance sheet have reported for inventories had the company used FIFO inventory costing?

c. What cumulative effect has GE's choice of LIFO over FIFO had on its pretax income as of year-end 2010? Explain.

d. Assume GE has a 35% income tax rate. As of the 2010 year-end, how much has GE saved in taxes by choosing LIFO over FIFO method for costing inventory? Has the use of LIFO increased or decreased GE's cumulative taxes paid?

e. What effect has the use of LIFO inventory costing had on GE's pretax income and tax expense for 2010 only (assume a 35% income tax rate)?

 E6-29.   Computing Cost of Sales and Ending Inventory   (LO2)

Stocken Company has the following financial records for the current period.

	Units	Unit Cost
Beginning inventory	100	$46
Purchases: #1	650	42
#2	550	38
#3	200	36

Ending inventory is 350 units. Compute the ending inventory and the cost of goods sold for the current period using (a) first-in, first out, (b) average cost, and (c) last-in, first-out.

E6-30.   Analyzing an Inventory Footnote Disclosure   (LO2)

Deere & Co. (DE)

The inventory footnote from the Deere & Company's 2010 10-K follows.

Inventories   Most inventories owned by Deere & Company and its U.S. equipment subsidiaries are valued at cost, on the "last-in, first-out" (LIFO) basis. Remaining inventories are generally valued at the lower of cost, on the "first-in, first-out" (FIFO) basis, or market. The value of gross inventories on the LIFO basis represented 59 percent of worldwide gross inventories at FIFO value on October 31, 2010 and 2009. If all inventories had been valued on a FIFO basis, estimated inventories by major classification at October 31 in millions of dollars would have been as follows:

($ millions)	2010	2009
Raw materials and supplies	$1,201	$ 940
Work-in-process	483	387
Finished goods and parts	2,777	2,437
Total FIFO value	4,461	3,764
Less adjustment to LIFO value	1,398	1,367
Inventories	$3,063	$2,397

This footnote reveals that not all of Deere's inventories are reported using the same inventory costing method (companies can use different inventory costing methods for different inventory pools).

a. What amount does Deere report for inventories on its 2010 balance sheet?

b. What would Deere have reported as inventories on its 2010 balance sheet had the company used FIFO inventory costing for all of its inventories?

c. What cumulative effect has the use of LIFO inventory costing had, as of year-end 2010, on Deere's pretax income compared with the pretax income it would have reported had it used FIFO inventory costing for all of its inventories? Explain.

d. Assuming a 35% income tax rate, by what cumulative dollar amount has Deere's tax expense been affected by use of LIFO inventory costing as of year-end 2010? Has the use of LIFO inventory costing increased or decreased Deere's cumulative tax expense?

e. What effect has the use of LIFO inventory costing had on Deere's pretax income and tax expense for 2010 only (assume a 35% income tax rate)?

 E6-31.   Computing Straight-Line and Double-Declining-Balance Depreciation   (LO3)

On January 2, Haskins Company purchases a laser cutting machine for use in fabrication of a part for one of its key products. The machine cost $80,000, and its estimated useful life is five years, after which the expected salvage value is $5,000. For both parts *a* and *b* below: (1) Compute depreciation expense for *each year* of the machine's five-year useful life under that depreciation method. (2) Use the financial statements effects template to show the effect of depreciation for the first year only for that method.

a. Straight-line
b. Double-declining-balance

E6-32.   Computing Depreciation, Net Book Value, and Gain or Loss on Asset Sale   (LO3)

Sloan Company owns an executive plane that originally cost $800,000. It has recorded straight-line depreciation on the plane for six full years, calculated assuming an $80,000 expected salvage value at the end of its estimated 10-year useful life. Sloan disposes of the plane at the end of the sixth year.

a. At the disposal date, what is the (1) cumulative depreciation expense and (2) net book value of the plane?
b. How much gain or loss is reported at disposal if the sales price is:
1. A cash amount equal to the plane's net book value.
2. $195,000 cash.
3. $600,000 cash.

E6-33.   Computing Straight-Line and Double-Declining-Balance Depreciation   (LO3)

On January 2, 2011, Dechow Company purchases a machine that manufactures a part for one of its key products. The machine cost $218,700 and is estimated to have a useful life of six years, with an expected salvage value of $23,400. Compute depreciation expense for 2011 and 2012 for the following depreciation methods. (When equipment is used exclusively in the manufacturing process, the depreciation is more accurately recorded as part of cost of goods sold and not as depreciation expense.)

a. Straight-line.
b. Double-declining-balance.

E6-34.   Computing Depreciation, Net Book Value, and Gain or Loss on Asset Sale   (LO3)

Palepu Company owns and operates a delivery van that originally cost $27,200. Palepu has recorded straight-line depreciation on the van for three years, calculated assuming a $2,000 expected salvage value at the end of its estimated six-year useful life. Depreciation was last recorded at the end of the third year, at which time Palepu disposes of this van.

a. Compute the net book value of the van on the disposal date.
b. Compute the gain or loss on sale of the van if the disposal proceeds are:
1. A cash amount equal to the van's net book value.
2. $15,000 cash.
3. $12,000 cash.

E6-35.   Estimating Useful Life and Percent Used Up   (LO3)

The property and equipment footnote from the Deere & Company balance sheet follows.   Deere & Co. (DE)

Property and Depreciation   A summary of property and equipment at October 31 follows:

Property and Equipment ($ millions)	Useful Lives (Years)	2010	2009
Land		$ 113	$ 116
Buildings and building equipment	23	2,226	2,144
Machinery and equipment	11	3,972	3,826
Dies, patterns, tools, etc.	7	1,105	1,081
All other	5	685	672
Construction in progress		478	362
Total at cost		8,579	8,201
Less accumulated depreciation		4,856	4,744
Total		$3,723	$3,457

Property and equipment is stated at cost less accumulated depreciation. Total property and equipment additions in 2010, 2009 and 2008 were $802 million, $798 million and $1,147 million and depreciation was $540 million, $513 million and $467 million, respectively.

a. Compute the estimated useful life of Deere's depreciable assets at year-end 2010. (Hint: Exclude land and construction in progress.) How does this estimate compare with the useful lives reported in Deere's footnote disclosure?
b. Estimate the percent used up of Deere's depreciable assets at year-end 2010. How do you interpret this figure?

E6-36.   Computing and Evaluating Receivables, Inventory and PPE Turnovers (LO1, 2, 3)

Intel Corp. (INTC)

Intel Corporation reports the following financial statement amounts in its 2010 10-K report.

$ millions	Sales	Cost of Goods Sold	Receivables, net	Inventories	Plant, property and equipment, net
2008	$37,586	$16,742	$1,712	$3,744	$17,544
2009	35,127	15,566	2,273	2,935	17,225
2010	43,623	15,132	2,867	3,757	17,899

a. Compute the receivables, inventory, and PPE turnover ratios for both 2009 and 2010.

b. What changes are evident in the turnover rates of Intel for these years? Discuss ways in which a company such as Intel can improve receivables, inventory, and PPE turnover ratios.

E6-37.   Computing and Assessing Plant Asset Impairment (LO3)

On July 1, Zeibart Company purchases equipment for $225,000. The equipment has an estimated useful life of 10 years and expected salvage value of $25,000. The company uses straight-line depreciation. Four years later, economic factors cause the fair value of the equipment to decline to $90,000. On this date, Zeibart examines the equipment for impairment and estimates $125,000 in undiscounted expected cash inflows from this equipment.

a. Compute the annual depreciation expense relating to this equipment.

b. Compute the equipment's net book value at the end of the fourth year.

c. Apply the test of impairment to this equipment as of the end of the fourth year. Is the equipment impaired? Show supporting computations.

d. If the equipment is impaired at the end of the fourth year, compute the impairment loss.

PROBLEMS

P6-38.   Evaluating Turnover Rates for Different Companies (LO1, 2, 3)

Best Buy (BBY)
Caterpillar (CAT)
Dell (DELL)
Verizon (VZ)
Walmart (WMT)

Following are asset turnover rates for accounts receivable; inventory; and property, plant, and equipment (PPE) for Best Buy (retailer), Caterpillar (manufacturer of heavy equipment), Dell (computers), Verizon (communications) and Walmart (department store).

Company Name	Accounts Receivable Turnover	Inventory Turnover	Plant, Property and Equipment Turnover
Best Buy Co	23.02	6.61	12.74
Caterpillar Inc	2.77	3.81	3.42
Dell	9.97	42.60	29.75
Verizon	8.75	34.53	1.19
Walmart	91.38	9.13	4.12

Required

a. Interpret and explain difference in receivables turnover for the retailer (Best Buy) vis-à-vis that for the manufacturer (Caterpillar). What reason can you give for a 91.38 turnover for Walmart?

b. Interpret and explain the difference in inventory turnover for Dell versus Caterpillar.

c. Why is the PPE turnover for Caterpillar and Verizon low compared with other companies on this list?

d. What are some general observations you might draw regarding the relative levels of these turnover rates across the different industries?

P6-39.   Interpreting Accounts Receivable and Its Footnote Disclosure (LO1)

W.W. Grainger, Inc. (GWW)

Following is the current asset section from the W.W. Grainger, Inc., balance sheet.

As of December 31 ($ 000s)	2010	2009	2008
Cash and cash equivalents	$ 313,454	$ 459,871	$ 396,290
Accounts receivable (less allowances for doubtful accounts of $24,552, $25,850 and $26,481, respectively)	762,895	624,910	589,416
Inventories—net	991,577	889,679	1,009,932
Prepaid expenses and other assets	87,125	88,364	73,359
Deferred income taxes	44,627	42,023	52,556
Prepaid income taxes	38,393	26,668	22,556
Total current assets	$2,238,071	$2,131,515	$2,144,109

Grainger reports the following footnote relating to its receivables.

Allowance for Doubtful Accounts The following table shows the activity in the allowance for doubtful accounts.

For Years Ended December 31 ($ 000s)	2010	2009	2008
Balance at beginning of period	$25,850	$26,481	$25,830
Provision for uncollectible accounts	6,718	10,748	12,924
Write-off of uncollectible accounts, less recoveries.	(8,302)	(12,254)	(11,501)
Foreign currency translation impact.	286	875	(772)
Balance at end of period	$24,552	$25,850	$26,481

Required

a. What amount do customers owe Grainger at each of the year-ends 2008 through 2010?

b. What percentage of its total accounts receivable does Grainger feel are uncollectible? (Hint: Percentage of uncollectible accounts = Allowance for uncollectible accounts/Gross accounts receivable)

c. What amount of bad debts expense did Grainger report in its income statement for each of the years 2008 through 2010?

d. Explain the change in the balance of the allowance for uncollectible accounts since 2008. Specifically, did the allowance increase or decrease as a percentage of gross accounts receivable, and why?

e. If Grainger had kept its 2010 allowance for uncollectible accounts at the same percentage of gross accounts receivable as it was in 2008, by what amount would its profit have changed (ignore taxes)? Explain.

f. Overall, what is your assessment of Grainger's allowance for uncollectible accounts and the related bad debts expense? As background, total assets were $3,904,377, $3,726,332 and $3,515,417 for 2010, 2009 and 2008, respectively, and net earnings attributable to the company were $510,865, $430,466 and $475,355 ($ 000s).

P6-40. Analyzing and Interpreting Receivables and Related Ratios (LO1)

Following is the current asset section from Intuit's balance sheet.   Intuit, Inc. (INTU)

July 31 ($ millions)	2010	2009
Cash and cash equivalents	$ 214	$ 679
Investments	1,408	668
Accounts receivable, net of allowance for doubtful accounts of $22 and $16, respectively.	135	135
Income taxes receivable.	27	67
Deferred income taxes	117	92
Prepaid expenses and other current assets.	57	43
Current assets of discontinued operations	—	12
Current assets before funds held for customers	1,958	1,696
Funds held for customers	337	272
Total current assets	$2,295	$1,968

Total revenues were $3,455 million ($1,412 million in product sales and $2,043 million in service revenues and other) in 2010.

Required

a. What are Intuit's gross accounts receivable at the end of 2010 and 2009?

b. For both 2010 and 2009, compute the ratio of the allowance for uncollectible accounts to gross receivables. What trend do you observe?

c. Compute the receivables turnover ratio and the average collection period for 2010 based on gross receivables computed in part a. Does the collection period (days sales in receivables) appear reasonable given Intuit's lines of business (Intuit's products include QuickBooks, TurboTax and Quicken, which it sells to consumers and small businesses)? Explain.

d. Is the percentage of Intuit's allowance for uncollectible accounts to gross accounts receivable consistent with what you expect for Intuit's line of business? Explain.

e. Intuit discloses the following table related to its allowance for uncollectible accounts from its 10-K. Comment on the change in the allowance account during 2008 through 2010.

(In millions)	Balance at Beginning of Period	Additions Charged to Expense	Deductions	Balance at End of Period	Net Income	Total Assets
Year ended July 31, 2010						
Allowance for doubtful accounts	$16	$23	$(17)	$22	$574	$5,198
Year ended July 31, 2009						
Allowance for doubtful accounts	$16	$14	$(14)	$16	447	4,826
Year ended July 31, 2008						
Allowance for doubtful accounts	$15	$15	$(14)	$16	477	4,667

P6-41. **Analyzing and Interpreting Inventories and Related Ratios and Disclosures** (LO2)

Dow Chemical (DOW)

The current asset section from The Dow Chemical Company's 2010 annual report follows.

December 31 (In millions)	2010	2009
Cash and cash equivalents	$ 7,039	$ 2,846
Accounts and notes receivable		
Trade (net of allowance for doubtful receivables—2010: $128; 2009: $160)	4,616	5,656
Other.	4,428	3,539
Inventories	7,087	6,847
Deferred income tax assets—current.	611	654
Total current assets	$23,781	$19,542

The Dow Chemical inventory footnote follows.

The following table provides a breakdown of inventories:

Inventories at December 31 (In millions)	2010	2009
Finished goods.	$4,289	$3,887
Work in process	1,498	1,593
Raw materials.	644	671
Supplies	656	696
Total inventories	$7,087	$6,847

The reserves reducing inventories from a FIFO basis to a LIFO basis amounted to $1,003 million at December 31, 2010 and $818 million at December 31, 2009. Inventories valued on a LIFO basis, principally hydrocarbon and U.S. chemicals and plastics product inventories, represented 29 percent of the total inventories at December 31, 2010 and December 31, 2009.

A reduction of certain inventories resulted in the liquidation of some of the Company's LIFO inventory layers, increasing pretax income $159 million in 2010 and $84 million in 2009 and decreasing pretax income $45 million in 2008.

Required

a. What inventory costing method does Dow Chemical use? As of 2010, what is the effect on cumulative pretax income and cash flow of using this inventory costing method? (Assume a 35% tax rate.) What is the effect on 2010 pretax income and cash flow of using this inventory costing method.

b. Compute inventory turnover and average inventory days outstanding for 2010 (2010 cost of goods sold is $45,780 million). Comment on the level of these two ratios. Is the level what you expect given Dow's industry? Explain.

c. Explain why a reduction of inventory quantities increased income in 2009 and 2010, but decreased income in 2008.

P6-42. **Estimating Useful Life and Percent Used Up**   (LO3)

The property and equipment section of the Abbott Laboratories 2010 balance sheet follows.

Abbott Laboratories (ABT)

	December 31		
Property and equipment, at cost ($ thousands)	2010	2009	2008
Land	$ 648,988	$ 546,204	$ 509,606
Buildings.	4,334,236	4,010,439	3,698,861
Equipment	11,813,618	11,325,450	10,366,267
Construction in progress	577,460	604,813	613,939
	17,374,302	16,486,906	15,188,673
Less: accumulated depreciation and amortization . .	9,403,346	8,867,417	7,969,507
Net property and equipment	$ 7,970,956	$ 7,619,489	$ 7,219,166

The company also provides the following disclosure relating to the useful lives of its depreciable assets.

Property and Equipment—Depreciation and amortization are provided on a straight-line basis over the estimated useful lives of the assets. The following table shows estimated useful lives of property and equipment.

Classification	Estimated Useful Lives
Buildings.	10 to 50 years (average 27 years)
Equipment	3 to 20 years (average 11 years)

During 2010, the company reported $1,207,450 ($ 000s) for depreciation expense.

Required

a. Compute the estimated useful life of Abbott Laboratories' depreciable assets. How does this compare with its useful lives footnote disclosure above?

b. Compute the estimated percent used up of Abbott Laboratories' depreciable assets. How do you interpret this figure?

P6-43. **Interpreting and Applying Disclosures on Property and Equipment**   (LO3)

Following are selected disclosures from the Rohm and Haas Company (a specialty chemical company) 2007 10-K.

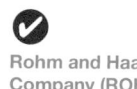

Rohm and Haas Company (ROH)

Land, Building and Equipment, Net

(in millions)	2007	2006
Land	$ 146	$ 142
Buildings and improvements	1,855	1,729
Machinery and equipment	6,155	5,721
Capitalized interest.	352	340
Construction in progress	271	218
Land, buildings, and equipment, gross	8,779	8,150
Less: Accumulated depreciation	5,908	5,481
Total	$2,871	$2,669

The principal lives (in years) used in determining depreciation rates of various assets are: buildings and improvement (10–50); machinery and equipment (5–20); automobiles, trucks and tank cars (3–10); furniture and fixtures, laboratory equipment and other assets (5–10); capitalized software (5–7). The principal life used in determining the depreciation rate for leasehold improvements is the years remaining in the lease term or the useful life (in years) of the asset, whichever is shorter.

continued

continued from prior page

Impairment of Long-lived Assets Long-lived assets, other than investments, goodwill and indefinite-lived intangible assets, are depreciated over their estimated useful lives, and are reviewed for impairment whenever changes in circumstances indicate the carrying value of the asset may not be recoverable. Such circumstances would include items such as a significant decrease in the market price of a long-lived asset, a significant adverse change in the manner the asset is being used or planned to be used or in its physical condition or a history of operating or cash flow losses associated with the use of the asset . . . When such events or changes occur, we assess the recoverability of the asset by comparing the carrying value of the asset to the expected future cash flows associated with the asset's planned future use and eventual disposition of the asset, if applicable . . . We utilize marketplace assumptions to calculate the discounted cash flows used in determining the asset's fair value . . . For the year ended December 31, 2007, we recognized approximately $24 million of fixed asset impairment charges.

Required

a. Compute the PPE turnover for 2007 (Sales in 2007 are $8,897 million). Does the level of its PPE turnover suggest that Rohm and Haas is capital intensive? Explain. (*Hint:* The median PPE turnover for all publicly traded companies is approximately 5.03 in 2007.)

b. Rohm and Haas reported depreciation expense of $412 million in 2007. Estimate the useful life, on average, for its depreciable PPE assets.

c. By what percentage are Rohm and Haas' assets "used up" at year-end 2007? What implication does the assets used up computation have for forecasting cash flows?

d. Rohm and Haas reports an asset impairment charge in 2007. How do companies determine if assets are impaired? How do asset impairment charges affect Rohm and Haas' cash flows for 2007? How would we treat these charges for analysis purposes?

Volkswagen Group
Daimler AG

IFRS APPLICATIONS

I6-44. Computing and Evaluating Inventory Turnover for Two Companies (LO2)

European car makers, Volkswagen Group (headquartered in Wolfsburg, Germany) and Daimler AG (headquartered in Stuttgart, Germany) report the following information.

(Euros in millions)	Volkswagen			Daimler		
	Sales	Cost of Goods Sold	Inventories	Sales	Cost of Goods Sold	Inventories
2008	€113,808	€96,612	€17,816	€98,469	€76,910	€16,805
2009	105,187	91,608	14,124	78,924	65,567	12,845

Required

a. Compute the 2009 inventory turnover and the 2009 gross profit margin (in %) for each of these two companies.

b. Discuss any difference in inventory turnover and gross profit margin between these two companies. Does the difference confirm expectations given their respective business models? Explain.

c. How could the companies improve inventory turnover?

I6-45. Estimating Useful Life and Percent Used Up (LO3)

Statoil ASA

Statoil ASA, headquartered in Stavanger, Norway, is a fully integrated petroleum company. The company uses IFRS to prepare its financial statements. During 2009, the company reported depreciation expense of NOK million 46,596. The property and equipment footnote from the Statoil balance sheet follows.

Equipment Operations (In NOK million, Norwegian Kroner)	2009	2008
Land and buildings..	15,735	16,528
Machinery, equipment, and transportation equipment	18,542	18,224
Production plants (including pipelines)	618,487	582,066
Refining and manufacturing plants	43,354	41,484
Vessels...	4,079	5,604
Assets under development..................................	89,221	77,883
Total at cost	789,418	741,789
Less accumulated depreciation.............................	448,583	411,948
Total	340,835	329,841

Required

a. Compute the estimated useful life of Statoil's depreciable assets at year-end 2009. Assume that land is 25% of "Land and buildings."

b. Estimate the percent used up of Statoil's depreciable assets at year-end 2009. How do we interpret this figure?

I6-46.   Computing and Evaluating Receivables, Inventory and PPE Turnovers (LO1, 2, 3)

Schneider Electric is a multinational energy company headquartered in Rueil-Malmaison, France.   Schneider Electric
Selected balance sheet and income statement information for 2007 through 2009 follows.

(€ in millions)	Sales	Cost of Goods Sold	Trade Receivables	Inventories	Plant, property, and equipment, net
2007.............	€17,309	€10,210	€3,463	€2,481	€1,856
2008.............	18,311	10,879	3,537	2,584	1,970
2009.............	15,793	9,572	3,071	2,174	1,965

Required

a. Compute the receivables, inventory, and PPE turnover ratios for both 2008 and 2009.

b. What changes are evident in the turnover rates of Schneider Electric for these years?

c. Discuss ways in which a company such as Schneider Electric can improve receivables, inventory, and PPE turnover ratios.

I6-47.   Analyzing and Interpreting Receivables and Related Ratios (LO1)

Unilever is a dual-listed company consisting of Unilever N.V. in Rotterdam, Netherlands and Unilever   Unilever
PLC in London, UK. Both Unilever companies have the same directors and effectively operate as a   Unilever N.V.
single business. Following is the current asset section of Unilever's balance sheet.   Unilever PLC

(€ million)	2009	2008
Inventories	€ 3,578	€ 3,889
Trade receivables, net of allowance for doubtful accounts of €129 and €120, respectively....................................	2,314	2,788
Prepayments, accrued income, and other receivables	1,115	1,035
Current tax assets	173	234
Cash and equivalents......................................	2,642	2,561
Other financial assets.....................................	972	632
Non-current assets held for sale	17	36
Total current assets	€10,811	€11,175

Required

a. What are Unilever's gross trade and other current receivables at the end of 2009 and of 2008?

b. For both 2009 and 2008, compute the ratio of the allowance for uncollectible accounts to gross receivables. What trend do we observe?

c. Is the ratio of Unilever's allowance for uncollectible accounts to gross accounts receivable consistent with what we expect for Unilever's line of business? Explain.

d. The company reported net sales of €39,823 in 2009. Compute the receivables turnover ratio and the average collection period for 2009 based on gross receivables computed in part a.

I6-48. **Analyzing and Interpreting Inventories and Related Ratios** (LO2)

Dr Reddy's Laboratories Limited is an Indian pharmaceutical manufacturer headquartered in Hyderabad, India. The company uses IFRS to prepare its financial statements. The 2010 balance sheet reported the following information.

Year ended March 31	2010 Rs. millions	2009 Rs. millions
Cash and cash equivalents	₹ 6,584	₹ 5,596
Investments	3,600	530
Trade receivables, net	11,960	14,592
Inventories	13,371	13,226
Derivative financial instruments	573	0
Current tax assets	530	58
Other current assets	5,445	5,008
Total current assets	**₹42,063**	**₹39,010**

Required

a. Compute inventory turnover and average inventory days outstanding for 2009 (2009 cost of goods sold is Rs. Millions ₹33,937). Comment on the level of these two ratios. Is the level what we expect given Dr Reddy's industry? Explain.

b. GAAP allows for FIFO, LIFO, and average cost inventory costing methods. How does IFRS differ?

c. In periods of rising prices, how will net income be affected under the different inventory costing methods?

MANAGEMENT APPLICATIONS

MA6-49. **Managing Operating Asset Reduction** (LO1, 2, 3)

Return on net operating assets (RNOA = NOPAT/Average NOA, see Module 4) is commonly used to evaluate financial performance. If managers cannot increase NOPAT, they can still increase this return by reducing the amount of net operating assets (NOA). List specific ways that managers could reduce the following assets:

a. Receivables
b. Inventories
c. Plant, property and equipment

MA6-50. **Ethics and Governance: Managing the Allowance for Uncollectible Accounts** (LO1)

Assume that you are the CEO of a publicly traded company. Your chief financial officer (CFO) informs you that your company will not be able to meet earnings per share targets for the current quarter. In that event, your stock price will likely decline. The CFO proposes reducing the quarterly provision for uncollectible accounts (bad debts expense) to increase your EPS to the level analysts expect. This will result in an allowance account that is less than it should be. The CFO explains that outsiders cannot easily detect a reduction in this allowance and that the allowance can be increased next quarter. The benefit is that your shareholders will not experience a decline in stock price.

a. Identify the parties that are likely to be affected by this proposed action.
b. How will reducing the provision for uncollectible accounts affect the income statement and the balance sheet?
c. How will reducing the provision for uncollectible accounts in the current period affect the income statement and the balance sheet in a future period?
d. What argument might the CFO use to convince the company's external auditors that this action is justified?
e. How might an analyst detect this earnings management activity?
f. How might this action affect the moral compass of your company? What repercussions might this action have?

SOLUTIONS TO REVIEW PROBLEMS

Mid-Module Review 1

Solution

1. As of December 31, 2012:

Current	$468,000 ×	1%	=	$ 4,680
1–60 days past due	244,000 ×	5%	=	12,200
61–180 days past due	38,000 ×	15%	=	5,700
Over 180 days past due.	20,000 ×	40%	=	8,000
Amount required.				30,580
Unused allowance balance				7,000
Provision.				$ 23,580 2012 bad debts expense

2. Current assets section of balance sheet:

Accounts receivable, net of $30,580 in allowances. . .	$739,420

3. The information here reveals that HP has markedly increased the percentage of the allowance for uncollectible accounts to gross accounts receivable; from the historical 2% to the current 4% ($30,580/$770,000). There are at least two possible interpretations:

   a. The quality of HP's receivables has declined. Possible causes include the following: (1) Sales have stagnated and the company is selling to lower-quality accounts to maintain sales volume; (2) It may have introduced new products for which average credit losses are higher; and (3) Its administration of accounts receivable has become lax.

   b. The company has intentionally increased its allowance account above the level needed for expected future losses so as to reduce current-period income and "bank" that income for future periods (income shifting).

Mid-Module Review 2

Solution

Preliminary computation: Units in ending inventory = 4,800 available − 2,800 sold = 2,000

1. First-in, first-out (FIFO)

Cost of goods sold computation:	Units		Cost		Total
	1,000	@	$18.00	=	$18,000
	1,800	@	$18.25	=	32,850
	2,800				$50,850

Cost of goods available for sale.	$88,450
Less: Cost of goods sold	50,850
Ending inventory ($22,800 + $14,800).	$37,600

2. Last-in, first-out (LIFO)

Cost of goods sold computation:	Units		Cost		Total
	1,200	@	$19.00	=	$22,800
	800	@	$18.50	=	14,800
	800	@	$18.25	=	14,600
	2,800				$52,200

Cost of goods available for sale.	$88,450
Less: Cost of goods sold	52,200
Ending inventory ($18,000 + [1,000 × $18.25]). . .	$36,250

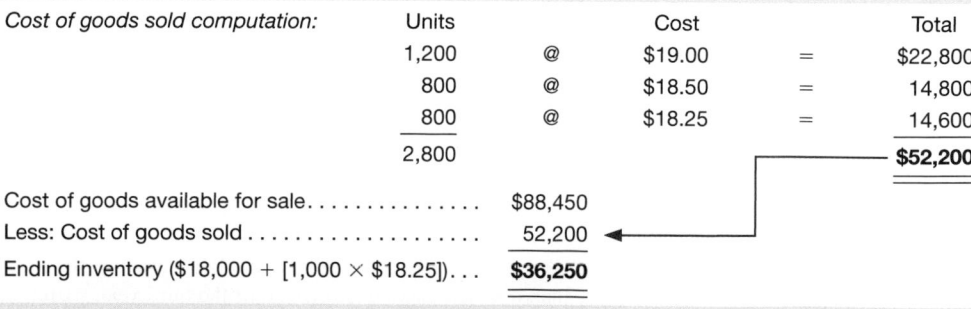

3. Average cost (AC)

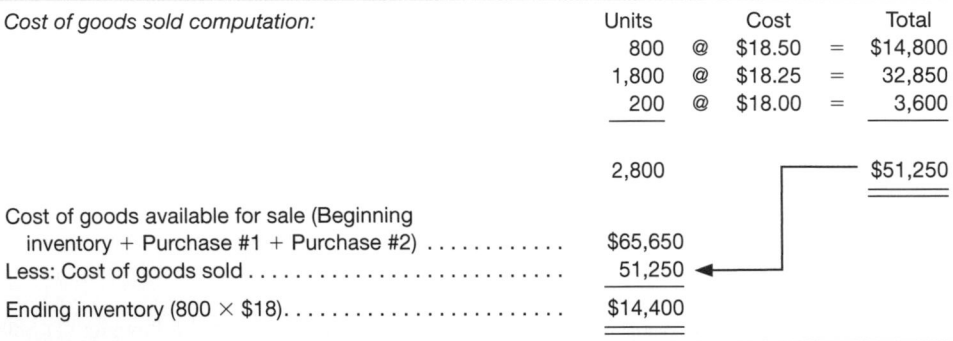

Average unit cost = $88,450/4,800 units = $18.427
Cost of goods sold = 2,800 × $18.427 = $51,596
Ending inventory   = 2,000 × $18.427 = $36,854

4. *a.* FIFO is normally the method that most closely reflects physical flow. For example, FIFO would apply to the physical flow of perishable units and to situations where the earlier units acquired are moved out first because of risk of deterioration or obsolescence.
   b. LIFO results in the highest cost of goods sold during periods of rising costs (as in the HP case); and, accordingly, LIFO yields the lowest net income and the lowest income taxes.
5. Last-in, first-out with LIFO liquidation

Cost of goods sold computation:	Units		Cost		Total
	800	@	$18.50	=	$14,800
	1,800	@	$18.25	=	32,850
	200	@	$18.00	=	3,600
	2,800				$51,250
Cost of goods available for sale (Beginning inventory + Purchase #1 + Purchase #2)	$65,650				
Less: Cost of goods sold	51,250				
Ending inventory (800 × $18).	$14,400				

The company's LIFO gross profit has increased by $950 ($52,200 − $51,250) because of the LIFO liquidation. The reduction of inventory quantities matched older (lower) cost layers against current selling prices. The company has, in effect, dipped into lower-cost layers to boost current-period profit—all from a simple delay of inventory purchases.

Module-End Review

Solution

1. *a.* Straight-line depreciation expense = ($95,000 − $10,000)/5 years = <u>$17,000 per year</u>

   b. Double-declining-balance (note: twice straight-line rate = 2 × [100%/5 years] = 40%)

Year	Net Book Value × Rate	Depreciation Expense	Accumulated Depreciation
1	$95,000 × 0.40 =	$38,000	$38,000
2	($95,000 − $38,000) × 0.40 =	22,800	60,800
3	($95,000 − $60,800) × 0.40 =	13,680	74,480
4	($95,000 − $74,480) × 0.40 =	8,208	82,688
5	($95,000 − $82,688) × 0.40 =	2,312*	85,000

*The formula value of $4,925 is not reported for Year 5 because doing so would depreciate the asset below the estimated salvage value; only the $2,312 needed to reach salvage value is depreciated.

2. HP reports the equipment on its balance sheet at its net book value of $44,000.

Equipment, cost.	$95,000
Less accumulated depreciation ($17,000 × 3)	51,000
Equipment, net (end of Year 3).	$44,000

3. The estimated useful life is computed as: Depreciable asset cost/Depreciation expense = $95,000/$17,000 = 5.6 years. Because companies do not usually disclose salvage values (not required disclosure), the useful-life estimate is a bit high for this asset. This estimate is still informative because companies typically only provide a range of useful lives for depreciable assets in the footnotes.

   The percent used up is computed as: Accumulated depreciation/Depreciable asset cost = $51,000/$95,000 = 53.7%. The equipment is more than one-half used up at the end of the third year. Again, the lack of knowledge of salvage value yields an underestimate of the percent used up. Still, this estimate is useful in that we know that the company's asset is over one-half used up and is likely to require replacement in about two years (estimated as less than one-half of its estimated useful life of 5.6 years). This replacement will require a cash outflow or financing and should be considered in our projections of future cash flows.

4. The equipment is impaired since the undiscounted expected cash flows ($40,000) are less than the net book value of the equipment ($44,000). HP must write down the equipment to its fair value of $36,000. The effect of this write-down is to reduce the net book value of the equipment by $8,000 ($44,000 − $36,000) and recognize a loss in the income statement.

5. HP must report a gain on this sale of $6,000, computed as proceeds of $50,000 less the net book value of the equipment of $44,000 (see part 2).

GOOGLE

How does Google make money? A recent *BusinessWeek* article explains: "everybody knows that Google Inc.'s innovations in search technology made it the No. 1 search engine. But Google didn't make money until it started auctioning ads that appear alongside the search results. Advertising today accounts for 99% of revenue." This seems to suggest that Google is a media company. Indeed, with a market capitalization of about $170 billion as of mid-2011, (over four times that of Time Warner), Google is the world's largest media company and among America's top 30 most valuable companies. Since its IPO in 2004, Google's (GOOG) stock price has increased more than tenfold making Google one of the fastest growing companies on any stock exchange.

Google's operations generated nearly $11 billion of operating cash flow in 2010, over four times the cash generated five years before. By the end of 2010, Google reported nearly $35 billion in cash and marketable securities on its balance sheet.

Google has considerable investments in government bonds. It holds these investments because it has excess cash awaiting deployment in other business activities. In the interim, the company expects to earn dividends and (potentially) capital gains from these securities. The accounting for these types of marketable securities differs markedly from the accounting for most other assets—Google's balance sheet reports these marketable securities at their current fair (or market) value instead of at their historical cost. As a result, the assets on Google's balance sheet fluctuate with the stock market. This causes stockholders' equity to fluctuate because, as we know from the accounting equation, assets equal liabilities plus equity.

We might wonder why Google would report these assets at fair value when nearly all other assets are reported at historical cost. As well, we might ask how these fluctuations in fair value affect Google's reported profit, if at all. This module answers both questions and explains the accounting for, and analysis of, such "passive" investments in marketable securities.

To expand its business activities beyond its current search-engine and advertising base, Google has strategically invested in the stock of other companies, which is a second category of investments. Through these strategic investments, Google can acquire substantial ownership of the companies such that Google can significantly influence their operations. The nature and purpose of these investments differs from Google's passive investment in marketable securities and, accordingly, the accounting reflects that difference. In particular, if Google owns enough voting stock to exert significant influence over another company, Google uses the *equity method* to account for those investments. Under the equity method, Google carries the investment on its balance sheet at an amount equal to its proportionate share of the investee company's equity. An equity method investment increases and decreases, not with changes in

Reporting and Analyzing Intercorporate Investments

LEARNING OBJECTIVES

LO1 Describe and illustrate accounting for passive investments. (p. 7-4)

LO2 Explain and illustrate accounting for equity method investments. (p. 7-11)

LO3 Describe and illustrate accounting for consolidations. (p. 7-16)

the stock's market value, but with changes in the investee company's stockholders' equity.

An interesting by-product of the equity method is that Google's balance sheet does not reflect the investee company's individual assets and liabilities, but only its net assets (its stockholders' equity). This is important because Google could be using the investee's assets and be responsible, to some extent, for the investee's liabilities. Yet, those liabilities are not detailed on Google's balance sheet. This creates what is called *off-balance-sheet financing*, potentially of great concern to accountants, analysts, creditors, and others who rely on financial reports. This module describes the equity method of accounting for investments, including the implications of this type of off-balance-sheet financing.

When an investor company acquires a sufficiently large proportion of the voting stock of another company, it can effectively control the other company. At that point, the acquired company is *consolidated*. Most of the financial statements of public companies are titled "consolidated." Consolidation essentially adds together the financial statements of two or more companies. It is important that we understand what consolidated financial statements tell us and what they do not. This module covers consolidation along with a discussion of its implications for analysis.

There was much consternation among investors when Google's stock price passed $100, then $200, then $600, then $700. At each milestone, investors became increas-

ingly concerned that Google's stock was overvalued. That concern still abounds. But, as Google continues to make strategic investments necessary to broaden its revenue base, its share price will likely increase. Google's management believes that investments are a crucial part of the company's strategic plan. Understanding the accounting for all three types of intercorporate investment is, thus, important to our understanding of Google's (and other companies') ongoing operations.

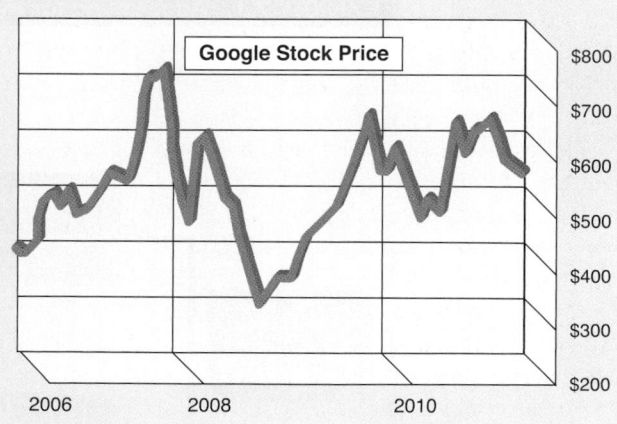

Sources: *Google Form 10-K*, 2010; *Google Annual Report*, 2010; *Business-Week*, 2006; and *Fortune*, 2006 and 2011.

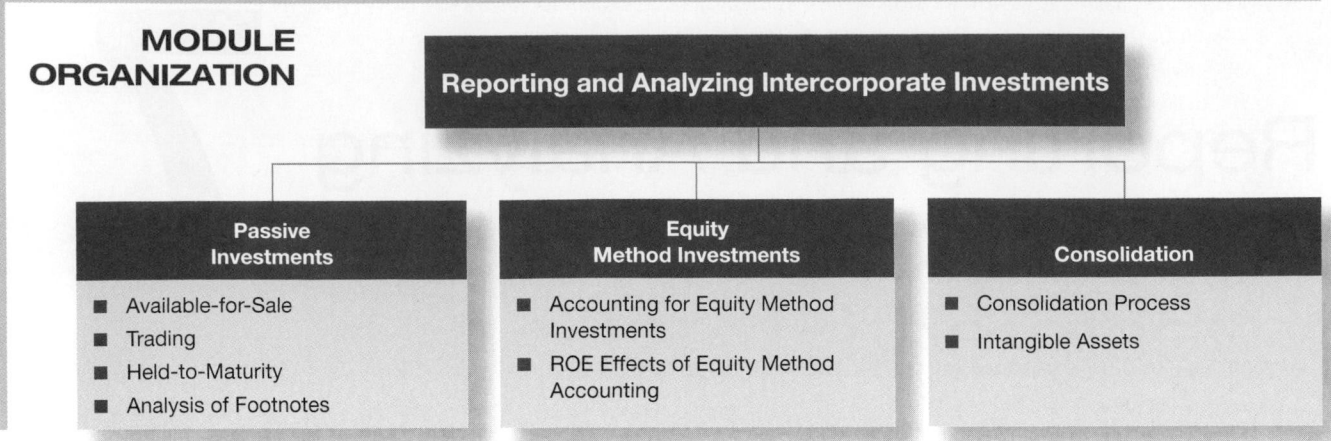

It is common for one company to purchase the voting stock of another. These purchases, called *intercorporate investments,* have the following strategic aims:

- **Short-term investment of excess cash.** Companies might invest excess cash to use during slow times of the year (after receivables are collected and before seasonal production begins) or to maintain liquidity (such as to counter strategic moves by competitors or to quickly respond to acquisition opportunities).

- **Alliances for strategic purposes.** Companies might acquire an equity interest in other companies for strategic purposes, such as gaining access to their research and development activities, to their supply or distribution markets, or to their production and marketing expertise.

- **Market penetration or expansion.** Companies might acquire control of other companies to achieve vertical or horizontal integration in existing markets or to penetrate new and growth markets.

Accounting for intercorporate investments follows one of three different methods, each of which affects the balance sheet and the income statement differently. These differences can be quite substantial. To help assimilate the materials in this module, Exhibit 7.1 graphically depicts the accounting for investments.

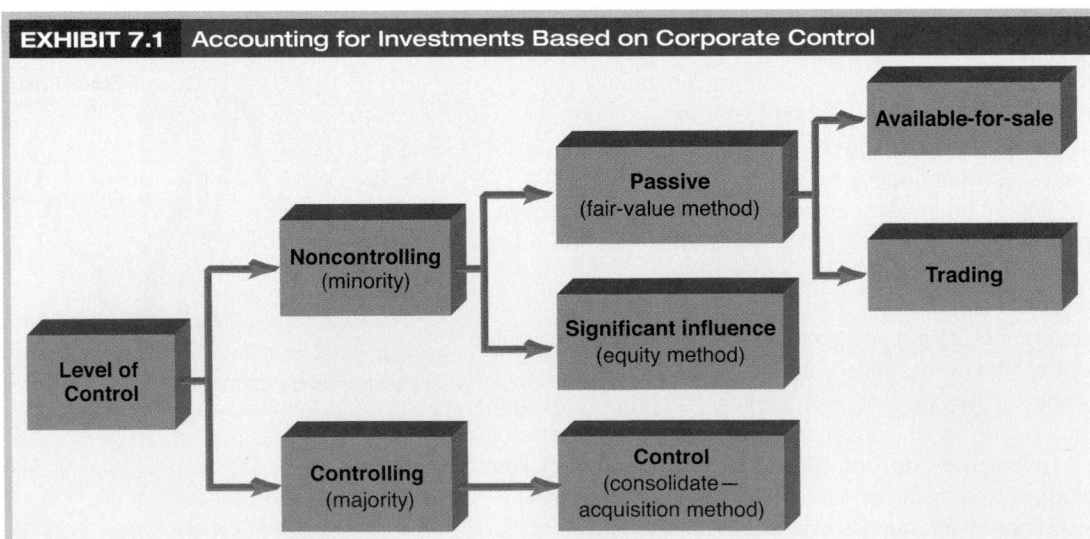

EXHIBIT 7.1   Accounting for Investments Based on Corporate Control

The degree of influence or control that the investor company (purchaser) can exert over the investee company (the company whose securities are being purchased) determines the accounting method. GAAP identifies three levels of influence/control.

1. **Passive.** A passive investment is one where the purchasing company has a relatively small investment and cannot exert influence over the investee company. The investor's goal is to realize dividends and capital gains. Generally, the investment is considered passive if the investor company owns less than 20% of the outstanding voting stock of the investee company.

2. **Significant influence.** A company can sometimes exert significant influence over, but not control, the activities of the investee company. Significant influence can result when the percentage of voting stock owned is greater than a passive, short-term investment. However, an investment can also exhibit "significant influence" if there exist legal agreements between the investor and investee, such as a license to use technology, a formula, or a trade secret like production know-how. Absent other contractual arrangements such as those described above, significant influence is presumed at investment levels between 20% and 50%.

3. **Control.** When a company has control over another, it has the ability to elect a majority of the board of directors and, as a result, the ability to affect the investee company's strategic direction and the hiring of executive management. Control is generally presumed if the investor company owns more than 50% of the outstanding voting stock of the investee company, but can sometimes occur at less than 50% stock ownership by virtue of legal agreements, technology licensing, or other contractual means.

The level of influence/control determines the specific accounting method applied and its financial statement implications as outlined in Exhibit 7.2.

EXHIBIT 7.2	Investment Type, Accounting Treatment, and Financial Statement Effects			
	Accounting	Balance Sheet Effects	Income Statement Effects	Cash Flow Effects
Passive	Fair-value method	Investment account is reported at fair value	Dividends and capital gains included in income. Interim changes in fair value affect income if the investor actively trades the securities. Sale of investment yields capital gain or loss	Dividends and sale proceeds are cash inflows from investing activities. Purchases are cash outflows from investing activities
Significant influence	Equity method	Investment account equals percent owned of investee company's equity*	Dividends reduce investment account. Investor reports income equal to percent owned of investee income. Sale of investment yields capital gain or loss	Dividends and sale proceeds are cash inflows from investing activities. Purchases are cash outflows from investing activities
Control	Consolidation	Balance sheets of investor and investee are combined	Income statements of investor and investee are combined. Sale of investee yields capital gain or loss	Cash flows of investor and investee are combined and retain original classification (operating, investing, or financing). Sale and purchase of investee are investing cash flows

*Investments are often acquired at purchase prices in excess of book value (the market price of S&P 500 companies was 1.9 times their book value as of mid 2011). In this case the investment account exceeds the proportionate ownership of the investee's equity.

There are two basic reporting issues with investments: (1) how investment income should be recognized in the income statement and (2) at what amount (cost or fair value) the investment should be reported on the balance sheet. We next discuss both of these issues as we consider the three investment types.

PASSIVE INVESTMENTS

Short-term investments of excess cash are typically passive investments. Passive investments can involve equity or debt securities. Equity securities involve an ownership interest such as common stock or preferred stock, whereas debt securities have no ownership interest. A voting stock investment is passive when the investor does not possess sufficient ownership to either influence or control the investee company. The *fair-value method* is used to account for passive investments in both debt and equity securities.

LO1 Describe and illustrate accounting for passive investments.

Acquisition and Sale

When a company makes a passive investment, it records the shares acquired on the balance sheet at fair value, that is, the purchase price. This is the same as accounting for the acquisition of other assets such as inventories or plant assets. Subsequent to acquisition, passive investments are carried on the balance sheet as current or long-term assets, depending on management's expectations about their ultimate holding period.

When investments are sold, any recognized gain or loss on sale is equal to the difference between the proceeds received and the book (carrying) value of the investment on the balance sheet as follows:

Gain or Loss on Sale = Proceeds from Sale − Book Value of Investment Sold

To illustrate the acquisition and sale of a passive investment, assume that Microsoft purchases 1,000 shares of Skype for $20 cash per share (this includes transaction costs such as brokerage fees). Microsoft, subsequently, sells 400 of the 1,000 shares for $23 cash per share. The following financial statement effects template shows how these transactions affect Microsoft.

		Balance Sheet								Income Statement		
	Transaction	Cash Asset	+	Noncash Assets	=	Liabil- ities	+	Contrib. Capital	+	Earned Capital		Rev- enues	−	Expen- ses	=	Net Income
	1. Purchase 1,000 shares of Skype common stock for $20 cash per share	−20,000 Cash		+20,000 Marketable Securities	=							−		=	
	2. Sell 400 shares of Skype common stock for $23 cash per share	+9,200 Cash		−8,000 Marketable Securities	=					+1,200 Retained Earnings		+1,200 Gain on Sale	−		=	+1,200

Income statements include the gain or loss on sale of marketable securities as a component of *other income*, which is typically reported separately from operating income and often aggregated with interest and dividend revenue. Accounting for the purchase and sale of passive investments is the same as for any other asset. Further, there is no difference in accounting for purchases and sales across the different types of passive investments discussed in this section. However, there are differences in accounting for different types of passive investments between their purchase and their sale. We next address this issue.

Fair Value versus Cost

If a passive investment in equity securities has an active market with published prices, that investment is reported on the balance sheet at fair value. Fair value is specifically defined under GAAP. It is the value a willing party would pay to buy the asset in a well-functioning market. Quoted market prices must be used when available, which are called *Level 1 fair values*. In the absence of quoted market prices, companies can use market prices for similar assets, which are called *Level 2 fair values* or, if market prices for similar assets are not available, an estimate of investment value using financial models, which are *Level 3 fair values*. For marketable securities, **fair value** is the published price (as listed on a stock exchange) multiplied by the number of shares owned. This is one of few assets that are reported at fair value instead of historical cost.[1] For marketable securities, the current market value is almost always equal to the "fair" value and, thus, the two terms are often used interchangeably. If there exists no active market with published prices for the stock, the investment is reported at its historical cost.

---

[1] Other assets reported at fair value include (1) derivative securities (such as forward contracts, options, and futures) that are purchased to provide a hedge against price fluctuations or to eliminate other business risks (such as interest or exchange rate fluctuations), and (2) inventories and long-term assets that must be written down to market when their values permanently decline.

Why are passive investments recorded at current fair value on the balance sheet? The answer lies in understanding the trade-off between the *objectivity* of historical cost and the *relevance* of market value. All things equal, current fair values of assets are more relevant in determining the market value of the company as a whole. However, for most assets, market values cannot be reliably determined. Adding unreliable "market values" to the balance sheet would introduce undue subjectivity into financial reports.

In the case of marketable securities, market prices result from numerous transactions between willing buyers and sellers. Market prices in this case provide an unbiased (objective) estimate of fair value to report on balance sheets. This reliability is the main reason GAAP allows passive investments to be recorded at fair value instead of at historical cost.

This fair-value method of accounting for securities causes asset values (the marketable securities) to fluctuate, with a corresponding change in equity (liabilities are unaffected). This is reflected in the following accounting equation:

$$\textbf{Assets} \blacktriangle \ = \ \textbf{Liabilities} \ + \ \textbf{Equity} \blacktriangle \qquad \textbf{or} \qquad \textbf{Assets} \blacktriangledown \ = \ \textbf{Liabilities} \ + \ \textbf{Equity} \blacktriangledown$$

An important issue is whether such changes in equity should be reported as income (with a consequent change in retained earnings), or whether they should bypass the income statement and directly impact equity via *accumulated other comprehensive income (AOCI)*. The answer differs depending on the classification of securities, which we explain next.

Investments Marked to Market

For accounting purposes, marketable securities are classified into two types, both of which are reported on the balance sheet at fair value. Remember that for marketable securities, current market value is usually synonymous with fair value, thus we say that marketable securities are *marked to market*.

1. **Available-for-sale (AFS).** These are securities that management intends to hold for capital gains and dividend revenue; although, they might be sold if the price is right.
2. **Trading (T).** These are investments that management intends to actively buy and sell for trading profits as market prices fluctuate.

Management classifies securities depending on the degree of turnover (transaction volume) it expects in the investment portfolio, which reflects management's intent to actively trade the securities or not. Available-for-sale portfolios exhibit less turnover than trading portfolios. (GAAP permits companies to have multiple portfolios, each with a different classification, and management can change portfolio classification provided it adheres to strict disclosure and reporting requirements about its expectations of turnover change.) The classification as either available-for-sale or trading determines the accounting treatment, as Exhibit 7.3 summarizes.

EXHIBIT 7.3	Accounting Treatment for Available-for-Sale and for Trading Investments	
Investment Classification	**Reporting of Fair-Value Changes**	**Reporting of Dividends Received and Gains and Losses on Sale**
Available-for-Sale (AFS)	Fair-value changes bypass the income statement and are reported in accumulated other comprehensive income (AOCI) as part of equity	Reported as *other income* in income statement
Trading (T)	Fair-value changes are reported in the income statement and impact equity via retained earnings	Reported as *other income* in income statement

The difference between the accounting treatment of available-for-sale and trading investments relates to how fair-value changes affect equity. Changes in the fair value of available-for-sale securities have no income effect; changes in fair value of trading securities have an income effect. The impact on total stockholders' equity is identical for both classifications. The only difference is whether the change is reflected in retained earnings or in the accumulated other comprehensive income (AOCI) component of stockholders' equity. Dividends and any gains or losses on security sales are reported in the other income section of the income statement for both classifications. (GAAP gives companies an option to account for available-for-sale securities like trading securities and report all changes in fair value on the income statement.) When sold, *unrealized* gains (losses) on available-for-sale investments are transferred ("reclassified") from AOCI into income and, thereby, become *realized* gains (losses).

Fair-Value Adjustments

To illustrate the accounting for changes in fair value subsequent to purchase (and before sale), assume that Microsoft's investment in Skype (600 remaining shares purchased for $20 per share) increases in value to $25 per share at year-end. The investment must be marked to market to reflect the $3,000 unrealized gain ($5 per share increase for 600 shares). The financial statement effects depend on whether the investment is classified as available-for-sale or as trading as follows:

Transaction	Balance Sheet							Income Statement		
	Cash Asset	+	Noncash Assets	=	Liabil- ities	+	Contrib. Capital	+	Earned Capital	Rev- enues	−	Expen- ses	=	Net Income

If classified as available-for-sale

MS 3,000
　AOCI 3,000

MS
3,000 |
　AOCI
　　| 3,000

| $5 increase in fair value of Skype investment | | +3,000 Marketable Securities | = | | | | +3,000 AOCI | − | = |

If classified as trading

MS 3,000
　UG 3,000

MS
3,000 |
　UG
　　| 3,000

| $5 increase in fair value of Skype investment | | +3,000 Marketable Securities | = | | +3,000 Retained Earnings | +3,000 Unrealized Gain | − | +3,000 = |

Under both classifications, the investment account increases by $3,000 to reflect the increase in the stock's market value. If Microsoft classifies these securities as available-for-sale, the unrealized gain increases the accumulated other comprehensive income (AOCI) account (which analysts typically view as a component of earned capital). However, if Microsoft classifies the securities as trading, the unrealized gain is recorded as income, thus increasing both reported income and retained earnings for the period. (Our illustration uses a portfolio with only one security for simplicity. Portfolios usually consist of multiple securities, and the unrealized gain or loss is computed based on the total cost and total market value of the entire portfolio.)

IFRS Alert
IFRS permits similar accounting for financial assets, including that for trading, available-for-sale, and held-to-maturity portfolios.

These fair-value adjustments only apply if market prices are available, that is, for publicly traded securities. Thus, this mark-to-market accounting does not apply to investments in start-up companies or privately held corporations. Investments in nonpublicly traded companies are accounted for at cost as we discuss later in this section.

Financial Statement Disclosures

Companies are required to disclose cost and fair values of their investment portfolios in footnotes to financial statements. Google reports the accounting policies for its investments in the following footnote to its 2010 10-K report:

Cash, Cash Equivalents, and Marketable Securities We invest our excess cash primarily in highly liquid debt instruments of the U.S. government and its agencies, municipalities in the U.S., debt instruments issued by foreign governments, time deposits, money market and other funds, including cash collateral received related to our securities lending program, mortgage-backed securities, and corporate securities. We classify all highly liquid investments with stated maturities of three months or less from date of purchase as cash equivalents and all highly liquid investments with stated maturities of greater than three months as marketable securities . . . We have classified and accounted for our marketable securities as available-for-sale . . . We carry these securities at fair value, and report the unrealized gains and losses, net of taxes, as a component of stockholders' equity, except for unrealized losses determined to be other-than-temporary which we record as interest and other income, net. We determine any realized gains or losses on the sale of marketable securities on a specific identification method, and we record such gains and losses as a component of interest and other income, net.

Google accounts for its investments in marketable securities at fair value. Because Google classifies those investments as "available-for-sale," unrealized gains and losses flow to the accumulated other comprehensive income component of stockholders' equity. When Google sells the securities, it will record any *realized* gains or losses in income.

Following is the current asset section of Google's 2010 balance sheet reflecting these investments.

December 31 ($ millions)	2009	2010
Cash and cash equivalents	$10,198	$13,630
Marketable securities	14,287	21,345
Total cash, cash equivalents, and marketable securities	24,485	34,975
Accounts receivable, net of allowance of $79 and $101	3,178	4,252
Receivable under reverse repurchase agreements	0	750
Deferred income taxes, net	644	259
Income taxes receivable, net	23	0
Prepaid revenue share, expenses and other assets	837	1,326
Total current assets	$29,167	$41,562

Google's investments in marketable securities that are expected to mature within 90 days of the balance sheet date are recorded together with cash as cash equivalents. Its remaining investments are reported as marketable securities.

Footnotes to the Google 10-K provide further information about the composition of its investment portfolio.

As of December 31 ($ millions)	2009	2010
Cash and cash equivalents:		
Cash	$ 4,303	$ 4,652
Cash equivalents:		
Time deposits	3,740	973
Money market and other funds	2,153	7,547
U.S. government agencies	2	0
U.S. government notes	0	300
Foreign government bonds	0	150
Corporate debt securities	0	8
Total cash and cash equivalents	10,198	13,630
Marketable securities:		
Time deposits	1,250	304
Money market mutual funds	28	3
U.S. government agencies	3,703	1,857
U.S. government notes	2,492	3,930
Foreign government bonds	37	1,172
Municipal securities	2,130	2,503
Corporate debt securities	2,822	5,742
Agency residential mortgage-backed securities	1,578	5,673
Commercial mortgage-backed securities	48	0
Marketable equity security	199	161
Total marketable securities	14,287	21,345
Total cash, cash equivalents, and marketable securities	$24,485	$34,975

The majority of Google's 2010 investments are in government debt securities such as bonds and T-bills, with a relatively small portion invested in equity securities. Google accounts for all of these investments as available-for-sale and reports them in the current asset section of the balance sheet because they mature within the coming year or can be readily sold, if necessary.

Google provides additional (required) disclosures on the costs, fair values, and unrealized gains and losses for its available-for-sale investments as follows:

December 31, 2010 ($ millions)	Adjusted Cost	Gross Unrealized Gains	Gross Unrealized Losses	Fair Value
Time deposits.	$ 304	$ 0	$ 0	$ 304
Money market mutual funds.	3	0	0	3
U.S. government agencies.	1,864	1	(8)	1,857
U.S. government notes	3,950	30	(50)	3,930
Foreign government bonds	1,154	23	(5)	1,172
Municipal securities	2,492	16	(5)	2,503
Corporate debt securities.	5,600	167	(25)	5,742
Agency residential mortgage-backed securities	5,649	56	(32)	5,673
Marketable equity security	150	11	0	161
Total	$21,166	$304	$(125)	$21,345

Google's net unrealized gain of $179 million ($304 million − $125 million) is reported net of tax in the accumulated other comprehensive income (AOCI) section of its stockholders' equity as follows ($ millions):

December 31 ($ millions)	2009	2010
Class A and Class B common stock	$15,817	$18,235
Accumulated other comprehensive income.	105	138
Retained earnings	20,082	27,868
Total stockholders' equity	36,004	46,241
Total liabilities and stockholders' equity.	$40,497	$57,851

Google does not identify the components of its 2010 accumulated other comprehensive income of $138 except to report that the other component, beyond the unrealized gains on available-for-sale investments, is the cumulative translation adjustment relating to subsidiaries whose balance sheets are denominated in currencies other than $US. This lack of information can be confusing because the amount of unrealized gain (loss) reported in the investment footnote and the amount reported in accumulated other comprehensive income differ. Part of this difference relates to taxes: the net unrealized gain of $179 reported in the investment footnote is pretax while the amount reported in the accumulated other comprehensive income section of stockholders' equity is after-tax.

Investments Reported at Cost

Companies often purchase debt securities, including bonds issued by other companies or by the U.S. government. Such debt securities have maturity dates—dates when the security must be repaid by the borrower. If a company buys debt securities, and *management intends to hold the securities to maturity* (as opposed to selling them early), the securities are classified as **held-to-maturity** (HTM). The cost method applies to held-to-maturity securities. Exhibit 7.4 identifies the reporting of these securities.

EXHIBIT 7.4	Accounting Treatment for Held-to-Maturity Investments	
Investment Classification	Reporting of Fair-Value Changes	Reporting Interest Received and the Gains and Losses on Sale
Held-to-Maturity (HTM)	Fair-value changes are *not* reported in either the balance sheet or income statement	Interest reported as *other income* in income statement IF sold before maturity (the exception), any gain or loss on sale is reported in income statement

Changes in fair value do not affect either the balance sheet or the income statement. The presumption is that these investments will indeed be held to maturity, at which time their market value will be exactly equal to their face value. Fluctuations in fair value, as a result, are less relevant for this investment classification. Finally, any interest received is recorded in current income. (GAAP gives companies an option to report held-to-maturity investments at fair value; if this fair-value option is elected, the accounting for held-to-maturity securities is like that for trading securities.)

Sometimes companies acquire held-to-maturity debt securities for more or less than the security's face value. Because the value of debt securities fluctuates with the prevailing rate of interest, the market value of the security will be greater than its face value if current market interest rates are lower than what the security pays for interest. In that case, the acquirer will pay a premium for the security. Conversely, if current market interest rates exceed what the security pays in interest, the acquirer will purchase the security at a discount. (We cover premiums and discounts on debt securities in more detail in Module 8.) Either way, the company records the investment at its acquisition cost (like any other asset) and amortizes any discount or premium over the remaining life of the held-to-maturity investment. At any point in time, the acquirer's balance sheet carries the investment at "amortized cost," which is never adjusted for subsequent market value changes.

Companies can acquire equity interests in other companies that are not traded on an organized exchange. These might be start-ups that have never issued stock or established privately held companies. Because there is no market for such securities, they cannot be classified as marketable securities and are carried at historical cost on the balance sheet. Google references one such investment in its 2010 10-K.

Non-Marketable Equity Securities   We have accounted for non-marketable equity security investments primarily at cost because we do not have significant influence over the underlying investees. We periodically review our marketable securities, as well as our non-marketable equity securities, for impairment. If we conclude that any of these investments are impaired, we determine whether such impairment is other-than-temporary. Factors we consider to make such determination include the duration and severity of the impairment, the reason for the decline in value and the potential recovery period, and our intent to sell, or whether it is more likely than not that we will be required to sell, the investment before recovery. If any impairment is considered other-than-temporary, we will write down the asset to its fair value and take a corresponding charge to our Consolidated Statements of Income.

Google uses historical cost to account for investments in non-marketable securities (equity investments where Google cannot exert significant influence over the investee company). Google monitors the value of these investments and writes them down to market value if they suffer a permanent decline in value. If such an investee company ever goes public, Google will change its accounting method. If Google's ownership percentage does not allow it to exert significant influence or control, Google will account for this investment following the procedures described above for marketable securities. However, if Google can exert significant influence or control, it will apply different accounting methods that we explain in later sections of this module.

MID-MODULE REVIEW 1

Assume that Google had the following four transactions involving investments in marketable securities. Use this information to answer requirements *a* and *b* below.

1. Purchased 1,000 shares of Yahoo! common stock for $15 cash per share.
2. Received cash dividend of $2.50 per share on Yahoo! common stock.
3. Year-end market price of Yahoo! common stock is $17 per share.
4. Sold all 1,000 shares of Yahoo! common stock for $17,000 cash in the next period.

Yahoo! reports the following table in the footnotes to its 2010 10-K. Use this information to answer requirements *c* and *d* below.

December 31, 2010 ($ Thousands)	Gross Amortized Costs	Gross Unrealized Gains	Gross Unrealized Losses	Estimated Fair Value
Government and agency securities	$1,353,064	$1,513	$ (514)	$1,354,063
Municipal bonds.	6,609	8	—	6,617
Corporate debt securities, commercial paper, and bank certificates of deposits.	740,043	1,608	(76)	741,575
Corporate equity securities	2,597	—	(1,128)	1,469
Total investments in available-for-sale securities. . .	$2,102,313	$3,129	$(1,718)	$2,103,724

Required

a. Using the financial statement effects template, enter the effects (amount and account) relating to the four transactions assuming the investments are classified as available-for-sale.
b. Using the financial statement effects template enter the effects (amount and account) relating to the four transactions assuming that the investments are classified as trading securities.
c. What amount does Yahoo! report as investments on its balance sheet? What does this balance represent?
d. How did the net unrealized gains affect reported income in 2010?

The solution is on page 7-51.

INVESTMENTS WITH SIGNIFICANT INFLUENCE

LO2 Explain and illustrate accounting for equity method investments.

Many companies make equity investments that yield them significant influence over the investee companies. These intercorporate investments are usually made for strategic reasons such as the following:

■ **Prelude to acquisition**. Significant ownership can allow the investor company to gain a seat on the board of directors from which it can learn much about the investee company, its products, and its industry.

■ **Strategic alliance**. Strategic alliances permit the investor to gain trade secrets, technical know-how, or access to restricted markets. For example, a company might buy an equity share in a company that provides inputs for the investor's production process. This relationship is closer than the usual supplier–buyer relationship and will convey benefits to the investor company.

■ **Pursuit of research and development**. Many research activities in the pharmaceutical, software, and oil and gas industries are conducted jointly. The common motivation is to reduce the investor's risk or the amount of capital investment. The investment often carries an option to purchase additional shares, which the investor can exercise if the research activities are fruitful.

A crucial feature in each of these investments is that the investor company has a level of ownership that is sufficient for it to exert *significant influence* over the investee company. GAAP requires that such investments be accounted for using the *equity method*.

Significant influence is the ability of the investor to affect the financing, investing and operating policies of the investee. Ownership levels of 20% to 50% of the outstanding common stock of the investee typically convey significant influence. Significant influence can also exist when ownership is less than 20%. Evidence of such influence can be that the investor company is able to gain a seat on the board of directors of the investee by virtue of its equity investment, or the investor controls technical know-how or patents that are used by the investee, or the investor is able to exert significant influence by virtue of legal contracts with the investee. (There is growing pressure from regulators for determining significant influence by the facts and circumstances of the investment instead of a strict ownership percentage rule.)

Accounting for Investments with Significant Influence

GAAP requires that investors use the **equity method** when significant influence exists. The equity method reports the investment on the balance sheet at an amount equal to the percentage of the investee's equity owned by the investor; hence, the name equity method. (This assumes acquisition at book value. Acquisition at an amount greater than book value is covered later in this section.) Contrary to passive investments whose carrying amounts increase or decrease with the market value of the investee's stock, equity method investments increase (decrease) with increases (decreases) in the investee's stockholders' equity.

Equity method accounting is summarized as follows:

- Investments are recorded at their purchase cost.

- Dividends received are treated as a recovery of the investment and, thus, reduce the investment balance (dividends are not reported as income).

- The investor reports income equal to its percentage share of the investee's reported net income; the investment account is increased by the percentage share of the investee's income or is decreased by the percentage share of any loss.

- Changes in fair value do not affect the investment's carrying value. (GAAP gives companies an option to report equity method investments at fair value unless those investments relate to consolidated subsidiaries; we discuss consolidation later in the module.)

> **IFRS Alert**
> There is no fair-value option for investments accounted for by the equity method under IFRS.

To illustrate the equity method, consider the following scenario: Assume that Google acquires a 30% interest in Mitel Networks, a company seeking to develop a new technology. This investment is a strategic alliance for Google. At the acquisition date, Mitel's balance sheet reports $1,000 of stockholders' equity, and Google purchases a 30% stake for $300, giving it the ability to exert significant influence over Mitel. At the first year-end, Mitel reports profits of $100 and pays $20 in cash dividends to its shareholders ($6 to Google). Following are the financial statement effects for Google from this investment using the equity method.

Transaction	Cash Asset	+	Noncash Assets	=	Liabilities	+	Contrib. Capital	+	Earned Capital		Revenues	−	Expenses	=	Net Income
1. Purchase 30% investment in Mitel for $300 cash	−300 Cash		+300 Investment in Mitel	=								−		=	
2. Mitel reports $100 income; Google's share is $30			+30 Investment in Mitel	=					+30 Retained Earnings		+30 Investment Income	−		=	+30
3. Mitel pays $20 cash dividends; $6 to Google	+6 Cash		−6 Investment in Mitel	=								−		=	
Ending balance of Google's investment account			324												

T-accounts (right margin):

1. EMI 300 / Cash 300
   EMI 300 | / Cash | 300

2. EMI 30 / EI 30
   EMI 30 | / EI | 30

3. Cash 6 / EMI 6
   Cash 6 | / EMI | 6

The investment is initially reported on Google's balance sheet at its purchase price of $300, representing a 30% interest in Mitel's total stockholders' equity of $1,000. During the year, Mitel's equity increases to $1,080 ($1,000 plus $100 income and less $20 dividends). Likewise, Google's investment increases by

$30 to reflect its 30% share of Mitel's $100 income, and decreases by $6, relating to its share of Mitel's dividends. After these transactions, Google's investment in Mitel is reported on Google's balance sheet at 30% of $1,080, or $324.

Google's investment in Mitel is an asset, just like any other asset. As such, it must be tested annually for impairment. If the investment is found to be permanently impaired, Google must reduce the investment amount on the balance sheet and report a loss on the write-down of the investment in its income statement. If and when Google sells Mitel, any gain or loss on the sale is reported in Google's income statement. The gain or loss is computed as the difference between the sales proceeds and the investment's carrying value on the balance sheet. For example, if Google sold Mitel for $500, Google would report a gain on sale of $176 ($500 proceeds − $324 balance sheet value).

Companies often pay more than book value when they make equity investments. For example, if Google paid $400 for its 30% stake in Mitel, Google would initially report its investment at its $400 purchase price. The $400 investment consists of two parts: the $300 equity investment described above and the $100 additional investment. Google is willing to pay the higher purchase price because it believes that Mitel's reported equity is below its current market value. Perhaps some of Mitel's assets are reported at costs that are below market values or Mitel has intangible assets like internally generated goodwill that are missing from the balance sheet. The $300 portion of the investment is accounted for as described above. Google's management must decide how to allocate the excess of the amount paid over the book value of the investee company's equity and account for the excess accordingly. For example, if management decides that the $100 relates to depreciable assets, the $100 is depreciated over the assets' estimated useful lives. Or, if it relates to identifiable intangible assets that have a determinable useful life (like patents), it is amortized over the useful lives of the intangible assets. If it relates to goodwill, however, it is not amortized and remains on the balance sheet at $100 unless and until it is deemed to be impaired. (See Appendix 7A for an expanded illustration.)

Two final points about equity method accounting: First, there can be a substantial difference between the book value of an equity method investment and its fair value. An increase in value is not recognized until the investment is sold. If the fair value of the investment has permanently declined, however, the investment is deemed impaired and it is written down to that lower fair value. Second, if the investee company reports income, the investor company reports its share. Recognition of equity income by the investor, however, does not mean that it has received that income in cash. Cash is only received if the investee pays a dividend. To highlight this, the investor's statement of cash flows will include a reconciling item (a deduction from net income in computing operating cash flow) for its percentage share of the investee's net income. This is typically reported net of any cash dividends received.

RESEARCH INSIGHT   **Equity Income and Stock Prices**

Under the equity method of accounting, the investor does not recognize as income any dividends received from the investee, nor any changes in the investee's fair value, until the investment is sold. However, research has found a positive relation between investors' and investees' stock prices at the time of investees' earnings and dividend announcements. This suggests that the market includes information regarding investees' earnings and dividends when assessing the stock prices of investor companies, and implies that the market looks beyond the book value of the investment account in determining stock prices of investor companies.

Equity Method Accounting and ROE Effects

The investor company reports equity method investments on the balance sheet at an amount equal to the percentage owned of the investee company's equity when that investment is acquired at book value. To illustrate, consider the case of **Abbott Laboratories, Inc.**, which owned 50% of **TAP Pharmaceutical Products Inc.** (TAP was a joint venture with Takeda Pharmaceutical Company, Limited of Japan that was terminated in 2008.) TAP Pharmaceuticals (TAP) develops and markets pharmaceutical products mainly for the U.S. and Canada. Abbott accounts for its investment in TAP using the equity method as described in the following footnote to its 2007 10-K report:

Equity Method Investments *($ millions)* Abbott's 50 percent-owned joint venture, TAP Pharmaceutical Products Inc. (TAP), is accounted for under the equity method of accounting. The investment in TAP was $159, $162 and $167 at December 31, 2007, 2006 and 2005, respectively, and dividends received from TAP were $502, $487 and $343 in 2007, 2006 and 2005, respectively. Abbott performs certain administrative and manufacturing services for TAP at negotiated rates that approximate fair value.

At the end of 2007, the TAP joint venture reported stockholders' equity of $318 million and net income of $996 million. (TAP's financial statements are included in an exhibit to Abbott's 2007 10-K; not reproduced here.) In the footnote above, Abbott reports an investment balance at December 31, 2007, of $159 million (TAP equity of $318 million × 50%). In its income statement (not shown here), Abbott reports income of $498 million (TAP net income of $996 million × 50%). Provided the investment was originally acquired at book value these relations will always hold.

Let's look a bit closer at TAP. TAP's balance sheet reports assets of $1,354.2 million, liabilities of $1,036.7 million, and stockholders' equity of $317.5 million. TAP is a highly leveraged company with considerable assets. The $159 million investment balance on Abbott's balance sheet does not provide investors with any clue about the level of TAP's total assets nor about the substantial amount of TAP's financial obligations. It reflects only Abbott's share of TAP's net assets (assets less liabilities, or equity).

Further, Abbott makes the following additional disclosure in its footnotes relating to the cumulative payment of dividends by TAP:

Undistributed earnings of investments accounted for under the equity method amounted to approximately $136 as of December 31, 2007.

Cumulatively, Abbott has recorded $136 million more of income than it has received in cash dividends from TAP. This shows that equity income does not necessarily equal cash inflow. This is particularly true for equity investments in growth-stage companies that do not pay dividends, or for foreign subsidiaries of U.S. nationals that might not pay dividends for tax reasons or other restrictions.

Another area of concern with equity method accounting relates to unreported liabilities. As described above, TAP reports total liabilities of $1,036.7 million as of 2007, none of which appear on Abbott's balance sheet (Abbott only reports its investment in TAP's equity as an asset). Pharmaceutical companies face large potential liabilities arising from drug sales. (For example, TAP reported a loss of $150 million relating to litigation that it settled in 2004.) Although Abbott might have no direct legal obligation for TAP's liabilities, it might need to fund settlement costs via additional investment or advances to maintain TAP's viability if the company is important to Abbott's strategic plan. Further, companies that routinely fund R&D activities through equity investments in other companies, a common practice in the pharmaceutical and software industries, can find themselves supporting underperforming equity investments to assure continued capital market funding for these entities. One cannot always assume, therefore, that the investee's liabilities will not adversely affect the investor.

The concern with unreported liabilities becomes particularly problematic when the investee company reports losses that are substantial. In extreme cases, the investee company can become insolvent (when equity is negative) as the growing negative balance in retained earnings more than offsets paid-in capital. Once the equity of the investee company reaches zero, the investor must discontinue accounting for the investment by the equity method. Instead, it accounts for the investment at cost with a zero balance and no further recognition of its proportionate share of investee company losses. In this case, the investor's income statement no longer includes the losses of the investee company and its balance sheet no longer reports the troubled investee company. Unreported liabilities can be especially problematic in this case.

To summarize, under equity method accounting, only the net equity owned is reported on the balance sheet (not the underlying assets and liabilities), and only the net equity in earnings is reported in the income statement (not the investee's sales and expenses). This is simply illustrated as follows using the (assumed) income statement and balance sheet from Mitel, the company in which Google invests $300 for a 30% ownership stake, at the end of the first year.

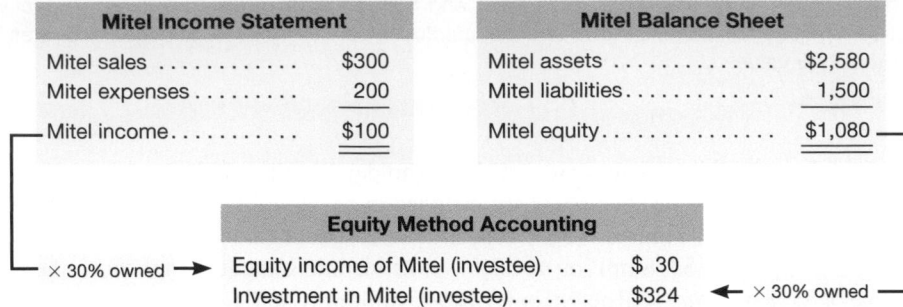

Mitel Income Statement	
Mitel sales	$300
Mitel expenses	200
Mitel income.	$100

Mitel Balance Sheet	
Mitel assets	$2,580
Mitel liabilities.	1,500
Mitel equity.	$1,080

Equity Method Accounting	
× 30% owned → Equity income of Mitel (investee)	$ 30
Investment in Mitel (investee).	$324 ← × 30% owned

From an analysis standpoint, because the assets and liabilities are left off the Google balance sheet, and because the sales and expenses are omitted from the Google income statement, the *components* of ROE are markedly affected as follows:

- **Net operating profit margin (NOPM = NOPAT/Sales).** Most analysts include equity income (sales less expenses) in NOPAT since it relates to operating investments. However, investee's sales are not included in the NOPM denominator. The reported NOPM is, thus, overstated.

- **Net operating asset turnover (NOAT = Sales/Average NOA).** Investee's sales are excluded from the NOAT numerator, and net operating assets in excess of the investment balance are excluded from the denominator. This means the impact on NOAT is *indeterminate*.

- **Financial leverage (FLEV = Net nonoperating obligations/Average equity).** Financial leverage is understated due to the absence of investee liabilities in the numerator.

Although ROE components are affected, ROE is unaffected by equity method accounting because the correct amount of investee net income and equity *is* included in the ROE numerator and denominator, respectively. Still, the evaluation of the quality of ROE is affected. Analysis using reported equity method accounting numbers would use an overstated NOPM and an understated FLEV because the numbers are based on net balance sheet and net income statement numbers. As we discuss in a later module, analysts should adjust reported financial statements for these types of items before conducting analysis. One such adjustment might be to consolidate (for analysis purposes) the equity method investee with the investor company.

IFRS INSIGHT   **Equity Method Investments and IFRS**

Like US GAAP, IFRS requires use of the equity method for investments in "associates" where the investor has significant influence. Unlike US GAAP, IFRS does not permit an investor that continues to have significant influence over an associate to cease applying the equity method when the associate is operating under severe long-term restrictions that impair its ability to transfer funds to the investor. Instead, significant influence must be lost before the equity method ceases to apply. US GAAP allows the equity method to cease once the investee's equity reaches zero.

MANAGERIAL DECISION   **You Are the Chief Financial Officer**

You are receiving capital expenditure requests for long-term operating asset purchases from various managers. You are concerned that capacity utilization is too low. What potential courses of action can you consider? Explain. [Answer, p. 7-32]

MID-MODULE REVIEW 2

Assume that Google had the following five transactions involving investments in marketable securities accounted for using the equity method. Use this information to answer requirement *a* below.

1. Purchased 5,000 shares of LookSmart common stock at $10 cash per share; these shares reflect 30% ownership of LookSmart.
2. Received a $2 per share cash dividend on LookSmart common stock.
3. Recorded an accounting adjustment to reflect $100,000 income reported by LookSmart.
4. Year-end market price of LookSmart has increased to $12 per common share.
5. Sold all 5,000 shares of LookSmart common stock for $90,000 cash in the next period.

Assume that Yahoo! reports a $637 million equity investment in Yahoo! Japan related to its 34% ownership interest, and Yahoo!'s footnotes reveal the following financial information about Yahoo! Japan ($ millions).

Twelve Months Ended September 30	2010	2011	2012
Operating data			
Revenues	$1,367	$1,671	$1,933
Gross profit.	1,252	1,584	1,836
Income from operations	656	807	984
Net income	382	451	508

September 30	2011	2012
Balance sheet data		
Current assets	$ 732	$1,131
Long-term assets	1,692	1,783
Current liabilities.	535	692
Long-term liabilities	509	348

Required

a. Use the financial statement effects template to enter the effects (amount and account) for the five Google transactions, above.
b. How much income does Yahoo! report in its 2012 income statement related to this equity investment?
c. Show the computations required to yield the $637 million balance in the equity investment account on Yahoo!'s balance sheet.

The solution is on page 7-52.

INVESTMENTS WITH CONTROL

This section discusses accounting for investments where the investor company "controls" the investee company. For example, in its footnote describing its accounting policies, Google reports the following:

> **Basis of Consolidations** The consolidated financial statements include the accounts of Google and wholly-owned subsidiaries. All intercompany balances and transactions have been eliminated.

LO3 Describe and illustrate accounting for consolidations.

This means that Google's financial statements are an aggregation (an adding up) of those of the parent company, Google, and all its subsidiary companies, less any intercompany activities such as intercompany sales or advances.

Accounting for Investments with Control

Accounting for business combinations (acquiring a controlling interest) goes one step beyond equity method accounting. Under the equity method, the investor's investment balance represents the proportion of the investee's equity owned by the investor, and the investor company's income statement

IFRS Alert
Consolidation accounting is generally similar with IFRS; differences exist in technical details, but not with presentation of consolidated financial statements.

includes its proportionate share of the investee's income. Once "control" over the investee company is achieved, GAAP requires consolidation for financial statements issued to the public (not for the internal financial records of the separate companies). Consolidation accounting includes 100% of the investee's assets and liabilities on the investor's balance sheet and 100% of the investee's sales and expenses on the investor's income statement. Specifically, the consolidated balance sheet includes the gross assets and liabilities of the investee company, and the income statement includes the investee's gross sales and expenses rather than just the investor's share of the investee company's net assets or income. All inter-company sales and expenses, and receivables and payables, are eliminated in the consolidation process to avoid double-counting when, for example, goods are sold from the investee (called a subsidiary) to the investor (called the parent company) for resale to the parent's ultimate customers.

Investments Purchased at Book Value: Subsidiary Wholly-Owned To illustrate, consider the following scenario. Penman Company acquires 100% of the common stock of Nissim Company by exchanging newly issued Penman shares for all of Nissim's common stock. The purchase price is equal to the $3,000 book value of Nissim's stockholders' equity (contributed capital of $2,000 and retained earnings of $1,000). On its balance sheet, Penman accounts for the investment in Nissim using the eq-uity method. This is important. Even if the investor (the parent) owns 100% of the investee, it records the investment on its (parent-company) balance sheet using the equity method described in the previous section. That is, Penman records an initial balance in the investment account of $3,000, equal to the purchase price. The balance sheets for Penman and Nissim immediately after the acquisition, together with the consolidated balance sheet, are shown in Exhibit 7.5.

Beginning on the date that Penman "controls" the activities of Nissim, GAAP requires consolidation of the two balance sheets, as well as the consolidation of the two income statements (not shown here). This process, shown in Exhibit 7.5, involves summing the individual lines for each balance sheet, after eliminating any intercompany transactions (such as investments and loans, and sales and purchases), within the consolidated group. The consolidated balances for accounts such as current assets, PPE, and liabilities are computed as the sum of those accounts from each balance sheet. The equity investment account, however, represents an intercompany transaction that Penman must eliminate during the con-solidation process. This is accomplished by removing the equity investment of $3,000 (from Penman's balance sheet), and removing Nissim's stockholders' equity to which Penman's investment relates.

EXHIBIT 7.5	Mechanics of Consolidation Accounting (Wholly-Owned Subsidiary, Purchased at Book Value)			
	Penman Company	Nissim Company	Consolidating Adjustments	Consolidated
Current assets	$ 5,000	$1,000		$ 6,000
Investment in Nissim	3,000	0	(3,000)	0
PPE, net	10,000	4,000		14,000
Total assets.	$18,000	$5,000		$20,000
Liabilities.	$ 5,000	$2,000		$ 7,000
Contributed capital.	10,000	2,000	(2,000)	10,000
Retained earnings	3,000	1,000	(1,000)	3,000
Total liabilities and equity	$18,000	$5,000		$20,000

Exhibit 7.5 shows the consolidated balance sheet in the far right column. It shows total assets of $20,000, total liabilities of $7,000 and stockholders' equity of $13,000. Notice that consolidated equity equals the equity of the parent company—this is always the case. (Likewise, consolidated net income always equals the parent company's net income as the subsidiary's net income is already reflected in the parent's income statement as equity income from its investment.)

Investments Purchased at Book Value: Subsidiary _Not_ Wholly-Owned In the event that Penman acquires less than 100% of the stock of Nissim, consolidated equity must increase to maintain the accounting equation. This equity account is titled **noncontrolling interest**. For example, assume that Penman acquires 80% of Nissim for $2,400 (80% of $3,000). The consolidating adjustments fol-low. The claim of noncontrolling shareholders on Nissim's net assets, is recognized in consolidated stockholders' equity, just like that of the majority shareholders. Exhibit 7.6 shows the consolidation adjustments and noncontrolling interest reported in the equity section of the consolidated balance sheet.

EXHIBIT 7.6	Mechanics of Consolidation Accounting (Subsidiary Not Wholly-Owned, Purchased at Book Value)			
	Penman Company	Nissim Company	Consolidating Adjustments	Consolidated
Current assets	$ 5,000	$1,000		$ 6,000
Investment in Nissim	2,400	0	(2,400)	0
PPE, net	10,000	4,000		14,000
Total assets.	$17,400	$5,000		$20,000
Liabilities.	$ 5,000	$2,000		$7,000
Contributed capital.	9,400	2,000	(2,000)	9,400
Retained earnings	3,000	1,000	(1,000)	3,000
Noncontrolling interest.			600	600
Total liability and equity	$17,400	$5,000		$20,000

The consolidated income statement lists the consolidated revenues, consolidated expenses, and consolidated net income. When less than 100% of the subsidiary is owned by the parent, the consolidated income statement allocates net income into that portion attributable to the parent's (controlling) shareholders and that which is attributable to the noncontrolling shareholders.

BUSINESS INSIGHT | Accounting for Noncontrolling Interests

When a company acquires less than 100% of a subsidiary, it must account for the interests of the noncontrolling shareholders separately from those of its own shareholders. This has two implications for consolidated financial statements:

1. The noncontrolling interest must be separately valued on the acquisition date. Consequently, the subsidiary is initially reported on the consolidated balance sheet at 100% of its fair value on the acquisition date (the fair value of the consideration paid plus the fair value of the noncontrolling interest on the acquisition date).
2. Consolidated net income is first computed for the company as a whole as revenues less expenses. Then, it is allocated to the portion attributable to the parent's shareholders and the noncontrolling shareholders in proportion to their respective ownership interests.

The balance of the noncontrolling interests is reported on the balance sheet in the stockholders' equity section. It is increased each year by the net income allocated to noncontrolling interests and is decreased by any dividends paid to those noncontrolling shareholders. A final point: if the subsidiary is acquired in a series of purchases, then once enough shares are purchased to gain control, the subsidiary is valued on the date control is achieved and any previously acquired shares are revalued on that acquisition date; this revaluation can result in recognition of a gain on previously acquired shares. (We describe reporting of noncontrolling interests in the balance sheet and income statement in Modules 5 and 9.)

Investments Purchased above Book Value The illustrations above assume that the purchase price of the acquisition equals the book value of the investee company. It is more often the case, however, that the purchase price exceeds the book value. This might arise, for example, if an investor company believes it is acquiring something of value that is not reported on the investee's balance sheet—such as tangible assets whose market values have risen above book value, or unrecorded intangible assets, like patents or corporate synergies. When the acquisition price exceeds book value, all net assets acquired (both tangible and intangible) must be recognized on the consolidated balance sheet.

To illustrate, assume that Penman Company acquires 100% of the voting stock of Nissim Company for $4,000. Also assume that in determining its purchase price, Penman paid the additional $1,000 because (1) Nissim's PPE is worth $300 more than its book value, and (2) Penman expects to realize $700 in additional value from corporate synergies (these "synergies" are an intangible asset with an indefinite useful life; they are classified as an asset called goodwill). The $4,000 investment account reflects two components: the book value acquired of $3,000 (as before) and an additional $1,000 of newly acquired assets. Exhibit 7.7 shows the post-acquisition balance sheets of the two companies, together with the consolidating adjustments and the consolidated balance sheet.

EXHIBIT 7.7	Mechanics of Consolidation Accounting (Purchase Price above Book Value)			
	Penman Company	Nissim Company	Consolidating Adjustments	Consolidated
Current assets	$ 5,000	$1,000		$ 6,000
Investment in Nissim	4,000	0	(4,000)	0
PPE, net	10,000	4,000	300	14,300
Goodwill			700	700
Total assets.	$19,000	$5,000		$21,000
Liabilities.	$ 5,000	$2,000		$ 7,000
Contributed capital.	11,000	2,000	(2,000)	11,000
Retained earnings	3,000	1,000	(1,000)	3,000
Total liabilities and equity	$19,000	$5,000		$21,000

The consolidated current assets and liabilities are the sum of those accounts on each company's balance sheet. The investment account, however, includes the $1,000 of additional newly acquired assets that must be reported on the consolidated balance sheet. The consolidation process in this case has two steps. First, the $3,000 equity of Nissim Company is eliminated against the investment account as before. Then, the remaining $1,000 of the investment account is eliminated and the newly acquired assets ($300 of PPE and $700 of goodwill not reported on Nissim's balance sheet) are added to the consolidated balance sheet. Thus, the consolidated balance sheet reflects the book value of Penman and the *fair market value* of Nissim (the book value plus the excess of Nissim's market value over its book value). For example, the consolidated PPE includes the book value of Penman's PPE ($10,000) along with the acquisition date fair value of Nissim's PPE ($4,300) for a total consolidated PPE of $14,300.

Consolidation is similar in successive periods. The excess purchase price assigned to depreciable assets, or identifiable intangible assets, must be amortized over the assets' useful lives. For example, if the additional $300 fair value of Nissim's PPE has an estimated life of 10 years with no salvage value, Penman would add $30 to depreciation expense on the consolidated income statement. This would reduce the consolidated PPE each year. And, as the excess of the purchase price over book value acquired is depreciated and/or amortized, the investment account on Penman's balance sheet gradually declines. Because goodwill is not amortized under GAAP, it remains at its carrying amount of $700 on the consolidated balance sheet unless it is impaired and written down (we discuss this below).

Consolidation Disclosures To illustrate consolidation mechanics with an actual case, consider the consolidated balance sheet (parent company, subsidiary, consolidating adjustments, and consolidated balance sheet) that Caterpillar (CAT) reports in a supplemental schedule to its 10-K report as shown in Exhibit 7.8. Caterpillar owns 100% of its financial products subsidiaries, principally Caterpillar Financial Services Corporation, whose stockholders' equity is $4,275 million as of 2010. The Investments in Financial Products account is also reported at $4,275 million on CAT's (parent company) balance sheet. This investment account is subsequently removed (eliminated) in the consolidation process, together with the equity of the subsidiaries to which it relates. Following this elimination, *and the elimination of all other intercompany transactions*, the adjusted balance sheets of the two companies are summed to yield the consolidated balance sheet that is reported in CAT's 10-K.

In sum, the consolidated balance sheet lists the consolidated assets, consolidated liabilities, and consolidated equity. (In some cases it also reports an additional equity account called *noncontrolling interests*, reflecting the ownership claim of the noncontrolling shareholders to the net assets of the subsidiary in which they are investors.)

EXHIBIT 7.8 Caterpillar Consolidated Balance Sheet

At December 31, 2010 (In millions)	Machinery and Engines (Parent)	Financial Products (Subsidiary)	Consolidating Adjustments	Consolidated
Assets				
Current assets:				
Cash and short-term investments	$ 1,825	$ 1,767	$ —	$ 3,592
Receivables—trade and other	5,893	482	2,119	8,494
Receivables—finance	—	11,158	(2,860)	8,298
Deferred and refundable income taxes	823	108	—	931
Prepaid expenses and other current assets	371	550	(13)	908
Inventories	9,587	—	—	9,587
Total current assets	18,499	14,065	(754)	31,810
Property, plant and equipment—net	9,662	2,877	—	12,539
Long-term receivables—trade and other	271	236	286	793
Long-term receivables—finance	—	11,586	(322)	11,264
Investments in unconsolidated affiliated companies	156	8	—	164
Investments in Financial Products subsidiaries	4,275	—	(4,275)	—
Noncurrent deferred and refundable income taxes	2,922	90	(519)	2,493
Intangible assets	795	10	—	805
Goodwill	2,597	17	—	2,614
Other assets	314	1,224	—	1,538
Total assets	$39,491	$30,113	$(5,584)	$64,020
Liabilities				
Current liabilities:				
Short-term borrowings	$ 306	$ 4,452	$ (702)	$ 4,056
Accounts payable	5,717	177	(38)	5,856
Accrued expenses	2,422	470	(12)	2,880
Accrued wages, salaries and employee benefits	1,642	28	—	1,670
Customer advances	1,831	—	—	1,831
Dividends payable	281	—	—	281
Other current liabilities	1,142	393	(14)	1,521
Long-term debt due within one year	495	3,430	—	3,925
Total current liabilities	13,836	8,950	(766)	22,020
Long-term debt due after one year	4,543	15,932	(38)	20,437
Liability for postemployment benefits	7,584	—	—	7,584
Other liabilities	2,203	956	(505)	2,654
Total liabilities	28,166	25,838	(1,309)	52,695
Commitments and contingencies				
Redeemable noncontrolling interest*	461	—	—	461
Stockholders' equity				
Common stock	3,888	902	(902)	3,888
Treasury stock	(10,397)	—	—	(10,397)
Profit employed in the business	21,384	3,027	(3,027)	21,384
Accumulated other comprehensive income (loss)	(4,051)	263	(263)	(4,051)
Noncontrolling interests	40	83	(83)	40
Total stockholders' equity	10,864	4,275	(4,275)	10,864
Total liabilities, redeemable noncontrolling interest and stockholders' equity	$39,491	$30,113	$(5,584)	$64,020

*This $461 is reported as mezzanine (temporary) equity because it relates to a CAT subsidiary, where another company has a noncontrolling interest, for which the CAT subsidiary has an option to purchase per a redemption agreement.

Reporting of Acquired Intangible Assets

As previously discussed, acquisitions are routinely made at a purchase price in excess of the book value of the investee company's equity. The purchase price is first allocated to the fair values of tangible assets and liabilities. Then, the remainder is allocated to acquired intangible assets: first to identifiable intangible assets, then, any remainder is allocated to goodwill. As of the acquisition date, the purchasing company values the tangible assets acquired and liabilities assumed in the purchase and records them on the consolidated balance sheet at fair market value. Common types of intangible assets recognized during acquisitions follow:

- Marketing-related assets like trademarks and Internet domain names
- Customer-related assets like customer lists and customer contracts
- Artistic-related assets like plays, books, and videos
- Contract-based assets like licensing, lease contracts, and franchise and royalty agreements
- Technology-based assets like patents, in-process research and development, software, databases, and trade secrets

To illustrate, Procter & Gamble (P&G) reported the following allocation of its $53.4 billion purchase price for Gillette in the footnotes to its 10-K report ($ millions).

Tangible assets	Current assets	$ 5,681
	Property, plant and equipment	3,655
	Other noncurrent assets	382
	Goodwill	35,298
Acquired intangible assets	Intangible assets	29,707
	Total assets acquired	74,723
Liabilities assumed	Current liabilities	5,346
	Noncurrent liabilities	15,951
	Total liabilities assumed	21,297
	Net assets acquired	53,426

Identifiable Intangible Assets (excluding goodwill) In its acquisition of Gillette, P&G allocated $29,707 million of its purchase price to identifiable intangible assets (other than goodwill), as described in the following footnote to P&G's 10-K ($ millions):

The purchase price allocation to the identifiable intangible assets included in these financial statements is as follows:

Intangible Assets with Determinable Lives		Average Life
Brands	$ 1,627	20
Patents and technology	2,716	17
Customer relationships	1,436	27
Brands with indefinite lives	23,928	Indefinite
Total intangible assets	29,707	

The majority of the intangible asset valuation relates to brands. Our assessment as to brands that have an indefinite life and those that have a determinable life was based on a number of factors, including the competitive environment, market share, brand history, product life cycles, operating plan and macroeconomic environment of the countries in which the brands are sold. The indefinite-lived brands include Gillette, Venus, Duracell, Oral-B and Braun. The determinable-lived brands include certain brand sub-names, such as Mach3 and Sensor in the blades and razors business, and other regional or local brands. The determinable-lived brands have asset lives ranging from 10 to 40 years. The patents and technology intangibles are concentrated in the blades and razors and oral care businesses and have asset lives ranging from 5 to 20 years. The customer relationship intangible asset useful lives ranging from 20 to 30 years reflect the very low historical and projected customer attrition rates among Gillette's major retailer and distributor customers.

P&G allocated a portion of the purchase price to the following identifiable intangible assets:

- Brands
- Patents and technology
- Customer relationships

P&G deemed these identifiable intangible assets as amortizable assets, which are those having a finite useful life. P&G will subsequently amortize them over their useful lives (similar to depreciation).

> **IFRS Alert**
> When a firm purchases in-process research and development in the course of an acquisition, those costs are capitalized as an intangible asset under both IFRS and U.S. GAAP.

BUSINESS INSIGHT   **Restructuring Liabilities**

Many acquisitions are accompanied by restructuring activities that are designed to maximize asset utilization. These restructuring activities typically involve relocation and retraining or termination of employees and the exiting of less profitable product lines resulting in costs from closure of manufacturing, retailing, and administrative facilities and the write-off of assets. Acquirers can recognize restructuring liabilities when they purchase a subsidiary *only* if that subsidiary has previously accrued those liabilities. It also requires the Board of Directors to approve a formal restructuring plan and to communicate that plan to affected employees. Restructuring activities beginning *after* acquisition must be accrued and the expense recognized in post-acquisition consolidated income statements.

Goodwill   Once the purchase price has been allocated to identifiable tangible and intangible assets (net of liabilities assumed), any remaining purchase price is allocated to goodwill. Goodwill, thus, represents the remainder of the purchase price that is not allocated to other assets. P&G allocated $35.3 billion (66%) of the Gillette purchase price to goodwill. The SEC scrutinizes companies that assign an excessive proportion of the purchase price to goodwill (companies might do this to avoid the future earnings drag from the amortization expense relating to identifiable intangible assets with useful lives).

BUSINESS INSIGHT   **Valuation of Earn-Outs**

Martha Stewart Living Omnimedia agreed to acquire some business units run by celebrity chef Emeril Lagasse for $50 million in cash and stock and a lucrative *earn-out* that could reach $20 million if Lagasse and company met specific profit goals. An earn-out is an incentive offered to key employees of a target company to entice them to remain with the company and increase value. Then, if the target company hits profit goals set by the buyer, the identified key employees earn a share of the profit. Under current GAAP, buyers must determine the estimated fair value of the future earn-out on the day of acquisition and record it as part of the purchase price. One impetus for an earn-out is when the buyer and seller cannot agree on a purchase price; in this way, the buyer is saying "I will pay if you make hay." Finally, any difference between the estimated fair value and the ultimate actual payout is recorded as an expense or gain.

Reporting of Goodwill

Goodwill is not amortized. Instead, GAAP requires companies to test the goodwill asset annually for impairment just like any other asset. The impairment test is a two-step process:

1. The fair value of the investee company is compared with the book value of the investor's equity investment account.[2]

2. If the fair value is less than the investment balance, the *investment* is deemed impaired. Next, one determines if the *goodwill* portion of the investment is impaired. The investor estimates the goodwill value as if the subsidiary were acquired at current fair value, and the imputed balance for goodwill becomes the balance in the goodwill account. If this imputed goodwill amount is

---

[2] GAAP allows firms to estimate fair value in three ways: using quoted market prices for identical assets, using quoted prices on similar assets, or using other valuation methods (such as the discounted cash flow model or residual operating income model—see Module 12). The FedEx footnote, which follows, provides an example of the third method of determining fair value: an income approach. A company can avoid the goodwill impairment test if qualitative indicators (see GAAP) suggest a likelihood that the fair value of the reporting unit is greater than its carrying value; if not, then the company must apply the two-step test.

less than its book value, the company writes goodwill down, resulting in an impairment loss on the consolidated income statement. (If not, no impairment of goodwill exists and no write-down is necessary; which, implies the impairment in this case relates to the investee's tangible assets, such as PPE, that must be tested separately for impairment.)

To illustrate the impairment computation, assume that an investment, currently reported at $1 million on the investor's balance sheet, has a current fair value of $900,000 (we know, therefore, that the investment is impaired); also assume the consolidated balance sheet reports goodwill at $300,000. Management's review reveals that the current fair value of the net assets of the investee company (absent goodwill) is $700,000. This indicates that the goodwill component of the investment account is impaired by $100,000, which is computed as follows:

Fair value of investee company	$ 900,000
Fair value of net assets (absent goodwill)	(700,000)
Implied goodwill	200,000
Current goodwill balance	(300,000)
Impairment loss	$(100,000)

This analysis implies that goodwill must be written down by $100,000. The impairment loss is reported in the consolidated income statement. The related footnote disclosure would describe the reasons for the write-down and the computations involved.

FedEx provides an example of a goodwill impairment disclosure in its 10-K report:

Our operating results include a charge of approximately $891 million ($696 million, net of tax, or $2.23 per diluted share) recorded during the fourth quarter, predominantly related to noncash impairment charges associated with the decision to minimize the use of the Kinko's trade name and goodwill resulting from the Kinko's acquisition. The components of the charge include the following (in millions):

Trade name	$515
Goodwill	367
Other	9
	$891

During the fourth quarter we decided to change the name of FedEx Kinko's to FedEx Office. The impairment of the Kinko's trade name was due to the decision to minimize the use of the Kinko's trade name and rebrand our centers over the next several years. In accordance with SFAS 142, "Goodwill and Other Intangible Assets," a two-step impairment test is performed on goodwill. In the first step, we compared the estimated fair value of the reporting unit to its carrying value. The valuation methodology to estimate the fair value of the FedEx Office reporting unit was based primarily on an income approach that considered market participant assumptions to estimate fair value. Key assumptions considered were the revenue and operating income forecast, the assessed growth rate in the periods beyond the detailed forecast period, and the discount rate. In the second step of the impairment test, we estimated the current fair values of all assets and liabilities to determine the amount of implied goodwill and consequently the amount of the goodwill impairment. Upon completion of the second step of the impairment test, we concluded that the recorded goodwill was impaired and recorded an impairment charge of $367 million during the fourth quarter.

FedEx determined that goodwill, reported on its balance sheet at $1,542 million, had a current (implied) market value $1,175 million. That is, FedEx's goodwill was impaired, resulting in a write-down of $367 million. In addition, FedEx recorded a $515 million charge to write off the Kinko's trade name that it had acquired four years earlier.

> **IFRS INSIGHT**   **Goodwill Impairment and Revaluation**
>
> Similar to GAAP, all long-term assets, including goodwill, must be periodically evaluated for impairment. But, under IFRS, any previous impairment losses must be reversed if the asset subsequently increases in value. However, this does not apply to goodwill; once it is impaired under IFRS, it can not be revalued upwards. This is consistent with GAAP. Impairment losses are typically larger in magnitude under IFRS because IFRS computes the impairment loss as the excess of the carrying amount of the goodwill over its recoverable amount. Under GAAP, the impairment is relative to the implied fair value of the goodwill, which by definition is higher than the recoverable amount. Thus, for identical circumstances, goodwill impairments will be larger under IFRS.

Reporting Subsidiary Stock Issuances

After subsidiaries are acquired, they can, and sometimes do, issue stock. If issued to outside investors, the result is an infusion of cash into the subsidiary and a reduction in the parent's percentage ownership. For example, Bristol-Myers Squibb's 10-K report discloses the following stock issuance by one of its subsidiaries.

> **MEAD JOHNSON NUTRITION COMPANY INITIAL PUBLIC OFFERING** In February 2009, Mead Johnson completed an initial public offering (IPO), in which it sold 34.5 million shares of its Class A common stock at $24 per share. Net proceeds of $782 million, after deducting $46 million of underwriting discounts, commissions and offering expenses, were allocated to noncontrolling interest and capital in excess of par value of stock. Upon completion of the IPO, 42.3 million shares of Mead Johnson Class A common stock and 127.7 million shares of Mead Johnson Class B common stock were held by the Company, representing an 83.1% interest in Mead Johnson and 97.5% of the combined voting power of the outstanding common stock...Various agreements related to the separation of Mead Johnson were entered into, including a separation agreement, a transitional services agreement, a tax matters agreement, a registration rights agreement and an employee matters agreement.

Prior to the IPO, Mead Johnson was a wholly-owned subsidiary of Bristol-Myers Squibb. The IPO resulted in the issuance of 34.5 million shares by Mead, representing 16.9% of the outstanding Class A common stock, for total proceeds of $782 million. As a result of the IPO, Bristol-Myers Squibb's stockholders' equity increased by $782 million, net of the noncontrolling interest that must now be recognized to reflect the claims of the noncontrolling shareholders to the net assets of Mead Johnson. This increase in stockholders' equity as a result of the IPO is not reflected in Bristol-Myers Squibb's retained earnings since it is not reflected in net income. Rather, it is reflected as an increase in additional paid-in capital.

> **BUSINESS INSIGHT**   **Pitfalls of Acquired Growth**
>
> One of the greatest destructions of shareholder value occurred during the bull market between 1995 and 2001 when market exuberance fueled a tidal wave of corporate takeovers. Companies often overpaid as a result of overestimating the cost-cutting and synergies their planned takeovers would bring. Then, acquirers failed to quickly integrate operations. The result? Subsequent years' market returns of most acquirers fell below those of their peers and were often negative. Indeed, 61% of corporate buyers saw their shareholders' wealth *decrease* after the acquisition. Who won? The sellers; the target-company shareholders who sold their stock within the first week of the takeover and reaped enormous profits at the expense of the acquirers' shareholders.

Reporting the Sale of Subsidiary Companies

Discontinued operations refer to any separately identifiable business unit that the company sells or intends to sell. The income or loss of the discontinued operations (net of tax), and the after-tax gain or loss on sale of the unit, are reported in the income statement below income from continuing operations. The segregation of discontinued operations means that revenues and expenses of the discontinued business unit are *not* reported with revenues and expenses from continuing operations.

To illustrate, assume that a company's recent periods' results were generated by both continuing and discontinued operations as follows:

	Continuing Operations	Discontinued Operations	Total
Revenues	$10,000	$3,000	$13,000
Expenses	7,000	2,000	9,000
Pretax Income	3,000	1,000	4,000
Tax expense (40%).	1,200	400	1,600
Net Income.	$ 1,800	$ 600	$ 2,400

The reported income statement would appear as follows—notice the separate disclosure for discontinued operations (as highlighted).

Revenues	$10,000
Expenses	7,000
Pretax income	3,000
Tax expense (40%).	1,200
Income from continuing operations	1,800
Income from discontinued operations, net of tax	**600**
Net income.	$ 2,400

Revenues and expenses reflect those of the continuing operations only, and the (persistent) income from continuing operations is reported net of its related tax expense. Results from the (transitory) discontinued operations are collapsed into one line item and reported separately net of its own tax (this includes any gain or loss from sale of the discontinued unit's net assets). The net income figure is unchanged by this presentation.

Importantly, results of the discontinued operations are segregated from those of continuing operations. This presentation facilitates the prediction of results from the (persistent) continuing operations. Discontinued operations are segregated (reported on one line) in the current year and for the two prior years. To illustrate, **Kraft Foods** reports the following footnote to its 2010 10-K relating to the decision to divest its North American frozen pizza business ($ millions).

Pizza Divestiture On March 1, 2010, we completed the sale of the assets of our North American frozen pizza business ("Frozen Pizza") to Nestlé USA, Inc. ("Nestlé") for $3.7 billion. Our Frozen Pizza business was a component of our U.S. Convenient Meals and Canada & N. A. Foodservice segments. The sale included the DiGiorno, Tombstone and Jack's brands in the U.S., the Delissio brand in Canada and the California Pizza Kitchen trademark license. It also included two Wisconsin manufacturing facilities (Medford and Little Chute) and the leases for the pizza depots and delivery trucks. Approximately 3,600 of our employees transferred with the business to Nestlé. As a result of the divestiture, we recorded a gain on discontinued operations of $1,596 million, or $0.92 per diluted share, in 2010. Summary results of operations for the Frozen Pizza business through March 1, 2010, were as follows. The after-tax results for Kraft include both the earnings from the discontinued operations and the gain on sale for a total of $1,644 million after tax.

For Years Ended December 31, (in millions)	2010	2009	2008
Net revenues	$ 335	$1,632	$1,440
Earnings before income taxes	73	341	267
Provisions for income taxes.	(25)	(123)	(97)
Gain on discontinued operations, net of income taxes	1,596	—	—
Earnings and gain from discontinued operations, net of income taxes	$1,644	$ 218	$ 170

This footnote highlights two important items. First, in 2010, the pizza operations had revenues of $335 million and net income of $48 million ($73 million before tax less tax of $25 million). Companies often discontinue profitable operations, selling them to recoup investments and/or to focus on other lines of business. Second, the sale of the frozen pizza operations generated a gain of $1,596 million after tax. The reported gain or loss on sale is equal to the proceeds received less the balance of the equity method investment reported on the parent's balance sheet at the sale date. Both of these two components—the net income or loss from operations during the year and any gain or loss on disposal of the discontinued operations—are reported, on one line, in Kraft's income statement. For comparative years (2009 and 2008) only the first component is included in the discontinued operations line item because the frozen pizza operations were not sold until 2010.

Limitations of Consolidation Reporting

Consolidation of financial statements is meant to present a financial picture of the entire set of companies under the control of the parent. Since investors typically purchase stock in the parent company, and not in the subsidiaries, a consolidated view is more relevant than the parent company merely reporting subsidiaries as equity investments in its balance sheet. Still, we must be aware of certain limitations of consolidation:

1. Consolidated income does not imply that the parent company has received any or all of the subsidiaries' net income as cash. The parent can only receive cash from subsidiaries via dividend payments. Conversely, the consolidated cash is not automatically available to the individual subsidiaries. It is quite possible, therefore, for an individual subsidiary to experience cash flow problems even though the consolidated group has strong cash flows. Likewise, unguaranteed debts of a subsidiary are not obligations of the consolidated group. Thus, even if the consolidated balance sheet is strong, creditors of a failing subsidiary are often unable to sue the parent or other subsidiaries to recoup losses.

2. Consolidated balance sheets and income statements are a mix of the various subsidiaries, often from different industries. Comparisons across companies, even if in similar industries, are often complicated by the different mix of subsidiary companies.

3. Segment disclosures on individual subsidiaries are affected by intercorporate transfer pricing policies relating to purchases of products or services that can artificially inflate the profitability of one segment at the expense of another. Companies also have considerable discretion in the allocation of corporate overhead to subsidiaries, which can markedly affect segment profitability.

> **BUSINESS INSIGHT** | **Determining the Parent Company in an Acquisition**
>
> Sensor, Inc., is acquiring Boston Instrument Company through an exchange of stock valued at $500 million. Sensor will survive as the continuing company, and the senior management of Boston Instrument will own 65% of the outstanding stock, reflecting a premium in the exchange ratios paid by Sensor to acquire Boston Instrument. Sensor's Chairman will remain as Chairman of the company, but the purchase agreement specifies that the board of directors will elect a new Chairman within six months of the deal's close. Boston Instrument's President and CFO will assume those same positions in the new entity. Following are the market values of the tangible and intangible net assets of both companies on the date of acquisition: Sensor, $400 million; and Boston Instrument, $200 million. Which of these two companies should be viewed as the acquiring firm (parent company) for purposes of consolidation, and how does this decision affect the amount of goodwill recorded on the consolidated balance sheet? Sensor is the larger firm, its name will survive, and its Chairman will serve in that capacity in the combined company. However, most accountants would likely conclude that Boston Instrument is the parent company for purposes of consolidation. This determination is based on the 65% ownership interest of the Boston Instrument shareholders who control the new entity. Further, these shareholders will be able to elect a new Chairman within six months. The amount of goodwill recorded following the acquisition is equal to the purchase price less the fair value of the net tangible and identifiable intangible assets acquired. If Sensor is the acquiring firm, $100 million ($500 million − $400 million) of goodwill will be recorded. If Boston Instrument is the acquiring firm, $300 million ($500 million − $200 million) of goodwill will be recorded. This decision will dramatically affect both the balance sheet (relative amounts of goodwill and other assets recorded) as well as the income statement (depreciation of tangible assets and amortization of identifiable intangible assets recognized vs. annual impairment testing for goodwill).

GLOBAL ACCOUNTING

Both U.S. GAAP and IFRS account similarly for investments by companies in the debt and equity securities of other companies. However, differences exist and we highlight the notable ones here.

Passive Investments Under both U.S. GAAP and IFRS, companies classify financial (passive) instruments as trading, available-for-sale, or held-to-maturity.

■ Under IFRS the definition of financial instrument is much broader, including for example loans to customers or associates. For analysis, such instruments are disclosed in the notes, which will aid our reclassification for comparison purposes.

■ Under U.S. GAAP, unlisted securities are not considered "marketable" and are carried at cost. Under IFRS, unlisted securities can be valued at fair value, if it can be reliably measured.

■ U.S. GAAP prohibits companies from reclassifying trading securities as available-for-sale or held-to-maturity but, under certain circumstances, requires companies to reclassify securities as trading (for example, if there has been a sale of a held-to-maturity security). Under IFRS, both reclassifications to and from the trading portfolio is prohibited. This provides opportunity for strategic reporting behavior under U.S. GAAP. We should review the notes that report reclassifications to assess such behavior and identify any reporting incentives managers might have.

Equity Method Investment One important difference exists with equity method accounting between U.S. GAAP and IFRS. That is, U.S. GAAP allows only the equity method in accounting for joint ventures, whereas IFRS allows the equity method or proportionate consolidation. Under the latter, the company's share of investee's assets and liabilities (and revenues and expenses) are added line-by-line on the balance sheet (and income statement). Proportionate consolidation means that every line on the IFRS financial statement is "grossed up" as compared to GAAP. The net numbers (equity and income) are identical but comparisons of individual line items between an IFRS and a GAAP report are problematic. This is similar to our concern about the effect of equity method accounting versus consolidation. There is currently a proposal to prohibit proportionate consolidation. In the interim, as discussed in the module, GAAP notes often disclose total revenue, assets, and liabilities of equity method investees. Thus, it is possible for us to amend certain GAAP accounts for comparative analysis.

Consolidation As part of their convergence effort, the FASB and IASB engaged in a joint project for business combinations (IFRS 3 and SFAS 141). Despite the common goal to develop a consistent and comprehensive standard, a few differences remain.

■ The most notable difference is how to measure noncontrolling interests. Under IFRS, companies can measure noncontrolling interests either at fair value (full goodwill approach) or at the proportionate share of the identifiable net assets acquired (purchased goodwill approach). U.S. GAAP permits fair value only. Relative to the proportionate method, the U.S. GAAP balance sheet reports a larger goodwill and a larger noncontrolling interest in equity. This difference is most pronounced when a company acquires significantly less than 100% of the target's stock or when goodwill is a larger proportion of the cost of acquisition. This IFRS-GAAP difference affects ratios based on operating assets, such as RNOA. Because goodwill is not routinely amortized, the difference will have no income statement impact (recall from Module 4 that we exclude noncontrolling interest from our calculation of return on equity).

■ Under U.S. GAAP, parent and subsidiaries' accounting policies do not need to conform. Under IFRS, parent and subsidiaries' accounting policies must conform.

■ IFRS fair-value impairments for intangible assets, excluding goodwill, can be later reversed (that is, written back up after being written down). Companies must have reliable evidence that the value of the intangible has been restored and the reversal cannot exceed the original impairment. While the original impairment was reported as a charge on the income statement, subsequent reversals do not affect income but, instead, are added to equity through a "reserve" much like that for accumulated other comprehensive income. IFRS notes disclose any reversals of a prior impairment (again, goodwill impairments cannot be reversed).

MODULE-END REVIEW

On January 1 of the current year, assume that Yahoo!, Inc., purchased all of the common shares of EarthLink for $600,000 cash—this is $200,000 more than the book value of EarthLink's stockholders' equity. Balance sheets of the two companies immediately after the acquisition follow:

	Yahoo! (Parent)	EarthLink (Subsidiary)	Consolidating Adjustments	Consolidated
Current assets	$1,000,000	$100,000		
Investment in EarthLink	600,000	—		
PPE, net	3,000,000	400,000		
Goodwill	—	—		
Total assets.	$4,600,000	$500,000		
Liabilities.	$1,000,000	$100,000		
Contributed capital.	2,000,000	200,000		
Retained earnings	1,600,000	200,000		
Total liabilities and equity	$4,600,000	$500,000		

During purchase negotiations, EarthLink's PPE was appraised at $500,000, and all of EarthLink's remaining assets and liabilities were appraised at values approximating their book values. Also, Yahoo! concluded that payment of an additional $100,000 was warranted because of anticipated corporate synergies. Prepare the consolidating adjustments and the consolidated balance sheet at acquisition.

The solution is on page 7-53.

APPENDIX 7A: Accounting for Derivatives

Although there is some speculative use of derivatives by U.S. companies (both industrial and financial), most companies use derivatives to shelter their income statements and cash flows from fluctuations in the market prices of currencies, commodities, and financial instruments, as well as for market rates of interest. Companies routinely face risk exposures that can markedly affect their balance sheets, profitability, and cash flows. These exposures can be grouped into two general categories:[3]

1. Exposure to changes in the **fair value** of an asset (such as accounts receivable, inventory, marketable securities, or a firm contract to sell an asset) or of a liability (such as accounts payable, a firm commitment to purchase an asset, or a fixed-rate liability).
2. Exposure to variation in **cash flows** relating to a forecasted transaction (such as *planned* inventory purchases or anticipated foreign revenues) or cash-flow exposure relating to a variable-rate debt obligation.

Both of these types of risks can be managed (hedged) with a variety of financial instruments, including futures, forward contracts, options, and swap contracts. For an example in the first risk category, consider a company with a fair-value exposure from a receivable denominated in a foreign currency. If the $US strengthens subsequently, the receivable declines in value and the company incurs a foreign-currency loss. To avoid this situation, the company can hedge the receivable with a foreign-currency derivative. Ideally, when the $US strengthens, the derivative will increase in value by an amount that exactly offsets the decrease in the value of the receivable. As a result, the company's net asset position (receivable less derivative) remains unaffected and no gain or loss arises when the $US weakens or strengthens. For accounting purposes, this is called a **fair-value hedge**.

---

[3] Risks relating to changes in the fair value of a recognized asset or liability, or the variation in cash flows relating to a contractual obligation or a forecasted transaction, that results from fluctuations in the exchange value of the $US vis-à-vis other world currencies are particularly troublesome for companies. The use of derivatives to mitigate **foreign-currency risk** can fall into either of the risk categories.

As an example for the second risk category, consider a company that routinely purchases a food commodity used in its manufacturing process. Any price increases during the coming year will flow to cost of goods sold and profit will decrease (unless the company can completely pass the price increase along to its customers, which is rarely the case). To avoid this situation, the company can hedge the inventory purchases with a commodity derivative contract that locks in a price today. When the price of the commodity increases, the derivative contract will shelter the company and, as a result, the company's cost of goods sold remains unaffected. For accounting purposes, this is called a **cash-flow hedge**.

Accounting for derivatives essentially boils down to this: all derivatives are reported at fair value on the balance sheet. For fair-value hedges, the asset or liability being hedged (the foreign receivable in the example above), is reported on the balance sheet at fair value. If the market value of the hedged asset or liability changes, the value of the derivative changes in the opposite direction if the hedge is effective and, thus, net assets and liabilities are unaffected. Likewise, the related gains and losses are largely offsetting, leaving income unaffected.

For cash-flow hedges, there is no hedged asset or liability on the books. In our example above, it is the anticipated commodity purchases that are being hedged. Thus, the company has no inventory yet and changes in the fair value of the derivative are not met with opposite changes in an asset or liability. For these cash-flow hedges, gains or losses from the fair value of the derivative are not reported on the income statement. Instead they are held in accumulated other comprehensive income (AOCI), as part of shareholders' equity. Later, when the hedged item impacts income (say, when the commodity cost is reflected in cost of goods sold), the derivative gain or loss is reclassified from AOCI to income. If the hedge was effective, the gain or loss on the hedged transaction is offset with the loss or gain on the derivative and income is unaffected.

For both fair-value and cash-flow hedges, income is impacted only to the extent that the hedging activities are ineffective. Naturally, if derivative use is for speculative activities, gains and losses are not offset and directly flow to income. It is this latter activity, in particular, that prompted regulators to formulate newer, tougher accounting standards for derivatives.

Disclosures for Derivatives

Companies must disclose both qualitative and quantitative information about derivatives in notes to their financial statements and elsewhere (in the Management's Discussion and Analysis section). The aim of these disclosures is to inform outsiders about potential risks associated with derivative use. We present footnotes relating to fair-value hedges and cash-flow hedges below as examples of common transactions relating to use of derivatives to mitigate risk. We discuss the accounting for each and how we should interpret these disclosures in our analysis of the company.

Fair-Value Hedge

Fair-value hedges are used to mitigate risks relating to the change in the fair values of existing assets and liabilities. These fair values can change, for example, with changes in commodity prices, interest rates, or foreign exchange rates. Following is an example from the Kellogg 2010 10-K.

> Our Company is exposed to fluctuations in foreign currency cash flows related primarily to third-party purchases, intercompany transactions, and when applicable, nonfunctional currency denominated third-party debt . . . Additionally, our Company is exposed to volatility in the translation of foreign currency denominated earnings to U.S. dollars. Primary exposures include the U.S. dollar versus the British pound, euro, Australian dollar, Canadian dollar, and Mexican peso. We assess foreign currency risk based on transactional cash flows and translational volatility and may enter into forward contracts, options, and currency swaps to reduce fluctuations in long or short currency positions. Forward contracts and options are generally less than 18 months duration. Our Company is exposed to price fluctuations primarily as a result of anticipated purchases of raw and packaging materials, fuel, and energy. Primary exposures include corn, wheat, soybean oil, sugar, cocoa, paperboard, natural gas, and diesel fuel. We have historically used the combination of long-term contracts with suppliers, and exchange-traded futures and option contracts to reduce price fluctuations in a desired percentage of forecasted raw material purchases over a duration of generally less than 18 months.

To illustrate the accounting for the Kellogg fair-value hedge, assume that the company sells goods for €3.7 million ($5 million equivalent) on account to a customer located in Ireland. The company is concerned about the potential effects of a strengthening or weakening of the $US and enters into a forward contract to hedge that foreign-currency (FX) risk. Before the receivable is collected, the $US weakens vis-à-vis the Euro, and the Euros received (€3.7 million) converts to $5.5 million. The transactions are accounted for as follows:

Transaction	Balance Sheet							Income Statement				
	Cash Asset	+	Noncash Assets	=	Liabil- ities	+	Contrib. Capital	+	Earned Capital	Rev- enues	−	Expen- ses	=	Net Income

Transaction	Cash Asset	Noncash Assets	Liabilities	Contrib. Capital	Earned Capital	Revenues	Expenses	Net Income
1. Credit sale for €3.7 mil. ($5 mil. equivalent)		+5.0 mil. Accounts Receivable			+5.0 mil. Retained Earnings	+5.0 mil. Sales		+5.0 mil.
2a. Receive €3.7 mil. ($5.5 mil. equivalent) per transaction 1	+5.5 mil. Cash	−5.0 mil. Accounts Receivable			+0.5 mil. Retained Earnings	+0.5 mil. Gain on Foreign Currency Transaction		+0.5 mil.
2b. Record loss on settlement of foreign exchange contract	−0.5 mil. Cash				−0.5 mil. Retained Earnings		+0.5 mil. Loss on Foreign Exchange Derivative Contract	−0.5 mil.

Margin T-accounts:

```
AR      5.0M
Sales          5.0M
    AR
5M |
    Sales
       | 5M

Cash    5.5M
AR             5.0M
GN             0.5M
    Cash
5.5M |
    AR
       | 5M
Gain on FX
       | 0.5M

LS      0.5M
Cash           0.5M
Loss on Contract
0.5M |
    Cash
       | 0.5M
```

In this transaction, the company hedged its foreign exchange exposure via a forward contract. As the $US weakens, the value of the accounts receivable increases by $0.5 million, resulting in a foreign exchange gain, and the fair value of the derivative contract decreases by $0.5 million, resulting in an offsetting loss. The net cash received is the $5.5 million from the receivable less the $0.5 million to settle the forward contract.

Why would the company want to enter into a contract such as this that resulted in a loss? After all, had the company not "hedged" the Euro receivable, the cash collected would have been $5.5 million and the company would have reported a gain. The answer is that a company does not know in advance which way currencies will move. As the Kellogg footnote indicates, sometimes the derivative suffers a loss, and at other times creates a gain. The purpose of the derivative is to lock in the operating profit on the sale and to shield the company from risk in the form of fluctuating foreign-currency exchange rates.

Cash-Flow Hedge

Following is Tiffany & Co.'s disclosures from its 2011 10-K report relating to its use of derivatives:

> **Precious Metal Collars & Forward Contracts** The Company periodically hedges a portion of its forecasted purchases of precious metals for use in its internal manufacturing operations in order to minimize the effect of volatility in precious metal prices. The Company may use a combination of call and put option contracts in net-zero-cost collar arrangements ("precious metal collars") or forward contracts. For precious metal collars, if the price of the precious metal at the time of the expiration of the precious metal collar is within the call and put price, the precious metal collar would expire at no cost to the Company. The Company accounts for its precious metal collars and forward contracts as cash flow hedges. The Company assesses hedge effectiveness based on the total changes in the precious metal collars and forward contracts' cash flows. The maximum term over which the Company is hedging its exposure to the variability of future cash flows for all forecasted transactions is 12 months. As of January 31, 2011, there were approximately 2,700 ounces of platinum and no silver precious metal derivative instruments outstanding.

Tiffany uses derivatives to hedge against the risk of fluctuations in the market price of precious metals that the company anticipates purchasing in future.

These derivatives are cash-flow hedges. Thus, unrealized gains and losses on these derivative contracts are added to the Accumulated Other Comprehensive Income (AOCI) (part of stockholders' equity) until the precious metal is purchased. Once that precious metal is purchased, any unrealized gains and losses are removed from AOCI and recognized in current-period income via cost of goods sold. The gain (loss) on the derivative contract offsets the increased (decreased) cost of the precious metal.

Although the market value of derivatives and their related assets or liabilities can be large, the net effect on stockholders' equity is usually minor. This is because companies use derivatives mainly to hedge and not to speculate. The FASB enacted SFAS 133, "Accounting for Derivative Instruments and Hedging Activities," to respond to concerns that speculative activities were not adequately disclosed. However, subsequent to the passage of SFAS 133, the financial effects have been minimal. Either companies were not speculating to the extent suspected, or they have since reduced their level of speculation in response to increased scrutiny from better disclosures.

To illustrate the accounting for cash-flow hedge, assume that Tiffany knows that it must purchase platinum over the coming year. The platinum would cost $1 million at the current market prices but Tiffany anticipates price increases. Simultaneously, Tiffany purchases call options to lock in the $1 million purchase price. (Tiffany would pay an option premium which would be recorded as an asset and amortized over time; to keep the example simple, we ignore this premium.) Delivery of the platinum takes place over the year and the market price of the platinum purchases is $1.686 million. During the year, Tiffany adjusts the option to fair value, the combined mark-to-market adjustments are $0.686 million. Those transactions are accounted for as follows:

Margin T-accounts:

```
Call Op   0.686M
    AOCI       0.686M
 ─── Call Option ───
 0.686M │
 ─────── AOCI ───────
          │ 0.686M

FE       1.686M
   Cash      1.686M
 ─── Platinum Exp ───
 1.686M │
 ─────── Cash ───────
          │ 1.686M

Cash     0.686M
  Call Op    0.686M
 ─────── Cash ───────
 0.686M │
 ─── Call Option ───
          │ 0.686M

AOCI     0.686M
   FE        0.686M
 ─────── AOCI ───────
 0.686M │
 ─── Platinum Exp ───
          │ 0.686M
```

Transaction	Balance Sheet					Income Statement		
	Cash Asset	+ Noncash Assets	= Liabil- ities	+ Contrib. Capital	+ Earned Capital	Rev- enues	− Expen- ses	= Net Income
1. Record unrealized fair-value gain on call option		+0.686 mil. Call Option =			+0.686 mil. AOCI		−	=
2a. Purchase and use platinum during the year	−1.686 mil. Cash	=			−1.686 mil. Retained Earnings		− +1.686 mil. COGS	= −1.686 mil.
2b. Exercise call option as Tiffany purchases platinum	+0.686 mil. Cash	−0.686 mil. Call Option =					−	=
2c. Recognize unrealized fair-value gain as Tiffany uses platinum		=			+0.686 mil. Retained Earnings −0.686 mil. AOCI		− −0.686 mil. COGS	= +0.686 mil.

In this transaction, Tiffany has hedged its platinum purchase via call options. As the price of platinum increases, so does the value of the call option. This unrealized gain on the option is reflected in AOCI until the platinum is consumed. At that time, the unrealized gain is removed from AOCI and expenses are reduced, thereby offsetting the increase in COGS resulting from the higher platinum cost. The net effect is that Tiffany reports $1 million for COGS. The net cash outlay for platinum is also $1 million as a result of the cash inflow related to the call option. The purpose of Tiffany's derivative program is to attempt to lock in the price of platinum. This is an operating activity and the gain on the derivative contract should be included in NOPAT to offset the increased cost of the platinum. Because Tiffany hedged the fuel purchases, there is no net effect on income.

In both of our illustrations, the derivative contract is perfectly correlated with the asset or cash flow to which it relates. In practice, this is unlikely. As a result, the change in the fair value of the derivatives might not exactly offset the change in the cost of the platinum. Only the effective portion of the hedge is deferred in AOCI. The ineffective portion of the hedge affects current income. Bottom line, some of the risk will impact net income if the company cannot perfectly hedge the risk or chooses not to manage 100% of the risk.

BUSINESS INSIGHT   Counter-Party Risk

The purpose of derivative financial instruments is to transfer risk from one company to another. For example, a company might be concerned about the possible decline in the $US value of a foreign-currency-denominated account receivable. In order to hedge that risk, the company might execute a forward contract to sell the foreign currency and receive $US. That forward contract only has value, however, if the party on the other side of the transaction (the counter-party) ultimately purchases the foreign currency for $US when the contract matures. If the counter-party fails to honor its part of the agreement, the forward contract is of no value. The risk that the other party might not live up to its part of the bargain is known as *counter-party risk*. The only justification for recognizing a gain in a forward contract to offset the loss in a foreign-currency-denominated receivable is the expectation that the counter-party has the intention and ability to purchase the foreign currency in exchange for $US when the contract matures. Counter-party risk is very real. Many companies require counter-parties to back up their agreement with cash collateral or other acceptable forms of guarantees (like a bank letter of credit, for example). As a result, there is a hidden risk in companies' use of derivatives that is difficult to quantify.

Analysis of Derivatives

Derivatives relate to a specific balance sheet account or forecasted transaction. The fair value of the derivatives and their ultimate gains (losses) should be classified with the account to which they relate. For example, in the Kellogg example, the fair value of the foreign exchange contract is grouped with the accounts receivable to which it relates, and the gain (loss) on that derivative is considered an operating item (part of NOPAT). The commodity derivative investments that Tiffany uses are treated similarly. In this case, both the balance sheet accounts and income statement effects are treated as operating.

Companies also frequently use a variety of derivative instruments to hedge exposure to interest rates. Companies can, for example, use swap contracts to convert floating-rate debt to fixed-rate debt and vice-versa. In this case, the fair values of the derivatives and their ultimate income statement effects are nonoperating because they relate to interest-bearing debt.

In addition to proper classification of balance sheet and income statement accounts for computation of NOPAT and NOA, we are interested in understanding the extent to which the company is hedged. That is, are there still risks over which the company has no control and that are not hedged? Unfortunately, footnote disclosures do not provide a completely satisfactory answer. We are not privy to the internal risk analysis that the company performs. As a result, we do not know, for example, the precise extent to which the hedges are ineffective, to what degree the company has decided to hedge, and whether the company is facing risks for which a derivative instrument is not available. To gain further insight into these questions, we must often look to other sources of information such as analyst reports, the financial press, and communications from the company.

GUIDANCE ANSWERS

MANAGERIAL DECISION   **You Are the Chief Financial Officer**

Capacity utilization is important. If long-term operating assets are used inefficiently, cost per unit produced is too high. Cost per unit does not relate solely to manufacturing products, but also applies to the cost of providing services and many other operating activities. However, if we purchase assets with little productive slack, our costs of production at peak levels can be excessive. Further, the company may be unable to service peak demand and risks losing customers. In response, the company might explore strategic alliances. These take many forms. Some require a simple contract to use another company's manufacturing, service, or administrative capability for a fee (note: these executory contracts are not recorded under GAAP). Another type of alliance is that of a joint venture to share ownership of manufacturing or IT facilities. In this case, if demand can be coordinated with that of a partner, perhaps operating assets can be more effectively used. Finally, a special purpose entity (SPE) can be formed to acquire the asset for use by the company and its partner—explained in Module 10.

Superscript ^A denotes assignments based on Appendix 7A.

DISCUSSION QUESTIONS

Q7-1. What measure (fair value or amortized cost) is on the balance sheet for (a) trading securities, (b) available-for-sale securities, and (c) held-to-maturity securities?

Q7-2. What is an unrealized holding gain (loss)? Explain.

Q7-3. Where are unrealized holding gains and losses related to trading securities reported in the financial statements? Where are unrealized holding gains and losses related to available-for-sale securities reported in the financial statements?

Q7-4. What does significant influence imply regarding intercorporate investments? Describe the accounting procedures used for such investments.

Q7-5. On January 1 of the current year, Yetman Company purchases 40% of the common stock of Livnat Company for $250,000 cash. This 40% ownership allows Yetman to exert significant influence over Livnat. During the year, Livnat reports $80,000 of net income and pays $60,000 in cash dividends. At year-end, what amount should appear in Yetman's balance sheet for its investment in Livnat?

Q7-6. What accounting method is used when a stock investment represents more than 50% of the investee company's voting stock and allows the investor company to "control" the investee company? Explain.

Q7-7. What is the underlying objective of consolidated financial statements?

Q7-8. Finn Company purchases all of the common stock of Murray Company for $750,000 when Murray Company has $300,000 of common stock and $450,000 of retained earnings. If a consolidated balance sheet is prepared immediately after the acquisition, what amounts are eliminated in consolidation? Explain.

Q7-9. Bradshaw Company owns 100% of Dee Company. At year-end, Dee owes Bradshaw $75,000 arising from a loan made during the year. If a consolidated balance sheet is prepared at year-end, how is the $75,000 handled? Explain.

Q7-10. What are some limitations of consolidated financial statements?

Assignments with the ⊘ in the margin are available in an online homework system. See the Preface of the book for details.

MINI EXERCISES

M7-11. Interpreting Disclosures of Available-for-Sale Securities (LO1)

Intel (INTC)

Use the following year-end footnote disclosure from Intel's 10-K report to answer parts *a* and *b*.

(Millions of Dollars)	2010
Cost of available-for-sale equity securities	$19,677
Gross unrealized gains.	648
Gross unrealized losses	(19)
Fair value of available-for-sale equity securities	$20,306

a. What amount does Intel report on its balance sheet as available-for-sale equity securities? Explain.
b. How does Intel report the net unrealized gain of $629 million ($648 million − $19 million) in its financial statements?

M7-12. Accounting for Available-for-Sale and Trading Securities (LO1)

Assume that Wasley Company purchases 6,000 common shares of Pincus Company for $12 cash per share. During the year, Wasley receives a cash dividend of $1.10 per common share from Pincus, and the year-end market price of Pincus common stock is $13 per share. How much income does Wasley report relating to this investment for the year if it accounts for the investment as:
a. Available-for-sale investment
b. Trading investment

M7-13. Interpreting Disclosures of Investment Securities (LO1)

Amgen (AMGN)

Amgen reports the following disclosure relating to its December 31 comprehensive income ($ millions). (*a*) How is Amgen accounting for its investment in marketable equity securities? How do you know? (*b*) Explain how its 2010 financial statements are impacted by Amgen's investment in marketable equity securities. (*c*) Explain the reclassification adjustments to income of $90 million.

	Foreign Currency Translation	Cash-Flow Hedges	Available-for-Sale Securities	Other	AOCI
Balance as of December 31, 2009	$40	$(82)	$ 95	$(8)	45
Other comprehensive income:					
Foreign currency translation adjustments . . .	(29)	—	—	—	(29)
Unrealized gains.	—	186	155	1	342
Reclassification adjustments to income.	—	(46)	(90)	—	(136)
Income taxes	11	(55)	(25)	—	(69)
Balance as of December 31, 2010	$22	$ 3	$135	$(7)	$153

M7-14. Analyzing and Interpreting Equity Method Investments (LO2)

Stober Company purchases an investment in Lang Company at a purchase price of $1 million cash, representing 30% of the book value of Lang. During the year, Lang reports net income of $100,000 and pays cash dividends of $40,000. At the end of the year, the market value of Stober's investment is $1.2 million.
a. What amount does Stober report on its balance sheet for its investment in Lang?
b. What amount of income from investments does Stober report? Explain.

c. Stober's $182,000 unrealized gain in the market value of the Lang investment (choose one and explain):
   (1) Is not reflected on either its income statement or balance sheet.
   (2) Is reported in its current income.
   (3) Is reported on its balance sheet only.
   (4) Is reported in its accumulated other comprehensive income.

M7-15. Computing Income for Equity Method Investments (LO2)
Kross Company purchases an equity investment in Penno Company at a purchase price of $5 million, representing 40% of the book value of Penno. During the current year, Penno reports net income of $600,000 and pays cash dividends of $200,000. At the end of the year, the fair value of Kross's investment is $5.3 million. What amount of income does Kross report relating to this investment in Penno for the year? Explain.

M7-16. Interpreting Disclosures on Investments in Affiliates (LO2)
Merck's 10-K report included the following footnote disclosure:

Merck & Co., Inc.
(MRK)

> Investments in affiliates accounted for using the equity method . . . totaled $494 million at December 31, 2010...These amounts are reported in *Other assets*.

a. At what amount are the equity method investments reported on Merck's balance sheet? Does this amount represent Merck's adjusted cost or fair value?
b. How does Merck account for the dividends received on these investments?
c. What sources of income does the company report for these investments?

M7-17. Computing Consolidating Adjustments and Noncontrolling Interest (LO3)
Philipich Company purchases 80% of Hirst Company's common stock for $600,000 cash when Hirst Company has $300,000 of common stock and $450,000 of retained earnings. If a consolidated balance sheet is prepared immediately after the acquisition, what amounts are eliminated when preparing that statement? What amount of noncontrolling interest appears in the consolidated balance sheet?

M7-18. Computing Consolidated Net Income (LO3)
Benartzi Company purchased a 90% interest in Liang Company on January 1 of the current year and the purchase price reflected 90% of Liang's book value of equity. Benartzi Company had $600,000 net income for the current year *before* recognizing its share of Liang Company's net income. If Liang Company had net income of $150,000 for the year, what is the consolidated net income for the year?

M7-19. Assigning Purchase Price in Acquisitions (LO3)
Weaver Company acquired 80% of Koonce Company at the beginning of the current year. Weaver paid $50,000 more than the book value of Koonce's shareholders' equity and determined that this excess purchase price related to intangible assets. How does the $50,000 appear on the consolidated Weaver Company balance sheet if the intangible assets acquired related to (*a*) patents, or alternatively (*b*) goodwill? How would the consolidated income statement be affected under each scenario?

EXERCISES

E7-20. Assessing Financial Statement Effects of Trading and Available-for-Sale Securities (LO1)
a. Use the financial statement effects template to record the following four transactions involving investments in marketable securities classified as trading.
   (1) Purchased 6,000 common shares of Liu, Inc., for $12 cash per share.
   (2) Received a cash dividend of $1.10 per common share from Liu.
   (3) Year-end market price of Liu common stock was $11.25 per share.
   (4) Sold all 6,000 common shares of Liu for $66,900.
b. Using the same transaction information as above, complete the financial statement effects template (with amounts and accounts) assuming the investments in marketable securities are classified as available-for-sale.

E7-21. Assessing Financial Statement Effects of Trading and Available-for-Sale Securities (LO1)
Use the financial statement effects template to record the accounts and amounts for the following four transactions involving investments in marketable securities:

(1) Ohlson Co. purchases 5,000 common shares of Freeman Co. at $16 cash per share.

(2) Ohlson Co. receives a cash dividend of $1.25 per common share from Freeman.

(3) Year-end market price of Freeman common stock is $17.50 per share.

(4) Ohlson Co. sells all 5,000 common shares of Freeman for $86,400 cash.

 a. Assume the investments are classified as trading.

 b. Assume the investments are classified as available-for-sale.

E7-22.   Interpreting Footnotes on Security Investments   (LO1)

Cisco Systems (CSCO)

Cisco Systems reports the following in its 10-K report.

(In millions)	Shares of Common Stock	Common Stock and Additional Paid-In Capital	Retained Earnings	Accumulated Other Comprehensive Income	Total Cisco Shareholders' Equity	Noncontrolling Interests	Total Equity
BALANCE AT JULY 25, 2009	5,785	$34,344	$3,868	$435	$38,647	$30	$38,677
Net income.	—	—	7,767	—	7,767	—	7,767
Change in:							
Unrealized gains and losses on investments.	—	—	—	195	195	(12)	183
Derivative instruments	—	—	—	48	48	—	48
Cumulative translation adjustment and other	—	—	—	(55)	(55)	—	(55)
Comprehensive income (loss)					7,955	(12)	7,943
Issuance of common stock	201	3,278	—	—	3,278	—	3,278
Repurchase of common stock.	(331)	(2,148)	(5,784)	—	(7,932)	—	(7,932)
Tax benefits from employee stock incentive plans, including transfer pricing adjustments	—	719	—	—	719	—	719
Purchase acquisitions	—	83	—	—	83	—	83
Share-based compensation expense . . .	—	1,517	—	—	1,517	—	1,517
BALANCE AT JULY 31, 2010	5,655	$37,793	$5,851	$623	$44,267	$18	$44,285

Summary of Available-for-Sale Investments

The following table summarizes the Company's available-for-sale investments (in millions):

July 31, 2010	Amortized Cost	Gross Unrealized Gains	Gross Unrealized Losses	Fair Value
Fixed income securities:				
U.S. government securities	$16,570	$ 42	$ —	$16,612
U.S. government agency securities	13,511	68	—	13,579
Non-U.S. government and agency securities. . .	1,452	15	—	1,467
Corporate debt securities.	2,179	64	(21)	2,222
Asset-backed securities	145	9	(5)	149
Total fixed income securities.	33,857	198	(26)	34,029
Publicly traded equity securities	889	411	(49)	1,251
Total.	$34,746	$609	$(75)	$35,280

 a. At what amount does Cisco report its investment portfolio on its balance sheet? Does that amount include any unrealized gains or losses? Explain.

 b. How is Cisco accounting for its investment portfolio—as an available-for-sale or trading portfolio? How do you know?

 c. What does the number $195 represent in the Accumulated Other Comprehensive Income column? Explain.

E7-23. **Interpreting Footnote Disclosures for Investments** (LO1)

CNA Financial Corporation provides the following footnote to its 2010 10-K report.

CNA Financial
Corporation (CNA)

> **Valuation of investments** CNA classifies its fixed maturity securities and its equity securities as either available-for-sale or trading, and as such, they are carried at fair value. Changes in fair value of trading securities are reported within net investment income on the Consolidated Statements of Operations. Changes in fair value related to available-for-sale securities are reported as a component of other comprehensive income. . . . Investment valuations are adjusted and losses may be recognized as Net realized investment losses on the Consolidated Statements of Operations when a decline in value is determined by the Company to be other-than-temporary.

The following table provides a summary of fixed maturity and equity securities.

Summary of Fixed Maturity and Equity Securities				
December 31, 2010 (In millions)	Cost or Amortized Cost	Gross Unrealized Gains	Gross Unrealized Losses	Estimated Fair Value
Fixed maturity securities available-for-sale				
U.S. Treasury and obligations of government agencies....	$ 122	$ 16	$ 1	$ 137
Asset-backed:				
Residential mortgage-backed......................	6,254	101	265	6,090
Commercial mortgage-backed.....................	994	40	41	993
Other asset-backed	753	18	8	763
Total asset-backed.............................	8,001	159	314	7,846
States, municipalities and political subdivisions	8,157	142	410	7,889
Foreign government	602	18	—	620
Corporate and other bonds	19,492	1,603	70	21,025
Redeemable preferred stock	47	7	—	54
Total fixed maturity securities available-for-sale	36,421	1,945	795	37,571
Total fixed maturity securities trading	6	—	—	6
Equity securities available-for-sale:				
Common stock...................................	90	25	—	115
Preferred stock.................................	332	2	9	325
Total equity securities available-for-sale	422	27	9	440
Total	$36,849	$1,972	$804	$38,017

    a. At what amount does CNA report its investment portfolio on its balance sheet? In your answer identify the portfolio's fair value, cost, and any unrealized gains and losses.

    b. How do CNA's balance sheet and income statement reflect any unrealized gains and/or losses on the investment portfolio?

    c. How do CNA's balance sheet and income statement reflect gains and losses realized from the sale of available-for-sale securities?

E7-24. **Assessing Financial Statement Effects of Equity Method Securities** (LO2)

Use the financial statement effects template (with amounts and accounts) to record the following transactions involving investments in marketable securities accounted for using the equity method:

    a. Purchased 12,000 common shares of Barth Co. at $9 per share; the shares represent 30% ownership in Barth.

    b. Received a cash dividend of $1.25 per common share from Barth.

    c. Barth reported annual net income of $80,000.

    d. Sold all 12,000 common shares of Barth for $120,500.

E7-25. **Assessing Financial Statement Effects of Equity Method Securities** (LO2)

Use the financial statement effects template (with amounts and accounts) to record the following transactions involving investments in marketable securities accounted for using the equity method:

    a. Healy Co. purchases 15,000 common shares of Palepu Co. at $8 per share; the shares represent 25% ownership of Palepu.

b. Healy receives a cash dividend of $0.80 per common share from Palepu.

c. Palepu reports annual net income of $120,000.

d. Healy sells all 15,000 common shares of Palepu for $140,000.

 E7-26. Assessing Financial Statement Effects of Passive and Equity Method Investments (LO1, 2)

On January 1, Ball Corporation purchased shares of Leftwich Company common stock.

a. Assume that the stock acquired by Ball represents 15% of Leftwich's voting stock and that Ball classifies the investment as available-for-sale. Use the financial statement effects template (with amounts and accounts) to record the following transactions:

1. Ball purchased 10,000 common shares of Leftwich at $15 cash per share.
2. Leftwich reported annual net income of $80,000.
3. Ball received a cash dividend of $1.10 per common share from Leftwich.
4. Year-end market price of Leftwich common stock is $19 per share.

b. Assume that the stock acquired by Ball represents 30% of Leftwich's voting stock and that Ball accounts for this investment using the equity method since it is able to exert significant influence. Use the financial statement effects template (with amounts and accounts) to record the following transactions:

1. Ball purchased 10,000 common shares of Leftwich at $15 cash per share.
2. Leftwich reported annual net income of $80,000.
3. Ball received a cash dividend of $1.10 per common share from Leftwich.
4. Year-end market price of Leftwich common stock is $19 per share.

E7-27. Interpreting Equity Method Investment Footnotes (LO2)

DuPont (DD)

DuPont's 2010 10-K report includes information relating to the company's equity method investments ($ millions). The following footnote reports summary balance sheets for affiliated companies for which DuPont uses the equity method of accounting. The information below is shown on a 100 percent basis followed by the carrying value of DuPont's investment in these affiliates.

Financial Position at December 31 (in millions)	2010	2009
Current assets	$1,972	$1,710
Noncurrent assets	1,397	1,416
Total assets	$3,369	$3,126
Short-term borrowings	$ 381	$ 375
Other current liabilities	841	768
Long-term borrowings	144	178
Other long-term liabilities	119	111
Total liabilities	$1,485	$1,432
DuPont's investment in affiliates (includes advances)	$1,041	$1,014

a. DuPont reports its investment in equity method affiliates on its balance sheet at $1,041 million. Does this reflect the adjusted cost or fair value of DuPont's interest in these companies?

b. What is the total stockholders' equity of the affiliates at the end of 2010? Approximately what percentage does DuPont own, on average, of these affiliates? Explain.

c. Should the balance of the equity investment be reduced to zero, say as a result of losses by the equity investee company, Dupont would cease accounting for the investment using the equity method. It would, instead, report the investments at a zero balance until the investee company would become solvent. Why might this cessation of accounting for this investment using the equity method impede our analysis and interpretation?

 E7-28. Analyzing and Interpreting Disclosures on Equity Method Investments (LO2)

Cummins, Inc. (CMI)

Cummins, Inc. (CMI) reports investments in affiliated companies, consisting mainly of investments in nine manufacturing joint ventures. Cummins reports those investments on its balance sheet at $734 million, and provides the following financial information of its investee companies in a footnote to its 10-K report:

Equity Investee Financial Summary

In millions	As of and for the years ended December 31,		
	2010	2009	2008
Net sales...	$7,107	$5,554	$6,610
Gross margin	1,651	1,365	1,509
Net income...	668	427	498
Cummins share of net income	$ 321	$ 196	$ 231
Royalty and interest income.........................	30	18	22
Total equity, royalty and interest income from investees ...	$ 351	$ 214	$ 253
Current assets	$2,741	$2,005	
Noncurrent assets	1,253	1,123	
Current liabilities..................................	(1,837)	(1,406)	
Noncurrent liabilities...............................	(499)	(390)	
Net assets	$1,658	$1,332	
Cummins share of net assets......................	$ 744	$ 587	

a. What assets and liabilities of unconsolidated affiliates are omitted from Cummins' balance sheet as a result of the equity method of accounting for those investments?

b. Do the liabilities of the unconsolidated affiliates affect Cummins directly? Explain.

c. How does the equity method impact Cummins' ROE and its RNOA components (net operating asset turnover and net operating profit margin)?

E7-29.   Reporting and Interpreting Stock Investment Performance   (LO1)

Kasznik Company began operations on June 15 of the current calendar year and, by year-end (December 31), had made six stock investments. Year-end information on these stock investments follows.

December 31	Cost or Equity Basis (as appropriate)	Year-End Fair Value	Market Classification
Barth, Inc.	$ 68,000	$ 65,300	Trading
Foster, Inc.	162,500	160,000	Trading
McNichols, Inc.	197,000	192,000	Available-for-sale
Patell Company	157,000	154,700	Available-for-sale
Ertimur, Inc.	100,000	102,400	Equity method
Soliman, Inc.	136,000	133,200	Equity method

a. What does Kasznik's balance sheet report for trading stock investments at December 31?

b. What does Kasznik's balance sheet report for available-for-sale investments at December 31?

c. What does Kasznik's balance sheet report for equity method investments at December 31?

d. What total amount of unrealized holding gains or unrealized holding losses related to investments appear in Kasznik's income statement?

e. What total amount of unrealized holding gains or unrealized holding losses related to investments appear in the stockholders' equity section of Kasznik's December 31 balance sheet?

f. What total amount of fair-value adjustment to investments appears in the December 31 balance sheet? Which category of investments does the fair-value adjustment relate to? Does the fair-value adjustment increase or decrease the carrying value of these investments?

E7-30.   Interpreting Equity Method Investment Footnotes   (LO2)

AT&T reports the following footnote to its 2005 10-K report ($ millions).   AT&T, Inc. (T)

Equity Method Investments We account for our nationwide wireless joint venture, Cingular, and our investments in equity affiliates under the equity method of accounting. The following table is a reconciliation of our investments in and advances to Cingular as presented on our Consolidated Balance Sheets.

continued

continued from prior page

($ millions)	2005	2004
Beginning of year	$33,687	$11,003
Contributions	—	21,688
Equity in net income.	200	30
Other adjustments	(2,483)	966
End of year	$31,404	$33,687

Undistributed earnings from Cingular were $2,711 and $2,511 at December 31, 2005 and 2004. "Other adjustments" in 2005 included the net activity of $2,442 under our revolving credit agreement with Cingular, consisting of a reduction of $1,747 (reflecting Cingular's repayment of their shareholder loan during 2005) and a decrease of $695 (reflecting Cingular's net repayment of their revolving credit balance during 2005). During 2004, we made an equity contribution to Cingular in connection with its acquisition of AT&T Wireless. "Other adjustments" in 2004 included the net activity of $972 under our revolving credit agreement with Cingular, consisting of a reduction of $30 (reflecting Cingular's repayment of advances during 2004) and an increase of $1,002 (reflecting the December 31, 2004 balance of advances to Cingular under this revolving credit agreement).

We account for our 60% economic interest in Cingular under the equity method of accounting in our consolidated financial statements since we share control equally (i.e., 50/50) with our 40% economic partner in the joint venture. We have equal voting rights and representation on the Board of Directors that controls Cingular. The following table presents summarized financial information for Cingular at December 31, or for the year then ended.

Cingular ($ millions)	2005	2004	2003
Income Statements			
Operating revenues . . .	$34,433	$19,565	$15,577
Operating income	1,824	1,528	2,254
Net income	333	201	977
Balance Sheets			
Current assets.	$ 6,049	$ 5,570	
Noncurrent assets.	73,270	76,668	
Current liabilities	10,008	7,983	
Noncurrent liabilities . . .	24,333	29,719	

We have made a subordinated loan to Cingular that totaled $4,108 and $5,855 at December 31, 2005 and 2004, which matures in June 2008. This loan bears interest at an annual rate of 6.0%. During 2005, Cingular repaid $1,747 to reduce the balance of this loan in accordance with the terms of a revolving credit agreement. We earned interest income on this loan of $311 during 2005, $354 in 2004 and $397 in 2003. This interest income does not have a material impact on our net income as it is mostly offset when we record our share of equity income in Cingular.

a. At what amount is the equity investment in Cingular reported on AT&T's balance sheet? (Hint: the table in the footnote reports AT&T's investment plus its "advances" of $4,108 to Cingular plus $311 of interest accrued on the advances.) Next, confirm (with computations) that this amount is equal to AT&T's proportionate share of Cingular's equity.

b. Did Cingular pay dividends in 2005? How do you know?

c. How much income did AT&T report in 2005 relating to this investment in Cingular?

d. Interpret the AT&T statement that "undistributed earnings from Cingular were $2,711 and $2,511 at December 31, 2005 and 2004."

e. How does use of the equity method impact AT&T's ROE and its RNOA components (net operating asset turnover and net operating profit margin)?

f. AT&T accounts for its investment in Cingular under the equity method, despite its 60% economic ownership position. Why?

g. In 2006, AT&T acquired Bell South, its joint venture partner in Cingular. What impact did this merger have on the way AT&T accounts for its investment in Cingular?

E7-31. **Interpreting Equity Method Investment Footnotes** (LO2)

On December 29, 2006, AT&T acquired Bell South. Prior to the acquisition, AT&T and Bell South jointly owned AT&T Mobility (formerly known as Cingular Wireless) and each accounted for its investment in AT&T Mobility under the equity method (see exercise E7-30). AT&T purchased Bell South for $66,834 million and reports the following allocation of the purchase price in its 2007 10-K:

AT&T (T)
Bell South

Bell South Purchase Price Allocation ($ millions)	As of 12/31/06	Adjustments	As of 12/29/07
Assets acquired			
Current assets.	$ 4,875	$ 6	$ 4,881
Property, plant and equipment	18,498	225	18,723
Intangible assets not subject to amortization			
Trademark/name	330	—	330
Licenses	214	100	314
Intangible assets subject to amortization			
Customer lists and relationships.	9,230	(25)	9,205
Patents	100	—	100
Trademark/name	211	—	211
Investments in AT&T Mobility	32,759	2,039	34,798
Other investments.	2,446	(3)	2,443
Other assets	11,211	(168)	11,043
Goodwill	26,467	(1,554)	24,913
Total assets acquired	106,341	620	106,961
Liabilities assumed			
Current liabilities, excluding current portion of long-term debt	5,288	(427)	4,861
Long-term debt.	15,628	(4)	15,624
Deferred income taxes	10,318	(89)	10,229
Postemployment benefit obligation	7,086	163	7,249
Other noncurrent liabilities	1,223	941	2,164
Total liabilities assumed.	39,543	584	40,127
Net assets acquired	$ 66,798	$ 36	$ 66,834

a. Describe how AT&T accounts for its investment in AT&T Mobility (formerly Cingular Wireless) following its acquisition of Bell South.

b. AT&T had the following disclosure in its 2007 10-K regarding the reporting of its investment in AT&T Mobility: "We recorded the consolidation of AT&T Mobility as a step acquisition, retaining 60% of AT&T Mobility's prior book value and adjusting the remaining 40% to fair value." Why is AT&T only adjusting 40% of its investment in AT&T Mobility to fair value?

c. AT&T adjusted the purchase price allocation for Bell South subsequent to the acquisition. Most of the allocation relates to an increased value placed on Bell South's equity investment in AT&T Mobility due to "increased value of licenses and customer lists and relationships acquired." Why did the increase in the allocation of the purchase price to Bell South's investment in AT&T Mobility decrease the allocation to goodwill? How will this increase in allocation to the equity investment impact AT&T's income statement?

d. More than half of the purchase price is allocated to intangible assets and goodwill. How is the fair value of customer lists and relationships estimated? How is the fair value of goodwill estimated? Why does it matter whether the allocation of the purchase price for intangible assets relates to "customer lists and relationships" or to goodwill?

E7-32. **Constructing the Consolidated Balance Sheet at Acquisition** (LO3)

On January 1 of the current year, Healy Company purchased all of the common shares of Miller Company for $500,000 cash. Balance sheets of the two firms immediately after the acquisition follow:

	Healy Company	Miller Company	Consolidating Adjustments	Consolidated
Current assets	$1,700,000	$120,000		
Investment in Miller	500,000	—		
Plant assets, net.	3,000,000	410,000		
Goodwill	—	—		
Total assets.	$5,200,000	$530,000		
Liabilities.	$ 700,000	$ 90,000		
Contributed capital.	3,500,000	400,000		
Retained earnings	1,000,000	40,000		
Total liabilities and equity	$5,200,000	$530,000		

During purchase negotiations, Miller's plant assets were appraised at $425,000 and all of its remaining assets and liabilities were appraised at values approximating their book values. Healy also concluded that an additional $45,000 (for goodwill) demanded by Miller's shareholders was warranted because Miller's earning power was better than the industry average. Prepare the consolidating adjustments and the consolidated balance sheet at acquisition.

E7-33. **Constructing the Consolidated Balance Sheet at Acquisition**   (LO3)

Rayburn Company purchased all of Kanodia Company's common stock for $600,000 cash on January 1, at which time the separate balance sheets of the two corporations appeared as follows:

	Rayburn Company	Kanodia Company	Consolidating Adjustments	Consolidated
Investment in Kanodia	$ 600,000	—		
Other assets	2,300,000	$700,000		
Goodwill	—	—		
Total assets.	$2,900,000	$700,000		
Liabilities.	$ 900,000	$160,000		
Contributed capital.	1,400,000	300,000		
Retained earnings	600,000	240,000		
Total liabilities and equity	$2,900,000	$700,000		

During purchase negotiations, Rayburn determined that the appraised value of Kanodia's Other Assets was $720,000; and, all of its remaining assets and liabilities were appraised at values approximating their book values. The remaining $40,000 of the purchase price was ascribed to goodwill. Prepare the consolidating adjustments and the consolidated balance sheet at acquisition.

E7-34. **Assessing Financial Statement Effects from a Subsidiary Stock Issuance**   (LO3)

Ryan Company owns 80% of Lev Company. Information reported by Ryan Company and Lev Company as of the current year end follows:

Ryan Company

Shares owned of Lev	40,000
Book value of investment in Lev.	$320,000

Lev Company

Shares outstanding.	50,000
Book value of equity	$400,000
Book value per share	$8

Assume Lev Company issues 30,000 additional shares of previously authorized but unissued common stock solely to outside investors (none to Ryan Company) for $12 cash per share. Indicate the financial statement effects of this stock issuance on Ryan Company using the financial statement effects template.

Ryan Company's Financial Statements

	Balance Sheet							Income Statement		
Transaction	Cash Asset	+	Noncash Assets	=	Liabil- ities	+	Contrib. Capital	+ Earned Capital	Rev- enues	− Expen- ses	= Net Income
Lev Co. issues 30,000 shares				=						−	=

E7-35. Estimating Goodwill Impairment (LO3)

On January 1 of the current year, Engel Company purchases 100% of Ball Company for $16.8 million. At the time of acquisition, the fair value of Ball's tangible net assets (excluding goodwill) is $16.2 million. Engel ascribes the excess of $600,000 to goodwill. Assume that the fair value of Ball declines to $12.5 million and that the fair value of Ball's tangible net assets is estimated at $12.3 million as of December 31.

  a. Determine if the goodwill has become impaired and, if so, the amount of the impairment.

  b. What impact does the impairment of goodwill have on Engel's financial statements?

E7-36. Allocating Purchase Price (LO3)

Adobe Systems, Inc., reports the following footnote to its 10-K report.

Adobe Systems (ADBE)

During fiscal 2006, we completed the acquisition of Macromedia, a provider of software technologies that enables the development of a wide range of Internet and mobile application solutions... The total $3.5 billion purchase price is allocated to the acquired net assets of Macromedia based on their estimated fair values as of December 3, 2005 and the associated estimated useful lives at that date:

(in 000s)	Amount	Estimated Useful Life
Net tangible assets	$ 713,164	N/A
Identifiable intangible assets		
Acquired product rights	365,500	4 years
Customer contracts and relationships	183,800	6 years
Non-competition agreements	500	2 years
Trademarks	130,700	5 years
Goodwill	1,993,898	N/A
Stock-based compensation	150,951	2.18 years
Total purchase price	$3,538,513	

  a. Of the total assets acquired, what portion is allocated to net tangible assets?

  b. Are the assets (both tangible and intangible) of Macromedia reported on the consolidated balance sheet at the book value or at the fair value on the date of the acquisition? Explain.

  c. How are the tangible and intangible assets accounted for subsequent to the acquisition?

  d. Describe the accounting for goodwill. Why is an impairment test difficult to apply?

E7-37. Constructing the Consolidated Balance Sheet at Acquisition (LO3)

Easton Company acquires 100 percent of the outstanding voting shares of Harris Company. To obtain these shares, Easton pays $210,000 in cash and issues 5,000 of its $10 par value common stock. On this date, Easton's stock has a fair value of $36 per share, and Harris's book value of stockholders' equity is $280,000. Easton is willing to pay $390,000 for a company with a book value for equity of $280,000 because it believes that (1) Harris's buildings are undervalued by $40,000, and (2) Harris has an unrecorded patent that Easton values at $30,000. Easton considers the remaining balance sheet items to be fairly valued (no book-to-market difference). The remaining $40,000 of the purchase price is ascribed to corporate synergies and other general unidentifiable intangible assets (goodwill). The balance sheets at the acquisition date follow:

	Easton Company	Harris Company	Consolidating Adjustments	Consolidated
Cash	$ 84,000	$ 40,000		
Receivables	160,000	90,000		
Inventory.	220,000	130,000		
Investment in Harris	390,000	—		
Land	100,000	60,000		
Buildings, net	400,000	110,000		
Equipment, net	120,000	50,000		
Total assets.	$1,474,000	$480,000		
Accounts payable.	$ 160,000	$ 30,000		
Long-term liabilities	380,000	170,000		
Common stock.	500,000	40,000		
Additional paid-in capital	74,000	—		
Retained earnings	360,000	240,000		
Total liabilities & equity	$1,474,000	$480,000		

a. Show the breakdown of the investment into the book value acquired, the excess of fair value over book value, and the portion of the investment representing goodwill.

b. Prepare the consolidating adjustments and the consolidated balance sheet on the date of acquisition.

c. How will the excess of the purchase price over book value acquired be treated in years subsequent to the acquisition?

E7-38.[A] **Reporting and Analyzing Derivatives** (LO1)

Johnson & Johnson (JNJ)

Johnson & Johnson reports the following schedule of other comprehensive income in its 2011 10-K report ($ millions):

(Dollars in Millions)	Foreign Currency Translation	Gains/ (Losses) on Securities	Employee Benefit Plans	Gains/ (Losses) on Derivatives & Hedges	Total Accumulated Other Comprehensive Income/(Loss)
January 3, 2010	$(508)	$(30)	$(2,665)	$145	$(3,058)
2010 changes.					
Unrealized gain (loss)	—	99	—	(333)	
Net amount reclassed to net earnings . . .	—	(45)	—	288	
Net 2010 changes	(461)	54	(21)	(45)	(473)
January 2, 2011	$(969)	$24	$(2,686)	$100	$(3,531)

a. Describe how firms like Johnson & Johnson typically use derivatives.

b. How does Johnson & Johnson report its derivatives designated as cash-flow hedges on its balance sheet?

c. By what amount have the unrealized losses of $(333) million on the cash-flow hedges affected current income? What are the analysis implications?

d. What does the $288 million classified as "Net amount reclassed to net earnings" relate to? How has this affected Johnson & Johnson's profit?

PROBLEMS

P7-39. **Analyzing and Interpreting Available-for-Sale Securities Disclosures** (LO1)

MetLife, Inc. (MET)

Following is a portion of the investments footnote from MetLife's 2010 10-K report. Investment earnings are a crucial component of the financial performance of insurance companies such as MetLife, and investments comprise a large part of MetLife's assets. MetLife accounts for its fixed maturity (debt security or bond) investments as available-for-sale securities.

December 31, 2010 (In millions)	Cost or Amortized Cost	Gross Unrealized			Estimated Fair Value
		Gain	Temporary Loss	OTTI* Loss	
Fixed Maturity Securities:					
U.S. corporate securities	$ 89,713	$ 4,486	$1,631	$ —	$ 92,568
Foreign corporate securities.	65,784	3,333	939	—	68,178
RMBS.	44,468	1,652	917	470	44,733
Foreign government securities.	42,154	1,856	610	—	43,400
U.S. Treasury, agency and government guaranteed securities	32,469	1,394	559	—	33,304
CMBS.	20,213	740	266	12	20,675
ABS	14,725	274	590	119	14,290
State and political subdivision securities	10,476	171	518	—	10,129
Other fixed maturity securities	6	1	—	—	7
Total fixed maturity securities	$320,008	$13,907	$6,030	$601	$327,284
Equity Securities:					
Common stock.	$ 2,060	$ 146	$ 12	$ —	$ 2,194
Non-redeemable preferred stock	1,565	76	229	—	1,412
Total equity securities	$ 3,625	$ 222	$ 241	$ —	$ 3,606

*OTTI refers to "Other-Than-Temporary Impairment" that MetLife does not expect to reverse.

December 31, 2009 (In millions)	Cost or Amortized Cost	Gross Unrealized			Estimated Fair Value
		Gain	Temporary Loss	OTTI* Loss	
Fixed Maturity Securities:					
U.S. corporate securities	$ 72,075	$2,821	$2,699	$ 10	$ 72,187
Foreign corporate securities.	37,254	2,011	1,226	9	38,030
RMBS.	45,343	1,234	1,957	600	44,020
Foreign government securities	11,010	1,076	139	—	11,947
U.S. Treasury, agency and government guaranteed securities	25,712	745	1,010	—	25,447
CMBS.	16,555	191	1,106	18	15,622
ABS	14,272	189	1,077	222	13,162
State and political subdivision securities	7,468	151	411	—	7,208
Other fixed maturity securities	20	1	2	—	19
Total fixed maturity securities	$229,709	$8,419	$9,627	$859	$227,642
Equity Securities:					
Common stock.	$ 1,537	$ 92	$ 8	$ —	$ 1,621
Non-redeemable preferred stock	1,650	80	267	—	1,463
Total equity securities	$ 3,187	$ 172	$ 275	$ —	$ 3,084

*OTTI refers to "Other-Than-Temporary Impairment" that MetLife does not expect to reverse.

Required

a. At what amount does MetLife report its fixed maturity securities on its balance sheets for 2010 and 2009?

b. What is the difference between realized and unrealized gains and losses?

c. What are the net unrealized gains (losses) for 2010 and 2009 on its fixed maturity securities? How did these unrealized gains (losses) affect the company's reported income in 2010 and 2009? (*Hint*: see the Google footnote excerpt on page 7-7 for an explanation of how OTTI losses affect income.)

P7-40. **Analyzing and Interpreting Disclosures on Equity Method Investments** (LO2)

General Mills invests in a number of joint ventures to manufacture and distribute its food products as discussed in the following footnote to its fiscal year 2010 10-K report:

General Mills (GIS)

> **INVESTMENTS IN JOINT VENTURES**   Our investments in companies over which we have the ability to exercise significant influence are stated at cost plus our share of undistributed

continued

continued from prior page

earnings or losses . . . We make advances to our joint ventures in the form of loans or capital investments. We also sell certain raw materials, semi-finished goods, and finished goods to the joint ventures, generally at market prices.

We have a 50 percent equity interest in Cereal Partners Worldwide (CPW), which manufactures and markets ready-to-eat cereal products in more than 130 countries and republics outside the United States and Canada . . . We also have a 50 percent equity interest in Häagen-Dazs Japan, Inc. (HDJ).

Joint venture balance sheet activity follows:

In Millions	May 30, 2010	May 31, 2009
Cumulative investments.	$398.1	$283.3
Goodwill and other intangibles.	512.6	593.9
Aggregate advances.	238.2	114.8

Joint venture earnings and cash flow activity follows:

	Fiscal Year		
In Millions	2010	2009	2008
Sales to joint ventures	$ 10.7	$14.2	$ 12.8
Net advances (repayments)	128.1	(8.2)	(75.2)
Dividends received.	88.0	68.5	108.7

Summary combined financial information for the joint ventures on a 100 percent basis follows:

	Fiscal Year		
In Millions	2010	2009	2008
Net sales.	$2,360.0	$2,280.0	$2,207.7
Gross margin	1,053.2	873.5	906.6
Earnings before income taxes	251.2	234.7	231.7
Earnings after income taxes.	202.3	175.3	190.4

In Millions	May 30, 2010	May 31, 2009
Current assets	$ 731.7	$ 835.4
Noncurrent assets	907.3	895.0
Current liabilities.	1,322.0	1,394.6
Noncurrent liabilities.	112.1	66.9

Required

a. How does General Mills account for its investments in joint ventures? How are these investments reflected on General Mills' balance sheet, and how, generally, is income recognized on these investments?

b. General Mills reports total equity method investments on its May 30, 2010, balance sheet at $159.9 million net of advances ($398.1 million − $238.2 million). Approximately what percent of these joint ventures does General Mills own, on average?

c. Does the $159.9 million investment reported on General Mills' balance sheet sufficiently reflect the assets and liabilities required to conduct these operations? Explain.

d. Do you believe that the liabilities of these joint venture entities represent actual obligations of General Mills? Explain.

e. What potential problem(s) does equity method accounting present for analysis purposes?

P7-41.   Analyzing and Interpreting Disclosures on Consolidations   (LO3)

Snap-on Incorporated consists of two business units: the manufacturing company (parent corporation) and a wholly-owned finance subsidiary. These two units are consolidated in Snap-on's 10-K report. Following is a supplemental disclosure that Snap-on includes in its 10-K report that shows the separate balance sheets of the parent and the subsidiary. This supplemental disclosure is not mandated under GAAP, but is voluntarily reported by Snap-on as useful information for investors and creditors. Using this disclosure, answer the following requirements:

Required

a. Do the parent and subsidiary companies each maintain their own financial statements? Explain. Why does GAAP require consolidation instead of separate financial statements of individual companies?

b. What is the balance of Investments in Financial Services as of December 31, 2010, on the parent's balance sheet? What is the equity balance of the financial services subsidiary to which this relates as of December 31, 2010? Do you see a relation? Will this relation always exist?

c. Refer to your answer for part a. How does the equity method of accounting for the investment in the subsidiary obscure the actual financial condition of the parent company that is revealed in the consolidated financial statements?

d. Recall that the parent company uses the equity method of accounting for its investment in the subsidiary, and that this account is eliminated in the consolidation process. What is the relation between consolidated net income and the net income of the parent company? Explain.

e. What is the implication for the consolidated balance sheet if the fair value of the Financial Services subsidiary (subsequent to acquisition) is greater than the book value of its stockholders' equity?

(Amounts in millions)	Operations* 2010	2009	Financial Services 2010	2009
ASSETS				
Current assets				
Cash and cash equivalents	$ 462.6	$ 577.1	$109.6	$122.3
Intersegment receivables	6.7	4.8	—	0.1
Trade and other accounts receivable—net	434.5	411.5	8.8	2.9
Finance receivables—net	—	—	215.3	122.3
Contract receivables—net	7.9	7.4	37.7	25.5
Inventories—net	329.4	274.7	—	—
Deferred income tax assets	82.4	69.3	4.6	0.2
Prepaid expenses and other assets	74.1	60.1	0.7	2.8
Total current assets	1,397.6	1,404.9	376.7	276.1
Property and equipment—net	343.0	346.4	1.0	1.4
Investment in Financial Services	134.4	205.6	—	—
Deferred income tax assets	75.7	73.6	15.8	14.6
Long-term finance receivables—net	—	—	345.7	177.9
Long-term contract receivables—net	8.4	10.9	110.9	59.8
Goodwill	798.4	814.3	—	—
Other intangibles—net	192.8	206.2	—	—
Other assets	72.8	65.2	0.5	1.0
Total assets	$3,023.1	$3,127.1	$850.6	$530.8
LIABILITIES AND SHAREHOLDERS' EQUITY				
Current liabilities				
Notes payable and current maturities of long-term debt	$ 216.0	$ 164.7	$ —	$ —
Accounts payable	129.6	119.3	16.5	0.5
Intersegment payables	—	4.2	6.7	0.7
Accrued benefits	45.0	48.4	—	0.3
Accrued compensation	83.4	61.6	3.3	3.2
Franchisee deposits	40.4	40.5	—	—
Other accrued liabilities	218.1	215.7	132.0	85.7
Total current liabilities	732.5	654.4	158.5	90.4
Long-term debt and intersegment long-term debt	418.8	674.8	536.0	227.3
Deferred income tax liabilities	94.3	97.8	0.1	—
Retiree health care benefits	59.6	60.7	—	—
Pension liabilities	246.1	255.9	—	—
Other long-term liabilities	67.4	77.9	21.6	7.5
Total liabilities	1,618.7	1,821.5	716.2	325.2
Total shareholders' equity attributable to Snap-on Inc.	1,388.5	1,290.0	134.4	205.6
Noncontrolling interests	15.9	15.6	—	—
Total shareholders' equity	1,404.4	1,305.6	134.4	205.6
Total liabilities and shareholders' equity	$3,023.1	$3,127.1	$850.6	$530.8

*Snap-on Incorporated with Financial Services on the equity method.

P7-42   Analyzing Reports and Disclosures on Noncontrolling Interests (LO3)

The following four items are reproduced from Verizon Communications' 2010 10-K: its income statement, its balance sheet's stockholders' equity section, its noncontrolling interest section from the statement of changes in stockholders' equity, and its footnotes relating to noncontrolling interests.

Years Ended December 31 (dollars in millions)	2010	2009	2008
Operating revenues	$106,565	$107,808	$97,354
Operating expenses			
Cost of services and sales			
(exclusive of items shown below)	44,149	44,579	38,615
Selling, general and administrative expense	31,366	30,717	41,517
Depreciation and amortization expense	16,405	16,534	14,610
Total operating expenses	91,920	91,830	94,742
Operating income	14,645	15,978	2,612
Equity in earnings of unconsolidated businesses	508	553	567
Other income and (expense), net	54	91	283
Interest expense	(2,523)	(3,102)	(1,819)
Income before (provision) benefit for income taxes	12,684	13,520	1,643
(Provision) benefit for income taxes	(2,467)	(1,919)	2,319
Net Income	$ 10,217	$ 11,601	$ 3,962
Net income attributable to noncontrolling interest	$ 7,668	$ 6,707	$ 6,155
Net income (loss) attributable to Verizon	2,549	4,894	(2,193)
Net Income	$ 10,217	$ 11,601	$ 3,962

At December 31 (dollars in millions, except per share amounts)	2010	2009
Equity		
Series preferred stock ($.10 par value; none issued)	$ —	$ —
Common stock ($.10 par value; 2,967,610,119 shares issued in both periods)	297	297
Contributed capital	37,922	40,108
Reinvested earnings	4,368	7,260
Accumulated other comprehensive income (loss)	1,049	(1,372)
Common stock in treasury, at cost	(5,267)	(5,000)
Deferred compensation—employee stock ownership plans and other	200	89
Noncontrolling interest	48,343	42,761
Total equity	$86,912	$84,143

Years Ended December 31 (dollars in millions)	2010	2009	2008
Noncontrolling Interest			
Balance at beginning of year	$42,761	$37,199	$32,266
Net income attributable to noncontrolling interest	7,668	6,707	6,155
Other comprehensive income (loss)	(35)	103	(30)
Total comprehensive income	7,633	6,810	6,125
Distributions and other	(2,051)	(1,248)	(1,192)
Balance at end of year	$48,343	$42,761	$37,199

Consolidation   The method of accounting applied to investments, whether consolidated, equity or cost, involves an evaluation of all significant terms of the investments that explicitly grant or suggest evidence of control or influence over the operations of the investee. The consolidated financial statements include our controlled subsidiaries. For controlled subsidiaries that are not wholly owned, the noncontrolling interest is included in Net income and Total equity.

Noncontrolling Interest Noncontrolling interests in equity of subsidiaries were as follows:

At December 31, (dollars in millions)	2010	2009
Noncontrolling interests in consolidated subsidiaries:		
Verizon Wireless.	$47,557	$41,950
Wireless partnerships.	786	811
	$48,343	$42,761

Wireless Joint Venture Our Domestic Wireless segment, Cellco Partnership doing business as Verizon Wireless (Verizon Wireless) is a joint venture formed in April 2000 by the combination of the U.S. wireless operations and interests of Verizon and Vodafone. Verizon owns a controlling 55% interest in Verizon Wireless and Vodafone owns the remaining 45%.

Required

a. What are noncontrolling interests and how are they accounted for?

b. The noncontrolling interests relate primarily to a joint venture between Verizon and Vodafone described in the footnote. Why does Verizon consolidate this joint venture rather than to account for its investment using the equity method? What are the financial reporting implications for the decision to consolidate the joint venture?

c. What does the significant amount of net income allocated to the noncontrolling interests imply about the profitability of the wireless subsidiary relative to other subsidiaries in the consolidated entity?

d. What does the "Distributions and other" line with an amount of $(2,051) million in the noncontrolling interest portion of the statement of changes in stockholders' equity relate to?

e. How should we treat noncontrolling interests in our return on equity (ROE) computation? Compute ROE for both the Verizon shareholders and for the noncontrolling interests.

IFRS APPLICATIONS

Groupe Auchan SA

I7-43. **Interpreting Equity Method Investment Footnotes** (LO2)

Groupe Auchan is a French retail corporation headquartered in Croix, France. The company included the following table in notes to its annual report.

Investment in Associates (in € millions)	2009	2008
At January 1.	€132	€152
Results for the period (share of profit and impairment)	(55)	(10)
Dividends received.	(1)	(7)
Equity interests acquired	10	25
Disposals and other	(5)	(28)
At December 31	€ 81	€132

Required

a. Groupe Auchan holds between 20% and 50% ownership of all its investments in associates. Groupe Auchan uses the equity method to account for these investments. Why?

b. What amount does Groupe Auchan report on its balance sheet for investments in associates at December 31, 2009? Is this a fair value or not?

c. For the fiscal period ended December 31, 2009, were Groupe Auchan's associates profitable, in the aggregate?

d. How do changes in the market value of the associates' stock affect the "Investment in associates" balance sheet account for Groupe Auchan?

e. How does use of the equity method impact Groupe Auchan's ROE and its RNOA components (net operating asset turnover and net operating profit margin) as compared with the assets and liabilities and the sales and expenses that would be recorded with consolidation?

I7-44. **Interpreting Equity Method Investment Footnotes** (LO2)

Ahold

Ahold, a food retailer headquartered in the Netherlands, reported in notes to its annual report that it owns 60% of the outstanding common shares in a joint venture, with ICA, a food retailer operating in Sweden, Norway and the Baltic states. Selected notes to Ahold's annual report (prepared under IFRS) follow:

> The 60% shareholding does not entitle Ahold to unilateral decision-making authority over ICA due to the shareholders' agreement with the joint venture partner, which provides that strategic, financial and operational decisions will be made only on the basis of mutual consent. On the basis of this shareholders' agreement, the Company concluded that it has no control over ICA and, consequently, does not consolidate ICA's financial statements.

Required

a. What is a joint venture?

b. Given that Ahold owns more than 50% of this joint venture, why does the company not consolidate this investment? Does this differ from U.S. GAAP?

c. What method does Ahold use to report the ICA joint venture? Explain how this method works.

I7-45. **Allocating Purchase Price Including Intangibles** (LO3)

Deutsche Telekom AG

Deutsche Telekom AG, headquartered in Bonn, Germany, is the largest telecommunications company in Europe. The company uses IFRS to prepare its financial statements. Assume that during 2011, Deutsche Telekom acquired a controlling interest in Hellenic Telecommunications Organization, S.A. (Hellenic). The table below shows the pre- and post-acquisition values of Hellenic's assets and liabilities.

(millions of €)	Fair value at acquisition date	Carrying amounts immediately prior to acquisition
Cash and cash equivalents	€ 1,558	€ 1,558
Non-current assets held for sale	195	158
Other assets	1,716	1,716
Current assets	3,469	3,432
Intangible assets	5,348	4,734
Goodwill	2,500	3,835
Property, plant, and equipment	6,965	5,581
Other assets	823	782
Non-current assets	15,636	14,932
Assets	€19,105	€18,364

Required

a. At the acquisition, which measurement does the company use, fair value or carrying value, to record the acquired tangible and intangible assets on its consolidated balance sheet?

b. At the acquisition date, why is fair value of goodwill less than its carrying value?

c. What are some possible reasons why intangible assets increased in value at the acquisition date?

d. Describe accounting for goodwill. Why is an impairment test difficult to apply?

e. What would Deutsche Telekom record if it determined at the end of fiscal 2011 that the goodwill purchased in the Hellenic acquisition had a reliably measured fair value of €2,000? Later, if in 2012 the company determined that the fair value of the Hellenic goodwill was €3,000, how would its balance sheet and income statement be affected?

I7-46. **Analyzing and Interpreting Available-for-Sale Securities Disclosures** (LO1)

Energias de Portugal

Energias de Portugal ranks among Europe's major electricity operators, as well as being one of Portugal's largest business groups. The company is headquartered in Lisbon, Portugal. At December 31, 2009, Energias de Portugal had an available-for-sale portfolio with original cost of €251,224 (in 000s). Its 2009 annual report disclosed the following for available-for-sale investments.

(€ in 000s)	Fair value 1 Jan 2009	Acquisitions	Disposals	Impairment	Increase in fair value	Fair value 31 Dec 2009
Ampla Energia e Servicos, S.A.	€ 68,939	€ —	€ —	€ —	€ 94,705	€163,644
Ampla Investimentos e Servicos, S.A.	9,073	—	—	—	5,965	15,038
Banco Comercial Portugues, S.A.	122,707	—	(17,351)	(29,274)	28,036	104,118
Denerge	—	15,193	—	—	370	15,563
EDA - Electricidade dos Acores, S.A.	6,006	—	—	—	2,207	8,213
REN - Rede Electrica Nacional, S.A.	52,332	—	—	—	3,551	55,883
Sociedade Eolica de Andalucia, S.A.	10,854	209	—	—	703	11,766
Sonaecom, S.A.	28,946	—	(28,946)	—	—	—
Tagusparque, S.A.	1,097	—	—	—	965	2,062
Tejo Energia, S.A.	18,200	—	—	—	7,436	25,636
Other	32,733	14,853	(7,368)	(15)	991	41,194
	€350,887	€30,255	€(53,665)	€(29,289)	€144,929	€443,117

Required

a. What were total unrealized gains or losses in the available-for-sale portfolio at year end 2009?

b. What is the historical cost of Energias de Portugal's investment in Denerge? Is there an unrealized gain or loss on this investment at year end 2009?

c. How would pretax income be affected if Energias de Portugal had instead classified all of its available-for-sale investments as trading?

I7-47. Interpreting Footnote Disclosures for Acquisitions (LO1)

Headquartered in Rome, Italy, Finmeccanica S.p.A. is a multinational conglomerate operating in the defense and aerospace sectors. The company uses IFRS for its financial reports and disclosed the following in its 2009 annual report.

Finmeccanica S.p.A.

Intangible assets acquired in the course of corporate combination operations decreased mainly as a result of amortisation and include the following items:

(€ million)	31 December 2009	31 December 2008
Know-how	€ 85	€ 88
Trademarks	45	45
Licenses	14	16
Backlog and commercial positioning*	831	875
Total	€975	€1,024

* This represents a customer-based intangible asset

Required

a. How do Trademarks and Licenses create an intangible asset for Finnmeccanica? How do customer-based intangible assets provide value to the company?

b. Explain how the company would select an amortization policy for these intangible assets.

c. What does the carrying value of these intangible assets represent?

d. Apart from routine amortization, does the company ever adjust the assets' carrying values? (*Hint*: Consider why the company might reduce or increase the carrying value of an intangible under IFRS.)

MANAGEMENT APPLICATIONS

MA7-48. Determining the Reporting of an Investment (LO1, 2, 3)

Assume that your company acquires 20% of the outstanding common stock of APEX Software as an investment. You also have an option to purchase the remaining 80%. APEX is developing software (its only activity) that it hopes to eventually package and sell to customers. You do not intend to exercise your option unless its software product reaches commercial feasibility. APEX has employed your software engineers to assist in the development efforts and you are integrally involved in its software design. Your ownership interest is significant enough to give you influence over APEX's software design specifications.

Required

a. Describe the financial statement effects of the three possible methods to accounting for this investment (fair-value, equity, or consolidation).

b. What method of accounting is appropriate for this investment (fair-value, equity, or consolidation)? Explain.

MA7-49.   Ethics and Governance: Establishing Corporate Governance   (LO2, 3)

Effective corporate governance policies are a crucial component of contemporary corporate management.

Required

What provisions do you believe should be incorporated into such a policy? How do such policies impact financial accounting?

SOLUTIONS TO REVIEW PROBLEMS

Mid-Module Review 1

a.

		Balance Sheet						Income Statement		
Transaction	Cash Asset	+ Noncash Assets	= Liabil-ities	+ Contrib. Capital	+ Earned Capital		Rev-enues	− Expen-ses	= Net Income
1. Purchased 1,000 shares of Yahoo! common stock for $15 cash per share	−15,000 Cash	+15,000 Marketable Securities	=					−	=
2. Received cash dividend of $2.50 per share on Yahoo! common stock	+2,500 Cash		=		+2,500 Retained Earnings		+2,500 Dividend Income	−	= +2,500
3. Year-end market price of Yahoo! common stock is $17 per share		+2,000 Marketable Securities	=		+2,000 AOCI			−	=
4. Sold 1,000 shares of Yahoo! common stock for $17,000 cash	+17,000 Cash	−17,000 Marketable Securities	=		−2,000 AOCI +2,000 Retained Earnings		+2,000 Gain on Sale	−	= +2,000

MS   15,000
  Cash   15,000

MS
15,000 |
    Cash
    | 15,000

Cash   2,500
  DI   2,500

Cash
2,500 |
    DI
    | 2,500

MS   2,000
  AOCI   2,000

MS
2,000 |
    AOCI
    | 2,000

Cash   17,000
AOCI   2,000
  MS   17,000
  GN   2,000

Cash
17,000 |
    AOCI
2,000 |
    MS
    | 17,000
    GN
    | 2,000

b.

Transaction	Balance Sheet									Income Statement					
	Cash Asset	+	Noncash Assets	=	Liabil- ities	+	Contrib. Capital	+	Earned Capital		Rev- enues	-	Expen- ses	=	Net Income
1. Purchased 1,000 shares of Yahoo! common stock for $15 cash per share	−15,000 Cash		+15,000 Marketable Securities	=								-		=	
2. Received cash dividend of $2.50 per share on Yahoo! common stock	+2,500 Cash			=					+2,500 Retained Earnings		+2,500 Dividend Income	-		=	+2,500
3. Year-end market price of Yahoo! common stock is $17 per share			+2,000 Marketable Securities	=					+2,000 Retained Earnings		+2,000 Unrealized Gain	-		=	+2,000
4. Sold 1,000 shares of Yahoo! common stock for $17,000 cash	+17,000 Cash		−17,000 Marketable Securities	=								-		=	

T-accounts (right margin):

```
1.  MS      15,000
       Cash      15,000
    MS
    15,000 |
       Cash
             | 15,000

2.  Cash    2,500
       DI        2,500
       Cash
    2,500 |
       DI
             | 2,500

3.  MS      2,000
       UG        2,000
    MS
    2,000 |
       UG
             | 2,000

4.  Cash    17,000
       MS        17,000
       Cash
    17,000 |
       MS
             | 17,000
```

c. Yahoo! reports an investment portfolio of $2,103,724. This represents the portfolio's current market value.

d. Yahoo! classifies these investments as available-for-sale. Consequently, the net unrealized gains of $1,411 thousand (computed as gross unrealized gains of $3,129 thousand less gross unrealized losses of $1,718 thousand), had no effect on Yahoo!'s reported income. Yahoo! will realize gains and losses only when it sells the investments. Then, Yahoo! will recognize the gains or losses in current-period income.

Mid-Module Review 2

a.

Transaction	Balance Sheet									Income Statement					
	Cash Asset	+	Noncash Assets	=	Liabil- ities	+	Contrib. Capital	+	Earned Capital		Rev- enues	-	Expen- ses	=	Net Income
1. Purchased 5,000 shares of LookSmart common stock at $10 cash per share; these shares reflect 30% ownership	−50,000 Cash		+50,000 Investments	=								-		=	
2. Received a $2 per share cash dividend on Look-Smart stock	10,000 Cash		−10,000 Investments	=								-		=	
3. Record 30% share of the $100,000 income reported by LookSmart			+30,000 Investments	=					+30,000 Retained Earnings		+30,000 Equity Income	-		=	+30,000
4. Market value has increased to $12 per share	NOTHING RECORDED														
5. Sold all 5,000 shares of LookSmart stock for $90,000	+90,000 Cash		−70,000 Investments	=					+20,000 Retained Earnings		+20,000 Gain on Sale	-		=	+20,000

T-accounts (right margin):

```
1.  EMI     50,000
       Cash      50,000
    EMI
    50,000 |
       Cash
             | 50,000

2.  Cash    10,000
       EMI       10,000
       Cash
    10,000 |
       EMI
             | 10,000

3.  EMI     30,000
       EI        30,000
    EMI
    30,000 |
       EI
             | 30,000

5.  Cash    90,000
       EMI       70,000
       GN        20,000
       CASH
    90,000 |
       EMI
             | 70,000
       GN
             | 20,000
```

    b. Yahoo! reports $173 million ($508 million × 34%) of equity income related to this investment in its 2012 income statement.

    c. Yahoo! Japan's stockholders' equity is $1,874 million (computed as $1,131 + $1,783 − $692 − $348, in $ millions), and Yahoo!'s investment account equals $637 million, computed as $1,874 million × 34%.

Module-End Review

Solution

	Yahoo! (Parent)	EarthLink (Subsidiary)	Consolidating Adjustments	Consolidated
Current assets	$1,000,000	$100,000		$1,100,000
Investment in EarthLink	600,000	—	$(600,000)	
PPE, net	3,000,000	400,000	100,000	3,500,000
Goodwill	—	—	100,000	100,000
Total assets.	$4,600,000	$500,000		$4,700,000
Liabilities.	$1,000,000	$100,000		$1,100,000
Contributed capital.	2,000,000	200,000	(200,000)	2,000,000
Retained earnings	1,600,000	200,000	(200,000)	1,600,000
Total liabilities and equity	$4,600,000	$500,000		$4,700,000

Explanation: The $600,000 investment account is eliminated together with the $400,000 book value of EarthLink's equity to which Yahoo's investment relates. The remaining $200,000 consists of the additional $100,000 in PPE assets and the $100,000 in goodwill from expected corporate synergies. Following these adjustments, the balance sheet items are summed to yield the consolidated balance sheet.

Getty Images

VERIZON COMMUNICATIONS

Verizon Communications, Inc., began doing business in 2000, when Bell Atlantic Corporation merged with GTE Corporation. Verizon is one of the world's leading providers of communications services. It is the largest provider of wireline and wireless communications in the U.S., and is the largest of the "Baby Bells" as of 2010 with over $107 billion in revenues and $220 billion in assets.

When Ivan Seidenberg became sole CEO of Verizon in mid-2002 (and its chairman in late 2003), the Internet frenzy had cooled and Verizon's stock price had plunged, falling from an all-time high of $70 in late 1999 to $27 in mid-2002. Since then, the stock has fluctuated between $25 and $45 per share.

Verizon survived the Internet and telecom downturn. Now it faces a formidable new challenger: cable. Cable companies spent billions upgrading their infrastructure to offer customers discounted bundled packages of local voice, high-speed Internet connections, and video (Verizon has spent over $50 billion in the past three years). Market analysts estimate that cable companies could capture a

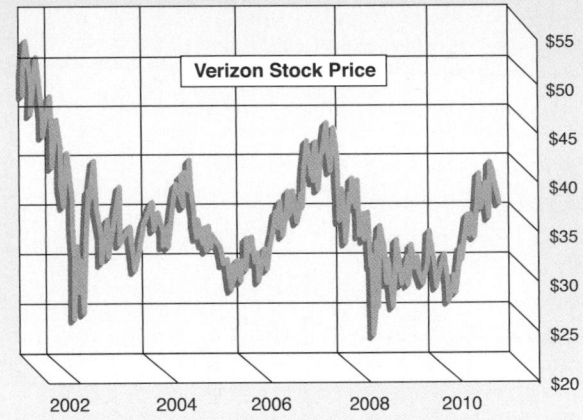

quarter of the local voice market over the next decade as they deploy new voice over Internet protocol (VOIP) technology.

While Verizon and the other traditional phone companies see their market positions erode, they also struggle to retain their image as innovators. They face creative pres-

Reporting and Analyzing Nonowner Financing

LEARNING OBJECTIVES

LO1 Describe the accounting for current operating liabilities, including accounts payable and accrued liabilities. (p. 8-4)

LO2 Describe the accounting for current and long-term nonoperating liabilities. (p. 8-10)

LO3 Explain how credit ratings are determined and identify their effect on the cost of debt. (p. 8-21)

sures from researchers and from companies (including Intel) who continue to develop new wireless technologies.

Competitors are rushing to build networks to deliver TV service and high-speed broadband access and Verizon is spending billions to roll out its FiOS phone, data, and video network to give its customers faster Internet service and an alternative to cable. Indeed, over the past three years, Verizon has spent $50 billion on capital expenditures. The demand for new capital spending is coming at an inopportune time. Verizon is currently saddled with a debt load of over $52 billion as of 2010 (a third of which matures over the next five years) and employee benefit obligations of over 28 billion. It is also paying over $5 billion in stock dividends annually. Faced with a question from a stockholder about why Verizon is not repurchasing its stock given its decline in value, Seidenberg said "our number-one priority for using free cash flow over the last two years has been reducing

debt." To that end, over the past two years, Verizon has repaid over $15 billion of its debt.

This module focuses on liabilities; that is, short-term and long-term obligations. Liabilities are one of two financing sources for a company. The other is shareholder financing. Bonds and notes are a major part of most companies' liabilities. In this module, we show how to price liabilities and how the issuance and subsequent payment of the principal and interest affect financial statements. We also discuss the required disclosures that enable us to effectively analyze a company's ability to pay its debts as they come due.

Verizon is now working harder than ever to transform itself in an era of fiber optics and wireless communication. The dilemma facing Seidenberg is how to allocate available cash flow between strategic investment and debt payments.

Source: *Verizon* 2010 10-K and Annual Report to Shareholders.

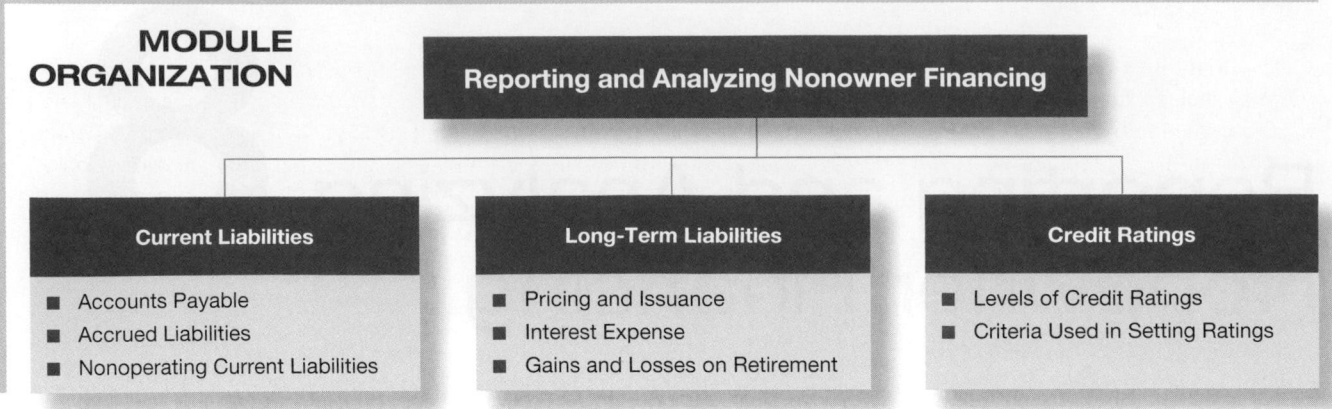

The accounting equation (Assets = Liabilities + Equity) is a useful tool in helping us think about how the balance sheet and income statement are constructed, the linkages among the financial statements, and the effects of transactions on financial statements. The accounting equation is also useful in helping us think about the statements from another perspective, namely, how the business is financed. Consider the following representation of the accounting equation:

$$\underbrace{\textbf{Assets}}_{\textbf{Uses of funds}} = \underbrace{\textbf{Liabilities + Equity}}_{\textbf{Sources of funds}}$$

Assets represent investments (uses of funds) that management has made. It includes current operating assets such as cash, accounts receivable, and inventories. It also includes long-term operating assets such as manufacturing and administrative facilities. Most companies also invest a portion of funds in nonoperating assets (marketable securities) that provide the liquidity a company needs to conduct transactions and to react to market opportunities and changes.

Just as asset disclosures provide us with information on where a company invests its funds, its liability and equity disclosures inform us as to how those assets are financed. These are the sources of funds. To be successful, a company must not only invest funds wisely, but must also be astute in the manner in which it raises funds. Companies strive to finance their assets at the lowest possible cost. Current liabilities (such as accounts payable and accrued liabilities) are generally non-interest-bearing. As a result, companies try to maximize the financing of their assets with these sources of funds.

Current liabilities, as the name implies, are short-term in nature, generally requiring payment within the coming year. As a result, they are not a suitable source of funding for long-term assets that generate cash flows over several years. Instead, companies often finance long-term assets with long-term liabilities that require payments over several years. Generally, companies try to link the pattern of the cash outflows of the financing source with the cash inflows of the related asset. As such, long-term financing is usually in the form of bonds, notes, and stock issuances.

When a company acquires assets, and finances them with liabilities, its financial leverage increases. Also, the required liability payments increase proportionally with the level of liabilities, and those larger payments imply a higher probability of default should a downturn in business occur. Greater levels of liabilities, then, make the company riskier to investors who, consequently, demand a higher return. Assessing the appropriate level of liabilities is part of liquidity and solvency analysis.

This module describes and analyzes *on-balance-sheet financing,* namely current and noncurrent liabilities that are reported on financial statements. If companies can find a way to purchase assets and have neither the asset, nor its related financing, appear on the balance sheet, they can report higher levels of asset turnover and appear less risky. This creates off-balance-sheet financing, which is the focus of Module 10.

CURRENT LIABILITIES

Current liabilities consist of both operating and nonoperating liabilities. Most *current operating liabilities* such as those related to inventory (accounts payable) or to utilities, wages, insurance, rent, and taxes (accrued liabilities), impact operating expenses such as cost of goods sold or selling, general and administrative expenses. *Current nonoperating liabilities* comprise short-term bank notes or the current portion of long-term debt. Verizon's balance sheet reports the following current liabilities:

LO1 Describe the accounting for current operating liabilities, including accounts payable and accrued liabilities.

At December 31 ($ millions)	2010	2009
Debt maturing within one year...................	$ 7,542	$ 7,205
Accounts payable and accrued liabilities............	15,702	15,223
Other.......................................	7,353	6,708
Total current liabilities	$30,597	$29,136

Verizon reports three categories of current liabilities: (1) long-term debt obligations that are scheduled for payment in the upcoming year, (2) accounts payable and accrued liabilities, and (3) other current liabilities, which consist mainly of customer deposits, dividends payable, and miscellaneous obligations.

Analysis and interpretation of the return on net operating assets (RNOA) requires that we separate current liabilities into operating and nonoperating components. In general, these two components consist of the following:

1. **Current operating liabilities**
   - **Accounts payable** Obligations to others for amounts owed on purchases of goods and services; these are usually non-interest-bearing.
   - **Accrued liabilities** Obligations for which there is no related external transaction in the current period. These include, for example, accruals for employee wages earned but yet unpaid, accruals for taxes (usually quarterly) on payroll and current period profits, and accruals for other liabilities such as rent, utilities, and insurance. Companies make accruals to properly reflect the liabilities owed as of the financial statement date and the expenses incurred for the period.
   - **Unearned revenue** Obligations to provide goods or services in the coming year; these arise from customers' deposits, subscriptions, or prepayments.
2. **Current nonoperating liabilities**
   - **Short-term interest-bearing debt** Short-term bank borrowings and notes expected to mature in whole or in part during the upcoming year; this item can include any accrued interest payable.
   - **Current maturities of long-term debt** Long-term borrowings that are scheduled to mature in whole or in part during the upcoming year; this current portion of long-term debt includes maturing principal payments only. Any unpaid interest is usually included in the prior item.

The remainder of this section describes, analyzes and interprets current operating liabilities followed by a discussion of current nonoperating liabilities.

Accounts Payable

Accounts payable arise from the purchase of goods and services from others. Accounts payable are normally non-interest-bearing and are, thus, an inexpensive financing source. Verizon does not break out accounts payable on its balance sheet but, instead, reports them with other accruals. It reports $15,702 million in accounts payable and accrued liabilities in 2010, and $15,223 million in 2009. The footnotes reveal that accounts payable represent $3,936 million in 2010, and $4,337 million in 2009, or 25% of the total each year.

The following financial statement effects template shows the accounting for a typical purchase of goods on credit and the ultimate sale of those goods. A series of four connected transactions illustrate the revenue and cost cycle.

	Balance Sheet						Income Statement		
Transaction	Cash Asset	+ Noncash Assets	= Liabil- ities	+ Contrib. Capital	+ Earned Capital		Rev- enues	− Expen- ses	= Net Income
1. Purchase $100 inventory on credit		+100 Inventory	= +100 Accounts Payable					−	=
2a. Sell inventory on credit for $140		+140 Accounts Receivable	=		+140 Retained Earnings		+140 Sales	−	= +140
2b. Record $100 cost of inventory sold in 2a		−100 Inventory	=		−100 Retained Earnings			+100 − Cost of Goods Sold	= −100
3. Collect $140 on accounts receivable	+140 Cash	−140 Accounts Receivable	=					−	=
4. Pay $100 cash for accounts payable	−100 Cash		= −100 Accounts Payable					−	=

(Left-margin T-accounts:)

```
INV     100
  AP          100
       INV
  100 |
       AP
          | 100

AR      140
  Sales       140
       AR
  140 |
       Sales
          | 140

COGS   100
  INV         100
       COGS
  100 |
       INV
          | 100

Cash   140
  AR          140
       Cash
  140 |
       AR
          | 140

AP     100
  Cash        100
       AP
  100 |
       Cash
          | 100
```

The financial statement effects template reveals several impacts related to the purchase of goods on credit and their ultimate sale.

1. Purchase of inventory is reflected on the balance sheet as an increase in inventory and an increase in accounts payable.

2a. Sale of inventory involves two components—revenue and expense. The revenue part reflects the increase in sales and the increase in accounts receivable (revenue is recognized when earned, even though cash is not yet received).

2b. The expense part of the sales transaction reflects the decrease in inventory and the increase in cost of goods sold (COGS). COGS is reported in the same income statement as the related sale (this expense is recognized because the inventory asset is sold, even though inventory-related payables may not yet be paid).

3. Collection of the receivable reduces accounts receivable and increases cash. It is solely a balance sheet transaction and does not impact the income statement.

4. Cash payment of accounts payable is solely a balance sheet transaction and does not impact income statement accounts (expense relating to inventories is recognized when the inventory is sold or used up, not when the liability is paid).

Accounts Payable Turnover (APT)

Inventories are financed, in large part, by accounts payable (also called *trade credit* or *trade payables*). Such payables usually represent interest-free financing and are, therefore, less expensive than using available cash or borrowed money to finance purchases or inventory production. Accordingly, companies use trade credit whenever possible. This is called *leaning on the trade*.

The **accounts payable turnover** reflects management's success in using trade credit to finance purchases of goods and services. It is computed as:

Accounts Payable Turnover (APT) = Cost of Goods Sold/Average Accounts Payable

Payables reflect the cost of inventory, not its retail value. Thus, to be consistent with the denominator, the ratio uses cost of goods sold (and not sales) in the numerator. Management desires to use trade credit to the greatest extent possible for financing. This means that *a lower accounts payable turnover is preferable*. Verizon's accounts payable turnover rate for 2010 is 10.7 times per year, computed as ($44,149 million/[($3,936 million + $4,337 million)/2]); this compares with 8.5 times three years earlier. This increase in accounts payable turnover indicates that Verizon is paying its obligations more quickly than it has in the past.

A metric analogous to accounts payable turnover is the **accounts payable days outstanding**, which is defined as follows:

Accounts Payable Days Outstanding (APDO) = Accounts Payable/Average Daily Cost of Goods Sold

Because accounts payable are a source of low-cost financing, *management desires to extend the accounts payable days outstanding as long as possible, provided that this action does not harm supply channel relations*. Verizon's accounts payable remain unpaid for 32.5 days in 2010, computed as ($3,936/[$44,149/365 days]), down from 43.7 days three years earlier. Verizon is paying its suppliers more quickly than it has in the past.[1]

Accounts payable reflect a source of interest-free financing. Increased payables reduce the amount of net operating working capital as payables (along with other current operating liabilities) are deducted from current operating assets in the computation of net operating working capital. Also, increased payables mean increased cash flow (as increased liabilities increase net cash from operating activities) and increased profitability (as the level of interest-bearing debt that is required to finance operating assets declines). RNOA increases when companies make use of this low-cost financing source.[2] Yet, companies must be careful to avoid excessive "leaning on the trade" as short-term income gains can yield long-term costs such as damaged supply channels.

MID-MODULE REVIEW 1

Verizon's accounts payable turnover (Cost of goods sold/Average accounts payable) increased from 8.5 in 2007 to 10.7 in 2010.

a. Does this change indicate that accounts payable have increased or decreased relative to cost of goods sold? Explain.
b. What effect does this change have on net cash flows from operating activities?
c. What management concerns, if any, might this change in accounts payable turnover pose?

The solution is on page 8-46.

Accrued Liabilities

Accrued liabilities reflect expenses that have been incurred during the period but not yet paid in cash. Accrued liabilities can also reflect unearned revenue as explained in Module 5. Verizon reports

---

[1] Excessive delays in payment of payables can result in suppliers charging a higher price for their goods or, ultimately, refusing to sell to certain buyers. Although a hidden "financing" cost is not interest, it is still a real cost.

[2] Accounts payable often carry credit terms such as 2/10, net 30. These terms give the buyer, for example, 2% off the invoice price of goods purchased if paid within 10 days. Otherwise the entire invoice is payable within 30 days. By failing to take a discount, the buyer is effectively paying 2% interest charge to keep its funds for an additional 20 days. Because there are approximately 18 such 20-day periods in a year (365/20), this equates to an annual rate of interest of about 36%. Thus, borrowing funds at less than 36% to pay this liability within the discount period would be cost effective.

details of its accrued liabilities (along with accounts payable) in the following footnote to its 2010 10-K report.

At December 31 ($ in millions)	2010	2009
Accounts payable............................	$ 3,936	$ 4,337
Accrued expenses	4,110	3,486
Accrued vacation, salaries and wages.............	5,686	5,084
Interest payable	813	872
Taxes payable	1,157	1,444
Total accounts payable and accrued liabilities	$15,702	$15,223

Accrued Liabilities (brace indicating Accrued expenses, Accrued vacation, salaries and wages, Interest payable, Taxes payable)

Verizon reports one nonoperating accrual: interest payable. Its other accrued liabilities are operating accruals that include miscellaneous accrued expenses, accrued vacation pay, accrued salaries and wages, and accrued taxes. Verizon's accruals are typical. To record accruals, companies recognize a liability on the balance sheet and a corresponding expense on the income statement. This means that liabilities increase, current income decreases, and equity decreases. When an accrued liability is ultimately paid, both cash and the liability decrease (but no expense is recorded because it was recognized previously).

Accounting for Accrued Liabilities

Accounting for a typical accrued liability such as accrued wages, for two consecutive periods, follows:

	Balance Sheet						Income Statement		
Transaction	Cash Asset	+ Noncash Assets	= Liabil- ities	+ Contrib. Capital	+ Earned Capital		Rev- enues	− Expen- ses	= Net Income
Period 1: Accrued $75 for employee wages earned at period-end			=	+75 Wages Payable		−75 Retained Earnings	−	+75 Wages Expense	= −75
Period 2: Paid $75 for wages earned in prior period	−75 Cash		=	−75 Wages Payable			−		=

The following financial statement effects result from this accrual of employee wages:

- Employees have worked during a period and have not yet been paid. The effect of this accrual is to increase wages payable on the balance sheet and to recognize wages expense on the income statement. Failure to recognize this liability and associated expense would understate liabilities on the balance sheet and overstate income in the current period and understate income in the subsequent period.

- When the company pays employees in the following period, cash and wages payable both decrease. This payment does not result in expense because the expense was recognized in the prior period when incurred.

The accrued wages illustration relates to events that are fairly certain. We know, for example, when wages are incurred but not paid. Other examples of accruals that are fairly certain are rental costs, insurance premiums, and taxes owed.

Contingent Accrued Liabilities Some accrued liabilities are less certain than others. Consider a company facing a lawsuit. Should it record the possible liability and related expense? The answer depends on the likelihood of occurrence and the ability to estimate the obligation. Specifically, if the obligation is *probable* and the amount *estimable* with reasonable certainty, then a company will recognize this obligation, called a **contingent liability**. If an obligation is only *reasonably possible* (or cannot be reliably estimated), the contingent liability is not reported on the balance sheet and is merely disclosed in the footnotes. All other contingent liabilities that are less than reasonably possible are not disclosed.

Management of Accrued Liabilities Managers have some latitude in determining the amount and timing of accruals. This latitude can lead to misreporting of income and liabilities (unintentional or otherwise). Here's how: If accruals are underestimated, then expenses are underestimated, income is overestimated, and retained earnings are overestimated. In subsequent periods when an understated accrued liability is settled (for more than the "under" estimate), reported income is lower than it should be; this is because prior-period income was higher than it should have been. (The reverse holds for overestimated accruals.) The misreporting of accruals, therefore, shifts income from one period into another. We must be keenly aware of this potential for income shifting as we analyze the financial condition of a company.

Experience tells us that accrued liabilities related to restructuring programs (including severance accruals and accruals for asset write-downs), or to legal and environmental liabilities, or business acquisitions are somewhat problematic. These accruals too often represent early recognition of expenses. Sometimes companies aggressively overestimate one-time accruals and record an even larger expense. This is called taking a *big bath*. The effect of a big bath is to depress current-period income, which relieves future periods of these expenses (thus, shifting income forward in time). Accordingly, we must monitor any change or unusual activity with accrued liabilities and view large one-time charges with skepticism.

IFRS INSIGHT | **Accruals and Contingencies under IFRS**

IFRS requires that a "provision" be recognized as a liability if a present obligation exists, if it is probable that an outflow of resources is required, and if the obligation can be reasonably estimated. These provisions are basically the same as accruals under GAAP. However, unlike GAAP, contingent liabilities are not recorded for IFRS. Contingencies do not meet the IFRS provisions definition because a present obligation does *not* exist as it may or may not be confirmed by uncertain future events. IFRS requires footnote disclosure of such contingent liabilities unless the eventual payment is remote in which case, no disclosure is required.

Estimating Accruals

Some accrued liabilities require more estimation than others. Warranty liabilities are an example of an accrual that requires managerial assumptions and estimates. Warranties are commitments that manufacturers make to their customers to repair or replace defective products within a specified period of time. The expected cost of this commitment can be reasonably estimated at the time of sale based on past experience. As a result, GAAP requires manufacturers to record the expected cost of warranties as a liability, and to record the related expected warranty expense in the income statement in the same period that the sales revenue is reported.

To illustrate, assume that a company estimates that its defective units amount to 1% of sales and that each unit costs $10 to replace. If sales during the period are $10,000, the estimated warranty expense is $1,000 ($10,000 × 1% × $10). The entries to accrue this liability and its ultimate payment follow.

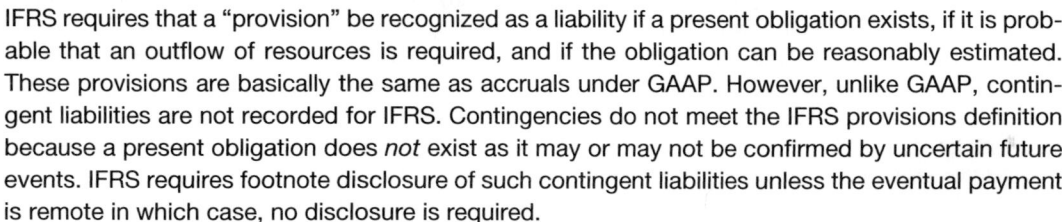

	Balance Sheet						Income Statement			
Transaction	Cash Asset	+ Noncash Assets	= Liabil- ities	+ Contrib. Capital	+ Earned Capital		Rev- enues	− Expen- ses	= Net Income	

Period 1: Accrued $1,000 of expected warranty costs on units sold during the period			= +1,000 Warranty Payable		−1,000 Retained Earnings			− +1,000 Warranty Expense	= −1,000	WRE 1,000
										  WRP 1,000
										  WRE
										1,000
										  WRP
										  1,000

Period 2: Delivered $1,000 in replacement products to cover warranty claims		−1,000 Inventory	= −1,000 Warranty Payable					−	=	WRP 1,000
										  INV 1,000
										  WRP
										1,000
										  INV
										  1,000

Accruing warranty liabilities has the same effect on financial statements as accruing wages expense in the previous section. That is, a liability is recorded on the balance sheet and an expense is reported in the income statement. When the defective product is later replaced (or repaired), the liability is reduced together with the cost of the inventory and/or the cash paid for other costs that were necessary to satisfy the claim. (Only a portion of the products estimated to fail does so in the current period; we expect other product failures in future periods. Management monitors this estimate and adjusts it if failure is higher or lower than expected.) As in the accrual of wages, the expense and the liability are reported when incurred and not when paid.

To illustrate, **Harley-Davidson** reports $54,134 thousand of warranty liability on its 2010 balance sheet. Its footnotes reveal the following additional information:

Product Warranty   Estimated warranty costs are reserved for each motorcycle at the time of sale. The warranty reserve is an estimated cost per unit sold based upon historical Company claim data used in combination with other known factors that may affect future warranty claims. The Company updates its warranty estimates quarterly to ensure that the warranty reserves are based on the most current information available. The Company believes that past claim experience is indicative of future claims; however, the factors affecting actual claims can be volatile. As a result, actual claims experience may differ from estimated which could lead to material changes in the Company's warranty provision and related reserves . . . The Company currently provides a standard two-year limited warranty on all new motorcycles sold worldwide, except for Japan, where the Company provides a standard three-year limited warranty on all new motorcycles sold. The warranty coverage for the retail customer includes parts and labor and generally begins when the motorcycle is sold to a retail customer. The Company maintains reserves for future warranty claims using an estimated cost per unit sold, which is based primarily on historical Company claim information. Additionally, the Company has from time to time initiated certain voluntary safety recall campaigns. The Company reserves for all estimated costs associated with safety recalls in the period that the safety recalls are announced. Changes in the Company's warranty and safety recall liability were as follows (in thousands):

Warranty and Safety Recall Liability (in thousands)	2010	2009	2008
Balance, beginning of period	$68,044	$64,543	$70,523
Warranties issued during the period	36,785	51,336	52,645
Settlements made during the period	(58,067)	(74,022)	(71,737)
Recalls and changes to pre-existing warranty liabilities	7,372	26,187	13,112
Balance, end of period	$54,134	$68,044	$64,543

Of the $68,044 thousand balance at the beginning of 2010, Harley incurred costs of $58,067 thousand to replace or repair defective motorcycles during 2010. This reduced Harley's liability by that amount. These costs include cash paid to customers, or to employees as wages, and the cost of parts used for repairs. Harley accrued an additional $44,157 thousand ($36,785 thousand + $7,372 thousand) in new warranty liabilities in 2010. It is important to understand that only the increase in the liability resulting from additional accruals impacts the income statement, reducing income through additional warranty expense. Payments made to settle warranty claims do not affect current-period income; they merely reduce the preexisting liability.

GAAP requires that the warranty liability reflects the estimated amount of cost that the company expects to incur as a result of warranty claims. This is often a difficult estimate to make and is prone to error. There is also the possibility that a company might underestimate its warranty liability to report higher current income, or overestimate it so as to depress current income and create an additional liability on the balance sheet (*cookie jar reserve*) that can be used to absorb future warranty costs and, thus, to reduce future expenses. The overestimation would shift income from the current-period to one or more future periods. Warranty liabilities must, therefore, be examined closely and compared with sales levels. Any deviations from the historical relation of the warranty liability to sales, or from levels reported by competitors, should be scrutinized.

MID-MODULE REVIEW 2

Assume that Verizon's employees worked during the current month and earned $10,000 in wages that Verizon will not pay until the first of next month. Must Verizon recognize any wages liability and expense for the current month? Explain. Use the financial statement effects template to show the effect of this accrual.

The solution is on page 8-47.

Current Nonoperating Liabilities

Current nonoperating liabilities include short-term bank loans, accrued interest on those loans, and the current maturities of long-term debt. Companies generally try to structure their financing so that debt service requirements (payments) coincide with the cash inflows from the assets financed. This means that current assets are usually financed with current liabilities, and that long-term assets are financed with long-term liabilities (and equity).

LO2 Describe the accounting for current and long-term nonoperating liabilities.

To illustrate, assume that a seasonal company's investment in current assets tends to fluctuate during the year as depicted in the graphic below:

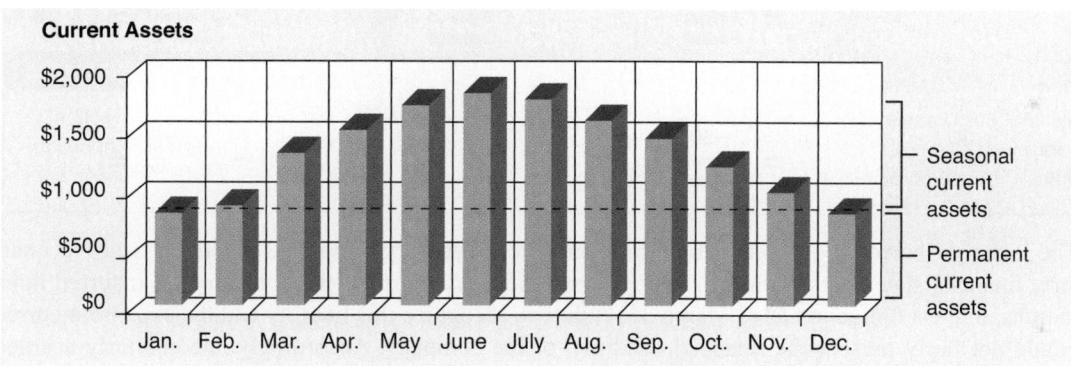

This company does most of its selling in the summer months. More inventory is purchased and manufactured in the early spring than at any other time of the year. High summer sales give rise to accounts receivable that are higher than normal during the fall. The company's working capital peaks at the height of the selling season and is lowest as the business slows in the off-season. There is a permanent level of working capital required for this business (about $750), and a seasonal component (maximum of about $1,000). Different businesses exhibit different patterns in their working capital requirements, but many have both permanent and seasonal components.

The existence of permanent and seasonal current operating assets often requires that financing sources also have permanent and seasonal components. Consider again the company depicted in the graphic above. A portion of the company's assets is in inventories that are financed, in part, with accounts payable and accruals. Thus, we expect that current operating liabilities also exhibit a seasonal component that fluctuates with the level of operations. These payables are generally non-interest-bearing and, thus, provide low-cost financing that should be used to the greatest extent possible. Additional financing needs are covered by short-term interest-bearing debt.

This section focuses on current nonoperating liabilities, which include short-term debt, current maturities of long-term liabilities, and accrued interest expenses.

Short-Term Interest-Bearing Debt

Seasonal swings in working capital are often financed with a bank line of credit (short-term debt). In this case the bank commits to lend up to a maximum amount with the understanding that the amounts borrowed will be repaid in full sometime during the year. An interest-bearing note evidences any such borrowing.

When the company borrows these short-term funds, it reports the cash received on the balance sheet together with an increase in liabilities (notes payable). The note is reported as a current liability because the company expects to repay it within a year. This borrowing has no effect on income or equity. The borrower incurs (and the lender earns) interest on the note as time passes. GAAP requires the borrower to accrue the interest liability and the related interest expense each time financial statements are issued.

To illustrate, assume that **Verizon** borrows $1,000 cash on January 1. The note bears interest at a 12% annual rate, and the interest (3% per quarter) is payable on the first of each subsequent quarter (April 1, July 1, October 1, January 1). Assuming that Verizon issues calendar-quarter financial statements, this borrowing results in the following financial statement effects for January 1 through April 1.

		Balance Sheet				Income Statement		
Transaction	Cash Asset	+ Noncash Assets	= Liabil- ities	+ Contrib. Capital	+ Earned Capital	Rev- enues	− Expen- ses	= Net Income
Jan 1: Borrow $1,000 cash and issue note payable	+1,000 Cash		= +1,000 Note Payable				−	=
Mar 31: Accrue quarterly interest on 12%, $1,000 note payable			= +30 Interest Payable		−30 Retained Earnings		+30 − Interest Expense	= −30
Apr 1: Pay $30 cash for interest due	−30 Cash		= −30 Interest Payable				−	=

Margin journal entries:

Cash   1,000
  NP   1,000

Cash	
1,000	

NP	
	1,000

IE   30
  IP   30

IE	
30	

IP	
	30

IP   30
  Cash   30

IP	
30	

Cash	
	30

The January 1 borrowing increases both cash and notes payable. On March 31, Verizon issues its quarterly financial statements. Although interest is not paid until April 1, the company has incurred three months' interest obligation as of March 31. Failure to recognize this liability and the expense incurred would not fairly present the financial condition of the company. Accordingly, the quarterly accrued interest payable is computed as follows:

$$\text{Interest Expense} = \text{Principal} \times \text{Annual Rate} \times \text{Portion of Year Outstanding}$$
$$\$30 \qquad = \quad \$1,000 \quad \times \quad 12\% \quad \times \qquad 3/12$$

The subsequent interest payment on April 1 reduces both cash and the interest payable that Verizon accrued on March 31. There is no expense reported on April 1, as it was recorded the previous day (March 31) when Verizon prepared its financial statements. (For fixed-maturity borrowings specified in days, such as a 90-day note, we assume a 365-day year for interest accrual computations, see Mid-Module Review 3.)

Current Maturities of Long-Term Debt

Principal payments that must be made during the upcoming 12 months on long-term debt (such as for a mortgage), or on bonds and notes that mature within the next year, are reported as current liabilities called *current maturities of long-term debt*. All companies must provide a schedule of the maturities of their long-term debt in the footnotes to the financial statements. To illustrate, Verizon reports $7,542 million in long-term debt due within one year in the current liability section of the balance sheet shown earlier in the module.

MID-MODULE REVIEW 3

Assume that on January 15, Verizon borrowed $10,000 on a 90-day, 6% note payable. The bank accrues interest daily based on a 365-day year. Use the financial statement effects template to show the January 31 interest accrual.

The solution is on page 8-47.

LONG-TERM NONOPERATING LIABILITIES

Companies often include long-term nonoperating liabilities in their capital structure to fund long-term assets. Smaller amounts of long-term debt can be readily obtained from banks, private placements with insurance companies, and other credit sources. However, when a large amount of financing is required, the issuance of bonds (and notes) in capital markets is a cost-efficient way to raise funds. The following discussion uses bonds for illustration, but the concepts also apply to long-term notes.

Bonds are structured like any other borrowing. The borrower receives cash and agrees to pay it back with interest. Generally, the entire **face amount** (principal) of the bond is repaid at maturity (at the end of the bond's life) and interest payments are made in the interim (usually semiannually).

Companies that raise funds in the bond market normally work with an underwriter (like Merrill Lynch) to set the terms of the bond issue. The underwriter then sells individual bonds (usually in $1,000 denominations) from this general bond issue to its retail clients and professional portfolio managers (like The Vanguard Group), and receives a fee for underwriting the bond issue. These bonds are investments for individual investors, other companies, retirement plans and insurance companies.

After they are issued, the bonds can trade in the secondary market just like stocks. Market prices of bonds fluctuate daily despite the fact that the company's obligation for payment of principal and interest normally remains fixed throughout the life of the bond. Then, why do bond prices change? The answer is that the bond's fixed rate of interest can be higher or lower than the interest rates offered on other securities of similar risk. Because bonds compete with other possible investments, bond prices are set relative to the prices of other investments. In a competitive investment market, a particular bond will become more or less desirable depending on the general level of interest rates offered by competing securities. Just as for any item, competitive pressures will cause bond prices to rise and fall.

This section analyzes and interprets the reporting for bonds. We also examine the mechanics of bond pricing and describe the accounting for, and reporting of, bonds.

Pricing of Debt

The following two different interest rates are crucial for pricing debt.

- **Coupon (contract or stated) rate** The coupon rate of interest is stated in the bond contract; it is used to compute the dollar amount of interest payments that are paid to bondholders during the life of the bond issue.

- **Market (yield or effective) rate** This is the interest rate that investors expect to earn on the investment in this debt security; this rate is used to price the bond.

The coupon (contract) rate is used to compute interest payments and the market (yield) rate is used to price the bond. The coupon rate and the market rate are nearly always different. This is because the coupon rate is fixed prior to issuance of the bond and normally remains fixed throughout its life. Market rates of interest, on the other hand, fluctuate continually with the supply and demand for bonds in the marketplace, general macroeconomic conditions, and the borrower's financial condition.

The bond price, both its initial sales price and the price it trades at in the secondary market subsequent to issuance, equals the present value of the expected cash flows to the bondholder. Specifically, bondholders normally expect to receive two different types of cash flows:

1. **Periodic interest payments** (usually semiannual) during the bond's life; these payments are called an *annuity* because they are equal in amount and made at regular intervals.

2. **Single payment** of the face (principal) amount of the bond at maturity; this is called a *lump-sum* because it occurs only once.

The bond price equals the present value of the periodic interest payments plus the present value of the single payment. If the present value of the two cash flows is equal to the bond's face value, the bond is sold at par. If the present value is less than or greater than the bond's face value, the bond sells at a discount or premium, respectively. We next illustrate the issuance of bonds at three different prices: at par, at a discount, and at a premium.

Bonds Issued at Par

To illustrate a bond issued (also said to be sold) at par, assume that a bond with a face amount of $10 million, has a 6% annual coupon rate payable semiannually (3% semiannual rate), and a maturity of 10 years. Semiannual interest payments are typical for bonds. This means that the issuer pays bondholders two interest payments per year. Each semiannual interest payment is equal to the bond's face value times the annual rate divided by two. Investors purchasing these bonds receive the following cash flows.

	Number of Payments	Dollars per Payment	Total Cash Flows
Semiannual interest payments.....	10 years × 2 = 20	$10,000,000 × 3% = $300,000	$ 6,000,000
Principal payment at maturity......	1	$10,000,000	10,000,000
			$16,000,000

Specifically, the bond agreement dictates that the borrower must make 20 semiannual payments of $300,000 each, computed as $10,000,000 × (6%/2). At maturity, the borrower must repay the $10,000,000 face amount. To price bonds, investors identify the *number* of interest payments and use that number when computing the present value of *both* the interest payments and the principal (face) payment at maturity.

The bond price is the present value of the periodic interest payments (the annuity) plus the present value of the principal payment (the lump sum). In our example, assuming that investors desire a 3% semiannual market rate (yield), the bond sells for $10,000,000, which is computed as follows:

Present value factors are from Appendix A

Calculator
N = 20
I/Yr = 3
PMT = 300,000
FV = 10,000,000
PV = 10,000,000

	Payment	Present Value Factor[a]	Present Value
Interest	$ 300,000	14.87747[b]	$ 4,463,200[d]
Principal	$10,000,000	0.55368[c]	5,536,800
			$10,000,000

[a] Mechanics of using tables to compute present values are explained in Appendix 8A; present value factors come from Appendix A near the end of the book.
[b] Present value of an ordinary annuity for 20 periods discounted at 3% per period.
[c] Present value of a single payment in 20 periods discounted at 3% per period.
[d] Rounded.

Because the bond contract pays investors a 3% semiannual rate when investors demand a 3% semiannual market rate, given the borrower's credit rating and the time to maturity, the investors purchase those bonds at the **par (face) value** of $10 million.

Discount Bonds

As a second illustration, assume investors demand a 4% semiannual return for the 3% semiannual coupon bond, while all other details remain the same. The bond now sells for $8,640,999, computed as follows:

Calculator
N = 20
I/Yr = 4
PMT = 300,000
FV = 10,000,000
PV = 8,640,967.37*
*rounding difference

	Payment	Present Value Factor	Present Value
Interest	$ 300,000	13.59033[a]	$4,077,099
Principal	$10,000,000	0.45639[b]	4,563,900
			$8,640,999

[a] Present value of an ordinary annuity for 20 periods discounted at 4% per period.
[b] Present value of a single payment in 20 periods discounted at 4% per period.

Because the bond carries a coupon rate *lower* than what investors demand, the bond is less desirable and sells at a **discount**. More generally, bonds sell at a discount whenever the coupon rate is less than the market rate.

Premium Bonds

As a third illustration, assume that investors demand a 2% semiannual return for the 3% semiannual coupon bonds, while all other details remain the same. The bond now sells for $11,635,129, computed as follows:

	Payment	Present Value Factor	Present Value
Interest	$ 300,000	16.35143[a]	$ 4,905,429
Principal	$10,000,000	0.67297[b]	6,729,700
			$11,635,129

[a] Present value of an ordinary annuity for 20 periods discounted at 2% per period.
[b] Present value of a single payment in 20 periods discounted at 2% per period.

> **Calculator**
> N = 20
> I/Yr = 2
> PMT = 300,000
> FV = 10,000,000
>
> PV = 11,635,143.33*
>
> *rounding difference

Because the bond carries a coupon rate *higher* than what investors demand, the bond is more desirable and sells at a **premium**. More generally, bonds sell at a premium whenever the coupon rate is greater than the market rate.[3] Exhibit 8.1 summarizes this relation for bond pricing.

EXHIBIT 8.1 Coupon Rate, Market Rate, and Bond Pricing		
Coupon rate > market rate	→	Bond sells at a **premium** (above face amount)
Coupon rate = market rate	→	Bond sells at **par** (at face amount)
Coupon rate < market rate	→	Bond sells at a **discount** (below face amount)

Exhibit 8.2 shows an announcement (called a *tombstone*) of a Union Pacific Corp $500 million debt issuance. It has a 4% coupon rate paying 2% semiannual interest, maturing in 2021, with an issue price of 99.525 (sold at a discount). Union Pacific Corp's underwriters took 0.65% in fees ($3.25 million) for underwriting and selling this debt issue.[4]

Effective Cost of Debt

When a bond sells for par, the cost to the issuing company is the cash interest paid. In our first illustration above, the *effective cost* of the bond is the 6% interest paid by the issuer.

When a bond sells at a discount, the issuer must repay more (the face value when the bond matures) than the cash received at issuance (the discounted bond proceeds). This means that the effective cost of a discount bond is greater than if the bond had sold at par. A discount is a cost and, like any other cost, must eventually be transferred from the balance sheet to the income statement as an expense.

When a bond sells at a premium, the borrower received more cash at issuance than it must repay. The difference, the premium, is a benefit that must eventually find its way into the income statement as a *reduction* of interest expense. As a result of the premium, the effective cost of a premium bond is less than if the bond had sold at par.

Bonds are priced to yield the return (market rate) demanded by investors. Consequently, the effective rate of a bond *always* equals the yield (market) rate demanded by investors, regardless of the coupon rate of the bond. This means that companies cannot influence the effective cost of debt by raising or lowering the coupon rate. Doing so will only result in a bond premium or discount. We discuss the factors affecting the yield demanded by investors later in the module.

The effective cost of debt is reflected in the amount of interest expense reported in the issuer's income statement. Because of bond discounts and premiums, interest expense is usually different from

---

[3] Bond prices are often stated in percent form. For example, a bond sold at par is said to be sold at 100 (that is, 100% of par). The bond sold at $8,640,999 is said to be sold at 86.41 (86.41% of par, computed as $8,640,999/$10,000,000). The bond sold for a premium is said to be sold at 116.35 (116.35% of the bond's face value).

[4] The tombstone makes clear that if we purchase any of these notes (in denominations of $1,000) after the semiannual interest date, we must pay accrued interest in addition to the purchase price. This interest is returned to us in the regular interest payment. (This procedure makes the bookkeeping easier for the issuer/underwriter because all interest payments are equal regardless of when Union Pacific actually sold the bond.)

EXHIBIT 8.2 Announcement (Tombstone) of Debt Offering to Public

$500,000,000

Union Pacific Corporation

4.00% Notes due 2021

We will pay interest on the notes each February 1 and August 1, commencing February 1, 2011. The notes will mature on February 1, 2021. We may redeem some or all of the notes at any time and from time to time at the redemption price described in this prospectus supplement. There is no sinking fund for the notes. See "Description of the Notes" for a description of the terms of the notes.

	Price to Public (1)	Underwriting Discount	Proceeds to the Company
Per Note	99.525%	0.650%	98.875%
Total	$497,625,000	$3,250,000	$494,375,000

(1) Plus accrued interest, if any, from August 2, 2010.

Neither the Securities and Exchange Commission nor any state securities commission has approved or disapproved of these securities or determined if this prospectus supplement or the accompanying prospectus is truthful or complete. Any representation to the contrary is a criminal offense. Delivery of the notes, in book-entry form only through The Depository Trust Company, will be made on or about August 2, 2010. The date of this prospectus supplement is July 28, 2010.

Joint Book-Running Managers

BofA Merrill Lynch   **J.P. Morgan**   **Morgan Stanley**

Senior Co-Managers

BNP PARIBAS   **Citi**

Co-Managers

    Mitsubishi UFJ Securities   **RBS**   **Sun Trust Robinson Humphrey**
    US Bancorp   **Wells Fargo Securities**

---

the cash interest paid. The next section discusses how management reports, and how we interpret, bonds on the balance sheet and interest expense on the income statement.

REPORTING OF DEBT FINANCING

This section identifies and describes the financial statement effects of bond transactions.

Financial Statement Effects of Debt Issuance

Bonds Issued at Par

When a bond sells at par, the issuing company receives the cash proceeds and accepts an obligation to make payments per the bond contract. Specifically, cash is increased and a long-term liability (bonds payable) is increased by the same amount. There is no revenue or expense at bond issuance. Using the facts from our $10 million bond illustration above, the issuance of bonds at par has the following financial statement effects:

Transaction	Balance Sheet						Income Statement		
	Cash Asset	+	Noncash Assets	=	Liabil- ities	+ Contrib. Capital + Earned Capital		Rev- enues	− Expen- ses = Net Income
Issue bonds at par for cash	+10,000,000 Cash				+10,000,000 = Long-Term Debt				− =

```
Cash   10,000,000
   LTD      10,000,000
        Cash
10,000,000 |
        LTD
        | 10,000,000
```

Discount Bonds

When a bond is sold at a discount, the cash proceeds and net bond liability are recorded at the amount of the proceeds received (not the face amount of the bond). Again, using the facts above from our bond discount illustration, the financial statement effects follow:

Transaction	Balance Sheet						Income Statement		
	Cash Asset	+	Noncash Assets	=	Liabil- ities	+ Contrib. Capital + Earned Capital		Rev- enues	− Expen- ses = Net Income
Issue bonds at discount for cash	+$8,640,999 Cash				+$8,640,999 = Long-Term Debt				− =

```
Cash   8,640,999
   LTD      8,640,999
        Cash
8,640,999 |
        LTD
        | 8,640,999
```

The net bond liability (long-term debt) reported on the balance sheet consists of two components as follows:

Bonds payable, face.	$10,000,000
Less bond discount	(1,359,001)
Bonds payable, net	$ 8,640,999

Bonds are reported on the balance sheet net of any discount. When the bond matures, however, the company is obligated to repay the face amount ($10 million). Accordingly, at maturity, the bonds payable account needs to read $10 million, the amount that is owed. This means that between the bond

BUSINESS INSIGHT   **Verizon's Zero-Coupon Debt**

Zero-coupon bonds and notes, called *zeros,* do not carry a coupon rate. Pricing of these bonds and notes is done in the same manner as those with coupon rates—the exception is the absence of an interest annuity. This means that the price is the present value of the principal payment at maturity; hence the bond is sold at a *deep discount.* Verizon reported on its zero-coupon debt in its 10-K (the bonds have since been paid off):

> *Zero-Coupon Convertible Notes* The previously issued $5.4 billion zero-coupon convertible notes due 2021, which resulted in gross proceeds of approximately $3 billion, were redeemable at the option of the holders on May 15th in each of the years 2004, 2006, 2011, and 2016. On May 15, 2004, $3,292 million of principal amount of the notes ($1,984 million after unamortized discount) were redeemed. On May 15, 2006, we redeemed the remaining $1,375 million accreted principal of the remaining outstanding zero-coupon convertible principal. The total payment on the date of redemption was $1,377 million.

When Verizon issued its zero-coupon convertible notes in May 2001, they had a maturity value of $5.4 billion and were slated to mature in 2021. No interest is paid in the interim. The notes sold for $3 billion. The difference between the $3 billion sales proceeds and the $5.4 billion maturity value represents Verizon's interest costs, which is the return to the investor. The effective cost of the debt is the interest rate that equates the issue price and maturity value, or approximately 3%.

issuance and its maturity, the discount must decline to zero. This reduction of the discount over the life of the bond is called **amortization**. The next section shows how discount amortization results in additional interest expense in the income statement. This amortization causes the effective interest expense to be greater than the periodic cash interest payments.

Premium Bonds

When a bond is sold at a premium, the cash proceeds and net bond liability are recorded at the amount of the proceeds received (not the face amount of the bond). Again, using the facts above from our premium bond illustration, the financial statement effects follow:

		Balance Sheet						Income Statement		
Transaction	**Cash Asset**	**+ Noncash Assets**	**= Liabil- ities**	**+ Contrib. Capital**	**+ Earned Capital**		**Rev- enues**	**− Expen- ses**	**= Net Income**
Issue bonds at premium for cash	+$11,635,129 Cash		= +$11,635,129 Long-Term Debt					−	=

Cash 11,635,129
  LTD 11,635,129
    Cash
11,635,129|
    LTD
      |11,635,129

The bond liability reported on the balance sheet, again, consists of two parts:

Bonds payable, face.........	$10,000,000
Add bond premium	1,635,129
Bonds payable, net	$11,635,129

The $10 million must be repaid at maturity, and the premium amortized to zero over the life of the bond. The premium represents a *benefit,* which *reduces* interest expense on the income statement.

Effects of Discount and Premium Amortization

For bonds issued at par, interest expense reported on the income statement equals the cash interest payment. However, for bonds issued at a discount or premium, interest expense reported on the income statement also includes any amortization of the bond discount or premium as follows:

Cash interest paid		Cash interest paid
+ Amortization of discount	or	− Amortization of premium
Interest expense		Interest expense

Specifically, periodic amortization of a discount is added to the cash interest paid to get interest expense. Amortization of the discount reflects the additional cost the issuer incurs from issuing the bonds at a discount. Over the bond's life, the discount is transferred from the balance sheet to the income statement via amortization, as an increase to interest expense. For a premium bond, the premium is a benefit the issuer receives at issuance. Amortization of the premium reduces interest expense over the bond's life. In both cases, interest expense on the income statement represents the *effective cost* of debt (the *nominal cost* of debt is the cash interest paid).

Companies amortize discounts and premiums using the effective interest method. To illustrate, assume that **Verizon** issues bonds with a face amount of $600,000, a 3% annual coupon rate payable semiannually (1.5% semiannual rate), a maturity of three years (six semiannual payment periods), and a market (yield) rate of 4% annual (2% semiannual). These facts yield a bond issue price of $583,195.71, which we round to $583,196 for the bond discount amortization table of Exhibit 8.3.

Calculator
N = 6
I/Yr = 2
PMT = 9,000
FV = 600,000

PV = 583,195.71

EXHIBIT 8.3	Bond Discount Amortization Table				
	[A] ([E] × market%) Interest	[B] (Face × coupon%) Cash	[C] ([A] – [B]) Discount	[D] (Prior bal – [C]) Discount	[E] (Face – [D]) Bond
Period	Expense	Interest Paid	Amortization	Balance	Payable, Net
0				$16,804	$583,196
1	$11,664	$ 9,000	$2,664	14,140	585,860
2	11,717	9,000	2,717	11,423	588,577
3	11,772	9,000	2,772	8,651	591,349
4	11,827	9,000	2,827	5,824	594,176
5	11,884	9,000	2,884	2,940	597,060
6	11,940	9,000	2,940	0	600,000
	$70,804	$54,000	$16,804		

During the bond life, carrying value is adjusted to par and the discount to zero

Cash paid plus discount amortization equals interest expense

The interest period is denoted in the left-most column. Period 0 is the point at which the bond is issued, and period 1 and following are successive six-month periods (recall, interest is paid semiannually). Column [A] is interest expense, which is reported in the income statement. Interest expense is computed as the bond's net balance sheet value (the carrying amount of the bond) at the beginning of the period (column [E]) multiplied by the 2% semiannual rate used to compute the bond issue price. Column [B] is cash interest paid, which is a constant $9,000 per the bond contract (face amount × coupon rate). Column [C] is discount amortization, which is the difference between interest expense and cash interest paid. Column [D] is the discount balance, which is the previous balance of the discount less the discount amortization in column [C]. Column [E] is the net bond payable, which is the $600,000 face amount less the unamortized discount from column [D].

The table shows amounts for the six interest payment periods. The amortization process continues until period 6, at which time the discount balance is 0 and the net bond payable is $600,000 (the maturity value). Each semiannual period, interest expense is recorded at 2%, the market rate of interest at the bond's issuance. This rate does not change over the life of the bond, even if the prevailing market interest rates change. An amortization table reveals the financial statement effects of the bond for its duration. Specifically, we see the income statement effects in column [A], the cash effects in column [B], and the balance sheet effects in columns [D] and [E].

To illustrate amortization of a premium bond, we assume that Verizon issues bonds with a $600,000 face value, a 3% annual coupon rate payable semiannually (1.5% semiannual rate), a maturity of three years (six semiannual interest payments), and a 2% annual (1% semiannual) market interest rate. These facts yield a bond issue price of $617,386.43, which we round to $617,386. Exhibit 8.4 shows the premium amortization table for this bond.

Calculator
N = 20
I/Yr = 1
PMT = 300,000
FV = 10,000,000
PV = 617,386

EXHIBIT 8.4	Bond Premium Amortization Table				
	[A] ([E] × market%) Interest	[B] (Face × coupon%) Cash	[C] ([B] – [A]) Premium	[D] (Prior bal – [C]) Premium	[E] (Face + [D]) Bond
Period	Expense	Interest Paid	Amortization	Balance	Payable, Net
0				$17,386	$617,386
1	$ 6,174	$ 9,000	$ 2,826	14,560	614,560
2	6,146	9,000	2,854	11,706	611,706
3	6,117	9,000	2,883	8,823	608,823
4	6,088	9,000	2,912	5,911	605,911
5	6,059	9,000	2,941	2,970	602,970
6	6,030	9,000	2,970	0	600,000
	$36,614	$54,000	$17,386		

During the bond life, carrying value is adjusted to par and the premium to zero

Cash paid less premium amortization equals interest expense

Interest expense is computed using the same process that we used for discount bonds. The difference is that the yield rate is 1% semiannual in the premium case. Also, cash interest paid follows from the bond contract (face amount × coupon rate), and the other columns' computations reflect the premium amortization. After period 6, the premium is fully amortized (equals zero) and the net bond payable balance is $600,000, the amount owed at maturity. Again, an amortization table reveals the financial statement effects of the bond—the income statement effects in column [A], the cash effects in column [B], and the balance sheet effects in columns [D] and [E].

Financial Statement Effects of Bond Repurchase

Companies report bonds payable at *historical (adjusted) cost*. Specifically, net bonds payable amounts follow from the amortization table, as do the related cash flows and income statement numbers. All financial statement relations are set when the bond is issued; they do not subsequently change.

Once issued, however, bonds trade in secondary markets. The yield rate used to compute bond prices for these subsequent transactions is the market interest rate prevailing at the time. These rates change daily based on the level of interest rates in the economy and the perceived creditworthiness of the bond issuer.

Companies can and sometimes do repurchase (or *redeem* or *retire*) their bonds prior to maturity. The bond indenture (contract agreement) can include provisions giving the company the right to repurchase its bonds directly from the bond holders. Or, the company can repurchase bonds in the open market. To illustrate, **Verizon**'s 10-K includes the following footnote relating to its repurchase of **MCI** debt in connection with the MCI acquisition:

Redemption of Debt Assumed in Merger On January 17, 2006, Verizon announced offers to purchase two series of MCI senior notes, MCI $1,983 million aggregate principal amount of 6.688% Senior Notes Due 2009 and MCI $1,699 million aggregate principal amount of 7.735% Senior Notes Due 2014, at 101% of their par value . . . In addition, on January 20, 2006, Verizon announced an offer to repurchase MCI $1,983 million aggregate principal amount of 5.908% Senior Notes Due 2007 at 101% of their par value . . . We recorded pretax charges of $26 million ($16 million after-tax) during the first quarter of 2006 resulting from the extinguishment of the debt assumed in connection with the completion of this merger.

When a bond repurchase occurs, a gain or loss usually results, and is computed as follows:

Gain or Loss on Bond Repurchase = Net Bonds Payable − Repurchase Payment

The net bonds payable, also referred to as the *book value,* is the net amount reported on the balance sheet. If the issuer pays more to retire the bonds than the amount carried on its balance sheet, it reports a loss on its income statement, usually called *loss on bond retirement.* The issuer reports a *gain on bond retirement* if the repurchase price is less than the net bonds payable.

GAAP prescribes that gains or losses on bond repurchases be reported as part of ordinary income unless the repurchase meets the criteria for treatment as an extraordinary item (unusual and infrequent, see Module 5). Relatively few debt retirements meet these criteria and, hence, most gains and losses on bond repurchases are reported as part of income from continuing operations.

How should we treat these gains and losses for analysis purposes? That is, do they carry economic effects? The answer is no—the gain or loss on repurchase is exactly offset by the present value of the future cash flow implications of the repurchase (Appendix 8B demonstrates this).

Another analysis issue involves assessing the fair value of bonds and other long-term liabilities. This information is relevant for some investors and creditors in revealing unrealized gains and losses (similar to that reported for marketable securities). GAAP requires companies to provide information about current fair values of their long-term liabilities in footnotes (see Verizon's fair value of debt disclosure in the next section). However, these fair values are *not* reported on the balance sheet and changes in these fair values are not reflected in net income. We must make our own adjustments to the balance sheet and income statement if we want to include changes in fair values of liabilities.

Financial Statement Footnotes

Companies are required to disclose details about their long-term liabilities, including the amounts borrowed under each debt issuance, the interest rates, maturity dates, and other key provisions. Following is **Verizon**'s disclosure for its long-term debt.

Long-Term Debt Outstanding long-term obligations are as follows:

At December 31 ($ millions)	Interest Rates %	Maturities	2010	2009
Verizon Communications—notes payable and other.	4.35 – 5.50	2011–2018	$ 6,062	$ 6,196
	5.55 – 6.90	2012–2038	10,441	10,386
	7.35 – 8.95	2012–2039	7,677	9,671
Verizon Wireless – notes payable and other	3.75 – 5.55	2011–2014	7,000	7,000
	7.38 – 8.88	2011–2018	5,975	6,118
	Floating	2011	1,250	6,246
Verizon Wireless—Alltel assumed notes	6.50 – 7.88	2012–2032	2,315	2,334
Telephone subsidiaries—debentures.	4.63 – 7.00	2011–2033	7,937	8,797
	7.15 – 7.88	2012–2032	1,449	1,449
	8.00 – 8.75	2011–2031	880	1,080
Other subsidiaries—debentures and other	6.84 – 8.75	2018–2028	1,700	1,700
Employee stock ownership plan loans.	—	—	—	23
Capital lease obligations (average rates of 6.8% and 6.3%, respectively).			332	397
Unamortized discount, net of premium			(224)	(241)
Total long-term debt, including current maturities			52,794	61,156
Less: debt maturing within one year			7,542	6,105
Total long-term debt.			$45,252	$55,051

Verizon reports a net book value for long-term debt of $52,794 million at year-end 2010. Of this amount, $7,542 million matures in the next year and is classified as a current liability (current maturities of long-term debt). The remainder of $45,252 matures after 2011. Verizon also reports $224 million in unamortized discount (net of premium) on this debt.

In addition to long-term debt amounts, rates, and due dates, and as required under GAAP, Verizon reports aggregate maturities for the five years subsequent to the balance sheet date as follows:

Maturities of Long-Term Debt Maturities of long-term debt outstanding at December 31, 2010, are as follows:

Years	(dollars in millions)
2011.	$ 7,542
2012.	5,902
2013.	5,915
2014.	3,529
2015.	1,201
Thereafter.	28,705

This reveals that Verizon is required to make principal payments that total $24,089 million in the next five years and an additional $28,705 million in principal payments thereafter. Such maturities are important information as a company must either meet its required payments, negotiate a rescheduling of the indebtedness, or refinance the debt to avoid default. Failing to repay debts (defaulting) usually has severe consequences as debt holders have legal remedies available to them that can bankrupt the company.

Verizon's disclosure on the fair value of its total debt follows:

At December 31, (dollars in millions)	2010 Carrying Amount	2010 Fair Value	2009 Carrying Amount	2009 Fair Value
Short- and long-term debt, excluding capital leases.....	$52,462	$59,020	$61,859	$67,359

As of 2010, indebtedness with a book value of $52,462 million had a fair value of $59,020 million, resulting in an unrecognized liability (which would be realized if Verizon redeemed the debt) of $6,558 million. The increase in fair value is due mainly to a decline in interest rates subsequent to the bonds' issuance (Verizon's credit ratings have not changed in recent years—see next section). The justification for not recognizing unrealized gains and losses on the balance sheet and income statement is that such amounts can reverse with future fluctuations in interest rates. Further, since only the face amount of debt is repaid at maturity, unrealized gains and losses that arise during intervening years do not affect the company's expected cash flows. This is the same logic for nonrecognition of gains and losses on held-to-maturity debt investments (see Module 7).

CREDIT RATINGS AND THE COST OF DEBT

LO3 Explain how credit ratings are determined and identify their effect on the cost of debt.

Earlier in the module we explained that the effective cost of debt to the issuing company is the market (yield) rate of interest used to price the bond, regardless of the bond coupon rate. The market rate of interest is usually defined as the yield on U.S. Government borrowings such as treasury bills, notes, and bonds, called the *risk-free rate,* plus a *risk premium* (also called a *spread*).

Yield Rate = Risk-Free Rate + Risk Premium

Both the treasury yield (the so-called risk-free rate) and the corporate yield vary over time as illustrated in the following graphic.

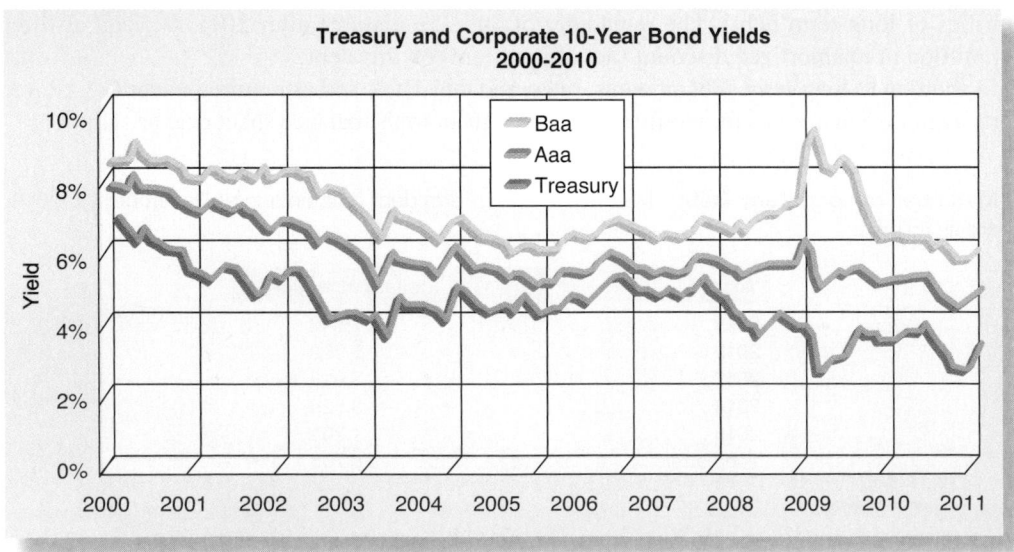

The rate of interest that investors expect for a particular bond is a function of the risk-free rate and the risk premium, where the latter depends on the creditworthiness of the issuing entity.

   The yield increases (shifts upward) as debt quality moves from Treasury securities (generally considered to be risk free), which is the highest-quality debt reflected in the lowest line in the graph, to the Aaa (highest) rated corporates and, finally, to the Baa (lower-rated) corporates shown in this graph. That is, higher credit-rated issuers warrant a lower rate than lower credit-rated issuers. This difference is substantial. For example, in December of 2010, the average 10-year treasury bond yield is 3.29%, while the Aaa corporate bond yield is 5.02% and the average Baa (the lowest investment grade corporate bond) yield is 6.10%.

RESEARCH INSIGHT | **Accounting Conservatism and Cost of Debt**

Research indicates that companies that use more conservative accounting policies incur a lower cost of debt. Research also suggests that while accounting conservatism can lead to lower-quality accounting income (because such income does not fully reflect economic reality), creditors are more confident in the numbers and view them as more credible. Evidence also implies that companies can lower the required return demanded by creditors (the risk premium) by issuing high-quality financial reports that include enhanced footnote disclosures and detailed supplemental reports.

What Are Credit Ratings?

A company's credit rating, also referred to as debt rating, credit quality, or creditworthiness, is related to default risk. **Default** refers to the nonpayment of interest and principal and/or the failure to adhere to the various terms and conditions (covenants) of the bond indenture. Companies that want to obtain bond financing from the capital markets, normally first seek a rating on their proposed debt issuance from one of several rating agencies such as Standard & Poor's, Moody's Investors Service, or Fitch Ratings. The aim of rating agencies is to rate debt so that its default risk is more accurately conveyed to, and priced by, the market. Each rating agency uses its own rating system, as Exhibit 8.5 shows. This exhibit includes the general description for each rating class—for example, AAA is assigned to debt of prime maximum safety (highest in creditworthiness).

EXHIBIT 8.5 Corporate Debt Ratings and Descriptions

Moody's	S&P	Fitch	Description
Aaa	AAA	AAA	Prime Maximum Safety
Aa1	AA+	AA+	High Grade, High Quality
Aa2	AA	AA	
Aa3	AA−	AA−	
A1	A+	A+	Upper-Medium Grade
A2	A	A	
A3	A−	A−	
Baa1	BBB+	BBB+	Lower-Medium Grade
Baa2	BBB	BBB	
Baa3	BBB−	BBB−	
Ba1	BB+	BB+	Non-Investment Grade
Ba2	BB	BB	Speculative
Ba3	BB−	BB−	
B1	B+	B+	Highly Speculative
B2	B	B	
B3	B−	B−	
Caa1	CCC+	CCC	Substantial Risk
Caa2	CCC		In Poor Standing
Caa3	CCC−		
Ca			Extremely Speculative
C			May be in Default
		DDD	Default
		DD	
	D	D	

MANAGERIAL DECISION | **You Are the Vice President of Finance**

Your company is currently rated B1/B+ by the Moody's and S&P credit rating agencies, respectively. You are considering restructuring to increase your company's credit rating. What types of restructurings might you consider? What benefits will your company receive from those restructurings? What costs will your company incur to implement such restructurings? [Answer, p. 8-33]

What Determines Credit Ratings?

Verizon bonds are rated A3, A−, and A by Moody's, S&P, and Fitch, respectively, as of 2010. It is this rating, in conjunction with the maturity of Verizon's bonds, that establishes the market interest rate and the bonds' selling price. There are a number of considerations that affect the rating of a bond. **Standard & Poor's** lists the following factors, categorized by business risk and financial risk, among its credit rating criteria:

Business Risk	**Financial Risk**
Industry characteristics	Financial characteristics
Competitive position (marketing, technology, efficiency, regulation)	Financial policy
	Profitability
	Capital structure
Management	Cash flow protection
	Financial flexibility

Debt ratings convey information primarily to debt investors who are interested in assessing the probability that the borrower will make interest and principal payments on time. If a company defaults on its debt, debt holders seek legal remedies, including forcing the borrower to liquidate its assets to settle obligations. However, in forced liquidations, debt holders rarely realize the entire amounts owed to them.

It's important to bear in mind that debt ratings are opinions. Rating agencies use several financial ratios to assess default risk. A partial listing of ratios utilized by Moody's, together with median averages for various ratings, is in Exhibit 8.6. In examining the ratios, recall that debt is increasingly more risky as we move from the first row, Aaa, to the last, C.

EXHIBIT 8.6 | Ratio Values for Different Risk Classes of Corporate Debt*

	EBITA/ Avg AT	EBITA/ Int Exp	EBITA Margin	Oper Margin	(FFO + Int Exp)/ Int Exp	FFO/ Debt	RCF/Net Debt	Debt/ EBITDA	Debt/ Book Cap	CAPEX/ Dep
Aaa......	20.6%	25.6	24.9%	22.8%	23.8	129.5%	83.2%	0.7	20.7%	1.2
Aa.......	12.6%	12.5	21.6%	20.5%	13.6	51.8%	39.4%	1.6	39.3%	1.2
A........	11.8%	7.5	15.0%	14.9%	8.3	40.2%	30.7%	1.9	43.7%	1.0
Baa......	9.0%	4.4	13.1%	12.4%	6.1	27.4%	26.6%	2.7	45.4%	1.1
Ba.......	8.3%	3.1	12.4%	10.9%	4.5	22.3%	23.5%	3.3	50.8%	1.1
B........	6.6%	1.4	9.1%	7.8%	2.6	11.7%	11.6%	5.1	73.8%	0.9
C........	2.3%	0.4	2.8%	3.1%	1.4	3.1%	3.2%	7.7	100.5%	0.7

* Table reports 2010 median values; from Moody's Financial Metrics™, Key Ratios by rating and industry for North American nonfinancial corporations: December 2010 (reproduced with permission).

Ratio	Definition
EBITA/Average Assets	EBITA/Average of Current and Previous Year Assets
EBITA/Interest Expense	EBITA/Interest Expense
EBITA Margin	EBITA/Net Revenue
Operating Margin	Operating Profit/Net Revenue
(FFO + Interest Exp)/Interest Exp	(Funds From Operations + Interest Expense)/Interest Expense
FFO/Debt	Funds From Operations/(Short-Term Debt + Long-Term Debt)
RCF/Debt	(FFO − Preferred Dividends − Common Dividends − Minority Dividends)/(Short-Term Debt + Long-Term Debt)
Debt/EBITDA	(Short-Term Debt + Long-Term Debt)/EBITDA
Debt/Book Capitalization	(Short-Term Debt + Long-Term Debt)/(Short-Term Debt + Long-Term Debt + Deferred Taxes + Minority Interest + Book Equity)
CAPEX/Depreciation Exp	Capital Expenditures/Depreciation Expense

where: EBITA = Earnings from continuing operations before interest, taxes, and amortization
        EBITDA = Earnings from continuing operations before interest and taxes, depreciation, and amortization
        FFO = Net income from continuing operations plus depreciation, amortization, deferred income taxes, and other noncash items

A review of these ratios indicates that Moody's considers the following factors, grouped by area of emphasis, as relevant in evaluating a company's ability to meet its debt service requirements:

1. Profitability ratios (first four metrics in footnote to Exhibit 8.6)
2. Cash flow ratios (metrics five, six and seven in footnote to Exhibit 8.6)
3. Solvency ratios (last three metrics in footnote to Exhibit 8.6)

Further, these ratios are variants of many of the ratios we describe in Module 4 and elsewhere in the book. Other relevant debt-rating factors include the following:

> **IFRS Alert**
> Unlike GAAP, IFRS requires that companies treat the conversion feature like an option and revalue it each period using the appropriate market rate. The difference in value each period is recorded as non-operating revenue or expense.

■ **Collateral** Companies can provide security for debt by pledging certain assets against the bond. This is like mortgages on assets. To the extent debt is secured, the debt holder is in a preferred position vis-à-vis other creditors.

■ **Covenants** Debt agreements (indentures) can restrict the behavior of the issuing company so as to protect debt holders. For example, covenants commonly prohibit excessive dividend payment, mergers and acquisitions, further borrowing, and commonly prescribe minimum levels for key liquidity and solvency ratios. These covenants provide debt holders an element of control over the issuer's operations because, unlike equity investors, debt holders have no voting rights.

■ **Options** Options are sometimes written into debt contracts. Examples are options to convert debt into stock (so that debt holders have a stake in value creation) and options allowing the issuing company to repurchase its debt before maturity (usually at a premium).

RESEARCH INSIGHT | **Valuation of Debt Options**

Debt instruments can include features such as conversion options, under which the debt can be converted to common stock. Such conversion features are not accounted for separately under GAAP. Instead, convertible debt is accounted for just like debt with no conversion features (unless the conversion option can be separately traded). However, option-pricing models can be used to estimate the value of such debt features even when no market for those features exists. Empirical results suggest that those debt features represent a substantial part of debt value. These findings contribute to the current debate regarding the separation of compound financial instruments into debt and equity portions for financial statement presentation and analysis.

Any Trends with Credit Ratings?

Companies strive to maintain an "investment-grade" credit rating. This allows them to sell their bonds to institutional investors such as pension, mutual and other investment funds. Many institutional investors will not invest in bonds that are rated below investment-grade rating of Baa3 (Moody's) or BBB- (S&P and Fitch). To achieve a higher credit rating, companies must have lower financial leverage and maintain greater liquidity. This is costly to shareholders. As a result, financial managers face a difficult task in finding the optimal capital structure that maximizes returns to shareholders while reducing the cost of debt capital.

The data suggest that corporate CFOs try to maintain investment-grade bond ratings but do not rely markedly on costly equity capital. Following is a graph of the distribution of companies across bond ratings. Ratings of A and Baa account for nearly half of all corporate issuers, while those issuers in the top ratings categories (Aaa and Aa) account for 14% of corporate issuers (source: Moody's financial metrics 2010).

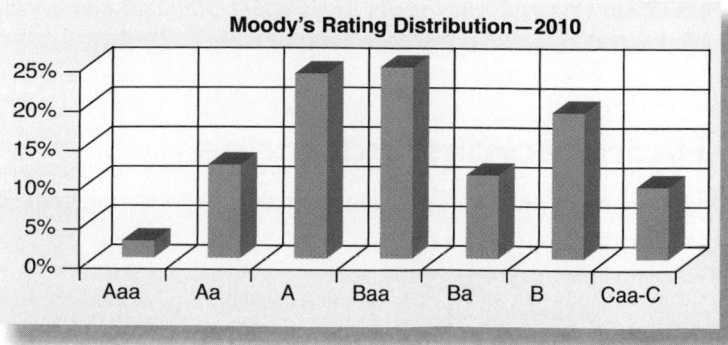

Trends in Financial Ratios Over Time

Many of the ratios we discuss above vary over time with changes in the level of macroeconomic activity. For example, financial leverage (as measured by, average assets / average equity) declined during the recovery following the recession of 2001, then increased as equity declined in the recessionary period of 2007–2008, see below. Measures of profitability and interest coverage exhibited similar trends.

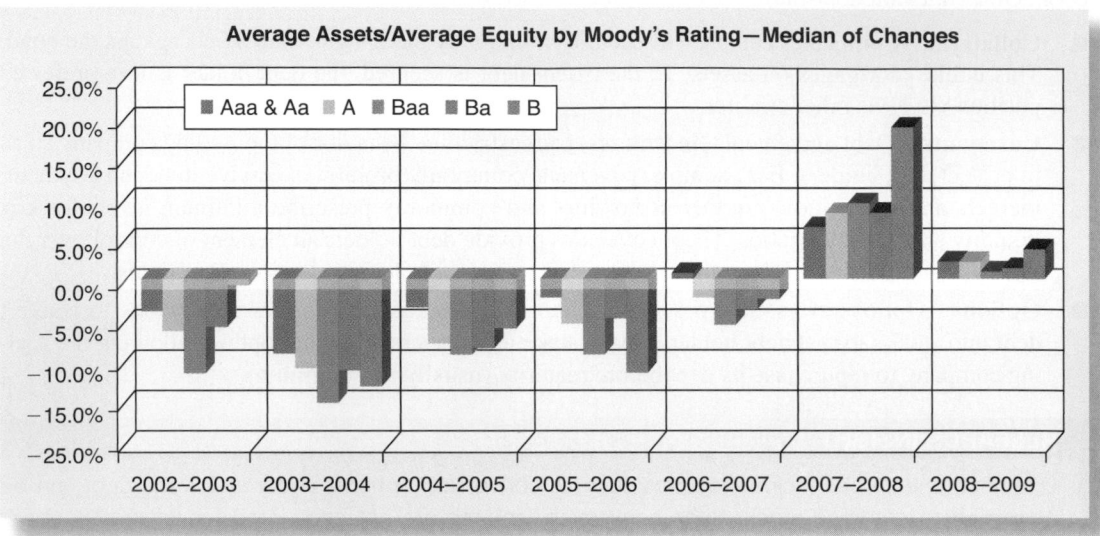

Changes in the level of financial leverage also differed across industries as shown below. Specifically, capital-intensive industries, such as transportation and capital goods reduced financial leverage during the recovery to a much greater extent than did retail and other consumer-related industries.

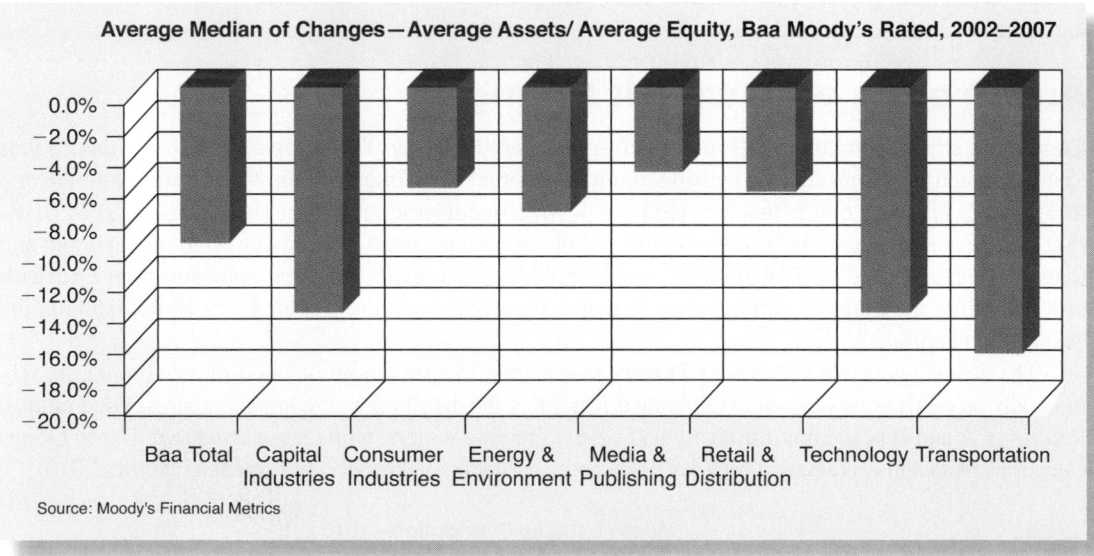

Financial Ratios across Industries

Financial ratios also differ across industries as demonstrated in the following graphic:

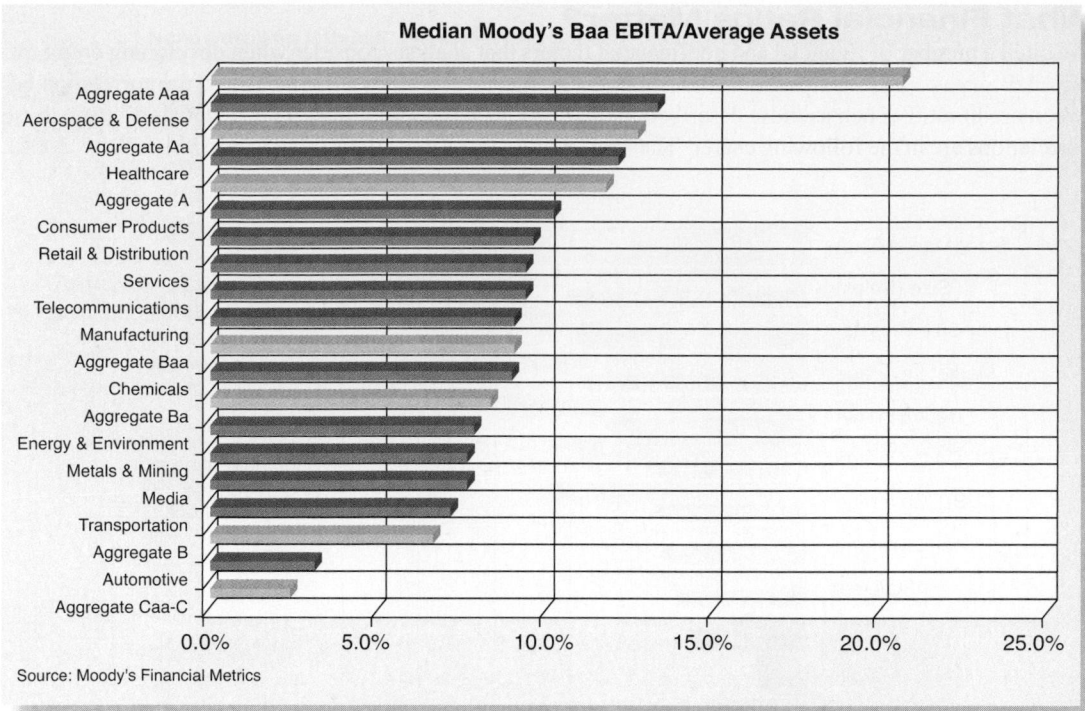

Median EBITA to average assets (a measure of return on assets) for Baa issuers is highest for defense contractors, healthcare, consumer products, and telecommunications industries. This probably reflects a larger required asset base in those industries as the median EBITA margin (EBITA as a percent of revenues) is highest for media companies, which rank much lower on the return measure, as shown in the following graphic.

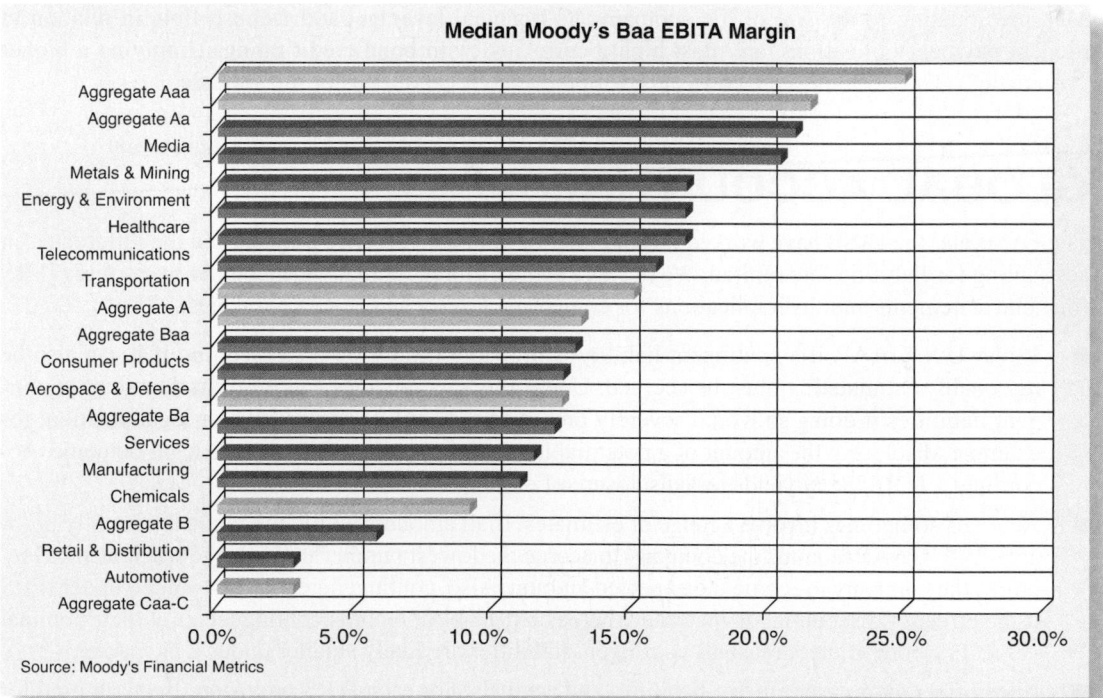

What Financial Ratios Matter?

We cited a number of financial and nonfinancial factors that analysts consider when developing credit ratings. **UBS** (www.UBS.com), global investment banking and securities firm, measured the correlation between credit ratios, such as those described in this section, and bond ratings. The "t-statistics" from those correlations are in the following chart ("The New World of Credit Ratings," *UBS Investment Bank*, 2004):

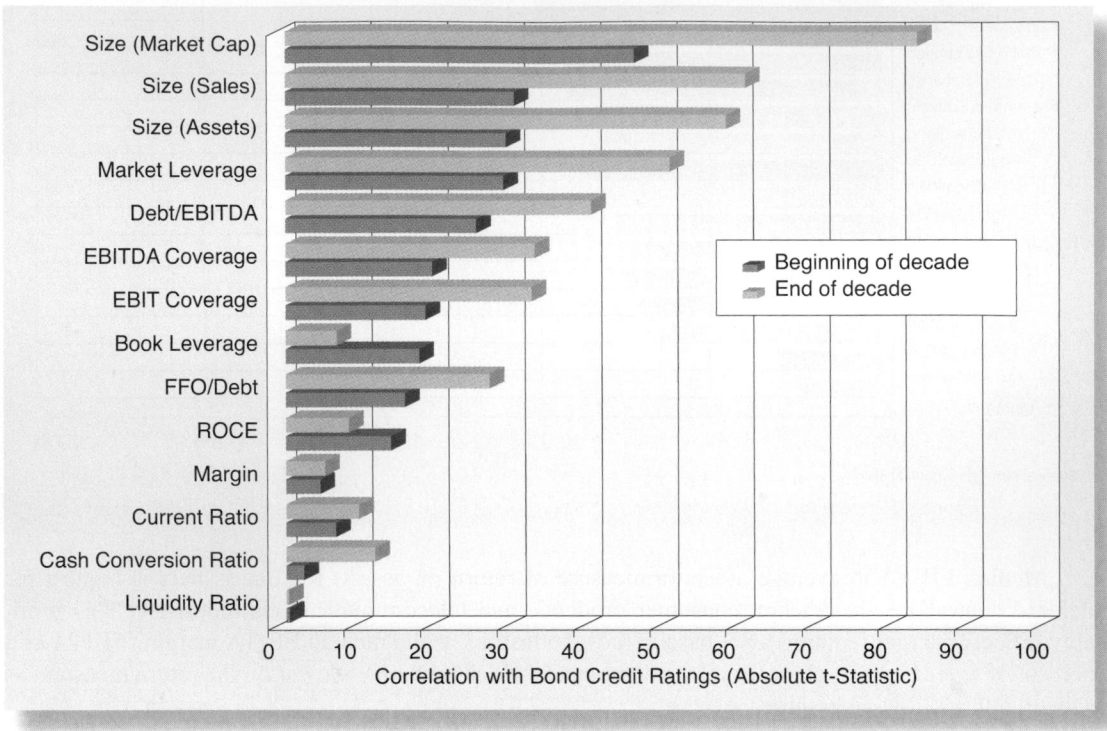

Measures relating to the size of the company, its financial leverage, and its cash flow in relation to its debt payment obligations, are most highly correlated with bond credit ratings (implying a higher "t-statistic"). These findings are consistent with the analysis and focus of this module.

GLOBAL ACCOUNTING

The FASB and the IASB have worked on a number of joint convergence projects and the differences in accounting for liabilities are limited. We list here some differences that we encounter in studying IFRS financial statements and the implications for comparing GAAP and IFRS companies.

■ Under U.S. GAAP, if a contingent liability is probable it must be disclosed *and* if it can also be reasonably estimated, it must be accrued. Under IFRS, companies can limit disclosure of contingent liabilities if doing so would severely prejudice the entity's competitive or legal position; for example, disclosing the amount of a potential loss on a lawsuit could sway the legal outcome. Accordingly, IFRS likely yields less disclosure of contingencies.

■ Accruals sometimes involve a range of estimates. If all amounts within the range are equally probable, U.S. GAAP requires the company to accrue the lowest number in the range whereas IFRS requires the company to accrue the expected amount. Also, contingencies are discounted under IFRS if the effect of discounting is material whereas U.S. GAAP records contingencies at their nominal value. For both of these reasons, contingent liabilities are likely smaller under U.S. GAAP.

■ IFRS offers more disclosure of liabilities and accruals. For each IFRS provision (the term used for accrued liabilities and expenses), the company must reconcile the opening and closing carrying amounts, describe any additional provision for the period, and explain any reversals for the period. Reconciliation is less prevalent under U.S. GAAP (required for example for allowance for doubtful accounts, warranty accruals, restructuring accruals). Recall that an over-accrual in one period shifts income to a subsequent period when the accrual is reversed. This increased transparency under IFRS might make it easier to spot earnings management.

■ U.S. GAAP classifies convertible debt as a liability. Under IFRS, convertible debt is split into two parts: debt and equity (reflecting the option to convert). The amount assigned to each part is based on fair values when the debt is issued. So, for equivalent convertible debt outstanding, IFRS balance sheets show a smaller amount for the debt portion.

MODULE-END REVIEW

On January 1, assume that Sprint Nextel Corporation issues $300,000 of 15-year, 10% bonds payable for $351,876, yielding an effective semiannual interest rate of 4%. Interest is payable semiannually on June 30 and December 31. (1) Show computations to confirm the issue price of $351,876, and (2) complete Sprint's financial statement effects template for (a) bond issuance, (b) semiannual interest payment and premium amortization on June 30 of the first year, and (c) semiannual interest payment and premium amortization on December 31 of the first year.

The solution is on page 8-47.

APPENDIX 8A: Compound Interest

This appendix explains the concepts of present and future value, which are useful for our analysis purposes.

Present Value Concepts

Would you rather receive a dollar now or a dollar one year from now? Most people would answer, a dollar now. Intuition tells us that a dollar received now is more valuable than the same amount received sometime in the future. Sound reasons exist for choosing the dollar now, the most obvious of which concerns risk. Because the future is uncertain, any number of events can prevent us from receiving the dollar a year from now. To avoid this risk, we choose the earlier date. Another reason is that the dollar received now could be invested. That is, one year from now, we would have the dollar and the interest earned on that dollar.

Present Value of a Single Amount

Risk and interest factors yield the following generalizations: (1) the right to receive an amount of money now, its **present value**, is worth more than the right to receive the same amount later, its **future value**; (2) the longer we must wait to receive an amount, the less attractive the receipt is; (3) the greater the interest rate the greater the amount we will receive in the future. (Putting 2 and 3 together we see that the difference between the present value of an amount and its future value is a function of both interest rate and time, that is, Principal × Interest Rate × Time); and (4) the more risk associated with any situation, the higher the interest rate.

To illustrate, let's compute the amount we would need to receive today (the present value) that would be equivalent to receiving $100 one year from now if money can be invested at 10%. We recognize intuitively that, with a 10% interest rate, the present value (the equivalent amount today) will be less than $100. The $100 received in the future must include 10% interest earned for the year. Thus, the $100 received in one year (the future value) must be 1.10 times the amount received today (the present value). Dividing $100/1.10, we obtain a present value of $90.91 (rounded). This means that we would do as well to accept $90.91 today as to wait one year and receive $100. To confirm the equality of the $90.91 receipt now to a $100 receipt one year later, we calculate the future value of $90.91 at 10% for one year as follows:

$90.91 × 1.10 × 1 year = $100 (rounded)

To generalize, we compute the present value of a future receipt by *discounting* the future receipt back to the present at an appropriate interest rate (also called the *discount rate*). We present this schematically below:

| Present Value
$90.91 | ← | Discounted for
1 year at 10% | ← | Future Value
$100 |

If either the time period or the interest rate were increased, the resulting present value would decrease. If more than one time period is involved, our future receipts include interest on interest. This is called *compounding*.

Time Value of Money Tables

Appendix A near the end of the book includes time value of money tables. Table 1 is a present value table that we can use to compute the present value of future amounts. A present value table provides present value factors (multipliers) for many combinations of time periods and interest rates that determine the present value of $1.

Present value tables are used as follows. First, determine the number of interest compounding periods involved (three years compounded annually are 3 periods, and three years compounded semiannually are 6 periods). The extreme left-hand column indicates the number of periods. It is important to distinguish between years and compounding periods. The table is for compounding periods (years × number of compounding periods per year).

Next, determine the interest rate per compounding period. Interest rates are usually quoted on a *per year* (annual) basis. The rate per compounding period is the annual rate divided by the number of compounding periods per year. For example, an interest rate of 10% *per year* would be 10% per period if compounded annually, and 5% *per period* if compounded semiannually.

Finally, locate the present value factor, which is at the intersection of the row of the appropriate number of compounding periods and the column of the appropriate interest rate per compounding period. Multiply this factor by the dollars that will be paid or received in the future.

All values in Table 1 are less than 1.0 because the present value of $1 received in the future is always smaller than $1. As the interest rate increases (moving from left to right in the table) or the number of periods increases (moving from top to bottom), the present value factors decline. This illustrates two important facts: (1) present values decline as interest rates increase, and (2) present values decline as the time lengthens. Consider the following three cases:

Calculator
N = 2
I/Yr = 5
PMT = 0
FV = 100
PV = 90.703

Case 1. Compute the present value of $100 to be received one year from today, discounted at 10% compounded semiannually:

> Number of periods (one year, semiannually) = 2
> Rate per period (10%/2) = 5%
> Multiplier = 0.90703
> Present value = $100.00 × 0.90703 = $90.70 (rounded)

Calculator
N = 4
I/Yr = 5
PMT = 0
FV = 100
PV = 82.270

Case 2. Compute the present value of $100 to be received two years from today, discounted at 10% compounded semiannually:

> Number of periods (two years, semiannually) = 4
> Rate per period (10%/2) = 5%
> Multiplier = 0.82270
> Present value = $100 × 0.82270 = $82.27 (rounded)

Calculator
N = 4
I/Yr = 6
PMT = 0
FV = 100
PV = 79.209

Case 3. Compute the present value of $100 to be received two years from today, discounted at 12% compounded semiannually:

> Number of periods (two years, semiannually) = 4
> Rate per period (12%/2) = 6%
> Multiplier = 0.79209
> Present value = $100 = 0.79209 = $79.21 (rounded)

In Case 2, the present value of $82.27 is less than for Case 1 ($90.70) because the time increased from two to four compounding periods—the longer we must wait for money, the lower its value to us today. Then in Case 3, the present value of $79.21 was lower than in Case 2 because, while there were still four compounding periods, the interest rate per year was higher (12% annually instead of 10%)—the higher the interest rate the more interest that could have been earned on the money and therefore the lower the value today.

Present Value of an Annuity

In the examples above, we computed the present value of a single amount (also called a lump sum) made or received in the future. Often, future cash flows involve the same amount being paid or received each period. Examples include semiannual interest payments on bonds, quarterly dividend receipts, or monthly insurance premiums. If the payment or the receipt (the cash flow) is equally spaced over time and each cash flow is the same dollar amount, we have an *annuity*. One way to calculate the present value of the annuity would be to calculate the present value of each future cash flow separately. However, there is a more convenient method.

To illustrate, assume $100 is to be received at the end of each of the next three years as an annuity. When annuity amounts occur at the *end of each period*, the annuity is called an *ordinary annuity*. As shown below, the present value of this ordinary annuity can be computed from Table 1 by computing the present value of each of the three individual receipts and summing them (assume a 5% annual rate).

Future Receipts (ordinary annuity)			PV Multiplier (Table 1)		Present Value
Year 1	Year 2	Year 3			
$100			× 0.95238	=	$ 95.24
	$100		× 0.90703	=	90.70
		$100	× 0.86384	=	86.38
			2.72325		$272.32

Calculator
N = 3
I/Yr = 5
PMT = 100
FV = 0

PV = 272.32

Table 2 in Appendix A provides a single multiplier for computing the present value of an ordinary annuity. Referring to Table 2 in the row for three periods and the column for 5%, we see that the multiplier is 2.72325. When applied to the $100 annuity amount, the multiplier gives a present value of $272.33. As shown above, the same present value (with 1 cent rounding error) is derived by summing the three separate multipliers from Table 1. Considerable computations are avoided by using annuity tables.

Bond Valuation

Recall that a bond agreement specifies a pattern of future cash flows—usually a series of interest payments and a single payment of the face amount at maturity, and bonds are priced using the prevailing market rate on the day the bond is sold. This is the case for the original bond issuance and for subsequent open-market sales. The market rate on the date of the sale is the rate we use to determine the bond's market value (its price). That rate is the bond's *yield*. The selling price of a bond is determined as follows:

1. Use Table 1 to compute the present value of the future principal payment at the prevailing market rate.
2. Use Table 2 to compute the present value of the future series of interest payments (the annuity) at the prevailing market rate.
3. Add the present values from steps 1 and 2.

We illustrate in Exhibit 8A.1 the price of $100,000, 8%, four-year bonds paying interest semiannually and sold when the prevailing market rate was (1) 8%, (2) 10% or (3) 6%. Note that the price of 8% bonds sold to yield 8%

EXHIBIT 8A.1   Calculation of Bond Price Using Present Value Tables

Future Cash Flows	Multiplier (Table 1)	Multiplier (Table 2)	Present Values at 4% Semiannually
(1) $100,000 of 8%, 4-year bonds with interest payable semiannually priced to yield 8%.			
Principal payment, $100,000 (a single amount received after 8 semiannual periods).	0.73069		$ 73,069
Interest payments, $4,000 at end of each of 8 semiannual periods.		6.73274	26,931
Present value (issue price) of bonds			$100,000

Calculator
N = 8
I/Yr = 4
PMT = 4,000
FV = 100,000

PV = 100,000

Future Cash Flows	Multiplier (Table 1)	Multiplier (Table 2)	Present Values at 5% Semiannually
(2) $100,000 of 8%, 4-year bonds with interest payable semiannually priced to yield 10%.			
Principal payment, $100,000 (a single amount received after 8 semiannual periods).	0.67684		$ 67,684
Interest payments, $4,000 at end of each of 8 semiannual periods.		6.46321	25,853
Present value (issue price) of bonds			$ 93,537

Calculator
N = 8
I/Yr = 5
PMT = 4,000
FV = 100,000

PV = 93,536.79

Future Cash Flows	Multiplier (Table 1)	Multiplier (Table 2)	Present Values at 3% Semiannually
(3) $100,000 of 8%, 4-year bonds with interest payable semiannually priced to yield 6%.			
Principal repayment, $100,000 (a single amount received after 8 semiannual periods).	0.78941		$ 78,941
Interest payments, $4,000 at end of each of 8 semiannual periods.		7.01969	28,079
Present value (issue price) of bonds			$107,020

Calculator
N = 8
I/Yr = 3
PMT = 4,000
FV = 100,000

PV = 107,019.69

is the face (or par) value of the bonds. A bond issue price of $93,537 (discount bond) yields 10%. A bond issue price of $107,020 (premium bond) yields 6%.

Time Value of Money Computations Using a Calculator

We can use a financial calculator for time value of money computations. There are five important function keys for these calculations. If we know values for four of those five, the calculator will compute the fifth. Those function keys are:

N	Number of compounding (or discounting) periods
I/Yr	Interest (yield) rate per period—entered in % terms, for example, 12% is entered as 12 and not as 0.12. This key is labeled "interest per year" but it can handle any rate per different compounding periods; for example, if we have semiannual interest payments, our compounding periods are semiannual and the interest rate is the semiannual rate.
FV	Future value of the cash flows, this is a lump sum
PMT	Annuity (coupon) per discount period
PV	Present value of the cash flows, this is a lump sum

Calculator inputs follow for the three examples in Exhibit 8A.1. In these examples, the unknown value is the bond price, which is the present value (PV) of the bond's cash flows. (For additional instruction on entering inputs into a specific calculator, or how to do more complicated computations, review the calculator's user manual or review online calculator tutorials.)

Example (1), Exhibit 8A.1: Bond priced to yield 8%.

N	=	8 (4 years × 2 periods per year = 8 semiannual periods)
I/Yr	=	4 (8% annual yield ÷ 2 periods per year = 4% semiannually)
FV	=	100,000 (face value, which is the lump sum that must be repaid in the future)
PMT	=	4,000 ($100,000 × 4% semiannual coupon rate)
PV	= 100,000	(output obtained from calculator)

Example (2), Exhibit 8A.1: Bond priced to yield 10%.

N = 8   I/Yr = 5   FV = 100,000   PMT = 4,000   PV = 93,537

Example (3), Exhibit 8A.1: Bond priced to yield 6%.

N = 8   I/Yr = 3   FV = 100,000   PMT = 4,000   PV = 107,020

Future Value Concepts

Future Value of a Single Amount

The **future value** of a single sum is the amount that a specific investment is worth at a future date if invested at a given rate of compound interest. To illustrate, suppose that we decide to invest $6,000 in a savings account that pays 6% annual interest and we intend to leave the principal and interest in the account for five years. We assume that interest is credited to the account at the end of each year. The balance in the account at the end of five years is determined using Table 3 in Appendix A, which gives the future value of a dollar, as follows:

Principal × Factor = Future Value
$6,000   × 1.33823 = $8,029

The factor 1.33823 is at the intersection of the row for five periods and the column for 6%.

Next, suppose that the interest is credited to the account semiannually rather than annually. In this situation, there are 10 compounding periods, and we use a 3% semiannual rate (one-half the annual rate because there are two compounding periods per year). The future value calculation follows:

Principal × Factor = Future Value
$6,000   × 1.34392 = $8,064

Calculator
N = 5
I/Yr = 6
PMT = 0
PV = 6,000

FV = 8,029

Calculator
N = 10
I/Yr = 3
PMT = 0
PV = 6,000

FV = 8,064

Future Value of an Annuity

If, instead of investing a single amount, we invest a specified amount *each period*, then we have an annuity. To illustrate, assume that we decide to invest $2,000 at the end of each year for five years at an 8% annual rate of return. To determine the accumulated amount of principal and interest at the end of five years, we refer to Table 4 in Appendix A, which furnishes the future value of a dollar invested at the end of each period. The factor 5.86660 is in the row for five periods and the column for 8%, and the calculation is as follows:

Periodic Payment	×	Factor	=	Future Value
$2,000	×	5.86660	=	$11,733

> **Calculator**
> N = 5
> I/Yr = 8
> PMT = 2,000
> PV = 0
> FV = 11,733

If we decide to invest $1,000 at the end of each six months for five years at an 8% annual rate of return, we would use the factor for 10 periods at 4%, as follows:

Periodic Payment	×	Factor	=	Future Value
$1,000	×	12.00611	=	$12,006

> **Calculator**
> N = 10
> I/Yr = 4
> PMT = 1,000
> PV = 0
> FV = 12,006

APPENDIX 8B: Economics of Gains and Losses on Bond Repurchases

Is a reported gain or loss on bond repurchases before maturity of economic substance? The short answer is no. To illustrate, assume that on January 1, a company issues $50 million face value bonds with an 8% annual coupon rate. The interest is to be paid semiannually (4% each semiannual period) for a term of five years (10 semiannual periods), at which time the principal will be repaid. If investors demand a 10% annual return (5% semiannually) on their investment, the bond price is computed as follows:

Present value of semiannual interest ($2,000,000 × 7.72173)	=	$15,443,460
Present value of principal ($50,000,000 × 0.61391)	=	30,695,500
Present value of bond	=	$46,138,960

> **Calculator**
> N = 10
> I/Yr = 5
> PMT = 2,000,000
> FV = 50,000,000
> PV = 46,138,132*
> *rounding difference

This bond's amortization table follows:

EXHIBIT 8B.1	Bond Discount Amortization Table				
	[A] ([E] × market%) Interest Expense	**[B]** (Face × coupon%) Cash Interest Paid	**[C]** ([A] − [B]) Discount Amortization	**[D]** (Prior bal − [C]) Discount Balance	**[E]** (Face − [D]) Bond Payable, Net
Period					
0				$3,861,040	$46,138,960
1	$2,306,948	$2,000,000	$306,948	3,554,092	46,445,908
2	2,322,295	2,000,000	322,295	3,231,797	46,768,203
3	2,338,410	2,000,000	338,410	2,893,387	47,106,613
4	2,355,331	2,000,000	355,331	2,538,056	47,461,944
5	2,373,097	2,000,000	373,097	2,164,959	47,835,041
6	2,391,752	2,000,000	391,752	1,773,207	48,226,793
7	2,411,340	2,000,000	411,340	1,361,867	48,638,133
8	2,431,907	2,000,000	431,907	929,960	49,070,040
9	2,453,502	2,000,000	453,502	476,458	49,523,542
10	2,476,458	2,000,000	476,458	0	50,000,000

Next, assume we are at period 6 (three years after issuance) and the market rate of interest for this bond has risen from 10% to 12%. The firm decides to retire (redeem) the outstanding bond issue and finances the retirement by issuing new bonds. That is, it issues bonds with a face amount equal to the market value of the old bonds and uses the proceeds to retire the existing (old) bonds. The new bond issue will have a term of two years (four semiannual periods), the remaining life of the existing bond issue.

At the end of the third year, there are four $2,000,000 semiannual interest payments remaining on the old bonds, plus the repayment of the face amount of the bond due at the end of the fourth semiannual period. The present value of this cash flow stream, discounted at the current 12% annual rate (6% semiannual rate) is:

<table>
<tr><td>Present value of semiannual interest ($2,000,000 × 3.46511)</td><td>=</td><td>$ 6,930,220</td></tr>
<tr><td>Present value of principal ($50,000,000 × 0.79209)</td><td>=</td><td>39,604,500</td></tr>
<tr><td>Present value of bond</td><td>=</td><td>$46,534,720</td></tr>
</table>

Calculator
N = 4
I/Yr = 6
PMT = 2,000,000
FV = 50,000,000

PV = 46,534,894*

*rounding difference

This means the company pays $46,534,720 to redeem a bond that is on its books at a carrying amount of $48,226,793. The difference of $1,692,073 is reported as a gain on repurchase (also called *redemption*). GAAP requires this gain be reported in income from continuing operations unless it meets the tests for treatment as an extraordinary item (the item is both unusual and infrequent).

Although the company reports a gain in its income statement, has it actually realized an economic gain? Consider that this company issues new bonds that carry a coupon rate of 12% (6% semiannually) for $46,534,720. If we assume that those bonds are sold with a coupon rate equal to the market rate, they will sell at par (no discount or premium). The interest expense per six-month period, therefore, equals the interest paid in cash, or $2,792,083 ($46,534,720 × 6%). Total expense for the four-period life of the bond is $11,168,333 ($2,792,083 × 4). That amount, plus the $46,534,720 face amount of bonds due at maturity, results in total bond payments of $57,703,053. Had this company not redeemed the bonds, it would have paid four additional interest payments of $2,000,000 each plus the face amount of $50,000,000 at maturity, for total bond payments of $58,000,000. On the surface, it appears that the firm is able to save $296,947 by redeeming the bonds and, therefore, reports a gain. (Also, total interest expense on the new bond issue is $3,168,333 [$11,168,333 − $8,000,000] more than it would have recorded under the old issue; so, although it is recording a present gain, it also incurs future higher interest costs which are not recognized under GAAP.)

However, this gain is misleading. Specifically, this gain has two components. First, interest payments increase by $792,083 per year ($2,792,083 − $2,000,000). Second, the face amount of the bond that must be repaid in four years decreases by $3,465,280 ($50,000,000 − $46,534,720). To evaluate whether a real gain has been realized, we must consider the present value of these cash outflows and savings. The present value of the increased interest outflow, a four-period annuity of $792,083 discounted at 6% per period, is **$2,744,655** ($792,083 × 3.46511). The present value of the reduced maturity amount, $3,465,280 in four periods, is **$2,744,814** ($3,465,280 × 0.79209)—note: the two amounts differ by $159, which is due to rounding. The conclusion is that the two amounts are the same.

This analysis shows there is no real economic gain from early redemption of debt. The present value of the increased interest payments exactly offsets the present value of the decreased amount due at maturity. Why, then, does GAAP yield a gain? The answer lies in use of historical costing. Bonds are reported at amortized cost, that is, the face amount less any applicable discount or plus any premium. These amounts are a function of the bond issue price and its yield rate at issuance, which are both fixed for the life of the bond. Market prices for bonds, however, vary continually with changes in market interest rates. Companies do not adjust bond liabilities for these changes in market value. As a result, when companies redeem bonds, their carrying amount differs from market value and GAAP reports a gain or loss equal to this difference.

GUIDANCE ANSWERS

MANAGERIAL DECISION **You Are the Vice President of Finance**

You might consider the types of restructuring that would strengthen financial ratios typically used to assess liquidity and solvency by the rating agencies. Such restructuring includes generating cash by reducing inventory, reallocating cash outflows from investing activities (PPE) to debt reduction, and issuing stock for cash and using the proceeds to reduce debt (an equity for debt recapitalization). These actions increase liquidity or reduce financial leverage and, thus, should improve debt rating. An improved debt rating will attract more investors because your current debt rating is below investment grade and is not a suitable investment for many professionally managed portfolios. An improved debt rating will also lower the interest rate on your debt. Offsetting these benefits are costs such as the following: (1) potential loss of sales from inventory stock-outs; (2) potential future cash flow reductions and loss of market power from reduced PPE investments; and (3) costs of equity issuances (equity costs more than debt because investors demand a higher return to compensate for added risk and, unlike interest payments, dividends are not tax deductible for the company), which can yield a net increase in the total cost of capital. All cost and benefits must be assessed before you pursue any restructuring.

Superscript ^A(^B) denotes assignments based on Appendix 8A (8B).

DISCUSSION QUESTIONS

Q8-1. What does the term *current liabilities* mean? What assets are usually used to settle current liabilities?

Q8-2. What is an accrual? How do accruals impact the balance sheet and the income statement?

Q8-3. What is the difference between a bond's coupon rate and its market interest rate (yield)?

Q8-4. Why do companies report a gain or loss when they repurchase their bonds? Is this a real economic gain or loss?

Q8-5. How do credit (debt) ratings affect the cost of borrowing for a company?

Q8-6. How would you interpret a company's reported gain or loss on the repurchase of its bonds?

**Assignments with the ● in the margin are available in an online homework system.
See the Preface of the book for details.**

MINI EXERCISES

M8-7. **Interpreting a Contingent Liability Footnote** (LO1)

NCI Building Systems reports the following footnote to one of its recent 10-Ks related to its manufac-turing of metal coil coatings and metal building components.

> We have discovered the existence of trichloroethylene in the ground water at our Southlake, Texas facility. Horizontal delineation concentrations in excess of applicable residential assess-ment levels have not been fully identified. We have filed an application with the Texas Commis-sion of Environmental Quality ("TCEQ") for entry into the voluntary cleanup program. The cost of required remediation, if any, will vary depending on the nature and extent of the contamina-tion. As of October 28, we have accrued $0.1 million to complete site analysis and testing. At this time, we cannot estimate a loss for any potential remediation costs, but we do not believe there will be a material adverse effect on our Consolidated Financial Statements.

NCI Building Systems (NCS)

a. How has NCI reported this potential liability on its balance sheet?

b. Does the $0.1 million accrual "to complete site analysis and testing" relate to a contingent liability? Explain.

M8-8. **Analyzing and Computing Financial Statement Effects of Interest** (LO2)

DeFond Company signed a 90-day, 8% note payable for $7,200 on December 16. Use the financial state-ment effects template to illustrate the year-end December 31 accounting adjustment DeFond must make.

M8-9. **Analyzing and Determining Liability Amounts** (LO1)

For each of the following situations, indicate the liability amount, if any, that is reported on the balance sheet of Basu, Inc., at December 31, 2012.

a. Basu owes $110,000 at year-end 2012 for inventory purchases.

b. Basu agreed to purchase a $28,000 drill press in January 2013.

c. During November and December of 2012, Basu sold products to a customer and warranted them against product failure for 90 days. Estimated costs of honoring this 90-day warranty during 2013 are $2,200.

d. Basu provides a profit-sharing bonus for its executives equal to 5% of reported pretax annual income. The estimated pretax income for 2012 is $600,000. Bonuses are not paid until January of the follow-ing year.

M8-10. **Interpreting Relations among Bond Price, Coupon, Yield, and Credit Rating** (LO2, 3)

The following appeared in Yahoo! Finance (reports.finance.yahoo.com) regarding outstanding bonds by Boston Scientific.

Boston Scientific (BSX)

Price	Coupon (%)	Maturity	Yield to Maturity (%)	Fitch Ratings
120.71	7.375	2040	5.873	BBB
108.42	6.000	2020	4.805	BBB

a. Discuss the relation among the coupon rate, price, and yield for the bond maturing in 2040.

b. Compare the yields on the two bonds. Why are the yields different when the credit ratings are the same?

M8-11. Determining Gain or Loss on Bond Redemption   (LO2)

On April 30, one year before maturity, Nissim Company retired $200,000 of its 9% bonds payable at the current market price of 101 (101% of the bond face amount, or $200,000 × 1.01 = $202,000). The bond book value on April 30 is $197,600, reflecting an unamortized discount of $2,400. Bond interest is currently fully paid and recorded up to the date of retirement. What is the gain or loss on retirement of these bonds? Is this gain or loss a real economic gain or loss? Explain.

M8-12. Interpreting Bond Footnote Disclosures   (LO2)

Bristol-Myers Squibb
Company (BMY)

Bristol-Myers Squibb reports the following long-term debt as part of its MD&A in its 2010 10-K.

		Obligations Expiring by Period					
Maturity Date	Total	2011	2012	2013	2014	2015	Later Years
Long-term debt ...	$4,749	—	—	$597	—	—	$4,152

a. What does the $597 million in 2013 indicate about Bristol-Myers Squibb's future payment obligations?

b. What implications does this payment schedule have for our evaluation of Bristol-Myers Squibb's liquidity and solvency?

M8-13. Classifying Liability-Related Accounts into Balance Sheet or Income Statement   (LO2)

Indicate the proper financial statement classification (balance sheet or income statement) for each of the following liability-related accounts.

a. Gain on Bond Retirement
b. Discount on Bonds Payable
c. Mortgage Notes Payable
d. Bonds Payable

e. Bond Interest Expense
f. Bond Interest Payable (due next period)
g. Premium on Bonds Payable
h. Loss on Bond Retirement

M8-14. Interpreting Bond Footnote Disclosures   (LO2)

Comcast Corporation
(CMCSA)

Comcast Corporation reports the following information from the Management Discussion and Analysis section of its 2010 10-K.

Debt Covenants   We and our cable subsidiaries that have provided guarantees are subject to the covenants and restrictions set forth in the indentures governing our public debt securities and in the credit agreements governing our bank credit facilities. We and the guarantors are in compliance with the covenants, and we believe that neither the covenants nor the restrictions in our indentures or loan documents will limit our ability to operate our business or raise additional capital. We test our compliance with our credit facilities' covenants on an ongoing basis. The only financial covenant in our $6.8 billion revolving credit facility due 2013 pertains to leverage (ratio of debt to operating income before depreciation and amortization). As of December 31, 2010, we met this financial covenant by a significant margin. We do not expect to have to further reduce debt or improve operating results in order to continue to comply with this financial covenant.

a. The financial ratios to which Comcast refers are similar to those discussed in the section on credit ratings and the cost of debt. What effects might these ratios have on the degree of freedom that management has in running Comcast?

b. Violation of debt covenants can be a serious event that could limit our ability to operate our business provision in the debt contract. What pressures might management face if the company's ratios are near covenant limits?

M8-15. Analyzing Financial Statement Effects of Bond Redemption   (LO2)

Holthausen Corporation issued $400,000 of 11%, 20-year bonds at 108 on January 1, 2007. Interest is payable semiannually on June 30 and December 31. Through January 1, 2012, Holthausen amortized $5,000 of the bond premium. On January 1, 2012, Holthausen retired the bonds at 103. Use the financial statement effects template to illustrate the bond retirement at January 1, 2012.

M8-16. Analyzing Financial Statement Effects of Bond Redemption (LO2)

Dechow, Inc., issued $250,000 of 8%, 15-year bonds at 96 on July 1, 2007. Interest is payable semiannually on December 31 and June 30. Through June 30, 2012, Dechow amortized $3,000 of the bond discount. On July 1, 2012, Dechow retired the bonds at 101. Use the financial statement effects template to illustrate the bond retirement.

M8-17. Analyzing and Computing Accrued Interest on Notes (LO2)

Compute any interest accrued for each of the following notes payable owed by Penman, Inc., as of December 31, 2012 (assume a 365-day year).

Lender	Issuance Date	Principal	Coupon Rate (%)	Term
Nissim......	11/21/2012	$18,000	10%	120 days
Klein	12/13/2012	14,000	9	90 days
Bildersee....	12/19/2012	16,000	12	60 days

M8-18. Interpreting Credit Ratings (LO3)

Cummins reports the following information in the Management Discussion & Analysis section of its 2010 10-K report.   Cummins (CMI)

> **Credit Ratings**   A number of our contractual obligations and financing agreements, such as our revolving credit facility, have restrictive covenants and/or pricing modifications that may be triggered in the event of downward revisions to our corporate credit rating. There were no downgrades of our credit ratings in 2010 that have impacted these covenants or pricing modifications. In January 2011, Fitch affirmed our ratings and upgraded our outlook to positive. In September 2010, Standard and Poor's raised our senior unsecured debt ratings to BBB+ and changed our outlook to stable. In July 2010, Moody's Investors Service, Inc. raised our senior unsecured debt ratings to Baa2 . . . Our ratings and outlook from each of the credit rating agencies as of the date of filing are shown in the table below.

Credit Rating Agency	Senior L-T Debt Rating	S-T Debt Rating	Outlook
Moody's Investors Service, Inc......	Baa2	Non-Prime	Stable
Standard and Poor's	BBB+	NR	Stable
Fitch	BBB+	BBB+	Positive

a. Cummins reduced the level of its financial leverage during 2010. Why does the reduction in financial leverage result in an increase in the credit ratings for Cummins' debt?

b. What effect will a higher credit rating have on Cummins' borrowing costs? Explain.

M8-19. Computing Bond Issue Price (LO2)

Bushman, Inc., issues $500,000 of 9% bonds that pay interest semiannually and mature in 10 years. Compute the bond issue price assuming that the prevailing market rate of interest is:

a. 8% per year compounded semiannually.

b. 10% per year compounded semiannually.

M8-20. Computing Issue Price for Zero Coupon Bonds (LO2)

Abarbanell, Inc., issues $500,000 of zero coupon bonds that mature in 10 years. Compute the bond issue price assuming that the bonds' market rate is:

a. 8% per year compounded semiannually.

b. 10% per year compounded semiannually.

M8-21. Determining the Financial Statement Effects of Accounts Payable Transactions (LO1)

Petroni Company had the following transactions relating to its accounts payable.

a. Purchases $300 of inventory on credit.

b. Sells inventory for $420 on credit.

c. Records $300 cost of sales for transaction *b.*

d. Receives $420 cash toward accounts receivable.

e. Pays $300 cash to settle accounts payable.

Use the financial statement effects template to identify the effects (both amounts and accounts) for these transactions.

M8-22.   Computing Bond Issue Price and Preparing an Amortization Table in Excel (LO2)
On January 1, 2012, Bushman, Inc., issues $500,000 of 9% bonds that pay interest semiannually and mature in 10 years (December 31, 2021).

a. Using the Excel PRICE function, compute the issue price assuming that the bonds' market rate is 8% per year compounded semiannually. (Use 100 for the redemption value to get a price as a percentage of the face amount, and use 1 for the basis.)

b. Prepare an amortization table in Excel to demonstrate the amortization of the book (carrying) value to the $500,000 maturity value at the end of the 20th semiannual period.

EXERCISES

E8-23.   Analyzing and Computing Accrued Warranty Liability and Expense (LO1)
Waymire Company sells a motor that carries a 60-day unconditional warranty against product failure. From prior years' experience, Waymire estimates that 2% of units sold each period will require repair at an average cost of $100 per unit. During the current period, Waymire sold 69,000 units and repaired 1,000 of those units.

a. How much warranty expense must Waymire report in its current-period income statement?

b. What warranty liability related to current-period sales will Waymire report on its current period-end balance sheet? (*Hint:* Remember that some units were repaired in the current period.)

c. What analysis issues must we consider with respect to reported warranty liabilities?

E8-24.   Analyzing Contingent and Other Liabilities (LO1)
The following independent situations represent various types of liabilities. Analyze each situation and indicate which of the following is the proper accounting treatment for the company: (a) record a liability on the balance sheet, (b) disclose the liability in a financial statement footnote, or (c) neither record nor disclose any liability.

1. A stockholder has filed a lawsuit against **Clinch Corporation**. Clinch's attorneys have reviewed the facts of the case. Their review revealed that similar lawsuits have never resulted in a cash award and it is highly unlikely that this lawsuit will either.

2. **Foster Company** signed a 60-day, 10% note when it purchased items from another company.

3. The Environmental Protection Agency notifies **Shevlin Company** that a state where it has a plant is filing a lawsuit for groundwater pollution against Shevlin and another company that has a plant adjacent to Shevlin's plant. Test results have not identified the exact source of the pollution. Shevlin's manufacturing process often produces by-products that can pollute groundwater.

4. **Sloan Company** manufactured and sold products to a retailer that later sold the products to consumers. The Sloan Company will replace the product if it is found to be defective within 90 days of the sale to the consumer. Historically, 1.2% of the products are returned for replacement.

E8-25.   Recording and Analyzing Warranty Accrual and Payment (LO1)
Refer to the discussion of and excerpt from the Harley-Davidson warranty reserve on page 8-9 to answer the following questions.

Harley-Davidson (HOG)

a. Using the financial statement effects template, record separately the accrual of warranty liability relating (1) to the "Warranties issued during the period" and (2) "Recalls and changes to preexisting warranty obligations" and (3) to the "Settlements made during the period."

b. Does the level of Harley-Davidson's warranty accrual appear to be reasonable?

E8-26.   Analyzing and Computing Accrued Wages Liability and Expense (LO1)
Demski Company pays its employees on the 1st and 15th of each month. It is March 31 and Demski is preparing financial statements for this quarter. Its employees have earned $25,000 since the 15th of March and have not yet been paid. How will Demski's balance sheet and income statement reflect the accrual of wages on March 31? What balance sheet and income statement accounts would be incorrectly reported if Demski failed to make this accrual (for each account indicate whether it would be overstated or understated)?

E8-27.   Analyzing and Reporting Financial Statement Effects of Bond Transactions (LO2)
On January 1, Hutton Corp. issued $300,000 of 15-year, 10% bonds payable for $351,876, yielding an effective interest rate of 8%. Interest is payable semiannually on June 30 and December 31. (a) Show computations to confirm the issue price of $351,876. (b) Indicate the financial statement effects using the template for (1) bond issuance, (2) semiannual interest payment and premium amortization on June 30 of the first year, and (3) semiannual interest payment and premium amortization on December 31 of the first year.

E8-28.   Analyzing and Reporting Financial Statement Effects of Mortgages   (LO2)

On January 1, Piotroski, Inc., borrowed $700,000 on a 12%, 15-year mortgage note payable. The note is to be repaid in equal semiannual installments of $50,854 (payable on June 30 and December 31). Each mortgage payment includes principal and interest. Interest is computed using the effective interest method. Indicate the financial statement effects using the template for (a) issuance of the mortgage note payable, (b) payment of the first installment on June 30, and (c) payment of the second installment on December 31.

E8-29.   Assessing the Effects of Bond Credit Rating Changes   (LO3)

Ford reports the following information from the Risk Factors and the Management Discussion and Analysis sections of its 2010 10-K report.

Ford (F)

> **Credit Ratings**   Our short-term and long-term debt is rated by four credit rating agencies designated as nationally recognized statistical rating organizations ("NRSROs") by the Securities and Exchange Commission:
> - Dominion Bond Rating Service Limited ("DBRS");
> - Fitch, Inc. ("Fitch");
> - Moody's Investors Service, Inc. ("Moody's"); and
> - Standard & Poor's Rating Services, a division of The McGraw-Hill Companies ("S&P").
>
> Lower credit ratings generally result in higher borrowing costs and reduced access to capital markets. In 2005 and 2006, the credit ratings assigned to Ford Credit were lowered to below investment grade, which increased its unsecured borrowing costs and restricted its access to the unsecured debt markets. In response, Ford Credit increased its use of securitization transactions (including other structured financings) and other sources of funding. In 2010, although Ford Credit experienced several credit rating upgrades and its credit spreads narrowed considerably, its credit ratings are still below investment grade. Ford Credit's higher credit ratings have provided it more economical access to the unsecured debt markets, but it is still utilizing asset-backed securitization transactions for a substantial amount of its funding . . . Over time, and particularly in the event of any credit rating downgrades, market volatility, market disruption, or other factors, Ford Credit may reduce the amount of receivables it purchases or originates because of funding constraints . . . A significant reduction in the amount of receivables Ford Credit purchases or originates would significantly reduce its ongoing profits and could adversely affect its ability to support the sale of Ford vehicles. The following ratings actions have been taken by these NRSROs since the filing of our Quarterly Report on Form 10-Q for the quarter ended September 30, 2010:
>
> **Ford**
> - On January 28, 2011, Moody's affirmed Ford Motor Company's ratings and changed the rating outlook to positive from stable.
> - On January 28, 2011, Fitch upgraded Ford's corporate rating to BB from BB- , the senior secured rating to BBB- from BB+, and the senior unsecured rating to BB- from B. Fitch also changed the outlook to positive from stable.
> - On February 1, 2011, S&P upgraded Ford's corporate credit rating to BB- from B+, the senior secured debt rating to BB+ from BB and the senior unsecured debt rating to B+ from B. The outlook remains positive.
>
> **Ford Credit**
> - On January 28, 2011, Moody's affirmed Ford Credit's ratings and changed the rating outlook to positive from stable.
> - On January 28, 2011, Fitch upgraded Ford Credit's corporate rating to BB from BB- . Fitch also affirmed the senior unsecured rating at BB- and the short-term rating at B. Fitch changed the outlook to positive from stable.
> - On February 1, 2011, S&P upgraded Ford Credit's corporate credit rating to BB- from B+ and its senior unsecured debt rating to BB- from B+. The outlook remains positive.

    a. What financial ratios do credit rating companies such as the four NRSROs listed above, use to evaluate the relative riskiness of borrowers?

    b. Why might an increase in credit ratings result in lower interest costs and increase Ford's access to credit markets?

    c. What type of actions can Ford take to improve its credit ratings?

E8-30.   Analyzing and Reporting Financial Statement Effects of Bond Transactions   (LO2)

Lundholm, Inc., reports financial statements each December 31 and issues $500,000 of 9%, 15-year bonds dated May 1, 2012, with interest payments on October 31 and April 30. Assuming the bonds are sold at par on May 1, 2012, complete the financial statement effects template to reflect the following events: (a) bond issuance, (b) the first semiannual interest payment, and (c) retirement of $300,000 of the bonds at 101 on November 1, 2012.

E8-31.   Analyzing and Reporting Financial Statement Effects of Bond Transactions   (LO2)

On January 1, 2012, McKeown, Inc., issued $250,000 of 8%, 9-year bonds for $220,776, which implies a market (yield) rate of 10%. Semiannual interest is payable on June 30 and December 31 of each year. (a) Show computations to confirm the bond issue price. (b) Indicate the financial statement effects using the template for (1) bond issuance, (2) semiannual interest payment and discount amortization on June 30, 2012, and (3) semiannual interest payment and discount amortization on December 31, 2012.

E8-32.   Analyzing and Reporting Financial Statement Effects of Bond Transactions   (LO2)

On January 1, 2012, Shields, Inc., issued $800,000 of 9%, 20-year bonds for $879,172, yielding a market (yield) rate of 8%. Semiannual interest is payable on June 30 and December 31 of each year. (a) Show computations to confirm the bond issue price. (b) Indicate the financial statement effects using the template for (1) bond issuance, (2) semiannual interest payment and premium amortization on June 30, 2012, and (3) semiannual interest payment and premium amortization on December 31, 2012.

Deere & Co (DE)

E8-33.   Determining Bond Prices, Interest Rates, and Financial Statement Effects   (LO2)

Deere & Company's 2010 10-K reports the following footnote relating to long-term debt for its equipment operations subsidiary. Deere's borrowings include $300 million, 7.125% notes, due in 2031 (highlighted below).

Long-term borrowings at October 31 consisted of the following in millions of dollars:

Notes and debentures	2010	2009
6.95% notes due 2014: ($700 principal) Swapped $300 to variable interest rate of 1.25%—2009	$ 763	$ 800
4.375% notes due 2019	750	750
8-1/2% debentures due 2022	105	105
6.55% debentures due 2028	200	200
5.375% notes due 2029	500	500
8.10% debentures due 2030	250	250
7.125% notes due 2031	300	300
Other notes	461	168
Total	$3,329	$3,073

A recent price quote (from Yahoo! Finance Bond Center) on Deere's 7.125% notes follows.

Type	Issuer	Price	Coupon (%)	Maturity	YTM (%)	Current Yield (%)	Fitch Rating	Callable
Corp	Deere & CO	131.84	7.125	2031	4.650	5.404	A	No

This price quote indicates that Deere's 7.125% notes have a market price of 131.84 (131.84% of face value), resulting in a yield to maturity of 4.65%.

a. Assuming that these notes were originally issued at par value, what does the market price reveal about interest rate changes since Deere issued its notes? (Assume that Deere's credit rating has remained the same.)

b. Does the change in interest rates since the issuance of these notes affect the amount of interest expense that Deere reports in its income statement? Explain.

c. How much cash would Deere have to pay to repurchase the 7.125% notes at the quoted market price of 131.84? (Assume no interest is owed when Deere repurchases the notes.) How would the repurchase affect Deere's current income?

d. Assuming that the notes remain outstanding until their maturity, at what market price will the notes sell on their due date in 2031?

E8-34.^A   Computing Present Values of Single Amounts and Annuities   (LO2)

Refer to Tables 1 and 2 in Appendix A near the end of the book to compute the present value for each of the following amounts:

a. $90,000 received 10 years hence if the annual interest rate is:

    1.   8% compounded annually.
    2.   8% compounded semiannually.

   b. $1,000 received at the end of each year for the next eight years discounted at 10% compounded annually.

   c. $600 received at the end of each six months for the next 15 years if the interest rate is 8% per year compounded semiannually.

   d. $500,000 received 10 years hence discounted at 10% per year compounded annually.

E8-35. Analyzing and Reporting Financial Statement Effects of Bond Transactions (LO2)
   On January 1, 2012, Trueman Corporation issued $600,000 of 20-year, 11% bonds for $554,860, yielding a market (yield) rate of 12%. Interest is payable semiannually on June 30 and December 31. (a) Confirm the bond issue price. (b) Indicate the financial statement effects using the template for (1) bond issuance, (2) semiannual interest payment and discount amortization on June 30, 2012, and (3) semiannual interest payment and discount amortization on December 31, 2012.

E8-36. Analyzing and Reporting Financial Statement Effects of Bond Transactions (LO2)
   On January 1, 2012, Verrecchia Company issued $400,000 of 5-year, 13% bonds for $446,329, yielding a market (yield) rate of 10%. Interest is payable semiannually on June 30 and December 31. (a) Confirm the bond issue price. (b) Indicate the financial statement effects using the template for (1) bond issuance, (2) semiannual interest payment and premium amortization on June 30, 2012, and (3) semiannual interest payment and premium amortization on December 31, 2012.

PROBLEMS

P8-37. Interpreting Term Structures of Coupon Rates and Yield Rates (LO2, 3)
   PepsiCo, Inc. reports $20,112 million of long-term debt outstanding as of December 2010 in the following schedule to its 10-K report.

PepsiCo, Inc.
(PEP)

Debt Obligations and Commitments

Short-Term Debt Obligations ($ millions)	2010	2009
Current maturities of long-term debt	$ 113	$102
Commercial paper (0.2%)	2,632	—
Notes due 2011 (4.4%)	1,513	—
Other borrowings (5.3% and 6.7%)	640	362
	$4,898	$464

Long-Term Debt Obligations ($ millions)	2010	2009
Notes due 2012 (3.1% and 1.9%)	$ 2,437	$1,079
Notes due 2013 (3.0% and 3.7%)	2,110	999
Notes due 2014 (5.3% and 4.0%)	2,888	1,026
Notes due 2015 (2.6%)	1,617	—
Notes due 2016-2040 (4.9% and 5.4%)	10,828	4,056
Zero coupon notes, due 2011–2012 (13.3%).	136	192
Other, due 2011–2019 (4.8% and 8.4%)	96	150
	20,112	7,502
Less: current maturities of long-term debt obligations	(113)	(102)
	$19,999	$7,400

In the first quarter of 2010, we issued . . . $1.0 billion of 5.50% senior notes maturing in 2040. A portion of the net proceeds from the issuance of these notes was used to finance our acquisitions of PBG and PAS and the remainder was used for general corporate purposes.

Long-Term Contractual Commitments

Payments Due by Period ($ millions)	Total	2011	2012–2013	2014–2015	2016 and beyond
Long-term debt obligations	$20,112	$113	$4,569	$4,322	$11,108

Credit Ratings   Our objective is to maintain credit ratings that provide us with ready access to global capital and credit markets at favorable interest rates. On February 24, 2010, Moody's

continued

continued from prior page

> Investors Service (Moody's) lowered the corporate credit rating of PepsiCo and its supported subsidiaries and the rating of PepsiCo's senior unsecured long-term debt to Aa3 from Aa2. Moody's rating for PepsiCo's short-term indebtedness was confirmed at Prime-1 and the outlook is stable. On March 17, 2010, Standard & Poor's Ratings Services (S&P) lowered PepsiCo's corporate credit rating to A from A+ and lowered the rating of PepsiCo's senior unsecured long-term debt to A- from A+. S&P's rating for PepsiCo's short-term indebtedness was confirmed at A-1 and the outlook is stable. Any downgrade of our credit ratings by either Moody's or S&P, including any downgrade to below investment grade, could increase our future borrowing costs or impair our ability to access capital markets on terms commercially acceptable to us or at all.

As of June 2011, the price of the $1 billion 5.5% senior notes maturing in 2040 follows (from **Yahoo! Finance, reports.finance.yahoo.com**):

Type	Issuer	Price	Coupon(%)	Maturity	YTM(%)	Fitch Ratings	Callable
Corp	PEPSICO INC	108.13	5.500	15-Jan-2040	4.965	AA	No

Required

a. PepsiCo reports current maturities of long-term debt of $113 million as part of short-term debt. Why is this amount reported that way? PepsiCo reports $4,569 million of long-term debt due in 2012-2013. What does this mean? Is this amount important to our analysis of PepsiCo? Explain.

b. The $1 billion 5.50% senior notes maturing in 2040 are priced at 108.13 (108.13% of face value, or $1.0813 billion) as of June 2011, resulting in a yield to maturity of 4.965%. Assuming that the credit rating of PepsiCo has not changed, what does the pricing of this 5.5% coupon bond imply about interest rate changes since PepsiCo issued the bond?

c. What does the schedule of long-term contractual commitments reveal that might be useful in analyzing PepsiCo's liquidity?

d. Moody's Investors Service lowered the corporate credit rating of PepsiCo in 2010. Why might a reduction in credit ratings result in higher interest costs and restrict PepsiCo's access to credit markets?

e. What type of actions can PepsiCo take to improve its credit ratings?

P8-38.   **Interpreting Debt Footnotes on Interest Rates and Interest Expense**   (LO2)

CVS Caremark Corporation (CVS)

CVS Caremark Corporation discloses the following as part of its long-term debt footnote in its 2010 10-K.

BORROWING AND CREDIT AGREEMENTS

The following table is a summary of the Company's borrowings as of December 31.

In millions	2010	2009
Commercial paper	$ 300	$ 315
Floating rate notes due 2010	—	350
Floating rate notes due 2010	—	1,750
5.75% senior notes due 2011	800	800
Floating rate notes due 2011	300	300
4.875% senior notes due 2014	550	550
3.250% senior notes due 2015	550	–
6.125% senior notes due 2016	700	700
5.75% senior notes due 2017	1,750	1,750
6.60% senior notes due 2019	1,000	1,000
4.75% senior notes due 2020	450	–
6.25% senior notes due 2027	1,000	1,000
6.125% note due 2039	1,500	1,500
6.302% Enhanced Capital Advantage Preferred Securities	1,000	1,000
Mortgage notes payable	6	6
Capital lease obligations	151	154
	10,057	11,175
Less:		
Short-term debt (commercial paper)	(300)	(315)
Current portion of long-term debt	(1,105)	(2,104)
	$ 8,652	$ 8,756

CVS also discloses the following information.

> **Interest expense, net**—Interest expense, net of capitalized interest, was $539 million, $530 million and $530 million in 2010, 2009 and 2008, respectively. Interest paid totalled $583, $542 and $574 in 2010, 2009 and 2008, respectively.
>
> **Maturities of long-term debt**—The aggregate maturities of long-term debt for each of the five years subsequent to December 31, 2010 are $1.1 billion in 2011, $2 million in 2012, $1 million in 2013, $550 million in 2014, and $550 million in 2015.

The price of the $1,500 million 6.125% senior note due 2039 as of 2011 follows (from Yahoo! finance).

Maturity Date	Issuer	Security Type	Coupon	Current Price	Current Yield	Fitch Rating	Callable
2039	CVS Caremark (NYSE: CVS)	Corporate Debentures	6.125	106.68	5.649	BBB	No

Required

a. What is the average coupon rate (interest paid) and the average effective rate (interest expense) on the long-term debt? (*Hint:* Use the disclosure for interest expense.)

b. Does your computation of the coupon rate in part *a* seem reasonable given the footnote disclosure relating to specific bond issues? Explain.

c. Explain how the amount of interest paid can differ from the amount of interest expense recorded in the income statement.

d. On its 2010 balance sheet, CVS reports current maturities of long-term debt of $1,105 million as part of short-term debt. Why is this amount reported that way? Is this amount important to our analysis of CVS? Explain.

e. The $1,500 million 6.125% senior note due in 2039 is priced at 106.68 (106.68% of face value, or $1,600.2 million) as of 2011, resulting in a yield to maturity of 5.649%. Assuming that the credit rating of CVS has not changed, what does the pricing of this 6.125% coupon bond imply about interest rate changes since CVS issued the bond?

P8-39.   Analyzing Debt Terms, Yields, Prices, and Credit Ratings   (LO2, 3)

Reproduced below is the debt footnote from the 2011 10-K report of Dell Inc.

Dell Inc.
(DELL)

Long-Term Debt (In millions)	January 28, 2011	January 29, 2010
Notes		
$400 million issued on June 10, 2009, at 3.375% due June 2012 ..	$400	$401
$600 million issued on April 17, 2008, at 4.70% due April 2013	609	599
$500 million issued on September 7, 2010, at 1.40% due September 2013	499	—
$500 million issued on April 1, 2009, at 5.625% due April 2014	500	500
$700 million issued on September 7, 2010, at 2.30% due September 2015	700	—
$500 million issued on April 17, 2008, at 5.65% due April 2018	499	499
$600 million issued on June 10, 2009, at 5.875% due June 2019 ..	600	600
$400 million issued on April 17, 2008, at 6.50% due April 2038	400	400
$300 million issued on September 7, 2010, at 5.40% due September 2040	300	—
Senior Debentures		
$300 million issued on April 3, 1998 at 7.10% due April 2028	389	394
Other		
India term loan: entered into on October 15, 2009 at 8.9% due October 2011	—	24
Structured financing debt.	250	—
Total long-term debt.	5,146	3,417

continued

continued from prior page

Long-Term Debt (In millions)	January 28, 2011	January 29, 2010
Short-Term Debt		
Commercial paper	—	496
Structured financing debt	850	164
Other	1	3
Total short-term debt	851	663
Total debt	$5,997	$4,080

Aggregate future maturities of long-term debt at face value were as follows at January 28, 2011:

(in millions)	Maturities by Fiscal Year						
	2012	2013	2014	2015	2016	Thereafter	Total
Aggregate future maturities of long-term debt outstanding	$ —	$595	$1,155	$500	$700	$2,100	$5,050

There is an $86 difference between the total referenced in this table and the $5,146 referenced for long-term debt in the table above. The difference arises because the maturity table reports the face value of the debt $(5,050). The first table above reports the carrying value (net book value) of the debt. Many of the notes are not carried at par. The largest difference is the senior debentures that have a premium of $89 (in millions).

Reproduced below is a summary of the market values of the Dell bonds maturing from 2021 to 2040 (from Morningstar, quicktake.morningstar.com).

Name	Maturity Date	Amount $	Price	Coupon %	Yield to Maturity %
Dell 5.4%	9/10/2040	300	94.8	5.4	5.77
Dell 6.5%	4/15/2038	400	111.9	6.5	5.63
Dell 4.625%	4/1/2021	400	104.9	4.625	4.01

Required

a. What is the amount of long-term debt reported on Dell's January 28, 2011, balance sheet? What are the scheduled maturities for this indebtedness? Why is information relating to a company's scheduled maturities of debt useful in an analysis of its financial condition?

b. Dell reported $199 million in interest expense in the notes to its 2011 income statement. In the note to its statement of cash flows, Dell indicates that the cash portion of this expense is $188 million. What could account for the difference between interest expense and interest paid? Explain.

c. Dell's long-term debt is rated A2 by Moody's, A− by S&P, and A by Fitch. What factors would be important to consider in attempting to quantify the relative riskiness of Dell compared with other borrowers? Explain.

d. Dell's $300 million 5.4% notes traded at 94.8, or 94.8% of par, as of December 2010. What is the market value of these notes on that date? How is the difference between this market value and the $300 million face value reflected in Dell's financial statements? What effect would the repurchase of this entire note issue have on Dell's financial statements? What does the 94.8 price tell you about the general trend in interest rates since Dell sold this bond issue? Explain.

e. Examine the yields to maturity of the three bonds in the table above. What relation do we observe between these yields and the maturities of the bonds? Also, explain why this relation applies in general.

P8-40. **Analyzing Notes, Yields, Financial Ratios, and Credit Ratings** (LO2, 3)

Comcast Corp. (CMCSA)

Comcast Corporation reports long-term senior notes totaling over $31 billion in its 2010 10-K. Following are selected ratios from Exhibit 8.6 computed for Comcast Corp. utilizing its 2010 data.

EBITA/Average assets	8.05%
EBITA/Interest expense	4.32
EBITA margin	24.52%
Operating margin	21.03%
(Funds from operations + Interest expense)/Interest expense	6.19
Funds from operations/Debt	35.58%
Debt/EBITDA	2.12
Debt/Book capitalization	30.18%

Required

This debt is rated "Baa" by Moody's, which is a lower medium grade. Examine the ratios provided above. *(Hint:* Compare Comcast's ratios to the ratio values reported in Exhibit 8.6.) What factors do you believe contribute to Comcast's credit rating being less than stellar?

IFRS APPLICATIONS

I8-41.   Interpreting a Contingent Liability Footnote   {LO1}

BP p.l.c.
(BP)

BP operates off-shore drilling rigs including rigs in the Gulf of Mexico. On April 20, 2010, explosions and fire on the Deepwater Horizon rig led to the death of 11 crew members and a 200-million-gallon oil spill in the Gulf of Mexico. BP's 2010 annual report (prepared under IFRS) included the following concerning estimates of contingent liabilities (provisions):

> In estimating the amount of the provision, BP has determined a range of possible outcomes for Individual and Business Claims, and State and Local Claims. . . . BP has concluded that a reasonable range of possible outcomes for the amount of the provision as at 31 December 2010 is $6 billion to $13 billion. BP believes that the provision recorded at 31 December 2010 of $9.2 billion represents a reliable best estimate from within this range of possible outcomes.

How did BP record the $9.2 billion estimate in its 2010 financial statements? How would the accounting for this provision differ if BP had prepared its financial statements in accordance with U.S. GAAP?

I8-42.   Interpreting Bond Footnote Disclosures   {LO2}

In May 2011, French real estate company Foncière des Régions issued convertible bonds with a total face value of €480 million. Each €1,000 bond included a conversion option whose fair value was estimated at €13. The average proceeds per €1,000 bond was €1,028.

a. Compute the total bond proceeds.
b. What portion of the bond proceeds is accounted for as debt under IFRS?
c. Had the company reported under U.S. GAAP what amount of the bond proceeds would be accounted for as debt?

I8-43.   Assessing the Effects of Bond Credit Rating Changes for Financial Statements   {LO3}

Deutsche Telekom AG

Deutsche Telekom AG, headquartered in Bonn, Germany, is the largest telecommunications company in Europe. The company uses IFRS to prepare its financial statements. The company's 2009 financial statements report the following:

> **Credit Quality**   In 2009, Fitch changed our long-term rating from A- to BBB+ with a stable outlook. Moody's Investor Service and Standard and Poor's maintained our long-term rating at Baa1 and BBB+ respectively with a stable outlook. A further decrease in our credit ratings below certain thresholds by various rating agencies would result in an increase in the interest rates on certain of our bonds and medium term notes due to step-up provisions and could raise the cost of our debt refinancing activities generally.
>
> **Step-up Provisions**   An improvement of our long-term senior unsecured debt ratings to A3 by Moody's and A- by Standard & Poor's would result in a 50 basis point decrease in interest rates due to relevant step-up provisions on bonds with an aggregate principal amount of approximately EUR 6.3 billion at December 31, 2009. A lowering of our long-term senior unsecured debt ratings below Baa1 by Moody's and BBB+ by Standard & Poor's would result in a 50 basis point increase in interest rates due to relevant step-up provisions on bonds and medium-term notes with an aggregate principal amount of approximately EUR 4.2 billion at December 31, 2009.

a. What is a credit rating in layperson terms?

b. Did the rating downgrade by Fitch move their credit rating closer to, or farther from, the Moody's and Standard & Poor's ratings? To answer this question, refer to Exhibit 8.5.

c. Based on the company's disclosures, conjecture about the purpose of a "step-up provision." Why would creditors add such a provision to a bond issue?

d. Compute the additional interest expense that Deutsche Telekom would incur if its credit ratings deteriorated by one notch. How much would be saved with a one-notch improvement in credit rating?

e. The company reported interest expense of €2,896 million in 2009. Would a credit deterioration impose significant income statement consequences? What other consequences could arise?

I8-44. **Analyzing Debt Terms, Yields, Prices, and Credit Ratings** (LO2, 3)

Statoil ASA (STO)

Statoil ASA, headquartered in Stavanger, Norway, is a fully integrated petroleum company. The company uses IFRS to prepare its financial statements. Reproduced below is the long-term debt note from its 2010 annual report.

At 31 December	Carrying amount in NOK million		Fair value in NOK million	
	2010	2009	2010	2009
Total financial liabilities.........	104,424	99,230	114,911	106,966
Less current portion............	4,627	3,268	4,627	3,268
Financial liabilities, non-current portion..........	99,797	95,962	110,284	103,698

Details of largest unsecured bonds

Bond agreement	Fixed interest rate	Issued (year)	Maturity (year)	Carrying amount in NOK million at 31 December	
				2010	2009
USD 1500 million	5.250%	2009	2019	8.738	8.613
USD 1250 million	3.125%	2010	2017	7.278	—
USD 900 million	2.900%	2009	2014	5.251	5.174
USD 750 million	5.100%	2010	2040	4.340	—
USD 500 million	3.875%	2009	2014	2.914	2.870
USD 500 million	5.125%	2004	2014	2.927	2.887
USD 500 million	6.500%	1998	2028	2.900	2.859
USD 481 million	7.250%	2000	2027	2.814	2.776
USD 300 million	7.750%	1993	2023	1.757	1.733
EUR 1300 million	4.375%	2009	2015	10.135	10.782
EUR 1200 million	5.625%	2009	2021	9.297	9.887
EUR 500 million	5.125%	1999	2011	3.903	4.148
GBP 800 million	6.875%	2009	2031	7.224	7.421
GBP 225 million	6.125%	1998	2028	2.040	2.096

Non-current financial liabilities maturity profile

At 31 December (in NOK million)	2010	2009
Years 2 and 3....................................	12,555	11,757
Years 4 and 5....................................	23,205	11,496
After 5 years....................................	64,037	72,709
Total repayment of non-current financial liabilities	99,797	95,962

Reproduced below is a summary of the market values, at December 2010, of the Statoil ASA bonds maturing from 2014 to 2040.

Currency	Maturity date	Amount Outstanding	Current price	Coupon	Yield
Statoil Asa USD	08/17/2017	1,250.0	101.4	3.125	2.90
Statoil Asa USD	08/17/2040	750.0	100.6	5.100	5.06
Statoil Asa USD	04/30/2014	500.0	111.2	3.875	1.74
Statoil Asa USD	04/30/2014	500.0	106.7	5.125	3.59

Required

a. What is the amount of total financial liabilities (debt) reported on Statoil's 2009 balance sheet? Of the total financial liabilities, what proportion is due within one year?

b. In what currencies has Statoil issued financial liabilities? Why do companies borrow money in foreign currencies?

c. What are the scheduled maturities for Statoil's indebtedness? Why is information relating to a company's scheduled maturities of debt useful in analyzing financial condition?

d. Statoil's long-term debt is rated AA- by Standard and Poor's and similarly by other credit agencies. What factors would be important to consider in quantifying the relative riskiness of Statoil compared to other borrowers? Explain.

e. Statoil's $1,250 million, 3.125% notes traded at 101.4, or 101.4% of par, as of December 2010. What is the market value of these notes on that date? How is the difference between this market value and the $1,250 million face value reflected on Statoil's financial statements? What does the 101.4 price tell you about the general trend in interest rates since Statoil sold this bond issue? Explain.

f. Examine the yields to maturity of the four bonds in the previous table. What relation do we observe between these yields and the maturities of the bonds? Explain why this relation applies in general.

MANAGEMENT APPLICATIONS

MA8-45.   Coupon Rate versus Effective Rate (LO2)

Assume that you are the CFO of a company that intends to issue bonds to finance a new manufacturing facility. A subordinate suggests lowering the coupon rate on the bond to lower interest expense and to increase the profitability of your company. Is the rationale for this suggestion a good one? Explain.

MA8-46.   Ethics and Governance: Bond Covenants (LO2)

Because lenders do not have voting rights like shareholders do, they often reduce their risk by invoking various bond covenants that restrict the company's operating, financing and investing activities. For example, debt covenants often restrict the amount of debt that the company can issue (in relation to its equity) and impose operating restrictions (such as the ability to acquire other companies or to pay dividends). Failure to abide by these restrictions can have serious consequences, including forcing the company into bankruptcy and potential liquidation. Assume that you are on the board of directors of a company that issues bonds with such restrictions. What safeguards can you identify to ensure compliance with those restrictions?

SOLUTIONS TO REVIEW PROBLEMS

Mid-Module Review 1

Solution

a. We know that accounts payable turnover is computed as cost of goods sold divided by average accounts payable. Thus, an increase in accounts payable turnover indicates that accounts payable have decreased relative to cost of goods sold (all else equal).

b. A decrease in accounts payable results in a decrease in net cash flows from operating activities because Verizon is using cash to pay bills more quickly.

c. Decreased accounts payable increases net operating working capital (all else equal), with a consequent decrease in cash flow. While unfavorable to cash flow, the more timely payment of accounts payable can improve supplier relations. Analysts must be aware of the costs and benefits of leaning on the trade to a greater or lesser extent.

Mid-Module Review 2

Solution

Yes. Verizon must recognize liabilities and expenses when incurred, regardless of when payment is made. Accruing expenses as incurred will match the expenses to the revenues they helped generate. Failure to recognize the wages owed to employees for the period would understate liabilities and overstate income. Verizon must reflect the wages earned and the related expense in its financial statements as follows:

	Balance Sheet							Income Statement		
Transaction	Cash Asset	+ Noncash Assets	= Liabil- ities	+ Contrib. Capital	+ Earned Capital		Rev- enues	− Expen- ses	= Net Income
Accrue $10,000 in wages expense			+10,000 Wages Payable		−10,000 Retained Earnings			+10,000 Wages Expense	= −10,000

WE 10,000
   WP 10,000
      WE
10,000 |
    WP
      | 10,000

Mid-Module Review 3

Solution

	Balance Sheet							Income Statement		
Transaction	Cash Asset	+ Noncash Assets	= Liabil- ities	+ Contrib. Capital	+ Earned Capital		Rev- enues	− Expen- ses	= Net Income
Jan 31: Accrue $26 interest expense*			+26 Interest Payable		−26 Retained Earnings			+26 Interest Expense	= −26

IE 26
  IP 26
     IE
26 |
   IP
     | 26

*Accrued interest = $10,000 × 0.06 × 16/365 = $26.

Module-End Review

Solution

1.

Calculator
N = 30
I/Yr = 4
PMT = 15,000
FV = 300,000

PV = 351,876.10

Issue price for $300,000, 15-year bonds that pay 10% interest semiannually, discounted at 8%:	
Present value of principal payment ($300,000 × 0.30832)	$ 92,496
Present value of semiannual interest payments ($15,000 × 17.29203).	259,380
Issue price of bonds.	$351,876

2.

Transaction	Balance Sheet						Income Statement			
	Cash Asset	+	Noncash Assets	=	Liabil- ities	+	Contrib. Capital	+	Earned Capital	
January 1: Issue 10% bonds	+351,876 Cash				+351,876 Long-Term Debt					
June 30: Pay interest and amortize bond premium[1]	−15,000 Cash				−925 Long-Term Debt				−14,075 Retained Earnings	
December 31: Pay interest and amortize bond premium[2]	−15,000 Cash				−962 Long-Term Debt				−14,038 Retained Earnings	

Rev- enues	−	Expen- ses	=	Net Income
	−		=	
	−	+14,075 Interest Expense	=	−14,075
	−	+14,038 Interest Expense	=	−14,038

```
Cash    351,876
  LTD        351,876
        Cash
351,876 |
        LTD
        | 351,876

IE        14,075
LTD          925
  Cash    15,000
        IE
14,075 |
        LTD
  925  |
        Cash
        | 15,000

IE        14,038
LTD          962
  Cash    15,000
        IE
14,038 |
        LTD
  962  |
        Cash
        | 15,000
```

[1] $300,000 × 0.10 × 6/12 = $15,000 cash payment; 0.04 × $351,876 = $14,075 interest expense; the difference of $925, is the bond premium amortization, which reduces the net bond carrying amount.

[2] 0.04 × ($351,876 − $925) = $14,038 interest expense. The difference between this amount and the $15,000 cash payment ($962) is the premium amortization, which reduces the net bond carrying amount.

Getty Images

AON CORPORATION

Aon Corporation provides risk management services, insurance and reinsurance brokerage, and human resource consulting and outsourcing. Aon aims to help its clients generate greater value from their employees by developing strategies to address human resource challenges, improve workforce performance, and streamline human resources operations. Its business has evolved as a result of organic growth and acquisitions, and it continues to extend, expand and create new human resources services that focus on its clients' changing workforce-related needs and challenges.

Aon serves its clients through the following two major segments:

- **Risk Solutions** Over 28,000 employees worldwide act as an advisor and insurance and reinsurance broker, helping clients manage their risks via consultation, as well as negotiation and placement of insurance risk

with insurance carriers through its global distribution network.

- **HR Solutions** Over 29,000 worldwide partners with organizations to tackle complex benefits, talent and related financial challenges, and improve business performance by designing, implementing, communicating and administering a range of human capital, retirement, investment management, health care, compensation and talent management strategies.

Each segment aims to help clients manage the complex human elements necessary to acquire, develop, motivate and retain the talent required to meet business objectives. As of 2011, Aon employed over 59,000 employees worldwide with nearly $8.5 billion in revenues.

Aon's value lies not in plant assets, such as land and buildings, but in the knowledge capital of its employees, most of whom are Aon shareholders. This module consid-

Reporting and Analyzing Owner Financing

LEARNING OBJECTIVES

LO1 Describe and illustrate accounting for contributed capital, including stock sales and repurchases, and equity-based compensation. (p. 9-4)

LO2 Explain and illustrate accounting for earned capital, including cash dividends, stock dividends, and comprehensive income. (p. 9-15)

LO3 Describe accounting for equity carve-outs and convertible debt. (p. 9-24)

ers how shareholders' investment is accounted for on a company's financial statements. We consider common stock features, stock options, share issuances, share repurchases, and dividend payments.

Aon has one class of stock. Of the 750 million shares that have been authorized for issuance, 385.9 million have been issued to date. It also has restricted stock and restricted stock units. This stock is awarded to employees as incentive compensation. As further incentive, it offers employee stock options. This module explains and assesses these various forms of equity-based compensation.

Aon has repurchased over 53.6 million shares of its stock at a purchase price of over $2 billion. Many companies routinely repurchase their common stock as it is the best use of excess cash when there exist no better outside investment opportunities. Some companies repurchase their stock to offset the dilutive effect of stock-based compensation programs. This module explains and analyzes stock repurchases. The module also discusses a variety

of equity transactions under the general heading of equity carve-outs and convertibles. These transactions include several methods by which companies seek to unlock hidden value for the benefit of their shareholders.

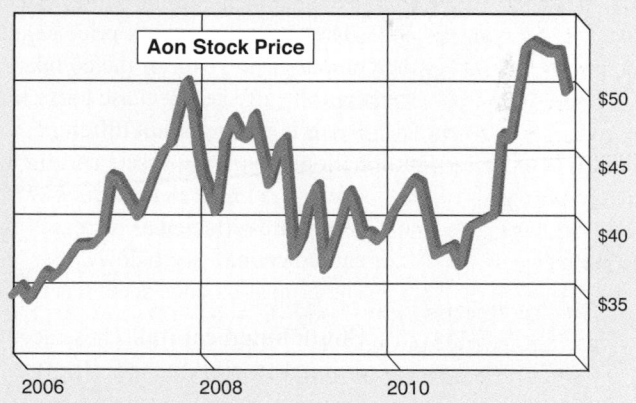

Source: Aon Corporation, 2010 Form 10-K; *The Wall Street Journal*, January 2012.

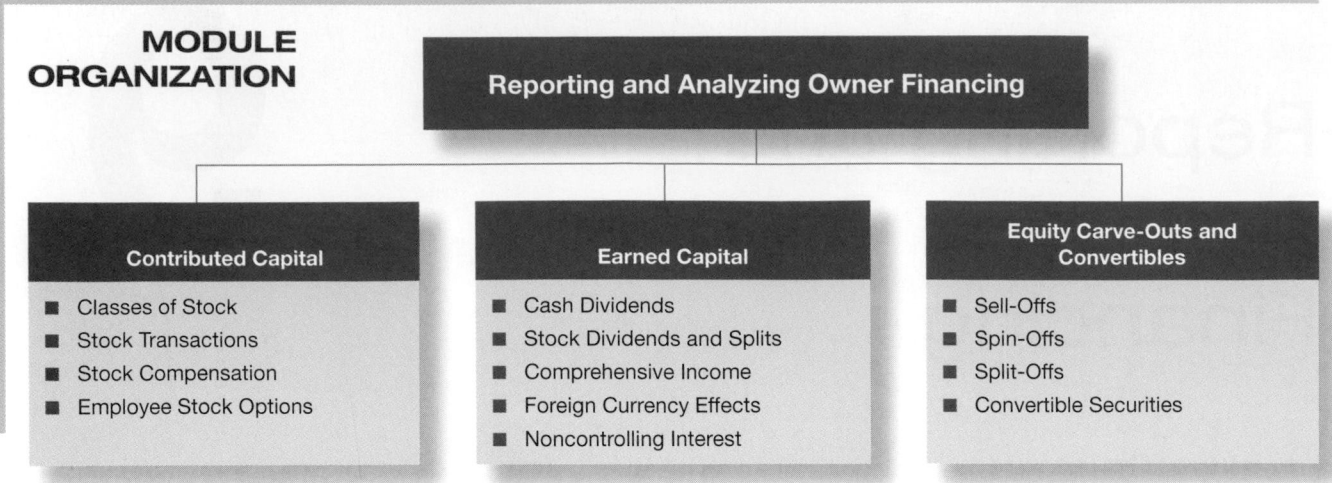

MODULE ORGANIZATION

Reporting and Analyzing Owner Financing

Contributed Capital
- Classes of Stock
- Stock Transactions
- Stock Compensation
- Employee Stock Options

Earned Capital
- Cash Dividends
- Stock Dividends and Splits
- Comprehensive Income
- Foreign Currency Effects
- Noncontrolling Interest

Equity Carve-Outs and Convertibles
- Sell-Offs
- Spin-Offs
- Split-Offs
- Convertible Securities

A company finances its assets through operating cash flows or it taps one or both of the following sources: either it borrows funds or it sells stock to shareholders. On average, companies obtain about half of their external financing from borrowed sources and the other half from shareholders. This module describes the issues relating to stockholders' equity, including the accounting for stock transactions (sales and repurchases of stock, dividends, stock-based compensation, and convertible securities). We also discuss equity carve-outs, a process by which companies can unlock substantial shareholder value via spin-offs and split-offs of business units into separate companies. Finally, we discuss the accumulated other comprehensive income and noncontrolling interest components of stockholders' equity.

When a company issues stock to the public, it records the receipt of cash (or other assets) and an increase in stockholders' equity, representing the shareholders' investment in the company. The increase in cash and equity is equal to the market price of the stock on the issue date multiplied by the number of shares sold.

Like bonds, stockholders' equity is accounted for at *historical cost*. Consequently, the company's financial statements do not reflect fluctuations in the market price of the stock subsequent to its issuance. The company's stock price results from market transactions that involve outside parties and not the company. However, if the company repurchases and/or resells shares of its own stock, the balance sheet will be affected because those transactions involve the company.

There is an important difference between accounting for stockholders' equity and accounting for transactions involving assets and liabilities: *there is never any gain or loss reported on the purchase and sale of a company's own stock or the payment of dividends to its shareholders*. Instead, these "gains and losses" are reflected as increases and decreases in stockholders' equity and do not affect net income (nor earned capital, see below).

The typical balance sheet has two broad categories of stockholders' equity:

1. **Contributed capital** These accounts report the proceeds received by the issuing company from original stock issuances. It often includes common stock, preferred stock, and additional paid-in capital. Netted against these contributed capital accounts is treasury stock, the amounts paid to repurchase shares of the issuer's stock from its investors, less the proceeds from the resale of such shares. Collectively, these accounts are referred to as contributed capital (or *paid-in capital*).

2. **Earned capital** This section consists of (a) retained earnings, which represent the cumulative income and losses of the company, less any dividends to shareholders, and (b) accumulated other comprehensive income (AOCI), which includes changes to equity that have not yet impacted income and are, therefore, not reflected in retained earnings.

In addition, many companies report an equity account called *noncontrolling interest*, which reflects the equity of minority shareholders. Exhibit 9.1 illustrates the stockholders' equity section of **Aon**'s balance sheet. Aon's balance sheet reports three equity accounts that make up contributed capital: common stock, additional paid-in capital, and treasury (repurchased) stock. Aon's balance sheet also reports two earned capital accounts: retained earnings and accumulated other comprehensive income (loss). The final component of Aon's stockholders' equity is the noncontrolling interest account.

EXHIBIT 9.1	Stockholders' Equity from Aon's Balance Sheet		
Stockholders' Equity (In millions except per share amounts)		December 31, 2010	December 31, 2009
Contributed Capital	Common stock-$1 par value Authorized: 750 shares (issued: 2010—385.9; 2009—362.7).	$ 386	$ 363
	Additional paid-in capital	4,000	3,215
	Treasury stock at cost (shares: 2010—53.6; 2009—96.4)	(2,079)	(3,859)
Earned Capital	Retained earnings.	7,861	7,335
	Accumulated other comprehensive loss	(1,917)	(1,675)
Noncontrolling Interest	Total Aon stockholders' equity	8,251	5,379
	Noncontrolling interest	55	52
	Total equity	$8,306	$5,431

* We list contributed and earned capital accounts together for learning purposes; in the Aon balance sheet, these accounts are grouped by positive and negative balances.

We discuss contributed capital, earned capital, and noncontrolling interest in order. For each section, we provide a graphic that displays the part of stockholders' equity in the balance sheet impacted by the discussion of that section.

CONTRIBUTED CAPITAL

Contributed capital represents the cumulative cash inflow that the company has received from the sale of various classes of stock, less the net cash that it has paid out to repurchase its stock from the market. The contributed capital of Aon is highlighted in the following graphic.

Stockholders' Equity (In millions except per share amounts)	December 31, 2010	December 31, 2009
Common stock-$1 par value Authorized: 750 shares (issued: 2010—385.9; 2009—362.7)	$ 386	$ 363
Additional paid-in capital.	4,000	3,215
Treasury stock at cost (shares: 2010—53.6; 2009—96.4)	(2,079)	(3,859)
Retained earnings	7,861	7,335
Accumulated other comprehensive loss	(1,917)	(1,675)
Total Aon stockholders' equity.	8,251	5,379
Noncontrolling interest.	55	52
Total equity	$8,306	$5,431

In 2010, Aon's contributed capital consists of par value and additional paid-in capital for the 385.9 million shares of its common stock that Aon has issued. Its contributed capital is reduced by the cost of treasury stock for the 53.6 million shares that Aon has repurchased.

Classes of Stock

There are two general classes of stock: preferred and common. The difference between the two lies in the legal rights conferred upon each class.

LO1 Describe and illustrate accounting for contributed capital, including stock sales and repurchases, and equity-based compensation.

Preferred Stock

Preferred stock generally has preference, or priority, with respect to common stock. Two usual preferences are:

1. **Dividend preference** Preferred shareholders receive dividends on their shares before common shareholders do. If dividends are not paid in a given year, those dividends are normally forgone. However, some preferred stock contracts include a *cumulative provision* stipulating that any forgone dividends (dividends in *arrears*) must first be paid to preferred shareholders, together with the current year's dividends, before any dividends are paid to common shareholders.

2. **Liquidation preference** If a company fails, its assets are sold (liquidated) and the proceeds are paid to the creditors and shareholders, in that order. Shareholders, therefore, have a greater risk of loss than creditors. Among shareholders, the preferred shareholders receive payment in full before common shareholders. This liquidation preference makes preferred shares less risky than common shares. Any liquidation payment to preferred shares is normally at par value, although sometimes the liquidation is specified in excess of par; called a *liquidating value*.

To illustrate the typical provisions contained in preferred stock agreements, consider the following stockholders' equity and related footnote disclosure from **Fortune Brands, Inc.** (2010 10-K).

December 31 (in millions, except per share amounts)	2010	2009
Fortune Brands stockholders' equity		
$2.67 convertible preferred stock	$ 4.9	$ 5.2
Common stock, par value $3.125 per share, 234.9 shares issued	734.0	734.0
Paid-in capital	820.2	755.6
Accumulated other comprehensive loss	(172.0)	(211.8)
Retained earnings	7,499.3	7,135.4
Treasury stock, at cost	(3,215.3)	(3,326.0)
Total Fortune Brands stockholders' equity	5,671.1	5,092.4
Noncontrolling interests	16.9	13.3
Total equity	$5,688.0	$5,105.7

$2.67 Convertible Preferred Stock—Redeemable at Company's Option We have 60 million authorized shares of Preferred stock. There were 160,729 and 171,138 shares of the $2.67 Convertible Preferred stock issued and outstanding at December 31, 2010 and 2009, respectively . . . The holders of $2.67 Convertible Preferred stock are entitled to cumulative dividends, three-tenths of a vote per share together with holders of common stock (in certain events, to the exclusion of the common shares), preference in liquidation over holders of common stock of $30.50 per share plus accrued dividends and to convert each share of Convertible Preferred stock into 6.601 shares of common stock . . . Holders converted 10,409 and 7,366 shares of Preferred stock into common stock during 2010 and 2009, respectively. The Company may redeem the Convertible Preferred stock at a price of $30.50 per share, plus accrued dividends. The Company paid cash dividends of $2.67 per share of Preferred stock in the aggregate amount of $0.4 million in the year ended December 31, 2010 and $0.5 million in each of the years ended December 31, 2009 and 2008.

Following are several important features of Fortune Brands' convertible preferred stock:

■ Preferred stock is typically reported before common stock to indicate that these shareholders will receive payments (dividends or payments if the company is liquidated) before common shareholders.

■ Holders of convertible preferred stock are entitled to $2.67 dividends per share; during 2010, the company paid dividends on preferred shares amounting to $429,146, computed as 160,729 shares × $2.67, which Fortune Brands rounds off to $0.4 million in the footnote.

■ Each share of convertible preferred stock is entitled to 3/10 of a vote per share.

■ Holders of convertible preferred stock have a preference in liquidation over common shareholders amounting to $30.50; this means that they receive $30.50 per share in liquidation before common shareholders receive a payment.

■ Each share of convertible preferred stock is convertible into 6.601 shares of common stock. Upon conversion, the preferred shareholder tenders preferred shares to the company and receives 6.601 shares of common in return for each preferred share tendered. Subsequent to conversion, then, the shareholder loses preferences accorded to preferred shareholders (for example, in dividends and liquidation) as well as the $2.67 of dividends per share. Instead, the shareholder is now able to participate in the wealth creation of the company with unlimited upside potential both for dividends and share price appreciation.

■ Fortune Brands has an option to redeem each share at a price of $30.50; upon redemption, the preferred shareholder will receive that cash amount and will surrender that share to the company.

Fortune Brands' convertible preferred shares carry a dividend $2.67 per share. This preferred dividend compares favorably with the $0.76 of dividends per share paid to its common shareholders in 2010 (which is a return of 1.26% based on year-end stock price of $60.25). Generally, preferred stock can be an attractive investment for shareholders seeking higher dividend yields, especially when tax laws wholly or partially exempt such dividends from taxation. (In comparison, interest payments received by debt holders are not tax exempt.)

In addition to the sorts of conversion features outlined above, preferred shares sometimes carry a *participation feature* that allows preferred shareholders to share ratably with common stockholders in dividends. The dividend preference over common shares can be a benefit when dividend payments are meager, but a fixed dividend yield limits upside potential if the company performs exceptionally well. A participation feature can overcome this limitation.

IFRS INSIGHT   Preferred Stock Under IFRS

Under IFRS, preferred stock (called *preference shares*) is classified according to its underlying characteristics. Preference shares are classified as equity if they are not redeemable, or redeemable at the option of the issuer. Preference shares are classified as liabilities if the company must redeem the shares (mandatorily redeemable) or if they are redeemable at the option of the shareholder. Accounting for payments to preference shareholders follows from the balance sheet classification: cash paid out is recorded as interest expense or dividends, when the shares are classified as liabilities or equity, respectively. Under US GAAP, preferred stock is classified as equity and cash paid out to preferred shareholders is classified as a dividend.

Common Stock

Aon has one class of common stock, Class A, which has the following important characteristics:

- Aon's Class A common stock has a par value of $1 per share. **Par value** is an arbitrary amount set by company organizers at the time of company formation and has no relation to, or impact on, the stock's market value. Generally, par value has no substance from a financial reporting perspective (there are some legal implications, which are usually minor). Its main impact is in specifying the allocation of proceeds from stock issuances between the two contributed capital accounts on the balance sheet: common stock and additional paid-in capital, as we describe below.

- Aon has 750 million shares of stock that have been **authorized** for issuance. The company cannot issue (sell) more shares than have been authorized. So, if more shares are needed, say for an acquisition or for one of its various stock purchase programs, it must first get additional authorization by its shareholders.

- To date, Aon's management has **issued** (sold) 385.9 million shares of stock. The number of issued shares is a cumulative amount. As of 2009, Aon had issued 362.7 million shares of stock and it issued an additional 23.2 million (385.9 million − 362.7 million) shares in 2010.

- Aon has repurchased 53.6 million shares from its shareholders at a cumulative cost of $2,079 million. These shares are currently held in the company's treasury, hence the name treasury stock. These shares neither have voting rights nor do they receive dividends.

- The number of **outstanding** shares is equal to the issued shares less treasury shares. There were 332.3 million (385.9 million − 53.6 million) shares outstanding at the end of 2010.

Accounting for Stock Transactions

We analyze the accounting for stock transactions in this section, including the accounting for stock issuances and repurchases.

Stock Issuance

Companies issue stock to obtain cash and other assets for use in their business. Stock issuances increase assets (cash) by the issue proceeds: the number of shares sold multiplied by the price of the stock on the issue date. Equity increases by the same amount, which is reflected in contributed capital accounts. If the stock has a par value, the common stock account increases by the number of shares sold multiplied by its par value. The additional paid-in capital account increases for the remainder. Stock can also be issued as "no-par" or as "no-par with a stated value." For no-par stock, the common stock account is increased by the entire proceeds of the sale and no amount is assigned to additional paid-in capital. For no-par stock with a stated value, the stated value is treated just like par value, that is, common stock is increased by the number of shares multiplied by the stated value, and the remainder is assigned to the additional paid-in capital account.

To illustrate, assume that Aon issues 100,000 shares of its $1 par value common stock at a market price of $43 cash per share. This stock issuance has the following financial statement effects:

		Balance Sheet							Income Statement		
Transaction	Cash Asset	+	Noncash Assets	=	Liabil- ities	+	Contrib. Capital	+	Earned Capital		Rev- enues	−	Expen- ses	=	Net Income
Issue 100,000 common shares with $1 par value for $43 cash per share	+4,300,000			=			+100,000 Common Stock +4,200,000 Additional Paid-In Capital				−		=

Cash 4,300,000
CS 100,000
APIC 4,200,000

Cash
4,300,000 |

CS
| 100,000

APIC
| 4,200,000

Specifically, the stock issuance affects the financial statements as follows:

1. Cash increases by $4,300,000 (100,000 shares × $43 per share)
2. Common stock increases by the par value of shares sold (100,000 shares × $1 par value = $100,000)
3. Additional paid-in capital increases by the $4,200,000 difference between the issue proceeds and par value ($4,300,000 − $100,000)

Once shares are issued, they are traded in the open market among investors. The proceeds of those sales and their associated gains and losses, as well as fluctuations in the company's stock price subsequent to issuance, do not affect the issuing company and are not recorded in its accounting records.

Refer again to the following report of common stock on Aon's balance sheet:

(In millions except for share amounts)	2010	2009
Common stock—$1 par value Authorized: 750 shares (issued: 2010—385.9; 2009—362.7)	$ 386	$ 363
Additional paid-in capital	4,000	3,215

IFRS Alert
Stock terminology commonly differs between IFRS and GAAP. Under IFRS, common stock is called *share capital* and additional paid-in capital (APIC) is called *share premium*. Accounting for these items is identical under both systems.

Aon common stock, in the amount of $4,386 million, equals the number of shares issued multiplied by the common stock's par value: 385.9 million × $1 = $385.9 million (rounded to $386 million). Total proceeds from its stock issuances are $4,386, the sum of the par value and additional paid-in capital. This implies that common shares were sold, on average, for $11.37 per share ($4,386 million / 385.9 million shares).

RESEARCH INSIGHT Stock Issuance and Stock Returns

Research shows that, historically, companies issuing equity securities experience unusually low stock returns for several years following those offerings. Evidence suggests that this poor performance is partly due to overly optimistic estimates of long-term growth for these companies by equity analysts. That optimism causes offering prices to be too high. This over-optimism is most pronounced when the analyst is employed by the brokerage firm that underwrites the stock issue. There is also evidence that companies manage earnings upward prior to an equity offering. This means the observed decrease in returns following an issuance likely reflects the market's negative reaction, on average, to lower earnings, especially if the company fails to meet analysts' forecasts.

Stock Repurchase

Aon has repurchased 53.6 million shares of its common stock for a cumulative cost of $2,079 million. One reason a company repurchases shares is because it believes that the market undervalues them. The logic is that the repurchase sends a favorable signal to the market about the company's financial condition that positively impacts its share price and, thus, allows it to resell those shares for a "gain." Any such gain on resale is *never* reflected in the income statement. Instead, any excess of the resale price over the repurchase price is added to additional paid-in capital. GAAP prohibits companies from reporting gains and losses from stock transactions with their own shareholders.

Another reason companies repurchase shares is to offset the dilutive effects of an employee stock option program. When an employee exercises stock options, the number of shares outstanding increases. These additional shares reduce earnings per share and are, therefore, viewed as *dilutive*. In response, many companies repurchase an equivalent number of shares in a desire to keep outstanding shares constant.

A stock repurchase reduces the size of the company (cash declines and, thus, total assets decline). A repurchase has the opposite financial statement effects from a stock issuance. That is, cash is reduced by the price of the shares repurchased (number of shares repurchased multiplied by the purchase price per share), and stockholders' equity is reduced by the same amount. The reduction in equity is achieved by increasing a contra equity (negative equity) account called **treasury stock**, which reduces stockholders' equity. Thus, when the treasury stock contra equity account increases, total equity decreases.

When the company subsequently reissues treasury stock there is no accounting gain or loss. Instead, the difference between the proceeds received and the original purchase price of the treasury stock is reflected as an increase or decrease to additional paid-in capital.

To illustrate, assume that 3,000 common shares of Aon previously issued for $43 are repurchased for $40. This repurchase has the following financial statement effects:

	Balance Sheet						Income Statement		
Transaction	Cash Asset	+ Noncash Assets	= Liabil- ities	+ Contrib. Capital	+ Earned Capital		Rev- enues	− Expen- ses	= Net Income
Repurchase 3,000 common shares for $40 cash per share	−120,000 Cash		=	−120,000 Treasury Stock				−	=

TS   120,000
   Cash   120,000

TS
120,000 |
   Cash
    | 120,000

Assets (cash) and equity both decrease. Treasury stock (a contra equity account) increases by $120,000, which reduces stockholders' equity by that amount.

Assume that these 3,000 shares are subsequently resold for $42 cash per share. This resale of treasury stock has the following financial statement effects:

	Balance Sheet						Income Statement		
Transaction	Cash Asset	+ Noncash Assets	= Liabil- ities	+ Contrib. Capital	+ Earned Capital		Rev- enues	− Expen- ses	= Net Income
Reissue 3,000 trea- sury (com- mon) shares for $42 cash per share	+126,000 Cash		=	+120,000 Treasury Stock +6,000 Additional Paid-In Capital				−	=

Cash   126,000
   TS   120,000
   APIC   6,000

Cash
126,000 |
   TS
    | 120,000
   APIC
    | 6,000

Cash assets increase by $126,000 (3,000 shares × $42 per share), the treasury stock account is reduced by the $120,000 cost of the treasury shares issued (thus increasing contributed capital), and the $6,000 excess (3,000 shares × $2 per share) is reported as an increase in additional paid-in capital. (If the reissue price is below the repurchase price, then additional paid-in capital is reduced until it reaches a zero balance, after

IFRS Alert
Accounting for stock repurchases under IFRS is similar to GAAP except that IFRS provides little guidance on how to allocate the treasury stock to equity accounts. Thus, repurchases can be recorded as an increase to treasury stock, or as a decrease to common stock and APIC (share capital and premium), retained earnings (reserves), or some combination.

which retained earnings are reduced.) Again, there is no effect on the income statement as companies are prohibited from reporting gains and losses from repurchases and reissuances of their own stock.

The treasury stock section of **Aon**'s balance sheet is reproduced below:

(In thousands except for share amounts)	2010	2009
Treasury stock at cost (shares: 2010 — 53.6; 2009 — 96.4)	$(2,079)	$(3,859)

Aon has repurchased a cumulative total of 53.6 million shares of its common stock for $2,079 million, an average repurchase price of $38.79 per share. This compares with total contributed capital of $4,386 million, see Exhibit 9.1. Thus, Aon has repurchased about 47% of its original contributed capital in dollar terms, which represents 14% of contributed capital in terms of shares (53.6 million / 385.9 million). Although some of Aon's treasury purchases were to meet stock option exercises, it appears that most of these purchases are motivated by a perceived low stock price by Aon management.

MANAGERIAL DECISION   **You Are the Chief Financial Officer**

As CFO, you believe that your company's stock price is lower than its real value. You are considering various alternatives to increase that price, including the repurchase of company stock in the market. What are some factors you should consider before making your decision? [Answer, p. 9-30]

Stock-Based Compensation

Common stock has been an important component of executive compensation for decades. The general idea follows: If the company executives own stock they will have an incentive to increase its value. This aligns the executives' interests with those of other shareholders. Although the strength of this alignment is the subject of much debate, its logic compels boards of directors of most American companies to use stock-based compensation.

Employee Stock Options

One popular incentive plan is to give an employee the right to purchase common stock at a pre-specified price for a given period of time. This is called a *stock option plan*. Options allow employees to purchase a predetermined number of shares at a fixed price (called the *exercise price* or *strike price*) for a specified period of time. Because there is a good chance of future stock price increases, options are valuable to employees when they receive them, even if the exercise price is exactly equal to the stock's market price the day the options are awarded. The intrinsic value of an option is the difference between the current stock price and the option's strike price. When an option is issued with a strike price equal to the current stock price, which is common practice among U.S. companies, the option has a $0 intrinsic value.

Companies use employee stock options (ESO) as a means to compensate employees and to better align the interests of employees and shareholders. The notion is that employees will work harder to increase their company's stock price when they can benefit directly from future price increases. Because an employee with stock options can purchase stock at a fixed price and resell it at the prevailing (expectedly higher) market price, the options create the possibility of a future gain. Unlike cash compensation, options give employees the same incentives as shareholders—to increase stock price.

Over the past 30 years, use of stock options has skyrocketed and options now make up the bulk of many executive compensation packages. Despite their popularity, stock options have a downside—they can create incentives for employees to increase stock price at any cost and by any means, including misstating earnings and engaging in transactions whose sole purpose is to inflate stock price. Options can also induce managerial myopia—managers want stock price to increase, at least until they can exercise their options and capture their gains.

Until recently, companies were not required to record the value of stock options as compensation expense. Previous GAAP (APB 25) held that options had value only to the extent that the predetermined purchase price (exercise price) was less than the market stock price on the date that the options were granted to the employee. If a company sets the exercise price equal to the market price on the date of grant, the view was that nothing of value had been given to the employee. This meant that no compensation expense was ever reported on such options. This reduced the quality of reported earnings because companies sheltered their income statements merely by setting the exercise price equal to the market price of the stock on the date of grant. Analysts and investors have long expressed serious concerns about accounting for stock options and the amount of unrecorded compensation expense tied to options.

Under considerable pressure and controversy, the FASB issued a pronouncement (SFAS 123R) that applies to stock options granted after 2005. Under the pronouncement, companies must expense the fair value of options and recognize an equivalent increase in stockholders' equity (to the additional paid-in capital account).

To illustrate the accounting for stock options, assume that Aon grants an employee 100,000 stock options with a strike price of $26, which will vest over a four-year period. The vesting period is the time over which an employee gains ownership of the shares, commonly over three to seven years. Employees usually acquire ownership ratably over time, such as 1/4 each year over four years, or acquire full (100%) vesting after the vesting period ends, called *cliff vesting*. Under SFAS 123R, Aon recognizes the fair value of the stock options granted over the employees' service period (generally interpreted as the options' vesting period).

A first step, then, is to determine the "fair value" of the option. SFAS 123R does not specify the method companies must use to estimate fair value, but most companies use the *Black-Scholes model* to estimate the value of exchange-traded options. This model, developed by professors Fischer Black and Myron Scholes, has six inputs, two of which are observable (the company's current stock price and the option's strike price). Companies must estimate the other four model inputs: option life, risk-free interest rate, stock price volatility, and dividend payout rate. These six inputs yield an estimate of the option's fair value. It is important we recognize that management selects the model inputs and, thus, can exercise some discretion over the reported fair value. The option's value computed using Black-Scholes increases with the estimated option life, risk-free interest rate, and stock price volatility; it decreases with the estimated dividend payout. (Free online Black-Scholes option calculators abound, which simplifies fair value estimation.) For analysis purposes, we can partly assess the quality of the reported fair values by comparing a company's model inputs to industry standards and to historical measures (of stock price volatility, for example).

Some companies have recently switched from the common Black-Scholes model to a more complicated binomial (or lattice-binomial) valuation method (currently fewer than 1,000 of the 17,000 publicly-traded U.S. companies use the binomial method). The basic mathematics of the Black-Scholes and binomial methods are identical, but the binomial method allows companies to insert additional assumptions into Black-Scholes and some claim that this provides a more accurate fair value. It also generally provides a lower fair value estimate than the Black-Scholes model, thus reducing the expense related to the options

Returning to our Aon example, assume that the Black-Scholes fair value of the 100,000 options granted is $1,000,000. Thus, Aon records fair value compensation expense of $250,000 each year (fair value of $1,000,000 spread over the four-year vesting period) and its additional paid-in capital increases by $250,000 each year (or $1,000,000 over the four years). Two points are worth noting. First, Aon expenses the entire fair value of the options granted ($1,000,000) regardless of whether the employee actually exercises the options. Second, subsequent changes in the options' value are *not* recognized in financial statements. Thus, the stock option expense and the increase to additional paid-in capital reflect the ESO fair value measured at the grant date.

As with any expense, there are tax consequences to stock option expense. That is, net income is affected on an after-tax basis—each dollar of expense is offset by a reduction in tax expense. Granting stock options creates a book-tax timing difference because the expense is recognized in the income statement at the grant date but is deductible for income tax purposes at the exercise date (see Module 5 for more details about book-tax timing differences). The general approach is that a deferred tax asset is recorded at the statutory rate for this timing difference. This difference reverses when the options are exercised. (Most companies grant *nonqualified stock options* (NQSOs), which are taxed like other compensation but *not* until the options are exercised; when NQSOs are exercised, the options' intrinsic value is taxed as ordinary income to the employee and the employer takes a corresponding tax deduction for the intrinsic value.)

Continuing with our Aon example, the company reports a deferred tax asset to recognize the future tax deduction of the compensation payment. Specifically, Aon reports a deferred tax benefit of $87,500 ($250,000 × 0.35) in each of the four years of the vesting period to reflect the expected reduction in future tax liability when the options are exercised. Thus, the after-tax stock option compensation expense is $162,500 (computed as $250,000 − $87,500). Each year, Aon increases the deferred tax asset account (on the balance sheet) by $87,500. The balance grows until the fourth year when the deferred tax asset balance is $350,000. When the employee exercises the options and Aon realizes the tax benefits, the company reduces taxes payable and reverses the deferred tax asset previously set up.[1] The financial statement effects template would record these transactions as follows in each of the four years of the vesting period.

		Balance Sheet					Income Statement		
Transaction	Cash Asset	+ Noncash Assets	= Liabil- ities	+ Contrib. Capital	+ Earned Capital		Rev- enues	− Expen- ses	= Net Income
Years 1,2,3,4: Grant 100,000 stock options with fair value of $10 per share, vesting over 4 years		+87,500 Deferred Tax Asset =		+250,000 Additional Paid-In Capital	−162,500 Retained Earnings			+250,000 Wages Expense − −87,500 Tax Expense =	−162,500 Net Income
At exercise: 100,000 stock options exercised at a $26 exercise price	+2,600,000 Cash		=	+2,600,000 Additional Paid-In Capital				−	=
At exercise: Tax effect of the exercised stock options		−350,000 Deferred Tax Asset =	−350,000 Taxes Payable					−	=

Left-margin T-accounts:

```
WE     250,000
DTA     87,500
   TE          87,500
   APIC       250,000
        WE
250,000 |
        DTA
 87,500 |
        TE
        | 87,500
        APIC
        | 250,000

Cash  2,600,000
  APIC       2,600,000
        Cash
2,600,000 |
        APIC
          | 2,600,000

TP    350,000
  DTA        350,000
        TP
350,000 |
        DTA
        | 350,000
```

Aon's following footnote discloses many details of its stock option activities. Aon reports that 143,000 options were granted in 2010 with an average strike price of $38.00. These options had a fair value of $10.37 per share. The company also reports how many of its options outstanding have already vested and could potentially be exercised. (Recall that outstanding options affect the company's diluted EPS calculation, see Module 5.)

> **Stock Compensation Costs** The Company recognizes compensation expense for all share-based payments to employees, including grants of employee stock options and restricted stock and restricted stock units ("RSUs"), as well as employee stock purchases related to the Employee Stock Purchase Plan, based on estimated fair value. Stock-based compensation expense recognized during the period is based on the value of the portion of stock-based payment awards that is ultimately expected to vest during the period, based on the achievement of service or performance conditions. Because the stock-based compensation expense recognized is based on awards ultimately expected to vest, it has been reduced for estimated forfeitures. Forfeitures are estimated at the time of grant and revised, if necessary, in subsequent periods if actual forfeitures differ from those estimates.

continued

---

[1] The tax benefit the company receives is based on the options' intrinsic value (current stock price less strike price) on the exercise date. Often, the exercise-date intrinsic value is greater than the grant-date fair value. Recall that deferred taxes are recorded based on grant-date fair value. Thus, the tax benefit received is often larger than the deferred tax asset on the company's balance sheet. In that case, any tax benefit in excess of the deferred tax asset is included in additional paid-in capital and not in net income. The excess tax benefit is classified as cash from financing activities on the statement of cash flows.

continued from prior page

Stock Options   Options to purchase common stock are granted to certain employees at 100% of market value on the date of grant. Commencing in 2010, the Company stopped granting stock options with the exception of historical contractual commitments...Aon uses a lattice-binomial option-pricing model to value stock options. Lattice-based option valuation models utilize a range of assumptions over the expected term of the options...The weighted average assumptions, the weighted average expected life and estimated fair value of employee stock options are summarized as follows:

Years ended December 31	2010		2009		2008	
	All Other Options	LPP Options	SSP Options	All Other Options	Executives	Key Employees
Weighted average volatility.....	28.5%	35.5%	34.1%	32.0%	29.4%	29.9%
Expected dividend yield.......	1.6%	1.3%	1.5%	1.5%	1.3%	1.4%
Risk-free rate	3.0%	1.5%	2.0%	2.6%	3.2%	3.0%
Weighted average expected life, in years..............	6.1	4.4	5.6	6.5	5.1	5.7
Weighted average estimated fair value per share........	$10.37	$12.19	$11.82	$12.34	$11.92	$12.87

A summary of the status of Aon's stock options and related information follows (shares in thousands).

Years ended December 31	2010		2009		2008	
	Shares	Weighted-Average Exercise Price Per Share	Shares	Weighted-Average Exercise Price Per Share	Shares	Weighted-Average Exercise Price Per Share
Beginning outstanding.............	15,937	$33	19,666	$31	26,479	$31
Options issued in connection with the Hewitt acquisition............	4,545	22	—	—	—	—
Granted......................	143	38	1,551	38	1,539	44
Exercised	(6,197)	27	(4,475)	27	(6,779)	30
Forfeited and expired	(509)	35	(805)	38	(1,573)	41
Outstanding at end of year.........	13,919	32	15,937	33	19,666	31
Exercisable at end of year	11,293	30	9,884	31	10,357	30
Shares available for grant..........	22,777		8,257		8,140	

Option grants and option exercises both affect the statement of cash flows. At grant, there is no cash inflow or outflow. However, the noncash stock option compensation expense is added back as a reconciling item in the operating section of the statement of cash flows (indirect method). Aon reported an add-back on its 2010 statement of cash flows of $221 million.

An interesting, often underappreciated, fact is that stock option expense pervades the income statement. Below is a footnote from Cisco System's 2010 10-K that details the allocation of its stock option expense to cost of sales, research and development, sales and marketing expenses, and general and administrative expenses.

Expense and Valuation Information for Share-Based Awards   Share-based compensation expense consists primarily of expenses for stock options, stock purchase rights, restricted stock, and restricted stock units granted to employees. The following table summarizes share-based compensation expense (in millions):

continued

continued from prior page

Years Ended	July 31, 2010	July 25, 2009	July 26, 2008
Cost of sales—product	$ 57	$ 46	$ 40
Cost of sales—service	164	128	108
Share-based compensation expense in cost of sales	221	174	148
Research and development	450	382	339
Sales and marketing.............................	536	441	438
General and administrative........................	310	234	187
Share-based compensation expense in operating expenses	1,296	1,057	964
Total share-based compensation expense	$1,517	$1,231	$1,112

Restricted Stock and Restricted Stock Units

Many companies, including Aon, compensate employees with restricted stock instead of with stock options. Increasingly, firms have moved away from stock options in favor of restricted stock as compensation for several reasons. First, stock options were seen as creating excess compensation during recent stock-market booms. Second, stock options can create incentives for managers to take on excessive firm risk because the value of an option increases with firm risk. Restricted stock does not create such severe risk-taking incentives. Third, there are certain tax advantages to restricted stock vis-a-vis stock options. Under a restricted stock plan, the company transfers shares to the employee, but the shares are restricted in that they cannot be sold until the end of a vesting period. Restricted stock units differ from restricted stock in two key ways: first, the company does not distribute shares of stock to employees until certain conditions are met; and second, the number of shares ultimately given to employees is typically a function of their performance relative to specified targets. Aon describes its restricted stock unit plan as follows:

Restricted stock unit awards   Employees may either receive service-based restricted stock units ("RSUs") or performance-based awards, which ultimately result in the receipt of RSUs, if the employee achieves his or her objectives . . . We account for service-based awards by expensing the total award value over the service period. We calculate the total award value by multiplying the estimated total number of shares to be delivered by the fair value on the date of grant . . . Performance-based RSUs may be immediately vested at the end of the performance period or may have a future additional service period. Generally, our performance awards are fixed, which means we determine the fair value of the award at the grant date, estimate the number of shares to be delivered at the end of the performance period, and recognize the expense over the performance or vesting period, whichever is longer . . . During 2010, the Company granted approximately 1.6 million shares in connection with the completion of the 2007 Leadership Performance Plan ("LPP") cycle and 84,000 shares related to other performance plans. During 2010, 2009 and 2008, the Company granted approximately 3.5 million, 3.7 million and 4.2 million restricted shares, respectively, in connection with the Company's incentive compensation plans.

A summary of the status of Aon's non-vested stock awards follows (shares in thousands).

	2010		2009		2008	
Years ended December 31	Shares	Fair Value(1)	Shares	Fair Value(1)	Shares	Fair Value(1)
Non-vested at beginning of year	12,850	$36	14,060	$35	14,150	$31
Granted	5,477	39	5,741	38	4,159	42
Vested.........................	(6,938)	35	(6,285)	35	(3,753)	28
Forfeited.......................	(715)	35	(666)	37	(496)	(34)
Non-vested at end of year	10,674	$38	12,850	$36	14,060	$35

(1) Represents per share weighted average fair value of award at date of grant.

continued

continued from prior page

Information regarding Aon's performance-based plans as of December 31, 2010, 2009 and 2008 follows (shares in thousands, dollars in millions):

	2010	2009	2008
Potential RSUs to be issued based on current performance levels.......	6,095	7,686	6,205
Unamortized expense, based on current performance levels	$69	$154	$82

The fair value of awards that vested during 2010, 2009 and 2008 was $235 million, $223 million, and $107 million, respectively.

The accounting for restricted stock and restricted stock units is similar to that which we describe for stock options. Specifically, compensation expense is recognized at an amount equal to the value of the shares given to employees as those shares are earned. The consequent decline in retained earnings is offset by an increase in paid-in capital. Stockholders' equity is, therefore, unaffected.

Accounting for restricted stock is illustrated in the following template:

Transaction	Balance Sheet					Income Statement		
	Cash Asset	+ Noncash Assets	= Liabil- ities	+ Contrib. Capital	+ Earned Capital	Rev- enues	− Expen- ses	= Net Income
Year 1: Company issues 100 shares of $10 par restricted stock with a market value of $30 per share, vesting ratably over 6 years			=	+1,000 Common Stock +2,000 Additional Paid-In Capital −3,000 Deferred Compensation			−	=
Years 1,2,3,4,5,6: Record compensation expense for year			=	+500 Deferred Compensation	−500 Retained Earnings		+500 Wage Expense	= −500

DC   3,000
    CS   1,000
    APIC   2,000

      DC
3,000 |
      CS
      | 1,000
      APIC
      | 2,000

WE   500
    DC   500

      WE
500 |
      DC
      | 500

The company records the restricted stock grants as a share issuance exactly as if the shares were sold. That is, the common stock account increases by the par value of the shares and additional paid-in capital increases for the remainder of the share value. However, instead of cash received, the company records a deferred compensation (contra equity) account for the value of the shares that have not yet been issued. This reduces equity. Thus, granting restricted shares leaves the total dollar amount of equity unaffected.

Subsequently, the value of shares given to employees is treated as compensation expense and recorded over the vesting period. Each year, the deferred compensation account is reduced by the vested shares and wage expense is recorded, thus reducing retained earnings. Total equity is unaffected by this transaction as the reduction of the deferred compensation contra equity account (thereby increasing stockholders' equity) is exactly offset by the decrease in retained earnings. The remaining deferred compensation account decreases total stockholders' equity until the end of the vesting period when the total restricted stock grant has been recognized as wage expense. Equity is, therefore, never increased when restricted stock is issued. As of 2010, Aon reports that "Unamortized deferred compensation expense, which includes both options and awards, amounted to $254 million as of December 31, 2010, with a remaining weighted-average amortization period of approximately 2.0 years."

MID-MODULE REVIEW 1

Part 1 Assume that Accenture (ACN) reported the following transactions relating to its stock accounts in 2012.

Jan   15   Issued 10,000 shares of $5 par value common stock at $17 cash per share
Mar   31   Purchased 2,000 shares of its own common stock at $15 cash per share.
June 25   Reissued 1,000 shares of its treasury stock at $20 cash per share.

Use the financial statement effects template to identify the effects of these stock transactions.

Part 2 Accenture reports the following table in its 10-K, which is related to its stock compensation plan.

	Number of Options	Weighted Average Exercise Price	Weighted Average Remaining Contractual Term (In Years)	Aggregate Intrinsic Value
Options outstanding as of August 31, 2009............	29,040,084	$19.35	3.6	$412,098
Granted.......................................	16,539	40.87		
Exercised	(8,010,117)	18.63		
Forfeited	(126,444)	21.72		
Options outstanding as of August 31, 2010............	20,920,062	19.63	2.6	356,341
Options exercisable as of August 31, 2010............	20,386,549	19.42	2.5	351,374
Options exercisable as of August 31, 2009............	28,150,454	19.11	3.4	406,360
Options exercisable as of August 31, 2008............	32,789,179	18.69	4.3	745,341

Required

a. Explain the terms "Granted," "Exercised," and "Forfeited." What is the meaning of "Weighted Average Exercise Price"?
b. Explain how the compensation cost related to the options above is recognized in financial statements.

The solution is on page 9-48.

EARNED CAPITAL

LO2 Explain and illustrate accounting for earned capital, including cash dividends, stock dividends, and comprehensive income.

We now turn to the earned capital portion of stockholders' equity. Earned capital represents the cumulative profit that the company has retained. Recall that earned capital increases each period by income earned and decreases by any losses incurred. Earned capital also decreases by dividends paid to shareholders. Not all dividends are paid in the form of cash. Companies can pay dividends in many forms, including property (land, for example) or additional shares of stock. We cover both cash and stock dividends in this section. Earned capital also includes the positive or negative effects of accumulated other comprehensive income (AOCI). The earned capital of Aon is highlighted in the following graphic.

Stockholders' Equity (In millions except per share amounts)	December 31, 2010	December 31, 2009
Common stock-$1 par value Authorized: 750 shares (issued: 2010—385.9; 2009—362.7)	$ 386	$ 363
Additional paid-in capital	4,000	3,215
Treasury stock at cost (shares: 2010—53.6; 2009—96.4)	(2,079)	(3,859)
Retained earnings	7,861	7,335
Accumulated other comprehensive loss	(1,917)	(1,675)
Total Aon stockholders' equity.......................................	8,251	5,379
Noncontrolling interest..	55	52
Total equity...	$8,306	$5,431

* We list contributed and earned capital accounts together for learning purposes; in the Aon balance sheet, these accounts are grouped by positive and negative balances.

Cash Dividends

Many companies, but not all, pay dividends. Their reasons for dividend payments are varied. Most dividends are paid in cash on a quarterly basis. Aon makes the following disclosure relating to dividends in its 2010 10-K:

> **Dividend** During 2010, 2009, and 2008, Aon paid dividends on its common stock of $175 million, $165 million and $171 million, respectively. Dividends paid per common share were $0.60 for each of the years ended December 31, 2010, 2009, and 2008.

Outsiders closely monitor dividend payments. It is generally perceived that the level of dividend payments is related to the company's expected long-term recurring income. Accordingly, dividend increases are usually viewed as positive signals about future performance and are accompanied by stock price increases. By that logic, companies rarely reduce their dividends unless absolutely necessary because dividend reductions are often met with substantial stock price declines.

Financial Effects of Cash Dividends

Cash dividends reduce both cash and retained earnings by the amount of the cash dividends paid. To illustrate, assume that Aon declares and pays cash dividends in the amount of $10 million. The financial statement effects of this cash dividend payment are as follows:

	Balance Sheet						Income Statement		
Transaction	**Cash Asset**	**+ Noncash Assets**	**= Liabil- ities**	**+ Contrib. Capital**	**+ Earned Capital**		**Rev- enues**	**− Expen- ses**	**= Net Income**
Payment of $10 million in cash dividends	−10 mil. Cash		**=**		−10 mil. Retained Earnings			**−**	**=**

RE   10 mil.
   Cash   10 mil.

RE	
10 mil.	
	Cash
	10 mil.

Dividend payments do not affect net income. They directly reduce retained earnings and bypass the income statement.

Dividends on preferred stock have priority over those on common stock, including unpaid prior years' preferred dividends (called *dividends in arrears*) when preferred stock is cumulative. To illustrate, assume that a company has 15,000 shares of $50 par value, 8% preferred stock outstanding; assume that the preferred stock is cumulative, which means that any unpaid dividends cumulate and must be paid before common dividends. The company also has 50,000 shares of $5 par value common stock outstanding. During its first three years in business, assume that the company declares $20,000 dividends in the first year, $260,000 of dividends in the second year, and $60,000 of dividends in the third year. Cash dividends paid to each class of stock in each of the three years follows:

	Preferred Stock	Common Stock
Year 1—$20,000 cash dividends paid		
Current-year dividend (15,000 shares × $50 par × 8%; but only $20,000 paid, leaving $40,000 in arrears)............	$20,000	
Balance to common...................................		$ 0
Year 2—$260,000 cash dividends paid		
Dividends in arrears from Year 1 ([15,000 shares × $50 par × 8%] − $20,000)	40,000	
Current-year dividend (15,000 shares × $50 par × 8%)	60,000	
Balance to common...................................		160,000
Year 3—$60,000 cash dividends paid		
Current-year dividend (15,000 shares × $50 par × 8%)	60,000	
Balance to common...................................		0

MID-MODULE REVIEW 2

Assume that Accenture (ACN) has outstanding 10,000 shares of $100 par value, 5% preferred stock and 50,000 shares of $5 par value common stock. During its first three years in business, assume that Accenture declared no dividends in the first year, $300,000 of cash dividends in the second year, and $80,000 of cash dividends in the third year.

a. If preferred stock is cumulative, determine the dividends paid to each class of stock for each of the three years.
b. If preferred stock is noncumulative, determine the dividends paid to each class of stock for each of the three years.

The solution is on page 9-49.

Stock Dividends and Splits

Dividends need not be paid in cash. Many companies pay dividends in the form of additional shares of stock. Companies can also distribute additional shares to their stockholders with a stock split. We cover both of these distributions in this section.

Stock Dividends

When dividends are paid in the form of the company's stock, retained earnings are reduced and contributed capital is increased. However, the amount by which retained earnings are reduced depends on the proportion of the outstanding shares distributed to the total outstanding shares on the dividend distribution date. Exhibit 9.2 illustrates two possibilities depending on whether stock dividends are classified as small stock dividends or large stock dividends. The break point between small and large is 20–25% of the outstanding shares. When the number of additional shares issued as a stock dividend is so great that it could materially reduce share price, the transaction is akin to a stock split. The 20–25% guideline is used as a rule of thumb to distinguish material stock price effects.

For *small stock dividends*, retained earnings are reduced by the *market* value of the shares distributed (dividend shares × market price per share), and par value and contributed capital together are increased by the same amount. For *large stock dividends*, retained earnings are reduced by the *par* value of the shares distributed (dividend shares × par value per share), and common stock is increased by the same amount (no change to additional paid-in capital).

EXHIBIT 9.2 Analysis of Stock Dividend Effects		
Percentage of Outstanding Shares Distributed	**Retained Earnings**	**Contributed Capital**
Less than 20-25% *(small stock dividend treated as a dividend)*	Reduce by **market value** of shares distributed	Common stock increased by: Dividend shares × Par value per share; Additional paid-in capital increased for the balance
More than 20-25% *(large stock dividend treated as a stock split)*	Reduce by **par value** of shares distributed	Common stock increased by: Dividend shares × Par value per share

To illustrate the financial statement effects of stock dividends, assume that BearingPoint has 1 million shares of $5 par common stock outstanding. It then declares a small stock dividend of 15% of the outstanding shares (1,000,000 shares × 15% = 150,000 shares) when the market price of the stock is $30 per share. This small stock dividend has the following financial statement effects:

	Balance Sheet						Income Statement		
Transaction	Cash Asset	+ Noncash Assets	= Liabil-ities	+ Contrib. Capital	+ Earned Capital		Rev-enues	− Expen-ses	= Net Income
Distribute 150,000 shares with a market value of $4.5 mil. as a *small* stock dividend			=	+750,000 Common Stock +$3,750,000 Additional Paid-In Capital	−$4,500,000 Retained Earnings			−	=

RE   4.5 mil.
  CS   0.75 mil.
  APIC   3.75 mil.

RE
4.5 mil. |
  CS
      | 0.75 mil.
  APIC
      | 3.75 mil.

The company reduces retained earnings by $4,500,000, which equals the market value of the small stock dividend (150,000 shares × $30 market price per share). The increase in contributed capital is split between the par value of $750,000 (150,000 shares × $5 par value) and additional paid-in capital ($3,750,000). Similar to cash dividend payments, stock dividends, whether large or small, never impact income.

Next, assume that instead, BearingPoint declares a large stock dividend of 70% of the 1 million outstanding common ($5 par) shares when the market price of the stock is $30 per share. This large stock dividend is treated like a stock split and has the following financial statement effects:

	Balance Sheet						Income Statement		
Transaction	Cash Asset	+ Noncash Assets	= Liabil-ities	+ Contrib. Capital	+ Earned Capital		Rev-enues	− Expen-ses	= Net Income
Distribute 700,000 shares as a *large* stock dividend			=	+$3,500,000 Common Stock	−$3,500,000 Retained Earnings			−	=

RE   3.5 mil.
  CS   3.5 mil.

RE
3.5 mil. |
  CS
      | 3.5 mil.

The company's retained earnings declines by $3,500,000, which equals the par value of the large stock dividend (700,000 shares × $5 par value per share). Common stock is increased by the par value of $3,500,000. There is no effect on additional paid-in capital since large stock dividends are reported at par value.

For both large and small stock dividends, companies are required to show comparable shares outstanding for all prior periods for which earnings per share (EPS) is reported in the statements. The reasoning is that a stock dividend has no effect on the ownership percentage of each common stockholder. As such, to show a dilution in reported EPS would erroneously suggest a decline in profitability when it is simply due to an increase in shares outstanding.

Stock Splits

A stock split is a proportionate distribution of shares and, as such, is similar in substance to a large stock dividend. A typical stock split is 2-for-1, which means that the company distributes one additional share for each share owned by a shareholder. Following the distribution, each investor owns twice as many shares, so that their percentage ownership in the company is unchanged.

A stock split is not a monetary transaction and, as such, there are no financial statement effects. However, companies must disclose the new number of shares outstanding for all periods presented in the financial statements. Further, many states require that the par value of shares be proportionately adjusted as well (for example, halved for a 2-for-1 split).

If state law requires that par value not be reduced for a stock dividend, this event should be described as a *stock split affected in the form of a dividend*. The following disclosure from John Deere's 2007 annual report provides such an example:

Stock Split in Form of Dividend On November 14, 2007, a special meeting of stockholders was held authorizing a two-for-one stock split effected in the form of a 100 percent stock dividend to holders of record on November 26, 2007, distributed on December 3, 2007. All share and per share data (except par value) have been adjusted to reflect the effect of the stock split for all periods presented. The number of shares of common stock issuable upon exercise of outstanding stock options, vesting of other stock awards, and the number of shares reserved for issuance under various employee benefit plans were proportionately increased in accordance with terms of the respective plans.

MID-MODULE REVIEW 3

Assume that the stockholders' equity of Arbitron, Inc. at December 31, 2011, follows.

5% preferred stock, $100 par value, 10,000 shares authorized; 4,000 shares issued and outstanding.	$ 400,000
Common stock, $5 par value, 200,000 shares authorized; 50,000 shares issued and outstanding	250,000
Paid-in capital in excess of par value-Preferred stock.	40,000
Paid-in capital in excess of par value-Common stock.	300,000
Retained earnings	656,000
Total stockholders' equity	$1,646,000

Use the template to identify the financial statement effects for each of the following transactions that occurred during 2012:

Apr. 1 Declared and issued a 100% stock dividend on all outstanding shares of common stock when the market value of the stock was $11 per share.

Dec. 7 Declared and issued a 3% stock dividend on all outstanding shares of common stock when the market value of the stock was $7 per share.

Dec. 31 Declared and paid a cash dividend of $1.20 per share on all outstanding shares.

The solution is on page 9-49.

Accumulated Other Comprehensive Income

Comprehensive income is a more inclusive notion of company performance than net income. It includes all changes in equity (assets less liabilities) that occur during a period except those resulting from contributions by and distributions to owners. It's important to note that comprehensive income includes both net income and other items, which collectively are called *other comprehensive income*.

Specifically, other comprehensive income includes (and net income excludes) foreign currency translation adjustments, unrealized changes in market values of available-for-sale securities, pension liability adjustments, and changes in market values of certain derivative investments. Comprehensive income, therefore, includes the effects of economic events that are often outside of management's control. Accordingly, some assert that net income measures management's performance, while comprehensive income measures company performance. Each period, net income or loss is added to retained earnings so that the balance sheet maintains a running total of the company's cumulative net income and losses (less any dividends paid out). In the same way, each period, comprehensive income items that are not included in net income (that is, all *other comprehensive income* items) are added to a balance sheet account called Accumulated Other Comprehensive Income (or Accumulated Other Comprehensive Loss if the comprehensive items are losses). This account maintains a running balance of the cumulative differences between net income and comprehensive income.

Aon reports the following components of its accumulated other comprehensive income in its 10-K report:

IFRS Alert
IFRS does not use the term "other comprehensive income" but reports that account in a *statement of recognized income and expenses* (SoRIE). As with GAAP's other comprehensive income, SoRIE includes all changes to equity, other than transactions with owners.

($ millions)	Net Derivative Gains (Losses)	Net Foreign Exchange Translation Adjustments*	Net Postretirement Benefit Obligations	Net Unrealized Investment Gains (Losses)	Accumulated Other Comprehensive Income
Balance as of January 1, 2008.........	$ 24	$284	$(1,110)	$76	$ (726)
Other comprehensive income	(37)	(182)	(497)	(20)	(736)
Balance as of December 31, 2008......	(13)	102	(1,607)	56	(1,462)
Other comprehensive income	13	199	(413)	(12)	(213)
Balance as of December 31, 2009......	0	301	(2,020)	44	(1,675)
Other comprehensive income	(24)	(133)	(41)	(44)**	(242)
Balance as of December 31, 2010......	$(24)	$168	$(2,061)	$ 0	$(1,917)

* Net of amount attributable to noncontrolling interest

** Relates to consolidation of a variable interest entity in 2010.

Aon's accumulated other comprehensive income for 2010 includes the four following items that affect stockholders' equity and are not reflected in net income:

1. **Net derivative losses**, $(24) million. Hedging transactions relate to the company's use of financial instruments (derivatives) to hedge exposure to various risks such as fluctuations in foreign currency exchange rates, commodity prices, and interest rates. This account relates to unrealized losses on cash flow hedges, which we discuss in the appendix to Module 7.

2. **Net foreign exchange translation adjustments**, $168 million. This is the cumulative translation adjustment for the net assets of foreign subsidiaries whose balance sheets are denominated in foreign currencies. A gain implies that the $US has weakened relative to foreign currencies; such as when assets denominated in foreign currencies translate to more $US. We discuss the effects of foreign currency translation adjustments on accumulated other comprehensive income in more detail below.

3. **Net postretirement benefit obligations**, $(2,061) million. This amount mainly relates to unrealized losses on pension investments or can derive from changes in pension plans that increase the pension liability. We discuss the accounting for pension plans and other postretirement benefit obligations in Module 10.

4. **Net unrealized investment gains**, $(0) this year. Unrealized gains and losses on available-for-sale securities are not reflected in net income. Instead, they are accumulated in a separate equity account, AOCI, until the securities are sold. We discuss the accounting for these unrealized gains (losses) in Module 7.

We discuss accounting for available-for-sale securities and derivatives in Module 7, pensions in Module 10, and the income statement effects of foreign currency translation adjustments in Module 5. In the next section, we discuss the balance sheet effects of foreign currency translation adjustments, specifically their impact on accumulated other comprehensive income. During 2010, Aon reported other comprehensive loss of $(242) million, which is the sum of the changes in each of the four components of AOCI, as shown on the statement above. This other comprehensive loss when added to the AOCI balance of $(1,675) at the beginning of the year yields the AOCI balance of $(1,917) at year-end.

Foreign Currency Translation Effects on Accumulated Other Comprehensive Income

Many companies have international transactions denominated in foreign currencies. They might purchase assets in foreign currencies, borrow money in foreign currencies, and transact business with their customers and suppliers in foreign currencies. Other companies might have subsidiaries whose entire balance sheets and income statements are stated in foreign currencies. Financial statements prepared according to U.S. GAAP must be reported in $US. This means that financial statements of foreign subsidiaries must be translated into $US before they are consolidated with those of the U.S. parent company. This translation process can markedly alter both the balance sheet and income statement. We discuss the income statement effects of foreign currency translation in Module 5 and the balance sheet effects in this section.

Consider a U.S. company with a foreign subsidiary that conducts its business in Euros. The subsidiary prepares its financial statements in Euros. Assume that the $US weakens vis-à-vis the Euro during the current period—that is, each Euro can now purchase more $US. When the balance sheet is translated into $US, the assets and liabilities are reported at higher $US than before the $US weakened. This result is shown in accounting equation format in Exhibit 9.3.[2]

EXHIBIT 9.3	Balance Sheet Effects of Changes in U.S. Dollar to Euro Exchange Rates					
Currency	**Assets**	**=**	**Liabilities**	**+**	**Equity**
$US weakens	Increase	=	Increase	+	Increase
$US strengthens.	Decrease	=	Decrease	+	Decrease

IFRS Alert
The IFRS counterpart to AOCI is the *General Reserve* and other reserve accounts. Reserves is the IFRS term for all equity accounts other than contributed capital. Retained earnings is typically the largest reserve. The components of AOCI are reported individually as additional reserve accounts rather than as one account.

The amount reflected as an increase (decrease) in equity is called a **foreign currency translation adjustment**. The *cumulative* foreign currency translation adjustment is included in accumulated other comprehensive income (or loss) as illustrated above for Aon. Foreign currency translation adjustments are direct adjustments to stockholders' equity; they do not impact reported net income. Because assets are greater than liabilities for solvent companies, the cumulative translation adjustment is positive when the $US weakens and negative when the dollar strengthens.

Referring to Aon's accumulated other comprehensive income table on the previous page, the cumulative foreign currency translation is a gain of $301 million at the beginning of 2010, which shrinks by $133 million (net of $2 million credited to noncontrolling shareholders) during the year to yield a cumulative year-end gain of $168 million. The $133 million reduction in Aon's equity reflects a strengthening of the $US vis-à-vis the foreign currencies in which Aon transacted in 2010. That is, as the $US strengthened, Aon's foreign assets and liabilities translated into fewer $US at year-end. This decreased Aon's equity (because assets are greater than liabilities for solvent companies). In general, unrealized losses (or gains) remain in other accumulated comprehensive income as long as the company owns the foreign subsidiaries to which the losses relate. The translation adjustments fluctuate between positive and negative amounts as the value of the $US fluctuates. However, when a subsidiary is sold, any remaining foreign currency translation adjustment (positive or negative) is immediately recognized in current income along with other gains or losses arising from sale of the subsidiary.

NONCONTROLLING INTEREST

Noncontrolling interest represents the equity of noncontrolling (minority) shareholders who only have a claim on the net assets of one or more of the subsidiaries in the consolidated entity. As we discuss in Module 7, if a company acquires a controlling interest in a subsidiary, it must consolidate that subsidiary when preparing its financial statements, thus reporting all of the subsidiary's assets and liabilities on the consolidated balance sheet and reporting all of the subsidiary's revenues and expenses in the consolidated income statement. If the company acquires less than 100% of the subsidiary, it must still include 100% of the subsidiary's assets, liabilities, revenues and expenses in its consolidated balance sheet and income statement, but now there are two groups of shareholders that have a claim on the net assets and earnings of the subsidiary company: the parent company and the noncontrolling shareholders (those shareholders who continue to own shares of the subsidiary company).

Consolidated stockholders' equity must now report the equity of these two groups of shareholders and consolidated net income must now be apportioned between the two groups. For Aon, the consolidated income statement apportions net income as follows:

---

[2] We assume that the company translates the subsidiary's financial statements using the more common **current rate method**, which is required for subsidiaries operating independently from the parent. Under the current rate method, most items in the balance sheet are translated using exchange rates in effect at the period-end consolidation date and the income statement is translated using the average exchange rate for the period. An alternative procedure is the *temporal method*, covered in advanced accounting courses, which uses historical exchange rates for some assets and liabilities.

Aon Consolidated Income Statement ($ millions)	
Revenues	$8,512
Expenses	7,780
Net income	732
Less: Net income attributable to noncontrolling interest	26
Net income attributable to Aon stockholders.	$ 706

Net income is apportioned between the portion attributable to the noncontrolling interest and the portion attributable to the parent company's shareholders. Although it can be more complicated, in its simplest form, if the noncontrolling shareholders own 20% of a subsidiary, 20% of the subsidary's net income is attributable to that shareholder group and the parent's shareholders received the balance of 80%.

The common stock, additional paid-in capital and retained earnings accounts we see on the consolidated balance sheet represent those of the parent's shareholders. The retained earnings attributable to the parent's shareholders is increased (decreased) by the income (loss) attributable to the parent's shareholders and is decreased by the dividends paid to the parent's shareholders in a reconciliation similar to the following for Aon:

Aon Retained Earnings Account ($ millions)	
Beginning balance of retained earnings.	$7,335
Net income attributable to parent	706
Dividends	(175)
Other adjustments	(5)
Ending balance of retained earnings	$7,861

The equity of the *noncontrolling* interest, however, is only represented by one equity account labeled Noncontrolling Interest. It is updated similarly to the stockholders' equity for the parent's shareholders, that is, it is increased (decreased) by the income (loss) attributable to the noncontrolling shareholders and is decreased by the dividends paid to the noncontrolling shareholders:

Aon Noncontrolling Interest Equity Account ($ millions)	
Beginning balance (fair value at acquisition date)	$52
Net income attributable to noncontrolling interest.	26
Dividends declared and paid to noncontrolling shareholders	(20)
Other adjustments	(3)
Ending balance.	$55

Again, although it can be more complicated, if the noncontrolling interest owns 20% of a subsidiary company, the balance in the noncontrolling interest equity account will equal 20% of the stockholders' equity of the subsidiary company. (This is not 20% of the consolidated company, only 20% of the subsidiary company.)

Finally, the noncontrolling interest equity account is reported as a separate line in the consolidated stockholders' equity as follows:

Aon Consolidated Balance Sheet	
Stockholders' Equity (In millions except per share amounts)	2010
Common stock—$1 par value Authorized: 750 shares (issued: 2010—385.9; 2009—362.7)	$ 386
Additional paid-in capital	4,000
Treasury stock at cost (shares: 2010—53.6; 2009—96.4)	(2,079)
Retained earnings	7,861
Accumulated other comprehensive loss	(1,917)
Total Aon stockholders' equity....................................	8,251
Noncontrolling interest...	55
Total equity...	$8,306

Analysis and Interpretation of Noncontrolling Interest

As we discuss more fully in Module 4, the return on equity (ROE) computation is usually performed from the perspective of the parent company's shareholders. Consequently, the numerator is usually the net income attributable to the parent company shareholders and the denominator includes only the equity of the parent company's shareholders (excluding noncontrolling interest equity). For the Aon financial statements shown above, that calculation follows (we use the year-end balance of equity, and not average equity, since we only illustrate one year in this example):

$$ROE = \frac{\$706}{\$8,251} = 8.6\%$$

Noncontrolling interest is reported as a component of stockholders' equity and represents the claim of the noncontrolling interest to their proportionate share of the net assets and net income *of the subsidiary in which they own stock*. These shareholders do not have a claim on the net assets or income of any other subsidiary or of the parent company. Further, their claim is a residual claim, like that of any other shareholder; that is, they are not entitled to a preference in dividends or payouts in liquidation.

Summary of Stockholders' Equity

The statement of shareholders' equity summarizes the transactions that affect stockholders' equity during the period. This statement reconciles the beginning and ending balances of important stockholders' equity accounts. Aon's statement of stockholders' equity is in Exhibit 9.4.

Aon's statement of shareholders' equity reveals the following key activities for 2010:

EXHIBIT 9.4   Aon's Statement of Stockholders' Equity

(millions)	Shares	Common Stock and Additional Paid-in Capital	Retained Earnings	Treasury Stock	Accumulated Other Comprehensive Loss, Net of Tax	Non-controlling Interest	Total	Comprehensive Income
Balance at December 31, 2009	362.7	$3,578	$7,335	$(3,859)	$(1,675)	$52	$5,431	$583
Adoption of new accounting guidance	—	—	44	—	(44)	—	—	(44)
Balance at January 1, 2010	362.7	3,578	7,379	(3,859)	(1,719)	52	5,431	539
Net income.	—	—	706	—	—	26	732	732
Shares issued—Hewitt acquisition.	61.0	2,474	—	—	—	—	2,474	—
Shares issued—employee benefit plans	2.2	135	—	—	—	—	135	—
Shares purchased	—	—	—	(250)	—	—	(250)	—
Shares reissued—employee benefit plans. . . .	—	(370)	(49)	370	—	—	(49)	—
Shares retired.	(40.0)	(1,660)	—	1,660	—	—	—	—
Tax benefit—employee benefit plans.	—	20	—	—	—	—	20	—
Stock compensation expense	—	221	—	—	—	—	221	—
Dividends to stockholders	—	—	(175)	—	—	—	(175)	—
Change in net derivative gains/losses	—	—	—	—	(24)	—	(24)	(24)
Net foreign currency translation adjustments	—	—	—	—	(133)	(2)	(135)	(135)
Net postretirement benefit obligation	—	—	—	—	(41)	—	(41)	(41)
Purchase of subsidiary shares from noncontrolling interest	—	(12)	—	—	—	(3)	(15)	—
Capital contribution by noncontrolling interest	—	—	—	—	—	2	2	—
Dividends paid to noncontrolling interest on subsidiary common stock.	—	—	—	—	—	(20)	(20)	—
Balance at December 31, 2010	385.9	$4,386	$7,861	$(2,079)	$(1,917)	$55	$8,306	$532

1. (Items bracketed: Shares issued—Hewitt acquisition, Shares issued—employee benefit plans, Shares purchased, Shares reissued—employee benefit plans, Shares retired)

2. (Items bracketed: Tax benefit—employee benefit plans, Stock compensation expense)

3. Dividends to stockholders

4. Change in net derivative gains/losses

5. Net foreign currency translation adjustments

6. Net postretirement benefit obligation

7. (Items bracketed: Purchase of subsidiary shares from noncontrolling interest, Capital contribution by noncontrolling interest, Dividends paid to noncontrolling interest on subsidiary common stock)

1 Shares issued are recorded as an increase in common stock (for the par value) and additional paid-in capital (for the excess of the value of the shares issued over the par value). Aon combines common stock and additional paid-in capital accounts into one column for total proceeds. The cost of shares repurchased is recorded as treasury stock. The cost of shares reissued and/or retired is recorded as a reduction of the treasury stock account since these are treasury shares. When shares are retired, the par value of the shares retired is removed from common stock and additional paid-in capital. Aon does not provide information relating to accounting for share reissuance for the employee benefit plans.

2 Tax benefits (in excess of the deferred tax asset previously recorded) arising from the exercise of employee stock options are recorded as an increase in additional paid-in capital (not as a reduction of tax expense).

3 Dividends are recorded as a reduction of retained earnings.

4 Change in the fair value of derivatives relates to cash flow derivatives. These unrealized gains (losses) are reflected as increases (decreases) in AOCI until the underlying transaction occurs, at which time they are removed from AOCI and transferred into the income statement. We discuss the accounting for derivatives in the appendix to Module 7.

5 Net foreign currency translation adjustments relate to the translation of foreign currency-denominated balance sheets at year-end into $US. The negative amount implied that the $US has strengthened vis-à-vis the currency in which the financial statements of foreign subsidiaries are maintained with a consequent decline in the $US value of the net assets of those subsidiaries.

6 The adjustment relating to postretirement benefit obligations relates to the financial statement effects of the changes in pension benefits or actuarial assumptions. We discuss the accounting for pension plans and other postretirement benefits in Module 10.

7 Proceeds from sales and repurchases of the stock of noncontrolling shareholders as well as dividends paid to noncontrolling shareholders are reflected in the noncontrolling equity account.

One final point: the financial press sometimes refers to a measure called **book value per share**. This is the net book value of the company that is available to common shareholders, defined as: stockholders' equity of the parent's shareholders less preferred stock (and preferred additional paid-in capital) divided by the number of common shares outstanding (issued common shares less treasury shares). Aon's book value per share of its common stock at the end of 2010 is computed as: $8,251 million/(385.9 million shares − 53.6 million shares) = $24.83 book value per share. In contrast, Aon's **market price per share** ranged from $36.81 to $42.32 in the 4th quarter of 2010.

EQUITY CARVE-OUTS AND CONVERTIBLES

Corporate divestitures, or **equity carve-outs**, are increasingly common as companies seek to augment shareholder value through partial or total divestiture of operating units. Generally, equity carve-outs are motivated by the notion that consolidated financial statements often obscure the performance of individual business units, thus complicating their evaluation by outsiders. Corporate managers are concerned that this difficulty in assessing the performance of individual business units limits their ability to reach full valuation. Shareholder value is, therefore, not maximized. In response, conglomerates have divested subsidiaries so that the market can individually price them.

LO3 Describe accounting for equity carve-outs and convertible debt.

Sell-Offs

Equity carve-outs take many forms. The first and simplest form of divestiture is the outright sale of a business unit, called a **sell-off**. In this case, the company sells its equity interest to an unrelated party. The sale is accounted for just like the sale of any other asset. Specifically, any excess (deficit) of cash received over the book value of the business unit sold is recorded as a gain (loss) on the sale.

To illustrate, in 2010, Conoco Phillips sold its Syncrude Canada Ltd. business for $4.6 billion and recorded a pretax gain on that sale of $2.9 billion as disclosed in the following excerpt from its 2010 annual report:

> On June 25, 2010, we sold our 9.03 percent interest in the Syncrude Canada Ltd. joint venture for $4.6 billion. The $2.9 billion before-tax gain was included in the "Gain on dispositions" line of our consolidated statement of operations. The cash proceeds were included in the "Proceeds from asset dispositions" line within the investing cash flow section of our consolidated statement of cash flows. At the time of disposition, Syncrude had a net carrying value of $1.75 billion, which included $1.97 billion of properties, plants and equipment. During 2010 until its disposition, Syncrude contributed $327 million in intercompany sales and other operating revenues, and generated income before taxes of $127 million and net income of $93 million for the E&P segment.

The financial statement effects of this transaction follow:

- Conoco received $4.6 billion in cash, which it reported as a component of cash flows from investing activities in its statement of cash flows.

- The Syncrude joint venture was reported on Conoco's balance sheet at $1.75 billion on the date of sale.

- Conoco's gain on sale equaled the proceeds ($4.6 billion) less the carrying amount of the business sold ($1.75 billion), or $2.85 billion which Conoco rounds to $2.9 billion in the footnote referenced above.

- Conoco subtracts the gain on sale in computing net cash flows from operating activities to remove the gain from net income; cash proceeds are reported as a cash inflow in the investing section.

Spin-Offs

A **spin-off** is a second form of divestiture. In this case, the parent company distributes the subsidiary shares that it owns as a dividend to its shareholders who, then, own shares in the subsidiary directly rather than through the parent company. In recording this dividend, the parent company reduces retained earnings by the book value of the equity method investment, thereby removing the investment in the subsidiary from the parent's balance sheet.

The spin-off of the Kraft Foods subsidiary by Altria is an example of this type of equity carve-out. Altria describes its spin-off of Kraft as follows:

> **Kraft Spin-Off** On March 30, 2007 (the "Kraft Distribution Date"), Altria Group, Inc. distributed all of its remaining interest in Kraft on a pro-rata basis to Altria Group, Inc. stockholders of record as of the close of business on March 16, 2007 (the "Kraft Record Date") in a tax-free distribution. The distribution ratio was 0.692024 of a share of Kraft for each share of Altria Group, Inc. common stock outstanding. Altria Group, Inc. stockholders received cash in lieu of fractional shares of Kraft. Following the distribution, Altria Group, Inc. does not own any shares of Kraft.

Altria treats the distribution of its Kraft shares as a dividend, which Altria reports in the following excerpt from its statement of stockholders' equity.

(In millions, except per share)	Common Stock	Additional Paid-in Capital	Earnings Reinvested in the Business	Currency Translation Adjustments	Other	Total	Cost of Repurchased Stock	Total Stock-holders' Equity
Balances, December 31, 2006	$935	$6,356	$59,879	$ (97)	$(3,711)	$(3,808)	$(23,743)	$39,619
Comprehensive earnings:								
Net earnings			9,786					9,786
Other comprehensive earnings (losses), net of income taxes:								
Currency translation adjustments				736		736		736
Change in net loss and prior service cost.					744	744		744
Change in fair value of derivatrives accounted for as hedges.					(18)	(18)		(18)
Total other comprehensive earnings.								1,462
Total comprehensive earnings								11,248
Adoption of FIN 48 and FAS 13-2			711					711
Exercise of stock options and issuance of other stock awards		528					289	817
Cash dividends declared ($3.05 per share)			(6,430)					(6,430)
Spin-off of Kraft Foods Inc.			(29,520)	89	2,020	2,109		(27,411)
Balances, December 31, 2007	$935	$6,884	$34,426	$728	$ (965)	$ (237)	$(23,454)	$18,554

The $29,520 million book value of the Kraft subsidiary (the amount at which this equity investment is reported on Altria's balance sheet) is removed from Altria's balance sheet when the shares are distributed to Altria's shareholders, and that amount is subtracted from Altria's retained earnings (titled

"Earnings Reinvested in the Business"). Altria also removes all amounts relating to Kraft that impacted its Accumulated Other Comprehensive Earnings (a net of $2,109 million). In total, the Kraft spin-off reduced Altria's equity by $27,411 million.

Split-Offs

The **split-off** is a third form of equity carve-out. In this case, the parent company buys back its own stock using the shares of the subsidiary company instead of cash. After completing this transaction, the subsidiary is an independent publicly traded company.

The parent treats the split-off like any other purchase of treasury stock. As such, the treasury stock account is increased and the equity method investment account is reduced, reflecting the distribution of that asset. The dollar amount recorded for this treasury stock depends on how the distribution is set up. There are two possibilities:

1. **Pro rata distribution**. Shares are distributed to stockholders on a pro rata basis. Namely, a shareholder owning 10% of the outstanding stock of the parent company receives 10% of the shares of the subsidiary. The treasury stock account is increased by the *book value* of the investment in the subsidiary. The accounting is similar to the purchase of treasury stock for cash, except that shares of the subsidiary are paid to shareholders instead of cash.

2. **Non pro rata distribution**. This case is like a tender offer where individual stockholders can accept or reject the distribution. The treasury stock account is recorded at the *market value* of the shares of the subsidiary distributed. Since the investment account can only be reduced by its book value, a gain or loss on distribution is recorded in the income statement for the difference. (The SEC allows companies to record the difference as an adjustment to additional paid-in capital; the usual practice, as might be expected, is for companies to report any gain as part of income.)

Bristol-Myers Squibb's non pro rata split-off of its subsidiary, Mead Johnson, provides an example. This transaction is described in the following excerpt from footnotes to Bristol-Myers' 10-K:

> **Mead Johnson Nutrition Company Split-off** The split-off of the remaining interest in Mead Johnson was completed on December 23, 2009. The split-off was effected through the exchange offer of previously held 170 million shares of Mead Johnson, after converting its Class B common stock to Class A common stock, for 269 million outstanding shares of the Company's stock resulting in a pre-tax gain of $7,275 million, $7,157 million net of taxes. The shares received in connection with the exchange were valued using the closing price on December 23, 2009, of $25.70 and reflected as treasury stock. The gain on the exchange was determined using the sum of the fair value of the shares received plus the net deficit of Mead Johnson attributable to the Company less taxes and other direct expenses related to the transaction, including a tax reserve of $244 million which was established.

From an accounting standpoint, the split-off of Mead Johnson is treated like the purchase of treasury stock, using the stock of Mead Johnson to fund the purchase instead of cash (such as exchanging Mead Johnson stock for Bristol-Myers stock). As a result of the transaction, the Treasury Stock account on Bristol-Myers' balance sheet increased (became more negative) by $6.9 billion (269 million shares × $25.70 per share), which reduced equity by $6.9 billion. This reduction was offset, however, by the recognition of a gain on the exchange amounting to $7.2 billion after tax. This split-off was affected by a tender offer with Bristol-Myers shareholders. Consequently, it is a non pro rata exchange and is, therefore, valued at market value with a resulting gain. The net effect on equity is minimal, but the income statement reports a substantial gain for that year.

Analysis of Equity Carve-Outs

Sell-offs, spin-offs, and split-offs all involve the divestiture of an operating segment. Although they are one-time occurrences, they can result in substantial gains that can markedly alter the income statement and balance sheet. Consequently, we need to interpret them carefully. This involves learning as many details about the carve out as possible from the annual report, the Management Discussion and Analysis, and other publicly available information.

Following an equity carve-out, the parent company loses the cash flows (positive or negative) of the divested business unit. As such, the divestiture should be treated like any other discontinued operation. Any recognized gain or loss from divestiture is treated as a nonoperating activity. The sale price of the divested unit reflects the valuation of *future expected* cash flows by the purchaser and is best viewed as a nonoperating activity. Income (and cash flows) of the divested unit up to the date of sale, however, is part of operations, although discontinued operations are typically segregated.

MID-MODULE REVIEW 4

Assume that BearingPoint announced the split-off of its Canadian subsidiary. BearingPoint reported a gain from the split-off. (1) Describe the accounting for a split-off. (2) Why was BearingPoint able to report a gain on this transaction?

The solution is on page 9-50.

Convertible Securities

Convertible securities are debt and equity securities that provide the holder with an option to convert those securities into other securities. In this section, we consider two specific types of convertibles: convertible debt securities, where debt is converted to common stock, and convertible preferred securities, where preferred stock is converted to common stock.

Convertible Debt Securities

Xilinx had convertible debt transactions in 2010, as explained in the following excerpt from footnotes to its 10-K report:

> **2.625% Senior Convertible Debentures** In June 2010, the Company issued $600.0 million principal amount of 2.625% Debentures to qualified institutional investors. The 2.625% Debentures are senior in right of payment to the Company's existing and future unsecured indebtedness... The 2.625% Debentures are initially convertible, subject to certain conditions, into shares of Xilinx common stock at a conversion rate of 33.0164 shares of common stock per $1 thousand principal amount of the 2.625% Debentures, representing an initial effective conversion price of approximately $30.29 per share of common stock.

The convertible debentures are reported as a long-term liability on Xilinx's balance sheet. To see the effects that conversion would have on Xilinx's financial statements, assume that the bonds are reported at their face amount of $600 (in $ millions) and that all of the bonds are subsequently converted into 19,809,840 shares ([$600 million/$1,000] × 33.0164 shares) of common stock with a par value of $0.01 per share. The financial statement effects of the conversion are as follows (Xilinx reports its balance sheet in $000s):

		Balance Sheet				Income Statement		
Transaction	Cash Asset	+ Noncash Assets	= Liabil- ities	+ Contrib. Capital	+ Earned Capital	Rev- enues	− Expen- ses	= Net Income
Conversion of convertible debt			−600,000 Long-Term Debt =	$198 Common Stock $599,802 Additional Paid-In Capital		−		=

L-T Debt 600,000
CS   198
APIC   599,802
LTD
600,000 |
        CS
        | 198
APIC
        | 599,802

Upon conversion, the debt is removed from the balance sheet at its book value ($600 million assumed in this case) and the common stock is issued for that amount, resulting in an increase in the Common Stock account of $198,000 (assuming 19,809,840 shares issued with a par value of $0.01 per share). Additional Paid-In Capital is increased for the remaining amount. No gain or loss (or cash inflow or outflow) is recognized as a result of the conversion.

Convertible Preferred Stock

Preferred stock can also contain a conversion privilege. Xerox provides an example in its 2010 10-K report:

> **Series A Convertible Preferred Stock** In connection with the acquisition of ACS in February 2010 (see Note 3 Acquisitions for additional information), we issued 300,000 shares of Series A convertible perpetual preferred stock with an aggregate liquidation preference of $300 and a fair value of $349 as of the acquisition date to the holder of ACS Class B common stock. The convertible preferred stock pays quarterly cash dividends at a rate of 8 percent per year and has a liquidation preference of $1,000 per share. Each share of convertible preferred stock is convertible at any time, at the option of the holder, into 89.8876 shares of common stock for a total of 26,966 thousand shares (reflecting an initial conversion price of approximately $11.125 per share of common stock . . .). On or after the fifth anniversary of the issue date, we have the right to cause, under certain circumstances, any or all of the convertible preferred stock to be converted into shares of common stock at the then applicable conversion rate. The convertible preferred stock is also convertible, at the option of the holder, upon a change in control, at the applicable conversion rate plus an additional number of shares determined by reference to the price paid for our common stock upon such change in control. In addition, upon the occurrence of certain fundamental change events, including a change in control or the delisting of Xerox's common stock, the holder of convertible preferred stock has the right to require us to redeem any or all of the convertible preferred stock in cash at a redemption price per share equal to the liquidation preference and any accrued and unpaid dividends to, but not including the redemption date.

Accounting for the conversion of preferred stock is essentially the same as that for convertible debt that we describe above: the preferred stock account is removed from the balance sheet and common stock is issued for the dollar amount of the preferred.

Conversion privileges offer an additional benefit to the holder of a security. That is, debtholders and preferred stockholders carry senior positions as claimants in bankruptcy, and also carry a fixed interest payment or dividend yield. Thus, they are somewhat protected from losses and their annual return is guaranteed. With a conversion privilege, debtholders or preferred stockholders can enjoy the residual benefits of common shareholders should the company perform well.

A conversion option is valuable and yields a higher price for the securities than they would otherwise command. However, conversion privileges impose a cost on common shareholders. That is, the higher market price received for convertible securities is offset by the cost imposed on the subordinate (common) securities.

One final note, diluted earnings per share (EPS) takes into account the potentially dilutive effect of convertible securities. Specifically, the diluted EPS computation assumes conversion at the beginning of the year (or when the security is issued if during the year). The earnings available to common shares in the numerator are increased by any forgone after-tax interest expense or preferred dividends, and the additional shares that would have been issued in the conversion, increase the shares outstanding in the denominator (see Module 5).

IFRS INSIGHT Convertible Securities under IFRS

Unlike GAAP, convertible securities (called *compound financial instruments* under IFRS) are split into separate debt and equity components. The idea is that the conversion premium is akin to a call option on the company's stock. This embedded option has a value of its own even if it is not legally detachable. Thus, under IFRS, the proceeds from the issuance are allocated between the liability component (at fair value) and an equity component (the residual amount).

GLOBAL ACCOUNTING

Under IFRS, accounting for equity is similar to that under U.S. GAAP. Following are a few terminology differences:

U.S. GAAP	IFRS
Common stock	Share capital
Preferred shares	Preference shares
Additional paid-in capital	Share premium
Retained earnings	Reserves
Accumulated other comprehensive income	Other equity or Other components of equity
—	Revaluation surplus or Revaluation reserve*

* In Modules 6 and 7, we noted that certain assets including fixed assets and intangible assets may be revalued upwards (and later, revalued downwards) under IFRS. These revaluations do not affect net income or retained earnings but, instead, are reported in a separate equity account. For comparative purposes our analysis might exclude revaluations from both equity and the asset accounts to which they relate.

U.S. GAAP has a more narrow definition of liabilities than IFRS. Therefore, more items are classified as liabilities under IFRS. For example, some preferred shares are deemed liabilities under IFRS and equity under GAAP. (Both systems classify preferred shares that are mandatorily redeemable or redeemable at the option of the shareholder, as liabilities.) For comparative purposes, we look at classification of preferred shares that are not mandatorily redeemable and make the numbers consistent. To do this we add preference shares classified as liabilities under IFRS to equity.

Treasury stock transactions are sometimes difficult to identify under IFRS because companies are not required to report a separate line item for treasury shares on the balance sheet. Instead treasury share transactions reduce share capital and share premium. We must review the statement of shareholders' equity to assess stock repurchases for IFRS companies.

For example, at March 31, 2011, British Telecom (BT) reports the following in the equity section of its IFRS balance sheet (in £ millions):

Ordinary shares	£ 408
Share premium	62
Capital redemption reserve	27
Other reserves	658
Retained earnings	770
Total parent shareholders' equity	**£1,925**

Its balance sheet reports no treasury stock line item, but footnotes disclose that the other reserves account (£658 million) includes the following:

(£ million)	Treasury shares
At 1 April 2010	**£(1,105)**
Net issue of treasury shares	27
At 31 March 2011	**£(1,078)**

The footnote reports that the treasury shares reserve is used to hold BT shares purchased by the company. During 2011 the company did not purchase any additional shares but did issue 12,335,580 shares from treasury to satisfy obligations under employee share schemes and executive share awards at a cost of £27 million . At March 31, 2011, 388,570,539 shares were held as treasury shares at cost.

Share-based compensation gives rise to timing differences and both IFRS and U.S. GAAP require companies to record deferred tax assets. Under IFRS, the deferred tax asset is adjusted each period to reflect fluctuations in the market price of equity. These market-value adjustments impact the income statement via tax expense. U.S. GAAP computes the deferred tax asset using the grant-date fair value and does not adjust for stock price fluctuations. This makes IFRS tax expense more volatile.

MODULE-END REVIEW

Assume that **Express Scripts, Inc.**, has issued the following convertible debentures: each $1,000 bond is convertible into 200 shares of $1 par common. Assume that the bonds were sold at a discount, and that each bond has a current unamortized discount equal to $150. Using the financial statements effect template, illustrate the effects on the financial statements of the conversion of one of these convertible debentures.

The solution is on page 9-50.

GUIDANCE ANSWERS

MANAGERIAL DECISION	You Are the Chief Financial Officer

Several points must be considered. (1) Buying stock back reduces the number of shares outstanding, which can prop up earnings per share (EPS). However, foregone earnings from the cash used for repurchases can dampen earnings. The net effect is that EPS is likely to increase because of the reduced shares in the denominator. (2) Another motivation is that, if the shares are sufficiently undervalued (in management's opinion), the stock repurchase and subsequent resale can provide a better return than alternative investments. (3) Stock repurchases send a strong signal to the market that management feels its stock is undervalued. This is more credible than merely making that argument with analysts. On the other hand, company cash is diverted from other investments. This is bothersome if such investments are mutually exclusive either now or in the future.

DISCUSSION QUESTIONS

Q9-1. Define *par value stock*. What is the significance of a stock's par value from an accounting and analysis perspective?

Q9-2. What are the basic differences between preferred stock and common stock? What are the typical features of preferred stock?

Q9-3. What features make preferred stock similar to debt? Similar to common stock?

Q9-4. What is meant by preferred dividends in arrears? If dividends are two years in arrears on $500,000 of 6% preferred stock, and dividends are declared at the end of this year, what amount of total dividends must the company pay to preferred shareholders before paying any dividends to common shareholders?

Q9-5. Distinguish between authorized shares and issued shares. Why might the number of shares issued be more than the number of shares outstanding?

Q9-6. Describe the difference between contributed capital and earned capital. Specifically, how can earned capital be considered as an investment by the company's shareholders?

Q9-7. How does the account "additional paid-in capital" (APIC) arise? Does the amount of APIC reported on the balance sheet relative to the common stock amount provide any information about the financial condition of the company?

Q9-8. Define *stock split*. What are the major reasons for a stock split?

Q9-9. Define *treasury stock*. Why might a corporation acquire treasury stock? How is treasury stock reported in the balance sheet?

Q9-10. If a corporation purchases 600 shares of its own common stock at $10 per share and resells them at $14 per share, where would the $2,400 increase in capital be reported in the financial statements? Why is no gain reported?

Q9-11. A corporation has total stockholders' equity of $4,628,000 and one class of $2 par value common stock. The corporation has 500,000 shares authorized; 300,000 shares issued; and 40,000 shares as treasury stock. What is its book value per share?

Q9-12. What is a stock dividend? How does a common stock dividend distributed to common shareholders affect their respective ownership interests?

Q9-13. What is the difference between the accounting for a small stock dividend and the accounting for a large stock dividend?

Q9-14. Employee stock options potentially dilute earnings per share (EPS). What can companies do to offset these dilutive effects and how might this action affect the balance sheet?

Q9-15. What information is reported in a statement of stockholders' equity?

Q9-16. What items are typically reported under the stockholders' equity category of accumulated other comprehensive income (AOCI)?

Q9-17. What is the difference between a spin-off and a split-off? Under what circumstances can either result in the recognition of a gain in the income statement?

Q9-18. Describe the accounting for a convertible bond. Can the conversion ever result in the recognition of a gain in the income statement?

Assignments with the ⊘ in the margin are available in an online homework system.
See the Preface of the book for details.

MINI EXERCISES

M9-19. Analyzing and Identifying Financial Statement Effects of Stock Issuances   (LO1)
During the current year, Beatty Company, (*a*) issues 8,000 shares of $50 par value preferred stock at $68 cash per share and (*b*) issues 12,000 shares of $1 par value common stock at $10 cash per share. Indicate the financial statement effects of these two issuances using the financial statement effects template.

M9-20. Analyzing and Identifying Financial Statement Effects of Stock Issuances   (LO1)
During the current year, Magliolo, Inc., (*a*) issues 18,000 shares of $10 par value preferred stock at $48 cash per share and (*b*) issues 120,000 shares of $2 par value common stock at $37 cash per share. Indicate the financial statement effects of these two issuances using the financial statement effects template.

M9-21. Distinguishing Between Common Stock and Additional Paid-in Capital   (LO1)

Cisco Systems, Inc.
(CSCO)

Following is the 2010 stockholders' equity section from the Cisco Systems, Inc., balance sheet.

Shareholders' Equity (in millions, except par value)	July 31, 2010
Preferred stock, no par value: 5 shares authorized; none issued and outstanding.......	$ —
Common stock and additional paid-in capital, $0.001 par value: 20,000 shares authorized; 5,655 and 5,785 shares issued and outstanding at July 31, 2010, and July 25, 2009, respectively	37,793
Retained earnings	5,851
Accumulated other comprehensive income....................................	623
Total Cisco shareholders' equity	44,267
Noncontrolling interests	18
Total equity...	$44,285

a. For the $37,793 million reported as "common stock and additional paid-in capital," what portion is common stock and what portion is additional paid-in capital?

b. Explain why Cisco does not report the two components described in part *a* separately.

M9-22. Identifying Financial Statement Effects of Stock Issuance and Repurchase   (LO1)
On January 1, Bartov Company issues 5,000 shares of $100 par value preferred stock at $250 cash per share. On March 1, the company repurchases 5,000 shares of previously issued $1 par value common stock at $83 cash per share. Use the financial statement effects template to record these two transactions.

M9-23. **Assessing the Financial Statement Effects of a Stock Split** (LO2)

Medco discloses the following footnote to its 10-K report.

Medco Health
Solutions, Inc.
(MHS)

> **Stock Split** In the first quarter of 2008, we completed a two-for-one stock split, which was
> effected in the form of a 100% stock dividend and distributed on January 24, 2008, to share-
> holders of record at the close of business on January 10, 2008. All share and per share amounts
> have been adjusted for the increase in issued and outstanding shares after giving effect to the
> stock split.

What restatements has Medco made to its balance sheet as a result of the stock split?

M9-24. **Reconciling Common Stock and Treasury Stock Balances** (LO1)

Following is the stockholders' equity section from the Abercrombie & Fitch balance sheet.

Abercrombie & Fitch
(ANF)

Stockholders' Equity ($ thousands, except par value amounts)	January 29, 2011	January 30, 2010
Class A common stock—$.01 par value: 150,000 shares authorized and 103,300 shares issued at each of January 29, 2011, and January 30, 2010	$ 1,033	$ 1,033
Paid-in capital	349,258	339,453
Retained earnings	2,272,317	2,183,690
Accumulated other comprehensive loss, net of tax........	(6,516)	(8,973)
Treasury stock at average cost: 16,054 and 15,314 shares at January 29, 2011, and January 30, 2010, respectively.....................	(725,308)	(687,286)
Total stockholders' equity	$1,890,784	$1,827,917

a. Show the computation to yield the $1,033 balance reported for common stock.

b. How many shares are outstanding at 2011 fiscal year-end?

c. Use the common stock and paid-in capital accounts to determine the average price at which Abercrombie & Fitch issued its common stock.

d. Use the treasury stock account to determine the average price Abercrombie & Fitch paid when it repurchased its common shares.

M9-25. **Identifying and Analyzing Financial Statement Effects of Cash Dividends** (LO2)

Freid Company has outstanding 6,000 shares of $50 par value, 6% preferred stock, and 40,000 shares of $1 par value common stock. The company has $328,000 of retained earnings. At year-end, the company declares and pays the regular $3 per share cash dividend on preferred stock and a $2.20 per share cash dividend on common stock. Use the financial statement effects template to indicate the effects of these two dividend payments.

M9-26. **Identifying and Analyzing Financial Statement Effects of Stock Dividends** (LO2)

Dutta Corp. has outstanding 70,000 shares of $5 par value common stock. At year-end, the company declares and issues a 4% common stock dividend when the market price of the stock is $21 per share. Use the financial statement effects template to indicate the effects of this stock dividend declaration and payment.

M9-27. **Identifying, Analyzing and Explaining the Effects of a Stock Split** (LO2)

On September 1, Weiss Company has 250,000 shares of $15 par value ($165 market value) common stock that are issued and outstanding. Its balance sheet on that date shows the following account balances relating to its common stock:

Common stock........................	$3,750,000
Paid-in capital in excess of par value........	2,250,000

On September 2, Weiss splits its stock 3-for-2 and reduces the par value to $10 per share.

a. How many shares of common stock are issued and outstanding immediately after the stock split?

b. What is the dollar balance of the common stock account immediately after the stock split?

c. What is the likely reason that Weiss Company split its stock?

M9-28.   Determining Cash Dividends to Preferred and Common Shareholders   (LO2)

Dechow Company has outstanding 20,000 shares of $50 par value, 6% cumulative preferred stock and 80,000 shares of $10 par value common stock. The company declares and pays cash dividends amounting to $160,000.

a. If there are no preferred dividends in arrears, how much in total dividends, and in dividends per share, does Dechow pay to each class of stock?

b. If there are one year's dividends in arrears on the preferred stock, how much in total dividends, and in dividends per share, does Dechow pay to each class of stock?

M9-29.   Reconciling Retained Earnings   (LO2)

Use the following data to reconcile the 2012 retained earnings for Bamber Company (that is, explain the change in retained earnings during the year).

Total retained earnings, December 31, 2011	$347,000
Stock dividends declared and paid in 2012	28,000
Cash dividends declared and paid in 2012	35,000
Net income for 2012	94,000

M9-30.   Interpreting a Spin-Off Disclosure   (LO3)

NCR Corp. (NCR)

NCR Corporation discloses the following in notes to its 2007 10-K report.

> **Spin-off of Teradata Data Warehousing Business** On September 30, 2007, NCR completed the spin-off of its Teradata Data Warehousing business through the distribution of a tax-free dividend to its stockholders. NCR distributed one share of common stock of Teradata Corporation (Teradata) for each share of NCR common stock to NCR stockholders of record as of the close of business on September 14, 2007. Upon the distribution of Teradata, NCR stockholders received 100% (approximately 181 million shares) of the common stock of Teradata, which is now an independent public company trading under the symbol "TDC" on the New York Stock Exchange.

a. Describe the difference between a spin-off and a split-off.

b. What effects did NCR's spin-off of Teradata have on NCR's balance sheet and income statement?

M9-31.   Interpreting a Proposed Split-Off Disclosure   (LO3)

Viacom, Inc. (VIA)

Viacom, Inc., reports the following footnote in its 2005 10-K.

> **Discontinued Operations** In 2004, Viacom completed the exchange offer for the split-off of Blockbuster Inc. ("Blockbuster") (NYSE: BBI and BBI.B). Under the terms of the offer, Viacom accepted 27,961,165 shares of Viacom common stock in exchange for the 144 million common shares of Blockbuster that Viacom owned. Each share of Viacom Class A or Class B common stock accepted for exchange by Viacom was exchanged for 5.15 shares of Blockbuster common stock, consisting of 2.575 shares of Blockbuster Class A common stock and 2.575 shares of Blockbuster Class B common stock.

a. Describe the accounting for a split-off.

b. How will the proposed split-off affect the number of Viacom shares outstanding?

c. Under what circumstances will Viacom be able to report a gain for this proposed split-off?

M9-32.   Interpreting Disclosure Related to Spin-Off   (LO3)

Altria Group, Inc. (MO)

Altria reports the following footnote to its 2008 10-K.

> On March 28, 2008, Altria Group, Inc. distributed all of its interest in Philip Morris International Inc. ("PMI") to Altria Group, Inc. stockholders of record as of the close of business on March 19, 2008, in a tax-free distribution. Altria Group, Inc. distributed one share of PMI common stock for every share of Altria Group, Inc. common stock outstanding as of the PMI Record Date. Following the PMI Distribution Date, Altria Group, Inc. does not own any shares of PMI stock. Altria Group, Inc. has reflected the results of PMI prior to the PMI Distribution Date as discontinued operations on the consolidated statements of earnings and the consolidated statements

continued

continued from prior page

of cash flows for all periods presented. The assets and liabilities related to PMI were reclassi-fied and reflected as discontinued operations on the consolidated balance sheet at December 31, 2007. The distribution resulted in a net decrease to Altria Group, Inc.'s total stockholders' equity of $14.4 billion on the PMI Distribution Date.

a. Describe the accounting for a spin-off.
b. What effects did this transaction have on Altria's balance sheet and income statement?

M9-33.   Analyzing Financial Statement Effects of Convertible Securities   (LO3)

JetBlue Airways Corporation reports the following footnote to its 2005 10-K.

JetBlue Airways
Corporation (JBLU)

In March 2005, we completed a public offering of $250 million aggregate principal amount of 3¾% convertible unsecured debentures due 2035, which are currently convertible into 14.6 million shares of our common stock at a price of approximately $17.10 per share.

a. Describe the effects on JetBlue's balance sheet if the convertible bonds are converted.
b. Would the conversion affect earnings? Explain.

EXERCISES

E9-34.   Identifying and Analyzing Financial Statement Effects of Stock Transactions   (LO1)

Lipe Company reports the following transactions relating to its stock accounts in the current year.

Feb.	20	Issued 10,000 shares of $1 par value common stock at $25 cash per share.
Feb.	21	Issued 15,000 shares of $100 par value, 8% preferred stock at $275 cash per share.
June	30	Purchased 2,000 shares of its own common stock at $15 cash per share.
Sep.	25	Sold 1,000 shares of its treasury stock at $21 cash per share.

Use the financial statement effects template to indicate the effects from each of these transactions.

E9-35.   Identifying and Analyzing Financial Statement Effects of Stock Transactions   (LO1)

McNichols Corp. reports the following transactions relating to its stock accounts in the current year.

Jan.	15	Issued 25,000 shares of $5 par value common stock at $17 cash per share.
Jan.	20	Issued 6,000 shares of $50 par value, 8% preferred stock at $78 cash per share.
Mar.	31	Purchased 3,000 shares of its own common stock at $20 cash per share.
June	25	Sold 2,000 shares of its treasury stock at $26 cash per share.
July	15	Sold the remaining 1,000 shares of treasury stock at $19 cash per share.

Use the financial statement effects template to indicate the effects from each of these transactions.

E9-36.   Analyzing and Computing Average Issue Price and Treasury Stock Cost   (LO1)

Following is the stockholders' equity section from the Campbell Soup Company balance sheet.

Campbell Soup (CPB)

Shareowners' Equity (millions, except per share amounts)	August 1, 2010	July 2, 2009
Preferred stock: authorized 40 shares; none issued	$ —	$ —
Capital stock, $.0375 par value; authorized 560 shares; issued 542 shares.	20	20
Additional paid-in capital	341	332
Earnings retained in the business	8,760	8,288
Capital stock in treasury, at cost	(7,459)	(7,194)
Accumulated other comprehensive loss	(736)	(718)
Total Campbell Soup Company shareowners' equity	926	728
Noncontrolling interest	3	3
Total equity	$ 929	$ 731

Campbell Soup Company also reports the following statement of stockholders' equity.

	CAMPBELL SOUP COMPANY Shareowners' Equity								
	Capital Stock				Additional Paid-in Capital	Earnings Retained in the Business	Accumulated Other Comprehensive Income (Loss)	Noncontrolling Interest	Total Equity
	Issued		In Treasury						
(Millions, except per share amounts)	Shares	Amount	Shares	Amount					
Balance at August 2, 2009.........	542	$20	(199)	$(7,194)	$332	$8,288	$(718)	$ 3	$731
Comprehensive income (loss)									
Net earnings..................						844		—	844
Foreign currency translation adjustments, net of tax.........							39	—	39
Cash-flow hedges, net of tax.....							2		2
Pension and postretirement benefits, net of tax							(59)		(59)
Other comprehensive income (loss)................							(18)	—	(18)
Total comprehensive income (loss) ..									826
Dividends ($1.075 per share).......						(372)			(372)
Treasury stock purchased			(14)	(472)					(472)
Treasury stock issued under management incentive and stock option plans.............			7	207	9				216
Balance at August 1, 2010.........	542	$20	(206)	$(7,459)	$341	$8,760	$(736)	$ 3	$929

a. Show the computation, using par value and share numbers, to arrive at the $20 million in the common stock account.

b. At what average price were the Campbell Soup shares issued?

c. Reconcile the beginning and ending balances of retained earnings.

d. Campbell Soup reports a $39 gain as part of Accumulated Other Comprehensive Income relating to foreign currency translation adjustments. Explain what foreign currency translation adjustments represent. What effect did foreign currency translation adjustments have on net earnings for the year?

e. Campbell Soup reports an increase in stockholders' equity relating to the exercise of stock options (titled "Treasury stock issued under management incentive and stock option plans"). This transaction involves the purchase of common stock by employees at a preset price. Describe how this set of transactions affects stockholders' equity.

f. Describe the transaction relating to the "Treasury stock purchased" line in the statement of stockholders' equity.

E9-37. Analyzing Cash Dividends on Preferred and Common Stock (LO2)

Moser Company began business on March 1, 2010. At that time, it issued 20,000 shares of $60 par value, 7% cumulative preferred stock and 100,000 shares of $5 par value common stock. Through the end of 2012, there has been no change in the number of preferred and common shares outstanding.

a. Assume that Moser declared and paid cash dividends of $0 in 2010, $183,000 in 2011, and $200,000 in 2012. Compute the total cash dividends and the dividends per share paid to each class of stock in 2010, 2011, and 2012.

b. Assume that Moser declared and paid cash dividends of $0 in 2010, $84,000 in 2011, and $150,000 in 2012. Compute the total cash dividends and the dividends per share paid to each class of stock in 2010, 2011, and 2012.

E9-38. Analyzing Cash Dividends on Preferred and Common Stock (LO2)

Potter Company has outstanding 15,000 shares of $50 par value, 8% preferred stock and 50,000 shares of $5 par value common stock. During its first three years in business, it declared and paid no cash dividends in the first year, $280,000 in the second year, and $60,000 in the third year.

a. If the preferred stock is cumulative, determine the total amount of cash dividends paid to each class of stock in each of the three years.

b. If the preferred stock is noncumulative, determine the total amount of cash dividends paid to each class of stock in each of the three years.

E9-39. **Analyzing and Computing Issue Price, Treasury Stock Cost, and Shares Outstanding** (LO1)
Following is the stockholders' equity section from Altria's 2010 balance sheet.

Altria Group, Inc.
(MO)

December 31 ($ million)	2010
Common stock, par value $0.33⅓ per share (2,805,961,317 shares issued)...........	$ 935
Additional paid-in capital...	5,751
Earnings reinvested in the business..	23,459
Accumulated other comprehensive losses	(1,484)
Cost of repurchased stock (717,221,651 shares in 2010)	(23,469)
Total stockholders' equity attributable to Altria Group, Inc....................	5,192
Noncontrolling interests..	3
Total stockholders' equity	$ 5,195

a. Show the computation to derive the $935 million for common stock.
b. At what average price has Altria issued its common stock?
c. How many shares of Altria common stock are outstanding as of December 31, 2010?
d. At what average cost has Altria repurchased its treasury stock as of December 31, 2010?
e. Why would a company such as Altria want to repurchase $23,469 million of its common stock?
f. What does the Noncontrolling Interests account of $3 million represent?

E9-40. **Analyzing Cash Dividends on Preferred and Common Stock** (LO2)
Skinner Company began business on June 30, 2010. At that time, it issued 18,000 shares of $50 par value, 6% cumulative preferred stock and 90,000 shares of $10 par value common stock. Through the end of 2012, there has been no change in the number of preferred and common shares outstanding.

a. Assume that Skinner declared and paid cash dividends of $63,000 in 2010, $0 in 2011, and $378,000 in 2012. Compute the total cash dividends and the dividends per share paid to each class of stock in 2010, 2011, and 2012.
b. Assume that Skinner declared and paid cash dividends of $0 in 2010, $108,000 in 2011, and $189,000 in 2012. Compute the total cash dividends and the dividends per share paid to each class of stock in 2010, 2011, and 2012.

E9-41. **Identifying and Analyzing Financial Statement Effects of Dividends** (LO2)
Chaney Company has outstanding 25,000 shares of $10 par value common stock. It also has $405,000 of retained earnings. Near the current year-end, the company declares and pays a cash dividend of $1.90 per share and declares and issues a 4% stock dividend. The market price of the stock the day the dividends are declared is $35 per share. Use the financial statement effects template to indicate the effects of these two separate dividend transactions.

E9-42. **Identifying and Analyzing Financial Statement Effects of Dividends** (LO2)
The stockholders' equity of Pagach Company at December 31, 2011, appears below.

Common stock, $10 par value, 200,000 shares authorized; 80,000 shares issued and outstanding......................	$800,000
Paid-in capital in excess of par value.........................	480,000
Retained earnings	305,000

During 2012, the following transactions occurred:

May 12 Declared and issued a 7% stock dividend; the common stock market value was $18 per share.
Dec. 31 Declared and paid a cash dividend of 75 cents per share.

a. Use the financial statement effects template to indicate the effects of these transactions.
b. Reconcile retained earnings for 2012 assuming that the company reports 2012 net income of $283,000.

E9-43.   Identifying and Analyzing Financial Statement Effects of Dividends   (LO2)

The stockholders' equity of Kinney Company at December 31, 2011, is shown below.

5% preferred stock, $100 par value, 10,000 shares authorized; 4,000 shares issued and outstanding.	$ 400,000
Common stock, $5 par value, 200,000 shares authorized; 50,000 shares issued and outstanding.	250,000
Paid-in capital in excess of par value—preferred stock.	40,000
Paid-in capital in excess of par value—common stock.	300,000
Retained earnings	656,000
Total stockholders' equity	$1,646,000

The following transactions, among others, occurred during 2012:

Apr. 1   Declared and issued a 100% stock dividend on all outstanding shares of common stock. The market value of the stock was $11 per share.

Dec. 7   Declared and issued a 3% stock dividend on all outstanding shares of common stock. The market value of the stock was $14 per share.

Dec. 20   Declared and paid (1) the annual cash dividend on the preferred stock and (2) a cash dividend of 80 cents per common share.

a. Use the financial statement effects template to indicate the effects of these separate transactions.

b. Compute retained earnings for 2012 assuming that the company reports 2012 net income of $253,000.

E9-44.   Identifying, Analyzing and Explaining the Effects of a Stock Split   (LO2)

On March 1 of the current year, Zhang Company has 400,000 shares of $20 par value common stock that are issued and outstanding. Its balance sheet shows the following account balances relating to common stock.

Common stock.	$8,000,000
Paid-in capital in excess of par value.	3,400,000

On March 2, Zhang Company splits its common stock 2-for-1 and reduces the par value to $10 per share.

a. How many shares of common stock are issued and outstanding immediately after the stock split?

b. What is the dollar balance in the common stock account immediately after the stock split?

c. What is the dollar balance in the paid-in capital in excess of par value account immediately after the stock split?

E9-45.   Analyzing and Computing Issue Price, Treasury Stock Cost, and Shares Outstanding   (LO1)

Caterpillar Inc.
(CAT)

Following is the stockholders' equity section of the 2010 Caterpillar Inc., balance sheet.

Stockholders' Equity ($ millions)	2010	2009	2008
Common stock of $1.00 par; Authorized shares: 2,000,000,000; Issued shares (2010, 2009 and 2008—814,894,624) at paid-in amount	$ 3,888	$ 3,439	$ 3,057
Treasury stock (2010—176,071,910 shares; 2009—190,171,905 shares; 2008—213,367,983 shares) at cost	(10,397)	(10,646)	(11,217)
Profit employed in the business.	21,384	19,711	19,826
Accumulated other comprehensive income (loss)	(4,051)	(3,764)	(5,579)
Noncontrolling interests	40	83	103
Total stockholders' equity	$10,864	$ 8,823	$ 6,190

a. How many shares of Caterpillar common stock are outstanding at year-end 2010?

b. What does the phrase "at paid-in amount" in the stockholders' equity section mean?

c. At what average cost has Caterpillar repurchased its stock as of year-end 2010?

d. Why would a company such as Caterpillar want to repurchase its common stock?

e. Explain how CAT's "issued shares" remains constant over the three-year period while the dollar amount of its common stock account increases.

E9-46. **Analyzing Equity Changes from Convertible Preferred Stock**   (LO3)

Xerox reports the following stockholders' equity information in its 10-K report.

Xerox Corporation (XRX)

Shareholders' Equity (In millions, except share data in thousands)	December 31 2006	2005
Series C mandatory convertible preferred stock	$ —	$ 889
Common stock, including additional paid-in capital	4,666	4,741
Treasury stock, at cost	(141)	(203)
Retained earnings	4,202	3,021
Accumulated other comprehensive loss	(1,647)	(1,240)

(In millions, except share data in thousands)	Common Stock Shares	Common Stock Amount	Additional Paid-in Capital	Treasury Stock Shares	Treasury Stock Amount	Retained Earnings	Accumulated Other Comprehensive Loss	Total
Balance at December 31, 2005	945,106	$945	$3,796	(13,917)	$ (203)	$3,021	$(1,240)	$6,319
Net income						1,210		1,210
Translation adjustments							485	485
Minimum pension liability							131	131
Other unrealized gains							1	1
Comprehensive income								$1,827
Adjustment to initially apply FAS No. 158, net							(1,024)	(1,024)
Stock option and incentive plans, net	10,256	11	156					167
Series C mandatory convertible preferred stock dividends ($6.25 per share)						(29)		(29)
Series C mandatory convertible preferred stock conversion	74,797	75	814					889
Payments to acquire treasury stock				(70,111)	(1,069)			(1,069)
Cancellation of treasury stock	(75,665)	(75)	(1,056)	75,665	1,131			—
Other	74							—
Balance, December 31, 2006	954,568	$956	$3,710	(8,363)	$ (141)	$4,202	$(1,647)	$7,080

Preferred Stock As of December 31, 2006, we had no preferred stock shares outstanding and one class of preferred stock purchase rights. We are authorized to issue approximately 22 million shares of cumulative preferred stock, $1.00 par value.

Series C Mandatory Convertible Preferred Stock Automatic Conversion: In July 2006, 9.2 million shares of 6.25% Series C Mandatory Convertible Preferred Stock were converted at a rate of 8.1301 shares of our common stock, or 74.8 million common stock shares. The recorded value of outstanding shares at the time of conversion was $889. The conversion occurred pursuant to the mandatory automatic conversion provisions set at original issuance of the Series C Preferred Stock. As a result of the automatic conversion, there are no remaining outstanding shares of our Series C Mandatory Convertible Preferred Stock.

Common Stock We have 1.75 billion authorized shares of common stock, $1 par value. At December 31, 2006, 106 million shares were reserved for issuance under our incentive compensation plans, 48 million shares were reserved for debt to equity exchanges, 15 million shares were reserved for the conversion of the Series C Mandatory Convertible Preferred Stock and 2 million shares were reserved for the conversion of convertible debt. The 15 million shares reserved for the conversion of the Series C Mandatory Convertible Preferred Stock are expected to be released in 2007, since conversion was completed in 2006.

Required

a. At December 31, 2005, Xerox reports $889 million of 6.25% Series C Mandatory Convertible Preferred stock. What is the dollar amount of dividends that Xerox must pay on this stock (assume a par value of $100 per share)? Some have argued that securities such as this are more like debt than equity. What is the basis for such an argument?

b. Describe the effects of conversion of the Series C Mandatory Convertible Preferred stock during 2006 on Xerox's balance sheet and its income statement.

c. What is the benefit, if any, to Xerox of issuing equity securities with a conversion feature? How are these securities treated in the computation of earnings per share (EPS)?

E9-47.   **Analyzing and Computing Issue Price, Treasury Stock Cost, and Shares Outstanding**   (LO1)
Following is the stockholders' equity and minority interest sections of the 2010 Merck & Co., Inc., balance sheet.

Stockholders' Equity ($ millions)	2010
Common stock, $0.50 par value; Authorized—6,500,000,000 shares; Issued—3,576,948,356 shares—2010	$ 1,788
Other paid-in capital.	40,701
Retained earnings	37,536
Accumulated other comprehensive loss	(3,216)
	76,809
Less treasury stock, at cost; 494,841,533 shares—2010	22,433
Total Merck & Co., Inc. stockholders' equity	54,376
Noncontrolling interests	2,429
Total equity.	$56,805

a. Show the computation of the $1,788 million in the common stock account.
b. At what average price were the Merck common shares issued?
c. At what average cost was the Merck treasury stock purchased?
d. How many common shares are outstanding as of December 31, 2010?

PROBLEMS

P9-48.   **Identifying and Analyzing Financial Statement Effects of Stock Transactions**   (LO1)
The stockholders' equity section of Gupta Company at December 31, 2011, follows:

8% preferred stock, $25 par value, 50,000 shares authorized; 6,800 shares issued and outstanding.	$170,000
Common stock, $10 par value, 200,000 shares authorized; 50,000 shares issued and outstanding.	500,000
Paid-in capital in excess of par value—preferred stock.	68,000
Paid-in capital in excess of par value—common stock.	200,000
Retained earnings	270,000

During 2012, the following transactions occurred:

Jan.   10   Issued 28,000 shares of common stock for $17 cash per share.
Jan.   23   Repurchased 8,000 shares of common stock at $19 cash per share.
Mar.   14   Sold one-half of the treasury shares acquired January 23 for $21 cash per share.
July   15   Issued 3,200 shares of preferred stock for $128,000 cash.
Nov.   15   Sold 1,000 of the treasury shares acquired January 23 for $24 cash per share.

Required
a. Use the financial statement effects template to indicate the effects from each of these transactions.
b. Prepare the December 31, 2012, stockholders' equity section of the balance sheet assuming the company reports 2012 net income of $59,000.

P9-49.   **Identifying and Analyzing Financial Statement Effects of Stock Transactions**   (LO1, 2)
The stockholders' equity of Sougiannis Company at December 31, 2011, follows:

7% Preferred stock, $100 par value, 20,000 shares authorized; 5,000 shares issued and outstanding.	$ 500,000
Common stock, $15 par value, 100,000 shares authorized; 40,000 shares issued and outstanding.	600,000
Paid-in capital in excess of par value—preferred stock.	24,000
Paid-in capital in excess of par value—common stock.	360,000
Retained earnings	325,000
Total stockholders' equity	$1,809,000

The following transactions, among others, occurred during the following year:

> Jan. 12 Announced a 3-for-1 common stock split, reducing the par value of the common stock to $5 per share. The authorized shares were increased to 300,000 shares.
>
> Sept. 1 Repurchased 10,000 shares of common stock at $10 cash per share.
>
> Oct. 12 Sold 1,500 treasury shares acquired September 1 at $12 cash per share.
>
> Nov. 21 Issued 5,000 shares of common stock at $21 cash per share.
>
> Dec. 28 Sold 1,200 treasury shares acquired September 1 at $9 cash per share.

Required

a. Use the financial statement effects template to indicate the effects from each of these transactions.

b. Prepare the December 31, 2012, stockholders' equity section of the balance sheet assuming that the company reports 2012 net income of $83,000.

P9-50. **Identifying and Analyzing Financial Statement Effects of Stock Transactions** (LO1)

The stockholders' equity of Verrecchia Company at December 31, 2011, follows:

Common stock, $5 par value, 350,000 shares authorized;	
150,000 shares issued and outstanding......................	$750,000
Paid-in capital in excess of par value.........................	600,000
Retained earnings	346,000

During 2012, the following transactions occurred:

> Jan.   5 Issued 10,000 shares of common stock for $12 cash per share.
>
> Jan. 18 Repurchased 4,000 shares of common stock at $14 cash per share.
>
> Mar. 12 Sold one-fourth of the treasury shares acquired January 18 for $17 cash per share.
>
> July 17 Sold 500 shares of treasury stock for $13 cash per share.
>
> Oct.   1 Issued 5,000 shares of 8%, $25 par value preferred stock for $35 cash per share. This is the first issuance of preferred shares from the 50,000 authorized preferred shares.

Required

a. Use the financial statement effects template to indicate the effects of each transaction.

b. Prepare the December 31, 2012, stockholders' equity section of the balance sheet assuming that the company reports net income of $72,500 for the year.

P9-51. **Identifying and Analyzing Financial Statement Effects of Stock Transactions** (LO1, 2)

Following is the stockholders' equity of Dennis Corporation at December 31, 2011:

8% preferred stock, $50 par value, 10,000 shares authorized;	
7,000 shares issued and outstanding..........................	$ 350,000
Common stock, $20 par value, 50,000 shares authorized;	
25,000 shares issued and outstanding........................	500,000
Paid-in capital in excess of par value—preferred stock..............	70,000
Paid-in capital in excess of par value—common stock..............	385,000
Retained earnings	238,000
Total stockholders' equity	$1,543,000

The following transactions, among others, occurred during 2012:

> Jan. 15 Issued 1,000 shares of preferred stock for $62 cash per share.
>
> Jan. 20 Issued 4,000 shares of common stock at $36 cash per share.
>
> May 18 Announced a 2-for-1 common stock split, reducing the par value of the common stock to $10 per share. The number of shares authorized was increased to 100,000 shares.
>
> June   1 Issued 2,000 shares of common stock for $60,000 cash.
>
> Sept. 1 Repurchased 2,500 shares of common stock at $18 cash per share.
>
> Oct. 12 Sold 900 treasury shares at $21 cash per share.
>
> Dec. 22 Issued 500 shares of preferred stock for $59 cash per share.

Required

Use the financial statement effects template to indicate the effects of each transaction.

P9-52.   Analyzing and Interpreting Equity Accounts and Comprehensive Income (LO2)
Following is the shareholders' equity section of the 2010 balance sheet for Procter & Gamble Company and its statement of shareholders' equity.

June 30 (In millions, except per share amounts)	2010	2009
Shareholders' Equity		
Convertible Class A preferred stock, stated value $1 per share (600 shares authorized)..	$ 1,277	$ 1,324
Non-Voting Class B preferred stock, stated value $1 per share (200 shares authorized)...	—	—
Common stock, stated value $1 per share (10,000 shares authorized; shares issued: 2010—4,007.6, 2009—4,007.3)	4,008	4,007
Additional paid-in capital	61,697	61,118
Reserve for ESOP debt retirement..................................	(1,350)	(1,340)
Accumulated other comprehensive income (loss)	(7,822)	(3,358)
Treasury stock, at cost (shares held: 2010—1,164.1, 2009—1,090.3)........	(61,309)	(55,961)
Retained earnings	64,614	57,309
Noncontrolling interest...	324	283
Total shareholders' equity	$61,439	$63,382

Consolidated Statement of Shareholders' Equity

Dollars in millions; Shares in thousands	Common Shares Outstanding	Common Stock	Preferred Stock	Additional Paid-in Capital	Reserve for ESOP Debt Retirement	Accumulated Other Comprehensive Income (Loss)	Non-controlling Interest	Treasury Stock	Retained Earnings	Total
Balance June 30, 2009...........	2,917,035	$4,007	$1,324	$61,118	$(1,340)	$(3,358)	$283	$(55,961)	$57,309	$63,382
Net earnings...................									12,736	12,736
Other comprehensive income:										
Financial statement translation....						(4,194)				(4,194)
Hedges and investment securities, net of $520 tax.....						867				867
Defined benefit retirement plans, net of $465 tax						(1,137)				(1,137)
Total comprehensive income										$8,272
Dividends to shareholders:										
Common....................									(5,239)	(5,239)
Preferred, net of tax benefits									(219)	(219)
Treasury purchases	(96,759)							(6,004)		(6,004)
Employee plan issuances.........	17,616	1		574				616		1,191
Preferred stock conversions.......	5,579		(47)	7				40		—
ESOP debt impacts					(10)				27	17
Noncontrolling interest........				(2)			41			39
Balance June 30, 2010...........	2,843,471	$4,008	$1,277	$61,697	$(1,350)	$(7,822)	$324	$(61,309)	$64,614	$61,439

Required

a. What does the term *convertible* (in reference to the company's Class A preferred stock) mean?

b. How many shares of common stock did Procter & Gamble issue when convertible Class A preferred stock was converted during fiscal 2010?

c. Describe the transactions relating to employee plan issuances. At what average price was the common stock issued as of year-end 2010?

d. What is other comprehensive income? What is the accumulated other comprehensive income account? Explain.

e. What cash dividends did Procter & Gamble pay in 2010 for each class of stock?

P9-53. **Analyzing and Interpreting Equity Accounts and Accumulated Other Comprehensive Income** (LO2)

Following is the stockholders' equity section of Fortune Brands balance sheet and its statement of stockholders' equity.

Fortune Brands, Inc. (FO)

December 31 (In millions, except per share amounts)	2010	2009
Stockholders' Equity		
$2.67 convertible preferred stock	$ 4.9	$ 5.2
Common stock, par value $3.125 per share, 234.9 shares issued	734.0	734.0
Paid-in capital	820.2	755.6
Accumulated other comprehensive loss	(172.0)	(211.8)
Retained earnings	7,499.3	7,135.4
Treasury stock, at cost	(3,215.3)	(3,326.0)
Total Fortune Brands stockholders' equity	5,671.1	5,092.4
Noncontrolling interests	16.9	13.3
Total equity	$5,688.0	$5,105.7

(In millions, except per share amounts)	$2.67 Convertible Preferred Stock	Common Stock	Paid-in Capital	Accumulated Other Comprehensive Income (Loss)	Retained Earnings	Treasury Stock At Cost	Non-controlling Interests	Total
Balance at December 31, 2009	$5.2	$734.0	$755.6	$(211.8)	$7,135.4	$(3,326.0)	$13.3	$5,105.7
Comprehensive income								
Net income	—	—	—	—	487.6	—	8.4	496.0
Translation adjustments (net of tax expense of $17.3 million)	—	—	—	26.0	—	—	—	26.0
Derivative instruments (net of tax benefit of $1.5 million)	—	—	—	2.8	—	—	—	2.8
Pension and postretirement benefit adjustments (net of tax expense of $8.1 million)	—	—	—	11.0	—	—	—	11.0
Total comprehensive Income	—	—	—	39.8	487.6	—	8.4	535.8
Dividends paid to noncontrolling interests	—	—	—	—	—	—	(4.8)	(4.8)
Dividends ($0.76 per Common share and $2.67 per Preferred share)	—	—	—	—	(116.2)	—	—	(116.2)
Shares issued from treasury stock for benefit plans			5.7		—	61.4	—	67.1
Stock-based compensation	—	—	55.2	—	(7.5)	46.6	—	94.3
Tax benefit on exercise of stock options	—	—	6.1	—	—	—	—	6.1
Conversion of preferred stock	(0.3)	—	(2.4)	—	—	2.7	—	—
Balance at December 31, 2010	$ 4.9	$734.0	$820.2	$(172.0)	$7,499.3	$(3,215.3)	$16.9	$5,688.0

Required

a. Explain the "$2.67" component of the convertible preferred stock account title.

b. Show (confirm) the computation that yields the $734.0 million common stock at year-end 2010.

c. Assuming that the convertible preferred stock was sold at par value, at what average price were Fortune Brands' common shares issued as of year-end 2010?

d. What is included in Fortune Brands' other comprehensive income for 2010? What other items are typically included in other comprehensive income?

e. Explain the $6.1 million tax benefit on exercise of stock options, reported in the statement of stockholders' equity.

P9-54. **Interpreting Footnote Disclosure on Convertible Debentures** (LO3)

Alloy, Inc., reports the following footnote related to its convertible debentures in its 2007 10-K ($ thousands).

Alloy, Inc. (ALOY)

In August 2003, Alloy completed the issuance of $69,300 of 20-Year 5.375% Senior Convertible Debentures due August 1, 2023. If converted, bondholders would currently receive 29.851 shares of Alloy common for each $1,000 face amount bond. Alloy continues to be responsible for repaying the Convertible Debentures in full if they are not converted into shares of Alloy

continued

continued from prior page

common stock. If not previously converted to common stock, Alloy may redeem the Convertible Debentures after August 1, 2008 at 103% of their face amount from August 1, 2008 through December 31, 2008 and at declining prices to 100% in January 2011 and thereafter, with accrued interest. From August 30, 2006 through December 7, 2006, holders converted approximately $67,903 face amount of their Debentures, in accordance with their terms, into approximately 2,026,000 shares of Alloy common stock. During fiscal 2006, the Company's additional paid-in capital increased by $67,883 as a result of the conversions. At January 31, 2007, the Company had $1,397 in principal amount of outstanding Convertible Debentures. At January 31, 2007, the fair value of the Convertible Debentures was approximately $1,504, which is estimated based on quoted market prices.

Required

a. How did Alloy initially account for the issuance of the 5.375% debentures, assuming that the conversion option cannot be detached and sold separately?

b. Consider the conversion terms reported in the footnote. At what minimum stock price would it make economic sense for debenture holders to convert to Alloy common stock?

c. Use the financial statement effects template to show how Alloy accounted for the conversion of the 5.375% debentures in 2006. The par value of the company's stock is $0.01.

d. Assume that the conversion feature is valued by investors and, therefore, results in a higher initial issuance price for the bonds. What effect will the conversion feature have on the amount of interest expense and net income that Alloy reports?

e. How are the convertible debentures treated in the computation of basic and diluted earnings per share (EPS)?

P9-55.   Interpreting Disclosure on Convertible Preferred Securities   (LO3)

Northrop Grumman
Corp. (NOC)

The 2008 annual report of Northrop Gruman Corporation includes the following disclosure in its shareholders' equity footnote:

Conversion of Preferred Stock   On February 20, 2008, the company's board of directors approved the redemption of all of the 3.5 million shares of mandatorily redeemable convertible preferred stock on April 4, 2008. Prior to the redemption date, substantially all of the preferred shares were converted into common stock at the election of shareholders. All remaining unconverted preferred shares were redeemed by the company on the redemption date. As a result of the conversion and redemption, the company issued approximately 6.4 million shares of common stock.

Required

a. Explain what is meant by "mandatorily redeemable" and "convertible" preferred stock.

b. The company's balance sheet reports preferred stock of $350 million at December 31, 2007 (and $0 at December 31, 2008). As is typical, Northrop Grumman originally sold these preferred at par. Confirm that the par value of the preferred stock is $100 per share.

c. Northrop's footnotes report that the fair value of the preferred shares was $146 per share at December 31, 2008. What would explain this large increase in its preferred stock's market price?

d. Use the financial statement effects template to record the conversion of the preferred stock on April 4, 2008. Assume that all 3.5 million shares were converted. The par value of the company's common stock is $1 per share.

P9-56.   Identifying and Analyzing Financial Statement Effects of Share-Based Compensation   (LO1)

Weaver Industries implements a new share-based compensation plan in 2009. Under the plan, the company's CEO and CFO each will receive non-qualified stock options to purchase 100,000, no par shares. The options vest ratably (1/3 of the options each year) over three years, expire in 10 years, and have an exercise (strike) price of $22 per share. Weaver uses the Black-Scholes model to estimate a fair value per option of $15. The company's tax rate is 40%.

Required

a. Use the financial statement effects template to record the compensation expense related to these options for each year 2009 through 2011. Include the effects of any anticipated deferred tax benefits.

b. In 2012, the company's stock price is $19. If you were the Weaver Industries CEO, would you exercise your options? Explain.

c. In 2014, the company's stock price is $40 and the CEO exercises all of her options. Use the financial statement effects template to record the exercise.

d. What tax benefit will Weaver Industries receive related to the CEO's exercise in part *c*? What will be the tax consequences to the CEO?

P9-57. Interpreting Disclosure on Employee Stock Options   (LO1)

Intel Corporation reported the following in its 2010 10-K report.

Intel Corporation
(INTC)

Share-Based Compensation Share-based compensation recognized in 2010 was $917 million ($889 million in 2009 and $851 million in 2008). . . . During 2010, the tax benefit that we realized for the tax deduction from share-based awards totaled $266 million ($119 million in 2009 and $147 million in 2008). . . . We use the Black-Scholes option pricing model to estimate the fair value of options granted under our equity incentive plans and rights to acquire stock granted under our stock purchase plan. We based the weighted average estimated values of employee stock option grants (excluding stock option grants in connection with the Option Exchange in 2009) and rights granted under the stock purchase plan, as well as the weighted average assumptions used in calculating these values, on estimates at the date of grant, as follows:

	Stock Options			Stock Purchase Plan		
	2010	2009	2008	2010	2009	2008
Estimated values	$4.82	$4.72	$5.74	$4.71	$4.14	$5.32
Expected life (in years)	4.9	4.9	5.0	0.5	0.5	0.5
Risk-free interest rate.	2.5%	1.8%	3.0%	0.2%	0.4%	2.1%
Volatility	28%	46%	37%	32%	44%	35%
Dividend yield.	2.7%	3.6%	2.7%	3.1%	3.6%	2.5%

Additional information with respect to stock option activity is as follows:

(In millions, except per option amounts)	Number of Options	Weighted Average Exercise Price
December 29, 2007	665.9	$27.76
Grants.	24.9	$20.81
Exercises	(33.6)	$19.42
Cancellations and forfeitures	(42.8)	$31.14
Expirations	(2.4)	$22.84
December 27, 2008	612.0	$27.70
Grants.	118.5	$18.01
Assumed in acquisition	9.0	$15.42
Exercises	(3.6)	$15.90
Cancellations and forfeitures	(29.6)	$28.16
Exchanged	(217.4)	$26.75
Expirations	(37.6)	$31.92
December 26, 2009	451.3	$25.08
Grants.	20.2	$23.25
Exercises	(16.6)	$18.36
Cancellations and forfeitures	(16.1)	$24.76
Expirations	(52.4)	$60.68
December 25, 2010	386.4	$20.45
Options exercisable as of:		
December 27, 2008	517.0	$28.78
December 26, 2009	297.7	$28.44
December 25, 2010	263.0	$21.03

Required

a. What did Intel expense for share-based compensation for 2010? How many options did Intel grant in 2010? Compute the fair value of all options granted during 2010. Why do the fair value of the option grants and the expense differ?

b. Intel used the Black-Scholes formula to estimate fair value of the options granted each year. How did the change in volatility from 2009 to 2010 affect share-based compensation in 2010? What about the change in risk-free rate?

c. How many options were exercised during 2010? Estimate the cash that Intel received from its employees when these options were exercised.

d. What was the intrinsic value per share of the options exercised in 2010? If employees who exercised options in 2010 immediately sold them, what "profit" did they make from the shares? (*Hint:* Assume that Intel grants options at-the-money.)

e. The tax benefit that Intel will receive on the options exercised is computed based on the intrinsic value of the options exercised. Estimate Intel's tax benefit from the 2010 option exercises assuming a tax rate of 37%.

f. What was the average exercise price of the options that expired in 2010? Explain why employees might have let these options expire without exercising them. (*Hint:* Assume that Intel grants options at-the-money.)

P9-58.   Interpreting Disclosure on Share-Based Compensation   (LO1)

Intel Corporation
(INTC)

Intel reported the following information in its 2010 10-K related to its restricted stock plan.

In 2009, we began issuing restricted stock units with both a market condition and a service condition (market-based restricted stock units), referred to in our 2010 Proxy Statement as out-performance stock units, to a small group of senior officers and non-employee directors. The number of shares of Intel common stock to be received at vesting will range from 33% to 200% of the target amount, based on total stockholder return (TSR) on Intel common stock measured against the benchmark TSR of a peer group over a three-year period. TSR is a measure of stock price appreciation plus any dividends paid in this performance period. As of December 25, 2010, there were 3 million market-based restricted stock units outstanding. These market-based restricted stock units accrue dividend equivalents and vest three years and one month from the grant date. Information with respect to outstanding restricted stock unit (RSU) activity is as follows:

(In Millions, Except Per RSU Amounts)	Number of RSUs	Weighted Average Grant-Date Fair Value
December 29, 2007	51.1	$20.24
Granted	32.9	$19.94
Vested	(12.1)	$19.75
Forfeited	(4.6)	$20.12
December 27, 2008	67.3	$20.18
Granted	60.0	$14.63
Assumed in acquisition	1.6	$17.52
Vested	(20.1)	$20.24
Forfeited	(3.4)	$18.19
December 26, 2009	105.4	$17.03
Granted	32.4	$22.56
Vested	(34.6)	$17.70
Forfeited	(3.4)	$17.98
December 25, 2010	99.8	$18.56
Expected to vest as of December 25, 2010	94.4	$18.54

The aggregate fair value of awards that vested in 2010 was $808 million ($320 million in 2009 and $270 million in 2008), which represents the market value of Intel common stock on the date that the restricted stock units vested. The grant date fair value of awards that vested in 2010

continued

continued from prior page

> was $612 million ($407 million in 2009 and $239 million in 2008). The number of restricted stock units vested includes shares that we withheld on behalf of employees to satisfy the minimum statutory tax withholding requirements. Restricted stock units that are expected to vest are net of estimated future forfeitures. As of December 25, 2010, there was $1.2 billion in unrecognized compensation costs related to restricted stock units granted under our equity incentive plans. We expect to recognize those costs over a weighted average period of 1.3 years.

Required

a. How do restricted stock and stock options differ? In what respects are they the same?

b. Why do companies impose vesting periods on restricted stock grants?

c. Use the financial statement effects template to record the restricted stock granted to senior executives during 2010. The common stock has a par value of $0.001 per share.

d. Use the financial statement effects template to record the 2010 compensation expense related to Intel's restricted stock awards assuming straight-line amortization of the deferred compensation over the 1.3-year amortization period.

IFRS APPLICATIONS

I9-59.   Analyzing Revaluation Reserve   (LO 2)

WorkCover Queensland offers workers compensation coverage to people in Queensland, Australia. Its 2010 notes (compliant with IFRS) reported the following information on the asset revaluation reserve, which is included in stockholders' equity on the balance sheet.

WorkCover
Queensland

(in 000 Australian dollars)	Land	Buildings	Total
Carrying amount at the beginning of fiscal 2009.	8,120	17,450	25,570
Revaluation increment (decrement)	1,000	(5,027)	(4,027)
Tax effect on revaluation.	(300)	1,508	1,208
Carrying amount at the end of fiscal 2009	8,820	13,931	22,751
Carrying amount at the beginning of fiscal 2010.	8,820	13,931	22,751
Revaluation increment (decrement)	(3,000)	(2,285)	(5,285)
Tax effect on revaluation.	900	686	1,586
Carrying amount at the end of fiscal 2010	6,720	12,332	19,052

Explain the concept of asset revaluation. What happened to the fair value of land during fiscal 2009 and fiscal 2010? Were the fair values of buildings similarly affected? How was the income statement affected by these revaluations?

I9-60.   Analyzing and Computing Average Issue Price and Treasury Stock Cost and Market Cap)
(LO 1, O2)

Ahold is a major international supermarket operator based in Zaandam, Netherlands. Following is information taken from Ahold's financial statements prepared in accordance with IFRS.

Ahold

Shareholders' Equity (€ millions)	January 3, 2010	December 28, 2008
Issued and paid-in share capital	358	358
Additional paid-in capital	9,916	9,916
Legal reserves	(236)	(311)
Accumulated deficit	(5,492)	(6,353)
Net income.	894	1,077
Shareholders' equity	5,440	4,687

Footnotes to financial statements disclose the following: At January 3, 2010, and December 28, 2008, there were 1,700,000,000 authorized and 1,191,888,000 shares issued. On those respective dates, the company had treasury stock of 10,674,000 shares and 15,203,000 shares, respectively, and the amount in shareholders' equity was €(112) million and €(159) million.

Required
a. How many shares are authorized at 2009 fiscal year-end?
b. How many shares are issued at 2009 fiscal year-end? At what average price were these shares issued at fiscal year-end 2009?
c. How many treasury shares are held as of fiscal 2009 year-end? At what average price did the company repurchase treasury shares as of fiscal 2009 year-end?
d. How many shares are outstanding as of January 3, 2010?
e. At January 3, 2010, the share price for Ahold was €9.32. Compute the company's market capitalization on that date. How does this compare to the net book value of equity?

I9-61.   **Analyzing and Interpreting Equity Accounts and Comprehensive Income**   (LO 1, 2)

Henkel AG & Co.

Henkel AG & Co. is an international, fast-moving consumer goods (FMCG) company headquartered in Düsseldorf, Germany. Following is its shareholders' equity statement, prepared using IFRS, from its 2010 annual report (in Euros millions).

Statement of changes in equity

| In millions euro | Issued capital | | | | | | Other components | | Shareholders | | |
	Ordinary shares	Pre-ferred shares	Capital reserve	Trea-sury shares	Retained earnings	Transla-tion dif-ferences	Financial instru-ments	of Henkel AG & Co. KGaA	Non-controlling Interests	Total
At January 1, 2009	260	178	652	(115)	6,920	(1,199)	(212)	6,484	51	6,535
Net income...................					602			602	26	628
Other comprehensive income					(285)	(102)	(11)	(398)	(2)	(400)
Total comprehensive income ...					*317*	*(102)*	*(11)*	*204*	*24*	*228*
Distributions					(224)			(224)	(12)	(236)
Sale of treasury shares.........				6	4			10		10
Other changes in equity					—				7	7
At December 31, 2009/										
January 1, 2010.............	260	178	652	(109)	7,017	(1,301)	(223)	6,474	70	6,544
Net income...................					1,118			1,118	25	1,143
Other comprehensive income					53	525	(59)	519	6	525
Total comprehensive income ...					*1,171*	*525*	*(59)*	*1,637*	*31*	*1,668*
Distribution...................					(225)			(225)	(19)	(244)
Sale of treasury shares.........				10	9			19		19
Other changes in equity					(46)			(46)	9	(37)
At December 31, 2010	260	178	652	(99)	7,926	(776)	(282)	7,859	91	7,950

Required
a. Did Henkel issue any additional ordinary or preferred shares during 2010?
b. Use the information above to infer how much Henkel paid in dividends during 2010. To whom were these dividends paid?
c. Did the company repurchase any stock during 2010? Did Henkel sell any treasury shares? If so, what did the company receive in exchange for the sale of treasury stock?
d. How much did Henkel make in economic profit or loss on the sale, relative to the original stock repurchase price? Was this recorded in net income as an accounting profit or loss?

I9-62.   **Analyzing and Computing Average Issue Price and Treasury Stock Transactions**   (LO 1)

ThyssenKrupp AG

ThyssenKrupp AG, is a German steelmaker and engineering company. The equity section of the company's 2010 statement of financial position reported the following:

(In million €)	September 30, 2009	September 30, 2010
Capital stock	1,317	1,317
Additional paid in capital	4,684	4,684
Retained earnings	3,643	3,703
Cumulative other comprehensive income	(296)	192
Treasury stock (51,015,552 and 50,094,707 shares)	(1,421)	(1,396)
Equity attributable to ThyssenKrupp AG's stockholders	7,927	8,500
Noncontrolling interest................................	1,769	1,888
Total equity..	9,696	10,388

Notes to financial statements reveal that the company sold treasury shares during 2010 for proceeds of €21 million cash. Also, on July 6, 2011, *Dow Jones Newswire* reported the following:

> Frankfurt—ThyssenKrupp AG (TKA.XE) said Wednesday it has decided to sell 49.48 million treasury shares, which correspond to 9.6% of its capital stock, as part of its strategy to reduce net debt. Analysts welcomed the share placement, saying it should help reduce debt and re-store confidence in the company's balance sheet, even though it puts short-term pressure on the stock. Net financial debt stood at around EUR6.5 billion, or around twice as high as earn-ings before interest, taxes, depreciation and amortization at the end of the company's fiscal year 2010, ended Sept. 30. At 0830 GMT, ThyssenKrupp traded lower EUR1.80 or 5.2% at EUR32.96, underperforming a broadly firmer market.

Required

a. Consider the treasury shares at September 30, 2009. At what average price had the company repur-chased these shares?

b. Use the information above to infer the number of treasury shares sold during fiscal 2010. How much cash did the company receive for these treasury shares? At what average price did the company sell these shares?

c. Use the financial statement effects template to record the sale of treasury shares during fiscal 2010.

d. Use the financial statement effects template to record the anticipated sale of treasury shares an-nounced in July 2011. Assume that the shares will be sold for EUR32.96.

e. Assume the company uses all the anticipated proceeds to reduce debt. Quantify the effect on the total debt to total equity ratio.

MANAGEMENT APPLICATIONS

MA9-63.   Ethics and Governance: Equity Carve-Outs (LO3)

Many companies use split-offs as a means to unlock shareholder value. The split-off effectively splits the company into two pieces, each of which can then be valued separately by the stock market. If man-agers are compensated based on reported profit, how might they strategically structure the split-off? What corporate governance issues does this present?

SOLUTIONS TO REVIEW PROBLEMS

Mid-Module Review 1

Part 1

Solution

Transaction	Balance Sheet							Income Statement				
	Cash Asset	+	Noncash Assets	=	Liabil-ities	+	Contrib. Capital	+	Earned Capital	Rev-enues	−	Expen-ses	=	Net Income
Jan. 15: Issue 10,000 shares, $5 par, common at $17 per share	+170,000 Cash			=			+50,000 Common Stock +120,000 Additional Paid-In Capital				−		=	
Mar. 31: Repurchase 2,000 shares of common at $15 per share	−30,000 Cash			=			−30,000 Treasury Stock				−		=	
June 25: Reissue 1,000 trea-sury shares at $20 per share	+20,000 Cash			=			+15,000 Treasury Stock +5,000 Additional Paid-In Capital				−		=	

Cash   170,000
    CS   50,000
    APIC   120,000

Cash
170,000	

CS
	50,000

APIC
	120,000

TS   30,000
    Cash   30,000

TS
30,000	

Cash
	30,000

Cash   20,000
    TS   15,000
    APIC   5,000

Cash
20,000	

TS
	15,000

APIC
	5,000

Part 2

Solution

a. *Granted* relates to the number of shares under option that have been awarded to employees for the year. *Exercised* refers to the number of shares that employees have purchased that were previously under option. *Forfeited* relates to the number of shares under option that are no longer exercisable because the options were not exercised before they expired. The "Weighted Average Exercise Price" is the average price at which employees can purchase shares of stock that are under option, weighted by the number of shares at each exercise price.

b. Compensation cost is computed as the total value of employee stock options spread over the vesting period. For example, if Accenture grants employees stock options with an estimated value of $1 billion that vest over a four-year period, the expense that is recognized over the subsequent four years is $250 million per year. The "unrecognized compensation cost" is that portion of the total estimated value of the stock options that has not yet been recognized as expense in the income statement.

Mid-Module Review 2

Solution

a.

Cumulative Preferred Stock	Preferred Stock	Common Stock
Year 1—$0 cash dividends paid.	$ 0	$ 0
Year 2—$300,000 cash dividends paid		
Dividends in arrears from Year 1 ($1,000,000 × 5%).	50,000	
Current-year dividend ($1,000,000 × 5%).	50,000	
Balance to common		200,000
Year 3—$80,000 cash dividends paid		
Current-year dividend ($1,000,000 × 5%).	50,000	
Balance to common		30,000

b.

Noncumulative Preferred Stock	Preferred Stock	Common Stock
Year 1—$0 cash dividends paid.	$ 0	$ 0
Year 2—$300,000 cash dividends paid		
Current-year dividend ($1,000,000 × 5%).	50,000	
Balance to common		250,000
Year 3—$80,000 cash dividends paid		
Current-year dividend ($1,000,000 × 5%).	50,000	
Balance to common		30,000

Mid-Module Review 3

Solution

	Balance Sheet						Income Statement		
Transaction	Cash Asset	+ Noncash Assets	= Liabil- ities	+ Contrib. Capital	+ Earned Capital		Rev- enues	− Expen- ses	= Net Income
Apr. 1: Declare and issue 100% stock dividend; stock is $11 per share			=	+250,000 Common Stock	−250,000[1] Retained Earnings			−	=
Dec. 7: Declare and issue 3% stock dividend; stock is $7 per share			=	+15,000 Common Stock +6,000 Additional Paid-In Capital	−21,000[2] Retained Earnings			−	=

(left margin journal entries)

RE 250,000
  CS 250,000

RE
250,000 |
  CS
      | 250,000

RE 21,000
  CS 15,000
  APIC 6,000

RE
21,000 |
  CS
      | 15,000
  APIC
      | 6,000

continued

continued from prior page

Transaction	Balance Sheet							Income Statement			
	Cash Asset	+	Noncash Assets	=	Liabil- ities	+	Contrib. Capital	+	Earned Capital		
									Rev- enues	− Expen- ses	= Net Income
Dec. 31: Declare and pay cash dividend of $1.20 per share	−123,600 Cash			=					−123,600[3] Retained Earnings	−	=

RE   123,600
   Cash   123,600

       RE
123,600 |
      Cash
         | 123,600

[1] This large stock dividend reduces retained earnings at the par value of shares distributed (50,000 shares × 100% × $5 par value = $250,000). Contributed capital (common stock) increases by the same amount.

[2] This small stock dividend reduces retained earnings at the market value of shares distributed (3% × 100,000 shares × $7 per share = $21,000). Contributed capital increases by the same amount ($15,000 to common stock and $6,000 to paid-in capital). Note that the number of common shares outstanding on December 7 was 100,000—the large stock dividend on April 7 doubled the number of common stock outstanding.

[3] At the time of the cash dividend, there are 103,000 shares outstanding. The cash paid is, therefore, 103,000 shares × $1.20 per share = $123,600.

Mid-Module Review 4

Solution

1. A split-off is like a treasury stock transaction, but instead of repurchasing stock with cash, shares of the parent company owned by the shareholders are exchanged for shares of the subsidiary owned by the parent. If the distribution is non pro rata, the parent can report a gain equal to the difference between the fair value of the subsidiary and its book value on the parent's balance sheet.
2. BearingPoint met the conditions for a split-off as described in part 1, which enabled it to report a gain.

Module-End Review

Solution

Transaction	Balance Sheet							Income Statement			
	Cash Asset	+	Noncash Assets	=	Liabil- ities	+	Contrib. Capital	+	Earned Capital		
									Rev- enues	− Expen- ses	= Net Income
Convert a bond with $850 book value into 200 common shares with $1 par value				=	−850 Long-Term Debt		+200 Common Stock +650 Additional Paid-In Capital			−	=

LTD   850
   CS   200
   APIC   650

      LTD
850 |
      CS
         | 200
     APIC
         | 650

DELTA AIR LINES

Delta Air Lines (DAL) is solvent and profitable, but confronts competing demands for its available cash flow as a result of a heavy debt load that includes borrowed money, aircraft leases, and pension and other post-employment obligations. The magnitude of obligations arising from aircraft leases often surprises those outside the industry. Many airlines do not own the planes that they fly. To a large extent, those planes are owned by commercial leasing companies like **General Electric Commercial Credit** (GE's financial subsidiary), and are leased by the airlines.

If structured in a specific way, neither the leased planes (the assets) nor the lease obligation (the liability) would be on Delta Air Lines' balance sheet. That exclusion can alter investors' perceptions of the capital investment Delta Air Lines needs to operate its business as well as the level of debt it carries. In this module, we describe an analytical procedure that provides an alternative view of the company's investing and financing activities.

The analytical adjustment increases the liability on Delta Air Lines' balance sheet: lease payment obligations on aircrafts total $7.09 billion in 2010, which is a staggering amount when compared to the company's net operating assets of $12.13 billion. This module discusses the accounting for leases and explains this analytical adjustment and how to apply it.

Reporting and Analyzing Off-Balance-Sheet Financing

LEARNING OBJECTIVES

LO1 Describe and illustrate the accounting for capitalized leases. (p. 10-4)

LO2 Describe and illustrate the accounting for pensions. (p. 10-12)

LO3 Explain the accounting for special purpose entities (SPEs). (p. 10-24)

Pensions and long-term health care plans are another large obligation for many large companies, including Delta Air Lines. Until recently, information about these pension and health care obligations was only in footnotes. Recent accounting rule changes now require companies to report that information on the balance sheet. In particular, the balance sheet now reports the net pension and health care liabilities (the total liability less related investments that fund the liabilities).

Delta Air Lines' 2010 net pension and health care liability exceeds pension assets by $11.4 billion. That amount represents 27% of Delta's total liabilities and equity. This module explains the accounting for both pensions and health care obligations and examines footnote disclosures that convey a wealth of information relating to assumptions underlying estimates of these obligations.

Methods that companies apply to avoid reporting potential liabilities (and expenses), are commonly referred to as *off-balance-sheet financing*. Although companies have long practiced off-balance-sheet financing, more recent techniques have become increasingly complex and require careful analysis. We explain one such off-balance-sheet technique, special purpose entities (SPEs), in Appendix 10B.

Sources: Delta Air Lines 2010 Form 10-K; *The Wall Street Journal*, January 2012.

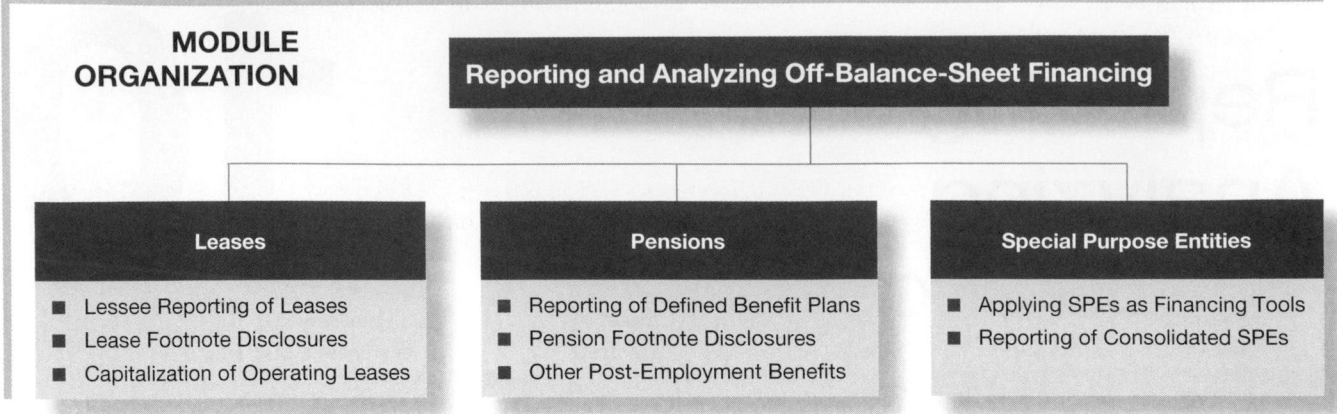

Company stakeholders pay attention to the composition of the balance sheet and its relation to the income statement. This attention extends to their analysis and valuation of both equity and debt securities. Of particular importance in this valuation process is the analysis of return on equity (ROE) and its components: return on net operating assets (RNOA)—including net operating profit margin (NOPM) and net operating asset turnover (NOAT)—and the degree of financial leverage (FLEV). Module 4 and its appendix explain these measures.

To value debt securities such as bonds and notes, one must consider a company's financial leverage (claims against assets) and the level of debt service (interest and principal payments), and compare them with expected cash flows. If analysis reveals that profitability (as measured by ROE and RNOA) and cash flows are inadequate, a company's credit rating could decline. The resulting higher cost of debt capital could limit the number of investment projects that yield a return greater than their financing cost. This restricts the company's growth and profitability.

Financial managers are aware of the importance of how financial markets perceive their companies. They also recognize the market attention directed at the quality of their balance sheets and income statements. This reality can pressure managers to *window dress* financial statements to present the company's financial condition and performance in the best possible light. To increase reported solvency and decrease the risk metrics, companies generally wish to present a balance sheet with low levels of debt. Companies that are more liquid and less financially leveraged are viewed as less likely to go bankrupt. As a result, the risk of default on their debt is less, resulting in a better credit rating and a lower interest rate.

Companies also generally wish to present a balance sheet with fewer assets. This is driven by return considerations. ROE has two components: operating return and nonoperating return. The latter is a function of the company's effective use of debt. Investors generally prefer a company's ROE to be derived from operations (RNOA) rather than from its use of debt. So, if a company can maintain a given level of profitability with fewer assets, the related increase in ROE is perceived to be driven by higher RNOA (asset turnover), and not by increased financial leverage.

Off-balance-sheet financing means that assets or liabilities, or both, are not reported on the balance sheet. Even though GAAP requires detailed footnote disclosures, managers generally believe that keeping such assets and liabilities off the balance sheet improves market perception of their operating performance and financial condition. This belief presumes that the market is somewhat inefficient, a notion that persists despite empirical evidence suggesting that analysts adjust balance sheets to include assets and liabilities that managers exclude.

This module explains and illustrates several types of off-balance-sheet financing. Major topics we discuss are leases, pensions, health care liabilities, and special purpose entities (SPEs). This is not an exhaustive list of the techniques that managers employ to achieve off-balance-sheet financing, but it includes the most common methods. We must keep one point in mind: the relevant information to assess off-balance-sheet financing is mainly in footnotes. While GAAP footnote disclosures on such financing are fairly good, we must have the analytic tools to interpret them and to understand the nature and the magnitude of assets and liabilities that managers have moved off of the balance sheet. This module provides those tools.

LEASES

We begin the discussion of off-balance-sheet financing with leases. The following graphic shows that leasing impacts both sides of the balance sheet (liabilities and assets) and the income statement (leasing expenses are often reported in selling, general and administrative expenses).

LO1 Describe and illustrate the accounting for capitalized leases.

Income Statement
Sales
Cost of goods sold
Selling, general and administrative expenses
Income taxes
Net income

Balance Sheet	
Cash	Current liabilities
Accounts receivable	**Long-term liabilities**
Inventory	
Long-term operating assets	Shareholders' equity
Investments	

A lease is a contract between the owner of an asset (the **lessor**) and the party desiring to use that asset (the **lessee**). Since this is a private contract between two willing parties, it is governed only by applicable commercial law, and can include whatever provisions the parties negotiate.

Leases generally provide for the following terms:

- Lessor allows the lessee the unrestricted right to use the asset during the lease term.
- Lessee agrees to make periodic payments to the lessor and to maintain the asset.
- Title to the asset remains with the lessor, who usually takes physical possession of the asset at lease-end unless the lessee negotiates the right to purchase the asset at its market value or other predetermined price.

From the lessor's standpoint, lease payments are set at an amount that yields an acceptable return on investment, commensurate with the lessee's credit rating. The lessor has an investment in the lease asset, and the lessee gains use of the asset.

The lease serves as a financing vehicle, similar to a secured bank loan. However, there are several advantages to leasing over bank financing:

- Leases often require less equity investment by the lessee (borrower) compared with bank financing. Leases usually require the first lease payment be made at the inception of the lease. For a 60-month lease, this amounts to a 1/60 (1.7%) investment by the lessee, compared with a typical bank loan of 70-80% of the asset cost (thus requiring 20-30% equity investment by the borrower).
- Because leases are contracts between two parties, their terms can be structured to meet both parties' needs. For example, a lease can allow variable payments to match the lessee's seasonal cash inflows or have graduated payments for start-up companies.
- A lease can be structured such that neither the lease asset nor the lease liability is reported on the balance sheet. Accordingly, leasing can be a form of off-balance-sheet financing.

Lessee Reporting of Leases

GAAP identifies two different approaches for the reporting of leases by the lessee:

- **Capital lease method**. This method requires that both the lease asset and the lease liability be reported on the balance sheet. The lease asset is depreciated like any other long-term asset. The lease liability is amortized like debt, where lease payments are separated into interest expense and principal repayment.
- **Operating lease method**. Under this method, neither the lease asset nor the lease liability is reported on the balance sheet. Lease payments are recorded as rent expense by the lessee.

The financial statement effects for the lessee of these methods are summarized in Exhibit 10.1.

EXHIBIT 10.1 Financial Statement Effects of Lease Type for the Lessee				
Lease Type	**Assets**	**Liabilities**	**Expenses**	**Cash Flows**
Capital	Lease asset reported	Lease liability reported	Depreciation and interest expense	Payments per lease contract
Operating	Lease asset **not** reported	Lease liability **not** reported	Rent expense	Payments per lease contract

GAAP defines criteria to determine whether a lease is capital or operating.[1] Managers seeking off-balance-sheet financing structure their leases around the GAAP rules so as to fail the "capitalization tests." (A proposal currently under review by the FASB and the IASB would require companies to record the rights and obligations related to *all* leases on their balance sheets. If approved, substantially all leases would be recorded on the balance sheet as an asset and a liability.)

Under the operating method, lease assets and lease liabilities are *not* recorded on the balance sheet. The company merely discloses key details of the transaction in the lease footnote. The income statement reports the lease payment as rent expense. And, the cash outflows (payments to lessor) per the lease contract are included in the operating section of the statement of cash flows.

For capital leases, both the lease asset and lease liability are reported on the balance sheet. In the income statement, depreciation and interest expense are reported instead of rent expense. (Because only depreciation is an operating expense, NOPAT is higher when a lease is classified as a capital lease.) Further, although the cash payments to the lessor are identical whether or not the lease is capitalized on the balance sheet, the cash flows are classified differently for capital leases—that is, each payment is part interest (operating cash flow) and part principal (financing cash flow). Operating cash flows are, therefore, greater when a lease is classified as a capital lease.

Classifying leases as "operating" has four financial reporting consequences for the lessee:

1. The lease asset is not reported on the balance sheet. This means that net operating asset turnover (NOAT) is higher because reported operating assets are lower and revenues are unaffected.

2. The lease liability is not reported on the balance sheet. This means that balance sheet measures of financial leverage (like the total liabilities-to-equity ratio) are improved; many managers believe the reduced financial leverage will result in a better credit rating and, consequently, a lower interest rate on borrowed funds.

3. Without analytical adjustments (see later section on capitalization of operating leases), the portion of ROE derived from operating activities (RNOA) appears higher, which improves the perceived quality of the company's ROE.

4. During the early years of the lease term, rent expense reported for an operating lease is less than the depreciation and interest expense reported for a capital lease.[2] This means that net income is higher in those early years with an operating lease.[3] Further, if the company is growing and continually adding operating lease assets, the level of profits will continue to remain higher during the growth period.

The benefits of applying the operating method for leases are obvious to managers, thus leading some to avoid lease capitalization. Furthermore, the lease accounting standard includes rigid requirements relating to capitalization. Whenever accounting standards are rigidly defined, managers can structure transactions to meet the letter of the standard to achieve a desired accounting result when the essence of the transaction would suggest a different accounting treatment. This is *form over substance*.

---

[1] Leases must be capitalized when one or more of the following four criteria are met: (1) The lease automatically transfers ownership of the lease asset from the lessor to the lessee at termination of the lease. (2) The lease provides that the lessee can purchase the lease asset for a nominal amount (a bargain purchase) at termination of the lease. (3) The lease term is at least 75% of the economic useful life of the lease asset. (4) The present value of the lease payments is at least 90% of the fair market value of the lease asset at inception of the lease.

[2] This is true even if the company employs straight-line depreciation for the lease asset since interest expense accrues on the outstanding balance of the lease liability, which is higher in the early years of the lease life. Total expense is the same *over the life of the lease*, regardless of whether the lease is capitalized or not. That is: Total rent expense (from operating lease) = Total depreciation expense (from capital lease) + Total interest expense (from capital lease).

[3] However, NOPAT is *lower* for an operating lease because rent expense is an operating expense whereas only depreciation expense (and not interest expense) is an operating expense for a capital lease.

IFRS INSIGHT	**Lease Accounting under IFRS**

U.S. GAAP and IFRS both require that leases be capitalized if the lease asset's risks and rewards are transferred to the lessee. The main difference between the two reporting systems is that IFRS are more principles based and GAAP is more rules based (as an example, see footnote 1). Given the broader application of principles, IFRS classify more leases as *finance leases* (termed "capital leases" under GAAP). Other small differences exist in the accounting for leases but these will not lead to materially different reporting outcomes in most cases.

Footnote Disclosure of Leases

Disclosures of expected payments for leases are required under both operating and capital lease methods. Delta Air Lines provides a typical disclosure from its 2010 annual report:

LEASE OBLIGATIONS We lease aircraft, airport terminals, maintenance facilities, ticket offices and other property and equipment from third parties. Rental expense for operating leases, which is recorded on a straight-line basis over the life of the lease term, totaled $1.2 billion, $1.3 billion and $798 million for the years ended December 31, 2010, 2009 and 2008, respectively. Amounts due under capital leases are recorded as liabilities on our Consolidated Balance Sheets. Assets acquired under capital leases are recorded as property and equipment on our Consolidated Balance Sheets. Amortization of assets recorded under capital leases is included in depreciation and amortization expense on our Consolidated Statements of Operations. The following tables summarize, as of December 31, 2010, our minimum rental commitments under capital leases and noncancelable operating leases (including certain aircraft under Contract Carrier agreements) with initial or remaining terms in excess of one year. At December 31, 2010, we operated 111 aircraft under operating leases and 113 aircraft under capital leases.

Capital Leases Year Ending December 31 (in millions)	
2011	$ 214
2012	193
2013	160
2014	130
2015	124
Thereafter	404
Total minimum lease payments	1,225
Less: amount of lease payments representing interest	(487)
Present value of minimum capital lease payments	738
Plus: unamortized premium, net	7
Less: current obligations under capital leases	(119)
Long-term capital lease obligations	$ 626

Operating Leases Year Ending December 31 (in millions)	Delta Lease Payments	Contract Carrier Aircraft Lease Payments	Total
2011	$ 899	$ 521	$ 1,420
2012	840	511	1,351
2013	816	504	1,320
2014	770	493	1,263
2015	688	481	1,169
Thereafter	7,096	1,327	8,423
Total minimum lease payments	$11,109	$3,837	$14,946

Lease disclosures such as this provide information concerning current and future payment obligations. These contractual obligations are similar to debt payments and must be factored into our evaluation of the company's financial condition.

Delta Air Lines' footnote disclosure reports minimum (base) contractual lease payment obligations for each of the next five years and the total lease payment obligations that come due in year six and beyond. This is similar to disclosures of future maturities for long-term debt. The company also must provide separate disclosures for operating leases and capital leases (Delta Air Lines has both operating and capital leases outstanding).

MANAGERIAL DECISION | **You Are the Division President**

You are the president of an operating division. Your CFO recommends operating lease treatment for asset acquisitions to reduce reported assets and liabilities on your balance sheet. To achieve this classification, you must negotiate leases with shorter base terms and lease renewal options that you feel are not advantageous to your company. What is your response? [Answer, p. 10-29]

Capitalization of Operating Leases

U.S. GAAP as of 2011 permits the classification of leases as operating or capital as explained above. As of the publication of this textbook, U.S. standard-setters are deliberating a new accounting standard that would require all leases to be accounted for much like capital leases currently (namely, lease assets and lease liabilities would be capitalized on the balance sheet following the procedures we outline below). However, until passage of the new standard, companies will report only capital leases on their balance sheets, whereas information on their operating leases will be in footnotes such as that shown above for Delta.

Although not recognized on-balance-sheet, leased properties arguably represent assets (and create liabilities) as defined under GAAP. That is, the company controls the assets and will profit from their future benefits. Also, lease liabilities represent real contractual obligations. Although the financial statements are prepared in conformity with current (2011) GAAP, the failure to capitalize operating lease assets and lease liabilities for analysis purposes distorts ROE analysis—specifically:

- Net operating profit margin (NOPM) is understated. Over the life of the lease, rent expense under operating leases equals depreciation plus interest expense under capital leases; however, only depreciation expense is included in net operating profit (NOPAT) as interest is a nonoperating expense. Operating expense is, therefore, overstated, and NOPM is understated. While cash payments are the same whether the lease is classified as operating or capital, *operating cash flow* is higher with capital leases since depreciation is an add-back, and the reduction of the capital lease obligation is classified as a *financing* outflow. Operating cash flows are, therefore, lower with operating leases than with capital leases.

- Net operating asset turnover (NOAT) is overstated due to nonreporting of lease assets.

- Financial leverage (FLEV) is understated by the omitted lease liabilities—recall that lease liabilities are nonoperating.

Although aggregate ROE is relatively unaffected (assuming that the leases are at their midpoint on average so that rent expense is approximately equal to depreciation plus interest) failure to capitalize an operating lease results in a balance sheet that, arguably, neither reflects all of the assets that are used in the business, nor the nonoperating obligations for which the company is liable. Such noncapitalization of leases makes ROE appear to be of higher quality because it derives from higher RNOA (due to higher NOA turnover) and not from higher financial leverage. This is, of course, the main reason why some managers want to exclude leases from the balance sheet.

Lease disclosures that are required under GAAP allow us to capitalize operating leases for analysis purposes. This capitalization process involves three steps (this is the same basic process that managers will use to capitalize leases under the proposed lease-accounting standard):

1. Determine the discount rate.

2. Compute the present value of future lease payments.

3. Adjust the balance sheet to include the present value from step 2 as both a lease asset and a lease liability. Adjust the income statement to include depreciation and interest in lieu of rent expense.

Step 1. There are at least two approaches to determine the appropriate discount rate for our analysis: (1) If the company discloses capital leases, we can impute (infer) an implicit rate of return: a rate that yields the present value computed by the company given the future capital lease payments (see Business Insight box below). (2) Use the rate that corresponds to the company's credit rating or the rate from any recent borrowings involving intermediate-term secured obligations. Companies typically disclose these details in their long-term debt footnote. To illustrate the capitalization of operating leases, we use the **Delta Air Lines** lease footnote reproduced above. Step 1 estimates the implicit rate for Delta's capital leases to be 14.31% (see the following Business Insight box on computing the imputed discount rate for leases).

BUSINESS INSIGHT | **Imputed Discount Rate Computation for Leases**

When companies report both operating and capital leases, the average rate used to discount capital leases can be imputed from disclosures in the lease footnote. **Delta Air Lines** reports total undiscounted minimum capital lease payments of $1,225 million and a discounted value for those lease payments of $738 million. Using Excel, we estimate the discount rate that Delta used for its capital lease computations with the IRR function (= **IRR (values**,guess)) as shown in the following spreadsheet. The entries in cells B2 through G2 are taken from Delta's reported schedule of lease maturities in the footnote shown earlier in this section, and those in cells H2 through K2 sum to $404 million, the total lease payments due after 2015 (year 5). We assume that Delta continues to pay $124 million per year (the same as in 2015) until the $404 is used up. This yields a smaller residual payment in year 9. The spreadsheet method yields an estimate of 14.31% for the discount rate that Delta implicitly used for capitalization of its capital leases in its 2010 balance sheet.

	A	B	C	D	E	F	G	H	I	J	K	L
1	N	0	1	2	3	4	5	6	7	8	9	
2	Amount	-738	214	193	160	130	124	124	124	124	32	
3	IRR	14.31% *										
4												
5			* Formula for cell B3 is =IRR(B2:K2,10%)							= 404		

(DAL Capitalized leases template.xlsx - Microsoft Excel)

Step 2. Compute the present value of future operating lease payments using the 14.31% discount rate that we estimated in Step 1, see Exhibit 10.2. We demonstrate this computation using a spreadsheet (without rounding of numbers); we show those same computations using both a financial calculator and present value tables in Appendix 10C. The spreadsheet (and calculator) method is more exact, but may or may not yield a material difference to the number obtained when using present value tables. Given the widespread use of spreadsheets such as Excel, we use the spreadsheet method hereafter.

EXHIBIT 10.2 | **Present Value of Operating Lease Payments ($ millions)**

Year	Operating Lease Payment	Discount Factor ($i = 0.1431$)	Present Value
1.................	$1,420	0.87481	$1,242
2.................	1,351	0.76530	1,034
3.................	1,320	0.66949	884
4.................	1,263	0.58568	740
5.................	1,169	0.51236	599
>5.................	8,423 ($1,169 × 7.205 years)	4.32210 × 0.51236	2,589
			$7,088

Remaining life......... $8,432/$1,169 = 7.205 years

Spreadsheet Method. The present value of the operating lease payments equals the sum of the present values for each of the lease payments Year 1 through Year 5 and the present value of the lease payments after Year 5. This two-step computation follows:

1. *Present values for Years 1 through 5.* The present value of each forecasted lease payment for Years 1 through 5 is computed as the product of (a) the lease payment for that year and (b) the present value factor for that year using the following formula: $\frac{1}{(1+i)^t}$ where i is the discount factor and t is the year (1, 2, 3, 4 and 5). To illustrate using Delta, we enter the discount rate of 14.31% and the year 1, 2, 3, 4 and 5 separately for each year to obtain a present value factor for each year. For example, for Year 1 the present value factor is 0.87481, computed as $\frac{1}{(1.1431)^1}$; and, for Year 2 the present value factor is 0.76530, computed as $\frac{1}{(1.1431)^2}$; and so forth. Thus, the present value ($ in millions) of the Year 1 lease payment equals $1,242, computed from: $1,420 \times \left[\frac{1}{(1.1431)^1}\right]$; the present value of the Year 2 lease payment equals $1,034, computed from: $1,351 \times \left[\frac{1}{(1.1431)^2}\right]$; and so forth. In Excel, for Year 2, the present value factor is entered as: 1/1.1431^2. The present values for Year 1 through Year 5 are in the far right column of Exhibit 10.2.

2. *Present value for Year 6 and thereafter.* To compute the present value of the lease payments remaining after Year 5, we make an assumption that the company continues to make lease payments at the Year 5 level for the remainder of the lease term. The remaining lease term is, therefore, estimated as: (Total payments for Year 6 and thereafter)/(Year 5 lease payment). This means the remaining payments are an annuity for the remainder of the lease term, the present value of which equals the product of (a) the lease payment for Year 5 and (b) the present value factor for that annuity using the following formula: $\frac{1-[1/(1+i)^n]}{i} \times \frac{1}{(1+i)^5}$, where i is the discount factor and n is the remainder of the lease term. To illustrate using Delta, we enter the 14.31% discount rate and the 7.205 years estimate of the remaining lease term (computed from $8,423/$1,169). The present value of the remaining lease payments equals $2,589, computed from:

$$\$1,169 \text{ million} \times \frac{1-[1/(1.1431)^{7.205}]}{0.1431} \times \frac{1}{(1.1431)^5}$$

The first term in this computation is the assumed annual payment after Year 5; the second term is the present value factor for the remaining annuity after Year 5; and the third term discounts the second term to the present. In Excel, the second and third terms are entered as ((1−(1/(1.1431)^7.205))/0.1431) * (1/1.1431^5). The present value of the lease payments for Year 6 and thereafter is in the sixth row of the far right column of Exhibit 10.2.

We sum the present values of Year 1 through Year 5 payments and the present value of the payments in Year 6 and beyond to obtain the present value of future operating lease payments; for Delta, this totals $7,088 ($ millions), computed as $1,242 + $1,034 + $884 + $740 + $599 + $2,589.

Step 3. Use the computed present value of future operating lease payments to adjust the balance sheet, income statement, and financial ratios as we illustrate below.

Balance Sheet Effects To adjust the balance sheet, add the present value from Step 2 to both operating assets (PPE) and nonoperating liabilities (long-term debt). Exhibit 10.3 shows the adjustments for **Delta Air Lines** at year-end 2010. The capitalization of operating leases has a marked impact on Delta Airlines' balance sheet. For the airline and retailing industries, in particular, lease assets (airplanes and real estate) comprise a large portion of net operating assets, which are typically accounted for using the operating lease method. Thus, companies in these industries usually have sizeable off-balance-sheet assets and liabilities.

EXHIBIT 10.3 Adjustments to Balance Sheet from Capitalization of Operating Leases				
Delta Air Lines ($ millions)	Reported Figures	Adjustments	Adjusted Figures	Percent Increase
Net operating assets	$12,130	$7,088	$19,218	58.4%
Net nonoperating obligations. . .	11,233	7,088	18,321	63.1%
Equity.	897	—	897	0.0%

Income Statement Effects Capitalizing operating leases affects the income statement via depreciation of the leased equipment and interest on the lease liability. Operating lease payments are reported as rent expense, typically included in selling, general and administrative expenses. The income statement adjustments relating to the capitalization of operating leases involve two steps:[4]

1. Remove "rent expense" of $1,420 million from operating expense.
2. Add depreciation expense from the lease assets to operating expense and add interest expense from the lease obligation as a nonoperating expense. Lease assets are estimated at $7,088 million (see Exhibit 10.3). GAAP requires companies to depreciate capital lease assets over their useful lives or the lease terms, whichever is less. For this example, we assume that the remaining lease term is 12.205 years (five years reported in the lease schedule plus 7.205 years after the fifth year). Using this term and zero salvage value results in estimated straight-line depreciation for lease assets of $581 million ($7,088 million/12.205 years). Interest expense on the $7,088 million lease liability at the 14.31% capitalization rate is $1,014 million ($7,088 million × 14.31%) for the first year.

Delta Air Lines reports NOPAT of $1,607 million, nonoperating expense of $1,014 million, and net income of $593 million. Assuming a tax rate of 37%, the net adjustment to NOPAT is $529 million ([$1,420 million rent expense − $581 million depreciation expense] × [1 − 0.37]), see Exhibit 10.4. The increase in nonoperating expense after-tax is $639 million ($1,014 × [1 − 0.37]), which is the additional after-tax interest expense on the capitalized lease obligation. Exhibit 10.4 summarizes those adjustments to Delta's profitability measures.

EXHIBIT 10.4 Adjustments to Income Statement from Capitalization of Operating Leases				
Delta Air Lines ($ millions)	**Reported Figures**	**Adjustments**	**Adjusted Figures**	**Percent Increase**
NOPAT........................	$1,607	$529	$2,136	32.9%
Nonoperating expense............	1,014	639	1,653	63.0%
Net income....................	$ 593	$(110)	$ 483	(18.5)%

ROE and Disaggregation Effects Adjustments to capitalize operating leases can alter our assessment of ROE components. Using the adjustments we describe in Exhibits 10.3 and 10.4, the impact for ROE and its components (defined in Module 4), is summarized in Exhibit 10.5 for Delta Air Lines.

EXHIBIT 10.5 Ratio Effects of Adjustments from Capitalization of Operating Leases			
Delta Air Lines ($ millions)	**Reported**	**Adjusted**	**Computations for Adjusted Numbers**
NOPM................................	5.1%	6.7%	$2,136/$31,755
NOAT	2.62	1.65	$31,755/$19,218*
RNOA................................	13.4%	11.1%	$2,136/$19,218*
Financial leverage (FLEV = NNO/Equity).......	12.52	20.42	$18,321/$897
ROE	66.1%	53.8%	$483/$897*
Nonoperating return.....................	52.7%	42.8%	ROE − RNOA

* For simplicity, we use year-end values for the denominator in lieu of average values.

Using *year-end* (reported and adjusted) data, and Delta Air Lines' total revenues of $31,755 million, adjusted RNOA is 11.1% (down from 13.4% reported). RNOA decreased because the increase in net operating profit margin (from 5.1% to 6.7%) was more than offset by a much lower net operating asset turnover (from 2.62 to 1.65). After capitalization of its operating leases, Delta Air Lines is

---

[4] This approach uses the operating lease payments from Year 1 of the projected payments to approximate the rent expense for operating leases. This approach also uses the computed present value of future lease payments (from Step 2) to compute the depreciation and interest expense for capital leases. An alternative approach is to use *actual* rent expense for the current year (disclosed in the lease footnote) together with depreciation and interest computed based on capitalization of the *prior* year's future lease payments. Although, arguably more exact, most analysts use the simplified approach illustrated here given the extent of other estimates involved (such as discount rates, depreciation lives, and salvage values).

more profitable (from an operating standpoint) and more capital intensive than we would infer from a review of its unadjusted income statement and balance sheet.

Delta's ROE decreases by 12.3% (from 66.1% to 53.8%).[5] The analysis reveals that the non-operating return component of its ROE decreases from 52.7% using reported figures to an adjusted 42.8%. The adjusted figures reveal that the lower spread is partially offset by much greater financial leverage from capitalized lease obligations that is not apparent prior to capitalization. Specifically, financial leverage is 20.42 times equity using adjusted figures versus 12.52 times using reported figures. Financial leverage is, therefore, revealed to play a greater role in ROE in partially offsetting the lower spread. In sum, Delta's adjusted figures reveal a company with a lower ROE and with more assets and more financial leverage than was apparent from reported figures.

Adjusted assets and liabilities arguably present a more realistic picture of the invested capital required to operate Delta Air Lines and of the amount of leverage represented by its leases. Similarly, operating profitability is revealed to be higher than reported, since a portion of Delta's rent payments represents repayment of the lease liability (a nonoperating cash outflow) rather than operating expense.

MID-MODULE REVIEW

Following is the leasing footnote disclosure from American Airlines' 2010 10-K report.

AMR's subsidiaries lease various types of equipment and property, primarily aircraft and airport facilities. The future minimum lease payments required under capital leases, together with the present value of such payments, and future minimum lease payments required under operating leases that have initial or remaining noncancelable lease terms in excess of one year as of December 31, 2010, were (in millions):

Year Ending December 31	Capital Leases	Operating Leases
2011	$186	$ 1,254
2012	136	1,068
2013	120	973
2014	98	831
2015	87	672
2016 and thereafter	349	6,006
	976	$10,804
Less amount representing interest	372	
Present value of net minimum lease payments	$604	

Required

1. Impute the discount rate that American uses, on average, to compute the present value of its capital leases.
2. What adjustments would we make to American's balance sheet to capitalize the operating leases at the end of 2010? (*Hint:* The implicit rate on its capital leases is approximately 13%; use this approximation to solve parts 2 and 3.)
3. Assuming the same facts as in part 2, what income statement adjustments might we consider?

The solution is on page 10-46.

---

[5] Delta's ROE (based on year-end equity) of 66.1% is high, which is an aberration resulting from the recessionary effects of the depressed economy in the late 2000s. During this period, U.S. airlines had huge losses that reduced equity and led to the bankruptcy of many carriers. Delta's high ROE for this year is due to its reduced equity base, and not to abnormally high profitability.

PENSIONS

Companies frequently offer pension plans as a benefit for their employees. There are two general types of pension plans:

LO2 Describe and illustrate the accounting for pensions.

1. **Defined contribution plan**. This plan requires the company make periodic contributions to an employee's account (usually with a third-party trustee like a bank), and many plans require an employee matching contribution. Following retirement, the employee makes periodic withdrawals from that account. A tax-advantaged 401(k) account is a typical example. Under a 401(k) plan, the employee makes contributions that are exempt from federal taxes until they are withdrawn after retirement.

2. **Defined benefit plan**. This plan also requires the company make periodic payments to a third party, which then makes payments to an employee after retirement. Payments are usually based on years of service and the employee's salary. The company may or may not set aside sufficient funds to cover these obligations (federal law does set minimum funding requirements). As a result, defined benefit plans can be overfunded or underfunded. All pension investments are retained by the third party until paid to the employee. In the event of bankruptcy, employees have the standing of a general creditor, but usually have additional protection in the form of government pension benefit insurance.

For a defined contribution plan, the company contribution is recorded as an expense in the income statement when the cash is paid or the liability accrued. For a defined benefit plan, it is not so simple. This is because while the company contributes cash or securities to the pension investment account, the pension obligation is not satisfied until the employee receives pension benefits, which may be many years into the future. This section focuses on how a defined benefit plan impacts financial statements, and how we assess company performance and financial condition when such a plan exists.

Reporting of Defined Benefit Pension Plans

There are two accounting issues concerning the reporting of defined benefit pension plans.

1. How are pension plans (assets and liabilities) reported in the balance sheet (if at all)?
2. How is the expense relating to pension plans reported in the income statement?

The following graphic shows where pensions appear on the balance sheet (liabilities and assets) and the income statement (pension expense is reported in the same expense accounts as employee wages; for example, pension expense for manufacturing employees is in cost of goods sold, whereas pension expense for salespeople is in SG&A).

Income Statement
Sales
Cost of goods sold
Selling, general and administrative expenses
Income taxes
Net income

Balance Sheet	
Cash	Current liabilities
Accounts receivable	**Long-term liabilities**
Inventory	
Long-term operating assets	Shareholders' equity
Investments	

Balance Sheet Effects

Pension plan assets are primarily investments in stocks and bonds (mostly of other companies, but it is not uncommon for companies to invest pension funds in their own stock). Pension liabilities (called the **projected benefit obligation** or **PBO**) are the company's obligations to pay current and former employees. The difference between the market value of the pension plan assets and the projected benefit obligation is called the **funded status** of the pension plan. If the PBO exceeds the pension plan assets, the pension is **underfunded**. Conversely, if pension plan assets exceed the PBO, the pension plan is **overfunded**. Under current GAAP, companies are required to record only the funded status on their balance sheets (namely, the *net* amount, not the pension plan assets and PBO separately), either as an asset if the plan is overfunded, or as a liability if it is underfunded.

Pension plan assets consist of stocks and bonds whose value changes each period in three ways. First, the value of the investments increases or decreases as a result of interest, dividends, and gains or losses on the stocks and bonds held. Second, the pension plan assets increase when the company contributes additional cash or stock to the investment account. Third, the pension plan assets decrease by the amount of benefits paid to retirees during the period. These three changes in the pension plan assets are articulated below.

Pension Plan Assets
Pension plan assets, beginning balance
+ Actual returns on investments (interest, dividends, gains and losses)
+ Company contributions to pension plan
− Benefits paid to retirees
= Pension plan assets, ending balance

The pension liability, or PBO (projected benefit obligation), is computed as the present value of the expected future benefit payments to employees. The present value of these future payments depends on the number of years the employee is expected to work (years of service), the employee's salary level at retirement, and the number of years the employee will receive benefits. Consequently, companies must estimate future wage increases, as well as the number of employees expected to reach retirement age with the company and how long they are likely to receive pension benefits following retirement. Once the future retiree pool is determined, the expected future payments under the plan are discounted to arrive at the present value of the pension obligation. This is the PBO. A reconciliation of the PBO from beginning balance to year-end balance follows.

Pension Obligation
Projected benefit obligation, beginning balance
+ Service cost
+ Interest cost
+/− Actuarial losses (gains)
− Benefits paid to retirees
= Projected benefit obligation, ending balance

As this reconciliation shows, the balance in the PBO changes during the period for four reasons.

■ First, as employees continue to work for the company, their pension benefits increase. The annual **service cost** represents the additional (future) pension benefits earned by employees during the current year.

■ Second, **interest cost** accrues on the outstanding pension liability, just as it would with any other long-term liability (see the accounting for bond liabilities in Module 8). Because there are no scheduled interest payments on the PBO, the interest cost accrues each year, that is, interest is added to the existing liability.

■ Third, the PBO can increase (or decrease) due to **actuarial losses (and gains)**, which arise when companies make changes in their pension plans or make *changes in actuarial assumptions* (such as the rate of wage inflation, termination and mortality rates, and the discount rate used to compute the present value of future obligations). For example, if a company increases the discount rate used to compute the present value of future pension plan payments from, say, 8% to 9%, the present value of future benefit payments declines (just like bond prices). Conversely, if the discount rate is reduced to 7%, the present value of the PBO increases. Other actuarial assumptions used to estimate the pension liability (such as the expected wage inflation rate or the expected life span of current and former employees) can also create similar actuarial losses or gains.

■ Fourth, pension benefit payments to retirees reduce the PBO (just as the payments reduce the pension plan assets).

Finally, companies are permitted to net the pension plan assets and the PBO and then report this net amount on the balance sheet. This net amount is called the **funded status** and is reported as an asset if pension assets exceed the PBO, and as a liability if the PBO exceeds pension assets.

Net Pension Asset (or Liability)
Pension plan assets (at market value)
− Projected benefit obligation (PBO)
Funded status

If the funded status is positive (assets exceed liabilities such that the plan is overfunded), the overfunded pension plan is reported on the balance sheet as an asset, typically called prepaid pension cost. If the funded status is negative (liabilities exceed assets and the plan is underfunded), it is reported as a liability.[6] During the late 2000s, long-term interest rates declined drastically and many companies lowered their discount rate for computing the present value of future pension payments. Lower discount rates meant higher PBO values. This period also witnessed a bear market and pension plan assets declined in value. The combined effect of the increase in PBO and the decrease in asset values caused many pension funds to become severely underfunded. Of the 710 publicly traded companies reporting pension plans in 2010 and with revenues over $500 million, a total of 662 (93%) were underfunded. (Delta Air Lines, for example, reports an underfunded pension plan of $9.257 billion in 2010.)

IFRS INSIGHT Reporting of Pension Funded Status under IFRS

Like U.S. GAAP, IFRS requires companies to report the funded status of their defined benefit pension plans on the balance sheet. The IFRS calculation of the unfunded status is slightly different than under GAAP. The IFRS unfunded status is calculated as projected benefit obligation minus the fair value of plan assets; but, unlike GAAP, any actuarial gains are added (losses are subtracted). There are other differences in detailed computations, which means that for pension assets and liabilities it is difficult to reliably compare GAAP and IFRS reports.

Income Statement Effects

A company's net pension expense is computed as follows.

Net Pension Expense
Service cost
+ Interest cost
− *Expected* return on pension plan assets
± Amortization of deferred amounts
Net pension expense

The net pension expense is rarely reported separately on the income statement. Instead, it is included with other forms of compensation expense. However, pension expense is disclosed separately in footnotes.

The net pension expense has four components. The previous PBO section described the first two components: service costs and interest costs. The third component of pension expense relates to the return on pension plan assets, which *reduces* total pension expense. To compute this component, companies use the long-term *expected* rate of return on the pension plan assets, rather than the *actual* return, and multiply that expected rate by the prior year's balance in the pension plan assets account (usually the average balance in the prior year). Use of the expected return rather than actual return is an important distinction. Company CEOs and CFOs dislike income variability because they believe that stockholders react negatively to it, and so company executives intensely (and successfully) lobbied the FASB to use the more stable expected long-term investment return, rather than the actual return, in

---

[6] Companies typically maintain many pension plans. Some are overfunded and others are underfunded. Current GAAP requires companies to separately group all of the overfunded and all of the underfunded plans, and to present a net asset for the overfunded plans and a net liability for the underfunded plans.

computing pension expense. Thus, the pension plan assets' expected return is deducted to compute net pension expense.[7]

Any difference between the expected and the actual return is accumulated, together with other deferred amounts, off-balance-sheet and reported in the footnotes. (Other deferred amounts include changes in PBO resulting from changes in estimates used to compute the PBO and from amendments to the pension plans made by the company.) However, if the deferred amount exceeds certain limits, the excess is recognized on-balance-sheet with a corresponding amount recognized (as amortization of deferred amounts) in the income statement.[8] This amortization is the fourth component of pension expense and can be either a positive or negative amount depending on the sign of the difference between expected and actual return on plan assets. (We discuss the amortization component of pension expense further in Appendix 10A.)

A final point to consider is the operating or nonoperating nature of the components of pension expense. Most analysts consider the service cost portion of pension expense to be an operating expense, similar to salaries and other benefits. However, the interest cost component is generally viewed as a nonoperating (financing) cost. Similarly, the expected return on plan assets is considered nonoperating.

Footnote Disclosures—Components of Plan Assets and PBO

GAAP requires extensive footnote disclosures for pensions (and other post-employment benefits which we discuss later). These notes provide details relating to the net pension liability reported in the balance sheet and for the components of pension expense on the income statement.

Delta Air Lines' pension footnote below indicates that the funded status of its pension plan is $(9,257) million on December 31, 2010. This means Delta's plan is underfunded. Following are the disclosures Delta Air Lines makes in its pension footnote, $ millions.

December 31 (in millions)	2010	2009
Benefit obligation at beginning of period	$17,031	$15,929
Service cost	—	—
Interest cost	982	1,002
Actuarial loss (gain)	570	1,170
Benefits paid, including lump sums and annuities	(1,013)	(1,021)
Participant contributions	—	—
Plan amendments	—	—
Special termination benefits	—	—
Settlements	(64)	(49)
Benefit obligation at end of period	$17,506	$17,031

continued

---

[7] The IASB has amended its standard on accounting for pensions and other postretirement benefits (OPEB), which potentially has important implications for U.S. GAAP. Those amendments take effect for years starting on or after January 1, 2013, and include the following key changes:

- *Elimination of deferred recognition.* The full value of the benefit obligation and plan assets will be reported in the balance sheet with changes arising from actuarial gains and losses recognized in full in other comprehensive income (OCI). Companies will not have an option to recognize those gains and losses in net income, either in the periods in which they occur or through amortization. Prior service cost will be recognized in full in determining net income in the period the plan amendment is made.

- *Disaggregation of benefit cost.* The components of pension and OPEB cost (service cost, finance cost, and remeasurement cost) will be reported separately in the footnotes. Separate or aggregate presentation of service and finance cost components will be permitted in the statement of comprehensive income.

- *Elimination of expected return on plan assets.* The discount rate would be applied to the net funded position to determine the net financing cost, which will include an implied return on assets. A separate expected long-term rate of return on plan assets will no longer be used.

[8] To avoid amortization, the deferred amounts must be less than 10% of the PBO or pension investments, whichever is less. The excess, if any, is amortized until no further excess remains. When the excess is eliminated (by investment returns or company contributions, for example), the amortization ceases.

continued from prior page

Fair value of plan assets at beginning of period	$ 7,623	$ 7,295
Actual (loss) gain on plan assets	975	1,198
Employer contributions	728	200
Participant contributions	—	—
Benefits paid, including lump sums and annuities	(1,013)	(1,021)
Settlements	(64)	(49)
Fair value of plan assets at end of period	$ 8,249	$ 7,623
Funded status at end of period	$ (9,257)	$ (9,408)

Delta Air Lines' PBO began the year with a balance of $17,031 million. It increased by the accrual of $982 million in interest cost (Delta froze its pension plans following the merger with Northwest Airlines; consequently, there is no current accrual for service cost as employees are not earning additional pension benefits). During the year, Delta realized an actuarial loss of $570 million, which increased the pension liability, and its PBO decreased as a result of $1,013 million in benefits paid to retirees, leaving a balance of $17,506 million at year-end.[9]

Pension plan assets began the year with a fair market value of $7,623 million, which increased by $975 million from investment returns and by $728 million from company contributions, and it decreased by $64 million for settlements to retirees. The company drew down its investments to make pension payments of $1,013 million to retirees. The $1,013 million payment reduced the PBO by the same amount, as discussed above, leaving the pension plan assets with a year-end balance of $8,249 million. The funded status of Delta Air Lines' pension plan at year-end was $(9,257) million, computed as $8,249 million − $17,506 million. The negative balance indicates that its pension plan is underfunded.

Delta Air Lines incurred $367 million of pension expense in 2010 and an additional $334 million of expense relating to defined contribution plans (companies typically maintain different types of retirement plans). The combined expense of $701 million is not broken out separately in the income statement. Details of this expense are found in its 2010 pension footnote, which follows ($ millions):

> We can treat the funded status as an operating item (either asset or liability).

Components of net periodic benefit cost	2010
Defined benefit plans	
Service cost	$ —
Interest cost	982
Expected return on plan assets	(677)
Amortization of prior service cost	—
Recognized net actuarial (gain) loss	48
Settlement charge, net	14
Special termination benefits	—
Net periodic cost	367
Defined contribution plan costs	334
Total cost	$701

The service and interest cost components of pension expense relate to the increase in the PBO of employees working another year for the company (expected benefits typically increase with longevity and salary, and the PBO increases because it is discounted for one less year). This expense is offset by the *expected* return on pension assets. Notice the use of expected returns rather than actual returns. Expected returns do not fluctuate as much as actual returns, and this yields a less volatile year-on-year pension expense and, consequently, less volatility in net income. The use of expected returns is in conformity with GAAP and companies lobbied for its use because of the reduced volatility for pension expense. Finally, because we cannot separate the operating and nonoperating components of a company's funded status and, hence, treat it entirely as operating, we do the same for pension expense and treat it entirely as operating. (We do this for consistency purposes even though

---

[9] This actuarial loss derives from: (1) a lower discount rate, from 5.93% to 5.69%—this change increased pension liability; and (2) a lower health care cost trend rate, from 7.5% to 7%—this change decreased pension liability. The lower discount rate dominated the lower cost trend and, thus, pension liability increased, yielding the actuarial loss.

we know that expense components related to interest cost, expected returns on plan assets, and many amortizations are nonoperating.)

RESEARCH INSIGHT | **Valuation Implications of Pension Footnote Disclosures**

The FASB requires footnote disclosure of the major components of pension cost presumably because it is useful for investors. Pension-related research has examined whether investors assign different valuation multiples to the components of pension cost when assessing company market value. Research finds that the market does, indeed, attach different interpretation to pension components, reflecting differences in information about perceived permanence in earnings.

Footnote Disclosures and Future Cash Flows

Companies use their pension plan assets to pay pension benefits to retirees. When markets are booming, as during the 1990s, pension plan assets can grow rapidly. However, when markets reverse, as in the bear markets of the early and late 2010s, the value of pension plan assets can decline. The company's annual pension plan contribution is an investment decision that is influenced, in part, by market conditions and minimum required contributions specified by law. Companies' cash contributions come from borrowed funds or operating cash flows.

RESEARCH INSIGHT | **Why Do Companies Offer Pensions?**

Research examines why companies choose to offer pension benefits. It finds that deferred compensation plans and pensions help align the long-term interests of owners and employees. Research also examines the composition of pension investments. It finds that a large portion of pension fund assets are invested in fixed-income securities, which are of lower risk than other investment securities. This implies that pension assets are less risky than nonpension assets. The FASB has mandated new pension disclosures that require firms (after 2009) to provide more detail about the types of assets held in pension plans. These disclosures presumably help investors better assess the riskiness of pension assets.

Delta Air Lines paid $1,013 million in pension benefits to retirees in 2010, yet it contributed only $728 million to pension assets that year. The remaining amount was paid out of available funds in the investment account. Cash contributions to the pension plan assets are the relevant amounts for an analysis of projected cash flows. Benefits paid in relation to the pension liability balance can provide a clue about the need for *future* cash contributions. Companies are required to disclose the expected benefit payments for five years after the statement date and the remaining obligations thereafter. Following is **Delta Air Lines**' benefit disclosure statement:

The following table summarizes the benefit payments that are scheduled to be paid in the following years ending December 31:

($ millions)	Pension
2011	$1,048
2012	1,036
2013	1,048
2014	1,059
2015	1,077
2016–2020	5,738

As of 2010, Delta Air Lines pension plan assets account reports a balance of $8,249 million, as discussed above, and during the year, the plan assets generated actual returns of $975 million. The pension plan asset account is currently generating investment returns that almost cover the $1 billion in projected benefit payments that Delta expects to pay to retirees as outlined in the schedule above. Should future investment returns decline, however, the company will have to use operating cash flow or borrow money to fund the deficit.

One application of the pension footnote is to assess the likelihood that the company will be required to increase its cash contributions to the pension plan. This estimate is made by examining the funded status of the pension plan and the projected payments to retirees. For severely underfunded plans, the projected payments to retirees might not be covered by existing pension assets and projected investment returns. In this case, the company might need to divert operating cash flow from other prospective projects to cover its pension plan. Alternatively, if operating cash flows are not available, it might need to borrow to fund those payments. This can be especially troublesome as the debt service payments include interest, which increase the required pension contribution. The decline in the financial condition and ultimate bankruptcy of General Motors was due in large part to its inability to meet its pension and health care obligations from pension assets. The company was forced to divert much needed operating cash flow and to borrow funds to meet its cash payment obligations.

Footnote Disclosures and Profit Implications

Recall the following earlier breakdown for pension expense:

Net Pension Expense
Service cost
+ Interest cost
− *Expected* return on pension plan assets
± Amortization of deferred amounts
Net pension expense

Interest cost is the product of the PBO and the discount rate. This discount rate is set by the company. The expected dollar return on pension assets is the product of the pension plan asset balance and the expected long-run rate of return on the investment portfolio. This rate is also set by the company. Further, PBO is affected by the expected rate of wage inflation, termination and mortality rates, all of which are estimated by the company.

GAAP requires disclosure of several rates used by the company in its estimation of PBO and the related pension expense. Delta Air Lines discloses the following in its pension footnote:

Net Periodic Benefit Cost (Year Ended December 31)	2010	2009	2008
Weighted average discount rate — pension benefit	5.93%	6.49%	7.19%
Weighted average discount rate — other postretirement benefit	5.75%	6.46%	6.46%
Weighted average discount rate — other postemployment benefit	5.88%	6.50%	6.95%
Weighted average expected long-term rate of return on plan assets	8.82%	8.83%	8.96%
Assumed health care cost trend rate................................	7.50%	8.00%	8.00%

During 2010, Delta Air Lines decreased its discount rate (used to compute the present value of its pension obligations, or PBO) by 0.56%, while leaving essentially unchanged its estimate of the expected return on plan assets. Delta also decreased its assumed health care cost trend rate by 0.50% and said it expects further declines in that rate to a level of about 5% by 2019 from its present rate of 7.5%.

Changes in these assumptions have the following general effects on pension expense and, thus, profitability. This table summarizes the effects of increases in the various rates. Decreases have the exact opposite effects.[10]

Assumption change	Probable effect on pension expense	Reason for effect
Discount rate ↑	↑	While the higher discount rate reduces the PBO, the lower PBO is multiplied by a higher rate when the company computes the interest component of pension expense. The rate effect is larger than the discount effect, resulting in increased pension expense.
Investment return ↑	↓	The dollar amount of expected return on plan assets is the product of the plan assets balance and the expected long-term rate of return. Increasing the return increases the expected return on plan assets, thus reducing pension expense.
Wage inflation ↑	↑	The expected rate of wage inflation affects future wage levels that determine expected pension payments. An increase, thus, increases PBO, which increases both the service and interest cost components of pension expense.

In the case of Delta Air Lines, the decrease in both the discount rate and the assumed health care cost trend rate, coupled with no change in the expected return on investments, served to decrease pension costs and increase profitability in that year. It is often the case that companies reduce the expected investment returns with a lag, but increase them without a lag, to favorably impact profitability. We must be aware of the impact of these changes in assumptions in our evaluation of company profitability.

Analysis Implications

There are two important analysis issues relating to pensions:

1. To what extent will the company's pension plans compete with investing and financing needs for the available cash flows?
2. In what ways has the company's choice of estimates affected its profitability?

Regarding the first issue, pension plan assets are the source of funds to pay benefits to retirees, and federal law (Employee Retirement Income Security Act) sets minimum standards for pension contributions. Consequently, if investment returns are insufficient, companies must make up the shortfall with additional contributions. Any such additional contributions compete for available operating cash flows with other investing and financing activities. This can be especially severe in a business downturn when operating cash flows are depressed. As debt payments are contractual, companies can be forced to postpone needed capital investment to make the contributions necessary to ensure funding of their pension plans as required by law or labor agreements. Analysts must be aware of funding requirements when projecting future cash flows.

---

[10] The effect of two hypothetical discount rates on the PBO and interest cost is seen in the following tables using the present values from an annuity of $1 for 10 and 40 years, respectively (dollar amounts are the present value factors from Appendix A; present value of an ordinary annuity, rounded to 2 decimal places).

	Discount rate	10 Years	40 Years
PBO	5%	$7.72	$17.16
	8%	6.71	11.92

As the discount rate increases, the PBO decreases. This is the discount effect. Second, the interest cost component of pension expense is computed as the PBO × Discount rate. For the four PBO amounts and related discount rates above, interest cost follows:

	Discount rate	10 Years	40 Years
Interest cost	5%	$0.39	$0.86
	8%	0.54	0.95

Interest cost increases with increases in the discount rate, regardless of the length of the liability. This is the rate effect.

Regarding the second issue, accounting for pensions requires several assumptions, including the expected return on pension investments, the expected rate of wage inflation, the discount rate used to compute the PBO, and other actuarial assumptions that are not reported in footnotes (mortality rates, for example). Each of these assumptions affects reported profit as already explained. Analysts must be aware of changes in these assumptions and their effects on profitability. An increase in reported profit that is due to an increase in the expected return on pension investments, for example, is not related to core operating activities and, further, might not be sustainable. Such changes in estimates must be considered in our evaluation of reported profitability.

BUSINESS INSIGHT   **How Pensions Confound Income Analysis**

Overfunded pension plans and boom markets can inflate income. Specifically, when the stock market is booming, pension investments realize large gains that flow to income (via reduced pension expense). Although pension plan assets do not belong to shareholders (as they are the legal entitlement of current and future retirees), the gains and losses from those plan assets are reported in income. The following graph plots the funded status of General Electric's pension plans together with pension expense (revenue) that GE reported from 1998 through 2010.

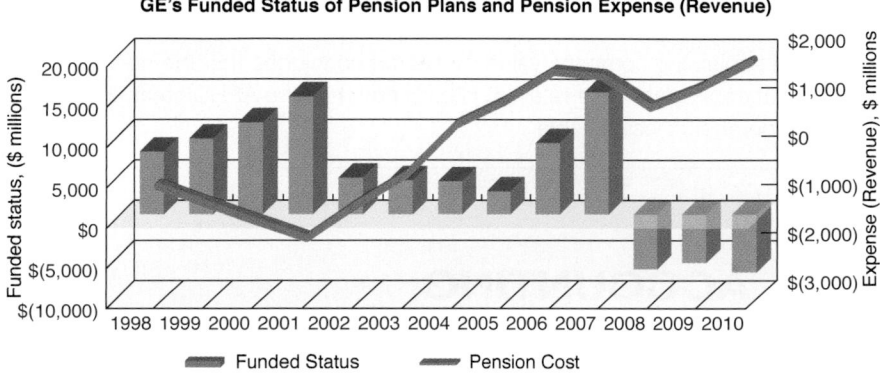

GE's Funded Status of Pension Plans and Pension Expense (Revenue)

GE's funded status has consistently been positive (indicating an overfunded plan) until the market decline of 2008. The degree of overfunding peaked in 2001 at the height of the stock market, and began to decline during the bear market of the early 2000s. GE reported pension *revenue* (not expense) during this period. In 2001, GE's reported pension *revenue* was $2,095 million (10.6% of its pretax income). Because of the plan's overfunded status, the expected return and amortization of deferred gains components of pension expense amounted to $5,288 million, far in excess of the service and interest costs of $3,193 million. In the mid to late 2000s, GE recorded pension expense (rather than revenue) as the pension plan's overfunding and expected long-term rates of return declined.

Other Post-Employment Benefits

In addition to pension benefits, many companies provide health care and insurance benefits to retired employees. These benefits are referred to as **other post-employment benefits (OPEB)**. These benefits present reporting challenges similar to pension accounting. However, companies most often provide these benefits on a "pay-as-you-go" basis and it is rare for companies to make contributions in advance for OPEB. As a result, this liability, known as the **accumulated post-employment benefit obligation (APBO)**, is largely, if not totally, unfunded. GAAP requires that the unfunded APBO liability, net of any unrecognized amounts, be reported in the balance sheet and the annual service costs and interest costs be accrued as expenses each year. This requirement is controversial for two reasons. First, future health care costs are especially difficult to estimate, so the value of the resulting APBO (the present value of the future benefits) is fraught with error. Second, these benefits are provided at the discretion of the employer and can be altered or terminated at any time. Consequently, employers argue that without a legal obligation to pay these benefits, the liability should not be reported in the balance sheet.

These other post-employment benefits can produce large liabilities. For example, **Delta Air Lines'** footnotes report a funded status for the company's health care obligation of $(2,178) million, consisting of an APBO liability of $3,298 million less health care plan investments with a market value of $1,120 million. Our analysis of cash flows related to pension obligations can be extended to other post-employment benefit obligations. For example, in addition to its pension payments, Delta Air Lines discloses that it is obligated to make health care payments to retirees totaling about $260 per year. Because health care obligations are rarely funded until payment is required (federal minimum funding standards do not apply to OPEB and there is no tax benefit to pre-funding), there are no investment returns to fund the payments. Our analysis of projected cash flows must consider this potential cash outflow in addition to that relating to pension obligations.

RESEARCH INSIGHT | **Valuation of Nonpension Post-Employment Benefits**

The FASB requires employers to accrue the costs of all nonpension post-employment benefits; known as *accumulated post-employment benefit obligation* (APBO). These benefits consist primarily of health care and insurance. This requirement is controversial due to concerns about the reliability of the liability estimate. Research finds that the APBO (alone) is associated with company value. However, when other pension-related variables are included in the research, the APBO liability is no longer useful in explaining company value. Research concludes that the pension-related variables do a better job at conveying value-relevant information than the APBO number alone, which implies that the APBO number is less reliable.

GLOBAL ACCOUNTING

We discussed three forms of off-balance-sheet financing. Moreover, there are several differences between U.S. GAAP and IFRS on these items, which we highlight below.

Leases   IFRS lease standards currently allow for operating leases, but the standards are such that it is very difficult for a lease agreement to qualify as an operating lease. IFRS standards are more principles based and so for lease accounting, there are no bright-line rules for lease classification. Instead the parties must consider the economic substance of the transaction. In addition, IFRS will classify as capital leases (labeled *financial leases*) various "arrangements" that convey the right to use an asset or compel the company to make specified payments, but that do not take the legal form of a lease. Examples include contracts where the company must make payments regardless of whether they take delivery of the contracted product or service (take-or-pay contracts) and outsourcing contracts. This will result in more capital leases under IFRS. A minor difference is that IFRS requires the separation of land and buildings for leases that involve both.

Pensions   For pension accounting, there are several disclosure differences and one notable accounting difference. The accounting difference pertains to actuarial gains and losses. As discussed in Appendix 10A, U.S. GAAP permits deferral of actuarial gains and losses and then amortizes them to net income over time. A notable difference is that IFRS companies can recognize all actuarial gains and losses in comprehensive income in the year they occur. These gains and losses are not deferred, and they are *never* reported on the IFRS income statement. Many IFRS companies select this option. Turning to disclosure, one difference is that pension expense is not reported as a single item under IFRS; various components can be aggregated with other expenses. For example, interest cost can be included with other interest expenses and reported as finance expense under IFRS. A second disclosure difference is that IFRS companies do not disclose the full funded status of their pension plan on the balance sheet as U.S. GAAP requires. However, they must do so in the footnotes. These disclosure differences make it more challenging to analyze IFRS pension costs and balance sheet items. FASB and IASB continue to work toward convergence on pension accounting.

Special Purpose Entities Companies use special purpose entities (SPE) to structure projects or transactions. Under U.S. GAAP, the primary beneficiary (the party with the power to direct SPE activities and with the obligation to absorb SPE losses) is required to consolidate the SPE. At the publication of this book, the IASB has not yet addressed the issue of SPEs. Instead, IFRS focuses on the general concept of "control" to determine if the SPE is consolidated.

MODULE-END REVIEW

Following is the pension disclosure footnote from American Airlines' 10-K report (in millions).

Pension Obligation and Assets	2010	2009
Reconciliation of benefit obligation		
Obligation at January 1	$12,003	$10,884
Service cost	366	333
Interest cost	737	712
Actuarial (gain) loss	442	675
Plan amendments	1	—
Benefit payments	(581)	(601)
Obligation at December 31	$12,968	$12,003
Reconciliation of fair value of plan assets		
Fair value of plan assets at January 1	$ 7,051	$ 6,714
Actual return on plan assets	837	928
Employer contributions	466	10
Benefit payments	(581)	(601)
Fair value of plan assets at December 31	$ 7,773	$ 7,051
Funded status at December 31	$ (5,195)	$ (4,952)

Following is American Airlines' footnote for its pension cost as reported in its income statement (in millions).

Pension Benefits	2010	2009
Components of net periodic benefit cost		
Defined benefit plans:		
Service cost	$366	$333
Interest cost	737	712
Expected return on assets	(593)	(566)
Amortization of:		
Prior service cost	13	13
Settlement	—	—
Unrecognized net loss	154	145
Net periodic benefit cost for defined benefit plans	677	637
Defined contribution plans	168	168
	$845	$805

Required

1. In general, what factors impact a company's pension benefit obligation during a period?
2. In general, what factors impact a company's pension plan investments during a period?
3. What amount is reported on the balance sheet relating to the American Airlines pension plan?
4. How does the expected return on plan assets affect pension cost?
5. How does American Airlines' expected return on plan assets compare with its actual return (in $s) for 2010?
6. How much net pension expense is reflected in American Airlines' 2010 income statement?
7. Assess American Airlines' ability to meet payment obligations to retirees.

The solution is on page 10-47.

APPENDIX 10A: Amortization Component of Pension Expense

One of the more difficult aspects of pension accounting relates to the issue of what is recognized on-balance-sheet and what is disclosed in the footnotes off-balance-sheet. This is an important distinction, and the FASB is moving toward more on-balance-sheet recognition and less off-balance-sheet disclosure. The FASB is considering whether to eliminate deferred gains and losses, and to require recognition in the income statement of *all* changes to pension assets and liabilities. Until this standard is enacted, deferred gains and losses will only impact reported pension expense via their amortization (the fourth component of pension expense described earlier in this module).

There are three sources of *unrecognized gains and losses*:

1. The difference between actual and expected return on pension investments.

2. Changes in actuarial assumptions such as expected wage inflation, termination and mortality rates, and the discount rate used to compute the present value of the projected benefit obligation.

3. Amendments to the pension plan to provide employees with additional benefits (called **prior service costs**).

Accounting for gains and losses resulting from these three sources is the same; specifically:

- Balance sheets report the net pension asset (overfunded status) or liability (underfunded status) irrespective of the magnitude of deferred gains and losses; that is, based solely on the relative balances of the pension assets and PBO accounts.

- Cumulative unrecognized gains and losses from all sources are recorded in one account, called deferred gains and losses, which is only disclosed in the footnotes, not on-balance-sheet.

- When the balance in the deferred gains and losses account exceeds prescribed levels, companies transfer a portion of the deferred gain or loss onto the balance sheet, with a matching expense on the income statement. This is the amortization process described in the text.

Recall that a company reports the *estimated* return on pension investments as a component (reduction) of pension expense. The pension assets, however, increase (decrease) by the *actual* return (loss). The difference between the two returns is referred to as a deferred (unrecognized) gain or loss. To illustrate, let's assume that the pension plan is underfunded at the beginning of the year by $200, with pension assets of $800, a PBO of $1,000, and no deferred gains or losses. Now, let's assume that actual returns for the year of $100 exceed the long-term expected return of $70. We can illustrate the accounting for the deferred gain as follows:

Year 1	Funded Status (Liabilities)	Earned Capital	Accumulated Other Comprehensive Income (AOCI)	Income Statement	Pension Assets	PBO
Balance, Jan. 1......	$200		$ 0	$ 0	$800	$1,000
Return.............	(100)	$70 (Retained Earnings) 30 (AOCI)	30	70	100	
Balance, Dec. 31	$100	$70 (Retained Earnings) 30 (AOCI)	$30	$70	$900	$1,000

The balance sheet at the beginning of the year reports the funded status of the pension plan as a $200 liability, reflecting the underfunded status of the pension plan. Neither the $800 pension asset account, nor the $1,000 PBO appear on-balance-sheet. Instead, their balances are only disclosed in a pension footnote.

During the year, pension assets (off-balance-sheet) increase by the actual return of $100 with no change in the PBO, thus decreasing the pension liability (negative funded status) by $100. The pension expense on the income statement, however, only reflects the expected return of $70, and retained earnings increase by that amount. The remaining $30 is recognized in accumulated other comprehensive income (AOCI), a component of earned capital.

These deferred gains and losses do not affect reported profit until they exceed prescribed limits, after which the excess is gradually recognized in income.[11] For example, assume that in the following year, $5 of the $30 deferred gain is amortized (recognized on the income statement as expense, which flows to retained earnings on the balance sheet). This amortization would result in the following effects:

Year 2	Funded Status (Liabilities)	Earned Capital	Accumulated Other Comprehensive Income (AOCI)	Income Statement	Pension Assets	PBO
		On Financial Statements			Footnotes	
Balance, Jan. 1.......	$100	$70 (Retained Earnings) 30 (AOCI)	$30	$ 0	$900	$1,000
Amortization.........		$ 5 (Retained Earnings)	(5)	5		
Balance, Dec. 31	$100	$75 (Retained Earnings) 25 (AOCI)	$25	$ 5	$900	$1,000

The deferred gain is reduced by $5 and is now recognized in reported income as a reduction of pension expense. (This amortization is the fourth item in the Net Pension Expense computation table from earlier in this module.) This is the only change, as the pension assets still report a balance of $900 and the PBO reports a balance of $1,000, for a funded status of $(100) that is reported as a liability on the balance sheet.

In addition to the difference between actual and expected gains (losses) on pension assets, the deferred gains (losses) account includes increases or decreases in the PBO balance that result from changes in assumptions used to compute it, namely, the expected rate of wage inflation, termination and mortality rates for employees, and changes in the discount rate used to compute the present value of the pension obligations. Some of these can be offsetting, and all accumulate in the same deferred gains (losses) account. Justification for off-balance-sheet treatment of these items was the expectation that their offsetting nature would combine to keep the magnitude of deferred gains (losses) small. It is only in relatively extreme circumstances that this account becomes large enough to warrant amortization and, consequently, on-balance-sheet recognition. Further, the amortization portion of reported pension expense is usually small.

APPENDIX 10B: Special Purpose Entities (SPEs)

Special purpose entities (SPEs) allow companies to structure projects or transactions with a number of financial advantages. SPEs have long been used and are an integral part of corporate finance. The SPE concept is illustrated by the following graphic that summarizes information taken from Ford's 2010 10-K relating to the SPE structure it uses to securitize the receivables of Ford Credit (its financing subsidiary):

LO3 Explain the accounting for special purpose entities (SPEs).

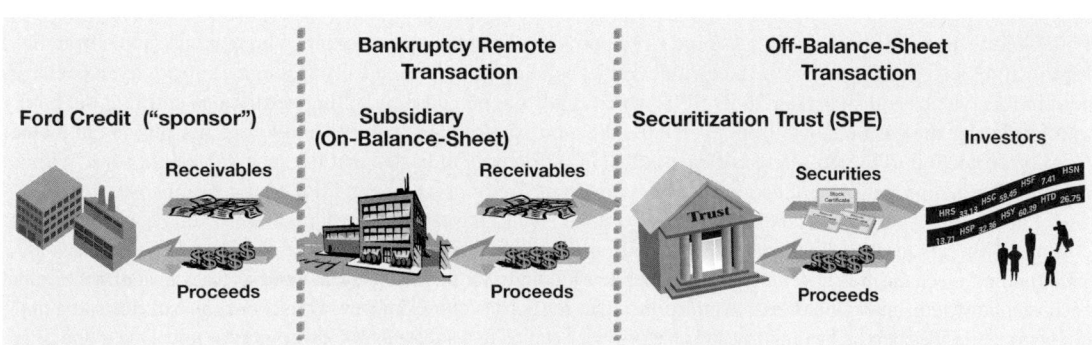

---

[11] The upper (lower) bound on the deferred gains (losses) account is 10% of the PBO or Plan Asset account balance, whichever is greater, at the beginning of the year. Once this limit is exceeded, the excess is amortized until the account balance is below that threshold, irrespective of whether such reduction results from amortization, or changes in the PBO or Pension Asset accounts (from changes in actuarial assumptions, company contributions, or positive investment returns).

This graphic is typical of many SPEs and has the following characteristics of all SPEs:

■ A sponsoring company (here, Ford Credit) forms a subsidiary that is capitalized entirely with equity; this creates a *bankruptcy remote* structure. This means that even if Ford Credit becomes bankrupt, neither it nor its creditors will be able to access the subsidiary's assets; this reduces the risk for subsequent investors.

■ The subsidiary purchases assets from the sponsoring company and sells them to a securitization (off-balance-sheet) trust (the SPE), which purchases the assets using borrowed funds (here, the SPE purchases receivables from Ford Credit's subsidiary using cash from investors).

■ Cash flows from the acquired assets are used by the SPE to repay its debt (here, the SPE collects receivables and uses the funds to repay any borrowings).

The sponsoring company benefits in two ways. First, SPEs create direct economic benefits by speeding up receipt of the company's operating cash flows and by mitigating certain types of risk. Second, SPEs create indirect economic benefits by providing financial reporting benefits and alternatives. These indirect benefits derive from having assets, and their related debt, moved off-balance-sheet. Also, the SPE owns the sponsoring company's former assets. Thus, the sponsoring company enjoys an improved asset turnover ratio (assets are typically less in the denominator of the turnover ratio) and an improved financial leverage ratio (liabilities are less in the numerator of the liabilities-to-equity ratio).

Applying SPEs as Financing Tools

This section describes two common means of using SPEs as financing tools.

Asset Securitization

Consumer finance companies, retailers, and financial subsidiaries of manufacturing companies commonly use SPEs to securitize (sell) their financial assets. Ford Credit, the finance subsidiary of Ford Motor Company, provides a common example as illustrated in the MD&A of Ford's 2010 10-K report.

Securitization In 2005 and 2006, the credit ratings assigned to Ford Credit were lowered to below investment grade, which increased its unsecured borrowing costs and restricted its access to the unsecured debt markets. In response, Ford Credit increased its use of securitization transactions (including other structured financings) and other sources of funding. In 2010, although Ford Credit experienced several credit rating upgrades and its credit spreads narrowed considerably, its credit ratings are still below investment grade. Ford Credit's higher credit ratings have provided it more economical access to the unsecured debt markets, but it is still utilizing asset-backed securitization transactions for a substantial amount of its funding. . .

In a securitization transaction, the securitized assets are generally held by a bankruptcy-remote special purpose entity ("SPE") in order to isolate the securitized assets from the claims of Ford Credit's other creditors and ensure that the cash flows on the securitized assets are available for the benefit of securitization investors. As a result, payments to securitization investors are based on the creditworthiness of the securitized assets and any enhancements, and not on Ford Credit's creditworthiness. Senior asset-backed securities issued by the SPEs generally receive the highest short-term credit ratings and among the highest long-term credit ratings from the rating agencies that rate them.

Ford Credit's use of SPEs is typical. As Ford Credit provides financing to customers who purchase autos from Ford Motor Company, it accumulates the receivables on its balance sheet. Periodically, through a subsidiary, it packages certain receivables and sells them to its SPE, which funds the purchase by selling certificates entitling the holder to a portion of the cash receipts from eventual collection of receivables. Ford Credit does not provide any other form of protection to the outside certificate holders (its footnote indicates that the receivables are sold "without recourse," meaning without collection rights against Ford Credit or its parent, Ford Motor Company).

Ford Motor Company's credit ratings have declined in recent years, thus making its unsecured borrowings more costly and limiting its availability to borrowed funds. In response, it has increased its use of SPEs as a financing source. This funding mechanism is now an important source of liquidity for the company, as Ford Credit's cost of debt capital is substantially less, and exhibits less volatility, than that for Ford Motor Company. Thus, Ford's use of SPEs as a funding source provides necessary liquidity and also provides capital at a substantially lower interest rate. Due to the SPE's limited scope of operations, and its isolation from the general business risk of the parent company, the SPE's lenders face lower risk of default and can, therefore, charge a comparatively lower rate of interest on money they lend to the SPE.

Project and Real Estate Financing

Another common use of SPEs is to finance construction projects. For example, a sponsoring company desires to construct a manufacturing plant. It establishes an SPE and executes a contract with the SPE to build the plant and to later purchase output from the plant. The SPE uses the contract, and the newly constructed manufacturing plant assets, to collateralize debt that it issues to finance the plant's construction. The sponsoring company obtains the benefits of the plant, but does not recognize either the PPE asset or the related liability on its balance sheet. The sponsoring company has commitments with the SPE, labeled executory contracts, but GAAP currently does not require such contracts be recognized in the balance sheet, nor does it even require footnote disclosure of these contracts.

Clothing retailers such as Gap and Abercrombie & Fitch use these types of executory contracts involving outside manufacturers. The manufacturing assets, and related liabilities, are reported on the balance sheet of the SPE and not of the company itself.

A slight variation is to add leasing to this transaction. To illustrate, assume a company desires to construct an office building. It establishes an SPE to construct and finance the building and then leases the building back from the SPE under an operating lease. As we explained earlier in this module, if the lease is structured as an operating lease, neither the lease asset nor the lease obligation is reported on the company's balance sheet. Thus, the company obtains the use and benefit of the building without recording either the building or the related debt on its balance sheet.

Reporting of SPEs

Special purpose entities, such as those that Ford uses to securitize its loan and lease assets, must be consolidated by whichever company has the power to direct the activities of the SPE and the right to receive its benefits (or absorb the losses). As we discuss in Module 7, for companies that issue common stock, consolidation means that the balance sheet and income statement of the SPE are reported together with that of the parent company. The consolidation of SPEs is no different and their financial statements must be combined with those of the sponsoring company (Ford Credit in this case).

The effect of consolidation of SPEs is to report both the loan and lease receivables on Ford's consolidated balance sheet as well as the liabilities of the SPE. Similarly, the loan and lease income is reported in Ford's income statement together with the SPE's expenses, including interest expense on borrowed funds. As a result, the securitization process is fully reflected in Ford's financial statements. Further, companies are required to provide extensive disclosures relating to the magnitude of the assets securitized and the effects (and risks) on their liquidity of reliable access to securitization credit markets.

IFRS INSIGHT	Consolidation of SPEs under IFRS

Under both U.S. GAAP and IFRS, SPEs are consolidated based on the transfer of risks and rewards. But unlike GAAP's more rules-based orientation, IFRS requires a more conceptual analysis of risks and rewards. This leads to consolidation of more special purpose entities under IFRS as compared to GAAP. The FASB and the IASB are working toward convergence on this standard.

Analysis Implications of SPEs

Despite that SPEs are consolidated in the financial statements of the sponsoring company, the securitization process continues to provide a lower-cost financing source to companies by reducing credit risk for the lenders. Accordingly, SPEs will continue to be part of the business landscape. As such, there are at least two analysis implications related to SPEs:

■ **Cost of capital.** As discussed, SPEs reduce business risk and bankruptcy risk for their lenders. Consequently, the sponsoring company is able to obtain capital at a lower cost. Ford Motor Company (a manufacturer), for example, has witnessed a reduction in its credit ratings and a consequent increase in its cost of borrowed funds. Ordinarily, its negative credit rating would be ascribed to its subsidiaries as well, including its finance subsidiary. Using SPEs, however, the finance subsidiary, Ford Credit, is able to obtain financing at lower interest rates, which allows it to pass along that lower cost in the form of lower interest rates on auto and other loans to its customers. Without that financing source, Ford Credit would be less competitive in the marketplace vis-à-vis other, financially stronger, financial institutions.

■ **Liquidity.** Financial institutions, and finance subsidiaries of manufacturing companies, rely on a business model of generating a high volume of loans, each of which carries a relatively small profit (spread of the interest rate over the cost of the funds). If they were forced to hold all of those loans on their own balance sheets, they would eventually need to raise costly equity capital to balance the increase in debt financing. That would also serve to reduce their competitiveness in the marketplace. These companies must, therefore, be able to package loans for sale, a crucial source of liquidity.

Given the importance of the cash flows contributed by its Ford Credit financing subsidiary to Ford Motor Company, analysts would be concerned about the welfare of the overall entity were there indications that its SPE financing sources would no longer be available (say, if further accounting standards limited Ford's ability to remove these loans from its consolidated balance sheet and record their transfer to the SPE as a sale). Analysts would also be concerned if the credit markets no longer favored this SPE structure as a financing mechanism (say, if the presumed bankruptcy protection of the SPEs was ultimately proven to be false following the bankruptcy of the sponsoring company and the consequent bankruptcy of an SPE that it sponsored). Neither of these events has occurred, and lenders rely on legal opinions that SPEs are "bankruptcy remote." Analysts must always assess these risks when assessing the financial strength of companies that rely on the SPE financial structure.

APPENDIX 10C: Lease Capitalization Using a Calculator and Present Value Tables

This Appendix identifies the keystrokes to compute both the present value of projected operating lease payments and the imputed discount rate using two popular financial calculators: Hewlett-Packard 10bII and Texas Instruments BA II Plus. It also computes the present value of projected lease payments using present value tables.

Hewlett-Packard 10bII: Present value of projected operating lease payments

Following are the keystrokes to compute the present value of the Delta Air Lines projected lease payments. This approach utilizes the same computational steps as our illustrations.

Enter #	Key[a]	
1	P/YR	Enter the number of periods per year
0	CF$_j$	Enter the cash flow in year 0 (current year)
1,420	CF$_j$	Enter the cash flow in year 1
1,351	CF$_j$	Enter the cash flow in year 2
1,320	CF$_j$	Enter the cash flow in year 3
1,263	CF$_j$	Enter the cash flow in year 4
1,169	CF$_j$	Enter the cash flow in year 5 (and assumed thereafter)
8	N$_j$	Enter the number of years the year 5 cash flow is repeated
240	CF$_j$	Enter the cash flow in final partial year ($1,169 × 0.205 years)
14.31	I/YR	Enter the annual discount rate
	NPV	Press **NPV** button to get present value ($7,085)

[a] To enter a number, type the number and then press the corresponding key; for example, to enter P/YR, type "1" and then press **P/YR**.

Hewlett-Packard 10bII: Imputed discount rate

This example computes the imputed discount rate given the capitalized lease disclosures in the lease footnote; we again use Delta Air Lines.

Enter #	Key[a]	
1	P/YR	Enter the number of periods per year
−738[a]	CF$_j$	Enter the cash flow in year 0 (current year)
214	CF$_j$	Enter the cash flow in year 1
193	CF$_j$	Enter the cash flow in year 2
160	CF$_j$	Enter the cash flow in year 3
130	CF$_j$	Enter the cash flow in year 4
124	CF$_j$	Enter the cash flow in year 5 (and assumed thereafter)
4	N$_j$	Enter the number of years the year 5 cash flow is repeated
32	CF$_j$	Enter the cash flow in final partial year ($124 × 0.258 years)
	IRR	Press **IRR** button to get implicit discount rate (14.31%)

[a] To enter a negative number, type in the absolute value of that number and then press +/− button; for example, to enter the initial cash flow in year 0, enter "738", press +/−, and then press **CF$_j$**.

Texas Instruments BA II Plus: Present value of projected operating lease payments

Following are the keystrokes to compute the present value of the Delta Air Lines projected lease payments. This approach utilizes the same computational steps as our illustrations.

Key	Enter # [a]	
FORMAT	0	Press the **FORMAT** button and enter decimal places desired
CF	0	Enter the cash flow in year 0 (**CF$_O$**)
↓	1,420	Enter the cash flow in year 1 (**CO1**)
↓		Frequency (**FO1**) should be pre-set at "1", so nothing need be entered
↓	1,351	Enter the cash flow in year 2 (**CO2**)
↓		Frequency (**FO2**) should be pre-set at "1"
↓	1,320	Enter the cash flow in year 3 (**CO3**)
↓		Frequency (**FO3**) should be pre-set at "1"
↓	1,263	Enter the cash flow in year 4 (**CO4**)
↓		Frequency (**FO4**) should be pre-set at "1"
↓	1,169	Enter the cash flow in year 5 (**CO5**) and assumed thereafter
↓	8	Enter the number of years the year 5 cash flow is repeated (**FO5**)
↓	240	Enter the cash flow in final partial year (1,169 × 0.205 years) (**CO6**)
↓		Frequency (**FO6**) should be pre-set at "1"
NPV	14.31	Press **NPV** button, the pre-set discount rate should say "0"; enter "14.31" the discount rate
↓, CPT	7,085	Press ↓ button and then press **CPT** to get present value

[a] After entering in a number from this column, press **ENTER**.

Texas Instruments BA II Plus: Imputed discount rate

Following are the keystrokes to compute the present value of the Delta Air Lines projected lease payments. This approach utilizes the same computational steps as our illustrations.

Key	Enter [a]	
CF	−738[b]	Enter the cash flow in year 0 (**CF$_O$**)
↓	214	Enter the cash flow in year 1 (CO1)
↓		Frequency (FO1) should be pre-set at "1"
↓	193	Enter the cash flow in year 2 (CO2)
↓		Frequency (FO2) should be pre-set at "1"
↓	160	Enter the cash flow in year 3 (CO3)
↓		Frequency (FO3) should be pre-set at "1"
↓	130	Enter the cash flow in year 4 (CO4)
↓		Frequency (FO4) should be pre-set at "1"
↓	124	Enter the cash flow in year 5 and assumed thereafter (CO5)
↓	4	Enter the number of years the year 5 cash flow is repeated (FO5)
↓	32	Enter the cash flow in final partial year (CO6)
↓		Frequency (FO6) should be pre-set at "1"
IRR		Press **IRR** button, the pre-set IRR should say "0"
↓, CPT		Press ↓ button and then press **CPT** to get implicit discount rate

[a] After typing in a number from this column, press **ENTER**.

[b] To enter a negative number, type in the absolute value of that number and then press +/− button; for example, to enter the initial cash flow in year 0, press **CF**, enter "738", press +/−, and then press **ENTER**.

Lease Capitalization Using Present Value Tables

Present value tables list the factors for selected interest rates and discount periods (often in whole numbers). To compute the present value of the operating lease payments using those tables (see Appendix A near the end of this book), we must first round the remaining lease term (7.205 for Delta) to the nearest whole year (7), and round the discount rate (14.31% for Delta) to its nearest whole interest rate (14%). After that, computation of the present value of future operating lease payments is identical to the spreadsheet method and is shown below. We see that the present value of each projected lease payment for Years 1 through 5 is computed using the present value factor for that particular year (taken from tables similar to Appendix A, Table 1, "Present Value of Single Amount") using a discount rate of 14%. To compute the present value of the lease payments remaining after Year 5, we again assume that lease payments continue at the Year 5 amount for the remainder of the lease term. Those payments represent an annuity, $672 million for 7 years (7.205 rounded to 7), that is discounted at 14% (taken from tables similar to Appendix A, Table 2, "Present Value of Ordinary Annuity"), which is then discounted back five more years to the present.

Year ($ millions)	Operating Lease Payment	Discount Factor ($i = 0.14$)	Present Value
1................	$1,420	0.87719	$1,246
2................	1,351	0.76947	1,040
3................	1,320	0.67497	891
4................	1,263	0.59208	748
5................	1,169	0.51937	607
>5................	8,423 [$1,169 for ~7.205 years]	4.28830 × 0.51937	2,604
			$7,136

Remaining life........ $8,423/$1,169 = 7.205 years, rounded to 7 years.

Regardless of the method used, the computed amount is the present value of future operating lease payments. That value is $7,088 million using the spreadsheet method, $7,085 million using a calculator, and $7,136 million using present value tables.

GUIDANCE ANSWERS

MANAGERIAL DECISION | **You Are the Division President**

Lease terms that are not advantageous to your company but are structured merely to achieve off-balance-sheet financing can destroy shareholder value. Long-term shareholder value is created by managing your operation well, including negotiating leases with acceptable terms. Lease footnote disclosures also provide sufficient information for skilled analysts to undo the operating lease treatment. This means that you can end up with de facto capitalization of a lease with lease terms that are not in the best interests of your company and with few benefits from off-balance-sheet financing. There is also the potential for lost credibility with stakeholders.

Superscript [A (B, C)] denotes assignments based on Appendix 10A (B, C).

DISCUSSION QUESTIONS

Q10-1. What are the financial reporting differences between an operating lease and a capital lease? Explain.

Q10-2. Are footnote disclosures sufficient to overcome nonrecognition on the balance sheet of assets and related liabilities for operating leases? Explain.

Q10-3. Is the expense of a lease over its entire life the same whether or not it is capitalized? Explain.

Q10-4. What are the economic and accounting differences between a defined contribution plan and a defined benefit plan?

Q10-5. Under what circumstances will a company report a net pension asset? A net pension liability?

Q10-6. What are the components of pension expense that are reported in the income statement?

Q10-7. What effect does the use of expected returns on pension investments and the deferral of unexpected gains and losses on those investments have on income?

Q10-8. What is a special purpose entity (SPE)? Provide an example of the use of an SPE as a financing vehicle.

Q10-9. What effect does consolidating SPEs have on both accounting for SPEs and the balance sheets of companies that sponsor them?

Assignments with the ✓ in the margin are available in an online homework system.
See the Preface of the book for details.

MINI EXERCISES

M10-10. Analyzing and Interpreting Lease Footnote Disclosures (LO1)

The GAP, Inc., discloses the following schedule to its 2011 10-K report relating to its leasing activities.   The GAP, Inc. (GPS)

The aggregate minimum noncancelable annual lease payments under leases in effect on January 29, 2011, are as follows:

Fiscal Year ($ millions)	
2011	$ 997
2012	841
2013	710
2014	602
2015	483
Thereafter	1,483
Total minimum lease commitments	$5,116

a. Compute the present value of GAP's operating leases using a 6% discount rate and round the remaining lease term to the nearest whole year.

b. What types of adjustments might we consider to GAP's balance sheet and income statement for analysis purposes?

M10-11. Analyzing and Capitalizing Operating Lease Payments Disclosed in Footnotes (LO1)

Costco Wholesale Corporation discloses the following in footnotes to its 10-K report relating to its leasing activities.

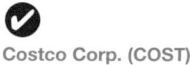

Costco Corp. (COST)

Future minimum payments . . . during the next five fiscal years and thereafter under non-cancelable leases with terms of at least one year, at the end of 2010, were as follows ($ millions):

2011	$ 162
2012	157
2013	155
2014	148
2015	134
Thereafter	1,572
Total minimum payments	$2,328

Operating leases are not reflected on-balance-sheet. In our analysis of a company, we often capitalize these operating leases, that is, add the present value of the future operating lease payments to both the reported assets and liabilities.

a. Compute the present value of Costco's operating lease payments assuming a 6% discount rate and round the remaining lease term to the nearest whole year.

b. What effect does capitalization of operating leases have on Costco's total liabilities and total assets (it reported total liabilities and total assets of $12,885 million and $23,815 million, respectively)?

M10-12. Analyzing and Interpreting Pension Disclosures—Expenses and Returns (LO2)

StanleyBlack & Decker discloses the following pension footnote in its 10-K report.   StanleyBlack & Decker (SWK)

($ millions)	2010
Service cost	$ 18.1
Interest cost	61.2
Expected return on plan assets	(52.5)
Amortization of prior service cost	1.0
Transition amount amortization	—
Actuarial loss amortization	2.0
Settlement/curtailment loss (gain)	(9.1)
Net periodic pension expense	$ 20.7

a. How much pension expense does StanleyBlack & Decker report in its 2010 income statement?

b. Explain, in general, how expected return on plan assets affects reported pension expense. How did expected return affect StanleyBlack & Decker's 2010 pension expense?

c. Explain use of the word "expected" as it relates to pension plan assets.

M10-13. Analyzing and Interpreting Pension Disclosures—PBO and Funded Status (LO2)

YUM! Brands, Inc.
(YUM)

YUM! Brands, Inc., discloses the following pension footnote in its 10-K report.

Pension Benefit Obligation ($ millions)	2010	2009
Change in benefit obligation		
Benefit obligation at beginning of year.	$1,010	$ 923
Service cost	25	26
Interest cost	62	58
Participant contributions.	—	—
Plan amendments.	—	1
Curtailment gain	(2)	(9)
Settlement loss.	1	2
Special termination benefits	1	4
Exchange rate changes	—	—
Benefits paid.	(57)	(47)
Settlement payments	(9)	(10)
Actuarial (gain) loss.	77	62
Benefit obligation at end of year	$1,108	$1,010

a. Explain the terms "service cost" and "interest cost."

b. How do actuarial losses arise?

c. The fair market value of YUM!'s pension assets is $907 million as of 2010. What is the funded status of the plan, and how will this be reflected on YUM!'s balance sheet?

M10-14. Analyzing and Interpreting Pension Disclosures—Plan Assets and Cash Flow (LO2)

YUM! Brands, Inc.
(YUM)

YUM! Brands, Inc., discloses the following pension footnote in its 10-K report.

Pension Plan Assets ($ millions)	2010	2009
Fair value of plan assets at beginning of year	$835	$513
Actual return on plan assets.	108	132
Employer contributions.	35	252
Participant contributions.	—	—
Settlement payments	(9)	(10)
Benefits paid.	(57)	(47)
Exchange rate changes	—	—
Administrative expenses.	(5)	(5)
Fair value of plan assets at end of year	$907	$835

a. How does the "actual return on plan assets" of $108 million affect YUM!'s reported profits for 2010?

 b. What are the cash flow implications of the pension plan for YUM! in 2010?

 c. YUM!'s pension plan paid out $57 million in benefits during 2010. Where else is this payment
   reflected?

M10-15. Analyzing and Interpreting Retirement Benefit Footnote   (LO2)

Abercrombie & Fitch discloses the following footnote relating to its retirement plans in its 2010 10-K
report.

                               Abercrombie & Fitch
                                (ANF)

> **RETIREMENT BENEFITS**   The Company maintains the Abercrombie & Fitch Co. Savings &
> Retirement Plan, a qualified plan. All U.S. associates are eligible to participate in this plan if they
> are at least 21 years of age and have completed a year of employment with 1,000 or more hours
> of service. In addition, the Company maintains the Abercrombie & Fitch Nonqualified Savings
> and Supplemental Retirement, composed of two sub-plans (Plan I and Plan II). Plan I contains
> contributions made through December 31, 2004, while Plan II contains contributions made on
> and after January 1, 2005. Participation in this plan is based on service and compensation.
> The Company's contributions are based on a percentage of associates' eligible annual
> compensation. The cost of the Company's contributions to these plans was $19.4 million in
> Fiscal 2010, $17.8 million in Fiscal 2009 and $24.7 million in Fiscal 2008.

 a. Does Abercrombie have a defined contribution or defined benefit pension plan? Explain.

 b. How does Abercrombie account for its contributions to its retirement plan?

 c. How does Abercrombie report its obligation for its retirement plan on the balance sheet?

M10-16. Analyzing and Interpreting Lease Disclosure   (LO1)

Dow Chemical Company provided the following footnote in its 2010 10-K report relating to
operating leases.

                               Dow Chemical
                               Company (DOW)

> **Leased Property**   The Company routinely leases premises for use as sales and adminis-
> trative offices, warehouses and tanks for product storage, motor vehicles, railcars, com-
> puters, office machines, and equipment under operating leases. In addition, the Company
> leases aircraft in the United States. At the termination of the leases, the Company has the
> option to purchase certain leased equipment and buildings based on a fair market value de-
> termination. In 2009, the Company purchased a previously leased ethylene plant in Canada
> for $713 million. Rental expenses under operating leases, net of sublease rental income,
> were $404 million in 2010, $459 million in 2009, and $439 million in 2008. Future minimum
> rental payments under operating leases with remaining noncancelable terms in excess of
> one year are as follows:
>
> | Minimum Operating Lease Commitments (in millions) | December 31, 2010 |
> | --- | --- |
> | 2011 . . . . | $ 202 |
> | 2012 . . . . | 163 |
> | 2013 . . . . | 149 |
> | 2014 . . . . | 126 |
> | 2015 . . . . | 115 |
> | 2016 and thereafter . . . . | 1,796 |
> | Total . . . . | $2,551 |

Required

 a. Dow describes all of its leases as "operating." What is the significance of this designation?

 b. How might we treat these operating leases in our analysis of the company?

M10-17. Analyzing and Interpreting Disclosure on Contract Manufacturers   (LO3)

Nike reports the following information relating to its manufacturing activities in footnotes to its fiscal
2010 10-K report for the year ended May 31, 2011.

Nike, Inc. (NKE)

Manufacturing Virtually all of our footwear is produced by factories we contract with outside of the United States. In fiscal 2010, contract factories in Vietnam, China, Indonesia, Thailand, and India manufactured approximately 37%, 34%, 23%, 2% and 1% of total NIKE Brand footwear, respectively. We also have manufacturing agreements with independent factories in Argentina, Brazil, India, and Mexico to manufacture footwear for sale primarily within those countries. The largest single footwear factory that we have contracted with accounted for approximately 5% of total fiscal 2010 footwear production. Almost all of NIKE Brand apparel is manufactured outside of the United States by independent contract manufacturers located in 33 countries. Most of this apparel production occurred in China, Thailand, Indonesia, Malaysia, Vietnam, Sri Lanka, Turkey, Cambodia, El Salvador, Mexico, and Taiwan. The largest single apparel factory that we have contracted with accounted for approximately 7% of total fiscal 2010 apparel production.

a. What effect does the use of contract manufacturers have on Nike's balance sheet?

b. How does Nike's use of contract manufacturers affect Nike's return on net operating assets (RNOA) and its components, net operating profit margin (NOPM) and net operating asset turnover (NOAT)? Explain.

c. Nike executes agreements with its contract manufacturers to purchase their output. How are such "executory contracts" reported under GAAP? Does your answer suggest a possible motivation for the use of contract manufacturing?

M10-18. **Analyzing and Interpreting Pension Plan Benefit Footnotes** (LO2)

Lockheed Martin Corp. (LMT)

Lockheed Martin Corporation discloses the following funded status for its defined benefit pension plans in its 10-K report.

Defined Benefit Pension Plans (In millions)	2010	2009
Unfunded status of the plans.............................	$(10,428)	$(10,663)

Lockheed contributed $2,240 million to its pension plan assets in 2010, up from $1,482 million in the prior year. The company also reports that it is obligated for the following expected payments to retirees in the next five years.

(In millions)	Qualified Pension Benefits
2011	$ 1,670
2012	1,740
2013	1,810
2014	1,900
2015	1,990
Years 2016–2020	11,580

a. How is this funded status reported in Lockheed's balance sheet under current GAAP?

b. How should we interpret this funded status in our analysis of the company?

c. What likely effect would a substantial decline in the financial markets have on Lockheed's contribution to its pension plans? Explain.

EXERCISES

E10-19. **Analyzing and Interpreting Leasing Footnote** (LO1)

Lowe's Companies (LOW)

Lowe's Companies, Inc., reports the following footnote relating to its leased facilities in its fiscal 2010 10-K report for the year ended January 28, 2011.

The Company leases facilities and land for certain facilities under agreements with original terms generally of 20 years. . . . The future minimum rental payments required under operating leases and capitalized lease obligations having initial or remaining noncancelable lease terms in excess of one year are summarized as follows:

(In millions)	Operating Leases	Capitalized Lease Obligations	Total
2011	$ 418	$ 68	$ 486
2012	416	69	485
2013	410	69	479
2014	399	64	463
2015	392	54	446
Later years	3,973	302	4,275
Total minimum lease payments	$6,008	$626	$6,634
Less amount representing interest.		(273)	
Present value of minimum lease payments		353	
Less current maturities.		(35)	
Present value of minimum lease payments, less current maturities		$318	

a. Using your financial calculator or Excel spreadsheet, confirm that Lowe's capitalized its capital leases using a rate of 12.2%.

b. What effect does the failure to capitalize operating leases have on Lowe's balance sheet? Over the life of the lease, what effect does this classification have on net income?

c. Compute the present value of these operating leases using a discount rate of 12% and round the remaining lease term to the nearest whole year. How might we use this information in our analysis of the company?

E10-20. **Analyzing and Interpreting Footnote on Operating and Capital Leases** (LO1)

Verizon Communications, Inc.
(VZ)

Verizon Communications, Inc., provides the following footnote relating to leasing activities in its 10-K report.

The aggregate minimum rental commitments under noncancelable leases for the periods shown at December 31, 2010, are as follows:

Years (dollars in millions)	Capital Leases	Operating Leases
2011	$ 97	$ 1,898
2012	74	1,720
2013	70	1,471
2014	54	1,255
2015	42	1,012
Thereafter.	81	5,277
Total minimum rental commitments.	418	$12,633
Less interest and executory costs	86	
Present value of minimum lease payments	332	
Less current installments	75	
Long-term obligation at December 31, 2010 . . .	**$257**	

a. Using your financial calculator or Excel spreadsheet, confirm that Verizon capitalized its capital leases using a rate of 7.4%.

b. What effect does the failure to capitalize operating leases have on Verizon's balance sheet? Over the life of its leases, what effect does this lease classification have on net income?

c. Compute the present value of Verizon's operating leases, assuming a 7.4% discount rate and rounding the remaining lease life to three decimal places. How might we use this additional information in our analysis of the company?

E10-21. Analyzing, Interpreting and Capitalizing Operating Leases (LO1)

Staples, Inc. (SPLS)

Staples, Inc., reports the following footnote relating to its capital and operating leases in its 10-K report for the fiscal year ended January 29, 2011 ($ thousands).

> Future minimum lease commitments due for retail and support facilities (including lease commitments for 76 retail stores not yet opened at January 29, 2011) and equipment leases under noncancelable operating leases are as follows (in thousands):

Year	Total
2011	$ 886,495
2012	798,958
2013	699,625
2014	594,819
2015	497,833
Thereafter	1,499,789
	$4,977,519

a. What dollar adjustment(s) might we consider to Staples' balance sheet and income statement given this information and assuming that Staples intermediate-term borrowing rate is 8% and rounding the remaining lease life to the nearest whole year? Explain.

b. Would the adjustment from part *a* make a substantial difference to Staples' total liabilities? (Staples reported total assets of nearly $14 billion and total liabilities of nearly $7 billion for 2011.)

E10-22. Analyzing, Interpreting and Capitalizing Operating Leases (LO1)

YUM! Brands, Inc. (YUM)

YUM! Brands, Inc., reports the following footnote relating to its capital and operating leases in its 2010 10-K report ($ millions).

> Future minimum commitments . . . under non-cancelable leases are set forth below. At December 25, 2010, and December 26, 2009, the present value of minimum payments under capital leases was $236 million and $249 million, respectively.

Commitments ($ millions)	Capital	Operating
2011	$ 26	$ 550
2012	63	514
2013	23	483
2014	23	447
2015	23	405
Thereafter	222	2,605
	$380	$5,004

a. Confirm that the implicit rate on YUM!'s capital leases is 7.63%. Using a 7.63% discount rate, compute the present value of YUM!'s operating leases and rounding the remaining lease life to three decimal places. Describe the adjustments we might consider to YUM!'s balance sheet and income statement using that information.

b. YUM! reported total liabilities of $6,647 million for 2010. Would the adjustment from part *a* make a substantial difference to YUM!'s total liabilities? Explain.

E10-23. Analyzing, Interpreting and Capitalizing Operating Leases (LO1)

TJX Companies (TJX)

TJX Companies reports the following footnote relating to its capital and operating leases in its 10-K report.

Following is a schedule of future minimum lease payments for continuing operations as of January 29, 2011:

Fiscal Year ($ 000s)	Operating Leases
2012	$1,092,709
2013	1,022,364
2014	915,656
2015	794,253
2016	670,437
Later years	2,304,674
Total future minimum lease payments	$6,800,093

Required

a. Using a 7% discount rate and rounding the remaining lease life to the nearest whole year, compute the present value of TJX's operating leases. Explain the adjustments we might consider to its balance sheet and income statement using that information.

b. TJX reported total liabilities of nearly $4.9 billion for fiscal 2011. Would the adjustment from part *a* make a substantial difference to the company's total liabilities? Explain.

E10-24. Analyzing and Interpreting Pension Disclosures (LO2)

General Mills reports the following pension footnote in its 10-K report.

General Mills (GIS)

Defined Benefit Pension Plans (In millions)	Fiscal Year	
	2010	2009
Change in Plan Assets		
Fair value at beginning of year	$3,157.8	$4,128.7
Actual return on assets	535.9	(1,009.1)
Employer contributions	17.1	220.2
Plan participant contributions	3.5	3.1
Benefits payments	(182.6)	(177.4)
Foreign currency	(1.9)	(7.7)
Fair value at end of year	$3,529.8	$3,157.8
Change in Projected Benefit Obligation		
Benefit obligation at beginning of year	$3,167.3	$3,224.1
Service cost	70.9	76.5
Interest cost	230.3	215.4
Plan amendment	25.8	0.3
Curtailment/other	—	—
Plan participant contributions	3.5	3.1
Medicare Part D reimbursements	—	—
Actuarial loss (gain)	716.4	(166.8)
Benefits payments	(182.6)	(177.4)
Foreign currency	(1.6)	(7.9)
Projected benefit obligation at end of year	$4,030.0	$3,167.3

Estimated benefit payments . . . are expected to be paid from fiscal 2011–2020 as follows:

(in millions)	Defined Benefit Pension Plans
2011	$ 194.8
2012	202.8
2013	211.9
2014	221.4
2015	231.4
2016–2020	1,331.7

   a. Describe what is meant by *service cost* and *interest cost.*

   b. What is the total amount paid to retirees during fiscal 2010? What is the source of funds to make these payments to retirees?

   c. Compute the 2010 funded status for the company's pension plan.

   d. What are actuarial gains and losses? What are the plan amendment adjustments, and how do they differ from the actuarial gains and losses?

   e. General Mills projects payments to retirees of over $200 million per year. How is the company able to contribute only $17.1 million to its pension plan?

   f. What effect would a substantial decline in the financial markets have on General Mills' contribution to its pension plans?

Xerox Corporation
(XRX)

E10-25. Analyzing and Interpreting Pension and Health Care Footnote (LO2)

Xerox reports the following pension and retiree health care ("Other") footnote as part of its 10-K report.

(in millions)	Pension Benefits 2010	Pension Benefits 2009	Retiree Health 2010	Retiree Health 2009
Change in Benefit Obligation				
Benefit obligation, January 1	$9,194	$8,495	$1,102	$1,002
Service cost	178	173	8	7
Interest cost	575	508	54	60
Plan participants' contributions	11	9	26	36
Plan amendments	(19)	4	(86)	1
Actuarial loss (gain)	477	209	13	124
Acquisitions	140	1	1	—
Currency exchange rate changes	(154)	373	6	15
Curtailments	(1)	—	—	—
Benefits paid/settlements	(670)	(578)	(118)	(143)
Benefit obligation, December 31	**$9,731**	**$9,194**	**$1,006**	**$1,102**
Change in Plan Assets				
Fair value of plan assets, January 1	$7,561	$6,923	$ —	$ —
Actual return on plan assets	846	720	—	—
Employer contribution	237	122	92	107
Plan participants' contributions	11	9	26	36
Acquisitions	107	—	—	—
Currency exchange rate changes	(144)	349	—	—
Benefits paid/settlements	(669)	(578)	(118)	(143)
Other	(9)	16	—	—
Fair value of plan assets, December 31	**$7,940**	**$7,561**	**$ —**	**$ —**
Net funded status at December 31	**$(1,791)**	**$(1,633)**	**$(1,006)**	**$(1,102)**

(in millions)	Pension Benefits 2010	Pension Benefits 2009	Pension Benefits 2008	Retiree Health 2010	Retiree Health 2009	Retiree Health 2008
Components of Net Periodic Benefit Cost						
Service cost	$ 178	$173	$209	$ 8	$ 7	$ 14
Interest cost	575	508	(5)	54	60	84
Expected return on plan assets	(570)	(523)	(80)	—	—	—
Recognized net actuarial loss	71	25	36	—	—	—
Amortization of prior service credit	(22)	(21)	(20)	(30)	(41)	(21)
Recognized settlement loss	72	70	34	—	—	—
Defined benefit plans	304	232	174	32	26	77
Defined contribution plans	51	38	80	—	—	—
Total net periodic benefit costs	**$ 355**	**$270**	**$254**	**$ 32**	**$ 26**	**$ 77**

continued

continued from prior page

**Other Changes in Plan Assets and Benefit Obligations
Recognized in Other Comprehensive Income**

Net actuarial loss (gain)	$ 198	$ 8	$1,062	$ 13	$126	$(244)
Prior service cost (credit)	(19)	—	1	(86)	1	(219)
Amortization of net actuarial (loss) gain	(143)	(95)	(70)	—	—	—
Amortization of prior service (cost) credit	22	21	20	30	41	21
Total recognized in other comprehensive income	$ 58	$ (66)	$1,013	$ (43)	$168	$(442)

> *a.* Describe what is meant by *service cost* and *interest cost* (the service and interest costs appear both in the reconciliation of the PBO and in the computation of pension expense).
>
> *b.* What is the actual return on the pension and the health care ("Other") plan investments in 2010? Was Xerox's profitability impacted by this amount?
>
> *c.* Provide an example under which an "actuarial loss," such as the $477 million loss in 2010 that Xerox reports, might arise.
>
> *d.* What is the source of funds to make payments to retirees?
>
> *e.* How much cash did Xerox contribute to its pension and health care plans in 2010?
>
> *f.* How much cash did retirees receive in 2010 from the pension plan and the health care plan? How much cash did Xerox pay these retirees in 2010?
>
> *g.* Show the computation of the 2010 funded status for the pension and health care plans.
>
> *h.[A]* The company reports $198 million "Net actuarial loss (gain)" in the table relating to Other Comprehensive Income, a credit of $19 million relating to "Prior service cost," a loss of $(143) million relating to "Amortization of net actuarial (loss) gain," and a credit of 22 million relating to "Amortization of prior service (cost) credit" in the net periodic benefit cost table. Describe the process by which these amounts are transferred from Other Comprehensive Income to pension expense in the income statement.

E10-26. Analyzing and Interpreting Pension and Health Care Disclosures (LO2)

Verizon reports the following pension and health care benefits footnote as part of its 10-K report.   Verizon (VZ)

	Pension		Health Care and Life	
At December 31 (dollars in millions)	**2010**	**2009**	**2010**	**2009**
Change in Benefit Obligations				
Beginning of year	$ 31,818	$ 30,394	$ 27,337	$ 27,096
Service cost	353	384	305	311
Interest cost	1,797	1,924	1,639	1,766
Plan amendments	(212)	—	(2,580)	(5)
Actuarial (gain) loss, net	748	2,056	826	(469)
Benefits paid	(1,996)	(2,565)	(1,675)	(1,740)
Termination benefits.	687	75	—	18
Curtailment (gain) loss, net.	61	1,245	132	352
Acquisitions and divestitures, net	(581)	192	(266)	8
Settlements paid	(3,458)	(1,887)	—	—
End of year.	$ 29,217	$ 31,818	$ 25,718	$ 27,337
Change in Plan Assets				
Beginning of year	$ 28,592	$ 27,791	$ 3,091	$ 2,555
Actual return on plan assets.	3,089	4,793	319	638
Company contributions	138	337	1,210	1,638
Benefits paid	(1,996)	(2,565)	(1,675)	(1,740)
Settlements paid	(3,458)	(1,887)	—	—
Acquisitions and divestitures, net	(551)	123	—	—
End of year.	$ 25,814	$ 28,592	$ 2,945	$ 3,091
Funded Status				
End of year	$ (3,403)	$ (3,226)	$(22,773)	$(24,246)

Years Ended December 31 (dollars in millions)	Pension			Health Care and Life		
	2010	2009	2008	2010	2009	2008
Service cost	$ 353	$ 384	$ 382	$ 305	$ 311	$ 306
Amortization of prior service cost	109	112	62	375	401	395
Subtotal	462	496	444	680	712	701
Expected return on plan assets	(2,176)	(2,216)	(3,444)	(252)	(205)	(331)
Interest cost	1,797	1,924	1,966	1,639	1,766	1,663
Subtotal	83	204	(1,034)	2,067	2,273	2,033
Remeasurement (gain) loss, net	(166)	(515)	13,946	758	(901)	1,069
Net periodic benefit (income) cost	(83)	(311)	12,912	2,825	1,372	3,102
Curtailment and termination benefits	860	1,371	32	386	532	31
Total	$ 777	$1,060	$12,944	$3,211	$1,904	$3,133

a. Describe what is meant by *service cost* and *interest cost*.
b. What payments did retirees receive during fiscal 2010 from the pension and health care plans? What is the source of funds to make payments to retirees?
c. Show the computation of Verizon's 2010 funded status for both the pension and health care plans.
d. What expense does Verizon's income statement report for both its pension and health care plans?

Harley-Davidson, Inc. (HOG)

E10-27.[B] **Analyzing and Interpreting Disclosure on Off-Balance-Sheet Financing** (LO3)

Harley-Davidson provides the following footnote in its 10-K report relating to the securitization of receivables by its finance subsidiary, Harley-Davidson Financial Services (HDFS).

Term Asset-Backed Securitization VIEs The Company transfers U.S. retail motorcycle finance receivables to SPEs which in turn issue secured notes to investors, with various maturities and interest rates, secured by future collections of the transferred U.S. retail motorcycle finance receivables. In 2010 and 2009, HDFS transferred $670.8 million and $3.08 billion, respectively, of U.S. retail motorcycle finance receivables to five separate SPEs. The SPEs in turn issued the following secured notes with the related maturity dates and interest rates (dollars in thousands):

Issue Date	Principal Amount	Weighted-Average Rate at Date of Issuance	Maturity Dates
November 2010	$600,000	1.05%	December 2011–April 2018
December 2009	562,499	1.55	December 2010–June 2017
October 2009	700,000	1.16	October 2010–April 2017
July 2009	700,000	2.11	July 2010–February 2017
May 2009	500,000	2.77	May 2010–January 2017

Each term asset-backed securitization SPE is a separate legal entity and the U.S. retail motorcycle finance receivables included in the term asset backed securitizations are only available for payment of the secured debt and other obligations arising from the term asset-backed securitization transactions and are not available to pay other obligations or claims of the Company's creditors until the associated secured debt and other obligations are satisfied. Cash and cash equivalent balances held by the SPEs are used only to support the securitizations. There are no amortization schedules for the secured notes; however, the debt is reduced monthly as available collections on the related U.S. retail motorcycle finance receivables are applied to outstanding principal. The Company was required to adopt the new guidance within ASC Topic 810 and ASC Topic 860 as of January 1, 2010. The Company determined that the formerly unconsolidated QSPEs that HDFS utilized were VIEs, of which the Company was the primary beneficiary, and consolidated them into the Company's financial statements beginning January 1, 2010.

a. Describe in your own words, the securitization process employed by HDFS.
b. What benefits does Harley-Davidson derive by securitizing receivables in this manner?
c. Current accounting standards require consolidation of the VIEs. What effect does this have on Harley-Davidson? Is there still a benefit to securitization? Explain.

PROBLEMS

P10-28. Analyzing, Interpreting and Capitalizing Operating Leases (LO1)

The Abercrombie & Fitch 10-K report contains the following footnote relating to leasing activities. This is the only information it discloses relating to its leasing activity.

Abercrombie & Fitch (ANF)

At January 29, 2011, the Company was committed to noncancelable leases with remaining terms of one to 17 years. A summary of operating lease commitments under noncancelable leases follows (thousands):

Fiscal 2011	$ 331,151
Fiscal 2012	319,982
Fiscal 2013	303,531
Fiscal 2014	285,337
Fiscal 2015	262,586
Thereafter	1,110,598

Required

a. What lease assets and lease liabilities does Abercrombie report on its balance sheet? How do we know?

b. What effect does the lease classification have on A&F's balance sheet? Over the life of the lease, what effect does this classification have on the company's net income?

c. Using a 6% discount rate and rounding the remaining lease life to the nearest whole year, estimate the assets and liabilities that A&F fails to report as a result of its off-balance-sheet lease financing.

d. What adjustments would we consider to A&F's income statement corresponding to the adjustments we would make to its balance sheet in part c?

e. Indicate the direction (increase or decrease) of the effect that capitalizing these leases would have on the following financial items and ratios for A&F: return on equity (ROE), net operating profit after tax (NOPAT), net operating assets (NOA), net operating profit margin (NOPM), net operating asset turnover (NOAT), and measures of financial leverage.

P10-29. Analyzing, Interpreting and Capitalizing Operating Leases (LO1)

The Best Buy 10-K report has the following footnote related to leasing activities.

Best Buy (BBY)

The future minimum lease payments under our capital and operating leases by fiscal year (not including contingent rentals) at February 26, 2011, were as follows:

Fiscal Year ($ millions)	Capital Leases	Operating Leases
2012	$18	$1,208
2013	16	1,166
2014	16	1,079
2015	14	992
2016	8	872
Thereafter	25	2,930
Subtotal	97	$8,247
Less: imputed interest	(18)	
Present value	$79	

Required

a. What is the balance of the lease liabilities reported on Best Buy's balance sheet?

b. What effect has the operating lease classification had on its balance sheet? Over the life of the lease, what effect does this classification have on the company's net income?

  c. Confirm that the implicit discount rate used by Best Buy for its capital leases is 5.73%. Use this
  discount rate to estimate the assets and liabilities that Best Buy fails to report as a result of its off
  balance-sheet lease financing. Round the remaining lease life to two decimals.

  d. What adjustments would we make to Best Buy's income statement corresponding to the
  adjustments we made to its balance sheet in part *c*?

  e. Indicate the direction (increase or decrease) of the effect that capitalizing the operating leases
  would have on the following financial items and ratios for Best Buy: return on equity (ROE),
  net operating profit after tax (NOPAT), net operating assets (NOA), net operating profit margin
  (NOPM), net operating asset turnover (NOAT), and measures of financial leverage.

P10-30. Analyzing, Interpreting and Capitalizing Operating Leases (LO1)

FedEx (FDX)

FedEx reports total assets of $24,902 and total liabilities of $11,091 for 2010 ($ millions). Its 10-K
report has the following footnote related to leasing activities.

A summary of future minimum lease payments under capital leases and noncancelable
operating leases with an initial or remaining term in excess of one year at May 31, 2010, is as
follows (in millions):

		Operating Leases		
	Capital Leases	Aircraft and Related Equipment	Facilities and Other	Total Operating Leases
2011	$ 20	$ 526	$1,250	$ 1,776
2012	8	504	1,085	1,589
2013	119	499	926	1,425
2014	2	473	786	1,259
2015	1	455	717	1,172
Thereafter	14	2,003	4,547	6,550
Total	164	$4,460	$9,311	$13,771
Less amount representing interest. . . .	23			
Present value of net minimum lease payments.	$141			

Required

  a. What is the balance of lease assets and lease liabilities reported on FedEx's balance sheet?
  Explain.

  b. Confirm that the implicit rate that FedEx uses to discount its capital leases is 4.6%. Use this
  discount rate and round the remaining lease life to three decimals to estimate the amount of
  assets and liabilities that FedEx fails to report as a result of its off-balance-sheet lease financing.

  c. What adjustments would we make to FedEx's income statement corresponding to the
  adjustments we make to its balance sheet in part *b*?

  d. Indicate the direction (increase or decrease) of the effect that capitalizing the operating leases
  would have on the following financial items and ratios for FedEx: return on equity (ROE), net
  operating profit after tax (NOPAT), net operating assets (NOA), net operating profit margin
  (NOPM), net operating asset turnover (NOAT), and measures of financial leverage.

  e. What portion of total lease liabilities did FedEx report on-balance-sheet and what portion is off-
  balance-sheet?

  f. Based on your analysis, do you believe that FedEx's balance sheet adequately reports its aircraft
  and facilities assets and related obligations? Explain.

P10-31. Analyzing and Interpreting Pension Disclosures (LO2)

DuPont (DD)

DuPont's 10-K report has the following disclosures related to its retirement plans ($ millions).

Obligations and Funded Status	Pension Benefits	
December 31 ($ millions)	2010	2009
Change in benefit obligation		
Benefit obligation at beginning of year.	$22,770	$21,506
Service cost	207	192
Interest cost	1,262	1,270
Plan participants' contributions	18	17
Actuarial loss	1,218	1,392
Benefits paid	(1,584)	(1,608)
Amendments	—	—
Net effects of acquisitions/divestitures	33	1
Benefit obligation at end of year	$23,924	$22,770
Change in plan assets		
Fair value of plan assets at beginning of year	$ 17,143	$ 16,209
Actual gain on plan assets	2,015	2,219
Employer contributions	782	306
Plan participants' contributions	18	17
Benefits paid	(1,584)	(1,608)
Net effects of acquisitions/divestitures	29	—
Fair value of plan assets at end of year	$ 18,403	$ 17,143
Funded status		
U.S. plans with plan assets	$ (3,408)	$ (3,594)
Non-U.S. plans with plan assets	(652)	(543)
All other plans.	(1,461)	(1,490)
Total	$ (5,521)	$ (5,627)

Components of net periodic benefit cost (credit) and amounts recognized in other comprehensive income	Pension Benefits (In millions)		
	2010	2009	2008
Net periodic benefit (credit) cost			
Service cost	$ 207	$ 192	$ 209
Interest cost	1,262	1,270	1,286
Expected return on plan assets	(1,435)	(1,603)	(1,932)
Amortization of loss	507	278	56
Amortization of prior service cost	16	18	18
Curtailment/settlement loss	—	—	1
Net periodic benefit (credit) cost	$ 557	$ 155	$ (362)
Changes in plan assets and benefit obligations recognized in other comprehensive income			
Net loss (gain).	634	781	6,397
Amortization of loss	(507)	(278)	(56)
Prior service cost	—	—	4
Amortization of prior service cost	(16)	(18)	(18)
Curtailment/settlement loss	—	—	(1)
Total recognized in other comprehensive income	$ 111	$ 485	$6,326
Total recognized in net periodic benefit cost and other comprehensive income	$ 668	$ 640	$5,964

Weighted-average assumptions used to determine net periodic benefit cost for years ended December 31	Pension Benefits		
	2010	2009	2008
Discount rate	5.80%	6.14%	6.01%
Expected return on plan assets	8.64%	8.75%	8.74%
Rate of compensation increase	4.24%	4.30%	4.28%

The following benefit payments, which reflect future service, as appropriate, are expected to be paid:

($ millions)	Pension Benefits
2011	$1,593
2012	1,528
2013	1,521
2014	1,527
2015	1,544
Years 2016–2020	8,002

Required

a. How much pension expense (revenue) does DuPont report in its 2010 income statement?

b. DuPont reports a $1,435 million expected return on pension plan assets as an offset to 2010 pension expense. Approximately, how is this amount computed (estimate from the numbers reported)? What is DuPont's actual gain or loss realized on its 2010 pension plan assets? What is the purpose of using this expected return instead of the actual gain or loss?

c. What main factors (and dollar amounts) affected DuPont's pension liability during 2010? What main factors (and dollar amounts) affected its pension plan assets during 2010?

d. What does the term *funded status* mean? What is the funded status of the 2010 DuPont pension plans?

e. DuPont decreased its discount rate from 6.14% to 5.80% in 2010. What effect(s) does this increase have on its balance sheet and its income statement?

f. How did DuPont's pension plan affect the company's cash flow in 2010? (Identify any inflows and outflows, including amounts.)

g. In 2010, DuPont contributed $782 million to its pension plan. Explain how the returns on pension assets affect the amount of cash that DuPont must contribute to fund the pension plan.

P10-32. Analyzing and Interpreting Pension Disclosures   (LO2)

Johnson & Johnson
(JNJ)

Johnson & Johnson provides the following footnote disclosures in its 10-K report relating to its defined benefit pension plans and its other post-retirement benefits.

($ in millions)	Retirement Plans 2010	Retirement Plans 2009	Other Benefit Plans 2010	Other Benefit Plans 2009
Change in Benefit Obligation				
Projected benefit obligation—beginning of year	$13,449	$11,923	$ 3,590	$ 2,765
Service cost	550	511	134	137
Interest cost	791	746	202	174
Plan participant contributions	42	50	—	—
Amendments	—	3	—	—
Actuarial losses	815	412	115	51
Divestitures & acquisitions	—	15	—	13
Curtailments & settlements & restructuring	(10)	(3)	—	748
Benefits paid from plan	(627)	(570)	(476)	(313)
Effect of exchange rates	(17)	362	7	15
Projected benefit obligation—end of year	$14,993	$13,449	$ 3,572	$ 3,590
Change in Plan Assets				
Plan assets at fair value—beginning of year	$10,923	$7,677	$ 16	$ 17
Actual return on plan assets	1,466	2,048	2	4
Company contributions	1,611	1,354	472	308
Plan participant contributions	42	50	—	—
Settlements	(7)	—	—	—
Benefits paid from plan assets	(627)	(570)	(476)	(313)
Effect of exchange rates	25	364	—	—
Plan assets at fair value—end of year	$13,433	$10,923	$ 14	$ 16
Funded status—end of year	$ (1,560)	$ (2,526)	$(3,558)	$(3,574)

($ in millions)	Retirement Plans			Other Benefit Plans		
	2010	2009	2008	2010	2009	2008
Service cost	$ 550	$511	$545	$134	$137	$142
Interest cost	791	746	701	202	174	166
Expected return on plan assets	(1,005)	(934)	(876)	(1)	(1)	(2)
Amortization of prior service cost	10	13	10	(4)	(5)	(4)
Amortization of net transition asset . . .	1	1	2	—	—	—
Recognized actuarial losses.	236	155	62	48	55	64
Curtailments and settlements	1	(11)	7	—	(1)	—
Net periodic benefit cost	$ 584	$481	$451	$379	$359	$366

($ in millions)	Retirement Plans			Other Benefit Plans		
	2010	2009	2008	2010	2009	2008
U.S. Benefit Plans						
Discount rate	5.98%	6.50%	6.50%	5.98%	6.50%	6.50%
Expected long-term rate of return on plan assets.	9.00	9.00	9.00	9.00	9.00	9.00
Rate of increase in compensation levels.	4.25	4.50	4.50	4.25	4.50	4.50

Required

a. How much pension expense does Johnson & Johnson report in its 2010 income statement?

b. The company reports a $1,005 million expected return on pension plan assets as an offset to 2010 pension expense. Approximately, how is this amount computed? What is the actual gain or loss realized on its 2010 pension plan assets? What is the purpose of using this expected return instead of the actual gain or loss?

c. What factors affected the company's pension liability during 2010? What factors affected the pension plan assets during 2010?

d. What does the term *funded status* mean? What is the funded status of the 2010 pension plans and postretirement benefit plans?

e. The company decreased its discount rate from 6.50% to 5.98% in 2010. What effect(s) does this increase have on its balance sheet and its income statement?

f. How did Johnson & Johnson's pension plan affect the company's cash flow in 2010?

IFRS APPLICATIONS

I10-33. **Analyzing and Capitalizing Operating Lease Payments Disclosed in Footnotes** (LO1)

GlaxoSmithKline plc, headquartered in London, United Kingdom, is the world's third largest pharmaceutical company. The company's 2009 balance sheet reported total assets of £42,862 and total liabilities of £32,120 (in millions). The footnotes disclosed the following information related to leasing activities.

Commitments under non-cancellable operating leases	2009 £m	2008 £m
Rental payments due within one year	£111	£140
Rental payments due between one and two yers	72	109
Rental payments due between two and three years	50	76
Rental payments due between three and four years	21	54
Rental payments due between four and five years	14	22
Rental payments due after five years.	69	47
Total commitments under non-cancellable operating leases . .	£337	£448

Operating leases are not reflected on-balance-sheet. In our analysis of a company, we often capitalize operating leases, that is, add the present value of the future operating lease payments to both the reported assets and liabilities.

    a. Compute the present value of GlaxoSmithKline's operating payments assuming a 6% discount rate and round the remaining lease life to three decimals.

    b. What effect would capitalization of operating leases have on GlaxoSmithKline's total liabilities and total assets?

I10-34. Analyzing, Interpreting and Capitalizing Operating Leases (LO1)

Total S.A. is a French multinational oil company and one of the six "supermajor" oil companies in the world. The company is headquartered in Courbevoie, France, and uses IFRS to prepare its financial statements. Total S.A. reports the following footnote relating to its finance and operating leases in its 2009 20-F report (€ millions).

The Group leases real estate, retail stations, ships, and other equipment. The future minimum lease payments on operating and finance leases to which the Group is committed are shown as follows:

For year ended December 31, 2009 (€ million)	Operating leases	Finance leases
2010	€ 523	€ 42
2011	377	43
2012	299	42
2013	243	41
2014	203	39
2015 and beyond	894	128
Total minimum payments	€2,539	€335

On December 31, 2009, the present value of minimum lease payments under capital leases was €282 million.

    a. Confirm that the implicit rate of Total's finance leases is 3.94%.

    b. Use 3.94% as the discount rate and round the remaining lease term to three decimals to compute the present value of Total's operating leases.

    c. Describe the adjustments we might consider to Total's balance sheet and income statement using the information from part *b*.

    d. Total reported total liabilities of €74,214 million for 2009. Are these finance leases substantial? Would capitalizing the operating leases make a difference to our assessment of Total's liquidity or solvency?

I10-35. Analyzing, Interpreting and Capitalizing Operating Leases (LO1)

Air Canada is the largest Canadian airline and is the world's ninth largest passenger airline by number of destinations. The company is headquartered in Montreal, Quebec. Air Canada used Canadian GAAP to prepare its 2010 financial statements. Its footnotes include the following:

Operating Lease Commitments The table below presents the future minimum lease payments under existing operating leases of aircraft and other property as at December 31, 2010.

CDN$ millions	2011	2012	2013	2014	2015	Thereafter	Total
Aircraft	335	316	295	230	178	554	1,908
Other property	47	39	38	36	32	117	309
	382	355	333	266	210	671	2,217

Required

a. Mandatory adoption of IFRS by European companies in 2005 caused many leases previously classified as operating to be treated as capital (finance) leases. This is due to the IFRS' conceptual approach to lease classification as compared to the rules-based approach taken by many country-specific GAAP. Use a discount rate of 10% and round the remaining years to 3 decimals to estimate the amount of assets and liabilities that Air Canada would likely need to capitalize had the company used IFRS in 2010.

b. What would the income statement effect have been given the balance sheet changes from part *a*?

I10-36. **Analyzing, Interpreting and Capitalizing Operating Leases** (LO1)

LM Ericsson, one of Sweden's largest companies, is a provider of telecommunication and data communication systems. The company reports total assets of SEK 269,809 and total liabilities of SEK 128,782 for 2009 (in millions). Its annual report has the following footnote related to leasing activities.

As of December 31, 2009, future minimum lease payment obligations for leases were distributed as follows:

In SEK millions	Finance Leases	Operating Leases
2010	177	3,185
2011	168	2,611
2012	166	2,102
2013	164	1,270
2014	209	935
2015 and later	1,186	2,371
Total	2,070	12,474
Future finance charges	(676)	n/a
Present value of finance lease liabilities	1,394	12,474

Required

a. What is reported on Ericsson's balance sheet as leased assets and lease liabilities?

b. Confirm that the implicit rate that Ericsson uses to discount its capital leases is 7.08%. Use this discount rate and round the remaining years to 3 decimals to estimate the amount of assets and liabilities that Ericsson fails to report as a result of its off-balance-sheet lease financing.

c. What adjustments would we make to Ericsson's income statement corresponding to the balance sheet adjustments implied in part b?

d. What portion of total lease liabilities did Ericsson report on-balance-sheet and what portion is off-balance-sheet?

e. Indicate the direction (increase or decrease) of the effect that capitalizing the operating leases would have on the following financial items and ratios for Ericsson: return on equity (ROE), net operating profit after tax (NOPAT), net operating assets (NOA), net operating profit margin (NOPM), net operating asset turnover (NOAT), and measures of financial leverage.

f. Based on your analysis, do you believe that Ericsson's balance sheet adequately reports its facilities assets and related obligations? Explain.

SOLUTIONS TO REVIEW PROBLEMS

Mid-Module Review

Solution

1. The interest rate that American uses in the computation of its capital lease balance is imputed to be 12.91%; this rate is determined as follows (using a spreadsheet).

		AMR Capitalized leases template.xlsx - Microsoft Excel									
Home	Insert	Page Layout	Formulas	Data	Review	View	Developer	Get Started	Acrobat		
A13		f_x									
	A	B	C	D	E	F	G	H	I	J	K	L
1	N	0	1	2	3	4	5	6	7	8	9	10
2	Amount	-604	186	136	120	98	87	87	87	87	87	1
3	IRR	12.91% *										
4												
5		* Formula for cell B3 is =IRR(B2:L2,10%)								=	349	

2. Using the 12.91% discount rate, the present value of American's operating leases follows ($ millions):

Year	Operating Lease Payment	Discount Factor (i = 12.91%)	Present Value
1	$ 1,254	0.88566	$1,111
2	1,068	0.78440	838
3	973	0.69471	676
4	831	0.61528	511
5	672	0.54493	366
>5	6,006	5.12909* × 0.54493	1,878**
			$5,380

Remaining life. . . . . . $6,006/$672 = 8.938 years

*The annuity factor for 9 years at 12.91% is 5.12909.
**$672 × 5.12909 × 0.54493 = $1,878

AMR's operating leases represent $5,380 million in both unreported operating assets and unreported non-operating liabilities. These amounts should be added to the balance sheet for analysis purposes.

3. Income statement adjustments relating to capitalization of operating leases involve two steps:
   a. Remove rent expense of $1,254 million from operating expense.
   b. Add depreciation expense from lease assets to operating expense and also reflect interest expense on the lease obligation as a nonoperating expense. We assume that the remaining lease term is 13.938 years (five years reported in the lease schedule plus 8.938 years after Year 5). Using this term and zero salvage value, we get an estimated straight-line depreciation for lease assets of $386 million ($5,380 million/13.938 years). Interest expense on the $5,380 million lease liability at the 12.91% capitalization rate is $695 million ($5,380 million × 12.91%). The net adjustment to NOPAT, reflecting the elimination of rent expense and the addition of depreciation expense, is $547 million, which is computed as: ($1,254 million rent expense − $386 million depreciation) × (1 − 0.37).

Module-End Review

Solution

1. A pension benefit obligation increases primarily by service cost, interest cost, and actuarial losses (which are increases in the pension liability as a result of changes in actuarial assumptions). It is decreased by the payment of benefits to retirees and by any actuarial gains.
2. Pension assets increase by positive investment returns for the period and cash contributions made by the company. Assets decrease by benefits paid to retirees and by investment losses.
3. American Airlines' funded status is $(5,195) million ($12,968 million PBO − $7,773 million Pension Assets) as of 2010. The negative amount indicates that the plan is underfunded. Consequently, this amount is reflected as a liability on American's balance sheet.
4. Expected return on plan assets acts as an offset to service cost and interest cost in computing net pension cost. As the expected return increases, net pension cost decreases.
5. American Airlines' expected return of $593 million is less than its actual return of $837 million in 2010.
6. American Airlines reports a net pension expense of $845 million in its 2010 income statement. Of this, $677 million pertained to the company's defined benefit plans, and $168 million to defined contribution plans.
7. American Airlines' funded status is negative, indicating an underfunded plan. In 2010, the company contributed $466 million to the pension plan, up from $10 million in the prior year. It is likely that the company will need to increase its future funding levels to cover the plan's requirements. This might have negative repercussions for its ability to fund other operating needs, and could eventually damage its competitive position.

Getty Images

PROCTER & GAMBLE (P&G)

Procter & Gamble (P&G), the world's largest consumer products company, is "one of the leaders in the race to harness massive streams of data for managing a business better. The company has been profit-forecasting on a monthly basis for about 40 years, trying to predict components such as sales, commodity prices and exchange rates. But the amount of real-time data it has been able to process has increased vastly . . . now P&G borrows liberally from tools born on the Web: ubiquitous high-speed networking, data visualization and high-speed analysis on multiple streams of information. The tools allow P&G to make in minutes the decisions that used to take weeks or months, when data had to be collated and passed through committees on their way to the top . . . . P&G is on the verge of having everyone's talents known and tracked, all information about sales decided at the executive level every week and production viewed in near real-time worldwide. The company talks in terms of increasing the amount of collected data sevenfold. The airy promises of networked technology are here, at a scale rarely, if ever, deployed before." (Forbes 2011)

P&G's financial performance has been impressive. In 2011, it generated over $13 billion of operating cash flow in one of the most severe recessions in recent memory. Its abundant cash flow allows it to fund the level of advertising and R&D necessary to remain a dominant force in the consumer products industry as well as to pay over $5.7 billion in dividends to shareholders.

P&G's product list is impressive. It consists of numerous well-recognized household brands. Total sales of Procter & Gamble products are distributed across its three business segments as illustrated in the chart to the side. A partial listing of its billion-dollar brands follows:

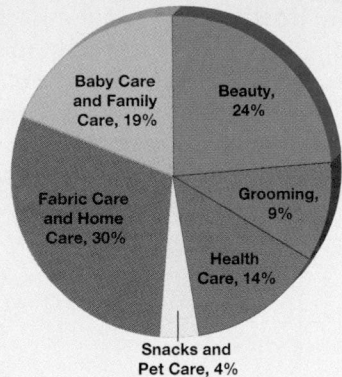

- **Beauty.** Head & Shoulders, Olay, Pantene, Wella
- **Grooming.** Braun, Fusion, Gillette, Mach3
- **Health Care.** Always, Crest, Oral-B
- **Snacks and Pet Care.** Iams, Pringles
- **Fabric Care and Home Care.** Ace, Ariel, Dawn, Downy, Duracell, Febreze, Gain, Tide
- **Baby Care and Family Care.** Bounty, Charmin, Pampers

P&G's recent successes have coincided with strong leadership. CEO Robert McDonald's innovations and market savvy have consistently propelled P&G. *BusinessWeek* explains that from its Swiffer mop to battery-powered Crest SpinBrush toothbrushes and Whitestrip tooth

Forecasting Financial Statements

LEARNING OBJECTIVES

LO1   Explain the process of forecasting financial statements. (p. 11-3)

LO2   Forecast revenues and the income statement. (p. 11-8)

LO3   Forecast the balance sheet. (p. 11-18)

LO4   Forecast the statement of cash flows. (p. 11-28)

LO5   Prepare multiyear forecasts of financial statements. (p. 11-30)

LO6   Implement a parsimonious method for multiyear forecasting of net operating profit and net operating assets. (p. 11-34)

whiteners, P&G has outshined its peers. Since assuming the CEO job, McDonald has guided P&G to successive increases in sales, income, and cash flows. Such increases have driven impressive gains in stock price as evident from the graph below:

Still, we know that *forecasts* of financial performance drive stock price. Historical financial statements are relevant to the extent that they provide information useful to forecast financial performance. Accordingly, considerable emphasis is placed on generating reliable forecasts.

This module explains the forecasting process, including the forecasting of the income statement, the balance sheet, and the statement of cash flows. From all accounts, the rebound in P&G's stock price following the market meltdown of 2009 reflects optimism about its future financial performance and condition.

Sources: *Procter & Gamble* 2011 10-K and Annual Report; *BusinessWeek,* April 2006; *Barron's,* November 2006; *Forbes,* 2011.

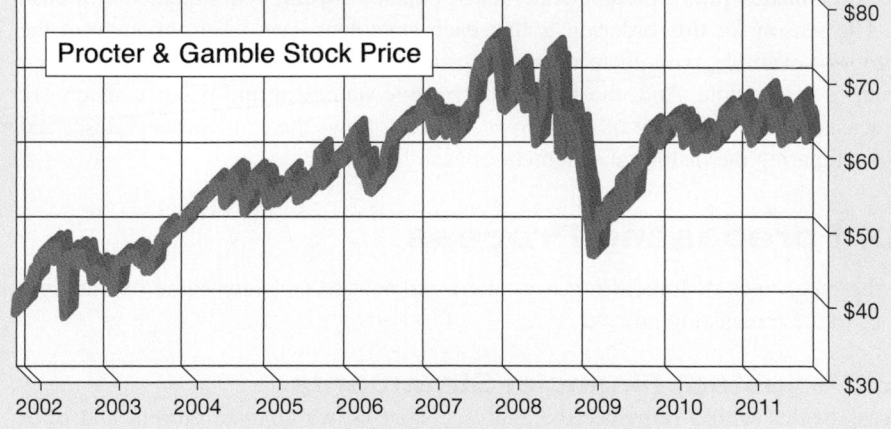

Procter & Gamble Stock Price

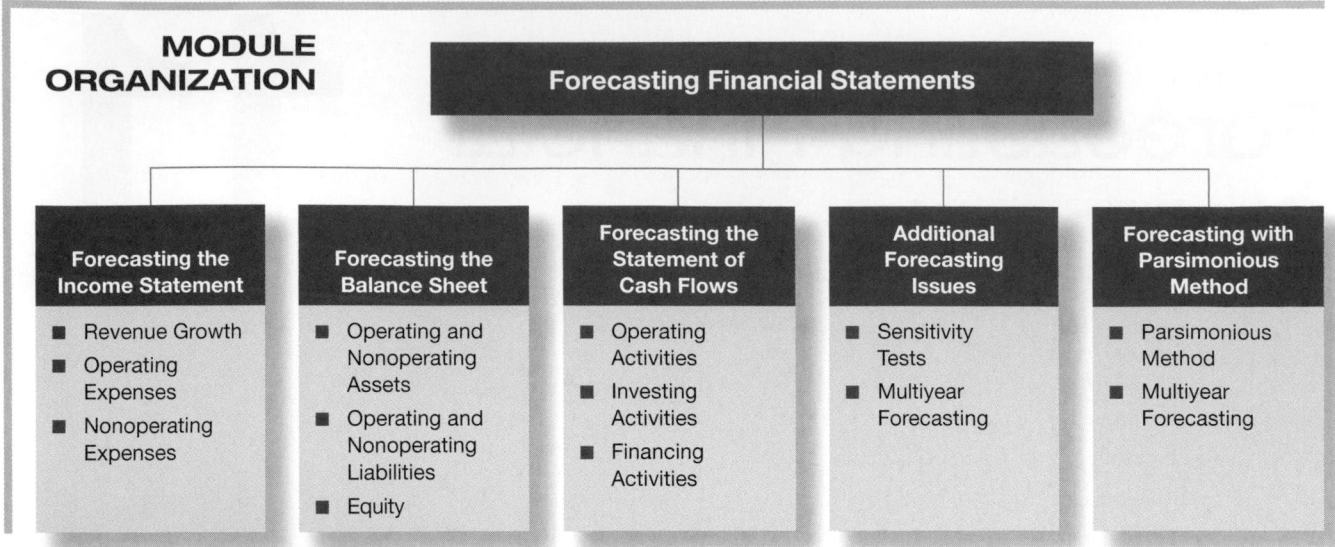

Forecasting financial performance is integral to a variety of business decisions ranging from investing to managing a company effectively. We might, for example, wish to value a company's common stock before purchasing its shares. To that end, we might use one of the valuation models we discuss in Module 12 that rely on financial statement forecasts as a crucial input. Or, we might be interested in evaluating the creditworthiness of a prospective borrower. In that case, we forecast the borrower's cash flows to estimate its ability to repay its obligations. We might also be interested in evaluating alternative strategic investment decisions. In this case, we can use our forecasts to evaluate the shareholder value that the strategic investment alternatives will create. All of these decisions require accurate financial forecasts. In this module, we illustrate the most common method to forecast the income statement, balance sheet, and statement of cash flows.

FORECASTING PROCESS

LO1 Explain the process of forecasting financial statements.

The forecasting process estimates future income statements, balance sheets, and statements of cash flows, in that order. The reason for this ordering is that each statement uses information from the preceding statement(s). For example, we update retained earnings on the balance sheet to reflect our forecast of the company's net income. And, the forecasted income statement and balance sheets are used in preparing forecasts for the statement of cash flows, which follows the same process described in Modules 2 and 3 for preparing the historical statement of cash flows.

Overview of Forecasting Process

Before we focus on the mechanics of forecasting, we take a moment to consider some overarching principles that guide us in the forecasting process.

Reformulated (Adjusted) Financial Statements

The forecasting process begins with a retrospective analysis. That is, we analyze current and prior years' statements to be sure that they accurately reflect the company's financial condition and performance. If we believe that they do not, we adjust those statements to reflect the company's net operating assets and the operating income that we expect to persist into the future. Once we've adjusted the historical results, we are ready to forecast future results. Why would we need to adjust historical results? The answer resides in the fact that financial statements prepared in conformity with GAAP do not always accurately reflect the "true" financial condition and performance of the company. This *adjusting process*, also referred to as recasting or reformulating (or *scrubbing the numbers*), is not "black and white." It requires judgment and estimation. Repeatedly in Modules 5 through 10, we have explained estimation, accounting choice, deliberate managerial intervention in reporting, and transitory versus persistent items. These concepts are integral to adjustments we make to financial statements. It is important to distinguish between the purposes of GAAP-based financial statements and the adjusting process for purposes of forecasting. Specifically, GAAP-based statements provide more than just information for forecasting. For example, financial statements are key inputs into contracts among business parties. This means that historical results, including any transitory activities, must be reported to meet management's fiduciary responsibilities. On the other hand, to forecast future performance, we need to create a set of financial statements that focus on those items that we expect to persist, with a special emphasis on persistent operating activities.

Garbage-In, Garbage-Out

All forecasts are based on a set of forecasting assumptions. For example, to forecast the income statement, we must make assumptions about revenue growth and other assumptions about how expenses will change in relation to changes in revenues. Then, to forecast the balance sheet, we make assumptions about the relation between balance sheet accounts and changes in revenues. Consequently, before we make business decisions based on forecasted financial statements, we must understand and agree with the underlying assumptions used to produce them. The old adage, "garbage-in, garbage-out," is apt. That is, the quality of our decision is only as good as the quality of the information on which it is based. We must be sure that our forecasting assumptions are consistent with our beliefs and predictions for future growth and key financial relations.

Optimism vs Conservatism

Many people believe that it is appropriate to be overly conservative in their financial forecasts so as to minimize the likelihood of making a bad decision. "Let's be conservative in our forecasts so that we are certain our forecast will be met" is a frequent prelude to the forecasting process. Although this approach might appear reasonable, being too conservative can result in missed valuable opportunities that, in the end, can be very costly. Instead, our objective is not to be overly optimistic or overly conservative. The objective for forecasting is accuracy.

Level of Precision

Computing forecasts out to the "nth decimal place" is easy using spreadsheets. This increased precision makes the resulting forecasts appear more "professional," but not necessarily more accurate. As we discuss in this module, our financial statement forecasts are highly dependent on our revenues forecast. Whether revenues are expected to grow by 4% or 5% can markedly impact profitability and other forecasts. Estimating cost of goods sold and other items to the nth decimal place is meaningless if we have imprecise revenue forecasts. Consequently, borderline decisions that depend on a high level of forecasting precision are probably ill-advised.

Smell Test

At the end of the forecasting process, we must step back and make sure that the numbers we predict pass the *smell test*. That is, we need to assess whether our forecasts are reasonable—do they make economic sense, do they fit with the underlying relations that drive financial forecasts? For example, if our forecasts are dependent on increasing selling prices, it is wise to explore the likely consequences of a price increase. Companies cannot raise prices without a consequent loss of demand unless the product in question is protected in some way from competitive attacks. Our forecasts must appear reasonable and consistent with basic business economics.

Internal Consistency

The forecasted income statement, balance sheet, and statement of cash flows are linked in the same way that historical financial statements are. That is, they must articulate (link together within and across time) as we explain in Module 2. Preparing a forecasted statement of cash flows, although tedious, is often a useful way to uncover forecasting assumptions that are inconsistently applied across financial statements (examples are CAPEX, depreciation, debt payments, and dividends). If the forecasted cash balance on the balance sheet agrees with that on the statement of cash flows, it is likely that our income statement and balance sheet articulate properly. We also must ensure that our forecast assumptions are internally consistent. It is nonsense to forecast an increased gross profit margin during an economic recession unless we can make compelling arguments based on economics.

Crucial Forecasting Assumptions

Analysts commonly perform sensitivity analyses following preparation of their forecasts. This entails increasing and decreasing the forecast assumptions to identify those assumptions that have the greatest impact. By "impact," we mean large enough to alter business decisions. Assumptions that are identified as crucial to a decision must be investigated thoroughly to ensure that forecast assumptions are as accurate as possible.

Summary of Forecasting Process

Some professionals assert that forecasting is more art than science. Whatever it is, it must begin with a business analysis, including an assessment of general economic activity and the competitive forces within the broader business environment that we discuss in Module 1. Ideally, forecasts should be developed at an individual-product level and consider competitive advantage, trends in manufacturing costs, logistical requirements, necessary marketing support, after-sale customer service, and so forth. The narrower the focus, the more we can focus on the business environment in which the company operates and the more informed our forecasts are. Unfortunately, as external users of financial statements, we only have access to general-purpose financial statements, which we adjust as we see fit, given publicly available information and our own assessments. Then, we formulate forecast assumptions that are reasonable and consistent with the economic realities defining that company.

All-Important Revenues Forecast

The revenues (sales) forecast is, arguably, the most crucial and difficult estimate in the forecasting process. It is a crucial estimate because other income statement and balance sheet accounts derive, either directly or indirectly, from the revenues forecast. As a result, both the income statement and balance sheet grow with increases in revenues. The income statement reflects this growth concurrently. However, different balance sheet accounts reflect revenue growth in different ways. Some balance sheet accounts anticipate (or lead) revenue growth (inventories are one example). Some accounts reflect this growth concurrently (accounts receivable). And some accounts reflect revenue growth with a lag (for example, companies usually expand plant assets only after growth is deemed sustainable). Conversely, when revenues decline, so do the income statement and balance sheet, as the company shrinks to cope with adversity. Such actions include reduction of overhead costs and divestiture of excess assets. Exhibit 11.1 highlights crucial relations that are impacted by the revenues forecast for both the income statement and the balance sheet.

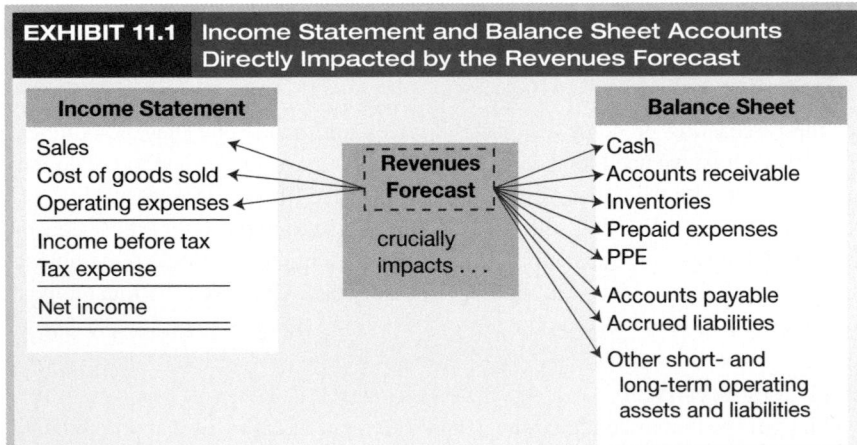

EXHIBIT 11.1   Income Statement and Balance Sheet Accounts Directly Impacted by the Revenues Forecast

Dynamics of Income Statement (and Balance Sheet) Growth

The following accounts are impacted directly, and with a relatively short lead or lag time, by the revenues forecast (for convenience, *our discussion assumes an increase in revenues*):

■ **Cost of goods sold** are impacted via increased inventory purchases, added manufacturing personnel, and greater depreciation from new manufacturing PPE.

- **Operating expenses** increase concurrently with, or in anticipation of, increased revenues; these expenses include increased costs for buyers, higher advertising costs, payments to sales personnel, costs of after-sale customer support, logistics costs, and administrative costs.
- **Cash** increases and decreases directly with increases in revenues as receivables are collected and as payables and accruals are paid.
- **Accounts receivable** increase directly with increases in revenues as more products and services are sold on credit.
- **Inventories** normally increase in anticipation of higher sales volume to ensure a sufficient stock of inventory available for sale.
- **Prepaid expenses** increase with increases in advertising and other expenditures made in anticipation of higher sales.
- **PPE** assets are usually acquired once the revenues increase is deemed sustainable and the capacity constraint is reached; thus, PPE assets increase with increased revenue, but with a lag.
- **Accounts payable** increase as additional inventories are purchased on credit.
- **Accrued liabilities** increase concurrent with increases in revenue-driven operating expenses.
- **Other operating assets and liabilities** such as deferred revenues, deferred taxes, and pensions, increase and decrease concurrent with revenues.

Dynamics of Balance Sheet Growth

To understand the dynamics of growth in the balance sheet, it is useful to view it in three sections as depicted in Exhibit 11.2. Each of these sections experiences growth at different rates. As evident from Exhibit 11.1, most net operating assets grow roughly concurrently with increases in revenues. As net operating assets are normally positive, the asset side of the balance sheet grows faster than the liability side, in dollar terms. This creates an imbalance that must be managed by the company's finance and treasury divisions.

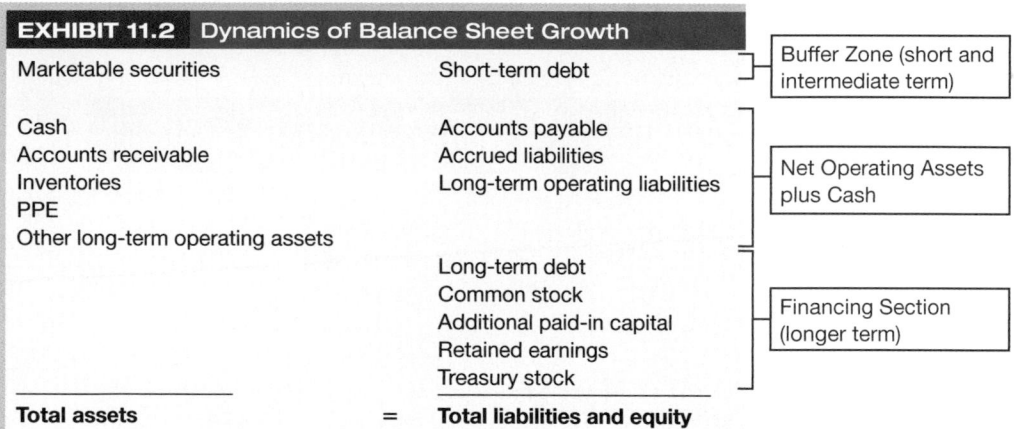

EXHIBIT 11.2   Dynamics of Balance Sheet Growth

Marketable securities	Short-term debt	Buffer Zone (short and intermediate term)
Cash	Accounts payable	
Accounts receivable	Accrued liabilities	Net Operating Assets plus Cash
Inventories	Long-term operating liabilities	
PPE		
Other long-term operating assets		
	Long-term debt	
	Common stock	
	Additional paid-in capital	Financing Section (longer term)
	Retained earnings	
	Treasury stock	
Total assets	= **Total liabilities and equity**	

The "buffer zone" represents that section of the balance sheet that responds to short- and intermediate-term imbalances. Cash declines as other operating assets increase, and companies typically finance that cash decline with short-term borrowings such as a seasonal line of credit from a bank. Conversely, companies typically invest excess cash in marketable securities (also titled short-term investments) to provide liquidity to meet future operating needs, investment opportunities, and similar near-term demands. Companies manage the "financing section" of the balance sheet on a long-term basis to provide funding for relatively permanent increases in net assets, such as PPE or even the acquisition of other companies. Further, income is reinvested in the business, long-term debt is borrowed, and equity securities are sold in proportions that are necessary to maintain the desired financial leverage for the company. Although the cash reinvestment decision is made continually, increases in long-term debt and equity occur relatively infrequently to meet longer-term funding needs. If the store of liquidity in the buffer zone is not needed for the foreseeable future, it can be used to retire long-term debt or to repurchase the company's outstanding shares.

Dynamics of Statement of Cash Flows Growth

The dynamics of the statement of cash flows mimic the dynamics of the income statement and balance sheet. This is because the statement of cash flows is prepared using both the income statement and balance sheet. Specifically, once we have forecasts of the income statement and balance sheet, we can compute the forecasted statement of cash flows just as we would its historical counterpart.

Identifying the Forecasting Steps

We apply the forecasting process in a four-step sequence:

1. **Forecast revenues.**
2. **Forecast operating and nonoperating expenses.** We assume a relation between revenue and each specific expense account.
3. **Forecast operating and nonoperating assets, liabilities and equity.** We assume a relation between revenue and each specific balance sheet account.
4. **Adjust short-term investments or short-term debt to balance the balance sheet.** We use marketable securities and short-term debt to balance the balance sheet. We then recompute net nonoperating expense (interest/dividend income or interest expense) to reflect any adjustments we make to nonoperating asset and liability account balances.

Morgan Stanley Research Report

We illustrate the forecasting process using Procter & Gamble and an actual research report (along with an accompanying analysis spreadsheet) prepared by Morgan Stanley analysts in August 2011, which coincides with P&G's August 10 filing of its fiscal year 2011 annual report with the SEC.[1] We also benefitted from conversations with Ruma Mukerji, one of the authors of the Morgan Stanley research report, and we are grateful for the background information that she provided us for the discussion of the forecasting process in this module. We begin our discussion by explaining forecasting of the income statement. P&G's income statement is reproduced in Exhibit 11.3 as a reference point.

EXHIBIT 11.3 Procter & Gamble Income Statement			
Year ended June 30, in millions except per share amounts	**2011**	**2010**	**2009**
Net sales.	$82,559	$78,938	$76,694
Cost of products sold.	40,768	37,919	38,690
Selling, general and administrative expense	25,973	24,998	22,630
Operating income.	15,818	16,021	15,374
Interest expense.	831	946	1,358
Other nonoperating income, net	202	(28)	397
Earnings from continuing operations before income taxes	15,189	15,047	14,413
Income taxes on continuing operations.	3,392	4,101	3,733
Net earnings from continuing operations.	11,797	10,946	10,680
Net earnings from discontinued operations.	—	1,790	2,756
Net earnings.	$11,797	$12,736	$13,436
Basic net earnings per common share.	$ 4.12	$ 4.32	$ 4.49
Diluted net earnings per common share	$ 3.93	$ 4.11	$ 4.26
Dividends per common share	$ 1.97	$ 1.80	$ 1.64

STEP 1: FORECASTING REVENUES

Forecasting revenues is the most difficult and crucial step in the forecasting process. Further, many of the remaining income statement and the balance sheet accounts are forecasted based on an assumed relation with forecasted revenues. We typically utilize both financial and nonfinancial information in developing forecasts. Each account must be separately analyzed using all relevant financial and nonfinancial information, including the insights gained from the first ten modules of this book.

LO2 Forecast revenues and the income statement.

To forecast revenues, then, we want to use all available, relevant information. But deciding what information is relevant and determining how to use the information varies across forecasters. As well, the level of information itself can vary across forecasters. For example, if we have access to inside information and we are developing forecasts as part of the strategic budgeting process for a company, we might have access to data regarding the competitive landscape, consumer trends and disposable income, new product introductions, production and marketing plans, and many other types of inside information. In this case, we can build our revenues forecast from the bottom up with unit sales and unit prices for each product or service sold. However, if we are a company outsider, we have much less information. In this case, we must rely on public statements by company management in conference calls and meetings in addition to the information disclosed in the management discussion and analysis (MD&A) section of the 10-K and the growth of individual product lines from segment disclosures. We also use publicly available information from competitors, suppliers, and customers for additional insight into broader trends that can impact future revenues. Companies often provide "guidance" to outsiders to help refine forecasts, which is usually valuable as companies have a vested interest in correct forecasts so that their securities are accurately priced. Generally, the revenues forecast is obtained from the following formula:

Forecasted revenues = Actual revenues × (1 + Revenue growth rate)

The revenue growth rate can be either positive or negative depending on numerous company and economic factors, described above. The remainder of this section identifies and explains key factors that impact revenue growth and illustrates their application to Procter & Gamble.

Factors Impacting Revenue Growth

Forecasts are made within the broader context of the general economic environment and the competitive landscape in which the company operates. There are a number of specific factors that impact a company's revenue growth.

Impact of Acquisitions When one company acquires another, the revenues and expenses of the acquired company are consolidated but only from the date of acquisition onward (we discuss consolidation in Module 7). Acquisitions can greatly impact the acquirer's income statement, especially if the acquisition occurs toward the beginning of the acquirer's fiscal year. **Procter & Gamble**'s acquisition of Gillette in October 2005 provides an example. In its June 30, 2006, fiscal year-end income statement (ending eight months following the acquisition), P&G reported the following for sales:

Years ended June 30 ($ millions)	2006	2005	2004
Net sales.	$68,222	$56,741	$51,407

These net sales amounts include Gillette product sales from October 2005 onward (for fiscal 2006), and none of Gillette's sales are reported in fiscal 2005 or fiscal 2004. P&G's 2006 sales growth of 20.2% ([$68,222/$56,741] − 1) was not P&G's organic growth, and we would have been remiss in forecasting a 20.2% increase for fiscal 2007.

Importantly, until all of the three comparative income statements in the 10-K include the acquired company, the acquirer is required to disclose what revenue and net income would have been had the acquired company been consolidated for all three years reported in the current income statement. This "what if" disclosure is called *pro forma* disclosure. Procter & Gamble's pro forma disclosure in 2006 includes the following discussion and table:

The following table provides pro forma results of operations for the years ended June 30, 2006, 2005, and 2004, as if Gillette had been acquired as of the beginning of each fiscal year presented.

Pro forma results; Years ended June 30	2006	2005	2004
Net sales (in millions)	$71,005	$67,920	$61,112
Net earnings (in millions)	8,871	8,522	7,504
Diluted net earnings per common share	2.51	2.29	1.98

Using this disclosure, we would have been able to compute the growth rate in sales for 2006 as 4.5% ([$71,005/$67,920] −1), and we would have used the pro forma net sales for 2006 as our forecasting base. That is, we would have forecasted 2007 net sales as $74,200 (calculated as $71,005 × 1.045). P&G was careful to point out, however, that the pro forma earnings estimate must be viewed with caution:

Pro forma results do not include any anticipated cost savings or other effects of the planned in-tegration of Gillette. Accordingly, such amounts are not necessarily indicative of the results if the acquisition had occurred on the dates indicated or that may result in the future.

Impact of Divestitures Companies are required to exclude sales and expenses of discontinued operations from the continuing operations portion of their income statements, and to present the net income and gain (loss) on sale of the divested entity, net of tax, below income from continuing opera-tions (we discuss accounting for divestitures in Module 5 and Module 7). Procter & Gamble's income statement in Exhibit 11.3 reports net earnings from discontinued operations of $1,790 million and $2,756 million for fiscal years 2010 and 2009, respectively. The following footnote from PG's 2011 10-K provides information about these two discontinued operations:

Discontinued Operations   In October 2009, the Company completed the divestiture of our global pharmaceuticals business to Warner Chilcott plc for $2.8 billion of cash, net of assumed and trans-ferred liabilities . . . . The Company recorded an after-tax gain on the transaction of $1,464, which is included in net earnings from discontinued operations in the Consolidated Statement of Earnings for the year ended June 30, 2010 . . .

In November 2008, the Company completed the divestiture of our coffee business through the merger of our Folgers coffee subsidiary into The J.M. Smucker Company . . . . The Company recorded an after-tax gain on the transaction of $2,011, which is included in net earnings from discontinued operations in the Consolidated Statement of Earnings for the year ended June 30, 2009 . . . .

Following is selected financial information included in net earnings from discontinued opera-tions for the pharmaceuticals and coffee businesses:

Year ended June 30 ($ millions)	2010			2009		
	Pharma	Coffee	Total	Pharma	Coffee	Total
Net sales............................	$ 751	$ —	$ 751	$2,335	$ 668	$3,003
Earnings from discontinued operations	306	—	306	912	212	1,124
Income tax expense....................	(101)	—	(101)	(299)	(80)	(379)
Gain on sale of discontinued operations	2,632	—	2,632	—	1,896	1,896
Income tax benefit (expense) on sale.......	(1,047)	—	(1,047)	—	115	115
Net earnings from discontinued operations..	$1,790	—	$1,790	$ 613	2,143	2,756

The net gain on the sale of the pharmaceuticals business, in the table above, for the year ended June 30, 2010, also includes an after-tax gain on the sale of the Actonel brand in Japan which oc-curred prior to the divestiture to Warner Chilcott.

The revenues, expenses, and earnings for Procter & Gamble in fiscal years 2010 and 2009, as reported in its income statement, *exclude* the revenues, expenses, and earnings from its discontinued operations. The detail relating to the revenues, expenses, and earnings of discontinued operations (and their gain on sale) is reported in the footnote disclosure shown above. This additional information allows us to better evaluate the drivers of observed growth of revenues and earnings, and we would be remiss if we included the revenues and gains relating to discontinued operations in our forecasts.

Impact of Existing vs New Store Growth Retailers typically derive revenue growth from two sources: (1) from *existing* stores (organic growth), and (2) from *new* stores. We are interested in the breakdown between these two growth sources as the latter is obtained at considerably more cost. **Target Corporation** provides the following footnote disclosure to its 10-K report.

Retail Segment Results (millions)	2010	2009	2008	Percent Change 2010/2009	2009/2008
Sales	$65,786	$63,435	$62,884	3.7%	0.9%
Cost of sales	45,725	44,062	44,157	3.8	(0.2)
Gross margin	20,061	19,373	18,727	3.5	3.5
SG&A expenses	13,367	12,989	12,838	2.9	1.2
EBITDA	6,694	6,384	5,889	4.9	8.4
Depreciation and amortization	2,065	2,008	1,808	2.8	11.0
EBIT	$ 4,629	$ 4,376	$ 4,081	5.8%	7.3%

Retail Segment Results (millions)	2010	2009	2008
Drivers of changes in comparable-store sales:			
Number of transactions	2.0%	(0.2)%	(3.1)%
Average transaction amount	0.1%	(2.3)%	0.2%
Units per transaction	2.5%	(1.5)%	(2.1)%
Selling price per unit	(2.3)%	(0.8)%	2.3%

Total sales for the Retail Segment for 2010 were $65,786 million, compared with $63,435 million in 2009 and $62,884 million in 2008. All periods were 52-week years. Growth in total sales between 2010 and 2009 resulted from higher comparable-store sales and additional stores opened, whereas between 2009 and 2008, growth in total sales resulted from sales from additional stores opened, partially offset by lower comparable-store sales.

At least three points in Target's footnote disclosure are noteworthy for forecasting purposes.

1. Retailers typically operate on a 52/53 week year, closing their books on a particular day of the week rather than on a constant date. Target has the following fiscal year-end policy:

Our fiscal year ends on the Saturday nearest January 31. Unless otherwise stated, references to years in this report relate to fiscal years, rather than to calendar years. Fiscal year 2010 ended January 29, 2011, and consisted of 52 weeks. Fiscal year 2009 ended January 30, 2010, and consisted of 52 weeks. Fiscal year 2008 ended January 31, 2009, and consisted of 52 weeks.

Target's sales for fiscal years 2008, 2009, and 2010 are all on a comparable 52-week year. Should a fiscal year include a 53-week year (as Target reported in 2006), the extra week's sales will make it appear as if sales are growing at a higher rate than they are. To accurately forecast revenue growth, we must use numbers and rates that reflect a consistent 52-week period each year. To do this, we assume that sales are recorded evenly each week and we adjust revenues for the 53-week year by multiplying reported sales by 52/53. We then use the adjusted 52-week pro forma sales to compute growth rates.

2. More than 43% ([3.7% − 2.1%]/3.7% = 43.2%) of Target's 2010 sales growth is attributable to new store openings.

3. The average per store planned capital expenditure is about $44 million ($574 million reported CAPEX for new stores/13 new stores opened in 2010 as reported in the 2011 MD&A). Although acquired growth provides the organic growth of the future, it comes at considerable cost per store.

Impact of Unit Sales and Price Disclosures Forecasts that are built from anticipated unit sales and current prices are generally more informative, and accurate, than those derived from historical dollar sales. Most companies, however, do not provide unit sales data in their 10-Ks. Apple, Inc., is an exception, and the following footnote disclosure from its 10-K provides useful information (like Target, Apple operates on a 52/53 week fiscal year):

Net Sales Fiscal years 2010, 2009 and 2008 each spanned 52 weeks. An additional week is included in the first fiscal quarter approximately every six years to realign fiscal quarters with calendar quarters.

The following table summarizes net sales and Mac unit sales by operating segment and net sales and unit sales by product during the three years ended September 25, 2010 (in millions, except unit sales in thousands and per unit amounts):

	2010	Change	2009	Change	2008
Net sales by product					
Desktops	$ 6,201	43%	$ 4,324	(23)%	$ 5,622
Portables	11,278	18%	9,535	9%	8,732
Total Mac net sales	17,479	26%	13,859	(3)%	14,354
iPod	8,274	2%	8,091	(12)%	9,153
Other music related products and services	4,948	23%	4,036	21%	3,340
iPhone and related products and services	25,179	93%	13,033	93%	6,742
iPad and related products and services	4,958	NM	0	NM	0
Peripherals and other hardware	1,814	23%	1,475	(13)%	1,694
Software, service, and other sales	2,573	7%	2,411	9%	2,208
Total net sales	$65,225	52%	$42,905	14%	$37,491
Unit sales by product					
Desktops	4,627	45%	3,182	(14)%	3,712
Portables	9,035	25%	7,214	20%	6,003
Total Mac unit sales	13,662	31%	10,396	7%	9,715
Net sales per Mac unit sold	$ 1,279	(4)%	$ 1,333	(10)%	$ 1,478
iPod unit sales	50,312	(7)%	54,132	(1)%	54,828
Net sales per iPod unit sold	$ 164	10%	$ 149	(11)%	$ 167
iPhone units sold	39,989	93%	20,731	78%	11,627
iPad units sold	7,458	NM	0	NM	0

From Apple's disclosure we can derive several useful insights for forecasting purposes.

1. On average, a Mac sells for $1,279 and the per unit selling price has decreased during the past three years; unit sales, however, have increased by 31% and 7% per year for the past two years.
2. The iPod unit sales are decreasing over the past two years, probably reflecting increased competition from other MP3 players and market saturation.
3. The average sales price of iPods in 2010 is $164, 10% higher than the average sales price in 2009.
4. iPhone unit sales are 39,989 thousand, up 93% from 2009 and 244% from 2008.
5. iPhone dollar sales are $25,179 million in 2010, 93% higher than 2009 and 273% greater than in 2008.
6. Apple has only begun to realize the effects of its iPad as of fiscal year 2010, with 7,458 thousand units sold and total revenues of about $4,958 million.

Detailed disclosures such as Apple's allow us to prepare more informed forecasts that consider both unit sales and selling prices.

Forecasting Revenue Growth

To illustrate the forecasting process, we forecast revenue growth for P&G. Our information includes public disclosures by management in meetings and conference calls with analysts and the company's published financial reports including the management discussion and analysis (MD&A) section of the 10-K. We discuss the information in each of these sources.

Public Disclosures via Meetings and Calls P&G held its first meeting with analysts on September 8, 2011, following the August 10 release of its fiscal year 2011 financial statements. Its presentation (publicly available on the "Investor Relations" section of P&G's Website) provides guidance in several areas that impact our forecasts and we include excerpts from that presentation in our discussion below.

Published Reports: Segment Disclosures and MD&A Companies are required to disclose summary financial results for each of their operating segments along with a discussion and analysis of each. (An operating segment is defined under GAAP as a component of the company for which financial information is available and disclosed to senior management.) P&G is organized into six operating segments as discussed in the following excerpt from its 2011 MD&A:

Our organizational structure is comprised of two Global Business Units (GBUs), Global Operations, Global Business Services (GBS) and Corporate Functions (CF) . . . Effective February 2011, our two GBUs are Beauty & Grooming and Household Care. The primary responsibility of the GBUs is to develop the overall strategy for our brands . . . Under U.S. GAAP, the business units comprising the GBUs are aggregated into six reportable segments: Beauty; Grooming; Health Care; Snacks and Pet Care; Fabric Care and Home Care; and Baby Care and Family Care.

Reportable Segment	% of Net Sales*	% of Net Earnings*	Categories	Billion-Dollar Brands
Beauty	24%	24%	Cosmetics, Female Antiperspirant and Deodorant, Female Personal Cleansing, Female Shave Care, Hair Care, Hair Color, Hair Styling, Pharmacy Channel, Prestige Products, Salon Professional, Skin Care	Head & Shoulders, Olay, Pantene, Wella
Grooming	9%	14%	Electronic Hair Removal Devices, Home Small Appliances, Male Blades and Razors, Male Personal Care	Braun, Fusion, Gillette, Mach3
Health Care	14%	16%	Feminine Care, Gastrointestinal, Incontinence, Rapid Diagnostics, Respiratory, Toothbrush, Toothpaste, Water Filtration, Other Oral Care	Always, Oral-B, Crest
Snacks and Pet Care	4%	2%	Pet Care, Snacks	Iams, Pringles
Fabric Care and Home Care	30%	27%	Laundry Additives, Air Care, Batteries, Dish Care, Fabric Enhancers, Laundry Detergents, Surface Care	Ace, Ariel, Dawn, Downy, Duracell, Febreze, Gain, Tide
Baby Care and Family Care	19%	17%	Baby Wipes, Diapers, Paper Towels, Tissue, Toilet Paper	Bounty, Charmin, Pampers

* Percent of net sales and net earnings from continuing operations for the year ended June 30, 2011 (excluding results held in Corporate).

P&G also reports a revenue history for each segment and its MD&A provides additional information relating to the breakdown of revenue increases for the current year into the portion relating to increases in unit volume sales, increases in prices, effects of foreign-currency translation, and changes in product mix. That disclosure and related discussion allow us to compile the following table:

Net Sales Change Drivers vs. Year Ago (2011 vs. 2010)	Volume with Acquisitions & Divestitures	Volume Excluding Acquisitions & Divestitures	Foreign Exchange	Price	Mix/Other	Net Sales Growth
Beauty	4%	4%	1%	0%	(2)%	3%
Grooming	3%	3%	0%	2%	0%	5%
Health Care	5%	5%	0%	0%	0%	5%
Snacks and Pet Care	1%	(2)%	1%	(1)%	0%	1%
Fabric Care and Home Care	7%	5%	(1)%	0%	(2)%	4%
Baby Care and Family Care	8%	8%	(1)%	1%	(2)%	6%
Total Company	6%	5%	0%	1%	(2)%	5%

Net sales percentage changes are approximations based on quantitative formulas that are consistently applied.

P&G's total sales volume increased by 6% in 2011, or 5% excluding acquisitions and divestitures. Revenues increased by 5% in total as a result of increases in units of product sold (although marked variation is evident across products) and 1% as a result of price increases. Revenues declined, however, as a result of changes in product mix (generally relating to an increase in the relative percentage of lower-priced products). This volume/price/mix analysis is potentially important as we are often more comfortable with revenue increases resulting from increased units sold than from price increases that might be unsustainable.

Although fluctuations in foreign-exchange rates affected individual product categories in 2011, the net effects on total revenues were largely offsetting in 2011 (see Module 5 for a discussion of foreign-exchange rate effects on sales). By comparison, however, during 2008, the $US weakened vis-à-vis other major world currencies. Thus, revenues denominated in foreign currencies, including P&G's, increased when translated into $US, resulting in an increase in revenue growth of about 5%. We must be aware of these foreign exchange fluctuations as reported fluctuations in revenues might not reflect underlying fluctuations in unit volumes.

Determining the Revenue Growth Forecast

As we saw, P&G disaggregated the sales growth for each business segment into volume, foreign exchange, price, and mix effects. Morgan Stanley analysts forecast each of those factors for each of P&G's segments to obtain an aggregate forecast of sales. To illustrate, following is an excerpt from the Morgan Stanley forecast spreadsheet for P&G's total sales and for its Beauty segment (the spreadsheet has similar forecasts for each segment).

	A	B	AF	AK	AP	AU	AV	AW	AX	AY	AZ	BA	BB	BC	BD	BE
1	Procter & Gamble Co (PG)															
2	Segment Breakdown		FY2007	FY2008	FY2009	FY2010	Sep-10	Dec-10	Mar-11	Jun-11	FY2011	Sep-11 E	Dec-11 E	Mar-12 E	Jun-12 E	FY2012E
3	Total Sales		76,476.0	81,748.0	76,694.0	78,938.0	20,122.0	21,347.0	20,230.0	20,860.0	82,559.0	21,555.2	22,136.4	20,843.3	21,786.9	86,321.8
4	Organic Sales Growth		6.0%	5.0%	2.0%	3.4%	4.0%	3.0%	4.0%	5.0%	4.0%	3.4%	4.9%	4.8%	4.6%	4.4%
5	Volume (Organic)		5.0%	5.0%	-2.0%	4.0%	7.0%	6.0%	5.0%	3.0%	5.2%	1.3%	2.8%	2.8%	4.1%	2.8%
6	Pricing		1.0%	1.0%	5.0%	0.5%	-1.0%	0.0%	1.0%	3.0%	0.4%	3.7%	3.6%	3.7%	2.0%	3.2%
7	Mix		0.0%	-1.0%	-1.0%	-1.1%	-2.0%	-2.0%	-2.0%	-1.0%	-1.6%	-1.5%	-1.5%	-1.5%	-1.5%	-1.5%
8	FX Impact		2.0%	5.0%	-4.0%	-0.4%	-3.0%	-2.0%	1.0%	5.0%	0.2%	3.8%	-1.2%	-1.8%	0.0%	0.1%
9	Acq/Div		4.0%	-1.0%	-0.8%	-0.1%	0.6%	0.0%	0.0%	0.0%	0.3%	0.0%	0.0%	0.0%	0.0%	0.0%
10	% Sales Growth		12.1%	9.2%	-2.8%	2.9%	1.6%	1.5%	5.5%	10.2%	4.6%	7.1%	3.7%	3.0%	4.4%	4.6%
11	Beauty															
12	Beauty Care		17,889.0	19,515.0	18,924.0	19,491.0	4,929.0	5,290.0	4,870.0	5,068.0	20,157.0	5,259.0	5,423.1	4,965.3	5,296.1	20,943.4
13	Organic Sales Growth			4.0%	1.0%	3.2%	2.0%	3.0%	4.0%	3.0%	3.0%	3.5%	3.5%	3.5%	4.5%	3.8%
14	Volume (Organic)			2.8%	-1.0%	3.3%	4.0%	6.0%	6.0%	2.0%	4.5%	1.5%	1.5%	1.5%	4.0%	2.1%
15	Pricing			0.5%	2.0%	0.9%	0.0%	-1.0%	1.0%	2.0%	0.5%	3.0%	3.0%	3.0%	1.5%	2.6%
16	Mix			0.5%	0.0%	-0.4%	-2.0%	-2.0%	-3.0%	-1.0%	-2.0%	-1.0%	-1.0%	-1.0%	-1.0%	-1.0%
17	FX Impact			5.5%	-4.0%	0.0%	-2.0%	-1.0%	2.0%	6.0%	1.2%	3.2%	-1.0%	-1.5%	0.0%	0.1%
18	Acq/Div			-0.3%	-0.5%	-0.5%	0.0%	-1.0%	-1.0%	-2.0%	-1.0%	0.0%	0.0%	0.0%	0.0%	0.0%
19	% Sales Growth		7.2%	9.1%	-3.7%	3.0%	0.2%	1.4%	5.3%	7.1%	3.4%	6.7%	2.5%	2.0%	4.5%	3.9%
20	Grooming		7,437.0	8,254.0	7,408.0	7,631.0	1,898.0	2,164.0	1,907.0	2,056.0	8,025.0	2,074.4	2,229.4	1,958.2	2,148.5	8,410.5
21	Organic Sales Growth			4.0%	-2.0%	3.0%	6.0%	6.0%	7.0%	1.0%	5.0%	4.5%	4.5%	5.0%	4.5%	4.6%
22	Volume (Organic)			5.5%	-5.0%	0.3%	5.0%	5.0%	2.0%	1.0%	3.3%	2.5%	2.5%	3.0%	4.0%	3.0%
23	Pricing			1.3%	5.0%	3.7%	1.0%	1.0%	5.0%	2.0%	2.2%	3.0%	3.0%	3.0%	1.5%	2.6%
24	Mix			-2.3%	-2.0%	-1.0%	0.0%	0.0%	0.0%	-2.0%	-0.5%	-1.0%	-1.0%	-1.0%	-1.0%	-1.0%
25	FX Impact			6.5%	-6.0%	0.0%	-4.0%	-3.0%	1.0%	6.0%	-0.1%	4.8%	-1.5%	-2.3%	0.0%	0.2%
26	Acq/Div			-0.3%	-0.3%	0.2%	0.0%	0.0%	0.0%	0.0%	0.0%	0.0%	0.0%	0.0%	0.0%	0.0%
27	% Sales Growth		45.4%	11.0%	-8.6%	3.0%	2.2%	3.3%	8.4%	7.1%	5.2%	9.3%	3.0%	2.7%	4.5%	4.8%

For fiscal year 2012, Morgan Stanley forecasts a total sales growth rate of 4.6%, which consists of the following:

Organic sales growth		4.5%*
Volume (organic)	2.8%	
Pricing	3.2%	
Mix	(1.5)%	
Foreign exchange impact		0.1%
Acquisitions & divestitures		0.0%
Sales growth %		4.6%

* Sum of volume (2.8%), pricing (3.2%), and mix (-1.5%), which is rounded down to 4.4 in the Excel spreadsheet as more digits are used than are printed.

Morgan Stanley forecasts organic sales growth for all of P&G at 4.5%, consisting of 2.8% growth in volume, a 3.2% increase in prices, a −1.5% decline in growth due to product mix (increasing percentage of lower-priced goods). Morgan Stanley analysts also forecast an increase in sales of 0.1% resulting from a weakening of the $US in countries in which PG sells its products.

Following are a few observations that Morgan Stanley analysts conveyed to us about the way in which their sales forecasts are developed:

1. Each product forecast is built from the bottom up; that is, analysts use information about a product's market share and the forecasted growth rate for the market of each product within each country the product is sold. Development of such forecasts uses information about product market, pricing strategy, and competitive landscape. With this information, analysts forecast overall market growth, the market share for each product, changes in product pricing, and changes in the product sales mix. The total sales forecast is the sum of individual product forecasts for each product market.

2. P&G, like many companies, provides analysts with its own forecasts of sales growth by products, disaggregated into price and volume. Morgan Stanley analysts also have internally-developed databases of commodity-price indices, inflation indices, and other macroeconomic indices against which to evaluate the reasonableness of company-provided forecasts.

3. Sales forecasts are determined by quantity and price along with growth forecasts of the product markets, the company-provided future pricing strategy, and forecasts of price elasticity of demand. Analysts commonly consider, for example, the effects of a current discount pricing strategy to increase market share or to gain entrance into a new market, which are followed by price increases once volume levels and customer loyalty is solidified.

Returning to P&G, we saw that Morgan Stanley forecasted no acquisitions or divestitures. Acquisition of brands is a normal component of P&G's operating activities, yet acquisitions are one-time occurrences and come at a cost. We, like Morgan Stanley, focus on revenue growth that is not acquired, and we believe that organic sales growth is the best predictor of core operating revenue growth. P&G defines organic sales growth as follows:

Organic Sales Growth Organic sales growth is a non-GAAP measure of sales growth excluding the impacts of acquisitions, divestitures and foreign exchange from year-over-year comparisons. We believe this provides investors with a more complete understanding of underlying sales trends by providing sales growth on a consistent basis. Organic sales is also one of the measures used to evaluate senior management and is a factor in determining their at-risk compensation.

Summary of Determining Revenue Growth Forecast To recap, each segment is disaggregated into its business units and product lines. The presumption is that determining the revenue forecasts from the sum of product forecasts is preferable to forecasting total sales growth because the former uses more information. This implies that we use as much detailed product information as reasonable (cost vs. benefit) to forecast revenue growth. For example, we saw Morgan Stanley analysts use data on the Beauty Care and Grooming units to aggregate into the Beauty segment. We also saw that these forecasts were determined from both price and volume for each product in each market. Finally, we saw that analysts forecasted from quarterly data and determined annual forecasts as the sum of quarterly forecasts for each unit and segment.

Data Sources in Forecasting Revenue Investors use a variety of data sources. Companies provide data in conference calls and meetings with analysts. P&G, for example, provided the following guidance on organic sales growth in its Barclay's Capital Conference from 2011:

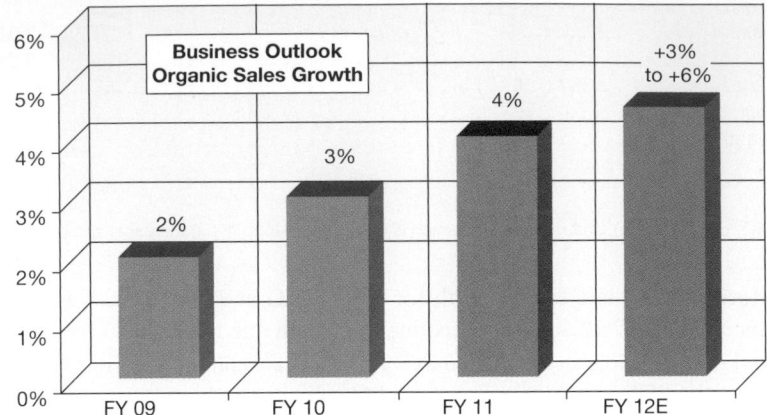

P&G's organic growth has ranged from 2% to 3% for the two most recent years, but it expects sales to recover as the world economy was expected to emerge from the recession in those previous years. Consequently, P&G's forecast of its revenue growth through fiscal year 2012 was in the range of 3% to 6%. Company expectations are an important input to our forecasts of revenue growth. Further, as we discuss above, total organic sales growth is a function of volume and price, and P&G provided the following quarterly information for forecasting these two variables:

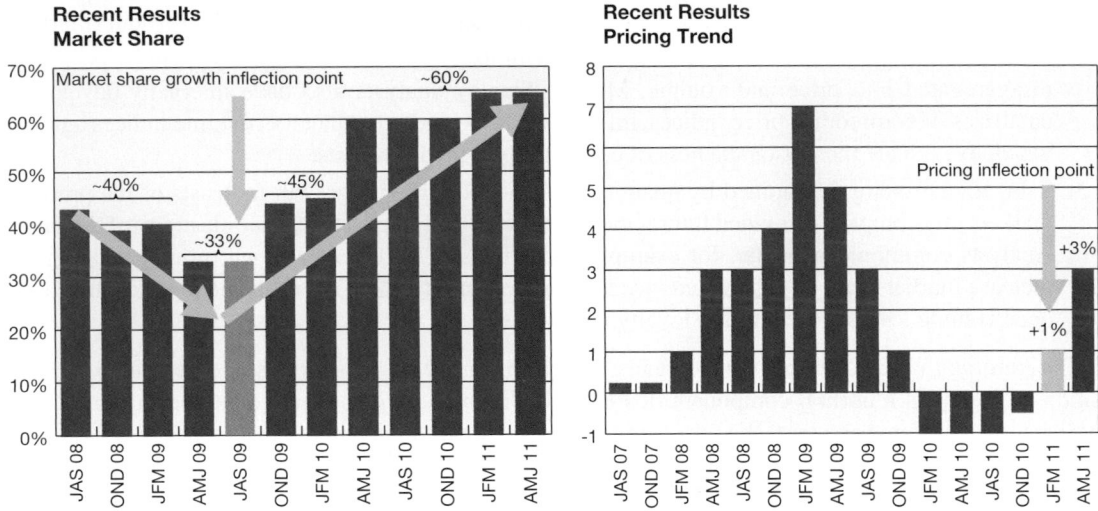

In addition to these company-provided sources of information, analysts can also use internally developed databases on macroeconomic data, commodity prices, and other inflation indices, along with data from competing companies, and other publicly available and proprietary databases. Most investors have access to similar information.

STEP 2: FORECASTING EXPENSES

The next step in the forecasting process is to predict expenses; for our purposes this includes operating expenses and nonoperating revenues and expenses.

Forecasting Operating Expenses

Generally, we use the following formula to forecast individual operating expenses:

Forecasted operating expense = Forecasted revenues × Forecasted operating expense margin

The forecasted operating expense margin is the expense expressed as a percent of sales (the common-sized expense). We normally start with the prior year's margin and then adjust it based on our business analysis. One exception to this general formula is for income taxes where we apply the following:

Forecasted income taxes = Forecasted income before taxes × Forecasted effective tax rate

In this case, we begin with forecasted income before taxes, not with sales, and the current effective tax rate is often a reasonable predictor of the company's long-term effective tax rate, taking into consideration any transitory items reported in the effective tax rate reconciliation in the tax footnote.

Forecasting Nonoperating Expenses

Generally, forecasts of individual line items of nonoperating expenses are obtained from the following "no change" forecast model:

Forecasted nonoperating expense = Nonoperating expense for prior period

This assumes no change in nonoperating expenses, with an exception of a "zero forecast" for items related to discontinued operations. If we make balance sheet financing or investment adjustments in Step 4, we must adjust one or more nonoperating expenses.

Forecasting Expenses for P&G

To illustrate the forecasting of operating expenses, we turn to Procter & Gamble. P&G's management forecasts an increase in operating profit and cash flow through fiscal year (FY) 2012 as shown in the following slide from the company's 2011 presentation to analysts.

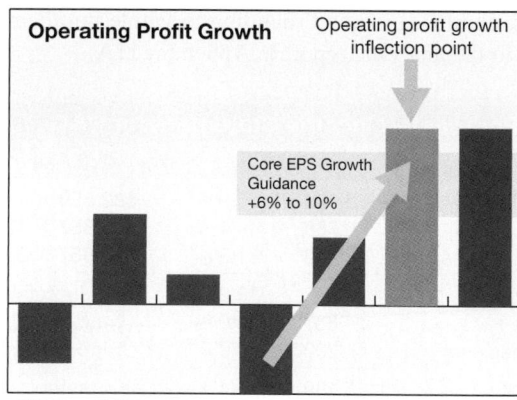

In addition to the 4.6% revenue growth, P&G's report to analysts also predicts an improved operating profit margin for FY2012.

Turning again to Morgan Stanley's analysts, we see that they forecast operating profit by business unit, consistent with how they determine sales forecasts. Following is an excerpt from the Morgan Stanley spreadsheet that has analysts' forecasts of pretax income:

	A	B	AF	AK	AP	AU	AV	AW	AX	AY	AZ	BA	BB	BC	BD	BE
1	Procter & Gamble Co (PG)															
2	Segment Breakdown		FY2007	FY2008	FY2009	FY2010	Sep-10	Dec-10	Mar-11	Jun-11	FY2011	Sep-11 E	Dec-11 E	Mar-12 E	Jun-12 E	FY2012E
66	Pretax Income By Segment		14,710.0	15,632.0	14,803.0	15,314.0	4,282.0	4,366.0	3,641.0	3,205.0	15,494.0	4,104.0	4,525.5	3,989.5	3,390.9	16,009.9
67	% Growth			6.3%	-5.3%	3.5%	2.3%	-8.1%	-3.2%	22.5%	1.2%	-4.2%	3.7%	9.6%	5.8%	3.3%
68	Beauty															
69	Beauty Care		3,440.0	3,528.0	3,558.0	3,648.0	1,081.0	1,141.0	762.0	623.0	3,607.0	982.5	1,196.8	851.4	704.0	3,734.6
70	% Growth					2.5%	5.3%	0.4%	-1.3%	-12.5%	-1.1%	-9.1%	4.9%	11.7%	13.0%	3.5%
71	Grooming		1,895.0	2,299.0	1,900.0	2,007.0	524.0	635.0	524.0	500.0	2,183.0	556.1	665.3	552.7	538.6	2,312.8
72	% Growth					5.6%	7.2%	3.6%	13.4%	12.9%	8.8%	1.0%	4.8%	5.5%	7.7%	5.9%

Total forecasted pretax income is the sum of forecasted pretax income for each business unit (which includes $3,734.6 million from the Beauty Care business unit and $2,312.8 million from the Grooming business unit as illustrated above).

Then, using the segment forecasts, Morgan Stanley analysts predict each line item of the income statement for each quarter of FY2012. We show the following excerpt from their spreadsheet as an illustration. (there are slight differences between the internal analyst spreadsheets reproduced in this module and the published report in the appendix due to timing and other differences)

	A	B	C	AQ	AV	AW	AX	AY	AZ	BA
1	Procter & Gamble Co (PG)									
2	Income Statement			FY2010	FY2011	Sep-11 E	Dec-11 E	Mar-12 E	Jun-12 E	FY2012E
3	**Sales**			**78,938.0**	**82,559.0**	**21,555.2**	**22,136.4**	**20,843.3**	**21,786.9**	**86,321.8**
4	% Growth			2.9%	4.6%	7.1%	3.7%	3.0%	4.4%	4.6%
	% Organic Growth			3.4%	4.0%	3.4%	4.9%	4.8%	4.6%	4.4%
6	Cost of Sales			-37,919.0	-40,768.0	-10,702.4	-10,833.4	-10,308.3	-11,213.5	-43.057.7
7	% of Sales			48.0%	49.4%	49.7%	48.9%	49.5%	51.5%	49.9%
8	% of Sales Bps Change			-241	134	150	75	0	-24	50
10	**Gross Profit**			**41,019.0**	**41,791.0**	**10,852.8**	**11,303.0**	**10,535.0**	**10,573.4**	**43,264.1**
11	Gross Margin %			52.0%	50.6%	50.3%	51.1%	50.5%	48.5%	50.1%
12	Gross Margin Bps Change			241	-134	-150	-75	0	24	-50
14	SG&A Expense (ex Incremental Restructuring)			-24,731.0	-25,668.0	-6,549.9	-6,575.3	-6,343.1	-6.983.1	-26,451.3
15	% of Sales			31.3%	31.1%	30.4%	29.7%	30.4%	32.1%	30.6%
16	% Growth			11.2%	3.8%	10.4%	1.2%	-1.7%	2.9%	3.1%
17	% of Sales Bps Change			233	-24	91	-72	-147	-49	-45
19	Operating Income (ex Incremental Restructuring)			16,288.0	16,123.0	4,302.9	4,727.7	4,191.9	3,590.3	16,812.7
20	Operating Margin			20.6%	19.5%	20.0%	21.4%	20.1%	16.5%	19.5%
21	% Growth			3.3%	-1.0%	-4.4%	3.6%	11.1%	9.3%	4.3%
22	Operating Margin Bps Change			8	-110	-241	-3	147	73	-5

The remainder of this section explains the details and logic behind these forecasts.

Our forecasted income statement is in Exhibit 11.4. We provide FY2011 actual income statement numbers along with our forecast assumptions and our forecasted numbers for FY2012. To simplify the exposition, we show only annual forecasts (not quarterly forecasts as estimated by Morgan Stanley analysts). Because of this simplification and rounding to whole numbers, the forecasts in this Exhibit differ slightly from those in the analysts' report in Appendix 11A.

EXHIBIT 11.4   Preliminary Forecasted Income Statement for P&G

($ millions)	2011		Forecast Assumptions	2012 Est.	
Net sales.	$82,559	100.0%	$82,559 × 1.046	$86,357	100.0%
Cost of products sold.	40,768	49.4%	$86,357 × 49.9%	43,092	49.9%
Selling, general and administrative expense . .	25,973	31.5%	$86,357 × 30.6%	26,425	30.6%
Operating income.	15,818	19.2%	subtotal	16,840	19.5%
Interest expense.	831	1.0%	no change	831	1.0%
Other nonoperating income (expense), net . . .	202	0.2%	no change	202	0.2%
Earnings before income taxes	15,189	18.4%	subtotal	16,211	18.8%
Income taxes on continuing operations.	3,392	4.1%	$16,211 × 25.0%	4,053	4.7%
Net earnings.	$11,797	14.3%	subtotal	$12,158	14.1%

Operating Expenses for P&G

This section describes the process of forecasting operating expenses (*we forecast nonoperating revenues and expenses following our adjustments to the balance sheet in Step 4*).

Forecasting Net Sales   Following our discussion above, we forecast net sales to increase by 4.6%, which is the forecasted outcome from a predicted 4.5% increase in organic sales, driven primarily by a 2.8% projected increase in volume and a 3.2% increase in selling prices, offset by a 1.5% decline in sales from changes in product mix (selling a greater proportion of lower priced products) and a positive 0.1% foreign exchange effect.

Forecasting Cost of Products Sold   Cost of products sold as a percent of sales increased from 48.0% in 2010 to 49.4% in 2011. Morgan Stanley analysts forecast an increase in the COGS percentage by 50 bp (basis points, or 100ths of a percent) to 49.9%. That forecast considers the proportion of raw materials and labor in the production process of each product along with forecasts of changes in commodity costs and wage rates. The 50bp increase in COGS, and the resulting decline in the gross profit margin described above, are reasonable given the recessionary climate and the product markets.

Subtotaling Gross Profit Gross profit is a subtotal, forecasted sales less forecasted cost of goods sold (as an alternative, in some cases, we might choose to forecast gross profit; in that case, cost of goods sold is the "plug" figure). P&G does not report this subtotal in its current income statement and we, therefore, do not include it in our statement (there is no requirement under GAAP to provide this subtotal, yet many companies do report it).

Forecasting Selling, General and Administrative Expense P&G has reduced SG&A expenses as a percent of sales from 31.3% in 2010 to 31.1% in 2011, and it cited further expected improvement during meetings with analysts. A recessionary climate encourages P&G to focus on further overhead reduction, and coupled with P&G's continued focus on manufacturing and supply chain improvements, justifies a forecast of reduced SG&A expenses as a percent of sales. Our forecast is for SG&A expenses to be 30.6% of sales, which is a 50bp improvement on 2011, and slightly more than the 20bp improvement P&G had from 2010 to 2011. This is a trend that P&G highlighted in meetings with analysts.

Subtotaling Operating Income Operating income is a subtotal, but we still check its reasonableness. Our forecasts imply a 19.5% operating income margin, which is close to the previous year's operating income margin of 19.2%. Further, it is reasonable to expect limited improvement in operating income margin as sales increase and expenses remain under control in the post-recessionary period 2012–2014.

Nonoperating Expenses for P&G To this point, we have forecasted sales and individual operating expenses, yielding a subtotal for operating income. The nonoperating section of the income statement requires estimates of nonoperating assets (which yield interest and/or dividend income) and nonoperating liabilities (which produce interest expense). We predict nonoperating revenue and expense once we estimate nonoperating assets and liabilities at the conclusion of the next section. Also, since we do not yet have forecasts of nonoperating revenues (expenses), we cannot forecast pretax income, tax expense, and net income. Thus, we complete our forecasts for the income statement at the conclusion of Step 4.

STEP 3: FORECASTING ASSETS, LIABILITIES AND EQUITY

Step 3 is to forecast balance sheet items, which consist of assets, liabilities, and equity. Special emphasis is on forecasts of operating assets and liabilities. We generally assume no change in nonoperating assets, liabilities, and equity (we discuss exceptions to this rule in this section and further adjustments to those accounts in Step 4). Step 3 proceeds with five steps as shown in Exhibit 11.5.

LO3 Forecast the balance sheet.

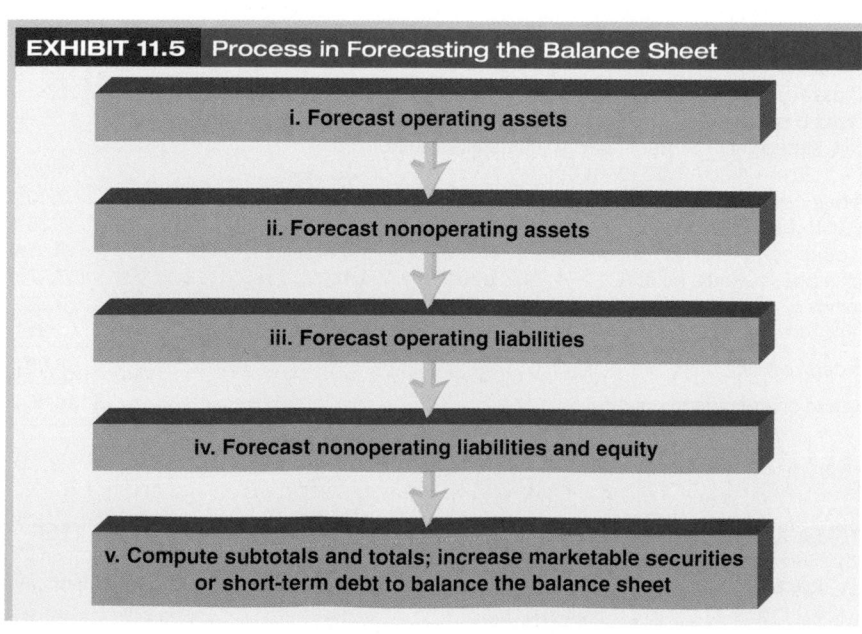

EXHIBIT 11.5 Process in Forecasting the Balance Sheet

i. Forecast operating assets

ii. Forecast nonoperating assets

iii. Forecast operating liabilities

iv. Forecast nonoperating liabilities and equity

v. Compute subtotals and totals; increase marketable securities or short-term debt to balance the balance sheet

As a starting point, we begin with **Procter & Gamble**'s balance sheet for 2011 in Exhibit 11.6. We will refer to these statements throughout this section.

EXHIBIT 11.6 Procter & Gamble Balance Sheet		
June 30, amounts in millions	2011	2010
Assets		
Current assets		
Cash and cash equivalents	$ 2,768	$ 2,879
Accounts receivable.	6,275	5,335
Inventories		
Materials and supplies	2,153	1,692
Work in process	717	604
Finished goods.	4,509	4,088
Total inventories	7,379	6,384
Deferred income taxes	1,140	990
Prepaid expenses and other current assets.	4,408	3,194
Total current assets	21,970	18,782
Property, plant and equipment		
Buildings.	7,753	6,868
Machinery and equipment	32,820	29,294
Land	934	850
Total property, plant and equipment.	41,507	37,012
Accumulated depreciation	(20,214)	(17,768)
Net property, plant and equipment	21,293	19,244
Goodwill and other intangible assets		
Goodwill.	57,562	54,012
Trademarks and other intangible assets, net	32,620	31,636
Net goodwill and other intangible assets.	90,182	85,648
Other noncurrent assets.	4,909	4,498
Total assets.	$138,354	$128,172
Liabilities and shareholders' equity		
Current liabilities		
Accounts payable.	$ 8,022	$ 7,251
Accrued and other liabilities.	9,290	8,559
Debt due within one year	9,981	8,472
Total current liabilities.	27,293	24,282
Long-term debt	22,033	21,360
Deferred income taxes	11,070	10,902
Other noncurrent liabilities	9,957	10,189
Total liabilities.	70,353	66,733
Shareholders' equity		
Convertible Class A preferred stock, stated value $1 per share (600 shares authorized)	1,234	1,277
Non-voting Class B preferred stock, stated value $1 per share (200 shares authorized)	—	—
Common stock, stated value $1 per share (10,000 shares authorized;		
shares issued: 2011—4,007.9, 2010—4,007.6)	4,008	4,008
Additional paid-in capital	62,405	61,697
Reserve for ESOP debt retirement.	(1,357)	(1,350)
Accumulated other comprehensive income (loss)	(2,054)	(7,822)
Treasury stock, at cost (shares held: 2011—1,242.2, 2010—1,164.1).	(67,278)	(61,309)
Retained earnings	70,682	64,614
Noncontrolling interest	361	324
Total shareholders' equity	68,001	61,439
Total liabilities and shareholders' equity.	$138,354	$128,172

Process of Forecasting Balance Sheet Items

We normally make one of three general assumptions when forecasting assets, liabilities, and equity.

1. **Forecast amounts with no change.** We can use a no-change forecast, which is common for nonoperating assets (investments in securities, discontinued operations, and other nonoperating investments). After we have generated forecasts of the balance sheet, we must reexamine the no-change forecasts to see if they are reasonable or if they require adjustment.

2. **Forecast contractual or specified amounts.** We can use contractual or other specified payment tables to forecast selected balance sheet items. For example, footnote disclosures contain scheduled maturities for long-term debt, capital leases, and mandatory redeemable preferred stock for a five-year period subsequent to the financial statement date. We can use those schedules and assume that the required payments are made as projected.

3. **Forecast amounts in relation to revenues.** We can use an item's relation to revenues to forecast that item. The underlying assumption is that, as revenues change, so does that item in some predictable manner. For example, in the case of operating assets, it is reasonable to assume that the required investment in receivables, inventories, and PPE is related, in some manner, to the level of revenues. Similarly, in the case of operating liabilities, it is reasonable to expect that accounts payable will grow with COGS (which grows with revenues), and accrued liabilities will grow with increases in payroll, utilities, advertising, and other expenses (which all grow with revenues).

When forecasting amounts in relation to revenues, the third forecasting assumption above, there are three common methods: (1) forecasts using the percent of revenues, (2) forecasts using turnover rates, and (3) forecasts using days outstanding ratios.

Forecasts Using Percent of Revenues Forecasts that use the percent of revenues build on the relation between revenues and the account being forecasted; this relation follows:

$$\textbf{Forecasted account balance = Forecasted revenues} \times \left(\frac{\textbf{Actual account balance}}{\textbf{Actual revenues}} \right)$$

For example, if the relation between the actual account balance to revenues is 10%, and forecasted revenues equal $100, then the forecasted account is $10, computed as $100 × 10%.

Forecasts Using Turnover Rates Turnover rates have the following general form: Turnover rate = Revenues (or COGS)/Average account balance. Using algebra to rearrange terms, we obtain: Average account balance = Revenues (or COGS)/Turnover rate. Substituting forecasted values we get:

$$\textbf{Forecasted account balance = Forecasted revenues (or COGS)/Turnover rate}$$

Consequently, if we have forecasted revenues (or COGS) and a forecasted turnover rate, we can forecast the account balance. However, there is a problem with this method if we use turnover rates as traditionally defined using average account balances; in this case the method would forecast the *average account balance*. Balance sheets report *ending account balances*. This issue is typically resolved in one of two ways:

1. Compute the turnover rate using ending balances rather than average balances; then, our forecast is for the ending account balance.

2. Multiply the forecasted average account balance by 2 and then subtract the beginning account balance; this yields the forecast for the ending account balance.

Forecasts Using Days Outstanding Days outstanding ratios have the following general form: Days outstanding = Account balance/Average daily revenues (or COGS), where Average daily revenues (or COGS) = Revenues (or COGS)/365. We can forecast the account balance by rearranging terms as follows:

$$\textbf{Forecasted account balance = Days outstanding} \times \textbf{[Forecasted revenues (or COGS)/365]}$$

If days outstanding is computed using the ending balance of the account, the resulting forecast is for the ending balance of that account. However, some analysts prefer a shortcut method to compute days outstanding as 365/Turnover rate. Their justification is based on the mathematical equality where [365/Turnover rate] = [365/(Revenues/Account balance)] = [(Account balance × 365)/Revenues] = [Account balance/(Revenues/365)]. Importantly, however, if this turnover rate is computed in the conventional way using the *average* account balance, we would forecast the average account balance rather than the ending account balance. In this case, we must make one of the two adjustments explained in the previous section.

Equivalence of the Three Forecasting Methods   If we compute the turnover rate and the days outstanding using ending account balances (meaning that we are properly forecasting the ending account balance), it does not matter which of these three forecasting methods we use. To illustrate, consider a company with current-period revenues of $1,000 and a forecasted revenue growth of 4% (or $1,040, computed as $1,000 × 1.04). Assume that the current accounts receivable ending balance is $200 and that we want to forecast accounts receivable for next year. Using each of the three methods above, our forecasted accounts receivable is $208 and is computed as follows:

Forecast Method	Forecast	Forecast Computation
Percent of revenues	$208	$1,040 × ($200/$1,000)
Turnover rate	$208	$1,040/($1,000/$200)
Days outstanding	$208	{[($200 × 365)/$1,000] × $1,040}/365

Each of these forecasting methods yields the same result. Analysts commonly use either percent of sales or days outstanding. The choice between percent of sales and days outstanding depends on the audience. Percent of sales is simple and intuitive. Days outstanding is well suited for analyses that are used in discussions with operating managers, as most managers are familiar with days outstanding ratios and can identify with projected changes (for example, what is the effect of collecting our receivables two days faster?). The choice is a matter of personal preference as all three methods yield the same result. *We use the percent of sales in our forecasts of balance sheet accounts because (1) it appears to be the most commonly used method, (2) it is the method that P&G management uses in its meetings with analysts, and (3) it is the method used by* Morgan Stanley *(and the majority of investment houses that we are familiar with) in the analysis illustration we provide in this module and in Appendix 11A.*

Forecasting Balance Sheet Items

We illustrate the forecasting of balance sheet items for Procter & Gamble.

Forecasting Operating Assets

This section describes the process of forecasting operating assets using the percent of revenues method. Morgan Stanley analysts forecast balance sheet items as a percentage of sales (except for Inventories and accounts payable that are forecasted as a percent of cost of goods sold). We provide an excerpt from the Morgan Stanley forecasting spreadsheet in Exhibit 11.7, which lists the forecasting assumptions (the entire spreadsheet is in the analysts' report in Appendix 11A).

Forecasting Accounts Receivable   P&G reports accounts receivable as a percentage of sales equal to 6.8% and 7.6% at year-end 2010 and 2011, respectively. Recall that Morgan Stanley's forecasts were prepared in a recessionary environment. It was reasonable, therefore, to expect a continuing decline in the financial condition of P&G customers; meaning that some P&G customers were likely to pay more slowly, if at all. This increases predicted accounts receivable relative to sales. Accordingly, Morgan Stanley analysts forecasted a slight increase in P&G's ratio of accounts receivables to sales for 2011 quarters, but returning to the FY2011 level of ~7.7% of projected sales by year-end 2012. Using 7.7% accounts receivable-to-sales and forecasted sales of $86,357 million, we forecast accounts receivable of $6,649 million ($86,357 million × 7.7%). The 7.7% equates to an average collection period of 28.1 days (0.077 × 365 days).

Forecasting Inventories   Morgan Stanley analysts forecast inventories as a percent of COGS rather than as a percent of sales. Either approach is fine and does not materially affect the forecasts as long as the method is used consistently. The motivation for use of COGS is that inventories are stated at cost, not at retail. As a result, many analysts use COGS to forecast inventories and the related accounts payable. *(In the assignments, we forecast inventories as a percent of sales so that all balance sheet items are forecasted based on the same basis.)* P&G's inventories increased in 2011 from 16.8% of COGS

EXHIBIT 11.7   Morgan Stanley Forecasted Balance Sheet Percents

	A	B	C	AQ	AV	AW	AX	AY	AZ	BA
1	Procter & Gamble Co (PG)									
2				FY2010	FY2011	Sep-11 E	Dec-11 E	Mar-12 E	Jun-12 E	FY2012E
161	Cash % of Sales			3.6%	3.4%	2.9%	2.8%	3.0%	2.9%	2.9%
162	AR % of Sales			6.8%	7.6%	7.8%	7.9%	7.9%	7.6%	7.7%
163	AR Days			24.7	27.7	28.3	28.7	29.0	27.8	28.1
164	Inventories % COGS			16.8%	18.1%	18.9%	18.1%	19.1%	17.2%	17.9%
165	Inventory Days			61.5	66.1	68.9	66.2	69.9	62.6	65.2
166	Deferred Inc Tax Assets % Sales			1.3%	1.4%	1.6%	1.6%	1.6%	1.6%	1.6%
167	Other CA % Sales			4.0%	5.3%	4.8%	4.5%	4.8%	4.5%	4.5%
168	Capex, net of dispositions			-3,067.0	-3,306.0	-663.7	-874.9	-938.8	-1,295.1	-3,772.5
169	Addition to PPE as % Sales			3.9%	4.0%	3.1%	4.0%	4.5%	5.9%	4.4%
170	Depreciation % opening PPE			16.0%	14.7%	14.3%	14.3%	14.1%	14.3%	14.3%
171	Depreciation % Net PPE			16.2%	13.3%	3.6%	3.6%	3.5%	3.5%	13.8%
172	AP % COGS			19.1%	19.7%	17.0%	15.1%	15.9%	18.3%	19.1%
173	AP Days			69.8	71.8	62.2	55.2	58.2	66.8	69.6
174	Accrued and Other liabilities % Sales			10.8%	11.3%	11.6%	11.4%	12.1%	11.0%	11.1%
175	Deferred Inc Tax Liabilities % Sales			13.8%	13.4%	12.9%	12.4%	13.2%	12.7%	12.8%
176	Other Liabilities			12.9%	12.1%	11.8%	10.9%	11.7%	10.9%	11.0%
177	Dividends Paid			$1.80	$1.97	$0.53	$0.53	$0.53	$0.57	$2.15
178										
179	Total Debt			29,832.0	32,014.0	32,231.7	32,884.1	32,271.4	31,949.6	31,949.6
180	Cash			2,879.0	2,768.0	2,500.0	2,500.0	2,500.0	2,500.0	2,500.0
181	**Net Debt**			**26,953.0**	**29,246.0**	**29,731.7**	**30,384.1**	**29,771.4**	**29,449.6**	**29,449.6**
182	Interest Rate on Debt			2.8%	2.7%	2.6%	2.6%	2.6%	2.6%	2.6%
183	Interest Rate on Cash					1.5%	1.5%	1.5%	1.5%	1.5%
184	**Net Debt/LTM EBITDA**			**1.4x**	**1.5x**	**1.6x**	**1.6x**	**1.5x**	**1.5x**	**1.5x**
186	**Capital Employed**			**109,483.0**	**118,274.0**	**119,312.2**	**119,958.7**	**119,777.8**	**118,945.0**	**118,945.0**

to 18.1% of COGS. In the MD&A section of its 10-K, P&G's management attributes the inventory increase to:

> higher commodity costs, business growth and increased stock levels in advance of initiatives and sourcing changes. Inventory days on hand increased by five days due to the impact of foreign exchange, higher commodity costs and increased safety stock levels.

Morgan Stanley analysts forecast a slight easing of these pressures to yield an annual level of 17.9% of COGS for FY2012 (they estimate inventories on a quarterly basis as: Quarterly COGS × 4 × Inventory %COGS; the year-end estimate, then, is the 4Q estimate, and the 17.9% is the ending 4Q inventory estimate divided by the annual COGS estimate). The 17.9% of COGS equates to an inventory days on hand of 65.3 (0.179 × 365 days, yielding a 0.1 rounding difference from the spreadsheet), which is down from 66.1 days at year-end 2011.

To be consistent with our approach of estimating balance sheet items in relation to the sales estimate, we forecast inventories at an equivalent rate of 8.6% of sales (computed from Morgan Stanley's estimate of ending inventories of $7,557.2 million divided by analysts' estimates of annual sales of $87,754.5 million—numbers from the FY2012E column of the forecasted balance sheet and income statement on pages 6 and 7 of the Morgan Stanley analysts' report in Appendix 11A). This results in forecasted inventories of $7,427 million ($86,357 million × 8.6%).

Forecasting Deferred Income Tax Assets and Other Current Assets   Morgan Stanley analysts forecast a slight increase in deferred tax assets to 1.6% of sales (up from 1.4% of sales in FY2011) and a reduction of other current assets from 5.3% of sales to 4.5% of sales. Companies generally provide little information about these accounts in their footnote and MD&A disclosures. We assume a continuation of these percentages in FY2012.

Forecasting Capital Expenditures, PPE, and Accumulated Depreciation   Capital expenditures (CAPEX) are often a large cash outflow and a major component of free cash flow, which is the focus of cash-flow-based equity valuation models. (Free cash flow is defined in Module 12 as [NOPAT − Increase in NOA] and is also defined in finance literature as [Net cash flow from operating activities − CAPEX].) CAPEX is used in forecasting PPE (gross), where Forecasted PPE (gross) = Actual PPE (gross) + Forecasted CAPEX. (We typically do not forecast dispositions of PPE unless they are specifically identified by management in the MD&A section of the 10-K or other source.) P&G reported CAPEX as a percent of sales for FY2010 of 3.9% and for FY2011 of 4.0%. In its meetings with analysts, P&G provided guidance for CAPEX as a percentage of sales of 4% to 5% of sales, and Morgan Stanley forecasts CAPEX at 4.4% of sales in their forecast. Based on our forecasted sales of $86,357 million, CAPEX is projected to be $3,800 million (computed as $86,357 million × 4.4%).

The forecast of net PPE is computed as: Beginning-year PPE, net + Forecasted CAPEX − Forecasted Depreciation. Morgan Stanley analysts combine amortization with depreciation; thus, for consistency, we will do the same. Depreciation and amortization are typically estimated by the percentage of reported depreciation and amortization expense (often reported in the statement of cash flows if not disclosed on the income statement) as a percentage of beginning-year PPE, net. This is the approach used by Morgan Stanley analysts. P&G's depreciation and amortization are 14.7% of the beginning-year balance for FY2011 ($2,838 million/$19,244 million). However, Morgan Stanley analysts forecast a slight decrease in that percentage to 14.3% for FY2012 and we use that rate in our forecast. Using the FY2011 net PPE of $21,293, our forecast of depreciation and amortization for FY2012 is $3,045 million ($21,293 million × 14.3%) and our forecast of FY2012 net PPE is $22,048 million as computed here:

Actual net PPE for FY2011	$21,293 million	
Add: CAPEX	3,800 million	($86,357 sales × 4.4% CAPEX-to-sales)
Less: Depreciation and amortization	(3,045) million	($21,293 PPE, net for FY2011 × 14.3%)
Forecasted net PPE for FY2012	$22,048 million	

We applied all amortization expense to net PPE as PPE assets are sometimes amortized as well as depreciated. Often amortization expense relates to intangible assets (see next section). In that case, we apportion depreciation and amortization between depreciable and intangible assets if we have sufficient information.

Forecasting Goodwill and Other Intangible Assets and Amortization Goodwill and other intangible assets arise mainly in connection with acquisitions of other companies. Unless an acquisition is pending at year-end, and we have sufficient information about its financial impact, we forecast no change for goodwill and other intangibles. Goodwill is not amortized, but some other intangible assets are (see Module 7). If we can identify the intangible assets that are amortized and can estimate their amortization expense, we can forecast that expense and reduce the intangible assets accordingly like we did for depreciable assets above. We forecast no change in these intangible assets in this case.

Forecasting Other Noncurrent Assets Other noncurrent assets are assumed to be part of operating assets unless information suggests otherwise. Since we have no information to suggest otherwise, we forecast no change in other noncurrent assets.

Forecasting Nonoperating Assets

This section forecasts nonoperating assets for P&G. Generally, we use the no-change forecast model for nonoperating assets.

Forecasting Cash Our forecasting process assumes that the cash on the balance sheet reflects an economically appropriate balance that we forecast similarly for the next fiscal year. Procter & Gamble's 2011 fiscal year-end cash balance is $2,768 million (3.4% of sales), down from $2,879 million (3.6% of sales) in the prior year. We assume 3.4% of sales in our forecast, resulting in a forecasted cash balance of $2,936 million ($86,357 million × 3.4%) for FY2012.

Forecasting Investment Securities The no-change forecast model applies to marketable securities. For P&G, it does not report marketable securities. We adjust the level of marketable securities (cash in this case) or short-term debt in Step 4 when we balance the balance sheet.

BUSINESS INSIGHT **Does Separately Forecasting Cash and Securities Matter?**

Our forecasting process, and that of the Morgan Stanley analysts, is to forecast a cash balance and adjust the level of investment securities or short-term debt to balance the balance sheet. We assume that cash consists of cash equivalents and then forecast interest income on the cash balance at the same rate as that for investment securities. Both cash and marketable securities are treated as nonoperating assets. This means it makes no difference whether we assume a larger balance for cash and a correspondingly smaller balance for investment securities or whether we assume a smaller balance for cash and a larger balance for investment securities. However, we see in recent years that cash balances have ballooned as companies face economic uncertainty. Still, we are indifferent as to whether that excess liquidity is reported as cash or as investment securities as they are both nonoperating assets. We see in the next module that changes in both cash and securities increase or decrease the value of a company dollar-for-dollar. Our focus is on net operating assets (NOA), which impact company value to a much greater extent. Bottom line: do not focus on the mix between cash and securities.

Summary of Asset Forecasts To this point, we have forecasted all of P&G's operating and non-operating assets. Following the forecast of liabilities and equity in the next section, we adjust the balance of investment securities or short-term debt to balance the balance sheet. This is Step 4.

Forecasting Operating Liabilities

This section describes the process of forecasting operating liabilities for P&G.

Forecasting Accounts Payable Morgan Stanley forecasts accounts payable as a percentage of COGS. The rationale is that inventories, which drive most accounts payable, are reported at wholesale cost and not retail. Another common method is to forecast accounts payable as a percentage of sales. Either method results in reasonable forecasts if consistently applied. For P&G, accounts payable as a percent of COGS increased from 19.1% in 2010 to 19.7% in 2011. P&G explains this increase as follows:

> Accounts payable, accrued and other liabilities increased primarily due to increased expenditures to support business growth, primarily related to the increased marketing investments.

Morgan Stanley forecasts a reduction of accounts payable as a percentage of COGS from 19.7% in FY2011 to 19.1% in FY2012. This corresponds to the reduction in inventory quantities previously discussed. As reported in Exhibit 11.7, Morgan Stanley's forecasts imply a decrease in accounts payable days outstanding from 71.8 (~19.7% × 365) to 69.6 days (~19.1% × 365). Consistent with our approach of forecasting balance sheet items in relation to forecasted sales, we forecast accounts payable at an equivalent rate of 9.2% of sales (using Morgan Stanley's estimate of accounts payable of $8,059.6 million divided by analysts' estimates of annual sales of $87,754.5 million—see the analysts' report in the appendix), resulting in an estimate for FY2012 accounts payable of $7,945 million ($86,357 million × 9.2%).

Forecasting Accrued and Other Liabilities Accruals as a percent of sales increased from 10.8% in 2010 to 11.3% in 2011. Footnotes reveal that P&G's accruals relate primarily to marketing and compensation expenses, although a large component is classified as "other." Morgan Stanley forecasts this account to remain fairly constant as a percentage of sales, decreasing slightly from 11.3% of sales to 11.1% of sales; similarly, we use 11.1% in our forecast.

Forecasting Taxes Payable Because taxes payable relate directly to tax expense, we prefer to express taxes payable as a percentage of tax expense for forecasting purposes. P&G does not separately identify income taxes payable on its balance sheet. Hence, this account is not included in our forecasts directly, but is forecasted as part of another account. When we encounter a balance sheet with taxes payable as a line item, we suggest forecasting that account using the historical percentage of taxes payable to tax expense.

Forecasting Deferred Income Tax Liabilities Deferred tax assets and deferred tax liabilities generally relate to the level of business activity. Accordingly, we can make a case to forecast these accounts as a percentage of sales. Indeed, Morgan Stanley follows this practice. That is, forecasted deferred tax liabilities are 12.8% of sales, down slightly from 13.4% of sales in FY2011.

Forecasting Other Noncurrent Liabilities Other noncurrent liabilities for P&G primarily relate to pension and other post-retirement benefits. We reasonably assume that these obligations grow with the size of the business. Following this notion, Morgan Stanley forecasts these liabilities as a percentage of sales. For P&G, these liabilities decreased as a percentage of sales, from 12.9% in FY2010 to 12.1% in FY2011. We, like Morgan Stanley, forecast a continuation of this decline to a level of 11.0% of sales for FY2012.

Forecasting Nonoperating Liabilities and Equity

This section forecasts nonoperating liabilities and equity for P&G.

Forecasting Debt Due Within One Year P&G discloses the following table for its debt due within one year:

June 30, in millions	2011	2010
Debt due within one year		
Current portion of long-term debt	$2,994	$ 564
Commercial paper	6,950	7,838
Other	37	70
Total	$9,981	$8,472

Of the $9,981 million total debt due within one year, $2,994 million represents contractual maturities of long-term debt and the $6,987 remainder represents other short-term borrowings. We assume that all contractual maturities of long-term debt will be repaid. Thus, we forecast the $2,994 million to be repaid. For the remaining short-term debt we assume no-change (Step 4 revisits this). Commercial paper represents short-term unsecured borrowings that are typically refinanced by newly issued commercial paper and are not repaid at maturity. Thus, we forecast $6,987 as short-term debt before any current portion of long-term debt. As we show below, the FY2012 current maturities of long-term debt are $3,839 million and, thus, we forecast total debt due within one year as $10,826 million ($6,987 million + $3,839 million).

Forecasting Long-Term Debt P&G's balance sheet reports long-term debt of $22,033. We use the no-change method to forecast long-term debt (and potentially modify this with optional Step 4). Companies are required to disclose the maturities of long-term debt for each of the five years subsequent to the statement date. Following is the disclosure by P&G in its long-term debt footnote:

Long-term debt maturities during the next five years are as follows:

June 30	2012	2013	2014	2015	2016
Debt maturities	$2,994	$3,839	$2,229	$3,021	$2,300

In our forecast for 2012, we classify the amount due in 2013, $3,839, as current maturities of long-term debt, and the remaining balance of $18,194 is forecasted as long-term debt. The $3,839 current maturities of long-term debt are, then, added to short-term debt as we discuss in the preceding section.

Forecasting Equity Accounts Prior to Step 4, we forecast FY2012 equity items with no change, with two exceptions. The first exception is retained earnings, which are increased by forecasted net income and are reduced by forecasted dividends. There are two approaches to forecasting dividends and either is acceptable:

1. Forecast dollar amount of dividends per share and multiply by the forecasted number of shares outstanding (and not the average number of shares outstanding as reported in the EPS calculations), or
2. Forecast a dividend payout ratio (dividends / net income) and multiply this dividend payout ratio by forecasted net income.

Morgan Stanley utilizes the first approach and forecasts dividends per share of $2.15 for the year, a 9.1% increase over the $1.97 per share paid in FY2011 (dividends per share for FY2011 increased by 9.4% over FY2010; so, this increase of 9.1% seems reasonable).

Morgan Stanley forecasts the number of shares outstanding after considering the effects of anticipated share issuances under employee stock option plans and share repurchases in treasury stock, resulting in estimated shares outstanding for FY2012 of 2,944.6 million.[2] Multiplying for forecasted dividends per share of $2.15 by the estimated number of shares outstanding of 2,944.6 million yields a forecasted dollar amount of dividends paid of $6,330.9 million. This is in line with guidance given by P&G of approximately $6 billion in dividends from its meeting with analysts.

Our initial forecast for ending FY2012 retained earnings is $76,509 million, computed as follows:

$70,682 million beginning retained earnings
+ 12,158 million forecasted net income
− 6,331 million forecasted dividends
_____
$76,509 million ending retained earnings

This forecast will likely change in Step 4 once we forecast the income (expense) related to new investments (borrowing), thus affecting our estimate of net income.

The second exception includes share repurchases (treasury stock) that are announced or planned by a company. In its Barclays capital conference, P&G provided the following slide that indicates its intentions to repurchase about $6 billion for treasury stock in the 2012 fiscal year:

Business Outlook
Cash Generation and Usage

Free Cash Flow Productivity:	+/− 90%
Capital Spending:	4% to 5% of sales
Share Repurchase:	~$6 Billion
Dividends:	~$6 Billion

This slide reflects continuation of P&G's share repurchase program that has resulted in the repurchase of $19.4 billion of treasury stock over the prior three years. Consistent with PG guidance, we forecast the purchase of treasury stock amounting to $6,000 million in 2012.

STEP 4: ADJUST FORECASTED STATEMENTS

Our (initial) forecasted balance sheet yields total assets of $139,419 million and total liabilities and equity of $134,932 million. Because total assets exceed the total of liabilities and equity, additional financing is required and we assume an increase of $4,487 million of short-term debt to balance. Another option would have been to reduce short-term investments, but P&G did not report short-term investments on its FY2011 balance sheet.) (Note some circularity here in that adjusting debt results in changes in interest expense that results in additional debt, and so on. Morgan Stanley allows for one

---

[2] Computation of shares outstanding requires estimates of anticipated share issuances and repurchases. We do not know the specific inputs that Morgan Stanley used in their computation, but can speculate that the share issuances relate to the exercise of employee stock options (footnotes usually disclose the number of shares issued for the current and prior two years). Share repurchases might be estimated by guidance provided by the company for the dollar amount of anticipated share repurchases divided by an estimate of the anticipated share price for the coming year. Thus, expected dollar amount of dividends is then: Estimate of ending basic shares outstanding (Beginning shares outstanding + Share issuances − Share repurchases) × Expected dividends per share (often disclosed by a company in guidance to analysts).

adjustment as we describe above, which is the $4,487 million of additional debt in our example and the related interest expense. Given the estimates involved in forecasting, additional precision of further iterations is unnecessary.) Had total liabilities and equity been greater than total assets, we could have reduced short-term debt or increased short-term investments to balance.[3]

Adjust Forecasted Income Statement: Nonoperating Expenses

Given our estimates of debt as a result of the "balancing" adjustment in Step 4, we can now finish our forecasts for the income statement (which we presented in Exhibit 11.4). Specifically, we can now forecast nonoperating expense (and revenue), compute pretax income, forecast tax expense, and compute net income. This section describes the process for forecasting those remaining items on the income statement.

Forecasting Interest Expense and "Other"   P&G's FY2010 interest expense of $831 million implies a 2.7% rate of interest based on average outstanding interest-bearing debt for that year of $30,923 million ([$29,832 million + $32,014 million]/2). This average interest rate was slightly less than the 2.8% rate reported for FY2010. Morgan Stanley analysts forecast a slight decline for FY2012 to 2.6% in their report (see Exhibit 11.7), and we also use 2.6% to forecast interest expense for FY2012.

Of the long-term debt outstanding as of the end of FY2011, footnotes reveal that $2,994 million is scheduled to mature during FY2012. Given our forecasted $4,487 million increase in short-term debt, then our forecast for interest expense must be adjusted accordingly (we would similarly increase interest income if we had projected an increase in short-term investments). This anticipated repayment of $2,994 million and borrowing of $4,487 million, assuming borrowing and repayment ratably over the year, results in a forecasted interest expense of $852 million ([$32,014 million + {−$2,994 million + $4,487 million}/2] × 2.6%). (Our amount is slightly higher than the Morgan Stanley estimate of $830 million, which they obtain from a detailed analysis of the debt payments and borrowings, vis-à-vis the simple average we assumed.)

Other nonoperating income for FY2011 of $202 million includes interest income on short-term investments (primarily cash balances invested in overnight investments) and net gains on divestitures. Since we are not forecasting any acquisitions or divestitures, nonoperating income is lower for FY2012. Morgan Stanley forecasts an investment rate of 1.5% on available cash balances (assumed to be approximately $2,900 million), which results in $44 million; alternatively, one can use an average of the beginning and ending balances ([$2,768 million + $2,936 million]/2 × 1.5%), which we demonstrate when computing the two-year-ahead forecasts in Exhibit 11.10.

Forecasting Income Taxes   Given our forecast of interest expense, we obtain a forecasted pretax income of $16,032 million. Our general method to forecast income taxes is to predict little change, if any, in a company's effective tax rate, *assuming* it is within reasonable limits and absent the company disclosing substantial transitory tax items in the reconciliation of the effective tax rate footnote or an anticipated rate change. Morgan Stanley forecasts a 25.0% effective tax rate for 2012–14, within the range of 25.7% and 23.5% that P&G reported for FY2010 and FY2011, respectively, and we use a 25% forecasted tax rate as well. Consequently, our forecast of tax expense is $4,008 million (computed as $16,032 million of pretax income × 25% forecasted tax rate).

Net Income   The resulting forecasted net income is $12,024 million for FY2012, or $4.08 per diluted share. This forecast is slightly below P&G's EPS guidance for FY2012 of $4.17–$4.33 per share, but greater than the $3.93 per diluted share reported in the P&G 10-K for FY2011.

Adjust Forecasted Balance Sheet

The forecasted balance sheet and the revised forecasted income statement for Procter & Gamble is in Exhibits 11.8A and 11.8B. We show the FY2011 balance for each account and the computations required to obtain the forecasted FY2012 balance, including the updated retained earnings computation reflecting the net income computed.

---

[3] When adjusting the balance sheet to balance, we must take care to not inadvertently alter a company's financial leverage. Recall that companies seek to maintain optimal levels of debt and equity to achieve a desired credit rating for their debt, among other objectives. Thus, we must maintain the past debt-to-equity relation within reasonable limits when balancing the forecasted balance sheet. For example, if our decision is to retire debt or to repurchase common stock, we should do it so that the historical debt-to-equity relation is roughly maintained.

EXHIBIT 11.8A   Forecasted Balance Sheet for P&G

($ millions)	2011	Forecast Assumptions	2012 Est.
Current Assets			
Cash and cash equivalents	$ 2,768	86,357 × 3.4%	$ 2,936
Accounts receivable...........................	6,275	86,357 × 7.7%	6,649
Inventories	7,379	86,357 × 8.6%	7,427
Deferred income taxes........................	1,140	86,357 × 1.6%	1,382
Prepaid expenses and other current assets........	4,408	86,357 × 4.5%	3,886
Total current assets	21,970	subtotal	22,280
Net property, plant and equipment	21,293	21,293 + 3,800 − 3,045	22,048
Goodwill and other intangible assets			
Goodwill...................................	57,562	no change	57,562
Trademarks and other intangible assets, net	32,620	no change	32,620
Net goodwill and other intangible assets...........	90,182	subtotal	90,182
Other noncurrent assets......................	4,909	no change	4,909
Total assets.................................	$138,354	subtotal	$139,419
Current Liabilities			
Accounts payable.............................	$ 8,022	86,357 × 9.2%	$ 7,945
Accrued and other liabilities....................	9,290	86,357 × 11.1%	9,586
Short-term debt (newly issued)	0	plug	4,621
Debt due within one year	9,981	9,981 − 2,994 + 3,839	10,826
Total current liabilities.........................	27,293	subtotal	32,978
Long-term debt	22,033	22,033 − 3,839	18,194
Deferred income taxes........................	11,070	86,357 × 12.8%	11,054
Other noncurrent liabilities	9,957	86,357 × 11.0%	9,499
Total liabilities...............................	70,353	subtotal	71,725
Shareholders' equity			
Preferred stock..............................	1,234	no change	1,234
Non-voting Class B preferred stock..............	0	no change	0
Common stock...............................	4,008	no change	4,008
Additional paid-in capital	62,405	no change	62,405
Reserve for ESOP debt retirement...............	(1,357)	no change	(1,357)
Accumulated other comprehensive income (loss)....	(2,054)	no change	(2,054)
Treasury stock	(67,278)	(67,278) − 6,000	(73,278)
Retained earnings	70,682	70,682 + 12,024 − 6,331	76,375
Noncontrolling interest........................	361	no change	361
Total shareholders' equity	68,001	subtotal	67,694
Total liabilities and shareholders' equity............	$138,354	subtotal	$139,419

EXHIBIT 11.8B   Revised Forecasted Income Statement for P&G

($ millions)	2011		Forecast Assumptions	Revised 2012 Est.	
Net sales..............................	$82,559	100.0%	$82,559 × 1.046	$86,357	100.0%
Cost of products sold....................	40,768	49.4%	$86,357 × 49.9%	43,092	49.9%
Selling, general and administrative expense ..	25,973	31.5%	$86,357 × 30.6%	26,425	30.6%
Operating income.......................	15,818	19.2%	subtotal	16,840	19.5%
Interest expense.......................	831	1.0%	(see computation in text)	852	1.0%
Other nonoperating income (expense), net ...	202	0.2%	(see computation in text)	44	0.1%
Earnings before income taxes	15,189	18.4%	subtotal	16,032	18.6%
Income taxes on continuing operations......	3,392	4.1%	$16,032 × 25.0%	4,008	4.6%
Net earnings...........................	$11,797	14.3%	subtotal	$12,024	13.9%

FORECASTING STATEMENT OF CASH FLOWS

We forecast the statement of cash flows using the forecasted income statement and forecasted balance sheet. We refer to the historical statement of cash flows mainly to check the reasonableness of our forecasts. We draw on the mechanics behind the preparation of the statement of cash flows, which we

LO4 Forecast the statement of cash flows.

discuss in Modules 2 and 3 and Appendix B. Specifically, once we have forecasts of the balance sheet and income statement, we can compute the forecasted statement of cash flows just as we would its historical counterpart.

Process of Forecasting the Statement of Cash Flows

To illustrate the forecasting of the statement of cash flows we again turn to Procter & Gamble. Given its forecasted balance sheet in Exhibit 11.8A and its forecasted income statement in Exhibit 11.8B, we prepare its forecasted statement of cash flows using the procedures for preparing the statement of cash flows explained in Modules 2 and 3 and Appendix B. Our forecasted statement of cash flows is in Exhibit 11.9.

EXHIBIT 11.9	Forecasted Statement of Cash Flows for P&G	
($ millions)	Forecast Assumptions	2012 Est.
Operating activities		
Net income...	via forecasted income stmt.	$12,024
Add: Depreciation and amortization......................	21,293 × 14.3%	3,045
Change in accounts receivable	6,275 − 6,649	(374)
Change in inventories.................................	7,379 − 7,427	(48)
Change in deferred income taxes	1,140 − 1,382	(242)
Change in prepaid expenses and other current..............	4,408 − 3,886	522
Change in accounts payable	7,945 − 8,022	(77)
Change in accrued compensation and other liabilities	9,586 − 9,290	296
Change in deferred income taxes	11,054 − 11,070	(16)
Change in other noncurrent liabilities.....................	9,499 − 9,957	(458)
Net cash from operating activities	subtotal	14,672
Investing activities		
Capital expenditures	86,357 × 4.4%	(3,800)
Net cash from investing activities.......................	subtotal	(3,800)
Financing activities		
Dividends..	computed as dividends per share	(6,331)
Increase in short-term debt	plug in balance sheet above	4,621
Decrease in long-term debt	current maturities via footnote	(2,994)
Purchase of treasury shares...........................	PG guidance to analysts	(6,000)
Net cash from financing activities	subtotal	(10,704)
Net change in cash..................................	subtotal	168
Beginning cash.....................................	from 2011 balance sheet	2,768
Ending cash	subtotal	$ 2,936

Forecasting Operating Activities We begin with the operating section and the forecasted net earnings of $12,024 million, which we compute above. We, then, adjust net earnings for operating expenses and revenues that do not impact cash, and for changes in current assets and liabilities. For the first category we have depreciation and amortization, which are in SG&A expense and are added back in the statement of cash flows because they do not use cash. (Computations for these expenses are explained in our discussion of forecasting capital expenditures and PPE, and forecasting goodwill and other intangibles.) (Appendix 11A shows that Morgan Stanley also forecasts $422.3 million of compensation expense related to stock-based compensation as an add-back to net income, as it is a noncash expense; we are not privy to data that analysts had in making this estimate and do not include it in our forecasts.)

For the second category we have four current assets and four current liabilities whose cash-flow effects we must consider. For example, the forecasted increase in accounts receivable reduces the available cash. We apply this logic to each of the other current assets and liabilities. Thus, net cash flow from operating activities is forecasted at $14,672 million for 2012.

Forecasting Investing Activities The forecasted investing section reports cash expenditures for short- and long-term investments as well as the purchase and sale of long-term operating assets. The only item for P&G is the forecasted $3,800 million outflow for capital expenditures (CAPEX). We discuss the computation of this amount in the section on forecasting capital expenditures and PPE, above. The remaining long-term assets are intangible and other nonoperating assets and we assumed no changes in those assets except for amortization of intangibles. Had we forecasted other changes in those assets, we would include the cash flow effects in the investing section.

Forecasting Financing Activities The forecasted financing section includes forecasted items that impact long-term nonoperating liabilities and equity. We forecast a reduction of long-term debt in the amount of $2,994 million relating to its contractual maturities. Those maturities are reported as part of debt due within one year on the 2011 balance sheet and we assume that all contractual obligations are paid as agreed.

This concludes our initial forecasts of the financial statements for Procter & Gamble. Appendix 11A reproduces an actual analyst forecast of P&G's financial statements from Morgan Stanley, which applies the percent of revenues approach that we describe. (Module 12 estimates the value of P&G's stock using our forecasts and compares our estimate to one that Oppenheimer develops from its forecasts and valuation model.)

ADDITIONAL FORECASTING ISSUES

Reassessing Financial Statement Forecasts

After preparing the forecasted financial statements, it is useful to reassess whether they are reasonable in light of current economic and company conditions. This task is subjective and benefits from the forecaster's knowledge of company, industry, and economic factors. Many analysts and managers prepare "what-if" forecasted financial statements. Specifically, they change key assumptions, such as the forecasted sales growth or key cost ratios and then recompute the forecasted financial statements. These alternative forecasting scenarios indicate the sensitivity of a set of predicted outcomes to different assumptions about future economic conditions. Such sensitivity estimates can be useful for setting contingency plans and in identifying areas of vulnerability for company performance and condition.

Multiyear Forecasting of Financial Statements

Many business decisions require forecasted financial statements for more than one year ahead. For example, managerial and capital budgeting, security valuation, and strategic analyses all benefit from reliable multiyear forecasts. Module 12 uses multiyear forecasts of financial results to estimate stock price for investment decisions.

LO5 Prepare multiyear forecasts of financial statements.

Forecasting the Income Statement We forecast two years ahead using the assumptions for our one-year-ahead forecasts and adjust those assumptions as necessary. To illustrate, we forecast P&G's 2013 sales as $90,329 million, computed as our forecasted FY2012 sales of $86,357 million × 1.046, the growth rate we used for FY2012. Operating expenses are forecasted from this sales level using the methodology we describe earlier for one-year-ahead forecasts. As before, we compute nonoperating income (expense) after we estimate nonoperating liabilities and, given our estimates of nonoperating revenue (expense), we compute pretax income, tax expense and net income.

Forecasting the Balance Sheet Assuming a continuation of the percent-of-revenues relation for current assets and liabilities, we can forecast current assets and current liabilities applying the same methodology used for one-year-ahead forecasts. For example, FY2013 accounts receivable are forecasted as $6,955 million, computed as $90,329 million × 7.7% (the same percentage we used to forecast FY2012 receivables). Similarly, we forecast CAPEX at $3,974 million ($90,329 × 4.4%) and depreciation expense at $3,153 million ($22,048 in FY2012 PPE, net × 14.3% depreciation rate used previously). Forecasted net PPE is, then, equal to $22,869 million (computed as $22,048 million + $3,974 million − $3,153 million).

Operating liabilities are estimated using the same percent of estimated sales that we use in FY2012. The long-term debt footnote (presented above) reveals that contractual maturities of long-term debt for FY2013 are $2,229 million, and we forecast long-term debt at $15,965 million ($18,194 million − current maturities of $2,229 million). As before, we assume that contractual maturities of long-term debt that were scheduled for FY2012 have been paid. Consequently, we forecast debt due within one year (which includes current maturities of long-term debt) at $9,216 million ($10,826 million for FY2012 − $3,839 in prior-year current maturities + $2,229 in FY2013 current maturities).

In the stockholders' equity section, we forecast a continuation of P&G's stated objective to repurchase $6,000 million of treasury stock. Retained earnings is updated for forecasted net income and decreased by forecasted dividends. For the latter, we highlight the alternative method in this example, that is, to forecast dividends as a percent of forecasted net income. For P&G, our dividend forecast for FY2012 is $6,333 or 52.7% of forecasted net income. Applying this percentage to forecasted net income for FY2013, yields dividends of $6,633 million ($12,587 million × 52.7%).

Adjust Forecasted Statements Our initial balance sheet yields estimated total assets of $141,264 million and total liabilities and equity of $132,664 million, indicating a financing need of $8,600 million. This represents an increase of $3,979 million over the $4,621 million we forecasted for FY2012.

Our estimate of interest expense begins with our FY2012 forecast for total interest-bearing debt of $33,641 million ($4,621 million + $10,826 million + $18,194 million). This debt will decrease by scheduled payments of $3,839 million and increase by new borrowings of $3,979 million. Assuming that these payments and borrowings (netting to an increase of $140 million) occur ratably over the year and that the borrowing rate continues at 2.6%, our estimate for interest expense is $876 million ([$33,641 million + ($140 million/2)] × 2.6%). And, given our estimated cash balance of $3,071 million and a 1.5% investment rate, our estimate of interest income is $45 million ([$2,936 million + $3,071 million]/2 × 1.5%).

Our forecasted income statement and balance sheet is presented in Exhibit 11.10 (FY2012 forecasts are shown in the first column). Given our forecasted nonoperating revenue (expense), we project pretax income at $16,783 million. Assuming a continuation of the 25% effective tax rate, we forecast tax expense of $4,196 million ($16,783 × 25%) and net income of $12,587 million. Exhibit 11.10 also reports the two-year-ahead forecasted statement of cash flows which is prepared using the forecasted FY2013 and FY2012 balance sheets and our forecasted FY2013 income statement. The Morgan Stanley forecast spreadsheet which we reproduce in our Appendix 11A provides forecasts through FY2014 using similar methodology.

EXHIBIT 11.10	Forecasted Two-Year-Ahead Financial Statements for P&G		
Income Statement ($ millions)	**2012 Est.**	**Forecast Assumptions**	**2013 Est.**
Net sales	$86,357	$86,357 × 1.046	$90,329
Cost of products sold.	43,092	90,329 × 49.9%	45,074
Selling, general and administrative expense	26,425	90,329 × 30.6%	27,641
Operating income.	16,840	subtotal	17,614
Interest expense.	852	computed	876
Other nonoperating income/(expense), net	44	computed	45
Earnings before income taxes	16,032	subtotal	16,783
Income taxes on continuing operations.	4,008	16,782 × 25.0%	4,196
Net earnings.	$12,024	subtotal	$12,587
Balance Sheet ($ millions)	**2012 Est.**	**Forecast Assumptions**	**2013 Est.**
Current assets			
Cash and cash equivalents	$2,936	90,329 × 3.4%	$3,071
Accounts receivable.	6,649	90,329 × 7.7%	6,955
Inventories	7,427	90,329 × 8.6%	7,768
Deferred income taxes.	1,382	90,329 × 1.6%	1,445
Prepaid expenses and other current assets.	3,886	90,329 × 4.5%	4,065
Total current assets	22,280	subtotal	23,304
Net property, plant and equipment	22,048	22,048 + 3,974 − 3,153	22,869
Goodwill and other intangible assets			
Goodwill.	57,562	no change	57,562
Trademarks and other intangible assets, net.	32,620	no change	32,620
Net goodwill and other intangible assets.	90,182	no change	90,182
Other noncurrent assets.	4,909	no change	4,909
Total assets.	$139,419	subtotal	$141,264

continued

continued from prior page

Balance Sheet—continued ($ millions)	2012 Est.	Forecast Assumptions	2013 Est.
Current liabilities			
Accounts payable.	$ 7,945	90,329 × 9.2%	$ 8,310
Accrued and other liabilities.	9,586	90,329 × 11.1%	10,027
Short-term debt	4,621	plug	8,600
Debt due within one year	10,826	10,826 − 3,839 + 2,229	9,216
Total current liabilities.	32,978	subtotal	36,153
Long-term debt	18,194	18,194 − 2,229	15,965
Deferred income taxes	11,054	90,329 × 12.8%	11,562
Other noncurrent liabilities	9,499	90,329 × 11.0%	9,936
Total liabilities	71,725	subtotal	73,616
Shareholders' equity			
Preferred stock	1,234	no change	1,234
Non–Voting Class B preferred stock	0	no change	0
Common stock.	4,008	no change	4,008
Additional paid-in capital	62,405	no change	62,405
Reserve for ESOP debt retirement.	(1,357)	no change	(1,357)
Accumulated other comprehensive income (loss)	(2,054)	no change	(2,054)
Treasury stock	(73,278)	(73,278) − 6,000	(79,278)
Retained earnings	76,375	76,375 + 12,587 − 6,633	82,329
Noncontrolling interest.	361	no change	361
Total shareholders' equity	67,694	subtotal	67,648
Total liabilities and shareholders' equity	$139,419	subtotal	$141,264

Statement of Cash Flows	2012 Est.	Forecast Assumptions	2013 Est.
Operating activities			
Net income.	$12,024	via forecasted income stmt.	$12,587
Add: Depreciation and amortization.	3,045	22,048 × 14.3%	3,153
Change in accounts receivable	(374)	6,649 − 6,955	(306)
Change in inventories.	(48)	7,427 − 7,768	(341)
Change in deferred income taxes	(242)	1,382 − 1,445	(63)
Change in prepaid expenses and other current.	522	3,886 − 4,065	(179)
Change in accounts payable	(77)	8,310 − 7,945	365
Change in accrued compensation and other liabilities	296	10,027 − 9,586	441
Change in deferred income taxes	(16)	11,562 − 11,054	508
Change in other noncurrent liabilities.	(458)	9,936 − 9,499	437
Net cash from operating activities	14,672	subtotal	16,602
Investing activities			
Capital expenditures	(3,800)	90,329 × 4.4%	(3,974)
Net cash from investing activities.	(3,800)	subtotal	(3,974)
Financing activities			
Dividends	(6,331)	$12,586 × 52.7%	(6,633)
Increase in short-term debt	4,621	plug	3,979
Decrease in long-term debt	(2,994)	current maturities via footnote	(3,839)
Purchase of treasury shares.	(6,000)	subtotal	(6,000)
Net cash from financing activities	(10,704)	subtotal	(12,493)
Net change in cash.	168	subtotal	135
Beginning cash.	2,768	from balance sheet	2,936
Ending cash	$ 2,936	subtotal	$ 3,071

MID-MODULE REVIEW

Following is financial statement information from Colgate-Palmolive Company.

Income Statement		
For year ended December 31 ($ millions)	2010	2009
Net sales.	$15,564	15,327
Cost of sales.	6,360	6,319
Gross profit.	9,204	9,008
Selling, general and administrative expenses	5,414	5,282
Other (income) expense, net	301	111
Operating profit	3,489	3,615
Interest expense, net	59	77
Income before income taxes	3,430	3,538
Provision for income taxes.	1,117	1,141
Net income including noncontrolling interests.	2,313	2,397
Less: Net income attributable to noncontrolling interests	110	106
Net income attributable to Colgate-Palmolive Company.	$ 2,203	$ 2,291

Balance Sheet		
As of December 31 ($ millions)	2010	2009
Assets		
Cash and cash equivalents	$ 490	$ 600
Receivables (net of allowances of $53 and $52, respectively).	1,610	1,626
Inventories	1,222	1,209
Other current assets.	408	375
Total current assets	3,730	3,810
Property, plant and equipment, net	3,693	3,516
Goodwill, net	2,362	2,302
Other intangible assets, net	831	821
Other assets.	556	685
Total assets.	$11,172	$11,134
Liabilities		
Notes and loans payable	$ 48	$ 35
Current portion of long-term debt	561	326
Accounts payable.	1,165	1,172
Accrued income taxes	272	387
Other accruals	1,682	1,679
Total current liabilities.	3,728	3,599
Long-term debt	2,815	2,821
Deferred income taxes.	108	82
Other liabilities	1,704	1,375
Total liabilities.	8,355	7,877
Commitments and contingent liabilities		
Shareholders' Equity		
Preference stock	0	169
Common stock, $1 par value (2,000,000,000 shares authorized, 732,853,180 shares issued)	733	733
Additional paid-in-capital.	1,132	1,764
Retained earnings	14,329	13,157
Accumulated other comprehensive income (loss)	(2,115)	(2,096)
Shareholders' equity before unearned compensation, treasury stock and noncontrolling interest	14,079	13,727
Unearned compensation	(99)	(133)
Treasury stock, at cost.	(11,305)	(10,478)
Total Colgate-Palmolive Company shareholders' equity	2,675	3,116
Noncontrolling interests.	142	141
Total shareholders' equity	2,817	3,257
Total liabilities and shareholders' equity.	$11,172	$11,134

Forecast the Colgate-Palmolive balance sheet, income statement, and statement of cash flows for 2011 using the following additional information; assume no change for all other accounts not listed below. All percentages, other than sales growth, are based on percent of revenues; assume all capital expenditures are purchases of PPE, and that depreciation and amortization are included as part of selling, general and administrative expenses.

Key Financial Relations and Measures ($ millions)	2010
Net sales growth.	3%
Cost of sales/Net sales	40.9%
Selling, general and administrative expenses/Net sales	34.8%
Depreciation for 2011.	$375
Amortization for 2011.	$19
Other (income) expense, net	$301
Interest expense, net	$59
Provision for income taxes/ Pretax income	32.6%
Net income attributable to noncontrolling interests.	$110
Cash and cash equivalents/Net sales	3.1%
Receivables /Net sales.	10.3%
Inventories/Net sales	7.9%
Other current assets/Net sales.	2.6%
Capital expenditures for 2010	$567
Goodwill, net	$2,362
Other assets/Net sales.	3.6%
Notes and loans payable	$48
Accounts payable/Net sales.	7.5%
Accrued income taxes/Provision for income taxes	24.4%
Other accruals/Net sales	10.8%
Deferred income taxes	$108
Other liabilities/Net sales	10.9%
Preference stock	$0
Common stock.	$733
Additional paid-in-capital	$1,132
Accumulated other comprehensive income (loss)	$(2,115)
Unearned compensation	$(99)
Treasury stock, at cost.	$(11,305)
Noncontrolling interests	$142
Dividends/Net income	52%
Long-term debt payments required in 2012.	$359

The solution is on page 11-71.

PARSIMONIOUS MULTIYEAR FORECASTING

The forecasting process described above uses a considerable amount of available information to derive accurate forecasts. We can, however, simplify the process by using less information. Stock valuation models commonly use more parsimonious methods to compute multiyear forecasts for an initial screening of prospective securities. For example, in Module 12 we introduce two stock valuation models that use parsimonious forecasting methods. One model utilizes forecasted free cash flows and the other uses forecasted net operating profits after tax (NOPAT) and net operating assets (NOA); see Module 4 for descriptions of these variables. Because free cash flows are equal to net operating profits after tax (NOPAT) less the change in net operating assets (NOA), we can accommodate both stock valuation models with forecasts of NOPAT and NOA.

LO6 Implement a parsimonious method for multiyear forecasting of net operating profit and net operating assets.

Parsimonious Method for Forecasting

Our parsimonious approach to forecast NOPAT and NOA requires three crucial inputs:

1. Sales growth
2. Net operating profit margin (NOPM); defined in Module 4 as NOPAT divided by sales
3. Net operating asset turnover (NOAT); defined in Module 4 as sales divided by average NOA. For forecasting purposes, we define NOAT as sales divided by *year-end* NOA instead of average NOA because we want to forecast year-end values.

Multiyear Forecasting with Parsimonious Method

The remainder of this module describes and illustrates this parsimonious approach. To illustrate, we use Procter & Gamble's 2011 income statement, from Exhibit 11.3, and its 2011 balance sheet, from Exhibit 11.6, to determine the following measures. We assume that P&G's statutory tax rate is 37% on nonoperating revenues and expenses.

($ millions)	2011
Sales.	$82,559
Net operating profit after tax ($15,818 − {$3,392 + [($831 − $202) × 37%]})	$12,193
NOA (($138,354 − $2,768) − ($27,293 − $9,981) − $11,070 − $9,957)*	$97,247
NOPM ($12,193/$82,559).	14.8%
NOAT ($82,559/$97,247)*	0.85

*We use ending balance sheet amounts rather than average amounts because we forecast *ending* balance sheet amounts.

Using these inputs, we forecast P&G's sales, NOPAT, and NOA. Each year's forecasted sales is the prior-year sales multiplied successively by (1+ Growth rate) and then rounded to whole digits. Consistent with our prior revenue growth rate assumptions for P&G, we define "1 + Growth rate" as 1.046 for 2012 and onward. NOPAT is computed using forecasted (and rounded) sales each year times the 2011 NOPM of 14.8%; and NOA is computed using forecasted (and rounded) sales divided by the 2011 NOAT of 0.85. Forecasted numbers for 2012 through 2015 are in Exhibit 11.11; supporting computations are in parentheses.

This forecasting process can be continued for any desired forecast horizon. Also, the forecast assumptions such as sales growth, NOPM, and NOAT can be varied by year, if desired. This alternative, parsimonious method is much simpler than the primary method illustrated in this module. However, its simplicity does forgo information that can impact forecast accuracy.

EXHIBIT 11.11 Procter & Gamble Multiyear Forecasts of Sales, NOPAT and NOA					
	Reported	**Forecast**			
($ millions)	2011	2012 Est.	2013 Est.	2014 Est.	2015 Est.
Net sales growth.		4.6%	4.6%	4.6%	4.6%
Net sales (unrounded) . .	$82,559	**$86,356.71** ($82,559 × 1.046)	**$90,329.12** ($86,356.71 × 1.046)	**$94,484.26** ($90,329.12 × 1.046)	**$98,830.54** ($94,484.26 × 1.046)
Net sales (rounded)	$82,559	**$86,357**	**$90,329**	**$94,484**	**$98,831**
NOPAT[1]	$12,193	**$12,781** ($86,357 × 0.148)	**$13,369** ($90,329 × 0.148)	**$13,984** ($94,484 × 0.148)	**$14,627** ($98,831 × 0.148)
NOA[2]	$97,247	**$101,596** ($86,357/0.85)	**$106,269** ($90,329/0.85)	**$111,158** ($94,484/0.85)	**$116,272** ($98,831/0.85)

[1] Forecasted NOPAT = Forecasted net sales (rounded) × 2011 NOPM
[2] Forecasted NOA = Forecasted net sales (rounded)/2011 NOAT

GLOBAL ACCOUNTING

There are no differences in forecasting financial statements prepared under IFRS versus U.S. GAAP. While factors influencing growth rates likely differ among countries across the globe, the method we use to assess growth is independent of the accounting principles applied. Similarly, the forecasting techniques and mechanics we describe in this module can be applied to any set of financial statements.

MODULE-END REVIEW

Johnson & Johnson (J&J) reports fiscal 2010 sales of $61,587 million, net operating profit after tax (NOPAT) of $13,065 million, and net operating assets (NOA) of $45,694 million. J&J's NOPM is computed as 21% ($13,065 million/$61,587 million) and its NOAT is computed as 1.35 ($61,587/$45,694).

Required

Use the parsimonious forecast model to project J&J's sales, NOPAT, and NOA for 2011 through 2014 assuming a sales growth rate of 4%.

The solution is on page 11-74.

APPENDIX 11A Morgan Stanley's Forecast Report on Procter & Gamble

Morgan Stanley analysts developed their forecasts of P&G shortly after attending the analyst meetings held by P&G management. We completed our analysis and developed our forecasts at about the same time. Thus, we have an opportunity to compare the analysis in this module with the Morgan Stanley analyst report. Following is the Morgan Stanley analysts' report on Procter & Gamble Co. that the firm issued on August 7, 2011 (Pages 9-14 of the report contain the customary disclosure information typical of analyst reports). *Please note that materials that are referenced comprise excerpts from research reports and should not be relied on as investment advice. This material is only as current as the publication date of the underlying Morgan Stanley research. For important disclosures, stock price charts, and equity rating histories regarding companies that are the subject of the underlying Morgan Stanley research, see www.morganstanley.com/researchdisclosures. Additionally, Morgan Stanley has provided their materials here as a courtesy. Therefore, Morgan Stanley and Cambridge Business Publishers do not undertake to advise you of changes in the opinions or information set forth in these materials.*

Morgan Stanley

MORGAN STANLEY RESEARCH
NORTH AMERICA

Morgan Stanley & Co. LLC

Dara Mohsenian, CFA
Dara.Mohsenian@morganstanley.com
+1 212 761 6575

Ruma Mukerji, CFA
Ruma.Mukerji@morganstanley.com
+1 212 761 6754

Kevin Grundy, CPA
Kevin.Grundy@morganstanley.com
+1 212 761 3645

Alison M. Lin, CFA
Alison.Lin@morganstanley.com
+1 212 761 7250

August 7, 2011

Stock Rating
Overweight

Industry View
In-Line

Procter & Gamble Co.

Raising 2012e EPS Despite Low Quality Q4

What's New: PG reported low-quality Q4 EPS, but the stock ended up outperforming the S&P 500 as we believe investors are appropriately looking ahead to an improved pricing/commodity cost scenario in 2012, particularly with stronger than expected 3% Q4 pricing ex-mix (MS was at +1.3%). In addition, FY12 guidance was in-line with consensus. Net, we were not enthused by Q4 results given the low quality nature of Q4, and a weak developed market consumer, as well as continued commodity pressure drove below consensus Q1 guidance, but we think the worst is now behind PG with improving pricing and declining spot commodity costs, and believe undemanding valuation of 13.2 times FY13e EPS is compelling, particularly with the market adopting a more defensive orientation.

In-line but low quality Q4: Q4 EPS of $0.84 was above our $0.81 estimate and the $0.82 consensus, but was boosted 2 cents by a lower than expected tax rate and 3 cents by higher than expected other non-operating income. PG's 5% organic sales growth result (+4% excluding pre-buying ahead of price increases) was solid, but higher than expected SG&A drove a 3% operating profit miss vs. our forecast and 4% miss vs. consensus. Segment profit results were also weak, up only 4.7% y-o-y despite an easy -11.1% comparison, while pretax profit was aided by a 60% y-o-y corporate expense decline

FY12 guidance OK: PG guided to $4.17-4.33 (current consensus at $4.26) in FY12 EPS, up 6-10% y-o-y (+8-12% excluding a higher tax rate), on +3-6% organic revenue growth. However, Q1 guidance of $1.00-1.04 was below the $1.14 consensus.

Raising FY12e EPS: We are raising our FY12e EPS slightly to $4.20 from $4.16 solely on a lower than expected tax rate. On an operating basis, Q4 downside is offset by a more favorable pricing/cost outlook for FY12. We are also lowering our price target slightly to $69 (15x 2013e EPS of $4.59) from $72 to reflect a lower market multiple.

Key Ratios and Statistics

Reuters: PG.N Bloomberg: PG US
Household & Personal Care / United States of America

Price target	**$69.00**
Shr price, close (Aug 5, 2011)	$60.59
Mkt cap, curr (mm)	$180,415
52-Week Range	$67.71-59.17

Fiscal Year ending	06/10	06/11	06/12e	06/13e
ModelWare EPS ($)	3.67	3.95	4.20	4.59
Prior ModelWare EPS ($)	-	3.92	4.15	4.59
P/E	16.3	16.1	14.4	13.2
Consensus EPS ($)§	4.11	3.93	4.28	4.58
Div yld (%)	3.0	3.1	3.5	3.9

Unless otherwise noted, all metrics are based on Morgan Stanley ModelWare framework (please see explanation later in this note).
§ = Consensus data is provided by FactSet Estimates.
e = Morgan Stanley Research estimates

Quarterly ModelWare EPS

Quarter	2010	2011 Prior	2011 Current	2012e Prior	2012e Current
Q1	0.97	-	1.02	-	1.04
Q2	1.10	-	1.13	-	1.18
Q3	0.89	-	0.96	-	1.05
Q4	0.71	-	0.84	-	0.93

e = Morgan Stanley Research estimates

MorganStanley

August 7, 2011
Procter & Gamble Co.

Risk-Reward Snapshot: Procter & Gamble (PG, $60.59, Overweight, PT $69)

Potential Long-Term Topline Reacceleration

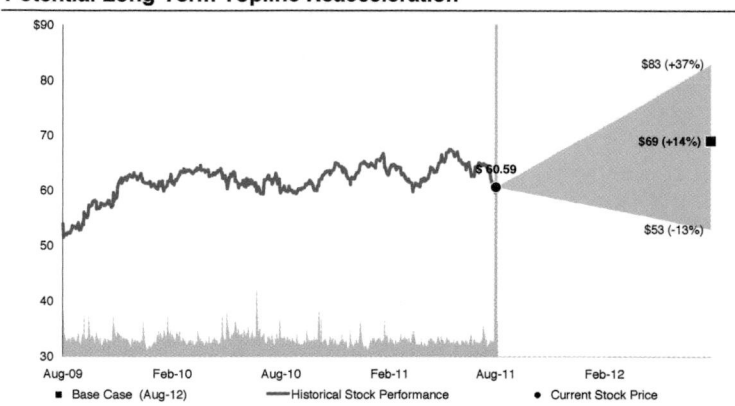

Price Target: $69		Based on 15x F2013e EPS, below PG's five-year historical NTM P/E average of 16.5x.
Bull Case $83	17x F2013e Bull Case EPS of $4.90	**Topline rebounds to 6% organic sales growth.** Revenue upside as PG's reinvigorated topline focus drives outsized market share gains and a macro rebound is stronger than expected. Cost cutting trims 50 bps from SG&A. Valuation expands to 17x C2012e EPS.
Base Case $69	15x F2013e Base Case EPS of $4.59	**Rebounding organic sales growth.** Organic sales growth of 4.4% through F2013, driven by emerging markets, higher marketing spending, and PG strategy changes. Average operating margin expansion of ~40 bps through F2013. Valuation expands to 15x F2013e EPS (10.2 times EV/EBITDA).
Bear Case $53	13x F2013e Bear Case EPS of $4.09	**Topline downside.** Pricing is 100 bps below our forecast due to a competitive environment and the macro rebound is slower than we expect, hurting volume by 200 bps. Margins miss by 50 bps due to negative mix. Valuation contracts to 13x F2013e EPS.

Bear to Bull: Competitive Environment and Macros Are the Key Drivers

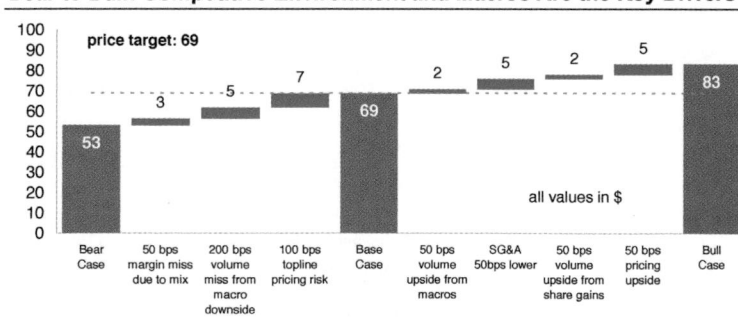

Source: Morgan Stanley Research, FactSet

Why Overweight?

- **LT Topline Re-Acceleration:** We expect PG's organic sales growth to re-accelerate to 4.5% over the next few years from 3% in F2008-11, aided by greater emerging markets focus.

- **Net Pricing/Cost Pressure Gap Eases:** With improving pricing trends despite commodity cost pressure, we expect PG's net commodity cost vs. pricing gap to ease to +1% of EPS in FY12e, versus -10% in FY11e.

- **Margin Expansion Potential:** We believe PG's focus on cost-cutting and productivity is increasing, which should provide margin flexibility to reinvest behind the business. We forecast ~50 bps of annual margin expansion in F2012-15.

Where We Could be Wrong

- **Macros Could Disappoint:** PG is sensitive to macro conditions given its skew to premium products, as each 100 basis point volume change drives an estimated 2% EPS impact.

- **Pricing:** We expect improved HPC industry pricing going forward, but if competition remains heightened, we estimate that each 100 bps of pricing pressure has a 5% EPS impact.

2

Morgan Stanley

MORGAN STANLEY RESEARCH

August 7, 2011
Procter & Gamble Co.

Q4 Results Were Weak Quality

Low quality Q4 EPS is not a surprise in a difficult environment: PG F4Q11 EPS of $0.84 was above our $0.81 estimate and the $0.82 consensus, but was aided by non-operating items, including a lower than expected tax rate (worth 2 cents to EPS), and higher than expected other income (worth 3 cents), while underlying operating profit missed consensus by 4% (MS est. by 3%).

Solid organic revenue growth: Q4 organic revenue growth of 5% was PG's best result in six quarters, but would have been 4% excluding 1% benefit from retailer load in ahead of price increases. This is in-line sequentially with Q3 trends, but still a solid result given a difficult industry environment. Organic growth was driven by +3% volumes, +3% pricing, partially offset by -1% mix.

Operating profit miss driven by higher than expected SG&A: Gross margin of 48.3% was down 120 bps YoY, and was ~60bps below consensus (in-line with our forecast). However, higher than expected SG&A expense as a % of sales resulted in a 4% operating profit miss versus consensus (3% vs. our forecast), which was more than offset by other non-operating income and a lower than expected tax rate, which in aggregate added 5 cents to EPS, driving more than all of the EPS upside. PG did disclose full-year ad spending was 40 bps higher than our forecast (PG does not disclose ad spend on a quarterly basis), which does mean FY EPS is higher quality. Please refer to Exhibit 1 and Exhibit 2 for more detail on the quarter's variance versus our forecast.

Exhibit 1
4Q11 EPS Summary

$ in millions, except EPS	MS Est. vs. Actual			Year-over-Year		
	MS Est. Jun-11 E	Actual Jun-11 E	+/-	Jun-10	Actual Jun-11 E	+/-
Sales	$20,812.0	$20,860.0	0.2%	$18,926.0	$20,860.0	10.2%
% Growth	10.0%	10.2%		4.7%	10.2%	
% Organic Growth	5.0%	5.0%		4.0%	5.0%	
Cost of Sales	-10,768.3	-10,787.0	0.2%	-9,560.0	-10,787.0	0.0%
% of Sales	51.7%	51.7%	(3) bps	50.5%	51.7%	120 bps
% of Sales Bps Change	123	120			120	
Gross Profit	10,043.8	10,073.0	0.3%	9,366.0	10,073.0	7.5%
Gross Margin %	48.3%	48.3%	(56) bps	49.5%	48.3%	(120) bps
Gross Margin Bps Change	-123	-120			-120	
SG&A Expense	-6,649.7	-6,788.0	2.1%	-6,416.0	-6,788.0	5.8%
% of Sales	32.0%	32.5%	59 bps	33.9%	32.5%	(136) bps
% Growth	3.6%	5.8%			5.8%	
% of Sales Bps Change	-195	-136			-136	
Operating Income	3,394.0	3,285.0	-3.2%	2,950.0	3,285.0	11.4%
Operating Margin	16.3%	15.7%	(56) bps	15.6%	15.7%	16 bps
% Growth	15.1%	11.4%			11.4%	
Operating Margin Bps Change	72	16			16	
Interest Expense	-204.2	-212.0	3.8%	-212.0	-212.0	0.0%
Other Non-Operating Income, Net	14.0	132.0	845.6%	-121.0	132.0	-209.1%
Pretax Income	3,204	3,205	0.0%	2,617	3,205	22.5%
Taxes	-769.3	-695.0		-432.0	-695.0	0.0%
Tax Rate	24.0%	21.7%		16.5%	21.7%	518 bps
Minority Interests	0.0	0.0		0.0	0.0	
Net Income	2,434.5	2,510.0	3.1%	2,185.0	2,510.0	14.9%
EPS Diluted (Core)	$0.81	$0.84	3.3%	$0.71	$0.84	18.2%
EPS % Growth	14.4%	18.2%		-9.4%	18.2%	
Diluted Shares	2,990.2	2,983.6	-0.2%	3,068.9	2,983.6	-2.8%

Source: Company data, Morgan Stanley Research

Exhibit 2
Low Quality Q4 EPS Beat

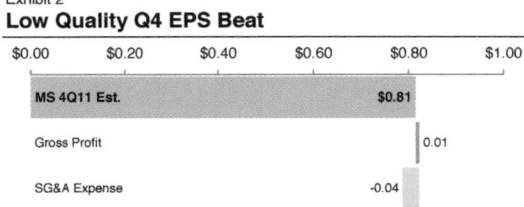

Source: Company data, Morgan Stanley Research

Q4 segment pretax profit results were weak: As shown in Exhibit 3, lower than expected revenue growth in grooming was offset by upside in baby/family. Each segment missed consensus profit estimates, except baby/ family, and total segment profit in aggregate was up only 4.7% y-o-y on an easy -11.1% comparison, offset by lower corporate pretax expense, which declined 60% y-o-y.

Exhibit 3
Segment Results – MS vs. Actual

$ in millions	MS Est. vs. Actual			Year-over-Year		
	MS Est. Jun-11 E	Actual Jun-11	+/-	Jun-10	Actual Jun-11	+/-
Total Sales	$20,812.0	$20,860.0	0.2%	$18,926.0	$20,860.0	10.2%
Organic Sales Growth	5.0%	5.0%	(4) bps	4.0%	5.0%	100bp
Volume (Organic)	4.5%	3.0%	(152) bps	8.0%	3.0%	-500bp
Pricing	1.3%	3.0%	171 bps	-1.0%	3.0%	400bp
Mix	-0.8%	-1.0%	(22) bps	-3.0%	-1.0%	200bp
FX Impact	5.0%	5.0%	0 bps	1.0%	5.0%	400bp
Segment Pretax Profit	$3,778.8	$3,492.0	-7.6%	$3,336.0	$3,492.0	4.7%
Beauty						
Beauty Care	$5,027.9	$5,068.0	0.8%	$4,730.0	$5,068.0	7.1%
Organic Sales Growth	2.0%	3.0%	100bp	5.0%	3.0%	-200bp
Pretax Profit	$691.5	$623.0	-9.9%	$712.0	$623.0	-12.5%
Grooming	$2,119.5	$2,056.0	-3.0%	$1,919.0	$2,056.0	7.1%
Organic Sales Growth	4.0%	1.0%	-300bp	12.0%	1.0%	-1100bp
Pretax Profit	$510.5	$500.0	-2.1%	$443.0	$500.0	12.9%
Household Care						
Fabric and Home Care	$6,238.9	$6,144.0	-1.5%	$5,552.0	$6,144.0	10.7%
Organic Sales Growth	7.0%	4.0%	-300bp	1.0%	4.0%	300bp
Pretax Profit	$1,190.4	$937.0	-21.3%	$965.0	$937.0	-2.9%
Baby and Family Care	$3,974.2	$4,056.0	2.1%	$3,562.0	$4,056.0	13.9%
Organic Sales Growth	7.5%	10.0%	250bp	5.0%	10.0%	500bp
Pretax Profit	$664.9	$798.0	20.0%	$571.0	$798.0	39.8%
Health & Well Being						
Health Care	$2,911.6	$2,949.0	1.3%	$2,638.0	$2,949.0	11.8%
Organic Sales Growth	5.0%	7.0%	200bp	2.0%	7.0%	500bp
Pretax Profit	$615.5	$542.0	-11.9%	$526.0	$542.0	3.0%
Snacks and Pets	$840.3	$850.0	1.2%	$798.0	$850.0	6.5%
Organic Sales Growth	1.0%	-1.0%	-200bp	3.0%	-1.0%	-400bp
Pretax Profit	$106.0	$92.0	-13.2%	$119.0	$92.0	-22.7%

Source: Company data, Morgan Stanley Research

Mixed cash flow and balance sheet results: PG reported solid Q4 cash flow results, with free cash flow up 17% y-o-y driven by sequential improvement versus weak Q3 balance sheet results and change in other assets/liabilities. Working capital results were still weak this quarter, with inventories up

Morgan Stanley

MORGAN STANLEY RESEARCH

August 7, 2011
Procter & Gamble Co.

16% and accounts receivables up 18% y-o-y, versus the 10% increase in reported sales.

Initial FY12 Guidance Relatively In-Line But Weak Q1 Guidance

PG guided to FY12 EPS of $4.17-4.33, in-line with the $4.26 consensus, up 6-10% (+8-12% excluding the higher 25% tax rate), on +3-6% organic revenue growth. Organic revenue guidance includes +3-4% pricing, -1% to -2% mix, with the rest of driven by volume. The relatively wide guidance range is driven by the current level of economic uncertainty. PG expects its organic revenue growth to be ahead of market growth of ~3%, including 4% growth in beauty/grooming, and 3% growth in household care. The company expects +1-2% growth in developed markets and +6-8% growth in emerging markets. FX is expected to contribute another +2-3% to FY12 revenue growth.

We expect PG's pricing/commodity cost gap to ease meaningfully in FY12: PG expects commodity cost inflation in FY12 to be similar to FY11 levels, which implies a $1.8B pretax headwind. PG expects to offset much of the dollar headwind through pricing, but still expects a net gross margin impact, which we estimate implies a 100-120 bps negative gross margin impact.

As shown in Exhibit 4, after assuming a 67-bp volume impact from each point of pricing, we estimate the net negative EPS impact from commodity costs versus pricing will abate

significantly to +4 cents in FY12 vs. -40 cents in FY11 (we assume 3% pricing in FY12 and commodity cost pressure in-line with what was experienced in 2011).

Exhibit 4
Price/Cost Gap (incl. Volume Impact) Should Improve Significantly in Fiscal 2012

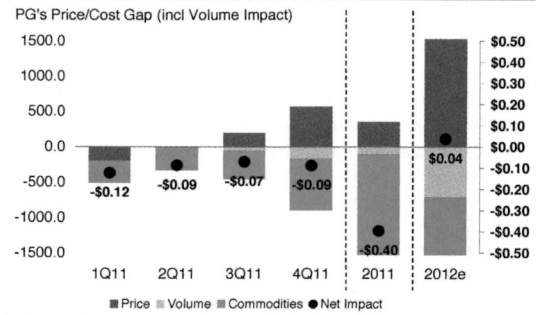

Source: Company data, Morgan Stanley Research

We are raising our FY12e EPS to $4.20 from $4.16 solely on a lower tax rate, with our Q1 estimate of $1.04 at the high end of PG's guidance.

Morgan Stanley

MORGAN STANLEY RESEARCH

August 7, 2011
Procter & Gamble Co.

Valuation and Risks

We rate PG Overweight. Our price target of $69 is based on a 15 times multiple on our FY13 EPS estimate of $4.59, below PG's 16.5x five-year average historical NTM P/E of 16.5x.

Key Risks to our Investment Thesis

Macro recovery stalls. Given Procter & Gamble's skew to premium products, the company's organic sales growth prospects will be significantly influenced by consumer spending going forward. PG's volume is sensitive to macro conditions as evidenced by its 2% volume decline in FY09. We estimate that a 100-bp change in volume is worth 2% to our FY12 EPS estimate.

Pricing environment does not improve as much as we expect. We expect improved HPC industry pricing going forward with selective list price increases in certain categories and less promotional spending. If the industry environment was more competitive than we expect, we estimate that each 100 bps of pricing pressure would be worth 5% to FY12 EPS.

Strong balance sheet could drive or hurt shareholder value. Procter & Gamble has a strong balance sheet with a net debt/EBITDA of 1.5 times at the end of F2Q11. The company has sufficient flexibility to increase its share buybacks above the $6-7 billion it did in FY11. In addition, PG may elect to pursue acquisitions which could boost or detract from shareholder value. If PG levers its balance sheet up to 2.0 times net debt/EBITDA by the end of FY12 to repurchase shares, we estimate EPS would increase by 2%.

Cost-cutting. PG's core SG&A as a percentage of sales (excluding shipping and handling, ad spending, R&D expense, and stock option expense) of 18% in FY10 was the highest in its large cap peer group despite PG's leading scale. As such, we believe PG has ample opportunity to pare back its SG&A spending, and also generate COGS cost savings/productivity. We also believe PG is more focused on cost cutting through simplifying the organization and streamlining bureaucracy, in order to better capitalize on its scale. Each 50 basis points change in core SG&A as a % of sales (about $400 million) versus our forecast would be worth an estimated 2% to FY12 EPS.

Market share vacillates. There may be upside to PG's FY12 EPS if market share gains accelerate with PG ramping up investment behind the business and a strong innovation

pipeline. On the other hand, market share could stall with higher pricing. We estimate each 100 basis points of incremental volume would be worth 2% to FY12 EPS.

Currency movements. 62% of PG's FY10 sales were derived from outside the US. As such, fluctuation in currencies could materially impact our EPS estimates. We estimate that a 5% change in the USD versus PG's basket of currencies would have a 3% impact on EPS. PG is more insulated from FX risk than its peers given relatively less international exposure. In addition, PG's significant manufacturing footprint outside the US mitigates the potential transaction impact of FX.

Commodity cost volatility. While PG's diversified product portfolio spreads out its raw material exposure across a wide variety of input costs, volatile commodity costs could significantly impact EPS. In past years, PG experienced significant margin pressure from commodities with input costs increasing $2 billion and $1 billion y-o-y in FY08 and FY09, respectively. In FY11, PG again experienced $1.8B in pretax commodity cost inflation, which is in-line with PG's forecast for FY12 as well. We estimate that each 200 bps change in overall commodity costs would impact EPS by 3%.

Morgan Stanley

MORGAN STANLEY RESEARCH

August 7, 2011
Procter & Gamble Co.

Exhibit 5
PG Income Statement

Income Statement	FY2008	FY2009	FY2010	Sep-10	Dec-10	Mar-11	Jun-11	FY2011	Sep-11 E	Dec-11 E	Mar-12 E	Jun-12 E	FY2012 E	FY2013E
Sales	81,748.0	76,694.0	78,938.0	20,122.0	21,347.0	20,230.0	20,860.0	82,559.0	21,612.4	22,828.8	21,503.0	21,810.3	87,754.5	91,795.6
% Growth	9.2%	-2.8%	2.9%	1.6%	1.5%	5.5%	10.2%	4.6%	7.4%	6.9%	6.3%	4.6%	6.3%	4.6%
% Organic Growth	5.0%	2.0%	3.4%	4.0%	3.0%	4.0%	5.0%	4.0%	3.0%	4.7%	4.7%	4.6%	4.3%	4.6%
Cost of Sales	-39,536.0	-36,690.0	-37,919.0	-9,689.0	-10,287.0	-10,005.0	-10,787.0	-40,768.0	-10,730.9	-11,172.3	-10,634.6	-11,015.2	-43,553.0	-45,099.6
% of Sales	48.4%	50.4%	48.0%	48.2%	48.2%	49.5%	51.7%	49.4%	49.7%	48.9%	49.5%	50.5%	49.6%	49.1%
% of Sales Bps Change	39	-241		70	189	135	120	134	150	75	0	-121	25	-50
Gross Profit	42,212.0	38,004.0	41,019.0	10,433.0	11,060.0	10,225.0	10,073.0	41,791.0	10,881.6	11,656.5	10,868.4	10,795.0	44,201.6	46,696.0
Gross Margin %	51.6%	49.6%	52.0%	51.8%	51.8%	50.5%	48.3%	50.6%	50.3%	51.1%	50.5%	49.5%	50.4%	50.9%
Gross Margin Bps Change	-39	241		-70	-189	-135	-120	-134	-150	-75	0	121	-25	50
SG&A Expense (ex Incremental Restructuring)	-25,575.0	-22,240.0	-24,731.0	-5,932.0	-6,495.0	-6,453.0	-6,788.0	-25,668.0	-6,579.5	-6,795.8	-6,564.2	-6,966.0	-26,905.4	-27,994.9
% of Sales	31.3%	29.0%	31.3%	29.5%	30.4%	31.9%	32.5%	31.1%	30.4%	29.8%	30.5%	31.9%	30.7%	30.5%
% Growth	5.1%		11.2%	-0.5%	2.0%	7.8%	5.8%	3.8%	10.9%	4.6%	1.7%	2.6%	4.8%	4.0%
% of Sales Bps Change	-54	233	8	-62	14	69	-136	-24	96	-66	-137	-60	-43	-16
Operating Income (ex Incremental Restructuring)	16,637.0	15,764.0	16,288.0	4,501.0	4,565.0	3,772.0	3,285.0	16,123.0	4,302.1	4,860.7	4,304.2	3,829.0	17,296.1	18,701.1
Operating Margin	20.4%	20.6%	20.6%	22.4%	21.4%	18.6%	15.7%	19.5%	19.9%	21.3%	20.0%	17.6%	19.7%	20.4%
% Growth	7.7%	-5.2%	3.3%	1.2%	-7.3%	-4.9%	11.4%	-1.0%	-4.4%	6.5%	14.1%	16.6%	7.3%	8.1%
Operating Margin Bps Change	15	20	8	-9	-202	-204	16	-110	-246	-9	137	181	18	66
Memo Item: D&A	3166	3082	3108.0	689.0	711.0	703.0	735.0	2838.0	762.4	758.2	751.9	772.1	3044.6	3141.7
Memo Item: EBITDA (excluding charges)	19,803.0	18,846.0	19,396.0	5,190.0	5,276.0	4,475.0	4,020.0	18,961.0	5,064.5	5,618.9	5,056.2	4,601.1	20,340.7	21,842.9
Memo Item: EBITDA Margin	24.2%	24.6%	24.6%	25.8%	24.7%	22.1%	19.3%	23.0%	23.4%	24.6%	23.5%	21.1%	23.2%	23.8%
Interest Expense	-1,467.0	-1,358.0	-946.0	-208.0	-209.0	-202.0	-212.0	-831.0	-208.6	-209.5	-207.6	-204.7	-830.4	-837.8
Other Non-Operating Income, Net	462.0	397.0	-28.0	-11.0	10.0	71.0	132.0	202.0	9.9	9.4	9.4	9.4	38.0	38.8
Pretax Income	15,632.0	14,803.0	15,314.0	4,282.0	4,366.0	3,641.0	3,205.0	15,494.0	4,103.4	4,660.6	4,106.1	3,633.7	16,503.8	17,902.1
Taxes	-4,309.0	-3,834.0	-3,931.0	-1,201.0	-980.0	-768.0	-695.0	-3,644.0	-1,025.8	-1,165.1	-1,026.5	-908.4	-4,125.9	-4,654.5
Tax Rate	27.6%	25.9%	25.7%	28.0%	22.4%	21.1%	21.7%	23.5%	25.0%	25.0%	25.0%	25.0%	25.0%	26.0%
Minority Interests	0.0	0.0	0.0	0.0	0.0	0.0	0.0	0.0	0.0	0.0	0.0	0.0	0.0	0.0
Net Income	11,323.0	10,969.0	11,383.0	3,081.0	3,386.0	2,873.0	2,510.0	11,850.0	3,077.5	3,495.4	3,079.6	2,725.3	12,377.8	13,247.6
EPS Diluted (Core)	$3.41	$3.48	$3.67	$1.02	$1.13	$0.96	$0.84	$3.95	$1.04	$1.18	$1.05	$0.93	$4.20	$4.59
EPS % Growth	12.2%	1.9%	5.6%	4.6%	3.0%	7.9%	18.2%	7.5%	1.8%	4.9%	9.5%	10.9%	6.5%	9.3%
Basic Shares	3,078.4	2,952.0	2,896.2	2,828.5	2,800.3	2,802.2	2,786.5	2,804.4	2,773.0	2,756.0	2,739.6	2,724.4	2,748.2	2,687.4
Diluted Shares	3,316.8	3,154.1	3,100.2	3,025.6	3,000.2	2,999.3	2,983.6	3,001.9	2,970.1	2,953.1	2,936.7	2,921.5	2,945.3	2,894.5

Source: Company data, Morgan Stanley Research estimates

6

Morgan Stanley

MORGAN STANLEY RESEARCH

August 7, 2011
Procter & Gamble Co.

Exhibit 6
PG Balance Sheet

Balance Sheet	FY2008	FY2009	FY2010	Sep-10	Dec-10	Mar-11	Jun-11	FY2011	Sep-11 E	Dec-11 E	Mar-12 E	Jun-12 E	FY2012E	FY2013E
Assets														
Surplus Cash	0.0	0.0	0.0	0.0	0.0	0.0	0.0	0.0	0.0	0.0	0.0	0.0	0.0	0.0
Cash & Equivalents	3,313.0	4,781.0	2,879.0	2,603.0	3,249.0	2,946.0	2,768.0	2,768.0	2,500.0	2,500.0	2,500.0	2,500.0	2,500.0	2,500.0
Investment Securities	228.0		00.0											
Receivables, Net	6,761.0	5,836.0	5,335.0	6,082.0	6,551.0	6,264.0	6,275.0	6,275.0	6,705.4	7,188.4	6,830.2	6,648.1	6,648.1	6,954.1
Inventories	8,416.0	6,880.0	6,384.0	7,277.0	7,423.0	7,619.0	7,379.0	7,379.0	8,102.4	8,106.5	8,141.0	7,557.2	7,557.2	7,826.8
Deferred Income Taxes	2,012.0	1,209.0	990.0	968.0	963.0	1,099.0	1,335.0	1,335.0	1,383.2	1,461.0	1,376.2	1,395.9	1,395.9	1,460.1
Prepaid Expenses and Other Current Assets	3,785.0	3,199.0	3194.0	3566.0	3644.0	3886.0	4213.0	4213.0	4175.9	4079.6	4130.5	3925.9	3925.9	4106.6
Total Current Assets	24,515.0	21,905.0	18,782.0	20,496.0	21,830.0	21,814.0	21,970.0	21,970.0	22,866.9	23,335.5	22,977.9	22,027.0	22,027.0	22,847.6
PP&E, Net	20,640.0	19,462.0	19,244.0	19,877.0	19,952.0	20,521.0	21,293.0	21,293.0	21,196.1	21,340.3	21,556.8	22,081.2	22,081.2	22,534.8
Goodwill, Net	59,767.0	56,512.0	54,012.0	56,171.0	55,760.0	57,030.0	57,030.0	57,030.0	57,030.0	57,030.0	57,030.0	57,030.0	57,030.0	57,030.0
Other Intangible Assets, Net	34,233.0	32,606.0	31,636.0	32,369.0	32,251.0	32,598.0	33,152.0	33,152.0	33,152.0	33,152.0	33,152.0	33,152.0	33,152.0	33,152.0
Other Assets	4,837.0	4,348.0	4,498.0	4,779.0	4,480.0	4,575.0	4,909.0	4,909.0	4,909.0	4,909.0	4,909.0	4,909.0	4,909.0	4,909.0
Total Assets	143,992.0	134,833.0	128,172.0	133,692.0	134,273.0	136,538.0	138,354.0	138,354.0	139,154.1	139,766.7	139,625.7	139,199.2	139,199.2	140,473.3
Liabilities														
Short-Term Debt	0.0	0.0	00.0	0.0	0.0	0.0	0.0	00.0	171.4	1,675.4	980.5	789.7	789.7	1,598.2
Notes and Loan Payable	0.0	0.0	0.0	0.0	0.0	0.0	0.0	0.0	0.0	0.0	0.0	0.0	0.0	0.0
Current Portion of Long-Term Debt	13,084.0	16,320.0	8,472.0	11,512.0	11,158.0	9,721.0	9,981.0	9,981.0	9,981.0	10,545.0	10,545.0	10,545.0	10,545.0	12,666.0
Accounts Payable	6,775.0	5,980.0	7,251.0	6,716.0	6,267.0	6,458.0	8,022.0	8,022.0	7,309.4	6,761.6	6,779.3	8,059.6	8,059.6	8,255.8
Accrued and Other Liabilities	11,099.0	8,601.0	8,559.0	9,412.0	9,816.0	9,996.0	9,290.0	9,290.0	10,022.7	10,406.0	10,410.0	9,626.0	9,626.0	9,977.8
Total Current Liabilities	30,958.0	30,901.0	24,282.0	27,640.0	27,241.0	26,175.0	27,293.0	27,293.0	27,484.5	29,388.1	28,714.8	29,020.2	29,020.2	32,517.9
Long-Term Debt	23,581.0	20,652.0	21,360.0	21,464.0	21,317.0	21,699.0	22,033.0	22,033.0	22,033.0	22,058.0	22,058.0	20,058.0	20,058.0	15,942.0
Deferred Income Taxes	11,805.0	10,752.0	10,902.0	10,709.0	10,867.0	10,923.0	10,847.2	10,847.2	11,156.4	11,347.4	11,352.3	11,079.6	11,079.6	11,589.6
Minority Interests	0.0	0.0	324.0	346.0	349.0	363.0	363.0	363.0	363.0	363.0	363.0	363.0	363.0	363.0
Other Liabilities	8,154.0	9,429.0	10,189.0	10,678.0	10,135.0	10,309.0	10,179.8	10,179.8	10,172.2	9,925.3	10,097.6	9,771.1	9,771.1	9,764.6
Total Liabilities	74,498.0	71,734.0	67,057.0	70,837.0	69,909.0	69,469.0	70,716.0	70,716.0	71,209.1	71,081.8	70,585.8	70,292.0	70,292.0	70,177.2
Shareholders' Equity														
Preferred Stock	1,366.0	1,324.0	1,277.0	1,260.0	1,253.0	1,241.0	1,241.0	1,241.0	1,241.0	1,241.0	1,241.0	1,241.0	1,241.0	1,241.0
Common Stock	4,002.0	4,007.0	4,008.0	4,008.0	4,008.0	4,008.0	4,008.0	4,008.0	4,008.0	4,008.0	4,008.0	4,008.0	4,008.0	4,008.0
Additional Paid-In Capital	60,307.0	61,118.0	61,697.0	61,839.0	61,985.0	62,180.0	62,180.0	62,180.0	62,180.0	62,180.0	62,180.0	62,180.0	62,180.0	62,180.0
Retained Earnings	48,986.0	57,309.0	64,614.0	66,282.0	68,212.0	69,692.0	71,582.7	71,582.7	73,101.0	75,046.1	76,583.8	77,629.7	77,629.7	84,087.9
Accumulated Other Comprehensive Income (Loss)	3,746.0	-3,358.0	-7,822.0	-5,007.0	-5,356.0	-3,495.0	-2,832.0	-2,832.0	-2,543.3	-2,248.4	-1,931.1	-1,609.7	-1,609.7	-379.0
Reserve for ESOP Debt Retirement	-1,325.0	-1,340.0	-1,350.0	-1,353.0	-1,355.0	-1,355.0	-1,355.0	-1,355.0	-1,355.0	-1,355.0	-1,355.0	-1,355.0	-1,355.0	-1,355.0
Treasury Stock	-47,588.0	-55,961.0	-61,309.0	-64,174.0	-64,383.0	-65,202.0	-67,186.7	-67,186.7	-68,686.7	-70,186.7	-71,686.7	-73,186.7	-73,186.7	-79,486.7
Total Shareholders' Equity	69,494.0	63,099.0	61,115.0	62,855.0	64,364.0	67,069.0	67,638.0	67,638.0	67,945.0	68,684.9	69,040.0	68,907.2	68,907.2	70,296.2
Total Liabilities & SE	143,992.0	134,833.0	128,172.0	133,692.0	134,273.0	136,538.0	138,354.0	138,354.0	139,154.1	139,766.7	139,625.7	139,199.2	139,199.2	140,473.3

Source: Company data, Morgan Stanley Research estimates

7

Morgan Stanley

MORGAN STANLEY RESEARCH

August 7, 2011
Procter & Gamble Co.

Exhibit 7
PG Cash Flow Statement

Cash Flow	FY2008	FY2009	FY2010	Sep-10	Dec-10	Mar-11	Jun-11	FY2011	Sep-11 E	Dec-11 E	Mar-12 E	Jun-12 E	FY2012E	FY2013E
Net Income	11,323.0	10,969.0	11,383.0	3,081.0	3,386.0	2,873.0	2,510.0	11,850.0	3077.5	3495.4	3079.6	2725.3	12,377.8	13,247.6
Adjustments:														
Depreciation and Amortization	3,166.0	3,082.0	3,108.0	689.0	711.0	703.0	735.0	2838.0	762.4	758.2	751.9	772.1	3044.6	3141.7
Stock-Based Compensation Expense	555.0	516.0	453.0	87.0	93.0	115.0	119.0	414.0	88.7	94.9	117.3	121.4	422.3	430.7
Deferred Income Taxes	1,214.0	596.0	36.0	48.0	94.0	44.0	-58.0	128.0	-48.2	-77.8	84.8	-19.7	-60.8	-64.3
Other	1,279.0	120.0	-1,121.0	2.0	-125.0	-797.0	680.0	-240.0	346.2	287.3	-46.0	-68.0	519.5	329.3
Changes in A/L														
Receivables	432.0	415.0	-14.0	-434.0	-497.0	436.0	69.0	-426.0	-430.4	-483.0	358.2	182.1	-373.1	-306.0
Inventories	-1,050.0	721.0	86.0	-604.0	-175.0	-38.0	316.0	-501.0	-723.4	-4.1	-34.5	583.8	-178.2	-269.6
A/P, Accrued and Other Liabilities	134.0	-742.0	2446.0	-303.0	-74.0	154.0	581.0	358.0	20.1	-164.4	21.6	496.2	373.5	548.1
Other Operating Assets and Liabilities	-1,239.0	-758.0	-305.0	-114.0	-536.0	566.0	-1,106.0	-1190.0	-07.6	-246.8	172.2	-326.5	-408.7	-6.5
Cash Provided by Operations	15,814.0	14,919.0	16,072.0	2,452.0	2,877.0	4,056.0	3,846.0	13,231.0	3,085.4	3,659.7	4,505.1	4,466.8	15,717.0	17,051.1
Cash Flows from Investing Activities:														
Capital Expenditures	-3,046.0	-3,238.0	-3,067.0	-519.0	-737.0	-810.0	-1,240.0	-3,306.0	-665.5	-902.3	-968.5	-1,296.5	-3,832.8	-3,595.3
Proceeds from Asset Sales	928.0	1,087.0	3068.0	14.0	8.0	67.0	136.0	225.0	0.0	0.0	0.0	0.0	0.0	0.0
Payment for Acquisitions	-381.0	-368.0	-425.0	-398.0	-37.0	-54.0	15.0	-474.0	0.0	0.0	0.0	0.0	0.0	0.0
Other	-50.0	166.0	-173.0	-25.0	153.0	-31.0	-24.0	73.0	0.0	0.0	0.0	0.0	0.0	0.0
Cash Used for Investing Activities	-2,549.0	-2,353.0	-597.0	-928.0	-613.0	-828.0	-1113.0	-3,482.0	-665.5	-902.3	-968.5	-1296.5	-3,832.8	-3,595.3
Cash Flows from Financing Activities:														
Change in Short-Term Debt	1,844.0	-2,420.0	-1,798.0	2,412.0	-1,464.0	-1,368.0	571.0	151.0	171.4	2068.0	-694.9	-190.8	1,353.7	2,949.5
Change in Long-Term Debt	-4,659.0	2,339.0	-4,716.0	-17.0	1,393.0	-28.0	-18.0	1,330.0	0.0	-1975.0	0.0	0.0	-1,975.0	-4,116.0
Dividends Paid	-4,655.0	-5,044.0	-5,458.0	-1,422.0	-1,412.0	-1,403.0	-1530.0	-5,761.0	-1559.3	-1550.4	-1541.8	-1679.5	-6,330.9	-6,789.3
Purchase of Treasury Shares	-10,047.0	-6,370.0	-6,004.0	-3,010.0	-518.0	-1,008.0	-2,503.0	-7,039.0	-1500.0	-1500.0	-1500.0	-1500.0	-6,000.0	-6,300.0
Proceeds From Stock Options, Other	1,867.0	681.0	721.0	136.0	374.0	248.0	544.0	1302.0	200.0	200.0	200.0	200.0	800.0	800.0
Cash Used for Financing Activities	-15,650.0	-10,814.0	-17,255.0	-1,901.0	-1,627.0	-3,559.0	-2,936.0	-10,023.0	-2,687.9	-2,757.4	-3,536.7	-3,170.3	-12,152.2	-13,455.8
Cash Provided by Discontinued Operations	0.0	0.0	0.0	0.0	0.0	0.0	0.0	0.0	0.0	0.0	0.0	0.0	0.0	0.0
Exchange Rate Effect on Cash / Other	344.0	-284.0	-122.0	101.0	9.0	28.0	25.0	163.0	0.0	0.0	0.0	0.0	0.0	0.0
Net Increase (Decrease) in Cash and Cash Equivs	-2041.0	1468.0	-1902.0	-276.0	646.0	-303.0	-178.0	-111.0	-268.0	0.0	0.0	0.0	-268.0	0.0
Cash and Cash Equivs, Beg	5,354.0	3,313.0	4,781.0	2,879.0	2,603.0	3,249.0	2,946.0	2,879.0	2,768.0	2,500.0	2,500.0	2,500.0	2,768.0	2,500.0
Cash and Cash Equivs, End	3,313.0	4,781.0	2,879.0	2,603.0	3,249.0	2,946.0	2,768.0	2,768.0	2,500.0	2,500.0	2,500.0	2,500.0	2,500.0	2,500.0

Source: Company data, Morgan Stanley Research estimates

8

Morgan Stanley

MORGAN STANLEY RESEARCH

August 7, 2011
Procter & Gamble Co.

Morgan Stanley

MORGAN STANLEY RESEARCH

August 7, 2011
Procter & Gamble Co.

MORGAN STANLEY
ModelWare

Morgan Stanley ModelWare is a proprietary analytic framework that helps clients uncover value, adjusting for distortions and ambiguities created by local accounting regulations. For example, ModelWare EPS adjusts for one-time events, capitalizes operating leases (where their use is significant), and converts inventory from LIFO costing to a FIFO basis. ModelWare also emphasizes the separation of operating performance of a company from its financing for a more complete view of how a company generates earnings.

Disclosure Section

The information and opinions in Morgan Stanley Research were prepared by Morgan Stanley & Co. LLC, and/or Morgan Stanley C.T.V.M. S.A., and/or Morgan Stanley Mexico, Casa de Bolsa, S.A. de C.V. As used in this disclosure section, "Morgan Stanley" includes Morgan Stanley & Co. LLC, Morgan Stanley C.T.V.M. S.A., Morgan Stanley Mexico, Casa de Bolsa, S.A. de C.V. and their affiliates as necessary.
For important disclosures, stock price charts and equity rating histories regarding companies that are the subject of this report, please see the Morgan Stanley Research Disclosure Website at www.morganstanley.com/researchdisclosures, or contact your investment representative or Morgan Stanley Research at 1585 Broadway, (Attention: Research Management), New York, NY, 10036 USA.

Analyst Certification

The following analysts hereby certify that their views about the companies and their securities discussed in this report are accurately expressed and that they have not received and will not receive direct or indirect compensation in exchange for expressing specific recommendations or views in this report: Dara Mohsenian.
Unless otherwise stated, the individuals listed on the cover page of this report are research analysts.

Global Research Conflict Management Policy

Morgan Stanley Research has been published in accordance with our conflict management policy, which is available at www.morganstanley.com/institutional/research/conflictpolicies.

Important US Regulatory Disclosures on Subject Companies

Within the last 12 months, Morgan Stanley managed or co-managed a public offering (or 144A offering) of securities of Colgate-Palmolive Co, Procter & Gamble Co..
Within the last 12 months, Morgan Stanley has received compensation for investment banking services from Avon Products Inc., Clorox Co, Colgate-Palmolive Co, Newell Rubbermaid Inc., Procter & Gamble Co., Weight Watchers International.
In the next 3 months, Morgan Stanley expects to receive or intends to seek compensation for investment banking services from Avon Products Inc., Church & Dwight Co., Inc., Clorox Co, Colgate-Palmolive Co, Energizer Holdings Inc, Newell Rubbermaid Inc., Procter & Gamble Co., Tupperware Brands Corp., Weight Watchers International.
Within the last 12 months, Morgan Stanley has received compensation for products and services other than investment banking services from Avon Products Inc., Church & Dwight Co., Inc., Clorox Co, Colgate-Palmolive Co, Energizer Holdings Inc, Procter & Gamble Co., Weight Watchers International.
Within the last 12 months, Morgan Stanley has provided or is providing investment banking services to, or has an investment banking client relationship with, the following company: Avon Products Inc., Church & Dwight Co., Inc., Clorox Co, Colgate-Palmolive Co, Energizer Holdings Inc, Newell Rubbermaid Inc., Procter & Gamble Co., Tupperware Brands Corp., Weight Watchers International.
Within the last 12 months, Morgan Stanley has either provided or is providing non-investment banking, securities-related services to and/or in the past has entered into an agreement to provide services or has a client relationship with the following company: Avon Products Inc., Church & Dwight Co., Inc., Clorox Co, Colgate-Palmolive Co, Energizer Holdings Inc, Newell Rubbermaid Inc., Procter & Gamble Co., Weight Watchers International.
Morgan Stanley & Co. LLC makes a market in the securities of Avon Products Inc., Church & Dwight Co., Inc., Clorox Co, Colgate-Palmolive Co, Energizer Holdings Inc, Newell Rubbermaid Inc., Procter & Gamble Co., Tupperware Brands Corp., Weight Watchers International.
The equity research analysts or strategists principally responsible for the preparation of Morgan Stanley Research have received compensation based upon various factors, including quality of research, investor client feedback, stock picking, competitive factors, firm revenues and overall investment banking revenues.
Morgan Stanley and its affiliates do business that relates to companies/instruments covered in Morgan Stanley Research, including market making, providing liquidity and specialized trading, risk arbitrage and other proprietary trading, fund management, commercial banking, extension of credit, investment services and investment banking. Morgan Stanley sells to and buys from customers the securities/instruments of companies covered in Morgan Stanley Research on a principal basis. Morgan Stanley may have a position in the debt of the Company or instruments discussed in this report.
Certain disclosures listed above are also for compliance with applicable regulations in non-US jurisdictions.

STOCK RATINGS

Morgan Stanley uses a relative rating system using terms such as Overweight, Equal-weight, Not-Rated or Underweight (see definitions below). Morgan Stanley does not assign ratings of Buy, Hold or Sell to the stocks we cover. Overweight, Equal-weight, Not-Rated and Underweight are not the equivalent of buy, hold and sell. Investors should carefully read the definitions of all ratings used in Morgan Stanley Research. In addition, since Morgan Stanley Research contains more complete information concerning the analyst's views, investors should carefully read Morgan Stanley Research, in its entirety, and not infer the contents from the rating alone. In any case, ratings (or research) should not be used or relied upon as investment advice. An investor's decision to buy or sell a stock should depend on individual circumstances (such as the investor's existing holdings) and other considerations.

Global Stock Ratings Distribution

(as of July 31, 2011)

For disclosure purposes only (in accordance with NASD and NYSE requirements), we include the category headings of Buy, Hold, and Sell alongside our ratings of Overweight, Equal-weight, Not-Rated and Underweight. Morgan Stanley does not assign ratings of Buy, Hold or Sell to the stocks we cover. Overweight, Equal-weight, Not-Rated and Underweight are not the equivalent of buy, hold, and sell but represent recommended relative weightings (see definitions below). To satisfy regulatory requirements, we correspond Overweight, our most positive stock rating, with a buy recommendation; we correspond Equal-weight and Not-Rated to hold and Underweight to sell recommendations, respectively.

Morgan Stanley

MORGAN STANLEY RESEARCH

August 7, 2011
Procter & Gamble Co.

Stock Rating Category	Coverage Universe		Investment Banking Clients (IBC)		
	Count	% of Total	Count	% of Total IBC	% of Rating Category
Overweight/Buy	**1107**	**40%**	**451**	**48%**	**41%**
Equal-weight/Hold	**1136**	**41%**	**372**	**40%**	**33%**
Not-Rated/Hold	**114**	**4%**	**20**	**2%**	**18%**
Underweight/Sell	**384**	**14%**	**97**	**10%**	**25%**
Total	**2,741**		**940**		

Data include common stock and ADRs currently assigned ratings. An investor's decision to buy or sell a stock should depend on individual circumstances (such as the investor's existing holdings) and other considerations. Investment Banking Clients are companies from whom Morgan Stanley received investment banking compensation in the last 12 months.

Analyst Stock Ratings
Overweight (O). The stock's total return is expected to exceed the average total return of the analyst's industry (or industry team's) coverage universe, on a risk-adjusted basis, over the next 12-18 months.
Equal-weight (E). The stock's total return is expected to be in line with the average total return of the analyst's industry (or industry team's) coverage universe, on a risk-adjusted basis, over the next 12-18 months.
Not-Rated (NR). Currently the analyst does not have adequate conviction about the stock's total return relative to the average total return of the analyst's industry (or industry team's) coverage universe, on a risk-adjusted basis, over the next 12-18 months.
Underweight (U). The stock's total return is expected to be below the average total return of the analyst's industry (or industry team's) coverage universe, on a risk-adjusted basis, over the next 12-18 months.
Unless otherwise specified, the time frame for price targets included in Morgan Stanley Research is 12 to 18 months.

Analyst Industry Views
Attractive (A): The analyst expects the performance of his or her industry coverage universe over the next 12-18 months to be attractive vs. the relevant broad market benchmark, as indicated below.
In-Line (I): The analyst expects the performance of his or her industry coverage universe over the next 12-18 months to be in line with the relevant broad market benchmark, as indicated below.
Cautious (C): The analyst views the performance of his or her industry coverage universe over the next 12-18 months with caution vs. the relevant broad market benchmark, as indicated below.
Benchmarks for each region are as follows: North America - S&P 500; Latin America - relevant MSCI country index or MSCI Latin America Index; Europe - MSCI Europe; Japan - TOPIX; Asia - relevant MSCI country index.

Stock Price, Price Target and Rating History (See Rating Definitions)

Morgan Stanley

M O R G A N   S T A N L E Y   R E S E A R C H

August 7, 2011
Procter & Gamble Co.

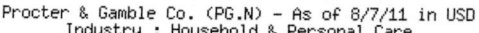

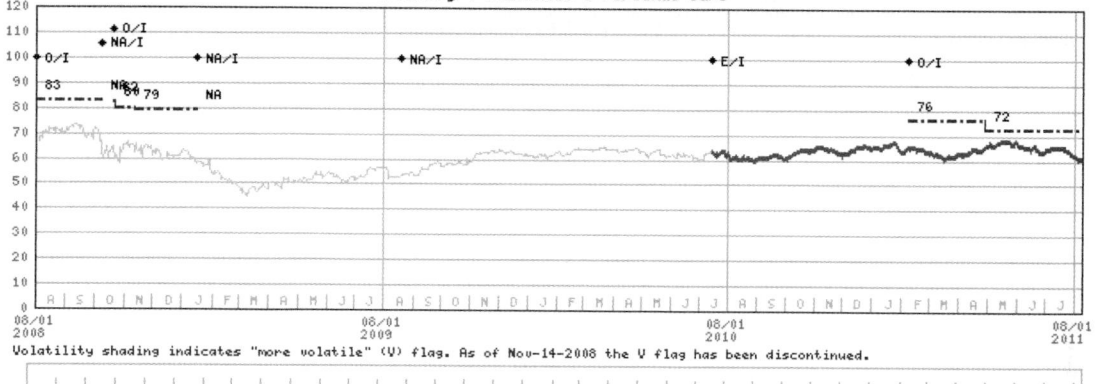

Procter & Gamble Co. (PG.N) - As of 8/7/11 in USD
Industry : Household & Personal Care

Volatility shading indicates "more volatile" (V) flag. As of Nov-14-2008 the V flag has been discontinued.

Stock Rating History: 8/1/08 : O/I; 10/8/08 : NA/I; 10/20/08 : O/I; 1/16/09 : NA/I; 8/19/09 : NA/I;
7/15/10 : E/I; 2/7/11 : O/I
Price Target History: 4/30/08 : 83; 10/8/08 : NA; 10/20/08 : 82; 10/22/08 : 80; 11/12/08 : 79; 1/16/09 : NA;
2/7/11 : 76; 4/28/11 : 72

Source: Morgan Stanley Research   Date Format : MM/DD/YY   Price Target ━•   No Price Target Assigned (NA)
Stock Price (Not Covered by Current Analyst) ━   Stock Price (Covered by Current Analyst) ▬
Stock and Industry Ratings (abbreviations below) appear as ◆ Stock Rating/Industry View
Stock Ratings: Overweight (O) Equal-weight (E) Underweight (U) Not-Rated (NR) More Volatile (V) No Rating Available (NA)
Industry View: Attractive (A)   In-line (I)   Cautious (C)   No Rating (NR)

Important Disclosures for Morgan Stanley Smith Barney LLC Customers

Citi Investment Research & Analysis (CIRA) research reports may be available about the companies or topics that are the subject of Morgan Stanley Research. Ask your Financial Advisor or use Research Center to view any available CIRA research reports in addition to Morgan Stanley research reports.

Important disclosures regarding the relationship between the companies that are the subject of Morgan Stanley Research and Morgan Stanley Smith Barney LLC, Morgan Stanley and Citigroup Global Markets Inc. or any of their affiliates, are available on the Morgan Stanley Smith Barney disclosure website at www.morganstanleysmithbarney.com/researchdisclosures.

For Morgan Stanley and Citigroup Global Markets, Inc. specific disclosures, you may refer to www.morganstanley.com/researchdisclosures and https://www.citigroupgeo.com/geopublic/Disclosures/index_a.html.

Each Morgan Stanley Equity Research report is reviewed and approved on behalf of Morgan Stanley Smith Barney LLC. This review and approval is conducted by the same person who reviews the Equity Research report on behalf of Morgan Stanley. This could create a conflict of interest.

Other Important Disclosures

Morgan Stanley & Co. International PLC and its affiliates have a significant financial interest in the debt securities of Avon Products Inc., Clorox Co, Colgate-Palmolive Co, Newell Rubbermaid Inc., Procter & Gamble Co..

Morgan Stanley is not acting as a municipal advisor and the opinions or views contained herein are not intended to be, and do not constitute, advice within the meaning of Section 975 of the Dodd-Frank Wall Street Reform and Consumer Protection Act.

Morgan Stanley produces an equity research product called a "Tactical Idea." Views contained in a "Tactical Idea" on a particular stock may be contrary to the recommendations or views expressed in research on the same stock. This may be the result of differing time horizons, methodologies, market events, or other factors. For all research available on a particular stock, please contact your sales representative or go to Client Link at www.morganstanley.com.

Morgan Stanley Research does not provide individually tailored investment advice. Morgan Stanley Research has been prepared without regard to the individual financial circumstances and objectives of persons who receive it. Morgan Stanley recommends that investors independently evaluate particular investments and strategies, and encourages investors to seek the advice of a financial adviser. The appropriateness of a particular investment or strategy will depend on an investor's individual circumstances and objectives. The securities, instruments, or strategies discussed in Morgan Stanley Research may not be suitable for all investors, and certain investors may not be eligible to purchase or participate in some or all of them.

The fixed income research analysts, strategists or economists principally responsible for the preparation of Morgan Stanley Research have received compensation based upon various factors, including quality, accuracy and value of research, firm profitability or revenues (which include fixed income trading and capital markets profitability or revenues), client feedback and competitive factors. Fixed Income Research analysts', strategists' or economists' compensation is not linked to investment banking or capital markets transactions performed by Morgan Stanley or the profitability or revenues of particular trading desks.

Morgan Stanley Research is not an offer to buy or sell or the solicitation of an offer to buy or sell any security/instrument or to participate in any particular trading strategy. The "Important US Regulatory Disclosures on Subject Companies" section in Morgan Stanley Research lists all companies mentioned where Morgan Stanley owns 1% or more of a class of common equity securities of the companies. For all other companies mentioned in Morgan Stanley Research, Morgan Stanley may have an investment of less than 1% in securities/instruments or derivatives of securities/instruments of companies and may trade them in ways different from those discussed in Morgan Stanley Research. Employees of Morgan Stanley not involved in the preparation of Morgan Stanley Research may have investments in securities/instruments or derivatives of securities/instruments of companies mentioned and may trade them in ways different from those discussed in Morgan Stanley Research. Derivatives may be issued by Morgan Stanley or associated persons.

With the exception of information regarding Morgan Stanley, Morgan Stanley Research is based on public information. Morgan Stanley makes every effort to use reliable, comprehensive information, but we make no representation that it is accurate or complete. We have no obligation to tell you when opinions or information in Morgan Stanley Research change apart from when we intend to discontinue equity research coverage of a subject company. Facts and views presented in Morgan Stanley Research have not been reviewed by, and may not reflect information known to, professionals in other Morgan Stanley business areas, including investment banking personnel.

Morgan Stanley

MORGAN STANLEY RESEARCH

August 7, 2011
Procter & Gamble Co.

Morgan Stanley

MORGAN STANLEY RESEARCH

The Americas	Europe	Japan	Asia/Pacific
1585 Broadway	20 Bank Street, Canary Wharf	4-20-3 Ebisu, Shibuya-ku	1 Austin Road West
New York, NY 10036-8293	London E14 4AD	Tokyo 150-6008	Kowloon
United States	**United Kingdom**	**Japan**	**Hong Kong**
Tel: +1 (1) 212 761 4000	Tel: +44 (0) 20 7 425 8000	Tel: +81 (0) 3 5424 5000	Tel: +852 2848 5200

Industry Coverage:Household & Personal Care

Company (Ticker)	Rating (as of)	Price* (08/05/2011)
Dara Mohsenian, CFA		
Avon Products Inc. (AVP.N)	E (10/04/2010)	$23.21
Church & Dwight Co., Inc. (CHD.N)	E (08/19/2009)	$38.54
Clorox Co (CLX.N)	E (07/15/2011)	$67.18
Colgate-Palmolive Co (CL.N)	E (07/15/2010)	$84.15
Energizer Holdings Inc (ENR.N)	E (02/02/2011)	$78.02
Newell Rubbermaid Inc. (NWL.N)	O (12/15/2010)	$13.16
Procter & Gamble Co. (PG.N)	O (02/07/2011)	$60.59
Tupperware Brands Corp. (TUP.N)	O (08/19/2009)	$56.47
Weight Watchers International (WTW.N)	E (02/18/2011)	$61.7

Stock Ratings are subject to change. Please see latest research for each company.
* Historical prices are not split adjusted.

DISCUSSION QUESTIONS

Q11-1. Identify at least two applications that use forecasted financial statements.

Q11-2. Forecasts of the income statement typically require estimates of cost of goods sold (gross profit) and operating and nonoperating expenses (revenues) as a percentage of revenues. Identify at least three financial statement adjustments that we discuss in previous modules that might affect our forecasts for gross profit margin and operating expense percentages.

Q11-3. Forecasts of the balance sheet commonly require estimates of the relative percentage of balance sheet accounts to revenues. Identify at least three financial statement adjustments to reported balance sheet items that can impact that item's relation to revenues. These can include adjustments to recognize assets and/or liabilities that are not recognized under GAAP.

Q11-4. What does the concept of financial statement articulation mean in the forecasting process?

Q11-5. Net operating assets typically move proportionately with revenues. How do the "buffer zone" and "financing" sections of the balance sheet offset some of these changes in net operating assets?

Q11-6. Identify and describe the four major steps in forecasting financial statements.

Q11-7. In addition to recent revenues trends, what other types and sources of information can we use to help us forecast revenues?

Q11-8. Describe the rationale for use of year-end balances in the computation of turnover rates (and other percentages) that are used to forecast selected balance sheet accounts.

Q11-9. What are "comparable store sales" for retailers and why are they important?

Q11-10. Capital expenditures are usually an important cash outflow for a company, and they figure prominently into forecasts of net operating assets. What are the sources of information about capital expenditures that we can draw upon?

Assignments with the ✓ logo in the margin are available in an online homework system. See the Preface of the book for details.

MINI EXERCISES

M11-11. Forecasting an Income Statement (LO2)

Abercrombie & Fitch
(ANF)

Abercrombie & Fitch reports the following income statements.

Income Statement, For Fiscal Years Ended ($ thousands)	Jan. 29, 2011	Jan. 30, 2010	Jan. 31, 2009
Net sales.	$3,468,777	$2,928,626	$3,484,058
Cost of goods sold.	1,256,596	1,045,028	1,152,963
Gross profit.	2,212,181	1,883,598	2,331,095
Stores and distribution expense.	1,589,501	1,425,950	1,436,363
Marketing, general and administrative expense.	400,804	353,269	405,248
Other operating income, net	(10,056)	(13,533)	(8,778)
Operating income.	231,932	117,912	498,262
Interest expense (income), net.	3,362	(1,598)	(11,382)
Income from continuing operations before taxes.	228,570	119,510	509,644
Tax expense from continuing operations.	78,287	40,557	201,475
Net income from continuing operations.	150,283	78,953	308,169
Loss from discontinued operations, net of tax.	—	(78,699)	(35,914)
Net Income.	$ 150,283	$ 254	$ 272,255

Forecast Abercrombie & Fitch's fiscal 2012 income statement assuming the following income statement relations. All percentages, other than sales growth and provision for income taxes, are based on percent of net sales.

Net Sales growth	10%
Cost of Goods Sold/Net sales	36%
Stores And Distribution Expense/Net sales	46%
Marketing, General And Administrative Expense/Net sales	12%
Other Operating Income, Net	10,056
Interest Expense (Income), Net	3,362
Tax Expense From Continuing Operations (% Of Pretax Income)	34%
Net Loss From Discontinued Operations (Net Of Taxes)	0

M11-12. Forecasting an Income Statement (LO2)

Best Buy reports the following income statements.

Best Buy (BBY)

Income Statement, Fiscal Years Ended ($ millions)	February 26, 2011	February 27, 2010	February 28, 2009
Revenue	$50,272	$49,694	$45,015
Cost of goods sold	37,611	37,534	34,017
Restructuring charges—cost of goods sold	24	—	—
Gross profit	12,637	12,160	10,998
Selling, general and administrative expenses	10,325	9,873	8,984
Restructuring charges	198	52	78
Goodwill and tradename impairment	—	—	66
Operating income	2,114	2,235	1,870
Other income (expense)			
Investment income and other	51	54	35
Investment impairment	—	—	(111)
Interest expense	(87)	(94)	(94)
Earnings before income tax expense and equity in income of affiliates . . .	2,078	2,195	1,700
Income tax expense	714	802	674
Equity in income of affiliates	2	1	7
Net earnings including noncontrolling interests	1,366	1,394	1,033
Net earnings attributable to noncontrolling interests	(89)	(77)	(30)
Net earnings attributable to Best Buy Co., Inc.	$ 1,277	$ 1,317	$ 1,003

Forecast Best Buy's fiscal 2012 income statement assuming the following income statement relations. All percentages (other than revenue growth, income tax expense, and net earnings attributable to noncontrolling interests) are based on percent of revenue.

Revenue growth	5%
Cost of goods sold/Revenue	75%
Restructuring charges − cost of goods sold	$0
Selling, general and administrative expenses/Revenue	21%
Restructuring charges	$0
Goodwill and tradename impairment	$0
Investment income and other	$51
Investment impairment	$0
Interest expense	$(87)
Income tax expense (% of pretax income)	34%
Equity in income of affiliates	$2
Net earnings attributable to noncontrolling interests (% of Net earnings including noncontrolling interests)	7%

M11-13. Forecasting an Income Statement (LO2)

General Mills reports the following fiscal year income statements.

General Mills (GIS)

Income Statement, Fiscal Years Ended (in millions)	May 29, 2011	May 30, 2010	May 31, 2009
Net sales.	$14,880.2	$14,635.6	$14,555.8
Cost of sales.	8,926.7	8,835.4	9,380.9
Selling, general and administrative expenses	3,192.0	3,162.7	2,893.2
Divestitures (gain), net	(17.4)	—	(84.9)
Restructuring, impairment, and other exit costs	4.4	31.4	41.6
Operating profit	2,774.5	2,606.1	2,325.0
Interest, net.	346.3	401.6	382.8
Earnings before income taxes and after-tax earnings from joint ventures	2,428.2	2,204.5	1,942.2
Income taxes	721.1	771.2	720.4
After-tax earnings from joint ventures	96.4	101.7	91.9
Net earnings, including earnings attributable to noncontrolling interests	1,803.5	1,535.0	1,313.7
Net earnings attributable to noncontrolling interests	5.2	4.5	9.3
Net earnings attributable to General Mills	$ 1,798.3	$ 1,530.5	$ 1,304.4

Forecast General Mills' fiscal year 2012 income statement assuming the following income statement relations. All percentages (other than net sales growth, income taxes, and net earnings attributable to noncontrolling interests) are based on percent of sales.

Net sales growth.	5%
Cost of sales/Net sales	60.0%
Selling, general, and administrative expenses/Net sales.	21.5%
Divestiture (gain), net	$0.0
Restructuring, impairment, and other exit costs	$0.0
Interest, net	$346.3
Income taxes (% pretax income)	29.7%
After-tax earnings from joint ventures	$96.4
Net earnings attributable to noncontrolling interests (% net earnings before attribution)	0.3%

M11-14. Analyzing, Forecasting, and Interpreting Working Capital Using Turnover Rates   (LO3)

Harley-Davidson
(HOG)

Harley-Davidson reports 2010 net operating working capital of $1,833 million and 2010 long-term operating assets of $2,679 million.

a. Forecast Harley-Davidson's 2011 net operating working capital and 2011 long-term operating assets. Assume forecasted 2011 net revenue of $4,938 million, net operating working capital turnover of 2.65 times, and long-term operating asset turnover of 1.81 times. (Both turnover rates are computed here using year-end balances. Finance receivables and related debt are considered operating under the assumption that they are an integral part of Harley's operating activities.)

b. Most of Harley's receivables arise from its financing activities relating to purchases of motorcycles by consumers and dealers. What effect will these receivables have on Harley's operating working capital turnover rate?

M11-15. Analyzing, Forecasting, and Interpreting Working Capital Using Turnover Rates   (LO3)

Nike (NKE)

Nike reports 2010 net operating working capital of $2,595 million and 2010 long-term operating assets of $3,460 million.

a. Forecast Nike's 2011 net operating working capital assuming forecasted sales of $19,451 million, net operating working capital turnover of 7.33 times, and long-term operating asset turnover of 5.50 times. (Both turnover rates are computed here using year-end balances.)

b. Nike's long-term operating asset turnover rate is comparatively high. Can you suggest a possible reason given Nike's business model? Explain.

M11-16. Forecasting the Balance Sheet Using Turnover Rates   (LO2, 3)

General Mills (GIS)

Refer to the General Mills information in M11-13. Assume the forecast of 2012 net sales is $15,624.2 million. Use the following financial statement relations to forecast General Mills' receivables, inventories, and accounts payable as of the end of May 2012.

Year-end turnover rates	2012
Year-end receivables/Net Sales	7.8%
Year-end inventories/Net Sales	10.8%
Year-end accounts payable/Net Sales	6.7%

M11-17. Adjusting the Income Statement (LO2)

Kraft Foods, Inc., reports the following footnote to its 2010 10-K.

Kraft Foods, Inc. (KFT)

> **Pizza Divestiture** On March 1, 2010, we completed the sale of the assets of our North American frozen pizza business ("Frozen Pizza") to Nestlé USA, Inc. ("Nestlé") for $3.7 billion. Our Frozen Pizza business was a component of our U.S. Convenient Meals and Canada & North America Foodservice segments. The sale included the *DiGiorno*, *Tombstone* and *Jack's* brands in the U.S., the *Delissio* brand in Canada and the *California Pizza Kitchen* trademark license. It also included two Wisconsin manufacturing facilities (Medford and Little Chute) and the leases for the pizza depots and delivery trucks. Approximately 3,600 of our employees transferred with the business to Nestlé. Accordingly, the results of our Frozen Pizza business have been reflected as discontinued operations on the consolidated statement of earnings, and prior period results have been revised in a consistent manner.

What adjustment(s) might we consider before we forecast Kraft's income for 2011? How would we treat the cash proceeds that Kraft realized on such a sale?

EXERCISES

E11-18. Analyzing, Forecasting, and Interpreting Income Statement and Balance Sheet (LO2, 3)

Following are the income statements and balance sheets of Abercrombie & Fitch.

Abercrombie & Fitch (ANF)

Income Statement, For Fiscal Years Ended ($ thousands)	January 29, 2011	January 30, 2010	January 31, 2009
Net sales.	$3,468,777	$2,928,626	$3,484,058
Cost of goods sold.	1,256,596	1,045,028	1,152,963
Gross profit.	2,212,181	1,883,598	2,331,095
Stores and distribution expense.	1,589,501	1,425,950	1,436,363
Marketing, general and administrative expense.	400,804	353,269	405,248
Other operating income, net	(10,056)	(13,533)	(8,778)
Operating income.	231,932	117,912	498,262
Interest expense (income), net	3,362	(1,598)	(11,382)
Income from continuing operations before taxes.	228,570	119,510	509,644
Tax expense from continuing operations	78,287	40,557	201,475
Net income from continuing operations.	150,283	78,953	308,169
Loss from discontinued operations, net of tax.	—	(78,699)	(35,914)
Net Income.	$ 150,283	$ 254	$ 272,255

Consolidated Balance Sheets		
(Thousands, except par value amounts)	January 29, 2011	January 30, 2010
Current Assets		
Cash and equivalents.	$ 826,353	$ 669,950
Marketable securities.	—	32,356
Receivables	81,264	90,865
Inventories	385,857	310,645
Deferred income taxes.	60,405	44,570
Other current assets.	79,389	77,297
Total current assets	1,433,268	1,225,683
Property and equipment, net	1,149,583	1,244,019
Noncurrent marketable securities	100,534	141,794
Other assets.	264,517	210,370
Total assets.	$2,947,902	$2,821,866

continued

continued from prior page

Liabilities and stockholders' equity
Current liabilities

Accounts payable.	$ 137,235	$ 150,134
Accrued expenses	306,587	246,289
Deferred lease credits	41,538	43,597
Income taxes payable	73,491	9,352
Total current liabilities.	558,851	449,372
Long-term liabilities		
Deferred income taxes.	33,515	47,142
Deferred lease credits	192,619	212,052
Long-term debt	68,566	71,213
Other liabilities	203,567	214,170
Total long-term liabilities.	498,267	544,577
Stockholders' equity:		
Class A common stock—$0.01 par value: 150,000 shares authorized and 103,300 shares issued at each of January 29, 2011 and January 30, 2010	1,033	1,033
Paid-in capital	349,258	339,453
Retained earnings	2,272,317	2,183,690
Accumulated other comprehensive loss, net of tax.	(6,516)	(8,973)
Treasury stock, at average cost 16,054 and 15,314 shares at January 29, 2011, and January 30, 2010, respectively.	(725,308)	(687,286)
Total stockholders' equity	1,890,784	1,827,917
Total liabilities and stockholders' equity.	$2,947,902	$2,821,866

a. Forecast Abercrombie & Fitch's fiscal 2012 income statement and balance sheet using the following relations (assume 'no change' for accounts not listed). Assume all capital expenditures are purchases of property and equipment.

Net sales growth.	10%
Cost of goods sold/Net sales.	36.20%
Stores and distribution expense/Net sales	45.80%
Marketing, general and administrative expense/Net sales	11.60%
Other operating income, net	$10,056
Interest expense (income), net.	$3,362
Tax expense from continuing operations (% of pretax income).	34.30%
Net loss from discontinued operations (net of taxes).	$0
Cash and equivalents/Net sales.	23.8%
Receivables/Net sales	2.3%
Inventories/Net sales	11.1%
Deferred income taxes/Net sales.	1.7%
Other current assets/Net sales.	2.3%
Other assets/Net sales.	7.6%
Accounts payable/Net sales.	4.0%
Accrued expenses/Net sales	8.8%
Deferred lease credits/Net sales	1.2%
Income taxes payable (% tax expense).	93.9%
Deferred income taxes/Net sales.	1.0%
Deferred lease credits/Net sales	5.6%
Capital expenditures (% Of Sales).	4.6%
Depreciation & amortization.	$229,153
Dividends (% Net income)	41.0%
Current maturities of long-term debt	$0

b. What does the forecasted adjustment to balance the accounting equation from part *a* reveal to us about the forecasted financing needs of the company? Explain.

E11-19. **Forecasting the Statement of Cash Flows** (LO4)

Refer to the Abercrombie & Fitch financial information in Exercise 11-18. Prepare a forecast of fiscal 2012 statement of cash flows.

Abercrombie & Fitch (ANF)

E11-20. **Analyzing, Forecasting, and Interpreting Both Income Statement and Balance Sheet** (LO2, 3)

Following are the income statements and balance sheets of Best Buy Co., Inc.

Best Buy Co., Inc. (BBY)

Income Statement, Fiscal Years Ended ($ millions)	February 26, 2011	February 27, 2010	February 28, 2009
Revenue	$50,272	$49,694	$45,015
Cost of goods sold	37,611	37,534	34,017
Restructuring charges—cost of goods sold	24	—	—
Gross profit	12,637	12,160	10,998
Selling, general and administrative expenses	10,325	9,873	8,984
Restructuring charges	198	52	78
Goodwill and tradename impairment	—	—	66
Operating income	2,114	2,235	1,870
Other income (expense)			
Investment income and other	51	54	35
Investment impairment	—	—	(111)
Interest expense	(87)	(94)	(94)
Earnings before income tax expense and equity in income of affiliates	2,078	2,195	1,700
Income tax expense	714	802	674
Equity in income of affiliates	2	1	7
Net earnings including noncontrolling interests	1,366	1,394	1,033
Net earnings attributable to noncontrolling interests	(89)	(77)	(30)
Net earnings attributable to Best Buy Co., Inc.	$ 1,277	$ 1,317	$ 1,003

Balance Sheet ($ millions, except per share and share amounts)	February 26, 2011	February 27, 2010
Assets		
Cash and cash equivalents	$ 1,103	$ 1,826
Short-term investments	22	90
Receivables	2,348	2,020
Merchandise inventories	5,897	5,486
Other current assets	1,103	1,144
Total current assets	10,473	10,566
Property and equipment		
Land and buildings	766	757
Leasehold improvements	2,318	2,154
Fixtures and equipment	4,701	4,447
Property under capital lease	120	95
	7,905	7,453
Less accumulated depreciation	4,082	3,383
Net property and equipment	3,823	4,070
Goodwill	2,454	2,452
Tradenames, net	133	159
Customer relationships, net	203	279
Equity and other investments	328	324
Other assets	435	452
Total assets	$17,849	$18,302

continued

continued from prior page

Liabilities and equity

Accounts payable	$ 4,894	$ 5,276
Unredeemed gift card liabilities	474	463
Accrued compensation and related expenses	570	544
Accrued liabilities	1,471	1,681
Accrued income taxes	256	316
Short-term debt	557	663
Current portion of long-term debt	441	35
Total current liabilities	8,663	8,978
Long-term liabilities	1,183	1,256
Long-term debt	711	1,104
Equity		
Best Buy Co., Inc. shareholders' equity		
Preferred stock, $1.00 par value: Authorized—400,000 shares; Issued and outstanding—none	—	—
Common stock, $0.10 par value: Authorized—1.0 billion shares; Issued and outstanding—392,590,000 and 418,815,000 shares, respectively	39	42
Additional paid-in capital	18	441
Retained earnings	6,372	5,797
Accumulated other comprehensive income	173	40
Total Best Buy Co., Inc. shareholders' equity	6,602	6,320
Noncontrolling interests	690	644
Total equity	7,292	6,964
Total liabilities and shareholders' equity	$17,849	$18,302

a. Forecast Best Buy's fiscal 2012 income statement and balance sheet using the following relations (assume 'no change' for accounts not listed). Assume that all capital expenditures are purchases of property and equipment.

Revenue growth	5%
Cost of goods sold/Revenue	74.8%
Restructuring charges - cost of goods sold	$0
Selling, general and administrative expenses/Revenue	20.5%
Restructuring charges	$0
Goodwill and tradename impairment	$0
Investment income and other	$51
Investment impairment	$0
Interest expense	$(87)
Income tax expense/Pretax income)	34.4%
Equity in income of affiliates	$2
Net earnings attributable to noncontrolling interests/Net earnings including noncontrolling interests	6.5%
Cash and cash equivalents/Revenue	2.2%
Receivables/Revenue	4.7%
Merchandise inventories/Revenue	11.7%
Other current assets/Revenue	2.2%
CAPEX (Increase in gross Property and equipment)/Revenue	1.5%
Goodwill	no chg
Tradenames, Net amortization	$25
Customer relationships, Net amortization	$38
Equity and other investments	no chg
Other assets/Revenue	0.9%

continued

continued from prior page

Accounts payable/Revenue	9.7%
Unredeemed gift card liabilities/Revenue.	0.9%
Accrued compensation and related expenses/Revenue	1.1%
Accrued liabilities/Revenue	2.9%
Accrued income taxes/Revenue	0.5%
Long-term liabilities	no chg
Noncontrolling interests	*
Capital expenditures/Revenue.	1.5%
Depreciation/Prior year gross PPE.	12.0%
Amortization/Prior year intangible asset balance.	18.7%
Dividends/Net income	18.6%
Long-term debt payments required in fiscal 2013	$37

* Increase by net income attributable to noncontrolling interests and assume no dividends

  b. What does the forecasted adjustment to balance the accounting equation from part *a* reveal to us
        about the forecasted financing needs of the company? Explain.

E11-21. **Forecasting the Statement of Cash Flows** (LO4)

Best Buy Co., Inc.
(BBY)

Refer to the Best Buy Co., Inc., financial information from Exercise 11-20. Prepare a forecast of its
fiscal year 2012 statement of cash flows. (*Hint:* Use net income before noncontrolling interests to begin
the statement of cash flows.)

E11-22. **Analyzing, Forecasting, and Interpreting Income Statement and Balance Sheet** (LO2, 3)

General Mills, Inc.
(GIS)

Following are the income statements and balance sheets of General Mills, Inc.

Income Statement, Fiscal Years Ended (in millions except per share data)	May 29, 2011	May 30, 2010	May 31, 2009
Net sales.	$14,880.2	$14,635.6	$14,555.8
Cost of sales.	8,926.7	8,835.4	9,380.9
Selling, general and administrative expenses	3,192.0	3,162.7	2,893.2
Divestitures (gain), net	(17.4)	—	(84.9)
Restructuring, impairment, and other exit costs	4.4	31.4	41.6
Operating profit	2,774.5	2,606.1	2,325.0
Interest, net.	346.3	401.6	382.8
Earnings before income taxes and after-tax earnings from joint ventures. . .	2,428.2	2,204.5	1,942.2
Income taxes	721.1	771.2	720.4
After-tax earnings from joint ventures	96.4	101.7	91.9
Net earnings, including earnings attributable to noncontrolling interests . . .	1,803.5	1,535.0	1,313.7
Net earnings attributable to noncontrolling interests	5.2	4.5	9.3
Net earnings attributable to General Mills	$ 1,798.3	$ 1,530.5	$ 1,304.4

Balance Sheet (In millions)	May 29, 2011	May 30, 2010
Assets		
Cash and cash equivalents	$ 619.6	$ 673.2
Receivables	1,162.3	1,041.6
Inventories	1,609.3	1,344.0
Deferred income taxes.	27.3	42.7
Prepaid expenses and other current assets.	483.5	378.5
Total current assets.	3,902.0	3,480.0
Land, buildings and equipment	3,345.9	3,127.7
Goodwill	6,750.8	6,592.8
Other intangible assets.	3,813.3	3,715.0
Other assets.	862.5	763.4
Total assets.	$18,674.5	$17,678.9

continued

continued from prior page

Liabilities and equity

Accounts payable..	$ 995.1	$ 849.5
Current portion of long-term debt	1,031.3	107.3
Notes payable	311.3	1,050.1
Other current liabilities..................................	1,321.5	1,762.2
Total current liabilities.................................	3,659.2	3,769.1
Long-term debt	5,542.5	5,268.5
Deferred income taxes..................................	1,127.4	874.6
Other liabilities	1,733.2	2,118.7
Total liabilities......................................	12,062.3	12,030.9
Stockholders' equity		
Common stock, 754.6 shares issued, $0.10 par value...........	75.5	75.5
Additional paid-in capital	1,319.8	1,307.1
Retained earnings......................................	9,191.3	8,122.4
Common stock in treasury, at cost, shares of 109.8 and 98.1......	(3,210.3)	(2,615.2)
Accumulated other comprehensive loss	(1,010.8)	(1,486.9)
Total stockholders' equity.............................	6,365.5	5,402.9
Noncontrolling interests.................................	246.7	245.1
Total equity...	6,612.2	5,648.0
Total liabilities and equity................................	$18,674.5	$17,678.9

a. Forecast **General Mills'** fiscal 2012 income statement and balance sheet using the following relations (assume 'no change' for accounts not listed). Assume all capital expenditures are purchases of land, buildings and equipment, net, and that depreciation and amortization expense is included as part of selling, general and administrative expense ($ millions).

Net sales growth...	5%
Cost of sales/Net sales	60.0%
Selling, general, and administrative expenses/Net sales..........................	21.5%
Divestiture (gain), net	$0.0
Restructuring, impairment, and other exit costs	$0.0
Interest, net	$346.3
Income taxes/Pretax income	29.7%
After-tax earnings from joint ventures	$96.4
Net earnings attributable to noncontrolling interests/Net earnings before attribution. . .	0.3%
Cash/Net sales...	4.2%
Receivables/Net sales	7.8%
Inventories/Net sales	10.8%
Deferred income taxes/Net sales....................................	0.2%
Prepaid expenses and other current assets/Net sales........................	3.2%
Other intangible assets...	$0 amortization
Other assets/Net sales...	5.8%
Accounts payable/Net sales..	6.7%
Other current liabilities/Net sales	8.9%
Current portion of long-term debt	$733.6
Deferred income taxes/Net sales....................................	7.6%
Other liabilities/Net sales	11.6%
Noncontrolling interests	*
Capital expenditures/Net sales	4.4%
Depreciation/Prior year net PPE.....................................	20.7%
Dividends/Net income	40.6%
Current maturities of long-term debt in fiscal 2013	$733.6

*Increase by net income attributable to noncontrolling interests and assume no dividends.

b. What does the forecasted adjustment to balance the accounting equation from part *a* reveal to us about the forecasted financing needs of the company? Explain.

E11-23. Forecasting the Statement of Cash Flows (LO4)

General Mills, Inc.
(GIS)

Refer to the **General Mills, Inc.,** financial information from Exercise 11-22. Forecast General Mills' fiscal 2012 statement of cash flows. (Use net income before noncontrolling interests to begin the statement of cash flows.)

E11-24. **Adjusting the Balance Sheet for Operating Leases** (LO1, 2, 3)

Delta Air Lines reports total net operating assets of $12,130 million, nonoperating liabilities of $11,233 million, and equity of $897 in its 2010 10-K. Footnotes reveal the existence of operating leases that have a present value of $7,088 million (see Module 10 for computations).

Delta Air Lines (DAL)

a. What balance sheet adjustment(s) might we consider relating to the leases before we forecast financial statements? (*Hint:* Consider the distinction between operating and nonoperating assets and liabilities.)

b. What income statement adjustment(s) might we consider? (*Hint:* Reflect on the operating and nonoperating distinction for lease-related expenses.)

E11-25. **Adjusting the Balance Sheet for Equity Method Investments** (LO3)

Abbott Laboratories, Inc., reports its 50% joint venture investment in TAP Pharmaceutical Products Inc. using the equity method of accounting in its 2007 10-K. The Abbott balance sheet reports an investment balance of $159 million. TAP has total assets of $1,354.2 million, liabilities of $1,036.7 million, and equity of $317.5 million. Abbott's investment balance is, thus, equal to its 50% interest in TAP's equity ($317.5 million × 50% = $158.75 million, rounded to $159 million). What adjustment(s) might we consider to Abbott's balance sheet before we forecast its financial statements? (*Hint:* Consider the distinction between operating and nonoperating assets and liabilities.) What risks might Abbott Laboratories face that are not revealed on the face of its balance sheet?

Abbott Laboratories, Inc. (ABT)

TAP Pharmaceutical Products Inc.

E11-26. **Analyzing, Forecasting, and Interpreting Income Statement and Balance Sheet** (LO2, 3)

Following are the income statement and balance sheet of Whole Foods Market, Inc.

Whole Foods Market, Inc. (WFM)

Income Statement, For Years Ended (in $ 000s)	2010	2009	2008
Sales.	$9,005,794	$8,031,620	$7,953,912
Cost of goods sold and occupancy costs	5,870,393	5,277,310	5,247,207
Gross profit.	3,135,401	2,754,310	2,706,705
Direct store expenses.	2,375,716	2,145,809	2,107,940
General and administrative expenses	272,449	243,749	270,428
Pre-opening expenses	38,044	49,218	55,554
Relocation, store closures and lease termination costs.	11,217	31,185	36,545
Operating income.	437,975	284,349	236,238
Interest expense.	(33,048)	(36,856)	(36,416)
Investment and other income.	6,854	3,449	6,697
Income before income taxes	411,781	250,942	206,519
Provision for income taxes.	165,948	104,138	91,995
Net income.	$ 245,833	$ 146,804	$ 114,524

Assets (in $ 000s)	2010	2009
Assets		
Cash and cash equivalents	$ 131,996	$ 430,130
Short-term investments—available-for-sale securities	329,738	—
Restricted cash	86,802	71,023
Accounts receivable.	133,346	104,731
Merchandise inventories	323,487	310,602
Prepaid expenses and other current assets.	54,686	51,137
Deferred income taxes.	101,464	87,757
Total current assets	1,161,519	1,055,380
Property and equipment, net of accumulated depreciation and amortization.	1,886,130	1,897,853
Long-term investments—available-for-sale securities.	96,146	—
Goodwill.	665,224	658,254
Intangible assets, net of accumulated amortization.	69,064	73,035
Deferred income taxes.	99,156	91,000
Other assets.	9,301	7,866
Total assets.	$3,986,540	$3,783,388

continued

continued from prior page

Liabilities and Shareholders' Equity				
Current installments of long-term debt and capital lease obligations	$	410	$	389
Accounts payable.		213,212		189,597
Accrued payroll, bonus and other benefits due team members		244,427		207,983
Dividends payable		—		8,217
Other current liabilities		289,823		277,838
Total current liabilities.		747,872		684,024
Long-term debt and capital lease obligations, less current installments.		508,288		738,848
Deferred lease liabilities		294,291		250,326
Other long-term liabilities		62,831		69,262
Total liabilities.		1,613,282		1,742,460
Series A redeemable preferred stock, $0.01 par value, 425 shares authorized; zero and 425 shares issued and outstanding at 2010 and 2009, respectively		—		413,052
Shareholders' equity:				
Common stock, no par value, 300,000 shares authorized; 172,033 and 140,542 shares issued and outstanding at 2010 and 2009, respectively.		1,773,897		1,283,028
Accumulated other comprehensive income (loss)		791		(13,367)
Retained earnings		598,570		358,215
Total shareholders' equity		2,373,258		1,627,876
Total liabilities and shareholders' equity.		$3,986,540		$3,783,388

a. Forecast Whole Foods Market's 2011 income statement and balance sheet using the following relations ($ 000)—assume 'no change' for accounts not listed.

Sales growth.	10.0%
Cost of goods sold and occupancy costs/Sales	65.2%
Direct store expenses/Sales.	26.4%
General and administrative expenses/Sales	3.0%
Pre-opening expenses/Sales	0.4%
Relocation, store closure and lease termination costs	$0
Interest expense.	$(33,048)
Investment and other income.	$6,854
Provision for income taxes/Pretax income.	40.3%
Cash and cash equivalents/Sales	1.5%
Restricted cash	$86,802
Accounts receivable/Sales.	1.5%
Merchandise inventories/Sales	3.6%
Prepaid expenses and other current assets/Sales.	0.6%
Deferred income taxes (current).	$101,464
Long-term investments—available-for-sale securities.	$96,146
Goodwill	$665,224
Intangible assets, net of accumulated amortization.	$69,064
Deferred income taxes (noncurrent).	$99,156
Other assets/Sales.	0.1%
Current installments of long-term debt and capital lease obligations	$410
Accounts payable/Sales.	2.4%
Accrued payroll, bonus and other benefits due team members/Sales	2.7%
Other current liabilities/Sales	3.2%
Current maturities of long-term debt and capital lease obligations.	$410
Deferred lease liabilities	$294,291
Other long-term liabilities/Sales.	0.7%
Series A redeemable preferred stock.	$0
Common stock.	$1,773,897
Accumulated other comprehensive income (loss)	$791
Capital expenditures/Prior year net PPE	13.5%
Depreciation & amortization/Prior year net PPE.	14.5%
Dividends/Net income	3.5%

b. What does the forecasted adjustment to balance the accounting equation from part *a* reveal to us about the forecasted financing needs of the company?

E11-27. Forecasting the Statement of Cash Flows (LO4)

Refer to the Whole Foods Market, Inc., financial information from Exercise 11-26. Prepare a forecast of its fiscal year 2011 statement of cash flows.

Whole Foods Market, Inc. (WFM)

E11-28. Projecting NOPAT and NOA Using Parsimonious Forecasting Method (LO6)

Following are Intel's sales, net operating profit after tax (NOPAT), and net operating assets (NOA) for its year ended December 31, 2010 ($ millions).

Intel (INTC)

Sales.	$43,623
Net operating profit after tax (NOPAT)	11,250
Net operating assets (NOA)	28,652

Forecast Intel's sales, NOPAT and NOA for years 2011 through 2014 using the following assumptions:

Sales growth per year.	10%
Net operating profit margin (NOPM).	25%
Net operating asset turnover (NOAT), based on NOA at December 31, 2010.	1.5

E11-29. Projecting NOPAT and NOA Using Parsimonious Forecasting Method (LO6)

Following are 3M's sales, net operating profit after tax (NOPAT), and net operating assets (NOA) for its fiscal year ended 2010 ($ millions).

3M Co. (MMM)

Sales.	$26,662
Net operating profit after tax (NOPAT)	$ 4,266
Net operating assets (NOA)	$16,305

Forecast 3M's sales, NOPAT and NOA for fiscal years 2011 through 2014 using the following assumptions:

Sales growth per year.	15%
Net operating profit margin (NOPM).	16%
Net operating asset turnover (NOAT), based on NOA at 2010 fiscal year-end.	1.6

PROBLEMS

P11-30. Forecasting the Income Statement, Balance Sheet, and Statement of Cash Flows (LO2, 3, 4)

Following are fiscal year financial statements of Oracle Corporation.

Oracle Corporation (ORCL)

Consolidated Statements of Operations			
Year ended May 31 (in millions)	**2011**	**2010**	**2009**
Revenues			
New software licenses	$ 9,235	$ 7,533	$ 7,123
Software license updates and product support.	14,796	13,092	11,754
Software revenues	24,031	20,625	18,877
Hardware systems products	4,382	1,506	—
Hardware systems support	2,562	784	—
Hardware systems revenues	6,944	2,290	—
Services	4,647	3,905	4,375
Total revenues	35,622	26,820	23,252

continued

continued from prior page

Operating expenses			
Sales and marketing	6,579	5,080	4,638
Software license updates and product support	1,264	1,063	1,088
Hardware systems products	2,057	880	—
Hardware systems support	1,259	423	—
Services	3,818	3,398	3,706
Research and development	4,519	3,254	2,767
General and administrative	970	911	785
Amortization of intangible assets	2,428	1,973	1,713
Acquisition related and other	208	154	117
Restructuring	487	622	117
Total operating expenses	23,589	17,758	14,931
Operating income	12,033	9,062	8,321
Interest expense	(808)	(754)	(630)
Non-operating income (expense), net	186	(65)	143
Income before provision for income taxes	11,411	8,243	7,834
Provision for income taxes	2,864	2,108	2,241
Net income	$ 8,547	$ 6,135	$ 5,593

Consolidated Balance Sheets		
May 31 (in millions, except per share data)	2011	2010
Assets		
Cash and cash equivalents	$16,163	$9,914
Marketable securities	12,685	8,555
Trade receivables, net of allowances for doubtful accounts of $372 and $305 as of May 31, 2011 and 2010, respectively	6,628	5,585
Inventories	303	259
Deferred tax assets	1,189	1,159
Prepaid expenses and other current assets	2,206	1,532
Total current assets	39,174	27,004
Non-current assets		
Property, plant and equipment, net	2,857	2,763
Intangible assets, net	7,860	9,321
Goodwill	21,553	20,425
Deferred tax assets	1,076	1,267
Other assets	1,015	798
Total non-current assets	34,361	34,574
Total assets	$73,535	$61,578
Liabilities and equity		
Notes payable, current and other current borrowings	$1,150	$3,145
Accounts payable	701	775
Accrued compensation and related benefits	2,320	1,895
Deferred revenues	6,802	5,900
Other current liabilities	3,219	2,976
Total current liabilities	14,192	14,691
Non-current liabilities		
Notes payable and other non-current borrowings	14,772	11,510
Income taxes payable	3,169	2,695
Deferred tax liabilities	59	424
Other non-current liabilities	1,098	1,059
Total non-current liabilities	19,098	15,688

continued

continued from prior page

Oracle Corporation stockholders' equity		
Preferred stock, $0.01 par value—authorized: 1.0 shares; outstanding: none	—	—
Common stock, $0.01 par value and additional paid in capital—authorized: 11,000 shares; outstanding: 5,068 shares and 5,026 shares as of May 31, 2011 and 2010, respectively	16,653	14,648
Retained earnings	22,581	16,146
Accumulated other comprehensive income	542	4
Total Oracle Corporation stockholders' equity	39,776	30,798
Noncontrolling interests	469	401
Total equity	40,245	31,199
Total liabilities and equity	$73,535	$61,578

Required

Forecast Oracle's fiscal 2012 income statement, balance sheet, and statement of cash flows; round forecasts to $ millions. *Hint*: We forecast total revenues by projecting a continuation of year-over-year percentage growth rates for each revenue category that Oracle includes in its income statement (rounded to the nearest whole percent). (*Note*: Oracle's long-term debt footnote reports that current maturities of long-term debt are $1,250 million for May 2012; Oracle includes the current maturities with "Notes payable, current and other current borrowings" on its balance sheet. Oracle reports capital expenditures of $450 million, dividends of $1,061 million, depreciation of $368 million, which it includes in G&A expense, and amortization of $2,428 million, which it reports separately. Identify all financial statement relations estimated and assumptions made; estimate forecasted income statement relations to 1 decimal (assume no change for: interest expense, nonoperating income, deferred tax assets and liabilities, goodwill, noncontrolling interest, common stock, and accumulated other comprehensive income). What do the forecasts imply about the financing needs of Oracle?

P11-31. Forecasting the Income Statement, Balance Sheet, and Statement of Cash Flows (LO2, 3, 4)
Following are the financial statements of Nike, Inc.

Nike, Inc. (NKE)

Consolidated Statements of Income			
Year ended May 31 (in millions)	2011	2010	2009
Revenues	$20,862	$19,014	$19,176
Cost of sales	11,354	10,214	10,572
Gross margin	9,508	8,800	8,604
Demand creation expense	2,448	2,356	2,352
Operating overhead expense	4,245	3,970	3,798
Total selling and administrative expense	6,693	6,326	6,150
Restructuring charges	—	—	195
Goodwill impairment	—	—	199
Intangible and other asset impairment	—	—	202
Interest expense (income), net	4	6	(10)
Other (income), net	(33)	(49)	(89)
Income before income taxes	2,844	2,517	1,957
Income taxes	711	610	470
Net income	$ 2,133	$ 1,907	$ 1,487

Consolidated Balance Sheets		
May 31 (in millions)	**2011**	**2010**
Assets		
Cash and equivalents..	$ 1,955	$ 3,079
Short-term investments	2,583	2,067
Accounts receivable, net	3,138	2,650
Inventories	2,715	2,041
Deferred income taxes.......................................	312	249
Prepaid expenses and other current assets.............	594	873
Total current assets	11,297	10,959
Property, plant and equipment, net	2,115	1,932
Identifiable intangible assets, net.........................	487	467
Goodwill..	205	188
Deferred income taxes and other assets	894	873
Total assets...	$14,998	$14,419
Liabilities and shareholders' equity		
Current portion of long-term debt	$ 200	$ 7
Notes payable	187	139
Accounts payable..	1,469	1,255
Accrued liabilities	1,985	1,904
Income taxes payable	117	59
Total current liabilities.......................................	3,958	3,364
Long-term debt	276	446
Deferred income taxes and other liabilities	921	855
Redeemable Preferred Stock...............................	—	—
Shareholders' equity		
Common stock at stated value		
Class A convertible — 90 and 90 shares outstanding.....................	—	—
Class B — 378 and 394 shares outstanding	3	3
Capital in excess of stated value	3,944	3,441
Accumulated other comprehensive income.............	95	215
Retained earnings	5,801	6,095
Total shareholders' equity	9,843	9,754
Total liabilities and shareholders' equity................	$14,998	$14,419

Required

Forecast Nike's fiscal year 2012 income statement, balance sheet, and statement of cash flows. Round the revenue growth rate to the nearest whole percent, and round forecasts to $ millions. Identify all financial statement relations estimated and assumptions made; estimate forecasted income statement relations to 1 decimal (assume no change for: other expense or income, interest expense, common stock, capital in excess of stated value, and accumulated other comprehensive income). For fiscal 2011, capital expenditures are $432 million, depreciation expense is $335 million, amortization is $23 million, and dividends are $555 million. Footnotes reveal that the current portion on long-term debt due in 2013 is $48 million. What do the forecasts imply about Nike's financing needs for the upcoming year?

P11-32. Forecasting the Income Statement, Balance Sheet, and Statement of Cash Flows (LO2, 3, 4)
Following are the financial statements of Home Depot, Inc.

Home Depot, Inc. (HD)

Consolidated Statements of Earnings			
	For Fiscal Year Ended		
Amounts in millions, except per share data	January 30, 2011	January 31, 2010	February 1, 2009
Net sales.	$67,997	$66,176	$71,288
Cost of sales.	44,693	43,764	47,298
Gross profit.	23,304	22,412	23,990
Operating expenses			
Selling, general and administrative	15,849	15,902	17,846
Depreciation and amortization	1,616	1,707	1,785
Total operating expenses	17,465	17,609	19,631
Operating income.	5,839	4,803	4,359
Interest and other (income) expense			
Interest and investment income.	(15)	(18)	(18)
Interest expense.	530	676	624
Other.	51	163	163
Interest and other, net	566	821	769
Earnings from continuing operations before provision for income taxes.	5,273	3,982	3,590
Provision for income taxes.	1,935	1,362	1,278
Earnings from continuing operations	3,338	2,620	2,312
Earnings (loss) from discontinued operations, net of tax.	—	41	(52)
Net earnings.	$ 3,338	$ 2,661	$ 2,260

Consolidated Balance Sheets		
Amounts in millions, except share and per share data	January 30, 2011	January 31, 2010
Assets		
Cash and cash equivalents	$ 545	$ 1,421
Receivables, net.	1,085	964
Merchandise inventories	10,625	10,188
Other current assets.	1,224	1,327
Total current assets	13,479	13,900
Property and equipment, at cost:		
Land	8,497	8,451
Buildings	17,606	17,391
Furniture, fixtures and equipment	9,687	9,091
Leasehold improvements	1,373	1,383
Construction in progress	654	525
Capital leases.	568	504
	38,385	37,345
Less accumulated depreciation and amortization	13,325	11,795
Net property and equipment	25,060	25,550
Notes receivable.	139	33
Goodwill	1,187	1,171
Other assets	260	223
Total assets.	$40,125	$40,877

continued

continued from prior page

Liabilities and stockholders' equity		
Accounts payable.	$ 4,717	$ 4,863
Accrued salaries and related expenses	1,290	1,263
Sales taxes payable	368	362
Deferred revenue	1,177	1,158
Income taxes payable	13	108
Current installments of long-term debt	1,042	1,020
Other accrued expenses	1,515	1,589
Total current liabilities.	10,122	10,363
Long-term debt, excluding current installments	8,707	8,662
Other long-term liabilities	2,135	2,140
Deferred income taxes	272	319
Total liabilities	21,236	21,484
Stockholders' equity		
Common stock, par value $0.05; authorized: 10 billion shares; issued: 1.722 billion shares at January 30, 2011 and 1.716 billion shares at January 31, 2010; outstanding: 1.623 billion shares at January 30, 2011 and 1.698 billion shares at January 31, 2010	86	86
Paid-in-capital	6,556	6,304
Retained earnings	14,995	13,226
Accumulated other comprehensive income	445	362
Treasury stock, at cost, 99 million shares at January 30, 2011 and 18 million shares at January 31, 2010	(3,193)	(585)
Total stockholders' equity	18,889	19,393
Total liabilities and stockholders' equity.	$40,125	$40,877

Required

Forecast Home Depot's fiscal year ended January 2012 income statement, balance sheet, and statement of cash flows . Round the revenue growth rate to the nearest whole percent, and round forecasts to $ millions. Estimate forecasted income statement relations to 1 decimal (assume no change for: notes receivable, goodwill, interest income and expense, deferred income taxes, common stock and additional paid-in capital, treasury stock, and accumulated other comprehensive income). Capital expenditures were $1,096 million and dividends were $1,569 million for fiscal year ended January 2011. Home Depot's long-term debt footnote indicates maturities of long-term debt of $29 million for 2012. What is our assessment of Home Depot's financial condition over the next year?

P11-33.   Two-Year-Ahead Forecasting of Financial Statements   (LO5)

Following are the financial statements of Target, Corp.

Target Corp. (TGT)

Consolidated Statements of Operations			
For fiscal year ended (millions, except per share data)	Jan. 29, 2011	Jan. 30, 2010	Jan. 31, 2009
Sales.	$65,786	$63,435	$62,884
Credit card revenues	1,604	1,922	2,064
Total revenues	67,390	65,357	64,948
Cost of sales.	45,725	44,062	44,157
Selling, general and administrative expenses	13,469	13,078	12,954
Credit card expenses	860	1,521	1,609
Depreciation and amortization	2,084	2,023	1,826
Earnings before interest expense and income taxes	5,252	4,673	4,402
Net interest expense			
Nonrecourse debt collateralized by credit card receivables. .	83	97	167
Other interest expense	677	707	727
Interest income.	(3)	(3)	(28)
Net interest expense	757	801	866
Earnings before income taxes	4,495	3,872	3,536
Provision for income taxes.	1,575	1,384	1,322
Net earnings	$2,920	$2,488	$2,214

Consolidated Statements of Financial Position		
(millions, except footnotes)	January 29, 2011	January 30, 2010
Assets		
Cash and cash equivalents, including marketable securities of $1,129 and $1,617....	$1,712	$2,200
Credit card receivables, net of allowance of $690 and $1,016	6,153	6,966
Inventory..	7,596	7,179
Other current assets...	1,752	2,079
Total current assets	17,213	18,424
Property and equipment		
Land..	5,928	5,793
Buildings and improvements	23,081	22,152
Fixtures and equipment	4,939	4,743
Computer hardware and software	2,533	2,575
Construction-in-progress...	567	502
Accumulated depreciation	(11,555)	(10,485)
Property and equipment, net	25,493	25,280
Other noncurrent assets..	999	829
Total assets...	$43,705	$44,533
Liabilities and shareholders' investment		
Accounts payable..	$6,625	$6,511
Accrued and other current liabilities..............................	3,326	3,120
Unsecured debt and other borrowings	119	796
Nonrecourse debt collateralized by credit card receivables	—	900
Total current liabilities...	10,070	11,327
Unsecured debt and other borrowings	11,653	10,643
Nonrecourse debt collateralized by credit card receivables	3,954	4,475
Deferred income taxes...	934	835
Other noncurrent liabilities	1,607	1,906
Total noncurrent liabilities..	18,148	17,859
Shareholders' investment...		
Common stock..	59	62
Additional paid-in-capital...	3,311	2,919
Retained earnings	12,698	12,947
Accumulated other comprehensive loss	(581)	(581)
Total shareholders' investment....................................	15,487	15,347
Total liabilities and shareholders' investment.....................	$43,705	$44,533

Consolidated Statements of Cash Flows			
For fiscal year ended (millions)	Jan. 29, 2011	Jan. 30, 2010	Jan. 31, 2009
Operating activities			
Net earnings......................................	$2,920	$2,488	$2,214
Reconciliation to cash flow			
Depreciation and amortization	2,084	2,023	1,826
Share-based compensation expense	109	103	72
Deferred income taxes............................	445	364	91
Bad debt expense	528	1,185	1,251
Non-cash (gains)/losses and other, net	(145)	143	316
Changes in operating accounts:			
Accounts receivable originated at Target.............	(78)	(57)	(458)
Inventory...	(417)	(474)	77
Other current assets..............................	(124)	(129)	(99)
Other noncurrent assets...........................	(212)	(114)	(55)
Accounts payable.................................	115	174	(389)
Accrued and other current liabilities................	149	257	(230)
Other noncurrent liabilities	(103)	(82)	(186)
Cash flow provided by operations	5,271	5,881	4,430

continued

continued from prior page

Investing activities			
Expenditures for property and equipment	(2,129)	(1,729)	(3,547)
Proceeds from disposal of property and equipment	69	33	39
Change in accounts receivable originated at third parties	363	(10)	(823)
Other investments	(47)	3	(42)
Cash flow required for investing activities	(1,744)	(1,703)	(4,373)
Financing activities			
Reductions of short-term notes payable	—	—	(500)
Additions to long-term debt	1,011	—	3,557
Reductions of long-term debt	(2,259)	(1,970)	(1,455)
Dividends paid	(609)	(496)	(465)
Repurchase of stock	(2,452)	(423)	(2,815)
Stock option exercises and related tax benefit	294	47	43
Other.	—	—	(8)
Cash flow required for financing activities	(4,015)	(2,842)	(1,643)
Net increase/(decrease) in cash and cash equivalents	(488)	1,336	(1,586)
Cash and cash equivalents at beginning of year	2,200	864	2,450
Cash and cash equivalents at end of year	$ 1,712	$ 2,200	$ 864

Required

Forecast Target's fiscal year ended January 2012 and 2013 income statements, balance sheets, and statements of cash flow. Round the revenue growth rate to the nearest whole percent, and round forecasts to $ millions. Use the same forecasting assumptions for both years; estimate forecasted income statement relations to 1 decimal (assume no change for: interest expense, deferred income tax liability, common stock, additional paid-in capital, and accumulated other comprehensive income). Target's long-term debt footnote indicates maturities of $2,251 million in fiscal year ended January 2012, and maturities of $3,812 million in fiscal year ended January 2013. Assume return on investments of 1.5% for average increase in investments. What investment or financing assumptions are required for forecasting purposes? What is our assessment of Target's financial condition over the next two years?

MANAGEMENT APPLICATIONS

MA11-34. Adjusting the Income Statement Prior to Forecasting (LO1, 2)

CBS Corporation
(CBS)

Following is the income statement of CBS Corporation, along with an excerpt from its MD&A section.

Income Statement Year ended December 31 ($ millions)	2005	2004	2003
Revenues	$14,536.4	$14,547.3	$13,554.5
Expenses			
Operating	8,671.8	8,643.6	8,165.4
Selling, general and administrative.	2,699.4	2,552.5	2,376.1
Impairment charges	9,484.4	17,997.1	—
Depreciation and amortization	498.7	508.6	501.7
Total expenses	21,354.3	29,701.8	11,043.2
Operating income (loss)	$ (6,817.9)	$(15,154.5)	$ 2,511.3

Operating Expenses: Table below presents consolidated operating expenses by type

Operating expenses by type Year ended December 31	2005	2004	Increase (Decrease) 2005 vs. 2004		2003	Increase (Decrease) 2004 vs. 2003	
Programming	$3,453.2	$3,441.8	$ 11.4	—%	$3,080.3	$361.5	12%
Production	2,453.5	2,584.7	(131.2)	(5)	2,661.9	(77.2)	(3)
Outdoor operations	1,134.2	1,102.7	31.5	3	1,012.6	90.1	9
Publishing operations.	525.0	517.6	7.4	1	486.3	31.3	6
Parks operations	243.8	232.7	11.1	5	212.2	20.5	10
Other.	862.1	764.1	98.0	13	712.1	52.0	7
Total operating expenses	$8,671.8	$8,643.6	$ 28.2	—%	$8,165.4	$478.2	6%

For 2005, operating expenses of $8.67 billion increased slightly over $8.64 billion in 2004. For 2004, operating expenses of $8.64 billion increased 6% over $8.17 billion in 2003. The major components and changes in operating expenses were as follows:

- Programming expenses represented approximately 40% of total operating expenses in 2005 and 2004 and 38% in 2003, and reflect the amortization of acquired rights of programs exhibited on the broadcast and cable networks, and television and radio stations. Programming expenses increased slightly to $3.45 billion in 2005 from $3.44 billion in 2004 principally reflecting higher costs for Showtime Networks theatrical titles. Programming expenses increased 12% to $3.44 billion in 2004 from $3.08 billion in 2003 reflecting higher program rights expenses for sports events and primetime series at the broadcast networks.
- Production expenses represented approximately 28% of total operating expenses in 2005, 30% in 2004, and 33% in 2003, and reflect the cost and amortization of internally developed television programs, including direct production costs, residuals and participation expenses, and production overhead, as well as television and radio costs including on-air talent and other production costs. Production expenses decreased 5% to $2.45 billion in 2005 from $2.58 billion in 2004 principally reflecting lower network costs due to the absence of *Frasier* partially offset by increased costs for new network series. Production expenses decreased 3% to $2.58 billion in 2004 from $2.66 billion in 2003 reflecting fewer network series produced in 2004 partially offset by higher news costs for political campaign coverage.
- Outdoor operations costs represented approximately 13% of total operating expenses in 2005 and 2004, and 12% in 2003, and reflect transit and billboard lease, maintenance, posting and rotation expenses. Outdoor operations expenses increased 3% to $1.13 billion in 2005 from $1.10 billion in 2004 principally reflecting higher billboard lease costs and maintenance costs associated with the impact of hurricanes in 2005. Outdoor operations costs increased 9% to $1.10 billion in 2004 from $1.01 billion in 2003 primarily reflecting higher transit and billboard lease costs.
- Publishing operations costs, which represented approximately 6% of total operating expenses in each of the years 2005, 2004 and 2003, reflect cost of book sales, royalties and other costs incurred with respect to publishing operations. Publishing operations expenses for 2005 increased 1% to $525.0 million and increased 6% to $517.6 million in 2004 from $486.3 million in 2003 primarily due to higher revenues.
- Parks operations costs, which represented approximately 3% of total operating expenses in each of the years 2005, 2004 and 2003, increased 5% to $243.8 million in 2005 from $232.7 million in 2004 principally reflecting the cost of fourth quarter 2005 winter events held at the parks and the impact of foreign currency translation. In 2004, Parks operations costs increased 10% to $232.7 million from $212.2 million in 2003 primarily from the impact of foreign currency translation.
- Other operating expenses, which represented approximately 10% of total operating expenses in 2005 and 9% in 2004 and 2003, primarily include distribution costs incurred with respect to television product, costs associated with digital media and compensation. Other operating expenses increased 13% to $862.1 million in 2005 from $764.1 million in 2004 primarily reflecting a 10% increase in distribution costs due to the DVD release of *Charmed* and increased costs associated with digital media from the inclusion of SportsLine.com, Inc. ("SportsLine.com") since its acquisition in December 2004. Other operating expenses for 2004 increased 7% to $764.1 million in 2004 from $712.1 million in 2003 principally reflecting 15% higher distribution costs due to additional volume of DVD releases of the *Star Trek* series and higher compensation.

continued

continued from prior page

Impairment Charges   SFAS 142 requires the Company to perform an annual fair value-based impairment test of goodwill. The Company performed its annual impairment test as of October 31, 2005, concurrently with its annual budgeting process which begins in the fourth quarter each year. The first step of the test examines whether or not the book value of each of the Company's reporting units exceeds its fair value. If the book value for a reporting unit exceeds its fair value, the second step of the test is required to compare the implied fair value of that reporting unit's goodwill with the book value of the goodwill. The Company's reporting units are generally consistent with or one level below the operating segments underlying the reportable segments. As a result of the 2005 annual impairment test, the Company recorded an impairment charge of $9.48 billion in the fourth quarter of 2005. The $9.48 billion reflects charges to reduce the carrying value of goodwill at the CBS Television reporting unit of $6.44 billion and the Radio reporting unit of $3.05 billion. As a result of the annual impairment test performed for 2004, the Company recorded an impairment charge of $18.0 billion in the fourth quarter of 2004. The $18.0 billion reflects charges to reduce the carrying value of goodwill at the Radio reporting unit of $10.94 billion and the Outdoor reporting unit of $7.06 billion as well as the reduction of the carrying value of intangible assets of $27.8 million related to the FCC licenses at the Radio segment. Several factors led to a reduction in forecasted cash flows and long-term growth rates for both the Radio and Outdoor reporting units. Radio and Outdoor both fell short of budgeted revenue and operating income growth targets in 2004. Competition from other advertising media, including Internet advertising and cable and broadcast television reduced Radio and Outdoor growth rates. Also, the emergence of new competitors and technologies necessitated a shift in management's strategy for the Radio and Outdoor businesses, including changes in composition of the sales force and operating management as well as increased levels of investment in marketing and promotion.

Required

Identify and explain any income statement line items over the past three years that you believe should be considered for potential adjustment in preparation for forecasting the income statement of CBS.

SOLUTIONS TO REVIEW PROBLEMS

Mid-Module Review

Solution

Forecasted 2011 financial statements for Colgate-Palmolive follow.

Forecasted Income Statement			
For year ended December 31 ($ millions)	2010	Forecast Assumptions	2011 Est.
Net sales.	$15,564	$15,564 × 1.03	$16,031
Cost of sales.	6,360	$16,031 × 40.9%	6,557
Gross profit.	9,204	subtotal	9,474
Selling, general and administrative expenses	5,414	$16,031 × 34.8%	5,579
Other (income) expense, net	301	no change	301
Operating profit	3,489	subtotal	3,594
Interest expense, net	59	no change	59
Income before income taxes	3,430	subtotal	3,535
Provision for income taxes.	1,117	$3,535 × 32.6%	1,152
Net income including noncontrolling interests.	2,313	subtotal	2,383
Less: Net income attributable to noncontrolling interests	110	no change	110
Net income attributable to Colgate-Palmolive Company.	$ 2,203	subtotal	$ 2,273

Forecasted Balance Sheet			
As of December 31 ($ millions)	2010	Forecast Assumptions	2011 Est.
Assets		computed	
Cash and cash equivalents	$ 490	16,031 × 3.1%	$ 497
Marketable securities		plug	373
Receivables	1,610	16,031 × 10.3%	1,651
Inventories	1,222	16,031 × 7.9%	1,266
Other current assets	408	16,031 × 2.6%	417
Total current assets	3,730	subtotal	4,204
Property, plant and equipment, net	3,693	3,693 + 567 − 375	3,885
Goodwill, net	2,362	no change	2,362
Other intangible assets, net	831	831 − 19	812
Other assets	556	16,031 × 3.6%	577
Total assets	$11,172	subtotal	$11,840
Liabilities			
Notes and loans payable	$ 48	no change	$ 48
Current portion of long-term debt	561	footnote disclosure	359
Accounts payable	1,165	16,031 × 7.5%	1,202
Accrued income taxes	272	1,152 × 24.4%	281
Other accruals	1,682	16,031 × 10.8%	1,731
Total current liabilities	3,728	subtotal	3,621
Long-term debt	2,815	2,815 − 359	2,456
Deferred income taxes	108	no change	108
Other liabilities	1,704	16,031 × 10.9%	1,747
Total liabilities	8,355	subtotal	7,932
Commitments and contingent liabilities			
Shareholders' Equity			
Preference stock	0	no change	0
Common stock, $1 par value (2,000,000,000 shares authorized, 732,853,180 shares issued)	733	no change	733
Additional paid-in-capital	1,132	no change	1,132
Retained earnings	14,329	14,329 + 2,273 − 1,182	15,420
Accumulated other comprehensive income (loss)	(2,115)	no change	(2,115)
Shareholders' equity before unearned compensation, treasury stock and noncontrolling interest	14,079	subtotal	15,170
Unearned compensation	(99)	no change	(99)
Treasury stock, at cost	(11,305)	no change	(11,305)
Total Colgate-Palmolive Company shareholders' equity	2,675	subtotal	3,766
Noncontrolling interests	142	no change	142
Total shareholders' equity	2,817	subtotal	3,908
Total liabilities and shareholders' equity	$11,172	subtotal	$11,840

Forecasted Statement of Cash Flows		
($ millions)	Forecast Assumptions	2011 Est.
Net income including noncontrolling interests...	via forecast income stmt.	$2,273
Add: Depreciation..........................	given	375
Add: Amortization..........................	given	19
Change in Accounts receivable.............	$1,610 − $1,651	(41)
Change in Inventories	$1,222 − $1,266	(44)
Change in Other current assets.............	$408 − $417	(9)
Change in Other long-term assets	$556 − $577	(21)
Change in Accounts payable...............	$1,202 − $1,165	37
Change in Accrued income taxes	$281 − $272	9
Change in Accrued liabilities	$1,731 − $1,682	49
Change in Other long-term liabilities	$1,747 − $1,704	43
Net cash from operating activities	subtotal	2,690
Capital expenditures	given	(567)
Increase in marketable securities............	plug	(373)
Net cash from investing activities.............	subtotal	(940)
Dividends	$2,273 × 52%	(1,182)
Payments of long-term debt	prior-year current portion	(561)
Net cash from financing activities	subtotal	(1,743)
Net change in cash.......................	subtotal	7
Beginning cash..........................	via prior bal. sheet	490
Ending cash	subtotal	$ 497

Our forecasts yield liabilities in excess of assets of $373 million. In this example, we assume that marketable securities are increased by that amount. We might have also assumed repayment of debt and/or purchase of treasury stock, being careful to maintain the company's debt-to-equity ratio. One further adjustment we might make at this point would be to increase interest income assuming an investment return on the marketable securities.

Module-End Review

Solution

	2010	2011E	2012E	2013E	2014E
Sales (unrounded)	$61,587	**$64,050.48** (61,587 × 1.04)	**$66,612.50** (64,050.48 × 1.04)	**$69,276.99** (66,612.50 × 1.04)	**$72,048.07** (69,276.99 × 1.04)
Sales (rounded)	61,587	**64,050**	**66,612**	**69,277**	**72,048**
NOPAT	13,065	**13,451** ($64,050 × 0.21)	**13,989** ($66,612 × 0.21)	**14,548** ($69,277 × 0.21)	**15,130** ($72,048 × 0.21)
NOA	45,694	**47,444** ($64,050/1.35)	**49,342** ($66,612/1.35)	**51,316** ($69,277/1.35)	**53,369** ($72,048/1.35)

JOHNSON & JOHNSON

In the three years prior to 2008, corporate earnings were steady and climbing, stock prices grew continuously, and growth appeared limitless. Then, the recession of 2008–2009 hit. Almost all companies saw revenues and profits decline. Healthcare companies, however, weathered the storm reasonably well. Compared to other sectors, healthcare tends to be less sensitive to economic changes for three reasons. First, demand for healthcare products persists as the U.S. population ages regardless of current events. Second, healthcare products are fairly immune to depressions in the economic cycle as consumers and patients need products and devices regardless of economic health. Third, government spending in healthcare is a large portion of overall healthcare spending, approaching $13 trillion in 2011. Government healthcare spending does not closely mirror economic changes as highlighted in the following graph.

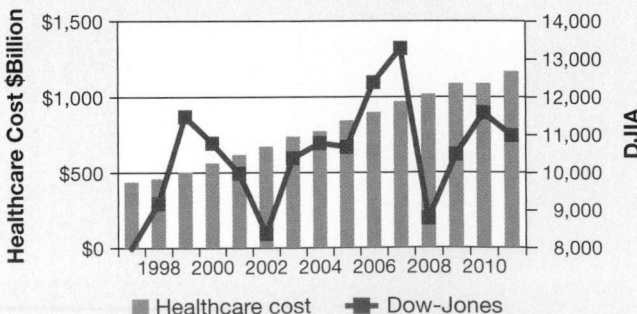

Johnson & Johnson (J&J) is a dominant company in the healthcare industry. The company engages in the research and development, manufacture, and sale of various healthcare products. Among healthcare firms, Johnson & Johnson often is a favorite for those who seek so-called ruler stocks. A *ruler stock* is one that has an earnings plot with an upward sloping line, as if drawn with a ruler. By this definition, Johnson & Johnson is a classic ruler stock, as the graph below shows.

Ruler stocks are arguably attractive because their steady earnings growth hints at more of the same for the future. Investors often have more confidence in continued earnings growth for a ruler stock than for a company with a history of erratic earnings.

How has Johnson & Johnson managed to create and sustain such steady earnings growth? Much of the answer

Analyzing and Valuing Equity Securities

LEARNING OBJECTIVES

LO1 Identify equity valuation models and explain the information required to value equity securities. (p. 12-3)

LO2 Describe and apply the discounted free cash flow model to value equity securities. (p. 12-4)

LO3 Describe and apply the residual operating income model to value equity securities. (p. 12-8)

LO4 Explain how equity valuation models can aid managerial decisions. (p. 12-10)

Sales by Segment (in billions of dollars)
- Consumer
- Pharmaceutical
- Medical Devices and Diagnostics

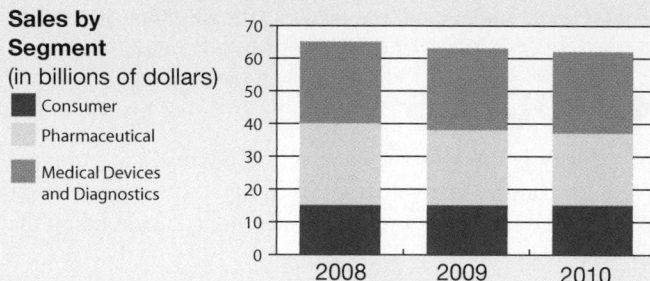

U.S. and International Sales for 10 Years (in billions of dollars)
- U.S.
- International

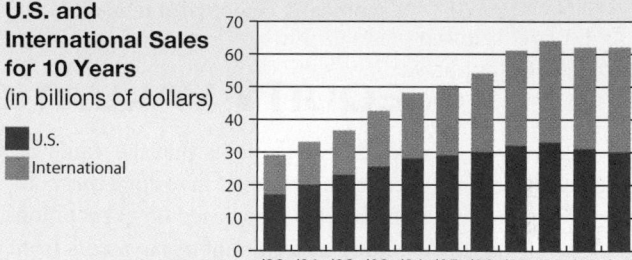

rests in its diversified portfolio of products, which includes consumer, pharmaceutical and medical devices. The company is also diversified geographically. The two charts above show Johnson & Johnson's balanced product portfolio and strong, growing international sales.

Johnson & Johnson's steady earnings are matched with solid dividend payments. In times of market turmoil, as during 2011, blue chip stocks with dependable dividends are perceived as providing good value to investors. Some might argue that Johnson & Johnson might not be the most "exciting" stock, but it is a solid bet in a volatile market.

Supported by its more diversified operations and fueled by a steady increase in operating profits, Johnson & Johnson's stock price has nearly completely rebounded from the decline of late 2007 and early 2008, as shown in the graph to the right.

This raises several questions. What factors drive the Johnson & Johnson stock price? Why do analysts expect its price to continue to rise? How do accounting measures of performance and financial condition impact stock price?

This module provides insights and answers to these questions. It explains how we can use forecasts of operating profits and cash flows to price equity securities such as Johnson & Johnson's stock.

Sources: *Johnson & Johnson* 10-K and Annual Reports; Yahoo Finance, www.usgovernmentspending.com.

Johnson & Johnson Stock Price

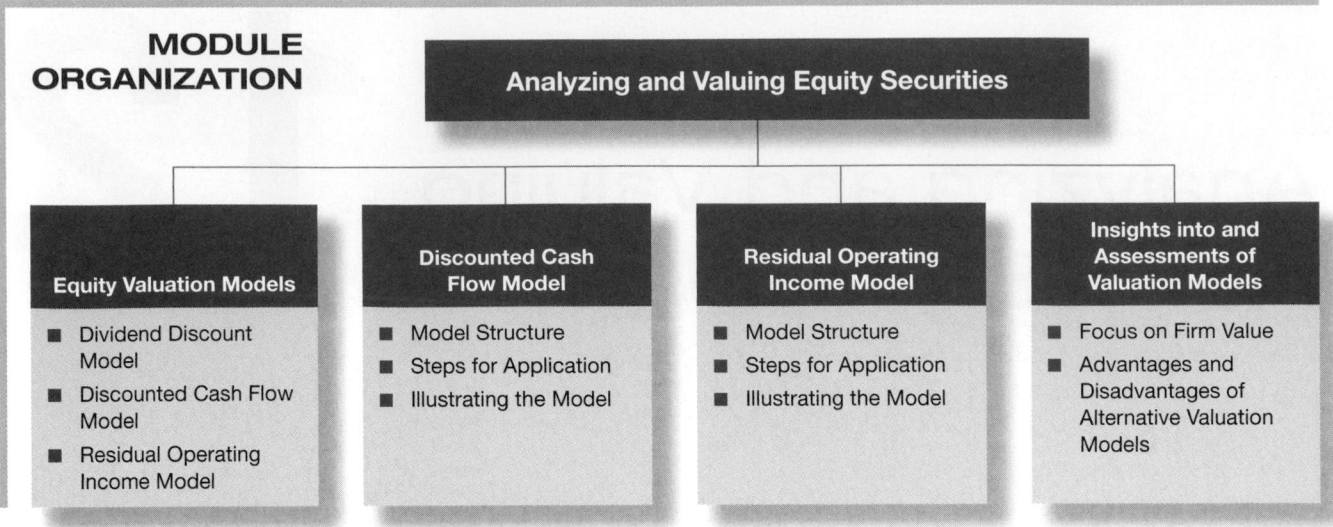

This module focuses on valuing equity securities (we explain the valuation of debt securities in Module 8). Specifically, we describe two approaches: the discounted free cash flow model (DCF) and residual operating income model (ROPI). We then conclude by discussing the management implications from an increased understanding of the factors that impact values of equity securities. It is important that we understand the determinants of equity value to make informed decisions. Employees at all levels of an organization, whether public or private, should understand the factors that create shareholder value so that they can work effectively toward that objective. For many senior managers, stock value serves as a scorecard. Successful managers are those who better understand the factors affecting that scorecard.

EQUITY VALUATION MODELS

LO1 Identify equity valuation models and explain the information required to value equity securities.

Module 8 explains that the value of a debt security is the present value of the interest and principal payments that the investor *expects* to receive in the future. The valuation of equity securities is similar in that it is also based on expectations. The difference lies in the increased uncertainty surrounding the timing and amount of payments from equity securities.

Dividend Discount Model

There are many equity valuation models in use today. Each of them defines the value of an equity security in terms of the present value of forecasted amounts. They differ primarily in terms of what is forecasted.

The basis of equity valuation is the premise that the value of an equity security is determined by the payments that the investor can expect to receive. Equity investments involve two types of payoffs: (1) dividends received during the holding period and (2) capital gains when the security is sold.[1] The value of an equity security is, then, based on the present value of expected dividends plus the present value of the security at the end of the forecasted holding period. This **dividend discount model** is appealing in its simplicity and its intuitive focus on dividend distribution. As a practical matter, however, the model is not always useful because many companies that have a positive stock price have never paid a dividend, and are not expected to pay a dividend in the foreseeable future.

Discounted Cash Flow Model

A more practical approach to valuing equity securities focuses on the company's operating and investing activities; that is, on the *generation* of cash rather than the *distribution* of cash. This approach is

---

[1] The future stock price is, itself, also assumed to be related to the expected dividends that the new investor expects to receive; as a result, the expected receipt of dividends is the sole driver of stock price under this type of valuation model.

called the **discounted cash flow (DCF)** model. The focus of the forecasting process for the DCF model is the company's expected *free cash flows to the firm*, which are defined as operating cash flows net of the expected new investments in net operating assets that are required to support the business.

Residual Operating Income Model

Another approach to equity valuation also focuses on operating and investing activities. It is known as the **residual operating income (ROPI)** model. This model uses both net operating profits after tax (NOPAT) and the net operating assets (NOA) to determine equity value; see Module 4 for complete descriptions of the NOPAT and NOA measures. This approach highlights the importance of return on net operating assets (RNOA), and the disaggregation of RNOA into net operating profit margin and NOA turnover. We discuss the implications of this insight for managers later in this module.

DISCOUNTED CASH FLOW (DCF) MODEL

The discounted cash flow (DCF) model defines firm value as follows:

LO2 Describe and apply the discounted free cash flow model to value equity securities.

Firm Value = Present Value of Expected Free Cash Flows to Firm

The expected free cash flows to the firm include cash flows arising from the operating side of the business; that is, cash generated from the firm's operating activities (but not from nonoperating activities such as interest paid on debt or dividends received on investments), and they do not include the cash flows from financing activities.

DCF Model Structure

Free cash flows to the firm (FCFF) equal net operating profit after tax that is not used to grow net operating assets. Using the terminology of Module 4 we can define FCFF as follows (see Business Insight box on next page for a more traditional definition):

FCFF = NOPAT − Increase in NOA

where

NOPAT = Net operating profit after tax

NOA = Net operating assets

Net operating profit after tax is normally positive and the net cash flows from increases in net operating assets are normally negative assuming that net operating assets increase each period. The sum of the two (positive or negative) represents the net cash flows available to creditors and shareholders. Positive FCFF imply that there are funds available for distribution to creditors and shareholders, either in the form of debt repayments, dividends, or stock repurchases (treasury stock). Negative FCFF imply that the firm requires additional funds from creditors and/or shareholders, in the form of new loans or equity investments, to support its business activities.

The DCF valuation model requires forecasts of *all* future free cash flows; that is, free cash flows for the remainder of the company's life. Generating an infinite stream of forecasts is not realistic. Consequently, analysts typically estimate FCFF over a horizon period, often 4 to 10 years, and then make simplifying assumptions about the FCFF subsequent to that horizon period.

MANAGERIAL DECISION   **You Are the Chief Financial Officer**

Assume that you are the CFO of a company that has a large investment in plant assets and sells its products on credit. Identify steps you can take to increase your company's cash flow and, hence, your company's firm value. [Answer p. 12-17]

BUSINESS INSIGHT	Definitions of Free Cash Flow

We often see free cash flows to the firm (unlevered free cash flow) defined as follows:

FCFF = Net cash flow from operating activities − Capital expenditures

Although somewhat similar to the definition in this book, NOPAT − Increase in NOA, there are important differences:

- Net cash flow from operating activities uses net income as the starting point; net income, of course, comingles both operating and nonoperating components (such as selling expense and interest expense). Analysts sometimes correct for this by adding back items such as after-tax net interest expense, which is the approach used by the Oppenheimer analysts in Appendix 12B.

- Income tax expense (in net income) includes the effect of the interest tax shield (see Module 4); the usual NOPAT definition includes only the tax on operating income.

- Net cash flow from operating activities also includes nonoperating items in working capital, such as changes in interest payable and dividends payable, as well as inflows from securitization of receivables (see Module 10); NOA focuses only on operating activities.

- The FCFF definition in this box consists of net income, changes in working capital accounts, and capital expenditures; the usual NOA consists of changes in operating working capital accounts, capital expenditures, *and* changes in long-term operating liabilities.

We must be attentive to differences in definitions for free cash flow so that we understand the analytical choices we make and their implications to equity valuation. It also aids us in drawing proper inferences from analyst research reports that might apply different definitions of free cash flow.

Steps in Applying the DCF Model

Application of the DCF model to equity valuation involves five steps:

1. Forecast and discount FCFF for the **horizon period**.[2]
2. Forecast and discount FCFF for the post-horizon period, called **terminal period**.[3]
3. Sum the present values of the horizon and terminal periods to yield firm (enterprise) value.
4. Subtract net nonoperating obligations (NNO), along with any noncontrolling interest, from firm value to yield firm equity value. If NNO is positive, the usual case, we subtract it in step 4; if NNO is negative, we add it. (For many, but not all, companies, NNO is positive because nonoperating liabilities exceed nonoperating assets; for convenience, any noncontrolling interest is often included in NNO.)
5. Divide firm equity value by the number of shares outstanding to yield stock value per share.

Illustrating the DCF Model

To illustrate, we apply the DCF model to Johnson & Johnson. J&J's recent financial statements are reproduced in Appendix 12A. Forecasted financials for J&J (forecast horizon of 2011–2014 and terminal period of 2015) are in Exhibit 12.1.[4] The forecasts (in bold) are for sales, NOPAT, and NOA.

---

[2] When discounting FCFF, the appropriate discount rate (r_w) is the **weighted average cost of capital (WACC)**, where the weights are the relative percentages of debt (d) and equity (e) in the capital structure applied to the expected returns on debt (r_d) and equity (r_e), respectively: WACC $= r_w = (r_d \times \%$ of debt$) + (r_e \times \%$ of equity$)$; see footnote 7 for an example.

[3] For an assumed growth, g, the terminal period (T) present value of FCFF in perpetuity (beyond the horizon period) is given by, $\frac{\text{FCFF}_T}{r_w - g}$, where FCFF_T is the free cash flow to the firm for the terminal period, r_w is WACC, and g is the assumed long-term growth rate of those cash flows. The resulting amount is then discounted back to the present using the horizon-end-period discount factor.

[4] We use a four-period horizon in the text and assignments to simplify the exposition and to reduce the computational burden. In practice, analysts use spreadsheets to forecast future cash flows and value the equity security, and typically have a forecast horizon of seven to ten periods.

These forecasts assume an annual 4.0% sales growth during the horizon period, a terminal period sales growth of 1%, net operating profit margin (NOPM) of 21%, and a year-end net operating asset turnover (NOAT) of 1.3 (which is the 2010 turnover rate based on year-end NOA; year-end amounts are used because we are forecasting year-end account balances, not average balances).[5,6]

EXHIBIT 12.1 Application of Discounted Cash Flow Model						
(In millions, except per share values and discount factors)	Reported 2010	Horizon Period				Terminal Period
		2011	2012	2013	2014	
Sales (unrounded)	$ 61,587	**$64,050.48** (61,587 × 1.04)	**$66,612.50** (64,050.48 × 1.04)	**$69,277.00** (66,612.50 × 1.04)	**$72,048.08** (69,277.00 × 1.04)	**$72,768.56** (72,048.08 × 1.01)
Sales (rounded)	61,587	**64,050**	**66,612**	**69,277**	**72,048**	**72,769**
NOPAT*	13,065	**13,451**	**13,989**	**14,548**	**15,130**	**15,281**
NOA**	45,694	**49,269**	**51,240**	**53,290**	**55,422**	**55,976**
Increase in NOA		3,575	1,971	2,050	2,132	554
FCFF (NOPAT − Increase in NOA)		9,876	12,018	12,498	12,998	14,727
Discount factor $[1/(1 + r_w)^t]$‡		0.92593	0.85734	0.79383	0.73503	
Present value of horizon FCFF		9,144	10,304	9,921	9,554	
Cum present value of horizon FCFF . . .	$ 38,923					
Present value of terminal FCFF	154,640					
Total firm value	193,563					
Less (plus) NNO†	(10,885)					
Firm equity value	$204,448					
Shares outstanding	2,738.1					
Stock value per share	$ 74.67					

*Given J&J's combined federal and state statutory tax rate of 36.0% as reported in the tax footnote to its 2010 10-K, NOPAT for 2010 is computed as follows ($ millions): ($61,587 − $18,792 − $19,424 − $6,844) − ($3,613 − {0.360 × [$455 − $107 − $768]}) = $13,065. A note on rounding: To forecast sales, we multiply prior year's unrounded sales by (1 + Growth rate); this is done for the horizon and terminal periods. Then, we round each year's forecasted sales to whole units and use rounded sales to compute NOPAT and NOA, where both are rounded to whole units. At each successive step, we round the number to whole units before proceeding to the next step.

**NOA computations for 2010 follow ($ millions): ($102,908 − $19,355 − $8,303) − ($46,329 − $7,617 − $9,156) = $45,694.

†NNO is the difference between NOA and total shareholders' equity; in this case NNO ($ millions) = $45,694 − $56,579 = $(10,885). J&J's NNO is negative because it carries substantial cash and securities that exceed its debt.

‡For simplification, present value computations use discount factors rounded to 5 decimal places.

The bottom line of Exhibit 12.1 is the estimated J&J equity value of $204,448 million, or a per share stock value of $74.67 (computed as $204,448/2,738.1 shares). The present value computations use an 8% WACC(r_w) as the discount rate.[7] Specifically, we obtain this stock valuation as follows:

1. **Compute present value of horizon period FCFF.** We compute the forecasted 2011 FCFF of $9,876 million from the forecasted 2011 NOPAT less the forecasted increase in 2011 NOA. The

---

[5] **NOPAT** equals revenues less operating expenses such as cost of goods sold, selling, general, and administrative expenses, and taxes. NOPAT excludes any interest revenue and interest expense and any gains or losses from financial investments. NOPAT reflects the operating side of the firm as opposed to nonoperating activities such as borrowing and security investment activities. **NOA** equals operating assets less operating liabilities. (See Module 4.)

[6] NOPAT and NOA are typically forecasted using the detailed forecasting procedures discussed in Module 11. In this module we use the parsimonious method to multiyear forecasting (see Module 11) to focus attention on the valuation process.

[7] The weighted average cost of capital (WACC) for J&J is computed using the following three-step process:

1. The cost of equity capital is given by the capital asset pricing model (CAPM): $r_e = r_f + \beta (r_m − r_f)$, where β is the beta of the stock (an estimate of stock price variability that is reported by several services such as Standard and Poors), r_f is the risk-free rate (commonly assumed as the 10-year treasury bond rate), and r_m is the expected return to the entire market. The expression $(r_m − r_f)$ is the "spread" of equities over the risk-free rate, often assumed to be about 5% to 7%. For J&J, given a beta of 1.00 and a 10-year treasury bond rate of 3.58% (r_f) as of February 28, 2011, r_e is estimated as 9.58%, computed as 3.58% + (1.00 × 6%).

2. Two alternative computations for pretax cost of debt capital are: (1) Interest expense/Average interest-bearing debt, and (2) Weighted-average effective interest rate on debt. For the latter, J&J reports its 5.25% rate in footnote 7 to its 10-K, which we use. To obtain J&J's after-tax cost of debt capital, we multiply 5.25% by 1 − 0.360, where 36.0% is the federal and state statutory tax rate from its tax footnote, yielding 3.36% (J&J's after-tax cost of debt).

3. WACC is the weighted average of the cost of equity capital and the cost of debt capital. J&J capital structure is 77% equity and 23% debt. Thus, J&J's weighted average cost of capital is (77% × 9.58%) + (23% × 3.36%) = 8.15%, rounded to 8%.

present value of this $9,876 million as of 2010 is $9,144.5 million, computed as $9,876 million × 0.92593 (the present value factor for one year at 8%). Similarly, the present value of 2012 FCFF (two years from the current date) is $10,303.5 million, computed as $12,018 million × 0.85734, and so on through 2014. The sum of these present values (*cumulative present value*) is $38,923 million.

2. **Compute present value of terminal period FCFF.** The present value of the terminal period

   FCFF is $154,640 million, computed as $\dfrac{\left(\dfrac{\$14,727 \text{ million}}{0.08 - 0.01}\right)}{(1.08)^4}$, or ($14,727/0.07) × 0.73503.

3. **Compute firm equity value.** Sum present values from the horizon and terminal period FCFF to get firm (enterprise) value of $193,563 million. Subtract the value of J&J's net nonoperating obligations of $(10,885) million to get firm equity value of $204,448. Dividing firm equity value by the 2,738.1 million shares outstanding (computed as 3,119,843,000 less 381,746,000) yields the estimated per share valuation of $74.67.

We perform this valuation as of February 25, 2011, which is the SEC filing date for J&J's 10-K. J&J's stock closed at $59.13 on February 25, 2011. Our valuation estimate of $74.67 indicates that the stock is undervalued as of that date. J&J's stock price climbed steadily through the spring of 2011 and was trading for $65 by July at which point J&J was still recommended as a strong BUY stock.

BUSINESS INSIGHT | **Analysts' Forecasts**

Earnings and cash-flow estimates are key to security valuation. Following are earnings estimates as of August 2011, for Johnson & Johnson from Yahoo.finance. About 20 analysts provided earnings estimates. The median (consensus) EPS estimate for 2011 (current year) is $4.97 per share, with a high of $5.02 and a low of $4.93. This compares to an actual diluted EPS of $4.78 in 2010. For 2012 (slightly more than one year ahead), the consensus EPS estimate is $5.29. The average buy rating for J&J stock is 2.2 on a scale that runs from 1.0 (Strong BUY) to 5.0 (Strong SELL).

Estimate Period	Total Analysts	Ave. EPS Est.	High EPS Est.	Low EPS Est.
2011 Fiscal Year.........	21	$4.97	$5.02	$4.93
2012 Fiscal Year.........	19	$5.29	$5.38	$5.19
Average recommendation: 2.2 (1 = Strong Buy, 3 = Hold, 5 = Strong Sell)				

MID-MODULE REVIEW

Following are forecasts of Procter & Gamble's sales, net operating profit after tax (NOPAT), and net operating assets (NOA). These are taken from our forecasting process in Module 11 and now include a terminal period forecast that reflects a long-term growth rate of 1%.

(In millions)	Reported 2011	Horizon Period 2012	2013	2014	2015	Terminal Period
Sales growth..........		4.6%	4.6%	4.6%	4.6%	1%
Net sales (unrounded) ...	$ 82,559	$86,356.71 ($82,559 × 1.046)	$90,329.12 ($86,356.71 × 1.046)	$94,484.26 ($90,329.12 × 1.046)	$98,830.54 ($94,484.26 × 1.046)	$99,818.84 ($98,830.54 × 1.01)
Net sales (rounded)	$ 82,559	$ 86,357	$ 90,329	$ 94,484	$ 98,831	$ 99,819
NOPAT	12,193	12,781	13,369	13,984	14,627	14,773
NOA	97,247	101,596	106,269	111,158	116,272	117,434

Use the forecasts above to compute P&G's free cash flows to the firm (FCFF) and an estimate of its stock value using the DCF model. Make the following assumptions: discount rate (WACC) of 8%, shares outstanding of 2,765.7 million, and net nonoperating obligations (NNO) of $29,607 million (which includes $361 million in noncontrolling interest).

The solution is on page 12-31.

RESIDUAL OPERATING INCOME (ROPI) MODEL

The residual operating income (ROPI) model focuses on net operating profit after tax (NOPAT) and net operating assets (NOA). This means it uses key measures from both the income statement and balance sheet in determining firm value.

LO3 Describe and apply the residual operating income model to value equity securities.

ROPI Model Structure

The ROPI model defines firm value as the sum of two components:

$$\textbf{Firm Value = NOA + Present Value of Expected ROPI}$$

where

> **NOA = Net operating assets**
>
> **ROPI = Residual operating income**

Net operating assets (NOA) are the foundation of firm value under the ROPI model. This is potentially problematic because we measure NOA using the balance sheet, which is unlikely to fully and contemporaneously capture the true (or intrinsic) value of all of a firm's operating assets.[8] However, the ROPI model adds an adjustment that corrects for the undervaluation or overvaluation of NOA. This adjustment is the present value of expected residual operating income, and is defined as follows:

$$\textbf{ROPI} = \textbf{NOPAT} - \underbrace{(\textbf{NOA}_{\textbf{Beg}} \times r_w)}_{\textbf{Expected NOPAT}}$$

where

> $\textbf{NOA}_{\textbf{Beg}}$ **= Net operating assets at beginning (*Beg*) of period**
>
> r_w **= Weighted average cost of capital (WACC)**

Residual operating income (ROPI) is the net operating profit a firm earns over and above the return that the operating assets are expected to earn given the firm's WACC. Shareholders expect the company to use NOA to generate, at least, a "hurdle" profit to cover the cost of capital (WACC). Companies that earn profits over and above that hurdle, create value for shareholders. This is the concept of residual income: that is, income earned over and above the minimum amount of return required by investors.

Understanding the ROPI model helps us reap the benefits from the disaggregation of return on net operating assets (RNOA) in Module 4. In addition, the ROPI model is the foundation for many internal and external performance evaluation and compensation systems marketed by management consulting and accounting services firms.[9]

Steps in Applying the ROPI Model

Application of the ROPI model to equity valuation involves five steps:

1. Forecast and discount ROPI for the horizon period.[10]

---

[8] If the assets earn more than expected, it could be because NOA does not capture all of the firms' assets. For example, R&D and advertising are not fully and contemporaneously reflected on the balance sheet as assets though they likely produce future cash inflows. Likewise, internally generated goodwill is not fully reflected on the balance sheet as an asset. Similarly, assets are generally not written up to reflect unrealized gains. Conversely, sometimes the balance sheet overstates the true value of NOA. For example, companies can delay the write-down of impaired assets and, thus, overstate their book values. These examples, and a host of others, can yield reported values of NOA that differ from the fair value of operating assets.

[9] Examples are economic value added (EVA™) from Stern Stewart & Company, the economic profit model from McKinsey & Co., the cash flow return on investment (CFROI™) from Holt Value Associates, the economic value management from KPMG, and the value builder from PricewaterhouseCoopers (PwC).

[10] The present value of expected ROPI uses the weighted average cost of capital (WACC) as its discount rate; same as with the DCF model.

2. Forecast and discount ROPI for the terminal period.[11]

3. Sum the present values from both the horizon and terminal periods; then add this sum to current NOA to get firm (enterprise) value.

4. Subtract net nonoperating obligations (NNO), along with any noncontrolling interest, from firm value to yield firm equity value.

5. Divide firm equity value by the number of shares outstanding to yield stock value per share.

Illustrating the ROPI Model

To illustrate application of the ROPI model, we again use Johnson & Johnson. Forecasted financials for J&J (forecast horizon of 2011–2014 and terminal period of 2015) are in Exhibit 12.2. The forecasts (in bold) are for sales, NOPAT, and NOA (the same forecasts from illustration of the DCF model). These forecasts assume an annual 4% sales growth for the horizon period, a terminal period sales growth of 1%, net operating profit margin (NOPM) of 21%, and a year-end net operating asset turnover (NOAT) of 1.30 (which is the 2010 turnover rate based on year-end NOA; year-end amounts are used because we are forecasting year-end account balances, not average balances).

EXHIBIT 12.2 Application of Residual Operating Income Model

(In millions, except per share values and discount factors)	Reported 2010	Horizon Period				Terminal Period
		2011	2012	2013	2014	
Sales (unrounded)	$ 61,587	$64,050.48 (61,587 × 1.04)	$66,612.49 (64,050.48 × 1.04)	$69,277.00 (66,612.49 × 1.04)	$72,048.08 (69,277.00 × 1.04)	$72,768.56 (72,048.08 × 1.01)
Sales (rounded)	61,587	64,050	66,612	69,277	72,048	72,769
NOPAT*	13,065	13,451	13,989	14,548	15,130	15,281
NOA**	45,694	49,269	51,240	53,290	55,422	55,976
ROPI (NOPAT − [NOA$_{Beg}$ × r_w])		9,795	10,047	10,449	10,867	10,847
Discount factor [1/(1 + r_w)^t]‡		0.92593	0.85734	0.79383	0.73503	
Present value of horizon ROPI		9,069	8,614	8,295	7,988	
Cum present value of horizon ROPI	$ 33,966					
Present value of terminal ROPI	113,898					
NOA	45,694					
Total firm value	193,558					
Less NNO†	(10,885)					
Firm equity value	$204,443					
Shares outstanding	2,738.1					
Stock value per share	$ 74.67					

*Given J&J's combined federal and state statutory tax rate of 36.0% as reported in the tax footnote to its 2010 10-K, NOPAT for 2010 is computed as follows ($ millions): ($61,587 − $18,792 − $19,424 − $6,844) − ($3,613 − {0.360 × [$455 − $107 − $768]}) = $13,065. A note on rounding: To forecast sales, we multiply prior year's unrounded sales by (1 + Growth rate); this is done for the horizon and terminal periods. Then, we round each year's forecasted sales to whole units and use rounded sales to compute NOPAT and NOA, where both are rounded to whole units. At each successive step, we round the number to whole units before proceeding to the next step.

**NOA computations for 2010 follow ($ millions): ($102,908 − $19,355 − $8,303) − ($46,329 − $7,617 − $9,156) = $45,694.

†NNO is the difference between NOA and total shareholders' equity; in this case NNO ($ millions) = 45,694 − 56,579 = $(10,885). J&J's NNO is negative because it carries substantial cash and securities that exceed its debt.

‡For simplification, present value computations use discount factors rounded to 5 decimal places.

The bottom line of Exhibit 12.2 is the estimated J&J equity value of $204,443 million, or a per share stock value of $74.67. The present value computations use an 8% WACC as the discount rate. Specifically, we obtain this stock valuation as follows:

1. **Compute present value of horizon period ROPI.** The forecasted 2011 ROPI of $9,795 million is computed from the forecasted 2011 NOPAT ($13,451) less the product of beginning

---

[11] For an assumed growth, g, the present value of the perpetuity of ROPI beyond the horizon period is given by $\frac{ROPI_T}{r_w - g}$, where $ROPI_T$ is the residual operating income for the terminal period, r_w is WACC for the firm, and g is the assumed growth rate of $ROPI_T$ following the horizon period. The resulting amount is then discounted back to the present using the WACC, computed over the length of the horizon period.

period NOA ($45,694) and WACC (0.08). The present value of this ROPI as of 2010 is $9,069 million, computed as $9,795 million $\times$ 0.92593 (the present value one year hence discounted at 8%). Similarly, the present value of 2012 ROPI (two years hence) is $8,614 million, computed as $10,047 million $\times$ 0.85734, and so on through 2015. The sum of these present values (*cumulative present value*) is $33,966 million.

2. **Compute present value of terminal period ROPI.** The present value of the terminal period ROPI is $113,898 million, computed as $\dfrac{\left(\dfrac{\$10{,}847\ \text{million}}{0.08 - 0.01}\right)}{(1.08)^4}$, or ($10,847/0.07) $\times$ 0.73503.

3. **Compute firm equity value.** We must sum the present values from the horizon period ($33,966 million) and terminal period ($113,898 million), plus NOA ($45,694 million), to get firm (enterprise) value of $193,558 million. We then subtract the value of net nonoperating obligations of $10,885 million to get firm equity value of $204,443. Dividing firm equity value by the 2,738.1 million shares outstanding yields the estimated per share valuation of $74.67.

We perform this valuation as of February 25, 2011, which is the SEC filing date for J&J's 10-K. J&J's stock closed at $59.13 on February 25, 2011. Our valuation estimate of $74.67 indicates that the company's stock is undervalued as of that date. J&J's stock price climbed steadily through the spring of 2011 and was trading for $65 by July. Our estimated price is higher than analysts' target price but J&J was still recommended as a strong BUY stock.

The ROPI model estimate is equal to that computed using the DCF model illustrated earlier in this module. This is the case so long as the firm is in a steady state, that is, NOPAT and NOA are growing at the same rate (for example, when RNOA is constant). When the steady-state condition is not met, for example, when a company has variable growth rates over time or when profit margins are changing from year to year, the two models yield different valuations. Analysts typically compute values from several models and use qualitative analysis to determine a final price estimate.

RESEARCH INSIGHT | **Power of NOPAT Forecasts**

Discounted cash flow (DCF) and residual operating income (ROPI) models yield identical estimates when the expected payoffs are forecasted for an infinite horizon. For practical reasons, we must use horizon period forecasts and a terminal period forecast. This truncation of the forecast horizon is a main cause of any difference in value estimates for these models. Importantly, if we can forecast (GAAP-based) NOPAT and NOA more accurately than forecasts of cash inflows and outflows, we will obtain more accurate estimates of firm value given a finite horizon.

MANAGERIAL INSIGHTS FROM THE ROPI MODEL

The ROPI model defines firm value as the sum of NOA and the present value of expected residual operating income as follows:

LO4 Explain how equity valuation models can aid managerial decisions.

$$\text{Firm Value} = \text{NOA} + \underbrace{\text{Present Value of } [\text{NOPAT} - (\text{NOA}_{\text{Beg}} \times r_w)]}_{\text{ROPI}}$$

Increasing ROPI, therefore, increases firm value. Managers can increase ROPI in two ways:

1. Decrease the NOA required to generate a given level of NOPAT (improve efficiency)
2. Increase NOPAT with the same level of NOA investment (improve profitability)

These are two very important observations. It means that achieving better performance requires effective management of *both* the balance sheet and the income statement. Most operating managers are accustomed to working with income statements. Further, they are often evaluated on profitability measures, such as achieving desired levels of sales and gross profit or efficiently managing operating expenses. The ROPI model focuses management attention on the balance sheet as well.

The two points above highlight two paths to increase ROPI and, accordingly, firm value. First, let's consider how management can reduce the level of NOA while maintaining a given level of NOPAT. Many managers begin by implementing procedures that reduce net operating working capital, such as:

- Reducing receivables through:
  - Better assessment of customers' credit quality
  - Better controls to identify delinquencies and automated payment notices
  - More accurate and timely invoicing
- Reducing inventories through:
  - Use of less costly components (of equal quality) and production with lower wage rates
  - Elimination of product features not valued by customers
  - Outsourcing to reduce product cost
  - Just-in-time deliveries of raw materials
  - Elimination of manufacturing bottlenecks to reduce work-in-process inventories
  - Producing to order rather than to estimated demand
- Increasing payables through:
  - Extending the payment of low or no-cost payables (so long as the supplier relationships are unharmed)

Management would next look at its long-term operating assets for opportunities to reduce unnecessary operating assets, such as the:

- Sale of unnecessary property, plant or equipment
- Acquisition of production and administrative assets in partnership with other entities for greater throughput
- Acquisition of finished or semifinished goods from suppliers to reduce manufacturing assets

The second path to increase ROPI and, accordingly, firm value is to increase NOPAT with the same level of NOA investment. Management would look to strategies that maximize NOPAT, such as:

- Increasing gross profit dollars through:
  - Better pricing and mix of products sold
  - Reduction of raw material and labor cost without sacrificing product quality, perhaps by outsourcing, better design, or more efficient manufacturing
  - Increase of throughput to minimize overhead costs per unit (provided inventory does not build up)
- Reducing selling, general, and administrative expenses through:
  - Better management of personnel
  - Reduction of overhead
  - Use of derivatives to hedge commodity and interest costs
  - Minimization of tax expense

Before undertaking any of these actions, managers must consider both short- and long-run implications for the company. The ROPI model helps managers assess company performance (income statement) relative to the net operating assets committed (balance sheet).

MANAGERIAL DECISION | **You Are the Chief Financial Officer**

The residual operating income (ROPI) model highlights the importance of increasing NOPAT and reducing net operating assets, which are the two major components of the return on net operating assets (RNOA). What specific steps can you take to improve RNOA through improvement of its components: net operating profit margin and net operating asset turnover? [Answer, p. 12-17]

ASSESSMENT OF VALUATION MODELS

Exhibit 12.3 provides a brief summary of the advantages and disadvantages of the DCF and ROPI models. Neither model dominates the other, and both are theoretically equivalent. Instead, professionals must choose the model that performs best under practical circumstances.

EXHIBIT 12.3	Advantages and Disadvantages of DCF and ROPI Valuation Models		
Model	Advantages	Disadvantages	Performs Best

DCF	• Popular and widely accepted model
	• Cash flows are unaffected by accrual accounting
	• FCFF is intuitive
		• Cash investments in plant assets are treated as cash outflows, even though they create shareholder value
		• Value not recognized unless evidenced by cash flows
		• Computing FCFF can be difficult as operating cash flows are affected by
		  – Cutbacks on investments (receivables, inventories, plant assets); can yield short-run benefits at long-run cost
		  – Securitization, which GAAP treats as an operating cash flow when many view it as a financing activity
			• When the firm reports positive FCFF
			• When FCFF grows at a relatively constant rate

ROPI	• Focuses on value drivers such as profit margins and asset turnovers • Uses both balance sheet and income statement, including accrual accounting information • Reduces weight placed on terminal period value	• Financial statements do not reflect all company assets, especially for knowledge-based industries (for example, R&D assets and goodwill) • Requires some knowledge of accrual accounting	• When financial statements reflect more of the assets and liabilities; including those items often reported off-balance-sheet

There are numerous other equity valuation models in practice. Many require forecasting, but several others do not. A quick review of selected models follows:

The **method of comparables** (often called *multiples*) **model** predicts equity valuation or stock value using price multiples. Price multiples are defined as stock price divided by some key financial statement number. That financial number varies across investors but is usually one of the following: net income, net sales, book value of equity, total assets, or cash flow. The method then compares companies' multiples to those of their competitors to assign value.

The **net asset valuation model** draws on the financial reporting system to assign value. That is, equity is valued as reported assets less reported liabilities. Some investors adjust reported assets and liabilities for several perceived shortcomings in GAAP prior to computing net asset value. This method is commonly applied when valuing privately held companies.

The **dividend discount model** predicts that equity valuation or stock values equal the present value of expected cash dividends. This model is founded on the dividend discount formula and depends on the reliability of forecasted cash dividends.

There are additional models applied in practice that involve dividends, cash flows, research and development outlays, accounting rates of return, cash recovery rates, and real option models. Further, some practitioners, called *chartists* and *technicians,* chart price behavior over time and use it to predict equity value.

RESEARCH INSIGHT | **Using Models to Identify Mispriced Stocks**

Implementation of the ROPI model can include parameters to capture differences in growth opportunities, persistence of ROPI, and the conservatism in accounting measures. Research finds differences in how such factors, across firms and over time, affect ROPI and changes in NOA. This research also hints that investors do not entirely understand the properties underlying these factors and, consequently, individual stocks can be mispriced for short periods of time. Other research contends that the apparent mispricing is due to an omitted valuation variable related to riskiness of the firm.

GLOBAL ACCOUNTING

There are no differences in the method or technique of valuing equity securities using IFRS financial statements. We can use the DCF or the ROPI method with IFRS data as inputs and determine intrinsic values. Regarding other inputs, it is important to note that WACC varies across countries. This is readily apparent when we recognize that the risk-free rate used to compute WACC is country specific; for example, following is the yield on 10-year government debt for several countries as of October 2011 (www.bloomberg.com/markets/rates-bonds/government-bonds/). In comparison to countries such as Japan and Germany, the countries such as Greece and Brazil are riskier because of their debt levels and economic troubles. The higher the country risk, the higher the yield demanded on that country's debt.

Country	Yield to maturity
Japan	0.99%
Germany	2.00%
United States	2.06%
United Kingdom	2.47%
Australia	4.24%
Brazil	11.52%
Greece	23.24%

MODULE-END REVIEW

Following are forecasts of Procter & Gamble's sales, net operating profit after tax (NOPAT), and net operating assets (NOA). These are taken from our forecasting process in Module 11 and now include a terminal period forecast that reflects a long-term growth rate of 1%.

(In millions)	Reported 2011	Horizon Period 2012	2013	2014	2015	Terminal Period
Sales growth		4.6%	4.6%	4.6%	4.6%	1%
Net sales (unrounded)	$ 82,559	$86,356.71 ($82,559 × 1.046)	$90,329.12 ($86,356.71 × 1.046)	$94,484.26 ($90,329.12 × 1.046)	$98,830.54 ($94,484.26 × 1.046)	$99,818.84 ($98,830.54 × 1.01)
Net sales (rounded)	$ 82,559	$ 86,357	$ 90,329	$ 94,484	$ 98,831	$ 99,819
NOPAT	12,193	12,781	13,369	13,984	14,627	14,773
NOA	97,247	101,596	106,269	111,158	116,272	117,434

Drawing on these forecasts, compute P&G's residual operating income (ROPI) and an estimate of its stock value using the ROPI model. Assume the following: discount rate (WACC) of 8%, shares outstanding of 2,765.7 million, and net nonoperating obligations (NNO) of $29,607 million (which includes $361 million in noncontrolling interest).

The solution is on page 12-32.

APPENDIX 12A: Johnson & Johnson Financial Statements

JOHNSON & JOHNSON Balance Sheet		
At Fiscal Year End ($ millions, except shares and per share)	2010	2009
Assets		
Cash and cash equivalents	$ 19,355	$15,810
Marketable securities	8,303	3,615
Accounts receivable trade, net of allowances for doubtful accounts $340 (2009, $333)	9,774	9,646
Inventories	5,378	5,180
Deferred taxes on income	2,224	2,793
Prepaid expenses and other receivables	2,273	2,497
Total current assets	47,307	39,541

continued

continued from prior page

Property, plant and equipment, net	$ 14,553	$14,759
Intangible assets, net	16,716	16,323
Goodwill	15,294	14,862
Deferred taxes on income	5,096	5,507
Other assets	3,942	3,690
Total assets	$102,908	$94,682

Liabilities and Shareholders' Equity

Loans and notes payable	$ 7,617	$ 6,318
Accounts payable	5,623	5,541
Accrued liabilities	4,100	4,625
Accrued rebates, returns and promotions	2,512	2,028
Accrued compensation	2,642	2,777
Accrued taxes on income	578	442
Total current liabilities	$ 23,072	$21,731
Long-term debt	9,156	8,223
Deferred taxes on income	1,447	1,424
Employee related obligations	6,087	6,769
Other liabilities	6,567	5,947
Total liabilities	$ 46,329	$44,094

Shareholders' equity

Preferred stock	$ —	$ —
Common stock—par value $1.00 per share (authorized 4,320,000,000 shares; issued 3,119,843,000 shares)	3,120	3,120
Accumulated other comprehensive income	(3,531)	(3,058)
Retained earnings	77,773	70,306
Less: common stock held in treasury, at cost (381,746,000 shares and 365,522,000 shares)	20,783	19,780
Total shareholders' equity	56,579	50,588
Total liabilities and shareholders' equity	$102,908	$94,682

JOHNSON & JOHNSON
Income Statement

For Fiscal Year Ended ($ millions)	2010	2009	2008
Sales to customers	$61,587	$61,897	$63,747
Cost of products sold	18,792	18,447	18,511
Gross profit	42,795	43,450	45,236
Selling, marketing and administrative expenses	19,424	19,801	21,490
Research and development expense	6,844	6,986	7,577
Purchased in-process research and development	—	—	181
Interest income	(107)	(90)	(361)
Interest expense, net of portion capitalized	455	451	435
Other (income) expense[1]	(768)	(526)	(1,015)
Restructuring	—	1,073	—
Earnings before provision for taxes on income	16,947	15,755	16,929
Provision for taxes on income	3,613	3,489	3,980
Net earnings	$13,334	$12,266	$12,949

[1] We classify Other (Income) Expense as nonoperating because it includes, among other items: royalty income; gains and losses related to the sale and write-down of investments in equity securities; currency gains and losses; non-controlling interests; and hedge ineffectiveness.

JOHNSON & JOHNSON Statement of Cash Flows			
For Fiscal Year Ended ($ millions)	2010	2009	2008
Cash flows from operating activities			
Net earnings	$13,334	$12,266	$12,949
Adjustments to reconcile net earnings to cash flows:			
Depreciation and amortization of property and intangibles	2,939	2,774	2,832
Stock based compensation	614	628	627
Purchased in-process research and development	—	—	181
Deferred tax provision	356	(436)	22
Accounts receivable allowances	12	58	86
Changes in assets and liabilities, net of effects from acquisitions:			
(Increase)/decrease in accounts receivable	(207)	453	(736)
(Increase)/decrease in inventories	(196)	95	(101)
Increase/(decrease) in accounts payable and accrued liabilities	20	(507)	(272)
(Increase)/decrease in other current and noncurrent assets	(574)	1,209	(1,600)
Increase in other current and noncurrent liabilities	87	31	984
Net cash flows from operating activities	16,385	16,571	14,972
Cash flows from investing activities			
Addition to property, plant and equipment	(2,384)	(2,365)	(3,066)
Proceeds from the disposal of assets	524	154	785
Acquisitions, net of cash acquired	(1,269)	(2,470)	(1,214)
Purchases of investments	(15,788)	(10,040)	(3,668)
Sales of investments	11,101	7,232	3,059
Other (primarily intangibles)	(38)	(109)	(83)
Net cash used by investing activities	(7,854)	(7,598)	(4,187)
Cash flows from financing activities			
Dividends to shareholders	(5,804)	(5,327)	(5,024)
Repurchase of common stock	(2,797)	(2,130)	(6,651)
Proceeds from short-term debt	7,874	9,484	8,430
Retirement of short-term debt	(6,565)	(6,791)	(7,319)
Proceeds from long-term debt	1,118	9	1,638
Retirement of long-term debt	(32)	(219)	(24)
Proceeds from the exercise of stock options/excess tax benefits	1,226	882	1,486
Net cash used by financing activities	(4,980)	(4,092)	(7,464)
Effect of exchange rate changes on cash and cash equivalents	(6)	161	(323)
Increase in cash and cash equivalents	3,545	5,042	2,998
Cash and cash equivalents, beginning of year	15,810	10,768	7,770
Cash and cash equivalents, end of year	$19,355	$15,810	$10,768

APPENDIX 12B: Oppenheimer Valuation of Procter & Gamble

We explain the forecasting process in Module 11 and reproduce an analyst report on forecasted financial statements for **Procter & Gamble** in Appendix 11A. In this appendix, we extend that report and reproduce an analyst forecasted stock price for P&G. We include below, two excerpts from the **Oppenheimer** valuation. The first excerpt provides a qualitative and quantitative analysis from Oppenheimer's report as of October 28, 2011 (*reproduced with permission*):

> **Investment Thesis** We remain confident in P&G's ability to execute in a challenging environment, as evidenced by its healthy organic growth outlook. In addition, P&G's anticipated pricing actions on commodity-intensive products and internal cost savings should help mitigate the risk of commodity cost inflation. Further, we expect the company to continue to gain global market share through higher spending on marketing and innovation. This growth profile and its solid handle on its cost structure should provide significant operating leverage and position the company well for meaningful EPS growth in 2011 and beyond, while valuation is compellling.

continued

continued from prior page

Price Target Calculation Our 12- to 18-month price target for P&G of $72 per share is derived from our five-year discounted cash flow analysis, using a weighted average cost of capital of 9.2%, a terminal (fiscal 2016) unlevered free cash flow estimate of $16.7 billion and a residual free cash flow growth rate into perpetuity of 2.50%.

Key Risks to Price Target Risks to the shares achieving our price target include, but are not limited to, management's ability to continue to deliver growth above market averages, achieve its targeted top- and bottom-line synergies from the Gillette acquisition, and weather intense competition through product innovation and marketing.

Our second excerpt is a set of assumptions and computations developed by Oppenheimer analysts to forecast P&G's target stock price reported as of October 2011 (*reproduced with permission*).

(In U.S. $ millions, except per share data)

Procter & Gamble DCF Model	F2012E	F2013E	F2014E	F2015E	F2016E	Assumptions:	
Net Income	12,435	13,318	14,141	15,017	15,955	Risk-free Rate	5.00%
Plus: Interest Expense (After-Tax)	598	652	730	805	870	Beta	0.90
Plus: Depreciation & Amortization	2,962	3,077	3,198	3,323	3,453	Market Risk Premium	6.00%
Less: Capital Expenditures	(3,845)	(3,584)	(3,724)	(3,869)	(4,021)	Cost of Equity	10.40%
Plus/Less: Changes in W/C & Other	526	399	399	981	421		
Unlevered Free Cash Flow	**12,676**	**13,862**	**14,743**	**16,256**	**16,678**	Tax Rate (Statutory)	35.00%
PV of Unlevered Free Cash Flow	**11,603**	**11,615**	**11,308**	**11,414**	**10,719**	Cost of Debt (Pre-Tax)	4.00%
						Cost of Debt (After-Tax)	2.60%
PV of Free Cash Flow	56,659						
Plus: PV of Residual Value	162,907					Cost of Preferred	5.00%
Enterprise Value	219,566						
Less: Total Debt/Preferred	(30,480)					Shares Outstanding	2,748
Equity Value	189,086					Price	$65
Mid-Year Adjustment Factor	1.05					Market Cap	179,319
Equity Value (Adjusted)	197,633					Total Debt	29,246
Shares Outstanding	2,748					Preferred	1,234
Value Per Share	**$72**					Total Capitalization	209,799

						Capitalization	Current	Target
						Equity	85%	85%
						Debt	14%	14%
						Preferred	1%	1%
						WACC		9.2%
						Residual FCF Growth Rate		2.50%

Terminal Free Cash Flow Growth Rate

		1.5%	2.0%	2.5%	3.0%	3.5%
W A C C	8.2%	$75	$80	$87	$94	$104
	8.7%	$69	$73	$79	$85	$93
	9.2%	$63	$67	**$72**	$77	$83
	9.7%	$59	$62	$66	$71	$76
	10.2%	$55	$58	$61	$65	$69

Sources: Company financial statements and Oppenheimer & Co. Inc. estimates.

We make four observations regarding this analyst report regarding P&G's target stock price.

1. The analyst report defines unlevered (before debt) free cash flow as follows. Earlier in this module we described differences in this type of FCFF computation from our FCFF definition.

> | | Net income |
> |---|---|
> | + | Interest expense |
> | + | Depreciation and amortization expense |
> | − | Capital expenditures |
> | + | Decreases in working capital |
> | = | Unlevered free cash flow |

2. This analyst report uses the same DCF computation we describe in this module. The analyst highlights the importance of the terminal year computation with a matrix that quantifies the impact on stock price of (1) growth rates subsequent to the forecasting horizon and (2) WACC. This type of sensitivity analysis is a useful way to identify crucial assumptions. We see that a 1 percentage point change in WACC results in a roughly 20% change in stock price estimate. Further, a 1 percentage point change in the terminal growth rate results in a roughly 15% change in stock price estimate.

3. The cost of equity capital is estimated using the capital asset pricing model (CAPM) as we describe in the module. The analyst's estimated WACC is 9.2%, higher than the WACC of 8% that we assumed in the module. It is not uncommon that model assumptions differ among analysts, and highlights the importance of sensitivity analyses that quantify the effects of varying model assumptions.

4. Bottom line: We see that this analyst's $72 stock price target is higher than the $51.62 stock price estimate that we independently determined in this module. There are a number of differences between our forecast and that of the Oppenheimer analyst. We assumed a constant horizon-period growth rate of 4.6% and a terminal growth rate of 1%. The Oppenheimer report shows a growth rate in unlevered free cash flow of 9.4% for 2013, 6.4% for 2014, 10.3% for 2015, and a terminal growth rate of 2.6%. These rates vary over time and are more optimistic than ours and contribute to the higher stock price target. Another difference is Oppenheimer's use of a mid-year adjustment factor (1.05 in the P&G report). The discount factors we use assume that the cash flows occur at year-end. However, firms generate cash flows throughout the year. The mid-year adjustment factor corrects for this. One simplified adjustment is to multiply the firm equity value by $\sqrt{(1 + WACC)}$ or in the P&G report by $\sqrt{(1.092)} = 1.045$, which Oppenheimer apparently rounded to 1.05. This yielded a 5% increase in the target stock price compared to our price. Again, stock prices are opinions about the intrinsic value of the stock and as with any opinion, they can differ.

APPENDIX 12C: Derivation of Free Cash Flow Formula

Derivation of the free cash flow formula follows; our thanks to Professor Jim Boatsman for this exposition:

$$\text{Assets} = \text{Liabilities} + \text{Stockholders' Equity (SE)}$$
$$\text{NOA} = \text{NNO} + \text{SE}$$
$$\Delta\text{NOA} = \Delta\text{NNO} + \Delta\text{SE} \quad \text{[in change form, where } \Delta \text{ refers to change]}$$
$$\Delta\text{NOA} = \Delta\text{NNO} + \Delta\text{Contributed Capital (CC)} + \text{Net Income} - \text{Dividends (DIV)} \text{[substituting for SE}$$
$$\Delta\text{NOA} = \Delta\text{NNO} + \Delta\text{CC} + (\text{NOPAT} - \text{NNE}) - \text{DIV} \quad \text{[substituting for NI]}$$
$$-\text{NOPAT} + \Delta\text{NOA} = \Delta\text{NNO} + \Delta\text{CC} - \text{NNE} - \text{DIV} \quad \text{[rearranging terms]}$$
$$\text{NOPAT} - \Delta\text{NOA} = \text{NNE} - \Delta\text{NNO} - \Delta\text{CC} + \text{DIV} \quad \text{[multiplying by } -1]$$

Free cash flows to the firm (FCFF)	Net payments to holders of net nonoperating obligations and stock

GUIDANCE ANSWERS

MANAGERIAL DECISION | **You Are the Chief Financial Officer**

Cash flow can be increased by reducing assets. For example, receivables can be reduced by the following:

- Encouraging up-front payments or progress billings on long-term contracts
- Increasing credit standards to avoid slow-paying accounts before sales are made
- Monitoring account age and sending reminders to past-due customers
- Selling accounts receivable to a financial institution or special purpose entity

As another example of asset reduction, plant assets can be reduced by the following:

- Selling unused or excess plant assets
- Forming alliances with other companies to share specialized plant assets
- Owning assets in a special purpose entity with other companies
- Selling production facilities to a contract manufacturer and purchasing the output

MANAGERIAL DECISION | **You Are the Chief Financial Officer**

RNOA can be disaggregated into its two key drivers: net operating profit margin and net operating asset turnover. Net operating profit margin can be increased by improving gross profit margins (better product pricing, lower-cost manufacturing, etc.) and closely monitoring and controlling operating expenses. Net operating asset turnover can be increased by reducing net operating working capital (better monitoring of receivables, better management of inventories, carefully extending payables, etc.) and making more effective use of plant assets (disposing of unused assets, forming corporate alliances to increase plant asset capacity, selling productive assets to contract producers and purchasing the output, etc.). The ROPI model effectively focuses managers on the balance sheet *and* income statement.

DISCUSSION QUESTIONS

Q12-1. Explain how information contained in financial statements is useful in pricing securities. Are there some components of earnings that are more useful than others in this regard? What nonfinancial information might also be useful?

Q12-2. In general, what role do expectations play in pricing equity securities? What is the relation between security prices and expected returns (the discount rate, or WACC, in this case)?

Q12-3. What are free cash flows to the firm (FCFF) and how are they used in the pricing of equity securities?

Q12-4. Define the weighted average cost of capital (WACC).

Q12-5. Define net operating profit after tax (NOPAT).

Q12-6. Define net operating assets (NOA).

Q12-7. Define the concept of residual operating income. How is residual operating income used in pricing equity securities?

Q12-8. What insight does disaggregation of RNOA into net operating profit margin and net operating asset turnover provide for managing a company?

Assignments with the ✓ logo in the margin are available in an online homework system.
See the Preface of the book for details.

MINI EXERCISES

M12-9. Interpreting Earnings Announcement Effects on Stock Prices (LO1, 2)

In a recent quarterly earnings announcement, Starbucks announced that its earnings had markedly increased (up 7 cents per share over the prior year) and were 1 cent higher than analysts' expectations. Starbucks' stock "edged higher," according to *The Wall Street Journal*, but did not markedly increase. Why do you believe that Starbucks' stock price did not markedly increase given the good news?

Starbucks (SBUX)

M12-10. Computing Residual Operating Income (ROPI) (LO3)

Halliburton Company reports net operating profit after tax (NOPAT) of $2,032 million in 2010. Its net operating assets at the beginning of 2010 are $9,937 million. Assuming a 10% weighted average cost of capital (WACC), what is Halliburton's residual operating income for 2010? Show computations.

Halliburton Company (HAL)

M12-11. Computing Free Cash Flows to the Firm (FCFF) (LO2)

Halliburton Company reports net operating profit after tax (NOPAT) of $2,032 million in 2010. Its net operating assets at the beginning of 2010 are $9,937 million and are $12,160 million at the end of 2010. What are Halliburton's free cash flows to the firm (FCFF) for 2010? Show computations.

Halliburton Company (HAL)

M12-12. Computing, Analyzing and Interpreting Residual Operating Income (ROPI) (LO3)

In its 2010 fiscal year annual report, CVS reports net operating income after tax (NOPAT) of $3,777 million. As of the beginning of fiscal year 2010 it reports net operating assets of $45,889 million.

CVS Caremark (CVS)

a. Did CVS earn positive residual operating income (ROPI) in 2010 if its weighted average cost of capital (WACC) is 7%? Explain.

b. At what level of WACC would CVS not report positive residual operating income for 2010? Explain.

M12-13. Estimating Share Value Using the DCF Model (LO1, 2)

Following are forecasts of Target Corporation's sales, net operating profit after tax (NOPAT), and net operating assets (NOA) as of January 29, 2011.

Target Corporation (TGT)

(In millions)	Reported 2011	Horizon Period				Terminal Period
		2012	2013	2014	2015	
Sales............	$67,390	$70,086	$72,889	$75,805	$78,837	$79,625
NOPAT	3,397	3,504	3,644	3,790	3,942	3,981
NOA	29,501	30,472	31,691	32,959	34,277	34,620

Answer the following requirements assuming a terminal period growth rate of 1%, discount rate (WACC) of 7%, shares outstanding of 704 million, and net nonoperating obligations (NNO) of $14,014 million.

a. Estimate the value of a share of Target common stock using the discounted cash flow (DCF) model as of January 29, 2011.

b. Target Corporation (TGT) stock closed at $49.99 on March 18, 2011. How does your valuation estimate compare with this closing price? What do you believe are some reasons for the difference?

Target Corporation (TGT)

M12-14. Estimating Share Value Using the ROPI Model (LO3)

Refer to the information in M12-13 to answer the following requirements.

a. Estimate the value of a share of Target common stock using the residual operating income (ROPI) model as of January 29, 2011.

b. Target Corporation (TGT) stock closed at $49.99 on March 18, 2011. How does your valuation estimate compare with this closing price? What do you believe are some reasons for the difference?

EXERCISES

Abercrombie & Fitch (ANF)

E12-15. Estimating Share Value Using the DCF Model (LO1, 2)

Following are forecasts of Abercrombie & Fitch's sales, net operating profit after tax (NOPAT), and net operating assets (NOA) as of January 29, 2011 (Current-year NOPAT is lower due to transitory items; we use a longer term estimate for NOPM of 8%.).

(In millions)	Reported 2011	Horizon Period				Terminal Period
		2012	2013	2014	2015	
Sales...........	$3,469	$3,989	$4,587	$5,275	$6,066	$6,187
NOPAT	152	319	367	422	485	495
NOA	1,032	1,173	1,349	1,551	1,784	1,820

Answer the following requirements assuming a discount rate (WACC) of 10%, a terminal period growth rate of 2%, common shares outstanding of 87.2 million, and net nonoperating obligations (NNO) of $(858) million (negative NNO reflects net nonoperating assets such as investments rather than net obligations).

a. Estimate the value of a share of Abercrombie & Fitch common stock using the discounted cash flow (DCF) model as of January 29, 2011.

b. Abercrombie & Fitch (ANF) stock closed at $56.71 on March 29, 2011. How does your valuation estimate compare with this closing price? What do you believe are some reasons for the difference?

Abercrombie & Fitch (ANF)

E12-16. Estimating Share Value Using the ROPI Model (LO3)

Refer to the information in E12-15 to answer the following requirements.

a. Estimate the value of a share of Abercrombie & Fitch common stock using the residual operating income (ROPI) model as of January 29, 2011.

b. Abercrombie & Fitch stock closed at $56.71 on March 29, 2011. How does your valuation estimate compare with this closing price? What do you believe are some reasons for the difference?

Best Buy (BBY)

E12-17. Estimating Share Value Using the DCF Model (LO1, 2)

Following are forecasts of sales, net operating profit after tax (NOPAT), and net operating assets (NOA) as of February 26, 2011, for Best Buy, Inc.

(In millions)	Reported 2011	Horizon Period				Terminal Period
		2012	2013	2014	2015	
Sales...........	$50,272	$52,786	$55,425	$58,196	$61,106	$61,717
NOPAT	1,389	1,584	1,663	1,746	1,833	1,852
NOA	7,876	8,248	8,660	9,093	9,548	9,643

Answer the following requirements assuming a discount rate (WACC) of 11%, a terminal period growth rate of 1%, common shares outstanding of 392.6 million, and net nonoperating obligations (NNO) of $1,274 million.

a. Estimate the value of a share of Best Buy's common stock using the discounted cash flow (DCF) model as of February 26, 2011.

b. Best Buy (BBY) stock closed at $30.20 on April 25, 2011. How does your valuation estimate compare with this closing price? What do you believe are some reasons for the difference?

E12-18. Estimating Share Value Using the ROPI Model (LO3)

Refer to the information in E12-17 to answer the following requirements.

Best Buy (BBY)

a. Estimate the value of a share of Best Buy common stock using the residual operating income (ROPI) model as of February 26, 2011.

b. Best Buy (BBY) stock closed at $30.20 on April 25, 2011. How does your valuation estimate compare with this closing price? What do you believe are some reasons for the difference?

E12-19. Identifying and Computing Net Operating Assets (NOA) and Net Nonoperating Obligations (NNO) (LO1, 2)

Following is the balance sheet for Halliburton Company.

Halliburton Company (HAL)

HALLIBURTON COMPANY Consolidated Balance Sheets		
At December 31 (Millions of dollars and shares)	2010	2009
Assets		
Cash and equivalents.	$ 1,398	$ 2,082
Receivables, net.	3,924	2,964
Inventories	1,940	1,598
Investments in markeatable securities.	653	1,312
Current deferred income taxes.	257	210
Other current assets.	714	472
Total current assets	8,886	8,638
Property, plant and equipment—net	6,842	5,759
Goodwill	1,315	1,100
Other assets.	1,254	1,041
Total assets.	$18,297	$16,538
Liabilities and Stockholders' Equity		
Accounts payable.	$ 1,139	$ 787
Current maturities of long-term debt	—	750
Accrued employee compensation and benefits.	716	514
Deferred revenue	266	215
Other current liabilities	636	623
Total current liabilities.	2,757	2,889
Long-term debt	3,824	3,824
Employee compensation and benefits.	487	462
Other liabilities	842	606
Total liabilities.	7,910	7,781
Shareholders' equity		
Common shares, par value $2.50 per share—authorized 2,000 shares, issued 1,069 shares and 1,067 shares.	2,674	2,669
Paid-in capital in excess of par value.	339	411
Accumulated other comprehensive loss	(240)	(213)
Retained earnings	12,371	10,863
Treasury stock, at cost—159 and 165 shares	(4,771)	(5,002)
Company shareholders' equity	10,373	8,728
Noncontrolling interest in consolidated subsidiaries	14	29
Total shareholders' equity	10,387	8,757
Total liabilities and shareholders' equity.	$18,297	$16,538

a. Compute net operating assets (NOA) and net nonoperating obligations (NNO) for 2010.

b. For 2010, show that: NOA = NNO + Stockholders' equity.

E12-20. **Identifying and Computing Net Operating Profit after Tax (NOPAT) and Net Nonoperating Expense (NNE)** (LO1, 2)

Halliburton Company
(HAL)

Following is the income statement for Halliburton Company.

HALLIBURTON COMPANY Consolidated Statements of Operations			
At December 31 (millions of dollars)	2010	2009	2008
Revenue			
Services	$13,779	$ 10,832	$13,391
Product sales	4,194	3,843	4,888
Total revenue	17,973	14,675	18,279
Operating costs and expenses			
Cost of services	11,237	9,224	10,079
Cost of sales.	3,508	3,255	3,970
General and administrative.	229	207	282
Gain on sale of operating assets, net.	(10)	(5)	(62)
Total operating costs and expenses.	14,964	12,681	14,269
Operating income.	3,009	1,994	4,010
Interest expense, net of interest income			
of $11, $12, and $39.	(297)	(285)	(128)
Other nonoperating expenses, net.	(57)	(27)	(33)
Income from continuing operations before			
income taxes	2,655	1,682	3,849
Provision for income taxes.	(853)	(518)	(1,211)
Income from continuing operations	1,802	1,164	2,638
Income (loss) from discontinued operations,			
net of income tax	40	(9)	(423)
Net income.	1,842	1,155	2,215
Noncontrolling interest in net income of subsidiaries	(7)	(10)	9
Net income attributable to company	$1,835	$ 1,145	$ 2,224

Compute net operating profit after tax (NOPAT) for 2010, assuming a federal and state statutory tax rate of 35%.

E12-21. **Estimating Share Value Using the DCF Model** (LO1, 2)

Halliburton Company
(HAL)

Following are forecasts of Halliburton Company's sales, net operating profit after tax (NOPAT), and net operating assets (NOA) as of December 31, 2010.

	Reported	Horizon Period				Terminal
(In millions)	2010	2011	2012	2013	2014	Period
Sales.	$17,973	$21,028	$24,603	$28,786	$33,680	$35,027
NOPAT	2,032	2,376	2,780	3,253	3,806	3,958
NOA	12,160	14,208	16,624	19,450	22,757	23,667

Answer the following requirements assuming a discount rate (WACC) of 10%, a terminal period growth rate of 4%, common shares outstanding of 910 million, and net nonoperating obligations (NNO) of $1,787 million.

a. Estimate the value of a share of Halliburton's common stock using the discounted cash flow (DCF) model as of February 17, 2011.

b. Halliburton Company (HAL) stock closed at $48.43 on February 17, 2011. How does your valuation estimate compare with this closing price? What do you believe are some reasons for the difference?

E12-22. Estimating Share Value Using the ROPI Model (LO3)

Refer to the information in E12-21 to answer the following requirements.

Halliburton Company
(HAL)

a. Estimate the value of a share of Halliburton Company common stock using the residual operating income (ROPI) model as of February 17, 2011.

b. Halliburton Company stock closed at $48.43 on February 17, 2011. How does your valuation estimate compare with this closing price? What do you believe are some reasons for the difference?

E12-23. Explaining the Equivalence of Valuation Models and the Relevance of Earnings (LO1, 2, 3)

This module focused on two different valuation models: the discounted cash flow (DCF) model and the residual operating income (ROPI) model. The models focus on free cash flows to the firm and on residual operating income, respectively. We stressed that these two models are theoretically equivalent.

a. What is the *intuition* for why these models are equivalent?

b. Some analysts focus on cash flows as they believe that companies manage earnings, which presumably makes earnings less relevant. Are earnings relevant? Explain.

E12-24. Applying and Interpreting Value Driver Components of RNOA (LO3)

The net operating profit margin and the net operating asset turnover components of return on net operating assets are often termed *value drivers*, which refers to their positive influence on stock value by virtue of their role as components of return on net operating assets (RNOA).

a. How do profit margins and asset turnover ratios influence stock values?

b. Assuming that profit margins and asset turnover ratios are value drivers, what insight does this give us about managing companies if the goal is to create shareholder value?

PROBLEMS

P12-25. Forecasting and Estimating Share Value Using the DCF Model (LO1, 2)

Following are the income statement and balance sheet for Intel Corporation.

Intel Corporation
(INTC)

INTEL CORPORATION Consolidated Statements of Income			
Year Ended (In millions)	December 25, 2010	December 26, 2009	December 27, 2008
Net revenue	$43,623	$35,127	$37,586
Cost of sales	15,132	15,566	16,742
Gross margin	28,491	19,561	20,844
Research and development	6,576	5,653	5,722
Marketing, general and administrative	6,309	7,931	5,452
Restructuring and asset impairment charges	—	231	710
Amortization of acquisition-related intangibles	18	35	6
Operating expenses	12,903	13,850	11,890
Operating income	15,588	5,711	8,954
Gains (losses) on equity method investments, net	117	(147)	(1,380)
Gains (losses) on other equity investments, net	231	(23)	(376)
Interest and other, net	109	163	488
Income before taxes	16,045	5,704	7,686
Provision for taxes	4,581	1,335	2,394
Net income	$11,464	$ 4,369	$ 5,292

INTEL CORPORATION Consolidated Balance Sheets		
As of Year-Ended (In millions, except par value)	December 25, 2010	December 26, 2009
Assets		
Current assets		
Cash and cash equivalents.	$ 5,498	$ 3,987
Short-term investments	11,294	5,285
Trading assets.	5,093	4,648
Accounts receivable, net	2,867	2,273
Inventories	3,757	2,935
Deferred tax assets.	1,488	1,216
Other current assets	1,614	813
Total current assets.	31,611	21,157
Property, plant and equipment, net	17,899	17,225
Marketable equity securities	1,008	773
Other long-term investments1	3,026	4,179
Goodwill	4,531	4,421
Other long-term assets	5,111	5,340
Total assets.	$63,186	$53,095
Liabilities		
Current liabilities		
Short-term debt	$ 38	$ 172
Accounts payable.	2,290	1,883
Accrued compensation and benefits	2,888	2,448
Accrued advertising	1,007	773
Deferred income on shipments to distributors	622	593
Other accrued liabilities	2,482	1,722
Total current liabilities	9,327	7,591
Long-term income taxes payable.	190	193
Long-term debt	2,077	2,049
Long-term deferred tax liabilities	926	555
Other long-term liabilities.	1,236	1,003
Total liabilities	13,756	11,391
Stockholders' equity		
Preferred stock, $0.001 par value.	—	—
Common stock, $0.001 par value, 10,000 shares authorized; 5,581 issued and 5,511 outstanding and capital in excess of par value	16,178	14,993
Accumulated other comprehensive income	333	393
Retained earnings.	32,919	26,318
Total stockholders' equity	49,430	41,704
Total liabilities and stockholders' equity.	$63,186	$53,095

[1] These investments are operating assets as they relate to associated companies.

Required

a. Compute Intel's net operating assets (NOA) for year-end 2010.

b. Compute net operating profit after tax (NOPAT) for 2010, assuming a federal and state statutory tax rate of 37%.

c. Forecast Intel's sales, NOPAT, and NOA for years 2011 through 2014 using the following assumptions:

Sales growth.	10%
Net operating profit margin (NOPM).	26%
Net operating asset turnover (NOAT) at year-end	1.50

Forecast the terminal period value assuming a 1% terminal period growth and using the NOPM and NOAT assumptions above.

d. Estimate the value of a share of Intel common stock using the discounted cash flow (DCF) model as of December 25, 2010; assume a discount rate (WACC) of 11%, common shares outstanding of

5,511 million, and net nonoperating obligations (NNO) of $(20,778) million (NNO is negative which means that Intel has net nonoperating investments).

   e. Intel (INTC) stock closed at $22.14 on February 18, 2011. How does your valuation estimate compare with this closing price? What do you believe are some reasons for the difference? What investment decision is suggested from your results?

P12-26. Estimating Share Value Using the ROPI Model (LO3)

Refer to the information in P12-25 to answer the following requirements.

Intel Corporation
(INTC)

Required

   a. Estimate the value of a share of Intel common stock using the residual operating income (ROPI) model as of December 25, 2010.

   b. Intel stock closed at $22.14 on February 18, 2011. How does your valuation estimate compare with this closing price? What do you believe are some reasons for the difference? What investment decision is suggested from your results?

P12-27. Forecasting and Estimating Share Value Using the DCF Model (LO1, 2)

Following are the income statement and balance sheet for CVS Caremark.

CVS Caremark (CVS)

CVS CAREMARK INC. Balance Sheets		
December 31 (In millions, except per share amounts)	2010	2009
Assets		
Cash and cash equivalents.	$ 1,427	$ 1,086
Short-term investments	4	5
Accounts receivable, net	4,925	5,457
Inventories	10,695	10,343
Deferred income taxes	511	506
Other current assets.	144	140
Total current assets.	17,706	17,537
Property and equipment, net	8,322	7,923
Goodwill	25,669	25,680
Intangible assets, net	9,784	10,127
Other assets	688	374
Total assets.	$62,169	$61,641
Liabilities		
Accounts payable.	$ 4,026	$ 3,560
Claims and discounts payable	2,569	3,075
Accrued expenses	3,070	3,246
Short-term debt	300	315
Current portion of long-term debt	1,105	2,104
Total current liabilities	11,070	12,300
Long-term debt.	8,652	8,756
Deferred income taxes	3,655	3,678
Other long-term liabilities	1,058	1,102
Redeemable noncontrolling interest.	34	37
Total liabilities	24,469	25,873
Shareholders' equity		
Common stock, par value $0.01: 3,200 shares authorized; 1,624 shares issued and 1,363 shares outstanding at December 31, 2010	16	16
Treasury stock at cost:	(9,030)	(7,610)
Shares held in trust.	(56)	(56)
Capital surplus	27,610	27,198
Retained earnings.	19,303	16,355
Accumulated other comprehensive loss	(143)	(135)
Total shareholders' equity.	37,700	35,768
Total liabilities and shareholders' equity	$62,169	$61,641

CVS CAREMARK INC. Consolidated Statements of Income			
For the year ended December 31 (In millions)	2010	2009	2008
Net revenues	$96,413	$98,729	$87,472
Cost of revenues	76,156	78,349	69,182
Gross profit	20,257	20,380	18,290
Operating expenses	14,092	13,942	12,244
Operating profit	6,165	6,438	6,046
Interest expense, net	536	525	509
Income before income tax provision	5,629	5,913	5,537
Income tax provision	2,190	2,205	2,193
Income from continuing operations	3,439	3,708	3,344
Loss from discontinued operations, net of income tax benefit	(15)	(12)	(132)
Net income	3,434	3,696	3,212
Net loss attributable to noncontrolling interest	3	—	—
Preference dividends, net of income tax benefit	—	—	(14)
Net income attributable to CVS Caremark	$ 3,427	$ 3,696	$ 3,198

Required

a. Compute net operating assets (NOA) as of December 31, 2010.

b. Compute net operating profit after tax (NOPAT) for fiscal year ended December 31, 2010, assuming a federal and state statutory tax rate of 37%.

c. Forecast CVS's sales, NOPAT, and NOA for 2011 through 2014 using the following assumptions:

Sales growth	5%
Net operating profit margin (NOPM)	4%
Net operating asset turnover (NOAT) at fiscal year-end	2.10

Forecast the terminal period value assuming a 1% terminal period growth and using the NOPM and NOAT assumptions above.

d. Estimate the value of a share of CVS common stock using the discounted cash flow (DCF) model as of December 31, 2010; assume a discount rate (WACC) of 7%, common shares outstanding of 1,363 million, and net nonoperating obligations (NNO) of $8,660 million.

e. CVS's stock closed at $33.06 on February 18, 2011. How does your valuation estimate compare with this closing price? What do you believe are some reasons for the difference?

CVS Caremark (CVS)

P12-28. Estimating Share Value Using the ROPI Model (LO3)

Refer to the information in P12-27 to answer the following requirements.

Required

a. Estimate the value of a share of CVS common stock using the residual operating income (ROPI) model as of December 31, 2010.

b. CVS stock closed at $33.06 on February 18, 2011. How does your valuation estimate compare with this closing price? What do you believe are some reasons for the difference? What investment decision is suggested from your results?

Abbott Laboratories (ABT)

P12-29. Forecasting and Estimating Share Value Using the DCF Model (LO1, 2)

Following are the income statement and balance sheet for Abbott Laboratories (ABT).

ABBOTT LABORATORIES Balance Sheet December 31 ($ millions)	2010	2009
Assets		
Cash and cash equivalents	$ 3,648.371	$ 8,809.339
Investments and restricted funds	3,675.569	1,122.709
Trade receivables, net	7,184.034	6,541.941
Total inventories	3,188.734	3,264.877
Deferred income taxes	3,076.051	2,364.142
Other prepaid expenses and receivables	1,544.770	1,210.883
Total current assets	22,317.529	23,313.891
Investments	302.049	1,132.866
Property and equipment, net	7,970.956	7,619.489
Intangible assets, net of amortization	12,151.628	6,291.989
Goodwill	15,930.077	13,200.174
Deferred income taxes and other assets	790.027	858.214
Total assets	$59,462.266	$52,416.623
Liabilities and Shareholders' Investment		
Short-term borrowings	$ 4,349.796	$ 4,978.438
Trade accounts payable	1,535.759	1,280.542
Salaries, wages and commissions	1,328.665	1,117.410
Other accrued liabilities	6,014.772	4,399.137
Dividends payable	680.749	620.640
Income taxes payable	1,307.723	442.140
Current portion of long-term debt	2,044.970	211.182
Total current liabilities	17,262.434	13,049.489
Long-term debt	12,523.517	11,266.294
Post-employment and other long-term obligations	7,199.851	5,202.111
Shareholders' investment		
Common shares, without par value. Authorized: 2,400,000,000 shares. Issued: 1,619,689,876 and 1,612,683,987	8,744.703	8,257.873
Common shares held in treasury: 72,705,928 and 61,516,398	(3,916.823)	(3,310.347)
Earnings employed in the business	18,927.101	17,054.027
Accumulated other comprehensive income (loss)	(1,366.846)	854.074
Total Abbott shareholders' investment	22,388.135	22,855.627
Noncontrolling interests in subsidiaries	88.329	43.102
Total shareholders' investment	22,476.464	22,898.729
Total liabilities and shareholders' investment	$59,462.266	$52,416.623

ABBOTT LABORATORIES AND SUBSIDIARIES			
Consolidated Statement of Earnings			
Year Ended December 31 (dollars in millions)	**2010**	**2009**	**2008**
Net sales.	$35,166.721	$30,764.707	$29,527.552
Cost of products sold.	14,665.192	13,209.329	12,612.022
Research and development	3,724.424	2,743.733	2,688.811
Acquired in-process research and development	313.200	170.000	97.256
Selling, general and administrative	10,376.324	8,405.904	8,435.624
Total operating cost and expenses	29,079.140	24,528.966	23,833.713
Operating earnings.	6,087.581	6,235.741	5,693.839
Interest expense.	553.135	519.656	528.474
Interest (income).	(105.453)	(137.779)	(201.229)
(Income) from the TAP Pharmaceutical joint venture	—	—	(118.997)
Other (income) expense, net	(72.935)	(1,339.910)	(370.695)
Earnings from continuing operations before taxes	5,712.834	7,193.774	5,856.286
Taxes on earnings from continuing operations	1,086.662	1,447.936	1,122.070
Earnings from continuing operations	4,626.172	5,745.838	4,734.216
Gain on sale of discontinued operations, net of taxes.	—	—	146.503
Net earnings.	$ 4,626.172	$ 5,745.838	$ 4,880.719

Required

a. Compute net operating assets (NOA) for year-end 2010.

b. Compute net operating profit after tax (NOPAT) for 2010 assuming a federal and state statutory tax rate of 35.4%.

c. Forecast Abbott Laboratories' sales, NOPAT, and NOA for 2011 through 2014 using the following assumptions:

Sales growth.	10%
Net operating profit margin (NOPM).	14%
Net operating asset turnover (NOAT), year-end	1.0

Forecast the terminal period value assuming a 1% terminal period growth and using the NOPM and NOAT assumptions above.

d. Estimate the value of a share of Abbott Laboratories' common stock using the discounted cash flow (DCF) model as of December 31, 2010; assume a discount rate (WACC) of 7%, common shares outstanding of 1,547 million, and net nonoperating obligations (NNO) of $12,061 million.

e. Abbott Laboratories (ABT) stock closed at $46.88 on February 18, 2011. How does your valuation estimate compare with this closing price? What do you believe are some reasons for the difference? What investment decision is suggested from your results?

P12-30. Estimating Share Value Using the ROPI Model   (LO3)

Abbott Laboratories
(ABT)

Refer to the information in P12-29 to answer the following requirements.

Required

a. Estimate the value of a share of Abbott Laboratories common stock using the residual operating income (ROPI) model as of December 31, 2010.

b. Abbott Laboratories stock closed at $46.88 on February 18, 2011. How does your valuation estimate compare with this closing price? What do you believe are some reasons for the difference? What investment decision is suggested from your results?

P12-31. **Forecasting and Estimating Share Value Using the DCF Model**   (LO1, 2)

Following are the income statement and balance sheet for Kellogg Company.

Kellogg Co. (K)

KELLOGG COMPANY AND SUBSIDIARIES Consolidated Statement of Income			
For Year Ended (in millions)	2010	2009	2008
Net sales.	$12,397	$12,575	$12,822
Cost of goods sold.	7,108	7,184	7,455
Selling, general and administrative expense	3,299	3,390	3,414
Operating profit	1,990	2,001	1,953
Interest expense.	248	295	308
Other income (expense), net	—	(22)	(14)
Income before income taxes	1,742	1,684	1,631
Income taxes	502	476	485
Net income.	1,240	1,208	1,146
Net loss attributable to noncontrolling interests	(7)	(4)	(2)
Net income attributable to Kellogg Company	$ 1,247	$ 1,212	$ 1,148

KELLOGG COMPANY AND SUBSIDIARIES Consolidated Balance Sheet		
(millions, except share data)	2010	2009
Current assets		
Cash and cash equivalents	$ 444	$ 334
Accounts receivable, net	1,190	1,093
Inventories	1,056	910
Other current assets.	225	221
Total current assets.	2,915	2,558
Property, net.	3,128	3,010
Goodwill	3,628	3,643
Other intangibles, net.	1,456	1,458
Other assets.	720	531
Total assets.	$11,847	$11,200
Current liabilities		
Current maturities of long-term debt	$ 952	$ 1
Notes payable	44	44
Accounts payable.	1,149	1,077
Other current liabilities	1,039	1,166
Total current liabilities	3,184	2,288
Long-term debt	4,908	4,835
Deferred income taxes	697	425
Pension liability.	265	430
Other liabilities	639	947
Equity		
Common stock, $.25 par value, 1,000,000,000 shares authorized Issued: 419,272,027 shares in 2010 and 419,058,168 shares in 2009	105	105
Capital in excess of par value	495	472
Retained earnings	6,122	5,481
Treasury stock at cost: 53,667,635 shares in 2010 and 37,678,215 shares in 2009.	(2,650)	(1,820)
Accumulated other comprehensive income (loss).	(1,914)	(1,966)
Total Kellogg Company equity	2,158	2,272
Noncontrolling interests	(4)	3
Total equity	2,154	2,275
Total liabilities and equity	$11,847	$11,200

Required

a. Compute net operating assets (NOA) as of year-end 2010.

b. Compute net operating profit after tax (NOPAT) for 2010, assuming a federal and state statutory tax rate of 36.4%.

c. Forecast Kellogg's sales, NOPAT, and NOA for 2011 through 2014 using the following assumptions:

Sales growth.	4%
Net operating profit margin (NOPM).	11%
Net operating asset turnover (NOAT), year-end	1.6

Forecast the terminal period value assuming a 1% terminal period growth and using the NOPM and NOAT assumptions above.

d. Estimate the value of a share of Kellogg common stock using the discounted cash flow (DCF) model; assume a discount rate (WACC) of 6%, common shares outstanding of 365.6 million, and net nonoperating obligations (NNO) of $5,456 million.

e. Kellogg's stock closed at $53.56 at February 28, 2011. How does your valuation estimate compare with this closing price? What do you believe are some reasons for the difference?

P12-32. Estimating Share Value Using the ROPI Model (LO3)

Kellogg Co. (K)

Refer to the information in P12-31 to answer the following requirements.

Required

a. Estimate the value of a share of Kellogg common stock using the residual operating income (ROPI) model.

b. Kellogg stock closed at $53.56 at February 28, 2011. How does your valuation estimate compare with this closing price? What do you believe are some reasons for the difference? What investment decision is suggested from your results?

IFRS APPLICATIONS

I12-33. Forecasting and Estimating Share Value Using the DCF Model (LO1, 2)

Tesco, PLC

Following are the income statement and balance sheet for Tesco, PLC, a UK-based grocery chain. The company's financial statements are prepared in accordance with IFRS.

Tesco, PLC Group Income Statement		
Year ended 26 February 2011	**52 weeks 2011 £m**	**52 weeks 2010 £m**
Continuing operations		
Revenue (sales excluding VAT).	£60,931	£56,910
Cost of sales.	(55,871)	(52,303)
Gross profit.	5,060	4,607
Administrative expenses	(1,676)	(1,527)
Profit arising on property-related items	427	377
Operating profit	3,811	3,457
Share of post-tax profits of joint ventures and associates	57	33
Finance income	150	265
Finance costs.	(483)	(579)
Profit before tax	3,535	3,176
Taxation	(864)	(840)
Profit for the year	£ 2,671	£ 2,336
Attributable to:		
Owners of the parent	£ 2,655	£ 2,327
Non-controlling interests	16	9
	£ 2,671	£ 2,336

TESCO PLC Group Balance Sheet	26 February 2011 £m	27 February 2010 £m
Non-current assets		
Goodwill and other intangible assets.....................	£ 4,338	£ 4,177
Property, plant and equipment...........................	24,398	24,203
Investments in joint ventures and associates..............	316	152
Other investments	2,971	2,594
Financial assets	3,266	3,094
Deferred tax assets	48	38
Total non-current assets	35,337	34,258
Current assets		
Inventories	3,162	2,729
Trade and other receivables...........................	2,314	1,888
Financial assets	3,066	2,636
Current tax assets	4	6
Short-term investments	1,022	1,314
Cash and cash equivalents	1,870	2,819
	11,438	11,392
Non-current assets classified as held for sale	431	373
Total current assets.................................	11,869	11,765
Current liabilities		
Trade and other payables.............................	(10,484)	(9,442)
Financial liabilities....................................	(1,641)	(1,675)
Customer prepayments and deposits	(5,110)	(4,387)
Current tax liabilities..................................	(432)	(472)
Provisions..	(64)	(39)
Total current liabilities	(17,731)	(16,015)
Non-current liabilities		
Financial liabilities....................................	(10,289)	(12,520)
Post-employment benefit obligations	(1,356)	(1,840)
Deferred tax liabilities................................	(1,094)	(795)
Provisions..	(113)	(172)
	(12,852)	(15,327)
Equity		
Share capital...	402	399
Share premium account...............................	4,896	4,801
Other reserves	40	40
Retained earnings	11,197	9,356
Equity attributable to owners of the parent	16,535	14,596
Non-controlling interests	88	85
Total equity..	£16,623	£14,681

Required

a. Compute net operating assets (NOA) as of year-end 2011.

b. Compute net operating profit after tax (NOPAT) for 2011, assuming a marginal tax rate of 25%.

c. Forecast Tesco's sales, NOPAT, and NOA for 2012 through 2015 using the following assumptions:

Sales growth......................................	6%
Net operating profit margin (NOPM)...................	4.8%
Net operating asset turnover (NOAT)	3.8

Estimate the terminal period value assuming a 1% terminal period growth and using the NOPM and NOAT assumptions, above.

    d. Estimate the value of a share of Tesco's common stock (which trades on the London Stock Exchange) using the discounted cash flow (DCF) model; assume a discount rate (WACC) of 8%, common shares outstanding of 8,046.5 million, and net nonoperating obligations (NNO) of £(608). (Note: NNO is negative which means that Tesco has net nonoperating investments and financial assets.)

    e. Tesco's stock price was £3.93 on April 19, 2011. How does your valuation estimate compare with this closing price? What do you believe are some reasons for the difference?

I12-34. Estimating Share Value Using the ROPI Model (LO1, 2)
Refer to the information in I12-33 to answer the following requirements.

Required

    a. Estimate the value of a share of Tesco's common stock (which trades on the London Stock Exchange) using the residual operating income (ROPI) model.

    b. Tesco's stock price was £3.93 on April 19, 2011. How does your valuation estimate compare with this closing price? What do you believe are some reasons for the difference? What investment decision do your results suggest?

MANAGEMENT APPLICATIONS

MA12-35. Management Application: Operating Improvement versus Financial Engineering (LO4)
Assume that you are the CEO of a small publicly traded company. The operating performance of your company has fallen below market expectations, which is reflected in a depressed stock price. At your direction, your CFO provides you with the following recommendations that are designed to increase your company's return on net operating assets (RNOA) and your operating cash flows, both of which will, presumably, result in improved financial performance and an increased stock price.

1. To improve net cash flow from operating activities, the CFO recommends that your company reduce inventories (raw material, work-in-progress, and finished goods) and receivables (through selective credit granting and increased emphasis on collection of past due accounts).

2. The CFO recommends that your company sell and lease back its office building. The lease will be structured so as to be classified as an operating lease under GAAP. The assets will, therefore, not be included in the computation of net operating assets (NOA), thus increasing RNOA.

3. The CFO recommends that your company lengthen the time taken to pay accounts payable (lean on the trade) to increase net cash flows from operating activities.

4. Because your company's operating performance is already depressed, the CFO recommends that you take a "big bath;" that is, write off all assets deemed to be impaired and accrue excessive liabilities for future contingencies. The higher current period expense will, then, result in higher future period income as the assets written off will not be depreciated and your company will have a liability account available to absorb future cash payments rather than recording them as expenses.

5. The CFO recommends that your company increase its estimate of expected return on pension investments. This will reduce pension expense and increase operating profit, a component of net operating profit after tax (NOPAT) and, thus, of RNOA.

6. The CFO recommends that your company share ownership of its outbound logistics (trucking division) with another company in a joint venture. This would have the effect of increasing throughput, thus spreading overhead over a larger volume base, and would remove the assets from your company's balance sheet since the joint venture would be accounted for as an equity method investment.

Evaluate each of the CFO's recommendations. In your evaluation, consider whether each recommendation will positively impact the operating performance of your company or whether it is cosmetic in nature.

SOLUTIONS TO REVIEW PROBLEMS

Mid-Module Review

Solution
The following DCF results yield a P&G stock value estimate of $51.63 as of August 10, 2011. P&G's stock closed at $58.51 on that date. This estimate suggests that P&G's stock is marginally overvalued on that date.

(In millions, except per share values and discount factors)	Reported 2011	Horizon Period				Terminal Period
		2012	2013	2014	2015	
Increase in NOA[a]		$ 4,349	$ 4,673	$ 4,889	$ 5,114	$ 1,162
FCFF (NOPAT − Increase in NOA)		8,432	8,696	9,095	9,513	13,611
Discount factor [$1/(1 + r_w)^t$]		0.92593	0.85734	0.79383	0.73503	
Present value of horizon FCFF		7,807	7,455	7,220	6,992	
Cum present value of horizon FCFF	$ 29,474					
Present value of terminal FCFF	142,921[b]					
Total firm value	172,395					
Less NNO	29,607					
Firm equity value	$142,788					
Shares outstanding	2,765.7					
Stock value per share	$ 51.63					

[a] NOA increases are viewed as a cash outflow.

[b] Computed as $\dfrac{\left(\dfrac{\$13,611 \text{ million}}{0.08 - 0.01}\right)}{(1.08)^4}$, or ($13,611 million/0.07) × 0.73503, where 8% is WACC and 1% is the long-term (terminal period) growth rate.

Module-End Review

Solution

Results from the ROPI model below yield a P&G stock value estimate of $51.62 as of August 10, 2011. P&G's stock closed at $58.51 on that date. This estimate suggests that P&G's stock is overvalued as of that date.

(In millions, except per share values and discount factors)	Reported 2011	Horizon Period				Terminal Period
		2012	2013	2014	2015	
ROPI (NOPAT − [$NOA_{Beg} \times r_w$])		$5,001	$5,241	$5,482	$5,734	$5,471
Discount factor [$1/(1 + r_w)^t$]		0.92593	0.85734	0.79383	0.73503	
Present value of horizon ROPI		4,631	4,493	4,352	4,215	
Cum present value of horizon ROPI	$ 17,691					
Present value of terminal ROPI	57,448[a]					
NOA	97,247					
Total firm value	172,386					
Less NNO	29,607					
Firm equity value	$142,779					
Shares outstanding (millions)	2,765.7					
Stock value per share	$ 51.62					

[a]Computed as $\dfrac{\left(\dfrac{\$5,471 \text{ million}}{0.08 - 0.01}\right)}{(1.08^4)}$, or ($5,471 million/0.07) × 0.73503.

The P&G stock price chart, extending from 2007 through 2011, follows.

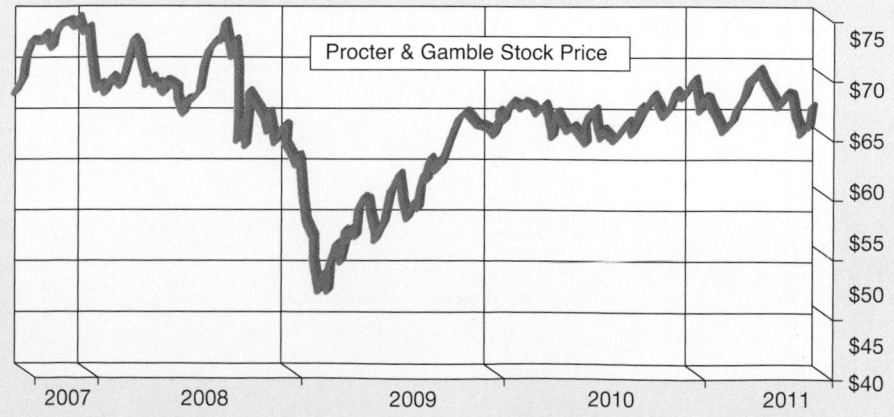

Procter & Gamble Stock Price

Getty Images

CARBON MOTORS CORPORATION

Recent years have seen rough times for the automobile industry with government bail-outs required to stabilize GM and Chrysler as a result of sagging sales and mounting losses. Despite this bleak environment for the automobile industry, a new start-up company, Carbon Motors Corporation, is revving up to fill their stated *mission* of building "the world's first purpose-built law enforcement patrol vehicle." By following a *strategy* focused on the needs of this narrow market segment or niche, marketing directly to government agencies, and utilizing innovative manufacturing approaches, management believes Carbon Motors can accomplish its profitability *goal* with an annual sales volume between 10,000 and 80,000 units.

According to Carbon Motors Chief Executive Officer (CEO) William Santana Li, current police cars are basically "a retail passenger car with some lights on it" purchased

through a local car dealer and then modified with between $5,000 and $35,000 of aftermarket equipment that was not designed, engineered, or manufactured by an automaker. Starting from scratch, Carbon Motors developed a set of criteria they believe reflects the needs and wants of the law enforcement personnel. They then designed a product to meet 95 percent of these criteria.

To achieve profitability at their anticipated scale of operations with competitive pricing, they plan to contain costs by selling directly to law enforcement agencies (rather than through dealers) and avoid inventory carrying costs by building only to fill customer orders. Management believes that direct sales to government agencies will also allow Carbon Motors to avoid major media advertising costs required for sales to the general public. Also avoided are the costs of annual "face-lifts" that are the

Managerial Accounting for MBAs

LEARNING OBJECTIVES

LO1 Contrast financial and managerial accounting and explain how managerial accounting is used by internal decision makers. (p. 13-3)

LO2 Explain how an organization's mission, goals, and strategies affect managerial accounting. (p. 13-6)

LO3 Discuss the factors determining changes in the nature of business competition. (p. 13-13)

LO4 Differentiate among structural, organizational, and activity cost drivers. (p. 13-13)

LO5 Explain the nature of the ethical dilemmas managers and accountants confront. (p. 13-17)

norm for passenger vehicles. And, to the extent possible, Carbon Motors plans to minimize investments in manufacturing facilities and all of the issues associated with operating such facilities. Instead, the production of many of the components included in completed vehicles will be accomplished by contract manufacturing. Carbon Motors will then assemble the final product at facilities in Connersville, Indiana.

The CEO and other members of the top-management team have many years of experience at established automobile companies, but they are sober about the challenges they face. Even though Carbon Motors is a privately held company, its lenders expect to receive interest and loan principal payments as provided for in the lending contracts, and its private investor shareholders expect to eventually receive a healthy return on their investment in

exchange for their willingness to take on the risk of investing in a start-up company. Financial accounting deals with the content and analysis of financial statements of organizations for which a primary objective is to provide an appropriate return to their stockholders and lenders. Managerial accounting provides tools that managers in organizations use to fulfill the expectations of stockholders and lenders.

We begin this module by considering how companies use financial and managerial accounting, and by examining the mission, goals, and strategies that provide broad guidelines for all members of the management team. We also discuss the relationships between organizational management and cost drivers to managerial accounting for internal decision making. We end this module with a discussion of ethics in managerial accounting.

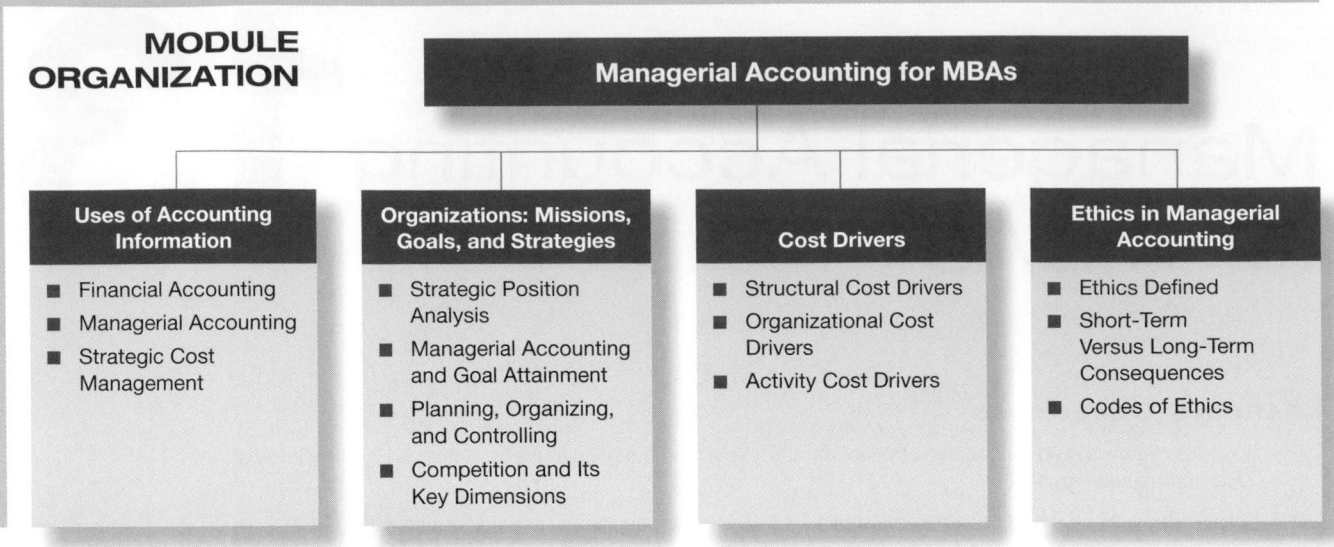

This module provides an overview of the factors that make managerial accounting increasingly important to successful businesses. **Managerial accounting** is defined as the activities carried out in a firm to provide its managers and other employees with financial and related information to help them make strategic, organizational, and operational decisions. We begin by distinguishing between financial and managerial (also called *management*) accounting and by investigating how competitive strategy affects the way organizations, such as **Carbon Motors**, use managerial accounting information. Next, we explore how the emergence of global competition and changes in technology have increased the need to understand managerial accounting concepts. We also provide an overview of factors that influence costs in an organization and how these factors have changed in recent years. Finally, we examine the interrelationships among measurement, management, and ethics.

USES OF ACCOUNTING INFORMATION

Financial Accounting

LO1 Contrast financial and managerial accounting and explain how managerial accounting is used by internal decision makers.

Financial accounting, as discussed in the first half of this text, is an information-processing system that generates general-purpose reports of financial operations (income statement and statement of cash flows) and financial position (balance sheet) for an organization. Although financial accounting is used by decision makers inside and outside the firm, financial accounting typically emphasizes external users, such as security investors, analysts, and lenders. Adding to this external orientation are external financial reporting requirements determined by law and generally accepted accounting principles.

Financial accounting is also concerned with keeping records of the organization's assets, obligations, and the collection and payment of cash. An organization cannot survive without converting sales into cash, paying for purchases, meeting payroll, and keeping track of its assets.

Managers often use income statements and balance sheets as a starting point in evaluating and planning the firm's overall activities. Managers learn a great deal by performing a comparative analysis of their firm and competing firms. Corporate goals are often stated using financial accounting numbers such as net income, or ratios such as return on investment and earnings per common share. However, internal decision makers often find the information provided in financial statements of limited value in managing day-to-day operating activities. They often complain that financial accounting information is too aggregated, prepared too late, based on irrelevant past costs, and not action oriented. For example, the costs of all items produced and sold or all services rendered are summarized in a single line in most financial statements, making it impossible to determine the costs of individual products or services. Financial accounting procedures, acceptable for costing inventories as a whole, often produce misleading information when applied to individual products. Even when they are accurately determined, the costs of individual products or services are rarely detailed enough in overall financial statements to provide the information needed for decisions concerning the factors that influence costs. Financial accounting reports, seldom prepared more than once a month, are not timely enough for use in the management of day-to-day activities that cause excess costs. Finally, financial accounting reports, to a great extent, are based on historical costs rather than on current or future costs. Managers are more interested in future costs than in historical costs such as last year's depreciation. While financial accounting information is useful in making some management decisions, its primary emphasis is not on internal decision making.

Managerial Accounting

Managers are constantly faced with the need to understand and control costs, make important product decisions, coordinate resources, and guide and motivate employees. Managerial accounting provides an information framework to organize, evaluate, and report proprietary data in light of an organization's goals. This information is directed to managers and other employees within the organization. Managerial accounting reports can be designed to meet the information needs of internal decision makers. Top management may need only summary information prepared once a month for each business unit. An engineer responsible for hourly production scheduling may need continuously updated and detailed information concerning the cost of alternative ways of producing a product.

Because of the intensity of competition and the shorter life cycles of new products and services, managerial accounting is crucial to an organization's success. All managers must understand the financial implications of their decisions. While accountants are available to assist in obtaining and evaluating relevant information, individual managers are responsible for requesting information, analyzing it, and making the final decisions. The increased use of accounting information is further examined in the Research Insight box that follows.

RESEARCH INSIGHT   **Managerial Accounting Is a Key to Success**

After studying several highly competitive, world-class companies, noted managerial accounting guru Robin Cooper observed that "with the emergence of the lean enterprise and increased global competition, companies must learn to be more proactive in the way they manage costs. For many, survival is dependent upon their abilities to develop sophisticated cost management systems that create intense pressure to reduce costs." He also observed that "as cost management becomes more critical to a company's survival, two trends emerge. First, new forms of cost management are required, and second, more individuals in the firm become actively involved in the cost management process." Cooper suggests that with the growing number of managers involved in the cost management process, there is an increased need for managerial accounting information (and people who know how to use it).

Source: Robin Cooper, "Look Out, Management Accountants," *Management Accounting*, May 1996, pp. 20–26.

Managerial accounting information exists to serve the needs of management. Hence, it is subject to a cost-benefit analysis and should be developed only if the perceived benefits exceed the costs of development and use. Also, while financial measures are often used in managerial accounting, they are not used to the exclusion of other measures. Money is simply a convenient way of expressing events in a form suitable to summary analysis. When this is not possible or appropriate, nonfinancial measures are used. Time, for example, is often an important element of quality or service. Hence, many performance measures focus on time, for example:

■ Internet vendors such as **Amazon.com** and **Netflix** track delivery time.

■ Fire departments and police departments measure the response time to emergency calls.

■ Airlines, such as **United Airlines** as well as the Federal Aviation Administration monitor the number of on-time departures and arrivals.

No external standards (such as requirements of the Securities and Exchange Commission) are imposed on information provided to internal users. Consequently, managerial accounting information may be quite subjective. In developing a budget, management is more interested in a subjective prediction of next year's sales than in an objective report on last year's sales. The significant differences between financial and managerial accounting are summarized in Exhibit 13.1.

EXHIBIT 13.1 Differences Between Financial and Managerial Accounting	
Financial Accounting	**Managerial Accounting**
Information for internal *and* external users	Information for internal users
General-purpose financial statements	Special-purpose information and reports
Statements are highly aggregated	Information is aggregated or detailed, depending on need
Relatively long reporting periods	Reporting periods are long or short, depending on need
Report on past decisions	Oriented toward current and future decisions
Follows generally accepted accounting principles	Not constrained by generally accepted accounting principles
Must conform to external standards	No external standards
Emphasizes objective data	Encourages subjective data, if relevant

Globalization of Accounting Standards

As indicated in Exhibit 13.1, a major difference between financial accounting and managerial accounting is that financial accounting must conform to a set of generally accepted accounting principles (GAAP), whereas managerial accounting is not subject to any external standards. As explained in Module 1, the creation of financial accounting standards in the United States, referred to as U.S. GAAP, is the purview of the Financial Accounting Standards Board (FASB), although the ultimate legal authority for accounting standards for publicly traded companies in the U.S. is held by the U.S. Securities and Exchange Commission (SEC). Over the past 25 years, a strong set of international accounting standards (IFRS) has been developed by the International Accounting Standards Board (IASB), which is based in the UK. With the emergence of IFRS, many countries, including all European Union countries, have adopted IFRS as a replacement of their domestic accounting standards for publicly traded companies.

For the past several years, the FASB and the IASB have cooperated to minimize the number of differences between U.S. GAAP and IFRS. It remains to be seen what impact this convergence of U.S. GAAP and IFRS will have on the financial reporting for privately owned companies.

Even though there is no existing regulation of managerial accounting systems, financial accounting standards invariably have some impact on managerial accounting. For example, in accounting for inventory costs, many companies use the same cost systems for both financial and managerial accounting purposes. One of the major differences between U.S. GAAP and IFRS is related to the accounting for inventory costs. It is widely anticipated in the financial accounting community that as the two sets of standards are harmonized further, some of the current inventory cost methods available under U.S. GAAP will no longer be acceptable for financial reporting purposes. This change will likely affect both the financial and managerial reporting systems in many companies.

The direct impact on managerial accounting of the convergence of U.S. GAAP and IFRS is expected to be rather limited. However, managers still need to be aware of major changes in financial accounting standards, because these standards affect how the results of their internal managerial decisions are reported to shareholders and other external constituencies. Financial reporting of managerial decisions affects earnings and earnings per share, and often affects stock valuations.

Strategic Cost Management

Most businesses are under constant pressure to reduce costs to remain competitive. A 2007 study by the accounting firm **KPMG** reported that more than 80 percent of survey participants viewed an efficient cost structure as a source of long-term competitive advantage.[1]

---

[1] Rethinking Cost Structures: Creating a Sustainable Cost Advantage, KPMG, 2007, p. 60.

During recent years, the rapid introduction of improved and new products and services has shortened the market lives of products and services. Some products, such as personal computers, can be obsolete within two or three years after introduction. At the same time, the increased use of complex automated equipment makes it difficult to change production procedures after production begins. Combining short product life cycles with automated production results in an environment where most costs are determined by decisions made before production begins (decisions concerning product design and production procedures).

In response to these trends, a strategic approach to managerial accounting, referred to as *strategic cost management* has emerged. Strategic cost management is a blending of three themes:

1. **Strategic position analysis**—an examination of an organization's basic way of competing to sell products or services.
2. **Cost driver analysis**—the study of factors that cause or influence costs.
3. **Value chain analysis**—the study of value-producing activities, stretching from basic raw materials to the final consumer of a product or service.[2]

We define **strategic cost management** as making decisions concerning specific cost drivers within the context of an organization's business strategy, internal value chain, and position in a larger value chain stretching from the development and use of resources to final consumers. Strategic position analysis is considered in this module as part of an organization's strategy. Cost driver analysis is also introduced in this module and examined further in Module 14. Value chain analysis is discussed in Module 20.

ORGANIZATIONS: MISSIONS, GOALS, AND STRATEGIES

An organization's **mission** is the basic purpose toward which its activities are directed. Carbon Motors' current mission is to build "the world's first purpose-built law enforcement patrol vehicle." Starbucks' mission is to "establish Starbucks as the premier purveyor of the finest coffee in the world while maintaining our uncompromising principles while we grow."[3] Organizations vary widely in their missions. One benefit of a mission statement is to help focus all the activities of an organization. For instance, the former chairman and CEO of Coca-Cola stated that the mission of The Coca-Cola Company is "to create value over time for the owners of our business." He went on to say:

LO2 Explain how an organization's mission, goals, and strategies affect managerial accounting.

> Our society is based on democratic capitalism. In such a society, people create specific institutions to help meet specific needs. Governments are created to help meet social needs. . . Businesses such as ours are created to meet economic needs. The common thread between these institutions is that they can flourish only when they stay focused on the specific need they were created to fulfill. When institutions try to broaden their scope beyond their natural realms, when for example they try to become all things to all people, they fail.[4]

The CEO of Coca-Cola believed that Coca-Cola best contributes to society and helps government and other organizations fulfill their missions by staying focused on shareholder value. He believed focusing on economics keeps a company financially healthy, and a healthy company fulfills its responsibilities. Conversely, a bankrupt company is incapable of paying taxes, employing people, serving customers, supporting charitable institutions, or making other contributions to society.

[2] John K. Shank, "Strategic Cost Management: New Wine, or Just New Bottles?" *Journal of Management Accounting Research,* Fall 1989, p. 50.
[3] www.starbucks.com
[4] Roberto Goizueta, "Why Shareholder Value?" *CEO Series Issue No. 13,* February 1997, Center for the Study of American Business, Washington University in St. Louis, p. 2.

We frequently distinguish between organizations on the basis of profit motive. **For-profit organizations** have profit as a primary objective, whereas **not-for-profit organizations** do not have profit as a primary objective. Clearly, the Coca-Cola Company is a for-profit organization, whereas the City of Chicago and the Red Cross are not-for-profit organizations. (The term *nonprofit* is frequently used to refer to what we have identified as not-for-profit organizations.) Regardless of whether a profit motive exists, organizations must use resources wisely. Every dollar United Way spends for administrative salaries is a dollar that cannot be used to support charitable activities. Not-for-profit organizations, including governments, can go bankrupt if they are unable to meet their financial obligations. All organizations, for-profit and not-for-profit, should use managerial accounting concepts to ensure that resources are used wisely.

A **goal** is a definable, measurable objective. Based on the organization's mission, management sets a number of goals. For-profit organizations have some measure of profitability or shareholder value as one of their stated or implicit goals. The mission of a paper mill located in a small town is to provide quality paper products in order to earn a profit for its owners. The paper mill's goals might include earning an annual profit equal to 10 percent of average total assets, maintaining annual dividends of $2 per share of common stock, developing a customer reputation for above-average quality and service, providing steady employment for area residents, and meeting or exceeding environmental standards.

A clear statement of mission and well-defined goals provides an organization with an identity and unifying purpose, thereby ensuring that all employees are heading in the same direction. Having developed a mission and a set of goals, employees are more apt to make decisions that move the organization toward its defined purpose.

A **strategy** is a course of action that will assist in achieving one or more goals. Much of this text will focus on the financial aspects of selecting strategies to achieve goals. For example, if an organization's goal is to improve product quality, possible strategies for achieving this goal include investing in new equipment, implementing additional quality inspections, prescreening suppliers, reducing batch size, redesigning products, training employees, and rearranging the shop floor. Managerial accounting information will assist in determining which of the many alternative strategies for achieving the goal of quality improvement are cost effective. The distinction between mission, goals, and strategies is illustrated in Exhibit 13.2.

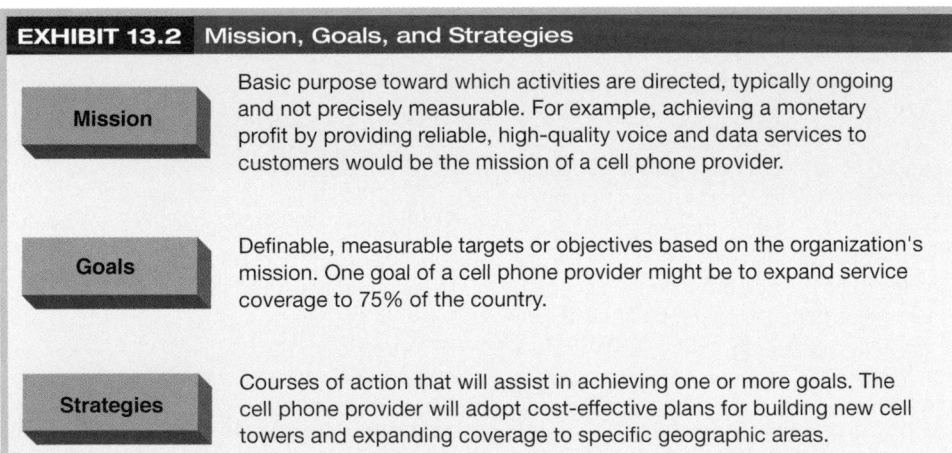

EXHIBIT 13.2   Mission, Goals, and Strategies

Mission	Basic purpose toward which activities are directed, typically ongoing and not precisely measurable. For example, achieving a monetary profit by providing reliable, high-quality voice and data services to customers would be the mission of a cell phone provider.
Goals	Definable, measurable targets or objectives based on the organization's mission. One goal of a cell phone provider might be to expand service coverage to 75% of the country.
Strategies	Courses of action that will assist in achieving one or more goals. The cell phone provider will adopt cost-effective plans for building new cell towers and expanding coverage to specific geographic areas.

Strategic Position Analysis

In competitive environments, managers must make a fundamental decision concerning their organization's goal for positioning itself in comparison to competitors. This goal is referred to as the organization's **strategic position**. Much of the organization's strategy depends on this strategic positioning goal. Michael Porter, a highly regarded expert on business strategy, has identified three possible strategic positions that lead to business success.[5]

1. Cost leadership
2. Product or service differentiation
3. Market niche

According to Porter, cost leadership

> requires aggressive construction of efficient-scale facilities, vigorous pursuit of cost reductions from experience, tight cost and overhead control, avoidance of marginal customer accounts, and cost minimization in areas like R&D [research and development], service, sales force, advertising, and so on. A great deal of managerial attention to cost control is necessary to achieve these aims. Low cost relative to competitors becomes the theme running through the entire strategy, though quality, service, and other areas cannot be ignored.[6]

Achieving cost leadership allows an organization to achieve higher profits selling at the same price as competitors or by allowing the firm to aggressively compete on the basis of price while remaining profitable. One of the first companies to successfully use a cost leadership strategy was **Carnegie Steel Company**.

> Carnegie's operating strategy was to push his own direct costs below his competitors so that he could charge prices that would always ensure enough demand to keep his plants running at full capacity. This strategy prompted him to require frequent information showing his direct costs in relation to those of his competitors. Possessing that information and secure in the knowledge that his costs were the lowest in the industry, Carnegie then mercilessly cut prices during economic recessions. While competing firms went under, he still made profits. In periods of prosperity, when customers' demands exceeded the industry's capacity to produce, Carnegie joined others in raising prices.[7]

Southwest Airlines and **Dell** are current examples of successful businesses competing with a strategy of cost leadership. Although **Amazon.com** uses the Internet to differentiate itself from traditional booksellers, its primary strategic position is price leadership.

Conversely, while an organization might compete primarily on the basis of price, management must take care to ensure their product or service remains attuned to changing customer needs and preferences. In the early twentieth century, **General Motors** employed a differentiation strategy, focusing on the rapid introduction of technological change in new automobile designs to overcome the market dominance of the Model T produced by **Ford Motor Company**. While successfully following a cost leadership strategy for years, Ford made the mistake of excluding other considerations such as vehicle performance and customer desires for different colors. The following Business Insight box reports on **Corning Corporation**'s strategy of product differentiation to achieve a competitive advantage.

---

[5] Michael E. Porter, *Competitive Strategy* (New York: The Free Press, 1980), p. 35.
[6] Porter, p. 35.
[7] H. Thomas Johnson and Robert S. Kaplan, Relevance Lost: *The Rise and Fall of Management Accounting* (Boston: Harvard Business School Press, 1987), pp. 33–34.

BUSINESS INSIGHT   A Century of Innovation Sets Corning Apart

Corning Incorporated, whose mission is to be "the world leader in specialty glass and ceramics," is a textbook example of a successful company with a strategy of product differentiation based on researching, developing, and manufacturing innovative products. The lengthy list of new products developed by Corning scientists and engineers include: A glass envelope for Thomas Edison's light bulb in 1870; heat-resistant Pyrex glass in 1915; processes for mass-producing television tubes in 1947; low-loss fiber optic cable in 1970; ceramic bases for automotive catalytic converters in 1972; LCD glass for flat-panel displays in 1984; and aluminum titanate filters for diesel vehicles in 2005.

To facilitate their product differentiation strategy Corning employs 1,700 scientists to work on hundreds of exploratory projects and is investing $300 million to refurbish and expand its research labs near Corning, New York. According to UBS analyst Nikos Theodosopoulos, "they're not afraid to invest and lose money for many years." Corning avoids outsourcing and owns dozens of factories producing thousands of different products. Its executives believe that retaining control of research and manufacturing provides a competitive advantage. Their strategy is to keep an array of products in the pipeline and, once a market develops, to quickly produce in volumes that keep rivals from getting traction.

Corning's strategy has produced major winners. The company is the world's largest producer of liquid-crystal-display glass used in flat-panel televisions and computers, which produced 100 percent of Corning's 2009 profit of $2.0 billion, offsetting losses in other divisions suffering during the recession. Corning's strategy also carries risks. Its investments in the development and production of optical fiber placed the company in financial difficulty after the dot.com collapse of the early 2000s. Looking ahead, Corning's new hit product is expected to be "Gorilla Glass," a hard-to-break, scratch-resistant glass, developed for the eyeglass industry, that is now being used for the growing market in touch-screen devices.

Source: Sara Silver, Corning's Biggest Bet Yet? Diesel-Filter Technologies," *The Wall Street Journal*, March 7, 2008, pp. B1–B2; Nancy Kelly, "Corning's Renaissance," *American Ceramic Society Bulletin*, February 2008; "Best Inventions of The Year," *Time Magazine*, November 12, 2007; Sara Silver, "Corning Profit Rises Sharply," *The Wall Street Journal*, April 29, 2010, p. B2. www.corning.com.

The third possible strategic position according to Porter, focuses on a specific market niche such as a buyer group, segment of the product line, or geographic market and

rests on the premise that the firm is thus able to serve its narrow strategic target more effectively or efficiently than competitors who are competing more broadly. As a result, the firm achieves either differentiation from better meeting the needs of the particular target, or lower costs in serving the target, or both. Even though the focus strategy does not achieve low costs or differentiation for the market as a whole, it does achieve one or both of these positions vis-à-vis its narrow market target.[8]

Carbon Motors is following a market niche strategy. Other examples of organizations successfully following a market niche strategy include regional breweries that cater to local tastes and **Gulfstream**, which follows a focused strategy in designing and building corporate aircraft, leaving the market for larger passenger aircraft to firms such as **Boeing** and the market for smaller private planes to firms such as **Piper Aircraft**.

The Research Insight box following considers cost leadership and product or service differentiation among the working principles for twenty-first century corporations.

---

[8] Porter, pp. 38–39.

A *Business Week* editorial reinforced the importance of competing on the basis of a business strategy of price or differentiation. However, recognizing the transitory nature of differentiation in a competitive environment, the editorial used the term "innovation" in place of "differentiation." According to Business Week, the first three working principles of the twenty-first century corporation are:

1. *Everything gets cheaper faster.* "The Net destroys corporate pricing power. It allows customers, suppliers, and partners to compare prices from 100 or 1,000 sources, not just two or three, and erases market inefficiencies. It rapidly commoditizes all that is new, reducing prices fast."

2. *Cutting costs is the answer.* "In an economic universe of downward pressure on margins, one path to profitability will be to reduce expenses."

3. *Innovation builds profits.* "There is one way for corporations to circumvent principle No. 1 and raise prices. In an information economy, companies can gain an edge through new ideas and products." This advantage is temporary, so corporations following this strategy must innovate rapidly and continuously.

The editorial asserts that human capital is the only asset. In a twenty-first century corporation, creativity is the sole source of growth and wealth. Consequently, the "value of education rises exponentially in an economy based on ideas and analytic thinking."

Source: Based on "The Twenty-First Century Corporation," *Business Week,* August 28, 2000, p. 278.

Managerial Accounting and Goal Attainment

A major purpose of managerial accounting is to support the achievement of goals. Hence, determining an organization's strategic position goal has implications for the operation of an organization's managerial accounting system.

Careful budgeting and cost control with frequent and detailed performance reports are critical with a goal of cost leadership. When the product is difficult to distinguish from that of competitors, price is the primary basis of competition. Under these circumstances, everyone in the organization should continuously apply managerial accounting concepts to achieve and maintain cost leadership. The managerial accounting system should constantly compare actual costs with budgeted costs and signal the existence of significant differences. A simplified version of a *performance report* for costs during a budget period is as follows:

Budgeted (planned) Costs	Actual Costs	Deviation from Budget	Percent Deviation
$560,000	$595,000	$35,000 unfavorable	6.25

Frequent and detailed comparisons of actual and budgeted costs are less important when a differentiation strategy is followed. This is especially true when products have short life cycles or production is highly automated. In these situations, most costs are determined before production begins and there is little opportunity to undertake cost reduction activities thereafter.

With short product lives or automated manufacturing, exceptional care must go into the initial design of a product or service and the determination of how it will be produced or delivered. Here, detailed cost information assists in design and scheduling decisions. A simplified version of the predicted costs of producing one batch of a specialty product is as follows:

Engineering and scheduling (12 hours @ $70)	$ 840
Materials (detail omitted)	3,500
Equipment setup (2.5 hours @ $100)	250
Machine operation (9.5 hours @ $90)	855
Materials movement	150
Packing and shipping	675
Total	$6,270

When a differentiation strategy is followed, it often pays to work closely with customers to find ways to enhance the perceived value of a product or service. This leads to an analysis of costs from the customer's viewpoint. The customer may not want a costly feature. Alternatively, the customer may be willing to pay more for an additional feature that will reduce subsequent operating costs.

In designing its 777 aircraft, Boeing invited potential customers to set up offices in Boeing plants and to work with Boeing employees designing the aircraft. Many design changes were made to reduce customer costs. United Airlines, for example, convinced Boeing to move the location of the 777's fuel tanks to reduce servicing costs.

Planning, Organizing, and Controlling

The process of selecting goals and strategies to achieve these goals is often referred to as **planning**. The implementation of plans requires the development of subgoals and the assignment of responsibility to achieve subgoals to specific individuals or groups within an organization. This process of making the organization into a well-ordered whole is called **organizing**. In organizing, the authority to take action to implement plans is delegated to other managers and employees.

Developing an **organization chart** illustrating the formal relationships that exist between the elements of an organization is an important part of organizing. An organization chart for Crown Department Stores is illustrated in Exhibit 13.3. The blocks represent organizational units, and the lines represent relationships between the units. Authority flows down through the organization. Top management delegates authority to use resources for limited purposes to subordinate managers who, in turn, delegate to their subordinates more limited authority for accomplishing more structured tasks. Responsibility flows up through the organization. People at the bottom are responsible for specific tasks, but the president is responsible for the operation of the entire organization.

A distinction is often made between line and staff departments. *Line departments* engage in activities that create and distribute goods and services to customers. *Staff departments* exist to facilitate the activities of line departments. In Exhibit 13.3, we see that Crown Department Stores has two levels of staff organizations—corporate and store. The corporate staff departments are Purchasing, Advertising, Treasurer, and Controller. Staff departments at the store level are Personnel, Accounting, and Maintenance. All other units are line departments. A change in plans can necessitate a change in the organization. For example, Crown's plan to discontinue the sale of hardware and add an art department during the coming year will necessitate an organizational change.

Controlling is the process of ensuring that results agree with plans. A brief example of a performance report for costs was presented previously. In the process of controlling operations, actual performance is compared with plans.

With a cost leadership strategy and long-lived products, if actual results deviate significantly from plans, an attempt is made to bring operations into line with plans, or the plans are adjusted. The original plan is adjusted if it is deemed no longer appropriate because of changed circumstances.

With a differentiation strategy and short-lived products, design and scheduling personnel will consider previous errors in predicting costs as they plan new products and services. Hence, the process of controlling feeds forward into the process of planning to form a continuous cycle coordinated through the management accounting system. This cycle is illustrated in Exhibit 13.4.

EXHIBIT 13.3   Crown Department Stores' Organization Chart

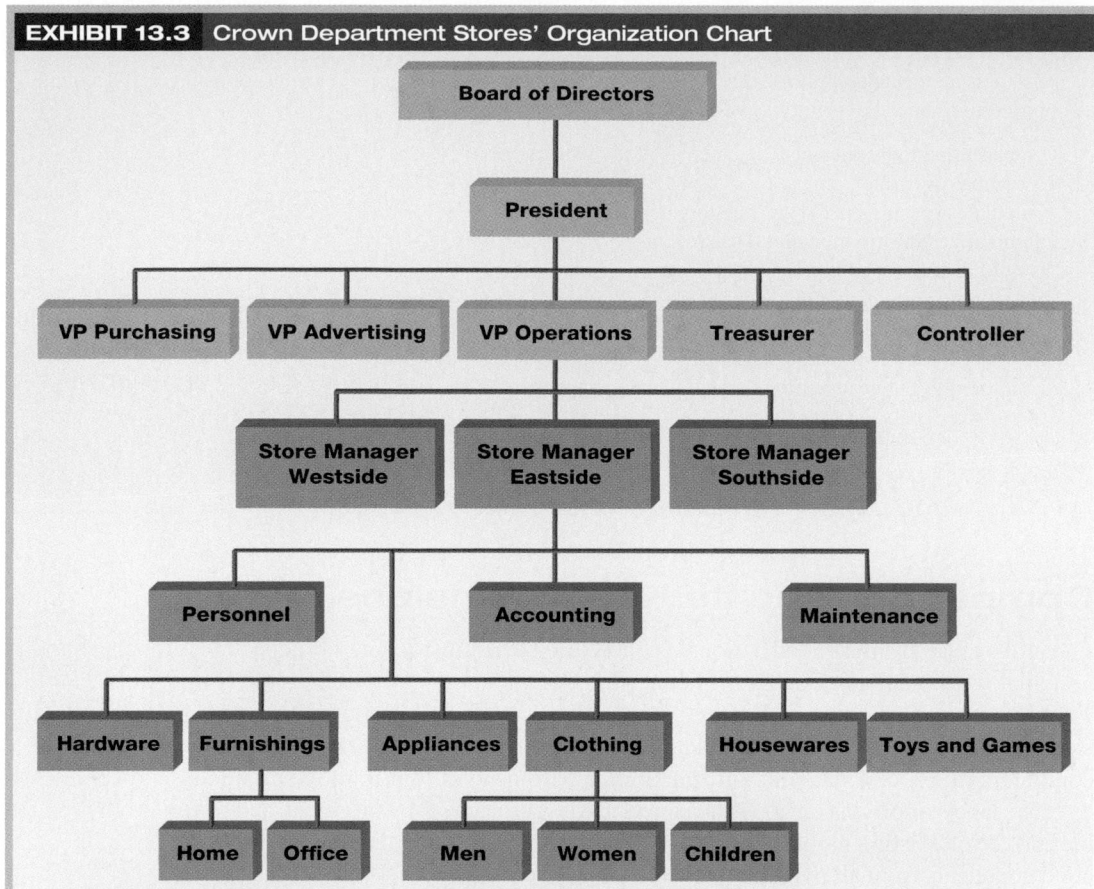

EXHIBIT 13.4   Planning, Organizating, & Control Cycle

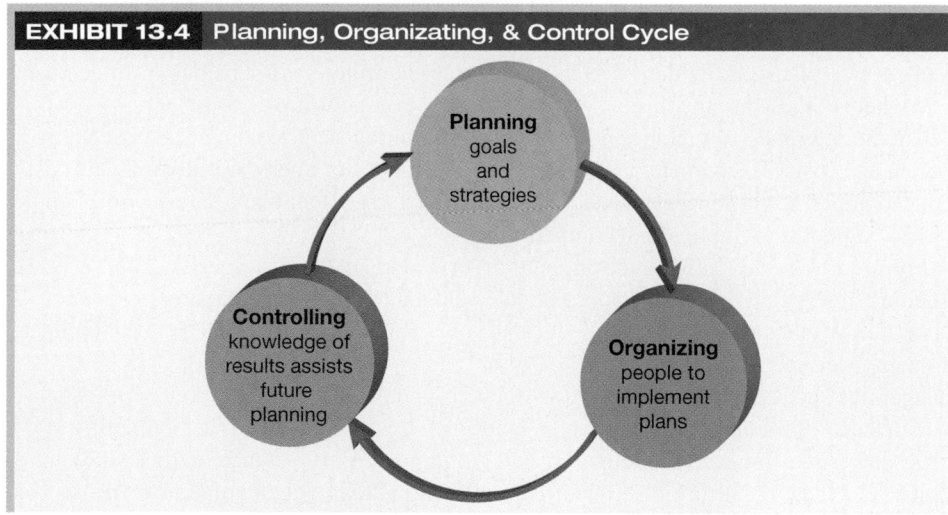

MID-MODULE REVIEW

The previous discussion has focused on understanding the difference between financial and managerial accounting and the broader context of managerial accounting within a company.

Required:

Identify the statements and phrases from the following list that are primarily relevant to managerial accounting, as opposed to financial accounting:

1. Preparing periodic financial statements
2. A company's strategic position
3. Calculates earnings per share for stockholders
4. Summarizes information about past events
5. Is not based on generally accepted accounting principles
6. Must conform to external standards
7. Helping managers make decisions is its primary purpose
8. Encourages use of selective data, if relevant
9. Is tailored to the needs of the company and its managers
10. Cost driver analysis

The solution is on page 13-26.

Competition and Its Key Dimensions

LO3 Discuss the factors determining changes in the nature of business competition.

The move away from isolated national economic systems toward an interdependent global economic system has become increasingly pronounced. International treaties, such as the North American Free Trade Agreement and the General Agreement on Tariffs and Trade, merely recognize an already existing and inevitable condition made possible by advances in telecommunications (to move data), computers (to process data into information), and transportation (to move products and people).

The labels of origins on goods (Japan, Germany, Canada, Taiwan, China, and so forth) only scratch the surface of existing global relationships. Behind labels designating a product's final assembly point are components from all over the world.

The move toward a global economy has heightened competition and reduced selling prices to such an extent that there is little or no room for error in managing costs or pricing products. Moreover, customers are not just looking for the best price. Well-informed buyers routinely search the world for the product or service that best fits their needs on the three interrelated dimensions of price/cost, quality, and service; hence, these are the three key dimensions of competition.

To customers, *price/cost* includes not only the initial purchase price but also subsequent operating and maintenance costs. To compete on the basis of price, the seller must carefully manage costs. Otherwise, reduced prices might squeeze product margins to such an extent that a sale becomes unprofitable. Hence, price competition implies cost competition.

Quality refers to the degree to which products or services meet the customer's needs. *Service* includes things such as timely delivery, helpfulness of sales personnel, and subsequent support. The Business Insight box below takes a look at how Federal Express and United Parcel Service compete on the basis of quality, service, and price.

Managers of successful companies know they compete in a global market with instant communications. Because the competition is hungry and always striving to gain a competitive advantage, world-class companies must continuously struggle to improve performance on these three interrelated dimensions: price/cost, quality, and service. Throughout this text, we examine how firms successfully compete on these three dimensions.

COST DRIVERS

LO4 Differentiate among structural, organizational, and activity cost drivers.

An **activity** is a unit of work. To serve a customer at a restaurant such as Outback Restaurants, a server might perform the following units of work:

- Seat customer and offer menu
- Take customer order
- Send order to kitchen

- Bring food to customer
- Serve and replenish beverages
- Determine and bring bill to customer
- Accept and process payment
- Clear and reset table

Each of these is an activity, and the performance of each activity consumes resources that cost money. To manage activities and their costs, it is necessary to understand how costs respond to **cost drivers**, which are the factors that cause or influence costs.

The most basic cost driver is customer demand. Without customer demand for products or services, the organization cannot exist. To serve customers, managers and employees make a variety of decisions and take numerous actions. These decisions and actions, undertaken to satisfy customer demand, drive costs. While these cost drivers may be classified in a variety of ways, we believe that dividing them into the three categories of structural, organizational, and activity cost drivers, as summarized in Exhibit 13.5, provides a useful foundation for the study of managerial accounting.

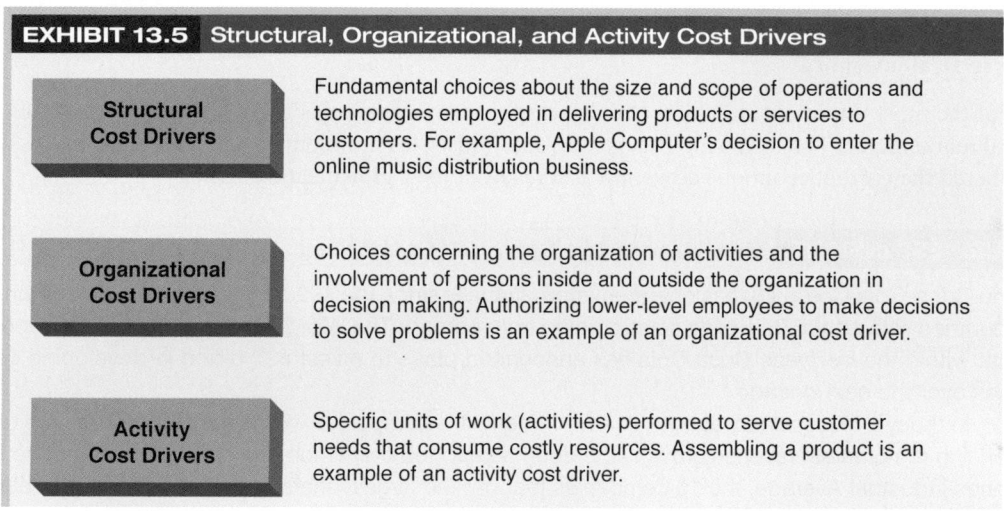

EXHIBIT 13.5 Structural, Organizational, and Activity Cost Drivers

Structural Cost Drivers	Fundamental choices about the size and scope of operations and technologies employed in delivering products or services to customers. For example, Apple Computer's decision to enter the online music distribution business.
Organizational Cost Drivers	Choices concerning the organization of activities and the involvement of persons inside and outside the organization in decision making. Authorizing lower-level employees to make decisions to solve problems is an example of an organizational cost driver.
Activity Cost Drivers	Specific units of work (activities) performed to serve customer needs that consume costly resources. Assembling a product is an example of an activity cost driver.

BUSINESS INSIGHT FedEx and UPS Stage Battle—Customer Is Sure to Win

To increase customer service in the express delivery business, Federal Express introduced a personal computer-based system that lets even its smallest customers go online to order pickups, print shipping labels, and track deliveries. "We have to stay ahead of the competition" was the theme of remarks describing this service by FedEx's chief information officer. Almost immediately, United Parcel Service announced a similar service. Responding to a reporter's question, the vice president of marketing at UPS, commented, "There's no question we track FedEx, just like they track us."

Both companies invest heavily in equipment and infrastructure to continue to meet increasingly tight delivery deadlines. This includes sorting hubs for air shipments and investments in new aircraft. FedEx even entered into an arrangement with the U.S. Postal Service to ship some USPS packages while the USPS placed FedEx boxes in selected Post Office buildings. A recent article in Business Week reports that UPS gained at least a temporary advantage by utilizing information technology to integrate its traditional strengths in ground transportation with its overnight air transportation system. According to the article, "UPS, like FedEx, still uses planes to make most (overnight) deliveries. But in the past two years, its logisticians have also figured out how to make quick mid-distance deliveries—as far as 500 miles in one night—by truck, which is much less expensive than by air." While both companies battle to improve or at least maintain profitability, customers benefit from continuously improving quality and service at lower and lower costs.

Source: Based on David Greising, "Watch Out for Flying Packages," *Business Week* (November 14, 1994), p. 40; and Charles Haddad, "Ground Wars: UPS's Rapid Ascent Leaves FedEx Scrambling," *Business Week* , May 21, 2001.

Structural Cost Drivers

The types of activities and the costs of activities performed to satisfy customer needs are influenced by an organization's size, its location, the scope of its operations, and the technologies used. Decisions affecting structural cost drivers are made infrequently, and once made, the organization is committed to a course of action that will be difficult to change. For a chain of discount stores such as Target, possible structural cost drivers include:

■ *Determining the size of stores.* This affects the variety of merchandise that can be carried and operating costs.

■ *Determining the type of construction.* While a lean warehouse type of construction is less expensive, it is not an appropriate setting for selling high-fashion clothing.

■ *Determining the location of stores.* Locating in a shopping mall can cost more and subject the store to mall regulations but provides for more customer traffic and shared advertising.

■ *Determining types of technology to employ in stores.* A computerized system for maintaining all inventory and sales data requires a large initial investment and fixed annual operating costs while providing more current information. However, the computerized inventory and sales systems can be less expensive at high sales volumes than a less costly system relying more on clerks taking physical inventory.

One of the most important structural cost drivers for many companies is the decision to reach out to a global marketplace. The following Business Insight illustrates how some companies have successfully weathered the current economic downturn as a result of their globalization strategy.

BUSINESS INSIGHT | **Globalization as a Structural Cost Driver**

The Coca-Cola Company has operated internationally since the 1920s. It operates in more than 100 countries with about 75% of its sales coming from abroad. The Wall Street Journal recently reported that within the last year, Coca-Cola has announced plans to invest $27 billion in developing countries over the next decade.

In today's recessionary economic environment, it is companies with a global focus that are experiencing the greatest revenue growth. The Journal reported that among the 30 companies in the Dow Jones Industrial Average, the 10 companies that get the largest share of their revenues from abroad saw revenue growth of 8.3%; whereas, the 10 companies with the least global revenues saw only a 1.6% growth. In tough economic times, with a weaker American economy, companies that have made structural cost decisions to go global are realizing significant payoff from those decisions.

Source: Justin Lahart, "Divided by a Two-Track Economy," *The Wall Street Journal Digital Network (WSJ.com)*, September 7, 2010.

Organizational Cost Drivers

Like structural cost drivers, organizational cost drivers influence costs by affecting the types of activities and the costs of activities performed to satisfy customer needs. Decisions that affect organizational cost drivers are made within the context of previous decisions affecting structural cost drivers. In a manufacturing organization, previous decisions about plant, equipment, and location are taken as a given when decisions impacting organizational cost drivers are made. Examples of organizational cost drivers at a manufacturing organization such as Harley-Davidson include making decisions regarding:

■ *Working closely with a limited number of suppliers.* This can help achieve proper materials in the proper quantities at the optimal time. Developing linkages with suppliers can also result in suppliers' initiatives that improve the profitability of both organizations.

■ *Providing employees with cost information and authorizing them to make decisions.* This helps improve decision speed and reduce costs while making employees more customer oriented. Production employees may, for example, offer product design suggestions that reduce manufacturing costs or reduce defects.

■ *Reorganizing the existing equipment in the plant so that sequential operations are closer.* This more efficient layout reduces the cost of moving inventory between workstations.

■ *Designing components of a product so they can fit together only in the correct manner.* This can reduce defects as well as assembly time and cost.

■ *Manufacturing a low-volume product on low-speed, general-purpose equipment rather than high-speed, special-purpose equipment.* Assuming the special-purpose equipment is more difficult and costly to set up for a new job, this decision can increase operating time and operating cost while reducing setup time and setup cost.

The following business insight illustrates how an innovative hospital in the suburbs of Seattle managed a key organizational cost driver to bring down costs and achieve profitability.

BUSINESS INSIGHT | **Managing an Organizational Cost Driver at Providence Hospital**

A key costing challenge for any hospital is how to manage the traffic flow of patients as they go from one level of care to another, from the patient room to laboratory, radiology, or testing location and back to the patient room, or to and from physical therapy or other treatment locations. Just as in any production environment, how the processes are organized is a key cost driver. Providence Hospital in Everett, Washington radically changed its patient movement practices resulting not only in significant cost savings, but also greatly improved patient satisfaction. In their "single stay" section of the hospital, the patient remains in the same room at all times as the level of care changes, or as testing or therapy takes place. Instead of moving the patient around, equipment is moved in and out of the patient room depending on the required level of care, the testing, or treatment to be performed.

Source: Based on Catherine Arnst, "Radical Surgery," *Bloomberg Business Week*, January 18, 2010.

Activity Cost Drivers

Activity cost drivers are specific units of work (activities) performed to serve customer needs that consume costly resources. Several examples of activities in a restaurant were mentioned previously. The customer may be outside the organization, such as a client of an advertising firm, or inside the organization, such as an accounting office that receives maintenance services. Because the performance of activities consumes resources and resources cost money, the performance of activities drives costs.

The basic decisions concerning which available activities will be used to respond to customer requests precede the actual performance of activities. At the activity level, execution of previous plans and following prescribed activities are important. All of the examples of structural and organizational cost drivers involved making decisions. In the following list of activity cost drivers for a manufacturing organization, note the absence of the decision-oriented words.

■ *Placing a purchase order for raw materials*

■ *Inspecting incoming raw materials*

■ *Moving items being manufactured between workstations*

■ *Setting up a machine to work on a product*

■ *Spending machine time working on a product*

■ *Spending labor time working on a product*

■ *Hiring and training a new employee*

■ *Packing an order for shipment*

■ *Processing a sales order*

■ *Shipping a product*

In managing costs, management makes choices concerning structural and organizational cost drivers. These decisions affect the types of activities required to satisfy customer needs. Because different types of activities have different costs, management's decisions concerning structural and organizational cost drivers ultimately affect activity costs and profitability. Good decision making at the level of structural and organizational cost drivers requires an understanding of the linkages among the types of cost drivers and the costs of different activities.

MANAGERIAL DECISION You are the CEO

How can you use information about structural, organizational, and activity cost drivers to help you in impementing the organization's strategy? [Answer, p. 13-20]

ETHICS IN MANAGERIAL ACCOUNTING

LO5 Explain the nature of the ethical dilemmas managers and accountants confront.

Ethics deals with the moral quality, fitness, or propriety of a course of action that can injure or benefit people. Ethics goes beyond legality, which refers to what is permitted under the law, to consider the moral quality of an action. Because situations involving ethics are not guided by well-defined rules, they are often subjective.

Although some actions are clearly ethical (working a full day in exchange for a full day's pay) and others are clearly unethical (pumping contaminants into an underground aquifer used as a source of drinking water), managers are often faced with situations that do not fall clearly into either category such as the following:

■ Accelerating or decelerating shipments at the end of the quarter to meet current earnings forecasts.

■ Keeping inventory that is unlikely to be used so as to avoid recording a loss.

■ Purchasing supplies from a relative or friend rather than seeking bids.

■ Basing a budget on an overly optimistic sales forecast.

■ Assigning some costs of Contract A to Contract B to avoid an unfavorable performance report on Contract A.

Many ethical dilemmas involve actions that are perceived to have desirable short-run consequences and highly probable undesirable long-run consequences. The ethical action is to face an undesirable situation now to avoid a worse situation later, yet the decision maker prefers to believe that things will work out in the long run, be overly concerned with the consequences of not doing well in the short run, or simply not care about the future because the problem will then belong to someone else. In a situation that is clearly unethical, the future consequences are known to be avoidable and undesirable. In situations involving questionable ethics, there is some hope that things will work out:

■ Next year's sales will more than make up for the accelerated shipments.

■ The obsolete inventory can be used in a new nostalgia line of products.

■ The relative or friend may charge more but provides excellent service.

■ A desire to have more confidence in the sales staff.

■ Making up for the cost shift by working extra hard and more efficiently with the remaining work on Contract B.

When forced to think about the situation, most employees want to act in an ethical manner. The problem faced by personnel involved in measurement and reporting is that while they may question the propriety of a proposed action, and the arguments may be plausible, they want to be team players, and their careers can be affected by "whistle-blowing." Of course, careers are also affected when individuals are identified as being involved in unethical behavior. The careers of people who fail to point out unethical behavior are also affected, especially if they have a responsibility for measurement and reporting.

Major ethical dilemmas often evolve from a series of small compromises, none of which appears serious enough to warrant taking a stand on ethical grounds. WorldCom is such a case, in which managers deferred expenses inappropriately over several periods to meet profit forecasts, expecting to recognize them at later time when sales improved. Unfortunately, these small compromises establish a pattern of behavior that is increasingly difficult to reverse. The key to avoiding these situations is recognizing the early warning signs of situations that involve questionable ethical behavior and taking whatever action is appropriate.

Codes of Ethics

Codes of ethics are often developed by professional organizations to increase members' awareness of the importance of ethical behavior and to provide a reference point for resisting pressures to engage in actions of questionable ethics. These professional organizations include the American Bar Association, the American Institute of Certified Public Accountants, the American Medical Association, and the Institute of Management Accountants (IMA).

Many corporations have established codes of ethics. A summary of General Motors Corporation's 20-page code of ethics, "Winning with Integrity" is presented in the following Business Insight box. One of the important goals of corporate codes of ethics is to provide employees with a common foundation for addressing ethical issues. These codes provide a summary of a company's policies that define ethical standards of employee conduct and they often include broad philosophical statements about behavior. A basic rule of thumb used by General Motors is that employees should never do anything they would be ashamed to explain to their families or to see in the front page of the local newspaper.

BUSINESS INSIGHT | **GM Code of Ethics: "Winning with Integrity"**

- GM hires, promotes, trains and pays based on merit, experience, or other work-related criteria and strives to create work environments that accept and tolerate differences while promoting productivity and teamwork.

- GM endeavors to protect the health and safety of each employee by creating and maintaining a healthy, injury-free work environment.

- All GM employees have an obligation to protect GM's assets, including information, and to ensure their proper use.

- Providing false or misleading information in any GM business record is strictly prohibited.

- As a general rule, GM employees should accept no gift, entertainment, or other gratuity from any supplier to GM or bidder for GM's business.

- GM employees must immediately disclose any situation that could result in an actual or potential conflict of interest, involving the employee or any member of his household, such as investing in a supplier, dealer, customer, or competitor.

- GM and all its employees must comply with all laws, including the U.S. Foreign Corrupt Practices Act, competition laws, and export control laws.

- To protect GM's reputation for integrity, it must communicate clearly and accurately to the public.

Source: http://www.gm.com/corporate/investor_information/docs/corp_gov/Winning_With_Integrity_March_2010.pdf

---

Corporate Governance

Corporate governance refers to the system of policies, processes, laws, and regulations that affect the way a company is directed and controlled. At the highest level, the system of corporate governance for a company is the responsibility of the board of directors, but it affects all stakeholders, including employees, creditors, customers, vendors, and the community at large. The large number of corporate failures of the last decade brought the topic of corporate governance to the forefront.

The collapse of Enron, along with its independent auditor, Arthur Andersen, prompted the U.S. Congress to pass the Sarbanes-Oxley Act of 2002 (or SOX), which was intended to address weaknesses affecting U.S. capital markets. Although SOX deals primarily with issues pertaining to the relationship between publicly traded companies and the capital markets, some of its requirements have become a standard for corporate responsibility and governance affecting both public and private companies, as well as not-for-profit organizations.

SOX consists of 66 sections, including such topics as external auditing standards, auditor conflicts of interest, codes of ethics for financial officers, review of internal controls, and criminal penalties for fraud. Probably the most important provisions of SOX, from a managerial accounting standpoint, are those related to internal control systems. **Internal control systems** generally are made up of the policies and procedures that exist to ensure that company objectives are achieved with regard to (a) effectiveness and efficiency of operations, (b) reliability of financial reporting, and (c) compliance with laws and regulations.

SOX imposes the requirement that CEOs and CFOs annually review and assess the effectiveness of their company's internal controls over financial reporting, and issue a report of their assessment. Although many CEOs and CFOs have argued that the cost of SOX compliance is unjustified by the benefits to investors, the following Research Insight provides evidence that SOX is improving the quality of financial reporting. Even though SOX limits the internal control review to aspects of the system related to financial reporting, in practice there is very little that takes place in any organization that does not impact the financial statements. Therefore, if SOX is resulting in improvements in data that goes into financial reports, it is likely that data supporting managerial accounting is also enhanced by a more reliable internal control system.

Many of the models and processes that we discuss in this text have either a direct or indirect impact on a company's financial statements; hence, they are likely subject to the SOX internal control review. An overlap often exists between the systems that produce the data for the external financial statements and those that produce data for internal decision making. For example, cost data produced by the product costing system is often used for both financial reporting and managerial decision making purposes. A more detailed discussion of SOX and internal control systems can typically be found in financial accounting and auditing textbooks.

RESEARCH INSIGHT | **SOX Improves Financial Reporting**

A recent study of about 1,000 firms reported that companies subject to Sarbanes-Oxley internal control system reviews were significantly less likely to issue materially misstated financial statements, thereby suggesting that the SOX legislation is probably meeting its objective of improving the quality of financial reports. The study based its conclusions on the fact that smaller companies exempt from the SOX internal control reviews were 40% more likely to have material misstatements in their financial statements than companies required to conduct internal control reviews. The study did not attempt to answer the question of whether the reduction in misstatements was sufficient to justify the expense incurred as a result of SOX requirements.

Source: Albert Nagy, "Section 404 Compliance and Financial Reporting Quality," Accounting Horizons, September, 2010, Vol. 24, Issue 3, p441-454.

Corporate Social Responsibility

Closely related to the concepts of ethics and corporate governance is the topic of **corporate social responsibility**, which can simply be defined as being a good corporate citizen. It entails balancing the objective of profitability with the objective of giving proper attention to issues such as environmental sustainability and energy conservation, and avoiding actions that would lower the quality of life in the communities in which a company operates and sells its products or services. In earlier generations it would have meant giving a day's wage for a day's labor, not hiring underage children, or not dumping untreated waste into the local river.

Managerial accounting includes a variety of models that help managers determine the cost of a particular activity or product, or the benefits and costs of various decision alternatives. Although such models in their current state of development may not take into account all external social costs, accountants are more aware today than in the past of the need to consider such costs. For example, when calculating the cost of building a new capital asset that is going to last for 25 years, it is necessary to include in that calculation the present value of the cost of the ultimate disposal of the asset, including any environmental cleanup.

Being a socially responsible company does not mean abandoning the profit motive or the goal of providing an attractive return to investors. It means that while pursuing these essential objectives, a for-profit company attempts to measure the total benefits and costs of its actions and accepts the responsibility for those actions. Also, being a good competitor should not be confused with social responsibility. For example, many companies offer certain fringe benefits, such as on-site childcare, because it attracts better employees, not because they feel they have a social responsibility to provide such services. Obviously, the line between being a good competitor and being socially responsible is sometimes blurred.

MODULE-END REVIEW

Classify each of the following as a structural, organizational, or activity cost driver.

a. Meals served to airplane passengers aboard Northwest Airlines.
b. General Motors' decision to manufacture the Volt, an all-electric automobile.
c. Zenith's decision to sell its computer operations and focus on the core television business.
d. Number of tax returns filed electronically by H&R Block.
e. Number of passenger cars in an Amtrak train.
f. Coors' decision to expand its market area east from the Rocky Mountains.
g. Boeing's decision to invite airlines to assist in designing the model 777 airplane.
h. Daimler Benz's decision to use cross-disciplinary teams to design a new automobile.
i. St.Jude Hospital's decision to establish review committees on the appropriateness and effectiveness of medical procedures for improving patient care.
j. Harley-Davidson's efforts to restructure production procedures to reduce inventories and machine setup times.

The solution is on page 13-26.

GUIDANCE ANSWER

MANAGERIAL DECISION **You are the CEO**

It is important that an organization's cost structure be aligned with its strategy. If your goal is to be a cost leader (such as Wal-Mart or Costco), you will want to make sure that the structural cost drivers, such as the type of buildings acquired and the displays used, are consistent with this strategy. As the CEO of Wal-Mart you would not permit many of the costs that would be incurred in an organization such as Tiffany or Nordstrom.

DISCUSSION QUESTIONS

Q13-1. Contrast financial and managerial accounting on the basis of user orientation, purpose of information, level of aggregation, length of time period, orientation toward past or future, conformance to external standards, and emphasis on objective data.

Q13-2. What three themes are a part of strategic cost management?

Q13-3. Distinguish between a mission and a goal.

Q13-4. Describe the three strategic positions that Porter views as leading to business success.

Q13-5. Distinguish between how managerial accounting would support the strategy of cost leadership and the strategy of product differentiation.

Q13-6. Why are the phases of planning, organizing, and controlling referred to as a *continuous cycle*?

Q13-7. Identify three advances that have fostered the move away from isolated national economic systems toward an interdependent global economy.

Q13-8.   What are the three interrelated dimensions of today's competition?

Q13-9.   Differentiate among structural, organizational, and activity cost drivers.

Q13-10. What is the link between performing activities and incurring costs?

Q13-11. How can top management establish an ethical tone in an organization?

Q13-12. Describe how pressures to have desirable short-run outcomes can lead to ethical dilemmas.

Assignments with the ✓ in the margin are available in an online homework system.
See the Preface of the book for details.

MINI EXERCISES

M13-13. Management Accounting Terminology   (LO1-5)

Match the following terms with the best descriptions. Each description is used only once.

Terms

1. Ethics	9. Organizational cost driver
2. Mission	10. Financial accounting
3. Controlling	11. Activity cost driver
4. Goal	12. Structural cost driver
5. Cost drivers	13. Managerial accounting
6. Quality	14. Resources
7. Balance sheet	15. Product differentiation
8. Income statement	

Description

a. Designing components so they are easily assembled

b. Factors that influence costs

c. Prepared as of a point in time

d. Accounting for external users

e. Increase year 2011 sales by 10 percent over year 2010 sales

f. Shows the results of operations for a period of time

g. Packing an order for shipment

h. Deciding to limit market focus to a region rather than the entire nation

i. The degree to which a new e-book reader meets a buyer's expectations

j. Used internally to make decisions

k. Consumed by activities

l. The propriety of taking some action

m. Reduces customer price sensitivity

n. Basic purpose toward which activities are directed

o. Comparing the budget with the actual results

M13-14. Financial and Managerial Accounting   (LO1)

Indicate whether each phrase is more descriptive of financial accounting or managerial accounting.

a. May be subjective

b. Often used to state corporate goals

c. Typically prepared quarterly or annually

d. May measure time or customer satisfaction

e. Future oriented

f. Has a greater emphasis on cost-benefit analysis

g. Keeps records of assets and liabilities

h. Highly aggregated statements

i. Must conform to external standards

j. Special-purpose reports

k. Decision-making tool

l. Income statement, balance sheet, and statement of cash flows

M13-15. Missions, Goals, and Strategies   (LO2)

Identify each of the following as a mission, goal, or strategy.

a. Budget time for study, sleep, and relaxation

b. Provide shelter for the homeless

    c. Provide an above-average return to investors

    d. Protect the public

    e. Locate fire stations so that the average response time is less than five minutes

    f. Overlap police patrols so that there are always police cars on major thoroughfares

    g. Achieve a 12 percent market share

    h. Lower prices and costs

    i. Select the most scenic route to drive between Las Vegas and Denver

    j. Graduate from college

M13-16. Line and Staff Organization (LO2)

Macy's Department Store (M)

Presented are the names of several departments often found in a merchandising organization such as **Macy's Department Store**.

a. Maintenance	*d.* Payroll
b. Home Furnishings	*e.* Human Resources
c. Store Manager	*f.* Advertising

Required

Identify each as a line or a staff department.

M13-17. Line and Staff Organization (LO2)

Kimberly-Clark (KMB)

Presented are the names of several departments often found in a manufacturing organization such as **Kimberly-Clark**.

a. Manager, Plant 2	*d.* Controller
b. Design Engineering	*e.* Property Accounting
c. President	*f.* Sales Manager, District 1

Required

Identify each as a line or a staff department.

M13-18. Classifying Cost Drivers (LO4)

Classify each of the following as structural, organizational, or activity cost drivers.

    a. Oneida Silversmiths reorganizes production facilities from a layout in which all similar types of machines are grouped together to a layout in which a set of machines is designated for the production of a particular product and that set of machines is grouped together.

    b. A cable television company decides to start offering telephone service.

    c. IBM decides to stop making personal computers.

    d. Canon decides to start making high-volume photocopy equipment to compete head-to-head with Xerox.

    e. The number of meals a cafeteria serves.

    f. The number of miles a taxi is driven.

    g. A company eliminates the position of supervisor and has each work group elect a team leader.

    h. Toyota empowers employees to halt production if a quality problem is identified.

    i. The number of tons of grain a ship loads.

    j. Crossgate Mall decides to build space for 80 additional stores.

IBM (IBM)

Canon (CAJ)

Toyota (TM)

M13-19. Classifying Cost Drivers (LO4)

Mesa Construction managers provide design and construction management services for various commercial construction projects. Senior managers are trying to apply cost driver concepts to their firm to better understand Mesa's costs.

Required

Classify each of the following actions or decisions as structural, organizational, or activity cost drivers.

    a. The decision to be a regional leader in computer-assisted design services.

    b. The decision to allow staff architects to follow a specific project through to completion.

    c. The daily process of inspecting the progress on various construction projects.

    d. The process of conducting extensive client interviews to assess the exact needs for Mesa services.

    e. The decision to expand the market area by establishing an office in another state.

    f. The decision to use only Mesa staff rather than relying on subcontractors.

    g. The process of receiving approval from government authorities along with appropriate permits for each project.

> *h.* The decision to organize the workforce into project teams.
> *i.* The decision to build a new headquarters facility with areas for design and administration as well as storage and maintenance of construction equipment.
> *j.* The process of grading building sites and preparing forms for foundations.

EXERCISES

General Electric (GE)

E13-20. Financial and Managerial Accounting (LO1)

Assume Alana Freeman has just been promoted to product manager at General Electric. Although she is an accomplished sales representative and well versed in market research, her accounting background is limited to reviewing her paycheck, balancing her checkbook, filing income tax returns, and reviewing the company's annual income statement and balance sheet. She commented that while the financial statements are no doubt useful to investors, she just doesn't see how accounting can help her be a good product manager.

Required

Based on her remarks, it is apparent that Alana's view of accounting is limited to financial accounting. Explain some of the important differences between financial and managerial accounting and suggest some ways managerial accounting can help Alana be a better product manager.

E13-21. Developing an Organization Chart (LO2)

Develop an organization chart for a three-outlet bakery chain with a central baking operation and deliveries every few hours. Assume the business is incorporated and that the president has a single staff assistant. Also assume that the delivery truck driver reports to the bakery manager.

E13-22. Identifying Monetary and Nonmonetary Performance Measures (LO2)

Identify possible monetary and nonmonetary performance measures for each of the following situations. One nonmonetary measure should relate to quality, and one should relate to time.

Cornell University
Cook County Hospital
L.L. Bean
Hilton Hotels (HLT)
United Parcel Service (UPS)

a. Cornell University wishes to evaluate the success of last year's graduating class.
b. Cook County Hospital wishes to evaluate the performance of its emergency room.
c. L.L. Bean wishes to evaluate the performance of its telephone order–filling operations.
d. Hilton Hotels wishes to evaluate the performance of registration activities at one of its hotels.
e. United Parcel Service wishes to evaluate the success of its operations in Knoxville.

E13-23. Identifying Monetary and Nonmonetary Performance Measures (LO2)

Identify possible monetary and nonmonetary performance measures for each of the following situations. One nonmonetary measure should relate to quality, and one should relate to time.

Verizon (VZ)
Time Warner Cable (TWTC)
Dell Computer (DELL)
Amazon.com (AMZN)
Emory University

a. Verizon's evaluation of the performance of its Internet service in Boston.
b. Time Warner Cable's evaluation of the performance of new customer cable installations in Rochester.
c. Dell Computer's evaluation of the performance of its logistical arrangements for delivering computers to residential customers.
d. Amazon.com's evaluation of the performance of its Web site.
e. Emory University's evaluation of the success of its freshman admissions activities.

E13-24. Identifying Information Needs of Different Managers (LO2)

Hyundai
Nissan

Manfred Pak operates a number of auto dealerships for Hyundai and Nissan. Identify possible monetary and nonmonetary performance measures for each of the following situations. One nonmonetary measure should relate to quality, and one should relate to time.

a. An individual sales associate.
b. The sales manager of a single dealership.
c. The general manager of a particular dealership.
d. The corporate chief financial officer.
e. The president of the corporation.

E13-25. Activities and Cost Drivers (LO4)

For each of the following activities, select the most appropriate cost driver. Each cost driver may be used only once.

Activity		Cost Driver	
1.	Pay vendors	a.	Number of different raw material items
2.	Receive material deliveries	b.	Number of classes offered
3.	Inspect raw materials	c.	Number of machine hours
4.	Plan for purchases of raw materials	d.	Number of employees
5.	Packaging	e.	Number of maintenance hours
6.	Supervision	f.	Number of units of raw materials received
7.	Employee training	g.	Number of new customers
8.	Operating machines	h.	Number of deliveries
9.	Machine maintenance	i.	Number of checks issued
10.	Opening accounts at a bank	j.	Number of customer orders

MANAGEMENT APPLICATIONS

MA13-26. Goals and Strategies (LO2)

a. What is your instructor's goal for students in this course? What strategies has he or she developed to achieve this goal?

b. What is your goal in this course? What strategies will help you achieve this goal?

c. What is your goal for this semester or term? What strategies will help you achieve this goal?

d. What is your next career goal? What strategies will help you achieve this goal?

MA13-27. Product Differentiation (LO3)

You are the owner of Lobster's Unlimited. You have no trouble catching lobsters, but you have difficulty in selling all that you catch. The problem is that all lobsters from all vendors look the same. You do catch high-quality lobsters, but you need to be able to tell your customers that your lobsters are better than those sold by other vendors.

Required

a. What are some possible ways of distinguishing your lobsters from those of other vendors?

b. Explain the possible results of this differentiation.

MA13-28. Ethics and Short-Term Borrowing (LO5)

Ashley, an administrative assistant, is in charge of petty cash for a local law firm. Normally, about $500 is kept in the petty cash box. When Ashley is short on cash and needs some for lunch or to pay her babysitter, she sometimes takes a few dollars from the box. Since she is in charge of the box, nobody knows that she takes the money, and she always replaces it within a few days.

Required

a. Is Ashley's behavior ethical?

b. Assume that Ashley has recently had major problems meeting her bills. She also is in charge of purchasing supplies for the office from petty cash. Last week when she needed $25 for the babysitter, she falsified a voucher for the amount of $25. Is this behavior ethical?

MA13-29. Ethics and Travel Reimbursement (LO5)

Scott takes many business trips throughout the year. All of his expenses are paid by his company. Last week he traveled to Rio De Janeiro, Brazil, and stayed there on business for five days. He is allowed a maximum of $50 per day for food and $150 per day for lodging. To his surprise, the food and accommodations in Brazil were much less than he expected. Being upset about traveling last week and having to sacrifice tickets he'd purchased to a Red Sox baseball game, he decided to inflate his expenses a bit. He increased his lodging expense from $75 per day to $100 per day and his food purchased from $30 per day to $40 per day. Therefore, for the five-day trip, he overstated his expenses by $175 total. After all, the allowance was higher than the amount he spent.

Required

Assume that the company would never find out that he had actually spent less. Are Scott's actions ethical? Are they acceptable?

MA13-30. Ethical Issues with Supplier-Buyer Partnerships (LO5)

John Snyder was excited to learn of his appointment as Circuit Electronics Corporation's sales representative to Household Appliance, Inc. For the past four years, Circuit Electronics has supplied all of the electric switches used in Household's washers and dryers. As Circuit Electronics' sales representative, John Snyder's job involves the following tasks.

1. Working with Household engineers to design electric switches that can be manufactured to meet Household's cost and quality requirements.
2. Assisting Household in resolving any problems related to electric switches.
3. Monitoring the inventory levels of electric switches at Household and placing orders for additional switches when appropriate.

This appointment will require John to move to Stutgart, Germany, for two years. Although John has mixed feelings about the move, he is familiar with the success of the program in improving Circuit Electronics' financial performance. He is also very much aware of the fact that the two previous sales representatives received promotions at the end of their appointments.

As John toured the Household factory in Stutgart with his predecessor, Janet Smith, his excitement turned to concern. It became apparent that Circuit Electronics had not been supplying Household with the best available switches at the lowest possible costs. Although the switches were adequate, they were more likely to wear out after five or six years of use than would switches currently on the market (and being used by Household's competitors). Furthermore, taking into account the current number of switches in transit by ship from North America to Europe, it also appeared that the inventory level of electric switches would soon be more than enough to satisfy Household's needs for the next four months.

Required

If you were John, what would you do?

MA13-31. Expected Values of Questionable Decisions   (LO5)

Exxon Mobil (XOM)

The members of the jury had to make a decision in a lawsuit brought by the State of Alabama against Exxon Mobil. The suit revolved around natural-gas wells that Exxon drilled in state-owned waters. After signing several leases obligating Exxon to share revenues with Alabama, company officials started questioning the terms of the agreement that prohibited deducting several types of processing costs before paying the state royalties.

Royal Dutch/Shell (RDS-B)

During the course of the trial, a memo by an in-house attorney of Exxon Mobil came to light. The memo noted that Royal Dutch/Shell, which had signed a similar lease, interpreted it "in the same manner as the state." The memo then presented arguments the company might use to claim the deduction, estimated the probability of the arguments being successful (less than 50 percent), and proceeded to consider whether Exxon should obey the law using a cost-benefit analysis. According to the memo, "If we adopt anything beyond a 'safe' approach, we should anticipate a quick audit and subsequent litigation." The memo also observed that "our exposure is 12 percent interest on underpayments calculated from the due date, and the cost of litigation." Deducting the questionable costs did, indeed, result in an audit and a lawsuit. Source: *Business Week*.[9]

Required

If you were a member of the jury, what would you do? Why?

MA13-32. Management Decisions Affecting Cost Drivers   (LO4)

An avid bicycle rider, you have decided to use an inheritance to start a new business to sell and repair bicycles. Two college friends have already accepted offers to work for you.

Required

a. What is the mission of your new business?
b. Suggest a strategic positioning goal you might strive for to compete with area hardware and discount stores that sell bicycles.
c. Identify two items that might be long-range goals.
d. Identify two items that might be goals for the coming year.
e. Mention two decisions that will be structural cost drivers.
f. Mention two decisions that will be organizational cost drivers.
g. Identify two activity cost drivers.

MA13-33. Success Factors and Performance Measurement   (LO2)

Three years ago, Vincent Chow completed his college degree. The economy was in a depressed state at the time, and Vincent managed to get an offer of only $35,000 per year as a bookkeeper. In addition to its relatively low pay, this job had limited advancement potential. Since Vincent was an enterprising

---

[9] Mike France, "When Big Oil Gets Too Slick," *Business Week*, April 9, 2001, p. 70.

and ambitious young man, he instead started a business of his own. He was convinced that because of changing lifestyles, a drive-through coffee establishment would be profitable. He was able to obtain backing from his parents to open such an establishment close to the industrial park area in town. Vincent named his business The Cappuccino Express and decided to sell only two types of coffee: cappuccino and decaffeinated.

As Vincent had expected, The Cappuccino Express was very well received. Within three years, Vincent had added another outlet north of town. He left the day-to-day management of each site to a manager and turned his attention toward overseeing the entire enterprise. He also hired an assistant to do the record keeping and other selected chores.[10]

Required

a. Develop an organization chart for The Cappuccino Express.

b. What factors can be expected to have a major impact on the success of The Cappuccino Express?

c. What major tasks must Vincent undertake in managing The Cappuccino Express?

d. What are the major costs of operating The Cappuccino Express?

e. Vincent would like to monitor the performance of each site manager. What measure(s) of performance should he use?

f. If you suggested more than one measure, which of these should Vincent select if he could use only one?

g. Suppose that last year, the original site had yielded total revenues of $146,000, total costs of $120,000, and hence, a profit of $26,000. Vincent had judged this profit performance to be satisfactory. For the coming year, Vincent expects that due to factors such as increased name recognition and demographic changes, the total revenues will increase by 20 percent to $175,200. What amount of profit should he expect from the site? Discuss the issues involved in developing an estimate of profit.

SOLUTIONS TO REVIEW PROBLEMS

Mid-Module Review

Solution
2, 5, 7, 8, 9, and 10

Module-End Review

Solution
a. Activity cost driver
b. Structural cost driver
c. Structural cost driver
d. Activity cost driver
e. Activity cost driver
f. Structural cost driver
g. Organizational cost driver
h. Organizational cost driver
i. Organizational cost driver
j. Organizational cost driver

---

[10] Based on Chee W. Chow, "Instructional Case: Vincent's Cappuccino Express—A Teaching Case to Help Students Master Basic Cost Terms and Concepts Through Interactive Learning," *Issues in Accounting Education*, Spring 1995, pp. 173–190.

Getty Images

WALMART

Retail giant **Walmart** operates more than 8,400 stores in 15 countries around the world. Its market success is built on low prices and one-stop shopping for a wide variety of goods in "discount centers" and "superstores." Its financial success is based on optimal store and distribution center locations, technology leadership in inventory management, obtaining volume discounts from suppliers, working directly with manufacturers to obtain low-cost merchandise, and operating efficiencies. These factors allow Walmart to minimize inventory investments and maintain a high inventory turnover (cost of goods sold/average inventory). Even with relatively low prices, Walmart's low inventory costs and high inventory turnover provide a healthy gross profit and bottom line. Walmart is an excellent example of a company successfully executing a strategy of cost leadership.

Success attracts competition and three chains of dollar stores (**Family Dollar**, **Dollar General**, and **Dollar Tree**)

have been successfully attracting customers from Walmart by adopting Walmart's approach to inventory management and operating efficiency, while differentiating themselves by focusing on low prices for a more limited number of high-volume items in smaller stores that provide customers more convenient access to their limited merchandise. Walmart discount centers average 108,000 square feet while its supercenters average 185,000 square feet. Dollar Tree's 3,800+ stores average a much smaller 8,580 square feet.

While Walmart custom builds its stores, these competitors often spend less per square foot by acquiring store space originally constructed for others. This provides the dollar stores with a lower cost per square foot than Walmart, thereby allowing them to cover their building costs at a lower sales volume per square foot.

Like Walmart, the dollar stores' key to success is high inventory turnover. And by focusing on a limited number

Cost Behavior, Activity Analysis, and Cost Estimation

LEARNING OBJECTIVES

LO1 Identify basic patterns of how costs respond to changes in activity cost drivers. (p. 14-3)

LO2 Determine a linear cost estimating equation. (p. 14-10)

LO3 Identify and discuss problems encountered in cost estimation. (p. 14-15)

LO4 Describe and develop alternative classifications for activity cost drivers. (p. 14-16)

of high-volume inventory items, it is possible for them to achieve a higher inventory turnover than Walmart with its much broader inventory. "We can make good money on an item we sell for a dollar," says Howard Levine, the CEO of Family Dollar. "We have 6,800 stores. If you sell one item a week in 6,800 stores, no matter what the price point, you've got a lot of velocity." And that velocity is growing. Between 2007 and 2010, sales per square foot at Dollar General, which currently operates almost 9,000 stores, grew from $165 to $199. Meanwhile, during the recent recession, Walmart's same-store sales declined.

Despite their success, the managers of dollar stores are quick to point out that they do not compete with Walmart. Instead, they claim to compete with convenience stores by offering a combination of convenience and value not available in large stores or other small convenience stores. "Walmart always worries me," says Levine of Family Dollar. "You can't out-Walmart Walmart. The dollar stores are not going after the same trip Walmart is going after. We are going after the fill-in trip. We live off the crumbs they leave us."

The success of Walmart and its smaller competitors, who claim not to be competitors, is built on a cost leadership strategy. Such a strategy necessarily requires a thorough understanding of cost behavior, activity analysis, and cost estimation, the topics of this module.[1]

---

[1] Based on Sean Gregory, "The Buck Shops Here", *Time*, December 20, 2010, pp. 54-56; and investor information available at www.dollargeneral.com, www.walmart.com, www.dollartree.com, www.familydollar.com.

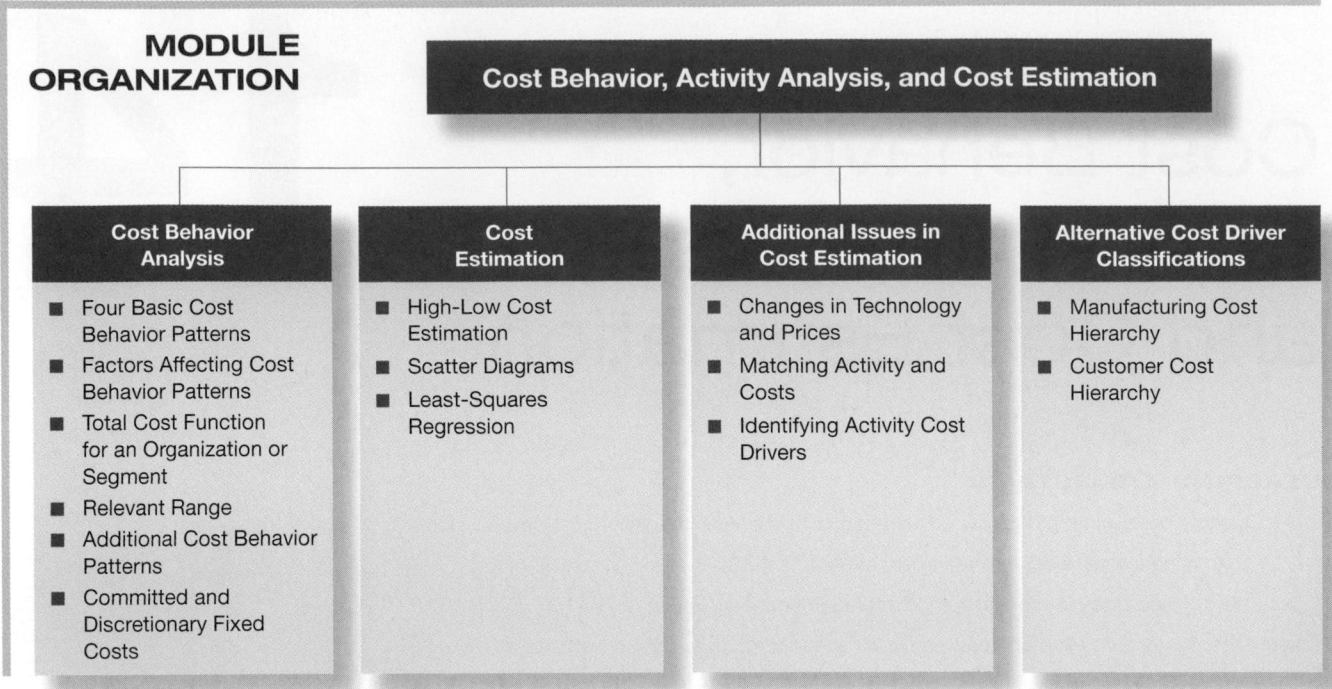

COST BEHAVIOR ANALYSIS

This module introduces **cost behavior**, which refers to the relationship between a given cost item and the quantity of its related cost driver. Cost behavior, therefore, explains how the total amount for various costs respond to changes in activity volume. Understanding cost behavior is essential for estimating future costs. In this module we examine several typical cost behavior patterns and methods for developing cost equations that are useful for predicting future costs.

Four Basic Cost Behavior Patterns

LO1 Identify basic patterns of how costs respond to changes in activity cost drivers.

Although there are an unlimited number of ways that costs can respond to changes in cost drivers, as a starting point it is useful to classify cost behavior into four categories: variable, fixed, mixed, and step. Graphs of each are presented in Exhibit 14.1. Observe that total cost (the dependent variable) is measured on the vertical axis, and total activity for the time period (the independent variable) is measured on the horizontal axis.

1. **Variable costs** change in total in direct proportion to changes in activity. Their total amount increases as activity increases, equaling zero dollars when activity is zero and increasing at a constant amount per unit of activity. The higher the variable cost per unit of activity, the steeper the slope of the line representing total cost. With the number of pizzas served as the activity cost driver for Pizza Hut restaurants, the cost of cheese is an example of a variable cost.

2. **Fixed costs** do not change in response to a change in activity volume. Hence, a line representing total fixed costs is flat with a slope (incline) of zero. With the number of Pizza Hut pizzas sold as the cost driver, annual depreciation, property taxes, and property insurance are examples of fixed costs. While fixed costs may respond to structural and organizational cost drivers over time, they do not respond to short-run changes in activity cost drivers.

3. **Mixed costs** (sometimes called **semivariable costs**) contain a fixed and a variable cost element. Total mixed costs are positive (like fixed costs) when activity is zero, and they increase in a linear fashion (like total variable costs) as activity increases. With the number of pizzas sold as the cost driver, the cost of electric power is an example of a mixed cost. Some electricity is required to provide basic lighting, while an increasing amount of electricity is required to prepare food as the number of pizzas served increases.

4. **Step costs** are constant within a narrow range of activity but shift to a higher level when activity exceeds the range. Total step costs increase in a steplike fashion as activity increases. With the number of pizzas served as the cost driver, employee wages is an example of a step cost. Up to a certain

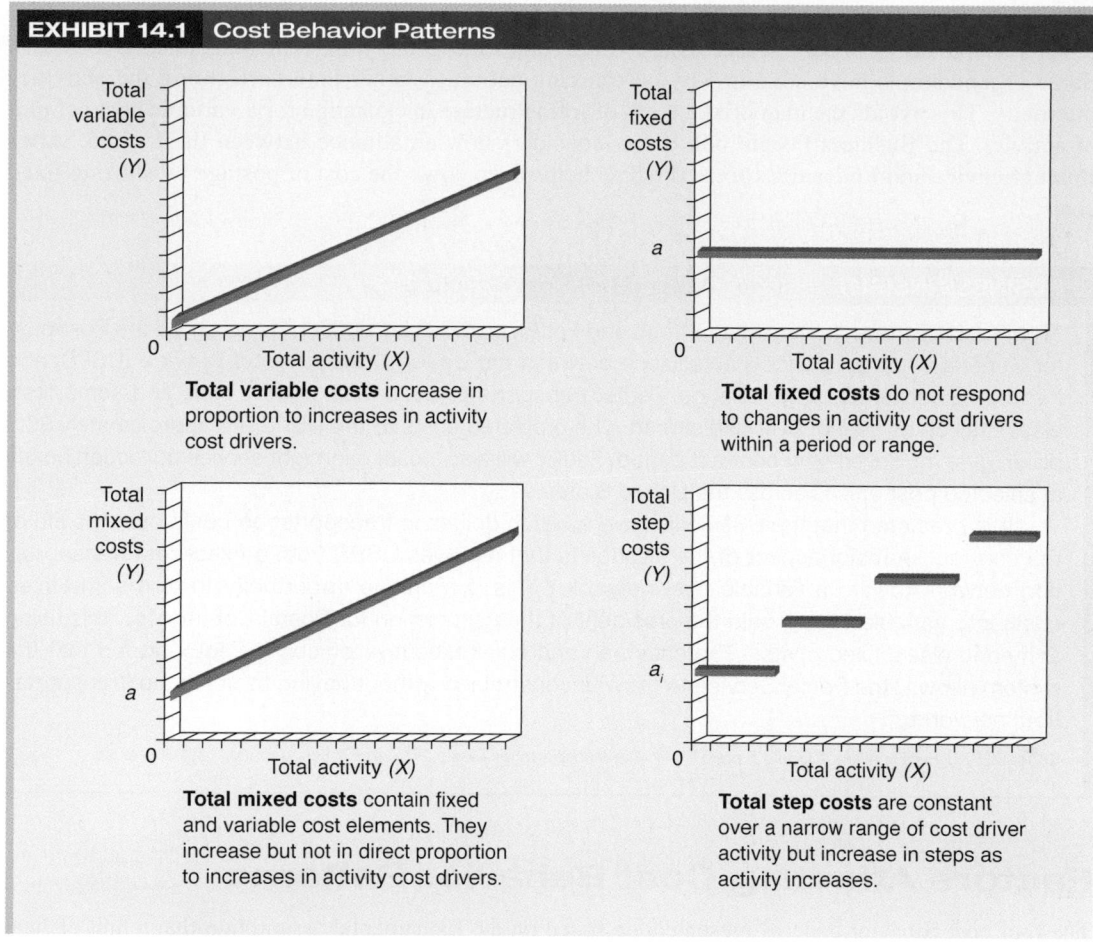

EXHIBIT 14.1   Cost Behavior Patterns

Total variable costs *(Y)* — Total activity *(X)*

Total variable costs increase in proportion to increases in activity cost drivers.

Total fixed costs *(Y)* — Total activity *(X)*

Total fixed costs do not respond to changes in activity cost drivers within a period or range.

Total mixed costs *(Y)* — Total activity *(X)*

Total mixed costs contain fixed and variable cost elements. They increase but not in direct proportion to increases in activity cost drivers.

Total step costs *(Y)* — Total activity *(X)*

Total step costs are constant over a narrow range of cost driver activity but increase in steps as activity increases.

number of pizzas, only a small staff needs to be on duty. Beyond that number, additional employees are needed for quality service and so forth.

The relationship between total cost (*Y* axis) and total activity (*X* axis) for the four cost behavior patterns is mathematically expressed as follows:

$$\text{Variable cost: } Y = bX$$

where

b = the variable cost per unit, sometimes referred to as the slope of the cost function.

$$\text{Fixed cost: } Y = a$$

where

a = total fixed costs. The slope of the fixed cost function is zero because fixed costs do not change with activity.

$$\text{Mixed cost: } Y = a + bX$$

where

a = total fixed cost element
b = variable cost element per unit of activity.

$$\text{Step cost: } Y = a_i$$

where

a_i = the step cost within a specific range of activity, identified by the subscript i.

The total cost function of most organizations has shifted in recent years toward more fixed costs and fewer variable costs, making it increasingly important for organizations to manage their fixed costs. Some organizations have done this by outsourcing activities rather than performing the activities internally. This avoids the many fixed costs of infrastructure in exchange for a variable cost per unit of activity. The Business Insight box below considers how an alliance between the United States Postal Service and Federal Express (FedEx) helps keep down the cost of postage by shifting fixed costs.

BUSINESS INSIGHT   Alliance Alters USPS Cost Structure

"The Postal Service delivers Main Street, and FedEx provides an air fleet," proclaimed the Postmaster General when announcing an alliance between the United States Postal Service (USPS) and FedEx. Under terms of the alliance, FedEx transports express mail, priority mail, and some first-class mail on its fleet of over 650 aircraft. The projected costs to the USPS are approximately $6.3 billion over the seven-year contract period. FedEx will also locate overnight service collection boxes at selected post offices across the United States.

It is predicted that the USPS will save a billion dollars in transportation costs over the life of the contract. A major aspect of the alliance is that it moves USPS from a fixed-cost transportation network toward a variable cost network. "This is a unique opportunity to turn some fixed costs into variable costs," said the president of the Association for Postal Commerce. "It is using someone else's fixed costs." The chairman and chief executive officer of FedEx added that the system allows "the Postal Service to grow unconstrained without having to put in big [transportation] networks."

Souce: USPS-FedEx Alliance Could Save $1 Billion in Transportation Costs," *Federal Times*, January 15, 2001, p. 4.

Factors Affecting Cost Behavior Patterns

The four cost behavior patterns presented are based on the fundamental assumption that a unit of final output is the primary cost driver. The implications of this assumption are examined later in this module.

Another important assumption is that the time period is too short to incorporate changes in strategic cost drivers such as the scale of operations. Although this assumption is useful for short-range planning, for the purpose of developing plans for extended time periods, it is more appropriate to consider possible variations in one or more strategic cost drivers. When this is done, many costs otherwise classified as fixed are better classified as variable.

Even the cost of depreciable assets can be viewed as variable if the time period is long enough. Assuming that the number of pizzas served is the cost driver, for a single month the depreciation on all Pizza Hut restaurants in the world is a fixed cost. Over several years, if sales are strong, a strategic decision will be made to open additional restaurants; if sales are weak, strategic decisions will likely be made to close some restaurants. Hence, over a multiple-year period, the number of restaurants varies with sales volume, making depreciation appear as a variable cost with sales revenue as the cost driver.

Total Cost Function for an Organization or Segment

To obtain a general understanding of an organization, to compare the cost structures of different organizations, or to perform preliminary planning activities, managers are often interested in how total costs respond to a single measure of overall activity such as units sold or sales revenue. This overview can be useful, but presenting all costs as a function of a single cost driver is seldom accurate enough to support decisions concerning products, services, or activities. Doing so implies that all of an organization's costs can be manipulated by changing a single cost driver. This is seldom true.

In developing a total cost function, the independent variable usually represents some measure of the goods or services provided customers, such as total student credit hours in a university, total sales revenue in a store, total guest-days in a hotel, or total units manufactured in a factory. The resulting cost function is illustrated in Exhibit 14.2.

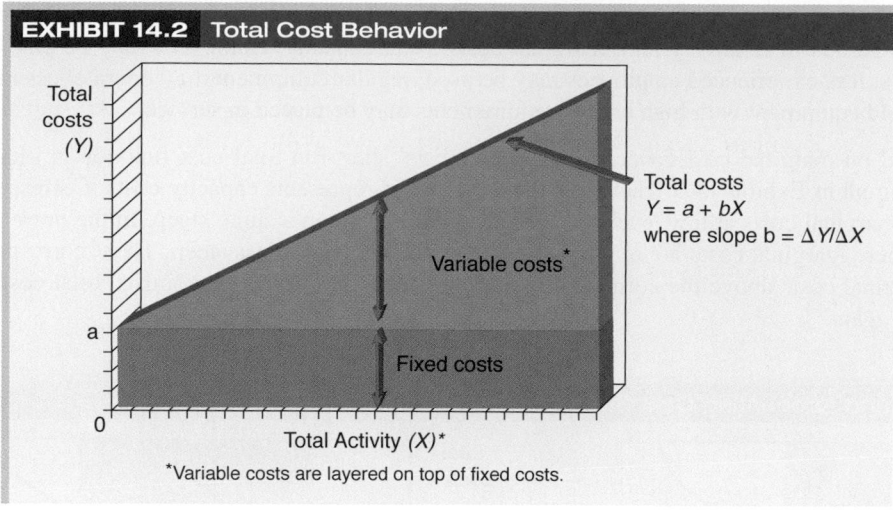

EXHIBIT 14.2 Total Cost Behavior

*Variable costs are layered on top of fixed costs.

The equation for total costs is:

$$Y = a + bX$$

where

Y = total costs
a = vertical axis intercept (an approximation of fixed costs)
b = slope (an approximation of variable costs per unit of X)
X = value of independent variable

In situations where the variable, fixed, and mixed costs, and the related cost functions, can be determined, a total cost equation can be useful in predicting future costs for various activity levels. However, generally, a total cost equation is useful for predicting costs in only a limited range of activity. The **relevant range** of a total cost equation is that portion of the range associated with the fixed cost of the current or expected capacity. For example, assume that a Dairy Queen ice cream shop's only fixed cost is the depreciation on its ice cream making machines, and that it is able to produce a maximum of 50 gallons of ice cream per day with a single ice cream making machine. If it has four machines in operation, and if it can readily adjust its fixed capacity cost by increasing or decreasing the number of ice cream machines, the relevant range of activity for the shop's current total cost equation is 151 to 200 gallons. In the future, if the shop expects to operate at more than 200 gallons per day, the current total cost equation would not predict total cost accurately, because fixed costs would have to be increased for additional machines. Conversely, if it expects to operate at 150 gallons or less, it may reduce the number of machines in the shop, thereby reducing total fixed costs.

Relevant Range

The use of straight lines in accounting models of cost behavior assumes a linear relationship between cost and activity with each additional unit of activity accompanied by a uniform increment in total cost. This uniform increment is known as the *variable cost of one unit.*

Economic models show a nonlinear relationship between cost and activity with each incremental unit of activity being accompanied by a varying increment in total cost. Economists identify the varying increment in total cost as the **marginal cost** *of one unit.*

It is useful to relate marginal costs to the following three levels of activity:

1. *Below the activity range for which the facility was designed,* the existence of excess capacity results in relatively high marginal costs. Having extra time, employees complete assignments at a leisurely pace, increasing the time and the cost to produce each unit above what it would be if employees were more pressed to complete work. Frequent starting and stopping of equipment may also add to costs.

2. *Within the activity range for which the facility was designed,* activities take place under optimal circumstances and marginal costs are relatively low.

3. *Above the activity range for which the facility was designed,* the existence of capacity constraints again results in relatively high marginal costs. Near capacity, employees may be paid overtime wages, less-experienced employees may be used, regular equipment may operate less efficiently, and old equipment with high energy requirements may be placed in service.

Based on marginal cost concepts, the economists' short-run total cost function is illustrated in the first graph in Exhibit 14.3. The vertical axis intercept represents capacity costs. Corresponding to the high marginal costs at low levels of activity, the initial slope is quite steep. In the normal activity range, where marginal costs are relatively low, the slope becomes less steep. Then, corresponding to high marginal costs above the normal activity range, the slope of the economists' total cost function increases again.

EXHIBIT 14.3 Economic and Accounting Cost Structures

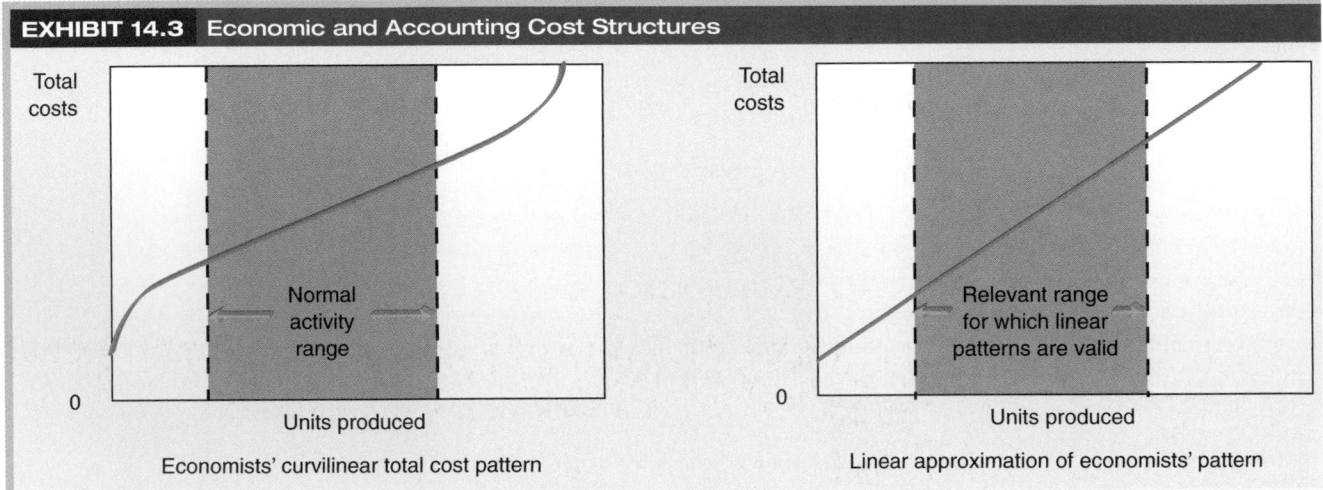

Economists' curvilinear total cost pattern   Linear approximation of economists' pattern

If the economists' total cost curve is valid, how can we reasonably approximate it with a straight line? The answer to this question is in the notion of a *relevant range*. A linear pattern may be a poor approximation of the economists' curvilinear pattern over the entire range of possible activity, but a linear pattern as illustrated in the right-hand graph in Exhibit 14.3 is often sufficiently accurate within the range of probable operations. The range of activity within which a linear cost function is valid is called the **relevant range**. Linear estimates of cost behavior are valid only within the relevant range. Extreme care must be exercised when making comments about cost behavior outside the relevant range.

Additional Cost Behavior Patterns

Although we have considered the most frequently used cost behavior patterns, remember that there are numerous ways that costs can respond to changes in activity. Avoid the temptation to automatically assume that the cost in question conforms to one of the patterns discussed in this module. As illustrated by the Research Insight box on the following page, it is important to think through each situation and then select a behavior pattern that seems logical and fits the known facts.

Particular care needs to be taken with the vertical axis. So far, all graphs have placed *total* costs on the vertical axis. Miscommunication is likely if one party is thinking in terms of *total* costs while the other is thinking in terms of *variable* or *average* costs. Consider the following cost function:

$$\text{Total costs} = \$3,000 + \$5X$$

where

X = customers served

The total, variable, and average costs at various levels of activity are computed here and graphed in Exhibit 14.4 on the following page. As the number of customers served increases, total costs increase, the variable costs of each unit remain constant, and the average cost decreases because fixed costs are spread over a larger number of units.

Customers Served	Total Costs	Average Cost*	Variable Costs per Customer
100	$3,500	$35.00	$5.00
200	4,000	20.00	5.00
300	4,500	15.00	5.00
400	5,000	12.50	5.00
500	5,500	11.00	5.00

* Total costs/customers served

To predict total costs for the coming period, management will use the first graph in Exhibit 14.4. To determine the minimum price required to avoid a loss on each additional customer served, management is interested in the variable costs per customer, yet if a manager inquired as to the cost of serving a customer, a financial accountant would probably provide average cost information, as illustrated in the third graph in Exhibit 14.4. The specific average cost would likely be a function of the number of customers served during the most recent accounting period.

Errors can occur if last period's average costs, perhaps based on a volume of 500 customers, were used to predict total costs for a future period when the anticipated volume was some other amount, say 300 units. Using average costs, the predicted total costs of 300 units are $3,300 ($11 × 300). In fact, using the proper total cost function, a more accurate prediction of total costs is $4,500 [$3,000 + ($5 × 300)]. The prediction error could cause a number of problems. If management budgeted $3,300 to pay bills and the bills actually totaled $4,500, the company might have to curtail activities or borrow under unfavorable terms to avoid running out of cash.

Committed and Discretionary Fixed Costs

Fixed costs are often classified as *committed* or *discretionary,* depending on their immediate impact on the organization if management attempts to change them. **Committed fixed costs**, sometimes referred to as **capacity costs**, are the fixed costs required to maintain the current service or production capacity or to fill previous legal commitments. Examples of committed fixed costs include depreciation, property taxes, rent, and interest on bonds.

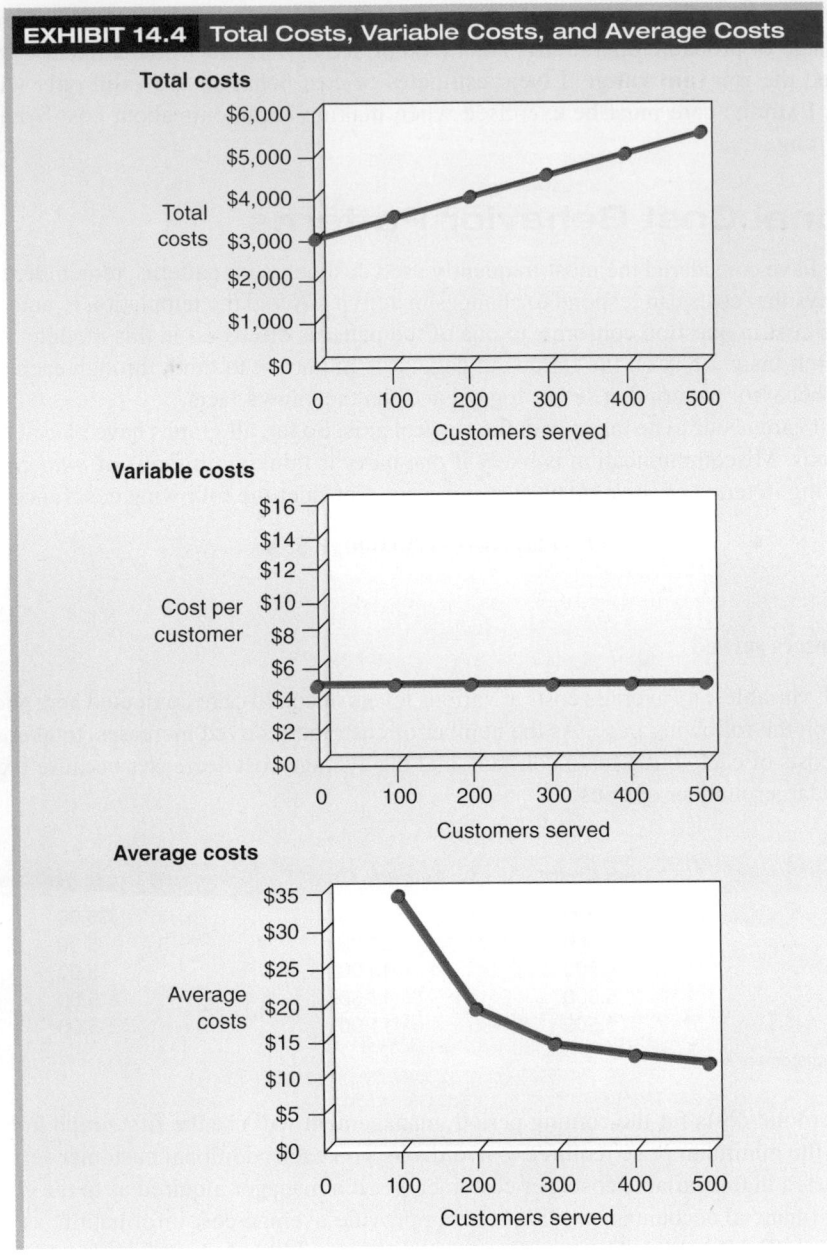

EXHIBIT 14.4 Total Costs, Variable Costs, and Average Costs

Committed fixed costs are often the result of structural decisions about the size and nature of an organization. For example, years ago the management of **Santa Fe Railroad** made decisions concerning what communities the railroad would serve. Track was laid on the basis of those decisions, and the Santa Fe Railroad now pays property taxes each year on the railroad's miles of track. These property taxes could be reduced by disposing of track. However, reducing track would also diminish the Santa Fe's capacity to serve.

Discretionary fixed costs, sometimes called **managed fixed costs**, are set at a fixed amount each period at the discretion of management. It is possible to reduce discretionary fixed costs without reducing production or service capacity in the short term. Typical discretionary fixed costs include advertising, maintenance, charitable contributions, employee training, and research and development.

Maintenance expenditures for discretionary fixed costs are frequently regarded as investments in the future. Research and development, for example, is undertaken to develop new or improved products that can be profitably produced and sold in future periods. During periods of financial well-being, organizations may make large expenditures on discretionary cost items. Conversely, during periods of financial stress, organizations likely reduce discretionary expenditures before reducing capacity costs.

Unfortunately, fluctuations in the funding of discretionary fixed costs may reduce the effectiveness of long-range programs. A high-quality research staff may be difficult to reassemble if key personnel are laid off. Even the contemplation of layoffs may reduce the staff's effectiveness. In all periods, discretionary costs are subject to debate and are likely to be changed in the budgeting process.

MID-MODULE REVIEW

Identify each of the following cost behavior patterns as variable, committed fixed, discretionary fixed, mixed, or step.

a. Total cost of bakery products used at a McDonald's restaurant when the number of meals served is the activity cost driver.

b. Total cost of operating the Mayo Clinic when the number of patients served is the cost driver.

c. Total property taxes for a Midas Muffler Shop when the number of vehicles serviced is the cost driver.

d. Total cost of motherboards used by Apple Computer when the number of computers manufactured and shipped is the cost driver.

e. Total cost of secretarial services at Indiana University with each secretary handling the needs of ten faculty members and where part-time secretarial help is not available. The number of faculty is the cost driver.

f. Total advertising costs for International Business Machines (IBM).

g. Automobile rental costs at Alamo in Orlando, Florida, when there is no mileage charge. The cost driver is the number of miles driven.

h. Automobile rental cost at Hertz in Dallas, Texas, which has a base charge plus a mileage charge. The cost driver is the number of miles driven.

i. Salaries paid to personnel while conducting on-campus employment interviews for Champion International. Number of on-campus interviews is the cost driver.

j. The cost of contributions to educational institutions by Xerox Corporation.

The solution is on page 14-31.

COST ESTIMATION

Cost estimation, the determination of the relationship between activity and cost, is an important part of cost management. In this section, we develop equations for the relationship between total costs and total activity.

LO2 Determine a linear cost estimating equation.

To properly estimate the relationship between activity and cost, we must be familiar with basic cost behavior patterns and cost estimating techniques. Costs known to have a variable or a fixed pattern are readily estimated by interviews or by analyzing available records. Sales commission per sales dollar, a variable cost, might be determined to be 15 percent of sales. In a similar manner, annual property taxes might be determined by consulting tax documents.

Mixed (semivariable) costs, which contain fixed and variable cost elements, are more difficult to estimate. According to a basic rule of algebra, two equations are needed to determine two unknowns. Following this rule, at least two observations are needed to determine the variable and fixed elements of a mixed cost.

High-Low Cost Estimation

The most straightforward approach to determining the variable and fixed elements of mixed costs is to use the **high-low method of cost estimation**. This method utilizes data from two time periods, a *representative* high-activity period and a *representative* low-activity period, to estimate fixed and variable costs. Assuming identical fixed costs in both periods, any difference in total costs between these two periods is due entirely to variable costs. The variable costs per unit are found by dividing the difference in total costs by the difference in total activity:

$$\text{Variable costs per unit} = \frac{\text{Difference in total costs}}{\text{Difference in activity}}$$

Once variable costs are determined, fixed costs, which are identical in both periods, are computed by subtracting the total variable costs of either the high or the low activity period from the corresponding total costs.

$$\textbf{Fixed costs} = \textbf{Total costs} - \textbf{Variable costs}$$

Assume a mail-order company such as **Lands' End** wants to develop a monthly cost function for its packaging department and that the number of shipments is believed to be the primary cost driver. The following observations are available for the first four months of 2011.

		Number of Shipments	Packaging Costs
(Low-activity period)	January.........	6,000	$17,000
	February........	9,000	26,000
(High-activity period)	March..........	12,000	32,000
	April	10,000	20,000

Equations for total costs for the packaging department in January and March (the periods of lowest and highest activity) follow:

$$\textbf{January: } \$17,\!000 = \textbf{a} + \textbf{b (6,000 shipments)}$$
$$\textbf{March: } \$32,\!000 = \textbf{a} + \textbf{b (12,000 shipments)}$$

where

$$\textbf{a} = \textbf{fixed costs per month}$$
$$\textbf{b} = \textbf{variable costs per shipment}$$

Solving for the estimated variable costs:

$$\textbf{b} = \frac{\textbf{Difference in total costs}}{\textbf{Difference in activity}}$$

$$\textbf{b} = \frac{\$32,\!000 - \$17,\!000}{12,\!000 - 6,\!000}$$

$$= \$2.50$$

Next, the estimated monthly fixed costs are determined by subtracting variable costs from total costs of *either* the January or March equation:

$$\textbf{a} = \textbf{Total costs} - \textbf{Variable costs}$$
$$\textbf{January: a} = \$17,\!000 - (\$2.50 \textbf{ per shipment} \times 6,\!000 \textbf{ shipments})$$
$$= \$2,\!000$$

or

$$\textbf{March: a} = \$32,\!000 - (\$2.50 \textbf{ per shipment} \times 12,\!000 \textbf{ shipments})$$
$$= \$2,\!000$$

The cost estimating equation for total packaging department costs is

$$\textbf{Y} = \$2,\!000 + \$2.50\textbf{X}$$

where

$$\textbf{X} = \textbf{number of shipments}$$
$$\textbf{Y} = \textbf{total costs for the packing department}$$

The concepts underlying the high-low method of cost estimation are illustrated in Exhibit 14.5.

Cost prediction, the forecasting of future costs, is a common purpose of cost estimation. Previously developed estimates of cost behavior are often the starting point in predicting future costs. Continuing the mail-order example, if 5,000 shipments are budgeted for June 2011, the predicted June 2011 packaging department costs are $14,500 [$2,000 + ($2.50 per shipment × 5,000 shipments)].

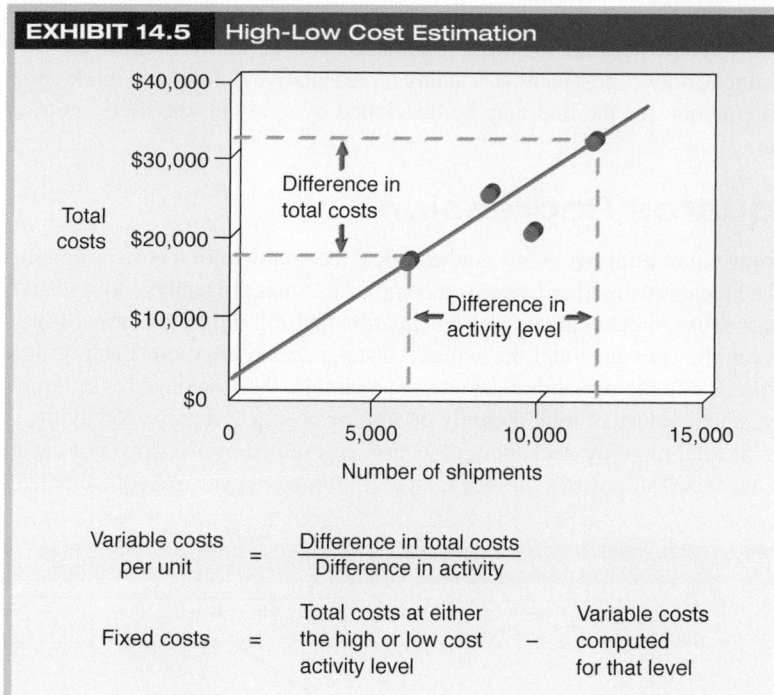

EXHIBIT 14.5   High-Low Cost Estimation

$$\frac{\text{Variable costs}}{\text{per unit}} = \frac{\text{Difference in total costs}}{\text{Difference in activity}}$$

$$\text{Fixed costs} = \frac{\text{Total costs at either}}{\text{the high or low cost}} - \frac{\text{Variable costs}}{\text{computed}} \text{ for that level}$$

Scatter Diagrams

A **scatter diagram** is a graph of past activity and cost data, with individual observations represented by dots. Plotting historical cost data on a scatter diagram is a useful approach to cost estimation, especially when used in conjunction with other cost-estimating techniques. As illustrated in Exhibit 14.6, a scatter diagram helps in selecting high and low activity levels representative of normal operating conditions. The periods of highest or lowest activity may not be representative because of the cost of overtime, the use of less efficient equipment, strikes, and so forth. If the goal is to develop an equation to predict costs under normal operating conditions, then the equation should be based on observations of normal operating conditions. A scatter diagram is also useful in determining whether costs can be reasonably approximated by a straight line.

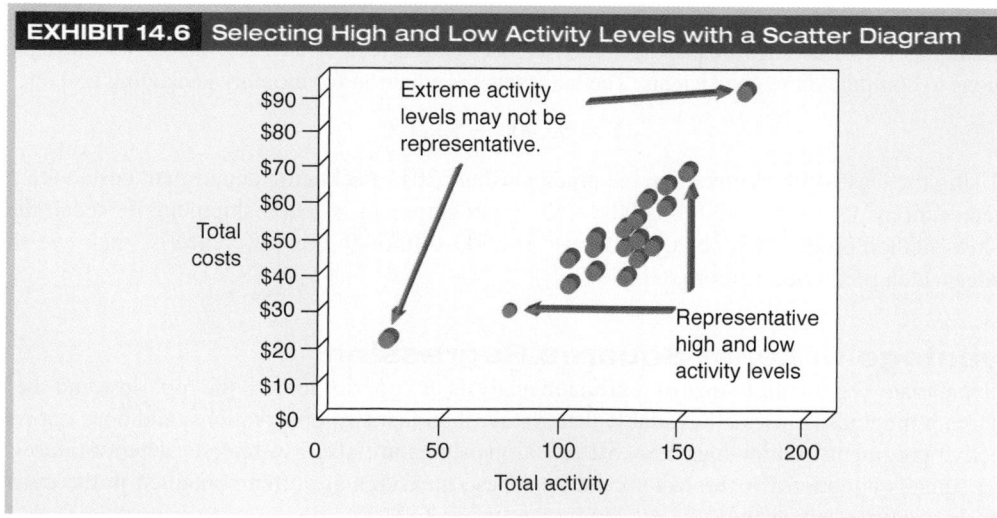

EXHIBIT 14.6   Selecting High and Low Activity Levels with a Scatter Diagram

Scatter diagrams are sometimes used alone as a basis of cost estimation. This requires the use of professional judgment to draw a representative straight line through the plot of historical data. Typically, the analyst tries to ensure that an equal number of observations are on either side of the line while minimizing the total vertical differences between the line and actual cost observations at each value of the independent variable. Once a line is drawn, cost estimates at any representative volume are made by studying the line. Alternatively, an equation for the line may be developed by applying the high-low method to any two points on the line.

Least-Squares Regression

Least-squares regression analysis uses a mathematical technique to fit a cost-estimating equation to the observed data. The technique mathematically accomplishes what the analyst does visually with a scatter diagram. The least-squares technique creates an equation that minimizes the sum of the vertical squared differences between the estimated and the actual costs at each observation. Each of these differences is an estimating error. Using the packaging department example, the least-squares criterion is illustrated in Exhibit 14.7. Estimated values of total monthly packaging costs are represented by the straight line, and the actual values of total monthly packaging costs are represented by the dots. For each dot, such as the one at a volume of 10,000 shipments, the line is fit to minimize the vertical squared differences.

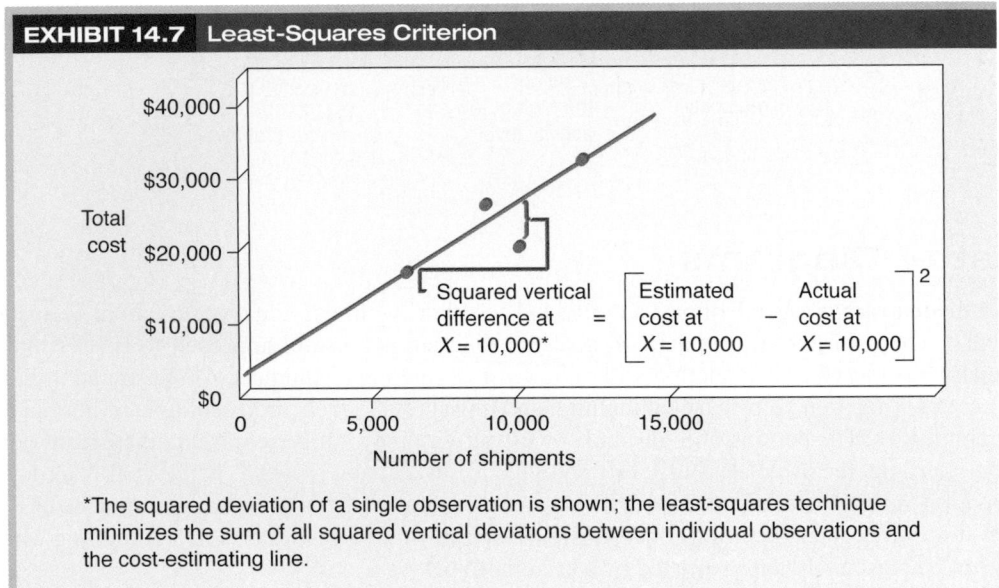

EXHIBIT 14.7   Least-Squares Criterion

*The squared deviation of a single observation is shown; the least-squares technique minimizes the sum of all squared vertical deviations between individual observations and the cost-estimating line.

Values of a and b can be manually calculated using a set of equations developed by mathematicians or by using spreadsheet software packages such as Microsoft Excel®. Many calculators also have built-in functions to compute these coefficients. The least-squares equation for monthly packaging costs is:

$$Y = \$3,400 + \$2.20X$$

Using the least-squares equation, the predicted June 2011 packaging department costs with 5,000 budgeted shipments are $14,400 [$3,400 + ($2.20 per shipment × 5,000 shipments)]. Recall that the high-low method predicted June 2011 costs of $14,500. Although this difference is small, we should consider which prediction is more reliable.

Advantage of Least-Squares Regression

Mathematicians regard least-squares regression analysis as superior to both the high-low and the scatter diagram methods. It uses all available data, rather than just two observations, and does not rely on subjective judgment in drawing a line. Statistical measures are also available to determine how well a least-squares equation fits the historical data. These measures are often contained in the output of spreadsheet software packages.

In addition to the vertical axis intercept and the slope, least-squares regression calculates the coefficient of determination. The **coefficient of determination** is a measure of the percent of variation in the dependent variable (such as total packaging department costs) that is explained by variations in the independent variable (such as total shipments). Statisticians often refer to the coefficient of determination as R-squared and represent it as R^2.

The coefficient of determination can have values between zero and one, with values close to zero suggesting that the equation is not very useful and values close to one indicating that the equation explains most of the variation in the dependent variable. When choosing between two cost-estimating equations, the one with the higher coefficient of determination is generally preferred. The coefficient of determination for the packaging department cost estimation equation, determined using least-squares regression analysis, is 0.68. This means that 68 percent of the variation in packaging department costs is explained by the number of shipments.

Managers, Not Models, Are Responsible

Although computers make least-squares regression easy to use, the generated output should not automatically be accepted as correct. Statistics and other mathematical techniques are tools to help managers make decisions. Managers, not mathematical models, are responsible for decisions. Judgment should always be exercised when considering the validity of the least-squares approach, the solution, and the data. If the objective is to predict future costs under normal operating conditions, observations reflecting abnormal operating conditions should be deleted. Also examine the cost behavior pattern to determine whether it is linear. Scatter diagrams assist in both of these judgments. Finally, the results should make sense. When the relationships between total cost and several activity drivers are examined, it is possible to have a high R-squared purely by chance. Even though the relationship has a high R-squared, if it "doesn't make sense" there is probably something wrong.

Simple and Multiple Regression

Least-squares regression analysis is identified as "simple regression analysis" when there is only one independent variable and as "multiple regression analysis" when there are two or more independent variables. The general form for simple regression analysis is:

$$Y = a + bX$$

The general form for multiple regression analysis is:

$$Y = a + \Sigma b_i X_i$$

In this case, the subscript i is a general representation of each independent variable. When there are several independent variables, i is set equal to 1 for the first, 2 for the second, and so forth. The total variable costs of each independent variable is computed as $b_i X_i$, with b_i representing the variable cost per unit of independent variable X_i. The Greek symbol sigma, Σ, indicates that the costs of all independent variables are summed in determining total variable costs.

As an illustration, assume that Walnut Desk Company's costs are expressed as a function of the unit sales of its two products: executive desks and task desks. Fixed costs are $18,000 per month and the variable costs are $250 per executive desk and $120 per task desk. The mathematical representation of monthly costs with two variables is:

$$Y = a + b_1 X_1 + b_2 X_2$$

where

$$a = \$18{,}000$$
$$b_1 = \$250$$
$$b_2 = \$120$$
$$X_1 = \text{unit sales of executive desks}$$
$$X_2 = \text{unit sales of task desks}$$

During a month when 105 executive desks and 200 task desks are sold, Walnut Desk Company's estimated total costs are:

$$Y = \$18,000 + \$250(105) + \$120(200)$$
$$= \$68,250$$

In addition to estimating costs, multiple regression analysis can be used to determine the effect of individual product features on the market value of a product or service. The following Research Insight reports on a low-cost approach, using a model similar to multiple regression analysis to predict future health and life expectancy.

RESEARCH INSIGHT   Is Social Data a Cost Effective and Acceptable Predictor of Health?

According to the insurance industry, the underwriting costs of issuing a life insurance policy range up to $1,000, with a significant portion spent on medical tests and exams. Using information on 60,000 insurance applicants gathered by data-assembly and mining firms, Deloitte Consulting LLP has developed a model that predicts a person's risk for diseases (and life expectancy) related to lifestyle. The information is gathered from a variety of sources including: public records, surveys, online behavior such as surfing and purchases, and social networking sites. Independent variables in the model include: activity indicators, financial indicators, purchases related to health or obesity, and television consumption. Although Deloitte estimates insurers could save an average of $125 per applicant by using the model, insurance companies are concerned that efforts to use the model for decision making will likely raise a number of privacy issues and objections from state insurance commissions.

Source: Leslie Scism and Mark Maremont, "Insurers Test Data Profiles to Identify Risky Clients," *The Wall Street Journal*, November 19, 2010, pp. A1, A16.

MANAGERIAL DECISION   You are the Purchasing Manager

Your department has been experiencing increased activity in recent periods as the company has grown, and you have observed that the average cost per purchase order processed has been declining, but not at a constant rate. You have been given an estimate by the production manager of the number of purchase orders that will be processed next period and have been asked by the accounting department to provide within one hour an estimate of the cost to process those orders. How can the scatter diagram method help you to meet this deadline? [Answer, p. 14-20]

ADDITIONAL ISSUES IN COST ESTIMATION

LO3 Identify and discuss problems encountered in cost estimation.

We have mentioned several items to be wary of when developing cost estimating equations:

- Data that are not based on normal operating conditions.
- Nonlinear relationships between total costs and activity.
- Obtaining a high R-squared purely by chance.

Additional items of concern include:

- Changes in technology or prices.
- Matching activity and cost within each observation.
- Identifying activity cost drivers.

Changes in Technology and Prices

Changes in technology and prices make cost estimation and prediction difficult. When telephone companies changed from using human operators to using automated switching equipment to place long-distance telephone calls, cost estimates based on the use of human operators were of little or no value in predicting future costs. Care must be taken to make sure that data used in developing cost estimates are based on the existing technology. When this is not possible, professional judgment is required to make appropriate adjustments.

Only data reflecting a single price level should be used in cost estimation and prediction. If prices have remained stable in the past but then uniformly increase by 20 percent, cost-estimating equations based on data from previous periods will not accurately predict future costs. In this case, all that is required is a 20 percent increase in the prediction. Unfortunately, adjustments for price changes are seldom this simple. The prices of various cost elements are likely to change at different rates and at different times. Furthermore, there are probably several different price levels included in the past data used to develop cost-estimating equations. If data from different price levels are used, an attempt should be made to restate them to a single price level.

Matching Activity and Costs

The development of accurate cost-estimating equations requires the matching of the activity to related costs within each observation. This accuracy is often difficult to achieve because of the time lag between an activity and the recording of the cost of resources consumed by the activity. Current activities usually consume electricity, but the electric bill won't be received and recorded until next month. Driving an automobile requires routine maintenance for items such as lubrication and oil, but the auto can be driven several weeks or even months before the maintenance is required. Consequently, daily, weekly, and perhaps even monthly observations of miles driven and maintenance costs are unlikely to match the costs of oil and lubrication with the cost-driving activity, miles driven.

In general, the shorter the time period, the higher the probability of error in matching costs and activity. The cost analyst must carefully review the database to verify that activity and cost are matched within each observation. If matching problems are found, it may be possible to adjust the data (perhaps by moving the cost of electricity from one observation to another). Under other circumstances, it may be necessary to use longer periods to match costs and activity.

Identifying Activity Cost Drivers

Identifying the appropriate activity cost driver for a particular cost requires judgment and professional experience. In general, the cost driver should have a logical, causal relationship with costs. In many cases, the identity of the most appropriate activity cost driver, such as miles driven for the cost of automobile gasoline, is apparent. In other situations, where different activity cost drivers might be used, scatter diagrams and statistical measures, such as the coefficient of determination, are helpful in selecting the activity cost driver that best explains past variations in cost. When scatter diagrams are used, the analyst can study the dispersion of observations around the cost-estimating line. In general, a small dispersion is preferred. If regression analysis is used, the analyst considers the coefficient of determination. In general, a higher coefficient of determination is preferred. The relationship between the activity cost driver and the cost must seem logical, and the activity data must be available.

ALTERNATIVE COST DRIVER CLASSIFICATIONS

So far we have examined cost behavior and cost estimation using only a unit-level approach, which assumes changes in costs are best explained by changes in the number of units of product or service provided customers. This approach may have worked for **Carnegie Steel Company**, but it is inappropriate for multiproduct organizations, such as **General Electric**. The unit-level approach becomes increasingly inaccurate for analyzing cost behavior when organizations experience the following types of changes:

LO4 Describe and develop alternative classifications for activity cost drivers.

■ From labor-based to automated manufacturing,

■ From a limited number of related products to multiple products, with variations in product volume and complexity (and related costs), and

■ From a set of similar customers to a diverse set of customers.

Exhibit 14.8 illustrates the composition of total manufacturing costs for the past century, illustrating changes in the percentage of manufacturing costs for three major cost categories.

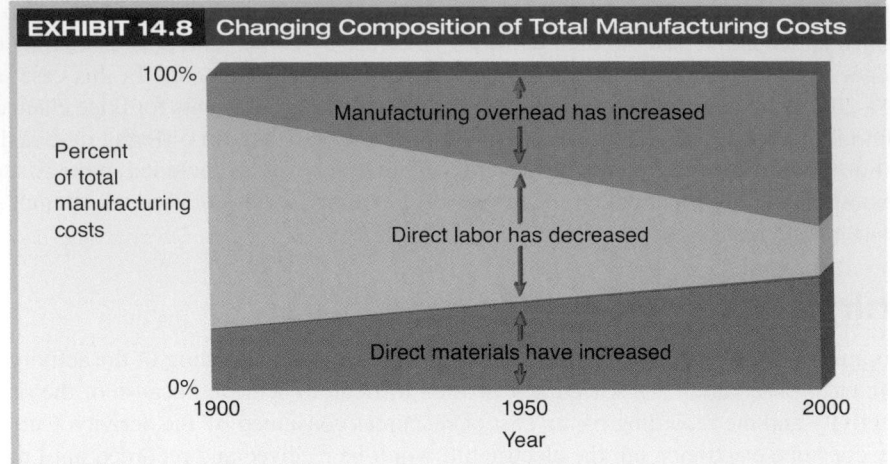

EXHIBIT 14.8   Changing Composition of Total Manufacturing Costs

1. **Direct materials**, the cost of primary raw materials converted into finished goods, have increased slightly as organizations purchase components they formerly fabricated. The word "direct" is used to indicate costs that are easily or directly traced to a finished product or service.

2. **Direct labor**, the wages earned by production employees for the time they spend converting raw materials into finished products, has decreased significantly as employees spend less time physically working on products and more time supporting automated production activities.

3. **Manufacturing overhead**, which includes all manufacturing costs other than direct materials and direct labor, has increased significantly due to automation, product diversity, and product complexity.

Changes in the composition of manufacturing costs have implications for the behavior of total costs and the responsiveness of costs to changes in cost drivers. Because direct materials and direct labor vary directly with the number of units, they are easy to measure. In the past, when manufacturing overhead was relatively small, it was possible to assume units of product or service was the primary cost driver. This is no longer true. Units of final product is no longer an adequate explanation of changes in manufacturing overhead for many organizations.

The past tendency to ignore overhead, while focusing on direct materials and direct labor, led one researcher to describe overhead-causing activities as "the hidden factory."[2] To better understand the hidden factory, several researchers have developed frameworks for categorizing cost-driving activities. The crucial feature of these frameworks is the inclusion of nonunit cost drivers. Depending on the characteristics of a particular organization, as well as management's information needs, there are an almost unlimited number of cost driver classification schemes. We consider two frequently applied cost driver classification schemes: one based on a manufacturing cost hierarchy and a second based on a customer cost hierarchy. We also illustrate variations of each.

Manufacturing Cost Hierarchy

The most well-known framework, developed by Cooper[3] and Cooper and Kaplan[4] for manufacturing situations, classifies activities into the following four categories.

1. A **unit-level activity** is performed *for each unit* of product produced. **Oneida Silversmiths** manufactures high-quality eating utensils. In the production of forks, the stamping of each fork into the prescribed shape is an example of a unit-level cost driver.

---

[2] Jeffrey G. Miller and Thomas E. Vollmann, "The Hidden Factory," *Harvard Business Review*, September-October 1985, pp. 142–150.

[3] Robin Cooper, "Cost Classification in Unit-Based and Activity-Based Manufacturing Cost Systems," *The Journal of Cost Management*, Fall 1990, pp. 4–14.

[4] Robin Cooper and Robert S. Kaplan, "Profit Priorities from Activity-Based Costing," *Harvard Business Review*, May-June 1991, pp. 130–135.

2. A **batch-level activity** is performed *for each batch* of product produced. At Oneida Silversmiths, a batch is a number of identical units (such as a fork of a specific design) produced at the same time. Batch-level activities include setting up the machines to stamp each fork in an identical manner, moving the entire batch between workstations (i.e., molding, stamping, and finishing), and inspecting the first unit in the batch to verify that the machines are set up correctly.

3. A **product-level activity** is performed *to support* the production of *each different type of product*. At Oneida Silversmiths, product-level activities for a specific pattern of fork include initially designing the fork, producing and maintaining the mold for the fork, and determining manufacturing operations for the fork.

4. A **facility-level activity** is performed *to maintain* general manufacturing capabilities. At Oneida Silversmiths, facility-level activities include plant management, building maintenance, property taxes, and electricity required to sustain the building.

Several additional examples of the costs driven by activities at each level are presented in Exhibit 14.9.

EXHIBIT 14.9	**Hierarchy of Activity Costs**	
Activity Level	**Reason for Activity**	**Examples of Activity Cost**
1. Unit level	Performed for each unit of product produced or sold	• Cost of raw materials • Cost of inserting a component • Utilities cost of operating equipment • Some costs of packaging • Sales commissions
2. Batch level	Performed for each batch of product produced or sold	• Cost of processing sales order • Cost of issuing and tracking work order • Cost of equipment setup • Cost of moving batch between workstations • Cost of inspection (assuming same number of units inspected in each batch)
3. Product level	Performed to support each different product that can be produced	• Cost of product development • Cost of product marketing such as advertising • Cost of specialized equipment • Cost of maintaining specialized equipment
4. Facility level	Performed to maintain general manufacturing capabilities	• Cost of maintaining general facilities such as buildings and grounds • Cost of nonspecialized equipment • Cost of maintaining nonspecialized equipment • Cost of real property taxes • Cost of general advertising • Cost of general administration such as the plant manager's salary

When using a cost hierarchy for analyzing and estimating costs, total costs are broken down into the different cost levels in the hierarchy, and a separate cost driver is determined for each level of cost. For example, using the above hierarchy, the costs that are related to the number of units produced (such as direct materials or direct labor) may have direct labor hours or machines hours as the cost driver; whereas, batch costs may be driven by the number of setups of production machines or the number of times materials are move from one machine to another. Other costs may be driven by the number of different products produced. Facility-level costs are generally regarded as fixed costs and do not vary unless capacity is increased or decreased.

Customer Cost Hierarchy

The manufacturing hierarchy presented is but one of many possible ways of classifying activities and their costs. Classification schemes should be designed to fit the organization and meet user needs. A merchandising organization or the sales division of a manufacturing organization might use the following hierarchy.

1. **Unit-level activity**: performed for each unit sold.
2. **Order-level activity**: performed for each sales order.
3. **Customer-level activity**: performed to obtain or maintain each customer.
4. **Facility-level activity**: performed to maintain the general marketing function

This classification scheme assists in answering questions concerning the cost of individual orders or individual customers.

If an organization sells to distinct market segments (for profit, not for profit, and government), the cost hierarchy can be modified as follows:

1. Unit-level activity
2. Order-level activity
3. Customer-level activity
4. **Market-segment-level activity**: performed to obtain or maintain operations in a segment.
5. Facility-level activity

The market-segment-level activities and their related costs differ with each market segment. This classification scheme assists in answering questions concerning the profitability of each segment.

Finally, an organization that completes unique projects for different market segments (such as buildings for **IBM** and the **U.S. Department of Defense**) can use the following hierarchy to determine the profitability of each segment:

1. **Project-level activity**: performed to support the completion of each project.
2. Market-segment-level activity
3. Facility-level activity

The possibilities are endless. The important point is that both the cost hierarchy and the costs included in the hierarchy be tailored to meet the specific circumstances of an organization and the interests of management. The following Business Insight box considers a possible cost hierarchy for the airline industry, with a closer examination of aircraft types as a cost driver.

BUSINESS INSIGHT   Aircraft Diversity is a Cost Driver

Cost hierarchies can be developed for almost any type of organization. The cost hierarchy for airlines might include seat miles, airports served, number of flights, point-to-point or hub and spoke scheduling, age of aircraft, and number of aircraft types. The diversity of aircraft impacts costs such as maintenance, parts inventories, ability to substitute aircraft and crew on a scheduled flight, pilot training, and crew assignments. Consider the differences between US Airways and AirTran in fleet complexity.

US Airways, formed through a series of mergers (the latest with America West), flies a wide variety of regional, national, and international routes. Because of its history of mergers and complex route structure, US Airways operates more than 450 aircraft consisting of 15 types, ranging from the De Havilland Dash 8-100 with 37 seats to the Airbus A330-300 with 266 seats. Although US Airways is striving to reduce the diversity of its fleet, which has been called a "hodgepodge," restructuring fixed assets takes many years. In the interim, US Airways struggles with high costs related to the number of aircraft types.

AirTran operates approximately 130 aircraft consisting of only two types, Boeing B717 and B737, from a single manufacturer. AirTran was the launch customer for the B717 that management regards as "ideally suited for the short-hall, high-frequency service that we primarily operate." Explaining the addition of the B737 to AirTran's fleet, management noted that Boeing discontinued the production of the B717 in 2006. By focusing on two types of Boeing aircraft, AirTran benefits from many efficiencies and avoids the types of costs US Airways incurs by having so many different types of planes.

Source: Christopher Palmeri, "A Cautionary Tale for Airline Mergers", *Business Week*, March 17, 2008, p. 66 and information in annual reports of AirTran and US Airways found at www.airtran.com and www.usairways.com.

MODULE-END REVIEW

Assume a local Subway reported the following results for April and May:

	April	May
Unit sales	2,100	2,700
Cost of food sold	$1,575	$2,025
Wages and salaries	1,525	1,675
Rent on building	1,500	1,500
Depreciation on equipment	200	200
Utilities	710	770
Supplies	225	255
Miscellaneous.	113	131
Total	$5,848	$6,556

Required

a. Identify each cost as being fixed, variable, or mixed.
b. Using the high-low method, estimate an equation for the cost of food, wages and salaries, rent on building, and total monthly costs.
c. Predict total costs for monthly volumes of 1,000 and 2,000 units.
d. Predict the average cost per unit at monthly volumes of 1,000 and 2,000 units. Explain why the average costs differ at these two volumes.

The solution is on page 14-31.

GUIDANCE ANSWER

MANAGERIAL DECISION You are the Purchasing Manager

One of the quickest methods for gaining a general understanding of the relationship between a given cost and its cost driver is to graph the relationship using data from several recent periods. As purchasing manager you could probably quickly obtain information about the amount of the total purchasing department costs and number of purchase orders processed for each of the most recent eight or ten periods. By graphing these data with costs on the vertical axis and number of purchase orders on the horizontal axis, you should be able to visually determine if there is an obvious behavioral pattern (variable, fixed, or mixed). Since costs have been declining as volume has increased, this would suggest that there are some fixed costs, and that they have been declining on a per unit basis as they are spread over an increasing number of purchase orders. Using two representative data points in the scatter diagram, you can plot a cost curve on the graph, and then use the data for those two points to calculate the estimated fixed and variable costs using the high-low cost estimation method. Using these cost estimates, you can predict the total cost for next period. This method may not give you a precise estimate of the cost, but coupled with your subjective estimate of cost based on your experience as manager of the department, it should give you more confidence than merely making a best guess. Hopefully, you will have an opportunity before presenting your budget for the next period to conduct additional analyses using more advanced methods.

DISCUSSION QUESTIONS

Q14-1. Briefly describe variable, fixed, mixed, and step costs and indicate how the total cost function of each changes as activity increases within a time period.

Q14-2. Why is presenting all costs of an organization as a function of a single independent variable, although useful in obtaining a general understanding of cost behavior, often not accurate enough to make specific decisions concerning products, services, or activities?

Q14-3. Explain the term "relevant range" and why it is important in estimating total costs.

Q14-4. How are variable and fixed costs determined using the high-low method of cost estimation?

Q14-5. Distinguish between cost estimation and cost prediction.

Q14-6.   Why is a scatter diagram helpful when used in conjunction with other methods of cost estimation?

Q14-7.   Identify two advantages of least-squares regression analysis as a cost estimation technique.

Q14-8.   Why is it important to match activity and costs within a single observation? When is this matching problem most likely to exist?

Q14-9.   During the past century, how have direct materials, direct labor, and manufacturing overhead changed as a portion of total manufacturing costs? What is the implication of the change in manufacturing overhead for cost estimation?

Q14-10. Distinguish between the unit-, batch-, product-, and facility-level activities of a manufacturing organization.

Assignments with the ✓ in the margin are available in an online homework system.
See the Preface of the book for details.

MINI EXERCISES

 M14-11. Classifying Cost Behavior   (LO1)
Classify the total costs of each of the following as variable, fixed, mixed, or step. Sales volume is the cost driver.

a. Salary of the department manager
b. Memory chips in a computer assembly plant
c. Real estate taxes
d. Salaries of quality inspectors when each inspector can evaluate a maximum of 1,000 units per day
e. Wages paid to production employees for the time spent working on products
f. Electric power in a factory
g. Raw materials used in production
h. Automobiles rented on the basis of a fixed charge per day plus an additional charge per mile driven
i. Sales commissions
j. Depreciation on office equipment

M14-12. Classifying Cost Behavior   (LO1)
Classify the total costs of each of the following as variable, fixed, mixed, or step.

a. Straight-line depreciation on a building
b. Maintenance costs at a hospital
c. Rent on a photocopy machine charged as a fixed amount per month plus an additional charge per copy
d. Cost of goods sold in a bookstore
e. Salaries paid to temporary instructors in a college as the number of course sessions varies
f. Lumber used by a house construction company
g. The costs of operating a research department
h. The cost of hiring a dance band for three hours
i. Laser printer paper for a department printer
j. Electric power in a restaurant

M14-13. Classifying Cost Behavior   (LO1)
For each of the following situations, select the most appropriate cost behavior pattern (as shown in the illustrations on the top of the next page) where the lines represent the cost behavior pattern, the vertical axis represents costs, the horizontal axis represents total volume, and the dots represent actual costs. Each pattern may be used more than once.

a. Variable costs per unit
b. Total fixed costs
c. Total mixed costs
d. Average fixed costs per unit
e. Total current manufacturing costs
f. Average variable costs
g. Total costs when employees are paid $10 per hour for the first 40 hours worked each week and $15 for each additional hour.
h. Total costs when employees are paid $10 per hour and guaranteed a minimum weekly wage of $200.

Graphs for Mini Exercise 14-13

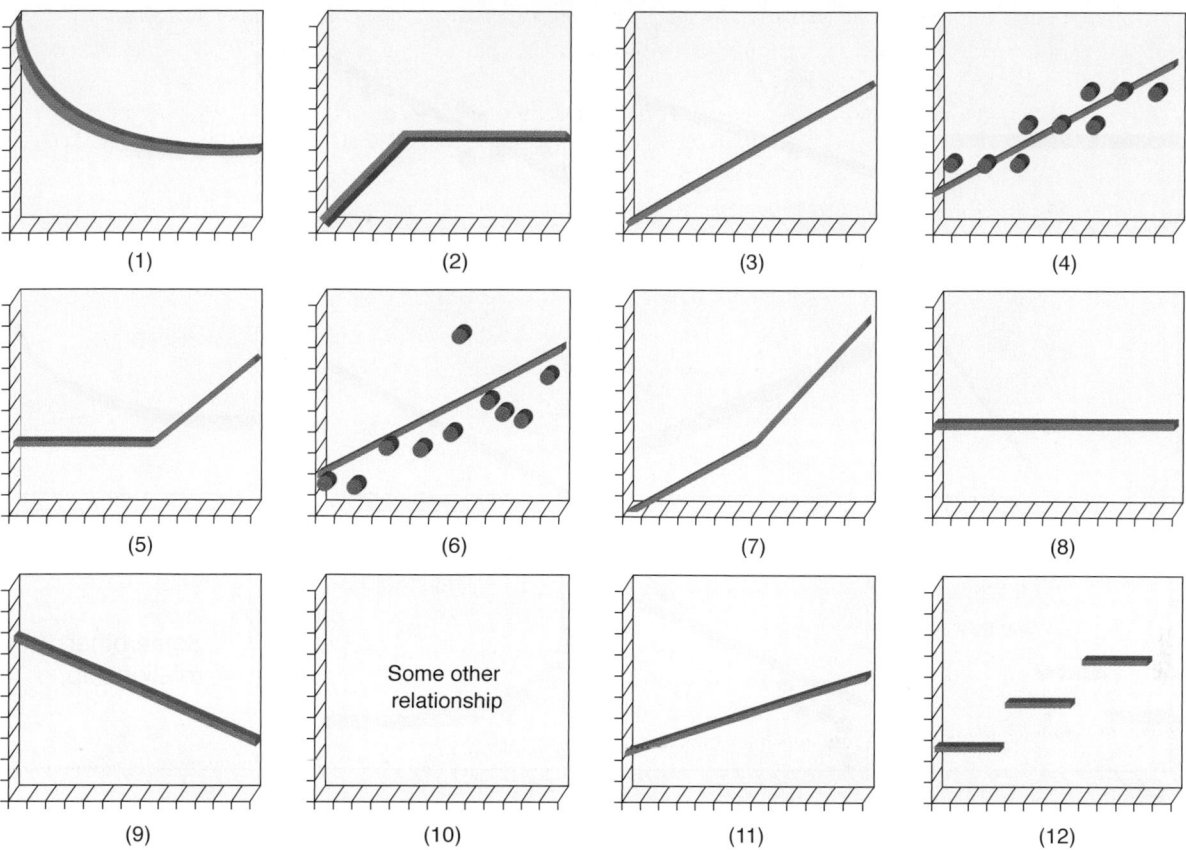

i. Total costs per day when a consultant is paid $200 per hour with a maximum daily fee of $1,000.
j. Total variable costs
k. Total costs for salaries of social workers where each social worker can handle a maximum of 20 cases
l. A water bill where a flat fee of $800 is charged for the first 100,000 gallons and additional water costs $0.005 per gallon
m. Total variable costs properly used to estimate step costs
n. Total materials costs
o. Rent on exhibit space at a convention

M14-14. Classifying Cost Behavior (LO1)

For each of the graphs displayed at the top of page 14-23, select the most appropriate cost behavior pattern where the lines represent the cost behavior pattern, the vertical axis represents total costs, the horizontal axis represents total volume, and the dots represent actual costs. Each pattern may be used more than once.

a. A cellular telephone bill when a flat fee is charged for the first 200 minutes of use per month and additional use costs $0.45 per minute
b. Total selling and administrative costs
c. Total labor costs when employees are paid per unit produced
d. Total overtime premium paid production employees
e. Average total cost per unit
f. Salaries of supervisors when each one can supervise a maximum of 10 employees
g. Total idle time costs when employees are paid for a minimum 40-hour week
h. Materials costs per unit
i. Total sales commissions
j. Electric power consumption in a restaurant
k. Total costs when high volumes of production require the use of overtime and obsolete equipment
l. A good linear approximation of actual costs
m. A linear cost estimation valid only within the relevant range

Graphs for Mini Exercise 14-14

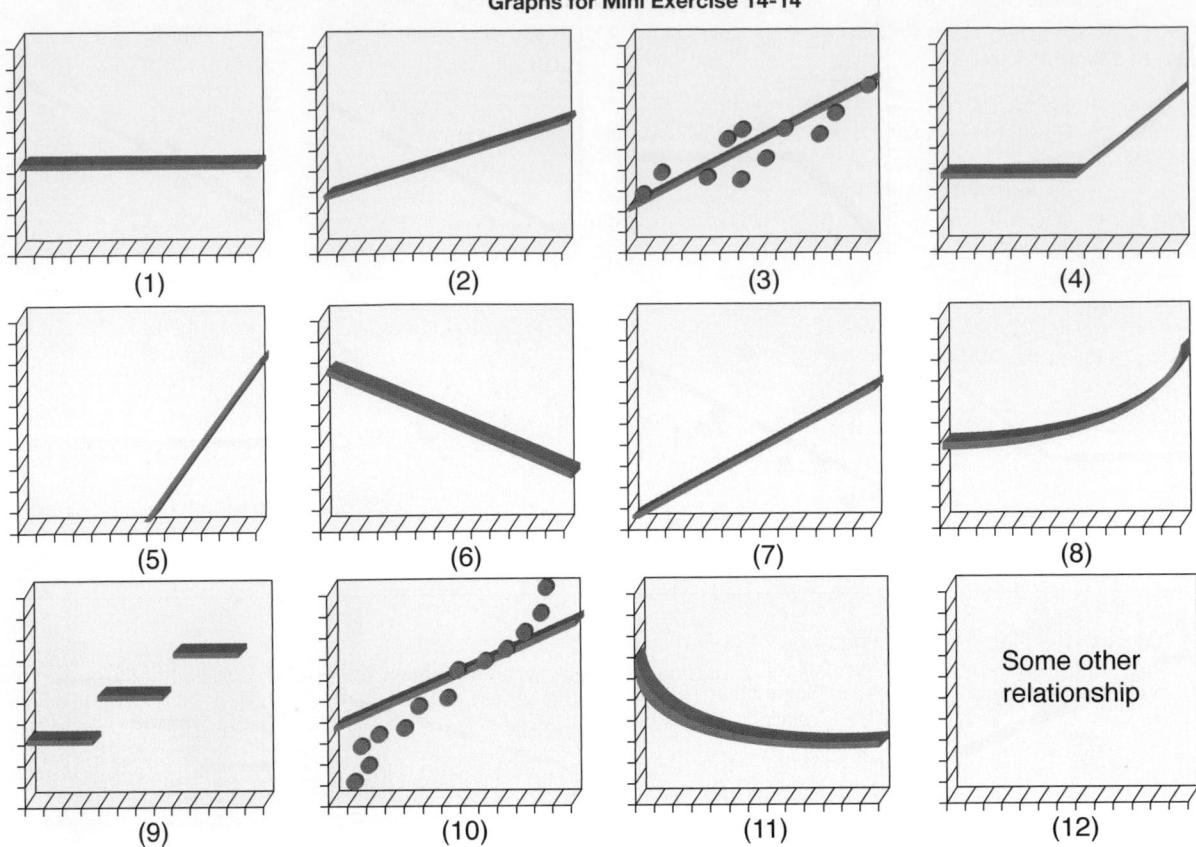

(1)   (2)   (3)   (4)

(5)   (6)   (7)   (8)

(9)   (10)   (11)   (12) Some other relationship

EXERCISES

E14-15.   Computing Average Unit Costs   (LO2)

The total monthly operating costs of Chili To Go are:

$$\$10,000 + \$0.40X$$

where

X = servings of chili

Required

a. Determine the average cost per serving at each of the following monthly volumes: 100; 1,000; 5,000; and 10,000

b. Determine the monthly volume at which the average cost per serving is $0.60.

E14-16.   Automatic versus Manual Processing   (LO2)

Photo Station Company operates a printing service for customers with digital cameras. The current service, which requires employees to download photos from customer cameras, has monthly operating costs of $5,000 plus $0.20 per photo printed. Management is evaluating the desirability of acquiring a machine that will allow customers to download and make prints without employee assistance. If the machine is acquired, the monthly fixed costs will increase to $10,000 and the variable costs of printing a photo will decline to $0.04 per photo.

Required

a. Determine the total costs of printing 20,000 and 50,000 photos per month:
   1. With the current employee-assisted process.
   2. With the proposed customer self-service process.

b. Determine the monthly volume at which the proposed process becomes preferable to the current process.

E14-17.   Automatic versus Manual Processing   (LO2)

Mid-Town Copy Service processes 1,800,000 photocopies per month at its mid-town service center. Approximately 50 percent of the photocopies require collating. Collating is currently performed by high school and college students who are paid $8 per hour. Each student collates an average of 5,000 copies per hour. Management is contemplating the lease of an automatic collating machine that has a monthly capacity of 5,000,000 photocopies, with lease and operating costs totaling $1,550, plus $0.05 per 1,000 units collated.

Required
a. Determine the total costs of collating 500,000 and 1,500,000 per month:
  1. With student help.
  2. With the collating machine.
b. Determine the monthly volume at which the automatic process becomes preferable to the manual process.

E14-18. High-Low Cost Estimation (LO2)
Assume the local DHL delivery service hub has the following information available about fleet miles and operating costs:

DHL (DHL)

Year	Miles	Operating Costs
2010	556,000	$177,000
2011	684,000	209,000

Required
Use the high-low method to develop a cost-estimating equation for total annual operating costs.

E14-19. Scatter Diagrams and High-Low Cost Estimation (LO2, 3)
Assume the local Pearle Vision has the following information on the number of sales orders received and order-processing costs.

Pearle Vision

Month	Sales Orders	Order-Processing Costs
1	3,000	$32,000
2	1,500	22,400
3	4,000	52,000
4	2,800	31,200
5	2,300	25,600
6	1,000	16,000
7	2,000	24,000

Required
a. Use information from the high- and low-volume months to develop a cost-estimating equation for monthly order-processing costs.
b. Plot the data on a scatter diagram. Using the information from representative high- and low-volume months, develop a cost-estimating equation for monthly production costs.
c. What factors might have caused the difference in the equations developed for requirements (a) and (b)?

E14-20. Scatter Diagrams and High-Low Cost Estimation (LO2, 3)
From April 1 through October 31, Knox County Highway Department hires temporary employees to mow and clean the right-of-way along county roads. The County Road Commissioner has asked you to help her in determining the variable labor cost of mowing and cleaning a mile of road. The following information is available regarding current-year operations:

Month	Miles Mowed and Cleaned	Labor Costs
April	350	$8,000
May	300	7,500
June	400	9,000
July	250	5,500
August	375	8,500
September	200	5,000
October	100	4,800

Required

a. Use the information from the high- and low-volume months to develop a cost-estimating equation for monthly labor costs.

b. Plot the data on a scatter diagram. Using the information from representative high- and low-volume months, use the high-low method to develop a cost-estimating equation for monthly labor costs.

c. What factors might have caused the difference in the equations developed for requirements (a) and (b)?

d. Adjust the equation developed in requirement (b) to incorporate the effect of an anticipated 7 percent increase in wages.

Papa John's (PZZA)

E14-21. Cost Behavior Analysis in a Restaurant: High-Low Cost Estimation (LO2)

Assume a Papa John's restaurant has the following information available regarding costs at representative levels of monthly sales:

	Monthly sales in units		
	5,000	8,000	10,000
Cost of food sold	$10,000	$16,000	$20,000
Wages and fringe benefits	4,250	4,400	4,500
Fees paid delivery help.............	1,250	2,000	2,500
Rent on building..................	1,200	1,200	1,200
Depreciation on equipment	600	600	600
Utilities	500	560	600
Supplies (soap, floor wax, etc.)	150	180	200
Administrative costs...............	1,300	1,300	1,300
Total	$19,250	$26,240	$30,900

Required

a. Identify each cost as being variable, fixed, or mixed.

b. Use the high-low method to develop a schedule identifying the amount of each cost that is fixed per month or variable per unit. Total the amounts under each category to develop an equation for total monthly costs.

c. Predict total costs for a monthly sales volume of 9,500 units.

E14-22. Developing an Equation from Average Costs (LO2)

The America Dog and Cat Hotel is a pet hotel located in Las Vegas. Assume that in March, when dog-days (occupancy) were at an annual low of 500, the average cost per dog-day was $21. In July, when dog-days were at a capacity level of 4,000, the average cost per dog-day was $7.

Required

a. Develop an equation for monthly operating costs.

b. Determine the average cost per dog-day at an annual volume of 24,000 dog-days.

E14-23. Selecting an Independent Variable: Scatter Diagrams (LO2, 3)

Peak Production Company produces backpacks that are sold to sporting goods stores throughout the Rocky Mountains. Presented is information on production costs and inventory changes for five recent months:

	January	February	March	April	May
Finished goods inventory in units:					
Beginning	30,000	40,000	50,000	30,000	60,000
Manufactured........	60,000	90,000	80,000	90,000	100,000
Available............	90,000	130,000	130,000	120,000	160,000
Sold	(50,000)	(80,000)	(100,000)	(60,000)	(120,000)
Ending	40,000	50,000	30,000	60,000	40,000
Manufacturing costs...	$250,000	$450,000	$400,000	$400,000	$500,000

Required

a. With the aid of scatter diagrams, determine whether units sold or units manufactured is a better predictor of manufacturing costs.

b. Prepare an explanation for your answer to requirement (a).

c. Which independent variable, units sold or units manufactured, should be a better predictor of selling costs? Why?

E14-24. Selecting a Basis for Predicting Shipping Expenses (Requires Computer Spreadsheet*) (LO2, 3)

Penn Company assembles and sells computer boards in western Pennsylvania. In an effort to improve the planning and control of shipping expenses, management is trying to determine which of three variables—units shipped, weight shipped, or sales value of units shipped—has the closest relationship with shipping expenses. The following information is available:

Month	Units Shipped	Weight Shipped (lbs.)	Sales Value of Units Shipped	Shipping Expenses
May.............	3,000	6,200	$100,000	$ 5,500
June	5,000	8,000	110,000	7,600
July.............	4,000	8,100	80,000	6,500
August	7,000	10,000	114,000	10,300
September	6,000	7,000	140,000	8,500
October	4,500	8,000	160,000	8,100

Required

a. With the aid of a spreadsheet program, determine whether units shipped, weight shipped, or sales value of units shipped has the closest relationship with shipping expenses.

b. Using the independent variable that appears to have the closest relationship to shipping expenses, develop a cost-estimating equation for total monthly shipping expenses.

c. Use the equation developed in requirement (b) to predict total shipping expenses in a month when 5,000 units, weighing 7,000 lbs., with a total sales value of $114,000 are shipped.

PROBLEMS

P14-25. High-Low and Scatter Diagrams with Implications for Regression (LO2, 3)

Trumpet Bagels produces and sells bagels at each of its restaurants. Presented is monthly cost and sales information for one of Trumpet's restaurants.

Month	Sales (Dozens)	Total Costs
January...............	8,000	$28,800
February..............	6,500	26,400
March	4,500	20,400
April	2,000	19,200
May..................	5,500	21,600
June	6,000	23,400

Required

a. Using the high-low method, develop a cost-estimating equation for total monthly costs.

b. 1. Plot the equation developed in requirement (a).

   2. Using the same graph, develop a scatter diagram of all observations for the bagel shop. Select representative high and low values and draw a second cost-estimating equation.

c. Which is a better predictor of future costs? Why?

d. If you decided to develop a cost-estimating equation using least-squares regression analysis, should you include all the observations? Why or why not?

e. Mention two reasons that the least-squares regression is superior to the high-low and scatter diagram methods of cost estimation.

---

* This exercise and several subsequent assignments require the use of a computer spreadsheet such as Excel® to solve. This assignment assumes previous knowledge of computer spreadsheets.

P14-26. Multiple Cost Drivers   (LO4)

Scottsdale Ltd. manufactures a variety of high-volume and low-volume products to customer demand. Presented is information on 2011 manufacturing overhead and activity cost drivers.

Level	Total Cost	Units of Cost Driver
Unit	$500,000	20,000 machine hours
Batch	100,000	1,000 customer orders
Product	200,000	50 products

Product X1 required 2,000 machine hours to fill 10 customer orders for a total of 8,000 units.

Required

a. Assuming all manufacturing overhead is estimated and predicted on the basis of machine hours, determine the predicted total overhead costs to produce the 8,000 units of product X1.

b. Assuming manufacturing overhead is estimated and predicted using separate rates for machine hours, customer orders, and products (a multiple-level cost hierarchy), determine the predicted total overhead costs to produce the 8,000 units of product X1.

c. Calculate the error in predicting manufacturing overhead using machine hours versus using multiple cost drivers. Indicate whether the use of only machine hours results in overpredicting or underpredicting the costs to produce 8,000 units of product X1.

d. Determine the error in the prediction of X1 batch-level costs resulting from the use of only machine hours. Indicate whether the use of only machine hours results in overpredicting or underpredicting the batch-level costs of product X1.

e. Determine the error in the prediction of X1 product-level costs resulting from the use of only machine hours. Indicate whether the use of only machine hours results in overpredicting or underpredicting the product-level costs of product X1.

 P14-27. Unit- and Batch-Level Cost Drivers   (LO4)

KC, a fast-food restaurant, serves fried chicken, fried fish, and French fries. The managers have estimated the costs of a batch of fried chicken for KC's all-you-can-eat Friday Fried Fiesta. Each batch must be 100 pieces. The chicken is precut by the chain headquarters and sent to the stores in 10-piece bags. Each bag costs $3. Preparing a batch of 100 pieces of chicken with KC's special coating takes one employee two hours. The current wage rate is $8 per hour. Another cost driver is the cost of putting fresh oil into the fryers. New oil, costing $5, is used for each batch.

Required

a. Determine the cost of preparing one batch of 100 pieces.

b. If management projects that it will sell 300 pieces of fried chicken, determine the total batch and unit costs.

c. If management estimates the sales to be 350 pieces, determine the total costs.

d. How much will the batch costs increase if the government raises the minimum wage to $10 per hour?

e. If management decided to reduce the number of pieces in a batch to 50, determine the cost of preparing 350 pieces. Assume that the batch would take half as long to prepare, and management wants to replace the oil after 50 pieces are cooked.

P14-28. Optimal Batch Size   (LO4)

This is a continuation of parts "c" and "e" of P14-27.

Required

Should management reduce the batch size to 50? Why or why not?

MANAGEMENT APPLICATIONS

MA14-29. Negative Fixed Costs   (LO3)

"This is crazy!" exclaimed the production supervisor as he reviewed the work of his new assistant. "You and that computer are telling me that my fixed costs are negative! Tell me, how did you get these negative fixed costs, and what am I supposed to do with them?"

Required

Explain to the supervisor the meaning of the negative "fixed costs" and what can be done with them.

MA14-30. Significance of High R-Squared (LO3)

Oliver Morris had always been suspicious of "newfangled mathematical stuff," and the most recent suggestion of his new assistant merely confirmed his belief that schools are putting a lot of useless junk in students' heads. It seems that after an extensive analysis of historical data, the assistant suggested that the number of pounds of scrap was the best basis for predicting manufacturing overhead. In response to Mr. Morris's rage, the slightly intimidated assistant indicated that of the 35 equations he tried, pounds of scrap had the highest coefficient of determination with manufacturing overhead.

Required

Comment on Morris's reaction. Is it justified? Is it likely that the number of pounds of scrap is a good basis for predicting manufacturing overhead? Is it a feasible basis for predicting manufacturing overhead?

MA14-31. Estimating Machine Repair Costs (LO3)

In an attempt to determine the best basis for predicting machine repair costs, the production supervisor accumulated daily information on these costs and production over a one-month period. Applying simple regression analysis to the data, she obtained the following estimating equation:

$$Y = \$800 - \$2.601X$$

where

$$Y = \textbf{total daily machine repair costs}$$
$$X = \textbf{daily production in units}$$

Because of the negative relationship between repair costs and production, she was somewhat skeptical of the results, even though the R-squared was a respectable 0.765.

Required

a. What is the most likely explanation of the negative variable costs?

b. Suggest an alternative procedure for estimating machine repair costs that might prove more useful.

MA14-32. Ethical Problem Uncovered by Cost Estimation (LO3)

Phoenix Management Company owns and provides management services for several shopping centers. After five years with the company, Mike Moyer was recently promoted to the position of manager of X-Town, an 18-store mall on the outskirts of a downtown area. When he accepted the assignment, Mike was told that he would hold the position for only a couple of years because X-Town would likely be torn down to make way for a new sports stadium. Mike was also told that if he did well in this assignment, he would be in line for heading one of the company's new 200-store operations that were currently in the planning stage.

While reviewing X-Town's financial records for the past few years, Mike observed that last year's oil consumption was up by 8 percent, even though the number of heating degree days was down by 4 percent. Somewhat curious, Mike uncovered the following information:

- X-Town is heated by forced-air oil heat. The furnace is five years old and has been well maintained.
- Fuel oil is kept in four 5,000-gallon underground oil tanks. The oil tanks were installed 25 years ago.
- Replacing the tanks would cost $80,000. If pollution was found, cleanup costs could go as high as $2,000,000, depending on how much oil had leaked into the ground and how far it had spread.
- Replacing the tanks would add more congestion to X-Town's parking situation.

Required

What should Mike do? Explain.

MA14-33. Activity Cost Drivers and Cost Estimation (LO3, 4)

Blue Ridge Ice Cream Company produces ten varieties of ice cream in large vats, several thousand gallons at a time. The ice cream is distributed to several categories of customers. Some ice cream is packaged in large containers and sold to college and university food services. Some is packaged in half-gallon or small containers and sold through wholesale distributors to grocery stores. Finally, some is packaged in a variety of individual servings and sold directly to the public from trucks owned and operated by Blue Ridge. Management has always assumed that costs fluctuated with the volume of ice cream, and cost-estimating equations have been based on the following cost function:

Estimated costs = Fixed costs + Variable costs per gallon × Production in gallons

Lately, however, this equation has not been a very accurate predictor of total costs. At the same time, management has noticed that the volumes and varieties of ice cream sold through the three distinct distribution channels have fluctuated from month to month.

Required
a. What *relevant* major assumption is inherent in the cost-estimating equation currently used by Blue Ridge?
b. Why might Blue Ridge wish to develop a cost-estimating equation that recognizes the hierarchy of activity costs? Explain.
c. Develop the general form of a more accurate cost-estimating equation for Blue Ridge. Clearly label and explain all elements of the equation, and provide specific examples of costs for each element.

MA14-34. Multiple Regression Analysis for a Special Decision (Requires Computer Spreadsheet) (LO2, 3)
For billing purposes, Central City Health Clinic classifies its services into one of four major procedures, X1 through X4. A local business has proposed that Central City provide health services to its employees and their families at the following set rates per procedure:

X1 . . . . . . $ 45
X2 90
X3 60
X4 105

Because these rates are significantly below the current rates charged for these services, management has asked for detailed cost information on each procedure. The following information is available for the most recent 12 months.

Month	Total Cost	X1	X2	X3	X4
1	$23,000	30	100	205	75
2	25,000	38	120	180	90
3	27,000	50	80	140	150
4	19,000	20	90	120	100
5	20,000	67	50	160	80
6	27,000	90	75	210	105
7	25,500	20	110	190	110
8	21,500	15	120	175	80
9	26,000	60	85	125	140
10	22,000	20	90	100	140
11	22,800	20	70	150	130
12	26,500	72	60	200	120

Required
a. Use multiple regression analysis to determine the unit cost of each procedure. How much variation in monthly cost is explained by your cost-estimating equation?
b. Evaluate the rates proposed by the local business. Assuming Central City has excess capacity and no employees of the local business currently patronize the clinic, what are your recommendations regarding the proposal?
c. Evaluate the rates proposed by the local business. Assuming Central City is operating at capacity and would have to turn current customers away if it agrees to provide health services to the local business, what are your recommendations regarding the proposal?

MA14-35. Cost Estimation, Interpretation, and Analysis (Requires Computer Spreadsheet) (LO2, 3)

Piedmont Table Company produces two styles of tables, dining room and kitchen. Presented is monthly information on production volume and manufacturing costs:

Period	Total Manufacturing Costs	Total Tables Produced	Dining Room Tables Produced	Kitchen Tables Produced
June 2010..........	$46,650	250	50	200
July...............	50,888	205	105	100
August	60,630	285	105	180
September	39,743	210	40	170
October	42,120	175	75	100
November..........	52,575	210	110	100
December..........	53,018	245	90	155
January 2011	47,325	250	50	200
February...........	47,235	220	70	150
March	44,475	180	80	100
April	97,800	315	180	135
May...............	59,933	280	105	175
June	52,043	255	75	180
July...............	55,380	235	110	125
August	46,223	195	85	110
September	60,435	260	120	140
October	53,708	250	90	160
November..........	57,600	270	100	170
December..........	37,650	165	60	105

Required

a. Use the high-low method to develop a cost-estimating equation for total manufacturing costs. Interpret the meaning of the "fixed" costs and comment on the results.

b. Use the chart feature of a spreadsheet to develop a scatter graph of total manufacturing costs and total units produced. Use the graph to identify any unusual observations.

c. Excluding any unusual observations, use the high-low method to develop a cost-estimating equation for total manufacturing costs. Comment on the results, comparing them with the results in requirement (a).

d. Use simple regression analysis to develop a cost-estimating equation for total manufacturing costs. What advantages does simple regression analysis have in comparison with the high-low method of cost estimation? Why must analysts carefully evaluate the data used in simple regression analysis?

e. A customer has offered to purchase 50 dining room tables for $220 per table. Management has asked your advice regarding the desirability of accepting the offer. What advice do you have for management? Additional analysis is required.

MA14-36. Simple and Multiple Regression (Requires Computer Spreadsheet) (LO2, 3)

Kevin Miller is employed by a mail-order distributor and reconditions used desktop computers, broadband routers, and laser printers. Kevin is paid $12 per hour, plus an extra $6 per hour for work in excess of 40 hours per week. The distributor just announced plans to outsource all reconditioning work. Because the distributor is pleased with the quality of Kevin's work, he has been asked to enter into a long-term contract to recondition used desktop computers at a rate of $40 per computer, plus all parts. The distributor also offered to provide all necessary equipment at a rate of $200 per month. Kevin has been informed that he should plan on reconditioning as many computers as he can handle, up to a maximum of 20 per week.

Kevin has room in his basement to set up a work area, but he is unsure of the economics of accepting the contract, as opposed to working for a local Radio Stuff store at $11 per hour. Data related to the time spent and the number of units of each type of electronic equipment Kevin has reconditioned in recent weeks is as follows:

Week	Laser Printers	Broadband Routers	Desktop Computers	Total Units	Total Hours
1.......	4	5	5	14	40
2.......	0	7	6	13	42
3.......	4	3	7	14	40
4.......	0	2	12	14	46
5.......	11	6	4	21	48
6.......	5	8	3	16	44
7.......	5	8	3	16	44
8.......	5	6	5	16	43
9.......	2	6	10	18	53
10.......	8	4	6	18	46
Total.......				160	446

Required

Assuming he wants to work an average of 40 hours per week, what should Kevin do?

SOLUTIONS TO REVIEW PROBLEMS

Mid-Module Review

Solution
a. Variable cost
b. Mixed cost
c. Committed fixed cost
d. Variable cost
e. Step cost
f. Discretionary fixed cost
g. Fixed cost (Without knowing the purpose of renting the car, the cost cannot be classified as committed or discretionary.)
h. Mixed cost
i. Step cost
j. Discretionary fixed cost

Module-End Review

Solution
a. Fixed costs are easily identified. They are the same at each activity level. Variable and mixed costs are determined by dividing the total costs for an item at two activity levels by the corresponding units of activity. The quotients of the variable cost items will be identical at both activity levels. The quotients of the mixed costs will differ, being lower at the higher activity level because the fixed costs are being spread over a larger number of units.

Cost	Behavior
Cost of food sold	Variable
Wages and salaries	Mixed
Rent on building...............	Fixed
Depreciation on equipment	Fixed
Utilities	Mixed
Supplies	Mixed
Miscellaneous................	Mixed

b. The cost of food sold was classified as a variable cost. Hence, the cost of food may be determined by dividing the total costs at either observation by the corresponding number of units.

$$b = \frac{\$1,575 \text{ total variable costs}}{2,100 \text{ units}}$$

$$= \$0.75X$$

Wages and salaries were previously classified as a mixed cost. Hence, the cost of wages and salaries is determined using the high-low method.

(variable cost) $b = \dfrac{\$1,675 - \$1,525}{2,700 - 2,100}$

$$= 0.25X$$

(fixed cost) $a = \$1,525 \text{ total cost} - (\$0.25 \times 2,100) \text{ variable cost}$

$$= \$1,000$$

Rent on building was classified as a fixed cost.

$$a = \$1,500$$

Total monthly costs most likely follow a mixed cost behavior pattern. Hence, they can be determined using the high-low method.

$$b = \frac{\$6,556 - \$5,848}{2,700 - 2,100}$$

$$= \$1.18X$$

$$a = \$5,848 - (\$1.18 \times 2,100)$$

$$= \$3,370$$

$$\text{Total costs} = \$3,370 + \$1.18X$$

where

$$X = \text{unit sales}$$

c. and *d.*

Volume	Total Costs	Average Cost per Unit
1,000	$3,370 + ($1.18 × 1,000) = $4,550	$4,550/1,000 = $4.550
2,000	$3,370 + ($1.18 × 2,000) = $5,730	$5,730/2,000 = $2.865

The average costs differ at 1,000 and 2,000 units because the fixed costs are being spread over a different number of units. The larger the number of units, the smaller the average fixed cost per unit.

NETFLIX

During the first decade of the 21st century, the profits of many established businesses were rocked by an economic downturn, soaring energy costs, and increased competition facilitated by innovation and technology. While many new businesses prospered by taking advantage of emerging technologies, innovations, and a competitive cost structure, many less innovative, established firms, utilizing older technologies and less competitive cost structures, struggled to survive. The success of Netflix, especially its rivalry with Blockbuster, is an example of the impact of technology, innovation, and cost structure on sales volume and firm profitability.

Established in the 1980s, Blockbuster, Inc., originally rented and sold VHS video tapes through a network of stores it owned or franchised. In 2002, Blockbuster's management described their company as "the world's leading provider of rentable home videocassettes, DVDs and video games, with nearly 8,000 stores in the United States, its territories and 26 other countries as of December 31, 2001."

Technological innovations, including the digitization of video and the dramatic increase in the use of the Internet, provided an opportunity for a new competitor, Netflix, to offer DVD rentals through the Internet. By using the Internet to market and the U.S. Postal Service to deliver videos to customers from a small number of distribution centers, Netflix was able to avoid the fixed costs of having physical stores, while providing individual customers a larger selection of DVDs, with a lower inventory investment. Additionally, using the Internet to order and the Postal Service to deliver and return videos, Netflix made it possible for customers to avoid trips to a store. With convenience, competitive pricing, and high levels of customer satisfaction, Netflix grew rapidly from fewer than 1 million subscribers in 2002 to more than 12 million by the end of 2010. Much of Netflix's growth came at the expense of Blockbuster, which struggled to remain competitive and profitable.

To reduce fixed costs and inventory investments, Blockbuster closed many retail outlets and implemented a service similar to Netflix's with online ordering and mail delivery/return of DVDs. In addition, Blockbuster offered customers the option of in-store pickup/return. Meanwhile, Netflix, using what its management describes as a "scalable, low-cost business model," opened more than 40 distribution centers providing one-day delivery to most of its customers. Raising the competitive bar, Netflix added video streaming to personal computers and televisions at a small additional charge. By the end of 2010, Blockbuster was operating under bankruptcy protection, and Netflix billed itself as "the world's largest subscription service streaming movies and TV episodes over the Internet and sending DVDs by mail."

After pushing Blockbuster to bankruptcy, Netflix mail-order and online streaming service is becoming a threat to premium cable services. In 2010, as Netflix reported a 52

Cost-Volume-Profit Analysis and Planning

LEARNING OBJECTIVES

LO1 Identify the uses and limitations of traditional cost-volume-profit analysis. (p. 15-3)

LO2 Prepare and contrast contribution and functional income statements. (p. 15-6)

LO3 Apply cost-volume-profit analysis to find a break-even point and for preliminary profit planning. (p. 15-8)

LO4 Analyze the profitability and sales mix of a multiple-product firm. (p. 15-13)

LO5 Apply operating leverage ratio to assess opportunities for profit and the risks of loss. (p. 15-16)

percent increase in subscribers during the past 12 months, Time Warner stated it anticipated losing 1.5 million HBO subscribers during the current year. Although Time Warner's management attributed the loss to difficult economic conditions, many industry analysts attributed at least some of the losses to competition from Netflix's online streaming service, which in 2010 became the largest source of U.S. Internet traffic during peak evening hours.

One key to business success is finding the best cost structure to profitably serve customers at a competitive price. When competing with Blockbuster in 2002, Netflix had a cost structure with relatively low fixed costs and relatively high variable costs. This low fixed, high variable cost structure provided Netflix with competitive average costs for their 2002 volume. At a much higher subscriber base, to compete with cable companies, Netflix added streaming services that have higher fixed costs for servers and licenses for the use of copyrighted materials and lower variable costs for videos delivered via Internet streaming rather than the Postal Service.

In September of 2011 Netflix announced plans to completely separate streaming and DVD mailing services with streaming services provided under the "Netflix" brand and DVD mailing services provided by "Qwickster." Explaining the change Netflix CEO Reed Hastings observed that: "streaming and DVD by mail are really becoming two different businesses, with very different cost structures, that

need to be marketed differently, and we need to let each grow and operate independently."

Subscribers and investors reacted negatively to the announcement, which would have required subscribers using both services to use two separate web sites for ordering and receive two separate bills. Realizing their public relations error, Netflix quickly backtracked. Apologizing to offended subscribers, Hastings indicated that both services would continue to be marketed under the Netflix brand and that customers who subscribe to both services would be able to use a single web site and would receive a single bill.

The financial success of Netflix illustrates that the optimal cost structure can vary over time, depending on competitive conditions, technology, and the volume of activity. This module focuses on the relationships among cost structures, volume, and profit and planning for future profits.

Sources: Nick Wingfield and Sam Schechner, "No Longer Tiny, Netflix Gets Respect—and Creates Fear," *The Wall Street Journal*, December 6, 2010, pp. B1, B5; Nat Worden, "Cable TV Loses Subscribers," *The Wall Street Journal*, November 10, 2010, p. B7; Peter Svensson (AP Technology Writer), "Cable subscribers flee, but is Internet to blame?" *YAHOO News*, November 5, 2010; Ronald Grover, "Netflix: Premium Cable's Worst Nightmare," *Bloomberg Businessweek*, September 20, 2010, pp.21-22; Cliff Edwards, "Netflix's Breakout Move," *Business Week Online*, January 3, 2008, p.2.; Ethan Smith, "Netflix Separates DVD and Streaming Services," *The Wall Street Journal*, September 19, 2011; Stu Woo, "Under Fire, Netflix Rewinds DVD Plan," *The Wall Street Journal*, October 11, 2011; annual reports and press releases available at *www.blockbuster.com, www.netflix.com*.

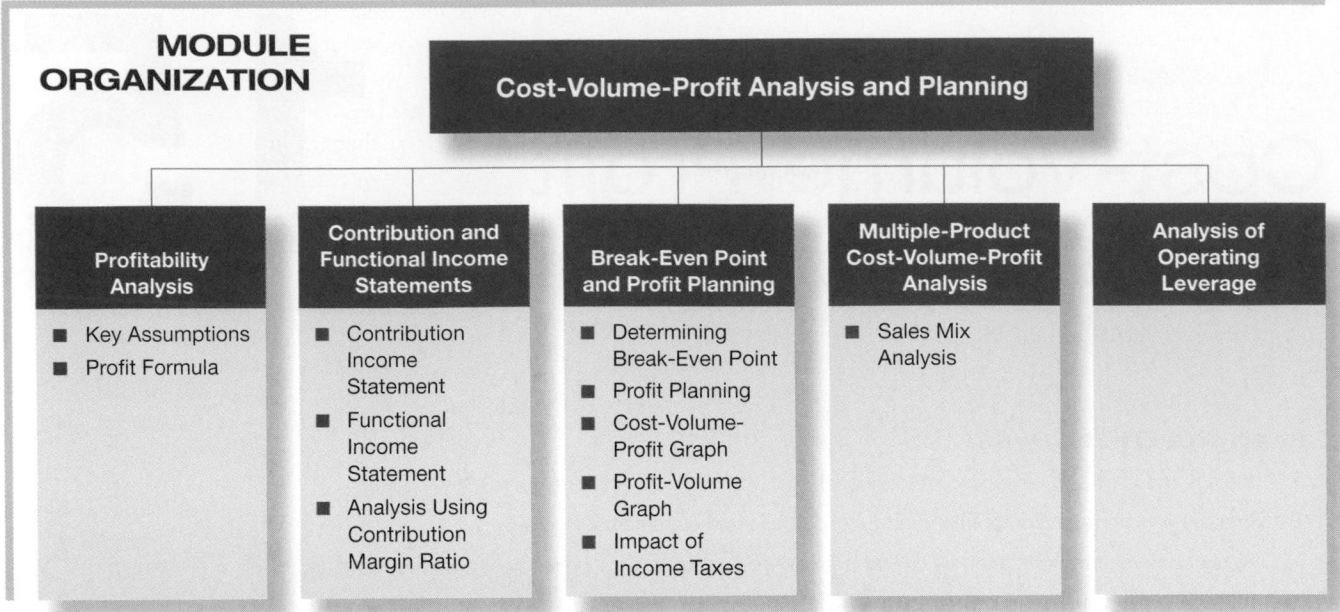

This module introduces basic approaches to profitability analysis and planning. We consider single-product, multiple-product, and service organizations; income taxes, sales mix, and the effects of cost structure on the relation between profit potential and the risk of loss.

PROFITABILITY ANALYSIS

LO1 Identify the uses and limitations of traditional cost-volume-profit analysis.

Profitability analysis involves examining the relationships among revenues, costs, and profits. Performing profitability analysis requires an understanding of selling prices and the behavior of activity cost drivers. Profitability analysis is widely used in the economic evaluation of existing or proposed products or services. Typically, it is performed before decisions are finalized in the operating budget for a future period.

Cost-volume-profit (CVP) analysis is a technique used to examine the relationships among the total volume of an independent variable, total costs, total revenues, and profits for a time period (typically a quarter or year). With CVP analysis, volume refers to a single activity cost driver, such as unit sales, that is assumed to correlate with changes in revenues, costs, and profits.

Cost-volume-profit analysis is useful in the early stages of planning because it provides an easily understood framework for discussing planning issues and organizing relevant data. CVP analysis is widely used by for-profit as well as not-for-profit organizations. It is equally applicable to service, merchandising, and manufacturing firms.

In for-profit organizations, CVP analysis is used to answer such questions as these: How many photocopies must the local **Kinko's** produce to earn a profit of $80,000? At what dollar sales volume will **Burger King's** total revenues and total costs be equal? What profit will **General Electric** earn at an annual sales volume of $60 billion? What will happen to the profit of **Red Lobster** if there is a 20 percent increase in the cost of food and a 10 percent increase in the selling price of meals? The Research Insight box on the following page indicates the importance of the concepts discussed in this and other modules to the success of new businesses.

In not-for-profit organizations, CVP analysis is used to establish service levels, plan fund-raising activities, and determine funding requirements. How many meals can the downtown **Salvation Army** serve with an annual budget of $600,000? How many tickets must be sold for the benefit concert to raise $20,000? Given the current cost structure, current tuition rates, and projected enrollments, how much money must **Cornell University** raise from other sources?

Key Assumptions

CVP analysis is subject to a number of assumptions. Although these assumptions do not negate the usefulness of CVP models, especially for a single product or service, they do suggest the need for further analysis before plans are finalized. Among the more important assumptions are:

1. *All costs are classified as fixed or variable.* This assumption is most reasonable when analyzing the profitability of a specific event (such as a concert) or the profitability of an organization that produces a single product or service on a continuous basis.

2. *The total cost function is linear within the relevant range.* This assumption is often valid within a relevant range of normal operations, but over the entire range of possible activity, changes in efficiency are likely to result in a nonlinear cost function.

3. *The total revenue function is linear within the relevant range.* Unit selling prices are assumed constant over the range of possible volumes. This implies a purely competitive market for final products or services. In some economic models in which demand responds to price changes, the revenue function is nonlinear. In these situations, the linear approximation is accurate only within a limited range of activity.

4. *The analysis is for a single product, or the sales mix of multiple products is constant.* The **sales mix** refers to the relative portion of unit or dollar sales derived from each product or service. If products have different selling prices and costs, changes in the mix affect CVP model results.

5. *There is only one cost driver: unit or sales dollar volume.* In a complex organization it is seldom possible to represent the multitude of factors that drive cost with a single cost driver.

When applied to a single product (such as pounds of potato chips), service (such as the number of pages printed), or event (such as the number of tickets sold to a banquet), it is reasonable to assume the single independent variable is the cost driver. The total costs associated with the single product, service, or event during a specific time period are often determined by this single activity cost driver.

Although cost-volume-profit analysis is often used to understand the overall operations of an organization or business segment, accuracy decreases as the scope of operations being analyzed increases.

RESEARCH INSIGHT | **Careless Financial Management Is a Primary Cause of Business Failure**

New small businesses, with fewer than 20 employees, have less than a twenty percent probability of surviving five years, with the highest failure rate occurring during the first year. Studies of business failure and testimony offered at the Securities and Exchange Commission's Government-Business Forum suggests that a leading cause of small businesses failures is the lack of knowledge about accounting, especially management accounting and internal control, by the owners and managers. "The antidote to small business failure," according to Samuel Bornstein writing in *Community Banker*, "is knowledge and understanding of practical accounting and its analytic tools and techniques, which provide the business owner indications of where the business has been, where it is, and where it is going."

Source: Samuel Bornstein, "Fighting Failure," *Community Banker*, May 2007, pp. 38–42.

Profit Formula

The profit associated with a product, service, or event is equal to the difference between total revenues and total costs as follows:

$$\pi = R - Y$$

where

$$\pi = \textbf{Profit}$$
$$R = \textbf{Total revenues}$$
$$Y = \textbf{Total costs}$$

The revenues are a function of the unit sales volume and the unit selling price, while total costs for a time period are a function of the fixed costs per period and the unit variable costs as follows:

$$R = pX$$
$$Y = a + bX$$

where

$$p = \text{Unit selling price}$$
$$a = \text{Fixed costs}$$
$$b = \text{Unit variable costs}$$
$$X = \text{Unit sales}$$

The equation for profit can then be expanded to include the above details of the total revenue and total cost equations as follows:

$$\pi = pX - (a + bX)$$

Using information on the selling price, fixed costs per period, and variable costs per unit, this formula is used to predict profit at any specified activity level.

To illustrate, assume that Benchmark Paper Company's only product is high-quality photocopy paper that it manufactures and sells to wholesale distributors at $8.00 per carton. Applying inventory minimization techniques, Benchmark does not maintain inventories of raw materials or finished goods. Instead, newly purchased raw materials are delivered directly to the factory, and finished goods are loaded directly onto trucks for shipment. Benchmark's variable and fixed costs follow.

1. **Direct materials** refer to the cost of the primary raw materials converted into finished goods. Because the consumption of raw materials increases as the quantity of goods produced increases, *direct materials represents a variable cost*. Benchmark's raw materials consist primarily of paper purchased in large rolls and packing supplies such as boxes. Benchmark also treats the costs of purchasing, receiving, and inspecting raw materials as part of the cost of direct materials. All together, these costs are $1.00 per carton of finished product.

2. **Direct labor** refers to wages earned by production employees for the time they spend working on the conversion of raw materials into finished goods. Based on Benchmark's manufacturing procedures, *direct labor represents a variable cost*. These costs are $0.25 per carton.

3. **Variable manufacturing overhead** includes all other variable costs associated with converting raw materials into finished goods. Benchmark's variable manufacturing overhead costs include the costs of lubricants for cutting and packaging machines, electricity to operate these machines, and the cost to move materials between receiving and shipping docks and the cutting and packaging machines. These costs are $1.25 per carton.

4. **Variable selling and administrative costs** include all variable costs other than those directly associated with converting raw materials into finished goods. At Benchmark, these costs include sales commissions, transportation of finished goods to wholesale distributors, and the cost of processing the receipt and disbursement of cash. These costs are $0.50 per carton.

5. **Fixed manufacturing overhead** includes all fixed costs associated with converting raw materials into finished goods. Benchmark's fixed manufacturing costs include the depreciation, property taxes, and insurance on buildings and machines used for manufacturing, the salaries of manufacturing supervisors, and the fixed portion of electricity used to light the factory. These costs are $5,000.00 per month.

6. **Fixed selling and administrative costs** include all fixed costs other than those directly associated with converting raw materials into finished goods. These costs include the salaries of Benchmark's president and many other staff personnel such as accounting and marketing. Also included are depreciation, property taxes, insurance on facilities used for administrative purposes, and any related utilities costs. These costs are $10,000.00 per month.

Benchmark's variable and fixed costs are summarized here.

Variable Costs per Carton			Fixed Costs per Month	
Manufacturing			Manufacturing overhead	$ 5,000.00
Direct materials	$1.00		Selling and administrative	10,000.00
Direct labor	0.25		Total	$15,000.00
Manufacturing overhead	1.25	$2.50		
Selling and administrative		0.50		
Total		$3.00		

The cost estimation techniques discussed in Module 14 can be used to determine many detailed costs. Least-squares regression, for example, might be used to determine the variable and monthly fixed amount of electricity used in manufacturing. Benchmark manufactures and sells a single product on a continuous basis with all sales to distributors under standing contracts. Therefore, it is reasonable to assume that in the short run, Benchmark's total monthly costs respond to a single cost driver, cartons sold. Combining all this information, Benchmark's profit equation is:

$$\text{Profit} = \$8.00X - (\$15,000.00 + \$3.00X)$$

where

$$X = \text{cartons sold}$$

Using this equation, Benchmark's profit at a volume of 5,400 units is \$12,000.00, computed as ($8.00 × 5,400) − [$15,000.00 + ($3.00 × 5,400)].

CONTRIBUTION AND FUNCTIONAL INCOME STATEMENTS

Contribution Income Statement

To provide more detailed information on anticipated or actual financial results at a particular sales volume, a contribution income statement is often prepared. Benchmark's contribution income statement for a volume of 5,400 units is in Exhibit 15.1. In a **contribution income statement**, costs are classified according to behavior as variable or fixed, and the **contribution margin** (the difference between total revenues and total variable costs) that goes toward covering fixed costs and providing a profit is emphasized.

LO2 Prepare and contrast contribution and functional income statements.

EXHIBIT 15.1 Contribution Income Statement		
BENCHMARK PAPER COMPANY Contribution Income Statement For a Monthly Volume of 5,400 Cartons		
Sales (5,400 × $8.00)		$43,200
Less variable costs		
Direct materials (5,400 × $1.00)	$ 5,400	
Direct labor (5,400 × $0.25)	1,350	
Manufacturing overhead (5,400 × $1.25)	6,750	
Selling and administrative (5,400 × $0.50)	2,700	(16,200)
Contribution margin		27,000
Less fixed costs		
Manufacturing overhead	5,000	
Selling and administrative	10,000	(15,000)
Profit		$12,000

Functional Income Statement

Contrast the contribution income statement in Exhibit 15.1 with the income statement in Exhibit 15.2 on the following page. This statement is called a **functional income statement** because costs are classified according to function (rather than behavior), such as manufacturing, selling, and administrative. This is the type of income statement typically included in corporate annual reports.

A problem with a functional income statement is the difficulty of relating it to the profit formula in which costs are classified according to behavior rather than function. The relationship between sales volume, costs, and profits is not readily apparent in a functional income statement. Consequently, we emphasize contribution income statements because they provide better information to internal decision makers.

EXHIBIT 15.2	Functional Income Statement

BENCHMARK PAPER COMPANY
Functional Income Statement
For a Monthly Volume of 5,400 Cartons

Sales (5,400 × $8.00)...............................		$43,200
Less cost of goods sold		
Direct materials (5,400 × $1.00)	$ 5,400	
Direct labor (5,400 × $0.25)........................	1,350	
Variable manufacturing overhead (5,400 × $1.25)	6,750	
Fixed manufacturing overhead	5,000	(18,500)
Gross margin		24,700
Less other expenses		
Variable selling and administrative (5,400 × $0.50).....	2,700	
Fixed selling and administrative..................	10,000	(12,700)
Profit...		$12,000

Analysis Using Contribution Margin Ratio

While the contribution income statement (shown in Exhibit 15.1) presents information on total sales revenue, total variable costs, and so forth, it is sometimes useful to present information on a per-unit or portion of sales basis.

	Total	Per Unit	Ratio to Sales
Sales (5,400 units)	$43,200	$8	1.000
Variable costs.............	(16,200)	(3)	(0.375)
Contribution margin	27,000	$5	0.625
Fixed costs..............	(15,000)		
Profit...................	$12,000		

The per-unit information assists in short-range planning. The **unit contribution margin** is the difference between the unit selling price and the unit variable costs. It is the amount, $5.00 in this case, that each unit contributes toward covering fixed costs and earning a profit.

The contribution margin is widely used in **sensitivity analysis** (the study of the responsiveness of a model to changes in one or more of its independent variables). Benchmark's income statement is an economic model of the firm, and the unit contribution margin indicates how sensitive Benchmark's income model is to changes in unit sales. If, for example, sales increase by 100 cartons per month, the increase in profit is readily determined by multiplying the 100-carton increase in sales by the $5 unit contribution margin as follows:

100 (carton sales increase) × $5 (unit contribution margin) = $500 (profit increase)

There is no increase in fixed costs, so the new profit level becomes $12,500 ($12,000 + $500) per month.

When expressed as a ratio to sales, the contribution margin is identified as the **contribution margin ratio**. It is the portion of each dollar of sales revenue contributed toward covering fixed costs and earning a profit. In the abbreviated income statement above, the portion of each dollar of sales revenue contributed toward covering fixed costs and earning a profit is $0.625 ($27,000 ÷ $43,200). This is Benchmark's contribution margin ratio. If sales revenue increases by $800 per month, the increase in profits is computed as follows:

$800 (sales increase) × 0.625 (contribution margin ratio) = $500 (profit increase)

The contribution margin ratio is especially useful in situations involving several products or when unit sales information is not available.

BREAK-EVEN POINT AND PROFIT PLANNING

The **break-even point** occurs at the unit or dollar sales volume when total revenues equal total costs. The break-even point is of great interest to management. Until break-even sales are reached, the product, service, event, or business segment of interest operates at a loss. Beyond this point, increasing levels of profits are achieved. Also, management often wants to know the **margin of safety**, the amount by which actual or planned sales exceed the break-even point. Other questions of interest include the probability of exceeding the break-even sales volume and the effect of some proposed change on the break-even point.

LO3 Apply cost-volume-profit analysis to find a break-even point and for preliminary profit planning.

Determining Break-Even Point

In determining the break-even point, the equation for total revenues is set equal to the equation for total costs and then solved for the break-even unit sales volume. Using the general equations for total revenues and total costs, the following results are obtained. Setting total revenues equal to total costs:

$$\text{Total revenues} = \text{Total costs}$$
$$pX = a + bX$$

Solving for the break-even sales volume:

$$pX - bX = a$$
$$(p - b)X = a$$
$$X = a/(p - b)$$

In words:

$$\text{Break-even unit sales volume} = \frac{\text{Fixed costs}}{\text{Selling price per unit} - \text{Variable costs per unit}}$$

Because the denominator is the unit contribution margin, the break-even point is also computed by dividing fixed costs by the unit contribution margin:

$$\text{Break-even unit sales volume} = \frac{\text{Fixed costs}}{\text{Unit contribution margin}}$$

With a $5 unit contribution margin and fixed costs of $15,000 per month, Benchmark's break-even point is 3,000 units per month ($15,000 ÷ $5). Stated another way, at a $5 per-unit contribution margin, 3,000 units of contribution are required to cover $15,000 of fixed costs. With a break-even point of 3,000 units, the monthly margin of safety and expected profit for a sales volume of 5,400 units are 2,400 units (5,400 expected unit sales − 3,000 break-even sales) and $12,000 (2,400 unit margin of safety × $5 unit contribution margin), respectively.

The break-even point concept is applicable to a wide variety of business and personal planning situations. The following Research Insight box illustrates how a personal financial planner might use break-even point concepts to assist a client making a retirement decision.

Profit Planning

Establishing profit objectives is an important part of planning in for-profit organizations. Profit objectives are stated in many ways. They can be set as a percentage of last year's profits, as a percentage of total assets at the start of the current year, or as a percentage of owners' equity. They might be based

---

RESEARCH INSIGHT **Determining the Cash Break-Even Point for Delaying Retirement**

Social Security retirement benefits are a function of years worked, contributions to the Social Security System, and the age at which the recipient files for Social Security retirement benefits. Currently, persons retiring at age 67 are entitled to "full" retirement benefits, while those retiring at age 62 are eligible for only 75 percent of "full" benefits. A person contemplating retirement at age 62 might ask: (1) how large is the reduction in benefits and (2) what is the break-even age at which the benefits from delaying retirement until age 67 equals the cumulative benefits from retiring at age 62?

An individual with the analytic skills obtained from a managerial accounting course can readily determine the answers to these questions after consulting the Social Security web site www.ssa.gov. Others might consult a personal financial planner.

(1) Assume the individual's full Social Security retirement benefits at age 67 are $2,265 per month. If that person started receiving benefits at age 62 their monthly benefits are reduced by 25 percent or $566.25 ($2,265 × 0.25) to $1,698.75.

(2) With retirement at age 62, the early retiree would receive total benefits of $101,925 ($1,698.75 × 12 months × 5 years) by age 67, the normal "full" age. Treating this as a fixed amount to be recovered by the subsequent incremental monthly benefits of $566.25 from delaying the receipt of monthly benefits to age 67, the break-even age is computed as follows:

Months beyond age 67 = $101,925/$566.25 = 180 months or 15 years.

Hence, the break-even age is 82 years (67 + 15).

The analysis suggests that life expectancy is an important consideration in deciding when to start taking Social Security benefits.

Note that this analysis does not consider any return on the $101,925 that might be earned by investing the benefits received during early retirement. Such returns would increase the break-even age. Nor does it consider the lost wages that could have been earned between age 62 and age 67.

Source: www.ssa.gov

---

on a profit trend, or they might be expressed as a percentage of sales. The economic outlook for the firm's products as well as anticipated changes in products, costs, and technology are also considered in establishing profit objectives.

Before incorporating profit plans into a detailed budget, it is useful to obtain some preliminary information on the feasibility of those plans. Cost-volume-profit analysis is one way of doing this. By manipulating cost-volume-profit relationships, management can determine the sales volume corresponding to a desired profit. Management might then evaluate the feasibility of this sales volume. If the profit plans are feasible, a complete budget might be developed for this activity level. The required sales volume might be infeasible because of market conditions or because the required volume exceeds production or service capacity, in which case management must lower its profit objective or consider other ways of achieving it. Alternatively, the required sales volume might be less than management believes the firm is capable of selling, in which case management might raise its profit objective.

Assume that Benchmark's management desires to know the unit sales volume required to achieve a monthly profit of $18,000. Using the profit formula, the required unit sales volume is determined by setting profits equal to $18,000 and solving for X, the unit sales volume.

$$\text{Profit} = \text{Total revenues} - \text{Total costs}$$
$$\$18,000 = \$8X - (\$15,000 + \$3X)$$

Solving for X

$$\$8X - \$3X = \$15,000 + \$18,000$$
$$X = (\$15,000 + \$18,000) \div \$5$$
$$= 6,600 \text{ units}$$

The total contribution must cover the desired profit as well as the fixed costs. Hence, the target sales volume required to achieve a desired profit is computed as the fixed costs plus the desired profit, all divided by the unit contribution margin.

$$\text{Target unit sales volume} = \frac{\text{Fixed costs} + \text{Desired profit}}{\text{Unit contribution margin}}$$

The Business Insight box below considers CVP analysis for Hewlett-Packard, a large manufacturer whose strategic position for personal computers focuses on cost leadership.

BUSINESS INSIGHT | **HP's High-Volume, Low-Price Break-Even Point**

"The wealthiest 1 billion people in the world are pretty well served by IT companies," says HP's director of its e-inclusion program. "We're targeting the next 4 billion." The goal of e-inclusion is for HP to be the leader in satisfying a demand for simple and economical computer products for technology-excluded regions of the world. HP already derives 60 percent of its sales overseas, and it plans to build on these beachheads to develop what may be the greatest marketing frontier of the coming decades. With worldwide operations and a low selling price, the HP strategy combines high fixed costs and a low contribution margin, leading to a high break-even point. While the final payoff is unclear, one HP official observed, "You don't get a harvest until you start planting."

Source: Pete Engardio and Geri Smith, "Hewlett-Packard," Business Week, August 27, 2001, p. 137.

Cost-Volume-Profit Graph

A **cost-volume-profit graph** illustrates the relationships among activity volume, total revenues, total costs, and profits. Its usefulness comes from highlighting the break-even point and depicting revenue, cost, and profit relationships over a range of activity. This representation allows management to view the relative amount of important variables at any graphed volume. Benchmark's monthly CVP graph is in Exhibit 15.3. Total revenues and total costs are measured on the vertical axis, with unit sales measured on the horizontal axis. Separate lines are drawn for total variable costs, total costs, and total revenues. The vertical distance between the total revenue and the total cost lines depicts the amount of profit or loss at a given volume. Losses occur when total revenues are less than total costs; profits occur when total revenues exceed total costs.

The total contribution margin is shown by the difference between the total revenue and the total variable cost lines. Observe that as unit sales increase, the contribution margin first goes to cover the fixed costs. Beyond the break-even point, any additional contribution margin provides a profit.

Profit-Volume Graph

In cost-volume-profit graphs, profits are represented by the difference between total revenues and total costs. When management is primarily interested in the impact of changes in sales volume on profits and less interested in the related revenues and costs, a **profit-volume graph** is sometimes used. A profit-volume graph illustrates the relationship between volume and profits; it does not show revenues and costs. Profits are read directly from a profit-volume graph, rather than being computed as the difference between total revenues and total costs. Profit-volume graphs are developed by plotting either unit sales or total revenues on the horizontal axis.

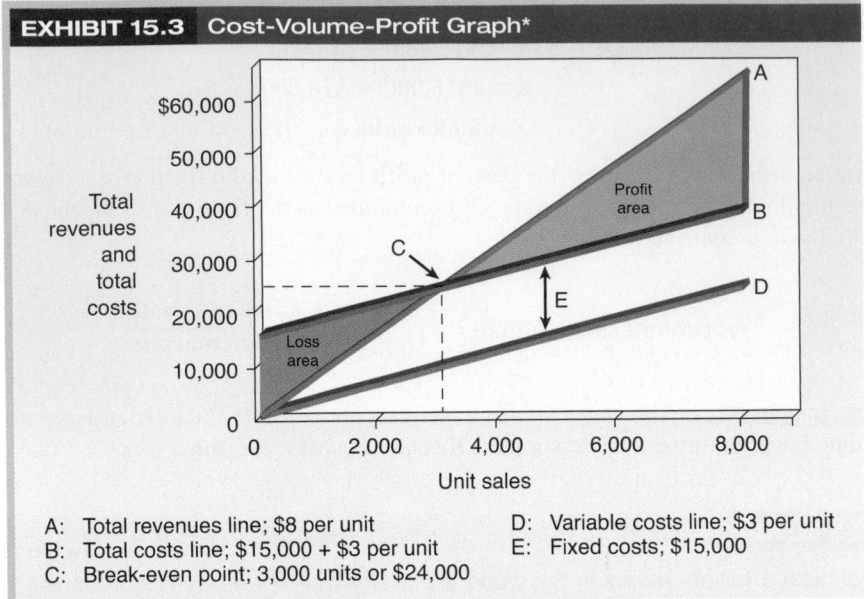

EXHIBIT 15.3   Cost-Volume-Profit Graph*

A: Total revenues line; $8 per unit
B: Total costs line; $15,000 + $3 per unit
C: Break-even point; 3,000 units or $24,000

D: Variable costs line; $3 per unit
E: Fixed costs; $15,000

* The three lines are developed as follows:

1. Total variable costs line, D, is drawn between the origin and total variable costs at an arbitrary sales volume. At 8,000 units, total variable costs are $24,000.
2. Total revenues line, A, is drawn through the origin and a point representing total revenues at some arbitrary sales volume. At 8,000 units, Benchmark's total revenues are $64,000.
3. Total cost line, B, is computed by layering fixed costs, $15,000 in this case, on top of total variable costs. This gives a vertical axis intercept of $15,000 and total costs of $39,000 at 8,000 units.

Benchmark's monthly profit-volume graph, is presented in Exhibit 15.4. Profit or loss is measured on the vertical axis, and volume (total revenues) is measured on the horizontal axis, which intersects the vertical axis at zero profit. A single line, representing total profit, is drawn intersecting the vertical axis at zero sales volume with a loss equal to the fixed costs. The profit line crosses the horizontal axis at the break-even sales volume. The profit or loss at any volume is depicted by the vertical difference between the profit line and the horizontal axis. The slope of the profit line is determined by the contribution margin. The greater the contribution margin ratio or the unit contribution margin, the steeper the slope of the profit line.

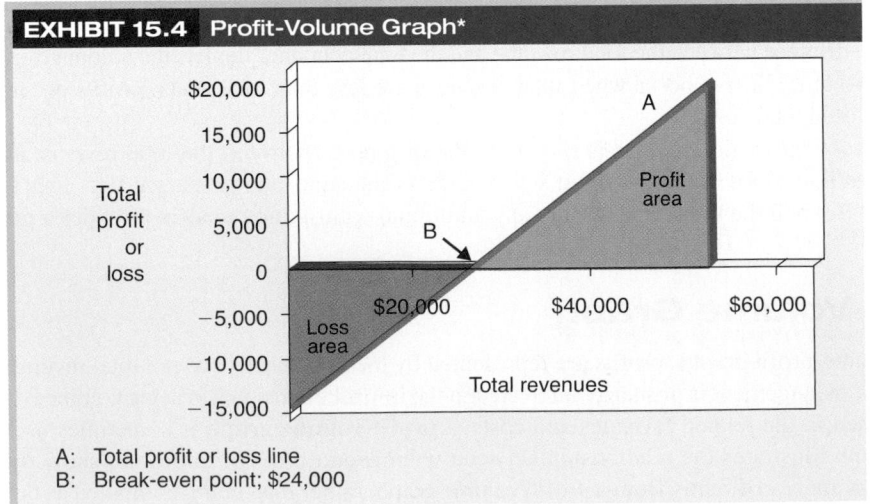

EXHIBIT 15.4   Profit-Volume Graph*

A: Total profit or loss line
B: Break-even point; $24,000

* The profit line is drawn by determining and plotting profit or loss at two different volumes and then drawing a straight line through the plotted values. Perhaps the easiest values to select are the loss at a volume of zero (with a loss equal to the fixed costs) and the volume at which the profit line crosses the horizontal axis (this is the break-even volume).

Impact of Income Taxes

Income taxes are imposed on individuals and for-profit organizations by government agencies. The amount of an individual's or organization's income tax is determined by laws that specify the calculation of taxable income (the income subject to tax) and the calculation of the amount of tax on taxable income. Income taxes are computed as a percentage of taxable income, with increases in taxable income usually subject to progressively higher tax rates. The laws governing the computation of taxable income differ in many ways from the accounting principles that guide the computation of accounting income. Consequently, taxable income and accounting income are seldom the same.

In the early stages of profit planning, income taxes are sometimes incorporated in CVP models by assuming that taxable income and accounting income are identical and that the tax rate is constant. Although these assumptions are seldom true, they are useful for assisting management in developing an early prediction of the sales volume required to earn a desired after-tax profit. Once management has developed a general plan, this early prediction should be refined with the advice of tax experts.

Assuming taxes are imposed at a constant rate per dollar of before-tax profit, income taxes are computed as before-tax profit multipled by the tax rate. After-tax profit is equal to before-tax profit minus income taxes.

$$\text{After-tax profit} = \text{Before-tax profit} - (\text{Before-tax profit} \times \text{Tax rate})$$

After-tax profit can also be expressed as before-tax profit times 1 minus the tax rate.

$$\text{After-tax profit} = \text{Before-tax profit} \times (1 - \text{Tax rate})$$

This formula can be rearranged to isolate before-tax profit as follows:

$$\text{Before-tax profit} = \frac{\text{After-tax profit}}{(1 - \text{Tax rate})}$$

Since all costs and revenues in the profit formula are expressed on a before-tax basis, the most straightforward way of determining the unit sales volume required to earn a desired after-tax profit is to:

1. Determine the required before-tax profit.
2. Substitute the required before-tax profit into the profit formula.
3. Solve for the required unit sales volume.

To illustrate, assume that Benchmark is subject to a 40 percent tax rate and that management desires to earn an after-tax profit of $18,000 for November 2012. The required before-tax profit is $30,000 [$18,000 ÷ (1 − 0.40)], and the unit sales volume required to earn this profit is 9,000 units [($15,000 + $30,000) ÷ $5].

Income taxes increase the sales volume required to earn a desired after-tax profit. A 40 percent tax rate increased the sales volume required for Benchmark to earn a profit of $18,000 from 6,600 to 9,000 units. These amounts are verified in Exhibit 15.5.

Another way to remember the computation of before-tax profit is shown on the right side of Exhibit 15.5. The before-tax profit represents 100 percent of the pie, with 40 percent going to income taxes and 60 percent remaining after taxes. Working back from the remaining 60 percent ($18,000), we can determine the 100 percent (before-tax profit) by dividing after-tax profit by 0.60.

EXHIBIT 15.5	Contribution Income Statement with Income Taxes		
BENCHMARK PAPER COMPANY **Contribution Income Statement** **Planned for the Month of November 2012**			
Sales (9,000 × $8.00).		$72,000	
Less variable costs			
Direct materials (9,000 × $1.00).	$ 9,000		
Direct labor (9,000 × $0.25).	2,250		
Manufacturing overhead (9,000 × $1.25). . . .	11,250		
Selling and administrative (9,000 × $0.50). . .	4,500	(27,000)	
Contribution margin		45,000	
Less fixed costs			
Manufacturing overhead.	5,000		
Selling and administrative.	10,000	(15,000)	
Before-tax profit		30,000	100%
Income taxes ($30,000 × 0.40)		(12,000)	(40)%
After-tax profit		$18,000	60%

MID-MODULE REVIEW

Memorabilia Cup Company produces keepsake 16-ounce beverage containers for educational institutions. Memorabilia sells the cups for $40 per box of 50 containers. Variable and fixed costs follow:

Variable Costs per Box			Fixed Costs per Month	
Manufacturing			Manufacturing overhead	$15,000
Direct materials.	$15		Selling and administrative	10,000
Direct labor	3		Total	$25,000
Manufacturing overhead. . .	10	$28		
Selling and administrative . . .		2		
Total		$30		

In September 2012, Memorabilia produced and sold 3,000 boxes of beverage containers.

Required

a. Prepare a contribution income statement for September 2012.
b. Prepare a cost-volume-profit graph with unit sales as the independent variable. Label the revenue line, total costs line, fixed costs line, loss area, profit area, and break-even point. The recommended scale for the horizontal axis is 0 to 5,000 units, and the recommended scale for the vertical axis is $0 to $200,000.
c. Determine Memorabilia's unit contribution margin and contribution margin ratio.
d. Determine Memorabilia's monthly break-even point in units.
e. Determine the monthly dollar sales required for a monthly profit of $5,000 (ignoring taxes).
f. Assuming Memorabilia is subject to a 40 percent income tax, determine the monthly unit sales required to produce a monthly after-tax profit of $4,500.

The solution is on page 15-35.

MULTIPLE-PRODUCT COST-VOLUME-PROFIT ANALYSIS

LO4 Analyze the profitability and sales mix of a multiple-product firm.

Unit cost information is not always available or appropriate when analyzing cost-volume-profit relationships of multiple-product firms. Assuming the sales mix is constant, the contribution margin ratio (the portion of each sales dollar contributed toward covering fixed costs and earning a profit) can be used to determine the break-even dollar sales volume or the dollar sales volume required to achieve a desired profit. Treating a dollar of sales revenue as a unit, the break-even point in dollars is computed as fixed costs divided by the contribution margin ratio (the number of cents from each dollar of revenue contributed to covering fixed costs and providing a profit).

$$\text{Dollar break-even point} = \frac{\text{Fixed costs}}{\text{Contribution margin ratio}}$$

If unit selling price and cost information were not available, Benchmark's dollar break-even point could be computed as $24,000 ($15,000 ÷ 0.625).

Corresponding computations can be made to find the dollar sales volume required to achieve a desired profit as follows.

$$\text{Target dollar sales volume} = \frac{\text{Fixed costs} + \text{Desired profit}}{\text{Contribution margin ratio}}$$

To achieve a desired profit of $12,000, Benchmark needs sales of $43,200 [($15,000 + $12,000) ÷ 0.625].

These relationships can be graphed by placing sales dollars, rather than unit sales, on the horizontal axis. The slope of the variable and total cost lines, identified as the **variable cost ratio**, presents variable costs as a portion of sales revenue. It indicates the number of cents from each sales dollar required to pay variable costs. The Business Insight box on the following page demonstrates how CVP information can be developed from the published financial statements of a multiple-product firm.

BUSINESS INSIGHT **Using CVP for Financial Analysis and Prediction**

Family Dollar operates a chain of more than 6,800 general merchandise retail discount stores in 44 states. Their mission is to provide customers with a compelling place to shop, employees with a compelling place to work, and investors with a compelling place to invest. Their vision is to be the best small-format convenience and value retailer serving the needs of families in our neighborhoods. Condensed 2008 and 2009 income statements in millions follow.

	For the Year Ending	
	August 29, 2009	August 30, 2008
Net sales.	$7,401	$6,984
Cost of sales and operating expenses.	(6,943)	(6,618)
Operating profit	$ 458	$ 366

We can determine Family Dollar's cost-volume-profit relationships and predict future profits for a given level of sales after using the high-low method to develop cost estimating equations. First determine variable costs as a percent of sales:

$$\text{Variable cost ratio} = \frac{\$6,943 - \$6,618}{\$7,401 - \$6,984} = \underline{\underline{0.7794}}$$

Next determine annual fixed costs by calculating and subtracting the variable costs of either period (revenues multiplied by the variable cost ratio) from the corresponding total costs. Using 2009 revenues and costs annual fixed costs are determined as follows:

$$\text{Annual fixed costs} = \$6,943 - (\$7,401 \times 0.7794) = \underline{\underline{\$1,175}} \text{ million}$$

Family Dollar's annual cost estimating equation is:

$$\text{Total annual costs} = \$1,175 \text{ million} + 0.7794 \text{ Net sales}$$

Using the fixed costs and the contribution margin ratio (1 minus the variable cost ratio) Family Dollar's break-even point in sales dollars is computed.

$$\text{Break-even point} = \$1,175 \text{ million}/(1 - 0.7794) = \underline{\underline{\$5,326}} \text{ million}$$

For 2010, Family Dollar's net sales and operating profits were $7,867 million and $576 million. Using the CVP relationships developed from 2008 and 2009 data, the predicted 2010 operating profits are $560 million $7,867 − [($7,867 × 0.7794) + $1,175]. In this case, because of Family Dollar's stable cost structure, the model error is small.

Sales Mix Analysis

Sales mix refers to the relative portion of unit or dollar sales that are derived from each product. One of the limiting assumptions of the basic cost-volume-profit model is that the analysis is for a single product or the sales mix is constant. When the sales mix is constant, managers of multiple-product organizations can use the average unit contribution margin, or the average contribution margin ratio, to determine the break-even point or the sales volume required for a desired profit. Often, however, management is interested in the effect of a change in the sales mix rather than a change in the sales volume at a constant mix. In this situation, it is necessary to determine either the average unit contribution margin or the average contribution margin ratio for each alternative mix.

Unit Sales Analysis

Assume the Eagle Card Company sells two kinds of greeting cards, regular and deluxe. At a 1:1 (one-to-one) unit sales mix in which Eagle sells one box of regular cards for every box of deluxe cards, the following revenue and cost information is available:

	Regular Box	Deluxe Box	Average Box*
Unit selling price.	$4	$12	$8
Unit variable costs	(3)	(3)	(3)
Unit contribution margin.	$1	$ 9	$5
Fixed costs per month			$15,000

* At a 1:1 sales mix, the average unit contribution margin is
$5[{($1 × 1 unit) + ($9 × 1 unit)} ÷ 2 units].

At a 1:1 mix, Eagle's current monthly break-even sales volume is 3,000 units ($15,000 ÷ $5), consisting of 1,500 boxes of regular cards and 1,500 boxes of deluxe cards. The top line in Exhibit 15.6 represents the current sales mix. Management wants to know the break-even sales volume if the unit sales mix became 3:1; that is, on average, a sale of 4 units contains 3 regular units and 1 deluxe unit. With no changes in the selling prices or variable costs of individual products, the average contribution margin becomes $3[{($1 × 3 units) + ($9 × 1 unit)} ÷ 4 units], and the revised break-even sales volume is 5,000 units ($15,000 ÷ $3). The revised break-even sales volume includes 3,750 boxes of regular cards [5,000 × $\frac{3}{4}$] and 1,250 boxes of deluxe cards [5,000 × $\frac{1}{4}$].

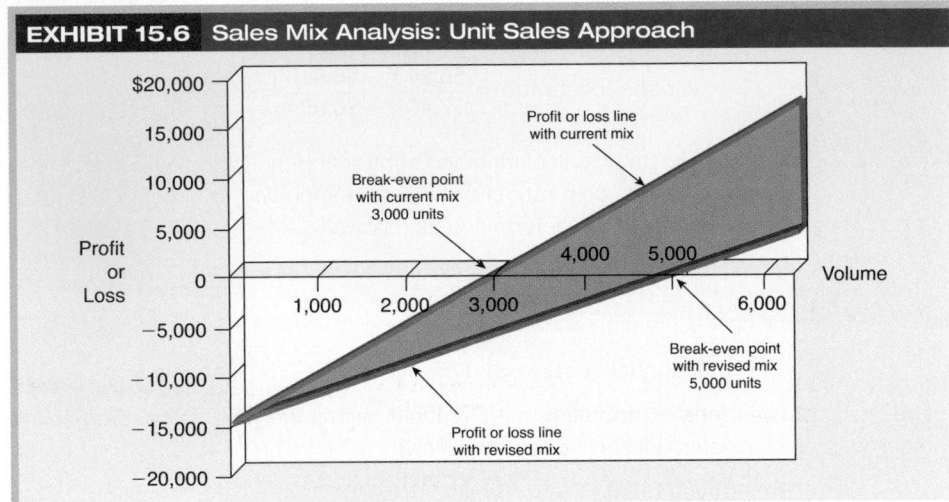

EXHIBIT 15.6   Sales Mix Analysis: Unit Sales Approach

The bottom line in Exhibit 15.6 represents the revised sales mix. Because a greater portion of the revised mix consists of lower contribution margin regular cards, the shift in the mix increases the break-even point.

Sales Dollar Analysis

The preceding analysis focused on units and the unit contribution margin. An alternative approach focuses on sales dollars and the contribution margin ratio. Following this approach, the sales mix is expressed in terms of sales dollars.

Eagle's current sales dollars are 25 percent from regular cards and 75 percent from deluxe cards. The following display indicates the contribution margin ratios at the current sales mix and monthly volume of 5,400 units.

	Regular	Deluxe	Total
Unit sales	2,700	2,700	
Selling price	$4.00	$12.00	
Sales.	$10,800	$32,400	$43,200
Variable costs	8,100	8,100	16,200
Contribution margin	$ 2,700	$24,300	$27,000
Contribution margin ratio	0.25	0.75	0.625

With monthly fixed costs of $15,000, Eagle's current break-even sales volume is $24,000 ($15,000 ÷ 0.625), consisting of $6,000 from regular cards ($24,000 × 0.25) and $18,000 from Deluxe cards ($24,000 × 0.75). The top line in Exhibit 15.7 illustrates the current sales mix.

Management wants to know the break-even sales volume if the dollar sales mix became 70 percent regular and 30 percent deluxe. With no changes in the selling prices or variable costs of individual products, the total contribution margin ratio becomes 0.40 [(0.25 × 0.70) + (0.75 × 0.30)], and the revised break-even sales volume is $37,500 ($15,000 ÷ 0.40). The revised break-even sales volume includes $26,250 from regular cards ($37,500 × 0.70) and $11,250 from deluxe cards (37,500 × 0.30).

The bottom line in Exhibit 15.7 represents the revised sales mix. Because a greater portion of the revised mix consists of lower contribution ratio regular cards, the shift in the mix increases the break-even point.

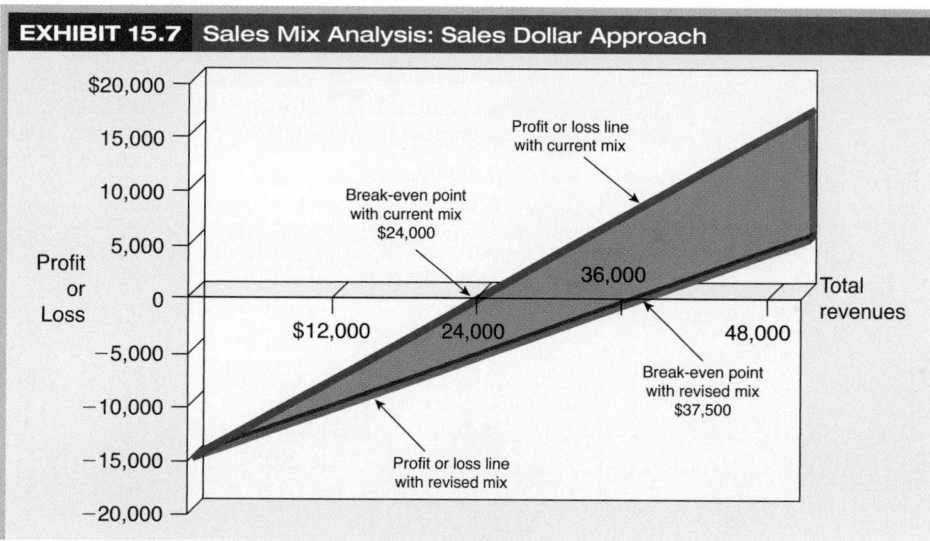

EXHIBIT 15.7 Sales Mix Analysis: Sales Dollar Approach

Sales mix analysis is important in multiple-product or service organizations. Management is just as concerned with the mix of products as with the total unit or dollar sales volume. A shift in the sales mix can have a significant impact on the bottom line. Profits may decline, even when sales increase, if the mix shifts toward products or services with lower unit margins. Conversely, profits may increase, even when sales decline, if the mix shifts toward products or services with higher unit margins. Other things being equal, managers of for-profit organizations strive to increase sales of high-margin products or services.

ANALYSIS OF OPERATING LEVERAGE

Operating leverage refers to the extent that an organization's costs are fixed. The **operating leverage ratio** is computed as the contribution margin divided by before-tax profit as follows.

$$\text{Operating leverage ratio} = \frac{\text{Contribution margin}}{\text{Before-tax profit}}$$

The rationale underlying this computation is that as fixed costs are substituted for variable costs, the contribution margin as a percentage of income before taxes increases. Hence, a high degree of operating leverage signals the existence of a high portion of fixed costs. As noted in Module 13, the shift from labor-based to automated activities has resulted in a decrease in variable costs and an increase in fixed costs, producing an increase in operating leverage.

Operating leverage is a measure of risk and opportunity. Other things being equal, the higher the degree of operating leverage, the greater the opportunity for profit with increases in sales. Conversely, a higher degree of operating leverage also magnifies the risk of large losses with a decrease in sales.

LO5 Apply operating leverage ratio to assess opportunities for profit and the risks of loss.

	Operating Leverage	
	High	Low
Profit opportunity with sales increase	High	Low
Risk of loss with sales decrease	High	Low

In addition to indicating the relative amount of fixed costs in the overall cost structure of a company, the operating leverage ratio can be used to measure the expected change in net income resulting from a change in sales. The operating leverage ratio multiplied times the percentage change in sales equals the percentage change in income before taxes. For example, if Benchmark Paper Company currently has an operating leverage ratio of 4.0, a change in sales of 12.5 percent will result in a 50 percent change in income before taxes; whereas, High-Fixed Paper Company, which has an operating leverage ratio of 5.2 will have an increase in sales of 65%.

	Current		Projected	
	Benchmark	High-Fixed	Benchmark	High-Fixed
Unit selling price...........................	$ 8.00	$ 8.00	$ 8.00	$ 8.00
Unit variable costs	(3.00)	(1.50)	(3.00)	(1.50)
Unit contribution margin...................	5.00	6.50	5.00	6.50
Unit sales	× 4,000	× 4,000	× 4,500	× 4,500
Contribution margin	20,000	26,000	22,500	29,250
Fixed costs...............................	(15,000)	(21,000)	(15,000)	(21,000)
Before-tax profit..........................	$ 5,000	$ 5,000	$ 7,500	$ 8,250
Contribution margin	$20,000	$26,000		
Before-tax profit..........................	÷ 5,000	÷ 5,000		
Operating leverage ratio...................	4.0	5.2		
Percent increase in sales			12.5%	12.5%
Percent increase in income before sales			50%	65%

Although both companies have identical before-tax profits at a sales volume of 4,000 units, High-Fixed has a higher degree of operating leverage and its profits vary more with changes in sales volume.

If sales are projected to increase by 12.5 percent, from 4,000 to 4,500 units, the percentage of increase in each firm's profits is computed as the percent change in sales multiplied by the degree of operating leverage.

	Benchmark	High-Fixed
Increase in sales..................	12.5%	12.5%
Degree of operating leverage........	× 4.0	× 5.2
Increase in profits................	50.0%	65.0%

As noted in the following Business Insight box, operating leverage was an important consideration in the proposed merger of **XM** and **Sirius** radio.

Management is interested in measures of operating leverage to determine how sensitive profits are to changes in sales. Risk-averse managers strive to maintain a lower operating leverage, even if this results in some loss of profits. One way to reduce operating leverage is to use more direct labor and less automated equipment. Another way is to contract outside organizations to perform tasks that could be done internally. This approach to reducing operating leverage is further considered in Module 16, where we examine the external acquisition of goods and services. While operating leverage is a useful analytic tool, long-run success comes from keeping the overall level of costs down, while providing customers with the products or services they want at competitive prices.

BUSINESS INSIGHT | **Operating Leverage Makes XM- Sirius Merger Attractive**

Together, Sirius Satellite Radio and XM Satellite Radio had 17.3 million subscribers and annual revenues of $2,062.1 million in 2007. Yet, primarily because of high fixed costs, they also had a combined net loss of $1,247.7 million. Writing in Money magazine, Pablo Galarza reported that because of high operating leverage analysts believed that both firms could be highly profitable as independent entities once they reached the break-even point, ". . . since it doesn't really cost more to broadcast to 50 million than it does to one million." Analysts determined that above break-even, 80 percent of incremental revenues would become profit.

　　High fixed costs, high operating leverage, and lack or profitability were among the considerations leading to a 2007 announcement of a merger agreement between XM Satellite Radio and Sirius Satellite Radio. The press release issued at the time of the announcement noted that the merger, "will enhance the long-term financial success of satellite radio by allowing the combined company to better manage its costs through sales and marketing and subscriber acquisition efficiencies, satellite fleet efficiencies, combined R&D, and other benefits from economies of scale."

Source: Pable Galarza, "Flying Off the Shelves," Money, February 2005, p. 56.; Rick Boucher, "Why the XM-Sirius Merger Makes Sense, Business Week Online, November 16, 2007, p.4.; 2007 annual reports and press releases available at www.sirius.com and www.XMradio.com

---

MANAGERIAL DECISION | **You are the Division Manager**

As manager of a division responsible for both production and sales of products and, hence, division profits, you are looking for ways to leverage the profits of your division to a higher level. You are considering changing your cost structure to include more fixed costs and less variable costs by automating some of the production activities currently performed by people. What are some of the considerations that you should keep in mind as you ponder this decision? [Answer, p. 15-22]

MODULE-END REVIEW

Joe's Brews is a new shop in Cambridge village shopping center that sells high-end teas and coffees. Recently, they have added smoothie drinks to their product line. Below are sales and cost data for the company:

	Coffee	Tea	Smoothie
Sales price per (12 oz.) serving	$1.35	$1.25	$1.95
Variable cost per serving	0.60	0.45	0.75
Fixed costs per month $8,000			

Currently the company sells each month an average of 6,000 servings of coffee, 3,750 servings of tea, and 2,250 servings of smoothies.

Required

a. Calculate the current before-tax profit, contribution margin ratio, and sales mix based on sales dollars.
b. Using a sales dollar analysis, calculate the monthly break-even point assuming the sales mix does not change.
c. Calculate Joe's operating leverage ratio. If sales increase by 20 percent, by how much will before-tax income be expected to change? If sales decrease by 20 percent, by how much will before-tax income be expected to change?

The solution is on page 15-36.

APPENDIX 15A: Profitability Analysis with Unit and Nonunit Cost Drivers

A major limitation of cost-volume-profit analysis and the related contribution income statement is the exclusive use of unit-level activity cost drivers. Even when multiple products are considered, the CVP approach either re-states volume in terms of an average unit or in terms of a dollar of sales volume. Additionally, CVP analysis does not consider other categories of cost drivers.

We now expand profitability analysis to incorporate nonunit cost drivers. While the addition of multiple levels of cost drivers makes it difficult to develop graphical relationships (illustrating the impact of cost driver changes on revenues, costs, and profits), it is possible to modify the traditional contribution income statement to incorporate a hierarchy of cost drivers. The expanded framework is not only more accurate, but it encourages management to ask important questions concerning costs and profitability.

Multi-Level Contribution Income Statement

To illustrate the use of profitability analysis with unit and nonunit cost drivers, consider General Distribution, a multiple-product merchandising organization with the following cost hierarchy:

Unit-level activities
    Cost of goods sold . . . . $0.80 per sales dollar
Order-level activities
    Cost of processing order. . . . . $20 per order
Customer-level activities
    Mail, phone, sales visits, recordkeeping, etc. . . . . $200 per customer per year
Facility-level costs
    Depreciation, manager salaries, insurance, etc. . . . . $120,000 per year

Assume that General Distribution, which is subject to a 40 percent income tax rate, has the following plans for the year 2012:

Sales.	$3,000,000
Number of sales orders	3,200
Number of customers.	400

While General Distribution's plans could be summarized in a functional income statement, we have previously considered the limitations of such statements for management. Contribution income statements are preferred because they correspond to the cost classification scheme used in CVP analysis. In this case, General Distribution's cost structure (unit level, order level, customer level, and facility level) does not correspond to the classification scheme used in traditional contribution income statements (variable and fixed). The problem occurs because traditional contribution income statements consider only unit-level cost drivers. When a larger set of unit and nonunit cost drivers is used for cost analysis, an expanded contribution income statement should be used for profitability analysis.

A multi-level contribution income statement for General Distribution is presented in Exhibit 15.8. Costs are separated using a cost hierarchy and there are several contribution margins, one for each level of costs that responds to a short-run change in activity. In the case of General Distribution, the contribution margins are at the unit level, order level, and customer level. Because the facility-level costs do not vary with short-run variations in activity, the final customer-level contribution goes to cover facility-level costs and to provide for a profit. If a company had a different activity cost hierarchy, it would use a different set of contribution margins.

A number of additional questions of interest to management can be formulated and answered using the multi-level hierarchy. Consider the following examples:

■ Holding the number of sales orders and customers constant, what is the break-even dollar sales volume? The answer is found by treating all other costs as fixed and dividing the total nonunit-level costs by the contribution margin ratio. Here the contribution margin ratio indicates how many cents of each sales dollar is available for profits and costs above the unit level.

$$\frac{\text{Unit-level break-even point in dollars with no changes in other costs}}{} = \frac{\text{Current order-level costs} + \text{Current customer-level costs} + \text{Facility-level costs}}{\text{Contribution margin ratio}}$$

$$= (\$64,000 + \$80,000 + \$120,000) \div (1 - 0.80)$$

$$= \$1,320,000$$

EXHIBIT 15.8	Multi-Level Contribution Income Statement with Taxes

GENERAL DISTRIBUTION
Multi-Level Contribution Income Statement
For Year 2012

Sales...	$3,000,000
Less unit-level costs	
Cost of goods sold ($3,000,000 × 0.80).....................................	(2,400,000)
Unit-level contribution margin..	600,000
Less order-level costs	
Cost of processing order (3,200 orders × $20)............................	(64,000)
Order-level contribution margin......................................	536,000
Less customer-level costs	
Mail, phone, sales visits, recordkeeping, etc. (400 customers × $200)...............	(80,000)
Customer-level contribution margin....................................	456,000
Less facility-level costs	
Depreciation, manager salaries, insurance, etc.............................	(120,000)
Before-tax profit...	336,000
Income taxes ($336,000 × 0.40)......................................	(134,400)
After-tax profit..	$ 201,600

■ What order size is required to break even on an individual order? Answering this question might help management to evaluate the desirability of establishing a minimum order size. To break even, each order must have a unit-level contribution equal to the order-level costs. Any additional contribution is used to cover customer- and facility-level costs and provide for a profit.

$$\text{Break-even order size} = \$20 \div (1 - 0.80)$$
$$= \$100$$

■ What sales volume is required to break even on an average customer? Answering this question might help management to evaluate the desirability of retaining certain customers. Based on the preceding information, an average customer places 8 orders per year (3,200 orders ÷ 400 customers). With costs of $20 per order and $200 per customer, the sales to an average customer must generate an annual contribution of $360 [($20 × 8) + $200]. Hence, the break-even level for an average customer is $1,800 [$360 ÷ (1 − 0.80)]. Management might consider discontinuing relations with customers with annual purchases of less than this amount. Alternatively, they might inquire as to whether such customers could be served in a less costly manner.

The concepts of multi-level break-even analysis and profitability analysis are finding increasing use as companies such as Federal Express, US West, and Bank of America strive to identify profitable and unprofitable customers. At FedEx, customers are sometimes rated as "the good, the bad, and the ugly." FedEx strives to retain the "good" profitable customers, turn the "bad" into profitable customers, and ignore the "ugly" who seem unlikely to become profitable. The following Business Insight box also advises managers to think in terms of customer profitability rather than in terms of sales volume.

BUSINESS INSIGHT	Think Customer Value Not Sales Volume

Marketing consultant and trainer Tom Reilly cautions against the exuberance that often accompanies a salesperson's announcement that he or she just landed a big account. According to Reilly, even if the sale results in celebration because sales quotas are met or exceeded, the sale might not be a good deal. "What happens when the big one is a low-margin sale? What if your cost of serving this customer is unusually high? How about the transactions cost of serving this customer? How much of your selling time will be consumed following up on this sale?"

Reilly cautions that high-volume customers such as Wal-Mart understand the lure of the big sale and strive to leverage volume to cut contribution margins to the bone. "You don't take volume to the bank—you take profit."

Source: Tom Reilly, "Think Value, Not Volume," *Industrial Distribution*, April 2007, p. 23.

Variations in Multi-Level Contribution Income Statement

Classification schemes should be designed to fit the organization and user needs. In Module 14, when analyzing the costs of a manufacturing company, we used a manufacturing cost hierarchy. While formatting issues can seem mundane and routine, format is important because the way information is presented encourages certain types of questions while discouraging others. Hence, management accountants must inquire as to user needs before developing management accounting reports, just as users of management accounting information should be knowledgeable enough to request appropriate information and know whether the information they are receiving is the information they need. With computers to reduce computational drudgery and to provide a wealth of available data, the most important issues involve identifying the important questions and presenting information to address those questions.

In the case of General Distribution, we used a customer cost hierarchy with information presented in a single column. A multiple-column format is also useful for presenting and analyzing information. Assume that General Distribution's managment believes that the differences between the government and private sector markets are such that these markets could be better served with separate marketing activities. They would have two market segments, one for the government sector and one for the private sector, giving the following cost hierarchy:

1. Unit-level activities
2. Order-level activities
3. Customer-level activities
4. Market segment activities
5. Facility-level activities

One possible way of presenting General Distribution's 2013 multi-level income statement with two market segments is shown in Exhibit 15.9. The details underlying the development of this statement are not presented. In developing the statement, we assume the mix of units sold, their cost structure, and the costs of processing an order are unchanged. Finally, we present new market segment costs and assume that the addition of the segments allows for some reduction in previous facility-level costs.

EXHIBIT 15.9 Multi-Level Contribution Income Statement with Segments and Taxes			
GENERAL DISTRIBUTION **Multi-Level Contribution Income Statement** **For Year 2013**	Government Segment	Private Segment	Total
Sales.	$1,500,000	$2,000,000	$3,500,000
Less unit-level costs			
Cost of goods sold (0.80).	(1,200,000)	(1,600,000)	(2,800,000)
Unit-level contribution margin	300,000	400,000	700,000
Less order-level costs			
Cost of processing order (1,000 × $20; 3,000 × $20).	(20,000)	(60,000)	(80,000)
Order-level contribution margin	280,000	340,000	620,000
Less customer-level costs			
Mail, phone, sales visits, recordkeeping, etc. (150 × $200, 300 × $200).	(30,000)	(60,000)	(90,000)
Customer-level contribution margin.	250,000	280,000	530,000
Less market segment-level costs.	(80,000)	(20,000)	(100,000)
Market segment-level contribution.	$ 170,000	$ 260,000	430,000
Less facility-level costs			
Depreciation, manager salaries, insurance, etc.			(90,000)
Before-tax profit			340,000
Income taxes ($340,000 × 0.40)			(136,000)
After-tax profit			$ 204,000

The information in the total column is all that is required for a multi-level contribution income statement. The information in the two detailed columns for the government and private segments can, however, prove useful in analyzing the profitability of each. Observe that the facility-level costs, incurred for the benefit of both segments, are not assigned to specific segments. Depending on the nature of the goods sold, it may be possible to further analyze the profitability of each product (or type of product) sold in each market segment. The profitability analysis of business segments is more closely examined in Module 23.

GUIDANCE ANSWER

MANAGERIAL DECISION **You are the Division Manager**

Fixed costs represent a two-edged sword. When a company is growing its sales, fixed costs cause profits to grow faster than sales; however, if a company should experience declining sales, the rate of reduction in profits is greater than the rate of reduction in sales. When sales decline, variable costs decline proportionately, while fixed costs continue. For this reason, when a company faces serious declines that are expected to continue, one of the first steps its top management should consider is reducing capacity in order to reduce fixed costs. The automobile companies in the U.S. have been employing this technique in recent years to try to offset the effect of sales lost to importers.

DISCUSSION QUESTIONS

Q15-1. What is cost-volume-profit analysis and when is it particularly useful?

Q15-2. Identify the important assumptions that underlie cost-volume-profit analysis.

Q15-3. When is it most reasonable to use a single independent variable in cost-volume-profit analysis?

Q15-4. Distinguish between a contribution and a functional income statement.

Q15-5. What is the unit contribution margin? How is it used in computing the unit break-even point?

Q15-6. What is the contribution margin ratio and when is it most useful?

Q15-7. How is the break-even equation modified to take into account the sales required to earn a desired profit?

Q15-8. How does a profit-volume graph differ from a cost-volume-profit graph? When is a profit-volume graph most likely to be used?

Q15-9. What impact do income taxes have on the sales volume required to earn a desired after-tax profit?

Q15-10. How are profit opportunities and the risk of losses affected by operating leverage?

**Assignments with the ✅ in the margin are available in an online homework system.
See the Preface of the book for details.**

MINI EXERCISES

M15-11. Profitability Analysis (LO3)

Assume a local Cost Cutters provides cuts, perms, and hairstyling services. Annual fixed costs are $120,000, and variable costs are 40 percent of sales revenue. Last year's revenues totaled $240,000.

Required

a. Determine its break-even point in sales dollars.

b. Determine last year's margin of safety in sales dollars.

c. Determine the sales volume required for an annual profit of $70,000.

M15-12. Cost-Volume-Profit Graph: Identification and Sensitivity Analysis (LO3)

A typical cost-volume-profit graph is presented below.

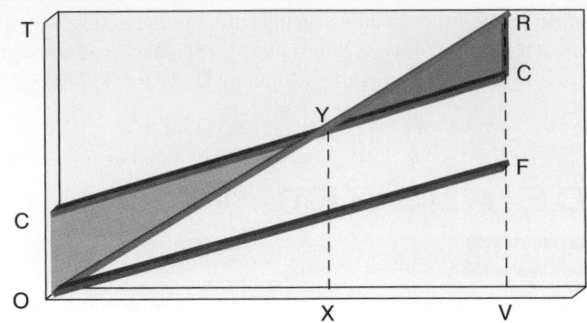

Required

a. Identify each of the following:
1. Line OF
2. Line OR
3. Line CC
4. The difference between lines OF and OV
5. The difference between lines CC and OF
6. The difference between lines CC and OV
7. The difference between lines OR and OF
8. Point X
9. Area CYO
10. Area RCY

b. Indicate the effect of each of the following independent events on lines CC, OR, and the break-even point:
1. A decrease in fixed costs
2. An increase in unit selling price
3. An increase in the variable costs per unit
4. An increase in fixed costs and a decrease in the unit selling price
5. A decrease in fixed costs and a decrease in the unit variable costs

M15-13. Profit-Volume Graph: Identification and Sensitivity Analysis (LO3)

A typical profit-volume graph follows.

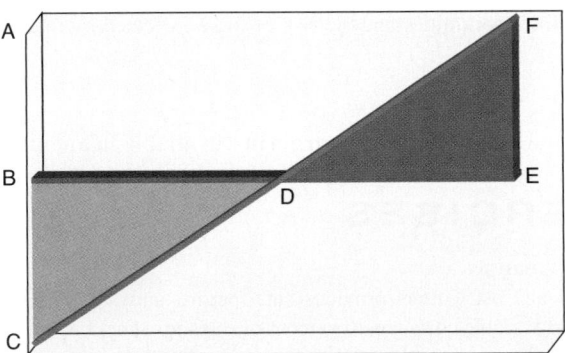

Required

a. Identify each of the following:
1. Area *BDC*
2. Area *DEF*
3. Point *D*
4. Line *AC*
5. Line *BC*
6. Line *EF*

b. Indicate the effect of each of the following on line *CF* and the break-even point:
1. An increase in the unit selling price
2. An increase in the variable costs per unit
3. A decrease in fixed costs
4. An increase in fixed costs and a decrease in the unit selling price
5. A decrease in fixed costs and an increase in the variable costs per unit

M15-14. Preparing Cost-Volume-Profit and Profit-Volume Graphs (LO3)

Assume a Domino's Pizza shop has the following monthly revenue and cost functions:

Domino's Pizza (DPZ)

$$\text{Total revenues} = \$10.00X$$
$$\text{Total costs} = \$18,000 + \$4.00X$$

Required

a. Prepare a graph (similar to that in Exhibit 15.3) illustrating Domino's cost-volume-profit relationships. The vertical axis should range from $0 to $72,000, in increments of $12,000. The horizontal axis should range from 0 units to 6,000 units, in increments of 2,000 units.

b. Prepare a graph (similar to that in Exhibit 15.4) illustrating Domino's profit-volume relationships. The horizontal axis should range from 0 units to 6,000 units, in increments of 2,000 units.

c. When is it most appropriate to use a profit-volume graph?

M15-15. Preparing Cost-Volume-Profit and Profit-Volume Graphs (LO3)

Hometown Dog Company is a hot dog concession business operating at five baseball stadiums. It sells hot dogs, with all the fixings, for $5.00 each. Variable costs are $3.50 per hot dog, and fixed operating costs are $750,000 per year.

Required

a. Determine the annual break-even point in hot dogs.

b. Prepare a cost-volume-profit graph for the company. Use a format that emphasizes the contribution margin. The vertical axis should vary between $0 and $5,000,000 in increments of $1,000,000. The horizontal axis should vary between 0 hot dogs and 1,000,000 hot dogs, in increments of 250,000 hot dogs. Label the graph in thousands.

c. Prepare a profit-volume graph for the company. The vertical axis should vary between $(750,000) and $750,000 in increments of $150,000. The horizontal axis should vary as described in requirement (b). Label the graph in thousands.

d. Evaluate the profit-volume graph. In what ways is it superior and in what ways is it inferior to the traditional cost-volume-profit graph?

M15-16. Multiple Product Break-Even Analysis (LO4)

Presented is information for Stafford Company's three products.

	A	B	C
Unit selling price..........	$5	$7	$6
Unit variable costs	(4)	(5)	(3)
Unit contribution margin....	$1	$2	$3

With monthly fixed costs of $112,500, the company sells two units of A for each unit of B and three units of B for each unit of C.

Required

Determine the unit sales of product A at the monthly break-even point.

EXERCISES

E15-17.   Contribution Income Statement and Cost-Volume-Profit Graph   (LO2, 3)

Alberta Company produces a product that is sold for $40 per unit. The company produced and sold 6,000 units during May 2012. There were no beginning or ending inventories. Variable and fixed costs follow.

Variable Costs per Unit			Fixed Costs per Month	
Manufacturing:			Manufacturing overhead	$40,000
Direct materials...........	$10		Selling and administrative ...	20,000
Direct labor..............	2		Total	$60,000
Manufacturing overhead....	5	$17		
Selling and administrative		5		
Total		$22		

Required

a. Prepare a contribution income statement for May.

b. Prepare a cost-volume-profit graph. Label the horizontal axis in units with a maximum value of 10,000. Label the vertical axis in dollars with a maximum value of $400,000. Draw a vertical line on the graph for the current (6,000) unit sales level, and label total variable costs, total fixed costs, and total profits at 6,000 units.

E15-18.   Contribution Margin Concepts   (LO3, 4)

The following information is taken from the 2012 records of Navajo Art Shop.

	Fixed	Variable	Total
Sales............			$750,000
Costs			
Goods sold		$337,500	
Labor..........	$160,000	60,000	
Supplies	2,000	5,000	
Utilities	12,000	13,000	
Rent	24,000	—	
Advertising	6,000	24,500	
Miscellaneous...	6,000	10,000	
Total costs......	$210,000	$450,000	(660,000)
Net income.......			$ 90,000

Required

a. Determine the annual break-even dollar sales volume.

b. Determine the current margin of safety in dollars.

c. Prepare a cost-volume-profit graph for the art shop. Label both axes in dollars with maximum values of $1,000,000. Draw a vertical line on the graph for the current ($750,000) sales level, and label total variable costs, total fixed costs, and total profits at $750,000 sales.

d. What is the annual break-even dollar sales volume if management makes a decision that increases fixed costs by $35,000?

 E15-19.   Multiple Product Planning with Taxes   (LO3, 4)

In the year 2012, Wiggins Processing Company had the following contribution income statement:

WIGGINS PROCESSING COMPANY Contribution Income Statement For the Year 2012		
Sales.		$1,000,000
Variable costs		
Cost of goods sold	$420,000	
Selling and administrative.	200,000	(620,000)
Contribution margin		380,000
Fixed costs		
Manufacturing overhead.	205,000	
Selling and administrative.	80,000	(285,000)
Before-tax profit		95,000
Income taxes (36%)		(34,200)
After-tax profit		$ 60,800

Required

a. Determine the annual break-even point in sales dollars.

b. Determine the annual margin of safety in sales dollars.

c. What is the break-even point in sales dollars if management makes a decision that increases fixed costs by $57,000?

d. With the current cost structure, including fixed costs of $285,000, what dollar sales volume is required to provide an after-tax net income of $200,000?

e. Prepare an abbreviated contribution income statement to verify that the solution to requirement (d) will provide the desired after-tax income.

E15-20. **Not-for-Profit Applications** (LO3)

Determine the solution to each of the following independent cases:

a. Hillside College has annual fixed operating costs of $12,500,000 and variable operating costs of $1,000 per student. Tuition is $8,000 per student for the coming academic year, with a projected enrollment of 1,500 students. Expected revenues from endowments and federal and state grants total $250,000. Determine the amount the college must obtain from other sources.

b. The Hillside College Student Association is planning a fall concert. Expected costs (renting a hall, hiring a band, etc.) are $30,000. Assuming 3,000 people attend the concert, determine the break-even price per ticket. How much will the association lose if this price is charged and only 2,700 tickets are sold?

c. City Hospital has a contract with the city to provide indigent health care on an outpatient basis for $25 per visit. The patient will pay $5 of this amount, with the city paying the balance ($20). Determine the amount the city will pay if the hospital has 10,000 patient visits.

d. A civic organization is engaged in a fund-raising program. On Civic Sunday, it will sell newspapers at $1.25 each. The organization will pay $0.75 for each newspaper. Costs of the necessary permits, signs, and so forth are $500. Determine the amount the organization will raise if it sells 5,000 newspapers.

e. Christmas for the Needy is a civic organization that provides Christmas presents to disadvantaged children. The annual costs of this activity are $5,000, plus $10 per present. Determine the number of presents the organization can provide with $20,000.

E15-21. **Alternative Production Procedures and Operating Leverage** (LO3, 5)

Assume Paper Mate is planning to introduce a new executive pen that can be manufactured using either a capital-intensive method or a labor-intensive method. The predicted manufacturing costs for each method are as follows:

Paper Mate

	Capital Intensive	Labor Intensive
Direct materials per unit..........................	$ 5.00	$ 6.00
Direct labor per unit	$ 5.00	$12.00
Variable manufacturing overhead per unit	$ 4.00	$ 2.00
Fixed manufacturing overhead per year.............	$2,440,000.00	$700,000.00

Paper Mate's market research department has recommended an introductory unit sales price of $30. The incremental selling costs are predicted to be $500,000 per year, plus $2 per unit sold.

Required
a. Determine the annual break-even point in units if Paper Mate uses the:
   1. Capital-intensive manufacturing method.
   2. Labor-intensive manufacturing method.
b. Determine the annual unit volume at which Paper Mate is indifferent between the two manufacturing methods.
c. Management wants to know more about the effect of each alternative on operating leverage.
   1. Explain operating leverage and the relationship between operating leverage and the volatility of earnings.
   2. Compute operating leverage for each alternative at a volume of 250,000 units.
   3. Which alternative has the higher operating leverage? Why?

 E15-22. Contribution Income Statement and Operating Leverage (LO3, 5)
Florida Berry Basket harvests early-season strawberries for shipment throughout the eastern United States in March. The strawberry farm is maintained by a permanent staff of 10 employees and seasonal workers who pick and pack the strawberries. The strawberries are sold in crates containing 100 individually packaged one-quart containers. Affixed to each one-quart container is the distinctive Florida Berry Basket logo inviting buyers to "Enjoy the berry best strawberries in the world!" The selling price is $90 per crate, variable costs are $80 per crate, and fixed costs are $275,000 per year. In the year 2012, Florida Berry Basket sold 45,000 crates.

Required
a. Prepare a contribution income statement for the year ended December 31, 2012.
b. Determine the company's 2012 operating leverage.
c. Calculate the percentage change in profits if sales decrease by 10 percent.
d. Management is considering the purchase of several berry-picking machines. This will increase annual fixed costs to $375,000 and reduce variable costs to $77.50 per crate. Calculate the effect of this acquisition on operating leverage and explain any change.

E15-23. Multiple Product Break-Even Analysis (LO4)
Yuma Tax Service prepares tax returns for low- to middle-income taxpayers. Its service operates January 2 through April 15 at a counter in a local department store. All jobs are classified into one of three categories: standard, multiform, and complex. Following is information for last year. Also, last year, the fixed cost of rent, utilities, and so forth were $45,000.

	Standard	Multiform	Complex
Billing rate.....................	$50	$125	$250
Average variable costs...........	(30)	(75)	(150)
Average contribution margin	$20	$50	$100
Number of returns prepared........	1,750	500	250

Required
a. Determine Yuma's break-even dollar sales volume.
b. Determine Yuma's margin of safety in sales dollars.
c. Prepare a profit-volume graph for Yuma's Tax Service.

E15-24. Cost-Volume-Profit Relations: Missing Data (LO3)
Following are data from 4 separate companies.

	Case 1	Case 2	Case 3	Case 4
Unit sales	1,000	800	?	?
Sales revenue.	$20,000	?	?	$60,000
Variable cost per unit	$10	$1	$12	?
Contribution margin	?	$800	?	?
Fixed costs.	$8,000	?	$80,000	?
Net income.	?	$400	?	?
Unit contribution margin.	?	?	?	$15
Break-even point (units)	?	?	4,000	2,000
Margin of safety (units).	?	?	300	1,000

Required
Supply the missing data in each independent case.

E15-25. Cost-Volume-Profit Relations: Missing Data (LO3)
Following are data from 4 separate companies.

	Case A	Case B	Case C	Case D
Sales revenue.	$100,000	$80,000	?	?
Contribution margin	$40,000	?	$20,000	?
Fixed costs.	$30,000	?	?	?
Net income.	?	$5,000	$10,000	?
Variable cost ratio.	?	0.50	?	0.20
Contribution margin ratio	?	?	0.40	?
Break-even point (dollars)	?	?	?	$25,000
Margin of safety (dollars)	?	?	?	$20,000

Required
Supply the missing data in each independent case.

E15-26.[A] Customer-Level Planning

7-Eleven operates a number of convenience stores worldwide. Assume that an analysis of operating   7-Eleven
costs, customer sales, and customer patronage reveals the following:

Fixed costs per store	$80,000.00/year
Variable cost ratio.	0.80
Average sale per customer visit	$15.00
Average customer visits per week	1.75
Customers as portion of city population	0.04

Required
Determine the city population required for a single 7-Eleven to earn an annual profit of $40,000.

E15-27.[A] Multiple-Level Break-Even Analysis
Nielsen Associates provides marketing services for a number of small manufacturing firms. Nielsen
receives a commission of 10 percent of sales. Operating costs are as follows:

Unit-level costs.	$0.02 per sales dollar
Sales-level costs	$200 per sales order
Customer-level costs	$1,000 per customer per year
Facility-level costs	$60,000 per year

Required

a. Determine the minimum order size in sales dollars for Nielsen to break even on an order.

b. Assuming an average customer places four orders per year, determine the minimum annual sales required to break even on a customer.

c. What is the average order size in (b)?

d. Assuming Nielsen currently serves 100 customers, with each placing an average of four orders per year, determine the minimum annual sales required to break even.

e. What is the average order size in (d)?

f. Explain the differences in the answers to (a), (c), and (e).

PROBLEMS

P15-28. Profit Planning with Taxes   (LO3)

Chandler Manufacturing Company produces a product that it sells for $35 per unit. Last year, the company manufactured and sold 20,000 units to obtain an after-tax profit of $54,000. Variable and fixed costs follow.

Variable Costs per Unit		Fixed Costs per Year	
Manufacturing	$18	Manufacturing	$ 80,000
Selling and administrative	7	Selling and administrative . . .	30,000
Total	$25	Total	$110,000

Required

a. Determine the tax rate the company paid last year.

b. What unit sales volume is required to provide an after-tax profit of $90,000?

c. If the company reduces the unit variable cost by $2.50 and increases fixed manufacturing costs by $20,000, what unit sales volume is required to provide an after-tax profit of $90,000?

d. What assumptions are made about taxable income and tax rates in requirements (a) through (c)?

 P15-29. Contribution Income Statement, Cost-Volume-Profit Graph, and Taxes   (LO2, 3)

New York Tours (NYT) provides daily sightseeing tours that include transportation, admission to selected attractions, and lunch. Ticket prices are $90 each. During June 2012, NYT provided 3,000 tours.

Variable Costs per Customer		Fixed Costs per Month	
Admission fees.	$30	Operations	$25,000
Lunch	20	Selling and administration	15,000
Overhead	12		
Selling and administrative	8		
Total	$70	Total	$40,000

NYT is subject to an income tax rate of 40 percent.

Required:

a. Prepare a contribution income statement for June.

b. Determine NYT's monthly break-even point in units.

c. Determine NYT's margin of safety for June 2012.

d. Determine the unit sales required for a monthly after-tax profit of $15,000.

e. Prepare a cost-volume-profit graph. Label the horizontal axis in units with a maximum value of 4,000. Label the vertical in dollars with a maximum value of $400,000. Draw a vertical line on the graph for the current (3,000) unit level and label total variable costs, total fixed costs, and total before-tax profits at 3,000 units.

 P15-30. High-Low Cost Estimation and Profit Planning   (LO3, 4)

Comparative 2011 and 2012 income statements for Dakota Products Inc. follow:

DAKOTA PRODUCTS INC. Comparative Income Statements For Years Ending December 31, 2011 and 2012		
	2011	2012
Unit sales	5,000	8,000
Sales revenue	$65,000	$104,000
Expenses	(70,000)	(85,000)
Profit (loss)	$ (5,000)	$ 19,000

Required

a. Determine the break-even point in units.

b. Determine the unit sales volume required to earn a profit of $10,000.

P15-31. CVP Analysis and Special Decisions (LO3, 4)

Sweet Grove Citrus Company buys a variety of citrus fruit from growers and then processes the fruit into a product line of fresh fruit, juices, and fruit flavorings. The most recent year's sales revenue was $4,200,000. Variable costs were 60 percent of sales and fixed costs totaled $1,300,000. Sweet Grove is evaluating two alternatives designed to enhance profitability.

- One staff member has proposed that Sweet Grove purchase more automated processing equipment. This strategy would increase fixed costs by $300,000 but decrease variable costs to 54 percent of sales.

- Another staff member has suggested that Sweet Grove rely more on outsourcing for fruit processing. This would reduce fixed costs by $300,000 but increase variable costs to 65 percent of sales.

Required

a. What is the current break-even point in sales dollars?

b. Assuming an income tax rate of 34 percent, what dollar sales volume is currently required to obtain an after-tax profit of $500,000?

c. In the absence of income taxes, at what sales volume will both alternatives (automation and outsourcing) provide the same profit?

d. Briefly describe one strength and one weakness of both the automation and the outsourcing alternatives.

P15-32. Break-Even Analysis in a Not-for-Profit Organization (LO3)

Melford Hospital operates a general hospital but rents space to separately owned entities rendering specialized services such as pediatrics and psychiatry. Melford charges each separate entity for patients' services (meals and laundry) and for administrative services (billings and collections). Space and bed rentals are fixed charges for the year, based on bed capacity rented to each entity. Melford charged the following costs to Pediatrics for the year ended June 30, 2011:

	Patient Services (Variable)	Bed Capacity (Fixed)
Dietary	$ 600,000	
Janitorial		$ 70,000
Laundry	300,000	
Laboratory	450,000	
Pharmacy	350,000	
Repairs and maintenance		30,000
General and administrative		1,300,000
Rent		1,500,000
Billings and collections	300,000	
Total	$2,000,000	$2,900,000

In addition to these charges from Melford Hospital, Pediatrics incurred the following personnel costs:

	Annual Salaries*
Supervising nurses.....	$100,000
Nurses	200,000
Assistants...........	180,000
Total	$480,000

*These salaries are fixed within the ranges of annual patient-days considered in this problem.

During the year ended June 30, 2011, Pediatrics charged each patient $300 per day, had a capacity of 60 beds, and had revenues of $6,000,000 for 365 days. Pediatrics operated at 100 percent capacity on 90 days during this period. It is estimated that during these 90 days, the demand exceeded 80 beds. Melford has 20 additional beds available for rent for the year ending June 30, 2012. This additional rental would proportionately increase Pediatrics' annual fixed charges based on bed capacity.

Required

a. Calculate the minimum number of patient-days required for Pediatrics to break even for the year ending June 30, 2012, if the additional beds are not rented. Patient demand is unknown, but assume that revenue per patient-day, cost per patient-day, cost per bed, and salary rates for the year ending June 30, 2012, remain the same as for the year ended June 30, 2011.

b. Assume Pediatrics rents the extra 20-bed capacity from Melford. Determine the net increase or decrease in earnings by preparing a schedule of increases in revenues and costs for the year ending June 30, 2012. Assume that patient demand, revenue per patient-day, cost per patient-day, cost per bed, and salary rates remain the same as for the year ended June 30, 2011.

(CPA adapted)

P15-33. CVP Analysis of Alternative Products (LO3)

Mountain Top Boot Company plans to expand its manufacturing capacity to allow up to 20,000 pairs of a new product each year. Because only one product can be produced, management is deciding between the production of the Sure Foot for backpacking and the Trail Runner for exercising. A marketing analysis indicates Mountain Top could sell between 8,000 and 14,000 pairs of either product.

The accounting department has developed the following price and cost information:

	Product	
	Sure Foot	Trail Runner
Selling price per pair.....	$ 80.00	$ 75.00
Variable costs per pair	50.00	50.00
Product costs.....	$130,000.00	$50,000.00

Facility costs for expansion, regardless of product, are $150,000. Mountain Top is subject to a 40 percent income tax rate.

Required

a. Determine the number of pairs of Sure Foot boots Mountain Top must sell to obtain an after tax profit of $30,000.

b. Determine the number of pairs of each product Mountain Top must sell to obtain identical before-tax profit.

c. For the solution to requirement b, calculate Mountain Top's after-tax profit or loss.

d. Which product should Mountain Top produce if both products were guaranteed to sell at least 13,000 pairs. Verify your solution with calculations.

e. How much would the variable costs per pair of the product *not* selected in requirement d have to fall before both products provide the same profit at sales of 13,000 pairs? Verify your solution with calculations.

P15-34. CVP Analysis Using Published Financial Statements (LO3, 4)

Netflix
NFLX

Condensed data in thousands of dollars (000) from Netflix's 2007 and 2008 income statements follow:

	2008	2007
Revenues	$1,364,661	$1,205,340
Cost of revenues and operating expenses.	(1,243,155)	(1,113,567)
Operating profit	$ 121,506	$ 91,773

Required

a. Develop a cost-estimation equation for Netflix's annual cost of revenues and operating expenses.

b. Determine Netflix's annual break-even point.

c. Predict operating profit for 2009, assuming 2009 sales of $1,670,269 thousand.

d. Identify the assumptions required to use the equations and amounts computed above.

P15-35.[A] **Multiple-Product Profitability Analysis, Multiple-Level Profitability Analysis**

College Avenue Bookstore sells new college textbooks at the publishers' suggested retail prices. It then pays the publishers an amount equal to 75 percent of the suggested retail price. The store's other variable costs average 5 percent of sales revenue and annual fixed costs amount to $360,000.

Required

a. Determine the bookstore's annual break-even point in sales dollars.

b. Assuming an average textbook has a suggested retail price of $120, determine the bookstore's annual break-even point in units.

c. College Avenue Bookstore is planning to add used book sales to its operations. A typical used book costs the store 25 percent of the suggested retail price of a new book. The bookstore plans to sell used books for 75 percent of the suggested retail price of a new book. Assuming unit sales are unchanged, describe the effect on bookstore profitability of shifting sales toward more used and fewer new textbooks.

d. College Publishing produces and sells new textbooks to college and university bookstores. Typical project-level costs total $325,000 for a new textbook. Production and distribution costs amount to 20 percent of the net amount the publisher receives from the bookstores. Textbook authors are paid a royalty of 15 percent of the net amount received from the bookstores. Determine the dollar sales volume required for College Publishing to break even on a new textbook. This is the amount the bookstore pays the publisher, not the bookstore's sales revenue.

e. For a project with predicted sales of 8,000 new books at $120 each, determine:
   1. The bookstores' contribution.
   2. The publisher's contribution.
   3. The author's royalties.

P15-36. **Multiple-Product Profitability Analysis** (LO3, 4)

Hearth Manufacturing Company produces two models of wood-burning stoves, Cozy Kitchen and All-House. Presented is sales information for the year 2012.

	Cozy Kitchen	All-House	Total
Units manufactured and sold.	1,000	1,500	2,500
Sales revenue.	$300,000	$750,000	$1,050,000
Variable costs.	(200,000)	(450,000)	(650,000)
Contribution margin	$100,000	$300,000	400,000
Fixed costs.			(240,000)
Before-tax profit.			160,000
Income taxes (40 percent)			(64,000)
After-tax profit			$ 96,000

Required

a. Determine the current break-even point in sales dollars.

b. With the current product mix and break-even point, determine the average unit contribution margin and unit sales.

c. Sales representatives believe that the total sales will increase to 3,000 units, with the sales mix likely shifting to 80 percent Cozy Kitchen and 20 percent All-House over the next few years. Evaluate the desirability of this projection.

P15-37. Multiple-Product Break-Even Analysis   (LO3, 4)

Currently, Corner Lunch Counter sells only Super Burgers for $2.50 each. During a typical month, the Counter reports a profit of $9,000 with sales of $50,000 and fixed costs of $21,000. Management is considering the introduction of a new Super Chicken Sandwich that will sell for $3 and have variable costs of $1.80. The addition of the Super Chicken Sandwich will require hiring additional personnel and renting additional equipment. These actions will increase monthly fixed costs by $7,760.

In the short run, management predicts that Super Chicken sales will average 10,000 sandwiches per month. However, almost all short-run sales of Super Chickens will come from regular customers who switch from Super Burgers to Super Chickens. Consequently, management predicts monthly sales of Super Burgers will decline by 10,000 units to $25,000. In the long run, management predicts that Super Chicken sales will increase to 15,000 sandwiches per month and that Super Burger sales will increase to 30,000 burgers per month.

Required

a. Determine each of the following:
  1. The current monthly break-even point in sales dollars.
  2. The short-run monthly profit and break-even point in sales dollars subsequent to the introduction of Super Chickens.
  3. The long-run monthly profit and break-even point in sales dollars subsequent to the introduction of Super Chickens.
b. Based on your analysis, what are your recommendations?

P15-38.ᴬ Multi-Level Profitability Analysis

AccuMeter manufactures and sells its only product (Z1) in lot sizes of 500 units. Because of this approach, lot (batch)-level costs are regarded as variable for CVP analysis. Presented is sales and cost information for the year 2012:

Sales revenue (50,000 units at $40)	$2,000,000
Direct materials (50,000 units at $10)	500,000
Processing (50,000 units at $15)	750,000
Setup (100 lots at $2,000)	200,000
Batch movement (100 lots at $400)	40,000
Order filling (100 lots at $200)	20,000
Fixed manufacturing overhead	800,000
Fixed selling and administrative	300,000

Required

a. Prepare a traditional contribution income statement in good form.
b. Prepare a multi-level contribution income statement in good form. (*Hint:* First determine the appropriate cost hierarchy.)
c. What is the current contribution per lot (batch) of 500 units?
d. Management is contemplating introducing a limited number of specialty products. One product would sell for $60 per unit and have direct materials costs of $12 per unit. All other costs and all production and sales procedures will remain unchanged. What lot (batch) size is required for a contribution of $700 per lot?

MANAGEMENT APPLICATIONS

MA15-39. Ethics and Pressure to Improve Profit Plans   (LO1)

Art Conroy is the assistant controller of New City Muffler, Inc., a subsidiary of New City Automotive, which manufactures tailpipes, mufflers, and catalytic converters at several plants throughout North America. Because of pressure for lower selling prices, New City Muffler has had disappointing financial performance in recent years. Indeed, Conroy is aware of rumblings from corporate headquarters threatening to close the plant.

One of Conroy's responsibilities is to present the plant's financial plans for the coming year to the corporate officers and board of directors. In preparing for the presentation, Conroy was intrigued to note that the focal point of the budget presentation was a profit-volume graph projecting an increase in profits and a reduction in the break-even point.

Curious as to how the improvement would be accomplished, Conroy ultimately spoke with Paula Mitchell, the plant manager. Mitchell indicated that a planned increase in productivity would reduce variable costs and increase the contribution margin ratio.

When asked how the productivity increase would be accomplished, Mitchell made a vague reference to increasing the speed of the assembly line. Conroy commented that speeding up the assembly line could lead to labor problems because the speed of the line was set by union contract. Mitchell responded that she was afraid that if the speedup were opened to negotiation, the union would make a big "stink" that could result in the plant being closed. She indicated that the speedup was the "only way to save the plant, our jobs, and the jobs of all plant employees." Besides, she did not believe employees would notice a 2 or 3 percent increase in speed. Mitchell concluded the meeting observing, "You need to emphasize the results we will accomplish next year, not the details of how we will accomplish those results. Top management does not want to be bored with details. If we accomplish what we propose in the budget, we will be in for a big bonus."

Required
What advice do you have for Art Conroy?

MA15-40. CVP Analysis with Changing Cost Structure (LO1, 3, 5)
Homestead Telephone was formed in the 1940s to bring telephone services to remote areas of the U.S. Midwest. The early equipment was quite primitive by today's standards. All calls were handled manually by operators, and all customers were on party lines. By the 1970s, however, all customers were on private lines, and mechanical switching devices handled routine local and long distance calls. Operators remained available for directory assistance, credit card calls, and emergencies. In the 1990s Homestead Telephone added local Internet connections as an optional service to its regular customers. It also established an optional cellular service, identified as the Home Ranger.

Required
a. Using a unit-level analysis, develop a graph with two lines, representing Homestead Telephone's cost structure (1) in the 1940s and (2) in the late 1990s. Be sure to label the axes and lines.
b. With sales revenue as the independent variable, what is the likely impact of the changed cost structure on Homestead Telephone's (1) contribution margin percent and (2) break-even point?
c. Discuss how the change in cost structure affected Homestead's operating leverage and how this affects profitability under rising or falling sales scenarios.

MA15-41. Cost Estimation and CVP Analysis (LO2, 3, 4)
Presented are the 2010 and 2011 functional income statements of Regional Distribution, Inc.:

REGIONAL DISTRIBUTION, INC. Functional Income Statements For Years Ending December 31, 2010 and 2011				
		2010		**2011**
Sales.		$5,520,000		$5,000,000
Expenses				
Cost of goods sold	$4,140,000		$3,750,000	
Shipping	215,400		200,000	
Sales order processing	52,500		50,000	
Customer relations	120,000		100,000	
Depreciation	80,000		80,000	
Administrative	250,000	(4,857,900)	250,000	(4,430,000)
Before-tax profit		662,100		570,000
Income taxes (40%)		(264,840)		(228,000)
After-tax profit		$ 397,260		$ 342,000

Required
a. Determine Regional Distribution's break-even point in sales dollars.
b. What dollar sales volume is required to earn an after-tax profit of $480,000?
c. Assuming budgeted 2012 sales of $6,000,000, prepare a 2012 contribution income statement.
d. Discuss the reliability of the calculations in requirements a-c, including the limitations of the CVP model and how they affect the reliability of the model.

SOLUTIONS TO REVIEW PROBLEMS

Mid-Module Review

Solution

a.

MEMORABILIA CUP COMPANY Contribution Income Statement For the Month of September 2012		
Sales (3,000 × $40)		$120,000
Less variable costs		
Direct materials (3,000 × $15)	$45,000	
Direct labor (3,000 × $3).	9,000	
Manufacturing overhead (3,000 × $10)	30,000	
Selling and administrative (3,000 × $2)	6,000	(90,000)
Contribution margin		30,000
Less fixed costs		
Manufacturing overhead.	15,000	
Selling and administrative.	10,000	(25,000)
Profit.		$ 5,000

b.

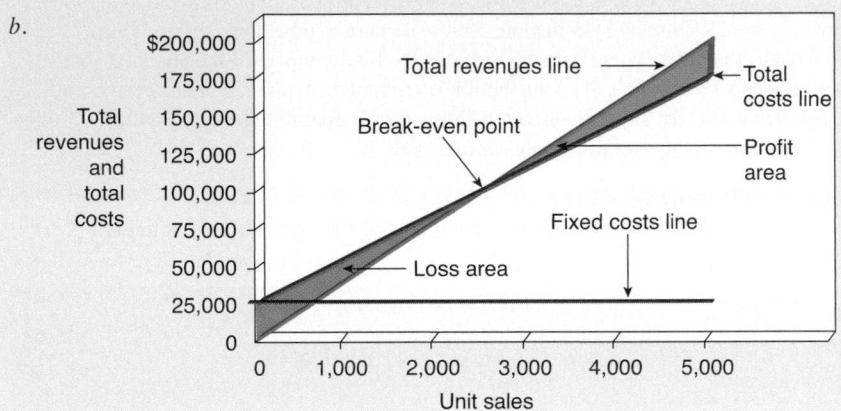

c.

Selling price	$40 per unit
Variable costs.	(30) per unit
Contribution margin	$10 per unit

$$\text{Contribution margin ratio} = \frac{\text{Unit contribution margin}}{\text{Unit selling price}}$$
$$= \$10 \div \$40$$
$$= 0.25$$

d.
$$\text{Break-even point} = \frac{\text{Fixed costs}}{\text{Unit contribution margin}}$$
$$= \$25,000 \div \$10$$
$$= 2,500 \text{ units}$$

e.
$$\text{Required dollar sales} = \frac{\text{Fixed costs} + \text{Desired profit}}{\text{Contribution margin ratio}}$$
$$= (\$25,000 + \$5,000) \div 0.25$$
$$= \$120,000$$

f.

$$\text{Required unit sales} = \frac{\text{Fixed costs} + \text{Desired before-tax profit}}{\text{Contribution margin per unit}}$$

$$\text{Desired before-tax profit} = \$4,500 \div (1 - 0.40) = \$7,500$$

$$\text{Required units sales} = (\$25,000 + \$7,500) \div \$10$$

$$= 3,250 \text{ units}$$

Module-End Review

Solution

a.

	Coffee	Tea	Smoothies	Total
Monthly unit sales	6,000	3,750	2,250	
Selling price	$1.35	$1.25	$1.95	
Sales	$8,100.00	$4,687.50	$4,387.50	$17,175.00
Variable cost	3,600.00	1,687.50	1,687.50	6,975.00
Contribution margin	$4,500.00	$3,000.00	$2,700.00	10,200.00
Fixed cost				8,000.00
Before-tax profit				$ 2,200.00
Contribution margin (CM) ratio	0.5556	0.640	0.6154	0.5939
Current sales mix (based on sales dollars)	47.16%	27.29%	25.55%	

b.

$$\text{Break-even} = \text{Fixed costs/Total contribution margin ratio}$$

$$= \$8,000/0.5939$$

$$= \$13,470$$

Proof:		Sales		C/M Ratio	
Coffee:	$13,470 × 47.16%	=	$ 6,352.45 ×	0.5556 =	$3,529.42
Tea:	$13,470 × 27.29%	=	3,675.96 ×	0.640 =	2,352.62*
Smoothies:	$13,470 × 25.55%	=	3,441.59 ×	0.6154 =	2,117.96*
			$13,470.00		
Total contribution margin					8,000.00
Fixed costs					8,000.00
Before-tax profit					–0–

* Amounts adjusted to correct for minor rounding error.

c. Joe's Brews has an operating leverage of 4.636, calculated as a contribution margin of $10,200 divided by before-tax profit of $2,200. Therefore, if sales dollars increase by 20% to $20,610, before-tax profit should increase by 4.636 times 20%, or 92.72%, to $4,240. Because of the leverage caused by fixed costs, a 20% increase in sales results in a 92.72% increase in before-tax profit. Conversely, a 20% decrease in sales would result in a 92.72% decrease in before-tax profits to $160.

Proof:	20% Sales Increase	20% Sales Decrease
Sales	$20,610	$13,740
CM %	× 0.5939	× 0.5939
Total CM	12,240	8,160
Fixed costs	8,000	8,000
Before-tax profit	$ 4,240	$ 160

Current before-tax profit of $2,200 × (1 + 0.9272) = $4,240
Current before-tax profit of $2,200 × (1 − 0.9272) = $160

Getty Images

NINTENDO

Companies are often confronted with decisions that involve multiple alternatives, such as when a new product is introduced. Consider some of the likely decisions that Nintendo's managers made surrounding the introduction of the Wii ® in 2006.

■ Like most other companies that produce and sell products, Nintendo had to make a decision about how to manufacture this product that its design engineers had developed—whether to make the product itself, or buy it from an outsourcing company. If you look on a Wii console, you will see that they decided to outsource the product from China. *Financial Times*1[1] reported that

---

[1] Robin Harding, "Nintendo Makes More Profit Per Employee Than Goldman," *Financial Times*, September, 18, 2008, p27.

Nintendo's outsourcing strategy was a key factor in achieving its world's best profit per staff person, even more than Goldman Sachs or Google.

■ Adding the Wii to its product line probably required Nintendo to add new employees to its workforce, including design engineers, logistics specialists, marketing managers, financial managers, and others. The company had to make a decision about whether to purchase new facilities to house the Wii staff, or lease them.

■ Another key decision for Nintendo was how to market the Wii. Previously, they had not introduced a product with such a large adult market potential. Would they use a limited distribution channel much like Apple initially did with the iPhone, or would they blanket the retail market by placing their product in as many outlets

Relevant Costs and Benefits for Decision Making

LEARNING OBJECTIVES

LO1   Distinguish between relevant and irrelevant revenues and costs. (p. 16-3)

LO2   Analyze relevant costs and indicate how they differ under alternative decision scenarios. (p. 16-6)

LO3   Apply differential analysis to decision scenarios, including whether to change plans; to accept a special order; to make, buy, or outsource; and to sell or further process a product. (p. 16-8)

LO4   Allocate limited resources for purposes of maximizing short-run profit. (p. 16-16)

as possible, or would they use a strategy somewhere between these two extremes?

■   One of the most important decisions is the price at which a new product is launched, because price has a major impact on the size of the market for the product. Nintendo had to balance the selling price against costs, and come up with a price that would meet their investment return requirements. After the initial launch phase for the product, any decision regarding adjustments to price or cost inputs must be evaluated in terms of the overall effects on profits.

These are just some of the types of decisions that Nintendo would have made in connection with introducing the Wii. In each case, the decision entails extensive cost and benefit analysis to enable the company's managers to make judgments about which alternative to recommend. With over 75 million units sold, Wii was one of the most successful new-product launches in history.

Obviously, Nintendo's decision making regarding the launch of Wii was very effective. In this module we will introduce the concept of **relevant costing**, which is a model that helps managers identify the costs and benefits that are relevant to a wide range of business decisions, including those discussed above for Nintendo.

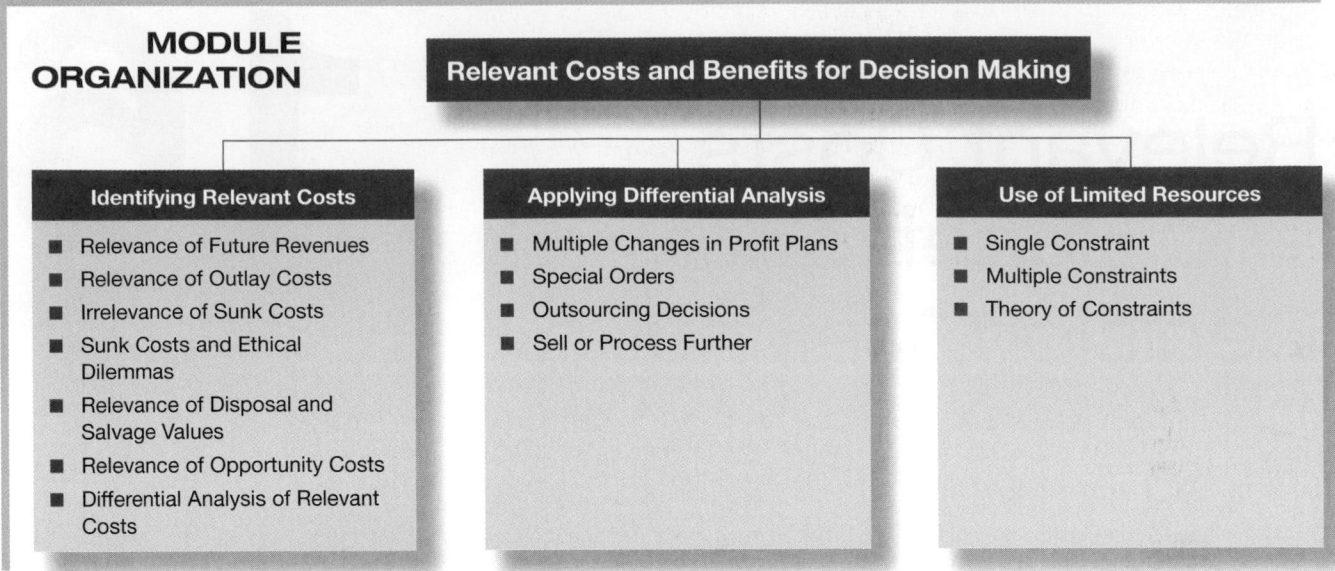

The purpose of this module is to examine approaches to identifying and analyzing revenue and cost information for specific decisions, such as the decision to outsource. Our emphasis is on identifying **relevant costs** (future costs that differ among competing decision alternatives) and distinguishing relevant costs from **irrelevant costs** that do not differ among competing decision alternatives. We consider a number of frequently encountered decisions: to make multiple changes in profit plans, to accept or reject a special order, to acquire a component or service internally or externally, to sell a product or process it further, and how to best use limited capacity. These decision situations are not exhaustive; they only illustrate relevant cost concepts. Once we understand these concepts, we can apply them to a variety of decision scenarios.

Although our focus in this module is on profit maximization, decisions should not be based solely on this criterion, especially maximizing profit in the short run. Managers must consider the implications decision alternatives have on long-run profit, as well as legal, ethical, social, and other nonquantitative factors. These factors can lead management to select a course of action other than that selected by financial information alone.

IDENTIFYING RELEVANT COSTS

LO1 Distinguish between relevant and irrelevant revenues and costs.

For a specific decision, the key to relevent cost analysis is first to identify the relevant costs (and revenues) and then to organize them in a manner that clearly indicates how they differ under each alternative. Consider the following equipment replacement decision.

Elektra, Inc. is a small start-up company that supplies high-quality components to manufacturers of wi-fi and bluetooth devices. One of its components used in wireless headsets is forecasted to sell 10,000 units during the coming year at a price of $20 per unit. Each of Elektra's components is manufactured with separate machines in a shared plant.

Headset Component Costs:	
Direct materials	$3.00 per unit
Conversion	5.00 per unit
Selling and distribution	1.00 per unit
Inspection and adjustment	$500 per batch
	(1,000 units)
Depreciation on machines	$15,000 per year
Machine maintenance	$200 per month
Advertising	$5,000 per year
Common Costs:	
Administrative salaries	$65,000 per year
Building operations	23,000 per year
Building rent	24,000 per year

The machine used in the manufacture of headset components is two years old and has a remaining useful life of four years. Its purchase price was $90,000 (new), and it has an estimated salvage value of zero dollars at the end of its useful life. Its current book value (original cost less accumulated depreciation) is $60,000, but it could be sold today for only $35,000.

Management is evaluating the desirability of replacing the machine with a new machine. The new machine costs $80,000, has a useful life of four years, and a predicted salvage value of zero dollars at the end of its useful life. Although the new machine has the same production capacity as the old machine, its predicted operating costs are lower because it consumes less electricity. Further, because of a computer control system, the new machine allows production of twice as many units between inspections and adjustments, and the cost of inspections and adjustments is lower. The new machine requires only annual, rather than monthly, overhauls. Hence, machine maintenance costs are lower. Costs for the new machine are predicted as follows:

Conversion costs	$4.00 per unit
Inspection and adjustment.	$300 per batch (2,000 units)
Machine maintenance	$200 per year

All other costs and all revenues remain unchanged.

The decision alternatives are to keep the old machine or to replace it with a new machine. An analysis of how costs and revenues differ under each alternative assists management in making the best choice. The first objective of this module is to study the distinction between relevant and irrelevant items. After evaluating the relevance of each item, we develop an analysis of relevant costs.

Relevance of Future Revenues

Revenues, which are inflows of resources from the sale of goods and services, are relevant to a decision only if they differ between alternatives. In this example, revenues are not relevant because they are identical under each alternative. They would be relevant if the new machine had greater capacity or if management intended to change the selling price should it acquire the new machine. (The $35,000 disposal value of the old machine is an inflow. However, *revenues* refer to resources from the sale of goods and services to customers in the normal course of business. We include the sale of the old machine under disposal and salvage values.)

The keep-or-replace decision facing Elektra's management might be called a **cost reduction proposal** because it is based on the assumption that the organization is committed to an activity and that management desires to minimize the cost of activities. Here, the two alternatives are either to continue operating with the old machine or to replace it with a new machine.

Although this approach is appropriate for many activities, managers should remember that they have another alternative—discontinue operations. To simplify the analysis, managers normally do not consider the alternative to discontinue when operations appear to be profitable. However, if there is any doubt about an operation's profitability, this alternative should be considered. Because revenues change if an operation is discontinued, revenues are relevant whenever this alternative is considered.

Relevance of Outlay Costs

Outlay costs are costs that require future expenditures of cash or other resources. Outlay costs that differ under the decision alternatives are relevant; outlay costs that do not differ are irrelevant. Elektra's relevant and irrelevant outlay costs for the equipment replacement decision follow.

Relevant Outlay Costs	Irrelevant Outlay Costs
Conversion Costs	Direct Materials
Inspection and Adjustment Costs	Selling and Distributon
Cost of New Machine	Advertising
Machine Maintenance	Common Outlay Costs

Irrelevance of Sunk Costs

Sunk costs result from past decisions that cannot be changed. Suppose we purchased a car for $15,000 five years ago. Today we must decide whether to purchase another car or have major maintenance performed on our current car. In making this decision, the purchase price of our current car is a sunk cost.

Although the relevance of outlay costs is determined by the decision scenario, sunk costs are never relevant. The cost of the old machine is a sunk cost, not a future cost. This cost and the related depreciation result from the past decision to acquire the old machine. Even though all the outlay costs discussed earlier would be relevant to a decision to continue or discontinue operations, the sunk cost of the old machine is not relevant even to this decision.

If management elects to keep the old machine, its book value will be depreciated over its remaining useful life of four years. However, if management elects to replace the old machine, its book value is written off when it is replaced. Even if management elects to discontinue operations, the book value of the old machine must be written off.

Sunk Costs Can Cause Ethical Dilemmas

Although the book value of the old machine has no economic significance, the accounting treatment of past costs may make it psychologically difficult for managers to regard them as irrelevant. If management replaces the old machine, a $25,000 accounting loss is recorded in the year of replacement:

Book value	$60,000
Disposal value	(35,000)
Loss on disposal	$25,000

The possibility of recording an accounting loss can create an ethical dilemma for managers. Although an action may be desirable from the long-run viewpoint of the organization, in the short run, choosing the action may result in an accounting loss. Fearing the loss will lead superiors to question her judgment, a manager might prefer to use the old machine (with lower total profits over the four-year period) as opposed to replacing it and being forced to record a loss on disposal. Although this action may avoid raising troublesome questions in the near term, the cumulative effect of many decisions of this nature is harmful to the organization's long-run economic health.

From an economic viewpoint, the analysis should focus on future costs and revenues that differ. The decision should not be influenced by sunk costs. Although there is no easy solution to this behavioral and ethical problem, managers and management accountants should be aware of its potential impact.

MANAGERIAL DECISION | **You are the Vice President of Manufacturing**

You recently made the decision to purchase a very expensive machine for your manufacturing plant that used technology that was well established over several years. The purchase of this machine was a major decision supported by the Chief Financial Officer, based solely on your recommendation. Shortly after making the purchase, you were attending a trade convention where you learned of new technology that is now available that essentially renders obsolete the machine you recently purchased. You feel that it may be best for the company to acquire the new technology since most of your competitors will be using it soon; however, you feel that this cannot be done now that you have recently purchased the new machine. What should you do? [Answer, p. 16-20]

Relevance of Disposal and Salvage Values

Elektra, Inc.'s revenues (inflows of resources from operations) from the sale of headset components were discussed earlier. The sale of fixed assets is also a source of resources. Because the sale of fixed assets is a nonoperating item, cash inflows obtained from these sales are discussed separately.

The disposal value of the old machine is a relevant cash inflow. It is obtained only if the replacement alternative is selected. Any salvage value available at the end of the useful life of either machine is also relevant. A loss on disposal can have a favorable tax impact if the loss can be offset against taxable gains or taxable income. To simplify the analysis, we ignore any tax implications at this point. The tax effects related to capital asset transactions are discussed in Module 24.

Relevance of Opportunity Costs

When making a decision between alternative courses of action, accepting one alternative results in rejecting the other alternative(s). Any benefit foregone as a result of rejecting one opportunity in favor of another opportunity is described as an **opportunity cost** of the accepted alternative. For example, if you are employed at a salary of $40,000 per year and you have the opportunity to continue to work or the opportunity to go back to school full-time for two years to earn a graduate degree, the cost of getting the degree includes not only all the outlay costs for tuition, books, and so forth, it also includes the salary foregone (or opportunity cost) of $40,000 per year. So, if your tuition and other outlay costs are going to be $25,000 per year for two years, the cost of earning the degree will be $50,000 of outlay costs and $80,000 of opportunity costs, for a total cost of earning the degree of $130,000. Opportunity costs are always relevant in making decisions among competing alternatives.

The following is a summary of all the relevant and irrelevant costs discussed in this section.

Relevant Costs		Irrelevant Costs	
Future costs that differ among competing alternatives		Future costs that do not differ among competing alternatives	
Opportunity Costs	**Relevant Outlay Costs**	**Irrelevant Outlay Costs**	**Sunk Costs**
Net benefits foregone of rejected alternatives	Future costs requiring future expenditures that differ	Future costs requiring future expenditures that do not differ	Historical costs resulting from past decisions

DIFFERENTIAL ANALYSIS OF RELEVANT COSTS

Differential cost analysis is an approach to the analysis of relevant costs that focuses on the costs that differ under alternative actions. A differential analysis of relevant costs for Elektra Inc.'s equipment replacement decision is in Exhibit 16.1. Replacement provides a net advantage of $17,800 over the life of both machines versus keeping the old machine.

An alternative analysis to that presented in Exhibit 16.1 is to present all revenues and costs (relevant and irrelevant) for each alternative in separate columns, such that the bottom line of the analysis is the total profit or loss for each alternative. This method is preferred if the goal is to determine the total profitability of each alternative. If the goal is to determine which of the two alternatives is most profitable, then a differential analysis is preferred.

Assuming the organization is committed to providing a particular product or service, a differential analysis of relevant costs (as shown in Exhibit 16.1) is preferred to a complete analysis of all costs and revenues for a number of reasons:

■ A differential analysis focuses on only those items that differ, providing a clearer picture of the impact of the decision. Management is less apt to be confused by this analysis than by one that combines relevant and irrelevant items.

■ A differential analysis contains fewer items, making it easier and quicker to prepare.

■ A differential analysis can help to simplify complex situations (such as those encountered by multiple-product or multiple-plant firms), when it is difficult to develop complete firmwide statements to analyze all decision alternatives.

LO2 Analyze relevant costs and indicate how they differ under alternative decision scenarios.

EXHIBIT 16.1 Differential Analysis of Relevant Costs

	Differential Analysis of Four-Year Totals		
	(1) Replace with New Machine	(2) Keep Old Machine	(1) − (2) Difference (effect of replacement on income)
Conversion:			
Old Machine (10,000 units × $5 × 4 years)		$200,000	
New Machine (10,000 units × $4 × 4 years)	$160,000		$40,000
Inspection and adjustment:			
Old Machine (10* setups × $500 × 4 years)		20,000	
New Machine (5** setups × $300 × 4 years).	6,000		14,000
Machine maintenance:			
Old Machine ($200 per month × 12 months × 4 years) .		9,600	
New Machine ($200 per month × 4 years).	800		8,800
Disposal of Old Machine	(35,000)		35,000
Cost of New Machine.	80,000		(80,000)
Totals	$211,800	$229,600	$17,800
Advantage of replacement.		$17,800	

* Old Machine: 10,000 units ÷ 1,000 units per batch
** New Machine: 10,000 units ÷ 2,000 units per batch

Before preparing a differential analysis, it is always desirable to reassess the organization's commitment to a product or service. This helps avoid "throwing good money after bad." If Elektra, Inc. currently had large annual losses, acquiring the new machine would merely reduce total losses over the next four years by $17,800. In this case, discontinuing operations (a third alternative) should also be considered.

MID-MODULE REVIEW

Tigertec Company manufactures golf clubs using a traditional process involving significant hand tooling and finishing. A European machine company has proposed to sell Tigertec a new highly automated machine that would reduce significantly the labor cost of producing its golf clubs. The cost of the machine is $1,000,000, and would have an expected life of 5 years, at the end of which it would have a residual value of $100,000. It has an estimated operating cost of $10,000 per month. The direct labor cost savings per club from using the machine is estimated to be $5 per club. In addition, one monthly salaried manufacturing manager, whose salary is $6,000 per month would no longer be needed. The Vice President of Manufacturing earns $10,000 per month. Also, the new machine would free up about 5,000 square feet of space from the displaced workers. Tigertec's building is held under a 10-year lease that has eight years remaining. The current lease cost is $1 per square foot per month. Tigertec may be able to use the space for other purposes, and it has received an offer to rent it to a nearby related company for $3,500 per month.

Required

a. Identify all of the costs described above as either "relevant" or "irrelevant" to the decision to acquire the new machine.
b. Assuming the new machine would be used to produce an average of 5,000 clubs per month, prepare a differential analysis of the relevant costs of buying the machine and using it for the next five years, versus continuing to use hand labor.
c. In addition to the quantitative analysis in requirement b., what qualitative considerations are important for making the right decision?

The solution is on page 16-34.

APPLYING DIFFERENTIAL ANALYSIS

Differential analysis is used to provide information for a variety of planning and decision-making situations. This section illustrates some of the more frequently encountered applications of differential analysis. To focus on differential analysis concepts, we will use a simple example involving the production of one product on a continuous basis with all output sold to distributors. From the viewpoint of our single-product firm, all costs can be classified as either (1) costs that vary with units produced and sold or (2) costs that are fixed in the short run.

LO3 Apply differential analysis to decision scenarios, including whether to change plans; to accept a special order; to make, buy, or outsource; and to sell or further process a product.

Multiple Changes in Profit Plans

Mind Trek, Limited, located in Dublin, Ireland, manufactures an electronic game sold to distributors for €22 per unit (the Euro, represented by the symbol €, is the basic unit of currency in the Republic of Ireland, which is a member of the European Union). Variable costs per unit and fixed costs per month follow:

Variable Costs per Unit		Fixed Costs per Month	
Direct materials	€ 5	Manufacturing overhead	€30,000
Direct labor	3	Selling and administrative ...	15,000
Manufacturing overhead ...	2	Total	€45,000
Selling	2		
Total	€12		

The unit contribution margin (UCM) is €10 (€22 selling price − €12 variable costs). Mind Trek's contribution income statement for April 2012 is presented in Exhibit 16.2. The April 2012 operations are typical. Monthly production and sales average 5,000 units, and monthly profits average €5,000.

Management wants to know the effect that each of the following three mutually exclusive alternatives would have on monthly profits.

1. Increasing the monthly advertising budget by €4,000, which should result in a 1,000-unit increase in monthly sales.
2. Increasing the selling price by €3, which should result in a 2,000-unit decrease in monthly sales.
3. Decreasing the selling price by €2, which should result in a 2,000-unit increase in monthly sales. However, because of capacity constraints, the last 1,000 units would be produced during overtime with the direct labor costs increasing by €1 per unit.

It is possible to develop contribution income statements for each alternative and then determine the profit impact of the proposed change by comparing the new income with the current income. A more direct approach is to use differential analysis and focus on only those items that differ under each alternative.

Alternative 1
Profit increase from increased sales
(1,000 additional unit sales × €10 UCM) €10,000
Profit decrease from increased advertising expenditures ....   (4,000)
Increase in monthly profit...   € 6,000

Alternative 2
Profit decrease from reduced sales given no changes in prices or costs
(2,000 lost unit sales × €10 UCM) ....   €(20,000)
Profit increase from increased selling price
[(5,000 current unit sales − 2,000 lost unit sales)
× €3 increase in unit selling price and UCM]   9,000
Decrease in monthly profit ....   €(11,000)

Alternative 3

Profit increase from increased sales given no changes in prices or costs	
(2,000 increased unit sales × €10 UCM)	€20,000
Profit decrease from reduced selling price of all units	
[(5,000 current unit sales + 2,000 additional unit sales)	
× €2 decrease in unit selling price and UCM]	(14,000)
Profit decrease from increased direct labor costs of the last 1,000 units	
(1,000 units × €1 increase in unit labor costs and decrease in UCM)	(1,000)
Increase in monthly profit	€ 5,000

Alternative 2 is undesirable because it would result in a decrease in monthly profit. Because Alternative 1 results in a larger increase in monthly profit, it is preferred to Alternative 3.

Special Orders

Assume an Australian distributor offered Mind Trek a reduced price of €12 per unit for a special, one-time order for 1,000 units. The Australian distributor will contract for a shipping company to handle all packing and transportation. Mind Trek has sufficient production capacity to produce the additional units without reducing sales to its regular distributors. Management desires to know the profit impact of accepting the order. The following analysis focuses on those costs and revenues that will differ if the order is accepted.

Increase in revenues (1,000 units × €12)......................		€12,000
Increase in costs		
Direct materials (1,000 units × €5)........................	€5,000	
Direct labor (1,000 units × €3)	3,000	
Variable manufacturing overhead (1,000 units × €2)...........	2,000	(10,000)
Increase in profits.......................................		€ 2,000

Accepting the special order will result in a profit increase of €2,000.

If management were unaware of relevant cost concepts, it might be tempted to compare the special order price to average unit cost information developed from accounting reports. Based on Mind Trek's April 2012 contribution income statement in Exhibit 16.2, the average cost of all manufacturing, selling, and administrative expenses was €21 per unit as follows.

Variable costs.....................	€ 60,000
Fixed costs.......................	45,000
Total costs	€105,000
Unit production and sales	÷ 5,000
Average unit cost	€ 21

Comparing the special order price of €12 per unit to the average unit cost of €21, management might conclude the order would result in a loss of €9 per unit.

It is apparent that the €21 figure encompasses variable costs of €12 per unit (including irrelevant selling and administrative costs of €2 per unit) and irrelevant fixed costs of €45,000 spread over 5,000 units. But remember, management may not have detailed cost information. To obtain appropriate information for decision-making purposes, management must ask its accounting staff for the specific information needed. Different configurations of cost information are provided for different purposes. In the absence of special instructions, the accounting staff might not supply relevant cost information.

EXHIBIT 16.2	Contribution Income Statement	

MIND TREK, LIMITED
Contribution Income Statement
For the Month of April 2012

Sales (5,000 units × €22)................................		€110,000
Less variable costs		
Direct materials (5,000 units × €5)......................	€25,000	
Direct labor (5,000 units × €3)...........................	15,000	
Manufacturing overhead (5,000 units × €2)................	10,000	
Selling and administrative (5,000 units × €2)..............	10,000	(60,000)
Contribution margin		50,000
Less fixed costs		
Manufacturing overhead...............................	30,000	
Selling and administrative.............................	15,000	(45,000)
Profit..		€ 5,000

Importance of Time Span and Opportunity Costs

The special order is a one-time order for 1,000 units that will use current excess capacity. Because no special setups or equipment are required to produce the order, it is appropriate to consider only variable costs in computing the order's profitability.

But what if the Australian distributor wanted Mind Trek to sign a multiyear contract to provide 1,000 units per month at €12 each? Under these circumstances, management would be well advised to reject the contract because there is a high probability that cost increases would make the order unprofitable in later years. At the very least, management should insist that a cost escalation clause be added to the purchase agreement, specifying that the selling price would increase to cover any cost increases and detailing the cost computation.

Of more concern is the variable nature of all long-run costs. Given adequate time, management must replace fixed assets and may adjust both the number of machines as well as the size of machines used in the manufacturing process. Accordingly, *in the long run, all costs (including costs classified as fixed in a given period) are relevant.* To remain in business in the long run, Mind Trek must replace equipment, pay property taxes, pay administrative salaries, and so forth. Consequently, management should consider *all costs* (fixed and variable, manufacturing and nonmanufacturing) in evaluating a long-term contract.

Full costs include all costs, regardless of their behavior pattern or activity level. The average full cost per unit is sometimes used to approximate long-run variable costs. If accepting a long-term contract increases the monthly production and sales volume to 6,000 units, the average full cost per unit will be €19.5.

Direct materials	€ 5.0
Direct labor...	3.0
Variable manufacturing overhead......................	2.0
Variable selling and administrative....................	2.0
Fixed manufacturing overhead (€30,000/6,000 units)	5.0
Fixed selling and administrative (€15,000/6,000 units)	2.5
Average full cost per unit	€19.5

If the Australian distributor agrees to pay separately all variable selling and administrative expenses associated with the contract, the estimated long-run variable costs are €17.5 per unit (€19.5 − €2). Many managers would say this is the minimum acceptable selling price, especially if the order extends over a long period of time.

Because Mind Trek has excess productive capacity, no opportunity cost is associated with accepting the Australian distributor's one-time order. There is no alternative use of the productive capacity in the short run, so there is no opportunity cost.

But what if Mind Trek were operating at capacity? In that case, accepting the special order would require reducing regular sales (assume overtime production is not possible). With an alternative use of the production capacity, an opportunity cost is associated with its use to fill the special order.

Each unit sold to the Australian distributor could otherwise generate a €10 contribution from regular customers. Accepting the special order would cause Mind Trek to incur an opportunity cost of €10,000 for the contribution margin lost from foregoing sales to regular customers.

Lost sales to regular customers (units)................	1,000
Regular unit contribution margin	× €10
Opportunity cost of accepting special order	€10,000

Because this opportunity cost exceeds the €2,000 contribution derived from the special order, management should reject the special order. Accepting the order will reduce profits by €8,000 (€2,000 contribution − €10,000 opportunity cost).

Qualitative Considerations

Although an analysis of cost and revenue information may indicate that a special order is profitable in the short run, management might still reject the order because of qualitative considerations. Any concerns regarding the order's impact on regular customers might lead management to reject the order even if there is excess capacity. If the order involves a special low price, regular customers might demand a similar price reduction and threaten to take their business elsewhere. Alternatively, management might accept the special order while operating at capacity if they believed there were long-term benefits associated with penetrating a new market. Legal factors must also be considered if the special order is from a buyer who competes with regular customers.

Outsourcing Decisions (Make or Buy)

One of the most common applications of relevant cost analysis involves the make-or-buy decision. Virtually any service, product, or component that can be produced or manufactured internally can also be acquired from an external source. The procurement of services, products or components from an external source is call **outsourcing**. For example, the management of the bookstore at your college or university is likely outsourced to Barnes and Noble or Follett, and the dining facilities may be outsourced to Marriott or ARA. Similarly, Dell and HP actually manufacture very few of the components of their computers. Instead the manufacture of components is outsourced to other firms such as Intel for computer chips and Seagate for storage devices. Virtually all computer manufacturers, with the exception of Apple, outsource their operating systems to Microsoft.

Any time you call a customer support call center, the representative reached is likely to be working in a different country. A growing number of companies even outsource employees from employee leasing companies. In the past 25 years, outsourcing of goods and services has expanded exponentially with the emergence of well-trained, low-cost labor forces in China and India and other parts of the world. Although reducing costs may be the most common reason for outsourcing, there are many other reasons for outsourcing, as discussed in the Research Insight on the next page.

As the above discussion reveals, the decision to outsource rather than to produce a service or product internally involves a vast array of qualitative issues. The quantitative issues surrounding the outsourcing (or make-or-buy) decision are often less challenging. To illustrate, we continue the Mind Trek example. Suppose a Canadian manufacturer offers a one-year contract to supply Mind Trek with an electronic component at a cost of 2 Euros per unit. Mind Trek is now faced with the decision to continue to make the electronic component internally or outsource the component from the Canadian company. An analysis of the materials and operations required to manufacture the component internally reveals that if Mind Trek accepts the offer, it will be able to reduce the following:

- Materials costs by 10 percent per unit.
- Direct labor and variable factory overhead costs by 20 percent per unit.
- Fixed manufacturing overhead by €20,000 per year.

A differential analysis of Mind Trek's make or buy decision is presented in Exhibit 16.3. Continuing to make the component has a net advantage of €10,000.

EXHIBIT 16.3   Differential Analysis of Make or Buy Decision

	(1) Cost to Make	(2) Cost to Buy	(1) − (2) Difference (income effect of buying)
Cost to buy (€2 × 60,000* units)		€120,000	€(120,000)
Cost to make			
Direct materials (€5 × 0.10 × 60,000 units)	€ 30,000		30,000
Direct labor (€3 × 0.20 × 60,000 units)	36,000		36,000
Variable manufacturing overhead (€2 × 0.20 × 60,000 units)	24,000		24,000
Fixed manufacturing overhead	20,000		20,000
Total	€110,000	€120,000	€ (10,000)
Advantage of making		€10,000	

* 5,000 units per month × 12 months

But what if the space currently used to manufacture the electronic component can be rented to a third party for €40,000 per year? In this case, the production capacity has an alternative use, and the net cash flow from this alternative use is an opportunity cost of making the component. Treating the rent Mind Trek will not receive if it continues to make the component as an opportunity cost, the analysis in Exhibit 16.4 indicates that buying now has a net advantage of €30,000.

EXHIBIT 16.4 Differential Analysis of Make or Buy Decision with Opportunity to Rent Facilities			
	(1) **Cost** **to** **Make**	**(2)** **Cost** **to** **Buy**	**(1) − (2)** **Difference** **(income effect** **of buying)**
Cost to buy (€2 × 60,000* units)		€120,000	€(120,000)
Cost to make			
Direct materials (€5 × 0.10 × 60,000 units)	€ 30,000		30,000
Direct labor (€3 × 0.20 × 60,000 units)	36,000		36,000
Variable manufacturing overhead			
(€2 × 0.20 × 60,000 units)	24,000		24,000
Fixed manufacturing overhead	20,000		20,000
Opportunity cost of lost rent income	40,000		
Total	€150,000	€120,000	€ (30,000)
Advantage of buying		€30,000	

* 5,000 units per month × 12 months

Although outsourcing has become widely accepted across virtually all industries, the results of outsourcing are not uniformly positive. Some companies that made a strong commitment to extensive outsourcing have discovered that there are many problems that can occur when they shift key processes and functions to other companies. It is usually easier to make major changes and to correct production problems related to in-house functions and processes than for those outsourced to other companies, especially if they are located offshore. The following Business Insight discusses the outsourcing experiences of Boeing, Sony, and Samsung.

BUSINESS INSIGHT **Outsourcing at Boeing, Sony, and Samsung**

The Boeing Company's design and manufacture of its new generation of passenger aircraft, the Boeing 787 Dreamliner®, represents one of the most extensive examples of outsourcing ever undertaken by a major company. Not only does it represent a radically new design for commercial aircraft, with extensive utilization of carbon-fiber instead of aluminum, it is the first jet in Boeing's history designed and built largely by other companies. Boeing enlisted 43 supplier partners from many countries, including Japan, Korea, Australia, France, Sweden, Italy, and Canada, to finalize the design at 135 sites around the world. Eleven partners have built 3 million square feet of manufacturing facilities to bring this new aircraft to market. The plan was to save about $10 billion of the cost of developing the plane by having parts suppliers from around the world design and build major sections that would be assembled at Boeing's Seattle factory.

The Wall Street Journal reported in late 2007 that, "outsourcing so much responsibility [by Boeing] has turned out to be far more difficult than anticipated. The supplier problems ranged from language barriers to snafus that erupted when some contractors themselves outsourced chunks of work. . . . The missteps underscore the hazards and limits of outsourcing." Boeing had originally planned for a maiden flight for the 787 Dreamliner in August 2007, but due to the unexpected delays, the actual maiden flight was in December 2009, delaying the delivery of the first production

continued

units to September of 2011. Still, Boeing is certain that the new airliner will be profitable, and is committed to its outsourcing strategy. Despite the problems of bringing the 787 to market, Boeing and its supplier partners still, "believe that this new method of developing planes is the model for future projects. Once the production line is running smoothly, they argue, it will be more efficient and profitable than existing construction methods."

Sony and Samsung are two of the largest producers in the television market, both offering very similar product lines. With a goal of outsourcing 40% of all production, Sony has adopted a policy of increasing dependence on outside manufacturers for its products. It recently sold its largest North American TV plant to a Taiwan-based company. On the other hand, Samsung's president is committed to the company making its own products, stating that "giving up manufacturing is tantamount to abandoning your brand." With Sony selling production facilities to other companies, Samsung is now the only major TV maker that produces computer chips for its digital TVs. Interestingly, Sony outsources the production of its digital TV computer chips to Samsung.

Sources: J. Lynn Lunsford, "Jet Blues: Boeing Scrambles to Repair Problems With New Plane—Layers of Outsourcing Slow 787 Production; 'Hostage to Suppliers'," *The Wall Street Journal*, December 7, 2007, p. A1. Dominic Gates, "Boeing Still Sure Delayed 787 Will Be Profitable," *The Seattle Times*, August 28, 2009. Moon Ihlwan, "Sony and Samsung's Strategic Split," *Bloomberg Businessweek*, January 18, 2010, p. 52.

Even if outsourcing appears financially advantageous in the short run, management should not decide to outsource before considering a variety of qualitative risk factors. Is the outside supplier interested in developing a long-term relationship or merely attempting to use some temporarily idle capacity? If so, what will happen at the end of the contract period? What impact would a decision to outsource have on the morale of Mind Trek's employees? Will Mind Trek have to rehire laid-off employees after the contract expires? Will the outside supplier meet delivery schedules? Does the supplied part meet Mind Trek's quality standards? Will it continue to meet them? Organizations often manufacture products or provide services they can obtain elsewhere in order to control quality, to have an assured supply source, to avoid dealing with a potential competitor, or to maintain a core competency. Some of these issues are discussed in the Business Insight that follows.

BUSINESS INSIGHT | **Rethinking Outsourcing**

Entrepreneur Farouk Shami's $1 billion dollar manufacturing company announced the decision to move all China-based production operations back to the United States. Citing "loss of control over manufacturing and distribution" as the primary reason for abandoning outsourcing, Shami said "we'll make more money this way because we'll have better quality and a better image" as a made-in-the-USA manufacturer.

Also reversing some of their offshore outsourcing decisions is General Electric, whose CEO, Jeffrey Immelt, stated that "overseas outsourcing had gone too far and that U.S. companies needed to expand domestic production." Daniel Meckstroth, with the Manufacturers Alliance, stated that "many U.S. producers got hurt when the recession hit and they were left holding large backlogs of goods ordered from overseas. Producing closer to customers—and limiting the inventory in the pipeline—is one solution."

Source: Timothy Aeppel, "Coming Home: Appliance Maker Drops China to Produce in Texas," *The Wall Street Journal*, August 24, 2009, p. B1.

The qualitative risk factors discussed above are often magnified when a company goes global, either as an outsourcing buyer or provider. Global outsourcing is often motivated by the desire to get projects completed "on time" and "within budget." However, as the study summarized in the Research Insight below showed, fewer than half of companies engaged in global outsourcing effectively manage their risks.

RESEARCH INSIGHT   **Global Assessment of Outsourcing Risks**

A survey by ESI International of more than 600 key outsourcing decision makers in organizations in North and South America, UK/Europe, Asia/Pacific, the Middle East, and India highlighted the risks faced by companies that buy and/or provide outsourcing services and functions. The top risks identified by the survey respondents are:

Diminished product or service quality	70%
Vendor delays	63
Failure to clearly define contract scope	61
Poor vendor management	50
Loss of in-house skills/capabilities	45
Regulatory compliance failures	40
Lack of financial viability of outsourcing partner	37
Poorly trained contract managers	32

The study found that fewer than half of the participating managers felt that their organization effectively manages the associated risks. More than half expressed a need for improvement in their outsourcing capabilities. Only 11 percent stated that they excel in managing outsourcing projects, thereby providing them with a potential competitive advantage.

Source: Caroline McDonald, "Firms Going Global Often Overlook Supply Chain Risks," *National Underwriter Buyers Report*, September 6/13, 2010, pp. 21-22.

Sell or Process Further

When a product is salable at various stages of completion, management must determine the product's most advantageous selling point. As each stage is completed, management must determine whether to sell the product then or to process it further. For example, petroleum companies have to determine how much crude oil to refine as diesel fuel and how much to process further as gasoline. We consider two types of sell or process further decisions: (1) for a single product and (2) for joint products.

Single Product Decisions

Assume that Scandinavian Furniture, Inc. manufactures modular wood furniture from precut and shaped wood. Although all units are salable before they are sanded and painted, Scandinavian Furniture, Inc. sands and paints all units before they are sold. Management wishes to know if this is the optimal selling point.

A complete listing of unit costs and revenues for the alternative selling points for a low-end stereo cabinet follows:

	Per Cabinet		
	Sell after Assembly	Sell after Painting	Difference (income effect of painting)
Selling price	$40	$75	$35
Assembly costs	(25)	(25)	
Sanding and painting costs		(12)	(12)
Contribution margin	$15	$38	$23
Advantage of painting		$23	

The sanding and painting operation has an additional contribution of $23 per unit. The stereo cabinets should be sold after they are painted.

The assembly costs are the same under both alternatives. This illustrates that *all costs incurred prior to the decision point are irrelevant*. Given the existence of an assembled chair, the decision alternatives are to sell it now or to process it further. A differential analysis for the decision to sell or process further should include only revenues and the incremental costs of further processing as follows.

Increase in revenues		
Sell after painting	$75	
Sell after assembly	(40)	$35
Additional costs of sanding and painting.		(12)
Advantage of sanding and painting		$23

The identical solution is obtained if the selling price without further processing is treated as an opportunity cost as follows.

Revenues after painting		$75
Additional costs of sanding and painting.	$12	
Opportunity cost of not selling after assembly . .	40	(52)
Advantage of sanding and painting		$23

By processing a chair further, Scandinavian Furniture has foregone the opportunity to receive $40 from its sale. Since the chair is already assembled, and the cost of assembly is an irrelevant sunk cost, this $40 is the net cash inflow from the most desirable alternative; it is the opportunity cost of painting.

Joint Product Decisions

Two or more products simultaneously produced by a single process from a common set of inputs are called **joint products**. Joint products are often found in basic industries that process natural raw materials such as dairy, chemical, meat, petroleum, and wood products. In the petroleum industry, crude oil is refined into fuel oil, gasoline, kerosene, diesel, lubricating oil, and other products.

The point in the process where the joint products become separately identifiable is called the **split-off point**. Materials and conversion costs incurred prior to the split-off point are called **joint costs**. For external reporting purposes, a number of techniques are used to allocate joint costs among joint products. We do not discuss these techniques here (interested students should consult a cost accounting textbook), except to note that none of the methods provide information useful for determining what to do with a joint product once it is produced. Because joint costs are incurred prior to the decision point, they are sunk costs. Consequently, *joint costs are irrelevant to a decision to sell a joint product or to process it further*. The only relevant factors are the alternative costs and revenues subsequent to the split-off point.

USE OF LIMITED RESOURCES

LO4 Allocate limited resources for purposes of maximizing short-run profit.

All of us have experienced time as a limiting or constraining resource. With two exams the day after tomorrow and a paper due next week, our problem is how to allocate limited study time. The solution depends on our objectives, our current status (grades, knowledge, skill levels, and so forth), and available time. Given this information, we devise a work plan to best meet our objectives.

Managers must also decide how to best use limited resources to accomplish organizational goals. A supermarket may lose sales because limited shelf space prevents stocking all available brands of soft drinks. A manufacturer may lose sales because limited machine hours or labor hours prevent filling all orders. Managers of for-profit organizations will likely find the problems of capacity constraints less troublesome than the problems of excess capacity; nonetheless, these problems are real. Ultimately, the problem often boils down to a product-mix decision, in which we must decide the mix of products or services we are going to offer our customers with the limited resources available to us.

If the limited resource is not a core business activity, it may be appropriate to outsource additional units of the limited resource externally. For example, many organizations have a small legal staff to handle routine activities; if the internal staff becomes fully committed, the organization seeks outside legal counsel. The external acquisition of such resources was discussed earlier in this module.

The long-run solution to the problem of limited resources to perform core activities may be to expand capacity. However, this is usually not feasible in the short run. Economic models suggest that another solution is to reduce demand by increasing the price. Again, this may not be desirable. A hotel, for example, may want to maintain competitive prices. A manufacturer might want to maintain a long-run price to retain customer goodwill to avoid attracting competitors, or to prevent accusations of "price gouging."

Single Constraint

The allocation of limited resources should be made only after a careful consideration of many qualitative factors. The following rule provides a useful starting point in making short-run decisions of how to best use limited resources: *To achieve short-run profit maximization, a for-profit organization should allocate limited resources in a manner that maximizes the contribution per unit of the limited resource.* The application of this rule is illustrated in the following example.

Luxury Auto Care Company offers three different service packages (A, B, and C) to its customers. These packages vary from a complete detailing of the automobile (wash, wax, carpet shampoo, etc.) to a simple hand wash. A limitation of 120 labor hours per week prevents Luxury from meeting the demand for its services. Information for the three service packages is as follows:

	A	B	C
Unit selling price.	$100	$80	$50
Unit variable costs	(60)	(35)	(25)
Unit contribution margin.	$ 40	$45	$25
Hours per unit.	4	3	1

Package A has the highest selling price and Package B has the highest unit contribution margin. Package C is shown below to have the highest contribution per hour.

	A	B	C
Unit contribution margin.	$40	$45	$25
Hours per unit.	÷ 4	÷ 3	÷ 1
Contribution per hour.	$10	$15	$25

Following the rule of maximizing the contribution per unit of a single constraining factor (labor hours), Luxury should use its limited labor hours to sell Package C. As shown in the following analysis, any other plan would result in lower profits:

	A Highest Selling Price per Unit	B Highest Contribution per Unit	C Highest Contribution per Constraining Factor
Hours available.	120	120	120
Hours per unit.	÷ 4	÷ 3	÷ 1
Weekly production in units	30	40	120
Unit contribution margin.	× $40	× $45	× $25
Total weekly contribution margin . . .	$1,200	$1,800	$3,000

Despite this analysis, management may decide on a product mix that includes some units of A or B or both to satisfy the requests of some "good" customers or to offer a full product line. However, such decisions sacrifice short-run profits.

Multiple Constraints

Continuing our illustration, assume a second constraint; that is, the maximum weekly demand for C is only 90 units, although the company is capable of producing 120 units of C each week. In this case, the limited labor resource should first be used to satisfy the demand for Package C, with any remaining capacity going to produce Package B, which has the next highest contribution per unit of constraining factor. This allocation provides a total weekly contribution of $2,700 as follows.

Available hours.............................	120
Required for C (90 units × 1 hour).............	(90)
Hours available for B	30
Labor hours per unit........................	÷ 3
Production of B in units	10
Unit contribution margin of B.................	× $45
Contribution from B	$ 450
Contribution from C ($25 per unit × 90 units)	2,250
Total weekly contribution margin	$2,700

When an organization has alternative uses for several limited resources, such as limited labor hours and limited space, the optimal use of those resources cannot be determined using the rule for short-run profit maximization. In these situations, techniques such as linear programming can be used to assist in determining the optimal mix of products or services.

Theory of Constraints

The **theory of constraints** states that every process has a bottleneck (constraining resource) and that production cannot take place faster than it is processed through that bottleneck. The goal of the theory of constraints is to maximize **throughput** (defined as sales revenue minus direct materials costs) in a constrained environment.[2] The theory has several implications for management.

- Management should identify the bottleneck. This is often difficult when several different products are produced in a facility containing many different production activities. One approach is to walk around and observe where inventory is building up in front of workstations. The bottleneck will likely have the largest piles of work that have been waiting for the longest time.

- Management should schedule production to maximize the efficient use of the bottleneck resource. Efficiently using the bottleneck resource might necessitate inspecting all units before they reach the bottleneck rather than after the units are completed. The bottleneck resource is too valuable to waste on units that may already be defective.

- Management should schedule production to avoid a buildup of inventory. Reducing inventory lowers the cost of inventory investments and the cost of carrying inventory. It also assists in improving quality by making it easier to identify quality problems that might otherwise be hidden in large piles of inventory. Reducing inventory will require a change in the attitude of managers who like to see machines and people constantly working. To avoid a buildup of inventory in front of the bottleneck, it may be necessary for people and equipment to remain idle until the bottleneck resource calls for additional input.

---

[2] *The Goal*, by Eliyah M. Goldratt and Jeff Cox, presents the concepts underlying the theory of constraints in the form of a novel.

■ Management should work to eliminate the bottleneck, perhaps by increasing the capacity of the bottleneck resource, redesigning products so they can be produced with less use of the bottleneck resource, rescheduling production procedures to substitute nonbottleneck resources, or outsourcing work performed by bottleneck resources.

The theory of constraints has implications for management accounting performance reports. Keeping people and equipment working on production full-time is often a goal of management. To support this goal, management accounting performance reports have traditionally highlighted underutilization as an unfavorable variance (see Module 22). This has encouraged managers to have people and equipment producing inventory, even if the inventory is not needed or cannot be further processed because of bottlenecks. The theory of constraints suggests that it is better to have non-bottleneck resources idle than it is to have them fully utilized. To support the theory of constraints, performance reports should:

■ Measure the utilization of bottleneck resources

■ Measure factory throughput

■ Not encourage the full utilization of nonbottleneck resources

■ Discourage the buildup of excess inventory

While the theory of constraints is *similar* to our general rule for how to best use limited resources, it emphasizes throughput (selling price minus direct materials) rather than contribution (selling price minus variable costs) in allocating the limited resource. The exclusion of direct labor and variable manufacturing overhead yields larger unit margins, and it may affect resource allocations based on throughput rankings. The result will likely be a reduction in profits from those that could be achieved using our general rule for how to allocate limited resources. Although the theory of constraints has not been widely embraced by companies, many of its users are enthusiastic about its benefits. See the following Business Insight for a discussion of one company's experience with adopting a theory of constraints approach to inventory management.

BUSINESS INSIGHT | **Fleetguard Sees Dramatic Improvements with Theory of Constraints**

Fleetguard is an international provider of filters and coolants for the auto and truck industries. After being convinced by its consultants to adopt a Theory of Constraints inventory management model, Fleetguard saw sales jump 30% without any increase in production capacity, at a time when the industry increase was only 10%. The consultant stated that "the idea was not to push sales with higher inventories." They worked on managing inventories to reduce stocks for 10 to 12 days, rather than the usual 40-day period, and they achieved this with a faster distribution network that helped them achieve 100% availability at the warehouse and at the retail level.

Source: Tanvi Shukla, "Downturn's the Time for Theory of Constraints," DNA – Daily News & Analysis, November 7, 2008.

Limitations of Decision Analysis Models

Analytical models, such as the relevant cost analysis model and applications presented in this module, are very useful in organizing information for purposes of determining the economics of a decision. However, it is important always to keep in mind that models do not make decisions—managers make decisions. The results of analytical models are an essential and necessary starting point in many decisions, but often there are other factors that weigh heavily on a decision that may cause the manager to go against the most economical alternative. There may be human resource, marketing, cultural, logistical, technological, or other factors that outweigh the analytics of a decision situation. It is in these situations where managers demonstrate leadership, problem-solving, and executive skill and potential, or the lack thereof.

MODULE-END REVIEW

ColorTek Company produces color cartridges for inkjet printers. The cartridges are sold to mail-order distributors for $4.80 each. Manufacturing and other costs are as follows:

Variable Costs per Unit		Fixed Costs per Month	
Direct materials	$2.00	Factory overhead	$15,000
Direct labor	0.20	Selling and administrative	5,000
Factory overhead	0.25	Total	$20,000
Distribution	0.05		
Total	$2.50		

The variable distribution costs are for transportation to mail-order distributors. The current monthly production and sales volume is 15,000. Monthly capacity is 20,000 units.

Required

Determine the effect of the following independent situations on monthly profits.

a. A $1.50 increase in the unit selling price should result in an 1,800 unit decrease in monthly sales.

b. A $1.80 decrease in the unit selling price should result in a 6,000 unit increase in monthly sales. However, because of capacity constraints, the last 1,000 units would be produced during overtime, when the direct labor costs increase by 50 percent.

c. A Russian distributor has proposed to place a special, one-time order for 4,000 units next month at a reduced price of $4.00 per unit. The distributor would pay all transportation costs. There would be additional fixed selling and administrative costs of $500.00

d. An Austrian distributor has proposed to place a special, one-time order for 8,000 units at a special price of $4.00 per unit. The distributor would pay all transportation costs. There would be additional fixed selling and administrative costs of $500.00. Assume overtime production is not possible.

e. A Mexican manufacturer has offered a one-year contract to supply ink for the cartridges at a cost of $1.00 per unit. If ColorTek accepts the offer, it will be able to reduce variable manufacturing costs by 40 percent and rent some of its factory space to another company for $1,000.00 per month.

f. The cartridges are currently unpackaged; that is, they are sold in bulk. Individual packaging would increase costs by $0.10 per unit. However, the units could then be sold for $5.05.

The solution is on page 16-35.

GUIDANCE ANSWER

MANAGERIAL DECISION   **You are the Vice President of Manufacturing**

This is a decision that has both economic and ethical dimensions. Economically, the cost of the old machine is a sunk cost, since the expenditure to acquire it has already been made. If it can be sold to another company to recover part of the initial cost, that amount would be relevant to the decision regarding the new technology. However, you should ignore the cost of the recently purchased machine and consider only the outlay costs that will differ between keeping the recently purchased machine and purchasing the new technology, plus any opportunity costs that may be involved with disposing of the existing machine and acquiring the new machine. From an ethical standpoint, managers are often hesitant to recommend an action that reflects poorly on their past decisions. The temptation is to try to justify the past decision. If you have evaluated all of the relevant costs and have considered all of the qualitative issues associated with upgrading the machine, these should be the basis for making your recommendation, not what it will do to your reputation with your superiors.

DISCUSSION QUESTIONS

Q16-1. Distinguish between relevant and irrelevant costs.

Q16-2. In evaluating a cost reduction proposal, what three alternatives are available to management?

Q16-3. When are outlay costs relevant and when are they irrelevant?

Q16-4. Relate the manufacturing cost hierarchy discussed in Module 14 to the concept of relevant costs. Under what conditions would product-level costs be relevant?

Q16-5. Why is a differential analysis of relevant items preferred to a detailed listing of all costs and revenues associated with each alternative?

Q16-6. How can cost predictions be made when the acquisition of new equipment results in a technological change?

Q16-7. When are opportunity costs relevant to the evaluation of a special order?

Q16-8. Identify some important qualitative considerations in evaluating a decision to make or buy a part.

Q16-9. In a decision to sell or to process further, of what relevance are costs incurred prior to the decision point? Explain your answer.

Q16-10. How should limited resources be used to achieve short-run profit maximization?

Q16-11. What should performance reports do in support of the theory of constraints?

Assignments with the ⊘ in the margin are available in an online homework system.
See the Preface of the book for details.

MINI EXERCISES

M16-12. Relevant Cost Terms: Matching (LO1)

A company that produces three products, M, N, and O, is evaluating a proposal that will result in doubling the production of N and discontinuing the production of O. The facilities currently used to produce O will be devoted to the production of N. Furthermore, additional machinery will be acquired to produce N. The production of M will not be affected. All products have a positive contribution margin.

Required

Presented below are a number of phrases related to the proposal followed by a list of cost terms. For each phrase, select the most appropriate cost term. Each term is used only once.

Phrases
1. Cost of equipment to produce O
2. Increased variable costs of N
3. Property taxes on the new machinery
4. Revenues from the sale of M
5. Increased revenue from the sale of N
6. Contribution margin of O
7. Variable costs of M
8. Company president's salary

Cost terms
a. Opportunity cost
b. Sunk cost
c. Irrelevant variable outlay cost
d. Irrelevant fixed outlay cost
e. Relevant variable outlay cost
f. Relevant fixed outlay cost
g. Relevant revenues
h. Irrelevant revenues

M16-13. Relevant Cost Terms: Matching (LO1)

A company that produces and sells 4,000 units per month, with the capacity to produce 5,000 units per month, is evaluating a one-time, special order for 2,000 units from a large chain store. Accepting the order will increase variable manufacturing costs and certain fixed selling and administrative costs. It will also require the company to forego the sale of 1,000 units to regular customers.

Required

Presented below are a number of statements related to the proposal followed by a list of cost terms. For each statement, select the most appropriate cost term. Each term is used only once.

Statements

1. Increased revenues from special order
2. Lost contribution margin from foregone sales to regular customers
3. Revenues from 4,000 units sold to regular customers
4. Variable cost of 4,000 units sold to regular customers
5. Increase in fixed selling and administrative expenses
6. Cost of existing equipment used to produce special order
7. Salary paid to current supervisor who oversees manufacture of special order
8. Increased variable costs of special order

Cost terms

a. Irrelevant variable outlay cost
b. Irrelevant fixed outlay cost
c. Sunk cost
d. Relevant variable outlay cost
e. Relevant fixed outlay cost
f. Opportunity cost
g. Relevant revenues
h. Irrelevant revenues

M16-14. Identifying Relevant Costs and Revenues (LO1)

The City of Bluffton operates a power plant on a river that flows through town. The village uses some of this generated electricity to operate a water treatment plant and sells the excess electricity to a local utility. The city council is evaluating two alternative proposals:

- *Proposal 1* calls for replacing the generators used in the plant with more efficient generators that will produce more electricity and have lower operating costs. The salvage value of the old generators is higher than their removal cost.
- *Proposal 2* calls for raising the level of the dam to retain more water for generating power and increasing the force of water flowing through the dam. This will significantly increase the amount of electricity generated by the plant. Operating costs will not be affected.

Required

Presented are a number of cost and revenue items. Indicate in the appropriate columns whether each item is relevant or irrelevant to proposals 1 and 2.

	Proposal 1	Proposal 2
1. Cost of new furniture for City Manager's office		
2. Cost of old generators		
3. Cost of new generators		
4. Operating cost of old generators		
5. Operating cost of new generators		
6. Police Chief's salary		
7. Depreciation on old generators		
8. Salvage value of old generators		
9. Removal cost of old generators		
10. Cost of raising dam		
11. Maintenance costs of water plant		
12. Revenues from sale of electricity		

M16-15. Classifying Relevant and Irrelevant Items (LO1)

The law firm of Taylor, Taylor, and Tower has been asked to represent a local client. All legal proceedings will be held out of town in Chicago.

Required

The law firm's accountant has asked you to help determine the incremental cost of accepting this client. Classify each of the following items on the basis of their relationship to this engagement. Items may have multiple classifications.

	Relevant costs		Irrelevant costs	
	Opportunity	Outlay	Outlay	Sunk

1. The case will require three attorneys to stay four nights in a Chicago hotel. The predicted hotel bill is $2,400.
2. Taylor, Taylor, and Tower's professional staff is paid $2,000 per day for out-of-town assignments.
3. Last year, depreciation on Taylor, Taylor, and Tower's office was $25,000.
4. Round-trip transportation to Chicago is expected to cost $250 per person.
5. The firm has recently accepted an engagement that will require partners to spend two weeks in Cincinnati. The predicted out-of-pocket costs of this trip are $8,500.
6. The firm has a maintenance contract on its computer equipment that will cost $2,200 next year.
7. If the firm accepts the client and sends attorneys to Chicago, it will have to decline a conflicting engagement in Miami that would have provided a net cash inflow of $15,000.
8. The firm's variable overhead is $80 per client hour.
9. The firm pays $250 per year for Mr. Tower's subscription to a law journal.
10. Last year the firm paid $3,500 to increase the insulation in its building.

M16-16. Relevant Costs for Equipment Replacement Decision (LO1, 2, 3)

Health Scan, Inc., paid $50,000 for X-ray equipment four years ago. The equipment was expected to have a useful life of 10 years from the date of acquisition with annual operating costs of $40,000. Technological advances have made the machine purchased four years ago obsolete with a zero salvage value. An improved X-ray device incorporating the new technology is available at an initial cost of $55,000 and annual operating costs of $26,000. The new machine is expected to last only six years before it, too, is obsolete. Asked to analyze the financial aspects of replacing the obsolete but still functional machine, Health Scan's accountant prepared the following analysis. After looking over these numbers, the company's manager rejected the proposal.

Six-year savings [($40,000 − $26,000) × 6]	$84,000
Cost of new machine	(55,000)
Undepreciated cost of old machine	(30,000)
Advantage (disadvantage) of replacement.	$ (1,000)

Required
Perform an analysis of relevant costs to determine whether the manager made the correct decision.

M16-17. Special Order (LO1, 2, 3)
Shanghai Exporters, LTD produces wall mounts for flat panel television sets. The forecasted income statement for 2012 is as follows:

SHANGHAI EXPORTERS, LTD Budgeted Income Statement For the Year 2012	
Sales ($44 per unit).	$4,400,000
Cost of good sold ($32 per unit).	(3,200,000)
Gross profit.	1,200,000
Selling expenses ($3 per unit)	(300,000)
Net income.	$ 900,000

Additional Information

(1) Of the production costs and selling expenses, $800,000 and $100,000, respectively, are fixed. (2) Shanghai Exporters, LTD received a special order from a hospital supply company offering to buy 12,500 wall mounts for $30. If it accepts the order, there will be no additional selling expenses, and there is currently sufficient excess capacity to fill the order. The company's sales manager argues for rejecting the order because "we are not in the business of paying $32 to make a product to sell for $30."

Required

Do you think the company should accept the special order? Should the decision be based only on the profitability of the sale, or are there other issues that Shanghai should consider? Explain.

M16-18. Sell or Process Further   (LO1, 2, 3)

Great Lakes Boat Company manufactures sailboat hulls at a cost of $4,200 per unit. The hulls are sold to boat- yards for $5,000. The company is evaluating the desirability of adding masts, sails, and rigging to the hulls prior to sale at an additional cost of $1,500. The completed sailboats could then be sold for $6,000 each.

Required

Determine whether the company should sell sailboat hulls or process them further into complete sailboats. Assume sales volume will not be affected.

EXERCISES

E16-19. Special Order   (LO1, 2, 3)

Healthy Foods Farms grows organic vegetables and sells them to local restaurants after processing. The firm's leading product is Salad-in-a-Bag, which is a mixture of organic green salad ingredients prepared and ready to serve. The company sells a large bag to restaurants for $23. It calculates the variable cost per bag at $15 (including $0.50 for local delivery), and the average total cost per bag is $18.10. Because the vegetables are perishable and Healthy Foods Farms is experiencing a large crop, the firm has extra capacity. A representative of a restaurant association in another city has offered to buy fresh salad stock from the company to augment its regular supply during an upcoming international festival. The restaurant association wants to buy 2,500 bags during the next month for $17 per bag. Delivery to restaurants in the other city will cost the company $0.75 per bag. It can meet most of the order with excess capacity but would sacrifice 400 bags of regular sales to fill this special order. Please assist Healthy Foods Farms' management by answering the following questions.

Required

a. Using differential analysis, what is the impact on profits of accepting this special order?

b. What nonquantitative issues should management consider before making a final decision?

c. How would the analysis change if the special order were for 2,500 bags per month for the next five years?

E16-20. Special Order   (LO1, 2, 3)

Nature's Garden, a new restaurant situated on a busy highway in Pomona, California, specializes in a chef's salad selling for $7. Daily fixed costs are $1,200, and variable costs are $4 per meal. With a capacity of 800 meals per day, the restaurant serves an average of 750 meals each day.

Required

a. Determine the current average cost per meal.

b. A busload of 30 Girl Scouts stops on its way home from the San Bernardino National Forest. The leader offers to bring them in if the scouts can all be served a meal for a total of $150. The owner refuses, saying he would lose $0.60 per meal if he accepted this offer. How do you think the owner arrived at the $0.60 figure? Comment on the owner's reasoning.

c. A local businessman on a break overhears the conversation with the leader and offers the owner a one-year contract to feed 300 of the businessman's employees one meal each day at a special price of $4.50 per meal. Should the restaurant owner accept this offer? Why or why not?

E16-21. Special Order: High-Low Cost Estimation   (LO1, 2, 3)

SafeRide, Inc. produces air bag systems that it sells to North American automobile manufacturers. Although the company has a capacity of 300,000 units per year, it is currently producing at an annual rate of 180,000 units. SafeRide, Inc. has received an order from a German manufacturer to purchase 60,000 units at $9.00 each. Budgeted costs for 180,000 and 240,000 units are as follows:

	180,000 Units	240,000 Units
Manufacturing costs		
Direct materials................	$ 450,000	$ 600,000
Direct labor....................	315,000	420,000
Factory overhead	1,215,000	1,260,000
Total	1,980,000	2,280,000
Selling and administrative	765,000	780,000
Total	$2,745,000	$3,060,000
Costs per unit		
Manufacturing................	$11.00	$ 9.50
Selling and administrative........	4.25	3.25
Total	$15.25	$12.75

Sales to North American manufacturers are priced at $20 per unit, but the sales manager believes the company should aggressively seek the German business even if it results in a loss of $3.75 per unit. She believes obtaining this order would open up several new markets for the company's product. The general manager commented that the company cannot tighten its belt to absorb the $225,000 loss ($3.75 × 60,000) it would incur if the order is accepted.

Required

a. Determine the financial implications of accepting the order.

b. How would your analysis differ if the company were operating at capacity? Determine the advantage or disadvantage of accepting the order under full-capacity circumstances.

E16-22. Outsourcing (Make-or-Buy) Decision   (LO1, 2, 3)

Hewlett-Packard
(HPQ)

Sanmina-SCI (SANM)

Assume a division of **Hewlett-Packard** currently makes 10,000 circuit boards per year used in producing diagnostic electronic instruments at a cost of $32 per board, consisting of variable costs per unit of $24 and fixed costs per unit of $8. Further assume **Sanmina-SCI** offers to sell Hewlett-Packard the 10,000 circuit boards for $32 each. If Hewlett-Packard accepts this offer, the facilities currently used to make the boards could be rented to one of Hewlett-Packard's suppliers for $25,000 per year. In addition, $5 per unit of the fixed overhead applied to the circuit boards would be totally eliminated.

Required

Should HP outsource this component from Samina-SCI? Support your answer with relevant cost calculations.

E16-23. Outsourcing (Make-or-Buy) Decision   (LO1, 2, 3)

Mountain Air Limited manufactures a line of room air purifiers. Management is currently evaluating the possible production of an air purifier for automobiles. Based on an annual volume of 10,000 units, the predicted cost per unit of an auto air purifier follows.

Direct materials	$ 8.00
Direct labor.............	1.50
Factory overhead	7.00
Total	$16.50

These cost predictions include $50,000 in fixed factory overhead averaged over 10,000 units.

The completed air purifier units include a battery-operated electric motor, which Mountain Air assembles with parts purchased from an outside vendor for $2.00 per motor. Mini Motor Company has offered to supply an assembled battery-operated motor at a cost of $5.00 per unit, with a minimum annual order of 5,000 units. If Mountain Air accepts this offer, it will be able to reduce the variable labor and variable overhead costs of the auto air purifier by 50 percent.

Required

a. Determine whether Mountain Air should continue to make the electric motor or outsource it from Mini Motor Company. (Hint: analyze the relevant costs of making the "motors," not the entire air purifier.)

   b. If it could otherwise rent the motor-assembly space for $20,000 per year, should it make or outsource this component?

   c. What additional factors should it consider in deciding whether to make or outsource the electric motors?

E16-24. **Make or Buy** (LO1, 2, 3)

Rashad Rahavy, M.D., is a general practitioner whose offices are located in the South Falls Professional Building. In the past, Dr. Rahavy has operated his practice with a nurse, a receptionist/secretary, and a part-time bookkeeper. Dr. Rahavy, like many small-town physicians, has billed his patients and their insurance companies from his own office. The part-time bookkeeper, who works 10 hours per week, is employed exclusively for this purpose.

    North Falls Physician's Service Center has offered to take over all of Dr. Rahavy's billings and collections for an annual fee of $10,000. If Dr. Rahavy accepts this offer, he will no longer need the bookkeeper. The bookkeeper's wages and fringe benefits amount to $12 per hour, and the bookkeeper works 50 weeks per year. With all the billings and collections done elsewhere, Dr. Rahavy will have two additional hours available per week to see patients. He sees an average of three patients per hour at an average fee of $30 per visit. Dr. Rahavy's practice is expanding, and new patients often have to wait several weeks for an appointment. He has resisted expanding his office hours or working more than 50 weeks per year. Finally, if Dr. Rahavy signs on with the center, he will no longer need to rent a records storage facility for $100 per month.

Required

Conduct a relevant cost analysis to determine if it is profitable to outsource the bookkeeping.

E16-25. **Sell or Process Further** (LO1, 2, 3)

Port Allen Chemical Company processes raw material D into joint products E and F. Raw material D costs $5 per liter. It costs $100 to convert 100 liters of D into 60 liters of E and 40 liters of F. Product F can be sold immediately for $5 per liter or processed further into Product G at an additional cost of $4 per liter. Product G can then be sold for $12 per liter.

Required

Determine whether Product F should be sold or processed further into Product G.

E16-26. **Limited Resources** (LO4)

Toledo Manufacturing Company, Ltd., produces three products: X, Y, and Z. A limitation of 220 labor hours per week prevents the company from meeting the sales demand for these products. Product information is as follows:

	X	Y	Z
Unit selling price.	$160	$100	$210
Unit variable costs	(100)	(50)	(180)
Unit contribution margin.	$ 60	$ 50	$ 30
Labor hours per unit.	4	2	4

Required

   a. Determine the weekly contribution from each product when total labor hours are allocated to the product with the highest
     1. Unit selling price.
     2. Unit contribution margin.
     3. Contribution per labor hour.
     (*Hint:* Each situation is independent of the others.)

   b. What generalization can be made regarding the allocation of limited resources to achieve short-run profit maximization?

   c. Determine the opportunity cost the company will incur if management requires the weekly production of 12 units of Z.

   d. Give reasons why a company may not allocate resources in the most economical way in some situations.

E16-27. Limited Resources (LO4)

Maria Pajet, a regional sales representative for UniTec Systems, Inc., has been working about 80 hours per week calling on a total of 123 regular customers each month. Because of family and health considerations, she has decided to reduce her hours to a maximum of 160 per month. Unfortunately, this cutback will require Maria to turn away some of her regular customers or, at least, serve them less frequently than once a month. Maria has developed the following information to assist her in determining how to best allocate time:

	Customer Classification		
	Large Business	Small Business	Individual
Number of customers.	8	35	80
Average monthly sales per customer. . . .	$2,500	$1,500	$600
Commission percentage	5%	8%	10%
Hours per customer per monthly visit . . .	5.0	3.0	2.5

Required

a. Develop a monthly plan that indicates the number of customers Maria should call on in each classification to maximize her monthly sales commissions.

b. Determine the monthly commissions Maria will earn if she implements this plan.

c. Give one or two reasons why Maria might decide not to follow the conclusions of the above analysis entirely?

PROBLEMS

P16-28. Multiple Changes in Profit Plans (LO1, 2, 3)

In an attempt to improve profit performance, Jacobson Company's management is considering a number of alternative actions. An August 2012 contribution income statement for Jacobson Company follows.

JACOBSON COMPANY Contribution Income Statement For Month of August 2012		
Sales (10,000 units × $40).		$400,000
Less variable costs		
Direct materials (10,000 units × $5)	$ 50,000	
Direct labor (10,000 units × $14)	140,000	
Variable factory overhead (10,000 units × $6)	60,000	
Selling and administrative (10,000 units × $5). . . .	50,000	(300,000)
Contribution margin (10,000 units × $10)		100,000
Less fixed costs		
Factory overhead	50,000	
Selling and administrative.	60,000	(110,000)
Net income (loss)		$ (10,000)

Required

Determine the effect of each of the following independent situations on monthly profit.

a. Purchasing automated assembly equipment, which should reduce direct labor costs by $5 per unit and increase variable overhead costs by $2 per unit and fixed factory overhead by $22,000 per month.

b. Reducing the selling price by $5 per unit. This should increase the monthly sales by 5,000 units. At this higher volume, additional equipment and salaried personnel would be required. This will increase fixed factory overhead by $2,800 per month and fixed selling and administrative costs by $2,500 per month.

c. Buying rather than manufacturing a component of Jacobson's final product. This will increase direct materials costs by $12 per unit. However, direct labor will decline $4 per unit, variable factory overhead will decline $1 per unit, and fixed factory overhead will decline $15,000 per month.

d. Increasing the unit selling price by $4 per unit. This action should result in a 1,000-unit decrease in monthly sales.

e. Combining alternatives (a) and (d).

P16-29. Multiple Changes in Profit Plans: Multiple Products (LO1, 2, 3)

Information on Guadalupe Ltd.'s three products follows:

	A	B	C
Unit sales per month	900	1,400	900
Selling price per unit.........	$ 5.00	$7.50	$4.00
Variable costs per unit	(5.20)	(6.00)	(2.00)
Unit contribution margin.......	$(0.20)	$1.50	$2.00

Required

Determine the effect each of the following situations would have on monthly profits. Each situation should be evaluated independently of all others.

a. Product A is discontinued.

b. Product A is discontinued, and the subsequent loss of customers causes sales of Product B to decline by 100 units.

c. The selling price of A is increased to $5.50 with a sales decrease of 150 units.

d. The price of Product B is increased to $8.00 with a resulting sales decrease of 200 units. However, some of these customers shift to Product A; sales of Product A increase by 140 units.

e. Product A is discontinued, and the plant in which A was produced is used to produce D, a new product. Product D has a unit contribution margin of $0.30. Monthly sales of Product D are predicted to be 600 units.

f. The selling price of Product C is increased to $4.50, and the selling price of Product B is decreased to $7.00. Sales of C decline by 200 units, while sales of B increase by 300 units.

P16-30. Relevant Costs and Differential Analysis (LO1, 2)

College Station Bank paid $50,000 for a check-sorting machine in January 2008. The machine had an estimated life of 10 years and annual operating costs of $45,000, excluding depreciation. Although management is pleased with the machine, recent technological advances have made it obsolete. Consequently, as of January 2012, the machine has a book value of $30,000, a remaining operating life of 6 years, and a salvage value of $0.

The manager of operations is evaluating a proposal to acquire a new optical scanning and sorting machine. The new machine would cost $90,000 and reduce annual operating costs to $25,000, excluding depreciation. Because of expected technological improvements, the manager believes the new machine will have an economic life of 6 years and no salvage value at the end of that life. Prior to signing the papers authorizing the acquisition of the new machine, the president of the bank prepared the following analysis:

Six-year savings [($45,000 − $25,000) × 6 years]......	$120,000
Cost of new machine	(90,000)
Loss on disposal of old machine	(30,000)
Advantage (disadvantage) of replacement...........	$ 0

After looking at these numbers, the manager rejected the proposal and commented that he was "tired of looking at marginal projects. This bank is in business to make a profit, not to break even. If you want to break even, go work for the government."

Required

a. Evaluate the president's analysis.

b. Prepare a differential analysis of six-year totals for the old and the new machines.

c. Speculate on some limitations of the model or other issues that might be a factor in making a final decision.

P16-31. Special Order (LO1, 2, 3)

Mobile Solutions Company produces a variety of electric scooters. Management follows a pricing policy of manufacturing cost plus 60 percent. In response to a request from Northern Cycles, LLC, the following price has been developed for an order of 300 scooters (the smallest scooter Mobile Solutions produces):

Manufacturing costs	
Direct materials........	$10,000
Direct labor...........	12,000
Factory overhead......	18,000
Total	40,000
Markup (60%)...........	24,000
Selling price	$64,000

Northern Cycles rejected this price and offered to purchase the 300 scooters at a price of $52,000. The following additional information is available:

- Mobile Solutions has sufficient excess capacity to produce the scooters.
- Factory overhead is applied on the basis of direct labor dollars.
- Budgeted factory overhead is $400,000 for the current year. Of this amount, $100,000 is fixed. Of the $18,000 of factory overhead assigned to the Northern Cycles order, only $13,500 is driven by the special order; $4,500 is a fixed cost.
- Selling and administrative expenses are budgeted as follows:

Fixed......	$90,000 per year
Variable....	$20 per unit manufactured and sold

Required

a. The president of Mobile Solutions wants to know if he should allow Northern Cycles to have the scooters for $52,000. Determine the effect on profits of accepting Northern Cycles' offer.

b. Briefly explain why certain costs should be omitted from the analysis in requirement (a).

c. Assume Mobile Solutions is operating at capacity and could sell the 300 scooters at its regular markup.
   1. Determine the opportunity cost of accepting Northern Cycles' offer.
   2. Determine the effect on profits of accepting Northern Cycles' offer.

d. What other factors should Mobile Solutions consider before deciding to accept the special order?

P16-32. Special Order (LO1, 2, 3)

Every Halloween, Glacier Ice Cream Shop offers a trick-or-treat package of 20 coupons for $3. The coupons are redeemable by children 12 years or under, for a single-scoop cone, with a limit of one coupon per child per visit. Coupon sales average 500 books per year. The printing costs are $60. A single-scoop cone of Glacier ice cream normally sells for $0.60. The variable costs of a single-scoop cone are $0.40.

Required

a. Determine the loss if all coupons are redeemed without any other effect on sales.

b. Assume all coupons will not be redeemed. With regular sales unaffected, determine the coupon redemption rate at which Glacier will break even on the offer.

c. Assuming regular sales are not affected and one additional single-scoop cone is sold at the regular price each time a coupon is redeemed, determine the coupon redemption rate at which Glacier will break even on the offer.

d. Determine the profit or loss incurred on the offer if the coupon redemption rate is 60 percent and:
   1. One-fourth of the redeemed coupons have no effect on sales.
   2. One-fourth of the redeemed coupons result in additional sales of two single-scoop cones.
   3. One-fourth of the redeemed coupons result in additional sales of three single-scoop cones.
   4. One-fourth of the redeemed coupons come out of regular sales of single-scoop cones.

P16-33. Applications of Differential Analysis (LO1, 2, 3)

Nantucket Optics Company manufactures high-end sunglasses that it sells to mail-order distributors for $50. Manufacturing and other costs follow:

Variable Costs per Unit		Fixed Costs per Month	
Direct materials	$ 8	Factory overhead..........	$20,000
Direct labor.............	7	Selling and administrative ...	10,000
Factory overhead........	2	Total	$30,000
Distribution.............	3		
Total	$20		

The variable distribution costs are for transportation to mail-order distributors. The current monthly production and sales volume is 5,000 units. Monthly capacity is 6,000 units.

Required

Determine the effect of each of the following independent situations on monthly profits.

a. A $2.00 increase in the unit selling price should result in a 1,200-unit decrease in monthly sales.

b. A 15% decrease in the unit selling price should result in a 2,000-unit increase in monthly sales. However, because of capacity constraints, the last 1,000 units would be produced during overtime with the direct labor costs increasing by 60 percent.

c. A British distributor has proposed to place a special, one-time order for 1,000 units at a reduced price of $45 per unit. The distributor would pay all transportation costs. There would be additional fixed selling and administrative costs of $1,000.

d. A Swiss distributor has proposed to place a special, one-time order for 2,500 units at a special price of $45 per unit. The distributor would pay all transportation costs. There would be additional fixed selling and administrative costs of $1,500. Assume overtime production is not possible.

e. Nantucket Optics provides a designer case for each pair of sunglasses that it manufactures. A Chinese manufacturer has offered a one-year contract to supply the cases at a cost of $4 per unit. If Nantucket Optics accepts the offer, it will be able to reduce variable manufacturing costs by 10%, reduce fixed costs by $1,500, and rent out some freed-up space for $2,000 per month.

f. The glasses also come with four different color inserts that allow the user to change the appearance of the glasses to match her or his clothing. Making the glasses in only one color without the color inserts would reduce the cost by $5, and Nantucket Optics believes the selling price would have to decrease to $45.

P16-34. Applications of Differential Analysis (LO1, 2, 3)

Trails Expeditions offers guided back-country hiking/camping trips in British Columbia. Trails provides a guide and all necessary food and equipment at a fee of $50 per person per day. Trails currently provides an average of 600 guide-days per month in June, July, August, and September. Based on available equipment and staff, maximum capacity is 800 guide-days per month. Monthly variable and fixed operating costs (valued in Canadian dollars) are as follows:

Variable Costs per Guide-Day		Fixed Costs per Month	
Food..................	$ 5	Equipment rental	$ 5,000
Guide salary	25	Administration	5,000
Supplies	2	Advertising	2,000
Insurance	8	Total	$12,000
Total	$40		

Required

Determine the effect of each of the following situations on monthly profits. Each situation is to be evaluated independently of all others.

a. A $12 increase in the daily fee should result in a 150-unit decrease in monthly sales.

b. A $7 decrease in the daily fee should result in a 300-unit increase in monthly sales. However, because of capacity constraints, the last 100 guide-days would be provided by subcontracting to another firm at a cost of $46 per guide-day.

c. A French tour agency has proposed to place a special, one-time order for 75 guide-days at a reduced fee of $45 per guide-day. The agency would pay all insurance costs. There would be additional fixed administrative costs of $200.

  d. An Italian tour agency has proposed to place a special, one-time order for 300 guide-days next month at a special fee of $40 per guide-day. The agency would pay all insurance costs. There would be additional fixed administrative costs of $200. Assume additional capacity beyond 800 guide-days is not available.

  e. An Alberta outdoor supply company has offered to supply all necessary food and camping equipment at $7.50 per guide-day. This eliminates the current food costs and reduces the monthly equipment rental costs to $1,800.

  f. Clients currently must carry a backpack and assist in camp activities such as cooking. Trails is considering the addition of mules to carry all food and equipment and the hiring of college students to perform camp activities such as cooking. This will increase variable costs by $12 per guide-day and fixed costs by $1,000 per month. However, 600 full-service guide-days per month could now be sold at $75 each.

P16-35.   **Continue or Discontinue**   (LO1, 2)

Lakeland Eye Clinic primarily performs three medical procedures: cataract removal, corneal implants, and laser keratotomy. At the end of the first quarter of this year, Dr. Pathaja, president of Lakeland, expressed grave concern about the cataract sector because it had reported a loss of $35,000. He rationalized that "since the cataract market is losing $35,000, and the overall practice is making $140,000, if we eliminate the cataract market, our total profits will increase to $175,000."

Required

  a. Is the president's analysis correct?

  b. Will total profits increase if the cataract section is dropped?

  c. Is it possible total profits will decline?

MANAGEMENT APPLICATIONS

MA16-36. **Assessing the Impact of an Incentive Plan**[3]   (LO1, 2, 3)

Overview

Ladbrecks is a major department store with fifty retail outlets. The company's stores compete with outlets run by companies such as Nordstrom, Macys, Marshall Fields, Bloomingdales and Saks Fifth Avenue. During the early nineties the company decided that providing excellent customer service was the key ingredient for success in the retail industry. Therefore, during the mid 1990s the company implemented an incentive plan for its sales associates in twenty of its stores. Your job is to assess the financial impact of the plan and to provide a recommendation to management to continue or discontinue the plan based on your findings.

Incentives in Retail

The past decade has evidenced a concerted effort by many firms to empower and motivate employees to improve performance. A recent New York Times article reported that more and more firms are offering bonus plans to hourly workers. An Ernst and Young survey of the retail industry indicates that virtually all department stores currently offer incentive programs such as straight commissions, base salary plus commission, and quota bonus programs. Although these programs can add to payroll costs, the survey respondents indicated that they believe these plans have contributed to major improvements in customer service.

Company's Background

Ladbrecks was founded by members of the Ladbreck family in the 1880s. The first store opened under the name Ladbreck Dry Goods. Growth was fueled through acquisitions as the industry consolidated during the 1960s. Over this hundred-year period, sales associates were paid a fixed hourly wage. Raises were based on seniority. Sales associates were expected to be neat and courteous to customers. The advent of specialty stores and the stated intention of an upscale west coast retailer to begin opening stores in the Midwest concerned Ladbreck's management. Building on its history of excellence in customer service, the company initiated its performance-based incentive plan to support its stated firm-wide strategy of "customer emphasis" with "employee empowerment." Management expected it to result in further enhancement of customer service and, consequently, in an increase in sales generated at its stores.

---

[3] Written to illustrate the use of relevant costs and revenues for decision making. This example is based on an actual company's experience with implementing an incentive plan. The company name and the financial numbers and key ratios have been altered.

Incentive Plan

The plan was implemented in stores sequentially as company managers intended to examine and evaluate the plan's impact on sales and profitability. Initially, the firm selected one store from a group of similar stores in the same general area to begin the implementation. By the end of 1994, ten stores had implemented the plan. In 1995, ten more stores implemented the plan, bringing the total to 20 out of a total of 50.

The performance-based incentive plan is best described as a bonus program. At the time of the plan's implementation, sales associates received little in the form of annual merit increases, and promotions were rare. The bonus payment became the only significant reward for high performance. Each week sales associates are paid a base hourly rate times hours worked. In addition, under the plan sales associates could increase their compensation by receiving a bonus at the end of each quarter. The contract provides sales-force personnel with a cash bonus only if the actual quarterly sales generated by the employee exceed a quarterly sales goal. Individualized pre-specified sales goals were established for each employee based only on the individual's base hourly rate, hours worked and a multiplier (multiplier = 1/bonus rate). The bonus is computed as a fixed percentage of the excess sales (actual sales minus a pre-specified sales goal) by the employee in a quarter (see exhibit one).

$$\textbf{Employee's Bonus} = .08 \times \frac{(\textbf{Employee's actual sales for quarter} - }{\textbf{employee's targeted sales for quarter})}$$

$$\frac{\textbf{Where employee's}}{\textbf{targeted sales for quarter}} = \frac{\textbf{Employee's}}{\textbf{hourly wage}} \times \textbf{Hours worked in quarter} \times \textbf{12.5}$$

Senior managers regarded the incentive plan as a major change for the firm and its sales force. Management expected that the new incentive scheme would motivate many changes in employee behavior that would enhance customer service. Sales associates were now expected to build a client base to generate repeat sales. Actions consistent with this approach include developing and updating customer address lists (including details of their needs and preferences), writing thank you notes and contacting customers about upcoming sales and new merchandise that matched their preferences.

Consultant's Task

Management decided to call you in to provide an independent assessment. While the company thought that sales had increased with the plan's implementation, the human resource department did not know exactly how to quantify the plan's impact on sales and expenses. It suspected that employee salaries, cost of goods sold, and inventory carrying costs, as well as sales, may have changed due to the plan's implementation. You, therefore, requested information on these financial variables.

Sales Analysis: Because each of the twenty stores implemented the plan at different dates, and store sales fluctuated greatly with the seasons and the economy, you could not simply plot store sales. Instead, for each of the twenty stores, you picked another Ladbreck store as a control and computed for 48 months the following series of monthly sales[4]:

$$\text{Percent Change in Sales} = \frac{[(\text{Plan Store Sales in Month t} \div \text{Plan Store Sales in Month t-24}) - }{(\text{Control Store Sales in Month t/ Control Store Sales in Month t-24})] \times 100}$$

The plan's implementation was denoted as month 25, so you had 24 months prior to the plan and 24 months after the plan. Averages were then taken for the twenty stores. If the control procedure worked then you expected that the first 24 months of the series would fluctuate around zero. The actual results are reported in Figure 1 below. Month 25 is denoted as the rollout month, the month the incentive plan began.

Expense Analysis: You then plotted wage expense/sales, cost of goods sold/sales, and inventory turnover for the twenty stores for the 24 months preceding the plan and the first 24 months after plan implementation. After pulling out seasonal effects these monthly series are presented in figures 2, 3 and 4. If the plan has no impact on these expenses then you would expect no dramatic change in the series around month 25.

Figure 2   plots (wage expense in month t/sales in month t)

Figure 3   plots (cost of goods sold in month t/sales in month t)

Figure 4   plots "annual" turnover computed as (12 × cost of goods sold in month t/inventory at beginning of month t)

> For example, if monthly cost of sales is $100 and the annual inventory turnover ratio is 4, it suggests a monthly turnover of 0.333 with the firm holding an average inventory of $300 throughout the year. (Note that a monthly inventory turnover of .333 implies an annual turnover of 4 (from 12 × 0.333).

---

[4] For instance, assume sales for plan store were $2,200 this January and $2,000 two Januarys ago. Also assume that sales in the control store were $4,400 this January and $4,000 two Januarys ago. Percent change = 2,200/2,000 − 4,400/4,000 = 0.

Financial Report for Store: A typical annual income statement for a pre-plan Ladbreck store before fixed charges, taxes and incidentals looks as follows.

	Total	Percent
Sales..	10,000,000	100
Cost of Goods Sold	6,300,000	63
Gross Profit	3,700,000	37
Employee salaries	800,000	8
Profit before fixed charges............................	2,900,000	29

A store also has substantial charges for rent, management salaries, insurance, etc. but they are fixed with respect to the incentive plan.

Required:

a. Suppose the goal of the firm is to now provide superior customer service by having the sales consultant identify and sell to the specific needs of the customer. What does this goal suggest about a change in managerial accounting and control systems?

b. Provide an estimate of the impact of the incentive plan on sales.

c. Did the sales impact occur all at once, or did it occur gradually?

d. What is the impact of the incentive plan on wage expense as a percent of sales?

e. What is the impact of the incentive plan on cost of good sold as a percent of sales?

f. What is the impact of incentive plan on inventory turnover (turnover = cost of goods sold ÷ inventory)? [If sales go up then stores are selling more goods; therefore, more goods need to be on the floor or those goods on floor need to turn over faster].

g. What is the additional dollar amount of inventory that must be held?

h. Using the information on sales and expenses for a typical store, provide an analysis of the additional store profit contributed by the plan. Assume that it costs 12% a year to carry the added inventory.

i. Look at Exhibit One which provides a partial listing of employee pay for one small department within a store. Which "type" of employee is receiving the bonus.

j. Should the company keep the plan? Explain your estimate of the financial impact of the plan and also incorporate any nonfinancial information you feel is relevant in justifying your decision.

EXHIBIT 1

Wages by subset of employees in Ladbreck's fashion department.

Name	Years of Service	Hourly Wage Rate	Hours Worked in Quarter	Regular Pay	Actual Sales for Quarter	Bonus	Total Pay Quarter
BOB MARLEY	2	4.00	400	1,600	25,000	400	2,000
JIMI HENDRIX	16	7.50	440	3,300	41,000	0	3,300
MILLIE SMALL................	24	9.99	440	4,396	40,000	0	4,396
AL GREEN	11	6.00	400	2,400	36,000	480	2,880
BOB DYLAN..................	4	5.00	400	2,000	30,000	400	2,400
JANIS JOPLIN	10	6.00	400	2,400	30,000	0	2,400
WILSON PICKETT	16	7.50	440	3,300	50,000	700	4,000
BRUCE SPRINGSTEEN	23	9.99	440	4,396	30,000	0	4,396
MICHIGAN & SMILEY...........	13	7.00	400	2,800	38,000	240	3,040
RICHIE FURAY................	22	9.90	400	3,960	30,000	0	3,960
JOHN LENNON	5	5.00	400	2,000	34,000	720	2,720
JULIO IGLESIAS...............	4	5.00	480	2,400	46,000	1,280	3,680
TOMMY PETTY	11	6.00	400	2,400	36,000	480	2,880
JOAN BAEZ	21	9.90	400	3,960	40,000	0	3,960
BB KING.....................	8	6.00	400	2,400	38,000	640	3,040
GLADYS KNIGHT..............	14	8.00	480	3,840	46,000	0	3,840
NEIL YOUNG	15	8.00	480	3,840	36,000	0	3,840
BO DIDDLEY	4	5.00	400	2,000	30,000	400	2,400

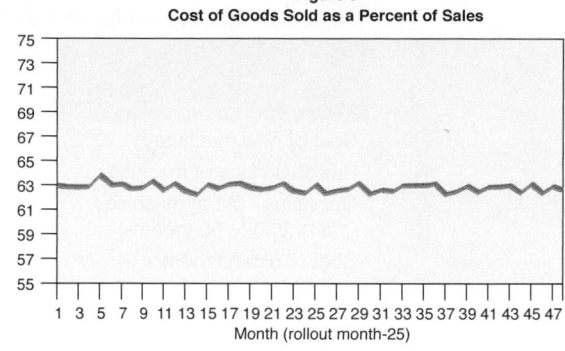

Figure 1
Percentage Change in Sales

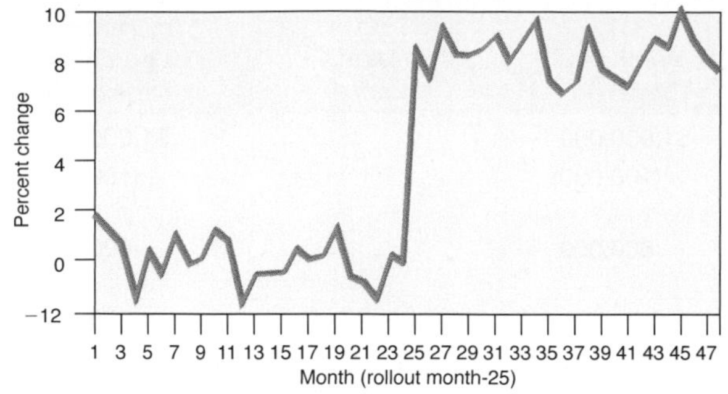

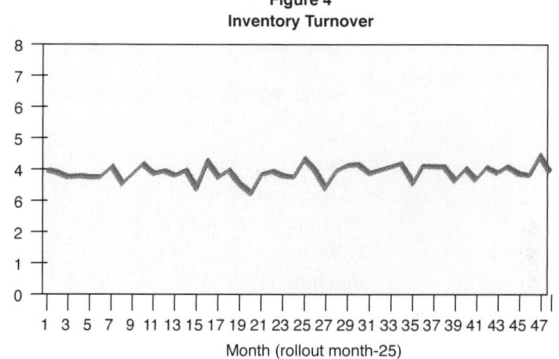

Figure 3
Cost of Goods Sold as a Percent of Sales

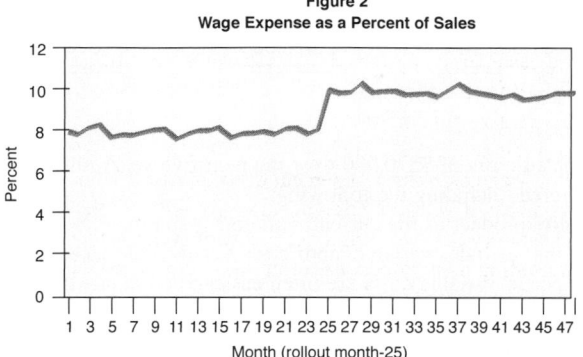

Figure 2
Wage Expense as a Percent of Sales

Figure 4
Inventory Turnover

SOLUTIONS TO REVIEW PROBLEMS

Mid-Module Review

Solution

a.

Relevant costs:	Irrelevant costs:
Cost of machine	Building lease cost
Residual value of machine	Vice President's salary
Operating cost of machine	
Direct labor savings	
Cost of manager	
Opportunity cost of renting released space	

b.

	(1) Purchase Machine	(2) Use Labor	(1) − (2) Difference (in total cost of purchasing machine)
Cost of new machine	$1,000,000		$1,000,000
Residual value of machine	(100,000)		(100,000)
Operating cost of machine ($10,000 × 60 months)	600,000		600,000
Cost of direct laborers (5,000 clubs × $5 × 60 months)		$1,500,000	(1,500,000)
Cost of one manager ($6,000 × 60 months)		360,000	(360,000)
Rental value of freed up space ($3,500 × 60 months)		210,000	(210,000)
Total costs	$1,500,000	$2,070,000	$ (570,000)
Advantage of purchasing machine.		$570,000	

c. Even though the new machine would save estimated costs of $570,000 over the next five years, there are several qualitative questions that should be answered, including the following:
  • Will the new machine provide the same quality product as the current workers?
  • How important is it to have a cost structure that includes variable labor costs versus more fixed machine costs? If a business decline should occur, variable costs are often easier to eliminate than fixed costs.
  • What is the expected effect on worker morale and community image of eliminating a significant number of jobs in the plant?
  • How important is it for the sales staff to be able to promote the product as primarily handmade, versus machine made?

Module-End Review

Solution

Unit selling price.	$4.80
Unit variable costs	(2.50)
Unit contribution margin.	$2.30

a.

Profit decrease from reduced sales given no changes in prices or costs (1,800 units × $2.30)	$ (4,140)
Profit increase from increase in selling price [(15,000 units − 1,800 units) × $1.50]	19,800
Increase in monthly profit.	$15,660

b.

Profit increase from increased sales given no changes in prices or costs (6,000 units × $2.30)	$13,800
Profit decrease from reduced selling price of all units [(15,000 units + 6,000 units) × $1.80]	(37,800)
Profit decrease from increased direct labor costs for the last 1,000 units [1,000 units × ($0.20 × 0.50)]	(100)
Decrease in monthly profit	$(24,100)

c.

Increase in revenues (4,000 units × $4.00)		$16,000
Increase in costs		
Direct materials (4,000 units × $2.00)	$ 8,000	
Direct labor (4,000 units × $0.20)	800	
Factory overhead (4,000 units × $0.25)	1,000	
Selling and administrative	500	(10,300)
Increase in profits		$ 5,700

d.

Increase in revenues (8,000 units × $4.00)		$32,000
Increase in costs		
Direct materials (8,000 units × $2.00)	$16,000	
Direct labor (8,000 units × $0.20)	1,600	
Factory overhead (8,000 units × $0.25)	2,000	
Selling and administrative	500	
Opportunity cost of lost regular sales		
[(15,000 units + 8,000 units −		
20,000 unit capacity) × $2.30]	6,900	(27,000)
Increase in profits		$ 5,000

e.

	Cost to Make	Cost to Buy	Difference (income effect of buying)
Cost to buy (15,000 units × $1.00)		$15,000	$(15,000)
Cost to make			
Direct materials			
(15,000 units × $2.00 × 0.40)	$12,000		12,000
Direct labor			
(15,000 units × $0.20 × 0.40)	1,200		1,200
Factory overhead			
(15,000 units × $0.25 × 0.40)	1,500		1,500
Opportunity cost	1,000		1,000
Totals	$15,700	$15,000	$ 700
Advantage of buying		$700	

f.

Increase in revenues			
Package individually (15,000 units × $5.05)		$75,750	
Sell in bulk (15,000 units × $4.80)		(72,000)	$3,750
Additional packaging costs (15,000 units × $0.10)			(1,500)
Advantage of individual packaging			$2,250

CATERPILLAR

Financial reporting is the process of preparing a firm's financial statements—income statement, balance sheet, and statement of cash flows—in accordance with generally accepted accounting principles (GAAP). GAAP requires that companies producing products measure the cost of products sold and the cost of ending inventory for each period. Caterpillar and Hershey Company present very different environments in which both the cost of products sold and ending inventory costs must be determined.

Caterpillar is a leading manufacturer of heavy moving equipment such as articulated trucks, pipe layers, scrapers, forest machines, and motor graders. Other products include marine engines and generator sets. Although some of Caterpillar's products are produced for inventory in anticipation of future sales, many are produced in single units or small batches in response to customer orders. Caterpillar reported an operating profit of $577 million on revenues of $32,396 million. To remain competitive the

Product Costing: Job and Process Operations

LEARNING OBJECTIVES

LO1 Describe inventory requirements and measurement issues for service, merchandising, and manufacturing organizations. (p. 17-3)

LO2 Explain the framework of inventory costing for financial reporting. (p. 17-4)

LO3 Describe the production environment as it relates to product costing systems. (p. 17-9)

LO4 Explain the operation of a job costing system. (p. 17-10)

LO5 Explain the operation of a process costing system. (p. 17-20)

company pursues "radical improvements in safety, quality, velocity, and costs."

The Hershey Company is the largest North American manufacturer of chocolate and sugar confectionery products. Hershey brands include Hershey's, Reese's, Hershey's Kisses, and Ice Breakers. Hershey's products are produced continuously with annual unit volumes in the tens of millions. With sales of $5,299 million, Hershey reported an operating profit of $762 million. To remain competitive Hershey must carefully control costs, especially anticipated increases in the costs of energy and raw materials.

These firms represent very different cost measurement environments. The volumes and products range from millions of units of an inexpensive commodity to limited numbers of highly customized, very expensive items. Although the specific accounting techniques and approaches differ for these firms, the intent of these accounting efforts is the same. That is, each product costing system must accumulate and assign the costs of the direct and indirect activities involved in manufacturing its products.

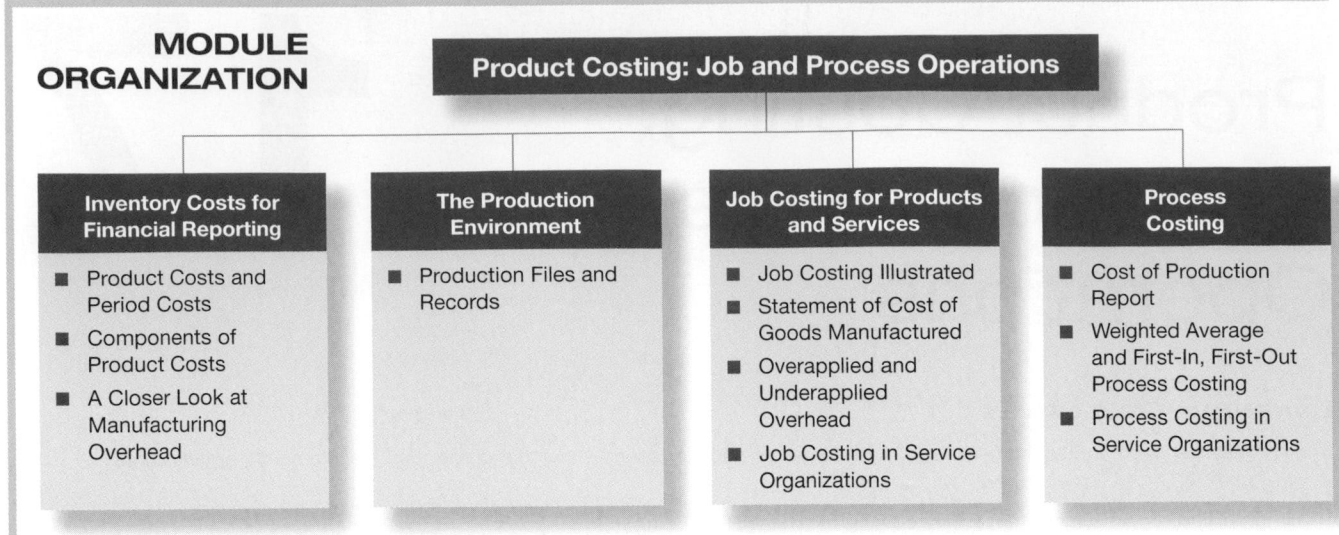

This module provides an overview of product costing systems and a framework for understanding costs in a production environment. It also examines aspects of the production environment that can affect product costing systems and discusses costing issues related to the production of physical products versus the production of services.

INVENTORY COSTS IN VARIOUS ORGANIZATIONS

LO1 Describe inventory requirements and measurement issues for service, merchandising, and manufacturing organizations.

Organizations can be classified as service, merchandising, or manufacturing. **Service organizations**, such as **Supercuts** hair salons, **Shriners Children's Hospitals**, **Cracker Barrel** restaurants, and **Delta Air Lines**, perform services for others. **Merchandising organizations**, such as **Wal-Mart**, **L. L. Bean**, and **Best Buy**, buy and sell goods. **Manufacturing organizations**, such as Caterpillar, **MillerCoors** brewing, and Hershey, process raw materials into finished products for sale to others.

Service organizations typically have a low percentage of their assets invested in inventory, which usually consists only of the supplies needed to facilitate their operations. In contrast, merchandising organizations usually have a high percentage of their assets invested in inventory. Their largest inventory investment is merchandise purchased for resale, but they also have supplies inventories.

Manufacturing organizations, like merchandisers, have a high percentage of their assets invested in inventories. However, rather than just one major inventory category, manufacturing organizations typically have three: raw materials, work-in-process, and finished goods. **Raw materials inventories** contain the physical ingredients and components that will be converted by machines and/or human labor into a finished product. **Work-in-process inventories** are the partially completed goods that are in the process of being converted into a finished product. **Finished goods inventories** are the completely manufactured products held for sale to customers. As of December 31, 2009, **MillerCoors** reported the following inventories:

Raw materials	$220.0 million
Work-in-progress	79.7 million
Finished goods	69.0 million
Other inventories	12.8 million
Total	$381.5 million

Manufacturing organizations also have supplies inventories used to facilitate production (see the "Other inventories" for MillerCoors shown above) and selling and administrative activities. Exhibit

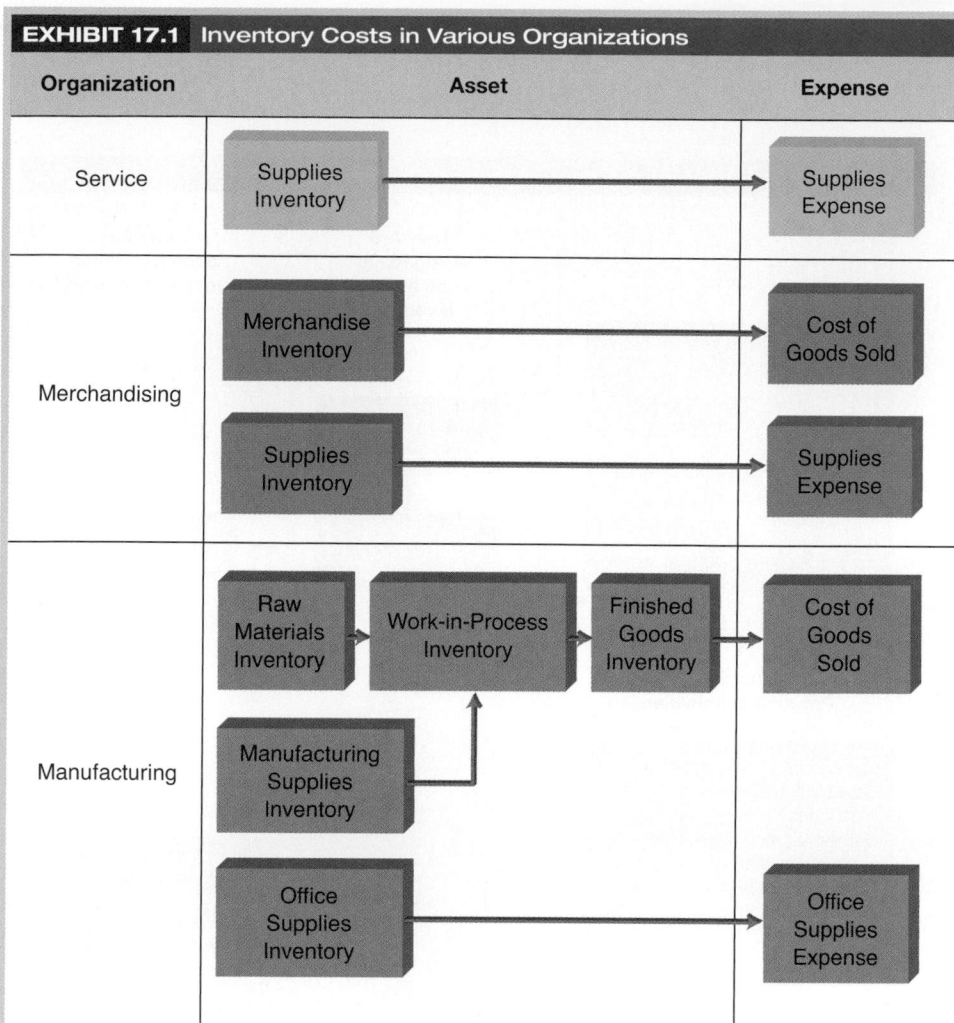

EXHIBIT 17.1 Inventory Costs in Various Organizations

17.1 illustrates the flow of inventory costs in service, merchandising, and manufacturing organizations. In all three types of organizations, the financial accounting system initially records costs of inventories as assets; when they are eventually consumed or sold, inventory costs are recorded as expenses.

Most formal inventory costing systems are designed to provide information for general purpose financial statements. Before the balance sheet and income statement are prepared, the cost of ending inventory and the cost of inventory sold or used during the period must be determined.

INVENTORY COSTS FOR FINANCIAL REPORTING

In financial reporting for manufacturing organizations, an important distinction is made between the cost of *producing* products and the cost of all other activities such as selling and administration.

LO2 Explain the framework of inventory costing for financial reporting.

Product Costs and Period Costs

For financial reporting, all costs incurred in the *manufacturing* of products are called **product costs**; these costs are carried in the accounts as an asset (inventory) until the product is sold, at which time they are recognized as an expense (cost of goods sold). Product costs include the costs of raw materials, production employee salaries and wages, and all other *manufacturing* costs incurred to transform raw materials into finished products. Expired costs (other than those related to manufacturing inventory) are called **period**

costs and are recognized as expenses when incurred. Period costs include the president's salary, sales commissions, advertising costs, and all other *nonmanufacturing* costs. Product and period costs are illustrated in Exhibit 17.2.

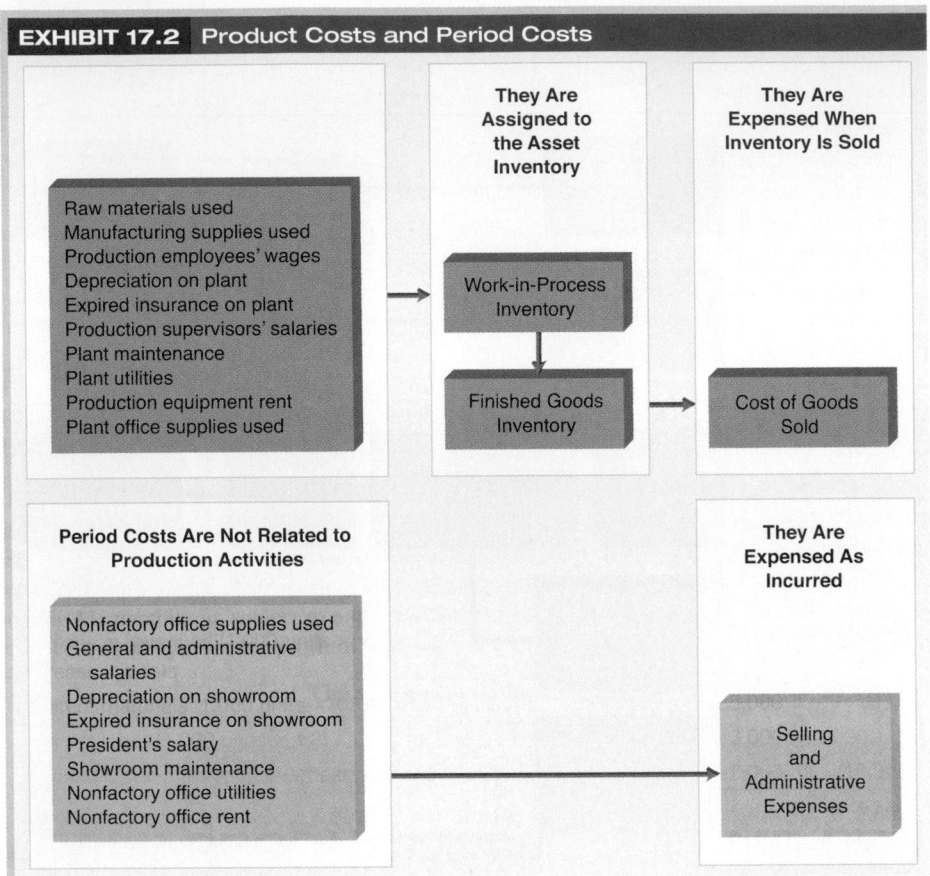

EXHIBIT 17.2 Product Costs and Period Costs

Costs such as research and development, marketing, distribution, and customer service are important for strategic analyses; however, since these costs are not incurred in the production process, they are not product costs for *financial reporting purposes*. For *internal managerial purposes,* accountants and managers often use the term *product costing* to embrace all costs incurred in connection with a product or service throughout the value chain.

To summarize, in the *product cost* versus *period cost* framework of *financial reporting,* costs are classified based on whether or not they are related to the production process. If they are related to the production process, they are product costs; otherwise, they are period costs. In this framework, costs that seem very similar may be treated quite differently. For example, note in Exhibit 17.2 that the expired cost of insurance on the *plant* is a *product cost,* but the expired cost of insurance on the *showroom* is a *period cost.* The reason is that the plant is used in production, but the showroom is not. This method of accounting for inventory that assigns all production costs to inventory is sometimes referred to as the **absorption cost** (or **full absorption cost**) method because all production costs are said to be fully absorbed into the cost of the product.

Three Components of Product Costs

The manufacture of even a simple product, such as a small wooden table, requires three basic ingredients: materials (wood), labor (the skill of a worker) and production facilities (a building to work in, a saw, and other tools). Corresponding to these three basic ingredients of any product are three basic categories of product costs: direct materials, direct labor, and manufacturing overhead.

Direct materials are the costs of the primary raw materials converted into finished goods. Examples of primary raw materials include iron ore to a steel mill, coiled aluminum to a manufacturer of aluminum siding, cow's milk to a dairy, logs to a sawmill, and lumber to a builder. The finished product of one firm may be the raw materials of another firm down the value chain. For example, rolled steel is a finished product of **U.S. Steel**, but it is the raw material of the **Maytag Company** for the manufacture of washers and dryers. **Direct labor** consists of wages earned by *production employees for the time they actually spend working on a product,* and **manufacturing overhead** includes all manufacturing costs other than direct materials and direct labor. (Manufacturing overhead is also called *factory overhead, burden, manufacturing burden,* and just *overhead.* Merchandising organizations occasionally refer to administrative costs as *overhead.*) **Conversion cost** consists of the combined costs of direct labor and manufacturing overhead incurred to convert raw materials into finished goods.

Examples of manufacturing overhead are manufacturing supplies, depreciation on manufacturing buildings and equipment, and the costs of plant taxes, insurance, maintenance, security, and utilities. Also included are production supervisors' salaries and all other manufacturing-related labor costs for employees who do not work directly on the product (such as maintenance, security, and janitorial personnel).

Just as raw materials, labor, and production facilities are combined to produce a finished product, direct materials costs, direct labor costs, and manufacturing overhead costs are accumulated to obtain the total cost of goods produced. Exhibit 17.3 illustrates that these product costs are accumulated in the general ledger in Work-in-Process Inventory (or just Work-in-Process) as production takes place and then are transferred to Finished Goods Inventory when production is completed. Product costs are finally assigned to Cost of Goods Sold when the finished goods are sold. (Account titles are capitalized to make it easier to determine when reference is being made to a physical item, such as work-in-process inventory, or to the account, Work-in-Process Inventory, in which costs assigned to the work-in-process inventory are accumulated.)

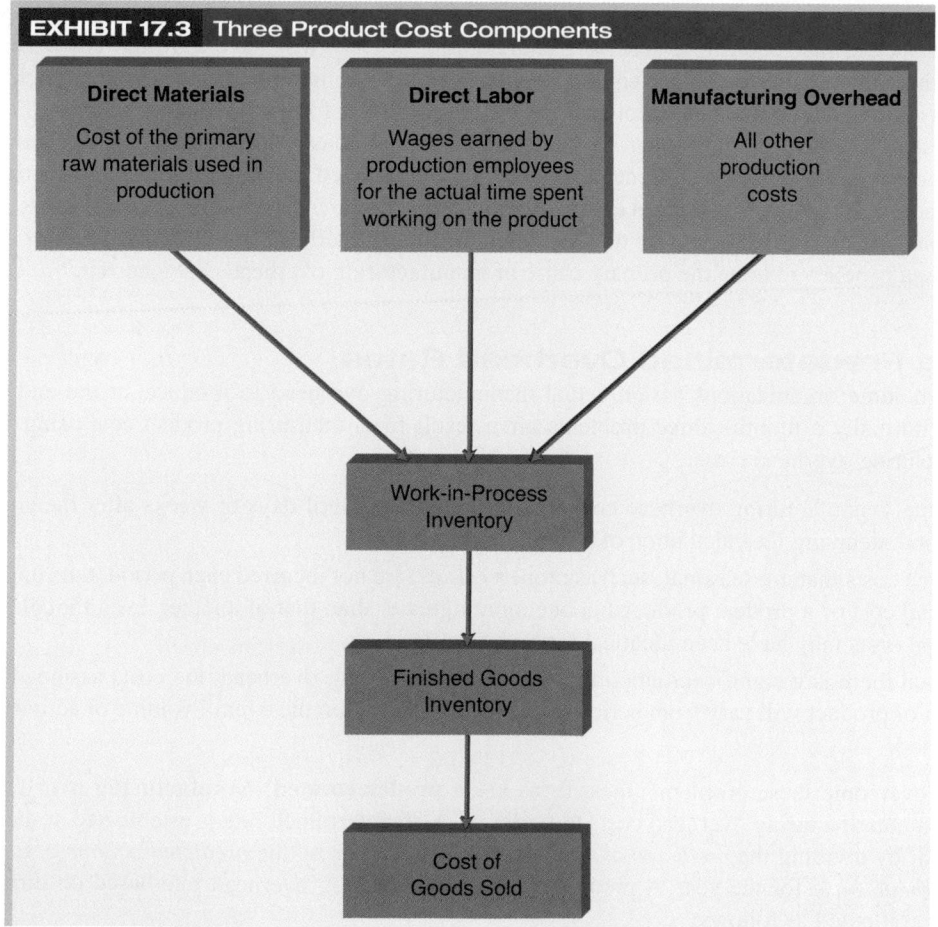

EXHIBIT 17.3 Three Product Cost Components

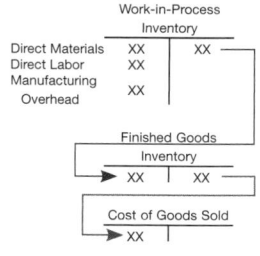

A Closer Look at Manufacturing Overhead

The biggest challenge in measuring the cost of a product is determining the amount of overhead incurred to produce it. Direct materials cost is driven by the number of raw materials units used; hence, its cost is simply the number of units of raw materials used multiplied by the related cost per unit. Direct labor cost is driven by the number of directly traceable labor hours worked on the product; so its cost is the number of direct labor hours used times the appropriate rate per hour. But what about manufacturing overhead? Manufacturing overhead often consists of dozens of different cost elements, potentially with many different cost drivers. Electricity cost is based on kilowatt-hours and water cost on gallons used; depreciation is usually measured in years of service and insurance in premium dollars per thousand dollars of coverage; and supervisors' salaries are a fixed amount per month.

Historically, accountants have believed that, even when possible, it is not cost effective to try to separately measure the cost incurred for each manufacturing overhead item to produce a unit of finished product. Instead of identifying separate cost drivers for each individual cost component in manufacturing overhead, all overhead costs for a department or plant are frequently placed in a cost pool and a single unit-level cost driver is used to assign (or apply) overhead to products.

If a company produced only one product, it would be simple to assign (or apply) overhead to the units produced because it would merely involve dividing total manufacturing overhead cost incurred by the number of units produced to get a cost per unit. For example, if total manufacturing overhead costs were $100,000 for a period when 20,000 units of product were produced, the overhead cost assigned to each unit would be $5.

Selecting a Basis (or Cost Driver) for Assigning Overhead

When multiple products are manufactured in the same facilities, using a simple average of manufacturing overhead cost per unit seldom provides a good estimate of the overhead costs incurred to produce each product. Units requiring extensive manufacturing activity will have too little cost assigned to them, while others requiring only a small amount of manufacturing effort will absorb too much cost. In these cases, units of production is not an appropriate cost driver for manufacturing overhead.

To solve this allocation problem, an overhead application base (or cost driver) other than number of units produced is used. The overhead application base selected is typically a unit-level activity that is common to all products and has a causal relationship with the incurrence of overhead costs. For example, *machine hours* may be used to assign manufacturing overhead costs if the *number of machine hours used* is believed to be the primary cause of manufacturing overhead cost incurred.

Using Predetermined Overhead Rates

Although some organizations assign actual manufacturing overhead to products at the end of each period (normally a month), three problems often result from measuring product cost using "actual" manufacturing overhead costs:

1. Actual manufacturing overhead cost may not be known until days or weeks after the end of the period, delaying the calculation of unit product cost.

2. Some costs that are seasonal, such as property taxes, are not incurred each period, thus making the actual cost of a product produced in one month greater than that of another, even though nonseasonal costs may have been identical for both months.

3. When there is a significant amount of fixed manufacturing overhead, the costs assigned to each unit of product will vary from period to period, depending on the overall volume of activity for the period.

To overcome these problems, most firms use a **predetermined manufacturing overhead rate** to assign manufacturing overhead costs to products. A predetermined rate is established at the start of each year by dividing the *predicted overhead costs for the year* by the *predicted volume of activity in the overhead base* for the year. A predetermined manufacturing overhead rate based on direct labor hours is computed as follows:

$$\text{Predetermined manufacturing overhead rate per direct labor hour} = \frac{\text{Predicted total manufacturing overhead cost for the year}}{\text{Predicted total direct labor hours for the year}}$$

If management believes machine hours is the major driver of manufacturing overhead, the denominator should be predicted machine hours.

Using a predetermined manufacturing overhead rate based on direct labor hours, we compute the assignment of overhead to Work-in-Process Inventory as follows:

$$\begin{array}{ccc} \text{Manufacturing} & \text{Actual} & \text{Predetermined manufacturing} \\ \text{overhead applied to} & = \text{direct labor} \times & \text{overhead assigned to direct} \\ \text{Work-in-Process Inventory} & \text{hours} & \text{labor hours} \end{array}$$

To illustrate, late in 2011, Harmon Manufacturing Company predicted a 2012 activity level of 25,000 direct labor hours with manufacturing overhead totaling $187,500. Using this information, its 2012 predetermined overhead rate per direct labor hour was computed as follows:

$$\begin{aligned} \text{Predetermined overhead rate} &= \frac{\$187{,}500}{25{,}000 \text{ direct labor hours}} \\ &= \$7.50 \text{ per direct labor hour} \end{aligned}$$

If 2,000 direct labor hours were used in September 2012, the applied overhead for September would be $15,000, as shown here:

$$2{,}000 \times \$7.50 = \$15{,}000$$

When a predetermined rate is used, monthly variations between actual and applied manufacturing overhead are expected because of the seasonality in costs and the variations in monthly activity. Hence, in some months overhead will be "overapplied" as applied overhead exceeds actual overhead; in other months overhead will be "underapplied" as actual overhead exceeds applied overhead. If the beginning-of-the-year estimates are accurate for annual overhead costs and annual activity, monthly over- and underapplied amounts during the year should offset each other by the end of the year. Later in this module, we consider accounting for any over- or underapplied manufacturing overhead balance that may exist at the end of the year.

Changing Cost Structures Affect the Basis of Overhead Application

By using a single overhead rate, we assume that overhead costs are primarily caused by a single cost driver. Historically, a single plantwide overhead application rate based on direct labor hours was widely used when direct labor was the predominant cost factor in production and manufacturing overhead costs were driven by the utilization of direct labor.

Changes in manufacturing processes have produced major shifts in the composition of conversion costs, resulting in significantly less direct labor and significantly more manufacturing overhead. An example of this shift is the automobile industry where firms such as Ford and Toyota have spent billions of dollars on robotics and other technologies, thereby reducing direct labor in the production process. In many cases, direct labor hours are no longer an appropriate basis for assigning manufacturing costs to products. In others, these changes mean there is no longer a single cost driver that is appropriate for assigning manufacturing overhead to products.

Although some companies continue to use a single manufacturing overhead rate because it is convenient, many companies no longer use this approach. Instead, they have adopted multiple overhead rates based on either major departments or activities within the organization. One method for using multiple overhead rates is activity-based costing, discussed in Module 18.

THE PRODUCTION ENVIRONMENT

LO3 Describe
the production
environment as it
relates to product
costing systems.

Production personnel need to know the specific products to produce on specific machines on a daily or even hourly basis. The detailed scheduling of products on machines is performed by production scheduling personnel. Exactly how production is scheduled depends on whether process manufacturing or job production is used and whether production is in response to a specific customer sales order or for the company's inventory in anticipation of future sales.

In **process manufacturing**, production of identical units is on a *continuous* basis; a production facility may be devoted exclusively to one product or to a set of closely related products. Companies where you would likely find a process manufacturing environment include **Exxon Mobil** and **Bowater Incorporated** (which makes rolled paper for the printing of daily newspapers such as the *Chicago Tribune*). Process manufacturing is discussed later in this module.

In **job production**, also called **job order production**, products are manufactured in single units or in batches of identical units. Of course, the products included in different jobs may vary considerably. Examples of single-unit jobs are found at **Hallco Builders**, a builder of custom-designed homes; **Metric Constructors Inc.**, which builds skyscrapers; and **Riverwood International**, which designs, produces, and installs packaging systems for food processors. Examples of multiple-unit jobs are found at **Hartmarx**, a clothing manufacturer; **Steelcase Furniture Company**, a large producer of office furnishings; and **Intermet Corporation**, a foundry company that makes parts for the automobile industry.

In a job production environment, when a customer's order is received, the marketing department forwards the order to production scheduling, where employees determine when and how the product is to be produced. Important scheduling considerations include the overall workload, raw materials availability, specific equipment or labor requirements, and the delivery date(s) of the finished product.

Important staff groups involved in production planning and control include engineering, scheduling, and accounting. Engineering is primarily concerned with determining how a product should be produced. Based on an engineering analysis and cost data, engineering personnel develop manufacturing specifications for each product. These manufacturing specifications are often summarized in two important documents: a bill of materials and an operations list. Each product's **bill of materials** specifies the kinds and quantities of raw materials required for one unit of product. The following Business Insight presents a bill of materials for a BlackBerry Smartphone. The **operations list** (sometimes called an **activities list**) specifies the manufacturing operations and related times required for one unit or batch of product. The operations list should also include information on any machine setup time, movements between work areas, and other scheduled activities, such as quality inspections.

BUSINESS INSIGHT   Reverse Engineering A Bill of Materials

Reverse engineering involves disassembling a device to determine its components, how it works, and how it is assembled. Companies and industry analysts use reverse engineering for competitive purposes or to stay abreast of industry trends. Using reverse engineering ISuppli analysts developed the following bill of materials for the Blackberry Torch 9800 shortly after its introduction in August of 2010:

Display and Touchscreen	$ 34.85
Memory	34.25
Mechanical/enclosures	23.35
Application processor	15.00
Radio/wireless	24.50
User interface	12.40
Battery/Power management	15.90
Camera	10.80
Total materials	$171.05

Because of the extensive use of components manufactured by other companies, ISuppli estimated conversion costs at only $12 per unit.

Source: Jennifer Valentino-Devries and Phred Dvorak, "Piece by Piece: The Suppliers Behind the New BlackBerry Torch Smartphone," *The Wall Street Journal*, August 16, 2010; Michelle Maisto, "BlackBerry Torch Smartphone Parts Cost $171.05: iSuppli" eweek.com, 2010-08-18; isuppli.com.

Scheduling personnel prepare a production order for each job. The **production order** contains a job's unique identification number and specifies such details as the quantity to be produced, raw materials requirements, manufacturing operations and other activities to be performed, and perhaps even the time when each manufacturing operation should be performed. In preparing a production order, scheduling personnel use the product's bill of materials and operations list to determine the materials, operations, and manufacturing times required for the job.

A **job cost sheet** is a document used to accumulate the costs for a specific job. The job cost sheet serves as the basic record for recording actual progress on the job. As production takes place, the materials, labor, and machine resources utilized are recorded on the job cost sheet along with the related costs. When a job is completed, the final cost of the job is determined by totalling the costs on the job cost sheet.

Production Files and Records

Certain files in the cost system (typically in a computer database) provide the necessary detail for amounts maintained in total in the general ledger. For example, the raw materials inventory file contains separate records for each type of raw materials, indicating increases, decreases, and the available balance for both units and costs. Every time there is a change in the Raw Materials Inventory general ledger account, there must be an equal change in one or more individual inventory records. Therefore, at any given time, the total of the balances in the raw materials inventory file for all raw materials inventory items should equal the balance in the Raw Materials Inventory general ledger account. Because of this relationship between the raw materials inventory file and Raw Materials Inventory in the general ledger, Raw Materials Inventory is called a *control account* and the raw materials file of detailed records is called a *subsidiary ledger*. Other general ledger accounts related to the product cost system that have subsidiary files are Work-in-Process, Finished Goods Inventory, and Cost of Goods Sold.

Other records required to operate a job cost system include production orders, job cost sheets, materials requisition forms, and work tickets. Production orders and job cost sheets were previously discussed. The production order serves as authorization for production supervisors to obtain materials from the storeroom and to issue work orders to production employees, and the job cost sheet accumulates the cost of the job.

A **materials requisition form** indicates the type and quantity of each raw material issued to the factory. This form is used to record the transfer of responsibility for materials and to record materials changes on raw materials and job cost sheet records. The materials requisition form has a place to record the job number; the job cost sheet has a place to record the requisition number. If a question arises regarding the issuance of materials, the requisition number and job number provide a trail for tracing the destination and the source of the materials. The materials requisition form also identifies the materials warehouse employee who issued the materials and the production employee who received them.

A **work ticket** is used to record the time a job spends in a specific manufacturing operation. Each manufacturing operation performed on a job is documented by a work ticket. The completed work tickets for a job should correspond to the operations specified on the job production order. Time information on the work tickets is used by production scheduling or expediting personnel to determine whether the job is on schedule, and to assign costs to the job.

A production operation can involve a single employee, a group of employees, a machine, or even heating, cooling, or aging processes. When the operation involves a single employee, the rate recorded on the work ticket is simply the employee's wage rate. When it involves a group of employees, the rate is composed of the wage rates of all employees in the group. When the work involves a machine operation, the rate includes a charge for machine time, as well as the time of any machine operators. Other operations, such as heating, cooling, or aging, will also have a rate for each unit of time.

JOB COSTING FOR PRODUCTS AND SERVICES

Exhibit 17.4 shows how inventory costs in a manufacturing organization flow in a logical pattern through the financial accounting system. Pay particular attention to the major inventory accounts (Raw Materials, Work-in-Process, and Finished Goods Inventory), Manufacturing Overhead, and the flow of costs through the inventory accounts. Each of the numbered items, representing a cost flow affecting an inventory account or Manufacturing Overhead, is explained here:

LO4 Explain the operation of a job costing system.

1. The costs of purchased raw materials and manufacturing supplies are recorded in Raw Materials and Manufacturing Supplies, respectively. An increase in Accounts Payable typically offsets these increases.

2. As primary raw materials are requisitioned to the factory, direct materials costs are transferred from Raw Materials to Work-in-Process.

3. Direct labor costs are assigned to Work-in-Process on the basis of the time devoted to processing raw materials. Indirect labor costs associated with production employees are initially assigned to Manufacturing Overhead.

4.–6. Other production related costs are also assigned to Manufacturing Overhead. Other Payables represents the incurrence of a variety of costs such as repairs and maintenance, utilities, and property taxes.

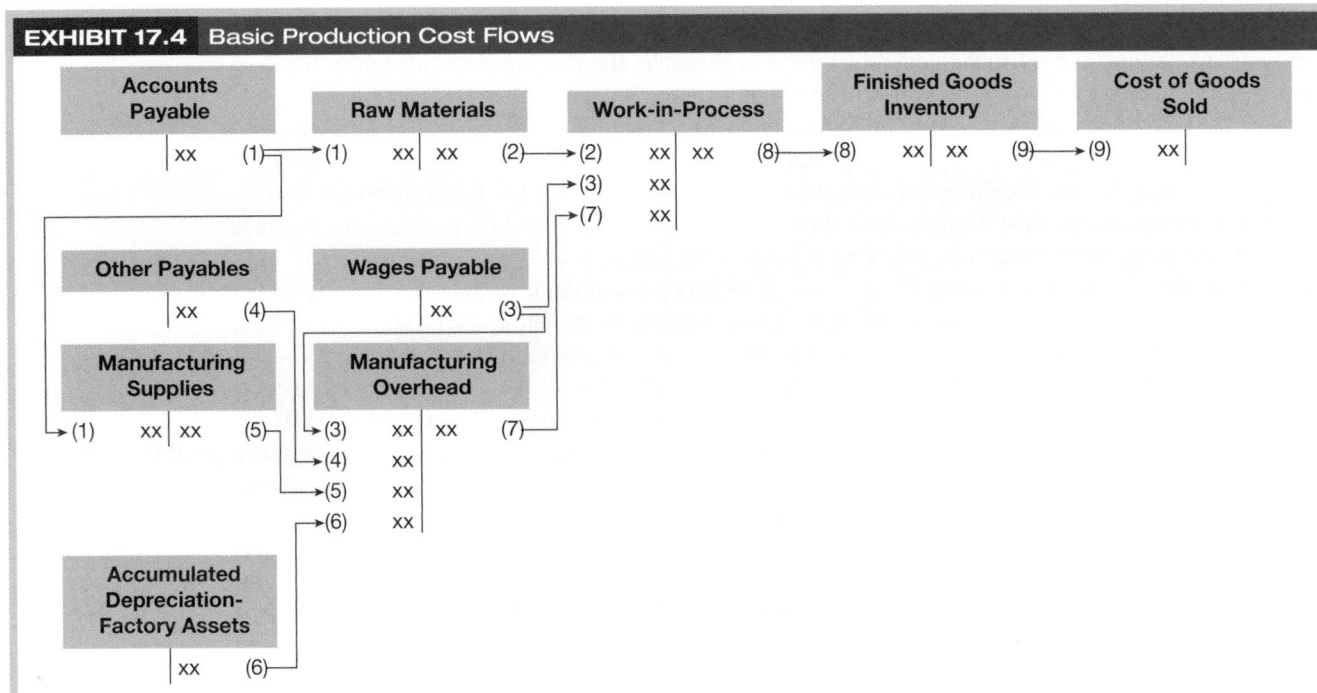

EXHIBIT 17.4 Basic Production Cost Flows

7. Costs assigned to Manufacturing Overhead are periodically reassigned (applied) to Work-in-Process, preferably with the use of a predetermined overhead rate such as direct labor hours, machine hours, or some other cost assignment base.

8. When products are completed, their accumulated product costs are totaled on a job cost sheet and transferred from Work-in-Process to Finished Goods Inventory.

9. When the completed products are sold, their costs are transferred from Finished Goods Inventory to Cost of Goods Sold.

Job Costing Illustrated

Even though data are almost always processed with computerized systems, data processing procedures are best illustrated within the context of a paper-based manual system. Outdoor Rainwear custom manufactures waterproof parkas for retail under store labels. Because variations in styles cause differences in costs, detailed records are kept concerning the costs assigned to specific jobs. Raw materials consist of Gore-Tex fabric, liner fabric, and zippers.

Total inventory on August 1, 2012, included Raw Materials, $71,000; Work-in-Process, $109,900; and Finished Goods, $75,000. In addition there were manufacturing supplies of $1,600, consisting of various items such as thread, needles, sheers, and machine lubricant. The August 1 balance in Manufacturing Overhead was $0.

Raw Materials			
Description	**Quantity**	**Unit Cost**	**Total Cost**
Gore-Tex fabric....................	3,000 square yards	$20	$60,000
Liner	2,000 square yards	3	6,000
Zippers.........................	1,000 units	5	5,000
Total			$71,000

Manufacturing Supplies	
Item	**Total Cost**
Various......................	$1,600

Work-in-Process	
Job	**Total Cost**
425	$ 58,600
426	51,300
Total	$109,900

Finished Goods Inventory	
Job	**Total Cost**
424	$75,000

To illustrate manufacturing cost flows in a job cost system, "T" accounts are presented in the margin for the cost system transactions for Outdoor Rainwear, for August 2012. Each cost assignment is supported by documented information that is recorded in subsidiary cost system records. The manufacturing cost transactions for Outdoor Rainwear for August 2012 are discussed here.

1. Raw materials and manufacturing supplies are purchased on account. The vendor's invoice totals $31,000, including $1,000 of manufacturing supplies and $30,000 of raw materials. The cost of the raw materials must be assigned to specific raw materials inventory records:

Gore-Tex fabric.....................................	850 square yards	×	$20 =	$17,000
Liner	2,000 square yards	×	$3 =	6,000
Zippers...	1,400 units	×	$5 =	7,000
Total				$30,000

Raw Materials Inventory
Beg. Bal. 71,000
(1) 30,000

Manufacturing Supplies
Beg. Bal. 1,600
(1) 1,000

Accounts Payable
31,000 (1)

2. Materials needed to complete Jobs 425 and 426 are requisitioned. Two new jobs, 427 and 428, were also started and direct materials were requisitioned for them. A total of $54,300 of raw materials was requisitioned:

	Job 425	Job 426	Job 427	Job 428	Total
Gore-Tex fabric...................					
975 sq. yds. × $20			$19,500		$19,500
955 sq. yds. × $20				$19,100	19,100
Liner					
500 sq. yds. × $3			1,500		1,500
1,100 sq. yds. × $3.............				3,300	3,300
Zippers........................					
960 units × $5.................	$4,800				4,800
720 units × $5.................		$3,600			3,600
500 × $5			2,500		2,500
Total	$4,800	$3,600	$23,500	$22,400	$54,300

Work-in-Process Inventory
Beg. Bal. 109,900
(2) 54,300

Raw Materials Inventory
Beg. Bal. 71,000 | 54,300 (2)
(1) 30,000

Work-in-Process Inventory

Beg. Bal.	109,900		
(2)	54,300		
(3)	34,450		

Manufacturing Overhead

Beg. Bal.	–0–		
(3)	7,200		

Wages Payable

		41,650	(3)

---

3. The August payroll liability was \$41,650, including \$34,450 for direct labor and \$7,200 for indirect labor. Direct labor was assigned to the jobs as follows:

	Job 425	Job 426	Job 427	Job 428	Total
Labor hours	600	900	1,000	945	
Labor rate........................	× \$10	× \$10	× \$10	× \$10	
Total	\$6,000	\$9,000	\$10,000	\$9,450	\$34,450

Note: The \$7,200 of indirect labor costs is assigned to products as part of applied overhead.

4.-6. In addition to indirect labor, Outdoor Rainwear incurred the following manufacturing overhead costs:

Manufacturing Overhead

Beg. Bal.	–0–		
(3)	7,200		
(4)	950		
(5)	2,400		
(6)	3,230		

Manufacturing Supplies

Beg. Bal.	1,600	950	(4)
(1)	1,000		

Accumulated Depreciation

		2,400	(5)

Other Payables

		3,230	(6)

Manufacturing Supplies	\$ 950
Accumulated Depreciation—Factory Assets	2,400
Miscellaneous (Other Payables)	3,230

7. Manufacturing overhead is applied to jobs using a predetermined rate of \$4 per direct labor hour. Assignments to individual jobs are as follows:

Work-in-Process Inventory

Beg. Bal.	109,900		
(2)	54,300		
(3)	34,450		
(7)	13,780		

Manufacturing Overhead

Beg. Bal.	–0–	13,780	(7)
(3)	7,200		
(4)	950		
(5)	2,400		
(6)	3,230		

	Job 425	Job 426	Job 427	Job 428	Total
Labor hours	600	900	1,000	945	
Overhead rate per labor hour........	× \$4	× \$4	× \$4	× \$4	
Total	\$2,400	\$3,600	\$4,000	\$3,780	\$13,780

8. Jobs 425, 426, and 427 are completed with the following costs:

Finished Goods Inventory

Beg. Bal.	75,000		
(8)	176,800		

Work-in-Process Inventory

Beg. Bal.	109,900	176,800	(8)
(2)	54,300		
(3)	34,450		
(7)	13,780		

	Job 425	Job 426	Job 427	Total
Beginning balance	\$58,600	\$51,300	\$ 0	\$109,900
Current costs:				
Direct materials (entry 2)	4,800	3,600	23,500	31,900
Direct labor (entry 3)......................	6,000	9,000	10,000	25,000
Applied overhead (entry 7).................	2,400	3,600	4,000	10,000
Total	\$71,800	\$67,500	\$37,500	\$176,800

Additional analysis for the completed jobs indicates the following:

	Job 425	Job 426	Job 427
Total cost of job	\$71,800	\$67,500	\$37,500
Units in job	÷ 1,200	÷ 900	÷ 500
Unit cost..	\$ 59.83	\$ 75.00	\$ 75.00

9. Jobs 424, 425, and 426 are delivered to customers for a sales price of \$400,000. Determining the costs transferred from Finished Goods Inventory to Cost of Goods Sold requires summing the total cost of jobs sold.

Cost of Goods Sold

(9)	214,300		

Finished Goods Inventory

Beg. Bal.	75,000	214,300	(9)
(8)	176,800		

Job 424	\$ 75,000
Job 425	71,800
Job 426	67,500
Total	\$214,300

At this point we can determine the gross profit on the completed jobs:

Sales.	$400,000
Cost of goods sold.	(214,300)
Gross profit.	$185,700

If inventory were produced in anticipation of future sales rather than in response to specific customer orders, it is likely that not all units in a job would be sold at the same time. In this case, the unit cost information is used to determine the amount transferred from Finished Goods Inventory to Cost of Goods Sold.

Exhibit 17.5 shows the cost system records supporting the ending balances in the major inventory accounts and Cost of Goods Sold. Note the importance of the job cost sheets for determining cost transfers affecting Work-in-Process and Finished Goods Inventory. The job cost sheets are also used in determining the ending balances of these accounts.

EXHIBIT 17.5 General Ledger Accounts and Subsidiary Records for Inventory Categories and Cost of Goods Sold

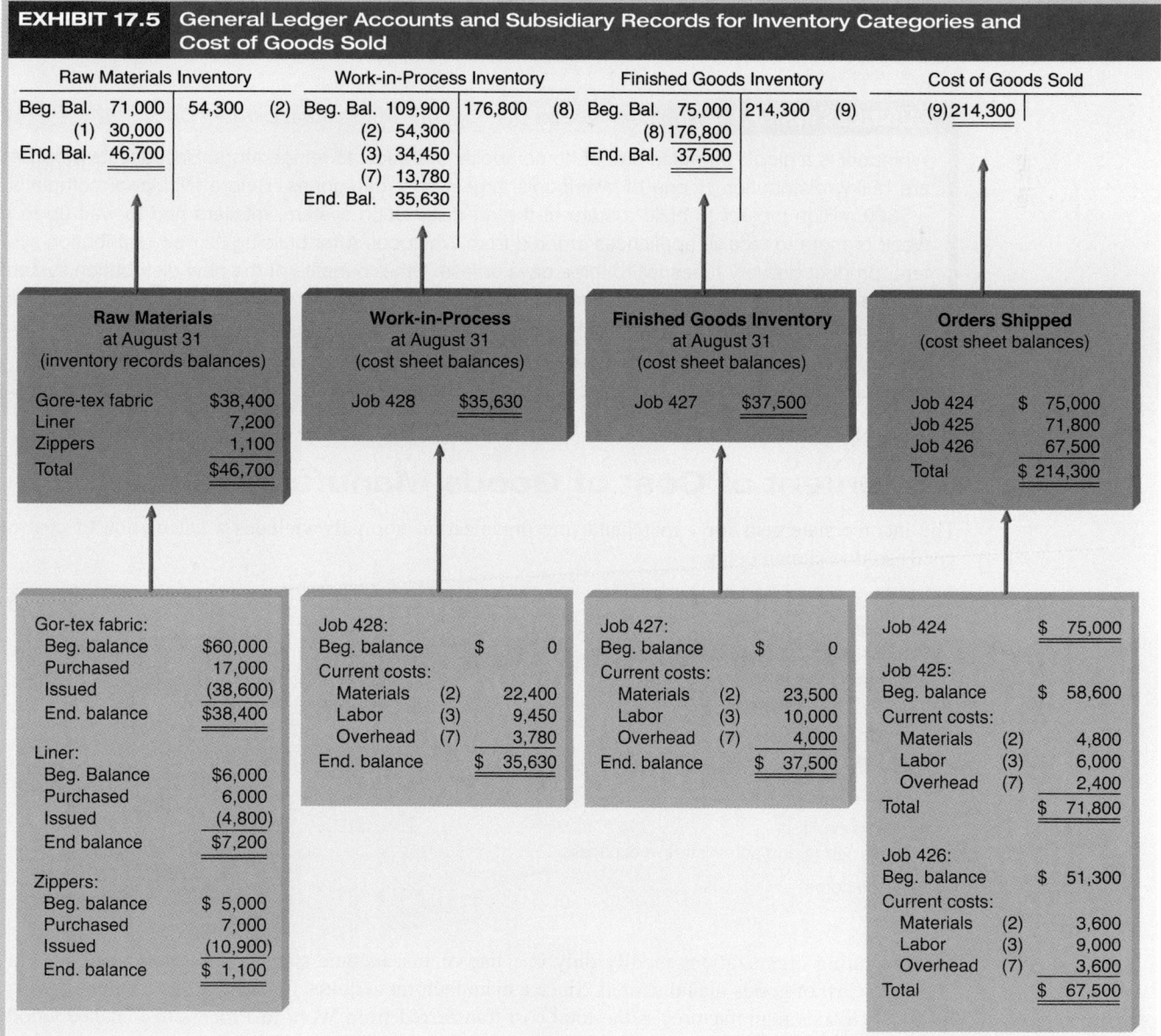

Raw Materials Inventory		
Beg. Bal. 71,000	54,300	(2)
(1) 30,000		
End. Bal. 46,700		

Work-in-Process Inventory		
Beg. Bal. 109,900	176,800	(8)
(2) 54,300		
(3) 34,450		
(7) 13,780		
End. Bal. 35,630		

Finished Goods Inventory		
Beg. Bal. 75,000	214,300	(9)
(8) 176,800		
End. Bal. 37,500		

Cost of Goods Sold	
(9) 214,300	

Raw Materials
at August 31
(inventory records balances)

Gore-tex fabric	$38,400
Liner	7,200
Zippers	1,100
Total	$46,700

Work-in-Process
at August 31
(cost sheet balances)

Job 428	$35,630

Finished Goods Inventory
at August 31
(cost sheet balances)

Job 427	$37,500

Orders Shipped
(cost sheet balances)

Job 424	$ 75,000
Job 425	71,800
Job 426	67,500
Total	$ 214,300

Gor-tex fabric:
Beg. balance	$60,000
Purchased	17,000
Issued	(38,600)
End. balance	$38,400

Liner:
Beg. Balance	$6,000
Purchased	6,000
Issued	(4,800)
End balance	$7,200

Zippers:
Beg. balance	$ 5,000
Purchased	7,000
Issued	(10,900)
End. balance	$ 1,100

Job 428:
Beg. balance		$ 0
Current costs:		
Materials	(2)	22,400
Labor	(3)	9,450
Overhead	(7)	3,780
End. balance		$ 35,630

Job 427:
Beg. balance		$ 0
Current costs:		
Materials	(2)	23,500
Labor	(3)	10,000
Overhead	(7)	4,000
End. balance		$ 37,500

Job 424		$ 75,000

Job 425:
Beg. balance		$ 58,600
Current costs:		
Materials	(2)	4,800
Labor	(3)	6,000
Overhead	(7)	2,400
Total		$ 71,800

Job 426:
Beg. balance		$ 51,300
Current costs:		
Materials	(2)	3,600
Labor	(3)	9,000
Overhead	(7)	3,600
Total		$ 67,500

Outdoor Rainwear's product costing system is adequate for determining the cost for each job for purposes of valuing ending inventories and cost of goods sold in its external financial statements. The costing system recognizes the differences in materials costs by carefully tracking each type of material as a separate cost pool. Because all direct labor employees are paid the same rate, it is necessary to maintain only one labor cost pool. Although there are three distinct operations in making parkas (cutting, sewing, and finishing), the various styles of parkas likely require the same proportionate times on each operation. Hence, even with only one plantwide manufacturing overhead cost pool applied on the basis of direct labor hours, individual product costs are reasonably accurate.

Although the Outdoor Rainwear's costing system may be adequate for inventory costing for financial statement purposes, the data it routinely generates do not provide management with information for many management decisions. To evaluate product or customer profitability, management needs additional information concerning marketing, distributing, selling, and customer service costs, which are not included in the product cost system. The following Business Insight illustrates the importance of distribution costs in decision making at Whirlpool.

Furthermore, the cost system does not provide information for decisions concerning individual operations, such as cutting. To answer questions regarding how best to perform operations, Outdoor Rainwear's accountants should perform a special cost study to obtain relevant activity-cost information.

BUSINESS INSIGHT   Whirlpool Scrubs Distribution—Its Second Largest Cost

Whirlpool is a global manufacturer of home appliances such as refrigerators. Because its products are bulky, distribution is one of Whirlpools largest cost categories. Before Whirlpool completed a $600 million project to build a state-of-the-art distribution system, retailers had to wait up to a week or more to receive appliances ordered from Whirlpool. After building its new distribution system, product delivery times fell to three days or less. Other benefits of the new distribution system include a $250 million reduction in warehoused finished goods inventory and annual reductions in distribution costs of approximately $100 million.

Source: Joe Barrett, "Whirlpool Cleans Up Its Delivery Act, *The Wall Street Journal*, September 23, 2009, pp. B1-B2.

Statement of Cost of Goods Manufactured

The income statement for a merchandising organization normally includes a calculation of cost of goods sold as shown below:

Sales.		$X,XXX
Less cost of goods sold		
Beginning inventory	$X,XXX	
Plus purchases	X,XXX	
Goods available for sale	X,XXX	
Less ending inventory	(X,XXX)	
Cost of goods sold		(X,XXX)
Gross profit		X,XXX
Less selling and administrative expenses		(X,XXX)
Net income		$X,XXX

Manufacturing organizations modify only one line of this income statement format, changing Purchases to Cost of goods manufactured. Since a manufacturer acquires finished goods from the factory, its cost of goods manufactured is the total cost transferred from Work-in-Process to Finished Goods Inventory during the period.

For internal reporting purposes, most companies prepare a separate **statement of cost of goods manufactured**, which summarizes the cost of goods completed and transferred into Finished Goods

Inventory during the period. A statement of cost of goods manufactured and an income statement for Outdoor Rainwear, are presented in Exhibit 17.6 for August 2012.

EXHIBIT 17.6	Statement of Cost of Goods Manufactured and Income Statement

OUTDOOR RAINWEAR
Statement of Cost of Goods Manufactured
For Month Ending August 31, 2012

Current manufacturing costs			
Cost of materials placed in production			
Raw materials, 8/1/12	$ 71,000		
Purchases	30,000		
Total available	101,000		
Raw materials, 8/31/12	(46,700)	$ 54,300	
Direct labor		34,450	
Manufacturing overhead		13,780	$102,530
Work-in-process, 8/1/12			109,900
Total costs in process			212,430
Work-in-process, 8/31/12			(35,630)
Cost of goods manufactured			$176,800

OUTDOOR RAINWEAR
Income Statement
For Month Ending August 31, 2012

Sales			$400,000
Cost of goods sold			
Finished goods inventory, 8/1/12		$ 75,000	
Cost of goods manufactured		176,800	
Total goods available for sale		251,800	
Finished goods inventory, 8/31/12		(37,500)	214,300
Gross profit			185,700
Selling and administrative expenses*			(90,000)
Net income			$ 95,700

* Selling and administrative expenses for Outdoor Rainwear are assumed to be $90,000.

Overapplied and Underapplied Overhead

In the Outdoor Rainwear example, assume that the predetermined manufacturing overhead rate of $4 per direct labor hour was based on predicted manufacturing overhead for the year of $100,000 and predicted direct labor hours of 25,000. Assume further that it was determined that the company actually incurred $100,000 in manufacturing overhead during the year and that actual direct labor hours for the year were 25,000, resulting in applied overhead of $100,000 (25,000 hours × $4). The activity in Manufacturing Overhead is summarized as follows:

Manufacturing Overhead	
Beginning balance	$ 0
Actual overhead	100,000
Total	100,000
Applied overhead	(100,000)
Ending balance	$ 0

With identical amounts of actual and applied overhead, the ending balance in Manufacturing Overhead is zero. However, if either the actual overhead cost or the actual level of the production activity base differed from its predicted value, there would be a balance in Manufacturing Overhead representing overapplied or underapplied overhead.

Assume, for example, that the prediction of 25,000 direct labor hours was correct but that actual overhead cost was $105,000. In this case, Manufacturing Overhead shows a $5,000 positive balance, representing underapplied manufacturing overhead:

Manufacturing Overhead	
Beginning balance	$ 0
Actual overhead	105,000
Total	105,000
Applied overhead	(100,000)
Ending balance.	$ 5,000*

* Underapplied; actual exceeds applied.

If actual manufacturing overhead were only $98,000, Manufacturing Overhead would be overapplied and show a $2,000 negative balance.

If the *prediction* of total manufacturing overhead cost is not accurate, there will be an underapplied or overapplied balance in Manufacturing Overhead at the end of the year. A similar result occurs when the *predicted* activity level used in computing the predetermined rate differs from the actual activity level. It is not uncommon for such differences to occur. Predictions are exactly that—predictions.

Month-to-month balances in Manufacturing Overhead are usually allowed to accumulate during the year. In the absence of evidence to the contrary, it is assumed that such differences result from seasonal variations in production or costs or both. However, any year-end balance in Manufacturing Overhead must be eliminated.

Theoretically, the disposition of any year-end balance in Manufacturing Overhead should be accomplished in a manner that adjusts every account to what its balance would have been if an actual, rather than a predetermined, overhead rate had been used. This involves adjusting the ending balances in Work-in-Process, Finished Goods Inventory, and Cost of Goods Sold. Procedures to do this are examined in cost accounting textbooks.

In most situations, the simple procedure of treating the remaining overhead as an adjustment to Cost of Goods Sold is adequate. Unless there are large ending balances in inventories and a large year-end balance in Manufacturing Overhead, this simple procedure produces acceptable results. Underapplied overhead indicates that the assigned costs are less than the actual costs, understating Cost of Goods Sold. Hence, disposing of an underapplied balance in Manufacturing Overhead increases the balance in Cost of Goods Sold.

Manufacturing Overhead	
Beginning balance	$ 0
Actual overhead	105,000
Total	105,000
Applied overhead	(100,000)
Ending balance.	$ 5,000* ← Increase Cost of Goods Sold

* Underapplied; actual exceeds applied.

Conversely, overapplied overhead indicates that the assigned costs are more than the actual costs, overstating Cost of Goods Sold. Hence, disposing of an overapplied balance in Manufacturing Overhead decreases Cost of Goods Sold.

Job Costing in Service Organizations

Service costing, the assignment of costs to services performed, uses job costing concepts to determine the cost of filling customer service orders in organizations such as automobile repair shops, charter airlines, CPA firms, hospitals, and law firms. Many of these organizations bill clients on the basis of resources consumed. Consequently, they maintain detailed records for billing purposes. On the invoice sent to the client, the organization itemizes any materials consumed on the job at a selling price per unit, the labor hours worked on the job at a billing rate per hour, and the time special facilities were used at a billing rate per unit of time. Employees with different capabilities and experience often have different billing rates. In a CPA firm, for example, a partner or a senior manager has a higher billing rate than a staff accountant.

The prices and rates must be high enough to cover costs not assigned to specific jobs and to provide for a profit. To evaluate the contribution to common costs and profit from a job, a comparison must be made between the price charged the customer and the actual cost of the job. This is easily done when the actual cost of resources itemized on the customer's invoice is presented on a job cost sheet. A CPA firm, for example, should accumulate the actual hardware and software costs of an accounting system installed for a client, along with the actual wages earned by employees while working on the job and any related travel costs. Comparing the total of these costs with the price charged, the client indicates the total contribution of the job to common costs and profit.

Although service organizations may identify costs with individual jobs for management accounting purposes, there is considerable variation in the way job cost information is presented in financial statements. Some organizations report the cost of jobs completed in their income statements using an account such as Cost of Services Provided. They use procedures similar to those outlined in Exhibit 17.6; the only major change involves replacing Cost of Goods Sold with Cost of Services Provided.

BUSINESS INSIGHT | **Service Contractors Learn Poor Cost Measurement Can Really Hurt**

Many service contractors bill on the basis of materials plus labor and a markup on labor. But what is the appropriate markup on labor? Twenty percent? Fifty percent? Seventy-five percent? If the employee's wage rate is $20 and the markup is one-hundred percent, the hourly charge, excluding materials, is $40. According to heating, ventilation, air conditioning (HVAC) consultant Bill Ligon, what contractors don't know about overhead costs can really hurt.

The Mechanical Service Contractors of America conducted a study of the total direct and indirect costs per labor hour and hourly billing rates. In addition to the obvious direct cost of the employee's wage rate, they considered the costs of: vacation pay, holiday pay, sick pay, non-billable time, benefits such as pension and health, payroll taxes such as Social Security and workers' compensation, and non-labor costs such as truck expense (lease, gas/oil, maintenance), communication equipment and charges, uniforms, and tools. By region of the U.S. they determined the average total non-materials costs varied between $47.22 per hour in the Southeast and $63.13 in the Southwest, making it apparent that a one-hundred percent markup on an hourly wage rate of $20 would really hurt.

Source: John R. Hall, "MSCA Examines Salaries, Costs," *Air Conditioning Heating & Refrigeration News*, January 27, 2003, p.8; Bill Ligon, "What You Don't Know Can Really Hurt," *Air Conditioning Heating & Refrigeration News,* October 9, 2006, p.46.

More often, however, service organizations do not formally establish detailed procedures to trace the flow of service costs. Instead, service job costs are left in their original cost categories such as materials expense, salaries and wages expense, travel expense, and so forth. Because all service costs are typically regarded as expenses rather than product costs, either procedure is acceptable for financial reporting. Regardless of the formal treatment of service costs in financial accounting records and statements, the managers of a well-run service organization need information regarding job cost and contribution. The previous Business Insight considers the importance of accurate cost estimation by service contractors.

All preceding examples of service costing involve situations in which the order is filled in response to a specific customer request. Job order costing can also be used to determine the cost of making services available even when the names of specific customers are not known in advance and the service is being provided on a speculative basis. A regularly scheduled airline flight, for example, could be regarded as a job. Management is interested in knowing the cost of the job in order to determine its profitability. This is but another example of the versatility of job order costing.

You have asked the accounting staff to provide you with cost information on each of the products manufactured by your company so you can conduct profitability analysis on each product. Accounting provided you with the costs that are used in the company's external financial statements. What additional information are you going to need before you can conduct a complete profitability analysis? [Answer p. 17-30]

MID-MODULE REVIEW

Tri-Star Printing Company prints sales fliers for retail and mail-order companies. Production costs are accounted for using a job cost system. At the beginning of June 2012, raw materials inventories totaled $7,000; manufacturing supplies amounted to $800; two jobs were in process—Job 225 with assigned costs of $13,750, and Job 226 with assigned costs of $1,800—and there were no finished goods inventories. There was no underapplied or overapplied manufacturing overhead on June 1. The following information summarized June manufacturing activities:

- Purchased raw materials costing $40,000 on account.
- Purchased manufacturing supplies costing $9,000 on account.
- Requisitioned materials needed to complete Job 226. Started two new jobs, 227 and 228, and requisitioned direct materials for them as follows:

Job 226	$ 2,600
Job 227	18,000
Job 228	14,400
Total	$35,000

- Incurred June salaries and wages as follows:

Job 225 (500 hours × $10 per hour)	$ 5,000
Job 226 (1,500 hours × $10 per hour).	15,000
Job 227 (2,050 hours × $10 per hour).	20,500
Job 228 (800 hours × $10 per hour)	8,000
Total direct labor.	48,500
Indirect labor	5,000
Total	$53,500

- Used manufacturing supplies costing $5,500.
- Recognized depreciation on factory fixed assets of $5,000.
- Incurred miscellaneous manufacturing overhead cost of $10,750 on account.
- Applied manufacturing overhead at the rate of $5 per direct labor hour.
- Completed Jobs 225, 226, and 227.
- Delivered Jobs 225 and 226 to customers.

Required

a. Prepare "T" accounts showing the flow of costs through the Work-in-Process, Finished Goods, and Cost of Goods Sold accounts.

b. Show the job cost details to support the June 30, 2012, balances in Work-in-Process, Finished Goods and Cost of Goods Sold.

c. Prepare a statement of cost of goods manufactured for June 2012.

The solution is on page 17-45.

PROCESS COSTING

A job costing system works well when products are made one at a time (building houses) or in batches of identical items (making blue jeans). However, if products are produced in a continuous manufacturing environment, where production does not have a distinct beginning and ending (refining fossil fuels such as gasoline or diesel), companies usually use a process costing system.

LO5 Explain the operation of a process costing system.

In job costing, the unit cost is the total cost of the "job" divided by the units produced in the job. Costs are accumulated for each job on a job cost sheet, and those costs remain in Work-in-Process until the job is completed, regardless of how long the job is in progress. A multiple-unit job is not considered completed until all units in the job are finished. The cost is not determined until the job is completed, which will not necessarily coincide with the end of an accounting period. Large jobs (such as construction projects) and jobs started near the end of the period frequently overlap two or more accounting periods.

In process costing, the cost of a single unit is equal to the total product costs assigned to a "process" or "department" during the accounting period (frequently a month) divided by the number of units produced. Since goods in the beginning and ending work-in-process inventory are only partially processed during the period, it is necessary to determine the total production for the period in terms of the equivalent number of completed units. For example, if 300 units were started and completed through 40 percent of the process during the period, then the equivalent of 120 fully completed units (300 units $\times$ 0.40) were produced. The average cost per unit is computed as total product costs divided by the number of equivalent units produced.

A good example of a process costing environment involving continuous production is the soft drink bottling process. At Coca-Cola's bottling facility in Atlanta, more than 2,000 twelve-ounce cans of Coca-Cola are produced per minute in a continuous process. The process adds the ingredients (concentrate syrup, water, sweetener, and the carbonation agent) at various points in the process and blends the ingredients in the can. At the end of the process, the cans are automatically wrapped in either 6-pack or 12-pack sizes. For another example, see the following Business Insight box for a discussion of the process costing environment at a large Japanese chemicals producer.

In a job cost system, job cost sheets are used to collect cost information for each and every job. In a process costing system, cost accumulation requires fewer records because each department's production is treated as the only job worked on during the period. In a department that has just one manufacturing process, process costing is particularly straightforward because the Work-in-Process account is, in effect, the departmental cost record. If a department has more than one manufacturing process, separate records should be maintained for each process.

BUSINESS INSIGHT | **Process Costing in a Japanese Dyestuffs Plant**

Nippon Kayaku is a large industrial company in Japan that produces a wide range of products, including industrial explosives, pharmaceuticals, agrochemicals, sophisticated products (resins, flame retardants, etc.) and dyestuffs. Nippon Kayaku's dyestuff division produces dyes that are particularly targeted to the polyester and cotton-blended textiles market.

The Fukuyama plant manufactures about 600 products for the sophisticated products and dyestuffs divisions, some of which are produced in continuous processes and others in batches. The costing system accumulates costs separately for the more than 1,000 processes, and product costs are determined for a particular product merely by adding the unit costs of the processes used to make that product. For example, the cost of the dyestuff product, Kayaset, consists of the costs of five processes: condensation, filtration, drying, grinding, and packaging. Nippon Kayaku uses these product costs for inventory valuation purposes and for managerial decision-making purposes.

Source: www.nipponkayaku.co.jp/english/

Cost of Production Report

To illustrate process costing procedures, consider Micro Systems Co., which manufactures memory chips for microcomputers in a one-step process using sophisticated machinery. Each finished unit requires one unit of raw materials added at the beginning of the manufacturing process. The production and cost data for the month of July 2012 for Micro Systems are as follows:

July Production Data	
Units in process, beginning of period (75% converted).............	4,000
Units started...	36,000
Completed and transferred to finished goods....................	35,000
Units in process, end of period (20% converted).................	5,000

July Cost Data		
Beginning work-in-process		
Materials costs.......................................		$ 16,000
Conversion costs		9,000
Total		$ 25,000
Current manufacturing costs		
Direct materials (36,000 × $4)		$144,000
Conversion costs		
Direct labor	$62,200	
Manufacturing overhead applied	46,700	108,900
Total		$252,900

Developing a cost of production report is a useful way of organizing and accounting for costs in a process costing environment. A **cost of production report**, which summarizes unit and cost data for each department or process for each period, consists of the following sections:

- Summary of units in process.
- Equivalent units.
- Total cost to be accounted for and cost per equivalent unit.
- Accounting for total costs.

The cost of production report for Micro Systems Co. is shown in Exhibit 17.7, and its four sections are discussed on next page.

Summary of Units in Process

This section of the cost of production report provides a summary of all units in the department during the period—both from an input and an output perspective—regardless of their stage of completion. From an input perspective, total units in process during the period consisted of the following:

- Units in process at the beginning of the period, plus
- Units started during the period.

From an output perspective, these units in process during the period were either

- Completed and transferred out of the department, or
- Still on hand at the end of the period.

In the summary of units in process, all units are treated as the same, regardless of the amount of processing that took place on them during the period. The objective here is to account for all discrete units of product in process at any time during the period. In the summary of units in process in Exhibit 17.7, 40,000 individual units were in process, including 4,000 partially completed units in the beginning inventory and 36,000 new units started during the month. During the period, 35,000 units were completed, and the remaining 5,000 were still in process at the end of the month.

Equivalent Units in Process

This section of the report translates the number of units in process during the period into equivalent completed units of production. The term **equivalent completed units** refers to the number of completed units that is equal, in terms of production effort, to a given number of partially completed units.

EXHIBIT 17.7 Cost of Production Report for Process Costing

MICRO SYSTEMS CO.
Cost of Production Report
For the Month Ending July 31, 2012

Summary of units in process

Beginning	4,000
Units started.	36,000
In process.	40,000
Completed	(35,000)
Ending	5,000

Equivalent units in process	Materials	Conversion	
Units completed.	35,000	35,000	
Plus equivalent units in ending inventory.	5,000	1,000*	
Equivalent units in process.	40,000	36,000	

Total cost to be accounted for and cost per equivalent unit in process	Materials	Conversion	Total
Beginning work-in-process	$ 16,000	$ 9,000	$ 25,000
Current cost	144,000	108,900**	252,900
Total cost in process	$160,000	$117,900	$277,900
Equivalent units in process.	÷ 40,000	÷ 36,000	
Cost per equivalent unit in process	$ 4.00	$ 3.275	$ 7.275

Accounting for total costs			
Transferred out (35,000 × $7.275).			$254,625
Ending work-in-process			
Materials (5,000 × $4.00).		$20,000	
Conversion (1,000 × $3.275)		3,275	23,275
Total cost accounted for.			$277,900

* 5,000 units, 20% converted

** Includes direct labor of $62,200 and applied manufacturing overhead of $46,700

For example, 80 units for which 50 percent of the expected total processing cost has been incurred is the equivalent of 40 completed units (80 × 0.50).

Frequently, direct materials costs are incurred largely, if not entirely, at the beginning of the process, whereas direct labor and manufacturing overhead costs are added throughout the production process. If direct labor and manufacturing costs are added to the process simultaneously, it is common to treat them jointly as conversion costs. Micro Systems Co. adds all materials at the beginning of the process; all conversion costs are added evenly throughout the process. Therefore, separate computations are made for equivalent units of materials and equivalent units of conversion. Although the department worked on 40,000 units during the period, the total number of equivalent units in process with respect to conversion costs was only 36,000 units, consisting of 35,000 finished units plus 1,000 equivalent units in ending inventory (5,000 units 20 percent converted). Because all materials are added at the start of the process, 40,000 equivalent units (35,000 finished and 5,000 in process) were in process with respect to materials costs.

Total Cost to Be Accounted for and Cost per Equivalent Unit in Process

This section of the report summarizes total costs in Work-in-Process during the period and calculates the cost per equivalent unit for materials, conversion, and in total. Total cost consists of the beginning Work-in-Process balance (if any) plus current costs incurred. For Micro Systems, the total cost to be accounted for during July was $277,900, consisting of $25,000 in Work-in-Process at the beginning of the period plus current costs of $252,900 incurred in July. Exhibit 17.7 shows these amounts broken down between materials costs and conversion costs.

To compute cost per equivalent unit, divide total cost in process by the equivalent units in process. This is done separately for materials cost and conversion cost. The total cost per equivalent unit is the sum of the unit costs for materials and conversion. Because the number of equivalent units in process was different for materials and conversion, it is not possible to get the total cost per unit by dividing total costs of $277,900 by some equivalent unit amount.

Accounting for Total Costs

This section shows the disposition of the total costs in process during the period divided between units completed (and sent to finished goods) and units still in process at the end of the period. As noted in the previous section, total cost in process is $277,900 and each equivalent unit in process has $4.00 of materials cost and $3.275 of conversion costs for a total of $7.275.

The first step in assigning total costs is to calculate the cost of units transferred out by multiplying the units completed during the period by the total cost per unit (35,000 units × $7.275). This assigns $254,625 of the total cost to units transferred out, leaving $23,275 ($277,900 − $254,625) to be assigned to ending Work-in-Process. To verify that $23,275 is the correct amount of cost remaining in ending Work-in-Process, the materials and conversion costs in ending Work-in-Process are calculated separately. Recall that the 5,000 units in process at the end of the period are 100 percent completed with materials costs, but only 20 percent completed with conversion costs. Therefore, in ending Work-in-Process, the materials cost component is $20,000 (5,000 × 1.00 × $4.00), the conversion cost component is $3,275 (5,000 × 0.20 × $3.275), and the total cost of ending Work-in-Process is $23,275 ($20,000 + $3,275).

The cost of production report summarizes manufacturing costs assigned to Work-in-Process during the period and provides information for determining the transfer of costs from Work-in-Process to Finished Goods Inventory. The supporting documents are similar to those previously illustrated for job costing, except that the single cost of production report replaces all the job cost sheets that flow through a department or process. The flow of costs through Work-in-Process is as follows:

Work-in-Process		
Beginning balance		$ 25,000
Current manufacturing costs		
Direct materials	$144,000	
Direct labor	62,200	
Applied overhead	46,700	252,900
Total		277,900
Cost of goods manufactured		(254,625)
Ending balance		$ 23,275

The reduction in Work-in-Process for the units completed during the period is determined in the cost of production report (see Exhibit 17.7). This amount is transferred to Finished Goods Inventory. The $23,275 ending balance in Work-in-Process is also determined in the cost of production report as the amount assigned to units in ending Work-in-Process.

Weighted Average and First-In, First-Out Process Costing

Because the costs of materials, labor, and overhead are constantly changing, unit costs are seldom exactly the same from period to period. Hence, if a unit is manufactured partially in one period and partially in the following period, its actual cost is seldom equal to the unit cost of units produced in either period.

In the cost of production report in Exhibit 17.7, we made no attempt to account separately for the completed units that came from beginning inventory and those that were started during the current period. The method illustrated in Exhibit 17.7 is called the **weighted average method**, and it simply spreads the combined beginning inventory cost and current manufacturing costs (for materials, labor, and overhead) over the units completed and those in ending inventory on an average basis. For example, the total cost in process for conversion ($117,900) included both beginning inventory cost and current costs; the 36,000 equivalent units in process for conversion included both units from beginning inventory and units started during the current period. Hence, the average cost per unit of $3.275 (or $117,900 ÷ 36,000) is a weighted average cost of the partially completed units in beginning inventory (prior period costs) and units started during the current period. It is not a precise cost per unit for the current period's production activity but an average cost that includes the cost of partially completed units in beginning inventory carried over from the previous period.

An alternative, more precise process costing method is the **first-in, first-out (FIFO) method**. It accounts for unit costs of beginning inventory units separately from those started during the current period. Under this method, the first costs incurred each period are assumed to have been used to complete the unfinished units carried over from the previous period. Hence, the cost of the beginning inventory is partially based on the prior period's unit costs and partially based on the current period's unit costs.

If unit costs are changing from period to period and beginning inventories are large in relation to total production for the period, the FIFO method is more accurate. However, with the current trend toward smaller inventories, the additional effort and cost of the FIFO method may not be justified. Detailed coverage of the FIFO method is included in cost accounting textbooks. Unless stated otherwise, weighted average process costing is used in module assignments.

Process Costing in Service Organizations

There are many applications of process costing for service organizations. Process costing in service organizations is similar to that in manufacturing organizations, the primary purpose being to assign costs to cost objectives. Generally, the use of process costing techniques for service organizations is easier than for manufacturing organizations because the raw materials element is not necessary. The applications for the labor and overhead costs are similar, if not identical, to those of a manufacturing firm.

Process costing for services is similar to job costing for batches in that an average cost for similar or identical services is determined. There are important differences, though, between batch and process costing. In a batch environment, a discrete group of services is identified, but in a process environment, services are performed on a continuous basis. Batch costing accumulates the cost for a specific group of services as the batch moves through the various activities that make up the service. Process service costing measures the average cost of identical or similar services performed each period (each month) in a department. An example of batch service costing is determining the cost of registering a student at your college during the fall term registration period; an example of process service costing is determining the cost each month of processing a check by a bank. If continuously performed services involved multiple processes, the total cost of the service would be the sum of the costs for each process.

After it is determined that process costing would be appropriate for a service activity, the actual decision to use it is generally contingent on two important factors about the items being evaluated. First, is average cost per unit acceptable as an input item to the decision process? For some activities, the answer is obvious. For instance, tracking the actual cost of processing each check through a bank would probably not be as useful as determining the average cost of processing checks for a given period; therefore, average cost is acceptable. For other activities, the answer is more difficult to determine. Should the decision model include average cost per patient-day or actual cost per individual patient?

The second issue relates to the benefits versus the costs of the resulting information. Normally, it is easier to track and record the cost of an activity or process than it is to track and record the cost of each individual item in the activity. Often actual cost tracking is impossible for practical reasons (the actual cost of processing a check through a banking system, for example). Although process costing will not work in every situation, it has many applications in service organizations. As illustrated in this text, there are many possibilities for applying either job or process costing to activities in service organizations.

MODULE-END REVIEW

Magnetic Media, Inc., manufactures data disks that are used in the computer industry. Since there is little product differentiation between Magnetic's products, it uses a process costing system to determine inventory costs. Production and manufacturing cost data for 2012 are as follows:

Production data (units)	
Units in process, beginning of period (60% converted).........	3,000,000
Units started...	27,000,000
Completed and transferred to finished goods................	25,000,000
Units in process, end of period (30% converted).............	5,000,000

Manufacturing costs	
Work-in-Process, beginning of period (materials, $468,000; conversion, $252,000)........................	$ 720,000
Current manufacturing costs:	
Raw materials transferred to processing	6,132,000
Direct labor for the period...............................	1,550,000
Overhead applied for the period.........................	3,498,000

Required

Prepare a cost of production report for Magnetic Media, Inc., for 2012.

The solution is on page 17-46.

APPENDIX 17A: Absorption and Variable Costing

Product costing for inventory valuation is the link between financial and managerial accounting. Product costing systems determine the cost-based valuation of the manufactured inventories used in making key financial accounting measurements (cost of goods sold and income on the income statement as well as inventory and total assets on the balance sheet). They also provide vital information to managers for setting prices, controlling costs, and evaluating management performance. The influence of financial accounting on product costing systems is apparent in the design of traditional job order and process costing systems. These systems reflect the requirement of financial accounting (i.e., generally accepted accounting principles) that all manufacturing costs be included in inventory valuations for external financial reporting purposes. In these systems, all other costs incurred, such as selling, general, and administrative costs, are treated as expenses of the period.

Basic Concepts

A debate exists over how to treat fixed manufacturing overhead costs in the valuation of inventory. The debate centers around whether fixed costs such as depreciation on manufacturing equipment should be considered an *inventoriable product cost* and treated as an asset cost until the inventory is sold, or as a *period cost* and recorded immediately as an operating expense. **Absorption costing** (also called **full costing**) treats fixed manufacturing overhead as a product cost, whereas **variable costing** (also called **direct costing**) treats it as a period cost. Therefore, fixed manufacturing overhead is recorded initially as an asset (inventory) under absorption costing but as an operating expense under variable costing.

> **Fixed manufacturing costs:**
>
> **Absorption costing** treats **fixed manufacturing costs** as **product costs**.
>
> **Variable costing** treats **fixed manufacturing costs** as **period costs**.

Since fixed product costs are eventually recorded as expenses under both variable and absorption costing by the time the inventory is sold, why does it matter whether fixed overhead is treated as a product cost or a period cost? It matters because the way it is treated affects the measurement of income for a particular period and the valuation assigned to inventory on the balance sheet at the end of the period. Because absorption costing presents fixed manufacturing overhead as a cost per unit rather than a total cost per period, management's perceptions of cost behavior, and decisions based on perceptions of cost behavior, may also be affected.

Inventory Valuations

To illustrate the difference in inventory valuations between absorption and variable costing, consider the following cost data for Nutech Company at a monthly volume of 4,000 units:

Direct materials	$ 5 per unit
Direct labor..............................	2 per unit
Variable manufacturing overhead............	3 per unit
Total variable cost........................	$ 10 per unit
Fixed manufacturing overhead..............	$8,000 per month

To determine the unit cost of inventory using absorption costing, an average fixed overhead cost per unit is calculated by dividing the monthly fixed manufacturing overhead by the monthly volume. Even though fixed manufacturing overhead is not a variable cost, under absorption costing it is applied to inventory on a per-unit basis, the same as variable costs. At a monthly volume of 4,000 units, Nutech's total inventory cost per unit, is $10 under variable costing, and $12 under absorption costing.

The $2 difference in total unit cost is attributed to the treatment of fixed overhead of $8,000 divided by 4,000 units. The difference in the total inventory valuation on the balance sheet between absorption and variable costing is the number of units in ending inventory times $2. So if 1,000 units are on hand at the end of the month, they are valued at $12,000 if absorption costing is used but at only $10,000 with variable costing.

Income Under Absorption and Variable Costing

The income statement formats used for variable and absorption costing are not the same. One benefit of variable costing is that it separates costs into variable and fixed costs, making it possible to present the income statement in a contribution format. As illustrated in Module 15, in a contribution income statement, variable costs are subtracted from revenues to compute contribution margin; fixed costs are then subtracted from contribution margin to calculate profit, also called net income or earnings.

When absorption costing is used, the income statement is usually formatted using the functional format, which classifies costs based on cost function, such as manufacturing, selling, or administrative. The functional income statement, used for financial reporting, subtracts manufacturing costs (represented by cost of goods sold) from revenues to calculate gross profit; selling and administrative costs are then subtracted from gross profit to calculate profit or income.

The contribution format provides information for determining the contribution margin ratio, which is calculated as total contribution margin divided by total sales. It also provides the total amount of fixed costs. These are the primary items of data needed to determine the break-even point and to conduct other cost-volume-profit analysis (see Module 15).

Not only is the income statement format different for absorption and variable costing methods, but also as illustrated in the following examples for Nutech Company, the amount of income reported on the income statement might not be the same because of the difference in the treatment of fixed manufacturing overhead. The following additional information is necessary for the Nutech Company examples:

Selling price	$30 per unit
Variable selling and administrative expenses...	$3 per unit
Fixed selling and administrative expenses.....	$10,000 per month

Production Equals Sales

Nutech has no inventory on June 1, 2012. Production and sales for the third quarter of 2012 are:

Month	Production	Sales
June	3,200 units	3,200 units
July......................	4,000 units	3,500 units
August	4,000 units	4,500 units
Third quarter..............	11,200 units	11,200 units

Production and sales both total 11,200 units for the third quarter. A summary of unit production, sales, and inventory levels is presented in Exhibit 17.8. Using previously presented cost and a selling price of $30 per unit, monthly contribution (variable costing) and functional (absorption costing) income statements are presented in Exhibit 17.8 parts B and C. An analysis of fixed manufacturing overhead with absorption costing is presented in part D.

In June, with 3,200 units produced and sold all $8,000 of fixed manufacturing overhead is deducted as a period cost under variable costing and expensed as part of the cost of goods sold under absorption costing. No costs were assigned to ending inventory under either method.

Production Exceeds Sales

July production of 4,000 units exceeded sales of 3,500 units by 500 units. The ending inventory under variable costing consisted of only the variable cost of production, $5,000 (500 × $10). The entire $8,000 of fixed manufacturing overhead is deducted as a period cost.

Under absorption costing, in addition to the variable cost of production, a portion of the fixed manufacturing overhead is assigned to the ending inventory. As shown in the July column of Exhibit 17.8D, absorption costing assigns $1,000 of the month's fixed manufacturing overhead to the July ending inventory and $7,000 to the cost of goods sold. Consequently, under absorption costing the July ending inventory is $1,000 higher, the July expenses are $1,000 lower, and the July net income is $1,000 higher than under variable costing.

Sales Exceed Production

In August just the opposite of July's situation occurred: sales of 4,500 units exceeded production of 4,000 units by 500 units. The additional units came from the July production. Under variable costing all current manufacturing costs are expensed either as the variable cost of goods sold or as part of the fixed expense. Additionally, the August variable cost of goods sold includes variable costs assigned the July ending inventory.

Under absorption costing all current manufacturing costs are expensed as part of the cost of goods sold. Additionally, the cost of goods sold includes the variable and fixed costs assigned the July ending inventory. The inclusion of the July fixed costs caused absorption costing net income to be $1,000 lower than the corresponding variable costing amount.

The above relationships between absorption and variable costing are summarized in Exhibit 17.9.

Exhibits 17.8 and 17.9 reveal several important relationships between absorption costing net income and variable costing net income, as well as the way net income responds to changes in sales and production under both methods.

For each period, the income differences between absorption and variable costing can be explained by analyzing the change in inventoried fixed manufacturing overhead under absorption costing net income. In general, the following relationship exists:

$$\begin{array}{ccccc} \text{Variable} & & \text{Increase (or minus decrease)} & & \text{Absorption} \\ \text{costing} & + & \text{in inventoried fixed} & = & \text{costing} \\ \text{net income} & & \text{manufacturing overhead} & & \text{net income} \end{array}$$

Using Nutech's July information, the equation is as follows:

$$\$41,500 + (500 \times \$2.00) = \$42,500$$

For any given time period, regardless of length, if total units produced equals total units sold, net income is the same for absorption costing and variable costing, all other things being equal. Under absorption costing, all fixed manufacturing overhead is released as a product cost through cost of goods sold when inventory is sold. Under variable costing, all fixed manufacturing overhead is reported as a period cost and expensed in the period incurred. Consequently, over the life of a product, the income differences within periods are offset since they occur only because of the timing of the release of fixed manufacturing overhead to the income statement.

Evaluating Alternatives to Inventory Valuation

The issue in the variable costing debate is whether or not fixed manufacturing costs add value to products. Proponents of variable costing argue that these costs do not add value to a product. They believe that fixed costs are incurred to provide the capacity to produce during a given period, and these costs expire with the passage of time regardless of whether the related capacity was used. Variable manufacturing costs, on the other hand, are incurred only if production takes place. Consequently, these costs are properly assignable to the units produced.

| EXHIBIT 17.8 | Contribution (Variable Costing) and Functional (Absorption Costing) Income Statements with Variations in Production and Sales |

	June (Production equals sales)	July (Production exceeds sales)	August (Sales exceed production)
A. NuTech Company: Summary of Unit Inventory Changes			
Beginning inventory	0	0	500
Production	3,200	4,000	4,000
Total available.	3,200	4,000	4,500
Sales.	(3,200)	(3,500)	(4,500)
Ending inventory.	0	500	0
B. Contribution (Variable Costing) Income Statements			
Sales ($30/unit).	$96,000	$105,000	$135,000
Less variable expenses:			
Cost of goods sold ($10/unit)	$32,000	$ 35,000	$ 45,000
Selling & admin. ($3/unit)	9,600	10,500	13,500
Total.	(41,600)	(45,500)	(58,500)
Contribution margin	54,400	59,500	76,500
Less fixed expenses.			
Manufacturing overhead.	8,000	8,000	8,000
Selling & admin.	10,000	10,000	10,000
Total.	(18,000)	(18,000)	(18,000)
Net income	$36,400	$ 41,500	$ 58,500
C. Functional (Absorption Costing) Income Statements			
Sales ($30/unit).	$96,000	$105,000	$135,000
Cost of goods sold (Part D.)	(40,000)	(42,000)	(54,000)
Gross profit.	56,000	63,000	81,000
Selling & admin. expenses			
Variable ($3/unit)	9,600	10,500	13,500
Fixed	10,000	10,000	10,000
Total.	(19,600)	(20,500)	(23,500)
Net income	$36,400	$ 42,500	$ 57,500
D. Analysis of Fixed Manufacturing Overhead under Absorption Costing			
Fixed manufacturing overhead.	$ 8,000	$ 8,000	$ 8,000
Units produced.	÷ 3,200	÷ 4,000	÷ 4,000
Absorption fixed cost per unit*.	$ 2.50	$ 2.00	$ 2.00
Units in ending inventory	× 0	× 500	× 0
Fixed costs in ending inv.	$ 0	$ 1,000	$ 0
Fixed cost of goods sold:			
From beginning inventory	$ 0	$ 0	$ 1,000
June (3,200 units × $2.50)	8,000		
July (3,500 units × $2.00).		7,000	
August (4,000 × $2.00).			8,000
Total fixed	8,000	7,000	9,000
Variable cost of goods sold	32,000	35,000	45,000
Absorption cost of goods sold.	$40,000	$ 42,000	$ 54,000

* To simplify the illustration, the example does not use a predetermined overhead rate. If a predetermined overhead rate were used, an increase or decrease in the balance of Manufacturing Overhead is treated as an adjustment to ending inventory.

EXHIBIT 17.9 Comparative Effects of Absorption and Variable Costing

Relationship between period production and sales	Effect on inventory costs	Effect on operating income	Explanation
Production = Sales	No change in inventory costs.	Absorption costing income = Variable costing income	All current fixed manufacturing costs are expensed under both absorption and variable costing.
Production > Sales	Absorption costing ending inventory increases more than variable costing inventory.	Absorption costing income > Variable costing income	Under absorption costing some current fixed manufacturing costs are assigned to ending inventory. Under variable costing all current fixed manufacturing costs are expensed.
Sales > Production	Absorption costing ending inventory declines more than variable costing inventory.	Absorption costing income < Variable costing income	Under absorption costing fixed manufacturing costs previously assigned to ending inventory are expenses along with current fixed manufacturing costs. Under variable costing only current fixed manufacturing costs are expensed.

Proponents of variable costing also argue that inventories have value only to the extent that they avoid the necessity of incurring costs in the future. Having inventory available for sale avoids the necessity of incurring some future variable costs, but the availability of finished goods inventory does not avoid the incurrence of future fixed manufacturing costs. Proponents conclude that inventories should be valued at their variable manufacturing cost, and fixed manufacturing costs should be expensed as incurred.

Opponents of variable costing argue that fixed manufacturing costs are incurred for only one purpose, namely, to manufacture the product. Because they are incurred to manufacture the product, they should be assigned to the product. It is also argued that in the long run all costs are variable. Consequently, by omitting fixed costs, variable costing understates long-run variable costs and misleads decision makers into underestimating true production costs.

On a pragmatic level, the central arguments for variable costing center around the fact that use of variable costing facilitates the development of contribution income statements and cost-volume-profit analysis. With costs accumulated on an absorption costing basis, contribution income statements are difficult to develop, and cost-volume-profit analysis becomes very complicated unless production and sales are equal.

Proponents of activity-based costing typically do not favor variable costing because ABC is based on the assumption that, in the long run, all costs are variable and that fixed costs should be assigned to products or services to represent long-run variable costs. Hence, inventory valuation using an ABC approach will tend to be closer to absorption costing values than variable costing values.

As modern manufacturing techniques have led to major reductions in inventory levels (see the following Research Insight) in many companies, the significance of the debate over absorption versus variable costing has declined. If a company has no inventories, all its costs are deducted as expenses (either as operating expenses or cost of goods sold expense) during the current period whether it uses absorption or variable costing. Hence, from an income determination standpoint, it does not matter in such cases whether fixed costs are considered a product or period cost.

RESEARCH INSIGHT Inventory Levels and Company Financial Performance

Professors Chen, Frank, and Wu examined inventory trends and related financial performance of American companies over a 20-year period and found that the average yearly rate of inventory reduction was two percent per year. Looking closer, they identified significant differences in the reductions of various types of inventories, with raw materials inventories declining three percent per year, work-in-process inventory declining by about six percent per year and finished goods inventory not declining at all.

They concluded "A firm that deals effectively with its suppliers will have low raw-materials inventories. A firm that has efficient internal operations will have low work-in-process inventories." They also observed that the type of supply chain management and information sharing required for reductions in finished goods inventory is more difficult to implement, suggesting further room for improvement.

As for profitability, "Firms with abnormally high inventories have abnormally poor long-term stock returns. Firms with slightly lower than average inventories have good stock returns, but firms with the lowest inventories have only ordinary returns."

Source: Chen, Hong; Murray Z. Frank; and Owen Q. Wu, "What Actually Happened to the Inventories of American Companies Between 1981 and 2000?", *Management Science*, Vol. 51, No. 7, July 2005, pp. 10117-1031.

GUIDANCE ANSWER

MANAGERIAL DECISION	**You are the Chief Financial Officer**

Inventory costs that are provided for financial statement purposes for external stockholders and lenders are required by generally accepted accounting principles to include only the manufacturing costs of the product for direct materials, direct labor, and manufacturing overhead. To conduct a complete profitability analysis, the CFO will need to gather data for all other costs that relate to the marketing, sales, and distribution of each product, as well as any costs related to providing service to customers who buy the products.

DISCUSSION QUESTIONS

Q17-1. Distinguish among service, merchandising, and manufacturing organizations on the basis of the importance and complexity of inventory cost measurement.

Q17-2. Distinguish between product costing and service costing.

Q17-3. When is depreciation a product cost? When is depreciation a period cost?

Q17-4. What are the three major product cost elements?

Q17-5. How are predetermined overhead rates developed? Why are they widely used?

Q17-6. Briefly distinguish between process manufacturing and job order production. Provide examples of products typically produced under each system.

Q17-7. Briefly describe the role of engineering personnel and production scheduling personnel in the production planning process.

Q17-8. Identify the primary records involved in the operation of a job cost system.

Q17-9. Describe the flow of costs through the accounting system of a labor-intensive manufacturing organization.

Q17-10. Identify two reasons that a service organization should maintain detailed job cost information.

Q17-11. What are the four major elements of a cost of production report?

Q17-12. What are equivalent completed units?

Q17-13. Under what conditions will equivalent units in process be different for materials and conversion costs?

**Assignments with the ⊘ in the margin are available in an online homework system.
See the Preface of the book for details.**

MINI EXERCISES

M17-14. Classification of Product and Period Costs (LO2)

Classify the following costs incurred by a manufacturer of golf clubs as product costs or period costs. Also classify the product costs as direct materials or conversion costs.

a. Depreciation on computer in president's office
b. Salaries of legal staff
c. Graphite shafts
d. Plant security department
e. Electricity for the corporate office
f. Rubber grips
g. Golf club heads
h. Wages paid assembly line maintenance workers
i. Salary of corporate controller
j. Subsidy of plant cafeteria
k. Wages paid assembly line production workers
l. National sales meeting in Orlando
m. Overtime premium paid assembly line workers
n. Advertising on national television
o. Depreciation on assembly line

M17-15. Developing and Using a Predetermined Overhead Rate   (LO2)

Assume that the following predictions were made for 2012 for one of the plants of Milliken & Company:

Total manufacturing overhead for the year..............	$40,000,000
Total machine hours for the year	2,000,000

Actual results for February 2012 were as follows:

Manufacturing overhead	$5,520,000
Machine hours	310,000

Required

a. Determine the 2012 predetermined overhead rate per machine hour.

b. Using the predetermined overhead rate per machine hour, determine the manufacturing overhead applied to Work-in-Process during February.

c. As of February 1, actual overhead was underapplied by $400,000. Determine the cumulative amount of any overapplied or underapplied overhead at the end of February.

M17-16. Job Order Costing and Process Costing Applications   (LO4, 5)

For each of the following manufacturing situations, indicate whether job order or process costing is more appropriate and why.

a. Manufacturer of chocolate candy bars

b. Manufacturer of carbonated beverages

c. Manufacturer of high-quality men's suits

d. Manufacturer of subway cars

e. Book printing

M17-17. Job Order Costing and Process Costing Applications   (LO4, 5)

For each of the following situations, indicate whether job order or process costing is more appropriate and why.

a. Building contractor for residential dwellings

b. Manufacturer of nylon yarn that sells to fabric-making textile companies

c. Evening gown manufacturer that makes gowns in several different fabrics, colors, styles, and sizes

d. Hosiery mill that manufactures a one-size-fits-all product

e. Vehicle battery manufacturer that has just received an order for 400,000 identical batteries to be delivered as completed over the next 12 months

M17-18. Process Costing   (LO5)

Tempe Manufacturing Company makes a single product that is produced on a continuous basis in one department. All materials are added at the beginning of production. The total cost per equivalent unit in process in March was $4.60, consisting of $3.00 for materials and $1.60 for conversion. During the month, 8,500 units of product were transferred to finished goods inventory; on March 31, 3,500 units were in process, 10 percent converted. The company uses weighted average costing.

Required

a. Determine the cost of goods transferred to finished goods inventory.

b. Determine the cost of the ending work-in-process inventory.

c. What was the total cost of the beginning work-in-process inventory plus the current manufacturing costs?

M17-19.[A]Absorption and Variable Costing; Inventory Valuation

Boxtel, Inc., has a highly automated assembly line that uses very little direct labor. Therefore, direct labor is part of variable overhead. For October, assume that it incurred the following unit costs:

Direct materials	$200
Variable overhead.......	180
Fixed overhead.........	70

The 100 units of beginning inventory for October had an absorption costing value of $45,000 and a variable costing value of $38,000. For October, assume that Boxtel, Inc. produced 500 units and sold 540 units.

Required
Compute Boxtel's October amount of ending inventory under both absorption and variable costing if the FIFO inventory method was used.

M17-20.[A]**Absorption and Variable Costing; Cost of Goods Sold**
Use data from Mini Exercise 17-19.[A]

Required
Compute Boxtel's October Cost of Goods Sold using both the variable and absorption costing methods.

EXERCISES

E17-21. Analyzing Activity in Inventory Accounts (LO2, 4)
Selected data concerning operations of Cascade Manufacturing Company for the past fiscal year follow:

Raw materials used	$300,000
Total manufacturing costs charged to production during the year (includes raw materials, direct labor, and manufacturing overhead applied at a rate of 60 percent of direct labor costs)	681,000
Cost of goods available for sale.	826,000
Selling and general expenses.	30,000

	Inventories	
	Beginning	**Ending**
Raw materials.	$70,000	$ 80,000
Work-in-process.	85,000	30,000
Finished goods.	90,000	110,000

Required
Determine each of the following:
a. Cost of raw materials purchased
b. Direct labor costs charged to production
c. Cost of goods manufactured
d. Cost of goods sold

E17-22. Statement of Cost of Goods Manufactured and Income Statement (LO4)
Information from the records of the Valley Manufacturing Company for August 2012 follows:

Sales.	$205,000
Selling and administrative expenses	85,000
Purchases of raw materials	25,000
Direct labor.	15,000
Manufacturing overhead	32,000

	Inventories	
	August 1	**August 31**
Raw materials.	$ 8,000	$ 5,000
Work-in-process.	14,000	11,000
Finished goods.	15,000	19,000

Required
Prepare a statement of cost of goods manufactured and an income statement for August 2012.

E17-23. Statement of Cost of Goods Manufactured from Percent Relationships (LO4)
Information about NuWay Products Company for the year ending December 31, 2012, follows:

- Sales equal $450,000.
- Direct materials used total $64,000.
- Manufacturing overhead is 150 percent of direct labor dollars.
- The beginning inventory of finished goods is 20 percent of the cost of goods sold.
- The ending inventory of finished goods is twice the beginning inventory.
- The gross profit is 20 percent of sales.
- There is no beginning or ending work-in-process.

Required

Prepare a statement of cost of goods manufactured for 2012. (*Hint:* Prepare an analysis of changes in Finished Goods Inventory.)

E17-24. Account Activity and Relationships (LO2, 4)

	Case 1	Case 2	Case 3	Case 4
Sales.	$80,000	?	$120,000	?
Direct materials	15,000	19,000	?	21,000
Direct labor.	5,000	?	20,000	?
Total direct costs	?	32,000	?	30,000
Conversion cost.	?	26,000	?	?
Manufacturing overhead	8,000	?	10,000	?
Current manufacturing costs	?	?	95,000	79,000
Work in process, beginning	7,000	10,000	?	21,000
Work in process, ending.	5,000	?	21,000	?
Cost of goods manufactured	?	32,000	?	82,000
Finished goods inventory, beginning	9,000	8,000	7,000	12,000
Finished goods inventory, ending.	6,000	?	8,000	?
Cost of goods sold.	?	35,000	?	80,000
Gross profit.	?	?	18,000	15,000
Selling and administrative expenses	20,000	15,000	?	?
Net income.	?	22,000	12,000	8,000

Required

Supply the missing data in each independent case.

E17-25. Developing and Using a Predetermined Overhead Rate: High-Low Cost Estimation (LO2)

For years, Daytona Parts Company has used an actual plantwide overhead rate and based its prices on cost plus a markup of 25 percent. Recently the marketing manager, Jan Arton, and the production manager, Sue Yount, confronted the controller with a common problem. The marketing manager expressed a concern that Daytona's prices seem to vary widely throughout the year. According to Arton, "It seems irrational to charge higher prices when business is bad and lower prices when business is good. While we get a lot of business during high-volume months because we charge less than our competitors, it is a waste of time to even call on customers during low-volume months because we are raising prices while our competitors are lowering them." Yount also believed that it was "folly to be so pushed that we have to pay overtime in some months and then lay employees off in others." She commented, "While there are natural variations in customer demand, the accounting system seems to amplify this variation."

Required

a. Evaluate the arguments presented by Arton and Yount. What suggestions do you have for improving the accounting and pricing procedures?

b. Assume that the Daytona Parts Company had the following total manufacturing overhead costs and direct labor hours in 2010 and 2011:

	2010	2011
Total manufacturing overhead	$200,000	$237,500
Direct labor hours.	20,000	27,500

Use the high-low method to develop a cost estimating equation for total manufacturing overhead.

c. Develop a predetermined rate for 2012, assuming 25,000 direct labor hours are budgeted for 2012.

d. Assume that the actual level of activity in 2012 was 30,000 direct labor hours and that the total 2012 manufacturing overhead was $250,000. Determine the underapplied or overapplied manufacturing overhead at the end of 2012.

e. Describe two ways of handling any underapplied or overapplied manufacturing overhead at the end of the year.

E17-26. Manufacturing Cost Flows with Machine Hours Allocation (LO4)

On November 1, Robotics Manufacturing Company's beginning balances in manufacturing accounts and finished goods inventory were as follows:

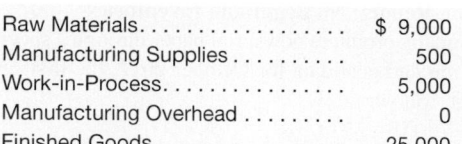

Raw Materials.	$ 9,000
Manufacturing Supplies	500
Work-in-Process.	5,000
Manufacturing Overhead	0
Finished Goods	25,000

During November, Robotics Manufacturing completed the following manufacturing transactions:

1. Purchased raw materials costing $58,000 and manufacturing supplies costing $3,000 on account.
2. Requisitioned raw materials costing $40,000 to the factory.
3. Incurred direct labor costs of $27,000 and indirect labor costs of $4,800.
4. Used manufacturing supplies costing $3,000.
5. Recorded manufacturing depreciation of $15,000.
6. Miscellaneous payables for manufacturing overhead totaled $3,600.
7. Applied manufacturing overhead, based on 2,250 machine hours, at a predetermined rate of $10 per machine hour.
8. Completed jobs costing $85,000.
9. Finished goods costing $96,000 were sold.

Required

a Prepare "T" accounts showing the flow of costs through all manufacturing accounts, Finished Goods Inventory, and Cost of Goods Sold.

b. Calculate the balances at the end of November for Work-in-Process Inventory and Finished Goods Inventory.

E17-27. Service Cost Flows (LO4)

Viva Marketing, Ltd., produces television advertisements for businesses that are marketing products in the western provinces of Canada. To achieve cost control, Viva Marketing uses a job cost system similar to that found in a manufacturing organization. It uses some different account titles:

Account	Replaces
Videos-in-Process	Work-in-Process
Video Supplies Inventory	Manufacturing Supplies Inventory
Cost of Videos Completed	Cost of Goods Sold
Accumulated Depreciation, Studio Assets	Accumulated Depreciation, Factory Assets
Studio Overhead	Manufacturing Overhead

Viva Marketing does not maintain Raw Materials or Finished Goods Inventory accounts. Materials, such as props needed for videos, are purchased as needed from outside sources and charged directly to Videos-in-Process and the appropriate job. Videos are delivered directly to clients upon completion. The October 1, balances were as follows:

Video Supplies	$ 300	
Videos-in-Process	1,000	
Studio Overhead	250	underapplied

During October, Viva Marketing completed the following production transactions:

1. Purchased video supplies costing $1,475 on account.
2. Purchased materials for specific jobs costing $27,000 on account.
3. Incurred direct labor costs of $65,000 and indirect labor costs of $3,200.
4. Used production supplies costing $850.

5. Recorded studio depreciation of $3,000.
6. Incurred miscellaneous payables for studio overhead of $1,800.
7. Applied studio overhead at a predetermined rate of $18 per studio hour, with 480 studio hours.
8. Completed jobs costing $100,000 and delivered them directly to clients.

Required
a. Prepare "T" accounts showing the flow of costs through all service accounts and Cost of Videos Completed.
b. Calculate the cost incurred as of the end of October for the incomplete jobs still in process.

E17-28. Cost of Production Report: No Beginning Inventories (LO5)
Oregon Paper Company produces newsprint paper through a special recycling process using scrap paper products. Production and cost data for October 2012, the first month of operations for the company's new Portland plant, follow:

Units of product started in process during October	90,000 tons
Units completed and transferred to finished goods	75,000 tons
Machine hours operated	10,000
Direct materials costs incurred	$486,000
Direct labor costs incurred	$190,530

Raw materials are added at the beginning of the process for each unit of product produced, and labor and manufacturing overhead are added evenly throughout the manufacturing process. Manufacturing overhead is applied to Work-in-Process at the rate of $24 per machine hour. Units in process at the end of the period were 65 percent converted.

Required
Prepare a cost of production report for Oregon Paper Company for October.

E17-29. Cost of Production Report: No Beginning Inventories (LO5)
Sure Grip Paving Products Company manufactures asphalt paving materials for highway construction through a one-step process in which all materials are added at the beginning of the process. During October 2012, the company accumulated the following data in its process costing system:

Production data	
Work-in-process, 10/1/12	0 tons
Raw materials transferred to processing	25,000 tons
Work-in-process, 10/31/12 (75% converted)	5,000 tons
Cost data	
Raw materials transferred to processing	$625,000
Conversion costs	
Direct labor cost incurred	$38,000
Manufacturing overhead applied	?

Manufacturing overhead is applied at the rate of $4 per equivalent unit (ton) processed.

Required
Prepare a cost of production report for October.

E17-30.ᴬ Absorption and Variable Costing Comparisons: Production Equals Sales
Assume that Smuckers manufactures and sells 15,000 cases of jelly each quarter. The following data are available for the third quarter of 2012.

J.M. Smucker Company (SJM)

Total fixed manufacturing overhead	$30,000
Fixed selling and administrative expenses	10,000
Sales price per case	28
Direct materials per case	12
Direct labor per case	5
Variable manufacturing overhead per case	3

Required
a. Compute the cost per case under both absorption costing and variable costing.

b. Compute net income under both absorption costing and variable costing.

c. Reconcile any differences in income. Explain.

E17-31.ᴬ Absorption and Variable Costing Income Statements: Production Exceeds Sales

Glendale Company sells its product at a unit price of $12.00. Unit manufacturing costs are direct materials, $2.00; direct labor, $3.00; and variable manufacturing overhead, $1.50. Total fixed manufacturing costs are $20,000 per year. Selling and administrative expenses are $1.00 per unit variable and $10,000 per year fixed. Though 25,000 units were produced during 2012, only 22,000 units were sold. There was no beginning inventory.

Required

a. Prepare a functional income statement using absorption costing.

b. Prepare a contribution income statement using variable costing.

E17-32.ᴬ Absorption and Variable Costing Comparisons: Sales Exceed Production

Eskew Development purchases, develops, and sells commercial building sites. As the sites are sold, they are cleared at an average cost of $2,500 per site. Storm drains and driveways are also installed at an average cost of $4,000 per site. Selling costs are 10 percent of sales price. Administrative costs are $425,000 per year. During 2011, the company bought 1,000 acres of land for $5,000,000 and divided it into 200 sites of equal size. The average selling price per site was $80,000 during 2011 when 50 sites were sold. During 2012, the company purchased and developed another 1,000 acres, divided into 200 sites. The purchase price was again $5,000.000. Sales totaled 300 sites in 2012 at an average price of $80,000.

Required

a. Prepare 2011 and 2012 functional income statements using absorption costing.

b. Prepare 2011 and 2012 contribution income statements using variable costing.

PROBLEMS

P17-33. Cost of Goods Manufactured and Income Statement   (L04)

Following is information from the records of the Calgary Company for July 2012.

Purchases	
Raw materials	$ 80,000
Manufacturing supplies	3,500
Office supplies	1,200
Sales.	425,700
Administrative salaries	12,000
Direct labor.	117,500
Production employees' fringe benefits*	4,000
Sales commissions.	50,000
Production supervisors' salaries	7,200
Plant depreciation	14,000
Office depreciation.	20,000
Plant maintenance	10,000
Plant utilities.	35,000
Office utilities	8,000
Office maintenance	2,000
Production equipment rent.	6,000
Office equipment rent.	1,300

* Classified as manufacturing overhead

Inventories	July 1	July 31
Raw materials.	$17,000	$25,000
Manufacturing supplies	1,500	3,000
Office supplies	600	1,000
Work-in-process.	51,000	40,000
Finished goods.	35,000	27,100

Required

Prepare a statement of cost of goods manufactured and an income statement. Actual overhead costs are assigned to products.

P17-34. Cost of Goods Manufactured and Income Statement with Predetermined Overhead and Labor Cost Classifications (LO2, 4)

Callaway Golf
Company (ELY)

Assume information pertaining to Callaway Golf Company for April 2012 follows.

Sales..............................	$200,000
Purchases	
Raw materials......................	37,000
Manufacturing supplies	800
Office supplies	500
Salaries (including fringe benefits)	
Administrative.....................	6,000
Production supervisors..............	3,600
Sales.............................	15,000
Depreciation	
Plant and machinery.................	8,000
Office and office equipment	4,000
Utilities	
Plant............................	5,250
Office	890

Inventories	April 1	April 30
Raw materials................	$3,000	$3,500
Manufacturing supplies	1,000	1,100
Office supplies	900	800
Work-in-process..............	2,000	2,300
Finished goods...............	8,000	9,000

Additional information follows:
- Manufacturing overhead is applied to products at 85 percent of direct labor dollars.
- Employee base wages are $12 per hour.
- Employee fringe benefits amount to 40 percent of the base wage rate. They are classified as manufacturing overhead.
- During April, production employees worked 5,600 hours, including 4,800 regular hours and 200 overtime hours spent working on products. There were 600 indirect labor hours.
- Employees are paid a 50 percent overtime premium. Any overtime premium is treated as manufacturing overhead.

Required

a. Prepare a statement of cost of goods manufactured and an income statement for April.
b. Determine underapplied or overapplied overhead for April.
c. Recompute direct labor and actual manufacturing overhead assuming employee fringe benefits for direct labor hours are classified as direct labor.

P17-35. Actual and Predetermined Overhead Rates (LO2, 4)

Allison's Engines, which builds high performance auto engines for race cars, started operations on January 1, 2012. During the month, the following events occurred:
- Materials costing $6,500 were purchased on account.
- Direct materials costing $3,000 were placed in process.
- A total of 380 direct labor hours was charged to individual jobs at a rate of $15 per hour.
- Overhead costs for the month of January were as follows:

Depreciation on building and equipment......	$ 500
Indirect labor	1,500
Utilities	600
Property taxes on building	650
Insurance on building....................	550

- On January 31, only one job (A06) was in process with materials costs of $600, direct labor charges of $450 for 30 direct labor hours, and applied overhead.
- The building and equipment were purchased before operations began and the insurance was prepaid. All other costs will be paid during the following month.

Note: Predetermined overhead rates are used throughout the module. An alternative is to accumulate actual overhead costs for the period in Manufacturing Overhead, and apply actual costs at the close of the period to all jobs in process during the period.

Required

a. Assuming Allison's Engines assigned actual monthly overhead costs to jobs on the basis of actual monthly direct labor hours, prepare an analysis of Work-in-Process for the month of January.

b. Assuming Allison's Engines uses a predetermined overhead rate of $10.50 per direct labor hour, prepare an analysis of Work-in-Process for the month of January. Describe the appropriate treatment of any overapplied or underapplied overhead for the month of January.

c. Review the overhead items and classify each as fixed or variable in relation to direct labor hours. Next, predict the actual overhead rates for months when 200 and 1,000 direct labor hours are used. Assuming jobs similar to A06 were in process at the end of each month, determine the costs assigned to these jobs. (*Hint:* Determine a variable overhead rate.)

d. Why do you suppose predetermined overhead rates are preferred to actual overhead rates?

P17-36. Job Costing with Predetermined Overhead Rate (LO2, 4)

Kubota Corporation manufactures equipment in batches for inventory stock. Assume that Kubota's production costs are accounted for using a job cost system. At the beginning of April raw materials inventories totaled $8,500,000, manufacturing supplies amounted to $1,200,000 and finished goods inventories totaled $6,000,000. Two jobs were in process: Job 522 with assigned costs of $5,640,000 and Job 523 with assigned costs of $2,400,000. The following information summarizes April manufacturing activities:

Kubota Corporation (KUB)

- Purchased raw materials costing $25,000,000 on account.
- Purchased manufacturing supplies costing $3,000,000 on account.
- Requisitioned materials needed to complete Job 523. Started two new jobs, 524 and 525, and requisitioned direct materials for them.

Direct materials

Job 523.	$ 3,000,000
Job 524.	12,900,000
Job 525.	9,600,000
Total	$25,500,000

- Recorded April salaries and wages as follows:

Direct labor

Job 522 (300,000 hours × $20 per hour)	$ 6,000,000
Job 523 (800,000 hours × $20 per hour)	16,000,000
Job 524 (1,200,000 hours × $20 per hour)	24,000,000
Job 525 (1,000,000 hours × $20 per hour)	20,000,000
Total direct labor.	66,000,000
Indirect labor	6,400,000
Total	$72,400,000

- Used manufacturing supplies costing $2,250,000.
- Recognized depreciation on factory fixed assets of $4,000,000.
- Incurred miscellaneous manufacturing overhead costs of $5,500,000 on account.
- Applied manufacturing overhead at the rate of $6 per direct labor hour.
- Completed Jobs 522, 523, and 524.

Required

Prepare a complete analysis of all activity in Work-in-Process. Be sure to show the beginning and ending balances, all increases and decreases, and label each item. Provide support information on decreases with job cost sheets.

P17-37. **Job Costing with Predetermined Overhead Rate**   (LO2, 4)

TruCut Mower Company manufactures a variety of gasoline-powered mowers for discount hardware and department stores. TruCut uses a job cost system and treats each customer's order as a separate job. The primary mower components (motors, chassis, and wheels) are purchased from three different suppliers under long-term contracts that call for the direct delivery of raw materials to the production floor as needed. When a customer's order is received, a raw materials purchase order is electronically placed with suppliers. The purchase order specifies the scheduled date that production is to begin as the delivery date for motors and chassis; the scheduled date production is to be completed is specified as the delivery date for the wheels. As a consequence, there are no raw materials inventories; raw materials are charged directly to Work-in-Process upon receipt. Upon completion, goods are shipped directly to customers rather than transferred to finished goods inventory. At the beginning of July TruCut had the following work-in-process inventories:

Job 365	$20,000
Job 366	16,500
Job 367	15,000
Job 368	9,000
Total	$60,500

During July, the following activities took place:
- Started Jobs 369, 370, and 371.
- Ordered and received the following raw materials for specified jobs:

Job	Motors	Chassis	Wheels	Total
366	$ 0	$ 0	$ 800	$ 800
367	0	0	1,200	1,200
368	0	0	1,600	1,600
369	12,000	4,000	1,000	17,000
370	9,000	3,500	900	13,400
371	8,500	3,800	0	12,300
Total	$29,500	$11,300	$5,500	$46,300

- Incurred July manufacturing payroll:

Direct labor	
Job 365.	$ 500
Job 366.	3,200
Job 367.	3,400
Job 368.	4,160
Job 369.	1,300
Job 370.	2,620
Job 371.	2,000
Total	17,180
Indirect labor	3,436
Total	$20,616

- Incurred additional manufacturing overhead costs for July:

Manufacturing supplies purchased on account and used	$ 2,800
Depreciation on factory fixed assets	6,000
Miscellaneous payables	5,100
Total	$13,900

- Applied manufacturing overhead using a predetermined rate based on predicted annual overhead of $190,000 and predicted annual direct labor of $200,000.
- Completed and shipped Jobs 365 through 370.

Required

Prepare a complete analysis of all activity in Work-in-Process. Be sure to show the beginning and ending balances, all increases and decreases, and label each item. Provide support information on decreases with job cost sheets.

P17-38. Weighted Average Process Costing (LO5)

Minot Processing Company manufactures one product on a continuous basis in two departments, Processing and Finishing. All materials are added at the beginning of work on the product in the Processing Department. During December 2012, the following events occurred in the Processing Department:

Units started.	16,000 units
Units completed and transferred to Finishing Department	15,000 units

Costs assigned to processing	
Raw materials (one unit of raw materials for each unit of product started)	$142,900
Manufacturing supplies used	18,000
Direct labor costs incurred	51,000
Supervisors' salaries.	12,000
Other production labor costs	14,000
Depreciation on equipment	6,000
Other production costs.	18,000

Additional information follows:
- Minot uses weighted average costing and applies manufacturing overhead to Work-in-Process at the rate of 100 percent of direct labor cost.
- Ending inventory in the Processing Department consists of 3,000 units that are one-third converted.
- Beginning inventory contained 2,000 units, one-half converted, with a cost of $27,300 ($17,300 for materials and $10,000 for conversion).

Required

a. Prepare a cost of production report for the Processing Department for December.
b. Prepare an analysis of all changes in Work-in-Process.

P17-39. Weighted Average Process Costing (LO5)

Assume that JIF, which is part of J.M. Smucker Company, processes its only product, 12-ounce jars of peanut butter, in a single process and uses weighted average process costing to account for inventory costs. All materials are added at the beginning of production. The following inventory, production, and cost data are provided for June 2012:

JIF

J.M. Smucker Company (SJM)

Production data	
Beginning inventory (25% converted).	210,000 units
Units started	650,000 units
Ending inventory (50% converted)	180,000 units

Manufacturing costs	
Beginning inventory in process:	
Materials cost	$146,000
Conversion cost	88,000
Raw materials cost added at beginning of process	739,800
Direct labor cost incurred	410,000
Manufacturing overhead applied	333,600

Required

a. Prepare a cost of production report for June.
b. Prepare a statement of cost of goods manufactured for June.

P17-40.   Weighted Average Process Costing with Error Correction   (LO5)

Blue Sky Manufacturing Company began operations on December 1. On December 31 a new accounting intern was assigned the task of calculating and costing ending inventories.

The intern estimated that the ending work-in-process inventory was 40 percent complete as to both materials and conversion, resulting in 2,000 equivalent units of materials and conversion. The ending work-in-process was then valued at $80,000, including $40,000 for materials and $40,000 for conversion. A subsequent review of the intern's work revealed that although the materials portion of the ending inventory was correctly estimated to be 40 percent complete, the units in ending inventory, on average, were only 20 percent complete as to conversion.

Required

a. Determine the number of units in the ending inventory.
b. How many equivalent units of conversion were in the ending inventory?
c. What cost per unit did the intern calculate for conversion?
d. Assuming 9,000 units were completed during the month of December, determine the correct cost per equivalent unit. *Hint:* Find the total conversion costs in process.
e. Determine the corrected cost of the ending inventory.
f. By how much was the cost of goods manufactured misstated as a result of the intern's error? Indicate whether the cost of goods manufactured was overstated or understated.

P17-41.ᴬ   Absorption and Variable Costing Comparisons

Never Quit Shoe Company is concerned with changing to the variable costing method of inventory valuation for making internal decisions. Functional income statements using absorption costing for January and February follow.

NEVER QUIT SHOE COMPANY Functional (Absorption Costing) Income Statements For January and February 2012		
	January	February
Sales (8,000 units)	$160,000	$160,000
Cost of goods sold.	(99,200)	(108,800)
Gross profit.	60,800	51,200
Selling and administrative expenses	(30,000)	(30,000)
Net income	$ 30,800	$ 21,200

Production data follow.

Production units.	10,000	6,000
Variable costs per unit	$10	$10
Fixed overhead costs.	$24,000	$24,000

The preceding selling and administrative expenses include variable costs of $1 per unit sold.

Required

a. Compute the absorption cost per unit manufactured in January and February.
b. Explain why the net income for January was higher than the net income for February when the same number of units was sold in each month.
c. Prepare contribution income statements for both months using variable costing.
d. Reconcile the absorption costing and variable costing net income figures for each month. (Start with variable costing net income.)

 P17-42.ᴬ   Absorption and Variable Costing Comparisons

Peachtree Company manufactures peach jam. Because of bad weather, its peach crop was small. The following data have been gathered for the summer quarter of 2012:

Beginning inventory (cases)	0
Cases produced	10,000
Cases sold	9,400
Sales price per case	$60
Direct materials per case	$8
Direct labor per case	$9
Variable manufacturing overhead per case	$3
Total fixed manufacturing overhead	$400,000
Variable selling and administrative cost per case	$2
Fixed selling and administrative cost	$48,000

Required

a. Prepare a functional income statement for the quarter using absorption costing.

b. Prepare a contribution income statement for the quarter using variable costing.

c. What is the value of ending inventory under absorption costing?

d. What is the value of ending inventory under variable costing?

e. Reconcile the difference in ending inventory under absorption costing and variable costing.

P17-43.[A] **Variable and Absorption Costing with High-Low Cost Estimation and CVP Analysis Including Taxes**

Presented are the Charger Company's functional income statements for January and February of 2012.

CHARGER COMPANY Functional (Absorption Costing) Income Statements For the Months of January and February 2012		
	January	**February**
Production and sales	40,000	50,000
Sales Revenue	$1,000,000	$1,250,000
Cost of goods manufactured and sold	(525,000)	(625,000)
Gross profit	475,000	625,000
General and administrative expenses	(235,000)	(235,000)
Net income before taxes	240,000	390,000
Income taxes at 0.40	(96,000)	(156,000)
Net income after taxes	$ 144,000	$ 234,000

Required

a. Using the high-low method, develop a cost estimating equation for total monthly manufacturing costs.

b. Determine Charger Company's monthly break-even point.

c. Determine the unit sales required to earn a monthly after-tax income of $150,000.

d. Prepare a January 2012 contribution income statement using variable costing.

e. If the January 2012 net income amounts differ using absorption and variable costing, explain why. If they are identical, explain why.

MANAGEMENT APPLICATIONS

MA17-44. Cost Data for Financial Reporting and Special Order Decisions (LO2, 4)

Friendly Greeting Card Company produces a full range of greeting cards sold through pharmacies and department stores. Each card is designed by independent artists. A production master is then prepared for each design. The production master has an indefinite life. Product designs for popular cards are deemed to be valuable assets. If a card sells well, many batches of the design will be manufactured over a period of years. Hence, Friendly Greeting maintains an inventory of production masters so that cards may be periodically reissued. Cards are produced in batches that may vary by increments of 1,000 units. An average batch consists of 10,000 cards. Producing a batch requires placing the production master on the printing press, setting the press for the appropriate paper size, and making other adjustments for colors and so forth. Following are facility-, product-, batch-, and unit-level cost information:

Product design and production master per new card	$ 1,500.00
Batch setup (typically per 10,000 cards)	150.00
Materials per 1,000 cards.	100.00
Conversion per 1,000 cards.	80.00
Shipping	
Per batch	20.00
Per card	0.01
Selling and administrative	
Companywide.	200,000.00
Per product design marketed.	500.00

Information from previous year:

Product designs and masters prepared for new cards	90
Product designs marketed.	120
Batches manufactured.	500
Cards manufactured and sold	5,000,000

Required
You may need to review materials in Modules 15 and 16 to complete the requirements.
a. Describe how you would determine the cost of goods sold and the value of any ending inventory for financial reporting purposes. (No computations are required.)
b. You have just received an inquiry from Mall-Mart department stores to develop and manufacture 20 special designs for sale exclusively in Mall-Mart stores. The cards would be sold for $1.50 each, and Mall-Mart would pay Friendly Greeting $0.30 per card. The initial order is for 20,000 cards of each design. If the cards sell well, Mall-Mart plans to place additional orders for these and other designs. Because of the preestablished sales relationship, no marketing costs would be associated with the cards sold to Mall-Mart. How would you evaluate the desirability of the Mall-Mart proposal?
c. Explain any differences between the costs considered in your answer to requirement (a) and the costs considered in your answer to requirement (b).

MA17-45. Continue or Discontinue: Plantwide Overhead with Labor- and Machine-Intensive Operations (LO2, 4)
When Dart Products started operation five years ago, its only product was a radar detector known as the Bear Detector. The production system was simple, with Bear Detectors manually assembled from purchased components. With no ending work-in-process inventories, unit costs were calculated once a month by dividing current manufacturing costs by units produced.

Last year, Dart Products began to manufacture a second product, code-named the Lion Tamer. The production of Lion Tamers involves both machine-intensive fabrication and manual assembly. The introduction of the second product necessitated a change in the firm's simple accounting system. Dart Products now separately assigns direct material and direct labor costs to each product using information contained on materials requisitions and work tickets. Manufacturing overhead is accumulated in a single cost pool and assigned on the basis of direct labor hours, which is common to both products. Following are last year's financial results by product:

	Bear Detector		Lion Tamer	
Sales				
Units		5,000		2,000
Dollars.		$ 500,000		$ 300,000
Cost of goods sold				
Direct materials.	$110,000		$65,000	
Direct labor	150,000		45,000	
Applied overhead	270,000		81,000	
Total		(530,000)		(191,000)
Gross profit.		$ (30,000)		$ 109,000

Management is concerned about the mixed nature of last year's financial performance. It appears that the Lion Tamer is a roaring success. The only competition, the Nittney Company, has been selling a competing product for considerably more than Dart's Lion Tamer; this company is in financial difficulty and is likely to file for bankruptcy. The management of Dart Products attributes the Lion Tamer's success to excellent production management. Management is concerned, however, about the future of the Bear Detector and is likely to discontinue that product unless its profitability can be improved. You have been asked to help with this decision and have obtained the following information:

- The labor rate is $15 per hour.
- Dart has two separate production operations, fabrication and assembly. Bear Detectors undergo only assembly operations and require 2.0 assembly hours per unit. Lion Tamers undergo both fabrication and assembly and require 1.0 fabrication hour and 0.5 assembly hour per unit.
- The annual Fabricating Department overhead cost function is:

$$\$200{,}000 + \$5 \text{ (labor hours)}$$

- The annual Assembly Department overhead cost function is:

$$\$20{,}000 + \$11 \text{ (labor hours)}$$

Required

You may need to review materials in Modules 15 and 16 to complete this case. Evaluate the profitability of Dart's two products and make any recommendations you believe appropriate.

MA17-46.[A] **Absorption Costing and Performance Evaluation**

On July 2, 2012 Innovative Financial acquired 90 percent of the outstanding stock of Medioker Industries in exchange for 2,000 shares of its own stock. Innovative Financial has a reputation as a "high flier" company that commands a high price-to-earnings ratio because its management team works wonders in improving the performance of ailing companies.

At the time of the acquisition, Medioker was producing and selling at an annual rate of 100,000 units per year. This is in line with the firm's average annual activity. Fifty thousand units were produced and sold during the first half of 2012.

Immediately after the acquisition Innovative Financial installed its own management team and increased production to practical capacity. One-hundred thousand units were produced during the second half of 2012.

At the end of the year, the new management declared another dramatic turnaround and a $100,000 cash dividend when the following set of income statements were issued:

MEDIOKER INDUSTRIES Income Statement For the first and second half-years of 2012			
	First	**Second**	**Total**
Sales.	$1,400,000	$1,400,000	$2,800,000
Cost of goods sold*	(1,200,000)	(700,000)	(1,900,000)
Gross profit.	200,000	700,000	900,000
Selling and administrative expenses	(200,000)	(400,000)	(600,000)
Net income	$ 0	$ 300,000	$ 300,000

* Absorption costing with any under-absorbed or over-absorbed overhead written off as an adjustment to cost of goods sold. Medioker applies manufacturing overhead using a predetermined overhead rate based on predicted annual fixed overhead of $1,000,000 and annual production of 100,000 units.

Required:

As the only representative of the minority interest on the board of directors, evaluate the performance of the new management team.

SOLUTIONS TO REVIEW PROBLEMS

Mid-Module Review

Solution

a.

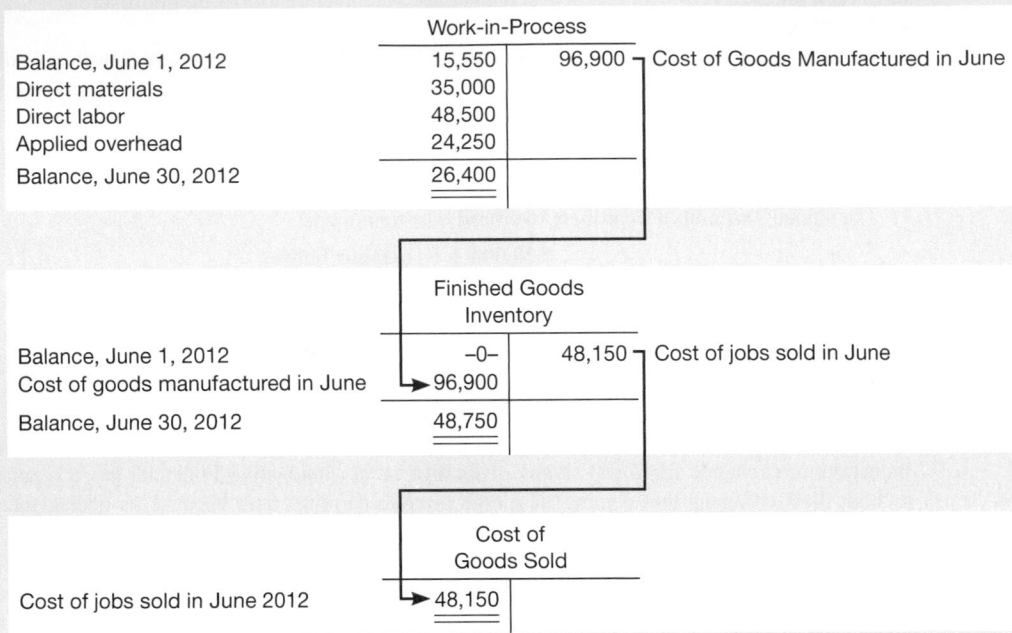

Work-in-Process

Balance, June 1, 2012	15,550	96,900	Cost of Goods Manufactured in June
Direct materials	35,000		
Direct labor	48,500		
Applied overhead	24,250		
Balance, June 30, 2012	26,400		

Finished Goods Inventory

Balance, June 1, 2012	–0–	48,150	Cost of jobs sold in June
Cost of goods manufactured in June	96,900		
Balance, June 30, 2012	48,750		

Cost of Goods Sold

Cost of jobs sold in June 2012	48,150

b. Job in Work-in-Process at June 30, 2012:

	Job 228
Direct materials	$14,400
Direct labor........................	8,000
Applied overhead (800 × $5).........	4,000
Total	$26,400

Job in Finished Goods at June 30, 2012:

	Job 227
Direct materials	$18,000
Direct labor........................	20,500
Applied overhead (2,050 × $5)	10,250
Total	$48,750

Jobs sold in June 2012:

	Job 225	Job 226	Total
Costs assigned from prior period......................	$13,750	$ 1,800	$15,550
June Costs: Direct materials	–0–	2,600	2,600
Direct labor............................	5,000	15,000	20,000
Applied overhead (500 & 1,500 × $5).........	2,500	7,500	10,000
Total	$21,250	$26,900	$48,150

c. Statement of cost of goods manufactured for June 2012.

TRI-STAR PRINTING COMPANY Statement of Cost of Goods Manufactured For Month Ending June 30, 2012			
Current manufacturing costs			
Cost of materials placed in production			
Raw materials, 6/1/12	$ 7,000		
Purchases	40,000		
Total available	47,000		
Raw materials, 6/30/12	(12,000)	$35,000	
Direct labor		48,500	
Manufacturing overhead applied		24,250	$107,750
Work-in-process, 6/1/12			15,550
Total costs in process			123,300
Work-in-process, 6/30/12			(26,400)
Cost of goods manufactured			$ 96,900

Module-End Review

Solution

MAGNETIC MEDIA, INC. Cost of Production Report For the Year 2012			
Summary of units in process:			
Beginning	3,000,000		
Units started	27,000,000		
In process	30,000,000		
Completed	−25,000,000		
Ending	5,000,000		

Equivalent units in process:	**Materials**	**Conversion**	
Units completed	25,000,000	25,000,000	
Plus equivalent units in ending inventory	5,000,000	1,500,000	
Equivalent units in process	30,000,000	26,500,000	

Total costs to be accounted for and cost per equivalent unit in process:	**Materials**	**Conversion**	**Total**
Work-in-Process, beginning	$ 468,000	$ 252,000	$ 720,000
Current cost	6,132,000	5,048,000	11,180,000
Total cost in process	$ 6,600,000	$ 5,300,000	$11,900,000
Equivalent units in process	÷ 30,000,000	÷26,500,000	
Cost per equivalent unit in process	$0.22	$0.20	$0.42
Accounting for total costs:			
Transferred out (25,000,000 × $0.42)			$10,500,000
Work-in-Process, ending:			
Materials (5,000,000 × $0.22)		$ 1,100,000	
Conversion (1,500,000 × $0.20)		300,000	1,400,000
Total cost accounted for			$11,900,000

Getty Images

UPS

Effective management of costs is a hallmark of sound financial management, and indirect costs (commonly referred to as overhead) are the most challenging costs to measure and manage. Direct costs, including direct materials and direct labor, can be readily traced to a job, product,[1] or other unit of work. Indirect costs, which are typically incurred for the benefit of several different products or cost objectives, are not as easily traced to specific units or projects. Managing indirect costs is a major concern of managers because this broad category of costs has grown from what was an overall average of about 10 percent of total sales several decades ago to about 35 percent today.

Many companies that once thrived have failed, arguably, because they did not manage effectively a growing pool of indirect costs. You might say they failed because they did not fully understand their business or their business model. If the true cost of producing and selling products is more than the revenues generated by those products, the business producing and selling those products will not succeed in the long-term.

It is well documented that for many years the **U.S. Postal Service** has struggled with mounting losses while its competitors, **UPS** and **FedEx**, have thrived in a highly competitive marketplace. At a meeting of the President's Commission on the United States Postal Service, (cre-

---

[1] Throughout this module, the term "product" should be interpreted to encompass both tangible products sold by a manufacturer, wholesaler, or retailer, as well as services sold by those companies, and services sold by professional or other service providers.

Activity-Based Costing, Customer Profitability, and Activity-Based Management

LEARNING OBJECTIVES

LO1 Explain the changes in the modern production environment that have affected cost structures. (p. 18-3)

LO2 Understand the concept of activity-based costing (ABC) and how it is applied. (p. 18-4)

LO3 Explain the difference between traditional plantwide and departmental overhead methods and ABC. (p. 18-6)

LO4 Describe the implementation of an activity-based costing system. (p. 18-13)

LO5 Explain customer profitability analysis based on ABC. (p. 18-14)

LO6 Explain the difference between ABC and activity-based management. (p. 18-17)

ated to examine the problems at USPS), the discussion focused on differences in the cost systems at the Postal Service and UPS. It was reported that the Postal Service cost system attributes only 58% of its operating costs to it various products; whereas, UPS attributes 100% of its costs to its products. The UPS representative on the panel stated that UPS does not price any product below its full cost. With only 58% of its costs attributed to products, the Postal Service cannot know whether any of its products, individually, is making a profit.[2]

_____
[2] James A. Johnson and Harry J. Pearce, Co-chairs, "Minutes of Meeting of the President's Commission on the U.S. Postal Service," May 28, 2003, p.3, http://www.ustreas.gov/offices/domestic-finance/usps/pdf/may_28_minutes.pdf

As competition from home and abroad puts increasing pressure on companies to price products more competitively, the importance of cost management is increasingly crucial. Organizations like UPS, Coca-Cola, IBM, the City of Indianapolis, and Toronto's Hospital for Sick Children have benefited greatly from a type of cost system referred to as **activity-based costing** (ABC). In this module we will define and discuss ABC systems, compare ABC with traditional costing systems, and demonstrate how ABC can be used to analyze customer profitability. Finally, we will introduce the notion of activity-based management, which uses activity-based costing information to better manage processes and activities within an organization.

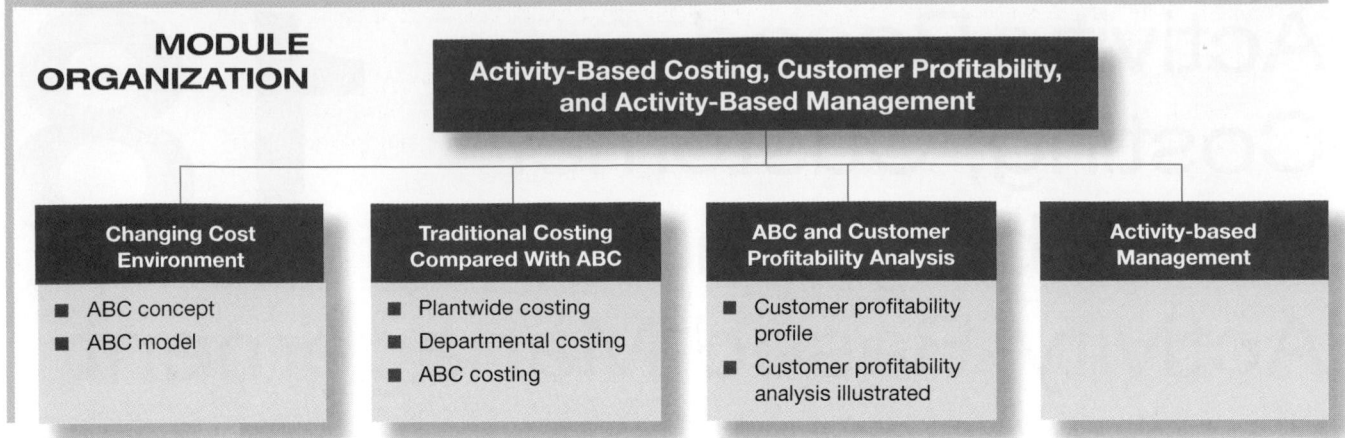

CHANGING COST ENVIRONMENT

LO1 Explain the changes in the modern production environment that have affected cost structures.

As technology has advanced and competition has intensified over the last century, there has been a fundamental shift in manufacturing organizations from labor-intensive to automated assembly techniques. These changes have influenced the activities performed to meet customer needs and, consequently, the costs of producing goods and services.

At the beginning of the twentieth century, products had long life cycles, production procedures were relatively straightforward, production was labor based, and only a limited number of related products were produced in a single plant. It was said of the Model T Ford that "you could have any color you wanted, as long as it was black." The largest cost elements of most manufactured goods were the cost of raw materials and the wages paid to production employees. Manufacturing overhead was a relatively small portion of the overall cost of manufacturing products.

The twentieth century saw an accelerating shift from traditional labor-based activities to production procedures requiring large investments in automated equipment. In the past, production employees used equipment to assist them in performing their jobs. Now employees spend considerable time scheduling, setting up, maintaining, and moving materials to and from, equipment. They spend relatively little time on actual production. The equipment does the work, and the employees keep it running efficiently. Increased complexity of production procedures and an increase in the variety of products produced in a single facility have also caused a shift toward more support personnel and fewer production employees. The result is a significant increase in manufacturing overhead as a percentage of total product cost. This change in the typical production cost structure over the past century is illustrated in Exhibit 18.1.

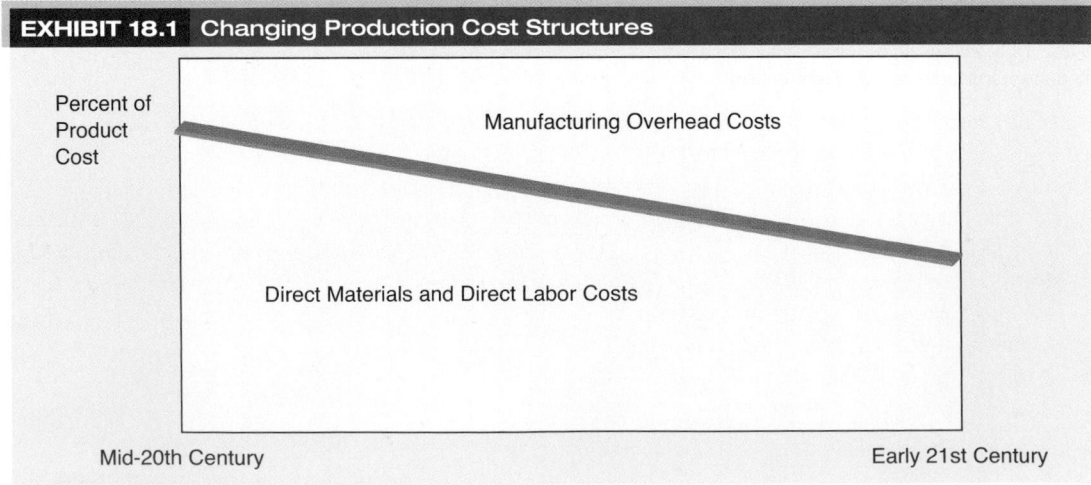

EXHIBIT 18.1 Changing Production Cost Structures

In the "low-tech," labor-intensive manufacturing environment, factors related to direct labor were often the primary drivers of manufacturing overhead costs; however, in today's "high-tech" automated environment there are many other factors that drive manufacturing overhead costs, and the specific set of cost drivers differs from organization to organization.

The previous module on product costing illustrated a simplified traditional system for allocating manufacturing overhead to products using a single, volume-based cost driver, such as direct labor hours. The following section introduces activity-based costing, which recognizes the multiple activities that drive manufacturing overhead costs in today's production environment.

ACTIVITY-BASED COSTING

The manufacturing overhead cost pool has been referred to as a "blob" of common costs. The constant growth of costs classified as overhead has forced us to search for increasingly detailed methods to ana-lyze these costs. If overhead costs are low in comparison with other costs and if factories produce few products in large production runs, the use of an overhead rate based on direct labor hours or machine hours may be adequate. However, as the amount of overhead costs continues to grow, as manufactur-ing facilities produce a wider variety of products, and as competition intensifies, the inadequacies of a single overhead rate based on a single cost driver such as direct labor hours become evident.

LO2 Understand the concept of activity-based costing (ABC) and how it is applied.

Fortunately, advances in information technology and the declining costs of computerized informa-tion systems have facilitated the development and maintenance of increasingly detailed databases. The increased complexity of the production environment, coupled with faster and cheaper computing technol-ogy, gave rise to the emergence and development of activity-based costing during the 1980s and 1990s.

Activity-based costing involves determining the cost of activities and tracing their costs to cost objectives on the basis of the cost objective's utilization of units of activity.

The concepts underlying ABC can be summarized in the following two statements and illustrations:

1. Activities performed to fill customer needs consume resources that cost money.

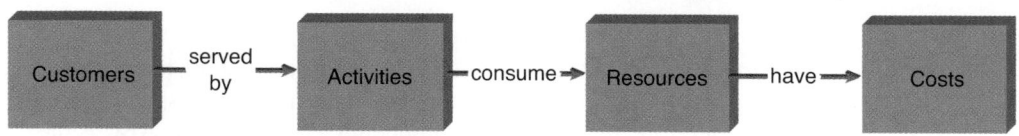

2. The cost of resources consumed by activities should be assigned to cost objectives on the basis of the units of activity consumed by the cost objective.

*Based on units of activity utilized by the cost objective.

The cost objective is typically a product or service provided to a customer. Depending on the informa-tion needs of decision makers, as we will discuss later in this module, the cost objective might be the customer.

To summarize, activity-based costing is a system of analysis that identifies and measures the cost of key activities, and then traces these activity costs to products or other cost objectives based on the quantity of activity consumed by the cost objectives. ABC is based on the premise that activities drive costs and that costs should be assigned to products (or other cost objectives) in proportion to the vol-ume of activities they consume. Although activity cost analysis is most often associated with product costing, it offers many benefits for controlling and managing costs, as we will see later in this module. As the following Research Insight box explains, ABC was actually used first to improve cost manage-ment before it was used for product costing.

ABC Product Costing Model

Traditional costing considers the cost of a product to be its direct costs for materials and labor plus some allocated portion of factory overhead, using overhead rates typically based on direct labor or machine hours. Activity-based costing is based on the notion that companies incur costs because of the activities they conduct in pursuit of their goals and objectives. For example, various activities

---

RESEARCH INSIGHT   **The History of ABC**

ABC came to the forefront in the 1980s and 1990s; however, it was beginning to evolve as early as the 1960s when General Electric's (GE) finance and accounting staff attempted to improve the usefulness of accounting information in controlling ever-increasing indirect costs. The GE staff noted that indirect costs were often the result of "upstream" decisions, such as engineering design and change orders, which were made long before the costs were actually incurred. Frequently, the engineering department was not informed of the consequences their actions had on the other parts of the organization.

The second phase of the development of ABC was accomplished by business consultants, professors, and manufacturing companies during the 1970s and early 1980s. By generating more accurate cost and profitability measures for the various products offered by companies, these consultants and professors hoped to improve product cost information used in pricing and product mix decisions. ABC has since been extended to assess customer profitability.

In the late 1980s and 1990s, ABC was being promoted by many of the leading consulting firms, and it almost became a fad, much as TQM and JIT had become before it. Consequently, many companies that jumped on the ABC bandwagon early in its life, later determined that it was not for them. Most of the companies that abandoned ABC, probably adopted it initially for the wrong reasons.

Knowledge of the historical development of activity-based costing is important in order to clearly understand what ABC analysis was intended to accomplish, as well as what it was not intended to accomplish.

Source: Latshaw, Craig A. Cortese-Danile, Teresa M., Activity-based costing: usage and pitfalls," *Review of Business*, Winter, 2002.

---

take place to produce a particular product, such as setting up, maintaining, or monitoring the machines to make the product, physically moving raw materials and work in process, and so forth. Each of these activities has a cost; therefore, the total cost of producing a product using ABC is the sum of the direct materials and direct labor costs of that product, plus the cost of other activities conducted to produce that product.

The general two-stage ABC product cost model is illustrated in Exhibit 18.2. The first stage includes the assignment of manufacturing overhead resource costs, such as indirect labor, depreciation, and utilities, to activity cost pools for the key activities identified. Typical activity cost pools in a manufacturing environment include pools for machine setup, material movement, and engineering. The second stage assigns those activity cost pools to products.

Notice in Exhibit 18.2 that direct product costs, such as direct materials and direct labor, are directly assigned to products and are excluded from the activity cost pools. Only indirect product costs (manufacturing overhead) are assigned to products via activity cost pools.

Probably the most critical step in ABC is identifying cost drivers. The activity cost driver for a particular cost (or cost pool) is the characteristic selected for measuring the quantity of the activity for a particular period of time. For example, if an activity cost pool is established for machine setup, it is necessary to select some basis for measuring the quantity of machine setup activity associated with the costs in the pool. The quantity of setup activity could be measured by the number of different times machines are set up to produce a different product, the amount of time used in completing machine setups, the number of staff working on setups, or some other measure. It is critical that the activity measure used has a logical causal relationship to the costs in the pool and that the quantity of the activity is highly correlated with the amount of cost in the pool. Statistical methods, such as regression analysis and correlation analysis, can be very useful in selecting activity cost drivers.

Once the total cost in the activity pool and the activity cost driver have been determined, the cost per unit of activity is calculated as the total cost divided by the total amount of activity. For example, if total costs assigned to the setup activity pool in July were $100,000 and 200 setups were completed in July, the cost per setup for the month would be $500. If during July machines were set up 10 times to make product JX2, the total setup cost that would be assigned to product JX2 would be $5,000 ($500 × 10).

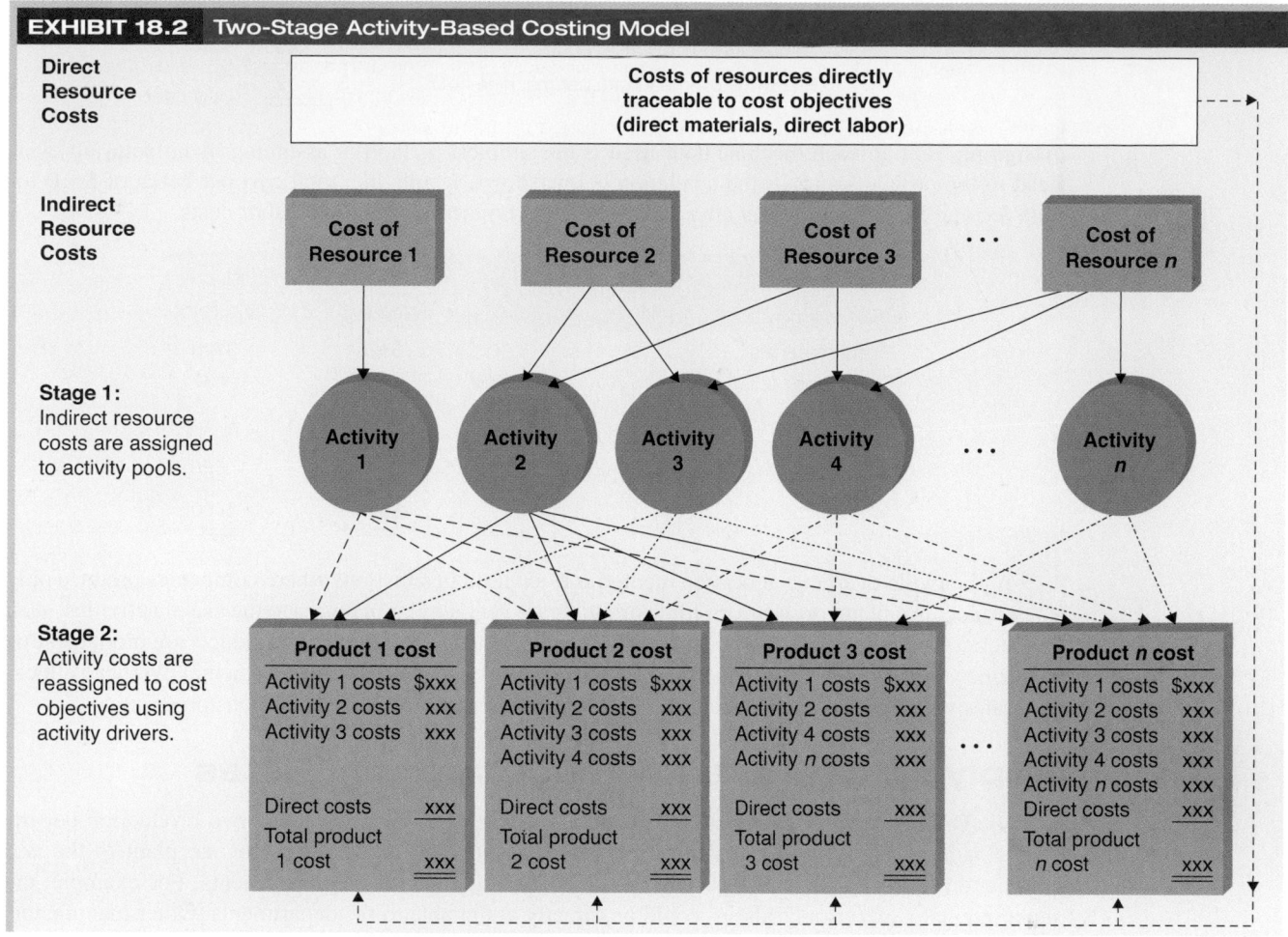

EXHIBIT 18.2 Two-Stage Activity-Based Costing Model

TRADITIONAL PRODUCT COSTING AND ABC COMPARED

Recall that Outdoor Rainwear in Module 17 recognized manufacturing overhead using a plantwide manufacturing overhead rate of $4 per direct labor hour. It was assumed that each hour of labor worked on product caused $4 of manufacturing overhead to be incurred. In that case, all manufacturing costs were assumed to be driven by one factor, direct labor hours. As discussed at the beginning of this module, such an assumption is often not appropriate with modern methods of producing goods (or services) where manufacturing overhead is related to a diverse set of activities and cost drivers.

LO3 Explain the difference between traditional plantwide and departmental overhead methods and ABC.

Applying Overhead with a Plantwide Rate

To illustrate, assume that VitaDrink, Inc. produces two beverages fortified with vitamins and minerals, VitaVeg and VitaFruit. VitaDrink has been facing intense competition from other health beverage producers in the vegetable drink market, and it is considering shifting its strategy entirely to the fruit drink market.

Each product is worked on in two departments, Mixing and Bottling. Both Mixing and Bottling operations are highly automated; therefore, the most common element of both products is machine hours in Mixing and Bottling. The products are produced in large 1,000-gallon batches. VitaVeg requires 3 machine hours per batch and VitaFruit requires 2 machine hours per batch. For July, 232 batches of VitaVeg and 400 batches of VitaFruit were produced, with total plantwide manufacturing overhead of $187,000 and 1,496 total machine hours. The plantwide overhead rate is calculated as $125 per machine hour in the following tabulation.

Total plantwide manufacturing overhead	$187,000
Total plantwide machine hours	÷ 1,496
Plantwide overhead rate per machine hour	$ 125

Assigning $125 to each machine hour used is the simplest method of assigning manufacturing over-head to the products and, as the tabulation below shows, results in a total cost per batch of $610 for VitaVeg and $400 for VitaFruit after adding the direct materials and direct labor costs.

	Unit Costs	
	VitaVeg	**VitaFruit**
Direct materials	$125	$120
Direct labor...............................	110	30
Manufacturing overhead		
Vegetable: 3 machine hours × $125	375	
Fruit: 2 machine hours × $125..............		250
Total unit cost............................	$610	$400

A plantwide overhead allocation method is often used in situations where companies produce only one product in a plant, or where multiple products are very similar in regard to the use of activities, such as machine or labor hours, that drive most of the overhead costs. If multiple products are produced that consume varying levels of activities in multiple production departments, departmental overhead alloca-tion rates will produce a more accurate allocation of overhead costs to the various products.

Applying Overhead with Department Rates

For VitaDrink to establish separate overhead allocation rates for each of the two production depart-ments, it is necessary first to assign the $187,000 of total overhead costs for the plant to the two production departments, some of which is directly assignable to the departments. For example, the departmental supervisors' salaries could be directly assignable to the departments. Other manufactur-ing overhead costs, such as support costs for maintenance, payroll, and so forth, are allocated to the production departments. Assume that after these allocations, the total costs assigned to the departments were $59,100 for Mixing and $127,900 for Bottling.

The next step in the product costing process is to assign the departmental costs to the products. Assume that the manufacturing process at VitaDrink is labor intensive in the Mixing Department and machine intensive in the Bottling Department, and that manufacturing overhead is applied to products as follows:

Department	Manufacturing Overhead Application Base
Mixing	Direct labor hours
Bottling	Machine hours

During the month of July, 500 direct labor hours were worked in Mixing, and Bottling used 800 machine hours. The department manufacturing overhead rates based on actual costs for July, and the total product costs using departmental overhead rates, are calculated in the following tables:

Overhead costs per unit for July	VitaVeg	VitaFruit
Total department manufacturing overhead (direct department costs plus allocated costs).........	$59,100	$127,900
Quantity of overhead application base		
Direct labor hours................................	÷ 500	
Machine hours		÷ 800
Department manufacturing overhead rates.............	$118.20	$159.875
	Per direct labor hour	Per machine hour

| Total costs per unit for July using department rates | Unit Costs per Batch | |
	VitaVeg	VitaFruit
Direct materials	$125	$120
Direct labor...	110	30
Manufacturing overhead		
Mixing: 1 labor hr. × $118.20.............................	118*	
0.67 labor hrs. × $118.20		79*
Bottling: 1 machine hr. × $159.875	160*	
1.42 machine hrs. × $159.875		227*
Total costs...	$513	$456

* Rounded

Allocating factory overhead costs based on department rates (rather than on a plantwide rate of $125 per machine hour) causes a shift in costs from VitaVeg to VitaFruit because VitaVeg's overhead activity is incurred evenly in both Mixing and Bottling (1.00 hour each) while VitaFruit incurs more of its overhead activity in Bottling (1.42 hours versus 0.67 hour).

The per-unit costs with multiple allocations are substantially different from the per-unit costs when using plantwide rates and, in fact, show the cost of VitaVeg to be slightly below a competitor's bid of $525 that was offered to one of VitaDrink's customers. Based on the plantwide rate, the cost of $610 for VitaVeg was higher than the competitor's price.

By creating separate manufacturing overhead cost allocation pools, allocation bases, and overhead application rates for Mixing and Bottling, it is possible to recognize overhead cost differences in various products based on differences in Mixing Department labor hours used and Bottling Department machine hours used for each product. In most multiproduct manufacturing environments, this approach represents a cost system improvement over using a single, plantwide overhead rate, and it reduces the likelihood of cost cross-subsidization, which occurs when one product is assigned too much cost as a result of another being assigned too little cost. While department overhead rates may improve product costing results for many organizations, and in fact may be satisfactory, this method does not attempt to reflect the actual activities used in producing the different product.

Applying Overhead with Activity-Based Costing

An even more precise method of measuring the cost of products than plantwide or departmental rates is the activity-based costing method. As stated earlier, activity-based costing involves determining the cost of activities associated with a particular cost objective. ABC for product costing identifies and measures the cost of activities used to produce the various products and sums the cost of those activities to determine the cost of the products. The following Business Insight compares three key benefits regarding the accuracy of cost systems for ABC users and non-ABC users.

For VitaDrink, Mixing and Bottling have overhead costs of $59,100 and $127,900, respectively. The overhead rates for each department were determined in the last section as $118.20 and $159.875, respectively, per relevant hour of use. The easiest way to assign these costs to products is by using one base and one rate for all products going through a given process (e.g., mixing). However, different products typically use different amounts of resources from a given process and using the same base and overhead rate for all may distort the cost for some or all products.

Overhead costs in the Mixing and Bottling departments consisted of two types of costs: direct department costs and allocated costs from other support departments. Direct department overhead costs are costs that are incurred directly by the department such indirect labor, indirect materials, depreciation on equipment, supervisory wages, and so forth. Allocated support costs are costs allocated from other departments (specifically, engineering, support services, and building and grounds) that provide services to both Mixing and Bottling. VitaDrink's accountants determined that the *direct* department overhead costs in Mixing were driven primarily by labor hours, whereas *direct* department overhead costs in Bottling were driven primarily by machine hours. It was also determined that each component of engineering, support services, and building and grounds represents a separate activity cost pool, and that these costs should be assigned to the products based on specific cost drivers rather than a single cost driver for the entire department.

BUSINESS INSIGHT **Key Benefits of Using ABC**

A 2009 study of 348 manufacturing and service companies worldwide indicated that activity-based costing continues to provide strategic and operational benefits. Although the study showed that there has been a decline in ABC users since the 1990s, when it was first widely adopted, the following graphics from the study report support the conclusion that users of ABC have a higher level of confidence than non-ABC users that their cost system provides more accurate cost measurements.

Comparisons of ABC to Non-ABC Users on Three Key Benefits

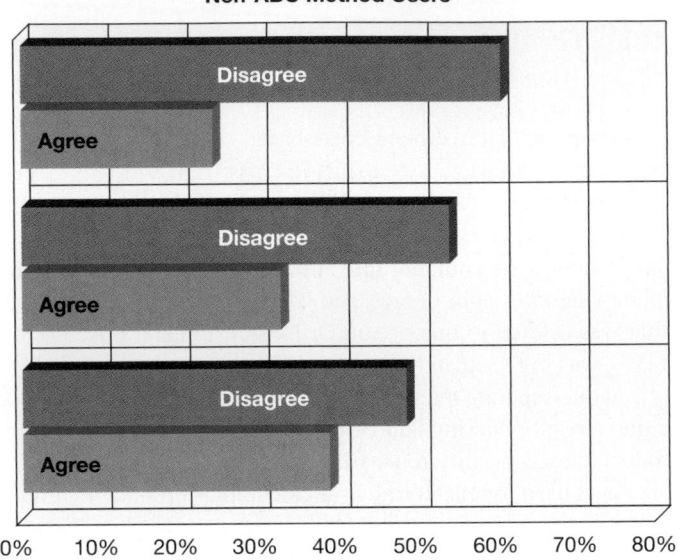

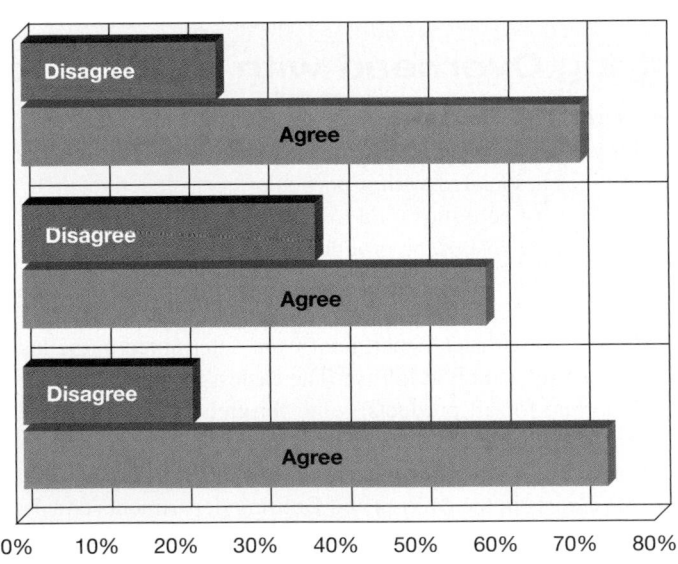

Source: William O. Stratton, Denis Desroches, Raef Lawson, and Toby Hatch, "Activity-Based Costing: Is It Still Relevant?" *Management Accounting Quarterly*, Spring 2009, Vol. 10, No. 3, pp. 31-40.

The following is a detailed analysis of overhead cost data for July's operations:

Overhead Activity	Total Activity Cost	Activity Cost Driver (number of)	Quantity of Activity	Unit Activity Rates
Direct departmental overhead costs				
Mixing	$ 40,000	Labor hours	500	$ 80.00
Bottling	90,000	Machine hours	800	112.50
Common overhead costs				
Support Services				
Receiving.	14,000	Purchase orders	100	140.00
Inventory control	13,000	Units produced.	632	20.57*
Engineering Resources				
Production setup.	12,000	Production runs	20	600.00
Engineering and testing	8,000	Machine hours	800	10.00
Building and Grounds				
Maintenance, machines	4,000	Machine hours	800	5.00
Depreciation, machines.	6,000	Units produced.	632	9.49*
Total	$187,000			

* Rounded

The amounts of activity attributed to VitaVeg and VitaFruit and the factory overhead cost per unit based on ABC costs are as follows:

	VitaVeg		VitaFruit	
Activity (cost per unit of driver activity)	Quantity of Activity	Cost of Activity	Quantity of Activity	Cost of Activity
Mixing ($80.00 per labor hour)	232	$18,560	268	$ 21,440
Bottling ($112.50 per machine hour)	174	19,575	626	70,425
Receiving ($140.00 per order)	40	5,600	60	8,400
Inventory control ($20.57 per unit produced)	232	4,772*	400	8,228
Production setup ($600.00 per run)	5	3,000	15	9,000
Engineering and testing ($10.00 per machine hour)	174	1,740	626	6,260
Maintenance, machines ($5.00 per machine hour)	174	870	626	3,130
Depreciation, machines ($9.49 per unit produced)	232	2,202*	400	3,796
Total factory overhead product cost.		$56,319		$130,679
Units produced.		÷ 232		÷ 400
Factory overhead cost per unit of product*		$ 243*		$327*
Direct materials cost per unit of product		125		120
Direct labor cost per unit of product		110		30
Total unit product cost using ABC		$ 478		$ 477

* Rounded

The following table summarizes the total product costs for VitaDrink's two products using the three different overhead cost assignment methods:

	VitaVeg	VitaFruit
Plantwide overhead rate.	$610	$400
Departmental overhead rates.	513	456
ABC	478	477

ABC product costing reveals a dramatically different cost picture. Using either a plantwide overhead rate or departmental rates, the VitaVeg drink is bearing more than its share of total overhead costs. Using either of these methods could lead the company into the very damaging strategy of abandoning the vegetable drink market. With an actual per-batch cost of $478, rather than $513 or $610, the company clearly has significant latitude to compete on price with other companies in this market and remain profitable. Obviously, the effect of adopting ABC is not always as significant as it was for VitaDrink in this example. However, even with less dramatic differences among the various cost methods, inaccurate costing can affect management's assessment of product profitability and its decisions regarding which products to continue to produce and which products to discontinue. Flawed product costing information can cause management mistakenly to decide to keep products that are losing money, while deciding to discontinue products that are profitable. Using a plantwide or departmental overhead allocation method could have led VitaDrink Management to shift its emphasis from the vegetable to the fruit drink market, a decision that could have been devastating to the company.

MANAGERIAL DECISION | **You are the Controller**

You have heard about companies that have adopted ABC and experienced significant differences in product costs compared with previous cost calculations using traditional costing methods. Consequently, you were surprised when your newly implemented ABC system provided product costs that were almost identical to those from the old costing system. You are, therefore, thinking about abandoning the ABC system, since it is quite costly to maintain. Should you abandon your ABC system? [Answer, p. 18-18]

MID-MODULE REVIEW

Slack Corporation has the following predicted indirect costs and cost drivers for 2012 for the given activity cost pools:

	Fabrication Department	Finishing Department	Cost Driver
Maintenance.............	$ 20,000	$10,000	Machine hours
Materials handling	30,000	15,000	Material moves
Machine setups	70,000	5,000	Machine setups
Inspections.............	—	25,000	Inspection hours
	$120,000	$55,000	

The following activity predictions were also made for the year:

	Fabrication Department	Finishing Department
Machine hours	10,000	5,000
Materials moves.......	3,000	1,500
Machine setups	700	50
Inspection hours.......	—	1,000

It is assumed that the cost per unit of activity for a given activity does not vary between departments.

Slack's president, Charles Slack, is trying to evaluate the company's product mix strategy regarding two of its five product models, ZX300 and SL500. The company has been using a plantwide overhead rate based on machine hours but is considering switching to either department rates or activity-based rates. The production manager has provided the following data for the production of a batch of 100 units for each of these models:

	ZX300	SL500
Direct materials cost.........	$12,000	$18,000
Direct labor cost.............	$5,000	$4,000
Machine hours (Fabrication)...	500	700
Machine hours (Finishing).....	200	100
Materials moves.............	30	50
Machine setups	5	9
Inspection hours.............	30	60

Required

a. Determine the cost of one unit each of ZX300 and SL500, assuming a plantwide overhead rate is used based on total machine hours.

b. Determine the cost of one unit of ZX300 and SL500, assuming department overhead rates are used. Overhead is assigned based on machine hours in both departments.

c. Determine the cost of one unit of ZX300 and SL500, assuming activity-based overhead rates are used for maintenance, materials handling, machine setup, and inspection activities.

d. Comment on the results of these cost calculations.

The solution is on page 18-35.

Limitations of ABC Illustration

Several limitations of the VitaDrink illustration should be mentioned. For the sake of simplicity, the example was limited to manufacturing cost considerations. A complete analysis would also require considerations of nonmanufacturing costs, such as marketing, distribution, and customer service, before a final determination of product profitability could be made. Finally, in calculating the activity cost per unit of activity, it is necessary to decide how to measure the total quantity of activity. For example, for VitaDrink, the receiving cost per purchase order was calculated as $140.00 based on the actual quantity of 100 purchase orders for the period. Alternatively, the receiving cost could have been calculated based on **practical capacity**, which is the maximum possible volume of activity, while allowing for normal downtime for repairs and maintenance. If the plant has a practical capacity to prepare 140 purchase orders per period, the cost per purchase order based on the practical capacity is $100 per purchase order, or $14,000 ÷ 140. Using this overhead rate in costing product, only $10,000 would have been assigned to the two products, which required only 100 purchase orders, and the remaining $4,000 for the 40 purchase orders of excess (or idle) capacity not used would be written off as an operating expense of the period as underapplied overhead. Practical capacity is generally regarded as better than actual capacity for calculating activity costs because it does not hide the cost of idle capacity within product costs, and it gives a truer cost of the activities used to produce the product.

Comparing Traditional and Activity-Based Costing

Procedurally, ABC is not a new method for assigning costs to cost objectives. Traditional costing systems have used a two-stage allocation model (similar to the ABC model) to assign costs to cost pools (such as departments) and subsequently assign those cost pools to products using an allocation base. In most traditional costing systems, overhead is assigned to one or more cost pools based on departments and functional characteristics (such as labor-related, machine-related, and space-related costs) and then reassigned to products using a general allocation base such as direct labor hours or machine hours. ABC is different in that it divides the overall manufacturing processes into activities. ABC accumulates costs in cost pools for the major activities and then assigns the costs of these activities to products or other cost objectives that benefit from these activities. *Conceptually,* ABC is different because of the way it views the operations of the company; *procedurally,* it uses a methodology that has been around for a long time.

The challenge in using ABC is specifying the model; that is, determining how many activity pools should be established for a given cost measurement purpose, which costs should be assigned to each activity pool, and the appropriate activity driver for each pool. Specifying the model also includes determining the resource cost drivers for assigning indirect resource costs to the various activity cost pools.

ABC IMPLEMENTATION ISSUES

LO4 Describe the implementation of an activity-based costing system.

The distortion in product costs for VitaDrink from using traditional cost systems based on plantwide or departmental rates, while hypothetical, is not uncommon. Studies have shown that distortions of this type occur regularly in traditional systems in which a significant variation exists in the volume and complexity of products and services produced.[3] Traditional systems tend to overcost high-volume, low-complexity products, and they tend to undercost low-volume, high-complexity products. These studies indicate that the typical amount of overcosting is up to 200 percent for high-volume products with low complexity and that the typical undercosting can be more than 1,000 percent for low-volume, highly complex products. In companies with a large number of different products, traditional costing can show that most products are profitable. After changing to ABC, however, these companies might find that 10 to 15 percent of the products are profitable while the remainder are unprofitable. Adopting ABC often leads to increased profits merely by changing the product mix to minimize the number of unprofitable products.

Most companies initially do not abandon their traditional cost system and move to a system that uses ABC for management and financial reporting purposes because financial statements must withstand the scrutiny of auditors and tax authorities. This scrutiny typically implies more demands on the cost accounting system for consistency, objectivity, and uniformity than required when the system is used only for management purposes. In addition, ABC systems must be built facility by facility rather than being embedded in a software program that can be used by all facilities within the company.[4] Often companies maintain traditional costing for external reporting purposes and ABC for pricing and other internal decision-making purposes.

Once an ABC system has been developed for a production facility, including an activities list (sometimes called an activities dictionary), identification of activity cost drivers, and calculation of cost per unit of driver activity, the activity costs of a current or proposed product can be readily determined. In ABC, as illustrated for VitaDrink, manufacturing a product is viewed simply as the combination of activities selected to make it; therefore, the activity cost of a product or service is the sum of the costs of those activities. This approach to viewing a product enables management to evaluate the importance of each of the activities consumed in making a product. Possibly some activities can be eliminated or a lower cost activity substituted for a more costly one without reducing the quality or performance of the product. In the 1980s, the Coca-Cola Company used ABC to determine that it was less costly—and thus, more profitable—to deliver soft drink concentrate to some fountain drink retailers (such as fast-food restaurants) in nonreturnable, disposable containers rather than in returnable stainless steel containers, which had been standard in the industry for many years.

Although an ABC system may be complex, it merely mirrors the complexity of an organization's design, manufacturing, and distribution systems. If a firm's products are diverse and its production and distribution procedures complex, the ABC system will also be complex; however, if its products are homogeneous and its production environment relatively simple, its ABC system should also be relatively simple. Even in highly complex manufacturing environments, ABC systems usually have no more than 10 to 20 cost pools. Many ABC experts in practice have observed that creating a large number of activity cost pools for a given costing application normally does not significantly improve cost accuracy above that of a smaller number of cost pools. As with any information system design, the costs of developing and maintaining the system must not exceed its benefits; hence, although adding more activity cost pools may result in some small amount of increased accuracy, it may be so small as not to be cost effective.

In addition to using ABC for product costing purposes, other important uses for ABC have also been found. One of the most useful applications for ABC discussed in the next section is in evaluating customer costs and distribution channel costs. Other applications include costing administrative functions such as processing accounts receivable or accounts payable; costing the process of hiring and training employees;

---

[3] Gary Cokins, Alan Stratton, and Jack Helbling, An ABC Manager's Primer (Montvale, NJ: Institute of Management Accountants, 1993).

[4] Robert S. Kaplan and Robin Cooper, *Cost and Effect* (Boston: Harvard Business School Press, 1998), p. 105.

and costing such menial tasks as processing a letter or copying a document. Any process, function, or activity performed in an organization, whether it is related to production, marketing and sales, finance and accounting, human resources, or even research and development, is a candidate for ABC analysis. In short, almost any cost objective that has more than an insignificant amount of indirect costs can be more effectively measured using ABC.

ABC AND CUSTOMER PROFITABILITY ANALYSIS

One of the most beneficial applications of activity-based costing is in the analysis of the profitability of customers. Companies that have a large number of diverse customers also usually have widely varied profits from serving those customers. Many companies never attempt to calculate the profit earned from individual customers. They merely assume that if they are selling products above their costs, and that overall the company is earning a profit, then each of the customers must be profitable. Unfortunately, the cost incurred to sell goods and services, and to provide service, to individual customers is not usually proportionate with the gross profits generated by those sales. Customers with high sales volume are not necessarily the most profitable. Profitability of individual customers depends on whether the gross profits from sales to those customers exceed the customer-specific costs of serving those customers. Some customers are simply more costly than others, and some may even be unprofitable, and the unprofitable customers are eating away at the total profits of the company. In an ideal world, only profitable customers would be retained, and unprofitable customers would be either converted to a profitable status or they would be dropped as customers.

LO5 Explain customer profitability analysis based on ABC.

Customer Profitability Profile

If a company knows the amount of profits (or losses) generated by each of its customers, a customer profitability profile can be prepared similar to the one illustrated in Exhibit 18.3.

This hypothetical company has 350 customers and has current total profits of $5 million, but only 200 of its customers are profitable. Cumulative profits reach $7.5 million when the 200th customer is added to the graph, but the 201st through the 350th customers cause cumulative profits to decline to $5 million because they are unprofitable. Once a company has profitability data on each of its customers (or categories of customers), only then can it proceed to try to convert them to profitability, or seek to terminate the relationship with those customers. Just as we saw that ABC provided a model for producing more accurate product cost data, ABC is also a valuable tool for generating customer profitability data.

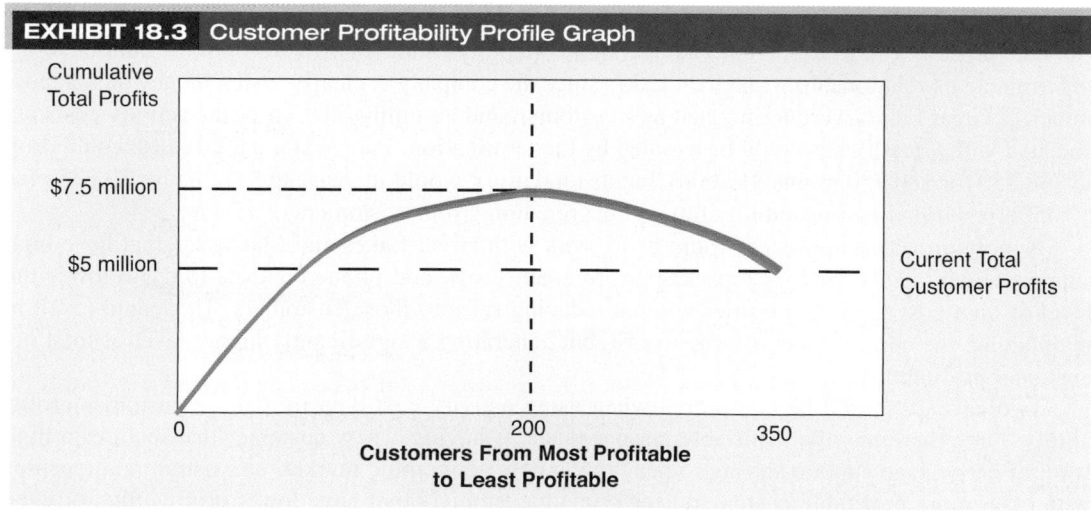

EXHIBIT 18.3 Customer Profitability Profile Graph

ABC Customer Profitability Analysis Illustrated

Pure Water Company is a "green" company located in the Midwest that manufactures and sells all-natural compounds for purifying water distributed through large public water systems. Rod James, the CEO and founder of Pure Water, personally developed the compounds using natural materials obtained from remote regions of the world. He knows that he has a product that is far superior to the traditional processes based on synthetic chemicals that have been used for generations to purify water. After five years in business, Pure Water has built a solid and growing customer base, but it has to invest significant time and expense servicing customers, especially those who have recently embraced its approach to water purification. Some customers require a lot of "hand-holding" with frequent visits and telephone calls, and they tend to purchase frequently in small amounts, often requiring repackaging. Other customers require little attention and support, and many of them purchase in large amounts once a year.

Although the company is making money, there is concern that profits could be higher if sales and other customer-related costs could be decreased. Pure Water's accountant, Mary West, has decided to conduct a customer profitability analysis using activity-based costing. As a first step, she determined that there were five primary activities related to serving customers: visits of customers by sales representatives, remote contacts (phone, email, fax), processing and shipping of customer orders, repackaging, and billing and collection. After extensive analysis, including numerous interviews and statistical analyses of activity and cost data, Mary determined the following cost drivers and cost per unit of activity for the five customer-related activities:

Activity	Activity Cost Driver	Cost per Unit of Driver Activity
Visits to customers.	Visits	$800
Remote contacts	Number of contacts	75
Processing & shipping	Customer orders	450
Repackaging	Number of requests	250
Billing & Collection	Invoices	90

After collecting activity driver data on each of these activities for its major customers, the accounting group prepared the customer activity cost and profitability analysis presented in Exhibit 18.4 for its five largest customers (in terms of sales dollars) in the order of greatest to least profit for the most recent year.

Since Pure Water is selling only one product to all of its customers, and has the same pricing policy for all customers, there is a constant 40% gross profit ratio across all customers, and the combined net profitability of these customers is 11.6% of sales. However, all customers are not equally profitable. The high level of support required by Manhattan and Great Lakes resulted in a net customer loss from sales to Great Lakes and only a 6.8% customer profitability ratio for Manhattan.

Armed with the information in the customer activity cost and profitability analysis, Pure Water can take proactive steps to increase its overall profitability ratio. An obvious option would be to try to terminate its relationship with Great Lakes since the company is clearly losing money on that customer. If Great Lakes were terminated as a customer, and assuming that all of the activity costs associated with Great Lakes could be avoided by the termination, Pure Water's total sales would drop to $68,750 (or $80,750 minus $12,000), but its total profit would increase to $11,785 (or $9,335 plus $2,450), resulting in a profitability ratio on the remaining four customers of 17.1%.

A more proactive approach would be to work with Great Lakes and Manhattan that have high support requirements, such as repackaging, frequent visits, and phone contacts to try to lower the level of high-cost support activities without reducing sales to those customers. This could result in maintaining the current level of gross profit, but generating a significantly higher level of total net customer profitability.

Two caveats should be considered when using activity cost data to manage customer profitability. First, there may be justifiable reasons (such as having a new customer that requires a high level of early-stage support, trying to penetrate a new geographic market, or existing relationships with other more profitable customers) for keeping customers that have lower profitability, or even customers that are not profitable. If so, these customers should be managed intensely to attempt to reduce the activities devoted to their support. Another caveat is that eliminating a customer may not immediately translate into an immediate reduction of activity costs. Some activity costs may not have a variable cost behavior pattern, and eliminating customers may merely create excess capacity

EXHIBIT 18.4 Pure Water Company

Customer Activity Cost and Profitability Analysis

	Seattle Water District	Manhattan Water Authority	Great Lakes Utility	Gulf Coast Utilities	Consoli- dated Water, Inc.	Total
Customer Activity Cost Analysis:						
Activity Cost Driver Data						
Visits to customers	3	5	4	1	1	
Remote contacts	5	7	8	2	3	
Processing & shipping	3	3	5	4	1	
Repackaging	0	2	3	0	0	
Billing & Collection.	3	3	5	4	1	
Customer Activity Cost						
Visits to customers	$ 2,400	$ 4,000	$ 3,200	$ 800	$ 800	
Remote contacts	375	525	600	150	225	
Processing & shipping	1,350	1,350	2,250	1,800	450	
Repackaging	0	500	750	0	0	
Billing & Collection.	270	270	450	360	90	
Total Activity Cost	$ 4,395	$ 6,645	$ 7,250	$ 3,110	$ 1,565	
Customer Profitability Analysis:						
Customer sales	$17,500	$20,000	$12,000	$15,000	$16,250	$80,750
Less cost of goods sold.	10,500	12,000	7,200	9,000	9,750	48,450
Gross profit on sales	7,000	8,000	4,800	6,000	6,500	32,300
Less activity costs	4,395	6,645	7,250	3,110	1,565	22,965
Customer profitability.	$ 2,605	$ 1,355	$ (2,450)	$2,890	$4,935	$ 9,335
Customer profitability ratio* . . .	14.9%	6.8%	(20.4%)	19.3%	30.4%	11.6%

* Customer profitability ÷ Sales

in the short term. Of course, as stated previously, activity-based costing views virtually all costs as variable in the longer term. As the following Business Insight following illustrates, despite these limitations, activity analysis of customer profitability analysis provides managers with valuable insights into the differences among customers that may otherwise not be apparent, and which can be used to enhance the overall performance of the organization.

BUSINESS INSIGHT | **Managing the Drivers of Customer Profitability**

The Chartered Institute of Management Accountants in the United Kingdom, along with the American Institute of CPAs and the Society of Management Accountants of Canada jointly published a Management Accounting Guideline titled "Customer Profitability Analysis." The following is a summary of that Guideline.

"The goal of business is not to improve customer or employee satisfaction at any cost, but rather to manage these relationships and the drivers of customer profitability to improve corporate performance. In order to do this, the company should identify the most and least profitable elements of its total customer base (and those in between), and manage these relationships accordingly. Customer profitability analysis (CPA) is the first stage in this process. Meeting the challenge of understanding the concept of customer profitability and conducting CPA requires a clear understanding of the causes of both revenues and costs. Strategic cost management tools such as activity-based costing (ABC) facilitate this understanding. The two models rely on the identification, measurement and understanding of the drivers and causal relationships among employee satisfaction, customer satisfaction, customer profitability and corporate profitability. Only with the specification and measurement of these relationships can the costs and revenues related to improving corporate performance be managed properly."

Source: Liz Murby, "Customer Profitability," *Financial Management,* December 2007, p. 33.

ACTIVITY-BASED MANAGEMENT

LO6 Explain the difference between ABC and activity-based management.

Activity-based costing has been highly touted as a technique for improving the measurement of the cost and profitability of products, customers, and other cost objectives. In the early development of ABC, it was discovered that a by-product of accurately measuring the cost using ABC is that management invariably gains a much better understanding of the processes and activities that are used to create cost objectives, such as products. Although ABC could be justified on the basis of its value as a tool in helping produce more accurate cost measurements for various cost objectives, its greatest potential value may be in its by-products. The access to ABC data enables managers to engage in **activity-based management (ABM),** defined as the identification and selection of activities to maximize the value of the activities while minimizing their cost from the perspective of the final consumer. In other words, ABM is concerned with how to efficiently and effectively manage activities and processes to provide value to the final consumer.

Defining processes and identifying key activities helps management better understand the business and to evaluate whether activities being performed add value to the customer. ABM focuses managerial attention on what is most important among the activities performed to create value for customers.

A helpful analogy in understanding what ABC can do for a company is to compare a company's operations with a large retail store, such as a Home Depot store. In a Home Depot store there is a clearly marked price on each of the tens of thousands of individual items that customers may decide to purchase. Similarly, every activity that takes place in any organization has a cost that can be determined and that management can use to make a judgment about the activity's value. In an ideal world, a manager could walk through the business and evaluate the cost of every activity being performed—maybe thousands of different activities—and then decide which ones are worth the cost and which ones are not adding value. Since generating ABC data has a cost, management must decide which ABC data are likely to be useful and cost beneficial. Our discussion here is only an introduction to activity-based costing and some of its applications. As the following Research Insight points out, over the past quarter of a century, ABC has matured well beyond merely accurately measuring cost of products and customers. More advanced topics such as those shown in the graphic are covered in advanced managerial accounting (or cost accounting) courses.

RESEARCH INSIGHT   The Maturing of Activity-Based Costing

One of the leading thinkers and authors on the topic of activity-based costing over the past 25 years has been Peter B. B. Turney. He recently traced the evolution of ABC within the context of a product life cycle showing how ABC functionality has expanded since it was first introduced in the 1980s.[7] As this graphic shows, ABC is now in its fourth generation, where it has become "an integral part of business performance management solutions, including profitability management, performance measurement, financial management, sustainability, and human capital management." In its current state of development, a single ABC model can support a number of needs, including historical cost measurement, resource planning, performance measurement, and other analyses.

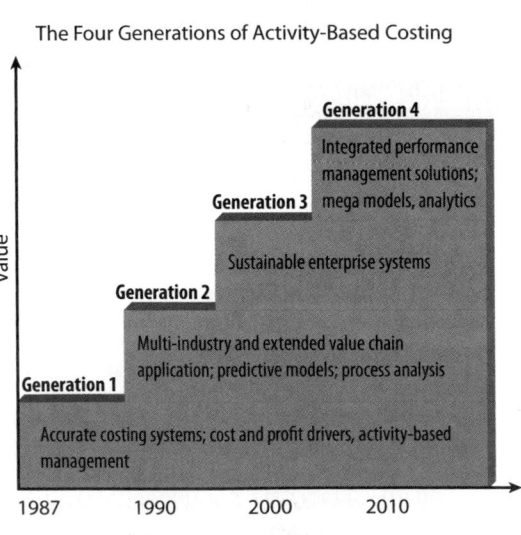

The Four Generations of Activity-Based Costing

Source: Peter B. B. Turney, "Activity-Based Costing: An Emerging Foundation for Performance Management," *Cost Management*, July/August 2010, pp. 33-42.

MODULE-END REVIEW

Customer Profitability Analysis

Systems Technology, Inc. (STI) is a small systems design and implementation firm that serves five different types of customers. STI's design and installation projects are fairly standardized and routine; hence, the pricing is also standardized for all customers. While the company is profitable overall, the CFO thinks the net margins should be higher. She is concerned that customer support costs are eating up some of the margin and has decided to do a customer profitability analysis based on the five different types of customers to see if some of the customer groups may actually be less profitable than others. The following data for the most recent period have been collected to support the analysis.

Support Activity		Driver	Cost per Driver Unit
A.	Minor systems maintenance	Hours on jobs	$160
B.	Visits to customer	Number of visits	$300
C.	Communication	Number of calls	$ 50

Customer Group	Activity A	Activity B	Activity C	Profit Before Support Costs
1	69	25	128	$80,000
2	141	42	205	85,000
3	74	19	99	83,000
4	61	28	106	90,000
5	136	39	189	78,000

Required

a. Calculate the customer profitability for each customer group taking into account the support activity required for each customer group.

b. Comment on the usefulness of this type of analysis. What reasonable actions might Roland take as a result of this analysis?

The solution is on page 18-37.

GUIDANCE ANSWER

MANAGERIAL DECISION	You are the Controller

It probably is not the right decision to abandon the ABC system because there are many benefits to using ABC other than just calculating product costs. Indeed, in cases where companies produce multiple products that are fairly homogeneous in terms of the use of resources, ABC may not produce more accurate costs than traditional methods; however, there are many uses of ABC information beyond just calculating the cost of products. Having detailed information about activities and their costs can significantly improve the management of those activities. Identifying key activities and measuring their costs often causes companies to seek more efficient processes, possibly considering outsourcing activities that are currently performed internally, or even looking for ways to eliminate activities altogether. Activity cost information can also be used to identify best practices within an organization, or to benchmark internal activity costs with other organizations.

DISCUSSION QUESTIONS

Q18-1. Summarize the concepts underlying activity-based costing in two sentences.

Q18-2. What steps are required to implement the two-stage activity-based costing model?

Q18-3. Define activity cost pool, activity cost driver, and cost per unit of activity.

Q18-4. Name two possible activity cost drivers for each of the following activities: maintenance, materials movement, machine setup, inspection, materials purchases, and customer service.

Q18-5. What is the premise of activity-based costing for product costing purposes?

Q18-6. In what ways does ABC product costing differ from traditional product cost methods?

Q18-7. Explain why ABC often reveals existing product cost cross-subsidization problems.

Q18-8. How can ABC be used to improve customer profitability analysis?

Q18-9. Explain activity-based management and how it differs from activity-based costing.

Assignments with the ✅ in the margin are available in an online homework system.
See the Preface of the book for details.

MINI EXERCISES

M18-10. Activities and Cost Drivers (LO2)

For each of the following activities, select the most appropriate cost driver. Each cost driver may be used only once.

Activity	Cost Driver
1. Pay vendors	*a.* Number of different kinds of raw materials
2. Evaluate vendors	*b.* Number of classes offered
3. Inspect raw materials	*c.* Number of tables
4. Plan for purchases of raw materials	*d.* Number of employees
5. Packaging	*e.* Number of operating hours
6. Supervision	*f.* Number of units of raw materials received
7. Employee training	*g.* Number of moves
8. Clean tables	*h.* Number of vendors
9. Machine maintenance	*i.* Number of checks issued
10. Move in-process product from one work station to the next	*j.* Number of customer orders

M18-11. Developing a List of Activities for Baggage Handling at an Airport (LO2)

As part of a continuous improvement program, you have been asked to determine the activities involved in the baggage-handling process of a major airline at one of the airline's hubs. Prior to conducting observations and interviews, you decide that a list of possible activities would help you to better observe key activities and ask meaningful questions.

Required

For incoming aircraft only, develop a sequential list of baggage-handling activities. Your list should contain between 8 and 10 activities.

M18-12. Stage 1 ABC at a College: Assigning Costs to Activities (LO2)

An economics professor at Prince Town University devotes 50 percent of her time to teaching, 35 percent of her time to research and writing, and 15 percent of her time to service activities such as committee work and student advising. The professor teaches two semesters per year. During each semester, she teaches one section of an introductory economics course (with a maximum enrollment of 50 students each) and one section of a graduate economics course (with a maximum enrollment of 30 students). Including course preparation, classroom instruction, and appointments with students, each course requires an equal amount of time. The economics professor is paid $135,000 per year.

Required

Determine the activity cost of instruction per student in both the introductory and the graduate economics courses.

M18-13. Stage 1 ABC for a Machine Shop: Assigning Costs to Activities (LO2)

As the chief engineer of a small fabrication shop, Brenda Tolliver refers to herself as a "jack-of-all-trades." When an order for a new product comes in, Brenda must do the following:

1. Design the product to meet customer requirements.
2. Prepare a bill of materials (a list of materials required to produce the product).
3. Prepare an operations list (a sequential list of the steps involved in manufacturing the product).

Each time the foundry manufactures a batch of the product, Brenda must perform these activities:

1. Schedule the job.
2. Supervise the setup of machines that will work on the job.
3. Inspect the first unit produced to verify that it meets specifications.

Brenda supervises the production employees who perform the actual work on individual units of product. She is also responsible for employee training, ensuring that production facilities are in proper operating condition, and attending professional meetings. Brenda's estimates (in percent) of time spent on each of these activities last year are as follows:

Designing product	12%
Preparing bills of materials.	5
Preparing operations lists.	12
Scheduling jobs	15
Supervising setups.	5
Inspecting first units	2
Supervising production	20
Training employees.	18
Maintaining facility	7
Attending professional meetings	4
	100%

Required
Assuming Brenda Tolliver's salary is $132,000 per year, determine the dollar amount of her salary assigned to unit-, batch-, product-, and facility-level activities. (You may need to review Module 14 before answering this question.)

M18-14. Stage 2 ABC for a Wholesale Company (LO2)
Information is presented for the activity costs of Oxford Wholesale Company:

Activity	Cost per Unit of Activity Driver
Customer relations.	$100.00 per customer per month
Selling.	0.06 per sales dollar
Accounting	5.00 per order
Warehousing.	0.50 per unit shipped
Packing.	0.25 per unit shipped
Shipping	0.20 per pound shipped

The following information pertains to Oxford Wholesale Company's activities in Massachusetts for the month of March 2012:

Number of orders	235
Sales revenue.	$122,200
Cost of goods sold.	$68,940
Number of customers.	25
Units shipped	4,700
Pounds shipped	70,500

Required
Determine the profitability of sales in Massachusetts for March 2012.

M18-15. Stage 2 ABC for Manufacturing: Reassigning Costs to Cost Objectives (LO2)
National Technology, LTD. has developed the following activity cost information for its manufacturing activities:

Activity	Activity Cost
Machine setup	$60.00 per batch
Movement	15.00 per batch move
	0.10 per pound
Drilling.	3.00 per hole
Welding.	4.00 per inch
Shaping	25.00 per hour
Assembly	18.00 per hour
Inspection.	2.00 per unit

Filling an order for a batch of 50 fireplace inserts that weighed 150 pounds each required the following:
- Three batch moves
- Two sets of inspections
- Drilling five holes in each unit
- Completing 80 inches of welds on each unit
- Thirty minutes of shaping for each unit
- One hour of assembly per unit

Required
Determine the activity cost of converting the raw materials into 50 fireplace inserts.

 M18-16. Two-Stage ABC for Manufacturing (LO2)
Detroit Foundry, a large manufacturer of heavy equipment components, has determined the following activity cost pools and cost driver levels for the year:

Activity Cost Pool	Activity Cost	Activity Cost Driver
Machine setup	$600,000	12,000 setup hours
Material handling	120,000	2,000 tons of materials
Machine operation	500,000	10,000 machine hours

The following data are for the production of single batches of two products, C23 Cams and U2 Shafts during the month of August:

	C23 Cams	U2 Shafts
Units produced.	500	300
Machine hours	4	5
Direct labor hours.	200	400
Direct labor cost.	$5,000	$10,000
Direct materials cost.	$30,000	$20,000
Tons of materials	12.5	8
Setup hours	3	7

Required
Determine the unit costs of C23 Cams and U2 Shafts using ABC.

M18-17. Two-Stage ABC for Manufacturing (LO2)
Assume Sherwin-Williams Company, a large paint manufacturer, has determined the following activity cost pools and cost driver levels for the latest period:

Activity Cost Pool	Activity Cost	Activity Cost Driver
Machine setup	$950,000	2,500 setup hours
Material handling	820,000	5,000 materials moves
Machine operation	200,000	20,000 machine hours

The following data are for the production of single batches of two products, Mirlite and Subdue:

	Mirlite	Subdue
Gallons produced.	50,000	30,000
Direct labor hours.	400	250
Machine hours	800	250
Direct labor cost.	$10,000	$7,500
Direct materials cost.	$350,000	$150,000
Setup hours	15	12
Material moves.	60	35

Required

Determine the batch and unit costs per gallon of Mirlite and Subdue using ABC.

M18-18. Customer Profitability Analysis (LO5)

HyStandard Services, Inc. provides residential painting services for three home building companies, Alpine, Blue Ridge, and Pineola, and it uses a job costing system for determining the costs for completing each job. The job cost system does not capture any cost incurred by HyStandard for return touchups and refinishes after the homeowner occupies the home. HyStandard paints each house on a square footage contract price, which includes painting as well as all refinishes and touchups required after the homes are occupied. Each year, the company generates about one-third of its total revenues and gross profits from each of the three builders. The HyStandard owner has observed that the builders, however, require substantially different levels of support following the completion of jobs. The following data have been gathered:

Support Activity	Driver	Cost per Driver Unit
Major refinishes	Hours on jobs	$ 60
Touchups	Number of visits	$100
Communication	Number of calls	$ 40

Builder	Major Refinishes	Touchups	Communication
Alpine	80	150	360
Blue Ridge	35	110	205
Pineola	42	115	190

Required

Assuming that each of the three customers produces gross profits of $100,000, calculate the profitability from each builder after taking into account the support activity required for each builder.

EXERCISES

E18-19. Two-Stage ABC for Manufacturing (LO2)

Merlot Company has determined its activity cost pools and cost drivers to be the following:

Cost pools

Setup	$ 56,000
Material handling	12,800
Machine operation.	240,000
Packing	60,000
Total indirect manufacturing costs.	$368,800

Cost drivers

Setups	350
Material moves.	640
Machine hours	20,000
Packing orders.	1,200

One product made by Merlot, metal casements, used the following activities during the period to produce 500 units:

Setups	20
Material moves.....................................	80
Machine hours	1,900
Packing orders	150

Required

a. Calculate the cost per unit of activity for each activity cost pool for Merlot Company.

b. Calculate the manufacturing overhead cost per metal casement manufactured during the period.

E18-20. Calculating Manufacturing Overhead Rates   (LO3)

Glassman Company, accumulated the following data for 2012:

Milling Department manufacturing overhead.............................	$344,000
Finishing Department manufacturing overhead..........................	$120,000
Machine hours used	
Milling Department	10,000 hours
Finishing Department	2,000 hours
Labor hours used	
Milling Department	1,000 hours
Finishing Department	1,000 hours

Required

a. Calculate the plantwide manufacturing overhead rate using machine hours as the allocation base.

b. Calculate the plantwide manufacturing overhead rate using direct labor hours as the allocation base.

c. Calculate department overhead rates using machine hours in Milling and direct labor hours in Finishing as the allocation bases.

d. Calculate department overhead rates using direct labor hours in Milling and machine hours in Finishing as the allocation bases.

e. Which of these allocation systems seems to be the most appropriate? Explain.

E18-21. Calculating Activity-Based Costing Overhead Rates   (LO2, 3, 4)

Assume that manufacturing overhead for Glassman Company in the previous exercise consisted of the following activities and costs:

Setup (1,000 setup hours)	$144,000
Production scheduling (400 batches)............	60,000
Production engineering (60 change orders)........	120,000
Supervision (2,000 direct labor hours)	56,000
Machine maintenance (12,000 machine hours)	84,000
Total activity costs	$464,000

The following additional data were provided for Job 845:

Direct materials costs.........................	$7,000
Direct labor cost (5 Milling direct labor hours;	
35 Finishing direct labor hours)	$1,000
Setup hours	5 hours
Production scheduling	1 batch
Machine hours used (25 Milling machine hours;	
5 Finishing machine hours)....................	30 hours
Production engineering	3 change orders

Required

a. Calculate the cost per unit of activity driver for each activity cost category.

b. Calculate the cost of Job 845 using ABC to assign the overhead costs.

c. Calculate the cost of Job 845 using the plantwide overhead rate based on machine hours calculated in the previous exercise.

d. Calculate the cost of Job 845 using a machine hour departmental overhead rate for the Milling Department and a direct labor hour overhead rate for the Finishing Department (see E18-20).

E18-22. Activity-Based Costing and Conventional Costs Compared (LO2, 3, 4)

Hickory Grill Company manufactures two types of cooking grills: the Gas Cooker and the Charcoal Smoker. The Cooker is a premium product sold in upscale outdoor shops; the Smoker is sold in major discount stores. Following is information pertaining to the manufacturing costs for the current month.

	Gas Cooker	Charcoal Smoker
Units.....................	1,000	5,000
Number of batches............	50	10
Number of batch moves........	80	20
Direct materials	$40,000	$100,000
Direct labor.................	$20,000	$25,000

Manufacturing overhead follows:

Activity	Cost	Cost Driver
Materials acquisition and inspection	$30,800	Amount of direct materials cost
Materials movement...................	16,200	Number of batch moves
Scheduling	36,000	Number of batches
	$83,000	

Required

a. Determine the total and per-unit costs of manufacturing the Gas Cooker and Charcoal Smoker for the month, assuming all manufacturing overhead is assigned on the basis of direct labor dollars.

b. Determine the total and per-unit costs of manufacturing the Gas Cooker and Charcoal Smoker for the month, assuming manufacturing overhead is assigned using activity-based costing.

E18-23. Activity-Based Costing Versus Conventional Costing (LO3, 4)

Refer to the previous exercise in E18-22 for Hickory Grill.

Required

a. Comment on the differences between the solutions to requirements (a) and (b). Which is more accurate? What errors might managers make if all manufacturing overhead costs are assigned on the basis of direct labor dollars?

b. Comment on the adequacy of the preceding data to meet management's needs

E18-24. Traditional Product Costing versus Activity-Based Costing (LO2, 3, 4)

Assume that Panasonic Company has determined its estimated total manufacturing overhead cost for one of its plants to be $204,000, consisting of the following activity cost pools for the current month:

Panasonic Company

Activity Centers	Activity Costs	Cost Drivers	Activity Level
Assembly setups	$ 45,000	Setup hours..............	1,500
Materials handling	15,000	Number of moves..........	300
Assembly	120,000	Assembly hours...........	12,000
Maintenance............	24,000	Maintenance hours........	1,200
Total	$204,000		

Total direct labor hours used during the month were 8,000. Panasonic produces many different electronic products, including the following two products produced during the current month:

	Model X301	Model Z205
Units produced..............	1,000	1,000
Direct materials costs.........	$15,000	$15,000
Direct labor costs............	$12,500	$12,500
Direct labor hours............	500	500
Setup hours	50	100
Materials moves.............	25	50
Assembly hours	800	800
Maintenance hours...........	10	40

Required

a. Calculate the total per-unit cost of each model using direct labor hours to assign manufacturing overhead to products.

b. Calculate the total per-unit cost of each model using activity-based costing to assign manufacturing overhead to products.

c. Comment on the accuracy of the two methods for determining product costs.

d. Discuss some of the strategic implications of your answers to the previous requirements.

E18-25. Traditional Product Costing versus Activity-Based Costing (LO2, 3, 4)

High Country Outfitters, Inc., makes backpacks for large sporting goods chains that are sold under the customers' store brand names. The accounting department has identified the following overhead costs and cost drivers for next year:

Overhead Item	Expected Costs	Cost Driver	Maximum Quantity
Setup costs	$ 936,000	Number of setups............	7,200
Ordering costs	240,000	Number of orders	60,000
Maintenance.........	1,200,000	Number of machine hours	80,000
Power..............	120,000	Number of kilowatt hours......	600,000

Total predicted direct labor hours for next year is 60,000. The following data are for two recently completed jobs:

	Job 201	Job 202
Cost of direct materials	$13,500	$15,000
Cost of direct labor................	$19,125	$71,250
Number of units completed	1,125	915
Number of direct labor hours........	270	330
Number of setups.................	18	22
Number of orders.................	24	45
Number of machine hours	540	450
Number of kilowatt hours...........	270	360

Required

a. Determine the unit cost for each job using a traditional plantwide overhead rate based on direct labor hours.

b. Determine the unit cost for each job using ABC. (Round answers to two decimal places.)

c. As the manager of High Country, is there additional information that you would want to help you evaluate the pricing and profitability of Jobs 201 and 202?

d. Assuming the company has been using the method required in part a, how should management react to the findings in part b.

E18-26. Customer Profitability Analysis (LO5, 6)

Gonalong, Inc., has 10 customers that account for all of its $4,500,000 of net income. Its activity-based costing system is able to assign all costs, except for $650,000 of general administrative costs, to key activities incurred in connection with serving its customers. A customer profitability analysis based on activity costing produced the following customer profits and losses:

Customer #1	$346,000
#2	624,000
#3	(257,000)
#4	969,000
#5	1,040,000
#6	872,000
#7	628,000
#8	322,000
#9	(105,000)
#10	711,000
Total	$5,150,000

Required

Prepare a customer profitability profile like the one in Exhibit 18.3.

E18-27. Customer Profitability Analysis (LO5)

Refer to the previous exercise E18-26 for Gonalong, Inc.

Required

a. If Gonalong were to notify customers 3 and 9 that it will no longer be able to provide them services in the future, will that increase company profits by $362,000? Why or why not?

b. What is the primary benefit of preparing a customer profitability analysis?

PROBLEMS

P18-28. Two-Stage ABC for Manufacturing with ABC Variances (LO2, 3, 4)

Montreat Manufacturing has developed the following activity cost pool information for its 2012 manufacturing activities:

	Budgeted Activity Cost	Activity Cost Driver at Practical Capacity
Purchasing and materials handling	$675,000	900,000 kilograms
Setup	700,000	1,120 setups
Machine operations	954,000	12,000 hours
First unit inspection	50,000	1,000 batches
Packaging	250,000	312,500 units

Actual 2012 production information is as follows:

	Standard Product A	Standard Product B	Specialty Products
Units	150,000	100,000	50,000
Batches	100	80	600
Setups*	300	160	900
Machine operations (hours)	6,000	3,000	2,000
Kilograms of raw materials	400,000	300,000	200,000
Direct materials costs	$900,000	$600,000	$820,000

* Some products require setups on two or more machines.

Required

a. Determine the unit cost of each product for Montreat Manufacturing.

b. Explain why the unit cost of the specialty products is so much higher than the unit cost of Standard Product A or Standard Product B.

P18-29.   ABC—A Service Application   (LO2, 3, 4)

Grand Haven is a senior living community that offers a full range of services including independent living, assisted living, and skilled nursing care. The assisted living division provides residential space, meals, and medical services (MS) to its residents. The current costing system adds the cost of all of these services (space, meals, and MS) and divides by total resident days to get a cost per resident day for each month. Recognizing that MS tends to vary significantly among the residents, Grand Haven's accountant recommended that an ABC system be designed to calculate more accurately the cost of MS provided to residents. She decided that residents should be classified into four categories (A, B, C, D) based on the level of services received, with group A representing the lowest level of service and D representing the highest level of service. Two cost drivers being considered for measuring MS costs are number of assistance calls and number of assistant contacts. A contact is registered each time an assistance professional provides medical services or aid to a resident. The accountant has gathered the following data for the most recent annual period:

Resident Classification	Annual Resident Days	Annual Assistance Hours	Number of Assistance Contacts
A	8,760	15,000	60,000
B	6,570	20,000	52,000
C	4,380	22,500	52,000
D	2,190	32,500	52,000
	21,900	90,000	216,000

Other data:

Total cost of medical services for the period.................	$2,500,000
Total cost of meals and residential space	$1,642,500

Required (round answers to the nearest dollar):

a. Determine the ABC cost of a resident day for each category of residents using assistance hours as the cost driver.

b. Determine the ABC cost of a resident day for each category of residents using assistance contacts as the cost driver.

c. Which cost driver do you think provides the more accurate measure of the cost per day for a Grand Haven resident?

P18-30.   ABC Costing for a Service Organization   (LO2, 3, 4)

Fairfield Mortgage Company is a full-service residential mortgage company in the Atlanta area that operates in a very competitive market. The CEO, Richard Sissom, is concerned about operating costs associated with processing mortgage applications and has decided to install an ABC costing system to help him get a handle on costs. Although labor hours seem to be the primary driver of the cost of processing a new mortgage, the labor cost for the different activities involved in processing new loans varies widely. The Accounting Department has provided the following data for the company's five major cost pools for 2012:

Activity Cost Pools		Activity Drivers	
Taking customer applications.....	$ 300,000	Time—assistant managers.......	12,000 hours
Conducting credit investigations ..	450,000	Time—credit managers	16,500 hours
Underwriting.................	525,000	Time—Underwriting Department ..	10,000 hours
Preparing loan packages	200,000	Time—Processing Department ...	8,000 hours
Closing loans	600,000	Time—Legal Department hours...	6,000 hours
	$2,075,000		52,500 hours

During 2012, the company processed and issued 5,000 new mortgages, two of which are summarized here with regard to activities used to process the mortgages:

	Loan 5066	Loan 5429
Application processing hours.	1.50	2.75
Credit investigating hours.	4.00	3.00
Underwriting hours.	2.50	4.75
Processing hours	3.50	3.00
Legal processing hours	1.50	1.50
Total hours	13.00	15.00

Required

a. Determine the cost per unit of activity for each activity cost pool.

b. Determine the cost of processing loans 5066 and 5429.

c. Determine the cost of preparing loans 5066 and 5429 assuming that an average cost per hour for all activities is used.

d. Compare and discuss your answers to requirements (b) and (c).

P18-31. Activity-Based Costing in a Service Organization (LO2, 3, 4, 6)

Red River Banking Company has ten automatic teller machines (ATMs) spread throughout the city maintained by the ATM Department. You have been assigned the task of determining the cost of operating each machine. Management will use the information you develop, along with other information pertaining to the volume and type of transactions at each machine, to evaluate the desirability of continuing to operate each machine and/or changing security arrangements for a particular machine.

The ATM Department consists of a total of six employees: a supervisor, a head cashier, two associate cashiers, and two maintenance personnel. The associate cashiers make between two and four daily trips to each machine to collect and replenish cash and to replenish supplies, deposit tickets, and so forth. Each machine contains a small computer that automatically summarizes and reports transactions to the head cashier. The head cashier reconciles the activities of the two associate cashiers to the computerized reports. The supervisor, who does not handle cash, reviews the reconciliation. When an automatic teller's computer, a customer, or a cashier reports a problem, the two maintenance employees and one cashier are dispatched immediately. The cashier removes all cash and transaction records, and the maintenance employees repair the machine.

Maintenance employees spend all of their time on maintenance-related activities. The associate cashiers spend approximately 50 percent of their time on maintenance-related activities and 50 percent on daily trips. The head cashier's time is divided, with 75 percent directly related to daily trips to each machine and 25 percent related to supervising cashiers on maintenance calls. The supervisor devotes 20 percent of the time to daily trips to each machine and 80 percent to the equal supervision of each employee. Cost information for a recent month follows:

Salaries	
Supervisor	$ 4,000
Head cashier	3,000
Other ($1,800 each)	7,200
Lease and operating costs	
Cashiers' service vehicle	1,200
Maintenance service vehicle	1,400
Office rent and utilities	2,300
Machine lease, space rent, and utilities ($1,500 each).	15,000
Total	$34,100

Related monthly activity information for this month follows:

Machine	Routine Trips	Maintenance Hours
1.	30	5
2.	90	17
3.	60	15
4.	60	30
5.	120	15
6.	30	10
7.	90	25
8.	120	5
9.	60	20
10.	60	18
Total	720	160

Additional information follows:

- The office is centrally located with about equal travel time to each machine.
- Maintenance hours include travel time.
- The cashiers' service vehicle is used exclusively for routine visits.
- The office space is divided equally between the supervisor and the head cashier.

Required

a. Determine the monthly operating costs of machines 7 and 8 when cost assignments are based on the number of machines.

b. Determine the activity cost of a routine trip and a maintenance hour for the month given. Round answers to the nearest cent.

c. Determine the operating costs assigned and reassigned to machines 7 and 8 when activity-based costing is used.

d. How can ABC cost information be used by Red River Banking Company to improve the overall management of monthly operating costs?

P18-32.   Product Costing: Plantwide Overhead versus Activity-Based Costing   (LO3, 4)

LaMesa produces machine parts as a contract provider for a large manufacturing company. LaMesa produces two particular parts, shafts and gears. The competition is keen among contract producers, and LeMesa's top management realizes how vulnerable its market is to cost-cutting competitors. Hence, having a very accurate understanding of costs is important to LeMesa's survival.

LeMesa's president, Jose Rodriguez, has observed that the company's current cost to produce shafts is $21.35, and the current cost to produce gears is $12.36. He indicated to the controller that he suspects some problems with the cost system because LaMesa is suddenly experiencing extraordinary competition on shafts, but it seems to have a virtual corner on the gears market. He is even considering dropping the shaft line and converting the company to a one-product manufacturer of gears. He asked the controller, Felix Bernhardt, to conduct a thorough cost study and to consider whether changes in the cost system are necessary. The controller collected the following data about the company's costs and various manufacturing activities for the most recent month:

	Shafts	Gears
Production units.	50,000	10,500
Selling price	$31.86	$24
Overhead per unit (based on direct labor hours)	$12.82	$6.10
Materials and direct labor cost per unit	$8.53	$6.26
Number of production runs	10	20
Number of purchasing and receiving orders processed	40	100
Number of machine hours	12,750	6,000
Number of direct labor hours	25,000	2,500
Number of engineering hours.	5,000	5,000
Number of material moves	50	40

The controller was able to summarize the company's total manufacturing overhead into the following pools:

Setup costs	$ 30,000
Machine costs	175,000
Purchasing and receiving costs	210,000
Engineering costs.	200,000
Materials handling costs	90,000
Total	$705,000

Required

a. Calculate LaMesa's current plantwide overhead rate based on direct labor hours.

b. Verify LaMesa's calculation of overhead cost per unit of $12.82 for shafts and $6.10 for gears.

c. Calculate the manufacturing overhead cost per unit for shafts and gears using activity-based costing, assuming each of the five cost pools represents a separate activity pool. Use the most appropriate activity driver for assigning activity costs to the two products.

d. Comment on LaMesa's current cost system and the reason the company is facing fierce competition for shafts but little competition for gears.

P18-33. Customer Profitability Analysis (LO2, 5, 6)

Roger's Aeronautics, LTD, is a British aeronautics subcontract company that designs and manufactures electronic control systems for commercial airlines. The vast majority of all commercial aircraft are manufactured by Boeing in the U.S. and Airbus in Europe; however, there is a relatively small group of companies that manufacture narrow-body commercial jets. Assume for this exercise that Roger's does contract work for the two major manufacturers plus three companies in the second tier.

Because competition is intense in the industry, Roger's has always operated on a fairly thin 20% gross profit margin; hence, it is crucial that it manage non-manufacturing overhead costs effectively in order to achieve an acceptable net profit margin. With declining profit margins in recent years, Roger's Aeronautics' CEO, Len Rogers, has become concerned that the cost of obtaining contracts and maintaining relations with its five major customers may be getting out of hand. You have been hired to conduct a customer profitability analysis.

Roger's Aeronautics' non-manufacturing overhead consists of $2.5 million of general and administrative (G&A) expense, (including, among other expenses, the CEO's salary and bonus and the cost of operating the company's corporate jet) and selling and customer support expenses of $3 million (including 5% sales commissions and $1,050,000 of additional costs).

The accounting staff determined that the $1,050,000 of additional selling and customer support expenses related to the following four activity cost pools:

Activity	Activity Cost Driver	Cost per Unit of Activity
1. Sales visits	Number of visit days	$1,200
2. Product adjustments	Number of adjustments	1,500
3. Phone and email contacts	Number of calls/contacts	150
4. Promotion and entertainment events.	Number of events	1,500

Financial and activity data on the five customers follows (Sales and Gross Profit data in millions):

Customer	Sales	Gross Profit	Quantity of Sales and Support Activity			
			Activity 1	Activity 2	Activity 3	Activity 4
#1	$17	$3.4	106	23	220	82
#2	12	2.4	130	36	354	66
#3	3	0.6	52	10	180	74
#4	4	0.8	34	6	138	18
#5	3	0.6	16	5	104	10
	$39	$7.8	338	80	996	250

In addition to the above, the sales staff used the corporate jet at a cost of $800 per hour for trips to customers as follows:

Customer #1	24 hours
Customer #2	36 hours
Customer #3	5 hours
Customer #4	0 hours
Customer #5	6 hours

The total cost of operating the airplane is included in general and administrative expense; none is included in selling and customer support costs.

Required:

a. Prepare a customer profitability analysis for Roger's Aeronautics that shows the gross profits less all expenses that can reasonably be assigned to the five customers.

b. Now assume that the remaining general and administrative costs are assigned to the five customers based on relative sales dollars, calculate net profit for each customer.

c. Discuss the merits of the analysis in part a. versus part b.

MANAGEMENT APPLICATIONS

MA18-34. Designing an ABC System for a Country Club   (LO2, 5, 6)

The Reserve Club is a traditional private golf and country club that has three different categories of memberships: golf, tennis & swimming, and social. Golf members have access to all amenities and programs in the Club, Tennis & Swimming members have access to all amenities and programs except use of the golf course, and Social members have access to only the social activities of the club, excluding golf, tennis, and swimming. All members have clubhouse privileges, including use of the bar and restaurant, which is operated by an outside contractor. During the past year, the average membership in each category, along with the number of club visits during the year, was

	Members	Visits
Golf	260	9,360
Tennis & Swimming	50	1,500
Social	120	2,160

Some members of the Club have been complaining that heavy users of the Club are not bearing their share of the costs through their membership fees. Dess Rosmond, General Manager of the Reserve Club, agrees that monthly fees paid by the various member groups should be based on the annual average amount of cost-related activities provided by the club for the three groups, and he intends to set fees on that basis for the coming year. The annual direct costs of operating the golf course, tennis courts, and swimming pool have been calculated by the Club's controller as follows:

Golf course	$900,000
Swimming pool	50,000
Tennis courts	25,000

The operation of the bar and restaurant and all related costs, including depreciation on the bar and restaurant facilities, are excluded from this analysis. In addition to the above costs, the Club incurs general overhead costs in the following amounts for the most recent (and typical) year:

General Ledger Overhead Accounts	Amounts
Indirect labor for the Club management staff (the general manager, assistant general manager, membership manager, and club controller)	$250,000
Utilities (other than those directly related to golf, swimming and tennis).	24,000
Website maintenance.	2,000
Postage	5,000
Computers and information systems maintenance	7,500
Clubhouse maintenance & depreciation	30,000
Liability insurance.	4,000
Security contract	12,000
	$334,500

Dess believes that the best way to assign most of the overhead costs to the three membership categories is with an activity-based system that recognizes four key activities that occur regularly in the club:

> Recruiting and providing orientation for new members
> Maintaining the membership roster and communicating with members
> Planning, scheduling and managing Club events
> Maintaining the financial records and reporting for the Club

Required

a. Identify and explain which overhead costs can reasonably be assigned to one or more of the four key activities, and suggest a basis for making the assignment.

b. Identify a cost driver for each activity cost pool that would seem to be suitable for assigning the activity cost pool to the three membership categories.

c. Suggest a method for assigning any overhead costs to the three membership categories that cannot reasonably be assigned to activity pools.

d. Comment on the suitability of ABC to this cost assignment situation.

MA18-35. Product Costing: Department versus Activity-Based Costing for Overhead   (LO2, 4, 6)

Advertising Technologies, Inc. (ATI) specializes in providing both published and online advertising services for the business marketplace. The company monitors its costs based on the cost per column inch of published space printed in print advertising media and based on the cost per minute of telephone advertising time delivered on "The AD Line," a computer-based, online advertising service. ATI has one new competitor, Tel-a-Ad, in its local teleadvertising market; and with increased competition, ATI has seen a decline in sales of online advertising in recent years. ATI's president, Robert Beard, believes that predatory pricing by Tel-a-Ad has caused the problem. The following is a recent conversation between Robert and Jane Minnear, director of marketing for ATI.

> *Jane:* I just received a call from one of our major customers concerning our advertising rates on "The AD Line" who said that a sales rep from another firm (it had to be Tel-a-Ad) had offered the same service at $1 per minute, which is $1.50 per minute less than our price.
>
> *Robert:* It's costing about $1.27 per minute to produce that product. I don't see how they can afford to sell it so cheaply. I'm not convinced that we should meet the price. Perhaps the better strategy is to emphasize producing and selling more published ads, which we're more experienced with and where our margins are high and we have virtually no competition.
>
> *Jane:* You may be right. Based on a recent survey of our customers, I think we can raise the price significantly for published advertising and still not lose business.
>
> *Robert:* That sounds promising; however, before we make a major recommitment to publishing, let's explore other possible explanations. I want to know how our costs compare with our competitors. Maybe we could be more efficient and find a way to earn a good return on teleadvertising.

After this meeting, Robert and Jane requested an investigation of production costs and comparative efficiency of producing published versus online advertising services. The controller, Tim Gentry, indicated that ATI's efficiency was comparable to that of its competitors and prepared the following cost data:

	Published Advertising	Online Advertising
Estimated number of production units...............	200,000	10,000,000
Selling price	$200	$2.50
Direct product costs.............................	$21,000,000	$5,000,000
Overhead allocation*	$9,800,000	$7,700,000
Overhead per unit................................	$49	$0.77
Direct costs per unit.............................	$105	$0.50
Number of customers.............................	180,000	25,000
Number of salesperson days	32,000	5,500
Number of art and design hours	35,000	5,000
Number of creative services subcontract hours	100,000	25,000
Number of customer service calls	72,000	8,000

* Based on direct labor costs

Upon examining the data, Robert decided that he wanted to know more about the overhead costs since they were such a high proportion of total production costs. He was provided the following list of overhead costs and told that they were currently being assigned to products in proportion to direct labor costs.

Selling costs...................	$7,500,000
Visual and audio design costs	3,000,000
Creative services costs	5,000,000
Customer service costs	2,000,000

Required

Using the data provided by the controller, prepare analyses to help Robert and Jane in making their decisions. (*Hint:* Prepare cost calculations for both product lines using ABC to see whether there is any significant difference in their unit costs). Should ATI switch from the fast-growing, online advertising market back into the well-established published advertising market? Does the charge of predatory pricing seem valid? Why are customers likely to be willing to pay a higher price to get published services? Do traditional costing and activity-based costing lead to the same conclusions?

MA18-36. Unit-Level and Multiple-Level Cost Assignments with Decision Implications (LO2, 3, 4, 6)
CarryAll Company[5] produces briefcases from leather, fabric, and synthetic materials in a single production department. The basic product is a standard briefcase made from leather and lined with fabric. CarryAll has a good reputation in the market because the standard briefcase is a high-quality item that has been produced for many years.

Last year, the company decided to expand its product line and produce specialty briefcases for special orders. These briefcases differ from the standard in that they vary in size, contain both leather and synthetic materials, and are imprinted with the buyer's logo (the standard briefcase is simply imprinted with the CarryAll name in small letters). The decision to use some synthetic materials in the briefcase was made to hold down the materials cost. To reduce the labor costs per unit, most of the cutting and stitching on the specialty briefcases is done by automated machines, which are used to a much lesser degree in the production of the standard briefcases. Because of these changes in the design and production of the specialty briefcases, CarryAll management believed that they would cost less to produce than the standard briefcases. However, because they are specialty items, they were priced slightly higher; standards are priced at $30 and specialty briefcases at $32.

After reviewing last month's results of operations, CarryAll's president became concerned about the profitability of the two product lines because the standard briefcase showed a loss while the specialty briefcase showed a greater profit margin than expected. The president is wondering whether the company should drop the standard briefcase and focus entirely on specialty items. Units and cost data for last month's operations as reported to the president are as follows:

---

[5] The CarryAll Company case, prepared by Professors Harold Roth and Imogene Posey, was originally published in the *Management Accounting Campus Report*.

	Standard	Specialty
Units produced..	10,000	2,500
Direct materials		
Leather (1 sq. yd. × $15.00; ½ sq. yd. × $15.00)............	$15.00	$ 7.50
Fabric (1 sq. yd. × $5.00; 1 sq. yd. × $5.00)	5.00	5.00
Synthetic		5.00
Total materials	20.00	17.50
Direct labor (½ hr. × $12.00, ¼ hr. × $12.00)	6.00	3.00
Manufacturing overhead (½ hr. × $8.98; ¼ hr. × $8.98)	4.49	2.25
Cost per unit.......................................	$30.49	$22.75

Factory overhead is applied on the basis of direct labor hours. The rate of $8.98 per direct labor hour was calculated by dividing the total overhead ($50,500) by the direct labor hours (5,625). As shown in the table, the cost of a standard briefcase is $0.49 higher than its $30 sales price; the specialty briefcase has a cost of only $22.75, for a gross profit per unit of $9.25. The problem with these costs is that they do not accurately reflect the activities involved in manufacturing each product. Determining the costs using ABC should provide better product costing data to help gauge the actual profitability of each product line.

The manufacturing overhead costs must be analyzed to determine the activities driving the costs. Assume that the following costs and cost drivers have been identified:

- The Purchasing Department's cost is $6,000. The major activity driving these costs is the number of purchase orders processed. During the month, the Purchasing Department prepared the following number of purchase orders for the materials indicated:

Leather	20
Fabric	30
Synthetic material......................................	50

- The cost of receiving and inspecting materials is $7,500. These costs are driven by the number of deliveries. During the month, the following number of deliveries were made:

Leather	30
Fabric	40
Synthetic material......................................	80

- Production line setup cost is $10,000. Setup activities involve changing the machines to produce the different types of briefcases. Each setup for production of the standard briefcases requires one hour; each setup for specialty briefcases requires two hours. Standard briefcases are produced in batches of 200, and specialty briefcases are produced in batches of 25. During the last month, there were 50 setups for the standard item and 100 setups for the specialty item.
- The cost of inspecting finished goods is $8,000. All briefcases are inspected to ensure that quality standards are met. However, the final inspection of standard briefcases takes very little time because the employees identify and correct quality problems as they do the hand cutting and stitching. A survey of the personnel responsible for inspecting the final products showed that 150 hours were spent on standard briefcases and 250 hours on specialty briefcases during the month.
- Equipment-related costs are $6,000. Equipment-related costs include repairs, depreciation, and utilities. Management has determined that a logical basis for assigning these costs to products is machine hours. A standard briefcase requires 1/2 hour of machine time, and a specialty briefcase requires two hours. Thus, during the last month, 5,000 hours of machine time relate to the standard line and 5,000 hours relate to the specialty line.
- Plant-related costs are $13,000. These costs include property taxes, insurance, administration, and others. For the purpose of determining average unit costs, they are to be assigned to products using machine hours.

Required

a. Using activity-based costing concepts, what overhead costs should be assigned to the two products?

b. What is the unit cost of each product using activity-based costing concepts?

c. Reevaluate the president's concern about the profitability of the two product lines.

d. Discuss the merits of activity-based management as it relates to CarryAll's ABC cost system.

SOLUTIONS TO REVIEW PROBLEMS

Mid-Module Review

Solution

a. **Plantwide overhead rate = Total manufacturing overhead ÷ Total machine hours**

$$= (\$120,\!000 + \$55,\!000) \div (10,\!000 + 5,\!000)$$

$$= \$175,\!000 \div 15,\!000$$

$$= \$11.67 \text{ per machine hour}$$

	ZX300	SL500
Product costs per unit		
Direct materials..................	$12,000	$18,000
Direct labor.....................	5,000	4,000
Manufacturing overhead		
700 machine hours × $11.67......	8,169	
800 machine hours × $11.67......		9,336
Total cost per batch...............	$25,169	$31,336
Number of units per batch........	÷ 100	÷ 100
Cost per unit.....................	$251.69	$313.36

b. **Departmental overhead rates = Total departmental overhead ÷ Dept. allocation base**

Fabrication = $120,000 ÷ 10,000 machine hours

$$= \$12 \text{ per machine hour}$$

Finishing = $55,000 ÷ 5,000 machine hours

$$= \$11 \text{ per machine hour}$$

	ZX300	SL500
Product costs per unit		
Direct materials..................	$12,000	$18,000
Direct labor.....................	5,000	4,000
Manufacturing overhead		
Fabrication Department		
500 machine hours × $12.....	6,000	
700 machine hours × $12.....		8,400
Finishing Department		
200 machine hours × $11.....	2,200	
100 machine hours × $11.....		1,100
Total cost per batch...............	$25,200	$31,500
Number of units per batch........	÷ 100	÷ 100
Cost per unit.....................	$252.00	$315.00

c. **Activity-based overhead rates = Activity cost pool ÷ Activity cost driver**

$$\text{Maintenance} = \$30{,}000 \div 15{,}000 \text{ machine hours}$$
$$= \$2 \text{ per machine hour}$$
$$\text{Materials handling} = \$45{,}000 \div 4{,}500 \text{ materials moves}$$
$$= \$10 \text{ per materials move}$$
$$\text{Machine setups} = \$75{,}000 \div 750 \text{ setups}$$
$$= \$100 \text{ per machine setup}$$
$$\text{Inspections} = \$25{,}000 \div 1{,}000 \text{ inspection hours}$$
$$= \$25 \text{ per inspection hour}$$

	ZX300	SL500
Product costs per unit		
Direct materials.	$12,000	$18,000
Direct labor	5,000	4,000
Manufacturing overhead		
Maintenance activity		
700 machine hours × $2.	1,400	
800 machine hours × $2.		1,600
Materials handling activity		
30 materials moves × $10.	300	
50 materials moves × $10.		500
Machine setups activity		
5 machine setups × $100	500	
9 machine setups × $100		900
Inspections activity		
30 inspection hours × $25	750	
60 inspection hours × $25		1,500
Total cost per batch	$19,950	$26,500
Number of units per batch	÷ 100	÷ 100
Cost per unit.	$199.50	$265.00

d. Following is a summary of product costs for ZX300 and SL500 assigning overhead costs based on a plantwide rate, department rates, and activity-based rates:

	ZX300	SL500
Plantwide rate.	$251.69	$313.36
Department rates	$252.00	$315.00
Activity rates.	$199.50	$265.00

Changing from a plantwide rate to department rates had little effect on unit costs because the department rates per machine hour are close to the plantwide rate per machine hour. Based on machine hours, both departments have similar cost structures.

When using activity rates, however, the cost of these two products drops dramatically because they use only a small portion (less than 2 percent) of the activities of setup (14 of 750) and materials moves (80 of 4,500). Neither a plantwide rate nor department rates recognize this fact, resulting in a large amount of cost cross-subsidization of other products by ZX300 and SL500 for these costs. Although this problem did not include cost analysis of the other three products, it shows that they are less profitable and that ZX300 and SL500 are much more profitable than management previously thought.

Module-End Review

Solution

a. Activity A—Minor systems maintenance

Activity B—Visits to customers

Activity C—Communications via phone

Activity	1	2	3	4	5
A (@ $160)	$11,040	$22,560	$11,840	$9,760	$21,760
B (@ $300)	7,500	12,600	5,700	8,400	11,700
C (@ $50)	6,400	10,250	4,950	5,300	9,450
Total support costs	$24,940	$45,410	$22,490	$23,460	$42,910
Profit before support Costs	80,000	85,000	83,000	90,000	78,000
Customer profits	$55,060	$39,590	$60,510	$66,540	$35,090
Ratio of support costs to profit before support costs:...	31%	53%	27%	26%	55%

b. This analysis is beneficial to Systems Technology because it shows that Groups 2 and 5 are outliers among the five customer groups in terms of support services required. Groups 2 and 5 are significantly larger consumers of activities for all three of the support activities. Note also that Group 4 customers are relatively light users of minor systems maintenance, and Group 3 are relatively light users of phone communications. Calculating the ratio of total support costs to profit before support costs provides additional insight into the relative profitability of the customer groups. All five customer groups are profitable; however, this analysis provides useful information for improving profits by working with groups 2 and 5 to control support activities and related costs and attempt to bring their support costs in line with the other customer groups.

WELLS FARGO BANK

Determining how much it costs to make a product or produce a service can be simple and straightforward for a company that has only one product or service; however, as the range of products and services offered expands, and as processes become more complex, the costing system also becomes more complex. The cost system is essentially a reflection of a company's product and production strategies.

Banking is an industry where the line of services has increased dramatically over the past two decades. This expansion was largely caused by the elimination of government regulations that once restricted banks from operating across state lines, as well the repeal of the Glass-Steagall Act in 1999 that removed the separation that previously existed between Wall Street investment banks and banks that hold customer deposits.

Just as a company that manufactures multiple *physical* products, banks or other service organizations that produce multiple *service* products must determine the costs and profit related to each product for purposes of evaluating performance and establishing the selling price. Banks have been on the forefront of service costing, and the Bank Administration Institute (BAI) and the American Bankers Association (ABA) for years have offered continuing education courses for bankers on how to control and measure costs in banks.

The fourth largest bank in the U.S. today is Wells Fargo Bank, with total assets of $1.2 trillion and total revenues of $88 billion. Much of Wells Fargo's recent growth was fueled by the banking crisis that led to its acquisition of failed Wachovia Bank in 2009. Like all the leading bank holding

Additional Topics in Product Costing

LEARNING OBJECTIVES

LO1   Differentiate between product and service department costs and direct and indirect department costs. (p. 19-3)

LO2   Describe the allocation of service department costs under the direct, step, and linear algebra methods. (p. 19-4)

LO3   Understand lean production and just-in-time inventory management. (p. 19-9)

LO4   Explain how lean production and just-in-time affect performance evaluation and recordkeeping. (p. 19-12)

companies, Wells Fargo offers a wide array of services. In its most recent annual report, Wells Fargo describes the following 11 major lines of service: community retail banking, credit cards, mortgage banking, wealth management, investment brokerage, institutional retirement management, commercial wholesale banking, mutual funds, investment banking, commercial real estate lending, and insurance.[11] Within each of these 11 lines of service there are likely multiple individual products.

Wells Fargo also lists in its annual report 19 categories of non-interest expense totaling $49 billion that are incurred to provide the wide range of services that it offers.[2] For the

company to determine the cost and profitability of each of its products, it must be able to distribute, or assign, these costs to the various products. Cost and profitability measurement of products is particularly crucial in light of the recent financial stress in the banking industry.

In the previous module we discussed how activity-based costing can assist in measuring the cost of products and services. In this module we will discuss how companies like Wells Fargo assign the cost of internal services, such as information technology or human resources, to their multiple product lines and products, and how both manufacturing and service organizations can benefit from adopting a lean operations philosophy.

---

[1] *Wells Fargo & Company Annual Report 2009*, pp. 3-7.

[2] *Wells Fargo & Company Annual Report 2009*, p. 44.

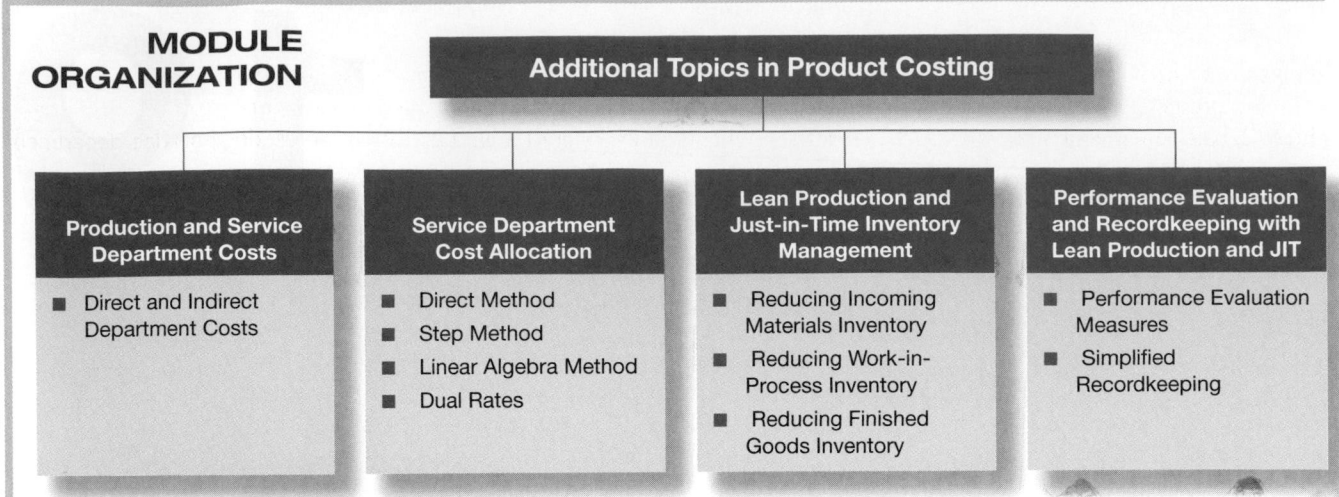

PRODUCTION AND SERVICE DEPARTMENT COSTS

LO1 Differentiate between product and service department costs and direct and indirect department costs.

In Module 17, we discussed two basic methods (job order costing and process costing) for accumulating, measuring and recording the costs of producing goods. In Module 18, we discussed both traditional and activity-based methods for assigning indirect costs to products. We now look in more detail at another aspect of assigning indirect costs.

In addition to *production* departments that actually perform work on a product, many companies have production *support* departments, such as payroll, human resources, information technology, security, and facilities, that provide support services for all of the production departments, and sometimes even for each other. These departments are typically called **service departments**. The cost of producing products, therefore, includes the costs incurred within production departments, as well as the cost of services received from service departments.

A **direct department cost** is a cost assigned directly to a department (production or service) when it is incurred. For a production department, direct department costs include both *direct* product costs (direct materials and direct labor) as well as *indirect* product costs (such as indirect labor and indirect materials) incurred directly in the department. An **indirect department cost** is a cost assigned to a department as a result of an indirect allocation, or reassignment, from another department, such as a service department.

The product costing system must include a policy for assigning to products the cost of services received from service departments. For companies that use a plantwide overhead rate, the costs of all service departments are added to the indirect product costs incurred within all of the producing departments to get total plantwide manufacturing overhead, which is then assigned to products using a single overhead rate based on a common factor such as direct labor hours. For companies that use departmental overhead rates, service department costs are allocated to the production departments that utilize their services, and the allocated service department costs are added to the indirect costs incurred within the department to arrive at total departmental overhead and allocation rates. Also, as illustrated in Module 18, service department costs may also be assigned to products using activity-based costing. As discussed in the following Business Insight, service department cost allocation can impact the amount of revenue received for some organizations.

BUSINESS INSIGHT **Cost Allocations in a Large University Setting**

A major research university, such as Emory University, encounters numerous cost allocation situations where the cost allocation system can substantially impact the University's financial well-being. Two examples are (1) cost allocation of various overhead costs for purposes of billing governmental and private insurance systems for services rendered to patients in University hospitals and clinics, and (2) cost allocations for indirect costs when seeking research and other grants. Failing to properly allocate service department costs can result in large revenue losses to such organizations. During times of economic recession, it is even more important to accurately measure the indirect service costs that are being passed on to other organizations to ensure maximum cost recovery.

SERVICE DEPARTMENT COST ALLOCATION

As discussed above, service departments (maintenance, administration, information technology, security, etc.) provide a wide range of support functions, primarily for one or more production departments. These departments, which are considered essential elements in the overall manufacturing process, do not work directly on the "product" but provide auxiliary support to the producing departments. In addition to providing support for the various producing departments, some service departments also provide services to *other service departments*. For example, the payroll and personnel departments typically provide services to all departments (producing and service), and engineering may provide services to only the producing departments. Services provided by one service department to other service departments are called **interdepartment services**.

LO2 Describe the allocation of service department costs under the direct, step, and linear algebra methods.

To illustrate service department cost allocations, consider the Manufacturing Division of Krown Drink Company, which has two producing departments, three service departments, and two products. The service departments and their respective service functions and cost allocation bases are as follows:

Department	Service Functions	Allocation Base
Support Services	Receiving and inventory control	Total amount of department capital investment
Engineering Resources	Production setup and engineering and testing	Number of employees
Building and Grounds	Machinery maintenance and depreciation	Amount of square footage occupied

Difficulty in choosing an allocation base for service department costs is not uncommon. For example, Krown Drink may have readily determined the appropriate allocation bases for the Engineering Resources and the Building and Grounds Departments but may have found the choice for Support Services to be less clear. Perhaps after conducting correlation studies, the most equitable base for allocating Support Services costs to other departments was determined to be total capital investment in the departments because they included expensive computer-tracking equipment, both manual and automated forklifts, and other material-moving equipment.

Direct department costs and allocation base information used to illustrate Krown Drink's July service department cost allocations are summarized as follows:

	Direct Department Costs	Number of Employees		Amount of Square Footage Occupied		Total Amount of Department Capital Investment	
Service departments							
Support Services	$ 27,000	15	15%	4,000	8%	—	—
Engineering Resources.	20,000	—	—	2,000	4	$ 45,000	8%
Building and Grounds.	10,000	5	5	—	—	50,000	9
Producing departments							
Mixing	40,000*	24	24	11,000	22	180,000	33
Bottling	90,000*	56	56	33,000	66	270,000	50
	$187,000	100	100%	50,000	100%	$545,000	100%

*Direct department overhead

The preceding information omitted the amount of capital investment in the Support Services Department, the number of employees in the Engineering Resources Department, and the amount of square footage used by the Building and Grounds Department. These data were omitted because a department normally does not allocate costs to itself; it allocates costs only to the departments it serves. The three methods commonly used for service department cost allocations—direct, step, and linear algebra—are discussed next.

Direct Method

The **direct method** allocates all service department costs based only on the amount of services provided to the producing departments. Exhibit 19.1 shows the flow of costs using the direct method. All arrows depicting the cost flows extend directly from service departments to producing departments; under the direct method there are no cost allocations between the service departments.

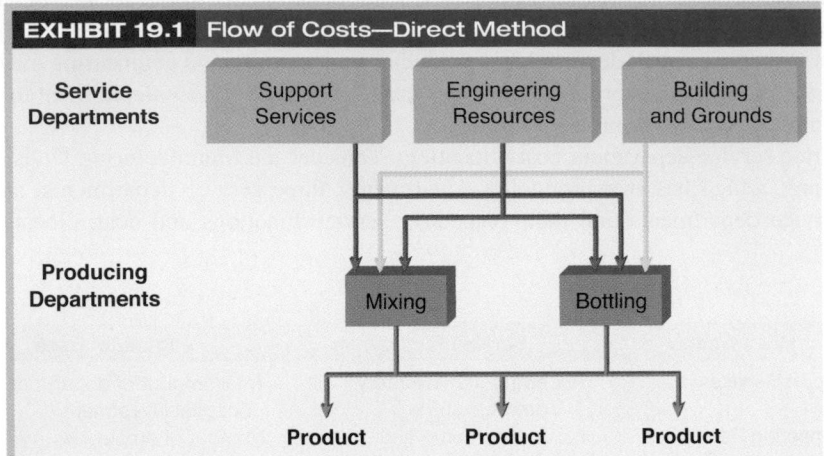

EXHIBIT 19.1 Flow of Costs—Direct Method

Exhibit 19.2 shows the service department cost allocations for the direct method. Notice the allocation base used to allocate Engineering Resources costs; only the employees in the producing departments are considered in computing the allocation percentages—24 in Mixing and 56 in Bottling, for a total of 80 employees in the allocation base. Thirty percent (24 ÷ 80) of the producing department employees work in Mixing; therefore, 30 percent of Engineering Resources costs are allocated to Mixing. Applying the same reasoning, 70 percent of Engineering Resources costs are allocated to Bottling. Similar logic is followed in computing the cost allocations for Building and Grounds and Support Services.

The cost allocation summary at the bottom of Exhibit 19.2 shows that all service department costs have been allocated, decreasing the service department costs to zero and increasing the producing

EXHIBIT 19.2 Service Department Cost Allocations—Direct Method

	Total	Mixing	Bottling
Support Services Department			
Allocation base (capital investment)........	$450,000	$180,000	$270,000
Percent of total base...................	100%	40%	60%
Cost allocations	$ 27,000	$ 10,800	$ 16,200
Engineering Resources Department			
Allocation base (number of employees).....	80	24	56
Percent of total base...................	100%	30%	70%
Cost allocations	$ 20,000	$ 6,000	$ 14,000
Building and Grounds Department			
Allocation base (square footage occupied) ..	44,000	11,000	33,000
Percent of total base...................	100%	25%	75%
Cost allocations	$ 10,000	$ 2,500	$ 7,500

Cost Allocation Summary

	Support Services	Engineering Resources	Building and Grounds	Mixing	Bottling	Total
Department cost before allocations..........	$27,000	$20,000	$10,000	$40,000	$ 90,000	$187,000
Cost allocations						
Support Services.....................	(27,000)			10,800	16,200	—
Engineering Resources................		(20,000)		6,000	14,000	—
Building and Grounds.................			(10,000)	2,500	7,500	—
Department costs after allocations.........	$ 0	$ 0	$ 0	$59,300	$127,700	$187,000

department overhead balances by the amounts of the respective allocations. Also, total costs are not affected by the allocations; the total of $187,000 was merely redistributed so that all costs are reassigned to the producing departments. Total department overhead costs of the producing departments after allocation of service costs are $59,300 for Mixing and $127,700 for Bottling.

The advantage of the direct method of allocating service department costs is that it is easy and convenient to use. Its primary disadvantage is that it does not recognize the costs for interdepartment services provided by one service department to another. Instead, any costs incurred to provide services to other service departments are passed directly to the producing departments. The step method improves on the allocation procedure by redirecting some of the costs to other service departments before they are finally allocated to the production departments.

Step Method

The **step method** gives partial recognition of interdepartmental services by using a methodology that allocates the service department costs *sequentially* both to the remaining service departments and the producing departments. Any indirect costs allocated to a service department in this process are added to that service department's direct costs to determine the total costs to allocate to the remaining departments. Through this procedure, all service department costs are assigned to the production departments and ultimately to the products.

To illustrate a problem that can result from using the direct method, assume that Ramso Company has two service departments, S1 and S2, and two producing departments, P1 and P2, that provide services as follows:

	Receiver of Services			
Provider of Services......	S1	S2	P1	P2
S1..............	0%	0%	70%	30%
S2..............	50%	0%	25%	25%

If the direct method is used to allocate service department costs to the producing departments, S2 total costs will be allocated equally to the producing departments because they use the same amount of S2 services (25 percent each). Is this an equitable allocation of S2 costs? S2 actually provides half of its services to the other service department (S1), which, in turn, provides the majority of its services to P1. Assume that S2 has total direct department costs of $100,000. If the direct method is used to allocate service department costs, the entire $100,000 will be divided equally among the two producing departments, each being allocated $50,000, with no allocation to S1.

	S1	S2	P1	P2
Direct allocation of S2 to P1 and P2	$0	$(100,000)	$50,000	$50,000

Consider the following alternative allocation of the $100,000 of S2 costs that takes into account interdepartment services. First, 25 percent, or $25,000, is allocated to each of the producing departments, and 50 percent, or $50,000, is allocated to S1. Next, the $50,000 allocated to S1 from S2 is reallocated to the producing departments in proportion to the amount of services provided to them by S1: 70 percent and 30 percent, respectively. In this scenario, the $100,000 of S2 costs is ultimately allocated $60,000 to P1 and $40,000 to P2 as follows:

	S1	S2	P1	P2
Step 1:				
Allocate S2 costs to S1, P1, and P2....	$50,000	$(100,000)	$25,000	$25,000
Step 2:				
Reallocate S1 costs to P1 and P2	(50,000)	0	35,000	15,000
Total allocation of S2				
costs via step method	$ 0	$ 0	$60,000	$40,000

This calculation shows only the ultimate allocation of S2 costs. Of course, any S1 direct department costs would also have to be allocated to P1 and P2 on a 70:30 basis. If interdepartmental services are

EXHIBIT 19.3	Flow of Costs—Step Method

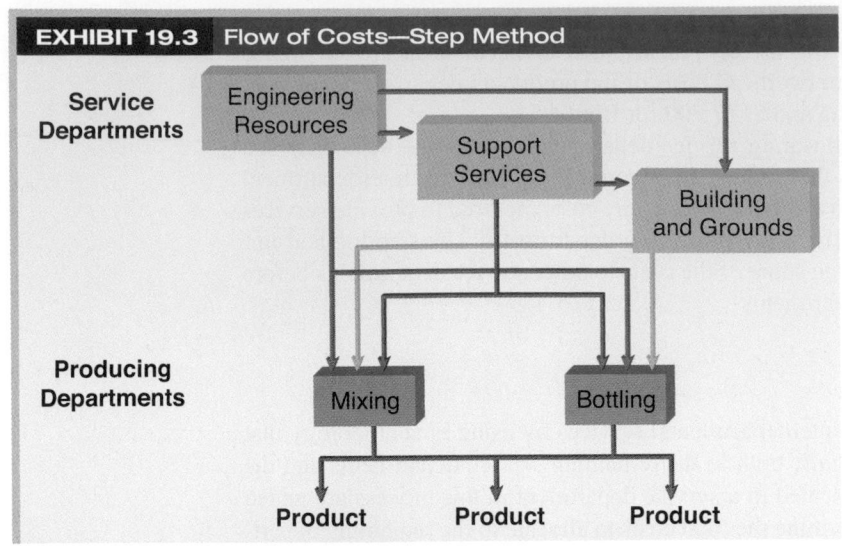

ignored, P1 is allocated only $50,000 of S2 costs; by considering interdepartmental services, P1 is allocated $60,000. Certainly, a more accurate measure of both the direct and indirect services received by P1 from S2 is $60,000, not $50,000.

As long as all producing departments use approximately the same percentage of services of each service department, the direct method provides a reasonably accurate cost assignment. In this example, the percentages of services used by the producing departments were quite different: 70 percent and 30 percent for S1, and 50 percent and 50 percent for S2. In such situations, the direct method can result in significantly different allocations.

The step method is illustrated graphically in Exhibit 19.3 for the Krown Drink Company. Notice the sequence of the allocations: Engineering Resources, Support Services, and Building and Grounds.

When using the step method, the sequence of allocation is typically based on the relative percentage of services provided to other service departments, with the largest provider of interdepartmental services allocated first and the smallest provider of interdepartmental services allocated last. For Krown Drink, Engineering Resources is allocated first because, of the three service departments, it provides the largest percentage (20 percent) of its services to other service departments: 15 percent to Support Services and 5 percent to Building and Grounds (see previous cost allocation data). Building and Grounds is allocated last because it provides the least amount (12 percent) of its services to other service departments: 8 percent to Support Services and 4 percent to Engineering Resources. The service department cost allocations for Krown Drink using the step method are shown in Exhibit 19.4.

EXHIBIT 19.4	Service Department Cost Allocations—Step Method

	Total	Support Services	Building and Grounds	Mixing	Bottling
Engineering Resources Department					
Allocation base (number of employees)	100	15	5	24	56
Percent of total base.	100%	15%	5%	24%	56%
Cost allocations	$20,000	$3,000	$1,000	$4,800	$11,200
Support Services Department					
Allocation base (capital investment).	$500,000		$50,000	$180,000	$270,000
Percent of total base.	100%		10%	36%	54%
Cost allocations	$30,000		$3,000	$10,800	$16,200
Building and Grounds Department					
Allocation base (square footage occupied) .	44,000			11,000	33,000
Percent of total base.	100%			25%	75%
Cost allocations	$14,000			$3,500	$10,500

Cost Allocation Summary						
	Engineering Resources	Support Services	Building and Grounds	Mixing	Bottling	Total
Department costs before allocations	$ 20,000	$ 27,000	$ 10,000	$40,000	$ 90,000	$187,000
Cost allocations						
Engineering Resources	(20,000)	3,000	1,000	4,800	11,200	—
Support Services.		(30,000)	3,000	10,800	16,200	—
Building and Grounds			(14,000)	3,500	10,500	—
Department costs after allocations.	$ 0	$ 0	$ 0	$59,100	$127,900	$187,000

Linear Algebra (Reciprocal) Method

The disadvantage of the step method is that it provides only partial recognition of interdepartmental services. For Krown Drink, the step method recognizes Engineering Resources services provided to the other two service departments; however, no services received by Engineering Resources from the other two departments are recognized. Similarly, services from Support Services to Building and Grounds are recognized, but not the reverse. To achieve the most mathematically accurate service department cost allocation, there should be full recognition of services between service departments as well as between service and producing departments. This requires using the linear algebra method, sometimes called the *reciprocal method*. The **linear algebra (reciprocal) method** uses a series of linear algebraic equations, which are solved simultaneously, to allocate service department costs both interdepartmentally and to the producing departments. This method is illustrated graphically in Exhibit 19.5 for a company that has two service departments and two producing departments. The cost allocation arrows run from each service department to the other service department as well as to the producing departments. Further discussion of this method can be found in Cost Accounting texts. Whether a company should use the direct method, step method, or linear algebra method depends on the extensiveness of interdepartmental services and how evenly services are used by the producing departments.

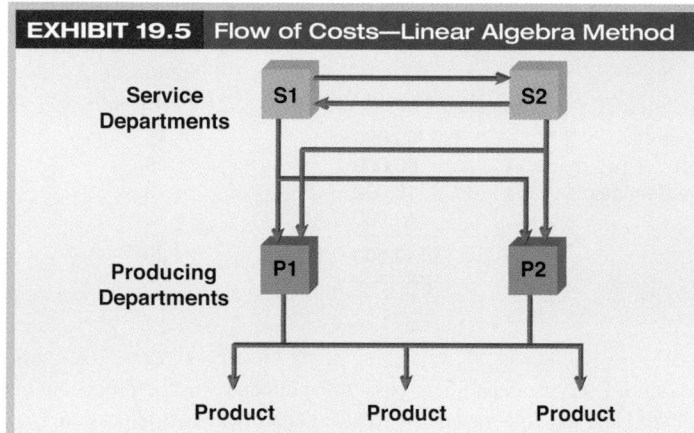

EXHIBIT 19.5 Flow of Costs—Linear Algebra Method

MANAGERIAL DECISION | **You are the Controller**

As the person responsible for the product costing system, you are trying to decide which method is best to use in allocating service department costs to the producing departments and to the products. Some of the service departments provide services only to producing departments; whereas, others provide services to both producing and service departments. You would like to use the method that provides reliable cost measurements, but without creating more costs than the benefits derived. Which method do you recommend? [Answer, p. 19-15]

Dual Rates

When allocating service department costs, it can be useful to provide separate allocations for fixed costs and variable costs. This will result in cost allocations that more accurately reflect the factors that drive costs. The capacity provided most often drives fixed costs, whereas some type of actual activity usually drives variable costs. Dual rates involve establishing separate bases for allocating fixed and variable costs. Dual rates may be used for one or all service departments, depending on the size and nature of the costs in each service department. They may also be used in conjunction with the direct, step, or linear algebra methods.

It is important to remember the relationship between capacity and cost when selecting the allocation method. Total variable costs change as activity changes. Fixed costs, however, are the same whether the activity is at or below capacity. Fixed costs should usually be allocated based on the relative capacity provided the benefiting department, while variable costs should be allocated on the basis of actual usage. The allocation methods and bases also may be different for variable and fixed costs.

Fixed costs based on capacity provided eliminates the possibility that the amount of the cost allocation to one department is affected by the level of services utilized by other departments. When fixed service department costs are allocated based on the capacity provided to the user department, managers of the user departments are charged for that capacity whether they use it or not, and their use of services has no effect on the amount of costs allocated to other departments. A benefit of this allocation system is that it reduces the temptation for managers to avoid or delay services to minimize fixed cost allocations to their departments. Dual rates are examined in more detail in most cost accounting texts.

MID-MODULE REVIEW

The Apparel Store, LTD, is organized into four departments: Women's Apparel, Men's Apparel, Administrative Services, and Facilities Services. The first two departments are the primary producing departments; the last two departments provide services to the producing departments as well as to each other. Top management has decided that, for internal reporting purposes, the cost of service department operations should be allocated to the producing departments. Administrative Services costs are allocated on the basis of the number of employees, and Facilities Services costs are allocated based on the amount of square footage of floor space occupied. Data pertaining to the cost allocations for February 2012 are as follows:

Department	Direct Department Cost	Number of Employees	Square Footage Occupied
Women's Apparel	$ 60,000	15	15,000
Men's Apparel.	50,000	9	7,500
Administrative Services	18,000	3	2,500
Facilities	12,000	2	1,000
Total	$140,000	29	26,000

Required

a. Determine the amount of service department costs to be allocated to the producing departments under both the *direct method* and the *step method* of service department cost allocation.

b. Discuss the *linear algebra method* of service department cost allocation, explaining circumstances when it should be considered over the direct and step methods.

c. Should The Apparel Store consider using the linear algebra method?

The solution is on page 19-25.

LEAN PRODUCTION AND JUST-IN-TIME INVENTORY MANAGEMENT

LO3 Understand lean production and just-in-time inventory management.

Previously, our discussions about inventories have centered around how to measure the cost of products. A related issue is how to manage the production process and physical inventory levels. Cost accounting textbooks, as well as operations management textbooks, usually discuss models that have been used for decades to determine the economic order quantities for products, given the particular level of inventory a company wants to maintain. Although these models are still relevant in many situations, managing the production process and inventory levels has changed dramatically for companies that have adopted a value chain approach to management. No longer do most managers consider only their company's strategies, goals, and objectives in deciding the characteristics and quantities of inventory that should be acquired or produced and maintained.

A value chain approach to inventory management requires that managers consider their suppliers' and customers' strategies, goals, and objectives as well if they hope to compete successfully in a global marketplace. Computer technology has affected the way inventories are manufactured and handled (using robotics, fully computerized manufacturing and product handling systems, bar code identification systems, etc.), and it is changing the way companies relate to other parties in the value chain. It has spawned worldwide use of alternative inventory production and management techniques and processes including just-in-time (JIT) inventory management and lean production methods.

Just-in-time (JIT) inventory management is a comprehensive inventory management philosophy that emerged in the 1970s that stresses policies, procedures, and attitudes by managers and other workers that result in the efficient production of high-quality goods while maintaining the minimum level of inventories. JIT is often described simply as an inventory model that maintains only the level of inventories required to meet current production and sales requirements, but it is, in reality, much more than that. The key elements of the JIT philosophy, which has come to be known as the "lean production" philosophy, include increased coordination throughout the value chain, reduced inventory, reduced production times, increased product quality, and increased employee involvement and empowerment.

In sum, JIT/lean production is a system aimed at reducing or eliminating waste, increasing cost efficiency, and securing a competitive advantage. Accordingly, it emphasizes a nimble production process with small lot sizes, short setup and changeover times, effective and efficient quality controls, a minimum number of bottlenecks and backups, and maximum efficiency of people.

Reducing Incoming Materials Inventory

The JIT/lean approach to reducing incoming materials includes these elements:

1. Developing long-term relationships with a limited number of vendors.
2. Selecting vendors on the basis of service and material quality, as well as price.
3. Establishing procedures for key employees to order materials for current needs directly from approved vendors.
4. Accepting vendor deliveries directly to the shop floor, and only as needed.

When fully implemented, these steps minimize or eliminate many materials inventories. Sufficient materials would be on hand to meet only immediate needs, and the materials inventories in the manufacturing setting are located on the shop floor.

To achieve this reduction, it is apparent that vendors and buyers must work as a team and that key employees must be involved in decision making. The goal of the JIT approach to purchasing is not to shift materials carrying costs to vendors. A close, long-term working relationship between purchasers and vendors should be beneficial to both. Purchasers' scheduling information is provided to vendors so that vendors also can reduce inventories and minimize costs. Vendors are therefore able to manufacture small batches frequently, rather than manufacturing large batches infrequently. Further, vendors are more confident of future sales. The following Business Insight discusses how a Kentucky home builder applied lean concepts to manage inventory acquisitions.

BUSINESS INSIGHT **Partnering with Vendors**

Bill and Brad Jagoe, the co-owners of a home building business in Owensboro, Kentucky, are strong advocates of "lean building," which applies lean operations concepts to the building industry. The following are excerpts from their interview with the Lean Building Forum on HousingZone.com/Lean:

> Brad: After working with our measurements and tracking systems, we began working specifically with our employees and trade partners on a higher and deeper level, and then the results really began to flow.

> Bill: For years this industry has liked using the term "trade partner" but for most builders it's just a buzzword. But when we got into lean thinking and processes and our people began to understand that lean mattered, we really established that strong trade partnership.

> Brad: That led us to our philosophy that we want a small number of extremely capable trades [partners] with low turnover. In a long-term relationship they have to be extremely competitive and make money. Lean gives both the builder and the trade partners the tools to eliminate waste, reduce cost and remain competitive, by working together.

> Brad: I don't think we have a person in our company right now – from laborers to architects to salespeople—that is not thinking lean. We have saved several million dollars the past few years, and everyone is now in the habit of asking: "Does that add value to the customer, or not?"

Source: Scott Sedam, *Professional Builder*, February 2010, p. 19.

Reducing Work-in-Process Inventory

Reducing the total time required to complete a process, or the **cycle time**, is the key to reducing work-in-process inventories and is central to a lean production approach. In a manufacturing organization, cycle time is composed of the time needed for setup, processing, movement, waiting, and inspection. **Setup time** is the time required to prepare equipment to produce a specific product, or to change from producing one product to another product. **Processing time** is the time spent working on units. **Movement time** is the time units spend moving between work or inspection stations. **Waiting time** is the time units spend in temporary storage waiting to be processed, moved, or inspected. **Inspection time** is the amount of time it takes units to be inspected. Of the five elements of cycle time, only processing time adds value to the product. Efforts to reduce cycle time are appropriate for both continuous and batch production.

Devising means of reducing setup times will directly reduce the cycle time for batch production and thus reduce setup costs. Setup times can also be reduced by shifting from batch to continuous production whenever practical. Rearranging the shop floor to eliminate unnecessary movements of materials can help reduce movement time for both continuous and batch production.

Many companies have created **quality circles**, which are groups of employees involved in production who have the authority, within certain parameters, to address and resolve quality problems as they occur, without seeking management approval. Giving employees more authority and responsibility for quality, including the right to stop production whenever quality problems are noted, can reduce the need for separate inspection time. The following Business Insight illustrates how a division of Daimler Trucks of North America benefits from lean manufacturing at one of its new plants.

BUSINESS INSIGHT   Daimler Trucks Emphasizes Lean Operations

During the lowest point of the worldwide recession, Daimler Trucks opened a new $300 million plant using advanced lean operations processing and techniques that incorporate continuous evaluation and improvement. It focuses on achieving more with fewer resources, by the continuous evaluation of waste. The focus at the new plant is on "getting it right the first time," and the Plant Manager, Mark Hernandez, stated that "Problems are solved within the assembly stations, not sent down the line.... If a problem can't be solved, the line is stopped until the issue has been solved." The Daimler CEO said that "the result is a culture that focuses on the problem and looks for ways to improve the process, while recognizing the value of employee initiative and insights."

Source: "New Freightliner Plant Opens in Mexico," *Refrigerated Transporter*, April 1, 2009, p. 28.

Waiting time can be reduced by moving from a materials push to a materials pull approach to production. Under a traditional **materials push system**, employees work to reduce the pile of inventory building up at their workstations. Workers at each station remove materials from an in-process storage area, complete their operation, and place the output in another in-process storage area. Hence, they *push* the work to the next workstation. The emphasis is on production efficiency at each station. In a push system, one of the functions of work-in-process inventory is to help make workstations independent of each other. Inventories are large enough to allow for variations in processing speeds, for discarding defective units without interrupting production, and for machine downtime.

Under a **materials pull system** (often called a **Kanban system**), employees at each station work to provide inventory for the next workstation only as needed. (*Kanban*, the Japanese word for *card*, is a system created in Japan that originally used cards to indicate that a department needed additional components.) The building of excess inventories is strictly prohibited. When the number of units in inventory reaches a specified limit, work at the station stops until workers at a subsequent station pull a unit from the in-process storage area. Hence, the *pull* of inventory by a subsequent station authorizes production to continue.

A pull, or Kanban, system's low inventory levels require a team effort. To avoid idle time, processing speeds must be balanced and equipment must be kept in good repair. Quality problems are identified immediately, and the low inventory levels require immediate correction of quality problems. To make a pull system work, management must accept the notion that it is better to have employees idle than to have them building excess inventory. A pull system also requires careful planning by management and active participation in decision making by employees. A lean production process involves minimizing cycle time, eliminating waste, producing inventory only as needed, and ensuring the highest level of quality and efficiency. To achieve these results on a continuing basis, there is a strong emphasis on continuous improvement programs (See Module 20).

Reducing Finished Goods Inventory

Finished goods inventory can be reduced by reducing cycle time and by better predicting customer demand for finished units. Lowering cycle times reduces the need for speculative inventories. If finished goods can be replenished quickly, the need diminishes for large inventory levels to satisfy customer needs and to provide for unanticipated fluctuations in customer orders. Anticipating customers' demand for goods can be improved by adopting a value chain approach to inventory management by which the manufacturer or supplier is working as a partner with its customers to meet their inventory needs. This frequently involves having online computer access to customers' inventory levels on a real-time basis and being able to synchronize changes in production with changes in customers' inventory levels as they occur.

Sharing this type of information obviously requires an enormous amount of mutual trust between a manufacturer or supplier and its customers, but it is becoming increasingly common among world-class organizations. An example of this type of vendor-customer relationship is the relationship between Procter & Gamble, one of the world's largest consumer products companies, and its largest customer, Wal-Mart. By having access to Wal-Mart's computer inventory system, Procter & Gamble is better able to determine and fill Wal-Mart's specific needs for products, such as disposable diapers.

PERFORMANCE EVALUATION AND RECORDKEEPING WITH LEAN PRODUCTION AND JIT

Movement toward a JIT/lean production philosophy requires changes in performance evaluation procedures and offers opportunities for significant reductions in recordkeeping costs. These changes are discussed in this section.

LO4 Explain how lean production and just-in-time affect performance evaluation and recordkeeping.

Performance Evaluation

JIT regards inventory as something to be eliminated. Hence, in a manufacturing organization, inventories are kept as small as possible. Under the JIT ideal, inventories do not exist because vendors deliver raw materials in small batches directly to the shop floor. JIT also strives to minimize, or eliminate, work-in-process inventory by minimizing the non-processing elements of cycle time and by having processing times as short as possible.

Dysfunctional Effects of Traditional Performance Measures

A potential conflict exists between the goals of JIT and lean production and those of traditional performance measures applied at the level of the department or cost center. Although lean production emphasizes overall efficiency, many traditional performance measures emphasize local (departmental) cost savings and local (departmental) efficiency. Consider the following traditional performance measures for a purchasing agent and a departmental production supervisor:

- To achieve quantity discounts and favorable prices, a purchasing agent might order excess inventory, thereby increasing subsequent storage, obsolescence, and handling costs.

- To obtain a low price, a purchasing agent might order from a supplier whose goods have not been certified as meeting quality specifications, thereby causing subsequent inspection, rework, and spoilage costs, and perhaps, dissatisfied customers further down the value chain.

- To avoid having idle employees and equipment, a supervisor might refuse to halt production to determine the cause of a quality problem, thereby increasing inspection, rework, and spoilage costs.

■ To obtain low fixed costs per unit under absorption costing, a supervisor might produce in excess of current needs (preferably in long production runs), thereby causing subsequent increases in storage, obsolescence, and handling costs.

Performance Measures Under Lean Production and JIT

In accordance with the goal of eliminating inventory and reducing cycle time to processing time, JIT supportive performance measures emphasize inventory turnover, cycle time, and **cycle efficiency** (the ratio of value-added to non-value-added manufacturing activities).

When applied to a specific item of raw materials or finished goods, **inventory turnover** is computed as the annual demand in units divided by the average inventory in units:

$$\text{Inventory turnover} = \frac{\text{Annual demand in units}}{\text{Average inventory in units}}$$

Progress toward the goal of reducing inventory is measured by comparing successive inventory turnover ratios. Generally, the higher the inventory turnover, the better.

When measured with inventory dollars instead of inventory units, inventory turnover can be used as a measure of the organization's overall success in reducing inventory, or in increasing sales in relation to inventories. This financial measure can be derived directly from a firm's financial statements.

$$\text{Inventory turnover} = \frac{\text{Cost of goods sold}}{\text{Average inventory (in dollars)}}$$

Another ratio often used to monitor the effectiveness of inventory levels in retail organizations, such as The Home Depot or Macy's, is gross margin return on inventory investment (GMROI), calculated as follows:

$$\text{GMROI} = \frac{\text{Gross margin (in dollars)}}{\text{Average inventory (in dollars)}}$$

Cycle time is a measure of the total time required to produce one unit of a product:

$$\frac{\text{Cycle}}{\text{time}} = \frac{\text{Setup}}{\text{time}} + \frac{\text{Processing}}{\text{time}} + \frac{\text{Movement}}{\text{time}} + \frac{\text{Waiting}}{\text{time}} + \frac{\text{Inspection}}{\text{time}}$$

Under ideal circumstances, cycle time would consist of only processing time, and processing time would be as low as possible. Only processing time adds value to the product; hence, the time required for all other activities should be driven toward zero. The use of flexible manufacturing systems, properly sequencing jobs, and properly placing tools will minimize setup time. If the shop floor is optimally arranged, workers pass products directly from one workstation to the next. If production is optimally scheduled, inventory will not wait in temporary storage between workstations. If raw materials are of high quality and products are manufactured so that they always conform to specifications, separate inspection activities are not needed.

Cycle efficiency is computed as the ratio of processing time to total cycle time:

$$\text{Cycle efficiency} = \frac{\text{Processing time}}{\text{Cycle time}}$$

The highest cycle efficiency possible is always sought. If all non-value-added activities are eliminated, this ratio equals one.

Simplified Recordkeeping

Lean Production and JIT enable significant reductions in the number of accounting transactions required for purchasing and production activities. This results in cost savings for bookkeeping activities and in shifting accounting resources from detailed bookkeeping to the development of more useful activity cost data.

Purchasing

In a traditional accounting system, every purchase results in the preparation of several documents. Additional documents are prepared for the issuance of raw materials to the factory. JIT, on the other hand, attempts to minimize inventory levels and stresses long-term relationships with a limited number of vendors who have demonstrated their ability to provide quality raw materials on a timely basis, as well as at a competitive price. Under a JIT inventory system, a company often has standing purchase orders for specified materials from specified vendors at specified prices. Production personnel are authorized to requisition materials directly from authorized vendors, who deliver limited quantities of materials as needed directly to the shop floor. Production personnel verify receipt of the raw materials. Periodically, each vendor sends an invoice for several shipments, which the company acknowledges and pays.

Product Costing

Another advantage of a lean production system is that it reduces the amount of detailed bookkeeping required for financial accounting purposes. If ending inventories are nonexistent, or so small that the costs assigned to them are insignificant in comparison with the costs assigned to Cost of Goods Sold, it makes little sense to track product costs through several inventory accounts. Instead of using a traditional product cost accounting system (as illustrated in Module 17), firms that have implemented JIT often use what is sometimes referred to as a backflush approach to accounting for product costs.

Under **backflush costing**, all costs of direct materials, direct labor, and manufacturing overhead are assigned as incurred to Cost of Goods Sold. If there are no inventories on hand at the end of the period, no additional steps are required. However, if there are inventories on hand at year-end, costs are backed out of Cost of Goods Sold and assigned to the appropriate inventory accounts. For a complete discussion of backflush costing, refer to a cost accounting text.

Also under a JIT inventory approach, many of the distinctions and arguments regarding absorption versus variable costing are moot (see Appendix 17A). If the quantity of inventory is insignificant, it matters little whether inventory cost includes only variable manufacturing costs or both variable and fixed manufacturing costs. Whether absorption or variable costing is used, the total cost assigned to inventory on the balance sheet will be small, and there is little difference in the amount of profit reported on the income statement.

As we discussed in previous modules, traditional product costing systems go to great lengths to calculate the materials, labor, and manufacturing overhead cost per unit for each unit produced. Overhead is typically assigned to inventory using a predetermined overhead rate based on an assumed volume-based driver such as direct labor hours or machine hours. If actual production is less than budgeted production, there will be underapplied overhead, which is usually written off as an expense of the period. To avoid this expense, managers are often motivated to overproduce product in order to ensure that all overhead is allocated to product. Also, by budgeting a large amount of produced units, fixed overhead cost is spread over more units, resulting in a lower cost per unit. Such overproduction is equivalent to a cardinal sin in a lean production company.

As we will see in Module 22, many companies also adopt standard cost systems where they account for product cost components on both an actual and budgeted cost basis, with variances between actual cost and standard (or allowed) costs reported on the internal performance reports as increased expenses if they are unfavorable and as a reduction of expenses if they are favorable. In such cases, managers are motivated to maximize favorable variances and minimize or eliminate unfavorable variances. Such systems of reporting often lead managers to actions that are contrary to the lean production philosophy.

MODULE-END REVIEW

The Champion Golf Company is trying to decide which automated production line to use to produce its new Pro XII golf balls. The two best systems under consideration have the following estimated performance characteristics, based on minutes per 1,000 balls produced:

	System A	System B
Setup time	25	10
Movement time from start to finish	10	14
Waiting time	3	16
Inspection time.	5	7
Processing time	40	30
Total time in minutes	83	77

Required

a. Determine the cycle time per batch for each system.
b. Determine the cycle efficiency for each system.
c. Which system do you recommend and why?
d. Assuming Champion is a "lean" manufacturer, what improvements in the selected system is it likely to pursue.

The solution is on page 19-26.

GUIDANCE ANSWER

MANAGERIAL DECISION **You are the Controller**

Designing any information processing system is a matter of weighing benefits with the costs of designing and operating the system. The same is true for a cost allocation system. Also, you have to decide how the cost information will be used. If it is used only for external financial reporting purposes, a high degree of precision may not be necessary. However, if it is used to determine the most profitable product mix, it may be crucial to have the most precise cost information. For the service departments that provide only services to producing departments and that receive no services from other service departments, a direct allocation method might be adequate. For departments that provide and/or receive interdepartmental services, you should consider using either a step or linear algebra approach to assigning costs. Whether you use a direct, step or linear algebra approach, you will have to decide whether to assign the costs using a single volume-based cost driver (such as square footage or number of employees) or using multiple cost drivers that reflect the actual activities performed. In most cases, the ABC approach (discussed in Module 18) will give a higher level of precision, but at considerably greater cost.

DISCUSSION QUESTIONS

Q19-1. Distinguish between the following sets of terms:

   a.   Direct product costs and indirect product costs.

   b.   Direct department costs and indirect department costs.

Q19-2. Define the terms direct cost and indirect cost.

Q19-3. Differentiate between cost assignment and cost allocation.

Q19-4. Explain how a cost item can be both a direct cost and an indirect cost.

Q19-5. What is the primary advantage of separately allocating fixed and variable indirect costs?

Q19-6. Define interdepartmental services.

Q19-7. To what extent are interdepartmental services recognized under the direct, step, and linear algebra methods of service department cost allocation?

Q19-8. Is it feasible to assign interdepartmental services to production departments using ABC?

Q19-9. Explain the concept of just-in-time inventory management.

Q19-10. What are the major elements of lean production?

Q19-11. What is the relationship between JIT and the lean production concept?

Q19-12. What role did Toyota have in the development of the lean production concept?

Q19-13. What elements of the JIT approach contribute to reducing materials inventories?

Q19-14. Define and identify the elements of cycle time. Which of these elements adds value to the product?

Q19-15. Explain briefly how JIT/lean production benefits organizations that take a value-chain approach to management.

Q19-16. Explain how traditional performance evaluation systems using standard costs conflict with the lean production concept.

**Assignments with the ⊘ in the margin are available in an online homework system.
See the Preface of the book for details.**

MINI EXERCISES

M19-17. Allocating Service Department Costs: Allocation Basis Alternatives (LO2)

Boston Fabricators has two producing departments, P1 and P2, and one service department, S1. Estimated direct overhead costs per month are as follows:

> P1 . . . . . . $125,000
> P2 200,000
> S1 66,000

Other data follow:

	P1	P2
Number of employees	75	25
Production capacity (units).	50,000	30,000
Space occupied (square feet).	2,500	7,500
Five-year average percent of		
S1's service output used	65%	35%

Required

a. For each of the following allocation bases, determine the total estimated overhead cost for P1 and P2 after allocating S1 cost to the producing departments.
  1. Number of employees
  2. Production capacity in units
  3. Space occupied
  4. Five-year average percentage of S1 services used
  5. Estimated direct overhead costs. (Round your answer to the nearest dollar.)

b. For each of the five allocation bases, explain the circumstances (including examples) under which each allocation base might be most appropriately used to allocate service department cost in a manufacturing plant such as Boston Fabricators. Also, discuss the advantages and disadvantages that might result from using each of the allocation bases.

M19-18. Indirect Cost Allocation: Direct Method (LO2)

Sprint Manufacturing Company has two production departments, Melting and Molding. Direct general plant management and plant security costs benefit both production departments. Sprint allocates general plant management costs on the basis of the number of production employees and plant security costs on the basis of space occupied by the production departments. In November, the following overhead costs were recorded:

Melting Department direct overhead	$150,000
Molding Department direct overhead.	300,000
General plant management	100,000
Plant security	35,000

Other pertinent data follow:

	Melting	Molding
Number of employees	25	45
Space occupied (square feet).	10,000	40,000
Machine hours	10,000	2,000
Direct labor hours.	4,000	20,000

Required

a. Prepare a schedule allocating general plant management costs and plant security costs to the Melting and Molding Departments.
b. Determine the total departmental overhead costs for the Melting and Molding Departments.
c. Assuming the Melting Department uses machine hours and the Molding Department uses direct labor hours to apply overhead to production, calculate the overhead rate for each production department.

M19-19. Interdepartment Services: Direct Method (LO2)

Tucson Manufacturing Company has five operating departments, two of which are producing departments (P1 and P2) and three of which are service departments (S1, S2, and S3). All costs of the service departments are allocated to the producing departments. The following table shows the distribution of services from the service departments.

Services provided from	Services Provided to				
	S1	S2	S3	P1	P2
S1.	—	5%	25%	50%	20%
S2.	10%	—	5	45	40
S3.	15	5	—	20	60

The direct operating costs of the service departments are as follows:

S1.	$42,000
S2.	85,000
S3.	19,000

Required

Using the direct method, prepare a schedule allocating the service department costs to the producing departments.

M19-20. Inventory Ratio Calculations (LO3, 4)

Delroi, Inc., provided the following data for 2011 and 2012:

Inventory	
December 31, 2010	$200,200
December 31, 2011	190,400
December 31, 2012	182,500
Cost of goods sold	
2011.	$654,000
2012.	724,000
Gross margin	
2011.	$340,000
2012.	410,000

Required

(round all calculations to two decimal places)

a. Calculate the inventory turnover ratio for 2011 and 2012.

b. Calculate the gross margin return on inventory investment for 2011 and 2012.

M19-21. Inventory Ratio Calculations (LO3, 4)

McMahan, LTD., provided the following data for 2011 and 2012:

Inventory	
December 31, 2010	$176,000
December 31, 2011	185,000
December 31, 2012	194,000
Cost of goods sold	
2011	$546,000
2012	589,000
Gross margin	
2011	$256,000
2012	287,000

Required

(round all calculations to two decimal places)

a. Calculate the inventory turnover ratio for 2011 and 2012.

b. Calculate the gross margin return on inventory investment for 2011 and 2012.

EXERCISES

E19-22. Interdepartment Services: Step Method (LO2)

Refer to the data in Mini-Exercise M19-19. Using the step method, prepare a schedule for Tucson Manufacturing Company allocating the service department costs to the producing departments. (Round calculations to the nearest dollar.)

E19-23. Interdepartment Services: Step Method (LO2)

O'Brian's Department Stores allocates the costs of the Personnel and Payroll departments to three retail sales departments, Housewares, Clothing, and Furniture. In addition to providing services to the operating departments, Personnel and Payroll provide services to each other. O'Brian's allocates Personnel Department costs on the basis of the number of employees and Payroll Department costs on the basis of gross payroll. Cost and allocation information for June is as follows:

	Personnel	Payroll	Housewares	Clothing	Furniture
Direct department cost.	$6,900	$3,200	$12,200	$20,000	$15,750
Number of employees	5	3	8	15	4
Gross payroll	$6,000	$3,300	$11,200	$17,400	$8,100

Required

a. Determine the percentage of total Personnel Department services that was provided to the Payroll Department.

b. Determine the percentage of total Payroll Department services that was provided to the Personnel Department.

c. Prepare a schedule showing Personnel Department and Payroll Department cost allocations to the operating departments, assuming O'Brian's uses the step method. (Round calculations to the nearest dollar.)

E19-24. Product Costing in a JIT/Lean Environment (LO3, 4)

Doll Computer manufactures laptop computers under its own brand, but acquires all the components from outside vendors. No computers are assembled until the order is received online from customers, so there is no finished goods inventory. When an order is received, the bill of materials required to fill the order is prepared automatically and sent electronically to the various vendors. All components are received from vendors within three days and the completed order is shipped to the customer immediately when completed, usually on the same day the components are received from vendors. The number of units in process at the end of any day is negligible.

The following data are provided for the most recent month of operations:

Actual components costs incurred	$905,000
Actual conversion costs incurred...........................	$192,000
Units in process, beginning of month	-0-
Units started in process during the month................	5,000
Units in process, end of month	-0-

Required

a. Assuming Doll uses traditional cost accounting procedures:
  1. How much cost was charged to Work-in-Process during the month?
  2. How much cost was charged to cost of goods sold during the month?
b. Assuming Doll is a lean production company and uses backflush costing method:
  1. How much cost was charged to Work-in-Process during the month?
  2. How much cost was charged to cost of goods sold during the month?

E19-25. Inventory Management Metrics (LO4)

Large retailers like The Home Depot and Wal-Mart typically use gross margin ratio (gross margin ÷ sales), inventory turnover (sometimes referred to as inventory turns), and gross margin return on investment (GMROI) to evaluate how well inventory has been managed. The goal is to maximize profits while minimizing the investment in inventory. Below are data for four scenarios, a base scenario (# 1) followed by three modifications (#s 2, 3, & 4) to the base scenario.

	Scenario 1	Scenario 2	Scenario 3	Scenario 4
Sales......................	$10,000	$20,000	$12,000	$10,000
Cost of goods sold...........	6,000	12,000	6,000	6,000
Gross profit.................	$ 4,000	$ 8,000	$ 6,000	$ 4,000
Average inventory............	$ 6,000	$ 6,000	$ 6,000	$ 5,000

Required

For each scenario calculate the gross margin percent, the inventory turnover, and GMROI.

E19-26. Evaluating Inventory Management Metrics (LO4)

Refer to E19-25.

Required

a. For Scenarios 2 though 4, explain what change occurred relative to Scenario 1 to cause GMROI to change. For example, was the change in GMROI caused by a change in inventory turns, a change in gross margin percent, or by reducing inventory levels.
b. What general conclusions can be made from the calculations and observations regarding the factors that influence GMROI.

PROBLEMS

P19-27. Selecting Cost Allocation Bases and Direct Method Allocations (LO2)

Nevada Company has three producing departments (P1, P2, and P3) for which direct department costs are accumulated. In January, the following indirect costs of operation were incurred.

Plant manager's salary and office expense	$14,400
Plant security	2,400
Plant nurse's salary and office expense	3,000
Plant depreciation	4,000
Machine maintenance	4,800
Plant cafeteria cost subsidy	3,600
	$32,200

The following additional data have been collected for the three producing departments:

	P1	P2	P3
Number of employees	10	15	5
Space occupied (square feet)	2,000	5,000	3,000
Direct labor hours	1,600	4,000	750
Machine hours	4,800	8,000	3,200
Number of nurse office visits	30	35	10

Required

a. Group the indirect cost items into cost pools based on the nature of the costs and their common basis for allocation. Identify the most appropriate allocation basis for each cost pool and determine the total January costs in the pool. (*Hint:* A cost pool may consist of one or more cost items.)

b. Allocate the cost pools directly to the three producing departments using the allocation bases selected in requirement (a).

c. How much indirect cost would be allocated to each producing department if Nevada Company were using a plantwide rate based on direct labor hours? Based on machine hours?

d. Comment on the benefits of allocating costs in pools compared with using a plantwide rate.

P19-28. Evaluating Allocation Bases and Direct Method Allocations (LO2)

Laramie Company has two service departments, Maintenance and Information Technology (IT), that serve two producing departments, Mixing and Packaging. The following data have been collected for these departments for the current year:

	IT	Maintenance	Mixing	Packaging
Direct department costs	$176,000	$140,000	$465,000	$295,000
Number of employees			50	30
Number of ethernet connections			90	70
Number of maintenance hours used			800	600
Number of maintenance orders			180	170

Required

a. Using the direct method, allocate the service department costs under the following independent assumptions:

1. IT costs are allocated based on the number of employees, and Maintenance costs are allocated based on the number of maintenance hours used.

2. IT costs are allocated based on the number of ethernet connections served, and Maintenance costs are allocated based on the number of maintenance orders.

b. Comment on the reasonableness of the bases used in the calculations in requirement (a). What considerations should determine which bases to use for allocating IT and Maintenance costs?

P19-29. Cost Reimbursement and Step Allocation Method (LO2)

Samaritan's Clinic is a not-for-profit outpatient facility that provides medical services to both fee-paying patients and low-income government-supported patients. Reimbursement from the government is based on total actual costs of services provided, including both direct costs of patient services and indirect operating costs. Patient services are provided through two producing departments, Medical Services and Ancillary Services (includes X-ray, therapy, etc.). In addition to the direct costs of these departments, the clinic incurs indirect costs in two service departments, Administration and Facilities. Administration costs are allocated first based on the number of full-time employees, and Facilities costs are then allocated based on space occupied. Costs and related data for the current month are as follows:

	Administration	Facilities	Medical Services	Ancillary Services
Direct costs	$24,000	$9,000	$121,400	$37,200
Number of employees	5	4	13	7
Amount of space occupied (square feet)	1,500	750	8,000	2,000
Number of patient visits.................	—	—	4,000	1,500

Required

a. Using the step method, prepare a schedule allocating the common service department costs to the producing departments.

b. Determine the amount to be reimbursed from the government for each low-income patient visit.

P19-30. Budgeted Service Department Cost Allocation: Pricing a New Product (LO2)

Pro-Trim Company is adding a new diet food concentrate called Body Trim to its line of bodybuilding and exercise products. A plant is being built for manufacturing the new product. Management has decided to price the new product based on a 100 percent markup on total manufacturing costs. A direct cost budget for the new plant projects that direct department costs of $2,450,000 will be incurred in producing an expected normal output of 700,000 pounds of finished product. In addition, indirect costs for Administration and Technical Support will be shared by Body Trim with the two exercise products divisions, Commercial Products and Retail Products. Budgeted annual data to be used in making the allocations are summarized here.

	Administration	Technical Support	Commercial Products	Retail Products	Body Trim
Number of employees	5	5	50	30	20
Amount of technical support time (hours)	500	—	1,500	1,250	750

Direct costs are budgeted at $202,500 for the Administration Department and $240,000 for the Technical Support Department.

Required

a. Using the step method, determine the total direct and indirect costs of Body Trim.

b. Determine the selling price per pound of Body Trim. (Round calculations to the nearest cent.)

P19-31. Allocation and Responsibility Accounting (LO2)

Timberland Company
(TBL)

Assume that Timberland Company uses a responsibility accounting system for evaluating its managers, and that abbreviated performance reports for the company's three divisions for the month of March are as follows (amounts in thousands).

	Total	East	Central	West
Income	$200,000	$70,000	$80,000	$50,000
Less allocated costs:				
Information Technology ...	(96,000)	(32,000)	(32,000)	(32,000)
Personnel	(75,000)	(28,125)	(28,125)	(18,750)
Division income	$ 29,000	$9,875	$19,875	$ (750)

The West Division manager is very disturbed over his performance report and recent rumors that his division may be closed because of its failure to report a profit in recent periods. He believes that the reported profit figures do not fairly present operating results because his division is being unfairly burdened with service department costs. He is particularly concerned over the amount of Information

Technology costs charged to his division. He believes that it is inequitable for his division to be charged with one-third of the total cost when it is using only 20 percent of the services. He believes that the Personnel Department's use of the Information Technology Department should also be considered in the cost allocations. Cost allocations were based on the following distributions of service provided:

| | | Services Receiver | | | |
| | | Computer | | | |
Services Provider	Personnel	Services	East	Central	West
Information Technology ...	40%	—	20%	20%	20%
Personnel.............	—	20%	30	30	20

Required

a. What method is the company using to allocate Personnel and Information Technology costs?
b. Recompute the cost allocations using the step method. (Round calculations to the nearest dollar.)
c. Revise the performance reports to reflect the cost allocations computed in requirement (b).
d. Comment on the complaint of the West Division's manager.

P19-32. **Allocating Service Department Costs: Direct and Step Methods; Department and Plantwide Overhead Rates** (LO2)

Assume that **Pennington Group**, a manufacturer of fine casual outdoor furniture, allocates Human Resources Department costs to the producing departments (Cutting and Welding) based on number of employees; Facilities Department costs are allocated based on the amount of square footage occupied. Direct department costs, labor hours, and square footage data for the four departments for October are as follows:

Pennington Group

	Human Resources	Facilities	Cutting	Welding
Direct department overhead costs...............	$60,000	$150,000	$800,000	$370,000
Number of employees	5	5	40	60
Number of direct labor hours......	—	—	8,000	10,000
Amount of square footage	10,000	3,000	100,000	50,000

Assume that two jobs, A1 and A2, were completed during October and that each job had direct materials costs of $1,200. Job A1 used 80 direct labor hours in the Cutting Department and 20 direct labor hours in the Welding Department. Job A2 used 20 direct labor hours in the Cutting Department and 80 direct labor hours in the Welding Department. The direct labor rate is $50 in both departments.

Required

a. Find the cost of each job using a plantwide rate based on direct labor hours.
b. Find the cost of each job using department rates with *direct* service department cost allocation.
c. Find the cost of each job using department rates with *step* service department cost allocation.
d. Explain the differences in the costs computed in requirements (a)–(c) for each job. Which costing method is better for product pricing and profitability analysis?

P19-33. **JIT/Lean Production and Product Costing** (LO4)

Presented is information pertaining to the standard or budgeted unit cost of a product manufactured in a JIT/Lean Production environment at Towry Systems Inc.:

Direct materials	$15
Conversion...	10
Total	$25

All materials are added at the start of the production process. All raw materials purchases and conversion costs are directly assigned to Cost of Goods Sold. At the end of the period, costs are backed out and assigned to Raw Materials in Process (only for materials still in the plant) and Finished Goods Inventory (for materials and conversion costs for completed units). Costs assigned to inventories are based on the standard or budgeted cost multiplied by the number of units in inventory. Conversion costs are assigned to inventories only for fully converted units. Since inventory levels tend to be small in this JIT environment, partially completed units are assigned no conversion costs. Towry had no beginning inventories on August 1, 2012. During the month, it incurred the following manufacturing-related costs:

Purchase of raw materials on account.	$300,000
Factory wages	130,000
Factory supervision salaries.	30,000
Utilities bill for month	17,000
Factory supplies purchased.	15,000
Depreciation.	9,500

The end-of-month inventory included raw materials in process of 750 units and finished goods of 500 units. One hundred units of raw materials were zero percent converted; the other 650 units averaged 60 percent converted.

Required

a. Calculate the total cost charged to Cost of Goods Sold during August.

b. Calculate the balances in Raw Materials in Process, Finished Goods Inventory, and Cost of Goods Sold at the end of August.

c. Assuming that August is a typical month, is it likely that using the company's shortcut backflush accounting procedures will produce misleading financial statements? Explain.

P19-34. Just-in-Time Performance Evaluation (LO5)

To control operations, Waymor Company makes extensive and exclusive use of financial performance reports for each department. Although all departments have been reporting favorable cost variances in most periods, management is perplexed by the firm's low overall return on investment. You have been asked to look into the matter. Believing the purchasing department is typical of the company's operations, you obtained the following information concerning the purchases of parts for a product it started producing in 2007:

Year	Purchase Price Variance	Quantity Used (units)	Average Inventory (units)
2007	$ 1,000 F	20,000	5,000
2008	10,000 F	30,000	7,500
2009	12,000 F	35,000	10,000
2010	20,000 U	25,000	6,250
2011	8,000 F	36,000	9,000
2012	9,500 F	29,000	7,250

Required

a. Compute the inventory turnover for each year. What conclusions can be drawn from a yearly comparison of the purchase price variance and the inventory turnover?

b. Identify problems likely to be caused by evaluating purchasing only on the basis of the purchase price variance.

c. Offer whatever recommendations you believe appropriate.

P19-35. Dual Allocation Approach and Charging for Services (LO2)

The Maintenance Department of Management Smart Suites Hotel has fixed costs of $600,000 a year. It also incurs $30 in out-of-pocket expenses for every hour of work. During the year the Rooms Department used 20,000 maintenance hours. The Food and Beverage (F&B) Department used 5,000 maintenance hours. When the Maintenance Department was established the Rooms and F&B departments estimated they would need 20,000 and 12,000 maintenance hours, respectively. It turns out F&B cut back on maintenance hours used to insure it would meet its budget.

Required:

a. Calculate the amount of Maintenance Department costs to allocate to Rooms and F&B based entirely on actual usage.

b. Calculate the amount of Maintenance Department costs to allocate to Rooms and F&B using a dual allocation approach where fixed cost is allocated based on estimated capacity needed and variable cost is allocated based on actual usage.

c. Which of the two methods applied in parts a. and b. is most fair to the two departments?

d. Assume that the maintenance department allocates costs to the producing departments using a user charge. What amount would you suggest for the user charge? Is it a good idea to use a user charge for allocating costs?

MANAGEMENT APPLICATIONS

MA19-36. Materials Push and Materials Pull Systems   (LO3, 4)

Data Storage Inc. produces three models of external storage devices for personal computers. Each model is produced on a separate assembly line. Production consists of several operations in separate work centers. Because of a high demand for Data's products, management is most interested in high-production volume and operating efficiency. Each work center is evaluated on the basis of its operating efficiency. To avoid idle time caused by defective units, variations in machine times, and machine breakdowns, significant inventories are maintained between each workstation.

At a recent administrative committee meeting, the director of research announced that the firm's engineers have made a dramatic breakthrough in designing a low-cost, read/write optical storage device. Data Storage's president is very enthusiastic, and the vice president of marketing wishes to add an assembly line for optical storage devices as soon as possible. The equipment necessary to manufacture the new product can be purchased and installed in less than 60 days. Unfortunately, all available plant space is currently devoted to the production of conventional storage devices, and expansion is not possible at the current plant location. It appears that adding the new product will require dropping a current product, relocating the entire operation, or manufacturing the optical storage devices at a separate location.

The vice president of marketing is opposed to dropping a current product. The vice president of finance is opposed to relocating the entire operation because of financing requirements and the associated financial risks. The vice president of production is opposed to splitting up production activities because of the loss of control and the added costs for various types of overhead.

Required

Explain how switching to a materials pull (Kanban) system can help solve Data Storage's space problems while improving quality and cycle time. Describe how a materials pull system works and the changes required in management attitude toward inventory and efficiency to make it work.

MA19-37. Product Costing Using Activity-Based Costing and Just-in-Time: A Value Chain Approach   (LO3, 4)

Wearwell Carpet Company is a small residential carpet manufacturer started by Don Stegall, a longtime engineer and manager in the carpet industry. Stegall began Wearwell in the early 1990s after learning about ABC, JIT, total quality management, and several other manufacturing concepts being used successfully in Japan and other parts of the world. Although it was a small company, he believed that with his many years of experience and by applying these advanced techniques, Wearwell could very quickly become a world-class competitor.

Stegall buys dyed carpet yarns for Wearwell from three different major yarn manufacturers with which he has done business for many years. He chose these companies because of their reputation for producing high-quality products and their state-of-the art research and development departments. He has arranged for two carpet manufacturing companies to produce (tuft) all of his carpets on a contractual basis. Both companies have their own brands, but they also do contract work for other companies. For each manufacturer, Stegall had to agree to use the full output of one manufacturing production line at least one day per month. Each production line was dedicated to producing only one style of carpet, but each manufacturer had production lines capable of running each type of carpet that Wearwell sold.

Stegall signed a contract with a large transport company (CTC), which specializes in carpet-related shipping, to pick up and deliver yarn from the yarn plants to the tufting mills. This company will then deliver the finished product from the tufting mills to Wearwell's ten customers, which are carpet retailers in the ten largest residential building markets in the country. These retailers pay the shipping charges to have the carpets delivered to them. Wearwell maintains a small sales staff (which also doubles as a customer service staff) to deal with the retailers and occasionally with the end customers on quality problems that arise.

Wearwell started selling only one line of carpet, a medium-grade plush, but as new carpet styles were developed, it added two additional lines, a medium-grade berber carpet and a medium-grade textured carpet. Three colors are offered in each carpet style. By selling only medium grades with limited color choices, Stegall felt that he would reach a very large segment of the carpet market without having to deal with a large number of different products. As textured (trackless) carpets have become more popular, sales of plush have diminished substantially.

Required

a. Describe the value chain for Wearwell Carpet Company, and identify the parties who compose this value chain.

b. Identify and discuss the cost categories that would be included in the cost of the product for financial reporting purposes.

c. Identify and discuss the cost categories that would be included in the cost of the product for pricing and other management purposes.

d. Discuss some of the challenges that Stegall will have trying to apply JIT to regulate the levels of control at Wearwell. Suggest changes that might be necessary to make JIT work.

e. Does Wearwell seem to be an appropriate setting for implementing ABC? If so, what are likely to be the most important activities and related cost drivers?

SOLUTIONS TO REVIEW PROBLEMS

Mid-Module Review

Solution
Service Department Cost Allocation

a. *Direct Method*

	Total	Women's	Men's
Administrative Services Department			
Allocation base (number of employees)	24	15	9
Percent of total base.	100%	62.5%	37.5%
Cost allocation	$18,000	$11,250	$6,750
Facilities Services Department			
Allocation base (square footage)	22,500	15,000	7,500
Percent of total base.	100%	66.7%	33.3%
Cost allocation	$12,000	$ 8,000	$4,000

Cost Allocation Summary					
	Administrative	Facilities	Women's	Men's	Total
Departmental costs					
before allocation	$18,000	$12,000	$60,000	$50,000	$140,000
Cost allocations					
Administrative.	(18,000)	—	11,250	6,750	0
Facilities	—	(12,000)	8,000	4,000	0
Departmental costs					
after allocation	$ 0	$ 0	$79,250	$60,750	$140,000

Step Method

Allocation Sequence		
	Administrative	Facilities
Allocation base.	Number of employees	Amount of square footage
Total base for other service and		
producing departments (a)	26	25,000
Total base for other service departments (b)	2	2,500
Percent of total services provided to other		
service departments (b ÷ a)	7.7%	10.0%
Order of allocation	Second	First

Step Allocations

	Total	Administrative	Women's	Men's
Facilities Services Department				
Allocation base (square footage)	25,000	2,500	15,000	7,500
Percent of total base.................	100%	10%	60%	30%
Cost allocation	$12,000	$1,200	$ 7,200	$3,600
Administrative Services Department				
Allocation base (number of employees)	24	—	15	9
Percent of total base.................	100%	—	62.5%	37.5%
Cost allocation ($18,000 + $1,200)	$19,200	—	$12,000	$7,200

Cost Allocation Summary

	Facilities	Administrative	Women's	Men's	Total
Departmental costs before allocation........	$12,000	$18,000	$60,000	$50,000	$140,000
Cost allocations					
Facilities	(12,000)	1,200	7,200	3,600	0
Administrative..........	—	(19,200)	12,000	7,200	0
Departmental costs after allocations	$ 0	$ 0	$79,200	$60,800	$140,000

b. Another service department cost allocation method is the *linear algebra method*. This method simultaneously allocates service department costs both to other service departments and to the producing departments. It has an advantage over the *step method* in that it fully recognizes interdepartmental services.

c. If The Apparel Store wants the most precise allocation of service department costs to the producing departments, considering both direct services and indirect services, it must use the linear algebra method of service department allocation. As indicated in the Allocation sequence section of the step method in (a), Facilities provides 10 percent of its services to Administrative, and Administrative provides 7.7 percent of its services to Facilities. The step method recognized the Facilities services provided to Administrative, but it did not recognize the Administrative services provided to Facilities.

In this case, the producing departments are using approximately the same proportion of services from each of the service departments (60.0 percent to 62.5 percent for the Women's Department and 30.0 percent to 37.5 percent for the Men's Department). Hence, using a more precise measure of cost allocation is not likely to produce significantly different results, especially since the interdepartmental services are so close (7.7 percent versus 10.0 percent). Just as the step method allocation results were quite close to the direct method results, the linear method results would likely be quite close to both the direct and step method results. Use of the linear algebra method is not recommended in this case. On the basis of simplicity and convenience, the direct method is probably the best method for The Apparel Store to use.

Module-End Review

Solution

a. Cycle time is the total time required to produce one batch, including both value-added and non-value-added activities: System A = 83; System B = 77

b. The cycle efficiency is the percent of total time used in value-added activities. In this case, only the processing time is adding value to the product. Cycle efficiency: System A = 40/83 = 0.48; System B = 30/77 = 0.39

c. In selecting between A and B, the system with the highest efficiency would not likely be chosen because it has the longest total cycle time. Assuming both systems produce products of equal quality and characteristics, B is appealing because it requires one-fourth less processing time than A and offers greater opportunity for continuous improvement.

d. In a lean environment, management and all employees involved will be seeking ways to reduce the cycle time while maintaining a high-quality product. For B, the most likely opportunity for significant reduction is to reduce the large amount of movement and waiting time. If these components of total cycle time can be reduced, B becomes even more attractive.

TOYOTA

For more than a decade, the major automobile manufacturers worldwide have been key players in the "green" movement with the introduction of about fifty hybrid automobile models. The first and most successful entry in this market by a major company was the Toyota Prius, with more than 2 million units sold in over 70 countries since 1997; but the other major manufacturers (including Honda, GM, Ford, and Daimler) all have established models in the hybrid cars market.

The second generation of green cars was introduced to the U.S. market in 2011 with the rollout of the Chevrolet Volt and the Nissan Leaf. The Volt is a plug-in hybrid electric vehicle with an on-board gas engine that can recharge the batteries and provide power to the electric motor. The Leaf (which stands for Leading, Environmentally friendly, Afford-able, Family car) is a true all-electric car that does not have any on-board power source other than the batteries. The Leaf carries the "green" commitment beyond just the drive train, as it uses recycled material for the interior, including seat covers made from recycled plastic bottles.

Initially, the ultimate green car envisioned by many in the automobile industry was a car powered by hydrogen fuel cells that combine hydrogen and oxygen to make electricity and water. Fuel cell technology has had limited success with larger vehicles such as buses and trucks, where size is not such a limiting factor. However, after major investments in this technology, most of the major auto manufacturers have either cancelled their hydrogen car efforts, or reduced them substantially, due to their inability to adapt the technology to a standard-sized car, and at a price the public is willing to pay.

Pricing and Other Product Management Decisions

LEARNING OBJECTIVES

LO1 Explain the importance of the value chain in managing products and identify the key components of an organization's internal and external value chain. (p. 20-3)

LO2 Distinguish between economic and cost-based approaches to pricing. (p. 20-7)

LO3 Explain target costing and its acceptance in highly competitive industries. (p. 20-11)

LO4 Describe the relation between target costing and continuous improvement costing. (p. 20-16)

LO5 Explain how benchmarking enhances quality management, continuous improvement, and process reengineering. (p. 20-17)

Price is a major factor when introducing any new technology to the market. As successful as the Prius and other hybrids have been, analysts have estimated that it takes seven to eight years for the higher purchase price and maintenance costs of a hybrid to be recovered by reduced fuel costs. With a suggested retail price of more than $40,000 for the Volt, and more than $32,000 for the Leaf, price will likely be a major barrier to their future success. However, with the current tax credits of $7,500 per car, they become more competitive with other mid-sized autos.

The introduction of new technology automobiles is a classic setting for applying the managerial accounting concepts of cost-based pricing, target costing, and continuous improvement costing. These managerial accounting tools, which are discussed in this module, are increasingly impor-

tant for managers involved in the development, manufacturing, and marketing of products and services. Companies that are successful in introducing new products, as well as managing existing products, invariably have a focus on the value chain for all of their products.[1]

---

[1] "Worldwide Prius Cumulative Sales Top 2M Mark; Toyota Reportedly Plans Two New Prius Variants for the US by End of 2012," *Green Car Congress*, October 7, 2010, http://www.greencarcongress.com/2010/10/; Chrissie Thompson, "GM Dealers: Chevy Volt Production Has Started," *Detroit Free Press*, November 16, 2010, http://www.freep.com/article/20101116/; "Nissan Rolls Out Leaf Electric Car in Japan," *Associated Press*, December 3, 2010, http://www.npr.org/templates/story/story.php?storyId=131771329; Anna Prior, "The Hidden Cost of Going Green," *Smart Money*, January 2011, p. 61.

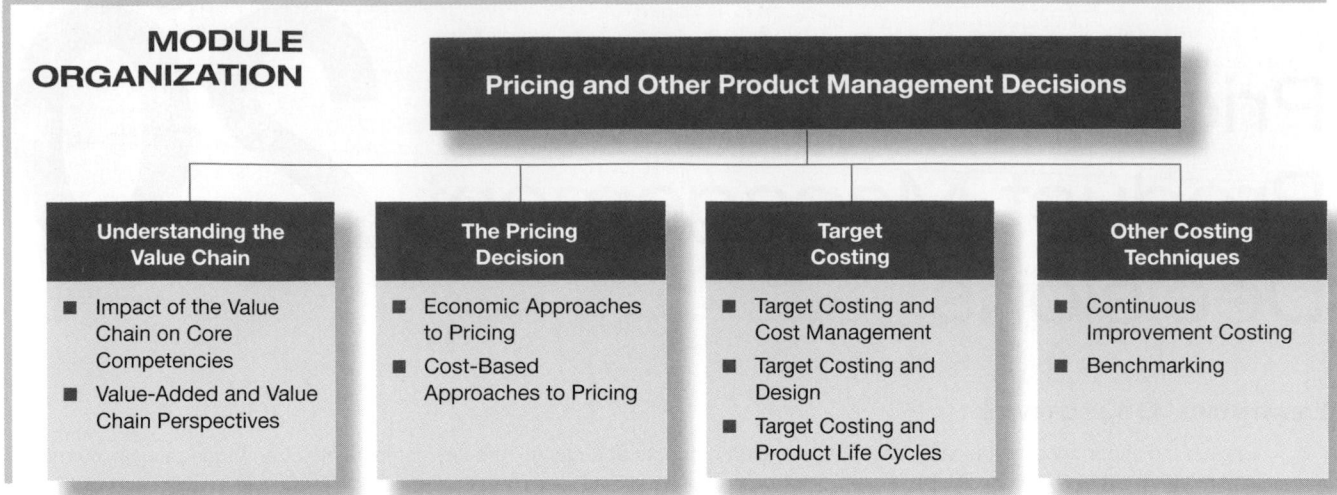

Strategic cost management techniques, such as *target costing* and *continuous improvement costing*, represent important concepts for product management professionals involved in the development, manufacture, and marketing of products and services. Virtually all such techniques are grounded in the notion of managing the value chain. This module examines pricing, the interrelation between price and cost, and the role of benchmarking in meeting customer needs at the lowest possible price.

We begin with a discussion of the value chain, followed by an overview of the pricing model economists use to explain price equilibrium. Given the limitations of this long-run equilibrium model for determining price of a product or service, we consider the widely used cost-plus approach to identifying initial prices. We then examine how intense competition (such as that for the green car market) has inverted the cost-plus pricing model into one that starts with an acceptable market price and subtracts a desired profit to determine a target cost. We also consider *life cycle costs* from the perspectives of both the seller, who increasingly plans for all costs before production begins, and the buyer, who regards subsequent operating, maintenance, repair, and disposal costs as important as price. Finally, we consider how *benchmarking* can assist in improving competitiveness and profitability.

UNDERSTANDING THE VALUE CHAIN

LO1 Explain the importance of the value chain in managing products and identify the key components of an organization's internal and external value chain.

The **value chain** for a product or service is the set of value-producing activities that stretches from basic raw materials to the final consumer. Each product or service has a distinct value chain, and all entities along the value chain depend on the final customer's perception of the value and cost of a product or service. It is the final customer who ultimately pays all costs and provides all profits to all organizations along the entire value chain. Consequently, *the goal of every organization is to maximize the value, while minimizing the cost, of a product or service to final customers*.

The value chain provides a viewpoint that encompasses all activities performed to deliver products and services to final customers. Depending on the needs of management, value chains are developed at varying levels of detail. Analyzing a value chain from the perspective of the final consumer requires working backward from the end product or service to the basic raw materials entering into the product or service. Analyzing a value chain from the viewpoint of an organization that is in the middle of a value chain requires working forward (downstream) to the final consumer and backward (upstream) to the source of raw materials. The paper industry provides a convenient context for illustrating the value chain concept.

Exhibit 20.1 presents the value chain for the paperboard cartons used to package beverages, such as Coca-Cola, Pepsi, or Evían products. The value chain is presented at three levels, with each successive level containing additional details. The first level depicts the various business entities in the value chain:

■ Timber producers grow the pulp wood (usually pine) used as the basic input into paper products. Some large paper companies, such as Boise Cascade and Georgia Pacific, harvest much of their pulp wood from timberlands that they manage. Other companies, including Riverwood Interna-

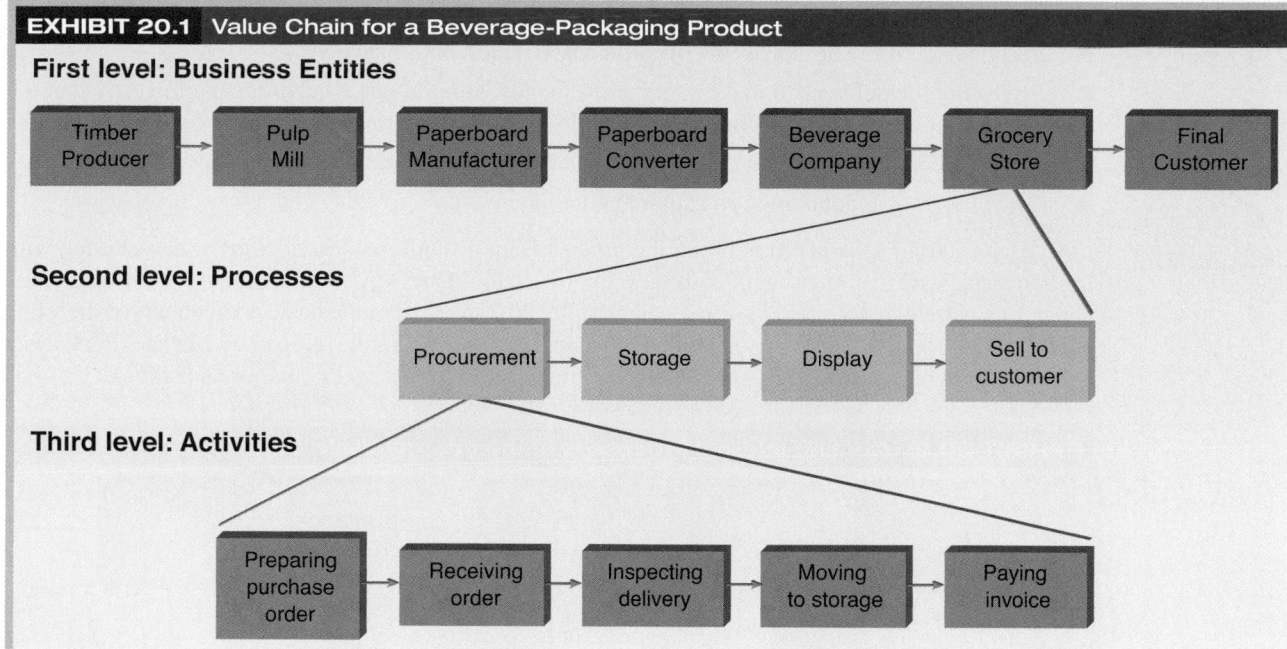

EXHIBIT 20.1 Value Chain for a Beverage-Packaging Product

First level: Business Entities

Timber Producer → Pulp Mill → Paperboard Manufacturer → Paperboard Converter → Beverage Company → Grocery Store → Final Customer

Second level: Processes

Procurement → Storage → Display → Sell to customer

Third level: Activities

Preparing purchase order → Receiving order → Inspecting delivery → Moving to storage → Paying invoice

tional (now **Graphic Packaging Holding Company**), which is a leading producer of paperboard for the beverage industry, do not manage their own timberlands, but purchase pulp for their mills on the open market through pulp intermediaries.

- Pulp mills produce the kraft (unbleached) paper used to produce the paperboard. Some of the smaller paperboard manufacturers purchase the kraft paper product from pulp mills; Graphic Packaging, however, owns its own paper mills that produce paper for its paperboard production facilities.

- Paperboard manufacturers perform a laminating process of coating paperboard material used to produce beverage packages. The paperboard consists of two layers of paper product plus three layers of coating that gives the top surface a high gloss finish that is water resistent and suitable for multicolor printing. Graphic Packaging is a manufacturer of paperboard for the beverage industry.

- The paperboard converter uses manufactured paperboard to print and produce the completed beverage packaging product, such as the cartons used to package the Diet **Coca-Cola** 12-pack.

- Beverage distributors, such as **Coca-Cola Enterprises** and **Anheuser-Busch**, purchase the completed paperboard packages from Graphic Packaging to package their many different brands in various package sizes and shapes.

- Grocery and convenience stores, such as **Safeway** and **7-Eleven**, display and sell beverages packaged in the paperboard containers.

- The final customer purchases beverages packaged in paperboard packages and uses the packages to carry the beverages and to store them until consumed. The packages not only perform a transport and storage function but also serve as an advertising medium for the beverage company. The beverage company's advertising on the paperboard packages is intended to entice customers to purchase the beverage company's product and to help create a sense of satisfaction for the customer.

To better understand how business entities within the chain add value and incur costs, management might further refine the value chain into **processes**, collections of related activities intended to achieve a common purpose. The second level in Exhibit 20.1 represents major processes concerning the procurement and sale of Coca-Cola products by a grocery store. To simplify our illustration, we show only the processes for the grocery store related to the purchase and sale of Coca-Cola products packaged in paperboard packages. These processes include procuring Coca-Cola products from the bottling company, storing and displaying the product, and selling the product to the final consumer.

An **activity** is a unit of work. In the third level of Exhibit 20.1, the grocery store process to procure Coca-Cola products is further broken up into the following activities:

- *Placing* a purchase order for Coca-Cola products packaged in paperboard packages.
- *Receiving* delivery of the Coca-Cola products in paperboard packages.
- *Inspecting* the delivery to make sure it corresponds with the purchase order and to verify that the products are in good condition.
- *Storing* Coca-Cola products in paperboard packages until needed for display.
- *Paying* for Coca-Cola products acquired after the invoice arrives.

Each of the activities involved in procuring product from a vendor is described by a word ending with *ing*. This suggests that most work activities involve action. One way to think about the internal value chain for a particular company is provided in Exhibit 20.2 in terms of the basic components of the value chain that are found in most organizations. This generic model, first developed by Michael Porter, is a good starting point in identifying the internal value chain links for a particular organization.

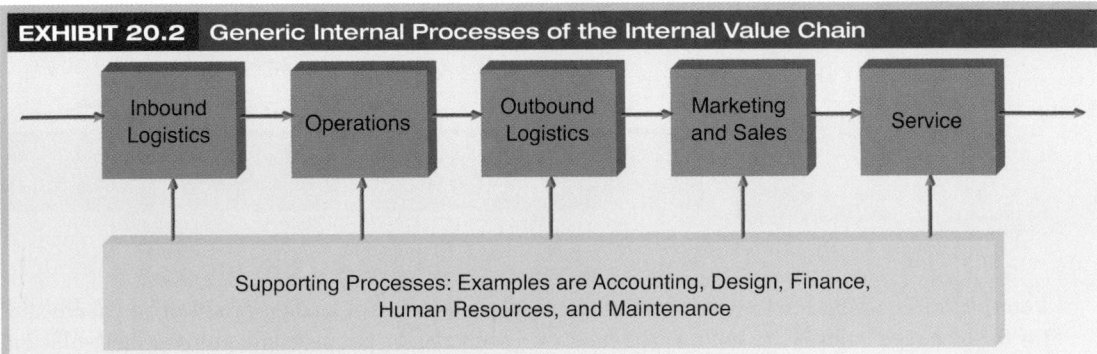

EXHIBIT 20.2 Generic Internal Processes of the Internal Value Chain

Usefulness of a Value Chain Perspective

The goal of maximizing final customer value while minimizing final customer cost leads organizations to examine *internal* and *external links* in the value chain rather than the departments, processes, or activities independently. From a value chain perspective, it is total cost across the entire value chain, not the cost of individual businesses, departments, processes, or activities that is most important. As the following Business Insight points out, value chain analysis can also be a valuable tool as companies pursue the goals of sustainability and environmental responsibility.

BUSINESS INSIGHT **A Green Analysis of a Value Chain**

Value chain and business process analysis has become an important tool in understanding "how work gets done" in an organization. According to a business process expert, the current emphasis on environmental concerns is now turning management's attention to "how can we change the way work gets done." If your company is a heavy consumer of electric energy, you should be asking what activities use energy. In the past, energy was probably managed with a cost reduction objective, but a green strategy would focus more on minimizing energy consumption or replacing electric energy with a more environmentally friendly energy source, or eliminating the energy-consuming activity entirely. For example, a rental car company with a policy, in winter climates, to keep the car (and heater) running until the customer picks it up, should ask the question: is it worth it, or could we accomplish the same level of customer satisfaction in a way that consumes less energy?

Source: "A Green Analysis of a Value Stream," *Business Process, Trends Email Advisor*, April 10, 2010, http://www.bptrends.com/publicationfiles/advisor20100427.pdf.

Value Chain Perspective Fosters Supplier-Buyer Partnerships

In the past, relationships between suppliers and buyers were often adversarial. Contact between suppliers and buyers was solely through the selling and purchasing departments. Suppliers attempted merely to meet purchasing contract specifications at the lowest possible cost. Buyers encouraged competition among suppliers with the primary—and often single—goal of obtaining the lowest purchase price.

As discussed in Module 19 with JIT and lean production, exploiting cost reduction and value-enhancing opportunities in the value chain has led many buyers and suppliers to view each other as partners rather than as adversaries. Buyers have reduced the number of suppliers they deal with, often developing long-term partnerships with a single supplier. Once they establish mutual trust, both proceed to share detailed information on internal operations and help each other solve problems. Partners work closely to examine mutual opportunities by studying their common value chain. Supplier engineers might determine that a minor relaxation in buyer specifications would significantly reduce supplier manufacturing costs with only minor increases in subsequent buyer processing costs. Working together, they determine how best to modify processes to reduce overall costs and share increased profits.

Companies such as Hewlett-Packard and Boeing involve suppliers in design, development, and manufacturing decisions. Motorola has even developed a survey asking suppliers to assess Motorola as a buyer. Among other questions, the survey asks sellers to evaluate Motorola's performance in helping suppliers to identify major cost drivers and to increase their profitability. These questions represent the concerns of a partner rather than those of an adversary. Michael Dell, at Dell Computers, stated that "rather than closely guarding our information databases, which took us years to develop, we used Internet browsers to essentially give that information to our customers and suppliers—bringing them into our business.[2] The following Business Insight box describes how Nestle assists coffee growers to make them more profitable while ensuring a supply of high-quality coffee beans.

BUSINESS INSIGHT   **Nestle Trains and Supplies Thousands of Farmers**

Nestle CEO, Paul Bulcke, said, "We shouldn't just be the world's largest coffee buyer, we should be involved upstream . . . . We're doing it for better quality and securing our raw material." Declining coffee bean production due to aging and poorly maintained trees prompted Nestle to adopt a program to provide a new generation of plants engineered for local climates, as well as providing advice and training to thousands of farmers worldwide. Nestle projects that it will distribute 220 million plants to coffee growers over the next ten years, even though the farmers are not obligated to sell their coffee beans to Nestle. The head of one coffee cooperative in Veracruz, Mexico, stated that "price is important, but so is the attention and the commitments they [Nestle] have shown to us."

Source: Christina Passariello and Laurence Iliff, "Nestle Plans Ground Attack Over Coffee Beans," *The Wall Street Journal*, August 26, 2010, p. b1.

On a smaller scale, the grocery store in Exhibit 20.1 should examine its external links. It may be willing to pay more for Coca-Cola products if the distributors cooperate to help reduce costs such as the following:

■ Making more frequent deliveries in small lots would reduce storage costs.

■ Being responsible for maintaining and changing the product displays would relieve store workers of these tasks.

■ Streamlining ordering and payment procedures would reduce bookkeeping costs.

If partnership arrangements with upstream suppliers enable the grocery store to reduce its total costs, the store can enhance or maintain its competitive position by reducing prices charged to its consumers. Remember that competitors are also striving to reduce costs and enhance their competitive position. Hence, failing to strive for improvements will likely result in reduced sales and profits.

Value Chain Perspective Fosters Focus on Core Competencies

Using value chain concepts, relationships with suppliers often begin to represent an extended family, allowing companies to focus on core competencies; this capability provides a distinct competitive advantage. In addition, a new breed of contract manufacturers, such as Solectron Corporation and Sanmina-SCI have emerged in recent years. These organizations manufacture products for other companies, ranging from Hewlett-Packard printers to Xerox photocopy machines, with such close partnership arrangements that they behave like a single company. This allows Hewlett-Packard and Xerox

---

[2] *Direct from Dell*, Michael Dell with Catherine Fredman, Harper Collins Publishers, 1999. Also, see http://money.cnn.com/magazines/fortune/fortune500/2007/full_list/index.html

to focus on marketing and product development while Solectron and SCI Systems focus on efficient, low-cost manufacturing.

Interestingly, because their facilities are available to all innovators with the necessary financing, the emergence of contract manufacturers may speed innovation. Michael Dell attributes much of Dell's rapid growth and profitability to virtual integration with suppliers. **Virtual integration** is the use of information technology and partnership concepts to allow two or more entities along a value chain to act as if they were a single economic entity.

Value-Added and Value Chain Perspectives

The value chain perspective is often contrasted with a value-added perspective. Under a value-added perspective, decision makers consider only the cost of resources to their organization and the selling price of products or services to their immediate customers. Using a value-added perspective, the goal is to maximize the value added (the difference between the selling price and costs) by the organization. To do this, the value-added perspective focuses primarily on internal activities and costs. Under a value chain perspective, the goal is to maximize value and minimize cost to final customers, often by developing linkages or partnerships with suppliers and customers.

Although initial efforts to enhance competitiveness might start with a value-added perspective, it is important to expand to a value chain perspective. World-class competitors utilize both a value-added and a value chain perspective. These firms always keep the final customer in mind and recognize that the profitability of each entity in the value chain depends on the overall value and cost of the products and services delivered to final customers.

The value-added perspective is the foundation of the make or buy (outsourcing) decision considered in Module 16. The key differences between the partnering decisions considered here and the make or buy decision in Module 16 concern time frame, perspective, and attitude. The make or buy decision is a stand-alone decision, often in the short run, that does not view vendors and customers as partners. In contrast, characteristics of the value chain perspective are as follows:

- Comprehensive.
- Focused on the final customers.
- Strategic.
- Basis for partnerships between vendors and customers.

Enhancing or maintaining a competitive position requires an understanding of the entire system used to develop and deliver value to final customers, including interactions among organizations along the value chain. All organizations in the value chain are in business together and should work together as partners rather than as adversaries.

THE PRICING DECISION

LO2 Distinguish between economic and cost-based approaches to pricing.

Pricing products and services is one of the most important and complex decisions facing management. Pricing decisions directly affect the salability of individual products or services, as well as the profitability, and even the survival, of the organization. Many economists have spent their entire careers examining the foundations of pricing. To respond to the needs of pricing hundreds or thousands of individual items, managers have developed pricing guidelines that are typically based on costs. More recently, global competition has turned cost-based approaches upside down. Managers of world-class organizations increasingly start with a price that customers are willing to pay and then determine allowable costs.

Economic Approaches to Pricing

In economic models, the firm has a profit-maximizing goal and known cost and revenue functions. Typically, increases in sales quantity require reductions in selling prices, causing **marginal revenue** (the varying increment in total revenue derived from the sale of an additional unit) to decline as sales increase. Increases in production cause an increase in **marginal cost** (the varying increment in total cost required to produce and sell an additional unit of product). In economic models, profits are maximized at the sales volume at which marginal revenues equal marginal costs. Firms continue to produce as long as the marginal revenue derived from the sale of each additional unit exceeds the marginal cost of producing that unit.

Economic models provide a useful framework for considering pricing decisions. The ideal price is the one that will lead customers to purchase all units a firm can provide up to the point at which the last unit has a marginal cost exactly equal to its marginal revenue.

Despite their conceptual merit, economic models are seldom used for day-to-day pricing decisions. Perfect information and an indefinite time period are required to achieve equilibrium prices at which marginal revenues equal marginal costs. In the short run, most for-profit organizations attempt to achieve a target profit rather than a maximum profit. One reason for this is an inability to determine the single set of actions that will lead to profit maximization. Furthermore, managers are more apt to strive to satisfy a number of goals (such as profits for investors, job security for themselves and their employees, and being a "good" corporate citizen) than to strive for the maximization of a single profit goal. In any case, to maximize profits, a company's management would have to know the cost and revenue functions of every product the firm sells. For most firms, this information cannot be developed at a reasonable cost.

Cost-Based Approaches to Pricing

Although cost is not the only consideration in pricing, it has traditionally been the most important for several reasons.

- *Cost data are available.* When hundreds or thousands of different prices must be set in a short time, cost could be the only feasible basis for product pricing.

- *Cost-based prices are defensible.* Managers threatened by legal action or public scrutiny feel secure using cost-based prices. They can argue that prices are set in a manner that provides a "fair" profit.

- *Revenues must exceed costs if the firm is to remain in business.* In the long run, the selling price must exceed the full cost of each unit.

Cost-based pricing is illustrated in Exhibit 20.3. The process begins with market research to determine customer wants. If the product requires components to be designed and produced by vendors, the process of obtaining prices can be time consuming. When some costs, such as those fixed costs at the facility level, are not assigned to specific products, a markup is added to cover these costs. An additional markup is added to achieve a desired profit. The selling price is then set as the sum of the assigned costs, the markup to cover unassigned costs, and the markup to achieve the desired profit.

The proposed selling price should be evaluated with regard to competitive information and what customers are willing to pay. If the price is acceptable, the product or service is produced. If the price is too high, the product might be redesigned, manufacturing procedures might be changed, and different types of materials might be considered until either an acceptable price is achieved or it is determined that the product cannot be produced at an acceptable price. On the other

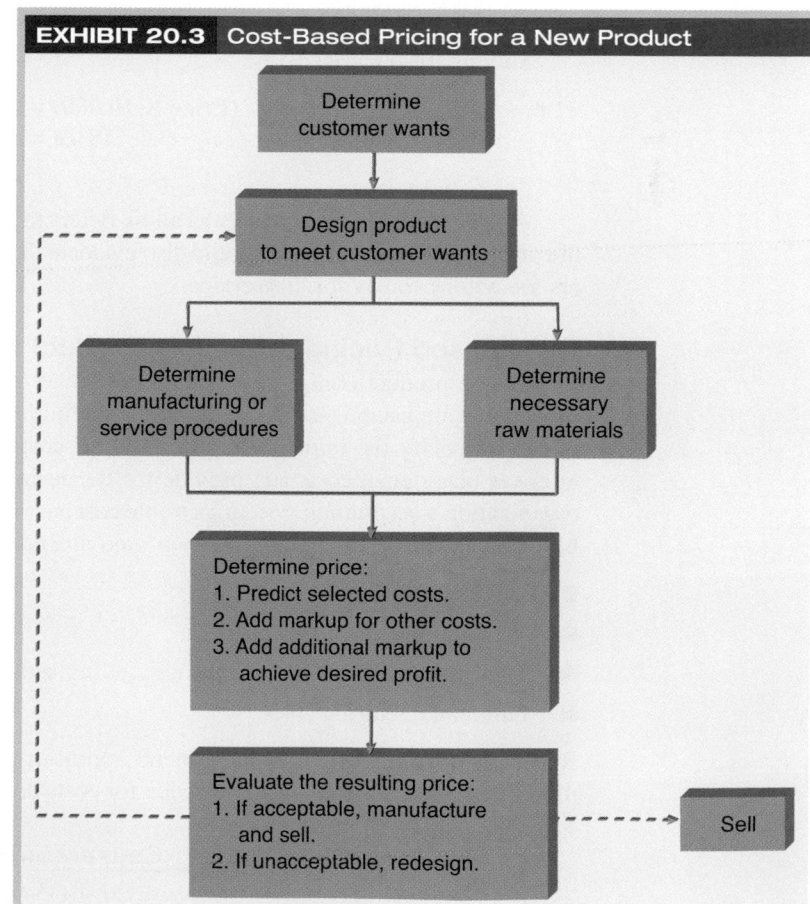

EXHIBIT 20.3   Cost-Based Pricing for a New Product

Determine customer wants

Design product to meet customer wants

Determine manufacturing or service procedures

Determine necessary raw materials

Determine price:
1. Predict selected costs.
2. Add markup for other costs.
3. Add additional markup to achieve desired profit.

Evaluate the resulting price:
1. If acceptable, manufacture and sell.
2. If unacceptable, redesign.

Sell

hand, as the Business Insight below shows, the price can sometimes be a major driver of a company's growth.

BUSINESS INSIGHT | **Subway Overtakes McDonald's**

What began as a promotion in an obscure Subway sandwich shop location in Miami, evolved into a corporate strategy for the Subway franchise organization. The small franchisee, Stuart Frankel, who owned two small Subway shops near one of Miami's major hospitals, decided to start selling footlong sandwiches for $5 to try to boost slow weekend sales. Soon the two shops had lines out the doors. A *Business Week* writer wrote: "Nobody, least of all Frankel, knew it at the time, but he had stumbled on a concept that has unexpectedly morphed from a short-term gimmick into a national phenomenon that has turbocharged Subway's performance." The biggest surprise to Frankel was that his profit margins did not decline, because the increased food costs were offset by increased volume and the increased productivity of employees who had less downtime. The $5 promotion was so successful that Subway has now overtaken McDonald's in worldwide locations numbering more than 32,000.

Source: Matthew Boyle, "The Accidental Hero," *Business Week*, November 2009, pp. 55-61.

Cost-Based Pricing in Single-Product Companies

Implementing cost-based pricing in a single-product company is straightforward if everything is known but the selling price. In this case, all known data are entered into the profit formula, which is then solved for the variable price. Assume that Bright Rug Cleaners' annual fixed facility-level costs are $200,000 and the unit cost of cleaning a rug is $10. Management desires to achieve an annual profit of $30,000 at an annual volume of 10,000 rugs. To simplify the example, assume that management charges the same price regardless of the type, size, or shape of the rug. Using the profit formula, the cost-based price is determined to be $33:

$$\textbf{Profit = Total revenues − Total costs}$$
$$\textbf{\$30,000 = (Price × 10,000 rugs) − (\$200,000 + [\$10 × 10,000 rugs])}$$

Solving for the price:

$$\textbf{(Price × 10,000) = \$300,000 + \$30,000}$$
$$\textbf{Price = \$330,000 ÷ 10,000}$$
$$\textbf{= \$33}$$

A price of $33 to clean a rug will allow Bright to achieve its desired profit. However, before setting the price at $33, management should also evaluate the competitive situation and consider what customers are willing to pay for this service.

Cost-Based Pricing in Multiple-Product Companies

In multiple-product companies, desired profits are determined for the entire company, and standard procedures are established for determining the initial selling price of each product. These procedures typically specify the initial selling price as the costs assigned to products or services plus a markup to cover unassigned costs and provide for the desired profit. Depending on the sophistication of the organization's accounting system, possible cost bases in a manufacturing organization include markups based on a *combination of cost behavior and function*. The possible cost bases include:

- Direct materials costs.
- Variable manufacturing costs.
- Total variable costs (manufacturing, selling, and administrative).
- Full manufacturing costs.

Regardless of the cost base, the general approach to developing a markup is to recognize that the markup must be large enough to provide for costs not included in the base plus the desired profit.

$$\textbf{Markup on cost base} = \frac{\textbf{Costs not included in the base + Desired profit}}{\textbf{Costs included in the base}}$$

First we illustrate a pricing decision with variable costs as the cost base; full manufacturing costs is the cost base in the second illustration.

1. When the markup is based on variable costs, it must be large enough to cover all fixed costs and the desired profit. Assume that the predicted annual variable and fixed costs for Magnum Enterprises are as follows:

Variable		Fixed	
Manufacturing	$600,000	Manufacturing	$300,000
Selling and		Selling and	
administrative	200,000	administrative	100,000
Total	$800,000	Total................	$400,000

Furthermore, assume that Magnum Enterprises has total assets of $1,250,000; management believes that an annual return of 16 percent on total assets is appropriate in Magnum's industry. A 16 percent return translates into a desired annual profit of $200,000 ($1,250,000 × 0.16). Assuming all cost predictions are correct, obtaining a profit of $200,000 requires a 75 percent markup on variable costs:

$$\textbf{Markup on variable costs} = \frac{\$400,000 + \$200,000}{\$800,000}$$
$$= 0.75$$

If the predicted variable costs for Product A1 are $12 per unit, the initial selling price for Product A1 is $21:

$$\textbf{Initial selling price} = \$12 + (\$12 \times 0.75)$$
$$= \$21$$

2. When the markup is based on full manufacturing costs, it must be large enough to cover selling and administrative expenses and to provide for the desired profit. Again, it is necessary to determine the desired profit and predict all costs for the pricing period. The initial prices of individual products are then determined as their unit manufacturing costs plus the markup. For Magnum, the markup on manufacturing costs would be 55.6 percent:

$$\textbf{Markup on manufacturing costs} = \frac{\$300,000 + \$200,000}{\$900,000}$$
$$= 0.556$$

If the predicted manufacturing costs for Product B1 are $10, the initial selling price for Product B1 is $15.56:

$$\textbf{Initial selling price} = \$10 + (\$10 \times 0.556)$$
$$= \$15.56$$

Cost-Based Pricing for Special Orders

Many organizations use cost-based pricing to bid on unique projects. If the project requires dedicated assets, the acquisition of new fixed assets, or an investment in employee training, the desired profit on the special order or project should allow for an adequate return on the dedicated assets or additional investment.

Critique of Cost-Based Pricing

Cost-based pricing has four major drawbacks:

1. Cost-based pricing requires accurate cost assignments. If costs are not accurately assigned, some products could be priced too high, losing market share to competitors; other products could be priced too low, gaining market share but being less profitable than anticipated.

2. The higher the portion of unassigned costs, the greater is the likelihood of over- or under-pricing individual products.

3. Cost-based pricing assumes that goods or services are relatively scarce and, generally, customers who want a product or service are willing to pay the price.

4. In a competitive environment, cost-based approaches increase the time and cost of bringing new products to market.

Cost-based pricing became the dominant approach to pricing during an era when products were relatively long-lived and there was relatively little competition. Also, these systems tend to focus on organizational units such as departments, plants, or divisions and not on activities or cost drivers. While easy to implement, reflecting the need to recover costs and earn a return on investment, and easily justified, cost-based prices might not be competitive. Competition puts intense downward pressure on prices and removes slack from pricing formulas. There is little margin for error in pricing. In a highly competitive market, small variations in pricing make significant differences in success.

MID-MODULE REVIEW

Presented is the 2012 contribution income statement of Knox Company.

KNOX COMPANY Contribution Income Statement For Year Ended December 31, 2012		
Sales (100,000 units at $12 per unit)		$1,200,000
Less variable costs		
Manufacturing.	$300,000	
Selling and administrative.	150,000	(450,000)
Contribution margin		750,000
Less fixed costs		
Manufacturing.	400,000	
Selling and administrative.	200,000	(600,000)
Net income.		$ 150,000

Knox has total assets of $2,000,000, and management desires an annual return of 10 percent on total assets.

Required

a. Determine the dollar amount by which Knox Company exceeded or fell short of the desired annual rate of return in 2012.

b. Given the current sales volume and cost structure, determine the unit selling price required to achieve an annual profit of $250,000.

c. Assume that management wants to state the selling price as a percentage of variable manufacturing costs. Given your answer to requirement (b) and the current sales volume and cost structure, determine the selling price as a percentage of variable manufacturing costs.

d. Restate your answer to requirement (c), dividing into two separate markup percentages:
1. The markup on variable manufacturing costs required to cover unassigned costs.
2. The additional markup on variable manufacturing costs required to achieve an annual profit of $250,000.

The solution is on page 20-26.

LO3 Explain target costing and its acceptance in highly competitive industries.

TARGET COSTING

Economists argue that cost-based prices are not realistic, because in the real world prices are determined by the confluence of supply and demand. However, when a new product is introduced into the market for which there is no previously existing supply or demand, there has to be a starting point. As discussed above, cost has often been the baseline for determining initial selling prices. All too often, however, companies introduce new products into the market based on what the designers and engineers "think" the market wants (or based on inadequate market research), only to find out later that either the market does not want the product, or it is not willing to buy the new product at a price sufficient to cover its cost plus an acceptable profit to the producer. This often leads to costly redesign, or in many cases, complete abandonment of the product, typically resulting in substantial financial losses.

Toyota, which has pioneered many of the innovations in manufacturing systems discussed in Module 19, turned the notion of cost-based pricing around and came up with the idea of price-based costing, referred to as target costing. Toyota determined that before a new product is introduced into the market, it must be able to be produced at a cost that will make it profitable when sold at a price acceptable to customers. The acceptable selling price to the marketplace determines the acceptable cost of producing the product.

Target Costing Is Proactive for Cost Management

Target costing starts with determining what customers are willing to pay for a product or service and then subtracts a desired profit on sales to determine the allowable, or target, cost of the product or service. This target cost is then communicated to a cross-functional team of employees representing such diverse areas as marketing, product design, manufacturing, and management accounting. Reflecting value chain concepts and the notion of partnerships up and down the value chain, suppliers of raw materials and components are often included in the teams. The target costing team is assigned the task of designing a product that meets customer price, function, and quality requirements while providing a desired profit. Its job is not completed until the target cost is met, or a determination is made that the product or service cannot be profitably introduced under the current circumstances. See Exhibit 20.4 for an overview of target costing.

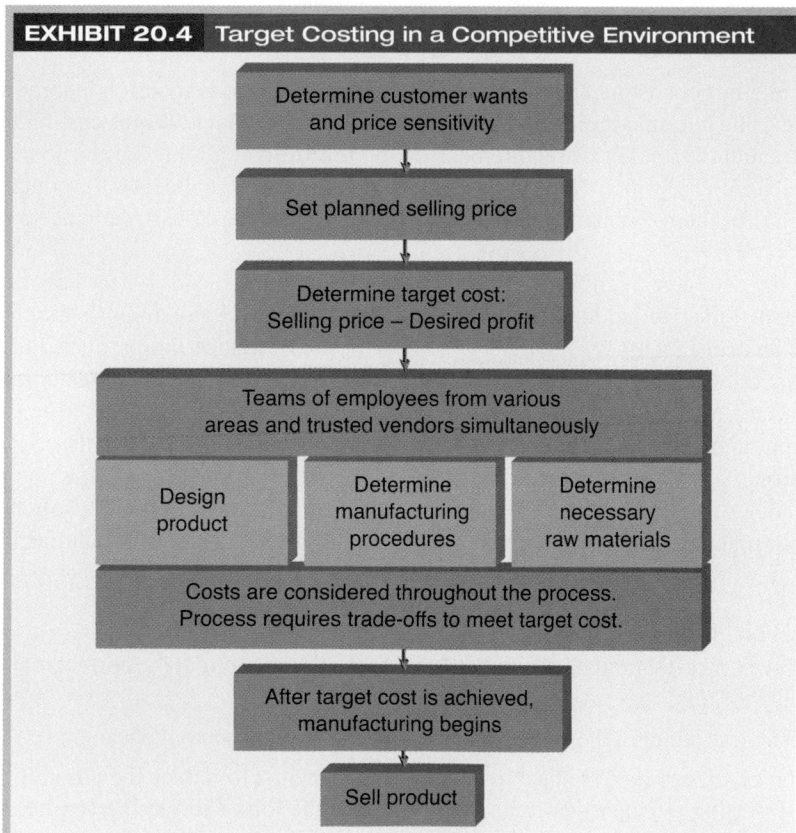

EXHIBIT 20.4 Target Costing in a Competitive Environment

Determine customer wants and price sensitivity

Set planned selling price

Determine target cost:
Selling price – Desired profit

Teams of employees from various areas and trusted vendors simultaneously

Design product | Determine manufacturing procedures | Determine necessary raw materials

Costs are considered throughout the process. Process requires trade-offs to meet target cost.

After target cost is achieved, manufacturing begins

Sell product

Although a formula can be used to determine a markup on cost, it is not possible to develop a formula indicating how to achieve a target cost. Hence, target costing is not a technique. It is more a philosophy or an approach to pricing and cost management. It takes a proactive approach to cost management, reflecting the belief that costs are best managed by decisions made during product development. This contrasts with the more passive cost-plus belief that costs result from design, procurement, and manufacture. Like the value chain, target costing helps orient employees toward the final customer and reinforces the notion that all departments within the organization and all organizations along the value chain must work together. Target costing also empowers employees who will be assigned the responsibility for carrying out activities necessary to deliver a product or service with the authority to determine what activities will be selected. Like process mapping, it helps employees to better understand their role in serving the customer. The following Research Insight discusses how target costing can improve margins for companies engaged in global sourcing.

RESEARCH INSIGHT Hitting a Moving Target in the Global Trade Economy

Global sourcing raises complex new commercial and operational challenges by exposing firms to an entirely new set of variables, resulting in sourcing initiatives that often do not meet targeted costs or profits. A report by a leading trade services company attributes this to the failure to understand, track, and manage "the risks and costs of longer, more complex cross-border supply chains." The report cites target costing as an opportunity for improving global trading, stating that "dynamically tracking actual costs against previously set targets quickly uncovers targets that are unrealistic or inaccurate. Early visibility into the delta between targets and actual allows shippers to quickly adjust targets and modify plans for downstream product pricing and marketing campaigns. By reducing the lag in discovering unrealistic targets from months to weeks or even days, companies can save millions in lost profits."

Source: Patrick Burnson, "Improving Import/Export Operations: How to Hit a Moving Target," *Logistics Management*, April 1, 2010, p. 40.

Target Costing Encourages Design for Production

In the absence of a target costing approach, design engineers are apt to focus on incorporating leading-edge technology and the maximum number of features in a product. Target costing keeps the customer's function, quality, and price requirements in the forefront at all times. If customers do not want leading-edge technology (which could be expensive and untested) and several product features, they will resist paying for them. Focusing on achieving a target cost keeps design engineers tuned in to the final customer.

Left on their own, design engineers might believe that their job ends when they design a product that meets the customer's functional requirements. The tendency is to simply pass on the design to manufacturing and let manufacturing determine how best to produce the product. Further down the line, if the product needs servicing, it becomes the service department's responsibility to determine how best to service the product. A target costing approach forces design engineers to explicitly consider the costs of manufacturing and servicing a product while it is being designed. This is known as **design for manufacture**.

Minor changes in design that do not affect the product's functioning can often produce dramatic savings in manufacturing and servicing costs. Examples of design for manufacture include the following:

- Using molded plastic parts to avoid assembling several small parts.
- Designing two parts that must be fit together so that joining them in the correct manner is obvious to assembly workers.
- Placing an access panel in the side of an appliance so service personnel can make repairs quickly.
- Using standard-size parts to reduce inventory requirements, to reduce the possibility of assembly personnel inserting the incorrect part, and to simplify the job of service personnel.
- Ensuring that tolerance requirements for parts that must fit together can be met with available equipment.
- Using manufacturing procedures that are common to other products.

The successful implementation of target costing requires employees from all involved disciplines to be familiar with costing concepts and the notions of value-added and non-value-added activities.

When considering the manufacturing process, team members should minimize non-value-added activities such as movement, storage, inspection, and setup. They should also select the lowest-cost value-added activities that do the job properly.

Target Costing Reduces Time to Introduce Products

By designing a product to meet a target cost (rather than evaluating the marketability of a product at a cost-plus price and having to recycle the design through several departments), target costing reduces the time required to introduce new products. Involving vendors in target costing design teams makes the vendors aware of the necessity of meeting a target cost. This facilitates the concurrent engineering of components to be produced outside the organization and reduces the time required to obtain components.

Target Costing Requires Cost Information

Implementing target costing requires detailed information on the cost of alternative activities. This information allows decision makers to select design and manufacturing alternatives that best meet function and price requirements. Tables that contain detailed databases of cost information for various manufacturing variables are occasionally used in designing products and selecting processes to meet target costs.

Target Costing Requires Coordination

Limitations of target costing are employee and supplier attitudes and the many meetings required to coordinate product design and to select manufacturing processes. All people involved must have a basic understanding of the overall processes required to bring a product to market and an appreciation of the cost consequences of alternative actions. They must also respect, cooperate, and communicate with other team members and be willing to engage in a negotiation process involving trade-offs. Finally, they must understand that although the total time required to bring a new product to market can be reduced, the countless coordinating meetings could be quite intrusive on the individuals' otherwise orderly schedule. See Exhibit 20.5 for an evaluation of target costing.

EXHIBIT 20.5 Pros and Cons of Target Costing
Pros
• Takes proactive approach to cost management.
• Orients organization toward customer.
• Breaks down barriers between departments.
• Enhances employee awareness and empowerment.
• Fosters partnerships with suppliers.
• Minimizes non-value-added activities.
• Encourages selection of lowest-cost value-added activities.
• Reduces time to market.
Cons
• To be effective, requires the development of detailed cost data.
• Requires willingness to cooperate.
• Requires many meetings for coordination.

This aspect of the process is even more difficult when suppliers must be brought in as part of the coordination process. This concept is frequently referred to as **chained target costing** because the supply chain's support is critical for the product to be both competitively priced and delivered to the final customer in a timely manner. When multiple suppliers are required, the organization must obtain everyone's support or the process will probably not be successful due to gaps in the reliability of delivery, quality, and cost control. Each organization and unit must understand that if the product is not brought to market within the defined constraints, all will lose. They must make firm commitments for the project undertaken and to have faith that each participant will carry out whatever part of the supply chain it has promised to fulfill. Coordination across the supply chain is vital in the overall process of continuous improvement as discussed later in this module.

Target Costing is Key for Products with Short Life Cycles

From a traditional marketing perspective, products with a relatively long life go through four distinct stages during their life cycle:

1. *Start-up.* Sales are low when a product is first introduced. Traditionally, initial selling prices are set high, and customers tend to be relatively affluent trendsetters.

2. *Growth.* Sales increase as the product gains acceptance. Traditionally, prices have remained high during this stage because of customer loyalty and the absence of competitive products.

3. *Maturity.* Sales level off as the product matures. Because of increased competition, pressure on prices is increasing; some price reductions could be necessary.

4. *Decline.* Sales decline as the product becomes obsolete. Significant price cuts could be required to sell remaining inventories.

Target costing is more important for products with a relatively short market life cycle. Products with a long life cycle present many opportunities to continuously improve design and manufacturing procedures that are not available when a product has a short life cycle. Hence, extra care must go into the initial planning for short-lived products. This is especially true when short product life cycles are combined with increased worldwide competition. It is important to introduce a product first and at a price that ensures rapid market penetration.

Target Costing Helps Manage Life Cycle Costs

An awareness of the impact of today's actions on tomorrow's costs underlies the notion of **life cycle costs**, which include all costs associated with a product or service ranging from those incurred with the initial conception through design, pre-production, production, and after-production support.

The lower line in Exhibit 20.6 illustrates the cumulative expenditure of funds over the life of a product. For low-technology products with relatively long product lives, decisions committing the organization to spend money are made at approximately the same time the money is spent. However, for high-technology products with relatively short product lives, most of the critical decisions affecting cost, such as product design and the selection of manufacturing procedures, are made before production begins. The top line in Exhibit 20.6 represents decisions committing the organization to expenditures for a product. It has been estimated that as much as 70% of the cost of the typical automobile, and 95% of the cost of high-technology products, is committed during the design stage.

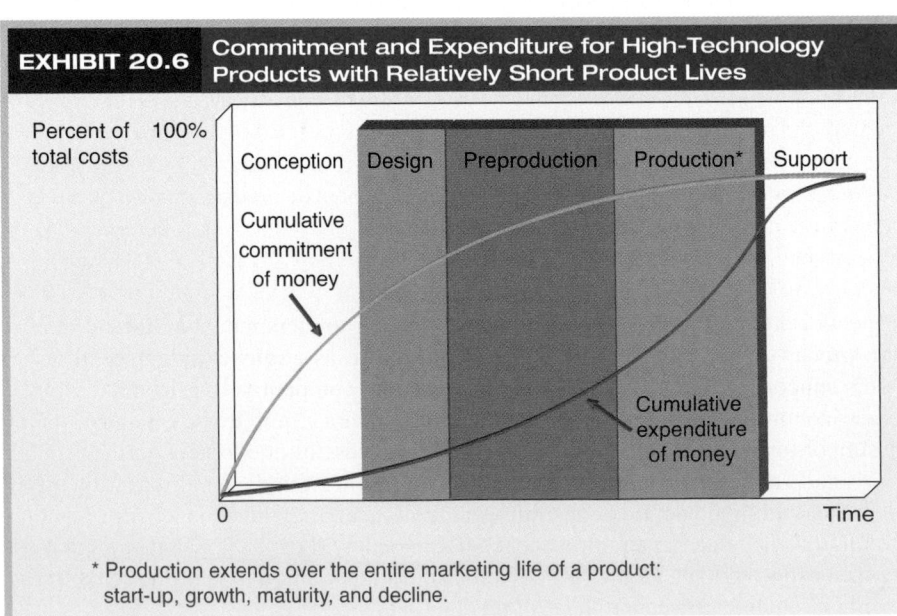

EXHIBIT 20.6 Commitment and Expenditure for High-Technology Products with Relatively Short Product Lives

* Production extends over the entire marketing life of a product: start-up, growth, maturity, and decline.

Reflecting significant changes in vehicle production since the time of Henry Ford and the Model T, General Motors estimates that 70 percent of the cost of manufacturing truck transmissions is determined during design. Others estimate that up to 95 percent of the total costs associated with high-technology products are committed before the first unit is produced.

Life cycle cost concepts have also been usefully applied to low-technology issues, such as repair versus replace decisions. The New York State Throughway Authority uses life cycle concepts to determine the point at which it is more expensive to repair than to replace bridges.

MANAGERIAL DECISION	**You are the Vice President of Product Development**

As head of new product development for your electronics company, you are concerned that so many of the ideas for new products coming from your research and development group are not succeeding in the market. Many recent attempts to take new products to market have failed, not because of technological deficiencies in the products, but because the market would not support the high prices for new products that were necessary to produce a satisfactory profit. What should you do to try to reverse this trend of new product failures? [Answer, p. 20-19]

CONTINUOUS IMPROVEMENT COSTING

Continuous improvement (Kaizen) costing calls for establishing cost reduction targets for products or services that an organization is currently providing to customers. Developed in Japan, this approach to cost management is often referred to as *Kaizen costing*. *Kaizen* means "continuous improvement" in Japanese. Continuous improvement costing begins where target costing ends. Target costing takes a proactive approach to cost management during the conception, design, and preproduction stages of a product's life; continuous improvement costing takes a proactive approach to cost management during the production stage of a product's life:

LO4 Describe the relation between target costing and continuous improvement costing.

			Time		
Conception	Design	Preproduction		Production
	Target costing			Continuous improvement costing

Continuous improvement costing adds a specific target to be achieved during a time period to the target costing concept previously discussed. Basically, the mathematics of the concept is quite simple, but its implementation is difficult. Assume that Home Depot wanted to reduce the cost of materials handling in each of its stores, and management set a target reduction of 2 percent a year. If a given store had current annual materials handling costs of $100,000 and expected an increase the next year due to 10 percent growth, the budget for the next year would be $107,800 [($100,000 × 1.10) × 0.98]. The budget for next year based on growth is $110,000 less the continuous improvement factor of 0.02.

Like target costing, Kaizen costing should be viewed as a serious attempt to make processes more efficient, while maintaining or improving quality, thereby making the company more competitive and profitable. In Kaizen costing, cost reductions can be achieved both internally and externally through continuous redesign and improved internal processes, and by working with vendors to improve their designs and processes. Kaizen is a team effort involving everyone who has an influence on costs. As stated in Module 19, Kaizen is typically found in companies that have adopted a lean production philosophy. The following Business Insight provides insight into Toshiba Corp.'s use of Kaizen in its procurement processes.

Successful companies use continuous improvement costing to avoid complacency. Competitors are constantly striving to win market share through better quality or lower prices. Hewlett-Packard studied Epson to determine its strengths and weaknesses. Isuzu Motors takes competitors' products apart to determine a target cost it must beat. To fend off competition, prices and costs must be continuously reduced. To maintain its competitive position, Hewlett-Packard has reduced the list price of the basic inkjet printer from nearly $400 when first introduced to less than $50 today. This could not have been done without continuous reductions in costs.

BUSINESS INSIGHT | **Kaizen for Procurement at Toshiba**

While Toshiba Corp.'s television business generated profits for the past three years, its primary rivals, Sony and Panasonic, were mired in red ink. Its success against makers of low-priced electronics is attributed largely to the use of Kaizen, or continuous improvement, in its procurement processes. This has led to several key changes in how it deals with suppliers. First, recognizing that the cost of making televisions is directly tied to the cost of acquiring the LCD panels, Toshiba made a first-in-the-industry decision to integrate the procurement of LCD panels for its television and personal computer divisions. Vice President of Procurement, Hisao Tanaka, said that "by combining procurement of the two products, our purchasing power is one of the strongest among global electronics makers." Toshiba also plans to cut costs by about 1 trillion yen (about $12 billion) over the next three years by expanding its business with original design manufacturers (ODMs), which are contract companies that manufacture products for many of the electronics firms, including Apple and HP. Other cost cutting measures at Toshiba include adopting design for improvement, where procurement staff is involved from the product planning and design stage, and assigning technology and procurement experts to factories to carry out kaizen to enhance product quality and reduce costs.

Source: Masamichi Hoshi, "Kaizen Can Be Applied to Procurement, Toshiba Finds," *Nikkei Weekly*, November 15, 2010.

The **Daihatsu Motor Company** sets Kaizen cost reduction targets for each cost element, including purchased parts per car, direct materials per car, labor hours per car, and office utilities. Performance reports developed at the end of each month compare targeted and actual cost reductions. If actual cost reductions are more than the targeted cost reductions, the results are favorable; if the actual cost reductions are less than the targeted cost reductions, the results are unfavorable.

Because cost reduction targets are set before it is known how they will be achieved, continuous improvement costing can be stressful to employees. To help reduce this stress at Daihatsu, a period of about three months following the introduction of a new product is allowed before organizational units are expected to meet target costs and Kaizen costing targets. A critical element in motivating employee cooperation and teamwork in aggressive cost management techniques, such as target and continuous improvement costing, is to avoid using performance reports to place blame for failure. The proper response to an unfavorable performance report must be an offer of assistance to correct the failure.

BENCHMARKING

LO5 Explain how benchmarking enhances quality management, continuous improvement, and process reengineering.

When Isuzu Motors takes a competitor's product apart to determine the competitor's manufacturing costs, or when Hewlett-Packard studies Epson to identify Epson's strengths and weaknesses, each company is engaging in *benchmarking*, a practice that has been around for centuries. In recent years, however, as globalization and increased competitiveness have forced businesses to more aggressively compete on the bases of cost, quality, and service, benchmarking has become more formalized and open. No longer regarded as spying, **benchmarking** is now a systematic approach to identifying the best practices to help an organization take action to improve performance.

The formalization of benchmarking is largely attributed to a book written in the 1980s by Robert Camp of **Xerox**. Since then, many managers have come to believe that benchmarking is a requirement for success. Although benchmarking can focus on anything of interest, it typically deals with target costs for a product, service, or operation, customer satisfaction, quality, inventory levels, inventory turnover, cycle time, and productivity. Benchmarking initially focused on studying competitors, but benchmarking efforts have changed dramatically in recent years to include competitors, as well as companies in very different industries. For example, a computer company like **Dell** may benchmark its order fulfillment processes against **Amazon**, or an electronics company like **Sony** may benchmark its inventory management processes against an apparel company like **Gap**.

In considering how to go about benchmarking, an organization must be careful because it must consider nonfinancial limitations. No single numerical measurement can completely describe the performance of a complex device such as a microprocessor or a television camera, but benchmarks can be useful tools for comparing different products, components, and systems. The only totally accurate way to measure the performance of a given product is to test it against other products while performing the exact same activity. The following Business Insight box describes how Intel Corporation makes benchmarks available with some information on how to use them.

Benchmarking provides measurements that are useful in setting goals. It can lead to dramatic innovations, and it can help overcome resistance to change. When presented with a major cost reduction target, employees often believe they are being asked to do the impossible. Benchmarking can be a psychological tool that helps overcome resistance to change by showing how others have already met the target.

Although each organization has its own approach to benchmarking, the following six steps are typical:

1. Decide what to benchmark.
2. Plan the benchmark project.
3. Understand your own performance.
4. Study others.
5. Learn from the data.
6. Take action.

In recent years, professional organizations, such as the Institute of Management Accountants, have set up clearinghouses for benchmark information or have performed benchmarking studies of interest to members as have certain corporations such as Intel.

BUSINESS INSIGHT | **Intel Benchmarks Performance**

Intel Corporation divides its benchmarks into two types, component and system. *Component benchmarks* measure the performance of specific parts of a computer system, such as a microprocessor or hard disk drive. *System benchmarks* typically measure the performance of the entire computer system. The performance obtained will almost certainly vary from benchmark performance for a number of reasons. First, individual components must usually be tested in a complete computer system, and it is not always possible to eliminate the considerable effects that differences in system design and configuration have on benchmark results. For instance, vendors sell systems with a wide variety of disk capabilities and speeds, system memory, and video and graphics capabilities, all of which influence how the system components perform in actual use. Differences in software, including operating systems and compilers, also affect component and system performance. Finally, benchmark tests are typically written to be exemplary for only a certain type of computer application, which might or might not be similar to what is being compared.

A benchmark is, at most, only one type of information that an organization might use during the purchasing or manufacturing process. To get a true picture of the performance of a component or system being considered, the organization should consult industry sources, publicly available research reports, and even government publications of related information.

Source: As described on the Intel website at http://www.intel.com/performance/resources/benchmark_limitations.htm

---

MODULE-END REVIEW

MBW, Inc. has been conducting early-stage research on hydrogen powered automobiles and is nearing the point where product development will soon begin. In order to determine the feasibility of the product, MBW has conducted marketing research that indicates that the price target for the product must be no more than $35,000 if it is to appeal to a large enough market segment to sell a minimum of 150,000 automobiles in the first year of production. The CFO has indicated that the new product must meet a 15% minimum profit margin requirement.

Required

a. Calculate the target cost per unit to produce the hydrogen powered automobile.
b. How would MBW go about determining whether the target cost can be achieved.
c. What should MBW do if the estimated cost to produce the product exceeds the target cost?

The solution is on page 20-27.

GUIDANCE ANSWER

MANAGERIAL DECISION   You are the Vice President of Product Development

You should consider adopting target costing methods for new product development. Great product research ideas are successful only when they translate into products that can be produced and sold for an acceptable profit. Creating and producing new products before determining what the customer wants and is willing to pay often leads to failure. Target costing methods reverse this process by applying value chain concepts to bring customers and suppliers along the value chain together to produce a product only if it has features and a selling price that are acceptable to potential customers, and if its production costs allow the seller to make an acceptable profit.

DISCUSSION QUESTIONS

Q20-1. What are the relationships among an organization's value chain, processes, and activities?

Q20-2. What should be the goal of every organization along the value chain?

Q20-3. Distinguish between the value-added perspective and the value chain perspective.

Q20-4. Why are economic models seldom used for day-to-day pricing decisions?

Q20-5. Identify three reasons that cost-based approaches to pricing have traditionally been important.

Q20-6. Identify four drawbacks to cost-based pricing.

Q20-7. How does target costing differ from cost-based pricing?

Q20-8. Why is cost-based pricing more a technique, and target costing is more a philosophy? Which approach takes a more proactive approach to cost management?

Q20-9. Distinguish between the marketing life cycles of products incorporating advanced technology (such as household electronic equipment) and those using more traditional technology (such as household paper products). Why would life cycle costing be more important to a manufacturer of household electronic equipment than to a manufacturer of household paper products?

Q20-10. What is the relationship between target costing and continuous improvement (Kaizen) costing?

Q20-11. Distinguish between the seller's and the buyer's perspective of life cycle costs.

Q20-12. What advantage is derived from benchmarking against firms other than competitors?

Assignments with the ⊘ in the margin are available in an online homework system.
See the Preface of the book for details.

MINI EXERCISES

M20-13. Developing a Value Chain from the Perspective of the Final Customer   (LO1)
Prepare a value chain for bottled orange juice that was purchased for personal consumption at an on-campus cafeteria.

M20-14. Developing a Value Chain: Upstream and Downstream Entities   (LO1)
Prepare a value chain for a firm that produces gasoline fuel. Clearly identify upstream and downstream entities in the value chain.

M20-15. Classifying Activities Using the Generic Internal Value Chain: Aluminum Cable Manufacturer   (LO1)
Using the generic internal value chain shown in Exhibit 20.2, classify each of the following activities of an aluminum cable manufacturer as inbound logistics, operations, outbound logistics, marketing and sales, service, or support.
a. Advertising in a construction magazine
b. Inspecting incoming aluminum ingots
c. Placing bar codes on coils of finished products
d. Borrowing money to finance a buildup of inventory
e. Hiring new employees

  f. Heating aluminum ingots
  g. Drawing wire from aluminum ingots
  h. Coiling wire
  i. Visiting a customer to determine the cause of cable breakage
  j. Filing tax returns

M20-16. Classifying Activities Using the Generic Internal Value Chain: Cable TV Company (LO1)
  Using the generic internal value chain shown in Exhibit 20.2, classify each of the following activities
  of a cable television company as inbound logistics, operations, outbound logistics, marketing and sales,
  service, or support.
  a. Installing coaxial cable in the apartment of a new customer
  b. Repairing coaxial cable after a windstorm
  c. Mailing brochures to prospective customers
  d. Discussing a rate increase with members of a regulatory agency
  e. Selling shares of stock in the company
  f. Monitoring the quality of reception at the company's satellite downlink
  g. Preparing financial statements
  h. Visiting a customer to determine the cause of poor-quality television reception
  i. Traveling to a conference to learn about technological changes affecting the industry
  j. Replacing old routers with updated technology

M20-17. Product Pricing: Single Product (LO2)
  Sue Bee Honey is one of the largest processors of its product for the retail market. Assume that one   Sue Bee Honey
  of its plants has annual fixed costs total $8,000,000, of which $3,000,000 is for administrative and
  selling efforts. Sales are anticipated to be 800,000 cases a year. Variable costs for processing are $40 per
  case, and variable selling expenses are 25 percent of selling price. There are no variable administrative
  expenses.

  Required
  If the company desires a profit of $5,000,000, what is the selling price per case?

M20-18. Product Pricing: Single Product (LO2)
  Assume that you plan to open a soft ice cream franchise in a resort community during the summer
  months. Fixed operating costs for the three-month period are projected to be $5,650. Variable costs
  per serving include the cost of the ice cream and cone, $0.45, and a franchise fee payable to Austrian
  Ice, AG, $0.10. A market analysis prepared by Austrian Ice indicates that summer sales in the resort
  community should total 27,000 units.

  Required
  Determine the price you should charge for each ice cream cone to achieve a $20,000 profit for the three-
  month period.

M20-19. Target Pricing (LO3)
  A few years ago, Marriott International, the large hotel chain, announced that because occupancy rates
  had declined during the previous quarter, it was raising room rates to cover the cost of its increase in
  vacant rooms. Although not referring to accounting or economics, several business journalists during the
  week following the announcement questioned the basis for the rate increases. One stated that "Marriott
  increases rates of vacant rooms."

  Required
  a. Did the journalist mean that vacant rooms would be more expensive? Explain.
  b. Do you think Marriott's action to raise room rates was based on economics, accounting, or both?

M20-20. Benchmarking (LO5)
  Your company is developing a new product for the computer printer industry. You have talked to several
  material vendors about being able to supply quality components for the new product. The product
  designers are satisfied with the company's ability to make the product in the current facilities. Numerous
  potential customers also have been surveyed, and most have indicated a willingness to buy the product
  if the price is competitive.

  Required
  What are some means of benchmarking the development and production of your new product?

EXERCISES

 E20-21.   Product Pricing: Single Product   (LO2)

Presented is the 2012 contribution income statement of Colgate Products.

COLGATE PRODUCTS Contribution Income Statement For Year Ended December 31, 2012		
Sales (12,000 units)		$1,440,000
Less variable costs		
Cost of goods sold	$480,000	
Selling and administrative.	132,000	(612,000)
Contribution margin		828,000
Less fixed costs		
Manufacturing overhead.	520,000	
Selling and administrative.	210,000	(730,000)
Net income.		$ 98,000

During the coming year, Colgate expects an increase in variable manufacturing costs of $8 per unit and in fixed manufacturing costs of $48,000.

Required

a. If sales for 2010 remain at 12,000 units, what price should Colgate charge to obtain the same profit as last year?

b. Management believes that sales can be increased to 16,000 units if the selling price is lowered to $107. Is this action desirable?

c. After considering the expected increases in costs, what sales volume is needed to earn a profit of $98,000 with a unit selling price of $107?

 E20-22.   Cost-Based Pricing and Markups with Variable Costs   (LO2)

Compu Services provides computerized inventory consulting. The office and computer expenses are $600,000 annually and are not assigned to specific jobs. The consulting hours available for the year total 20,000, and the average consulting hour has $30 of variable costs.

Required

a. If the company desires a profit of $80,000, what should it charge per hour?

b. What is the markup on variable costs if the desired profit is $120,000?

c. If the desired profit is $60,000, what is the markup on variable costs to cover (1) unassigned costs and (2) desired profit?

E20-23.   Computing Markups   (LO2)

The predicted 2012 costs for Osaka Motors are as follows:

Manufacturing Costs		Selling and Administrative Costs	
Variable.	$100,000	Variable.	$300,000
Fixed.	220,000	Fixed.	200,000

Average total assets for 2012 are predicted to be $6,000,000.

Required

a. If management desires a 12 percent rate of return on total assets, what are the markup percentages based on total variable costs and based on total manufacturing costs?

b. If the company desires a 10 percent rate of return on total assets, what is the markup percentage on total manufacturing costs for (1) unassigned costs and (2) desired profit?

E20-24.   Product Pricing: Two Products   (LO2)

Quality Data manufactures two products, CDs and DVDs, both on the same assembly lines and packaged 10 disks per pack. The predicted sales are 400,000 packs of CDs and 500,000 packs of DVDs. The predicted costs for the year 2012 are as follows:

	Variable Costs	Fixed Costs
Materials...............	$200,000	$500,000
Other..................	250,000	800,000

Each product uses 50 percent of the materials costs. Based on manufacturing time, 40 percent of the other costs are assigned to the CDs, and 60 percent of the other costs are assigned to the DVDs. The management of Quality Data desires an annual profit of $150,000.

Required

a. What price should Quality Data charge for each disk pack if management believes the DVDs sell for 20 percent more than the CDs?

b. What is the total profit per product using the selling prices determined in part a?

E20-25. Product Pricing: Two Products (LO2)

Refer to the previous exercise, E20-24. Based on your calculations of the selling price and profit for CDs and DVDs, how should Quality Data evaluate the status of these two products? Should either CDs or DVDs be discontinued? What additional information does the management of Quality Data need in order to make an appropriate judgment on the future status of these two products?

E20-26. Target Costing (LO3)

Oregon Equipment Company wants to develop a new log-splitting machine for rural homeowners. Market research has determined that the company could sell 5,000 log-splitting machines per year at a retail price of $600 each. An independent catalog company would handle sales for an annual fee of $2,000 plus $50 per unit sold. The cost of the raw materials required to produce the log-splitting machines amounts to $80 per unit.

Required

If company management desires a return equal to 10 percent of the final selling price, what is the target unit cost?

PROBLEMS

P20-27. Product Pricing: Two Products (LO2)

Macquarium Intelligent Communications provides computer-related services to its clients. Its two primary services are are Web page design (WPD), and Internet consulting services (ICS). Assume that Macquarium's management expects to earn a 20 percent annual return on the assets invested. Macquarium has invested $8 million since its opening. The annual costs for the coming year are expected to be as follows:

Macquarium Intelligent Communications

	Variable Costs	Fixed Costs
Consulting support.........	$600,000	$1,050,000
Sales and administration	100,000	850,000

The two services expend about equal costs per hour, and the predicted hours for the coming year are 50,000 for WPD and 30,000 for ICS.

Required

a. If markup is based on variable costs, how much revenue must each service generate to provide the profit expected by corporate headquarters? What is the anticipated revenue per hour for each service?

b. If the markup is based on total costs, how much revenue must each service generate to provide the expected profit?

c. Explain why answers in requirements (a) and (b) are either the same or different.

d. Comment on the advantages and disadvantages of using a cost-based pricing model.

P20-28. Target Costing (LO3)

Redback Networks, Inc., a subsidiary of Ericsson, provides networking services and related systems for 75% of the world's largest telephone companies. Assume that it is developing a new networking system for smaller, private telephone companies. To attract small companies, Redback must keep the price low without giving up too many of the features of larger networking systems. A marketing research study conducted on the company's behalf found that the price range must be $50,000 to $75,000. Management

Redback Networks, Inc.

has determined a target price to be $60,000. The company's minimum profit percentage of sales is normally 20 percent, but the company is willing to reduce it to 15 percent to get the new product on the market. The fixed costs for the first year are anticipated to be $8,000,000. If sales reach 500 installed networks, the company needs to know how much it can spend on variable costs, which are primarily related to installation.

Required

a. What is the amount of total cost allowed if the 15 percent profit target is allowed and the sales target is met? Show the amount for fixed and for variable costs.

b. What is the amount of total costs allowed if the 20 percent normal profit target is desired at the 500 sales target? Show the amount for fixed and for variable costs.

c. Discuss the advantages of using a target costing model versus using cost-based pricing.

P20-29. Continuous Improvement (Kaizen) Costing (LO4)

Patel Company does contract manufacturing of compact video cameras. At its Pacific plant, cost control has become a concern of management. The actual costs per unit for the years 2011 and 2012 were as follows:

	2011	2012
Direct materials		
Plastic case.	$ 4.00	$ 3.90
Lens set	17.00	17.20
Electrical component set	6.00	5.40
Film track	11.00	10.00
Direct labor.	32.00 (1.6 hours)	30.00 (1.5 hours)
Indirect manufacturing costs		
Variable.	7.50	7.10
Fixed.	2.00 (100,000 unit base)	1.90 (120,000 unit base)

The company manufactures all of the camera components except the lens sets, which it purchases from several vendors. The company has used target costing in the past but has not been able to meet the very competitive global pricing. Beginning in 2012, the company implemented a continuous improvement program that requires cost reduction targets.

Required

a. If continuous improvement (Kaizen) costing sets a first-year target of a 5 percent reduction of the 2011 base, how successful was the company in meeting 2012 per unit cost reduction targets? Support your answer with appropriate computations.

b. Evaluate and discuss Patel's use of Kaizen costing.

P20-30. Continuous Improvement (Kaizen) Costing (LO4)

General Electric

Assume that GE Capital, a division of General Electric, has been displeased with the costs of servicing its consumer loans. Assume that it has decided to implement a Kaizen-based cost improvement program. For 2012, GE Capital incurred the following costs:

Loan processing.	$14,500,000
Customer relations.	3,500,000
Printing, mailing, and postage	800,000

For the next two years, GE Capital expects an increase in consumer loans of 4 percent annually with related increases in costs.

Required

a. If the company has a continuous improvement goal of 2 percent each year, develop a budget for the next two years for the consumer loan department.

b. Identify some possible ways that GE Capital can achieve the Kaizen costing goal.

c. Discuss the potential benefits and limitations of GE's Kaizen costing model.

P20-31.   Price Setting: Multiple Products   (LO2)

Comtel Electronics Company's predicted 2012 variable and fixed costs are as follows:

	Variable Costs	Fixed Costs
Manufacturing	$400,000	$260,000
Selling and administrative	100,000	50,000
Total	$500,000	$310,000

Comtel Electronics, Inc., is a small company produces a wide variety of computer interface devices. Per-unit manufacturing cost information about one of these products, a high-capacity flash drive, is as follows:

Direct materials	$ 8
Direct labor.	7
Manufacturing overhead	
Variable.	5
Fixed.	7
Total manufacturing costs	$27

Variable selling and administrative costs for the flash drive is $3 per unit. Management has set a 2012 target profit of $150,000 on the sale of the flash drive.

Required

a. Determine the markup percentage on variable costs required to earn the desired profit.
b. Use variable cost markup to determine a suggested selling price for the flash drive.
c. For the flash drive, break the markup on variable costs into separate parts for fixed costs and profit. Explain the significance of each part.
d. Determine the markup percentage on manufacturing costs required to earn the desired profit.
e. Use the manufacturing costs markup to determine a suggested selling price for the flash drive.
f. Evaluate the variable and the manufacturing cost approaches to determine the markup percentage.

P20-32.   Price Setting: Multiple Products   (LO2)

Augusta Golf, Inc. produces a wide variety of golfing equipment. In the past, product managers set prices using their professional judgment. Jack Woods, the new controller, believes this practice has led to the significant underpricing of some products (with lost profits) and the significant overpricing of other products (with lost sales volume). You have been asked to assist Woods in developing a corporate approach to pricing. The output of your work should be a cost-based formula that can be used to develop initial selling prices for each product. Although product managers are allowed to adjust these prices to meet competition and to take advantage of market opportunities, they must explain such deviations in writing. The following 2012 cost information from the accounting records is available:

	Manufacturing Costs	Selling and Administrative Costs
Variable.	$350,000	$ 50,000
Fixed.	150,000	200,000

In 2012, Augusta Golf reported earnings of $120,000. However, the controller believes that proper pricing should produce earnings of at least $150,000 on the same sales mix and unit volume. Accordingly, you are to use the preceding cost information and a target profit of $150,000 in developing a cost-based pricing formula. Selling and administrative expenses are not currently associated with individual products. However, you have obtained the following unit production cost information for the Tiger Irons:

Variable manufacturing costs. . . .	$155
Fixed manufacturing costs.	60
Total	$215

Required

a. Determine the standard markup percentage for each of the following cost bases. Round answers to two decimal places.
   1. Full costs, including fixed and variable manufacturing costs, and fixed and variable selling and administrative costs.
   2. Manufacturing costs plus variable selling and administrative costs.
   3. Manufacturing costs.
   4. Variable costs.
   5. Variable manufacturing costs.

b. Explain why the markup percentages become progressively larger from requirement (a), parts (1) through (5).

c. Determine the initial price of a set of Tiger Irons using the manufacturing cost markup and the variable manufacturing cost markup.

d. Do you believe the controller's approach to product pricing is reasonable? Why or why not?

MANAGEMENT APPLICATIONS

MA20-33. Telephone Pole Rental Rates (LO2, 3)

Most utility poles carry electric and telephone lines. In areas served by cable television, they also carry television cables. However, cable television companies rarely own any utility poles. Instead, they pay utility companies a rental fee for the use of each pole on a yearly basis. The determination of the rental fee is a source of frequent disagreement between the pole owners and the cable television companies. In one situation, pole owners were arguing for a $10 annual rental fee per pole; this was the standard rate the electric and telephone companies charged each other for the use of poles.

"We object to that," stated the representative of the cable television company. "With two users, the $10 fee represents a rental fee for one-half the pole. This fee is too high because we only use about six inches of each 40-foot pole."

"You are forgetting federal safety regulations," responded a representative of the electric company. "They specify certain distances between different types of lines on a utility pole. Television cables must be a minimum of 40 inches below power lines and 12 inches above telephone lines. If your cable is added to the pole, the total capacity is reduced because this space cannot be used for anything else. Besides, we have an investment in the poles; you don't. We should be entitled to a fair return on this investment. Furthermore, speaking of fair, your company should pay the same rental fee that the telephone company pays us and we pay them. We do not intend to change this fee."

In response, the cable television company representative made two points. First, any fee represents incremental income to the pole owners because the cable company would pay all costs of moving existing lines. Second, because the electric and telephone companies both strive to own the same number of poles in a service area, their pole rental fees cancel themselves. Hence, the fee they charge each other is not relevant.

Required

Evaluate the arguments presented by the cable television and electric company representatives. What factors should be considered in determining a pole rental fee?

MA20-34. Target Costing (LO3)

The president of Houston Electronics was pleased with the company's newest product, the HE Versatile CVD. The product is portable and can be attached to a computer to play or record computer programs or sound, attached to an amplifier to play or record music, or attached to a television to play or record TV programs. It can even be attached to a camcorder to record videos directly on compact disks rather than on tape. It also can be used with a headset to play or record sound. The proud president announced that this unique and innovative product would be an important factor in reestablishing the North American consumer electronics industry.

Based on development costs and predictions of sales volume, manufacturing costs, and distribution costs, the cost-based price of the HE Versatile CVD was determined to be $425. Following a market-skimming strategy, management set the initial selling price at $525. The marketing plan was to reduce the selling price by $50 during each of the first two years of the product's life to obtain the highest contribution possible from each market segment.

The initial sales of the HE Versatile CVD were strong, and Houston Electronics found itself adding second and third production shifts. Although these shifts were expensive, at a selling price of $525, the product had ample contribution margin to remain highly profitable. The president was talking with the company's major investors about the desirability of obtaining financing for a major plant expansion when the bad news arrived. A foreign company had announced that it would shortly introduce a similar product that would incorporate new design features and sell for only $350. The president was shocked. "Why," she remarked, "it costs us $375 to put a complete unit in the hands of customers."

Required

How could the foreign competitor profitably sell a similar product for less than the manufacturing costs to Houston Electronics? What advice do you have for the president concerning the HE Versatile CVD? What advice would you have to help the company avoid similar problems in the future?

SOLUTIONS TO REVIEW PROBLEMS

Mid-Module Review

Solution

a.

Desired annual profit ($2,000,000 × 0.10)	$200,000
Actual profit	(150,000)
Amount actual profit fell short of achieving the desired return	$ 50,000

b.

Predicted costs		
Variable	$450,000	
Fixed	600,000	$1,050,000
Desired profit		250,000
Required revenue		$1,300,000
Unit sales		÷ 100,000
Required unit selling price		$ 13

c.

Variable manufacturing costs per unit ($300,000/100,000 unit)	= $3
Selling price as a percent of variable manufacturing costs	= $13/3
	= 433⅓%
Markup as a percent of variable manufacturing costs ($10/$3)	= 333⅓%

d. Detail of markup on variable manufacturing costs:

1. Unassigned costs

Variable selling and administrative	$150,000	
Fixed costs	600,000	$750,000
Variable manufacturing costs		÷300,000
Markup on variable manufacturing costs to cover unassigned costs		250%

2.

Desired profit	$250,000
Variable manufacturing costs	÷300,000
Additional markup on variable manufacturing costs to achieve desired profit ($250,000)	83⅓%

Module-End Review

Solution

a.

Total revenue (150,000 × $35,000)	$5,250,000,000
Required profit margin (15%).	−787,500,000
Total cost	$4,462,500,000
Number of units	÷ 150,000
Target cost per unit.	$ 29,750

b. A new product such as an automobile is an extremely complex product with hundreds, if not thousands, of different components, involving many different vendors. Once MBW has determined what product features potential customers want, its engineers must determine how best to provide those features, working with vendors and potential vendors. The idea is to determine how best to provide the final product that the customers want at a cost that will provide a reasonable profit to MBW and its vendors.

c. Teams of engineers, accountants, designers, etc. from MBW and its vendors should work together to try to achieve the target cost. If initial cost estimates are too high, they should explore every possibility, including redesign of the product, using components from existing products, developing new production systems, etc. to meet the target cost. If it is finally determined that the target cannot be reached, then management has to decide if it is willing to go forward with the product with a lower than desired initial profit margin. In some cases, managers will proceed with the idea that additional cost savings will be found (using Kaizen costing methods) after the product is in production.

APPLE

The annual sales revenue of Apple Inc. exceeds $65 billion. Apple's well-known products include Mac computers, iPhones, iPods, iTunes, iPads, and Internet software. To manage its international sales activities, Apple has four organizational segments, including the Americas (North and South America), Europe (including the Middle East and Africa), Japan, and worldwide Retail (for Apple-owned retail stores).

To plan and control the company, Apple's management uses budgets that integrate the activities related to its many products sold through its various organizational segments. By linking marketing, suppliers, internal operations, distribution, and finance, Apple's budgeting process assists top management in synchronizing business activities.

Operating budgets are typically prepared for yearly increments, broken down into months or quarters. The sales forecast is a key starting point in the budget process. Apple's managers must predict the volume of physical products, such as iPads, or services, like MobleMe, that customers will purchase. These volumes, in turn, drive budgets for the levels of activities and costs the firm incurs to provide the products and services. After incorporating other key information for things such as research and development, capital expenditures for new plant and equipment, and financing, management is then able to predict financial results for the budget period. If the predicted results are feasible and accepted by management, the budget is approved and implemented. If the results of the first attempt at budgeting are not feasible or acceptable, the budgeting process continues. One indication of feasibility is having adequate cash available to finance budgeted operations. One indication of acceptability is meeting profit goals.

Operational Budgeting and Profit Planning

LEARNING OBJECTIVES

LO1 Discuss the importance of budgets. (p. 21-3)

LO2 Describe basic approaches to budgeting. (p. 21-4)

LO3 Explain the relations among elements of a master budget and develop a basic budget. (p. 21-7)

LO4 Explain and develop a basic manufacturing budget. (p. 21-15)

LO5 Describe the relationship between budget development and manager behavior. (p. 21-18)

To effectively forecast sales, managers must evaluate leading economic indicators, potential changes in consumer preferences, and possible changes in competition. Macroeconomic variables such as income levels and interest rates provide basic information for sales forecasters. Many of Apple's segments rely on specialized economic indicators for specific product lines, like iPhones, as well as in-house analyses of competitors, such as Amazon.

The competitive environment can change quickly. Consider the impact of e-readers, like Apple's iPad and Amazon's Kindle, on traditional booksellers, such as Barnes and Noble, Borders, and Waldenbooks. To remain competitive, the traditional bookstores are forced to reinvent themselves with new products, like Barnes and Noble's Nook, while facing declines in sales and cash flows from traditional products. Periods of change, such as business growth and new competitive pressures faced by existing companies, require careful budgeting.

Things seldom proceed exactly according to plan, and well managed organizations consider these risks in budgeting. Budget models are used to obtain insight into the impact of changed circumstances in sales, costs, and other variables. Managers can then develop plans for the best approaches to handling such risks.

Source: Apple 10-K Reports

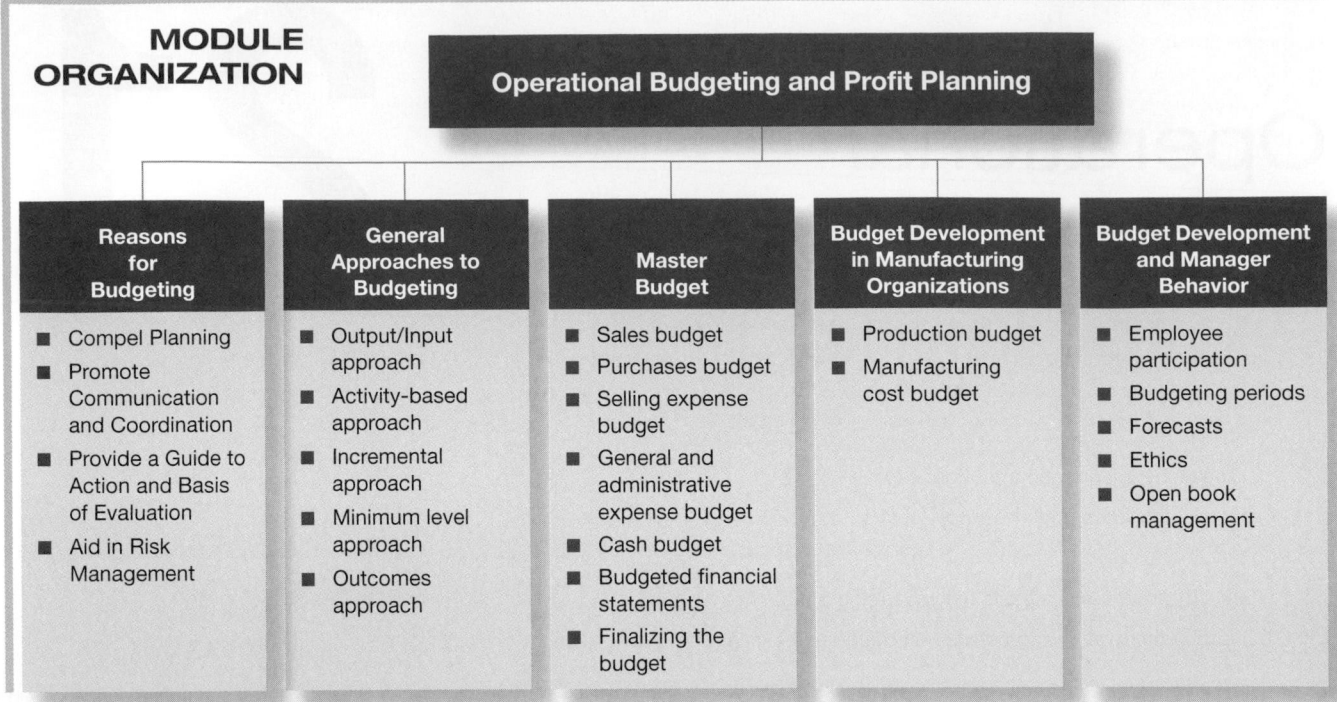

A **budget** is a formal plan of action expressed in monetary terms. The purpose of this module is to examine the concepts, relationships, and procedures used in budgeting. Our emphasis is on **operating budgets**, which concern the development of detailed plans to guide operations throughout the budget period. We consider the reasons that organizations budget and alternative approaches to budget development. We also examine budget assembly and consider issues related to manager behavior and the budgeting process.

REASONS FOR BUDGETING

LO1 Discuss the importance of budgets.

Operating managers frequently regard budgeting as a time-consuming task that diverts attention from current problems. Indeed, the development of an effective budget is a difficult job. It is also a necessary one. Organizations that do not plan are likely to wander aimlessly and ultimately succumb to the swirl of current events. The formal development of a budget helps to ensure both success and survival. As discussed below, budgeting compels planning; it improves communications and coordination among organizational elements; it provides a guide to action; and it provides a basis of performance evaluation. Budget models are also used to analyze and prepare for various business risks.

Compel Planning

Formal budgeting procedures require people to think about the future. Without the discipline of formal planning procedures, busy operating managers would not find time to plan. Immediate needs would consume all available time. Formal budgeting procedures, with specified deadlines, force managers to plan for the future by making the completion of the budget another immediate need. Budgeting moves an organization from an informal "reactive" style to a formal "proactive" style of management. As a result, management and other employees spend less time solving unanticipated problems and more time on positive measures and preventative actions.

Promote Communication and Coordination

When operating responsibilities are divided, it is difficult to synchronize activities. Production must know what marketing intends to sell. Purchasing and personnel must know the factory's material and labor requirements. The treasurer must plan to ensure the availability of the cash to support receivables, inventories, and capital expenditures. Budgeting forces the managers of these diverse functions to communicate their plans and coordinate their activities. It helps ensure that plans are feasible (Can purchasing obtain adequate inventories to support projected sales?) and that they are synchronized (Will inventory be available in advance of an advertising campaign?). The final version of the budget emerges after an extensive (often lengthy) process of communication and coordination.

Provide a Guide to Action and Basis of Evaluation

Once the budget has been finalized, the various operating managers know what is expected of them, and they can set about doing it. If employees do not have a guide to action, their efforts could be wasted on unproductive or even counterproductive activities.

After employees accept the budget as a guide to action, they can be held responsible for their portion of the budget. When results do not agree with plans, managers attempt to determine the cause of the divergence. This information is then used to adjust operations or to modify plans. More generally, budgeting is an important part of **management by exception**, whereby management directs attention only to those activities not proceeding according to plan. Without the budget, management might spend an inordinate amount of time seeking explanation of past activities and not enough time planning future activities.

Aid in Risk Management

The models used for budgeting are also used in managing risk. **Risk** is the danger that things will not go according to plan. Although some risk results from anticipated events having a positive impact, such as an increase in sales volume or selling prices, risk is more typically associated with events that have a negative impact, like a work stoppage at a key supplier, a fire, or hackers shutting down a retail Web site for an extended period of time.

Risk management (also called **enterprise risk management**) is the process of identifying, evaluating, and planning possible responses to risks that could impede an organization from achieving its plans. It also involves monitoring the sources of risk. An organization's budget model can be used to evaluate the financial impact of a risk and to determine, from a financial perspective, the best response to a risk. The Research Insight on the following page summarizes a proposed approach to risk management. The performance evaluation procedures considered in Module 22, if completed on a timely basis, assist in monitoring risk.

The lead responsibility for risk management is often part of the finance function. In the State of Washington, for example, the Risk Management Division is included in the Office of Financial Management. Washington's Risk Management Division defines risk as "anything that poses a potential barrier to an agency achieving, on time, its mandated and strategic objectives/goals." Examples include: financial/budget risk, reputation risk, operational risk, safety/security risk, legal risk, regulatory/compliance risk, and document/management risk.[1]

GENERAL APPROACHES TO BUDGETING

Before an organization can develop operating budgets, management must decide which approaches to budget planning will be used for the various revenue and expenditure activities and organizational units. Widely used planning approaches to budgeting include the input/output, activity-based, incremental, and minimum level approaches.

LO2 Describe basic approaches to budgeting.

Output/Input Approach

The **output/input approach** budgets physical inputs and costs as a function of planned unit-level activities. This approach is often used for service, merchandising, manufacturing, and distribution activities that have defined relationships between effort and accomplishment. If each unit produced requires

---

[1] "Guide for Section 13.1—Risk Management and Self-Insurance Premiums 2011-2013 Budget," Risk Management Division, Office of Financial Management, State of Washington.

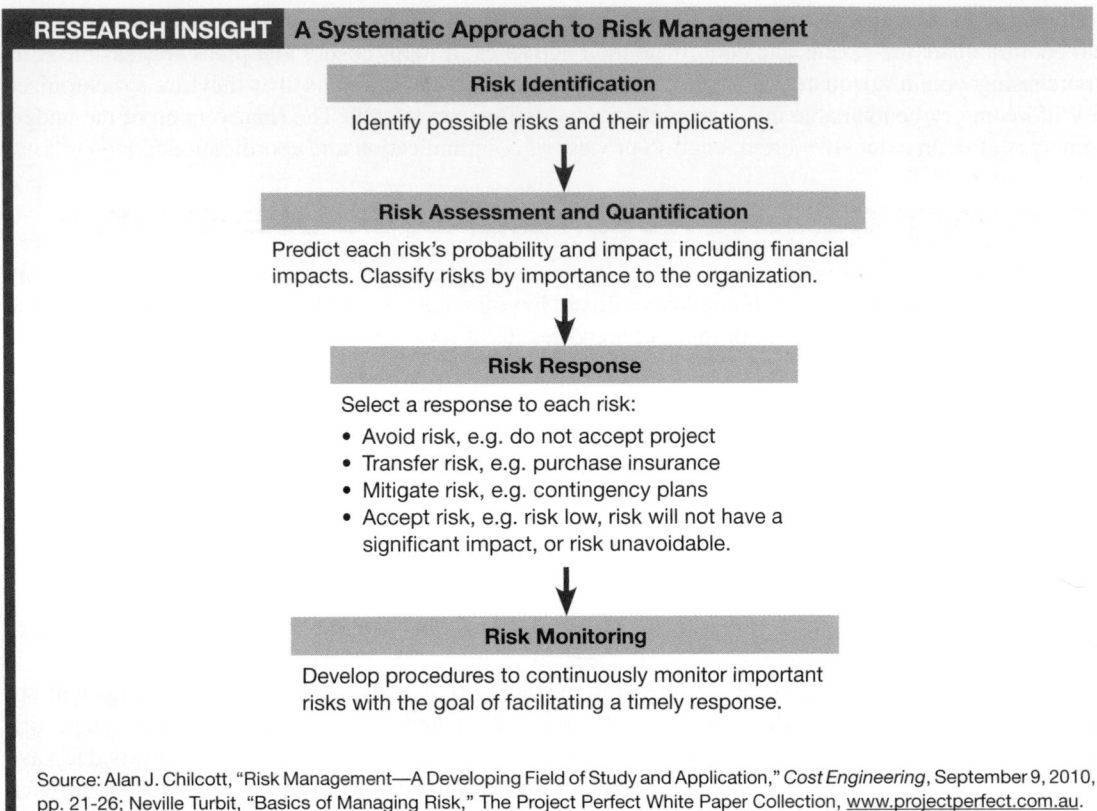

Source: Alan J. Chilcott, "Risk Management—A Developing Field of Study and Application," *Cost Engineering*, September 9, 2010, pp. 21-26; Neville Turbit, "Basics of Managing Risk," The Project Perfect White Paper Collection, www.projectperfect.com.au.

2 pounds of direct materials that cost $5 each, and the planned production volume is 25 units, the budgeted inputs and costs for direct materials are 50 pounds (25 units × 2 pounds per unit) and $250 (50 pounds × $5 per pound).

The budgeted inputs are a function of the planned outputs. The output/input approach starts with the planned outputs and works backward to budget the inputs. It is difficult to use this approach for costs that do not respond to changes in unit-level cost drivers.

Activity-Based Approach

The **activity-based approach** is a type of output/input method, but it reduces the distortions in the transformation through emphasis on the expected cost of the planned activities that will be consumed for a process, department, service, product, or other budget objective. Overhead costs are budgeted on the basis of the cost objective's anticipated consumption of activities, not based only on some broad-based cost driver such as direct labor hours or machine hours.

The amount of each activity cost driver used by each budget objective (for example, product or service) is determined and multiplied by the cost per unit of the activity cost driver. The result is an estimate of the costs of each product or service based on cost drivers such as assembly-line setup or inspections, as well as the traditional volume-based drivers such as direct labor hours or units of direct materials consumed. Activity-based budgeting predicts costs of budget objectives by adding all costs of the activity cost drivers that each product or service is budgeted to consume. In evaluating the proposed budget, management would focus their attention on identifying the optimal set of activities rather than just the output/input relationships.

Incremental Approach

The **incremental approach** budgets costs for a coming period as a dollar or percentage change from he amount budgeted for (or spent during) some previous period. This approach is often used when the re-lationships between inputs and outputs are weak or nonexistent. For example, it is difficult to establish a clear relationship between sales volume and advertising expenditures. Consequently, the budgeted amount of advertising for a future period is often based on the budgeted or actual advertising expenditures in a previous period. If budgeted advertising expenditures for 2011 were $200,000, the budgeted expenditures for 2012 would be some increment, say 5 percent, above $200,000. In evaluating the proposed 2012 budget, management would accept the $200,000 base and focus attention on justifying the increment.

The incremental approach is widely used in government and not-for-profit organizations. In seeking a budget appropriation, a manager using the incremental approach need only justify proposed expenditures in excess of the previous budget. The primary advantage of the incremental approach is that it simplifies the budget process by considering only the increments in the various budget items. A major disadvantage is that existing waste and inefficiencies could escalate year after year.

Minimum Level Approach

Using the **minimum level approach**, an organization establishes a base amount for budget items and requires explanation or justification for any budgeted amount above the minimum (base). This base is usually significantly less than the base used in the incremental approach. It likely is the minimum amount necessary to keep a program or organizational unit viable. For example, the corporate director of product development would need some basic amount to avoid canceling ongoing projects. Additional increments might also be included, first to support the current level of product development and second to undertake desirable new projects.

Some organizations, especially units of government, employ a variation of the minimum level approach, identified as zero-based budgeting. Under **zero-based budgeting** every dollar of expenditure must be justified. The essence of zero-based budgeting is breaking an organizational unit's total budget into program packages with related costs. Management then ranks all program packages on the basis of the perceived benefits in relationship to their costs. Program packages are then funded for the budget

---

BUSINESS INSIGHT | **Fort Collins Budgets for Outcomes**

When Daren Atteberry became city manager of Fort Collins, Colorado, he was faced with declining tax revenues and inflation in the cost of providing city services. Using an incremental approach to budgeting that focused on budget allocations to city departments, department budgets had been cut by six percent, services reduced, and employee compensation frozen for three years. Clearly it was time for a change.

Responding to the financial mess, city officials put away the budget axe and adopted "Budgeting for Objectives (BFO)." Instead of starting with the previous year's budget and justifying incremental changes, BFO starts by asking what results matter most to citizens. The Government Finance Officers Association outlines the steps in budgeting for objectives as follows:

1. Determine how much money is available.
2. Prioritize the results.
3. Allocate resources among high priority results.
4. Conduct analysis to determine what strategies, programs, and activities will best achieve the desired results.
5. Budget available dollars to the most significant programs and activities.
6. Set measures of annual progress, monitor, and close the feedback loop.
7. Check what actually happened.

This results-oriented approach considers processes and activities that cut across the city's departmentalized organization structure, resulting in changes in what is done and in how objectives are accomplished. Evaluating this new approach, Fort Collins Mayor Doug Hutchinson observed "Previous budget processes focused primarily on funding city departments, rather than on providing services to citizens. With BFO, council had an unprecedented level of involvement, setting the priorities and identifying the outcomes that matter most to our citizens."

Source: Camille Cates Barnett and Darin Atteberry, "Your Budget: From Axe to Aim," *Public Management*, May 2007, pp 6-12.

period using this ranking. High-ranking packages are most likely to be funded and low-ranking packages are least likely to be funded.

Budgeting for objectives is a variation on the minimum level approach that combines elements of activity-based and zero-based budgeting with a need to live within fixed financial constraints. The Business Insight that follows examines the implementation of budgeting for objectives by the city management of Fort Collins, Colorado.

The minimum level approach improves on the incremental approach by questioning the necessity for costs included in the base of the incremental approach, but it is very time consuming. All three approaches are often used within the same organization. A pharmaceutical company might use the output/input or the activity-based approach to budget distribution expenditures, the incremental approach to budget administrative salaries, and the minimum level approach to budget research and development.

MID-MODULE REVIEW

To illustrate the various approaches to budgeting discussed above, assume that Alpha Company manufactures two products, Beta and Gamma. Last period, Alpha produced 18,000 units of Beta and 45,000 units of Gamma at a total unit cost of $38 for Beta and $32 for Gamma. During the current period, overall costs are expected to rise about 3.5 percent over the last period. Total estimated overhead costs of $408,500 for the next period include the cost of assembly-line setups, engineering and maintenance, and inspections. Total estimated assembly hours is 50,000 hours; therefore, the estimated overhead cost per assembly hour is $8.17. Other predicted data for the next period follow:

	Beta	Gamma
Direct materials (per unit)	$20.00	$14.50
Direct labor hours of assembly time (per unit)	0.5	0.8
Assembly labor cost (per hour)	$18	$18
Total estimated production (in units)	20,000	50,000
Total setup hours	1,000	1,500
Total engineering and maintenance hours	500	600
Total inspections.	650	580
Setup cost (per setup hour)	$25	$25
Engineering and maintenance (per hour)	$35	$35
Inspection cost (per inspection).	$250	$250

Required

a. Calculate Alpha's budgeted cost per unit to produce Beta and Gamma during the next period, assuming it uses an output/input approach and budgets overhead cost based only on assembly hours.
b. Repeat a., assuming Alpha uses an activity-based approach and budgets overhead cost based on budgeted activity costs.
c. Repeat a., assuming Alpha uses an incremental approach for budgeting overhead cost.
d. Explain how the minimum level approach differs from the above methods.

The solution is on page 21-37.

MASTER BUDGET

LO3 Explain the relations among elements of a master budget and develop a basic budget.

The culmination of the budgeting process is the preparation of a master budget for the entire organization that considers all interrelationships among organization units. The master budget groups together all budgets and supporting schedules and coordinates all financial and operational activities, placing them into an organization-wide set of budgets for a given time period.

Because it explicitly considers organizational interrelationships, the master budget is more complex than budgets developed for products, services, organization units, or specific processes. The elements of the master budget depend on the nature of the business, its products or services, processes and organization, and management needs.

A major goal of developing a master budget is to ensure the smooth functioning of a business throughout the budget period and the organization's operating cycle. As shown in Exhibit 21.1, the operating cycle involves the conversion of cash into other assets, which are intended to produce revenues in excess of their costs. The cycle generally follows a path from cash, to inventories, to receivables (via sales or services), and back to cash. There are, of course, intermediate processes such as the purchase or manufacture of inventories, payments of accounts payable, and the collection of receivables. The master budget is merely a detailed model of the firm's operating cycle that includes all internal processes.

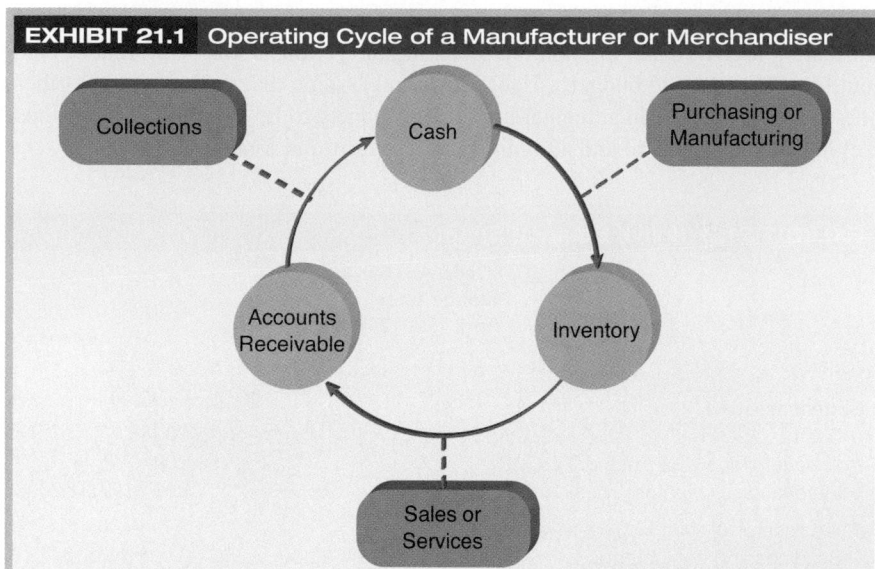

EXHIBIT 21.1 Operating Cycle of a Manufacturer or Merchandiser

Most for-profit organizations begin the budgeting process with the development of the sales budget and conclude with the development of budgeted financial statements. Exhibit 21.2 depicts the annual budget assembly process in a retail merchandising organization. Most of the budget data flow from sales toward cash and then toward the budgeted financial statements.

To illustrate the procedures involved in budget assembly, a monthly budget for the second quarter of 2012 is developed for Blue Mountain Sports (BMS), a retail organization specializing in outdoor clothing and equipment. The assembly sequence follows the overview illustrated in Exhibit 21.2. Each element of the budget process in Exhibit 21.2 is illustrated in a separate exhibit. Because of the numerous elements in the budget process illustrated for BMS, you will find it useful to refer to Exhibit 21.2 often.

The activities of a business can be summarized under three broad categories: operating activities, financing activities, and investing activities. To simplify the illustration, assume that Blue Mountain Sports engaged in no investing activities during the budget period and that the only anticipated financing activity is short-term borrowing. Normal profit-related activities performed in conducting the daily affairs of an organization are called **operating activities**. The operating activities of Blue Mountain Sports include the following:

1. Purchasing inventory intended for sale.
2. Selling goods or services.

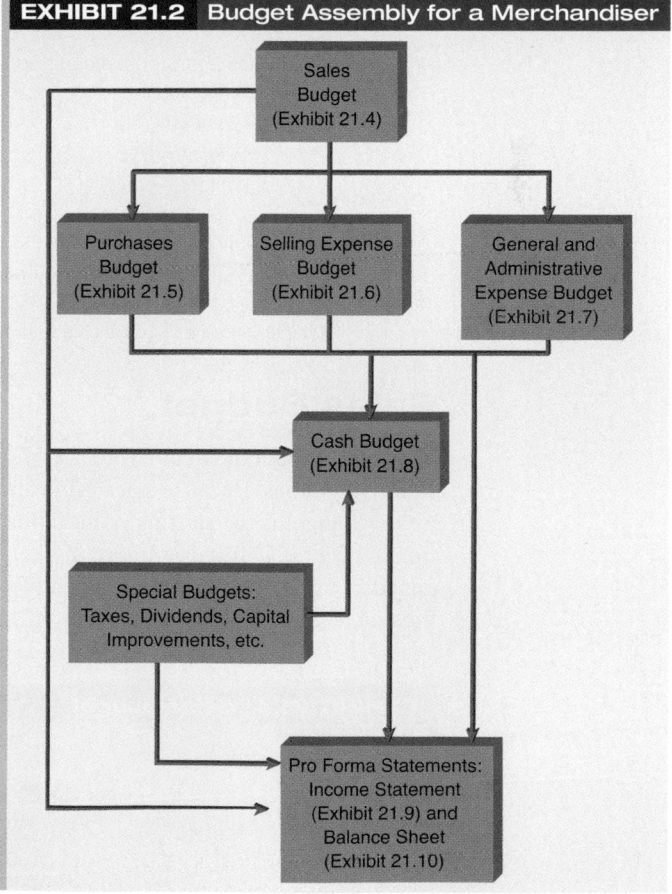

EXHIBIT 21.2 Budget Assembly for a Merchandiser

3. Purchasing and using goods and services classified as selling expenses.
4. Purchasing and using goods and services classified as general and administrative expenses.

In addition to preparing the budget for each operating activity, companies prepare a cash budget for cash receipts and disbursements related to their operating activities as well as for financing and investing activities. The importance of cash planning makes this budget a vital part of the total budget process. Management must, for example, be aware in advance of the need to borrow and have some idea when borrowed funds can be repaid.

The balance sheet for April 1, 2012, the start of the second quarter, is presented in Exhibit 21.3. It contains information used as a starting point in preparing the various budgets. To reduce complexity, we use the output/input approach to budget variable costs and assume that the budgets for other costs were previously developed using the incremental approach. Budgets to be prepared include those for sales, purchases, selling expense, general and administrative expense, and cash.

EXHIBIT 21.3 Initial Balance Sheet

BLUE MOUNTAIN SPORTS
Balance Sheet
April 1, 2012

Assets

Current assets
Cash	$ 15,000	
Accounts receivable, net	59,200	
Merchandise Inventory	157,000	$231,200

Fixed assets
Buildings and equipment	$460,000		
Less accumulated depreciation	(124,800)	335,200	
Land		60,000	395,200
Total assets			$626,400

Liabilities and Stockholders' Equity
Current liabilities
Accounts payable		$ 84,000	
Taxes payable*		35,000	$119,000

Stockholders' equity
Capital stock		350,000	
Retained earnings		157,400	507,400
Total liabilities and stockholders' equity			$626,400

*Quarterly income taxes are paid within 30 days of the end of each quarter.

Sales Budget

The **sales budget** includes a forecast of sales revenue, and it can also contain a forecast of unit sales and sales collections. Because sales drive almost all other activities in a for-profit organization, developing a sales budget is the starting point in the budgeting process. Managers use the best available information to accurately forecast future market conditions. These forecasts, when considered along with merchandise available, promotion and advertising plans, and expected pricing policies, should lead to the most dependable sales budget. The sales budget of BMS is in Exhibit 21.4.

EXHIBIT 21.4 Sales Budget

BLUE MOUNTAIN SPORTS
Sales Budget
For the Second Quarter Ending June 30, 2012

	April	May	June	Quarter Total	July
Sales.	$190,000	$228,000	$250,000	$668,000	$309,000

The information in the sales budget along with predictions of the expected portion of cash sales and the timing of collections from credit sales are used to calculate cash receipts. In the event of a projected cash shortfall, management could consider ways to increase cash sales or to accelerate the collection of receipts from credit sales.

Purchases Budget

The **purchases budget** indicates the merchandise that must be acquired to meet sales needs and ending inventory requirements. It can be referred to as a merchandise budget if it contains only purchases of merchandise for sale. However, for a manufacturer it would include purchase of raw materials. The purchases budget, shown in Exhibit 21.5, includes only purchases of merchandise.

EXHIBIT 21.5 Purchases Budget

BLUE MOUNTAIN SPORTS
Purchases Budget
For the Second Quarter Ending June 30, 2012

	April	May	June	Quarter Total	July
Budgeted sales (Exhibit 21.4)	$190,000	$228,000	$250,000	$668,000	$309,000
Current cost of goods sold*	$114,000	$136,800	$150,000	$400,800	
Desired ending inventory**	168,400	175,000	192,700	192,700	
Total needs	282,400	311,800	342,700	593,500	
Less beginning inventory***	(157,000)	(168,400)	(175,000)	(157,000)	
Purchases	$125,400	$143,400	$167,700	$436,500	

*Cost of goods sold is 60 percent of selling price
**Fifty percent of inventory required for next month's budgeted sales plus base inventory of $100,000.
 April: ($228,000 May sales x 0.60 cost x 0.50 desired ending inventory) + $100,000
 May: ($250,000 June sales x 0.60 cost x 0.50 desired ending inventory) + $100,000
 June :($309,000 July sales x 0.60 cost x 0.50 desired ending inventory) + $100,000
***Fifty percent of current month sales plus base inventory of $100,000. Note monthly beginning inventory.
 Same as previous month's ending inventory.

In reviewing BMS's purchases budget, note the following:

- Because BMS sells a wide variety of items, the purchases budget is expressed in terms of sales dollars, with the cost of merchandise averaging 60 percent of the selling price. Management also keeps detailed records for budgeting the number of units of items carried. An organization that only sold a small number of items might present the sales budget in units as well as dollars.

- Management desires to have 50 percent of the inventory needed to fill the following month's sales in stock at the end of the previous month.

- To provide for a possible delay in the receipt of inventory and to meet variations in customer demand, BMS maintains an additional base inventory of $100,000.

- The total inventory needs equal current sales plus desired ending inventory, including the base inventory.

- Budgeted purchases are computed as total inventory needs less the beginning inventory.

The information in the purchases budget and the information on expected timing of payments for purchases are used to budget cash disbursements for purchases. In the event of a projected cash shortfall, management can consider ways to delay the purchase of inventory or the payment for inventory purchases.

Selling Expense Budget

The **selling expense budget** presents the expenses the organization plans to incur in connection with sales and distribution. In the selling expense budget, Exhibit 21.6, the budgeted variable selling expenses are determined as a percentage of budgeted sales dollars. The budgeted fixed selling expenses are based on amounts obtained from the manager of the sales department. To simplify the presentation of the cash budget, assume BMS pays its selling expenses in the month they are incurred.

EXHIBIT 21.6 Selling Expense Budget

BLUE MOUNTAIN SPORTS
Selling Expense Budget
For the Second Quarter Ending June 30, 2012

	April	May	June	Quarter Total
Budgeted sales (Exhibit 21.4)...........	$190,000	$228,000	$250,000	$668,000
Variable selling expenses				
Setup/Display (1% sales)............	$ 1,900	$ 2,280	$ 2,500	$ 6,680
Commissions (2% sales).............	3,800	4,560	5,000	13,360
Miscellaneous (1% sales)............	1,900	2,280	2,500	6,680
Total.........................	7,600	9,120	10,000	26,720
Fixed selling expenses				
Advertising....................	2,250	2,250	2,250	6,750
Office........................	1,250	1,250	1,250	3,750
Miscellaneous..................	1,000	1,000	1,000	3,000
Total.........................	4,500	4,500	4,500	13,500
Total selling expenses..............	$ 12,100	$ 13,620	$ 14,500	$ 40,220

General and Administrative Expense Budget

The **general and administrative expense budget** presents the expenses the organization plans to incur in connection with the general administration of the organization. Included are expenses for the accounting department, the computer center, and the president's office, for example. Blue Mountain's general and administrative expense budget is presented in Exhibit 21.7.

The depreciation of $2,000 per month is a noncash item and is not carried forward to the cash budget. No variable general and administrative costs are included because most expenditures categorized as general and administrative are related to top-management operations that do not vary with unit-level cost drivers. To simplify the presentation of the cash budget, assume that general and administrative expenses, except depreciation, are paid in the month they are incurred.

EXHIBIT 21.7 General and Administrative Expense Budget

BLUE MOUNTAIN SPORTS
General and Administrative Expense Budget
For the Second Quarter Ending June 30, 2012

	April	May	June	Quarter Total
General and administrative expenses				
Compensation..........................	$25,000	$25,000	$25,000	$75,000
Insurance.............................	2,000	2,000	2,000	6,000
Depreciation...........................	2,000	2,000	2,000	6,000
Utilities...............................	3,000	3,000	3,000	9,000
Miscellaneous..........................	1,000	1,000	1,000	3,000
Total general and administrative expenses..........	$33,000	$33,000	$33,000	$99,000

Cash Budget

The **cash budget** summarizes all cash receipts and disbursements expected to occur during the budget period. Cash is critical to survival. Income is like food and cash is like water. Food is necessary to survive and prosper over time, but you can get along without food for a short period of time. You cannot survive very long without water. Hence, cash budgeting is very important, especially in a small business where cash receipts from sales lag purchases of inventory. As pointed out in the following Business Insight, cash budgets are also critical in large organizations undergoing restructuring.

BUSINESS INSIGHT | **Cash Is King as Kodak Restructures**

For many decades **Kodak**'s success was built on selling film. Although Kodak scientists were leaders in pioneering digital imagery, not wanting to undercut current sales, the firm lagged in developing, producing, and selling digital cameras. The result was a significant decline in sales and layoffs in the tens of thousands of employees, as the firm played catch-up and restructured in the 2000s. During this period Kodak's reported income was dismal. Although Kodak reported large annual losses, its annual cash flows remained positive because depreciation expense and losses on discontinued operations do not require the use of cash. With positive cash flows, management turned its attention to reinventing the company with a focus on digital cameras, printing, and related products. Ulysses Yannas, a Wall Street broker who has tracked Kodak for decades, observed that the company managed cash well during the 2008 recession and was well positioned to turn a profit when sales rebound.

Source: Mike Dickinson, "For Wall Street Cash Is Kodak's Key Benchmark," *Rochester Business Journal*, July 24, 2009, pp. 1 and 7.

After it makes sales predictions, an organization uses information regarding credit terms, collections policy, and prior collection experience to develop a cash collections budget. Collections on sales normally include receipts from the current period's sales and collections from sales of prior periods. An allowance for bad debts, which reduces each period's collections, is also predicted. Other items often included are cash sales, sales discounts, allowances for volume discounts, and seasonal changes of sales prices and collections. BMS's cash budget is in Exhibit 21.8. Note the following important points:

- Management estimates that one-half of all sales are for cash and the other half are on the company's credit card. (When sales are on bank credit cards, the collection is immediate, less any bank user fee; however, charges using Blue Mountain's credit card are collected by the company from the customer.) Twenty-five percent of the credit card sales are collected in the month of sale, and 74 percent are collected in the following month. Bad debts are budgeted at 1 percent of credit sales. This resource flow is graphically illustrated as follows:

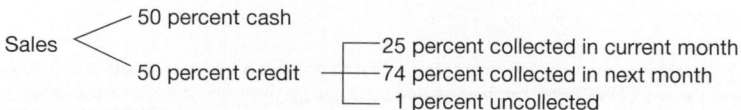

- Payments for purchases are made 20 percent in the month purchased and 80 percent in the next month.

- Information on cash expenditures for selling expenses and for general and administrative expenses is based on budgets for these items. The monthly cash expenditures for general and administrative expenses are $31,000 rather than $33,000. The $2,000 difference relates to depreciation, which does not require use of cash.

- Blue Mountain's accountant provided tax information. Income taxes are determined on the basis of predicted taxable income following IRS rules. Estimated tax payments are made during the month following the end of each quarter. Hence, the taxes payable on April 1 are paid during April.

- The cash budget shows cash operating deficiencies and surpluses expected to occur at the end of each month; this is used to plan for borrowing and loan payment.

- The cash maintenance policy for Blue Mountain specifies that a minimum balance of $15,000 is to be maintained.

- BMS has a line of credit with a bank, with any interest on borrowed funds computed at the simple interest rate of 12.0 percent per year, or 1.0 percent per month. All necessary borrowing is assumed to occur at the start of each month in increments of $1,000. Repayments are assumed to occur at the end of the month. Interest is paid when loans are repaid.

EXHIBIT 21.8 Cash Budget

BLUE MOUNTAIN SPORTS
Cash Budget
For the Second Quarter Ending June 30, 2012

	April	May	June	Quarter Total
Budgeted sales (Exhibit 21.4)...................	$190,000	$228,000	$250,000	$668,000
Cash balance, beginning	$ 15,000	$ 15,770	$ 44,850	$ 15,000
Collections on sales				
Cash sales (50% sales)......................	95,000	114,000	125,000	
Credit sales				
Current month (25% credit sales).............	23,750	28,500	31,250	
Prior month (74% credit sales)..............	59,200*	70,300	84,360	
Total......................................	177,950	212,800	240,610	631,360
Cash available for operations....................	192,950	228,570	285,460	646,360
Disbursements				
Purchases (Exhibit 21.5)				
Current month (20% purchases)..............	25,080	28,680	33,540	
Prior month (80% purchases)...............	84,000**	100,320	114,720	
Total......................................	109,080	129.000	148,260	386,340
Selling expenses (Exhibit 21.6)................	12,100	13,620	14,500	40,220
General & Administrative Expenses				
(Exhibit 21.7, excluding depreciation)..........	31,000	31,000	31,000	93,000
Taxes (Exhibit 21.3).........................	35,000			35,000
Total	(187,180)	(173,620)	(193,760)	(554,560)
Excess (deficiency) cash available over	5,770	54,950	91,700	91,800
disbursements				
Short-term financing***				
New loans.................................	10,000			10,000
Repayments		(10,000)		(10,000)
Interest	—	(100)	—	(100)
Net cash from financing.......................	10,000	(10,100)	—	(100)
Cash balance, ending.........................	$ 15,770	$ 44,850	$ 91,700	$ 91,700

*April 1 accounts receivable.
**April 1 accounts payable.
***Loans are obtained in $1,000 increments at the start of the month to maintain a minimum balance of $15,000 at all times. Repayments are made at the end of the month, as soon as adequate cash is available. Interest of 12 percent per year (1 percent per month) is paid when the loan is repaid.

■ The cash budget indicates Blue Mountain needs to borrow $10,000 in April. The $10,000 plus interest is repaid in May.

If Blue Mountain had any cash disbursements for dividends or capital expenditures they would be included in the cash budget. These items, along with information on income taxes, would be shown in special budgets.

Budgeted Financial Statements

The preparation of the master budget culminates in the preparation of budgeted financial statements. **Budgeted financial statements** are pro forma statements that reflect the "as-if" effects of the budgeted activities on the actual financial position of the organization. That is, the statements reflect the results of operations assuming all budget predictions are correct. Spreadsheets that permit the user to immediately determine the impact of any assumed changes facilitate developing budgeted financial statements. The budgeted income statement can follow the functional format traditionally used for financial accounting or the contribution format introduced in Module 15. In either case, the balance sheet amounts reflect the corresponding budgeted entries.

Exhibit 21.9 presents the budgeted income statement for the quarter ending June 30, 2012. If all predictions made in the operating budget are correct, BMS will produce a net income of $51,540 for the quarter. Almost every item on the budgeted income statement comes from one of the budget schedules.

EXHIBIT 21.9 Budgeted Income Statement

BLUE MOUNTAIN SPORTS
Budgeted Income Statement
For the Second Quarter Ending June 30, 2012

Sales (Exhibit 21.4)...		$668,000
Cost of goods sold:*		
Beginning inventory (Exhibit 21.3)	$157,000	
Purchases (Exhibit 21.5)..	436,500	
Cost of merchandise available	593,500	
Ending inventory (Exhibit 21.5)......................................	(192,700)	(400,800)
Gross profit..		267,200
Other expenses:...		
Bad debt (1% of credit sales)**....................................	3,340	
Selling (Exhibit 21.6)...	40,220	
General and administrative (Exhibit 21.7)............................	99,000	(142,560)
Income from operations..		124,640
Interest expense (Exhibit 21.8)......................................		(100)
Net income from operations...		124,540
Allowance for income taxes***......................................		(73,000)
Net income...		$ 51,540

*Also computed at sales x 0.6
**$668,000 x 0.5 credit sales x 0.01 bad debts
***Provided by accounting

The budgeted balance sheet, presented in Exhibit 21.10 shows Blue Mountain's financial position as of June 30, 2012, assuming that all budget predictions are correct. Sources of the budgeted balance sheet data are included as part of the exhibit.

EXHIBIT 21.10 Budgeted Balance Sheet

BLUE MOUNTAIN SPORTS
Balance Sheet
June 30, 2012

Assets:			
Current assets			
Cash (Exhibit 21.8)		$ 91,700	
Accounts receivable, net*		92,500	
Merchandise inventory (Exhibit 21.5 and 21.9)...............		192,700	$376,900
Fixed assets			
Buildings and equipment (Exhibit 21.3)	$460,000		
Less accumulated depreciation			
(Exhibit 21.3 plus depreciation Exhibit 21.7)...............	(130,800)	329,200	
Land (Exhibit 21.3)		60,000	389,200
Total assets..			$766,100
Liabilities and Stockholders' Equity			
Current liabilities			
Accounts payable**..		$134,160	
Taxes payable (Exhibit 21.9)		73,000	$207,160
Stockholders' equity			
Capital stock (Exhibit 21.3)...............................		350,000	
Retained earnings (Exhibit 21.3 plus net income Exhibit 21.9)....		208,940	558,940
Total liabilities and stockholders' equity..........................			$766,100

*June credit sales collected in July, $250,000 x 0.50 x 0.74.
**June purchases paid in July, $167,700 x 0.80.

Finalizing the Budget

After studying the BMS example, you might conclude that developing the master budget is a mechanical process. That is not the case. Understanding the basics of budget assembly is not the end; it is a tool to assist in efficient and effective budgeting. Before finalizing the budget, the following two questions must be addressed:

- Is the proposed budget feasible?
- Is the proposed budget acceptable?

To be feasible, the organization must be able to actually implement the proposed budget. Without the line of credit, Blue Mountain's budget is not feasible because the company would run out of cash sometime in April. Knowing this, management can take timely corrective action. Possible actions include obtaining equity financing, issuing long-term debt, reducing the amount of inventory on hand at the end of each quarter, or obtaining a line of credit. Other constraints that would make the budget infeasible include the availability of merchandise and, in the case of a manufacturing organization, production capacity.

Once management determines that the budget is feasible, they still need to determine if it is acceptable. To evaluate acceptability, management might consider various financial ratios, such as return on assets. They might compare the return provided by the proposed budget with past returns, industry averages, or some organizational goal.

BUDGET DEVELOPMENT IN MANUFACTURING ORGANIZATIONS

LO4 Explain and develop a basic manufacturing cost budget.

The importance of inventory in various organizations was introduced in Module 17 where Exhibit 17.1 (page 17-4) summarized inventory and related expense accounts for service, merchandising, and manufacturing organizations. Recall that service organizations usually have a low percentage of their assets invested in inventory, usually consisting of the supplies needed to facilitate operations. In contrast, merchandising organizations usually have a high percentage of their total assets invested in inventory, with the largest inventory investment in merchandise purchased for resale. The preceding illustration of the development of a master budget was for a merchandising organization.

Production Budget

Because manufacturing organizations convert raw materials into finished goods that are sold to customers, there are additional steps in developing their master budget. Contrast the assembly of a budget for a merchandiser in Exhibit 21.2 with the assembly of a budget for a manufacturer in Exhibit 21.11. The management of a manufacturing organization must determine the production volume required to support sales and finished goods ending inventory requirements (production budget). Then, based on available inventories or raw materials and the raw materials required for production, management develops a purchases budget.

Manufacturing Cost Budget

In addition to a selling expense budget and a general and administrative expense budget, management needs also to develop a manufacturing cost budget, which is similar in design to a statement of cost of goods manufactured (see Exhibit 17.6, page 17-16) except that it is prepared in advance of production rather than after production. Reflecting these additional steps, the cash budget includes payments for direct labor and manufacturing overhead, based on information in the manufacturing cost budget, and payments for purchases of raw materials based on the purchases budget. Note cash disbursements are for materials purchased rather than materials used in production.

Continuing our Blue Mountain Sports example, assume that management is considering the option of manufacturing a high-quality backpack, tentatively named the "Trekpack" as an alternative to

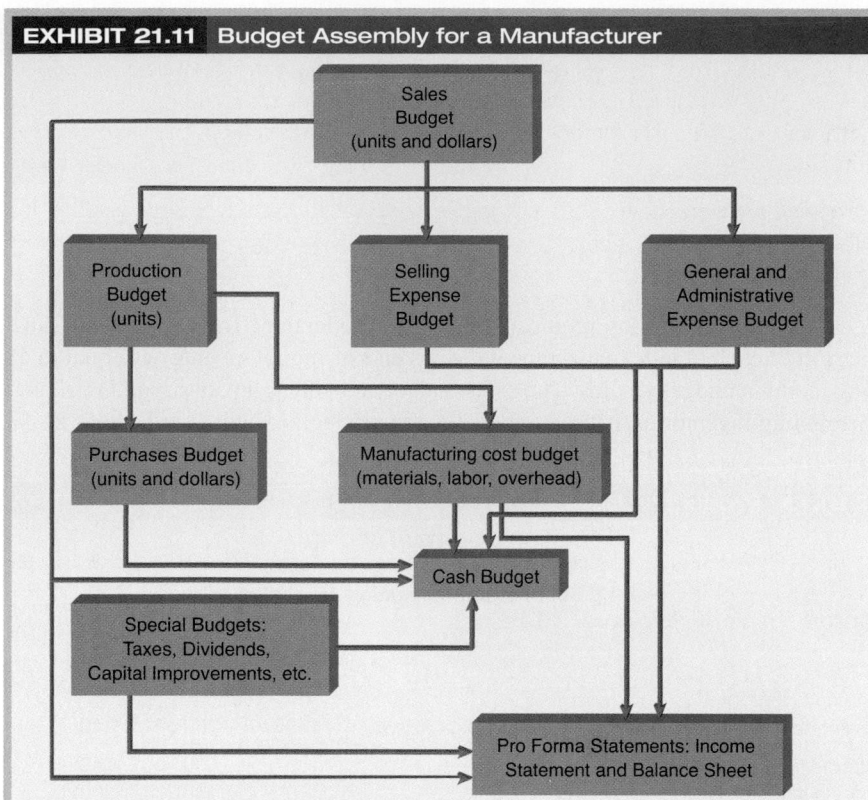

EXHIBIT 21.11 Budget Assembly for a Manufacturer

purchasing a similar item from an outside vendor. Unit variable and monthly fixed cost estimates associated with the manufacture of Trekpacks follow:

Unit costs:
Direct materials:

Fabric: 2 square yards at $10 per yard	$20	
Hardware kits (buckles, straps, etc.)	5	$ 25
Direct labor 0.5 hours at $30 per hour		15
Variable overhead, per unit		8
Total variable costs per unit		$ 48
Fixed costs per month (rent, utilities, supervision)		$6,000

Because management anticipates an average monthly production volume of 500 Trekpacks, the average fixed cost per unit, a predetermined overhead rate, is $12 ($6,000/500).

For budgeting purposes, management uses a standard cost, a budget per unit of product, for valuing inventories and forecasting the cost of goods sold. The standard cost of a Trekpack is $60:

Direct materials	$25
Direct labor	15
Variable overhead	8
Fixed overhead	12
Standard cost	$60

Management, planning to introduce this new product in May, developed the sales budget shown in Exhibit 21.12. In this case, because unit information is necessary to determine production requirements, the sales budget is expressed in units as well as dollars.

EXHIBIT 21.12   Sales Budget

BLUE MOUNTAIN SPORTS
Sales Budget (Trekpacks)
For the Second Quarter Ending June 30, 2012

	April	May	June	Quarter Total	July
Sales - Units.....................	0	400	500	900	600
Sales - Dollars ($100 each).............	0	$40,000	$50,000	$90,000	$60,000

Introducing Trekpacks in May requires some April production. To meet the initial sales requirement for the start of each month, management desires end-of-month inventories equal to 40 percent of the following month's budgeted sales. The sales budget and ending inventory plans, along with information on beginning inventories, is used to develop the production budget in Exhibit 21.13.

EXHIBIT 21.13   Production Budget

BLUE MOUNTAIN SPORTS
Production Budget (Trekpacks)
For the Second Quarter Ending June 30, 2012

	April	May	June	Quarter Total
Budgeted Sales	0	400	500	900
Desired ending inventory				
40% following month sales........................	160	200	240	240
Total requirements	160	600	740	1,140
Less beginning inventory...........................	0	(160)	(200)	0
Budgeted production................................	160	440	540	1,140

The production budget, along with information on beginning inventories of raw materials and planned ending inventory levels (500 square yards of fabric and 200 kits) is then used to budget the purchases in Exhibit 21.14 for raw materials in units and dollars. The production budget, along with standard variable and predicted fixed cost information is also used to develop the manufacturing cost budget in Exhibit 21.15.

EXHIBIT 21.14   Purchase Budget

BLUE MOUNTAIN SPORTS
Purchases Budget
For the Second Quarter Ending June 30, 2012

	April	May	June	Quarter Total
Fabric:				
Current needs (2 yards per unit)	320	880	1,080	2,280
Desired ending inventory (500 yards)	500	500	500	500
Total requirements.............................	820	1,380	1,580	2,780
Less beginning inventory.......................	−0	−500	−500	−0
Fabric purchases in yards	820	880	1,080	2,780
Assembly kits:				
Current needs (1 per unit)	160	440	540	1,140
Desired ending inventory (200 kits)	200	200	200	200
Total requirements.............................	360	640	740	1,340
Less beginning inventory.......................	−0	−200	−200	−0
Kit purchases in units.........................	360	440	540	1,340
Purchases (Dollars)				
Fabric at $10 per yard	$ 8,200	$ 8,800	$10,800	$27,800
Kits at $5 each...............................	1,800	2,200	2,700	6,700
Total purchases in dollars......................	$10,000	$11,000	$13,500	$34,500

Because it does not require the introduction of new concepts, the cash budget and the pro-forma financial statements for Blue Mountain Sports with the manufacturing of Trekpacks are not presented. Keep in mind that the cash budget will include disbursements for purchases shown in Exhibit 21.14 and for direct labor, variable overhead, and fixed overhead shown in Exhibit 21.15. A pro-forma functional income statement using absorption costing will include the predicted cost of goods sold for Trekpacks at a $60 standard cost per unit. A contribution income statement using variable costing would include the cost of goods sold for Trekpacks at a $48 standard cost per unit with all fixed manufacturing costs expensed in the period incurred. Finally, the pro-forma balance sheet will include standard costs of any June raw materials (500 square yards at $10 per yard and 200 kits at $5 each), work in process (none), and finished goods. Any unpaid liabilities for purchases of raw materials, direct labor, and manufacturing overhead would also be shown under current liabilities. Note that completing the cash budget and the pro-forma statements requires information on the timing of payments for the purchases of raw materials, direct labor, and manufacturing overhead.

EXHIBIT 21.15 Manufacturing Cost Budget

BLUE MOUNTAIN SPORTS
Manufacturing Cost Budget
For the Second Quarter Ending June 30, 2012

	April	May	June	Quarter Total
Direct materials				
Fabric used in production (production × 2 yards × $10) .	$ 3,200	$ 8,800	$10,800	$22,800
Kits used in production (production × 1 kit × $5).	800	2,200	2,700	5,700
Total	4,000	11,000	13,500	28,500
Direct labor (production × 1/2 hour × $30)	2,400	6,600	8,100	17,100
Manufacturing overhead				
Variable ($8 per unit)	1,280	3,520	4,320	9,120
Fixed	6,000	6,000	6,000	18,000
Total	7,280	9,520	10,320	27,120
Total manufacturing costs	$13,680	$27,120	$31,920	$72,720

BUDGET DEVELOPMENT AND MANAGER BEHAVIOR

Organizations are composed of individuals who perform a wide variety of activities in pursuit of the organization's goals. To accomplish these goals, management must recognize the effects that budgeting and performance evaluation methods have on the behavior of the organization's employees.

LO5 Describe the relationship between budget development and manager behavior.

Employee Participation

Budgeting should be used to promote productive employee behavior directed toward meeting the organization's goals. While no two organizations use exactly the same budgeting procedures, two approaches to employee involvement in budgeting represent possible end points on a continuum. These approaches are sometimes referred to as top-down and bottom-up methods.

With a **top-down** or **imposed budget**, top management identifies the primary goals and objectives for the organization and communicates them to lower management levels. Because relatively few people are involved in top-down budgeting, an imposed budget saves time. It also minimizes the slack that managers at lower organizational levels are sometimes prone to build into their budgets. However, this nonparticipative approach to budgeting can have undesirable motivational consequences. Personnel who do not participate in budget preparation might lack a commitment to achieve their part of the budget.

With a **bottom-up** or **participative budget**, managers at all levels—and in some cases, even nonmanagers—are involved in budget preparation. Budget proposals originate at the lowest level of management possible and are then integrated into the proposals for the next level, and so on, until the proposals reach the top level of management, which completes the budget.

Participation helps ensure that important issues are considered and that employees understand the importance of their roles in meeting the organization's goals. It also provides opportunities for problem solving and fosters employee commitment to agreed-upon goals. Hence, budget predictions are likely to be more accurate, and the people responsible for the budget are more likely to strive to accomplish its objectives. These self-imposed budgets reinforce the concept of participative management and should strengthen the overall budgeting process.

Participative approaches to budgeting have a few disadvantages. Because they require the involvement of many people, the preparation period is longer than that for an imposed budget. Another disadvantage is the tendency of some managers to intentionally understate revenues or overstate expenses to provide **budgetary slack**. A manager might do this to reduce his or her concern regarding unfavorable performance reviews or to make it easier to obtain favorable performance reviews. If a department consistently produces favorable variances (actual results versus budget) with little apparent effort, this might be a symptom of budgetary slack. On the other hand, as discussed in the following Business Insight, budgetary slack can produce favorable results under certain circumstances.

MANAGERIAL DECISION   **You are the Chief Financial Officer**

As the CFO of a relatively new and fast-growing entrepreneurial enterprise, you and the other top managers have previously emphasized technical and marketing innovation and creativity over planning and budgeting. But now with growing competition and the maturing of the company's products, you recognized that a culture of better financial planning must be established if the company is to succeed in the long run. You feel that the financial staff have the best expertise and understanding of the business to prepare effective budgets, but you are concerned about the motivational effects of excluding the lower-level managers from the process and are seeking advice. [Answer, p. 21-23.]

Budgeting Periods

Although most organizations use a one-year budget period, some organizations budget for shorter or longer periods. In addition to fixed-length budget periods, two other types of budget periods commonly used are life cycle budgeting and continuous budgeting.

When a fixed time period is not particularly relevant to planning, an organization can use **life cycle budgeting**, which involves developing a budget for a project's entire life. An ice cream vendor at the beach might develop a budget for the season. A general contractor might budget costs for the entire (multiple-year) time required to construct a building.

Under **continuous budgeting**, the budget (sometimes called a **rolling budget**) is based on a moving time frame. For example, an organization on a continuous four-quarter budget system adds a quarter to the budget at the end of each quarter of operations, thereby always maintaining a budget for four quarters into the future. Under this system, plans for a full year into the future are always available, whereas under a fixed annual budget, operating plans for a full year ahead are available only at the beginning of the budget year. Because managers are constantly involved in this type of budgeting, the budget process becomes an active and integral part of the management process. Managers are forced to be future oriented throughout the year rather than just once each year.

Forecasts

Budget preparation requires the development of a variety of forecasts. The sales forecast is based on a variety of interrelated factors such as historical trends, product innovation, general economic conditions, industry conditions, and the organization's strategic position for competing on the basis of price, product differentiation, or market niche. Many organizations first determine the industry forecast for a given product or service and then extract from it their sales estimations.

Although the sales forecast is primary to most organizations, there are many other forecasts of varying importance that must be made, including (a) the collection period for sales on account, (b) percent of uncollectable sales on account, (c) cost of materials, supplies, utilities, and so forth, (d) employee turnover, (e) time required to perform activities, (f) interest rates, and (g) development time for new products or services.

BUSINESS INSIGHT	Budgetary Slack May Provide Flexibility for Innovation and Improve Control in Unstructured Environments

When one of the authors became responsible for budgeting and financial control of a business school, department budgets were developed using the incremental approach. There were two major problems. First, there was inadequate information on the activities and programs financed by college funds. Second, department heads with budget authority frequently requested additional funds for special projects and overspent their budget, causing the college to dip into discretionary funds contributed by alumni and friends.

Practicing what is taught in this book, the author implemented different approaches to budgeting different costs. For example average salary increases were budgeted on an incremental basis, instructional supplies and photocopying were budgeted using the output/input approach, and various student and alumni events were budgeted per event using budgeting for objectives. Funds were then allocated to the budget of the department responsible for the activity or event. This approach demystified the budgeting process and allowed personnel to understand what was accomplished with college's funds.

The availability of dollars in regular budgets almost always expires at the end of the budget year, leading managers to spend all of their funds, and even a bit more. To provide flexibility for department managers to undertake new initiatives during the year, each department was provided an additional budget allocation, funded by college alumni and friends for unspecified discretionary items. If the manager spent more than the regular budget, the overspending would be taken from the allocated discretionary funds. If the manager spent less than the regular budget plus the allocated discretionary funds, the unspent discretionary funds were carried forward to the following year.

The availability of the discretionary funds reduced the tendency of managers to make special requests throughout the year. Interestingly, department managers saw the discretionary funds as a savings account that they were reluctant to spend without good reason. The result was a significant decline in overspending of the regular budget.

Ethics

Because most wrongful activities related to budgeting are unethical, rather than illegal, organizations often have difficulty dealing with them. However, when managers' actions cross the gray area between ethical and fraudulent behavior, organizations are not reluctant to dismiss employees or even pursue legal actions against them.

Although most managers have a natural inclination to be conservative in developing their budgets, at some level the blatant padding or building slack into the budget becomes unethical. In an extreme case, it might even be considered theft if an inordinate level of budgetary slack creates favorable performance variances that lead to significant bonuses or other financial gain for the manager. Another form of falsifying budgets occurs when managers include expense categories in their budgets that are not needed in their operations and subsequently use the funds to pad other budget categories. The deliberate falsification of budgets is unethical behavior and is grounds for dismissal in most organizations.

Ethical issues might also arise in the reporting of performance results, which usually compares actual data with budgeted data. Examples of unethical reporting of actual performance data include misclassification of expenses, overstating revenues or understating expenses, postponing or accelerating the recording of activities at the end of the accounting period, or creating fictitious activities.

Open Book Management

If an organization is to obtain the full benefit of budgeting, support for the budget must be obtained from employees at all levels. Many organizations, especially smaller ones, have used open book management to obtain employee support for the budget. **Open book management** involves sharing financial and related information with employees, teaching employees to understand financial numbers, encouraging employees to use the information in their work, and sharing financial results with employees, perhaps through a bonus program. The following Research Insight examines the success of open book management in small companies.

RESEARCH INSIGHT   Open Book Management Opens the Door to Profits

Research performed by Dr. Jody Heymann and others at the McGill University Institute for Health and Social Policy shows that "sharing financial information with low-skilled workers helps build efficiency and profits." This is especially true at smaller companies with profit sharing plans. Examples cited by Dr. Heymann include Great Little Box, a Canadian packaging company with 213 employees, and Dancing Deer Baking, a gourmet bakery with 63 employees in Boston.

At Great Little Box, fifteen percent of the profits are split equally among all employees, and the firm's finances, production, and sales performance are discussed at monthly meetings attended by employees ranging from machine operators to senior managers. "As a result, even the lowest-level employees act like managers, looking for ways to reduce costs and improve productivity."

At Dancing Deer Baking, employees are offered "options" that are sold back to the company when workers leave or retire. When discussing finances and operations, production workers noted that fifteen percent of the brownies were scrapped because the shape of the pans required edges to be cut after baking. To alleviate this problem the company purchased new pans costing $35,000. The investment was recouped in three months.

Source: Jody Heymann, "Bootstrapping Profits by Opening the Books," *Bloomberg Businessweek*, September 27, 2010, p. 62; Jody Heymann with Magda Barrera, "Profit at the Bottom of the Ladder," *Harvard Business School Press*, 2010.

Properly used, an operating budget is an effective mechanism for motivating employees to higher levels of performance and productivity. Improperly developed and administered, budgets can foster feelings of animosity toward management and the budget process. Behavioral research has generally concluded that when employees participate in the preparation of budgets and believe that the budgets represent fair standards for evaluating their performance, they receive personal satisfaction from accomplishing the goals set in the budgets.

MODULE-END REVIEW 1: BUDGET FOR A MERCHANDISING ORGANIZATION

Stumphouse Cheese Company is a wholesale distributor of blue cheese and ice cream. The following information is available for April 2012.

Estimated sales	
Blue cheese	160,000 hoops at $10 each
Ice cream	240,000 gallons at $5 each

Estimated costs	
Blue cheese	$8 per hoop
Ice cream	$2 per gallon

	Beginning	Ending
Desired inventories		
Blue cheese	10,000	12,000
Ice cream	4,000	5,000

Financial information follows:

- Beginning cash balance is $400,000.
- Purchases of merchandise are paid 60 percent in the current month and 40 percent in the following month. Purchases totaled $1,800,000 in March and are estimated to be $2,000,000 in May.
- Employee wages, salaries, and commissions are paid for in the current month. Employee expenses for April totaled $156,000.
- Overhead expenses are paid in the next month. The accounts payable amount for these expenses from March is $80,000 and for May will be $90,000. April's overhead expenses total $80,000.

- Sales are on credit and are collected 70 percent in the current period and the remainder in the next period. March's sales were $3,000,000, and May's sales are estimated to be $3,200,000. Bad debts average 1 percent of sales.
- Selling and administrative expenses are paid monthly and total $450,000, including $40,000 of depreciation.
- All unit costs for April are the same as they were in March.

Required

Prepare the following for April:
  a. Sales budget in dollars.
  b. Purchases budget.
  c. Cash budget.
  d. Budgeted income statement.

The solution is on page 21-38.

MODULE-END REVIEW 2: BUDGET FOR A MANUFACTURER

Handy Company manufactures and sells two industrial products in a single plant. The new manager wants to have quarterly budgets and has prepared the following information for the first quarter of 2012:

Budgeted sales

Drills..	60,000 at $100 each
Saws	40,000 at $125 each

Budgeted inventories

	Beginning	Ending
Drills, finished.....................	20,000 units	25,000 units
Saws, finished	8,000 units	10,000 units
Metal, direct materials	32,000 pounds	36,000 pounds
Plastic, direct materials	29,000 pounds	32,000 pounds
Handles, direct materials	6,000 each	7,000 each

Standard variable costs per unit

	Drills		Saws	
Direct materials				
Metal	5 pounds × $8.00	$40.00	4 pounds × $8.00	$32.00
Plastic	3 pounds × $5.00	15.00	3 pounds × $5.00	15.00
Handles	1 handle × $3.00	3.00		
Total		58.00		47.00
Direct labor.............	2 labor hours × $12.00	24.00	3 labor hours × $16.00	48.00
Variable manufacturing				
Overhead	2 hours × $1.50	3.00	3 hours × $1.50	4.50
Total		$85.00		$99.50

Fixed manufacturing overhead is $214,000 per quarter (including noncash expenditures of $156,000) and is allocated on total units produced. Financial information follows:

- Beginning cash balance is $1,800,000.
- Sales are on credit and are collected 50 percent in the current period and the remainder in the next period. Last quarter's sales were $8,400,000. There are no bad debts.
- Purchases of direct materials and labor costs are paid for in the quarter acquired.
- Manufacturing overhead expenses are paid in the quarter incurred.
- Selling and administrative expenses are all fixed and are paid in the quarter incurred. They are budgeted at $340,000 per quarter, including $90,000 of depreciation.

Required

For the first quarter of 2012, prepare the following:

a. Sales budget in dollars.

b. Production budget in units.

c. Purchases budget.

d. Manufacturing cost budget.

e. Cash budget.

f. Budgeted contribution income statement. (Hint: See Module 15.)

The solution is on page 21-39.

GUIDANCE ANSWER

MANAGERIAL DECISION   **You are the Chief Financial Officer**

You seem to be leaning toward using a top-down approach to budgeting. While this method may produce an effective set of benchmarks for planning and evaluation, it does not maximize the benefits of budgeting. A key element in any effective budgeting system is that it must be embraced by the managers whose performance will be evaluated by it. If the budget is imposed from the top down, it is far less likely to be embraced by managers than if they have participated from the beginning of the budget development process. The most effective budgeting systems are those that are strongly embraced by managers at all levels, which is most readily achieved through a participative (bottom-up) approach.

DISCUSSION QUESTIONS

Q21-1. What are the primary phases in the planning and control cycle?

Q21-2. Does budgeting require formal or informal planning? What are some advantages of this style of management?

Q21-3. Identify the advantages and disadvantages of the incremental approach to budgeting.

Q21-4. Explain the minimum level approach to budgeting.

Q21-5. How does activity-based budgeting predict a cost objective's budget?

Q21-6. Explain the continuous improvement concept of budgeting.

Q21-7. Which budget brings together all other budgets? How is this accomplished?

Q21-8. What budgets are normally used to support the cash budget? What is the net result of cash budget preparations?

Q21-9. Define *budgeted financial statements*.

Q21-10. Identify the two budgets that are part of the master budget of a manufacturing organization but not part of the master budget of a merchandising organization.

Q21-11. Contrast the top-down and bottom-up approaches to budget preparation.

Q21-12. Is budgetary slack a desirable feature? Can it be prevented? Why or why not?

Q21-13. Why are annual budgets not always desirable? What are some alternative budget periods?

Q21-14. Explain how continuous budgeting works.

Q21-15. In addition to the sales forecast, what forecasts are used in budgeting?

Q21-16. Why should motivational considerations be a part of budget planning and utilization? List several ways to motivate employees with budgets.

Assignments with the ⊘ in the margin are available in an online homework system.
See the Preface of the book for details.

MINI EXERCISES

M21-17. Output/Input Budget (LO2)

Fifth Street Health Center has the following resource input information available for a routine physical examination.

- Each exam normally requires 1.25 hours of examining room time, including:
  - ○ 45 minutes of nursing services,
  - ○ 30 minutes of physician services
- Each exam also utilizes one package of examination supplies costing $15 each.
- Including benefits, physicians earn $60/hour and nurses earn $25/hour.
- Variable overhead is budgeted at $20 per examining room hour and fixed overhead is budgeted at $5,000 per month.

Required

Prepare an output/input budget for October when 500 routine examinations are planned.

M21-18. Incremental Budget (LO2)

Smith County uses an incremental approach to budgeting. The 2011 cash budget for the Smith County Department of Motor Vehicles is presented below:

Supplies	$12,000
Temporary and seasonal wages.	18,000
Wages of full-time employees	180,000
Supervisor salaries.	42,000
Rent	36,000
Insurance	16,000
Utilities	18,000
Miscellaneous.	6,000
Contingencies and equipment	30,000
Total	$358,000

Required

Prepare an incremental cash budget for 2012, assuming the planned total budget increase is 2.5 percent. Budget details include a budget increment for salaries and wages of 3.5 percent, no change in rent, and 2 percent increases in the budget for supplies and miscellaneous. Utility companies have received approvals for rate increases amounting to 4 percent and insurance companies have announced an increase in premiums of 6 percent.

M21-19. Purchases Budget in Units and Dollars (LO3)   ⊘

Budgeted sales of The Music Shop for the first six months of 2012 are as follows:

Month	Unit Sales	Month	Unit Sales
January.	130,000	April.	210,000
February	160,000	May	180,000
March	200,000	June	240,000

Beginning inventory for 2012 is 40,000 units. The budgeted inventory at the end of a month is 40 percent of units to be sold the following month. Purchase price per unit is $5.

Required

Prepare a purchases budget in units and dollars for each month, January through May.

M21-20. Cash Budget (LO3)

Wilson's Retail Company is planning a cash budget for the next three months. Estimated sales revenue is as follows:

Month	Sales Revenue	Month	Sales Revenue
January..........	$300,000	March............	$200,000
February.........	225,000	April	175,000

All sales are on credit; 60 percent is collected during the month of sale, and 40 percent is collected during the next month. Cost of goods sold is 80 percent of sales. Payments for merchandise sold are made in the month following the month of sale. Operating expenses total $41,000 per month and are paid during the month incurred. The cash balance on February 1 is estimated to be $30,000.

Required

Prepare monthly cash budgets for February, March, and April.

M21-21. Production and Purchases Budgets in Units (LO4)

At the end of business on June 30, 2012, the Wooly Rug Company had 100,000 square yards of rugs and 400,000 pounds of raw materials on hand. Budgeted sales for the third quarter of 2012 are:

Month	Sales
July...	200,000 sq. yards
August	180,000 sq. yards
September	150,000 sq. yards
October	160,000 sq. yards

The Wooly Rug Company wants to have sufficient square yards of finished product on hand at the end of each month to meet 40 percent of the following month's budgeted sales and sufficient pounds of raw materials to meet 30 percent of the following month's production requirements. Five pounds of raw materials are required to produce one square yard of carpeting.

Required

Prepare a production budget for the months of July, August, and September and a purchases budget in units for the months of July and August.

M21-22. Manufacturing Cost Budget (LO4)

Henrietta Products produces a product with the following standard costs:

Unit costs:			
Direct materials:			
Wood: 20 square feet at $3	$60		
Hardware kits (screws, etc)	5	$	65
Direct labor 0.5 hours at $26 per hour........................			13
Variable overhead, per unit			5
Total variable costs per unit..................................		$	83
Fixed costs per month (rent, utilities, supervision).................			$50,000

Management plans to produce 8,000 units in April 2012.

Required

Prepare a manufacturing cost budget for April 2012.

EXERCISES

E21-23. Activity-Based Budget (LO2)

Macon Industries has the following budget information available for February:

Units manufactured	18,000
Factory administration	$40,000
Assembly	½ hour per unit × $8
Direct materials	2 pounds per unit × $3
Inspection.	$200 per batch of 1,000 units
Manufacturing overhead	$2 per unit
Product development.	$15,000
Setup cost	$10 per batch of 1,000 units

Required

Use activity based costing to prepare a manufacturing cost budget for February. Clearly distinguish between unit, batch, and facility-level costs.

E21-24. Product and Department Budgets Using Activity-Based Approach (LO2) ✔

The following data are from the general records of the Loading Department of Bowman Freight Company for November.
- Cleaning incoming trucks, 20 minutes.
- Obtaining and reviewing shipping documents for loading truck and instructing loaders, 30 minutes.
- Loading truck, 1 hour and 30 minutes.
- Cleaning shipping dock and storage area after each loading, 10 minutes.
- Employees perform both cleaning and loading tasks and are currently averaging $16 per hour in wages and benefits.
- The supervisor spends 10 percent of her time overseeing the cleaning activities; 60 percent overseeing various loading activities; and the remainder of her time making general plans and managing the department. Her current salary is $4,000 per month.
- Other overhead of the department amounts to $10,000 per month, 20 percent for cleaning and 80 percent for loading.

Required

Prepare an activities budget for cleaning and loading in the Loading Department for November, assuming 20 working days and the loading of an average of 14 trucks per day.

E21-25. Activity-Based Budgeting (LO2)

St. Mary's Hospital is preparing its budget for the coming year. It uses an activity-based approach for all costs except physician care. Its emergency room has three activity areas with cost drivers as follows:
1. *Reception*—paperwork of incoming patients. Cost driver is the number of forms completed.
2. *Treatment*—initial diagnosis and treatment of patients. Cost driver is the number of diagnoses treated.
3. *Cleaning*—general cleaning plus preparing treatment facilities for next patient. Cost driver is the number of people visiting emergency room (patients plus person(s) accompanying them).

Activity Area	Cost Driver Rates	Budgeted Amount of Cost Driver	
		Outpatients	Admitted Patients
Reception	$30	7,400 forms	5,500 forms
Treatment	90	7,000 diagnoses	4,400 diagnoses
Cleaning	12	6,400 people	2,400 people

Required

a. Prepare the total budgeted cost for each activity.

b. How might you adjust the budget approach if you found that outpatients were kept in the emergency room for one hour on average while admitted patients remained for two hours?

c. What advantage does an activity-based approach have over the hospital's former budgeting method of basing the next year's budget on the last year's actual amount plus a percentage increase?

E21-26. Sales Budget (LO3)

Summer Fun T-Shirt Shop has very seasonal sales. For 2012, management is trying to decide whether to establish a sales budget based on average sales or on sales estimated by quarter. The unit sales for 2012 are expected to be 10 percent higher than 2011 sales. Unit shirt sales by quarter for 2011 were as follows:

	Children's	Women's	Men's	Total
Winter quarter..........	200	200	100	500
Spring quarter	200	250	200	650
Summer quarter........	400	300	200	900
Fall quarter............	200	250	100	550
Total	1,000	1,000	600	2,600

Children's T-shirts sell for $5 each, women's sell for $9, and men's sell for $10.

Required

Assuming a 10 percent increase in sales, prepare a sales budget for each quarter of 2012 using the following:
a. Average quarterly sales. (*Hint:* Winter quarter children's shirts are 275 [1,000 × 1.10 ÷ 4].)
b. Actual quarterly sales. (*Hint:* Winter quarter children's shirts are 220 [200 × 1.10].)
c. Suggest advantages of each method.

E21-27. Cash Budget & Short-Term Financing (LO3)

Presented are partial October, November, and December cash budgets for Seasonal Parties:

Seasonal Parties Partial Cash Budgets For the Months of October, November, and December				
	October	November	December	Total
Cash balance, beginning	$11,000	$?	$?	$?
Collections on sales	20,000	30,000	60,000	?
Cash available for operations....................	?	?	?	?
Disbursements for operations	(40,000)	(50,000)	(20,000)	?
Ending cash before borrowings or replacements	?	?	?	?
Short-term finance:	?	?	?	?
New loans..................................	?	?	?	?
Repayments	?	?	?	?
Interest	?	?	?	?
Cash balance, ending..........................	$?	$?	$?	$?

Loans are obtained in increments of $1,000 at the start of each month to maintain a minimum end-of-month balance of $10,000. Interest is one percent simple interest (no compounding) per month, payable when the loan is repaid. Repayments are made as soon as possible, subject to the minimum end-of-month balance.

Required

Complete the short-term financing section of the cash budget.

E21-28. Purchases and Cash Budgets (LO3)

On July 1, Five Corners Wholesalers had a cash balance of $145,000 and accounts payable of $77,000. Actual sales for May and June, and budgeted sales for July, August, September, and October are:

Month	Sales	Month	Sales
May............	$120,000	September........	$ 80,000
June	140,000	October	100,000
July............	80,000		
August	60,000		

All sales are on credit with 75 percent collected during the month of sale, 20 percent collected during the next month, and 5 percent collected during the second month following the month of sale. Cost of goods sold averages 70 percent of sales revenue. Ending inventory is one-half of the next month's predicted cost of sales. The other half of the merchandise is acquired during the month of sale. All purchases are paid for in the month after purchase. Operating costs are estimated at $20,000 each month and are paid during the month incurred.

Required
Prepare purchases and cash budgets for July, August, and September.

E21-29. Cash Receipts (LO3)
The sales budget for Perrier Inc. is forecasted as follows:

Month	Sales Revenue
May.	$120,000
June	160,000
July.	180,000
August	120,000

To prepare a cash budget, the company must determine the budgeted cash collections from sales. Historically, the following trend has been established regarding cash collection of sales:
- 60 percent in the month of sale.
- 20 percent in the month following sale.
- 15 percent in the second month following sale.
- 5 percent uncollectible.

  The company gives a 2 percent cash discount for payments made by customers during the month of sale. The accounts receivable balance on April 30 is $24,000, of which $7,000 represents uncollected March sales and $17,000 represents uncollected April sales.

Required
Prepare a schedule of budgeted cash collections from sales for May, June, and July. Include a three-month summary of estimated cash collections.

E21-30. Cash Disbursements (LO3)
Montana Timber Company is in the process of preparing its budget for next year. Cost of goods sold has been estimated at 70 percent of sales. Lumber purchases and payments are to be made during the month preceding the month of sale. Wages are estimated at 15 percent of sales and are paid during the month of sale. Other operating costs amounting to 10 percent of sales are to be paid in the month following the month of sale. Additionally, a monthly lease payment of $12,000 is paid to BMI for computer services. Sales revenue is forecast as follows:

Month	Sales Revenue
February	$100,000
March	160,000
April	180,000
May.	210,000
June	180,000
July.	230,000

Required
Prepare a schedule of cash disbursements for April, May, and June.

E21-31. Cash Disbursements (LO3)
Assume that Waycross Manufacturing manages its cash flow from its home office. Waycross controls cash disbursements by category and month. In setting its budget for the next six months, beginning in July, it used the following managerial guidelines:

Category	Guidelines
Purchases.	Pay half in current and half in following month.
Payroll.	Pay 80 percent in current month and 20 percent in following month.
Loan payments. . .	Pay total amount due each month.

Predicted activity for selected months follow:

Category	May	June	July	August
Purchases.	$ 30,000	$ 44,000	$ 48,000	$ 50,000
Payroll.	100,000	110,000	120,000	100,000
Loan payments.	10,000	10,000	15,000	15,000

Required

Prepare a schedule showing cash disbursements by account for July and August.

E21-32. **Budgeted Income Statement** (LO3)

Pendleton Company, a merchandising company, is developing its master budget for 2013. The income statement for 2012 is as follows:

PENDLETON COMPANY Income Statement For Year Ending December 31, 2012	
Gross sales.	$750,000
Less estimated uncollectible accounts	(7,500)
Net sales.	742,500
Cost of goods sold.	(430,000)
Gross profit.	312,500
Operating expenses (including $25,000 depreciation).	(200,500)
Net income.	$112,000

The following are management's goals and forecasts for 2013:

1. Selling prices will increase by 8 percent, and sales volume will increase by 5 percent.
2. The cost of merchandise will increase by 4 percent.
3. All operating expenses are fixed and are paid in the month incurred. Price increases for operating expenses will be 10 percent. The company uses straight-line depreciation.
4. The estimated uncollectibles are 1 percent of budgeted sales.

Required

Prepare a budgeted functional income statement for 2013.

E21-33. **Budgeted Income Statement with CVP** (LO3)

Wisconsin Booksellers is planning a budget for 2013. The estimate of sales revenue is $1,200,000 and of cost of goods sold is 70 percent of sales revenue. Depreciation on the office building and fixtures is budgeted at $50,000. Salaries and wages are budgeted at $90,000. Advertising has been budgeted at $80,000, and utilities should amount to $70,000. Income tax is estimated at 40 percent of operating income.

Required

a. Prepare a budgeted income statement for 2013.
b. Assuming management desired an after-tax income of $100,000, determine the necessary sales volume. (*Hint:* refer to Module 15.)

E21-34. **Production and Purchases Budgets** (LO4)

At the beginning of October, Company Cushion had 1,600 cushions and 7,740 pounds of raw materials on hand. Budgeted sales for the next three months are:

Month	Sales
October	8,000 cushions
November.	10,000 cushions
December.	12,000 cushions

Company Cushion wants to have sufficient raw materials on hand at the end of each month to meet 25 percent of the following month's production requirements and sufficient cushions on hand at the end of each month to meet 20 percent of the following month's budgeted sales. Three pounds of raw materials, at a standard cost of $0.80 per pound, are required to produce each cushion.

Required
a. Prepare a production budget for October and November.
b. Prepare a purchases budget in units and dollars for October.

E21-35. Production and Purchases Budgets (LO4)
Rocky Mountain Culvert produces small culverts for water drainage under two-lane dirt roads. Budgeted unit sales for the next several months are:

Month	Sales
September	2,500
October	1,500
November	1,000
December	500

At the beginning of September, 200 units of finished goods were in inventory. During the final third of the year, as road construction declines, plans are to have an inventory of finished goods equal to 25 percent of the following month's sales. Each unit of finished goods requires 500 pounds of raw materials at a cost of $5 per pound. Management wishes to maintain month-end inventories of raw materials equal to 50 percent of the following month's needs. Five hundred thousand pounds of raw materials were on hand at the start of September.

Required:
a. Prepare a production budget for September, October, and November.
b. Prepare a purchases budget in units and dollars for September and October.

PROBLEMS

P21-36. Cash Budget (LO3)
Cash budgeting for Carolina Apple, a merchandising firm, is performed on a quarterly basis. The company is planning its cash needs for the third quarter of 2012, and the following information is available to assist in preparing a cash budget. Budgeted income statements for July through October 2012 are as follows:

	July	August	September	October
Sales	$18,000	$24,000	$28,000	$36,000
Cost of goods sold	(10,000)	(14,000)	(16,000)	(20,000)
Gross profit	8,000	10,000	12,000	16,000
Less other expenses				
Selling	2,300	3,000	3,400	4,200
Administrative	2,600	3,000	3,200	3,600
Total	(4,900)	(6,000)	(6,600)	(7,800)
Net income	$ 3,100	$ 4,000	$ 5,400	$ 8,200

Additional information follows:

1. Other expenses, which are paid monthly, include $1,000 of depreciation per month.
2. Sales are 30 percent for cash and 70 percent on credit.
3. Credit sales are collected 20 percent in the month of sale, 70 percent one month after sale, and 10 percent two months after sale. May sales were $15,000, and June sales were $16,000.
4. Merchandise is paid for 50 percent in the month of purchase; the remaining 50 percent is paid in the following month. Accounts payable for merchandise at June 30 totaled $6,000.
5. The company maintains its ending inventory levels at 25 percent of the cost of goods to be sold in the following month. The inventory at June 30 is $2,500.

6. An equipment note of $5,000 per month is being paid through August.
7. The company must maintain a cash balance of at least $5,000 at the end of each month. The cash balance on June 30 is $5,100.
8. The company can borrow from its bank as needed. Borrowings and repayments must be in multiples of $100. All borrowings take place at the beginning of a month, and all repayments are made at the end of a month. When the principal is repaid, interest on the repayment is also paid. The interest rate is 12 percent per year.

Required

a. Prepare a monthly schedule of budgeted operating cash receipts for July, August, and September.
b. Prepare a monthly purchases budget and a schedule of budgeted cash payments for purchases for July, August, and September.
c. Prepare a monthly cash budget for July, August, and September. Show borrowings from the company's bank and repayments to the bank as needed to maintain the minimum cash balance.

P21-37. Cash Budget (LO3)

The Peoria Supply Company sells for $30 one product that it purchases for $20. Budgeted sales in total dollars for next year are $720,000. The sales information needed for preparing the July budget follows:

Month	Sales Revenue
May.............	$30,000
June.............	42,000
July.............	48,000
August	50,000

Account balances at July 1 include these:

Cash.........................	$20,000
Merchandise inventory............	16,000
Accounts receivable (sales)	23,000
Accounts payable (purchases)......	15,000

The company pays for one-half of its purchases in the month of purchase and the remainder in the following month. End-of-month inventory must be 50 percent of the budgeted sales in units for the next month. A 2 percent cash discount on sales is allowed if payment is made during the month of sale. Experience indicates that 50 percent of the billings will be collected during the month of sale, 40 percent in the following month, 8 percent in the second following month, and 2 percent will be uncollectible. Total budgeted selling and administrative expenses (excluding bad debts) for the fiscal year are estimated at $186,000, of which one-half is fixed expense (inclusive of a $20,000 annual depreciation charge). Fixed expenses are incurred evenly during the year. The other selling and administrative expenses vary with sales. Expenses are paid during the month incurred.

Required

a. Prepare a schedule of estimated cash collections for July.
b. Prepare a schedule of estimated July cash payments for purchases. (Round calculations to the nearest dollar.)
c. Prepare schedules of July selling and administrative expenses, separately identifying those requiring cash disbursements.
d. Prepare a cash budget in summary form for July.

P21-38. Budgeting Purchases, Revenues, Expenses, and Cash in a Service Organization (LO3)

Round Lake Medical Center is located in a summer resort community. During the summer months the center operates an outpatient clinic for the treatment of minor injuries and illnesses. The clinic is administered as a separate department within the hospital. It has its own staff and maintains its own financial records. All patients requiring extensive or intensive care are referred to other hospital departments.

An analysis of past operating data for the out-patient clinic reveals the following:

• Staff: Seven full-time employees with total monthly salaries of $40,000. On a monthly basis, one additional staff member is hired for every 500 budgeted patient visits in excess of 3,000, at a cost of $4,000 per month.

- Facilities: Monthly facility costs, including depreciation of $2,000, total $9,000.
- Supplies: The supplies expense averages $10 per patient visit. The center maintains an end-of-month supplies inventory equal to ten percent of the predicted needs of the following month, with a minimum ending inventory of $3,000, which is also the desired inventory at the end of August.
- Additional variable patient costs, such as medications, are charged directly to the patient by the hospital pharmacy.
- Payments: All staff and maintenance expenses are paid in the month the cost is incurrent. Supplies are purchased at cost directly from the hospital with an immediate transfer of cash from the clinic cash account to the hospital cash account.
- Collections: The average bill for services rendered is $55. Of the total bills, 40 percent are paid in cash at the time the service is rendered, 10 percent are never paid, and the remaining 50 percent are covered by insurance. In the past, insurance companies have disallowed 20 percent of the claims filed and paid the balance two months after services are rendered.
- May 30 status: At the end of May, the clinic had $12,000 in cash and supplies costing $3,000.

Budgeted patient visits for next summer are as follows:

Month	Patient visits
June	2,000
July	3,500
August	4,000

Required:
For the Round Lake Outpatient Clinic:

a. Prepare a supplies purchases budget for June, July, and August, with a total column.
b. Prepare a revenue and expense budget for June, July, and August with a total column.
c. Prepare a cash budget for June, July and August with a total column. Hint: See requirement d.
d. Explain why you were unable to develop a feasible cash budget and make any appropriate recommendations for management's consideration.

P21-39. Developing a Master Budget for a Merchandising Organization (LO3)
Peyton Department Store prepares budgets quarterly. The following information is available for use in planning the second quarter budgets for 2012.

PEYTON DEPARTMENT STORE
Balance Sheet
March 31, 2012

Assets		Liabilities and Stockholders' Equity	
Cash	$ 3,000	Accounts payable	$26,000
Accounts receivable	25,000	Dividends payable	17,000
Inventory	30,000	Rent payable	2,000
Prepaid insurance	2,000	Stockholders' equity	40,000
Fixtures	25,000		
Total assets	$85,000	Total liabilities and equity	$85,000

Actual and forecasted sales for selected months in 2012 are as follows:

Month	Sales Revenue
January	$60,000
February	50,000
March	40,000
April	50,000
May	60,000
June	70,000
July	90,000
August	80,000

Monthly operating expenses are as follows:

Wages and salaries	$25,000
Depreciation	100
Utilities	1,000
Rent	2,000

Cash dividends of $17,000 are declared during the third month of each quarter and are paid during the first month of the following quarter. Operating expenses, except insurance, rent, and depreciation are paid as incurred. Rent is paid during the following month. The prepaid insurance is for five more months. Cost of goods sold is equal to 50 percent of sales. Ending inventories are sufficient for 120 percent of the next month's sales. Purchases during any given month are paid in full during the following month. All sales are on account, with 50 percent collected during the month of sale, 40 percent during the next month, and 10 percent during the month thereafter. Money can be borrowed and repaid in multiples of $1,000 at an interest rate of 12 percent per year. The company desires a minimum cash balance of $3,000 on the first of each month. At the time the principal is repaid, interest is paid on the portion of principal that is repaid. All borrowing is at the beginning of the month, and all repayment is at the end of the month. Money is never repaid at the end of the month it is borrowed.

Required

a. Prepare a purchases budget for each month of the second quarter ending June 30, 2012.
b. Prepare a cash receipts schedule for each month of the second quarter ending June 30, 2012. Do not include borrowings.
c. Prepare a cash disbursements schedule for each month of the second quarter ending June 30, 2012. Do not include repayments of borrowings.
d. Prepare a cash budget for each month of the second quarter ending June 30, 2012. Include budgeted borrowings and repayments.
e. Prepare an income statement for each month of the second quarter ending June 30, 2012.
f. Prepare a budgeted balance sheet as of June 30, 2012.

P21-40. Developing a Master Budget for a Manufacturing Organization (LO4)
Jacobs Incorporated manufactures a product with a selling price of $50 per unit. Units and monthly cost data follow:

Variable:	
Selling and administrative	$ 5 per unit sold
Direct materials	10 per unit manufactured
Direct labor	10 per unit manufactured
Variable manufacturing overhead	5 per unit manufactured
Fixed:	
Selling and administrative	$20,000 per month
Manufacturing (including depreciation of $10,000)	30,000 per month

Jacobs pays all bills in the month incurred. All sales are on account with 50 percent collected the month of sale and the balance collected the following month. There are no sales discounts or bad debts.

Jacobs desires to maintain an ending finished goods inventory equal to 20 percent of the following month's sales and a raw materials inventory equal to 10 percent of the following month's production. January 1, 2012, inventories are in line with these policies.

Actual unit sales for December and budgeted unit sales for January, February, and March of 2012 are as follows:

JACOBS INCORPORATED				
Sales Budget				
For the Months of January, February, and March 2012				
Month	December	January	February	March
Sales - Units	6,250	5,000	10,000	8,000
Sales - Dollars	$312,500	$250,000	$500,000	$400,000

Additional information:
- The January 1 beginning cash is projected as $5,000.
- For the purpose of operational budgeting, units in the January 1 inventory of finished goods are valued at variable manufacturing cost.
- Each unit of finished product requires one unit of raw materials.
- Jacobs intends to pay a cash dividend of $10,000 in January

Required

a. A production budget for January and February.
b. A purchases budget in units for January.
c. A manufacturing cost budget for January.
d. A cash budget for January.
e. A budgeted contribution income statement for January.

P21-41. Risk Management in a Manufacturing Organization (LO4)

Required:

Continuing problem P21-40, management is concerned that their supplier of raw materials will have a strike. Determine the budget implications if management plans to increase the January-end raw materials inventory to 100 percent of February's production needs. Offer any recommendations you believe appropriate.

P21-42. Developing a Master Budget for a Manufacturing Organization: Challenge Problem (LO4)

Banana Computer Accessories assembles a computer networking device from kits of imported components. You have been asked to develop a quarterly and annual operating budget and pro-forma income statements for 2012. You have obtained the following information:

Beginning-of-year balances

Cash.	$40,000.00
Accounts receivable (previous quarter's sales)	$15,000.00
Raw materials	300 kits
Finished goods	400 units
Accounts payable	$40,000.00
Borrowed funds	$10,000.00

Desired end-of-year inventory balances

Raw materials	500 kits
Finished goods	200 units

Desired end-of-quarter balances

Cash.	$10,000.00
Raw materials as a portion of the following quarter's production.	0.2
Finished goods as a portion of the following quarter's sales	0.15

Manufacturing costs

Standard cost per unit	Units	Unit price	Total
Raw materials.	1 kit	$40.00	$40.00
Direct labor hours at rate	0.8 hour	$20.00	16.00
Variable overhead/labor hour	0.8 hour	$10.00	8.00
Total standard variable cost			$64.00

Fixed cost per quarter

Cash	$40,000.00
Depreciation	10,000.00
Total	$50,000.00

Selling and administrative costs

Variable cost per unit	$5.00

Fixed costs per quarter

Cash	$20,000.00
Depreciation	5,000.00
Total	$25,000.00

continued

continued from prior page

Interest rate per quarter	0.04			
Portion of sales collected				
Quarter of sale	0.75			
Subsequent quarter	0.24			
Bad debts	0.01			
Portion of purchases paid				
Quarter of purchase	0.75			
Subsequent quarter	0.25			
Unit selling price	$110.00			
Sales forecast				
Quarter	First	Second	Third	Fourth
Unit sales	2,400	1,500	2,000	3,100

Additional information
- All cash payments except purchases are made quarterly as incurred.
- All borrowings occur at the start of the quarter.
- All repayments on borrowings occur at the end of the quarter.
- All interest on borrowed funds is paid at the end of each quarter.
- Borrowings and repayments may be made in any amount.

Required:

a. A sales budget for each quarter and the year. Hint: Use of spreadsheet software strongly recommended for this problem.
b. A production budget for each quarter and the year.
c. A purchases budget for each quarter and the year.
d. A manufacturing cost budget for each quarter and the year.
e. A selling and administrative expense budget for each quarter and the year.
f. A cash budget for each quarter and the year.
g. A pro-forma contribution income statement for each quarter and the year.

MANAGEMENT APPLICATIONS

MA21-43. Behavioral Implications of Budgeting (LO5)

Andrea Rawls, controller of Data Scientific, believes that effective budgeting greatly assists in meeting the organization's goals and objectives. She argues that the budget serves as a blueprint for the operating activities during each reporting period, making it an important control device. She believes that sound management evaluations can be based on the comparisons of performance and budgetary schedules and that employees respond more favorably when they participate in the budgetary process. Jeff Cooke, treasurer of Data Scientific, agrees that budgeting is essential for overall organization success, but he argues that human resources are too valuable to spend much time planning and preparing the budgetary process. He thinks that the roles people play in budgetary preparation are not important in the final analysis of a budget's effectiveness.

Required
Contrast the participative versus imposed budgeting concepts and indicate how the ideas of Rawls and Cooke fit the two categories.

MA21-44. Behavioral Considerations and Budgeting (LO5)

Scott Weidner, the controller in the Division of Social Services for the state, recognizes the importance of the budgetary process for planning, control, and motivation purposes. He believes that a properly implemented participative budgeting process for planning purposes and a management by exception reporting procedure based on that budget will motivate his subordinates to improve productivity within their particular departments. Based on this philosophy, Weidner has implemented the following budget procedures.
- An appropriation target figure is given to each department manager. This amount is the maximum funding that each department can expect to receive in the next fiscal year.
- Department managers develop their individual budgets within the following spending constraints as directed by the controller's staff.
  1. Expenditure requests cannot exceed the appropriation target.

2. All fixed expenditures should be included in the budget; these should include items such as contracts and salaries at current levels.

3. All government projects directed by higher authority should be included in the budget in their entirety.

- The controller consolidates the departmental budget requests from the various departments into one budget that is to be submitted for the entire division.

- Upon final budget approval by the legislature, the controller's staff allocates the appropriation to the various departments on instructions from the division manager. However, a specified percentage of each department's appropriation is held back in anticipation of potential budget cuts and special funding needs. The amount and use of this contingency fund are left to the discretion of the division manager.

- Each department is allowed to adjust its budget when necessary to operate within the reduced appropriation level. However, as stated in the original directive, specific projects authorized by higher authority must remain intact.

- The final budget is used as the basis of control for a management by exception form of reporting. Excessive expenditures by account for each department are highlighted on a monthly basis. Department managers are expected to account for all expenditures over budget. Fiscal responsibility is an important factor in the overall performance evaluation of department managers.

Weidner believes that his policy of allowing the department managers to participate in the budget process and then holding them accountable for their performance is essential, especially during these times of limited resources. He also believes that department managers will be positively motivated to increase the efficiency and effectiveness of their departments because they have provided input into the initial budgetary process and are required to justify any unfavorable performances.

Required

a. Explain the operational and behavioral benefits that generally are attributed to a participative budgeting process.

b. Identify deficiencies in Weidner's participative budgetary policy for planning and performance evaluation purposes. For each deficiency identified, recommend how the deficiency can be corrected.

(CMA Adapted)

MA21-45. Budgetary Slack with Ethical Considerations (LO5)

Alene Adams was promoted to department manager of a production unit in Dallas Industries three years ago. She enjoys her job except for the evaluation measures that are based on the department's budget. After three years of consistently poor annual evaluations based on a set annual budget, she has decided to improve the evaluation situation. At a recent budget meeting of junior-level managers, the topic of budgetary slack was discussed as a means to maintain some consistency in budgeting matters. As a result of this meeting, Adams decided to take the following steps in preparing the upcoming year's budget:

1. Use the top quartile for all wage and salary categories.

2. Select the optimistic values for the estimated production ranges for the coming year. These are provided by the marketing department.

3. Use the average of the three months in the current year with poorest production efficiency as benchmarks of success for the coming year.

4. Base equipment charges (primarily depreciation) on replacement values furnished by the purchasing department.

5. Base other fixed costs on current cost plus an inflation rate estimated for the coming year.

6. Use the average of the ten newly hired employees' performance as a basis of labor efficiency for the coming year.

Required

a. For each item on Adams' list, explain whether it will create budgetary slack. Use numerical examples as necessary to illustrate.

b. Given the company's use of static budgets as one of the performance evaluation measures of its managers, can the managers justify the use of built-in budgetary slack?

c. What would you recommend as a means for Adams to improve the budgeting situation in the company? Provide some specific examples of how the budgeting process might be improved.

MA21-46. Budgetary Slack with Ethical Considerations (LO5)

Norton Company, a manufacturer of infant furniture and carriages, is in the initial stages of preparing the annual budget for next year. Scott Ford recently joined Norton's accounting staff and is interested to learn as much as possible about the company's budgeting process. During a recent lunch with Marge Atkins, sales manager, and Pete Granger, production manager, Ford initiated the following conversation:

Ford: Since I'm new around here and am going to be involved with the preparation of the annual budget, I'd be interested to learn how the two of you estimate sales and production numbers.

Atkins: We start out very methodically by looking at recent history, discussing what we know about current accounts, potential customers, and the general state of consumer spending. Then we add that usual dose of intuition to come up with the best forecast we can.

Granger: I usually take the sales projections as the basis for my projections. Of course, we have to make an estimate of what this year's closing inventories will be, which is sometimes difficult.

Ford: Why does that present a problem? There must have been an estimate of closing inventories in the budget for the current year.

Granger: Those numbers aren't always reliable since Marge makes some adjustments to the sales numbers before passing them on to me.

Ford: What kind of adjustments?

Atkins: Well, we don't want to fall short of the sales projections, so we generally give ourselves a little breathing room by lowering the initial sales projection anywhere from 5 to 10 percent.

Granger: So, you can see why this year's budget is not a very reliable starting point. We always have to adjust the projected production rates as the year progresses; of course, this changes the ending inventory estimates. By the way, we make similar adjustments to expenses by adding at least 10 percent to the estimates; I think everyone around here does the same thing.

Required

a. Marge Atkins and Pete Granger have described the use of budgetary slack.
   1. Explain why Atkins and Granger behave in this manner, and describe the benefits they expect to realize from the use of budgetary slack.
   2. Explain how the use of budgetary slack can adversely affect Atkins and Granger.
b. As a management accountant, Scott Ford believes that the behavior described by Marge Atkins and Pete Granger could be unethical and that he might have an obligation not to support this behavior. Explain why the use of budgetary slack could be unethical.

(CMA Adapted)

SOLUTIONS TO REVIEW PROBLEMS

Mid-Module Review

Solution

a. Under the output/input approach, the output of units dictates the expected cost inputs. Here budgeted overhead costs are based on the number of budgeted assembly hours.

	Beta	Gamma
Direct materials (20,000 × $20)	$400,000	
(50,000 × $14.50)		$ 725,000
Direct assembly labor (20,000 × 0.5 × $18)	180,000	
(50,000 × 0.8 × $18)		720,000
Overhead (20,000 × 0.5 × $8.17)	81,700	
(50,000 × 0.8 × $8.17)		326,800
Total budgeted cost	$661,700	$1,771,800
Unit Cost	$33.085	$35.436

b. Under the activity-based approach, budgeted overhead costs are based on expected activities to produce the products, not only on assembly hours.

Direct materials (20,000 × $20)	$400,000	
(50,000 × $14.50)		$ 725,000
Direct assembly labor (20,000 × 0.5 × $18)...........	180,000	
(50,000 × 0.8 × $18)..........		720,000
Setup (1,000 hours × $25)........................	25,000	
(1,500 hours × $25)........................		37,500
Engineering and Maintenance (500 hours × $35)	17,500	
(600 hours × $35)		21,000
Inspections (650 inspections × $250)...............	162,500	
(580 inspections × $250)...............		145,000
Total budgeted cost	$785,000	$1,648,500
Unit cost......................................	$39.25	$32.97

c. Under the incremental approach to budgeting, the cost per unit would be budgeted at last period's cost, plus an increment for expected additional costs in the current period. Based on last period's actual cost of $38 for Beta and $32 for Gamma, and using the 3.5 percent overall expected increase in costs, the current period's budgeted cost would be $39.33 for Beta and $33.12 for Gamma.

d. Under the minimum level approach, the company begins with either a zero or very low cost estimate, and then requires all additional costs beyond this minimum to be justified by the production managers. This approach forces managers to evaluate thoroughly all elements of cost each period.

Module-End Review 1

Solution to Module-End Review 1

a.

STUMPHOUSE CHEESE COMPANY
Sales Budget
For Month of April 2012

	Units	Price	Sales
Blue cheese	160,000	$10	$1,600,000
Ice cream	240,000	5	1,200,000
Total			$2,800,000

b.

STUMPHOUSE CHEESE COMPANY
Purchases Budget
For Month of April 2012

	Blue Cheese	Ice Cream	Total
Units			
Sales needs	160,000	240,000	
Desired ending inventory	12,000	5,000	
Total	172,000	245,000	
Less beginning inventory	(10,000)	(4,000)	
Purchases......................	162,000	241,000	
Dollars			
Sales needs	$1,280,000	$480,000	
Desired ending inventory	96,000	10,000	
Total	1,376,000	490,000	
Less beginning inventory	(80,000)	(8,000)	
Purchases needed	$1,296,000	$482,000	$1,778,000

c.

STUMPHOUSE CHEESE COMPANY Cash Budget For Month of April 2012		
Cash balance, beginning		$ 400,000
Collections on sales		
Current month's sales ($2,800,000 × 0.70)	$1,960,000	
Previous month's sales ($3,000,000 × 0.29).	870,000	2,830,000
Cash available from operations		3,230,000
Less budgeted disbursements		
March purchases ($1,800,000 × 0.40).	720,000	
April purchases ($1,778,000 × 0.60)	1,066,800	
Labor.	156,000	
Overhead (March)	80,000	
Selling and administrative		
($450,000 − $40,000 depreciation).	410,000	(2,432,800)
Cash balance, ending.		$ 797,200

d.

STUMPHOUSE CHEESE COMPANY Budgeted Income Statement For Month of April 2012			
Sales (sales budget).			$2,800,000
Allowance for bad debts			(28,000)
Net sales.			2,772,000
Costs of merchandise sold			
Blue cheese (160,000 × $8)	$1,280,000		
Ice cream (240,000 × $2)	480,000	$1,760,000	
Wages and salaries	156,000		
Overhead	80,000		
Selling and administrative	450,000	686,000	(2,446,000)
Net income.			$ 326,000

Module-End Review 2:

Solution Module-End Review 2

a.

HANDY COMPANY Sales Budget For First Quarter of 2012			
	Units	Price	Sales
Drills	60,000	$100	$ 6,000,000
Saws.	40,000	125	5,000,000
Total			$11,000,000

b.

HANDY COMPANY Production Budget For First Quarter of 2012	Drills	Saws
Budget sales..	60,000	40,000
Plus desired ending inventory	25,000	10,000
Total inventory requirements	85,000	50,000
Less beginning inventory	(20,000)	(8,000)
Budgeted production......................................	65,000	42,000

c.

HANDY COMPANY Purchases Budget For First Quarter of 2012	Drills	Saws	Total
Metal purchases			
Production units (production budget)	65,000	42,000	
Metal (pounds)............................	× 5	× 4	
Production needs (pounds).................	325,000	168,000	493,000
Desired ending inventory (pounds)			36,000
Total metal needs (pounds).......................................			529,000
Less beginning inventory (pounds)			(32,000)
Purchases needed (pounds)			497,000
Cost per pound			× $8
Total metal purchases			$3,976,000
Plastic purchases			
Production units (production budget)	65,000	42,000	107,000
Plastic (pounds)...			× 3
Production needs (pounds)			321,000
Desired ending inventory (pounds)			32,000
Total plastic needs (pounds)			353,000
Less beginning inventory (pounds)			(29,000)
Purchases needed (pounds)			324,000
Cost per pound			× $5
Total plastic purchases.....................................			$1,620,000
Handle purchases			
Production units (production budget)	65,000		65,000
Handles			× 1
Production needs......................................			65,000
Desired ending inventory................................			7,000
Total handle needs......................................			72,000
Less beginning inventory...................................			(6,000)
Purchases needed......................................			66,000
Cost per handle...			× $3
Total handle purchases			$198,000
Total purchases			
Metal			$3,976,000
Plastic			1,620,000
Handles			198,000
Total purchases			$5,794,000

d.

HANDY COMPANY Manufacturing Cost Budget For First Quarter of 2012	Drills	Saws	Total
Direct materials			
Metal			
Production units (production budget)	65,000	42,000	
Metal per unit of product (pounds)	× 5	× 4	
Production needs for metal (pounds)	325,000	168,000	
Unit cost	× $8	× $8	
Cost of metal issued to production	$2,600,000	$1,344,000	$3,944,000
Plastic			
Production units (production budget)	65,000	42,000	
Plastic (pounds)	× 3	× 3	
Production needs for plastic (pounds).	195,000	126,000	
Unit cost.	× $5	× $5	
Cost of plastic issued to production	$ 975,000	$ 630,000	1,605,000
Handles			
Production units (production budget)	65,000		
Handles	× 1		
Production needs for handles	65,000		
Unit cost.	× $3		
Cost of handles issued to production	$ 195,000		195,000
Total			5,744,000
Direct labor			
Budgeted production.	65,000	42,000	
Direct labor hours per unit	× 2	× 3	
Total direct labor hours	130,000	126,000	
Labor rate.	× $12	× $16	
Labor expenditures	$1,560,000	$2,016,000	3,576,000
Variable manufacturing overhead			
Direct labor hours	130,000	126,000	
Variable manufacturing overhead rate.	× $1.50	× $1.50	
Total variable overhead	$ 195,000	$ 189,000	384,000
Fixed manufacturing overhead.			214,000
Total			$9,918,000

e.

HANDY COMPANY Cash Budget For First Quarter of 2012		
Cash balance, beginning		$ 1,800,000
Collections on sales		
Current quarter's sales ($11,000,000 × 0.50)	$5,500,000	
Previous quarter's sales ($8,400,000 × 0.50)	4,200,000	9,700,000
Cash available from operations		11,500,000
Less budgeted disbursements		
Materials (purchases budget)	5,794,000	
Labor (manufacturing cost budget)	3,576,000	
Manufacturing overhead (manufacturing cost budget)		
([$384,000 + 214,000] − 156,000 noncash)	442,000	
Selling and administrative		
($340,000 − $90,000 depreciation)	250,000	(10,062,000)
Cash balance, ending.		$ 1,438,000

f.

HANDY COMPANY Contribution Income Statement For First Quarter of 2012		
Sales (sales budget)		$11,000,000
Less variable costs of goods sold		
Drills (60,000 × $85.00)	$5,100,000	
Saws (40,000 × $99.50)	3,980,000	(9,080,000)
Gross profit		1,920,000
Less fixed costs		
Manufacturing overhead	214,000	
Selling and administrative expenses	340,000	(554,000)
Net income		$ 1,366,000

Getty Images

HOME DEPOT

Passed over for promotion to Chief Executive Officer (CEO) of General Electric, Robert Nardelli left to accept the top job at Home Depot. Believing "facts are friendly," he brought with him a desire to measure almost everything and to hold executives strictly accountable for performance. To enhance financial performance by reducing costs, he replaced thousands of experienced full-time employees with large numbers of part-time employees. Managers not meeting performance targets were also replaced. Indeed, between 2001 and 2007, 98 percent of Home Depot's top 170 executives were new, with more than half coming from outside the company.

Driven by a strategy that included cost cutting, as well as a housing and home improvement boom, Home Depot sales rose from $46 billion in 2000 to $81.5 billion in 2005. Gross profit also increased from 30 percent to 33.8% of sales, and profits more than doubled to $5.8 billion. Unfortunately, Home Depot's stock price did not show similar improvements, even though the stock prices of arch rival Lowes continued to build higher. Savvy investors may have

realized that the 2000 to 2005 financial improvements came with a long-term price.

Employees were alienated by cost cutting and the "replacement" of full-time employees with part-time help. Customers were alienated by the decline in customer service. Do-it-yourself customers complained that the Depot went from "great help" to "no help." Meanwhile, arch-rival Lowes was making great strides in customer service and building strong customer relations.

By late 2006, Home Depot and Nardelli were under pressure as sales and profits declined. Employees, shareholders, and financial analysts were also displeased with his arrogant style, lack of stock performance, and excessive compensation. When Nardelli left in early 2007, employees' cell phones lit up with text-messaged happy-faces.

Later in 2007, new Home Depot CEO Frank Blake announced plans to commit $2.2 billion to efforts to improve stores, customer service, and sales. According to Blake, "We plan to continue our reinvestment plans for the long-run

Standard Costs and Performance Reports

LEARNING OBJECTIVES

LO1 Explain responsibility accounting. (p. 22-3)

LO2 Differentiate between static and flexible budgets for performance reporting. (p. 22-7)

LO3 Determine and interpret direct materials, direct labor, and overhead cost variances. (p. 22-10)

LO4 Calculate revenue variances and prepare a performance report for a revenue center. (p. 22-17)

health of the business, understanding that it will put short-term pressure on earnings."

By early 2009, the number of reports required from individual stores and directives handed down to individual stores were slashed and store managers were given just three goals: cleaner stores, stocked shelves, and top customer service. Home Depot also instituted what it called "power hours," when employees were supposed to do nothing but serve customers.

In a 2010 letter to shareholders, Frank Blake announced a dividend increase, made possible by an increase in market share, that was driven by a significant improvement in customer satisfaction, as measured by customer surveys. Stressing the importance of experienced and knowledgeable employees in providing superior customer service, Blake also reported that for 2009 Home Depot issued "success sharing" checks in excess of $146 million to hourly associates.

Understanding and properly using financial performance reports is necessary for an organization to succeed.

This module introduces the fundamentals of responsibility accounting and the measurement of financial performance. However, as underscored by events at Home Depot, while an understanding of financial performance is necessary for success, it is not sufficient. In addition to financial performance, managers must consider a myriad of quantifiable and non-quantifiable, short-term and long-term factors. Some of these other factors are discussed in this module and incorporated into the balanced scorecard, considered in Module 23.[1]

---

[1] Frank C. Blake, "Letter to Shareholders," 2009 *Home Depot Annual Report*, March 25, 2010; Jena McGregor, "Putting Home Depot's House in Order," *Business Week*, May 18, 2009, p. 54. "Out at Home Depot," Brian Grow; Dean Foust; Emily Thornton; Roben Farzad; Jena McGregor; Susan Zegal; and Eamon Javers, *Business Week*, January 15, 2007, pp. 56-62. "Being Mean Is So Last Millennium," Diane Brady, *Business Week*, January 15, 2007, p. 62. "Nardelli's Tear-Down Job," John Hollon, *Workforce Management*, January 15, 2007, p. 34. "Home Depot: Blues for Big Orange," *Business Week* Online, May 16, 2007, p. 16.

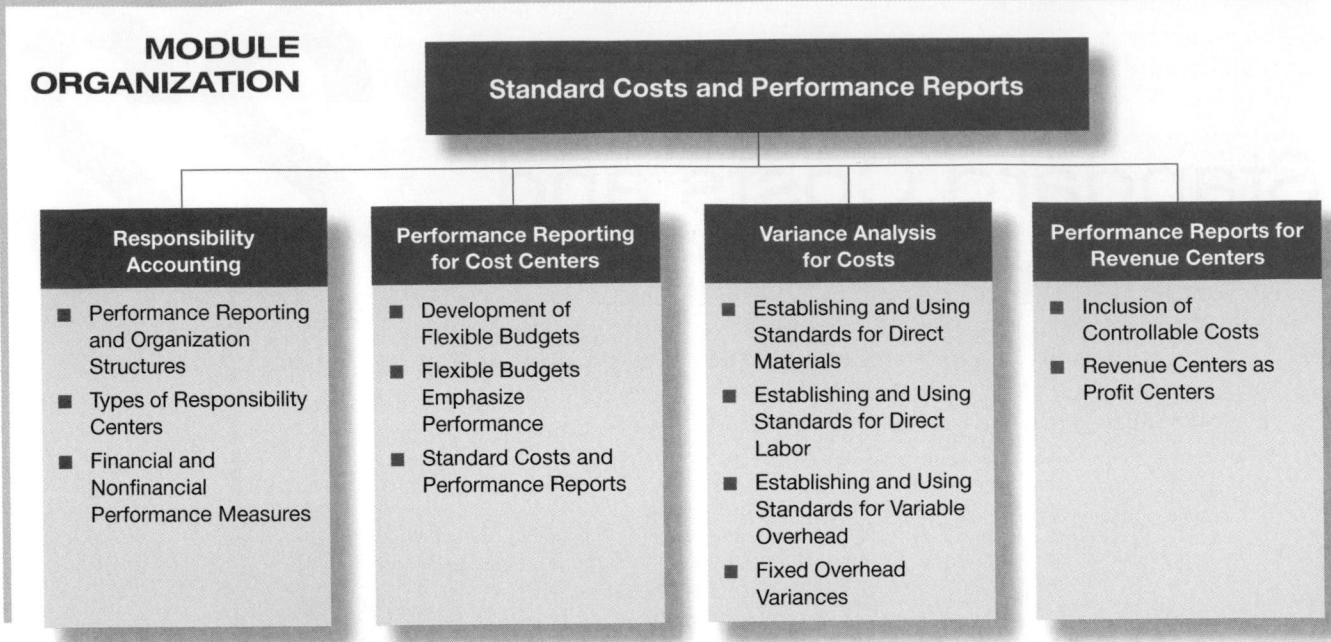

Management accounting tools aid in the assessment of the performance of the firm as a whole and all of its various components. Feedback in the form of performance reports is essential if the benefits of budgeting and other types of planning are to be fully realized. To control current operations and to improve future operations managers must know how actual results compare with the current budget. These performance reports should be prepared in accordance with the concept of **responsibility accounting**, which is the structuring of performance reports addressed to individual (or group) members of an organization to emphasize the factors they control.

This module focuses on responsibility accounting and performance assessment. We examine responsibility accounting and identify various types of responsibility centers. We then take a close look at performance assessment for cost centers and conclude by considering performance reports for revenue centers. Responsibility accounting for major business segments is considered in Module 23.

RESPONSIBILITY ACCOUNTING

LO1 Explain responsibility accounting.

Performance reports that include comparisons of actual results with plans or budgets serve as assessment tools and attention-directors to help managers control activities. According to the concept of *management by exception,* the absence of significant differences indicates that activities are proceeding as planned whereas the presence of significant differences indicates a need to either take corrective action or revise plans. These evaluations and actions are made within the framework of an organization's overall mission, goals, and strategies.

Responsibility accounting reports are customized to emphasize the activities of specific organizational units. For example, a performance report addressed to the head of a production department contains manufacturing costs controllable by the department head; it should not contain costs (such as advertising, sales commissions, or the president's salary) that the head of the production department cannot control. Including noncontrollable costs in the report distracts the manager's attention from the controllable costs, thereby diluting a manager's efforts to deal with controllable items.

If too much pressure is placed on managers to meet performance targets, they may take actions that are not in the best interest of the organization. The Business Insight that follows presents examples of such actions involving a vice president of Bausch & Lomb and the CEO of Sunbeam who forced sales into one year to the detriment of the companies' sales the following year. The designers of an organization's responsibility accounting system need to be aware of the potential pressures that such a system can place on managers. The decision-making model of the organization should be such that managers are not influenced to make undesirable decisions just to receive bonuses or promotions.

BUSINESS INSIGHT | **Ethics and Responsibility Accounting**

A few years ago, the contact lens division of Bausch & Lomb, Inc., was experiencing lower-than-anticipated sales levels. The head of the division called a meeting of its independent distributors and told them that the company had changed its sales strategy. Effective immediately, each distributor would have to boost its inventory of contact lenses if it wanted to remain a distributor of Bausch & Lomb products. The strategy was for distributors to buy only in very large quantities (some as much as a two-year supply) with prices increased by amounts up to 50 percent. Also, the distributors had to place these large orders by year-end. As one distributor stated, "When your No. 1 vendor says you'd better take it or else, what're you going to do?" All but two of Bausch & Lomb's distributors complied with the new sales strategy demands; and those two were subsequently dropped as customers.

Initially the strategy paid off; the sales in the last few days of the year totaled about $25 million and amounted to one-half of the division's profit for the entire year. The division manager was delighted. However, the long-term results were not favorable. By the following mid-year, the company announced that the high inventories of its distributors would severely reduce sales and profits for that year. The profit decline was approximately 37 percent. After the announcement, the company's stock fell from $50 to $32. The manager was forced to step down, and stockholders filed a class-action lawsuit accusing the company of falsely inflating sales and earnings.

History repeated itself when the CEO of Sunbeam followed the Bausch & Lomb plan to force sales to show how well his management style (firing employees and closing plants) was working. Sunbeam instituted a "bill and hold" plan that called for products to be produced in large quantities and sold to customers for delivery at a later date. While this made the financial report for that first year very favorable, it had a detrimental effect on the next year's report. In late March of that following year, Sunbeam acknowledged that first-quarter income would be below expectations, and in fact, a loss. Stockholders quickly filed lawsuits charging deception, and the CEO was fired.

Source: "Numbers Game at Bausch & Lomb?" *Business Week,* December 19, 1994, pp. 108–10; and "How Al Dunlap Self-Destructed," *Business Week,* July 6, 1998, pp. 58–61, 64.

Performance Reporting and Organization Structures

Before implementing a responsibility accounting system, all areas of authority and responsibility within an organization must be clearly defined. Organization charts and other documents should be examined to determine an organization's authority and responsibility structure. **Organization structure** is the arrangement of lines of authority and responsibility within an organization. These structures vary widely. Some companies have functional-based structures along the lines of marketing, production, research, and so forth; others use products, services, customers, or geography as the basis of organization. When an attempt is made to implement a responsibility accounting system, management could find instances of overlapping duties, authority not commensurate with responsibility, and expenditures for which no one appears responsible. The identification and resolution of these problems can be a major benefit of implementing a responsibility accounting system.

Although performance reports can be developed for areas of responsibility as narrow as a single worker, the basic responsibility unit in most organizations begins with the department and progresses to division and corporate levels. In manufacturing plants, separate performance reports may be prepared for each production and service department, and then summarized into a performance report for all manufacturing activities. In large universities, reports may be prepared for individual departments such as history, philosophy, and English, and then summarized into a performance report of a college, such as Liberal Arts.

Types of Responsibility Centers

Based on the nature of their responsibility, responsibility centers can be classified as cost centers, revenue centers, profit centers, or investment centers.

Cost Center

A **cost center** manager is only responsible for costs; there is no revenue responsibility. A cost center can be as small as a segment of a department or large enough to include a major aspect of the organization, such as all manufacturing activities. Typical examples of cost centers include the following:

Organization	Cost Center
Manufacturing plant	Tooling department
	Assembly activities
Retail store	Inventory control function
	Maintenance department
Hospital	Radiology
	Emergency room
College	History department
	Registrar's office
City government.	Public safety (police and fire)
	Road maintenance

Revenue Center

A **revenue center** manager is responsible for the generation of sales revenues. Even though the basic performance report of a revenue center emphasizes sales, revenue centers are likely to be assigned responsibility for the controllable costs they incur in generating revenues. If revenues and costs are evaluated separately, the center has dual responsibility as a revenue center and as a cost center. If controllable costs are deducted from revenues to obtain some bottom-line contribution, the center is, in fact, being treated more like a profit center than a revenue center.

Profit Center

A **profit center** manager is responsible for revenues, costs, and the resulting profits. A profit center could be an entire organization, but it is more frequently a segment of an organization such as a product line, marketing territory, or store. In the context of performance evaluation, the word "profit" does not necessarily refer to the bottom line of an income statement; instead, it likely refers to the profit center's contribution to common corporate costs and profit. Profit is computed as the center's revenues less all costs directly associated with operating the center. Having limited authority regarding the size of total assets, the profit center manager is not held responsible for the relationship between profits and assets. In recent years many hospitals have been treating treating critical care and clinical service departments as profit centers to encourage physician chiefs to manage their departments as small businesses. The following Research Insight examines some of issues associated with this movement.

Investment Center

An **investment center** manager is responsible for the relationship between its profits and the total assets invested in the center. Investment center managers have a high degree of organization autonomy. In general, the management of an investment center is expected to earn a target profit per dollar invested. Investment center managers are evaluated on the basis of how well they use the total resources entrusted to their care to earn a profit. An investment center is the broadest and most inclusive type of responsibility center. Managers of these centers have more authority and responsibility than other managers and are primarily responsible for planning, organizing, and controlling firm activities. Because of their authority regarding the size of corporate assets, they are held responsible for the relationship between profits and assets. Investment centers are discussed further in Module 23.

RESEARCH INSIGHT   **Hospital Researcher Questions Use of Profit Centers**

As hospitals attempt to improve fiscal management many have designated critical care departments such as cardiovascular surgery, orthopedics, and pediatrics as profit centers. After examining this movement, Professor David Young concludes that hospitals and patients would be better served by treating critical care departments as standard expense (cost) centers. Problems Young identified with designating critical care departments as profit centers include:

- Bad feelings between departments that are inherently more lucrative such as cardiovascular surgery and departments that are normally poor financial performers such as pediatrics. According to Young, the intensity of feeling is illustrated by a cardiovascular surgeon at a large medical center who blurted out "I'm tired of subsidizing those lazy pediatricians."

- Problems determining the proper relationships between critical care (line) departments such as orthopedics and clinical service departments such as radiology. Should a critical care department such as orthopedics be allowed to obtain radiology services outside the hospital? How much should orthopedics pay for radiology services obtained inside the hospital, and who should determine the amount they pay? (See transfer pricing discussed in Module 23.)

- Many hospitals are now shifting their strategy toward service lines such as women's health that require historically independent critical care and clinical service departments to work seamlessly together toward a common goal. Treating individual departments as profit centers may be incompatible with such a strategy.

- Critical care departments, seeking an operating profit, may try to avoid treating low-income or poorly insured patients even when treating such patients is part of the hospital's mission.

Professor Young concludes that the physician managers of standard expense (cost) centers should focus their attention on striving to provide quality medical care while meeting a flexible budget, thereby avoiding the additional decisions and conflicts associated with efforts to obtain a department operating surplus.

Source: David W. Young, "Profit Centers in Clinical Care Departments An Idea Whose Time Has Gone," *Healthcare Financial Management*, March 2008, pp. 66–71.

Financial and Nonfinancial Performance Measures

This module's emphasis is on financial performance reports. Dollar-based financial reports have several advantages over other financial measures. Their "bottom line" impact is readily apparent. If actual fixed costs exceed budgeted fixed costs by $10,000, the before-tax income of an organization is $10,000 less than it would be without the extra fixed costs. Additionally, because dollars are additive and applicable to all organizational units, financial measures are easily summarized and reported up the organization chart.

It is important to keep in mind that although financial measures may indicate results are not in accordance with the budget, they do not indicate the root cause of financial deviations. The identification and analysis of the root cause of financial variances requires asking questions and, frequently, the use of nonfinancial data. Managers and employees at lower levels of the organization are often better served by performance reports focusing on data directly related to their job, such as units processed or customers served per hour. Although financial performance is still critical to Home Depot's top management and still used to evaluate individual stores, the focus for the evaluation of store managers and employees is now on clean stores, stocked shelves, and customer satisfaction. Other examples of nonfinancial performance measures include: defects per thousand units in a manufacturing plant, average and longest waiting time in a restaurant, nursing staff hours per patient day in a hospital, response time for a fire department, and customer satisfaction at a retail store or bank.

When organizations seek to improve financial performance beyond what is possible with current products, procedures, or services, the initial focus is most often on nonfinancial measures. Kroger grocery stores might benchmark the length of their cash-register waiting times against Winn Dixie's. A systematic process improvement such as six sigma, discussed in the following Business Insight, might be used to improve service or product quality.

Six sigma is a process used to improve product or service quality by identifying errors and removing their causes. Six sigma is also used to minimize process variability and streamline processes by removing unnecessary, especially non-value-added, activities. Six sigma received its name from its original goal of reducing the probability of a defect to the probability of having an event six standard deviations away from the mean of a normal distribution. As initially implemented in companies such as Motorola and General Electric six sigma has five basic steps:

1. Define: Identify and define problems related to a process.
2. Measure: Determine what is wrong with the current process.
3. Analyze: Determine the root cause or reason for what is wrong.
4. Improve: Develop and implement a plan to improve the process.
5. Control: Develop and implement procedures to monitor operations to ensure they proceed as planned.

In recent years six sigma has moved from manufacturing firms to service organizations and, especially, retail firms. Target claims savings of more than $100 million over the past five years from six sigma and Best Buy projects significant cost savings from streamlining appliance installation using six sigma.

Source: Brian Burnsed and Emily Thornton, "The Six Sigma Black Belts Are Back," *Business Week*, September 21, 2009; Sridhar Seshadri and Gregory T. Lucier, "GE Takes Six Sigma Beyond the Bottom Line," *Strategic Finance*, May 2001, pp. 40–46.

PERFORMANCE REPORTING FOR COST CENTERS

LO2 Differentiate between static and flexible budgets for performance reporting.

Financial performance reports for cost centers include a comparison of actual and budgeted (or allowed) costs and identify the difference as a **variance**. *Allowed costs* in performance reports are the flexible budget amounts for the actual level of activity. The variance is favorable if actual costs are less than budgeted (or allowed) costs and unfavorable if actual costs are more than budgeted (or allowed) costs. These comparisons are made in total and individually for each type of controllable cost assigned to the cost center.

Development of Flexible Budgets

A budget that is based on a prediction of sales and production is called a **static budget**. The operating budget explained in Module 21 is a static budget. Budgets can also be set for a series of possible production and sales volumes, or budgets can be adjusted to a particular level of production after the fact. These budgets, based on cost-volume relationships, are called **flexible budgets**; they are used to determine what costs should be for a level of activity. For example, if the college cafeteria budgets $15,000 for food during April for 5,000 meals but provides 6,000 meals, the budget needs to be adjusted by the original food budget rate of $3 ($15,000/5,000 meals). If $17,500 was spent on food during the month, the analysis might appear as follows:

Budget Item	Actual	Budget	Difference
Static analysis			
Food.............	$17,500	5,000 meals × $3 = $15,000	$2,500 over budget
Flexible analysis			
Food.............	$17,500	6,000 meals × $3 = $18,000	$500 under budget

The cafeteria manager is better evaluated based on what actually happened with the flexible budget than with the static budget, especially if the manager had no control over how many student meals were requested.

For a complete example of a flexible budget, assume that McMillan Company, which produces high-quality computer carrying cases, has three departments: Production, Sales, and Administration. Focusing on the Production Department, the flexible budget cost-estimating equations for total monthly production costs of cases are based on the production standards for variable and fixed costs. The standards follow:

> Variable costs
> Direct materials—2 pounds per unit at $5 per pound, or $10 per unit
> Direct labor—0.25 hour per unit at $24 per hour, or $6 per unit
> Variable overhead - 2 pounds per unit at $4 per pound, or $8 per unit
> Fixed costs—$52,000

If management plans to produce 10,000 cases in July, the budgeted manufacturing costs are $292,000:

McMILLAN COMPANY Manufacturing Cost Budget For Month of July	
Manufacturing costs	
Variable costs	
Direct materials (10,000 units × 2 pounds × $5) . . .	$100,000
Direct labor (10,000 units × 0.25 hours × $24)	60,000
Variable overhead (10,000 units × 2 pounds × $4) .	80,000
Fixed costs	52,000
Total	$292,000

Flexible Budgets Emphasize Performance

If actual production happened to equal budgeted production, the Production Department is evaluated by comparing the actual and budgeted costs. If production needs change, perhaps due to an unexpected increase or decrease in sales volume, the Production Department should attempt to make appropriate changes. When the actual production volume is anything other than the originally budgeted amount, the Production Department's financial responsibility for costs should be based on the actual level of production.

For the purpose of evaluating the financial performance of cost centers, a flexible budget is tailored, after the fact, to the actual level of activity. A **flexible budget variance** is computed for each cost as the difference between the actual cost and the flexible budget cost. Assume actual production for July totaled 11,000 units rather than 10,000 units. Examples of a performance report for July manufacturing costs based on static and flexible budgets are presented in Exhibit 22.1. When the Production Department's financial performance is evaluated using the static budget, the actual cost of producing 11,000 units is compared to the budgeted cost of producing 10,000 units. The result is a series of unfavorable static budget variances totaling $20,000.

EXHIBIT 22.1 Flexible Budgets and Performance Evaluation

McMILLAN COMPANY
Production Department Performance Report
For Month of July

	Based on Static Budget			Based on Flexible Budget		
	Actual	Original Budget	Static Budget Variance	Actual	Flexible Budget*	Flexible Budget Variance
Volume	11,000	10,000		11,000	11,000	
Variable costs						
Direct materials	$108,000	$100,000	$ 8,000 U	$108,000	$110,000	$2,000 F
Direct labor	70,000	60,000	10,000 U	70,000	66,000	4,000 U
Variable overhead	81,000	80,000	1,000 U	81,000	88,000	7,000 F
Fixed costs	53,000	52,000	1,000 U	53,000	52,000	1,000 U
Totals	$312,000	$292,000	$20,000 U	$312,000	$316,000	$4,000 F

*Flexible budget manufacturing costs: (Actual level × Budgeted unit cost)
Direct materials (11,000 units × 2 pounds × $5)
Direct labor (11,000 units × 0.25 labor hour × $24)
Variable overhead (11,000 units × 2 pounds × $4)

When the Production Department's financial performance is evaluated by comparing actual costs with costs allowed in a flexible budget drawn up for the actual production volume, the results are mixed. Direct materials have a $2,000 favorable variance. Direct labor has a $4,000 unfavorable variance. The variable overhead variance is $7,000 favorable. The fixed overhead variance remains $1,000 unfavorable since the static and flexible fixed budgets stay the same. The net flexible budget variance is $4,000 favorable, a substantial change from the static variance of $20,000 unfavorable.

Flexible budget variances provide a much better indicator of performance than static budget variances that do not consider the increased level of production (11,000 units rather than 10,000 units). When production exceeds the planned level, the static budget variances are usually unfavorable. Likewise, when actual production is substantially below the planned level of activity, the static variances are usually favorable. While it is important to isolate and determine the cause of any variation between planned and actual production, the financial-based performance report is not the appropriate place to mix volume-created variances with those related to the actual production levels.

MID-MODULE REVIEW

Ron Gilette received the following performance report from the accounting department for his first month as plant manager for a new company. Ron's supervisor, the vice president of manufacturing, has concerns that the report does not provide an accurate picture of Ron's performance in the area of cost control.

	Actual	Budgeted	Variance
Units.....................	10,000	12,000	2,000 U
Costs			
Direct materials	$ 299,000	$ 360,000	$ 61,000 F
Direct labor...............	345,500	432,000	86,500 F
Variable factory overhead.....	180,000	216,000	36,000 F
Fixed factory overhead	375,000	360,000	15,000 U
Total costs	$1,199,500	$1,368,000	$168,500 F

Required
Prepare a revised budget that better reflects Ron Gilette's performance.

The solution is on page 23-36.

Standard Costs and Performance Reports

A **standard cost** indicates what it should cost to provide an activity or produce one batch or unit of product under planned and efficient operating conditions. In a standard costing environment, the flexible budget is based on standard unit costs. Traditionally, standard costs have been developed from an engineering analysis or from an analysis of historical data adjusted for expected changes in the product, production technology, or costs. When standards are developed using historical data, management must be careful to ensure that past inefficiencies are excluded from current standards.

To obtain the full benefit of standard costs, the standards must be based on realistic expectations. The standard cost for direct labor for McMillan Company is $6.00 per unit, (computed as 0.25 direct labor hours × $24 per hour). Some organizations intentionally set "tight" standards to motivate employees toward higher levels of production. The management of McMillan Company might set their standards for direct labor at 0.22 hours per unit rather than at the expected 0.25 hours per unit, hoping that employees will strive toward the lower time and, consequently, the lower cost of $5.28 ($24 × 0.22). The use of tight standards often causes planning and behavioral problems. Management expects them to result in unfavorable variances. Accordingly, tight standards should not be used to budget input requirements and cash flows because management expects to incur more labor costs than the standards allow. The use of tight standards can have undesirable behavioral effects if employees find that a second set of standards is used in the "real" budget or if they are constantly subject to unfavorable performance reports. These employees could come to distrust the entire budgeting and performance evaluation system, or they may quit trying to achieve any of the organization's standards.

Tight standards are more likely to occur in an imposed budget than in a participation budget. In a participation budget, the problem may be to avoid overstating the costs required to produce a product. Loose standards may fail to properly motivate employees and can make the company uncompetitive due to costs that are higher than competitors'.

VARIANCE ANALYSIS FOR COSTS

To use and interpret standard cost variances properly, managers must understand the processes and activities that drive costs. Cost variances are merely signals. They do not explain why costs differ from expectations. Underlying causes of variances must be investigated before final judgment is passed on the effectiveness and efficiency of an operation or activity.

LO3 Determine and interpret direct materials, direct labor, and overhead cost variances.

Standard cost variance analysis is a systematic approach to examining flexible budget variances. Actual costs are determined from the organization's financial transactions. Flexible budget costs are determined by multiplying standard quantities allowed for the output times the standard price per unit. For a company using activity-based costing, each manufacturing activity could have its own standard costs that focus on underlying concepts and cost drivers, and companies even develop their own set of variances as discussed in the following Business Insight.

Standard cost variance analysis identifies the general causes of the total flexible budget variance by breaking it into separate price and quantity variances for each production component. Two possible reasons that actual cost could differ from flexible budget cost for a given amount of output produced are (1) a difference between actual and standard prices paid for the production components—the price variance—and (2) a difference between the actual quantity and the standard quantity allowed for the production components—the quantity variance. Variances have different names for different cost categories as follows:

Cost Component	Price Variance Name	Quantity Variance Name
Direct materials	Materials price variance	Materials quantity variance
Direct labor	Labor rate variance	Labor efficiency variance
Variable overhead	Variable overhead spending variance	Variable overhead efficiency variance

Fixed overhead is excluded from the unit standard costs because, within the relevant range of normal activity, it does not vary with the volume of production. To facilitate product costing, however, many organizations develop a standard fixed overhead cost per unit.

In the following sections, we analyze the flexible budget cost variances for materials, labor and variable overhead. Our illustration is based on the following July activity and costs of McMillan Company's Production Department.

McMILLAN COMPANY—PRODUCTION DEPARTMENT Actual Manufacturing Costs For Month of July	
Actual units completed....................	11,000
Manufacturing costs	
Unit level costs	
Direct materials (24,000 pounds × $4.50) ..	$108,000
Direct labor (2,800 hours × $25.00)	70,000
Variable overhead	81,000
Fixed overhead costs	53,000
Total	$312,000

BUSINESS INSIGHT   **Companies Design Cost Variances to Meet Needs**

The variances in this book are not the only ones used by managers. Many companies develop their own variances to meet the needs of their managers when confronted with unusual activities. Such is the case with Parker Brass. Two concerns of the production managers at Parker Brass are the timing of product cost information and providing an effective cost control system. As managers were struggling with new and different decisions, they decided that additional information was needed. They developed three new variances: standard run quantity variance, materials substitution variance, and method variance.

The *standard run quantity variance* measures the amount of setup cost that was not recovered because the batch size was smaller than the predetermined optimal batch size. Because the company had been including setup cost with labor, the managers were having difficulty explaining all of the labor variances. By pulling out the amounts related to batch sizes, the remainder of the analysis became easier to explain. The *materials substitute variance* is relevant when the standard materials have to be substituted because of lack of inventory or because a customer wants something different than normal. This often helps explain both materials price variances and usage variances so these two variances do not have to be used to justify all differences between standard and actual cost. The *method variance* is used when different machines or processes can be used to produce the same output. For example, if a process requires three labor hours and two machine hours but due to machine demand by other products, the process can be completed with seven labor hours and one machine hour, the resulting standard versus actual cost variances will be different even when all costs are perfectly controlled.

When managers know that the accounting system is flexible, there is more coordination between those who develop the system and those who use it. Parker Brass modified its standard costing system to better meet the needs of its managers without disrupting the traditional cost accounting system.

Source: David Johnsen and Parvez Sopariwala, "Standard Costing Is Alive and Well at Parker Brass, *Management Accounting Quarterly,* Winter 2000, pp. 12–20.

Note that detailed information on actual pounds and an actual rate is not provided for variable overhead. That is because variable overhead represents a pool of related costs driven by a number of factors rather than a single cost with a single driver. Although the basis used in budgeting variable overhead may, and should, have a high correlation with actual variable overhead, it is a surrogate for the multiple cost elements that comprise variable overhead. Issues related to variable overhead are discussed in greater detail later in this module.

Establishing and Using Standards for Direct Materials

The two basic elements contained in the standards for direct materials are the *standard price* and the *standard quantity*. Materials standards indicate how much an organization should pay for each input unit of direct materials and the quantity of direct materials it should use to produce one unit of output. The standard price per unit of direct materials should include all reasonable costs necessary to acquire the materials. These costs include the invoice price of materials, less planned discounts plus freight, insurance, special handling, and any other costs related to the acquisition of the materials. The standard quantity represents the number of units of raw materials allowed for the production of one unit of finished product. This amount should include the amount dictated by the physical characteristics of the process and the product, plus a reasonable allowance for normal spoilage, waste, and other inefficiencies. The quantity standard can be determined by engineering analysis, professional judgment, or by averaging the actual amount used for several periods. An average of actual past materials usage may not be a good standard because it could include excessive wastes and inefficiencies in the standard quantity.

Direct Materials Variances

The **materials price variance** is the difference between the actual materials cost and the standard cost of actual materials inputs. The **materials quantity variance** is the difference between the standard cost of actual materials inputs and the flexible budget cost for materials. The direct materials variances for McMillan Company follow.

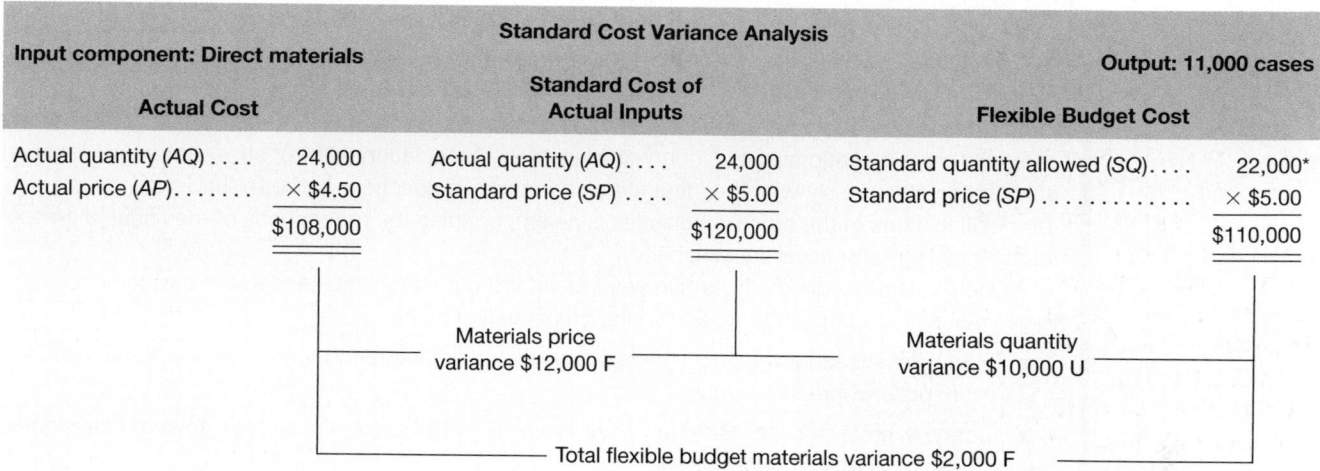

*11,000 units × 2 pounds per unit

McMillan Company had a favorable materials price variance of $12,000 because the actual cost of materials used ($108,000) was less than the standard cost of actual materials used ($120,000). The price variance can also be computed using a formula approach as the actual quantity (*AQ*) used times the difference between the actual price (*AP*) and the standard price (*SP*). McMillan Company paid $0.50 per pound below the standard price for 24,000 pounds for a total savings of $12,000:

$$\text{Materials price variance} = AQ(AP - SP)$$
$$= 24,000(\$4.50 - \$5.00)$$
$$= 24,000 \times \$0.50$$
$$= \$12,000 \text{ F}$$

The unfavorable quantity variance of $10,000 occurred because the standard cost of actual materials used, $120,000 (24,000 × $5), was higher than the cost of materials allowed by the flexible budget, $110,000 (22,000 × $5). A total of 22,000 pounds of materials is allowed to produce 11,000 units of finished outputs. This is computed as 11,000 finished units times 2.0 pounds of direct materials per unit. The materials quantity variance can also be computed using a formula approach as the standard price (*SP*) per pound times the difference between the number of pounds actually used (*AQ*) and the number of pounds allowed (*SQ*):

$$\text{Materials quantity variance} = SP(AQ - SQ)$$
$$= \$5(24,000 - 22,000)$$
$$= \$5 \times 2,000$$
$$= \$10,000 \text{ U}$$

Interpreting Materials Variances

As highlighted in the following Business Insight, after computing variances, managers must understand how to use them in making decisions relevant to the items being evaluated. A *favorable materials price variance* indicates that the employee responsible for materials purchases paid less per unit than the price allowed by the standards. This could result from receiving discounts for purchasing more than the normal quantities, effective bargaining by the employee, purchasing substandard-quality materials, purchasing from a distress seller, or other factors. Ordinarily, when a favorable price variance is reported, the employee's performance is interpreted as favorable. However, if the favorable price variance results from the purchase of materials of lower than standard quality or from a purchase in more than desirable quantities, the employee's performance would be questionable. All large variances, including favorable variances, should be thoroughly investigated for causes and corrections.

BUSINESS INSIGHT   It's All in the Questions

Writing for local governments officials, Jon Johnson and Chris Fabian, senior management advisors with the International City/County Management Association (ICMA), stress the need for such officials to work closely with their finance officer and ask questions to better understand "not only the positive signs of the organization's fiscal health, but also the root causes of the fiscal 'dis-ease' impacting long-term fiscal sustainability."

One of their key questions is "Do we understand our variances – especially budget versus actual?" According to the authors, answering this question helps:

- Determine reasons variances have occurred and adjust the budget or eliminate the source of variances where appropriate.

- Identify areas where resources have been over-allocated with an eye toward reassigning those resources to other needs.

- Reduce budget contingencies included in multiple department budgets by consolidation into a unified contingency budget.

- Improve the accuracy to budgets by better identifying emerging trends.

Source: Jon Johnson and Chris Fabian, "It's All in the Questions: The Manager's Role in Achieving Fiscal Health," *Public Management*, September 2009, pp. 22-15, 33.

An *unfavorable materials price variance* means that the purchasing employee paid more per unit for materials than the price allowed by the standards. This could be caused by failure to buy in sufficient quantities to receive normal discounts; purchase of higher-quality materials than called for in the product specifications; failure to place materials orders on a timely basis; failure to bargain for the best available prices; or other factors. An unfavorable variance does not always mean that the employee performed unfavorably. Many noncontrollable factors surround the purchasing function, including unanticipated price increases, the need to increase production to meet unanticipated sales, and supply chain problems such as a work stoppage at a vendor.

A *favorable materials quantity variance* means that the actual quantity of raw materials used was less than the quantity allowed for the units produced. This could result from factors such as less materials waste than allowed by the standards, better than expected machine efficiency, direct materials of higher quality than required by the standards, and more efficient use of direct materials by employees. An *unfavorable materials quantity variance* occurs when the quantity of raw materials used exceeds the quantity allowed for the units produced. This could result from incurring more waste than provided for in the standards, poorly maintained machinery requiring larger amounts of raw materials, raw materials of lower quality than required by the standards, or poorly trained employees who were unable to use the materials at the level of efficiency required by the standards.

Establishing and Using Standards for Direct Labor

To evaluate management performance in controlling labor costs, it is necessary to determine the *standard labor rate* for each hour allowed and the *standard time allowed* to produce a unit. Setting labor rate standards can be quite simple or extremely complex. If all employees have the same wage rate, determining the standard cost is relatively easy: Simply adopt the normal wage rate as the standard labor rate. If there are variations in employee wage rates, the standard labor rate should be based on the expected mix of employee wage rates.

The standard labor time per unit can be determined by an engineering approach or an empirical observation approach. When using an engineering approach, industrial engineers ascertain the amount of time required to produce a unit of finished product by applying time and motion methods or other available techniques. Normal operating conditions are assumed in arriving at the labor standard. Therefore, allowances must be made for normal machine downtime, employee personal breaks, and so forth. Under the empirical approach, the average time required to produce a unit under normal operating conditions is used as a basis for the standard.

Direct Labor Variances

Using the general variance model that was used for materials, we can compute the labor rate and efficiency variances. The **labor rate variance** is the difference between the actual cost and the standard cost of actual labor inputs. The **labor efficiency variance** is the difference between the standard cost of actual inputs and the flexible budget cost for labor.

McMillan Company's labor standards provide for 0.25 hour of labor per unit produced at $24 per hour. During July, 2,800 hours were used at a cost of $25 per hour. Using these data, the labor rate (price) variance and labor efficiency (quantity) variance can be computed as shown in the following illustration.

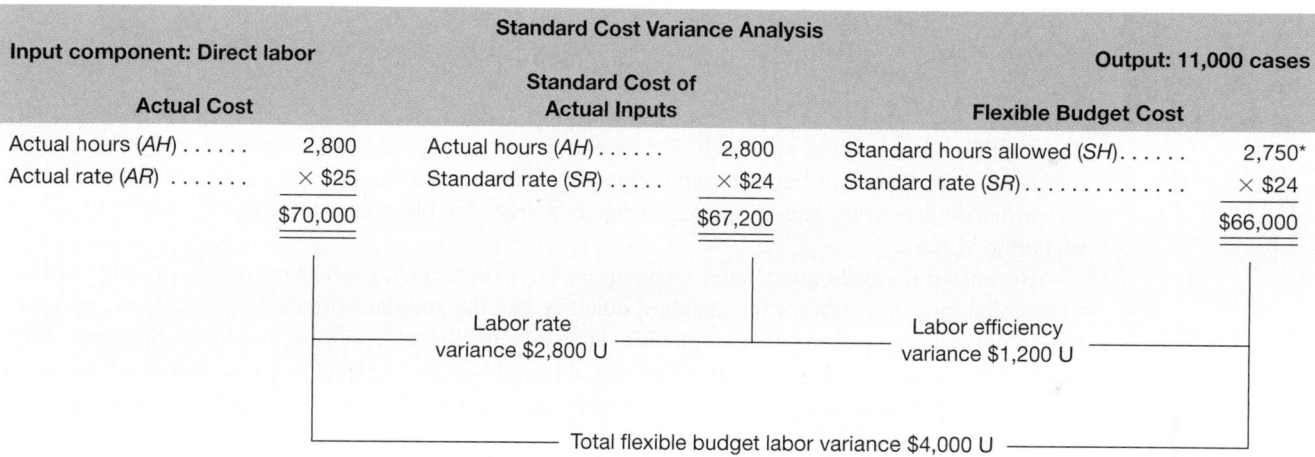

*11,000 units × 0.25 hour per unit

The labor rate variance can also be computed in formula form as the actual number of hours used times the difference between the actual rate and the standard rate.

$$\text{Labor rate variance} = \text{AH(AR} - \text{SR)}$$
$$= 2{,}800(\$25 - \$24)$$
$$= 2{,}800 \times \$1$$
$$= \$2{,}800 \text{ U}$$

This computation of the labor rate variance shows that the company paid $1 more than the standard rate for each of the 2,800 hours worked.

Since 11,000 units of product were finished during the period and 0.25 hour of labor was allowed for each unit, the total number of standard hours allowed was 2,750 (11,000 units × 0.25 hours). The labor efficiency variance can also be computed as the standard rate times the difference between the actual labor hours and the standard hours allowed:

$$\text{Labor efficiency variance} = \text{SR(AH} - \text{SH)}$$
$$= \$24(2{,}800 - 2{,}750)$$
$$= \$24 \times 50$$
$$= \$1{,}200 \text{ U}$$

McMillian's labor efficiency variance indicates that the company used 50 more labor hours than allowed. By itself, this inefficiency caused an unfavorable variance of $1,200.

Interpreting Labor Variances

The possible explanations for labor rate variances are rather limited. An *unfavorable labor rate variance* can be caused by the use of higher paid laborers than the standards provided. An increase in wage rates not reflected in the standards can also cause an unfavorable labor rate variance. A *favorable labor rate variance* occurs if lower paid workers were used or if actual wage rates declined.

Unfavorable labor efficiency variances occur when the actual labor hours exceed the number of hours allowed for the actual output. This could be caused by using poorly trained workers or poorly maintained machinery or by the use of low-quality materials. Low employee morale and generally poor working conditions could also adversely affect the efficiency.

Favorable labor efficiency variances occur when the actual labor hours are less than the number of hours allowed for the actual output. This above-normal efficiency can be caused by the company's use of higher-skilled (and higher-paid) workers, better machinery, or higher-quality raw materials than the standards require. High employee morale, improved job satisfaction, or generally improved working conditions could also account for the above-normal efficiency of the workers.

Establishing and Using Standards for Variable Overhead

The traditional unit-level approach to cost estimation, budgeting, and variance analysis separates overhead costs into fixed and variable elements. This separation is necessary because fixed costs are primarily driven by factors related to capacity and variable costs are primarily driven by factors related to volume.

Because it includes many heterogeneous costs, manufacturing overhead poses a unique problem in establishing standards for the standard quantity and the standard price of inputs. Direct materials have a natural physical measure of quantity such as tons, barrels, pounds, and liters. Similarly, labor or assembly is measurable in hours. However, no single quantity measure is common to all overhead items. Overhead is a cost group that can simultaneously include costs measurable in hours, pounds, liters and kilowatts.

The most frequent approach to dealing with the problem of multiple quantity measures in variable manufacturing overhead is to use a single surrogate (or substitute) measure to represent the quantity of all items in a given group. Typical substitute measures include machine hours, units of finished product, direct labor hours, and direct labor dollars. The variable overhead standard is then stated in terms of this surrogate measure.

Variable Overhead Variances

The **variable overhead spending variance** is the difference between the actual variable overhead cost and the standard variable overhead cost for the actual inputs of the surrogate measure. The **variable overhead efficiency variance** is the difference between the standard variable overhead cost for the actual inputs of the surrogate measure and the flexible budget cost allowed for variable overhead based on outputs.

For McMillan Company, the actual variable overhead in July was $81,000. This represents the actual cost of overhead items such as indirect materials and indirect labor. Pounds of materials is McMillian's surrogate measure for quantity for variable overhead allowed and used. This means that the standard costs allowed for variable overhead varies with the pounds of direct materials allowed. Hence the standard cost of actual inputs is calculated as actual pounds of direct materials (AP) times the standard variable overhead rate per pound (SRP):

$$\text{Standard cost of actual inputs} = (AP \times SRP)$$
$$= 24,000 \times \$4$$
$$= \$96,000$$

The flexible budget cost for variable overhead allowed for the actual outputs is based on the 22,000 pounds of direct materials allowed (*SP*) for the units produced during the period (11,000 units × 2 pounds). The allowed quantities are multiplied by the standard variable overhead rate (*SRP*). The resulting variable overhead flexible budget cost is $88,000:

$$\textbf{Flexible budget cost} = \textbf{(SP} \times \textbf{SRP)}$$
$$= \textbf{22,000} \times \textbf{\$4}$$
$$= \textbf{\$88,000}$$

Using these data, the variable overhead spending (price) variance and the variable overhead efficiency (quantity) variance follow.

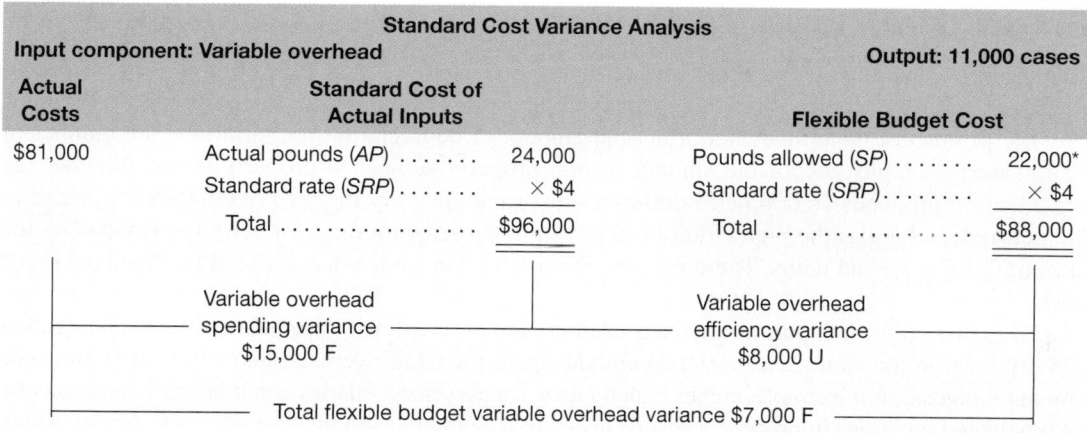

*11,000 × 2 lbs.

An alternative to the computation of the variable overhead effectiveness variance follows:

$$\textbf{Variable overhead efficiency variance} = \textbf{SRP(AP} - \textbf{SP)}$$
$$= \textbf{\$4(24,000} - \textbf{22,000)}$$
$$= \textbf{\$8,000 U}$$

This approach emphasizes that the 2,000 extra pounds used should have increased variable overhead by $8,000 at the standard rate of $4 per pound.

Interpreting Variable Overhead Variances

A *favorable spending variance* encompasses all factors that cause actual expenditures to be less than the amount expected for the actual inputs of the measurement base, including consumption and payment. Conversely, an *unfavorable spending variance* results when the actual expenditures are more than expected for the inputs of the measurement base. This is caused by consuming more overhead items than expected, or by paying more than the expected amount for overhead items consumed, or by both. Thus, the term *spending variance* is used instead of *price variance*.

The key to understanding the variable overhead spending variance is recognizing that the amount of variable overhead cost allowed is determined by the level of the surrogate measurement base used. Any deviation from this spending budget causes a spending variance to occur.

The variable overhead efficiency variance measures the difference between the standard variable overhead cost for the actual quantity of the surrogate measurement base and the standard variable overhead cost for the allowed quantity of the surrogate measurement base. This variance measures the amount of variable overhead that should have been saved (or incurred) because of the efficient (or inefficient) use of the surrogate measurement base. It provides no information about the degree of efficiency in using variable overhead items such as indirect materials and indirect labor. This information is reflected in the spending variance.

Fixed Overhead Variances

By definition, the quantity of goods and services purchased by fixed expenditures is not expected to change in proportion to short-run changes in the level of production. For example, in the short run, the production level does not affect the amount of depreciation on buildings, the number of fixed salaried employees, or the amount of real property subject to property taxes. Whether the organization produces 10,000 or 15,000 cases, the same quantity of fixed overhead is expected to be incurred, as long as the production level is within the relevant range of activity provided by the current fixed overhead items. Therefore, an efficiency variance is not computed for fixed overhead costs.

Even though the components of fixed overhead are not expected to be affected by the production activity level in the short run, the actual amount spent for fixed overhead items can differ from the amount budgeted. For example, higher than budgeted supervisors' salaries could be paid, there may be unanticipated increases in property taxes or insurance premiums, and the cost of leased facilities may increase. Fixed overhead costs in excess of the amount budgeted are reflected in the fixed overhead budget variance. The **fixed overhead budget variance** is, simply, the difference between budgeted and actual fixed overhead. Using the fixed costs of McMillan Company as an example:

$$\text{Fixed overhead budget variance} = \text{Actual fixed overhead} - \text{Budgeted fixed overhead}$$
$$= \$53,000 - \$52,000$$
$$= \$1,000\ U$$

The fixed overhead budget variance is always the same as the total fixed overhead flexible budget variance. Because budgeted fixed overhead is the same for all outputs within the relevant range, the budget variance explains the total flexible budget variance between actual and allowed fixed overhead. Similar to variable overhead, fixed overhead variances can be caused by a combination of price and quantity factors. Fixed overhead variances are examined further in Appendix 22A.

PERFORMANCE REPORTS FOR REVENUE CENTERS

LO4 Calculate revenue variances and prepare a performance report for a revenue center.

The financial performance reports for revenue centers include a comparison of actual and budgeted revenues. Controllable costs can be deducted from revenues to obtain some bottom-line contribution margin. If the center is then evaluated on the basis of this contribution, it is being treated as a profit center.

If the organization is to meet its budgeted profit goal for a period, with its budgeted fixed and variable costs, the organization's revenue centers must meet their original revenue budgets. Consequently, the original budget (a static budget) rather than a flexible budget is used to evaluate the financial performance of revenue centers.

Assume that McMillan Company's July sales budget called for the sale of 10,000 units at $40.00 each. If McMillan Company actually sold 11,000 units at $38.50 each, the total revenue variance is $23,500 favorable:

Actual revenues (11,000 × $38.50)	$423,500
Budgeted revenues (10,000 × $40)	(400,000)
Revenue variance.	$ 23,500 F

The **revenue variance** is the difference between the budgeted sales volume at the budgeted selling price and the actual sales volume at the actual selling price. Because McMillian's actual revenues exceeded budgeted revenues, the revenue variance is favorable. It can be presented as follows:

Revenue variance = (Actual volume × Actual price) − (Budgeted volume × Budgeted price)

The separate impact of changing prices and volume on revenue is analyzed with the sales price and sales volume variances. The **sales price variance** is computed as the change in selling price times the actual sales volume:

Sales price variance = (Actual selling price − Budgeted selling price) × Actual sales volume

For McMillan, the sales price variance for July follows:

$$\textbf{Sales price variance} = (\$38.50 - \$40.00) \times 11{,}000 \textbf{ units}$$
$$= \$16{,}500 \textbf{ U}$$

The **sales volume variance** indicates the impact of the change in sales volume on revenues, assuming there was no change in selling price. The sales volume variance is computed as the difference between the actual and the budgeted sales volumes times the budgeted selling price:

Sales volume variance = (Actual sales volume − Budgeted sales volume) × Budgeted selling price

For McMillan, the sales volume variance for July follows:

$$\textbf{Sales volume variance} = (11{,}000 \textbf{ units} - 10{,}000 \textbf{ units}) \times \$40$$
$$= \$40{,}000 \textbf{ F}$$

The net of the sales price and the sales volume variances is equal to the revenue variance:

Sales price variance.	$16,500 U
Sales volume variance	40,000 F
Revenue variance.	$23,500 F

Interpretation of these variances is subjective. In this case, we could say that if the increase in sales volume had not been accompanied by a decline in selling price, revenues would have increased $40,000 instead of $23,500. The $1.50 per unit decline in selling price cost the company $16,500 in revenues. Alternatively, we might note that a $1.50 reduction in the unit selling price was more than offset by an increase in sales volume. An economic analysis could explain the relationship as volume being sensitive to price (price elasticity).

In any case, variances are merely signals that actual results are not proceeding according to plan. They help managers identify potential problems and opportunities. An investigation into their cause(s) could even indicate that a manager who received a favorable variance was doing a poor job, whereas a manager who received an unfavorable variance was doing an outstanding job. Consider McMillan

Company's favorable revenue variance. This occurred because actual sales exceeded budgeted sales by 1,000 units (10 percent), which on the surface indicates good performance. But what if the total market for the company's products exceeded the company's forecast by 15 percent? In this case, McMillan Company's sales volume falls below its expected percentage share of the market; the favorable variance could occur (despite a poor marketing effort) because of strong customer demand that competitors could not fill.

Inclusion of Controllable Costs

Controllable costs should also be considered when evaluating the overall performance of revenue centers. A failure to consider costs could encourage uneconomic selling practices, such as excessive advertising and entertaining, and spending too much time on small accounts. The controllable costs of revenue centers include variable and fixed selling costs. These costs are sometimes further classified into order-getting and order-filling costs. **Order-getting costs** are incurred to obtain customers' orders (for example, advertising, salespersons' salaries and commissions, travel, telephone, and entertainment). **Order-filling costs** are distribution costs incurred to place finished goods in the hands of purchasers (for example, storing, packaging, and transportation).

The performance of a revenue center in controlling costs can be evaluated with the aid of a flexible budget drawn up for the actual level of activity. Assume that the McMillan Company's July budget for the Sales Department calls for fixed costs of $10,000 and variable costs of $5 per unit sold. If the actual fixed and variable selling expenses for July are $9,500 and $65,000, respectively, the total cost variances assigned to the Sales Department, detailed in Exhibit 22.2, are $9,500 unfavorable. In evaluating the Sales Department's performance as both a cost center and a revenue center, management should consider these cost variances as well as the revenue variances. Although the revenue variances are based on the original budget, the cost variances are based on the flexible budget.

EXHIBIT 22.2	Sales Department Performance Report for Controllable Costs		
McMILLAN COMPANY Sales Department Performance Report for Controllable Costs For Month of July			
		Based on Flexible Budget	
	Actual	Flexible Budget*	Flexible Budget Variance
Units...............................	11,000	11,000	
Selling expenses			
Variable...........................	$65,000	$55,000	$10,000 U
Fixed.............................	9,500	10,000	500 F
Total..............................	$74,500	$65,000	$ 9,500 U

* Flexible budget formulas:
  Variable selling expenses ($5 per unit)
  Fixed selling expenses($10,000 per month)

Revenue Centers as Profit Centers

Even though we have computed revenue and cost variances for McMillan's Sales Department, we are still left with an incomplete picture of this revenue center's performance. Is the Sales Department's performance best represented by the $23,500 favorable revenue variance, by the $9,500 unfavorable cost variance, or by the net favorable variance of $14,000 ($23,500 F − $9,500 U)? Actually, it is inappropriate to attempt to obtain an overall measure of the Sales Department's performance by combining these separate revenue and selling cost variances. The combination of revenue and cost variances is appropriate only for a profit center; so far, we have left out one important cost that must be assigned to the Sales Department before it can be treated as a profit center. That cost is the *standard variable cost of goods sold*.

As a profit center, the Sales Department acquires units from the Production Department and sells them outside the firm. Its total responsibilities include revenues, the standard variable cost of goods sold, and actual selling expenses. The Sales Department is assigned the *standard*, rather than the *actual, variable cost of goods sold*. Because the Sales Department does not control production activities, it should not be assigned actual production costs. Doing so results in passing the Production Department's variances on to the Sales Department. Fixed manufacturing costs are not assigned to the Sales Department because short-run variations in sales volume do not normally affect the total amount of these costs.

To evaluate the Sales Department as a profit center, the net sales volume variance must be computed. The **net sales volume variance** indicates the impact of a change in sales volume on the contribution margin given the budgeted selling price *and* the standard variable costs. It is computed as the difference between the actual and the budgeted sales volumes times the budgeted unit contribution margin.

Net sales volume variance = (Actual volume − Budgeted volume) × Budgeted contribution margin

Using the $40 budgeted selling price, the standard variable manufacturing costs, and the standard variable selling expenses, the budgeted contribution margin is $11.00:

Sales.		$40.00
Direct materials	$10.00	
Direct labor.	6.00	
Variable manufacturing overhead.	8.00	
Selling.	5.00	(29.00)
Contribution margin		$11.00

The net sales volume variance is computed as follows:

$$\text{Net sales volume variance} = (11{,}000 - 10{,}000) \times \$11.00$$
$$= \$11{,}000 \text{ F}$$

As a profit center, the Sales Department has responsibility for the sales price variance, the net sales volume variance, and any cost variances associated with its operations. As shown in Exhibit 22.3, the Sales Department variances, as a profit center, net to $15,000 unfavorable:

EXHIBIT 22.3 Sales Department Profit Center Performance Report

McMILLIAN COMPANY Sales Department Profit Center Performance Report For Month of July	
Sales price variance.	$16,500 U
Net sales volume variance.	11,000 F
Selling expense variance.	9,500 U
Sales Department variances, net.	$15,000 U

In an attempt to improve their overall performance, managers often commit themselves to unfavorable variances in some areas, believing that these variances will be more than offset by favorable variances in other areas. When the Sales Department is evaluated as a revenue center, the favorable sales volume variance more than offsets the price reductions and the higher selling expenses. The more complete evaluation of the Sales Department as a profit center (with a $15,000 unfavorable variance) gives a very different impression than the evaluation of the Sales Department as a pure revenue center (with a $23,500 favorable variance) or as a revenue center responsible only for its own direct costs with net favorable variances of $14,000, computed as $23,500 F minus $9,500 U. The performance reports of all the organization's responsibility centers are summarized to reconcile budgeted and actual income in Appendix 22B.

MODULE-END REVIEW

The flexible budget performance report for Sunset Enterprises Inc. for March follows. The company manufactures only one product, folding chairs.

	Actual Costs	Flexible Budget Cost	Flexible Budget Variances
Output units	5,000	5,000	
Direct materials	$104,125	$100,000	$ 4,125 U
Direct labor.	82,400	75,000	7,400 U
Variable manufacturing overhead			
Category 1	31,000	30,000	1,000 U
Category 2	18,000	20,000	2,000 F
Fixed manufacturing overhead.	42,000	40,000	2,000 U
Total	$277,525	$265,000	$12,525 U

The standard unit cost for folding chairs follows:

Direct materials (4 pounds × $5.00 per pound).	$20
Direct labor (1.25 hours × $12.00 per hour).	15
Variable overhead, Category 1 (1.25 hours × $4.80). . . .	6
Variable overhead, Category 2 ($4 per finished unit)	4
Total standard variable cost per unit	$45

Actual cost of materials is based on 21,250 pounds of direct materials purchased and used at $4.90 per pound; actual cost of assembly is based on 7,000 labor hours. Variable overhead is applied on labor hours for Category 1 and finished units for Category 2.

Required

a. Calculate all standard cost variances for direct materials and direct labor.
b. Calculate all standard cost variances for variable manufacturing overhead.

The solution is on page 22-37.

APPENDIX 22A: Fixed Overhead Variances

By definition, the quantity of goods and services purchased by fixed expenditures is not expected to change in proportion to short-run changes in the level of production. For example, in the short run, the production level does not affect the amount of depreciation on buildings, the number of fixed salaried employees, or the amount of real property subject to property taxes.

Even though the components of fixed overhead are not expected to be affected by the production activity level in the short run, the actual amount spent for fixed overhead items can differ from the amount budgeted. For example, higher than budgeted supervisors' salaries could be paid, insurance premiums may increase unexpectedly, and price increases could cause the amounts paid for equipment to be higher than expected. Fixed overhead costs in excess of the amount budgeted are reflected in the fixed overhead budget variance. The McMillian Company's fixed overhead budget variance was previously determined as:

Fixed overhead budget variance = Actual fixed overhead − Budgeted fixed overhead
= $53,000 − $52,000
= $1,000 U

The fixed overhead budget variance is always the same as the total fixed overhead flexible budget variance. Because budgeted fixed overhead is the same for all outputs within the relevant range, the budget variance explains the total flexible budget variance between actual and allowed fixed overhead.

Recall that predetermined overhead rates are computed by dividing the predicted overhead costs for the period by the predicted activity of the period. The motivation for using a standard fixed overhead rate is the same as the motivation for using a predetermined overhead rate; namely, quicker product costing and assigning identical fixed costs to identical products, regardless of when they are produced during the year.

When a standard fixed overhead rate is used, total fixed overhead costs assigned to production behave as variable costs. As production increases, the total fixed overhead assigned to production increases. Because total budgeted fixed overhead does not vary, differences arise between budgeted and assigned fixed overhead, and managers often inquire about the cause of the differences.

The standard fixed overhead rate is computed as the budgeted fixed costs divided by some budgeted standard level of activity. Assume McMillian applies fixed manufacturing overhead on the basis of machine hours and that 0.40 machine hours are allowed to produce one carrying case. Further assume that the budgeted production is 10,000 carrying cases per month, a level that allows 4,000 (10,000 × 0.40) machine hours. The standard fixed overhead rate per machine hour is $13.

Standard fixed overhead rate = Budgeted total fixed overhead ÷ Budgeted activity level
= $52,000 ÷ 4,000 hours
= $13 per machine hour

The total fixed overhead assigned to production is computed as the standard rate of $13 multiplied by the standard hours allowed for the units produced. Note that assigned fixed overhead cost equals budgeted fixed overhead only if the allowed activity equals the budgeted activity of 4,000 hours. If less than 4,000 hours are allowed the fixed overhead assigned to production is less than the $52,000 budgeted; if more than 4,000 hours are allowed the fixed overhead assigned to production is more than the amount budgeted.

Even though budgeted fixed overhead is not affected by production below or above 4,000 hours, the fixed overhead assigned to production increases at the rate of $13 per allowed machine hour. The difference between budgeted fixed overhead and fixed overhead assigned to production is called the **fixed overhead volume variance**. This variance is sometimes referred to as the **capacity variance**, a term that emphasizes the maximum output of an operation. The fixed overhead volume variance indicates neither good nor poor performance. Instead, it indicates the difference between the activity allowed for the actual output and the budget level used as the denominator in computing the standard fixed overhead rate.

To explain the difference between actual fixed overhead and fixed overhead assigned to production, two fixed overhead variances are computed: the fixed overhead budget variance and the fixed overhead volume variance. As previously explained, the fixed overhead budget variance represents the difference between actual fixed overhead and budgeted fixed overhead. The fixed overhead budget variance is caused by a combination of price and quantity factors related to the use of fixed overhead goods and services (e.g., depreciation, insurance, supervisors' salaries). The $1,000 unfavorable budget variance for McMillan was caused either by using higher quantities of fixed overhead goods and services, or by paying higher prices than expected for those items, or both.

The fixed overhead volume variance represents the difference between budgeted and assigned fixed overhead and is caused by a difference between the activity level allowed for the actual output and the budgeted activity used in computing the fixed overhead rate. For McMillan, actual July output of 11,000 units resulted in 4,400 allowed machine hours and applied fixed overhead of $57,200 (11,000 units × 0.40 hours × $13). The $5,200 favorable fixed overhead volume variance (budgeted costs of $52,000 minus applied costs of $57,200) indicates that the activity level allowed for the actual output was more than the budgeted activity level. As previously stated, this variance ordinarily cannot be used to control costs. If the budgeted activity is based on production capacity, an unfavorable variance alerts management that facilities are underutilized, and a favorable variance alerts management that facilities are utilized above their expectations. A summary standard cost variance analysis for fixed costs is shown below.

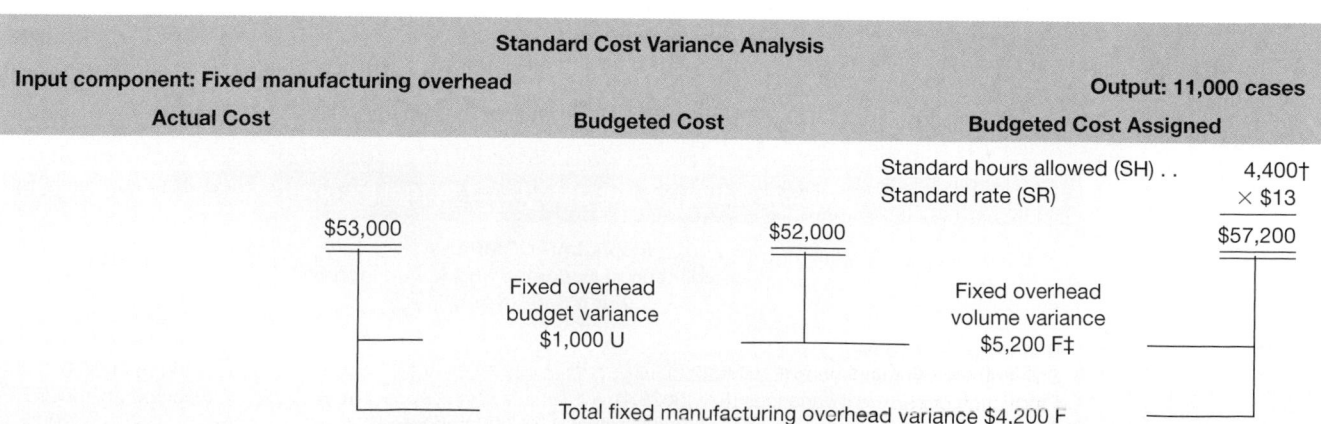

Standard Cost Variance Analysis

Input component: Fixed manufacturing overhead — Output: 11,000 cases

Actual Cost	Budgeted Cost	Budgeted Cost Assigned
		Standard hours allowed (SH) . . 4,400†
		Standard rate (SR) × $13
$53,000	$52,000	$57,200

Fixed overhead budget variance $1,000 U

Fixed overhead volume variance $5,200 F‡

Total fixed manufacturing overhead variance $4,200 F

†11,000 units × 0.40
‡ Also computed as: (4,400 allowed hours − 4,000 budget hours) × $13 standard rate per hour

APPENDIX 22B: Reconciling Budgeted and Actual Income

Using a contribution format, it is possible to reconcile the difference between budgeted and actual net income for an entire organization. This is done by assigning all costs and revenues to responsibility centers and summarizing the financial performance of each responsibility center. McMillan Company's budgeted and actual income statements, in a contribution format, for July are presented in Exhibit 22.4.

EXHIBIT 22.4	Budgeted and Actual Income Statements: Contribution Format

McMILLAN COMPANY
Budgeted Income Statement
For Month of July

Sales (10,000 units × $40)			$400,000
Less variable costs			
Variable cost of goods sold			
Direct materials (10,000 units × $10)	$100,000		
Direct labor (10,000 units × $6)	60,000		
Manufacturing overhead (10,000 × $8)	80,000	$240,000	
Selling (10,000 units × $5)		50,000	(290,000)
Contribution margin			110,000
Less fixed costs			
Manufacturing overhead		52,000	
Selling		10,000	
Administrative		4,000	(66,000)
Net income			$ 44,000
Sales (11,000 units × $38.50)			$423,500
Less variable costs			
Variable cost of goods sold			
Direct materials	$108,000		
Direct labor	70,000		
Manufacturing overhead	81,000	$259,000	
Selling		65,000	(324,000)
Contribution margin			99,500
Less fixed costs			
Manufacturing overhead		53,000	
Selling		9,500	
Administrative		3,800	(66,300)
Net income			$ 33,200

McMillan Company contains three responsibility centers: a Production Department, a Sales Department, and an Administration Department. The Sales Department variances in Exhibit 22.3 net to $15,000 U. The Production Department's variances in Exhibit 22.1 net to $4,000 F. The only variance for the Administration Department is the $200 difference between actual and budgeted fixed administrative costs ($3,800 actual − $4,000 budget). Because the Administration Department is a discretionary cost center, this variance is best identified as being underbudget. For consistency in the performance reports, however, it is labeled favorable. By assigning all variances to these three responsibility centers, the reconciliation of budgeted and actual income is as shown in Exhibit 22.5.

EXHIBIT 22.5	Reconciliation of Budgeted and Actual Income

McMILLAN COMPANY
Reconciliation of Budgeted and Actual Income
For Month of July

Budgeted net income	$44,000
Sales department variances (Exhibit 22.3)	15,000 U
Production department variances (Exhibit 22.1)	4,000 F
Administration department variances ($3,800 actual − $4,000 budgeted)	200 F
Actual net income	$33,200

GUIDANCE ANSWER

MANAGERIAL DECISION You Are the Vice President of Manufacturing

It appears that direct labor hours may no longer be a reliable basis for budgeting variable overhead in your company. If actual variable overhead costs do not appear to correlate closely with direct labor hours, this could be an indication that the components of variable overhead have changed since direct labor hours was selected as the cost driver. Your cost accountants should consider other unit-level cost drivers for budgeting variable overhead costs. However, an activity-based costing method using multiple overhead cost pools with separate cost drivers might provide a more reliable basis for budgeting and controlling variable overhead costs.

DISCUSSION QUESTIONS

Q22-1. What is responsibility accounting? Why should noncontrollable costs be excluded from performance reports prepared in accordance with responsibility accounting?

Q22-2. How can responsibility accounting lead to unethical practices?

Q22-3. Responsibility accounting reports must be expanded to include what nonfinancial areas? Give some examples of nonfinancial measures.

Q22-4. What is a cost center? Give some examples.

Q22-5. How is a cost center different from either an investment or a profit center?

Q22-6. What problems can result from the use of tight standards?

Q22-7. What is a standard cost variance, and what is the objective of variance analysis?

Q22-8. Standard cost variances can usually be broken down into two basic types of variances. Identify and describe these two types of variances.

Q22-9. Identify possible causes for (1) a favorable materials price variance; (2) an unfavorable materials price variance; (3) a favorable materials quantity variance; and (4) an unfavorable materials quantity variance.

Q22-10. How is standard labor time determined? Explain the two ways.

Q22-11. In the standard cost system, what is the appropriate treatment of a change in wage rates (per new labor union contract) that dominate the cost of labor?

Q22-12. Explain the difference between the revenue variance and the sales price variance.

Q22-13. Explain the net sales volume variance and list its components.

Q22-14. Explain the difference between how the *actual costs* and the *standard cost of actual inputs* are computed in variable overhead analysis.

Q22-15. Explain what the net sales volume variance measures.

Assignments with the ✅ in the margin are available in an online homework system.
See the Preface of the book for details.

MINI EXERCISES

M22-16. Flexible Budgets and Performance Evaluation (LO2)

Presented is the January performance report for the Production Department of Newport Company.

NEWPORT COMPANY Production Department Performance Report For Month of January			
	Actual	**Budget**	**Variance**
Volume	30,000	28,000	
Manufacturing costs			
Direct materials.	$ 88,000	$ 84,000	$ 4,000 U
Direct labor	165,000	140,000	25,000 U
Variable overhead	62,000	56,000	6,000 U
Fixed overhead	27,500	28,000	500 F
Total	$342,500	$308,000	$34,500 U

Required

a. Evaluate the performance report.

b. Prepare a more appropriate performance report.

 M22-17. Materials Variances (LO3)

North Wind manufactures decorative weather vanes that have a standard materials cost of two pounds of raw materials at $1.50 per pound. During September 10,000 pounds of raw materials costing $1.55 per pound were used in making 4,800 weather vanes.

Required

Determine the materials price and quantity variance.

M22-18. Materials Variances (LO3)

 Pearle Vision

Assume that **Pearle Vision** uses standard costs to control the materials in its made-to-order sunglasses. The standards call for 2 ounces of material for each pair of lenses. The standard cost per ounce of material is $15. During July, the Santa Clara location produced 4,800 pairs of sunglasses and used 9,000 ounces of materials. The cost of the materials during July was $15.25 per ounce, and there were no beginning or ending inventories.

Required

a. Determine the flexible budget materials cost for the completion of the 4,800 pairs of glasses.

b. Determine the actual materials cost incurred for the completion of the 4,800 pairs of glasses and compute the total materials variance.

c. How much of the total variance was related to the price paid to purchase the materials?

d. How much of the difference between the answers to requirements (a) and (b) was related to the quantity of materials used?

 M22-19. Direct Labor Variances (LO3)

Nortel (NT)

Assume that **Nortel** manufactures specialty electronic circuitry through a unique photoelectronic process. One of the primary products, Model ZX40, has a standard labor time of 0.5 hour and a standard labor rate of $13.50 per hour. During February, the following activities pertaining to direct labor for ZX40 were recorded:

Direct labor hours used	2,180
Direct labor cost.	$34,000
Units of ZX40 manufactured . . .	4,600

Required

a. Determine the labor rate variance.

b. Determine the labor efficiency variance.

c. Determine the total flexible budget labor cost variance.

M22-20. Significance of Direct Labor Variances (LO3)

The Morgan Company's April budget called for labor costs of $125,000. Because the actual labor costs were exactly $125,000, management concluded there were no labor variances.

Required:

Comment on management's conclusion.

 M22-21. Variable Overhead Variances (LO3)

Sony

Assume that the best cost driver that **Sony** has for variable factory overhead in the assembly department is machine hours. During April, the company budgeted 480,000 machine hours and $5,000,000 for its Texas plant's assembly department. The actual variable overhead incurred was $5,200,000, which was related to 500,000 machine hours.

Required

a. Determine the variable overhead spending variance.

b. Determine the variable overhead effectiveness variance.

M22-22. Sales Variances (LO4)

Presented is information pertaining to an item sold by Winding Creek General Store:

	Actual	Budget
Unit sales	150	125
Unit selling price.	$26	$25
Unit standard variable costs.	(20)	(20)
Unit contribution margin	$ 6	$ 5
Revenues	$3,900	$3,125
Standard variable costs	(3,000)	(2,500)
Contribution margin at standard costs	$ 900	$ 625

Required

Compute the revenue, sales price, and the sales volume variances.

M22-23.[A]**Fixed Overhead Variances** (LO3)

Assume that Marathon Oil uses a standard cost system for each of its refineries. For the Texas City refinery, the monthly fixed overhead budget is $5,800,000 for a planned output of 2,000,000 barrels. For September, the actual fixed cost was $6,000,000 for 2,100,000 barrels.

Marathon Oil

Required

a. Determine the fixed overhead budget variance.

b. If fixed overhead is applied on a per-barrel basis, determine the volume variance.

M22-24.[B]**Reconciling Budgeted and Actual Income**

Midstate Supply Company has three responsibility centers: sales, production, and administration. The following information pertains to the November activities of Midstate Supply:

Budgeted contribution income.	$16,000
Actual contribution income	25,500
Sales price variance	24,000 F
Sales volume variance	40,000 F
Net sales price variance	6,000 F
Sales department variable expense variance.	18,000 U
Sales department fixed expense variance	1,000 U
Administration department variances	500 F
Production department variances	2,000 U

Required

Prepare a reconciliation of budgeted and actual contribution income.

EXERCISES

E22-25. **Elements of a Flexible Budget** (LO2)

Presented are partial flexible cost budgets for various levels of output.

	Rate per unit	Units		
		10,000	15,000	20,000
Direct materials	a.	$100,000	b.	c.
Direct labor.	d.	e.	30,000	f.
Variable overhead.	$5	g.	h.	i.
Fixed overhead.		j.	k.	l.
Total		m.	n.	$400,000

Required:

Solve for items "a" though "n."

E22-26.   Elements of Labor and Variable Overhead Variances   (LO3)

Charlotte Fabricating applies variable overhead to products on the basis of standard direct labor hours. Presented is selected information for last month when 8,000 units were produced.

	Direct labor	Variable overhead
Actual..	a.	f.
Standard hours/unit.............................	b.	b.
Actual hours (total).............................	2,100	2,100
Standard rate/hour..............................	$12.00	$8.00
Actual rate.....................................	$12.30	
Flexible budget.................................	$24,000	$16,000
Labor rate or variable overhead spending variance......	c.	g.
Efficiency variances.............................	d.	h.
Total flexible budget variance.....................	e.	$1,000 F

Required:

Solve for items "a" through" h."

E22-27.   Causes of Standard Cost Variances (Comprehensive)   (LO3)

Following are ten unrelated situations that would ordinarily be expected to affect one or more standard cost variances:

1. A salaried production supervisor is given a raise, but no adjustment is made in the labor cost standards.

2. The materials purchasing manager gets a special reduced price on raw materials by purchasing a train carload. A warehouse had to be rented to accommodate the unusually large amount of raw materials. The rental fee was charged to Rent Expense, a fixed overhead item.

3. An unusually hot August caused the company to use 25,000 kilowatts more electricity than provided for in the variable overhead standards.

4. The local electric utility company raised the charge per kilowatt-hour. No adjustment was made in the variable overhead standards.

5. The plant manager traded in his leased company car for a new one in July, increasing the monthly lease payment by $150.

6. A machine malfunction on the assembly line (caused by using cheap and inferior raw materials) resulted in decreased output by the machine operator and higher than normal machine repair costs. Repairs are treated as variable overhead costs.

7. The production maintenance supervisor decreased routine maintenance checks, resulting in lower maintenance costs and lower machine production output per hour. Maintenance costs are treated as fixed costs.

8. An announcement that vacation benefits had been increased resulted in improved employee morale. Consequently, raw materials pilferage and waste declined, and production efficiency increased.

9. The plant manager reclassified her secretary to administrative assistant and gave him an increase in salary.

10. A union contract agreement calling for an immediate 5 percent increase in production worker wages was signed. No changes were made in the standards.

Required

For each of these situations, indicate by letter which of the following standard cost variances would be affected. More than one variance will be affected in some cases.

a. Materials price variance.

b. Materials quantity variance.

c. Labor rate variance.

d. Labor efficiency variance.

e. Variable overhead spending variance.

f. Variable overhead efficiency variance.

g. Fixed overhead budget variance.

E22-28. Sales Variances (LO4)

Assume that Casio Computer Company, LTD. sells handheld communication devices for $110 during August as a back-to-school special. The normal selling price is $150. The standard variable cost for each device is $70. Sales for August had been budgeted for 400,000 units nationwide; however, due to the slowdown in the economy, sales were only 350,000.

Casio Computer
Company, LTD.

Required

Compute the revenue, sales price, sales volume variance, and net sales volume variance.

E22-29.[A] Fixed Overhead Variances (LO3)

Auburn Company uses standard costs for cost control and internal reporting. Fixed costs are budgeted at $20,000 per month at a normal operating level of 10,000 units of production output. During October, actual fixed costs were $21,000, and actual production output was 12,000 units.

Required

a. Determine the fixed overhead budget variance.
b. Assume that the company applied fixed overhead to production on a per-unit basis. Determine the fixed overhead volume variance.
c. Was the fixed overhead budget variance from requirement (a) affected because the company operated above the normal activity level of 10,000 units? Explain.
d. Explain the possible causes for the volume variance computed in requirement (b). How is reporting of the volume variance useful to management?

PROBLEMS

P22-30. Multiple Product Performance Report (LO2)

Storage Products manufactures two models of DVD storage cases: regular and deluxe. Presented is standard cost information for each model:

Cost Components	Regular		Deluxe	
Direct materials				
Lumber	2 board feet × $3 =	$ 6.00	3 board feet × $3 =	$ 9.00
Assembly kit	=	2.00	=	2.00
Direct labor.	1 hour × $4 =	4.00	1.25 hours × $4 =	5.00
Variable overhead. .	1 labor hr. × $2 =	2.00	1.25 labor hrs. × $2 =	2.50
Total		$14.00		$18.50

Budgeted fixed manufacturing overhead is $15,000 per month. During July, the company produced 5,000 regular and 3,000 deluxe storage cases while incurring the following manufacturing costs:

Direct materials	$ 80,000
Direct labor.	36,000
Variable overhead.	14,000
Fixed overhead.	17,500
Total	$147,500

Required

Prepare a flexible budget performance report for the July manufacturing activities.

P22-31. Computation of Variable Cost Variances (LO3)

The following information pertains to the standard costs and actual activity for Tyler Company for September:

Standard cost per unit	
Direct materials.	4 units of material A × $2.00 per unit
	1 unit of material B × $3.00 per unit
Direct labor	3 hours × $8.00 per hour

continued

continued from prior page

Activity for September
Materials purchased
  Material A . . . .   4,500 units × $2.05 per unit
  Material B . . . .   1,100 units × $3.10 per unit
Materials used
  Material A . . . .   4,150 units
  Material B . . . .   1,005 units
Direct labor used . . . .   2,950 hours × $8.20 per hour
Production output. . . . .   1,000 units

There were no beginning direct materials inventories.

Required
a. Determine the materials price and quantity variances.
b. Determine the labor rate and efficiency variances.

P22-32. Variance Computations and Explanations (LO3)
Outdoor Company manufactures camping tents from a lightweight synthetic fabric. Each tent has a standard materials cost of $20, consisting of 4 yards of fabric at $5 per yard. The standards call for 2 hours of assembly at $12 per hour. The following data were recorded for October, the first month of operations:

Fabric purchased . . . .   9,000 yards × $4.90 per yard
Fabric used in production of 1,700 tents . . . .   7,000 yards
Direct labor used . . . .   3,600 hours × $12.50 per hour

Required
a. Compute all standard cost variances for materials and labor.
b. Give one possible reason for each of the preceding variances.
c. Determine the standard variable cost of the 1,700 tents produced, separated into direct materials and labor.

P22-33. Determining Unit Costs, Variance Analysis, and Interpretation (LO2, 3)
Big Dog Company, a manufacturer of dog food, produces its product in 1,000-bag batches. The standard cost of each batch consists of 8,000 pounds of direct materials at $0.30 per pound, 48 direct labor hours at $8.50 per hour, and variable overhead cost (based on machine hours) at the rate of $10 per hour with 16 machine hours per batch. The following variable costs were incurred for the last 1,000-bag batch produced:

Direct materials . . . .   8,300 pounds costing $2,378 were purchased and used
Direct labor. . . . .   45 hours costing $450
Variable overhead. $225
Machine hours used. . . . .   18 hours

Required
a. Determine the actual and standard variable costs per bag of dog food produced, separated into direct materials, direct labor, and variable overhead.
b. For the last 1,000-bag batch, determine the standard cost variances for direct materials, direct labor, and variable overhead.
c. Explain the possible causes for each of the variances determined in requirement (b).

P22-34. Computation of Variances and Other Missing Data (LO3)
The following data for O'Keefe Company pertain to the production of 300 units of Product X during December. Selected data items are omitted.

Direct materials (all materials purchased were used during period)

Standard cost per unit: (a) pounds at $3.20 per pound

Total actual cost: (b) pounds costing $5,673

Standard cost allowed for units produced: $5,760

Materials price variance: (c)

Materials quantity variance: $96 U

Direct labor

Standard cost: 2 hours at $7.00

Actual cost per hour: $7.25

Total actual cost: (d)

Labor rate variance: (e)

Labor efficiency variance: $140 U

Variable overhead

Standard costs: (f) hours at $4.00 per direct labor hour

Actual cost: $2,250

Variable overhead spending variance: (g)

Variable overhead efficiency variance: (h)

Required

Complete the missing amounts lettered (a) through (h).

P22-35. Flexible Budgets and Performance Evaluation (LO3)

Anna Van Degna, supervisor of housecleaning for Hotel Dell, was surprised by her summary performance report for March given below.

HOTEL DELL Housekeeping Performance Report For the Month of March			
Actual	**Budget**	**Variance**	**%Variance**
$164,423	$154,000	$10,423 U	6.768% U

Anna was disappointed. She thought she had done a good job controlling housekeeping labor and towel usage, but her performance report revealed an unfavorable variance of $10,423. She had been hoping for a bonus for her good work, but now expected a series of questions from her manager.

The cost budget for housekeeping is based on standard costs. At the beginning of a month, Anna receives a report from Hotel Dell's Sales Department outlining the planned room activity for the month. Anna then schedules labor and purchases using this information. The budget for the housekeeping was based on 8,000 room nights. Each room night is budgeted based on the following standards for various materials, labor, and overhead:

Shower supplies . . . . 3 bottles @ $0.25 each
Towels* . . . . 1 @ $2.00
Laundry . . . . 10 lbs. @ $0.35 a lb.
Labor . . . . ½ hour @ $12.00 an hour
VOH . . . . $6.00 per labor hour
FOH . . . . $4 a room night (based on 8,000 room nights)

*Replacements for towels evaluated by housekeeping as inappropriate for cleaning and reuse.

With 8,900 room nights sold, actual costs and usage for housekeeping during April were:

$6,890 for 26,500 bottles of shower supplies.
$15,563 for 7,900 towels.
$31,329 for 88,500 lbs. of laundry.
$51,591 for 4,350 labor hours.
$25,839 in total VOH.
$33,211 in FOH.

Required

a. Develop a complete budget column for the above performance report presented to Anna. Break it down by expense category. The following format, with additional lines for expense categories, is suggested:

Account	Actual	Budget	Variance
Shower Supplies	$ 6,890	?	?
...		...	...	...
Total	$164,423	$154,000	$10,423 U

b. Evaluate the usefulness of the cost center performance report presented to Anna.

c. Prepare a more logical performance report where standard allowed is based on actual output. Also, split each variance into its price/rate/spending and quantity/efficiency components (except fixed of course). The following format, with additional lines for expense categories, is suggested:

Account	Actual	Flexible Budget	Total Variance	Price/Rate/ Spending Variance	Quantity/ Efficiency Variance
Shower Supplies	$ 6,890	?	?	?	?
...	—	—	—		
Total	$164,423	?	?		

d. Explain to Anna's boss what your report suggests about Anna's department performance.

e. Identify additional nonfinancial performance measures management might consider when evaluating the performance of the housekeeping department and Anna as a manager.

P22-36. Flexible Budget Performance Evaluation with Process Costing (LO3)

Note: This problem requires knowledge of process costing concepts covered in Module 17.

The Davis Company produces a single product on a continuous basis. On July 1, 400 units, 75 percent complete as to materials and 50 percent complete as to conversion, were in process. During January, 1,000 units were started and 1,200 units were completed. The July 31 ending work-in-process inventory contained 200 units, 50 percent complete as to materials and 25 percent complete as to conversion.

Davis uses standard costs for planning and control. The following standard costs are based on a monthly volume of 800 equivalent units with fixed budgeted at $6,000 per month.

Direct materials [(2 square meters per unit × $8.50 per meter) × 800]............	$13,600
Direct labor [(1.5 hours per unit × $20 per hour) × 800]......................	24,000
Variable overhead [(1.5 labor hours per unit × $5.00 per hour) × 800]...........	6,000
Fixed manufacturing overhead..	6,000

Actual July production costs were:

Direct materials	$20,800
Direct labor..	31,400
Manufacturing overhead	11,250

Required

a. Determine the equivalent units of materials and conversion manufactured during July.

b. Based on the July equivalent units of materials and conversion, prepare a July performance report for the Davis Company.

c. Explain the treatment of overhead in the July performance report.

P22-37. Measuring the Effects of Decisions on Standard Cost Variances (Comprehensive) (LO3)

The following five unrelated situations affect one or more standard cost variances for materials, labor (assembly), and overhead:

1. Lois Jones, a production worker, announced her intent to resign to accept another job paying $1.20 more per hour. To keep Lois, the production manager agreed to raise her salary from $7.00 to $8.50 per hour. Lois works an average of 175 regular hours per month.

2. At the beginning of the month, a supplier of a component used in our product notified us that, because of a minor design improvement, the price will be increased by 15 percent above the current standard price of $100 per unit. As a result of the improved design, we expect the number of defective

components to decrease by 80 units per month. On average, 1,200 units of the component are purchased each month. Defective units are identified prior to use and are not returnable.

3. In an effort to meet a deadline on a rush order in Department A, the plant manager reassigned several higher-skilled workers from Department B, for a total of 300 labor hours. The average salary of the Department B workers was $1.85 more than the standard $7.00 per hour rate of the Department A workers. Since they were not accustomed to the work, the average Department B worker was able to produce only 36 units per hour instead of the standard 48 units per hour. (Consider only the effect on Department A labor variances.)

4. Rob Celiba is an inspector who earns a base salary of $700 per month plus a piece rate of 20 cents per bundle inspected. His company accounts for inspection costs as manufacturing overhead. Because of a payroll department error in June, Rob was paid $500 plus a piece rate of 30 cents per bundle. He received gross wages totaling $1,100.

5. The materials purchasing manager purchased 5,000 units of component K2X from a new source at a price $12 below the standard unit price of $200. These components turned out to be of extremely poor quality with defects occurring at three times the standard rate of 5 percent. The higher rate of defects reduced the output of workers (who earn $8 per hour) from 20 units per hour to 15 units per hour on the units containing the discount components. Each finished unit contains one K2X component. To appease the workers (who were irate at having to work with inferior components), the production manager agreed to pay the workers an additional $0.25 for each of the components (good and bad) in the discount batch. Variable manufacturing overhead is applied at the rate of $4 per direct labor hour. The defective units also caused a 20-hour increase in total machine hours. The actual cost of electricity to run the machines is $2 per hour.

Required

For each of the preceding situations, determine which standard cost variance(s) will be affected, and compute the amount of the effect for one month on each variance. Indicate whether the effect is favorable or unfavorable. Assume that the standards are not changed in response to these situations. (Round calculations to two decimal places.)

P22-38.[A] **Fixed Overhead Budget and Volume Variance**

Lucky Seven Company assigns fixed overhead costs to inventory for external reporting purposes by using a predetermined standard overhead rate based on direct labor hours. The standard rate is based on a normal activity level of 10,000 standard allowed direct labor hours per year. There are five standard allowed hours for each unit of output. Budgeted fixed overhead costs are $200,000 per year. During 2009, the company produced 2,200 units of output, and actual fixed costs were $210,000.

Required

a. Determine the standard fixed overhead rate used to assign fixed costs to inventory.
b. Determine the amount of fixed overhead assigned to inventory in 2009.
c. Determine the fixed overhead budget variance.

P22-39.[B] **Profit Center Performance Report**

Bach-by-Net is a classical music retailer specializing in the Internet sale of MP3 albums of the works of J. S. Bach. Although prices vary with album popularity and file sizes, the albums sell for an average of $7.75 each and Bach-by-Net pays a fixed royalty of $4.25 per MP3 album. With the exception of royalty fees, the operating costs of Bach-by-Net are fixed. Presented are budgeted and actual income statements for the month of September.

BACH-BY-NET Budgeted and Actual Contribution Statements For Month of September		
	Actual	Budget
Unit sales	4,200	4,000
Unit selling price.	$7.25	$7.75
Sales revenue.	$30,450	$31,000
Cost of goods sold.	(17,850)	(17,000)
Gross profit.	12,600	14,000
Operating costs	(5,000)	(6,000)
Contribution to corporate costs and profits.	$ 7,600	$ 8,000

Required

Compute variances to assist in evaluating the performance of Bach-by-Net as a profit center. What was the likely cause of the shortfall in profits?

P22-40[B]. Profit Center Performance Report

Chili Town operates fast food restaurants in the food courts of shopping malls. It's main product is a serving of chili that requires beans (direct material) and food preparation (direct labor). The April budget for Chili Town's Riverside Mall restaurant was:

- Sales 21,000 servings at $1.25 each
- Standard food cost of $0.20 per serving (1/3 pound @ $0.60 per pound)
- Standard direct labor of $0.30 per serving (1/30th hour @ $9.00 per hour)
- Fixed occupancy expenses (equip and rent) of $7,000

Actual April performance of the Riverside Mall restaurant was:

- Sales 18,000 servings at $1.30 each
- Food cost of $3,136 for 5,600 pounds
- Direct labor cost of $6,720 for 800 hours
- Fixed occupancy expenses of $7,200

In early May, the manager received the following financial performance report:

CHILI TOWN— RIVERSIDE MALL Performance Report For the Month of April			
	Actual	**Budgeted**	**Variance**
Revenues	$23,400	$26,250	$2,850 U
Food Cost.	(3,136)	(4,200)	1,064 F
Labor Cost	(6,720)	(6,300)	420 U
Occupancy	(7,200)	(7,000)	200 U
Profit.	$ 6,344	$ 8,750	$2,406 U

Required

a. Partition variance into variances for 1) selling price and net sales volume, 2) food variances for price and quantity, and 3) labor variances for rate and efficiency.
b. Using the results of your analysis, prepare an alternative reconciliation of budgeted and actual profit. Be sure to include the occupancy variance.
c. Explain why the total variances for sales, food, and labor in your reconciliation differ from those originally presented to the restaurant manager.

P22-41[B]. Comprehensive Performance Report

Laptop Computing is a contract manufacturer of laptop computers sold under brand named companies. Presented are Laptop's budgeted and actual contribution income statements for October. The company has three responsibility centers: Production, Selling and Distribution, and Administration. Production and Administration are cost centers while Selling and Distribution is a profit center.

LAPTOP COMPUTING Budgeted Contribution Income Statement For Month of October		
Sales (900 × $300).		$270,000
Less variable costs		
Variable cost of goods sold		
Direct materials (900 × $50)	$45,000	
Direct labor (900 × $20)	18,000	
Manufacturing overhead (900 × $30)	27,000	$ 90,000
Selling and Distribution (900 × $70).	63,000	(153,000)
Contribution margin		117,000
Less fixed costs		
Manufacturing overhead.	40,000	
Selling and Distribution.	50,000	
Administrative	10,500	(100,500)
Net income.		$ 16,500

LAPTOP COMPUTING Actual Contribution Income Statement For Month of October			
Sales (1,000 × $330)			$330,000
Less variable costs			
Cost of goods sold			
Direct materials	$50,000		
Direct labor	25,000		
Manufacturing overhead	35,000	$110,000	
Selling and Distribution.		100,000	(210,000)
Contribution margin			120,000
Less fixed costs			
Manufacturing overhead.		38,000	
Selling and Distribution.		65,000	
Administrative.		22,000	(125,000)
Net income (loss)			$ (5,000)

Required

a. Prepare a performance report for Production that compares actual and allowed costs.

b. Prepare a performance report for Selling and Distribution that compares actual and allowed costs.

c. Determine the sales price and the net sales volume variances.

d. Prepare a report that summarizes the performance of Selling and Distribution.

e. Determine the amount by which Administration was over or under budget.

f. Prepare a report reconciling budgeted and actual net income. Your report should focus on the performance of each responsibility center.

MANAGEMENT APPLICATIONS

MA22-42. Discretionary Cost Center Performance Reports (LO1)

TruckMax had been extremely profitable, but the company has been hurt in recent years by competition and a failure to introduce new consumer products. In 2008, Tom Lopez became head of Consumer Products Research (CPR) and began a number of product development projects. Under his leadership the group had good ideas that led to the introduction of several promising products. Nevertheless, when 2009 financial results were reviewed, CPR's report revealed large unfavorable variances leading management to criticize Lopez for poor cost control. Management was quite concerned about cost control because profits were low, and the company's cash budget indicated that additional borrowing would be required throughout 2010 to cover out-of-pocket costs. Because of his inability to exert proper cost control, Lopez was relieved of his responsibilities in 2010, and Gabriella Garcia became head of Consumer Products Research. Garcia vowed to improve the performance of CPR and scaled back CPR's development activities to obtain favorable financial performance reports.

By the end of 2011, the company had improved its market position, profitability, and cash position. At this time, the board of directors promoted Garcia to president, congratulating her for the contribution CPR made to the revitalization of the company, as well as her success in improving the financial performance of CPR. Garcia assured the board that the company's financial performance would improve even more in the future as she applied the same cost-reducing measures that had worked so well in CPR to the company as a whole.

Required

a. For the purpose of evaluating financial performance, what responsibility center classification should be given to the Consumer Products Research Department? What unique problems are associated with evaluating the financial performance of this type of responsibility center?

b. Compare the performances of Lopez and Garcia in the role as head of Consumer Products Research. Did Garcia do a much better job, thereby making her deserving of the promotion? Why or why not?

MA22-43. Developing Cost Standards for Materials and Labor (LO2)

After several years of operating without a formal system of cost control, DeWalt Company, a tools manufacturer, has decided to implement a standard cost system. The system will first be established for the department that makes lug wrenches for automobile mechanics. The standard production batch size is 100 wrenches. The actual materials and labor required for eight randomly selected batches from last year's production are as follows:

Batch	Materials Used (in pounds)	Labor Used (in hours)
1	504.0	10.00
2	508.0	9.00
3	506.0	9.00
4	521.0	5.00
5	516.0	8.00
6	518.0	7.00
7	520.0	6.00
8	515.0	8.00
Average	513.5	7.75

Management has obtained the following recommendations concerning what the materials and labor quantity standards should be:

- The manufacturer of the equipment used in making the wrenches advertises in the toolmakers' trade journal that the machine the company uses can produce 100 wrenches with 500 pounds of direct materials and 5 labor hours. Company engineers believe the standards should be based on these facts.
- The accounting department believes more realistic standards would be 505 pounds and 5 hours.
- The production supervisor believes the standards should be 512 pounds and 7.75 hours.
- The production workers argue for standards of 522 pounds and 8 hours.

Required

a. State the arguments for and against each of the recommendations, as well as the probable effects of each recommendation on the quantity variance for materials and labor.

b. Which recommendation provides the best combination of cost control and motivation to the production workers? Explain.

MA22-44. Behavioral Effect of Standard Costs (LO1, 2, 3)

Delaware Corp. has used a standard cost system for evaluating the performance of its responsibility center managers for three years. Top management believes that standard costing has not produced the cost savings or increases in productivity and profits promised by the accounting department. Large unfavorable variances are consistently reported for most cost categories, and employee morale has fallen since the system was installed. To help pinpoint the problem with the system, top management asked for separate evaluations of the system by the plant department manager, the accounting department manager, and the personnel department manager. Their responses are summarized here.

Plant Manager—The standards are unrealistic. They assume an ideal work environment that does not allow materials defects or errors by the workers or machines. Consequently, morale has gone down and productivity has declined. Standards should be based on expected actual prices and recent past averages for efficiency. Thus, if we improve over the past, we receive a favorable variance.

Accounting Manager—The goal of accounting reports is to measure performance against an absolute standard and the best approximation of that standard is ideal conditions. Cost standards should be comparable to "par" on a golf course. Just as the game of golf uses a handicap system to allow for differences in individual players' skills and scores, it could be necessary for management to interpret variances based on the circumstances that produced the variances. Accordingly, in one case, a given unfavorable variance could represent poor performance; in another case, it could represent good performance. The managers are just going to have to recognize these subtleties in standard cost systems and depend on upper management to be fair.

Personnel Manager—The key to employee productivity is employee satisfaction and a sense of accomplishment. A set of standards that can never be met denies managers of this vital motivator. The current standards would be appropriate in a laboratory with a controlled environment but not in the factory with its many variables. If we are to recapture our old "team spirit," we must give the managers a goal that they can achieve through hard work.

Required

Discuss the behavioral issues involved in Delaware Corp.'s standard cost dilemma. Evaluate each of the three responses (pros and cons) and recommend a course of action.

MA22-45.[B] **Evaluating a Companywide Performance Report**

Mr. Micawber, the production supervisor, bursts into your office, carrying the company's 2012 performance report and thundering, "There is villainy here, sir! And I shall get to the bottom of it. I will not stop searching until I have found the answer! Why is Mr. Heep so down on my department? I thought we did a good job last year. But Heep claims my production people and I cost the company $31,500! I plead with you, sir, explain this performance report to me." Trying to calm Micawber, you take the report from him and ask to be left alone for 15 minutes. The report is as follows:

DICKENS COMPANY, LIMITED Performance Report For Year 2012	Actual	Budget	Variance
Unit sales	7,500	5,000	
Sales	$262,500	$225,000	$37,500 F
Less manufacturing costs			
Direct materials	55,500	47,500	8,000 U
Direct labor	48,000	32,500	15,500 U
Manufacturing overhead	40,000	32,000*	8,000 U
Total	(143,500)	(112,000)	(31,500) U
Gross profit	119,000	113,000	6,000 F
Less selling and administrative expenses			
Selling (all fixed)	57,800	40,000	17,800 U
Administrative (all fixed)	55,000	50,000	5,000 U
Total	(112,800)	(90,000)	(22,800)
Net income	$ 6,200	$ 23,000	$16,800 U
Performance summary			
Budgeted net income			$23,000
Sales department variances			
Sales revenue	$ 37,500 F		
Selling expenses	17,800 U	$19,700 F	
Administration department variances		5,000 U	
Production department variances		31,500 U	16,800 U
Actual net income			$ 6,200

*Includes fixed manufacturing overhead of $22,000.

Required

a. Evaluate the performance report. Is Mr. Heep correct, or is there "villainy here"?

b. Assume that the Sales Department is a profit center and that the Production and Administration Departments are cost centers. Determine the responsibility of each for cost, revenue, and income variances, and prepare a report reconciling budgeted and actual net income. Your report should focus on the performance of each responsibility center.

SOLUTIONS TO REVIEW PROBLEMS

Mid-Module Review

Solution

The performance report prepared by the accounting department was based on a "static" budget. A better basis for evaluating Ron Gilette's performance is to compare actual performance with a flexible budget. By dividing the budgeted sales and variable costs amounts by 12,000 units, the budgeted unit variable costs amounts can be determined as follows:

Direct materials cost............	$360,000 ÷ 12,000 units = $30 per unit
Direct labor..................	$432,000 ÷ 12,000 units = $36 per unit
Variable factory overhead.......	$216,000 ÷ 12,000 units = $18 per unit

Using these budgeted unit values, a flexible budget can be prepared as follows:

	Actual	Flexible Budget	Variance
Units.....................	10,000	10,000	
Costs			
Direct materials	$ 299,000	$ 300,000	$ 1,000 F
Direct labor...............	345,500	360,000	14,500 F
Variable factory overhead.....	180,000	180,000	
Fixed factory overhead.......	375,000	360,000	15,000 U
Total plant costs............	$1,199,500	$1,200,000	$ 500 F

The plant did not produce the number of units originally budgeted. Therefore, from a cost control standpoint, a flexible budget is a better basis for evaluating Ron's performance because it compares the actual cost of producing 10,000 units with a budget also based on 10,000 units. Based on the flexible budget, his performance is still quite good; however, it is much less favorable than it appeared using a static budget.

Module-End Review

Solution

a.

Standard Cost Variance Analysis		
Input component: Direct materials		**Output: 5,000 units**
Actual Cost	**Standard Cost of Actual Inputs**	**Flexible Budget Cost**
Actual quantity (AQ)............ 21,250	Actual quantity (AQ) 21,250	Standard quantity allowed (SQ) 20,000*
Actual price (AP)..... × $4.90	Standard price (SP) ... × $5.00	Standard price (SP) . × $5.00
$104,125	$106,250	$100,000

Materials price variance $2,125 F   Materials quantity variance $6,250 U

Total flexible budget materials variance $4,125 U

*5,000 units × 4 pounds per unit produced

Input component: Direct labor			**Output: 5,000 units**	
Actual Costs	**Standard Cost of Actual Inputs**		**Flexible Budget Cost**	
$82,400	Actual hours (AH)	7,000	Standard hours allowed (SH)	6,250*
	Standard rate (SR).....	× $12	Standard rate (SR)	× $12
	Total.............	$84,000	Total......................	$75,000

Labor rate variance $1,600 F   Labor efficiency variance $9,000 U

Total flexible budget labor variance $7,400 U

*5,000 units × 1.25 hours per unit

b.

Standard Cost Variance Analysis				
Input component: Variable overhead				**Output: 5,000 units**
Actual Costs		**Standard Cost of Actual Inputs**		**Flexible Budget Cost**
Category 1	$31,000	Actual labor hours	7,000	Standard hours
Category 2	18,000	Standard rate	× $4.80	allowed 6,250
Total	$49,000	Driver total	$33,600	Standard rate . . . . . . × $4.80
				Driver total. $30,000
		Finished units.	5,000	
		Standard rate	× $4.00	Finished units 5,000
		Driver total	$20,000	Standard rate . . . . . . × $4.00
		Total	$53,600	Driver total $20,000
				Total. $50,000

Variable overhead spending variance $4,600 F

Variable overhead efficiency variance $3,600 U

Total flexible budget variable overhead variance $1,000 F

smarter together

IBM

Getty Images

IBM

The "Letter from the Chairman" in the 2009 IBM Annual Report included the following paragraph:

> IBM's gross profit margin rose for the sixth consecutive year—to 45.7 percent, up 9.2 points since 2003. Our pre-tax income margin rose to 18.9 percent. Both margins are at their highest in more than a decade. We achieved this by driving productivity and continuing to shift our business mix to more profitable segments.[1]

IBM's 2009 annual report goes on to tell the story of a major re-making of the world's oldest and best-known major computer company over the past decade. The bar charts that follow show how IBM "divested commoditizing businesses like personal computers and hard drives, and strengthened its position through strategic investments and acquisitions in areas such as analytics, next-generation data centers, cloud computing and green solutions."[2]

---

[1] 2009 *IBM Annual Report*, p. 3.
[2] 2009 *IBM Annual Report*, p. 10.

Segment Pre-tax Income*
($ in billions)*

2000

| 2.7 | 1.2 | 4.5 | | 2.8 |

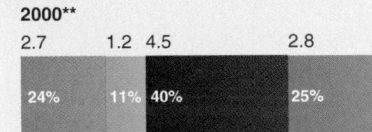

2009

| 1.4 | 1.7 | 8.1 | | 8.1 |

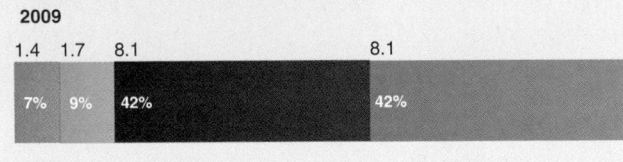

— Hardware   — Financing   ▬ Services   — Software

*Sum of external segment pre-tax income not equal to IBM
**Excludes Enterprise Investments and stock-based compensation

Source: 2009 IBM Annual Report, p. 10.

Since its beginning in the 19th century as Computing-Tabulating-Recording Corporation, when it manufactured

Segment Reporting, Transfer Pricing, and Balanced Scorecard

LEARNING OBJECTIVES

LO1 Define a strategic business segment, and prepare and use segment reports. (p. 23-3)

LO2 Explain transfer pricing and assess alternative transfer-pricing methods. (p. 23-7)

LO3 Determine and contrast return on investment and residual income. (p. 23-12)

LO4 Describe the balanced scorecard as a comprehensive performance measurement system. (p. 23-19)

a wide range of products, including time-keeping systems, weighing scales, automatic meat slicers, coffee grinders, and punched card equipment that tabulated and sorted data, IBM has adapted its products and services to the needs of the marketplace. Its punch card system was the standard method of processing data in large organizations for many decades until IBM introduced the first commercial computer in the early 1950s, followed soon after with the development of the first magnetic hard drive, and then its revolutionary System/360 mainframe computer in the mid-1960s. In the early 1980s, IBM introduced the Personal Computer and immediately became the leader in the PC industry, but later lost that lead with the development of major competitors Dell, Compaq, and HP. In 2004 IBM sold its last PC group to Lenova, having lost nearly a billion dollars in its personal computers segment in the previous 3½ years. Today, with more than half of its revenues and profits derived from services, IBM has evolved into a major business and technology consulting enterprise.[3]

To survive and thrive in a changing and highly competitive environment, companies must continually assess their operations to determine how well they are performing in the various segments of the marketplace in which they are operating. Few companies today can succeed by selling a single product to a narrow market segment. Even though most successful companies, including companies like Google and Amazon, began by operating in a fairly narrow niche, as they developed, they branched out into other strategic product or customer segments. This module will introduce some of the models that companies, such as IBM, Google, and Amazon, use to evaluate their business segments.

---

[3] History of IBM, http://www-03.ibm.com/ibm/history/history/history_intro.html

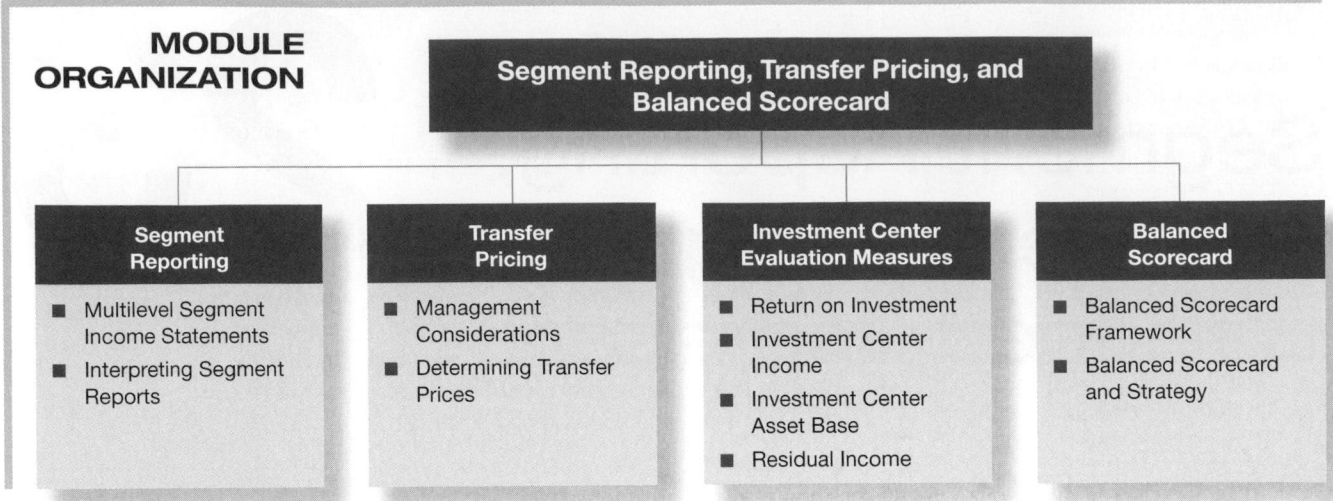

Organizations that maintain multiple product lines or that operate in several industries or in multiple markets often adopt a decentralized organization structure in which managers of major business units or strategic segments enjoy a high degree of autonomy. Examples of strategic business segments include the **Acura Division of Honda** and the Asia Pacific Group of **The Coca-Cola Company**. Sometimes companies establish segments within segments such as at Coca-Cola, whose Asia Pacific Group has separate business units for individual countries (Japan, Korea, etc.). In organizations such as Honda and Coca-Cola, upper management typically sets specific performance and profitability objectives for each segment and allows the manager of the segment the decision-making freedom to achieve those objectives.

This module explains the ways that an organization evaluates strategic business segments. It also considers transfer pricing and some of the problems that occur when one segment provides goods or services to another segment in the same organization.

STRATEGIC BUSINESS SEGMENTS AND SEGMENT REPORTING

LO1 Define a strategic business segment, and prepare and use segment reports.

A **strategic business segment** has its own mission and set of goals. Its mission influences the decisions that top managers make in both short-run and long-run situations. The organization structure dictates to a large extent the type of financial segment reporting and other measures used to evaluate the segment and its managers. In decentralized organizations, for example, the reporting units (typically called *divisions*) normally are quasi-independent companies, often having their own computer system, cost accounting system, and administrative and marketing staffs. With this type structure, top management monitors the segments to ensure that these independent units are functioning for the benefit of the entire organization.

Although segment reports are normally produced to coincide with managerial lines of responsibility, some companies also produce segment reports for smaller slices of the business that do not represent separate responsibility centers. These parts of the business are not significant enough to be identified as "strategic" business units as defined, but management could want information about them on a continuing basis.

For example, **AT&T** has several strategic business units, including wireless, wireline, and advertising solutions (see the following Business Insight). Financial reports are prepared for each of these units. Within the wireline segment, AT&T can also prepare segment reports on a more detailed basis to determine the profitability of its smaller segments, such as phone-only and data service customers. As the Business Insight below shows, many public companies are required to provide some segment information in their annual reports.

The point is that segment reporting is not constrained by lines of responsibility. A segment report can be prepared for any part of the business for which management believes more detailed information is useful in managing that portion of the business.

All publicly traded companies are required to include income statement information by segment in their annual reports if their business consists of more than one major business segment. For example, AT&T reports segment information for three major segments: Wireless, Wireline, and Advertising Solutions. The reported income statement information (in billions) for these three segments in AT&T's 2009 Annual Report was as follows:

At December 31, 2009 or for the year ended	Wireless	Wireline	Advertising Solutions
Revenues from external customers	$53,504	$63,331	$4,724
Intersegment revenues.	93	2,339	85
Total segment operating revenues	53,597	65,670	4,809
Operations and support expenses.	34,561	44,646	2,922
Depreciation and amortization expenses.	5,765	13,093	649
Total segment operating expenses	40,326	57,739	3,571
Segment operating income	13,271	7,931	1,238
Interest expense.	—	—	—
Equity in net income of affiliates.	9	18	—
Other income (expense)—net.	—	—	—
Segment income before income taxes.	$13,280	$7,949	$1,238

Segment reports are income statements for portions or segments of a business. Segment reporting is used primarily for internal purposes, although generally accepted accounting principles also require some disclosure of segment information for public corporations. Even though there are many different types of segment reports, at least three steps are basic to the preparation of all segment reports:

1. Identify the segments.
2. Assign direct costs to segments.
3. Allocate indirect costs to segments.

The format of segment income statements varies depending on the approach adopted by a company for reporting income statements internally. The income statement formats illustrated earlier in this text, including the functional format and the contribution format, can be used for segment reporting. Data availability can, however, dictate the format used. Regardless of the format adopted, it is essential that costs be separable into those directly traceable to the segments and those not directly traceable to segments.

Determining the segment reporting structure is often a more difficult decision than choosing the format for the segment income statements. Companies must decide whether to structure segment reporting along the lines of responsibility reporting, and whether segment reports will be prepared only on one level or on several levels.

For example, consider the hypothetical case of Digital Communications Company (DCC) that has two market divisions, three products, and two geographic territories. DCC's two divisions include the National Division (serving large national accounts) and the Regional Division (serving smaller regional and local accounts). DCC's three product lines are fiber optic cable, twisted pair cable, and coaxial cable. The company is organized into two geographic territories, Atlantic and Pacific. If DCC were using only a single-level segment reporting approach for all three groupings, one report would show the total company income statement broken down into the two divisions, a second report would show the total company income statement broken down into the three products, and a third report would show the total company income statement broken down into the two geographic territories.

Multilevel Segment Income Statements

If top management of DCC wants to know how much a particular product is contributing to the income of one of the two divisions or how much income a particular product in one of its two geographic territories contributes, it is necessary to prepare multilevel segment income statements. Since DCC sells three products and operates through two divisions in two territories, many combinations of divisions, products, and territories could be used in structuring the company's multilevel segment reporting. The goal is not to slice and dice the revenue and cost data in as many ways as possible but to provide useful and meaningful information to management. Therefore, deciding what type of reporting structure is most useful in managing the company is important.

This decision will be constrained to a great extent by data availability and cost. If there were no data constraints, DCC could look at the company's net income for every possible combination of division, product, and territory. The more data required to support a reporting system, however, the more costly it is to maintain the system, so management must determine the value and the cost of the additional information and make an appropriate cost-benefit judgment.

Panel A of Exhibit 23.1 illustrates multilevel segment reporting for DCC in which the first level shows the total company income statement segmented into the two market divisions, National Accounts and Regional Accounts. Panel B of Exhibit 23.1 shows a second-level report for DCC in which the National Division's segment income statement is broken down into its three product lines, fiber optic cable, twisted pair cable, and coaxial cable. Panel C then provides a third-level income statement for the National Division's fiber optic sales in each of the company's two geographic territories, the Atlantic and Pacific territories. The example in Exhibit 23.1 shows only part of the segment reports for DCC. The complete three-level set of segment reports would also break down the Regional Accounts Division into its product lines and all product lines for both divisions into geographic territories.

In the DCC example in Exhibit 23.1, the first reporting level is the company's divisions, its second reporting level is product lines, and the third is geographic territories. Another approach could be to structure the segment reports with product lines as the first level, geographic territories as the second level, and divisions as the third level. Still another approach would be to make product lines the first level, divisions the second level, and geographic territories the third level.

Regardless of how many different ways the company segments the income statements, at least one set of segment reports follows the company's responsibility reporting system; therefore, one of the segment reports has the operating divisions as the first level. If each division has a product manager for each product, the division segment reports are broken down by products. Finally, if each product within each division has a territory manager, the product segment reports are broken down by territories.

Interpreting Segment Reports

Exhibit 23.1 reports costs in four categories: variable costs, direct fixed costs, allocated common costs, and unallocated common costs. Variable costs vary in proportion to the level of sales and are subtracted from sales in calculating contribution margin. **Direct segment fixed costs** are nonvariable costs directly traceable to the segments incurred for the specific benefit of the respective segments. **Segment margin** equals the contribution margin minus the direct segment fixed costs. For DCC, segment margins are referred to as *division margins, product margins,* and *territory margins.* Segment margins represent the amount that a segment contributes directly to the company's profitability in the short run.

Common segment costs are incurred for the common benefit of all related segments shown on a segment income statement. In some cases, allocating some common costs is reasonable even though they cannot be directly traced to the various segments based on benefits received. For example, if segments share common space, allocating all space-related costs to the segments based on building space occupied could be appropriate. If there is no reasonable basis for allocating common costs, they should not be allocated to the segments. In Panel C of Exhibit 23.1, if advertising costs to promote the company's fiber optic products on national television could not be reasonably allocated to the two geographic territories, they would be charged to the fiber optic product line as an unallocated common cost, not to the individual territories.

If some portion of common costs can be reasonably allocated to the segments, those allocated costs are subtracted from the segment margins to determine segment income. Hence, **segment income** represents all revenues of the segment minus all costs directly or indirectly charged to it.

To properly interpret segment income, we should ask whether segment income represents the amount by which net income of the company will change if that segment is discontinued. For example, if DCC discontinues the coaxial product line in the National Division, does this mean that DCC's net

EXHIBIT 23.1	Multilevel Segment Reports

Panel A: First-Level Segment Report of Digital Communications Company—For Divisions (in thousands)

	Segments (Divisions)		
	National Accounts	Regional Accounts	Company Total
Sales.	$100,000	$ 200,000	$300,000
Less variable costs.	(55,000)	(95,000)	(150,000)
Contribution margin	45,000	105,000	150,000
Less direct fixed costs	(20,000)	(60,000)	(80,000)
Division margin.	25,000	45,000	70,000
Less allocated segment costs	(10,000)	(25,000)	(35,000)
Division income	$ 15,000	$ 20,000	35,000
Less unallocated common costs			(12,000)
Net income			$ 23,000

Panel B: Second-Level Segment Report of the National Division—For Products (in thousands)

	Segments (Products)			National Accounts Total
	Fiber Optic	Twisted Pair	Coaxial	
Sales.	$30,000	$40,000	$30,000	$100,000
Less variable costs.	(15,000)	(19,000)	(21,000)	(55,000)
Contribution margin	15,000	21,000	9,000	45,000
Less direct fixed costs	(9,000)	(4,000)	(2,000)	(15,000)
Product margin.	6,000	17,000	7,000	30,000
Less allocated segment costs	(5,000)	(4,000)	(1,000)	(10,000)
Product income	$ 1,000	$13,000	$ 6,000	20,000
Less unallocated common costs				(5,000)
National Division income				$ 15,000

Panel C: Third-Level Segment Report of the Fiber Optic Product Line in the National Division—For Geographic Territories (in thousands)

	Segments (Territories)		Fiber Optic Total
	Atlantic	Pacific	
Sales.	$20,000	$10,000	$30,000
Less variable costs.	(11,000)	(4,000)	(15,000)
Contribution margin	9,000	6,000	15,000
Less direct fixed costs	(3,000)	(4,000)	(7,000)
Territory margin.	6,000	2,000	8,000
Less allocated segment costs	(2,000)	(3,000)	(5,000)
Territory income	$ 4,000	$(1,000)	3,000
Less unallocated common costs			(2,000)
Fiber optic income			$ 1,000

income will decrease by $6 million? Also, does it mean that if the National Division stops selling fiber optic cable in the Pacific territory, DCC's net income will increase by $1 million?

The answer to these questions depends on whether the costs allocated to the segments are avoidable. **Avoidable common costs** are allocated common costs that eventually can be avoided (that is, can be eliminated) if a segment is discontinued. If all allocated common costs are avoidable, the effect of discontinuing the segment on corporate profitability equals the amount of segment income. In most cases, the short-term impact of discontinuing a segment equals the segment margin because allocated costs are capacity costs that cannot be adjusted in the short run. Over time, the company should be able to adjust capacity and eliminate some, or possibly all, of the allocated common costs or find productive uses for that capacity in other segments of the business. The unallocated common costs cannot be changed readily in the short term or the long term without causing major disruptions to the company and its strategy. Therefore, over the long term, the impact of discontinuing a segment should be, approximately, it's segment income.

If DCC discontinues selling fiber optic cable in the Pacific territory (see Exhibit 23.1, Panel C) the short-term effect on the company's profits will probably be a $2 million reduction of profits, which equals the Pacific territory's margin. The revenues and costs that make up the Pacific territory margin would all be lost if fiber optic sales were discontinued in the Pacific territory, but the $3 million of common costs allocated to the Pacific territory would continue, at least in the short term. Over the long term, however, after adjusting the capacity for selling this product in the Pacific territory and eliminating the $3 million of allocated common costs, the effect of discontinuing fiber optics in the Pacific territory on profits should be an increase of about $1 million, which is the amount of the segment loss for fiber optics in the Pacific territory.

To summarize, generally, segment margin is relevant for measuring the short-term effects of decisions to continue or discontinue a segment; however, segment income is relevant for measuring the long-term effects of decisions to continue or discontinue.

MID-MODULE REVIEW

Refer to the Digital Communications (DCC) example in Exhibit 23.1, Panel B. The following additional information is provided for the Coaxial product line in the National Division:

Sales—Atlantic territory	$12,000
Sales—Pacific territory	18,000
Direct fixed cost—Atlantic territory	500
Direct fixed cost—Pacific territory	800
Allocated segment costs—Atlantic territory	200
Allocated segment costs—Pacific territory	600

Required:
a. Prepare a geographic territory segment report of the Coaxial product line in the National division.
b. Explain why the total of the Territory Margins for geographic segments of the Coaxial product line does not equal the product margin of the Coaxial product segment in Panel B of Exhibit 23.1.

The solution is on page 23-38.

TRANSFER PRICING

LO2 Explain transfer pricing and assess alternative transfer-pricing methods.

To determine whether each division is achieving its organizational objectives, managers must be accountable for the goods and services they acquire, both externally and internally. When goods or services are exchanged internally between segments of a decentralized organization, the way that the transferor and the transferee will report the transfer must be determined, either by negotiations between the two segments or by corporate policy. A **transfer price** is the internal value assigned a product or service that one division provides to another. The transfer price is recognized as revenue by the division providing goods or services and as expense (or cost) by the division receiving them. Transfer-pricing transactions normally occur between profit or investment centers rather than between cost centers of an organization; however, managers often consider cost allocations between cost centers as a type of transfer price. The focus in this module is on transfers between responsibility centers that are evaluated based on profits.

Management Considerations

The desire of the selling and buying divisions of the same company to maximize their individual performance measures often creates transfer-pricing conflicts within an organization. Acting as independent units, divisions could take actions that are not in the best interest(s) of the organization as a whole. The three examples that follow illustrate the need for organizations to maintain a *corporate* profit-maximizing viewpoint while attempting to allow *divisional* autonomy and responsibility.

OmniTech, Inc., has five divisions, some of which transfer products and product components to other OmniTech divisions. The BioTech Division manufactures two products, Alpha and Beta. It sells Alpha externally for $50 per unit and transfers Beta to the GenTech Division for $60 per unit. The costs associated with the two products follow:

Product	Alpha	Beta
Variable costs		
Direct materials.................	$15	$14
Direct labor.....................	5	10
Variable manufacturing overhead......	5	16
Selling.........................	4	0
Fixed Costs		
Fixed manufacturing overhead........	6	15
Total	$35	$55

An external company has just proposed to supply a Beta substitute product to the GenTech Division at a price of $52. From the company's viewpoint, this is merely a make or buy decision. The relevant costs are the differential outlay costs of the alternative actions. Assuming that the fixed manufacturing costs of the BioTech Division are unavoidable, the relevant costs of this proposal from the company's perspective are as follows:

Buy		$52
Make		
Direct materials......................	$14	
Direct labor.........................	10	
Variable manufacturing overhead..........	16	(40)
Difference..................................		$12

From the corporate viewpoint, the best decision is for the product to be transferred since the relevant cost is $40 rather than to buy it from an external source for $52. The decision for the GenTech Division management is basically one of cost minimization: Buy from the source that charges the lowest price. If BioTech is not willing to transfer Beta at a price of $52 or less, the GenTech management could go to the external supplier to maximize the division's profits. (Although GenTech's managers are concerned about the cost of Beta, they are also concerned about the quality of the goods. If the $52 product does not meet its quality standards, GenTech could decide to buy from BioTech at the higher price. For this discussion, assume that the internal and external products are identical; therefore, acting in its best interest, GenTech purchases Beta for $52 from the external source unless BioTech can match the price.)

Prior to GenTech's receipt of the external offer, BioTech had been transferring Beta to GenTech for $60. BioTech must decide whether to reduce the contribution margin on its transfers of Beta to GenTech and, therefore, lower divisional profits or to try to find an alternative use for its resources. Of course, corporate management could intervene and require the internal transfer even though it would hurt BioTech's profits.

As the second example, assume that the BioTech Division has the option to sell an equivalent amount of Beta externally for $60 per unit if the GenTech Division discontinues its transfers from BioTech. Now the decision for BioTech's management is simple: Sell to the buyer willing to pay the most. From the corporate viewpoint, it is best for BioTech to sell to the external buyer for $60 and for GenTech to purchase from the external provider for $52.

To examine a slightly different transfer-pricing conflict, assume that the BioTech Division can sell all the Alpha that it can produce (it is operating at capacity). Also assume that there is no external market for Beta, but there is a one-to-one trade-off between the production of Alpha and Beta, which use equal amounts of the BioTech Division's limited capacity.

The corporation still regards this as a make or buy decision, but the costs of producing Beta have changed. The cost of Beta now includes an outlay cost and an opportunity cost. The outlay cost of Beta is its variable cost of $40 ($14 + $10 + $16), as previously computed. Beta's opportunity cost is the net benefit foregone if the BioTech Division's limited capacity is used to produce Beta rather than Alpha:

Selling price of Alpha		$50
Outlay costs of Alpha		
Direct materials	$15	
Direct labor	5	
Variable manufacturing overhead	5	
Variable selling	4	(29)
Opportunity cost of making Beta		$21

Accordingly, the relevant costs in the make or buy decision follow.

Make		
Outlay cost of Beta	$40	
Opportunity cost of Beta	21	$61
Buy		$52

From the corporate viewpoint, GenTech should purchase Beta from the outside supplier for $52 because in this case it costs $61 to make the product. If there were no outside suppliers, the corporation's relevant cost of manufacturing Beta would be $61. This is another way of saying that the GenTech Division should not acquire Beta internally unless its revenues cover all outlay costs (including the $40 in the BioTech Division) and provide a contribution of at least $21 ($61 − $40). From the corporate viewpoint, the relevant costs in make or buy decisions are the external price, the outlay costs to manufacture, and the opportunity cost to manufacture. The opportunity cost is zero if there is excess capacity.

The transfer of goods and services between divisions of a company located in different countries that have unequal tax structures often attracts the attention of the taxing authorities. Companies are sometimes accused of trying to minimize their total tax costs by setting transfer prices that shift profits from the division in the higher-tax-rate country to the division in the lower-tax-rate country. For example, assume that IBM has a division in Denmark that produces software that it sells to its systems division in the U.S. Denmark's corporate tax rate is about 50 percent; whereas, the U.S. rate is about 35 percent. By setting a transfer price at the lowest possible level, the profits of the Danish division will be less, and those of the American division will be higher, resulting in lower overall taxes for the company. The taxing authorities in the high-tax-rate country always insist that the transfer price for goods and services sold to divisions in other countries be at least as high as fair market value of the goods or services transferred out. The following Business Insight discusses a recent attempt by the IRS to collect taxes of more than $500 million from **Guidant Corp.** related to improper transfer prices.

BUSINESS INSIGHT | **International Transfer Pricing at Guidant Corp.**

Boston Scientific Corp. reported that the IRS ruled that its Guidant Corp. division owes $521.1 million in taxes plus interest as a result of an audit of Guidant's prior years' tax returns. The company said "the IRS is assessing additional taxes related to transfer prices on technology license agreements between some of Guidant's U.S. and foreign businesses." Boston Scientific said it disagrees with the methodology the IRS used in determining the additional taxes and will fight the ruling through the legal process. The methodology used by the IRS was not disclosed.

Source: "Boston Scientific owes half billion in taxes, IRS says ; Company vows to fight ruling on Guidant division," *Boston Globe*, December 22, 2010, p. B9

Determining Transfer Prices

As illustrated, the transfer price of goods or services can be subject to much controversy. The most widely used and discussed transfer prices are covered in this section. Although a price must be agreed upon for each item or service transferred between divisions, the selection of the pricing method depends on many factors. The conditions surrounding the transfer determine which of the alternative methods discussed subsequently is selected.

Although no method is likely to be ideal, one must be selected if the profit or investment center concept is used. In considering each method, observe that each transfer results in a revenue entry on the supplier's books and a cost entry on the receiver's books. Transfers can be considered as sales by the supplier and as purchases by the receiver.

Market Price

When there is an existing market with established prices for an intermediate product and the transfer actions of the company will not affect prices, market prices are ideal transfer prices. If divisions are free to buy and sell outside the firm, the use of market prices preserves divisional autonomy and leads divisions to act in a manner that maximizes corporate goal congruence. Unfortunately, not all product transfers have equivalent external markets. Furthermore, the divisions should carefully evaluate whether the market price is competitive or controlled by one or two large companies. When substantial selling expenses are associated with outside sales, many firms specify the transfer price as market price less selling expenses. The internal sale may not require the incurrence of costs to get and fill the order.

To illustrate using the OmniTech example, assume that product Alpha of the BioTech Division can be sold competitively at $50 per unit or transferred to a third division, the Quantum Division, for additional processing. Under most situations, the BioTech Division will never sell Alpha for less than $50, and the Quantum Division will likewise never pay more than $50 for it. However, if any variable expenses related to marketing and shipping can be eliminated by divisional transfers, these costs are generally subtracted from the competitive market price. In our illustration in which variable selling expenses are $4 for Alpha, the transfer price could be reduced to $46 ($50 − $4). A price between $46 and $50 would probably be better than either extreme price. To the extent that these transfer prices represent a nearly competitive situation, the profitability of each division can then be fairly evaluated.

Variable Costs

If excess capacity exists in the supplying division, establishing a transfer price equal to variable costs leads the purchasing division to act in a manner that is optimal from the corporation's viewpoint. The buying division has the corporation's variable cost as its own variable cost as it enters the external market. Unfortunately, establishing the transfer price at variable cost causes the supplying division to report zero profits or a loss equal to any fixed costs. If excess capacity does not exist, establishing a transfer price at variable cost would not lead to optimal action because the supplying division would have to forego external sales that include a markup for fixed costs and profits. If Beta could be sold externally for $60, the BioTech Division would not want to transfer Beta to the GenTech Division for a $40 transfer price based on the following variable costs:

Direct materials	$14
Direct labor	10
Variable manufacturing overhead	16
Total variable costs	$40

The BioTech Division would much rather sell outside the company for $60, which covers variable costs and provides a profit contribution margin of $20:

Selling price of Beta	$60
Variable costs	(40)
Contribution margin	$20

Variable Costs Plus Opportunity Costs

From the organization's viewpoint, this is the optimal transfer price. Because all relevant costs are included in the transfer price, the purchasing division is led to act in a manner optimal for the overall company, whether or not excess capacity exists.

With excess capacity in the supplying division, the transfer price is the variable cost per unit. Without excess capacity, the transfer price is the sum of the variable and opportunity costs. Following this rule in the previous example, if the BioTech Division had excess capacity, the transfer price of Beta would be set at Beta's variable costs of $40 per unit. At this transfer price, the GenTech Division would buy Beta internally, rather than externally at $52 per unit. If the BioTech Division cannot sell Beta externally but can sell all the Alpha it can produce and is operating at capacity, the transfer price per unit would be set at $61, the sum of Beta's variable and opportunity costs ($40 + $21). (Refer back two pages.) At this transfer price, the GenTech Division would buy Beta externally for $52. In both situations, the management of the GenTech Division has acted in accordance with the organization's profit-maximizing goal.

There are two problems with this method. First, when the supplying division has excess capacity, establishing the transfer price at variable cost causes the supplying division to report zero profits or a loss equal to any fixed costs. Second, determining opportunity costs when the supplying division produces several products is difficult. If the problems with the previously mentioned transfer-pricing methods are too great, three other methods can be used: absorption cost plus markup, negotiated prices, and dual prices.

Absorption Cost Plus Markup

According to absorption costing, all variable and fixed manufacturing costs are product costs. Pricing internal transfers at absorption cost eliminates the supplying division's reported loss on each product that can occur using a variable cost transfer price. Absorption cost plus markup provides the supplying division a contribution toward unallocated costs. In "cost-plus" transfer pricing, "cost" should be defined as standard cost rather than as actual cost. This prevents the supplying division from passing on the cost of inefficient operations to other divisions, and it allows the buying division to know its cost in advance of purchase. Even though cost-plus transfer prices may not maximize company profits, they are widely used. Their popularity stems from several factors, including ease of implementation, justifiability, and perceived fairness. Once everyone agrees on absorption cost plus markup pricing rules, internal disputes are minimized.

Negotiated Prices

Negotiated transfer prices are used when the supplying and buying divisions independently agree on a price. As with market-based transfer prices, negotiated transfer prices are believed to preserve divisional autonomy. Negotiated transfer prices can lead to some suboptimal decisions, but this is regarded as a small price to pay for other benefits of decentralization. When they use negotiated transfer prices, some corporations establish arbitration procedures to help settle disputes between divisions. However, the existence of an arbitrator with any real or perceived authority reduces divisional autonomy.

Negotiated prices should have market prices as their ceiling and variable costs as their floor. Although frequently used when an external market for the product or component exists, the most common use of negotiated prices occurs when no identical-product external market exists. Negotiations could start with a floor price plus add-ons such as overhead and profit markups or with a ceiling price less adjustments for selling and administrative expenses and allowances for quantity discounts. When no identical-product external market exists, the market price for a similar completed product can be used, less the estimated cost of completing the product from the transfer stage to the completed stage.

Dual Prices

Dual prices exist when a company allows a difference in the supplier's and receiver's transfer prices for the same product. This method should minimize internal squabbles of division managers and problems of conflicting divisional and corporate goals. The supplier's transfer price normally approximates market price, which allows the selling division to show a "normal" profit on items that it transfers internally. The receiver's price is usually the internal cost of the product or service, calculated as variable cost plus opportunity cost. This ensures that the buying division will make an internal transfer when it is in the best interest of the company to do so.

In most cases, a market-based transfer price achieves the optimal outcome for both the divisions and the company as a whole. As discussed earlier, an exception occurs when a division is operating below full capacity and has no alternative use for its excess capacity. In this case, it is best for the company to have an internal transfer; therefore, to ensure that the receiving division makes an internal transfer, the company must require the internal transfer as long as its price does not exceed the established market rate. The only time an external price is more attractive when excess capacity exists is when the external price is below the variable cost of the providing internal division, and that scenario is highly unlikely.

A potential transfer-pricing problem exists when divisions exchange goods or services for which no established market exists. For example, suppose that a company is operating its information technology (IT) service department as a profit center that transfers services to other profit center departments using a cost-plus transfer price. If the departments using IT services can choose to use those services or to replicate them inside their departments, users might not make a decision that is best for the company. It could be best for the company to have all IT services come from the IT department, but other profit centers could believe that they can provide those services for themselves at lower cost. In this case, the company must decide how important it is to maintain the independence of its profit center. In the interest of maintaining a strong profit center philosophy, top management can decide that it is acceptable to suboptimize by allowing profit centers to provide IT services for themselves.

The ideal transfer-pricing arrangement is seldom the same for both the providing and receiving divisions for every situation. In these cases, what is good for one division is likely not to be good for the other division resulting in no transfer, even though a transfer could achieve corporate goals. These conflicts are sometimes overcome by having a higher-ranking manager impose a transfer price and insist that a transfer be made. Managers in organizations that have a policy of decentralization, however, often regard these orders as undermining their autonomy. Therefore, the imposition of a price could solve the corporate profit optimization problem but create other problems regarding the company's organization strategy. Transfer pricing thus becomes a problem with no ideal solutions.

The previous discussion has focused on the challenges of establishing transfer prices that motivate managers to make decisions that are beneficial to their divisions as well as the overall company. However, recent research, discussed in the following Research Insight box, concluded that there are often price benefits when dealing with outside vendors, if the company has the option of acquiring the goods or services internally.

RESEARCH INSIGHT	Transfer Pricing and External Competition

Researchers found that a firm can glean benefits from discussing transfer-pricing problems with external suppliers. Though transfer prices above marginal cost introduce interdivision coordination problems, they also reduce a firm's willingness to pay outside suppliers. Knowing that costly internal transfers will eat into demand, the supplier is more willing to set lower prices. Such supplier discounts can make decentralization worthwhile for the firm. The benefit of decentralization is shown to be robust in both downstream and upstream competition.

Source: "Anil Arya and Brian Mittendorf, "Interacting Supply Chain Distortions: The Pricing of Internal Transfers and External Procurement," *The Accounting Review*, May 2007.

INVESTMENT CENTER EVALUATION MEASURES

LO3 Determine and contrast return on investment and residual income.

Two of the most common measures of investment center performance, return on investment and residual income, are discussed in the following sections. Several supporting components of these measures that help clarify the applications are also presented. (Earlier in the book, we explained the advantages of separating operating and nonoperating items to compute sales, assets, income, and so forth. We can similarly separate operating and nonoperating items for performance measurement. In this case, all measures would be adjusted to yield operating sales, operating assets, operating income, and so forth. Then, the following analysis would apply to those operating metrics and would reflect the operating performance of each center.)

Return on Investment

Return on investment (ROI) is a measure of the earnings per dollar of investment. This assumes that financing decisions are made at the corporate level rather than the division level. Hence, the corporation's investment in the division equals the division's asset base. The return on investment of an investment center is computed by dividing the income of the center by its asset base (usually total assets):

$$\text{ROI} = \frac{\text{Investment center income}}{\text{Investment center asset base}}$$

ROI can be disaggregated into investment turnover times the return-on-sales ratio:

$$\text{ROI} = \text{Investment turnover} \times \text{Return-on-sales}$$

where

$$\text{Investment turnover} = \frac{\text{Sales}}{\text{Investment center asset base}}$$

and

$$\text{Return-on-sales} = \frac{\text{Investment center income}}{\text{Sales}}$$

When investment turnover is multiplied by return-on-sales, the product is the same as investment center income divided by investment center asset base:

$$\text{ROI} = \frac{\text{Sales}}{\text{Investment center base}} \times \frac{\text{Investment center income}}{\text{Sales}} = \frac{\text{Investment center income}}{\text{Investment center asset base}}$$

Once ROI has been computed, it is compared to some previously identified performance criteria. These include the investment center's previous ROI, overall company ROI, the ROI of similar divisions, or the ROI of nonaffiliated companies that operate in similar markets. The breakdown of ROI into investment turnover and return-on-sales is useful in determining the source of variance in overall performance.

To illustrate the computation and use of ROI, the following information is available concerning the 2012 operations of North American Steel:

Division	Asset Base	Sales	Divisional Income
Maine	$8,000,000	$12,000,000	$1,440,000
Alberta	4,000,000	8,000,000	960,000
Missouri	7,500,000	5,000,000	1,650,000
Tijuana	3,800,000	5,700,000	1,026,000

Using this information and the preceding equations, a set of performance measures are shown in Exhibit 23.2. To illustrate, Maine Division earned a return on its investment base of 18 percent ($1,440,000 ÷ $8,000,000), consisting of an investment turnover of 1.50 ($12,000,000 ÷ $8,000,000) and a return-on-sales of 0.12 ($1,440,000 ÷ $12,000,000). Using such an analysis, the company has three measurement criteria with which to evaluate the performance of Maine Division: (1) ROI, (2) investment turnover, and (3) return-on-sales.

For 2012, North American chose to evaluate its divisions based on company ROI and its interrelated components of investment turnover and return-on-sales. Because each division is different in size, the company evaluation standard is not a simple average of the divisions but is based on desired relationships between assets, sales, and income.

Based on ROI, the Tijuana Division had the best performance, the Alberta Division excelled in investment turnover, and the Missouri Division had the highest return-on-sales. From Exhibit 23.2, the Tijuana Division had the best year because it was the only division that exceeded each of the company's performance criteria. For 2012, each division equaled or exceeded the minimum ROI established by the company even though the component criteria of ROI were not always achieved.

EXHIBIT 23.2 Performance Evaluation Data			
NORTH AMERICAN STEEL Performance Measures For Year Ending June 30, 2012			
	Performance Measures		
	Investment Turnover	× Return-on-Sales	= ROI
Operating unit			
Maine	1.50	0.12	0.18
Alberta	2.00	0.12	0.24
Missouri	0.67	0.33	0.22
Tijuana	1.50	0.18	0.27
Company performance criteria			
Projected minimums.	1.20	0.15	0.18

To properly evaluate each division, the company should study the underlying components of ROI. For the Maine Division, management would want to know why the minimum investment turnover was exceeded while the return-on-sales minimum was not. The Maine Division could have incurred unfavorable cost variances by producing inefficiently. As a result of inefficient production, the return-on-sales declined to a point below the minimum desired level. Evaluating a large operating division based on one financial indicator is difficult. Management should select several key indicators of performance when conducting periodic reviews of its operating segments.

A similar analysis of ROI and its components is useful for planning. In developing plans for 2013, management wants to know the possible effect of changes in the major elements of ROI for the Maine Division. Sensitivity analysis can be used to predict the impact of changes in sales, the investment center asset base, or the investment center income.

Assuming the investment asset base is unchanged, a projected ROI can be determined for the Maine Division for a sales goal of $16,000,000 and an income goal of $1,600,000:

$$\text{ROI} = \frac{\text{Sales}}{\text{Investment center asset base}} \times \frac{\text{Investment center income}}{\text{Sales}}$$

$$= \frac{\$16,000,000}{\$8,000,000} \times \frac{\$1,600,000}{\$16,000,000}$$

$$= 2.0 \times 0.10$$

$$= 0.20, \text{ or } 20 \text{ percent.}$$

ROI increased from 18 to 20 percent, even though the return-on-sales decreased from 12 to 10 percent. The change in turnover from 1.5 to 2.0 more than offset the reduced return-on-sales.

Sensitivity analysis can involve changing only one factor or a combination of factors in the ROI model. When more than one factor is changed, it is important to analyze exactly how much change is caused by each factor.

Statistics such as ROI, investment turnover, and return-on-sales mean little by themselves. They take on meaning only when compared with an objective, a trend, another division, a competitor, or an industry average. Many businesses establish minimum ROIs for each of their divisions, expecting them to attain or exceed this minimum return. The salaries, bonuses, and promotions of division managers can be tied directly to their division's ROI. Without other evaluation techniques, managers often strive for ROI maximization, sometimes to the long-run detriment of the entire organization.

Investment Center Income

Despite the relevance and conceptual simplicity of ROI, a division's ROI cannot be determined until management decides how to measure divisional income and investment. Divisional income equals divisional revenues less divisional operating expenses. Determining divisional revenues is usually a relatively easy task since revenues are typically generated and recorded at the division level, but determining total operating expenses for divisions is more complicated. Because many expenses are incurred at the corporate level for the common benefit of the various operating divisions and to support corporate headquarters operations, the cost assignment issues discussed early in this module affect investment center income.

Direct division expenses are always included in division operating expenses, but there are conflicting viewpoints about how to deal with common corporate expenses. As stated earlier in this module, in corporate annual reports, many companies are required to provide segment revenues and expenses segmented by product lines, geographic territories, customer markets, and so on. Companies also show operating income for their various segments in their annual reports, but they include a category called *corporate* or *unallocated* for company expenses that cannot be reasonably allocated to the various segments. ("Unallocated" typically includes costs for corporate staffs, certain goodwill writeoffs, and non-operational gains and losses.) For example, the Ericsson, Inc., annual report for a recent year includes the following breakdown of its operating income by segments (stated in millions of Swedish kronas):

Networks	6,879 SEK
Professional services	6,990
Multi-media	655
Sony Ericsson	(10,820)
ST-Ericsson	(2,615)
Unallocated	(855)
Inter-segment eliminations	5,684
Total operating income	5,918 SEK

For internal segment reporting, some companies do not allocate corporate costs that cannot be associated closely with individual segments. Other companies insist on allocating all common corporate costs to the operating divisions to emphasize that the company does not earn a profit until revenues have covered all costs. Some top managers believe that since only operating divisions produce revenues, they should also bear all costs, including corporate costs. These managers want to ensure that the sum of the division income for the various segments equals the total income for the company.

Division managers do not control corporate costs; therefore, these costs are seldom relevant in evaluating a division manager's performance. To deal with this conflict, some companies allocate some, or possibly all, common corporate costs in reporting segment operating income, but for ROI calculation purposes exclude allocated corporate costs that are not closely associated with the divisions. These companies include in the ROI calculation costs that represent an identifiable benefit to the divisions but not general corporate costs that provide no identifiable benefits to the divisions. In practice, the treatment of corporate costs for division performance evaluation varies widely.

Investment Center Asset Base

Because the primary purpose for computing ROI is to evaluate the effectiveness of a division's operating management in using the assets entrusted to them, most organizations define *investment* as the average total assets of a division during the evaluation period. For most companies, the *investment base* is defined as each division's operating assets. These normally include those assets held for productive use, such as accounts receivable, inventory, and plant and equipment. Nonproductive assets, such as land for a future plant site, are not included in the investment base of a division but in the investment base for the company.

General corporate assets allocated to divisions should not be included in their bases. Although the divisions might need additional administrative facilities if they were truly independent, they have no control over the headquarters' facilities. The joint nature and use of corporate facility-level expenses make any allocation arbitrary.

Other Valuation Issues

Once divisional investment and income have been operationally defined and ROI computations have been made, the significance of the resulting ratios can still be questioned. Return on investment can be overstated in terms of constant dollars because inflation as well as arbitrary inventory and depreciation procedures cause an undervaluation of the inventory and fixed assets included in the investment center asset base. Asset measurement is particularly troublesome if inventories are valued at last-in, first-out (LIFO) cost and fixed assets were acquired many years ago. A division manager could hesitate to replace an old, inefficient asset with a new, efficient one because the replacement could lower income and ROI through an increased investment base and increased depreciation.

To improve the comparability between divisions with old and new assets when computing ROI, some firms value assets at original cost rather than at net book value (cost less accumulated depreciation). This procedure does not reflect inflation, however. An old asset that cost $120,000 ten years ago is still being compared with an asset that costs $200,000 today. A better solution could be to value old assets at their replacement cost, although replacement costs are often difficult to determine.

> **MANAGERIAL DECISION** **You are the Division Vice President**
>
> Division managers in your company are evaluated primarily based on division return on investment, and you recently received financial reports for your division for the most recent period and discovered that the ROI for your division was 14.5%; whereas, the target ROI for your division set by the CFO and the CEO was 15%. What action can you take to try to avoid missing your performance target for the next period? [Answer, p. 23-23]

Residual Income

Residual income is an often-mentioned alternative to ROI for measuring investment center performance. **Residual income** is the excess of investment center income over the minimum rate or dollar of return. The *minimum rate of return* represents the rate that can be earned on alternative investments of similar risks, which is the opportunity cost of the investment. The *minimum dollar return* is computed as a percentage of the investment center's asset base. When residual income is the primary basis of evaluation, the management of each investment center is encouraged to maximize residual income rather than ROI. (We can again measure assets, sales, income, and so forth, as excluding all nonoperating components; similarly, the investment base can be measured as operating assets less operating liabilities.)

To illustrate the computation, assume that a company requires a minimum return of 12 percent on each division's investment base. The residual income of a division with an annual net operating income of $2,000,000 and an investment base of $15,000,000 is $200,000 as computed here:

Division income	$2,000,000
Minimum return ($15,000,000 × 0.12)	(1,800,000)
Residual income	$ 200,000

Economic Value Added

A variation of residual income, referred to as **economic value added** or **EVA®**, is also often used as a basis for evaluating investment center performance. (The term EVA is a registered trademark of the financial consulting firm of Stern Stewart and Company.) EVA is equal to income after taxes less the cost of capital employed. The three significant changes from the residual income computation in applying EVA are the use of an organization's weighted average cost of capital as the minimum return, *net assets* as the evaluation base, and after-tax income. **Weighted average cost of capital** is an average of the after-tax cost of all long-term borrowing and the cost of equity[4]; **net assets** are total assets less current liabilities. Economic value is added only if a division's taxable income exceeds its net cost of

---

[4] Weighted average cost of capital computations are covered in introductory corporate finance textbooks.

investing. (We can again measure assets, sales, income, and so forth, as excluding all nonoperating components; similarly, the net asset base can be measured as operating assets less operating liabilities.)

Using the preceding situation, assume that the company has a cost of capital of 10 percent, $1,800,000 in current liabilities, and a 30 percent tax rate. The economic value-added is $80,000, computed as follows:

Division income after taxes ($2,000,000 × 0.70)	$1,400,000
Cost of capital employed [($15,000,000 − $1,800,000) × 0.10]	(1,320,000)
Economic value added	$ 80,000

Another differentiating characteristic of the EVA model is that it usually corrects for potential distortions in economic net income caused by generally accepted accounting principles (GAAP). In calculating EVA, the user can abandon any accounting principles that are viewed as distorting the measurement of wealth creation. In practice, EVA consultants have identified up to 150 different adjustments to GAAP income and equity that must be made to restore equity and income to their true economic values. Most companies use no more than about five adjustments (such as the capitalization of research and development cost and the elimination of goodwill write-offs).

Proponents of EVA argue that it is the best measure of managerial performance from the standpoint of maximizing the market value added to a firm through managerial decisions. They maintain that **market value added (MVA)**, which is the increase in market value of the firm for the period, is the definitive measure of wealth creation and that MVA is maximized by maximizing EVA. By maximizing the excess of economic net income over the cost of all outside capital invested in the firm, the firm should maximize its MVA in the long run.

One might ask why we should use EVA to estimate managerial contribution to the maximization of MVA, when we could simply measure how much market value has been added to the firm by considering changes in stock prices. In practice this does not work well because of short-run changes in market prices caused by overall market factors, not just firm-specific factors, and the inability of market prices to reflect divisional wealth creation that is not transparent. Also, many firms are not publicly traded, which makes determining market value changes problematic. Finally, companies want to measure managerial performance over specific segments of a firm, as well as the firm as a whole, but market values for individual segments are seldom available.

EVA provides a good operational metric for assessing managers' performance in terms of maximizing MVA over time. It is a model that can be used to guide managerial action. Companies that use EVA for evaluating performance use it in making a broad range of decisions such as evaluating capital expenditure proposals, adding or dropping a product line, or acquiring another company. Only alternatives that provide economic value are accepted. The following Businesss Insight box discusses the impact of adopting an EVA financial management system at Ryder Systems.

BUSINESS INSIGHT   **Ryder System Touts Its EVA Performance**

At a recent investment conference sponsored by the financial services firm of Robert W. Baird & Co., the CEO of Ryder Systems, Greg Swienton, stated that "we have not only maintained, but we have increased our economic value added per unit sold even during the downturn." When asked why the EVA is up, Swienton attributed it to managerial discipline of only investing in assets with a high EVA, but also to the sales force. He stated that "they earn more money when they sell higher EVA.... So I think the fact [is] that they will look to try to get every additional dollar they can, sell additional add-on services, [and] get more EVA per unit, because that's how they earn a better living, not just moving units or selling revenue." These statements reflect a deep commitment to the EVA model at Ryder and to having the model deeply imbedded in the managerial performance evaluation and compensation system throughout the company.

Source: Ryder System, Inc. at Baird Industrial Conference," *CQ Transcriptions*, November 9, 2010.

Which Measure Is Best?

Many executives view residual income or EVA as a better measure of managers' performance than ROI. They believe that residual income and EVA encourages managers to make profitable investments that managers might reject if being measured exclusively by ROI.

To illustrate, assume that three divisions of Color Company have an opportunity to make an investment of $100,000 that requires $10,000 of additional current liabilities and that will generate a return of 20 percent. The manager of the Paint Division is evaluated using ROI, the manager of the Ink Division is evaluated using residual income, and the manager of the Dye Division is evaluated using economic value added. The current ROI of each division is 24 percent. Each division has a current income of $120,000, a minimum return of 18 percent on invested capital, and a cost of capital of 14 percent. If each division has a current investment base of $500,000, current liabilities of $40,000, and a tax rate of 30 percent, the effect of the proposed investment on each division's performance is as follows:

	Current	+	Proposed	=	Total
Paint Division					
Investment center income	$120,000		$ 20,000		$140,000
Asset base	$500,000		$100,000		$600,000
ROI	24%		20%		23.3%
Ink Division					
Asset base	$500,000		$100,000		$600,000
Investment center income	$120,000		$ 20,000		$140,000
Minimum return (0.18 × base)	(90,000)		(18,000)		(108,000)
Residual income	$ 30,000		$ 2,000		$ 32,000
Dye Division					
Assets	$500,000		$100,000		$600,000
Current liabilities	(40,000)		(10,000)		(50,000)
Evaluation base	$460,000		$ 90,000		$550,000
Investment center income	$120,000		$ 20,000		$140,000
Income taxes (30%)	(36,000)		(6,000)		(42,000)
Income after taxes	84,000		14,000		98,000
Cost of capital (0.14 × base)	(64,400)		(12,600)		(77,000)
Economic value added	$ 19,600		$ 1,400		$ 21,000

The Paint Division manager will not want to make the new investment because it reduces the current ROI from 24 percent to 23.3 percent. This is true, even though the company's minimum return is only 18 percent. Not wanting to explain a decline in the division's ROI, the manager will probably reject the opportunity even though it could have benefited the company as a whole.

The Ink Division manager will probably be happy to accept the new project because it increases residual income by $2,000. Any investment that provides a return more than the required minimum of 18 percent will be acceptable to the Ink Division manager. Given a profit maximization goal for the organization, the residual income method is preferred over ROI evaluations because it encourages division managers to accept all projects with returns above the 18 percent cutoff. The same is true for the Dye Division manager, although the EVA increase is not as high as that of the residual income because it has a different base.

The primary disadvantage of the residual income and EVA methods as comparative evaluation tools is that they measure performance in absolute dollars rather than percentages. Although they can be used to compare period-to-period results of the same division or with similar-size divisions, they cannot be used effectively to compare the performance of divisions of substantially different sizes. For example, the residual income of a multimillion dollar sales division should be higher than that of a half-million-dollar sales division. Because most performance evaluations and comparisons are made between units or alternative investments of different sizes, ROI continues to be extensively used. The following Business Insight box discusses the use of multiple evaluation models for assessing IT projects.

BUSINESS INSIGHT	Methods used to Evaluate IT Projects at Harrah's

A recent article in *Computer World* discusses the methods used to evaluate IT project proposals by IT managers and corporate executives. The article outlines the differences between "operational projects" aimed at saving money, and "strategic projects" aimed at making money. Harrah's Entertainment was one of several companies cited in the article. Harrah's Entertainment uses three metrics to prioritize IT projects: net present value, internal rate of return, and economic value added. "Increased sales is usually the key benefit to be measured, but the business sponsor of a project works with IT to measure softer benefits such as increased guest visits at Harrah's hotels and casinos, customer satisfaction, and even employee satisfaction." Using more than one metric has pros and cons, says Harrah's CIO Tim Stanley. "Using multiple criteria to assess a project provides a robust framework for decisions," he says. "Each tool takes into consideration the investment and the expected business value or return, and we are not limited to a single point of view." But, he adds, "the prospect of sophisticated financial analyses can inhibit some people from submitting ideas for consideration."

Source: Gary Anthes, "What's Your Project Worth? Figuring it out isn't easy. But you can't manage what you don't measure," *Computer World*, March 10, 2008.

BALANCED SCORECARD

LO4 Describe the balanced scorecard as a comprehensive performance measurement system.

Although financial measures have been emphasized throughout this text, several sections stress that other measures, specifically qualitative measures, are important in evaluating managerial performance. This section examines one popular method of performance evaluation using *both* financial and nonfinancial information.

We might ask: why not use just financial measures? First, no single financial measure captures all performance aspects of an organization. More than one measure must be used. Second, financial measures have reporting time lags that could hinder timely decision making. Third, financial measures might not accurately capture the information needed for current decision making because of the delay that sometimes occurs between making financial investments and receiving their results. For example, building a new nuclear power plant can take several years with the investment in total assets increasing the entire time without generating any revenues.

Balanced Scorecard Framework

Comprehensive performance measurement systems are one suggested solution. The basic premise is to establish a set of diverse key performance indicators to monitor performance. The **balanced scorecard** is a performance measurement system that includes financial and operational measures related to a firm's goals and strategies. The balanced scorecard comprises several categories of measurements, the most common of which include the following:

- Financial
- Customer satisfaction
- Internal processes
- Innovation and learning

A balanced scorecard is usually a set of reports required of all common operating units in an organization. To facilitate the periodic evaluation of performance, a cover sheet (or sheets for a large operation) can be used to summarize the performance of each area using the established criteria for each category.

For example, a chain of bagel shops might have a balanced scorecard that looks something like the one in Exhibit 23.3. This balanced scorecard uses four categories for evaluation and includes financial and nonfinancial information. Each category being monitored has information from the previous period and the standard related to the category. The report should always include the current period, at least one previous period, and some standard. Each store manager should attach documentation and an appropriate explanation as to the change in the measurements during the reporting period.

EXHIBIT 23.3 Balanced Scorecard Illustration			
	Standard	Prior Period	Current Period
Key financial indicators			
Cash flow	$ 25,000	$ 28,000	$ 21,000
Return on investment (ROI).	0.18	0.22	0.19
Sales.	$4,400,000	$4,494,000	$4,342,000
Key customer indicators			
Average customers per hour	75	80	71
Number of customer complaints per period.	22	21	17
Number of sales returns per period	10	8	5
Key operating indicators			
Bagels sold/produced per day ratio	0.96	0.93	0.91
Daily units lost (burned, dropped, etc.).	25	32	34
Employee turnover per period	0.10	0.07	0.00
Key growth and innovation indicators			
New products introduced during period.	1	1	0
Products discontinued during period	1	1	1
Number of sales promotions	3	3	2
Special offers, discounts, etc.	4	5	3

In making assessments with the evaluation categories, it is important to consider both trailing and leading performance measures. *Trailing measures* look backward at historical data while *leading measures* provide some idea of what to expect currently or in the near future. For example, in the financial category, ROI is a trailing indicator while a budget of production units and costs for the next period is a leading indicator. In the customer category, the number of sales invoices per store might tell us whether each store is maintaining its customer base (a trailing indicator) while the number of product complaints per 1000 invoices might be a leading indicator of customer satisfaction, quality control problems, and future sales.

The use of balanced scorecard systems to monitor and assess managerial and organizational performance is increasing worldwide. The following Research Insight discusses characteristics of successful balanced scorecard implementations.

RESEARCH INSIGHT   Implementing a Successful Balanced Scorecard

A group of professors researched balanced scorecard systems and identified five crucial characteristics of a successful scorecard implementation:

1. Fairness, or equality, in the assessment process—the system must be perceived by managers to be fair, regarding both the fairness of outcomes and the fairness of the process that generates those outcomes.

2. Communication—there must be communication of corporate goals to ensure an understanding of the linkages between daily actions and those goals.

3. Involvement—evaluations are more effective if users develop their own scorecards, rather than using one developed by someone else higher up in the organization.

4. Stretch goals—there is a de-motivating effect when goals are seen as either too easy or two aggressive.

5. Meaningful rewards systems—scorecard performance of individuals or business units should be linked to specific rewards such as bonuses, raises, and promotions.

Source: Thomas L. Albright, Christopher M. Burgess, Aleecia R. Hibbets, and Michael L. Roberts, "How to Transition from Assessing Performance to Enhancing Performance With Balanced Scorecard Goal Action Plans," *The Journal of Corporate Accounting & Finance*, September/October 2010, pp 69-74.

A balanced scorecard gives management a perspective of the organization's performance on a recurring set of criteria. Since each reporting unit knows what reports are expected, no one is surprised by changing monthly requests for data. Because the multiple perspectives provide management a broad analysis of the organization's performance, it allows them to determine how and where the goals and objectives are either being achieved or not achieved.

For most management teams, the balanced scorecard highlights trade-offs between measures. For example, a substantial increase in customer satisfaction can result in a short-run decrease in ROI because the extra effort to please customers is expensive, thereby reducing ROI. A balanced scorecard can be filtered down the organization with successively lower-level operating units having their own scorecards that mimic those of the higher-level units. This provides all levels of management an opportunity to evaluate operations from more than just a financial perspective.

As with all management tools and techniques, the use of the balanced scorecard must be incorporated with the other information sources within the organization. Just as the accounting information system cannot stand alone in managing a business, neither can the balanced scorecard. Some areas could need extensive accounting information in great detail to make the best possible decision while other areas need great detail in production or service integration to be at the right place at the right time. By using a multi-faceted approach to managing, the organization should be able to better establish an operating strategy that coincides with its overall goals and objectives.

Balanced Scorecard and Strategy

When a balanced scorecard system is fully utilized to monitor and evaluate an organization's progress, it becomes a system for operationalizing the organization's strategy. Having a goal to maximize shareholder value or generate a certain income does not constitute a strategy. Maximizing shareholder value can be an overarching corporate goal, but it will not likely be realized without a well-developed strategy that identifies and establishes a balanced set of goals on various dimensions of performance.

A balanced scorecard can be the primary vehicle for translating strategy into action and establishing accountability for performance. The balanced scorecard identifies the areas of managerial action that are believed to be the drivers of corporate achievement. If the corporate goal is to increase ROI or residual income, the balanced scorecard should include key performance indicators that drive these measures.

An interesting parallel to the successful management of a company can be drawn by considering the key performance indicators the manager of a professional baseball team uses in setting goals and evaluating progress. The manager of the New York Yankees does not just tell his players and managers at the beginning of the baseball season that the team's goal is to win the World Series or even a certain number of ball games. The win-loss record is only one metric used to set goals and evaluate performance for a baseball team. The manager looks at many different drivers of success related to hitting, pitching, and fielding, including the earned-run averages of the pitchers, the batting and on-base averages of hitters, the number of errors per game by fielders, and the number of bases stolen by base runners. At the end of the season, the manager measures success not just by whether the Yankees won the World Series, but also by the batting average, number of home runs, and number of bases stolen by individual players, and whether or not a team member won a Golden Glove award or the Cy Young award. These are all measures by which to evaluate achievement and strategic accomplishment. By achieving the goals for each of these areas of the game, the win-loss ratio will take care of itself. If the win-loss results are not acceptable, then the manager adjusts his strategic goals with respect to the key performance indicators (or the manager is dismissed).

Like a baseball team, a company can use a balanced scorecard to develop performance metrics for managers from the top of the company to the lowest-level department. The scorecard becomes a vehicle for communicating the factors that are key to the success of managers, factors that upper management will monitor in evaluating the success of lower managers in carrying out the corporate strategy. To make balanced scorecards more user friendly, several companies use performance monitoring **dashboards**, which are computer generated graphics that present scorecard results using graphics, some of which mimic the instrument displays on an automobile dashboard.

The following Business Insight provides an illustration of dashboard graphics.

BUSINESS INSIGHT **Balanced Scorecard Dashboard**

Balanced scorecard dashboards provide information about an organization in an "at-a-glance" format. Many software companies now provide utilities for generating dashboards from SAP, Excel, Quick-Books, and other databases. The following is an example of a dashboard for Sonatica, a fictional company, designed by Dundas Dashboard for executive assessment of financial performance. The shaded tabs present financial information graphics for Sales and Support (students may visit the web page referenced below to view these tabs). Additional screens would provide performance data on other scorecard dimensions such as internal processes, customers, and innovation and growth.

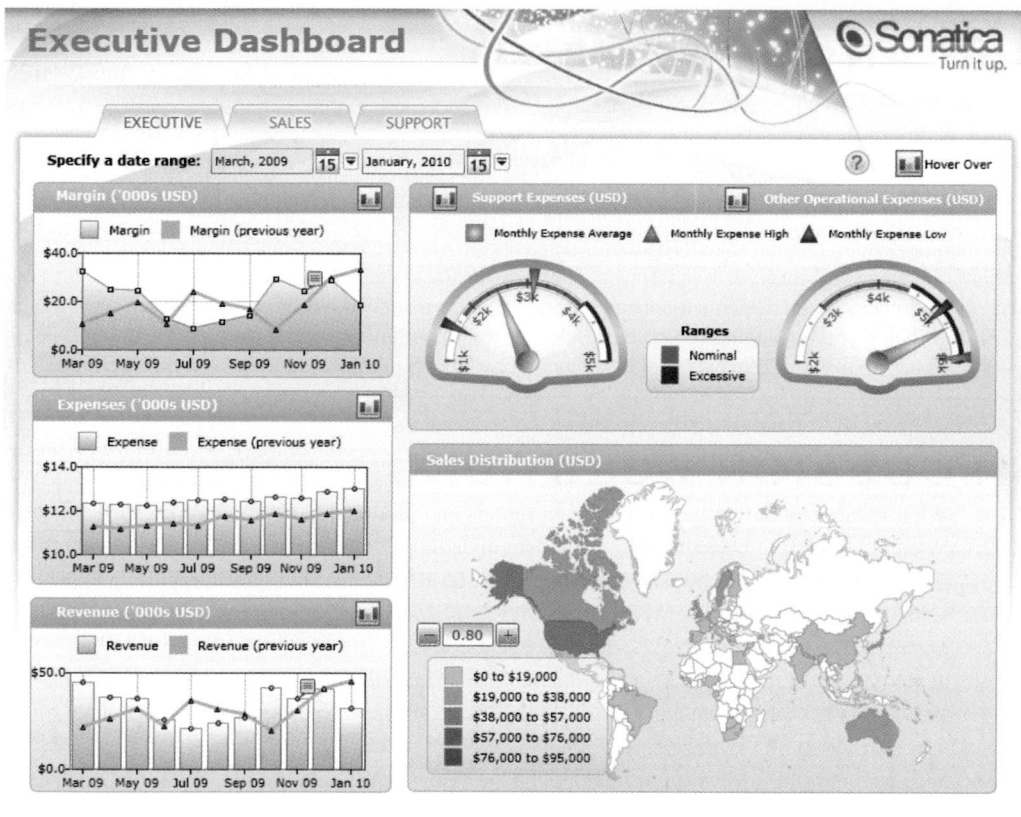

Source: *http://media1.dundas.com/DashboardDemo/Viewer.aspx?view=Sonatica Performance Dashboards*

MODULE-END REVIEW

Pareto International, a decentralized organization that manufactures specialty construction products, has three divisions, Commercial, Industrial, and Residential. Corporate management desires a minimum return of 15 percent on its investments and has a 20 percent tax rate. The divisions' 2012 results follow (in thousands):

Division	Income	Investment
Commercial	$30,000	$200,000
Industrial..........	50,000	250,000
Residential	22,000	100,000

The company is planning an expansion project in 2013 that will cost $50,000,000 and return $9,000,000 per year.

Required

a. Compute the ROI for each division for 2012.

b. Compute the residual income for each division for 2012.

c. Rank the divisions according to their ROI and residual income.

d. Assume that other income and investments will remain unchanged. Determine the effect of the project by itself. What is the effect on ROI and residual income, if the new project is added to each division?

The solution is on page 23-38.

GUIDANCE ANSWER

MANAGERIAL DECISION   **You are the Division Vice President**

ROI is primarily a measure of the profitability of a division's assets, which is in turn a measure of how effectively the investment in assets was used to generate sales, and how profitable those sales were. ROI is driven by investment (or asset) turnover (which is division sales divided by assets) and return on sales (which is division net income divided division sales). Therefore, increasing ROI is similar to a simultaneous balancing act involving controlling sales, expenses, and asset investment. You can increase ROI by increasing sales more than expenses, while holding asset investment constant, or by other combinations of these three variables that ultimately increase ROI. If you adjust one of these variables, at the same time you must keep your eye on the other two variables or you may not achieve your goal of increasing ROI.

DISCUSSION QUESTIONS

Q23-1. What is the relationship between segment reports and product reports?

Q23-2. What is a reporting objective? How is it determined?

Q23-3. Can a company have more than one type of first-level statement in segment reporting?

Q23-4. Explain the relationships between any two levels of statements in segment reporting.

Q23-5. Distinguish between direct and indirect segment costs.

Q23-6. What types of information are needed before management should decide to drop a segment?

Q23-7. In what types of organizations and for what purpose are transfer prices used?

Q23-8. What problems arise when transfer pricing is used?

Q23-9. When do transfer prices lead to suboptimization? How can suboptimization be minimized? Can it be eliminated? Why or why not?

Q23-10. For what purpose do organizations use return on investment? Why is this measure preferred to net income?

Q23-11. What advantages do residual income and EVA have over ROI for segment evaluations?

Q23-12. Contrast the difference between residual income and EVA.

Q23-13. Explain how a balanced scorecard helps with the evaluation process of internal operations.

Q23-14. How can a balanced scorecard be used as a strategy implementation tool?

Assignments with the ✓ in the margin are available in an online homework system.
See the Preface of the book for details.

MINI EXERCISES

M23-15. Multiple Levels of Segment Reporting   (LO1)

Sisco, Inc., manufactures four different lines of computer devices: modems, routers, servers, and drives. Each of the product lines is produced in all of the company's three plants: Abbeyville, Bakersville, and Charlottesville. Marketing efforts of the company are divided into five regions: East, West, South, North, and Central.

Required

a. Develop a reporting schematic that illustrates how the company might prepare single-level reports segmented on three different bases.

b. Develop a segment reporting schematic that has three different levels. Be sure to identify each segment's level. Briefly explain why you chose the primary-level segment.

M23-16. Income Statements Segmented by Territory (LO1)

Script, Inc., has two product lines. The September income statements of each product line and the company are as follows:

SCRIPT, INC.			
Product Line and Company Income Statements			
For Month of September			
	Pens	**Pencils**	**Total**
Sales..........................	$25,000	$30,000	$55,000
Less variable expenses	(10,000)	(12,000)	(22,000)
Contribution margin	15,000	18,000	33,000
Less direct fixed expenses..........	(9,000)	(7,000)	(16,000)
Product margin...................	$ 6,000	$11,000	17,000
Less common fixed expenses			(6,000)
Net income...			$11,000

Pens and pencils are sold in two territories, Florida and Alabama, as follows:

	Florida	**Alabama**
Pen sales	$15,000	$10,000
Pencil sales	9,000	21,000
Total sales........	$24,000	$31,000

The preceding common fixed expenses are traceable to each territory as follows:

Florida fixed expenses.......................	$2,000
Alabama fixed expenses	3,000
Home office administration fixed expenses........	1,000
Total common fixed expenses	$6,000

The direct fixed expenses of pens, $9,000, and of pencils, $7,000, cannot be identified with either territory. The company's accountants were unable to allocate any of the common fixed expenses to the various segments.

Required

Prepare income statements segmented by territory for September, including a column for the entire firm.

M23-17. Income Statements Segmented by Products (LO1)

Clay Consulting Firm provides three types of client services in three health-care-related industries. The income statement for July is as follows:

Clay Consulting Firm		
Income Statement		
For Month of July		
Sales........................		$900,000
Less variable costs..............		(605,000)
Contribution margin		295,000
Less fixed expenses		
Service	$70,000	
Selling and administrative........	65,000	(135,000)
Net income...................		$160,000

The sales, contribution margin ratios, and direct fixed expenses for the three types of services are as follows:

	Hospitals	Physicians	Nursing Care
Sales.....................................	$350,000	$250,000	$300,000
Contribution margin ratio	30%	40%	30%
Direct fixed expenses of services..............	$ 20,000	$ 18,000	$ 16,000
Allocated common fixed services expense	$ 1,000	$ 1,000	$ 1,500

Required
Prepare income statements segmented by client categories. Include a column for the entire firm in the statement.

 M23-18. Internal or External Acquisitions: No Opportunity Costs   (LO2)
The Van Division of MotoCar Corporation has offered to purchase 180,000 wheels from the Wheel Division for $42 per wheel. At a normal volume of 500,000 wheels per year, production costs per wheel for the Wheel Division are as follows:

Direct materials	$15
Direct labor...........	10
Variable overhead......	6
Fixed overhead........	18
Total	$49

The Wheel Division has been selling 500,000 wheels per year to outside buyers at $58 each. Capacity is 700,000 wheels per year. The Van Division has been buying wheels from outside suppliers at $55 per wheel.

Required
a. Should the Wheel Division manager accept the offer? Show computations.
b. From the standpoint of the company, will the internal sale be beneficial?

M23-19. Transfer Prices at Full Cost with Excess Capacity: Divisional Viewpoint   (LO2)
Koji Cameras, Inc., has a Disposables Division that produces a camera that sells for $10 per unit in the open market. The cost of the product is $6 (variable manufacturing of $4, plus fixed manufacturing of $2). Total fixed manufacturing costs are $140,000 at the normal annual production volume of 70,000 units. The Overseas Division has offered to buy 15,000 units at the full cost of $6. The Disposables Division has excess capacity, and the 15,000 units can be produced without interfering with the current outside sales of 70,000 units. The total fixed cost of the Disposables Division will not change.

Required
Explain whether the Disposables Division should accept or reject the offer. Show calculations.

M23-20. Transfer Pricing with Excess Capacity: Divisional and Corporate Viewpoints   (LO2)
Eclectic Art Company has a Print Division that is currently producing 100,000 prints per year but has a capacity of 150,000 prints. The variable costs of each print are $30, and the annual fixed costs are $1,350,000. The prints sell for $45 in the open market. The company's Retail Division wants to buy 50,000 prints at $27 each. The Print Division manager refuses the order because the price is below variable cost. The Retail Division manager argues that the order should be accepted because it will lower the fixed cost per print from $9 to $6.

Required
a. Should the Retail Division order be accepted? Why or why not?
b. From the viewpoints of the Print Division and the company, should the order be accepted if the manager of the Retail Division intends to sell each print in the outside market for $42 after incurring additional costs of $10 per print?
c. What action should the company take, assuming it believes in divisional autonomy?

 M23-21. ROI and Residual Income: Impact of a New Investment   (LO3)
The Mustang Division of Detroit Motors had an operating income of $900,000 and net assets of $4,000,000. Detroit Motors has a target rate of return of 16 percent.

Required

a. Compute the return on investment.

b. Compute the residual income.

c. The Mustang Division has an opportunity to increase operating income by $200,000 with an $850,000 investment in assets.

    1. Compute the Mustang Division's return on investment if the project is undertaken. (Round your answer to three decimal places.)

    2. Compute the Mustang Division's residual income if the project is undertaken.

M23-22. ROI: Fill in the Unknowns (LO3)

Provide the missing data in the following situations:

	North American Division	Asian Division	European Division
Sales.	?	$5,000,000	?
Net operating income.	$100,000	$ 200,000	$144,000
Operating assets	?	?	$800,000
Return on investment.	16%	10%	?
Return on sales	0.04	?	0.12
Investment turnover	?	?	1.5

M23-23. Selection of Balanced Scorecard Items (LO4)

The International Accountants' Association is a professional association. Its current membership totals 97,600 worldwide. The association operates from a central headquarters in New Zealand but has local membership units throughout the world. The local units hold monthly meetings to discuss recent developments in accounting and to hear professional speakers on topics of interest. The association's journal, *International Accountant,* is published monthly with feature articles and topical interest areas. The association publishes books and reports and sponsors continuing education courses. A statement of revenues and expenses follows:

INTERNATIONAL ACCOUNTANTS' ASSOCIATION Statement of Revenues and Expenses For Year Ending November 30, 2012		
Revenues		$26,700,000
Expenses		
Salaries.	$14,000,000	
Other personnel costs	3,400,000	
Occupancy costs	2,000,000	
Reimbursement to local units.	800,000	
Other membership services	500,000	
Printing and paper	320,000	
Postage and shipping.	114,000	
General and administrative.	538,000	(21,672,000)
Excess of revenues over expenses		$ 5,028,000

Additional information follows:

• Membership dues are $200 per year, of which $50 is considered to cover a one-year subscription to the association's journal. Other benefits include membership in the association and unit affiliation.

• One-year subscriptions to *International Accountant* are sold to nonmembers for $80 each. A total of 2,500 of these subscriptions were sold. In addition to subscriptions, the journal generated $200,000 in advertising revenue. The cost per magazine was $20.

• A total of 30,000 technical reports were sold by the Books and Reports Department at an average unit selling price of $45. Average costs per publication were $12.

• The association offers a variety of continuing education courses to both members and nonmembers. During 2012, the one-day course, which cost participants an average of $250 each, was attended by 31,300 people. A total of 1,985 people took two-day courses at a cost of $400 per person.

• General and administrative expenses include all other costs incurred by the corporate staff to operate the association.

- The organization has net capital assets of $44,000,000 and had an actual cost of capital of 11 percent.

Required

a. Give some examples of key financial performance indicators (no computations needed) that could be part of a balanced scorecard for the IAA.

b. Give some examples of key customer and operating performance indicators (no computations needed) that could be part of a balanced scorecard for IAA.

EXERCISES

 E23-24. Appropriate Transfer Prices: Opportunity Costs   (LO2)

Plains Peanut Butter Company recently acquired a peanut-processing company that has a normal annual capacity of 4,000,000 pounds and that sold 2,800,000 pounds last year at a price of $2.00 per pound. The purpose of the acquisition is to furnish peanuts for the peanut butter plant, which needs 1,600,000 pounds of peanuts per year. It has been purchasing peanuts from suppliers at the market price. Production costs per pound of the peanut-processing company are as follows:

Direct materials	$0.50
Direct labor	0.25
Variable overhead	0.12
Fixed overhead at normal capacity	0.20
Total	$1.07

Management is trying to decide what transfer price to use for sales from the newly acquired Peanut Division to the Peanut Butter Division. The manager of the Peanut Division argues that $2.00, the market price, is appropriate. The manager of the Peanut Butter Division argues that the cost price of $1.07 (or perhaps even less) should be used since fixed overhead costs should be recomputed. Any output of the Peanut Division up to 2,800,000 pounds that is not sold to the Peanut Butter Division could be sold to regular customers at $2.00 per pound.

Required

a. Compute the annual gross profit for the Peanut Division using a transfer price of $2.00.

b. Compute the annual gross profit for the Peanut Division using a transfer price of $1.07.

c. What transfer price(s) will lead the manager of the Peanut Butter Division to act in a manner that will maximize company profits?

E23-25. Negotiating a Transfer Price with Excess Capacity   (LO2)

The Foundry Division of Augusta Pumps, Inc., produces metal parts that are sold to the company's Assembly Division and to outside customers. Operating data for the Foundry Division for 2012 are as follows:

	To the Assembly Division	To Outside Customers	Total
Sales			
400,000 parts × $5.50	$2,200,000		
300,000 parts × $6.00		$1,800,000	$4,000,000
Variable expenses at $2.00	(800,000)	(600,000)	(1,400,000)
Contribution margin	1,400,000	1,200,000	2,600,000
Fixed expenses*	(700,000)	(525,000)	1,225,000
Net income	$ 700,000	$ 675,000	$1,375,000

*Allocated on the basis of unit sales.

The Assembly Division has just received an offer from an outside supplier to supply parts at $3.50 each. The Foundry Division manager is not willing to meet the $3.50 price. She argues that it costs her $3.75 per part to produce and sell to the Assembly Division, so she would show no profit on the Assembly Division sales. Sales to outside customers are at a maximum, 300,000 parts.

Required

a. Verify the Foundry Division's $3.75 unit cost figure.

b. Should the Foundry Division meet the outside price of $3.50 for Assembly Division sales? Explain.

c. Could the Foundry Division meet the $3.50 price and still show a net profit for sales to the Assembly Division? Show computations.

E23-26. Dual Transfer Pricing (LO2)

The Greek Company has two divisions, Beta and Gamma. Gamma Division produces a product at a variable cost of $6 per unit, and sells 150,000 units to outside customers at $10 per unit and 40,000 units to Beta Division at variable cost plus 40 percent. Under the dual transfer price system, Beta Division pays only the variable cost per unit. Gamma Division's fixed costs are $250,000 per year. Beta Division sells its finished product to outside customers at $23 per unit. Beta has variable costs of $5 per unit, in addition to the costs from Gamma Division. Beta Division's annual fixed costs are $170,000. There are no beginning or ending inventories.

Required

a. Prepare the income statements for the two divisions and the company as a whole.

b. Why is the income for the company less than the sum of the profit figures shown on the income statements for the two divisions? Explain.

E23-27. ROI and Residual Income: Basic Computations (LO3)

Watkins Associated
Industries

Watkins Associated Industries is a highly diversified company with three divisions: Trucking, Seafood, and Construction. Assume that the company uses return on investment and residual income as two of the evaluation tools for division managers. The company has a minimum desired rate of return on investment of 10 percent with a 30 percent tax rate. Selected operating data for three divisions of the company follow.

	Trucking Division	Seafood Division	Construction Division
Sales......................	$1,200,000	$750,000	$900,000
Operating assets	600,000	250,000	350,000
Net operating income..........	102,000	56,000	59,000

Required

a. Compute the return on investment for each division. (Round answers to three decimal places.)

b. Compute the residual income for each division.

E23-28. ROI and Residual Income: Assessing Performance (LO3)

Refer to the computations in the previous exercise E23-27. Assess the performance of the division managers, basing your conclusions on ROI. Assess the performance of the division managers, basing your conclusions on Residual Income. Which manager is doing the best job?

E23-29. ROI, Residual Income, and EVA with Different Bases (LO3)

Paradyme Company has a target return on capital of 12 percent. The following financial information is available for October ($ thousands):

	Software Division (Value Base)		Consulting Division (Value Base)		Venture Capital Division (Value Base)	
	Book	Current	Book	Current	Book	Current
Sales..............	$100,000	$100,000	$200,000	$200,000	$800,000	$800,000
Income	12,000	10,000	16,000	17,000	50,000	52,000
Assets.............	60,000	80,000	90,000	100,000	600,000	580,000
Liabilities...........	10,000	10,000	14,000	14,000	40,000	40,000

Required

a. Compute the return on investment using both book and current values for each division. (Round answers to three decimal places.)

b. Compute the residual income for both book and current values for each division.

c. Compute the economic value added income for both book and current values for each division if the tax rate is 35 percent and the weighted average cost of capital is 11 percent.

d. Does book value or current value provide a better basis for performance evaluation? Which division do you consider the most successful?

E23-30. Balanced Scorecard Preparation (LO4)

The following information is in addition to that presented in Mini Exercise 23-23 for the International Accountants' Association. For the year ended November 30, 2012, the organization had set a membership goal of 100,000 members with the following anticipated results:

INTERNATIONAL ACCOUNTANTS' ASSOCIATION Planned Revenues and Expenses For Year Ending November 30, 2012		
Revenues		$28,000,000
Expenses		
Salaries	$13,950,000	
Other personnel costs	3,450,000	
Occupancy costs	1,900,000	
Reimbursement to local units	780,000	
Other membership services	525,000	
Printing and paper	300,000	
Postage and shipping	110,000	
General and administrative	550,000	(21,565,000)
Excess of revenues over expenses		$ 6,435,000

Additional information follows:
- Membership dues were increased from $180 to $200 at the beginning of the year.
- One-year subscriptions to *International Accountant* were anticipated to be 2,400 units.
- Advertising revenue was budgeted at $225,000. Each magazine was budgeted at $18.
- A total of 28,000 technical reports were anticipated at an average price of $40 with average costs of $11.
- The budgeted one-day courses had an anticipated attendance of 32,000 with an average fee of $225. The two-day courses had an anticipated attendance of 3,000 with an average fee of $385 per person.
- The organization began the year with net capital assets of $40,000,000 with a planned cost of capital of 11 percent.

Required

a. Prepare a balanced scorecard for IAA for November 2012 with calculated key performance indicators presented in two columns for planned performance and actual performance—include key financial, customer, and operating performance indicators.

b. Which of the evaluation areas you selected indicated success and which indicated failure?

c. Give some explanations of the successes and failures.

E23-31. Balanced Scorecard (LO4)

The following alphabetically ordered list of financial and nonfinancial performance metrics is provided for Midwest, Inc.

Average call wait	New product acceptance rate
Average customer survey rating	New product revenue
Employee turnover ratio	New product ROI
Expense as a % of revenue	Net profit
Expense variance %	Net profit margin
Fulfillment %	Number of complaints
Headcount growth	Number of defects reported
Industry quality rating	Service error rate
Job offer acceptance rate	Time to market on new products
Market share	Unique repeat customer count
New customer count	Year over year revenue growth
New customer sales value	

Required:

a. Assign the above metrics to the four balanced scorecard categories of (1) Financial Success, (2) Customer Satisfaction and Brand Improvement, (3) Business Process Improvement, (4) Learning and Growth of Motivated Workforce.

b. Comment on the use of balanced scorecard versus a single financial measure such as ROI or EVA.

PROBLEMS

P23-32. Multiple Segment Reports   (LO1)

International Enterprises, Incorporated, sells telecommunication products throughout the world in three sales territories: Europe, Asia, and the Americas. For July, all $500,000 of administrative expense is traceable to the territories, except $100,000, which is common to all units and cannot be traced or allocated to the sales territories. The percentage of product line sales made in each of the sales territories and the assignment of traceable fixed expenses follow:

	Sales Territory			
	Europe	Asia	The Americas	Total
Handset sales..................	40%	50%	10%	100%
Switchboard sales	40	40	20	100
Automated switches sales........	20	20	60	100
Fixed administrative expense......	$150,000	$150,000	$100,000	$ 400,000
Fixed selling expense............	$300,000	$600,000	$600,000	$1,500,000

The manufacturing takes place in one large facility with three distinct manufacturing operations. Selected product-line cost data follow.

	Handset	Switchboard	Automated Switches	Total
Variable costs...........................	$ 18	$ 790	$ 1,975	
Depreciation and supervision..............	150,000	150,000	120,000	$450,000*
Other mfg. overhead (common)...				100,000
Fixed administrative expense (common).......................................				500,000
Fixed selling expense (common)				1,500,000

*Includes common costs of $30,000

The unit sales and selling prices for each product follow.

	Unit Sales	Selling Price
Handset	10,000	$45
Switchboard.....	2,000	1,500
Automated	1,500	3,200

Required

a. Prepare an income statement for July segmented by product line. Include a column for the entire firm.

b. Prepare an income statement for July segmented by sales territory. Include a column for the entire firm.

c. Prepare an income statement for July by product line for The Americas sales territory. Include a column for the territory as a whole.

d. Discuss the value of multilevel segment reporting as a managerial tool. Compare and contrast the benefits of the reports generated in parts a, b, and c.

P23-33. Segment Reporting and Analysis   (LO1)

Minnesota Bread Company bakes three products: donuts, bread, and pasteries. It sells them in the cities of Minneapolis and St. Paul. For March, its first month of operation, the following income statement was prepared:

MINNESOTA BREAD COMPANY Territory and Company Income Statements For Month of March			
	Minneapolis	St. Paul	Total
Sales...............................	$2,100	$500	$2,600
Cost of goods sold....................	(1,500)	(300)	(1,800)
Gross profit.........................	600	200	800
Selling and administrative expenses	(400)	(225)	(625)
Net income.........................	$ 200	$ (25)	$ 175

Sales and selected variable expense data are as follows:

	Products		
	Donuts	Bread	Pastries
Fixed baking expenses................................	$200	$140	$100
Variable baking expenses as a percentage of sales	50%	50%	60%
Variable selling expenses as a percentage of sales...........	4%	4%	5%
City of Minneapolis, sales	$800	$900	$400
City of St. Paul, sales.................................	$200	$100	$200

The fixed selling expenses were $385 for March, of which $160 was a direct expense of the Minneapolis market and $225 was a direct expense of the St. Paul market. Fixed administrative expenses were $130, which management has decided not to allocate when using the contribution approach.

Required

a. Prepare a segment income statement showing the territory margin for each sales territory for March. Include a column for the entire firm.

b. Prepare segment income statements showing the product margin for each product. Include a column for the entire firm.

c. If the pastries line is dropped and fixed baking expenses do not change, what is the product margin for donuts and bread?

d. What other type of segmentation might be useful to Minnesota Bread. Explain.

P23-34. Segment Reporting and Analysis (LO1)

University Publishers, Inc., has prepared income statements segmented by divisions, but management is still uncertain about actual performance. Financial information for May is given as follows:

	Textbook Division	Professional Division	Company Total
Sales............................	$200,000	$410,000	$610,000
Less variable expenses			
Manufacturing....................	32,000	205,000	237,000
Selling and administrative..........	4,000	20,500	24,500
Total	(36,000)	(225,500)	(261,500)
Contribution margin	164,000	184,500	348,500
Less direct fixed expenses...........	(15,000)	(205,000)	(220,000)
Net income......................	$149,000	$(20,500)	$ 128,500

Management is concerned about the Professional Division and requests additional analysis. Additional information regarding May operations of the Professional Division is as follows:

	Accounting	Executive	Management
Sales....................................	$140,000	$140,000	$130,000
Variable manufacturing expenses as a percentage of sales..................	60%	40%	50%
Other variable expenses as a percentage of sales..................	5%	5%	5%
Direct fixed expenses.....................	$50,000	$75,000	$50,000
Allocated common fixed expenses	$5,000	$2,000	$7,000

The professional accounting books are sold to auditors and controllers. The current information on these markets is as follows:

	Sales Market	
	Auditors	Controllers
Sales......................................	$30,000	$110,000
Variable manufacturing expenses as a percentage of sales.....................	60%	60%
Other variable expenses as a percentage of sales.....................	16%	2%
Direct fixed expenses.........................	$10,000	$ 25,000
Allocated common fixed expenses	$ 4,000	$ 8,000

Required

a. Prepare an income statement segmented by product for the Professional Division. Include a column for the division as a whole.

b. Prepare an income statement segmented by market for the accounting books of the Professional Division.

c. Evaluate which accounting books the Professional Division should keep or discontinue in the short run.

d. What is the correct long-run decision? Explain fully, including any possible risks associated with your recommendation.

P23-35. Segment Reports and Cost Allocations (LO1)

Great Lakes, Inc., has three sales divisions. One of the key evaluation inputs for each division manager is the performance of his or her division based on division income. The division statements for August are as follows:

	Superior	Ontario	Michigan	Total
Sales......................	$400,000	$500,000	$450,000	$1,350,000
Cost of sales................	200,000	240,000	230,000	670,000
Division overhead.............	100,000	110,000	110,000	320,000
Division expenses.............	(300,000)	(350,000)	(340,000)	(990,000)
Division contribution...........	100,000	150,000	110,000	360,000
Corporate overhead...........	(70,000)	(90,000)	(80,000)	(240,000)
Division income	$ 30,000	$ 60,000	$ 30,000	$ 120,000

The Michigan manager is unhappy that his profitability is the same as that of the Superior Division and one-half that of the Ontario Division when his sales are halfway between these two divisions. The manager knows that his division must carry more product lines because of customer demands, and many of these additional product lines are not very profitable. He has not dropped these marginal product lines because of idle capacity; all of the products cover their own variable costs. After analyzing the product lines with the lowest profit margins, the divisional controller for Michigan provided the following to the manager:

Sales of marginal products........................		$90,000
Cost of sales........................	$50,000	
Avoidable fixed costs.................	22,000	(72,000)
Product margin.......................		18,000
Proportion of corporate overhead		(16,000)
Product income		$ 2,000

Although these products were 20 percent of Michigan's total sales, they contributed only about 7 percent of the division's profits. The controller also noted that the corporate overhead allocation was based on a formula of sales and divisional contribution margin.

Required

a. Prepare a set of segment statements for August assuming that all facts remain the same except that Michigan's weak product lines are dropped and corporate overhead is allocated as follows: Superior, $80,000; Ontario, $95,000; and Michigan, $65,000. Does the Michigan Division appear better after this action? What will be the responses of the other two division managers?

b. Suggest improvements for Great Lakes' reporting process that will better reflect the actual operations of the divisions. Keep in mind the utilization of the reporting process to assist in the evaluation of the managers. What other changes could be made to improve the manager evaluation process?

P23-36. ROI, Residual Income, and EVA: Impact of a New Investment   (LO3)

RCI Inc. is a decentralized organization with four autonomous divisions. The divisions are evaluated on the basis of the change in their return on invested assets. Operating results in the Commercial Division for 2012 follow:

RCI INC.—COMMERCIAL DIVISION **Income Statement** **For Year Ending December 31, 2012**	
Sales....................................	$3,125,000
Less variable expenses	(1,600,000)
Contribution margin	1,525,000
Less fixed expenses......................	(1,000,000)
Net operating income....................	$ 525,000

Operating assets for the Commercial Division currently average $2,500,000. The Commercial Division can add a new product line for an investment of $300,000. Relevant data for the new product line are as follows:

Sales....................................	$800,000
Variable expenses (% of sales).	0.60
Fixed expenses	$275,000
Increase in current liabilities.................	$ 20,000

Required

a. Determine the effect on ROI of accepting the new product line. (Round calculations to three decimal places.)

b. If a return of 6 percent is the minimum that any division should earn and residual income is used to evaluate managers, would this encourage the division to accept the new product line? Explain and show computations.

c. If EVA is used to evaluate managers, should the new product line be accepted if the weighted average cost of capital is 8 percent and the income tax rate is 40 percent?

P23-37. Valuing Investment Center Assets (LO3)

Six Flags Theme Parks, Inc. (SIX)

Six Flags Theme Parks, Inc., operates theme parks in the United States, Mexico, and Europe. One of its first theme parks, Six Flags over Georgia, was built in the 1960s in Atlanta on a large tract of land that has appreciated enormously over the years. Although most of the rides and other attractions have a fairly short life, some of the major buildings that are still in use on the property have been fully depreciated since they were built. Assume that Six Flags over Georgia operates as an investment center with total assets that have a book value of $150 million and current liabilities of $20 million. Assume also that in 2012, this particular theme park had sales of $120 million and pretax division income of $40 million. The replacement cost of all the assets in this park is estimated to be $250 million. The company has a 35 percent tax rate and a target return of 10% and a cost of capital of 8%.

Required

a. Calculate the ROI, residual income, and EVA for Six Flags over Georgia using book value as the valuation basis for the investment center asset base.
b. Repeat requirement (a) using replacement cost as the investment center asset value.
c. Which valuation, accounting book value or replacement cost do you think the company uses to evaluate the managers of its various theme parks? Discuss.

P23-38. Transfer Pricing with and without Capacity Constraints (LO2)

Elite Carpets, Inc., has just acquired a new backing division that produces a rubber backing, which it sells for $2.10 per square yard. Sales are about 1,200,000 square yards per year. Since the Backing Division has a capacity of 2,000,000 square yards per year, top management is thinking that it might be wise for the company's Tufting Division to start purchasing from the newly acquired Backing Division. The Tufting Division now purchases 600,000 square yards per year from an outside supplier at a price of $1.90 per square yard. The current price is lower than the competitive $2.10 price as a result of the large quantity discounts. The Backing Division's cost per square yard follows.

Direct materials	$1.00
Direct labor	0.20
Variable overhead	0.25
Fixed overhead (1,200,000 level)	0.10
Total cost	$1.55

Required

a. If both divisions are to be treated as investment centers and their performance evaluated by the ROI formula, what transfer price would you recommend? Why?
b. Determine the effect on corporate profits of making the backing.
c. Based on your transfer price, would you expect the ROI in the Backing Division to increase, decrease, or remain unchanged? Explain.
d. What would be the effect on the ROI of the Tufting Division using your transfer price? Explain.
e. Assume that the Backing Division is now selling 2,000,000 square yards per year to retail outlets. What transfer price would you recommend? What will be the effect on corporate profits?
f. If the Backing Division is at capacity and decides to sell to the Tufting Division for $1.90 per square yard, what will be the effect on the company's profits?

P23-39. Transfer Pricing and Special Orders (LO2)

Silicone Valley Products has several manufacturing divisions. The Palo Alto Division produces a component part that is used in the manufacture of electronic equipment. The cost per part for July is as follows:

Variable cost	$ 90
Fixed cost (at 2,000 units per month capacity)	60
Total cost per part	$150

Some of Palo Alto Division's output is sold to outside manufacturers, and some is sold internally to the Berkeley Division. The price per part is $200. The Berkeley Division's cost and revenue structure follow.

Selling price per unit.		$1,000
Less variable costs per unit		
Cost of parts from the Palo Alto Division	$200	
Other variable costs	400	(600)
Contribution margin per unit		400
Less fixed costs per unit (at 200 units per month)		(100)
Net income per unit		$ 300

The Berkeley Division received a one-time order for 10 units. The buyer wants to pay only $500 per unit.

Required

a. From the perspective of the Berkeley Division, should the $500 price be accepted? Explain.

b. If both divisions have excess capacity, would the Berkeley Division's action benefit the company as a whole? Explain.

c. If the Berkeley Division has excess capacity but the Palo Alto Division does not and can sell all of its parts to outside manufacturers, what would be the advantage or disadvantage of accepting the ten-unit order at the $500 price to the Berkeley Division?

d. To make a decision that is in the best interest of the company, what transfer-pricing information does the Berkeley Division need?

P23-40. Balanced Scorecard (LO4)

The Summersworth Community Bank recently decided to adopt a balanced scorecard system of performance evaluation. Below is a list of primary performance goals for four major performance categories that have been identified by corporate management and the board of directors.

1. Financial Perspective–Maintain and grow the bank financially
    a. Increase customer deposits
    b. Manage financial risk
    c. Provide profits for the stockholders
2. Customer Perspective – Maintain and grow the customer base
    a. Increase customer satisfaction
    b. Increase number of depositors & customer retention
    c. Increase quality of deposits
3. Internal Perspective – Improve internal processes
    a. Achieve best practices for processing transactions
    b. Improve employee satisfaction
    c. Improve employee promotion opportunities
4. Learning and Innovation – Improve market differentiation
    a. Beat competitors in introducing new products
    b. Become first mover in establishing customer benefit for customers
    c. Become recognized as an innovator in the industry

Required:

a. For each of the 12 goals above suggest at least one measure of performance to measure the achievement of the goal.

b. At what level of the organization should the balanced scorecard be implemented as a means of evaluating performance? Explain.

MANAGEMENT APPLICATIONS

MA23-41. Transfer Price Decisions (LO2)

IBM Corporation (IBM)

The Consulting Division of **IBM Corporation** is often involved in assignments for which IBM computer equipment is sold as part of a systems installation. The Computer Equipment Division is frequently a vendor of the Consulting Division in cases for which the Consulting Division purchases the equipment from the Computer Equipment Division. The Consulting Division does not view itself as a sales arm of the Computer Equipment Division but as a strong competitor to the major consulting firms of information systems. The Consulting Division's goal is to maximize its profit contribution to the company, not necessarily to see how much IBM equipment it can sell. If the Consulting Division is truly an autonomous investment center, it has the freedom to purchase equipment from competing vendors if the consultants believe that a competitor's products serve the needs of a client better than the comparable IBM product in a particular situation.

Required

a. In this situation, should corporate management be concerned about whether the Consulting Division sells IBM products or those of other computer companies? Should the Consulting Division be required to sell only IBM products?

b. Discuss the transfer-pricing issues that both the Computer Equipment Division manager and the Consulting Division manager should consider. If top management does not have a policy on pricing transfers between these two divisions, what alternative transfer prices should the division managers consider?

c. What is your recommendation regarding how the managers of the Consulting and Computer Equipment Divisions can work together in a way that will benefit each of them individually and the company as a whole?

MA23-42. Transfer Pricing at Absorption Cost (LO2)

The Injection Molding Division of Universal Sign Company produces molded parts that are sold to the Sign Division. This division uses the parts in constructing signs that are sold to various businesses. The Molding Division contains two operations, injection and finishing. The unit variable cost of materials and labor used in the injection operation is $100. The fixed injection overhead is $800,000 per year. Current production (20,000 units) is at full capacity. The variable cost of labor used in the finishing operation is $14 per part. The fixed overhead in this operation is $340,000 per year. The company uses an absorption-cost transfer price. The price data for each operation presented to the Sign Division by the Molding Division follow.

Injection		
Variable cost per unit	$100	
Fixed overhead cost per unit ($800,000 ÷ 20,000 units)	40	$140
Finishing		
Labor cost per unit	14	
Fixed overhead cost per unit ($340,000 ÷ 20,000 units)	17	31
Total cost per unit.		$171

An outside company has offered to lease machinery to the Sign Division that would perform the finishing portion of the parts manufacturing for $200,000 per year. With the new machinery, the labor cost per part would remain at $14. If the Molding Division transfers the units for $140, the following analysis can be made:

Current process		
Finishing process costs (20,000 × $31)		$620,000
New process		
Machine rental cost per year	$200,000	
Labor cost ($14 × 20,000 units).	280,000	(480,000)
Savings.		$140,000

The manager of the Sign Division wants approval to acquire the new machinery.

Required

a. How would you advise the company concerning the proposed lease?

b. How could the transfer-pricing system be modified or the transfer-pricing problem eliminated?

MA23-43. Transfer Pricing Dispute (LO2)

MBR Inc. consists of three divisions that were formerly three independent manufacturing companies. Bader Corporation and Roper Company merged in 2011, and the merged corporation acquired Mitchell

Company in 2012. The name of the corporation was subsequently changed to MBR Inc., and each company became a separate division retaining the name of its former company.

The three divisions have operated as if they were still independent companies. Each division has its own sales force and production facilities. Each division management is responsible for sales, cost of operations, acquisition and financing of divisional assets, and working capital management. The corporate management of MBR evaluates the performance of the divisions and division management on the basis of return on investment.

Mitchell Division has just been awarded a contract for a product that uses a component manufactured by the Roper Division and also by outside suppliers. Mitchell used a cost figure of $3.80 for the component manufactured by Roper in preparing its bid for the new product. Roper supplied this cost figure in response to Mitchell's request for the average variable cost of the component; it represents the standard variable manufacturing cost and variable selling and distribution expenses.

Roper has an active sales force that is continually soliciting new prospects. Roper's regular selling price for the component Mitchell needs for the new product is $6.50. Sales of this component are expected to increase. The Roper management has indicated, however, that it could supply Mitchell the required quantities of the component at the regular selling price less variable selling and distribution expenses. Mitchell's management has responded by offering to pay standard variable manufacturing cost plus 20 percent.

The two divisions have been unable to agree on a transfer price. Corporate management has never established a transfer-pricing policy because interdivisional transactions have never occurred. As a compromise, the corporate vice president of finance suggested a price equal to the standard full manufacturing cost (i.e., no selling and distribution expenses) plus a 15 percent markup. The two division managers have also rejected this price because each considered it grossly unfair.

The unit cost structure for the Roper component and the three suggested prices follow.

Standard variable manufacturing cost	$3.20
Standard fixed manufacturing cost	1.20
Variable selling and distribution expenses	0.60
	$5.00
Regular selling price less variable selling and distribution expenses ($6.50 − $0.60)	$5.90
Standard full manufacturing cost plus 15% ($4.40 × 1.15)	$5.06
Variable manufacturing plus 20% ($3.20 × 1.20)	$3.84

Required

a. What should be the attitude of the Roper Division's management toward the three proposed prices?

b. Is the negotiation of a price between the Mitchell and Roper Divisions a satisfactory method of solving the transfer-pricing problem? Explain your answer.

c. Should the corporate management of MBR Inc. become involved in this transfer-price controversy? Explain your answer.

(CMA Adapted)

SOLUTIONS TO REVIEW PROBLEMS

Mid-Module Review

Solution

a.

	Segments (Territories)		Coaxial Total
	Atlantic	Pacific	
Sales.....................................	$12,000	$18,000	$30,000
Less variable costs........................	(8,400)	(12,600)	(21,000)
Contribution margin	3,600	5,400	9,000
Less direct fixed costs	(500)	(800)	(1,300)
Territory margin............................	3,100	4,600	7,700
Less allocated segment costs	(200)	(600)	(800)
Territory income	$ 2,900	$ 4,000	6,900
Less unallocated common costs			(900)
Fiber optic income			$ 6,000

b. The Product Margin for the Coaxial product line in Panel B was $7,000 and reflected $2,000 of direct fixed costs that were attributable to that product line in the National Division. However, when the Coaxial product segment income statement is further segmented into geographic segments, only $1,300 of the $2,000 could be directly traced to the two geographic territories. Therefore, $700 of costs that were direct costs at the product segment level became common costs (either allocated or unallocated) at the territory segment level. This reflects the general notion that as segmentation is extended down to lower and lower levels, the total amount of common costs increase and direct costs decrease. Hence, segmentation rarely is extended to more than three levels.

Module-End Review

Solution

a.
$$\text{Return on investment} = \frac{\text{Investment center income}}{\text{Investment center asset base}}$$

$$\text{Commercial Division} = \$30,000 \div \$200,000$$
$$= 0.15, \text{ or 15 percent}$$
$$\text{Industrial Division} = \$50,000 \div \$250,000$$
$$= 0.20, \text{ or 20 percent}$$
$$\text{Residential Division} = \$22,000 \div \$100,000$$
$$= 0.22, \text{ or 22 percent}$$

b. **Residual income = Investment center income − (Investment center asset base × Minimum return)**

$$\text{Commercial Division} = \$30,000 - (0.15 \times \$200,000)$$
$$= \$0.00$$
$$\text{Industrial Division} = \$50,000 - (0.15 \times \$250,000)$$
$$= \$12,500$$
$$\text{Residential Division} = \$22,000 - (0.15 \times \$100,000)$$
$$= \$7,000$$

c. ROI ranks the Residential Division first, the Industrial Division second, and the Commercial Division third. Residual income ranks the Industrial Division first, the Residential Division second, and the Commercial Division third. Because the investments for each division are different, it is somewhat misleading to rank the divisions according to residual income. The Industrial Division had the highest residual income, but it also had the largest investment. The Residential Division's residual income was 56 percent of the Industrial Division's income but only 40 percent of the investment of the Industrial Division. This fact, along with the best ROI ranking, probably justifies the Residential Division being evaluated as the best division of Pareto Company.

d. Return on investment:

$$
\begin{aligned}
\textbf{Investment} &= \$9,000 \div \$50,000 \\
&= \textbf{0.18, or 18 percent} \\
\textbf{Commercial Division} &= (\$30,000 + \$9,000) \div (\$200,000 + \$50,000) \\
&= \textbf{0.156, or 15.6 percent} \\
\textbf{Industrial Division} &= (\$50,000 + \$9,000) \div (\$250,000 + \$50,000) \\
&= \textbf{0.1967, or 19.67 percent} \\
\textbf{Residential Division} &= (\$22,000 + \$9,000) \div (\$100,000 + \$50,000) \\
&= \textbf{0.2067, or 20.67 percent}
\end{aligned}
$$

ROI will increase for the Commercial Division but decrease for the Industrial and Residential Divisions, even though the project's ROI of 18 percent exceeds the company's minimum return of 15 percent. Residual income:

$$
\begin{aligned}
\textbf{Commercial Division} &= (\$30,000 + \$9,000) - [0.15 \times (\$200,000 + \$50,000)] \\
&= \textbf{\$1,500} \\
\textbf{Industrial Division} &= (\$50,000 + \$9,000) - [0.15 \times (\$250,000 + \$50,000)] \\
&= \textbf{\$14,000} \\
\textbf{Residential Division} &= (\$22,000 + \$9,000) - [0.15 \times (\$100,000 + \$50,000)] \\
&= \textbf{\$8,500}
\end{aligned}
$$

Because the project's ROI exceeds the company's minimum return, the residual income of all divisions will increase.

Getty Images

VIKING AIR

Although the last Twin Otter turboprop was built in 1988 more than 600 of these 19-seat aircraft remain in service, primarily in remote regions without scheduled commercial air travel. Twin Otters are used in deserts, jungles, mountains, and the arctic, where rugged reliability, versatility, and short takeoffs and landings are required. The planes can be outfitted with wheels, skis, and pontoons. Owners include NASA, British Antarctic Survey, parachute clubs, sightseeing firms, charter airlines, and companies engaged in oil and gas exploration. In 2001, when a scientist had to be evacuated from the South Pole because of a medical emergency, the Twin Otter was chosen as the only aircraft capable of landing and taking off in -60 F temperatures.

In 2010 Canadian parts supplier Viking Air Ltd., one of the firms keeping the Twin Otter aloft with replacement parts, announced it was expanding its mission to include the production of an updated Twin Otter 400. Brian Mandrusiak, head mechanic at Viking, stated that he had been dreaming of this day. "When they stopped building them we thought it was a big mistake. I've been working on Twin Otters for 22 years. You can do things with this airplane that people can only imagine."

Key to reviving the Twin Otter was purchasing the rights to, and copies of, the aircraft's design from de Havilland Aircraft of Canada (now part of Bombardier). According to Viking's executive officer, David Curtis, designing a plane from scratch would cost $200 million. Starting from the old

Capital Budgeting Decisions

LEARNING OBJECTIVES

LO1 Explain the role of capital budgeting in long-range planning. (p. 24-4)

LO2 Apply capital budgeting models, such as net present value and internal rate of return, that consider the time value of money. (p. 24-6)

LO3 Apply capital budgeting models, such as payback period and accounting rate of return, that do not consider the time value of money. (p. 24-11)

LO4 Evaluate the strengths and weaknesses of alternative capital budgeting models. (p. 24-14)

LO5 Discuss the importance of judgment, attitudes toward risk, and relevant cash flow information for capital budgeting decisions. (p. 24-16)

LO6 Determine the net present value of investment proposals with consideration of taxes. (p. 24-20)

design reduced design costs to a third of that. Although the new version, with a list price of $4.5 million, is similar in overall design to the old, it uses composite materials, more-powerful engines, and modern cockpit electronics.

Before committing to the new venture, David Curtis also commissioned an independent marketing study that estimated worldwide demand over the next ten years at 440 new Twin Otters. With a planned production of 24 planes a year, 50 planes on order, and other owners of the old version waiting in the wings to see how the new Twin Otter 400 performs, early signs point to success for Viking's expanded mission and related capital expenditure of many millions for design and manufacture.

Viking Air's decisions to expand its mission and make a strategic investment in the design, production, and market-

ing of the Twin Otter 400 are high stakes. In reviewing Viking Air's decision process, note their experience and industry knowledge, their attention to cost management, and their use of independent marketing surveys. Although no analytical tools can relieve Viking's management of responsibility for decisions or eliminate the inherent uncertainty of those decisions, management accounting tools such as those discussed in this text, and for capital expenditures, this module, are key to successfully identifying, organizing and analyzing relevant information.[1]

---

[1] Susan Carey, "Viking Air Breathes New Life Into Old Plane," *The Wall Street Journal*, July 8, 2010, pp. B1-B2; Laura Cameron, "Relaunch of a Legend," *Canadian Business*, December 7, 2009, p. 18; www.Vikingair.com.

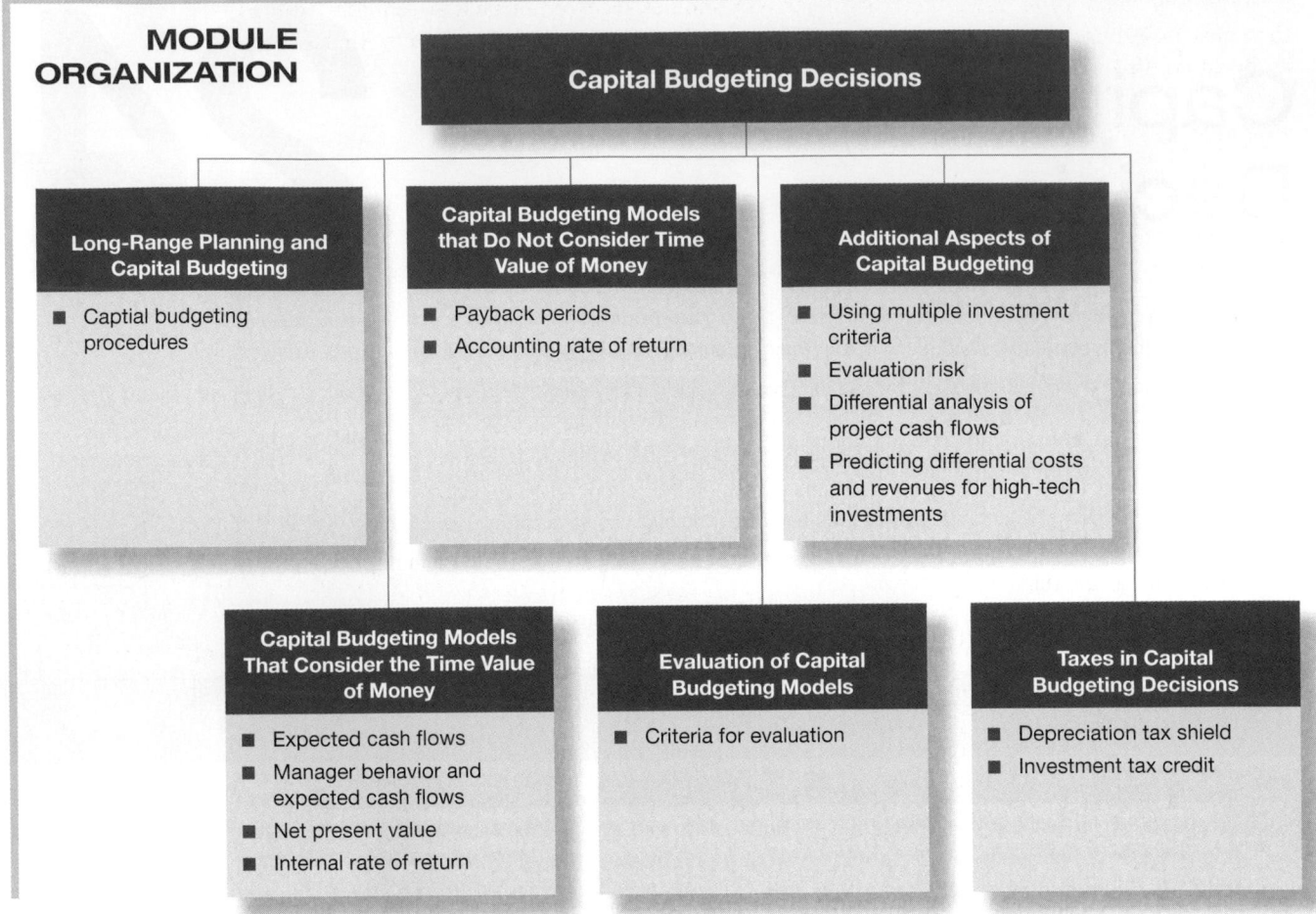

MODULE ORGANIZATION

Capital Budgeting Decisions

Long-Range Planning and Capital Budgeting
- Captial budgeting procedures

Capital Budgeting Models that Do Not Consider Time Value of Money
- Payback periods
- Accounting rate of return

Additional Aspects of Capital Budgeting
- Using multiple investment criteria
- Evaluation risk
- Differential analysis of project cash flows
- Predicting differential costs and revenues for high-tech investments

Capital Budgeting Models That Consider the Time Value of Money
- Expected cash flows
- Manager behavior and expected cash flows
- Net present value
- Internal rate of return

Evaluation of Capital Budgeting Models
- Criteria for evaluation

Taxes in Capital Budgeting Decisions
- Depreciation tax shield
- Investment tax credit

Capital expenditures are investments of financial resources in projects to develop or introduce new products or services, to expand current production or service capacity, or to change current production or service facilities. Capital expenditures are made with the expectation that the new product, process, or service will generate future financial inflows that exceed the initial costs. Capital expenditure decisions affect structural cost drivers. They are made infrequently but once made are difficult to change. They commit the organization to the use of certain facilities and activities to satisfy customer needs. In making large capital expenditure decisions, such as for the Airbus A380 or the Boeing 787, management is risking the future existence of the company.

Although capital expenditure decisions are fraught with risk, management accounting provides the concepts and tools needed to organize information and evaluate the alternatives. This systematic organization and analysis is the essence of capital budgeting. This Module introduces important capital budgeting concepts and models, and it explains the proper use of accounting data in these models.

Capital budgeting is a process that involves identifying potentially desirable projects for capital expenditures, evaluating capital expenditure proposals, and selecting proposals that meet minimum criteria. A number of quantitative models are available to assist managers in evaluating capital expenditure proposals.

The best capital budgeting models are conceptually similar to the short-range planning models used in Modules 15 and 16. They all emphasize cash flows and focus on future costs (and revenues) that differ among decision alternatives. The major difference is that capital budgeting models involve cash flows over several years, whereas short-range planning models involve cash flows for a year or less. When the cash flows associated with a proposed activity extend over several years, an adjustment is necessary to make the cash flows comparable when they are expected to occur at different points in time.

The *time value of money concept* explains why monies received or paid at different points in time must be adjusted to comparable values. The time value of money is introduced in Appendix 24A at the end of this Module.

LONG-RANGE PLANNING AND CAPITAL BUDGETING

Most organizations plan not only for operations in the current period but also for the longer term, perhaps 5, 10, or even 20 years in the future. Most planning beyond the next budget year is called *long-range planning*.

LO1 Explain the role of capital budgeting in long-range planning.

Increased uncertainty and business alternatives add to the difficulty of planning as the horizon lengthens. Even though long-range planning is difficult and involves uncertainties, management must make long-range planning and capital expenditure decisions. Capital expenditure decisions will be made. The question is: How will they be made? Will they be made on the basis of the best information available? Will care be taken to ensure that capital expenditure decisions are in line with the organization's long-range goals? Will the potential consequences, both positive and negative, of capital expenditures be considered?

Will important alternative uses of the organization's limited financial resources be considered in a systematic manner? Will managers be held accountable for the capital expenditure programs they initiate? The alternative to a systematic approach to capital budgeting is the haphazard expenditure of resources on the basis of a hunch, immediate need, or persuasion—without accountability by the person(s) making the decisions.

The steps of an effective capital budgeting process are outlined in Exhibit 24.1. A basic requirement for a systematic approach to capital budgeting is a defined mission, a set of long-range goals, and a business strategy. These elements provide focus and boundaries that reduce the types of capital expenditure decisions management considers. If, for example, KFC's goal is to become the largest fast-food restaurant chain in North America, its management should not consider a proposal to purchase and operate a bus line.

A well-defined business strategy will likewise guide capital expenditure decisions. If Cisco Systems is following a strategy to obtain technological leadership, it might seriously consider a proposal to meet customer needs by investing in innovative production facilities but would not consider a proposal to purchase and refurbish used (but seemingly cost-efficient) equipment. In the following Business Insight Heineken identified reducing energy consumption as a strategic goal, thereby drawing attention to an aspect of business that might otherwise go unnoticed.

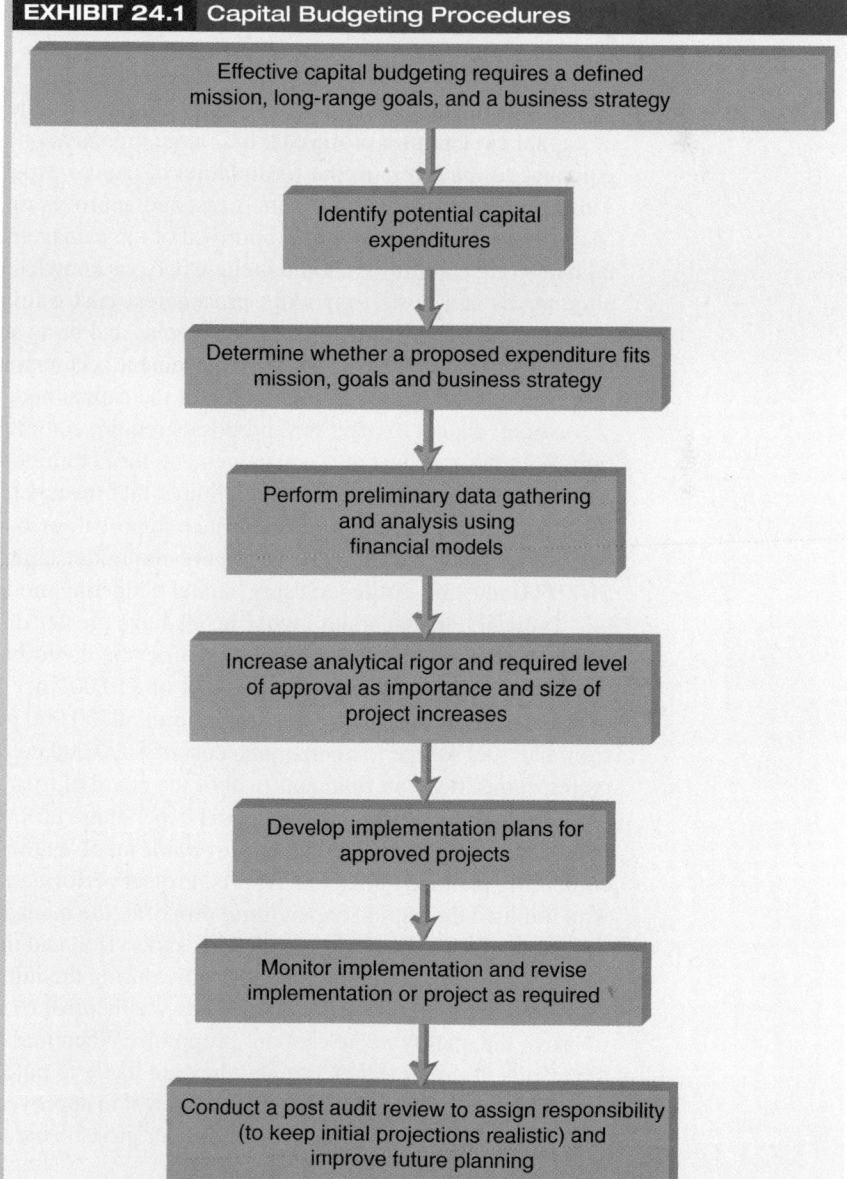

EXHIBIT 24.1 Capital Budgeting Procedures

Effective capital budgeting requires a defined mission, long-range goals, and a business strategy

Identify potential capital expenditures

Determine whether a proposed expenditure fits mission, goals and business strategy

Perform preliminary data gathering and analysis using financial models

Increase analytical rigor and required level of approval as importance and size of project increases

Develop implementation plans for approved projects

Monitor implementation and revise implementation or project as required

Conduct a post audit review to assign responsibility (to keep initial projections realistic) and improve future planning

---

BUSINESS INSIGHT   **Energy Reduction as a Corporate Goal Fosters Green Investments**

With the manufacturing sector accounting for more than one-third of global energy use and energy prices soaring, there are countless opportunities for green investments that reduce energy consumption and costs. Yet, according to energy-expert Paul Waide of the International Energy Agency, corporate structure can be an obstacle. No one person is in charge of minimizing energy use. "The purchasing department might be looking for the cheapest motor to install in terms of upfront costs . . . The energy bill gets paid out of some other budget, so unless the company as a whole focuses on the issue, nothing gets done."

Netherlands-based Heineken, Europe's largest beer maker, overcame this obstacle by establishing corporate goals for reducing energy consumption. The company plans to use 15 percent less energy in 2010 than it used in 2002. This direction from the top has been important in focusing attention on projects that reduce energy consumption, according to Jasko Bakker, who leads environmental initiatives for Heineken.

HSBC Holdings, an international bank, has committed $90 million to become more energy efficient, with a seven percent targeted reduction in power consumption. HSBC investments to support this goal include software that automatically turns off desktop computers if employees leave them on at night and replacing computer monitors with more efficient models.

Source: Leila Abboud and John Biers, "Business Goes on an Energy Diet," *The Wall Street Journal*, August 27, 2007, pp. R1, R4.

Management should also develop procedures for the review, evaluation, approval, and post-audit of capital expenditure proposals. In a large organization, a capital budgeting committee that provides guidance to managers in the formulation of capital expenditure proposals is key to these procedures. This committee also reviews, analyzes, and approves or rejects major capital expenditure proposals. Major projects often require the approval of top management and even the board of directors. The capital budgeting committee should include persons knowledgeable in capital budgeting models; financing alternatives and costs; operating procedures; cost estimation and prediction methods; research and development efforts; the organization's goals and basic strategy; and the expectations of the organization's stockholders or owners. A management accountant who is generally expert in data collection, retrieval, and analysis is normally part of the capital budgeting committee.

Not all capital expenditure proposals require committee approval or are subject to formal evaluation. With the approval of top management, the committee might provide guidelines indicating the type and dollar amount of capital expenditures that managers at each level of the organization can make without formal evaluation or committee approval, or both. The guidelines might state that expenditures of less than $20,000 do not require committee approval and that only expenditures of more than $100,000 must be evaluated using capital budgeting models.

Typically, managers at higher levels have greater discretion in making capital expenditures. In a college or university, a department chairperson could have authority to purchase office and instructional equipment with a maximum limit of $10,000 per year. A dean may have authority to renovate offices or classrooms with a maximum limit of $50,000 per year, but the conversion of the power plant from one fuel source to another at a cost of $400,000 could require the formal review of a capital budgeting committee and final approval of the board of trustees.

The post-audit of approved capital expenditure proposals is an important part of a well-formulated approach to capital budgeting. A *post-audit* involves the development of project performance reports comparing planned and actual results. Project performance reports should be provided to the manager who initiated the capital expenditure proposal, the manager assigned responsibility for the project (if a different person), the project manager's supervisor, and the capital budgeting committee. These reports help keep the project on target (especially during the initial investment phase), identify the need to re-evaluate the project if the initial analysis was in error or significant environmental changes occur, and improve the quality of investment proposals. When managers know they will be held accountable for the results of projects they initiate, they are likely to put more care into the development of capital expenditure proposals and take a greater interest in approved projects. Problems can occur when decision makers are rewarded for undertaking major projects but are not held responsible for the consequences that occur several years later.

A post-audit review of approved projects also helps the capital budgeting committee do a better job in evaluating new proposals. The committee might learn how to adjust proposals for the biases of individual managers, learn of new factors that should be considered in evaluating proposals, and avoid the routine approval of projects that appear desirable by themselves but are related to larger projects that are not meeting management's expectations. As summarized in the following Research Insight, an analysis of the findings of post-audit reviews reveals that sales forecasting is the most error-prone element in the financial analysis of capital budgeting.

RESEARCH INSIGHT | **Where the Errors Are**

After conducting a study of post-audits of capital expenditures, Professors Sores, Coutinho, and Martins reached the following conclusions:

■ Forecasts of operating costs were remarkably accurate.

■ There was a high degree of variability in the actual investments when compared to budgeted investments, which may be related to delays in the execution of projects.

■ Forecasts of sales were overstated seventy percent of the time, with actual sales, on average, being nine percent below forecasted sales.

Source: Joao Oliveira Sores, Maria Cristina Coutinho, and Carlos V. Martina, "Forecasting Errors in Capital Budgeting: A multi-firm Post-audit Study, *The Engineering Economist*, Vol 52, 2007, pp. 21–39.

MANAGERIAL DECISION | **You Are the Vice President of Finance**

You have recently accepted the position of VP of finance for a rapidly growing biotech company. Last year the company made capital expenditures of $10 million and you anticipate that annual capital expenditures will exceed $30 million in a couple of years. You believe it is time to develop a more formal approach to making capital expenditure decisions. Where do you begin? [Answer p. 24-29]

CAPITAL BUDGETING MODELS THAT CONSIDER TIME VALUE OF MONEY

The capital budgeting models in this Module have gained wide acceptance by for-profit and not-for-profit organizations. Our primary focus is on the *net present value* and the *internal rate of return models*, which are superior because they consider the time value of money. Later discussions will consider more traditional capital budgeting models, such as the payback period and the accounting rate of return that, while useful under certain circumstances, do not consider the time value of money. Although we briefly consider the cost of financing capital expenditures, we leave a detailed treatment of this topic, as well as a detailed examination of the sources of funds for financing investments, to books on financial management.

LO2 Apply capital budgeting models, such as net present value and internal rate of return, that consider the time value of money.

Expected Cash Flows

The focus of capital budgeting models that consider the time value of money is on future cash receipts and future cash disbursements that differ under decision alternatives. It is often convenient to distinguish between the following three phases of a project's cash flows:

■ Initial investment
■ Operation
■ Disinvestment

All cash expenditures necessary to begin operations are classified as part of the project's *initial investment phase*. Expenditures to acquire property, plant, and equipment are part of the initial investment.

Less obvious, but equally important, are expenditures to acquire working capital to purchase inventories and recruit and train employees. Although the initial investment phase often extends over many years, in our examples, we assume that the initial investment takes place at a single point in time.

Cash receipts from sales of goods or services, as well as normal cash expenditures for materials, labor, and other operating expenses, occur during the operation phase. The *operation phase* is typically broken down into one-year periods; for each period, operating cash expenditures are subtracted from operating cash receipts to determine the net operating cash inflow or outflow for the period.

The *disinvestment phase* occurs at the end of the project's life when assets are disposed of for their salvage value and any initial investment of working capital is recovered. Also included are any expenditures to dismantle facilities and dispose of waste. Although this phase might extend over many years, in our examples, we assume disinvestment takes place at a single point in time.

To illustrate the analysis of a project's cash flows, assume the management of Mobile Yogurt Shoppe is considering a capital expenditure proposal to operate a new shop in a resort community in the Ozark Mountains. Each Mobile Yogurt Shoppe is located in a specially constructed motor vehicle that moves on a regular schedule throughout the community it serves. The predicted cash flows associated with the project, which has an expected life of five years, are presented in Exhibit 24.2.

EXHIBIT 24.2	Analysis of a Project's Predicted Cash Flows		
Initial investment (at time 0)			
Vehicle and equipment..			$ 90,554
Inventories and other working capital			4,000
Total			$ 94,554
Operation (per year for 5 years)			
Sales...			$175,000
Cash expenditures			
Food		$47,000	
Labor...		65,000	
Supplies		9,000	
Fuel and utilities		8,000	
Advertising		4,000	
Miscellaneous...		12,000	(145,000)
Net annual cash inflow.....................................			$ 30,000
Disinvestment (at the end of 5 years)			
Sale of vehicle and equipment...............................			$ 8,000
Recovery of investment in inventories and other working capital			4,000
Total			$ 12,000

Manager Behavior and Expected Cash Flows

Accurately predicting the cash flows associated with a capital expenditure proposal is critical to properly evaluating the proposal. Managers might be overly optimistic with their predictions, and they are sometimes tempted to modify predictions to justify capital expenditures. Perhaps they are interested in personal rewards. They might also want to avoid a loss of prestige or employment for themselves or to keep a local facility operating for the benefit of current employees and the local economy. Unfortunately, if a major expenditure does not work out, not only the local plant but also the entire company could be forced out of business. For example, under pressure to increase current sales, automobile leasing companies could be tempted to overstate cash receipts during the disinvestment phase of a lease. The following Business Insight considers the financial consequences of overstating residual values for automobile leases.

BUSINESS INSIGHT	Profits Today, Losses Tomorrow When Managers Overstate Residual Values

To increase current sales and profits, automobile company managers are incented to lower monthly lease rates. Important factors in setting vehicle lease rates include vehicle cost, interest rate, lease period, and the residual value of the vehicle at lease-end. The most difficult item to predict is residual value. That value, the future market price of the vehicle, is a function of its condition, economic climate, actions of competitors, and its popularity when the lease expires. If residual values are predicted to be high, monthly leases can be set low enough to attract customers and earn a profit.

In the 1990s, favorable lease terms based on high residual values helped bring down monthly payments of then-popular Ford Explorers and Jeep Grand Cherokees. When market prices of used vehicles fell in the late 1990s, automobile companies suffered significant losses as leases expired. Again, in the mid-2000s, automakers overestimated residual values when leasing millions of gas guzzling SUVs, pickup trucks and luxury cars. As leases expired in 2008, while the economy went in the tank, consumers opted for more fuel efficient and less expensive vehicles. Manufacturers were again forced to unload used vehicles at a loss as leases expired. BMW reported a loss of almost $400 million in lease-related losses, while Ford's loss on expiring leases was estimated at more than $1 billion. To make up for the losses, and perhaps repeat the cycle, manufacturers began to aggressively market leases for small cars.

Source; Kathleen Lansing, "Painful Math for Leasing Companies," *Business Week*, May 19, 1997, p. 38; David Welch, "Nobody Loves a Three-Year-Old SUV," *Business Week*, August 4, 2008, p. 64; "Crash," *Economist*, December 13, 2008, pp. 76-78.

Net Present Value

A project's **net present value**, usually computed as of the time of the initial investment, is the present value of the project's net cash inflows from operations and disinvestment less the amount of the initial investment. Module Appendix 24A contains an introduction to the time value of money, including net present value fundamentals. In computing a project's net present value, the cash flows occurring at different points in time are adjusted for the time value of money using a **discount rate** that is the minimum rate of return required for the project to be acceptable. Projects with positive net present values (or values at least equal to zero) are acceptable, and projects with negative net present values are unacceptable. Two methods to compute net present value follow.

Table Approach

Assuming that management uses a 12 percent discount rate, the net present value of the proposed investment in a Mobile Yogurt Shoppe is shown in Exhibit 24.3 (a) to be $20,400. Since the net present value is more than zero, the investment in the Mobile Yogurt Shoppe is expected to be profitable, even when adjusted for the time value of money.

We can verify the amounts and computations in Exhibit 24.3. Start by tracing the cash flows back to Exhibit 24.2. Next, verify the 12 percent present value factors in Tables 24A.1 and 24A.2 in module Appendix 24A. The initial investment is assumed to occur at a single point in time (identified as time 0), the start of the project. In net present value computations, all cash flows are restated in terms of their value at time 0. Hence, time 0 cash flows have a present value factor of 1. To simplify computations, all other cash flows are assumed to occur at the end of years 1 through 5, even if they occurred during the year. Although further refinements could be made to adjust for cash flows occuring throughout each year, such adjustments are seldom necessary. Observe that net operating cash inflows are treated as an *annuity*, whereas cash flows for the initial investment and disinvestment are treated as *lump-sum amounts*. If net operating cash flows varied from year to year, we would treat each year's cash flow as a separate amount.

Spreadsheet Approach

Spreadsheet software contains functions that compute the present value of a series of cash flows. With this software, simply enter a column or row containing the net cash flows for each period and the appropriate formula. The discount rate of 0.12 is entered as part of the formula. Sample spreadsheet input to determine the net present value of the proposed investment in a Mobile Yogurt Shoppe is shown on the left in Exhibit 24.3 (b). The spreadsheet output is shown on the right, in Exhibit 24.3 (b).

Two cautionary notes follow:

1. The spreadsheet formula for the net present value assumes that the first cash flow occurs at time "1," rather than at time "0." Hence, we cannot include the initial investment in the data set analyzed by the spreadsheet formula when computing the net present value. Instead, the initial investment is subtracted from the present value of future cash flows.

2. Arrange the cash flows subsequent to the initial investment from *top* to bottom in a column, or *left* to right in a row.

EXHIBIT 24.3 Net Present Value of a Project's Predicted Cash Flows

(a) Table approach:

	Predicted Cash Inflows (outflows) (A)	Year(s) of Cash Flows (B)	12% Present Value Factor (C)	Present Value of Cash Flows (A) × (C)
Initial investment	$(94,554)	0	1.000	$ (94,554)
Operation	30,000	1–5	3.605	108,150
Disinvestment	12,000	5	0.567	6,804
Net present value of all cash flows				$ 20,400

(b) Spreadsheet approach:

Input:

	A	B
1	Year of cash flow	Cash flow
2	1	$30,000
3	2	30,000
4	3	30,000
5	4	30,000
6	5	42,000
7	Present value	=NPV(0.12,B2:B6)
8	Initial investment at time 0	(94,554)
9	Net present value	=B7+B8

Output:

	A	B
1	Year of cash flow	Cash flow
2	1	$ 30,000
3	2	30,000
4	3	30,000
5	4	30,000
6	5	42,000
7	Present value	$114,952.41
8	Initial investment at time 0	(94,554.00)
9	Net present value	$ 20,398.41

Internal Rate of Return

The **internal rate of return (IRR)**, often called the **time-adjusted rate of return**, is the discount rate that equates the present value of a project's cash inflows with the present value of the project's cash outflows. Other ways to describe IRR include: (1) The minimum rate that could be paid for the money invested in a project without losing money, and (2) The discount rate that results in a project's net present value equaling zero.

All practical applications of the IRR model use a calculator or spreadsheet. Thus, we illustrate determining an IRR with a spreadsheet. A table approach to determining a project's internal rate of return is illustrated in Appendix 24B of this Module.

With spreadsheet software, simply enter a column or row containing the net cash flows for each period and the appropriate formula. Spreadsheet input for Mobile Yogurt Shoppe's investment proposal is shown in Exhibit 24.4. The spreadsheet formula for the IRR assumes that the first cash flow occurs at time "0."

The spreadsheet approach requires an initial prediction or guess of the project's internal rate of return. Although the closeness of the prediction to the final solution affects computational speed, for textbook examples almost any number can be used. We use an initial estimate of 0.08 in all illustrations. Because the IRR formula assumes that the first cash flow occurs at time 0, the initial investment is included in the data analyzed by the IRR formula. Again, we must order the cash flows from top to bottom in a column or left to right in a row. As shown on the right column in Exhibit 24.4, the spreadsheet software computes the IRR as 20 percent.

Although a project's IRR should be compared to the discount rate established by management, such a discount rate is often unknown. In these situations, computing the IRR still provides insights into a project's profitability.

EXHIBIT 24.4 Spreadsheet Approach to Determining Internal Rate of Return

Input:

	A	B
	Year of cash flow	**Cash flow**
1	Year of cash flow	Cash flow
2	0	$(94,554)
3	1	30,000
4	2	30,000
5	3	30,000
6	4	30,000
7	5	42,000
8	IRR	=IRR(B2:B7,0.08)*

Output:

	A	B
	Year of cash flow	**Cash flow**
1	Year of cash flow	Cash flow
2	0	$(94,554)
3	1	30,000
4	2	30,000
5	3	30,000
6	4	30,000
7	5	42,000
8	IRR	0.20

The formula is "=IRR(Input data range, guess)." The guess, which is any likely rate of return, is used as an initial starting point in determining the solution. We use 0.08 in all illustrations.

The calculated internal rate of return is compared to the discount rate established by management to evaluate investment proposals. If the proposal's IRR is greater than or equal to the discount rate, the project is acceptable; if it is less than the discount rate, the project is unacceptable. Because Mobile Yogurt Shoppes has a 12 percent discount rate, the project is acceptable using the IRR model.

Although a computer and appropriate software quickly and accurately perform tedious computations, computational ease increases the opportunity for inappropriate use. The ability to plug numbers into a computer or calculator and obtain an output labeled NPV or IRR could mislead the unwary into believing that capital budgeting models are easy to use. This is not true. Training and professional judgment are required to identify relevant costs, to implement procedures to obtain relevant cost information, and to make a good decision once results are available. Capital budgeting models are merely decision aids. Managers, not models, make the decisions. To better illustrate underlying concepts, all subsequent textbook illustrations use a table approach.

Cost of Capital

When discounting models are used to evaluate capital expenditure proposals, management must determine the discount rate (1) used to compute a proposal's net present value or (2) used as the standard for evaluating a proposal's IRR. An organization's cost of capital is often used as this discount rate.

The **cost of capital** is the average cost an organization pays to obtain the resources necessary to make investments. This average rate considers items such as the:

- Effective interest rate on debt (notes or bonds).
- Effective dividend rate on preferred stock.
- Discount rate that equates the present value of all dividends expected on common stock over the life of the organization to the current market value of the organization's common stock.

The cost of capital for a company that has no debt or preferred stock equals the cost of equity capital, computed as follows:

$$\text{Cost of equity capital} = \frac{\text{Current annual dividend per common share}}{\text{Current market price per common share}} + \begin{array}{c}\text{Expected dividend}\\ \text{growth rate}\end{array}$$

Procedures for determining the cost of capital for more complex capital structures are covered in finance books. Investing in a project that has an internal rate of return equal to the cost of capital should not affect the market value of the firm's securities. Investing in a project that has a return higher than the cost of capital should increase the market value of a firm's securities. If, however, a firm invests in a project that has a return less than the cost of capital, the market value of the firm's securities should fall.

The cost of capital is the minimum return acceptable for investment purposes. Any investment proposal not expected to yield this minimum rate should normally be rejected. Because of difficulties encountered in determining the cost of capital, many organizations adopt a discount rate or a target rate of return without complicated mathematical analysis.

MID-MODULE REVIEW

Consider the following investment proposal:

Initial investment	
Depreciable assets	$27,740
Working capital	3,000
Operations (per year for 4 years)	
Cash receipts	25,000
Cash expenditures	15,000
Disinvestment	
Salvage value of plant and equipment	2,000
Recovery of working capital	3,000

Required
Determine each of the following:

a. Net present value at a 10 percent discount rate.
b. Internal rate of return. (Refer to Appendix 24B if using the table approach.)

The solution is on page 24-41.

CAPITAL BUDGETING MODELS THAT DO NOT CONSIDER TIME VALUE OF MONEY

LO3 Apply capital budgeting models, such as payback period and accounting rate of return, that do not consider the time value of money.

Years ago, capital budgeting models that do not consider the time value of money were more widely used than discounting models. Although most large organizations use net present value or internal rate of return as their primary evaluation tool, they often use nondiscounting models as an initial screening device. Further, as discussed in the following Research Insight, nondiscounting models remain entrenched in small businesses. We consider two nondiscounting models, the *payback period* and the *accounting rate of return*.

Payback Period

The **payback period** is the time required to recover the initial investment in a project from operations. The payback decision rule states that acceptable projects must have less than some maximum payback period designated by management. Payback emphasizes management's concern with liquidity and the need to minimize risk through a rapid recovery of the initial investment. It is frequently used for small expenditures having such obvious benefits that the use of more sophisticated capital budgeting models is not required or justified.

When a project is expected to have equal annual operating cash inflows, its payback period is computed as follows:

$$\text{Payback period} = \frac{\textbf{Initial investment}}{\textbf{Annual operating cash inflows}}$$

For Mobile Yogurt Shoppe's investment proposal, outlined in Exhibit 24.2, the payback period is 3.15 years:

$$\text{Payback period} = \frac{\$94,554}{\$30,000}$$
$$= 3.15$$

RESEARCH INSIGHT Size and Education Matter in Capital Budgeting

Danielson and Scott, after surveying the owners of small business, concluded that small businesses (an average of ten employees) use much less sophisticated methods in making capital expenditure decisions than recommended by theory. In their survey the most frequently used approach to making capital expenditure decisions was "gut feel" followed by payback period and the accounting rate of return, with few firms using discounted cash flow methods. Commenting on their results, Danielson and Scott observed that:

- Many small business owners have limited formal education and limited staff support. What's more, the investments made by small business are often not discretionary. The firm either makes the investment, say in a new delivery truck, or goes out of business.

- The use of payback appears to increase with the formal education of the business owner as well as the use of basic budgeting techniques such as forecasting cash flows.

- The use of the accounting rate of return increases with the growth or expansion plans of small firms, especially if the firm is required to provide banks with periodic financial information.

- Small businesses with owners having advanced degrees are most likely to use discounted cash flow approaches. They are also most likely to have written business plans and most likely to consider the tax implications of decisions.

Graham and Harvey surveyed chief financial officers (CFOs) of Fortune 500 firms as well as CFOs of smaller firms belonging to the Financial Executives Institute (FEI). CFO's and members of the FEI are likely to have formal education in capital budgeting and they are likely to network with finance professionals through organizations such as the FEI.

Of the CFOs responding to the survey, 46 percent were at firms with sales of more than $1 billion. The majority of respondents to the Graham-Harvey survey used multiple capital budgeting models:

- 75.7 percent used internal rate of return.
- 74.9 percent used net present value.
- More than 50 percent used payback.
- Approximately 20 percent used the accounting rate of return.

Even though the firms included in the Graham-Harvey study were much larger than those in the Danielson-Scott study, Graham and Harvey also noted that "small firms" (firms with sales of less than $100 million) are less likely to use net present value than large firms.

Source: Morris G. Danielson and Jonathan A. Scott, "The Capital Budgeting Decisions of Small Businesses." *Journal of Applied Finance*, Fall/Winter 2006, pp. 45-56. John R. Graham and Campbell R. Harvey, "The Theory and Practice of Corporate Finance: Evidence from the Field," *Journal of Financial Economics*, May-June, 2001, pp: 187-243.

Determining the payback period for a project having unequal cash flows is slightly more complicated. Assume that Alderman Company is evaluating a capital expenditure proposal that requires an initial investment of $50,000 and has the following expected net cash inflows:

Year	Net Cash Inflow
1	$15,000
2	25,000
3	40,000
4	20,000
5	10,000

To compute the payback period, we must determine the net unrecovered amount at the end of each year. In the year of full recovery, the net cash inflows are assumed to occur evenly and are prorated based on the unrecovered investment at the start of the year. Full recovery of Alderman Company's investment proposal is expected to occur in Year 3:

Year	Net Cash Inflow	Unrecovered Investment
0	$ - 0	$50,000
1	15,000	35,000
2	25,000	10,000
3	40,000	0

Therefore, $10,000 of $40,000 is needed in Year 3 to complete the recovery of the initial investment. This provides a proportion of 0.25 ($10,000 ÷ $40,000) and a payback period of 2.25 years (2 years plus 0.25 of Year 3). This project is acceptable if management specified a maximum payback period of three years. Because they occur after the payback period, the net cash inflows of Years 4 and 5 are ignored.

Accounting Rate of Return

The **accounting rate of return** is the average annual increase in net income that results from the acceptance of a capital expenditure proposal divided by either the initial investment or the average investment in the project. This method differs from other capital budgeting models in that it focuses on accounting income rather than on cash flow. In most capital budgeting applications, accounting net income is approximated as net cash inflow from operations minus expenses not requiring the use of cash, such as depreciation.

Consider Mobile Yogurt Shoppe's capital expenditure proposal whose cash flows were outlined in Exhibit 24.2. The vehicle and equipment cost $90,554 and have a disposal value of $8,000 at the end of five years, resulting in an average annual increase in net income of $13,489:

Annual net cash inflow from operations....................................	$30,000
Less average annual depreciation [($90,554 − $8,000) ÷ 5]....................	(16,511)
Average annual increase in net income	$13,489

Considering the investment in inventories and other working capital, the initial investment is $94,554 ($90,554 + $4,000), and the *accounting rate of return on initial investment* is 14.27 percent:

$$\frac{\text{Accounting rate of return}}{\text{on initial investment}} = \frac{\text{Average annual increase in net income}}{\text{Initial investment}} = \frac{\$13,489}{\$94,554} = 0.1427$$

The average investment, computed as the initial investment plus the expected value of any disinvestment, all divided by 2, is $53,277 [($94,554 + $12,000) ÷ 2]. The *accounting rate of return on average investment* is 25.32 percent:

$$\frac{\text{Accounting rate of return}}{\text{on average investment}} = \frac{\text{Average annual increase in net income}}{\text{Average investment}} = \frac{\$13,489}{\$53,277} = 0.2532$$

When using the accounting rate of return, management specifies either the initial investment or average investment plus some minimum acceptable rate. Management rejects capital expenditure proposals with a lower accounting rate of return but accepts proposals with an accounting rate of return higher than or equal to the minimum.

EVALUATION OF CAPITAL BUDGETING MODELS

As a single criterion for evaluating capital expenditure proposals, capital budgeting models that consider the time value of money are superior to models that do not consider it. The payback model concerns merely how long it takes to recover the initial investment from a project, yet investments are not made with the objective of merely getting the money back. Indeed, not investing has a payback period of 0. Investments are made to earn a profit. Hence, what happens after the payback period is more important than is the payback period itself. The payback period model, when used as the sole investment criterion, has a fatal flaw in that it fails to consider cash flows after the payback period. Despite this flaw, payback is a rough-and-ready approach to getting a handle on investment proposals. Sometimes a project is so attractive using payback that, when its life is considered, no further analysis is necessary. This appears to be the situation with the investments in energy-saving renovations detailed in the following Business Insight. But note how financial reward systems interfere.

LO4 Evaluate the strengths and weaknesses of alternative capital budgeting models.

BUSINESS INSIGHT   **Green Renovations with Low Payback Period and Low Business Appeal**

As reported in *Business Week*, a McKinsey and Company study suggests that energy-saving renovations in large/high buildings have long lives and very rapid payback periods:

- Investing in sensors that turn off lights in empty rooms and hallways has a payback period of less than one year.
- Changing to more efficient light bulbs has a payback period of one year.
- Switching to variable speed water pumps and air circulating motors has a payback period of one year.
- Replacing single-pane for multiple-pane windows has a payback period of less than three years.

Although these energy-saving investments appear to be "no brainers", a New York City proposal calling for energy audits and energy-saving renovations in large buildings has met with resistance from owners of buildings occupied by tenants with long-term leases. It seems while the building owner pays for energy renovations, the financial benefits of lower electric, water, and gas bills accrue to tenants who often pay separately for the actual cost of energy consumption. "Without a better reward on the table, the landlords will drag their feet," predicts Jennifer Henry of the Natural Resources Defense Council.

Source: Adam Aston, "Should Landlords Save the Earth?," *Business Week*, May 18, 2009, pp. 46-49.

For total life evaluations, the accounting rate of return is superior to the payback period because it does consider a capital expenditure proposal's profitability. Using the accounting rate of return, a project that merely returns the initial investment will have an average annual increase in net income of 0 and an accounting rate of return of 0. The problem with the accounting rate of return is that it fails to consider the timing of cash flows. It treats all cash flows within the life of an investment proposal equally despite the fact that cash flows occurring early in a project's life are more valuable than cash flows occurring late in a project's life. Early period cash flows can earn additional profits by being invested elsewhere. Consider the two investment proposals summarized in Exhibit 24.5. Both have an accounting rate of return of 5 percent, but Proposal A is superior to Proposal B because most of its cash flows occur in the first two years. Because of the timing of the cash flows when discounted at an annual rate of 10 percent, Proposal A has a net present value of $1,140 while Proposal B has a negative net present value of $(10,940).

EXHIBIT 24.5   Evaluating Capital Budgeting Models with Differences in Cash Flow Timing

Accounting rate of return analysis of Projects A and B

	Project A	Project B
Predicted net cash inflow from operations		
Year 1	$ 50,000	$ 10,000
Year 2	50,000	10,000
Year 3	10,000	50,000
Year 4	10,000	50,000
Total	120,000	120,000
Total depreciation	(100,000)	(100,000)
Total net income	$ 20,000	$ 20,000
Project life	÷ 4 years	÷ 4 years
Average annual increase in net income	$ 5,000	$ 5,000
Initial investment	÷ 100,000	÷ 100,000
Accounting rate of return on initial investment	0.05	0.05

Net present value analysis of Project A

	Predicted Cash Inflows (outflows)	Year(s) of Cash Flows	10% Present Value Factor	Present Value of Cash Flows
Initial investment	$(100,000)	0	1.000	$(100,000)
Operation	50,000	1–2	1.736	86,800
Operation	10,000	3–4	3.170–1.736	14,340
Net present value of all cash flows				$ 1,140

Net present value analysis of Project B

	Predicted Cash Inflows (outflows)	Year(s) of Cash Flows	10% Present Value Factor	Present Value of Cash Flows
Initial investment	$(100,000)	0	1.000	$(100,000)
Operation	10,000	1–2	1.736	17,360
Operation	50,000	3–4	3.170–1.736	71,700
Net present value of all cash flows				$ (10,940)

The net present value and the internal rate of return models both consider the time value of money and project profitability. They almost always provide the same evaluation of individual projects whose acceptance or rejection will not affect other projects. (An exception can occur when periods of net cash outflows are mixed with periods of net cash inflows. Under these circumstances, an investment proposal could have multiple internal rates of return.) The net present value and the internal rate of return models, however, have two basic differences that often lead to differences in the evaluation of competing investment proposals:

1. The net present value model gives explicit consideration to investment size. The internal rate of return model does not.

2. The net present value model assumes that all net cash inflows are reinvested at the discount rate; the internal rate of return model assumes that all net cash inflows are reinvested at the project's internal rate of return.

When there is a difference in the size of competing investment proposals and funds not invested in the accepted proposal can only be invested at the cost of capital, the net present value method is superior.

ADDITIONAL ASPECTS OF CAPITAL BUDGETING

The capital budgeting models discussed do not make investment decisions. Rather, they help managers separate capital expenditure proposals that meet certain criteria from those that do not. Managers then focus on those proposals that pass the initial screening.

LO5 Discuss the importance of judgment, attitudes toward risk, and relevant cash flow information for capital budgeting decisions.

Using Multiple Investment Criteria

In performing this initial screening, management can use a single capital budgeting model or multiple models, including some we have not discussed. Management might specify that proposals must be in line with the organization's long-range goals and business strategy, have a maximum payback period of three years, have a positive net present value when discounted at 14 percent, and have an initial investment of less than $500,000. The maximum payback period might be intended to reduce risk, the present value criterion might be to ensure an adequate return to investors, and the maximum investment size might reflect the resources available for investment.

Nonquantitative factors such as market position, operational performance improvement, and strategy implementation often play a decisive role in management's final decision to accept or reject a capital expenditure proposal that has passed the initial screening. Also important at this point are top management's attitudes toward risk and financing alternatives, their confidence in the professional judgment of other managers making investment proposals, their beliefs about the future direction of the economy, and their evaluation of alternative investments. In the following sections, we will focus on evaluating risk, differential analysis of project cash flows, predicting differential costs and revenues for high-tech investments, and evaluating mutually exclusive investments.

Evaluating Risk

All capital expenditure proposals involve risk, including risk related to

- Cost of the initial investment.
- Time required to complete the initial investment and begin operations.
- Whether the new facilities will operate as planned.
- Life of the facilities.
- Customers' demand for the product or service.
- Final selling price.
- Operating costs.
- Disposal values.

Projected cash flows (such as those summarized for the Mobile Yogurt Shoppe proposal in Exhibit 24.2) are based on management's best predictions. Although these predictions are likely to reflect the professional judgment of economists, marketing personnel, engineers, and accountants, they are far from certain.

Many techniques have been developed to assist in the analysis of the risks inherent in capital budgeting. Suggested approaches include the following:

- *To adjust the discount rate for individual projects based on management's perception of the risks associated with a project.* A project perceived as being almost risk free might be evaluated using a discount rate of 12 percent; a project perceived as having moderate risk may be evaluated using a discount rate of 16 percent; and a project perceived as having high risk might be evaluated using a discount rate of 20 percent.

- *To compute several internal rates of return and/or net present values for a project.* For example, a project's net present value might be computed three times: first assuming the most optimistic projections of cash flows; second assuming the most likely projections of cash flows; and third assuming the most pessimistic projections of cash flows. The final decision is then based on management's attitudes toward risk. A project whose most likely outcome is highly profitable would probably be rejected if its pessimistic outcome might lead to bankruptcy.

■ *To subject a capital expenditure proposal to sensitivity analysis*, a study of the responsiveness of a model's dependent variable(s) to changes in one or more of its independent variables. Management might want to know, for example, the minimum annual net cash inflows that will provide an internal rate of return of 12 percent with other cost and revenue projections being as expected.

Differential Analysis of Project Cash Flows

All previous examples assume that capital expenditure proposals produce additional net cash inflows, but this is not always the case. Units of government and not-for-profit organizations might provide services that do not produce any cash inflows. For-profit organizations might be required to make capital expenditures to maintain product quality or to bring facilities up to environmental or safety standards. In these situations, it is impossible to compute a project's payback period, accounting rate of return, or internal rate of return. It is possible, however, to compute the present value of all life cycle costs associated with alternative ways of providing the service or meeting the environmental or safety standard. Here, the alternative with the smallest negative net present value is preferred.

Capital expenditure proposals to reduce operating costs by upgrading facilities might not provide any incremental cash inflows. Again, we can use a total cost approach and calculate the present value of the costs associated with each alternative, with the low-cost alternative being preferred. Alternatively, we can perform a differential analysis of cash flows and, treating any reduced operating costs as if they were cash inflows, compute the net present value or the internal rate of return of the cost reduction proposal. Recall from Module 16 that a relevant cost analysis focuses on the costs that differ under alternative actions. Once the differential amounts have been determined, they can be adjusted for the time value of money. To illustrate the differential approach, we consider an example introduced in Module 16.

Elektra, Inc. produces a variety of electronic components, including 10,000 units per year of a component used in wireless headsets. The machine currently used in manufacturing the headset components is two years old and has a remaining useful life of four years. It cost $90,000 and has an estimated salvage value of zero dollars at the end of its useful life. Its current book value (original cost less accumulated depreciation) is $60,000, but its current disposal value is only $35,000.

Management is evaluating the desirability of replacing the machine with a new machine. The new machine costs $80,000, has a useful life of four years, and a predicted salvage value of zero dollars at the end of its useful life. Although the new machine has the same productive capacity as the old machine, its predicted operating costs are lower because it requires less electricity. Furthermore, because of a computer control system, the new machine will require less frequent and less expensive inspections and adjustments. Finally, the new machine requires less maintenance.

An analysis of the cash flows associated with this cost reduction proposal, separated into the three phases of the project's life, are presented in Exhibit 24.6. Because the proposal does not have a disposal value, this portion of the analysis could have been omitted. (A detailed explanation of the relevant costs included in this analysis is in Exhibit 16.1 and the accompanying Module 16 discussion of relevant costs.) Assuming that Elektra, Inc. has a discount rate of 12 percent, the proposal's net present value (computed in Exhibit 24.7) is $2,681, and the proposal is acceptable.

Predicting Differential Costs and Revenues for High-Tech Investments

Care must be taken when evaluating proposals for investments in the technological innovations such as flexible manufacturing systems and computer integrated manufacturing. The three types of errors to consider are: (1) investing in unnecessary or overly complex equipment, (2) overestimating cost saving, and (3) underestimating incremental sales.

Investing in Unnecessary or Overly Complex Equipment

A common error is to simply compare the cost associated with the current inefficient way of doing things with the predicted cost of performing the identical operations with more modern equip-

EXHIBIT 24.6 Differential Analysis of Predicted Cash Flows

	Differential Analysis of Predicted Cash Flows		
	Keep Old Machine (A)	**Replace with New Machine (B)**	**Difference (income effect of replacement) (A) – (B)**
Initial investment			
Cost of new machine		$80,000	$80,000
Disposal value of old machine		(35,000)	(35,000)
Net initial investment			$45,000
Annual operating cash savings			
Conversion			
Old machine (10,000 units × $5)	$50,000		
New machine (10,000 units × $4)		$40,000	$10,000
Inspection and adjustment			
Old machine (10 setups × $500 per setup)	5,000		
New machine (5 setups × $300 per setup)		1,500	3,500
Machine maintenance			
Old machine ($200 per month × 12 months).	2,400		
New machine ($200 per year).		200	2,200
Net annual cost savings.			$15,700
Disinvestment at end of life			
Old machine	$ 0		
New machine		$ 0	

EXHIBIT 24.7 Differential Analysis of Predicted Cash Flows

	Predicted Cash Inflows (outflows) (A)	**Year(s) of Cash Flows (B)**	**12% Present Value Factor (C)**	**Present Value of Cash Flows (A) × (C)**
Initial investment	$(45,000)	0	1.000	$(45,000)
Operation	15,700	1–4	3.037	47,681
Disinvestment.	0	4	0.636	0
Net present value of all cash flows.				$ 2,681

ment. Although capital budgeting models might suggest that such investments are justifiable, the result could be the costly and rapid completion of non-value-added activities. Consider the following examples.

■ A company invests in an automated system to speed the movement of work in process between workstations without first evaluating the plant layout. The firm is still unable to compete with other companies having better organized plants that allow lower cycle times, lower work-in-process inventories, and lower manufacturing costs. Management should have evaluated the plant layout before investing in new equipment. They may have found that rearranging the factory floor would have reduced materials movement and eliminated the need for the investment.

■ A company invests in an automated warehouse to permit the rapid storage and retrieval of goods while competitors work to eliminate excess inventory. The firm is left with large inventories and a large investment in the automated warehouse while competitors, not having to earn a return on similar investments, are able to charge lower prices. Management should have evaluated the need for current inventory levels and perhaps shifted to a just-in-time approach to inventory management before considering the investment in an automated warehouse.

■ A company hires staff to perform quality inspections while competitors implement total quality management and seek to eliminate the need for quality inspections. While defective products or services are now identified before they affect customers, they still exist. Furthermore, the company has higher expenditures than competitors, resulting in a less competitive cost structure. The inspections might not have been needed if management had shifted from inspecting for conformance to an emphasis on "doing it right the first time."

■ A company invests in automated welding equipment to more efficiently produce printer casings while competitors simplify the product design and shift from welded to molded plastic casings. Although the cost of producing the welded casings might be lower, the company's cost structure is still not competitive.

All of these examples illustrate the limitations of capital budgeting models and the need for good judgment. *In the final analysis, managers, not models, make decisions.* Management must carefully evaluate the situations and determine whether they have considered the proper alternatives and all important cash flows.

Overestimating Cost Savings

When a number of activities drive manufacturing overhead costs, estimates of overhead cost savings based on a single activity cost driver can significantly overestimate cost savings. Assume, for example, that a company containing both machine-intensive and labor-intensive operations develops a cost-estimating equation for overhead with labor as the only independent variable. Because of this, all overhead costs are associated with labor. The predicted cost savings can be computed as the sum of predicted reductions in labor plus predicted reductions in overhead; the predicted reductions in overhead are computed as the overhead per direct labor dollar or labor hour multiplied by the predicted reduction in direct labor dollars or labor hours. Because a major portion of the overhead is driven by factors other than direct labor, reducing direct labor will not provide the predicted savings. Capital budgeting models might suggest that the investment is acceptable, but the models are based on inaccurate cost data.

Management should beware of overly simplistic computations of cost savings. This is an area in which management needs the assistance of well-trained management accountants and engineers.

Underestimating Incremental Sales or Cost Savings

In evaluating proposals for investments in new equipment, management often assumes that the baseline for comparison is the current sales level, but this might not be the case. If competitors are investing in equipment to better meet customer needs and to reduce costs, a failure to make similar investments might result in uncompetitive prices and declining, rather than steady, sales. Hence, the baseline for sales without the investment is overstated, and the incremental sales of the investment is understated. Not considering the likely decline in sales understates the incremental sales associated with the investment and biases the results against the proposed investment.

Investments in manufacturing technologies, such as flexible manufacturing systems (FMS) and computer integrated manufacturing (CIM), do more than simply allow the efficient production of current products. Such investments also make possible the rapid, low-cost switching to new products. The result is expanded sales opportunities.

Such investments might also produce cost savings further down the value chain, either within or outside the company. Elektra's decision to acquire a new machine might have the unanticipated consequence of reducing customer warranty claims or increasing sales because customers are attracted to a higher-quality product.

Unfortunately, because such opportunities are difficult to quantify, they are often ignored in the evaluation of capital expenditure proposals. The solution to this dilemma involves the application of management's professional judgment, a willingness to take risks based on this professional judgment, and recognition that certain investments transcend capital budgeting models in that they involve strategic as well as long-range planning. At this level of planning, qualitative decisions concerning the nature of the organization are at least as important as quantified factors.

TAXES IN CAPITAL BUDGETING DECISIONS

To focus on capital budgeting concepts, we deferred consideration of the impact of taxes. Because income taxes affect cash flows and income, their consideration is important in evaluating investment proposals in for-profit organizations.

LO6 Determine the net present value of investment proposals with consideration of taxes.

The cost of investments in plant and equipment is not deducted from taxable revenues in determining taxable income and income taxes at the time of the initial investment. Instead, the amount of the initial investment is deducted as depreciation over the operating life of an asset. To illustrate the impact of taxes on cash flows, assume:

- Revenues and operating cash receipts are the same each year.
- Depreciation is the only noncash expense of an organization.

Depreciation Tax Shield

Depreciation does not require the use of cash (the funds were spent at the initial investment), but depreciation is said to provide a "tax shield" because it reduces cash payments for income taxes. The **depreciation tax shield** (the reduction in taxes due to the deductibility of depreciation from taxable revenues) is computed as follows:

Depreciation tax shield = Depreciation × Tax rate

The value of the depreciation tax shield is illustrated using Mobile Yogurt Shoppe's capital expenditure proposal summarized in Exhibit 24.2. Mobile Yogurt Shoppe's annual straight line depreciation of $16,511 is computed as the initial investment of $90,554 minus the predicted disposal value of $8,000, all divided by the predicted five year life $16,511 [($90,554 − $8,000)/5]. With an assumed tax rate of 34 percent, the annual depreciation tax shield is $5,614 ($16,511 depreciation × 0.34 tax rate). The increase in annual cash flows provided by the depreciation tax shield is illustrated in Exhibit 24.8. Examine this exhibit, paying particular attention to the lines for depreciation, income taxes, and net annual cash flow.

The U.S. Tax Code contains guidelines concerning the depreciation of various types of assets. (Analysis of these guidelines is beyond the scope of this text.) Tax guidelines allow organizations a choice in tax depreciation procedures between straight-line depreciation and an accelerated depreciation method detailed in the Tax Code. Because of the time value of money, profitable businesses should usually select the tax depreciation procedure that provides the earliest depreciation. To illustrate the effect of accelerated depreciation on taxes and capital budgeting, we use double-declining balance depreciation rather than the accelerated method detailed in the Code. When making capital expenditure decisions, managers should, of course, refer to the most current version of the Tax Code to determine the specific depreciation guidelines in effect at that time.

Exhibits 24.9 and 24.10 illustrate the effect of two alternative depreciation procedures, straight-line and double-declining balance, on the net present value of Mobile Yogurt Shoppe's proposed investment. The cash flows for this investment were presented in Exhibit 24.2, and the effect of taxes on the investment's annual cash flows were examined in Exhibit 24.8. Ignoring taxes, the investment was shown (in Exhibit 24.3) to have a positive net present value of $20,400 at a discount rate of 12 percent. With taxes, the investment has a positive net present value of $3,867 using straight-line depreciation and $6,084 using double-declining balance depreciation. Although taxes and cash flows are identical over the entire life of the project, the use of double-declining balance depreciation for taxes results in a higher net present value because it results in lower cash expenditures for taxes in the earlier years of an asset's life.

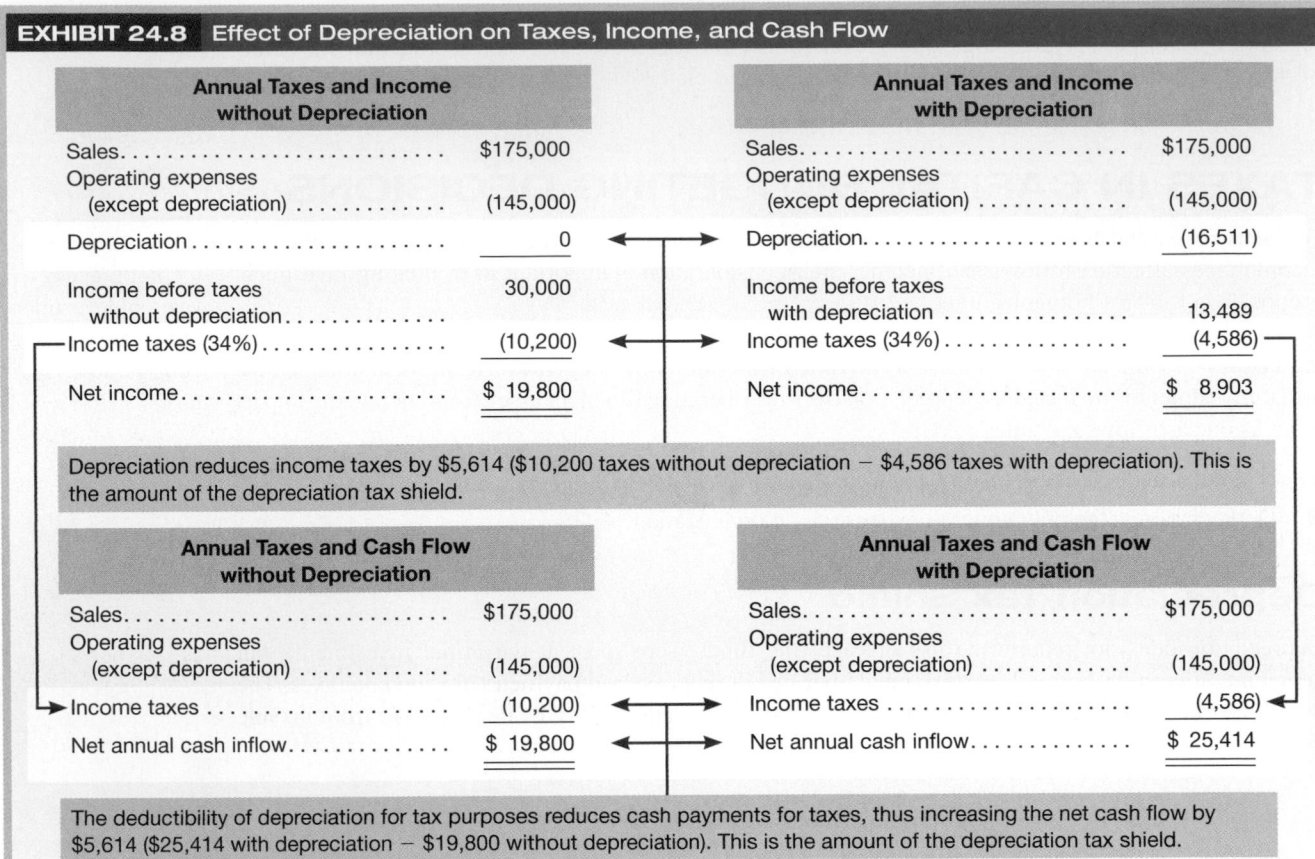

EXHIBIT 24.8   Effect of Depreciation on Taxes, Income, and Cash Flow

Annual Taxes and Income without Depreciation		Annual Taxes and Income with Depreciation	
Sales..........................	$175,000	Sales..........................	$175,000
Operating expenses (except depreciation)	(145,000)	Operating expenses (except depreciation)	(145,000)
Depreciation.....................	0	Depreciation.....................	(16,511)
Income before taxes without depreciation.............	30,000	Income before taxes with depreciation	13,489
Income taxes (34%)...............	(10,200)	Income taxes (34%)...............	(4,586)
Net income.....................	$ 19,800	Net income.....................	$ 8,903

Depreciation reduces income taxes by $5,614 ($10,200 taxes without depreciation − $4,586 taxes with depreciation). This is the amount of the depreciation tax shield.

Annual Taxes and Cash Flow without Depreciation		Annual Taxes and Cash Flow with Depreciation	
Sales..........................	$175,000	Sales..........................	$175,000
Operating expenses (except depreciation)	(145,000)	Operating expenses (except depreciation)	(145,000)
Income taxes	(10,200)	Income taxes	(4,586)
Net annual cash inflow.............	$ 19,800	Net annual cash inflow.............	$ 25,414

The deductibility of depreciation for tax purposes reduces cash payments for taxes, thus increasing the net cash flow by $5,614 ($25,414 with depreciation − $19,800 without depreciation). This is the amount of the depreciation tax shield.

EXHIBIT 24.9   Analysis of Capital Expenditures Including Tax Effects: Straight-Line Depreciation

	Predicted Cash Inflows (outflows) (A)	Year(s) of Cash Flows (B)	12% Present Value Factor (C)	Present Value of Cash Flows (A) × (C)
Initial investment				
Vehicle and equipment............................	$(90,554)	0	1.000	$ (90,554)
Inventory and other working capital....................	(4,000)	0	1.000	(4,000)
Operations				
Annual taxable income without depreciation............	30,000	1–5	3.605	108,150
Taxes on income ($30,000 × 0.34)...................	(10,200)	1–5	3.605	(36,771)
Depreciation tax shield*	5,614	1–5	3.605	20,238
Disinvestment				
Sale of vehicle and equipment......................	8,000	5	0.567	4,536
Inventory and other working capital..................	4,000	5	0.567	2,268
Net present value of all cash flows				$ 3,867

*Computation of depreciation tax shield:

Annual straight-line depreciation	$16,511
Tax rate..	× 0.34
Depreciation tax shield	$ 5,614

Investment Tax Credit

From time to time, for the purpose of stimulating investment and economic growth, the U.S. federal government has implemented an investment tax credit. An **investment tax credit** reduces taxes in the year a new asset is placed in service by some stated percentage of the cost of the asset. In recent years tax credits, such as the credits for purchasing hybrid automobiles, have been used to stimulate

EXHIBIT 24.10	Analysis of Capital Expenditures Including Tax Effects: DDB Depreciation			
	Predicted Cash Inflows (outflows) (A)	Year(s) of Cash Flows (B)	12% Present Value Factor (C)	Present Value of Cash Flows (A) × (C)
Initial investment				
Vehicle and equipment.............................	$(90,554)	0	1.000	$ (90,554)
Inventory and other working capital..................	4,000	0	1.000	(4,000)
Operations				
Annual taxable income without depreciation............	30,000	1–5	3.605	108,150
Taxes on income ($30,000 × 0.34)...................	(10,200)	1–5	3.605	(36,771)
Depreciation tax shield*				
Year 1	12,315	1	0.893	10,997
Year 2	7,389	2	0.797	5,889
Year 3	4,434	3	0.712	3,157
Year 4	2,660	4	0.636	1,692
Year 5	1,270	5	0.567	720
Disinvestment				
Sale of vehicle and equipment.....................	8,000	5	0.567	4,536
Inventory and other working capital..................	4,000	5	0.567	2,268
Net present value of all cash flows				$ 6,084

*Computation of depreciation tax shield:

Year	Depreciation Base† (A)	Annual Rate (B)	Annual Depreciation (C) = (A) × (B)	Tax Rate (D)	Tax Shield (E) = (C) × (D)
1 ...	$90,554	2/5	$36,222	0.34	$12,315
2 ...	54,332	2/5	21,733	0.34	7,389
3 ...	32,599	2/5	13,040	0.34	4,434
4 ...	19,559	2/5	7,824	0.34	2,660
5 ...	11,735	balance	3,735	0.34	1,270

†The depreciation base is reduced by the amount of all previous depreciation. The annual rate is twice the straight-line rate. For simplicity, we depreciated the remaining balance in the fifth year and did not switch to straight-line depreciation when the straight-line amount exceeds the double-declining balance amount. This would happen in the fourth year, when $19,559 ÷ 2 = $9,780. Although the depreciable base excludes the predicted disposal value of $8,000, under double declining balance depreciation, an asset is only depreciated down to its disposal value. Hence, year 8 depreciation is computed as the $11,735 depreciable base minus the $8,000 disposal value.

investments that reduce the emission of greenhouses gases. Typically, this is done without reducing the depreciation base of the asset for tax purposes. An investment tax credit reduces cash payments for taxes and, hence, is treated as a cash inflow for capital budgeting purposes. This additional cash inflow increases the probability that a new asset will meet a taxpayer's capital expenditure criteria.

MODULE-END REVIEW

Consider the following investment proposal:

Initial investment	
Depreciable assets	$27,740
Working capital	3,000
Operations (per year for 4 years)	
Cash receipts	25,000
Cash expenditures	15,000
Disinvestment	
Salvage value of plant and equipment	2,000
Recovery of working capital	3,000

Required
Determine each of the following:
  a. Payback period.
  b. Accounting rate of return on initial investment and on average investment.

The solution is on page 24-42.

APPENDIX 24A: Time Value of Money

When asked to choose between $500 today or an IOU for $500 to be paid one year later, rational decision makers choose the $500 today. Two reasons for this involve the time *value of money* and the *risk*. A dollar today is worth more than a dollar tomorrow or at some future time. Having a dollar provides flexibility. It can be spent, buried, or invested in a number of projects. If invested in a savings account, it will amount to more than one dollar at some future time because of the effect of interest. The interest paid by a bank (or borrower) for the use of money is analogous to the rent paid for the use of land, buildings, or equipment. Furthermore, we live in an uncertain world, and, for a variety of reasons, the possibility exists that an IOU might not be paid.

Future Value

Future value is the amount that a current sum of money earning a stated rate of interest will accumulate to at the end of a future period. Suppose we deposit $500 in a savings account at a financial institution that pays interest at the rate of 10 percent per year. At the end of the first year, the original deposit of $500 will total $550 ($500 × 1.10). If we leave the $550 for another year, the amount will increase to $605 ($550 × 1.10). It can be stated that $500 today has a future value in one year of $550, or conversely, that $550 one year from today has a present value of $500. Interest of $55 ($605 − $550) was earned in the second year, whereas interest of only $50 was earned in the first year. This happened because interest during the second year was earned on the principal plus interest from the first year ($550). When periodic interest is computed on principal plus prior periods' accumulated interest, the interest is said to be *compounded*. Compound interest is used throughout this text.

To determine future values at the end of one period (usually a year), multiply the beginning amount (present value) by 1 plus the interest rate. When multiple periods are involved, the future value is determined by repeatedly multiplying the beginning amount by 1 plus the interest rate for each period. When $500 is invested for two years at an interest rate of 10 percent per year, its future value is computed as $500 × 1.10 × 1.10. The following equation is used to figure future value:

$$\mathbf{fv = pv(1 + i)^n}$$

where:

$$fv = \text{future value amount}$$
$$pv = \text{present value amount}$$
$$i = \text{interest rate per period}$$
$$n = \text{number of periods}$$

For our $500 deposit, the equation becomes:

$$\mathbf{fv \text{ of } \$500 = pv(1 + i)^n}$$
$$\mathbf{= \$500(1 + 0.10)^2}$$
$$\mathbf{= \$605}$$

In a similar manner, once the interest rate and number of periods are known, the future value amount of any present value amount is easily determined.

Present Value

Present value is the current worth of a specified amount of money to be received at some future date at some interest rate. Solving for *pv* in the future value equation, the new present value equation is determined as follows:

$$\mathbf{pv = \frac{fv}{(1 + i)^n}}$$

Using this equation, the present value of $8,800 to be received in one year, discounted at 10 percent, is computed as follows:

$$\text{pv of } \$8{,}800 = \frac{\$8{,}800}{(1 + 0.10)^1}$$
$$= \frac{\$8{,}800}{(1.10)}$$
$$= \$8{,}000$$

Thus, when the discount rate is 10 percent, the present value of $8,800 to be received in one year is $8,000. The present value equation is often expressed as the future value amount times the present value of $1:

$$\text{pv} = \text{fv} \times \frac{\$1}{(1 + i)^n}$$

Using the equation for the present value of $1, the present value of $8,800 to be received in one year, discounted at 10 percent, is computed as follows:

$$\text{pv of } \$8{,}800 = \$8{,}800 \times \frac{\$1}{(1 + 0.10)^1}$$
$$= \$8{,}800 \times 0.909$$
$$= \$8{,}000$$

The present value of $8,800 two periods from now is $7,273, computed as [$8,800 ÷ (1.10)^2] or [$8,800 × $1 ÷ (1.10)^2].

  If a calculator or computer with spreadsheet software is not available, present value computations can be done by hand. Tables, such as Table 24A.1 for the present value of $1 at various interest rates and time periods, can be used to simplify hand computations. Using the factors in Table 24A.1, the present value of any future amount can be determined. For example, with an interest rate of 10 percent, the present value of the following future amounts to be received in one period are as follows:

Future Value Amount		Present Value Factor of $1		Present Value
$ 100	×	0.909	=	$ 90.90
628	×	0.909	=	570.85
4,285	×	0.909	=	3,895.07
9,900	×	0.909	=	8,999.10

  To further illustrate the use of Table 24A.1, consider the following application. Alert Company wants to invest its surplus cash at 12 percent to have $10,000 to pay off a long-term note due at the end of five years. Table 24A.1 shows that the present value factor of $1, discounted at 12 percent per year for five years, is 0.567. Multiplying $10,000 by 0.567, the present value is determined to be $5,670:

$$\text{pv of } \$10{,}000 = \$10{,}000 \times \text{Present value factor for } \$1$$
$$= \$10{,}000 \times 0.567$$
$$= \$5{,}670$$

Therefore, if Alert invests $5,670 today, it will have $10,000 available to pay off its note in five years.

  Managers also use present value tables to make investment decisions. Assume that Monroe Company can make an investment that will provide a cash flow of $12,000 at the end of eight years. If the company demands a rate of return of 14 percent per year, what is the most it will be willing to pay for this investment? From Table 24A.1, we find that the present value factor for $1, discounted at 14 percent per year for eight years, is 0.351:

$$\text{pv of } \$12{,}000 = \$12{,}000 \times \text{Present value factor for } \$1$$
$$= \$12{,}000 \times 0.351$$
$$= \$4{,}212$$

If the company demands an annual return of 14 percent, the most it would be willing to invest today is $4,212.

Annuities

Not all investments provide a single sum of money. Many investments provide periodic cash flows called *annuities*. An **annuity** is a series of equal cash flows received or paid over equal intervals of time. Suppose that $100 will be received at the end of each of the next three years. If the discount rate is 10 percent, the present value of this annuity can be determined by summing the present value of each receipt:

$$\text{Year 1 } \$100 \times \$1 \div (1 + 0.10)1 = \$\ 90.90$$
$$\text{Year 2 } \$100 \times \$1 \div (1 + 0.10)2 = \quad 82.65$$
$$\text{Year 3 } \$100 \times \$1 \div (1 + 0.10)3 = \quad \underline{75.13}$$
$$\text{Total} \ldots\ldots\ldots\ldots\ldots\ldots\ldots\ldots \$248.68$$

Alternatively, the following equation can be used to compute the present value of an annuity with cash flows at the end of each period:

$$pva = \frac{a}{i} \times \left[1 - \frac{1}{(1 + 0.10)^n}\right]$$

where:

pva = present value of an annuity (also called the annuity factor)
i = prevailing rate per period
n = number of periods
a = annuity amount

This equation was used to compute the factors presented in Table 24A.2 for an annuity amount of $1. The present value of an annuity of $1 per period for three periods discounted at 10 percent per period is as follows:

$$pva \text{ of } \$1 = \frac{1}{0.10} \times \left[1 - \frac{1}{(1 + 0.10)^3}\right]$$
$$= 2.4868$$

Using this factor, the present value of a $100 annuity can be computed as $100 × 2.4868, which yields $248.68. To determine the present value of an annuity of any amount, the annuity factor for $1 can be multiplied by the annuity amount.

To further illustrate the use of Table 24A.2, assume that Red Kite Company is considering an investment in a piece of equipment that will produce net cash inflows of $2,000 at the end of each year for five years. If the company's desired rate of return is 12 percent, an investment of $7,210 will provide such a return:

$$pva \text{ of } \$2,000 = \$2,000 \times \begin{array}{l} \textbf{Present value factor for an annuity of} \\ \textbf{\$1 for five periods discounted at 12\%} \end{array}$$
$$= \$2,000 \times 3.605$$
$$= \$7,210$$

Here, the $2,000 annuity is multiplied by 3.605, the factor for an annuity of $1 for five periods found in Table 24A.2, discounted at 12 percent per period.

Another use of Table 24A.2 is to determine the amount that must be received annually to provide a desired rate of return on an investment. Assume that Burnsville Company invests $33,550 and desires a return of the investment plus interest of 8 percent in equal year-end payments for ten years. The minimum amount that must be received each year is determined by solving the equation for the present value of an annuity:

$$pva = a \times (pva \text{ of } \$1)$$
$$a = \frac{pva}{pva \text{ of } \$1}$$

From Table 24A.2, we see that the 8 percent factor for ten periods is 6.710. Dividing the $33,550 investment by 6.710, the required annuity is computed to be $5,000:

$$a = \frac{\$33,550}{6.710}$$
$$= \$5,000$$

TABLE 24A.1 Present Value of $1

$$\text{Present value of } \$1 = \frac{1}{(1 + r)^n}$$

Discount rate (r)

Periods (n)	6%	8%	10%	12%	14%	16%	18%	20%	22%	24%	26%	28%	30%
1	0.943	0.926	0.909	0.893	0.877	0.862	0.847	0.833	0.820	0.806	0.794	0.781	0.769
2	0.890	0.857	0.826	0.797	0.769	0.743	0.718	0.694	0.672	0.650	0.630	0.610	0.592
3	0.840	0.794	0.751	0.712	0.675	0.641	0.609	0.579	0.551	0.524	0.500	0.477	0.455
4	0.792	0.735	0.683	0.636	0.592	0.552	0.516	0.482	0.451	0.423	0.397	0.373	0.350
5	0.747	0.681	0.621	0.567	0.519	0.476	0.437	0.402	0.370	0.341	0.315	0.291	0.269
6	0.705	0.630	0.564	0.507	0.456	0.410	0.370	0.335	0.303	0.275	0.250	0.227	0.207
7	0.665	0.583	0.513	0.452	0.400	0.354	0.314	0.279	0.249	0.222	0.198	0.178	0.159
8	0.627	0.540	0.467	0.404	0.351	0.305	0.266	0.233	0.204	0.179	0.157	0.139	0.123
9	0.592	0.500	0.424	0.361	0.308	0.263	0.225	0.194	0.167	0.144	0.125	0.108	0.094
10	0.558	0.463	0.386	0.322	0.270	0.227	0.191	0.162	0.137	0.116	0.099	0.085	0.073
11	0.527	0.429	0.350	0.287	0.237	0.195	0.162	0.135	0.112	0.094	0.079	0.066	0.056
12	0.497	0.397	0.319	0.257	0.208	0.168	0.137	0.112	0.092	0.076	0.062	0.052	0.043
13	0.469	0.368	0.290	0.229	0.182	0.145	0.116	0.093	0.075	0.061	0.050	0.040	0.033
14	0.442	0.340	0.263	0.205	0.160	0.125	0.099	0.078	0.062	0.049	0.039	0.032	0.025
15	0.417	0.315	0.239	0.183	0.140	0.108	0.084	0.065	0.051	0.040	0.031	0.025	0.020
16	0.394	0.292	0.218	0.163	0.123	0.093	0.071	0.054	0.042	0.032	0.025	0.019	0.015
17	0.371	0.270	0.198	0.146	0.108	0.080	0.060	0.045	0.034	0.026	0.020	0.015	0.012
18	0.350	0.250	0.180	0.130	0.095	0.069	0.051	0.038	0.028	0.021	0.016	0.012	0.009
19	0.331	0.232	0.164	0.116	0.083	0.060	0.043	0.031	0.023	0.017	0.012	0.009	0.007
20	0.312	0.215	0.149	0.104	0.073	0.051	0.037	0.026	0.019	0.014	0.010	0.007	0.005

TABLE 24A.2 Present Value of an Annuity of $1

$$\text{Present value of an annuity of } \$1 = \frac{1}{r}\left[1 - \frac{1}{(1 + r)^n}\right]$$

Discount rate (r)

Periods (n)	6%	8%	10%	12%	14%	16%	18%	20%	22%	24%	25%	26%	28%	30%
1	0.943	0.926	0.909	0.893	0.877	0.862	0.847	0.833	0.820	0.806	0.800	0.794	0.781	0.769
2	1.833	1.783	1.736	1.690	1.647	1.605	1.566	1.528	1.492	1.457	1.440	1.424	1.392	1.361
3	2.673	2.577	2.487	2.402	2.322	2.246	2.174	2.106	2.042	1.981	1.952	1.923	1.868	1.816
4	3.465	3.312	3.170	3.037	2.914	2.798	2.690	2.589	2.494	2.404	2.362	2.320	2.241	2.166
5	4.212	3.993	3.791	3.605	3.433	3.274	3.127	2.991	2.864	2.745	2.689	2.635	2.532	2.436
6	4.917	4.623	4.355	4.111	3.889	3.685	3.498	3.326	3.167	3.020	2.951	2.885	2.759	2.643
7	5.582	5.206	4.868	4.564	4.288	4.039	3.812	3.605	3.416	3.242	3.161	3.083	2.937	2.802
8	6.210	5.747	5.335	4.968	4.639	4.344	4.078	3.837	3.619	3.421	3.329	3.241	3.076	2.925
9	6.802	6.247	5.759	5.328	4.946	4.607	4.303	4.031	3.786	3.566	3.463	3.366	3.184	3.019
10	7.360	6.710	6.145	5.650	5.216	4.833	4.494	4.192	3.923	3.682	3.571	3.465	3.269	3.092
11	7.887	7.139	6.495	5.938	5.453	5.029	4.656	4.327	4.035	3.776	3.656	3.544	3.335	3.147
12	8.384	7.536	6.814	6.194	5.660	5.197	4.793	4.439	4.127	3.851	3.725	3.606	3.387	3.190
13	8.853	7.904	7.103	6.424	5.842	5.342	4.910	4.533	4.203	3.912	3.780	3.656	3.427	3.223
14	9.295	8.244	7.367	6.628	6.002	5.468	5.008	4.611	4.265	3.962	3.824	3.695	3.459	3.249
15	9.712	8.559	7.606	6.811	6.142	5.575	5.092	4.675	4.315	4.001	3.859	3.726	3.483	3.268
16	10.106	8.851	7.824	6.974	6.265	5.669	5.162	4.730	4.357	4.033	3.887	3.751	3.503	3.283
17	10.477	9.122	8.022	7.120	6.373	5.749	5.222	4.775	4.391	4.059	3.910	3.771	3.518	3.295
18	10.828	9.372	8.201	7.250	6.467	5.818	5.273	4.812	4.419	4.080	3.928	3.786	3.529	3.304
19	11.158	9.604	8.365	7.366	6.550	5.877	5.316	4.844	4.442	4.097	3.942	3.799	3.539	3.311
20	11.470	9.818	8.514	7.469	6.623	5.929	5.353	4.870	4.460	4.110	3.954	3.808	3.546	3.316

Unequal Cash Flows

Many investment situations do not produce equal periodic cash flows. When this occurs, the present value for each cash flow must be determined independently because the annuity table can be used only for equal periodic cash flows. Table 24A.1 is used to determine the present value of each future amount separately. To illustrate, assume that the Atlanta Braves wish to acquire the contract of a popular baseball player who is known to attract large crowds. Management believes this player will return incremental cash flows to the team at the end of each of the next three years in the amounts of $2,500,000, $4,000,000, and $1,500,000. After three years, the player anticipates retiring. If the team's owners require a minimum return of 14 percent on their investment, how much would they be willing to pay for the player's contract?

To solve this problem, it is necessary to determine the present value of the expected future cash flows. Here we use Table 24A.1 to find the $1 present value factors at 14 percent for Periods 1, 2, and 3. The cash flows are then multiplied by these factors:

Year	Annual Cash Flow		Present Value of $1 at 14 Percent		Present Value Amount
1	$2,500,000	×	0.877	=	$2,192,500
2	4,000,000	×	0.769	=	3,076,000
3	1,500,000	×	0.675	=	1,012,500
Total					$6,281,000

The total present value of the cash flows for the three years, $6,281,000, represents the maximum amount the team would be willing to pay for the player's contract.

Deferred Returns

Many times, organizations make investments for which they receive no cash until several periods have passed. The present value of an investment discounted at 12 percent per year, which has a $2,000 return only at the end of Years 4, 5, and 6, can be determined as follows:

Year	Amount		Present Value of $1 at 12 Percent		Present Value Amount
1	$ 0	×	0.893	=	$ 0
2	0	×	0.797	=	0
3	0	×	0.712	=	0
4	2,000	×	0.636	=	1,272
5	2,000	×	0.567	=	1,134
6	2,000	×	0.507	=	1,014
Total					$3,420

Computation of the present value of the deferred annuity can also be performed using the annuity tables if the cash flow amounts are equal for each period. The present value of an annuity for six years minus the present value of an annuity for three years yields the present value of an annuity for Years 4 through 6.

Present value of an annuity for 6 years at 12 percent: $2,000 × 4.111 = $8,222

Present value of an annuity for 3 years at 12 percent: 2,000 × 2.402 = (4,804)

Present value of the deferred annuity. $3,418*

*The difference between the $3,420 above and the $3,418 here is due to rounding.

APPENDIX 24B: Table Approach to Determining Internal Rate of Return

We consider the use of present value tables to determine the internal rate of return of a series of cash flows with (1) equal net cash flows after the initial investment and (2) unequal net cash flows after the initial investment.

Equal Cash Inflows

An investment proposal's internal rate of return is easily determined when a single investment is followed by a series of equal annual net cash flows. The general relationship between the initial investment and the equal annual cash inflows is expressed as follows:

$$\text{Initial investment} = \text{Present value factor for an annuity of \$1} \times \text{Annual net cash inflow}$$

Solve for the appropriate present value factor as follows:

$$\text{Present value factor for an annuity of \$1} = \frac{\text{Initial investment}}{\text{Annual net cash inflows}}$$

Once the present value factor is calculated, use Table 24A.2 and go across the row corresponding to the expected life of the project until a table factor equal to or closest to the project's computed present value factor is found. The corresponding percentage for the present value factor is the proposal's internal rate of return. If a table factor does not exactly equal the proposal's present value factor, a more accurate answer can be obtained by interpolation (which is not discussed in this text).

To illustrate, assume that Mobile Yogurt Shoppe's proposed investment has a zero disinvestment value. Using all information in Exhibit 24.2 (except that for disinvestment), the proposal's present value factor is 3.152:

$$\text{Present value factor for an annuity of \$1} = \frac{\text{Initial investment}}{\text{Annual net cash inflows}}$$

$$= \frac{\$94,554}{\$30,000}$$

$$= 3.152$$

Using Table 24A.2, go across the row for five periods; the closest table factor is 3.127, which corresponds to an internal rate of return of 18 percent.

Unequal Cash Inflows

If periodic cash flows subsequent to the initial investment are unequal, the simple procedure of determining a present value factor and looking up the closest corresponding factor in Table 24A.2 cannot be used. Instead, a trial-and-error approach must be used to determine the internal rate of return.

The first step is to select a discount rate estimated to be close to the proposal's IRR and to compute the proposal's net present value. If the resulting net present value is zero, the selected discount rate is the actual rate of return. However, it is unlikely that the first rate selected will be the proposal's IRR. If the computation results in a positive net present value, the actual IRR is higher than the initially selected rate. In this case, the next step is to compute the proposal's net present value using a higher rate. If the second computation produces a negative net present value, the actual IRR is less than the selected rate. Therefore, the actual IRR is between the first and the second rates. This trial-and-error approach continues until a discount rate is found that equates the proposal's cash inflows and outflows. For Mobile Yogurt Shoppe's investment proposal outlined in Exhibit 24.2, the details of the trial-and-error approach are presented in Exhibit 24B.1.

In Exhibit 24B.1 the first rate produced a negative net present value, indicating that the proposal's IRR is less than 24 percent. To produce a positive net present value, a smaller rate was selected for the second trial. Since the second rate produced a positive net present value, the proposal's true IRR must be between 16 and 24 percent. The 20 percent rate selected for the third trial produced a net present value of zero, indicating that this is the proposal's IRR.

EXHIBIT 24B.1 Internal Rate of Return with Unequal Cash Flows

First trial with a 24 percent discount rate

	Predicted Cash Inflows (outflows) (A)	Year(s) of Cash Flows (b)	24% Present Value Factor (C)	Present Value of Cash Flows (A) × (C)
Initial investment.	$(94,554)	0	1.000	$(94,554)
Operation	30,000	1–5	2.745	82,350
Disinvestment.	12,000	5	0.341	4,092
Net present value of all cash flows.				$ (8,112)

Second trial with a 16 percent discount rate

	Predicted Cash Inflows (outflows) (A)	Year(s) of Cash Flows (b)	16% Present Value Factor (C)	Present Value of Cash Flows (A) × (C)
Initial investment.	$(94,554)	0	1.000	$(94,554)
Operation	30,000	1–5	3.274	98,220
Disinvestment.	12,000	5	0.476	5,712
Net present value of all cash flows.				$ 9,378

Third trial with a 20 percent discount rate

	Predicted Cash Inflows (outflows) (A)	Year(s) of Cash Flows (b)	20% Present Value Factor (C)	Present Value of Cash Flows (A) × (C)
Initial investment.	$(94,554)	0	1.000	$(94,554)
Operation	30,000	1–5	2.991	89,730
Disinvestment.	12,000	5	0.402	4,824
Net present value of all cash flows.				$ 0

GUIDANCE ANSWER

MANAGERIAL DECISION You Are the Vice President of Finance

There is no single correct response to this question. It is useful to start by learning how other companies in similar circumstances handle capital expenditure decisions. This might be done through personal contacts or through professional organizations, such as the Financial Executives Institute. Another starting point might be the formation of a small capital budgeting committee, which could be expanded as necessary once formal procedures were in place. Early tasks of the committee might include developing guidelines for the size of expenditures at various organizational levels subject to committee review and developing guidelines for the criteria used in formal reviews. You would want to ensure that the CEO is in agreement with these proposals. If the company has a board of directors, you would also want some mutual understanding of the board's role in the approval of capital expenditures. Finally, you would want to make clear the importance of a post-audit review.

Superscript [A] denotes assignments based on Appendix.

DISCUSSION QUESTIONS

Q24-1. What is the relationship between long-range planning and capital budgeting?

Q24-2. What tasks are often assigned to the capital budgeting committee?

Q24-3. What purposes are served by a post-audit of approved capital expenditure proposals?

Q24-4. Into what three phases are a project's cash flows organized?

Q24-5. State three alternative definitions or descriptions of the internal rate of return.

Q24-6. Why is the cost of capital an important concept when discounting models are used for capital budgeting?

Q24-7. What weakness is inherent in the payback period when it is used as the sole investment criterion?

Q24-8. What weakness is inherent in the accounting rate of return when it is used as an investment criterion?

Q24-9. Why are the net present value and the internal rate of return models superior to the payback period and the accounting rate of return models?

Q24-10. State two basic differences between the net present value and the internal rate of return models that often lead to differences in the evaluation of competing investment proposals.

Q24-11. Identify several nonquantitative factors that are apt to play a decisive role in the final selection of projects for capital expenditures.

Q24-12. In what way does depreciation affect the analysis of cash flows for a proposed capital expenditure?

Assignments with the ✓ in the margin are available in an online homework system.
See the Preface of the book for details.

MINI EXERCISES

M24-13.ᴬ Time Value of Money: Basics (LO2)   ✓

Using the equations and tables in Appendix 24A of this Module, determine the answers to each of the following independent situations:
  a. The future value in two years of $1,000 deposited today in a savings account with interest compounded annually at 6 percent.
  b. The present value of $9,000 to be received in four years, discounted at 12 percent.
  c. The present value of an annuity of $2,000 per year for five years discounted at 14 percent.
  d. An initial investment of $32,010 is to be returned in eight equal annual payments. Determine the amount of each payment if the interest rate is 10 percent.
  e. A proposed investment will provide cash flows of $20,000, $8,000, and $6,000 at the end of Years 1, 2, and 3, respectively. Using a discount rate of 20 percent, determine the present value of these cash flows.
  f. Find the present value of an investment that will pay $4,000 at the end of Years 10, 11, and 12. Use a discount rate of 14 percent.

M24-14.ᴬ Time Value of Money: Basics   (LO2)

Using the equations and tables in Appendix 24A of this Module, determine the answers to each of the following independent situations:
  a. The future value in two years of $4,000 invested today in a certificate of deposit with interest compounded annually at 10 percent.
  b. The present value of $6,000 to be received in five years, discounted at 8 percent.
  c. The present value of an annuity of $20,000 per year for four years discounted at 12 percent.
  d. An initial investment of $29,480 is to be returned in six equal annual payments. Determine the amount of each payment if the interest rate is 16 percent.
  e. A proposed investment will provide cash flows of $6,000, $8,000, and $20,000 at the end of Years 1, 2, and 3, respectively. Using a discount rate of 18 percent, determine the present value of these cash flows.
  f. Find the present value of an investment that will pay $6,000 at the end of Years 8, 9, and 10. Use a discount rate of 12 percent.

M24-15. NPV and IRR: Equal Annual Net Cash Inflows   (LO2)   ✓

Apache Junction Company is evaluating a capital expenditure proposal that requires an initial investment of $9,350, has predicted cash inflows of $2,000 per year for 15 years, and has no salvage value.

Required
  a. Using a discount rate of 16 percent, determine the net present value of the investment proposal.
  b. Determine the proposal's internal rate of return. (Refer to Appendix 24B if you use the table approach.)
  c. What discount rate would produce a net present value of zero?

M24-16. NPV and IRR: Equal Annual Net Cash Inflows (LO2)
Snow Devil Company is evaluating a capital expenditure proposal that requires an initial investment of $32,312, has predicted cash inflows of $8,000 per year for seven years, and has no salvage value.

Required
a. Using a discount rate of 12 percent, determine the net present value of the investment proposal.
b. Determine the proposal's internal rate of return. (Refer to Appendix 24B if you use the table approach.)
c. What discount rate would produce a net present value of zero?

M24-17. Payback Period and Accounting Rate of Return: Equal Annual Operating Cash Flows without Disinvestment (LO3)
Amanda is considering an investment proposal with the following cash flows:

Initial investment—depreciable assets.	$90,000
Net cash inflows from operations (per year for 6 years).	20,000
Disinvestment.	0

Required
a. Determine the payback period
b. Determine the accounting rate of return on initial investment
c. Determine the accounting rate of return on average investment

M24-18. Payback Period and Accounting Rate of Return: Equal Annual Operating Cash Flows with Disinvestment (LO3)
Hoi is considering an investment proposal with the following cash flows:

Initial investment—depreciable assets.	$120,000
Net cash inflows from operations (per year for 5 years).	30,000
Disinvestment—depreciable assets.	20,000

Required
a. Determine the payback period
b. Determine the accounting rate of return on initial investment
c. Determine the accounting rate of return on average investment

M24-19. Payback Period and Accounting Rate of Return: Equal Annual Operating Cash Flows with Disinvestment (LO3)
Khazanchi is considering an investment proposal with the following cash flows:

Initial investment—depreciable assets.	$100,000
Initial investment—working capital.	12,500
Net cash inflows from operations (per year for 8 years).	25,000
Disinvestment—depreciable assets.	10,000
Disinvestment—working capital.	12,500

Required
a. Determine the payback period
b. Determine the accounting rate of return on initial investment
c. Determine the accounting rate of return on average investment

EXERCISES

E24-20. NPV and IRR: Unequal Annual Net Cash Inflows (LO2)
Goodrich Corporation

Assume that Goodrich Corporation is evaluating a capital expenditure proposal that has the following predicted cash flows:

Initial investment.	$(85,160)
Operation	
Year 1	36,000
Year 2	50,000
Year 3	40,000
Salvage.	0

Required

a. Using a discount rate of 12 percent, determine the net present value of the investment proposal.

b. Determine the proposal's internal rate of return. (Refer to Appendix 24B if you use the table approach.)

E24-21. NPV and IRR: Unequal Annual Net Cash Inflows (LO2)

Salt River Company is evaluating a capital expenditure proposal that has the following predicted cash flows:

Initial investment.	$(43,270)
Operation	
Year 1	20,000
Year 2	30,000
Year 3	10,000
Salvage.	0

Required

a. Using a discount rate of 14 percent, determine the net present value of the investment proposal.

b. Determine the proposal's internal rate of return. (Refer to Appendix 24B if you use the table approach.)

E24-22. Payback Period, IRR, and Minimum Cash Flows (LO2, 3)

The management of Mesquite Limited is currently evaluating the following investment proposal:

	Time 0	Year 1	Year 2	Year 3	Year 4
Initial investment.	$240,000	—	—	—	—
Net operating cash inflows	—	$100,000	$100,000	$100,000	$100,000

Required

a. Determine the proposal's payback period.

b. Determine the proposal's internal rate of return. (Refer to Appendix 24B if you use the table approach.)

c. Given the amount of the initial investment, determine the minimum annual net cash inflows required to obtain an internal rate of return of 14 percent. Round the answer to the nearest dollar.

E24-23. Time-Adjusted Cost-Volume-Profit Analysis (LO2, 3)

Boardwalk Treat Shop is considering the desirability of producing a new chocolate candy called Pleasure Bombs. Before purchasing the new equipment required to manufacture Pleasure Bombs, Marty Dey, the shop's proprietor performed the following analysis:

Unit selling price.	$1.45
Variable manufacturing and selling costs.	(1.15)
Unit contribution margin.	$0.30
Annual fixed costs	
Depreciation (straight-line for 4 years)	$15,000
Other (all cash)	30,000
Total	$45,000

Annual break-even sales volume = $45,000 ÷ $0.30 = 150,000 units

Because the expected annual sales volume is 160,000 units, Dey decided to undertake the production of Pleasure Bombs. This required an immediate investment of $60,000 in equipment that has a life of four years and no salvage value. After four years, the production of Pleasure Bombs will be discontinued.

Required
a. Evaluate the analysis performed by Dey.
b. If Boardwalk Treat Shop has a time value of money of 14 percent, should it make the investment with projected annual sales of 160,000 units?
c. Considering the time value of money, what annual unit sales volume is required to break even?

E24-24. Time-Adjusted Cost-Volume-Profit Analysis with Income Taxes (LO6)
Assume the same facts as given in Exercise E24-23 for the Boardwalk Treat Shop.

Required
With a 40 percent tax rate and a 14 percent time value of money, determine the annual unit sales required to break even on a time-adjusted basis. Assume straight-line depreciation is used to determine tax payments.

E24-25. Payback Period and IRR of a Cost Reduction Proposal—Differential Analysis (LO2, 3)
A light-emitting diode (LED) is a semiconductor diode that emits narrow-spectrum light. Although relatively expensive when compared to incandescent bulbs, they use significantly less energy and last six to ten times longer, with a slow decline in performance rather than an abrupt failure.

New York City currently has 80,000 incandescent bulbs in traffic lights at approximately 12,000 intersections. It is estimated that replacing all the incandescent bulbs with LED will cost $28 million. However, the investment is also estimated to save the City $6.3 million per year in energy costs.[2]

Required:
a. Determine the payback period of converting New York City traffic lights to LEDs.
b. If the average life of an incandescent streetlight is one year and the average life of an LED street-light is seven years, should the City finance the investment in LED's at an interest rate of five percent per year? Justify your answer.

E24-26. Payback Period and NPV of a Cost Reduction Proposal—Differential Analysis (LO2, 3)
Mary Zimmerman decided to purchase a new automobile. Being concerned about environmental issues, she is leaning toward the hybrid rather than the gasoline only model. Nevertheless, as a new business school graduate, she wants to determine if there is an economic justification for purchasing the hybrid, which costs $1,300 more than the regular model. She has determined that city/highway combined gas mileage of the hybrid and regular models are 27 and 23 miles per gallon respectively. Mary anticipates she will travel an average of 12,000 miles per year for the next several years.

Required:
a. Determine the payback period of the incremental investment if gasoline costs $3.50 per gallon.
b. Assuming that Mary plans to keep the care five years and does not believe there will be a trade-in premium associated with the hybrid model, determine the net present value of the incremental investment at an eight percent time value of money.
c. Determine the cost of gasoline required for a payback period of three years.
d. At $3.50 per gallon, determine the gas mileage required for a payback period of three years.

E24-27. Payback Period and NPV of Alternative Automobile Purchase (LO2, 3)
Bob Wu decided to purchase a new Honda Civic. Being concerned about environmental issues he is leaning toward a Honda Civic Hybrid rather than the completely gasoline-powered LX model. Nevertheless, he wants to determine if there is an economic justification for purchasing the Hybrid, which costs $6,000 more than the LX. Based on a mix of city and highway driving he predicts that the average gas mileage of each car is 42 MPG for the Hybrid and 30 MPG for the LX. Bob also anticipates he will drive an average of 12,000 miles per year and that gasoline will cost an average of $3.50 per gallon over the next five years. He also plans to replace whichever car he purchases at the end of five years when the resale values of the Hybrid and the LX are predicted to be $11,000 and $8,500 respectively.[3]

---

[2] Based on "Mayors Take the Lead," *Newsweek*, April 16, 2007, pp. 68-73.

[3] Based on Robert L. Barker, Ronald Clouse, Thomas G. Stout, and Gary R. Stout, "The Economics of Buying a More Fuel Efficient Automobile: An Interactive Analysis," *Journal of Financial Planning*, June 2009, pp.62-71.

Required

a. Determine the payback period of the incremental investment associated with purchasing the Hybrid.

b. Determine the net present value of the incremental investment associated with purchasing the Hybrid at an eight percent time value of money.

c. Determine the cost of gasoline required for a payback period of three years on the incremental investment.

d. Identify other factors Bob should consider before making his decision.

PROBLEMS

P24-28. Ranking Investment Proposals: Payback Period, Accounting Rate of Return, and Net Present Value (LO2, 3, 4)

Presented is information pertaining to the cash flows of three mutually exclusive investment proposals:

	Proposal X	Proposal Y	Proposal Z
Initial investment.	$45,000	$45,000	$45,000
Cash flow from operations			
Year 1	40,000	22,500	45,000
Year 2	5,000	22,500	
Year 3	22,500	22,500	
Disinvestment.	0	0	0
Life (years)	3 years	3 years	1 year

Required

a. Rank these investment proposals using the payback period, the accounting rate of return on initial investment, and the net present value criteria. Assume that the organization's cost of capital is 14 percent. Round calculations to four decimal places.

b. Explain the difference in rankings. Which investment would you recommend?

P24-29. Cost Reduction Proposal: IRR, NPV, and Payback Period (LO2, 3)

JB Chemical currently discharges liquid waste into Calgary's municipal sewer system. However, the Calgary municipal government has informed JB that a surcharge of $4 per thousand cubic liters will soon be imposed for the discharge of this waste. This has prompted management to evaluate the desirability of treating its own liquid waste.

A proposed system consists of three elements. The first is a retention basin, which would permit unusual discharges to be held and treated before entering the downstream system. The second is a continuous self-cleaning rotary filter required where solids are removed. The third is an automated neutralization process required where materials are added to control the alkalinity-acidity range.

The system is designed to process 500,000 liters a day. However, management anticipates that only about 200,000 liters of liquid waste would be processed in a normal workday. The company operates 300 days per year. The initial investment in the system would be $450,000, and annual operating costs are predicted to be $150,000. The system has a predicted useful life of ten years and a salvage value of $50,000.

Required

a. Determine the project's net present value at a discount rate of 14 percent.

b. Determine the project's approximate internal rate of return. (Refer to Appendix 24B if you use the table approach.)

c. Determine the project's payback period.

P24-30. NPV with Income Taxes: Straight-Line versus Accelerated Depreciation (LO2, 6)

John Paul Jones Inc. is a conservatively managed boat company whose motto is, "The old ways are the good ways." Management has always used straight-line depreciation for tax and external reporting purposes. Although they are reluctant to change, they are aware of the impact of taxes on a project's profitability.

Required

For a typical $100,000 investment in equipment with a five-year life and no salvage value, determine the present value of the advantage resulting from the use of double-declining balance depreciation as opposed to straight-line depreciation. Assume an income tax rate of 40 percent and a discount rate of 16 percent. Also assume that there will be a switch from double-declining balance to straight-line depreciation in the fourth year.

P24-31. Payback Period and NPV: Taxes and Straight-Line Depreciation   (LO2, 3, 6)

United Technologies

Assume that United Technologies is evaluating a proposal to change the company's manual design system to a computer-aided design (CAD) system. The proposed system is expected to save 10,000 design hours per year; an operating cost savings of $40 per hour. The annual cash expenditures of operating the CAD system are estimated to be $200,000. The CAD system requires an initial investment of $500,000. The estimated life of this system is five years with no salvage value. The tax rate is 40 percent, and United Technologies uses straight-line depreciation for tax purposes. United Technologies has a cost of capital of 16 percent.

Required
a. Compute the annual after-tax cash flows related to the CAD project.
b. Compute each of the following for the project:
   1. Payback period.
   2. Net present value.

P24-32. NPV: Taxes and Accelerated Depreciation   (LO6)

Assume the same facts as given in P24-31, except that management intends to use double-declining balance depreciation with a switch to straight-line depreciation (applied to any undepreciated balance) starting in Year 4.

Required
Determine the project's net present value.

P24-33. NPV Total and Differential Analysis of Replacement Decision   (LO2)

Gusher Petro is evaluating a proposal to purchase a new processor that would cost $120,000 and have a salvage value of $12,000 in five years. Gusher's cost of capital is 16 percent. It would provide annual operating cash savings of $15,000, as follows:

	Old Processor	New Processor
Salaries.	$34,000	$44,000
Supplies	6,000	5,000
Utilities	13,000	6,000
Cleaning and maintenance.	22,000	5,000
Total cash expenditures	$75,000	$60,000

If the new processor is purchased, Gusher will sell the old processor for its current salvage value of $30,000. If the new processor is not purchased, the old processor will be disposed of in five years at a predicted scrap value of $2,000. The old processor's present book value is $50,000. If kept, the old processor will require repairs predicted to cost $40,000 in one year.

Required
a. Use the total cost approach to evaluate the alternatives of keeping the old processor and purchasing the new processor. Indicate which alternative is preferred.
b. Use the differential cost approach to evaluate the desirability of purchasing the new processor.

P24-34. NPV Total and Differential Analysis of Replacement Decision   (LO2)

White Snow Automatic Laundry must either have a complete overhaul of its current dry-cleaning system or purchase a new one. Its cost of capital is 20 percent. White Snow's accountant has developed the following cost projections:

	Present System	New System
Purchase cost (new).	$40,000	$50,000
Remaining book value	15,000	
Overhaul needed	20,000	
Annual cash operating costs	35,000	20,000
Current salvage value.	10,000	
Salvage value in 5 years.	2,500	10,000

If White Snow keeps the old system, it will have to be overhauled immediately. With the overhaul, the old system will have a useful life of five more years.

Required

a. Use the total cost approach to evaluate the alternatives of keeping the old system and purchasing the new system. Indicate which alternative is preferred.

b. Use the differential cost approach to evaluate the desirability of purchasing the new system.

P24-35. NPV Differential Analysis of Replacement Decision (LO2, 5)

The management of Essen Manufacturing Company is currently evaluating a proposal to purchase a new, innovative drill press as a replacement for a less efficient piece of similar equipment, which would then be sold. The cost of the equipment, including delivery and installation, is $175,000. If the equipment is purchased, Essen will incur a $5,000 cost in removing the present equipment and revamping service facilities. The present equipment has a book value of $100,000 and a remaining useful life of ten years. Because of new technical improvements that have made the present equipment obsolete, it now has a disposal value of only $40,000. Management has provided the following comparison of manufacturing costs:

	Present Equipment	New Equipment
Annual production (units)	400,000	400,000
Annual costs		
Direct labor (per unit)	$0.075	$0.05
Overhead		
Depreciation (10% of asset's book value)	$10,000	$17,500
Other	$48,000	$20,000

Additional information follows:

- Management believes that if the current equipment is not replaced now, it will have to wait ten years before replacement is justifiable.
- Both pieces of equipment are expected to have a negligible salvage value at the end of ten years.
- Management expects to sell the entire annual production of 400,000 units.
- Essen's cost of capital is 14 percent.

Required

Evaluate the desirability of purchasing the new equipment

MANAGEMENT APPLICATIONS

MA24-36. Payback, ARR, and IRR: Evaluating the Sale of Government Assets (Requires Spreadsheet) (LO2, 3, 5)

In 2008 the City of Chicago agreed to lease 35,000 parking meters to a Morgan Stanley-led partnership for a one-time sum of $1.15 billion. The lease has been criticized as an example of "one-shot" deals arrived at behind closed doors to balance a current budget at the expense of future generations. Some have observed that deals such as this are akin to individuals using their retirement savings to meet current needs, instead of planning for the future. "These deals are rarely done under the light of public scrutiny," says Richard G. Little, director of the Keston Institute for Public Finance at the University of Southern California. "Often the facts come out long after the deal is done."

Morgan Stanley

Since the lease was signed, helped by parking-fee hikes, the partnership has earned a profit before taxes and depreciation of $0.80 per dollar of revenue. Projected revenues over the 75-year life of the lease are now projected at $11.6 billion.

Defending the city's action, Gene Saffold, Chicago's chief financial officer, stated that "The concession agreement was absolutely the best deal for Chicagoans. ... The net present value of $11.6 billion in revenue over the life of the 75-year agreement is consistent with $1.15 billion.[4]

Required

Evaluate the 75-year lease and determine if the projected revenues are consistent with the initial investment. To simplify your analysis assume equal revenues and operating costs in all periods, no investment required in working capital, and no salvage value at the end of the lease. Suggested elements of your solution include:

---

[4] "Windfall for Investors, A Loss for the Windy City," *Bloomberg Businessweek*, August 29, 2010, pp. 44-45; Ianthe Jeanne Dugan, "Facing Budget Gaps, Cities Sell Parking, Airports, Zoo," *The Wall Street Journal*, August 23, 2010, pp. A1, A12.

a. Determine the payback period in the absence of taxes.
b. Determine the accounting rate of return on the initial investment in the absence of taxes.
c. Determine the accounting rate of return on the initial investment with a tax rate of 0.34.
d. Determine the internal rate of return in the absence of taxes.
e. Determine the internal rate of return with a tax rate of 0.34.
f. Summary of analysis and conclusions.

MA24-37. Determining Terms of Automobile Leases (Requires Spreadsheet) (LO2, 5)

Avant-Garde Motor Company has asked you to develop lease terms for the firm's popular Avant-Garde Challenger, which has an average selling price (new) of $25,000. You know that leasing is attractive because it assists consumers in obtaining new vehicles with a small down payment and "reasonable" monthly payments. Market analysts have told you that to attract the widest number of young professionals, the Challenger must have an initial down payment of no more than $1,000, monthly payments of no more than $450, and lease terms of no more than three years. When the lease expires, Avant-Garde will sell the used Challengers at the automobile's resale market price at that time. It is difficult to predict the future price of the increasingly popular Challenger, but you have obtained the following information on the average resale prices of used Challengers:

Age	Resale Price
1 year	$20,000
2 years	18,500
3 years	16,000
4 years	13,500
5 years	12,500

Avant-Garde's cost of capital is 18 percent per year, or 1.5 percent per month.

Required

a. With the aid of spreadsheet software, develop a competitive and profitable lease payment program. Assume the down payment and the first lease payment are made immediately and that all subsequent lease payments are made at the start of the month. [Hint: Most software packages include a function such as the following: PMT (rate,nper,pv,fv,type), where rate = the time value of money; nper = the number of periods; pv = the present value; fv = the future value; and type = 0 (when the payment is at the end of the period) or 1 (when the payment is at the beginning of the period). For monthly payments, rate should be set at the annual rate divided by 12, and npr should be set at the number of months in the lease. Here, fv is the residual value. Consider the residual value as a future value and enter it as a negative number, indicating the lessor has not paid the full cost of the car.]
b. Reevaluate the lease program assuming a down payment of $2,000.
c. Reevaluate the lease program assuming a down payment of $1,000 and a $2,000 increase in residual values.
d. Reevaluate the lease program assuming a down payment of $2,000 and a $2,000 increase in residual values.
e. What is your final recommendation? What risks are associated with your recommendation? Are there any other actions to consider?

MA24-38. Evaluating Data and Using Payback Period for an Investment Proposal (LO3, 5)

To determine the desirability of investing in a 21-inch monitor (as opposed to the typical 17-inch monitor that comes with a new personal computer), researchers developed an experiment testing the time required to perform a set of tasks. The tasks included the following:

- Setting up a meeting using electronic mail.
- Reviewing meeting requests.
- Checking an on-line schedule.
- Embedding a video file into a document.
- Searching a customer database to find a specific set of contracts.
- Copying a database into a spreadsheet.
- Modifying a slide presentation.

The researchers assumed this was a typical set of tasks performed by a manager. They determined that there was a 9 percent productivity gain using the 21-inch monitor. One test manager commented that the largest productivity gain came from being able to have multiple applications open at the same time and from being able to view several files at once.

Required

Accepting the 9 percent productivity gain as accurate, what additional information is needed to determine the payback period of an investment in one 21-inch monitor that is to be used by a manager? Make any necessary assumptions and obtain whatever data you can (perhaps from computer component advertisements) to determine the payback period for the proposed investment.

MA24-39. IRR and NPV with Performance Evaluation Conflict (LO2, 4, 5)

Pepperoni Pizza Company owns and operates fast-service pizza parlors throughout North America. The firm operates on a regional basis and provides almost complete autonomy to the manager of each region. Regional managers are responsible for long-range planning, capital expenditures, personnel policies, pricing, and so forth. Each year the performance of regional managers is evaluated by determining the accounting return on fixed assets in their regions; a return of 14 percent is expected. To determine this return, regional net income is divided by the book value of fixed assets at the start of the year. Managers of regions earning a return of more than 16 percent are identified for possible promotion, and managers of regions with a return of less than 12 percent are subject to replacement.

Mr. Light, with a degree in hotel and restaurant management, is the manager of the Northeast region. He is regarded as a "rising star" and will be considered for promotion during the next two years. Light has been with Pepperoni for a total of three years. During that period, the return on fixed assets in his region (the oldest in the firm) has increased dramatically. He is currently considering a proposal to open five new parlors in the Boston area. The total project involves an investment of $640,000 and will double the number of Pepperoni pizzas sold in the Northeast region to a total of 600,000 per year. At an average price of $6 each, total sales revenue will be $3,600,000.

The expenses of operating each of the new parlors include variable costs of $4 per pizza and fixed costs (excluding depreciation) of $80,904 per year. Because each of the new parlors has only a five-year life and no salvage value, yearly straight-line depreciation will be $25,600 [($640,000 ÷ 5 parlors) ÷ 5 years].

Required

a. Evaluate the desirability of the $640,000 investment in new pizza parlors by computing the internal rate of return and the net present value. Assume a time value of money of 14 percent. (Refer to Appendix 24B if you use the table approach.)

b. If Light is shrewd, will he approve the expansion? Why or why not? (Additional computations are suggested.)

MA24-40. NPV and Project Reevaluation with Taxes, Straight-Line Depreciation (LO2, 5, 6)

In 2010, the Bayside Chemical Company prepared the following analysis of an investment proposal for a new manufacturing facility:

	Predicted Cash Inflows (outflows) (A)	Year(s) of Cash Flows (B)	12% Present Value Factor (C)	Present Value of Cash Flows (A) × (C)
Initial investment				
Fixed assets	$(800,000)	0	1.000	$ (800,000)
Working capital.	(100,000)	0	1.000	(100,000)
Operations				
Annual taxable income				
without depreciation	300,000	1–5	3.605	1,081,500
Taxes on income				
($300,000 × 0.34)	(102,000)	1–5	3.605	(367,710)
Depreciation tax shield	54,400*	1–5	3.605	196,112
Disinvestment				
Site restoration	80,000	5	0.567	(45,360)
Tax shield of restoration				
($80,000 × 0.34)	27,200	5	0.567	15,422
Working capital.	100,000	5	0.567	56,700
Net present value of all cash flows.				$ 36,664

*Computation of depreciation tax shield:

Annual straight-line depreciation ($800,000 ÷ 5)	$160,000
Tax rate	× 0.34
Depreciation tax shield	$ 54,400

Because the proposal had a positive net present value when discounted at Bayside's cost of capital of 12 percent, the project was approved; all investments were made at the end of 2011. Shortly after production began in January 2012, a government agency notified Bayside of required additional expenditures totaling $200,000 to bring the plant into compliance with new federal emission regulations. Bayside has the option either to comply with the regulations by December 31, 2012, or to sell the entire operation (fixed assets and working capital) for $250,000 on December 31, 2012. The improvements will be depreciated over the remaining four-year life of the plant using straight-line depreciation. The cost of site restoration will not be affected by the improvements. If Bayside elects to sell the plant, any book loss can be treated as an offset against taxable income on other operations. This tax reduction is an additional cash benefit of selling.

Required

a. Should Bayside sell the plant or comply with the new federal regulations? To simplify calculations, assume that any additional improvements are paid for on December 31, 2012.

b. Would Bayside have accepted the proposal in 2011 if it had been aware of the forthcoming federal regulations?

c. Do you have any suggestions that might increase the project's net present value? (No calculations are required.)

MA24-41. Post-Audit and Reevaluation of Investment Proposal: NPV (LO1, 2, 5)

Anthony Company's capital budgeting committee is evaluating a capital expenditure proposal for the production of a high definition television receiver to be sold as an add-on feature for personal computers. The proposal calls for an independent contractor to construct the necessary facilities by December 31, 2012, at a total cost of $250,000. Payment for all construction costs will be made on that date. An additional $50,000 in cash will also be made available on December 31, 2012, for working capital to support sales and production activities.

Management anticipates that the receiver has a limited market life; there is a high probability that by 2019 all new PCs will have built-in high definition receivers. Accordingly, the proposal specifies that production will cease on December 31, 2018. The investment in working capital will be recovered on that date, and the production facilities will be sold for $30,000. Predicted net cash inflows from operations for 2013 through 2018 are as follows:

2013	$100,000
2014	100,000
2015	100,000
2016	40,000
2017	40,000
2018	40,000

Anthony Company has a time value of money of 16 percent. For capital budgeting purposes, all cash flows are assumed to occur at the end of each year.

Required

a. Evaluate the capital expenditure proposal using the net present value method. Should Anthony accept the proposal?

b. Assume that the capital expenditure proposal is accepted, but construction delays caused by labor problems and difficulties in obtaining the necessary construction permits delay the completion of the project. Payments totaling $200,000 were made to the construction company on December 31, 2012, for that year's construction. However, completion is now scheduled for December 31, 2013, and an additional $100,000 will be required to complete construction. If the project is continued, the additional $100,000 will be paid at the end of 2013, and the plant will begin operations on January 1, 2014.

Because of the cost overruns, the capital budgeting committee requests a reevaluation of the project in early 2013, before agreeing to any additional expenditures. After much effort, the following revised predictions of net operating cash inflows are developed:

2014	$120,000
2015	100,000
2016	40,000
2017	40,000
2018	40,000

The working capital investment and disinvestment and the plant salvage values have not changed, except that the cash for working capital would now be made available on December 31, 2013. Use the net present value method to reevaluate the initial decision to accept the proposal. Given the information currently available about the project, should it have been accepted in 2012? (Hint: Determine the net present value as of December 31, 2012, assuming management has not committed Anthony to the proposal.)

c. Given the situation that exists in early 2013, should management continue or cancel the project? Assume that the facilities have a current salvage value of $50,000. (Hint: Assume that the decision is being made on January 1, 2013.)

MA24-42. Post-Audit and Reevaluation of Investment Proposal: IRR (LO1, 2, 5)

Throughout his four years in college, Ronald King worked at the local Beef Burger Restaurant in College City. Although the working conditions were good and the pay was not bad, Ron believed he could do a much better job of managing the restaurant than the current owner-manager. In particular, Ron believed that the proper use of marketing campaigns and sales incentives, such as selling a second burger for a 25 percent discount, could increase annual sales by 50 percent.

Just before graduation in 2011, Ron inherited $500,000 from his great uncle. He seriously considered buying the restaurant. It seemed like a good idea because he liked the town and its college atmosphere, knew the business, and always wanted to work for himself. He also knew that the current owner wanted to sell the restaurant and retire to Florida. As part of a small business management course, Ron developed the following income statement for the restaurant's 2010 operations:

BEEF BURGER RESTAURANT: COLLEGE CITY		
Income Statement		
For Year Ended December 31, 2010		
Sales.		$450,000
Expenses		
Cost of food	$150,000	
Supplies	20,000	
Employee expenses	140,000	
Utilities	28,000	
Property taxes.	20,000	
Insurance	10,000	
Advertising	8,000	
Depreciation	60,000	436,000
Net income.		$ 14,000

Ron believed that the cost of food and supplies were all variable, the employee expenses and utilities were one-half variable and one-half fixed in 2010, and all other expenses were fixed. If Ron purchased the restaurant and followed through on his plans, he believed there would be a 50 percent increase in unit sales volume and all variable costs. Of the fixed costs, only advertising would increase by $12,000. The use of discounts and special promotions would, however, limit the increase in sales revenue to only 40 percent even though sales volume increased 50 percent.

Required

a. Determine

  1. The current annual net cash inflow.

  2. The predicted annual net cash inflow if Ron executes his plans and his assumptions are correct.

b. Ron believes his plan would produce equal net cash inflows during each of the next 15 years, the period remaining on a long-term lease for the land on which the restaurant is built. At the end of that time, the restaurant would have to be demolished at a predicted net cost of $80,000. Assuming Ron would otherwise invest the money in stock expected to yield 12 percent, determine the maximum amount he should pay for the restaurant.

c. Assume that Ron accepts an offer from the current owner to buy the restaurant for $400,000. Unfortunately, although the expected increase in sales volume does occur, customers make much more extensive use of the promotions than Ron had anticipated. As a result, total sales revenues are 8 percent below projections. Furthermore, to improve employee attitudes, Ron gave a 10 percent raise immediately after purchasing the restaurant. Reevaluate the initial decision using the actual sales revenue and the increase in labor costs, assuming conditions will remain unchanged over the remaining life of the project. Was the investment decision a wise one? (Round calculations to the nearest dollar.)

d. Ron can sell the restaurant to a large franchise operator for $300,000. Alternatively, he believes that additional annual marketing expenditures and changes in promotions costing $20,000 per year could bring the sales revenues up to their original projections, with no other changes in costs. Should Ron sell the restaurant or keep it and make the additional expenditures? (Round calculations to the nearest dollar.) (*Hint:* Ron has just bought the restaurant.)

SOLUTIONS TO REVIEW PROBLEMS

Mid-Module Review

Solution
Basic computations:

Initial investment	
Depreciable assets	$27,740
Working capital	3,000
Total	$30,740
Operation	
Cash receipts	$25,000
Cash expenditures	(15,000)
Net cash inflow	$10,000
Disinvestment	
Sale of depreciable assets	$ 2,000
Recovery of working capital	3,000
Total	$ 5,000

a. Net present value at a 10 percent discount rate:

	Predicted Cash Inflows (outflows) (A)	Year(s) of Cash Flows (B)	10% Present Value Factor (C)	Present Value of Cash Flows (A) × (C)
Initial investment	$(30,740)	0	1.000	$(30,740)
Operation	10,000	1–4	3.170	31,700
Disinvestment	5,000	4	0.683	3,415
Net present value of all cash flows				$ 4,375

b. Internal rate of return:
   Using a spreadsheet, the proposal's internal rate of return is readily determined to be 16 percent:

	A	B
1	Year of cash flow	Cash flow
2	0	$(30,740)
3	1	10,000
4	2	10,000
5	3	10,000
6	4	15,000
7	IRR	0.16

The table approach requires additional analysis. Because the proposal has a positive net present value when discounted at 10 percent, its internal rate of return must be higher than 10 percent. Through a trial-and-error approach, the internal rate of return is determined to be 16 percent.

	Predicted Cash Inflows (outflows) (A)	Year(s) of Cash Flows (B)	16% Present Value Factor (C)	Present Value of Cash Flows (A) × (C)
Initial investment	$(30,740)	0	1.000	$(30,740)
Operation	10,000	1–4	2.798	27,980
Disinvestment.	5,000	4	0.552	2,760
Net present value of all cash flows.				$ 0

Module-End Review

Solution
Basic computations:

Initial investment	
Depreciable assets	$27,740
Working capital	3,000
Total	$30,740
Operation	
Cash receipts	$25,000
Cash expenditures	(15,000)
Net cash inflow.	$10,000
Disinvestment	
Sale of depreciable assets	$ 2,000
Recovery of working capital	3,000
Total	$ 5,000

a. Payback period = $30,740 ÷ $10,000
= 3.074 years

b. Accounting rate of return on initial and average investments:

Annual net cash inflow from operations.	$10,000
Less average annual depreciation [($27,740 − $2,000) ÷ 4]	(6,435)
Average annual increase in net income.	$ 3,565

Average investment = ($30,740 + $5,000) ÷ 2
= $17,870

$$\text{Accounting rate of return on initial investment} = \frac{\$3,565}{\$30,740}$$

= 0.1160, or 11.6%

$$\text{Accounting rate of return on average investment} = \frac{\$3,565}{\$17,870}$$

= 0.1995, or 19.95%

Appendix

A

Compound Interest Tables

TABLE 1 Present Value of Single Amount $p = 1/(1 + i)^t$

Period	0.01	0.02	0.03	0.04	0.05	0.06	0.07	0.08	0.09	0.10	0.11	0.12
1	0.99010	0.98039	0.97087	0.96154	0.95238	0.94340	0.93458	0.92593	0.91743	0.90909	0.90090	0.89286
2	0.98030	0.96117	0.94260	0.92456	0.90703	0.89000	0.87344	0.85734	0.84168	0.82645	0.81162	0.79719
3	0.97059	0.94232	0.91514	0.88900	0.86384	0.83962	0.81630	0.79383	0.77218	0.75131	0.73119	0.71178
4	0.96098	0.92385	0.88849	0.85480	0.82270	0.79209	0.76290	0.73503	0.70843	0.68301	0.65873	0.63552
5	0.95147	0.90573	0.86261	0.82193	0.78353	0.74726	0.71299	0.68058	0.64993	0.62092	0.59345	0.56743
6	0.94205	0.88797	0.83748	0.79031	0.74622	0.70496	0.66634	0.63017	0.59627	0.56447	0.53464	0.50663
7	0.93272	0.87056	0.81309	0.75992	0.71068	0.66506	0.62275	0.58349	0.54703	0.51316	0.48166	0.45235
8	0.92348	0.85349	0.78941	0.73069	0.67684	0.62741	0.58201	0.54027	0.50187	0.46651	0.43393	0.40388
9	0.91434	0.83676	0.76642	0.70259	0.64461	0.59190	0.54393	0.50025	0.46043	0.42410	0.39092	0.36061
10	0.90529	0.82035	0.74409	0.67556	0.61391	0.55839	0.50835	0.46319	0.42241	0.38554	0.35218	0.32197
11	0.89632	0.80426	0.72242	0.64958	0.58468	0.52679	0.47509	0.42888	0.38753	0.35049	0.31728	0.28748
12	0.88745	0.78849	0.70138	0.62460	0.55684	0.49697	0.44401	0.39711	0.35553	0.31863	0.28584	0.25668
13	0.87866	0.77303	0.68095	0.60057	0.53032	0.46884	0.41496	0.36770	0.32618	0.28966	0.25751	0.22917
14	0.86996	0.75788	0.66112	0.57748	0.50507	0.44230	0.38782	0.34046	0.29925	0.26333	0.23199	0.20462
15	0.86135	0.74301	0.64186	0.55526	0.48102	0.41727	0.36245	0.31524	0.27454	0.23939	0.20900	0.18270
16	0.85282	0.72845	0.62317	0.53391	0.45811	0.39365	0.33873	0.29189	0.25187	0.21763	0.18829	0.16312
17	0.84438	0.71416	0.60502	0.51337	0.43630	0.37136	0.31657	0.27027	0.23107	0.19784	0.16963	0.14564
18	0.83602	0.70016	0.58739	0.49363	0.41552	0.35034	0.29586	0.25025	0.21199	0.17986	0.15282	0.13004
19	0.82774	0.68643	0.57029	0.47464	0.39573	0.33051	0.27651	0.23171	0.19449	0.16351	0.13768	0.11611
20	0.81954	0.67297	0.55368	0.45639	0.37689	0.31180	0.25842	0.21455	0.17843	0.14864	0.12403	0.10367
21	0.81143	0.65978	0.53755	0.43883	0.35894	0.29416	0.24151	0.19866	0.16370	0.13513	0.11174	0.09256
22	0.80340	0.64684	0.52189	0.42196	0.34185	0.27751	0.22571	0.18394	0.15018	0.12285	0.10067	0.08264
23	0.79544	0.63416	0.50669	0.40573	0.32557	0.26180	0.21095	0.17032	0.13778	0.11168	0.09069	0.07379
24	0.78757	0.62172	0.49193	0.39012	0.31007	0.24698	0.19715	0.15770	0.12640	0.10153	0.08170	0.06588
25	0.77977	0.60953	0.47761	0.37512	0.29530	0.23300	0.18425	0.14602	0.11597	0.09230	0.07361	0.05882
30	0.74192	0.55207	0.41199	0.30832	0.23138	0.17411	0.13137	0.09938	0.07537	0.05731	0.04368	0.03338
35	0.70591	0.50003	0.35538	0.25342	0.18129	0.13011	0.09366	0.06763	0.04899	0.03558	0.02592	0.01894
40	0.67165	0.45289	0.30656	0.20829	0.14205	0.09722	0.06678	0.04603	0.03184	0.02209	0.01538	0.01075

TABLE 2 Present Value of Ordinary Annuity $p = \{1 - [1/(1 + i)^t]\}/i$

Period	0.01	0.02	0.03	0.04	0.05	0.06	0.07	0.08	0.09	0.10	0.11	0.12
1	0.99010	0.98039	0.97087	0.96154	0.95238	0.94340	0.93458	0.92593	0.91743	0.90909	0.90090	0.89286
2	1.97040	1.94156	1.91347	1.88609	1.85941	1.83339	1.80802	1.78326	1.75911	1.73554	1.71252	1.69005
3	2.94099	2.88388	2.82861	2.77509	2.72325	2.67301	2.62432	2.57710	2.53129	2.48685	2.44371	2.40183
4	3.90197	3.80773	3.71710	3.62990	3.54595	3.46511	3.38721	3.31213	3.23972	3.16987	3.10245	3.03735
5	4.85343	4.71346	4.57971	4.45182	4.32948	4.21236	4.10020	3.99271	3.88965	3.79079	3.69590	3.60478
6	5.79548	5.60143	5.41719	5.24214	5.07569	4.91732	4.76654	4.62288	4.48592	4.35526	4.23054	4.11141
7	6.72819	6.47199	6.23028	6.00205	5.78637	5.58238	5.38929	5.20637	5.03295	4.86842	4.71220	4.56376
8	7.65168	7.32548	7.01969	6.73274	6.46321	6.20979	5.97130	5.74664	5.53482	5.33493	5.14612	4.96764
9	8.56602	8.16224	7.78611	7.43533	7.10782	6.80169	6.51523	6.24689	5.99525	5.75902	5.53705	5.32825
10	9.47130	8.98259	8.53020	8.11090	7.72173	7.36009	7.02358	6.71008	6.41766	6.14457	5.88923	5.65022
11	10.36763	9.78685	9.25262	8.76048	8.30641	7.88687	7.49867	7.13896	6.80519	6.49506	6.20652	5.93770
12	11.25508	10.57534	9.95400	9.38507	8.86325	8.38384	7.94269	7.53608	7.16073	6.81369	6.49236	6.19437
13	12.13374	11.34837	10.63496	9.98565	9.39357	8.85268	8.35765	7.90378	7.48690	7.10336	6.74987	6.42355
14	13.00370	12.10625	11.29607	10.56312	9.89864	9.29498	8.74547	8.24424	7.78615	7.36669	6.98187	6.62817
15	13.86505	12.84926	11.93794	11.11839	10.37966	9.71225	9.10791	8.55948	8.06069	7.60608	7.19087	6.81086
16	14.71787	13.57771	12.56110	11.65230	10.83777	10.10590	9.44665	8.85137	8.31256	7.82371	7.37916	6.97399
17	15.56225	14.29187	13.16612	12.16567	11.27407	10.47726	9.76322	9.12164	8.54363	8.02155	7.54879	7.11963
18	16.39827	14.99203	13.75351	12.65930	11.68959	10.82760	10.05909	9.37189	8.75563	8.20141	7.70162	7.24967
19	17.22601	15.67846	14.32380	13.13394	12.08532	11.15812	10.33560	9.60360	8.95011	8.36492	7.83929	7.36578
20	18.04555	16.35143	14.87747	13.59033	12.46221	11.46992	10.59401	9.81815	9.12855	8.51356	7.96333	7.46944
21	18.85698	17.01121	15.41502	14.02916	12.82115	11.76408	10.83553	10.01680	9.29224	8.64869	8.07507	7.56200
22	19.66038	17.65805	15.93692	14.45112	13.16300	12.04158	11.06124	10.20074	9.44243	8.77154	8.17574	7.64465
23	20.45582	18.29220	16.44361	14.85684	13.48857	12.30338	11.27219	10.37106	9.58021	8.88322	8.26643	7.71843
24	21.24339	18.91393	16.93554	15.24696	13.79864	12.55036	11.46933	10.52876	9.70661	8.98474	8.34814	7.78432
25	22.02316	19.52346	17.41315	15.62208	14.09394	12.78336	11.65358	10.67478	9.82258	9.07704	8.42174	7.84314
30	25.80771	22.39646	19.60044	17.29203	15.37245	13.76483	12.40904	11.25778	10.27365	9.42691	8.69379	8.05518
35	29.40858	24.99862	21.48722	18.66461	16.37419	14.49825	12.94767	11.65457	10.56682	9.64416	8.85524	8.17550
40	32.83469	27.35548	23.11477	19.79277	17.15909	15.04630	13.33171	11.92461	10.75736	9.77905	8.95105	8.24378

TABLE 3 Future Value of Single Amount $f = (1 + i)^t$

						Interest Rate						
Period	0.01	0.02	0.03	0.04	0.05	0.06	0.07	0.08	0.09	0.10	0.11	0.12
1	1.01000	1.02000	1.03000	1.04000	1.05000	1.06000	1.07000	1.08000	1.09000	1.10000	1.11000	1.12000
2	1.02010	1.04040	1.06090	1.08160	1.10250	1.12360	1.14490	1.16640	1.18810	1.21000	1.23210	1.25440
3	1.03030	1.06121	1.09273	1.12486	1.15763	1.19102	1.22504	1.25971	1.29503	1.33100	1.36763	1.40493
4	1.04060	1.08243	1.12551	1.16986	1.21551	1.26248	1.31080	1.36049	1.41158	1.46410	1.51807	1.57352
5	1.05101	1.10408	1.15927	1.21665	1.27628	1.33823	1.40255	1.46933	1.53862	1.61051	1.68506	1.76234
6	1.06152	1.12616	1.19405	1.26532	1.34010	1.41852	1.50073	1.58687	1.67710	1.77156	1.87041	1.97382
7	1.07214	1.14869	1.22987	1.31593	1.40710	1.50363	1.60578	1.71382	1.82804	1.94872	2.07616	2.21068
8	1.08286	1.17166	1.26677	1.36857	1.47746	1.59385	1.71819	1.85093	1.99256	2.14359	2.30454	2.47596
9	1.09369	1.19509	1.30477	1.42331	1.55133	1.68948	1.83846	1.99900	2.17189	2.35795	2.55804	2.77308
10	1.10462	1.21899	1.34392	1.48024	1.62889	1.79085	1.96715	2.15892	2.36736	2.59374	2.83942	3.10585
11	1.11567	1.24337	1.38423	1.53945	1.71034	1.89830	2.10485	2.33164	2.58043	2.85312	3.15176	3.47855
12	1.12683	1.26824	1.42576	1.60103	1.79586	2.01220	2.25219	2.51817	2.81266	3.13843	3.49845	3.89598
13	1.13809	1.29361	1.46853	1.66507	1.88565	2.13293	2.40985	2.71962	3.06580	3.45227	3.88328	4.36349
14	1.14947	1.31948	1.51259	1.73168	1.97993	2.26090	2.57853	2.93719	3.34173	3.79750	4.31044	4.88711
15	1.16097	1.34587	1.55797	1.80094	2.07893	2.39656	2.75903	3.17217	3.64248	4.17725	4.78459	5.47357
16	1.17258	1.37279	1.60471	1.87298	2.18287	2.54035	2.95216	3.42594	3.97031	4.59497	5.31089	6.13039
17	1.18430	1.40024	1.65285	1.94790	2.29202	2.69277	3.15882	3.70002	4.32763	5.05447	5.89509	6.86604
18	1.19615	1.42825	1.70243	2.02582	2.40662	2.85434	3.37993	3.99602	4.71712	5.55992	6.54355	7.68997
19	1.20811	1.45681	1.75351	2.10685	2.52695	3.02560	3.61653	4.31570	5.14166	6.11591	7.26334	8.61276
20	1.22019	1.48595	1.80611	2.19112	2.65330	3.20714	3.86968	4.66096	5.60441	6.72750	8.06231	9.64629
21	1.23239	1.51567	1.86029	2.27877	2.78596	3.39956	4.14056	5.03383	6.10881	7.40025	8.94917	10.80385
22	1.24472	1.54598	1.91610	2.36992	2.92526	3.60354	4.43040	5.43654	6.65860	8.14027	9.93357	12.10031
23	1.25716	1.57690	1.97359	2.46472	3.07152	3.81975	4.74053	5.87146	7.25787	8.95430	11.02627	13.55235
24	1.26973	1.60844	2.03279	2.56330	3.22510	4.04893	5.07237	6.34118	7.91108	9.84973	12.23916	15.17863
25	1.28243	1.64061	2.09378	2.66584	3.38635	4.29187	5.42743	6.84848	8.62308	10.83471	13.58546	17.00006
30	1.34785	1.81136	2.42726	3.24340	4.32194	5.74349	7.61226	10.06266	13.26768	17.44940	22.89230	29.95992
35	1.41660	1.99989	2.81386	3.94609	5.51602	7.68609	10.67658	14.78534	20.41397	28.10244	38.57485	52.79962
40	1.48886	2.20804	3.26204	4.80102	7.03999	10.28572	14.97446	21.72452	31.40942	45.25926	65.00087	93.05097

TABLE 4 Future Value of an Ordinary Annuity $f = [(1 + i)^t - 1]/i$

						Interest Rate						
Period	0.01	0.02	0.03	0.04	0.05	0.06	0.07	0.08	0.09	0.10	0.11	0.12
1	1.00000	1.00000	1.00000	1.00000	1.00000	1.00000	1.00000	1.00000	1.00000	1.00000	1.00000	1.00000
2	2.01000	2.02000	2.03000	2.04000	2.05000	2.06000	2.07000	2.08000	2.09000	2.10000	2.11000	2.12000
3	3.03010	3.06040	3.09090	3.12160	3.15250	3.18360	3.21490	3.24640	3.27810	3.31000	3.34210	3.37440
4	4.06040	4.12161	4.18363	4.24646	4.31013	4.37462	4.43994	4.50611	4.57313	4.64100	4.70973	4.77933
5	5.10101	5.20404	5.30914	5.41632	5.52563	5.63709	5.75074	5.86660	5.98471	6.10510	6.22780	6.35285
6	6.15202	6.30812	6.46841	6.63298	6.80191	6.97532	7.15329	7.33593	7.52333	7.71561	7.91286	8.11519
7	7.21354	7.43428	7.66246	7.89829	8.14201	8.39384	8.65402	8.92280	9.20043	9.48717	9.78327	10.08901
8	8.28567	8.58297	8.89234	9.21423	9.54911	9.89747	10.25980	10.63663	11.02847	11.43589	11.85943	12.29969
9	9.36853	9.75463	10.15911	10.58280	11.02656	11.49132	11.97799	12.48756	13.02104	13.57948	14.16397	14.77566
10	10.46221	10.94972	11.46388	12.00611	12.57789	13.18079	13.81645	14.48656	15.19293	15.93742	16.72201	17.54874
11	11.56683	12.16872	12.80780	13.48635	14.20679	14.97164	15.78360	16.64549	17.56029	18.53117	19.56143	20.65458
12	12.68250	13.41209	14.19203	15.02581	15.91713	16.86994	17.88845	18.97713	20.14072	21.38428	22.71319	24.13313
13	13.80933	14.68033	15.61779	16.62684	17.71298	18.88214	20.14064	21.49530	22.95338	24.52271	26.21164	28.02911
14	14.94742	15.97394	17.08632	18.29191	19.59863	21.01507	22.55049	24.21492	26.01919	27.97498	30.09492	32.39260
15	16.09690	17.29342	18.59891	20.02359	21.57856	23.27597	25.12902	27.15211	29.36092	31.77248	34.40536	37.27971
16	17.25786	18.63929	20.15688	21.82453	23.65749	25.67253	27.88805	30.32428	33.00340	35.94973	39.18995	42.75328
17	18.43044	20.01207	21.76159	23.69751	25.84037	28.21288	30.84022	33.75023	36.97370	40.54470	44.50084	48.88367
18	19.61475	21.41231	23.41444	25.64541	28.13238	30.90565	33.99903	37.45024	41.30134	45.59917	50.39594	55.74971
19	20.81090	22.84056	25.11687	27.67123	30.53900	33.75999	37.37896	41.44626	46.01846	51.15909	56.93949	63.43968
20	22.01900	24.29737	26.87037	29.77808	33.06595	36.78559	40.99549	45.76196	51.16012	57.27500	64.20283	72.05244
21	23.23919	25.78332	28.67649	31.96920	35.71925	39.99273	44.86518	50.42292	56.76453	64.00250	72.26514	81.69874
22	24.47159	27.29898	30.53678	34.24797	38.50521	43.39229	49.00574	55.45676	62.87334	71.40275	81.21431	92.50258
23	25.71630	28.84496	32.45288	36.61789	41.43048	46.99583	53.43614	60.89330	69.53194	79.54302	91.14788	104.60289
24	26.97346	30.42186	34.42647	39.08260	44.50200	50.81558	58.17667	66.76476	76.78981	88.49733	102.17415	118.15524
25	28.24320	32.03030	36.45926	41.64591	47.72710	54.86451	63.24904	73.10594	84.70090	98.34706	114.41331	133.33387
30	34.78489	40.56808	47.57542	56.08494	66.43885	79.05819	94.46079	113.28321	136.30754	164.49402	199.02088	241.33268
35	41.66028	49.99448	60.46208	73.65222	90.32031	111.43478	138.23688	172.31680	215.71075	271.02437	341.58955	431.66350
40	48.88637	60.40198	75.40126	95.02552	120.79977	154.76197	199.63511	259.05652	337.88245	442.59256	581.82607	767.09142

Getty Images

STARBUCKS

Starbucks Corporation is the leading retailer, roaster, and brander of specialty coffee. The company has broad geographic reach. At last count, Starbucks operated 11,131 stores in the U.S. and another 5,727 stores in scores of countries around the world. In 2011, the company reported strong operating results: net income of $1,248.0 million on revenue of $11.7 billion. Income is up for the third straight year, up by 32% compared to 2010.

The company was hard hit during the 2008–2009 recession when customers switched from "luxury" goods such as premium coffees to more economical items. The company recorded restructuring charges, made significant changes to its operations, and has not looked back. As Starbucks' income declined and then recovered, so too has the company's stock price as the following chart illustrates:

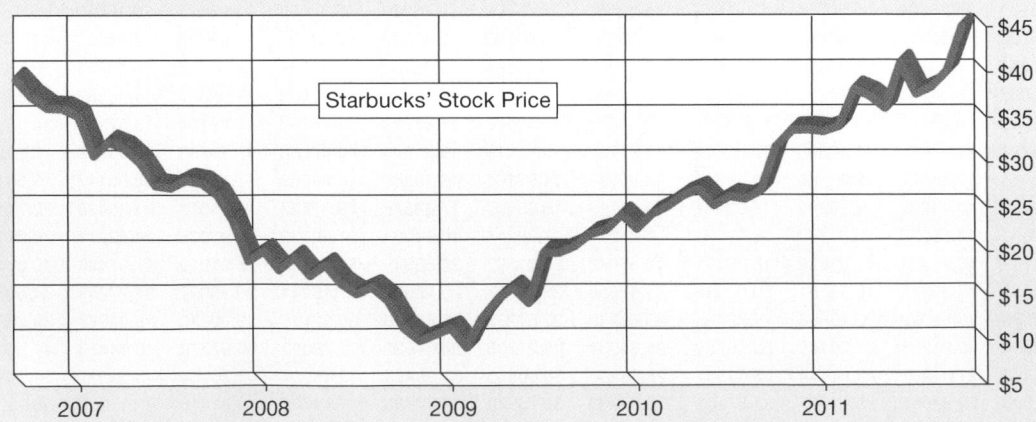

Constructing the Statement of Cash Flows

LEARNING OBJECTIVES

LO1 Define and describe the framework for the statement of cash flows. (p. B-3)

LO2 Define and explain net cash flows from operating activities. (p. B-6)

LO3 Define and explain net cash flows from investing activities. (p. B-11)

LO4 Define and explain net cash flows from financing activities. (p. B-12)

LO5 Describe and apply ratios based on operating cash flows. (p. B-16)

Although Starbucks' income declined by 53% in 2008, operating cash flow declined by only 5%. Similarly, when income recovered by 140% in 2010, the increase in cash flows was a more modest 20%. Over the 2006 to 2011 period, Starbucks' cash flows have been far less volatile than its net income, as the graphic below reveals. What is behind this relation? What does it mean? This appen-

dix helps answer these and other questions. It begins by describing the process of constructing the statement of cash flows. Next, it explains how we use and interpret the statement of cash flows to aid both internal and external business decisions.

Sources: Starbucks 2011 10-K and Annual Report.

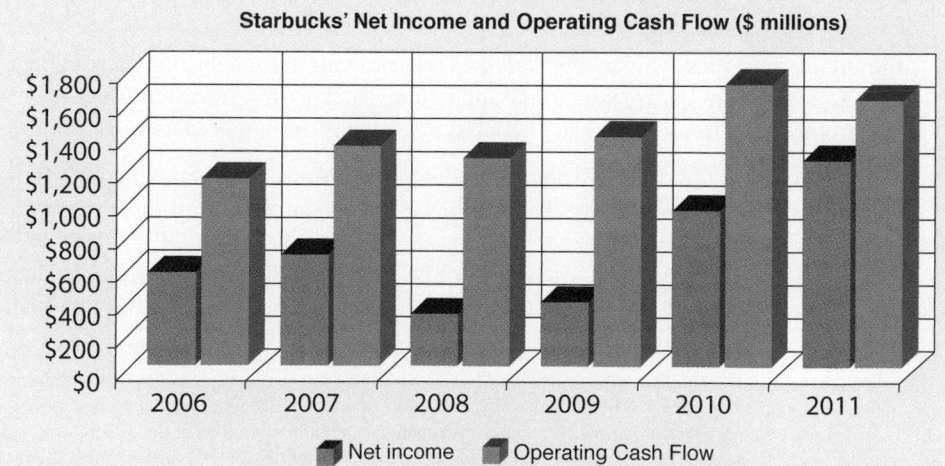

Starbucks' Net Income and Operating Cash Flow ($ millions)

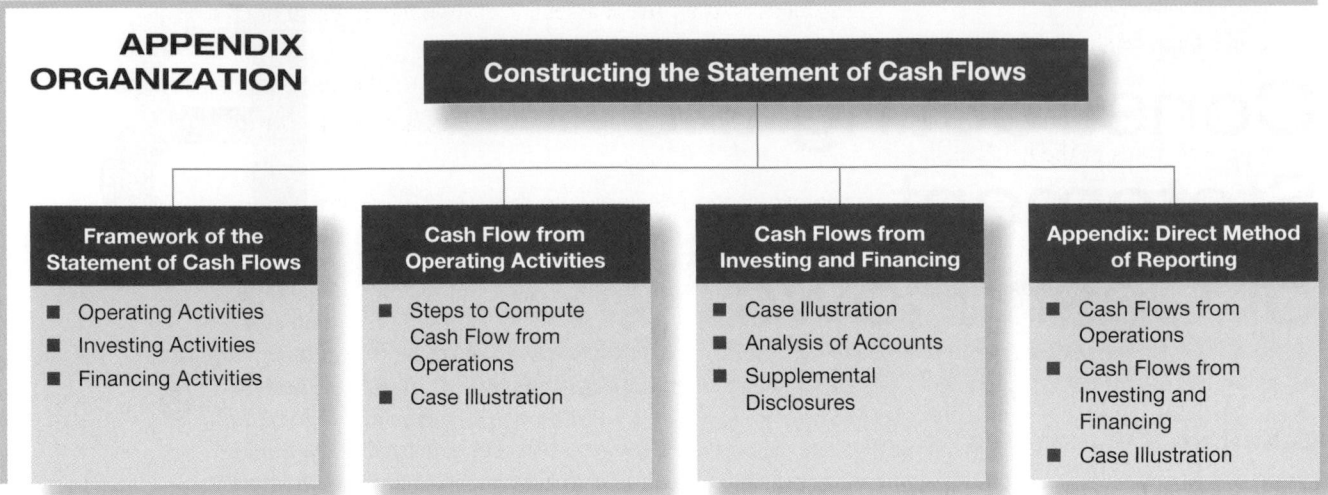

The **statement of cash flows** is a financial statement that summarizes information about the flow of cash into and out of a company. In this appendix, we discuss the preparation, analysis, and interpretation of the statement of cash flows. The statement of cash flows complements the balance sheet and the income statement. The balance sheet reports the company's financial position at a point in time (the end of each period) whereas the statement of cash flows explains the change in one of its components—cash—from one balance sheet date to the next. The income statement reveals the results of the company's operating activities for the period, and these operating activities are a major contributor to the change in cash as reported in the statement of cash flows.

FRAMEWORK FOR STATEMENT OF CASH FLOWS

LO1 Define and describe the framework for the statement of cash flows.

The statement of cash flows classifies cash receipts and cash payments into one of three categories:

- **Operating activities** Operating activities measure the net cash inflows and outflows as a result of the company's transactions with its customers. We generally prefer operating cash flows to be positive, although companies can report net cash outflows for operating activities in the short run during periods of growth (as outflows to increase working capital accounts outstrip inflows from profits).

- **Investing activities** Investing activities relate to net cash flows generally relating to long-term assets. Outflows occur when a company purchases long-term assets and inflows occur when long-term assets are sold.

- **Financing activities** Financing activities relate to long-term debt and stockholders' equity. Cash inflows result from borrowing money and issuing stock to investors. Outflows occur when a company repays debt, repurchases stock, or pays dividends to shareholders.

Classifying cash flows into these categories readily identifies the effects on cash from each of these three major activities of a company. The combined effects on cash of all three categories explain the net change in cash for that period.[1]

Preparation of the statement of cash flows draws mainly on information from the income statement and the balance sheet. Specifically, the three sections draw generally on the following information:

---

[1] The statement of cash flows explains the change in a firm's cash *and* cash equivalents. **Cash equivalents** are short-term, highly liquid investments that are (1) easily convertible into a known cash amount and (2) close enough to maturity so that their market value is not sensitive to interest rate changes (generally, investments with initial maturities of three months or less). Treasury bills, commercial paper (short-term notes issued by corporations), and money market funds are typical examples of cash equivalents.

When preparing a statement of cash flows, the cash and cash equivalents are added together and treated as a single sum. This is done because the purchase and sale of investments in cash equivalents are considered to be part of a firm's overall management of cash rather than a source or use of cash. As statement users evaluate and project cash flows, for example, it should not matter whether the cash is readily available, deposited in a bank account, or invested in cash equivalents. Transfers back and forth between a firm's cash account and its investments in cash equivalents, therefore, are not treated as cash inflows and cash outflows in its statement of cash flows. When discussing the statement of cash flows, managers generally use the word *cash* rather than the term *cash and cash equivalents*. We follow the same practice in this appendix.

- **Net cash flows from operating activities** draws on the current asset and current liabilities sections of the balance sheet.
- **Net cash flows from investing activities** draws on the long-term assets section of the balance sheet.
- **Net cash flows from financing activities** draws on the long-term liabilities and stockholders' equity sections of the balance sheet.

These relations do not hold exactly, but they provide us a useful way to visualize the construction of the statement of cash flows.

Exhibit B.1 reproduces Starbucks' statement of cash flows ($ millions). During 2011, Starbucks reported net income of $1,248.0 million and generated $1,612.4 million of cash from operating activities.

EXHIBIT B.1 Statement of Cash Flows for Starbucks

(in millions) Year Ended	October 2, 2011	October 3, 2010	September 27, 2009
OPERATING ACTIVITIES:			
Net earnings including noncontrolling interests.	1,248.0	948.3	391.5
Adjustments to reconcile net earnings to net cash provided by operating activities:			
Depreciation and amortization	550.0	540.8	563.3
Gain on sale of properties.	(30.2)	—	—
Provision for impairments and asset disposals	36.2	67.7	224.4
Deferred income taxes, net.	106.2	(42.0)	(69.6)
Equity in income of investees.	(118.5)	(108.6)	(78.4)
Distributions of income from equity investees	85.6	91.4	53.0
Gain resulting from acquisition of joint ventures	(55.2)	(23.1)	—
Stock-based compensation	145.2	113.6	83.2
Excess tax benefit from exercise of stock options.	(103.9)	(36.9)	(15.9)
Other.	(2.9)	7.8	5.4
Cash provided/(used) by changes in operating assets and liabilities:			
Accounts receivable	(88.7)	(33.4)	59.1
Inventories.	(422.3)	123.2	28.5
Accounts payable	227.5	(3.6)	(53.0)
Accrued taxes	104.0	0.6	59.2
Deferred revenue.	35.8	24.2	16.3
Other operating assets	(22.5)	17.3	61.4
Other operating liabilities	(81.9)	17.6	60.6
Net cash provided by operating activities	1,612.4	1,704.9	1,389.0
INVESTING ACTIVITIES:			
Purchase of available-for-sale securities	(966.0)	(549.0)	(129.2)
Maturities and calls of available-for-sale securities	430.0	209.9	111.0
Sales of available-for-sale securities	—	1.1	5.0
Acquisitions, net of cash acquired	(55.8)	(12.0)	—
Net purchases of equity, other investments and other assets.	(13.2)	1.2	(4.8)
Additions to property, plant and equipment.	(531.9)	(440.7)	(445.6)
Proceeds from sale of property, plant and equipment.	117.4	—	42.5
Net cash used by investing activities	(1,019.5)	(789.5)	(421.1)
FINANCING ACTIVITIES:			
Proceeds from (repayments of) short-term borrowings	30.8	—	(713.1)
Purchase of noncontrolling interest	(27.5)	(45.8)	—
Proceeds from issuance of common stock	235.4	127.9	57.3
Excess tax benefit from exercise of stock options.	103.9	36.9	15.9
Principal payments on long-term debt.	(4.3)	(6.6)	(0.7)
Cash dividends paid.	(389.5)	(171.0)	—
Repurchase of common stock	(555.9)	(285.6)	—
Other.	(0.9)	(1.8)	(1.6)
Net cash used by financing activities.	(608.0)	(346.0)	(642.2)
Effect of exchange rate changes on cash and cash equivalents.	(0.8)	(5.2)	4.3
Net increase/(decrease) in cash and cash equivalents	(15.9)	564.2	330.0
CASH AND CASH EQUIVALENTS:			
Beginning of period	1,164.0	599.8	269.8
End of the period	1,148.1	1,164.0	599.8

The company used $1,019.5 million of cash for investing activities and $608.0 million of cash for financing activities. In sum, Starbucks decreased its cash reserves by $15.9 million (including foreign exchange effects), from $1,164.0 million at the beginning of fiscal 2011 to $1,148.1 million at the end of fiscal 2011.

Operating Activities

A company's income statement reflects primarily the transactions and events that constitute its operating activities. Generally, the cash effects of these operating transactions and events determine the net cash flow from operating activities. The usual focus of a firm's **operating activities** is on selling goods or rendering services, but the activities are defined broadly enough to include any cash receipts or payments that are not classified as investing or financing activities. For example, cash received from collection of receivables and cash payments to purchase inventories are treated as cash flows from operating activities. The following are examples of cash inflows and outflows relating to operating activities.

Operating Activities	
Cash Inflows	**Cash Outflows**
■ Receipts from customers for sales made or services rendered.	■ Payments to employees or suppliers.
■ Receipts of interest and dividends.	■ Payments to purchase inventories.
■ Other receipts that are not related to investing or financing activities, such as lawsuit settlements and refunds received from suppliers.	■ Payments of interest to creditors.
	■ Payments of taxes to government.
	■ Other payments that are not related to investing or financing activities, such as contributions to charity.

Investing Activities

A firm's transactions involving (1) the acquisition and disposal of property, plant, and equipment (PPE) assets and intangible assets, (2) the purchase and sale of stocks, bonds, and other securities (that are not cash equivalents), and (3) the lending and subsequent collection of money constitute the basic components of its **investing activities**. The related cash receipts and payments appear in the investing activities section of the statement of cash flows. Examples of these cash flows follow.

Investing Activities	
Cash Inflows	**Cash Outflows**
■ Receipts from sales of property, plant, and equipment (PPE) assets and intangible assets.	■ Payments to purchase property, plant, and equipment (PPE) assets and intangible assets.
■ Receipts from sales of investments in stocks, bonds, and other securities (other than cash equivalents).	■ Payments to purchase stocks, bonds, and other securities (other than cash equivalents).
■ Receipts from repayments of loans by borrowers.	■ Payments made to lend money to borrowers.

Financing Activities

A firm engages in **financing activities** when it obtains resources from owners, returns resources to owners, borrows resources from creditors, and repays amounts borrowed. Cash flows related to these transactions are reported in the financing activities section of the statement of cash flows. Examples of these cash flows follow.

Financing Activities	
Cash Inflows ▲	**Cash Outflows ▼**
■ Receipts from issuances of common stock and preferred stock and from sales of treasury stock. ■ Receipts from issuances of bonds payable, mortgage notes payable, and other notes payable.	■ Payments to acquire treasury stock. ■ Payments of dividends. ■ Payments to settle outstanding bonds payable, mortgage notes payable, and other notes payable.

CASH FLOW FROM OPERATING ACTIVITIES

The first section of a statement of cash flows presents a firm's net cash flow from operating activities. Two alternative formats are used to report the net cash flow from operating activities: the *indirect method* and the *direct method*. *Both methods report the same amount of net cash flow from operating activities*. (Net cash flows from investing and financing activities are prepared in the same manner under both the indirect and direct methods; only the format for cash flows from operating activities differs.)

LO2 Define and explain net cash flows from operating activities.

The *indirect method* starts with net income and applies a series of adjustments to net income to convert it to a cash-basis income number, which is the net cash flow from operating activities. Accountants estimate that *more than 98% of companies preparing the statement of cash flows use the indirect method*. The indirect method is popular because (1) it is easier and less expensive to prepare than the direct method and (2) the direct method requires a supplemental disclosure showing the indirect method (thus, essentially reporting both methods).

The remainder of this appendix discusses the preparation of the statement of cash flows. The indirect method is presented in this section, and the direct method is presented in Appendix B1. (These discussions are independent of each other; both provide complete coverage of the preparation of the statement of cash flows.)

To prepare a statement of cash flows, we need a firm's income statement, comparative balance sheets, and some additional data taken from the accounting records. Exhibit B.2 presents this information for Java House. We use these data to prepare Java's 2011 statement of cash flows using the indirect method. Java's

EXHIBIT B.2 Financial Data of Java House

JAVA HOUSE Income Statement For Year Ended December 31, 2011		
Sales.		$250,000
Cost of goods sold. . . .	$148,000	
Wages expense	52,000	
Insurance expense. . . .	5,000	
Depreciation expense. .	10,000	
Income tax expense. . .	11,000	
Gain on sale of land . . .	(8,000)	218,000
Net income.		$ 32,000

Additional Data for 2011

1. Purchased the entirety of long-term stock investments for cash at year-end.
2. Sold land costing $20,000 for $28,000 cash.
3. Acquired $60,000 patent at year-end by issuing common stock at par.
4. All accounts payable relate to merchandise purchases.
5. Issued common stock at par for $10,000 cash.
6. Declared and paid cash dividends of $13,000.

JAVA HOUSE Balance Sheet	Dec. 31, 2011	Dec. 31, 2010
Assets		
Cash.	$ 35,000	$ 10,000
Accounts receivable.	39,000	34,000
Inventory.	54,000	60,000
Prepaid insurance	17,000	4,000
Long-term investments	15,000	—
PPE assets	180,000	200,000
Accumulated depreciation . . .	(50,000)	(40,000)
Patent.	60,000	—
Total assets	$350,000	$268,000
Liabilities and Equity		
Accounts payable.	$ 10,000	$ 19,000
Income tax payable	5,000	3,000
Common stock.	260,000	190,000
Retained earnings	75,000	56,000
Total liabilities and equity. . . .	$350,000	$268,000

statement of cash flows explains the $25,000 increase in cash that occurred during 2011 (from $10,000 to $35,000) by classifying the firm's cash flows into operating, investing, and financing categories.

Steps to Compute Net Cash Flow from Operating Activities

The following four steps are applied to construct the net cash flows from operating activities section of the statement of cash flows:

1. **Begin with net income** The first line of the operating section of the statement of cash flows is net income, which is the bottom line from the income statement. This amount is recorded as a positive amount for net income and as a negative amount for a net loss.

2. **Adjust net income (loss) for** *noncash* **revenues, expenses, gains and losses**
   a. **Noncash revenues and expenses** The income statement often includes noncash expenses such as depreciation and amortization. These expenses are allocations of asset costs over their useful lives to match the revenues generated from those assets. The cash outflow normally occurs when the asset is acquired, which is reported in the *investing* section. Depreciation and amortization expenses do not have cash outflows. Hence, we must eliminate them from the statement of cash flows by adding them back (to "zero them out" because they are negative amounts in the net income computation).
   b. **Gains and losses** Gains and losses on sales of assets are part of investing activities, not operating activities (unless the company is in the business of buying and selling assets). Thus, we must zero them out in the operating section and record the net cash inflows or outflows in the investing section; namely, gains on sales are subtracted from income and losses on sales are added to income.

3. **Adjust net income (loss) for changes in current assets and current liabilities** Net income must be adjusted for changes in current assets and current liabilities (the operating section of the balance sheet). A decrease (from prior year to current year) in a noncash current asset is identified as a cash inflow and an increase is identified as a cash outflow. Conversely, an increase in a current liability is identified as a cash inflow and a decrease as a cash outflow. To make this computation, we use the following guide:

Balance Sheet Account	Cash flow increases from	Cash flow decreases from
Current assets (excluding cash)...	Account decreases	Account increases
Current liabilities.............	Account increases	Account decreases

4. **Sum the amounts from steps 1, 2 and 3 to get net cash flows from operating activities.**

   Exhibit B.3 summarizes the adjustments to net income in determining operating cash flows. These are the adjustments applied under the indirect method of computing cash flow from operations.

EXHIBIT B.3 Converting Net Income to Net Cash Flow from Operating Activities	Add (+) or Subtract (−) from Net Income
Net income	$ #
Add depreciation and amortization	+
Add (subtract): Losses (gains) on asset and liability dispositions	±
Adjust for changes in noncash current assets	
Subtract increases in noncash current assets	−
Add decreases in noncash current assets	+
Adjust for changes in current liabilities	
Add increases in current liabilities..	+
Subtract decreases in current liabilities	−
Net cash flow from operating activities	$ #

Adjustments for noncash revenues, expenses, gains & losses

Adjustments for changes in noncash current assets and current liabilities

To better understand the adjustments for current assets and liabilities, the following table provides brief explanations of adjustments for receivables, inventories, payables and accruals.

	Change in account balance . . .	Means that . . .	Which requires this adjustment to net income to yield cash profit . . .
Receivables	Increase	Sales and net income increase, but cash is not yet received	Deduct increase in receivables from net income
	Decrease	More cash is received than is reported in sales and net income	Add decrease in receivables to net income
Inventories	Increase	Cash is paid for inventories that are not yet reflected in cost of goods sold	Deduct increase in inventories from net income
	Decrease	Cost of goods sold includes inventory costs that were paid for in a prior period	Add decrease in inventories to net income
Payables and accruals	Increase	More goods and services are acquired on credit, delaying cash payment	Add increase in payables and accruals to net income
	Decrease	More cash is paid than that reflected in cost of goods sold or operating expenses	Deduct decrease in payables and accruals from net income

Java House Case Illustration

We next explain and illustrate these adjustments with Java House's data from Exhibit B.2.

Depreciation and Amortization Expenses

Depreciation and amortization expenses represent write-offs of previously recorded assets; so-called noncash expenses. Because depreciation and amortization expenses are subtracted in computing net income, we add these expenses to net income as we convert it to a related net operating cash flow. Adding these expenses to net income eliminates them from the income statement and is a necessary adjustment to obtain cash income. Java House had $10,000 of 2011 depreciation expense, so this amount is added to Java's net income of $32,000.

Net income.	$32,000
Add: Depreciation.	**10,000**

Gains and Losses Related to Investing or Financing Activities

The income statement can contain gains and losses that relate to investing or financing activities. Gains and losses from the sale of investments, PPE assets, or intangible assets illustrate gains and losses from investing (not operating) activities. A gain or loss from the retirement of bonds payable is an example of a financing gain or loss. The full cash flow effect from these types of events is reported in the investing or financing sections of the statement of cash flows. Therefore, the related gains or losses must be eliminated as we convert net income to net cash flow from operating activities. To eliminate their impact on net income, gains are subtracted and losses are added to net income. Java House had an $8,000 gain from the sale of land in 2011. This gain relates to an investing activity, so it is subtracted from Java's net income.

Net income.	$32,000
Add: Depreciation.	10,000
Deduct: Gain on sale of land	**(8,000)**

Accounts Receivable Change

Credit sales increase accounts receivable; cash collections on account decrease accounts receivable. If, overall, accounts receivable decrease during a year, then cash collections from customers exceed credit sales revenue by the amount of the decrease. Because sales are added in computing net income, the decrease in accounts receivable is added to net income. In essence, this adjustment replaces the sales amount with the larger amount of cash collections from customers. If accounts receivable increase during a year, then sales revenue exceeds the cash collections from customers by the amount of the increase. Because sales are added in computing net income, the increase in accounts receivable is subtracted from net income as we convert it to a net cash flow from operating activities. In essence, this adjustment replaces the sales amount with the smaller amount of cash collections from customers. Java's accounts receivable increased $5,000 during 2011, so this increase is subtracted from net income under the indirect method.

Net income.	$32,000
Add: Depreciation.	10,000
Deduct: Gain on sale of land	(8,000)
Deduct: Accounts receivable increase.	**(5,000)**

Inventory Change

The adjustment for an inventory change is one of two adjustments to net income that together cause the cost of goods sold expense to be replaced by an amount representing the cash paid during the period for merchandise purchased. The second adjustment, which we examine shortly, is for the change in accounts payable. The effect of the inventory adjustment alone is to adjust net income for the difference between the cost of goods sold and the cost of merchandise purchased during the period. The cost of merchandise purchased increases inventory; the cost of goods sold decreases inventory. An overall decrease in inventory during a period must mean, therefore, that the cost of merchandise purchased was less than the cost of goods sold by the amount of the decrease. Because cost of goods sold was subtracted in computing net income, the inventory decrease is added to net income. After this adjustment, the effect of the cost of goods sold on net income has been replaced by the smaller cost of merchandise purchased. Similarly, if inventory increased during a period, the cost of merchandise purchased is larger than the cost of goods sold by the amount of the increase. To replace the cost of goods sold with the cost of merchandise purchased, the inventory increase is subtracted from net income. Java's inventory decreased $6,000 during 2011, so this decrease is added to net income.

Net income.	$32,000
Add: Depreciation.	10,000
Deduct: Gain on sale of land	(8,000)
Deduct: Accounts receivable increase.	(5,000)
Add: Inventory decrease	**6,000**

Prepaid Expenses Change

Cash prepayments of various expenses increase a firm's prepaid expenses. When the related expenses for the period are subsequently recorded, the prepaid expenses decrease. An overall decrease in prepaid expenses for a period means that the cash prepayments were less than the related expenses. Because the expenses were subtracted in determining net income, the indirect method adds the decrease in prepaid expenses to net income as it is converted to a cash flow amount. The effect of the addition is to replace the expense amount with the smaller cash payment amount. Similarly, an increase in prepaid expenses is subtracted from net income because an increase means that the cash prepayments during the year were more than the related expenses. Java's prepaid insurance increased $13,000 during 2011, so this increase is deducted from net income.

Net income.	$32,000
Add: Depreciation.	10,000
Deduct: Gain on sale of land	(8,000)
Deduct: Accounts receivable increase.	(5,000)
Add: Inventory decrease	6,000
Deduct: Prepaid insurance increase	**(13,000)**

Accounts Payable Change

When merchandise is purchased on account, accounts payable increase by the amount of the goods' cost. Accounts payable decrease when cash payments are made to settle the accounts. An overall decrease in accounts payable during a year means that cash payments for purchases were more than the cost of the purchases. An accounts payable decrease, therefore, is subtracted from net income under the indirect method. The deduction, in effect, replaces the cost of merchandise purchased with the larger cash payments for merchandise purchased. (Recall that the earlier inventory adjustment replaced the cost of goods sold with the cost of merchandise purchased.) In contrast, an increase in accounts payable means that cash payments for purchases were less than the cost of purchases for the period. Thus, an accounts payable increase is added to net income as it is converted to a cash flow amount. Java House shows a $9,000 decrease in accounts payable during 2011. This decrease is subtracted from net income.

Net income.	$32,000
Add: Depreciation.	10,000
Deduct: Gain on sale of land	(8,000)
Deduct: Accounts receivable increase.	(5,000)
Add: Inventory decrease	6,000
Deduct: Prepaid insurance increase	(13,000)
Deduct: Accounts payable decrease	**(9,000)**

Accrued Liabilities Change

Changes in accrued liabilities are interpreted the same way as changes in accounts payable. A decrease means that cash payments exceeded the related expense amounts; an increase means that cash payments were less than the related expenses. Decreases are subtracted from net income; increases are added to net income. Java has one accrued liability, income tax payable, and it increased by $2,000 during 2011. The $2,000 increase is added to net income.

Net income.	$32,000
Add: Depreciation.	10,000
Deduct: Gain on sale of land	(8,000)
Deduct: Accounts receivable increase.	(5,000)
Add: Inventory decrease	6,000
Deduct: Prepaid insurance increase	(13,000)
Deduct: Accounts payable decrease.	(9,000)
Add: Income tax payable increase	**2,000**

We have now identified the adjustments to convert Java's net income to its net cash flow from operating activities. The operating activities section of the statement of cash flows appears as follows under the indirect method:

Net income.	$32,000
Add (deduct) items to convert net income to cash basis:	
Depreciation	10,000
Gain on sale of land	(8,000)
Accounts receivable increase.	(5,000)
Inventory decrease	6,000
Prepaid insurance increase	(13,000)
Accounts payable decrease	(9,000)
Income tax payable increase	2,000
Net cash provided by operating activities	**$15,000**

To summarize, net cash flows from operating activities begins with net income (loss) and eliminates noncash expenses (such as depreciation) and any gains and losses that are properly reported in the investing and financing sections. Next, cash inflows (outflows) relating to changes in the level of current operating assets and liabilities are added (subtracted) to yield net cash flows from operating activities. During the period, Java earned cash operating profits of $34,000 ($32,000 + $10,000 − $8,000), but used $19,000 of cash (−$5,000 + $6,000 − $13,000 − $9,000 + $2,000) to increase net working capital. Cash outflows relating to the increase in net working capital are a common occurrence for growing companies, and this net asset increase must be financed just like the increase in PPE assets.

BUSINESS INSIGHT   Starbucks' Addbacks for Operating Cash Flow

Starbucks reports $1,248.0 million of net income for 2011 and $1,612.4 million of operating cash inflows. The difference between these numbers is mainly due to $550.0 million of depreciation and amortization expense that is included in net income. Depreciation is a noncash charge; an expense not requiring cash payment. It is added back to income in computing operating cash flows. Starbucks also reports a $36.2 million asset impairment (write-down). This, too, is a noncash charge and is an addback in computing operating cash flows. Starbucks adds $106.2 million for deferred taxes, indicating that cash payments of taxes are less than tax expense reported in income. It also subtracts $118.5 million for equity in income of investees, meaning that it received less in dividends from affiliated companies than it reported in equity income (see Module 7). Starbucks also adds back its $145.2 million of stock option expense since that compensation is paid in stock, not in cash, and reclassifies the $103.9 million of tax benefits it receives for the exercise of these options from operating activities to financing activities as required under current GAAP.

MANAGERIAL DECISION   You Are the Securities Analyst

You are analyzing a company's statement of cash flows. The company has two items relating to its accounts receivable. First, the company finances the sale of its products to some customers; the increase to notes receivable is classified as an investing activity. Second, the company sells its accounts receivable to a separate entity, such as a trust. As a result, sale of receivables is reported as an asset sale; this reduces receivables and yields a gain or loss on sale (in this case, the company is not required to consolidate the trust as a Primary Beneficiary of a Variable Interest Entity). This action increases its operating cash flows. How should you interpret this cash flow increase? [Answer, p. B-23]

CASH FLOWS FROM INVESTING ACTIVITIES

Analyze Remaining Noncash Assets

LO3 Define and explain net cash flows from investing activities.

Investing activities cause changes in asset accounts. Usually the accounts affected (other than cash) are noncurrent asset accounts such as property, plant and equipment assets and long-term investments, although short-term investment accounts can also be affected. To determine the cash flows from investing activities, *we analyze changes in all noncash asset accounts not used in computing net cash flow from operating activities*. Our objective is to identify any investing cash flows related to these changes.

As before, changes in long-term assets accounts (and investment accounts) are classified as cash inflows and cash outflows according to the following decision rule:

Balance Sheet Account	Cash flow increases from	Cash flow decreases from
Noncurrent assets	Account decreases	Account increases

Increases in long-term assets and investment accounts are identified as cash outflows. Decreases are identified as cash inflows.

Java House Case Illustration

Analyze Change in Long-Term Investments

Java's comparative balance sheets show that long-term investments increased $15,000 during 2011. The increase means that investments must have been purchased, and the additional data reported indicates that cash was spent to purchase long-term stock investments. Purchasing stock is an investing activity. Thus, a $15,000 purchase of stock investments is reported as a cash outflow from investing activities in the statement of cash flows.

Analyze Change in Property, Plant and Equipment Assets

Java's PPE assets decreased $20,000 during 2011. PPE assets decrease as the result of disposals, and the additional data for Java House indicate that land was sold for cash in 2011. Selling land is an investing activity. Thus, the sale of land for $28,000 is reported as a cash inflow from investing activities in the statement of cash flows. (Recall that the $8,000 gain on sale of land was deducted as a reconciling item in the operating section; see above.)

Analyze Change in Accumulated Depreciation

Java's accumulated depreciation increased $10,000 during 2011. Accumulated depreciation increases when depreciation expense is recorded. Java's 2011 depreciation expense was $10,000, so the total change in accumulated depreciation is the result of the recording of depreciation expense. As previously discussed, there is no cash flow related to the recording of depreciation expense, and we have previously adjusted for this expense in our computation of net cash flows from operating activities.

Analyze Change in Patent

We see from the comparative balance sheets that Java had an increase of $60,000 in a patent. The increase means that a patent was acquired, and the additional data indicate that common stock was issued to obtain a patent. This event is a noncash investing (acquiring a patent) and financing (issuing common stock) transaction that must be disclosed as supplementary information to the statement of cash flows.

BUSINESS INSIGHT | **Starbucks' Investing Activities**

Starbucks used $1,019.5 million cash for investing activities in 2011. Of this, $536 million ($966 million − $430 million) is related to the purchase of securities. Starbucks also spent $55.8 million on acquisitions of other companies, which is the cash portion of the acquisition cost. It might also have issued debt and stock to finance this acquisition, which would be excluded from this statement and would be identified as noncash financing and investing activities in a footnote. Starbucks invested $531.9 million in property, plant, and equipment (PPE) and received cash of $117.4 on sales of PPE during the year. These expenditures might have been for owned property or for leasehold improvements on leased property. It also spent $13.2 million on other investments. Investing activities on the statement of cash flows can involve investments in operating assets (such as purchases of PPE or acquisitions of other companies) or investments in nonoperating assets (such as purchases and sales of marketable securities and other investments).

CASH FLOWS FROM FINANCING ACTIVITIES

Analyze Remaining Liabilities and Equity

Financing activities cause changes in liability and stockholders' equity accounts. Usually the accounts affected are noncurrent accounts such as bonds payable and common stock, although a current liability such as short-term notes payable can also be affected. To determine the cash flows from financing activities, *we analyze changes in all liability and stockholders' equity accounts that were not used in computing net cash flow from operating activities.* Our objective is to identify any financing cash flows related to these changes.

LO4 Define and explain net cash flows from financing activities.

As before, changes in long-term liability and equity accounts are classified as cash inflows and cash outflows according to the following decision rule:

Balance Sheet Account	Cash flow increases from	Cash flow decreases from
Noncurrent liabilities and equity....	Account increases	Account decreases

Increases in long-term liabilities and equity accounts are identified as cash inflows. Decreases are identified as cash outflows.

Java House Case Illustration

Analyze Change in Common Stock

Java's common stock increased $70,000 during 2011. Common stock increases when shares of stock are issued. As noted in discussing the patent increase, common stock with a $60,000 par value was issued in exchange for a patent. This event is disclosed as a noncash investing and financing transaction. The other $10,000 increase in common stock, as noted in the additional data, resulted from an issuance of stock for cash. Issuing common stock is a financing activity, so a $10,000 cash inflow from a stock issuance appears as a financing activity in the statement of cash flows.

Analyze Change in Retained Earnings

Retained earnings grew from $56,000 to $75,000 during 2011—a $19,000 increase. This increase is the net result of Java's $32,000 of net income (which increased retained earnings) and a $13,000 cash dividend (which decreased retained earnings). Because every item in Java's income statement was considered in computing the net cash provided by operating activities, only the cash dividend remains to be considered. Paying a cash dividend is a financing activity. Thus, a $13,000 cash dividend appears as a cash outflow from financing activities in the statement of cash flows. We have now completed the analysis of all of Java's noncash balance sheet accounts and can prepare the 2011 statement of cash flows. Exhibit B.4 shows this statement.

If there are cash inflows and outflows from similar types of investing and financing activities, the inflows and outflows are reported separately (rather than reporting only the net difference). For example, proceeds from the sale of plant assets are reported separately from outlays made to acquire plant assets. Similarly, funds borrowed are reported separately from debt repayments, and proceeds from issuing stock are reported separately from outlays to acquire treasury stock.

BUSINESS INSIGHT **Starbucks' Financing Activities**

Starbucks realized cash *outflows* of $320.5 million ($235.4 million − $555.9 million) from issuance of common stock, net of repurchases. Only stock issued for cash is reflected in the statement of cash flows. Stock issued in connection with acquisitions is not reflected because it does not involve cash. Issuance of stock is often related to the exercise of employee stock options, and companies frequently repurchase stock to offset the dilutive effect of granting the options and to have stock to sell to employees when they exercise their options. Starbucks also reports a cash inflow of $30.8 million from borrowings during the year. Starbucks also realized a net cash outflow of $389.5 million for dividend payments. The net effect is a decrease in cash of $608.0 million from financing activities.

SUMMARY OF NET CASH FLOW REPORTING

Income statement accounts are all identified within the operating section of the statement of cash flows. Balance sheet items are classified as follows:

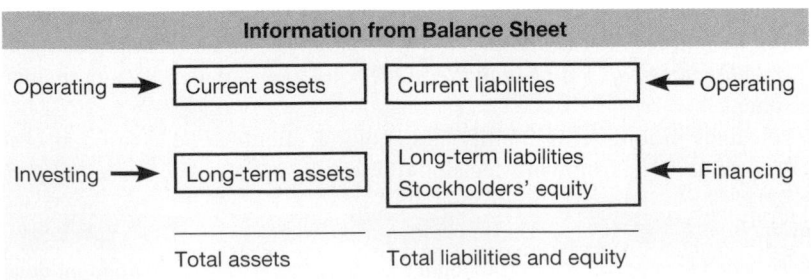

More specifically, and drawing on the Java House illustration, we can summarize the cash flow effects of the income statement and balance sheet information and categorize them into the operating, investing and financing classifications in the following table:

Account	Change	Source or Use	Cash flow effect	Classification on SCF
Current assets				
Accounts receivable	+5,000	Use	−5,000	Operating
Inventories	−6,000	Source	+6,000	Operating
Prepaid insurance.	+13,000	Use	−13,000	Operating
Noncurrent assets				
PPE related				Investing
Accumulated depreciation . . .	+10,000	Neither	+10,000	Operating
Sale of land				
Proceeds	+28,000	Source	+28,000	Investing
Gain	−8,000	Neither	−8,000	Operating
Investments	+15,000	Use	−15,000	Investing
Current liabilities				
Accounts payable	−9,000	Use	−9,000	Operating
Income tax payable	+2,000	Source	+2,000	Operating
Long-term liabilities				Financing
Stockholders' equity				
Common stock	+10,000	Source	+10,000	Financing
Retained earnings				
Net income	+32,000	Source	+32,000	Operating
Dividends	+13,000	Use	−13,000	Financing
Total (net cash flow)			+25,000	

The current year's cash balance increases by $25,000, from $10,000 to $35,000. Formal preparation of the statement of cash flows can proceed once we have addressed one final issue: required supplemental disclosures. We discuss that topic in the next section.

Supplemental Disclosures for Indirect Method

When the indirect method is used in the statement of cash flows, three separate disclosures are required: (1) two specific operating cash outflows—cash paid for interest and cash paid for income taxes, (2) a schedule or description of all noncash investing and financing transactions, and (3) the firm's policy for determining which highly liquid, short-term investments are treated as cash equivalents. Noncash investing and financing activities include the issuance of stocks, bonds, or leases in exchange for property, plant, and equipment (PPE) assets or intangible assets; the exchange of long-term assets for other long-term assets; and the conversion of long-term debt into common stock.

Java House Case Illustration

Java House incurred no interest cost during 2011. It did pay income taxes. Our discussion of the $2,000 change in income tax payable during 2011 revealed that the increase meant that cash tax payments were less than income tax expense by the amount of the increase. Income tax expense was $11,000, so the cash paid for income taxes was $2,000 less than $11,000, or $9,000.

Java House did have one noncash investing and financing event during 2011: the issuance of common stock to acquire a patent. This event, as well as the cash paid for income taxes, is disclosed as supplemental information to the statement of cash flows in Exhibit B.4.

EXHIBIT B.4   Statement of Cash Flows for Indirect Method with Supplemental Disclosures

JAVA HOUSE
Statement of Cash Flows
For Year Ended December 31, 2011

Net cash flow from operating activities		
Net income.	$32,000	
Add (deduct) items to convert net income to cash basis		
Depreciation.	10,000	
Gain on sale of land	(8,000)	
Accounts receivable increase.	(5,000)	
Inventory decrease	6,000	
Prepaid insurance increase	(13,000)	
Accounts payable decrease.	(9,000)	
Income tax payable increase	2,000	
Net cash provided by operating activities		$15,000
Cash flows from investing activities		
Purchase of stock investments.	(15,000)	
Sale of land.	28,000	
Net cash provided by investing activities.		13,000
Cash flows from financing activities		
Issuance of common stock.	10,000	
Payment of dividends.	(13,000)	
Net cash used by financing activities.		(3,000)
Net increase in cash.		25,000
Cash at beginning of year		10,000
Cash at end of year		$35,000
Supplemental cash flow disclosures		
Cash paid for income taxes		$ 9,000
Schedule of noncash investing and financing activities		
Issuance of common stock to acquire patent		$60,000

APPLICATIONS OF CASH FLOW INFORMATION

Usefulness of Classifications

The classification of cash flows into three categories of activities helps financial statement users interpret cash flow data. To illustrate, assume that companies D, E, and F are similar companies operating in the same industry. Each company reports a $100,000 cash increase during the current year. Information from their statements of cash flows is summarized below.

	Company D	Company E	Company F
Net cash provided by operating activities	$100,000	$ 0	$ 0
Cash flows from investing activities			
Sale of property, plant, and equipment (PPE)	0	100,000	0
Cash flows from financing activities			
Issuance of notes payable	0	0	100,000
Net increase in cash.	$100,000	$100,000	$100,000

Although each company's net cash increase was the same, the source of the increase varied by company. This variation affects the analysis of the cash flow data, particularly for potential short-term creditors who must evaluate the likelihood of obtaining repayment in the future for any funds loaned to the company. Based only on these cash flow data, a potential creditor would feel more comfortable lending money to D than to either E or F. This is because D's cash increase came from its operating activities, whereas both E and F could only break even on their cash flows from operations. Also, E's cash increase came from the sale of property, plant, and equipment (PPE) assets, a source that is not likely to recur regularly. F's cash increase came entirely from borrowed funds. This means F faces additional cash burdens in the future when the interest and principal payments on the note payable become due.

BUSINESS INSIGHT | **Objectivity of Cash**

Usefulness of financial statements is enhanced when the underlying data are objective and verifiable. Measuring cash and the changes in cash are among the most objective measurements that accountants make. Thus, the statement of cash flows is arguably the most objective financial statement. This characteristic of the statement of cash flows is welcomed by those investors and creditors interested in evaluating the quality of a firm's income.

Usefulness of the Statement of Cash Flows

A statement of cash flows shows the periodic cash effects of a firm's operating, investing, and financing activities. Distinguishing among these different categories of cash flows helps users compare, evaluate, and predict cash flows. With cash flow information, creditors and investors are better able to assess a firm's ability to settle its liabilities and pay its dividends. A firm's need for outside financing is also better evaluated when using cash flow data. Over time, the statement of cash flows permits users to observe and access management's investing and financing policies.

A statement of cash flows also provides information useful in evaluating a firm's financial flexibility. *Financial flexibility* is a firm's ability to generate sufficient amounts of cash to respond to unanticipated needs and opportunities. Information about past cash flows, particularly cash flows from operations, helps in assessing financial flexibility. An evaluation of a firm's ability to survive an unexpected drop in demand, for example, should include a review of its past cash flows from operations. The larger these cash flows, the greater is the firm's ability to withstand adverse changes in economic conditions. Other financial statements, particularly the balance sheet and its notes, also contain information useful for judging financial flexibility.

Some investors and creditors find the statement of cash flows useful in evaluating the quality of a firm's income. As we know, determining income under accrual accounting procedures requires many accruals, deferrals, allocations, and valuations. These adjustment and measurement procedures introduce more subjectivity into income determination than some financial statement users prefer. These users relate a more objective performance measure—cash flow from operations—to net income. To these users, the higher this ratio is, the higher is the quality of income.

In analyzing the statement of cash flows, we must not necessarily conclude that the company is better off if cash increases and worse off if cash decreases. It is not the cash change that is most important, but the sources of that change. For example, what are the sources of cash inflows? Are these sources transitory? Are these sources mainly from operating activities? We must also review the uses of cash. Has the company invested its cash in operating areas to strengthen its competitive position? Is it able to comfortably meet its debt obligations? Has it diverted cash to creditors or investors at the expense of the other? Such questions and answers are key to properly interpreting the statement of cash flows for business decisions.

Ratio Analyses of Cash Flows

Data from the statement of cash flows enter into various financial ratios. Two such ratios are the operating cash flow to current liabilities ratio and the operating cash flow to capital expenditures ratio.

LO5 Describe and apply ratios based on operating cash flows.

Operating Cash Flow to Current Liabilities Ratio

Two measures previously introduced—the current ratio and the quick ratio—emphasize the relation of current assets to current liabilities in an attempt to measure the ability of the firm to liquidate current liabilities when they become due. The **operating cash flow to current liabilities ratio** is another measure of the ability to liquidate current liabilities and is calculated as follows:

Operating Cash Flow to Current Liabilities = Cash Flow from Operating Activities/Average Current Liabilities

Net cash flow from operating activities is obtained from the statement of cash flows; it represents the excess amount of cash derived from operations during the year after deducting working capital needs and payments required on current liabilities. The denominator is the average of the beginning and ending current liabilities for the year.

To illustrate, the following amounts are taken from the 2011 financial statements for Cisco Systems, Inc.

Net cash flow from operating activities	$10,079 million
Current liabilities at beginning of the year	19,233 million
Current liabilities at end of the year	17,506 million

Its operating cash flow to current liabilities ratio of 0.54 is computed as follows:

$$\$10,079 \text{ million}/[(\$19,233 \text{ million} + \$17,506 \text{ million})/2] = 0.54$$

The higher this ratio, the stronger is a firm's ability to settle current liabilities as they come due. A ratio of 0.5 is considered a good ratio, so, Cisco's ratio of 0.54 is above average.

Operating Cash Flow to Capital Expenditures Ratio

To remain competitive, an entity must be able to replace, and expand when appropriate, its property, plant, and equipment. A ratio that helps assess a firm's ability to do this from internally generated cash flow is the **operating cash flow to capital expenditures ratio**, which is computed as follows:

Operating Cash Flow to Capital Expenditures = Cash Flow from Operating Activities/Annual Capital Expenditures

The numerator in this ratio comes from the first section of the statement of cash flows—the section reporting the net cash flow from operating activities. Information for the denominator can be found in one or more places in the financial statements and related disclosures. Data on capital expenditures are part of the required industry segment disclosures in notes to the financial statements. Capital expenditures are often also shown in the investing activities section of the statement of cash flows. Also, capital expenditures often appear in the comparative selected financial data presented as supplementary information to the financial statements. Finally, management's discussion and analysis of the statements commonly identify the annual capital expenditures.

A ratio in excess of 1.0 means that the firm's current operating activities are providing cash in excess of the amount needed to provide the desired level of plant capacity and would normally be considered a sign of financial strength. This ratio is also viewed as an indicator of long-term solvency—a ratio exceeding 1.0 means that there is operating cash flow in excess of capital needs that can then be used to repay outstanding long-term debt.

The interpretation of this ratio for a firm is influenced by its trend in recent years, the ratio size being achieved by other firms in the same industry, and the stage of the firm's life cycle. A firm in the early stages of its life cycle, when periods of rapid expansion occur, is expected to experience a lower ratio than a firm in the mature stage of its life cycle, when maintenance of plant capacity is more likely than expansion of capacity.

To illustrate the ratio's computation, Cicso Systems reported capital expenditures in 2011 of $1,174 million. Cisco's operating cash flow to capital expenditures ratio for that same year is 8.59, computed as $10,079 million/$1,174 million. Following are recent operating cash flow to capital expenditures ratios for several companies:

Colgate-Palmolive (consumer grocery products).	5.84
Lockheed Martin (aerospace).	4.33
Verizon Communications (telecommunications)	2.03
Harley-Davidson (motorcycle manufacturer)	6.80
Home Depot (home products).	4.18

APPENDIX-END REVIEW 1

Part A

1. Which of the following is not disclosed in a statement of cash flows?
   - a.   A transfer of cash to a cash equivalent investment
   - b.   The amount of cash at year-end
   - c.   Cash outflows from investing activities during the period
   - d.   Cash inflows from financing activities during the period

2. Which of the following events appears in the cash flows from investing activities section of the statement of cash flows?
   - a.   Cash received as interest
   - b.   Cash received from issuance of common stock
   - c.   Cash purchase of equipment
   - d.   Cash payment of dividends

3. Which of the following events appears in the cash flows from financing activities section of the statement of cash flows?
   - a.   Cash purchase of equipment
   - b.   Cash purchase of bonds issued by another company
   - c.   Cash received as repayment for funds loaned
   - d.   Cash purchase of treasury stock

4. Tyler Company has a net income of $49,000 and the following related items:

Depreciation expense.	$ 5,000
Accounts receivable increase	2,000
Inventory decrease.	10,000
Accounts payable decrease.	4,000

Using the indirect method, what is Tyler's net cash flow from operations?

    a. $42,000   b. $46,000   c. $58,000   d. $38,000

Part B

Expresso Royale's income statement and comparative balance sheets follow:

EXPRESSO ROYALE Income Statement For Year Ended December 31, 2011		
Sales.		$385,000
Dividend income.		5,000
		390,000
Cost of goods sold.	$233,000	
Wages expense	82,000	
Advertising expense.	10,000	
Depreciation expense.	11,000	
Income tax expense.	17,000	
Loss on sale of investments.	2,000	355,000
Net income.		$ 35,000

EXPRESSO ROYALE Balance Sheets		
	Dec. 31, 2011	Dec. 31, 2010
Assets		
Cash.	$ 8,000	$ 12,000
Accounts receivable.	22,000	28,000
Inventory.	94,000	66,000
Prepaid advertising.	12,000	9,000
Long-term investments—Available-for-sale.	30,000	41,000
Fair value adjustment to investments.	—	(1,000)
Plant assets	178,000	130,000
Accumulated depreciation	(72,000)	(61,000)
Total assets	$272,000	$224,000
Liabilities and Equity		
Accounts payable.	$ 27,000	$ 14,000
Wages payable.	6,000	2,500
Income tax payable	3,000	4,500
Common stock.	139,000	125,000
Retained earnings	97,000	79,000
Unrealized loss on investments	—	(1,000)
Total liabilities and equity.	$272,000	$224,000

Cash dividends of $17,000 were declared and paid during 2011. Plant assets were purchased for cash in 2011, and, later in the year, additional common stock was issued for cash. Investments costing $11,000 were sold for cash at a $2,000 loss in 2011; an unrealized loss of $1,000 on these investments had been recorded in 2010 (at December 31, 2011, the cost and fair value of unsold investments are equal).

Required

a. Compute the change in cash that occurred during 2011.

b. Prepare a 2011 statement of cash flows using the indirect method.

The solution is on page B-40.

APPENDIX B1: Direct Method Reporting for the Statement of Cash Flows

To prepare a statement of cash flows, we need a firm's income statement, comparative balance sheets, and some additional data taken from the accounting records. Exhibit B.2 presents this information for Java House. We use these data to prepare Java's 2011 statement of cash flows using the direct method. Java's statement of cash flows explains the $25,000 increase in cash that occurred during 2011 (from $10,000 to $35,000) by classifying the firm's cash flows into operating, investing, and financing categories. To get the information to construct the statement, we do the following:

1. **Use the direct method to determine individual cash flows from operating activities.** We use changes that occurred during 2011 in various current asset and current liability accounts.
2. **Determine cash flows from investing activities.** We do this by analyzing changes in noncurrent asset accounts.
3. **Determine cash flows from financing activities.** We do this by analyzing changes in liability and stockholders' equity accounts.

The net cash flows from investing and financing are identical to those prepared using the indirect method. Only the format of the net cash flows from operating activities differs between the two methods, not the total amount of cash generated from operating activities.

Cash Flows from Operating Activities

The **direct method** presents net cash flow from operating activities by showing the major categories of operating cash receipts and payments. The operating cash receipts and payments are usually determined by converting the accrual revenues and expenses to corresponding cash amounts. It is efficient to do it this way because the accrual revenues and expenses are readily available in the income statement.

Converting Revenues and Expenses to Cash Flows

Exhibit B.5 summarizes the procedures for converting individual income statement items to corresponding cash flows from operating activities.

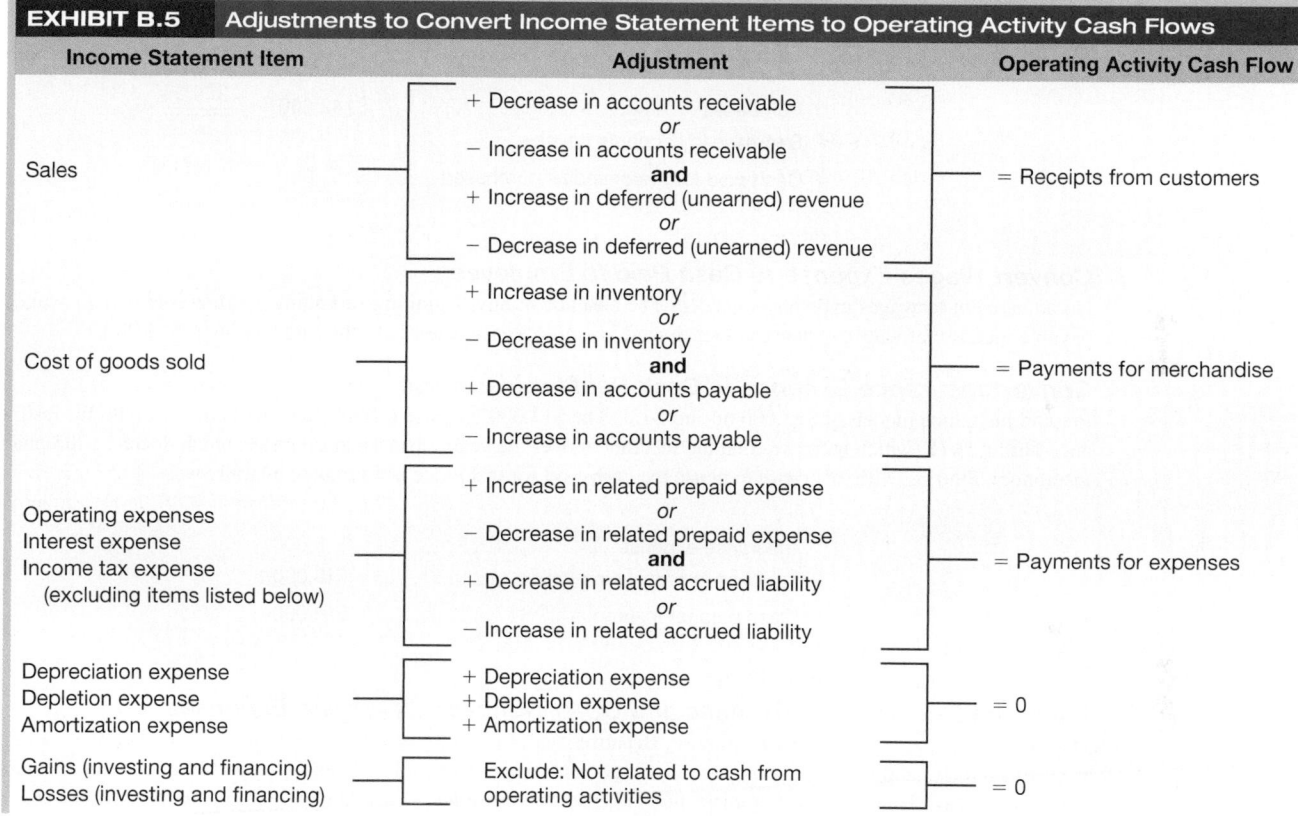

EXHIBIT B.5	Adjustments to Convert Income Statement Items to Operating Activity Cash Flows	
Income Statement Item	**Adjustment**	**Operating Activity Cash Flow**
Sales	+ Decrease in accounts receivable or − Increase in accounts receivable **and** + Increase in deferred (unearned) revenue or − Decrease in deferred (unearned) revenue	= Receipts from customers
Cost of goods sold	+ Increase in inventory or − Decrease in inventory **and** + Decrease in accounts payable or − Increase in accounts payable	= Payments for merchandise
Operating expenses Interest expense Income tax expense (excluding items listed below)	+ Increase in related prepaid expense or − Decrease in related prepaid expense **and** + Decrease in related accrued liability or − Increase in related accrued liability	= Payments for expenses
Depreciation expense Depletion expense Amortization expense	+ Depreciation expense + Depletion expense + Amortization expense	= 0
Gains (investing and financing) Losses (investing and financing)	Exclude: Not related to cash from operating activities	= 0

Java House Case Illustration

We next explain and illustrate the process of converting Java House's 2011 revenues and expenses to corresponding cash flows from operating activities under the direct method.

Convert Sales to Cash Received from Customers

During 2011, accounts receivable increased $5,000. This increase means that during 2011, cash collections on account (which decrease accounts receivable) were less than credit sales (which increase accounts receivable). We compute cash received from customers as follows (this computation assumes that no accounts were written off as uncollectible during the period):

Sales	$250,000
− Increase in accounts receivable	(5,000)
= Cash received from customers	$245,000

Convert Cost of Goods Sold to Cash Paid for Merchandise Purchased

The conversion of cost of goods sold to cash paid for merchandise purchased is a two-step process. First, cost of goods sold is adjusted for the change in inventory to determine the amount of purchases during the year. Then the purchases amount is adjusted for the change in accounts payable to derive the cash paid for merchandise purchased. Inventory decreased from $60,000 to $54,000 during 2011. This $6,000 decrease indicates that the cost of goods sold exceeded the cost of goods purchased during the year. The year's purchases amount is computed as follows:

	Cost of goods sold	$148,000
−	Decrease in inventory	(6,000)
=	Purchases	$142,000

During 20011, accounts payable decreased $9,000. This decrease reflects the fact that cash payments for merchandise purchased on account (which decrease accounts payable) exceeded purchases on account (which increase accounts payable). The cash paid for merchandise purchased, therefore, is computed as follows:

	Purchases	$142,000
+	Decrease in accounts payable	9,000
=	Cash paid for merchandise purchased	$151,000

Convert Wages Expense to Cash Paid to Employees

No adjustment to wages expense is needed. The absence of any beginning or ending accrued liability for wages payable means that wages expense and cash paid to employees as wages are the same amount: $52,000.

Convert Insurance Expense to Cash Paid for Insurance

Prepaid insurance increased $13,000 during 2011. The $13,000 increase reflects the excess of cash paid for insurance during 2011 (which increases prepaid insurance) over the year's insurance expense (which decreases prepaid insurance). Starting with insurance expense the cash paid for insurance is computed as follows:

	Insurance expense	$ 5,000
+	Increase in prepaid insurance	13,000
=	Cash paid for insurance	$18,000

Eliminate Depreciation Expense and Other Noncash Operating Expenses

Depreciation expense is a noncash expense. Because it does not represent a cash payment, depreciation expense is eliminated (by adding it back) as we convert accrual expense amounts to the corresponding amounts of cash payments. If Java House had any amortization expense or depletion expense, it would eliminate them for the same reason. The amortization of an intangible asset and the depletion of a natural resource are noncash expenses.

Convert Income Tax Expense to Cash Paid for Income Taxes

The increase in income tax payable from $3,000 at December 31, 2010, to $5,000 at December 31, 2011, means that 2011's income tax expense (which increases income tax payable) was $2,000 more than 2011's tax payments (which decrease income tax payable). If we start with income tax expense, then we calculate cash paid for income taxes as follows:

	Income tax expense	$11,000
−	Increase in income tax payable	(2,000)
=	Cash paid for income taxes	$ 9,000

Omit Gains and Losses Related to Investing and Financing Activities

The income statement may contain gains and losses related to investing or financing activities. Examples include gains and losses from the sale of plant assets and gains and losses from the retirement of bonds payable. Because these gains and losses are not related to operating activities, we omit them as we convert income statement items to various cash flows from operating activities. The cash flows relating to these gains and losses are reported in the investing activities or financing activities sections of the statement of cash flows. Java House had an $8,000 gain from the sale of land in 2011. This gain is excluded; no related cash flow appears within the operating activities category.

We have now applied the adjustments to convert each accrual revenue and expense to the corresponding operating cash flow. We use these individual cash flows to prepare the operating activities section of the statement of cash flows; see Exhibit B.6

EXHIBIT B.6 Direct Method Operating Section of Statement of Cash Flows		
Cash received from customers		$245,000
Cash paid for merchandise purchased	$151,000	
Cash paid to employees.	52,000	
Cash paid for insurance	18,000	
Cash paid for income taxes	9,000	230,000
Net cash provided by operating activities		$ 15,000

Cash Flows from Investing and Financing

The reporting of investing and financing activities in the statement of cash flows is identical under the indirect and direct methods. Thus, we simply refer to the previous sections in this appendix for explanations.

Supplemental Disclosures

When the direct method is used for the statement of cash flows, three separate disclosures are required: (1) a reconciliation of net income to the net cash flow from operating activities, (2) a schedule or description of all noncash investing and financing transactions, and (3) the firm's policy for determining which highly liquid, short-term investments are treated as cash equivalents. The firm's policy regarding cash equivalents is placed in the financial statement notes. The other two separate disclosures are reported either in the notes or at the bottom of the statement of cash flows.

The required reconciliation is essentially the indirect method of computing cash flow from operating activities. *Thus, when the direct method is used in the statement of cash flows, the indirect method is a required separate disclosure.* We discussed the indirect method earlier in this appendix.

Java House did have one noncash investing and financing event during 2011: the issuance of common stock to acquire a patent. This event is disclosed as supplemental information to the statement of cash flows in Exhibit B.4.

APPENDIX-END REVIEW 2

Expresso Royale's income statement and comparative balance sheets follow:

EXPRESSO ROYALE Income Statement For Year Ended December 31, 2011		
Sales.		$385,000
Dividend income.		5,000
		390,000
Cost of goods sold.	$233,000	
Wages expense	82,000	
Advertising expense.	10,000	
Depreciation expense.	11,000	
Income tax expense.	17,000	
Loss on sale of investments.	2,000	355,000
Net income.		$ 35,000

EXPRESSO ROYALE Balance Sheets	Dec. 31, 2011	Dec. 31, 2010
Assets		
Cash..	$ 8,000	$ 12,000
Accounts receivable.........................	22,000	28,000
Inventory....................................	94,000	66,000
Prepaid advertising..........................	12,000	9,000
Long-term investments—Available-for-sale........	30,000	41,000
Fair value adjustment to investments............	—	(1,000)
Plant assets	178,000	130,000
Accumulated depreciation	(72,000)	(61,000)
Total assets	$272,000	$224,000
Liabilities and Equity		
Accounts payable...........................	$ 27,000	$ 14,000
Wages payable..............................	6,000	2,500
Income tax payable	3,000	4,500
Common stock..............................	139,000	125,000
Retained earnings	97,000	79,000
Unrealized loss on investments	—	(1,000)
Total liabilities and equity.....................	$272,000	$224,000

Cash dividends of $17,000 were declared and paid during 2011. Plant assets were purchased for cash in 2011, and later in the year, additional common stock was issued for cash. Investments costing $11,000 were sold for cash at a $2,000 loss in 2011; an unrealized loss of $1,000 on these investments had been recorded in 2010 (at December 31, 2011, the cost and fair value of unsold investments are equal).

Required

a. Compute the change in cash that occurred during 2011.

b. Prepare a 2011 statement of cash flows using the direct method.

The solution is on page B-42.

GUIDANCE ANSWERS

MANAGERIAL DECISION   You Are the Securities Analyst

Many companies, but not all, treat customers' notes receivable as an investing activity. In 2005, the SEC became concerned with this practice and issued letters to a number of companies objecting to this accounting classification. "Presenting cash receipts from receivables generated by the sale of inventory as investing activities in the company's consolidated statements of cash flows is not in accordance with GAAP," wrote the chief accountant for the SEC's division of corporation finance, in her letter to the companies ("Little Campus Lab Shakes Big Firms—Georgia Tech Crew's Report Spurs Change in Accounting for Operating Cash Flow," March 1, 2005, *The Wall Street Journal*). The SEC's position is that these notes receivable are an operating activity and analysts are certainly justified in treating them likewise. Concerning the sale of receivables, so long as the separate entity (a trust in this case) is properly structured, the transaction can be treated as a sale (rather than require consolidation) with a consequent reduction in receivables and a gain or loss on the sale recorded in the income statement. Many analysts treat this as a financing activity and argue that the cash inflow should not be regarded as an increase in operating cash flows. Bottom line: many argue that operating cash flows do not increase as a result of these two transactions and analysts should adjust the statement of cash flows to properly classify the financing of receivables as an operating activity and the sale of receivables as a financing activity.

Superscript ᴮ¹ denotes assignments based on Appendix B1.

DISCUSSION QUESTIONS

Q B-1.   What is the definition of *cash equivalents?* Give three examples of cash equivalents.

Q B-2.   Why are cash equivalents included with cash in a statement of cash flows?

Q B-3.   What are the three major types of activities classified on a statement of cash flows? Give an example of a cash inflow and a cash outflow in each classification.

Q B-4.   In which of the three activity categories of a statement of cash flows would each of the following items appear? Indicate for each item whether it represents a cash inflow or a cash outflow:
   a.   Cash purchase of equipment.
   b.   Cash collection on loans.
   c.   Cash dividends paid.
   d.   Cash dividends received.
   e.   Cash proceeds from issuing stock.
   f.   Cash receipts from customers.
   g.   Cash interest paid.
   h.   Cash interest received.

Q B-5.   Traverse Company acquired a $3,000,000 building by issuing $3,000,000 worth of bonds payable. In terms of cash flow reporting, what type of transaction is this? What special disclosure requirements apply to a transaction of this type?

Q B-6.   Why are noncash investing and financing transactions disclosed as supplemental information to a statement of cash flows?

Q B-7.   Why is a statement of cash flows a useful financial statement?

Q B-8.   What is the difference between the direct method and the indirect method of presenting net cash flow from operating activities?

Q B-9.   In determining net cash flow from operating activities using the indirect method, why must we add depreciation back to net income? Give an example of another item that is added back to net income under the indirect method.

Q B-10.   Vista Company sold for $98,000 cash land originally costing $70,000. The company recorded a gain on the sale of $28,000. How is this event reported in a statement of cash flows using the indirect method?

Q B-11.   A firm uses the indirect method. Using the following information, what is its net cash flow from operating activities?

Net income.	$88,000
Accounts receivable decrease.	13,000
Inventory increase	9,000
Accounts payable decrease.	3,500
Income tax payable increase	1,500
Depreciation expense.	6,000

Q B-12.   What separate disclosures are required for a company that reports a statement of cash flows using the indirect method?

Q B-13.   If a business had a net loss for the year, under what circumstances would the statement of cash flows show a positive net cash flow from operating activities?

Q B-14.ᴮ¹   A firm is converting its accrual revenues to corresponding cash amounts using the direct method. Sales on the income statement are $925,000. Beginning and ending accounts receivable on the balance sheet are $58,000 and $44,000, respectively. What is the amount of cash received from customers?

Q B-15.ᴮ¹   A firm reports $86,000 wages expense in its income statement. If beginning and ending wages payable are $3,900 and $2,800, respectively, what is the amount of cash paid to employees?

Q B-16.ᴮ¹   A firm reports $43,000 advertising expense in its income statement. If beginning and ending prepaid advertising are $6,000 and $7,600, respectively, what is the amount of cash paid for advertising?

Q B-17.ᴮ¹   Rusk Company sold equipment for $5,100 cash that had cost $35,000 and had $29,000 of accumulated depreciation. How is this event reported in a statement of cash flows using the direct method?

Q B-18.[B1] What separate disclosures are required for a company that reports a statement of cash flows using the direct method?

Q B-19. How is the operating cash flow to current liabilities ratio calculated? Explain its use.

Q B-20. How is the operating cash flow to capital expenditures ratio calculated? Explain its use.

Q B-21. The statement of cash flows provides information that may be useful in predicting future cash flows, evaluating financial flexibility, assessing liquidity, and identifying financing needs. It is not, however, the best financial statement for learning about a firm's financial performance during a period; information about periodic financial performance is provided by the income statement. Two basic principles—the revenue recognition principle and the matching concept—work to distinguish the income statement from the statement of cash flows. (a) Define the revenue recognition principle and the matching concept. (b) Briefly explain how these two principles work to make the income statement a better report on periodic financial performance than the statement of cash flows.

Assignments with the ✓ logo in the margin are available in an online homework system.
See the Preface of the book for details.

MINI EXERCISES

M B-22. Classification of Cash Flows   (LO1)

For each of the items below, indicate whether the cash flow relates to an operating activity, an investing activity, or a financing activity.

a. Cash receipts from customers for services rendered.
b. Sale of long-term investments for cash.
c. Acquisition of plant assets for cash.
d. Payment of income taxes.
e. Bonds payable issued for cash.
f. Payment of cash dividends declared in previous year.
g. Purchase of short-term investments (not cash equivalents) for cash.

M B-23. Classification of Cash Flows   (LO1)

For each of the items below, indicate whether it is (1) a cash flow from an operating activity, (2) a cash flow from an investing activity, (3) a cash flow from a financing activity, (4) a noncash investing and financing activity, or (5) none of the above.

a. Paid cash to retire bonds payable at a loss.
b. Received cash as settlement of a lawsuit.
c. Acquired a patent in exchange for common stock.
d. Received advance payments from customers on orders for custom-made goods.
e. Gave large cash contribution to local university.
f. Invested cash in 60-day commercial paper (a cash equivalent).

M B-24. Net Cash Flow from Operating Activities (Indirect Method)   (LO2)

The following information was obtained from Galena Company's comparative balance sheets. Assume that Galena Company's 2011 income statement showed depreciation expense of $8,000, a gain on sale of investments of $9,000, and a net income of $45,000. Calculate the net cash flow from operating activities using the indirect method.

	Dec. 31, 2011	Dec. 31, 2010
Cash..............................	$ 19,000	$ 9,000
Accounts receivable.................	44,000	35,000
Inventory.........................	55,000	49,000
Prepaid rent	6,000	8,000
Long-term investments	21,000	34,000
Plant assets	150,000	106,000
Accumulated depreciation............	40,000	32,000
Accounts payable..................	24,000	20,000
Income tax payable	4,000	6,000
Common stock.....................	121,000	92,000
Retained earnings	106,000	91,000

M B-25. Net Cash Flow from Operating Activities (Indirect Method) (LO2)

Cairo Company had a $21,000 net loss from operations for 2012. Depreciation expense for 2012 was $8,600 and a 2012 cash dividend of $6,000 was declared and paid. Balances of the current asset and current liability accounts at the beginning and end of 2012 follow. Did Cairo Company's 2012 operating activities provide or use cash? Use the indirect method to determine your answer.

	Ending	Beginning
Cash.......................	$ 3,500	$ 7,000
Accounts receivable..........	16,000	25,000
Inventory...................	50,000	53,000
Prepaid expenses............	6,000	9,000
Accounts payable............	12,000	8,000
Accrued liabilities	5,000	7,600

M B-26.[B1] Operating Cash Flows (Direct Method) (LO2)

Calculate the cash flow for each of the following cases.

  a. Cash paid for rent:

Rent expense...................	$60,000
Prepaid rent, beginning year	10,000
Prepaid rent, end of year	8,000

  b. Cash received as interest:

Interest income..................	$16,000
Interest receivable, beginning year ...	3,000
Interest receivable, end of year	3,700

  c. Cash paid for merchandise purchased:

Cost of goods sold................	$98,000
Inventory, beginning year...........	19,000
Inventory, end of year.............	22,000
Accounts payable, beginning year....	11,000
Accounts payable, end of year.......	7,000

M B-27.[B1] Operating Cash Flows (Direct Method) (LO2)

Howell Company's current year income statement reports the following:

Sales..........................	$825,000
Cost of goods sold...............	550,000
Gross profit.....................	$275,000

Howell's comparative balance sheets show the following (accounts payable relate to merchandise purchases):

	End of Year	Beginning of Year
Accounts receivable.........	$ 71,000	$60,000
Inventory..................	109,000	96,000
Prepaid expenses...........	3,000	8,000
Accounts payable...........	31,000	37,000

Compute Howell's current-year cash received from customers and cash paid for merchandise purchased.

EXERCISES

 E B-28. Net Cash Flow from Operating Activities (Indirect Method) (LO2)

Lincoln Company owns no plant assets and reported the following income statement for the current year:

Sales..........................		$750,000
Cost of goods sold..............	$470,000	
Wages expense	110,000	
Rent expense...................	42,000	
Insurance expense..............	15,000	637,000
Net income....................		$113,000

Additional balance sheet information about the company follows:

	End of Year	Beginning of Year
Accounts receivable.........	$54,000	$49,000
Inventory.................	60,000	66,000
Prepaid insurance	8,000	7,000
Accounts payable...........	22,000	18,000
Wages payable............	9,000	11,000

Use the information to calculate the net cash flow from operating activities under the indirect method.

E B-29. Statement of Cash Flows (Indirect Method) (LO2, 3, 4)

Use the following information about Lund Corporation for 2011 to prepare a statement of cash flows under the indirect method.

Accounts payable increase	$ 9,000
Accounts receivable increase	4,000
Accrued liabilities decrease	3,000
Amortization expense.............................	6,000
Cash balance, beginning of 2011....................	22,000
Cash balance, end of 2011	15,000
Cash paid as dividends	29,000
Cash paid to purchase land........................	90,000
Cash paid to retire bonds payable at par..............	60,000
Cash received from issuance of common stock	35,000
Cash received from sale of equipment	17,000
Depreciation expense.............................	29,000
Gain on sale of equipment.........................	4,000
Inventory decrease...............................	13,000
Net income.....................................	76,000
Prepaid expenses increase	2,000

 E B-30. Operating Section of Statement of Cash Flows (Indirect Method) (LO2)

Oracle, Corp. (ORCL)

Following are the income statement and balance sheet for Oracle, Corp. for the year ended May 31, 2011, and a forecasted income statement and balance sheet for 2012.

Income Statement

($ millions)	2011 Actual	2012 Est.
Total revenues	$35,622	$47,794
Operating Expenses		
Sales and marketing	6,579	8,842
Software license updates and product support	1,264	1,673
Hardware systems products	2,057	2,772
Hardware systems support	1,259	1,673
Services	3,818	5,114
Research and development	4,519	6,070
General and administrative	970	1,290
Amortization of intangible assets	2,428	2,044
Acquisition related and other	208	—
Restructuring	487	—
Total operating expenses	23,589	29,478
Operating income	12,033	18,316
Interest income	(808)	(808)
Non-operating income (expense), net	186	186
Income before provision for income taxes	11,411	17,694
Provision for income taxes	2,864	4,441
Net income	$ 8,547	$13,253

Balance Sheet

($ millions)	2011 Actual	2012 Est.
Cash and cash equivalents	$16,163	$29,013
Marketable securities	12,685	12,685
Trade receivables	6,628	8,890
Inventories	303	430
Deferred tax assets	1,189	1,189
Prepaid expenses and other current assets	2,206	2,963
Total current assets	39,174	55,170
Property, plant and equipment, net	2,857	4,962
Intangible assets, net	7,860	5,816
Goodwill	21,553	21,553
Deferred tax assets	1,076	1,076
Other operating assets	1,015	1,338
Total non-current assets	34,361	34,745
Total assets	$73,535	$89,915
Notes payable, current and other current borrowings	$ 1,150	$ 1,250
Accounts payable	701	956
Accrued compensation and related benefits	2,320	3,107
Deferred revenues	6,802	9,129
Other current liabilities	3,219	4,301
Total current liabilities	14,192	18,743
Notes payable and other non-current borrowings	14,772	13,522
Income taxes payable	3,169	4,254
Deferred tax liabilities	59	59
Other non-current liabilities	1,098	1,482
Total non-current liabilities	19,098	19,317

continued

continued from prior page

Oracle Corporation stockholders' equity:		
Preferred stock..	0	0
Common stock..	16,653	16,653
Retained earnings	22,581	34,191
Accumulated other comprehensive income.....................	542	542
Total Oracle Corporation stockholders' equity	39,776	51,386
Noncontrolling interests.......................................	469	469
Total equity...	40,245	51,855
Total liabilities and equity.....................................	$73,535	$89,915

Prepare the net cash flows from operating activities section of a forecasted statement of cash flows for 2012 using the indirect method. Treat current and noncurrent deferred tax assets and liabilities as operating. Operating expenses (such as Sales and marketing, and General and administrative expense) for 2012 include estimated depreciation expense of $380 million.

E B-31. **Operating Section of Statement of Cash Flows (Indirect Method)**   (LO2)

General Mills, Inc. (GIS)

Following are the income statement and balance sheet for General Mills for the year ended May 29, 2011, and a forecasted income statement and balance sheet for 2012.

Income Statement		
($ millions)	2011 Actual	2012 Est.
Net sales..	$14,880.2	$15,624.2
Cost of sales.......................................	8,926.7	9,374.5
Selling, general, and administrative expenses............................	3,192.0	3,359.2
Divestiture (gain), net	(17.4)	0.0
Restructuring, impairment, and other exit costs	4.4	0.0
Operating profit	2,774.5	2,890.5
Interest, net	346.3	346.3
Earnings before income taxes and after-tax earnings from joint ventures	2,428.2	2,544.2
Income taxes	721.1	755.6
After-tax earnings from joint ventures	96.4	96.4
Net earnings, including earnings attributable to noncontrolling interests	1,803.5	1,885.0
Net earnings attributable to noncontrolling interests.........................	5.2	5.7
Net earnings attributable to General Mills	$ 1,798.3	$ 1,879.3

Balance Sheet		
($ millions)	2011 Actual	2012 Est.
Cash and cash equivalents	$ 619.6	$ 776.8
Marketable securities		
Receivables	1,162.3	1,218.7
Inventories	1,609.3	1,687.4
Deferred income taxes.....................................	27.3	31.2
Prepaid expenses and other	483.5	500.0
Total current assets	3,902.0	4,214.1
Land, buildings, and equipment..............................	3,345.9	3,340.8
Goodwill..	6,750.8	6,750.8
Other intangible assets.....................................	3,813.3	3,813.3
Other assets...	862.5	906.2
Total assets	$18,674.5	$19,025.2

continued

Current liabilities		
Accounts payable.	$995.1	$1,046.8
Current portion of long-term debt	1,031.3	733.6
Notes payable	311.3	311.3
Other current liabilities	1,321.5	1,390.6
Total current liabilities	3,659.2	3,482.3
Long-term debt	5,542.5	4,808.9
Deferred income taxes.	1,127.4	1,187.4
Other liabilities	1,733.2	1,812.4
Total liabilities.	12,062.3	11,291.0
Stockholders' equity		
Common stock.	75.5	75.5
Additional paid-in capital	1,319.8	1,319.8
Retained earnings	9,191.3	10,307.6
Common stock in treasury.	(3,210.3)	(3,210.3)
Accumulated other comprehensive loss	(1,010.8)	(1,010.8)
Total stockholders' equity	6,365.5	7,481.8
Noncontrolling interests.	246.7	252.4
Total equity.	6,612.2	7,734.2
Total liabilities and equity.	$18,674.5	$19,025.2

Prepare the net cash flows from operating activities section of a forecasted statement of cash flows for 2012 using the indirect method. Operating expenses (such as Cost of sales and Selling, general and administrative expenses) for 2012 include estimated depreciation expense of $692.6 million. Estimated 2012 retained earnings includes dividends of $768.7 million.

E B-32.[B1] **Operating Cash Flows (Direct Method)** (LO2)

Calculate the cash flow for each of the following cases.

a. Cash paid for advertising:

Advertising expense.	$62,000
Prepaid advertising, beginning of year.	11,000
Prepaid advertising, end of year	15,000

b. Cash paid for income taxes:

Income tax expense.	$29,000
Income tax payable, beginning of year	7,100
Income tax payable, end of year	4,900

c. Cash paid for merchandise purchased:

Cost of goods sold.	$180,000
Inventory, beginning of year.	30,000
Inventory, end of year.	25,000
Accounts payable, beginning of year.	10,000
Accounts payable, end of year.	12,000

E B-33.[B1] **Statement of Cash Flows (Direct Method)** (LO2, 3, 4)

Use the following information about the 2011 cash flows of Mason Corporation to prepare a statement of cash flows under the direct method.

Cash balance, end of 2011	$ 12,000
Cash paid to employees and suppliers	148,000
Cash received from sale of land.	40,000
Cash paid to acquire treasury stock	10,000
Cash balance, beginning of 2011.	16,000
Cash received as interest.	6,000
Cash paid as income taxes	11,000
Cash paid to purchase equipment.	89,000
Cash received from customers	194,000
Cash received from issuing bonds payable. .	30,000
Cash paid as dividends	16,000

✓ **E B-34.**[B1] **Operating Cash Flows (Direct Method)** (LO2)

Refer to the information in Exercise B-28. Calculate the net cash flow from operating activities using the direct method. Show a related cash flow for each revenue and expense.

E B-35. **Investing and Financing Cash Flows** (LO3, 4)

During 2012, Paxon Corporation's long-term investments account (at cost) increased $15,000, which was the net result of purchasing stocks costing $80,000 and selling stocks costing $65,000 at a $6,000 loss. Also, its bonds payable account decreased $40,000, the net result of issuing $100,000 of bonds at $103,000 and retiring bonds with a face value (and book value) of $140,000 at a $9,000 gain. What items and amounts appear in the (a) cash flows from investing activities and (b) cash flows from financing activities sections of its 2012 statement of cash flows?

PROBLEMS

P B-36. **Statement of Cash Flows (Indirect Method)** (LO2, 3, 4)

Wolff Company's income statement and comparative balance sheets follow.

WOLFF COMPANY Income Statement For Year Ended December 31, 2011		
Sales.		$635,000
Cost of goods sold.	$430,000	
Wages expense	86,000	
Insurance expense.	8,000	
Depreciation expense.	17,000	
Interest expense.	9,000	
Income tax expense.	29,000	579,000
Net income.		$ 56,000

WOLFF COMPANY Balance Sheets	Dec. 31, 2011	Dec. 31, 2010
Assets		
Cash.	$ 11,000	$ 5,000
Accounts receivable.	41,000	32,000
Inventory.	90,000	60,000
Prepaid insurance	5,000	7,000
Plant assets	250,000	195,000
Accumulated depreciation	(68,000)	(51,000)
Total assets	$329,000	$248,000

	Dec. 31, 2011	Dec. 31, 2010
Liabilities and Stockholders' Equity		
Accounts payable....................	$ 7,000	$ 10,000
Wages payable.....................	9,000	6,000
Income tax payable	7,000	8,000
Bonds payable.....................	130,000	75,000
Common stock.....................	90,000	90,000
Retained earnings	86,000	59,000
Total liabilities and equity.............	$329,000	$248,000

Cash dividends of $29,000 were declared and paid during 2011. Also in 2011, plant assets were purchased for cash, and bonds payable were issued for cash. Bond interest is paid semiannually on June 30 and December 31. Accounts payable relate to merchandise purchases.

Required

a. Compute the change in cash that occurred during 2011.

b. Prepare a 2011 statement of cash flows using the indirect method.

P B-37. **Statement of Cash Flows (Indirect Method)** (LO2, 3, 4)

Following are the income statement and balance sheet for Best Buy for the year ended February 26, 2011, and a forecasted income statement and balance sheet for 2012.

Best Buy (BBY)

Income Statement		
($ millions)	2011 Actual	2012 Est.
Revenue	$50,272	$52,786
Cost of goods sold..	37,611	39,484
Restructuring charges	24	0
Gross profit..	12,637	13,302
Selling, general and administrative expenses	10,325	10,821
Restructuring charges	198	0
Goodwill and tradename impairment............................	0	0
Operating income...	2,114	2,481
Other income (expense)......................................	0	0
Investment income and other..................................	51	51
Interest expense..	(87)	(87)
Earnings before income tax expense and equity in income of affiliates .	2,078	2,445
Income tax expense...	714	841
Equity in income of affiliates..................................	2	2
Net earnings including noncontrolling interests....................	1,366	1,606
Net earnings attributable to noncontrolling interests................	(89)	104
Net earnings attributable to Best Buy Co., Inc.	$ 1,277	$ 1,502

Balance Sheet		
($ millions)	2011 Actual	2012 Est.
Cash and cash equivalents	$ 1,103	$ 2,005
Short-term investments	22	22
Receivables	2,348	2,481
Merchandise inventories	5,897	6,176
Other current assets	1,103	1,161
Total current assets	10,473	11,845
Property and Equipment		
Land and buildings	766	843
Leasehold improvements	2,318	2,550
Fixtures and equipment	4,701	5,172
Property under capital lease	120	132
Gross property and equipment	7,905	8,697
Less accumulated depreciation	4,082	5,031
Net property and equipment	3,823	3,666
Goodwill	2,454	2,454
Tradenames, Net	133	108
Customer Relationships, Net	203	165
Equity and Other Investments	328	328
Other Assets	435	475
Total Assets	$17,849	$19,041
Current Liabilities		
Accounts payable	$ 4,894	$ 5,120
Unredeemed gift card liabilities	474	475
Accrued compensation and related expenses	570	581
Accrued liabilities	1,471	1,531
Accrued income taxes	256	264
Short-term debt	557	557
Current portion of long-term debt	441	37
Total current liabilities	8,663	8,565
Long-Term Liabilities	1,183	1,183
Long-Term Debt	711	674
Shareholders' Equity		
Common stock	39	39
Additional paid-in capital	18	18
Retained earnings	6,372	7,595
Accumulated other comprehensive income	173	173
Total Best Buy Co., Inc. shareholders' equity	6,602	7,825
Noncontrolling interests	690	794
Total equity	7,292	8,619
Total Liabilities and Equity	$17,849	$19,041

Required

Prepare a forecasted statement of cash flows for 2012 using the indirect method. Operating expenses for 2012 (such as Cost of goods sold and General and administrative expenses) include estimated depreciation and amortization expense of $1,012 million; and estimated retained earnings assume the payment of $279 million in dividends.

P B-38.   Statement of Cash Flows (Indirect Method)   (LO2, 3, 4)

Arctic Company's income statement and comparative balance sheets follow.

ARCTIC COMPANY Income Statement For Year Ended December 31, 2011		
Sales.		$ 728,000
Cost of goods sold.	$534,000	
Wages expense	190,000	
Advertising expense.	31,000	
Depreciation expense.	22,000	
Interest expense.	18,000	
Gain on sale of land	(25,000)	770,000
Net loss		$(42,000)

ARCTIC COMPANY Balance Sheets		
	Dec. 31, 2011	**Dec. 31, 2010**
Assets		
Cash.	$ 49,000	$ 28,000
Accounts receivable.	42,000	50,000
Inventory.	107,000	113,000
Prepaid advertising.	10,000	13,000
Plant assets	360,000	222,000
Accumulated depreciation	(78,000)	(56,000)
Total assets	$490,000	$370,000
Liabilities and Stockholders' Equity		
Accounts payable.	$ 17,000	$ 31,000
Interest payable	6,000	—
Bonds payable	200,000	—
Common stock.	245,000	245,000
Retained earnings	52,000	94,000
Treasury stock	(30,000)	—
Total liabilities and equity.	$490,000	$370,000

During 2011, Arctic sold land for $70,000 cash that had originally cost $45,000. Arctic also purchased equipment for cash, acquired treasury stock for cash, and issued bonds payable for cash in 2011. Accounts payable relate to merchandise purchases.

Required

a. Compute the change in cash that occurred during 2011.

b. Prepare a 2011 statement of cash flows using the indirect method.

P B-39. **Statement of Cash Flows (Indirect Method)** (LO2, 3, 4)

Dair Company's income statement and comparative balance sheets follow.

DAIR COMPANY Income Statement For Year Ended December 31, 2011		
Sales...		$700,000
Cost of goods sold.........................	$440,000	
Wages and other operating expenses............	95,000	
Depreciation expense........................	22,000	
Amortization expense........................	7,000	
Interest expense............................	10,000	
Income tax expense.........................	36,000	
Loss on bond retirement	5,000	615,000
Net income.................................		$ 85,000

DAIR COMPANY Balance Sheets	Dec. 31, 2011	Dec. 31, 2010
Assets		
Cash.............................	$ 27,000	$ 18,000
Accounts receivable................	53,000	48,000
Inventory.........................	103,000	109,000
Prepaid expenses...................	12,000	10,000
Plant assets	360,000	336,000
Accumulated depreciation............	(87,000)	(84,000)
Intangible assets	43,000	50,000
Total assets	$511,000	$487,000
Liabilities and Stockholders' Equity		
Accounts payable...................	$ 32,000	$ 26,000
Interest payable	4,000	7,000
Income tax payable	6,000	8,000
Bonds payable.....................	60,000	120,000
Common stock.....................	252,000	228,000
Retained earnings	157,000	98,000
Total liabilities and equity.............	$511,000	$487,000

During 2011, the company sold for $17,000 cash old equipment that had cost $36,000 and had $19,000 accumulated depreciation. Also in 2011, new equipment worth $60,000 was acquired in exchange for $60,000 of bonds payable, and bonds payable of $120,000 were retired for cash at a loss. A $26,000 cash dividend was declared and paid in 2011. Any stock issuances were for cash.

Required

a. Compute the change in cash that occurred in 2011.

b. Prepare a 2011 statement of cash flows using the indirect method.

c. Prepare separate schedules showing (1) cash paid for interest and for income taxes and (2) noncash investing and financing transactions.

P B-40. **Statement of Cash Flows (Indirect Method)** (LO2, 3, 4)

Whole Foods Market (WFMI)

Following are the income statement and balance sheet for Whole Foods Market, for the year ended September 26, 2010, and a forecasted income statement and balance sheet for 2011.

Balance Sheet		
($ thousands)	2010 Actual	2011 Est.
Cash and cash equivalents	$ 131,996	$ 448,245
Short-term investments	329,738	329,738
Restricted cash	86,802	86,802
Accounts receivable	133,346	148,596
Merchandise inventories	323,487	356,629
Prepaid expenses and other	54,686	59,438
Deferred income taxes	101,464	101,464
Total current assets	1,161,519	1,530,912
Property and equipment, net	1,886,130	1,867,269
Long-term investments	96,146	96,146
Goodwill	665,224	665,224
Intangible assets, net	69,064	69,064
Deferred income taxes	99,156	99,156
Other assets	9,301	9,906
Total assets	$3,986,540	$4,337,677
Current installments of long-term debt and capital lease obligations	$ 410	$ 410
Accounts payable	213,212	237,753
Accrued payroll and other	244,427	267,472
Other current liabilities	289,823	317,004
Total current liabilities	747,872	822,639
Long-term debt and capital lease obligations	508,288	507,878
Deferred lease liabilities	294,291	294,291
Other long-term liabilities	62,831	69,345
Total liabilities	1,613,282	1,694,153
Common stock	1,773,897	1,773,897
Accumulated other comprehensive income	791	791
Retained earnings	598,570	868,836
Total shareholders' equity	2,373,258	2,643,524
Total liabilities and shareholders' equity	$3,986,540	$4,337,677

Income Statement		
($ millions)	2010	2011
Sales	$9,005,794	$9,906,373
Cost of goods sold and occupancy costs	5,869,519	6,458,955
Gross profit	3,136,275	3,447,418
Direct store expenses	2,376,590	2,615,282
General and administrative expenses	272,449	297,191
Pre-opening expenses	38,044	39,625
Relocation, store closure and lease termination costs	11,217	0
Operating income	437,975	495,320
Interest expense	(33,048)	(33,048)
Investment and other income	6,854	6,854
Income before income taxes	411,781	469,126
Provision for income taxes	165,948	189,058
Net income	$ 245,833	$ 280,068

Required

Prepare a forecasted statement of cash flows for 2011 using the indirect method. Assume the following:
- Operating expenses for 2011 (such as General and administrative) include depreciation and amortization expense of $273,489 thousand.
- The company did not dispose of or write-down any long-term assets during the year.

- The company paid dividends of $9,802 thousand in 2011.

P B-41. **Statement of Cash Flows (Indirect Method)** (LO2, 3, 4)
Rainbow Company's income statement and comparative balance sheets follow.

RAINBOW COMPANY Income Statement For Year Ended December 31, 2011		
Sales.		$750,000
Dividend income.		15,000
		765,000
Cost of goods sold.	$440,000	
Wages and other operating expenses	130,000	
Depreciation expense.	39,000	
Patent amortization expense	7,000	
Interest expense.	13,000	
Income tax expense.	44,000	
Loss on sale of equipment.	5,000	
Gain on sale of investments.	(10,000)	668,000
Net income.		$ 97,000

RAINBOW COMPANY Balance Sheets	Dec. 31, 2011	Dec. 31, 2010
Assets		
Cash and cash equivalents	$ 19,000	$ 25,000
Accounts receivable.	40,000	30,000
Inventory.	103,000	77,000
Prepaid expenses.	10,000	6,000
Long-term investments—Available-for-sale.	—	50,000
Fair value adjustment to investments.	—	7,000
Land.	190,000	100,000
Buildings.	445,000	350,000
Accumulated depreciation—Buildings.	(91,000)	(75,000)
Equipment	179,000	225,000
Accumulated depreciation—Equipment	(42,000)	(46,000)
Patents.	50,000	32,000
Total assets	$903,000	$781,000
Liabilities and Stockholders' Equity		
Accounts payable.	$ 20,000	$ 16,000
Interest payable	6,000	5,000
Income tax payable	8,000	10,000
Bonds payable.	155,000	125,000
Preferred stock ($100 par value)	100,000	75,000
Common stock ($5 par value)	379,000	364,000
Paid-in capital in excess of par value—Common	133,000	124,000
Retained earnings	102,000	55,000
Unrealized gain on investments.	—	7,000
Total liabilities and equity.	$903,000	$781,000

During 2011, the following transactions and events occurred in addition to the company's usual business activities:

1. Sold long-term investments costing $50,000 for $60,000 cash. Unrealized gains totaling $7,000 related to these investments had been recorded in earlier years. At year-end, the fair value adjustment and unrealized gain account balances were eliminated.
2. Purchased land for cash.
3. Capitalized an expenditure made to improve the building.
4. Sold equipment for $14,000 cash that originally cost $46,000 and had $27,000 accumulated depreciation.
5. Issued bonds payable at face value for cash.
6. Acquired a patent with a fair value of $25,000 by issuing 250 shares of preferred stock at par value.
7. Declared and paid a $50,000 cash dividend.
8. Issued 3,000 shares of common stock for cash at $8 per share.
9. Recorded depreciation of $16,000 on buildings and $23,000 on equipment.

Required

a. Compute the change in cash and cash equivalents that occurred during 2011.
b. Prepare a 2011 statement of cash flows using the indirect method.
c. Prepare separate schedules showing (1) cash paid for interest and for income taxes and (2) noncash investing and financing transactions.

P B-42.^{B1} **Statement of Cash Flows (Direct Method)**   (LO2, 3, 4)
Refer to the data for Wolff Company in Problem B-36.

Required

a. Compute the change in cash that occurred during 2011.
b. Prepare a 2011 statement of cash flows using the direct method.

P B-43.^{B1} **Statement of Cash Flows (Direct Method)**   (LO2, 3, 4)
Refer to the data for Arctic Company in Problem B-38.

Required

a. Compute the change in cash that occurred during 2011.
b. Prepare a 2011 statement of cash flows using the direct method.

P B-44.^{B1} **Statement of Cash Flows (Direct Method)**   (LO2, 3, 4)
Refer to the data for Dair Company in Problem B-39.

Required

a. Compute the change in cash that occurred in 2011.
b. Prepare a 2011 statement of cash flows using the direct method. Use one cash outflow for "cash paid for wages and other operating expenses." Accounts payable relate to inventory purchases only.
c. Prepare separate schedules showing (1) a reconciliation of net income to net cash flow from operating activities (see Exhibit B.3) and (2) noncash investing and financing transactions.

P B-45.^{B1} **Statement of Cash Flows (Direct Method)**   (LO2, 3, 4)
Refer to the data for Rainbow Company in Problem B-41.

Required

a. Compute the change in cash that occurred in 2011.
b. Prepare a 2011 statement of cash flows using the direct method. Use one cash outflow for "cash paid for wages and other operating expenses." Accounts payable relate to inventory purchases only.
c. Prepare separate schedules showing (1) a reconciliation of net income to net cash flow from operating activities (see Exhibit B.3) and (2) noncash investing and financing transactions.

P B-46. **Interpreting the Statement of Cash Flows**   (LO1, 5)
Following is the statement of cash flows of Amgen, Inc.

Amgen, Inc. (AMGN)

Year Ended December 31 (In millions)	2010	2009	2008
Cash flows from operating activities:			
Net income.	$ 4,627	$ 4,605	$ 4,052
Depreciation and amortization	1,017	1,049	1,073
Stock-based compensation expense	353	284	262
Deferred income taxes.	(167)	47	(137)
Property, plant and equipment impairments	118	21	59
Dividend received from equity investee	—	110	8
Other items, net	140	111	244
Changes in operating assets and liabilities, net of acquisitions:			
Trade receivables, net	(210)	(36)	65
Inventories	153	(134)	(59)
Other current assets.	36	(3)	15
Accounts payable.	142	71	95
Accrued income taxes	(656)	(142)	14
Other accrued liabilities	152	320	(30)
Deferred revenue	82	33	327
Net cash provided by operating activities	5,787	6,336	5,988
Cash flows from investing activities:			
Purchases of property, plant and equipment.	(580)	(530)	(672)
Cash paid for acquisitions, net of cash acquired.	—	—	(56)
Purchases of marketable securities	(14,602)	(12,418)	(10,345)
Proceeds from sales of marketable securities.	10,485	8,252	6,762
Proceeds from maturities of marketable securities	642	1,443	1,018
Other.	(97)	51	128
Net cash used in investing activities	(4,152)	(3,202)	(3,165)
Cash flows from financing activities:			
Repurchases of common stock	(3,786)	(3,208)	(2,268)
Repayment of debt.	—	(1,000)	(2,000)
Net proceeds from issuance of debt	2,471	1,980	991
Net proceeds from issuance of common stock in connection			
with Company's equity award programs	80	171	155
Other.	3	33	49
Net cash used in financing activities	(1,232)	(2,024)	(3,073)
Increase (decrease) in cash and cash equivalents.	403	1,110	(250)
Cash and cash equivalents at beginning of period	2,884	1,774	2,024
Cash and cash equivalents at end of period	$ 3,287	$ 2,884	$ 1,774

Required

a. Amgen reports that it generated $5,787 million in net cash from operating activities in 2010. Yet, its net income for the year amounted to only $4,627 million. Much of this difference is the result of depreciation. Why is Amgen adding depreciation to net income in the computation of operating cash flows?

b. In determining cash provided by operating activities, Amgen adds $353 million relating to stock-based compensation expense in 2010. What is the purpose of this addition?

c. Amgen reports $(210) million relating to trade receivables. What does the sign (positive or negative) on this amount signify about the change in receivables during the year compared with the sign on the amount for 2008?

d. Amgen reports $118 relating to property, plant and equipment impairments. Explain why this amount is on the statement of cash flows.

e. Does the composition of Amgen's cash flow present a "healthy" picture for 2010? Explain.

P B-47.   **Interpreting the Statement of Cash Flows**   (LO1, 5)

Staples, Inc. (SPLS)

Following is the statement of cash flows of Staples, Inc.

For Year Ended, In thousands	January 29, 2011
Operating activities:	
Consolidated net income, including income from the noncontrolling interests............	$ 888,569
Adjustments to reconcile net income to net cash provided by operating activities:	
Depreciation and amortization..	498,863
Stock-based compensation..	146,879
Deferred income taxes..	172,630
Other.......................................	5,418
Change in assets and liabilities, net of companies acquired:	
(Increase) decrease in receivables..	(95,656)
(Increase) decrease in merchandise inventories	(46,450)
(Increase) decrease in prepaid expenses and other assets................	(70,600)
Increase (decrease) in accounts payable.................................	63,305
(Decrease) increase in accrued expenses and other current liabilities	(191,917)
Increase (decrease) in other long-term obligations	75,450
Net cash provided by operating activities	1,446,491
Investing activities:	
Acquisition of property and equipment	(408,889)
Acquisition of businesses and investments in joint ventures, net of cash acquired	(63,066)
Net cash used in investing activities	(471,955)
Financing activities:	
Proceeds from the exercise of stock options and the sale of stock under	
employee stock purchase plans..	85,429
Proceeds from borrowings.......................................	201,566
Payments on borrowings, including payment of deferred financing fees	(207,478)
Purchase of noncontrolling interest	(360,595)
Cash dividends paid..	(258,746)
Purchase of treasury stock, net	(398,582)
Net cash (used in) provided by financing activities	(938,406)
Effect of exchange rate changes on cash and cash equivalents..............	9,308
Net increase (decrease) in cash and cash equivalents	45,438
Cash and cash equivalents at beginning of period	1,415,819
Cash and cash equivalents at end of period	$1,461,257

Required

a. Staples reports net income of $888,569 thousand and net cash inflows from operating activities of $1,446,491 thousand. Part of the difference relates to depreciation and amortization of $498,863 thousand. Why does Staples add this amount in the computation of operating cash flows?

b. Staples reports a positive amount of $146,879 thousand relating to stock-based compensation. What does this positive amount signify?

c. Staples reports a cash outflow of $408,889 thousand relating to the acquisition of property, plant and equipment. Is this cash outflow a cause for concern? Explain.

d. Staples' net cash flows from financing activities is $(938,406) thousand. For what purposes is Staples using this cash?

e. Staples' cash balance increased by $45,438 thousand during the year. Does Staples present a "healthy" cash flow picture for the year? Explain.

SOLUTIONS TO REVIEW PROBLEMS

Appendix-End Review 1

Part A: Solution

1. *a*   2. *c*   3. *d*   4. *c*

Part B: Solution

a. $8,000 ending balance − $12,000 beginning balance = $4,000 decrease in cash

b. (1) Use the indirect method to determine the net cash flow from operating activities.

- Adjustments to convert Expresso Royale's net income of $35,000 to a net cash provided by operating activities of $38,000 are shown in the following statement of cash flows.

(2) Analyze changes in remaining noncash asset (and contra asset) accounts to determine cash flows from investing activities.

- Long-Term Investments: $11,000 decrease resulted from sale of investments for cash at a $2,000 loss. Cash received from sale of investments = $9,000 ($11,000 cost − $2,000 loss).
- Fair Value Adjustment to Investments: $1,000 decrease resulted from the elimination of this account balance (and the Unrealized Loss on Investments) at the end of 2011. No cash flow effect.
- Plant Assets: $48,000 increase resulted from purchase of plant assets for cash. Cash paid to purchase plant assets = $48,000.
- Accumulated Depreciation: $11,000 increase resulted from the recording of 2011 depreciation. No cash flow effect.

(3) Analyze changes in remaining liability and stockholders' equity accounts to determine cash flows from financing activities.

- Common Stock: $14,000 increase resulted from the issuance of stock for cash. Cash received from issuance of common stock = $14,000.
- Retained Earnings: $18,000 increase resulted from net income of $35,000 and dividend declaration of $17,000. Cash dividends paid = $17,000.
- Unrealized Loss on Investments: $1,000 decrease resulted from the elimination of this account balance (and the Fair Value Adjustment to Investments) at the end of 2011. No cash flow effect.

The statement of cash flows follows:

EXPRESSO ROYALE		
Statement of Cash Flows		
For Year Ended December 31, 2011		
Net cash flow from operating activities		
Net income...............................	$35,000	
Add (deduct) items to convert net income to cash basis		
Depreciation	11,000	
Loss on sale of investments.................	2,000	
Accounts receivable decrease	6,000	
Inventory increase........................	(28,000)	
Prepaid advertising increase	(3,000)	
Accounts payable increase..................	13,000	
Wages payable increase....................	3,500	
Income tax payable decrease................	(1,500)	
Net cash provided by operating activities		$38,000
Cash flows from investing activities		
Sale of investments	9,000	
Purchase of plant assets	(48,000)	
Net cash used by investing activities............		(39,000)
Cash flows from financing activities		
Issuance of common stock..................	14,000	
Payment of dividends......................	(17,000)	
Net cash used by financing activities............		(3,000)
Net decrease in cash		(4,000)
Cash at beginning of year		12,000
Cash at end of year		$ 8,000

Appendix-End Review 2

Solution

a. $8,000 ending balance − $12,000 beginning balance = $4,000 decrease in cash

b. (1) Use the direct method to determine the individual cash flows from operating activities.
- $385,000 sales + $6,000 accounts receivable decrease = $391,000 cash received from customers
- $5,000 dividend income = $5,000 cash received as dividends
- $233,000 cost of goods sold + $28,000 inventory increase − $13,000 accounts payable increase = $248,000 cash paid for merchandise purchased
- $82,000 wages expense − $3,500 wages payable increase = $78,500 cash paid to employees
- $10,000 advertising expense + $3,000 prepaid advertising increase = $13,000 cash paid for advertising
- $17,000 income tax expense + $1,500 income tax payable decrease = $18,500 cash paid for income taxes

(2) Analyze changes in remaining noncash asset (and contra asset) accounts to determine cash flows from investing activities.
- Long-term investments: $11,000 decrease resulted from sale of investments for cash at a $2,000 loss. Cash received from sale of investments = $9,000 ($11,000 cost − $2,000 loss).
- Fair value adjustment to investments: $1,000 decrease resulted from the elimination of this account balance (and the unrealized loss on investments) at the end of 2011. No cash flow effect.
- Plant assets: $48,000 increase resulted from purchase of plant assets for cash. Cash paid to purchase plant assets = $48,000.
- Accumulated depreciation: $11,000 increase resulted from the recording of 2011 depreciation. No cash flow effect.

(3) Analyze changes in remaining liability and stockholders' equity accounts to determine cash flows from financing activities.
- Common stock: $14,000 increase resulted from the issuance of stock for cash. Cash received from issuance of common stock = $14,000.
- Retained earnings: $18,000 increase resulted from net income of $35,000 and dividend declaration of $17,000. Cash dividends paid = $17,000.
- Unrealized loss on investments: $1,000 decrease resulted from the elimination of this account balance (and the fair value adjustment to investments) at the end of 2011. No cash flow effect.

The statement of cash flows under the direct method follows:

EXPRESSO ROYALE
Statement of Cash Flows
For Year Ended December 31, 2011

Cash flows from operating activities		
Cash received from customers	$391,000	
Cash received as dividends	5,000	
Cash paid for merchandise purchased	(248,000)	
Cash paid to employees	(78,500)	
Cash paid for advertising	(13,000)	
Cash paid for income taxes	(18,500)	
Net cash provided by operating activities		$ 38,000
Cash flows from investing activities		
Sale of investments	9,000	
Purchase of plant assets	(48,000)	
Net cash used by investing activities		(39,000)
Cash flows from financing activities		
Issuance of common stock	14,000	
Payment of dividends	(17,000)	
Net cash used by financing activities		(3,000)
Net decrease in cash		(4,000)
Cash at beginning of year		12,000
Cash at end of year		$ 8,000

KIMBERLY-CLARK

The past decade has seen a shift in the competitive landscape for consumer products companies. Gone are numerous competitors. Many were gobbled up in the industry's consolidation trend. Also gone is media control. Now, hundreds of different media outlets and venues compete for promotion space and scarce consumer time.

Another development is in-store branding. Companies such as Costco, with its Kirkland Signature brand on everything from candy to apparel, threaten the powerhouse brands from Kimberly-Clark, Procter & Gamble, Colgate-Palmolive, and other consumer products companies.

Ten years ago, when Thomas J. Falk assumed the top spot at Kimberly-Clark, the nation's largest disposable diaper producer, he inherited some extra baggage: a company in the throes of an identity crisis, a decades-long rivalry with consumer-products behemoth Procter & Gamble, and

a group of investors short on patience following a series of earnings misses.

In a move aimed at boosting its stock price and its return on equity, Kimberly-Clark spun off its paper and pulp businesses in 2004, and began a strategic investment and streamlining initiative in 2005. Under Falk's leadership, the company has steadily improved its focus on its health and hygiene segments.

Kimberly-Clark has also moved to shore up its brand images across its immense product line. With sales of nearly $20 billion, the company manufactures such well-recognized brands as Huggies and Pull-Ups disposable diapers, Kotex and Lightdays feminine products, Kleenex facial tissue, Viva paper towels, and Scott bathroom tissue.

The rocky ride that Kimberly-Clark investors have endured over the past few years is unlikely to subside—

Appendix

C

Comprehensive Case

LEARNING OBJECTIVES

LO1 Explain and illustrate a review of financial statements and their components. (p. C-4)

LO2 Assess company profitability and creditworthiness. (p. C-29)

LO3 Forecast financial statements. (p. C-32)

LO4 Describe and illustrate the valuation of firm equity and stock. (p. C-35)

see the following stock price chart. Competition is fierce and well-armed, and the purchase of Gillette by Procter & Gamble further muddies the future of the industry.

On the positive side, Kimberly-Clark's earnings performance is consistent, and its financial position is solid. Kimberly-Clark's RNOA for 2010 was 17.6%, and its non-operating return increased RNOA to yield a robust 32.6% in return on equity. It also reported $19.9 billion in assets, 42% of which is concentrated in plant, property, and equipment, and another 18.6% in intangible assets.

This module presents a financial accounting analysis and interpretation of Kimberly-Clark. It is intended to illustrate the key financial reporting topics covered in the book. We begin with a detailed review of Kimberly-Clark's financial statements and notes, followed by the forecasting of key accounts that we use to value its common stock.

Source: *Kimberly-Clark* 10-K Filings and Annual Report to Shareholders.

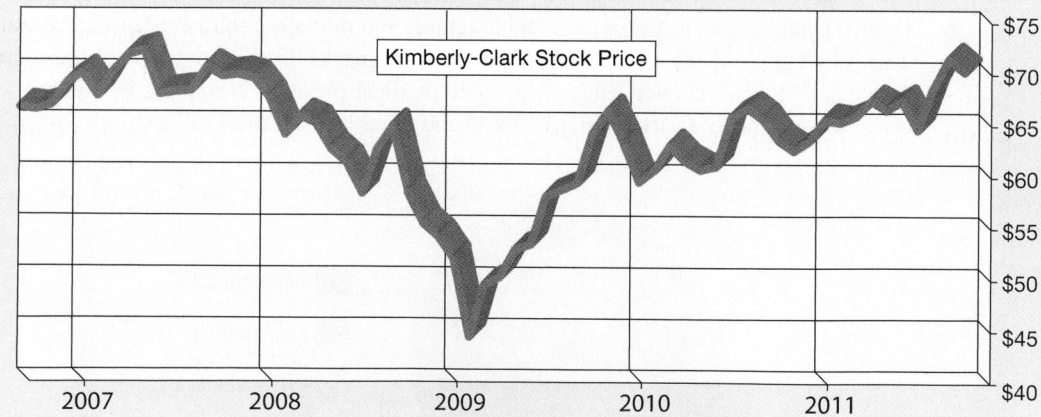

Kimberly-Clark Stock Price

2007 2008 2009 2010 2011

$75, $70, $65, $60, $55, $50, $45, $40

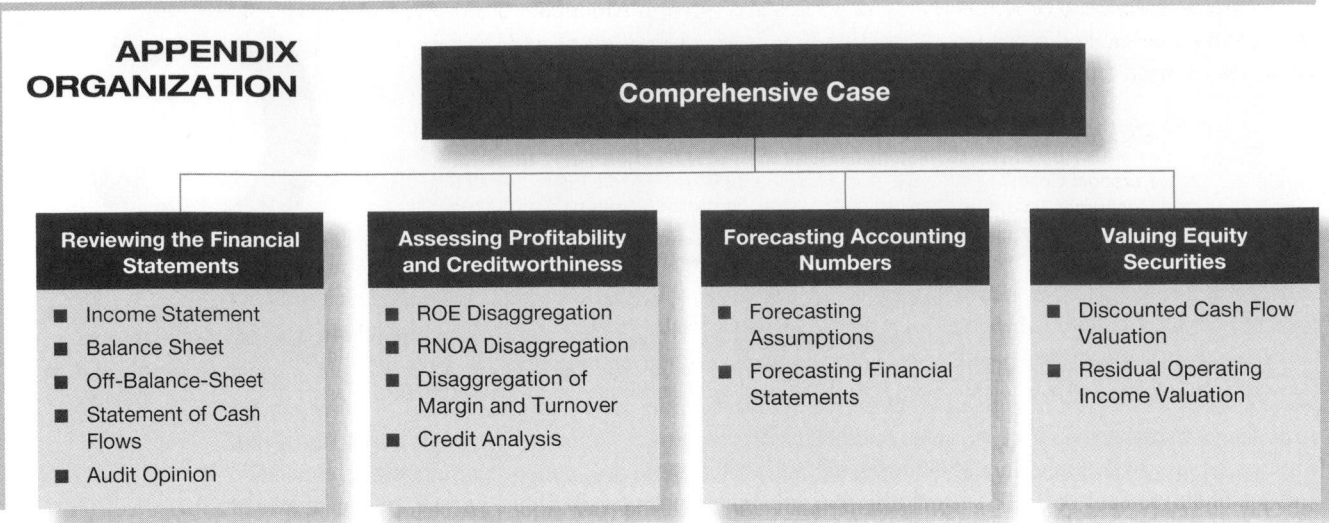

APPENDIX ORGANIZATION

Comprehensive Case

Reviewing the Financial Statements
- Income Statement
- Balance Sheet
- Off-Balance-Sheet
- Statement of Cash Flows
- Audit Opinion

Assessing Profitability and Creditworthiness
- ROE Disaggregation
- RNOA Disaggregation
- Disaggregation of Margin and Turnover
- Credit Analysis

Forecasting Accounting Numbers
- Forecasting Assumptions
- Forecasting Financial Statements

Valuing Equity Securities
- Discounted Cash Flow Valuation
- Residual Operating Income Valuation

INTRODUCTION

Kimberly-Clark is one of the largest consumer products companies in the world. It is organized into four general business segments (percentages are for 2010):

- **Personal Care** (44% of sales), which manufactures and markets disposable diapers, training and youth pants, swim pants, baby wipes, feminine and incontinence care products, and related products. Products in this segment are primarily for household use and are sold under a variety of brand names, including Huggies, Pull-Ups, Little Swimmers, GoodNites, Kotex, Lightdays, Depend, Poise and other brand names.

- **Consumer Tissue** (33% of sales), which manufactures and markets facial and bathroom tissue, paper towels, napkins and related products for household use. Products in this segment are sold under the Kleenex, Scott, Cottonelle, Viva, Andrex, Scottex, Hakle, Page and other brand names.

- **Professional & Other** (16% of sales), which manufactures and markets facial and bathroom tissue, paper towels, napkins, wipes and a range of safety products for the away-from-home marketplace. Products in this segment are sold under the Kimberly-Clark, Kleenex, Scott, WypAll, Kimtech, KleenGuard, Kimcare and Jackson brand names.

- **Health Care** (7% of sales), which manufactures and markets health care products such as surgical drapes and gowns, infection control products, face masks, exam gloves, respiratory products, pain management products and other disposable medical products. Products in this segment are sold under the Kimberly-Clark, Ballard, ON-Q and other brand names.

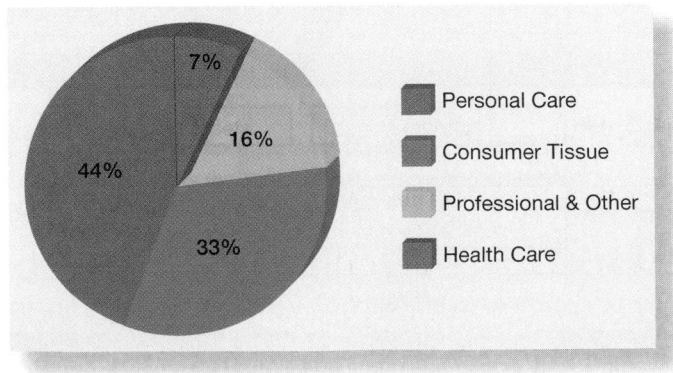

Approximately 52% of Kimberly-Clark's sales are in North America, 16% in Europe and 32% in Asia, Latin America, and other areas. Shown below is the proportion of its U.S. sales in each of these categories for each of the years 2008 through 2010:

Product Category	2010	2009	2008
Personal Care...................	43.9%	43.7%	42.6%
Consumer Tissue	32.9%	33.5%	34.8%
Professional & Other.............	15.8%	15.7%	16.3%
Health Care	7.4%	7.2%	6.3%

In addition, approximately 13% of Kimberly-Clark's sales are made to **Wal-Mart**, primarily in the personal care and consumer tissue businesses (source: Kimberly-Clark 2010 10-K).

In the MD&A section of its 10-K, Kimberly-Clark describes its competitive environment as follows:

We compete in intensely competitive markets against well-known, branded products and low-cost or private label products both domestically and internationally. Inherent risks in our competitive strategy include uncertainties concerning trade and consumer acceptance, the effects of consolidation within retailer and distribution channels, and competitive reaction. Our competitors for these markets include not only our traditional competitors but also private label manufacturers, low-cost manufacturers and rapidly-expanding international manufacturers. These competitors may have greater financial resources and greater market penetration, which enable them to offer a wider variety of products and services at more competitive prices. Alternatively, some of these competitors may have significantly lower product development and manufacturing costs, allowing them to offer products at a lower cost. The actions of these competitors could adversely affect our financial results. It may be necessary for us to lower prices on our products and increase spending on advertising and promotions, each of which could adversely affect our financial results.

Our ability to develop new products is affected by whether we can successfully anticipate consumer needs and preferences, develop and fund technological innovations, and receive and maintain necessary patent and trademark protection. In addition, we incur substantial development and marketing costs in introducing new and improved products and technologies. The introduction of a new consumer product (whether improved or newly developed) usually requires substantial expenditures for advertising and marketing to gain recognition in the marketplace. If a product gains consumer acceptance, it normally requires continued advertising and promotional support to maintain its relative market position. Some of our competitors are larger and have greater financial resources. These competitors may be able to spend more aggressively on advertising and promotional activities, introduce competing products more quickly and respond more effectively to changing business and economic conditions.

Beyond the competitive business risks described above, Kimberly-Clark faces fluctuating prices for cellulose fiber, the company's principle raw material, uncertain energy costs for manufacturing operations, foreign currency translation risks, and risks resulting from fluctuating interest rates.

Given this background, we begin the accounting analysis of Kimberly-Clark with a discussion of its financial statements.

REVIEWING THE FINANCIAL STATEMENTS

This section reviews and analyzes the financial statements of Kimberly-Clark.

L01 Explain and illustrate a review of financial statements and their components.

Income Statement Reporting and Analysis

Kimberly-Clark's income statement is reproduced in Exhibit C.1. The remainder of this section provides a brief review and analysis for Kimberly-Clark's income statement line items.

EXHIBIT C.1 Kimberly-Clark Income Statement

KIMBERLY-CLARK CORPORATION AND SUBSIDIARIES
Consolidated Income Statement

Year Ended December 31 (Millions of dollars, except per share amounts)	2010	2009	2008
Net sales.	$19,746	$19,115	$19,415
Cost of products sold.	13,196	12,695	13,557
Gross profit.	6,550	6,420	5,858
Marketing, research and general expenses	3,673	3,498	3,291
Other (income) and expense, net	104	97	20
Operating profit	2,773	2,825	2,547
Interest income.	20	26	46
Interest expense	(243)	(275)	(304)
Income before income taxes, equity interests and extraordinary loss.	2,550	2,576	2,289
Provision for income taxes	(788)	(746)	(618)
Income before equity interests and extraordinary loss	1,762	1,830	1,671
Share of net income of equity companies	181	164	166
Income before extraordinary loss.	1,943	1,994	1,837
Extraordinary loss, net of income taxes, attributable to Kimberly-Clark Corporation	—	—	(8)
Net income.	1,943	1,994	1,829
Net income attributable to noncontrolling interests	(100)	(110)	(139)
Net income attributable to Kimberly-Clark Corporation.	$ 1,843	$ 1,884	$ 1,690
Per share basis			
Basic			
Before extraordinary loss	$ 4.47	$ 4.53	$ 4.06
Extraordinary loss	—	—	(.02)
Net income attributable to Kimberly-Clark Corporation	$ 4.47	$ 4.53	$ 4.04
Diluted			
Before extraordinary loss	$ 4.45	$ 4.52	$ 4.05
Extraordinary loss	—	—	(.02)
Net income attributable to Kimberly-Clark Corporation	$ 4.45	$ 4.52	$ 4.03

Net Sales

Exhibit C.1 reveals that sales increased 3.3% in 2010 to $19,746 million, following a 1.5% sales decrease in the prior year. In its 2010 MD&A report, management attributes the increase equally to volume, price and mix effects.

Kimberly-Clark describes its revenue recognition policy as follows:

> Sales revenue is recognized at the time of product shipment or delivery, depending on when title passes, to unaffiliated customers, and when all of the following have occurred: a firm sales agreement is in place, pricing is fixed or determinable, and collection is reasonably assured. Sales are reported net of returns, consumer and trade promotions, rebates and freight allowed. Taxes imposed by governmental authorities on our revenue-producing activities with customers, such as sales taxes and value-added taxes, are excluded from net sales.

Its revenue recognition conditions are taken directly from GAAP and SEC guidelines, which recognize revenues when "earned and realizable." For Kimberly-Clark, *earned* means when title to the goods passes to the customer, and *realizable* means an account receivable whose collection is reasonably assured.

Sales for retailers and manufacturers are straightforward: revenue is recognized when the product is transferred to the buyer, an obligation for payment exists and collection of that payment is reasonably assured. In that case, the revenue is deemed to have been "earned." The primary issue for retailers and manufacturers relates to sales return allowances. These allowances pertain to product return or sales discounts (sometimes called *mark-downs*). Companies can only report sales when earned, that is, past the return allowance period. Further, companies can only report *net* sales as revenue (i.e., gross sales less any sales discounts, including volume discounts). K-C's footnotes provide the following table relating to sales allowances:

| December 31, 2010 ($ millions) | Balance at Beginning of Period | Additions | | Deductions | |
		Charged to Costs and Expenses	Charged to Other Accounts	Write-Offs and Reclassifications	Balance at End of Period
Allowances for sales discounts	$21	$266	—	$269	$18

K-C's balance sheet includes a contra-asset related to sales discounts. The table indicates that the company had $21 million in sales discounts accrued at the start of the year that relate to sales in the prior year. During 2010, K-C granted its customers $266 million in additional sales discounts, $269 million of which had been taken by the customers by the end of the year. The remaining amount of $18 million, relates to discounts granted, but not yet taken, and is held over to the following year. These year-end amounts typically relate to discounts given toward the end of the year that are ultimately taken in the first quarter of the following year.

The sales discount process affects net sales and, thus, profit. This allowance works just like any other allowance. If K-C underestimated the sales discount allowance, net sales and profit in the current year would be increased. Overestimation of the sales discount allowance would have the opposite effect: current sales and profit would be depressed. K-C's allowance has not changed appreciably in 2010 and is, therefore, not of concern.

Revenue recognition in service industries and those industries that use the percentage-of-completion method can be problematic. Often, determining when a service contract has been "earned" can be difficult and revenue can easily be mis-estimated, either intentionally or not. Sanjay Kumar, former CEO of Computer Associates, was sentenced to 12 years in jail for his role in an accounting scandal relating primarily to misrepresentation of revenues and profit for the computer services company he headed up. The percentage-of-completion method is difficult to implement because it requires estimates of total costs or revenues of the project. Underestimation of costs results in overestimation of revenues. These estimation errors are often hidden from view because details in footnote disclosures are often vague or completely missing.

Cost of Products Sold and Gross Profit

Kimberly-Clark's 2010 gross profit margin is 33.2% ($6,550/$19,746), which is about 3.0 percentage points above what it was in 2008 (30.2%). As a benchmark, Procter & Gamble, the company's principle competitor, recently reported sales of $82.6 billion, over four times the level of K-C's sales, and a gross profit margin of 50.6%. This comparison highlights the intense competition that K-C faces from its much larger rival.

The choice of inventory costing method affects cost of goods sold. K-C uses the LIFO method to cost its inventory. In 2011, the company's LIFO reserve increased by $37 million (see inventory discussion later in this Appendix). This increased cost of goods sold and reduced gross profit by $37 million. COGS can also be increased by inventory write-downs, typically related to restructuring efforts. For example, Cisco Systems, Inc. reported a $2.1 billion inventory write-down in 2001 when the tech bubble burst. This write-down increased COGS and reduced gross profit by that amount.

Marketing, Research and General Expenses

Kimberly-Clark's marketing, research and general expenses have increased to 18.6% of sales from 18.3% in the prior year. This increase resulted from general cost inflation as well as from the company's restructuring efforts designed to improve long-run manufacturing and operating costs. K-C reports 2010 net operating profit after taxes (NOPAT) of $2,083 million [($2,773 + $181) − ($788 + {$243 − $20} × 37%)] and a net operating profit margin (NOPM) of 10.5% ($2,083 million/$19,746 million) of sales.[1] P&G, by contrast, is able to use its higher gross profit margin to fund a higher level of advertising and other SGA expenditures, resulting in a NOPM of 14.8%.

Pension Costs. Kimberly-Clark's marketing, research and general expenses include $133 million of pension expense. This is reported in the following table in the pension footnote:

	Components of Net Periodic Benefit Cost					
	Pension Benefits			Other Benefits		
Year Ended December 31 (Millions of dollars)	2010	2009	2008	2010	2009	2008
Service cost	$ 56	$ 68	$ 73	$ 14	$ 14	$ 15
Interest cost	309	310	324	44	47	49
Expected return on plan assets	(336)	(269)	(370)	—	—	—
Curtailments	—	21	—	—	—	—
Amortization of prior service cost and transition amount	2	3	6	3	2	2
Recognized net actuarial loss	99	111	56	1	—	1
Other	3	7	8	—	—	(1)
Net periodic benefit cost	$133	$251	$ 97	$ 62	$ 63	$ 66

For 2010, the expected return on pension investments ($336 million) provides an offset to the company's pension service and interest costs ($56 million and $309 million, respectively). Footnotes reveal that Kimberly-Clark's pension investments realized an *actual* return of $473 million in 2010 (from the pension footnote in its 10-K report). So, for 2010, use of the expected return results in an unrecognized *gain* that is deferred, along with other unrecognized gains and losses, in the computation of reported profit.

Kimberly-Clark describes how it determines the expected return in its footnotes. It is instructive to review the company's rationale and, thus, the footnote follows:

Strategic asset allocation decisions are made with the intent of maximizing return at an acceptable level of risk. Risk factors considered in setting the strategic asset allocation include, among other things, plan participants' retirement benefit security, the estimated payments of the associated liabilities, the plan funded status, and Kimberly-Clark's financial condition. The resulting strategic asset allocation is a diversified blend of equity and fixed income investments. Equity investments are typically diversified across geography and market capitalization. Fixed income investments are diversified across multiple sectors including government issues, corporate debt instruments, mortgage backed securities and asset backed securities with a portfolio duration that is consistent with the estimated payment of the associated liability. Actual asset allocation is regularly reviewed and periodically rebalanced to the strategic allocation when considered appropriate.

The expected long-term rate of return is evaluated on an annual basis. In setting this assumption, we consider a number of factors including projected future returns by asset class, current asset allocation and historical long-term market performance.

The weighted-average expected long-term rate of return on pension fund assets used to calculate pension expense for the Principal Plans was 8.19 percent in 2010 compared with 8.47 percent in 2009 and will be 7.35 percent in 2011. The expected long-term rate of return on the assets in the Principal Plans is based on an asset allocation assumption of about 60 percent with equity managers, with expected long-term rates of return ranging from 9 to 10 percent, and about 40 percent with fixed income managers, with an expected long-term rate of return ranging from 5 to 6 percent.

The expected return on pension assets offsets service and interest costs, and serves to reduce pension expense. In general, increasing (decreasing) the expected return on pension assets, increases (de-

---

[1] We include equity income of $181 million (labeled as "share of net income of equity companies" in K-C's income statement) as operating because it relates to investments in paper-related companies and it, therefore, aligns with K-C's primary operating activities. This amount is reported by K-C net of tax, and therefore, no tax adjustment is necessary when computing NOPAT. We consider K-C's noncontrolling interests share of subsidiaries' net income, as nonoperating.

creases) profit. In 2010, K-C reduced its expected return from 8.17% to 7.96%. The discount rate (used to compute the PBO and the interest cost component of pension expense) declined by 55 basis points (6.40% to 5.85%). It is not uncommon for the expected return rate to be "stickier" on the downside (thus propping up profits) and more quickly adjusted on the upside (to take advantage of increasing returns). We need to be mindful of these effects when assessing operating profits.

Transitory versus Persistent Line Items

Expenses relating to restructuring activities have become increasingly common in the past two decades. In a subsequent event footnote to its 2010 10-K, Kimberly-Clark announced the following restructuring plan:

> The restructuring plan will commence in the first quarter of 2011 and is expected to be completed by December 31, 2012. The restructuring is expected to result in cumulative charges of approximately $400 million to $600 million before tax ($280 million to $420 million after tax) over that period. We anticipate that the charges will fall into the following categories and approximate dollar ranges: workforce reduction costs ($50 million to $100 million); incremental depreciation ($300 million to $400 million); and other associated costs ($50 million to $100 million). Cash costs related to the streamlining of operations, sale or closure, relocation of equipment, severance and other expenses are expected to account for approximately 25 percent to 50 percent of the charges. Noncash charges will consist primarily of incremental depreciation.

These initiatives are designed to further improve the company's competitive position by accelerating investments in targeted growth opportunities and strategic cost reductions to streamline manufacturing and administrative operations.

Classification of these charges as transitory or persistent is a judgment call. In K-C's case, these charges relate to a multi-year program that is expected to continue through 2012. Therefore, we might classify these expenses as persistent. Our review of the financial statements did not identify any other transitory items and thus, we classified all other activity as persistent.

Earnings per Share

Net income for Kimberly-Clark has increased from $1,690 million in 2008 to $1,843 million in 2010. Basic (diluted) earnings per share, however, has increased from $4.04 ($4.03) to $4.47 ($4.45). Following is Kimberly-Clark's computation of earnings per share:

Earnings Per Share A reconciliation of the average number of common shares outstanding used in the basic and diluted EPS computations follows:

(Millions)	Average Common Shares Outstanding		
	2010	2009	2008
Average shares outstanding.	411.3	414.6	416.7
Participating securities	1.1	1.5	1.8
Basic.	412.4	416.1	418.5
Dilutive effect of stock options.	1.1	.4	.9
Dilutive effect of restricted share and restricted share unit awards	.9	.3	.2
Diluted	414.4	416.8	419.6

Options outstanding that were not included in the computation of diluted EPS mainly because their exercise price was greater than the average market price of the common shares are summarized below:

continued

continued from prior page

Description	2010	2009	2008
Average number of share equivalents (millions).......	13.9	21.8	15.6
Weighted-average exercise price.................	$66.00	$64.12	$66.31
Expiration date of options	2010 to 2020	2009 to 2019	2008 to 2018
Options outstanding at year-end (millions)	14.7	20.3	16.0

The number of common shares outstanding as of December 31, 2010, 2009 and 2008 was 406.9 million, 416.9 million and 413.6 million, respectively.

Most of the difference between basic and diluted earnings per share usually arises from the dilutive effects of employee stock options. (We should note that if stock options are *under water*, meaning that K-C's stock price is lower than the exercise price of the options, they are considered *antidilutive*, meaning that including them would increase EPS. Accordingly, they are excluded in the diluted EPS computation, but remain potentially dilutive if K-C's stock price subsequently rises above the exercise price of the options.) (Although not present for Kimberly-Clark, convertible debt and preferred shares are also potentially dilutive for many companies.)

Income Taxes

Kimberly-Clark's net income has been negatively affected over the past three years by an increase in its effective tax rate from 27.0% to 30.9% as K-C describes in the following footnote:

Year Ended December 31	2010	2009	2008
Tax at U.S. statutory rate applied to income before income taxes..............................	35.0%	35.0%	35.0%
State income taxes, net of federal tax benefit	1.8	(0.3)	0.9
Statutory rates other than U.S. statutory rate	(3.0)	(2.4)	(2.4)
Other—net	(2.9)	(3.3)	(6.5)
Effective income tax rate	30.9%	29.0%	27.0%

Common-Size Income Statement

It is useful for analysis purposes to prepare common-size statements. Exhibit C.2 shows Kimberly-Clark's common-size income statement covering the two most recent years.

EXHIBIT C.2 Kimberly-Clark Common-Size Income Statement

Year Ended December 31	2010	2009
Net sales........	100.0%	100.0%
Cost of products sold.	66.8	66.4
Gross profit.	33.2	33.6
Marketing, research and general expenses.	18.6	18.3
Other (income) and expense, net.	0.5	0.5
Operating profit	14.0	14.8
Interest income.	0.1	0.1
Interest expense.	(1.2)	(1.4)
Income before income taxes and equity interests.	12.9	13.5
Provision for income taxes.	(4.0)	(3.9)
Income before equity interests.	8.9	9.6
Share of net income of equity companies.	0.9	0.9
Net income.	9.8	10.4
Net income attributable to noncontrolling interests.	(0.5)	(0.6)
Net income attributable to Kimberly-Clark Corporation.	9.3%	9.9%

Note: All percentages are computed by dividing each income statement line item by that year's net sales.

The gross profit margin declined in 2010 from 33.6% in 2009 to 33.2%. This most likely reflects the competitive environment in which K-C operates. Companies typically offset a declining gross profit margin with reductions in SG&A expense. K-C has been unable to do that, however, as its marketing, research and general (SG&A) expense in 2010 actually exceeds its 2009 level as a percentage of sales. Accordingly, 2010 income before taxes declined by 0.6 percentage points relative to 2009, from 13.5% of sales to 12.9%. Further, income from equity companies (reported net of tax) remained constant as a percentage of sales at 0.9%. Finally, net income as a percentage of sales declined by 0.6 percentage points from 9.9% of sales to 9.3%.

Management Discussion and Analysis

The Management Discussion and Analysis section of a 10-K is usually informative for interpreting company financial statements and for additional insights into company operations. To illustrate, Kimberly-Clark provides the following analysis of its operating results in the MD&A section of its 2010 10-K:

Overview of 2010 Results

- Net sales increased 3.3 percent because of an increase in sales volumes, net selling prices and improvements in product mix.

- Operating profit decreased 1.8 percent, and net income attributable to Kimberly-Clark and diluted earnings per share decreased 2.2 percent and 1.5 percent, respectively. The benefits of the net sales increase, cost savings, a decrease in pension expense, and the effect of the 2009 organization optimization severance and related charges, were more than offset by inflation in key input costs, increased marketing, research and general expenses, and the charge related to the adoption of highly inflationary accounting for Venezuela.

- Cash flow from operations was $2.7 billion, a decrease of 21 percent.

Results of Operations and Related Information   *2010 versus 2009*

- Personal care net sales in North America increased about 4 percent due to an increase in sales volumes and net selling prices of 3 percent and 1 percent, respectively. The sales volume increases resulted from higher sales of feminine care and adult incontinence products, including benefits from innovation by Kotex, Poise and Depend brands and higher sales of training pants and baby wipes, partially offset by lower sales of Huggies diapers.

  In Europe, personal care net sales decreased about 2 percent due to unfavorable currency effects of 2 percent and a decrease in net selling prices of 1 percent, partially offset by increases in sales volumes of 1 percent.

  In K-C's International operations in Asia, Latin America, the Middle East, Eastern Europe and Africa ("K-C International"), net sales increased about 6 percent driven by a 5 percent increase in sales volumes and a 1 percent favorable currency effect. The growth in sales volumes was broad-based, with particular strength in Asia and Latin America, excluding Venezuela.

- Consumer tissue net sales in North America decreased 1 percent as an increase in net selling prices of 2 percent and improvements in product mix of 1 percent were more than offset by a sales volume decline of 4 percent. Sales volumes were down low single-digits in bath tissue and double-digits in paper towels, primarily as a result of continued consumer trade-down to lower-priced product offerings.

  In Europe, consumer tissue net sales decreased 2 percent due to unfavorable currency effects of 2 percent and a decrease in sales volumes of 2 percent, partially offset by an increase in net selling prices of 2 percent.

  In K-C International, consumer tissue net sales increased about 8 percent due to an increase in net selling prices of 4 percent, favorable currency effects of 2 percent and improvements in product mix of 1 percent. Increases in net selling prices were broad-based, with particular strength in Latin America and Russia.

- K-C Professional's net sales in North America increased 3 percent due to higher net selling prices of about 2 percent and favorable currency effects of 1 percent. Volume comparisons benefited from the Jackson Products, Inc. ("Jackson") acquisition in 2009 and growth in the wipes and safety categories, while washroom product volumes declined in a continued

continued

continued from prior page

challenging economic environment. In Europe, sales of K-C Professional products decreased 1 percent, as an increase in sales volumes of 3 percent was more than offset by unfavorable currency effects of 3 percent and lower net selling prices of 1 percent.

- The increased sales volumes for health care products were primarily due to a 9 percent benefit from the acquisition of I-Flow Corporation ("I-Flow") in late November 2009, as well as volume increases in other medical devices, which were more than offset by declines in supplies, including the impact from increased face mask demand in 2009 related to the H1N1 influenza virus.

Business Segments

Generally accepted accounting principles require that companies disclose the composition of their operating profit by business segment. Segments are investment centers (those having both income statement and balance sheet data) that the company routinely evaluates at the chief executive level.

We outlined and discussed Kimberly-Clark's business segments at the beginning of the appendix: personal care, consumer tissue, professional & other, and health care. Following are its GAAP disclosures for each of its business segments:

(Millions of dollars)	Personal Care	Consumer Tissue	Professional & Other	Health Care	Corporate & Other	Consolidated Total
Consolidated Operations by Business Segment						
Net sales						
2010	$8,670	$6,497	$3,110	$1,460	9	$19,746
2009	8,365	6,409	3,007	1,371	(37)	19,115
2008	8,272	6,748	3,174	1,224	(3)	19,415
Operating profit						
2010	1,764	660	468	174	(293)	2,773
2009	1,739	736	464	244	(358)	2,825
2008	1,649	601	428	143	(274)	2,547
Depreciation and amortization						
2010	277	329	142	56	9	813
2009	255	314	148	50	16	783
2008	239	319	136	52	29	775
Assets						
2010	6,316	6,106	2,962	2,410	2,070	19,864
2009	5,895	5,871	2,969	2,558	1,916	19,209
2008	5,480	5,809	2,710	2,139	1,951	18,089
Capital spending						
2010	436	331	156	40	1	964
2009	440	271	97	38	2	848
2008	375	351	130	49	1	906

Given these data, it is possible for us to perform a rudimentary return analysis for each segment. This analysis provides insight into a company's dependence on any one segment. Following is a brief summary analysis of K-C's segment return disaggregation for 2010:

(Millions of dollars)	Personal Care	Consumer Tissue	Professional & Other	Health Care
Net sales	8,670	6,497	3,110	1,460
Operating profit	1,764	660	468	174
Assets	6,316	6,106	2,962	2,410
Operating profit margin	20.3%	10.2%	15.0%	11.9%
Year-end asset turnover	1.37	1.06	1.05	0.61
Operating profit divided by year-end assets	27.9%	10.8%	15.8%	7.2%

The intensely competitive nature and capital intensity of the health care market is evident in its low profit margin (11.9%) and low return on ending operating assets (7.2%). K-C relies, to a great extent, on its personal care segment to generate income.

Balance Sheet Reporting and Analysis

Kimberly-Clark's balance sheet is reproduced in Exhibit C.3.

EXHIBIT C.3 Kimberly-Clark Balance Sheet

KIMBERLY-CLARK CORPORATION AND SUBSIDIARIES
Consolidated Balance Sheet

December 31 (Millions of dollars)	2010	2009
ASSETS		
Current assets		
Cash and cash equivalents.	$ 876	$ 798
Accounts receivable, net	2,472	2,566
Note receivable.	218	—
Inventories	2,373	2,033
Deferred income taxes	187	136
Other current assets.	202	331
Total current assets.	6,328	5,864
Property, plant and equipment, net.	8,356	8,033
Investments in equity companies.	374	355
Goodwill.	3,403	3,275
Other intangible assets.	287	310
Long-term notes receivable	393	607
Other assets.	723	765
Total assets	$19,864	$19,209
LIABILITIES AND STOCKHOLDERS' EQUITY		
Current liabilities		
Debt payable within one year.	$ 344	$ 610
Redeemable preferred securities of subsidiary	506	—
Trade accounts payable.	2,206	1,920
Accrued expenses	1,909	2,064
Accrued income taxes	104	79
Dividends payable	269	250
Total current liabilities.	5,338	4,923
Long-term debt	5,120	4,792
Noncurrent employee benefits.	1,810	1,989
Long-term income taxes payable.	260	168
Deferred income taxes.	369	377
Other liabilities	224	218
Redeemable preferred and common securities of subsidiaries.	541	1,052
Stockholders' Equity		
Kimberly-Clark Corporation stockholders' equity		
Preferred stock—no par value—authorized 20.0 million shares, none issued.	—	—
Common stock—$1.25 par value—authorized 1.2 billion shares; issued 478.6 million shares at December 31, 2010 and 2009	598	598
Additional paid-in capital	425	399
Common stock held in treasury, at cost—71.7 million and 61.6 million shares at December 31, 2010 and 2009.	(4,726)	(4,087)
Accumulated other comprehensive income (loss)	(1,466)	(1,833)
Retained earnings.	11,086	10,329
Total Kimberly-Clark Corporation stockholders' equity	5,917	5,406
Noncontrolling interests	285	284
Total stockholders' equity.	6,202	5,690
Total liabilities and stockholders' equity	$19,864	$19,209

Kimberly-Clark reports total assets of $19,864 million in 2010. Its net working capital is relatively illiquid because a large proportion of current assets consists of accounts receivable and inventories, and its cash is 4.4% ($876 million/$19,864 million) of total assets at year-end 2010, up from 4.1% in 2009. It also reports no marketable securities that can serve as another source of liquidity, if needed. The lack of liquidity is usually worrisome, but is not a serious concern in this case given Kimberly-Clark's moderate financial leverage and high level of free cash flow (see later discussion in this section).

Following is a brief review and analysis for each of Kimberly-Clark's balance sheet line items.

Accounts Receivable

Kimberly-Clark reports $2,472 million in net accounts receivable at year-end 2010. This represents 12.4% ($2,472 million/$19,864 million) of total assets, down from 13.4% in the previous year. Footnotes reveal the following additional information:

Summary of Accounts Receivable ($ millions), December 31	2010	2009
Accounts Receivable		
From customers	$2,231	$2,290
Other	321	365
Less allowance for doubtful accounts and sales discounts	(80)	(89)
Total	$2,472	$2,566

Most accounts receivables are from customers. This means we must consider the following two issues:

1. **Magnitude**—Receivables are generally non-interest-bearing and, therefore, do not earn a return. Further, the company incurs costs to finance them. Accordingly, a company wants to optimize its level of investment in receivables—that is, keep them as low as possible while still meeting industry specific credit policies to meet customer demands.

2. **Collectibility**—Receivables represent unsecured loans to customers. It is critical therefore, to understand the creditworthiness of these borrowers. Receivables are reported at net realizable value, that is, net of the allowance for doubtful accounts. Kimberly-Clark reports an allowance of $80 million. In addition, the footnotes reveal the following history of the company's allowance versus its write-offs:

		Additions		Deductions	
Description (December 31, 2010)	Balance at Beginning of Period	Charged to Costs and Expenses	Charged to Other Accounts	Write-Offs and Reclassifications	Balance at End of Period
Allowance for doubtful accounts	$68	$7	—	$13	$62

The company reported a balance in the allowance for doubtful accounts of $68 million at the beginning of 2010, which is 2.6% of gross receivables [$68/($2,566 million + $68 million)]. During 2010, it increased this allowance account by $7 million. This is the amount of bad debt expense that is reported in the income statement. Write-offs and reclassifications of uncollectible accounts amounted to $13 million during the year, yielding a $62 million balance at year-end, which is 2.4% of gross receivables [$62 million/($2,472 million + $62 million)]. It appears, therefore, that the company's receivables were less adequately reserved at year-end relative to the beginning of the year, but the difference is not substantial.

The allowance for doubtful accounts should always reflect the company's best estimate of the potential loss in its accounts receivable. This amount should not be overly conservative (which would understate profit), and it should not be inadequate (which would overstate profit). K-C's estimate of its potential losses results from its own (unaudited) review of the age of its receivables (older receivables are at greater risk of uncollectibility).

Inventories

Kimberly-Clark reports $2,373 million in inventories as of 2010. Footnote disclosures reveal the following inventory costing policy:

> **Inventories and Distribution Costs** For financial reporting purposes, most U.S. inventories are valued at the lower of cost, using the Last-In, First-Out (LIFO) method, or market. The balance of the U.S. inventories and inventories of consolidated operations outside the U.S. are valued at the lower of cost, using either the First-In, First-Out (FIFO) or weighted-average cost methods, or market. Distribution costs are classified as Cost of Products Sold.

Most of its U.S. inventories are reported on a LIFO basis. Some of its U.S. inventories, as well as those outside of the U.S., are valued at FIFO or weighted-average. The use of multiple inventory costing methods for different pools of inventories is common and acceptable under GAAP.

Kimberly-Clark provides the following footnote disclosure relating to the composition of its inventories:

Summary of Inventories ($ millions), December 31	2010 LIFO	2010 Non-LIFO	2010 Total	2009 LIFO	2009 Non-LIFO	2009 Total
Inventories by Major Class:						
At the lower of cost determined on the FIFO or weighted-average cost methods or market:						
Raw materials	$ 154	$ 350	$ 504	$ 137	$ 282	$ 419
Work in process	195	144	339	177	111	288
Finished goods	715	763	1,478	573	685	1,258
Supplies and other	—	298	298	—	277	277
	1,064	1,555	2,619	887	1,355	2,242
Excess of FIFO or weighted-average cost over:						
LIFO cost	(246)	—	(246)	(209)	—	(209)
Total	$ 818	$1,555	$2,373	$ 678	$1,355	$2,033

Companies aim to optimize their investment in inventories because inventory is a non-income-producing asset until sold. Inventories must also be financed, stored, moved, and insured at some cost. Kimberly-Clark reports $504 million of raw materials, which is 19% of the total of $2,619 million FIFO inventories (see table above). Work-in-process inventories amount to another $339 million, and supplies and other amount to $298 million. The bulk of its inventories, or $1,478 million (56% of total inventories), is in finished goods.

Kimberly-Clark reports its total inventory cost *at FIFO* is $2,619 million then subtracts $246 million from this amount (the *LIFO reserve*) to yield the inventories balance of $2,373 million at LIFO as reported on the balance sheet. This means that, over time, Kimberly-Clark has reduced gross profit and pretax operating profit by a cumulative amount of $246 million. This has also reduced pretax income and saved federal income tax, and generated cash flow, of approximately $86.1 million (assuming a 35% statutory federal tax rate and computed as $246 million × 35%). During 2010, its LIFO reserve increased by $37 million, resulting in a $37 million decrease in gross profit and pretax operating profit, and a $13.0 million ($37 million × 35%) *increase* in cash flow from decreased federal income taxes.

Property, Plant, and Equipment

Kimberly-Clark reports Property, Plant, and Equipment, net, of $8,356 million at year-end 2010; PPE makes up 42.1% of total assets and is the largest single asset category. Given the cost of depreciable assets of $17,877 million and accumulated depreciation of $9,521 million (not reported here), PPE is 53.3% depreciated assuming straight-line depreciation ($9,521 million/$17,877 million) as of 2010. This suggests these assets are about the average age that we would expect assuming a regular replacement policy. Footnotes reveal a useful life range of 40 years for buildings and 16 to 20 years for machinery as follows:

> **Property and Depreciation**   For financial reporting purposes, property, plant and equipment are stated at cost and are depreciated principally on the straight-line method. Buildings are depreciated over their estimated useful lives, primarily 40 years. Machinery and equipment are depreciated over their estimated useful lives, primarily ranging from 16 to 20 years. For income tax purposes, accelerated methods of depreciation are used. Purchases of computer software are capitalized. External costs and certain internal costs (including payroll and payroll-related costs of employees) directly associated with developing significant computer software applications for internal use are capitalized. Training and data conversion costs are expensed as incurred. Computer software costs are amortized on the straight-line method over the estimated useful life of the software, which generally does not exceed five years...The cost of major maintenance performed on manufacturing facilities, composed of labor, materials and other incremental costs, is charged to operations as incurred. Start-up costs for new or expanded facilities are expensed as incurred.

Again, assuming straight-line depreciation, Kimberly-Clark's 2010 depreciation expense of $790 million ($813 depreciation and amortization expense reported in its statement of cash flows, Exhibit C.5, less $23 million reported as amortization expense in footnotes not reproduced in the text, but equal to the difference in accumulated amortization) reveals that its long-term depreciable assets, as a whole, are being depreciated over an average useful life of about 21.7 years, computed as $17,877 million − $220 million of nondepreciable land and $553 million of construction in progress divided by $790 million depreciation expense.

Each year, Kimberly-Clark tests PPE for impairment and records a write-down to net realizable value if the PPE is deemed to be impaired. Following is Kimberly-Clark's discussion relating to its impairment testing:

> Estimated useful lives are periodically reviewed and, when warranted, changes are made to them. Long-lived assets, including computer software, are reviewed for impairment whenever events or changes in circumstances indicate that their carrying amount may not be recoverable. An impairment loss would be indicated when estimated undiscounted future cash flows from the use and eventual disposition of an asset group, which are identifiable and largely independent of the cash flows of other asset groups, are less than the carrying amount of the asset group. Measurement of an impairment loss would be based on the excess of the carrying amount of the asset over its fair value. Fair value is measured using discounted cash flows or independent appraisals, as appropriate. When property is sold or retired, the cost of the property and the related accumulated depreciation are removed from the Consolidated Balance Sheet and any gain or loss on the transaction is included in income.

The company did not report any impairment losses in the periods covered by its recent 10-K.

If present, impairment losses should be treated as a transitory item. Further, we must consider the effects of such losses on current and future income statements. An impairment loss depresses current period income. Further, depreciation expense in future years is decreased because it is computed based on the asset's lower net book value (cost less accumulated depreciation) following the write-down. This will increase future period profitability. The net effect of an impairment charge, therefore, is to shift profit from the current period into future periods.

Investments in Equity Companies

K-C's balance sheet reports equity investments of $374 million at year-end 2010. This amount represents the book value of its investments in affiliated companies over which Kimberly-Clark can exert significant influence, but not control. Footnotes reveal investments in the following companies:

> **Investments in Equity Companies**   Investments in companies over which we have the ability to exercise significant influence and that, in general, are at least 20 percent owned by us, are stated at cost plus equity in undistributed net income. These investments are evaluated for impairment when warranted. An impairment loss would be recorded whenever a decline in value of an equity investment below its carrying amount is determined to be other than temporary. In judging "other

continued

than temporary," we would consider the length of time and extent to which the fair value of the equity company investment has been less than the carrying amount, the near-term and longer-term operating and financial prospects of the equity company, and our longer-term intent of retaining the investment in the equity company.

Consolidation is not required unless the affiliate is "controlled." Generally, control is presumed at an ownership level of more than 50%. By this rule, Kimberly-Clark does not control any of these companies. Thus, the company uses the equity method to account for these investments. This means that only the net equity owned of these companies is reported on the balance sheet. We further discuss these investments in the section on off-balance-sheet financing.

Goodwill

Kimberly-Clark reports $3,403 million of goodwill at year-end 2010. This amount represents the excess of the purchase price for acquired companies over the fair market value of the acquired tangible and identifiable intangible assets (net of liabilities assumed). Under GAAP, goodwill is not systematically amortized, but is annually tested for impairment.

Other Assets

Kimberly-Clark reports $723 million as "other assets." There is no table detailing what assets are included in this total, but footnotes reveal the following: $15 million of long-term marketable securities, $70 million of assets related to derivative financial instruments, and $312 million of noncurrent deferred income tax assets. No information is given on the remaining $330 million of other assets, most likely because this amount represents several assets each of which is not determined to be material and, therefore, subject to disclosure.

Concerning the deferred income tax assets, Kimberly-Clark provides the following disclosure relating to its composition ($ millions):

December 31 (Millions of dollars)	2010	2009
Net current deferred income tax asset attributable to:		
Accrued expenses	$ 103	$ 102
Pension, postretirement and other employee benefits	82	86
Loss carryforwards	72	—
Installment sales	(72)	—
Inventory	(21)	(45)
Other	46	8
Valuation allowances	(23)	(15)
Net current deferred income tax asset	$ 187	$ 136
Net current deferred income tax liability included in accrued expenses	$ (28)	$ (31)
Net noncurrent deferred income tax asset attributable to:		
Tax credits and loss carryforwards	$ 447	$ 405
Pension and other postretirement benefits	153	228
Property, plant and equipment, net	(97)	(86)
Other	42	37
Valuation allowances	(233)	(211)
Net noncurrent deferred income tax asset included in other assets	$ 312	$ 373
Net noncurrent deferred income tax liability attributable to:		
Property, plant and equipment, net	$(1,081)	$(976)
Pension, postretirement and other employee benefits	550	546
Tax credits and loss carryforwards	447	462
Installment sales	(112)	(180)
Provision for unremitted earnings	(88)	(70)
Intangible assets	(43)	(63)
Other	(13)	(78)
Valuation allowances	(29)	(18)
Net noncurrent deferred income tax liability	$ (369)	$(377)

Most of this deferred tax asset (benefit) results from tax loss carryforwards. The IRS allows companies to carry forward losses to offset future taxable income, thereby reducing future tax expense. This benefit can only be realized if the company expects taxable income in the specific entity that generated the tax losses before the carryforwards expire. If the company deems it more likely than not that the carryforwards will *not* be realized, a valuation allowance for the unrealizable portion is required (this is similar to establishing an allowance for uncollectible accounts receivable). As of 2010, Kimberly-Clark has such a valuation allowance (of $285 million). Following is its discussion relating to this allowance:

> Valuation allowances increased $43 million in 2010 and decreased $75 million in 2009. Valuation allowances at the end of 2010 primarily relate to tax credits and income tax loss carryforwards of $1.2 billion. If these items are not utilized against taxable income, $210 million of the loss carryforwards will expire from 2011 through 2030. The remaining $981 million has no expiration date. Realization of income tax loss carryforwards is dependent on generating sufficient taxable income prior to expiration of these carryforwards. Although realization is not assured, we believe it is more likely than not that all of the deferred tax assets, net of applicable valuation allowances, will be realized. The amount of the deferred tax assets considered realizable could be reduced or increased due to changes in the tax environment or if estimates of future taxable income change during the carryforward period.

Tax loss carryforwards reduce income tax expense in the year they are recognized, similar to tax loss carry-backs. However, companies often establish a deferred tax asset valuation allowance which increases tax expense. It is common that companies establish both the loss carryforward and the valuation allowance concurrently. The net effect is to leave tax expense (and net income) unchanged. In future years, however, a reduction of the deferred tax asset valuation account, in anticipation of utilization of the tax carry-forwards (and not as a result of their expiration), reduces tax expense and increases net income. This is a transitory increase in profit and should not be factored into projections.

Current Liabilities

Kimberly-Clark reports current liabilities of $5,338 million on its year-end balance sheet for 2010 ($4,923 million in 2009), which consists of the following:

Current Liabilities ($ millions), December 31	2010	2009
Debt payable within one year.	$ 344	$ 610
Redeemable preferred securities of subsidiary	506	—
Trade accounts payable.	2,206	1,920
Accrued expenses	1,909	2,064
Accrued income taxes	104	79
Dividends payable	269	250
Total Current Liabilities.	$5,338	$4,923

Regarding K-C's current liabilities, $1,119 of this amount relates to financial items, such as maturing long-term debt ($344 million), an obligation to repurchase redeemable preferred stock of a subsidiary ($506 million) and dividends payable ($269 million). The remaining items in current liabilities arise from common external transactions, such as trade accounts payable and taxes payable. These transactions are less prone to management reporting bias. We must, however, determine the presence of excessive "leaning on the trade" as a means to boost operating cash flow. K-C's trade accounts payable have increased as a percentage of total liabilities and equity from 10.0% ($1,920 million/$19,209 million) in 2009 to 11.1% ($2,206 million/$19,864 million) in 2010. While this change is not drastic, and the level is not excessive, we need to monitor K-C's balance sheet for a continuation of this trend.

The possibility of management reporting bias is typically greater for accrued liabilities, which are often estimated (and difficult to audit), involve no external transaction, and can markedly impact reported balance sheet and income statement amounts. One of Kimberly-Clark's accrued liabilities involves promotions and rebates, reported at $352 million in the footnotes as of 2010. Following is the description of its accrual policy in this area:

Promotion and Rebate Accruals   Among those factors affecting the accruals for promotions are estimates of the number of consumer coupons that will be redeemed and the type and number of activities within promotional programs between us and our trade customers. Rebate accruals are based on estimates of the quantity of products distributors have sold to specific customers. Generally, the estimates for consumer coupon costs are based on historical patterns of coupon redemption, influenced by judgments about current market conditions such as competitive activity in specific product categories. Estimates of trade promotion liabilities for promotional program costs incurred, but unpaid, are generally based on estimates of the quantity of customer sales, timing of promotional activities and forecasted costs for activities within the promotional programs. Settlement of these liabilities sometimes occurs in periods subsequent to the date of the promotion activity. Trade promotion programs include introductory marketing funds such as slotting fees, co-operative marketing programs, temporary price reductions, favorable end-of-aisle or in-store product displays and other activities conducted by our customers to promote our products. Promotion accruals as of December 31, 2010 and 2009 were $352 million and $364 million, respectively. Rebate accruals as of December 31, 2010 and 2009 were $353 million and $365 million, respectively.

The company also reports accruals relating to its insurance risks as described in the following footnote:

Retained Insurable Risks   Selected insurable risks are retained, primarily those related to property damage, workers' compensation, and product, automobile and premises liability based upon historical loss patterns and management's judgment of cost effective risk retention. Accrued liabilities for incurred but not reported events, principally related to workers' compensation and automobile liability, are based upon undiscounted loss development factors.

All of these accruals have similar effects on the financial statements: when the accrual is established the company recognizes both an expense in the income statement and a liability on the balance sheet. The company subsequently reduces the liability as payments are made. Companies can (and do) use accruals to shift income from one period to another, say by over-accruing in one period to intentionally depress current period profits, and later reducing the liability account, rather than recording an expense, to increase future period profits. Accruals are sometimes referred to as "pads." They represent a cost that has previously been charged to the income statement. They also represent an account that can absorb future costs. We need to monitor accrual accounts carefully for evidence of earnings management.

Long-Term Debt

Kimberly-Clark reports $5,385 million of long-term debt as of 2010. Footnotes reveal the following:

Long-term debt is composed of the following:

($ millions)	Weighted-Average Interest Rate	Maturities	December 31 2010	2009
Notes and debentures	5.97%	2012–2037	$4,286	$4,483
Dealer remarketable securities.	4.43%	2011–2016	200	—
Industrial development revenue bonds	0.35%	2015–2037	280	280
Bank loans and other financings in various currencies.	2.61%	2011–2045	619	532
Total long-term debt.			5,385	5,295
Less current portion			265	503
Long-term portion			$5,120	$4,792

Most of its long-term financing is in the form of notes and debentures, specifically $4,286 million in 2010, which mature over the next 25 years. GAAP requires disclosure of scheduled maturities for each of the five years subsequent to the balance sheet date. Kimberly-Clark's five-year maturity schedule follows:

> Scheduled maturities of long-term debt for the next five years are $265 million in 2011, $427 million in 2012, $550 million in 2013, $516 million in 2014 and $355 million in 2015.

Our concern with debt maturity dates is whether or not a company is able to repay debt as it comes due. Alternatively, a company can refinance the debt. If a company is unable or unwilling to repay or refinance its debt, it must approach creditors for a modification of debt terms for those issuances coming due. Creditors are often willing to oblige but will likely increase interest rates or impose additional debt covenants and restrictions. However, if creditors deny default waivers, the company might face the prospect of bankruptcy. This highlights the importance of long-term debt maturity disclosures.

We have little concern about Kimberly-Clark's debt maturity schedule as the company has strong cash flows. Still, it is worth noting that **Standard & Poor's** (S&P) debt rating for K-C is A. This rating is solid (described as "upper-medium grade" debt).

Noncurrent Employee Benefit and Other Obligations

Kimberly-Clark reports a (negative) funded status of its pension plan of $(1,058) million at year-end 2010 (disclosed in footnotes). This means that the company's pension plans are underfunded by that amount. This underfunding is computed as the difference between the pension benefit obligation (PBO) of $5,658 million and the fair market value of the company's pension assets of $4,600 million (these amounts are also reported in the pension footnote not reproduced here).

The central issue with respect to pensions and other post-retirement obligations is the potential demand they present on operating cash flows. Companies can tap cash from two sources to pay pension and other post-retirement obligations: from the returns on plan assets (i.e., the cumulative contributions and investment returns that have not yet been paid out to beneficiaries) and/or from operating cash flow. To the extent that plan assets are insufficient to meet retirement obligations, companies must divert operating cash flows from other investment activities, potentially reducing the dollar amount of capital projects that can be funded.

We can gain insight into potential cash flow issues by comparing expected future benefit payments to the funds available to make those payments. Companies must provide these disclosures in a schedule to the pension footnotes. K-C provides the following schedule of expected payments in the footnotes to its 10-K:

Estimated Future Benefit Payments   Over the next ten years, we expect that the following gross benefit payments and related Medicare Part D reimbursements will occur:

(Millions of dollars)	Pension Benefits	Other Benefits	Medicare Part D Reimbursements
2011	$ 360	$ 68	$ (4)
2012	362	67	(4)
2013	362	66	(5)
2014	367	67	(5)
2015	373	69	(5)
2016–2020	1,996	370	(26)

The schedule shows that K-C expects to pay out $360 million in benefits to pension beneficiaries and $68 million in health care and other post-retirement benefits (OPEB) to its former employees in 2010. The schedule also reveals that the company expects these amounts to remain fairly constant over the next five years.

K-C also reports the following table relating to its pension and other post-retirement benefit plans' assets:

| Change in Plan Assets | Pension Benefits | | Other Benefits | |
Year Ended December 31 (Millions of dollars)	2010	2009	2010	2009
Fair value of plan assets at beginning of year	$4,244	$3,101	—	—
Actual gain on plan assets.........................	473	520	—	—
Employer contributions	245	845	—	—
Currency and other	(6)	134	—	—
Benefit payments................................	(356)	(356)	—	—
Fair value of plan assets at end of year	$4,600	$4,244	—	—

In 2010, K-C contributed $245 million to its pension plan. That amount, when combined with investment returns of $473 million, was more than sufficient to cover 2010 benefit payments of $356 million (K-C expects this amount to be $360 million in 2011). Should pension assets decline markedly as a result of severe underfunding or investment losses, K-C will need to divert operating cash flows from other investment activities into pension contributions, or to borrow funds to meet its pension obligations. Although K-C's pension obligations are under-funded (as represented by the negative funded status), its current contribution levels and investment returns are sufficient to meet its anticipated pension obligations, at least in the near future.

Other post-retirement benefit obligations (future health care payments) present a different picture. Because federal law does not require minimum funding of these plans, and companies do not receive a tax deduction for such contributions, companies rarely fund OPEB plans. All of the OPEB payments to beneficiaries, therefore, must be funded by concurrent company contributions. These payments amounted to $64 million in 2010. Given K-C's $2.7 billion in operating cash flow for 2010, the $64 million cash requirement is not material. However, OPEB funding requirements have been a burden for many companies, most notably General Motors prior to its bankruptcy.

Deferred Income Taxes

Kimberly-Clark reports deferred income tax assets and liabilities as follows:

Deferred income tax assets (liabilities) are composed of the following:

December 31 (Millions of dollars)	2010	2009
Net current deferred income tax asset attributable to:		
Accrued expenses	$ 103	$ 102
Pension, postretirement and other employee benefits...............	82	86
Loss carryforwards......................................	72	—
Installment sales.......................................	(72)	—
Inventory..	(21)	(45)
Other...	46	8
Valuation allowances	(23)	(15)
Net current deferred income tax asset...........................	$ 187	$ 136
Net current deferred income tax liability included in accrued expenses	$ (28)	$ (31)
Net noncurrent deferred income tax asset attributable to:		
Tax credits and loss carryforwards	$ 447	$ 405
Pension and other postretirement benefits	153	228
Property, plant and equipment, net	(97)	(86)
Other...	42	37
Valuation allowances	(233)	(211)
Net noncurrent deferred income tax asset included in other assets	$ 312	$ 373

continued

continued from prior page

Net noncurrent deferred income tax liability attributable to:		
Property, plant and equipment, net	$(1,081)	$(976)
Pension, postretirement and other employee benefits	550	546
Tax credits and loss carryforwards	447	462
Installment sales	(112)	(180)
Provision for unremitted earnings	(88)	(70)
Intangible assets	(43)	(63)
Other	(13)	(78)
Valuation allowances	(29)	(18)
Net noncurrent deferred income tax liability	$ (369)	$(377)

Most of the noncurrent deferred tax liability ($1,081 million) arises from K-C's use of straight-line depreciation for GAAP reporting and accelerated depreciation for tax reporting. As a result, tax depreciation expense is higher in the early years of the assets' lives. This will reverse in later years for individual assets, resulting in higher taxable income and tax liability. The deferred tax liability account reflects this future expected tax.

Although depreciation expense for an individual asset declines over time, thus increasing taxable income and tax liability, if K-C adds new assets at a sufficient rate, the additional first-year depreciation on those assets will more than offset the reduction of depreciation expense on older assets, resulting in a long-term reduction of tax liability. That is, the deferred tax liability is unlikely to reverse in the aggregate. For this reason, many analysts treat the deferred tax liability as a "quasi-equity" account.

Still, while deferred taxes can be postponed, they cannot be eliminated. If the company's asset growth slows markedly, it will realize higher taxable income and tax liability. We need to be mindful of the potential for a "real" tax liability (requiring cash payment) when companies begin to downsize.

K-C also reports a long-term deferred tax asset valuation allowance of $285 million for 2010 ($23 million + $233 million + $29 million), an increase of $41 million over the $244 million ($15 million + $211 million + $18 million) of the prior year. This valuation allowance is related to deferred tax assets that arise from the company's tax loss carry-forwards. The valuation allowance indicates that the company does not expect to fully realize cash flows relating to deferred tax assets, such as tax loss carry-forwards before their scheduled expiration. Increases in the deferred tax asset valuation allowance impact tax expense, and, thus, net income, dollar for dollar. K-C's net income (and net operating income after tax or NOPAT) was reduced by $41 million in 2010 as a result of the increase in this valuation allowance. In future years, we need to be aware that profit can increase if and when the allowance account is reversed with no offsetting expense (unless the reversal is related to the expiration of tax loss carryforwards).

Noncontrolling Interests in Subsidiaries

K-C reports $285 million for the equity interests of noncontrolling shareholders in subsidiaries. Noncontrolling interests are shareholder claims against the net assets and cash flows of subsidiaries of the company (after all senior claims are settled). Consequently, we treat noncontrolling interest as a component of stockholders' equity.

Redeemable Preferred Securities of Subsidiary

Redeemable preferred securities represent the sale of preferred stock by a subsidiary of Kimberly-Clark to outside interests. Because these securities are redeemable, they are not reported in K-C's stockholders' equity but, instead, are reported between liabilities and equity.

Stockholders' Equity

Kimberly-Clark reports the following statement of stockholders' equity for 2010:

Dollars in million, shares in thousands	Common Stock Issued		Additional Paid-in Capital	Treasury Stock		Retained Earnings	Accumulated Other Comprehensive Income (Loss)	Noncontrolling Interests
	Shares	Amount		Shares	Amount			
Balance at Dec. 31, 2009	478,597	$598	$399	61,649	$(4,087)	$10,329	$(1,833)	$284
Net income in stockholders' equity	—	—	—	—	—	1,843	—	44
Other comprehensive income:								
Unrealized translation	—	—	—	—	—	—	326	7
Employee postretirement benefits, net of tax	—	—	—	—	—	—	57	(2)
Other	—	—	—	—	—	—	(16)	—
Stock-based awards exercised or vested	—	—	(37)	(2,862)	170	—	—	—
Income tax benefits on stock-based compensation	—	—	2	—	—	—	—	—
Shares repurchased	—	—	—	12,954	(809)	—	—	—
Recognition of stock-based compensation	—	—	52	—	—	—	—	—
Dividends declared	—	—	—	—	—	(1,085)	—	(47)
Other	—	—	9	—	—	(1)	—	(1)
Balance at Dec. 31, 2010 . . .	478,597	$598	$425	71,741	$(4,726)	$11,086	$(1,466)	$285

K-C has issued 478,597,000 shares of its $1.25 par value common stock. The common stock account is, therefore, equal to $598 million, computed as 478,597,000 shares × $1.25. The additional paid-in capital (APIC) represents the excess of proceeds from stock issuance over par value. It includes adjustments relating to the recognition of stock-based compensation and the exercise of stock-based awards and other minor adjustments.

Kimberly-Clark's stockholders' equity is reduced by $809 million relating to repurchases of common stock, less the reissuance of those securities from the exercise of stock options in the amount of $170 million. These treasury shares are the result of a stock purchase plan approved by K-C's board of directors, and evidences K-C's conviction that its stock is undervalued by the marketplace. The repurchased shares are held in treasury and reduce stockholders' equity by the purchase price until such time as they are reissued, perhaps to fund an acquisition or to compensate employees under a stock purchase or stock option plan (treasury shares can also be retired).

K-C compensates employees via restricted stock in addition to other forms of compensation. Under its restricted stock plan, eligible employees are issued stock, which is restricted as to sale until fully vested (owned). When issued, the market value of the restricted stock is deducted from stockholders' equity. As the employees gain ownership of the shares (that is, the restricted stock vests), a portion of this account is transferred to the income statement as compensation expense. The consequent reduction in retained earnings offsets the reduction (and increase in equity) of the restricted stock account. Stockholders' equity is, therefore, unaffected in total, although its components change.

Retained earnings reflect a $1,843 million increase relating to net income and a $1,085 million decrease from declaration of dividends. Accumulated other comprehensive income (AOCI), which is often aggregated with retained earnings for analysis purposes, began 2010 with a balance of $(1,833) million; this negative balance reduces stockholders' equity. During the period, this AOCI account was further increased (less negative) by $326 million relating to the increase in the $US value of net assets of foreign subsidiaries. This increase in net asset value resulted from a weakened $US vis-à-vis other currencies in which the company conducts its operations in 2010. In addition, the AOCI account was increased by $57 million relating to employee postretirement benefits adjustments and decreased (made more negative) by $16 million for activities designated as "other." Finally, K-C's comprehensive income equals net income plus (minus) the components of other comprehensive income.

Common-Size Balance Sheet

Similar to our analysis of the income statement, it is useful to compute common-size balance sheets. Such statements can reveal changes or relations masked by other analyses. Kimberly-Clark's common-size balance sheet covering its recent two years is shown in Exhibit C.4.

EXHIBIT C.4 Kimberly-Clark Common-Size Balance Sheet		
December 31	**2010**	**2009**
Current assets		
Cash and cash equivalents	4.4%	4.2%
Accounts receivable, net	12.4	13.4
Note receivable	1.1	0.0
Inventories	11.9	10.6
Deferred income taxes	0.9	0.7
Other current assets	1.0	1.7
Total current assets	31.9	30.5
Property, plat and equipment, net	42.1	41.8
Investments in equity companies	1.9	1.8
Goodwill	17.1	17.0
Other intangible assets	1.4	1.6
Long-term notes receivable	2.0	3.2
Other assets	3.6	4.0
Total assets	100.0%	100.0%
Current liabilities		
Debt payable within one year	1.7%	3.2%
Redeemable preferred securities of subsidiary	2.5	0.0
Trade accounts payable	11.1	10.0
Accrued expenses	9.6	10.7
Accrued income taxes	0.5	0.4
Dividends payable	1.4	1.3
Total current liabilities	26.9	25.6
Long-term debt	25.8	24.9
Noncurrent employee benefits	9.1	10.4
Long-term income taxes payable	1.3	0.9
Deferred income taxes	1.9	2.0
Other liabilities	1.1	1.1
Redeemable preferred and common securities of subsidiaries	2.7	5.5
Stockholders' equity		
Preferred stock-no par value-authorized 20.0 million shares, none issued	0.0	0.0
Common stock- $1.25 par value-authorized 1.2 billion shares; issued 478.6 million shares at December 31, 2010 and 2009	3.0	3.1
Additional paid-in capital	2.1	2.1
Common stock held in treasury, at cost-71.7 million and 61.6 million shares at December 31, 2010 and 2009	(23.8)	(21.3)
Accumulated other comprehensive income (loss)	(7.4)	(9.5)
Retained earnings	55.8	53.8
Total Kimberly-Clark Corporation stockholders' equity	29.8	28.1
Noncontrolling interests	1.4	1.5
Total stockholders' equity	31.2	29.6
Liabilities and stockholders' equity, total	100.0%	100.0%

Note: Percentages are computed by dividing each balance sheet line item by that year's total assets.

Total current assets increased from 30.5% of total assets in 2009 to 31.9% in 2010. The 1.3% increase in inventories as a percent to total assets was largely offset by a 1.0 reduction of accounts receivable. The increase in current assets is largely due to the emergence of a note receivable in the amount of $218 million, 1.1% of total assets. Net PPE also increased as a percent of total assets, from 41.8% in 2009 to 42.1% in 2010. This was largely offset by a reduction of long-term notes receivable from 3.2% of total assets in 2009 to 2.0% in 2010.

On the liability side, current liabilities increased as a percent of the total from 25.6% in 2009 to 26.9% in 2010. This was largely due to an increase in accounts payable (from 10.0% to 11.1%) and the emergence of a current liability relating to redeemable preferred stock of a subsidiary. On balance, K-C became somewhat less financially leveraged in 2010 as stockholders' equity rose from 29.6% of the total in 2009 to 31.2%. The relative proportions of debt and equity do not appear out of line at a ratio of 2.2:1.0.

Off-Balance-Sheet Reporting and Analysis

There are numerous assets and liabilities that do not appear on the balance sheet. Some are excluded because managers and accounting professionals only report what they can reliably measure. Others are excluded because of the rigidity of accounting standards. Following are some areas we might consider in our evaluation and adjustment of the Kimberly-Clark balance sheet.

Internally Developed Intangible Assets

Many brands and their corresponding values are excluded from the balance sheet. For example, consider the brand "Kleenex." Many individuals actually refer to facial tissues as Kleenex–that is successful branding! So, is the Kleenex brand reported and valued on Kimberly-Clark's balance sheet? No. That brand value cannot be reliably measured and, hence, is not included on K-C's balance sheet.

Likewise, other valuable assets are excluded from the company's balance sheet. Examples are the value of a competent management team, high employee morale, innovative production know-how, a superior supply chain, customer satisfaction, and a host of other assets.

R&D activities often create internally generated intangible assets that are mostly excluded from the balance sheet. Footnotes reveal that Kimberly-Clark spends over $317 million (1.6% of sales) on R&D to remain competitive—and, this is for an admittedly non-high-tech company. Further, K-C reveals that it spends $698 million (3.5% of sales) on advertising. Both R&D and advertising costs are expensed under GAAP as opposed to being capitalized on the balance sheet as tangible assets. These unrecognized intangible assets often represent a substantial part of a company's market value.

Equity Method Investments

Kimberly-Clark reports equity investments of $374 million at year-end 2010. These are unconsolidated affiliates over which K-C can exert significant influence (but not control) and, hence, are accounted for using the equity method. The amount reported on the balance sheet represents the initial cost of the investment, plus (minus) the percentage share of investee earnings and losses, and minus any cash dividends received. Consequently, the investment balance equals the percentage owned of the affiliates' stockholders' equity (plus any unamortized excess purchase price).

Footnotes reveal that, in sum, these K-C affiliates have total assets of $2,117 million, liabilities of $1,502 million, and stockholders' equity of $615 million. K-C's reported investment balance of $374 in the balance sheet does not reveal the extent of the investment (assets) required to manage these companies, nor the level of potential liability exposure. For instance, if one of these affiliates falters financially, K-C might have to invest additional cash to support it rather than let it fail. Failure of an important affiliate might affect K-C's ability to finance another such venture in the future.

These investments are reported at cost, not at fair market value as are passive investments. This means that unrecognized gains and losses can be buried in such investment accounts. For example, K-C footnotes reveal the following:

> Kimberly-Clark de Mexico, S.A.B. de C.V. is partially owned by the public and its stock is publicly traded in Mexico. At December 31, 2010, our investment in this equity company was $269 million, and the estimated fair value of the investment was $3.1 billion based on the market price of publicly traded shares.

Thus, for at least one of its investments, there is an unrecognized gain of $2,831 million ($3,100 million − $269 million).

Operating Leases

Kimberly-Clark has leases classified as "operating" for financial reporting purposes. As a result, neither the lease asset nor the lease obligation are reported on its balance sheet. For example, K-C reports the following disclosure relating to its operating leases:

Leases We have entered into operating leases for certain warehouse facilities, automobiles and equipment. The future minimum obligations under operating leases having a noncancelable term in excess of one year as of December 31, 2010 are as follows:

Year Ending December 31	(Millions of dollars)
2011	$194
2012	143
2013	118
2014	103
2015	84
Thereafter	153
Future minimum obligations	$795

These leases represent an unreported asset and an unreported liability; both amounting to $711 million. This amount is computed as follows and assumes a 4% discount rate ($ millions):

Year	Operating Lease Payment	Discount Factor (i = 0.04)	Present Value
1	$194	0.96154	$187
2	143	0.92456	132
3	118	0.88900	105
4	103	0.85480	88
5	84	0.82193	69
>5	153 [$84 for ~1.821 years]	1.88609* × 0.82193	130**
			$711

Remaining life = $153/84 = 1.821 or ~2 years
*The annuity factor for 2 years at 4% is 1.88609.
**1.88609 × 0.82193 × $84 = $130

The classification of leases as operating for financial reporting purposes often involves a rigid application of accounting rules that depend solely on the structure of the lease. A large amount of assets and liabilities is excluded from many companies' balance sheets because leases are structured as operating leases. For K-C, these excluded assets amount to $711 million. The valuation of K-C common stock (shown later) uses net operating assets (NOA) as one of its inputs. Our adjustment to the K-C balance sheet, then, would entail the addition of these assets to NOA and the inclusion of $711 million in *non-operating* liabilities.

Pensions

Kimberly-Clark's pension plan is underfunded as explained earlier. Total pension obligations are $5,658 million and pension assets have a market value of $4,600 million at year-end 2010. Neither of these amounts appears on the balance sheet, but are reported in the footnotes. Only the net amount of $(1,058) appears on the balance sheet via three component amounts as identified in the following footnote disclosure:

Amounts Recognized in the Balance Sheet	
Noncurrent asset—Prepaid benefit cost	$ 21
Current liability—Accrued benefit cost	(11)
Noncurrent liability—Accrued benefit cost	(1,068)
Net amount recognized	$(1,058)

Variable Interest Entities

Footnotes reveal that Kimberly-Clark owns investments in entities that are considered to be a variable interest entity (VIE) under GAAP. These entities are typically non-stock entities, such as joint ventures, partnerships and trusts, and the accounting for these entities depends upon whether the investor is deemed to be the primary beneficiary. If so, the investor must consolidate the VIE. If not, the investor accounts for its investment using the equity method. Following is K-C's footnote disclosure relating to these investments:

> We consolidate real estate entities in which we are the primary beneficiary. In most of these entities we also have voting control. We determined we are the primary beneficiary of these variable interests based on qualitative analysis. The assets of these entities are classified principally as property, plant and equipment and have a carrying amount aggregating $37 million at December 31, 2010, that serves as collateral for the obligations of these ventures. The obligations have a carrying amount aggregating $25 million, of which $23 million is included in debt payable within one year and $2 million is included in long-term debt… We have significant interests in other variable interest real estate entities in which we are not the primary beneficiary. We account for our interests in these nonconsolidated real estate entities by the equity method of accounting, and have accounted for the related income tax credits and other tax benefits as a reduction in our income tax provision. As of December 31, 2010, we had net equity of $6 million in our nonconsolidated real estate entities. We have made noncontractual cash infusions to certain of the entities aggregating $8 million principally to provide cash flow to support debt payment.

K-C invests in a number of real estate-related entities that own properties, borrow money, and provide K-C with tax benefits. These entities consist of companies that issue common stock together with partnerships and funds in which K-C is an investor. Regardless of their organizational form, and because K-C is deemed the primary beneficiary, it must consolidate the financial statements of these entities. As a result, it reports assets and liabilities of these entities of $37 million and $25 million, respectively, on its balance sheet. Had these entities *not* been consolidated, but reported as equity investments, only the proportion of the *net equity* that K-C owns would be reported in its statements (because we do not know the percentage of the entities that K-C owns, we do not know what amount would have been reported, but it would have been less than $12 million ($37 million - $25 million).

Entities that are consolidated present little analysis concerns because all of their assets and liabilities (and their revenues and expenses) are included in the financial statements of the primary beneficiary. Those that are accounted for as equity method investments, however, present analysis concerns that we must address. K-C reports the following investments in non-consolidated entities:

> We have significant interests in other variable interest real estate entities in which we are not the primary beneficiary. We account for our interests in these nonconsolidated real estate entities by the equity method of accounting . . . As of December 31, 2010, we had net equity of $6 million in our nonconsolidated real estate entities. We have made noncontractual cash infusions to certain of the entities aggregating $8 million principally to provide cash flow to support debt payments.

These nonconsolidated investments are accounted for under the equity method of accounting and, thus, K-C reports only the percentage of their equity that it owns on the balance sheet. Further, only its portion of the net income of these entities is reported in the income statement (not their revenues and expenses). K-C reports these investments at $6 million on its balance sheet. As we discuss in Module 7, however, this investment can belie a larger investment in assets and liabilities and K-C's footnote disclosures do not report the detail relating to the assets and liabilities of these entities. We do know, however, that K-C has made additional cash infusion into these entities of $8 million "to provide cash flow to support debt payments." In other words, these entities did not generate sufficient cash flow to make required debt payments and K-C felt compelled to invest additional cash into the entities to provide that funding.

Derivatives

Kimberly-Clark is exposed to a number of market risks as outlined in the following footnote to its 10-K:

> As a multinational enterprise, we are exposed to risks such as changes in foreign currency exchange rates, interest rates and commodity prices. A variety of practices are employed to manage these risks, including operating and financing activities and, where deemed appropriate, the use of derivative instruments. Derivative instruments are used only for risk management purposes and not for speculation. All foreign currency derivative instruments are entered into with major financial institutions. Our credit exposure under these arrangements is limited to agreements with a positive fair value at the reporting date. Credit risk with respect to the counterparties is actively monitored but is not considered significant since these transactions are executed with a diversified group of financial institutions.

The company hedges these risks using derivatives, including forwards, options, and swap contracts. This hedging process transfers risk from K-C to another entity (called the counterparty), which assumes that risk for a fee.

The accounting for derivatives is summarized in an appendix to Module 7. In brief, the derivative contracts, and the assets or liabilities to which they relate, are reported on the balance sheet at fair market value. Any unrealized gains and losses are ultimately reflected in net income, although they can be accumulated in AOCI for a short time. To the extent that a company's hedging activities are effective, the market values of the derivatives and the assets or liabilities to which they relate are largely offsetting, as are the net gains or losses on the hedging activities. As a result, the effect of derivative activities is generally minimal on both income and equity. (It is generally only when companies use derivatives for speculative purposes that these investments markedly affect income and equity. The aim of the derivatives standard was to highlight these speculative activities and we need to read risk footnotes carefully to assess whether companies are hedging or speculating with derivatives.)

Statement of Cash Flows Reporting and Analysis

The statement of cash flows for **Kimberly-Clark** is shown in Exhibit C.5.

In 2010, K-C generated $2,744 million of operating cash flow, primarily from income (net income plus the depreciation add-back equals $2,756 million). This amount is well in excess of K-C's capital expenditures of $964 million. K-C used excess cash to pay $1,066 million in dividends to shareholders.

Kimberly-Clark offers the following commentary regarding its 2010 operating cash flow:

> Cash provided by operations decreased $737 million primarily due to a lower level of working capital improvements as compared to the prior year, partially offset by decreased pension plan contributions.

Overall, the cash flow picture for Kimberly-Clark is strong: operating cash flows are more than sufficient to cover capital expenditures and acquisitions, leaving excess cash that is being returned to the shareholders in the form of dividends and share repurchases. The strength of its operating cash flows mitigates any concerns we might have regarding its relative lack of liquidity on the balance sheet.

EXHIBIT C.5 Kimberly-Clark Statement of Cash Flows

KIMBERLY-CLARK CORPORATION AND SUBSIDIARIES
Consolidated Cash Flow Statement

Year Ended December 31 (Millions of dollars)	2010	2009	2008
Operating Activities			
Net income	$ 1,943	$ 1,994	$ 1,829
Extraordinary loss, net of income taxes, attributable to Kimberly-Clark Corporation	—	—	8
Depreciation and amortization	813	783	775
Stock-based compensation	52	86	47
Deferred income taxes	(12)	141	151
Net losses on asset dispositions	26	36	51
Equity companies' earnings in excess of dividends paid	(48)	(53)	(34)
Decrease (increase) in operating working capital	24	1,105	(335)
Postretirement benefits	(125)	(609)	(38)
Other	71	(2)	62
Cash provided by operations	2,744	3,481	2,516
Investing Activities			
Capital spending	(964)	(848)	(906)
Acquisitions of businesses, net of cash acquired	—	(458)	(98)
Investments in marketable securities	1	—	(9)
Proceeds from sales of investments	47	40	48
Investments in time deposits	(131)	(270)	(238)
Maturities of time deposits	248	223	314
Proceeds from disposition of property	9	25	28
Other	9	—	14
Cash used for investing	(781)	(1,288)	(847)
Financing Activities			
Cash dividends paid	(1,066)	(986)	(950)
Net decrease in short-term debt	(28)	(312)	(436)
Proceeds from issuance of long-term debt	515	2	551
Repayments of long-term debt	(506)	(278)	(274)
Cash paid on redeemable preferred securities of subsidiary	(54)	(53)	(47)
Proceeds from exercise of stock options	131	165	113
Acquisitions of common stock for the treasury	(803)	(7)	(653)
Shares purchased from noncontrolling interests	—	(293)	—
Other	(48)	(26)	(51)
Cash used for financing	(1,859)	(1,788)	(1,747)
Effect of exchange rate changes on cash and cash equivalents	(26)	29	(31)
Increase (decrease) in cash and cash equivalents	78	434	(109)
Cash and cash equivalents, beginning of year	798	364	473
Cash and cash equivalents, end of year	$ 876	$ 798	$ 364

Independent Audit Opinion

Kimberly-Clark is subject to various audit requirements. Its independent auditor is Deloitte & Touche LLP, which issued the following clean opinion on K-C's 2010 financial statements:

REPORT OF INDEPENDENT REGISTERED PUBLIC ACCOUNTING FIRM

To the Board of Directors and Stockholders of Kimberly-Clark Corporation:

We have audited the accompanying consolidated balance sheets of Kimberly-Clark Corporation and subsidiaries (the "Corporation") as of December 31, 2010 and 2009, and the related consolidated statements of income, stockholders' equity, comprehensive income, and cash flows for each of the three years in the period ended December 31, 2010. Our audits also included the financial statement

continued

continued from prior page

schedule listed in the Index at Item 15. These financial statements and financial statement schedule are the responsibility of the Corporation's management. Our responsibility is to express an opinion on the financial statements and financial statement schedule based on our audits.

We conducted our audits in accordance with the standards of the Public Company Accounting Oversight Board (United States). Those standards require that we plan and perform the audit to obtain reasonable assurance about whether the financial statements are free of material misstatement. An audit includes examining, on a test basis, evidence supporting the amounts and disclosures in the financial statements. An audit also includes assessing the accounting principles used and significant estimates made by management, as well as evaluating the overall financial statement presentation. We believe that our audits provide a reasonable basis for our opinion.

In our opinion, such consolidated financial statements present fairly, in all material respects, the financial position of Kimberly-Clark Corporation and subsidiaries as of December 31, 2010 and 2009, and the results of their operations and their cash flows for each of the three years in the period ended December 31, 2010, in conformity with accounting principles generally accepted in the United States of America. Also, in our opinion, the financial statement schedule, when considered in relation to the basic consolidated financial statements taken as a whole, presents fairly, in all material respects, the information set forth therein.

As discussed in Note 1 to the consolidated financial statements, the Corporation adopted new accounting standards for variable interest entities effective January 1, 2010. The Corporation also adopted new accounting standards for business combinations and noncontrolling interests in consolidated financial statements effective January 1, 2009.

We have also audited, in accordance with the standards of the Public Company Accounting Oversight Board (United States), the Corporation's internal control over financial reporting as of December 31, 2010, based on the criteria established in *Internal Control—Integrated Framework* issued by the Committee of Sponsoring Organizations of the Treadway Commission, and our report dated February 23, 2011, expressed an unqualified opinion on the Corporation's internal control over financial reporting.

/s/ DELOITTE & TOUCHE LLP
Deloitte & Touche LLP
Dallas, Texas
February 23, 2011

Although this report is a routine disclosure, it should not be taken for granted. Exceptions to a clean audit report must be scrutinized. Also, any disagreements between management and the independent auditor must be documented in an SEC filing. If this occurs, it is a "red flag" that must be investigated. Management activities and reports that cannot meet usual audit standards raise serious concerns about integrity and credibility. At a minimum, the riskiness of investments and relationships with such a company markedly increases.

ASSESSING PROFITABILITY AND CREDITWORTHINESS

L02 Assess company profitability and creditworthiness.

This section reports a profitability analysis of Kimberly-Clark. We begin by computing several key measures that are used in the ROE disaggregation, which is the overriding focus of this section. The ROE disaggregation process is defined in Module 4, and a listing of the ratio acronyms and definitions is in the review section at the end of the book.

K-C's 2010 net operating profit after-tax, or NOPAT, is $2,083 million, computed as ($2,773 million + $181 million) − ($788 million + [{$243 million − $20 million} × 37%]). In 2010, K-C's net operating assets, or NOA, total $12,106 million, computed as $19,864 − $876 − $2,206 − $1,909 − $104 − $1,810 − $260 − $369 − $224 ($ millions). For 2009, NOA totals $11,596 million.

ROE Disaggregation

Our first step is to compute the ROE and, then, disaggregate it into its operating (return on net operating assets or RNOA) and nonoperating components. Using the computations in the previous section, the 2010 disaggregation analysis of ROE for Kimberly-Clark follows. (Many of these ratios require computation of averages, such as average assets. If we wanted to compute ratios for years prior to 2010, then we would obtain information from prior 10-Ks to compute the necessary averages for these ratios.)

$$\textbf{ROE} \ = \ \textbf{RNOA} \ + \ \textbf{Nonoperating return}$$
$$32.55\% \ = \ 17.58\% \ + \ 14.97\%$$

where

ROE = $1,843 million /[($5,917 million + $5,406 million)/2]*
RNOA = $2,083 million/[$12,106 million + $11,596 million)/2]

*We use net income and stockholders' equity attributed to K-C shareholders.

RNOA accounts for 54% (17.58%/32.55%) of K-C's ROE. K-C successfully uses its nonoperating activities to increase its 17.58% RNOA to produce a 32.55% ROE.

Disaggregation of RNOA—Margin and Turnover

The next level analysis of ROE focuses on RNOA disaggregation. Kimberly-Clark's net operating profit margin (NOPM) and net operating asset turnover (NOAT) are as follows:

RNOA = NOPAT/Average Net Operating Assets = NOPAT/Sales × Sales/Average Net Operating Assets

	NOPM	NOAT
17.58% =	10.55% ×	1.67 (0.0004 rounding error)

where

NOPM = $2,083 million/$19,746 million
NOAT = $19,746 million/[($12,106 million + $11,596 million)/2]

Kimberly-Clark's RNOA of 17.58% consists of a net operating profit margin of 10.55% and a net operating asset turnover of 1.67 times.

Disaggregation of Margin and Turnover

This section focuses on the disaggregation of profit margin and asset turnover to better understand the drivers of RNOA. Again, understanding the drivers of financial performance (RNOA) is key to predicting future company performance. Our analysis of the drivers of operating profit margin and asset turnover for Kimberly-Clark follows:

Disaggregation of NOPM
Gross profit margin (GPM) ($6,550 mil./$19,746 mil.) 33.2%
Marketing, research and general expense margin [($3,673 mil)/$19,746 mil] 18.6%

Disaggregation of NOAT
Accounts receivable turnover (ART) { $19,746 mil./[($2,534 mil. + $2,634 mil.)/2]} 7.64
Inventory turnover (INVT) {$13,196 mil./[($2,373 mil. + $2,033 mil.)/2]} 5.99
PPE turnover (PPET) { $19,746 mil./[($8,356 mil. + $8,033 mil.)/2]} 2.41
Accounts payable turnover (APT) {$13,196 mil./[($2,206 mil. + $1,920 mil.)/2]} 6.40

Related turnover measures
Average collection period [$2,534 mil./($19,746 mil./365)] . . . . 46.84 days
Average inventory days outstanding [$2,373 mil./($13,196 mil./365)] . . . . 65.64 days
Average payable days outstanding [$2,206 mil./($13,196 mil./365)] . . . . 61.02 days

First, let's look at the disaggregation of NOPM. K-C reports a decrease in its gross profit margin from 33.6% in 2009 to 33.2% in 2010. As K-C points out in the excerpt from its MD&A that we reproduce on page C-4, the company operates in a very competitive market that makes gross profit margins difficult to maintain.

In its commentary, K-C explains that it might increase its advertising budget in the face of shrinking gross profit margins. That is, in fact, what happened in 2010. As gross profit margins decreased from 33.6% to 33.2%, K-C increased marketing, research and general expenses as a percentage of sales from 18.3% to 18.6%. Part of this increase was due to higher advertising expense, which increased by $139 million from 2.8% of sales to 3.5% of sales.

Next, we consider the disaggregation of NOAT. K-C's receivables turnover rate of 7.64 times corresponds to an average collection period of 46.8 days, which is reasonable considering normal credit terms. However, the more important issue here is asset productivity (turnover) instead of credit quality. This is because most of K-C's sales are to large retailers; for example, 13% of Kimberly-Clark's sales are to Wal-Mart.

Inventories turn over 5.99 times a year, resulting in an average inventory days outstanding of 65.6 days in 2010. Inventories are an important (and large) asset for companies like Kimberly-Clark. Improved turnover is always a goal so long as the company maintains sufficient inventories to meet market demand.

K-C's Property, plant, and equipment are turning over 2.41 times a year, which is about average for publicly traded companies. The issue with respect to PPET is throughput, and K-C does not discuss this aspect of its business in its financial filings.

K-C's trade accounts payable turnover is 6.40, resulting in an average payable days outstanding of 61.0 days. Since payables represent a low cost source of financing, we would prefer to see its days payable lengthened so long as K-C is not endangering its relationships with suppliers.

Credit Analysis

Credit analysis is an important part of a complete company analysis. Following is a selected set of measures for 2010 that can help us gauge the relative credit standing of Kimberly-Clark ($ millions):

Current ratio ($6,328/$5,338) 1.19
Quick ratio ([$876 + $2,472]/$5,338) 0.63
Total liabilities/Equity* ([$19,864 − $6,202]/$6,202) 2.20
Long-term debt/Equity ($5,120/$6,202) 0.83
Earnings before interest and taxes/Interest expense ($2,773/$243) 11.41
Net operating cash flows/Total liabilities ($2,744/[$19,864 − $6,202]) 0.20

*Includes noncontrolling interest as equity as we analyze the company from the perspective of all equity holders; if we prefer to examine the company from the perspective of the company's equity holders only, then we would exclude noncontrolling interest.

K-C's current and quick ratios are not particularly high, and both have decreased slightly over the past two years (not shown here). These ratios do not imply any excess liquidity, and probably do not suggest any room for a further decrease in liquidity.

K-C's financial leverage, as reflected in both the liability-to-equity and long-term-debt-to-equity ratios, is slightly above the median for all publicly traded companies. Normally, this is cause for some concern. However, Kimberly-Clark has strong operating and free cash flows that mitigate this concern.

K-C's times interest earned ratio of 11.41 is healthy, indicating a sufficient buffer to protect creditors if earnings decline. It also has relatively little off-balance-sheet exposure. Thus, we do not have any serious concerns about K-C's ability to repay its maturing debt obligations.

Summarizing Profitability and Creditworthiness

An increasingly competitive environment has diminished Kimberly-Clark's gross profit margin. Operating expense reductions have not offset this decline and its NOPAT has declined slightly as a result. Its level of net operating asset turnover is acceptable, although not stellar. K-C does not provide sufficient information for us to further assess the throughput performance of its operating assets. Finally, its leverage, although higher than average, is not of great concern given K-C's strong cash flows.

FORECASTING FINANCIAL STATEMENT NUMBERS

The valuation of K-C's common stock requires forecasts of NOPAT and NOA over a forecast horizon period and a forecast terminal period. Our approach is to project individual income statement and balance sheet items using the methodology we discuss in Module 11. K-C presented its 4Q results and 2011 guidance to analysts on January 25, 2011, and provided the following slide relative to its expectations for 2011 (posted on the K-C investor relations Website).

L03 Forecast financial statements.

> ### *Planning Assumptions*
>
> - **Sales increase 3 to 4 percent**
>   - Organic growth 2 to 3 percent: volume growth 1 to 2 percent, combination of net selling prices and product mix +1 percent
>   - Volume estimate includes combined 1 point negative impact from continued declines in Venezuela and impact of pulp and tissue restructuring
>   - Currency benefit approximately 1 percent
> - **Adjusted operating profit growth 3 to 5 percent**
>   - Adjusted gross profit expected to grow at a faster rate
>   - Strategic marketing increase faster than sales growth
> - **FORCE cost savings $200 to $250 million**

We use the mid-point of K-C's 3.5% sales growth prediction in our forecast of the company's sales for 2011. Additional slides in its presentation provide the following forecast assumptions:

1. The effective tax rate is likely to increase to 30%–32%. We use 31% in our forecast.
2. Capital spending (CAPEX) is expected to be $950–$1,050 million. In 2010, the CAPEX was 4.9% of sales. Using that percentage and expected sales growth of 3.5%, our forecast of CAPEX is $1,001 million, computed as 2010 sales of $19,746 million × 1.035 × 4.9%. Our estimate is within the range provided by K-C.
3. Share repurchases are expected to be $1,500 million per year and we use that amount in our forecast.
4. Dividends are expected to increase by 6%, resulting in forecasted dividends of $1,130 million, computed as 2010 dividends of $1,066 million × 1.06.

We assume that expenses retain their 2010 relation to sales and that all assets and liabilities, other than CAPEX referenced above, retain their relations to sales as well.

Our initial forecast results in total assets of $20,240 million and total liabilities and equity of $19,165 million. Since K-C does not report marketable securities on its balance sheet, we assume that the difference is made up with additional financing in the amount of $1,075 million. K-C reports that it issued $250 million of 3.625% Notes in the 4Q of 2010. We assume that the $1,075 million in additional financing is drawn on evenly over the year and that K-C continues to borrow at 3.625%. This means that interest expense is expected to increase by $19 million ([$1,075 million / 2] × 3.625%), from $243 million to $262 million. The resulting forecasts of the K-C income statement and balance sheet for 2011, reflecting these assumptions, are in Exhibit C.6.

The forecasted statement of cash flows is in Exhibit C.7. This forecasted statement utilizes the forecasted income statement and comparative balance sheets as presented in Exhibit C.6 and is prepared as explained in Module 11.

We forecast that K-C will generate $2,923 million in cash from operating activities in 2011, a 7% increase from the $2,744 million reported in 2010. Given projected CAPEX of $1,001 million, divi-

EXHIBIT C.6 Forecasts of Income Statement and Balance Sheet of Kimberly-Clark

Consolidated Income Statement ($ millions)	2010	Forecast Assumptions	2011 Est.
Net sales...	$19,746	19,746 × 1.035	$20,437
Cost of products sold................................	13,196	20,437 × 66.8%	13,652
Gross profit..	6,550	Subtotal	6,785
Marketing, research and general expenses............	3,673	20,437 × 18.6%	3,801
Other (income) and expense, net....................	104	20,437 × 0.5%	102
Operating profit	2,773	Subtotal	2,882
Interest income.....................................	20	no change	20
Interest expense....................................	(243)	(243) − 19	(262)
Income before income taxes, equity interests and extraordinary loss..........	2,550	Subtotal	2,640
Provision for income taxes.........................	(788)	2,640 × 31.0%	(818)
Income before equity interests and extraordinary loss	1,762	Subtotal	1,822
Share of net income of equity companies	181	no change	181
Net income...	1,943	Subtotal	2,003
Net income attributable to noncontrolling interests......	(100)	no change	(100)
Net income attributable to Kimberly-Clark Corporation....................	$ 1,843	Subtotal	$ 1,903

Consolidated Balance Sheet ($ millions)	2010	Forecast Assumptions	2011 Est.
Assets			
Cash and cash equivalents	$ 876	20,437 × 4.4%	$ 899
Accounts receivable, net	2,472	20,437 × 12.5%	2,555
Note receivable	218	no change	218
Inventories	2,373	20,437 × 12.0%	2,452
Deferred income taxes.............................	187	20,437 × 0.9%	184
Other current assets...............................	202	20,437 × 1.0%	204
Total current assets	6,328	Subtotal	6,512
Property, plant and equipment, net.................	8,356	8,356 + 1,001 − 819	8,538
Investments in equity companies...................	374	no change	374
Goodwill	3,403	no change	3,403
Other intangible assets............................	287	287 − 23	264
Long-term notes receivable	393	no change	393
Other assets.......................................	723	20,437 × 3.7%	756
Total assets	$19,864	Subtotal	$20,240
Liabilities and Stockholders' Equity			
New financing......................................	$ 0	plug	$ 1,075
Debt payable within one year.......................	344	from debt footnote	427
Redeemable preferred securities of subsidiary	506	no change	506
Trade accounts payable............................	2,206	20,437 × 11.2%	2,289
Accrued expenses	1,909	20,437 × 9.7%	1,982
Accrued income taxes	104	818 × 13.2%	108
Dividends payable	269	1,130 × 25.2%	285
Total current liabilities	5,338	Subtotal	6,672
Long-term debt	5,120	5,120 − 427	4,693
Noncurrent employee benefits......................	1,810	20,437 × 9.2%	1,880
Long-term income taxes payable...................	260	20,437 × 1.3%	266
Deferred income taxes.............................	369	20,437 × 1.9%	388
Other liabilities....................................	224	20,437 × 1.1%	225
Redeemable preferred and common securities of subsidiaries..............	541	no change	541
Stockholders' equity			
Preferred stock, no par value, authorized 20.0 million shares, none issued	0	no change	0
Common stock, $1.25 par value, authorized 1.2 billion shares; issued 478.6 million shares at December 31, 2010 and 2009....................	598	no change	598
Additional paid-in capital	425	no change	425
Common stock held in treasury, at cost: 71.7 million and 61.6 million shares at December 31, 2010 and 2009.................	(4,726)	(4,726) − 1,500	(6,226)
Accumulated other comprehensive income (loss)	(1,466)	no change	(1,466)
Retained earnings	11,086	11,086 + 1,903 − 1,130	11,859
Total Kimberly-Clark Corporation stockholders' equity....................	5,917	Subtotal	5,190
Noncontrolling interests	285	285 + 100	385
Total stockholders' equity	6,202	Subtotal	5,575
Liabilities and stockholders' equity, total............	$19,864	Subtotal	$20,240

EXHIBIT C.7 Forecast of Statement of Cash Flows for Kimberly-Clark

$ millions	Forecast Assumptions	2011 Est.
Operating activities		
Net income including noncontrolling interests...........	via forecasted income statement	$2,003
Add: Depreciation................................	8,356 × 9.8%	819
Add: Amortization................................	287 × 8.1%	23
Accounts receivable.............................	2,472 − 2,555	(83)
Inventories	2,373 − 2,452	(79)
Deferred income taxes	187 − 184	3
Other current assets............................	202 − 204	(2)
Other long-term assets..........................	723 − 756	(33)
Accounts payable...............................	2,289 − 2,206	83
Accrued expenses	1,982 − 1,909	73
Accrued income taxes	108 − 104	4
Dividends payable	285 − 269	16
Noncurrent employee benefits	1,880 − 1,810	70
Long-term income taxes payable..................	266 − 260	6
Deferred income taxes	388 − 369	19
Other liabilities	225 − 224	1
Net cash from operating activities	subtotal	2,923
Investing activities		
Capital expenditures	20,437 × 4.9%	(1,001)
Net cash from investing activities	subtotal	(1,001)
Financing activities		
Dividends......................................	1,066 × 1.06	(1,130)
Stock purchase	company guidance	(1,500)
Payments of long-term debt	prior year current maturities of LTD	(344)
New financing..................................	plug	1,075
Net cash from financing activities	subtotal	(1,899)
Net change in cash..............................	subtotal	23
Beginning cash.................................	from balance sheet	876
Ending cash	subtotal	$ 899

dends of $1,130 million, and stock repurchases of $1,500 million, we forecast that K-C will require external financing of $1,075 million. The forecasted year-end cash balance of $899 million is equal to 4.4% of estimated sales, the same relation to sales that the company reported in 2010.

VALUING EQUITY SECURITIES

L04 Describe and illustrate the valuation of firm equity and stock.

This section estimates the values of Kimberly-Clark's equity and common stock per share.

Multiyear Forecasting

For valuation purposes we must forecast the financial statements for more than one year ahead. Exhibits C.8A and C.8B, respectively, show the 2010 reported statements and the results of forecasting the income statement and the balance sheet for four years ahead. The methods used in this forecasting process follow those described in the module on forecasting.

EXHIBIT C.8A Four Year Ahead Forecasts of Income Statement of Kimberly-Clark

Consolidated Income Statement ($ millions)	2010	2011E	2012E	2013E	2014E
Net sales.	$19,746	$20,437	$21,152	$21,892	$22,658
Cost of products sold.	13,196	13,652	14,130	14,624	15,136
Gross profit.	6,550	6,785	7,022	7,268	7,522
Marketing, research and general expenses	3,673	3,801	3,934	4,072	4,214
Other (income) and expense, net.	104	102	106	109	113
Operating profit	2,773	2,882	2,982	3,087	3,195
Interest income.	20	20	20	20	20
Interest expense.	(243)	(262)	(281)	(300)	(319)
Income before income taxes, equity interests and extraordinary loss	2,550	2,640	2,721	2,807	2,896
Provision for income taxes.	(788)	(818)	(844)	(870)	(898)
Income before equity interests and extraordinary loss	1,762	1,822	1,877	1,937	1,998
Share of net income of equity companies	181	181	181	181	181
Net income.	1,943	2,003	2,058	2,118	2,179
Net income attributable to noncontrolling interests.	(100)	(100)	(100)	(100)	(100)
Net income attributable to Kimberly-Clark Corporation.	$ 1,843	$ 1,903	$ 1,958	$ 2,018	$ 2,079
NOPAT.	$ 2,083	$ 2,155	$ 2,222	$ 2,294	$ 2,367

EXHIBIT C.8B Four Year Ahead Forecasts of Balance Sheet of Kimberly-Clark

Consolidated Balance Sheet ($ millions)	2010	2011E	2012E	2013E	2014E
Assets					
Cash and cash equivalents	$ 876	$ 899	$ 931	$ 963	$ 997
Accounts receivable, net	2,472	2,555	2,644	2,737	2,832
Note receivable	218	218	218	218	218
Inventories	2,373	2,452	2,538	2,627	2,719
Deferred income taxes	187	184	190	197	204
Other current assets	202	204	212	219	227
Total current assets	6,328	6,512	6,733	6,961	7,197
Property, plant and equipment, net	8,356	8,538	8,737	8,954	9,187
Investments in equity companies	374	374	374	374	374
Goodwill	3,403	3,403	3,403	3,403	3,403
Other intangible assets	287	264	241	218	195
Long-term notes receivable	393	393	393	393	393
Other assets	723	756	783	810	838
Total assets	$19,864	$20,240	$20,664	$21,113	$21,587
Liabilities and Stockholders' Equity					
New financing	$ 0	$ 1,075	$ 2,299	$ 3,673	$ 5,043
Debt payable within one year	344	427	550	516	355
Redeemable preferred securities of subsidiary	506	506	506	506	506
Trade accounts payable	2,206	2,289	2,369	2,452	2,538
Accrued expenses	1,909	1,982	2,052	2,124	2,198
Accrued income taxes	104	108	111	115	119
Dividends payable	269	285	302	320	339
Total current liabilities	5,338	6,672	8,189	9,706	11,098
Long-term debt	5,120	4,693	4,143	3,627	3,272
Noncurrent employee benefits	1,810	1,880	1,946	2,014	2,085
Long-term income taxes payable	260	266	275	285	295
Deferred income taxes	369	388	402	416	431
Other liabilities	224	225	233	241	249
Redeemable preferred and common securities of subsidiaries	541	541	541	541	541
Stockholders' equity					
Preferred stock, no par value, authorized 20.0 million shares,					
none issued	0	0	0	0	0
Common stock, $1.25 par value, authorized 1.2 billion shares;					
issued 478.6 million shares at December 31, 2010 and 2009	598	598	598	598	598
Additional paid-in capital	425	425	425	425	425
Common stock held in treasury, at cost: 71.7 million and					
61.6 million shares at December 31, 2010 and 2009	(4,726)	(6,226)	(7,726)	(9,226)	(10,726)
Accumulated other comprehensive income (loss)	(1,466)	(1,466)	(1,466)	(1,466)	(1,466)
Retained earnings	11,086	11,859	12,619	13,367	14,100
Total Kimberly-Clark Corporation stockholders' equity	5,917	5,190	4,450	3,698	2,931
Noncontrolling interests	285	385	485	585	685
Total stockholders' equity	6,202	5,575	4,935	4,283	3,616
Liabilities and stockholders' equity, total	$19,864	$20,240	$20,664	$21,113	$21,587
NOA	$12,106	$12,203	$12,345	$12,503	$12,675

Discounted Cash Flow Valuation

Exhibit C.9 shows the discounted cash (DCF) model results. In addition to the forecasted NOPAT and NOA from Exhibits C.8A and C.8B, these results use a discount (WACC) rate of 5%, shares outstanding of 406.9 million, and net nonoperating obligations (NNO) of $6,989 million. For the terminal year, we use a 1% long-term growth rate and estimate NOPAT and NOA using the NOPM and NOAT ratios from 2014 as we expained in the parsimonious forecasting method section of Module 11 as follows ($ millions): sales is $22,885 ($22,658 × 1.01), NOPAT is $2,391 ($22,885 × 10.45%, where 10.45% is from $2,367 ÷ $22,658), and NOA is $12,785 ($22,885 ÷ 1.79, where 1.79 is from $22,658/$12,675).

EXHIBIT C.9 Kimberly-Clark Discounted Cash Flow (DCF) Valuation

(In millions, except per share values and discount factors)	Reported 2010	2011	2012	2013	2014	Terminal Year
NOPAT		$2,155	$2,222	$2,294	$2,367	$2,391
Change NOA		97	142	158	172	110
FCFF (NOPAT − Increase in NOA)		2,058	2,080	2,136	2,195	2,281
Discount factor $[1/(1+r_w)^t]$		0.95238	0.90703	0.86384	0.82270	
Present value of horizon FCFF		1,960	1,887	1,845	1,806	
Cum present value of horizon FCFF	$ 7,498					
Present value of terminal FCFF	46,914[a]					
Total firm value	54,412					
Less (plus) NNO	6,989					
Firm equity value	47,423					
Shares outstanding	406.9					
Stock value per share	$116.55					

[a] Computed as $\dfrac{\left(\dfrac{\$2,281\text{ million}}{0.05-0.01}\right)}{(1.05)^4}$

Residual Operating Income Valuation

Exhibit C.10 reports estimates of the values of Kimberly-Clark's equity and common stock per share using the residual operating income (ROPI) model. As with the DCF valuation, we use a discount (WACC) rate of 5%, shares outstanding of 406.9 million, and net nonoperating obligations (NNO) of $6,989 million; for the terminal year, we use a 1% long-term growth rate and estimate the following ($ millions): sales of $22,885 ($22,658 × 1.01), NOPAT of $2,391 ($22,885 × 10.45%, where 10.45% is from $2,367/$22,658), and NOA of $12,785 ($22,885/1.79, where 1.79 is from $22,658/$12,675).

EXHIBIT C.10 Kimberly-Clark Residual Operating Income (ROPI) Valuation

(In millions, except per share values and discount factors)	Reported 2010	2011	2012	2013	2014	Terminal Year
NOPAT		$ 2,155	$ 2,222	$ 2,294	$ 2,367	$ 2,391
NOA	$12,106	12,203	12,345	12,503	12,675	12,785
ROPI (NOPAT − [NOA_Beg × r_w])		1,550	1,612	1,677	1,742	1,757
Discount factor $[1/(1+r_w)^t]$		0.95238	0.90703	0.86384	0.82270	
Present value of horizon ROPI		1,476	1,462	1,448	1,433	
Cum present value of horizon ROPI	5,819					
Present value of terminal ROPI	36,137[a]					
Total firm value	54,062					
Less NNO	6,989					
Firm equity value	47,073					
Shares outstanding	406.9					
Stock value per share	$115.69					

($0.86 difference from DCF due to rounding terminal period NOPM and NOAT)

[a] Computed as $\dfrac{\left(\dfrac{\$1,757\text{ million}}{0.05-0.01}\right)}{(1.05)^4}$

Sensitivity Analysis of Valuation Parameters

We estimate Kimberly-Clark's equity value at $47,073 million as of December 2010, which implies a per share value estimate of $115.69. As expected, equity value estimates are identical (minor difference due to rounding) for both models (because K-C is assumed to be in a steady state, that is, NOPAT and NOA growing at the same rate and, therefore, RNOA is constant).

Our stock price estimate uses only one set of assumptions and derives only one stock price. We illustrate the sensitivity of our stock price estimate to changes in input assumptions for WACC and terminal growth rate in the following table. We can expand this sensitivity analysis to any assumption or estimate we use in our financial statement adjusting, forecasting, and valuing process.

		Terminal Growth Rate				
		0.0%	0.5%	1.0%	1.5%	2.0%
	6.0%	77.62	82.78	88.97	96.53	105.98
W	5.5%	86.41	92.91	100.84	110.76	123.51
A C C	5.0%	96.97	105.28	**115.69**	129.05	146.88
	4.5%	109.87	120.76	134.77	153.45	179.60
	4.0%	126.00	140.67	160.22	187.60	228.66

Assessment of the Valuation Estimate

The closing stock price on December 31, 2010, for Kimberly-Clark (KMB) was $63.04 per share. Our model's estimates, therefore, suggest that K-C stock is undervalued as of that date. As it turns out, this valuation proved prophetic as its stock price increased to the low $70s in the continuing bear market subsequent to that date as shown in the following graph:

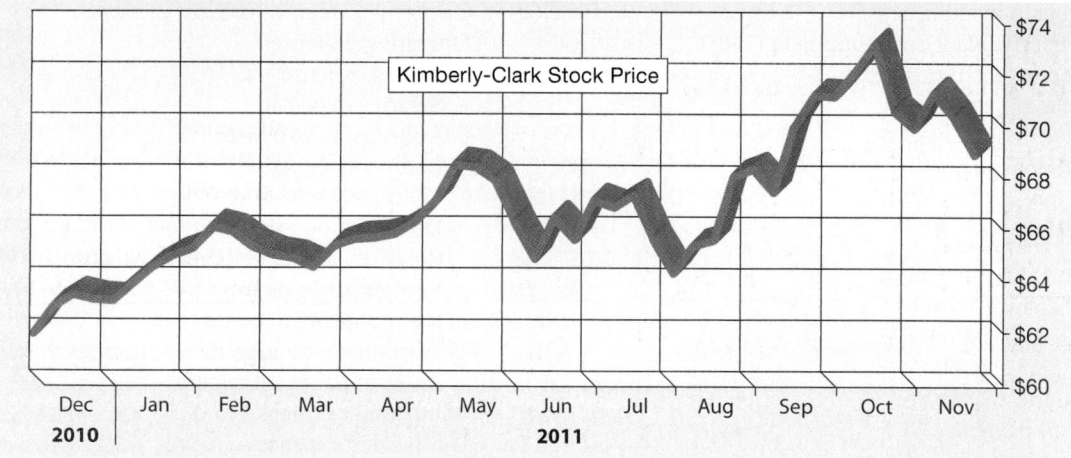

Summary Observations

Overall, this appendix presents a financial accounting analysis and interpretation of Kimberly-Clark's performance and position. It illustrates many of the key financial reporting topics covered in the book. We review the company's financial statements and notes, forecast key accounts, and conclude with estimates of K-C's equity value.

The Kimberly-Clark case provides an opportunity for us to apply many of the procedures conveyed in the book in a comprehensive manner. With analyses of additional companies, we become more comfortable with, and knowledgeable of, variations in financial reporting, which enhances our analysis and business decision-making skills. Our analysis of a company must go beyond the accounting numbers to include competitor and economic factors, and we must appreciate that estimation and judgment are key ingredients in financial accounting.

Chart of Accounts with Acronyms

Assets

Cash	Cash
MS	Marketable securities
EMI	Equity method investments
AR	Accounts receivable
AU	Allowance for uncollectible accounts
INV	Inventory (or Inventories)
SUP	Supplies
PPD	Prepaid expenses
PPDA	Prepaid advertising
PPRNT	Prepaid rent
PPI	Prepaid insurance
PPE	Property, plant and equipment (PPE)
AD	Accumulated depreciation
INT	Intangible assets
DTA	Deferred tax assets
OA	Other assets

Liabilities

NP	Notes payable
AP	Accounts payable
ACC	Accrued expenses
WP	Wages payable
SP	Salaries payable
RNTP	Rent payable
RSL	Restructuring liability
UP	Utilities payable
TP	Taxes payable
WRP	Warranty payable
IP	Interest payable
CMLTD	Current maturities of long-term debt
UR	Unearned (or deferred) revenues
LTD	Long-term debt
CLO	Capital lease obligations
DTL	Deferred tax liabilities

Equity

EC	Earned capital
CS	Common stock
APIC	Additional paid-in capital
RE	Retained earnings
DIV	Dividends
TS	Treasury stock
AOCI	Accumulated other comprehensive income
DC	Deferred compensation expense

Revenues and Expenses

Sales	Sales
REV	Revenues
COGS	Cost of goods sold (or Cost of sales)
OE	Operating expenses
WE	Wages expense
SE	Salaries expense
AE	Advertising expense
BDE	Bad debts expense
UTE	Utilities expense
DE	Depreciation expense
RDE	Research and development expense
RNTE	Rent expense
RSE	Restructuring expense
WRE	Warranty expense
AIE	Asset impairment expense
INSE	Insurance expense
SUPE	Supplies expense
GN (LS)	Gain (loss)–operating
TE	Tax expense
ONI (E)	Other nonoperating income (expense)
IE	Interest expense
UG (UL)	Unrealized gain (loss)
DI	Dividend income (or revenue)
EI	Equity income (or revenue)
GN (LS)	Gain (loss)–nonoperating

Closing Account

IS	Income summary

Glossary

A

absorption costing an approach to product costing that treats both variable and fixed manufacturing costs as product costs.

accelerated cost recovery system (ACRS, MACRS) A system of accelerated depreciation for tax purposes introduced in 1981 (ACRS) and modified starting in 1987 (MACRS); it prescribes depreciation rates by asset classification for assets acquired after 1980

accelerated depreciation method Any depreciation method under which the amounts of depreciation expense taken in the early years of an asset's life are larger than the amounts expensed in the later years; includes the double-declining balance method

access control matrix A computerized file that lists the type of access that each computer user is entitled to have to each file and program in the computer system

account A record of the additions, deductions, and balances of individual assets, liabilities, equity, revenues, and expenses

accounting The process of measuring the economic activity of an entity in money terms and communicating the results to interested parties; the purpose is to provide financial information that is useful in making economic decisions

accounting adjustments (adjusting entries) Entries made at the end of an accounting period under accrual accounting to ensure the proper recording of expenses incurred and revenues earned for the period

accounting cycle A series of basic steps followed to process accounting information during a fiscal year

accounting entity An economic unit that has identifiable boundaries and that is the focus for the accumulation and reporting of financial information

accounting equation An expression of the equivalency of the economic resources and the claims upon those resources of a specific entity; often stated as Assets = Liabilities + Owners' Equity

accounting period The time period, typically one year (or quarter), for which periodic accounting reports are prepared

accounting rate of return the average annual increase in net income that results from acceptance of a capital expenditure proposal divided by either the initial investment or the average investment in the project.

accounting system The structured collection of policies, procedures, equipment, files, and records that a company uses to collect, record, classify, process, store, report, and interpret financial data

accounts payable turnover The ratio obtained by dividing cost of goods sold by average accounts payable

accounts receivable A current asset that is created by a sale on a credit basis; it represents the amount owed the company by the customer

accounts receivable aging method A procedure that uses an aging schedule to determine the year-end balance needed in the allowance for uncollectible accounts

accounts receivable turnover Annual net sales divided by average accounts receivable (net)

accrual accounting Accounting procedures whereby revenues are recorded when they are earned and realized and expenses are recorded in the period in which they help to generate revenues

accruals Adjustments that reflect revenues earned but not received or recorded and expenses incurred but not paid or recorded

accrued expense An expense incurred but not yet paid; recognized with an accounting adjustment

accrued revenue Revenue earned but not yet billed or received; recognized with an accounting adjustment (adjusting entry)

accumulated depreciation The sum of all depreciation expense recorded to date; it is subtracted from the cost of the asset in order to derive the asset's net book value

accumulated other comprehensive income (AOCI) current accumulation of all prior other comprehensive income; *see* definition for other comprehensive income

acid test ratio more specific than the current ratio as a test of short-term solvency, the acid test ratio (also known as the quick ratio) measures the availability of cash and other current monetary assets that can be quickly generated into cash to pay current liabilities. The general equation for the acid test ratio is: (Cash + Marketable securities + Current receivables)/Current liabilities.

activities list *see* operations list.

activity a unit of work.

activity cost drivers specific units of work (activities) performed to serve customer needs that consume costly resources.

activity costing the determination of the cost of specific activities performed to fill customer needs.

activity dictionary a standardized list of processes and related activities.

activity-based budgeting an approach to budgeting that uses an activity cost hierarchy to budget physical inputs and costs as a function of planned activity. It is mechanically similar to the output/input approach to budgeting where physical inputs and costs are budgeted as a function of planned activity.

activity-based costing (ABC) used to develop cost information by determining the cost of activities and tracing their costs to cost objectives on the basis of the cost objective's utilization of units of activity.

activity-based management (ABM) the identification and selection of activities to maximize the value of the activities while minimizing their cost from the perspective of the final consumer.

adjusted trial balance A list of general ledger accounts and their balances taken after accounting adjustments have been made

adjusting The process of adjusting the historical financial statements prior to the projection of future results; also called recasting and reformulating

adjusting entries Entries made at the end of an accounting period under accrual accounting to ensure the proper matching of expenses incurred with revenues earned for the period

aging schedule An analysis that shows how long customers' accounts receivable balances have remained unpaid

allowance for uncollectible accounts A contra asset account with a normal credit balance shown on the balance sheet as a deduction from accounts receivable to reflect the expected realizable amount of accounts receivable

allowance method An accounting procedure whereby the amount of uncollectible accounts expense is estimated and recorded in the period in which the related credit sales occur

Altman's Z-score A predictor of potential bankruptcy based on multiple ratios

amortization The periodic writing off of an account balance to expense; similar to depreciation and usually refers to the periodic writing off of an intangible asset

annuity a series of equal cash flows received or paid over equal intervals of time.

appraisal costs quality costs incurred to identify nonconforming products or services before they are delivered to customers.

articles of incorporation A document prepared by persons organizing a corporation in the United States that sets forth the structure and purpose of the corporation and specifics regarding the stock to be issued

articulation The linkage of financial statements within and across time

assembly efficiency variance the difference between the standard cost of actual assembly inputs and the flexible budget cost for assembly.

assembly rate variance the difference between the actual cost and the standard cost of actual assembly inputs.

asset turnover a measure of performance, the asset turnover ratio measures the firm's ability to use its assets to generate sales. The general equation for asset turnover is: Sales/Average total assets.

asset turnover Net income divided by average total assets

asset write-downs Adjustment of carrying value of assets down to their current fair value

assets The economic resources of an entity that are owned or controlled will provide future benefits and can be reliably measured

audit An examination of a company's financial statements by a firm of independent certified public accountants

audit report A report issued by independent auditors that includes the final version of the financial statements, accompanying notes, and the auditor's opinion on the financial statements

authorized stock The maximum number of shares in a class of stock that a corporation may issue

automatic identification systems (AIS) the use of bar coding of products and production processes that allows inventory and production information to be entered into a computer without writing or keying.

available-for-sale securities Investments in securities that management intends to hold for capital gains and dividend income; although it may sell them if the price is right

average cash conversion cycle Average collection period + average inventory days outstanding − average payable days outstanding

average cash cycle Average collection period + modified average inventory days outstanding + modified average payable days outstanding

average collection period Determined by dividing accounts receivable by average daily sales, sometimes referred to as days sales outstanding or DSO

average inventory days outstanding (AIDO) An indication of how long, on average, inventories are on the shelves, computed as inventory divided by average daily cost of goods sold

B

backflush costing an inventory accounting system used in conjunction with JIT in which costs are assigned initially to cost of goods sold. At the end of the period, costs are backed out of cost of goods sold and assigned to appropriate inventory accounts for any inventories that may exist.

balance sheet A financial statement showing an entity's assets, liabilities, and stockholders' equity at a specific date; sometimes called a statement of financial position

balance sheet A financial statement showing an entity's assets, liabilities, and owners' equity at a specific date; sometimes called a statement of financial position

balanced scorecard a performance measurement system that includes financial and operational measures which are related to the organizational goals. The basic premise is to establish a set of indicators that can be used to monitor performance progress and then compare the goals that are established with the results.

batch level activity an activity performed for each batch of product produced.

bearer One of the terms that may be used to designate the payee on a promissory note; means the note is payable to whoever holds the note

benchmarking a systematic approach to identifying the best practices to help an organization take action to improve performance.

bill of materials a document that specifies the kinds and quantities of raw materials required to produce one unit of product.

bond A long-term debt instrument that promises to pay interest periodically and a principal amount at maturity, usually issued by the borrower to a group of lenders; bonds may incorporate a wide variety of provisions relating to security for the debt involved, methods of paying the periodic interest, retirement provisions, and conversion options

book value The dollar amount carried in the accounts for a particular item; the book value of a depreciable asset is cost less accumulated depreciation; the *book value of an entity* is assets less liabilities

book value per share The dollar amount of net assets represented by one share of stock; computed by dividing the amount of stockholders' equity associated with a class of stock by the outstanding shares of that class of stock

borrows at a discount When the face amount of the note is reduced by a calculated cash discount to determine the cash proceeds

bottom-up budget a budget where managers at all levels—and in some cases even non-managers—become involved in the budget preparation.

break-even point the unit or dollar sales volume where total revenues equal total costs.

budget a formal plan of action expressed in monetary terms.

budget committee a committee responsible for super-vising budget preparation. It serves as a review board for evaluating requests for discretionary cost items and new projects.

budget office an organizational unit responsible for the preparation, distribution, and processing of forms used in gathering budget data. It handles most of the work of actually formulating the budget schedules and reports.

budgetary slack occurs when managers intentionally understate revenues or overstate expenses in order to produce favorable variances for the department.

budgeted financial statements hypothetical statements that reflect the "as if" effects of the budgeted activities on the actual financial position of the organization. They reflect what the results of operations will be if all the predictions in the budget are correct.

budgeting projecting the operations of an organization and their financial impact on the future.

C

calendar year A fiscal year that ends on December 31

call provision A bond feature that allows the borrower to retire (call in) the bonds after a stated date

capacity costs *see* committed fixed costs.

capital budgeting a process that involves the identification of potentially desirable projects for capital expenditures, the subsequent evaluation of capital expenditure proposals, and the selection of proposals that meet certain criteria.

capital expenditures Expenditures that increase the book value of long-term assets; sometimes abbreviated as CAPEX

capital expenditures investments of significant financial resources in projects to develop or introduce new products or services, to expand current production or service capacity, or to change current production or service facilities.

capital lease A lease that transfers to the lessee substantially all of the benefits and risks related to ownership of the property; the lessee records the leased property as an asset and establishes a liability for the lease obligation

capital markets Financing sources, which are formalized when companies issue securities that are traded on organized exchanges; they are informal when companies are funded by private sources

capitalization The recording of a cost as an asset on the balance sheet rather than as an expense on the income statement; these costs are transferred to expense as the asset is used up

capitalization of interest A process that adds interest to an asset's initial cost if a period of time is required to prepare the asset for use

cash An asset category representing the amount of a firm's available cash and funds on deposit at a bank in checking accounts and savings accounts

cash (operating) conversion cycle The period of time (typically measured in days) from when cash is invested in inventories until inventory is sold and receivables are collected

cash and cash equivalents The sum of cash plus short-term, highly liquid investments such as treasury bills and money market funds; includes marketable securities maturing within 90 days of the financial statement date

cash budget summarizes all cash receipts and disbursements expected to occur during the budget period.

cash discount An amount that a purchaser of merchandise may deduct from the purchase price for paying within the discount period

cash equivalents short-term, highly liquid investments that are readily convertible into known amounts of cash and so near their maturity date that they present insignificant risk of change in value from interest or money market rate changes; generally, only investments with original maturities of three months or less are considered as possible cash equivalents.

cash-basis accounting Accounting procedures whereby revenues are recorded when cash is received from operating activities and expenses are recorded when cash payments related to operating activities are made

centralization when top management controls the major functions of an organization (such as manufacturing, sales, accounting, computer operations, marketing, research and development, and management control).

certificate of deposit (CD) An investment security available at financial institutions generally offering a fixed rate of return for a specified period of time

chained target costing bringing in suppliers as part of the coordination process to attain a competitively priced product that is delivered to the customer in a timely manner.

change in accounting estimate Modification to a previous estimate of an uncertain future event, such as the useful life of a depreciable asset, uncollectible accounts receivable, and warranty expenses; applied currently and prospectively only

changes in accounting principles Cumulative income or loss from changes in accounting methods (such as depreciation or inventory costing methods)

chart of accounts A list of all the general ledger account titles and their numerical code

clean surplus accounting Income that explains successive equity balances

closing procedures A step in the accounting cycle in which the balances of all temporary accounts are transferred to the retained earnings account, leaving the temporary accounts with zero balances

coefficient of determination (R2) a measure of the percent of variation in the dependent variable that is explained by variations in the independent variable when the least-squares estimation equation is used.

commitments A contractual arrangement by which both parties to the contract still have acts to perform

committed fixed costs (capacity costs) costs required to maintain the current service or production capacity or to fill a previous legal commitment.

common cost a cost incurred for the benefit of two or more cost objectives—an indirect cost.

common segment costs costs related to more than one segment and not directly traceable to a particular segment. These costs are referred to as common costs because they are incurred at one level for the benefit of two or more segments at a lower level.

common size statement a financial statement that has had all its accounts converted into percentages. As such, a common size statement is very useful for detecting items that are out of line, that deviate from some present amount, or that may be indications of other problems.

common stock The basic ownership class of corporate capital stock, carrying the rights to vote, share in earnings, participate in future stock issues, and share in any liquidation proceeds after prior claims have been settled

common-size financial statement A financial statement in which each item is presented as a percentage of a key figure such as sales or total assets

comparative financial statements A form of horizontal analysis involving comparison of two or more periods' financial statements showing dollar and/or percentage changes

compensating balance A minimum amount that a financial institution requires a firm to maintain in its account as part of a borrowing arrangement complex capital structure

comprehensive income The total income reported by the company, including net profit and all other changes to stockholders' equity other than those arising from capital (stock) transactions; typical components of *other comprehensive income* (OCI) are unrealized gains (losses) on available-for-sale securities and derivatives, minimum pension liability adjustment, and foreign currency translation adjustments

computer-aided design (CAD) a method of design that involves the use of computers to design products.

computer-aided manufacturing (CAM) a manufacturing method that involves the use of computers to control the operation of machines.

computer-integrated manufacturing (CIM) the ultimate extension of the CAD, CAM, and FMS concepts to a completely automated and computer-controlled factory where production is self-operating once a product is designed and the decision to produce is made.

conceptual framework A cohesive set of interrelated objectives and fundamentals for external financial reporting developed by the FASB

conservatism An accounting principle stating that judgmental determinations should tend toward understatement rather than overstatement of net assets and income

consistency An accounting principle stating that, unless otherwise disclosed, accounting reports should be prepared on a basis consistent with the preceding period

consolidated financial statements Financial statements reflecting a parent company and one or more subsidiary companies and/or a variable interest entity (VIE) and its primary beneficiary

contingency A possible future event; significant contingent liabilities must be disclosed in the notes to the financial statements

contingent liabilities A potential obligation, the eventual occurrence of which usually depends on some future event beyond the control of the firm; contingent liabilities may originate with such events as lawsuits, credit guarantees, and environmental damages

continuous budgeting budgeting based on a moving time frame that extends over a fixed period. The budget system adds an identical time period to the budget at the end of each period of operations, thereby always maintaining a budget of exactly the same time length.

continuous improvement an approach to activity-based management where the employees constantly evaluate products, services, and processes, seeking ways to do better.

continuous improvement (Kaizen) budgeting an approach to budgeting that incorporates a targeted improvement (reduction) in costs; management requests that a given process will be improved during the budgeting process. This may be applied to every budget category or to specific areas selected by management. Kaizen budgeting is based upon prior performance and anticipated operating conditions during the upcoming period.

continuous improvement (Kaizen) costing establishing cost reduction targets for products or services that an organization is currently providing to customers.

contra account An account related to, and deducted from, another account when financial statements are prepared or when book values are computed

contract rate The rate of interest stated on a bond certificate

contributed capital The net funding that a company receives from issuing and acquiring its equity shares

contribution income statement an income statement format in which variable costs are subtracted from revenues to figure contribution margin, and fixed costs are then subtracted from contribution margin to calculate net income.

contribution margin the difference between total revenues and total variable costs; this amount goes toward covering fixed costs and providing a profit.

contribution margin ratio the portion of each dollar of sales revenue contributed toward covering fixed costs and earning a profit.

controlling the process of ensuring that results agree with plans.

conversion cost the combined costs of direct labor and manufacturing overhead incurred to convert raw materials into finished goods.

convertible bond A bond incorporating the holder's right to convert the bond to capital stock under prescribed terms

convertible securities Debt and equity securities that provide the holder with an option to convert those securities into other securities

copyright An exclusive right that protects an owner against the unauthorized reproduction of a specific written work or artwork

core income A company's income from its usual business activities that is expected to continue (persist) into the future

corporation A legal entity created by the granting of a charter from an appropriate governmental authority and owned by stockholders who have limited liability for corporate debt

cost allocation base a measure of volume of activity, such as direct labor hours or machine hours, that determines how much of a cost pool is assigned to each cost objective.

cost behavior how costs respond to changes in an activity cost driver.

cost center a responsibility center whose manager is responsible only for managing costs.

cost driver a factor that causes or influences costs.

cost driver analysis the study of factors that influence costs.

cost estimation the determination of the relationship between activity and cost.

cost method An investment is reported at its historical cost, and any cash dividends and interest received are recognized in current income

cost method An investment is reported at its historical cost, and any cash dividends and interest received are recognized in current income

cost objective an object to which costs are assigned. Examples include departments, products, and services.

cost of capital the average cost of obtaining the resources necessary to make investments.

cost of goods sold The total cost of merchandise sold to customers during the accounting period

cost of goods sold percentage The ratio of cost of goods sold divided by net sales

cost of production report used in a process costing system; summarizes unit and cost data for each department or process for each period.

cost pool a collection of related costs, such as departmental manufacturing overhead, that is assigned to one or more cost objectives, such as products.

cost prediction the forecasting of future costs.

cost prediction error the difference between a predicted future cost and the actual amount of the cost when, or if, it is incurred.

cost principle An accounting principle stating that asset measures are based on the prices paid to acquire the assets

cost reduction proposal a proposed action or investment intended to reduce the cost of an activity that the organization is committed to keeping.

cost-volume-profit (CVP) analysis a technique used to examine the relationships among total volume of some independent variable, total costs, total revenues, and profits during a time period (typically a month or a year).

cost-volume-profit graph an illustration of the relationships among activity volume, total revenues, total costs, and profits.

coupon (contract or stated) rate The coupon rate of interest is stated in the bond contract; it is used to compute the dollar amount of (semiannual) interest payments that are paid to bondholder during the life of the bond issue

coupon bond A bond with coupons for interest payable to bearer attached to the bond for each interest period; whenever interest is due, the bondholder detaches a coupon and deposits it with his or her bank for collection

covenants Contractual requirements put into loan or bond agreements by lenders

credit (entry) An entry on the right side (or in the credit column) of any account

credit card fee A fee charged retailers for credit card services provided by financial institutions; the fee is usually stated as a percentage of credit card sales

credit guarantee A guarantee of another company's debt by cosigning a note payable; a guarantor's contingent liability that is usually disclosed in a balance sheet footnote

credit memo A document prepared by a seller to inform the purchaser that the seller has reduced the amount owed by the purchaser due to a return or an allowance

credit period The maximum amount of time, usually stated in days, that the purchaser of merchandise has to pay the seller

credit rating An opinion formed by a credit-rating agency (such as Standard & Poor's, Moody's or Fitch) concerning the creditworthiness of a borrower (a corporation or a government) based on an assessment of the borrower's likelihood of default

credit terms The prescribed payment period for purchases on credit with discount specified for early payment

cumulative (preferred stock) A feature associated with preferred stock whereby any dividends in arrears must be paid before dividends may be paid on common stock

cumulative effect of a change in principle The cumulative effect on net income to the date of a change in accounting principle

cumulative translation adjustment The amount recorded in the equity section as necessary to balance the accounting equation when assets and liabilities of foreign subsidiaries are translated into $US at the rate of exchange prevailing at the statement date

current assets Cash and other assets that will be converted to cash or used up during the normal operating cycle of the business or one year, whichever is longer

current liabilities Obligations that will require within the coming year or operating cycle, whichever is longer, (1) the use of existing current assets or (2) the creation of other current liabilities

current rate method Method of translating foreign currency transactions under which balance sheet amounts are translated using exchange rates in effect at the period-end consolidation date and income statement amounts using the average exchange rate for the period

current ratio Current assets divided by current liabilities; a measure of liquidity

customer level activity an activity performed to obtain or maintain each customer.

customer profitability analysis a presentation showing the profits of individual or categories of customers net of the cost of serving and supporting those customers.

customer profitability profile a graphical presentation showing the cumulative profits from the most profitable to the least profitable customer

cycle efficiency the ratio of value-added to nonvalue-added manufacturing activities.

cycle time the total time required to complete a process. It is composed of the times needed for setup, processing, movement, waiting, and inspection.

D

Dashboards software programs that tabulate and display scorecard results using graphics that mimic the instrument displays on an automobile dashboard

days sales in inventory Inventories divided by average cost of goods sold

days sales in receivables a measure of both solvency and performance, the days receivable outstanding tells how long it takes to convert accounts receivable into cash or how well the firm is managing the credit extended to customers. The general equation for days receivable outstanding is: Ending receivables/Average daily sales.

days' sales in inventory Inventories divided by average cost of goods sold

debenture bond A bond that has no specific property pledged as security for the repayment of funds borrowed

debit (entry) An entry on the left side (or in the debit column) of any account

debt-to-equity ratio A firm's total liabilities divided by its total owners' equity; a measure of long-term solvency

decentralization the delegation of decision-making authority to successively lower management levels in an organization. The lower in the organization the authority is delegated, the greater the decentralization.

declining-balance method An accelerated depreciation method that allocates depreciation expense to each year by applying a constant percentage to the declining book value of the asset

default The nonpayment of interest and principal and/or the failure to adhere to the various terms and conditions of the bond indenture

deferrals Adjustments that allocate various assets and revenues received in advance to the proper accounting periods as expenses and revenues

deferred revenue A liability representing revenues received in advance; also called unearned revenue

deferred tax liability A liability representing the estimated future income taxes payable resulting from an existing temporary difference between an asset's book value and its tax basis

deferred tax valuation allowance Reduction in a reported deferred tax asset to adjust for the amount that is not likely to be realized

defined benefit plan A type of retirement plan under which the company promises to make periodic payments to the employee after retirement

defined contribution plan A retirement plan under which the company makes cash contribution into an employee's account (usually with a third-party trustee like a bank) either solely or as a matching contribution

degree of operating leverage a measure of operating leverage, often computed as the contribution margin divided by income before taxes.

denominator variance *see* fixed overhead volume variance.

depletion The allocation of the cost of natural resources to the units extracted and sold or, in the case of timberland, the board feet of timber cut

depreciation The decline in economic potential (using up) of plant assets originating from wear, deterioration, and obsolescence

depreciation accounting The process of allocating the cost of equipment, vehicles, and buildings (not land) to expense over the time period benefiting from their use

depreciation base The acquisition cost of an asset less estimated salvage value

depreciation rate An estimate of how the asset will be used up over its useful life—evenly over its useful life, more heavily in the early years, or in proportion to its actual usage

depreciation tax shield the reduction in taxes due to the deductibility of depreciation from taxable revenues.

derivatives Financial instruments such as futures, options, and swaps that are commonly used to hedge (mitigate) some external risk, such as commodity price risk, interest rate risk, or risks relating to foreign currency fluctuations

descriptive model a model that merely specifies the relationships between a series of independent and dependent variables.

design for manufacture explicitly considering the costs of manufacturing and servicing a product while it is being designed.

differential cost analysis an approach to the analysis of relevant costs that focuses on the costs that differ under alternative actions.

diluted earnings per share The earnings per share computation taking into consideration the effects of dilutive securities

dilutive securities Securities that can be exchanged for shares of common stock and, thereby, increase the number of common shares outstanding

direct costing *see* variable costing.

direct department cost a cost directly traceable to a department upon its incurrence.

direct labor wages earned by production employees for the time they spend working on the conversion of raw materials into finished goods.

direct materials the costs of primary raw materials that are converted into finished goods.

direct method (for cost allocation) a method of allocating service department costs to producing departments based only on the amount of services provided to the producing departments; it does not recognize any interdepartmental services.

direct method (for statement of cash flow) a reporting format for the operating section of the statement of cash flows; where basically, the income statement is reconstructed on a cash basis so that the primary categories of cash inflows and outflows from operating activities are reported.

direct segment fixed costs costs that would not be incurred if the segment being evaluated were discontinued. They are specifically identifiable with a particular segment.

discontinued operations Net income or loss from business segments that are up for sale or have been sold in the current period

discount bond A bond that is sold for less than its par (face) value

discount on notes payable A contra-account that is subtracted from the Notes Payable amount on the balance sheet; as the life of the note elapses, the discount is reduced and charged to interest expense

discount period The maximum amount of time, usually stated in days, that the purchaser of merchandise has to pay the seller if the purchaser wants to claim the cash discount

discount rate the minimum rate of return required for the project to be acceptable.

discounted cash flow (DCF) model The value of a security is equal to the present value of the expected free cash flows to the firm, discounted at the weighted average cost of capital (WACC)

discounting The exchanging of notes receivable for cash at a financial institution at an amount that is less than the face value of the notes

discretionary cost center a cost center that does not have clearly defined relationships between effort and accomplishment.

discretionary fixed costs costs set at a fixed amount each period at the discretion of management.

dividend discount model The value of a security today is equal to the present value of that security's expected dividends, discounted at the weighted average cost of capital

dividend payout ratio Annual dividends per share divided by the earnings per share or by net income

dividend yield Annual dividends per share divided by the market price per share

dividends account A temporary equity account used to accumulate owner dividends from the business

division margin the amount each division contributes toward covering common corporate expenses and generating corporate profits. It is computed by subtracting all direct fixed expenses identifiable with each division from the contribution margin.

double-entry accounting system A method of accounting that recognizes the duality of a transaction such that the analysis results in a recording of equal amounts of debits and credits

E

earned When referring to revenue, the seller's execution of its duties under the terms of the agreement, with the resultant passing of title to the buyer with no right of return or other contingencies

earned capital The cumulative net income (losses) retained by the company (not paid out to shareholders as dividends)

earnings per share (EPS) Net income less preferred stock dividends divided by the weighted average common shares outstanding for the period

earnings quality The degree to which reported earnings represent how well the firm has performed from an economic standpoint

earnings smoothing Earnings management with a goal to provide an earnings stream with less variability

EBIT Earnings before interest and taxes

EBITDA Earnings before interest, taxes, depreciation and amortization

economic profit The number of inventory units sold multiplied by the difference between the sales price and the replacement cost of the inventories (approximated by the cost of the most recently purchased inventories)

economic value added (EVA) Net operating profits after tax less a charge for the use of capital equal to beginning capital utilized in the business multiplied by the weighted average cost of capital ($EVA = NOPAT - [r_w \times$ Net operating assets$]$)

effective interest method A method of amortizing bond premium or discount that results in a constant rate of interest each period and varying amounts of premium or discount amortized each period

effective interest rate The rate determined by dividing the total discount amount by the cash proceeds on a note payable when the borrower borrowed at a discount

effective rate The current rate of interest in the market for a bond or other debt instrument; when issued, a bond is priced to yield the market (effective) rate of interest at the date of issuance

efficient markets hypothesis Capital markets are said to be efficient if at any given time, current equity (stock) prices reflect all relevant information that determines those equity prices

electronic data interchange (EDI) the electronic communication of data between organizations.

employee severance costs Accrued (estimated) costs for termination of employees as part of a restructuring program

employee stock options A form of compensation that grants a select group of employees the right to purchase a fixed number of company shares at a fixed price for a predetermined time period

enterprise resource planning (ERP) enterprise management information systems that provide organizations an integrated set of operating, financial, and management systems.

equity carve out A corporate divestiture of operating units

equity method The prescribed method of accounting for investments in which the investor company has a significant influence over the investee company (usually taken to be ownership between 20-50% of the outstanding common stock of the investee company)

equivalent completed units the number of completed units that is equal, in terms of production effort, to a given number of partially completed units.

ethics the moral quality, fitness, or propriety of a course of action that can injure or benefit people; also, the values, rules, and justifications that governs one's way of life.

executory contract A contract where a party has a material unperformed obligation that, if not performed, will result in a breach of contract

expenses Decreases in owners' equity incurred by a firm in the process of earning revenues

external failure costs quality costs incurred when nonconforming products or services are delivered to customers.

extraordinary items Revenues and expenses that are both unusual and infrequent and are, therefore, excluded from income from continuing operations

F

face amount The principal amount of a bond or note to be repaid at maturity

facility level activity an activity performed to maintain general manufacturing or marketing capabilities.

factoring Selling an account receivable to another company, typically a finance company or a financial institution, for less than its face value

fair value Value that an asset could be sold for (or an obligation discharged) in an orderly market, between willing buyers and sellers; often, but not always, is current market value

fair value method Method of accounting that records on the balance sheet, the asset or liabilities fair value, and records on the income statement, changes in the fair value

file a collection of related records.

financial accounting an information processing system that generates general-purpose reports of financial operations (income statement and cash flows statement) and financial position (balance sheet) for an organization.

Financial Accounting Standards Board (FASB) The organization currently responsible for setting accounting standards for reporting financial information by U.S. entitites

financial assets Normally consist of excess resources held for future expansion or unexpected needs; they are usually invested in the form of other companies' stock, corporate or government bonds, and real estate

financial leverage The proportionate use of borrowed funds in the capital structure, computed as net nonoperating obligations (NNO) divided by average equity

financial reporting the process of preparing financial statements (income statement, balance sheet, and statement of cash flows) for a firm in accordance with generally accepted accounting principles.

financial reporting objectives A component of the conceptual framework that specifies that financial statements should provide information (1) useful for investment and credit decisions, (2) helpful in assessing an entity's ability to generate future cash flows, and (3) about an entity's resources, claims to those resources, and the effects of events causing changes in these items

financial statement analysis the process of interpreting and evaluating financial statements by using the data contained in them to produce additional financial measures. Financial statement analysis involves comparing financial statements for the current period with those of the previous periods, studying the internal composition of the financial statements, and studying relationships within and among the financial statements.

financial statement elements A part of the conceptual framework that identifies the significant components—such as assets, liabilities, equity, revenues, and expenses—used to guide financial statement preparation

financing activities business activities that involve (1) resource transfers between the entity and its owners and (2) the securement of loans from and the repayment of them to nonowners (creditors).

financing activities Methods that companies use to raise the funds to pay for resources such as land, buildings, and equipment

finished goods inventory The dollar amount of inventory that has completed the production process and is awaiting sale to customers

finished goods inventory The dollar amount of inventory that has completed the production process and is awaiting sale

first-in, first-out (FIFO) method One of the prescribed methods of inventory costing; FIFO assumes that the first costs incurred for the purchase or production of inventory are the first costs relieved from inventory when goods are sold

first-in, first-out (FIFO) method in process costing A costing method that accounts for unit costs of beginning inventory units separately from those started during the current period. The first costs incurred each period are assumed to have been used to complete the unfinished units left over from the previous period.

fiscal year The annual accounting period used by a business firm

fiscal year The annual accounting period used by a business firm

five forces of competitive intensity Industry competition, bargaining power of buyers, bargaining power of suppliers, threat of substitution, threat of entry

fixed assets An alternate label for long-term assets; may also be called property, plant, and equipment (PPE)

fixed costs Costs that do not change with changes in sales volume (over a reasonable range); with a unit level cost driver as the independent variable, fixed costs are a constant amount per period of time

fixed manufacturing overhead all fixed costs associated with converting raw materials into finished goods.

fixed overhead budget variance the difference between budgeted and actual fixed overhead.

fixed overhead volume variance the difference between total budgeted fixed overhead and total standard fixed overhead assigned to production.

fixed selling and administrative costs all fixed costs other than those directly associated with converting raw materials into finished goods.

flexible budget variance computed for each cost as the difference between the actual cost and the flexible budget cost of producing a given quantity of product or service.

flexible budgets budgets that are drawn up for a series of possible production and sales volumes or adjusted to a particular level of production after the fact. These budgets, based on cost-volume or cost-activity relationships, are used to determine what costs should have been for an attained level of activity.

flexible manufacturing systems (FMS) an extension of computer-aided manufacturing techniques through a series of manufacturing operations. These operations include the automatic movement of units between operations and the automatic and rapid setup of machines to produce each product.

forecast The projection of financial results over the forecast horizon and terminal periods

foreign currency transaction The $US equivalent of an asset or liability denominated in a foreign currency

foreign exchange gain or loss The gain (loss) recognized in the income statement relating to the change in the $US equivalent of an asset or liability denominated in a foreign currency

for-profit organization an organization that has profit as a primary mission.

forward earnings earnings expected to be reported in the next period.

franchise Generally, an exclusive right to operate or sell a specific brand of products in a given geographic area

free cash flow This excess cash flow (above that required to manage its growth and development) from which dividends can be paid; computed as NOPAT − Increase in NOA

full absorption cost see absorption costing.

full costing see absorption costing.

full costs include all costs, regardless of their behavior patterns (variable or fixed) or activity level.

full disclosure principle An accounting principle stipulating the disclosure of all facts necessary to make financial statements useful to readers

fully diluted earnings per share See diluted earnings per share

functional currency The currency representing the primary currency in which a business unit conducts its operations

functional income statement a type of income statement where costs are classified according to function, rather than behavior. It is typically included in external financial reports.

fundamental analysis Uses financial information to predict future valuation and, hence, buy-sell stock strategies

funded status The difference between the pension obligation and the fair market value of the pension investments

future value the amount a current sum of money (or series of monies) earning a stated rate of interest will accumulate to at the end of a future period.

G

general and administrative expense budget presents the expenses the organization plans to incur in connection with the general administration of the organization. Included are expenses for such things as the accounting department, the computer center, and the president's office.

general journal A journal with enough flexibility so that any type of business transaction can be recorded in it

general ledger A grouping of all of an entity's accounts that are used to prepare the basic financial statements

generally accepted accounting principles (GAAP) A set of standards and procedures that guide the preparation of financial statements

goal a definable, measurable objective.

going concern concept An accounting principle that assumes that, in the absence of evidence to the contrary, a business entity will have an indefinite life

goodwill The value that derives from a firm's ability to earn more than a normal rate of return on the fair market value of its specific, identifiable net assets; computed as the residual of the purchase price less the fair market value of the net tangible and intangible assets acquired

gross margin The difference between net sales and cost of goods sold; also called gross profit

gross profit margin (GPM) (percentage) The ratio of gross profit on sales divided by net sales

gross profit on sales The difference between net sales and cost of goods sold; also called gross margin

H

held-to-maturity securities The designation given to a portfolio of bond investments that are expected to be held until they mature

high-low method of cost estimation utilizes data from two time periods, a representative high activity period and a representative low activity period, to estimate fixed and variable costs.

historical cost Original acquisition or issuance costs

holding company The parent company of a subsidiary

holding gain The increase in replacement cost since the inventories were acquired, which equals the number of units sold multiplied by the difference between the current replacement cost and the original acquisition cost

horizon period The forecast period for which detailed estimates are made, typically 5–10 years

horizontal analysis Analysis of a firm's financial statements that covers two or more years

I

IASB International Accounting Standards Board, independent, privately funded accounting standard-setter based in London, responsible for developing IFRS and promoting the use and application of these standards.

IFRS International Financial Reporting Standards, a body of accounting standards developed by the International Accounting Standards Board and used for financial reports across much of the world

impairment A reduction in value from that presently recorded

impairment loss A loss recognized on an impaired asset equal to the difference between its book value and current fair value

imposed budget *see* top-down budget.

income statement a summary of economic events during a period of time, showing the revenues generated by operating activities, the expenses incurred in generating those revenues, and any gains or losses attributed to the period.

incremental budgeting an approach to budgeting where costs for a coming period are budgeted as a dollar or percentage change from the amount budgeted for (or spent during) some previous period.

indirect department cost a cost reassigned, or allocated, to a department from another cost objective.

indirect method A presentation format for the statement of cash flows that refers to the operating section only; that section begins with net income and converts it to cash flows from operations

indirect segment costs *see* common segment costs.

inspection time the amount of time it takes units to be inspected.

intangible assets A term applied to a group of long-term assets, including patents, copyrights, franchises, trademarks, and goodwill, that benefit an entity but do not have physical substance

integer programming a variation of linear programming that determines the solution in whole numbers.

interdepartmental services services provided by one service department to other service departments.

interest cost (pensions) The increase in the pension obligation due to the accrual of an additional year of interest

internal auditing A company function that provides independent appraisals of the company's financial statements, its internal controls, and its operations

internal controls The measures undertaken by a company to ensure the reliability of its accounting data, protect its assets from theft or unauthorized use, make sure that employees are following the company's policies and procedures, and evaluate the performance of employees, departments, divisions, and the company as a whole

internal failure costs quality costs incurred when materials, components, products, or services are identified as defective before delivery to customers.

internal rate of return (IRR) (often called the time-adjusted rate of return) the discount rate that equates the present value of a project's cash inflows with the present value of the project's cash outflows.

inventory carrying costs Costs of holding inventories, including warehousing, logistics, insurance, financing, and the risk of loss due to theft, damage, or technological or fashion change

inventory shrinkage The cost associated with an inventory shortage; the amount by which the perpetual inventory exceeds the physical inventory

inventory turnover Cost of goods sold divided by average inventory

inventory turnover (in dollars) often regarded as a measure of both solvency and performance, inventory turnover tells how long it takes to convert inventory into current monetary assets and how well the firm is managing investments in inventory. The general equation for inventory turnover is: Cost of goods sold/Average inventory cost.

inventory turnover (in units) the annual demand in units divided by the average inventory in units.

investing activities The acquiring and disposing of resources (assets) that a company uses to acquire and sell its products and services

investing creditors Those who primarily finance investing activities

investment center a responsibility center whose manager is responsible for the relationship between its profits and the total assets invested in the center. In general, the management of an investment center is expected to earn a target profit per dollar invested.

investment returns The increase in pension investments resulting from interest, dividends, and capital gains on the investment portfolio

investment tax credit a reduction in income taxes of a percent of the cost of a new asset in the year the new asset is placed in service.

invoice A document that the seller sends to the purchaser to request payment for items that the seller shipped to the purchaser

invoice price The price that a seller charges the purchaser for merchandise

IOU A slang term for a receivable

irrelevant costs costs that do not differ among competing decision alternatives.

IRS Internal Revenue Service, the U.S. taxing authority

issued stock Shares of stock that have been sold and issued to stockholders; issued stock may be either outstanding or in the treasury

J

job cost sheet a document used to track the status of and accumulate the costs for a specific job in a job cost system.

job order production the manufacturing of products in single units or in batches of identical units.

job production *see* job order production.

joint costs all materials and conversion costs of joint products incurred prior to the split-off point.

joint products two or more products simultaneously produced by a single process from a common set of inputs.

journal A tabular record in which business transactions are analyzed in debit and credit terms and recorded in chronological order

just-in-time (JIT) inventory Receive inventory from suppliers into the production process just at the point it is needed

just-in-time (JIT) inventory management a comprehensive inventory management philosophy that stresses policies, procedures, and attitudes by managers and other workers that result in the efficient production of high-quality goods while maintaining the minimum level of inventories.

just-in-time (JIT) inventory philosophy Receive inventory from suppliers into the production process just at the point it is needed

K

Kaizen costing *see* continuous improvement costing.

kanban system *see* materials pull system.

L

labor efficiency variance the difference between the standard cost of actual labor inputs and the flexible budget cost for labor.

labor rate (spending) variance the difference between the actual cost and the standard cost of actual labor inputs.

land improvements Improvements with limited lives made to land sites, such as paved parking lots and driveways

last-in, first-out (LIFO) method One of the prescribed methods of inventory costing; LIFO assumes that the last costs incurred for the purchase or production of inventory are the first costs relieved form inventory when goods are sold

lean accounting a system of product cost assignment where costs are assigned to value streams of multiple products rather than to individual products

lean production a philosophy of inventory production and management that emphasizes increased coordination throughout the value chain, reduced inventory, reduced production times, increased product quality, and increased employee involvement and empowerment

lease A contract between a lessor (owner) and lessee (tenant) for the rental of property

leasehold The rights transferred from the lessor to the lessee by a lease

leasehold improvements Expenditures made by a lessee to alter or improve leased property

least-squares regression analysis uses a mathematical technique to fit a cost estimating equation to the observed data in a manner that minimizes the sum of the vertical squared estimating errors between the estimated and actual costs at each observation.

lessee The party acquiring the right to the use of property by a lease

lessor The owner of property who transfers the right to use the property to another party by a lease

leveraging The use of borrowed funds in the capital structure of a firm; the expectation is that the funds will earn a return higher than the rate of interest on the borrowed funds

liabilities The obligations, or debts, that an entity must pay in money or services at some time in the future because of past transactions or events

life-cycle budgeting an approach to budgeting when the entire life of the project represents a more useful planning horizon than an artificial period of one year.

life-cycle costs from the seller's perspective, all costs associated with a product or service ranging from those incurred with initial conception through design, pre-production, production, and after-production support. From the buyer's perspective, all costs associated with a purchased product or service, including initial acquisition costs and subsequent costs of operation, maintenance, repair, and disposal.

LIFO conformity rule IRS requirement to cost inventories using LIFO for tax purposes if they are costed using LIFO for financial reporting purposes

LIFO liquidation The reduction in inventory quantities when LIFO costing is used; LIFO liquidation yields an increase in gross profit and income when prices are rising

LIFO reserve The difference between the cost of inventories using FIFO and the cost using LIFO

linear algebra method (reciprocal) method a method of allocating service department costs using a series of linear algebraic equations, which are solved simultaneously, to allocate service department costs both interdepartmentally among service departments and to the producing departments.

linear programming an optimizing model used to assist managers in making decisions under constrained conditions when linear relationships exist between all variables.

liquidation value per share The amount that would be received by a holder of a share of stock if the corporation liquidated

liquidity How much cash the company has, how much is expected, and how much can be raised on short notice

list price The suggested price or reference price of merchandise in a catalog or price list

long-term liabilities Debt obligations not due to be settled within the normal operating cycle or one year, whichever is longer

lower of cost or market (LCM) GAAP requirement to write down the carrying amount of inventories on the balance sheet if the reported cost (using FIFO, for example) exceeds market value (determined by current replacement cost)

M

maker The signer of a promissory note

managed fixed costs *see* discretionary fixed costs.

management accounting a discipline concerned with financial and related information used by managers and other persons inside specific organizations to make strategic, organizational, and operational decisions.

management by exception an approach to performance assessment whereby management directs attention only to those activities not proceeding according to plan.

management discussion and analysis (MD&A) The section of the 10-K report in which a company provides a detailed discussion of its business activities

managerial accounting The accounting activities carried out by a firm's accounting staff primarily to furnish managers and other employees with accounting data for decisions related to the firm's operations

manufacturers Companies that convert raw materials and components into finished products through the application of skilled labor and machine operations

manufacturing costs The costs of direct materials, direct labor, and manufacturing overhead incurred in the manufacture of a product

manufacturing cost budget a budget detailing the direct materials, direct labor, and manufacturing overhead costs that should be incurred by manufacturing operations to produce the number of units called for in the production budget.

manufacturing margin the result when direct manufacturing costs (variable costs) are deducted from product sales.

manufacturing organizations organizations that process raw materials into finished products for sale to others.

manufacturing overhead all manufacturing costs other than direct materials and direct labor.

margin of safety the amount by which actual or planned sales exceed the break-even point.

marginal cost the varying increment in total cost required to produce and sell an additional unit of product.

marginal revenue the varying increment in total revenue derived from the sale of an additional unit.

market (yield) rate This is the interest rate that investors expect to earn on the investment in this debt security; this rate is used to price the bond issue

market cap Market capitalization of the firm, or value as perceived by investors; computed as market value per share multiplied by shares outstanding

market method accounting Securities are reported at current market values (marked-to-market) on the statement date

market segment level activity performed to obtain or maintain operations in a market segment.

market value The published price (as listed on a stock exchange)

market value per share The current price at which shares of stock may be bought or sold

master budget the grouping together of all budgets and supporting schedules. This budget coordinates all the financial and operational activities and places them into an organization wide set of budgets for a given time period.

matching principle An accounting guideline that states that income is determined by relating expenses, to the extent feasible, with revenues that have been recorded

materiality An accounting guideline that states that transactions so insignificant that they would not affect a user's actions or perception of the company may be recorded in the most expedient manner

materials inventory The physical component of inventory; the other components of manufactured inventory are labor costs and overhead costs

materials price variance the difference between the actual materials cost and the standard cost of actual materials inputs.

materials pull system an inventory production flow system in which employees at each station work to replenish the inventory used by employees at subsequent stations. The building of excess inventories is strictly prohibited. When the number of units in inventory reaches a specified limit, work at the station stops until workers at a subsequent station pull a unit from the in-process storage area.

materials push system an inventory production flow system in which employees work to reduce the pile of inventory building up at their work stations. Workers at each station remove materials from an in-process storage area, complete their operation, and place the output in another in-process storage area. Hence, they push the work to the next work station.

materials quantity variance the difference between the standard cost of actual materials inputs and the flexible budget cost for materials.

materials requisition form a document used to record the type and quantity of each raw material issued to the factory.

maturity date The date on which a note or bond matures

measuring unit concept An accounting guideline noting that the accounting unit of measure is the basic unit of money

merchandise inventory A stock of products that a company buys from another company and makes available for sale to its customers

merchandising firm A company that buys finished products, stores the products for varying periods of time, and then resells the products

merchandising organizations organizations that buy and sell goods without performing manufacturing operations.

method of comparables model Equity valuation or stock values are predicted using price multiples, which are defined as stock price divided by some key financial statement number such as net income, net sales, book value of equity, total assets, or cash flow; companies are then compared with their competitors

minimum level budgeting an approach to budgeting that establishes a base amount for all budget items and requires explanation or justification for any budgeted amount above the minimum (base).

minority interest See noncontrolling interest

mission the basic purpose toward which an organization's activities are directed.

mixed costs costs that contain a fixed and a variable cost element.

model a simplified representation of some real-world phenomenon.

modified accelerated cost recovery system (MACRS) *See* accelerated cost recovery system

movement time the time units spend moving between work or inspection stations.

multiple element arrangements sales (revenue) arrangements containing multiple deliverables and, in some cases, multiple cash-flow streams

mutually exclusive investments two or more capital expenditure proposals where the acceptance of one investment automatically causes the rejection of the other(s).

N

natural resources Assets occurring in a natural state, such as timber, petroleum, natural gas, coal, and other mineral deposits

net asset based valuation model Equity is valued as reported assets less reported liabilities

net assets The difference between an entity's assets and liabilities; net assets are equal to stockholders' equity

net book value (NBV) The cost of the asset less accumulated depreciation; also called carrying value

net financial obligations (NFO) net total of all financial (nonoperating) obligations less financial (nonoperating) assets

net income The excess of a firm's revenues over its expenses

net loss The excess of a firm's expenses over its revenues

net nonoperating expense (NNE) Nonoperating expenses and losses (including the portion of net income attributable to noncontrolling interests) less nonoperating income and gains

net nonoperating expense percentage (NNEP) Net nonoperating expense divided by net nonoperating obligations (NNO)

net nonoperating obligations (NNO) All nonoperating obligations (including noncontrolling interests) less nonoperating assets

net operating asset turnover (NOAT) Ratio obtained by dividing sales by net operating assets

net operating assets (NOA) Current and long-term operating assets less current and long-term operating liabilities; or net operating working capital plus long-term net operating assets

net operating profit after tax (NOPAT) Sales less operating expenses (including taxes)

net operating profit margin (NOPM) ratio obtained by dividing net operating profit after tax (NOPAT) by sales

net present value the present value of a project's net cash inflows from operations and disinvestment less the amount of the initial investment.

net operating working capital (NOWC) Current operating assets less current operating liabilities

net realizable value The value at which an asset can be sold, net of any costs of disposition

net sales The total revenue generated by a company through merchandise sales less the revenue given up through sales returns and allowances and sales discounts

net sales volume variance indicates the impact of a change in sales volume on the contribution margin, given the budgeted selling price and the standard variable costs. It is computed as the difference between the actual and the budgeted sales volumes times the budgeted unit contribution margin.

net working capital Current assets less current liabilities

nominal rate The rate of interest stated on a bond certificate or other debt instrument

noncash investing and financing activities Significant business activities during the period that do not impact cash inflows or cash outflows

noncontrolling interest The portion of equity (net assets) in a subsidiary not attributable, directly or indirectly, to a parent. A noncontrolling interest (formerly called minority interest) typically represents the ownership interest of shareholders other than those of the parent company.

noncurrent liabilities Obligations not due to be paid within one year or the operating cycle, whichever is longer

nonoperating expenses Expenses that relate to the company's financing activities and include interest income and interest expense, gains and losses on sales of securities, and income or loss on discontinued operations

non-value-added activity an activity that does not add value to a product or service from the viewpoint of the customer.

no-par stock Stock that does not have a par value

NOPAT Net operating profit after tax

normal operating cycle For a particular business, the average period of time between the use of cash in its typical operating activity and the subsequent collection of cash from customers

note receivable A promissory note held by the note's payee

notes to financial statements Footnotes in which companies discuss their accounting policies and estimates used in preparing the statements

not-for-profit organization an organization that does not have profit as a primary goal.

not-sufficient-funds check A check from an individual or company that had an insufficient cash balance in the bank when the holder of the check presented it to the bank for payment

O

objective function in linear programming models, the goal to be minimized or maximized.

objectivity principle An accounting principle requiring that, whenever possible, accounting entries are based on objectively determined evidence

off-balance-sheet financing The structuring of a financing arrangement so that no liability shows on the borrower's balance sheet

operating activities business activities related to a company's normal income-earning activity (research, develop, produce, purchase, market, and distribute company products and services)

operating asset turnover The ratio obtained by dividing sales by average net operating assets

operating budget detailed plans to guide operations throughout the budget period.

operating cash flow to capital expenditures ratio A firm's net cash flow from operating activities divided by its annual capital expenditures

operating cash flow to current liabilities ratio A firm's net cash flow from operating activities divided by its average current liabilities

operating creditors Those who primarily finance operating activities

operating cycle The time between paying cash for goods or employee services and receiving cash from customers

operating expense margin (OEM) The ratio obtained by dividing any operating expense item or category by sales

operating expenses The usual and customary costs that a company incurs to support its main business activities; these include cost of goods sold, selling expenses, depreciation expense, amortization expense, research and development expense, and taxes on operating profits

operating lease A lease by which the lessor retains the usual risks and rewards of owning the property

operating leverage a measure of the extent that an organization's costs are fixed.

operating profit margin The ratio obtained by dividing NOPAT by sales

operational audit An evaluation of activities, systems, and internal controls within a company to determine their efficiency, effectiveness, and economy

operations list a document that specifies the manufacturing operations and related times required to produce one unit or batch of product.

opportunity cost the net cash inflow that could be obtained if the resources committed to one action were used in the most desirable other alternative.

optimal solution in linear programming models, the feasible solution than maximizes or minimizes the value of the objective function, depending on the decision maker's goal.

optimizing model a model that suggests a specific choice between decision alternatives.

order level activity an activity performed for each sales order.

order-filling costs costs incurred to place finished goods in the hands of purchasers (for example, storing, packaging, and transportation).

order-getting costs costs incurred to obtain customers' orders (for example, advertising, salespersons' salaries and commissions, travel, telephone, and entertainment).

organization chart an illustration of the formal relationships existing between the elements of an organization.

organization costs Expenditures incurred in launching a business (usually a corporation), including attorney's fees and various fees paid to the state

organization structure the arrangement of lines of responsibility within the organization.

organizational cost drivers choices concerning the organization of activities and the involvement of persons inside and outside the organization in decision making.

organizational-based cost systems used for financial reporting, these systems focus on organizational units such as a company, plant, or department rather than on processes and activities.

organizing the process of making the organization into a well-ordered whole.

outcomes assessment *see* performance measurement.

outlay costs costs that require future expenditures of cash or other resources.

output/input budgeting an approach to budgeting where physical inputs and costs are budgeted as a function of planned unit level activities. The budgeted inputs are a function of the planned outputs.

outsourcing the external acquisition of services or components.

other comprehensive income (OCI) The change in stockholders' equity other than those arising from capital (stock) transactions and those included in net income; typical OCI components are unrealized gains (losses) on available-for-sale securities and derivatives, minimum pension liability adjustment, and foreign currency translation adjustments

outstanding checks Checks issued by a firm that have not yet been presented to its bank for payment

outstanding stock Shares of stock that are currently owned by stockholders (excludes treasury stock)

owners' equity The interest of owners in the assets of an entity; equal to the difference between the entity's assets and liabilities; also called *stockholders' equity* or *equity*

P

packing list A document that lists the items of merchandise contained in a carton and the quantity of each item; the packing list is usually attached to the outside of the carton

paid-in capital The amount of capital contributed to a corporation by various transactions; the primary source of paid-in capital is from the issuance of shares of stock

par (bonds) Face value of the bond

par value (stock) An amount specified in the corporate charter for each share of stock and imprinted on the face of each stock certificate, often determines the legal capital of the corporation

parent company A company owning one or more subsidiary companies

parsimonious method to multiyear forecasting Forecasting multiple years using only sales growth, net operating profit margin (NOPM), and the turnover of net operating assets (NOAT)

participation budget *see* bottom-up budget.

partnership A voluntary association of two or more persons for the purpose of conducting a business

password A string of characters that a computer user enters into a computer terminal to prove to the computer that the person using the computer is truly the person named in the user identification code

patent An exclusive privilege granted for 20 years to an inventor that gives the patent holder the right to exclude others from making, using, or selling the invention

payback period the time required to recover the initial investment in a project from operations.

payee The company or individual to whom a promissory note is made payable

payment approval form A document that authorizes the payment of an invoice

pension plan A plan to pay benefits to employees after they retire from the company; the plan may be a defined contribution plan or a defined benefit plan

percentage of net sales method A procedure that determines the uncollectible accounts expense for the year by multiplying net credit sales by the estimated uncollectible percentage

percentage-of-completion method Recognition of revenue by determining the costs incurred per the contract as compared to its total expected costs

performance measurement the determination of the extent to which actual outcomes correspond to planned outcomes.

period costs expired costs not related to manufacturing inventory; they are recognized as expenses when incurred.

performance obligation a promise in a contract with a customer to transfer a good or service to the customer; includes promises that are implied by business practices, published policies, or explicit statements if those promises create an expectation of the customer that the entity will perform.

period statement A financial statement accumulating information for a specific period of time; examples are the income statement, the statement of stockholders' equity, and the statement of cash flows

permanent account An account used to prepare the balance sheet; that is, asset, liability, and equity capital (capital stock and retained earnings) accounts; any balance in a permanent account at the end of an accounting period is carried forward to the next period

physical inventory A year-end procedure that involves counting the quantity of each inventory item, determining the unit cost of each item, multiplying the unit cost times quantity, and summing the costs of all the items to determine the total inventory at cost

physical model a scaled-down version or replica of physical reality.

planning the process of selecting goals and strategies to achieve those goals.

plant assets Land, buildings, equipment, vehicles, furniture, and fixtures that a firm uses in its operations; sometimes referred to by the acronym PPE

pooling of interests method A method of accounting for business combinations under which the acquired company is recorded on the acquirer's balance sheet at its book value, rather than market value; this method is no longer acceptable under GAAP for acquisitions occurring after 2001

position statement A financial statement, such as the balance sheet, that presents information as of a particular date

post-closing trial balance A list of general ledger accounts and their balances after closing entries have been recorded and posted

postdated check A check from another person or company with a date that is later than the current date; a postdated check does not become cash until the date of the check

practical capacity the maximum possible activity, allowing for normal repairs and maintenance.

predetermined manufacturing overhead rate an overhead rate established at the start of each year by dividing the predicted overhead costs for the year by the predicted volume of activity in the overhead base for the year.

preemptive right The right of a stockholder to maintain his or her proportionate interest in a corporation by having the right to purchase an appropriate share of any new stock issue

preferred stock A class of corporate capital stock typically receiving priority over common stock in dividend payments and distribution of assets should the corporation be liquidated

premium bond A bond that is sold for more than its par (face) value

present value the current worth of a specified amount of money to be received at some future date at some specified interest rate.

present value index the present value of the project's subsequent cash flows divided by the initial investment.

prevention costs quality costs incurred to prevent nonconforming products from being produced or nonconforming services from being performed.

price discrimination illegally charging different purchasers different prices.

price earnings ratio a measure of performance, price earnings ratio compares the current market price with earnings per share of stock and arrives at a multiple of earnings represented by the selling price.

price fixing the organized setting of prices by competitors.

price-earnings ratio Current market price per common share divided by earnings per share

pro forma income A computation of income that begins with the GAAP income from continuing operations (that excludes discontinued operations, extraordinary items and changes in accounting principle), but then excludes other transitory items (most notably, restructuring charges), and some additional items such as expenses arising from acquisitions (goodwill amortization and other acquisition costs), compensation expense in the form of stock options, and research and development expenditures; pro forma income is not GAAP

process a collection of related activities intended to achieve a common purpose.

process manufacturing a manufacturing environment where production is on a continuous basis.

process map (or process flowchart) a schematic overview of all the activities required to complete a process. Each major activity is represented by a rectangle on the map.

process reengineering the fundamental redesign of a process to serve internal or external customers.

processing time the time spent working on units.

product costs all costs incurred in the manufacturing of products; they are carried in the accounts as an asset (inventory) until the product is sold, at which time they are recognized as an expense (cost of goods sold).

product level activity an activity performed to support the production of each different type of product.

product margin computed as product sales less direct product costs.

production order a document that contains a job's unique identification number and specifies details for the job such as the quantity to be produced, the total raw materials requirements, the manufacturing operations and other activities to be performed, and perhaps even the time when each manufacturing operation should be performed.

productivity the relationship between outputs and inputs.

profit center a responsibility center whose manager is responsible for revenues, costs, and resulting profits. It may be an entire organization, but it is more frequently a segment of an organization such as a product line, marketing territory, or store.

profitability analysis an examination of the relationships between revenues, costs, and profits.

profit-volume graph illustrates the relationship between volume and profits; it does not show revenues and costs.

project-level activity an activity performed to support the completion of each project.

promissory note A written promise to pay a certain sum of money on demand or at a determinable future time

purchase method The prescribed method of accounting for business combinations; under the purchase method, assets and liabilities of the acquired company are recorded at fair market value, together with identifiable intangible assets; the balance is ascribed to goodwill

purchase order A document that formally requests a supplier to sell and deliver specific quantities of particular items of merchandise at specified prices

purchase requisition An internal document that requests that the purchasing department order particular items of merchandise

purchases budget indicates the merchandise or materials that must be acquired to meet current needs and ending inventory requirements.

Q

qualitative characteristics of accounting information The characteristics of accounting information that contribute to decision usefulness; the primary qualities are relevance and reliability

quality conformance to customer expectations.

quality circles groups of employees involved in the production of products who have the authority, within certain parameters, to address and resolve quality problems as they occur, without seeking management approval.

quality costs costs incurred because poor quality of conformance does (or may) exist.

quality of conformance the degree of conformance between a product and its design specifications.

quality of design the degree of conformance between customer expectations for a product or service and the design specifications of the product or service.

quantitative model a set of mathematical relationships.

quarterly data Selected quarterly financial information that is reported in annual reports to stockholders

quick ratio defined as quick assets (cash and cash equivalents, short-term investments, and current receivables) divided by current liabilities. *See acid test ratio.*

R

raw materials inventories the physical ingredients and components that will be converted by machines and/or human labor into a finished product.

realized (or realizable) When referring to revenue, the receipt of an asset or satisfaction of a liability or performance obligation as a result of a transaction or event

recognition criteria The criteria that must be met before a financial statement element may be recorded in the accounts; essentially, the item must meet the definition of an element and must be measurable

record a related set of alphabetic and/or numeric data items.

registered bond A bond for which the issuer (or the trustee) maintains a record of owners and, at the appropriate times, mails out interest payments

relational (cause-and-effect) cost center a cost center that has clearly defined relationships between effort and accomplishment (cause and effect).

relevance A qualitative characteristic of accounting information; relevant information contributes to the predictive and evaluative decisions made by financial statement users

relevant costs future costs that differ between competing decision alternatives.

relevant range the range of activity within which a linear cost function is valid.

reliability A qualitative characteristic of accounting information; reliable information contains no bias or error and faithfully portrays what it intends to represent

remeasurement The computation of gain or loss in the translation of subsidiaries denominated in a foreign currency into $US when the temporal method is used

residual income for investment center excess of investment center income over the minimum rate of return set by top management. The minimum dollar return is computed as a percentage of the investment center's asset base.

residual net operating income (ROPI) model An equity valuation approach that equates the firm's value to the sum of its net operating assets (NOA) and the present value of its residual operating income (ROPI)

residual operating income Net operating profits after tax (NOPAT) less the product of net operating assets (NOA) at the beginning of the period multiplied by the weighted average cost of capital (WACC)

residual operating income (ROPI) model An equity valuation approach that equates the firm's value to the sum of its net operating assets (NOA) and the present value of its residual operating income (ROPI)

responsibility accounting the structuring of performance reports addressed to individual (or group) members of an organization in a manner that emphasizes the factors they are able to control. The focus is on specific units within the organization that are responsible for the accomplishment of specific activities or objectives.

retailers Companies that buy products from wholesale distributors and sell the products to individual customers, the general public

retained earnings Earned capital, the cumulative net income and loss, of the company (from its inception) that has not been paid to shareholders as dividends

retained earnings reconciliation The reconciliation of retained earnings from the beginning to the end of the year; the change in retained earnings includes, at a minimum, the net income (loss) for the period and dividends paid, if any, but may include other components as well; also called statement of retained earnings

return The amount earned on an investment; also called yield

return on assets (ROA) A financial ratio computed as net income divided by average total assets

return on common stockholders' equity (ROCE) A financial ratio computed as net income less preferred stock dividends divided by average common stockholders' equity

return on equity (ROE) The ultimate measure of performance from the shareholders' perspective; computed as net income divided by average equity

return on investment The ratio obtained by dividing income by average investment; sometimes referred to by the acronym ROI

return on investment for investment center a measure of the earnings per dollar of investment. The return on investment of an investment center is computed by dividing the income of the center by its asset base (usually average total assets). It can also be computed as investment turnover times the return-on-sales ratio.

return on net operating assets (RNOA) The ratio obtained by dividing NOPAT by average net operating assets

return on sales (ROS) The ratio obtained by dividing net income by net sales

revenue center a responsibility center whose manager is responsible for the generation of sales revenues.

revenue recognition principle An accounting principle requiring that revenue be recognized when earned and realized (or realizable)

revenue variance the difference between the budgeted sales volume at the budgeted selling price and the actual sales volume at the actual selling price.

revenues inflows of earned resources from providing goods and services to customers; reflected as increases in equity

Robinson-Patman Act prohibits price discrimination when purchasers compete with one another in the sale of their products or services to third parties.

rolling budget *see* continuous budgeting.

s

sale on account A sale of merchandise made on a credit basis

sales budget a forecast of sales revenue for a future period. It may also contain a forecast of sales collections.

sales mix the relative portion of unit or dollar sales derived from each product or service.

sales price variance the impact on revenues of a change in selling price, given the actual sales volume. It is computed as the change in selling price times the actual sales volume.

sales volume variance indicates the impact on revenues of change in sales volume, assuming there was no change in selling price. It is computed as the difference between the actual and the budgeted sales volumes times the budgeted selling price.

salvage value The expected net recovery when a plant asset is sold or removed from service; also called residual value

scatter diagram a graph of past activity and cost data, with individual observations represented by dots.

secured bond A bond that pledges specific property as security for meeting the terms of the bond agreement

Securities and Exchange Commission (SEC) The commission, created by the 1934 Securities Act, that has broad powers to regulate the issuance and trading of securities, and the financial reporting of companies issuing securities to the public

segment income all revenues of a segment minus all costs directly or indirectly charged to it.

segment margin the amount that a segment contributes toward the common (indirect) costs of the organization and toward profits. It is computed as segment sales less direct segment costs.

segment reports income statements that show operating results for portions or segments of a business. Segment reporting is used primarily for internal purposes, although generally accepted accounting principles also require disclosure of segment information for some public corporations.

segments Subdivisions of a firm for which supplemental financial information is disclosed

selling expense budget presents the expenses the organization plans to incur in connection with sales and distribution.

semi-variable costs *see* mixed costs.

sensitivity analysis the study of the responsiveness of a model to changes in one or more of its independent variables.

serial bond A bond issue that staggers the bond maturity dates over a series of years

service cost (pensions) The increase in the pension obligation due to employees working another year for the employer

service costing the process of assigning costs to services performed.

service department a department that provides support services to production and/or other support departments.

service organizations nonmanufacturing organizations that perform work for others, including banks, hospitals, and real estate agencies.

setup time the time required to prepare equipment to produce a specific product.

share-based payment Payment for a good or service using the entity's equity securities; an example is restricted stock used to compensate employees

Sherman Antitrust Act prohibits price fixing.

significant influence The ability of the investor to affect the financing or operating policies of the investee

simplex method a mathematical approach to solving linear programming models containing three or more variables.

sinking fund provision A bond feature that requires the borrower to retire a portion of the bonds each year or, in some cases, to make payments each year to a trustee who is responsible for managing the resources needed to retire the bonds at maturity

solvency The ability to meet obligations, especially to long-term creditors

source document Any written document or computer record evidencing an accounting transaction, such as a bank check or deposit slip, sales invoice, or cash register tape

special purpose entity (*See* variable interest entity)

spin-off A form of equity carve out in which divestiture is accomplished by distribution of a company's shares in a subsidiary to the company's shareholders who then own the shares in the subsidiary directly rather than through the parent company

split-off A form of equity carve out in which divestiture is accomplished by the parent company's exchange of stock in the subsidiary in return for shares in the parent owned by its shareholders

split-off point the point in the process where joint products become separately identifiable.

spread The difference between the return on net operating activities (RNOA) and the net nonoperating expense percentage (NNEP)

standard cost a budget that indicates what it should cost to provide an activity or produce one batch or unit of product under efficient operating conditions.

standard cost variance analysis a system for examining the flexible budget variance, which is the difference between the actual cost and flexible budget cost of producing a given quantity of product or service.

stated value A nominal amount that may be assigned to each share of no-par stock and accounted for much as if it were a par value

statement of cash flows a financial statement that reports the major sources and uses of cash classified into operating, investing, and financing activities and that indicates the net increase or decrease in cash; the statement also includes a schedule of any significant noncash investing and financing activities that occur during the period.

statement of cost of goods manufactured a report that summarizes the cost of goods completed and transferred into finished goods inventory during the period.

statement of equity *See* statement of stockholders' equity

statement of financial position A financial statement showing a firm's assets, liabilities, and stockholders' equity at a specific date; also called a balance sheet

statement of owner's equity A financial statement presenting information on the events causing a change in stockholders' equity during a period; the statement presents the beginning balance, additions to, deductions from, and the ending balance of stockholders' equity for the period

statement of retained earnings *See* retained earnings reconciliation

statement of stockholders' equity The financial statement that reconciles all of the components of stockholders' equity; *see statement of owner's equity*

static budget a budget based on a prior prediction of expected sales and production.

step costs costs that are constant within a narrow range of activity but shift to a higher level with an increased range of activity. Total step costs increase in a step-like fashion as activity increases.

step method A method of allocating service department costs that gives partial recognition to interdepartmental services by using a methodology that allocates service department costs sequentially to both the remaining service departments and the producing departments.

stock dividends The payment of dividends in shares of stock

stock split Additional shares of its own stock issued by a corporation to its current stockholders in proportion to their current ownership interests without changing the balances in the related stockholders' equity accounts; a formal stock split increases the number of shares outstanding and reduces proportionately the stock's per share par value

storyboard a process map developed by employees who perform the component activities within a process.

straight-line depreciation A depreciation procedure that allocates uniform amounts of depreciation expense to each full period of a depreciable asset's useful life

strategic business segment a segment that has its own mission and set of goals to be achieved. The mission of the segment influences the decisions that its top managers make in both short-run and long-run situations.

strategic cost management making decisions concerning specific cost drivers within the context of an organization's business strategy, its internal value chain, and its place in a larger value chain stretching from the development and use of resources to the final consumers.

strategic plan a guideline or framework for making specific medium-range or short-run decisions.

strategic position how an organization wants to place itself in comparison to the competition.

strategic position analysis an organization's basic way of competing to sell products or services.

strategy a course of action that will assist in achieving one or more goals.

structural cost drivers fundamental choices about the size and scope of operations and technologies employed in delivering products or services to customers. These choices affect the types of activities and the costs of activities performed to satisfy customer needs.

suboptimization when managers or operating units, acting in their own best interests, make decisions that are not in the best interest of the organization as a whole.

subsequent events Events occurring shortly after a fiscal year-end that will be reported as supplemental information to the financial statements of the year just ended

subsidiaries Companies that are owned by the parent company

subsidiary ledger A set of accounts or records that contains detailed information about the items included in the balance of one general ledger account

summary of significant accounting policies A financial statement disclosure, usually the initial note to the statements, which identifies the major accounting policies and procedures used by the firm

sum-of-the-years'-digits method An accelerated depreciation method that allocates depreciation expense to each year in a fractional proportion, the denominator of which is the sum of the years' digits in the useful life of the asset and the numerator of which is the remaining useful life of the asset at the beginning of the current depreciation period

sunk costs costs resulting from past decisions that cannot be changed.

T

T account An abbreviated form of the formal account that is set in the shape of a T; use is usually limited to illustrations of accounting techniques and analysis

target costing establishes the allowable cost of a product or service by starting with determining what customers are willing to pay for the product or service and then subtracting a desired profit on sales.

temporary account An account used to gather information for an accounting period; at the end of the period, the balance is transferred to a permanent stockholders' equity account; in contrast, the revenue, expense, and dividends accounts are temporary accounts

term loan A long-term borrowing, evidenced by a note payable, which is contracted with a single lender

terminal period The forecast period following the horizon period

theory of constraints every process has a bottleneck (constraining resource), and production cannot take place faster than it is processed through the bottleneck. The theory's goal is to maximize throughput in a constrained environment.

throughput sales revenue minus direct materials costs. *See* also theory of constraints.

time-adjusted rate of return *see* internal rate of return.

times interest earned ratio Income before interest expense and income taxes divided by interest expense

top-down budget a budget where top management decides on the primary goals and objectives for the organization and communicates them to lower management levels.

total compensation cost The sum of gross pay, payroll taxes, and fringe benefits paid by the employer

trade credit Inventories purchased on credit from other companies

trade discount An amount, usually based on quantity of merchandise purchased, that the seller subtracts from the list price of merchandise to determine the invoice price

trade name An exclusive and continuing right to use a certain term or name to identify a brand or family of products

trademark An exclusive and continuing right to use a certain symbol to identify a brand or family of products

trading on the equity The use of borrowed funds in the capital structure of a firm; the expectation is that the funds will earn a return higher than the rate of interest on the borrowed funds

trading securities Investments in securities that management intends to actively trade (buy and sell) for trading profits as market prices fluctuate

trailing earnings Earnings reported in the prior period

transfer price the internal value assigned a product or service that one division provides to another.

transitory items Transactions or events that are not likely to recur

translation adjustment The change in the value of the net assets of a subsidiary whose assets and liabilities are denominated in a foreign currency

treasury stock Shares of outstanding stock that have been acquired (and not retired) by the issuing corporation; treasury stock is recorded at cost and deducted from stockholders' equity in the balance sheet

trend percentages A comparison of the same financial item over two or more years stated as a percentage of a base-year amount

trial balance A list of the account titles in the general ledger, their respective debit or credit balances, and the totals of the debit and credit amounts

U

unadjusted trial balance A list of general ledger accounts and their balances taken before accounting adjustments are made

uncollectible accounts expense The expense stemming from the inability of a business to collect an amount previously recorded as a receivable; sometimes called bad debts expense; normally classified as a selling or administrative expense

unearned revenue A liability representing revenues received in advance; also called deferred revenue

unit contribution margin the difference between the unit selling price and the unit variable costs.

unit level activity an activity performed for each unit of product produced or sold.

unit level approach an approach to analyzing cost behavior that assumes changes in costs are best explained by changes in the number of units or sales dollars of products or services provided for customers.

units-of-production method A depreciation method that allocates depreciation expense to each operating period in proportion to the amount of the asset's expected total production capacity used each period

useful life The period of time an asset is used by an entity in its operating activities, running from date of acquisition to date of disposal (or removal from service)

V

value the worth in usefulness or importance of a product or service to the customer.

value chain the set of value-producing activities stretching from basic raw materials to the final consumer.

value chain analysis the study of value-producing activities, stretching from basic raw materials to the final consumer of a product or service.

value stream consists of the production processes for similar products. Each value stream in a lean company not only has lean processes; it also has a lean accounting system because most costs should be directly traceable to one of the value streams.

value-added activity an activity that adds value to a product or service from the viewpoint of the customer.

variable cost ratio variable costs as a portion of sales revenue.

variable costing an approach to product costing that treats variable manufacturing costs as product costs and fixed manufacturing costs as period costs.

variable costs Those costs that change in proportion to changes in sales volume; equaling zero dollars when activity is zero and increasing at a constant amount per unit of activity.

variable interest entity (VIE) Any form of business organization (such as corporation, partnership, trust) that is established by a sponsoring company and provides benefits to that company in the form of asset securitization or project financing; VIEs were formerly known as special purpose entities (SPEs)

variable manufacturing overhead all variable costs, except direct labor and direct materials, associated with converting raw materials into finished goods.

variable overhead effectiveness variance the difference between the standard variable overhead cost for the actual inputs and the flexible budget cost for variable overhead based on outputs.

variable overhead spending variance the difference between the actual variable overhead cost and the standard variable overhead cost for the actual inputs.

variable selling and administrative costs all variable costs other than those directly associated with converting raw materials into finished goods.

variance a comparison of actual and budgeted (or allowed) costs or revenues which are usually identified in financial performance reports.

vertical analysis Analysis of a firm's financial statements that focuses on the statements of a single year; restates amounts in the current financial statements as a percentage of some base measure such as sales

virtual integration the use of information technology and partnership concepts to allow two or more entities along a value chain to act as if they were a single economic entity.

voucher Another name for the payment approval form

W

waiting time the time units spend in temporary storage waiting to be processed, moved, or inspected.

warranties Guarantees against product defects for a designated period of time after sale

wasting assets Another name for natural resources; *see* natural resources

weighted average cost of capital (WACC) The discount rate where the weights are the relative percentages of debt and equity in the capital structure and are applied to the expected returns on debt and equity respectively; an average of the after-tax cost of long-term borrowings and the cost of equity

weighted average method in process costing, a costing method that spreads the combined beginning inventory cost and current manufacturing costs (for materials, labor, and overhead) over the units completed and those in ending inventory on an average basis.

work in process inventory The cost of inventories that are in the manufacturing process and have not yet reached completion

work ticket a document used to record the time a job spends in a specific manufacturing operation.

working capital The difference between current assets and current liabilities

work-in-process inventories partially completed goods consisting of raw materials that are in the process of being converted into a finished product.

Z

zero coupon bond A bond that offers no periodic interest payments but that is issued at a substantial discount from its face value

zero-based budgeting a variation of the minimum level approach to budgeting where every dollar of expenditure must be justified.

z-score The outcome of the Altman Z-score bankruptcy prediction model

Index

A

Abbott Laboratories, Inc., 5:16, 7:13–15
ABC. *See* activity-based costing
Abercrombie & Fitch, 10:26
absorption cost
 defined, 17:5
 overview, 17:25–29e, 28e
 transfer price and, 23:11–12
accelerated depreciation, 5:20e–22, 6:29
accounting
 constructing financial statements, 2:25–28
 quality of, 5:30–33
 for transactions, 3:4e–7
accounting adjustments. *See* accrual accounting
accounting cycle, 3:3e, 20–21
accounting rate of return, 24:13–14
accounting standards. *See also* IFRS Insight;
  IFRS (International Financial Accounting
  Standards)
 choices in, 1:16–17
 financial statements, 2:29
 globalization of, 13:5
 international standards, overview, 1:7, 8–9
 principles and governance, 1:25–30
 Sarbanes-Oxley Act, 1:9
accounting year, 1:10
accounts, closing of, 3:20–21
accounts payable
 accounts payable days outstanding, 8:6
 accounts payable turnover (APT), 8:5–6
 balance sheet, 2:7e–9, 8e
 current liabilities, 8:4–5
 forecasting, 11:6, 24
 net operating capital and, 12:11
 operating items, balance sheet, 4:8e–11e
 settling, 2:27
 statement of cash flows, 3:17–20, B:9–10
accounts receivable
 accounts receivable turnover (ART), 6:10–11
 analysis of, 6:8–12
 asset turnover and, 4:15–16e
 balance sheet, 2:5e
 Cisco Systems, Inc., overview, 6:1–2
 collecting, 2:27
 footnote and MD&A disclosures, 6:7–8e
 forecasting, 11:6, 22
 global accounting, 6:35
 operating items, balance sheet, 4:8e–11e
 overview, 6:3–5
 quick ratio, 4:27
 reducing net operating capital, 12:11
 statement of cash flows, 3:17–20, B:8–9
 uncollectible amounts, 6:5e–7e, 6e
accrual, defined, 2:8
accrual accounting
 accruals, estimating, 8:8–9
 accrued expenses, 2:24, 3:8–11, 9e
 accrued revenues, 2:24, 3:9e, 11
 income statements, 2:12–13
 overview, 3:3e–4, 8–9e

prepaid expenses, 3:9
 transaction analysis, 2:22–28, 3:5–7
 trial balance, 3:12–15, 14e
 unearned revenues, 3:9–10
accrued liabilities
 balance sheet, 2:7e–9, 8e
 current liabilities, 8:4, 6–8
 forecasting, 11:6, 25
 operating items, balance sheet, 4:8e–11e
 statement of cash flows, B:10–11
accumulated depreciation, 6:28, 11:23–24, B:12
accumulated income or loss, 2:9
accumulated other comprehensive income
  (AOCI), 7:6e–7, 29, 9:29
Accumulated Other Comprehensive Income (or
  Loss), 9:19–21
accumulated post-employment benefit obligation
  (APBO), 10:20–21
ACP (average collection period), 6:10–11
acquisition
 acquired growth, pitfalls of, 7:24
 intangible assets, 7:20–22
 intercorporate investments, 7:11–15
 passive investments, 7:5
 revenue growth forecasts, 11:9
activity
 activities list, 17:9
 as cost drivers, 13:13–14e, 16–17
 value chain, 20:4e–5e
activity-based budgeting, 21:5
activity-based costing (ABC)
 activity-based management, 18:17
 cost environment, changes in, 18:3e–4
 customer profitability analysis, 18:14e–16e
 department overhead rates, 18:7–8
 implementation issues, 18:13–14
 indirect costs and, 18:1–2
 limitations of, 18:12
 overhead, applying, 18:8–11
 overview of, 18:4–6e
 plantwide overhead rate, 18:6–7
 vs. traditional costing, 18:12–13
activity-based management (ABM), 18:17
actual cost, goal attainment and, 13:10–11
actuarial losses (and gains), pensions, 10:13
Acura Division of Honda, 23:3
additional paid-in capital, 2:9, 9:29
Adelphia Communications (ADELQ), 1:16, 1:30
adjusted trial balance, 3:14
adjustments, accounting. *See* accrual accounting
adjustments, accounts, 2:21–28
administrative costs, 15:5. *See also* service
  departments
administrative expense budget, 21:11e
administrative expenses, 5:3–4
advance payments, 5:11–13
advertising expense, 6:22
AFS (available-for-sale), 7:6e–7
after-tax profits, 15:12e
aging analysis, 6:5e–7e, 6e

AIDO (average inventory days outstanding),
  6:21–24
AirTran, 14:19
alliances, strategic, 7:3–4e, 11–15
Amazon.com, 13:8, 20:17, 21:2
American Bankers Association (ABA), 19:1
American Institute of CPAs, 13:5, 18:16
America West, 14:19
amortization, B:8, 8:17–19, 18e, 10:15n8,
  23–24, 11:24
analyst reports
 financial statements, use of, 1:6
 forecasts, meeting or beating, 5:33
 Morgan Stanley, balance sheet forecasting,
  11:22–27
 Morgan Stanley, expense forecasting, 11:17–
  19, 18e
 Morgan Stanley, income statement, 11:7–8e
 Morgan Stanley, Procter & Gamble forecast,
  11:37–51
 Morgan Stanley, revenue forecasts, 11:13–16
 Oppenheimer valuation, J&J, 12:15–17
 overview, 2:31
Anheuser-Busch, 20:4
annuities, 8:29–30, 24:25–26e
antidilutive securities, 5:30n9
AOCI (accumulated other comprehensive
  income), 7:6e–7, 29, 9:29
Aon Corporation
 cash dividends, 9:16
 common stock, 9:6
 contributed capital, 9:4
 earned capital, 9:15
 noncontrolling interest, 9:21–24, 23e
 other comprehensive income, 9:19–21
 owner financing, overview, 9:1–2
 restricted stock, 9:13–14
 stock-based compensation, 9:9–14
 stockholder's equity, 9:3–4e
 stock issuance, 9:7
 stock repurchase, 9:8–9
 treasury stock, 9:9
Apple, Inc. (AAPL)
 accounting adjustments, 3:9–15
 articulation of financial statements, 2:19–20e
 balance sheet, 2:4–6, 5e, 3:16
 budgeting and planning, 21:1–2
 business strategy, 1:4
 debt level, 2:10
 Form 10-K, 2:30
 income statement, 2:11–14, 12e, 13e,
  3:15–16
 liabilities and equity, balance sheet, 2:6–11,
  7e, 8e
 market and book value, 2:6, 11
 operating activities, 1:13
 outsourcing decisions, 16:11
 overview, 2:1–2, 3:1–2
 return on assets, 1:19
 revenue forecasts, 11:11–12
 statement of cash flows, 2:15–18, 16e

Note: The letter "e" refers to an exhibit on the stated page, and the letter "n" indicates that the information is included in a footnote on the given page. For example, 15n7 means footnote 7 on page 15.

statement of stockholders' equity, 2:14e–15, 3:17
transaction analysis, 2:21–28, 3:5–7
trial balance, 3:12–15, 14e
unearned revenue, recognition of, 5:11–13
APT (accounts payable turnover), 8:5–6
ARA, 16:11
Arthur Andersen, 13:19
articulation of financial statements, 2:19–20e
asset financing
balance sheet, overview, 1:10e–12
leases, 10:4–11, 5e, 8e, 9e, 10e
leverage across industries, 4:17–19
long-term nonoperating liabilities, 8:12–15e, 14e
special purpose entities, 10:24–27
assets. *See also* cash; depreciation; off-balance-sheet financing; property, plant and equipment (PPE)
acquisition of, 3:6
asset base, investment centers, 23:16
balance sheet, overview, 1:10e–12
capitalization of asset costs, 6:26–27
Cisco Systems, Inc., overview, 6:1–2
consolidation disclosures, 7:19–20e
costs, flow of, 2:4
current ratio, 4:26–27
deferred tax assets, 5:22, 35–37, 36e
depreciation, 5:20e–22
DuPont disaggregation analysis, 4:30–33e
economic value added, 12:17–18
forecasting, 11:6, 19–27, 20e, 22e
global accounting, 6:35–36
impairments, 6:31–32
intangible, 7:20–22
leases, 10:5e
pension assets, 10:12–14
return on, 1:18–19e
return on net operating assets (RNOA), 4:1, 5–7
sales and impairments, 6:30–32
statement of cash flows, 2:15–18, 16e, 3:17–20, B:11–12
transactions, posting, 3:4e–5
trial balance, 3:12–15, 14e
asset turnover (AT), 1:18–19e, 4:11–14, 13e, 30–33e, 6:11
asset write-downs, 5:16–19
Atlanta Braves, 24:27
AT&T, 23:3, 4
audit reports, 1:26–28e
authorized shares, 9:6
automated production processes, 13:6
automobiles, pricing for, 20:1–2
available-for-sale (AFS), 7:6e–7
average collection period (ACP), 6:10–11
average cost, inventory, 6:16, 18e–20
average inventory days outstanding (AIDO), 6:21–24
avoidable common costs, 23:6e–7

B

backflush costing, 19:14
balanced scorecard, 23:19–22, 20e

balance sheet. *See also* accrual accounting; off-balance-sheet financing
accounts payable, overview, 8:5
accounts receivable, overview, 6:3–5, 7e
accrued liabilities, 8:7, 8:8–9
articulation of, 2:19–20e
assets, 2:4–6, 5e
cash dividends, 9:16
cash flow from financing activities, B:12–13
cash flow from investing activities, B:11–12
cash flow from operating activities, B:6e–11, 7e
closing accounts, 3:20–21
consolidated disclosures, 7:19–20e
consolidation reporting, 7:26
debt issuance, 8:15–21, 18e
depreciation, 6:28, 6:29
flow of costs, 2:3e–4
forecasting, 11:19–27, 20e, 22e, 30–33e, 32e
global standards, 2:29, 4:19–20
Google, investments, 7:2
growth dynamics, 11:6e
intercorporate investments, 7:12
inventory, 6:13, 15–20, 18e
Johnson & Johnson, 12:13–15
leases, present value, 10:9e–10
lease types, 10:4–5e
liabilities and equity, 2:6–11, 7e, 8e
noncontrolling interest, 9:22
nonoperating return, 4:23
operating items, 4:8e–11e
overview, 1:10e–12
passive investments, 7:5, 7
pension plans, 10:12–14, 23–24
preparation, 3:16
property, plant, and equipment (PPE), 6:26
restricted stock compensation, 9:14
short-term debt, 8:11
statement of cash flows, B:13–15e
stock-based compensation, 9:11
stock dividends, 9:17e–18
stockholder's equity, 9:3–4e
stock issuance, 9:7
stock repurchase, 9:8–9
transaction analysis, 2:21–28
Bank Administration Institute (BAI), 19:1
Bank of America, 15:20
banks, financial statement use, 1:6
banks, product costing, 19:1–2
Barnes and Noble, 16:11, 21:2
barriers to entry, 1:21
barter transactions, 5:8
basis, manufacturing overhead, 17:7
batch-level activity, 14:18
Bausch & Lomb, 22:3–4
Bayer Construction, 5:9–11
BDO Seidman, 1:26
Bearing Point, 9:17e–18
before-tax profits, 15:12e, 17–19
Bell Atlantic Corporation, 8:1
below-the-line items, 5:28–30
benchmarking, 20:17–18
benefit cost, pension plans, 10:15n7
benefits, 10:20–21. *See also* pension plans
Berkshire Hathaway
acquisition criteria, 4:1

assessing SEC filings, 1:23–25
audit report, 1:27e
balance sheet, 1:10–12
earnings per share, 5:30
income statement, 1:12e–13
McLane Company, Inc., 1:21
overview, 1:1–2
statement of cash flows, overview, 1:15e
statement of stockholders' equity, overview, 1:14e
Best Buy Co. Inc. (BBY), 1:10, 19, 5:4, 17:3, 22:7
big bath, 5:17, 8:8
bill of materials, 17:9
Black-Scholes option calculations, 9:10
Blake, Franke, 22:1–2
Blockbuster, Inc., 15:1
BMW, 24:8
board of directors, 1:28e
Boeing, 13:9, 13:11, 16:13–14, 20:6
Boise Cascade, 20:3
Bombardier, 24:1–2
bonds
bond valuation, 8:30e–31
issued at par, 8:15–17
noncurrent liabilities, 2:9
overview, 8:12
pricing, 8:12–14
repurchase, 8:19–20, 32e, 33
book value
bond repurchase, 8:19–20
book value per share, 9:24
market-to-book ratio, 2:15
purchases above book value, 7:18–19e
subsidiary not wholly owned, 7:17–18e
subsidiary wholly-owned, 7:17e
vs. market value, 2:10–11
Borders, 21:2
Boston Scientific Corp., 23:10
bottom-up budget, 21:18
Bowater Incorporated, 17:9
break-even point
multi-level contribution income statement, 15:19–20
multiple-product cost-volume-profit analysis, 15:14–17e, 16e
profit planning and, 15:8–12e, 11e
Bristol-Myers Squibb (BMY), 1:16, 5:16, 7:24, 9:26
British Telecom (BT), 9:29
budgetary slack, 21:19, 20
budgets. *See also* capital budgeting
activity-based approach, 21:5
Apple, overview, 21:1–2
budgeted financial statements, 21:13–14e
budget period, 21:19
cash budget, 21:11–13e
employee participation, 21:18–19
ethics, 21:20
finalizing, 21:15
flexible budgets
development of, 22:7–9, 8e
direct materials, 22:11–13
overhead cost variance, 22:15–17
standard cost variance analysis, 22:9–11
forecasts, 21:19

Note: The letter "e" refers to an exhibit on the stated page, and the letter "n" indicates that the information is included in a footnote on the given page. For example, 15n7 means footnote 7 on page 15.

general and administrative expense, 21:11
goal attainment and, 13:10–11
income reconciliation, budget *vs.* actual,
    22:23
incremental approach, 21:5–6
manufacturing and production costs, 21:15–
    18e, 16e, 17e
master budget, overview, 21:7–9e, 8e
minimum level approach, 21:6–7
open book management, 21:20–21
for outcomes, 21:6
output/input approach, 21:4–5
purchase budget, 21:10e, 17e
reasons for, 21:3–4
sales budgets, 21:9e–10, 17e
selling expense budgets, 21:10–11e
buffer zone, balance sheet, 11:6e
Buffett, Warren
    acquisition criteria, 4:1
    on audit committees, 1:29
    on financial reports, 1:13
    overview, 1:1–2
    on pro forma income, 5:34
    return on equity, 4:4
burden. *See* manufacturing overhead
Burger King, 15:3
business activity reports, 1:4–5e
business analysis, 1:20e–22
business failure, causes of, 15:4
Business Insight
    accounting quality, 1:9
    acquired growth, pitfalls of, 7:24
    analyst forecasts, meeting or beating, 5:33
    analyst forecasts, security valuation, 12:7
    audit committees, Buffett on, 1:29
    cash, nonoperating assets, 4:9
    cash, objectivity of, B:16
    cash and securities forecasting, 11:24
    controlling and noncontrolling interest, 2:28
    counter-party risk, 7:31
    debt levels, 2:10
    earn-outs, valuation of, 7:22
    financial reports, Buffett on, 1:13
    free cash flows, 12:5
    gross *vs.* net revenue, 5:9
    imputed discount rate, leases, 10:8
    net income and stockholder equity, 4:4
    net operating asset turnover (NOAT), 4:12
    net operating profit margin (NOPM), 4:12
    noncontrolling interests, 7:18
    parent company acquisition, 7:26
    pensions and income analysis, 10:20
    Pfizer restructuring, 5:17
    pro forma income, 5:34
    ratios across industries, 5:4
    restructuring liabilities, 7:22
    revenue recognition standard, 5:13
    Sears cookie jar reserve, 6:10
    Starbuck's addbacks, operating cash flow,
        B:11
    Starbuck's financing activities, B:13
    Starbuck's investing activities, B:12
    statement of cash flows, Apple, 2:18
    tax rates, net operating profit after tax, 4:7
    tax shield, 4:7
    Verizon's zero-coupon debt, 8:16

Walt Disney Company, 5:11
WorldCom, cost capitalization, 6:26
business plan, 1:4–5
business segments. *See* segment reporting
business strategy, 1:4
buyers
    competitive analysis, 1:22
    competitive environment, 1:20e–22

C

calendar-year, 1:10
Camp, Robert, 20:17
capital. *See also* contributed capital
    capital asset pricing model (CAPM), 12:6n7
    capital expenditures, forecasting, 11:23–24
    capital investment, 3:5–6
    capitalization, operating leases, 10:7–11, 9e,
        10e
    capitalization of inventory cost, 6:13–14
    capitalized lease assets, 4:8e–11e, 10:5e
    capital lease method, 10:4–11, 5e, 8e, 9e, 10e
    cost of, special purpose entities and, 10:26–
        27
    distributions, 3:7
    equity, balance sheet, 2:6–11, 7e, 8e
    operating cash flow to capital expenditure
        ratio, B:17
    stockholders' equity, types of, 2:9
    weighted average cost of capital, 12:6n7
capital budgeting
    accounting rate of return, 24:13–14
    cash flow, expected, 24:6–7e
    cash flows, differential analysis, 24:17–18e
    cost of capital, 24:10–11
    high-tech investments, 24:18–19
    internal rate of return (IRR), 24:9–10e
    long-range planning and, 24:4e–6
    models, evaluation of, 24:14–15e
    multiple investment criteria, 24:16
    net present value, 24:8–9e
    overview, 24:3–4
    payback period, 24:11–13
    risk, evaluating, 24:16–17
    taxes and, 24:20–22e, 21e
    Viking Air, overview, 24:1–2
capital expenditures, 24:3. *See also* capital
    budgeting
Capital IQ, 2:32
capital markets, 1:7–8, 22
CAPM (capital asset pricing model), 12:6n7
Carbon Motors Corporation, 13:1–2, 13:6, 13:9
Carnegie Steel Company, 13:8, 14:16
carry forwards, tax loss, 5:22
carrying value, 6:28
cars, pricing, 20:1–2
cash. *See also* cash flow; statement of cash flows
    balance sheet, overview, 1:10e–12, 2:5e
    cash accounting, 3:8
    cash conversion cycle, 2:8e–9
    cash cycle, 2:8
    cash equivalents, B:3n1
    forecasting, 11:5–6, 24
    intercorporate investments, 7:3e–4e
    lease payments, 10:7
    operating assets, 4:9–11e

passive investments, 7:3e, 4e–10, 6e, 9e
quick ratio, 4:27
statement of stockholders' equity, overview,
    1:14e
stock issuance, 9:6–7
stock repurchase, 9:8–9
cash budget, 21:11–13e
cash flow. *See also* contributed capital;
        statement of cash flows
    bond valuation, 8:30e
    cash-flow hedge, 7:29–32
    derivatives, 7:28–32
    discounted cash flow model, equity
        valuation, 12:3–4
    forecasting, 11:29e–30
    lease types, 10:4–5e
    from operating activity, B:6e–11, 7e
    pension plan assets, 10:17–18
cash flows
    annuities, 24:25–26e
    capital budgeting, differential analysis,
        24:17–18e
    capital budgeting and, 24:6–7e, 14–15e
    depreciation and, 24:20–21e
    internal rate of return, table approach,
        24:28–29e
    net present value, 24:8–9e
    unequal cash flows, time value of money,
        24:27
cash shortfall, purchases budget, 21:10
Caterpillar, Inc. (CAT), 1:11, 4:13–14, 5:4,
    6:19–20, 7:19–20e, 17:1–2
chained target costing, 20:14
Chambers, John, 6:2
changes in accounting principles, 5:28n7
channel stuffing, 5:7
charge-offs, 5:16–19
Chartered Institute of Management Accountants,
    18:16
Cheesecake Factory Inc. (CAKE), 5:4
Chevrolet, 20:1–2
Chicago Tribune, 17:9
Chrysler, 24:8
Cisco Systems, Inc. (CSCO)
    accounts receivable, 6:3, 11
    capital budgeting, 24:4
    financing activities, 1:11
    footnote and MD&A disclosures, 6:7–8e
    footnotes, inventory, 6:17–18
    gross profit margin, 6:20e–21
    inventory turnover, 6:21–24
    operating activities, 1:13, 5:4
    operating assets, overview, 6:1–2
    operating cash flow to current liabilities ratio,
        B:17
    PPE asset amounts, 6:33
    PPE turnover, 6:33–35
    stock-based compensation, 9:12–13
City of Chicago, 13:7
City of Indianapolis, 18:2
class action law suits, 1:30
cliff vesting, 9:10
closing process, 3:20–23
Coca-Cola Company, The, 13:6, 13:15, 17:20,
    18:2, 13, 20:3–4, 6, 23:3
codes of ethics, 13:18. *See also* ethics

coefficient of determination, 14:13–14
Colgate-Palmolive, B:17
collateral, 8:24
collectibility risk, 6:3
Comcast, 1:11
committed fixed costs, 14:8–10, 9e
common segment costs, 23:5–7, 6e
common stock. *See also* stock
    dividends in arrears, 9:16
    global accounting, 9:29
    overview, 9:6
    shareholders' equity, 2:9
    statement of cash flows, B:13
    stock-based compensation, 9:9–14
communication, budgets and, 21:3–4
compensation, stock-based, 9:9–14
competition, key dimensions, 13:13
competitive environment, analysis of, 1:20e–22
compound financial instruments, 9:28
compound interest, 8:28–32, 24:23
conglomerates, 4:13, 4:19
Conoco Phillips, 9:24–25
consignment sales, 5:7, 8
consolidation accounting, 7:16–26, 17e, 18e,
    19e, 20e, 27
constraints, resource use, 16:16–19
contingency sales, 5:7
contingent liabilities, 8:7–8
continuous budgeting, 21:19
continuous improvement (Kaizen) costing,
    20:16–17
contract-based assets, 7:21
contract rate, 8:12
contributed capital
    defined, 9:3
    overview, 9:4
    restricted stock, 9:13–14
    stock, classes of, 9:4–6
    stock-based compensation, 9:9–14
    stockholders' equity, 1:14e, 2:9
    stock repurchase, 9:8–9
    stock transactions, 9:6–9
contribution income statements, 15:6e–7e
contribution margin
    income statements, 15:6e–7e
    multiple-product cost-volume-profit analysis,
      15:14–17e, 16e
    operating leverage ratio, 15:17–19
control, investments, 7:3e–4e
control account, production files and records,
    17:10
controlling, overview of, 13:11, 12e
controlling interest, 2:28, 7:16–26, 17e, 18e,
    19e, 20e
conversion cost, defined, 17:6
convertible securities, 9:27–29
cookie jar reserve, 6:9–10, 8:9
Cooper, Robin, 13:4
core competencies, value chain and, 20:6–7
Cornell University, 15:3
Corning Corporation, 13:8, 9
corporate governance, ethics and, 13:18–20
corporate social responsibility, 13:19–20
cost behavior
    basic patterns, 14:3–5, 4e
    committed fixed costs, 14:8–10, 9e

defined, 14:3
discretionary fixed costs, 14:8–10, 9e
factors affecting, 14:5
total cost function, 14:5–6e
variable and average costs, 14:8
cost centers, 22:5, 7–9, 8e
Costco (COST), 1:19
cost competition, 13:13, 14:1–2, 17:1–2
cost drivers
    activity cost drivers, 13:14e, 16–17
    analysis, 13:6, 17:7
    organizational costs, 13:14e, 15–16
    overview, 13:13–14e
    structural cost drivers, 13:14e, 15
cost estimation
    activity and, 14:16
    alternative classifications, 14:16–19, 17e, 18e
    customer cost hierarchy, 14:18–19
    defined, 14:10
    high-low cost estimation, 14:11–12e
    least-squares regression, 14:13e–15
    manufacturing cost hierarchy, 14:17–18e
    scatter diagrams, 14:12e–13
    technology and price, changes in, 14:15–16
cost leadership, defined, 13:8
cost of goods manufactured, product costing,
    17:15–16e
cost of goods sold (COGS)
    accounts payable, 8:5
    defined, 2:4
    forecasting, 11:5–6, 18
    income statements, overview, 1:12e–13,
      2:12e–14, 13e, 4:5–6
    inventory, 6:13–14, 21–24, 22n7
    operating activities, overview, 4:5–6, 5:3–4
    product costing, 17:6e, 10–15, 11e, 14e
    statement of cash flows, B:19–22e, 20e
cost of production report, 17:20–24, 22e
cost of services provided, 17:17–19
cost per equivalent unit in process, 17:21–22
cost prediction, defined, 14:12
cost reduction proposal, 16:4
costs. *See also* activity-based costing; budgets;
    capital budgeting; cost of goods sold
    (COGS); cost-volume-profit analysis and
    planning; operation costs; performance
    reporting; product costing; transfer pricing
    break-even point, 15:8, 14–17e, 16e, 19–20e
    of capital, 24:10–11
    capitalization of asset costs, 6:26–27
    continuous improvement (Kaizen) costing,
      20:16–17
    contribution income statements, 15:6e–7e
    cost capitalization, WorldCom, 6:26
    cost estimates, 5:11
    cost of sales, income statements, 1:12e–13
    differential cost analysis, 16:6–7e
    division operating expenses, 23:15–16
    effective cost of debt, 8:14–15e
    flow of, balance sheet, 2:3e–4
    full costs, 16:10–11
    functional income statements, 15:6e–7e
    general and administrative expense budget,
      21:11e
    incremental approach, budgeting, 21:5–6
    joint costs, 16:16

management, overview of, 13:5–6
manufacturing cost budget, 21:15–18e, 16e,
    17e
minimum level approach, budgeting, 21:6–7
multiple-product cost-volume-profit analysis,
    15:14–17e, 16e
opportunity costs, 16:6
outlay costs, relevance of, 16:4
output/input approach, budgeting, 21:4–5
passive investments, 7:5–6
performance reports, 13:10–11
pricing and, 20:7–11, 8e
profit analysis, unit and nonunit cost drivers,
    15:19–21e, 20e
profit centers, performance reports, 22:19–20
profit formula, 15:4–6
purchases budgets, 21:10e
relevant costs, identifying, 16:3–6
responsibility accounting, 22:3–7
segment reports, 23:5–7, 6e
selling expense budget, 21:10–11e
standard costs, 22:9
sunk costs, 16:5
variance analysis, 22:10–11
costs and benefits, decisions about
    differential cost analysis
      outsourcing, 16:11–15, 12e, 13e
      overview, 16:6–7e
      profit plans, changes in, 16:8–9
      sell or process further, 16:15–16
      special orders, 16:9–11, 10e
    limited resources, use of, 16:16–19
    model limitations, 16:19
    new product introduction, 16:1–2
    relevant costs, identifying, 16:3–6
cost structure, Netflix example, 15:1–2
cost-volume-profit (CVP) analysis and planning
    break-even point and profit planning, 15:8–
      12e, 11e
    income statements, contribution and
      functional, 15:6e–7e
    income taxes, impact of, 15:12e
    multiple-product analysis, 15:14–17e, 16e
    Netflix, overview, 15:1–2
    operating leverage analysis, 15:17–19
    profitability analysis, 15:3–6
    unit and nonunit cost drivers, 15:19–21e,
      20e
counter-party risk, 7:31
coupon rate, 8:12
courts, 1:30
covenants, 1:6, 8:24
Cracker Barrel, 17:3
credit. *See also* accounts receivable
    compound interest, 8:28–32
    credit ratings and debt cost, 8:21–27
    credit sales, 6:3–5
    credit services, 2:31–32
    inventory purchases, 2:26–27
    leverage across industries, 4:17–19
    terms of, 8:6n2
creditors
    balance sheet, overview, 1:11–12
    financial statements, use of, 1:6
    liabilities and equity, balance sheet, 2:6–11,
      7e, 8e

Note: The letter "e" refers to an exhibit on the stated page, and the letter "n" indicates that the information is included in a footnote on the given page. For example, 15n7 means footnote 7 on page 15.

credits
    T-account, 3:5
    trial balance, 3:12–15, 14e
Crown Department Stores, 13:11–12e
cumulative provision, dividends, 9:4–5
currency
    foreign currency translation effects, 5:26–27e
    risk, 7:28n3
    Statement of Stockholders' Equity, 9:23e–24
    translation adjustment, 9:20–21
    translation effects, 5:3–4, 26–27e
current assets, 2:4–6, 5e, 4:26–27. See also
        assets
current liabilities. See also liabilities
    balance sheet, 2:7e–9, 8e
    liquidity analysis, 4:26–27
    nonowner financing, 8:3
    operating cash flow to current liabilities ratio,
        B:17
    types of, 8:4–11
current maturities of long-term debt, 8:4
current method rate, 9:21n2
current nonoperating liabilities, 8:4, 10–11
current ratio, 4:26–27, 6:35–36
current tax expense, 5:22–26e, 23e
Curtis, David, 24:1–2
customer cost hierarchy, 14:18–19
customer demand, as cost driver, 13:14e
customer feedback, cost management and, 13:11
customer-level activity, 14:19
customer profitability analysis, 18:14e–16e
customers, financial statement use, 1:6
customer value, 15:20
cycle efficiency, 19:12–13
cycle time, 19:11–12

D

Daihatsu Motor Company, 20:17
Daimler, 20:1–2
Daimler Trucks, 19:11
Dairy Queen, 14:6
Dancing Deer Baking, 21:21
data services, 2:32
days outstanding, forecasting and, 11:21
DCF. See discounted cash flow (DCF) model,
        valuation
debits
    T-account, 3:5
    trial balance, 3:12–15, 14e
debt. See also off-balance-sheet financing
    convertible securities, 9:27–29
    credit ratings and debt cost, 8:21–27
    current nonoperating liabilities, 8:10–11
    effective cost of, 8:14–15e
    as extraordinary item, 5:28n8
    financing, reporting of, 8:15–21, 18e
    footnotes, 8:20–21
    forecasting, 11:25–27
    global accounting, 8:27–28
    income shifting, 6:9–10
    levels of, 2:10
    leverage across industries, 4:17–19
    long-term, 2:9
    long-term nonoperating liabilities, 8:12–15e,
        14e

nonoperating return, 4:16–17
operating items, balance sheet, 4:8e–11e
pricing, 8:12–14
short-term interest-bearing, 8:4
transaction analysis, 2:26–27
debt financing. See also financing activities
    balance sheet, overview, 1:11–12
    liabilities and equity, balance sheet, 2:6–11,
        7e, 8e
    nonoperating return, 4:21–26
    vs. equity financing, 4:17
debt securities, passive investments, 7:3e, 4e–10,
        6e, 9e
decline, product life cycle, 20:15
default, 8:22
deferred gains (and losses), pension plans,
        10:23–24
deferred income tax assets, 4:8e–11e, 5:25–26e,
        9:10–11
deferred income tax liabilities, 4:8e–11e, 11:25
deferred recognition, pension obligations,
        10:15n7
deferred returns, 24:27
deferred tax asset valuation allowance, 5:22,
        25–26e, 11:23
deferred tax expense, 5:22–26e, 23e
deferred tax liability, 5:20e–22, 35–37, 36e
defined benefit plan, pensions, 10:12. See also
        pension plans
defined contribution plan, pensions, 10:12. See
        also pension plans
de Havilland Aircraft of Canada, 24:1–2
deliberate manager intervention, 5:32
Dell, Inc. (DELL), 1:28, 5:4, 6:22, 23–24
Dell Computers, 13:8, 16:11, 20:6, 17
Deloitte, 1:26
Delta Air Lines (DAL)
    capitalization of operating leases, 10:8e–11,
        9e, 10e
    inventory costs, 17:3
    lease disclosure footnotes, 10:6–7
    off-balance-sheet financing, overview, 10:1–2
    pension footnotes, 10:15–16
    pension footnotes, future cash flows,
        10:17–18
    pension funding, 10:14
    pensions, profit implications, 10:18–19
demand, as cost driver, 13:14e
departmental overhead rates, 19:3
deposits for future service, 5:11–13
depreciation
    deferred tax liability, 5:35–37, 36e
    defined, 2:4
    depreciation base, 6:27
    depreciation method, 6:27
    depreciation rate, 6:27
    forecasting, 11:23–24
    income statements, 2:12e–14, 13e
    leases, 10:10e–11
    manufacturing equipment, 17:6e
    operating activities, overview, 5:3–4
    percent used up, 6:35
    property, plant, and equipment, 6:27–30e
    recording, 2:27
    sale of equipment, 5:4n2
    statement of cash flows, B:8, 12, 19–22e, 20e

straight line vs. accelerated, 5:20e
    useful life, 6:35
depreciation tax shield, 24:20–21e
derivative securities, 7:5n1, 28–32, 9:20, 23e–24
description of the business, Form 10-K, 2:30
design for manufacture, 20:13
differential cost analysis
    multiple change in profit plans, 16:8–9
    outsourcing, 16:11–15e, 12e, 13e
    overview of, 16:6–7e
    sell or process further, 16:15–16
    special orders, 16:9–11
dilutive securities, 5:30n9
direct costs, cost-based pricing, 20:9–10
direct department cost, product costing, 19:3
direct labor
    cost estimation, 14:17e
    cost reporting, 17:4–5e
    cost variance, standards for, 22:13–15
    manufacturing overhead and, 17:7–8
    profit formula, 15:5
directly linked costs, 6:27
direct materials
    cost estimation, 14:17e
    cost reporting, 17:4–5e
    cost variance analysis, 22:12–13
    manufacturing overhead and, 17:7–8
    profit formula, 15:5
direct method, cash flow reports, 3:17–20,
        B:6e–11, 7e, 19–22e, 20e
direct method, service department cost
        allocation, 19:5e–6
directors, financial statement use, 1:6
direct resource costs. activity-based costing,
        18:4–6e
direct segment fixed costs, 23:5–7, 6e
disclosure
    benefits and costs, 1:7–8
    statement of cash flows, B:22
discontinued operations, 2:13e–14, 4:25,
        5:28–29
discount amortization, 8:17–19, 18e
discount bonds, 8:13, 16
discounted cash flow (DCF) model, valuation,
        12:3–7, 6e, 12e
discounted value, 1:1–2
discount rate
    annuities, 24:25–26e
    cost of capital, 24:10–11
    lease capitalization, 10:27–29
    leases, 10:8–10
    net present value, 24:8–9e
    pension expense and profit, 10:18–19
    present value of money, 24:23–24
    risk assessments and, 24:16–17
discretionary fixed costs, 14:8–10, 9e
disinvestment phase, capital expenditures, 24:7e
disposal values, 16:5–6
distribution costs, 17:15
distribution costs, income statements, 1:12e–13
divestitures, revenue and, 11:9–10
dividend discount model, valuation, 12:3, 12e
dividend rate, 24:10–11
dividends. See also earned capital
    cash dividends, 9:16
    dividend preference, 9:4–5

dividends in arrears, 9:16
earnings per share, 5:29e–30
effects of, 9:17e–18
income statements, 2:12e–14, 13e
Johnson & Johnson, 12:2
passive investments, 7:6e–7
recording, 3:7
statement of stockholders' equity, 1:14e, 9:23e–24
stock splits, 9:18–19
Dodd-Frank Act, 1:17
Dollar General, 14:1
Dollar Tree, 14:1
double-declining-balance depreciation, 6:29–30e, 24:20–21e
double-entry accounting, 3:5–6
dual prices, transfer pricing, 23:12–13
dual rates, service department cost allocation, 19:8–9
DuPont disaggregation analysis, 4:30–33e

E

earned capital
cash dividends, 9:16
defined, 9:3
other comprehensive income, 9:19–21e
overview, 9:15
stock dividends, 9:17e–18
stockholders' equity, 1:14e, 2:9
stock splits, 9:18–19
earned revenue, 3:6–7, 5:6
earnings
earnings per share (EPS), 5:2, 29e–30, 9:18, 28–29
forecasts, meeting or beating, 5:33
importance of, 1:14
income statements, 2:11–14, 12e, 13e
Johnson & Johnson, 12:2
statement of stockholders' equity, overview, 1:14e
earn-outs, valuation of, 7:22
Ebbers, Bernie, 6:26
economic models, pricing decisions, 20:7–8
economic value added (EVA), 23:17–19
economies of scale, 1:21
effective cost of debt, 8:17
effective rate, 8:12
effective tax rate, 5:24
E.L. DuPont de Nemours and Company, 4:30–33e
electric cars, pricing for, 20:1–2
7-Eleven, 20:4
Eli Lilly, 5:16
employees. See also pension plans
employee participation, budgeting, 21:18–19
financial statements, use of, 1:6
severance or relocation cost, 5:16–19
stock options, 9:8–14
Enron, 1:9, 16, 17, 25, 30, 2:4, 13:19
enterprise risk management, 21:4
Epson, 20:16, 17
equipment, 17:6e. See also capital budgeting; manufacturing overhead; property, plant and equipment (PPE)

equity. See also earned capital; owner financing
balance sheet, 1:10e–12, 2:6–11, 7e, 8e
consolidation disclosures, 7:19–20e
defined, 1:10
DuPont disaggregation analysis, 4:30–33e
equity carve outs and convertibles, 9:24–28
forecasting, 11:19–27, 20e, 22e
leverage across industries, 4:17–19
liabilities-to-equity ratio, 4:27
noncontrolling interest, 9:21–24, 23e
passive investments, 7:3e, 4e–10, 6e, 9e
return on equity (ROE), 1:19, 4:1, 4
statement of cash flows, 3:17–20, B:12–13
statement of stockholders' equity, 1:14e, 2:14e–15
stock issuance, 9:6–7
stock repurchase, 9:8–9
transaction analysis, 2:21–28
transactions, posting, 3:4e–5
equity financing
nonoperating return, 4:16–17
vs. debt financing, 4:17
equity method accounting, ROE effects, 7:13–15
equity method investments, 4:8e–11e, 7:1–2, 11–15, 27
equity securities
discounted cash flow (DFC) model, 12:4–7, 6e
equity valuation models, 12:3–4
Johnson & Johnson (J&J), 12:1–2
residual operating income (ROPI) model, 12:8–11, 9e
valuation model comparison, 12:12e
equity value, computing, 12:7
equivalent completed units, 17:21–22
Ericcson, Inc., 23:15
Ernst & Young, 1:26
errors, unintentional, 5:31
estimates, accrued liabilities, 8:8–9
ethics
budgeting, 21:20
overview of, 13:17–20
responsibility accounting, 22:4
sunk costs and, 16:5
evaluation, budgets and, 21:4
Evían, 20:3
exercise price, 9:9–14
existing stores, revenue forecasting, 11:10–11
expense management, 4:31–32
expenses. See also off-balance-sheet financing
accrued, 3:8–11, 9e
depreciation, 2:4
expense recognition principle, 2:12–13
forecasting, 11:16–19, 18e
income statements, overview, 1:12e–13, 2:11–14, 12e, 13e
operating items, balance sheet, 4:8e–11e
prepaid, 2:5e, 3:8–9e
recording, 3:6–7
statement of cash flows, 2:15–18, 16e
transaction analysis, 2:27
external accounting standards, 13:4
extraordinary items, 2:13e–14, 5:3–4, 28–29
Exxon Mobil, 17:9

F

face amount, 8:12
facility-level activity, 14:18, 14:19
factory overhead. See manufacturing overhead
failure to take delivery, 5:8
fair market value
derivatives, 7:28–32
noncontrolling interest purchases, 7:19
fair value, goodwill reporting, 7:22–24
fair value, stock-based compensation, 9:10
fair-value hedge, derivatives, 7:28–32
fair-value method, 7:4e–10, 6e, 9e
Family Dollar, 14:1, 15:15
FASB. See Financial Accounting Standards Board (FASB)
FCFF (free cash flows to the firm), 12:4–7, 6e, 17
federal tax rates, 4:6
FedEx, 7:23, 13:13, 14, 14:5, 15:20, 18:1–2
fees, nonrefundables, 5:8
FIFO (first-in, first-out), 6:15–16, 18e–20
FIFO (first-in, first-out) process costing, 17:23–24
financial accounting
choices in use, 1:16–17
defined, 13:2
globalization of standards, 13:5
overview, 1:3
principles and governance, 1:25–30
uses of, 13:3–4, 5e
Financial Accounting Standards Board (FASB), 13:5
lease types, 10:5e
overview, 1:7, 8–9, 26
pension expense, 10:23–24
revenue recognition standard, 5:13
financial flexibility, B:16
financial institutions, product costing, 19:1–2
financial leverage (FLEV). See also off-balance-sheet financing
across industries, 4:17–19
DuPont disaggregation analysis, 4:30–33e
leases, 10:7
nonoperating return framework, 4:21–26
return on equity, 7:15
financial ratios, 8:25–27
financial reporting, defined, 17:1
financial statement effects template, 2:21–28, 3:4e–5
financial statements. See also specific statement names
analysis of, 1:18–19e
articulation of, 2:19–20e
balance sheet, overview, 1:10e–12
business activities, 1:4–5e
business analysis, 1:20e–22
choices in use, 1:16–17
constructing, 2:25–28
debt issuance, 8:15–21, 18e
demand and supply, 1:5–9
global accounting, 1:22–23, 2:29
income statements, overview, 1:12e–13
linkages, 1:15–16
other information sources, 1:16
overview, 1:9e–10

principles and governance, 1:25–30
statement of cash flows, overview, 1:15e
statement of stockholders' equity, overview, 1:14e
trial balance, 3:12–15, 14e
financial statements, budgeted, 21:13–14e
financing activities. *See also* equity; nonowner financing; off-balance-sheet financing; owner financing
  balance sheet, overview, 1:11–12
  equity *vs.* debt financing, 4:17
  forecasting, 11:29e–30
  leases, 10:4–11, 5e, 8e, 9e, 10e
  net cash flows, 2:15–18, 16e
  nonoperating return, 4:16–17
  special purpose entities, 10:24–27
  statement of cash flows, B:3–6, 4e, 8, 12–13, 22
  transaction analysis, 2:26–28
  Verizon Communications, Inc., overview, 8:1–2
  weighted average cost of capital, 12:6n7
financing outflow, leases, 10:7
finished goods, 6:18
finished goods inventories
  cost of production report, 17:20–23, 22e
  inventory costing, overview, 17:3–4e
  job costing, 17:10–16e, 11e, 14e
  product cost reporting, 17:6e
  production files and records, 17:10
  reducing, 19:12
Finmeccanica S.p.A., 5:6
first-in, first-out (FIFO), 6:15–16, 18e–20
first-in, first-out (FIFO) process costing, 17:23–24
fiscal year, 1:10
Fitch Ratings, 2:31–32, 8:22e
fixed administrative costs, profit formula, 15:5
fixed assets. *See* property, plant and equipment (PPE)
fixed costs
  committed and discretionary, 14:8–10, 9e
  cost behavior, 14:3–4e
  high-low cost estimation, 14:11–12e
  profit formula, 15:5
  total cost function, 14:5–6e
fixed overhead budget variance, 22:17
Fleetguard, 16:19
flexible budgets
  budget development, 22:8e–9
  direct materials, 22:12–13
  overhead costs, 22:15–17
  standard cost variance analysis, 22:9–11
Follett, 16:11
footnotes
  accounts receivable, 6:7–8e
  inventory, 6:17–18
  lease disclosure, 10:6–7
  nonowner financing, 8:20–21
  off-balance-sheet financing, 10:3
  pension plans, 10:15–16
  pension plans and future cash flows, 10:17–18
  PPE assets, 6:33
  stock option activities, 9:11–12

Ford Motor Company, 10:24–27, 13:8, 17:8, 20:1–2, 24:8
forecasting financial statements. *See also* equity securities
  adjusting forecasted statements, 11:27–28e
  assets, liabilities and equity, 11:19–27, 20e, 22e
  expense forecasts, 11:16–19, 18e
  forecasted balance sheet, 11:27–28e
  forecasting process, 11:3–8e, 5e, 6e
  Morgan Stanley Research Report on P&G, 11:37–51
  multiyear forecasts, 11:30–33e, 32e
  parsimonious multiyear forecasting, 11:35–36e
  Procter & Gamble, overview, 11:1–2
  reassessing, 11:30
  revenue forecasts, 11:8–16
  statement of cash flows, 11:29e–30
forecasts, budgets and, 21:19–20
foreign currency
  risk, 7:28n3
  Statement of Stockholders' Equity, 9:23e–24
  translation adjustment, 9:20–21
  translation effects, 5:3–4, 26–27e
foreign subsidiaries, 3:21, 9:20
Form 8-K, SEC, 2:31
Form 10-K, SEC, 1:7, 23–25, 28, 2:30–31
Form 10-Q, 2:30
Form 10-Q, SEC, 1:7
for-profit organizations, 13:7, 15:3
Fortune Brands, Inc., 2:5, 9:5–6
forward contracts, 7:5n1, 28–32
free cash flows to the firm (FCFF), 12:4–7, 6e, 17
full absorption cost, defined, 17:5
full costs, 16:10–11
functional income statements, cost-volume-profit (CVP) analysis, 15:6e–7e
fundamental analysis, 1:6
funded status, pensions, 10:12, 13–14
future performance, 2:13e–14
futures, derivatives, 7:28–32
future value, 8:28–32, 24:23

G

GAAP. *See* Generally Accepted Accounting Principles (GAAP)
gains
  asset sales, 6:31
  bond repurchase, 8:32e–33
  gain on bond retirement, 8:19–20
  other comprehensive income, 9:20
  passive investments, 7:6e–7
  Statement of Stockholders' Equity, 9:23e–24
Gap, 10:26, 20:17
General Electric, 14:16, 15:3, 16:14, 18:5, 22:1–2, 7
General Electric Commercial Credit, 10:1
general expense budget, 21:11e
general ledger, entries to, 3:4e–5
Generally Accepted Accounting Principles (GAAP)
  balance sheets, 2:14
  book value, 2:10–11

deferred tax liability, 5:35–37, 36e
economic net income distortions, 23:17–18
extraordinary items, 5:28–30
income statements, 2:14
lease disclosure, 10:7
lease types, 10:5e
market value, 2:10–11
one-time events, 5:31–32
overview, 1:7, 26
overview of, 13:5
pro forma earnings, 5:32
ratio analysis, 4:18–19
research and development expenses, 5:15
General Motors Company, 10:18, 13:8, 18, 20:1–2, 16
General Reserve, 9:21
Georgia Pacific, 20:3
gift card payments, 5:11–13
Gillette, 7:21–22
Glass, Lewis and Co., 1:9
global accounting. *See also* IFRS (International Financial Reporting Standards)
  equity valuation, 12:13
  intercorporate investments, 7:27
  leases, 10:21–22
  multiyear forecasts, 11:36
  nonowner financing, 8:27–28
  operating assets, 6:35–36
  owner financing, 9:29
  pensions, 10:21–22
  special purpose entities, 10:22
Global Crossing (GLBC), 1:16
globalization
  accounting standards, 13:5
  target costing, 20:13
goals
  managerial accounting and, 13:10–11
  overview, 13:6–7e
  planning, organizing and controlling, 13:11, 12e
  role of, 13:1–2
goodwill assets, 4:8e–11e, 7:22–24, 11:24
Google
  financing activities, 1:11
  income statement, 1:13
  intercorporate investments, overview, 7:1–2
  investments with control, 7:16–26, 17e, 18e, 19e, 20e
  passive investments, 7:7–9
  sale of subsidiaries, 7:25–26
  significant influence, 7:12–13
governance, corporate, 1:22, 13:18–20
government, incremental budgeting, 21:5–6
government agencies, financial statement use, 1:7
Grant Thornton, 1:26
Graphic Packaging Holding Company, 20:4
Great Little Box, 21:21
green investment, 24:5, 14
Green Mountain Coffee, 5:33
gross margin, 1:12e–13, 4:15–16e
gross margin return on inventory investment (GMROI), 19:13
gross profit, 1:12e–13, 6:13–14, 11:18. *See also* profit
gross profit margin (GPM), 4:31, 6:20e–21

gross revenues, 5:8–9. *See also* revenue
Groupon, Inc., 5:9
growth, product life cycle, 20:15
GTE Corporation, 8:1
Guidant Corp., 23:10
Gulfstream, 13:9

H

Hallco Builders, 17:9
Halliburton (HAL), 1:17
Harley-Davidson, 8:9, 13:15–16, B:17
Harrah's Entertainment, 23:19
Hartmarx, 17:9
health care plans, 10:20–21. *See also* off-balance-sheet financing
Heineken, 24:4, 5
held-to-maturity (HTM), 7:9e–10
Hershey Company, 17:1–2
Hewlett-Packard, 10:27–29, 15:10, 16:11, 20:6, 16
Heymann, Jody, 21:21
high-low cost estimation, 14:11–12e
historical costs, 2:6
Home Depot, Inc. (HD), 1:13, 5:4, B:17, 18:17, 20:16, 22:1–2, 6
Honda, 20:1–2, 23:3
horizon period, 12:5
horizontal analysis, 4:28, 29e, 30e
HSBC Holdings, 24:5
HTM (held-to-maturity), 7:9e–10
human capital, as asset, 13:10

I

IASB (International Accounting Standards Board)
    lease types, 10:5e
    overview, 1:7, 8–9, 13:5
    pension plan reporting, 10:15n7
    revenue recognition standard, 5:13
IBM, 14:19, 18:2, 23:1–2
IFRS Insight
    accruals and contingencies, 8:8
    balance sheet presentation, 1:12, 2:14
    convertible securities, 9:28
    equity method investments, 7:15
    extraordinary items, 5:29
    goodwill impairment and revaluation, 7:24
    income statements, 2:14, 5:6
    international standards, 1:7
    inventory measurement, 6:17
    lease accounting, 10:6
    pension funded status, 10:14
    PPE valuation, 6:32
    preferred stock, 9:6
    research and development expenses, 5:14
    revenue recognition, 5:7
    special purpose entities, 10:26
IFRS (International Financial Reporting Standards). *See also* global accounting
    accumulated other comprehensive income, 9:21
    common stock terminology, 9:7
    consolidation accounting, 7:16
    financial statements, 2:29, 3:21

intercorporate investments, 7:27
    nonowner financing, 8:27–28
    operating and nonoperating items, 4:19–20
    operating assets, 6:35–36
    operating income, 5:33–35
    other comprehensive income, 9:19
    overview, 1:7, 8–9, 22–23, 13:5
    stock repurchase, 9:9
impairments, PPE assets, 6:31–32
imposed budget, 21:18
imputed discount rate, leases, 10:8
income. *See also* operating income
    accounting rate of return, 24:13–14
    depreciation and, 24:20–21e
    DuPont disaggregation analysis, 4:30–33e
    forecasting, 11:27–28e
    investment centers, 23:15–16
    passive investments, 7:5
    pensions, analysis of, 10:20
    residual income, 23:16–17
    sale of subsidiaries, 7:25–26
    statement of cash flows, 2:15–18, 16e
income shifting, 6:9–10
income statements. *See also* accrual accounting
    absorption and variable costing, 17:25–26
    accounts payable, overview, 8:5
    accounts receivable, overview, 6:3–5, 7e
    accrued liabilities, 8:7, 8–9
    articulation of, 2:19–20e
    budgeted income statement, 21:13–14e
    capitalization of operating leases, 10:9e–11, 10e
    cash dividends, 9:16
    cash flow from operating activities, B:6e–11, 7e
    closing accounts, 3:20–21
    costs, flow of, 2:4
    cost-volume-profit (CVP) analysis, 15:6e–7e
    debt issuance, 8:15–21, 18e
    depreciation, 6:28, 29
    forecasting, 11:5–6, 30–33e, 32e
    global standards, 2:29
    intercorporate investments, 7:12
    inventory, 6:13, 15–16, 17, 18e–20
    Johnson & Johnson, 12:13–15
    lease types, 10:4–5e
    multi-level contribution, 15:19–21e, 20e
    noncontrolling interest, 9:22
    operating income, global accounting, 5:35
    operating items, 4:5–7, 5:3–4
    overview, 1:12e–13, 2:11–14, 12e, 13e
    passive investments, 7:5, 7:7
    pension plans, 10:12, 14–15
    Pfizer, Inc. (PFE), 5:5e
    preparation, 3:15–16
    property, plant, and equipment (PPE), 6:26
    reconciling budgeted and actual income, 22:23
    restricted stock compensation, 9:14
    restructuring expense and incentives, 5:16–19
    segment reporting, 23:3–7, 6e
    short-term debt, 8:11
    statement of cash flows, B:13–15e, 19–22e, 20e
    stock-based compensation, 9:11
    stock dividends, 9:17e–18

    stock issuance, 9:7
    stock repurchase, 9:8–9
    transaction analysis, 2:21–28
income tax assets, balance sheet, 4:8e–11e
income taxes, 15:12e, 19–20e
income taxes, forecasting, 11:27–28e
income tax expense, 5:3–4, 5:19–26, 20e, 21e, 23e, B:21
incremental approach, budgeting, 21:5–6
incremental sales, estimating, 24:19–20
incurred expenses, 3:6–7
indirect costs, 18:1–2, 4–6e, 19:3
indirect method, cash flow reports, 3:18–20, B:6e–11, 7e, 14
industry competition, 1:20e–22
information technology departments. *See* service departments
initial investment phase, capital expenditures, 24:6–7e
inputs, competitive analysis, 1:22
inspection time, 19:11–12, 13
insurance, product cost reporting, 17:6e
insurance benefits, retirees, 10:20–21
intangible assets
    acquisition, reporting, 7:20–22
    balance sheet, 2:5e–6
    forecasting, 11:24
    operating items, balance sheet, 4:8e–11e
Intel Corporation (INTC), 5:4, 16:11, 20:18
intellectual assets, 2:6
intercorporate investments. *See* investments, intercorporate
interdepartment services, 19:4. *See also* service departments
interest
    cost of capital, 24:10–11
    future value, 24:23
interest expense
    bond issuance, 8:17–19, 18e
    credit terms, 8:6n2
    DuPont disaggregation analysis, 4:31–33e
    effective cost of debt, 8:14–15e
    forecasting, 11:27–28e
    income statement, 2:12e–14, 13e
    interest-bearing debt, 8:4
    interest cost, pensions, 10:13
    nonoperating assets, 4:5–6
    pension expense and profit, 10:18–19
    times interest earned, 4:28
interest income, 2:12e–14, 13e
Intermet Corporation, 17:9
internal control systems, 13:19
internal rate of return (IRR), 24:9–10e, 16, 28–29e
international accounting standards, 13:5. *See also* accounting standards
International Accounting Standards Board (IASB), 13:5
    lease types, 10:5e
    overview, 1:7, 8–9
    pension plan reporting, 10:15n7
    revenue recognition standard, 5:13
International Energy Agency, 24:5
International Financial Reporting Standards. *See* IFRS (International Financial Reporting Standards)

Note: The letter "e" refers to an exhibit on the stated page, and the letter "n" indicates that the information is included in a footnote on the given page. For example, 15n7 means footnote 7 on page 15.

International Paper Company, 6:31
international standards, 1:7, 8–9. *See also*
        global accounting; IFRS Insight; IFRS
        (International Financial Reporting
        Standards)
intrinsic value, 1:1–2
inventory
        absorption and variable costing, 17:25–29e,
                28e
        accounts payable turnover (APT), 8:5–6
        analysis of, 6:20e–25
        balance sheet, 1:10e–12, 2:5e, 8e
        Cisco Systems, Inc., overview, 6:1–2
        cost flow, 2:4
        costing of, 6:13–17, 14e, 15e
        cost of good sold, 4:15–16e
        divisional investment valuation, 23:16
        footnotes, 6:17–18
        forecasting, 11:6, 23
        global accounting, 6:36
        income statements, overview, 1:12e–13
        inventory levels, financial performance and,
                17:29
        inventory turnover, 6:21–24
        job costing, 17:10–15, 11e, 14e
        just-in-time inventory management, 19:9–12
        manufacturing overhead, 17:7–8
        operating items, balance sheet, 4:8e–11e
        overview, 6:3, 17:3–4e
        product cost, components of, 17:5–6e
        product costs and period costs, 17:4–5e
        reducing net operating capital, 12:11
        statement of cash flows, B:9
        transaction analysis, 2:26–27
        turnover, 19:13
investing activities
        balance sheet, overview, 1:10e–12
        forecasting, 11:29e–30
        net cash flows, 2:15–18, 16e
        net unrealized investment gains, 9:20
        pensions, 10:13
        statement of cash flows, B:3–6, 4e, 8, 11–12,
                22
investment analysts, financial statement use, 1:6
investment centers
        asset base, 23:16
        balanced scorecard, 23:19–22, 20e
        economic value added (EVA), 23:17–18
        overview of, 22:5
        residual income, 23:16–17
        return on investment (ROI)
                investment center income, 23:15–16
                measurement comparison, 23:18–19
                overview, 23:13–15, 14e
                valuation issues, 23:16
investment-grade ratings, 8:24
investment income, recording, 2:27
investments, intercorporate. *See also* capital
        budgeting
        financial statement disclosures, 7:7–9
        global accounting, 7:27
        Google, overview, 7:1–2
        investments reported at cost, 7:9e–10
        investments with control, 7:16–26, 17e, 18e,
                19e, 20e
        marked to market, 7:6e–7

overview, 7:3e–4e
        passive investments, 7:3e, 4e–10, 6e, 9e
        significant influence, 7:11–15
investment securities, forecasting, 11:24
investment tax credit, 24:21–22
irrelevant costs, defined, 16:3
IRR (internal rate of return), 24:9–10e, 16,
        28–29e
issued shares, 9:6
ISuppli, 17:9
Isuzu Motors, 20:16

J

JIT (just-in-time), 6:22
job costing
        absorption and variable costing, 17:25–29e,
                28e
        job cost sheet, 17:10
        joint product decisions, 16:16
        overhead, overapplied and underapplied,
                17:16–17
        overview of, 17:10–15, 11e, 14e
        service organizations, 17:17–19
        statement of cost of goods manufactured,
                17:15–16e
job order environment, 17:9
job production environment, 17:9
Jobs, Steve, 2:1–2
John Deere, 9:18–19
Johnson & Johnson (JNJ), 1:19
        discounted cash flow, 12:5–6e
        equity securities, overview, 12:1–2
        financial statements, 12:13–15
        Oppenheimer valuation of, 12:15–17
        residual operating income (ROPI) model,
                valuation, 12:9e–10
joint product decisions, 16:16
journal entries
        capital investment, 3:5–6
        closing process, 3:22–23
        transactions, 3:4e–5
J.P. Morgan, 2:31
just-in-time (JIT) inventory management, 6:22,
        19:9–12

K

401k accounts, 10:12. *See also* pension plans
Kaizen costing, 20:16–17
Kanban system, 19:11–12
Kellogg, 7:29–30, 32
KFC, 24:4
Kinko's, 15:3
knowledge-based assets, 2:6
Kodak, 21:12
KPMG, 1:26, 13:5–6
Kraft Foods, 7:25–26, 9:25–26
Kroger, 22:6

L

labor
        competitive analysis, 1:22
        cost variance, standards for, 22:14–15
        income statements, overview, 1:12e–13
        labor efficiency variance, 22:14–15

labor rate variance, 22:14–15
        manufacturing costs, 6:13–14
        overhead, overapplied and underapplied,
                17:16–17
        savings estimates, 24:19–20
        wages, balance sheet, 2:7e–9, 8e
Lands' end, 14:11–12
last-in, first-out (LIFO), 6:15–16, 18e–20, 25, 36
leaning on the trade, 8:5–6
lean production, product costing, 19:9–12
leases
        capitalization, present value tables, 10:27–29
        Delta Air Lines, overview, 10:1–2
        global accounting, 10:21
        off-balance-sheet financing, 10:4–11, 5e, 8e,
                9e, 10e
        operating items, balance sheet, 4:8e–11e
least-squares regression analysis, 14:13e–15
lenders, financial statements use, 1:6
leverage, 4:30–33e, 10:1–3, 5e. *See also*
        financing activities
Li, William Santana, 13:1
liabilities. *See also* nonowner financing; off-
        balance-sheet financing
        accrued expenses, 3:10–11
        accrued liabilities, 8:6–8
        balance sheet, 1:10e–12, 2:6–11, 7e, 8e,
                4:8e–11e
        consolidation disclosures, 7:19–20e
        convertible debentures, 9:27–29
        current nonoperating liabilities, 8:10–11
        current ratio, 4:26–27
        deferred taxes, 5:35–37, 36e
        equity method investments, 7:14–15
        forecasting, 11:6, 19–27, 20e, 22e
        liabilities-to-equity ratio, leases, 10:5e
        long-term nonoperating liabilities, 8:12–15e,
                14e
        nonowner financing, global accounting,
                8:27–28
        operating cash flow to current liabilities ratio,
                B:17
        preference shares, 9:6
        restructuring, 7:22
        statement of cash flows, 3:17–20, B:12–13
        transaction analysis, 2:21–28
        transactions, posting, 3:4e–5
        trial balance, 3:12–15, 14e
liabilities-to-equity ratio, 4:27
life cycle, 1:22, 20:15e–16
life cycle budgeting, 21:19
LIFO liquidation, 6:25
LIFO reserve, 6:19–20
linear algebra (reciprocal) costing method, 19:8
line departments, 13:11, 12e
liquidation, LIFO, 6:25
liquidation preference, dividends, 9:5
liquidity
        current assets, 2:4–6, 5e
        liquidity analysis, 4:18–19, 26–30e, 29e
        net working capital, 2:8
        special purpose entities, 10:26–27
L.L. Bean, 17:3
loans. *See also* debt; financing activities
        current nonoperating liabilities, 8:10–11
        financial statements, use of, 1:6

Note: The letter "e" refers to an exhibit on the stated page, and the letter "n" indicates that the information is included in a footnote on the given page. For example, 15n7 means footnote 7 on page 15.

operating items, balance sheet, 4:8e–11e
Lockheed Martin, B:17
logistic costs, 1:12e–13
long-range planning, capital budgeting and,
    24:4e–6
long-term assets. *See also* assets
    balance sheet, overview, 1:10e–12, 2:4–6, 5e
    leases, 10:4–11, 5e, 8e, 9e, 10e
    pensions, 10:12
    sales and, 4:15–16e
long-term debt, 2:7e–9, 8e, 8:4, 11:25–27
long-term investments, 2:5e–6
long-term liabilities, 2:9, 8:15–21, 18e, 9:27–29
long-term nonoperating liabilities, 8:12–15e, 14e
long-term sales contracts, 5:9–11
losses
    asset sales, 6:31
    bond repurchases, 8:32e–33
    other comprehensive income, 9:20
    passive investments, 7:6e–7
    Statement of Stockholders' Equity, 9:23e–24
loss on bond retirement, 8:19–20
lower of cost or market, 6:16–17
Lowes, 22:1

M

MACRS (Modified Accelerated Cost Recovery
    System), 5:20n5, 6:30n9
maintenance costs, product cost reporting, 17:6e
managed fixed costs. *See* discretionary fixed
    costs
management by exception, 21:4, 22:3
management discussion and analysis (MD&A),
    2:30–31, 11:12–13
managerial accounting, overview
    competition, key dimensions, 13:13
    cost drivers, 13:13–17, 14e
    defined, 13:2, 3
    ethics, 13:17–20
    goal attainment and, 13:10–11
    missions, goals and strategies, role of, 13:1–2
    planning, organizing and controlling, 13:11,
        12e
    standards, globalization of, 13:5
    strategic cost management, 13:5–6
    strategic position analysis, 13:7–10
    uses of, 13:4–6e
manager intervention, accounting, 5:32
managers, financial statements, use of, 1:6
Mandrusiak, Brian, 24:1
manufacturing burden. *See* manufacturing
    overhead
manufacturing cost hierarchy, 14:17–18e
manufacturing costs, 6:13–14
manufacturing costs, cost-based pricing, 20:9–10
manufacturing organizations, 17:3–5, 4e
manufacturing overhead. *See also* indirect costs;
    service departments
    activity-based budgeting, 21:5
    activity-based costing
        applying overhead, 18:8–11
        department overhead rates, 18:7–8
        implementation issues, 18:13–14
        limitations of, 18:12
        overview of, 18:4–6e

plantwide overhead rate, 18:6–7
production environment changes and,
    18:3e–4
vs. traditional costing, 18:12–13
cost estimation, 14:17e
cost reporting, 17:4–5e
cost savings, estimating, 24:19–20
cost variance, standards for, 22:15–17
job costing
    overhead, overapplied and underapplied,
        17:16–17
    overview of, 17:10–15, 11e, 14e
product cost reporting, 17:7–8
profit formula, 15:5
Marathon Oil, 5:32
Marathon Petroleum, 5:32
marginal cost of one unit, 14:6
marginal costs, pricing and, 20:7–8
marginal revenue, pricing and, 20:7–8
margin of safety, 15:8
marked to market, 7:6e–7
market capitalization, 2:10–11
market expansion, 7:3–4e
marketing assets, 7:21
marketing expenses, 1:12e–13
market method, passive investments, 7:3e–4e
market penetration, 7:3–4e
market price, as transfer price, 23:10–11
market price, debt, 5:28n8
market price per share, 9:24
market rate, 8:12
market-segment-level activity, 14:19
market-to-book ratio, 2:15
market value
    derivatives, 7:29–32
    lower of cost or market, 6:16–17
    marked to market, 7:6e–7
    market-to-book ratio, 2:15
    measuring assets, 2:6, 10–11
market value added (MVA), 23:17–18
Marriott, 16:11
Martha Stewart Living Omnimedia, 7:22
master budget, 21:7–9e, 8e. *See also* budgets
material costs, 1:12e–13, 5:4n3
materials price variance, 22:11–13
materials pull system, 19:11
materials push system, 19:11
materials quantity variance, 22:11–13
materials requisition forms, 17:10
maturities of long-term debt, 8:4
maturity, product life cycle, 20:15e–16
McDonalds, 20:9
MCI, 8:19–20
McKinsey and company, 24:14
McLane Company, Inc., 1:21
MD&A disclosures, 6:7–8e
Mead Johnson Nutrition Company, 7:24, 9:26
Mechanical Service Contractors of America,
    10:18
media, financial statements use, 1:6
merchandise budget, 21:9e–10
merchandising organizations, 10:3–4e
Merck & Co., Inc., 5:16, 31–32
Merrill Lynch, 8:12
method of comparables model, 12:12e
Metric Constructors Inc., 17:9

Microsoft, 7:5, 7, 16:11
MillerCoors, 17:3–4
minimum level approach, budgeting, 21:6–7
mission
    overview, 13:6–7e
    role of, 13:1–2
Mitel Networks, 7:12–13
mixed costs, 14:3–6e, 4e
Modified Accelerated Cost Recovery System
    (MACRS), 5:20n5, 6:30n9
Moody's Investor Service, 2:31–32, 8:22e
Morgan Stanley Research Report
    balance sheet items, forecasting, 11:22–27
    expense forecasting, 11:17–19, 18e
    income statement, 11:7–8e
    Procter & Gamble forecast report, 11:37–51
    revenue forecasts, 11:13–16
mortgages, 2:9, 4:8e–11e
Motorola, 20:6, 22:7
movement time, 19:11–12, 13
MTV, 3:9
multi-element contracts, 5:11–13
multi-level contribution income statement,
    15:19–21e, 20e
multilevel segment income statements, 23:4–7,
    6e
multi-national companies, 3:21
multiple-product companies, pricing, 20:9–10
multiple-product cost-volume-profit analysis,
    15:14–17e, 16e
multiple regression analysis, 14:14

N

Nardelli, Robert, 22:1
natural resources, balance sheet, 4:8e–11e
negotiated transfer price, 23:12
Nestle, 20:6
net assets, economic value added, 23:17–18
net asset valuation model, 12:12e
net book value, 5:35–37, 36e, 6:28
net cash flow from financing activity, B:4
net cash flow from investing activity, B:4
net cash flow from operating activity, B:4
net derivative losses, 9:20
Netflix, 15:1–2
net foreign exchange translation adjustments,
    9:20
net income
    DuPont disaggregation analysis, 4:30–33e
    forecasting, 11:27–28e
    income statements, overview, 1:12e–13,
        2:11–14, 12e, 13e
    return on equity, 4:4
    sale of subsidiaries, 7:25–26
net loss, income statements, 2:11–14, 12e, 13e
net nonoperating expense (NNE), 4:11e, 21–26
net nonoperating expense percent. *See* NNEP
    (net nonoperating expense percent)
net nonoperating obligations (NNO), 4:21–26,
    12:5
net nonoperating revenue, 4:6
net operating assets (NOA)
    balance sheet, 4:8e–11e
    defined, 4:11e
    free cash flows to firm (FCFF), 12:4

Note: The letter "e" refers to an exhibit on the stated page, and the letter "n" indicates that the information is included in a footnote on the given page. For example, 15n7 means footnote 7 on page 15.

overview, 4:1, 5–7
residual operating income (ROPI) model,
    valuation, 12:8–11, 9e
net operating asset turnover (NOAT), 4:8–14,
    11e, 13e, 6:10–11, 7:15, 10:5e, 7. *See also*
    off-balance-sheet financing
net operating profit after tax (NOPAT), 4:6–7
    defined, 4:11e
    free cash flows to firm (FCFF), 12:4
    leases, 10:7
    overview, 4:5–7
    residual operating income (ROPI) model,
        valuation, 12:8–11, 9e
net operating profit before tax (NOPBT), 4:6–7
net operating profit margin (NOPM), 4:2, 11–14,
    13e, 7:15, 10:7. *See also* off-balance-sheet
    financing
net operating working capital (NOWCT),
    4:15–16e
net pension expense, 10:14–15
net postretirement benefit obligations, 9:20
net present value, 24:8–9e, 16–17
net realizable value, 6:3
net revenues, recognition of, 5:8–9. *See also*
    revenue
net sales, forecasting, 11:18. *See also* sales
net sales volume variance, 22:20
net unrealized investment gains, 9:20
net working capital, 2:8
Newell Rubbermaid, 6:25
new store growth, 11:10–11
Nike Inc. (NKE), 5:4
Nintendo, 16:1–2
Nippon Kayaku, 17:20
Nissan, 20:1–2
NNE (net nonoperating expense), 4:11e
NNEP (net nonoperating expense percent),
    4:21–26
NNO (net nonoperating obligations), 4:21–26
NOA. *See* net operating assets (NOA)
NOAT. *See* net operating asset turnover (NOAT)
nominal cost of debt, 8:17
noncash assets, 1:10e–12, 2:27, B:11–12. *See
    also* assets
noncontrolling interest, 2:28, 4:25, 7:17e–18e,
    9:3–4e, 21–24, 23e
noncurrent assets, forecasting, 11:24
noncurrent liabilities, 2:9, 11:25
nonoperating activities
    current nonoperating liabilities, 8:10–11
    defined, 4:3
    global standards, 4:19–20
    income statement, 4:5–7
    long-term nonoperating liabilities, 8:12–15e,
        14e
    overview of, 5:3–4
nonoperating assets, forecasting, 11:24
nonoperating expenses, 2:12e–14, 13e, 11:16–
    19, 18e
nonoperating return, 4:16–17, 24
nonoperating return framework, 4:21–26
nonowner financing
    balance sheet, 1:10, 11–12
    bond repurchase, 8:19–20, 32e–33
    compound interest, 8:28–32
    credit ratings and debt cost, 8:21–27

current liabilities, 8:4–11
    footnotes, 8:20–21
    global accounting, 8:27–28
    long-term nonoperating liabilities, 8:12–15e,
        14e
    overview, 8:3
    reporting of, 8:15–21, 18e
    Verizon Communications, Inc., overview,
        8:1–2
non pro rata distribution, 9:26
nonqualified stock options (NQSOs), 9:10–11
nonrecoverable cost, 6:27
nonrefundable fees, 5:8
NOPAT (net operating profit after tax), 4:6–7,
    11e, 12:8–11, 9e
NOPBT (net operating profit before tax), 4:6–7,
    10:7
NOPM (net operating profit margin), 4:2, 11–14,
    13e, 7:15
not-for-profit organizations
    capital budgeting, 24:16–20, 18e
    cost-volume-profit (CVP) analysis, 15:3
    defined, 13:7
    incremental approach, budgeting, 21:5–6
NOWCT (net operating working capital),
    4:15–16e
NQSOs (nonqualified stock options), 9:10–11

O

obsolescence, 6:27
off-balance-sheet financing
    Delta Air Lines (DAL), overview, 10:1–2
    Enron, 1:17
    global accounting, 10:21–22
    Google, 7:2
    lease capitalization computations, 10:27–29
    leases, 10:4–11, 5e, 8e, 9e, 10e
    other post-employment benefits, 10:20–21
    overview, 10:1–3
    pensions, 10:12–21, 23–24
    special-purpose entities, 10:24–27
on account purchases, 2:26–27
on credit purchases, 2:26–27
Oneida Silversmiths, 14:17–18
one-time events, 5:31–32
open book management, 21:20
operating activities. *See also* operating income
    balance sheet, 4:8e–11e
    budgets and, 21:8e–9e
    defined, 4:3
    extraordinary items, 5:28–29
    forecasting, 11:29e–30
    global standards, 4:19–20
    income statements, overview, 1:12e–13
    net cash flows, 2:15–18, 16e
    overview of, 5:3–4
    Pfizer, overview, 5:1–2
    ratio behavior over time, 4:17
    return on net operating assets, 4:1
    statement of cash flows, B:3–11, 4e, 6e, 7e,
        19–22e, 20e
operating assets
    accounts receivable, 6:3–5, 8–12
    analysis, PPE, 6:33–35

asset sales and impairments, 6:30–32
    balance sheet, 4:8e–11e
    capitalization of asset costs, 6:26–27
    Cisco Systems, Inc., overview, 6:1–2
    depreciation, 6:27–30e
    footnote and MD&A disclosures, 6:7–8e
    footnotes, inventory, 6:17–18
    footnotes, PPE assets, 6:33
    forecasting, 11:22e
    global accounting, 6:35–36
    inventory, costing, 6:13–17, 14e, 15e
    inventory, financial statement effects,
        6:18e–20
    inventory analysis, 6:20e–25
    lower of cost or market, 6:16–17
    margin and turnover, 4:11–14, 13e
    operating activities, overview, 5:3–4
    overview, 6:3
    property, plant, and equipment, overview,
        6:26
    return on, 4:5–7
    uncollectible accounts, 6:5e–7e, 6e
operating budget. *See also* budgets
    activity-based approach, 21:5
    budgeted financial statements, 21:13–14e
    budget period, 21:19
    cash budget, 21:11–13e
    employee participation, 21:18–19
    ethics, 21:20
    finalizing, 21:15
    forecasts, 21:19
    general and administrative expense, 21:11e
    incremental approach, 21:5–6
    manufacturing, 21:15–18e, 16e, 17e
    master budget, overview, 21:7–9e, 8e
    minimum level approach, 21:6–7
    open book management, 21:20–21
    output/input approach, 21:4–5
    production budgets, 21:15, 16e
    purchases budget, 21:10e, 17e
    reasons for, 21:3–4
    sales budget, 21:10–11e, 17e
    selling expense budget, 21:10–11e
operating cash flow to capital expenditure ratio,
    B:17
operating cash flow to current liabilities ratio,
    B:16–17
operating cycle, 2:8, 21:7–8e
operating expenses
    forecasting, 11:16–19, 18e
    income statements, 2:12e–14, 13e
    sales and, 4:15–16e
operating income
    accounting quality, 5:30–33
    components of, 5:5
    deferred tax liability, 5:35–37, 36e
    extraordinary items, 5:28–29
    forecasting, 11:18
    foreign currency translation effects, 5:26–27e
    global accounting, 5:33–35
    income tax expenses and allowance, 5:19–26,
        20e, 21e, 23e
    overview of, 5:3–5
    research and development expenses, 5:13–16
    restructuring expense and incentives, 5:16–19
    revenue, recognition of, 5:5e–13

Note: The letter "e" refers to an exhibit on the stated page, and the letter "n" indicates that the information is included in a footnote on the given page. For example, 15n7 means footnote 7 on page 15.

operating lease method, 10:4–11, 5e, 8e, 9e, 10e
operating leverage ratio, 15:17–19
operating liabilities
  balance sheet, 4:8e–11e
  types of, 8:4
operating profit, 4:6–7
operation costs
  absorption and variable costing, 17:25–29e, 28e
  cost competition and success, 17:1–2
  inventory costing
    manufacturing overhead, 17:7–8
    overview, 17:4–5e
    product costs, components of, 17:5–6e
    product costs and period costs, 17:4–5e
  job costing
    overhead, overapplied and underapplied, 17:16–17
    overview of, 17:10–15, 11e, 14e
    service organizations, 17:17–19
    statement of cost of goods manufactured, 17:15–16e
  process costing
    cost of production report, 17:20–23, 22e
    overview, 17:20
    service organizations, 17:24
    weighted average and FIFO method, 17:23–24
  production environment, 17:9–10
operation phase, capital expenditures, 24:7e
operations list, 17:9
Oppenheimer valuation, Johnson & Johnson, 12:15–17
opportunity, assessing, 15:17–19
opportunity costs, 16:6, 10–11, 23:11
options
  debt contracts, 8:24
  derivatives, 7:28–32
  fair value, 7:5n1
  restricted stock compensation, 9:13–14
  stock-based compensation, 9:9–14
  underwater, 5:30n9
order-filling costs, 22:19
order-getting costs, 22:19
order-level activity, 14:19
organizational cost drivers, 13:14e, 15–16
organizational structure, performance reporting and, 22:4
organization chart, 13:11, 12e
organizing, process of, 13:11, 12e
other components of equity, global accounting, 9:29
other comprehensive income, 9:19–21e, 29
other income, passive investments, 7:5
other post-employment benefits (OPEB), 10:15n7–16, 20–21
Outback Restaurants, 13:13–14
outcomes, budgeting for, 21:6
outlay costs, relevance of, 6:4
output/input approach, budgeting, 21:4–5
output markets, 1:12e–13, 22
outsourcing, 16:11–15, 12e, 13e
outstanding shares, 9:6
overfunded pensions, 10:12

overhead. See also indirect costs; service departments
  activity-based budgeting, 21:5
  activity-based costing
    applying overhead, 18:8–11
    department overhead rates, 18:7–8
    implementation issues, 18:13–14
    limitations of, 18:12
    overview of, 81:4–6e
    plantwide overhead rate, 18:6–7
    production environment changes and, 18:3e–4
    vs. traditional costing, 18:12–13
  cost estimation, 14:17e
  cost reporting, 17:4–5e
  cost savings, estimating, 24:19–20
  cost variance, standards for, 22:15–17
  job costing
    overhead, overapplied and underapplied, 17:16–17
    overview of, 17:10–15, 11e, 14e
  product cost reporting, 17:7–8
  profit formula, 15:5
  variance costs, standards for, 22:15–17
overhead costs, 1:12e–13, 6:13–14
owner financing
  Aon Corporation, overview, 9:1–2
  balance sheet, 1:10–12
  cash dividends, 9:16
  contributed capital, overview, 9:4
  earned capital, overview, 9:15
  equity carve outs and convertibles, 9:24–28
  global accounting, 9:29
  noncontrolling interest, 9:21–24, 23e
  other comprehensive income, 9:19–21e
  overview, 9:3–4e
  restricted stock, 9:13–14
  stock, classes of, 9:4–6
  stock-based compensation, 9:9–14
  stock dividends, 9:17e–18
  stock repurchase, 9:8–9
  stock splits, 9:18–19
  stock transactions, 9:6–9
  transaction analysis, 2:26

P

paid-in capital, 2:9, 9:7
par (face) value, 8:13, 9:6–7
Parker Brass, 22:11
parsimonious multiyear forecasting, 11:35–36e
participation feature, preferred stock, 9:6
participative budget, 21:18–19
partners, strategic, 1:6
passive investments, 7:3e, 4e–10, 6e, 9e, 27
patents, Pfizer, 5:1–2
payback period, capital budgeting, 24:11–13
payroll department. See service departments
pending sales agreements, 5:8
pension plans. See also off-balance-sheet financing
  amortization of, 10:23–24
  analysis of, 10:19–20
  future cash flows, 10:17–18
  global accounting, 10:21
  income statement, 10:14–15

operating items, balance sheet, 4:8e–11e
  pension liabilities, 10:13–14
  pension plan assets, 10:12–14
  postretirement benefit obligations, 9:20
  profit implications, 10:18–19
  reporting, 10:12
Pepsi, 20:3
percentage-of-completion revenue, 5:9–11
percentage of sales method, 6:6n2
percent used up, 6:35
performance measures. See also financial statement analysis; return on investment (ROI)
  balanced scorecard, 23:19–22, 20e
  overview, 4:1
  transfer pricing and, 23:8–9
performance reporting
  capital expenditures, 24:5
  cost centers, 22:7–9, 8e
  financial and nonfinancial measures, 22:6–7
  goal attainment and, 13:10–11
  Home Depot, overview, 22:1–2
  lean production and just-in-time inventory, 19:13
  responsibility accounting, 22:3–6
  revenue center reports, 22:17–20e, 19e
  variance analysis, costs
    direct labor, 22:13–15
    direct materials, 22:11–13
    overhead, 22:15–17
    overview, 22:9–11
period costs, reporting, 17:4–5e
periodic interest payments, 8:12
period-of-time statements, 1:9e–10
permanent accounts, 2:3
personnel department. See service departments
Pfizer, Inc. (PFE)
  depreciation, 5:20e
  earnings per share, 5:29e–30
  foreign currency translation effects, 5:27e
  income statement, 5:5e
  income tax expense, 5:22–26e, 23e
  operating activities, 5:1–2
  ratios across industries, 5:4
  research and development expenses, 5:13–16
  return on assets, 1:19
  revenue, recognition of, 5:5e–13
physical obsolescence, 6:27
Piper Aircraft, 13:9
Pizza Hut, 14:3, 14:5
planning, overview of, 13:11, 12e. See also budgets
plants. See property, plant and equipment (PPE)
plantwide overhead rate, 18:6–7, 19:3. See also overhead
point-in-time statements, 1:9e, 10e–12
Porter, Michael, 13:8, 9
position analysis, strategic, 13:6, 7–10
post-employment liabilities
  operating items, balance sheet, 4:8e–11e
  Statement of Stockholders' Equity, 9:23e–24
posting transactions, 3:4e–5
PPE. See property, plant and equipment (PPE)
predetermined manufacturing overhead rate, 17:7–8

Note: The letter "e" refers to an exhibit on the stated page, and the letter "n" indicates that the information is included in a footnote on the given page. For example, 15n7 means footnote 7 on page 15.

preferred stock
    convertible preferred stock, 9:28–29
    defined, 2:9
    dividends in arrears, 9:16
    global accounting, 9:29
    overview of, 9:4–6
    return on equity, 4:25
premium amortization, 8:17–19, 18e
premium bonds, 8:14e, 17
prepaid expenses
    adjusting accounts, 2:23, 3:8–9e
    balance sheet, 2:5e
    forecasting, 11:6
    operating items, balance sheet, 4:8e–11e
    statement of cash flows, B:9
present value
    concepts, 8:28–32, 30e, 10:8–11
    pension liabilities, 10:13–14
    present value factors, 8:13
    present value tables, 10:27–29
    of terminal period, 12:7
present value of money
    deferred returns, 24:27
    internal rate of return, table approach,
        24:28–29e
    overview, 24:23–24, 26e
    unequal cash flows, 24:27
price disclosure, revenue forecasts, 11:11–12
PricewaterhouseCoopers, 1:26
pricing decisions
    benchmarking, 20:17–18
    business example, green cars, 20:1–2
    continuous improvement (Kaizen) costing,
        20:16–17
    cost-based approaches, 13:13, 14:1–2,
        20:8e–11
    cost estimation and, 14:15–16
    economic approaches, 20:7–8
    target costing
        coordination for, 20:14
        cost information for, 20:14
        design, influence on, 20:13–14
        overview of, 20:11–12e
        product introduction time, 20:13–14
        product life cycles and, 20:15
    transfer price
        defined, 23:8
        management considerations, 23:8–9
        methods for determining, 23:10–13
    value chain
        overview, 20:3–5e, 4e
        usefulness of, 20:5–7
        value-added perspective, 20:7
pricing of debt, 8:12–14
printers, buying decisions about, 14:7
prior service costs, 10:23–24
process costing
    absorption and variable costing, 17:25–29e,
        28e
    cost competition and success, 17:1–2
    cost of production report, 17:20–23, 22
    inventory costs
        manufacturing overhead, 17:7–8
        overview, 17:3–4e
        product costs, components of, 17:5–6e
        product costs and period costs, 17:4–5e

job costing
    overhead, overapplied and underapplied,
        17:16–17
    overview of, 17:10–15, 11e, 14e
    statement of cost of goods manufactured,
        17:15–16e
overview, process costing, 17:20
production environment, 17:9–10
service organizations, 17:24
weighted average and FIFO method,
    17:23–24
processes, value chain, 20:4e
processing time, 19:11–12, 13
process manufacturing environment, 17:9–10
Procter & Gamble (P&G)
    assets, liabilities, and equity forecasts, 11:19–
        27, 20e, 22e
    balance sheet, 1:11
    debt level, 2:10
    expense forecasts, 11:16–19, 18e
    finished good inventory, 19:12
    forecasted balance sheet, 11:27–28e
    forecasted statement of cash flows, 11:29e–
        30
    forecasting, overview, 11:1–2
    intangible assets, acquisition of, 7:21–22
    Morgan Stanley Research Report, 11:37–51
    multiyear forecasts, 11:30–33e, 32e
    parsimonious multiyear forecasting, 11:35–
        36e
    research report, 11:7–8e
    revenue growth forecasts, 11:9–16
product costing. See also activity-based costing
    absorption and variable costing, 17:25–29e,
        28e
    banks and financial institutions, 19:1–2
    cost competition, 17:1–2
    inventory costs
        components of, 17:5–6e
        manufacturing overhead, 17:7–8
        overview, 17:3–4e
        product costs and period costs, 17:4–5e
        reporting, 17:4–5e
    job costing
        overhead, overapplied and underapplied,
            17:16–17
        overview, 17:10–15, 11e, 14e
        service organizations, 17:17–19
        statement of cost of goods manufactured,
            17:15–16e
    lean production (just-in-time inventory
        management)
        overview of, 19:9–12
        performance evaluation, 19:12–14
        recordkeeping and, 19:14
    plantwide overhead rate, 18:6–7
    process costing
        cost of production report, 17:20–23, 22
        overview, 17:20
        service organizations, 17:24
        weighted average and FIFO method,
            17:23–24
    production department costs, overview, 19:3
    production environment, 17:9–10
    service department costing
        direct method, 19:5e–6

dual rates, 19:8–9
linear algebra (reciprocal) method, 19:8e
overview, 19:3, 4
step method, 19:6–7e
product design, target costing and, 20:13–14
product distribution costs, 1:12e–13
product introduction time, 20:14
production budgets, 21:15, 16e, 17e
production environment, product cost and,
    17:9–10
production files and records, 17:10
production order, 17:10
productivity, 4:13, 32
product-level activity, 14:18
product life cycles
    continuous improvement costing, 20:16–17
    impact on cost, 13:6
    target costing and, 20:15–16
product substitutes, 1:20e–22
profit. See also earned capital
    analysis with unit and non unit cost drivers,
        15:19–21e, 20e
    break-even point, 15:8–12e, 11e, 14–17e,
        16e, 19–21e
    competitive environment, 1:20e–22
    cost-volume-profit (CVP) analysis, 15:6e–7e,
        10, 11e
    customer profitability analysis, 18:14e–16e
    free cash flows to firm (FCFF), 12:4
    gross profit margin, 6:20e–21
    income statements, 2:11–14, 12e, 13e
    income statements, overview, 1:12e–13
    Netflix, overview, 15:1–2
    operating leverage, 15:17–19
    pension expense and, 10:18–19
    as percent of sales, 4:15–16e
    profitability analysis, 15:3–6
    profitability and productivity, 4:13
    profit centers, 22:5, 6
    profit formula, 15:4–6
    profit margin, 4:11–14, 13e
    profit plans, differential cost analysis, 16:8–9
    profit-volume graph, 15:10–11e
    residual operating income (ROPI) model,
        valuation, 12:8–11, 9e
    residual value, overstatement of, 24:8
    return on assets, 1:18–19e
    return on net operating assets (RNOA), 4:1–2
    statement of cash flows, 2:15–18, 16e
    tax on operating profit, 4:6–7
profitability, 4:31
profit margin (PM), 1:18–19e, 4:30–33e
pro forma earnings, 5:32
pro forma income, 5:34
projected benefit obligation (PBO), 10:12–14
project-level activity, 14:19
property, plant and equipment (PPE)
    analysis of, 6:33–35
    asset costs, capitalization of, 6:26–27
    asset sales and impairments, 6:30–32
    balance sheet, 1:10e–12, 2:5e–6
    balance sheet, overview, 1:10e–12
    Cisco Systems, Inc., overview, 6:1–2
    cost recording, 2:4
    depreciation, 6:27–30e
    footnote disclosures, 6:33

Note: The letter "e" refers to an exhibit on the stated page, and the letter "n" indicates that the information is included in a footnote on the given page. For example, 15n7 means footnote 7 on page 15.

forecasting, 11:6, 23–24
global accounting, 6:36
operating items, balance sheet, 4:8e–11e
overview, 6:3, 26
sale of, 5:4n2
statement of cash flows, B:12
transaction analysis, 2:26
pro rata distribution, 9:26
Providence Hospital, 13:16
Public Company Accounting Oversight Board
    (PCAOB), 1:28
purchases budget, 21:10e, 17e
purchasing, just-in-time inventory, 19:14
pure-play firms, 4:13

Q

quality, defined, 13:13
quality circles, 19:11–12
quick ratio, 4:27
Qwest Communications International (Q), 1:17

R

ratio analysis, 4:18–19, 8:25–27, B:16–17
ratio behavior, 4:17
ratio values, debt risk classes, 8:23e
raw materials
    footnote disclosures, 6:18
    inventories, 17:3–4e, 10
    job costing, overview of, 17:10–15, 11e, 14e
    product cost reporting, 17:6e
    production files and records, 17:10
Raytheon Company, 5:10
real estate financing, 10:25–26
realized revenue, 3:6–7, 5:6
receivables. See accounts receivable
reciprocal method, service department costing,
    19:8
records, production, 17:10, 19:12–14
Red Cross, 13:7
Red Lobster, 15:3
reduction of interest expense, 8:14–15e
regression analysis, least-square, 14:13e–15
Regulation FD, SEC, 1:8
regulators, financial statement use, 1:6–7
reinvested capital, 1:14e
relevance, market value, 2:6
relevant, information, 5:30–31
relevant costs
    differential cost analysis
        multiple changes in profit plans, 16:8–9
        outsourcing, 16:11–15, 12e, 13e
        overview of, 16:6–7e
        sell or process further, 16:15–16
        special orders, 16:9–11, 10e
    identifying, 16:3–6
    limited resources, use of, 16:16–19
    model limitations, 16:19
    Nintendo, overview, 16:1–2
relevant range, total cost function, 14:6–8, 7e
reliability, market value, 2:6
reliable information, 5:30
relocation costs, 5:16–19
rent expense, leases, 10:10e–11

reports, uses of, 13:3–6. See also cost of
    production report; performance reporting;
    segment reporting
repurchase, stock, 9:8–9
research and development, intercorporate
    investments, 7:11–15
research and development expense
    capitalization of, 6:27
    income statements, 2:12e–14, 13e
    operating activities, overview, 5:3–4
    operating income and, 5:13–16
    Pfizer, 5:1–2
Research Insight
    accruals, 3:12
    cost of debt, 8:22
    debt option valuations, 8:24
    earnings, importance of, 1:14
    earnings quality, 11:7
    equity income and stock price, 7:13
    LIFO and stock price, 6:20
    market-to-book ratio, 2:15
    NOPAT forecasts, 12:9e–10
    NOPM, NOAT and stock prices, 4:14
    other post-employment benefits, valuation
        of, 10:21
    pension plans, 10:17
    pro forma earnings, 5:32
    ration behavior over time, 4:17
    restructuring costs and incentives, 5:17
    stock issuance and returns, 9:7
    stock mispricing, 12:12e
reserve accounts, 9:21
reserves, global accounting, 9:29
residual income, 23:16–19
residual interest, 2:9
residual operating income (ROPI) model,
    valuation, 12:4, 8–11, 9e, 12e
residual value, overstatement of, 24:8
resources
    activity-based costing, overview of, 18:4–6e
    limited, use of, 16:16–19
responsibility accounting. See also performance
    reporting
    financial and nonfinancial performance
        measures, 22:6–7
    organizational structure and, 22:4
    overview, 22:3–4
    responsibility centers, 22:5–6
restricted stock, 9:13–14
restructuring expense, 5:3–4, 16–19, 34
restructuring liabilities, 7:22
retained earnings
    earned capital, 9:15
    global accounting, 9:29
    income statement, 3:16
    reconciliation, 2:19–20e
    statement of cash flows, B:13
    stockholders' equity, 1:14e, 2:9–11
retirement, break-even point, 15:9
return on assets (ROA), 1:18–19e, 4:31–33e,
    7:13–15, 10:15n7
return on equity (ROE). See also off-balance-
    sheet financing
    defined, 4:11e
    DuPont disaggregation analysis, 4:30–33e
    equity method investments, 7:13–15

leases, 10:5e, 7
noncontrolling interest, 9:23e–24
nonoperating return, 4:16–17, 21–26
overview, 1:19, 4:1, 4
ratio behavior, 4:17
return on investment (ROI)
    asset base, 23:16
    economic value added (EVA), 23:17–18
    investment center income, 23:15–16
    measurement comparison, 23:18–19
    overview, 23:13–15, 14e
    residual income, 23:16–17
    valuation issues, 23:16
return on net operating assets (RNOA). See also
    off-balance-sheet financing
    disaggregation, 4:15–16e
    leases, 10:5e
    margin and turnover, 4:11–14, 13e
    nonoperating return framework, 4:21–26
    overview, 4:1–2, 5–7
    ratio behavior, 4:17
    Target, 4:4
revaluation, goodwill impairment and, 7:24
revaluation reserve or surplus, global
    accounting, 9:29
revenue. See also budgets; costs and benefits,
    decisions about; performance reporting
    accrued, 3:9e
    break-even point, 15:8
    forecasting, 11:5e, 8–16, 21
    future, relevance of, 16:4
    income statements, overview, 1:12e–13,
        2:11–14, 12e, 13e
    pricing and, 20:7–8
    profitability analysis, 15:3–6
    profit formula, 15:4–6
    reconciling budgeted and actual income,
        22:23
    revenue centers, 22:5, 17–20e, 19e
    revenue recognition criteria, 5:6–13, 34
    revenue recognition principle, 2:12–13,
        3:6–7, 5:13
    revenue variance, 22:17–20e, 19e
    sales budgets, 21:9e–10, 17e
    segment reports, 23:5–7, 6e
    unearned, 2:7e–9, 8e, 3:8–10, 9e
reverse engineering, 17:9
rights of return, 5:7
risk. See also time value of money
    business environment, 1:22
    capital expenditures, evaluating, 24:16–17
    operating leverage, 15:17–19
    of outsourcing, 16:13–15e
    revenue recognition and risk exposure, 5:7–8
    risk management, 21:4, 5
risk-free rate, 8:21–27
risk premium rate, 8:21–27
Riverwood International, 17:9, 20:3–4
RNOA. See return on net operating assets
    (RNOA)
ROA (return on assets), 1:18–19e, 4:31–33e,
    7:13–15, 10:15n7
ROE. See return on equity (ROE)
rolling budget, 21:19
ROPI (residual operating income) model,
    valuation, 12:4, 8–11, 9e, 12e

Note: The letter "e" refers to an exhibit on the stated page, and the letter "n" indicates that the information is included in a footnote on the given page. For example, 15n7 means footnote 7 on page 15.

RSM McGladry, 1:26
ruler stock, 12:1
Ryder Systems, 23:18

S

Safeway, 20:4
salaries. *See also* stock-based compensation
    balance sheet, 2:7e–9, 8e
    income statements, 1:12e–13
    job costing, 17:10–17, 11e, 14e
    pension expense and profit, 10:18–19
    product costs and period costs, 17:4–5e
    statement of cash flows, B:21
    transaction analysis, 2:24
sale of subsidiaries, reporting, 7:24–26
sales
    asset turnover, 1:18–19e
    DuPont disaggregation analysis, 4:30–33e
    forecasting, 11:5e, 18, 21:19
    income statements, overview, 1:12e–13
    operating activities, overview, 5:3–4
    PPE turnover, 6:33–35
    profit as percent of sales, 4:15–16e
    sales agreements, 5:8
    sales budgets, 21:9e–10, 17e
    sales dollar analysis, 15:16–17e
    sales mix, defined, 15:4
    sales mix analysis, 15:15–17e, 16e
    sales on account, 6:3–5
    sales price variance, 22:17–20e, 19e
    sales volume, 15:1–2, 15:20
    sales volume variance, 22:17–20e, 19e
    statement of cash flows, B:19–22e, 20e
salvage value, 6:27, 16:5–6
Salvation Army, 15:3
Samsung, 16:13–14
Sanmina-SCI, 20:6
Sante Fe Railroad, 14:9
Sarbanes-Oxley Act (SOX), 1:9, 17, 5:32, 13:19
scatter diagrams, cost estimation, 14:12e–13
Seagate, 16:11
Sears, 6:10
seasonal swings, 8:10–11
SEC. *See* Securities Exchange Commission
        (SEC)
securities. *See also* equity securities
    forecasting, 11:24
    income statements, 2:12e–14, 13e
    quick ratio, 4:27
Securities Act (1933), 1:25
Securities Exchange Commission (SEC). *See
        also* Form 8-K, SEC; Form 10-K, SEC
    accessing filings, 1:23–25
    accounting principles and governance,
        1:25–30
    global standards, 13:5
    international standards, 1:7, 8–9
    revenue recognition, 5:7–8
security, product cost reporting, 17:6e
segment income, 23:5–7, 6e
segment margins, 23:5–7, 6e
segment reporting
    balanced scorecard, 23:19–22, 20e
    economic value added (EVA), 23:17–18
    IBM, overview, 23:1–2

overview, 23:3–4
return on investment
    asset base, 23:16
    investment center income, 23:15–16
    measurement comparison, 23:18–19
    overview, 23:13–15, 14e
    residual income, 23:16–17
    valuation issues, 23:16
segment income statements, multilevel,
        23:4–7, 6e
transfer pricing
    management considerations, 23:8–9
    methods for determining, 23:10–13
    overview, 23:8
Seidenberg, Ivan, 8:1
selling expense
    income statements, 2:12e–14, 13e
    leases, 10:4–11, 5e, 8e, 9e, 10e
    operating activities, overview, 5:3–4
    selling, general and administrative expense,
        10:12, 11:18
    selling costs, profit formula, 15:5
    selling expense budget, 21:10–11e
sell-offs, 9:24–25
semivariable costs, 4e, 14:3–6e
sensitivity analysis, 15:7
service cost, pensions, 10:13
service departments
    cost allocation
        direct method, 19:5e–6
        dual rates, 19:8–9
        linear algebra (reciprocal) method, 19:8
        overview, 19:4
        step method, 19:6–7e
    product costing, 19:3
service organizations
    defined, 13:13
    inventory, 17:3–4e
    job costing, 17:17–19
    process costing, 17:24
    product costing, 19:1–2
    service (job) costing, 17:17–19
setup time, 19:11, 13
severance costs, 5:16–19
share capital, 9:7, 29
shareholders
    financial statements, use of, 1:6
    statement of stockholders' equity, overview,
        1:14e
share premium, 9:7, 29
short-range planning. *See* capital budgeting
short-term assets, 1:10e–12, 2:5e. *See also* assets
short-term interest-bearing debt, 8:4, 10–11
short-term notes payable, 2:7e–9, 8e
Shriners Children's Hospital, 17:3
significant influence, investments, 7:3e–4e,
        11–15
simple regression analysis, 14:14
single payment, 8:12
Sirius Satellite Radio, 15:18, 19
six sigma, 22:7
Skype, 7:5, 7
social responsibility, corporate, 13:19–20
Society of Management Accountants of Canada,
        18:16
Solectron Corporation, 20:6

solvency analysis, 4:18–19, 26–30e, 29e
Sony, 16:13–14, 20:17
Southwest Airlines, 1:13, 13:8
SOX (Sarbanes-Oxley Act, 2002), 13:19
special orders, 16:9–11, 10, 20:10
special purpose entities (SPEs), 1:17, 10:21,
        24–27
spin-offs, 9:25–26
split-off, 9:26
split-off point, 16:16
spread, 8:21–27
spreadsheet approach, net present value, 24:8–9e
spreadsheet method, lease present value,
        10:9–10
staff departments, 13:11, 12e
standard cost, 22:9
standard cost variance analysis, 22:9–11
standard labor rate, 22:13–15
Standard & Poor's, 2:31–32, 8:22e
standard price, direct materials, 22:11–13
standard quantity, direct materials, 22:11–13
standards. *See* accounting standards; IFRS
        Insight; IFRS (International Financial
        Reporting Standards)
standard time allowed, 22:13–15
Stanley, Tim, 23:19
Starbucks Corporation
    addbacks for operating cash flow, B:11
    asset impairments, 6:32
    cash flow from operating activity, B:6e–11,
        7e
    financing activities, B:13
    framework for, B:3–6, 4e
    investing activities, B:12
    mission of, 13:6
    overview, B:1–2
start-up, product life cycle, 20:15
stated rate, 8:12
statement of cash flows
    applications of, B:15–17
    cash flow from financing activities, B:12–13
    cash flow from investing activities, B:11–12
    cash flow from operating activity, B:6e–11,
        7e
    direct method reporting, B:19–22e, 20e
    forecasted, 11:29e–30
    framework for, B:3–6, 4e
    global standards, 2:29
    growth dynamics, 11:7
    lease types, 10:4–5e
    overview, 1:15e, 2:15–18, 16e
    preparation, 3:17–20
    Starbucks, overview, B:1–2
    stock-based compensation, 9:12–13
    summary of net cash flow reporting, B:13–
        15e
statement of cost of goods manufactured,
        17:15–16e
statement of recognized income and expenses
        (SoRIE), 9:19
statement of stockholders' equity, 1:14e, 2:14e–
        15, 3:17, 9:23e–24
state tax rates, 4:6
static budgets, 22:7
statutory tax rate, 5:24
Steelcase Furniture Company, 17:9

Note: The letter "e" refers to an exhibit on the stated page, and the letter "n" indicates that the information is included in a footnote on the given page. For example, 15n7 means footnote 7 on page 15.

step costs, 14:3–4e
step method, service department cost allocation, 19:6–7e
stock. *See also* common stock; equity securities; investments, intercorporate; owner financing
  capital distributions, 3:7
  capital investment entries, 3:5–6
  cash dividends, 9:16
  classes of, 9:4–6
  dividends, 9:17e–18
  earnings per share, 5:2, 29e–30
  equity, balance sheet, 2:6–11, 7e, 8e
  income statements, 2:12e–14, 13e
  liabilities-to-equity ratio, 4:27
  LIFO and, 6:20
  passive investments, 7:3e, 4e–10, 6e, 9e
  pricing, 4:14, 12:12e
  repurchase, 9:8–9
  restricted stock compensation, 9:13–14
  return on equity (ROE), 1:19, 4:4
  statement of cash flows, 3:20
  statement of stockholders' equity, 1:14e, 2:14e–15, 3:17
  stock issuance, 9:6–7
  stock splits, 9:18–19
  subsidiary stock issuance, 7:24
stock-based compensation, 9:9–14
stockholders' equity, 1:14e, 2:9, 14e–15, 3:17, 4:30–33e, 9:21–24, 23e. *See also* equity
stock options, 9:8–9
Stone, David, 14:7
straight-line depreciation, 5:20e–22, 6:28–29, 24:20–21e
strategic business segments, 23:3. *See also* segment reporting
strategic cost management, overview of, 13:5–6
strategic partners, 1:6, 7:3–4e, 11–15
strategic planning, 1:4–5
strategic position analysis, 13:6, 8–10
strategies, overview, 1:4–5, 13:1–2, 6–7
strike price, 9:9–14
structural cost drivers, 13:14e, 15
subscription payment, 5:11–13
subsidiaries
  foreign, translation adjustments, 9:20
  global accounting, 3:21
  noncontrolling interest, 9:21–24, 23e
  not wholly owned, 7:17–18e
  sale of, reporting, 7:24–26
  sell-offs, 9:24–25
  spin-offs, 9:25–26
  stock issuance, reporting, 7:24
  wholly owned, 7:17e
subsidiary ledger, 17:10
Subway, 20:9
Sullivan, Scott, 6:26
summary of significant accounting policies, 6:33
Sunbeam, 22:3–4
sunk costs, 16:5, 16:16
Supercuts, 17:3
supplemental disclosures, B:22
supplier-buyer partnerships, value chain and, 20:5–6
suppliers, 1:6, 20e–22
supplies, 6:18

support functions, costing. *See* service departments
swap contracts, derivatives, 7:28–32
Swienton, Greg, 23:18
Symantec Corporation, 3:21–22
Syncrude Canada, Ltd., 9:24–25

T

table approach, internal rate of return, 24:28–29e
table approach, net present value, 24:8
T-accounts, 3:4e–6
TAP Pharmaceutical Products Inc. (TAP), 7:13–15
Target Corp. (TGT)
  balance sheets, 4:9–11
  cost drivers, 13:15
  current ratio, 4:26–27
  debt level, 2:10
  DuPont disaggregation analysis, 4:33e
  income statement, 4:6–7
  market value, 2:6
  nonoperating return, 4:23
  performance measures, 4:1–2
  profit margin and asset turnover, 4:11–14, 13e
  quick ratio, 4:27
  ratios across industries, 5:4
  return on equity (ROE), 4:4
  return on net operating assets (RNOA), 4:4
  revenue forecasting, 11:10–11
  Six Sigma improvements, 22:7
  tax shield, 4:7
  times interest earned, 4:28
  vertical and horizontal analysis, 4:28, 29e, 30e
target costing
  coordination for, 20:14
  cost information for, 20:14
  design, influence on, 20:13–14
  global trade, 20:13
  overview of, 20:11–12e
  product introduction time, 20:14
  product life cycles and, 20:15
tax agencies, financial statement use, 1:6–7
taxes
  capital budgeting and, 24:20–22e, 21e
  corporate rates, 4:6
  deferred tax liability, 5:35–37, 36e
  DuPont disaggregation analysis, 4:31–33e
  forecasting, 11:23, 25, 27–28e
  impact on profit, 15:12e
  investment tax credit, 24:21–22e
  multi-level contribution income statements, 15:19–20e
  net operating profit after tax (NOPAT), 4:6–7
  product costs reporting, 17:6e
  Statement of Stockholders' Equity, 9:23e–24
  stock-based compensation, 9:10–11
  tax basis, deferred tax liability, 5:35–37, 36e
  tax computation, operating profit, 4:6–7
  tax loss carryforwards, 5:22
  tax shield, 4:6–7
technical obsolescence, 6:27
technology
  cost estimation and, 14:15–16

investment in, capital budgeting, 24:18–19
  manufacturing overhead costs and, 17:8
temporal method, 9:21n2
terminal period, 12:5
terms, credit, 8:6n2
Texas Instrument BA II Plus, 10:27–29
theory of constraints, 16:16–19
Thomson Reuters Corporation, 2:32
threat of entry, 1:20e–22
throughput, 16:17
Tiffany & Co., 7:30–32
time
  opportunity cost and, 16:10–11
  performance measures of, 13:4
time-adjusted rate of return, 24:9–10e
times interest earned, 4:28
time value of money, 8:29, 31
  annuities, 24:25–26e
  capital budgeting models
    cost of capital, 24:10–11
    expected cash flows, 24:6–7e
    internal rate of return (IRR), 24:9–10e
    net present value, 24:8–9e
  deferred returns, 24:27
  future value, 24:23
  present value, 24:23–24, 26e
  unequal cash flows, 24:27
Time Warner (TWX), 1:16, 15:2
TJX Companies (TJX), 1:19
tombstone, 8:14, 15e
top-down budget, 21:18
Toronto's Hospital for Sick Children, 18:2
Toshiba Corporation, 20:17
total cost function, 14:5–6e, 15:4
total costs, cost of production report, 17:20–23, 22e
total revenues, profit formula, 15:4–6
Toyota, 17:8, 20:1–2, 12
trade credit, 2:8e, 8:5–6
trade payables, 8:5–6
trading (T), investment class, 7:6e–7
transaction analysis, 2:21–28, 3:5–7
transactions, accounting for, 3:4e–7
transfer pricing
  management considerations, 23:8–9
  methods for determining, 23:10–13
  overview, 23:8
transitory items, income statements, 2:13e–14
transitory operating income, 6:31
Treasury stock, 2:9, 8:21–27, 9:8–9
trial balance, 3:12–15, 14e
turnover, assets, 4:11–14, 13e, 6:35–36
turnover rates, forecasting and, 11:21
Tyco (TYC), 1:9, 17

U

UBS, 8:27
unadjusted trial balance, 3:14
uncollectible amounts, 6:5e–7e, 6e, 9–10
underfunded pensions, 10:12
underwater options, 5:30n9
unearned revenues
  adjusting accounts, 2:23, 3:8–10, 9e
  balance sheet, 2:7e–9, 8e
  current liabilities, 8:4

Note: The letter "e" refers to an exhibit on the stated page, and the letter "n" indicates that the information is included in a footnote on the given page. For example, 15n7 means footnote 7 on page 15.

operating items, balance sheet, 4:8e–11e
  recognition of, 5:11–13
unintentional errors, 5:31
Union Pacific Corp, 8:14, 15e
unit contribution margin, 15:7
unit cost drivers, 15:19–21e, 20e
United Airlines, 13:11
United Parcel Service, 13:13, 14
United States Postal Service, 14:5
United Way, 13:7
unit-level activity, 14:17–18e, 14:19
unit sales, revenue forecasts, 11:11–12
unit sales analysis, 15:15–16e
units in process, cost of production report, 17:21
units-of-production, 6:30n10
university settings, cost allocation, 19:3
unrecognized gains (and losses), pension plans,
  10:23–24
unsecured liabilities, 6:3
UPS, 18:1–2
U.S. Department of Defense, 14:19
U.S. GAAP, 13:5, 23:17–18
U.S. Postal Service, 18:1–2
U.S. Securities and Exchange Commission, 13:5
US Airways, 14:19
useful life, 6:27, 35
USPS (United States Postal Service), 18:1–2
US West, 15:20
utilities
  job costing, overview of, 17:10–15, 11e, 14e
  product cost reporting, 17:6e

V

valuation, segment reporting, 23:16
value, assets, 2:6, 10–11, 15
value-added perspective, 20:7
value chain
  inventory management, 19:9–12
  overview, 20:3–5e, 4e
  usefulness of, 20:5–7
  value-added perspective, 20:7
value chain analysis, defined, 13:6
Vanguard Group, 8:12
variable costs
  absorption and, 17:25–29e, 28e
  administrative costs, 15:5
  cost-based pricing, 20:9–10
  cost behavior, 14:3–4e
  high-low cost estimation, 14:11–12e

total cost function, 14:5–6e
  as transfer price, 23:11
  variable cost of one unit, 14:6
  variable cost ratio, 15:14–17e, 16e
variable manufacturing overhead, 15:5
variable overhead efficiency variance, 22:15–17
variable overhead spending variance, 22:15–17
variable selling costs, 15:5
variance, defined, 22:7
variance analysis, costs
  direct labor, 22:13–15
  direct materials, 22:11–13
  overhead, 22:15–17
  overview, 22:9–11
Verizon Communications, Inc.
  accounts payable turnover, 8:6
  accrued liabilities, 8:6–8
  bond issuance, 8:17–19, 18e
  bond rating, 8:23
  bond repurchase, 8:19–20
  controlling vs. noncontrolling interest, 2:28
  current liabilities, 8:4–11
  long-term liabilities, footnotes, 8:20–21
  nonowner financing, overview, 8:1–2
  operating cash flow to current liabilities ratio,
    B:17
  short-term debt, 8:10–11
  zero-coupon debt, 8:16
Verizon Wireless, 2:28
vertical analysis, 4:28, 29e, 30e
vesting, 9:10, 13–14
Viking Air Ltd., 24:1–2
Vodafone, 2:28
volume. See cost-volume-profit analysis and
  planning
voters, use of financial statements, 1:7

W

WACC (weighted average cost of capital),
  12:6n7
Wachovia Bank, 19:2
wages
  balance sheet, 2:7e–9, 8e
  direct labor costs, 17:4–5e
  job costing, 17:10–17, 11e, 14e
  pension expense and profit, 10:18–19
  product costs and period costs, 17:4–5e
  statement of cash flows, B:21
  transaction analysis, 2:24

waiting time, 19:11–12, 13
Waldenbooks, 21:2
Wall Street Reform and Consumer Protection
  Act (2010), 1:17
Walmart
  balance sheet, 4:14–15
  current ratio, 4:27
  finished goods inventory, 19:12
  inventory costs, 17:3
  noncontrolling interest, 4:4, 25–26
  overview, 14:1–2
  return on net operating assets (RNOA), 10
warranty liabilities, 8:8–9
weighted average cost of capital, 23:17–18
weighted average cost of capital (WACC),
  12:6n7
weighted average process costing, 17:23–24
Wells Fargo Bank, 19:1–2
wholly owned subsidiaries, 7:17e–18e
Wii, 16:1–2
Winn Dixie, 22:6
working capital management, 2:18
work in process, defined, 6:18
work-in-process inventories
  cost of production report, 17:20–23
  defined, 17:3–4e
  job costing, 17:10–16e, 11e, 14e
  product cost reporting, 17:6e
  production files and records, 17:10
work tickets, 17:10
WorldCom, Inc., 1:9, 17, 30, 2:4, 5:33, 6:26,
  13:18
write-down, inventory, 6:16–17
write-downs, asset impairments, 6:31–32
write-offs, 5:16–19, 6:6e–7e

X

Xerox (XRX), 1:17, 9:28–29, 20:6, 17
Xilinx, 9:27–29
XM Satellite Radio, 15:18, 19

Y

yield rate, 8:12, 21–27
Young, David, 22:6

Z

zero-based budgeting, 21:6–7
zero-coupon debt, 8:16

Note: The letter "e" refers to an exhibit on the stated page, and the letter "n" indicates that the information is included in a footnote on the given page. For example, 15n7 means footnote 7 on page 15.